سورة العلق مكية وآياتها تسع عشرة

بسم الله الرحمن الرحيم

اقرأ باسم ربك

الذي خلق

بسم الله الرحمن الرحيم

AL - AZHAR AL - SHARIF
ISLAMIC RESEARCH ACADEMY
GENERAL DEPARTMENT
For Research, Writting & Translation

الأزهـــر الشريف
مجمـــع البحـــوث الاســـلامية
الادارة العـــامة
للبحـــوث والتـــأليف والترجمـــة

السيد الأستاذ/ ياسر رأفت محمد

السلام عليكم ورحمة الله وبركاته...   وبعـــد،

فإشارة إلى الطلب المقدم من سيادتكم بشأن أبداء الرأى فى شأن تداول ترجمة محمد أسد الإنجليزية لمعانى القرآن الكريم وبها النطق الصوتى لكلمات القرآن الكريم.

تفيد الإدارة العامة للبحوث والتأليف والترجمة بمجمع البحوث الإسلامية بأن الترجمة المذكورة ليس فيها ما يتعارض مع ثوابت العقيدة الإسلامية ولا مانع من الاستفادة العلمية بها لعموم فائدتها على كافة المسلمين وذلك دون أدنى مسئولية على الأزهر تجاه حقوق القارئ أو المترجم.

والسلام عليكم ورجمة الله وبركاته.

إدارة الترجمة

ضياء
٢٢/٧/٢٠٠٧

مدير عام الإدارة العامة
البحوث والتأليف والترجمة
(ضياء)
٢٢/٧/٢٠٠٧

The Message of
THE QURʾĀN

THE FULL ACCOUNT OF THE REVEALED ARABIC TEXT

ACCOMPANIED BY PARALLEL TRANSLITERATION

TRANSLATED AND EXPLAINED

by

Muhammad Asad

Compliments of

Council on American-Islamic Relations (CAIR)

www.cair.com

With Special Thanks to the State of Qatar

The Book Foundation

England

Complete Edition published 2003
by
The Book Foundation
London, England

www.thebook.org

British Library Cataloguing in Publication Data
A catalogue record for this book is
available from the British Library.

ISBN No. 978-1-904510-35-2

First published, without transliteration 1980
Republished 1984, 1993, 1997
Present Format published 2008
Present Format reprinted 2012

Printed by Oriental Press
Dubai

. . . **wa ᵓinnahū laKitābun ᶜazīz. (41) Lā yaᵓtīhil-bāṭilu mim-bayni yadayhi wa lā min khalfihī tañzīlum-min Ḥakīmin Ḥamīd. (42)**

. . . وَإِنَّهُۥ لَكِتَٰبٌ عَزِيزٌ ﴿٤١﴾ لَّا يَأْتِيهِ
ٱلْبَٰطِلُ مِنۢ بَيْنِ يَدَيْهِ وَلَا مِنْ خَلْفِهِۦ
تَنزِيلٌ مِّنْ حَكِيمٍ حَمِيدٍ ﴿٤٢﴾

. . . for, behold, it is a sublime divine writ: ‹41› no falsehood can ever attain to it openly, and neither in a stealthy manner, [since it is] bestowed from on high by One who is truly wise, ever to be praised. ‹42›

Sūrah 41, *verses* 41-42. *Volume* 5, *page* 832

Endpaper Illustration:

التصوّر الداخلي للغلاف:

Reference to the first verses in the chronological order of the Quᵓranic revelations to the Prophet Muḥammad (Peace Be Upon Him).

مستلهم من نصّ الآيات الأولى طبقاً للنظام الزمني في وحي القرآن الكريم إلى محمد رسول الله ﷺ.

READ in the name of thy Sustainer, who has created – created man out of a germ-cell! Read – for thy Sustainer is the Most Bountiful One who has taught [man] the use of the pen – taught man what he did not know.

ٱقْرَأْ بِٱسْمِ رَبِّكَ ٱلَّذِى خَلَقَ ﴿١﴾
خَلَقَ ٱلْإِنسَٰنَ مِنْ عَلَقٍ ﴿٢﴾ ٱقْرَأْ وَرَبُّكَ ٱلْأَكْرَمُ ﴿٣﴾
ٱلَّذِى عَلَّمَ بِٱلْقَلَمِ ﴿٤﴾ عَلَّمَ ٱلْإِنسَٰنَ مَا لَمْ يَعْلَمْ ﴿٥﴾

Surah 96, verses 1-5

سورة العلق 96

Project Initiation
Hisham A. Alireza
The Book Foundation

Project Concept and Development
Dr. Ahmed Moustafa

Project Consultants
Dr. Jeremy Henzell-Thomas, Abder-Razzaq Pérez, Subhana Ansari,
Sammi M. Hanafy, Dr. Mohammed Abdul-Haleem,
Dr. Stefan Sperl, Dr. Edmund Bosworth,
Kabir Helminski, Hasan Gai Eaton,
Dr. Ibrahim Allawi, Adil Allawi,
Dr. Ali Gomᶜa

Transliteration
Dr. Ahmed Moustafa

Design
Dr. Ahmed Moustafa

Design Implementation
Mark Brady, Moustafa M. Hassan, Tawhid ar-Rahman
at Fe-Noon Ahmed Moustafa (UK) Ltd

Project Co-ordination
Dr. Ahmed Moustafa, Mark Brady

Essential Tools
Origination of Boulaq Arabic typeface by Dr. Ahmed Moustafa
Digitisation and production of Boulaq Arabic software font by Diwan Software Ltd.
Layout program used – Al Nashir Al Sahafi Dibaj by Diwan Software Ltd.

Technical Support
A Bigger Splash, Advanced Graphics, Diwan Software, Oriental Press, Prudence Cuming Associates

Artwork Origination
All calligraphic compositions © Ahmed Moustafa
Special Western Kufic typeface (Andalusian) © Ahmed Moustafa

A special thanks to Mrs Pola Hamida Asad for entrusting the Book Foundation
with the sole rights of the publication of "The Message of The Qurʾān".

Contents

Prologue i

Foreword vi

Works of Reference xiv

Explanatory Notes on Arabic Alphabets and Transliteration System used xvi

Key to Layout xxiii

SŪRAH

1	*Al-Fātiḥah* (The Opening) – 7 verses	الفاتحة	4
2	*Al-Baqarah* (The Cow) – 286 verses	البقرة	7
3	*ᵓĀl ᶜImrān* (The House of ᶜImrān) – 200 verses	آل عمران	78
4	*An-Nisāaᵓ* (Women) – 176 verses	النساء	116
5	*Al-Māaᵓidah* (The Repast) – 120 verses	المائدة	162
6	*Al-ᵓAnᶜām* (Cattle) – 165 verses	الأنعام	196
7	*Al-ᵓAᶜrāf* (The Faculty of Discernment) – 206 verses	الأعراف	230
8	*Al-ᵓAñfāl* (Spoils of War) – 75 verses	الأنفال	268
9	*At-Tawbah* (Repentance) – 129 verses	التوبة	287
10	*Yūnus* (Jonah) – 109 verses	يونس	324
11	*Hūd* – 123 verses	هود	349
12	*Yūsuf* (Joseph) – 111 verses	يوسف	376
13	*Ar-Raᶜd* (Thunder) – 43 verses	الرعد	398
14	*ᵓIbrāhīm* (Abraham) – 52 verses	إبراهيم	413
15	*Al-Ḥijr* – 99 Verses	الحجر	426
16	*An-Naḥl* (The Bee) – 128 verses	النحل	438
17	*Al-ᵓIsrāaᵓ* (The Night Journey) – 111 verses	الإسراء	464
18	*Al-Kahf* (The Cave) – 110 verses	الكهف	486
19	*Maryam* (Mary) – 98 verses	مريم	510
20	*Ṭā Hā* (O Man) – 135 verses	طه	524
21	*Al-ᵓAmbiyāaᵓ* (The Prophets) – 112 verses	الأنبياء	543
22	*Al-Ḥajj* (The Pilgrimage) – 78 verses	الحج	561
23	*Al-Muᵓminūn* (The Believers) – 118 verses	المؤمنون	578
24	*An-Nūr* (The Light) – 64 verses	النور	593
25	*Al-Furqān* (The Standard of True and False) – 77 verses	الفرقان	612
26	*Ash-Shuᶜarāaᵓ* (The Poets) – 227 verses	الشعراء	624
27	*An-Naml* (The Ants) – 93 verses	النمل	642
28	*Al-Qaṣaṣ* (The Story) – 88 verses	القصص	657

SŪRAH

29	*Al-ᶜAñkabūt* (The Spider) – 69 verses	العنكبوت	676
30	*Ar-Rūm* (The Byzantines) – 60 verses	الروم	692
31	*Luqmān* – 34 verses	لقمان	704
32	*As-Sajdah* (Prostration) – 30 verses	السجدة	711
33	*Al-ᵓAḥzāb* (The Confederates) – 73 verses	الأحزاب	716
34	*Sabaᵓ* (Sheba) – 54 verses	سبإ	734
35	*Fāṭir* (The Originator) – 45 verses	فاطر	748
36	*Yā Sīn* (O Thou Human Being) – 83 verses	يس	757
37	*Aṣ-Ṣāaffāt* (Those Ranged in Ranks) – 182 verses	الصافات	768
38	*Ṣād* – 88 verses	ص	782
39	*Az-Zumar* (The Throngs) – 75 verses	الزمر	794
40	*Ghāfir* (Forgiving) – 85 verses	غافر	810
41	*Fuṣṣilat* (Clearly Spelled Out) – 45 verses	فصلت	825
42	*Ash-Shūrā* (Consultation) – 53 verses	الشورى	835
43	*Az-Zukhruf* (Gold) – 89 verses	الزخرف	847
44	*Ad-Dukhān* (Smoke) – 59 verses	الدخان	860
45	*Al-Jāthiyah* (Kneeling Down) – 37 verses	الجاثية	866
46	*Al-ᵓAḥqāf* (The Sand-Dunes) – 35 verses	الأحقاف	874
47	*Muḥammad* – 38 verses	محمد	882
48	*Al-Fatḥ* (Victory) – 29 verses	الفتح	891
49	*Al-Ḥujurāt* (The Private Apartments) – 18 verses	الحجرات	901
50	*Qāf* – 45 verses	ق	906
51	*Adh-Dhāriyāt* (The Dust-Scattering Winds) – 60 verses	الذاريات	913
52	*Aṭ-Ṭūr* (Mount Sinai) – 49 verses	الطور	919
53	*An-Najm* (The Unfolding) – 62 verses	النجم	924
54	*Al-Qamar* (The Moon) – 55 verses	القمر	931
55	*Ar-Raḥmān* (The Most Gracious) – 78 verses	الرحمن	937
56	*Al-Wāqiᶜah* (That Which Must Come to Pass) – 96 verses	الواقعة	943
57	*Al-Ḥadīd* (Iron) – 29 verses	الحديد	950
58	*Al-Mujādalah* (The Pleading) – 22 verses	المجادلة	958
59	*Al-Ḥashr* (The Gathering) – 24 verses	الحشر	966
60	*Al-Mumtaḥanah* (The Examined One) – 13 verses	الممتحنة	974
61	*Aṣ-Ṣaff* (The Ranks) – 14 verses	الصف	980
62	*Al-Jumuᶜah* (The Congregation) – 11 verses	الجمعة	984
63	*Al-Munāfiqūn* (The Hypocrites) – 11 verses	المنافقون	987
64	*At-Taghābun* (Loss and Gain) – 18 verses	التغابن	990

65	*Aṭ-Ṭalāq* (Divorce) – 12 verses	الطلاق	994
66	*At-Taḥrīm* (Prohibition) – 12 verses	التحريم	998
67	*Al-Mulk* (Dominion) – 30 verses	الملك	1002
68	*Al-Qalam* (The Pen) – 52 verses	القلم	1008
69	*Al-Ḥāaqqah* (The Laying-Bare of the Truth) – 52 verses	الحاقة	1014
70	*Al-Maᶜārij* (The Ways of Ascent) – 44 verses	المعارج	1018
71	*Nūh* (Noah) – 28 verses	نوح	1022
72	*Al-Jinn* (The Unseen Beings) – 28 verses	الجن	1026
73	*Al-Muzzammil* (The Enwrapped One) – 20 verses	المزمل	1031
74	*Al-Muddaththir* (The Enfolded One) – 52 verses	المدثر	1035
75	*Al-Qiyāmah* (Resurrection) – 40 verses	القيامة	1042
76	*Al-ᵓInsān* (Man) – 31 verses	الإنسان	1045
77	*Al-Mursalāt* (Those Sent Forth) – 50 verses	المرسلات	1049
78	*An-Nabaᵓ* (The Tiding) – 40 verses	النبإ	1053
79	*An-Nāziᶜāt* (Those That Rise) – 46 verses	النازعات	1057
80	*ᶜAbasa* (He Frowned) – 42 verses	عبس	1061
81	*At-Takwīr* (Shrouding in Darkness) – 29 verses	التكوير	1064
82	*Al-Infiṭār* (The Cleaving Asunder) – 19 verses	الانفطار	1067
83	*Al-Muṭaffifīn* (Those Who Give Short Measure) – 36 verses	المطففين	1069
84	*Al-Inshiqāq* (The Splitting Asunder) – 25 verses	الانشقاق	1073
85	*Al-Burūj* (The Great Constellations) – 22 verses	البروج	1075
86	*Aṭ-Ṭāriq* (That Which Comes in the Night) – 17 verses	الطارق	1078
87	*Al-ᵓAᶜlā* (The All-Highest) – 19 verses	الأعلى	1080
88	*Al-Ghāshiyah* (The Overshadowing Event) – 26 verses	الغاشية	1082
89	*Al-Fajr* (The Daybreak) – 30 verses	الفجر	1084
90	*Al-Balad* (The Land) – 20 verses	البلد	1087
91	*Ash-Shams* (The Sun) – 15 verses	الشمس	1089
92	*Al-Layl* (The Night) – 21 verses	الليل	1091
93	*Aḍ-Ḍuḥā* (The Bright Morning Hours) – 11 verses	الضحى	1093
94	*Ash-Sharḥ* (The Opening-Up of the Heart) – 8 verses	الشرح	1095
95	*At-Tīn* (The Fig) – 8 verses	التين	1096
96	*Al-ᶜAlaq* (The Germ-Cell) – 19 verses	العلق	1098
97	*Al-Qadr* (Destiny) – 5 verses	القدر	1101
98	*Al-Bayyinah* (The Evidence of the Truth) – 8 verses	البينة	1102
99	*Az-Zalzalah* (The Earthquake) – 8 verses	الزلزلة	1104
100	*Al-ᶜĀdiyāt* (The Chargers) – 11 verses	العاديات	1105

SŪRAH

101	*Al-Qāriʿah* (The Sudden Calamity) – 11 verses	القارعة	1107
102	*At-Takāthur* (Greed for More and More) – 8 verses	التكاثر	1108
103	*Al-ʿAṣr* (The Flight of Time) – 3 verses	العصر	1111
104	*Al-Humazah* (The Slanderer) – 9 verses	الهمزة	1112
105	*Al-Fīl* (The Elephant) – 5 verses	الفيل	1114
106	*Quraysh* – 4 verses	قريش	1116
107	*Al-Māʿūn* (Assistance) – 7 verses	الماعون	1118
108	*Al-Kawthar* (Good in Abundance) – 3 verses	الكوثر	1119
109	*Al-Kāfirūn* (Those Who Deny the Truth) – 6 verses	الكافرون	1120
110	*An-Naṣr* (Succour) – 3 verses	النصر	1121
111	*Al-Masad* (The Twisted Strands) – 5 verses	المسد	1122
112	*Al-ʾIkhlāṣ* (The Declaration of [God's] Perfection) – 4 verses	الإخلاص	1124
113	*Al-Falaq* (The Rising Dawn) – 5 verses	الفلق	1125
114	*An-Nās* (Men) – 6 verses	الناس	1127

Appendices:

I	Symbolism and Allegory in the Qurʾān	1129
II	*Al-Muqaṭṭaʿāt*	1133
III	On the Term and Concept of *Jinn*	1135
IV	The Night Journey	1137

Index:

General Index 1141

بِسْمِ ٱللَّهِ ٱلرَّحْمَٰنِ ٱلرَّحِيمِ

Prologue

It is axiomatic from the Islamic perspective that the Qurʾān cannot be translated, because the *form* of God's revelation, that is the Arabic itself, is not merely incidental to its meaning, but essential to it. The Arabic of the Qurʾān does not, however, limit the Qurʾān to one "literal" interpretation, but by virtue of the power of its vocabulary allows for a depth of meaning that would be lost in any translation. A rendering into another language, therefore, is not and never can be the Qurʾān as such, but merely an interpretation of it.

There are a number of reasons for this, not least the nature of the Arabic language in which almost every word is derived from a root of three (rarely four) consonants. This root has a great number of branches but its basic meaning penetrates all of them although the derivatives may often appear to have quite different and even contrary meanings. There is a subtle inter-relationship between all of them so that each individual word has resonances which enrich it for the Arabic speaker as though, when one string is plucked, many others vibrate in unison. These are lost beyond recovery in translation and can only be recovered by the inclusion of extensive notes. We might take as an example one of the "Ninety-nine Names of God" through which the Qurʾān delineates the qualities of the Divine and the relationship which the Creator has with His creation.

The Name in question is *aṣ-Ṣamad*. The standard Saudi version (produced by a committee) gives "the Eternal, Absolute", while Picthall suggests "The eternally besought of all" and Arberry gives "The Everlasting Refuge"; Muhammad Ali has "He on Whom all Depend", Majid Fakhry in "*The Quran, a Modern English Version*" favours "The Everlasting", while Abdalḥaqq and Aisha Bewley have "The Everlasting Sustainer of all". Finally there is Muhammad Asad with "The Uncaused Cause of all Being", but he warns in a note that "this rendering gives no more than an approximate meaning of the term *aṣ-Ṣamad*" and explains that "it comprises the concepts of Primary Cause, and eternal independent Being combined with the idea that everything existing or conceivable goes back to Him as its source . . ." It is not difficult to see why, for many who seek to understand the Qurʾān in depth, Asad's "translation" is the more helpful.

There is, however, an even more important reason for insisting that the Qurʾān, which specifically defines itself as "an Arabic recitation", is no longer the Qurʾān when it is "translated". The divine Word is embodied in the language of the text, a language which the Muslim believes was chosen by God as the most suitable vehicle for His message of mercy, inspiration and guidance. The calligraphy, though it varies from one part of the Islamic world to another, is part of the message, a major art form in itself, and to copy it by hand is a form of prayer. This is equally true of the sound. The majority of Muslims do not understand Arabic, though all will have learned a number of verses for purposes of prayer, but the very sound of the Qurʾān when it is recited moves them, often to tears, by its majestic beauty as though they were privileged to hear God speaking directly to them. The fact that they may not be consciously aware of the meaning of what is recited becomes irrelevant. Music is music and communicates what it communicates. The very idea of the Creator communicating with His creatures, trapped as they are in the non-eternal, or of the Absolute communicating with the relative seems rationally impossible. The fact that this has happened is therefore a miracle and is perceived by Muslims as such.

The Qurʾān is to be studied and understood as a whole, one might almost say an organic whole, not as a collection of separate sections and verses. This is why some theologians have held the view that the Book descended into the substance – today one might speak of the "unconscious" – of the Messenger of God in a single moment on the "Night of Power" like a lightning flash, becoming articulate over the course of 23 years when and as required by circumstances. This might suggest that the revelation was dependent on passing events, but that would contradict the unitarian perspective of Islam. Events occur as willed by God, and the connection between inward and outward is seamless. Modern thought functions by separating, Islamic thought by uniting, and there is a perfect match between revelation and destiny; in other words these events occurred so that the verses which they provoked might emerge at a particular moment. Time, from beginning to end, is but a single moment in the divine knowledge and there is no discontinuity in that knowledge.

The revelation, however, is not seen as an incursion of something foreign and entirely unfamiliar into human awareness. The Qurʾān came as a "reminder" of truths inherent at the deepest level of our being but forgotten since man is, by definition, forgetful and drifts away from the Truth implanted in him unless he is constantly reminded. Islam does not claim to be a "new" religion, on the contrary it presents itself as a restoration or re-statement of the *Din-ul-Fitrah*, the perennial religion of mankind, so we read in the Qurʾān that Adam, after the fall from Paradise, received from his Lord "words [of revelation], and his Lord relented toward him, for He is the Relenting, the Merciful". This passage continues: "We said, 'Go down from hence, but truly there comes to you from Me a guidance, and whosoever follows My guidance, no fear shall come upon them neither shall they grieve'".

For the believer, the encounter with the Qurʾān is an act of recognition: *Hadhā huwa*, "That's it!" In the Christian tradition it has been said that "the truth is native to man" however deeply it may have been overlaid by debris, by falsehood and illusion. According to Islamic doctrine such "reminders" have been sent repeatedly to humanity since the beginning of the human story although these previous revelations have either been forgotten or falsified in the course of time. This explains the determination of Muslims to hold fast to the Qurʾān in its integrity and to allow no innovations to corrupt that integrity.

Muslims are often asked why they refuse to adapt their scripture to the "needs of the modern age". The Qurʾān itself answers this question: "There is no changing the words of God". The fact that it was sent down in the seventh century of the Christian era is irrelevant. You do not wear out a diamond by constant handling and the passage of the centuries cannot erode the words of God. That, after all, is the whole point of a divine intervention in the affairs of the world. The act – the revelation – is necessarily located in a particular period of time but it is, in itself, timeless, and Islamic theology defines the essence of the Qurʾān as "uncreated", therefore eternal.

Western (Christian or post-Christian) incomprehension of the Qur'ān has been exacerbated by attempts to compare it with the Bible. The two scriptures are of a totally different nature and comparisons are therefore fruitless. The Qur'ān, as we have seen, is a single revelation which descended upon Muhammad, either instantly or over a very brief period, transforming the hearts of a large sector of humanity and creating a worldwide civilisation The Bible, on the other hand, is a collection of writings relating to very different levels of inspiration. The Gospels themselves do not, as Muslims see the matter, have the character of direct revelation which is accorded to the Qur'ān. They are comparable to the *hadith* literature which records the reported sayings of Muhammad, both spiritual and practical, and here is a key to the very notion of revelation in the two religions. For Christians the divine Word became incarnate in the person of Jesus whereas, for Islam, the Word became "inlibrate"; it entered the world as a Book or, to be more precise, as a Recitation recorded in a script which some have compared with the physical body of Jesus. It follows therefore that the Westerner, including the new "convert" to Islam, has to put aside preconceived notions in approaching the Qur'ān (particularly if he or she was raised on the Bible) and set foot in an unfamiliar landscape.

The Book is indeed comparable to a landscape. For the Muslim there are in truth two divine revelations. There is the Qur'ān and there is the Book of Nature replete with "signs" which point back to the source of all life and being. The Arabic term for these "signs", *ayat*, is the same as the term used for the Qur'ānic verses. The revealed text is a tissue of "signs", and they are equally present everywhere in creation; in the forests, the mountains, the ocean, the lakes and the rivers, as also in the wind, in the rain which descends upon us, in the storms which refresh the earth, in the lighting flash and in the sun and the moon. Nature implicitly obeys the commands of its Creator. Man alone has the freedom to wander away in blind disobedience. Whether we understand them or not these precious "signs" are reminders for those prepared to be reminded and a cure for the blindness which afflicts the "deniers".

The messages contained in the two complementary books are clothed in beauty. Muhammad is reported to have said in one of his divinely inspired statements that "God is beautiful and He loves beauty". It might be said that beauty was the presiding principle of traditional Islamic civilisation at its height, starting with the beauty of the Qur'ān itself. The Qur'ān's beauty is not intrinsic to itself, but becomes a mode of aesthetic expression through the arts of calligraphy and recitation. In Arabic the word for "beautiful" is the same as the word for "good" and this is clearly of the greatest significance. A good character is by its very nature a beautiful character, a good action has its own beauty, and this is true also of the human environment – the mosque, the city, the home – which cannot be described as good unless it is also beautiful. The ugliness of the modern Western environment, now spreading throughout the world, afflicts the soul of the Muslim even when he or she is unaware of its pernicious influence and, in effect, makes it more difficult to be good and to remember the divine Presence which is perceptible in all that it beautiful but concealed in ugliness.

This brings us back to the impossibility of translating the Qur'ān. In "The Koran Interpreted" Arthur Arberry, a noted Arabist, attempted at least to reproduce the rhythms of the original in English but with little success. The structure of the two languages is too different for this to be possible and there is always the danger that those who aim to honour the original by adopting poetic language in their "translation" will fall short of conveying the meaning in so far as it can be conveyed without extensive notes. This is where Muhammad Asad triumphs. The title of his rendition is "The Meaning of the Qur'ān" and that is precisely what it offers. Moreover his explanatory notes are, to a large extent, based on the great commentaries written by some of the wisest Islamic scholars over the centuries. These commentaries are inaccessible to those who do not have Arabic, and even Arabic speakers have difficulty with them, but they are essential for a full understanding of the text. A "translation" without explanatory notes is inevitably open to misunderstanding or misuse. It is said that a group of young converts to Islam in America who had decided to rob a bank set themselves to find, in an English text, a Qur'ānic verse that would justify their action. No doubt they found one. The story may be apocryphal, but it makes a point.

Asad has been criticised for occasionally employing terms which differ from those in common use when translating a key word in the text, but he always has a note to explain his reasons. A particular example of this occurs in the first line of the opening chapter of the Qur'ān. *Ar-Raḥmān* is the most important and the most significant of the "Names of God". It is usually given as "The Merciful" or the "All-Merciful". Asad prefers "The Most Gracious". The term *raḥmah* from which it is derived, as is the accompanying Name, *ar-Raḥīm*, signifies, he explains, "mercy, compassion, loving tenderness and, more comprehensively, grace. From the very earliest times, Islamic scholars have endeavoured to define the exact shades of meaning which differentiate the two terms. The best and simplest of these explanations is undoubtedly the one advanced by Ibn al-Qayyim; "the term *raḥmān* circumscribes the quality of abounding grace inherent in, and inseparable from, the concept of God's Being, whereas *raḥīm* expresses the manifestation of that grace, . . . an aspect of His activity".

When powerful emotions come into play, as they are bound to do in the religious sphere, disputes are likely to arise and, with so much at stake, these may be bitter, but Asad's critics must be asked if they could do any better. So far no one has succeeded – or come closer to succeeding – in conveying the meaning of the Qur'ān to readers who do not have access to the Arabic text, that is to say to the Qur'ān as such, or to the classical commentaries. If one had to find terms to define the principal virtue of this great work we might say that it combines good sense with meticulous precision. There exists no more useful guide to the Qur'ān in the English language and, after a period of many years during which it was difficult to obtain, this new edition at last makes it readily accessible at the very time when its value is becoming widely and deservedly appreciated.

*

MUHAMMAD ASAD was born Leopold Weiss in Lwow (now in Western Ukraine, but at that time part of the Austrian Empire) in 1900, the grandson of an Orthodox Rabbi. After service in the Austrian army he joined the United Telegraph news agency at the early age of 21, leaving it soon afterwards to travel in the Middle East. He was appointed special correspondent of the *Frankfurter Zeitung*, edited by a relative, and he took advantage of the opportunity to study Arabic at al-Azhar University in Cairo. He converted to Islam in 1926 and, for six formative years, he travelled the length and breadth of Arabia with the Bedouin. This experience had an unforeseen consequence. Many words which occur in the Qur'ān had fallen out of common usage and were unfamiliar to scholars but still used, as they had been in the time of the Prophet, by bedouin tribes. He became the close friend of King Abdul Azīz (Ibn Saud), a friendship which, as he wrote many years later, "has lain like a warm shimmer over my life".

Later, in British India, he formed a close friendship with the poet Iqbal, the "spiritual father" of what was to be Pakistan and, after independence, he was appointed the country's Minister

Plenipotentiary to the newly created United Nations, an extraordinary tribute to a European of Jewish origin whose conversion to Islam had been, he said, "a conscious, whole-hearted transference of allegiance from one cultural environment to another". The autobiography which he wrote at this time or soon afterwards, *The Road to Mecca,* still in print after so many years, has had a remarkable and enduring influence. On the surface a simple and often touching story of his early life and his adventures in Arabia, the book presents a vision of Islam which has drawn a number of Europeans and Americans to the Faith.

Subsequently he lived in Morocco for 19 years with his third wife and there he began his great work though finding time to write "The Principles of State and Government in Islam" which many Muslims still regard as the most authoritative work on the political dimension of Islam. His influence, especially in Pakistan, was widespread, not least his advocacy of the rights of women, but his opinions often aroused opposition, particularly those expressed in his notes to "The Meaning of the Qurʾān". His views concerning "Islamic punishments" appealed to many Muslims who were uneasy about the application of punishments such as amputation for theft in societies which fall far short of the Islamic ideal which is primarily concerned with mercy, social justice, equity and the relief of poverty, but these views enraged others. The great mistake of those who dream of creating a truly Islamic State based on *Shariʿah,* he pointed out, "is that most of these leaders start with the *hudud* punishment. This is the end result [of Islamic law], not the beginning. The beginning is the rights of people. There is no punishment in Islam which has no corresponding right". The hostility of what are commonly described as "Fundamentalists" cast a shadow over his later years and led to his self-imposed "exile" from the Muslim world. He died in Spain at the age of 92 and his interpretation of the Qurʾān was neglected for some years until Muslims of very different persuasions came to recognise it as an unrivalled aid to the understanding of the Faith.

Hasan Gai Eaton
London
Spring 2003

بسم الله الرحمن الرحيم

Foreword

> ***READ in the name of thy Sustainer, who has created – created man out of a germ-cell!***
> ***Read – for thy Sustainer is the Most Bountiful One who has taught [man] the use of the pen – taught man what he did not know.***

With these opening verses of the ninety-sixth *sūrah* – with an allusion to man's humble biological origin as well as to his consciousness and intellect – began, early in the seventh century of the Christian era, the revelation of the Qurʾān to the Prophet Muḥammad, destined to continue during the twenty-three years of his ministry and to end, shortly before his death, with verse 281 of the second *sūrah*:

> ***And be conscious of the Day on which you shall be brought back unto God, whereupon every human being shall be repaid in full for what he has earned, and none shall be wronged.***

Between these first and last verses (the first and the last in the chronological order of their revelation)[1] unfolds a book which, more than any other single phenomenon known to us, has fundamentally affected the religious, social and political history of the world. No other sacred scripture has ever had a similarly immediate impact upon the lives of the people who first heard its message and, through them and the generations that followed them, on the entire course of civilization. It shook Arabia, and made a nation out of its perennially warring tribes; within a few decades, it spread its world-view far beyond the confines of Arabia and produced the first ideological society known to man; through its insistence on consciousness and knowledge, it engendered among its followers a spirit of intellectual curiosity and independent inquiry, ultimately resulting in that splendid era of learning and scientific research which distinguished the world of Islam at the height of its cultural vigour; and the culture thus fostered by the Qurʾān penetrated in countless ways and by-ways into the mind of medieval Europe and gave rise to that revival of Western culture which we call the Renaissance, and thus became in the course of time largely responsible for the birth of what is described as the "age of science": the age in which we are now living.

All this was, in the final analysis, brought about by the message of the Qurʾān: and it was brought about through the medium of the people whom it inspired and to whom it supplied a basis for all their ethical valuations and a direction for all their worldly endeavours: for, never has any book – not excluding the Bible – been read by so many with a comparable intensity and ven-

---

1 It is to be borne in mind that, in its final compilation, the Qurʾān is arranged in accordance with the inner requirements of its message as a whole, and not in the chronological order in which the individual *sūrahs* or passages were revealed.

eration; and never has any other book supplied to so many, and over so long a span of time, a similarly comprehensive answer to the question, "How shall I behave in order to achieve the good life in this world and happiness in the life to come?" However often individual Muslims may have misread this answer, and however far many of them may have departed from the spirit of its message, the fact remains that to all who believed and believe in it, the Qur'ān represents the ultimate manifestation of God's grace to man, the ultimate wisdom, and the ultimate beauty of expression: in short, the true Word of God.

This attitude of the Muslims towards the Qur'ān perplexes, as a rule, the Westerner who approaches it through one or another of the many existing translations. Where the believer, reading the Qur'ān in Arabic, sees beauty, the non-Muslim reader often claims to discern "crudeness"; the coherence of the Qur'ānic world-view and its relevance to the human condition escape him altogether and assume the guise of what, in Europe's and America's orientalist literature, is frequently described as "incoherent rambling";[2] and passages which, to a Muslim, are expressive of sublime wisdom, often sound "flat" and "uninspiring" to the Western ear. And yet, not even the most unfriendly critics of the Qur'ān have ever denied that it did, in fact, provide the supreme source of inspiration – in both the religious and cultural senses of this word – to innumerable millions of people who, in their aggregate, have made an outstanding contribution to man's knowledge, civilization and social achievement. How can this paradox be explained?

It cannot be explained by the too-facile argument, so readily accepted by many modern Muslims, that the Qur'ān has been "deliberately misrepresented" by its Western translators. For, although it cannot be denied that among the existing translations in almost all of the major European languages there is many a one that has been inspired by malicious prejudice and – especially in earlier times – by misguided "missionary" zeal, there is hardly any doubt that some of the more recent translations are the work of earnest scholars who, without being actuated by any conscious bias, have honestly endeavoured to render the meaning of the Arabic original into this or that European language; and, in addition, there exist a number of modern translations by Muslims who, by virtue of their being Muslims, cannot by any stretch of the imagination be supposed to have "misrepresented" what, to them, was a sacred revelation. Still, none of these translations – whether done by Muslims or by non-Muslims – has so far brought the Qur'ān nearer to the hearts or minds of people raised in a different religious and psychological climate and revealed something, however little, of its real depth and wisdom. To some extent this may be due to the conscious and unconscious prejudice against Islam which has pervaded Western cultural notions ever since the time of the Crusades – an intangible heritage of thought and feeling which has left its mark on the attitude towards all things Islamic on the part not only of the Western "man in the street" but also, in a more subtle manner, on the part of scholars bent on objective research. But even this psychological factor does not sufficiently explain the complete lack of appreciation of the Qur'ān in the Western world, and this in spite of its undeniable and ever-increasing interest in all that concerns the world of Islam.

---

2 Thus, for instance, Western critics of the Qur'ān frequently point to the allegedly "incoherent" references to God – often in one and the same phrase – as "He", "God", "We" or "I", with the corresponding changes of the pronoun from "His" to "Ours" or "My", or from "Him" to "Us" or "Me". They seem to be unaware of the fact that these changes are not accidental, and not even what one might describe as "poetic licence", but are obviously *deliberate*: a linguistic device meant to stress the idea that God is not a "person" and cannot, therefore, be really circumscribed by the pronouns applicable to finite beings.

It is more than probable that one of the main reasons for this lack of appreciation is to be found in that aspect of the Qur᾽ān which differentiates it fundamentally from all other sacred scriptures: its stress on *reason* as a valid way to faith as well as its insistence on the inseparability of the spiritual and the physical (and, therefore, also social) spheres of human existence: the inseparability of man's daily actions and behaviour, however "mundane", from his spiritual life and destiny. This absence of any division of reality into "physical" and "spiritual" compartments makes it difficult for people brought up in the orbit of other religions, with their accent on the "supernatural" element allegedly inherent in every true religious experience, to appreciate the predominantly rational approach of the Qur᾽ān to all religious questions. Consequently, its constant interweaving of spiritual teachings with practical legislation perplexes the Western reader, who has become accustomed to identifying "religious experience" with a thrill of numinous awe before things hidden and beyond all intellectual comprehension, and is suddenly confronted with the claim of the Qur᾽ān to being a guidance not only towards the spiritual good of the hereafter but also towards the good life – spiritual, physical and social – attainable in this world. In short, the Westerner cannot readily accept the Qur᾽anic thesis that all life, being God-given, is a unity, and that problems of the flesh and of the mind, of sex and economics, of individual righteousness and social equity are intimately connected with the hopes which man may legitimately entertain with regard to his life after death. This, in my opinion, is one of the reasons for the negative, uncomprehending attitude of most Westerners towards the Qur᾽ān and its teachings. But still another – and perhaps even more decisive – reason may be found in the fact that *the Qur᾽ān itself has never yet been presented in any European language in a manner which would make it truly comprehensible.*

When we look at the long list of translations – beginning with the Latin works of the high Middle Ages and continuing up to the present in almost every European tongue – we find one common denominator between their authors, whether Muslims or non-Muslims: all of them were – or are – people who acquired their knowledge of Arabic through academic study alone: that is, from books. None of them, however great his scholarship, has ever been familiar with the Arabic language as a person is familiar with his own, having absorbed the nuances of its idiom and its phraseology with an active, associative response within himself, and hearing it with an ear spontaneously attuned to the *intent* underlying the acoustic symbolism of its words and sentences. For, the words and sentences of a language – any language – are but symbols for meanings conventionally, and subconsciously, agreed upon by those who express their perception of reality by means of that particular tongue. Unless the translator is able to reproduce within himself the conceptual symbolism of the language in question – that is, unless he hears it "sing" in his ear in all its naturalness and immediacy – his translation will convey no more than the outer shell of the literary matter to which his work is devoted, and will miss, to a higher or lesser degree, the inner meaning of the original: and the greater the depth of the original, the farther must such a translation deviate from its spirit.

No doubt, some of the translators of the Qur᾽ān whose works are accessible to the Western public can be described as outstanding scholars in the sense of having mastered the Arabic grammar and achieved a considerable knowledge of Arabic literature; but this mastery of grammar and this acquaintance with literature cannot by itself, in the case of a translation from Arabic (and especially the Arabic of the Qur᾽ān), render the translator independent of that intangible communion with the spirit of the language which can be achieved only by living with and in it.

Arabic is a Semitic tongue: in fact, it is the only Semitic tongue which has remained uninterruptedly alive for thousands of years; and it is the only living language which has remained entirely unchanged for the last fourteen centuries. These two factors are extremely relevant to the problem which we are considering. Since every language is a framework of symbols expressing its people's particular sense of life-values and their particular way of conveying their perception of reality, it is obvious that the language of the Arabs – a Semitic language which has remained unchanged for so many centuries – must differ widely from anything to which the Western mind is accustomed. The difference of the Arabic idiom from any European idiom is not merely a matter of its syntactic cast and the mode in which it conveys ideas; nor is it exclusively due to the well-known, extreme flexibility of the Arabic grammar arising from its peculiar system of verbal "roots" and the numerous stem-forms which can be derived from these roots; nor even to the extraordinary richness of the Arabic vocabulary: it is a difference of spirit and life-sense. And since the Arabic of the Qur᾽ān is a language which attained to its full maturity in the Arabia of fourteen centuries ago, it follows that in order to grasp its spirit correctly, one must be able to feel and hear this language as the Arabs felt and heard it at the time when the Qur᾽ān was being revealed, and to understand the meaning which *they* gave to the linguistic symbols in which it is expressed.

We Muslims believe that the Qur᾽ān is the Word of God, revealed to the Prophet Muḥammad through the medium of a human language. It was the language of the Arabian Peninsula: the language of a people endowed with that peculiar quick-wittedness which the desert and its feel of wide, timeless expanses bestows upon its children: the language of people whose mental images, flowing without effort from association to association, succeed one another in rapid progression and often vault elliptically over intermediate – as it were, "self-understood" – sequences of thought towards the idea which they aim to conceive or express. This ellipticism (called *ījāz* by the Arab philologists) is an integral characteristic of the Arabic idiom and, therefore, of the language of the Qur᾽ān – so much so that it is impossible to understand its method and inner purport without being able to reproduce within oneself, instinctively, something of the same quality of elliptical, associative thought. Now this ability comes to the educated Arab almost automatically, by a process of mental osmosis, from his early childhood: for, when he learns to speak his tongue properly, he subconsciously acquires the mould of thought within which it has evolved and, thus, imperceptibly grows into the conceptual environment from which the Arabic language derives its peculiar form and mode of expression. Not so, however, the non-Arab who becomes acquainted with Arabic only at a mature age, in result of a conscious effort, that is, through study: for, what he acquires is but a ready-made, outward structure devoid of that intangible quality of ellipticism which gives to the Arabic idiom its inner life and reality.

This does not, however, mean that a non-Arab can never understand Arabic in its true spirit: it means no more and no less than that he cannot really master it through academic study alone, but needs, in addition to philological learning, an instinctive "feel" of the language. Now it so happens that such a "feel" cannot be achieved by merely living among the modern Arabs of the cities. Although many of them, especially the educated ones, may have subconsciously absorbed the spirit of their language, they can only rarely communicate it to an outsider – for the simple reason that, however high their linguistic education, their daily speech has become, in the course of centuries, largely corrupted and estranged from pristine Arabic. Thus, in order to obtain the requisite "feel" of the Arabic language, a non-Arab must have lived in long and intimate association with people whose daily speech mirrors the genuine spirit of their language, and whose mental processes are similar to those of the Arabs who lived at the time when the Arabic tongue received its final colouring and inner form. In our day, such people are only the bedouin of the Arabian Peninsula, and particularly those of Central and Eastern Arabia. For, notwith- standing the many dialectical peculiarities in which their speech may differ from the classical Arabic of the Qur'ān, it has remained – so far – very close to the idiom of the Prophet's time and has preserved all its intrinsic characteristics.[3] In other words, familiarity with the bedouin speech of Central and Eastern Arabia – in addition, of course, to academic knowledge of classical Arabic – is the only way for a non-Arab of our time to achieve an intimate understanding of the diction of the Qur'ān. And because none of the scholars who have previously translated the Qur'ān into European languages has ever fulfilled this prerequisite, their translations have remained but distant, and faulty, echoes of its meaning and spirit.

*

THE WORK which I am now placing before the public is based on a lifetime of study and of many years spent in Arabia. It is an attempt – perhaps the first attempt – at a really idiomatic, explanatory rendition of the Qur'anic message into a European language.

None the less, I do not claim to have "translated" the Qur'ān in the sense in which, say, Plato or Shakespeare can be translated. Unlike any other book, its meaning and its linguistic presentation form one unbreakable whole. The position of individual words in a sentence, the rhythm and sound of its phrases and their syntactic construction, the manner in which a metaphor flows almost imperceptibly into a pragmatic statement, the use of acoustic stress not merely in the service of rhetoric but as a means of alluding to unspoken but clearly implied ideas: all this makes the Qur'ān, in the last resort, unique and untranslatable – a fact that has been pointed out by many earlier translators and by all Arab scholars. But although it is impossible to "reproduce" the Qur'ān as such in any other language, it is none the less possible to render its message comprehensible to people who, like most Westerners, do not know Arabic at all or – as is the case with most of the educated non-Arab Muslims – not well enough to find their way through it unaided.

To this end, the translator must be guided throughout by the linguistic usage prevalent at the time of the revelation of the Qur'ān, and must always bear in mind that some of its expressions – especially such as relate to abstract concepts – have in the course of time undergone a subtle change in the popular mind and should not, therefore, be translated in accordance with the sense given to them by post-classical usage. As has been pointed out by that great Islamic scholar, Muḥammad ʿAbduh,[4] even some of the renowned, otherwise linguistically reliable Qur'ān-

3 It is to be noted that under the impact of modern economic circumstances, which radically changed the time-honoured way of life of the bedouin and brought them, by means of school education and the radio, into direct contact with the Levantine culture of the cities, the purity of their language is rapidly disappearing and may soon cease to be a living guide to students of the Arabic tongue.

4 The reader will find in my explanatory notes frequent references to views held by Muḥammad ʿAbduh (1849-1905). His importance in the context of the modern world of Islam can never be sufficiently stressed. It may be stated without exaggeration that every single trend in contemporary Islamic thought can be traced back to the influence, direct or indirect, of this most outstanding of all modern Islamic thinkers. The Qur'ān-commentary planned and begun by him was interrupted by his death in 1905; it was continued (but unfortunately also left incomplete) by his pupil Rashīd Riḍā' under the title *Tafsīr al-Manār*, and has been extensively used by me. See also Rashīd Riḍā', *Ta'rīkh al-Ustādh al-Imām ash-Shaykh Muḥammad ʿAbduh* (Cairo 1350-1367 H.), the most authoritative biography of ʿAbduh hitherto published, as well as C. C. Adams, *Islam and Modernism in Egypt* (London 1933).

commentators have occasionally erred in this respect; and their errors, magnified by the inadequacy of modern translators, have led to many a distortion, and sometimes to a total incomprehensibility, of individual Qurʾanic passages in their European renditions.

Another (and no less important) point which the translator must take fully into account is the *ījāz* of the Qurʾān: that inimitable ellipticism which often deliberately omits intermediate thought-clauses in order to express the final stage of an idea as pithily and concisely as is possible within the limitations of a human language. This method of *ījāz* is, as I have explained, a peculiar, integral aspect of the Arabic language, and has reached its utmost perfection in the Qurʾān. In order to render its meaning into a language which does not function in a similarly elliptical manner, the thought-links which are missing – that is, *deliberately omitted* – in the original must be supplied by the translator in the form of frequent interpolations between brackets; for, unless this is done, the Arabic phrase concerned loses all its life in the translation and often becomes a meaningless jumble.

Furthermore, one must beware of rendering, in each and every case, the religious terms used in the Qurʾān in the sense which they have acquired after Islam had become "institutionalized" into a definite set of laws, tenets and practices. However legitimate this "institutionalization" may be in the context of Islamic religious history, it is obvious that the Qurʾān cannot be correctly understood if we read it merely in the light of later ideological developments, losing sight of its original purport and the meaning which it had – and was intended to have – for the people who first heard it from the lips of the Prophet himself. For instance, when his contemporaries heard the words *islām* and *muslim*, they understood them as denoting man's "self-surrender to God" and "one who surrenders himself to God", without limiting these terms to any specific community or denomination – e.g., in 3 : 67, where Abraham is spoken of as having "surrendered himself unto God" (*kāna musliman*), or in 3 : 52, where the disciples of Jesus say, "Bear thou witness that we have surrendered ourselves unto God (*bi-annā muslimūn*)". In Arabic, this original meaning has remained unimpaired, and no Arab scholar has ever become oblivious of the wide connotation of these terms. Not so, however, the non-Arab of our day, believer and non-believer alike: to him, *islām* and *muslim* usually bear a restricted, historically circumscribed significance, and apply exclusively to the followers of the Prophet Muḥammad. Similarly, the terms *kufr* ("denial of the truth") and *kāfir* ("one who denies the truth") have become, in the conventional translations of the Qurʾān, unwarrantably simplified into "unbelief" and "unbeliever" or "infidel", respectively, and have thus been deprived of the wide spiritual meaning which the Qurʾān gives to these terms. Another example is to be found in the conventional rendering of the word *kitāb*, when applied to the Qurʾān, as "book": for, when the Qurʾān was being revealed (and we must not forget that this process took twenty-three years), those who listened to its recitation did not conceive of it as a "book" – since it was compiled into one only some decades after the Prophet's death – but rather, in view of the derivation of the noun *kitāb* from the verb *kataba* ("he wrote" or, tropically, "he ordained"), as a "divine writ" or a "revelation". The same holds true with regard to the Qurʾanic use of this term in its connotation of earlier revealed scriptures: for the Qurʾān often stresses the fact that those earlier instances of divine writ have largely been corrupted in the course of time, and that the extant holy "books" do not really represent the original revelations. Consequently, the translation of *ahl al-kitāb* as "people of the book" is not very meaningful; in my opinion, the term should be rendered as "followers of earlier revelation".

In short, if it is to be truly comprehensible in another language, the message of the Qur'ān must be rendered in such a way as to reproduce, as closely as possible, the sense which it had for the people who were as yet unburdened by the conceptual images of later Islamic developments: and this has been the overriding principle which has guided me throughout my work.

With the exception of two terms, I have endeavoured to circumscribe every Qur'anic concept in appropriate English expressions – an endeavour which has sometimes necessitated the use of whole sentences to convey the meaning of a single Arabic word. The two exceptions from this rule are the terms *al-qur'ān* and *sūrah*, since neither of the two has ever been used in Arabic to denote anything but the title of this particular divine writ and each of its sections or "chapters", respectively: with the result that it would have been of no benefit whatsoever to the reader to be presented with "translations" of these two terms.[5]

Apart from these linguistic considerations, I have tried to observe consistently two fundamental rules of interpretation.

Firstly, the Qur'ān must not be viewed as a compilation of individual injunctions and exhortations but as *one integral whole*: that is, as an exposition of an ethical doctrine in which every verse and sentence has an intimate bearing on other verses and sentences, all of them clarifying and amplifying one another. Consequently, its real meaning can be grasped only if we correlate every one of its statements with what has been stated elsewhere in its pages, and try to explain its ideas by means of frequent cross-references, always subordinating the particular to the general and the incidental to the intrinsic. Whenever this rule is faithfully followed, we realize that the Qur'ān is – in the words of Muḥammad ʿAbduh – "its own best commentary".

Secondly, no part of the Qur'ān should be viewed from a purely *historical* point of view: that is to say, all its references to historical circumstances and events – both at the time of the Prophet and in earlier times – must be regarded as illustrations of the *human condition* and not as ends in themselves. Hence, the consideration of the historical occasion on which a particular verse was revealed – a pursuit so dear, and legitimately so, to the hearts of the classical commentators – must never be allowed to obscure the underlying *purport* of that verse and its inner relevance to the ethical teaching which the Qur'ān, taken as a whole, propounds.

In order to bring out, to the best of my ability, the many facets of the Qur'anic message, I have found it necessary to add to my translation a considerable number of explanatory notes. Certain observations relating to the symbolism of the Qur'ān as well as to its eschatology are separately dealt with in Appendix I at the end of this work. In both the notes and the appendices I have tried no more than to elucidate the message of the Qur'ān and have, to this end, drawn amply on the works of the great Arab philologists and of the classical commentators. If, on occasion, I have found myself constrained to differ from the interpretations offered by the latter, let the reader remember that the very uniqueness of the Qur'ān consists in the fact that the more our worldly knowledge and historical experience increase, the more meanings, hitherto unsuspected, reveal themselves in its pages.

---

5 Etymologically, the word *al-qur'ān* is derived from the verb *qara'a* ("he read" or "recited"), and is to be understood as "the reading [*par excellence*]", while the noun *sūrah* might be rendered as "a step [leading to another step]" and – tropically – as "eminence in degree" (cf. Lane IV, 1465). It should be noted, however, that when the noun *qur'ān* appears without the definite article *al*, it usually has its primary meaning of "recitation" or "discourse", and may be rendered accordingly.

The great thinkers of our past understood this problem fully well. In their commentaries, they approached the Qur'ān with their *reason*: that is to say, they tried to explain the purport of each Qur'ānic statement in the light of their superb knowledge of the Arabic language and of the Prophet's teachings – forthcoming from his *sunnah* – as well as by the store of general knowledge available to them and by the historical and cultural experiences which had shaped human society until their time. Hence, it was only natural that the way in which one commentator understood a particular Qur'anic statement or expression differed occasionally – and sometimes very incisively – from the meaning attributed to it by this or that of his predecessors. In other words, they often contradicted one another in their interpretations: but they did this without any animosity, being fully aware of the element of relativity inherent in all human reasoning, and of each other's integrity. And they were fully aware, too, of the Prophet's profound saying, "The differences of opinion (*ikhtilāf*) among the learned men of my community are [an outcome of] divine grace (*raḥmah*)" – which clearly implies that such differences of opinion are the basis of all progress in human thinking and, therefore, a most potent factor in man's acquisition of knowledge.

But although none of the truly original, classical Qur'ān-commentators ever made any claim to "finality" concerning his own interpretations, it cannot be often enough stressed that *without* the work of those incomparably great scholars of past centuries, no modern translation of the Qur'ān – my own included – could ever be undertaken with any hope of success; and so, even where I differ from their interpretations, I am immeasurably indebted to their learning for the impetus it has given to my own search after truth.

*

AS REGARDS the style of my translation, I have consciously avoided using unnecessary archaisms, which would only tend to obscure the meaning of the Qur'ān to the contemporary reader. On the other hand, I did not see any necessity of rendering the Qur'anic phrases into a deliberately "modern" idiom, which would conflict with the spirit of the Arabic original and jar upon any ear attuned to the solemnity inherent in the concept of revelation. With all this, however, I make no claim to having reproduced anything of the indescribable rhythm and rhetoric of the Qur'ān. No one who has truly experienced its majestic beauty could ever be presumptuous enough to make such a claim or even to embark upon such an attempt.

And I am fully aware that my rendering does not and could not really "do justice" to the Qur'ān and the layers upon layers of its meaning: for,

> *if all the sea were ink for my Sustainer's words, the sea would indeed be exhausted ere my Sustainer's words are exhausted.*
>
> (Qur'ān 18 : 109).

Muhammad Asad

Works of Reference

THIS WORK is based on the recension of Ḥafṣ ibn Sulaymān al-Asadī, as it appears in the so-called "Royal Egyptian" edition of the Qurʾān, first published in Cairo in 1337 H. and regarded by Arab scholars as the most exact of all existing editions.

When referring in the explanatory notes to a particular Qurʾanic passage, the number of the *sūrah* is followed by a colon and the verse-number: e.g. 3 : 28 signifies *sūrah* 3, verse 28; similarly, 6 : 138-140 and 142 stands for *sūrah* 6, verses 138-140 and verse 142. (It should be noted that in the translation the verse-numbers – corresponding to those of the Arabic text – have been placed within parentheses at the end of each verse, and not, as in the Cairo edition, at its beginning.)

Inasmuch as many of the works mentioned below – and referred to in the explanatory notes – have been published in several editions, no useful purpose would have been served by indicating the edition utilized by the translator. As for works which exist in single or easily identifiable editions, the place and date of publication have been stated below.

The explanations of the classical Qurʾān-commentators referred to in the notes will be found, unless otherwise indicated, in the context of the particular author's commentary on the Qurʾān-verse under consideration. References to dictionaries relate – unless otherwise indicated – to the article dealing with the root-form of the word concerned.

All references to the Bible relate to the Authorized King James Version.

ʾAbū Dāʾūd	ʾAbū Dāʾūd Sulaymān al-ʾAshʿath (d. 275 H.), *Kitāb as-Sunan.*
Asās	Maḥmūd ibn ʿUmar az-Zamakhsharī (d. 538 H.), *Asās al-Balāghah.*
Baghawī	Al-Ḥusayn ibn Masʿūd al-Farrāʾ al-Baghawī (d. 516 H.), *Maʿālim at-Tanzīl.*
Bayḍāwī	ʿAbd Allāh ibn ʿUmar al-Bayḍāwī (d. 685 or 691 H.), *Anwār at-Tanzīl wa-Asrār at-Taʾwīl.*
Bayhaqī	Abū Bakr ʾAḥmad ibn al-Ḥusayn al-Bayhaqī (d. 458 H.), *Kitāb as-Sunan al-Kubrā.*
Bidāyat al-Mujtahid	Muḥammad ibn ʾAḥmad ibn Rushd (d. 595 H.), *Bidāyat al-Mujtahid wa-Nihāyat al-Muqtaṣid*, Cairo n.d.
Bukhārī	Muḥammad ibn ʾIsmāʿīl al-Bukhārī (d. 256 H.), *Al-Jāmiʿ aṣ-Ṣaḥīḥ.*
Dārimī	Abū Muḥammad ʿAbd Allāh ad-Dārimī (d. 255 H.), *Kitāb as-Sunan.*
Dārquṭnī	ʿAli ibn ʿUmar ad-Dārquṭnī (d. 385 H.), *Kitāb as-Sunan.*
Encyclopaedia of Islam	(1st ed.) Leyden 1913-38.
Fāʾiq	Maḥmūd ibn ʿUmar az-Zamakhsharī (d. 538 H.), *Kitāb al-Fāʾiq fī Gharīb al-Ḥadīth*, Hyderabad 1324 H.
Fatḥ al-Bārī	ʾAḥmad ibn ʿAlī ibn Ḥajar al-ʿAsqalānī (d. 852 H.), *Fatḥ al-Bārī bi-Sharḥ Ṣaḥīḥ al-Bukhārī*, Cairo 1348 H.
Ḥākim	see *Mustadrak.*
Ibn Ḥanbal	ʾAḥmad ibn Muḥammad ibn Ḥanbal (d. 241 H.), *Al-Musnad.*
Ibn Ḥazm	see *Muḥallā.*
Ibn Ḥibbān	Muḥammad ibn ʾAḥmad ibn Ḥibbān (d. 354 H.), *Kitāb at-Taqāsīm wa'l-Anwāʿ.*
Ibn Ḥishām	ʿAbd al-Malik ibn Hishām (d. 243 H.), *Sīrat an-Nabī.*
Ibn Kathīr	Abu 'l-Fidāʾ ʾIsmāʿīl ibn Kathīr (d. 774 H.), *Tafsīr al-Qurʾān*, Cairo 1343-47 H.

Ibn Khallikān	Aḥmad ibn Ibrāhīm ibn Khallikān (d. 681 H.), *Wafāyāt al-Aʿyān wa-Anbāʾ Abnāʾ az -Zamān*, Cairo 1310 H.
Ibn Mājah	Muḥammad ibn Yazīd ibn Mājah al-Qazwīnī (d. 273 or 275 H.), *Kitāb as-Sunan.*
Ibn Qayyim	ʾAbū ʿAbd Allāh Muḥammad ibn Qayyim al-Jawziyyah (d. 751 H.), *Zād al-Maʿād fī Ḥajj Khayr al-ʿIbād*, Cairo 1347 H.
Ibn Saʿd	Muḥammad ibn Saʿd (d. 230 H.), *Kitāb aṭ-Ṭabaqāt al-Kabīr*, Leyden 1904-28.
Ibn Taymiyyah	Taqī ad-Dīn Aḥmad ibn Taymiyyah al-Ḥarrānī (d. 728 H.), *Tafsīr Sitt Suwar*, Bombay 1954.
Itqān	ʿAbd ar-Raḥmān Jalāl ad-Dīn as-Suyūṭī (d. 911 H.), *Al-Itqān fī ʿUlūm al-Qurʾān.*
Jawharī	ʾAbū Naṣr ʾIsmāʿīl ibn Ḥammād al-Jawharī (d. about 400 H.), *Tāj al-Lughah wa-Ṣiḥāḥ al-ʿArabiyyah*, Būlāq 1292 H.
Kashshāf	see Zamakhsharī.
Lane	William Edward Lane, *Arabic-English Lexicon*, London 1863-93.
Lisān al-ʿArab	ʾAbu 'l-Faḍl Muḥammad ibn Mukarram al-ʾIfrīqī (d. 711 H.), *Lisān al-ʿArab.*
Manār	Muḥammad Rashīd Riḍāʾ, *Tafsīr al-Qurʾān* (known as *Tafsīr al-Manār*), Cairo 1367-72 H.
Mufradāt	see Rāghib.
Mughnī	Jamāl ad-Dīn ʿAbd Allāh ibn Yūsuf al-Anṣārī (d. 761 H.), *Mughni 'l-Labīb ʿan Kutub al-Aʿārīb.*
Muḥallā	ʾAbū Muḥammad ʿAlī ibn Ḥazm (d. 456 H.), *Al-Muḥallā*, Cairo 1347-52 H.
Muslim	Muslim ibn al-Ḥajjāj an-Nīsābūrī (d. 261 H.), *Kitāb aṣ-Ṣaḥīḥ.*
Mustadrak	Muḥammad ibn ʿAbd Allāh al-Ḥākim (d. 405 H.), *Al-Mustadrak ʿala 'ṣ-Ṣaḥīḥayn fi 'l-Ḥadīth*, Hyderabad 1334-41 H.
Muwaṭṭaʾ	Mālik ibn Anas (d. 179 H.), *Al-Muwaṭṭaʾ.*
Nasāʾī	Aḥmad ibn Shuʿayb an-Nasāʾī (d. 303 H.), *Kitāb as-Sunan.*
Nayl al-Awṭār	Muḥammad ibn ʿAlī ash-Shawkānī (d. 1255 H.), *Nayl al-Awṭār Sharḥ Muntaqā al-Akhbār*, Cairo 1344 H.
Nihāyah	ʿAlī ibn Muḥammad ibn al-ʾAthīr (d. 630 H.), *An-Nihāyah fī Gharīb al-Ḥadīth.*
Qāmūs	ʾAbu 'ṭ-Ṭāhir Muḥammad ibn Yaʿqūb al-Fīrūzābādī (d. 817 H.), *Al-Qāmūs.*
Rāghib	ʾAbu 'l-Qāsim Ḥusayn ar-Rāghib (d. 503 H.), *Al-Mufradāt fī Gharīb al-Qurʾān.*
Rāzī	ʾAbu 'l-Faḍl Muḥammad Fakhr ad-Dīn ar-Rāzī (d. 606 H.), *At-Tafsīr al-Kabīr.*
Shawkānī	see *Nayl al-Awṭār.*
State and Government	Muḥammad Asad, *The Principles of State and Government in Islam*, University of California Press, 1961.
Suyūṭī	see *Itqān.*
Ṭabaqāt	see Ibn Saʿd.
Ṭabarī	ʾAbū Jaʿfar Muḥammad ibn Jarīr aṭ-Ṭabarī (d. 310 H.), *Jāmiʿ al-Bayān ʿan Taʾwīl al-Qurʾān.*
Tāj al-ʿArūs	Murtaḍā az-Zabīdī (d. 1205 H.), *Tāj al-ʿArūs.*
Tirmidhī	Muḥammad ibn ʿĪsā at-Tirmidhī (d. 275 or 279 H.), *Al-Jāmiʿ aṣ-Ṣaḥīḥ.*
Wāqidī	Muḥammad ibn ʿUmar al-Wāqidī (d. 207 H.), *Kitāb al-Maghāzī.*
Zamakhsharī	Maḥmūd ibn ʿUmar az-Zamakhsharī (d. 538 H.), *Al-Kashshāf ʿan Ḥaqāʾiq Ghawāmiḍ at-Tanzīl.* (For the same author's lexicographic works, see *Asās* and *Fāʾiq.*)

Explanatory Notes on the Transliteration and Pronunciation of the Arabic Alphabet

THE FOLLOWING CHART sets out the shapes and names of the twenty-eight Arabic consonants with their Romanised transliterations and a guide to pronunciation, which is supplemented by further practical guidance on the pronunciation of sounds for which there are no English equivalents. The explanatory notes as a whole are designed to assist the reader to recite as correctly as possible the sound of the original Arabic text of the Qurʾān.

An accompanying book marker is provided to help the reciter keep in mind the key elements of the transliteration system. Additional information can be found at http://www.thebook.org.

1. Consonants

No.	Shapes and names of Arabic character	Transliteration into Roman character	Guide to pronunciation
1	ء *Hamzah*	ʾ (in superior position) - see Note 1 and also Further Guidance A	a glottal stop
1a	ا *Alif*	ā - see Note 2	as in 'fat', 'hat'
1b	آ *Alif madd*	ʾā initially; āa elsewhere - see Note 2	
	ءا *Hamzah + Alif*	ʾā	
2	ب *Bāʾ*	b	as in 'big'
3	ت *Tāʾ*	t	as in 'tell'
4	ث *Thāʾ*	th	as in 'think'
5	ج *Jīm*	j	as in 'judge'
6	ح *Ḥāʾ*	ḥ - see Further Guidance B	no English equivalent / a breathy, strong 'h'
7	خ *Khāʾ*	kh - see Further Guidance C	as in Scottish 'loch'
8	د *Dāl*	d	as in 'dad'
9	ذ *Dhāl*	dh	as in 'that'
10	ر *Rāʾ*	r	rolled 'r' / as in Spanish 'arriba'

No.	Shapes and names of Arabic character		Transliteration into Roman character	Guide to pronunciation
11	ز	*Zāy*	z	as in 'zone'
12	س	*Sīn*	s	as in 'sea'
13	ش	*Shīn*	sh	as in 'sheet'
14	ص	*Ṣād*	ṣ - see Further Guidance D	no English equivalent / strong, emphatic '**s**'
15	ض	*Ḍād*	ḍ - see Further Guidance E	no English equivalent / strong, emphatic '**d**'
16	ط	*Ṭā᾽*	ṭ - see Further Guidance F	no English equivalent / strong, emphatic '**t**'
17	ظ	*Ẓā᾽*	ẓ - see Further Guidance G	no English equivalent / strong, emphatic '**dh**'
18	ع	*ᶜAyn*	ᶜ (in superior position) - see Further Guidance H	no English equivalent
19	غ	*Ghayn*	gh - see Further Guidance I	no English equivalent
20	ف	*Fā᾽*	f	as in 'foot'
21	ق	*Qāf*	q - see Further Guidance J	no English quivalent
22	ك	*Kāf*	k	as in 'kitten'
23	ل	*Lām*	l	as in 'love'
24	م	*Mīm*	m	as in 'mask'
25	ن	*Nūn*	n	as in 'never'
26	ه	*Hā᾽*	h	as in 'happy'
26a	ة	*Tā᾽ (marbūṭah)*	t - see Notes 5 and 8	
27	و	*Wāw*	w - see No. 30 and Notes 1, 3 and 9)	as in 'wet'
28	ي	*Yā᾽*	y - see also No. 31 and Notes 1, 3 and 9)	as in 'yet'

2. Vowels and Diphthongs

No.	Short Vowels Arabic	Short Vowels Roman	Long Vowels Arabic	Long Vowels Roman	Extn. Long Vowels Arabic	Extn. Long Vowels Roman	Nunation Arabic	Nunation Roman	Diphthongs Arabic	Diphthongs Roman
29	...َ...	a	...َا	ā	...آ	āa	...ءً ، ...اً	an		
30	...ُ...	u	...ُو	ū	...وٓ	ūu	...ٌ...	un	...َوْ	aw
31	...ِ...	i	...ِي	ī	...ىٓ	īi	...ٍ...	in	...َيْ	ay

3. Other Conventional Signs

No.	Arabic designation	Arabic character	Transliteration
32	*Sukūn*	...ْ...	ignored in transliteration
33	*Shaddah*	...ّ...	rendered by doubling the consonant
34	*Hamzatul-waṣl* (*Alif waṣl*)	...ٱ...	see Note 7

A. General Notes

Note	Arabic character	Position	Transliteration	Examples
1	*Hamzah* ء	a) initially	may be transliterated as ᵓ where necessary to distinguish from *Hamzatul-waṣl* ..ٱ..	ᵓamīn
		b) elsewhere	rendered by ᵓ	fuᵓād
		c) when ا, ي and و are bearers of *hamzah*	not transliterated	raᵓā, riᵓāaᵓ, suᵓāl
2	*Alif* ا	having a purely orthographical value	not transliterated see No. 1b and 29 and note 7	miᵓah, faᶜalū
3	*wāw* and *yā*ᵓ و، ي	with *shaddah*, even after vowels **u** and **i**, respectively	always transliterated **ww** and **yy**	quwwah, ᵓIyyāka
4	*Al* ال	definite article	assimilated with "*sun*" letters: ت ث د ذ ر ز س ش ص ض ط ظ ل ن	wash-shamsi

B. Notes on Transliteration with I^c^rāb

Note	Arabic character	Position	Transliteration	Examples
5	*Tā*ʾ (*marbūṭah*) (ة)		rendered by t	ʾalqāriʿatu jannatul-khuldi

C. Notes on Transliteration without Iʿrāb

Note	Arabic character	Position	Transliteration	Examples
6	Short vowels in the nominal inflection *Fatḥah* ..... a *Ḍammah* ..... u *Kasrah* i	a) followed by *tanwīn*	are transliterated	Naṣrāniyyan, kitāban
		b) after a pronominal suffix	transliterated exceptionally	ʾAllāhu, Lillāhi
		c) at the end of name or title	the pronominal suffix is transliterated in its pausal form (without the final vowel)	mir-Rabbih
7	*Alif waṣl* ٱ	transliterated by its original vowel in initial position or after a word ending in a consonant; otherwise omitted		wa minan-nās lahul-mulk ʾUdkhulul-jannah wad-khulul-bāba
8	*Tā*ʾ (*marbūṭah*) (ة)	in the absolute state	rendered by **h**	lahumul-jannah
		in the construct state	rendered by **t**	jannatul-khuldi
9	*-iyy* and *-uww* *-iyy* (ـِيّ) preceded by a letter voweled with a *Kasrah* .... *-uww* (ـُوّ) preceded by a letter voweled with a *Ḍammah*	final	transliterated (**iyy**) and (**uww**), respectively	ʿarabiyy, ʿaduww

Further Guidance*

A. ***Hamzah*** – ء – the glottal stop used in Cockney English for the **tt** in 'bottle' or 'butter'. In standard English it is heard as the initial or attacking sound in the emphatic pronunciation of such phrases as 'Absolutely **aw**ful'.

B. *Ḥā*ʾ – ح – to approximate to this sound, try a very deep and forceful sigh with mouth wide open and constrict your throat in the region of the Adam's apple. At the same time, slightly tense the tongue and tuck the tip of the tongue behind the lower teeth.

C. ***Khā*ʾ** – خ – is like Scottish lo**ch**, or German Ba**ch**, but more rasping. It is produced by closing the back of the tongue against the palate as in pronouncing the letter '**k**', then forcing the breath through the constriction.

D. A strong, emphatic '**s**' for the '**s**' of ***Ṣād*** – ص – is required. This sound is "velarized", i.e. pronounce a regular English '**s**', similar to Arabic ***Sīn*** – س – but depress the middle of the tongue, creating a larger space between the tongue and the roof of the mouth. This produces a distinctive 'hollow' sound which also affects the surrounding vowels. In English, the difference between 'Sam' and 'psalm' gives a clue, although this is not an exact parallel. Tense the tongue muscles in pronouncing 'psalm' and this begins to approximate closely to the '**s**' of ***Ṣād***. This method of articulation applies also to ***Ḍād***, ***Ṭā*ʾ** and ***Ẓā*ʾ**.

E. ***Ḍād*** – ض – a velarized, emphatic '**d**'. Start with a regular English '**d**' and follow the method for pronouncing ***Ṣād*** above. The difference between English 'Dan' and 'darn' gives a clue. Tense the tongue muscles in pronouncing 'darn' and this begins to come close to the sound of ***Ḍād***.

F. ***Ṭā*ʾ** – ط – a velarized, emphatic '**t**'. Start with a regular English '**t**' and follow the method for pronouncing ***Ṣād*** above. The difference between English 'tan' and 'tarn' gives a clue. Tense the tongue muscles in pronouncing 'tarn' and this begins to come close to the sound of ***Ṭā*ʾ**.

G. ***Ẓā*ʾ** – ظ – a velarized, emphatic '**dh**'. Start with a regular voiced English '**th**' (as in '**th**at') and follow the method for pronouncing ***Ṣād*** above. There are no corresponding pairs like 'Sam' and 'psalm' or 'Dan' and 'darn' to help here because the voiced '**th**' sound in English never precedes a long '**a**' sound, except in a very few, obscure words derived from Scots. The best way to get around this is to pronounce the '**th**' as in '**th**at' before the '**a**' in 'psalm' and tense the tongue muscles. This begins to come close to the sound of ***Ẓā*ʾ**.

H. ***ʿAyn*** – ع – can be described non-technically as 'a violent, tense glottal stop'. The passage of breath is blocked deep in the throat by constricting the muscles near the Adams' apple, then suddenly opened under pressure and with the vocal chords in action. The only time English speakers use these muscles is in vomiting. (Note: the ordinary glottal stop is used in pronouncing ***Hamzah***).

I. Similarly, ***Ghayn*** – غ – is simply the voiced version of ***Khā*ʾ**, produced by pronouncing **kh** and activating the vocal chords. It is vaguely similar to a French '**r**' but with more of a scrape than a trill.

J. ***Qāf*** – ق – pronounce English 'calm' repeatedly, trying to force the point at which the tongue meets the palate further back into the throat and keeping the mouth well open to produce an open-vowel effect. (English 'calm' is the starting-point here because it is a back '**k**' sound, unlike 'kill' which is further forward).

---

* We are indebted to the practical guidance for speakers of English in the opening chapter on The Arabic Script and Pronunciation in *Teach Yourself Arabic*, by J.R. Smart (London: Hodder Headline, 1986).

General Rules and Exceptions

After well researched observation of other transliterations it was realised that a general rule need not be applied as a 'straitjacket' but should accommodate exceptional cases.

A good example is a hyphen after the Arabic article '*al-*', which is the case generally speaking, when the enunciation of such an article is assimilated to the preceding word; for example, if you say '*qīlal-ḥamdu*' the hyphen indicates a silent pause between two words. In the case of '*ᵓAlḥamdu*' at the beginning of a sentence, such a silent pause is redundant because it will interrupt the flow of the utterance. But if the same word on its own is used as a heading, the hyphen can be used since the reader has time to give the word its due articulation.

Another example of a general and exceptional case is the word '*Kitāb*'. If the word refers to a book of divine guidance, it is always capitalised. Since the Qurᵓān makes no distinction between any of God's apostles (*Sūrah* 2, *verse* 285) and His books, we should always maintain a capital 'K' for any use of the word.

In order to preserve the meaning and intonation of the original Qurᵓanic text, whenever the mark for a comma (,) is used to replace the mark for a full stop or period sign (.) at the end of some verses, the recitation should not be stopped but carried on to the succeeding verse, which in these cases begins with a lower case letter.
For example:
ᶜAbasa wa tawallāa, ۝ **ᵓan-jāaᵓahul-ᵓaᶜmā.** ۝ (*Sūrah* 80 *verse* 1-2)

Further features of the transliteration system

1. Punctuation marks
Like the original text, the transliterated text is free of any interrogation (?), interjection (!) and quotation marks ("...").

2. The nasal sound (*Ghunnah*) sign (ñ)
The '*Ghunnah*' (nasal sound), transliterated by **ñ**, as in 'uncle', is a sound which occurs with great frequency throughout the Qurᵓān.

3. Extn. Long Vowel
Extended long vowels, i.e. **āa, ūu, īi**, are applicable in the following cases:
a) if any of the letters ***Alif*** – ا, ***Wāw*** – و, or ***Yāᵓ*** – ي, are succeded by ***Hamzah*** – ء, either in the same word or at the beginning of the following word, e.g.
mā shāaᵓ, ᵓalladhīi ᵓkhraja, mālahūu ᵓkhladah.
b) if the letter Alif is succeded by a double consonant, e.g.
ᵓaṣṣāaffāt, ᵓaṭṭāammah.

4. The hyphen sign (-)
This is used mainly to articulate the recitation of utterance according to the following rules:
a) as a bridge between two words where they are linked by a suspended Alif (*Alif wasl*), e.g.
Bismil-lāh (*Sūrah* 1, *verse* 1)
b) as a bridge connecting two words connected by a nasal sound (*Ghunnah*), e.g.
miñ-qablik (*Sūrah* 2, *verse* 4), **mim-baᶜdi** (*Sūrah* 2, *verse* 56),
raᶜduñw-wa barquñy-yajᶜalūna (*Sūrah* 2, *verse* 19)
c) as a bridge between two words where the first word terminates with the same letter as the first letter of the second word, in which case it is also doubled in sound, e.g.
fī qulūbihim-maraḍuñ (*Sūrah* 2, *verse* 10)

5. It is worth mentioning the adoption of using a word space instead of the hyphen sign to separate a word preceded by one or more of a particular letter, which in Arabic has grammatical impact on the word, such as the letter *'Bāʾ'*, *'Fāʾ'*, *'Lām'*, *'Sīn'*, *'Kāf'*. For example, the words *'falā tajᶜalū'* are correct in sound, rather than *'falā-tajᶜalū'* which may confuse the reader and interrupt the flow of his pronunciation. The following letters and words are succeeded by a word space:

wa mā fī ʾalā ʾila min yāa lā ʾilla ʾanna ʾinna ʾan kāna kaʾanna lākinna lākin laᶜalla laysa layta maᶜa law ʾam ʾamma lam lima hal ʾidh ʾidhā qad lan thumma ᶜan

For example:

wa kulla ʾIñsānin ʾalzamnāhu ṭāaʾirahu fī ᶜunuqih. (*Sūrah* 17 *verse* 13)

6. Generally there should not be a break in the pronunciation of a sound composed of the following letter combinations: *'dh', 'gh', 'kh', 'th', 'sh'.* However, a separator is sometimes necessary between two of these letters within a word to avoid misreading the two letters as one sound. For example:

ʾakhadhat-hul – in this example, there is a distinct break between the *'t'* and following *'h'*, whereby the break is represented by a hyphen. (*Sūrah* 2, *verse* 206)

7. **Capital letters are used for:**

a) The beginning of verses, except for those occasions when a verse is separated from the preceding verse by a comma

b) God and all His attributes of Divine Perfection, e.g.
...Huwar-Raḥmānur-Raḥīm (*Sūrah* 59, *verse* 22)

c) Names of prophets, messengers, apostles, and people, e.g.
Muḥammad, ʾIbrāhīm, Mūsā, ᶜĪsā, Zayd, Yaʾjūj, Maʾjūj.

d) The Holy books, e.g.
Tawrāh, ʾIñjīl, Zabūr, Qurʾān, Furqān, Kitāb, Dhikr, ʾĀyatul-lāh, Āyah, Kalimatul-lāh, or any word referring to Divine writings.

e) Communities named by their creed, e.g.
Muslimūn, Naṣārā, Yahūd, Ṣābiʾūn, Majūs

f) Names of rituals and foundations of Islam, e.g.
Shahādah, Ṣalāh, Zakāh, Ṣiyām, Hajj

g) Names of places, e.g.
...al-Kaᶜbatul-Baytul-Harām, wal-Baytul-Maᶜmūr, ...al-Baytul-ᶜAtīq, ...al-Masjidul-ʾAqṣā, ...aṣ-Ṣafā wal-Marwah, ...al-Mashᶜarul-Harām, Bakkah, Makkah, ᶜArafāt, Ṭuwā.

h) Words to define classes of created beings, such as angels, genies, Satan:
Malak, Malāaʾikah, Jinn, Shayṭān, ʾIblīs, ʾIñsān

i) The day of Resurrection, the Hour, the Hereafter – any word or phrase referring to the Last Day, e.g.
Yawmul-Qiyāmah, Ākhirah, was-Sāᶜah, Yawmud-Dīn, wal-Yawmul-ʾĀkhir

j) Chapters of the Qurʾān, e.g.
Al-Fātiḥah, Al-Baqarah, ʾĀl-ᶜImrān, An-Nisāaʾ etc.

Key to Layout

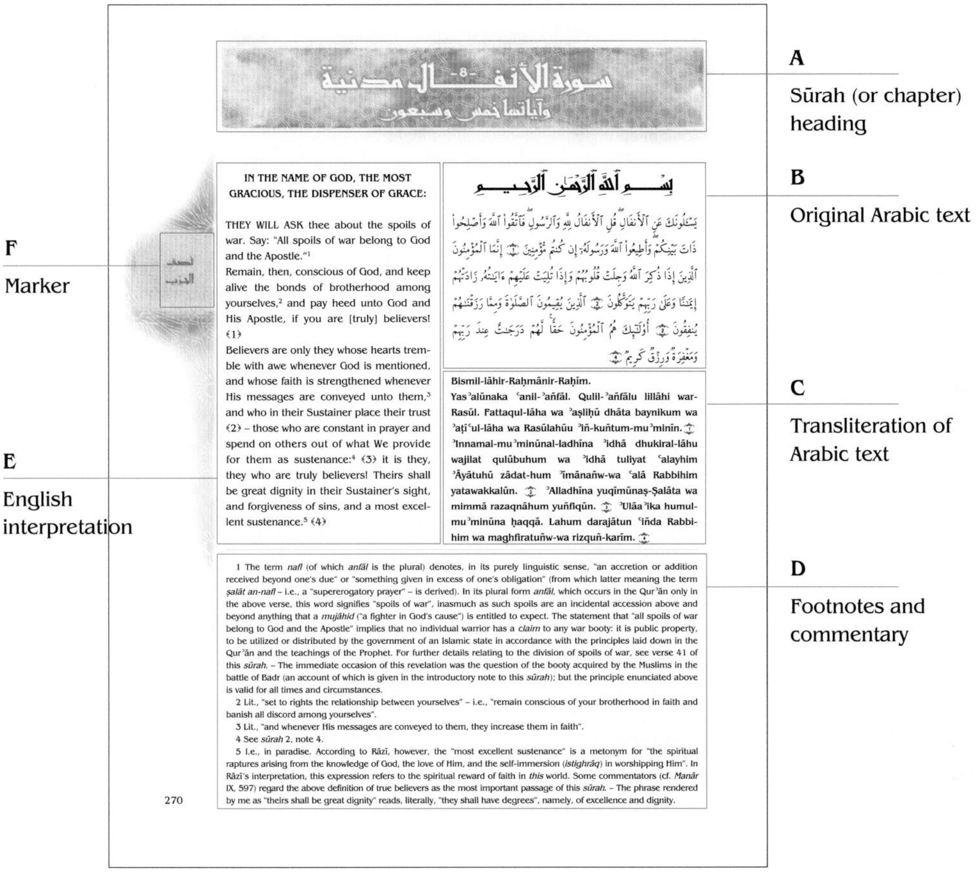

■ This marker (F) is a visual reference to the original Qurʾanic Arabic text which falls into 30 Sections (ʾAjzāʾ), each of which is sub-divided into two Parts (Aḥzāb). Each Part is further portioned into four Quarters (ʾArbāʿ), all of which are symbolized by the sign. The same marker will occasionally include a reference to a due prostration (Sajdah) by the reciter. It is indicated in the Arabic text by the sign (which comes at the end of the relevant Arabic verse). The *reason* for prostration is indicated by a line running above the relevant Arabic word.

■ The content of the main components, B, C, D, and E consistently match one another, on each page, throughout this publication.

■ Qurʾanic verses in components B, C, and E are numbered at the end of each verse using the universally known shapes of Arabic numbers (i.e. 1, 2, 3, 4, 5, . . .).

THE MESSAGE OF THE QUR'ĀN

لقوم يتفكرون

FOR PEOPLE WHO THINK

لتكون من المنذرين بلسان
عربي مبين وإنه لفي زبر

وإياك نستعين اهدنا الصراط
المستقيم صراط الذين أنعمت عليهم
غير المغضوب عليهم ولا الضالين

الأولين أولم يكن لهم
آية أن يعلمه علماء بني إسرائيل

سورة فاتحة الكتاب
وهي سبع ايات مكية
بسم الله الرحمن الرحيم
الحمد لله رب العلمين الرحمن الرحيم
ملك يوم الدين اياك نعبد
وانه لتنزيل رب العلمين
نزل به الروح الامين على قلبك

The First Sūrah

Al-Fātiḥah (The Opening)

Mecca Period

THIS SŪRAH is also called *Fātiḥat al-Kitāb* ("The Opening of the Divine Writ"), *Umm al-Kitāb* ("The Essence of the Divine Writ"), *Sūrat al-Ḥamd* ("The *Sūrah* of Praise"), *Asās al-Qur'ān* ("The Foundation of the Qur'ān"), and is known by several other names as well. It is mentioned elsewhere in the Qur'ān as *As-Sab' al-Mathānī* ("The Seven Oft-Repeated [Verses]") because it is repeated several times in the course of each of the five daily prayers. According to Bukhārī, the designation *Umm al-Kitāb* was given to it by the Prophet himself, and this in view of the fact that it contains, in a condensed form, all the fundamental principles laid down in the Qur'ān: the principle of God's oneness and uniqueness, of His being the originator and fosterer of the universe, the fount of all life-giving grace, the One to whom man is ultimately responsible, the only power that can really guide and help; the call to righteous *action* in the life of this world ("guide us the straight way"); the principle of life after death and of the organic consequences of man's actions and behaviour (expressed in the term "Day of Judgment"); the principle of guidance through God's message-bearers (evident in the reference to "those upon whom God has bestowed His blessings") and, flowing from it, the principle of the continuity of all true religions (implied in the allusion to people who have lived – and erred – in the past); and, finally, the need for voluntary self-surrender to the will of the Supreme Being and, thus, for worshipping Him alone. It is for this reason that this *sūrah* has been formulated as a prayer, to be constantly repeated and reflected upon by the believer.

"The Opening" was one of the earliest revelations bestowed upon the Prophet. Some authorities (for instance, 'Alī ibn Abī Ṭālib) were even of the opinion that it was the very first revelation; but this view is contradicted by authentic Traditions quoted by both Bukhārī and Muslim, which unmistakably show that the first five verses of *sūrah* 96 ("The Germ-Cell") constituted the beginning of revelation. It is probable, however, that whereas the earlier revelations consisted of only a few verses each, "The Opening" was the first *sūrah* revealed to the Prophet in its entirety at one time: and this would explain the view held by 'Alī.

سورة الفاتحة -1- مكية
وآياتها سبع

IN THE NAME OF GOD, THE MOST GRACIOUS, THE DISPENSER OF GRACE:[1] (1)

ALL PRAISE is due to God alone, the Sustainer of all the worlds,[2] ‹2› the Most Gracious, the Dispenser of Grace, ‹3› Lord of the Day of Judgment! ‹4›
Thee alone do we worship; and unto Thee alone do we turn for aid. ‹5›
Guide us the straight way ‹6› – the way of those upon whom Thou hast bestowed Thy blessings,[3] not of those who have been condemned [by Thee], nor of those who go astray![4] ‹7›

بِسۡمِ ٱللَّهِ ٱلرَّحۡمَٰنِ ٱلرَّحِيمِ ١

ٱلۡحَمۡدُ لِلَّهِ رَبِّ ٱلۡعَٰلَمِينَ ٢ ٱلرَّحۡمَٰنِ ٱلرَّحِيمِ ٣ مَٰلِكِ يَوۡمِ
ٱلدِّينِ ٤ إِيَّاكَ نَعۡبُدُ وَإِيَّاكَ نَسۡتَعِينُ ٥ ٱهۡدِنَا ٱلصِّرَٰطَ
ٱلۡمُسۡتَقِيمَ ٦ صِرَٰطَ ٱلَّذِينَ أَنۡعَمۡتَ عَلَيۡهِمۡ غَيۡرِ ٱلۡمَغۡضُوبِ عَلَيۡهِمۡ
وَلَا ٱلضَّآلِّينَ ٧

Bismil-lāhir-Raḥmānir-Raḥīm. 1
ʾAlḥamdu lillāhi Rabbil-ʿālamīn. 2 **ʾArraḥmānir-Raḥīm.** 3 **Māliki Yawmid-Dīn.** 4 **ʾIyyāka naʿbudu wa ʾIyyāka nastaʿīn.** 5 **ʾIhdinaṣ-ṣirāṭal-mustaqīm.** 6 **Ṣirāṭal-ladhīna ʾanʿamta ʿalayhim ghayril-maghḍūbi ʿalayhim wa laḍ-ḍāallīn.** 7

---

1 According to most of the authorities, this invocation (which occurs at the beginning of every *sūrah* with the exception of *sūrah* 9) constitutes an integral part of "The Opening" and is, therefore, numbered as verse 1. In all other instances, the invocation "in the name of God" precedes the *sūrah* as such, and is not counted among its verses. – Both the divine epithets *raḥmān* and *raḥīm* are derived from the noun *raḥmah*, which signifies "mercy", "compassion", "loving tenderness" and, more comprehensively, "grace". From the very earliest times, Islamic scholars have endeavoured to define the exact shades of meaning which differentiate the two terms. The best and simplest of these explanations is undoubtedly the one advanced by Ibn Qayyim (as quoted in *Manār* I, 48): the term *raḥmān* circumscribes the quality of abounding grace inherent in, and inseparable from, the concept of God's *Being*, whereas *raḥīm* expresses the manifestation of that grace in, and its effect upon, His creation – in other words, an aspect of His *activity*.

2 In this instance, the term "worlds" denotes all categories of existence both in the physical and the spiritual sense. The Arabic expression *rabb* – rendered by me as "Sustainer" – embraces a wide complex of meanings not easily expressed by a single term in another language. It comprises the ideas of having a just claim to the possession of anything and, consequently, authority over it, as well as of rearing, sustaining and fostering anything from its inception to its final completion. Thus, the head of a family is called *rabb ad-dār* ("master of the house") because he has authority over it and is responsible for its maintenance; similarly, his wife is called *rabbat ad-dār* ("mistress of the house"). Preceded by the definite article *al*, the designation *rabb* is applied, in the Qurʾān, exclusively to God as the sole fosterer and sustainer of all creation – objective as well as conceptual – and therefore the ultimate source of all authority.

3 I.e., by vouchsafing to them prophetic guidance and enabling them to avail themselves thereof.

4 According to almost all the commentators, God's "condemnation" (*ghaḍab*, lit., "wrath") is synonymous with the evil consequences which man brings upon himself by wilfully rejecting God's guidance and acting contrary to His injunctions. Some commentators (e.g., Zamakhsharī) interpret this passage as follows: ". . . the way of those upon whom Thou hast bestowed Thy blessings – those who have not been condemned [by Thee], and who do not go astray": in other words, they regard the last two expressions as *defining* "those upon whom Thou hast bestowed Thy blessings". Other commentators (e.g., Baghawī and Ibn Kathīr) do not subscribe to this interpretation – which would imply the use of negative definitions – and understand the last verse of the *sūrah* in the manner rendered by me

above. As regards the two categories of people following a wrong course, some of the greatest Islamic thinkers (e.g., Al-Ghazālī or, in recent times, Muḥammad ᶜAbduh) held the view that the people described as having incurred "God's condemnation" – that is, having deprived themselves of His grace – are those who have become fully cognizant of God's message and, having understood it, have rejected it; while by "those who go astray" are meant people whom the truth has either not reached at all, or to whom it has come in so garbled and corrupted a form as to make it difficult for them to recognize it as the truth (see ᶜAbduh in *Manār* I, 68 ff.).

The Second Sūrah

Al-Baqarah (The Cow)

Medina Period

THE TITLE of this *sūrah* is derived from the story narrated in verses 67-73. It is the first *sūrah* revealed in its entirety after the Prophet's exodus to Medina, and most of it during the first two years of that period; verses 275-281, however, belong to the last months before the Prophet's death (verse 281 is considered to be the very last revelation which he received).

Starting with a declaration of the purpose underlying the revelation of the Qur'ān as a whole – namely, man's guidance in all his spiritual and worldly affairs – *Al-Baqarah* contains, side by side with its constant stress on the necessity of God-consciousness, frequent allusions to the errors committed by people who followed the earlier revelations, in particular the children of Israel. The reference, in verse 106, to the abrogation of all earlier messages by that granted to the Prophet Muḥammad is of the greatest importance for a correct understanding of this *sūrah*, and indeed of the entire Qur'ān. Much of the legal ordinances provided here (especially in the later part of the *sūrah*) – touching upon questions of ethics, social relations, warfare, etc. – are a direct consequence of that pivotal statement. Again and again it is pointed out that the legislation of the Qur'ān corresponds to the true requirements of man's nature, and as such is but a continuation of the ethical guidance offered by God to man ever since the beginning of human history. Particular attention is drawn to Abraham, the prophet-patriarch whose intense preoccupation with the idea of God's oneness lies at the root of the three great monotheistic religions; and the establishment of Abraham's Temple, the Ka'bah, as the direction of prayer for "those who surrender themselves to God" which is the meaning of the word *muslimūn*, sing. *muslim*), sets a seal, as it were, on the conscious self-identification of all true believers with the faith of Abraham.

Throughout this *sūrah* runs the five-fold Qur'anic doctrine that God is the self-sufficient fount of all being (*al-qayyūm*); that the fact of His existence, reiterated by prophet after prophet, is accessible to man's intellect; that righteous living – and not merely believing – is a necessary corollary of this intellectual perception; that bodily death will be followed by resurrection and judgment; and that all who are truly conscious of their responsibility to God "need have no fear, and neither shall they grieve".

سورة البقرة مدنية -2-

وآياتها ست وثمانون ومائتان

IN THE NAME OF GOD, THE MOST GRACIOUS, THE DISPENSER OF GRACE:

Alif. Lām. Mīm.[1] ‹1›

THIS DIVINE WRIT – let there be no doubt about it – is [meant to be] a guidance for all the God-conscious[2] ‹2› who believe in [the existence of] that which is beyond the reach of human perception,[3] and are constant in prayer, and spend on others out of what We provide for them as sustenance;[4] ‹3› and who believe in that which has been bestowed from on high upon thee, [O Prophet,] as well as in that which was bestowed before thy time:[5] for it is they who in their innermost are certain of the life to come! ‹4›

It is they who follow the guidance [which comes] from their Sustainer; and it is they, they who shall attain to a happy state! ‹5›

بِسۡمِ ٱللَّهِ ٱلرَّحۡمَٰنِ ٱلرَّحِيمِ

الٓمٓ ﴿١﴾ ذَٰلِكَ ٱلۡكِتَٰبُ لَا رَيۡبَۛ فِيهِۛ هُدٗى لِّلۡمُتَّقِينَ ﴿٢﴾ ٱلَّذِينَ
يُؤۡمِنُونَ بِٱلۡغَيۡبِ وَيُقِيمُونَ ٱلصَّلَوٰةَ وَمِمَّا رَزَقۡنَٰهُمۡ يُنفِقُونَ ﴿٣﴾ وَٱلَّذِينَ
يُؤۡمِنُونَ بِمَآ أُنزِلَ إِلَيۡكَ وَمَآ أُنزِلَ مِن قَبۡلِكَ وَبِٱلۡأٓخِرَةِ هُمۡ يُوقِنُونَ ﴿٤﴾
أُوْلَٰٓئِكَ عَلَىٰ هُدٗى مِّن رَّبِّهِمۡۖ وَأُوْلَٰٓئِكَ هُمُ ٱلۡمُفۡلِحُونَ ﴿٥﴾

Bismil-lāhir-Raḥmānir-Raḥīm.
ʾAlif-Lāam-Mīim. (1) Dhālikal-Kitābu lā rayba fīh.
Hudal-lilmuttaqīn. (2) ʾAlladhīna yuʾminūna bil-
ghaybi wa yuqīmūnaṣ-Ṣalāta wa mimmā razaqnā-
hum yuñfiqūn. (3) Wal-ladhīna yuʾminūna bimāa
ʾuñzila ʾilayka wa māa ʾuñzila miñ-qablika wa bil-
ʾĀkhirati hum yūqinūn. (4) ʾUlāaʾika ʿalā hudam-
mir-Rabbihim wa ʾulāaʾika humul-mufliḥūn. (5)

---

1 Regarding the possible significance of the single letters called *al-muqaṭṭaʿāt,* which occur at the beginning of some *sūrahs* of the Qurʾan, see Appendix II, where the various theories bearing on this subject are discussed.

2 The conventional translation of *muttaqī* as "God-fearing" does not adequately render the *positive* content of this expression – namely, the awareness of His all-presence and the desire to mould one's existence in the light of this awareness; while the interpretation adopted by some translators, "one who guards himself against evil" or "one who is careful of his duty", does not give more than one particular aspect of the concept of God-consciousness.

3 *Al-ghayb* (commonly, and erroneously, translated as "the Unseen") is used in the Qurʾān to denote all those sectors or phases of reality which lie beyond the range of human perception and cannot, therefore, be proved or disproved by scientific observation or even adequately comprised within the accepted categories of speculative thought: as, for instance, the existence of God and of a definite purpose underlying the universe, life after death, the real nature of time, the existence of spiritual forces and their inter-action, and so forth. Only a person who is convinced that the ultimate reality comprises far more than our *observable* environment can attain to belief in God and, thus, to a belief that life has meaning and purpose. By pointing out that it is "a guidance for those who believe in the existence of that which is beyond human perception", the Qurʾān says, in effect, that it will – of necessity – remain a closed book to all whose minds cannot accept this fundamental premise.

4 *Ar-rizq* ("provision of sustenance") applies to all that may be of benefit to man, whether it be concrete (like food, property, offspring, etc.) or abstract (like knowledge, piety, etc.). The "spending on others" is mentioned here in one breath with God-consciousness and prayer because it is precisely in such selfless acts that true piety comes to its full fruition. It should be borne in mind that the verb *anfaqa* (lit., "he spent") is always used in the Qurʾān to denote spending freely on, or as a gift to, others, whatever the motive may be.

5 This is a reference to one of the fundamental doctrines of the Qurʾān: the doctrine of the historical continuity of divine revelation. Life – so the Qurʾān teaches us – is not a series of unconnected jumps but a continuous, organic process: and this law applies also to the life of the mind, of which man's religious experience (in its cumulative sense)

سورة البقرة مدنية

بِسْمِ اللَّهِ الرَّحْمَٰنِ الرَّحِيمِ

الٓمٓ ذَٰلِكَ الْكِتَابُ لَا رَيْبَ فِيهِ

هُدًى لِلْمُتَّقِينَ الَّذِينَ يُؤْمِنُونَ

وآياتها ست وثمانون ومائتان

بالغيب ويقيمون الصلوة ومما رزقناهم

ينفقون والذين يومنون بما انزل اليك

وما انزل من قبلك وبالاخرة هم يوقنون

اولئك على هدى من ربهم واولئك

هم المفلحون ان الذين كفروا

BEHOLD, as for those who are bent on denying the truth[6] – it is all one to them whether thou warnest them or dost not warn them: they will not believe. ‹6› God has sealed their hearts and their hearing, and over their eyes is a veil;[7] and awesome suffering awaits them. ‹7›

And there are people who say, "We do believe in God and the Last Day," the while they do not [really] believe. ‹8› They would deceive God and those who have attained to faith – the while they deceive none but themselves, and perceive it not. ‹9› In their hearts is disease, and so God lets their disease increase; and grievous suffering awaits them because of their persistent lying.[8] ‹10›

And when they are told, "Do not spread corruption on earth," they answer, "We are but improving things!" ‹11› Oh, verily, it is they, they who are spreading corruption – but they perceive it not![9] ‹12›

إِنَّ ٱلَّذِينَ كَفَرُواْ سَوَآءٌ عَلَيۡهِمۡ ءَأَنذَرۡتَهُمۡ أَمۡ لَمۡ تُنذِرۡهُمۡ لَا يُؤۡمِنُونَ ﴿6﴾
خَتَمَ ٱللَّهُ عَلَىٰ قُلُوبِهِمۡ وَعَلَىٰ سَمۡعِهِمۡۖ وَعَلَىٰٓ أَبۡصَٰرِهِمۡ غِشَٰوَةٞۖ وَلَهُمۡ عَذَابٌ
عَظِيمٞ ﴿7﴾ وَمِنَ ٱلنَّاسِ مَن يَقُولُ ءَامَنَّا بِٱللَّهِ وَبِٱلۡيَوۡمِ ٱلۡأٓخِرِ وَمَا هُم
بِمُؤۡمِنِينَ ﴿8﴾ يُخَٰدِعُونَ ٱللَّهَ وَٱلَّذِينَ ءَامَنُواْ وَمَا يَخۡدَعُونَ إِلَّآ أَنفُسَهُمۡ
وَمَا يَشۡعُرُونَ ﴿9﴾ فِي قُلُوبِهِم مَّرَضٞ فَزَادَهُمُ ٱللَّهُ مَرَضٗاۖ وَلَهُمۡ عَذَابٌ أَلِيمُۢ
بِمَا كَانُواْ يَكۡذِبُونَ ﴿10﴾ وَإِذَا قِيلَ لَهُمۡ لَا تُفۡسِدُواْ فِي ٱلۡأَرۡضِ قَالُوٓاْ إِنَّمَا
نَحۡنُ مُصۡلِحُونَ ﴿11﴾ أَلَآ إِنَّهُمۡ هُمُ ٱلۡمُفۡسِدُونَ وَلَٰكِن لَّا يَشۡعُرُونَ ﴿12﴾

**ʾInnal-ladhīna kafarū sawāaʾun ʿalayhim ʾaʾañdhar-
tahum ʾam lam tuñdhirhum lā yuʾminūn. (6) Khata-
mal-lāhu ʿalā qulubihim wa ʿalā samʿihim; wa ʿalāa
ʾabṣārihim ghishāwatuñw-wa lahum ʿadhābun ʿaẓīm.
(7) Wa minan-nāsi mañy-yaqūlu ʾāmannā billāhi
wa bilYawmil-ʾĀkhiri wa mā hum bimuʾminīn. (8)
Yukhādiʿūnal-lāha wal-ladhīna ʾāmanū wa mā yakh-
daʿūna ʾillāa ʾañfusahum wa mā yashʿurūn. (9) Fī
qulūbihim maraḍuñ-fazādahumul-lāhu maraḍā. Wa
lahum ʿadhābun ʾalīmum-bimā kānū yakdhibūn. (10)
Wa ʾidhā qīla lahum lā tufsidū fil-ʾarḍi qālūu
ʾinnamā naḥnu muṣliḥūn. (11) ʾAlāa ʾinnahum hu-
mul-mufsidūna wa lākil-lā yashʿurūn. (12)**

is a part. Thus, the religion of the Qurʾān can be properly understood only against the background of the great monotheistic faiths which preceded it, and which, according to Muslim belief, culminate and achieve their final formulation in the faith of Islam.

6 In contrast with the frequently occurring term *al-kāfirūn* ("those who deny the truth"), the use of the past tense in *alladhīna kafarū* indicates conscious intent, and is, therefore, appropriately rendered as "those who are bent on denying the truth". This interpretation is supported by many commentators, especially Zamakhsharī (who, in his commentary on this verse, uses the expression, "those who have deliberately resolved upon their *kufr*"). Elsewhere in the Qurʾān such people are spoken of as having "hearts with which they fail to grasp the truth, and eyes with which they fail to see, and ears with which they fail to hear" (7 : 179). – For an explanation of the terms *kufr* ("denial of the truth"), *kāfir* ("one who denies the truth"), etc., see note 4 on 74 : 10, where this concept appears for the first time in Qurʾanic revelation.

7 A reference to the natural law instituted by God, whereby a person who persistently adheres to false beliefs and refuses to listen to the voice of truth gradually loses the *ability* to perceive the truth "so that finally, as it were, a seal is set upon his heart" (Rāghib). Since it is God who has instituted all laws of nature – which, in their aggregate, are called *sunnat Allāh* ("the way of God") – this "sealing" is attributed to Him: but it is obviously a consequence of man's free choice and not an act of "predestination". Similarly, the suffering which, in the life to come, is in store for those who during their life in this world have wilfully remained deaf and blind to the truth, is a natural consequence of their free choice – just as happiness in the life to come is the natural consequence of man's endeavour to attain to righteousness and inner illumination. It is in this sense that the Qurʾanic references to God's "reward" and "punishment" must be understood.

8 I.e., before God and man – and to themselves. It is generally assumed that the people to whom this passage alludes in the first instance are the hypocrites of Medina who, during the early years after the *hijrah,* outwardly professed their adherence to Islam while remaining inwardly unconvinced of the truth of Muḥammad's message. However, as is always the case with Qurʾanic allusions to contemporary or historical events, the above and the following verses have a general, timeless import inasmuch as they refer to all people who are prone to deceive themselves in order to evade a spiritual commitment.

9 It would seem that this is an allusion to people who oppose any "intrusion" of religious considerations into the

And when they are told, "Believe as other people believe," they answer, "Shall we believe as the weak-minded believe?" Oh, verily, it is they, they who are weak-minded – but they know it not! ‹13›
And when they meet those who have attained to faith, they assert, "We believe [as you believe]"; but when they find themselves alone with their evil impulses,[10] they say, "Verily, we are with you; we were only mocking!" ‹14›
God will requite them for their mockery,[11] and will leave them for a while in their overweening arrogance, blindly stumbling to and fro: ‹15› [for] it is they who have taken error in exchange for guidance; and neither has their bargain brought them gain, nor have they found guidance [elsewhere]. ‹16›
Their parable is that of people who kindle a fire: but as soon as it has illumined all around them, God takes away their light and leaves them in utter darkness, wherein they cannot see: ‹17› deaf, dumb, blind – and they cannot turn back. ‹18›
Or [the parable] of a violent cloudburst in the sky, with utter darkness, thunder and lightning: they put their fingers into their ears to keep out the peals of thunder, in terror of death; but God encompasses [with His might] all who deny the truth. ‹19› The lightning well-nigh takes away their sight; whenever it gives them light, they advance therein, and whenever darkness falls around them, they stand still.

وَإِذَا قِيلَ لَهُمْ ءَامِنُوا۟ كَمَآ ءَامَنَ ٱلنَّاسُ قَالُوٓا۟ أَنُؤْمِنُ كَمَآ ءَامَنَ
ٱلسُّفَهَآءُ ۗ أَلَآ إِنَّهُمْ هُمُ ٱلسُّفَهَآءُ وَلَـٰكِن لَّا يَعْلَمُونَ ﴿١٣﴾ وَإِذَا لَقُوا۟
ٱلَّذِينَ ءَامَنُوا۟ قَالُوٓا۟ ءَامَنَّا وَإِذَا خَلَوْا۟ إِلَىٰ شَيَـٰطِينِهِمْ قَالُوٓا۟ إِنَّا مَعَكُمْ
إِنَّمَا نَحْنُ مُسْتَهْزِءُونَ ﴿١٤﴾ ٱللَّهُ يَسْتَهْزِئُ بِهِمْ وَيَمُدُّهُمْ فِى طُغْيَـٰنِهِمْ
يَعْمَهُونَ ﴿١٥﴾ أُو۟لَـٰٓئِكَ ٱلَّذِينَ ٱشْتَرَوُا۟ ٱلضَّلَـٰلَةَ بِٱلْهُدَىٰ فَمَا رَبِحَت
تِّجَـٰرَتُهُمْ وَمَا كَانُوا۟ مُهْتَدِينَ ﴿١٦﴾ مَثَلُهُمْ كَمَثَلِ ٱلَّذِى ٱسْتَوْقَدَ نَارًا
فَلَمَّآ أَضَآءَتْ مَا حَوْلَهُۥ ذَهَبَ ٱللَّهُ بِنُورِهِمْ وَتَرَكَهُمْ فِى ظُلُمَـٰتٍ لَّا
يُبْصِرُونَ ﴿١٧﴾ صُمٌّۢ بُكْمٌ عُمْىٌ فَهُمْ لَا يَرْجِعُونَ ﴿١٨﴾ أَوْ كَصَيِّبٍ مِّنَ
ٱلسَّمَآءِ فِيهِ ظُلُمَـٰتٌ وَرَعْدٌ وَبَرْقٌ يَجْعَلُونَ أَصَـٰبِعَهُمْ فِىٓ ءَاذَانِهِم مِّنَ
ٱلصَّوَٰعِقِ حَذَرَ ٱلْمَوْتِ ۚ وَٱللَّهُ مُحِيطٌۢ بِٱلْكَـٰفِرِينَ ﴿١٩﴾ يَكَادُ ٱلْبَرْقُ
يَخْطَفُ أَبْصَـٰرَهُمْ ۖ كُلَّمَآ أَضَآءَ لَهُم مَّشَوْا۟ فِيهِ وَإِذَآ أَظْلَمَ عَلَيْهِمْ قَامُوا۟

Wa ʾidhā qīla lahum ʾāminū kamāa ʾāmanan-nāsu qālūu ʾanuʾminu kamāa ʾāmanas-sufahāaʾ. ʾAlāa ʾinnahum humus-sufahāaʾu wa lākil-lā yaʿlamūn. (13) Wa ʾidhā laqul-ladhīna ʾāmanū qālūu ʾāmannā wa ʾidhā khalaw ʾilā Shayāṭīnihim qālūu ʾinnā maʿakum ʾinnamā naḥnu mustahziʾūn. (14) ʾAllāhu yastahziʾu bihim wa yamudduhum fī ṭughyānihim yaʿmahūn. (15) ʾUlāaʾikal-ladhīnash-tarawuḍ-ḍalālata bilhudā famā rabiḥat-tijāratuhum wa mā kānū muhtadīn. (16) Mathaluhum kamathalil-ladhis-tawqada nārañ-falammāa ʾaḍāaʾat mā ḥawlahū dhahabal-lāhu binūrihim wa tarakahum fī ẓulumātil-lā yubṣirūn. (17) Ṣummum-bukmun ʿumyuñ-fahum lā yarjiʿūn. (18) ʾAw kaṣayyibim-minas-samāaʾi fīhi ẓulumātuñw-wa raʿduñw-wa barquñy-yajʿalūna ʾaṣābiʿahum fīi ʾādhānihim minaṣ-ṣawāʿiqi ḥadharal-mawt. Wallāhu muḥīṭum-bilkāfirīn. (19) Yakādul-barqu yakhṭafu ʾabṣārahum; kullamāa ʾaḍāaʾa lahum mashaw fīhi wa ʾidhāa ʾaẓlama ʿalayhim qāmū.

---

realm of practical affairs, and thus – often unwittingly, thinking that they are "but improving things" – contribute to the moral and social confusion referred to in the subsequent verse.

10 Lit., "their satans" (*shayāṭīn*, pl. of *shayṭān*). In accordance with ancient Arabic usage, this term often denotes people "who, through their insolent persistence in evildoing (*tamarrud*), have become like satans" (Zamakhsharī): an interpretation of the above verse accepted by most of the commentators. However, the term *shayṭān* – which is derived from the verb *shaṭana,* "he was [or "became"] remote [from all that is good and true]" (*Lisān al-ʿArab, Tāj al-ʿArūs*) – is often used in the Qurʾān to describe the "satanic" (i.e., exceedingly evil) propensities in man's own soul, and especially all impulses which run counter to truth and morality (Rāghib).

11 Lit., "God will mock at them". My rendering is in conformity with the generally accepted interpretation of this phrase.

وَلَوْ شَآءَ ٱللَّهُ لَذَهَبَ بِسَمْعِهِمْ وَأَبْصَٰرِهِمْ ۚ إِنَّ ٱللَّهَ عَلَىٰ كُلِّ شَىْءٍ
قَدِيرٌ ﴿٢٠﴾ يَٰٓأَيُّهَا ٱلنَّاسُ ٱعْبُدُوا۟ رَبَّكُمُ ٱلَّذِى خَلَقَكُمْ وَٱلَّذِينَ مِن
قَبْلِكُمْ لَعَلَّكُمْ تَتَّقُونَ ﴿٢١﴾ ٱلَّذِى جَعَلَ لَكُمُ ٱلْأَرْضَ فِرَٰشًا وَٱلسَّمَآءَ
بِنَآءً وَأَنزَلَ مِنَ ٱلسَّمَآءِ مَآءً فَأَخْرَجَ بِهِۦ مِنَ ٱلثَّمَرَٰتِ رِزْقًا لَّكُمْ ۖ فَلَا
تَجْعَلُوا۟ لِلَّهِ أَندَادًا وَأَنتُمْ تَعْلَمُونَ ﴿٢٢﴾ وَإِن كُنتُمْ فِى رَيْبٍ مِّمَّا نَزَّلْنَا عَلَىٰ
عَبْدِنَا فَأْتُوا۟ بِسُورَةٍ مِّن مِّثْلِهِۦ وَٱدْعُوا۟ شُهَدَآءَكُم مِّن دُونِ ٱللَّهِ إِن كُنتُمْ
صَٰدِقِينَ ﴿٢٣﴾ فَإِن لَّمْ تَفْعَلُوا۟ وَلَن تَفْعَلُوا۟ فَٱتَّقُوا۟ ٱلنَّارَ ٱلَّتِى وَقُودُهَا
ٱلنَّاسُ وَٱلْحِجَارَةُ ۖ أُعِدَّتْ لِلْكَٰفِرِينَ ﴿٢٤﴾

Wa law shāaʾal-lāhu ladhahaba bisamᶜihim wa ʾabṣārihim; ʾinnal-lāha ᶜalā kulli shayʾiñ-Qadīr. (20) Yāa ʾayyuhan-nāsuᶜ-budū Rabbakumul-ladhī khalaqakum wal-ladhīna miñ-qablikum laᶜallakum tattaqūn. (21) ʾAlladhī jaᶜala lakumul-ʾarḍa firāshañw-was-samāaʾa bināaʾñw-wa ʾañzala minas-samāaʾi māaʾañ-faʾakhraja bihī minath-thamarāti rizqal-lakum; falā tajᶜalū lillāhi ʾañdādañw-waʾañtum taᶜlamūn. (22) Wa ʾiñ-kuñtum fī raybim-mimmā nazzalnā ᶜalā ᶜabdinā faʾtū bisūratim-mim-mithlihī wad-ᶜū shuhadāaʾakum-miñ-dūnil-lāhi ʾiñ-kuñtum ṣādiqīn. (23) Faʾil-lam tafᶜalū wa lañ-tafᶜalū fattaqun-nāral-latī waqūduhan-nāsu wal-ḥijāratu ʾuᶜiddat lilkāfirīn. (24)

And if God so willed, He could indeed take away their hearing and their sight:[12] for, verily, God has the power to will anything. ‹20›

O MANKIND! Worship your Sustainer, who has created you and those who lived before you, so that you might remain conscious of Him ‹21› who has made the earth a resting-place for you and the sky a canopy, and has sent down water from the sky and thereby brought forth fruits for your sustenance: do not, then, claim that there is any power that could rival God,[13] when you know [that He is One]. ‹22›
And if you doubt any part of what We have bestowed from on high, step by step, upon Our servant [Muḥammad],[14] then produce a *sūrah* of similar merit, and call upon any other than God to bear witness for you[15] – if what you say is true! ‹23› And if you cannot do it – and most certainly you cannot do it – then be conscious of the fire whose fuel is human beings and stones[16] which awaits all who deny the truth! ‹24›

12 The obvious implication is: "but He does not will this" – that is, He does not preclude the possibility that "those who have taken error in exchange for guidance" may one day perceive the truth and mend their ways. The expression "their hearing and their sight" is obviously a metonym for man's instinctive ability to discern between good and evil and, hence, for his moral responsibility. – In the parable of the "people who kindle a fire" we have, I believe, an allusion to some people's exclusive reliance on what is termed the "scientific approach" as a means to illumine and explain all the imponderables of life and faith, and the resulting arrogant refusal to admit that anything could be beyond the reach of man's intellect. This "overweening arrogance", as the Qurʾān terms it, unavoidably exposes its devotees – and the society dominated by them – to the lightning of disillusion which "well-nigh takes away their sight", i.e., still further weakens their moral perception and deepens their "terror of death".

13 Lit., "do not give God any compeers" (*andād,* pl. of *nidd*). There is full agreement among all commentators that this term implies any object of adoration to which some or all of God's qualities are ascribed, whether it be conceived as a deity "in its own right" or a saint supposedly possessing certain divine or semi-divine powers. This meaning can be brought out only by a free rendering of the above phrase.

14 I.e., the message of which the doctrine of God's oneness and uniqueness is the focal point. By the use of the word "doubt" (*rayb*), this passage is meant to recall the opening sentence of this *sūrah*: "This divine writ – let there be no doubt about it . . .", etc. The gradualness of revelation is implied in the grammatical form *nazzalnā* – which is important in this context inasmuch as the opponents of the Prophet argued that the Qurʾān could not be of divine origin because it was being revealed gradually, and not in one piece (Zamakhsharī).

15 Lit., "come forward with a *sūrah* like it, and call upon your witnesses other than God" – namely, "to attest that your hypothetical literary effort could be deemed equal to any part of the Qurʾān." This challenge occurs in two other places as well (10 : 38 and 11 : 13, in which latter case the unbelievers are called upon to produce ten chapters of comparable merit); see also 17 : 88.

16 This evidently denotes all objects of worship to which men turn instead of God – their powerlessness and inefficacy being symbolized by the lifelessness of stones – while the expression "human beings" stands here for

ربع
الحزب

But unto those who have attained to faith and do good works give the glad tiding that theirs shall be gardens through which running waters flow. Whenever they are granted fruits therefrom as their appointed sustenance, they will say, "It is this that in days of yore was granted to us as our sustenance!" – for they shall be given something that will recall that [past].[17] And there shall they have spouses pure, and there shall they abide. ‹25›
Behold, God does not disdain to propound a parable of a gnat, or of something [even] less than that.[18] Now, as for those who have attained to faith, they know that it is the truth from their Sustainer – whereas those who are bent on denying the truth say, "What could [your] God mean by this parable?"
In this way does He cause many a one to go astray, just as He guides many a one aright: but none does He cause thereby to go astray save the iniquitous, ‹26› who break their bond with God after it has been established [in their nature][19] and cut asunder what God has bidden to be joined, and spread corruption on earth: these it is that shall be the losers. ‹27›

وَبَشِّرِ ٱلَّذِينَ ءَامَنُوا۟ وَعَمِلُوا۟ ٱلصَّٰلِحَٰتِ أَنَّ لَهُمْ جَنَّٰتٍ تَجْرِى مِن
تَحْتِهَا ٱلْأَنْهَٰرُ ۖ كُلَّمَا رُزِقُوا۟ مِنْهَا مِن ثَمَرَةٍ رِّزْقًا ۙ قَالُوا۟ هَٰذَا ٱلَّذِى رُزِقْنَا مِن
قَبْلُ ۖ وَأُتُوا۟ بِهِۦ مُتَشَٰبِهًا ۖ وَلَهُمْ فِيهَآ أَزْوَٰجٌ مُّطَهَّرَةٌ ۖ وَهُمْ فِيهَا خَٰلِدُونَ ﴿٢٥﴾
۞ إِنَّ ٱللَّهَ لَا يَسْتَحْىِۦٓ أَن يَضْرِبَ مَثَلًا مَّا بَعُوضَةً فَمَا فَوْقَهَا ۚ فَأَمَّا
ٱلَّذِينَ ءَامَنُوا۟ فَيَعْلَمُونَ أَنَّهُ ٱلْحَقُّ مِن رَّبِّهِمْ ۖ وَأَمَّا ٱلَّذِينَ كَفَرُوا۟ فَيَقُولُونَ
مَاذَآ أَرَادَ ٱللَّهُ بِهَٰذَا مَثَلًا ۘ يُضِلُّ بِهِۦ كَثِيرًا وَيَهْدِى بِهِۦ كَثِيرًا ۚ وَمَا يُضِلُّ بِهِۦٓ
إِلَّا ٱلْفَٰسِقِينَ ﴿٢٦﴾ ٱلَّذِينَ يَنقُضُونَ عَهْدَ ٱللَّهِ مِنۢ بَعْدِ مِيثَٰقِهِۦ وَيَقْطَعُونَ مَآ
أَمَرَ ٱللَّهُ بِهِۦٓ أَن يُوصَلَ وَيُفْسِدُونَ فِى ٱلْأَرْضِ ۚ أُو۟لَٰٓئِكَ هُمُ ٱلْخَٰسِرُونَ ﴿٢٧﴾

Wa bashshiril-ladhīna ʾāmanū wa ʿamiluṣ-ṣāliḥāti ʾanna lahum jannātiñ-tajrī miñ-taḥtihal-ʾanhār kullamā ruziqū minhā miñ-thamaratir-rizqañ-qālū hādhal-ladhī ruziqnā miñ-qablu wa ʾutū bihī mutashābihañw-wa lahum fīhāa ʾazwājum-muṭahharatuñw-wa hum fīhā khālidūn. (25) ۞ ʾInnal-lāha lā yastaḥyīi ʾañy-yaḍriba mathalam-mā baʿūḍatañ-famā fawqahā. Faʾammal-ladhīna ʾāmanū fayaʿlamūna ānnahul-ḥaqqu mir-Rabbihim; wa ʾammal-ladhīna kafarū fayaqūlūna mādhāa ʾarādal-lāhu bihādhā mathalā. Yuḍillu bihī kathīrañw-wa yahdī bihī kathīrā. Wa mā yuḍillu bihīi ʾillal-fāsiqīn. (26) ʾAlladhīna yañquḍūna ʿahdal-lāhi mim-baʿdi mīthāqihī wa yaqṭaʿūna māa ʾamaral-lāhu bihīi ʾañy-yūṣala wa yufsidūna fil-ʾarḍi ʾulāaʾika humul-khāsirūn. (27)

human actions deviating from the way of truth (cf. *Manār* I, 197): the remembrance of all of which is bound to increase the sinner's suffering in the hereafter, referred to in the Qurʾān as "hell".

17 Lit., "something resembling it". Various interpretations, some of them of an esoteric and highly speculative nature, have been given to this passage. For the manner in which I have translated it I am indebted to Muḥammad ʿAbduh (in *Manār* I, 232 f.), who interprets the phrase, "It is this that in days of yore was granted to us as our sustenance" as meaning: "It is this that we have been promised during our life on earth as a requital for faith and righteous deeds." In other words, man's actions and attitudes in this world will be mirrored in their "fruits", or consequences, in the life to come – as has been expressed elsewhere in the Qurʾān in the verses, "And he who shall have done an atom's weight of good, shall behold it; and he who shall have done an atom's weight of evil, shall behold it" (99 : 7-8). As regards the reference to "spouses" in the next sentence, it is to be noted that the term *zawj* (of which *azwāj* is the plural) signifies either of the two components of a couple – that is, the male as well as the female.

18 Lit., "something above it", i.e., relating to the quality of *smallness* stressed here – as one would say, "such-and-such a person is the lowest of people, and even more than that" (Zamakhsharī). The reference to "God's parables", following as it does immediately upon a mention of the gardens of paradise and the suffering through hell-fire in the life to come, is meant to bring out the allegorical nature of this imagery.

19 The "bond with God" (conventionally translated as "God's covenant") apparently refers here to man's moral obligation to use his inborn gifts – intellectual as well as physical – in the way intended for them by God. The "establishment" of this bond arises from the faculty of reason which, if properly used, must lead man to a realization of his own weakness and dependence on a causative power and, thus, to a gradual cognition of God's will with reference to his own behaviour. This interpretation of the "bond with God" seems to be indicated by the fact that there is no mention of any specific "covenant" in either the preceding or the subsequent verses of the passage under consideration. The deliberate

How can you refuse to acknowledge God, seeing that you were lifeless and He gave you life, and that He will cause you to die and then will bring you again to life, whereupon unto Him you will be brought back? ‹28›
He it is who has created for you all that is on earth, and has applied His design to the heavens and fashioned them into seven heavens;[20] and He alone has full knowledge of everything. ‹29›

AND LO![21] Thy Sustainer said unto the angels: "Behold, I am about to establish upon earth one who shall inherit it."[22]
They said: "Wilt Thou place on it such as will spread corruption thereon and shed blood – whereas it is we who extol Thy limitless glory, and praise Thee, and hallow Thy name?"
[God] answered: "Verily, I know that which you do not know." ‹30›
And He imparted unto Adam the names of all things;[23] then He brought them within the ken of the angels and said: "Declare unto Me the names of these [things], if

كَيْفَ تَكْفُرُونَ بِٱللَّهِ وَكُنتُمْ أَمْوَٰتًا فَأَحْيَٰكُمْ ثُمَّ يُمِيتُكُمْ ثُمَّ
يُحْيِيكُمْ ثُمَّ إِلَيْهِ تُرْجَعُونَ ﴿٢٨﴾ هُوَ ٱلَّذِى خَلَقَ لَكُم مَّا فِى ٱلْأَرْضِ
جَمِيعًا ثُمَّ ٱسْتَوَىٰٓ إِلَى ٱلسَّمَآءِ فَسَوَّىٰهُنَّ سَبْعَ سَمَٰوَٰتٍ وَهُوَ بِكُلِّ شَىْءٍ
عَلِيمٌ ﴿٢٩﴾ وَإِذْ قَالَ رَبُّكَ لِلْمَلَٰٓئِكَةِ إِنِّى جَاعِلٌ فِى ٱلْأَرْضِ خَلِيفَةً
قَالُوٓا۟ أَتَجْعَلُ فِيهَا مَن يُفْسِدُ فِيهَا وَيَسْفِكُ ٱلدِّمَآءَ وَنَحْنُ نُسَبِّحُ
بِحَمْدِكَ وَنُقَدِّسُ لَكَ قَالَ إِنِّىٓ أَعْلَمُ مَا لَا تَعْلَمُونَ ﴿٣٠﴾ وَعَلَّمَ ءَادَمَ
ٱلْأَسْمَآءَ كُلَّهَا ثُمَّ عَرَضَهُمْ عَلَى ٱلْمَلَٰٓئِكَةِ فَقَالَ أَنۢبِـُٔونِى بِأَسْمَآءِ هَٰٓؤُلَآءِ إِن

Kayfa takfurūna billāhi wa kuntum ʾamwātañ-faʾaḥyākum; thumma yumītukum thumma yuḥyīkum thumma ʾilayhi turjaʿūn. (28) Huwal-ladhī khalaqa lakum-mā fil-ʾarḍi jamīʿañ-thummas-tawāa ʾilas-samāaʾi fasawwāhunna sabʿa samāwāt. Wa huwa bi-kulli shayʾiñ-ʿAlīm. (29) Wa ʾidh qāla Rabbuka lil-Malāaʾikati ʾInnī jāʿiluñ-fil-ʾarḍi khalīfah. Qālūu ʾatajʿalu fīhā mañy-yufsidu fīhā wa yasfikud-dimāaʾa wa naḥnu nusabbiḥu biḥamdika wa nuqaddisu lak. Qāla ʾInnīi ʾaʿlamu mālā taʿlamūn. (30) Wa ʿallama ʾĀdamal-ʾasmāaʾa kullahā thumma ʿaraḍahum ʿalal-Malāaʾikati faqāla ʾambiʾūnī biʾasmāaʾi hāaʾulāaʾi ʾiñ-

omission of any explanatory reference in this connection suggests that the expression "bond with God" stands for something that is rooted in the human situation as such, and can, therefore, be perceived instinctively as well as through conscious experience: namely, that innate relationship with God which makes Him "closer to man than his neck-vein" (50 : 16). For an explanation of the subsequent reference to "what God has bidden to be joined", see *sūrah* 13, note 43.

20 The term *samāʾ* ("heaven" or "sky") is applied to anything that is spread like a canopy above any other thing. Thus, the visible skies which stretch like a vault above the earth and form, as it were, its canopy, are called *samāʾ*: and this is the *primary* meaning of this term in the Qurʾān; in a wider sense, it has the connotation of "cosmic system". As regards the "seven heavens", it is to be borne in mind that in Arabic usage – and apparently in other Semitic languages as well – the number "seven" is often synonymous with "several" (see *Lisān al-ʿArab*), just as "seventy" or "seven hundred" often means "many" or "very many" (*Tāj al-ʿArūs*). This, taken together with the accepted linguistic definition that "every *samāʾ* is a *samāʾ* with regard to what is below it" (Rāghib), may explain the "seven heavens" as denoting the multiplicity of cosmic systems. – For my rendering of *thumma*, at the beginning of this sentence, as "and", see *sūrah* 7, first part of note 43.

21 The interjection "lo" seems to be the only adequate rendering, in this context, of the particle *idh*, which is usually – and without sufficient attention to its varying uses in Arabic construction – translated as "when". Although the latter rendering is often justified, *idh* is also used to indicate "the sudden, or unexpected, occurrence of a thing" (cf. Lane I, 39), or a sudden turn in the discourse. The subsequent allegory, relating as it does to the faculty of reason implanted in man, is logically connected with the preceding passages.

22 Lit., "establish on earth a successor" or a "vice-gerent". The term *khalīfah* – derived from the verb *khalafa*, "he succeeded [another]" – is used in this allegory to denote man's rightful supremacy on earth, which is most suitably rendered by the expression "he shall inherit the earth" (in the sense of being given possession of it). See also 6 : 165, 27 : 62 and 35 : 39, where all human beings are spoken of as *khalāʾif al-arḍ*.

23 Lit., "all the names". The term *ism* ("name") implies, according to all philologists, an expression "conveying the knowledge [of a thing] . . . applied to denote a substance or an accident or an attribute, for the purpose of distinction" (Lane IV, 1435): in philosophical terminology, a "concept". From this it may legitimately be inferred that

what you say is true."[24] ‹31›

They replied: "Limitless art Thou in Thy glory! No knowledge have we save that which Thou hast imparted unto us. Verily, Thou alone art all-knowing, truly wise." ‹32›

Said He: "O Adam, convey unto them the names of these [things]."

And as soon as [Adam] had conveyed unto them their names, [God] said: "Did I not say unto you, 'Verily, I alone know the hidden reality of the heavens and the earth, and know all that you bring into the open and all that you would conceal'?" ‹33›

And when We told the angels, "Prostrate yourselves before Adam!"[25] – they all prostrated themselves, save Iblīs, who refused and gloried in his arrogance: and thus he became one of those who deny the truth.[26] ‹34›

And We said: "O Adam, dwell thou and thy wife in this garden,[27] and eat freely thereof, both of you, whatever you may wish; but do not approach this one tree, lest you become wrongdoers."[28] ‹35›

But Satan caused them both to stumble therein, and thus brought about the loss of their erstwhile state.[29] And so We said:

كُنتُمْ صَـٰدِقِينَ ﴿31﴾ قَالُوا۟ سُبْحَـٰنَكَ لَا عِلْمَ لَنَآ إِلَّا مَا عَلَّمْتَنَآ ۖ إِنَّكَ أَنتَ
ٱلْعَلِيمُ ٱلْحَكِيمُ ﴿32﴾ قَالَ يَـٰٓـَٔادَمُ أَنۢبِئْهُم بِأَسْمَآئِهِمْ ۖ فَلَمَّآ أَنۢبَأَهُم بِأَسْمَآئِهِمْ قَالَ
أَلَمْ أَقُل لَّكُمْ إِنِّىٓ أَعْلَمُ غَيْبَ ٱلسَّمَـٰوَٰتِ وَٱلْأَرْضِ وَأَعْلَمُ مَا تُبْدُونَ وَمَا
كُنتُمْ تَكْتُمُونَ ﴿33﴾ وَإِذْ قُلْنَا لِلْمَلَـٰٓئِكَةِ ٱسْجُدُوا۟ لِـَٔادَمَ فَسَجَدُوٓا۟ إِلَّآ إِبْلِيسَ
أَبَىٰ وَٱسْتَكْبَرَ وَكَانَ مِنَ ٱلْكَـٰفِرِينَ ﴿34﴾ وَقُلْنَا يَـٰٓـَٔادَمُ ٱسْكُنْ أَنتَ وَزَوْجُكَ
ٱلْجَنَّةَ وَكُلَا مِنْهَا رَغَدًا حَيْثُ شِئْتُمَا وَلَا تَقْرَبَا هَـٰذِهِ ٱلشَّجَرَةَ فَتَكُونَا مِنَ
ٱلظَّـٰلِمِينَ ﴿35﴾ فَأَزَلَّهُمَا ٱلشَّيْطَـٰنُ عَنْهَا فَأَخْرَجَهُمَا مِمَّا كَانَا فِيهِ ۖ وَقُلْنَا

kuñtum ṣādiqīn. 31 Qālū subḥānaka lā ᶜilma lanāa ˀillā mā ᶜallamtanā. ˀInnaka ˀAñtal-ᶜAlīmul-Ḥakīm. 32 Qāla yāa ˀĀdamu ˀambiˀhum biˀasmāaˀihim. Falammāa ˀambaˀahum biˀasmāaˀihim qāla ˀalam ˀaqullakum ˀinnīi ˀaᶜlamu ghaybas-samāwāti wal-ˀarḍi wa ˀaᶜlamu mā tubdūna wa mā kuñtum taktumūn. 33 Wa ˀidh qulnā lilMalāaˀikatis-judū liˀĀdama fasajadūu ˀillāa ˀIblīsa ˀabā was-takbara wa kāna minal-kāfirīn. 34 Wa qulnā yāa ˀĀdamus-kun ˀañta wa zawjukal-jannata wa kulā minhā raghadan ḥaythu shiˀtumā wa lā taqrabā hādhihish-shajarata fatakūnā minaẓ-ẓālimīn. 35 Faˀazallahumash-Shayṭānu ᶜanhā faˀakhrajahumā mimmā kānā fīh. Wa qulnah-

the "knowledge of all the names" denotes here man's faculty of logical definition and, thus of conceptual thinking. That by "Adam" the whole human race is meant here becomes obvious from the preceding reference, by the angels, to "such as will spread corruption on earth and will shed blood", as well as from 7 : 11.

24 Namely, that it was they who, by virtue of their purity, were better qualified to "inherit the earth".

25 To show that, by virtue of his ability to think conceptually, man is superior in this respect even to the angels.

26 For an explanation of the name of the Fallen Angel, see *sūrah* 7, note 10. The fact of this "rebellion", repeatedly stressed in the Qurˀān, has led some of the commentators to the conclusion that he could not have been one of the angels, since these are incapable of sinning: "they do not bear themselves with false pride . . . and they do whatever they are bidden to do" (16 : 49-50). As against this, other commentators point to the Qurˀānic phrasing of God's command to the angels and of Iblīs' refusal to obey, which makes it absolutely clear that at the time of that command he was indeed one of the heavenly host. Hence, we must assume that his "rebellion" has a purely symbolic significance and is, in reality, the outcome of a specific *function* assigned to him by God (see note 31 on 15 : 41).

27 Lit., "the garden". There is a considerable difference of opinion among the commentators as to what is meant here by "garden": a garden in the earthly sense, or the paradise that awaits the righteous in the life to come, or some special garden in the heavenly regions? According to some of the earliest commentators (see *Manār* I, 277), an *earthly* abode is here alluded to – namely, an environment of perfect ease, happiness and innocence. In any case, this story of Adam is obviously one of the allegories referred to in 3 : 7.

28 This tree is alluded to elsewhere in the Qurˀān (20 : 120) as "the tree of life eternal", and in the Bible (Genesis ii, 9) as "the tree of life" and "the tree of knowledge of good and evil". For a tentative explanation of this allegory, see note 106 on 20 : 120.

29 Lit., "brought them out of what they had been in": i.e., by inducing them to eat the fruit of the forbidden tree.

"Down with you, [and be henceforth] enemies unto one another; and on earth you shall have your abode and your livelihood for a while!"[30] «36»
Thereupon Adam received words [of guidance] from his Sustainer, and He accepted his repentance: for, verily, He alone is the Acceptor of Repentance, the Dispenser of Grace. «37» [For although] We did say, "Down with you all from this [state]," there shall, none the less, most certainly come unto you guidance from Me: and those who follow My guidance need have no fear, and neither shall they grieve; «38» but those who are bent on denying the truth and giving the lie to Our messages – they are destined for the fire, and therein shall they abide. «39»

O CHILDREN of Israel![31] Remember those blessings of Mine with which I graced you, and fulfil your promise unto Me, [whereupon] I shall fulfil My promise unto you; and of Me, of Me stand in awe! «40»
Believe in that which I have [now] bestowed from on high, confirming the truth already in your possession, and be not foremost among those who deny its truth; and do not barter away My messages for a trifling gain;[32] and of Me, of Me be conscious! «41»
And do not overlay the truth with falsehood, and do not knowingly suppress the truth;[33] «42» and be constant in prayer,

ٱهْبِطُوا۟ بَعْضُكُمْ لِبَعْضٍ عَدُوٌّ ۖ وَلَكُمْ فِى ٱلْأَرْضِ مُسْتَقَرٌّ وَمَتَـٰعٌ إِلَىٰ
حِينٍ ﴿٣٦﴾ فَتَلَقَّىٰٓ ءَادَمُ مِن رَّبِّهِۦ كَلِمَـٰتٍ فَتَابَ عَلَيْهِ ۚ إِنَّهُۥ هُوَ ٱلتَّوَّابُ
ٱلرَّحِيمُ ﴿٣٧﴾ قُلْنَا ٱهْبِطُوا۟ مِنْهَا جَمِيعًا ۖ فَإِمَّا يَأْتِيَنَّكُم مِّنِّى هُدًى فَمَن تَبِعَ
هُدَاىَ فَلَا خَوْفٌ عَلَيْهِمْ وَلَا هُمْ يَحْزَنُونَ ﴿٣٨﴾ وَٱلَّذِينَ كَفَرُوا۟ وَكَذَّبُوا۟
بِـَٔايَـٰتِنَآ أُو۟لَـٰٓئِكَ أَصْحَـٰبُ ٱلنَّارِ ۖ هُمْ فِيهَا خَـٰلِدُونَ ﴿٣٩﴾ يَـٰبَنِىٓ إِسْرَٰٓءِيلَ
ٱذْكُرُوا۟ نِعْمَتِىَ ٱلَّتِىٓ أَنْعَمْتُ عَلَيْكُمْ وَأَوْفُوا۟ بِعَهْدِىٓ أُوفِ بِعَهْدِكُمْ وَإِيَّـٰىَ
فَٱرْهَبُونِ ﴿٤٠﴾ وَءَامِنُوا۟ بِمَآ أَنزَلْتُ مُصَدِّقًا لِّمَا مَعَكُمْ وَلَا تَكُونُوٓا۟ أَوَّلَ
كَافِرٍۭ بِهِۦ ۖ وَلَا تَشْتَرُوا۟ بِـَٔايَـٰتِى ثَمَنًا قَلِيلًا وَإِيَّـٰىَ فَٱتَّقُونِ ﴿٤١﴾ وَلَا تَلْبِسُوا۟
ٱلْحَقَّ بِٱلْبَـٰطِلِ وَتَكْتُمُوا۟ ٱلْحَقَّ وَأَنتُمْ تَعْلَمُونَ ﴿٤٢﴾ وَأَقِيمُوا۟ ٱلصَّلَوٰةَ

biṭū baʿḍukum libaʿḍin ʿaduww. Wa lakum fil-ʾarḍi mustaqarruñw-wa matāʿun ʾilā ḥīn. (36) Fatalaqqāa ʾĀdamu mir-Rabbihī Kalimātiñ-fatāba ʿalayhi ʾinnahū Huwat-Tawwābur-Raḥīm. (37) Qulnah-biṭū minhā jamīʿañ-faʾimmā yaʾtiyannakum-minnī hudañ-famañ-tabiʿa hudāya falā khawfun ʿalayhim wa lā hum yaḥzanūn. (38) Wal-ladhīna kafarū wa kadhdhabū biʾĀyātināa ʾulāaʾika ʾaṣḥābun-nāri hum fīhā khālidūn. (39) Yā banīi ʾIsrāaʾīladh-kurū niʿmatiyal-latīi ʾanʿamtu ʿalaykum wa ʾawfū biʿahdīi ʾūfi bi ʿahdikum wa ʾIyyāya farhabūn. (40) Wa ʾāminū bimāa ʾañzaltu muṣaddiqal-limā maʿakum wa lā takūnūu ʾawwala kāfirim-bih. Wa lā tashtarū biʾĀyātī thamanañ-qalīlañw-wa ʾIyyāya fattaqūn. (41) Wa lā talbisul-ḥaqqa bilbāṭili wa taktumul-ḥaqqa wa ʾañtum taʿlamūn. (42) Wa ʾaqīmuṣ-Ṣalāta

---

30 With this sentence, the address changes from the hitherto-observed dual form to the plural: a further indication that the moral of the story relates to the human race as a whole. See also *sūrah* 7, note 16.

31 This passage connects directly with the preceding passages in that it refers to the continuous guidance vouchsafed to man through divine revelation. The reference to the children of Israel at this point, as in so many other places in the Qurʾān, arises from the fact that their religious beliefs represented an earlier phase of the monotheistic concept which culminates in the revelation of the Qurʾān.

32 A reference to the persistent Jewish belief that they alone among all nations have been graced by divine revelation. The "trifling gain" is their conviction that they are "God's chosen people" – a claim which the Qurʾān consistently refutes.

33 By "overlaying the truth with falsehood" is meant the corrupting of the Biblical text, of which the Qurʾān frequently accuses the Jews (and which has since been established by objective textual criticism), while the "suppression of the truth" refers to their disregard or deliberately false interpretation of the words of Moses in the Biblical passage, "The Lord thy God will raise up unto thee a prophet from the midst of thee, of thy brethren, like unto me; unto him ye shall hearken" (Deuteronomy xviii, 15), and the words attributed to God Himself, "I will raise them up a prophet from among thy brethren, like unto thee, and will put My words in his mouth" (Deuteronomy xviii, 18). The

نصف الحزب

and spend in charity,[34] and bow down in prayer with all who thus bow down. ⟨43⟩
Do you bid other people to be pious, the while you forget your own selves – and yet you recite the divine writ? Will you not, then, use your reason? ⟨44⟩
And seek aid in steadfast patience and prayer: and this, indeed, is a hard thing for all but the humble in spirit, ⟨45⟩ who know with certainty that they shall meet their Sustainer and that unto Him they shall return. ⟨46⟩
O children of Israel! Remember those blessings of Mine with which I graced you, and how I favoured you above all other people; ⟨47⟩ and remain conscious of [the coming of] a Day when no human being shall in the least avail another, nor shall intercession be accepted from any of them, nor ransom taken from them,[35] and none shall be succoured. ⟨48⟩
And [remember the time] when We saved you from Pharaoh's people, who afflicted you with cruel suffering, slaughtering your sons and sparing [only] your women[36] – which was an awesome trial from your Sustainer; ⟨49⟩ and when We cleft the sea before you, and thus saved you and caused Pharaoh's people to drown before your very eyes; ⟨50⟩

وَءَاتُواْ ٱلزَّكَوٰةَ وَٱرۡكَعُواْ مَعَ ٱلرَّٰكِعِينَ ﴿٤٣﴾ ۞ أَتَأۡمُرُونَ ٱلنَّاسَ بِٱلۡبِرِّ
وَتَنسَوۡنَ أَنفُسَكُمۡ وَأَنتُمۡ تَتۡلُونَ ٱلۡكِتَٰبَۚ أَفَلَا تَعۡقِلُونَ ﴿٤٤﴾ وَٱسۡتَعِينُواْ
بِٱلصَّبۡرِ وَٱلصَّلَوٰةِۚ وَإِنَّهَا لَكَبِيرَةٌ إِلَّا عَلَى ٱلۡخَٰشِعِينَ ﴿٤٥﴾ ٱلَّذِينَ يَظُنُّونَ
أَنَّهُم مُّلَٰقُواْ رَبِّهِمۡ وَأَنَّهُمۡ إِلَيۡهِ رَٰجِعُونَ ﴿٤٦﴾ يَٰبَنِيٓ إِسۡرَٰٓءِيلَ ٱذۡكُرُواْ
نِعۡمَتِيَ ٱلَّتِيٓ أَنۡعَمۡتُ عَلَيۡكُمۡ وَأَنِّي فَضَّلۡتُكُمۡ عَلَى ٱلۡعَٰلَمِينَ ﴿٤٧﴾ وَٱتَّقُواْ
يَوۡمٗا لَّا تَجۡزِي نَفۡسٌ عَن نَّفۡسٖ شَيۡـٔٗا وَلَا يُقۡبَلُ مِنۡهَا شَفَٰعَةٞ وَلَا يُؤۡخَذُ
مِنۡهَا عَدۡلٞ وَلَا هُمۡ يُنصَرُونَ ﴿٤٨﴾ وَإِذۡ نَجَّيۡنَٰكُم مِّنۡ ءَالِ فِرۡعَوۡنَ
يَسُومُونَكُمۡ سُوٓءَ ٱلۡعَذَابِ يُذَبِّحُونَ أَبۡنَآءَكُمۡ وَيَسۡتَحۡيُونَ نِسَآءَكُمۡۚ وَفِي
ذَٰلِكُم بَلَآءٞ مِّن رَّبِّكُمۡ عَظِيمٞ ﴿٤٩﴾ وَإِذۡ فَرَقۡنَا بِكُمُ ٱلۡبَحۡرَ فَأَنجَيۡنَٰكُمۡ
وَأَغۡرَقۡنَآ ءَالَ فِرۡعَوۡنَ وَأَنتُمۡ تَنظُرُونَ ﴿٥٠﴾

wa ʾātuz-Zakāta war-kaʿū maʿar-rākiʿīn. ﴿43﴾ ۞
ʾAtaʾmurūnan-nāsa bilbirri wa tañsawna ʾañfusa-
kum wa ʾañtum tatlūnal-Kitāb. ʾAfalā taʿqilūn. ﴿44﴾
Was-taʿīnū biṣṣabri waṣ-Ṣalāta wa ʾinnahā laka-
bīratun ʾillā ʿalal-khāshiʿīn. ﴿45﴾ ʾAlladhīna yaẓun-
nūna ʾannahum mulāqū Rabbihim wa ʾannahum
ʾilayhi rājiʿūn. ﴿46﴾ Yā banīi ʾIsrāaʾīladh-kurū niʿ-
matiyal-latīi ʾanʿamtu ʿalaykum wa ʾannī faḍḍal-
tukum ʿalal-ʿālamīn. ﴿47﴾ Wat-taqū Yawmal-lā tajzī
nafsun ʿañ-nafsiñ-shayʾañw-wa lā yuqbalu minhā
shafāʿatuñw-wa lā yuʾkhadhu minhā ʿadluñw-wa lā
hum yuñṣarūn. ﴿48﴾ Wa ʾidh najjaynākum-min ʾāli-
Firʿawna yasūmūnakum sūuʾal-ʿadhābi yudhab-
biḥūna ʾabnāaʾakum wa yastaḥyūna nisāaʾakum;
wa fī dhālikum balāaʾum-mir-Rabbikum ʿaẓīm. ﴿49﴾
Wa ʾidh faraqnā bikumul-baḥra faʾañjaynākum wa
ʾaghraqnāa ʾāla Firʿawna wa ʾañtum tañẓurūn. ﴿50﴾

"brethren" of the children of Israel are obviously the Arabs, and particularly the *mustaʿribah* ("Arabianized") group among them, which traces its descent to Ishmael and Abraham: and since it is to this group that the Arabian Prophet's own tribe, the Quraysh, belonged, the above Biblical passages must be taken as referring to his advent.

34 In Islamic Law, *zakāh* denotes an obligatory tax, incumbent on Muslims, which is meant to purify a person's capital and income from the taint of selfishness (hence the name). The proceeds of this tax are to be spent mainly, but not exclusively, on the poor. Whenever, therefore, this term bears the above legal implication, I translate it as "the purifying dues". Since, however, in this verse it refers to the children of Israel and obviously implies only acts of charity towards the poor, it is more appropriate to translate it as "almsgiving" or "charity". I have also adopted this latter rendering in all instances where the term *zakāh*, though relating to Muslims, does not apply specifically to the obligatory *tax* as such (e.g., in 73 : 20, where this term appears for the first time in the chronology of revelation).

35 The "taking of ransom (*ʿadl*)" is an obvious allusion to the Christian doctrine of vicarious redemption as well as to the Jewish idea that "the chosen people" – as the Jews considered themselves – would be exempt from punishment on the Day of Judgment. Both these ideas are categorically refuted in the Qurʾān.

36 See Exodus i, 15-16, 22.

and when We appointed for Moses forty nights [on Mount Sinai], and in his absence you took to worshipping the [golden] calf, and thus became evildoers: ‹51› yet, even after that, We blotted out this your sin, so that you might have cause to be grateful.[37] ‹52›

And [remember the time] when We vouchsafed unto Moses the divine writ – and [thus] a standard by which to discern the true from the false[38] – so that you might be guided aright; ‹53› and when Moses said unto his people: "O my people! Verily, you have sinned against yourselves by worshipping the calf; turn, then, in repentance to your Maker and mortify yourselves;[39] this will be the best for you in your Maker's sight."

And thereupon He accepted your repentance: for, behold, He alone is the Acceptor of Repentance, the Dispenser of Grace. ‹54›

And [remember] when you said, "O Moses, indeed we shall not believe thee until we see God face to face!" – whereupon the thunderbolt of punishment[40] overtook you before your very eyes. ‹55›

But We raised you again after you had been as dead,[41] so that you might have cause to be grateful. ‹56›

وَإِذْ وَٰعَدْنَا مُوسَىٰٓ أَرْبَعِينَ لَيْلَةً ثُمَّ ٱتَّخَذْتُمُ ٱلْعِجْلَ مِنۢ بَعْدِهِۦ وَأَنتُمْ
ظَٰلِمُونَ ﴿٥١﴾ ثُمَّ عَفَوْنَا عَنكُم مِّنۢ بَعْدِ ذَٰلِكَ لَعَلَّكُمْ تَشْكُرُونَ ﴿٥٢﴾
وَإِذْ ءَاتَيْنَا مُوسَى ٱلْكِتَٰبَ وَٱلْفُرْقَانَ لَعَلَّكُمْ تَهْتَدُونَ ﴿٥٣﴾ وَإِذْ قَالَ
مُوسَىٰ لِقَوْمِهِۦ يَٰقَوْمِ إِنَّكُمْ ظَلَمْتُمْ أَنفُسَكُم بِٱتِّخَاذِكُمُ ٱلْعِجْلَ فَتُوبُوٓا۟
إِلَىٰ بَارِئِكُمْ فَٱقْتُلُوٓا۟ أَنفُسَكُمْ ذَٰلِكُمْ خَيْرٌ لَّكُمْ عِندَ بَارِئِكُمْ فَتَابَ
عَلَيْكُمْ إِنَّهُۥ هُوَ ٱلتَّوَّابُ ٱلرَّحِيمُ ﴿٥٤﴾ وَإِذْ قُلْتُمْ يَٰمُوسَىٰ لَن نُّؤْمِنَ لَكَ
حَتَّىٰ نَرَى ٱللَّهَ جَهْرَةً فَأَخَذَتْكُمُ ٱلصَّٰعِقَةُ وَأَنتُمْ تَنظُرُونَ ﴿٥٥﴾ ثُمَّ
بَعَثْنَٰكُم مِّنۢ بَعْدِ مَوْتِكُمْ لَعَلَّكُمْ تَشْكُرُونَ ﴿٥٦﴾

Wa ʾidh wāʿadnā Mūsāa ʾarbaʿīna laylatañ-thummat-takhadhtumul-ʿijla mim-baʿdihī wa ʾañtum ẓālimūn. (51) Thumma ʿafawnā ʿañkum mim-baʿdi dhālika laʿallakum tashkurūn. (52) Wa ʾidh ʾātaynā Mūsal-Kitāba wal-Furqāna laʿallakum tahtadūn. (53) Wa ʾidh qāla Mūsā liqawmihī yā qawmi ʾinnakum ẓalamtum ʾañfusakum bittikhādhikumul-ʿijla fatūbūu ʾilā Bāriʾikum faqtulūu ʾañfusakum; dhālikum khayrul-lakum ʿiñda Bāriʾikum fatāba ʿalaykum. ʾInnahū Huwat-Tawwābur-Raḥīm. (54) Wa ʾidh qultum yā Mūsā lañ-nuʾmina laka ḥattā naral-lāha jahratañ-faʾakhadhatkumuṣ-ṣāʿiqatu wa ʾañtum tañẓurūn. (55) Thumma baʿathnākum mim-baʿdi mawtikum laʿallakum tashkurūn. (56)

37 the story of the golden calf is dealt with at greater length in 7 : 148 ff. and 20 : 85 ff. Regarding the crossing of the Red Sea, to which verse 50 above alludes, see 20 : 77-78 and 26 : 63-66, as well as the corresponding notes. The forty nights (and days) which Moses spent on Mount Sinai are mentioned again in 7 : 142.

38 Muḥammad ʿAbduh amplifies the above interpretation of *al-furqān* (adopted by Ṭabarī, Zamakhsharī and other great commentators) by maintaining that it applies also to "human reason, which enables us to distinguish the true from the false" (*Manār* III, 160), apparently basing this wider interpretation on 8 : 41, where the battle of Badr is described as *yawm al-furqān* ("the day on which the true was distinguished from the false"). While the term *furqān* is often used in the Qurʾān to describe one or another of the revealed scriptures, and particularly the Qurʾān itself, it has undoubtedly also the connotation pointed out by ʿAbduh: for instance, in 8 : 29, where it clearly refers to the faculty of moral valuation which distinguishes every human being who is truly conscious of God.

39 Lit., "kill yourselves" or, according to some commentators, "kill one another". This literal interpretation (probably based on the Biblical account in Exodus xxxii, 26-28) is not, however, convincing in view of the immediately preceding call to repentance and the subsequent statement that this repentance was accepted by God. I incline, therefore, to the interpretation given by ʿAbd al-Jabbār (quoted by Rāzī in his commentary on this verse) to the effect that the expression "kill yourselves" is used here in a metaphorical sense (*majāzan*), i.e., "mortify yourselves".

40 The Qurʾān does not state what form this "thunderbolt of punishment" (*aṣ-ṣāʿiqah*) took. The lexicographers give various interpretations to this word, but all agree on the element of vehemence and suddenness inherent in it (see Lane IV, 1690).

41 Lit., "after your death". the expression *mawt* does not always denote physical death. Arab philologists – e.g., Rāghib – explain the verb *māta* (lit., "he died") as having, in certain contexts, the meaning of "he became deprived of sensation, dead as to the senses"; and occasionally as "deprived of the intellectual faculty, intellectually dead"; and sometimes even as "he slept" (see Lane VII, 2741).

ثلاثة ارباع الحزب

وَظَلَّلۡنَا عَلَيۡكُمُ ٱلۡغَمَامَ وَأَنزَلۡنَا عَلَيۡكُمُ ٱلۡمَنَّ وَٱلسَّلۡوَىٰۖ كُلُواْ مِن طَيِّبَٰتِ
مَا رَزَقۡنَٰكُمۡۚ وَمَا ظَلَمُونَا وَلَٰكِن كَانُوٓاْ أَنفُسَهُمۡ يَظۡلِمُونَ ﴿٥٧﴾ وَإِذۡ قُلۡنَا
ٱدۡخُلُواْ هَٰذِهِ ٱلۡقَرۡيَةَ فَكُلُواْ مِنۡهَا حَيۡثُ شِئۡتُمۡ رَغَدٗا وَٱدۡخُلُواْ ٱلۡبَابَ
سُجَّدٗا وَقُولُواْ حِطَّةٞ نَّغۡفِرۡ لَكُمۡ خَطَٰيَٰكُمۡۚ وَسَنَزِيدُ ٱلۡمُحۡسِنِينَ ﴿٥٨﴾ فَبَدَّلَ
ٱلَّذِينَ ظَلَمُواْ قَوۡلًا غَيۡرَ ٱلَّذِي قِيلَ لَهُمۡ فَأَنزَلۡنَا عَلَى ٱلَّذِينَ ظَلَمُواْ رِجۡزٗا مِّنَ
ٱلسَّمَآءِ بِمَا كَانُواْ يَفۡسُقُونَ ﴿٥٩﴾ ۞ وَإِذِ ٱسۡتَسۡقَىٰ مُوسَىٰ لِقَوۡمِهِۦ فَقُلۡنَا
ٱضۡرِب بِّعَصَاكَ ٱلۡحَجَرَۖ فَٱنفَجَرَتۡ مِنۡهُ ٱثۡنَتَا عَشۡرَةَ عَيۡنٗاۖ قَدۡ عَلِمَ كُلُّ
أُنَاسٖ مَّشۡرَبَهُمۡۖ كُلُواْ وَٱشۡرَبُواْ مِن رِّزۡقِ ٱللَّهِ وَلَا تَعۡثَوۡاْ فِي ٱلۡأَرۡضِ
مُفۡسِدِينَ ﴿٦٠﴾ وَإِذۡ قُلۡتُمۡ يَٰمُوسَىٰ لَن نَّصۡبِرَ عَلَىٰ طَعَامٖ وَٰحِدٖ فَٱدۡعُ لَنَا رَبَّكَ
يُخۡرِجۡ لَنَا مِمَّا تُنۢبِتُ ٱلۡأَرۡضُ مِنۢ بَقۡلِهَا وَقِثَّآئِهَا وَفُومِهَا وَعَدَسِهَا وَبَصَلِهَاۖ

Wa ẓallalnā ᶜalaykumul-ghamāma wa ᵓañzalnā ᶜalaykumul-manna was-salwā; kulū miñ-ṭayyibāti mā razaqnākum; wa mā ẓalamūnā wa lākiñ-kānūu ᵓañfusahum yaẓlimūn. (57) Wa ᵓidh qulnad-khulū hādhihil-qaryata fakulū minhā ḥaythu shiᵓtum ra-ghadañw-wad-khulul-bāba sujjadañw-wa qūlū ḥiṭṭatuñ-naghfir lakum khaṭāyākum; wa sanazīdul-muḥsinīn. (58) Fabaddalal-ladhīna ẓalamū qawlañ-ghayral-ladhī qīla lahum faᵓañzalnā ᶜalal-ladhīna ẓalamū rijzam-minas-samāaᵓi bimā kānū yaf-suqūn. (59) ۞ Wa ᵓidhis-tasqā Mūsā liqawmihī faqul-naḍ-rib biᶜaṣākal-ḥajar. Fañfajarat minhuth-natā ᶜashrata ᶜaynā. Qad ᶜalima kullu ᵓunāsim-mashra-bahum. Kulū wash-rabū mir-rizqil-lāhi wa lā taᶜthaw fil-ᵓarḍi mufsidīn. (60) Wa ᵓidh qultum yā Mūsā lañ-naṣbira ᶜalā ṭaᶜāmiñw-wāḥidiñ-fadᶜu lanā Rabbaka yukhrij lanā mimmā tumbitul-ᵓarḍu mim-baqlihā wa qiththāaᵓihā wa fūmihā wa ᶜadasihā wa baṣalihā.

And We caused the clouds to comfort you with their shade, and sent down unto you manna and quails, [saying,] "Partake of the good things which We have provided for you as sustenance."

And [by all their sinning] they did no harm unto Us – but [only] against their own selves did they sin. «57»

And [remember the time] when We said: "Enter this land,[42] and eat of its food as you may desire, abundantly; but enter the gate humbly and say, 'Remove Thou from us the burden of our sins',[43] [whereupon] We shall forgive you your sins, and shall amply reward the doers of good." «58»

But those who were bent on evildoing substituted another saying for that which had been given them:[44] and so We sent down upon those evildoers a plague from heaven in requital for all their iniquity. «59»

And [remember] when Moses prayed for water for his people and We replied, "Strike the rock with thy staff!" – whereupon twelve springs gushed forth from it, so that all the people knew whence to drink.[45] [And Moses said:] "Eat and drink the sustenance provided by God, and do not act wickedly on earth by spreading corruption." «60»

And [remember] when you said: "O Moses, indeed we cannot endure but one kind of food; pray, then, to thy Sustainer that He bring forth for us aught of what grows from the earth – of its herbs, its cucumbers, its garlic, its lentils, its onions."

---

42 The word *qaryah* primarily denotes a "village" or "town", but is also used in the sense of "land". Here it apparently refers to Palestine.

43 This interpretation of the word *ḥiṭṭah* is recorded by most of the lexicographers (cf. Lane II, 592) on the basis of what many Companions of the Prophet said about it (for the relevant quotations, see Ibn Kathīr in his commentary on this verse). Thus, the children of Israel were admonished to take possession of the promised land ("enter the gate") in a spirit of humility (lit., "prostrating yourselves"), and not to regard it as something that was "due" to them.

44 According to several Traditions (extensively quoted by Ibn Kathīr), they played, with a derisive intent, upon the word *ḥiṭṭah* substituting for it something irrelevant or meaningless. Muḥammad ᶜAbduh, however, is of the opinion that the "saying" referred to in verse 58 is merely a metaphor for an *attitude of mind* demanded of them, and that, correspondingly, the "substitution" signifies here a wilful display of arrogance in disregard of God's command (see *Manār* I, 324 f.).

45 I.e., according to their tribal divisions.

Said [Moses]: "Would you take a lesser thing in exchange for what is [so much] better?[46] Go back in shame to Egypt, and then you can have what you are asking for."[47]
And so, ignominy and humiliation overshadowed them, and they earned the burden of God's condemnation: all this, because they persisted in denying the truth of God's messages and in slaying the prophets against all right: all this, because they rebelled [against God], and persisted in transgressing the bounds of what is right.[48] ﴾61﴿

VERILY, those who have attained to faith [in this divine writ], as well as those who follow the Jewish faith, and the Christians, and the Sabians[49] – all who believe in God and the Last Day and do righteous deeds – shall have their reward with their Sustainer; and no fear need they have, and neither shall they grieve.[50] ﴾62﴿

قَالَ أَتَسْتَبْدِلُونَ ٱلَّذِى هُوَ أَدْنَىٰ بِٱلَّذِى هُوَ خَيْرٌ ٱهْبِطُوا۟ مِصْرًا فَإِنَّ لَكُم
مَّا سَأَلْتُمْ وَضُرِبَتْ عَلَيْهِمُ ٱلذِّلَّةُ وَٱلْمَسْكَنَةُ وَبَآءُو بِغَضَبٍ مِّنَ ٱللَّهِ
ذَٰلِكَ بِأَنَّهُمْ كَانُوا۟ يَكْفُرُونَ بِـَٔايَٰتِ ٱللَّهِ وَيَقْتُلُونَ ٱلنَّبِيِّـۧنَ بِغَيْرِ ٱلْحَقِّ
ذَٰلِكَ بِمَا عَصَوا۟ وَّكَانُوا۟ يَعْتَدُونَ ﴿٦١﴾ إِنَّ ٱلَّذِينَ ءَامَنُوا۟ وَٱلَّذِينَ هَادُوا۟
وَٱلنَّصَٰرَىٰ وَٱلصَّٰبِـِٔينَ مَنْ ءَامَنَ بِٱللَّهِ وَٱلْيَوْمِ ٱلْءَاخِرِ وَعَمِلَ صَٰلِحًا
فَلَهُمْ أَجْرُهُمْ عِندَ رَبِّهِمْ وَلَا خَوْفٌ عَلَيْهِمْ وَلَا هُمْ يَحْزَنُونَ ﴿٦٢﴾

Qāla ᵓatastabdilūnal-ladhī huwa ᵓadnā billadhī huwa khayr. ᵓIhbiṭū miṣrañ-faᵓinna lakum-mā saᵓaltum. Wa ḍuribat ᶜalayhimudh-dhillatu wal-maskanatu wa bāaᵓū bighaḍabim-minal-lāh. Dhālika biᵓannahum kānū yakfurūna biᵓāyātil-lāhi wa yaqtulūnan-Nabiyyīna bighayril-ḥaqq. Dhālika bimā ᶜaṣaw-wa kānū yaᶜtadūn. ﴾61﴿ ᵓInnal-ladhīna ᵓāmanū wal-ladhīna Hādū wan-Naṣārā waṣ-Ṣābiᵓīna man ᵓāmana billāhi wal-Yawmil-ᵓĀkhiri wa ᶜamila ṣāliḥañ-falahum ᵓajruhum ᶜiñda Rabbihim wa lā khawfun ᶜalayhim wa lā hum yaḥzanūn. ﴾62﴿

---

46 I.e., "Would you exchange your freedom for the paltry comforts which you enjoyed in your Egyptian captivity?" In the course of their wanderings in the desert of Sinai, many Jews looked back with longing to the comparative security of their life in Egypt, as has been explicitly stated in the Bible (Numbers xi), and is, moreover, evident from Moses' allusion to it in the next sentence of the above Qurᵓanic passage.

47 The verb *habaṭa* means, literally, "he went down a declivity"; it is also used figuratively in the sense of falling from dignity and becoming mean and abject (cf. Lane VIII, 2876). Since the bitter exclamation of Moses cannot be taken literally, both of the above meanings of the verb may be combined in this context and agreeably translated as "go back in shame to Egypt".

48 This passage obviously refers to a later phase of Jewish history. That the Jews actually did kill some of their prophets is evidenced, for instance, in the story of John the Baptist, as well as in the more general accusation uttered, according to the Gospel, by Jesus: "O Jerusalem, Jerusalem, thou that killest the prophets, and stonest them which are sent unto thee" (Matthew xxiii, 37). See also Matthew xxiii, 34-35, Luke xi, 51 – both of which refer to the murder of Zachariah – and I Thessalonians ii, 15. The implication of continuity in, or persistent repetition of, their wrongdoing transpires from the use of the auxiliary verb *kānū* in this context.

49 The Sabians seem to have been a monotheistic religious group intermediate between Judaism and Christianity. Their name (probably derived from the Aramaic verb *tsĕbhaᶜ*, "he immersed himself [in water]") would indicate that they were followers of John the Baptist – in which case they could be identified with the Mandaeans, a community which to this day is to be found in ᶜIrāq. They are not to be confused with the so-called "Sabians of Ḥarrān", a gnostic sect which still existed in the early centuries of Islam, and which may have deliberately adopted the name of the true Sabians in order to obtain the advantages accorded by the Muslims to the followers of every monotheistic faith.

50 The above passage – which recurs in the Qurᵓān several times – lays down a fundamental doctrine of Islam. With a breadth of vision unparalleled in any other religious faith, the idea of "salvation" is here made conditional upon three elements only: belief in God, belief in the Day of Judgment, and righteous action in life. The statement of this doctrine at this juncture – that is, in the midst of an appeal to the children of Israel – is warranted by the false Jewish belief that their descent from Abraham entitles them to be regarded as "God's chosen people".

وَإِذْ أَخَذْنَا مِيثَٰقَكُمْ وَرَفَعْنَا فَوْقَكُمُ ٱلطُّورَ خُذُوا۟ مَآ ءَاتَيْنَٰكُم بِقُوَّةٍ
وَٱذْكُرُوا۟ مَا فِيهِ لَعَلَّكُمْ تَتَّقُونَ ﴿٦٣﴾ ثُمَّ تَوَلَّيْتُم مِّنۢ بَعْدِ ذَٰلِكَ ۖ فَلَوْلَا
فَضْلُ ٱللَّهِ عَلَيْكُمْ وَرَحْمَتُهُۥ لَكُنتُم مِّنَ ٱلْخَٰسِرِينَ ﴿٦٤﴾ وَلَقَدْ عَلِمْتُمُ
ٱلَّذِينَ ٱعْتَدَوْا۟ مِنكُمْ فِى ٱلسَّبْتِ فَقُلْنَا لَهُمْ كُونُوا۟ قِرَدَةً خَٰسِـِٔينَ ﴿٦٥﴾
فَجَعَلْنَٰهَا نَكَٰلًا لِّمَا بَيْنَ يَدَيْهَا وَمَا خَلْفَهَا وَمَوْعِظَةً لِّلْمُتَّقِينَ ﴿٦٦﴾ وَإِذْ
قَالَ مُوسَىٰ لِقَوْمِهِۦٓ إِنَّ ٱللَّهَ يَأْمُرُكُمْ أَن تَذْبَحُوا۟ بَقَرَةً ۖ قَالُوٓا۟ أَتَتَّخِذُنَا
هُزُوًا ۖ قَالَ أَعُوذُ بِٱللَّهِ أَنْ أَكُونَ مِنَ ٱلْجَٰهِلِينَ ﴿٦٧﴾ قَالُوا۟ ٱدْعُ لَنَا رَبَّكَ
يُبَيِّن لَّنَا مَا هِىَ ۚ قَالَ إِنَّهُۥ يَقُولُ إِنَّهَا بَقَرَةٌ لَّا فَارِضٌ وَلَا بِكْرٌ عَوَانٌۢ بَيْنَ
ذَٰلِكَ ۖ فَٱفْعَلُوا۟ مَا تُؤْمَرُونَ ﴿٦٨﴾ قَالُوا۟ ٱدْعُ لَنَا رَبَّكَ يُبَيِّن لَّنَا مَا لَوْنُهَا ۚ
قَالَ إِنَّهُۥ يَقُولُ إِنَّهَا بَقَرَةٌ صَفْرَآءُ فَاقِعٌ لَّوْنُهَا تَسُرُّ ٱلنَّٰظِرِينَ ﴿٦٩﴾

Wa ʾidh ʾakhadhnā mīthāqakum wa rafaʿnā fawqa-kumuṭṭūra khudhū māa ʾātaynākum-biquwwatiñw-wadh-kurū mā fīhi laʿallakum tattaqūn. (63) **Thumma tawallaytum mim-baʿdi dhālik. Falawlā faḍlul-lāhi ʿalaykum wa raḥmatuhū lakuñtum-minal-khāsirīn.** (64) **Wa laqad ʿalimtumul-ladhīnaʿ-tadaw miñkum fis-sabti faqulnā lahum kūnū qiradatañ-khāsiʾīn.** (65) **Fajaʿalnāhā nakālal-limā bayna yadayhā wa mā khalfahā wa mawʿiẓatal-lilmuttaqīn.** (66) **Wa ʾidh qāla Mūsā liqawmihīi ʾinnal-lāha yaʾmurukum ʾañ-tadhbaḥū baqarah. Qālūu ʾatattakhidhunā huzuwā. Qāla ʾaʿūdhu billāhi ʾan ʾakūna minal-jāhilīn.** (67) **Qālud-ʿu lanā Rabbaka yubayyil-lanā mā hī. Qāla ʾinnahū yaqūlu ʾinnahā baqaratul-lā fāriḍuñw-wa lā bikruñ-ʿawānum-bayna dhālika fafʿalū mā tuʾmarūn.** (68) **Qālud-ʿu lanā Rabbaka yubayyil-lanā mā lawnuhā. Qāla ʾinnahū yaqūlu ʾinnahā baqaratuñ-ṣafrāaʾu fāqiʿul-lawnuhā tasurrun-nāẓirīn.** (69)

AND LO! We accepted your solemn pledge, raising Mount Sinai high above you,[51] [and saying,] "Hold fast with [all your] strength unto what We have vouchsafed you, and bear in mind all that is therein, so that you might remain conscious of God!" «63»
And you turned away after that! And had it not been for God's favour upon you and His grace, you would surely have found yourselves among the lost; «64» for you are well aware of those from among you who profaned the Sabbath, whereupon We said unto them, "Be as apes despicable!" «65» – and set them up as a warning example for their time and for all times to come, as well as an admonition to all who are conscious of God.[52] «66»

AND LO! Moses said unto his people: "Behold, God bids you to sacrifice a cow."[53]
They said: "Dost thou mock at us?"
He answered: "I seek refuge with God against being so ignorant!"[54] «67»
Said they: "Pray on our behalf unto thy Sustainer that He make clear to us what she is to be like."
[Moses] replied: "Behold, He says it is to be a cow neither old nor immature, but of an age in-between. Do, then, what you have been bidden!" «68»
Said they: "Pray on our behalf unto thy Sustainer that He make clear to us what her colour should be."
[Moses] answered: "Behold, He says it is to be a yellow cow, bright of hue, pleasing to the beholder." «69»

---

51 Lit., "and We raised the mountain (*aṭ-ṭūr*) above you": i.e., letting the lofty mountain bear witness, as it were, to their solemn pledge, spelled out in verse 83 below. Throughout my translation of the Qurʾān, I am rendering the expression *aṭ-ṭūr* as "Mount Sinai", since it is invariably used in this sense alone.

52 For the full story of the Sabbath-breakers, and the metaphorical allusion to "apes", see 7 : 163-166. The expression *mā bayna yadayhā*, rendered here as "their time", is explained in *sūrah* 3, note 3.

53 As is evident from verse 72, the story related in this and the subsequent passages almost certainly refers to the Mosaic law which ordains that in certain cases of unresolved murder a cow should be sacrificed, and the elders of the town or village nearest to the place of the murder should wash their hands over it and declare, "Our hands have not shed this blood, neither have our eyes seen it" – whereupon the community would be absolved of collective responsibility. For the details of this Old Testament ordinance, see Deuteronomy xxi, 1-9.

54 Lit., "lest I be one of the ignorant". The imputation of mockery was obviously due to the fact that Moses promulgated the above ordinance in very general terms, without specifying any details.

Said they: "Pray on our behalf unto thy Sustainer that He make clear to us what she is to be like, for to us all cows resemble one another; and then, if God so wills, we shall truly be guided aright!" ‹70›
[Moses] answered: "Behold, He says it is to be a cow not broken-in to plough the earth or to water the crops, free of fault, without markings of any other colour."
Said they: "At last thou hast brought out the truth!" – and thereupon they sacrificed her, although they had almost left it undone.[55] ‹71›
For, [O children of Israel,] because you had slain a human being and then cast the blame for this [crime] upon one another – although God will bring to light what you would conceal[56] ‹72› – We said: "Apply this [principle] to some of those [cases of unresolved murder]:[57] in this way God saves lives from death and shows you His will,

قَالُوا۟ ٱدْعُ لَنَا رَبَّكَ يُبَيِّن لَّنَا مَا هِىَ إِنَّ ٱلْبَقَرَ تَشَٰبَهَ عَلَيْنَا وَإِنَّآ إِن شَآءَ ٱللَّهُ
لَمُهْتَدُونَ ﴿٧٠﴾ قَالَ إِنَّهُۥ يَقُولُ إِنَّهَا بَقَرَةٌ لَّا ذَلُولٌ تُثِيرُ ٱلْأَرْضَ وَلَا تَسْقِى
ٱلْحَرْثَ مُسَلَّمَةٌ لَّا شِيَةَ فِيهَا قَالُوا۟ ٱلْـَٰٔنَ جِئْتَ بِٱلْحَقِّ فَذَبَحُوهَا وَمَا كَادُوا۟
يَفْعَلُونَ ﴿٧١﴾ وَإِذْ قَتَلْتُمْ نَفْسًا فَٱدَّٰرَْٰٔتُمْ فِيهَا وَٱللَّهُ مُخْرِجٌ مَّا كُنتُمْ تَكْتُمُونَ ﴿٧٢﴾
فَقُلْنَا ٱضْرِبُوهُ بِبَعْضِهَا كَذَٰلِكَ يُحْىِ ٱللَّهُ ٱلْمَوْتَىٰ وَيُرِيكُمْ ءَايَٰتِهِۦ

Qālud-ᶜu lanā Rabbaka yubayyil-lanā mā hiya ᵓinnal-baqara tashābaha ᶜalaynā wa ᵓinnāa ᵓiñ-shāaᵓal-lāhu lamuhtadūn. (70) Qāla ᵓinnahū yaqūlu ᵓinnahā baqaratul-lā dhalūluñ-tuthīrul-ᵓarḍa wa lā tasqil-ḥartha musallamatul-lā shiyata fīhā. Qālul-ᵓāna jiᵓta bilḥaqq. Fadhabaḥūhā wa mā kādū yafᶜalūn. (71) Wa ᵓidh qataltum nafsañ-faddāraᵓtum fīhā; wal-lāhu mukhrijum-mā kuñtum taktumūn. (72) Faqulnaḍ-ribūhu bibaᶜḍihā. Kadhālika yuḥyil-lāhul-mawtā wa yurīkum ᵓĀyātihī

55 I.e., their obstinate desire to obtain closer and closer definitions of the simple commandment revealed to them through Moses had made it almost impossible for them to fulfil it. In his commentary on this passage, Ṭabarī quotes the following remark of Ibn ᶜAbbās: "If [in the first instance] they had sacrificed any cow chosen by themselves, they would have fulfilled their duty; but they made it complicated for themselves, and so God made it complicated for them." A similar view has been expressed, in the same context, by Zamakhsharī. It would appear that the moral of this story points to an important problem of all (and, therefore, also of Islamic) religious jurisprudence: namely, the inadvisability of trying to elicit additional details in respect of any religious law that had originally been given in general terms – for, the more numerous and multiform such details become, the more complicated and rigid becomes the law. This point has been acutely grasped by Rashīd Riḍāᵓ, who says in his commentary on the above Qurᵓanic passage (see *Manār* I, 345 f.): "Its lesson is that one should not pursue one's [legal] inquiries in such a way as to make laws more complicated. . . . This was how the early generations [of Muslims] visualized the problem. They did not make things complicated for themselves – and so, for them, the religious law (*dīn*) was natural, simple and liberal in its straightforwardness. But those who came later added to it [certain other] injunctions which they had deduced by means of their own reasoning (*ijtihād*); and they multiplied those [additional] injunctions to such an extent that the religious law became a heavy burden on the community." For the sociological reason why the genuine ordinances of Islamic Law – that is, those which have been *prima facie* laid down as such in the Qur'an and the teachings of the Prophet – are almost always devoid of details, I would refer the reader to my book *State and Government in Islam* (pp. 11 ff. and *passim*). The importance of this problem, illustrated in the above story of the cow – and correctly grasped by the Prophet's Companions – explains why this *sūrah* has been entitled "The Cow". (See also 5 : 101 and the corresponding notes 120-123.)

56 See note 53 above. The use of the plural "you" implies the principle of collective, communal responsibility stipulated by Mosaic Law in cases of murder by a person or persons unknown. God's bringing the guilt to light obviously refers to the Day of Judgment.

57 The phrase *iḍribūhu bi-baᶜḍihā* can be literally translated as "strike him [or "it"] with something of her [or "it"]" – and this possibility has given rise to the fanciful assertion by many commentators that the children of Israel were commanded to strike the corpse of the murdered man with some of the flesh of the sacrificed cow, whereupon he was miraculously restored to life and pointed out his murderer! Neither the Qurᵓān, nor any saying of the Prophet, nor even the Bible offers the slightest warrant for this highly imaginative explanation, which must, therefore, be rejected – quite apart from the fact that the pronoun *hu* in *iḍribūhu* has a masculine gender, while the noun *nafs* (here translated as "human being") is feminine in gender: from which it follows that the imperative *iḍribūhu* cannot possibly refer to *nafs*. On the other hand, the verb *ḍaraba* (lit., "he struck") is very often used in a figurative or metonymic sense, as, for instance, in the expression *ḍaraba fi 'l-arḍ* ("he journeyed on earth"), or *ḍaraba 'sh-shayᵓ bi'sh-shayᵓ*

so that you might [learn to] use your reason."[58] ⟨73⟩
And yet, after all this, your hearts hardened and became like rocks, or even harder: for, behold, there are rocks from which streams gush forth; and, behold, there are some from which, when they are cleft, water issues; and, behold, there are some that fall down for awe of God.[59] And God is not unmindful of what you do! ⟨74⟩

حزب 2

CAN YOU, then, hope that they will believe in what you are preaching[60] – seeing that a good many of them were wont to listen to the word of God and then, after having understood it, to pervert it knowingly?[61] ⟨75⟩ For, when they meet those who have attained to faith, they say, "We believe [as you believe]" – but when they find themselves alone with one another, they say, "Do you inform them of what God has disclosed to you, so that they might use it in argument against you, quoting the words of your Sustainer?[62] Will you not, then, use your reason?" ⟨76⟩

لَعَلَّكُمۡ تَعۡقِلُونَ ﴿٧٣﴾ ثُمَّ قَسَتۡ قُلُوبُكُم مِّنۢ بَعۡدِ ذَٰلِكَ فَهِيَ كَٱلۡحِجَارَةِ
أَوۡ أَشَدُّ قَسۡوَةٗۚ وَإِنَّ مِنَ ٱلۡحِجَارَةِ لَمَا يَتَفَجَّرُ مِنۡهُ ٱلۡأَنۡهَٰرُۚ وَإِنَّ مِنۡهَا لَمَا
يَشَّقَّقُ فَيَخۡرُجُ مِنۡهُ ٱلۡمَآءُۚ وَإِنَّ مِنۡهَا لَمَا يَهۡبِطُ مِنۡ خَشۡيَةِ ٱللَّهِۗ وَمَا ٱللَّهُ بِغَٰفِلٍ
عَمَّا تَعۡمَلُونَ ﴿٧٤﴾ ۞ أَفَتَطۡمَعُونَ أَن يُؤۡمِنُواْ لَكُمۡ وَقَدۡ كَانَ فَرِيقٞ مِّنۡهُمۡ
يَسۡمَعُونَ كَلَٰمَ ٱللَّهِ ثُمَّ يُحَرِّفُونَهُۥ مِنۢ بَعۡدِ مَا عَقَلُوهُ وَهُمۡ يَعۡلَمُونَ ﴿٧٥﴾ وَإِذَا
لَقُواْ ٱلَّذِينَ ءَامَنُواْ قَالُوٓاْ ءَامَنَّا وَإِذَا خَلَا بَعۡضُهُمۡ إِلَىٰ بَعۡضٖ قَالُوٓاْ أَتُحَدِّثُونَهُم
بِمَا فَتَحَ ٱللَّهُ عَلَيۡكُمۡ لِيُحَآجُّوكُم بِهِۦ عِندَ رَبِّكُمۡۚ أَفَلَا تَعۡقِلُونَ ﴿٧٦﴾

laʿallakum taʿqilūn. ⟨73⟩ Thumma qasat qulūbukum-mim-baʿdi dhalika fahiya kalḥijārati ʾaw ʾashaddu qaswah. Wa ʾinna minal-ḥijārati lamā yatafajjaru minhul-ʾanhār. Wa ʾinna minhā lamā yashshaqqaqu fayakhruju minhul-māaʾ. Wa ʾinna minhā lamā yahbiṭu min khashyatil-lāh. Wa mal-lāhu bighāfilin ʿammā taʿmalūn. ⟨74⟩ ۞ ʾAfataṭmaʿūna ʾañy-yuʾminū lakum wa qad kāna farīqum-minhum yasmaʿūna Kalāmal-lāhi thumma yuḥarrifūnahū mim-baʿdi mā ʿaqalūhu wa hum yaʿlamūn. ⟨75⟩ Wa ʾidhā laqul-ladhīna ʾāmanū qālūu ʾāmannā wa ʾidhā khalā baʿḍuhum ʾilā baʿḍiñ-qālūu ʾatuḥaddithūnahum-bimā fataḥal-lāhu ʿalaykum liyuḥāajjūkum-bihī ʿiñda Rabbikum. ʾAfalā taʿqilūn. ⟨76⟩

("he mixed one thing with another thing"), or *ḍaraba mathal* ("he coined a similitude" or "propounded a parable" or "gave an illustration"), or *ʿalā ḍarb wāḥid* ("similarly applied" or "in the same manner"), or *ḍuribat ʿalayhim adh-dhillah* ("humiliation was imposed on them" or "applied to them") and so forth. Taking all this into account, I am of the opinion that the imperative *iḍribūhu* occurring in the above Qurʾanic passage must be translated as "apply it" or "this" (referring, in this context, to the principle of communal responsibility). As for the feminine pronoun *hā* in *baʿḍihā* ("some of it"), it must necessarily relate to the nearest preceding feminine noun – that is, to the *nafs* that has been murdered, or the act of murder itself about which (*fīhā*) the community disagreed. Thus, the phrase *iḍribūhu bi-baʿḍihā* may be suitably rendered as "apply this [principle] to some of those [cases of unresolved murder]": for it is obvious that the principle of communal responsibility for murder by a person or persons unknown can be applied only to some and not to all such cases.

58 Lit., "God gives life to the dead and shows you His messages" (i.e., He shows His will by means of such messages or ordinances). The figurative expression "He gives life to the dead" denotes the *saving* of lives, and is analogous to that in 5 : 32. In this context it refers to the prevention of bloodshed and the killing of innocent persons (*Manār* I, 351), be it through individual acts of revenge, or in result of an erroneous judicial process based on no more than vague suspicion and possibly misleading circumstantial evidence.

59 For an explanation of this allusion, see 7 : 143. The simile of "the rocks from which streams gush forth" or "from which water issues" serves to illustrate its *opposite*, namely, dryness and lack of life, and is thus an allusion to the spiritual barrenness with which the Qurʾān charges the children of Israel.

60 Here the Muslims are addressed. In the early period of Islam – and especially after their exodus to Medina, where many Jews were then living – the Muslims expected that the Jews, with their monotheistic beliefs, would be the first to rally to the message of the Qurʾān: a hope that was disappointed because the Jews regarded their own religion as a kind of national heritage reserved to the children of Israel alone, and did not believe in the necessity – or possibility – of a new revelation.

61 Cf. Jeremiah xxiii, 36 – "Ye have perverted the words of the living God".

62 Lit., "before [or "in the sight of"] your Sustainer". Most of the commentators (e.g., Zamakhsharī, Baghawī, Rāzī)

Do they not know, then, that God is aware
of all that they would conceal as well as of
all that they bring into the open? «77»
And there are among them unlettered
people who have no real knowledge of the
divine writ,[63] [following] only wishful beliefs and depending on nothing but conjecture. «78» Woe, then, unto those who
write down, with their own hands, [some-
thing which they claim to be] divine writ,
and then say, "This is from God," in order
to acquire a trifling gain thereby;[64] woe,
then, unto them for what their hands have
written, and woe unto them for all that
they may have gained! «79»
And they say, "The fire will most certainly
not touch us for more than a limited
number of days."[65] Say [unto them]: "Have
you received a promise from God – for
God never breaks His promise – or do you
attribute to God something which you
cannot know?" «80»
Yea! Those who earn evil and by their
sinfulness are engulfed – they are destined
for the fire, therein to abide; «81» whereas
those who attain to faith and do righteous
deeds – they are destined for paradise,
therein to abide. «82»

AND LO! We accepted this solemn pledge
from [you,] the children of Israel:[66] "You
shall worship none but God; and you shall
do good unto your parents and kinsfolk,
and the orphans, and the poor; and you shall

أَوَلَا يَعْلَمُونَ أَنَّ ٱللَّهَ يَعْلَمُ مَا يُسِرُّونَ وَمَا يُعْلِنُونَ (77) وَمِنْهُمْ أُمِّيُّونَ لَا
يَعْلَمُونَ ٱلْكِتَٰبَ إِلَّآ أَمَانِىَّ وَإِنْ هُمْ إِلَّا يَظُنُّونَ (78) فَوَيْلٌ لِّلَّذِينَ يَكْتُبُونَ
ٱلْكِتَٰبَ بِأَيْدِيهِمْ ثُمَّ يَقُولُونَ هَٰذَا مِنْ عِندِ ٱللَّهِ لِيَشْتَرُوا۟ بِهِۦ ثَمَنًا قَلِيلًا
فَوَيْلٌ لَّهُم مِّمَّا كَتَبَتْ أَيْدِيهِمْ وَوَيْلٌ لَّهُم مِّمَّا يَكْسِبُونَ (79) وَقَالُوا۟ لَن
تَمَسَّنَا ٱلنَّارُ إِلَّآ أَيَّامًا مَّعْدُودَةً قُلْ أَتَّخَذْتُمْ عِندَ ٱللَّهِ عَهْدًا فَلَن يُخْلِفَ
ٱللَّهُ عَهْدَهُۥٓ أَمْ تَقُولُونَ عَلَى ٱللَّهِ مَا لَا تَعْلَمُونَ (80) بَلَىٰ مَن كَسَبَ سَيِّئَةً
وَأَحَٰطَتْ بِهِۦ خَطِيٓـَٔتُهُۥ فَأُو۟لَٰٓئِكَ أَصْحَٰبُ ٱلنَّارِ هُمْ فِيهَا خَٰلِدُونَ (81)
وَٱلَّذِينَ ءَامَنُوا۟ وَعَمِلُوا۟ ٱلصَّٰلِحَٰتِ أُو۟لَٰٓئِكَ أَصْحَٰبُ ٱلْجَنَّةِ هُمْ فِيهَا
خَٰلِدُونَ (82) وَإِذْ أَخَذْنَا مِيثَٰقَ بَنِىٓ إِسْرَٰٓءِيلَ لَا تَعْبُدُونَ إِلَّا ٱللَّهَ
وَبِٱلْوَٰلِدَيْنِ إِحْسَانًا وَذِى ٱلْقُرْبَىٰ وَٱلْيَتَٰمَىٰ وَٱلْمَسَٰكِينِ وَقُولُوا۟

**ʾAwalā yaʿlamūna ʾannal-lāha yaʿlamu mā yusirrūna
wa mā yuʿlinūn. (77) Wa minhum ʾummiyyūna lā
yaʿlamūnal-Kitāba ʾillāa ʾamāniyya wa ʾin hum
ʾillā yaẓunnūn. (78) Fawaylul-lilladhīna yaktubūnal-
Kitāba biʾaydīhim thumma yaqūlūna hādhā min
ʿiñdil-lāhi liyashtarū bihī thamanañ-qalīlā. Fawaylul-
lahum-mimmā katabat ʾaydīhim wa waylul-lahum-
mimmā yaksibūn. (79) Wa qālū lañ-tamassanan-nāru
ʾillāa ʾayyāmam-maʿdūdah. Qul ʾattakhadhtum
ʿiñdal-lāhi ʿahdañ-falañy-yukhlifal-lāhu ʿahdahūu
ʾam taqūlūna ʿalal-lāhi mā lā taʿlamūn. (80) Balā
mañ-kasaba sayyiʾatañw-wa ʾaḥāṭat bihī
khaṭīiʾatuhū faʾulāaʾika ʾaṣḥābun-nāri hum fīhā
khālidūn. (81) Wal-ladhīna ʾāmanū wa ʿamiluṣ-ṣāliḥāti
ʾulāaʾika ʾaṣḥābul-jannati hum fīhā khālidūn. (82)
Wa ʾidh ʾakhadhnā mīthāqa banīi ʾIsrāaʾīla lā
taʿbudūna ʾillal-lāha wa bilwālidayni ʾiḥsānañw-wa
dhil-qurbā wal-yatāmā wal-masākīni wa qūlū**

agree in that the expression "your Sustainer" stands here for "that which your Sustainer has revealed", namely, the Biblical prophecy relating to the coming of a prophet "from among the brethren" of the children of Israel, and that, therefore, the above phrase implies an argument on the basis of the Jews' own scriptures. (See also note 33 above.)

63 In this case, the Old Testament.

64 The reference here is to the scholars responsible for corrupting the text of the Bible and thus misleading their ignorant followers. The "trifling gain" is their feeling of pre-eminence as the alleged "chosen people".

65 According to popular Jewish belief, even the sinners from among the children of Israel will suffer only very limited punishment in the life to come, and will be quickly reprieved by virtue of their belonging to "the chosen people": a belief which the Qurʾān rejects.

66 In the preceding passages, the children of Israel have been reminded of the favours that were bestowed on them. Now, however, the Qurʾān, reminds them of the fact that the way of righteousness has indeed been shown to them by means of explicit social and moral injunctions: and this reminder flows directly from the statement that the human condition in the life to come depends exclusively on the manner of one's life in this world, and not on one's descent.

speak unto all people in a kindly way; and you shall be constant in prayer; and you shall spend in charity."[67]

And yet, save for a few of you, you turned away: for you are obstinate folk![68] ‹83›

And lo! We accepted your solemn pledge that you would not shed one another's blood, and would not drive one another from your homelands – whereupon you acknowledged it; and thereto you bear witness [even now]. ‹84› And yet, it is you who slay one another and drive some of your own people from their homelands, aiding one another against them in sin and hatred; but if they come to you as captives, you ransom them – although the very [act of] driving them away has been made unlawful to you!"[69]

Do you, then, believe in some parts of the divine writ and deny the truth of other parts? What, then, could be the reward of those among you who do such things but ignominy in the life of this world and, on the Day of Resurrection, commitment to most grievous suffering? For God is not unmindful of what you do. ‹85›

All who buy the life of this world at the price of the life to come – their suffering shall not be lightened, nor shall they be succoured! ‹86›

For, indeed, We vouchsafed unto Moses the divine writ and caused apostle after apostle to follow him;[70] and We vouch-

لِلنَّاسِ حُسْنًا وَأَقِيمُوا۟ ٱلصَّلَوٰةَ وَءَاتُوا۟ ٱلزَّكَوٰةَ ثُمَّ تَوَلَّيْتُمْ إِلَّا قَلِيلًا
مِّنكُمْ وَأَنتُم مُّعْرِضُونَ ﴿٨٣﴾ وَإِذْ أَخَذْنَا مِيثَٰقَكُمْ لَا تَسْفِكُونَ دِمَآءَكُمْ
وَلَا تُخْرِجُونَ أَنفُسَكُم مِّن دِيَٰرِكُمْ ثُمَّ أَقْرَرْتُمْ وَأَنتُمْ تَشْهَدُونَ ﴿٨٤﴾ ثُمَّ أَنتُمْ
هَٰٓؤُلَآءِ تَقْتُلُونَ أَنفُسَكُمْ وَتُخْرِجُونَ فَرِيقًا مِّنكُم مِّن دِيَٰرِهِمْ تَظَٰهَرُونَ
عَلَيْهِم بِٱلْإِثْمِ وَٱلْعُدْوَٰنِ وَإِن يَأْتُوكُمْ أُسَٰرَىٰ تُفَٰدُوهُمْ وَهُوَ مُحَرَّمٌ عَلَيْكُمْ
إِخْرَاجُهُمْ أَفَتُؤْمِنُونَ بِبَعْضِ ٱلْكِتَٰبِ وَتَكْفُرُونَ بِبَعْضٍ فَمَا جَزَآءُ مَن
يَفْعَلُ ذَٰلِكَ مِنكُمْ إِلَّا خِزْىٌ فِى ٱلْحَيَوٰةِ ٱلدُّنْيَا وَيَوْمَ ٱلْقِيَٰمَةِ يُرَدُّونَ إِلَىٰٓ
أَشَدِّ ٱلْعَذَابِ وَمَا ٱللَّهُ بِغَٰفِلٍ عَمَّا تَعْمَلُونَ ﴿٨٥﴾ أُو۟لَٰٓئِكَ ٱلَّذِينَ ٱشْتَرَوُا۟
ٱلْحَيَوٰةَ ٱلدُّنْيَا بِٱلْءَاخِرَةِ فَلَا يُخَفَّفُ عَنْهُمُ ٱلْعَذَابُ وَلَا هُمْ يُنصَرُونَ ﴿٨٦﴾
وَلَقَدْ ءَاتَيْنَا مُوسَى ٱلْكِتَٰبَ وَقَفَّيْنَا مِنۢ بَعْدِهِۦ بِٱلرُّسُلِ وَءَاتَيْنَا

linnāsi ḥusnañw-wa ᵓaqīmuṣ-Ṣalāta wa ᵓātuz-Zakāta thumma tawallaytum ᵓillā qalīlam-miñkum wa ᵓañtummuᶜriḍūn. (83) Wa ᵓidh ᵓakhadhnā mīthāqakum lā tasfikūna dimāaᵓakum wa lā tukhrijūna ᵓañfusakum-miñ-diyārikum thumma ᵓaqrartum wa ᵓañtum tashhadūn. (84) Thumma ᵓañtum hāaᵓulāaᵓi taqtulūna ᵓañfusakum wa tukhrijūna farīqam-miñkum-miñ-diyārihim taẓāharūna ᶜalayhim-bilᵓithmi wal-ᶜudwāni wa ᵓiñy-yaᵓtūkum ᵓusārā tufādūhum wa huwa muḥarramun ᶜalaykum ᵓikhrājuhum. ᵓAfatuᵓminūna bibaᶜḍil-Kitābi wa takfurūna bibaᶜḍ. Famā jazāaᵓu mañy-yafᶜalu dhālika miñkum ᵓillā khizyuñ-fil-ḥayātid-dunyā; wa Yawmal-Qiyāmati yuraddūna ᵓilāa ashad-dil-ᶜadhāb. Wa mal-lāhu bighāfilin ᶜammā taᶜmalūn. (85) ᵓUlāaᵓikal-ladhīnash-tarawul-ḥayātad-dunyā bil-ᵓĀkhirati falā yukhaffafu ᶜanhumul-ᶜadhābu wa lā hum yuñṣarūn. (86) Wa laqad ᵓātaynā Mūsal-Kitāba wa qaffaynā mimbaᶜdihī birRusuli wa ᵓātaynā

67 See note 34 above.

68 The Old Testament contains many allusions to the waywardness and stubborn rebelliousness of the children of Israel – e.g., Exodus xxxii, 9, xxxiii, 3, xxxiv, 9; Deuteronomy ix, 6-8, 23-24, 27.

69 This is a reference to the conditions prevailing at Medina at the time of the Prophet's *hijrah*. The two Arab tribes of Medina – Al-Aws and Khazraj – were in pre-Islamic times permanently at war with one another; and out of the three Jewish tribes living there – the Banū Qaynuqāᶜ, Banu 'n-Naḍīr and Banū Qurayẓah – the first-named two were allied with Khazraj, while the third was allied with Al-Aws. Thus, in the course of their warfare, Jew would kill Jew in alliance with pagans ("aiding one another in sin and hatred"): a twofold crime from the viewpoint of Mosaic Law. Nevertheless, they would subsequently ransom their mutual captives in obedience to that very same Law – and it is this glaring inconsistency to which the Qurᵓān alludes in the next sentence.

70 Lit., "We caused him to be followed, after his time, by [all] the other apostles": a stress upon the continuous succession of prophets among the Jews (see Ṭabarī, Zamakhsharī, Rāzī, Ibn Kathīr), which fact deprives them of any excuse of ignorance.

safed unto Jesus, the son of Mary, all evidence of the truth, and strengthened him with holy inspiration.[71] [Yet] is it not so that every time an apostle came unto you with something that was not to your liking, you gloried in your arrogance, and to some of them you gave the lie, while others you would slay?[72] ‹87›

But they say, "Our hearts are already full of knowledge."[73] Nay, but God has rejected them because of their refusal to acknowledge the truth: for, few are the things in which they believe."[74] ‹88›

And whenever there came unto them a [new] revelation from God, confirming the truth already in their possession – and [bear in mind that] aforetime they used to pray for victory over those who were bent on denying the truth: – whenever there came unto them something which they recognized [as the truth], they would deny it. And God's rejection is the due of all who deny the truth. ‹89›

Vile is that [false pride] for which they have sold their own selves by denying the truth of what God has bestowed from on high, out of envy that God should bestow aught of His favour upon whomsoever He wills of His servants:[75] and thus have they earned the burden of God's condemnation, over and over. And for those who deny the truth there is shameful suffering in store. ‹90›

عِيسَى ٱبْنَ مَرْيَمَ ٱلْبَيِّنَٰتِ وَأَيَّدْنَٰهُ بِرُوحِ ٱلْقُدُسِ ۗ أَفَكُلَّمَا جَآءَكُمْ
رَسُولٌۢ بِمَا لَا تَهْوَىٰٓ أَنفُسُكُمُ ٱسْتَكْبَرْتُمْ فَفَرِيقًا كَذَّبْتُمْ وَفَرِيقًا
تَقْتُلُونَ ﴿٨٧﴾ وَقَالُوا۟ قُلُوبُنَا غُلْفٌۢ ۚ بَل لَّعَنَهُمُ ٱللَّهُ بِكُفْرِهِمْ فَقَلِيلًا مَّا
يُؤْمِنُونَ ﴿٨٨﴾ وَلَمَّا جَآءَهُمْ كِتَٰبٌ مِّنْ عِندِ ٱللَّهِ مُصَدِّقٌ لِّمَا مَعَهُمْ وَكَانُوا۟
مِن قَبْلُ يَسْتَفْتِحُونَ عَلَى ٱلَّذِينَ كَفَرُوا۟ فَلَمَّا جَآءَهُم مَّا عَرَفُوا۟ كَفَرُوا۟ بِهِۦ ۚ
فَلَعْنَةُ ٱللَّهِ عَلَى ٱلْكَٰفِرِينَ ﴿٨٩﴾ بِئْسَمَا ٱشْتَرَوْا۟ بِهِۦٓ أَنفُسَهُمْ أَن يَكْفُرُوا۟
بِمَآ أَنزَلَ ٱللَّهُ بَغْيًا أَن يُنَزِّلَ ٱللَّهُ مِن فَضْلِهِۦ عَلَىٰ مَن يَشَآءُ مِنْ عِبَادِهِۦ ۖ
فَبَآءُو بِغَضَبٍ عَلَىٰ غَضَبٍ ۚ وَلِلْكَٰفِرِينَ عَذَابٌ مُّهِينٌ ﴿٩٠﴾

ᶜĪsab-na Maryamal-bayyināti wa ᵓayyadnāhu birūḥil-qudus. ᵓAfakullamā jāaᵓakum Rasūlum-bimā lā tahwāa ᵓañfusukumus-takbartum. Fafarīqañ-kadhdhabtum wa farīqañ-taqtulūn. (87) Wa qālū qulūbunā ghulf. Bal-laᶜanahumul-lāhu bikufrihim faqalīlam-mā yuᵓminūn. (88) Wa lammā jāaᵓahum Kitābum-min ᶜiñdil-lāhi muṣaddiqul-limā maᶜahum wa kānū miñ-qablu yastaftiḥūna ᶜalal-ladhīna kafarū falam-mā jāaᵓahum-mā ᶜarafū kafarū bihī falaᶜnatul-lāhi ᶜalal-kāfirīn. (89) Biᵓsamash-taraw bihīi ᵓañfusahum ᵓañy-yakfurū bimāa ᵓañzalal-lāhu baghyan ᵓañy-yunazzilal-lāhu miñ-faḍlihī ᶜalā mañy-yashāaᵓu min ᶜibādih. Fabāaᵓū bighaḍabin ᶜalā ghaḍab. Wa lilkāfirīna ᶜadhābum-muhīn. (90)

71 This rendering of *rūḥ al-qudus* (lit., "the spirit of holiness") is based on the recurring use in the Qurᵓān of the term *rūḥ* in the sense of "divine inspiration". It is also recorded that the Prophet invoked the blessing of the *rūḥ al-qudus* on his Companion, the poet Ḥassān ibn Thābit (Bukhārī, Muslim, Abū Dāᵓūd and Tirmidhī): just as the Qurᵓān (58 : 22) speaks of *all* believers as being "strengthened by inspiration (*rūḥ*) from Him".

72 Lit., "and some you are slaying". The change from the past tense observed throughout this sentence to the present tense in the verb *taqtulūn* ("you are slaying") is meant to express a conscious intent in this respect and, thus, a persistent, ever-recurring trait in Jewish history (*Manār* I, 377), to which also the New Testament refers (Matthew xxiii, 34-35, 37), and I Thessalonians ii, 15).

73 Lit., "our hearts are repositories [of knowledge]" – an allusion to the boast of the Jews that in view of the religious knowledge which they already possess, they are in no need of any further preaching (Ibn Kathīr, on the authority of Ibn ᶜAbbās; identical explanations are mentioned by Ṭabarī and Zamakhsharī).

74 I.e., all their beliefs are centred on themselves and their alleged "exceptional" status in the sight of God.

75 I.e., out of envy that God should bestow revelation upon anyone but a descendant of Israel – in this particular instance, upon the Arabian Prophet, Muḥammad.

وَإِذَا قِيلَ لَهُمْ ءَامِنُوا۟ بِمَآ أَنزَلَ ٱللَّهُ قَالُوا۟ نُؤْمِنُ بِمَآ أُنزِلَ عَلَيْنَا
وَيَكْفُرُونَ بِمَا وَرَآءَهُۥ وَهُوَ ٱلْحَقُّ مُصَدِّقًا لِّمَا مَعَهُمْ ۗ قُلْ فَلِمَ تَقْتُلُونَ
أَنۢبِيَآءَ ٱللَّهِ مِن قَبْلُ إِن كُنتُم مُّؤْمِنِينَ ﴿٩١﴾ ۞ وَلَقَدْ جَآءَكُم مُّوسَىٰ
بِٱلْبَيِّنَٰتِ ثُمَّ ٱتَّخَذْتُمُ ٱلْعِجْلَ مِنۢ بَعْدِهِۦ وَأَنتُمْ ظَٰلِمُونَ ﴿٩٢﴾ وَإِذْ أَخَذْنَا
مِيثَٰقَكُمْ وَرَفَعْنَا فَوْقَكُمُ ٱلطُّورَ خُذُوا۟ مَآ ءَاتَيْنَٰكُم بِقُوَّةٍ وَٱسْمَعُوا۟ ۖ
قَالُوا۟ سَمِعْنَا وَعَصَيْنَا وَأُشْرِبُوا۟ فِى قُلُوبِهِمُ ٱلْعِجْلَ بِكُفْرِهِمْ ۚ قُلْ بِئْسَمَا
يَأْمُرُكُم بِهِۦٓ إِيمَٰنُكُمْ إِن كُنتُم مُّؤْمِنِينَ ﴿٩٣﴾ قُلْ إِن كَانَتْ لَكُمُ ٱلدَّارُ
ٱلْءَاخِرَةُ عِندَ ٱللَّهِ خَالِصَةً مِّن دُونِ ٱلنَّاسِ فَتَمَنَّوُا۟ ٱلْمَوْتَ إِن كُنتُمْ
صَٰدِقِينَ ﴿٩٤﴾ وَلَن يَتَمَنَّوْهُ أَبَدًۢا بِمَا قَدَّمَتْ أَيْدِيهِمْ ۗ وَٱللَّهُ عَلِيمٌۢ
بِٱلظَّٰلِمِينَ ﴿٩٥﴾ وَلَتَجِدَنَّهُمْ أَحْرَصَ ٱلنَّاسِ عَلَىٰ حَيَوٰةٍ وَمِنَ ٱلَّذِينَ أَشْرَكُوا۟ ۚ

Wa ʾidhā qīla lahum ʾāminū bimāa ʾañzalal-lāhu
qālū nuʾminu bimāa ʾuñzila ʿalaynā wa yakfurūna
bimā warāaʾahū wa huwal-ḥaqqu muṣaddiqal-limā
maʿahum. Qul falima taqtulūna ʾAmbiyāaʾal-lāhi
miñ-qablu ʾiñ-kuñtum-muʾminīn. (91) ۞ Wa laqad
jāaʾakum Mūsā bilbayyināti thummat-takhadhtu-
mul-ʿijla mim-baʿdihī wa ʾañtum ẓālimūn. (92) Wa
ʾidh ʾakhadhnā mīthāqakum wa rafaʿnā fawqaku-
muṭ-ṭūra khudhū māa ʾātaynākum-biquwwatiñw-
was-maʿū. Qālū samiʿnā wa ʿaṣaynā wa ʾushribū fī
qulūbihimul-ʿijla bikufrihim. Qul biʾsamā yaʾmuru-
kum bihīi ʾĪmānukum ʾiñ-kuñtum-muʾminīn. (93)
Qul ʾiñ-kānat lakumud-dārul-ʾĀkhiratu ʿiñdal-lāhi
khāliṣatam-miñ-dūnin-nāsi fatamannawul-mawta
ʾiñ-kuñtum ṣādiqīn. (94) Wa lañy-yatamannawhu
ʾabadam-bimā qaddamat ʾaydīhim. Wal-lāhu
ʿAlīmum-biẓẓālimīn. (95) Wa latajidannahum ʾaḥraṣan-
nāsi ʿalā ḥayātiñw-wa minal-ladhīna ʾashrakū

ربع
الحزب

For when they are told, "Believe in what God has bestowed from on high," they reply, "We believe [only] in what has been bestowed on *us*" – and they deny the truth of everything else, although it be a truth confirming the one already in their possession.

Say: "Why, then, did you slay God's prophets aforetime, if you were [truly] believers?"[76] «91»

And indeed, there came unto you Moses with all evidence of the truth – and thereupon, in his absence, you took to worshipping the [golden] calf, and acted wickedly. «92»

And, lo, We accepted your solemn pledge, raising Mount Sinai high above you, [saying,] "Hold fast with [all your] strength unto what We have vouchsafed you, and hearken unto it!"

[But] they say, "We have heard, but we disobey"[77] – for their hearts are filled to overflowing with love of the [golden] calf because of their refusal to acknowledge the truth.[78]

Say: "Vile is what this [false] belief of yours enjoins upon you – if indeed you are believers!" «93»

Say: "If an afterlife with God is to be for you alone, to the exclusion of all other people,[79] then you should long for death – if what you say is true!" «94»

But never will they long for it, because [they are aware] of what their hands have sent ahead in this world: and God has full knowledge of evildoers. «95» And thou wilt most certainly find that they cling to life more eagerly than any other people, even more than those who are bent on

76 A reference to their assertion that they believe in what has been revealed to *them* – i.e., the Law of Moses, which obviously prohibits the killing not only of prophets but of any innocent human being. See also the concluding sentences of verses 61 and 87, and the corresponding notes.

77 It is obvious that they did not actually *utter* these words; their subsequent behaviour, however, justifies the above metonymical expression.

78 Lit., "into their hearts has been instilled the calf because of their denial of the truth": i.e., as soon as they turned away from the genuine message propounded by Moses, they fell into worshipping material goods, symbolized by the "golden calf".

79 An allusion to the Jewish belief that paradise is reserved for the children of Israel alone (cf. verse 111 of this *sūrah*).

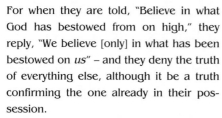

يَوَدُّ أَحَدُهُمْ لَوْ يُعَمَّرُ أَلْفَ سَنَةٍ وَمَا هُوَ بِمُزَحْزِحِهِۦ مِنَ ٱلْعَذَابِ أَن
يُعَمَّرَ ۗ وَٱللَّهُ بَصِيرٌۢ بِمَا يَعْمَلُونَ ﴿٩٦﴾ قُلْ مَن كَانَ عَدُوًّا لِّجِبْرِيلَ فَإِنَّهُۥ
نَزَّلَهُۥ عَلَىٰ قَلْبِكَ بِإِذْنِ ٱللَّهِ مُصَدِّقًا لِّمَا بَيْنَ يَدَيْهِ وَهُدًى وَبُشْرَىٰ
لِلْمُؤْمِنِينَ ﴿٩٧﴾ مَن كَانَ عَدُوًّا لِّلَّهِ وَمَلَٰٓئِكَتِهِۦ وَرُسُلِهِۦ وَجِبْرِيلَ
وَمِيكَىٰلَ فَإِنَّ ٱللَّهَ عَدُوٌّ لِّلْكَٰفِرِينَ ﴿٩٨﴾ وَلَقَدْ أَنزَلْنَآ إِلَيْكَ ءَايَٰتٍۭ
بَيِّنَٰتٍ ۖ وَمَا يَكْفُرُ بِهَآ إِلَّا ٱلْفَٰسِقُونَ ﴿٩٩﴾ أَوَكُلَّمَا عَٰهَدُوا۟ عَهْدًا نَّبَذَهُۥ
فَرِيقٌ مِّنْهُم ۚ بَلْ أَكْثَرُهُمْ لَا يُؤْمِنُونَ ﴿١٠٠﴾ وَلَمَّا جَآءَهُمْ رَسُولٌ مِّنْ عِندِ ٱللَّهِ
مُصَدِّقٌ لِّمَا مَعَهُمْ نَبَذَ فَرِيقٌ مِّنَ ٱلَّذِينَ أُوتُوا۟ ٱلْكِتَٰبَ كِتَٰبَ ٱللَّهِ
وَرَآءَ ظُهُورِهِمْ كَأَنَّهُمْ لَا يَعْلَمُونَ ﴿١٠١﴾

**yawaddu ʾaḥaduhum law yuᶜammaru ʾalfa sanatiñw-wa mā huwa bimuzaḥziḥihī minal-ᶜadhābi añy-yuᶜammar. Wal-lāhu Baṣīrum-bimā yaᶜmalūn. (96)
Qul mañ-kāna ᶜaduwwal-liJibrīla faʾinnahū nazzalahū ᶜalā qalbika biʾidhnil-lāhi muṣaddiqal-limā bayna yadayhi wa hudañw-wa bushrā lilmuʾminīn. (97) Mañ-kāna ᶜaduwwal-lillāhi wa Malāaʾikatihī wa Rusulihī wa Jibrīla wa Mīkāla faʾinnal-lāha ᶜaduwwul-lilkāfirīn. (98) Wa laqad ʾañzalnāa ʾilayka ʾĀyātim-bayyināt. Wa mā yakfuru bihāa ʾillal-fāsiqūn. (99) ʾAwa kullamā ᶜāhadū ᶜahdañ-nabadhahū farīqum-minhum. Bal ʾaktharuhum lā yuʾminūn. (100) Wa lammā jāaʾahum Rasūlum-min ᶜiñdil-lāhi muṣaddiqul-limā maᶜahum nabadha farīqum-minal-ladhīna ʾūtul-Kitāba Kitābal-lāhi warāaʾa ẓuhūrihim kaʾannahum lā yaᶜlamūn. (101)**

ascribing divinity to other beings beside God: every one of them would love to live a thousand years, although the grant of long life could not save him from suffering [in the hereafter]: for God sees all that they do. ‹96›

SAY [O Prophet]: "Whosoever is an enemy of Gabriel" – who, verily, by God's leave, has brought down upon thy heart this [divine writ] which confirms the truth of whatever there still remains [of earlier revelations], and is a guidance and a glad tiding for the believers: ‹97› – "whosoever is an enemy of God and His angels and His message-bearers, including Gabriel and Michael, [should know that,] verily, God is the enemy of all who deny the truth."[80] ‹98›

For, clear messages indeed have We bestowed upon thee from on high; and none denies their truth save the iniquitous. ‹99›

Is it not so that every time they made a promise [unto God], some of them cast it aside? Nay, indeed: most of them do not believe. ‹100›

And [even now,] when there has come unto them an apostle from God, confirming the truth already in their possession, some of those who were granted revelation aforetime cast the divine writ behind their backs as though unaware [of what it says][81] ‹101›

80 According to several authentic Traditions, some of the learned men from among the Jews of Medina described Gabriel as "the enemy of the Jews", and this for three reasons: firstly, all the prophecies of the misfortune which was to befall the Jews in the course of their early history were said to have been transmitted to them by Gabriel, who thus became in their eyes a "harbinger of evil" (in contrast to the angel Michael, whom they regarded as a bearer of happy predictions and, therefore, as their "friend"); secondly, because the Qurʾān states repeatedly that it was Gabriel who conveyed its message to Muḥammad, whereas the Jews were of the opinion that only a descendant of Israel could legitimately claim divine revelation; and, thirdly, because the Qurʾān – revealed through Gabriel – abounds in criticism of certain Jewish beliefs and attitudes and describes them as opposed to the *genuine* message of Moses. (For details of these Traditions, see Ṭabarī, Zamakhsharī, Baghawī, Rāzī, Bayḍāwī, Ibn Kathīr.) As regards my rendering of *mā bayna yadayhi* in verse 97 as "whatever there still remains of earlier revelations", see *sūrah* 3, note 3.

81 The divine writ referred to here is the Torah. By disregarding the prophecies relating to the coming of the Arabian Prophet, contained in Deuteronomy xviii, 15, 18 (see note 33 above), the Jews rejected, as it were, the whole of the revelation granted to Moses (Zamakhsharī; also ᶜAbduh in *Manār* I, 397).

and follow [instead] that which the evil ones used to practice during Solomon's reign – for it was not Solomon who denied the truth, but those evil ones denied it by teaching people sorcery;[82] – and [they follow] that which has come down through the two angels in Babylon, Hārūt and Mārūt – although these two never taught it to anyone without first declaring, "We are but a temptation to evil: do not, then, deny [God's] truth!"[83] And they learn from these two how to create discord between a man and his wife; but whereas they can harm none thereby save by God's leave, they acquire a knowledge that only harms themselves and does not benefit them – although they know, indeed, that he who acquires this [knowledge] shall have no share in the good of the life to come.[84] For, vile indeed is that [art] for which they have sold their own selves – had they but known it! ‹102›

And had they but believed and been conscious of Him, reward from God would indeed have brought them good – had they but known it! ‹103›

وَٱتَّبَعُواْ مَا تَتْلُواْ ٱلشَّيَٰطِينُ عَلَىٰ مُلْكِ سُلَيْمَٰنَ ۖ وَمَا كَفَرَ سُلَيْمَٰنُ
وَلَٰكِنَّ ٱلشَّيَٰطِينَ كَفَرُواْ يُعَلِّمُونَ ٱلنَّاسَ ٱلسِّحْرَ وَمَآ أُنزِلَ عَلَى
ٱلْمَلَكَيْنِ بِبَابِلَ هَٰرُوتَ وَمَٰرُوتَ ۚ وَمَا يُعَلِّمَانِ مِنْ أَحَدٍ حَتَّىٰ يَقُولَآ
إِنَّمَا نَحْنُ فِتْنَةٌ فَلَا تَكْفُرْ ۖ فَيَتَعَلَّمُونَ مِنْهُمَا مَا يُفَرِّقُونَ بِهِۦ بَيْنَ ٱلْمَرْءِ
وَزَوْجِهِۦ ۚ وَمَا هُم بِضَآرِّينَ بِهِۦ مِنْ أَحَدٍ إِلَّا بِإِذْنِ ٱللَّهِ ۚ وَيَتَعَلَّمُونَ مَا
يَضُرُّهُمْ وَلَا يَنفَعُهُمْ ۚ وَلَقَدْ عَلِمُواْ لَمَنِ ٱشْتَرَىٰهُ مَا لَهُۥ فِى ٱلْءَاخِرَةِ مِنْ
خَلَٰقٍ ۚ وَلَبِئْسَ مَا شَرَوْاْ بِهِۦٓ أَنفُسَهُمْ ۚ لَوْ كَانُواْ يَعْلَمُونَ ﴿١٠٢﴾ وَلَوْ أَنَّهُمْ
ءَامَنُواْ وَٱتَّقَوْاْ لَمَثُوبَةٌ مِّنْ عِندِ ٱللَّهِ خَيْرٌ ۖ لَّوْ كَانُواْ يَعْلَمُونَ ﴿١٠٣﴾

Wat-tabaᶜū mā tatlush-Shayāṭīnu ᶜalā mulki Sulaymān. Wa mā kafara Sulaymānu wa lākinnash-Shayāṭīna kafarū yuᶜallimūnan-nāsas-siḥra wa māa ʾuñzila ᶜalal-Malakayni biBābila Hārūta wa Mārūt. Wa mā yuᶜallimāni min ʾaḥadin ḥattā yaqūlāa ʾinnamā naḥnu fitnatuñ-falā takfur. Fayataᶜallamūna minhumā mā yufarriqūna bihī baynal-marʾi wa zawjih. Wa mā hum-biḍāarrīna bihī min ʾaḥadin ʾillā biʾidhnil-lāh. Wa yataᶜallamūna mā yaḍurruhum wa lā yañfaᶜuhum. Wa laqad ᶜalimū lamanish-tarāhu mā lahū fil-ʾĀkhirati min khalāq. Wa labiʾsa mā sharaw bihīi ʾañfusahum law kānū yaᶜlamūn. ﴿102﴾ Wa law ʾannahum ʾāmanū wat-taqaw lamathūbatum-min ᶜiñdil-lāhi khayrul-law kānū yaᶜlamūn. ﴿103﴾

82 The expression *ash-shayāṭīn*, here rendered as "the evil ones", apparently refers to human beings, as has been pointed out by Ṭabarī, Rāzī, etc., but may also allude to the evil, immoral impulses within man's heart (see note 10 on verse 14 of this *sūrah*). The above parenthetic sentence constitutes the Qurʾanic refutation of the Biblical statement that Solomon had been guilty of idolatrous practices (see I Kings xi, 1-10), as well as of the legend that he was the originator of the magic arts popularly associated with his name.

83 This "declaration" circumscribes, metonymically, man's moral duty to reject every attempt at "sorcery" inasmuch as – irrespective of whether it succeeds or fails – it aims at subverting the order of nature as instituted by God. – As regards the designation of Hārūt and Mārūt, most of the readings of the Qurʾan give the spelling *malakayn* ("the two angels"); but it is authentically recorded (see Ṭabarī, Zamakhsharī, Baghawī, Rāzī, etc.) that the great Companion of the Prophet, Ibn ᶜAbbās, as well as several learned men of the next generation – e.g., Al-Ḥasan al-Baṣrī, Abu 'l-Aswad and Aḍ-Ḍaḥḥāk – read it as *malikayn* ("the two kings"). I myself incline to the latter reading; but since the other is more generally accepted, I have adopted it here. Some of the commentators are of the opinion that, whichever of the two readings is followed, it ought to be taken in a metaphorical sense, namely, "the two kingly persons", or "the two angelic persons": in this they rely on a saying of Ibn ᶜAbbās to the effect that Hārūt and Mārūt were "two *men* who practiced sorcery in Babylon" (Baghawī; see also *Manār* I, 402). At any rate, it is certain that from very ancient times Babylon was reputed to be the home of magic arts, symbolized in the legendary persons – perhaps kings – Hārūt and Mārūt; and it is to this legend that the Qurʾān refers with a view to condemning every attempt at magic and sorcery, as well as all preoccupation with occult sciences in general.

84 The above passage does not raise the question as to whether there is an objective truth in the occult phenomena loosely described as "magic", or whether they are based on self-deception. The intent here is no more and no less than to warn man that any attempt at influencing the course of events by means which – at least in the mind of the person responsible for it – have a "supernatural" connotation is a spiritual offence, and must inevitably result in a most serious damage to their author's spiritual status.

O YOU who have attained to faith! Do not say [to the Prophet], "Listen to us," but rather say, "Have patience with us," and hearken [unto him], since grievous suffering awaits those who deny the truth.[85] ‹104›
Neither those from among the followers of earlier revelation who are bent on denying the truth, nor those who ascribe divinity to other beings beside God, would like to see any good[86] ever bestowed upon you from on high by your Sustainer; but God singles out for His grace whom He wills – for God is limitless in His great bounty. ‹105›
Any message which We annul or consign to oblivion We replace with a better or a similar one.[87]
Dost thou not know that God has the power to will anything? ‹106› Dost thou not know that God's is the dominion over the heavens and the earth, and that besides God you have none to protect you or bring you succour? ‹107›

يَٰٓأَيُّهَا ٱلَّذِينَ ءَامَنُوا۟ لَا تَقُولُوا۟ رَٰعِنَا وَقُولُوا۟ ٱنظُرْنَا وَٱسْمَعُوا۟ ۗ
وَلِلْكَٰفِرِينَ عَذَابٌ أَلِيمٌ ﴿١٠٤﴾ مَّا يَوَدُّ ٱلَّذِينَ كَفَرُوا۟ مِنْ أَهْلِ ٱلْكِتَٰبِ
وَلَا ٱلْمُشْرِكِينَ أَن يُنَزَّلَ عَلَيْكُم مِّنْ خَيْرٍ مِّن رَّبِّكُمْ ۗ وَٱللَّهُ يَخْتَصُّ
بِرَحْمَتِهِۦ مَن يَشَآءُ ۚ وَٱللَّهُ ذُو ٱلْفَضْلِ ٱلْعَظِيمِ ﴿١٠٥﴾ ۞ مَا نَنسَخْ مِنْ ءَايَةٍ
أَوْ نُنسِهَا نَأْتِ بِخَيْرٍ مِّنْهَآ أَوْ مِثْلِهَآ ۗ أَلَمْ تَعْلَمْ أَنَّ ٱللَّهَ عَلَىٰ كُلِّ شَىْءٍ
قَدِيرٌ ﴿١٠٦﴾ أَلَمْ تَعْلَمْ أَنَّ ٱللَّهَ لَهُۥ مُلْكُ ٱلسَّمَٰوَٰتِ وَٱلْأَرْضِ ۗ وَمَا لَكُم
مِّن دُونِ ٱللَّهِ مِن وَلِىٍّ وَلَا نَصِيرٍ ﴿١٠٧﴾

نصف الحزب

Yāa ᵓayyuhal-ladhīna ᵓāmanū lā taqūlū rāᶜinā wa qūluñ-ẓurnā was-maᶜū. Wa lilkāfirīna ᶜadhābun ᵓalīm. (104) Mā yawaddul-ladhīna kafarū min ᵓahlil-Kitābi wa lal-mushrikīna ᵓañy-yunazzala ᶜalaykum-min khayrim-mir-Rabbikum. Wal-lāhu yakhtaṣṣu biraḥmatihī mañy-yashāaᵓu wal-lāhu Dhul-faḍlil-ᶜaẓīm. (105) ۞ Mā nañsakh min ᵓāyatin ᵓaw nuñsihā naᵓti bikhayrim-minhāa ᵓaw mithlihā. ᵓAlam taᶜlam ᵓannal-lāha ᶜalā kull shayᵓiñ-Qadīr. (106) Alam taᶜlam ᵓannal-lāha lahū mulkus-samāwāti wal-ᵓarḍ. Wa mā lakum miñ-dūnil-lāhi miñw-waliyyiñw-wa lā naṣīr. (107)

---

85 This admonition, addressed in the first instance to the contemporaries of the Prophet, has – as so often in the Qurᵓān – a connotation that goes far beyond the historical circumstances that gave rise to it. The Companions were called upon to approach the Prophet with respect and to subordinate their personal desires and expectations to the commandments of the Faith revealed through him: and this injunction remains valid for every believer and for all times.

86 I.e., revelation – which is the highest good. The allusion here is to the unwillingness of the Jews and the Christians to admit that revelation could have been bestowed on any community but their own.

87 The principle laid down in this passage – relating to the supersession of the Biblical dispensation by that of the Qurᵓān – has given rise to an erroneous interpretation by many Muslim theologians. The word *āyah* ("message") occurring in this context is also used to denote a "verse" of the Qurᵓān (because every one of these verses contains a message). Taking this restricted meaning of the term *āyah*, some scholars conclude from the above passage that certain verses of the Qurᵓān have been "abrogated" by God's command before the revelation of the Qurᵓān was completed. Apart from the fancifulness of this assertion – which calls to mind the image of a human author correcting, on second thought, the proofs of his manuscript, deleting one passage and replacing it with another – there does not exist a single reliable Tradition to the effect that the Prophet ever declared a verse of the Qurᵓān to have been "abrogated". At the root of the so-called "doctrine of abrogation" may lie the inability of some of the early commentators to reconcile one Qurᵓanic passage with another: a difficulty which was overcome by declaring that one of the verses in question had been "abrogated". This arbitrary procedure explains also why there is no unanimity whatsoever among the upholders of the "doctrine of abrogation" as to which, and how many, Qurᵓān-verses have been affected by it; and, furthermore, as to whether this alleged abrogation implies a total elimination of the verse in question from the *context* of the Qurᵓān, or only a cancellation of the specific ordinance or statement contained in it. In short, the "doctrine of abrogation" has no basis whatever in historical fact, and must be rejected. On the other hand, the apparent difficulty in interpreting the above Qurᵓanic passage disappears immediately if the term *āyah* is understood, correctly, as "message", and if we read this verse in conjunction with the preceding one, which states that the Jews and the Christians refuse to accept any revelation which might supersede that of the Bible: for, if read in this way, the abrogation relates to the earlier divine messages and not to any part of the Qurᵓān itself.

Would you, perchance, ask of the Apostle who has been sent unto you what was asked aforetime of Moses? But whoever chooses to deny the [evidence of the] truth, instead of believing in it,[88] has already strayed from the right path. ⟨108⟩ Out of their selfish envy, many among the followers of earlier revelation would like to bring you back to denying the truth after you have attained to faith – [even] after the truth has become clear unto them. None the less, forgive and forbear, until God shall make manifest His will: behold, God has the power to will anything. ⟨109⟩ And be constant in prayer, and render the purifying dues; for, whatever good deed you send ahead for your own selves, you shall find it with God: behold, God sees all that you do. ⟨110⟩

AND THEY claim,[89] "None shall ever enter paradise unless he be a Jew" – or, "a Christian". Such are their wishful beliefs! Say: "Produce an evidence for what you are claiming,[90] if what you say is true!" ⟨111⟩ Yea, indeed: everyone who surrenders his whole being unto God,[91] and is a doer of good withal, shall have his reward with his Sustainer; and all such need have no fear, and neither shall they grieve.[92] ⟨112⟩

أَمْ تُرِيدُونَ أَن تَسْـَٔلُوا۟ رَسُولَكُمْ كَمَا سُئِلَ مُوسَىٰ مِن قَبْلُ ۗ وَمَن يَتَبَدَّلِ
ٱلْكُفْرَ بِٱلْإِيمَٰنِ فَقَدْ ضَلَّ سَوَآءَ ٱلسَّبِيلِ ﴿١٠٨﴾ وَدَّ كَثِيرٌ مِّنْ أَهْلِ
ٱلْكِتَٰبِ لَوْ يَرُدُّونَكُم مِّنۢ بَعْدِ إِيمَٰنِكُمْ كُفَّارًا حَسَدًا مِّنْ عِندِ أَنفُسِهِم
مِّنۢ بَعْدِ مَا تَبَيَّنَ لَهُمُ ٱلْحَقُّ ۖ فَٱعْفُوا۟ وَٱصْفَحُوا۟ حَتَّىٰ يَأْتِىَ ٱللَّهُ بِأَمْرِهِۦٓ ۗ إِنَّ
ٱللَّهَ عَلَىٰ كُلِّ شَىْءٍ قَدِيرٌ ﴿١٠٩﴾ وَأَقِيمُوا۟ ٱلصَّلَوٰةَ وَءَاتُوا۟ ٱلزَّكَوٰةَ ۚ وَمَا تُقَدِّمُوا۟
لِأَنفُسِكُم مِّنْ خَيْرٍ تَجِدُوهُ عِندَ ٱللَّهِ ۗ إِنَّ ٱللَّهَ بِمَا تَعْمَلُونَ بَصِيرٌ ﴿١١٠﴾
وَقَالُوا۟ لَن يَدْخُلَ ٱلْجَنَّةَ إِلَّا مَن كَانَ هُودًا أَوْ نَصَٰرَىٰ ۗ تِلْكَ أَمَانِيُّهُمْ ۗ
قُلْ هَاتُوا۟ بُرْهَٰنَكُمْ إِن كُنتُمْ صَٰدِقِينَ ﴿١١١﴾ بَلَىٰ مَنْ أَسْلَمَ وَجْهَهُۥ لِلَّهِ
وَهُوَ مُحْسِنٌ فَلَهُۥٓ أَجْرُهُۥ عِندَ رَبِّهِۦ وَلَا خَوْفٌ عَلَيْهِمْ وَلَا هُمْ يَحْزَنُونَ ﴿١١٢﴾

ʾAm turīdūna ʾañ-tasʾalū Rasūlakum kamā suʾila Mūsā miñ-qabl. Wa mañy-yatabaddalil-kufra bilʾīmāni faqad-ḍalla sawāaʾas-sabīl. (108) Wadda kathīrum-min ʾahlil-Kitābi law yaruddūnakum mim-baᶜdi ʾīmānikum kuffārañ-ḥasadam-min ᶜiñdi ʾañfusihim mim-baᶜdi mā tabayyana lahumul-ḥaqq. Faᶜfū waṣ-faḥū ḥattā yaʾtiyal-lāhu biʾamrih. ʾInnal-lāha ᶜalā kulli shayʾiñ-Qadīr. (109) Wa aqīmuṣ-Ṣalāta wa ʾātuz-Zakāh. Wa mā tuqaddimū liʾañfusikum-min khayriñ-tajidūhu ᶜiñdal-lāh. ʾInnal-lāha bimā taᶜmalūna Baṣīr. (110) Wa qālū lañy-yadkhulal-jannata ʾillā mañ-kāna Hūdan ʾaw Naṣārā. Tilka ʾamāniyyuhum. Qul hātū burhānakum ʾiñ-kuñtum ṣādiqīn. (111) Balā man ʾaslama wajhahū lillāhi wa huwa muḥsinuñ-falahūu ʾajruhū ᶜiñda Rabbihī wa lā khawfun ᶜalayhim wa lā hum yaḥzanūn. (112)

88 Lit., "whoever takes a denial of the truth in exchange for belief" – i.e., whoever refuses to accept the internal evidence of the truth of the Qurʾanic message and demands, instead, an "objective" proof of its divine origin (*Manār* I, 416 f.). – That which was "asked of Moses aforetime" was the demand of the children of Israel to "see God face to face" (cf. 2 : 55). The expression rendered by me as "the Apostle who has been sent unto you" reads, literally, "*your* Apostle", and obviously refers to the Prophet Muḥammad, whose message supersedes the earlier revelations.

89 This connects with verse 109 above: "Many among the followers of earlier revelation would like to bring you back to denying the truth", etc.

90 Lit., "produce your evidence" – i.e., "from your own scriptures".

91 Lit., "who surrenders his face unto God". Since the face of a person is the most expressive part of his body, it is used in classical Arabic to denote one's whole personality, or whole being. This expression, repeated in the Qurʾān several times, provides a perfect definition of *islām*, which – derived from the root-verb *aslama*, "he surrendered himself" – means "self-surrender [to God]": and it is in this sense that the terms *islām* and *muslim* are used throughout the Qurʾān. (For a full discussion of this concept, see my note on 68 : 35, where the expression *muslim* occurs for the first time in the chronological order of revelation.)

92 Thus, according to the Qurʾān salvation, is not reserved for any particular "denomination", but is open to everyone who consciously realizes the oneness of God, surrenders himself to His will and, by living righteously, gives practical effect to this spiritual attitude.

Furthermore, the Jews assert, "The Christians have no valid ground for their beliefs," while the Christians assert, "The Jews have no valid ground for their beliefs" – and both quote the divine writ! Even thus, like unto what they say, have [always] spoken those who were devoid of knowledge;[93] but it is God who will judge between them on Resurrection Day with regard to all on which they were wont to differ.[94] ‹113›

Hence, who could be more wicked than those who bar the mention of God's name from [any of] His houses of worship and strive for their ruin, [although] they have no right to enter them save in fear [of God]?[95] For them, in this world, there is ignominy in store; and for them, in the life to come, awesome suffering. ‹114›

And God's is the east and the west: and wherever you turn, there is God's countenance. Behold, God is infinite, all-knowing. ‹115›

And yet some people assert, "God has taken unto Himself a son!" Limitless is He in His glory![96]

Nay, but His is all that is in the heavens and on earth; all things devoutly obey His will. ‹116› The Originator is He of the heavens and the earth: and when He wills a thing to be, He but says unto it, "Be" – and it is. ‹117›

وَقَالَتِ ٱلْيَهُودُ لَيْسَتِ ٱلنَّصَٰرَىٰ عَلَىٰ شَىْءٍ وَقَالَتِ ٱلنَّصَٰرَىٰ لَيْسَتِ
ٱلْيَهُودُ عَلَىٰ شَىْءٍ وَهُمْ يَتْلُونَ ٱلْكِتَٰبَ كَذَٰلِكَ قَالَ ٱلَّذِينَ لَا يَعْلَمُونَ
مِثْلَ قَوْلِهِمْ فَٱللَّهُ يَحْكُمُ بَيْنَهُمْ يَوْمَ ٱلْقِيَٰمَةِ فِيمَا كَانُوا۟ فِيهِ
يَخْتَلِفُونَ ﴿١١٣﴾ وَمَنْ أَظْلَمُ مِمَّن مَّنَعَ مَسَٰجِدَ ٱللَّهِ أَن يُذْكَرَ فِيهَا ٱسْمُهُۥ
وَسَعَىٰ فِى خَرَابِهَآ أُو۟لَٰٓئِكَ مَا كَانَ لَهُمْ أَن يَدْخُلُوهَآ إِلَّا خَآئِفِينَ لَهُمْ فِى
ٱلدُّنْيَا خِزْىٌ وَلَهُمْ فِى ٱلْءَاخِرَةِ عَذَابٌ عَظِيمٌ ﴿١١٤﴾ وَلِلَّهِ ٱلْمَشْرِقُ وَٱلْمَغْرِبُ
فَأَيْنَمَا تُوَلُّوا۟ فَثَمَّ وَجْهُ ٱللَّهِ إِنَّ ٱللَّهَ وَٰسِعٌ عَلِيمٌ ﴿١١٥﴾ وَقَالُوا۟ ٱتَّخَذَ ٱللَّهُ وَلَدًا
سُبْحَٰنَهُۥ بَل لَّهُۥ مَا فِى ٱلسَّمَٰوَٰتِ وَٱلْأَرْضِ كُلٌّ لَّهُۥ قَٰنِتُونَ ﴿١١٦﴾ بَدِيعُ
ٱلسَّمَٰوَٰتِ وَٱلْأَرْضِ وَإِذَا قَضَىٰٓ أَمْرًا فَإِنَّمَا يَقُولُ لَهُۥ كُن فَيَكُونُ ﴿١١٧﴾

Wa qālatil-Yahūdu laysatin-Naṣārā ʿalā shayʾiñw-wa qālatin-Naṣārā laysatil-Yahūdu ʿalā shayʾiñw-wa hum yatlūnal-Kitāb. Kadhālika qālal-ladhīna lā yaʿlamūna mithla qawlihim. Fallāhu yaḥkumu baynahum Yawmal-Qiyāmati fīmā kānū fīhi yakhtalifūn. (113) Wa man ʾaẓlamu mimmam-manaʿa masājidal-lāhi ʾañy-yudhkara fīhas-muhū wa saʿā fī kharābihā. ʾUlāaʾika māa kāna lahum ʾañy-yadkhulūhāa ʾillā khāaʾifīn. Lahum fid-dunyā khizyuñw-wa lahum fil-ʾĀkhirati ʿadhābun ʿaẓīm. (114) Wa lillāhil-mashriqu wal-maghrib. Faʾaynamā tuwallū fathamma wajhul-lāh. ʾInnal-lāha Wāsiʿun ʿAlīm. (115) Wa qālut-takhadhal-lāhu waladañ-subḥānah. Bal-lahū mā fis-samā-wāti wal-ʾarḍi kullul-lahū qānitūn. (116) Badīʿus-samāwāti wal-ʾarḍi wa ʾidhā qaḍāa ʾamrañ-faʾinnamā yaqūlu lahū kuñ-fayakūn. (117)

93 An allusion to all who assert that only the followers of their own denomination shall partake of God's grace in the hereafter.

94 In other words, "God will confirm the truth of what was true [in their respective beliefs] and show the falseness of what was false [therein]" (Muḥammad ʿAbduh in *Manār* I, 428). The Qurʾān maintains throughout that there is a substantial element of truth in all faiths based on divine revelation, and that their subsequent divergencies are the result of "wishful beliefs" (2 : 111) and of a gradual corruption of the original teachings. (See also 22 : 67-69.)

95 It is one of the fundamental principles of Islam that every religion which has belief in God as its focal point must be accorded full respect, however much one may disagree with its particular tenets. Thus, the Muslims are under an obligation to honour and protect any house of worship dedicated to God, whether it be a mosque or a church or a synagogue (cf. the second paragraph of 22 : 40); and any attempt to prevent the followers of another faith from worshipping God according to their own lights is condemned by the Qurʾān as a sacrilege. A striking illustration of this principle is forthcoming from the Prophet's treatment of the deputation from Christian Najrān in the year 10 H. They were given free access to the Prophet's mosque, and with his full consent celebrated their religious rites there, although their adoration of Jesus as "the son of God" and of Mary as "the mother of God" was fundamentally at variance with Islamic beliefs (see Ibn Saʿd I/1, 84 f.).

96 I.e., far from any imperfection such as would be implied in the necessity (or logical possibility) of having "progeny" either in a literal or a metaphorical sense. The expression *subḥāna* – applied exclusively to God – connotes His utter remoteness from any imperfection and any similarity, however tenuous, with any created being or thing.

وَقَالَ ٱلَّذِينَ لَا يَعْلَمُونَ لَوْلَا يُكَلِّمُنَا ٱللَّهُ أَوْ تَأْتِينَآ ءَايَةٌۗ كَذَٰلِكَ قَالَ
ٱلَّذِينَ مِن قَبْلِهِم مِّثْلَ قَوْلِهِمْۘ تَشَٰبَهَتْ قُلُوبُهُمْۗ قَدْ بَيَّنَّا ٱلْءَايَٰتِ لِقَوْمٍ
يُوقِنُونَ ﴿118﴾ إِنَّآ أَرْسَلْنَٰكَ بِٱلْحَقِّ بَشِيرًا وَنَذِيرًاۖ وَلَا تُسْـَٔلُ عَنْ أَصْحَٰبِ
ٱلْجَحِيمِ ﴿119﴾ وَلَن تَرْضَىٰ عَنكَ ٱلْيَهُودُ وَلَا ٱلنَّصَٰرَىٰ حَتَّىٰ تَتَّبِعَ مِلَّتَهُمْۗ
قُلْ إِنَّ هُدَى ٱللَّهِ هُوَ ٱلْهُدَىٰۗ وَلَئِنِ ٱتَّبَعْتَ أَهْوَآءَهُم بَعْدَ ٱلَّذِى جَآءَكَ
مِنَ ٱلْعِلْمِۙ مَا لَكَ مِنَ ٱللَّهِ مِن وَلِىٍّ وَلَا نَصِيرٍ ﴿120﴾ ٱلَّذِينَ ءَاتَيْنَٰهُمُ
ٱلْكِتَٰبَ يَتْلُونَهُۥ حَقَّ تِلَاوَتِهِۦٓ أُوْلَٰٓئِكَ يُؤْمِنُونَ بِهِۦۗ وَمَن يَكْفُرْ بِهِۦ
فَأُوْلَٰٓئِكَ هُمُ ٱلْخَٰسِرُونَ ﴿121﴾ يَٰبَنِىٓ إِسْرَٰٓءِيلَ ٱذْكُرُواْ نِعْمَتِىَ ٱلَّتِىٓ
أَنْعَمْتُ عَلَيْكُمْ وَأَنِّى فَضَّلْتُكُمْ عَلَى ٱلْعَٰلَمِينَ ﴿122﴾ وَٱتَّقُواْ يَوْمًا لَّا
تَجْزِى نَفْسٌ عَن نَّفْسٍ شَيْـًٔا وَلَا يُقْبَلُ مِنْهَا عَدْلٌ وَلَا تَنفَعُهَا شَفَٰعَةٌ
وَلَا هُمْ يُنصَرُونَ ﴿123﴾

AND [only] those who are devoid of knowledge say, "Why does God not speak unto us, nor is a [miraculous] sign shown to us?" Even thus, like unto what they say, spoke those who lived before their time:[97] their hearts are all alike. Indeed, We have made all the signs manifest unto people who are endowed with inner certainty. ‹118›
Verily, We have sent thee [O Prophet] with the truth, as a bearer of glad tidings and a warner: and thou shalt not be held accountable for those who are destined for the blazing fire. ‹119›
For, never will the Jews be pleased with thee, nor yet the Christians, unless thou follow their own creeds. Say: "Behold, God's guidance is the only true guidance." And, indeed, if thou shouldst follow their errant views after all the knowledge that has come unto thee, thou wouldst have none to protect thee from God, and none to bring thee succour. ‹120›
Those unto whom We have vouchsafed the divine writ [and who] follow it as it ought to be followed[98] – it is they who [truly] believe in it; whereas all who choose to deny its truth – it is they, they who are the losers! ‹121›

O CHILDREN of Israel! Remember those blessings of Mine with which I graced you, and how I favoured you above all other people; ‹122› and remain conscious of [the coming of] a Day when no human being shall in the least avail another, nor shall ransom be accepted from any of them, nor shall intercession be of any use to them, and none shall be succoured.[99] ‹123›

Wa qālal-ladhīna lā yaᶜlamūna lawlā yukallimunal-lāhu ʾaw taʾtīnāa ʾĀyah. Kadhālika qālal-ladhīna miñ-qablihim-mithla qawlihim. Tashābahat qulūbuhum. Qad bayyannal-ʾĀyāti liqawmiñy-yūqinūn. (118) ʾInnāa ʾarsalnāka bilḥaqqi bashīrañw-wa nadhīrañw-wa lā tusʾalu ᶜan ʾaṣḥābil-jaḥīm. (119) Wa lañ-tarḍā ᶜañkal-Yahūdu wa lan-Naṣārā ḥattā tattabiᶜa millatahum. Qul ʾinna hudal-lāhi huwal-hudā. Wa laʾinittabaᶜta ʾahwāaʾahum baᶜdal-ladhī jāaʾaka minal-ᶜilmi mā laka minal-lāhi miñw-waliyyiñw-wa lā naṣīr. (120) ʾAlladhīna ʾātaynāhumul-Kitāba yatlūnahū ḥaqqa tilāwatihīi ʾulāaʾika yuʾminūna bih. Wa mañy-yakfur bihī faʾulāaʾika humul-khāsirūn. (121) Yā banīi-ʾIsrāaʾīladh-kurū niᶜmatiyal-latīi ʾanᶜamtu ᶜalaykum wa ʾannī faḍḍaltukum ᶜalal-ᶜālamīn. (122) Wat-taqū Yawmal-lā tajzī nafsun ᶜañ-nafsiñ-shayʾañw-wa lā yuqbalu minhā ᶜadluñw-wa lā tañfaᶜuhā shafāᶜatuñw-wa lā hum yuñṣarūn. (123)

97 I.e., people who were not able to perceive the intrinsic truth of the messages conveyed to them by the prophets, but rather insisted on a miraculous "demonstration" that those messages really came from God, and thus failed to benefit from them. – This verse obviously connects with verse 108 above and, thus, refers to the objections of the Jews and the Christians to the message of the Qurʾān. (See also note 29 on 74 : 52.)

98 Or: "apply themselves to it with true application" – i.e., try to absorb its meaning and to understand its spiritual design.

99 See 2 : 48. In the above context, this refers, specifically, to the belief of the Jews that their descent from Abraham would "ransom" them on the Day of Judgment – a belief which is refuted in the next verse.

۞ وَإِذِ ٱبْتَلَىٰٓ إِبْرَٰهِـۧمَ رَبُّهُۥ بِكَلِمَـٰتٍ فَأَتَمَّهُنَّ ۖ قَالَ إِنِّى جَاعِلُكَ لِلنَّاسِ
إِمَامًا ۖ قَالَ وَمِن ذُرِّيَّتِى ۖ قَالَ لَا يَنَالُ عَهْدِى ٱلظَّـٰلِمِينَ ﴿124﴾ وَإِذْ جَعَلْنَا
ٱلْبَيْتَ مَثَابَةً لِّلنَّاسِ وَأَمْنًا وَٱتَّخِذُوا۟ مِن مَّقَامِ إِبْرَٰهِـۧمَ مُصَلًّى ۖ وَعَهِدْنَآ
إِلَىٰٓ إِبْرَٰهِـۧمَ وَإِسْمَـٰعِيلَ أَن طَهِّرَا بَيْتِىَ لِلطَّآئِفِينَ وَٱلْعَـٰكِفِينَ وَٱلرُّكَّعِ
ٱلسُّجُودِ ﴿125﴾

ثلاثة ارباع الحزب

۞ **Wa ʾidhib-talāa ʾIbrāhīma Rabbuhū biKalimātiñ-faʾatammahunn. Qāla ʾinnī jāʿiluka linnāsi ʾImāmā. Qāla wa miñ-dhurriyyatī. Qāla lā yanālu ʿahdiẓ-ẓālimīn. (124) Wa ʾidh jaʿalnal-Bayta mathābatal-linnāsi wa ʾamnañw-wat-takhidhū mim-maqāmi ʾIbrāhīma muṣallā. Wa ʿahidnāa ʾilāa ʾIbrāhīma wa ʾIsmāʿīla ʾañ-ṭahhirā Baytiya liṭṭāaʾifīna wal-ʿākifīna war-rukkaʿis-sujūd. (125)**

And [remember this:] when his Sustainer tried Abraham by [His] commandments and the latter fulfilled them,[100] He said: "Behold, I shall make thee a leader of men." Abraham asked: "And [wilt Thou make leaders] of my offspring as well?" [God] answered: "My covenant does not embrace the evildoers."[101] ‹124›

AND LO! We made the Temple a goal to which people might repair again and again, and a sanctuary:[102] take, then, the place whereon Abraham once stood as your place of prayer.[103] And thus did We command Abraham and Ishmael: "Purify My Temple for those who will walk around it,[104] and those who will abide near it in meditation, and those who will bow down and prostrate themselves [in prayer]." ‹125›

100 The classical commentators have indulged in much speculation as to what these commandments (*kalimāt*, lit., "words") were. Since, however, the Qurʾān does not specify them, it must be presumed that what is meant here is simply Abraham's complete submission to whatever commandments he received from God.

101 This passage, read in conjunction with the two preceding verses, refutes the contention of the children of Israel that by virtue of their descent from Abraham, whom God made "a leader of men", they are "God's chosen people". The Qurʾān makes it clear that the exalted status of Abraham was not something that would automatically confer a comparable status on his physical descendants, and certainly not on the sinners among them.

102 The Temple (*al-bayt*) – lit., "the House [of Worship]" – mentioned here is the Kaʿbah in Mecca. In other places the Qurʾān speaks of it as "the Ancient Temple" (*al-bayt al-ʿatīq*), and frequently also as "the Inviolable House of Worship" (*al-masjid al-ḥarām*). Its prototype is said to have been built by Abraham as the first temple ever dedicated to the One God (see 3 : 96), and which for this reason has been instituted as the direction of prayer (*qiblah*) for all Muslims, and as the goal of the annually recurring pilgrimage (*ḥajj*). It is to be noted that even in pre-Islamic times the Kaʿbah was associated with the memory of Abraham, whose personality had always been in the foreground of Arabian thought. According to very ancient Arabian traditions, it was at the site of what later became Mecca that Abraham, in order to placate Sarah, abandoned his Egyptian bondwoman Hagar and their child Ishmael after he had brought them there from Canaan. This is by no means improbable if one bears in mind that for a camel-riding bedouin (and Abraham was certainly one) a journey of twenty or even thirty days has never been anything out of the ordinary. At first glance, the Biblical statement (Genesis xxi, 14) that it was "in the wilderness of Beersheba" (i.e., in the southernmost tip of Palestine) that Abraham left Hagar and Ishmael would seem to conflict with the Qurʾanic account. This seeming contradiction, however, disappears as soon as we remember that to the ancient, town-dwelling Hebrews the term "wilderness of Beersheba" comprised all the desert regions south of Palestine, including the Ḥijāz. It was at the place where they had been abandoned that Hagar and Ishmael, after having discovered the spring which is now called the Well of Zamzam, eventually settled; and it may have been that very spring which in time induced a wandering group of bedouin families belonging to the South-Arabian (Qaḥṭānī) tribe of Jurhum to settle there. Ishmael later married a girl of this tribe, and so became the progenitor of the *mustaʿribah* ("Arabianized") tribes – thus called on account of their descent from a Hebrew father and a Qaḥṭānī mother. As for Abraham, he is said to have often visited Hagar and Ishmael; and it was on the occasion of one of these periodic visits that he, aided by Ishmael, erected the original structure of the Kaʿbah. (For more detailed accounts of the Abrahamic tradition, see Bukhārī's *Ṣaḥīḥ, Kitāb al-ʿIlm*, Ṭabarī's *Taʾrīkh al-Umam*, Ibn Saʿd, Ibn Hishām, Masʿūdī's *Murūj adh-Dhahab*, Yāqūt's *Muʿjam al-Buldān*, and other early Muslim historians.)

103 This may refer to the immediate vicinity of the Kaʿbah or, more probably (*Manār* I, 461 f.), to the sacred precincts (*ḥaram*) surrounding it. The word *amn* (lit., "safety") denotes in this context a sanctuary for all living beings.

104 The seven-fold circumambulation (*ṭawāf*) of the Kaʿbah is one of the rites of the pilgrimage, symbolically indicating that all human actions and endeavours ought to have the idea of God and His oneness for their centre.

And, lo, Abraham prayed: "O my Sustainer! Make this a land secure, and grant its people fruitful sustenance – such of them as believe in God and the Last Day."

[God] answered: "And whoever shall deny the truth, him will I let enjoy himself for a short while – but in the end I shall drive him to suffering through fire: and how vile a journey's end!" ﴾126﴿

And when Abraham and Ishmael were raising the foundations of the Temple, [they prayed:] "O our Sustainer! Accept Thou this from us: for, verily, Thou alone art all-hearing, all-knowing! ﴾127﴿

"O our Sustainer! Make us surrender ourselves unto Thee, and make out of our offspring"[105] a community that shall surrender itself unto Thee, and show us our ways of worship, and accept our repentance: for, verily, Thou alone art the Acceptor of Repentance, the Dispenser of Grace! ﴾128﴿

"O our Sustainer! Raise up from the midst of our offspring[106] an apostle from among themselves, who shall convey unto them Thy messages, and impart unto them revelation as well as wisdom, and cause them to grow in purity: for, verily, Thou alone art almighty, truly wise!" ﴾129﴿

And who, unless he be weak of mind, would want to abandon Abraham's creed, seeing that We have indeed raised him high in this world, and that, verily, in the life to come he shall be among the righteous? ﴾130﴿

When his Sustainer said to him, "Surrender thyself unto Me!" – he answered, "I have surrendered myself unto [Thee,] the Sustainer of all the worlds." ﴾131﴿

And this very thing did Abraham bequeath unto his children, and [so did] Jacob: "O my children! Behold, God has granted you the purest faith; so do not allow death to

وَإِذْ قَالَ إِبْرَٰهِـۧمُ رَبِّ ٱجْعَلْ هَـٰذَا بَلَدًا ءَامِنًا وَٱرْزُقْ أَهْلَهُۥ مِنَ ٱلثَّمَرَٰتِ
مَنْ ءَامَنَ مِنْهُم بِٱللَّهِ وَٱلْيَوْمِ ٱلْـَٔاخِرِ ۖ قَالَ وَمَن كَفَرَ فَأُمَتِّعُهُۥ قَلِيلًا ثُمَّ
أَضْطَرُّهُۥٓ إِلَىٰ عَذَابِ ٱلنَّارِ ۖ وَبِئْسَ ٱلْمَصِيرُ ﴿١٢٦﴾ وَإِذْ يَرْفَعُ إِبْرَٰهِـۧمُ
ٱلْقَوَاعِدَ مِنَ ٱلْبَيْتِ وَإِسْمَـٰعِيلُ رَبَّنَا تَقَبَّلْ مِنَّآ ۖ إِنَّكَ أَنتَ ٱلسَّمِيعُ
ٱلْعَلِيمُ ﴿١٢٧﴾ رَبَّنَا وَٱجْعَلْنَا مُسْلِمَيْنِ لَكَ وَمِن ذُرِّيَّتِنَآ أُمَّةً مُّسْلِمَةً لَّكَ وَأَرِنَا
مَنَاسِكَنَا وَتُبْ عَلَيْنَآ ۖ إِنَّكَ أَنتَ ٱلتَّوَّابُ ٱلرَّحِيمُ ﴿١٢٨﴾ رَبَّنَا وَٱبْعَثْ فِيهِمْ
رَسُولًا مِّنْهُمْ يَتْلُوا۟ عَلَيْهِمْ ءَايَـٰتِكَ وَيُعَلِّمُهُمُ ٱلْكِتَـٰبَ وَٱلْحِكْمَةَ وَيُزَكِّيهِمْ ۚ
إِنَّكَ أَنتَ ٱلْعَزِيزُ ٱلْحَكِيمُ ﴿١٢٩﴾ وَمَن يَرْغَبُ عَن مِّلَّةِ إِبْرَٰهِـۧمَ إِلَّا مَن سَفِهَ
نَفْسَهُۥ ۚ وَلَقَدِ ٱصْطَفَيْنَـٰهُ فِى ٱلدُّنْيَا ۖ وَإِنَّهُۥ فِى ٱلْـَٔاخِرَةِ لَمِنَ ٱلصَّـٰلِحِينَ ﴿١٣٠﴾
إِذْ قَالَ لَهُۥ رَبُّهُۥٓ أَسْلِمْ ۖ قَالَ أَسْلَمْتُ لِرَبِّ ٱلْعَـٰلَمِينَ ﴿١٣١﴾ وَوَصَّىٰ بِهَآ
إِبْرَٰهِـۧمُ بَنِيهِ وَيَعْقُوبُ يَـٰبَنِىَّ إِنَّ ٱللَّهَ ٱصْطَفَىٰ لَكُمُ ٱلدِّينَ فَلَا تَمُوتُنَّ

Wa ʾidh qāla ʾIbrāhīmu Rabbij-ʿal hādhā baladan ʾāminañw-war-zuq ʾahlahū minath-thamarāti man ʾāmana minhum-billāhi wal-Yawmil-ʾĀkhir. Qāla wa mañ-kafara faʾumattiʿuhū qalīlañ-thumma ʾaḍṭarruhūu ʾilā ʿadhābin-nār wa biʾsal-maṣīr. (126) Wa ʾidh yarfaʿu ʾIbrāhīmul-qawāʿida minal-Bayti wa ʾIsmāʿīlu Rabbanā taqabbal minnāa ʾinnaka ʾAñtas-Samīʿul-ʿAlīm. (127) Rabbanā waj-ʿalnā-Muslimayni laka wa miñ-dhurriyyatināa ʾummatam-Muslimatal-laka wa ʾarinā manāsikanā wa tub ʿalaynāa ʾinnaka ʾAñtat-Taw-wābur-Raḥīm. (128) Rabbanā wab-ʿath fīhim Rasūlam-minhum yatlū ʿalayhim ʾĀyātika wa yuʿallimuhumul-Kitāba wal-ḥikmata wa yuzakkīhim. ʾInnaka ʾAñtal-ʿAzīzul-Ḥakīm. (129) Wa mañy-yarghabu ʿam-millati ʾIbrāhīma ʾillā mañ-safiha nafsah. Wa laqadiṣ-ṭafaynāhu fid-dunyā; wa ʾinnahū fil-ʾĀkhirati laminaṣ-ṣāliḥīn. (130) ʾIdh qāla lahū Rabbuhūu ʾaslim qāla ʾaslamtu liRabbil-ʿālamīn. (131) Wa waṣṣā bihāa ʾIbrāhīmu banīhi wa Yaʿqūbu yā baniyya ʾinnal-lāhaṣ-ṭafā lakumud-dīna falā tamūtunna

105 The expression "*our* offspring" indicates Abraham's progeny through his first-born son, Ishmael, and is an indirect reference to the Prophet Muḥammad, who descended from the latter.

106 Lit., "within them".

overtake you ere you have surrendered yourselves unto Him." ⟨132⟩
Nay, but you [yourselves, O children of Israel,] bear witness[107] that when death was approaching Jacob, he said unto his sons: "Whom will you worship after I am gone?"
They answered: "We will worship thy God, the God of thy forefathers Abraham and Ishmael[108] and Isaac, the One God; and unto Him will we surrender ourselves." ⟨133⟩
Now those people have passed away; unto them shall be accounted what they have earned, and unto you, what you have earned; and you will not be judged on the strength of what they did.[109] ⟨134⟩

AND THEY say, "Be Jews" – or, "Christians" – "and you shall be on the right path." Say: "Nay, but [ours is] the creed of Abraham, who turned away from all that is false,[110] and was not of those who ascribe divinity to aught beside God." ⟨135⟩
Say: "We believe in God, and in that which has been bestowed from on high upon us, and that which has been bestowed upon Abraham and Ishmael and Isaac and Jacob and their descendants,[111] and that

إِلَّا وَأَنتُم مُّسْلِمُونَ ﴿١٣٢﴾ أَمْ كُنتُمْ شُهَدَآءَ إِذْ حَضَرَ يَعْقُوبَ ٱلْمَوْتُ إِذْ قَالَ
لِبَنِيهِ مَا تَعْبُدُونَ مِنۢ بَعْدِى قَالُوا۟ نَعْبُدُ إِلَـٰهَكَ وَإِلَـٰهَ ءَابَآئِكَ إِبْرَٰهِـۧمَ
وَإِسْمَـٰعِيلَ وَإِسْحَـٰقَ إِلَـٰهًا وَٰحِدًا وَنَحْنُ لَهُۥ مُسْلِمُونَ ﴿١٣٣﴾ تِلْكَ أُمَّةٌ قَدْ
خَلَتْ لَهَا مَا كَسَبَتْ وَلَكُم مَّا كَسَبْتُمْ وَلَا تُسْـَٔلُونَ عَمَّا كَانُوا۟ يَعْمَلُونَ ﴿١٣٤﴾
وَقَالُوا۟ كُونُوا۟ هُودًا أَوْ نَصَـٰرَىٰ تَهْتَدُوا۟ قُلْ بَلْ مِلَّةَ إِبْرَٰهِـۧمَ حَنِيفًا
وَمَا كَانَ مِنَ ٱلْمُشْرِكِينَ ﴿١٣٥﴾ قُولُوٓا۟ ءَامَنَّا بِٱللَّهِ وَمَآ أُنزِلَ إِلَيْنَا وَمَآ
أُنزِلَ إِلَىٰٓ إِبْرَٰهِـۧمَ وَإِسْمَـٰعِيلَ وَإِسْحَـٰقَ وَيَعْقُوبَ وَٱلْأَسْبَاطِ وَمَآ

ʾillā wa ʾañtum-Muslimūn. (132) ʾAm kuñtum shuha-
dāaʾa ʾidh ḥaḍara Yaʿqūbal-mawtu ʾidh qāla libanīhi
mā taʿbudūna mim-baʿdī qālū naʿbudu ʾIlāhaka wa
ʾIlāha ʾābāaʾika ʾIbrāhīma wa ʾIsmāʿīla wa ʾIsḥāqa
ʾIlāhañw-Wāḥidañw-wa naḥnu lahū Muslimūn. (133)
Tilka ʾummatuñ-qad khalat. Lahā mā kasabat wa
lakum-mā kasabtum. Wa lā tusʾalūna ʿammā kānū
yaʿmalūn. (134) Wa qālū kūnū Hūdan ʾaw Naṣārā tah-
tadū. Qul bal millata ʾIbrāhīma ḥanīfañw-wa mā
kāna minal-mushrikīn. (135) Qūlūu ʾāmannā billāhi wa
māa ʾuñzila ʾilaynā wa māa ʾuñzila ʾilāa ʾIbrāhīma wa
ʾIsmāʿīla wa ʾIsḥāqa wa Yaʿqūba wal-ʾasbāṭi wa māa

107 I.e., "in the religious traditions to which you adhere". It is to be noted that the conjunction *am* which stands at the beginning of this sentence is not always used in the interrogative sense ("is it that . . . ?"): sometimes – and especially when it is syntactically unconnected with the preceding sentence, as in this case – it is an equivalent of *bal* ("rather", or "nay, but"), and has no interrogative connotation.

108 In classical Arabic, as in ancient Hebrew usage, the term *ab* ("father") was applied not only to the direct male parent but also to grandfathers and even more distant ancestors, as well as to paternal uncles: which explains why Ishmael, who was Jacob's uncle, is mentioned in this context. Since he was the first-born of Abraham's sons, his name precedes that of Isaac.

109 Lit., "you will not be asked about what they did". This verse, as well as verse 141 below, stresses the fundamental Islamic tenet of individual responsibility, and denies the Jewish idea of their being "the chosen people" by virtue of their descent, as well as – by implication – the Christian doctrine of an "original sin" with which all human beings are supposedly burdened because of Adam's fall from grace.

110 The expression *ḥanīf* is derived from the verb *ḥanafa*, which literally means "he inclined [towards a right state or tendency]" (cf. Lane II, 658). Already in pre-Islamic times, this term had a definitely monotheistic connotation, and was used to describe a man who turned away from sin and worldliness and from all dubious beliefs, especially idol-worship; and *taḥannuf* denoted the ardent devotions, mainly consisting of long vigils and prayers, of the unitarian God-seekers of pre-Islamic times. Many instances of this use of the terms *ḥanīf* and *taḥannuf* occur in the verses of pre-Islamic poets, e.g., Umayyah ibn Abi 'ṣ-Ṣalt and Jīrān al-ʿAwd (cf. *Lisān al-ʿArab*, art. *ḥanafa*).

111 Lit., "the grandchildren" (*al-asbāṭ*, sing. *sibṭ*) – a term used in the Qurʾān to describe, in the first instance, Abraham's, Isaac's and Jacob's immediate descendants, and, consequently, the twelve tribes which evolved from this ancestry.

which has been vouchsafed to Moses and Jesus, and that which has been vouchsafed to all the [other] prophets by their Sustainer: we make no distinction between any of them.[112] And it is unto Him that we surrender ourselves." ‹136›

And if [others] come to believe in the way you believe, they will indeed find themselves on the right path; and if they turn away, it is but they who will be deeply in the wrong, and God will protect thee from them: for He alone is all-hearing, all-knowing. ‹137›

[Say: "Our life takes its] hue from God! And who could give a better hue [to life] than God, if we but truly worship Him?" ‹138›

Say [to the Jews and the Christians]: "Do you argue with us about God?[113] But He is our Sustainer as well as your Sustainer – and unto us shall be accounted our deeds, and unto you, your deeds; and it is unto Him alone that we devote ourselves. ‹139›

"Do you claim that Abraham and Ishmael and Isaac and Jacob and their descendants were 'Jews' or 'Christians'?"[114] Say: "Do you know more than God does? And who could be more wicked than he who suppresses a testimony given to him by God?[115] Yet God is not unmindful of what you do. ‹140›

"Now those people have passed away; unto them shall be accounted what they have earned, and unto you, what you have earned; and you will not be judged on the strength of what they did." ‹141›

أُوتِىَ مُوسَىٰ وَعِيسَىٰ وَمَآ أُوتِىَ ٱلنَّبِيُّونَ مِن رَّبِّهِمْ لَا نُفَرِّقُ بَيْنَ أَحَدٍ مِّنْهُمْ
وَنَحْنُ لَهُۥ مُسْلِمُونَ ﴿١٣٦﴾ فَإِنْ ءَامَنُوا۟ بِمِثْلِ مَآ ءَامَنتُم بِهِۦ فَقَدِ ٱهْتَدَوا۟
وَّإِن تَوَلَّوْا۟ فَإِنَّمَا هُمْ فِى شِقَاقٍ فَسَيَكْفِيكَهُمُ ٱللَّهُ وَهُوَ ٱلسَّمِيعُ
ٱلْعَلِيمُ ﴿١٣٧﴾ صِبْغَةَ ٱللَّهِ وَمَنْ أَحْسَنُ مِنَ ٱللَّهِ صِبْغَةً وَنَحْنُ لَهُۥ
عَٰبِدُونَ ﴿١٣٨﴾ قُلْ أَتُحَآجُّونَنَا فِى ٱللَّهِ وَهُوَ رَبُّنَا وَرَبُّكُمْ وَلَنَآ أَعْمَٰلُنَا
وَلَكُمْ أَعْمَٰلُكُمْ وَنَحْنُ لَهُۥ مُخْلِصُونَ ﴿١٣٩﴾ أَمْ تَقُولُونَ إِنَّ إِبْرَٰهِۦمَ
وَإِسْمَٰعِيلَ وَإِسْحَٰقَ وَيَعْقُوبَ وَٱلْأَسْبَاطَ كَانُوا۟ هُودًا أَوْ نَصَٰرَىٰ قُلْ
ءَأَنتُمْ أَعْلَمُ أَمِ ٱللَّهُ وَمَنْ أَظْلَمُ مِمَّن كَتَمَ شَهَٰدَةً عِندَهُۥ مِنَ ٱللَّهِ وَمَا ٱللَّهُ
بِغَٰفِلٍ عَمَّا تَعْمَلُونَ ﴿١٤٠﴾ تِلْكَ أُمَّةٌ قَدْ خَلَتْ لَهَا مَا كَسَبَتْ وَلَكُم مَّا
كَسَبْتُمْ وَلَا تُسْـَٔلُونَ عَمَّا كَانُوا۟ يَعْمَلُونَ ﴿١٤١﴾

ʾūtiya Mūsā wa ʿĪsā wa māa ʾūtiyan-Nabiyyūna mir-Rabbihim. Lā nufarriqu bayna ʾaḥadim-minhum wa naḥnu lahū Muslimūn. (136) Faʾin ʾāmanū bimithli māa ʾāmañtum-bihī faqadih-tadaw. Wa ʾiñ-tawallaw faʾinnamā hum fī shiqāqiñ-fasayakfīkahumul-lāhu wa Huwas-Samīʿul-ʿAlīm. (137) Ṣibghatal-lāhi wa man ʾaḥsanu minal-lāhi ṣibghah. Wa naḥnu lahū ʿābidūn. (138) Qul ʾatuḥāajjūnanā fil-lāhi wa Huwa Rabbunā wa Rabbukum wa lanāa ʾaʿmālunā wa lakum ʾaʿmālukum wa naḥnu lahū mukhliṣūn. (139) ʾAm taqūlūna ʾinna ʾIbrāhīma wa ʾIsmāʿīla wa ʾIsḥāqa wa Yaʿqūba wal-ʾasbāṭa kānū Hūdan ʾaw Naṣārā. Qul ʾaʾañtum ʾaʿlamu ʾamil-lāh. Wa man ʾaẓlamu mimmañ-katama shahādatan ʿiñdahū minal-lāh. Wa mal-lāhu bighāfilin ʿammā taʿmalūn. (140) Tilka ʾummatuñ-qad khalat. Lahā mā kasabat wa lakum-mā kasabtum. Wa lā tusʾalūna ʿammā kānū yaʿmalūn. (141)

112 I.e., "we regard them all as true prophets of God".

113 I.e., about God's will regarding the succession of prophethood and man's ultimate salvation. The Jews believe that prophethood was a privilege granted to the children of Israel alone, while the Christians maintain that Jesus – who, too, descended from the children of Israel – was God's final manifestation on earth; and each of these two denominations claims that salvation is reserved to its followers alone (see 2 : 111 and 135). The Qurʾān refutes these ideas by stressing, in the next sentence, that God is the Lord of *all* mankind, and that every individual will be judged on the basis of his own beliefs and his own behaviour alone.

114 Regarding the term *asbāṭ* (rendered here as well as in verse 136 as "descendants"), see note 111 above. In the above words the Qurʾān alludes to the fact that the concept of "Jewry" came into being many centuries after the time of the Patriarchs, and even long after the time of Moses, while the concepts of "Christianity" and "Christians" were unknown in Jesus' time and represent later developments.

115 A reference to the Biblical prediction of the coming of the Prophet Muḥammad, (see note 33 on verse 42 of this *sūrah*), which effectively contradicts the Judaeo-Christian claim that all true prophets, after the Patriarchs, belonged to the children of Israel.

THE WEAK-MINDED among people will say, "What has turned them away from the direction of prayer which they have hitherto observed?"[116]
Say: "God's is the east and the west; He guides whom He wills onto a straight way"[117] ⟨142⟩
And thus have We willed you to be a community of the middle way,[118] so that [with your lives] you might bear witness to the truth before all mankind, and that the Apostle might bear witness to it before you.[119]
And it is only to the end that We might make a clear distinction between those who follow the Apostle and those who turn about on their heels that We have appointed [for this community] the direction of prayer which thou [O Prophet] hast formerly observed: for this was indeed a hard test for all but those whom God has guided aright.[120] But God will

۞ سَيَقُولُ ٱلسُّفَهَآءُ مِنَ ٱلنَّاسِ مَا وَلَّىٰهُمْ عَن قِبْلَتِهِمُ ٱلَّتِى كَانُوا۟ عَلَيْهَا ۚ قُل
لِّلَّهِ ٱلْمَشْرِقُ وَٱلْمَغْرِبُ ۚ يَهْدِى مَن يَشَآءُ إِلَىٰ صِرَٰطٍ مُّسْتَقِيمٍ ﴿١٤٢﴾ وَكَذَٰلِكَ
جَعَلْنَٰكُمْ أُمَّةً وَسَطًا لِّتَكُونُوا۟ شُهَدَآءَ عَلَى ٱلنَّاسِ وَيَكُونَ ٱلرَّسُولُ عَلَيْكُمْ
شَهِيدًا ۗ وَمَا جَعَلْنَا ٱلْقِبْلَةَ ٱلَّتِى كُنتَ عَلَيْهَآ إِلَّا لِنَعْلَمَ مَن يَتَّبِعُ ٱلرَّسُولَ مِمَّن
يَنقَلِبُ عَلَىٰ عَقِبَيْهِ ۚ وَإِن كَانَتْ لَكَبِيرَةً إِلَّا عَلَى ٱلَّذِينَ هَدَى ٱللَّهُ ۗ وَمَا كَانَ ٱللَّهُ

۞ Sayaqūlus-sufahāaʾu minan-nāsi mā wallāhum ʿañ-qiblatihimul-latī kānū ʿalayhā. Qul-lillāhil-mashriqu wal-maghrib. Yahdī mañy-yashāaʾu ʾilā ṣirāṭim-mustaqīm. ﴿142﴾ Wa kadhālika jaʿalnākum ʾummatañw-wasaṭal-litakūnū shuhadāaʾa ʿalan-nāsi wa yakūnar-Rasūlū ʿalaykum shahīdā. Wa mā jaʿalnal-qiblatal-latī kuñta ʿalayhāa ʾillā linaʿlama mañy-yattabiʿur-Rasūla mim-mañy-yañqalibu ʿalā ʿaqibayh. Wa ʾiñ-kānat lakabīratan ʾillā ʿalal-ladhīna hadal-lāh. Wa mā kānal-lāhu

حزب 3
جزء 2

116 Before his call to prophethood, and during the early Meccan period of his ministry, the Prophet – and his community with him – used to turn in prayer towards the Kaʿbah. This was not prompted by any specific revelation, but was obviously due to the fact that the Kaʿbah – although it had in the meantime been filled with various idols to which the pre-Islamic Arabs paid homage – was always regarded as the first temple ever dedicated to the One God (cf. 3 : 96). Since he was aware of the sanctity of Jerusalem – the other holy centre of the unitarian faith – the Prophet prayed, as a rule, before the southern wall of the Kaʿbah, towards the north, so as to face both the Kaʿbah and Jerusalem. After the exodus to Medina he continued to pray northwards, with only Jerusalem as his *qiblah* (direction of prayer). About sixteen months after his arrival at Medina, however, he received a revelation (verses 142-150 of this *sūrah*) which definitively established the Kaʿbah as the *qiblah* of the followers of the Qurʾān. This "abandonment" of Jerusalem obviously displeased the Jews of Medina, who must have felt gratified when they saw the Muslims praying towards their holy city; and it is to them that the opening sentence of this passage refers. If one considers the matter from the historical point of view, there had never been any *change* in the divine commandments relating to the *qiblah*: there had simply been no ordinance whatever in this respect before verses 142-150 were revealed. Their logical connection with the preceding passages, which deal, in the main, with Abraham and his creed, lies in the fact that it was Abraham who erected the earliest structure of the temple which later came to be known as the Kaʿbah.

117 Or: "He guides onto a straight way him that wills [to be guided]".

118 Lit., "middlemost community" – i.e., a community that keeps an equitable balance between extremes and is realistic in its appreciation of man's nature and possibilities, rejecting both licentiousness and exaggerated asceticism. In tune with its oft-repeated call to moderation in every aspect of life, the Qurʾān exhorts the believers not to place too great an emphasis on the physical and material aspects of their lives, but postulates, at the same time, that man's urges and desires relating to this "life of the flesh" are God-willed and, therefore, legitimate. On further analysis, the expression "a community of the middle way" might be said to summarize, as it were, the Islamic attitude towards the problem of man's existence as such: a denial of the view that there is an inherent conflict between the spirit and the flesh, and a bold affirmation of the natural, God-willed unity in this twofold aspect of human life. This balanced attitude, peculiar to Islam, flows directly from the concept of God's oneness and, hence, of the unity of purpose underlying all His creation: and thus, the mention of the "community of the middle way" at this place is a fitting introduction to the theme of the Kaʿbah, a symbol of God's oneness.

119 I.e., "that your way of life be an example to all mankind, just as the Apostle is an example to you".

120 I.e., "whom He has given understanding" (Rāzī). The "hard test" (*kabīrah*) consisted in the fact that ever since their exodus to Medina the Muslims had become accustomed to praying towards Jerusalem – associated in their

surely not lose sight of your faith – for, behold, God is most compassionate towards man, a dispenser of grace. ⟨143⟩
We have seen thee [O Prophet] often turn thy face towards heaven [for guidance]: and now We shall indeed make thee turn in prayer in a direction which will fulfil thy desire. Turn, then, thy face towards the Inviolable House of Worship; and wherever you all may be, turn your faces towards it [in prayer].
And, verily, those who have been vouchsafed revelation aforetime know well that this [commandment] comes in truth from their Sustainer; and God is not unaware of what they do. ⟨144⟩
And yet, even if thou wert to place all evidence[121] before those who have been vouchsafed earlier revelation, they would not follow thy direction of prayer; and neither mayest thou follow their direction of prayer, nor even do they follow one another's direction. And if thou shouldst follow their errant views after all the knowledge that has come unto thee, thou wouldst surely be among the evildoers. ⟨145⟩
They unto whom We have vouchsafed revelation aforetime know it as they know their own children: but, behold, some of them knowingly suppress the truth ⟨146⟩ – the truth from thy Sustainer![122]
Be not, then, among the doubters: ⟨147⟩ for, every community faces a direction of its own, of which He is the focal point.[123]

لِيُضِيعَ إِيمَـٰنَكُمْ إِنَّ ٱللَّهَ بِٱلنَّاسِ لَرَءُوفٌ رَّحِيمٌ ﴿١٤٣﴾ قَدْ نَرَىٰ تَقَلُّبَ
وَجْهِكَ فِى ٱلسَّمَآءِ فَلَنُوَلِّيَنَّكَ قِبْلَةً تَرْضَىٰهَا فَوَلِّ وَجْهَكَ شَطْرَ ٱلْمَسْجِدِ
ٱلْحَرَامِ وَحَيْثُ مَا كُنتُمْ فَوَلُّوا۟ وُجُوهَكُمْ شَطْرَهُۥ وَإِنَّ ٱلَّذِينَ أُوتُوا۟
ٱلْكِتَـٰبَ لَيَعْلَمُونَ أَنَّهُ ٱلْحَقُّ مِن رَّبِّهِمْ وَمَا ٱللَّهُ بِغَـٰفِلٍ عَمَّا
يَعْمَلُونَ ﴿١٤٤﴾ وَلَئِنْ أَتَيْتَ ٱلَّذِينَ أُوتُوا۟ ٱلْكِتَـٰبَ بِكُلِّ ءَايَةٍ مَّا تَبِعُوا۟
قِبْلَتَكَ وَمَآ أَنتَ بِتَابِعٍ قِبْلَتَهُمْ وَمَا بَعْضُهُم بِتَابِعٍ قِبْلَةَ بَعْضٍ وَلَئِنِ
ٱتَّبَعْتَ أَهْوَآءَهُم مِّنۢ بَعْدِ مَا جَآءَكَ مِنَ ٱلْعِلْمِ إِنَّكَ إِذًا لَّمِنَ
ٱلظَّـٰلِمِينَ ﴿١٤٥﴾ ٱلَّذِينَ ءَاتَيْنَـٰهُمُ ٱلْكِتَـٰبَ يَعْرِفُونَهُۥ كَمَا يَعْرِفُونَ
أَبْنَآءَهُمْ وَإِنَّ فَرِيقًا مِّنْهُمْ لَيَكْتُمُونَ ٱلْحَقَّ وَهُمْ يَعْلَمُونَ ﴿١٤٦﴾ ٱلْحَقُّ مِن
رَّبِّكَ فَلَا تَكُونَنَّ مِنَ ٱلْمُمْتَرِينَ ﴿١٤٧﴾ وَلِكُلٍّ وِجْهَةٌ هُوَ مُوَلِّيهَا

liyuḍīʿa ʾīmānakum. ʾInnal-lāha binnāsi laRaʾūfur-Raḥīm. (143) Qad narā taqalluba wajhika fis-samāaʾi falanuwalliyannaka qiblatañ-tarḍāhā. Fawalli wajhaka shaṭral-Masjidil-Ḥarām. Wa ḥaythu mā kuñtum fawallū wujūhakum shaṭrah. Wa ʾinnal-ladhīna ʾūtul-Kitāba layaʿlamūna ʾannahul-ḥaqqu mir-Rabbihim. Wa mal-lāhu bighāfilin ʿammā yaʿmalūn. (144) Wa laʾin ʾataytal-ladhīna ʾūtul-Kitāba bikulli ʾĀyatim-mā tabiʿū qiblataka wa māa ʾañta bitābiʿiñ-qiblatahum; wa mā baʿḍuhum-bitābiʿiñ-qiblata baʿḍ. Wa laʾinit-tabaʿta ʾahwāaʾahum-mim-baʿdi mā jāaʾaka minal-ʿilmi ʾinnaka ʾidhal-laminaẓ-ẓālimīn. (145) ʾAlladhīna ʾātaynāhumul-Kitāba yaʿrifūnahū kamā yaʿrifūna ʾabnāaʾahum; wa ʾinna farīqam-minhum layaktumūnal-ḥaqqa wa hum yaʿlamūn. (146) ʾAlḥaqqu mir-Rabbika falā takūnanna minal-mumtarīn. (147) Wa likulliñw-wijhatun huwa muwallīhā

minds with the teachings of most of the earlier prophets mentioned in the Qurʾān – and were now called upon to turn in their prayers towards the Kaʿbah, which at that time (in the second year after the *hijrah*) was still used by the pagan Quraysh as a shrine dedicated to the worship of their numerous idols. As against this, the Qurʾān states that true believers would not find it difficult to adopt the Kaʿbah once again as their *qiblah*: they would instinctively realize the divine wisdom underlying this commandment which established Abraham's Temple as a symbol of God's oneness and a focal point of the ideological unity of Islam. (See also note 116 above.)

121 Lit., "every sign (*āyah*)", i.e., of its being a revealed commandment.

122 This refers, in the first instance, to the fact that the Kaʿbah was Abraham's *qiblah*, as well as to the Biblical prophecies relating to Ishmael as the progenitor of a "great nation" (Genesis xxi, 13 and 18) from whom a prophet "like unto Moses" would one day arise: for it was through Ishmael's descendant, the Arabian Prophet, that the commandment relating to the *qiblah* was revealed. (Regarding the still more explicit predictions of the future advent of the Prophet Muḥammad, forthcoming from the canonical Gospels, see 61 : 6 and the corresponding note.)

123 Lit., "everyone has a direction . . .", etc. Almost all of the classical commentators, from the Companions of the Prophet downwards, interpret this as a reference to the various religious communities and their different

فَاسْتَبِقُوا الْخَيْرَاتِ ۚ أَيْنَ مَا تَكُونُوا يَأْتِ بِكُمُ اللَّهُ جَمِيعًا ۚ إِنَّ اللَّهَ عَلَىٰ
كُلِّ شَيْءٍ قَدِيرٌ ﴿١٤٨﴾ وَمِنْ حَيْثُ خَرَجْتَ فَوَلِّ وَجْهَكَ شَطْرَ الْمَسْجِدِ
الْحَرَامِ ۖ وَإِنَّهُ لَلْحَقُّ مِن رَّبِّكَ ۗ وَمَا اللَّهُ بِغَافِلٍ عَمَّا تَعْمَلُونَ ﴿١٤٩﴾ وَمِنْ
حَيْثُ خَرَجْتَ فَوَلِّ وَجْهَكَ شَطْرَ الْمَسْجِدِ الْحَرَامِ ۚ وَحَيْثُ مَا كُنتُمْ
فَوَلُّوا وُجُوهَكُمْ شَطْرَهُ لِئَلَّا يَكُونَ لِلنَّاسِ عَلَيْكُمْ حُجَّةٌ إِلَّا الَّذِينَ ظَلَمُوا
مِنْهُمْ فَلَا تَخْشَوْهُمْ وَاخْشَوْنِي وَلِأُتِمَّ نِعْمَتِي عَلَيْكُمْ وَلَعَلَّكُمْ تَهْتَدُونَ ﴿١٥٠﴾
كَمَا أَرْسَلْنَا فِيكُمْ رَسُولًا مِّنكُمْ يَتْلُو عَلَيْكُمْ آيَاتِنَا وَيُزَكِّيكُمْ
وَيُعَلِّمُكُمُ الْكِتَابَ وَالْحِكْمَةَ وَيُعَلِّمُكُم مَّا لَمْ تَكُونُوا تَعْلَمُونَ ﴿١٥١﴾
فَاذْكُرُونِي أَذْكُرْكُمْ وَاشْكُرُوا لِي وَلَا تَكْفُرُونِ ﴿١٥٢﴾

Vie, therefore, with one another in doing good works. Wherever you may be, God will gather you all unto Himself: for, verily, God has the power to will anything. ‹148›

Thus, from wherever thou mayest come forth, turn thy face [in prayer] towards the Inviolable House of Worship – for, behold, this [commandment] comes in truth from thy Sustainer; and God is not unaware of what you do. ‹149› Hence, from wherever thou mayest come forth, turn thy face [in prayer] towards the Inviolable House of Worship; and wherever you all may be, turn your faces towards it, so that people should have no argument against you unless they are bent upon wrongdoing.[124] And hold not them in awe, but stand in awe of Me, and [obey Me,] so that I might bestow upon you the full measure of My blessings, and that you might follow the right path. ‹150›

Even as We have sent unto you an apostle from among yourselves to convey unto you Our messages, and to cause you to grow in purity, and to impart unto you revelation and wisdom, and to teach you that which you knew not: ‹151› so remember Me, and I shall remember you; and be grateful unto Me, and deny Me not. ‹152›

fastabiqul-khayrāt. ʾAyna mā takūnū yaʾti bikumul-lāhu jamīʿā. ʾInnal-lāha ʿalā kulli shayʾiñ-Qadīr. (148) Wa min ḥaythu kharajta fawalli wajhaka shaṭral-Masjidil-Ḥarām. Wa ʾinnahū lalḥaqqu mir-Rabbik. Wa mal-lāhu bighāfilin ʿammā taʿmalūn. (149) Wa min ḥaythu kharajta fawalli wajhaka shaṭral-Masjidil-Ḥarām. Wa ḥaythu mā kuñtum fawallū wujūhakum shaṭrahū liʾallā yakūna linnāsi ʿalaykum ḥujjatun ʾillal-ladhīna ẓalamū minhum falā takhshawhum wakh-shawnī wa liʾutimma niʿmatī ʿalaykum wa laʿallakum tahtadūn. (150) Kamāa ʾarsalnā fīkum Rasūlam-miñkum yatlū ʿalaykum ʾĀyātinā wa yuzakkīkum wa yuʿallimukumul-Kitāba wal-ḥikmata wa yuʿallimukum-mā lam takūnū taʿlamūn. (151) Fadh-kurūnīi ʾadhkurkum wash-kurū lī wa lā takfurūn. (152)

modes of "turning towards God" in worship. Ibn Kathīr, in his commentary on this verse, stresses its inner resemblance to the phrase occurring in 5 : 48: "unto every one of you have We appointed a [different] law and way of life". The statement that "every community faces a direction of its own" in its endeavour to express its submission to God implies, firstly, that at various times and in various circumstances man's desire to approach God in prayer has taken different forms (e.g., Abraham's choice of the Kaʿbah as his *qiblah*, the Jewish concentration on Jerusalem, the eastward orientation of the early Christian churches, and the Qurʾanic commandment relating to the Kaʿbah); and, secondly, that the direction of prayer – however important its symbolic significance may be – does not represent the essence of faith as such: for, as the Qurʾān says, "true piety does not consist in turning your faces towards the east or the west" (2 : 177), and, "God's is the east and the west" (2 : 115 and 142). Consequently, the revelation which established the Kaʿbah as the *qiblah* of the Muslims should not be a matter of contention for people of other faiths, nor a cause of their disbelief in the truth of the Qurʾanic revelation as such (*Manār* II, 21 f.).

124 Lit., "except such among them as are bent upon wrongdoing" (regarding the *intent* implied in the use of the past tense in expressions like *alladhīna ẓalamū* or *alladhīna kafarū*, see note 6 on verse 6 of this *sūrah*). The Qurʾān stresses repeatedly that the Muslims are true followers of Abraham. This claim, however, might have been open to objection so long as they prayed in a direction other than Abraham's *qiblah*, the Kaʿbah. The establishment of the latter as the *qiblah* of the followers of the Qurʾān would invalidate any such argument and would leave it only to "those who are bent upon wrongdoing" (in this case, distorting the truth) to challenge the message of the Qurʾān on these grounds.

ربع
الحزب

O YOU who have attained to faith! Seek aid in steadfast patience and prayer: for, behold, God is with those who are patient in adversity. ‹153›

And say not of those who are slain in God's cause, "They are dead": nay, they are alive, but you perceive it not. ‹154›

And most certainly shall We try you by means[125] of danger, and hunger, and loss of worldly goods, of lives and of [labour's] fruits. But give glad tidings unto those who are patient in adversity ‹155› – who, when calamity befalls them, say, "Verily, unto God do we belong and, verily, unto Him we shall return." ‹156› It is they upon whom their Sustainer's blessings and grace are bestowed, and it is they, they who are on the right path! ‹157›

[Hence,] behold, Aṣ-Ṣafā and Al-Marwah are among the symbols set up by God;[126] and thus, no wrong does he who, having come to the Temple on pilgrimage or on a pious visit, strides to and fro between these two:[127] for, if one does more good than he is bound to do – behold, God is responsive to gratitude, all-knowing.[128] ‹158›

يَٰٓأَيُّهَا ٱلَّذِينَ ءَامَنُوا۟ ٱسْتَعِينُوا۟ بِٱلصَّبْرِ وَٱلصَّلَوٰةِ ۚ إِنَّ ٱللَّهَ مَعَ
ٱلصَّٰبِرِينَ ﴿١٥٣﴾ وَلَا تَقُولُوا۟ لِمَن يُقْتَلُ فِى سَبِيلِ ٱللَّهِ أَمْوَٰتٌۢ ۚ بَلْ أَحْيَآءٌ
وَلَٰكِن لَّا تَشْعُرُونَ ﴿١٥٤﴾ وَلَنَبْلُوَنَّكُم بِشَىْءٍ مِّنَ ٱلْخَوْفِ وَٱلْجُوعِ
وَنَقْصٍ مِّنَ ٱلْأَمْوَٰلِ وَٱلْأَنفُسِ وَٱلثَّمَرَٰتِ ۗ وَبَشِّرِ ٱلصَّٰبِرِينَ ﴿١٥٥﴾
ٱلَّذِينَ إِذَآ أَصَٰبَتْهُم مُّصِيبَةٌ قَالُوٓا۟ إِنَّا لِلَّهِ وَإِنَّآ إِلَيْهِ رَٰجِعُونَ ﴿١٥٦﴾
أُو۟لَٰٓئِكَ عَلَيْهِمْ صَلَوَٰتٌ مِّن رَّبِّهِمْ وَرَحْمَةٌ ۖ وَأُو۟لَٰٓئِكَ هُمُ
ٱلْمُهْتَدُونَ ﴿١٥٧﴾ ۞ إِنَّ ٱلصَّفَا وَٱلْمَرْوَةَ مِن شَعَآئِرِ ٱللَّهِ ۖ فَمَنْ حَجَّ ٱلْبَيْتَ
أَوِ ٱعْتَمَرَ فَلَا جُنَاحَ عَلَيْهِ أَن يَطَّوَّفَ بِهِمَا ۚ وَمَن تَطَوَّعَ خَيْرًا فَإِنَّ ٱللَّهَ
شَاكِرٌ عَلِيمٌ ﴿١٥٨﴾

Yāa ʾayyuhal-ladhīna ʾāmanus-taʿīnū biṣṣabri
waṣ-Ṣalāh. ʾInnal-lāha maʿaṣ-ṣābirīn. ﴿153﴾ Wa lā
taqūlū li-mañy-yuqtalu fī sabīlil-lāhi ʾamwāt. Bal
ʾaḥyāa-ʾuñw-wa lākil-lā tashʿurūn. ﴿154﴾ Wa lanablu-
wanna-kum-bishayʾim-minal-khawfi wal-jūʿi wa
naqṣim-minal-ʾamwāli wal-ʾañfusi wath-thamarāt.
Wa bashshiriṣ-ṣābirīn. ﴿155﴾ ʾAlladhīna ʾidhāa ʾaṣābat-
hum muṣībatuñ-qālūu ʾinnā lillāhi wa ʾinnāa ʾilayhi
rajiʿūn. ﴿156﴾ ʾUlāaʾika ʿalayhim ṣalawātum-mir-Rab-
bihim wa raḥmah. Wa ʾulāaʾika humul-muhtadūn.
﴿157﴾ ۞ ʾInnaṣ-Ṣafā wal-Marwata miñ-Shaʿāaʾiril-lāh.
Faman ḥajjal-Bayta ʾawiʿ-tamara falā junāḥa ʿalayhi
ʾañy-yaṭṭawwafa bihimā. Wa mañ-taṭawwaʿa khay-
rañ-faʾinnal-lāha Shākirun ʿAlīm. ﴿158﴾

125 Lit., "with something".

126 Lit., "God's symbols". The space between the two low outcrops of rock called Aṣ-Ṣafā and Al-Marwah, situated in Mecca in the immediate vicinity of the Kaʿbah, is said to have been the scene of Hagar's suffering when Abraham, following God's command, abandoned her and their infant son Ishmael in the desert (see note 102 above). Distraught with thirst and fearing for the life of her child, Hagar ran to and fro between the two rocks and fervently prayed to God for succour: and, finally, her reliance on God and her patience were rewarded by the discovery of a spring – existing to this day and known as the Well of Zamzam – which saved the two from death through thirst. It was in remembrance of Hagar's extreme trial, and of her trust in God, that Aṣ-Ṣafā and Al-Marwah had come to be regarded, even in pre-Islamic times, as symbols of faith and patience in adversity: and this explains their mention in the context of the passages which deal with the virtues of patience and trust in God (Rāzī).

127 It is in commemoration of Hagar's running in distress between Aṣ-Ṣafā and Al-Marwah that the Mecca pilgrims are expected to walk, at a fast pace, seven times between these two hillocks. Because of the fact that in pre-Islamic times certain idols had been standing there, some of the early Muslims were reluctant to perform a rite which seemed to them to be associated with recent idolatry (Rāzī, on the authority of Ibn ʿAbbās). The above verse served to reassure them on this score by pointing out that this symbolic act of remembrance was much older than the idolatry practiced by the pagan Quraysh.

128 From the phrase "if one does more good than he is bound to do", read in conjunction with "no wrong does he who. . ." (or, more literally, "there shall be no blame upon him who . . ."), some of the great Islamic scholars – e.g., Imām Abū Ḥanīfah – conclude that the walking to and fro between Aṣ-Ṣafā and Al-Marwah is not one of the obligatory rites of pilgrimage but rather a supererogatory act of piety (see Zamakhsharī and Rāzī). Most scholars, however, hold the view that it is an integral part of the pilgrimage.

BEHOLD, as for those who suppress aught of the evidence of the truth and of the guidance which We have bestowed from on high, after We have made it clear unto mankind through the divine writ – these it is whom God will reject, and whom all who can judge will reject.[129] ‹159› Excepted, however, shall be they that repent, and put themselves to rights, and make known the truth: and it is they whose repentance I shall accept – for I alone am the Acceptor of Repentance, the Dispenser of Grace. ‹160›
Behold, as for those who are bent on denying the truth and die as deniers of the truth – their due is rejection by God, and by the angels, and by all [righteous] men. ‹161› In this state shall they abide; [and] neither will their suffering be lightened, nor will they be granted respite. ‹162›

AND YOUR GOD is the One God: there is no deity save Him, the Most Gracious, the Dispenser of Grace. ‹163›
Verily, in the creation of the heavens and of the earth, and the succession of night and day: and in the ships that speed through the sea with what is useful to man: and in the waters which God sends down from the sky, giving life thereby to the earth after it had been lifeless, and causing all manner of living creatures to multiply thereon: and in the change of the winds, and the clouds that run their appointed courses between sky and earth: [in all this] there are messages indeed for people who use their reason.[130] ‹164›

إِنَّ ٱلَّذِينَ يَكْتُمُونَ مَآ أَنزَلْنَا مِنَ ٱلْبَيِّنَٰتِ وَٱلْهُدَىٰ مِنۢ بَعْدِ مَا بَيَّنَّٰهُ
لِلنَّاسِ فِى ٱلْكِتَٰبِ أُو۟لَٰٓئِكَ يَلْعَنُهُمُ ٱللَّهُ وَيَلْعَنُهُمُ ٱللَّٰعِنُونَ ﴿159﴾ إِلَّا
ٱلَّذِينَ تَابُوا۟ وَأَصْلَحُوا۟ وَبَيَّنُوا۟ فَأُو۟لَٰٓئِكَ أَتُوبُ عَلَيْهِمْ ۚ وَأَنَا ٱلتَّوَّابُ
ٱلرَّحِيمُ ﴿160﴾ إِنَّ ٱلَّذِينَ كَفَرُوا۟ وَمَاتُوا۟ وَهُمْ كُفَّارٌ أُو۟لَٰٓئِكَ عَلَيْهِمْ لَعْنَةُ
ٱللَّهِ وَٱلْمَلَٰٓئِكَةِ وَٱلنَّاسِ أَجْمَعِينَ ﴿161﴾ خَٰلِدِينَ فِيهَا ۖ لَا يُخَفَّفُ عَنْهُمُ
ٱلْعَذَابُ وَلَا هُمْ يُنظَرُونَ ﴿162﴾ وَإِلَٰهُكُمْ إِلَٰهٌ وَٰحِدٌ ۖ لَّآ إِلَٰهَ إِلَّا هُوَ
ٱلرَّحْمَٰنُ ٱلرَّحِيمُ ﴿163﴾ إِنَّ فِى خَلْقِ ٱلسَّمَٰوَٰتِ وَٱلْأَرْضِ وَٱخْتِلَٰفِ
ٱلَّيْلِ وَٱلنَّهَارِ وَٱلْفُلْكِ ٱلَّتِى تَجْرِى فِى ٱلْبَحْرِ بِمَا يَنفَعُ ٱلنَّاسَ وَمَآ
أَنزَلَ ٱللَّهُ مِنَ ٱلسَّمَآءِ مِن مَّآءٍ فَأَحْيَا بِهِ ٱلْأَرْضَ بَعْدَ مَوْتِهَا وَبَثَّ فِيهَا مِن
كُلِّ دَآبَّةٍ وَتَصْرِيفِ ٱلرِّيَٰحِ وَٱلسَّحَابِ ٱلْمُسَخَّرِ بَيْنَ ٱلسَّمَآءِ وَٱلْأَرْضِ
لَءَايَٰتٍ لِّقَوْمٍ يَعْقِلُونَ ﴿164﴾

ʾInnal-ladhīna yaktumūna māa ʾañzalnā minal-bayyināti wal-hudā mim-baʿdi mā bayyannāhu linnāsi fil-Kitābi ʾulāaʾika yalʿanuhumul-lāhu wa yalʿanuhumul-lāʿinūn. (159) ʾIllal-ladhīna tābū wa ʾaṣlaḥū wa bayyanū faʾulāaʾika atūbu ʿalayhim; wa ʾAnat-Tawwābur-Raḥīm. (160) ʾInnal-ladhīna kafarū wa mātū wa hum kuffārun ʾulāaʾika ʿalayhim laʿnatul-lāhi wal-Malāaʾikati wan-nāsi ʾajmaʿīn. (161) Khālidīna fīhā; lā yukhaffafu ʿanhumul-ʿadhābu wa lā hum yuñẓarūn. (162) Wa ʾIlāhukum ʾIlāhuñw-Wāḥiduñ-lāa ʾilāha ʾillā Huwar-Raḥmānur-Raḥīm. (163) ʾInna fī khalqis-samāwāti wal-ʾarḍi wakh-tilāfil-layli wan-nahāri wal-fulkil-latī tajrī fil-baḥri bimā yañfaʿun-nāsa wa māa ʾañzalal-lāhu minas-samāaʾi mim-māaʾiñ-faʾaḥyā bihil-ʾarḍa baʿda mawtihā wa bath-tha fīhā miñ-kulli dāabbatiñw-wa taṣrīfir-riyāḥi was-saḥābil-musakhkhari baynas-samāaʾi wal-ʾarḍi la-ʾĀyātil-liqawmiñy-yaʿqilūn. (164)

129 Lit., "whom all who reject will reject" – i.e., all righteous persons who are able to judge moral issues. God's rejection (*laʿnah*) denotes "exclusion from His grace" (*Manār* II, 50). In classical Arabic usage, the primary meaning of *laʿnah* is equivalent to *ibʿād* ("estrangement" or "banishment"); in the terminology of the Qurʾān, it signifies "rejection from all that is good" (*Lisān al-ʿArab*). According to Ibn ʿAbbās and several outstanding scholars of the next generation, the divine writ mentioned here is the Bible; thus, the above verse refers to the Jews and the Christians.

130 This passage is one of the many in which the Qurʾān appeals to "those who use their reason" to observe the daily wonders of nature, including the evidence of man's own ingenuity ("the ships that speed through the sea"), as so many indications of a conscious, creative Power pervading the universe.

وَمِنَ ٱلنَّاسِ مَن يَتَّخِذُ مِن دُونِ ٱللَّهِ أَندَادًا يُحِبُّونَهُمْ كَحُبِّ ٱللَّهِ
وَٱلَّذِينَ ءَامَنُوٓاْ أَشَدُّ حُبًّا لِّلَّهِ وَلَوْ يَرَى ٱلَّذِينَ ظَلَمُوٓاْ إِذْ يَرَوْنَ ٱلْعَذَابَ
أَنَّ ٱلْقُوَّةَ لِلَّهِ جَمِيعًا وَأَنَّ ٱللَّهَ شَدِيدُ ٱلْعَذَابِ ﴿١٦٥﴾ إِذْ تَبَرَّأَ ٱلَّذِينَ ٱتُّبِعُواْ
مِنَ ٱلَّذِينَ ٱتَّبَعُواْ وَرَأَوُاْ ٱلْعَذَابَ وَتَقَطَّعَتْ بِهِمُ ٱلْأَسْبَابُ ﴿١٦٦﴾ وَقَالَ
ٱلَّذِينَ ٱتَّبَعُواْ لَوْ أَنَّ لَنَا كَرَّةً فَنَتَبَرَّأَ مِنْهُمْ كَمَا تَبَرَّءُواْ مِنَّا كَذَٰلِكَ
يُرِيهِمُ ٱللَّهُ أَعْمَٰلَهُمْ حَسَرَٰتٍ عَلَيْهِمْ وَمَا هُم بِخَٰرِجِينَ مِنَ ٱلنَّارِ ﴿١٦٧﴾
يَٰٓأَيُّهَا ٱلنَّاسُ كُلُواْ مِمَّا فِى ٱلْأَرْضِ حَلَٰلًا طَيِّبًا وَلَا تَتَّبِعُواْ خُطُوَٰتِ
ٱلشَّيْطَٰنِ إِنَّهُۥ لَكُمْ عَدُوٌّ مُّبِينٌ ﴿١٦٨﴾ إِنَّمَا يَأْمُرُكُم بِٱلسُّوٓءِ وَٱلْفَحْشَآءِ
وَأَن تَقُولُواْ عَلَى ٱللَّهِ مَا لَا تَعْلَمُونَ ﴿١٦٩﴾

Wa minan-nāsi mañy-yattakhidhu miñ-dūnil-lāhi ʾañdādañy-yuḥibbūnahum kaḥubbil-lāh. Wal-ladhīna ʾāmanūu ʾashaddu ḥubbal-lillāh. Wa law yaral-ladhīna ẓalamūu ʾidh yarawnal-ʿadhāba ʾannal-quwwata lillāhi jamīʿañw-wa ʾannal-lāha Shadīdul-ʿadhāb. (165) ʾIdh tabarraʾal-ladhīnat-tubiʿū minal-ladhīnat-tabaʿū wa raʾawul-ʿadhāba wa taqaṭṭaʿat bihimul-ʾasbāb. (166) Wa qālal-ladhīnat-tabaʿū law ʾanna lanā karratañ-fanatabarraʾa minhum kamā tabarraʾū minnā. Kadhālika yurīhimul-lāhu ʾaʿmālahum ḥasarātin ʿalayhim. Wa mā hum-bikhārijīna minan-nār. (167) Yāa ʾayyuhan-nāsu kulū mimmā fil-ʾarḍi ḥalālañ-ṭayyibañw-wa lā tattabiʿū khuṭuwātish-Shayṭāni ʾinnahū lakum ʿaduwwum-mubīn. (168) ʾInnamā yaʾmurukum-bissūuʾi wal-faḥshāaʾi wa ʾañ-taqūlū ʿalal-lāhi mā lā taʿlamūn. (169)

And yet there are people who choose to believe in beings that allegedly rival God,[131] loving them as [only] God should be loved: whereas those who have attained to faith love God more than all else.

If they who are bent on evildoing could but see – as see they will when they are made to suffer[132] [on Resurrection Day] – that all might belongs to God alone, and that God is severe in [meting out] punishment! ‹165›

[On that Day] it will come to pass that those who had been [falsely] adored[133] shall disown their followers, and the latter shall see the suffering [that awaits them], with all their hopes[134] cut to pieces! ‹166›

And then those followers shall say: "Would that we had a second chance [in life],[135] so that we could disown them as they have disowned us!"

Thus will God show them their works [in a manner that will cause them] bitter regrets; but they will not come out of the fire.[136] ‹167›

O MANKIND! Partake of what is lawful and good on earth, and follow not Satan's footsteps: for, verily, he is your open foe, ‹168› and bids you only to do evil, and to commit deeds of abomination, and to attribute unto God something of which you have no knowledge.[137] ‹169›

131 Lit., "there are among the people such as take [to worshipping] compeers beside God". Regarding the term *andād*, see note 13 on verse 22 of this *sūrah*.

132 Lit., "when they see the suffering" (or "chastisement").

133 Lit., "followed" – i.e., as saints or alleged "divine personalities".

134 *Asbāb* (sing. *sabab*) denotes, in its primary meaning, "ties" or "attachments", and in a tropical sense, "means [towards any end]" (cf. *Lisān al-ʿArab*, and Lane IV, 1285). In the above context, *asbāb* obviously refers to means of salvation, and may thus be rendered as "hopes".

135 Lit., "Would that there were a return for us".

136 Sc., back to the life of this world, with a second chance before them (*Manār* II, 81).

137 This refers to an arbitrary attribution to God of commandments or prohibitions in excess of what has been clearly ordained by Him (Zamakhsharī). Some of the commentators (e.g., Muḥammad ʿAbduh in *Manār* II, 89 f.) include within this expression the innumerable supposedly "legal" injunctions which, without being clearly warranted by the wording of the Qurʾān or an authentic Tradition, have been obtained by individual Muslim scholars through subjective methods of deduction and then put forward as "God's ordinances". The connection between this passage and the preceding ones is obvious. In verses 165-167 the Qurʾān speaks of those "who choose to believe in beings that supposedly rival God": and this implies also a false attribution, to those beings, of a right to issue quasi-religious

But when they are told, "Follow what God has bestowed from on high," some answer, "Nay, we shall follow [only] that which we found our forefathers believing in and doing." Why, even if their forefathers did not use their reason at all, and were devoid of all guidance? ‹170›

And so, the parable of those who are bent on denying the truth is that of the beast which hears the shepherd's cry, and hears in it nothing but the sound of a voice and a call.[138] Deaf are they, and dumb, and blind: for they do not use their reason. ‹171›

O you who have attained to faith! Partake of the good things which We have provided for you as sustenance, and render thanks unto God, if it is [truly] Him that you worship. ‹172›

He has forbidden to you only carrion, and blood, and the flesh of swine, and that over which any name other than God's has been invoked;[139] but if one is driven by necessity – neither coveting it nor exceeding his immediate need – no sin shall be upon him: for, behold, God is much-forgiving, a dispenser of grace. ‹173›

VERILY, as for those who suppress aught of the revelation[140] which God has bestowed from on high, and barter it away for a trifling gain – they but fill their bellies with fire. And God will not speak unto them on the Day of Resurrection, nor will He cleanse them [of their sins]; and grievous suffering awaits them. ‹174› It is they who take error in exchange for guidance, and suffering in exchange for forgiveness: yet how little do they seem to fear the fire! ‹175›

وَإِذَا قِيلَ لَهُمُ ٱتَّبِعُوا۟ مَآ أَنزَلَ ٱللَّهُ قَالُوا۟ بَلْ نَتَّبِعُ مَآ أَلْفَيْنَا عَلَيْهِ
ءَابَآءَنَآ ۗ أَوَلَوْ كَانَ ءَابَآؤُهُمْ لَا يَعْقِلُونَ شَيْـًٔا وَلَا يَهْتَدُونَ ﴿١٧٠﴾ وَمَثَلُ
ٱلَّذِينَ كَفَرُوا۟ كَمَثَلِ ٱلَّذِى يَنْعِقُ بِمَا لَا يَسْمَعُ إِلَّا دُعَآءً وَنِدَآءً ۚ صُمٌّۢ
بُكْمٌ عُمْىٌ فَهُمْ لَا يَعْقِلُونَ ﴿١٧١﴾ يَـٰٓأَيُّهَا ٱلَّذِينَ ءَامَنُوا۟ كُلُوا۟ مِن طَيِّبَـٰتِ
مَا رَزَقْنَـٰكُمْ وَٱشْكُرُوا۟ لِلَّهِ إِن كُنتُمْ إِيَّاهُ تَعْبُدُونَ ﴿١٧٢﴾ إِنَّمَا حَرَّمَ
عَلَيْكُمُ ٱلْمَيْتَةَ وَٱلدَّمَ وَلَحْمَ ٱلْخِنزِيرِ وَمَآ أُهِلَّ بِهِۦ لِغَيْرِ ٱللَّهِ ۖ فَمَنِ ٱضْطُرَّ
غَيْرَ بَاغٍ وَلَا عَادٍ فَلَآ إِثْمَ عَلَيْهِ ۚ إِنَّ ٱللَّهَ غَفُورٌ رَّحِيمٌ ﴿١٧٣﴾ إِنَّ ٱلَّذِينَ
يَكْتُمُونَ مَآ أَنزَلَ ٱللَّهُ مِنَ ٱلْكِتَـٰبِ وَيَشْتَرُونَ بِهِۦ ثَمَنًا قَلِيلًا ۙ أُو۟لَـٰٓئِكَ
مَا يَأْكُلُونَ فِى بُطُونِهِمْ إِلَّا ٱلنَّارَ وَلَا يُكَلِّمُهُمُ ٱللَّهُ يَوْمَ ٱلْقِيَـٰمَةِ وَلَا
يُزَكِّيهِمْ وَلَهُمْ عَذَابٌ أَلِيمٌ ﴿١٧٤﴾ أُو۟لَـٰٓئِكَ ٱلَّذِينَ ٱشْتَرَوُا۟ ٱلضَّلَـٰلَةَ
بِٱلْهُدَىٰ وَٱلْعَذَابَ بِٱلْمَغْفِرَةِ ۚ فَمَآ أَصْبَرَهُمْ عَلَى ٱلنَّارِ ﴿١٧٥﴾

Wa ʾidhā qīla lahumut-tabiʿū māa ʾañzalal-lāhu qālū bal nattabiʿu māa ʾalfaynā ʿalayhi ʾābāaʾanā. ʾAwa law kāna ʾābāaʾuhum lā yaʿqilūna shayʾañw-wa lā yahtadūn. (170) Wa mathalul-ladhīna kafarū kamathalil-ladhī yanʿiqu bimā lā yasmaʿu ʾillā duʿāaʾañw-wa nidāaʾ. Ṣummum-bukmun ʿumyuñfahum lā yaʿqilūn. (171) Yāa ʾayyuhal-ladhīna ʾāmanū kulū miñ-ṭayyibāti mā razaqnākum wash-kurū lillāhi ʾiñ-kuñtum ʾIyyāhu taʿbudūn. (172) ʾInnamā ḥarrama ʿalaykumul-maytata wad-dama wa laḥmal-khinzīri wa māa ʾuhilla bihī lighayril-lāh. Famaniḍ-ṭurra ghayra bāghiñw-wa lā ʿādiñ-falāa ʾithma ʿalayh. ʾInnal-lāha Ghafūrur-Raḥīm. (173) ʾInnal-ladhīna yaktumūna māa ʾañzalal-lāhu minal-Kitābi wa yashtarūna bihī thamanañ-qalīlan ʾulāaʾika mā yaʾkulūna fī buṭūnihim ʾillan-nāra wa lā yukallimuhumul-lāhu Yawmal-Qiyāmati wa lā yuzakkīhim wa lahum ʿadhābun ʾalīm. (174) ʾUlāaʾikal-ladhīnash-tarawuḍ-ḍalālata bilhudā wal-ʿadhāba bilmaghfirah. Famāa ʾaṣbarahum ʿalan-nār. (175)

ordinances of their own, as well as an attribution of religious validity to customs sanctioned by nothing but ancient usage (see next verse).

138 This is a very free rendering of the elliptic sentence which, literally, reads thus: "The parable of those who are bent on denying the truth is as that of him who cries unto what hears nothing but a cry and a call." The verb *naʿaqa* is mostly used to describe the inarticulate cry with which the shepherd drives his flock.

139 I.e., all that has been dedicated or offered in sacrifice to an idol or a saint or a person considered to be "divine". For a more comprehensive enumeration of the forbidden kinds of flesh, see 5 : 3.

140 This term is used here in its generic sense, comprising both the Qurʾān and the earlier revelations.

ذَٰلِكَ بِأَنَّ ٱللَّهَ نَزَّلَ ٱلْكِتَٰبَ بِٱلْحَقِّ ۗ وَإِنَّ ٱلَّذِينَ ٱخْتَلَفُوا۟ فِى ٱلْكِتَٰبِ
لَفِى شِقَاقٍۭ بَعِيدٍ ﴿١٧٦﴾ ۞ لَّيْسَ ٱلْبِرَّ أَن تُوَلُّوا۟ وُجُوهَكُمْ قِبَلَ ٱلْمَشْرِقِ
وَٱلْمَغْرِبِ وَلَٰكِنَّ ٱلْبِرَّ مَنْ ءَامَنَ بِٱللَّهِ وَٱلْيَوْمِ ٱلْءَاخِرِ وَٱلْمَلَٰٓئِكَةِ
وَٱلْكِتَٰبِ وَٱلنَّبِيِّۦنَ وَءَاتَى ٱلْمَالَ عَلَىٰ حُبِّهِۦ ذَوِى ٱلْقُرْبَىٰ وَٱلْيَتَٰمَىٰ
وَٱلْمَسَٰكِينَ وَٱبْنَ ٱلسَّبِيلِ وَٱلسَّآئِلِينَ وَفِى ٱلرِّقَابِ وَأَقَامَ ٱلصَّلَوٰةَ
وَءَاتَى ٱلزَّكَوٰةَ وَٱلْمُوفُونَ بِعَهْدِهِمْ إِذَا عَٰهَدُوا۟ ۖ وَٱلصَّٰبِرِينَ فِى ٱلْبَأْسَآءِ
وَٱلضَّرَّآءِ وَحِينَ ٱلْبَأْسِ ۗ أُو۟لَٰٓئِكَ ٱلَّذِينَ صَدَقُوا۟ ۖ وَأُو۟لَٰٓئِكَ هُمُ ٱلْمُتَّقُونَ ﴿١٧٧﴾

نصف الحزب

Thus it is: since it is God who bestows[141] the divine writ from on high, setting forth the truth, all those who set their own views against the divine writ[142] are, verily, most deeply in the wrong. ‹176›
True piety does not consist in turning your faces towards the east or the west[143] – but truly pious is he who believes in God, and the Last Day, and the angels, and revelation,[144] and the prophets; and spends his substance – however much he himself may cherish it – upon his near of kin, and the orphans, and the needy, and the wayfarer,[145] and the beggars, and for the freeing of human beings from bondage;[146] and is constant in prayer, and renders the purifying dues; and [truly pious are] they who keep their promises whenever they promise, and are patient in misfortune and hardship and in time of peril: it is they that have proved themselves true, and it is they, they who are conscious of God. ‹177›

Dhālika biʾannal-lāha nazzalal-Kitāba bilḥaqq. Wa ʾinnal-ladhīnakh-talafū fil-Kitābi lafī shiqāqim-baʿīd. ﴿١٧٦﴾ ۞ Laysal-birra ʾañ-tuwallū wujūhakum qibalal-mashriqi wal-maghribi wa lākinnal-birra man ʾāmana billāhi wal-Yawmil-ʾĀkhiri wal-Malāaʾikati wal-Kitābi wan-Nabiyyīna wa ʾātal-māla ʿalā ḥubbihī dhawil-qurbā wal-yatāmā wal-masākīna wab-nas-sabīli was-sāaʾilīna wa fir-riqābi wa ʾaqāmaṣ-Ṣalāta wa ʾātaz-Zakāta wal-mūfūna biʿahdihim ʾidhā ʿāhadū; waṣ-ṣābirīna fil-baʾsāaʾi wad-ḍarrāaʾi wa ḥīnal-baʾs. ʾUlāaʾikal-ladhīna ṣadaqū; wa ʾulāaʾika humul-muttaqūn. ﴿١٧٧﴾

141 Lit., "has been bestowing". Since the form *nazzala* implies gradualness and continuity in the process of revelation, it can best be rendered by the use of the present tense.

142 Lit., "who hold discordant views about the divine writ" – i.e., either suppressing or rejecting parts of it, or denying its divine origin altogether (Rāzī).

143 Thus, the Qurʾān stresses the principle that mere compliance with outward forms does not fulfil the requirements of piety. The reference to the turning of one's face in prayer in this or that direction flows from the passages which dealt, a short while ago, with the question of the *qiblah*.

144 In this context, the term "revelation" (*al-kitāb*) carries, according to most of the commentators, a generic significance: it refers to the *fact* of divine revelation as such. As regards belief in angels, it is postulated here because it is through these spiritual beings or forces (belonging to the realm of *al-ghayb*, i.e., the reality which is beyond the reach of human perception) that God reveals His will to the prophets and, thus, to mankind at large.

145 The expression *ibn as-sabīl* (lit., "son of the road") denotes any person who is far from his home, and especially one who, because of this circumstance, does not have sufficient means of livelihood at his disposal (cf. Lane IV, 1302). In its wider sense it describes a person who, for any reason whatsoever, is unable to return home either temporarily or permanently: for instance, a political exile or refugee.

146 *Ar-raqabah* (of which *ar-riqāb* is the plural) denotes, literally, "the neck", and signifies also the whole of a human person. Metonymically, the expression *fi 'r-riqāb* denotes "in the cause of freeing human beings from bondage", and applies to both the ransoming of captives and the freeing of slaves. By including this kind of expenditure within the essential acts of piety, the Qurʾān implies that the freeing of people from bondage – and, thus, the abolition of slavery – is one of the social objectives of Islam. At the time of the revelation of the Qurʾān, slavery was an established institution throughout the world, and its sudden abolition would have been economically impossible. In order to obviate this difficulty, and at the same time to bring about an eventual abolition of all slavery, the Qurʾān ordains in 8 : 67 that henceforth only captives taken in a just war (*jihād*) may be kept as slaves. But even with regard to persons enslaved in this or – before the revelation of 8 : 67 – in any other way, the Qurʾān stresses the great merit inherent in the freeing of slaves, and stipulates it as a means of atonement for various transgressions (see, e.g., 4 : 92, 5 : 89, 58 : 3). In addition, the Prophet emphatically stated on many occasions that, in the sight of God, the unconditional freeing of a human being from bondage is among the most praiseworthy acts which a Muslim

O YOU who have attained to faith! Just retribution is ordained for you in cases of killing: the free for the free, and the slave for the slave, and the woman for the woman.[147] And if something [of his guilt] is remitted to a guilty person by his brother,[148] this [remission] shall be adhered to with fairness, and restitution to his fellow-man shall be made in a goodly manner.[149]

يَٰٓأَيُّهَا ٱلَّذِينَ ءَامَنُوا۟ كُتِبَ عَلَيْكُمُ ٱلْقِصَاصُ فِى ٱلْقَتْلَى ۖ
ٱلْحُرُّ بِٱلْحُرِّ وَٱلْعَبْدُ بِٱلْعَبْدِ وَٱلْأُنثَىٰ بِٱلْأُنثَىٰ ۚ فَمَنْ عُفِىَ
لَهُۥ مِنْ أَخِيهِ شَىْءٌ فَٱتِّبَاعٌۢ بِٱلْمَعْرُوفِ وَأَدَآءٌ إِلَيْهِ بِإِحْسَٰنٍ ۗ

Yāa ʾayyuhal-ladhīna ʾāmanū kutiba ʿalaykumul-qiṣāṣu fil-qatlā. ʾAlḥurru bilḥurri wal-ʿabdu bilʿabdi wal-ʾuñthā bilʾuñthā. Faman ʿufiya lahū min ʾakhīhi shayʾuñ-fattibāʿum-bilmaʿrūfi wa ʾadāaʾun ʾilayhi biʾiḥsān.

could perform. (For a critical discussion and analysis of all the authentic Traditions bearing on this problem, see *Nayl al-Awṭār* VI, 199 ff.)

147 After having pointed out that true piety does not consist in mere adherence to outward forms and rites, the Qurʾān opens, as it were, a new chapter relating to the problem of man's behaviour. Just as piety cannot become effective without righteous action, individual righteousness cannot become really effective in the social sense unless there is agreement within the community as to the social rights and obligations of its members: in other words, as to the practical *laws* which should govern the behaviour of the individual within the society and the society's attitude towards the individual and his actions. This is the innermost reason why legislation plays so great a role within the ideology of Islam, and why the Qurʾān consistently intertwines its moral and spiritual exhortation with ordinances relating to practical aspects of social life. Now one of the main problems facing any society is the safeguarding of the lives and the individual security of its members: and so it is understandable that laws relating to homicide and its punishment are dealt with prominently at this place. (It should be borne in mind that "The Cow" was the first *sūrah* revealed in Medina, that is, at the time when the Muslim community had just become established as an independent social entity.)

As for the term *qiṣāṣ* occurring at the beginning of the above passage, it must be pointed out that – according to all the classical commentators – it is almost synonymous with *musāwāh*, i.e., "making a thing equal [to another thing]": in this instance, making the punishment equal (or appropriate) to the crime – a meaning which is best rendered as "just retribution" and not (as has been often, and erroneously, done) as "retaliation". Seeing that the Qurʾān, speaks here of "cases of killing" (*fī 'l-qatlā*, lit., "in the matter of the killed") in general, and taking into account that this expression covers all possible cases of homicide – premeditated murder, murder under extreme provocation, culpable homicide, accidental manslaughter, and so forth – it is obvious that the taking of a life for a life (implied in the term "retaliation") would not in every case correspond to the demands of equity. (This has been made clear, for instance, in 4 : 92, where legal restitution for unintentional homicide is dealt with.) Read in conjunction with the term "just retribution" which introduces this passage, it is clear that the stipulation "the free for the free, the slave for the slave, the woman for the woman" cannot – and has not been intended to – be taken in its literal, restrictive sense: for this would preclude its application to many cases of homicide, e.g., the killing of a free man by a slave, or of a woman by a man, or *vice-versa.* Thus, the above stipulation must be regarded as an example of the elliptical mode of expression (*ījāz*) so frequently employed in the Qurʾān, and can have but one meaning, namely: "if a free man has committed the crime, the free man must be punished; if a slave has commited the crime . . .", etc. – in other words, whatever the status of the guilty person, he or she (and he or she alone) is to be punished in a manner appropriate to the crime.

148 Lit., "and he to whom [something] is remitted by his brother". There is no linguistic justification whatever for attributing – as some of the commentators have done – the adjective "his" to the victim and, thus, for assuming that the expression "brother" stands for the victim's "family" or "blood relations". The adjective "his" refers, unquestionably, to the guilty person; and since there is no reason for assuming that by "his brother" a *real* brother is meant, we cannot escape the conclusion that it denotes here "his brother in faith" or "his fellow-man" – in either of which terms the whole community is included. Thus, the expression "if something is remitted to a guilty person by his brother" (i.e., by the community or its legal organs) may refer either to the establishment of mitigating circumstances in a case of murder, or to the finding that the case under trial falls within the categories of culpable homicide or manslaughter – in which cases no capital punishment is to be exacted and restitution is to be made by the payment of an indemnity called *diyyah* (see 4 : 92) to the relatives of the victim. In consonance with the oft-recurring Qurʾanic exhortation to forgiveness and forbearance, the "remission" mentioned above may also (and especially in cases of accidental manslaughter) relate to a partial or even total waiving of any claim to indemnification.

149 Lit., "and restitution to him in a goodly manner", it being understood that the pronoun in *ilayhi* ("to him") refers to the "brother in faith" or "fellow-man" mentioned earlier in this sentence. The word *adāʾ* (here translated as "restitution") denotes an act of acquitting oneself of a duty or a debt (cf. Lane I, 38), and stands here for the act of

This is an alleviation from your Sustainer, and an act of His grace. And for him who, none the less,[150] wilfully transgresses the bounds of what is right, there is grievous suffering in store: ‹178› for, in [the law of] just retribution, O you who are endowed with insight, there is life for you, so that you might remain conscious of God![151] ‹179›

IT IS ordained for you, when death approaches any of you and he is leaving behind much wealth, to make bequests in favour of his parents and [other] near of kin in accordance with what is fair:[152] this is binding on all who are conscious of God. ‹180› And if anyone alters such a provision after having come to know it, the sin of acting thus shall fall only upon those who have altered it.[153] Verily, God is all-hearing, all-knowing. ‹181›
If, however, one has reason to fear that the testator has committed a mistake or a [deliberate] wrong, and thereupon brings about a settlement between the heirs,[154] he will incur no sin [thereby]. Verily, God is much-forgiving, a dispenser of grace. ‹182›

O YOU who have attained to faith! Fasting is ordained for you as it was ordained for those before you, so that you might remain conscious of God: ‹183›

ذَٰلِكَ تَخۡفِيفٞ مِّن رَّبِّكُمۡ وَرَحۡمَةٞۗ فَمَنِ ٱعۡتَدَىٰ بَعۡدَ ذَٰلِكَ فَلَهُۥ
عَذَابٌ أَلِيمٞ ﴿178﴾ وَلَكُمۡ فِي ٱلۡقِصَاصِ حَيَوٰةٞ يَٰٓأُوْلِي ٱلۡأَلۡبَٰبِ لَعَلَّكُمۡ
تَتَّقُونَ ﴿179﴾ كُتِبَ عَلَيۡكُمۡ إِذَا حَضَرَ أَحَدَكُمُ ٱلۡمَوۡتُ إِن تَرَكَ خَيۡرًا
ٱلۡوَصِيَّةُ لِلۡوَٰلِدَيۡنِ وَٱلۡأَقۡرَبِينَ بِٱلۡمَعۡرُوفِۖ حَقًّا عَلَى ٱلۡمُتَّقِينَ ﴿180﴾ فَمَنۢ
بَدَّلَهُۥ بَعۡدَمَا سَمِعَهُۥ فَإِنَّمَآ إِثۡمُهُۥ عَلَى ٱلَّذِينَ يُبَدِّلُونَهُۥٓۚ إِنَّ ٱللَّهَ سَمِيعٌ
عَلِيمٞ ﴿181﴾ فَمَنۡ خَافَ مِن مُّوصٖ جَنَفًا أَوۡ إِثۡمٗا فَأَصۡلَحَ بَيۡنَهُمۡ فَلَآ إِثۡمَ
عَلَيۡهِۚ إِنَّ ٱللَّهَ غَفُورٞ رَّحِيمٞ ﴿182﴾ يَٰٓأَيُّهَا ٱلَّذِينَ ءَامَنُواْ كُتِبَ عَلَيۡكُمُ
ٱلصِّيَامُ كَمَا كُتِبَ عَلَى ٱلَّذِينَ مِن قَبۡلِكُمۡ لَعَلَّكُمۡ تَتَّقُونَ ﴿183﴾

Dhālika takhfīfum-mir-Rabbikum wa raḥmah. Famaniʿ-tadā baʿda dhālika falahū ʿadhābun ʾalīm. (178) Wa lakum fil-qiṣāṣi ḥayātuñy-yāa ʾulil-ʾalbābi laʿallakum tattaqūn. (179) Kutiba ʿalaykum ʾidhā ḥaḍara ʾaḥadakumul-mawtu ʾiñ-taraka khayranil-waṣiyyatu lilwālidayni wal-ʾaqrabīna bilmaʿrūfi ḥaqqan ʿalal-muttaqīn. (180) Famam-baddalahū baʿda mā samiʿahū faʾinnamāa ʾithmuhū ʿalal-ladhīna yubaddilūnah. ʾInnal-lāha Samīʿun ʿAlīm. (181) Faman khāfa mim-mūṣiñ-janafan ʾaw ʾithmañ-faʾaṣlaḥa baynahum falāa ʾithma ʿalayh. ʾInnal-lāha Ghafūrur-Raḥīm. (182) Yāa ʾayyuhal-ladhīna ʾāmanū kutiba ʿalaykumuṣ-Ṣiyāmu kamā kutiba ʿalal-ladhīna miñ-qablikum laʿallakum tattaqūn. (183)

legal reparation imposed on the guilty person. This reparation or restitution is to be made "in a goodly manner" – by taking into account the situation of the accused and, on the latter's part, by acquitting himself of his obligation willingly and sincerely (cf. *Manār* II, 129).

150 Lit., "after this" – i.e., after the meaning of what constitutes "just retribution" (*qiṣāṣ*) has been made clear in the above ordinance (Rāzi).

151 I.e., "there is a safeguard for you, as a community, so that you might be able to live in security, as God wants you to live". Thus, the objective of *qiṣāṣ* is the protection of the society, and not "revenge".

152 The word *khayr* occurring in this sentence denotes "much wealth" and not simply "property": and this explains the injunction that one who leaves much wealth behind should make bequests to particularly deserving members of his family in addition to – and preceding the distribution of – the legally-fixed shares mentioned in 4: 11-12. This interpretation of *khayr* is supported by sayings of ʿĀʾishah and ʿAlī ibn Abī Ṭālib, both of them referring to this particular verse (cf. Zamakhsharī and Bayḍāwī).

153 Lit., "and as for him who alters it" – i.e., after the testator's death – "after having heard it, the sin thereof is only upon those who alter it": that is, not on anyone who may have unwittingly benefited by this alteration. It is to be noted that the verb *samiʿa* (lit., "he heard") has also the connotation of "he came to know".

154 Lit., "between them" – i.e., a settlement overriding the testamentary provisions which, by common consent of the parties concerned, are considered unjust.

[fasting] during a certain number of days.[155] But whoever of you is ill, or on a journey, [shall fast instead for the same] number of other days; and [in such cases] it is incumbent upon those who can afford it to make sacrifice by feeding a needy person.[156]
And whoever does more good than he is bound to do[157] does good unto himself thereby; for to fast is to do good unto yourselves – if you but knew it. ‹184›
It was the month of Ramaḍān in which the Qurᵓān was [first] bestowed from on high as a guidance unto man and a self-evident proof of that guidance, and as the standard by which to discern the true from the false. Hence, whoever of you lives to see[158] this month shall fast throughout it; but he that is ill, or on a journey, [shall fast instead for the same] number of other days. God wills that you shall have ease, and does not will you to suffer hardship; but [He desires] that you complete the number [of days required], and that you extol God for His having guided you aright, and that you render your thanks [unto Him]. ‹185›

AND IF My servants ask thee about Me – behold, I am near; I respond to the call of him who calls, whenever he calls unto Me: let them, then, respond unto Me, and believe in Me, so that they might follow the right way. ‹186›

أَيَّامًا مَّعْدُودَٰتٍ فَمَن كَانَ مِنكُم مَّرِيضًا أَوْ عَلَىٰ سَفَرٍ فَعِدَّةٌ مِّنْ أَيَّامٍ
أُخَرَ وَعَلَى ٱلَّذِينَ يُطِيقُونَهُۥ فِدْيَةٌ طَعَامُ مِسْكِينٍ فَمَن تَطَوَّعَ خَيْرًا فَهُوَ
خَيْرٌ لَّهُۥ وَأَن تَصُومُوا۟ خَيْرٌ لَّكُمْ إِن كُنتُمْ تَعْلَمُونَ ﴿184﴾ شَهْرُ رَمَضَانَ
ٱلَّذِىٓ أُنزِلَ فِيهِ ٱلْقُرْءَانُ هُدًى لِّلنَّاسِ وَبَيِّنَٰتٍ مِّنَ ٱلْهُدَىٰ وَٱلْفُرْقَانِ
فَمَن شَهِدَ مِنكُمُ ٱلشَّهْرَ فَلْيَصُمْهُ وَمَن كَانَ مَرِيضًا أَوْ عَلَىٰ سَفَرٍ فَعِدَّةٌ
مِّنْ أَيَّامٍ أُخَرَ يُرِيدُ ٱللَّهُ بِكُمُ ٱلْيُسْرَ وَلَا يُرِيدُ بِكُمُ ٱلْعُسْرَ وَلِتُكْمِلُوا۟
ٱلْعِدَّةَ وَلِتُكَبِّرُوا۟ ٱللَّهَ عَلَىٰ مَا هَدَىٰكُمْ وَلَعَلَّكُمْ تَشْكُرُونَ ﴿185﴾ وَإِذَا
سَأَلَكَ عِبَادِى عَنِّى فَإِنِّى قَرِيبٌ أُجِيبُ دَعْوَةَ ٱلدَّاعِ إِذَا دَعَانِ فَلْيَسْتَجِيبُوا۟
لِى وَلْيُؤْمِنُوا۟ بِى لَعَلَّهُمْ يَرْشُدُونَ ﴿186﴾

ᵓAyyāmam-maᶜdūdātiñ-famañ-kāna miñkum-marīḍan ᵓaw ᶜalā safariñ-faᶜiddatum-min ᵓayyāmin ᵓukhar. Wa ᶜalal-ladhīna yuṭīqūnahū fidyatuñ-ṭaᶜāmu miskīn. Famañ-taṭawwaᶜa khayrañ-fahuwa khayrul-lah. Wa ᵓañ-taṣūmū khayrul-lakum ᵓiñ-kuñtum taᶜlamūn. (184) Shahru Ramaḍānal-ladhīi ᵓuñzila fīhil-Qurᵓānu hudal-linnāsi wa bayyinātim-minal-hudā wal-Furqān. Famañ-shahida miñkumush-shahra falyaṣumhu wa mañ-kāna marīḍan ᵓaw ᵓalā safariñ-faᶜiddatum-min ᵓayyāmin ᵓukhar. Yurīdul-lāhu bikumul-yusra wa lā yurīdu bikumul-ᶜusr. Wa litukmilul-ᶜiddata wa litukabbirul-lāha ᶜalā mā hadākum wa laᶜallakum tashkurūn. (185) Wa ᵓidhā saᵓalaka ᶜibādī ᶜannī faᵓinnī qarībun ᵓujību daᶜwatad-dāᶜi ᵓidhā daᶜān. Falyastajībū lī wal-yuᵓminū bī laᶜallahum yarshudūn. (186)

155 I.e., during the twenty-nine or thirty days of Ramaḍān, the ninth month of the Islamic lunar calendar (see next verse). It consists of a total abstention from food, drink and sexual intercourse from dawn until sunset. As the Qurᵓān points out, fasting has been widely practiced at all times of man's religious history. The extreme rigour and the long duration of the Islamic fast – which is incumbent on every healthy adult, man or woman – fulfils, in addition to the general aim of spiritual purification, a threefold purpose: (1) to commemorate the beginning of the Qurᵓanic revelation, which took place in the month of Ramaḍān about thirteen years before the Prophet's exodus to Medina; (2) to provide an exacting exercise of self-discipline; and (3) to make everyone realize, through his or her own experience, how it feels to be hungry and thirsty, and thus to gain a true appreciation of the needs of the poor.

156 This phrase has been subject to a number of conflicting and sometimes highly laboured interpretations. My rendering is based on the *primary* meaning of *alladhīna yuṭīqūnahu* ("those who are capable of it" or "are able to do it" or "can afford it"), with the pronoun *hu* relating to the act of "feeding a needy person".

157 Some commentators are of the opinion that this refers to a voluntary feeding of more than one needy person, or to feeding the needy for more than the number of days required by the above ordinance. Since, however, the remaining part of the sentence speaks of the benefits of fasting as such, it is more probable that "doing more good than one is bound to do" refers, in this context, to supererogatory fasting (such as the Prophet sometimes undertook) apart from the obligatory one during the month of Ramaḍān.

158 Lit., "witnesses" or "is present in".

ثلاثة ارباع الحزب

IT IS lawful for you to go in unto your wives during the night preceding the [day's] fast: they are as a garment for you, and you are as a garment for them. God is aware that you would have deprived yourselves of this right,[159] and so He has turned unto you in His mercy and removed this hardship from you. Now, then, you may lie with them skin to skin, and avail yourselves of that which God has ordained for you,[160] and eat and drink until you can discern the white streak of dawn against the blackness of night,[161] and then resume fasting until nightfall; but do not lie with them skin to skin when you are about to abide in meditation in houses of worship.[162]
These are the bounds set by God: do not, then, offend against them – [for] it is thus that God makes clear His messages unto mankind, so that they might remain conscious of Him. ‹187›

AND DEVOUR NOT one another's possessions wrongfully, and neither employ legal artifices[163] with a view to devouring sinfully, and knowingly, anything that by right belongs to others.[164] ‹188›

THEY WILL ASK thee about the new moons. Say: "They indicate the periods for [various doings of] mankind, including the pilgrimage."[165]

أُحِلَّ لَكُمۡ لَيۡلَةَ ٱلصِّيَامِ ٱلرَّفَثُ إِلَىٰ نِسَآئِكُمۡۚ هُنَّ لِبَاسٞ لَّكُمۡ وَأَنتُمۡ
لِبَاسٞ لَّهُنَّۗ عَلِمَ ٱللَّهُ أَنَّكُمۡ كُنتُمۡ تَخۡتَانُونَ أَنفُسَكُمۡ فَتَابَ عَلَيۡكُمۡ
وَعَفَا عَنكُمۡۖ فَٱلۡـَٰٔنَ بَٰشِرُوهُنَّ وَٱبۡتَغُواْ مَا كَتَبَ ٱللَّهُ لَكُمۡۚ وَكُلُواْ
وَٱشۡرَبُواْ حَتَّىٰ يَتَبَيَّنَ لَكُمُ ٱلۡخَيۡطُ ٱلۡأَبۡيَضُ مِنَ ٱلۡخَيۡطِ ٱلۡأَسۡوَدِ مِنَ
ٱلۡفَجۡرِۖ ثُمَّ أَتِمُّواْ ٱلصِّيَامَ إِلَى ٱلَّيۡلِۚ وَلَا تُبَٰشِرُوهُنَّ وَأَنتُمۡ عَٰكِفُونَ فِي
ٱلۡمَسَٰجِدِۗ تِلۡكَ حُدُودُ ٱللَّهِ فَلَا تَقۡرَبُوهَاۗ كَذَٰلِكَ يُبَيِّنُ ٱللَّهُ ءَايَٰتِهِۦ
لِلنَّاسِ لَعَلَّهُمۡ يَتَّقُونَ ١٨٧ وَلَا تَأۡكُلُوٓاْ أَمۡوَٰلَكُم بَيۡنَكُم بِٱلۡبَٰطِلِ
وَتُدۡلُواْ بِهَآ إِلَى ٱلۡحُكَّامِ لِتَأۡكُلُواْ فَرِيقٗا مِّنۡ أَمۡوَٰلِ ٱلنَّاسِ بِٱلۡإِثۡمِ وَأَنتُمۡ
تَعۡلَمُونَ ١٨٨ ۞ يَسۡـَٔلُونَكَ عَنِ ٱلۡأَهِلَّةِۖ قُلۡ هِيَ مَوَٰقِيتُ لِلنَّاسِ وَٱلۡحَجِّۗ

ʾUḥilla lakum laylataṣ-Ṣiyāmir-rafathu ʾilā nisāaʾikum. Hunna libāsul-lakum wa ʾañtum libāsul-lahunn. ʿAlimal-lāhu ʾannakum kuñtum takhtānūna ʾañfusakum fatāba ʿalaykum wa ʿafā ʿañkum; falʾāna bāshirūhunna wab-taghū mā katabal-lāhu lakum. Wa kulū wash-rabū ḥattā yatabayyana lakumul-khayṭul-ʾabyaḍu minal-khayṭil-ʾaswadi minal-fajr. Thumma ʾatimmuṣ-Ṣiyāma ʾilal-layli wa lā tubāshirūhunna wa ʾañtum ʿākifūna fil-masājid. Tilka ḥudūdul-lāhi falā taqrabūhā. Kadhālika yubayyinul-lāhu ʾĀyātihī linnāsi laʿallahum yattaqūn.
187
Wa lā taʾkulūu ʾamwālakum baynakum-bilbāṭili wa tudlū bihāa ʾilal-ḥukkāmi litaʾkulū farīqam-min ʾamwālin-nāsi bilʾithmi wa ʾañtum taʿlamūn.
188
۞ Yasʾalūnaka ʿanil-ʾahillati qul hiya mawāqītu linnāsi wal-Ḥajj.

159 Lit., "deceived" or "defrauded yourselves [in this respect]": an allusion to the idea prevalent among the early Muslims, before the revelation of this verse, that during the period of fasting all sexual intercourse should be avoided, even at night-time, when eating and drinking are allowed (Rāzī). The above verse removed this misconception.

160 Lit., "and seek that which God has ordained for you": an obvious stress on the God-willed nature of sexual life.

161 Lit., "the white line of dawn from the black line [of night]". According to all Arab philologists, the "black line" (*al-khayṭ al-aswad*) signifies "the blackness of night" (Lane II, 831); and the expression *al-khayṭān* ("the two lines" or "streaks") denotes "day and night" (*Lisān al-ʿArab*).

162 It was the practice of the Prophet to spend several days and nights during Ramaḍān – and occasionally also at other times – in the mosque, devoting himself to prayer and meditation to the exclusion of all worldly activities; and since he advised his followers as well to do this from time to time, seclusion in a mosque for the sake of meditation, called *iʿtikāf*, has become a recognized – though optional – mode of devotion among Muslims, especially during the last ten days of Ramaḍān.

163 Lit., "and do not throw it to the judges" – i.e., with a view to being decided by them contrary to what is right (Zamakhsharī, Bayḍāwī).

164 Lit., "a part of [other] people's possessions".

165 The reference, at this stage, to lunar months arises from the fact that the observance of several of the religious obligations instituted by Islam – like the fast of Ramaḍān, or the pilgrimage to Mecca (which is dealt with in verses

However, piety does not consist in your entering houses from the rear, [as it were,] but truly pious is he who is conscious of God.[166] Hence, enter houses through their doors, and remain conscious of God, so that you might attain to a happy state. ‹189›

AND FIGHT in God's cause against those who wage war against you, but do not commit aggression – for, verily, God does not love aggressors.[167] ‹190› And slay them wherever you may come upon them, and drive them away from wherever they drove you away – for oppression is even worse than killing.[168] And fight not against them near the Inviolable House of Worship unless they fight against you there first;[169] but if they fight against you, slay them: such shall be the recompense of those who deny the truth. ‹191›

وَلَيْسَ الْبِرُّ بِأَن تَأْتُوا الْبُيُوتَ مِن ظُهُورِهَا وَلَٰكِنَّ الْبِرَّ مَنِ اتَّقَىٰ ۗ وَأْتُوا
الْبُيُوتَ مِنْ أَبْوَابِهَا ۚ وَاتَّقُوا اللَّهَ لَعَلَّكُمْ تُفْلِحُونَ ﴿١٨٩﴾ وَقَاتِلُوا فِي سَبِيلِ
اللَّهِ الَّذِينَ يُقَاتِلُونَكُمْ وَلَا تَعْتَدُوا ۚ إِنَّ اللَّهَ لَا يُحِبُّ الْمُعْتَدِينَ ﴿١٩٠﴾
وَاقْتُلُوهُمْ حَيْثُ ثَقِفْتُمُوهُمْ وَأَخْرِجُوهُم مِّنْ حَيْثُ أَخْرَجُوكُمْ ۚ وَالْفِتْنَةُ
أَشَدُّ مِنَ الْقَتْلِ ۚ وَلَا تُقَاتِلُوهُمْ عِندَ الْمَسْجِدِ الْحَرَامِ حَتَّىٰ يُقَاتِلُوكُمْ فِيهِ ۖ
فَإِن قَاتَلُوكُمْ فَاقْتُلُوهُمْ ۗ كَذَٰلِكَ جَزَاءُ الْكَافِرِينَ ﴿١٩١﴾

Wa laysal-birru biʾañ-taʾtul-buyūta miñ-ẓuhūrihā wa lākinnal-birra manit-taqā. Waʾ-tul-buyūta min ʾabwābihā; wat-taqul-lāha laʿallakum tufliḥūn. ﴿189﴾ Wa qātilū fī sabīlil-lāhil-ladhīna yuqātilūnakum wa lā taʿtadū; ʾinnal-lāha lā yuḥibbul-muʿtadīn. ﴿190﴾ Waq-tulūhum ḥaythu thaqiftumūhum wa ʾakhrijūhum-min ḥaythu ʾakhrajūkum; wal-fitnatu ʾashaddu mi-nal-qatl. Wa lā tuqātilūhum ʿiñdal-Masjidil-Ḥarāmi ḥattā yuqātilūkum fīhi faʾiñ qātalūkum faqtulūhum. Kadhālika jazāaʾul-kāfirīn. ﴿191﴾

196-203) – is based on the lunar calendar, in which the months rotate through the seasons of the solar year. This fixation on the lunar calendar results in a continuous variation of the seasonal circumstances in which those religious observances are performed (e.g., the length of the fasting-period between dawn and sunset, heat or cold at the time of the fast or the pilgrimage), and thus in a corresponding, periodical increase or decrease of the hardship involved. In addition to this, reckoning by lunar months has a bearing on the tide and ebb of the oceans, as well as on human physiology (e.g., a woman's monthly courses – a subject dealt with later on in this *sūrah*).

166 I.e., true piety does not consist in approaching questions of faith through a "back door", as it were – that is, through mere observance of the forms and periods set for the performance of various religious duties (cf. 2 : 177). However important these forms and time-limits may be in themselves, they do not fulfil their real purpose unless every act is approached through its spiritual "front door", that is, through God-consciousness. Since, metonymically, the word *bāb* ("door") signifies "a means of access to, or of attainment of, a thing" (see Lane I, 272), the metaphor of "entering a house through its door" is often used in classical Arabic to denote a proper approach to a problem (Rāzī).

167 This and the following verses lay down unequivocally that only self-defence (in the widest sense of the word) makes war permissible for Muslims. Most of the commentators agree in that the expression *lā taʿtadū* signifies, in this context, "do not commit aggression"; while by *al-muʿtadīn* "those who commit aggression" are meant. The defensive character of a fight "in God's cause" – that is, in the cause of the ethical principles ordained by God – is, moreover, self-evident in the reference to "those who wage war against you", and has been still further clarified in 22 : 39 – "permission [to fight] is given to those against whom war is being wrongfully waged" – which, according to all available Traditions, constitutes the earliest (and therefore fundamental) Qurʾānic reference to the question of *jihād*, or holy war (see Ṭabarī and Ibn Kathīr in their commentaries on 22 : 39). That this early, fundamental principle of self-defence as the only possible justification of war has been maintained throughout the Qurʾān is evident from 60 : 8, as well as from the concluding sentence of 4 : 91, both of which belong to a later period than the above verse.

168 In view of the preceding ordinance, the injunction "slay them wherever you may come upon them" is valid only within the context of hostilities *already in progress* (Rāzī), on the understanding that "those who wage war against you" are the aggressors or oppressors (a war of liberation being a war "in God's cause"). The translation, in this context, of *fitnah* as "oppression" is justified by the application of this term to any affliction which may cause man to go astray and to lose his faith in spiritual values (cf. *Lisān al-ʿArab*).

169 This reference to warfare in the vicinity of Mecca is due to the fact that at the time of the revelation of this verse the Holy City was still in the possession of the pagan Quraysh, who were hostile to the Muslims. However – as is always the case with historical references in the Qurʾān – the above injunction has a general import, and is valid for all times and circumstances.

But if they desist – behold, God is much-forgiving, a dispenser of grace. ‹192›
Hence, fight against them until there is no more oppression and all worship is devoted to God alone;[170] but if they desist, then all hostility shall cease, save against those who [wilfully] do wrong. ‹193›
Fight during the sacred months if you are attacked:[171] for a violation of sanctity is [subject to the law of] just retribution. Thus, if anyone commits aggression against you, attack him just as he has attacked you – but remain conscious of God, and know that God is with those who are conscious of Him.[172] ‹194›
And spend [freely] in God's cause, and let not your own hands throw you into destruction;[173] and persevere in doing good: behold, God loves the doers of good. ‹195›

AND PERFORM the pilgrimage and the pious visit [to Mecca][174] in honour of God; and if you are held back, give instead whatever offering you can easily afford. And do not shave your heads until the offering has been sacrificed;[175] but he from among you who is ill or suffers from an ailment of the head shall redeem himself by fasting, or alms, or [any other] act of worship. And if you are hale and

فَإِنِ ٱنتَهَوْا۟ فَإِنَّ ٱللَّهَ غَفُورٌ رَّحِيمٌ ﴿١٩٢﴾ وَقَـٰتِلُوهُمْ حَتَّىٰ لَا تَكُونَ فِتْنَةٌ
وَيَكُونَ ٱلدِّينُ لِلَّهِ ۖ فَإِنِ ٱنتَهَوْا۟ فَلَا عُدْوَٰنَ إِلَّا عَلَى ٱلظَّـٰلِمِينَ ﴿١٩٣﴾
ٱلشَّهْرُ ٱلْحَرَامُ بِٱلشَّهْرِ ٱلْحَرَامِ وَٱلْحُرُمَـٰتُ قِصَاصٌ ۚ فَمَنِ ٱعْتَدَىٰ
عَلَيْكُمْ فَٱعْتَدُوا۟ عَلَيْهِ بِمِثْلِ مَا ٱعْتَدَىٰ عَلَيْكُمْ ۚ وَٱتَّقُوا۟ ٱللَّهَ وَٱعْلَمُوٓا۟ أَنَّ
ٱللَّهَ مَعَ ٱلْمُتَّقِينَ ﴿١٩٤﴾ وَأَنفِقُوا۟ فِى سَبِيلِ ٱللَّهِ وَلَا تُلْقُوا۟ بِأَيْدِيكُمْ
إِلَى ٱلتَّهْلُكَةِ ۛ وَأَحْسِنُوٓا۟ ۛ إِنَّ ٱللَّهَ يُحِبُّ ٱلْمُحْسِنِينَ ﴿١٩٥﴾ وَأَتِمُّوا۟ ٱلْحَجَّ
وَٱلْعُمْرَةَ لِلَّهِ ۚ فَإِنْ أُحْصِرْتُمْ فَمَا ٱسْتَيْسَرَ مِنَ ٱلْهَدْىِ ۖ وَلَا تَحْلِقُوا۟
رُءُوسَكُمْ حَتَّىٰ يَبْلُغَ ٱلْهَدْىُ مَحِلَّهُۥ ۚ فَمَن كَانَ مِنكُم مَّرِيضًا أَوْ بِهِۦٓ
أَذًى مِّن رَّأْسِهِۦ فَفِدْيَةٌ مِّن صِيَامٍ أَوْ صَدَقَةٍ أَوْ نُسُكٍ ۚ فَإِذَآ أَمِنتُمْ

Faʾiniñ-tahaw faʾinnal-lāha Ghafūrur-Raḥīm. (192) Wa qātilūhum ḥattā lā takūna fitnatuñw-wa yakūnad-dīnu lillāhi faʾiniñ-tahaw falā ʿudwāna ʾillā ʿalaẓ-ẓālimīn. (193) ʾAshShahrul-Ḥarāmu bishShahril-Ḥarāmi wal-ḥurumātu qiṣāṣ. Famaniʿ-tadā ʿalaykum faʿtadū ʿalayhi bimithli maʿ-tadā ʿalaykum. Wattaqul-lāha waʿ-lamūu ʾannal-lāha maʿal-muttaqīn. (194) Wa ʾañfiqū fī sabīlil-lāhi wa lā tulqū biʾaydīkum ʾilat-tahlukah. Wa ʾaḥsinūu ʾinnal-lāha yuḥibbul-muḥsinīn. (195) Wa ʾatimmul-Ḥajja wal-ʿUmrata lillāh. Faʾin ʾuḥṣirtum famas-taysara minal-hadyi wa lā taḥliqū ruʾūsakum ḥattā yablughal-hadyu maḥillah. Famañ-kāna miñkum marīḍan ʾaw bihīi ʾadham-mir-raʾsihī fafidyatum-miñ-Ṣiyāmin ʾaw Ṣadaqatin ʾaw Nusuk. Faʾidhāa ʾamiñtum

170 Lit.,"and religion belongs to God [alone]" – i.e., until God can be worshipped without fear of persecution, and none is compelled to bow down in awe before another human being. (See also 22 : 40.) The term *dīn* is in this context more suitably translated as "worship" inasmuch as it comprises here both the doctrinal and the moral aspects of religion: that is to say, man's faith as well as the obligations arising from that faith.

171 This is a free rendering of the phrase "the sacred month for the sacred month", which is interpreted by all commentators in the sense given above. The "sacred months" during which, according to ancient Arab custom, all fighting was deemed utterly wrong, were the first, seventh, eleventh and twelfth months of the lunar calendar.

172 Thus, although the believers are enjoined to fight back whenever they are attacked, the concluding words of the above verse make it clear that they must, when fighting, abstain from all atrocities, including the killing of non-combatants.

173 I.e., "you might bring about your own destruction by withholding your personal and material contribution to this common effort".

174 The Mecca pilgrimage (*ḥajj*) takes place once a year, in the month of Dhu 'l-Ḥijjah, whereas a pious visit (*ʿumrah*) may be performed at any time. In both *ḥajj* and *ʿumrah*, the pilgrims are required to walk seven times around the Kaʿbah and seven times between Aṣ-Ṣafā and Al-Marwah (see notes 127 and 128 above); in the course of the *ḥajj*, they must, in addition, attend the gathering on the plain of ʾArafāt on the 9th of Dhu 'l-Ḥijjah, (see note 182 below). Irrespective of whether they are performing a full *ḥajj* or only an *ʿumrah*, the pilgrims must refrain from cutting or even trimming the hair on their heads from the time they enter the state of pilgrimage (*iḥrām*) until the end of the pilgrimage, respectively the pious visit. As mentioned in the sequence, persons who are ill or suffer from an ailment which *necessitates* the cutting or shaving of one's hair are exempted from this prohibition.

175 Lit., "until the offering has reached its destination" – i.e., in time or in place; according to Rāzī, the *time* of

secure,[176] then he who takes advantage of a pious visit before the [time of] pilgrimage shall give whatever offering he can easily afford;[177] whereas he who cannot afford it shall fast for three days during the pilgrimage and for seven days after your return: that is, ten full [days]. All this relates to him who does not live near the Inviolable House of Worship.[178]

And remain conscious of God, and know that God is severe in retribution.[179] «196»

The pilgrimage shall take place in the months appointed for it.[180] And whoever undertakes the pilgrimage in those [months] shall, while on pilgrimage, abstain from lewd speech, from all wicked conduct, and from quarrelling; and whatever good you may do, God is aware of it.

And make provision for yourselves – but, verily, the best of all provisions is God-consciousness: remain, then, conscious of Me, O you who are endowed with insight! «197» [However,] you will be committing no sin if [during the pilgrimage] you seek to obtain any bounty from your Sustainer.[181]

And when you surge downward in multitudes from ʿArafāt,[182] remember God at the holy place, and remember Him as

فَمَن تَمَتَّعَ بِٱلْعُمْرَةِ إِلَى ٱلْحَجِّ فَمَا ٱسْتَيْسَرَ مِنَ ٱلْهَدْيِ ۚ فَمَن لَّمْ يَجِدْ
فَصِيَامُ ثَلَـٰثَةِ أَيَّامٍ فِى ٱلْحَجِّ وَسَبْعَةٍ إِذَا رَجَعْتُمْ ۗ تِلْكَ عَشَرَةٌ كَامِلَةٌ ۗ ذَٰلِكَ
لِمَن لَّمْ يَكُنْ أَهْلُهُۥ حَاضِرِى ٱلْمَسْجِدِ ٱلْحَرَامِ ۚ وَٱتَّقُوا۟ ٱللَّهَ وَٱعْلَمُوٓا۟ أَنَّ
ٱللَّهَ شَدِيدُ ٱلْعِقَابِ ﴿١٩٦﴾ ٱلْحَجُّ أَشْهُرٌ مَّعْلُومَـٰتٌ ۚ فَمَن فَرَضَ فِيهِنَّ
ٱلْحَجَّ فَلَا رَفَثَ وَلَا فُسُوقَ وَلَا جِدَالَ فِى ٱلْحَجِّ ۗ وَمَا تَفْعَلُوا۟ مِنْ خَيْرٍ
يَعْلَمْهُ ٱللَّهُ ۗ وَتَزَوَّدُوا۟ فَإِنَّ خَيْرَ ٱلزَّادِ ٱلتَّقْوَىٰ ۚ وَٱتَّقُونِ يَـٰٓأُو۟لِى
ٱلْأَلْبَـٰبِ ﴿١٩٧﴾ لَيْسَ عَلَيْكُمْ جُنَاحٌ أَن تَبْتَغُوا۟ فَضْلًا مِّن رَّبِّكُمْ ۚ فَإِذَآ
أَفَضْتُم مِّنْ عَرَفَـٰتٍ فَٱذْكُرُوا۟ ٱللَّهَ عِندَ ٱلْمَشْعَرِ ٱلْحَرَامِ ۖ وَٱذْكُرُوهُ كَمَا

famañ-tamattaʿa bilʿUmrati ʾilal-Ḥajji famas-taysara minal-hady. Famal-lam yajid faṢiyāmu thalāthati ʾayyāmiñ-fil-Ḥajji wa sabʿatin ʾidhā rajaʿtum. Tilka ʿasharatuñ-kāmilah. Dhālika limal-lam yakun ʾahluhū ḥāḍiril-Masjidil-Ḥarām. Wat-taqul-lāha waʿ-lamūu ʾannal-lāha Shadīdul-ʿiqāb. (196) ʾAlḤajju ʾashhurum-maʿlūmāt. Famañ-faraḍ fīhinnal-Ḥajja falā rafatha wa lā fusūqa wa lā jidāla fil-Ḥajj. Wa mā tafʿalū min khayriñy-yaʿlamhul-lāh. Wa tazawwadū faʾinna khayraz-zādit-taqwā. Wat-taqūni yāa ʾulil-ʾalbāb. (197) Laysa ʿalaykum junāḥun ʾañ-tabtaghū faḍlam-mir-Rabbikum. Faʾidhāa ʾafaḍtum-min ʿArafātiñ-fadhkurul-lāha ʿiñdal-Mashʿaril-Ḥarām. Wadh-kurūhu kamā

sacrifice is meant here, namely, the conclusion of the pilgrimage, when those who participate in the *ḥajj* are expected – provided they can afford it – to sacrifice a sheep, a goat, or the like, and to distribute most of its flesh in charity.

176 The expression *idhā amantum* (lit., "when you are safe") refers here to safety both from external dangers (e.g., war) and from illness, and is, therefore, best rendered as "hale and secure" – the implication being that the person concerned is in a position, and intends, to participate in the pilgrimage.

177 This relates to an interruption, for the sake of personal comfort, of the state of pilgrimage (*iḥrām*) during the time intervening between the completion of an *ʿumrah* and the performance of the *ḥajj* (cf. *Manār* II, 222). The pilgrim who takes advantage of this facility is obliged to sacrifice an animal (see note 175 above) at the termination of the pilgrimage or, alternatively, to fast for ten days.

178 Lit., "whose people are not present at the Inviolable House of Worship" – i.e., do not permanently reside there: for, obviously, the inhabitants of Mecca cannot remain permanently in the state of *iḥrām*.

179 This refers not merely to a possible violation of the sanctity of the pilgrimage but also, in a more general way, to all deliberate violations of God's ordinances.

180 Lit., "in the well-known months". Since the *ḥajj* culminates in one particular month (namely, Dhu 'l-Ḥijjah), the plural apparently refers to its annual recurrence. It should, however, be noted that some commentators understand it as referring to the last three months of the lunar year.

181 I.e., by trading while in the state of *iḥrām*. Muḥammad ʿAbduh points out (in *Manār* II, 231) that the endeavour "to obtain any bounty *from Your Sustainer*" implies God-consciousness and, therefore, constitutes a kind of worship – provided, of course, that this endeavour does not conflict with any other, more prominent religious requirement.

182 The gathering of all pilgrims on the plain of ʿArafāt, east of Mecca, takes place on the 9th of Dhu 'l-Ḥijjah and constitutes the climax of the pilgrimage. The pilgrims are required to remain until sunset on that plain, below the

the One who guided you after you had indeed been lost on your way;[183] ‹198› and surge onward together with the multitude of all the other people who surge onward,[184] and ask God to forgive you your sins: for, verily, God is much-forgiving, a dispenser of grace. ‹199›

And when you have performed your acts of worship, [continue to] bear God in mind as you would bear your own fathers in mind – nay, with a yet keener remembrance![185] For there are people who [merely] pray, "O our Sustainer! Give us in this world" – and such shall not partake in the blessings of the life to come. ‹200› But there are among them such as pray "O our Sustainer! Grant us good in this world and good in the life to come, and keep us safe from suffering through the fire": ‹201› it is these that shall have their portion [of happiness] in return for what they have earned. And God is swift in reckoning. ‹202›

حزب 4

And bear God in mind during the appointed days;[186] but he who hurries away within two days shall incur no sin, and he who tarries longer shall incur no sin, provided that he is conscious of God. Hence, remain conscious of God, and know that unto Him you shall be gathered. ‹203›

هَدَىٰكُمْ وَإِن كُنتُم مِّن قَبْلِهِۦ لَمِنَ ٱلضَّآلِّينَ ﴿١٩٨﴾ ثُمَّ أَفِيضُوا۟ مِنْ حَيْثُ
أَفَاضَ ٱلنَّاسُ وَٱسْتَغْفِرُوا۟ ٱللَّهَ ۚ إِنَّ ٱللَّهَ غَفُورٌ رَّحِيمٌ ﴿١٩٩﴾ فَإِذَا قَضَيْتُم
مَّنَٰسِكَكُمْ فَٱذْكُرُوا۟ ٱللَّهَ كَذِكْرِكُمْ ءَابَآءَكُمْ أَوْ أَشَدَّ ذِكْرًا ۗ فَمِنَ
ٱلنَّاسِ مَن يَقُولُ رَبَّنَآ ءَاتِنَا فِى ٱلدُّنْيَا وَمَا لَهُۥ فِى ٱلْءَاخِرَةِ مِنْ
خَلَٰقٍ ﴿٢٠٠﴾ وَمِنْهُم مَّن يَقُولُ رَبَّنَآ ءَاتِنَا فِى ٱلدُّنْيَا حَسَنَةً وَفِى ٱلْءَاخِرَةِ
حَسَنَةً وَقِنَا عَذَابَ ٱلنَّارِ ﴿٢٠١﴾ أُو۟لَٰٓئِكَ لَهُمْ نَصِيبٌ مِّمَّا كَسَبُوا۟ ۚ وَٱللَّهُ
سَرِيعُ ٱلْحِسَابِ ﴿٢٠٢﴾ ۞ وَٱذْكُرُوا۟ ٱللَّهَ فِىٓ أَيَّامٍ مَّعْدُودَٰتٍ ۚ فَمَن تَعَجَّلَ
فِى يَوْمَيْنِ فَلَآ إِثْمَ عَلَيْهِ وَمَن تَأَخَّرَ فَلَآ إِثْمَ عَلَيْهِ ۚ لِمَنِ ٱتَّقَىٰ ۗ وَٱتَّقُوا۟ ٱللَّهَ
وَٱعْلَمُوٓا۟ أَنَّكُمْ إِلَيْهِ تُحْشَرُونَ ﴿٢٠٣﴾

hadākum wa ʾiñ-kuñtum-miñ-qablihī laminaḍ-ḍāallīn. ﴿198﴾ Thumma ʾafīḍū min ḥaythu ʾafāḍan-nāsu was-taghfirul-lāh. ʾInnal-lāha Ghafūrur-Raḥīm. ﴿199﴾ Faʾidhā qaḍaytum-manāsikakum fadhkurul-lāha kadhikrikum ʾābāaʾakum ʾaw ʾashadda dhikrā. Faminan-nāsi mañy-yaqūlu Rabbanāa ʾātinā fid-dunyā wa mā lahū fil-ʾĀkhirati min khalāq. ﴿200﴾ Wa minhum-mañy-yaqūlu Rabbanāa ʾātinā fid-dunyā ḥasanatañw-wa fil-ʾĀkhirati ḥasanatañw-wa qinā ʿadhāban-nār. ﴿201﴾ ʾUlāaʾika lahum naṣībum-mimmā kasabū; wal-lāhu Sarīʿul-ḥisāb. ﴿202﴾ ۞ Wadh-kurul-lāha fii ʾayyāmim-maʿdūdāt. Famañ-taʾajjala fī yawmayni falāa ʾithma ʿalayhi wa mañ-taʾakhkhara falāa ʾithma ʿalayhi limanit-taqā. Wat-taqul-lāha waʿ-lamūu ʾannakum ʾilayhi tuḥsharūn. ﴿203﴾

hillock known as Jabal ar-Raḥmah ("the Mount of Grace") – a symbolic act meant to bring to mind that ultimate gathering on Resurrection Day, when every soul will await God's judgment. Immediately after sunset, the multitudes of pilgrims move back in the direction of Mecca, stopping overnight at a place called Muzdalifah, the "holy place" referred to in the next clause of this sentence.

183 Lit.,"and remember Him as He has guided you, although before that you had indeed been among those who go astray".

184 Lit., "surge onward in multitudes whence the people surge onward in multitudes": thus the pilgrims are called upon to submerge their individualities, at that supreme moment of the pilgrimage, in the consciousness of belonging to a community of people who are all equal before God, with no barrier of race or class or social status separating one person from another.

185 Most of the commentators see in this passage a reference to the custom of the pre-Islamic Arabs to extol, on the occasion of various gatherings, the greatness and the supposed virtues of their ancestors. Some of the earliest Islamic scholars, however – e.g., Aḍ-Ḍaḥḥāk, Ar-Rabīʿ and Abū Muslim – are of the opinion that what is meant here are actual fathers (or, by implication, both parents), whom a child usually considers to be the embodiment of all that is good and powerful (see Rāzī's commentary on this verse).

186 These are the days following the "Festival of Sacrifices" (*ʿīd al-aḍḥāʾ*), which takes place on the 10th of Dhu 'l-Ḥijjah. The pilgrims are obliged to spend at least two of these days in the valley of Minā, about half-way between ʿArafāt and Mecca.

NOW THERE IS a kind of man[187] whose views on the life of this world may please thee greatly, and [the more so as] he cites God as witness to what is in his heart and is, moreover, exceedingly skillful in argument.[188] ‹204› But whenever he prevails, he goes about the earth spreading corruption and destroying [man's] tilth and progeny:[189] and God does not love corruption. ‹205› And whenever he is told, "Be conscious of God," his false pride drives him into sin: wherefore hell will be his allotted portion – and how vile a resting-place! ‹206›

But there is [also] a kind of man who would willingly sell his own self in order to please God:[190] and God is most compassionate towards His servants. ‹207›

وَمِنَ ٱلنَّاسِ مَن يُعْجِبُكَ قَوْلُهُۥ فِى ٱلْحَيَوٰةِ ٱلدُّنْيَا وَيُشْهِدُ ٱللَّهَ عَلَىٰ مَا فِى
قَلْبِهِۦ وَهُوَ أَلَدُّ ٱلْخِصَامِ ﴿٢٠٤﴾ وَإِذَا تَوَلَّىٰ سَعَىٰ فِى ٱلْأَرْضِ لِيُفْسِدَ فِيهَا
وَيُهْلِكَ ٱلْحَرْثَ وَٱلنَّسْلَ ۗ وَٱللَّهُ لَا يُحِبُّ ٱلْفَسَادَ ﴿٢٠٥﴾ وَإِذَا قِيلَ لَهُ
ٱتَّقِ ٱللَّهَ أَخَذَتْهُ ٱلْعِزَّةُ بِٱلْإِثْمِ ۚ فَحَسْبُهُۥ جَهَنَّمُ ۚ وَلَبِئْسَ ٱلْمِهَادُ ﴿٢٠٦﴾ وَمِنَ
ٱلنَّاسِ مَن يَشْرِى نَفْسَهُ ٱبْتِغَآءَ مَرْضَاتِ ٱللَّهِ ۗ وَٱللَّهُ رَءُوفٌۢ بِٱلْعِبَادِ ﴿٢٠٧﴾

Wa minan-nāsi mañy-yuʿjibuka qawluhū fil-ḥayātid-dunyā wa yushhidul-lāha ʿalā mā fī qalbihī wa huwa ʾaladdul-khiṣām. (204) Wa ʾidhā tawallā saʿā fil-ʾarḍi liyufsida fīhā wa yuhlikal-ḥartha wan-nasl. Wal-lāhu lā yuḥibbul-fasād. (205) Wa ʾidhā qīla lahut-taqil-lāha ʾakhadhat-hul-ʿizzatu bilʾithm. Faḥasbuhū jahannamu wa labiʾsal-mihād. (206) Wa minan-nāsi mañy-yashrī nafsahub-tighāaʾa marḍātil-lāh. Wal-lāhu Raʾūfum-bilʿibād. (207)

187 Lit., "among the people there is he" (or "such as"). Since there is no valid reason to suppose, as some commentators do, that this refers to a particular person – a contemporary of the Prophet – the most reliable authorities hold that the above passage has a general meaning (cf. Rāzī). As the context shows, it is a further elaboration of the allusion, made in 2 : 200-201, to two contrasting attitudes: the attitude of people whose only real concern is the life of this world, and that of people who are mindful of the hereafter as well as, or even more than, their present life.

188 Lit., "the most contentious of adversaries in a dispute". According to Az-Zajjāj (quoted by Rāzī), this signifies a person who is always able to defeat his opponent in a controversy by the use of extremely adroit and often misleading arguments. It is obvious that this passage refers to people who hold plausible and even admirable views regarding a possible improvement of human society and of man's lot on earth, but at the same time refuse to be guided by what they regard as "esoteric" considerations – like belief in a life after death – and justify their exclusive preoccupation with the affairs of this world by seemingly sound arguments and a stress on their own ethical objectives ("they cite God as witness to what is in their hearts"). There is an inescapable affinity between the mental attitude described in the above passage and the one spoken of in 2 : 8-12.

189 Lit., "he hastens about the earth [or "strives on earth"] to spread corruption therein and to destroy tilth and progeny". Most of the commentators see in this sentence an indication of a conscious *intent* on the part of the person thus described; but it is also possible that the particle *li* in *li-yufsida* (generally taken to mean "in order that he might spread corruption") plays in this context the role of what the grammarians call a *lām al-ʿāqibah*, "the [letter] *lām* used to denote a consequence" – i.e., regardless of the existence or non-existence of a conscious intent. (By rendering the sentence the way I do it, both possibilities are left open.) As regards the expression *ḥarth* (rendered by me as "tilth"), its primary significance is "gain" or "acquisition" through labour; and thus it often signifies "worldly goods" (see Lane II, 542), and especially the crops obtained by tilling land, as well as the tilled land itself. If *ḥarth* is understood in this context as "tilth", it would apply, metaphorically, to human endeavours in general, and to social endeavours in particular. However, some commentators – basing their opinion on the Qurʾanic sentence, "your wives are your tilth" (2 : 223) – maintain that *ḥarth* stands here for "wives" (cf. Rāzī, and the philologist Al-Azharī, as quoted in *Manār* II, 248): in which case the "destruction of tilth and progeny" would be synonymous with an upsetting of family life and, consequently, of the entire social fabric. According to either of these two interpretations, the passage has the following meaning: As soon as the mental attitude described above is generally accepted and made the basis of social behaviour, it unavoidably results in widespread moral decay and, consequently, social disintegration.

190 Lit., "there is such as would sell his own self out of a desire for God's pleasure": i.e., would give up all his personal interests if compliance with God's will were to demand it.

O you who have attained to faith! Surrender yourselves wholly unto God,[191] and follow not Satan's footsteps, for, verily, he is your open foe. «208» And if you should stumble after all evidence of the truth has come unto you, then know that, verily, God is almighty, wise. «209»

Are these people[192] waiting, perchance, for God to reveal Himself unto them in the shadows of the clouds, together with the angels – although [by then] all will have been decided, and unto God all things will have been brought back?[193] «210»

Ask the children of Israel how many a clear message We have given them! And if one alters God's blessed message[194] after it has reached him – verily, God is severe in retribution! «211»

Unto those who are bent on denying the truth the life of this world [alone] seems goodly;[195] hence, they scoff at those who have attained to faith: but they who are conscious of God shall be above them on Resurrection Day.

And God grants sustenance unto whom He wills, beyond all reckoning.[196] «212»

ALL MANKIND were once one single community; [then they began to differ –] whereupon God raised up the prophets as heralds of glad tidings and as warners,

يَٰٓأَيُّهَا ٱلَّذِينَ ءَامَنُوا۟ ٱدْخُلُوا۟ فِى ٱلسِّلْمِ كَآفَّةً وَلَا تَتَّبِعُوا۟ خُطُوَٰتِ
ٱلشَّيْطَٰنِ ۚ إِنَّهُۥ لَكُمْ عَدُوٌّ مُّبِينٌ ﴿٢٠٨﴾ فَإِن زَلَلْتُم مِّنۢ بَعْدِ مَا جَآءَتْكُمُ
ٱلْبَيِّنَٰتُ فَٱعْلَمُوٓا۟ أَنَّ ٱللَّهَ عَزِيزٌ حَكِيمٌ ﴿٢٠٩﴾ هَلْ يَنظُرُونَ إِلَّآ أَن
يَأْتِيَهُمُ ٱللَّهُ فِى ظُلَلٍ مِّنَ ٱلْغَمَامِ وَٱلْمَلَٰٓئِكَةُ وَقُضِىَ ٱلْأَمْرُ ۚ وَإِلَى ٱللَّهِ
تُرْجَعُ ٱلْأُمُورُ ﴿٢١٠﴾ سَلْ بَنِىٓ إِسْرَٰٓءِيلَ كَمْ ءَاتَيْنَٰهُم مِّنْ ءَايَةٍۭ بَيِّنَةٍ ۗ
وَمَن يُبَدِّلْ نِعْمَةَ ٱللَّهِ مِنۢ بَعْدِ مَا جَآءَتْهُ فَإِنَّ ٱللَّهَ شَدِيدُ ٱلْعِقَابِ ﴿٢١١﴾
زُيِّنَ لِلَّذِينَ كَفَرُوا۟ ٱلْحَيَوٰةُ ٱلدُّنْيَا وَيَسْخَرُونَ مِنَ ٱلَّذِينَ ءَامَنُوا۟ ۘ وَٱلَّذِينَ
ٱتَّقَوْا۟ فَوْقَهُمْ يَوْمَ ٱلْقِيَٰمَةِ ۗ وَٱللَّهُ يَرْزُقُ مَن يَشَآءُ بِغَيْرِ حِسَابٍ ﴿٢١٢﴾
كَانَ ٱلنَّاسُ أُمَّةً وَٰحِدَةً فَبَعَثَ ٱللَّهُ ٱلنَّبِيِّـۧنَ مُبَشِّرِينَ وَمُنذِرِينَ

Yāa ʾayyuhal-ladhīna ʾāmanud-khulū fis-silmi kāaffatanw-wa lā tattabiᶜū khuṭuwātish-Shayṭān. ʾInnahū lakum ᶜaduwwum-mubīn. 208 Faʾin-zalaltum-mim-baᶜdi mā jāaʾatkumul-bayyinātu faᶜlamūu ʾannal-lāha ᶜAzīzun-Ḥakīm. 209 Hal yanẓurūna ʾillāa ʾany-yaʾtiyahumul-lāhu fī ẓulalim-minal-ghamāmi wal-Malāaʾikatu wa quḍiyal-ʾamr. Wa ʾilal-lāhi turjaᶜul-ʾumūr. 210 Sal banīi ʾIsrāaʾīla kam ʾātaynāhum-min ʾĀyatim-bayyinah. Wa many-yubaddil niᶜmatal-lāhi mim-baᶜdi mā jāaʾat-hu faʾinnal-lāha Shadīdul-ᶜiqāb. 211 Zuyyina lilladhīna kafarul-ḥayātud-dunyā wa yaskharūna minal-ladhīna ʾāmanū. Wal-ladhīnat-taqaw fawqahum Yawmal-Qiyāmah. Wal-lāhu yarzuqu many-yashāaʾu bighayri ḥisāb. 212 Kānan-nāsu ʾummatanw-wāḥidatan-fabaᶜathal-lāhun-Nabiyyīna mubashshirīna wa mundhirīna

191 Lit., "enter wholly into self-surrender". Since self-surrender to God is the basis of all true belief, some of the greatest commentators (e.g., Zamakhsharī, Rāzī) hold that the address, "O you who have attained to faith" cannot refer here to *Muslims* – a designation which, throughout the Qurʾān, literally means "those who have surrendered themselves to God" – but must relate to people who have not yet achieved such complete self-surrender: that is, to the Jews and the Christians, who do believe in most of the earlier revelations but do not regard the message of the Qurʾān as true. This interpretation would seem to be borne out by the subsequent passages.

192 Lit., "they" – obviously referring to the people addressed in the preceding two verses.

193 I.e., it will be too late for repentance. All commentators agree in that the "decision" relates to the unequivocal manifestation of God's will on the Day of Judgment, which is alluded to in the words, "when unto God all things will have been brought back". Since, in the next verse, the children of Israel are addressed, it is possible that this rhetorical question is connected with their refusal, in the time of Moses, to believe in the divine message unless they "see God face to face" (cf. 2 : 55).

194 Lit., "God's blessing".

195 Lit., "has been made beauteous".

196 I.e., He cannot be called to account for the way in which He distributes worldly benefits, sometimes granting them to the morally deserving and sometimes to sinners.

and through them bestowed revelation from on high, setting forth the truth, so that it might decide between people with regard to all on which they had come to hold divergent views.[197] Yet none other than the selfsame people who had been granted this [revelation] began, out of mutual jealousy, to disagree about its meaning after all evidence of the truth had come unto them. But God guided the believers unto the truth about which, by His leave, they had disagreed: for God guides onto a straight way him that wills [to be guided].[198] ‹213›

[But] do you think that you could enter paradise without having suffered like those [believers] who passed away before you?[199] Misfortune and hardship befell them, and so shaken were they that the apostle, and the believers with him, would exclaim, "When will God's succour come?"[200]

Oh, verily, God's succour is [always] near! ‹214›

وَأَنزَلَ مَعَهُمُ ٱلْكِتَٰبَ بِٱلْحَقِّ لِيَحْكُمَ بَيْنَ ٱلنَّاسِ فِيمَا ٱخْتَلَفُوا۟ فِيهِ
وَمَا ٱخْتَلَفَ فِيهِ إِلَّا ٱلَّذِينَ أُوتُوهُ مِنۢ بَعْدِ مَا جَآءَتْهُمُ ٱلْبَيِّنَٰتُ بَغْيًۢا
بَيْنَهُمْ ۖ فَهَدَى ٱللَّهُ ٱلَّذِينَ ءَامَنُوا۟ لِمَا ٱخْتَلَفُوا۟ فِيهِ مِنَ ٱلْحَقِّ بِإِذْنِهِۦ ۗ
وَٱللَّهُ يَهْدِى مَن يَشَآءُ إِلَىٰ صِرَٰطٍ مُّسْتَقِيمٍ ﴿٢١٣﴾ أَمْ حَسِبْتُمْ أَن تَدْخُلُوا۟
ٱلْجَنَّةَ وَلَمَّا يَأْتِكُم مَّثَلُ ٱلَّذِينَ خَلَوْا۟ مِن قَبْلِكُم ۖ مَّسَّتْهُمُ ٱلْبَأْسَآءُ
وَٱلضَّرَّآءُ وَزُلْزِلُوا۟ حَتَّىٰ يَقُولَ ٱلرَّسُولُ وَٱلَّذِينَ ءَامَنُوا۟ مَعَهُۥ مَتَىٰ نَصْرُ
ٱللَّهِ ۗ أَلَآ إِنَّ نَصْرَ ٱللَّهِ قَرِيبٌ ﴿٢١٤﴾

wa ʾan̄zala maᶜahumul-Kitāba bilḥaqqi liyaḥkuma baynan-nāsi fīmakh-talafū fīh. Wa makh-talafa fīhi ʾillal-ladhīna ʾūtūhu mim-baᶜdi mā jāaʾat-humul-bayyinātu baghyam-baynahum. Fahadal-lāhul-ladhīna ʾāmanū limakh-talafū fīhi minal-ḥaqqi biʾidhnih. Wal-lāhu yahdī man̄y-yashāaʾu ʾilā ṣirāṭim-mustaqīm. (213) ʾAm ḥasibtum ʾan̄-tadkhulul-jannata wa lammā yaʾtikum-mathalul-ladhīna khalaw min̄-qablikum. Massat-humul-baʾsāaʾu waḍ-ḍarrāaʾu wa zulzilū ḥattā yaqūlar-Rasūlu wal-ladhīna ʾamanū maᶜahū matā naṣrul-lāh. ʾAlāa ʾinna naṣral-lāhi qarīb. (214)

197 By using the expression *ummah wāḥidah* ("one single community") to describe the original state of mankind, the Qurʾān does not propound, as might appear at first glance, the idea of a mythical "golden age" obtaining at the dawn of man's history. What is alluded to in this verse is no more than the relative homogeneity of instinctive perceptions and inclinations characteristic of man's primitive mentality and the primitive social order in which he lived in those early days. Since that homogeneity was based on a lack of intellectual and emotional differentiation rather than on a conscious agreement among the members of human society, it was bound to disintegrate in the measure of man's subsequent development. As his thought-life became more and more complex, his emotional capacity and his individual needs, too, became more differentiated, conflicts of views and interests came to the fore, and mankind ceased to be "one single community" as regards their outlook on life and their moral valuations: and it was at this stage that divine guidance became necessary. (It is to be borne in mind that the term *al-kitāb* refers here – as in many other places in the Qurʾān – not to any particular scripture but to divine revelation as such.) This interpretation of the above Qurʾanic passage is supported by the fact that the famous Companion ᶜAbd Allāh ibn Masᶜūd used to read it thus: "All mankind were once one single community, and then they began to differ (*fakhtalafū*) – whereupon God raised up . . .", etc. Although the word *fakhtalafū* interpolated here by Ibn Masᶜūd does not appear in the generally-accepted text of the Qurʾān, almost all of the authorities are of the opinion that it is implied in the context.

198 Or: "God guides whomever He wills onto a straight way." As is made clear in the second part of verse 253 of this *sūrah*, man's proneness to intellectual dissension is not an accident of history but an integral, God-willed aspect of human nature as such: and it is this natural circumstance to which the words "by His leave" allude. For an explanation of the phrase "out of mutual jealousy", see 23 : 53 and the corresponding note 30.

199 Lit., "while yet there has not come to you the like of [what has come to] those who passed away before you". This passage connects with the words, "God guides onto a straight way him that wills [to be guided]", which occur at the end of the preceding verse. The meaning is that intellectual cognition of the truth cannot, by itself, be a means of attaining to ultimate bliss: it must be complemented by readiness to sacrifice and spiritual purification through suffering.

200 The preceding reference to "those who passed away before you" makes it obvious that the term "the apostle" is used here in a generic sense, applying to all the apostles (*Manār* II, 301).

THEY WILL ASK thee as to what they should spend on others. Say: "Whatever of your wealth you spend shall [first] be for your parents, and for the near of kin, and the orphans, and the needy, and the wayfarer; and whatever good you do, verily, God has full knowledge thereof." ‹215›

FIGHTING is ordained for you, even though it be hateful to you; but it may well be that you hate a thing the while it is good for you, and it may well be that you love a thing the while it is bad for you: and God knows, whereas you do not know.[201] ‹216› They will ask thee about fighting in the sacred month.[202] Say: "Fighting in it is an awesome thing; but turning men away from the path of God and denying Him, and [turning them away from] the Inviolable House of Worship and expelling its people therefrom – [all this] is yet more awesome in the sight of God, since oppression is more awesome than killing." [Your enemies] will not cease to fight against you till they have turned you away from your faith, if they can. But if any of you should turn away from his faith and die as a denier of the truth – these it is whose works will go for nought in this world and in the life to come; and these it is who are destined for the fire, therein to abide. ‹217›

Verily, they who have attained to faith, and they who have forsaken the domain of evil[203] and are striving hard in God's cause – these it is who may look forward to God's grace: for God is much-forgiving, a dispenser of grace. ‹218›

يَسْـَٔلُونَكَ مَاذَا يُنفِقُونَ قُلْ مَآ أَنفَقْتُم مِّنْ خَيْرٍ فَلِلْوَٰلِدَيْنِ وَٱلْأَقْرَبِينَ
وَٱلْيَتَٰمَىٰ وَٱلْمَسَٰكِينِ وَٱبْنِ ٱلسَّبِيلِ وَمَا تَفْعَلُوا۟ مِنْ خَيْرٍ فَإِنَّ ٱللَّهَ بِهِۦ
عَلِيمٌ ﴿٢١٥﴾ كُتِبَ عَلَيْكُمُ ٱلْقِتَالُ وَهُوَ كُرْهٌ لَّكُمْ وَعَسَىٰٓ أَن تَكْرَهُوا۟ شَيْـًٔا
وَهُوَ خَيْرٌ لَّكُمْ وَعَسَىٰٓ أَن تُحِبُّوا۟ شَيْـًٔا وَهُوَ شَرٌّ لَّكُمْ وَٱللَّهُ يَعْلَمُ وَأَنتُمْ لَا
تَعْلَمُونَ ﴿٢١٦﴾ يَسْـَٔلُونَكَ عَنِ ٱلشَّهْرِ ٱلْحَرَامِ قِتَالٍ فِيهِ قُلْ قِتَالٌ فِيهِ كَبِيرٌ
وَصَدٌّ عَن سَبِيلِ ٱللَّهِ وَكُفْرٌۢ بِهِۦ وَٱلْمَسْجِدِ ٱلْحَرَامِ وَإِخْرَاجُ أَهْلِهِۦ مِنْهُ
أَكْبَرُ عِندَ ٱللَّهِ وَٱلْفِتْنَةُ أَكْبَرُ مِنَ ٱلْقَتْلِ وَلَا يَزَالُونَ يُقَٰتِلُونَكُمْ حَتَّىٰ
يَرُدُّوكُمْ عَن دِينِكُمْ إِنِ ٱسْتَطَٰعُوا۟ وَمَن يَرْتَدِدْ مِنكُمْ عَن دِينِهِۦ فَيَمُتْ
وَهُوَ كَافِرٌ فَأُو۟لَٰٓئِكَ حَبِطَتْ أَعْمَٰلُهُمْ فِى ٱلدُّنْيَا وَٱلْءَاخِرَةِ وَأُو۟لَٰٓئِكَ أَصْحَٰبُ
ٱلنَّارِ هُمْ فِيهَا خَٰلِدُونَ ﴿٢١٧﴾ إِنَّ ٱلَّذِينَ ءَامَنُوا۟ وَٱلَّذِينَ هَاجَرُوا۟ وَجَٰهَدُوا۟
فِى سَبِيلِ ٱللَّهِ أُو۟لَٰٓئِكَ يَرْجُونَ رَحْمَتَ ٱللَّهِ وَٱللَّهُ غَفُورٌ رَّحِيمٌ ﴿٢١٨﴾

Yasˀalūnaka mādhā yuñfiqūn. Qul māa ˀañfaqtum-min khayriñ-falilwālidayni wal-ˀaqrabīna wal-yatāmā wal-masākīni wab-nis-sabīl. Wa mā tafˁalū min khayriñ-faˀinnal-lāha bihī ˁAlīm. (215) Kutiba ˁalaykumul-qitālu wa huwa kurhul-lakum. Wa ˁasāa ˀañ takrahū shayˀañw-wa huwa khayrul-lakum. Wa ˁsāa ˀañ-tuḥibbū shayˀañw-wa huwa sharrul-lakum. Wal-lāhu yaˁlamu wa ˀañtum lā taˁlamūn. (216) Yasˀalūnaka ˁanish-Shahril-Ḥarāmi qitāliñ-fīh. Qul qitāluñ-fīhi kabīr. Wa ṣaddun ˁañ-sabīlil-lāhi wa kufrum-bihī wal-Masjidil-Ḥarāmi wa ˀikhrāju ˀahlihī minhu ˀakbaru ˁiñdal-lāh. Wal-fitnatu ˀakbaru minal-qatl. Wa lā yazālūna yuqātilūnakum ḥattā yaruddūkum ˁañ-dīnikum ˀinis-taṭāˁū. Wa mañy-yartadid miñkum ˁañ-dīnihī fayamut wa huwa kāfiruñ-faˀulāaˀika ḥabiṭat ˀaˁmāluhum fid-dunyā wal-ˀĀkhirah. Wa ˀulāaˀika ˀaṣḥābun-nāri hum fīhā khālidūn. (217) ˀInnal-ladhīna ˀāmanū wal-ladhīna hājarū wa jāhadū fī sabīlil-lāhi ˀulāaˀika yarjūna raḥmatal-lāhi wal-lāhu Ghafūrur-Raḥīm. (218)

201 Insofar as it relates to fighting, this verse must be read in conjunction with 2 : 190-193 and 22 : 39: but it expresses, in addition, a general truth applicable to many situations.

202 For an explanation of the "sacred months", see note 171 above.

203 The expression *alladhīna hājarū* (lit., "those who have forsaken their homelands") denotes, primarily, the early Meccan Muslims who migrated at the Prophet's bidding to Medina – which was then called Yathrib – in order to be able to live in freedom and in accordance with the dictates of Islam. After the conquest of Mecca by the Muslims in the year 8 H., this exodus (*hijrah*) from Mecca to Medina ceased to be a religious obligation. Ever since the earliest days of Islam, however, the term *hijrah* has had a spiritual connotation as well – namely, a "forsaking of the domain of evil" and turning towards God: and since this spiritual connotation applies both to the historical *muhājirūn* ("emigrants") of early Islam and to all believers of later times who forsake all that is sinful and "migrate unto God", I am using this expression frequently.

THEY WILL ASK thee about intoxicants and games of chance. Say: "In both there is great evil[204] as well as some benefit for man; but the evil which they cause is greater than the benefit which they bring."[205]
And they will ask thee as to what they should spend [in God's cause]. Say: "Whatever you can spare."
In this way God makes clear unto you His messages, so that you might reflect ‹219›
on this world and on the life to come.
And they will ask thee about [how to deal with] orphans. Say: "To improve their condition is best." And if you share their life, [remember that] they are your brethren:[206] for God distinguishes between him who spoils things and him who improves. And had God so willed, He would indeed have imposed on you hardships which you would not have been able to bear:[207] [but,] behold, God is almighty, wise! ‹220›

AND DO NOT marry women who ascribe divinity to aught beside God ere they attain to [true] belief: for any believing bondwoman [of God][208] is certainly better than a woman who ascribes divinity to aught beside God, even though she please you greatly. And do not give your women in marriage to men who ascribe divinity to aught beside God ere they attain to [true] belief: for any believing bondman [of God] is certainly better than a man who ascribes divinity to aught beside God, even though he please you greatly.

۞ يَسْـَٔلُونَكَ عَنِ ٱلْخَمْرِ وَٱلْمَيْسِرِ ۖ قُلْ فِيهِمَآ إِثْمٌ كَبِيرٌ وَمَنَٰفِعُ
لِلنَّاسِ وَإِثْمُهُمَآ أَكْبَرُ مِن نَّفْعِهِمَا ۗ وَيَسْـَٔلُونَكَ مَاذَا يُنفِقُونَ قُلِ
ٱلْعَفْوَ ۗ كَذَٰلِكَ يُبَيِّنُ ٱللَّهُ لَكُمُ ٱلْـَٔايَٰتِ لَعَلَّكُمْ تَتَفَكَّرُونَ ﴿٢١٩﴾ فِى
ٱلدُّنْيَا وَٱلْـَٔاخِرَةِ ۗ وَيَسْـَٔلُونَكَ عَنِ ٱلْيَتَٰمَىٰ ۖ قُلْ إِصْلَاحٌ لَّهُمْ خَيْرٌ ۖ وَإِن
تُخَالِطُوهُمْ فَإِخْوَٰنُكُمْ ۚ وَٱللَّهُ يَعْلَمُ ٱلْمُفْسِدَ مِنَ ٱلْمُصْلِحِ ۚ وَلَوْ شَآءَ
ٱللَّهُ لَأَعْنَتَكُمْ ۚ إِنَّ ٱللَّهَ عَزِيزٌ حَكِيمٌ ﴿٢٢٠﴾ وَلَا تَنكِحُوا۟ ٱلْمُشْرِكَٰتِ
حَتَّىٰ يُؤْمِنَّ ۚ وَلَأَمَةٌ مُّؤْمِنَةٌ خَيْرٌ مِّن مُّشْرِكَةٍ وَلَوْ أَعْجَبَتْكُمْ ۗ وَلَا تُنكِحُوا۟
ٱلْمُشْرِكِينَ حَتَّىٰ يُؤْمِنُوا۟ ۚ وَلَعَبْدٌ مُّؤْمِنٌ خَيْرٌ مِّن مُّشْرِكٍ وَلَوْ أَعْجَبَكُمْ ۗ

ربع الحزب

۞ Yasʾalūnaka ʿanil-khamri wal-maysir. Qul fīhimāa ʾithmuñ-kabīruñw-wa manāfiʿu linnās. Wa ʾithmuhumāa ʾakbaru miñ-nafʿihimā. Wa Yasʾalūnaka mādhā yuñfiqūna qulil-ʿafw. Kadhālika yubayyinul-lāhu lakumul-ʾĀyāti laʿallakum tatafakkarūna, 219 fid-dunyā wal-ʾĀkhirah. Wa yasʾalūnaka ʿanil-yatāmā. Qul ʾiṣlāḥul-lahum khayr. Wa ʾiñtukhāliṭūhum faʾikhwānukum. Wal-lāhu yaʿlamul-mufsida minnal-muṣliḥ. Wa law shāaʾal-lāhu la-ʾaʿnatakum. ʾInnal-lāha ʿAzīzun Ḥakīm. 220 Wa lā tañkiḥul-mushrikāti ḥattā yuʾminna wa laʾamatum-muʾminatun khayrum-mim-mushrikatiñw-wa law ʾaʿjabatkum. Wa lā tuñkiḥul-mushrikīna ḥattā yuʾminū; wa laʿabdum-muʾminun khayrum-mim-mushrikiñw-wa law ʾaʿjabakum.

204 Lit., "sin", or anything that is conducive to sinning. As some of the classical commentators (e.g., Rāzī) point out, the term *ithm* is used in this verse as the antithesis of *manāfi*ʿ ("benefits"); it can, therefore, be suitably rendered as "evil".

205 Lit., "their evil is greater than their benefit". For a clear-cut prohibition of intoxicants and games of chance, see 5 : 90-91 and the corresponding notes.

206 The implication is that if one shares the life of an orphan in his charge, one is permitted to benefit by such an association – for instance, through a business partnership – provided this does not damage the orphan's interests in any way.

207 I.e., "by putting you under an obligation to care for the orphans, and at the same time prohibiting you from sharing their life" (see preceding note).

208 Although the majority of the commentators attribute to the term *amah*, occurring in this context, its usual connotation of "slave-girl", some of them are of the opinion that it stands here for "*God's* bondwoman". Thus,

[Such as] these invite unto the fire, whereas God invites unto paradise, and unto [the achievement of] forgiveness by His leave; and He makes clear His messages unto mankind, so that they might bear them in mind. ‹221›

AND THEY will ask thee about [woman's] monthly courses. Say: "It is a vulnerable condition. Keep, therefore, aloof from women during their monthly courses, and do not draw near unto them until they are cleansed; and when they are cleansed, go in unto them as God has bidden you to do."[209]
Verily, God loves those who turn unto Him in repentance,[210] and He loves those who keep themselves pure. ‹222›
Your wives are your tilth; go, then, unto your tilth as you may desire, but first provide something for your souls,[211] and remain conscious of God, and know that you are destined to meet Him. And give glad tidings unto those who believe. ‹223›

AND DO NOT allow your oaths in the name of God to become an obstacle to virtue and God-consciousness and the promotion of peace between men:[212] for God is all-hearing, all-knowing. ‹224›
God will not take you to task for oaths which you may have uttered without thought, but will take you to task [only] for what your hearts have conceived [in earnest]: for God is much-forgiving, forbearing. ‹225›

أُوْلَـٰٓئِكَ يَدْعُونَ إِلَى ٱلنَّارِ ۖ وَٱللَّهُ يَدْعُوٓا۟ إِلَى ٱلْجَنَّةِ وَٱلْمَغْفِرَةِ بِإِذْنِهِۦ ۖ
وَيُبَيِّنُ ءَايَـٰتِهِۦ لِلنَّاسِ لَعَلَّهُمْ يَتَذَكَّرُونَ ﴿٢٢١﴾ وَيَسْـَٔلُونَكَ عَنِ
ٱلْمَحِيضِ ۖ قُلْ هُوَ أَذًى فَٱعْتَزِلُوا۟ ٱلنِّسَآءَ فِى ٱلْمَحِيضِ ۖ وَلَا تَقْرَبُوهُنَّ
حَتَّىٰ يَطْهُرْنَ ۖ فَإِذَا تَطَهَّرْنَ فَأْتُوهُنَّ مِنْ حَيْثُ أَمَرَكُمُ ٱللَّهُ ۚ إِنَّ ٱللَّهَ يُحِبُّ
ٱلتَّوَّٰبِينَ وَيُحِبُّ ٱلْمُتَطَهِّرِينَ ﴿٢٢٢﴾ نِسَآؤُكُمْ حَرْثٌ لَّكُمْ فَأْتُوا۟ حَرْثَكُمْ
أَنَّىٰ شِئْتُمْ ۖ وَقَدِّمُوا۟ لِأَنفُسِكُمْ ۚ وَٱتَّقُوا۟ ٱللَّهَ وَٱعْلَمُوٓا۟ أَنَّكُم مُّلَـٰقُوهُ ۗ وَبَشِّرِ
ٱلْمُؤْمِنِينَ ﴿٢٢٣﴾ وَلَا تَجْعَلُوا۟ ٱللَّهَ عُرْضَةً لِّأَيْمَـٰنِكُمْ أَن تَبَرُّوا۟ وَتَتَّقُوا۟
وَتُصْلِحُوا۟ بَيْنَ ٱلنَّاسِ ۗ وَٱللَّهُ سَمِيعٌ عَلِيمٌ ﴿٢٢٤﴾ لَّا يُؤَاخِذُكُمُ ٱللَّهُ بِٱللَّغْوِ فِىٓ
أَيْمَـٰنِكُمْ وَلَـٰكِن يُؤَاخِذُكُم بِمَا كَسَبَتْ قُلُوبُكُمْ ۗ وَٱللَّهُ غَفُورٌ حَلِيمٌ ﴿٢٢٥﴾

ʾUlāaʾika yadʿūna ʾilan-nār. Wal-lāhu yadʿūu ʾilal-jannati wal-maghfirati biʾidhnihi wa yubayyinu ʾĀyātihī linnāsi laʿallahum yatadhakkarūn. (221) Wa yasʾalūnaka ʿanil-maḥīḍ. Qul huwa ʾadhañ-faʿtazilun-nisāaʾa fil-maḥīḍi wa lā taqrabūhunna ḥattā yaṭhurn. Faʾidhā taṭahharna faʾtūhunna min ḥaythu ʾamarakumul-lāh. ʾInnal-lāha yuḥibbut-tawwābīna wa yuḥibbul-mutaṭahhirīn. (222) Nisāaʾukum ḥarthul-lakum faʾtū ḥarthakum ʾannā shiʾtum; wa qaddimū liʾañfusikum; wat-taqul-lāha waʿ-lamūu ʾannakum-mulāqūh. Wa bashshiril-muʾminīn. (223) Wa lā tajʿalul-lāha ʿurḍatal-liʾaymānikum ʾañ-tabarrū wa tattaqū wa tuṣliḥū baynan-nās. Wal-lāhu Samīʿun ʿAlīm. (224) Lā yuʾākhidhukumul-lāhu bil-laghwi fīi ʾaymānikum wa lākiñy-yuʾākhidhukum bimā kasabat qulūbukum. Wal-lāhu Ghafūrun Ḥalīm. (225)

Zamakhsharī explains the words *amah muʾminah* (lit., "a believing bondwoman") as denoting "any believing woman, whether she be free or slave; and this applies to [the expression] 'believing bondman' as well: for all human beings are God's bondmen and bondwomen". My rendering of the above passage is based on this eminently plausible interpretation.

209 This is one of the many references in the Qurʾān to the positive, God-ordained nature of sexuality.

210 I.e., if they have transgressed against the above restriction.

211 In other words, a spiritual relationship between man and woman is postulated as the indispensable basis of sexual relations.

212 Lit., "do not make God, because of your oaths . . .", etc. As can be seen from verse 226, this injunction refers primarily to oaths relating to divorce but is, nevertheless, general in its import. Thus, there are several authentic Traditions to the effect that the Prophet Muḥammad said: "If anyone takes a solemn oath [that he would do or refrain from doing such-and-such a thing], and thereupon realizes that something else would be a more righteous course, then let him do that which is more righteous, and let him break his oath and then atone for it" (Bukhārī and Muslim; and other variants of the same Tradition in other compilations). As regards the method of atonement, see 5 : 89.

Those who take an oath that they will not approach their wives shall have four months of grace; and if they go back [on their oath][213] – behold, God is much-forgiving, a dispenser of grace. «226» But if they are resolved on divorce – behold, God is all-hearing, all-knowing. «227»
And the divorced women shall undergo, without remarrying,[214] a waiting-period of three monthly courses: for it is not lawful for them to conceal what God may have created in their wombs,[215] if they believe in God and the Last Day. And during this period their husbands are fully entitled to take them back, if they desire reconciliation; but, in accordance with justice, the rights of the wives [with regard to their husbands] are equal to the [husbands'] rights with regard to them, although men have precedence over them [in this respect].[216] And God is almighty, wise. «228»
A divorce may be [revoked] twice, whereupon the marriage must either be resumed in fairness or dissolved in a goodly manner.[217]
And it is not lawful for you to take back anything of what you have ever given to your wives unless both [partners] have cause to fear that they may not be able to keep within the bounds set by God: hence, if you have cause to fear that the two may not be able to keep within the bounds set by God, there shall be no sin upon either of them for what the wife may give up [to her husband] in order to free herself.[218]
These are the bounds set by God; do not,

لِّلَّذِينَ يُؤْلُونَ مِن نِّسَآئِهِمْ تَرَبُّصُ أَرْبَعَةِ أَشْهُرٍ فَإِن فَآءُو فَإِنَّ ٱللَّهَ غَفُورٌ
رَّحِيمٌ ﴿٢٢٦﴾ وَإِنْ عَزَمُوا۟ ٱلطَّلَٰقَ فَإِنَّ ٱللَّهَ سَمِيعٌ عَلِيمٌ ﴿٢٢٧﴾ وَٱلْمُطَلَّقَٰتُ
يَتَرَبَّصْنَ بِأَنفُسِهِنَّ ثَلَٰثَةَ قُرُوٓءٍ وَلَا يَحِلُّ لَهُنَّ أَن يَكْتُمْنَ مَا
خَلَقَ ٱللَّهُ فِىٓ أَرْحَامِهِنَّ إِن كُنَّ يُؤْمِنَّ بِٱللَّهِ وَٱلْيَوْمِ ٱلْءَاخِرِ وَبُعُولَتُهُنَّ
أَحَقُّ بِرَدِّهِنَّ فِى ذَٰلِكَ إِنْ أَرَادُوٓا۟ إِصْلَٰحًا وَلَهُنَّ مِثْلُ ٱلَّذِى عَلَيْهِنَّ
بِٱلْمَعْرُوفِ وَلِلرِّجَالِ عَلَيْهِنَّ دَرَجَةٌ وَٱللَّهُ عَزِيزٌ حَكِيمٌ ﴿٢٢٨﴾ ٱلطَّلَٰقُ مَرَّتَانِ
فَإِمْسَاكٌۢ بِمَعْرُوفٍ أَوْ تَسْرِيحٌۢ بِإِحْسَٰنٍ وَلَا يَحِلُّ لَكُمْ أَن تَأْخُذُوا۟ مِمَّآ
ءَاتَيْتُمُوهُنَّ شَيْـًٔا إِلَّآ أَن يَخَافَآ أَلَّا يُقِيمَا حُدُودَ ٱللَّهِ فَإِنْ خِفْتُمْ أَلَّا
يُقِيمَا حُدُودَ ٱللَّهِ فَلَا جُنَاحَ عَلَيْهِمَا فِيمَا ٱفْتَدَتْ بِهِۦ تِلْكَ حُدُودُ ٱللَّهِ فَلَا

Lilladhīna yuʾlūna min-nisāaʾihim tarabbuṣu ʾarbaʿati ʾashhuriñ-faʾiñ-fāaʾū faʾinnal-lāha Ghafūrur-Raḥīm. (226) Wa ʾin ʿazamuṭ-ṭalāqa faʾinnal-lāha Samīʿun ʿAlīm. (227) Wal-muṭallaqātu yatarabbaṣna biʾañfusihinna thalāthata qurūuʾ. Wa lā yaḥillu lahunna ʾañy-yaktumna mā khalaqal-lāhu fīi ʾarḥāmihinna ʾiñ-kunna yuʾminna billāhi wal-Yawmil-ʾĀkhir. Wa buʿūlatuhunna ʾaḥaqqu biraddihinna fī dhālika ʾin ʾarādūu ʾiṣlāḥā. Wa lahunna mithlul-ladhī ʿalayhinna bilmaʿrūf. Wa lirrijāli ʿalayhinna darajah. Wal-lāhu ʿAzīzun Ḥakīm. (228) ʾAṭṭalāqu marratāni faʾimsākum-bimaʿrūfin ʾaw tasrīḥum-biʾiḥsān. Wa lā yaḥillu lakum ʾañ-taʾkhudhū mimmāa ʾātaytumūhunna shayʾan ʾillāa ʾañy-yakhāfāa ʾallā yuqīmā ḥudūdal-lāh. Faʾin khiftum ʾallā yuqīmā ḥudūdal-lāhi falā junāḥa ʿalayhimā fīmaf-tadat bih. Tilka ḥudūdul-lāhi falā

213 I.e., during this period of grace.

214 Lit., "by themselves".

215 The primary purpose of this waiting-period is the ascertainment of possible pregnancy, and thus of the parentage of the as yet unborn child. In addition, the couple are to be given an opportunity to reconsider their decision and possibly to resume the marriage. See also 65 : 1 and the corresponding note 2.

216 A divorced wife has the right to refuse a resumption of marital relations even if the husband expresses, before the expiry of the waiting-period, his willingness to have the provisional divorce rescinded; but since it is the husband who is responsible for the maintenance of the family, the first option to rescind a provisional divorce rests with him.

217 Lit., "whereupon either retention in fairness or release in a goodly manner". In other words, a third pronouncement of divorce makes it final and irrevocable.

218 All authorities agree in that this verse relates to the unconditional right on the part of the wife to obtain a divorce from her husband; such a dissolution of marriage at the wife's instance is called *khulʿ*. There exist a number of highly-authenticated Traditions to the effect that the wife of Thābit ibn Qays, Jamīlah, came to the Prophet and

تَعْتَدُوهَا وَمَن يَتَعَدَّ حُدُودَ ٱللَّهِ فَأُو۟لَٰٓئِكَ هُمُ ٱلظَّٰلِمُونَ ﴿٢٢٩﴾ فَإِن طَلَّقَهَا
فَلَا تَحِلُّ لَهُۥ مِنۢ بَعْدُ حَتَّىٰ تَنكِحَ زَوْجًا غَيْرَهُۥ فَإِن طَلَّقَهَا فَلَا جُنَاحَ
عَلَيْهِمَآ أَن يَتَرَاجَعَآ إِن ظَنَّآ أَن يُقِيمَا حُدُودَ ٱللَّهِ وَتِلْكَ حُدُودُ ٱللَّهِ يُبَيِّنُهَا
لِقَوْمٍ يَعْلَمُونَ ﴿٢٣٠﴾ وَإِذَا طَلَّقْتُمُ ٱلنِّسَآءَ فَبَلَغْنَ أَجَلَهُنَّ فَأَمْسِكُوهُنَّ
بِمَعْرُوفٍ أَوْ سَرِّحُوهُنَّ بِمَعْرُوفٍ وَلَا تُمْسِكُوهُنَّ ضِرَارًا لِّتَعْتَدُوا۟ وَمَن
يَفْعَلْ ذَٰلِكَ فَقَدْ ظَلَمَ نَفْسَهُۥ وَلَا تَتَّخِذُوٓا۟ ءَايَٰتِ ٱللَّهِ هُزُوًا وَٱذْكُرُوا۟
نِعْمَتَ ٱللَّهِ عَلَيْكُمْ وَمَآ أَنزَلَ عَلَيْكُم مِّنَ ٱلْكِتَٰبِ وَٱلْحِكْمَةِ يَعِظُكُم
بِهِۦ وَٱتَّقُوا۟ ٱللَّهَ وَٱعْلَمُوٓا۟ أَنَّ ٱللَّهَ بِكُلِّ شَىْءٍ عَلِيمٌ ﴿٢٣١﴾ وَإِذَا طَلَّقْتُمُ
ٱلنِّسَآءَ فَبَلَغْنَ أَجَلَهُنَّ فَلَا تَعْضُلُوهُنَّ أَن يَنكِحْنَ أَزْوَٰجَهُنَّ إِذَا
تَرَٰضَوْا۟ بَيْنَهُم بِٱلْمَعْرُوفِ ذَٰلِكَ يُوعَظُ بِهِۦ مَن كَانَ مِنكُمْ يُؤْمِنُ بِٱللَّهِ

taʿtadūhā. Wa mañy-yataʿadda ḥudūdal-lāhi faʾulāaʾika humuẓ-ẓālimūn. (229) Faʾiñ-ṭallaqahā falā taḥillu lahū mim-baʿdu ḥattā tañkiḥa zawjan ghayrah. Faʾiñ-ṭallaqahā falā junāḥa ʿalayhimāa ʾañy-yatarājaʿāa ʾiñ-ẓannāa ʾañy-yuqīmā ḥudūdal-lāh. Wa tilka ḥudūdul-lāhi yubayyinuhā liqawmiñy-yaʿlamūn. (230) Wa ʾidhā ṭallaqtumun-nisāaʾa fabalaghna ʾajalahunna faʾamsikūhunna bimaʿrūfin ʾaw sarriḥūhunna bimaʿrūf. Wa lā tumsikūhunna ḍirāral-litaʿtadū. Wa mañy-yafʿal dhālika faqad ẓalama nafsah. Wa lā tattakhidhūu ʾĀyātil-lāhi huzuwā. Wadh-kurū niʿmatal-lāhi ʿalaykum wa māa ʾañzala ʿalaykum-minal-Kitābi wal-ḥikmati yaʿiẓukum-bih. Wat-taqul-lāha waʿ-lamūu ʾannal-lāha bikulli shayʾin ʿAlīm. (231) Wa ʾidhā ṭallaqtumun-nisāaʾa fabalaghna ʾajalahunna falā taʿḍulūhunna ʾañy-yañkiḥna ʾazwājahunna ʾidhā tarāḍaw baynahum bilmaʿrūf. Dhālika yūʿaẓu bihī mañ-kāna miñkum yuʾminu billāhi

then, transgress them: for they who transgress the bounds set by God – it is they, they who are evildoers! «229»

And if he divorces her [finally], she shall thereafter not be lawful unto him unless she first takes another man for husband; then, if the latter divorces her, there shall be no sin upon either of the two if they return to one another – provided that both of them think that they will be able to keep within the bounds set by God: for these are the bounds of God which He makes clear unto people of [innate] knowledge. «230»

And so, when you divorce women and they are about to reach the end of their waiting-term, then either retain them in a fair manner or let them go in a fair manner. But do not retain them against their will in order to hurt [them]: for he who does so sins indeed against himself.

And do not take [these] messages of God in a frivolous spirit; and remember the blessings with which God has graced you, and all the revelation and the wisdom which He has bestowed on you from on high in order to admonish you thereby; and remain conscious of God, and know that God has full knowledge of everything. «231»

And when you divorce women, and they have come to the end of their waiting-term, hinder them not from marrying other men if they have agreed with each other in a fair manner. This is an admonition unto every one of you who believes in God

demanded a divorce from her husband on the ground that, in spite of his irreproachable character and behaviour, she "disliked him as she would dislike falling into unbelief after having accepted Islam". Thereupon the Prophet ordained that she should return to Thābit the garden which he has given her as her dower (*mahr*) at the time of their wedding, and decreed that the marriage should be dissolved. (Several variants of this Tradition have been recorded by Bukhārī, Nasāʾī, Tirmidhī, Ibn Mājah and Bayhaqī, on the authority of Ibn ʿAbbās.) Similar Traditions, handed down on the authority of ʿĀʾishah and relating to a woman called Ḥubaybah bint Sahl, are to be found in the *Muwaṭṭaʾ* of Imām Mālik, in the *Musnad* of Imām Aḥmad, and in the compilations of Nasāʾī and Abū Dāʾūd (in one variant, the latter gives the woman's name as Ḥafṣah bint Sahl). In accordance with these Traditions, Islamic Law stipulates that whenever a marriage is dissolved at the wife's instance *without* any offence on the part of the husband against his marital obligations, the wife is the contract-breaking party and must, therefore, return the dower which she received from him at the time of concluding the marriage: and in this event "there shall be no sin upon either of them" if the husband takes back the dower which the wife gives up of her own free will. An exhaustive discussion of all these Traditions and their legal implications is found in *Nayl al-Awṭār* VII, pp. 34-41. For a summary of the relevant views of the various schools of Islamic jurisprudence, see *Bidāyat al-Mujtahid* II, pp. 54-57.

and the Last Day; it is the most virtuous [way] for you, and the cleanest. And God knows, whereas you do not know. «232»

And the [divorced] mothers may nurse their children for two whole years, if they wish to complete the period of nursing; and it is incumbent upon him who has begotten the child to provide in a fair manner for their sustenance and clothing. No human being shall be burdened with more than he is well able to bear: neither shall a mother be made to suffer because of her child, nor, because of his child, he who has begotten it. And the same duty rests upon the [father's] heir.

And if both [parents] decide, by mutual consent and counsel, upon separation [of mother and child],[219] they will incur no sin [thereby]; and if you decide to entrust your children to foster-mothers, you will incur no sin provided you ensure, in a fair manner, the safety of the child which you are handing over.[220] But remain conscious of God, and know that God sees all that you do. «233»

And if any of you die and leave wives behind, they shall undergo, without remarrying[221] a waiting period of four months and ten days; whereupon, when they have reached the end of their waiting-term, there shall be no sin[222] in whatever they may do with their persons in a lawful manner. And God is aware of all that you do. «234»

وَٱلْيَوْمِ ٱلْءَاخِرِ ذَٰلِكُمْ أَزْكَىٰ لَكُمْ وَأَطْهَرُ وَٱللَّهُ يَعْلَمُ وَأَنتُمْ لَا تَعْلَمُونَ ﴿٢٣٢﴾
۞ وَٱلْوَٰلِدَٰتُ يُرْضِعْنَ أَوْلَٰدَهُنَّ حَوْلَيْنِ كَامِلَيْنِ لِمَنْ أَرَادَ أَن يُتِمَّ ٱلرَّضَاعَةَ
وَعَلَى ٱلْمَوْلُودِ لَهُۥ رِزْقُهُنَّ وَكِسْوَتُهُنَّ بِٱلْمَعْرُوفِ لَا تُكَلَّفُ نَفْسٌ إِلَّا وُسْعَهَا
لَا تُضَآرَّ وَٰلِدَةٌۢ بِوَلَدِهَا وَلَا مَوْلُودٌ لَّهُۥ بِوَلَدِهِۦ وَعَلَى ٱلْوَارِثِ مِثْلُ ذَٰلِكَ فَإِنْ
أَرَادَا فِصَالًا عَن تَرَاضٍ مِّنْهُمَا وَتَشَاوُرٍ فَلَا جُنَاحَ عَلَيْهِمَا وَإِنْ أَرَدتُّمْ أَن
تَسْتَرْضِعُوٓا۟ أَوْلَٰدَكُمْ فَلَا جُنَاحَ عَلَيْكُمْ إِذَا سَلَّمْتُم مَّآ ءَاتَيْتُم بِٱلْمَعْرُوفِ
وَٱتَّقُوا۟ ٱللَّهَ وَٱعْلَمُوٓا۟ أَنَّ ٱللَّهَ بِمَا تَعْمَلُونَ بَصِيرٌ ﴿٢٣٣﴾ وَٱلَّذِينَ يُتَوَفَّوْنَ مِنكُمْ
وَيَذَرُونَ أَزْوَٰجًا يَتَرَبَّصْنَ بِأَنفُسِهِنَّ أَرْبَعَةَ أَشْهُرٍ وَعَشْرًا فَإِذَا بَلَغْنَ أَجَلَهُنَّ فَلَا
جُنَاحَ عَلَيْكُمْ فِيمَا فَعَلْنَ فِىٓ أَنفُسِهِنَّ بِٱلْمَعْرُوفِ وَٱللَّهُ بِمَا تَعْمَلُونَ خَبِيرٌ ﴿٢٣٤﴾

نصف الحزب

wal-Yawmil-ʾĀkhir. Dhālikum ʾazkā lakum wa ʾaṭhar. Wal-lāhu yaʿlamu wa ʾañtum lā taʿlamūn. (232) ۞ Wal-wālidātu yurḍiʿna ʾawlādahunna ḥawlayni kāmilayni liman ʾarāda añy-yutimmar-raḍāʿah. Wa ʿalal-mawlūdi lahū rizquhunna wa kiswatuhunna bil-maʿrūf. Lā tukallafu nafsun ʾillā wusʿahā. Lā tuḍāarra wālidatum-biwaladihā wa lā mawlūdul-lahū biwaladihī wa ʿalal-wārithi mithlu dhālik. Faʾin ʾarādā fiṣālan ʿañ-tarāḍim-minhummā wa tashāwuriñ-falā junāḥa ʿalayhimā. Wa ʾin ʾarattum ʾañ-tastarḍiʿūu ʾawlādakum falā junāḥa ʿalaykum ʾidhā sallamtum-māa ʾātaytum bilmaʿrūf. Wat-taqul-lāha waʿ-lamūu ʾannal-lāha bimā taʿmalūna Baṣīr. (233) Wal-ladhīna yutawaffawna miñkum wa yadharūna ʾazwājañy-yatarabbaṣna biʾañfusihina ʾarbaʿata ʾashhuriñw-wa ʿashrā. Faʾidhā balaghna ʾajalahunna falā junāḥa ʿalaykum fīmā faʿalna fii ʾañfusihinna bilmaʿrūf. Wal-lāhu bimā taʿmalūna Khabīr. (234)

219 Most of the commentators understand the word *fiṣāl* as being synonymous with "weaning" (i.e., before the end of the maximum period of two years). Abū Muslim, however, is of the opinion that it stands here for "separation" – i.e., of the child from its mother (Rāzī). It appears to me that this is the better of the two interpretations inasmuch as it provides a solution for cases in which both parents agree that, for some reason or other, it would not be fair to burden the divorced mother with the upbringing of the child despite the father's obligation to support them materially, while, on the other hand, it would not be feasible for the father to undertake this duty single-handed.

220 Lit., "provided you make safe [or "provided you surrender"] in a fair manner that which you are handing over". While it cannot be denied that the verb *sallamahu* can mean "he surrendered it" as well as "he made it safe", it seems to me that the latter meaning (which is the primary one) is preferable in this context since it implies the necessity of assuring the child's future safety and well-being. (The commentators who take the verb *sallamtum* in the sense of "you surrender" interpret the phrase *idhā sallamtum mā ātaytum bi'l-maʿrūf* as meaning "provided you hand over the agreed-upon [wages to the foster-mothers] in a fair manner" – which, to my mind, unduly limits the purport of the above injunction.)

221 Lit., "by themselves".

222 Lit., "you will incur no sin". Since, obviously, the whole community is addressed here (Zamakhsharī), the rendering "there shall be no sin" would seem appropriate.

وَلَا جُنَاحَ عَلَيْكُمْ فِيمَا عَرَّضْتُم بِهِۦ مِنْ خِطْبَةِ ٱلنِّسَآءِ أَوْ أَكْنَنتُمْ فِىٓ أَنفُسِكُمْ ۚ
عَلِمَ ٱللَّهُ أَنَّكُمْ سَتَذْكُرُونَهُنَّ وَلَـٰكِن لَّا تُوَاعِدُوهُنَّ سِرًّا إِلَّآ أَن تَقُولُوا۟ قَوْلًا
مَّعْرُوفًا ۚ وَلَا تَعْزِمُوا۟ عُقْدَةَ ٱلنِّكَاحِ حَتَّىٰ يَبْلُغَ ٱلْكِتَـٰبُ أَجَلَهُۥ ۚ وَٱعْلَمُوٓا۟ أَنَّ ٱللَّهَ
يَعْلَمُ مَا فِىٓ أَنفُسِكُمْ فَٱحْذَرُوهُ ۚ وَٱعْلَمُوٓا۟ أَنَّ ٱللَّهَ غَفُورٌ حَلِيمٌ ﴿٢٣٥﴾ لَّا جُنَاحَ
عَلَيْكُمْ إِن طَلَّقْتُمُ ٱلنِّسَآءَ مَا لَمْ تَمَسُّوهُنَّ أَوْ تَفْرِضُوا۟ لَهُنَّ فَرِيضَةً ۚ وَمَتِّعُوهُنَّ
عَلَى ٱلْمُوسِعِ قَدَرُهُۥ وَعَلَى ٱلْمُقْتِرِ قَدَرُهُۥ مَتَـٰعًۢا بِٱلْمَعْرُوفِ ۖ حَقًّا عَلَى
ٱلْمُحْسِنِينَ ﴿٢٣٦﴾ وَإِن طَلَّقْتُمُوهُنَّ مِن قَبْلِ أَن تَمَسُّوهُنَّ وَقَدْ فَرَضْتُمْ لَهُنَّ
فَرِيضَةً فَنِصْفُ مَا فَرَضْتُمْ إِلَّآ أَن يَعْفُونَ أَوْ يَعْفُوَا۟ ٱلَّذِى بِيَدِهِۦ عُقْدَةُ ٱلنِّكَاحِ ۚ
وَأَن تَعْفُوٓا۟ أَقْرَبُ لِلتَّقْوَىٰ ۚ وَلَا تَنسَوُا۟ ٱلْفَضْلَ بَيْنَكُمْ ۚ إِنَّ ٱللَّهَ بِمَا تَعْمَلُونَ
بَصِيرٌ ﴿٢٣٧﴾ حَـٰفِظُوا۟ عَلَى ٱلصَّلَوَٰتِ وَٱلصَّلَوٰةِ ٱلْوُسْطَىٰ وَقُومُوا۟ لِلَّهِ قَـٰنِتِينَ ﴿٢٣٨﴾

Wa lā junāḥa ʿalaykum fīmā ʿarraḍtum-bihī min khiṭbatin-nisāaʾi ʾaw ʾaknañtum fii ʾañfusikum. ʿAlimal-lāhu ʾannakum satadhkurūnahunna wa lākil-lā tuwāʿidūhunna sirran ʾillāa ʾañ-taqūlū qawlam-maʿrūfā. Wa lā taʿzimū ʿuqdatan-nikāḥi ḥattā yablughal-kitābu ʾajalah. Waʿ-lamūu ʾannal-lāha yaʿlamu mā fii ʾañfusikum faḥdharūhu waʿ-lamūu ʾannal-lāha Ghafūrun Ḥalīm. (235) Lā junāḥa ʿalaykum ʾiñ-ṭallaqtumun-nisāaʾa mā lam tamassūhunna ʾaw tafriḍū lahunna farīḍah. Wa mattiʿūhunna ʿalal-mūsiʿi qadaruhū wa ʿalal-muqtiri qadaruhu matāʿam-bilmaʿrūfi ḥaqqan ʿalal-muḥsinīn. (236) Wa ʾiñ-ṭallaqtumūhunna miñ-qabli ʾañ-tamassūhunna wa qad faraḍtum lahunna farīḍatañ-faniṣfu mā faraḍtum ʾillāa ʾañy-yaʿfūna ʾaw yaʿfuwal-ladhī biyadihī ʿuqdatun-nikāḥ. Wa ʾañ-taʿfūu ʾaqrabu littaqwā. Wa lā tañsawul-faḍla baynakum. ʾInnal-lāha bimā taʿmalūna Baṣīr. (237) Ḥāfiẓu ʿalaṣ-Ṣalawāti waṣ-Ṣalātil-wusṭā wa qūmū lillāhi qānitīn. (238)

But you will incur no sin if you give a hint of [an intended] marriage-offer to [any of] these women, or if you conceive such an intention without making it obvious: [for] God knows that you intend to ask them in marriage.[223] Do not, however, plight your troth with them in secret, but speak only in a decent manner; and do not proceed with tying the marriage-knot ere the ordained [term of waiting] has come to its end. And know that God knows what is in your minds, and therefore remain conscious of Him; and know, too, that God is much-forgiving, forbearing. ‹235›

You will incur no sin if you divorce women while you have not yet touched them nor settled a dower upon them;[224] but [even in such a case] make provision for them – the affluent according to his means, and the straitened according to his means – a provision in an equitable manner: this is a duty upon all who would do good.[225] ‹236›

And if you divorce them before having touched them, but after having settled a dower upon them, then [give them] half of what you have settled – unless it be that they forgo their claim or he in whose hand is the marriage-tie[226] forgoes his claim [to half of the dower]: and to forgo what is due to you is more in accord with God-consciousness. And forget not [that you are to act with] grace towards one another: verily, God sees all that you do. ‹237›

BE EVER mindful of prayers, and of praying in the most excellent way;[227] and stand before God in devout obedience. ‹238›

223 Lit., "if you conceal [such an intention] within yourselves: [for] God knows that you will mention [it] to them". In classical Arabic usage, the expression *dhakarahā* ("he mentioned [it] to her") is often idiomatically synonymous with "he demanded her in marriage" (see Lane III, 969). The above passage relates to a marriage-offer – or to an intention of making such an offer – to a newly-widowed or divorced woman before the expiry of the prescribed waiting-term.

224 The term *farīḍah* denotes the dower (often also called *mahr*) which must be agreed upon by bridegroom and bride before the conclusion of the marriage-tie. While the amount of this dower is left to the discretion of the two contracting parties (and may even consist of no more than a token gift), its stipulation is an essential part of an Islamic marriage contract. For exceptions from this rule, see 33 : 50 and the corresponding note 58.

225 Lit., "upon the doers of good" – i.e., all who are determined to act in accordance with God's will.

226 According to some of the most prominent Companions of the Prophet (e.g., ʿAlī) and their immediate successors (e.g., Saʿīd ibn al-Musayyab and Saʿīd ibn Jubayr), this term denotes the *husband* (cf. Ṭabarī, Zamakhsharī, Baghawī, Rāzī and Ibn Kathīr).

227 Lit., "the midmost [or "the most excellent"] prayer". It is generally assumed that this refers to the mid-

But if you are in danger, [pray] walking or riding;[228] and when you are again secure, bear God in mind – since it is He who taught you what you did not previously know. ‹239›

AND IF any of you die and leave wives behind, they bequeath thereby to their widows [the right to] one year's maintenance without their being obliged to leave [the dead husband's home].[229] If, however, they leave [of their own accord], there shall be no sin in whatever they may do with themselves in a lawful manner.[230] And God is almighty, wise. ‹240›

And the divorced women, too, shall have [a right to] maintenance in a goodly manner:[231] this is a duty for all who are conscious of God. ‹241›

In this way God makes clear unto you His messages, so that you might [learn to] use your reason. ‹242›

ART THOU NOT aware of those who forsook their homelands in their thousands for fear of death – whereupon God said unto them, "Die," and later brought them back to life?[232]

Behold, God is indeed limitless in His bounty unto man – but most people are ungrateful. ‹243›

فَإِنْ خِفْتُمْ فَرِجَالًا أَوْ رُكْبَانًا فَإِذَآ أَمِنتُمْ فَٱذْكُرُوا۟ ٱللَّهَ كَمَا عَلَّمَكُم مَّا
لَمْ تَكُونُوا۟ تَعْلَمُونَ ﴿٢٣٩﴾ وَٱلَّذِينَ يُتَوَفَّوْنَ مِنكُمْ وَيَذَرُونَ أَزْوَٰجًا وَصِيَّةً
لِّأَزْوَٰجِهِم مَّتَٰعًا إِلَى ٱلْحَوْلِ غَيْرَ إِخْرَاجٍ فَإِنْ خَرَجْنَ فَلَا جُنَاحَ
عَلَيْكُمْ فِى مَا فَعَلْنَ فِىٓ أَنفُسِهِنَّ مِن مَّعْرُوفٍ وَٱللَّهُ عَزِيزٌ حَكِيمٌ ﴿٢٤٠﴾
وَلِلْمُطَلَّقَٰتِ مَتَٰعٌۢ بِٱلْمَعْرُوفِ حَقًّا عَلَى ٱلْمُتَّقِينَ ﴿٢٤١﴾ كَذَٰلِكَ يُبَيِّنُ
ٱللَّهُ لَكُمْ ءَايَٰتِهِۦ لَعَلَّكُمْ تَعْقِلُونَ ﴿٢٤٢﴾ ۞ أَلَمْ تَرَ إِلَى ٱلَّذِينَ خَرَجُوا۟ مِن
دِيَٰرِهِمْ وَهُمْ أُلُوفٌ حَذَرَ ٱلْمَوْتِ فَقَالَ لَهُمُ ٱللَّهُ مُوتُوا۟ ثُمَّ أَحْيَٰهُمْ إِنَّ
ٱللَّهَ لَذُو فَضْلٍ عَلَى ٱلنَّاسِ وَلَٰكِنَّ أَكْثَرَ ٱلنَّاسِ لَا يَشْكُرُونَ ﴿٢٤٣﴾

ثلاثة ارباع الحزب

Faʾin khiftum farijālan ʾaw rukbānā. Faʾidhāa ʾamiñtum fadhkurul-lāha kamā ʿallamakum-mā lam takūnū taʿlamūn. (239) Wal-ladhīna yutawaffawna miñkum wa yadharūna ʾazwājañw-waṣiyyatal-liʾazwājihim-matāʿan ʾilal-ḥawli ghayra ʾikhrāj. Faʾin kharajna falā junāḥa ʿalaykum fīmā faʿalna fīi ʾañfusihinna mim-maʿrūf. Wal-lāhu ʿAzīzun-Ḥakīm. (240) Wa lilmuṭallaqāti matāʿum-bilmaʿrūfi ḥaqqan ʿalal-muttaqīn. (241) Kadhālika yubayyinul-lāhu lakum ʾĀyātihī laʿallakum taʿqilūn. (242) ۞ ʾAlam tara ʾilal-ladhīna kharajū miñ-diyārihim wa hum ʾulūfun ḥadharal-mawti faqāla lahumul-lāhu mūtū thumma ʾaḥyāhum. ʾInnal-lāha ladhū-faḍlin ʿalan-nāsi wa lākinna ʾaktharan-nāsi lā yashkurūn. (243)

afternoon (*ʿasr*) prayer, although some authorities believe that it denotes the prayer at dawn (*fajr*). Muḥammad ʿAbduh, however, advances the view that it may mean "the *noblest* kind of prayer – that is, a prayer from the fullness of the heart, with the whole mind turned towards God, inspired by awe of Him, and reflecting upon His word" (*Manār* II, 438). – In accordance with the system prevailing throughout the Qurʾān, any lengthy section dealing with social laws is almost invariably followed by a call to God-consciousness: and since God-consciousness comes most fully to its own in prayer, this and the next verse are interpolated here between injunctions relating to marital life and divorce.

228 This relates to any dangerous situation – for instance, in war – where remaining for any length of time at one place would only increase the peril: in such an event, the obligatory prayers may be offered in any way that is feasible, even without consideration of the *qiblah*.

229 Lit., "[it is] a bequest to their wives [of] one year's maintenance without being dislodged". (As regards the justification of the rendering adopted by me, see *Manār* II, 446 ff.). The question of a widow's residence in her dead husband's house arises, of course, only in the event that it has not been bequeathed to her outright under the provisions stipulated in 4 : 12.

230 For instance, by remarrying – in which case they forgo their claim to additional maintenance during the remainder of the year. Regarding the phrase "there shall be no sin", see note 222 above.

231 This obviously relates to women who are divorced without any legal fault on their part. The amount of alimony – payable unless and until they remarry – has been left unspecified since it must depend on the husband's financial circumstances and on the social conditions of the time.

232 After the conclusion of the injunctions relating to marital life, the Qurʾān returns here to the problem of warfare in a just cause by alluding to people who – obviously under a hostile attack – "forsook their homelands for fear of death".

Fight, then, in God's cause,[233] and know that God is all-hearing, all-knowing. ‹244›
Who is it that will offer up unto God a goodly loan,[234] which He will amply repay, with manifold increase? For, God takes away, and He gives abundantly; and it is unto Him that you shall be brought back. ‹245›
Art thou not aware of those elders of the children of Israel, after the time of Moses, how they said unto a prophet of theirs,[235] "Raise up a king for us, [and] we shall fight in God's cause"?
Said he: "Would you, perchance, refrain from fighting if fighting is ordained for you?"
They answered: "And why should we not fight in God's cause when we and our children have been driven from our homelands?"[236]
Yet, when fighting was ordained for them, they did turn back, save for a few of them; but God had full knowledge of the evildoers. ‹246›
And their prophet said unto those elders:[237] "Behold, now God has raised up Saul to be your king."
They said: "How can he have dominion over us when we have a better claim to dominion than he, and he has not [even] been endowed with abundant wealth?"
[The prophet] replied: "Behold, God has exalted him above you, and endowed him abundantly with knowledge and bodily perfection. And God bestows His

وَقَٰتِلُوا۟ فِى سَبِيلِ ٱللَّهِ وَٱعْلَمُوٓا۟ أَنَّ ٱللَّهَ سَمِيعٌ عَلِيمٌ ﴿٢٤٤﴾ مَّن ذَا ٱلَّذِى
يُقْرِضُ ٱللَّهَ قَرْضًا حَسَنًا فَيُضَٰعِفَهُۥ لَهُۥٓ أَضْعَافًا كَثِيرَةً ۚ وَٱللَّهُ يَقْبِضُ
وَيَبْصُۜطُ وَإِلَيْهِ تُرْجَعُونَ ﴿٢٤٥﴾ أَلَمْ تَرَ إِلَى ٱلْمَلَإِ مِنۢ بَنِىٓ إِسْرَٰٓءِيلَ مِنۢ
بَعْدِ مُوسَىٰٓ إِذْ قَالُوا۟ لِنَبِىٍّ لَّهُمُ ٱبْعَثْ لَنَا مَلِكًا نُّقَٰتِلْ فِى سَبِيلِ ٱللَّهِ ۖ قَالَ
هَلْ عَسَيْتُمْ إِن كُتِبَ عَلَيْكُمُ ٱلْقِتَالُ أَلَّا تُقَٰتِلُوا۟ ۖ قَالُوا۟ وَمَا لَنَآ أَلَّا
نُقَٰتِلَ فِى سَبِيلِ ٱللَّهِ وَقَدْ أُخْرِجْنَا مِن دِيَٰرِنَا وَأَبْنَآئِنَا ۖ فَلَمَّا كُتِبَ عَلَيْهِمُ
ٱلْقِتَالُ تَوَلَّوْا۟ إِلَّا قَلِيلًا مِّنْهُمْ ۗ وَٱللَّهُ عَلِيمٌۢ بِٱلظَّٰلِمِينَ ﴿٢٤٦﴾ وَقَالَ لَهُمْ
نَبِيُّهُمْ إِنَّ ٱللَّهَ قَدْ بَعَثَ لَكُمْ طَالُوتَ مَلِكًا ۚ قَالُوٓا۟ أَنَّىٰ يَكُونُ لَهُ ٱلْمُلْكُ
عَلَيْنَا وَنَحْنُ أَحَقُّ بِٱلْمُلْكِ مِنْهُ وَلَمْ يُؤْتَ سَعَةً مِّنَ ٱلْمَالِ ۚ قَالَ إِنَّ ٱللَّهَ
ٱصْطَفَىٰهُ عَلَيْكُمْ وَزَادَهُۥ بَسْطَةً فِى ٱلْعِلْمِ وَٱلْجِسْمِ ۖ وَٱللَّهُ يُؤْتِى

Wa qātilū fī sabīlil-lāhi waᶜ-lamūu ᵓannal-lāha Samīᶜun ᶜAlīm. (244) Mañ-dhal-ladhī yuqriḍul-lāha qarḍan ḥasanañ-fayuḍāᶜifahū lahūu ᵓaḍᶜāfañ-kathīrah. Wal-lāhu yaqbiḍu wa yabsuṭu wa ᵓilayhi turjaᶜūn. (245) ᵓAlam tara ᵓilal-malaᵓi mim-banīi ᵓIsrāaᵓīla mim-baᶜdi Mūsāa ᵓidh qālū liNabiyyil-lahumub-ᵓath lanā Malikañ-nuqātil fī sabīlil-lāh. Qāla hal ᶜasaytum ᵓiñ-kutiba ᶜalaykumul-qitālu ᵓallā tuqātilū. Qālū wa mā lanāa ᵓallā nuqātila fī sabīlil-lāhi wa qad ᵓukhrijnā miñ-diyārinā wa ᵓabnāaᵓinā. Falammā kutiba ᶜalay-himul-qitālu tawallaw ᵓillā qalīlam-minhum. Wal-lāhu ᶜAlīmum-biẓẓālimīn. (246) Wa qāla lahum Nabiy-yuhum ᵓinnal-lāha qad baᶜatha lakum Ṭālūta malikā. Qālūu ᵓannā yakūnu lahul-mulku ᶜalaynā wa naḥnu ᵓaḥaqqu bilmulki minhu wa lam yuᵓta saᶜatam-minal-māl. Qāla ᵓinnal-lāhaṣ-ṭafāhu ᶜalaykum wa zādahū basṭatañ-fil-ᶜilmi wal-jism. Wal-lāhu yuᵓtī

Now, neither the Qurᵓān nor any authentic Tradition offers any indication as to who the people referred to in this verse may have been. The "historical" explanations given by some of the commentators are most contradictory; they seem to have been derived from Talmudic stories current at the time, and cannot be used in this context with any justification. We must, therefore, assume (as Muḥammad ᶜAbduh does in *Manār* II, 455 ff.) that the above allusion is parabolically connected with the subsequent call to the faithful to be ready to lay down their lives in God's cause: an illustration of the fact that fear of physical death leads to the moral death of nations and communities, just as their regeneration (or "coming back to life") depends on their regaining their moral status through overcoming the fear of death. This is undoubtedly the purport of the elliptic story of Samuel, Saul and David told in verses 246-251.

233 I.e., in a just war in self-defence against oppression or unprovoked aggression (cf. 2 : 190-194).

234 I.e., by sacrificing one's life in, or devoting it to, His cause.

235 The prophet referred to here is Samuel (cf. Old Testament, I Samuel viii ff.).

236 Obviously a reference to the many invasions of their homelands by their perennial enemies, the Philistines, Amorites, Amalekites and other Semitic and non-Semitic tribes living in and around Palestine; and, by implication, a reminder to believers of all times that "fighting in God's cause" (as defined in the Qurᵓān) is an act of faith.

237 Lit., "to them" – but the next sentence shows that the *elders* were thus addressed by Samuel.

dominion[238] upon whom He wills: for God is infinite, all-knowing." ‹247›

And their prophet said unto them: "Behold, it shall be a sign of his [rightful] dominion that you will be granted a heart[239] endowed by your Sustainer with inner peace and with all that is enduring in the angel-borne heritage left behind by the House of Moses and the House of Aaron.[240] Herein, behold, there shall indeed be a sign for you if you are [truly] believers." ‹248›

And when Saul set out with his forces, he said: "Behold, God will now try you by a river: he who shall drink of it will not belong to me, whereas he who shall refrain from tasting it – he, indeed, will belong to me; but forgiven shall be he[241] who shall scoop up but a single handful." However, save for a few of them, they all drank [their fill] of it.

And as soon as he and those who had kept faith with him had crossed the river, the others said: "No strength have we today [to stand up] against Goliath and his forces!"

[Yet] those who knew with certainty that they were destined to meet God, replied: "How often has a small host overcome a great host by God's leave! For God is with those who are patient in adversity." ‹249›

مُلْكَهُۥ مَن يَشَآءُ ۚ وَٱللَّهُ وَٰسِعٌ عَلِيمٌ ﴿٢٤٧﴾ وَقَالَ لَهُمْ نَبِيُّهُمْ إِنَّ ءَايَةَ
مُلْكِهِۦٓ أَن يَأْتِيَكُمُ ٱلتَّابُوتُ فِيهِ سَكِينَةٌ مِّن رَّبِّكُمْ وَبَقِيَّةٌ مِّمَّا تَرَكَ
ءَالُ مُوسَىٰ وَءَالُ هَٰرُونَ تَحْمِلُهُ ٱلْمَلَٰٓئِكَةُ ۚ إِنَّ فِى ذَٰلِكَ لَءَايَةً لَّكُمْ إِن
كُنتُم مُّؤْمِنِينَ ﴿٢٤٨﴾ فَلَمَّا فَصَلَ طَالُوتُ بِٱلْجُنُودِ قَالَ إِنَّ ٱللَّهَ مُبْتَلِيكُم
بِنَهَرٍ فَمَن شَرِبَ مِنْهُ فَلَيْسَ مِنِّى وَمَن لَّمْ يَطْعَمْهُ فَإِنَّهُۥ مِنِّىٓ إِلَّا مَنِ
ٱغْتَرَفَ غُرْفَةًۢ بِيَدِهِۦ ۚ فَشَرِبُوا۟ مِنْهُ إِلَّا قَلِيلًا مِّنْهُمْ ۚ فَلَمَّا جَاوَزَهُۥ هُوَ
وَٱلَّذِينَ ءَامَنُوا۟ مَعَهُۥ قَالُوا۟ لَا طَاقَةَ لَنَا ٱلْيَوْمَ بِجَالُوتَ وَجُنُودِهِۦ ۚ قَالَ
ٱلَّذِينَ يَظُنُّونَ أَنَّهُم مُّلَٰقُوا۟ ٱللَّهِ كَم مِّن فِئَةٍ قَلِيلَةٍ غَلَبَتْ فِئَةً كَثِيرَةًۢ بِإِذْنِ
ٱللَّهِ ۗ وَٱللَّهُ مَعَ ٱلصَّٰبِرِينَ ﴿٢٤٩﴾

mulkahū mañy-yashāaʾ. Wal-lāhu Wāsiʿun ʿAlīm. ‹247› Wa qāla lahum Nabiyyuhum ʾinna ʾĀyata-mulkihīi ʾañy-yaʾtiyakumut-tābūtu fīhi sakīnatum-mir-Rabbikum wa baqiyyatum-mimmā taraka ʾālu Mūsā wa ʾālu Hārūna taḥmiluhul-Malāaʾikah. ʾInna fī dhālika laʾĀyatal-lakum ʾiñ- kuñtum-muʾminīn. ‹248› Falammā faṣala Ṭālūtu biljunūdi qāla ʾinnal-lāha mubtalīkum-binahariñ-famañ-shariba minhu falaysa minnī wa mal-lam yaṭʿamhu faʾinnahū minnīi ʾillā manighṭarafa ghurfatam-biyadih. Fasharibū minhu ʾillā qalīlam-minhum. Falammā jāwazahū huwa walladhīna ʾāmanū maʿahū qālū lā ṭāqata lanal-yawma biJālūta wa junūdih. Qālal-ladhīna yaẓunnūna ʾannahum-mulāqul-lāhi kam-miñ-fiʾatiñ-qalīlatin ghalabat fiʾatañ-kathīratam-biʾidhnil-lāh. Wal-lāhu maʿaṣ-ṣābirīn. ‹249›

238 An allusion to the Qurʾanic doctrine that all dominion and all that may be "owned" by man belongs to God alone, and that man holds it only in trust from Him.

239 Lit., "that there will come to you the heart". The word *tābūt* – here rendered as "heart" – has been conventionally interpreted as denoting the Ark of the Covenant mentioned in the Old Testament, which is said to have been a highly-ornamented chest or box. The explanations offered by most of the commentators who adopt the latter meaning are very contradictory, and seem to be based on Talmudic legends woven around that "ark". However, several authorities of the highest standing attribute to *tābūt* the meaning of "bosom" or "heart" as well: thus, Bayḍāwī in one of the alternatives offered in his commentary on this verse, as well as Zamakhsharī in his *Asās* (though not in the *Kashshāf*), Ibn al-Athīr in the *Nihāyah*, Rāghib, and *Taj al-ʿArūs* (the latter four in the article *tabata*); see also Lane I, 321, and IV, 1394 (art. *sakīnah*). If we take this to be the meaning of *tābūt* in the above context, it would be an allusion to the Israelites' coming change of heart (a change already indicated, in general terms, in verse 243 above). In view of the subsequent mention of the "inner peace" in the *tābūt*, its rendering as "heart" is definitely more appropriate than "ark".

240 Lit., "and the remainder of that which the House (*āl*) of Moses and the House of Aaron left behind, borne by the angels". The expression "borne by the angels" or "angel-borne" is an allusion to the God-inspired nature of the spiritual heritage left by those two prophets; while the "remainder" (*baqiyyah*) denotes that which is "lasting" or "enduring" in that heritage.

241 Lit., "excepting him". The symbolic implication is that faith – and, thus, belief in the justice of one's cause – has no value unless it is accompanied by heightened self-discipline and disregard of one's material interests.

حزب 5
جزء 3

وَلَمَّا بَرَزُوا۟ لِجَالُوتَ وَجُنُودِهِۦ قَالُوا۟ رَبَّنَآ أَفْرِغْ عَلَيْنَا صَبْرًا وَثَبِّتْ
أَقْدَامَنَا وَٱنصُرْنَا عَلَى ٱلْقَوْمِ ٱلْكَـٰفِرِينَ ﴿٢٥٠﴾ فَهَزَمُوهُم بِإِذْنِ ٱللَّهِ وَقَتَلَ
دَاوُۥدُ جَالُوتَ وَءَاتَىٰهُ ٱللَّهُ ٱلْمُلْكَ وَٱلْحِكْمَةَ وَعَلَّمَهُۥ مِمَّا يَشَآءُ ۗ وَلَوْلَا
دَفْعُ ٱللَّهِ ٱلنَّاسَ بَعْضَهُم بِبَعْضٍ لَّفَسَدَتِ ٱلْأَرْضُ وَلَـٰكِنَّ ٱللَّهَ ذُو
فَضْلٍ عَلَى ٱلْعَـٰلَمِينَ ﴿٢٥١﴾ تِلْكَ ءَايَـٰتُ ٱللَّهِ نَتْلُوهَا عَلَيْكَ بِٱلْحَقِّ ۚ وَإِنَّكَ
لَمِنَ ٱلْمُرْسَلِينَ ﴿٢٥٢﴾ ۞ تِلْكَ ٱلرُّسُلُ فَضَّلْنَا بَعْضَهُمْ عَلَىٰ بَعْضٍ ۘ مِّنْهُم
مَّن كَلَّمَ ٱللَّهُ ۖ وَرَفَعَ بَعْضَهُمْ دَرَجَـٰتٍ ۚ وَءَاتَيْنَا عِيسَى ٱبْنَ مَرْيَمَ ٱلْبَيِّنَـٰتِ
وَأَيَّدْنَـٰهُ بِرُوحِ ٱلْقُدُسِ ۗ وَلَوْ شَآءَ ٱللَّهُ مَا ٱقْتَتَلَ ٱلَّذِينَ مِنۢ بَعْدِهِم مِّنۢ بَعْدِ
مَا جَآءَتْهُمُ ٱلْبَيِّنَـٰتُ وَلَـٰكِنِ ٱخْتَلَفُوا۟ فَمِنْهُم مَّنْ ءَامَنَ وَمِنْهُم مَّن كَفَرَ ۚ
وَلَوْ شَآءَ ٱللَّهُ مَا ٱقْتَتَلُوا۟ وَلَـٰكِنَّ ٱللَّهَ يَفْعَلُ مَا يُرِيدُ ﴿٢٥٣﴾

Wa lammā barazū liJālūta wa junūdihī qālū Rabbanāa ʾafrigh ᶜalaynā ṣabrañw-wa thabbit ʾaqdāmanā wañ-ṣurnā ᶜalal-qawmil-kāfirīn. (250) Fa-hazamūhum-biʾidhnil-lāhi wa qatala Dāwūdu Jālūta wa ʾātāhul-lāhul-mulka wal-ḥikmata wa ᶜallamahū mimmā yashāaʾ. Wa lawlā dafᶜul-lāhin-nāsa baᶜḍahum-bibaᶜḍil-lafasadatil-ʾarḍu wa lākinnal-lāha Dhū-faḍlin ᶜalal-ᶜālamīn. (251) Tilka ʾĀyātul-lāhi natlūhā ᶜalayka bilḥaqq. Wa ʾinnaka laminal-Mursalīn. (252) ۞ Tilkar-Rusulu faḍḍalnā baᶜḍahum ᶜalā baᶜḍ. Minhum-mañ-kallamal-lāhu wa rafaᶜa baᶜḍahum darajāt. Wa ʾātaynā ᶜĪsab-na Maryamal-bayyināti wa ʾayyadnāhu biRūḥil-Qudus. Wa law shāaʾal-lāhu maq-tatalal-ladhīna mim-baᶜdihim-mim-baᶜdi mā jāaʾat-humul-bayyinātu wa lākinikh-talafū faminhum-man ʾāmana wa minhum-mañ-kafar. Wa law shāaʾal-lāhu maq-tatalū wa lākinnal-lāha yafᶜalu mā yurīd. (253)

And when they came face to face with Goliath and his forces, they prayed: "O our Sustainer! Shower us with patience in adversity, and make firm our steps, and succour us against the people who deny the truth!" ‹250›

And thereupon, by God's leave, they routed them. And David slew Goliath; and God bestowed upon him dominion, and wisdom, and imparted to him the knowledge of whatever He willed.

And if God had not enabled people to defend themselves against one another,[242] corruption would surely overwhelm the earth: but God is limitless in His bounty unto all the worlds. ‹251›

THESE are God's messages: We convey them unto thee, [O Prophet,] setting forth the truth – for, verily, thou art among those who have been entrusted with a message. ‹252› Some of these apostles have We endowed more highly than others: among them were such as were spoken to by God [Himself], and some He has raised yet higher.[243] And We vouchsafed unto Jesus, the son of Mary, all evidence of the truth, and strengthened him with holy inspiration.[244]

And if God had so willed, they who succeeded those [apostles] would not have contended with one another after all evidence of the truth had come to them; but [as it was,] they did take to divergent views, and some of them attained to faith, while some of them came to deny the truth. Yet if God had so willed, they would not have contended with one another: but God does whatever He wills.[245] ‹253›

242 Lit., "were it not that God repels some people by means of others": an elliptic reference to God's enabling people to defend themselves against aggression or oppression. Exactly the same phrase occurs in 22 : 40, which deals with fighting in self-defence.

243 This appears to be an allusion to Muḥammad inasmuch as he was the Last Prophet and the bearer of a universal message applicable to all people and to all times. By "such as were spoken to by God" Moses is meant (see the last sentence of 4 : 164).

244 The mention, in this context, of Jesus by name is intended to stress the fact of his having been a prophet, and to refute the claims of those who deify him. For an explanation of the term *rūḥ al-qudus* (rendered by me as "holy inspiration"), see note 71 on verse 87 of this *sūrah*.

245 Once again – as in verse 213 above – the Qurʾān alludes to the inevitability of dissension among human beings: in other words, it is the will of God that their way to the truth should be marked by conflicts and trial by error.

O YOU who have attained to faith! Spend [in Our way] out of what We have granted you as sustenance ere there come a Day[246] when there will be no bargaining, and no friendship, and no intercession. And they who deny the truth – it is they who are evildoers! ‹254›

GOD – there is no deity save Him, the Ever-Living, the Self-Subsistent Fount of All Being.
Neither slumber overtakes Him, nor sleep. His is all that is in the heavens and all that is on earth. Who is there that could intercede with Him, unless it be by His leave?
He knows all that lies open before men and all that is hidden from them,[247] whereas they cannot attain to aught of His knowledge save that which He wills [them to attain].
His eternal power[248] overspreads the heavens and the earth, and their upholding wearies Him not. And He alone is truly exalted, tremendous. ‹255›

THERE SHALL BE no coercion in matters of faith.[249]
Distinct has now become the right way from [the way of] error: hence, he who rejects

يَٰٓأَيُّهَا ٱلَّذِينَ ءَامَنُوٓاْ أَنفِقُواْ مِمَّا رَزَقۡنَٰكُم مِّن قَبۡلِ أَن يَأۡتِيَ يَوۡمٞ لَّا بَيۡعٞ
فِيهِ وَلَا خُلَّةٞ وَلَا شَفَٰعَةٞۗ وَٱلۡكَٰفِرُونَ هُمُ ٱلظَّٰلِمُونَ ﴿٢٥٤﴾ ٱللَّهُ لَآ إِلَٰهَ
إِلَّا هُوَ ٱلۡحَيُّ ٱلۡقَيُّومُۚ لَا تَأۡخُذُهُۥ سِنَةٞ وَلَا نَوۡمٞۚ لَّهُۥ مَا فِي ٱلسَّمَٰوَٰتِ
وَمَا فِي ٱلۡأَرۡضِۗ مَن ذَا ٱلَّذِي يَشۡفَعُ عِندَهُۥٓ إِلَّا بِإِذۡنِهِۦۚ يَعۡلَمُ مَا بَيۡنَ
أَيۡدِيهِمۡ وَمَا خَلۡفَهُمۡۖ وَلَا يُحِيطُونَ بِشَيۡءٖ مِّنۡ عِلۡمِهِۦٓ إِلَّا بِمَا شَآءَۚ وَسِعَ
كُرۡسِيُّهُ ٱلسَّمَٰوَٰتِ وَٱلۡأَرۡضَۖ وَلَا يَـُٔودُهُۥ حِفۡظُهُمَاۚ وَهُوَ ٱلۡعَلِيُّ
ٱلۡعَظِيمُ ﴿٢٥٥﴾ لَآ إِكۡرَاهَ فِي ٱلدِّينِۖ قَد تَّبَيَّنَ ٱلرُّشۡدُ مِنَ ٱلۡغَيِّۚ فَمَن يَكۡفُرۡ

Yāa ʾayyuhal-ladhīna ʾāmanūu ʾañfiqū mimmā razaqnākum miñ-qabli ʾañy-yaʾtiya Yawmul-lā bayʿuñ-fīhi wa lā khullatuñw-wa lā shafāʿah. Wal-kāfirūna humuẓ-ẓālimūn. ‹254› ʾAllāhu lāa ʾilāha ʾillā Huwal-Ḥayyul-Qayyūm. Lā taʾkhudhuhū sinatuñw-wa lā nawm. Lahū mā fis-samāwāti wa mā fil-ʾarḍ. Mañ-dhal-ladhī yashfaʿu ʿiñdahūu ʾillā biʾidhnih. Yaʿlamu mā bayna ʾaydīhim wa mā khalfahum; wa lā yuḥīṭūna bishayʾim-min ʿilmihīi ʾillā bimā shāaʾ. Wasiʿa kursiyyuhus-samāwāti wal-ʾarḍa wa lā yaʾūduhū ḥifẓuhumā. Wa Huwal-ʿAliyyul-ʿAẓīm. ‹255› Lāa ʾikrāha fid-dīn. Qat-tabayyanar-rushdu minal-ghayy. Famañy-yakfur

246 I.e., the Day of Judgment. With this exhortation, the Qurʾān returns to the subject of verse 245: "Who is it that will offer up unto God a goodly loan?" We may, therefore, infer that the "spending in God's way" relates here to every kind of sacrifice in God's cause, and not merely to the spending of one's possessions.

247 Lit., "that which is between their hands and that which is behind them". The commentators give most conflicting interpretations to this phrase. Thus, for instance, Mujāhid and ʿAṭāʾ assume that "that which is between their hands" means "that which has happened to them in this world", while "that which is behind them" is an allusion to "that which will happen to them in the next world"; Aḍ-Ḍaḥḥāk and Al-Kalbī, on the other hand, assume the exact opposite and say that "that which is between their hands" refers to the next world, "because they are going towards it", while "that which is behind them" means this world, "because they are leaving it behind" (Rāzī). Another explanation is "that which took place before them and that which will take place after them" (Zamakhsharī). It would seem, however, that in all these interpretations the obvious meaning of the idiomatic expression *mā bayna yadayhi* ("that which *lies open* between one's hands") is lost sight of: namely, that which is evident, or known, or perceivable; similarly, *mā khalfahu* means that which is beyond one's ken or perception. Since the whole tenor of the above Qurʾan-verse relates to God's omnipotence and omniscience, the translation given by me seems to be the most appropriate.

248 Lit., "His seat [of power]". Some of the commentators (e.g., Zamakhsharī) interpret this as "His sovereignty" or "His dominion", while others take it to mean "His knowledge" (see Muḥammad ʿAbduh in *Manār* III, 33); Rāzī inclines to the view that this word denotes God's majesty and indescribable, eternal glory.

249 The term *dīn* denotes both the contents of and the compliance with a morally binding law; consequently, it signifies "religion" in the widest sense of this term, extending over all that pertains to its doctrinal contents and their practical implications, as well as to man's attitude towards the object of his worship, thus comprising also the concept of "faith". The

the powers of evil[250] and believes in God has indeed taken hold of a support most unfailing, which shall never give way: for God is all-hearing, all-knowing. ‹256›

God is near unto those who have faith, taking them out of deep darkness into the light – whereas near unto those who are bent on denying the truth are the powers of evil that take them out of the light into darkness deep: it is they who are destined for the fire, therein to abide. ‹257›

ART THOU NOT aware of that [king] who argued with Abraham about his Sustainer, [simply] because God had granted him kingship?

Lo! Abraham said: "My Sustainer is He who grants life and deals death."

[The king] replied: "I [too] grant life and deal death!"

Said Abraham: "Verily, God causes the sun to rise in the east; cause it, then, to rise in the west!"

Thereupon he who was bent on denying the truth remained dumbfounded: for God does not guide people who [deliberately] do wrong.[251] ‹258›

Or [art thou, O man, of the same mind] as he[252] who passed by a town deserted by its people, with its roofs caved in, [and] said, "How could God bring all this back to life after its death?"[253]

Thereupon God caused him to be dead for a hundred years; whereafter He brought him back to life [and] said: "How long hast thou remained thus?"

بِٱلطَّٰغُوتِ وَيُؤْمِنۢ بِٱللَّهِ فَقَدِ ٱسْتَمْسَكَ بِٱلْعُرْوَةِ ٱلْوُثْقَىٰ لَا ٱنفِصَامَ لَهَا ۗ وَٱللَّهُ
سَمِيعٌ عَلِيمٌ ﴿٢٥٦﴾ ٱللَّهُ وَلِىُّ ٱلَّذِينَ ءَامَنُوا۟ يُخْرِجُهُم مِّنَ ٱلظُّلُمَٰتِ إِلَى ٱلنُّورِ ۖ
وَٱلَّذِينَ كَفَرُوٓا۟ أَوْلِيَآؤُهُمُ ٱلطَّٰغُوتُ يُخْرِجُونَهُم مِّنَ ٱلنُّورِ إِلَى ٱلظُّلُمَٰتِ ۗ
أُو۟لَٰٓئِكَ أَصْحَٰبُ ٱلنَّارِ ۖ هُمْ فِيهَا خَٰلِدُونَ ﴿٢٥٧﴾ أَلَمْ تَرَ إِلَى ٱلَّذِى حَآجَّ
إِبْرَٰهِۦمَ فِى رَبِّهِۦٓ أَنْ ءَاتَىٰهُ ٱللَّهُ ٱلْمُلْكَ إِذْ قَالَ إِبْرَٰهِۦمُ رَبِّىَ ٱلَّذِى يُحْىِۦ
وَيُمِيتُ قَالَ أَنَا۠ أُحْىِۦ وَأُمِيتُ ۖ قَالَ إِبْرَٰهِۦمُ فَإِنَّ ٱللَّهَ يَأْتِى بِٱلشَّمْسِ مِنَ
ٱلْمَشْرِقِ فَأْتِ بِهَا مِنَ ٱلْمَغْرِبِ فَبُهِتَ ٱلَّذِى كَفَرَ ۗ وَٱللَّهُ لَا يَهْدِى ٱلْقَوْمَ
ٱلظَّٰلِمِينَ ﴿٢٥٨﴾ أَوْ كَٱلَّذِى مَرَّ عَلَىٰ قَرْيَةٍ وَهِىَ خَاوِيَةٌ عَلَىٰ عُرُوشِهَا قَالَ أَنَّىٰ
يُحْىِۦ هَٰذِهِ ٱللَّهُ بَعْدَ مَوْتِهَا ۖ فَأَمَاتَهُ ٱللَّهُ مِا۟ئَةَ عَامٍ ثُمَّ بَعَثَهُۥ ۖ قَالَ كَمْ لَبِثْتَ

biṭṭāghūti wa yuʾmim-billāhi faqadis-tamsaka bilʿurwatil-wuthqā lañ-fiṣāma lahā. Wal-lāhu Samīʿun ʿAlīm. ﴿256﴾ ʾAllāhu Waliyyul-ladhīna ʾāmanū yukhrijuhum-minaẓ-ẓulumāti ʾilan-nūr. Wal-ladhīna kafarūu ʾawliyāaʾuhumuṭ-ṭāghūtu yukhrijūnahum minannūri ʾilaẓ-ẓulumāt. ʾUlāaʾika ʾaṣḥābun-nāri hum fīhā khālidūn. ﴿257﴾ ʾAlam tara ʾilal-ladhī ḥāajja ʾIbrāhīma fī Rabbihīi ʾan ʾātāhul-lāhul-mulka ʾidh qāla ʾIbrāhīmu Rabbiyal-ladhī yuḥyī wa yumītu qāla ʾana ʾuḥyī wa ʾumīt. Qāla ʾIbrāhīmu faʾinnal-lāha yaʾtī bishshamsi minal-mashriqi faʾti bihā minal-maghribi fabuhital-ladhī kafar. Wal-lāhu lā yahdil-qawmaẓ-ẓālimīn. ﴿258﴾ ʾAw kalladhī marra ʿalā qaryatiñw-wa hiya khāwiyatun ʿalā ʿurūshihā qāla ʾannā yuḥyī hādhihil-lāhu baʿda mawtihā. Faʾamātahul-lāhu miʾata ʿāmiñ-thumma baʿathah. Qāla kam labitht.

rendering of *dīn* as "religion", "faith", "religious law" or "moral law" (see note 3 on 109 : 6) depends on the context in which this term is used. – On the strength of the above categorical prohibition of coercion (*ikrāh*) in anything that pertains to faith or religion, all Islamic jurists (*fuqahāʾ*), without any exception, hold that forcible conversion is under all circumstances null and void, and that any attempt at coercing a non-believer to accept the faith of Islam is a grievous sin: a verdict which disposes of the widespread fallacy that Islam places before the unbelievers the alternative of "conversion or the sword".

250 *Aṭ-ṭāghūt* denotes, primarily, anything that is worshipped instead of God and, thus, all that may turn man away from God and lead him to evil. It has both a singular and a plural significance (Rāzī) and is, therefore, best rendered as "the powers of evil".

251 According to Muḥammad ʿAbduh, the wrong (*ẓulm*) referred to here consists in "one's deliberately turning away from the light [of guidance] provided by God" (*Manār* III, 47).

252 Lit., "Or like him". The words interpolated by me between brackets are based on Zamakhsharī's interpretation of this passage, which connects with the opening of the preceeding verse.

253 The story told in this verse is obviously a parable meant to illustrate God's power to bring the dead back to life:

He answered: "I have remained thus a day, or part of a day."
Said [God]: "Nay, but thou hast remained thus for a hundred years! But look at thy food and thy drink – untouched is it by the passing of years – and look at thine ass![254] And [We did all this] so that We might make thee a symbol unto men. And look at the bones [of animals and men] – how We put them together and then clothe them with flesh!"[255]
And when [all this] became clear to him, he said: "I know [now] that God has the power to will anything!" ‹259›
And, lo, Abraham said: "O my Sustainer! Show me how Thou givest life unto the dead!"
Said He: "Hast thou, then, no faith?"
[Abraham] answered: "Yea, but [let me see it] so that my heart may be set fully at rest".
Said He: "Take, then, four birds and teach them to obey thee;[256] then place them separately on every hill [around thee]; then summon them: they will come flying to thee. And know that God is almighty, wise."[257] ‹260›

THE PARABLE of those who spend their possessions for the sake of God is that of a grain out of which grow seven ears, in every ear a hundred grains: for God grants manifold increase unto whom He wills; and God is infinte, all-knowing. ‹261›

قَالَ لَبِثْتُ يَوْمًا أَوْ بَعْضَ يَوْمٍ قَالَ بَل لَّبِثْتَ مِاْئَةَ عَامٍ فَٱنظُرْ إِلَىٰ
طَعَامِكَ وَشَرَابِكَ لَمْ يَتَسَنَّهْ وَٱنظُرْ إِلَىٰ حِمَارِكَ وَلِنَجْعَلَكَ ءَايَةً لِّلنَّاسِ
وَٱنظُرْ إِلَى ٱلْعِظَامِ كَيْفَ نُنشِزُهَا ثُمَّ نَكْسُوهَا لَحْمًا فَلَمَّا تَبَيَّنَ لَهُۥ قَالَ
أَعْلَمُ أَنَّ ٱللَّهَ عَلَىٰ كُلِّ شَىْءٍ قَدِيرٌ ﴿259﴾ وَإِذْ قَالَ إِبْرَٰهِـۧمُ رَبِّ أَرِنِى
كَيْفَ تُحْىِ ٱلْمَوْتَىٰ قَالَ أَوَلَمْ تُؤْمِن قَالَ بَلَىٰ وَلَـٰكِن لِّيَطْمَئِنَّ قَلْبِى قَالَ
فَخُذْ أَرْبَعَةً مِّنَ ٱلطَّيْرِ فَصُرْهُنَّ إِلَيْكَ ثُمَّ ٱجْعَلْ عَلَىٰ كُلِّ جَبَلٍ مِّنْهُنَّ
جُزْءًا ثُمَّ ٱدْعُهُنَّ يَأْتِينَكَ سَعْيًا وَٱعْلَمْ أَنَّ ٱللَّهَ عَزِيزٌ حَكِيمٌ ﴿260﴾ مَّثَلُ
ٱلَّذِينَ يُنفِقُونَ أَمْوَٰلَهُمْ فِى سَبِيلِ ٱللَّهِ كَمَثَلِ حَبَّةٍ أَنۢبَتَتْ سَبْعَ سَنَابِلَ
فِى كُلِّ سُنۢبُلَةٍ مِّاْئَةُ حَبَّةٍ وَٱللَّهُ يُضَـٰعِفُ لِمَن يَشَآءُ وَٱللَّهُ وَٰسِعٌ عَلِيمٌ ﴿261﴾

Qāla labiththu yawman ʾaw baʿḍa yawm. Qāla bal-labiththa miʾata ʿāmiñ-fañẓur ʾilā ṭaʿāmika wa sharābika lam yatasannah. Wañ-ẓur ʾilā ḥimārika wa linajʿalaka ʾāyatal-linnāsi wañ-ẓur ʾilal-ʿiẓāmi kayfa nuñshizuhā thumma naksūhā laḥmā. Falammā tabayyana lahū qāla ʾaʿlamu ʾannal-lāha ʿalā kulli shayʾiñ-Qadīr. (259) Wa ʾidh qāla ʾIbrāhīmu Rabbi ʾarinī kayfa tuḥyil-mawtā. Qāla ʾawa lam tuʾmin. Qāla balā wa lākil-liyaṭmaʾinna qalbī. Qāla fakhudh ʾarbaʿatam-minaṭ-ṭayri faṣurhunna ʾilayka thummajʿal ʿalā kulli jabalim-minhunna juzʾañ-thummadʿuhunna yaʾtīnaka saʿyā. Waʿ-lam ʾannal-lāha ʿAzīzun Ḥakīm. (260) Mathalul-ladhīna yuñfiqūna ʾamwālahum fī sabīlil-lāhi kamathali ḥabbatin ʾambatat sabʿa sanābila fī kulli sumbulatim-miʾatu ḥabbah. Wal-lāhu yuḍāʿifu limañy-yashāaʾ. Wal-lāhu Wāsiʿun ʿAlīm. (261)

and, thus, it is significantly placed between Abraham's words in verse 258, "My Sustainer is He who grants life and deals death", and his subsequent request, in verse 260, to be shown *how* God resurrects the dead. The speculations of some of the earlier commentators as to the "identity" of the man and the town mentioned in this story are without any substance, and may have been influenced by Talmudic legends.

254 Sc., "and observe that it is alive": thus pointing out that God has the power to grant life indefinitely, as well as to resurrect the dead.

255 The Qurʾān frequently points to the ever-recurring miracle of birth, preceded by the gradual evolution of the embryo in its mother's womb, as a visible sign of God's power to create – and therefore also to re-create – life.

256 Lit., "make them incline towards thee" (Zamakhsharī; see also Lane IV, 1744).

257 My rendering of the above parable is based on the primary meaning of the imperative *ṣurhunna ilayka* ("make them incline towards thee", i.e., "teach them to obey thee"). The moral of this story has been pointed out convincingly by the famous commentator Abū Muslim (as quoted by Rāzī): "If man is able – as he undoubtedly is – to train birds in such a way as to make them obey his call, then it is obvious that God, whose will all things obey, can call life into being by simply decreeing, 'Be!'"

They who spend their possessions for the sake of God and do not thereafter mar[258] their spending by stressing their own benevolence and hurting [the feelings of the needy] shall have their reward with their Sustainer, and no fear need they have, and neither shall they grieve. ‹262›
A kind word and the veiling of another's want[259] is better than a charitable deed followed by hurt; and God is self-sufficient, forbearing. ‹263›
O you who have attained to faith! Do not deprive your charitable deeds of all worth by stressing your own benevolence and hurting [the feelings of the needy], as does he who spends his wealth only to be seen and praised by men, and believes not in God and the Last Day: for his parable is that of a smooth rock with [a little] earth upon it – and then a rainstorm smites it and leaves it hard and bare. Such as these shall have no gain whatever from all their [good] works: for God does not guide people who refuse to acknowledge the truth. ‹264›
And the parable of those who spend their possessions out of a longing to please God, and out of their own inner certainty, is that of a garden on high, fertile ground: a rainstorm smites it, and thereupon it brings forth its fruit twofold; and if no rainstorm smites it, soft rain [falls upon it]. And God sees all that you do. ‹265›
Would any of you like to have a garden of date-palms and vines, through which running waters flow, and have all manner of fruit therein – and then be overtaken by old age, with only weak children to [look after] him – and then [see] it smitten by a fiery whirlwind and utterly scorched?
In this way God makes clear His messages unto you, so that you might take thought. ‹266›

ربع الحزب

ٱلَّذِينَ يُنفِقُونَ أَمْوَٰلَهُمْ فِى سَبِيلِ ٱللَّهِ ثُمَّ لَا يُتْبِعُونَ مَآ أَنفَقُوا۟ مَنًّا وَلَآ أَذًى
لَّهُمْ أَجْرُهُمْ عِندَ رَبِّهِمْ وَلَا خَوْفٌ عَلَيْهِمْ وَلَا هُمْ يَحْزَنُونَ ﴿262﴾ ۞ قَوْلٌ
مَّعْرُوفٌ وَمَغْفِرَةٌ خَيْرٌ مِّن صَدَقَةٍ يَتْبَعُهَآ أَذًى ۗ وَٱللَّهُ غَنِىٌّ حَلِيمٌ ﴿263﴾ يَٰٓأَيُّهَا
ٱلَّذِينَ ءَامَنُوا۟ لَا تُبْطِلُوا۟ صَدَقَٰتِكُم بِٱلْمَنِّ وَٱلْأَذَىٰ كَٱلَّذِى يُنفِقُ مَالَهُۥ
رِئَآءَ ٱلنَّاسِ وَلَا يُؤْمِنُ بِٱللَّهِ وَٱلْيَوْمِ ٱلْءَاخِرِ ۖ فَمَثَلُهُۥ كَمَثَلِ صَفْوَانٍ عَلَيْهِ
تُرَابٌ فَأَصَابَهُۥ وَابِلٌ فَتَرَكَهُۥ صَلْدًا ۖ لَّا يَقْدِرُونَ عَلَىٰ شَىْءٍ مِّمَّا كَسَبُوا۟ ۗ وَٱللَّهُ
لَا يَهْدِى ٱلْقَوْمَ ٱلْكَٰفِرِينَ ﴿264﴾ وَمَثَلُ ٱلَّذِينَ يُنفِقُونَ أَمْوَٰلَهُمُ ٱبْتِغَآءَ
مَرْضَاتِ ٱللَّهِ وَتَثْبِيتًا مِّنْ أَنفُسِهِمْ كَمَثَلِ جَنَّةٍۭ بِرَبْوَةٍ أَصَابَهَا وَابِلٌ فَـَٔاتَتْ
أُكُلَهَا ضِعْفَيْنِ فَإِن لَّمْ يُصِبْهَا وَابِلٌ فَطَلٌّ ۗ وَٱللَّهُ بِمَا تَعْمَلُونَ بَصِيرٌ ﴿265﴾ أَيَوَدُّ
أَحَدُكُمْ أَن تَكُونَ لَهُۥ جَنَّةٌ مِّن نَّخِيلٍ وَأَعْنَابٍ تَجْرِى مِن تَحْتِهَا ٱلْأَنْهَٰرُ
لَهُۥ فِيهَا مِن كُلِّ ٱلثَّمَرَٰتِ وَأَصَابَهُ ٱلْكِبَرُ وَلَهُۥ ذُرِّيَّةٌ ضُعَفَآءُ فَأَصَابَهَآ إِعْصَارٌ
فِيهِ نَارٌ فَٱحْتَرَقَتْ ۗ كَذَٰلِكَ يُبَيِّنُ ٱللَّهُ لَكُمُ ٱلْءَايَٰتِ لَعَلَّكُمْ تَتَفَكَّرُونَ ﴿266﴾

ʾAlladhīna yuñfiqūna ʾamwālahum fī sabīlil-lāhi thumma lā yutbiʿūna māa ʾañfaqū mannañw-wa lāa ʾadhal-lahum ʾajruhum ʿiñda Rabbihim wa lā khawfun ʿalayhim wa lā hum yaḥzanūn. (262) ◈ Qawlum-maʿrūfuñw-wa maghfiratun khayrum-miñ-ṣadaqatiñy-yatbaʿuhāa ʾadhā. Wal-lāhu Ghaniyyun Ḥalīm. (263) Yāa ʾayyuhal-ladhīna ʾāmanū lā tubṭilū ṣadaqātikum-bilmanni wal-ʾadhā kalladhī yuñfiqu mālahū riʾāaʾan-nāsi wa lā yuʾminu billāhi wal-Yawmil-ʾĀkhir. Famathaluhū kamathali ṣafwānin ʿalayhi turābuñ-faʾaṣābahū wābiluñ-fatarakahū ṣaldā. Lā yaqdirūna ʿalā shayʾim-mimmā kasabū. Wal-lāhu lā yahdil-qawmal-kāfirīn. (264) Wa mathalul-ladhīna yuñfiqūna ʾamwālahumub-tighāaʾa marḍātil-lāhi wa tathbītam-min ʾañfusihim kamathali jannatim-birabwatin ʾaṣābahā wābiluñ-faʾātat ʾukulahā ḍiʿfayn. Faʾil-lam yuṣibhā wābiluñ-faṭall. Wal-lāhu bimā taʿmalūna Baṣīr. (265) ʾAyawaddu ʾaḥadukum ʾañ-takūna lahū jannatum-min-nakhīliñw-wa ʾaʿnābiñ-tajrī miñ-taḥtihal-ʾanhāru lahū fīhā miñ-kullith-thamarāti wa ʾaṣābahul-kibaru wa lahū dhurriyyatuñ-ḍuʿafāaʾu faʾaṣābahāaʾiʿṣāruñ-fīhi nāruñ-faḥtaraqat. Kadhālika yubayyinul-lāhu lakumul-ʾĀyāti laʿallakum tatafakkarūn. (266)

258 Lit., "do not follow up".
259 For the rendering of *maghfarah* (lit., "forgiveness") in this context as "veiling another's want" I am indebted to Baghawī's explanation of this verse.

يَـٰٓأَيُّهَا ٱلَّذِينَ ءَامَنُوٓا۟ أَنفِقُوا۟ مِن طَيِّبَـٰتِ مَا كَسَبْتُمْ وَمِمَّآ أَخْرَجْنَا لَكُم مِّنَ
ٱلْأَرْضِ ۖ وَلَا تَيَمَّمُوا۟ ٱلْخَبِيثَ مِنْهُ تُنفِقُونَ وَلَسْتُم بِـَٔاخِذِيهِ إِلَّآ أَن تُغْمِضُوا۟
فِيهِ ۚ وَٱعْلَمُوٓا۟ أَنَّ ٱللَّهَ غَنِىٌّ حَمِيدٌ ﴿٢٦٧﴾ ٱلشَّيْطَـٰنُ يَعِدُكُمُ ٱلْفَقْرَ وَيَأْمُرُكُم
بِٱلْفَحْشَآءِ ۖ وَٱللَّهُ يَعِدُكُم مَّغْفِرَةً مِّنْهُ وَفَضْلًا ۗ وَٱللَّهُ وَٰسِعٌ عَلِيمٌ ﴿٢٦٨﴾ يُؤْتِى
ٱلْحِكْمَةَ مَن يَشَآءُ ۚ وَمَن يُؤْتَ ٱلْحِكْمَةَ فَقَدْ أُوتِىَ خَيْرًا كَثِيرًا ۗ وَمَا يَذَّكَّرُ
إِلَّآ أُو۟لُوا۟ ٱلْأَلْبَـٰبِ ﴿٢٦٩﴾ وَمَآ أَنفَقْتُم مِّن نَّفَقَةٍ أَوْ نَذَرْتُم مِّن نَّذْرٍ فَإِنَّ ٱللَّهَ
يَعْلَمُهُۥ ۗ وَمَا لِلظَّـٰلِمِينَ مِنْ أَنصَارٍ ﴿٢٧٠﴾ إِن تُبْدُوا۟ ٱلصَّدَقَـٰتِ فَنِعِمَّا هِىَ ۖ وَإِن
تُخْفُوهَا وَتُؤْتُوهَا ٱلْفُقَرَآءَ فَهُوَ خَيْرٌ لَّكُمْ ۚ وَيُكَفِّرُ عَنكُم مِّن سَيِّـَٔاتِكُمْ ۗ وَٱللَّهُ
بِمَا تَعْمَلُونَ خَبِيرٌ ﴿٢٧١﴾ ۞ لَّيْسَ عَلَيْكَ هُدَىٰهُمْ وَلَـٰكِنَّ ٱللَّهَ يَهْدِى مَن يَشَآءُ ۗ
وَمَا تُنفِقُوا۟ مِنْ خَيْرٍ فَلِأَنفُسِكُمْ ۚ وَمَا تُنفِقُونَ إِلَّا ٱبْتِغَآءَ وَجْهِ ٱللَّهِ ۚ وَمَا تُنفِقُوا۟
مِنْ خَيْرٍ يُوَفَّ إِلَيْكُمْ وَأَنتُمْ لَا تُظْلَمُونَ ﴿٢٧٢﴾

نصف الحزب

Yāa ᵓayyuhal-ladhīna ᵓāmanūu ᵓañfiqū miñ-ṭayyibāti mā kasabtum wa mimmāa ᵓakhrajnā lakum-minal-ᵓarḍ. Wa lā tayammamul-khabītha minhu tuñfiqūna wa lastum-biᵓākhidhīhi ᵓillāa ᵓañ-tughmiḍū fīh. Waᶜ-lamūu ᵓannal-lāha Ghaniyyun Ḥamīd. (267) ᵓAsh-Shayṭānu yaᶜidukumul-faqra wa yaᵓmurukum bil-faḥshāaᵓ. Wal-lāhu yaᶜidukum maghfiratam-minhu wa faḍlā. Wal-lāhu Wāsiᶜun ᶜAlīm. (268) Yuᵓtil-ḥikmata mañy-yashāaᵓu wa mañy-yuᵓtal-ḥikmata faqad ᵓūtiya khayrañ-kathīrā. Wa mā yadhdhakkaru ᵓillāa ᵓulul-ᵓalbāb. (269) Wa māa ᵓañfaqtum-miñ-nafaqatin ᵓaw nadhartum miñ-nadhriñ-faᵓinnal-lāha yaᶜlamuh. Wa mā liẓẓālimīna min ᵓañṣār. (270) ᵓIñ-tubduṣ-ṣadaqāti faniᶜimmā hiya wa ᵓiñ-tukhfūhā wa tuᵓtūhal-fuqarāaᵓa fahuwa khayrul-lakum; wa yukaffiru ᶜañkum-miñ-sayyiᵓātikum. Wal-lāhu bimā taᶜmaluna Khabīr. (271) ۞ Laysa ᶜalayka hudāhum wa lākinnal-lāha yahdī mañy-yashāaᵓ. Wa mā tuñfiqū min khayriñ-faliᵓañfusikum; wa mā tuñfiqūna ᵓillab-tighāaᵓa Wajhil-lāh. Wa mā tuñfiqū min khayriñy-yuwaffa ᵓilaykum wa ᵓañtum lā tuẓlamūn. (272)

O you who have attained to faith! Spend on others out of the good things which you may have acquired, and out of that which We bring forth for you from the earth; and choose not for your spending the bad things which you yourselves would not accept without averting your eyes in disdain. And know that God is self-sufficient, ever to be praised. ‹267›
Satan threatens you with the prospect of poverty and bids you to be niggardly, whereas God promises you His forgiveness and bounty; and God is infinite, all-knowing, ‹268› granting wisdom unto whom He wills: and whoever is granted wisdom has indeed been granted wealth abundant. But none bears this in mind save those who are endowed with insight. ‹269›
For, whatever you may spend on others, or whatever you may vow [to spend], verily, God knows it; and those who do wrong [by withholding charity] shall have none to succour them. ‹270›
If you do deeds of charity openly, it is well; but if you bestow it upon the needy in secret, it will be even better for you, and it will atone for some of your bad deeds. And God is aware of all that you do. ‹271›
It is not for thee [O Prophet] to make people follow the right path,[260] since it is God [alone] who guides whom He wills.
And whatever good you may spend on others is for your own good, provided that you spend only out of a longing for God's countenance: for, whatever good you may spend will be repaid unto you in full, and you shall not be wronged. ‹272›

260 Lit., "their guidance is not upon thee" – i.e., "thou art responsible only for conveying God's message to them, and not for their reaction to it": the people referred to being the needy spoken of in the preceding verses. It appears that in the early days after his migration to Medina, the Prophet – faced by the great poverty prevalent among his own community – advised his Companions that "charity should be bestowed only on the followers of Islam" – a view that was immediately corrected by the revelation of the above verse (a number of Traditions to this effect are quoted by Ṭabarī, Rāzī and Ibn Kathīr, as well as in *Manār* III, 82 f.). According to several other Traditions (recorded, among others, by Nasāᵓi and Abū Dāᵓūd and quoted by all the classical commentators), the Prophet thereupon explicitly enjoined upon his followers to disburse charities upon all who needed them, irrespective of the faith of the person concerned. Consequently, there is full agreement among all the commentators that the above verse of the Qurᵓān –

لِلْفُقَرَآءِ ٱلَّذِينَ أُحْصِرُوا۟ فِى سَبِيلِ ٱللَّهِ لَا يَسْتَطِيعُونَ ضَرْبًا فِى ٱلْأَرْضِ
يَحْسَبُهُمُ ٱلْجَاهِلُ أَغْنِيَآءَ مِنَ ٱلتَّعَفُّفِ تَعْرِفُهُم بِسِيمَـٰهُمْ لَا يَسْـَٔلُونَ
ٱلنَّاسَ إِلْحَافًا ۗ وَمَا تُنفِقُوا۟ مِنْ خَيْرٍ فَإِنَّ ٱللَّهَ بِهِۦ عَلِيمٌ ﴿٢٧٣﴾ ٱلَّذِينَ يُنفِقُونَ
أَمْوَٰلَهُم بِٱلَّيْلِ وَٱلنَّهَارِ سِرًّا وَعَلَانِيَةً فَلَهُمْ أَجْرُهُمْ عِندَ رَبِّهِمْ وَلَا
خَوْفٌ عَلَيْهِمْ وَلَا هُمْ يَحْزَنُونَ ﴿٢٧٤﴾ ٱلَّذِينَ يَأْكُلُونَ ٱلرِّبَوٰا۟ لَا يَقُومُونَ
إِلَّا كَمَا يَقُومُ ٱلَّذِى يَتَخَبَّطُهُ ٱلشَّيْطَـٰنُ مِنَ ٱلْمَسِّ ۚ ذَٰلِكَ بِأَنَّهُمْ قَالُوٓا۟
إِنَّمَا ٱلْبَيْعُ مِثْلُ ٱلرِّبَوٰا۟ ۗ وَأَحَلَّ ٱللَّهُ ٱلْبَيْعَ وَحَرَّمَ ٱلرِّبَوٰا۟ ۚ فَمَن جَآءَهُۥ
مَوْعِظَةٌ مِّن رَّبِّهِۦ فَٱنتَهَىٰ فَلَهُۥ مَا سَلَفَ وَأَمْرُهُۥٓ إِلَى ٱللَّهِ ۖ وَمَنْ عَادَ فَأُو۟لَـٰٓئِكَ
أَصْحَـٰبُ ٱلنَّارِ ۖ هُمْ فِيهَا خَـٰلِدُونَ ﴿٢٧٥﴾ يَمْحَقُ ٱللَّهُ ٱلرِّبَوٰا۟ وَيُرْبِى ٱلصَّدَقَـٰتِ

Lilfuqarāaʾil-ladhīna ʾuḥṣirū fī sabīlil-lāhi lā yastaṭīʿūna ḍarbañ-fil-ʾarḍi yaḥsabuhumul-jāhilu ʾaghniyāaʾa minat-taʿaffufi taʿrifuhum-bisīmāhum lā yasʾalūnan-nāsa ʾilḥāfā. Wa mā tuñfiqū min khayriñ-faʾinnal-lāha bihī ʿAlīm. (273) ʾAlladhīna yuñfiqūna ʾamwālahum-billayli wan-nahāri sirrañw-wa ʿalāniyatañ-falahum ʾajruhum ʿiñda Rabbihim wa lā khawfun ʿalayhim wa lā hum yaḥzanūn. (274) ʾAlladhīna yaʾkulūnar-ribā lā yaqūmūna ʾillā kamā yaqūmul-ladhī yatakhabbaṭuhsh-Shayṭānu minal-mass. Dhālika biʾannahum qālūu ʾinnamal-bayʿu mithlur-ribā. Wa ʾaḥallal-lāhul-bayʿa wa ḥarramar-ribā. Famañ-jāaʾahū mawʿiẓatum-mir-Rabbihī fañtahā falahū mā salafa wa ʾamruhūu ʾilal-lāh. Wa man ʿāda faʾulāaʾika ʾaṣḥābun-nāri hum fīhā khālidūn. (275) Yamḥaqul-lāhur-ribā wa yurbiṣ-ṣadaqāt.

[And give] unto [such of] the needy who, being wholly wrapped up in God's cause, are unable to go about the earth [in search of livelihood].[261] He who is unaware [of their condition] might think that they are wealthy, because they abstain [from begging]; [but] thou canst recognize them by their special mark: they do not beg of men with importunity. And whatever good you may spend [on them], verily, God knows it all. ⟨273⟩

Those who spend their possessions [for the sake of God] by night and by day, secretly and openly, shall have their reward with their Sustainer; and no fear need they have, and neither shall they grieve. ⟨274⟩

THOSE who gorge themselves on usury[262] behave but as he might behave whom Satan has confounded with his touch; for they say, "Buying and selling is but a kind of[263] usury" – the while God has made buying and selling lawful and usury unlawful. Hence, whoever becomes aware of his Sustainer's admonition,[264] and thereupon desists [from usury], may keep his past gains, and it will be for God to judge him; but as for those who return to it – they are destined for the fire, therein to abide! ⟨275⟩

God deprives usurious gains of all blessing, whereas He blesses charitable

---

although expressed in the singular and, on the face of it, addressed to the Prophet – lays down an injunction binding upon all Muslims. Rāzī, in particular, draws from it the additional conclusion that charity – or the threat to withhold it – must never become a means of attracting unbelievers to Islam: for, in order to be valid, faith must be an outcome of inner conviction and free choice. This is in consonance with verse 256 of this *sūrah*: "There shall be no coercion in matters of faith."

261 I.e., those who have devoted themselves entirely to working in the cause of the Faith – be it by spreading, elucidating or defending it physically or intellectually – or to any of the selfless pursuits extolled in God's message, such as search for knowledge, work for the betterment of man's lot, and so forth; and, finally, those who, having suffered personal or material hurt in such pursuits, are henceforth unable to fend for themselves.

262 For a discussion of the concept of *ribā* ("usury"), see note 35 on 30 : 39, where this term occurs for the first time in the chronological order of revelation. The passage dealing with the prohibition of *ribā*, which follows here, is believed to have been among the last revelations received by the Prophet. The subject of usury connects logically with the preceding long passage on the subject of charity because the former is morally the exact opposite of the latter: true charity consists in giving without an expectation of material gain, whereas usury is based on an expectation of gain without any corresponding effort on the part of the lender.

263 Lit., "like".

264 Lit., "he to whom an admonition has come from his Sustainer".

deeds with manifold increase.[265] And God does not love anyone who is stubbornly ingrate and persists in sinful ways. ‹276›
Verily, those who have attained to faith and do good works, and are constant in prayer, and dispense charity – they shall have their reward with their Sustainer, and no fear need they have, and neither shall they grieve. ‹277›
O you who have attained to faith! Remain conscious of God, and give up all outstanding gains from usury, if you are [truly] believers;[266] ‹278› for if you do it not, then know that you are at war with God and His Apostle. But if you repent, then you shall be entitled to [the return of] your principal:[267] you will do no wrong, and neither will you be wronged. ‹279› If, however, [the debtor] is in straitened circumstances, [grant him] a delay until a time of ease; and it would be for your own good – if you but knew it – to remit [the debt entirely] by way of charity. ‹280›
And be conscious of the Day on which you shall be brought back unto God, whereupon every human being shall be repaid in full for what he has earned, and none shall be wronged.[268] ‹281›

O YOU who have attained to faith! Whenever you give or take credit[269] for a stated term, set it down in writing. And let a scribe write it down equitably between you; and no scribe shall refuse to write as God has taught him:[270] thus shall he write. And let him who contracts the debt dictate; and let him be conscious of God, his Sustainer, and not weaken anything of

وَٱللَّهُ لَا يُحِبُّ كُلَّ كَفَّارٍ أَثِيمٍ ﴿٢٧٦﴾ إِنَّ ٱلَّذِينَ ءَامَنُوا۟ وَعَمِلُوا۟ ٱلصَّٰلِحَٰتِ
وَأَقَامُوا۟ ٱلصَّلَوٰةَ وَءَاتَوُا۟ ٱلزَّكَوٰةَ لَهُمْ أَجْرُهُمْ عِندَ رَبِّهِمْ وَلَا خَوْفٌ عَلَيْهِمْ وَلَا
هُمْ يَحْزَنُونَ ﴿٢٧٧﴾ يَٰٓأَيُّهَا ٱلَّذِينَ ءَامَنُوا۟ ٱتَّقُوا۟ ٱللَّهَ وَذَرُوا۟ مَا بَقِىَ مِنَ ٱلرِّبَوٰٓا۟ إِن
كُنتُم مُّؤْمِنِينَ ﴿٢٧٨﴾ فَإِن لَّمْ تَفْعَلُوا۟ فَأْذَنُوا۟ بِحَرْبٍ مِّنَ ٱللَّهِ وَرَسُولِهِۦ ۖ وَإِن تُبْتُمْ
فَلَكُمْ رُءُوسُ أَمْوَٰلِكُمْ لَا تَظْلِمُونَ وَلَا تُظْلَمُونَ ﴿٢٧٩﴾ وَإِن كَانَ ذُو عُسْرَةٍ
فَنَظِرَةٌ إِلَىٰ مَيْسَرَةٍ ۚ وَأَن تَصَدَّقُوا۟ خَيْرٌ لَّكُمْ ۖ إِن كُنتُمْ تَعْلَمُونَ ﴿٢٨٠﴾ وَٱتَّقُوا۟ يَوْمًا
تُرْجَعُونَ فِيهِ إِلَى ٱللَّهِ ۖ ثُمَّ تُوَفَّىٰ كُلُّ نَفْسٍ مَّا كَسَبَتْ وَهُمْ لَا يُظْلَمُونَ ﴿٢٨١﴾
يَٰٓأَيُّهَا ٱلَّذِينَ ءَامَنُوٓا۟ إِذَا تَدَايَنتُم بِدَيْنٍ إِلَىٰٓ أَجَلٍ مُّسَمًّى فَٱكْتُبُوهُ ۚ وَلْيَكْتُب
بَّيْنَكُمْ كَاتِبٌۢ بِٱلْعَدْلِ ۚ وَلَا يَأْبَ كَاتِبٌ أَن يَكْتُبَ كَمَا عَلَّمَهُ ٱللَّهُ ۚ
فَلْيَكْتُبْ وَلْيُمْلِلِ ٱلَّذِى عَلَيْهِ ٱلْحَقُّ وَلْيَتَّقِ ٱللَّهَ رَبَّهُۥ وَلَا يَبْخَسْ مِنْهُ

Wal-lāhu lā yuḥibbu kulla kaffārin ʾathīm. (276) ʾInnal-
ladhīna ʾāmanū wa ʿamiluṣ-ṣāliḥāti wa ʾaqāmuṣ-
Ṣalāta wa ʾātawuz-Zakāta lahum ʾajruhum ʿiñda
Rabbihim wa lā khawfun ʿalayhim wa lā hum
yaḥzanūn. (277) Yāa ʾayyuhal-ladhīna ʾāmanut-taqul-
lāha wa dharū mā baqiya minar-ribāa ʾiñ-kuñtum-
muʾminīn. (278) Faʾil-lam tafʿalū faʾdhanū biḥarbim-
minal-lāhi wa Rasūlihi wa ʾiñ-tubtum falakum ruʾūsu
ʾamwālikum lā taẓlimūna wa lā tuẓlamūn. (279) Wa ʾiñ-
kāna dhū ʿusratiñ-fanaẓiratun ʾilā maysarah. Wa
ʾañ-taṣaddaqū khayrul-lakum ʾiñ-kuñtum taʿlamūn.
(280) Wat-taqū Yawmañ-turjaʿūna fīhi ʾilal-lāhi thum-
ma tuwaffā kullu nafsim-mā kasabat wa hum lā
yuẓlamūn. (281) Yāa ʾayyuhal-ladhīna ʾāmanūu ʾidhā
tadāyañtum-bidaynin ʾilāa ʾajalim-musammañ-
faktubūh. Wal-yaktub-baynakum kātibum-bilʿadl.
Wa lā yaʾba kātibun ʾañy-yaktuba kamā ʿallamahul-
lāh. Falyaktub wal-yumlilil-ladhī ʿalayhil-ḥaqqu wal-
yattaqil-lāha Rabbahū wa lā yabkhas minhu

265 Lit., "whereas He causes [the merit of] charitable deeds to increase with interest (*yurbī*)".

266 This refers not merely to the believers at the time when the prohibition of usury was proclaimed, but also to people of later times who may come to believe in the Qurʾanic message.

267 I.e., without interest.

268 According to the uncontested evidence of Ibn ʿAbbās, the above verse was the last revelation granted to the Prophet, who died shortly afterwards (Bukhārī; see also *Fatḥ al -Bārī* VIII 164 f.).

269 The above phrase embraces any transaction on the basis of credit, be it an outright loan or a commercial deal. It relates (as the grammatical form *tadāyantum* shows) to both the giver and taker of credit, and has been rendered accordingly.

270 I.e., in accordance with the laws promulgated in the Qurʾān.

ثلاثة ارباع الحزب

his undertaking.[271] And if he who contracts the debt is weak of mind or body, or is not able to dictate himself,[272] then let him who watches over his interests dictate equitably. And call upon two of your men to act as witnesses; and if two men are not available, then a man and two women from among such as are acceptable to you as witnesses, so that if one of them should make a mistake, the other could remind her.[273] And the witnesses must not refuse [to give evidence] whenever they are called upon.

And be not loath to write down every contractual provision,[274] be it small or great, together with the time at which it falls due; this is more equitable in the sight of God, more reliable as evidence, and more likely to prevent you from having doubts [later]. If, however [the transaction] concerns ready merchandise which you transfer directly unto one another, you will incur no sin if you do not write it down.

And have witnesses whenever you trade with one another, but neither scribe nor witness must suffer harm;[275] for if you do [them harm], behold, it will be sinful conduct on your part. And remain conscious of God, since it is God who teaches you [herewith] – and God has full knowledge of everything. ‹282›

And if you are on a journey and cannot find a scribe, pledges [may be taken] in hand: but if you trust one another, then let him who is trusted fulfil his trust, and let him be conscious of God, his Sustainer.

شَيْـًٔا ۚ فَإِن كَانَ ٱلَّذِى عَلَيْهِ ٱلْحَقُّ سَفِيهًا أَوْ ضَعِيفًا أَوْ لَا يَسْتَطِيعُ أَن يُمِلَّ
هُوَ فَلْيُمْلِلْ وَلِيُّهُۥ بِٱلْعَدْلِ ۚ وَٱسْتَشْهِدُوا۟ شَهِيدَيْنِ مِن رِّجَالِكُمْ ۖ فَإِن لَّمْ يَكُونَا
رَجُلَيْنِ فَرَجُلٌ وَٱمْرَأَتَانِ مِمَّن تَرْضَوْنَ مِنَ ٱلشُّهَدَآءِ أَن تَضِلَّ إِحْدَىٰهُمَا
فَتُذَكِّرَ إِحْدَىٰهُمَا ٱلْأُخْرَىٰ ۚ وَلَا يَأْبَ ٱلشُّهَدَآءُ إِذَا مَا دُعُوا۟ ۚ وَلَا تَسْـَٔمُوٓا۟ أَن
تَكْتُبُوهُ صَغِيرًا أَوْ كَبِيرًا إِلَىٰٓ أَجَلِهِۦ ۚ ذَٰلِكُمْ أَقْسَطُ عِندَ ٱللَّهِ وَأَقْوَمُ لِلشَّهَـٰدَةِ
وَأَدْنَىٰٓ أَلَّا تَرْتَابُوٓا۟ ۖ إِلَّآ أَن تَكُونَ تِجَـٰرَةً حَاضِرَةً تُدِيرُونَهَا بَيْنَكُمْ فَلَيْسَ
عَلَيْكُمْ جُنَاحٌ أَلَّا تَكْتُبُوهَا ۗ وَأَشْهِدُوٓا۟ إِذَا تَبَايَعْتُمْ ۚ وَلَا يُضَآرَّ كَاتِبٌ وَلَا
شَهِيدٌ ۚ وَإِن تَفْعَلُوا۟ فَإِنَّهُۥ فُسُوقٌۢ بِكُمْ ۗ وَٱتَّقُوا۟ ٱللَّهَ ۖ وَيُعَلِّمُكُمُ ٱللَّهُ ۗ وَٱللَّهُ بِكُلِّ
شَىْءٍ عَلِيمٌ ﴿٢٨٢﴾ ۞ وَإِن كُنتُمْ عَلَىٰ سَفَرٍ وَلَمْ تَجِدُوا۟ كَاتِبًا فَرِهَـٰنٌ مَّقْبُوضَةٌ ۖ
فَإِنْ أَمِنَ بَعْضُكُم بَعْضًا فَلْيُؤَدِّ ٱلَّذِى ٱؤْتُمِنَ أَمَـٰنَتَهُۥ وَلْيَتَّقِ ٱللَّهَ رَبَّهُۥ

shayʾā. Faʾiñ-kānal-ladhī ʿalayhil-ḥaqqu safīhan ʾaw ḍaʿīfan ʾaw lā yastaṭīʿu ʾañy-yumilla huwa falyumlil waliyyuhū bilʿadl. Was-tashhidū shahīdayni mir-rijālikum; faʾil-lam yakūnā rajulayni farajuluñw-wamraʾatāni mimmañ-tarḍawna minash-shuhadāaʾi ʾañ-taḍilla ʾiḥdāhumā fatudhakkira ʾiḥdāhumal-ʾukhrā. Wa lā yaʾbash-shuhadāaʾu ʾidhā mā duʿū. Wa lā tasʾamūu ʾañ-taktubūhu ṣaghīran ʾaw kabīran ʾilāa ʾajalih. Dhālikum ʾaqsaṭu ʿiñdal-lāhi wa ʾaqwamu lish-shahādati wa ʾadnāa ʾallā tartābūu ʾillāa ʾañ-takūna tijāratan ḥāḍiratañ-tudīrūnahā baynakum falaysa ʿalaykum junāḥun ʾallā taktubūhā. Wa ʾashhidūu ʾidhā tabāyaʿtum. Wa lā yuḍāarra kātibuñw-wa lā shahīd. Wa ʾiñ-tafʿalū faʾinnahū fusūqum-bikum. Wat-taqlul-lāha wa yuʿallimukumul-lāh. Wallāhu bikulli shayʾin ʿAlīm. ﴿٢٨٢﴾ Wa ʾiñ-kuñtum ʿalā safariñw-wa lam tajidū kātibañ-farihānum-maqbūḍah. Faʾin ʾamina baʿḍukum baʿḍañ-falyuʾaddil-ladhiʾ-utumina ʾamānatahū wal-yattaqil-lāha Rabbah.

271 Lit., "and do not diminish anything thereof". Thus, the formulation of the undertaking is left to the weaker party, i.e., to the one who contracts the debt.

272 E.g., because he is physically handicapped, or does not fully understand the business terminology used in such contracts, or is not acquainted with the language in which the contract is to be written. The definition "weak of mind or body" (lit., "lacking in understanding or weak") applies to minors as well as to very old persons who are no longer in full possession of their mental faculties.

273 The stipulation that two women may be substituted for one male witness does not imply any reflection on woman's moral or intellectual capabilities: it is obviously due to the fact that, as a rule, women are less familiar with business procedures than men and, therefore, more liable to commit mistakes in this respect (see ʿAbduh in *Manār* III, 124 f.).

274 Lit., "to write it down" – i.e., all rights and obligations arising from the contract.

275 E.g., by being held responsible for the eventual consequences of the contract as such, or for the non-fulfilment of any of its provisions by either of the contracting parties.

And do not conceal what you have witnessed[276] – for, verily, he who conceals it is sinful at heart; and God has full knowledge of all that you do. ⟨283⟩

Unto God belongs all that is in the heavens and all that is on earth. And whether you bring into the open what is in your minds or conceal it, God will call you to account for it; and then He will forgive whom He wills, and will chastise whom He wills: for God has the power to will anything. ⟨284⟩

THE APOSTLE, and the believers with him, believe in what has been bestowed upon him from on high by his Sustainer: they all believe in God, and His angels, and His revelations, and His apostles, making no distinction between any of His apostles;[277] and they say:

"We have heard, and we pay heed. Grant us Thy forgiveness, O our Sustainer, for with Thee is all journeys' end! ⟨285⟩

"God does not burden any human being with more than he is well able to bear: in his favour shall be whatever good he does, and against him whatever evil he does.

"O our Sustainer! Take us not to task if we forget or unwittingly do wrong!

"O our Sustainer! Lay not upon us a burden such as Thou didst lay upon those who lived before us![278] O our Sustainer! Make us not bear burdens which we have no strength to bear!

"And efface Thou our sins, and grant us forgiveness, and bestow Thy mercy upon us! Thou art our Lord Supreme: succour us, then, against people who deny the truth!" ⟨286⟩

وَلَا تَكْتُمُواْ ٱلشَّهَٰدَةَ وَمَن يَكْتُمْهَا فَإِنَّهُۥٓ ءَاثِمٌ قَلْبُهُۥ وَٱللَّهُ بِمَا تَعْمَلُونَ عَلِيمٌ ۝ لِّلَّهِ مَا فِى ٱلسَّمَٰوَٰتِ وَمَا فِى ٱلْأَرْضِ وَإِن تُبْدُواْ مَا فِىٓ أَنفُسِكُمْ أَوْ تُخْفُوهُ يُحَاسِبْكُم بِهِ ٱللَّهُ فَيَغْفِرُ لِمَن يَشَآءُ وَيُعَذِّبُ مَن يَشَآءُ وَٱللَّهُ عَلَىٰ كُلِّ شَىْءٍ قَدِيرٌ ۝ ءَامَنَ ٱلرَّسُولُ بِمَآ أُنزِلَ إِلَيْهِ مِن رَّبِّهِۦ وَٱلْمُؤْمِنُونَ كُلٌّ ءَامَنَ بِٱللَّهِ وَمَلَٰٓئِكَتِهِۦ وَكُتُبِهِۦ وَرُسُلِهِۦ لَا نُفَرِّقُ بَيْنَ أَحَدٍ مِّن رُّسُلِهِۦ وَقَالُواْ سَمِعْنَا وَأَطَعْنَا غُفْرَانَكَ رَبَّنَا وَإِلَيْكَ ٱلْمَصِيرُ ۝ لَا يُكَلِّفُ ٱللَّهُ نَفْسًا إِلَّا وُسْعَهَا لَهَا مَا كَسَبَتْ وَعَلَيْهَا مَا ٱكْتَسَبَتْ رَبَّنَا لَا تُؤَاخِذْنَآ إِن نَّسِينَآ أَوْ أَخْطَأْنَا رَبَّنَا وَلَا تَحْمِلْ عَلَيْنَآ إِصْرًا كَمَا حَمَلْتَهُۥ عَلَى ٱلَّذِينَ مِن قَبْلِنَا رَبَّنَا وَلَا تُحَمِّلْنَا مَا لَا طَاقَةَ لَنَا بِهِۦ وَٱعْفُ عَنَّا وَٱغْفِرْ لَنَا وَٱرْحَمْنَآ أَنتَ مَوْلَىٰنَا فَٱنصُرْنَا عَلَى ٱلْقَوْمِ ٱلْكَٰفِرِينَ ۝

Wa lā taktumush-shahādah. Wa mañy-yaktumhā faʾinnahūu ʾāthimuñ-qalbuh. Wal-lāhu bimā taʿmalūna ʿAlīm. ۝ Lillāhi mā fis-samāwāti wa mā fil-ʾarḍ. Wa ʾiñ-tubdū mā fii ʾañfusikum ʾaw tukhfūhu yuḥāsibkum-bihil-lāh. Fayaghfiru limañy-yashāaʾu wa yuʿadhdhibu mañy-yashāaʾ. Wal-lāhu ʿalā kulli shay-ʾiñ-Qadīr. ۝ ʾĀmanar-Rasūlu bimāa ʾuñzila ʾilayhi mir-Rabbihī wal-muʾminūn. Kullun ʾāmana billāhi wa Malāaʾikatihī wa Kutubihī wa Rusulihī lā nufarriqu bayna ʾaḥadim-mir-Rusulih. Wa qālū samiʿnā wa ʾaṭaʿnā; ghufrānaka Rabbanā wa ʾilaykal-maṣīr. ۝ Lā yukalliful-lāhu nafsan ʾillā wusʿahā lahā mā kasabat wa ʿalayhā mak-tasabat. Rabbanā lā tuʾākhidhnāa ʾiñ-nasīnāa ʾaw ʾakhṭaʾnā. Rabbanā wa lā taḥmil ʿalaynāa ʾiṣrañ-kamā ḥamaltahū ʿalal-ladhīna miñ-qablinā. Rabbanā wa lā tuḥammilnā mā lā ṭāqata lanā bihī waʿ-fu ʿannā wagh-fir lanā war-ḥamnā. ʾAñta Mawlānā fañṣurnā ʿalal-qawmil-kāfirīn. ۝

---

276 Lit., "do not conceal testimony". This relates not only to those who have witnessed a business transaction, but also to a debtor who has been given a loan on trust – without a written agreement and without witnesses – and subsequently denies all knowledge of his indebtedness.

277 Lit., "we make no distinction between any of His apostles": these words are put, as it were, in the mouths of the believers. Inasmuch as all the apostles were true bearers of God's messages, there is no distinction between them, albeit some of them have been "endowed more highly than others" (see verse 253).

278 A reference to the heavy burden of rituals imposed by the Law of Moses upon the children of Israel, as well as the world-renunciation recommended by Jesus to his followers.

The Third Sūrah

ᵓĀl ᶜImrān (The House of ᶜImrān)

Medina Period

THIS SŪRAH is the second or (according to some authorities) the third to have been revealed at Medina, apparently in the year 3 H.; some of its verses, however, belong to a much later period, namely, to the year preceding the Prophet's death (10 H.). The title "The House of ᶜImrān" has been derived from references, in verses 33 and 35, to this common origin of a long line of prophets.

Like the preceding *sūrah*, this one begins with the mention of divine revelation and men's reactions to it. In *Al-Baqarah* the main stress is laid on the contrasting attitudes of those who accept the truth revealed by God and those who reject it; the opening verses of *ᵓĀl ᶜImrān,* on the other hand, refer to the inclination of many misguided believers to interpret the allegorical passages of the Qurᵓān – and, by implication, of the earlier revealed scriptures as well – in an arbitrary manner, and thus to arrive at esoteric propositions which conflict with the true nature and purpose of the divine message. Since the deification of Jesus by his later followers is one of the most outstanding instances of such an arbitrary interpretation of a prophet's original message, the *sūrah* relates the story of Mary and Jesus, as well as of Zachariah, the father of John the Baptist, all of whom belonged to the House of ᶜImrān. Here the Qurᵓān takes issue with the Christian doctrine of the divinity of Jesus: he himself is quoted as calling upon his followers to worship God alone; his purely human nature and mortality are stressed again and again; and it is described as "inconceivable that a human being unto whom God had granted revelation, and sound judgment, and prophethood, should thereafter have said unto people, 'Worship *me* beside God'" (verse 79).

The principle of God's oneness and uniqueness and of man's utter dependence on Him is illumined from many angles, and leads logically to the problem of man's faith and to the temptations, arising out of human frailty, to which that faith is continually exposed: and this brings the discourse to the subject of the battle of Uḥud – that near-disaster which befell the small Muslim community in the year 3 H., and provided a wholesome, if bitter, lesson for all its future development. More than one-third of *ᵓĀl ᶜImrān* deals with this experience and the many-sided moral to be derived from it.

سورة آل عمران مدنية -3- وآياتها مائتان

IN THE NAME OF GOD, THE MOST GRACIOUS, THE DISPENSER OF GRACE:

بِسْمِ ٱللَّهِ ٱلرَّحْمَٰنِ ٱلرَّحِيمِ

Alif. Lām. Mīm.[1] ‹1›
GOD – there is no deity save Him, the Ever-Living, the Self-Subsistent Fount of All Being! ‹2›
Step by step has He bestowed upon thee from on high this divine writ,[2] setting forth the truth which confirms whatever there still remains [of earlier revelations]:[3] for it is He who has bestowed from on high the Torah and the Gospel ‹3› aforetime, as a guidance unto mankind, and it is He who has bestowed [upon man] the standard by which to discern the true from the false.[4]
Behold, as for those who are bent on denying God's messages – grievous suffering awaits them: for God is almighty, an avenger of evil. ‹4›

الٓمٓ ﴿١﴾ ٱللَّهُ لَآ إِلَٰهَ إِلَّا هُوَ ٱلْحَىُّ ٱلْقَيُّومُ ﴿٢﴾ نَزَّلَ عَلَيْكَ ٱلْكِتَٰبَ
بِٱلْحَقِّ مُصَدِّقًا لِّمَا بَيْنَ يَدَيْهِ وَأَنزَلَ ٱلتَّوْرَىٰةَ وَٱلْإِنجِيلَ ﴿٣﴾ مِن قَبْلُ
هُدًى لِّلنَّاسِ وَأَنزَلَ ٱلْفُرْقَانَ ۗ إِنَّ ٱلَّذِينَ كَفَرُوا۟ بِـَٔايَٰتِ ٱللَّهِ لَهُمْ
عَذَابٌ شَدِيدٌ ۗ وَٱللَّهُ عَزِيزٌ ذُو ٱنتِقَامٍ ﴿٤﴾

Bismil-lāhir-Raḥmānir-Raḥīm.
ʾAlif-Lāam-Mīim. (1) ʾAllāhu lāa ʾilāha ʾillā Huwal-Ḥayyul-Qayyūm. (2) Nazzala ʿalaykal-Kitāba bilḥaqqi muṣaddiqal-limā bayna yadayhī wa ʾañzalat-Tawrāta wal-ʾIñjīl. (3) Miñ-qablu hudal-linnāsi wa ʾañzalal-Furqān. ʾInnal-ladhīna kafarū biʾĀyātil-lāhi lahum ʿadhābuñ-shadīd. Wal-lāhu ʿAzīzuñ-Dhuñ-tiqām. (4)

---

1 See Appendix II.

2 The gradualness of the Qurʾanic revelation is stressed here by means of the grammatical form *nazzala*.

3 Most of the commentators are of the opinion that *mā bayna yadayhi* – lit., "that which is between its hands" – denotes here "the revelations which came before it", i.e., before the Qurʾān. This interpretation is not, however, entirely convincing. Although there is not the least doubt that in this context the pronominal *mā* refers to earlier revelations, and particularly the Bible (as is evident from the parallel use of the above expression in other Qurʾanic passages), the idiomatic phrase *mā bayna yadayhi* does not, in itself, mean "that which came before it" – i.e., in time – but, rather (as pointed out by me in *sūrah* 2, note 247), "that which *lies open* before it". Since, however, the pronoun "it" relates here to the Qur'ān, the metaphorical expression "between its hands" or "before it" cannot possibly refer to "knowledge" (as it does in 2 : 255), but must obviously refer to an objective reality with which the Qur'ān is "confronted": that is, something that was *coexistent in time* with the revelation of the Qurʾān. Now this, taken together (a) with the fact – frequently stressed in the Qurʾān and since established by objective scholarship – that in the course of the millennia the Bible has been subjected to considerable and often arbitrary alteration, and (b) with the fact that many of the laws enunciated in the Qurʾān differ from the laws of the Bible, brings us forcibly to the conclusion that the "confirmation" of the latter by the Qurʾān can refer only to the basic truths still discernible in the Bible, and not to its time-bound legislation or to its present text – in other words, a confirmation of *whatever was extant* of its basic teachings at the time of the revelation of the Qurʾān: and it is this that the phrase *mā bayna yadayhi* expresses in this context as well as in 5 : 46 and 48 or in 61 : 6 (where it refers to *Jesus'* confirming the truth of "whatever there still remained [i.e., in his lifetime] of the Torah").

4 It is to be borne in mind that the Gospel frequently mentioned in the Qurʾān is not identical with what is known today as the Four Gospels, but refers to an original, since lost, revelation bestowed upon Jesus and known to his contemporaries under its Greek name of *Evangelion* ("Good Tiding"), on which the Arabicized form *Injīl* is based. It was probably the source from which the Synoptic Gospels derived much of their material and some of the teachings attributed to Jesus. The fact of its having been lost and forgotten is alluded to in the Qurʾān in 5 : 14. – Regarding my rendering of *al-furqān* as "the standard by which to discern the true from the false", see also note 38 on the identical phrase occurring in 2 : 53.

Verily, nothing on earth or in the heavens is hidden from God. ⟨5⟩ He it is who shapes you in the wombs as He wills. There is no deity save Him, the Almighty, the Truly Wise. ⟨6⟩

He it is who has bestowed upon thee from on high this divine writ, containing messages that are clear in and by themselves – and these are the essence of the divine writ – as well as others that are allegorical.[5] Now those whose hearts are given to swerving from the truth go after that part of the divine writ[6] which has been expressed in allegory, seeking out [what is bound to create] confusion,[7] and seeking [to arrive at] its final meaning [in an arbitrary manner]; but none save God knows its final meaning.[8] Hence, those who are deeply rooted in knowledge say: "We believe in it; the whole [of the divine writ] is from our Sustainer – albeit none takes this to heart save those who are endowed with insight. ⟨7⟩

"O our Sustainer! Let not our hearts swerve from the truth after Thou hast guided us; and bestow upon us the gift of Thy grace: verily, Thou art the [true] Giver of Gifts. ⟨8⟩

إِنَّ ٱللَّهَ لَا يَخْفَىٰ عَلَيْهِ شَىْءٌ فِى ٱلْأَرْضِ وَلَا فِى ٱلسَّمَآءِ ﴿٥﴾ هُوَ ٱلَّذِى
يُصَوِّرُكُمْ فِى ٱلْأَرْحَامِ كَيْفَ يَشَآءُ لَآ إِلَٰهَ إِلَّا هُوَ ٱلْعَزِيزُ
ٱلْحَكِيمُ ﴿٦﴾ هُوَ ٱلَّذِىٓ أَنزَلَ عَلَيْكَ ٱلْكِتَٰبَ مِنْهُ ءَايَٰتٌ مُّحْكَمَٰتٌ
هُنَّ أُمُّ ٱلْكِتَٰبِ وَأُخَرُ مُتَشَٰبِهَٰتٌ فَأَمَّا ٱلَّذِينَ فِى قُلُوبِهِمْ زَيْغٌ فَيَتَّبِعُونَ
مَا تَشَٰبَهَ مِنْهُ ٱبْتِغَآءَ ٱلْفِتْنَةِ وَٱبْتِغَآءَ تَأْوِيلِهِۦ وَمَا يَعْلَمُ تَأْوِيلَهُۥٓ إِلَّا ٱللَّهُ
وَٱلرَّٰسِخُونَ فِى ٱلْعِلْمِ يَقُولُونَ ءَامَنَّا بِهِۦ كُلٌّ مِّنْ عِندِ رَبِّنَا وَمَا يَذَّكَّرُ إِلَّآ
أُو۟لُوا۟ ٱلْأَلْبَٰبِ ﴿٧﴾ رَبَّنَا لَا تُزِغْ قُلُوبَنَا بَعْدَ إِذْ هَدَيْتَنَا وَهَبْ لَنَا مِن
لَّدُنكَ رَحْمَةً إِنَّكَ أَنتَ ٱلْوَهَّابُ ﴿٨﴾

ʾInnal-lāha lā yakhfā ʿalayhi shayʾuñ-fil-ʾarḍi wa lā fis-samāaʾ. ⟨5⟩ Huwal-ladhī yuṣawwirukum fil-ʾarḥāmi kayfa yashāaʾ. Lāa ʾilāha ʾilla Huwal-ʿAzīzul-Ḥakīm. ⟨6⟩ Huwal-ladhīi ʾañzala ʿalaykal-Kitāba minhu ʾāyātum-muḥkamātun hunna ʾummul-Kitābi wa ʾukharu mutashābihāt. Faʾammal-ladhīna fī qulūbihim zayghuñ-fayattabiʿūna mā tashābaha minhub-tighāaʾal-fitnati wab-tighāaʾa taʾwīlih. Wa mā yaʿlamu taʾwīlahūu ʾillal-lāh. War-rāsikhūna fil-ʿilmi yaqūlūna ʾāmannā bihī kullum-min ʿiñdi Rabbinā. Wa mā yadhdhakkaru ʾillāa ʾulul-ʾalbāb. ⟨7⟩ Rabbanā lā tuzigh qulūbanā baʿda ʾidh hadaytanā wa hab lanā mil-laduñka raḥmatan ʾinnaka ʾAñtal-Wahhāb. ⟨8⟩

---

5 The above passage may be regarded as a key to the understanding of the Qurʾān. Ṭabarī identifies the *āyāt muḥkamāt* ("messages that are clear in and by themselves") with what the philologists and jurists describe as *naṣṣ* – namely, ordinances or statements which are self-evident (*ẓāhir*) by virtue of their wording (cf. *Lisān al-ʿArab*, art. *naṣṣ*). Consequently, Ṭabarī regards as *āyāt muḥkamāt* only those statements or ordinances of the Qurʾān which do not admit of more than one interpretation (which does not, of course, preclude differences of opinion regarding the *implications* of a particular *āyah muḥkamah*). In my opinion, however, it would be too dogmatic to regard any passage of the Qurʾān which does not conform to the above definition as *mutashābih* ("allegorical"): for there are many statements in the Qurʾrān which are liable to more than one interpretation but are, nevertheless, not allegorical – just as there are many expressions and passages which, despite their allegorical formulation, reveal to the searching intellect only one possible meaning. For this reason, the *āyāt mutashābihāt* may be defined as those passages of the Qurʾān which are expressed in a figurative manner, with a meaning that is metaphorically implied but not directly, in so many words, stated. The *āyāt muḥkamāt* are described as the "essence of the divine writ" (*umm al-kitāb*) because they comprise the fundamental principles underlying its message and, in particular, its ethical and social teachings: and it is only on the basis of these clearly enunciated principles that the allegorical passages can be correctly interpreted. (For a more detailed discussion of symbolism and allegory in the Qurʾān, see Appendix I.)

6 Lit., "that of it".

7 The "confusion" referred to here is a consequence of interpreting allegorical passages in an "arbitrary manner" (Zamakhsharī).

8 According to most of the early commentators, this refers to the interpretation of allegorical passages which deal with metaphysical subjects – for instance, God's attributes, the ultimate meaning of time and eternity, the resurrection of the dead, the Day of Judgment, paradise and hell, the nature of the beings or forces described as

"O our Sustainer! Verily, Thou wilt gather mankind together to witness the Day about [the coming of] which there is no doubt: verily, God never fails to fulfil His promise." ‹9›

BEHOLD, as for those who are bent on denying the truth – neither their worldly possessions nor their offspring will in the least avail them against God; and it is they, they who shall be the fuel of the fire! ‹10› [To them shall happen] the like of what happened to Pharaoh's people and those who lived before them: they gave the lie to Our messages – and so God took them to task for their sins: for God is severe in retribution. ‹11›

Say unto those who are bent on denying the truth: "You shall be overcome and gathered unto hell – and how evil a resting-place!" ‹12›

You have already had a sign in the two hosts that met in battle, one host fighting in God's cause and the other denying Him; with their own eyes [the former] saw the others as twice their own number: but God strengthens with His succour whom He wills. In this, behold, there is indeed a lesson for all who have eyes to see.[9] ‹13›

رَبَّنَآ إِنَّكَ جَامِعُ ٱلنَّاسِ لِيَوْمٍ لَّا رَيْبَ فِيهِ إِنَّ ٱللَّهَ لَا يُخْلِفُ ٱلْمِيعَادَ ﴿٩﴾
إِنَّ ٱلَّذِينَ كَفَرُوا۟ لَن تُغْنِىَ عَنْهُمْ أَمْوَٰلُهُمْ وَلَآ أَوْلَٰدُهُم مِّنَ ٱللَّهِ شَيْـًٔا
وَأُو۟لَٰٓئِكَ هُمْ وَقُودُ ٱلنَّارِ ﴿١٠﴾ كَدَأْبِ ءَالِ فِرْعَوْنَ وَٱلَّذِينَ مِن قَبْلِهِمْ
كَذَّبُوا۟ بِـَٔايَٰتِنَا فَأَخَذَهُمُ ٱللَّهُ بِذُنُوبِهِمْ وَٱللَّهُ شَدِيدُ ٱلْعِقَابِ ﴿١١﴾ قُل
لِّلَّذِينَ كَفَرُوا۟ سَتُغْلَبُونَ وَتُحْشَرُونَ إِلَىٰ جَهَنَّمَ وَبِئْسَ ٱلْمِهَادُ ﴿١٢﴾ قَدْ
كَانَ لَكُمْ ءَايَةٌ فِى فِئَتَيْنِ ٱلْتَقَتَا فِئَةٌ تُقَٰتِلُ فِى سَبِيلِ ٱللَّهِ وَأُخْرَىٰ كَافِرَةٌ
يَرَوْنَهُم مِّثْلَيْهِمْ رَأْىَ ٱلْعَيْنِ وَٱللَّهُ يُؤَيِّدُ بِنَصْرِهِۦ مَن يَشَآءُ إِنَّ فِى ذَٰلِكَ
لَعِبْرَةً لِّأُو۟لِى ٱلْأَبْصَٰرِ ﴿١٣﴾

Rabbanāa ʾinnaka jāmiʿun-nāsi liYawmil-lā rayba fīh. ʾInnal-lāha lā yukhliful-mīʿād. (9) ʾInnal-ladhīna kafarū lan-tughniya ʿanhum ʾamwāluhum wa lāa ʾawlāduhum-minal-lāhi shayʾā; wa ʾulāaʾika hum waqūdun-nār. (10) Kadaʾbi ʾāli Firʿawna wal-ladhīna miñ-qablihim. Kadhdhabū biʾāyātinā faʾakhadhahumul-lāhu bidhunūbihim. Wal-lāhu Shadīdul-ʿiqāb. (11) Qul-lilladhīna kafarū satughlabūna wa tuḥsharūna ʾilā jahannama wa biʾ-sal-mihād. (12) Qad kāna lakum ʾāyatuñ-fī fiʾataynil-taqatā. Fiʾatuñ-tuqātilu fī sabīlil-lāhi wa ʾukhrā kāfiratuñy-yarawnahum-mithlayhim raʾyal-ʿayn. Wal-lāhu yuʾayyidu binaṣrihī mañy-yashāaʾ. ʾInna fī dhālika laʿibratal-liʾulil-ʾabṣār. (13)

angels, and so forth – all of which fall within the category of *al-ghayb*, i.e., that sector of reality which is beyond the reach of human perception and imagination and cannot, therefore, be conveyed to man in other than allegorical terms. This view of the classical commentators, however, does not seem to take into account the many Qurʾanic passages which do *not* deal with metaphysical subjects and yet are, undoubtedly, allegorical in intent and expression. To my mind, one cannot arrive at a correct understanding of the above passage without paying due attention to the nature and function of allegory as such. A true allegory – in contrast with a mere pictorial paraphrase of something that could equally well be stated in direct terms – is always meant to express in a figurative manner something which, because of its complexity, *cannot* be adequately expressed in direct terms or propositions and, because of this very complexity, can be grasped only intuitively, as a general mental image, and not as a series of detailed "statements": and this seems to be the meaning of the phrase, "none save God knows its final meaning".

9 It is generally assumed that this is an allusion to the battle of Badr, in the third week of Ramaḍān, 2 H., in which three hundred and odd poorly-equipped Muslims, led by the Prophet, utterly routed a well-armed Meccan force numbering nearly one thousand men, seven hundred camels and one hundred horses; it was the first open battle between the pagan Quraysh and the young Muslim community of Medina. According to some commentators, however (e.g., *Manār* III, 234), the above Qurʾanic passage has a general import and alludes to an occurrence often witnessed in history – namely, the victory of a numerically weak and ill-equipped group of people, filled with a burning belief in the righteousness of their cause, over a materially and numerically superior enemy lacking a similar conviction. The fact that in this Qurʾān-verse the believers are spoken of as being faced by an enemy "twice their number" (while at the battle of Badr the pagan Quraysh were more than three times the number of the Muslims) lends great plausibility to this explanation – and particularly so in view of the allusion, in the next verse, to material riches and worldly power.

ALLURING unto man is the enjoyment of worldly desires through women, and children, and heaped-up treasures of gold and silver, and horses of high mark, and cattle, and lands. All this may be enjoyed in the life of this world – but the most beauteous of all goals is with God. ‹14›
Say: "Shall I tell you of better things than those [earthly joys]? For the God-conscious there are, with their Sustainer, gardens through which running waters flow, therein to abide, and spouses pure, and God's goodly acceptance."
And God sees all that is in [the hearts of] His servants ‹15› – those who say, "O our Sustainer! Behold, we believe [in Thee]; forgive us, then, our sins and keep us safe from suffering through the fire:" ‹16› – those who are patient in adversity, and true to their word, and truly devout, and who spend [in God's way], and pray for forgiveness from their innermost hearts.[10] ‹17›

GOD [Himself] proffers evidence[11] – and [so do] the angels and all who are endowed with knowledge – that there is no deity save Him, the Upholder of Equity: there is no deity save Him, the Almighty, the Truly Wise. ‹18›
Behold, the only [true] religion in the sight of God is [man's] self-surrender unto Him; and those who were vouchsafed revelation aforetime[12] took, out of mutual jealousy, to divergent views [on this point] only

الحزب ٥

زُيِّنَ لِلنَّاسِ حُبُّ ٱلشَّهَوَٰتِ مِنَ ٱلنِّسَآءِ وَٱلْبَنِينَ وَٱلْقَنَٰطِيرِ ٱلْمُقَنطَرَةِ
مِنَ ٱلذَّهَبِ وَٱلْفِضَّةِ وَٱلْخَيْلِ ٱلْمُسَوَّمَةِ وَٱلْأَنْعَٰمِ وَٱلْحَرْثِ ۗ ذَٰلِكَ مَتَٰعُ
ٱلْحَيَوٰةِ ٱلدُّنْيَا ۖ وَٱللَّهُ عِندَهُۥ حُسْنُ ٱلْمَـَٔابِ ﴿١٤﴾ ۞ قُلْ أَؤُنَبِّئُكُم بِخَيْرٍ
مِّن ذَٰلِكُمْ ۚ لِلَّذِينَ ٱتَّقَوْا۟ عِندَ رَبِّهِمْ جَنَّٰتٌ تَجْرِى مِن تَحْتِهَا ٱلْأَنْهَٰرُ
خَٰلِدِينَ فِيهَا وَأَزْوَٰجٌ مُّطَهَّرَةٌ وَرِضْوَٰنٌ مِّنَ ٱللَّهِ ۗ وَٱللَّهُ بَصِيرٌۢ
بِٱلْعِبَادِ ﴿١٥﴾ ٱلَّذِينَ يَقُولُونَ رَبَّنَآ إِنَّنَآ ءَامَنَّا فَٱغْفِرْ لَنَا ذُنُوبَنَا وَقِنَا
عَذَابَ ٱلنَّارِ ﴿١٦﴾ ٱلصَّٰبِرِينَ وَٱلصَّٰدِقِينَ وَٱلْقَٰنِتِينَ وَٱلْمُنفِقِينَ
وَٱلْمُسْتَغْفِرِينَ بِٱلْأَسْحَارِ ﴿١٧﴾ شَهِدَ ٱللَّهُ أَنَّهُۥ لَآ إِلَٰهَ إِلَّا هُوَ وَٱلْمَلَٰٓئِكَةُ
وَأُو۟لُوا۟ ٱلْعِلْمِ قَآئِمًۢا بِٱلْقِسْطِ ۚ لَآ إِلَٰهَ إِلَّا هُوَ ٱلْعَزِيزُ ٱلْحَكِيمُ ﴿١٨﴾ إِنَّ
ٱلدِّينَ عِندَ ٱللَّهِ ٱلْإِسْلَٰمُ ۗ وَمَا ٱخْتَلَفَ ٱلَّذِينَ أُوتُوا۟ ٱلْكِتَٰبَ إِلَّا مِنۢ

Zuyyina linnāsi ḥubbush-shahawāti minan-nisāaᵓi wal-banīna wal-qanāṭīril-muqañṭarati minadh-dhahabi wal-fiḍḍati wal-khaylil-musawwamati wal-ᵓanᶜāmi wal-ḥarth. Dhālika matāᶜul-ḥayātid-dunyā; wal-lāhu ᶜiñdahū ḥusnul-maᵓāb. (14) Qul ᵓaᵓunabbiᵓukum-bikhayrim-miñ-dhālikum. Lilladhīnat-taqaw ᶜiñda Rabbihim jannātuñ-tajrī miñ-taḥtihal-ᵓanhāru khālidīna fīhā wa ᵓazwājum-muṭahharatuñw-wa riḍwānum-minal-lāh. Wal-lāhu Baṣīrum-bilᶜibād. (15) ᵓAlladhīna yaqūlūna Rabbanāa ᵓinnanāa ᵓāmannā faghfir lanā dhunūbanā wa qinā ᶜadhāban-nār. (16) Aṣṣābirīna waṣ-ṣādiqīna wal-qānitīna wal-muñfiqī-na wal-mustaghfirīna bilᵓasḥār. (17) Shahidal-lāhu ᵓannahū lāa ᵓilāha ᵓillā Huwa wal-Malāaᵓikatu wa ᵓulul-ᶜilmi qāaᵓimam-bilqisṭ. Lāa ᵓilāha ᵓillā Huwal-ᶜAzīzul-Ḥakīm. (18) ᵓInnad-dīna ᶜiñdal-lāhil-ᵓIslām. Wa makh-talafal-ladhīna ᵓūtul-Kitāba ᵓillā mim-

10 The expression *biʾl-asḥār* is usually taken to mean "at the times before daybreak", or simply "before daybreak". This is in agreement with the Prophet's recommendation to his followers (forthcoming from several authentic Traditions) to devote the latter part of the night, and particularly the time shortly before dawn, to intensive prayer. But while the word *saḥar* (also spelled *saḥr* and *suḥr*), of which *asḥār* is the plural, undoubtedly denotes "the time before daybreak," it also signifies – in the spellings *saḥar* and *suḥr* – "the core of the heart", "the inner part of the heart", or simply "heart" (cf. *Lisān al-ᶜArab*; also Lane IV, 1316). It seems to me that in the context of the above Qurᵓān-verse – as well as of 51 : 18 – this latter rendering is preferable to the conventional one: for, although the value of praying before daybreak has undoubtedly been stressed by the Prophet, it is not very plausible that the Qurᵓān should have tied the *prayer for forgiveness* to a particular time of day.

11 Lit., "bears witness" – i.e., through the nature of His creation, which shows plainly that it has been brought into being by a consciously planning Power.

12 Most of the classical commentators are of the opinion that the people referred to are the followers of the Bible, or of parts of it – i.e., the Jews and the Christians. It is, however, highly probable that this passage bears a wider import and relates to all communities which base their views on a revealed scripture, extant in a partially corrupted form, with parts of it entirely lost.

بَعْدِ مَا جَآءَهُمُ ٱلْعِلْمُ بَغْيَۢا بَيْنَهُمْ ۗ وَمَن يَكْفُرْ بِـَٔايَـٰتِ ٱللَّهِ فَإِنَّ ٱللَّهَ سَرِيعُ
ٱلْحِسَابِ ﴿١٩﴾ فَإِنْ حَآجُّوكَ فَقُلْ أَسْلَمْتُ وَجْهِىَ لِلَّهِ وَمَنِ ٱتَّبَعَنِ ۗ وَقُل
لِّلَّذِينَ أُوتُوا۟ ٱلْكِتَـٰبَ وَٱلْأُمِّيِّـۧنَ ءَأَسْلَمْتُمْ ۚ فَإِنْ أَسْلَمُوا۟ فَقَدِ ٱهْتَدَوا۟ ۖ وَّإِن
تَوَلَّوْا۟ فَإِنَّمَا عَلَيْكَ ٱلْبَلَـٰغُ ۗ وَٱللَّهُ بَصِيرٌۢ بِٱلْعِبَادِ ﴿٢٠﴾ إِنَّ ٱلَّذِينَ يَكْفُرُونَ
بِـَٔايَـٰتِ ٱللَّهِ وَيَقْتُلُونَ ٱلنَّبِيِّـۧنَ بِغَيْرِ حَقٍّ وَيَقْتُلُونَ ٱلَّذِينَ يَأْمُرُونَ بِٱلْقِسْطِ
مِنَ ٱلنَّاسِ فَبَشِّرْهُم بِعَذَابٍ أَلِيمٍ ﴿٢١﴾ أُو۟لَـٰٓئِكَ ٱلَّذِينَ حَبِطَتْ أَعْمَـٰلُهُمْ فِى
ٱلدُّنْيَا وَٱلْـَٔاخِرَةِ وَمَا لَهُم مِّن نَّـٰصِرِينَ ﴿٢٢﴾ أَلَمْ تَرَ إِلَى ٱلَّذِينَ أُوتُوا۟ نَصِيبًا
مِّنَ ٱلْكِتَـٰبِ يُدْعَوْنَ إِلَىٰ كِتَـٰبِ ٱللَّهِ لِيَحْكُمَ بَيْنَهُمْ ثُمَّ يَتَوَلَّىٰ فَرِيقٌ مِّنْهُمْ
وَهُم مُّعْرِضُونَ ﴿٢٣﴾ ذَٰلِكَ بِأَنَّهُمْ قَالُوا۟ لَن تَمَسَّنَا ٱلنَّارُ إِلَّآ أَيَّامًا
مَّعْدُودَٰتٍ ۖ وَغَرَّهُمْ فِى دِينِهِم مَّا كَانُوا۟ يَفْتَرُونَ ﴿٢٤﴾ فَكَيْفَ إِذَا جَمَعْنَـٰهُمْ
لِيَوْمٍ لَّا رَيْبَ فِيهِ وَوُفِّيَتْ كُلُّ نَفْسٍ مَّا كَسَبَتْ وَهُمْ لَا يُظْلَمُونَ ﴿٢٥﴾

baʿdi mā jāaʾahumul-ʿilmu baghyam-baynahum. Wa mañy-yakfur biʾĀyātil-lāhi faʾinnal-lāha Sarīʿul-ḥisāb. (19) Faʾin ḥāajjūka faqul ʾaslamtu wajhiya lillāhi wa manit-tabaʿan. Wa qul-lilladhīna ʾūtul-Kitāba wal-ʾummiyyīna ʾaʾaslamtum. Faʾin ʾaslamū faqadih-tadaw. Wa ʾiñ-tawallaw faʾinnamā ʿalaykal-balāgh. Wal-lāhu Baṣīrum-bilʿibād. (20) ʾInnal-ladhīna yakfurūna biʾāyātil-lāhi wa yaqtulūnan-Nabiyyīna bighayri ḥaqqiñw-wa yaqtulūnal-ladhīna yaʾmurūna bilqisṭi minan-nāsi fabashshirhum-biʿadhābin ʾalīm. (21) ʾUlāaʾikal-ladhīna ḥabiṭat ʾaʿmāluhum fid-dunyā wal-Ākhirati wa mā lahum-miñ-nāṣirīn. (22) ʾAlam tara ʾilal-ladhīna ʾūtū naṣībam-minal-Kitābi yudʿawna ʾilā Kitābil-lāhi liyaḥkuma baynahum thumma yatawallā farīqum-minhum wa hum-muʿ-riḍūn. (23) Dhālika biʾannahum qālū lañ-tamassa-nan-nāru ʾillāa ʾayyāmam-maʿdūdāt. Wa gharrahum fī dīnihim-mā kānū yaftarūn. (24) Fakayfa ʾidhā jamaʿnāhum liYawmil-lā rayba fīhi wa wuffiyat kullu nafsim-mā kasabat wa hum lā yuẓlamūn. (25)

after knowledge [thereof] had come unto them.[13] But as for him who denies the truth of God's messages – behold, God is swift in reckoning! ‹19›
Thus, [O Prophet,] if they argue with thee, say, "I have surrendered my whole being unto God, and [so have] all who follow me!" – and ask those who have been vouchsafed revelation aforetime, as well as all unlettered people,[14] "Have you [too] surrendered yourselves unto Him?"
And if they surrender themselves unto Him, they are on the right path; but if they turn away – behold, thy duty is no more than to deliver the message: for God sees all that is in [the hearts of] His creatures. ‹20›
Verily, as for those who deny the truth of God's messages, and slay the prophets against all right, and slay people who enjoin equity[15] – announce unto them a grievous chastisement. ‹21› It is they whose works shall come to nought both in this world and in the life to come; and they shall have none to succour them. ‹22›
Art thou not aware of those who have been granted their share of revelation [aforetime]? They have been called upon to let God's writ be their law[16] – and yet some of them turn away [from it] in their obstinacy, ‹23› simply because they claim, "The fire will most certainly not touch us for more than a limited number of days":[17] and thus the false beliefs which they invented have [in time] caused them to betray their faith.[18] ‹24›
How, then, [will they fare] when We shall gather them all together to witness the Day about [the coming of] which there is no doubt, and every human being shall be repaid in full for what he has done, and none shall be wronged? ‹25›

13 I.e., all these communities at first subscribed to the doctrine of God's oneness and held that man's self-surrender to Him (*islām* in its original connotation) is the essence of all true religion. Their subsequent divergencies were an outcome of sectarian pride and mutual exclusiveness.

14 According to Rāzī, this refers to people who have no revealed scripture of their own.

15 See *sūrah* 2, note 48.

16 Lit., "decide [all disputes] between them" – the reference being to the Torah.

17 Cf. 2 : 80, and the corresponding note.

18 Lit., "that which they were wont to invent has deluded them in their faith".

SAY: "O God, Lord of all dominion! Thou grantest dominion unto whom Thou willest, and takest away dominion from whom Thou willest; and Thou exaltest whom Thou willest, and abasest whom Thou willest. In Thy hand is all good. Verily, Thou hast the power to will anything. ‹26›
"Thou makest the night grow longer by shortening the day, and Thou makest the day grow longer by shortening the night. And Thou bringest forth the living out of that which is dead, and Thou bringest forth the dead out of that which is alive. And Thou grantest sustenance unto whom Thou willest, beyond all reckoning." ‹27›

LET NOT the believers take those who deny the truth for their allies in preference to the believers[19] – since he who does this cuts himself off from God in everything – unless it be to protect yourselves against them in this way.[20] But God warns you to beware of Him: for with God is all journeys' end. ‹28›
Say: "Whether you conceal what is in your hearts[21] or bring it into the open, God knows it: for He knows all that is in the heavens and all that is on earth; and God has the power to will anything." ‹29›
On the Day when every human being will find himself faced with all the good that he has done, and with all the evil that he has done, [many a one] will wish that there were a long span of time between himself and that [Day]. Hence, God warns you to beware of Him; but God is most compassionate towards His creatures. ‹30›
Say [O Prophet]: "If you love God, follow me, [and] God will love you and forgive you your sins; for God is much-forgiving, a dispenser of grace." ‹31›

قُلِ ٱللَّهُمَّ مَـٰلِكَ ٱلْمُلْكِ تُؤْتِى ٱلْمُلْكَ مَن تَشَآءُ وَتَنزِعُ ٱلْمُلْكَ مِمَّن تَشَآءُ
وَتُعِزُّ مَن تَشَآءُ وَتُذِلُّ مَن تَشَآءُ ۖ بِيَدِكَ ٱلْخَيْرُ ۖ إِنَّكَ عَلَىٰ كُلِّ شَىْءٍ قَدِيرٌ ﴿٢٦﴾
تُولِجُ ٱلَّيْلَ فِى ٱلنَّهَارِ وَتُولِجُ ٱلنَّهَارَ فِى ٱلَّيْلِ ۖ وَتُخْرِجُ ٱلْحَىَّ مِنَ ٱلْمَيِّتِ
وَتُخْرِجُ ٱلْمَيِّتَ مِنَ ٱلْحَىِّ ۖ وَتَرْزُقُ مَن تَشَآءُ بِغَيْرِ حِسَابٍ ﴿٢٧﴾ لَّا
يَتَّخِذِ ٱلْمُؤْمِنُونَ ٱلْكَـٰفِرِينَ أَوْلِيَآءَ مِن دُونِ ٱلْمُؤْمِنِينَ ۖ وَمَن يَفْعَلْ ذَٰلِكَ
فَلَيْسَ مِنَ ٱللَّهِ فِى شَىْءٍ إِلَّآ أَن تَتَّقُوا۟ مِنْهُمْ تُقَىٰةً ۗ وَيُحَذِّرُكُمُ ٱللَّهُ نَفْسَهُۥ ۗ
وَإِلَى ٱللَّهِ ٱلْمَصِيرُ ﴿٢٨﴾ قُلْ إِن تُخْفُوا۟ مَا فِى صُدُورِكُمْ أَوْ تُبْدُوهُ يَعْلَمْهُ
ٱللَّهُ ۗ وَيَعْلَمُ مَا فِى ٱلسَّمَـٰوَٰتِ وَمَا فِى ٱلْأَرْضِ ۗ وَٱللَّهُ عَلَىٰ كُلِّ شَىْءٍ قَدِيرٌ ﴿٢٩﴾
يَوْمَ تَجِدُ كُلُّ نَفْسٍ مَّا عَمِلَتْ مِنْ خَيْرٍ مُّحْضَرًا وَمَا عَمِلَتْ مِن سُوٓءٍ تَوَدُّ لَوْ
أَنَّ بَيْنَهَا وَبَيْنَهُۥٓ أَمَدًۢا بَعِيدًا ۗ وَيُحَذِّرُكُمُ ٱللَّهُ نَفْسَهُۥ ۗ وَٱللَّهُ رَءُوفٌۢ بِٱلْعِبَادِ ﴿٣٠﴾
قُلْ إِن كُنتُمْ تُحِبُّونَ ٱللَّهَ فَٱتَّبِعُونِى يُحْبِبْكُمُ ٱللَّهُ وَيَغْفِرْ لَكُمْ ذُنُوبَكُمْ ۗ
وَٱللَّهُ غَفُورٌ رَّحِيمٌ ﴿٣١﴾

Qulil-lāhumma Mālikal-mulki tuʾtil-mulka mañ-tashāaʾu wa tañziʿul-mulka mimmañ-tashāaʾu wa tuʿizzu mañ-tashāaʾu wa tudhillu mañ-tashāaʾu bi-yadikal-khayr. ʾInnaka ʿalā kulli shayʾiñ-Qadīr. (26)
Tūlijul-layla fin-nahāri wa tūlijun-nahāra fil-layl. Wa tukhrijul-ḥayya minal-mayyiti wa tukhrijul-mayyita minal-ḥayy. Wa tarzuqu mañ-tashāaʾu bighayri ḥisāb. (27)
Lā yattakhidhil-muʾminūnal-kāfirīna ʾawliyāaʾa miñ-dūnil-muʾminīn. Wa mañy-yafʿal dhālika falaysa minal-lāhi fī shayʾin ʾillāa ʾañ-tattaqū minhum tuqāh. Wa yuḥadhdhirukumul-lāhu Nafsah. Wa ʾilal-lāhil-maṣīr. (28)
Qul ʾiñ-tukhfū mā fī ṣudūrikum ʾaw tubduhu yaʿlamhul-lāh. Wa yaʿlamu mā fis-samāwāti wa mā fil-ʾarḍ. Wal-lāhu ʿalā kulli shayʾiñ-Qadīr. (29)
Yawma tajidu kullu nafsim-mā ʿamilat miñ-khayrim-muḥḍarañw-wa mā ʿamilat miñ-sūuʾiñ-tawaddu law ʾanna baynahā wa baynahūu ʾamadam-baʿīdā. Wa yuḥadhdhirukumul-lāhu Nafsah. Wal-lāhu Raʾūfum-bilʿibād. (30)
Qul ʾiñ-kuñtum tuḥibbūnal-lāha fattabiʿūnī yuḥbibkumul-lāhu wa yaghfir lakum dhunūbakum. Wal-lāhu Ghafūrur-Raḥīm. (31)

19 I.e., in cases where the interests of those "deniers of the truth" clash with the interests of believers (*Manār* III, 278). Regarding the deeper implications of the term "allies" (*awliyāʾ*), see 4 : 139 and the corresponding note.

20 Lit., "unless you fear from them something that is to be feared". Zamakhsharī explains this phrase as meaning, "unless you have reason to fear that they might do something which ought to be guarded against" – obviously referring to situations in which "those who deny the truth" are more powerful than the Muslims, and are therefore in a position to damage the latter unless they become their "allies" in a political or moral sense.

21 Lit., "breasts". This is a reference to the real motives underlying the decision of a Muslim group or power to form

Say: "Pay heed unto God and the Apostle." And if they turn away – verily, God does not love those who deny the truth. ‹32›

BEHOLD, God raised Adam, and Noah, and the House of Abraham, and the House of ʿImrān above all mankind, ‹33› in one line of descent.[22]

And God was all-hearing, all-knowing[23] ‹34› when a woman of [the House of] ʿImrān prayed: "O my Sustainer! Behold, unto Thee do I vow [the child] that is in my womb, to be devoted to Thy service. Accept it, then, from me: verily, Thou alone art all-hearing, all-knowing!" ‹35›

But when she had given birth to the child,[24] she said: "O my Sustainer! Behold, I have given birth to a female" – the while God had been fully aware of what she would give birth to, and [fully aware] that no male child [she might have hoped for] could ever have been like this female[25] – "and I have named her Mary. And, verily, I seek Thy protection for her and her offspring against Satan, the accursed." ‹36›

And so her Sustainer accepted her with goodly acceptance, and caused her to grow up in goodly growth, and placed her in the care of Zachariah.[26]

قُلْ أَطِيعُوا۟ ٱللَّهَ وَٱلرَّسُولَ ۖ فَإِن تَوَلَّوْا۟ فَإِنَّ ٱللَّهَ لَا يُحِبُّ ٱلْكَٰفِرِينَ ﴿٣٢﴾ ۞
إِنَّ ٱللَّهَ ٱصْطَفَىٰٓ ءَادَمَ وَنُوحًا وَءَالَ إِبْرَٰهِيمَ وَءَالَ عِمْرَٰنَ عَلَى ٱلْعَٰلَمِينَ ﴿٣٣﴾
ذُرِّيَّةًۢ بَعْضُهَا مِنۢ بَعْضٍ ۗ وَٱللَّهُ سَمِيعٌ عَلِيمٌ ﴿٣٤﴾ إِذْ قَالَتِ ٱمْرَأَتُ عِمْرَٰنَ رَبِّ
إِنِّى نَذَرْتُ لَكَ مَا فِى بَطْنِى مُحَرَّرًا فَتَقَبَّلْ مِنِّىٓ ۖ إِنَّكَ أَنتَ ٱلسَّمِيعُ ٱلْعَلِيمُ ﴿٣٥﴾
فَلَمَّا وَضَعَتْهَا قَالَتْ رَبِّ إِنِّى وَضَعْتُهَآ أُنثَىٰ وَٱللَّهُ أَعْلَمُ بِمَا وَضَعَتْ وَلَيْسَ
ٱلذَّكَرُ كَٱلْأُنثَىٰ ۖ وَإِنِّى سَمَّيْتُهَا مَرْيَمَ وَإِنِّىٓ أُعِيذُهَا بِكَ وَذُرِّيَّتَهَا مِنَ ٱلشَّيْطَٰنِ
ٱلرَّجِيمِ ﴿٣٦﴾ فَتَقَبَّلَهَا رَبُّهَا بِقَبُولٍ حَسَنٍ وَأَنۢبَتَهَا نَبَاتًا حَسَنًا وَكَفَّلَهَا زَكَرِيَّا ۖ

ربع الحزب

Qul ʾaṭīʿul-lāha war-Rasūla faʾiñ-tawallaw faʾinnal-lāha lā yuḥibbul-kāfirīn. (32) ۞ ʾInnal-lāhaṣ-ṭafāa ʾĀdama wa Nūḥañw-wa ʾĀla ʾIbrāhīma wa ʾĀla ʿImrāna ʿalal-ʿālamīn. (33) Dhurriyyatam-baʿḍuhā mim-baʿḍ. Wal-lāhu Samīʿun ʿAlīm. (34) ʾIdh qālatim-raʾatu ʿImrana Rabbi ʾinnī nadhartu laka mā fī baṭnī muḥarrarañ-fataqabbal minni ʾinnaka ʾAñtas-Samīʿul-ʿAlīm. (35) Falammā waḍaʿat-hā qālat Rabbi ʾinnī waḍaʿtuhāa uñthā; wal-lāhu ʾaʿlamu bimā waḍaʿat wa laysadh-dhakaru kalʾuñthā. Wa ʾinnī sammaytuhā Maryama wa ʾinnīi ʾuʿīdhuhā bika wa dhurriyātahā minash-Shayṭānir-rajīm. (36) Fataqabbalahā Rabbuhā biqabūlin ḥasaniñw-wa ʾambatahā nabātan ḥasanañw-wa kaffalahā Zakariyyā.

---

an alliance with "those who deny the truth" in preference to, or against the legitimate interests of, other believers.

22 Lit., "offspring of one another" – an allusion not merely to the physical descent of those prophets but also to the fact that all of them were spiritually linked with one another and believed in one and the same fundamental truth (Ṭabarī). Thus, the above passage is a logical sequence to verses 31-32, which make God's approval contingent upon obedience to His chosen message-bearers. The names which appear in this sentence circumscribe, by implication, all the prophets mentioned in the Qurʾān inasmuch as most of them were descendants of two or more of these patriarchs. The House of ʿImrān comprises Moses and Aaron, whose father was ʿImrān (the Amram of the Bible), and Aaron's descendants, the priestly caste among the Israelites – thus including John the Baptist, both of whose parents were of the same descent (cf. the reference, in Luke i, 5, to John's mother Elisabeth as one "of the daughters of Aaron"), as well as Jesus, whose mother Mary – a close relation of John – is spoken of elsewhere in the Qurʾān (19 : 28) as a "sister of Aaron": in both cases embodying the ancient Semitic custom of linking a person's or a people's name with that of an illustrious forebear. The reference to the House of ʿImrān serves as an introduction to the stories of Zachariah, John, Mary, and Jesus.

23 My joining of this phrase with the following passage is in agreement with the interpretation advanced by Muḥammad ʿAbduh and Rashīd Riḍāʾ (*Manār* III, 289).

24 Lit., "to her" – implying that it was a girl.

25 Lit., "and the male is not [or "could not be"] like the female". Zamakhsharī reads these words as forming part of the parenthetic sentence relating to God's knowledge, and explains them thus: "The male [child] which she had prayed for could not have been like the female which she was granted" – which implies that Mary's excellence would go far beyond any hopes which her mother had ever entertained.

26 As is evident from verse 44 of this *sūrah*, the guardianship of Mary was entrusted to Zachariah – who was not only her relative but also a priest attached to the Temple – after lots had been drawn to decide which of the priests

Whenever Zachariah visited her in the sanctuary, he found her provided with food. He would ask: "O Mary, whence came this unto thee?"
She would answer: "It is from God; behold, God grants sustenance unto whom He wills, beyond all reckoning."[27] ‹37›
In that self-same place, Zachariah prayed unto his Sustainer, saying: "O my Sustainer! Bestow upon me [too], out of Thy grace, the gift of goodly offspring; for Thou, indeed, hearest all prayer." ‹38›
Thereupon, as he stood praying in the sanctuary, the angels called out unto him: "God sends thee the glad tiding of [the birth of] John, who shall confirm the truth of a word from God,[28] and [shall be] outstanding among men, and utterly chaste, and a prophet from among the righteous." ‹39›
[Zachariah] exclaimed: "O my Sustainer! How can I have a son when old age has already overtaken me, and my wife is barren?"
Answered [the angel]: "Thus it is: God does what He wills." ‹40›
[Zachariah] prayed: "O my Sustainer! Appoint a sign for me!"
Said [the angel]: "Thy sign shall be that for three days thou wilt not speak unto men other than by gestures.[29] And remember

كُلَّمَا دَخَلَ عَلَيْهَا زَكَرِيَّا ٱلْمِحْرَابَ وَجَدَ عِندَهَا رِزْقًا قَالَ يَٰمَرْيَمُ أَنَّىٰ
لَكِ هَٰذَا قَالَتْ هُوَ مِنْ عِندِ ٱللَّهِ إِنَّ ٱللَّهَ يَرْزُقُ مَن يَشَآءُ بِغَيْرِ حِسَابٍ ﴿٣٧﴾
هُنَالِكَ دَعَا زَكَرِيَّا رَبَّهُۥ قَالَ رَبِّ هَبْ لِى مِن لَّدُنكَ ذُرِّيَّةً طَيِّبَةً إِنَّكَ
سَمِيعُ ٱلدُّعَآءِ ﴿٣٨﴾ فَنَادَتْهُ ٱلْمَلَٰٓئِكَةُ وَهُوَ قَآئِمٌ يُصَلِّى فِى ٱلْمِحْرَابِ أَنَّ
ٱللَّهَ يُبَشِّرُكَ بِيَحْيَىٰ مُصَدِّقًۢا بِكَلِمَةٍ مِّنَ ٱللَّهِ وَسَيِّدًا وَحَصُورًا وَنَبِيًّا مِّنَ
ٱلصَّٰلِحِينَ ﴿٣٩﴾ قَالَ رَبِّ أَنَّىٰ يَكُونُ لِى غُلَٰمٌ وَقَدْ بَلَغَنِىَ ٱلْكِبَرُ
وَٱمْرَأَتِى عَاقِرٌ قَالَ كَذَٰلِكَ ٱللَّهُ يَفْعَلُ مَا يَشَآءُ ﴿٤٠﴾ قَالَ رَبِّ ٱجْعَل لِّىٓ
ءَايَةً قَالَ ءَايَتُكَ أَلَّا تُكَلِّمَ ٱلنَّاسَ ثَلَٰثَةَ أَيَّامٍ إِلَّا رَمْزًا وَٱذْكُر

Kullamā dakhala ʿalayhā Zakariyyal-miḥrāba wajada ʿiñdahā rizqā. Qāla yā Maryamu ʾannā laki hādhā. Qālat huwa min ʿiñdil-lāh. ʾInnal-lāha yarzuqu mañy-yashāaʾu bighayri ḥisāb. (37) Hunālika daʿā Zakariyyā Rabbah. Qāla Rabbi hab lī mil-laduñka dhurriyyatañ-ṭayyibah. ʾInnaka Samīʿud-duʿāaʾ. (38) Fanādat-hul-Malāaʾikatu wa huwa qāaʾimuñy-yuṣallī fil-miḥrābi ʾannal-lāha yubashshiruka bi-Yaḥyā muṣaddiqam-bikalimatim-minal-lāhi wa sayyidañw-wa ḥaṣūrañw-wa Nabiyyam-minaṣ-ṣāliḥīn. (39) Qāla Rabbi ʾannā yakūnu lī ghulāmuñw-wa qad balaghaniyal-kibaru wam-raʾatī ʿāqir. Qāla kadhālikal-lāhu yafʿalu mā yashāaʾ. (40) Qāla Rabbij-ʿal-līi ʾĀyah. Qāla ʾĀyatuka ʾallā tukallimannāsa thalāthata ʾayyāmin ʾillā ramzā. Wadh-kur-

should have the responsibility for this girl who, in consequence of her mother's vow, was to be dedicated to Temple service (Ṭabarī).

27 In spite of all the legends quoted in this connection by most of the commentators, there is no indication whatsoever either in the Qurʾān or in any authentic Tradition that these provisions were of a miraculous origin. On the other hand, Ṭabarī quotes a story to the effect that when, in his old age, Zachariah became unable to support Mary by his own means, the community decided to assume this responsibility through another of its members, who thereupon provided her daily with food. Whether this story is authentic or not, Mary's answer to Zachariah reflects no more and no less than her deep consciousness of God as the ultimate Provider.

28 In view of the fact that the expression *kalimah* is often used in the Qurʾān to denote an announcement from God, or a statement of His will, or His promise (e.g., 4 : 171, 6 : 34 and 115, 10 : 64, 18 : 27, and so forth), we must conclude that in the above passage, too, the "word from God" which would be confirmed by the birth of John (described in the Gospels as "John the Baptist") refers to a divine *promise* given through revelation: and this, indeed, is the interpretation adopted by the famous philologist Abū ʿUbaydah Maʿmar ibn al-Muthannā, who lived in the second century H. and devoted most of his labours to the study of rare expressions in the Arabic language; his identification, in the context under discussion, of *kalimah* with *kitāb* ("revelation" or "divine writ") has been quoted by Rāzī in his commentary on this verse and is, moreover, agreeable with a similar announcement conveyed to Mary regarding the birth of Jesus (see verse 45 of this *sūrah*).

29 According to Abū Muslim (quoted with approval by Rāzī), Zachariah was merely *enjoined* not to speak to anyone during the period of three days, and not struck dumb as in the New Testament narrative (Luke i, 20-22): thus the "sign" was purely spiritual, and was to consist in Zachariah's utter self-abandonment to prayer and contemplation.

thy Sustainer unceasingly, and extol His limitless glory by night and by day." ‹41›

AND LO! The angels said: "O Mary! Behold, God has elected thee and made thee pure, and raised thee above all the women of the world. ‹42› O Mary! Remain thou truly devout unto thy Sustainer, and prostrate thyself in worship, and bow down with those who bow down [before Him]." ‹43›

This account of something that was beyond the reach of thy perception We [now] reveal unto thee,[30] for thou wert not with them when they drew lots as to which of them should be Mary's guardian,[31] and thou wert not with them when they contended [about it] with one another. ‹44›

Lo! The angels said: "O Mary! Behold, God sends thee the glad tiding, through a word from Him, [of a son] who shall become known as the Christ[32] Jesus, son of Mary, of great honour in this world and in the life to come, and [shall be] of those who are drawn near unto God. ‹45› And he shall speak unto men in his cradle,[33] and as a grown man, and shall be of the righteous." ‹46›

رَبَّكَ كَثِيرًا وَسَبِّحْ بِالْعَشِيِّ وَالْإِبْكَارِ ﴿41﴾ وَإِذْ قَالَتِ الْمَلَٰٓئِكَةُ
يَٰمَرْيَمُ إِنَّ اللَّهَ اصْطَفَىٰكِ وَطَهَّرَكِ وَاصْطَفَىٰكِ عَلَىٰ نِسَآءِ الْعَٰلَمِينَ ﴿42﴾
يَٰمَرْيَمُ اقْنُتِي لِرَبِّكِ وَاسْجُدِي وَارْكَعِي مَعَ الرَّٰكِعِينَ ﴿43﴾ ذَٰلِكَ مِنْ
أَنۢبَآءِ الْغَيْبِ نُوحِيهِ إِلَيْكَ وَمَا كُنتَ لَدَيْهِمْ إِذْ يُلْقُونَ أَقْلَٰمَهُمْ أَيُّهُمْ
يَكْفُلُ مَرْيَمَ وَمَا كُنتَ لَدَيْهِمْ إِذْ يَخْتَصِمُونَ ﴿44﴾ إِذْ قَالَتِ الْمَلَٰٓئِكَةُ
يَٰمَرْيَمُ إِنَّ اللَّهَ يُبَشِّرُكِ بِكَلِمَةٍ مِّنْهُ اسْمُهُ الْمَسِيحُ عِيسَى ابْنُ مَرْيَمَ
وَجِيهًا فِي الدُّنْيَا وَالْأَخِرَةِ وَمِنَ الْمُقَرَّبِينَ ﴿45﴾ وَيُكَلِّمُ النَّاسَ فِي
الْمَهْدِ وَكَهْلًا وَمِنَ الصَّٰلِحِينَ ﴿46﴾

Rabbaka kathīrañw-wa sabbiḥ bilʿashiyyi wal-ʾibkār. ﴿41﴾ Wa ʾidh qālatil-Malāaʾikatu yā Maryamu ʾinnal-lāhaṣ-ṭafāki wa ṭahharaki waṣ-ṭafāki ʿalā nisāaʾil-ʿālamīn. ﴿42﴾ Yā Maryamuq-nutī liRabbiki was-judī war-kaʿī maʿar-rākiʿīn. ﴿43﴾ Dhālika min ʾambāaʾil-ghaybi nūḥīhi ʾilayk. Wa mā kuñta ladayhim ʾidh yulqūna ʾaqlāmahum ʾayyuhum yakfulu Maryam. Wa mā kuñta ladayhim ʾidh yakhtaṣimūn. ﴿44﴾ ʾIdh qālatil-Malāaʾikatu yā Maryamu ʾinnal-lāha yubash-shiruki biKalimatim-minhus-muhul-Masīḥu ʿĪsab-nu Maryama wajīhañ-fid-dunyā wal-ʾĀkhirati wa minal-muqarrabīn. ﴿45﴾ Wa yukallimun-nāsa fil-mahdi wa kahlañw-wa minaṣ-ṣāliḥīn. ﴿46﴾

30 This parenthetic passage, addressed to the Prophet, is meant to stress the fact that the story of Mary, as narrated in the Qurʾān, is a direct outcome of revelation and, therefore, inherently true in spite of all the differences between this account and that given in the scriptures regarded by the Christians as authentic (Muḥammad ʿAbduh in *Manār* III, 301 f.).

31 See note 26 above. The phrase rendered above as "they drew lots" reads literally, "they cast their reeds" – obviously a reference to an ancient Semitic custom, perhaps similar to the divination by means of blunt arrows practiced by the pre-Islamic Arabs and comprehensively described in Lane III, 1247. The pronoun "they" relates to the priests, of whom Zachariah was one.

32 Lit., "whose name shall be 'the Anointed' (*al-masīḥ*)". The designation *al-masīḥ* is the Arabicized form of the Aramaic *mĕshīḥā* which, in turn, is derived from the Hebrew *māhsīaḥ*, "the anointed" – a term frequently applied in the Bible to the Hebrew kings, whose accession to power used to be consecrated by a touch with holy oil taken from the Temple. This anointment appears to have been so important a rite among the Hebrews that the term "the anointed" became in the course of time more or less synonymous with "king". Its application to Jesus may have been due to the widespread conviction among his contemporaries (references to which are found in several places in the Synoptic Gospels) that he was descended in direct – and obviously legitimate – line from the royal House of David. (It is to be noted that this could not have related to his mother's side, because Mary belonged to the priestly class descending from Aaron, and thus to the tribe of Levi, while David descended from the tribe of Judah). Whatever may have been the historical circumstances, it is evident that the honorific "the Anointed" was applied to Jesus in his own lifetime. In the Greek version of the Gospels – which is undoubtedly based on a now-lost Aramaic original – this designation is correctly translated as *Christos* (a noun derived from the Greek verb *chriein*, "to anoint"): and since it is in this form – "the Christ" – that the designation *al-masīḥ* has achieved currency in all Western languages, I am using it throughout in my translation.

33 A metaphorical allusion to the prophetic wisdom which was to inspire Jesus from a very early age. As regards the expression *min al-muqarrabīn* ("of those who are drawn near", i.e., unto God), see 56 : 11, where the most excellent among the inmates of paradise are thus described.

Said she: "O my Sustainer! How can I have a son when no man has ever touched me?"
[The angel] answered: "Thus it is: God creates what He wills:[34] when He wills a thing to be, He but says unto it, 'Be' – and it is. ‹47› And He will impart unto thy son[35] revelation, and wisdom, and the Torah, and the Gospel, ‹48› and [will make him] an apostle unto the children of Israel."[36]

"I HAVE COME unto you with a message from your Sustainer. I shall create for you out of clay, as it were, the shape of [your] destiny, and then breathe into it, so that it might become [your] destiny by God's leave;[37] and I shall heal the blind and the leper, and bring the dead back to life by God's leave:[38] and I shall let you know what you may eat and what you should store up in your houses.[39] Behold, in all this there is indeed a message for you, if you are [truly] believers. ‹49›
"And [I have come] to confirm the truth of whatever there still remains[40] of the Torah,

قَالَتْ رَبِّ أَنَّىٰ يَكُونُ لِي وَلَدٌ وَلَمْ يَمْسَسْنِي بَشَرٌ قَالَ كَذَٰلِكِ ٱللَّهُ يَخْلُقُ
مَا يَشَآءُ إِذَا قَضَىٰٓ أَمْرًا فَإِنَّمَا يَقُولُ لَهُۥ كُن فَيَكُونُ ﴿٤٧﴾ وَيُعَلِّمُهُ
ٱلْكِتَٰبَ وَٱلْحِكْمَةَ وَٱلتَّوْرَىٰةَ وَٱلْإِنجِيلَ ﴿٤٨﴾ وَرَسُولًا إِلَىٰ بَنِىٓ إِسْرَٰٓءِيلَ
أَنِّى قَدْ جِئْتُكُم بِـَٔايَةٍ مِّن رَّبِّكُمْ أَنِّىٓ أَخْلُقُ لَكُم مِّنَ ٱلطِّينِ كَهَيْـَٔةِ
ٱلطَّيْرِ فَأَنفُخُ فِيهِ فَيَكُونُ طَيْرًۢا بِإِذْنِ ٱللَّهِ وَأُبْرِئُ ٱلْأَكْمَهَ وَٱلْأَبْرَصَ وَأُحْىِ
ٱلْمَوْتَىٰ بِإِذْنِ ٱللَّهِ وَأُنَبِّئُكُم بِمَا تَأْكُلُونَ وَمَا تَدَّخِرُونَ فِى بُيُوتِكُمْ إِنَّ فِى
ذَٰلِكَ لَءَايَةً لَّكُمْ إِن كُنتُم مُّؤْمِنِينَ ﴿٤٩﴾ وَمُصَدِّقًا لِّمَا بَيْنَ يَدَىَّ مِنَ ٱلتَّوْرَىٰةِ

Qālat Rabbi ʾannā yakūnu lī waladuñw-wa lam yamsasnī basharuñ-qāla kadhālikil-lāhu yakhluqu mā yashāaʾ. ʾIdhā qaḍāa ʾamrañ-faʾinnamā yaqūlu lahū kuñ-fayakūn. ﴿47﴾ Wa yuʿallimuhul-Kitāba wal-ḥikmata wat-Tawrāta wal-ʾIñjīl. ﴿48﴾ Wa Rasūlan ʾilā banīi ʾIsrāaʾīla ʾannī qad jiʾtukum-biʾĀyatim-mir-Rabbikum ʾannīi ʾakhluqu lakum-minaṭ-ṭīni kahayʾatiṭ-ṭayri faʾañfukhu fīhi fayakūnu ṭayram-biʾidhnil-lāh. Wa ʾubriʾul-ʾakmaha wal-ʾabraṣa wa ʾuḥyil-mawtā biʾidhnil-lāh. Wa ʾunabbiʾukum-bimā taʾkulūna wa mā taddakhirūna fī buyūtikum. ʾInna fī dhālika laʾĀyatal-lakum ʾiñ-kuñtum muʾminīn. ﴿49﴾ Wa muṣaddiqal-limā bayna yadayya minat-Tawrāti

34 See 19 : 16-22 and the corresponding notes. In the context of the story of Mary in *Āl ʿImrān*, the announcement made to her, as well as the parallel one to Zachariah (verses 39-40 above), is meant to stress God's unlimited power of creation – specifically, in both cases, His power to create the circumstances in which His will is to manifest itself – and thus to bring about any event, however unexpected or even improbable it might seem at the time of the announcement.

35 Lit., "to him".

36 The passage which follows here – up to the end of verse 51 – may be understood in either of two ways: as part of the announcement made to Mary (implying that he would thus speak in the *future*) or, alternatively, as a statement of what, at a later time, he actually *did* say to the children of Israel. In view of the narrative form adopted in verses 52 ff., the second of these two alternatives seems preferable.

37 Lit., "[something] like the shape of a bird (*ṭayr*); and then I shall breathe into it, so that it might [or "whereupon it will"] become a bird . . .". The noun *ṭayr* is a plural of *ṭaʾir* ("flying creature" or "bird"), or an infinitive noun ("flying") derived from the verb *ṭāra* ("he flew"). In pre-Islamic usage, as well as in the Qurʾān, the words *ṭāʾir* and *ṭayr* often denote "fortune" or "destiny", whether good or evil (as, for instance, in 7 : 131, 27 : 47 or 36 : 19, and still more clearly in 17 : 13). Many instances of this idiomatic use of *ṭayr* and *ṭāʾir* are given in all the authoritative Arabic dictionaries; see also Lane V, 1904 f. Thus, in the parabolic manner so beloved by him, Jesus intimated to the children of Israel that out of the humble clay of their lives he would fashion for them the vision of a soaring destiny, and that this vision, brought to life by his God-given inspiration, would become their real destiny by God's leave and by the strength of their faith (as pointed out at the end of this verse).

38 It is probable that the "raising of the dead" by Jesus is a metaphorical description of his giving new life to people who were spiritually dead; cf. 6 : 122 – "Is then he who was dead [in spirit], and whom We thereupon gave life, and for whom We set up a light whereby he can see his way among men – [is then he] like unto one [who is lost] in darkness deep, out of which he cannot emerge?" If this interpretation is – as I believe – correct, then the "healing of the blind and the leper" has a similar significance: namely, an inner regeneration of people who were spiritually diseased and blind to the truth.

39 I.e., "what good things you may partake of in the life of this world, and what good deeds you should lay up as a treasure for the life to come".

40 Lit., "whatever there is between my hands": for an explanation, see note 3 on verse 3 of this *sūrah*.

and to make lawful unto you some of the things which [aforetime] were forbidden to you. And I have come unto you with a message from your Sustainer; remain, then, conscious of God, and pay heed unto me. ‹50›
"Verily, God is my Sustainer as well as your Sustainer; so worship Him [alone]: this is a straight way." ‹51›
And when Jesus became aware of their refusal to acknowledge the truth,[41] he asked: "Who will be my helpers in God's cause?"
The white-garbed ones[42] replied: "We shall be [thy] helpers [in the cause] of God! We believe in God: and bear thou witness that we have surrendered ourselves unto Him! ‹52› O our Sustainer! We believe in what Thou hast bestowed from on high, and we follow this Apostle; make us one,[43] then, with all who bear witness [to the truth]!" ‹53›
And the unbelievers schemed [against Jesus];[44] but God brought their scheming to nought: for God is above all schemers. ‹54›
Lo! God said: "O Jesus! Verily, I shall cause thee to die, and shall exalt thee unto Me, and cleanse thee of [the presence of] those who are bent on denying the truth; and I shall place those who follow thee [far] above those who are bent on denying the truth, unto the Day of Resurrection. In the end, unto Me you all must return, and I shall judge between you with regard to all on which you were wont to differ.[45] ‹55›

وَلِأُحِلَّ لَكُم بَعْضَ ٱلَّذِى حُرِّمَ عَلَيْكُمْ ۚ وَجِئْتُكُم بِـَٔايَةٍ مِّن رَّبِّكُمْ
فَٱتَّقُوا۟ ٱللَّهَ وَأَطِيعُونِ ﴿50﴾ إِنَّ ٱللَّهَ رَبِّى وَرَبُّكُمْ فَٱعْبُدُوهُ ۗ هَـٰذَا صِرَٰطٌ
مُّسْتَقِيمٌ ﴿51﴾ ۞ فَلَمَّآ أَحَسَّ عِيسَىٰ مِنْهُمُ ٱلْكُفْرَ قَالَ مَنْ أَنصَارِىٓ إِلَى
ٱللَّهِ ۖ قَالَ ٱلْحَوَارِيُّونَ نَحْنُ أَنصَارُ ٱللَّهِ ءَامَنَّا بِٱللَّهِ وَٱشْهَدْ بِأَنَّا
مُسْلِمُونَ ﴿52﴾ رَبَّنَآ ءَامَنَّا بِمَآ أَنزَلْتَ وَٱتَّبَعْنَا ٱلرَّسُولَ فَٱكْتُبْنَا مَعَ
ٱلشَّـٰهِدِينَ ﴿53﴾ وَمَكَرُوا۟ وَمَكَرَ ٱللَّهُ ۖ وَٱللَّهُ خَيْرُ ٱلْمَـٰكِرِينَ ﴿54﴾ إِذْ قَالَ
ٱللَّهُ يَـٰعِيسَىٰٓ إِنِّى مُتَوَفِّيكَ وَرَافِعُكَ إِلَىَّ وَمُطَهِّرُكَ مِنَ ٱلَّذِينَ كَفَرُوا۟
وَجَاعِلُ ٱلَّذِينَ ٱتَّبَعُوكَ فَوْقَ ٱلَّذِينَ كَفَرُوٓا۟ إِلَىٰ يَوْمِ ٱلْقِيَـٰمَةِ ۖ ثُمَّ إِلَىَّ
مَرْجِعُكُمْ فَأَحْكُمُ بَيْنَكُمْ فِيمَا كُنتُمْ فِيهِ تَخْتَلِفُونَ ﴿55﴾

نصف الحزب

wa liʾuḥilla lakum baʿḍal-ladhī ḥurrima ʿalaykum wa jiʾtukum-biʾĀyatim-mir-Rabbikum; fattaqul-lāha wa ʾaṭīʿūn. (50) ʾInnal-lāha Rabbī wa Rabbukum faʿbudūhu hādhā ṣirāṭum-mustaqīm. (51) ۞ Falammāa ʾaḥassa ʿĪsā minhumul-kufra qāla man ʾanṣārīi ʾilal-lāh. Qālal-Ḥawāriyyūna naḥnu ʾanṣārul-lāhi ʾāmannā bil-lāhi wash-had biʾannā Muslimūn. (52) Rabbanāa ʾāmannā bimāa ʾanzalta wat-tabaʿnar-Rasūla faktubnā maʿash-shāhidīn. (53) Wa makarū wa makaral-lāhu wal-lāhu khayrul-mākirīn. (54) ʾIdh qālal-lāhu yā ʿĪsāa ʾinnī mutawaffīka wa rāfiʿuka ʾilayya wa muṭahhiruka minal-ladhīna kafarū wa jāʿilul-ladhīnat-tabaʿūka fawqal-ladhīna kafarūu ʾilā Yawmil-Qiyāmah. Thumma ʾilayya marjiʿukum faʾaḥkumu baynakum fīmā kuntum fīhi takhtalifūn. (55)

41 This relates to a later time, when Jesus was being opposed by the majority of his people, particularly the Pharisees.

42 *Al-ḥawāriyyūn* (sing. *ḥawārī*) is the designation applied in the Qurʾān to the disciples of Jesus. Many interpretations of this term (derived from *ḥawar*, "whiteness") are given by the commentators, ranging from "one who whitens clothes by washing them" (because this was allegedly the occupation of some of Jesus' disciples) to "one who wears white garments", or "one whose heart is white", i.e., pure (cf. Ṭabarī, Rāzī, Ibn Kathīr). It is, however, most probable – and the evidence provided by the recently discovered Dead Sea Scrolls strongly supports this view – that the term *ḥawārī* was popularly used to denote a member of the Essene Brotherhood, a Jewish religious group which existed in Palestine at the time of Jesus, and to which, possibly, he himself belonged. The Essenes were distinguished by their strong insistence on moral purity and unselfish conduct, and always wore white garments as the outward mark of their convictions; and this would satisfactorily explain the name given to them. The fact that the Prophet once said, "Every prophet has his *ḥawārī*" (Bukhārī and Muslim) does not conflict with the above view, since he obviously used this term figuratively, recalling thereby Jesus' "helpers in God's cause".

43 Lit., "write us down" or "inscribe us". It must, however, be borne in mind that the verb *kataba* means also "he drew together" or "brought together": hence the noun *katībah*, "a body of men".

44 Lit., "they schemed" – here referring to those among the Jews who refused to acknowledge Jesus as a prophet and tried to destroy him.

45 This refers to all who revere Jesus (i.e., the Christians, who believe him to be "the son of God", and the Muslims,

"And as for those who are bent on denying the truth, I shall cause them to suffer a suffering severe in this world and in the life to come, and they shall have none to succour them; ‹56› whereas unto those who attain to faith and do good works He will grant their reward in full: for God does not love evildoers." ‹57›

THIS MESSAGE do We convey unto thee, and this tiding full of wisdom:[46] ‹58›
Verily, in the sight of God, the nature of Jesus is as the nature of Adam, whom He created out of dust and then said unto him, "Be" – and he is.[47] ‹59› [This is] the truth from thy Sustainer; be not, then, among the doubters! ‹60›
And if anyone should argue with thee about this [truth] after all the knowledge that has come unto thee, say: "Come! Let us summon our sons and your sons, and our women and your women, and ourselves and yourselves; and then let us pray [together] humbly and ardently, and let us invoke God's curse upon those [of us] who are telling a lie."[48] ‹61›
Behold, this is indeed the truth of the matter, and there is no deity whatever save God; and, verily, God – He alone – is almighty, truly wise. ‹62› And if they turn away [from this truth] – behold, God has full knowledge of the spreaders of corruption. ‹63›

فَأَمَّا ٱلَّذِينَ كَفَرُواْ فَأُعَذِّبُهُمْ عَذَابًا شَدِيدًا فِى ٱلدُّنْيَا وَٱلْأَخِرَةِ وَمَا لَهُم مِّن
نَّٰصِرِينَ ﴿56﴾ وَأَمَّا ٱلَّذِينَ ءَامَنُواْ وَعَمِلُواْ ٱلصَّٰلِحَٰتِ فَيُوَفِّيهِمْ أُجُورَهُمْ
وَٱللَّهُ لَا يُحِبُّ ٱلظَّٰلِمِينَ ﴿57﴾ ذَٰلِكَ نَتْلُوهُ عَلَيْكَ مِنَ ٱلْأَيَٰتِ وَٱلذِّكْرِ
ٱلْحَكِيمِ ﴿58﴾ إِنَّ مَثَلَ عِيسَىٰ عِندَ ٱللَّهِ كَمَثَلِ ءَادَمَ خَلَقَهُۥ مِن تُرَابٍ ثُمَّ قَالَ
لَهُۥ كُن فَيَكُونُ ﴿59﴾ ٱلْحَقُّ مِن رَّبِّكَ فَلَا تَكُن مِّنَ ٱلْمُمْتَرِينَ ﴿60﴾ فَمَنْ
حَآجَّكَ فِيهِ مِنۢ بَعْدِ مَا جَآءَكَ مِنَ ٱلْعِلْمِ فَقُلْ تَعَالَوْاْ نَدْعُ أَبْنَآءَنَا وَأَبْنَآءَكُمْ
وَنِسَآءَنَا وَنِسَآءَكُمْ وَأَنفُسَنَا وَأَنفُسَكُمْ ثُمَّ نَبْتَهِلْ فَنَجْعَل لَّعْنَتَ ٱللَّهِ عَلَى
ٱلْكَٰذِبِينَ ﴿61﴾ إِنَّ هَٰذَا لَهُوَ ٱلْقَصَصُ ٱلْحَقُّ وَمَا مِنْ إِلَٰهٍ إِلَّا ٱللَّهُ وَإِنَّ
ٱللَّهَ لَهُوَ ٱلْعَزِيزُ ٱلْحَكِيمُ ﴿62﴾ فَإِن تَوَلَّوْاْ فَإِنَّ ٱللَّهَ عَلِيمٌۢ بِٱلْمُفْسِدِينَ ﴿63﴾

Faʾammal-ladhīna kafarū faʾuᶜadhdhibuhum ᶜadhābañ-shadīdañ-fid-dunyā wal-ʾĀkhirati wa mā lahum-miñ-nāṣirīn. (56) Wa ʾammal-ladhīna ʾāmanū wa-ᶜamiluṣ-ṣāliḥāti fayuwaffīhim ʾujūrahum. Wallāhu lā yuḥibbuẓ-ẓālimīn. (57) Dhālika natlūhu ᶜalayka minal-ʾĀyāti wadh-Dhikril-ḥakīm. (58) ʾInna mathala ʾĪsā ᶜiñdal-lāhi kamathali ʾĀdama khalaqahū miñ-turābiñ-thumma qāla lahū kuñ-fayakūn. (59) ʾAlḥaqqu mir-Rabbika falā takum-minal-mumtarīn. (60) Faman ḥāajjaka fīhi mim-baᶜdi mā jāaʾaka minal-ᶜilmi faqul taᶜālaw nadᶜu ʾabnāaʾanā wa ʾabnāaʾakum wa nisāaʾanā wa nisāaʾakum wa ʾañfusanā wa ʾañfusakum thumma nabtahil fanajᶜal-laᶜnatal-lāhi ᶜalal-kādhibīn. (61) ʾInna hādhā lahuwal-qaṣaṣul-ḥaqq. Wa mā min-ʾilāhin-ʾillal-lāhu wa ʾinnal-lāha laHuwal-ᶜAzīzul-Ḥakīm. (62) Faʾiñ-tawallaw faʾinnal-lāha ᶜAlīmum-bilmufsidīn. (63)

who regard him as a prophet) as well as to those who deny him altogether. Regarding God's promise to Jesus, "I shall exalt thee unto Me", see *sūrah* 4, note 172.

46 Lit., "This We convey unto thee of the messages and of the wise tiding." The expression "this of the messages" bears, to my mind, the connotation of one particular message – namely, the one which follows immediately after this sentence.

47 Lit., "The parable of Jesus is as the parable of Adam . . .", etc. The expression *mathal* (rendered above as "nature") is often metaphorically employed to denote the state or condition (of a person or a thing), and is in this sense – as the commentators have pointed out – synonymous with *ṣifah* (the "quality" or "nature" of a thing). As is evident from the sequence, the above passage is part of an argument against the Christian doctrine of the divinity of Jesus. The Qurʾān stresses here, as in many other places, the fact that Jesus, like Adam – by which name, in this context, the whole human race is meant – was only a mortal "created out of dust", i.e., out of substances, both organic and inorganic, which are found in their elementary forms on and in the earth. Cf. also 18 : 37, 22 : 5, 30 : 20, 35 : 11, 40 : 67, where the Qurʾān speaks of all human beings as "created out of dust". That "Adam" stands here for the human race is clearly implied in the use of the present tense in the last word of this sentence.

48 I.e., regarding the true nature of Jesus. According to all the reliable authorities, verses 59-63 of this *sūrah* were revealed in the year 10 H., on the occasion of a dispute between the Prophet and a deputation of the Christians of Najrān who, like all other Christians, maintained that Jesus was "the son of God" and, therefore, God incarnate. Although they refused the "trial through prayer" (*mubāhalah*) proposed to them by the Prophet, the latter accorded to them a treaty guaranteeing all their civic rights and the free exercise of their religion.

Say: "O followers of earlier revelation! Come unto that tenet which we and you hold in common:[49] that we shall worship none but God, and that we shall not ascribe divinity to aught beside Him, and that we shall not take human beings for our lords beside God."[50]
And if they turn away, then say: "Bear witness that it is we who have surrendered ourselves unto Him." ‹64›

O FOLLOWERS of earlier revelation! Why do you argue about Abraham,[51] seeing that the Torah and the Gospel were not revealed till [long] after him? Will you not, then, use your reason? ‹65› Lo! You are the ones who would argue about that which is known to you; but why do you argue about something which is unknown to you?[52]
Yet God knows [it], whereas you do not know: ‹66› Abraham was neither a "Jew" nor a "Christian", but was one who turned away from all that is false, having surrendered himself unto God; and he was not of those who ascribe divinity to aught beside Him. ‹67›
Behold, the people who have the best claim to Abraham are surely those who follow him – as does this Prophet and all who believe [in him] – and God is near unto the believers. ‹68›
Some of the followers of earlier revelation would love to lead you astray: yet none do they lead astray but themselves, and perceive it not. ‹69›

قُلْ يَٰٓأَهْلَ ٱلْكِتَٰبِ تَعَالَوْاْ إِلَىٰ كَلِمَةٍ سَوَآءٍ بَيْنَنَا وَبَيْنَكُمْ أَلَّا نَعْبُدَ
إِلَّا ٱللَّهَ وَلَا نُشْرِكَ بِهِۦ شَيْـًٔا وَلَا يَتَّخِذَ بَعْضُنَا بَعْضًا أَرْبَابًا مِّن دُونِ ٱللَّهِ
فَإِن تَوَلَّوْاْ فَقُولُواْ ٱشْهَدُواْ بِأَنَّا مُسْلِمُونَ ﴿٦٤﴾ يَٰٓأَهْلَ ٱلْكِتَٰبِ لِمَ
تُحَآجُّونَ فِىٓ إِبْرَٰهِيمَ وَمَآ أُنزِلَتِ ٱلتَّوْرَىٰةُ وَٱلْإِنجِيلُ إِلَّا مِنۢ بَعْدِهِۦٓ أَفَلَا
تَعْقِلُونَ ﴿٦٥﴾ هَٰٓأَنتُمْ هَٰٓؤُلَآءِ حَٰجَجْتُمْ فِيمَا لَكُم بِهِۦ عِلْمٌ فَلِمَ تُحَآجُّونَ
فِيمَا لَيْسَ لَكُم بِهِۦ عِلْمٌ وَٱللَّهُ يَعْلَمُ وَأَنتُمْ لَا تَعْلَمُونَ ﴿٦٦﴾ مَا كَانَ
إِبْرَٰهِيمُ يَهُودِيًّا وَلَا نَصْرَانِيًّا وَلَٰكِن كَانَ حَنِيفًا مُّسْلِمًا وَمَا كَانَ مِنَ
ٱلْمُشْرِكِينَ ﴿٦٧﴾ إِنَّ أَوْلَى ٱلنَّاسِ بِإِبْرَٰهِيمَ لَلَّذِينَ ٱتَّبَعُوهُ وَهَٰذَا ٱلنَّبِىُّ
وَٱلَّذِينَ ءَامَنُواْ وَٱللَّهُ وَلِىُّ ٱلْمُؤْمِنِينَ ﴿٦٨﴾ وَدَّت طَّآئِفَةٌ مِّنْ أَهْلِ ٱلْكِتَٰبِ
لَوْ يُضِلُّونَكُمْ وَمَا يُضِلُّونَ إِلَّآ أَنفُسَهُمْ وَمَا يَشْعُرُونَ ﴿٦٩﴾

Qul yāa ʾahlal-Kitābi taʿālaw ʾilā kalimatiñ-sawāa-ʾim-baynanā wa baynakum ʾallā naʿbuda ʾillal-lāha wa lā nushrika bihī shayʾañw-wa lā yattakhidha baʿḍuna baʿḍan ʾarbābam-miñ-dūnil-lāh. Faʾiñ-tawallaw faqūlush-hadū biʾannā Muslimūn. (64) Yāa ʾahlal-Kitābi lima tuḥāajjūna fīi ʾIbrāhīma wa māa ʾuñzilatit-Tawrātu wal-ʾIñjīlu ʾillā mim-baʿdih. ʾAfalā taʿqilūn. (65) Hāa ʾañtum hāaʾulāaʾi ḥājajtum fīmā lakum-bihī ʿilmuñ-falima tuḥāajjūna fīmā laysa lakum-bihī ʿilm. Wal-lāhu yaʿlamu wa ʾañtum lā taʿlamūn. (66) Mā kāna ʾIbrāhīmu Yahūdiyyañw-wa lā Naṣrāniyyañw-wa lākiñ-kāna ḥanīfañ-Muslimā. Wa mā kāna minal-mush-rikīn. (67) ʾInna ʾawlan-nāsi biʾIbrāhīma lalladhīnat-tabaʿūhu wa hādhan-Nabiyyu wal-ladhina ʾāmanū. Wal-lāhu Waliyyul-muʾminīn. (68) Waddaṭ-ṭāaʾifatum-min ʾahlil-Kitābi law yuḍillūnakum wa mā yuḍillūna ʾillāa ʾañfusa-hum wa mā yashʿurūn. (69)

49 Lit., "a word [that is] equitable between us and you". The term *kalimah*, primarily meaning "word" or "utterance", is often used in the philosophical sense of "proposition" or "tenet".

50 Lit., "that we shall not take one another for lords beside God". Since the personal pronoun "we" obviously applies to human beings, the expression "one another" necessarily bears the same connotation. In its wider implication, the above call is addressed not merely to the Christians, who attribute divinity to Jesus and certain aspects of divinity to their saints, but also to the Jews, who assign a quasi-divine authority to Ezra and even to some of their great Talmudic scholars (cf. 9 : 30-31).

51 I.e., as to whether the principles he followed were those of the Jewish faith, according to which the Torah is considered to be the final Law of God, or of the Christian faith, which conflicts with the former in many respects.

52 I.e., as to what was the true creed of Abraham. "That which is known to you" is an allusion to their knowledge of the obvious fact that many of the teachings based on the extant versions of the Torah and the Gospels conflict with the teachings of the Qurʾān (Rāzī).

ثلاثة ارباع الحزب

O followers of earlier revelation! Why do you deny the truth of God's messages to which you yourselves bear witness?[53] ‹70›
O followers of earlier revelation! Why do you cloak the truth with falsehood and conceal the truth of which you are [so well] aware? ‹71›
And some of the followers of earlier revelation say [to one another]: "Declare your belief in what has been revealed unto those who believe [in Muḥammad] at the beginning of the day, and deny the truth of what came later,[54] so that they might go back [on their faith]; ‹72› but do not [really] believe anyone who does not follow your own faith."
Say: "Behold, all [true] guidance is God's guidance, consisting in one's being granted [revelation] such as you have been granted."[55] Or would they contend against you before your Sustainer?
Say: "Behold, all bounty is in the hand of God; He grants it unto whom He wills:[56] for God is infinite, all-knowing, ‹73› singling out for His grace whom He wills. And God is limitless in His great bounty." ‹74›

AND AMONG the followers of earlier revelation there is many a one who, if thou entrust him with a treasure, will [faithfully] restore it to thee; and there is among them many a one who, if thou entrust him with a tiny gold coin, will not restore it to thee unless thou keep standing over him –

يَٰٓأَهۡلَ ٱلۡكِتَٰبِ لِمَ تَكۡفُرُونَ بِـَٔايَٰتِ ٱللَّهِ وَأَنتُمۡ تَشۡهَدُونَ ﴿٧٠﴾ يَٰٓأَهۡلَ
ٱلۡكِتَٰبِ لِمَ تَلۡبِسُونَ ٱلۡحَقَّ بِٱلۡبَٰطِلِ وَتَكۡتُمُونَ ٱلۡحَقَّ وَأَنتُمۡ تَعۡلَمُونَ ﴿٧١﴾
وَقَالَت طَّآئِفَةٞ مِّنۡ أَهۡلِ ٱلۡكِتَٰبِ ءَامِنُواْ بِٱلَّذِيٓ أُنزِلَ عَلَى ٱلَّذِينَ ءَامَنُواْ
وَجۡهَ ٱلنَّهَارِ وَٱكۡفُرُوٓاْ ءَاخِرَهُۥ لَعَلَّهُمۡ يَرۡجِعُونَ ﴿٧٢﴾ وَلَا تُؤۡمِنُوٓاْ إِلَّا لِمَن
تَبِعَ دِينَكُمۡ قُلۡ إِنَّ ٱلۡهُدَىٰ هُدَى ٱللَّهِ أَن يُؤۡتَىٰٓ أَحَدٞ مِّثۡلَ مَآ أُوتِيتُمۡ أَوۡ
يُحَآجُّوكُمۡ عِندَ رَبِّكُمۡۗ قُلۡ إِنَّ ٱلۡفَضۡلَ بِيَدِ ٱللَّهِ يُؤۡتِيهِ مَن يَشَآءُۗ وَٱللَّهُ
وَٰسِعٌ عَلِيمٞ ﴿٧٣﴾ يَخۡتَصُّ بِرَحۡمَتِهِۦ مَن يَشَآءُۗ وَٱللَّهُ ذُو ٱلۡفَضۡلِ
ٱلۡعَظِيمِ ﴿٧٤﴾ ۞ وَمِنۡ أَهۡلِ ٱلۡكِتَٰبِ مَنۡ إِن تَأۡمَنۡهُ بِقِنطَارٖ يُؤَدِّهِۦٓ إِلَيۡكَ
وَمِنۡهُم مَّنۡ إِن تَأۡمَنۡهُ بِدِينَارٖ لَّا يُؤَدِّهِۦٓ إِلَيۡكَ إِلَّا مَا دُمۡتَ عَلَيۡهِ قَآئِمٗاۗ

Yāa ʾahlal-Kitābi lima takfurūna biʾĀyātil-lāhi wa ʾañtum tashhadūn. ﴿70﴾ Yāa ʾahlal-Kitābi lima talbisūnal-ḥaqqa bilbāṭili wa taktumūnal-ḥaqqa wa ʾañtum taʿlamūn. ﴿71﴾ Wa qālaṭ-ṭāaʾifatum-min ʾahlil-Kitābi ʾāminū billadhīi ʾuñzila ʿalal-ladhīna ʾāmanū wajhan-nahāri wak-furūu ʾākhirahū laʿallahum yarjiʿūn. ﴿72﴾ Wa lā tuʾminūu ʾillā limañ-tabiʿa dīnakum. Qul ʾinnal-hudā hudal-lāhi ʾañy-yuʾtāa ʾaḥadum-mithla māa ʾūtītum ʾaw yuḥāajjūkum ʿiñda Rabbikum. Qul ʾinnal-faḍla biyadil-lāhi yuʾtīhi mañy-yashāaʾ. Wal-lāhu Wāsiʿun ʿAlīm. ﴿73﴾ Yakhtaṣṣu biraḥmatihī mañy-yashāaʾ. Wal-lāhu Dhul-faḍlil-ʿaẓīm. ﴿74﴾ ۞ Wa min ʾahlil-Kitābi man ʾiñ-taʾmanhu biqiñṭāriñy-yuʾaddihīi ʾilayk. Wa minhum-man ʾiñ-taʾmanhu bidīnāril-lā yuʾaddihīi ʾilayka ʾillā mā dumta ʿalayhi qāaʾimā.

53 Lit., "when you [yourselves] bear witness": an allusion to the Biblical prophecies relating to the coming of the Prophet Muḥammad.

54 Most of the commentators, relying on views current among some of the *tābiʿūn* (i.e., the generation that came after the Companions of the Prophet), understand this passage thus: "Declare at the beginning of the day your belief in what has been revealed unto those who believe in Muḥammad, and deny the truth [thereof] in its latter part." This rendering would imply that the Judaeo-Christian attempts at confusing the Muslims, to which the above verse refers, consisted in alternatingly declaring belief and disbelief in the Qurʾanic message. On the other hand, the rendering adopted by me (and supported by Al-Aṣam, whose interpretation has been quoted by Rāzī in his commentary on this verse) implies that some Jews and Christians have been and are hoping to achieve this end by admitting, however reluctantly, that there may be "some truth" in the early Qurʾanic revelations ("that which has been revealed at the beginning of the day"), while they categorically reject its later parts inasmuch as they clearly contradict certain Biblical teachings.

55 This refers to the Jews and the Christians, who are not prepared to accept the Qurʾanic message on the ground that it conflicts with parts of their own scriptures.

56 In this context, the term *faḍl* ("bounty") is synonymous with the bestowal of divine revelation.

which is an outcome of their assertion,[57] "No blame can attach to us [for anything that we may do] with regard to these unlettered folk": and [so] they tell a lie about God, being well aware [that it is a lie].[58] ‹75›
Nay, but [God is aware of] those who keep their bond with Him,[59] and are conscious of Him: and, verily, God loves those who are conscious of Him. ‹76›
Behold, those who barter away their bond with God and their own pledges for a trifling gain – they shall not partake in the blessings of the life to come; and God will neither speak unto them nor look upon them on the Day of Resurrection, nor will He cleanse them of their sins; and grievous suffering awaits them. ‹77›
And, behold, there are indeed some among them who distort the Bible with their tongues, so as to make you think that [what they say] is from the Bible, the while it is not from the Bible; and who say, "This is from God," the while it is not from God: and thus do they tell a lie about God, being well aware [that it is a lie].[60] ‹78›

ذَٰلِكَ بِأَنَّهُمْ قَالُوا۟ لَيْسَ عَلَيْنَا فِى ٱلْأُمِّيِّـۧنَ سَبِيلٌ وَيَقُولُونَ عَلَى ٱللَّهِ
ٱلْكَذِبَ وَهُمْ يَعْلَمُونَ ﴿٧٥﴾ بَلَىٰ مَنْ أَوْفَىٰ بِعَهْدِهِۦ وَٱتَّقَىٰ فَإِنَّ ٱللَّهَ يُحِبُّ
ٱلْمُتَّقِينَ ﴿٧٦﴾ إِنَّ ٱلَّذِينَ يَشْتَرُونَ بِعَهْدِ ٱللَّهِ وَأَيْمَـٰنِهِمْ ثَمَنًا قَلِيلًا
أُو۟لَـٰٓئِكَ لَا خَلَـٰقَ لَهُمْ فِى ٱلْـَٔاخِرَةِ وَلَا يُكَلِّمُهُمُ ٱللَّهُ وَلَا يَنظُرُ إِلَيْهِمْ
يَوْمَ ٱلْقِيَـٰمَةِ وَلَا يُزَكِّيهِمْ وَلَهُمْ عَذَابٌ أَلِيمٌ ﴿٧٧﴾ وَإِنَّ مِنْهُمْ لَفَرِيقًا
يَلْوُۥنَ أَلْسِنَتَهُم بِٱلْكِتَـٰبِ لِتَحْسَبُوهُ مِنَ ٱلْكِتَـٰبِ وَمَا هُوَ مِنَ
ٱلْكِتَـٰبِ وَيَقُولُونَ هُوَ مِنْ عِندِ ٱللَّهِ وَمَا هُوَ مِنْ عِندِ ٱللَّهِ وَيَقُولُونَ عَلَى
ٱللَّهِ ٱلْكَذِبَ وَهُمْ يَعْلَمُونَ ﴿٧٨﴾

Dhālika biʾannahum qālū laysa ʿalaynā fil-ʾummiyyīna sabīluñw-wa yaqūlūna ʿalal-lāhil-kadhiba wa hum yaʿlamūn. ﴿75﴾ Balā man ʾawfā biʿahdihī wattaqā faʾinnal-lāha yuḥibbul-muttaqīn. ﴿76﴾ ʾInnal-ladhīna yashtarūna biʿahdil-lāhi wa ʾaymānihim thamanañ-qalīlan ʾulāaʾika lā khalāqa lahum fil-ʾĀkhirati wa lā yukallimuhumul-lāhu wa lā yañẓuru ʾilayhim Yawmal-Qiyāmati wa lā yuzakkīhim; wa lahum ʿadhābun ʾalīm. ﴿77﴾ Wa ʾinna minhum lafarīqañy-yalwūna ʾalsinatahum-bilKitābi litaḥsabūhu minal-Kitābi wa mā huwa minal-Kitābi wa yaqūlūna huwa min ʿiñdil-lāhi wa mā huwa min ʿiñdil-lāhi wa yaqūlūna ʿalal-lāhil-kadhiba wa hum yaʿlamūn. ﴿78﴾

57 Lit., "this, because they say". In Arabic usage, the verb *qāla* (lit., "he said") often signifies "he asserted" or "expressed an opinion". As is evident from many Traditions, the people referred to are the Jews.

58 I.e., they falsely claim that God Himself has exempted them from all moral responsibility towards non-Jews (contemptuously described as "unlettered folk"), knowing well that their own scriptures provide no basis whatever for such a claim.

59 Some of the commentators relate the personal pronoun in *ʿahdihi* to the person or persons concerned, and therefore take *ʿahd* as meaning "promise" – thus: "[as for] him who fulfils his promise . . .", etc. It is, however, obvious from the next verse that the pronoun in *ʿahdihi* refers to God; consequently, the phrase must be rendered either as "those who fulfil their duty towards Him" or "those who keep their bond with Him" – the latter being, in my opinion, preferable. (For the meaning of man's "bond with God", see *sūrah* 2, note 19.)

60 Most of the commentators assume that this refers specifically to the Jews, whom the Qurʾān frequently accuses of having deliberately corrupted the Old Testament. However, since the next two verses clearly relate to Jesus and to the false beliefs of the Christians regarding his nature and mission, we must conclude that both Jews and Christians are referred to in this passage. For this reason, the term *al-kitāb*, which occurs three times in this sentence, has been rendered here as "the Bible". – According to Muḥammad ʿAbduh (*Manār* III, 345), the above-mentioned distortion of the Bible does not necessarily presuppose a corruption of the text as such: it can also be brought about "by attributing to an expression a meaning other than the one which was originally intended". As an example, ʿAbduh quotes the metaphorical use, in the Gospels, of the term "my Father" with reference to God – by which term, as is evident from the Lord's Prayer, was obviously meant the "Father" – i.e., the Originator and Sustainer – of all mankind. Subsequently, however, some of those who claimed to be followers of Jesus lifted this expression from the realm of metaphor and "transferred it to the realm of positive reality with reference to Jesus alone": and thus they gave currency to the idea that he was literally "the son of God", that is, God incarnate.

It is not conceivable that a human being unto whom God had granted revelation, and sound judgment, and prophethood, should thereafter have said unto people,[61] "Worship *me* beside God" but rather [did he exhort them], "Become men of God[62] by spreading the knowledge of the divine writ, and by your own deep study [thereof]." ‹79› And neither did he bid you to take the angels and the prophets for your lords:[63] [for] would he bid you to deny the truth after you have surrendered yourselves unto God? ‹80›

AND, LO, God accepted, through the prophets, this solemn pledge [from the followers of earlier revelation]:[64] "If, after all the revelation and the wisdom which I have vouchsafed unto you, there comes to you an apostle confirming the truth already in your possession, you must believe in him and succour him. Do you" – said He – "acknowledge and accept My bond on this condition?"
They answered: "We do acknowledge it."
Said He: "Then bear witness [thereto], and I shall be your witness.[65] ‹81› And, henceforth, all who turn away [from this pledge] – it is they, they who are truly iniquitous!" ‹82›
Do they seek, perchance, a faith other than in God,[66] although it is unto Him that whatever is in the heavens and on earth surrenders itself, willingly or unwillingly, since unto Him all must return?[67] ‹83›
Say: "We believe in God, and in that which has been bestowed from on high upon us,

مَا كَانَ لِبَشَرٍ أَن يُؤْتِيَهُ ٱللَّهُ ٱلْكِتَـٰبَ وَٱلْحُكْمَ وَٱلنُّبُوَّةَ ثُمَّ يَقُولَ
لِلنَّاسِ كُونُوا۟ عِبَادًا لِّى مِن دُونِ ٱللَّهِ وَلَـٰكِن كُونُوا۟ رَبَّـٰنِيِّـۧنَ بِمَا كُنتُمْ
تُعَلِّمُونَ ٱلْكِتَـٰبَ وَبِمَا كُنتُمْ تَدْرُسُونَ ﴿٧٩﴾ وَلَا يَأْمُرَكُمْ أَن تَتَّخِذُوا۟
ٱلْمَلَـٰٓئِكَةَ وَٱلنَّبِيِّـۧنَ أَرْبَابًا ۗ أَيَأْمُرُكُم بِٱلْكُفْرِ بَعْدَ إِذْ أَنتُم
مُّسْلِمُونَ ﴿٨٠﴾ وَإِذْ أَخَذَ ٱللَّهُ مِيثَـٰقَ ٱلنَّبِيِّـۧنَ لَمَآ ءَاتَيْتُكُم مِّن كِتَـٰبٍ
وَحِكْمَةٍ ثُمَّ جَآءَكُمْ رَسُولٌ مُّصَدِّقٌ لِّمَا مَعَكُمْ لَتُؤْمِنُنَّ بِهِۦ وَلَتَنصُرُنَّهُۥ ۚ
قَالَ ءَأَقْرَرْتُمْ وَأَخَذْتُمْ عَلَىٰ ذَٰلِكُمْ إِصْرِى ۖ قَالُوٓا۟ أَقْرَرْنَا ۚ قَالَ فَٱشْهَدُوا۟
وَأَنَا۠ مَعَكُم مِّنَ ٱلشَّـٰهِدِينَ ﴿٨١﴾ فَمَن تَوَلَّىٰ بَعْدَ ذَٰلِكَ فَأُو۟لَـٰٓئِكَ هُمُ
ٱلْفَـٰسِقُونَ ﴿٨٢﴾ أَفَغَيْرَ دِينِ ٱللَّهِ يَبْغُونَ وَلَهُۥٓ أَسْلَمَ مَن فِى ٱلسَّمَـٰوَٰتِ
وَٱلْأَرْضِ طَوْعًا وَكَرْهًا وَإِلَيْهِ يُرْجَعُونَ ﴿٨٣﴾ قُلْ ءَامَنَّا بِٱللَّهِ وَمَآ أُنزِلَ عَلَيْنَا

Mā kāna libasharin ʾañy-yuʾtiyahul-lāhul-Kitāba wal-ḥukma wan-Nubuwwata thumma yaqūla linnāsi kūnū ʿibādal-lī miñ-dūnil-lāhi wa lākiñ-kūnū Rabbāniyyīna bimā kuñtum tuʿallimūnal-Kitāba wa bimā kuñtum tadrusūn. (79) Wa lā yaʾmurakum ʾañ-tattakhidhul-Malāaʾikata wan-Nabiyyīna ʾarbābā. ʾAyaʾmurukum-bilkufri baʿda ʾidh ʾañtum-Muslimūn. (80) Wa ʾidh ʾakhadhal-lāhu mīthāqan-Nabiyyīna lamāa ʾātaytukum-miñ-Kitābiñw-wa ḥikmatiñ-thumma jāaʾakum Rasūlum-muṣaddiqul-limā maʿakum latuʾminunna bihī wa latañṣurunnah. Qāla ʾaʾaqrartum wa ʾakhadhtum ʿalā dhālikum ʾiṣrī. Qālūu ʾaqrarnā. Qāla fashhadū wa ʾana maʿakum-minash-shāhidīn. (81) Famañ-tawallā baʿda dhālika faʾulāaʾika humul-fāsiqūn. (82) ʾAfaghayra dīnil-lāhi yabghuna wa lahūu ʾaslama mañ-fis-samāwāti wal-ʾarḍi ṭawʿañw-wa karhañw-wa ʾilayhi yurjaʿūn. (83) Qul ʾāmannā billāhi wa māa ʾuñzila ʿalaynā

61 This obvious reference to Jesus reads, literally, "It is not [possible] for a human being that God should grant him . . . and that thereafter he should say . . .". Zamakhsharī regards the term *ḥukm* ("judgment" or "sound judgment") occurring in the above sentence as synonymous, in this context, with *ḥikmah* ("wisdom").

62 According to Sībawayh (as quoted by Rāzī), a *rabbānī* is "one who devotes himself exclusively to the endeavour to know the Sustainer (*ar-rabb*) and to obey Him": a connotation fairly close to the English expression "a man of God".

63 I.e., to attribute divine or semi-divine powers to them: a categorical rejection of the adoration of saints and angelic beings.

64 Lit., "the solemn pledge of the prophets". Zamakhsharī holds that what is meant here is a pledge taken from the community as a whole: a pledge consisting in their acceptance of the messages conveyed through the prophets.

65 Lit., "and I am with you among the witnesses".

66 Lit., "[any] other than God's religion".

67 Lit., "will be returned". For an explanation of this sentence, see 13 : 15 and the corresponding notes.

and that which has been bestowed upon Abraham and Ishmael and Isaac and Jacob and their descendants, and that which has been vouchsafed by their Sustainer unto Moses and Jesus and all the [other] prophets: we make no distinction between any of them.[68] And unto Him do we surrender ourselves." ‹84›
For, if one goes in search of a religion other than self-surrender unto God, it will never be accepted from him, and in the life to come he shall be among the lost. ‹85›
How would God bestow His guidance upon people who have resolved to deny the truth after having attained to faith, and having borne witness that this Apostle is true, and [after] all evidence of the truth has come unto them?[69] For, God does not guide such evildoing folk. ‹86› Their requital shall be rejection by God, and by the angels, and by all [righteous] men. ‹87› In this state shall they abide; [and] neither will their suffering be lightened, nor will they be granted respite. ‹88›
But excepted shall be they that afterwards repent and put themselves to rights: for, behold, God is much-forgiving, a dispenser of grace. ‹89›
Verily, as for those who are bent on denying the truth after having attained to faith, and then grow [ever more stubborn] in their refusal to acknowledge the truth, their repentance [of other sins] shall not be accepted:[70] for it is they who have truly gone astray. ‹90› Verily, as for those who are bent on denying the truth and die as deniers of the truth – not all the gold on earth could ever be their ransom.[71] It is they for whom grievous suffering is in store; and they shall have none to succour them. ‹91›

وَمَآ أُنزِلَ عَلَىٰٓ إِبْرَٰهِيمَ وَإِسْمَٰعِيلَ وَإِسْحَٰقَ وَيَعْقُوبَ وَٱلْأَسْبَاطِ وَمَآ
أُوتِىَ مُوسَىٰ وَعِيسَىٰ وَٱلنَّبِيُّونَ مِن رَّبِّهِمْ لَا نُفَرِّقُ بَيْنَ أَحَدٍ مِّنْهُمْ وَنَحْنُ
لَهُۥ مُسْلِمُونَ ﴿٨٤﴾ وَمَن يَبْتَغِ غَيْرَ ٱلْإِسْلَٰمِ دِينًا فَلَن يُقْبَلَ مِنْهُ وَهُوَ فِى
ٱلْءَاخِرَةِ مِنَ ٱلْخَٰسِرِينَ ﴿٨٥﴾ كَيْفَ يَهْدِى ٱللَّهُ قَوْمًا كَفَرُوا۟ بَعْدَ
إِيمَٰنِهِمْ وَشَهِدُوٓا۟ أَنَّ ٱلرَّسُولَ حَقٌّ وَجَآءَهُمُ ٱلْبَيِّنَٰتُ ۚ وَٱللَّهُ لَا يَهْدِى
ٱلْقَوْمَ ٱلظَّٰلِمِينَ ﴿٨٦﴾ أُو۟لَٰٓئِكَ جَزَآؤُهُمْ أَنَّ عَلَيْهِمْ لَعْنَةَ ٱللَّهِ وَٱلْمَلَٰٓئِكَةِ
وَٱلنَّاسِ أَجْمَعِينَ ﴿٨٧﴾ خَٰلِدِينَ فِيهَا لَا يُخَفَّفُ عَنْهُمُ ٱلْعَذَابُ وَلَا هُمْ
يُنظَرُونَ ﴿٨٨﴾ إِلَّا ٱلَّذِينَ تَابُوا۟ مِنۢ بَعْدِ ذَٰلِكَ وَأَصْلَحُوا۟ فَإِنَّ ٱللَّهَ غَفُورٌ
رَّحِيمٌ ﴿٨٩﴾ إِنَّ ٱلَّذِينَ كَفَرُوا۟ بَعْدَ إِيمَٰنِهِمْ ثُمَّ ٱزْدَادُوا۟ كُفْرًا لَّن تُقْبَلَ
تَوْبَتُهُمْ وَأُو۟لَٰٓئِكَ هُمُ ٱلضَّآلُّونَ ﴿٩٠﴾ إِنَّ ٱلَّذِينَ كَفَرُوا۟ وَمَاتُوا۟ وَهُمْ كُفَّارٌ
فَلَن يُقْبَلَ مِنْ أَحَدِهِم مِّلْءُ ٱلْأَرْضِ ذَهَبًا وَلَوِ ٱفْتَدَىٰ بِهِۦٓ ۗ أُو۟لَٰٓئِكَ لَهُمْ
عَذَابٌ أَلِيمٌ وَمَا لَهُم مِّن نَّٰصِرِينَ ﴿٩١﴾

**wa māa ʾuñzila ʿalāa ʾIbrāhīma wa ʾIsmāʿīla wa
ʾIsḥāqa wa Yaʿqūba wal-ʾasbāṭi wa māa ʾūtiya Mūsā
wa ʿĪsā wan-Nabiyyūna mir-Rabbihim. Lā nufarriqu
bayna ʾaḥadim-minhum wa naḥnu lahū Muslimūn.
84 Wa mañy-yabtaghi ghayral-ʾIslāmi dīnañ-falañy-
yuqbala minhu wa huwa fil-ʾĀkhirati minal-khāsirīn.
85 Kayfa yahdil-lāhu qawmañ-kafarū baʿda ʾīmānihim
wa shahidūu ʾannar-Rasūla ḥaqquñw-wa jāaʾahu-
mul-bayyināt. Wal-lāhu lā yahdil-qawmaẓ-ẓālimīn. 86
ʾUlāaʾika jazāaʾuhum ʾanna ʿalayhim laʿnatal-lāhi
wal-Malāaʾikati wan-nāsi ʾajmaʿīn. 87 Khālidīna
fīhā; lā yukhaffafu ʿanhumul-ʿadhābu wa lā hum
yuñẓarūn. 88 ʾIllal-ladhīna tābū mim-baʿdi dhālika
wa ʾaṣlaḥū faʾinnal-lāha Ghafūrur-Raḥīm. 89 ʾInnal-
ladhīna kafarū baʿda ʾīmānihim thummaz-dādū ku-
fral-lan tuqbala tawbatuhum wa ʾulāaʾika humuḍ-
ḍāallūn. 90 ʾInnal-ladhīna kafarū wa mātū wa hum
kuffāruñ-falañy-yuqbala min ʾaḥadihim milʾul-ʾarḍi
dhahabañw-wa lawif-tadā bih. ʾUlāaʾika lahum
ʿadhābun ʾalīmuñw-wa mā lahum-miñ-nāṣirīn. 91**

68 See 2 : 136 and the corresponding note 112.

69 The people referred to are the Jews and the Christians. Their acceptance of the Bible, which predicts the coming of the Prophet Muḥammad, has made them "witnesses" to the truth of his prophethood. See also verses 70 and 81 above.

70 My interpolation, between brackets, of the words "of other sins" is based on Ṭabarī's convincing explanation of this passage.

71 Lit., "there shall not be accepted from any of them the earth full of gold, were he to proffer it in ransom". The meaning of this sentence is obviously metaphorical; but in view of the mention of "ransom", some of the

لَن تَنَالُواْ ٱلۡبِرَّ حَتَّىٰ تُنفِقُواْ مِمَّا تُحِبُّونَۚ وَمَا تُنفِقُواْ مِن شَيۡءٖ فَإِنَّ ٱللَّهَ بِهِۦ
عَلِيمٞ ﴿92﴾ ۞ كُلُّ ٱلطَّعَامِ كَانَ حِلّٗا لِّبَنِيٓ إِسۡرَٰٓءِيلَ إِلَّا مَا حَرَّمَ إِسۡرَٰٓءِيلُ
عَلَىٰ نَفۡسِهِۦ مِن قَبۡلِ أَن تُنَزَّلَ ٱلتَّوۡرَىٰةُۗ قُلۡ فَأۡتُواْ بِٱلتَّوۡرَىٰةِ فَٱتۡلُوهَآ إِن
كُنتُمۡ صَٰدِقِينَ ﴿93﴾ فَمَنِ ٱفۡتَرَىٰ عَلَى ٱللَّهِ ٱلۡكَذِبَ مِنۢ بَعۡدِ ذَٰلِكَ
فَأُوْلَٰٓئِكَ هُمُ ٱلظَّٰلِمُونَ ﴿94﴾ قُلۡ صَدَقَ ٱللَّهُۗ فَٱتَّبِعُواْ مِلَّةَ إِبۡرَٰهِيمَ حَنِيفٗا
وَمَا كَانَ مِنَ ٱلۡمُشۡرِكِينَ ﴿95﴾ إِنَّ أَوَّلَ بَيۡتٖ وُضِعَ لِلنَّاسِ لَلَّذِي بِبَكَّةَ

Lañ-tanālul-birra ḥattā tuñfiqū mimmā tuḥibbūn. Wa mā tuñfiqū miñ-shayʾiñ-faʾinnal-lāha bihī ʿAlīm. (92) ۞ Kulluṭ-ṭaʿāmi kāna ḥillal-libanīi ʾIsrāaʾīla ʾillā mā ḥarrama ʾIsrāaʾīlu ʿalā nafsihī miñ-qabli ʾañ-tunazzalat-Tawrāh. Qul faʾtū bitTawrāti fatlūhāa ʾiñ-kuñtum ṣādiqīn. (93) Famanif-tarā ʿalal-lāhil-kadhiba mim-baʿdi dhālika faʾulāaʾika humuẓ-ẓālimūn. (94) Qul ṣadaqal-lāh. Fattabiʿū millata ʾIbrā-hīma ḥanīfañw-wa mā kāna minal-mushrikīn. (95) ʾInna ʾawwala Baytiñw-wuḍiʿa linnāsi lalladhī biBakkata

[But as for you, O believers,] never shall you attain to true piety unless you spend on others out of what you cherish yourselves; and whatever you spend – verily, God has full knowledge thereof.[72] ⟨92⟩

ALL FOOD was lawful unto the children of Israel, save what Israel had made unlawful unto itself [by its sinning] before the Torah was bestowed from on high.[73] Say: "Come forward, then, with the Torah and recite it, if what you say is true!" ⟨93⟩

حزب 7
جزء 4

And all who henceforth invent lies about God – it is they, they who are evildoers![74] ⟨94⟩

Say: "God has spoken the truth: follow, then, the creed of Abraham, who turned away from all that is false, and was not of those who ascribe divinity to aught beside God." ⟨95⟩

Behold, the first Temple ever set up for mankind was indeed the one at Bakkah:[75]

commentators are of the opinion that what is meant here are otherwise good actions in this world (and, in particular, efforts and possessions spent for the sake of helping one's fellow-men), on the strength of which such stubborn "deniers of the truth" might plead for God's clemency on the Day of Judgment – a plea that would be rejected on the ground of their deliberate denial of fundamental truths.

72 After telling those who deliberately deny the truth that even their benevolent spending of efforts and possessions during their lifetime will be of no avail to them on the Day of Judgment, the Qurʾān reminds the believers that, on the other hand, their faith in God cannot be considered complete unless it makes them conscious of the material needs of their fellow-beings (cf. 2 : 177).

73 Up to this point, most of this *sūrah* dealt with the divine origin of the Qurʾān and was meant to establish the true nature of the mission entrusted to the Prophet – namely, his call to an acknowledgement of God's oneness and uniqueness. Now, verses 93-97 are devoted to a refutation of two objections on the part of the Jews to what they consider to be an infringement, by the Qurʾān, of Biblical laws, in spite of the oft-repeated Qurʾanic claim that this revelation confirms the truth inherent in the teachings of the earlier prophets. These two objections relate to (a) the Qurʾanic annulment of certain dietary injunctions and prohibitions laid down in the Torah, and (b) the alleged "substitution" of Mecca for Jerusalem as the direction of prayer (*qiblah*) – see *sūrah* 2, note 116. In order to answer the objection relating to Jewish food laws, the Qurʾān calls to mind that originally all wholesome foods were lawful to the children of Israel, and that the severe restrictions subsequently imposed upon them in the Torah were but a punishment for their sins (cf. 6 : 146), and were, therefore, never intended for a community that truly surrenders itself to God. For an answer to the second objection, see verse 96.

74 This is a reference to the unwarranted Jewish belief that the Mosaic food restrictions were an eternal law decreed by God. As against this claim, the Qurʾān stresses that no food restrictions had been imposed before the time of Moses and, secondly, that the restrictions arising from the Mosaic Law were imposed on the children of Israel alone. To claim that they represent an eternal divine law is described here as "inventing lies about God".

75 All authorities agree that this name is synonymous with Mecca (which, correctly transliterated, is spelt *Makkah*). Various etymologies have been suggested for this very ancient designation; but the most plausible explanation is given by Zamakhsharī (and supported by Rāzī): in some old Arabic dialects the labial consonants *b* and *m*, being phonetically close to one another, are occasionally interchangeable. The mention, in this context, of the Temple in Mecca – that is, the Kaʿbah – arises from the fact that it is the direction of prayer (*qiblah*) stipulated in the Qurʾān. Since the prototype of the Kaʿbah was built by Abraham and Ishmael (see 2 : 125 ff.) – and is, therefore, much older than the Temple of Solomon in Jerusalem – its establishment as the *qiblah* of the followers of the Qurʾān does not only not imply any break with the Abrahamic tradition (on which, ultimately, the whole Bible rests), but, on the

rich in blessing, and a [source of] guidance unto all the worlds, «96» full of clear messages.[76] [It is] the place whereon Abraham once stood; and whoever enters it finds inner peace.[77] Hence, pilgrimage unto the Temple is a duty owed to God by all people who are able to undertake it. And as for those who deny the truth – verily, God does not stand in need of anything in all the worlds. «97»

SAY: "O followers of earlier revelation! Why do you refuse to acknowledge the truth of God's messages, when God is witness to all that you do?" «98»
Say: "O followers of earlier revelation! Why do you [endeavour to] bar those who have come to believe [in this divine writ] from the path of God by trying to make it appear crooked, when you yourselves bear witness[78] [to its being straight]? For, God is not unaware of what you do." «99»
O you who have attained to faith! If you pay heed to some of those to whom revelation was vouchsafed aforetime, they might cause you to renounce the truth after you have come to believe [in it]. «100» And how could you deny the truth when it is unto you that God's messages are being conveyed, and it is in your midst that His Apostle lives? But he who holds fast unto God has already been guided onto a straight way. «101»
O you who have attained to faith! Be conscious of God with all the consciousness that is due to Him, and do not allow death to overtake you ere you have surrendered yourselves unto Him. «102»

مُبَارَكًا وَهُدًى لِّلْعَٰلَمِينَ ﴿96﴾ فِيهِ ءَايَٰتُۢ بَيِّنَٰتٌ مَّقَامُ إِبْرَٰهِيمَ وَمَن
دَخَلَهُۥ كَانَ ءَامِنًا وَلِلَّهِ عَلَى ٱلنَّاسِ حِجُّ ٱلْبَيْتِ مَنِ ٱسْتَطَاعَ إِلَيْهِ سَبِيلًا
وَمَن كَفَرَ فَإِنَّ ٱللَّهَ غَنِىٌّ عَنِ ٱلْعَٰلَمِينَ ﴿97﴾ قُلْ يَٰٓأَهْلَ ٱلْكِتَٰبِ لِمَ
تَكْفُرُونَ بِـَٔايَٰتِ ٱللَّهِ وَٱللَّهُ شَهِيدٌ عَلَىٰ مَا تَعْمَلُونَ ﴿98﴾ قُلْ يَٰٓأَهْلَ
ٱلْكِتَٰبِ لِمَ تَصُدُّونَ عَن سَبِيلِ ٱللَّهِ مَنْ ءَامَنَ تَبْغُونَهَا عِوَجًا وَأَنتُمْ
شُهَدَآءُ وَمَا ٱللَّهُ بِغَٰفِلٍ عَمَّا تَعْمَلُونَ ﴿99﴾ يَٰٓأَيُّهَا ٱلَّذِينَ ءَامَنُوٓا۟ إِن تُطِيعُوا۟
فَرِيقًا مِّنَ ٱلَّذِينَ أُوتُوا۟ ٱلْكِتَٰبَ يَرُدُّوكُم بَعْدَ إِيمَٰنِكُمْ كَٰفِرِينَ ﴿100﴾
وَكَيْفَ تَكْفُرُونَ وَأَنتُمْ تُتْلَىٰ عَلَيْكُمْ ءَايَٰتُ ٱللَّهِ وَفِيكُمْ رَسُولُهُۥ وَمَن
يَعْتَصِم بِٱللَّهِ فَقَدْ هُدِىَ إِلَىٰ صِرَٰطٍ مُّسْتَقِيمٍ ﴿101﴾ يَٰٓأَيُّهَا ٱلَّذِينَ ءَامَنُوا۟
ٱتَّقُوا۟ ٱللَّهَ حَقَّ تُقَاتِهِۦ وَلَا تَمُوتُنَّ إِلَّا وَأَنتُم مُّسْلِمُونَ ﴿102﴾

mubārakañw-wa hudal-lilʿālamīn. (96) Fīhī ʾĀyātum-
bayyinātum-maqāmu ʾIbrāhīma wa mañ-dakhalahū
kāna ʾāminā. Wa lillāhi ʿalan-nāsi ḥijjul-bayti manis-
taṭāʿa ʾilayhi sabīlā. Wa mañ-kafara faʾinnal-lāha
Ghaniyyun ʿanil-ʿālamīn. (97) Qul yāa ʾahlal-Kitābi
lima takfurūna biʾāyātil-lāhi wal-lāhu shahīdun ʿalā
mā taʿmalūn. (98) Qul yāa ʾahlal-Kitābi lima
taṣuddūna ʿañ-sabīlil-lāhi man ʾāmana tabghūnahā
ʿiwajañw-wa ʾañtum shuhadāaʾ. Wa mal-lāhu
bighāfilin ʿammā taʿmalūn. (99) Yāa ʾayyuhal-la-
dhīna ʾāmanūu ʾiñ-tuṭīʿū farīqam-minal-ladhīna ʾūtul-
Kitāba yaruddūkum baʿda ʾīmānikum kāfirīn. (100)
Wa kayfa takfurūna wa ʾañtum tutlā ʿalaykum
ʾĀyātul-lāhi wa fīkum Rasūluh. Wa mañy-yaʿtaṣim-
billāhi faqad hudiya ʾilā ṣirāṭim-mustaqīm. (101) Yāa
ʾayyuhal-ladhīna ʾāmanut-taqul-lāha ḥaqqa tuqātihī
wa lā tamūtunna ʾillā wa ʾañtum-Muslimūn. (102)

contrary, re-establishes the direct contact with that Patriarch: and herein lies the answer to the second of the two Jewish objections mentioned in note 73 above.

76 Lit., "in it [are] clear messages" – such as the messages relating to God's oneness and uniqueness (symbolized by the Kaʿbah), to the continuity of mankind's religious experience ("the *first* Temple set up for mankind") and, finally, to the brotherhood of all believers (who, wherever they may be, turn their faces in prayer towards this one focal point).

77 Or: "is secure" – i.e., in the original sense of *amn*, which implies "ease of mind and freedom from fear" (cf. Lane I, 100 f.).

78 I.e., "through your own scriptures" (see note 69 above, as well as note 33 on 2 : 42). This is an allusion to the attempts of Jews and Christians to "prove" that Muḥammad had "borrowed" the main ideas of the Qurʾān from the Bible and twisted them out of context so as to suit his own alleged "ambitions".

And hold fast, all together, unto the bond with God, and do not draw apart from one another. And remember the blessings which God has bestowed upon you: how, when you were enemies, He brought your hearts together, so that through His blessing you became brethren; and [how, when] you were on the brink of a fiery abyss,[79] He saved you from it.
In this way God makes clear His messages unto you, so that you might find guidance, ‹103› and that there might grow out of you a community [of people] who invite unto all that is good, and enjoin the doing of what is right and forbid the doing of what is wrong: and it is they, they who shall attain to a happy state! ‹104›
And be not like those who have drawn apart from one another and have taken to conflicting views after all evidence of the truth has come unto them:[80] for these it is for whom tremendous suffering is in store ‹105› on the Day [of Judgment] when some faces will shine [with happiness] and some faces will be dark [with grief]. And as for those with faces darkened, [they shall be told:] "Did you deny the truth after having attained to faith? Taste, then, this suffering for having denied the truth!" ‹106› But as for those with faces shining, they shall be within God's grace, therein to abide. ‹107›
These are God's messages: We convey them unto thee, setting forth the truth, since God wills no wrong to His creation.[81] ‹108›
And unto God belongs all that is in the heavens and all that is on earth; and all things go back to God [as their source]. ‹109›

YOU ARE indeed the best community that has ever been brought forth for [the good

وَٱعۡتَصِمُواْ بِحَبۡلِ ٱللَّهِ جَمِيعٗا وَلَا تَفَرَّقُواْۚ وَٱذۡكُرُواْ نِعۡمَتَ ٱللَّهِ عَلَيۡكُمۡ
إِذۡ كُنتُمۡ أَعۡدَآءٗ فَأَلَّفَ بَيۡنَ قُلُوبِكُمۡ فَأَصۡبَحۡتُم بِنِعۡمَتِهِۦٓ إِخۡوَٰنٗا وَكُنتُمۡ
عَلَىٰ شَفَا حُفۡرَةٖ مِّنَ ٱلنَّارِ فَأَنقَذَكُم مِّنۡهَاۗ كَذَٰلِكَ يُبَيِّنُ ٱللَّهُ لَكُمۡ
ءَايَٰتِهِۦ لَعَلَّكُمۡ تَهۡتَدُونَ (103) وَلۡتَكُن مِّنكُمۡ أُمَّةٞ يَدۡعُونَ إِلَى ٱلۡخَيۡرِ
وَيَأۡمُرُونَ بِٱلۡمَعۡرُوفِ وَيَنۡهَوۡنَ عَنِ ٱلۡمُنكَرِۚ وَأُوْلَٰٓئِكَ هُمُ
ٱلۡمُفۡلِحُونَ (104) وَلَا تَكُونُواْ كَٱلَّذِينَ تَفَرَّقُواْ وَٱخۡتَلَفُواْ مِنۢ بَعۡدِ مَا
جَآءَهُمُ ٱلۡبَيِّنَٰتُۚ وَأُوْلَٰٓئِكَ لَهُمۡ عَذَابٌ عَظِيمٞ (105) يَوۡمَ تَبۡيَضُّ وُجُوهٞ
وَتَسۡوَدُّ وُجُوهٞۚ فَأَمَّا ٱلَّذِينَ ٱسۡوَدَّتۡ وُجُوهُهُمۡ أَكَفَرۡتُم بَعۡدَ إِيمَٰنِكُمۡ
فَذُوقُواْ ٱلۡعَذَابَ بِمَا كُنتُمۡ تَكۡفُرُونَ (106) وَأَمَّا ٱلَّذِينَ ٱبۡيَضَّتۡ وُجُوهُهُمۡ
فَفِي رَحۡمَةِ ٱللَّهِۖ هُمۡ فِيهَا خَٰلِدُونَ (107) تِلۡكَ ءَايَٰتُ ٱللَّهِ نَتۡلُوهَا عَلَيۡكَ
بِٱلۡحَقِّۗ وَمَا ٱللَّهُ يُرِيدُ ظُلۡمٗا لِّلۡعَٰلَمِينَ (108) وَلِلَّهِ مَا فِي ٱلسَّمَٰوَٰتِ وَمَا فِي
ٱلۡأَرۡضِۚ وَإِلَى ٱللَّهِ تُرۡجَعُ ٱلۡأُمُورُ (109) كُنتُمۡ خَيۡرَ أُمَّةٍ أُخۡرِجَتۡ

Waʿ-taṣimū biḥablil-lāhi jamīʿañw-wa lā tafarraqū. Wadh-kurū niʿmatal-lāhi ʿalaykum ʾidh kuñtum ʾaʿdāaʾañ-faʾallafa bayna qulūbikum faʾaṣbaḥtum-biniʿmatihīi ʾikhwānañw-wa kuñtum ʿalā shafā ḥufratim-minan-nāri faʾañqadhakum-minhā. Kadhālika yubayyinul-lāhu lakum ʾĀyātihī laʿallakum tahtadūn. (103) Wal-takum-miñkum ʾummatuñy-yadʿūna ʾilal-khayri wa yaʾmurūna bilmaʿrūfi wa yanhawna ʿanil-muñkari wa ʾulāaʾika humul-mufliḥūn. (104) Wa lā takūnū kalladhīna tafarraqū wakh-talafū mim-baʿdi mā jāaʾahumul-bayyinātu wa ʾulāaʾika lahum ʿadhābun ʿaẓīm, (105) Yawma tabyaḍḍu wujūhuñw-wa taswaddu wujūh. Faʾammal-ladhīnas-waddat wujūhuhum ʾakafartum-baʿda ʾīmānikum fadhūqul-ʿadhāba bimā kuñtum takfurūn. (106) Wa ʾammal-ladhīnab-yaḍḍat wujūhuhum fafī raḥmatil-lāhi hum fīhā khālidūn. (107) Tilka ʾĀyātul-lāhi natlūhā ʿalayka bilḥaqq. Wa mal-lāhu yurīdu ẓulmal-lilʿālamīn. (108) Wa lillāhi mā fis-samāwāti wa mā fil-ʾarḍi wa ʾilal-lāhi turjaʿul-ʾumūr. (109) Kuñtum khayra ʾummatin ʾukhrijat

79 Lit., "a pit of fire" – a metaphor of the sufferings which are the inescapable consequence of spiritual ignorance. The reminder of their one-time mutual enmity is an allusion to man's lot on earth (cf. 2 : 36 and 7 : 24), from which only God's guidance can save him (see 2 : 37-38).

80 I.e., like the followers of the Bible, who became "Jews" and "Christians" in spite of the fact that their beliefs have a common source and are based on the same spiritual truths (see also 6 : 159 and the corresponding note).

81 Lit., "to the worlds". For an explanation of this sentence, see 6 : 131-132 and note 117.

of] mankind: you enjoin the doing of what is right and forbid the doing of what is wrong, and you believe in God.
Now if the followers of earlier revelation had attained to [this kind of] faith, it would have been for their own good; [but only few] among them are believers, while most of them are iniquitous: ‹110› [but] these can never inflict more than a passing hurt on you; and if they fight against you, they will turn their backs upon you [in flight], and will not be succoured.[82] ‹111›
Overshadowed by ignominy are they wherever they may be, save [when they bind themselves again] in a bond with God and a bond with men;[83] for they have earned the burden of God's condemnation, and are overshadowed by humiliation: all this [has befallen them] because they persisted in denying the truth of God's messages and in slaying the prophets against all right: all this, because they rebelled [against God], and persisted in transgressing the bounds of what is right.[84] ‹112›
[But] they are not all alike: among the followers of earlier revelation there are upright people,[85] who recite God's messages throughout the night, and prostrate themselves [before Him]. ‹113› They believe in God and the Last Day, and enjoin the doing of what is right and forbid the doing of what is wrong, and vie with one another in doing good works: and these are among the righteous. ‹114› And whatever good they do, they shall never be denied the reward thereof: for, God has full knowledge of those who are conscious of Him. ‹115›

لِلنَّاسِ تَأْمُرُونَ بِٱلْمَعْرُوفِ وَتَنْهَوْنَ عَنِ ٱلْمُنكَرِ وَتُؤْمِنُونَ بِٱللَّهِ ۗ وَلَوْ
ءَامَنَ أَهْلُ ٱلْكِتَـٰبِ لَكَانَ خَيْرًا لَّهُم ۚ مِّنْهُمُ ٱلْمُؤْمِنُونَ وَأَكْثَرُهُمُ
ٱلْفَـٰسِقُونَ ﴿١١٠﴾ لَن يَضُرُّوكُمْ إِلَّآ أَذًى ۖ وَإِن يُقَـٰتِلُوكُمْ يُوَلُّوكُمُ ٱلْأَدْبَارَ
ثُمَّ لَا يُنصَرُونَ ﴿١١١﴾ ضُرِبَتْ عَلَيْهِمُ ٱلذِّلَّةُ أَيْنَ مَا ثُقِفُوٓا۟ إِلَّا بِحَبْلٍ مِّنَ
ٱللَّهِ وَحَبْلٍ مِّنَ ٱلنَّاسِ وَبَآءُو بِغَضَبٍ مِّنَ ٱللَّهِ وَضُرِبَتْ عَلَيْهِمُ ٱلْمَسْكَنَةُ ۚ
ذَٰلِكَ بِأَنَّهُمْ كَانُوا۟ يَكْفُرُونَ بِـَٔايَـٰتِ ٱللَّهِ وَيَقْتُلُونَ ٱلْأَنۢبِيَآءَ بِغَيْرِ حَقٍّ ۚ
ذَٰلِكَ بِمَا عَصَوا۟ وَّكَانُوا۟ يَعْتَدُونَ ﴿١١٢﴾ ۞ لَيْسُوا۟ سَوَآءً ۗ مِّنْ أَهْلِ ٱلْكِتَـٰبِ
أُمَّةٌ قَآئِمَةٌ يَتْلُونَ ءَايَـٰتِ ٱللَّهِ ءَانَآءَ ٱلَّيْلِ وَهُمْ يَسْجُدُونَ ﴿١١٣﴾ يُؤْمِنُونَ بِٱللَّهِ
وَٱلْيَوْمِ ٱلْـَٔاخِرِ وَيَأْمُرُونَ بِٱلْمَعْرُوفِ وَيَنْهَوْنَ عَنِ ٱلْمُنكَرِ وَيُسَـٰرِعُونَ فِى
ٱلْخَيْرَٰتِ ۖ وَأُو۟لَـٰٓئِكَ مِنَ ٱلصَّـٰلِحِينَ ﴿١١٤﴾ وَمَا يَفْعَلُوا۟ مِنْ خَيْرٍ فَلَن
يُكْفَرُوهُ ۗ وَٱللَّهُ عَلِيمٌۢ بِٱلْمُتَّقِينَ ﴿١١٥﴾

ربع الحزب

linnāsi taᵓmurūna bilmaᶜrūfi wa tanhawna ᶜanil-muñkari wa tuᵓminūna billāh. Wa law ᵓāmana ᵓahlul-Kitābi lakāna khayral-lahum; minhumul-muᵓminūna wa ᵓaktharuhumul-fāsiqūn. (110) Lañy-yaḍurrūkum ᵓillāa ᵓadhañw-wa ᵓiñy-yuqātilūkum yuwallūkumul-ᵓadbāra thumma lā yuñṣarūn. (111) Ḍuribat ᶜalayhimudh-dhillatu ᵓayna mā thuqifūu ᵓillā biḥablim-minal-lāhi wa ḥablim-minan-nāsi wa bāaᵓū bighaḍabim-minal-lāhi wa ḍuribat ᶜalayhimul-maskanah. Dhālika biᵓannahum kānū yakfurūna biᵓĀyātil-lāhi wa yaqtulūnal-ᵓAmbiyāaᵓa bighayri ḥaqq. Dhālika bimā ᶜaṣaw-wa kānū yaᶜtadūn. (112) ◈ Laysū sawāaᵓ. Min ᵓahlil-Kitābi ᵓummatuñ-qāaᵓimatuñy-yatlūna ᵓĀyātil-lāhi ᵓānāaᵓal-layli wa hum yasjudūn. (113) Yuᵓminūna billāhi wal-Yawmil-ᵓĀkhiri wa yaᵓmurūna bilmaᶜrūfi wa yanhawna ᶜanil-muñkari wa yusāriᶜūna fil-khayrāti wa ᵓulāaᵓika minaṣ-ṣāliḥīn. (114) Wa mā yafᶜalū min khayriñ-falañy-yukfarūh. Wal-lāhu ᶜAlīmum-bilmuttaqīn. (115)

82 As is obvious from the opening sentence of verse 110, this promise to the followers of the Qurᵓān is conditional upon their being, or remaining, a community of people who "enjoin the doing of what is right and forbid the doing of what is wrong, and [truly] believe in God"; and – as history has shown – this promise is bound to lapse whenever the Muslims fail to live up to their faith.

83 I.e., if they return to the concept of God as the Lord and Sustainer of all mankind, and give up the idea of being "God's chosen people" which creates a barrier between them and all other believers in the One God.

84 The above passage – as the very similar one in 2 : 61 – relates specifically to the children of Israel, although this section as a whole (verses 110-115) obviously refers to the followers of the Bible in general, that is, to both the Jews and the Christians.

85 Lit., "an upright community": a reference to those among the followers of the Bible who are truly believers (cf. the last sentence of verse 110 above) and observe the "bond with God and with men" (verse 112).

[But,] behold, as for those who are bent on denying the truth – neither their worldly possessions nor their children will in the least avail them against God: and it is they who are destined for the fire, therein to abide. ‹116›

The parable of what they spend on the life of this world is that of an icy wind which smites the tilth of people who have sinned against themselves, and destroys it: for, it is not God who does them wrong, but it is they who are wronging themselves.[86] ‹117›

O YOU who have attained to faith! Do not take for your bosom-friends people who are not of your kind.[87] They spare no effort to corrupt you; they would love to see you in distress.[88] Vehement hatred has already come into the open from out of their mouths, but what their hearts conceal is yet worse. We have indeed made the signs [thereof] clear unto you, if you would but use your reason. ‹118›

Lo! It is you who [are prepared to] love them, but they will not love you, although you believe in all of the revelation.[89] And when they meet you, they assert, "We believe [as you believe]"; but when they find themselves alone, they gnaw their fingers in rage against you.

Say: "Perish in your rage! Behold, God has full knowledge of what is in the hearts [of men]!" ‹119›

إِنَّ ٱلَّذِينَ كَفَرُواْ لَن تُغۡنِيَ عَنۡهُمۡ أَمۡوَٰلُهُمۡ وَلَآ أَوۡلَٰدُهُم مِّنَ ٱللَّهِ شَيۡـٔٗاۖ
وَأُوْلَٰٓئِكَ أَصۡحَٰبُ ٱلنَّارِۖ هُمۡ فِيهَا خَٰلِدُونَ ﴿١١٦﴾ مَثَلُ مَا يُنفِقُونَ فِي هَٰذِهِ
ٱلۡحَيَوٰةِ ٱلدُّنۡيَا كَمَثَلِ رِيحٖ فِيهَا صِرٌّ أَصَابَتۡ حَرۡثَ قَوۡمٖ ظَلَمُوٓاْ أَنفُسَهُمۡ
فَأَهۡلَكَتۡهُۚ وَمَا ظَلَمَهُمُ ٱللَّهُ وَلَٰكِنۡ أَنفُسَهُمۡ يَظۡلِمُونَ ﴿١١٧﴾ يَٰٓأَيُّهَا ٱلَّذِينَ
ءَامَنُواْ لَا تَتَّخِذُواْ بِطَانَةٗ مِّن دُونِكُمۡ لَا يَأۡلُونَكُمۡ خَبَالٗا وَدُّواْ مَا عَنِتُّمۡ
قَدۡ بَدَتِ ٱلۡبَغۡضَآءُ مِنۡ أَفۡوَٰهِهِمۡ وَمَا تُخۡفِي صُدُورُهُمۡ أَكۡبَرُۚ قَدۡ بَيَّنَّا لَكُمُ
ٱلۡأٓيَٰتِۖ إِن كُنتُمۡ تَعۡقِلُونَ ﴿١١٨﴾ هَٰٓأَنتُمۡ أُوْلَآءِ تُحِبُّونَهُمۡ وَلَا يُحِبُّونَكُمۡ
وَتُؤۡمِنُونَ بِٱلۡكِتَٰبِ كُلِّهِۦ وَإِذَا لَقُوكُمۡ قَالُوٓاْ ءَامَنَّا وَإِذَا خَلَوۡاْ عَضُّواْ
عَلَيۡكُمُ ٱلۡأَنَامِلَ مِنَ ٱلۡغَيۡظِۚ قُلۡ مُوتُواْ بِغَيۡظِكُمۡۗ إِنَّ ٱللَّهَ عَلِيمُۢ بِذَاتِ
ٱلصُّدُورِ ﴿١١٩﴾

ʾInnal-ladhīna kafarū lañ-tughniya ʿanhum ʾamwāluhum wa lāa ʾawlāduhum minal-lāhi shayʾā. Wa ʾulāaʾika ʾaṣḥābun-nāri hum fīhā khālidūn. (116)
Mathalu mā yuñfiqūna fī hādhihil-ḥayātid-dunyā kamathali rīḥiñ-fīhā ṣirrun ʾaṣābat ḥartha qawmiñ-ẓalamūu ʾañfusahum faʾahlakat-hu wa mā ẓalamahumul-lāhu wa lākin ʾañfusahum yaẓlimūn. (117)
Yāa ʾayyuhal-ladhīna ʾāmanū lā tattakhidhū biṭānatam-miñ-dūnikum lā yaʾlūnakum khabālañw-waddū mā ʿanittum qad badatil-baghḍāaʾu min ʾafwāhihim wa mā tukhfī ṣudūruhum ʾakbar. Qad bayyannā lakumul-ʾĀyāti ʾiñ-kuñtum taʿqilūn. (118)
Hāaʾañtum ʾulāaʾi tuḥibbūnahum wa lā yuḥib-būnakum wa tuʾminūna bilkitābi kullihī wa ʾidhā laqūkum qālūu ʾāmannā; wa ʾidhā khalaw ʿaḍḍū ʿalaykumul-ʾanāmila-minal-ghayẓ. Qul mūtū bigh-ayẓikum; ʾinnal-lāha ʿAlīmum-bidhātiṣ-ṣudūr. (119)

86 In a marginal note connected with his commentary on this verse, Zamakhsharī explains this parable thus: "If the 'tilth' (i.e., the gainful achievement] of those who deny the truth is lost, it is lost in its entirety, with nothing remaining to them in this world and in the life to come; while, on the other hand, the 'tilth' of a believer is never lost in its entirety: for even if it is seemingly lost, there remains to him the expectation of a reward, in the life to come, for his patience in adversity." In other words, the above Qurʾanic phrase is meant to stress the completeness of loss of all efforts in the case of those who are bent on denying the truth.

87 Lit., "from among others than yourselves". Some of the commentators incline to the view that this expression comprises all non-Muslims: but this view obviously conflicts with 60 : 8-9, where the believers are expressly allowed to form friendships with such of the non-believers as are not hostile to them and to their faith. Moreover, the sequence makes it clear that by "those who are not of your kind" are meant only people whose enmity to Islam and its followers has become apparent from their behaviour and their utterances (Ṭabarī). The rendering adopted by me, "people who are not of your kind", implies that their outlook on life is so fundamentally opposed to that of the Muslims that genuine friendship is entirely out of the question.

88 Lit., "they love that which causes you distress".

89 I.e., including the revelation of the Bible.

If good fortune comes to you, it grieves them; and if evil befalls you, they rejoice in it. But if you are patient in adversity and conscious of God, their guile cannot harm you at all: for, verily, God encompasses [with His might] all that they do. ‹120›

إِن تَمْسَسْكُمْ حَسَنَةٌ تَسُؤْهُمْ وَإِن تُصِبْكُمْ سَيِّئَةٌ يَفْرَحُوا۟ بِهَا ۖ وَإِن
تَصْبِرُوا۟ وَتَتَّقُوا۟ لَا يَضُرُّكُمْ كَيْدُهُمْ شَيْـًٔا ۗ إِنَّ ٱللَّهَ بِمَا يَعْمَلُونَ
مُحِيطٌ ﴿١٢٠﴾ وَإِذْ غَدَوْتَ مِنْ أَهْلِكَ تُبَوِّئُ ٱلْمُؤْمِنِينَ مَقَٰعِدَ
لِلْقِتَالِ ۗ وَٱللَّهُ سَمِيعٌ عَلِيمٌ ﴿١٢١﴾ إِذْ هَمَّت طَّآئِفَتَانِ مِنكُمْ أَن تَفْشَلَا

AND [remember, O Prophet, the day] when thou didst set out from thy home at early morn to place the believers in battle array.[90] And God was all-hearing, all-knowing ‹121› when two groups from among you were about to lose heart,[91]

ʾIñ-tamsaskum ḥasanatuñ-tasuʾhum wa ʾiñ-tuṣibkum sayyiʾatuñy-yafraḥū bihā. Wa ʾiñ-taṣbirū wa tattaqū lā yaḍurrukum kayduhum shayʾā. ʾInnal-lāha bimā yaᶜmalūna muḥīṭ. (120) Wa ʾidh ghadawta min ʾahlika tubawwiʾul-Muʾminīna maqāᶜida lilqitāl. Wal-lāhu Samīᶜun ᶜAlīm. (121) ʾIdh hammaṭ-ṭāaʾifatāni miñkum ʾañ-tafshalā

90 This reference to the battle of Uḥud, to which many verses of this *sūrah* are devoted, connects with the exhortation implied in the preceding verse, "if you are patient in adversity and conscious of God, their guile cannot harm you at all". Since this and the subsequent references cannot be fully understood without a knowledge of the historical background, a brief account of the battle would seem to be indicated.

In order to avenge their catastrophic defeat at Badr in the second year after the *hijrah*, the pagan Meccans – supported by several tribes hostile to the Muslims – mustered in the following year an army comprising ten thousand men under the command of Abū Sufyān and marched against Medina. On hearing of their approach, in the month of Shawwāl 3 H., the Prophet held a council of war at which the tactics to be adopted were discussed. In view of the overwhelming cavalry forces at the disposal of the enemy, the Prophet himself was of the opinion that the Muslims should give battle from behind the fortifications of Medina and, if need be, fight in its narrow streets and lanes; and his plan was supported by some of the most outstanding among his Companions. However, the majority of the Muslim leaders who participated in the council strongly insisted on going forth and meeting the enemy in the open field. In obedience to the Qurʾanic principle that all communal affairs must be transacted on the basis of mutually-agreed decisions (see verse 159 of this *sūrah*, as well as 42 : 38), the Prophet sorrowfully gave way to the will of the majority and set out with his followers towards the plain below the mountain of Uḥud, a little over three miles from Medina. His army consisted of less than one thousand men; but on the way to Mount Uḥud this number was still further reduced by the defection of some three hundred men led by the hypocritical ᶜAbd Allāh ibn Ubayy, who pretended to be convinced that the Muslims did not really intend to fight. Shortly before the battle, two other groups from among the Prophet's forces – namely, the clans of Banū Salamah (of the tribe of Al-Aws) and Banū Ḥārithah (of the tribe of Khazraj) almost lost heart and were about to join the defectors (3 : 122) on the plea that because of their numerical weakness the Muslims must now avoid giving battle; but at the last moment they decided to follow the Prophet. Having less than seven hundred men with him, the Prophet arrayed the bulk of his forces with their backs to the mountain and posted all his archers – numbering fifty – on a nearby hill in order to provide cover against an outflanking manoeuvre by the enemy cavalry; these archers were ordered not to leave their post under any circumstances. In their subsequent, death-defying assault upon the greatly superior forces of the pagan Quraysh, the Muslims gained a decisive advantage over the former and almost routed them. At that moment, however, most of the archers, believing that the battle had been won and fearing lest they lose their share of the spoils, abandoned their covering position and joined the melée around the encampment of the Quraysh. Seizing this opportunity, the bulk of the Meccan cavalry under the command of Khālid ibn al-Walīd (who shortly after this battle embraced Islam and later became one of the greatest Muslim generals of all times) veered round in a wide arc and attacked the Muslim forces from the rear. Deprived of the cover of the archers, and caught between two fires, the Muslims retreated in disorder, with the loss of many lives. The Prophet himself and a handful of his most stalwart Companions defended themselves desperately; and the Prophet was seriously injured and fell to the ground. The cry immediately arose, "The Apostle of God has been killed!" Many of the Muslims began to flee; some among them were even prepared to throw themselves upon the mercy of the enemy. But a few of the Companions – among them ᶜUmar ibn al-Khaṭṭāb and Ṭalḥah – called out, "What good are your lives without him, O believers? Let us die as he has died!" – and threw themselves with the strength of despair against the Meccans. Their example at once found an echo among the rest of the Muslims, who in the meantime had learnt that the Prophet was alive: they rallied and counter-attacked the enemy, and thus saved the day. But the Muslims were now too exhausted to exploit their chances of victory, and the battle ended in a draw, with the enemy retreating in the direction of Mecca. On the next day the Prophet started in pursuit of them at the head of seventy of his Companions. But when the Muslims reached the place called Ḥamrāʾ al-Asad, about eight miles south of Medina, it became obvious that the Meccans were in no mood to risk another encounter and were rapidly marching home; and thereupon the tiny Muslim army returned to Medina.

91 I.e., the clans of Banū Salamah and Banū Ḥārithah, who had almost joined the deserters led by ᶜAbd Allāh ibn

وَٱللَّهُ وَلِيُّهُمَا ۗ وَعَلَى ٱللَّهِ فَلْيَتَوَكَّلِ ٱلْمُؤْمِنُونَ ﴿١٢٢﴾ وَلَقَدْ نَصَرَكُمُ ٱللَّهُ بِبَدْرٍ وَأَنتُمْ
أَذِلَّةٌ ۖ فَٱتَّقُوا۟ ٱللَّهَ لَعَلَّكُمْ تَشْكُرُونَ ﴿١٢٣﴾ إِذْ تَقُولُ لِلْمُؤْمِنِينَ أَلَن يَكْفِيَكُمْ أَن
يُمِدَّكُمْ رَبُّكُم بِثَلَٰثَةِ ءَالَٰفٍ مِّنَ ٱلْمَلَٰٓئِكَةِ مُنزَلِينَ ﴿١٢٤﴾ بَلَىٰٓ ۚ إِن تَصْبِرُوا۟
وَتَتَّقُوا۟ وَيَأْتُوكُم مِّن فَوْرِهِمْ هَٰذَا يُمْدِدْكُمْ رَبُّكُم بِخَمْسَةِ ءَالَٰفٍ مِّنَ
ٱلْمَلَٰٓئِكَةِ مُسَوِّمِينَ ﴿١٢٥﴾ وَمَا جَعَلَهُ ٱللَّهُ إِلَّا بُشْرَىٰ لَكُمْ وَلِتَطْمَئِنَّ قُلُوبُكُم
بِهِۦ ۗ وَمَا ٱلنَّصْرُ إِلَّا مِنْ عِندِ ٱللَّهِ ٱلْعَزِيزِ ٱلْحَكِيمِ ﴿١٢٦﴾ لِيَقْطَعَ طَرَفًا مِّنَ ٱلَّذِينَ
كَفَرُوٓا۟ أَوْ يَكْبِتَهُمْ فَيَنقَلِبُوا۟ خَآئِبِينَ ﴿١٢٧﴾ لَيْسَ لَكَ مِنَ ٱلْأَمْرِ شَىْءٌ أَوْ
يَتُوبَ عَلَيْهِمْ أَوْ يُعَذِّبَهُمْ فَإِنَّهُمْ ظَٰلِمُونَ ﴿١٢٨﴾ وَلِلَّهِ مَا فِى ٱلسَّمَٰوَٰتِ وَمَا
فِى ٱلْأَرْضِ ۚ يَغْفِرُ لِمَن يَشَآءُ وَيُعَذِّبُ مَن يَشَآءُ ۚ وَٱللَّهُ غَفُورٌ رَّحِيمٌ ﴿١٢٩﴾

although God was near unto them and it is in God that the believers must place their trust: ‹122› for, indeed, God did succour you at Badr, when you were utterly weak.[92] Remain, then, conscious of God, so that you might have cause to be grateful. ‹123›
[And remember] when thou didst say unto the believers: "Is it not enough for you [to know] that your Sustainer will aid you with three thousand angels sent down [from on high]? ‹124› Nay, but if you are patient in adversity and conscious of Him, and the enemy should fall upon you of a sudden, your Sustainer will aid you with five thousand angels swooping down!"[93] ‹125›
And God ordained this [to be said by His Apostle[94]] only as a glad tiding for you, and that your hearts should thereby be set at rest – since no succour can come from any save God, the Almighty, the Truly Wise ‹126› – [and] that [through you] He might destroy some of those who were bent on denying the truth, and so abase the others[95] that they would withdraw in utter hopelessness. ‹127›
[And] it is in no wise for thee [O Prophet] to decide whether He shall accept their repentance or chastise them – for, behold, they are but wrongdoers, ‹128› whereas unto God belongs all that is in the heavens and all that is on earth: He forgives whom He wills, and He chastises whom He wills; and God is much-forgiving, a dispenser of grace.[96] ‹129›

wal-lāhu Waliyyuhumā. Wa ʿalal-lāhi falyatawakkalil-muʾminūn. 122 Wa laqad naṣarakumul-lāhu biBa-
driñw-wa ʾañtum ʾadhillah. Fattaqul-lāha laʿallakum tashkurūn. 123 ʾIdh taqūlu lilmuʾminīna
ʾalañy-yakfiyakum ʾañy-yumiddakum Rabbukum bi-
thalāthati ʾālāfim-minal-Malāaʾikati muñzalīn. 124
Balāa ʾiñ-taṣbirū wa tattaqū wa yaʾtūkum miñ-
fawrihim hādhā yumdidkum Rabbukum bikhamsati
ʾālāfim-minal-Malāaʾikati musawwimīn. 125 Wa mā
jaʿalahul-lāhu ʾillā bushrā lakum wa litaṭmaʾinna
qulūbukum bih. Wa man-naṣru ʾillā min ʿiñdil-lāhil-
ʿAzīzil-Ḥakīm 126 Liyaqṭaʿa ṭarafam-minal-ladhīna
kafarūu ʾaw yakbitahum fayañqalibū khāaʾibīn. 127
Laysa laka minal-ʾamri shayʾun ʾaw yatūba ʿalayhim
ʾaw yuʿadhdhibahum faʾinnahum ẓālimūn. 128 Wa
lillāhi mā fis-samāwāti wa mā fil-ʾarḍ. Yaghfiru
limañy-yashāaʾu wa yuʿadh-dhibu mañy-yashāaʾu
wal-lāhu Ghafūrur-Raḥīm. 129

Ubayy (see preceding note).

92 A reference to the battle of Badr, in 2 H., which is dealt with extensively in *sūrah* 8.

93 As is evident from the next verse, the Prophet's allusion to God's aiding the believers with thousands of angels signifies, metaphorically, a strengthening of the believers' hearts through spiritual forces coming from God (*Manār* IV 112 ff., and IX, 612 ff.). A very similar announcement – relating to the battle of Badr – occurs in 8 : 9-10, where "one thousand" angels are mentioned. As regards these varying numbers (one, three and five thousand), they would seem to indicate the unlimited nature of God's aid to those who are "patient in adversity and conscious of Him". It is reasonable to assume that the Prophet thus exhorted his followers immediately before the battle of Uḥud, that is, after three hundred men under the leadership of ʿAbd Allāh ibn Ubayy had deserted him and some of the others "almost lost heart" in the face of the greatly superior enemy forces.

94 According to many commentators (see *Manār* IV 112), this interpolation is justified by the preceding two verses, which show that it was the Prophet who, under divine inspiration, made this promise to his followers. See also 8 : 9, where a similar promise is voiced on the occasion of the battle of Badr.

95 Lit., "that He might destroy some . . . or [so] abase them". It is obvious that the particle *aw* ("or") does not, in this context, denote an alternative but, rather, a specification (*tanwīʿ*) – as, for instance, in the phrase "ten persons were killed or injured": meaning that some of them were killed and others injured.

96 As recorded in several authentic Traditions, the Prophet invoked, during the battle of Uḥud, God's curse upon

O YOU who have attained to faith! Do not gorge yourselves on usury, doubling and re-doubling it[97] – but remain conscious of God, so that you might attain to a happy state; ‹130› and beware of the fire which awaits those who deny the truth! ‹131›
And pay heed unto God and the Apostle, so that you might be graced with mercy. ‹132› And vie with one another to attain to your Sustainer's forgiveness and to a paradise as vast as the heavens and the earth, which has been readied for the God-conscious ‹133› who spend [in His way] in time of plenty and in time of hardship, and hold in check their anger, and pardon their fellow-men because God loves the doers of good; ‹134› and who, when they have committed a shameful deed or have [otherwise] sinned against themselves, remember God and pray that their sins be forgiven – for who but God could forgive sins? – and do not knowingly persist in doing whatever [wrong] they may have done. ‹135›
These it is who shall have as their reward forgiveness from their Sustainer, and gardens through which running waters flow, therein to abide: and how excellent a reward for those who labour! ‹136›

[MANY] WAYS of life have passed away before your time.[98] Go, then, about the earth and behold what happened in the end to those who gave the lie to the truth: ‹137›

يَـٰٓأَيُّهَا ٱلَّذِينَ ءَامَنُوا۟ لَا تَأْكُلُوا۟ ٱلرِّبَوٰٓا۟ أَضْعَـٰفًا مُّضَـٰعَفَةً ۖ وَٱتَّقُوا۟ ٱللَّهَ
لَعَلَّكُمْ تُفْلِحُونَ ﴿١٣٠﴾ وَٱتَّقُوا۟ ٱلنَّارَ ٱلَّتِىٓ أُعِدَّتْ لِلْكَـٰفِرِينَ ﴿١٣١﴾
وَأَطِيعُوا۟ ٱللَّهَ وَٱلرَّسُولَ لَعَلَّكُمْ تُرْحَمُونَ ﴿١٣٢﴾ ۞ وَسَارِعُوٓا۟ إِلَىٰ مَغْفِرَةٍ
مِّن رَّبِّكُمْ وَجَنَّةٍ عَرْضُهَا ٱلسَّمَـٰوَٰتُ وَٱلْأَرْضُ أُعِدَّتْ لِلْمُتَّقِينَ ﴿١٣٣﴾
ٱلَّذِينَ يُنفِقُونَ فِى ٱلسَّرَّآءِ وَٱلضَّرَّآءِ وَٱلْكَـٰظِمِينَ ٱلْغَيْظَ وَٱلْعَافِينَ عَنِ
ٱلنَّاسِ ۗ وَٱللَّهُ يُحِبُّ ٱلْمُحْسِنِينَ ﴿١٣٤﴾ وَٱلَّذِينَ إِذَا فَعَلُوا۟ فَـٰحِشَةً أَوْ
ظَلَمُوٓا۟ أَنفُسَهُمْ ذَكَرُوا۟ ٱللَّهَ فَٱسْتَغْفَرُوا۟ لِذُنُوبِهِمْ وَمَن يَغْفِرُ ٱلذُّنُوبَ إِلَّا
ٱللَّهُ وَلَمْ يُصِرُّوا۟ عَلَىٰ مَا فَعَلُوا۟ وَهُمْ يَعْلَمُونَ ﴿١٣٥﴾ أُو۟لَـٰٓئِكَ جَزَآؤُهُم مَّغْفِرَةٌ
مِّن رَّبِّهِمْ وَجَنَّـٰتٌ تَجْرِى مِن تَحْتِهَا ٱلْأَنْهَـٰرُ خَـٰلِدِينَ فِيهَا ۚ وَنِعْمَ أَجْرُ
ٱلْعَـٰمِلِينَ ﴿١٣٦﴾ قَدْ خَلَتْ مِن قَبْلِكُمْ سُنَنٌ فَسِيرُوا۟ فِى ٱلْأَرْضِ فَٱنظُرُوا۟
كَيْفَ كَانَ عَـٰقِبَةُ ٱلْمُكَذِّبِينَ ﴿١٣٧﴾

نصف الحزب

Yāa ˀayyuhal-ladhīna ˀāmanū lā taˀkulur-ribāa
ˀaḍᶜāfam-muḍāᶜafatañw-wat-taqul-lāha laᶜallakum
tufliḥūn. (130) Wat-taqun-nāral-latīi ˀuᶜiddat lilkāfirīn.
(131) Wa ˀaṭīᶜul-lāha war-Rasūla laᶜallakum turḥamūn.
(132) ۞ Wa sāriᶜūu ˀilā maghfiratim-mir-Rabbikum wa
jannatin ᶜarḍuhas-samāwātu wal-ˀarḍu ˀuᶜidat lil-
muttaqīn. (133) ˀAlladhīna yuñfiqūna fis-sarrāaˀi waḍ-
ḍarrāaˀi wal-kāẓimīnal-ghayẓa wal-ᶜāfīna ᶜanin-nās.
Wal-lāhu yuḥibbul-muḥsinīn. (134) Wal-ladhīna ˀidhā
faᶜalū fāḥishatan ˀaw ẓalamūu ˀañfusahum dhaka-
rul-lāha fastaghfarū lidhunūbihim wa mañy-
yaghfirudh-dhunūba ˀillal-lāhu wa lam yuṣirrū ᶜalā
mā faᶜalū wa hum yaᶜlamūn. (135) ˀUlāaˀika jazā-
aˀuhum-maghfiratum-mir-Rabbihim wa jannātuñ-
tajrī miñ-taḥtihal-ˀanhāru khālidīna fīhā; wa niᶜma
ˀajrul-ᶜāmilīn. (136) Qad khalat miñ-qablikum suna-
nuñ-fasīrū fil-ˀarḍi fañẓurū kayfa kāna ᶜāqibatul-
mukadhdhibīn. (137)

the leaders of the pagan Quraysh (Bukhārī, Tirmidhī, Nasāˀī and Aḥmad ibn Ḥanbal); and when he lay on the ground severely injured, he exclaimed, "How could those people prosper after having done this to their prophet, who but invites them to [acknowledge] their Sustainer?" – whereupon the above two verses were revealed (Muslim and Ibn Ḥanbal).

97 For a definition of *ribā* ("usury"), see note 35 on 30 : 39, the earliest Qurˀanic reference to this term. As for the connection of the above verse with the subject-matter dealt with in the foregoing, the best explanation is, to my mind, the one offered by Qiffāl (as quoted by Rāzī): Since it was mainly through usurious gains that the pagan Meccans had acquired the wealth which enabled them to equip their powerful army and almost to defeat the poorly-armed Muslims at Uḥud the latter might have been tempted to emulate their enemies in this respect; and it was to remove this temptation – from them as well as from later generations of believers – that the prohibition of usury was once again stressed through revelation.

98 The word *sunnah* (of which *sunan* is the plural) denotes a "way of life" or "conduct" (hence its application, in

this [should be] a clear lesson unto all men, and a guidance and an admonition unto the God-conscious. ‹138›
Be not, then, faint of heart, and grieve not:[99] for you are bound to rise high if you are [truly] believers. ‹139›
If misfortune[100] touches you, [know that] similar misfortune has touched [other] people as well; for it is by turns that We apportion unto men such days [of fortune and misfortune]: and [this] to the end that God might mark out those who have attained to faith, and choose from among you such as [with their lives] bear witness to the truth[101] – since God does not love evildoers ‹140› – and that God might render pure of all dross those who have attained to faith, and bring to nought those who deny the truth. ‹141›
Do you think that you could enter paradise unless God takes cognizance of your having striven hard [in His cause], and takes cognizance of your having been patient in adversity?[102] ‹142› For, indeed, you did long for death [in God's cause] before you came face to face with it; and now you have seen it with your own eyes![103] ‹143›

هَٰذَا بَيَانٌ لِّلنَّاسِ وَهُدًى وَمَوْعِظَةٌ لِّلْمُتَّقِينَ ﴿١٣٨﴾ وَلَا تَهِنُوا۟ وَلَا تَحْزَنُوا۟
وَأَنتُمُ ٱلْأَعْلَوْنَ إِن كُنتُم مُّؤْمِنِينَ ﴿١٣٩﴾ إِن يَمْسَسْكُمْ قَرْحٌ فَقَدْ مَسَّ
ٱلْقَوْمَ قَرْحٌ مِّثْلُهُۥ ۚ وَتِلْكَ ٱلْأَيَّامُ نُدَاوِلُهَا بَيْنَ ٱلنَّاسِ وَلِيَعْلَمَ ٱللَّهُ ٱلَّذِينَ
ءَامَنُوا۟ وَيَتَّخِذَ مِنكُمْ شُهَدَآءَ ۗ وَٱللَّهُ لَا يُحِبُّ ٱلظَّٰلِمِينَ ﴿١٤٠﴾ وَلِيُمَحِّصَ
ٱللَّهُ ٱلَّذِينَ ءَامَنُوا۟ وَيَمْحَقَ ٱلْكَٰفِرِينَ ﴿١٤١﴾ أَمْ حَسِبْتُمْ أَن تَدْخُلُوا۟
ٱلْجَنَّةَ وَلَمَّا يَعْلَمِ ٱللَّهُ ٱلَّذِينَ جَٰهَدُوا۟ مِنكُمْ وَيَعْلَمَ ٱلصَّٰبِرِينَ ﴿١٤٢﴾
وَلَقَدْ كُنتُمْ تَمَنَّوْنَ ٱلْمَوْتَ مِن قَبْلِ أَن تَلْقَوْهُ فَقَدْ رَأَيْتُمُوهُ وَأَنتُمْ
تَنظُرُونَ ﴿١٤٣﴾

Hādhā bayānul-linnāsi wa hudañw-wa mawʿiẓatul-lilmuttaqīn. (138) Wa lā tahinū wa lā taḥzanū wa ʾañtumul-ʾaʿlawna ʾiñ-kuñtum muʾminīn. (139) ʾIñy-yamsaskum qarḥuñ-faqad massal-qawma qarḥum-mithluh. Wa tilkal-ʾayyāmu nudāwiluhā baynan-nāsi wa liyaʿlamal-lāhul-ladhīna ʾāmanū wa yattakhidha miñkum shuhadāaʾ. Wal-lāhu lā yuḥibbuẓ-ẓālimīn. (140) Wa liyumaḥḥiṣal-lāhul-ladhīna ʾāmanū wa yamḥa-qal-kāfirīn. (141) ʾAm ḥasibtum ʾañ-tadkhulul-jannata wa lammā yaʿlamil-lāhul-ladhīna jāhadū miñkum wa yaʿlamaṣ-ṣābirīn. (142) Wa laqad kuñtum tamannawnal-mawta miñ-qabli ʾañ-talqawhu faqad raʾaytumūhu wa ʾañtum tañẓurūn. (143)

Islamic terminology, to the way of life of the Prophet as an example for his followers). In the above passage, the term *sunan* refers to the "conditions (*aḥwāl*) characteristic of past centuries" (Rāzī), in which, despite all the continuous changes, an ever-recurring pattern can be discerned: a typically Qurʾanic reference to the possibility, and necessity, of learning from man's past experiences.

99 A reference to the near-disaster at Uḥud and the heavy loss of lives (about seventy men) which the Muslims had suffered.

100 Lit., "a wound" (*qarḥ*) or, according to some philologists, "pain caused by a wound".

101 I.e., "His decision to let some of you die as martyrs in His cause is not due to love of the sinful enemies who oppose you, but to His love for you." The term *shuhadāʾ* (pl. of *shahīd*) denotes "witnesses" as well as "martyrs". The rendering adopted by me comprises both the concepts of "bearing witness to the truth" and of "martyrdom" in God's cause.

102 Lit., "while God has not yet taken cognizance of those of you who have striven . . . and those who are patient in adversity". Since God is all-knowing, His "not taking cognizance" implies, of course, that the thing or happening referred to has not come about or is non-existent (Zamakhsharī).

103 In Zamakhsharī's opinion, this is a twofold reproach addressed to the majority of the Companions who took part in the battle of Uḥud: firstly, on account of their insistence, against the Prophet's advice, on giving battle to the enemy in the open field and thereby unnecessarily courting a deadly danger, and, secondly, on account of their failure to live up to their faith during the earlier part of the battle (see note 90 above). This passage may have yet another, more positive implication: namely, a reference to the lesson which the believers should draw from their near-defeat, and a reminder of the fact that their future depends on the strength of their faith in God (cf. verse 139 above) and not on a fleeting desire for self-sacrifice.

AND MUḤAMMAD is only an apostle; all the [other] apostles have passed away before him: if, then, he dies or is slain, will you turn about on your heels?[104] But he that turns about on his heels can in no wise harm God – whereas God will requite all who are grateful [to Him]. ‹144›
And no human being can die save by God's leave, at a term pre-ordained.
And if one desires the rewards of this world, We shall grant him thereof, and if one desires the rewards of the life to come, We shall grant him thereof; and We shall requite those who are grateful [to Us]. ‹145›
And how many a prophet has had to fight [in God's cause], followed by many God-devoted men: and they did not become faint of heart for all that they had to suffer in God's cause, and neither did they weaken, nor did they abase themselves [before the enemy], since God loves those who are patient in adversity; ‹146› and all that they said was this: "O our Sustainer! Forgive us our sins and the lack of moderation in our doings! And make firm our steps, and succour us against people who deny the truth!" ‹147› – whereupon God granted them the rewards of this world, as well as the goodliest rewards of the life to come: for God loves the doers of good. ‹148›

O YOU who have attained to faith! If you pay heed to those who are bent on denying the truth, they will cause you to turn back on your heels, and you will be the losers. ‹149›

وَمَا مُحَمَّدٌ إِلَّا رَسُولٌ قَدْ خَلَتْ مِن قَبْلِهِ ٱلرُّسُلُ أَفَإِيْن مَّاتَ أَوْ قُتِلَ ٱنقَلَبْتُمْ
عَلَىٰٓ أَعْقَـٰبِكُمْ وَمَن يَنقَلِبْ عَلَىٰ عَقِبَيْهِ فَلَن يَضُرَّ ٱللَّهَ شَيْـًٔا وَسَيَجْزِى ٱللَّهُ
ٱلشَّـٰكِرِينَ ﴿١٤٤﴾ وَمَا كَانَ لِنَفْسٍ أَن تَمُوتَ إِلَّا بِإِذْنِ ٱللَّهِ كِتَـٰبًا مُّؤَجَّلًا وَمَن
يُرِدْ ثَوَابَ ٱلدُّنْيَا نُؤْتِهِۦ مِنْهَا وَمَن يُرِدْ ثَوَابَ ٱلْـَٔاخِرَةِ نُؤْتِهِۦ مِنْهَا وَسَنَجْزِى
ٱلشَّـٰكِرِينَ ﴿١٤٥﴾ وَكَأَيِّن مِّن نَّبِىٍّ قَـٰتَلَ مَعَهُۥ رِبِّيُّونَ كَثِيرٌ فَمَا وَهَنُوا۟ لِمَآ
أَصَابَهُمْ فِى سَبِيلِ ٱللَّهِ وَمَا ضَعُفُوا۟ وَمَا ٱسْتَكَانُوا۟ وَٱللَّهُ يُحِبُّ ٱلصَّـٰبِرِينَ ﴿١٤٦﴾
وَمَا كَانَ قَوْلَهُمْ إِلَّآ أَن قَالُوا۟ رَبَّنَا ٱغْفِرْ لَنَا ذُنُوبَنَا وَإِسْرَافَنَا فِىٓ أَمْرِنَا وَثَبِّتْ
أَقْدَامَنَا وَٱنصُرْنَا عَلَى ٱلْقَوْمِ ٱلْكَـٰفِرِينَ ﴿١٤٧﴾ فَـَٔاتَىٰهُمُ ٱللَّهُ ثَوَابَ ٱلدُّنْيَا
وَحُسْنَ ثَوَابِ ٱلْـَٔاخِرَةِ وَٱللَّهُ يُحِبُّ ٱلْمُحْسِنِينَ ﴿١٤٨﴾ يَـٰٓأَيُّهَا ٱلَّذِينَ ءَامَنُوٓا۟ إِن
تُطِيعُوا۟ ٱلَّذِينَ كَفَرُوا۟ يَرُدُّوكُمْ عَلَىٰٓ أَعْقَـٰبِكُمْ فَتَنقَلِبُوا۟ خَـٰسِرِينَ ﴿١٤٩﴾

Wa mā Muḥammadun ᵓillā Rasūluñ-qad khalat miñ-qablihir-Rusul. ᵓAfaᵓim-māta ᵓaw qutilañ-qalabtum ᶜalāa ᵓaᶜqābikum. Wa mañy-yañqalib ᶜalā ᶜaqibayhi falañy-yaḍurral-lāha shayᵓā. Wa sayajzil-lāhush-shākirīn. 144 Wa mā kāna linafsin ᵓañ-tamūta ᵓillā biᵓidhnil-lāhi kitābam-muᵓajjalā. Wa mañy-yurid thawābad-dunyā nuᵓtihī minhā wa mañy-yurid thawābal-ᵓĀkhirati nuᵓtihī minhā. Wa sanajzish-shākirīn. 145 Wa kaᵓayyim-miñ-Nabiyyiñ-qātala maᶜahū ribbiyyūna kathīruñ-famā wahanū limāa ᵓaṣābahum fī sabīlil-lāhi wa mā ḍaᶜufū wa mastakānū. Wal-lāhu yuḥibbuṣ-ṣābirīn. 146 Wa mā kāna qawlahum ᵓillāa ᵓañ-qālū Rabbanagh-fir lanā dhunūbanā wa ᵓisrāfanā fīi ᵓamrinā wa thabbit ᵓaqdāmanā wañ-ṣurnā ᶜalal-qawmil-kāfirīn. 147 Faᵓātāhumul-lāhu thawābad-dunyā wa ḥusna thawābil-ᵓĀkhirah. Wal-lāhu yuḥibbul-muḥsinīn. 148 Yāa ᵓayyuhal-ladhīna ᵓāmanūu ᵓiñ-tuṭīᶜul-ladhīna kafarū yaruddūkum ᶜalāa ᵓaᶜqābikum fatañqalibū khāsirīn. 149

104 This stress on the mortality of the Prophet – and that of all the other prophets who preceded him in time – connects, in the first instance, with the battle of Uḥud and the rumour of his death, which caused many Muslims to abandon the fight and even brought some of them close to apostasy (Ṭabarī; see also note 90 above). In its wider implication, however, the above verse re-states the fundamental Islamic doctrine that adoration is due to God alone, and that no human being – not even a prophet – may have any share in it. It was this very passage of the Qurᵓān which Abū Bakr, the first Caliph, recited immediately after the Prophet's death, when many faint-hearted Muslims thought that Islam itself had come to an end; but as soon as Abū Bakr added, "Behold, whoever has worshipped Muḥammad may know that Muḥammad has died; but whoever worships God may know that God is ever-living, and never dies" (Bukhāri), all confusion was stilled. – The expression "turning about on one's heels" denotes – according to circumstances – either actual apostasy or a deliberate withdrawal from efforts in the cause of God.

ثلاثة ارباع الحزب

Nay, but God alone is your Lord Supreme, and His is the best succour.[105] ‹150›
Into the hearts of those who are bent on denying the truth We shall cast dread in return for their ascribing divinity, side by side with God, to other beings – [something] for which He has never bestowed any warrant from on high;[106] and their goal is the fire – and how evil that abode of evildoers! ‹151›

AND, INDEED, God made good His promise unto you when, by His leave, you were about to destroy your foes[107] – until the moment when you lost heart and acted contrary to the [Prophet's] command,[108] and disobeyed after He had brought you within view of that [victory] for which you were longing. There were among you such as cared for this world [alone], just as there were among you such as cared for the life to come:[109] whereupon, in order that He might put you to a test, He prevented you from defeating your foes.[110] But now He has effaced your sin: for God is limitless in His bounty unto the believers. ‹152›
[Remember the time] when you fled, paying no heed to anyone, while at your rear the Apostle was calling out to you – wherefore He requited you with woe in return for [the Apostle's] woe, so that you should not grieve [merely] over what had escaped you, nor over what had befallen you: for God is aware of all that you do.[111] ‹153›
Then, after this woe, He sent down upon you a sense of security, an inner calm

بَلِ ٱللَّهُ مَوْلَىٰكُمْ وَهُوَ خَيْرُ ٱلنَّٰصِرِينَ ﴿١٥٠﴾ سَنُلْقِى فِى قُلُوبِ ٱلَّذِينَ
كَفَرُوا۟ ٱلرُّعْبَ بِمَآ أَشْرَكُوا۟ بِٱللَّهِ مَا لَمْ يُنَزِّلْ بِهِۦ سُلْطَٰنًا وَمَأْوَىٰهُمُ ٱلنَّارُ
وَبِئْسَ مَثْوَى ٱلظَّٰلِمِينَ ﴿١٥١﴾ وَلَقَدْ صَدَقَكُمُ ٱللَّهُ وَعْدَهُۥٓ إِذْ تَحُسُّونَهُم
بِإِذْنِهِۦ حَتَّىٰٓ إِذَا فَشِلْتُمْ وَتَنَٰزَعْتُمْ فِى ٱلْأَمْرِ وَعَصَيْتُم مِّنۢ بَعْدِ مَآ أَرَىٰكُم
مَّا تُحِبُّونَ مِنكُم مَّن يُرِيدُ ٱلدُّنْيَا وَمِنكُم مَّن يُرِيدُ ٱلْءَاخِرَةَ ثُمَّ صَرَفَكُمْ
عَنْهُمْ لِيَبْتَلِيَكُمْ وَلَقَدْ عَفَا عَنكُمْ وَٱللَّهُ ذُو فَضْلٍ عَلَى ٱلْمُؤْمِنِينَ ﴿١٥٢﴾ ۞
إِذْ تُصْعِدُونَ وَلَا تَلْوُۥنَ عَلَىٰٓ أَحَدٍ وَٱلرَّسُولُ يَدْعُوكُمْ فِىٓ أُخْرَىٰكُمْ
فَأَثَٰبَكُمْ غَمًّۢا بِغَمٍّ لِّكَيْلَا تَحْزَنُوا۟ عَلَىٰ مَا فَاتَكُمْ وَلَا مَآ أَصَٰبَكُمْ وَٱللَّهُ
خَبِيرٌۢ بِمَا تَعْمَلُونَ ﴿١٥٣﴾ ثُمَّ أَنزَلَ عَلَيْكُم مِّنۢ بَعْدِ ٱلْغَمِّ أَمَنَةً نُّعَاسًا

Balil-lāhu Mawlākum; wa Huwa khayrun-nāṣirīn. ﴿150﴾ Sanulqī fī qulūbil-ladhīna kafarur-ruʿba bimāa ʾashrakū billāhi mā lam yunazzil bihī sulṭānā. Wa maʾwāhumun-nāru wa biʾsa mathwaẓ-ẓālimīn. ﴿151﴾ Wa laqad ṣadaqakumul-lāhu waʿdahūu ʾidh taḥussūnahum biʾidhnihī ḥattāa ʾidhā fashiltum wa tanāzaʿtum fil-ʾamri wa ʿaṣaytum-mim-baʿdi māa ʾarākum mā tuḥibbūn. Miñkum mañy-yurīdud-dunyā wa miñkum-mañy-yurīdul-ʾĀkhirah. Thumma ṣarafakum ʿanhum liyabtaliyakum; wa laqad ʿafā ʿañkum. Wal-lāhu Dhū faḍlin ʿalal-muʾminīn. ﴿152﴾ ۞ ʾIdh tuṣʿidūna wa lā talwūna ʿalāa ʾaḥadiñw-war-Rasūlu yadʿūkum fīi ʾukhrākum faʾathābakum ghammam-bighammil-likaylā taḥzanū ʿalā mā fātakum wa lā māa ʾaṣābakum. Wal-lāhu Khabīrum-bimā taʿmalūn. ﴿153﴾ Thumma ʾañzala ʿalaykum-mim-baʿdil-ghammi ʾamanatañ-nuʿāsañy-

105 Lit., "He is the best of all who bring succour".

106 I.e., something which He never permits. The use of the adverb "never" in my rendering is based on the grammatical form *lam yunazzil* (lit., "He has not been sending down" or "bestowing from on high"), which implies continuity in time.

107 Lit., "when you were destroying them": a reference to the opening stages of the battle of Uḥud. Regarding the promise alluded to, see verses 124-125 of this *sūrah*.

108 Lit., "you disagreed with one another regarding the [Prophet's] command" – an allusion to the abandonment of their post by most of the archers at the moment when it seemed that victory had been won (see note 90 above).

109 Out of the fifty Muslim archers less than ten remained at their post, and were killed by Khālid's cavalry. It is to them, as well as the few Companions who went on fighting after the bulk of the Muslims had fled, that the second part of the above sentence refers.

110 Lit., "He turned you away from them".

111 I.e., the realization of how shamefully they had behaved at Uḥud (see note 90 above) would be, in the end, more painful to them than the loss of victory and the death of so many of their comrades: and this is the meaning of

which enfolded some of you,[112] whereas the others, who cared mainly for themselves, entertained wrong thoughts about God – thoughts of pagan ignorance – saying, "Did we, then, have any power of decision [in this matter]?"[113]
Say: "Verily, all power of decision does rest with God"[114] – [but as for them,] they are trying to conceal within themselves that [weakness of faith] which they would not reveal unto thee, [O Prophet, by] saying, "If we had any power of decision, we would not have left so many dead behind."[115]
Say [unto them]: "Even if you had remained in your homes, those [of you] whose death had been ordained would indeed have gone forth to the places where they were destined to lie down."
And [all this befell you] so that God might put to a test all that you harbour in your bosoms, and render your innermost hearts[116] pure of all dross: for God is aware of what is in the hearts [of men]. ‹154›
Behold, as for those of you who turned away [from their duty] on the day when the two hosts met in battle – Satan caused them to stumble only by means of something that they [themselves] had done.[117] But now God has effaced this sin of theirs: verily, God is much-forgiving, forbearing. ‹155›
O you who have attained to faith! Be not like those who are bent on denying the truth and say of their brethren [who die]

يَغۡشَىٰ طَآئِفَةٗ مِّنكُمۡۖ وَطَآئِفَةٞ قَدۡ أَهَمَّتۡهُمۡ أَنفُسُهُمۡ يَظُنُّونَ بِٱللَّهِ غَيۡرَ ٱلۡحَقِّ ظَنَّ
ٱلۡجَٰهِلِيَّةِۖ يَقُولُونَ هَل لَّنَا مِنَ ٱلۡأَمۡرِ مِن شَيۡءٖۗ قُلۡ إِنَّ ٱلۡأَمۡرَ كُلَّهُۥ لِلَّهِۗ
يُخۡفُونَ فِيٓ أَنفُسِهِم مَّا لَا يُبۡدُونَ لَكَۖ يَقُولُونَ لَوۡ كَانَ لَنَا مِنَ ٱلۡأَمۡرِ شَيۡءٞ مَّا
قُتِلۡنَا هَٰهُنَاۗ قُل لَّوۡ كُنتُمۡ فِي بُيُوتِكُمۡ لَبَرَزَ ٱلَّذِينَ كُتِبَ عَلَيۡهِمُ ٱلۡقَتۡلُ إِلَىٰ
مَضَاجِعِهِمۡۖ وَلِيَبۡتَلِيَ ٱللَّهُ مَا فِي صُدُورِكُمۡ وَلِيُمَحِّصَ مَا فِي قُلُوبِكُمۡۚ وَٱللَّهُ
عَلِيمُۢ بِذَاتِ ٱلصُّدُورِ ١٥٤ إِنَّ ٱلَّذِينَ تَوَلَّوۡاْ مِنكُمۡ يَوۡمَ ٱلۡتَقَى ٱلۡجَمۡعَانِ إِنَّمَا
ٱسۡتَزَلَّهُمُ ٱلشَّيۡطَٰنُ بِبَعۡضِ مَا كَسَبُواْۖ وَلَقَدۡ عَفَا ٱللَّهُ عَنۡهُمۡۗ إِنَّ ٱللَّهَ غَفُورٌ
حَلِيمٞ ١٥٥ يَٰٓأَيُّهَا ٱلَّذِينَ ءَامَنُواْ لَا تَكُونُواْ كَٱلَّذِينَ كَفَرُواْ وَقَالُواْ لِإِخۡوَٰنِهِمۡ

yaghshā ṭāaʾifatam-miñkum wa ṭāaʾifatuñ-qad ʾahammat-hum ʾañfusuhum yaẓunnūna billāhi ghayral-ḥaqqi ẓannal-jāhiliyyah. Yaqūlūna hal lanā minal-ʾamri miñ-shayʾ. Qul ʾinnal-ʾamra kullahū lillāh. Yukhfūna fii ʾañfusihim mā lā yubdūna lak. Yaqūlūna law kāna lanā minal-ʾamri shayʾum-mā qutilnā hāhunā. Qul law kuñtum fī buyūtikum labarazal-ladhīna kutiba ʿalayhimul-qatlu ʾilā maḍājiʿihim; wa liyabtaliyal-lāhu mā fī ṣudūrikum wa liyumaḥḥiṣa mā fī qulūbikum. Wal-lāhu ʿAlīmum-bidhātiṣ-ṣudūr. (154) ʾInnal-ladhīna tawallaw miñkum yawmal-taqal-jamʿāni ʾinnamas-tazallahumush-Shayṭānu bibaʿḍi mā kasabū. Wa laqad ʿafal-lāhu ʿanhum; ʾinnal-lāha Ghafūrun Ḥalīm. (155) Yāa ʾayyuhal-ladhīna ʾāmanū lā takūnū kalladhīna kafarū wa qālū liʾikhwānihim

the "test" mentioned in the preceding verse.

112 I.e., those who had remained steadfast throughout the battle. According to some commentators – in particular Rāghib – the term *nuʿās* (lit., "the drowsiness which precedes sleep") is used here metaphorically, and denotes "inner calm".

113 I.e., in the matter of victory or defeat. The "thoughts of pagan ignorance" is obviously an allusion to the initial reluctance of those faint-hearted people to admit their moral responsibility for what had happened, and to their excusing themselves by saying that their failure to live up to their faith had been "predestined". See also *sūrah* 5, note 71.

114 I.e., while it is for God alone to apportion actual success or failure to whomever He wills, "nought shall be accounted unto man but what he is [or "was"] striving for" (53 : 39).

115 Lit., "we would not have been killed here".

116 Lit., "all that is in your hearts".

117 This is an illustration of a significant Qurʾanic doctrine, which can be thus summarized: "Satan's influence" on man is not the primary *cause* of sin but its *first consequence*: that is to say, a consequence of a person's own attitude of mind which in moments of moral crisis induces him to choose the easier, and seemingly more pleasant, of the alternatives open to him, and thus to become guilty of a sin, whether by commission or omission. Thus, God's "causing" a person to commit a sin is conditional upon the existence, in the individual concerned, of an attitude of mind which makes him prone to commit such a sin: which, in its turn, presupposes man's free will – that is, the ability to make, within certain limitations, a conscious choice between two or more possible courses of action.

after having set out on a journey to faraway places[118] or gone forth to war, "Had they but remained with us, they would not have died," or, "they would not have been slain" – for God will cause such thoughts to become[119] a source of bitter regret in their hearts, since it is God who grants life and deals death. And God sees all that you do. ‹156›
And if indeed you are slain or die in God's cause, then surely forgiveness from God and His grace are better than all that one[120] could amass [in this world]: ‹157› for, indeed, if you die or are slain, it will surely be unto God that you shall be gathered. ‹158›
And it was by God's grace that thou [O Prophet] didst deal gently with thy followers:[121] for if thou hadst been harsh and hard of heart, they would indeed have broken away from thee. Pardon them, then, and pray that they be forgiven.
And take counsel with them in all matters of public concern; then, when thou hast decided upon a course of action, place thy trust in God: for, verily, God loves those who place their trust in Him.[122] ‹159›
If God succours you, none can ever overcome you; but if He should forsake you, who could succour you thereafter? In God, then, let the believers place their trust! ‹160›

إِذَا ضَرَبُواْ فِى ٱلْأَرْضِ أَوْ كَانُواْ غُزًّى لَّوْ كَانُواْ عِندَنَا مَا مَاتُواْ وَمَا قُتِلُواْ
لِيَجْعَلَ ٱللَّهُ ذَٰلِكَ حَسْرَةً فِى قُلُوبِهِمْ ۗ وَٱللَّهُ يُحْىِۦ وَيُمِيتُ ۗ وَٱللَّهُ بِمَا
تَعْمَلُونَ بَصِيرٌ ﴿١٥٦﴾ وَلَئِن قُتِلْتُمْ فِى سَبِيلِ ٱللَّهِ أَوْ مُتُّمْ لَمَغْفِرَةٌ مِّنَ ٱللَّهِ
وَرَحْمَةٌ خَيْرٌ مِّمَّا يَجْمَعُونَ ﴿١٥٧﴾ وَلَئِن مُّتُّمْ أَوْ قُتِلْتُمْ لَإِلَى ٱللَّهِ تُحْشَرُونَ ﴿١٥٨﴾
فَبِمَا رَحْمَةٍ مِّنَ ٱللَّهِ لِنتَ لَهُمْ ۖ وَلَوْ كُنتَ فَظًّا غَلِيظَ ٱلْقَلْبِ لَٱنفَضُّواْ
مِنْ حَوْلِكَ ۖ فَٱعْفُ عَنْهُمْ وَٱسْتَغْفِرْ لَهُمْ وَشَاوِرْهُمْ فِى ٱلْأَمْرِ ۖ فَإِذَا عَزَمْتَ
فَتَوَكَّلْ عَلَى ٱللَّهِ ۚ إِنَّ ٱللَّهَ يُحِبُّ ٱلْمُتَوَكِّلِينَ ﴿١٥٩﴾ إِن يَنصُرْكُمُ ٱللَّهُ فَلَا غَالِبَ
لَكُمْ ۖ وَإِن يَخْذُلْكُمْ فَمَن ذَا ٱلَّذِى يَنصُرُكُم مِّنۢ بَعْدِهِۦ ۗ وَعَلَى ٱللَّهِ
فَلْيَتَوَكَّلِ ٱلْمُؤْمِنُونَ ﴿١٦٠﴾

ʾidhā ḍarabū fil-ʾarḍi ʾaw kānū ghuzzal-law kānū ʿiñdanā mā mātū wa mā qutilū liyajʿalal-lāhu dhalika ḥasratañ-fī qulūbihim. Wal-lāhu yuḥyī wa yumīt. Wal-lāhu bimā taʿmalūna Baṣīr. (156) Wa laʾiñ-qutiltum fī sabīlil-lāhi ʾaw muttum la-maghfiratum-minal-lāhi wa raḥmatun khayrum-mimmā yajmaʿūn. (157) Wa laʾim-muttum ʾaw qutiltum laʾilal-lāhi tuḥsharūn. (158) Fabimā raḥmatim-minal-lāhi liñta lahum. Wa law kuñta faẓẓan ghalīẓal-qalbi lañfaḍḍū min ḥawlik. Faʿfu ʿanhum was-taghfir lahum wa shāwirhum fil-ʾamr. Faʾidhā ʿazamta fatawakkal ʿalal-lāh. ʾInnal-lāha yuḥibbul-mutawakkilīn. (159) ʾIñy-yañṣurkumul-lāhu falā ghāliba lakum; wa ʾiñy-yakhdhulkum famañ-dhal-ladhī yañṣurukum mimbaʿdih. Wa ʿalal-lāhi falyatawakkalil-muʾminūn. (160)

118 Lit., "when they travel on earth".

119 Lit., "so that God causes this to be": but since the particle *li* in *li-yajʿal* is obviously a *lām al-ʿāqibah* (i.e., the letter *lām* denoting a causal sequence), it is best rendered in this context by the conjunctive particle "for", combined with the future tense.

120 Lit., "they".

121 Lit., "with them" – i.e., with those of his followers who had failed in their duty before and during the disaster at Uḥud. According to all available accounts the Prophet did not even reproach any of them for what they had done.

122 This injunction, implying government by consent and council, must be regarded as one of the fundamental clauses of all Qurʾanic legislation relating to statecraft. The pronoun "them" relates to the believers, that is, to the whole community; while the word *al-amr* occurring in this context – as well as in the much earlier-revealed phrase *amruhum shūrā baynahum* in 42 : 38 – denotes all affairs of public concern, including state administration. All authorities agree in that the above ordinance, although addressed in the first instance to the Prophet, is binding on all Muslims and for all times. (For its wider implications see *State and Government in Islam*, pp. 44 ff.) Some Muslim scholars conclude from the wording of this ordinance that the leader of the community, although obliged to take counsel, is nevertheless free to accept or to reject it; but the arbitrariness of this conclusion becomes obvious as soon as we recall that even the Prophet considered himself bound by the decisions of his council (see note 90 above). Moreover, when he was asked – according to a Tradition on the authority of ʿAlī ibn Abī Ṭālib – to explain the implications of the word *ʿazm* ("deciding upon a course of action") which occurs in the above verse, the Prophet replied, "[It means] taking counsel with knowledgeable people (*ahl ar-raʾy*) and thereupon following them [therein]" (see Ibn Kathīr's commentary on this verse).

AND IT IS not conceivable that a prophet should deceive[123] – since he who deceives shall be faced with his deceit on the Day of Resurrection, when every human being shall be repaid in full for whatever he has done, and none shall be wronged. «161» Is then he[124] who strives after God's goodly acceptance like unto him who has earned the burden of God's condemnation[125] and whose goal is hell? – and how vile a journey's end! «162» They are on [entirely] different levels in the sight of God; for God sees all that they do. «163» Indeed, God bestowed a favour upon the believers when he raised up in their midst an apostle from among themselves, to convey His messages unto them, and to cause them to grow in purity, and to impart unto them the divine writ as well as wisdom – whereas before that they were indeed, most obviously, lost in error. «164»

AND DO YOU, now that a calamity has befallen you after you had inflicted twice as much [on your foes],[126] ask yourselves, "How has this come about?" Say: "It has come from your own selves."[127] Verily, God has the power to will anything: «165» and all that befell you on the day when the two hosts met in battle happened by God's leave, so that He might mark out the [true] believers, «166» and mark out those who were tainted with hypocrisy and, when they were told, "Come, fight in God's cause" – or, "Defend yourselves"[128] – answered, "If we but knew

وَمَا كَانَ لِنَبِيٍّ أَن يَغُلَّ وَمَن يَغْلُلْ يَأْتِ بِمَا غَلَّ يَوْمَ ٱلْقِيَـٰمَةِ ثُمَّ تُوَفَّىٰ كُلُّ
نَفْسٍ مَّا كَسَبَتْ وَهُمْ لَا يُظْلَمُونَ ﴿١٦١﴾ أَفَمَنِ ٱتَّبَعَ رِضْوَٰنَ ٱللَّهِ كَمَنۢ
بَآءَ بِسَخَطٍ مِّنَ ٱللَّهِ وَمَأْوَىٰهُ جَهَنَّمُ وَبِئْسَ ٱلْمَصِيرُ ﴿١٦٢﴾ هُمْ دَرَجَـٰتٌ عِندَ
ٱللَّهِ وَٱللَّهُ بَصِيرٌۢ بِمَا يَعْمَلُونَ ﴿١٦٣﴾ لَقَدْ مَنَّ ٱللَّهُ عَلَى ٱلْمُؤْمِنِينَ إِذْ بَعَثَ
فِيهِمْ رَسُولًا مِّنْ أَنفُسِهِمْ يَتْلُوا۟ عَلَيْهِمْ ءَايَـٰتِهِۦ وَيُزَكِّيهِمْ وَيُعَلِّمُهُمُ
ٱلْكِتَـٰبَ وَٱلْحِكْمَةَ وَإِن كَانُوا۟ مِن قَبْلُ لَفِى ضَلَـٰلٍ مُّبِينٍ ﴿١٦٤﴾ أَوَلَمَّآ
أَصَـٰبَتْكُم مُّصِيبَةٌ قَدْ أَصَبْتُم مِّثْلَيْهَا قُلْتُمْ أَنَّىٰ هَـٰذَا قُلْ هُوَ مِنْ عِندِ
أَنفُسِكُمْ إِنَّ ٱللَّهَ عَلَىٰ كُلِّ شَىْءٍ قَدِيرٌ ﴿١٦٥﴾ وَمَآ أَصَـٰبَكُمْ يَوْمَ ٱلْتَقَى
ٱلْجَمْعَانِ فَبِإِذْنِ ٱللَّهِ وَلِيَعْلَمَ ٱلْمُؤْمِنِينَ ﴿١٦٦﴾ وَلِيَعْلَمَ ٱلَّذِينَ نَافَقُوا۟
وَقِيلَ لَهُمْ تَعَالَوْا۟ قَـٰتِلُوا۟ فِى سَبِيلِ ٱللَّهِ أَوِ ٱدْفَعُوا۟ قَالُوا۟ لَوْ نَعْلَمُ

Wa mā kāna liNabiyyin ʾañy-yaghull. Wa mañy-yaghlul yaʾti bimā ghalla Yawmal-Qiyāmah. Thumma tuwaffā kullu nafsim-mā kasabat wa hum lā yuẓlamūn. (161) ʾAfamanit-tabaᶜa riḍwānal-lāhi kamam-bāaʾa bisakhatim-minal-lāhi wa maʾwāhu jahannamu wa biʾsal-maṣīr. (162) Hum darajātun ᶜiñdal-lāh. Wal-lāhu Baṣīrum-bimā yaᶜmalūn. (163) Laqad mannal-lāhu ᶜalal-muʾminīna ʾidh baᶜatha fīhim Rasūlam-min ʾañfusihim yatlū ᶜalayhim ʾāyātihī wa yuzakkīhim wa yuᶜallimu-humul-Kitāba wal-ḥikmata wa ʾiñ-kānū miñ-qablu lafī ḍalālim-mubīn. (164) ʾAwa lammāa ʾaṣābatkum-muṣībatuñ-qad ʾaṣabtum-mithlayhā qultum ʾannā hādhā. Qul huwa min ʾiñdi ʾañfusikum. ʾInnal-lāha ᶜalā kulli shayʾiñ-Qadīr. (165) Wa māa ʾaṣābakum yawmal-taqal-jamᶜāni fabiʾidhnil-lāhi wa liyaᶜlamal-muʾminīn. (166) Wa liyaᶜlamal-ladhīna nāfaqū wa qīla lahum taᶜālaw qātilū fī sabīlil-lāhi ʾawid-faᶜū. Qālū law naᶜlamu

123 I.e., by attributing his own opinions to God, and then appealing to the believers to place their trust in Him alone. However contrary to reason such deceit may be, it is a common view among non-believers that the Prophet himself "composed" the Qur'an and thereupon falsely attributed it to divine revelation.

124 An allusion, in this case, to the Prophet Muḥammad as well as to prophets in general.

125 I.e., by falsely attributing his own views to God or distorting His messages by arbitrary interpolations and deliberate changes in the wording of a revelation – an accusation often levelled in the Qurʾān (e.g., 2 : 79 and 3 : 78) against the followers of earlier revelations.

126 I.e., at the battle of Badr, in the year 2 H.

127 Many of the followers of the Prophet had been convinced that, whatever the circumstances, God would grant them victory on account of their faith alone. The bitter experience at Uḥud came as a shock to them; and so the Qurʾān reminds them that this calamity was a consequence of their own doings.

128 Only a fight in self-defence – in the widest meaning of this term – can be considered a "fight in God's cause" (see 2 : 190-194, and the corresponding notes); and, thus, the particle "or" between these two phrases is almost synonymous with the expression "in other words".

[that it would come to a] fight, we would indeed follow you."
Unto apostasy were they nearer on that day than unto faith, uttering with their mouths something which was not in their hearts,[129] the while God knew fully well what they were trying to conceal: ‹167› they who, having themselves held back [from fighting, later] said of their [slain] brethren, "Had they but paid heed to us, they would not have been slain."
Say: "Avert, then, death from yourselves, if what you say is true!" ‹168›
But do not think of those that have been slain in God's cause as dead. Nay, they are alive! With their Sustainer have they their sustenance, ‹169› exulting in that [martyrdom] which God has bestowed upon them out of His bounty. And they rejoice in the glad tiding given to those [of their brethren] who have been left behind and have not yet joined them, that no fear need they have, and neither shall they grieve: ‹170› they rejoice in the glad tiding of God's blessings and bounty, and [in the promise] that God will not fail to requite the believers ‹171› who responded to the call of God and the Apostle after misfortune had befallen them.[130]
A magnificent requital awaits those of them who have persevered in doing good and remained conscious of God: ‹172› those who have been warned by other people,[131]

حزب 8

قِتَالًا لَّاتَّبَعْنَٰكُمْ هُمْ لِلْكُفْرِ يَوْمَئِذٍ أَقْرَبُ مِنْهُمْ لِلْإِيمَٰنِ يَقُولُونَ بِأَفْوَٰهِهِم
مَّا لَيْسَ فِى قُلُوبِهِمْ وَٱللَّهُ أَعْلَمُ بِمَا يَكْتُمُونَ ﴿١٦٧﴾ ٱلَّذِينَ قَالُوا۟ لِإِخْوَٰنِهِمْ
وَقَعَدُوا۟ لَوْ أَطَاعُونَا مَا قُتِلُوا۟ قُلْ فَٱدْرَءُوا۟ عَنْ أَنفُسِكُمُ ٱلْمَوْتَ إِن كُنتُمْ
صَٰدِقِينَ ﴿١٦٨﴾ وَلَا تَحْسَبَنَّ ٱلَّذِينَ قُتِلُوا۟ فِى سَبِيلِ ٱللَّهِ أَمْوَٰتًۢا بَلْ أَحْيَآءٌ عِندَ
رَبِّهِمْ يُرْزَقُونَ ﴿١٦٩﴾ فَرِحِينَ بِمَآ ءَاتَىٰهُمُ ٱللَّهُ مِن فَضْلِهِۦ وَيَسْتَبْشِرُونَ بِٱلَّذِينَ
لَمْ يَلْحَقُوا۟ بِهِم مِّنْ خَلْفِهِمْ أَلَّا خَوْفٌ عَلَيْهِمْ وَلَا هُمْ يَحْزَنُونَ ﴿١٧٠﴾ ۞
يَسْتَبْشِرُونَ بِنِعْمَةٍ مِّنَ ٱللَّهِ وَفَضْلٍ وَأَنَّ ٱللَّهَ لَا يُضِيعُ أَجْرَ ٱلْمُؤْمِنِينَ ﴿١٧١﴾
ٱلَّذِينَ ٱسْتَجَابُوا۟ لِلَّهِ وَٱلرَّسُولِ مِنۢ بَعْدِ مَآ أَصَابَهُمُ ٱلْقَرْحُ لِلَّذِينَ
أَحْسَنُوا۟ مِنْهُمْ وَٱتَّقَوْا۟ أَجْرٌ عَظِيمٌ ﴿١٧٢﴾ ٱلَّذِينَ قَالَ لَهُمُ ٱلنَّاسُ إِنَّ ٱلنَّاسَ

qitālal-lattabaᶜnākum. Hum lilkufri yawmaᵓidhin ᵓaqrabu minhum lilᵓīmān. Yaqūlūna biᵓafwāhihim mā laysa fī qulūbihim. Wal-lāhu ᵓaᶜlamu bimā yak-tumūn. (167) ᵓAlladhīna qālū liᵓikhwānihim wa qaᶜadū law ᵓaṭā-ᶜūnā mā qutilū. Qul fadraᵓū ᶜan ᵓañfusiku-mul-mawta ᵓiñ-kuñtum ṣādiqīn. (168) Wa lā taḥsabannal-ladhīna qutilū fī sabīlil-lāhi ᵓamwātā. Bal ᵓaḥyāaᵓun ᶜiñda Rabbihim yurzaqūn. (169) Fariḥīna bimāa ᵓātā-humul-lāhu miñ-faḍlihī wa yastabshirūna billadhīna lam yalḥaqū bihim min khalfihim ᵓallā khawfun ᶜalayhim wa lā hum yaḥzanūn. (170) ۞ Yastabshirūna biniᶜmatim-minal-lāhi wa faḍliñw-wa ᵓannal-lāha lā yuḍīᶜu ᵓajral-muᵓminīn. (171) ᵓAlladhīnas-tajābū lillāhi war-Rasūli mim-baᶜdi māa ᵓaṣābahumul-qarḥ. Lilladhīna ᵓaḥsanū minhum wat-taqaw ᵓajrun ᶜaẓīm. (172) ᵓAlladhīna qāla lahumun-nāsu ᵓinnan-nāsa

129 This is an allusion to the three hundred men who, on the way from Medina to Mount Uḥud, forsook the Prophet on the specious plea that he did not really intend to give battle (see note 90 above). But since they knew in their hearts that it would come to a fight, their defection from God's cause almost amounted to a denial of Him (*kufr*, here rendered as "apostasy").

130 Lit., "after injury had afflicted them". Most of the commentators assume that this is an allusion to the losses sustained by the Muslims at the battle of Uḥud. It is, however, probable that the implication is much wider, the more so since this passage connects directly with the preceding verses which speak, in general terms, of the martyrs who die in God's cause. There is a distinct tendency on the part of most of the classical commentators to read minute historical references into many Qurᵓanic passages which express ideas of a far wider import and apply to the human condition as such. Verses 172-175 are an instance of this. Some commentators are of the opinion that they refer to the fruitless expedition to Ḥamrāᵓ al-Asad on the day following the battle of Uḥud, while others see in it an allusion to the Prophet's expedition, in the following year, known to history as the "Little Badr" (*Badr aṣ-Ṣughrā*); others, again, think that verse 172 refers to the former and verses 173-174 to the latter. In view of this obvious lack of unanimity – due to the absence of a really authoritative support, either in the Qurᵓān itself or in authentic Traditions, for any of these speculative assumptions – there is every reason for concluding that the whole passage under consideration expresses a general moral, rounding off, as it were, the historical references to the battle of Uḥud and the lessons to be drawn therefrom.

131 Lit., "those to whom people said".

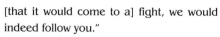

"Behold, a host has gathered against you; so beware of them!" – whereupon this only increased their faith, so that they answered, "God is enough for us; and how excellent a guardian is He!" ﴾173﴿ – and returned [from the battle] with God's blessings and bounty, without having been touched by evil:[132] for they had been striving after God's goodly acceptance – and God is limitless in His great bounty. ﴾174﴿

It is but Satan who instils [into you] fear of his allies:[133] so fear them not, but fear Me, if you are [truly] believers! ﴾175﴿

And be not grieved by those who vie with one another in denying the truth: verily, they can in no wise harm God. It is God's will that they shall have no share[134] in the [blessings of the] life to come; and tremendous suffering awaits them. ﴾176﴿

Verily, they who have bought a denial of the truth at the price of faith can in no wise harm God, whereas grievous suffering awaits them. ﴾177﴿ And they should not think – they who are bent on denying the truth – that Our giving them rein is good for them: We give them rein only to let them grow in sinfulness; and shameful suffering awaits them.[135] ﴾178﴿

It is not God's will [O you who deny the truth] to abandon the believers to your way of life:[136] [and] to that end He will set apart the bad from the good. And it is not God's will to give you insight into that which is beyond the reach of human perception:

قَدْ جَمَعُوا۟ لَكُمْ فَٱخْشَوْهُمْ فَزَادَهُمْ إِيمَٰنًا وَقَالُوا۟ حَسْبُنَا ٱللَّهُ وَنِعْمَ
ٱلْوَكِيلُ ﴿١٧٣﴾ فَٱنقَلَبُوا۟ بِنِعْمَةٍ مِّنَ ٱللَّهِ وَفَضْلٍ لَّمْ يَمْسَسْهُمْ سُوٓءٌ وَٱتَّبَعُوا۟
رِضْوَٰنَ ٱللَّهِ ۗ وَٱللَّهُ ذُو فَضْلٍ عَظِيمٍ ﴿١٧٤﴾ إِنَّمَا ذَٰلِكُمُ ٱلشَّيْطَٰنُ يُخَوِّفُ
أَوْلِيَآءَهُۥ فَلَا تَخَافُوهُمْ وَخَافُونِ إِن كُنتُم مُّؤْمِنِينَ ﴿١٧٥﴾ وَلَا يَحْزُنكَ ٱلَّذِينَ
يُسَٰرِعُونَ فِى ٱلْكُفْرِ ۚ إِنَّهُمْ لَن يَضُرُّوا۟ ٱللَّهَ شَيْـًٔا ۗ يُرِيدُ ٱللَّهُ أَلَّا يَجْعَلَ لَهُمْ
حَظًّا فِى ٱلْءَاخِرَةِ ۖ وَلَهُمْ عَذَابٌ عَظِيمٌ ﴿١٧٦﴾ إِنَّ ٱلَّذِينَ ٱشْتَرَوُا۟ ٱلْكُفْرَ
بِٱلْإِيمَٰنِ لَن يَضُرُّوا۟ ٱللَّهَ شَيْـًٔا وَلَهُمْ عَذَابٌ أَلِيمٌ ﴿١٧٧﴾ وَلَا يَحْسَبَنَّ
ٱلَّذِينَ كَفَرُوٓا۟ أَنَّمَا نُمْلِى لَهُمْ خَيْرٌ لِّأَنفُسِهِمْ ۚ إِنَّمَا نُمْلِى لَهُمْ لِيَزْدَادُوٓا۟
إِثْمًا ۚ وَلَهُمْ عَذَابٌ مُّهِينٌ ﴿١٧٨﴾ مَّا كَانَ ٱللَّهُ لِيَذَرَ ٱلْمُؤْمِنِينَ عَلَىٰ مَآ أَنتُمْ
عَلَيْهِ حَتَّىٰ يَمِيزَ ٱلْخَبِيثَ مِنَ ٱلطَّيِّبِ ۗ وَمَا كَانَ ٱللَّهُ لِيُطْلِعَكُمْ عَلَى ٱلْغَيْبِ

qad jamaᶜū lakum fakhshawhum fazādahum ʾīmānañw-wa qālū ḥasbunal-lāhu wa niᶜmal-Wakīl. (173) Fañqalabū biniᶜmatim-minal-lāhi wa faḍlil-lam yamsas-hum sūuʾuñw-wat-tabaᶜū riḍwānal-lāh. Wal-lāhu Dhū faḍlin ᶜAẓīm. (174) ʾInnamā dhālikumush-Shayṭānu yukhawwifu ʾawliyāaʾah. Falā takhāfūhum wa khāfūni ʾiñ-kuñtum muʾminīn. (175) Wa lā yaḥzuñkal-ladhīna yusāriᶜūna fil-kufri ʾinnahum lañy-yaḍurrul-lāha shayʾā. Yurīdul-lāhu ʾallā yajᶜala lahum ḥaẓẓañ-fil-ʾĀkhirati wa lahum ᶜadhābun ᶜaẓīm. (176) ʾInnal-ladhīnash-tarawul-kufra bilʾīmāni lañy-yaḍurrul-lāha shayʾañw-wa lahum ᶜadhābun ʾalīm. (177) Wa lā yaḥsabannal-ladhīna kafarūu ʾannamā numlī lahum khayrul-liʾañfusihim; ʾinnamā numlī lahum liyazdādūu ʾithmañw-wa lahum ᶜadhābum-muhīn. (178) Mā kānal-lāhu liyadharal-muʾminīna ᶜalā māa ʾañtum ᶜalayhi ḥattā yamīzal-khabītha minaṭ-ṭayyib. Wa mā kānal-lāhu liyuṭliᶜakum ᶜalal-ghaybi

132 I.e., the moral evil arising out of weakness of faith and loss of courage: an allusion to what happened to many Muslims at Uḥud.

133 I.e., people who "ally themselves with Satan" by deliberately doing wrong.

134 Lit., "that He will not assign to them a share".

135 This is an allusion to the doctrine of natural law (in Qurʾanic terminology, *sunnat Allāh*, "God's way") to which man's inclinations and actions – as well as all other happenings in the universe – are subject. The above verse says, as it were, "Since these people are bent on denying the truth, Our giving them rein [that is, freedom of choice and time for a reconsideration of their attitude] will not work out for their benefit but will, on the contrary, cause them to grow in false self-confidence and, thus, in sinfulness." As in many similar passages in the Qurʾān, God attributes here their "growing in sinfulness" to His own will because it is He who has imposed on all His creation the natural law of cause and effect. (See also note 4 on 14 : 4.)

136 Some commentators (e.g., Rāzī) assume that the expression *mā antum ᶜalayhi* (lit., "that upon which you are") denotes here "the condition in which you are" – i.e., the state of weakness and confusion in which the Muslim community found itself after the battle of Uḥud – and that, therefore, this passage is addressed to the believers. This

but [to that end] God elects whomsoever He wills from among His apostles.[137] Believe, then, in God and His apostles; for if you believe and are conscious of Him, a magnificent requital awaits you. ‹179›

AND THEY should not think – they who niggardly cling to all that God has granted them out of His bounty – that this is good for them: nay, it is bad for them.[138] That to which they [so] niggardly cling will, on the Day of Resurrection, be hung about their necks: for unto God [alone] belongs the heritage of the heavens and of the earth; and God is aware of all that you do. ‹180›

God has indeed heard the saying of those who said, "Behold, God is poor while we are rich!"[139] We shall record what they have said, as well as their slaying of prophets against all right,[140] and We shall say [unto them on Judgment Day]: "Taste suffering through fire ‹181› in return for what your own hands have wrought – for never does God do the least wrong to His creatures!" ‹182›

As for those who maintain, "Behold, God has bidden us not to believe in any apostle unless he comes unto us with burnt offerings"[141] – say [unto them, O Prophet]: "Even before me there came

وَلَٰكِنَّ ٱللَّهَ يَجْتَبِى مِن رُّسُلِهِۦ مَن يَشَآءُ ۖ فَـَٔامِنُوا۟ بِٱللَّهِ وَرُسُلِهِۦ ۚ وَإِن تُؤْمِنُوا۟
وَتَتَّقُوا۟ فَلَكُمْ أَجْرٌ عَظِيمٌ ﴿١٧٩﴾ وَلَا يَحْسَبَنَّ ٱلَّذِينَ يَبْخَلُونَ بِمَآ ءَاتَىٰهُمُ ٱللَّهُ
مِن فَضْلِهِۦ هُوَ خَيْرًا لَّهُم ۖ بَلْ هُوَ شَرٌّ لَّهُمْ ۖ سَيُطَوَّقُونَ مَا بَخِلُوا۟ بِهِۦ يَوْمَ
ٱلْقِيَٰمَةِ ۗ وَلِلَّهِ مِيرَٰثُ ٱلسَّمَٰوَٰتِ وَٱلْأَرْضِ ۗ وَٱللَّهُ بِمَا تَعْمَلُونَ خَبِيرٌ ﴿١٨٠﴾
لَّقَدْ سَمِعَ ٱللَّهُ قَوْلَ ٱلَّذِينَ قَالُوٓا۟ إِنَّ ٱللَّهَ فَقِيرٌ وَنَحْنُ أَغْنِيَآءُ ۘ سَنَكْتُبُ مَا قَالُوا۟
وَقَتْلَهُمُ ٱلْأَنۢبِيَآءَ بِغَيْرِ حَقٍّ وَنَقُولُ ذُوقُوا۟ عَذَابَ ٱلْحَرِيقِ ﴿١٨١﴾ ذَٰلِكَ بِمَا
قَدَّمَتْ أَيْدِيكُمْ وَأَنَّ ٱللَّهَ لَيْسَ بِظَلَّامٍ لِّلْعَبِيدِ ﴿١٨٢﴾ ٱلَّذِينَ قَالُوٓا۟ إِنَّ ٱللَّهَ
عَهِدَ إِلَيْنَآ أَلَّا نُؤْمِنَ لِرَسُولٍ حَتَّىٰ يَأْتِيَنَا بِقُرْبَانٍ تَأْكُلُهُ ٱلنَّارُ ۗ قُلْ قَدْ جَآءَكُمْ

wa lākinnal-lāha yajtabī mir-Rusulihī mañy-yashāaʾ. Faʾāminū billāhi wa Rusulih. Wa ʾiñ-tuʾminū wa tattaqū falakum ʾajrun ʿaẓīm. (179) Wa lā yaḥsabannal-ladhīna yabkhalūna bimāa ʾātāhumul-lāhu miñ-faḍlihī huwa khayral-lahum; bal huwa sharrul-lahum; sayuṭawwaqūna mā bakhilū bihī Yawmal-Qiyāmah. Wa lillāhi mīrāthus-samāwāti wal-ʾarḍ. Wal-lāhu bimā taʿmalūna Khabīr. (180) Laqad samiʿal-lāhu qawlal-ladhīna qālūu ʾinnal-lāha faqīruñw-wa naḥnu ʾaghniyāaʾ. Sanaktubu mā qālū wa qatlahumul-ʾAmbiyāaʾa bighayri ḥaqqiñw-wa naqūlu dhūqū ʿadhābal-ḥarīq. (181) Dhālika bimā qaddamat ʾaydīkum wa ʾannal-lāha laysa biẓallāmil-lilʿabīd. (182) ʾAlladhīna qālūu ʾinnal-lāha ʿahida ʾilaynāa ʾallā nuʾmina liRasūlin ḥattā yaʾtiyanā biqurbāniñ-taʾkuluhun-nār. Qul qad jāaʾakum

interpretation, however, is not plausible. Apart from the fact that the believers are here referred to in the third person, while *mā antum ʿalayhi* is in the second person plural, the latter expression denotes almost invariably, both in the Qurʾān and in the Traditions, people's mode of life and beliefs. Moreover, we have reliable reports to the effect that Ibn ʿAbbās, Qatādah, Aḍ-Ḍaḥḥāk, Muqātil and Al-Kalbī unhesitatingly declared that the people addressed here are "those who deny the truth" to whom the preceding passages refer (see Ṭabarī's and Baghawī's commentaries on this verse). Read in this sense, the above passage implies that the believers would, in time, differ from the unbelievers not only in their convictions but also in their social aims and their manner of living.

137 I.e., it is through these apostles that God vouchsafes to man a partial glimpse of the reality of which He alone has full knowledge.

138 This is an allusion to the way of life of the unbelievers mentioned in verse 179 above: a way of life characterized by extreme attachment to the material things of this world – a materialism based on a lack of belief in anything that transcends the practical problems of life.

139 According to several authentic Traditions, the Jews of Medina were given to satirizing the phraseology of the Qurʾān, and especially 2 : 245 – "Who is it that will offer up unto God a goodly loan, which He will amply repay, with manifold increase?"

140 Regarding this accusation levelled against the Jews, see *sūrah* 2, note 48.

141 Lit., "with an offering which the fire consumes" – in other words, unless he conforms to Mosaic Law, which prescribes burnt offerings as an essential part of divine services. Although this aspect of the Law had been left in abeyance ever since the destruction of the Second Temple in Jerusalem, the Jews of post-Talmudic times were convinced that the Messiah promised to them would restore the Mosaic rites in their entirety; and so they refused to

unto you apostles with all evidence of the truth, and with that whereof you speak: why, then, did you slay them, if what you say is true?"[142] «183»

And if they give thee the lie – even so, before thy time, have [other] apostles been given the lie when they came with all evidence of the truth, and with books of divine wisdom, and with light-giving revelation. «184»

Every human being is bound to taste death: but only on the Day of Resurrection will you be requited in full [for whatever you have done] – whereupon he that shall be drawn away from the fire and brought into paradise will indeed have gained a triumph: for the life of this world is nothing but an enjoyment of self-delusion. «185»

You shall most certainly be tried in your possessions and in your persons; and indeed you shall hear many hurtful things from those to whom revelation was granted before your time, as well as from those who have come to ascribe divinity to other beings beside God. But if you remain patient in adversity and conscious of Him – this, behold, is something to set one's heart upon. «186»

AND LO, God accepted a solemn pledge from those who were granted earlier revelation [when He bade them]: "Make it known unto mankind, and do not conceal it!"[143]

But they cast this [pledge] behind their backs, and bartered it away for a trifling gain: and how evil was their bargain![144] «187»

رُسُلٌ مِّن قَبۡلِي بِٱلۡبَيِّنَٰتِ وَبِٱلَّذِي قُلۡتُمۡ فَلِمَ قَتَلۡتُمُوهُمۡ إِن كُنتُمۡ
صَٰدِقِينَ (183) فَإِن كَذَّبُوكَ فَقَدۡ كُذِّبَ رُسُلٞ مِّن قَبۡلِكَ جَآءُو
بِٱلۡبَيِّنَٰتِ وَٱلزُّبُرِ وَٱلۡكِتَٰبِ ٱلۡمُنِيرِ (184) كُلُّ نَفۡسٖ ذَآئِقَةُ ٱلۡمَوۡتِۗ
وَإِنَّمَا تُوَفَّوۡنَ أُجُورَكُمۡ يَوۡمَ ٱلۡقِيَٰمَةِۖ فَمَن زُحۡزِحَ عَنِ ٱلنَّارِ وَأُدۡخِلَ
ٱلۡجَنَّةَ فَقَدۡ فَازَۗ وَمَا ٱلۡحَيَوٰةُ ٱلدُّنۡيَآ إِلَّا مَتَٰعُ ٱلۡغُرُورِ (185) ۞ لَتُبۡلَوُنَّ فِيٓ
أَمۡوَٰلِكُمۡ وَأَنفُسِكُمۡ وَلَتَسۡمَعُنَّ مِنَ ٱلَّذِينَ أُوتُواْ ٱلۡكِتَٰبَ مِن قَبۡلِكُمۡ
وَمِنَ ٱلَّذِينَ أَشۡرَكُوٓاْ أَذٗى كَثِيرٗاۚ وَإِن تَصۡبِرُواْ وَتَتَّقُواْ فَإِنَّ ذَٰلِكَ مِنۡ عَزۡمِ
ٱلۡأُمُورِ (186) وَإِذۡ أَخَذَ ٱللَّهُ مِيثَٰقَ ٱلَّذِينَ أُوتُواْ ٱلۡكِتَٰبَ لَتُبَيِّنُنَّهُۥ
لِلنَّاسِ وَلَا تَكۡتُمُونَهُۥ فَنَبَذُوهُ وَرَآءَ ظُهُورِهِمۡ وَٱشۡتَرَوۡاْ بِهِۦ ثَمَنٗا قَلِيلٗاۖ
فَبِئۡسَ مَا يَشۡتَرُونَ (187)

ربع الحزب

Rusulum-miñ-qablī bilbayyināti wa billadhī qultum falima qataltumūhum ʾiñ-kuñtum ṣādiqīn. (183) Faʾiñ-kudhdhabūka faqad kudhdhiba Rusulum-miñ-qablika jāaʾū bilbayyināti waz-Zuburi wal-Kitābil-munīr. (184) Kullu nafsiñ-dhāaʾiqatul-mawt. Wa ʾinnamā tuwaffawna ʾujūrakum Yawmal-Qiyāmah. Famañ-zuḥziḥa ʿanin-nāri wa ʾudkhilal-jannata faqad fāz. Wa mal-ḥayātud-dunyāa ʾillā matāʿul-ghurūr. (185) ۞ Latublawunna fīi ʾamwālikum wa ʾañfusikum wa latasmaʿunna minal-ladhīna ūtul-Kitāba miñ-qablikum wa minal-ladhīna ʾashrakūu ʾadhañ-kathīrā. Wa ʾiñ-taṣbirū wa tattaqū faʾinna dhālika min ʿazmil-ʾumūr. (186) Wa ʾidh ʾakhadhal-lāhu mīthāqal-ladhīna ʾūtul-Kitāba latubayyinunnahū linnāsi wa lā taktumūnahū fanabadhūhu warāaʾa ẓuhūrihim wash-taraw bihī thamanañ-qalīlā. Fabiʾsa mā yash-tarūn. (187)

accept as a prophet anyone who did not conform to the Law of the Torah in every detail.

142 At the time of the martyrdom of John the Baptist and of Zachariah, of Jesus' exclamation, "O Jerusalem, Jerusalem, thou that killest the prophets" (Matthew xxiii, 37), and of the reference of Paul of Tarsus to the Jews "who killed their own prophets" (I Thessalonians ii, 15), the Second Temple was still in existence, and burnt offerings were a daily practice: thus, the refusal of the Jews to accept the prophets alluded to, culminating in their killing, could not be attributed to those prophets' lack of conformity with Mosaic Law.

143 This connects with verses 183-184, where the Jews are spoken of as refusing to accept the message of the Qurʾān. The implication of verse 187 above is that the advent of the Prophet Muḥammad was predicted in both the Old and New Testaments, and that the followers of the Bible had been called upon to spread this prophecy and not – as they actually have done – to suppress it.

144 Lit., "that which they are buying" – an allusion to the belief of the Jews that they are "God's chosen people", and to the conviction of the Christians that their belief in Jesus' "vicarious atonement" automatically assures to them

لَا تَحْسَبَنَّ ٱلَّذِينَ يَفْرَحُونَ بِمَآ أَتَوا۟ وَّيُحِبُّونَ أَن يُحْمَدُوا۟ بِمَا لَمْ يَفْعَلُوا۟
فَلَا تَحْسَبَنَّهُم بِمَفَازَةٍ مِّنَ ٱلْعَذَابِ ۖ وَلَهُمْ عَذَابٌ أَلِيمٌ ﴿١٨٨﴾ وَلِلَّهِ
مُلْكُ ٱلسَّمَـٰوَٰتِ وَٱلْأَرْضِ ۗ وَٱللَّهُ عَلَىٰ كُلِّ شَىْءٍ قَدِيرٌ ﴿١٨٩﴾ إِنَّ فِى خَلْقِ
ٱلسَّمَـٰوَٰتِ وَٱلْأَرْضِ وَٱخْتِلَـٰفِ ٱلَّيْلِ وَٱلنَّهَارِ لَـَٔايَـٰتٍ لِّأُو۟لِى
ٱلْأَلْبَـٰبِ ﴿١٩٠﴾ ٱلَّذِينَ يَذْكُرُونَ ٱللَّهَ قِيَـٰمًا وَقُعُودًا وَعَلَىٰ جُنُوبِهِمْ وَيَتَفَكَّرُونَ
فِى خَلْقِ ٱلسَّمَـٰوَٰتِ وَٱلْأَرْضِ رَبَّنَا مَا خَلَقْتَ هَـٰذَا بَـٰطِلًا سُبْحَـٰنَكَ
فَقِنَا عَذَابَ ٱلنَّارِ ﴿١٩١﴾ رَبَّنَآ إِنَّكَ مَن تُدْخِلِ ٱلنَّارَ فَقَدْ أَخْزَيْتَهُۥ ۖ وَمَا
لِلظَّـٰلِمِينَ مِنْ أَنصَارٍ ﴿١٩٢﴾ رَّبَّنَآ إِنَّنَا سَمِعْنَا مُنَادِيًا يُنَادِى لِلْإِيمَـٰنِ أَنْ
ءَامِنُوا۟ بِرَبِّكُمْ فَـَٔامَنَّا ۚ رَبَّنَا فَٱغْفِرْ لَنَا ذُنُوبَنَا وَكَفِّرْ عَنَّا سَيِّـَٔاتِنَا وَتَوَفَّنَا
مَعَ ٱلْأَبْرَارِ ﴿١٩٣﴾ رَبَّنَا وَءَاتِنَا مَا وَعَدتَّنَا عَلَىٰ رُسُلِكَ وَلَا تُخْزِنَا يَوْمَ
ٱلْقِيَـٰمَةِ ۗ إِنَّكَ لَا تُخْلِفُ ٱلْمِيعَادَ ﴿١٩٤﴾

Lā taḥsabannal-ladhīna yafraḥūna bimāa ʾataw wa yuḥibbūna ʾañy-yuḥmadū bimā lam yafʿalū falā taḥsabannahum bimafāzatim-minal-ʿadhāb. Wa lahum ʿadhābun ʾalīm. (188) Wa lillāhi mulkus-samāwāti wal-ʾarḍ. Wal-lāhu ʿalā kulli shayʾiñ-Qadīr. (189) ʾInna fī khalqis-samāwāti wal-ʾarḍi wakh-tilāfil-layli wan-nahāri laʾāyātil-liʾulil-ʾalbāb. (190) ʾAlladhīna yadh-kurūnal-lāha qiyāmañw-wa quʿūdañw-wa ʿalā junūbihim wa yatafakkarūna fī khalqis-samāwāti wal-ʾarḍi Rabbanā mā khalaqta hādhā bāṭilañ-subḥānaka faqinā ʿadhāban-nār. (191) Rabbanāa ʾinnaka mañ-tudkhilin-nāra faqad ʾakh-zaytah. Wa mā lizẓālimīna min ʾañṣār. (192) Rabbanāa ʾinnanā samiʿnā munādiyañy-yunādī lilʾīmāni ʾan ʾāminū bi-Rabbikum faʾāmannā. Rabbanā faghfir lanā dhunūbanā wa kaffir ʿannā sayyiʾātinā wa tawaffanā maʿal-ʾabrār. (193) Rabbanā wa ʾātinā mā waʿattanā ʿalā Rusulika wa lā tukhzinā Yawmal-Qiyāmah. ʾInnaka lā tukhliful-mīʿād. (194)

Think not that those who exult in what they have thus contrived, and who love to be praised for what they have not done[145] – think not that they will escape suffering: for grievous suffering does await them [in the life to come]. ‹188›

AND UNTO GOD belongs the dominion over the heavens and the earth: and God has the power to will anything. ‹189›

Verily, in the creation of the heavens and the earth, and in the succession of night and day, there are indeed messages for all who are endowed with insight, ‹190› [and] who remember God when they stand, and when they sit, and when they lie down to sleep,[146] and [thus] reflect on the creation of the heavens and the earth:

"O our Sustainer! Thou hast not created [aught of] this without meaning and purpose.[147] Limitless art Thou in Thy glory! Keep us safe, then, from suffering through fire! ‹191›

"O our Sustainer! Whomsoever Thou shalt commit to the fire, him, verily, wilt Thou have brought to disgrace [in this world];[148] and such evildoers will have none to succour them. ‹192›

"O our Sustainer! Behold, we heard a voice[149] call [us] unto faith, 'Believe in your Sustainer!' – and so we came to believe. O our Sustainer! Forgive us, then, our sins, and efface our bad deeds; and let us die the death of the truly virtuous! ‹193›

"And, O our Sustainer, grant us that which Thou hast promised us through Thy apostles, and disgrace us not on Resurrection Day! Verily, Thou never failest to fulfil Thy promise!" ‹194›

---

salvation: the "bargain" being, in both cases, an illusion of immunity in the life to come.

145 I.e., they have not, in spite of all their claims, preserved the integrity of the Bible and of Abraham's faith (Rāzī).

146 Lit., "and [lying] on their sides".

147 Lit., "in vain" (*bāṭilan*): see note 11 on 10 : 5.

148 I.e., the suffering which a sinner will have to undergo in the life to come will be a consequence of the spiritual disgrace which he has already brought upon himself by his actions in this world.

149 Lit., "a caller".

And thus does their Sustainer answer their prayer:
"I shall not lose sight of the labour of any of you who labours [in My way], be it man or woman: each of you is an issue of the other."[150] Hence, as for those who forsake the domain of evil,[151] and are driven from their homelands, and suffer hurt in My cause, and fight [for it], and are slain – I shall most certainly efface their bad deeds, and shall most certainly bring them into gardens through which running waters flow, as a reward from God: for with God is the most beauteous of rewards." ‹195›

LET IT NOT deceive thee that those who are bent on denying the truth seem to be able to do as they please on earth: ‹196› it is [but] a brief enjoyment, with hell thereafter as their goal – and how vile a resting place! ‹197› – whereas those who remain conscious of their Sustainer shall have gardens through which running waters flow, therein to abide: a ready welcome from God. And that which is with God is best for the truly virtuous. ‹198›
And, behold, among the followers of earlier revelation there are indeed such as [truly] believe in God, and in that which has been bestowed from on high upon you as well as in that which has been bestowed upon them. Standing in awe of God, they do not barter away God's messages for a trifling gain. They shall have their reward with their Sustainer – for, behold, God is swift in reckoning! ‹199›
O you who have attained to faith! Be patient in adversity, and vie in patience with one another, and be ever ready [to do what is right], and remain conscious of God, so that you might attain to a happy state! ‹200›

فَٱسۡتَجَابَ لَهُمۡ رَبُّهُمۡ أَنِّي لَآ أُضِيعُ عَمَلَ عَٰمِلٖ مِّنكُم مِّن ذَكَرٍ أَوۡ
أُنثَىٰۖ بَعۡضُكُم مِّنۢ بَعۡضٖۖ فَٱلَّذِينَ هَاجَرُواْ وَأُخۡرِجُواْ مِن دِيَٰرِهِمۡ وَأُوذُواْ
فِي سَبِيلِي وَقَٰتَلُواْ وَقُتِلُواْ لَأُكَفِّرَنَّ عَنۡهُمۡ سَيِّـَٔاتِهِمۡ وَلَأُدۡخِلَنَّهُمۡ جَنَّٰتٖ
تَجۡرِي مِن تَحۡتِهَا ٱلۡأَنۡهَٰرُ ثَوَابٗا مِّنۡ عِندِ ٱللَّهِۚ وَٱللَّهُ عِندَهُۥ حُسۡنُ
ٱلثَّوَابِ ﴿١٩٥﴾ لَا يَغُرَّنَّكَ تَقَلُّبُ ٱلَّذِينَ كَفَرُواْ فِي ٱلۡبِلَٰدِ ﴿١٩٦﴾ مَتَٰعٞ
قَلِيلٞ ثُمَّ مَأۡوَىٰهُمۡ جَهَنَّمُۖ وَبِئۡسَ ٱلۡمِهَادُ ﴿١٩٧﴾ لَٰكِنِ ٱلَّذِينَ ٱتَّقَوۡاْ رَبَّهُمۡ
لَهُمۡ جَنَّٰتٞ تَجۡرِي مِن تَحۡتِهَا ٱلۡأَنۡهَٰرُ خَٰلِدِينَ فِيهَا نُزُلٗا مِّنۡ عِندِ ٱللَّهِۗ
وَمَا عِندَ ٱللَّهِ خَيۡرٞ لِّلۡأَبۡرَارِ ﴿١٩٨﴾ وَإِنَّ مِنۡ أَهۡلِ ٱلۡكِتَٰبِ لَمَن يُؤۡمِنُ بِٱللَّهِ
وَمَآ أُنزِلَ إِلَيۡكُمۡ وَمَآ أُنزِلَ إِلَيۡهِمۡ خَٰشِعِينَ لِلَّهِ لَا يَشۡتَرُونَ بِـَٔايَٰتِ ٱللَّهِ
ثَمَنٗا قَلِيلًاۚ أُوْلَٰٓئِكَ لَهُمۡ أَجۡرُهُمۡ عِندَ رَبِّهِمۡۗ إِنَّ ٱللَّهَ سَرِيعُ ٱلۡحِسَابِ ﴿١٩٩﴾
يَٰٓأَيُّهَا ٱلَّذِينَ ءَامَنُواْ ٱصۡبِرُواْ وَصَابِرُواْ وَرَابِطُواْ وَٱتَّقُواْ ٱللَّهَ لَعَلَّكُمۡ
تُفۡلِحُونَ ﴿٢٠٠﴾

Fastajāba lahum Rabbuhum ᵓannī lāa ᵓuḍīᶜu ᶜamala ᶜāmilim-miñkum miñ-dhakarin ᵓaw ᵓuñthā baᶜḍukum mim-baᶜḍ. Falladhīna hājarū wa ᵓukhrijū miñ-diyārihim wa ᵓūdhū fī sabīlī wa qātalū wa qutilū laᵓukaffiranna ᶜanhum sayyiᵓātihim wa laᵓudkhilannahum jannātiñ-tajrī miñ-taḥtihal-ᵓanhāru thawābam-min ᶜiñdil-lāh. Wal-lāu ᶜiñdahū ḥusnuth-thawāb. (195) Lā yaghurrannaka taqallubul-ladhīna kafarū fil-bilād. (196) Matāᶜuñ-qalīluñ thumma maᵓwāhum jahannama wa biᵓsal-mihād. (197) Lākinil-ladhīnat-taqaw Rabbahum lahum jannātuñ-tajrī miñ-taḥtihal-ᵓanhāru khālidīna fīhā nuzulam-min ᶜiñdil-lāh. Wa mā ᶜiñdal-lāhi khayrul-lilᵓabrār. (198) Wa ᵓinna min ᵓahlil-Kitābi lamañy-yuᵓminu billāhi wa māa ᵓuñzila ᵓilaykum wa māa ᵓuñzila ᵓilayhim khāshiᶜīna lillāhi lā yashtarūna biᵓĀyātil-lāhi thamanañ-qalīlā. ᵓUlāaᵓika lahum ᵓajruhum ᶜiñda Rabbihim; ᵓinnal-lāha Sarīᶜul-ḥisāb. (199) Yāa ᵓayyuhal-ladhīna ᵓāmanuṣ-birū wa ṣābirū wa rābiṭū wat-taqul-lāha laᶜallakum tufliḥūn. (200)

150 I.e., "you all are members of one and the same human race, and therefore equal to one another".
151 See *sūrah* 2, note 203, and *sūrah* 4, note 124.

The Fourth Sūrah

*An-Nisāa*ᵓ (Women)

Medina Period

THE TITLE *An-Nisāa*ᵓ has been given to this *sūrah* because many of its passages deal with the rights of women and with questions relating to family life in general, including laws of inheritance, prohibition of marriage within certain degrees of consanguinity, marital relations, and so forth. The opening verse stresses the essential unity of the human race and the mutual obligations, arising from this kinship, of men and women towards one another. A large part of the *sūrah* is devoted to practical legislation bearing on problems of peace and war, as well as to relations of believers with unbelievers, especially with hypocrites. Verses 150-152 refute the possibility of believing in God without believing in His prophets; and this, in turn, leads to the subject of the Jews, who deny the prophethood not only of Muḥammad but also of Jesus, as well as of the Christians, who deny Muḥammad and deify Jesus although he "never felt too proud to be God's servant" (verse 172). And, finally, as if to stress the inseparability of man's beliefs from his social behaviour, the last verse refers, again, to laws of inheritance.

There is no doubt that this *sūrah* belongs in its entirety to the Medina period. In the order of revelation it either follows immediately upon *ᵓĀl ᶜImrān* or – according to some authorities – is separated from the latter, in point of time, by *Al-ᵓAḥzāb* and *Al-Mumtaḥanah*. On the whole, however, it is most probable that it was revealed in the fourth year after the *hijrah*, although a few of its verses may belong to an earlier, and verse 58 to a later, period.

سورة النساء مدنية -4-
وآياتها ست وسبعون ومائة

بِسۡمِ ٱللَّهِ ٱلرَّحۡمَٰنِ ٱلرَّحِيمِ

يَٰٓأَيُّهَا ٱلنَّاسُ ٱتَّقُواْ رَبَّكُمُ ٱلَّذِي خَلَقَكُم مِّن نَّفۡسٖ وَٰحِدَةٖ وَخَلَقَ
مِنۡهَا زَوۡجَهَا وَبَثَّ مِنۡهُمَا رِجَالٗا كَثِيرٗا وَنِسَآءٗۚ وَٱتَّقُواْ ٱللَّهَ ٱلَّذِي
تَسَآءَلُونَ بِهِۦ وَٱلۡأَرۡحَامَۚ إِنَّ ٱللَّهَ كَانَ عَلَيۡكُمۡ رَقِيبٗا ﴿١﴾ وَءَاتُواْ
ٱلۡيَتَٰمَىٰٓ أَمۡوَٰلَهُمۡۖ وَلَا تَتَبَدَّلُواْ ٱلۡخَبِيثَ بِٱلطَّيِّبِۖ وَلَا تَأۡكُلُوٓاْ
أَمۡوَٰلَهُمۡ إِلَىٰٓ أَمۡوَٰلِكُمۡۚ إِنَّهُۥ كَانَ حُوبٗا كَبِيرٗا ﴿٢﴾ وَإِنۡ خِفۡتُمۡ أَلَّا
تُقۡسِطُواْ فِي ٱلۡيَتَٰمَىٰ فَٱنكِحُواْ مَا طَابَ لَكُم مِّنَ ٱلنِّسَآءِ مَثۡنَىٰ

نصف الحزب

Bismil-lāhir-Raḥmānir-Raḥīm.
Yāa ᵓayyuhan-nāsut-taqū Rabbakumul-ladhī khalaqakum-miñ-nafsiñw-wāḥidatiñw-wa khalaqa minhā zawjahā wa baththa minhumā rijālañ-kathīrañw-wa nisāaᵓ. Wat-taqul-lāhal-ladhī tasāaᵓalūna bihī wal-ᵓarḥām; ᵓinnal-lāha kāna ᶜalaykum Raqībā. ⟨1⟩ **Wa ᵓātul-yatāmāa ᵓamwālahum wa lā tatabaddalul-khabītha biṭ-ṭayyib. Wa lā taᵓkulūu ᵓamwālahum ᵓilāa ᵓamwālikum. ᵓInnahu kāna ḥūbañ-kabīrā.** ⟨2⟩ **Wa ᵓiñ-khiftum ᵓallā tuqsiṭū fil-yatāmā fañkiḥū mā ṭāba lakum-minan-nisāaᵓi mathnā**

IN THE NAME OF GOD, THE MOST GRACIOUS, THE DISPENSER OF GRACE;

O MANKIND! Be conscious of your Sustainer, who has created you out of one living entity, and out of it created its mate, and out of the two spread abroad a multitude of men and women.[1] And remain conscious of God, in whose name you demand [your rights] from one another, and of these ties of kinship. Verily, God is ever watchful over you! ⟨1⟩
Hence, render unto the orphans their possessions, and do not substitute bad things [of your own] for the good things [that belong to them], and do not consume their possessions together with your own:[2] this, verily, is a great crime. ⟨2⟩
And if you have reason to fear that you might not act equitably towards orphans, then marry from among [other] women such as are lawful to you[3] – [even] two,

---

1 Out of the many meanings attributable to the term *nafs* – soul, spirit, mind, animate being, living entity, human being, person, self (in the sense of a personal identity), humankind, life-essence, vital principle, and so forth – most of the classical commentators choose "human being", and assume that it refers here to Adam. Muḥammad ᶜAbduh, however, rejects this interpretation (*Manār* IV, 323 ff.) and gives, instead, his preference to "humankind" inasmuch as this term stresses the common origin and brotherhood of the human race (which, undoubtedly, is the purport of the above verse), without, at the same time, unwarrantably tying it to the Biblical account of the creation of Adam and Eve. My rendering of *nafs*, in this context, as "living entity" follows the same reasoning. – As regards the expression *zawjahā* ("its mate"), it is to be noted that, with reference to animate beings, the term *zawj* ("a pair", "one of a pair" or "a mate") applies to the male as well as to the female component of a pair or couple; hence, with reference to human beings, it signifies a woman's mate (husband) as well as a man's mate (wife). Abū Muslim – as quoted by Rāzī – interprets the phrase "He created out of it (*minhā*) its mate" as meaning "He created its mate [i.e., its sexual counterpart] out of its own kind (*min jinsihā*)", thus supporting the view of Muḥammad ᶜAbduh referred to above. The literal translation of *minhā* as "out of it" clearly alludes, in conformity with the text, to the biological fact that both sexes have originated from "one living entity".

2 This relates to the legal guardians of orphans during the latters' minority.

3 Lit., "such as are good for you" – i.e., women outside the prohibited degrees enumerated in verses 22-23 of this *sūrah* (Zamakhsharī, Rāzī). According to an interpretation suggested by ᶜĀᵓishah, the Prophet's widow, this refers to the (hypothetical) case of orphan girls whom their guardians might wish to marry without, however, being prepared

وَثُلَٰثَ وَرُبَٰعَ فَإِنْ خِفْتُمْ أَلَّا تَعْدِلُوا۟ فَوَٰحِدَةً أَوْ مَا مَلَكَتْ أَيْمَٰنُكُمْ
ذَٰلِكَ أَدْنَىٰٓ أَلَّا تَعُولُوا۟ ﴿٣﴾ وَءَاتُوا۟ ٱلنِّسَآءَ صَدُقَٰتِهِنَّ نِحْلَةً فَإِن طِبْنَ
لَكُمْ عَن شَىْءٍ مِّنْهُ نَفْسًا فَكُلُوهُ هَنِيٓـًٔا مَّرِيٓـًٔا ﴿٤﴾

wa thulātha wa rubāʿ. Faʾin khiftum ʾallā taʿdilū fawāḥidatan ʾaw mā malakat ʾaymānukum. Dhālika ʾadnāa ʾallā taʿūlū. ﴾3﴿ Wa ʾātun-nisāaʾa ṣaduqātihinna niḥlah. Faʾiñ-ṭibna lakum ʿañ-shayʾim-minhu nafsañ-fakulūhu haniiʾam-mariiʾā. ﴾4﴿

or three, or four; but if you have reason to fear that you might not be able to treat them with equal fairness, then [only] one – or [from among] those whom you rightfully possess.[4] This will make it more likely that you will not deviate from the right course. ‹3›

And give unto women their marriage portions in the spirit of a gift;[5] but if they, of their own accord, give up unto you aught thereof, then enjoy it with pleasure and good cheer. ‹4›

---

or able to give them an appropriate marriage-portion – the implication being that they should avoid the temptation of committing such an injustice and should marry other women instead (cf. Bukhārī, *Kitāb at-Tafsīr*, as well as Muslim and Nasāʾī). However, not all of ʿĀʾishah's contemporaries subscribed to her explanation of this verse. Thus, according to Saʿid ibn Jubayr, Qatādah, and other successors of the Companions, the purport of the above passage is this: "Just as you are, rightly, fearful of offending against the interests of orphans, you must apply the same careful consideration to the interests and rights of the women whom you intend to marry." In his commentary on this passage, Ṭabarī quotes several variants of the above interpretation and gives it his unequivocal approval.

4 Lit., "whom your right hands possess" – i.e., from among the captives taken in a war in God's cause (regarding which see *sūrah* 2, notes 167 and 168, and *sūrah* 8, note 72). It is obvious that the phrase "two, or three, or four: but if you have reason to fear . . .", etc. is a *parenthetic clause* relating to both the free women mentioned in the first part of the sentence and to female slaves – for both these nouns are governed by the imperative verb "marry". Thus, the whole sentence has this meaning: "Marry from among [other] women such as are lawful to you, or [from among] those whom you rightfully possess – [even] two, or three, or four: but if you have reason to fear that you might not be able to treat them with equal fairness, then [only] one" – implying that, irrespective of whether they are free women or, originally, slaves, the number of wives must not exceed four. It was in this sense that Muḥammad ʿAbduh understood the above verse (see *Manār* IV, 350). This view is, moreover, supported by verse 25 of this *sūrah* as well as by 24 : 32, where *marriage* with female slaves is spoken of. Contrary to the popular view and the practice of many Muslims in the past centuries, neither the Qurʾān nor the life-example of the Prophet provides any sanction for sexual intercourse *without* marriage.

As regards the permission to marry more than one wife (up to the maximum of four), it is so restricted by the condition, "if you have reason to fear that you might not be able to treat them with equal fairness, then [marry only] one", as to make such plural marriages possible only in quite exceptional cases and under exceptional circumstances (see also the first clause of 24 : 32 and the corresponding note 42). Still, one might ask why the same latitude has not been given to women as well; but the answer is simple. Notwithstanding the spiritual factor of *love* which influences the relations between man and woman, the determinant *biological* reason for the sexual urge is, in both sexes, procreation: and whereas a woman can, at one time, conceive a child from one man only and has to carry it for nine months before she can conceive another, a man can beget a child every time he cohabits with a woman. Thus, while nature would have been merely wasteful if it had produced a polygamous instinct in woman, man's polygamous inclination is biologically justified. It is, of course, obvious that the biological factor is only one – and by no means always the most important – of the aspects of marital love: none the less, it is a basic factor and, therefore, decisive in the institution of marriage as such. With the wisdom that always takes human nature fully into account, Islamic Law undertakes no more than the safeguarding of the socio-biological function of marriage (which includes also care of the progeny), allowing a man to have more than one wife and not allowing a woman to have more than one husband at one time; while the spiritual problem of marriage, being imponderable and therefore outside the scope of law, is left to the discretion of the partners. In any event – since marriage in Islam is a purely civil contract – recourse to divorce is always open to either of the two partners. (Regarding the dissolution of a marriage at the wife's instance, see *sūrah* 2, note 218.)

5 The expression *niḥlah* signifies the giving of something willingly, of one's own accord, without expecting a return for it (Zamakhsharī). It is to be noted that the amount of the marriage-portion, or dower, which the bridegroom has to give to the bride has not been circumscribed by the Law: it depends entirely on the agreement of the two parties, and may consist of anything, even a mere token. According to several authentic Traditions recorded in most of the compilations, the Prophet made it clear that "even an iron ring" may be enough if the bride is willing to accept it, or, short of that, even "the imparting to thy bride of a verse of the Qurʾān".

And do not entrust to those who are weak of judgment the possessions which God has placed in your charge[6] for [their] support; but let them have their sustenance therefrom, and clothe them, and speak unto them in a kindly way. ‹5› And test the orphans [in your charge] until they reach a marriageable age; then, if you find them to be mature of mind, hand over to them their possessions; and do not consume them by wasteful spending, and in haste, ere they grow up. And let him who is rich abstain entirely [from his ward's property]; and let him who is poor partake thereof in a fair manner. And when you hand over to them their possessions, let there be witnesses on their behalf – although none can take count as God does. ‹6›

MEN SHALL have a share in what parents and kinsfolk leave behind, and women shall have a share in what parents and kinsfolk leave behind, whether it be little or much – a share ordained [by God]. ‹7› And when [other] near of kin and orphans and needy persons[7] are present at the distribution [of inheritance], give them something thereof for their sustenance, and speak unto them in a kindly way. ‹8› And let them stand in awe [of God], those [legal heirs] – who, if they [themselves] had to leave behind weak offspring, would feel fear on their account – and let them remain conscious of God, and let them speak [to the poor] in a just manner. ‹9› Behold, those who sinfully devour the possessions of orphans but fill their bellies with fire; for [in the life to come] they will have to endure a blazing flame! ‹10›

وَلَا تُؤْتُوا۟ ٱلسُّفَهَآءَ أَمْوَٰلَكُمُ ٱلَّتِى جَعَلَ ٱللَّهُ لَكُمْ قِيَـٰمًا وَٱرْزُقُوهُمْ فِيهَا
وَٱكْسُوهُمْ وَقُولُوا۟ لَهُمْ قَوْلًا مَّعْرُوفًا ﴿5﴾ وَٱبْتَلُوا۟ ٱلْيَتَـٰمَىٰ حَتَّىٰٓ إِذَا
بَلَغُوا۟ ٱلنِّكَاحَ فَإِنْ ءَانَسْتُم مِّنْهُمْ رُشْدًا فَٱدْفَعُوٓا۟ إِلَيْهِمْ أَمْوَٰلَهُمْ وَلَا
تَأْكُلُوهَآ إِسْرَافًا وَبِدَارًا أَن يَكْبَرُوا۟ وَمَن كَانَ غَنِيًّا فَلْيَسْتَعْفِفْ وَمَن
كَانَ فَقِيرًا فَلْيَأْكُلْ بِٱلْمَعْرُوفِ فَإِذَا دَفَعْتُمْ إِلَيْهِمْ أَمْوَٰلَهُمْ فَأَشْهِدُوا۟
عَلَيْهِمْ وَكَفَىٰ بِٱللَّهِ حَسِيبًا ﴿6﴾ لِّلرِّجَالِ نَصِيبٌ مِّمَّا تَرَكَ ٱلْوَٰلِدَانِ
وَٱلْأَقْرَبُونَ وَلِلنِّسَآءِ نَصِيبٌ مِّمَّا تَرَكَ ٱلْوَٰلِدَانِ وَٱلْأَقْرَبُونَ مِمَّا قَلَّ مِنْهُ
أَوْ كَثُرَ نَصِيبًا مَّفْرُوضًا ﴿7﴾ وَإِذَا حَضَرَ ٱلْقِسْمَةَ أُو۟لُوا۟ ٱلْقُرْبَىٰ
وَٱلْيَتَـٰمَىٰ وَٱلْمَسَـٰكِينُ فَٱرْزُقُوهُم مِّنْهُ وَقُولُوا۟ لَهُمْ قَوْلًا مَّعْرُوفًا ﴿8﴾
وَلْيَخْشَ ٱلَّذِينَ لَوْ تَرَكُوا۟ مِنْ خَلْفِهِمْ ذُرِّيَّةً ضِعَـٰفًا خَافُوا۟ عَلَيْهِمْ فَلْيَتَّقُوا۟
ٱللَّهَ وَلْيَقُولُوا۟ قَوْلًا سَدِيدًا ﴿9﴾ إِنَّ ٱلَّذِينَ يَأْكُلُونَ أَمْوَٰلَ ٱلْيَتَـٰمَىٰ ظُلْمًا
إِنَّمَا يَأْكُلُونَ فِى بُطُونِهِمْ نَارًا وَسَيَصْلَوْنَ سَعِيرًا ﴿10﴾

Wa lā tuʾtus-sufahāaʾa ʾamwālakumul-latī jaʿalal-lāhu lakum qiyāmañw-war-zuqūhum fīhā waksūhum wa qūlū lahum qawlam-maʿrūfā. (5) Wabtalul-yatāmā ḥattāa ʾidhā balaghun-nikāḥa faʾin ʾānastum-minhum rushdañ-fadfaʿūu ʾilayhim ʾamwālahum; wa lā taʾkulūhāa ʾisrāfañw-wa bidāran ʾañy-yakbarū. Wa mañ-kāna ghaniyyañ-falyastaʿfif. Wa mañ-kāna faqīrañ-falyaʾkul bilmaʿrūf. Faʾidhā dafaʿtumʾilayhim ʾamwālahum faʾashhidū ʿalayhim; wa kafā billāhi Ḥasībā. (6) Lirrijāli naṣībum-mimmā tarakal-wālidāni wal-ʾaqrabūna wa linnisāaʾi naṣībum-mimmā tarakal-wālidāni wal-ʾaqrabūna mimmā qalla minhu ʾaw kathura naṣībam-mafrūḍā. (7) Wa ʾidhā ḥaḍaral-qismata ʾulul-qurbā wal-yatāmā wal-masākīnu farzuqūhum-minhu wa qūlū lahum qawlam-maʿrūfā. (8) Wal-yakhshal-ladhīna law tarakū min khalfihim dhurriyyatañ-ḍiʿāfan khāfū ʿalayhim falyattaqul-lāha wal-yaqūlū qawlañ-sadīdā. (9) ʾInnal-ladhīna yaʾkulūna ʾamwālal-yatāmā ẓulman ʾinnamā yaʾkulūna fī buṭūnihim nārañw-wa sayaṣlawna saʿīrā. (10)

6 Lit., "your possessions which God has assigned to you". The context makes it obvious that this relates to the property of orphans who have not yet reached the age of discretion and are, therefore, "weak of judgment" (lit., "weak-minded").

7 I.e., people who do not have any *legal* claim to the inheritance, but nevertheless deserve to be considered.

ثلاثة ارباع الحزب

يُوصِيكُمُ ٱللَّهُ فِىٓ أَوْلَٰدِكُمْ ۖ لِلذَّكَرِ مِثْلُ حَظِّ ٱلْأُنثَيَيْنِ ۚ فَإِن كُنَّ نِسَآءً
فَوْقَ ٱثْنَتَيْنِ فَلَهُنَّ ثُلُثَا مَا تَرَكَ ۖ وَإِن كَانَتْ وَٰحِدَةً فَلَهَا ٱلنِّصْفُ ۚ وَلِأَبَوَيْهِ
لِكُلِّ وَٰحِدٍ مِّنْهُمَا ٱلسُّدُسُ مِمَّا تَرَكَ إِن كَانَ لَهُۥ وَلَدٌ ۚ فَإِن لَّمْ يَكُن لَّهُۥ
وَلَدٌ وَوَرِثَهُۥٓ أَبَوَاهُ فَلِأُمِّهِ ٱلثُّلُثُ ۚ فَإِن كَانَ لَهُۥٓ إِخْوَةٌ فَلِأُمِّهِ ٱلسُّدُسُ ۚ مِنۢ
بَعْدِ وَصِيَّةٍ يُوصِى بِهَآ أَوْ دَيْنٍ ۗ ءَابَآؤُكُمْ وَأَبْنَآؤُكُمْ لَا تَدْرُونَ أَيُّهُمْ أَقْرَبُ
لَكُمْ نَفْعًا ۚ فَرِيضَةً مِّنَ ٱللَّهِ ۗ إِنَّ ٱللَّهَ كَانَ عَلِيمًا حَكِيمًا ﴿١١﴾ ۞ وَلَكُمْ
نِصْفُ مَا تَرَكَ أَزْوَٰجُكُمْ إِن لَّمْ يَكُن لَّهُنَّ وَلَدٌ ۚ فَإِن كَانَ لَهُنَّ وَلَدٌ فَلَكُمُ
ٱلرُّبُعُ مِمَّا تَرَكْنَ ۚ مِنۢ بَعْدِ وَصِيَّةٍ يُوصِينَ بِهَآ أَوْ دَيْنٍ ۚ وَلَهُنَّ ٱلرُّبُعُ مِمَّا تَرَكْتُمْ
إِن لَّمْ يَكُن لَّكُمْ وَلَدٌ ۚ فَإِن كَانَ لَكُمْ وَلَدٌ فَلَهُنَّ ٱلثُّمُنُ مِمَّا تَرَكْتُم ۚ مِّنۢ بَعْدِ
وَصِيَّةٍ تُوصُونَ بِهَآ أَوْ دَيْنٍ ۗ وَإِن كَانَ رَجُلٌ يُورَثُ كَلَٰلَةً أَوِ ٱمْرَأَةٌ وَلَهُۥٓ
أَخٌ أَوْ أُخْتٌ فَلِكُلِّ وَٰحِدٍ مِّنْهُمَا ٱلسُّدُسُ ۚ فَإِن كَانُوٓا۟ أَكْثَرَ مِن ذَٰلِكَ

Yūṣīkumul-lāhu fīi ᵓawlādikum; lidhdhakari mithlu ḥaẓẓil-ᵓuñthayayn; faᵓiñ kunna nisāaᵓañ-fawqathnatayni falahunna thulutha mā taraka wa ᵓiñ-kānat wāḥidatañ-falahan-niṣf. Wa liᵓabawayhi likulli wāḥidim-minhumas-sudusu mimmā taraka ᵓiñ-kāna lahū walad. Faᵓil-lam yakul-lahū waladuñw-wa warithahūu ᵓabawāhu faliᵓummihith-thuluth. Faᵓiñ kāna lahūu ᵓikhwatuñ-faliᵓummihis-sudusu mimbaᶜdi waṣiyyatiñy-yūṣī bihāa ᵓaw dayn. ᵓĀbāaᵓukum wa ᵓabnāaᵓukum lā tadrūna ᵓayyuhum aqrabu lakum nafᶜā. Farīḍatam-minal-lāh. ᵓInnal-lāha kāna ᶜAlīman Ḥakīmā. ﴾11﴿ ۞ Wa lakum niṣfu mā taraka ᵓazwājukum ᵓillam-yakul-lahunna walad. Faᵓiñ-kāna lahunna waladuñ-falakumur-rubuᶜu mimmā tarakna mim-baᶜdi waṣyyatiñy-yūṣīna bihāa ᵓaw dayn. Wa lahunnar-rubuᶜu mimmā taraktum ᵓil-lam yakul-lakum walad. Faᵓiñ-kāna lakum waladuñ-falahunnath-thumunu mimmā taraktum-mimbaᶜdi waṣiyyatiñ-tūṣūna bihāa ᵓaw dayn. Wa ᵓiñ-kāna rajuluñy-yūrathu kalālatan ᵓawim-raᵓatuñw-wa lahūu ᵓakhun ᵓaw ᵓukhtuñ-falikulli wāḥidim-minhumas-sudus. Faᵓiñ-kānūu ᵓakthara miñ-dhālika

CONCERNING [the inheritance of] your children, God enjoins [this] upon you:[8] The male shall have the equal of two females' share; but if there are more than two females, they shall have two-thirds of what [their parents] leave behind; and if there is only one, she shall have one-half thereof.

And as for the parents [of the deceased], each of them shall have one-sixth of what he leaves behind, in the event of his having [left] a child; but if he has left no child and his parents are his [only] heirs, then his mother shall have one-third; and if he has brothers and sisters, then his mother shall have one-sixth after [the deduction of] any bequest he may have made, or any debt [he may have incurred].

As for your parents and your children – you know not which of them is more deserving of benefit from you; [therefore this] ordinance from God. Verily, God is all-knowing, wise. ﴾11﴿

And you shall inherit one-half of what your wives leave behind, provided they have left no child; but if they have left a child, then you shall have one-quarter of what they leave behind, after [the deduction of] any bequest they may have made, or any debt [they may have incurred]. And your widows[9] shall have one-quarter of what you leave behind, provided you have left no child; but if you have left a child, then they shall have one-eighth of what you leave behind, after [the deduction of] any bequest you may have made, or any debt [you may have incurred].

And if a man or a woman has no heir in the direct line, but has a brother or a sister, then each of these two shall inherit one-sixth; but if there are more than two,[10]

8 In my notes on verses 11-12, which spell out the legal shares of inheritance due to the next of kin, no attempt has been made to analyze all the legal implications of this ordinance. The laws of inheritance are the subject of a special, and very elaborate, branch of Islamic jurisprudence, and their full elucidation would go far beyond the scope of explanatory notes which aim at no more than making the text of the Qurᵓān accessible to the understanding of the non-specialized reader.

9 Lit., "they".

10 Lit., "more than that". According to most of the classical commentators, this passage refers to half-brothers and half-sisters. The inheritance of full brothers and sisters is dealt with at the end of this *sūrah* (verse 176).

then they shall share in one-third [of the inheritance], after [the deduction of] any bequest that may have been made, or any debt [that may have been incurred], neither of which having been intended to harm [the heirs].[11]
[This is] an injunction from God; and God is all-knowing, forbearing. ‹12›
These are the bounds set by God. And whoever pays heed unto God and His Apostle, him will He bring into gardens through which running waters flow, therein to abide; and this is a triumph supreme. ‹13› And whoever rebels against God and His Apostle and transgresses His bounds, him will He commit unto fire, therein to abide; and shameful suffering awaits him. ‹14›

AND AS FOR those of your women who become guilty of immoral conduct, call upon four from among you who have witnessed their guilt; and if these bear witness thereto, confine the guilty women[12] to their houses until death takes them away or God opens for them a way [through repentance]. ‹15› And punish [thus] both of the guilty parties;[13] but if they both repent and mend their ways, leave them alone: for, behold, God is an acceptor of repentance, a dispenser of grace.[14] ‹16›

فَهُمْ شُرَكَآءُ فِى ٱلثُّلُثِ مِنۢ بَعْدِ وَصِيَّةٍ يُوصَىٰ بِهَآ أَوْ دَيْنٍ غَيْرَ مُضَآرٍّ
وَصِيَّةً مِّنَ ٱللَّهِ وَٱللَّهُ عَلِيمٌ حَلِيمٌ ﴿١٢﴾ تِلْكَ حُدُودُ ٱللَّهِ وَمَن يُطِعِ ٱللَّهَ
وَرَسُولَهُۥ يُدْخِلْهُ جَنَّٰتٍ تَجْرِى مِن تَحْتِهَا ٱلْأَنْهَٰرُ خَٰلِدِينَ فِيهَا
وَذَٰلِكَ ٱلْفَوْزُ ٱلْعَظِيمُ ﴿١٣﴾ وَمَن يَعْصِ ٱللَّهَ وَرَسُولَهُۥ وَيَتَعَدَّ حُدُودَهُۥ
يُدْخِلْهُ نَارًا خَٰلِدًا فِيهَا وَلَهُۥ عَذَابٌ مُّهِينٌ ﴿١٤﴾ وَٱلَّٰتِى يَأْتِينَ ٱلْفَٰحِشَةَ
مِن نِّسَآئِكُمْ فَٱسْتَشْهِدُوا۟ عَلَيْهِنَّ أَرْبَعَةً مِّنكُمْ فَإِن شَهِدُوا۟ فَأَمْسِكُوهُنَّ
فِى ٱلْبُيُوتِ حَتَّىٰ يَتَوَفَّىٰهُنَّ ٱلْمَوْتُ أَوْ يَجْعَلَ ٱللَّهُ لَهُنَّ سَبِيلًا ﴿١٥﴾ وَٱلَّذَانِ
يَأْتِيَٰنِهَا مِنكُمْ فَـَٔاذُوهُمَا فَإِن تَابَا وَأَصْلَحَا فَأَعْرِضُوا۟ عَنْهُمَآ إِنَّ ٱللَّهَ
كَانَ تَوَّابًا رَّحِيمًا ﴿١٦﴾

fahum shurakāaʾu fith-thuluthi mim-baᶜdi waṣiy-yatiñy-yūṣā bihāa ʾaw daynin ghayra muḍāarr. Waṣiyyatam-minal-lāh. Wal-lāhu ᶜAlīmun Ḥalīm. ﴿12﴾ Tilka ḥudūdul-lāh. Wa mañy-yuṭiᶜil-lāha wa Rasūlahū yudkhilhu jannātiñ-tajrī miñ-taḥtihal-ʾanhāru khālidīna fīhā; wa dhālikal-fawzul-ᶜaẓīm. ﴿13﴾ Wa mañy-yaᶜṣil-lāha wa Rasūlahū wa yataᶜadda ḥudūdahū yudkhilhu nāran khālidañ-fīhā; wa lahū ᶜadhābum-muhīn. ﴿14﴾ Wal-lātī yaʾtīnal-fāḥishata miñ-nisāaʾikum fastashhidū ᶜalayhinna ʾarbaᶜatam-miñkum; faʾiñ shahidū faʾamsikūhunna fil-buyūti ḥattā yatawaffāhunnal-mawtu ʾaw yajᶜalal-lāhu la-hunna sabīlā. ﴿15﴾ Wal-ladhāni yaʾtiyānihā miñkum faʾādhūhumā. Faʾiñ-tābā wa ʾaṣlaḥā faʾaᶜriḍū ᶜanhumā. ʾInnal-lāha kāna Tawwābar-Raḥīmā. ﴿16﴾

11 This refers to bequests and fictitious debts meant to deprive the heirs of their legal shares. According to several authentic Traditions, the Prophet forbade, in cases where there are legal heirs, the making of bequests to other persons in excess of one-third of one's estate (Bukhārī and Muslim). If, however, there are no near of kin legally entitled to a share of the inheritance, the testator is free to bequeath his fortune in any way he desires.

12 Lit., "them".

13 Lit., "and the two from among you who become guilty thereof, punish them both". According to most of the commentators, this refers to immoral conduct on the part of a man and a woman as well as to homosexual relations.

14 Some of the commentators attribute to the term *fāḥishah* (here rendered as "immoral conduct") the meaning of "adultery" or "fornication" and are, consequently, of the opinion that this verse has been "abrogated" by 24 : 2, which lays down the punishment of one hundred stripes for each of the guilty parties. This unwarranted assumption must, however, be rejected. Quite apart from the impossibility of admitting that any passage of the Qurʾān could have been "abrogated" by another of its passages (see *sūrah* 2, note 87), the expression *fāḥishah* does not, by itself, connote illicit sexual intercourse: it signifies anything that is grossly immodest, unseemly, lewd, indecent or abominable in word or in deed (cf. Lane VI, 2344 f.), and is by no means restricted to sexual transgressions. Read in this context, and in conjunction with 24 : 2, this expression obviously denotes here immoral conduct not necessarily amounting to what is termed *zinā* (i.e., "adultery" or "fornication"), and therefore redeemable by sincere repentance (in contrast to a proven act of *zinā* which is punishable by flogging). – It is noteworthy that in all cases of alleged sexual transgressions or misbehaviour the Qurʾān stipulates the *direct evidence of four witnesses* (instead of the two required in all other judicial cases) as a *sine qua non* of conviction. For the reasons underlying this injunction, as well as for its judicial implications, see note 7 on 24 : 4.

Verily, God's acceptance of repentance relates only to those who do evil out of ignorance and then repent before their time runs out:[15] and it is they unto whom God will turn again in His mercy – for God is all-knowing, wise; ‹17› whereas repentance shall not be accepted from those who do evil deeds until their dying hour and then say,[16] "Behold, I now repent"; nor from those who die as deniers of the truth; it is these for whom We have readied grievous suffering. ‹18›

O YOU who have attained to faith! It is not lawful for you to [try to] become heirs to your wives [by holding onto them] against their will;[17] and neither shall you keep them under constraint with a view to taking away anything of what you may have given them, unless it be that they have become guilty, in an obvious manner, of immoral conduct.[18]

And consort with your wives[19] in a goodly manner; for if you dislike them, it may well be that you dislike something which God might yet make a source of[20] abundant good. ‹19›

But if you desire to give up a wife and to take another in her stead, do not take away anything of what you have given the first one, however much it may have been.[21]

إِنَّمَا ٱلتَّوۡبَةُ عَلَى ٱللَّهِ لِلَّذِينَ يَعۡمَلُونَ ٱلسُّوٓءَ بِجَهَٰلَةٖ ثُمَّ يَتُوبُونَ مِن قَرِيبٖ
فَأُوْلَٰٓئِكَ يَتُوبُ ٱللَّهُ عَلَيۡهِمۡۗ وَكَانَ ٱللَّهُ عَلِيمًا حَكِيمٗا ﴿١٧﴾ وَلَيۡسَتِ
ٱلتَّوۡبَةُ لِلَّذِينَ يَعۡمَلُونَ ٱلسَّيِّـَٔاتِ حَتَّىٰٓ إِذَا حَضَرَ أَحَدَهُمُ ٱلۡمَوۡتُ قَالَ
إِنِّي تُبۡتُ ٱلۡـَٰٔنَ وَلَا ٱلَّذِينَ يَمُوتُونَ وَهُمۡ كُفَّارٌۚ أُوْلَٰٓئِكَ أَعۡتَدۡنَا لَهُمۡ
عَذَابًا أَلِيمٗا ﴿١٨﴾ يَٰٓأَيُّهَا ٱلَّذِينَ ءَامَنُواْ لَا يَحِلُّ لَكُمۡ أَن تَرِثُواْ ٱلنِّسَآءَ
كَرۡهٗاۖ وَلَا تَعۡضُلُوهُنَّ لِتَذۡهَبُواْ بِبَعۡضِ مَآ ءَاتَيۡتُمُوهُنَّ إِلَّآ أَن يَأۡتِينَ
بِفَٰحِشَةٖ مُّبَيِّنَةٖۚ وَعَاشِرُوهُنَّ بِٱلۡمَعۡرُوفِۚ فَإِن كَرِهۡتُمُوهُنَّ فَعَسَىٰٓ أَن
تَكۡرَهُواْ شَيۡـٔٗا وَيَجۡعَلَ ٱللَّهُ فِيهِ خَيۡرٗا كَثِيرٗا ﴿١٩﴾ وَإِنۡ أَرَدتُّمُ ٱسۡتِبۡدَالَ
زَوۡجٖ مَّكَانَ زَوۡجٖ وَءَاتَيۡتُمۡ إِحۡدَىٰهُنَّ قِنطَارٗا فَلَا تَأۡخُذُواْ مِنۡهُ شَيۡـًٔاۚ

ʾInnamat-tawbatu ʿalal-lāhi lilladhīna yaʿmalūnas-sūuʾa bijahālatiñ-thumma yatūbūna miñ-qarībiñ-faʾulāaʾika yatūbul-lāhu ʿalayhim. Wa kānal-lāhu ʿAlīman Ḥakīmā. (17) Wa laysatit-tawbatu lilladhīna yaʿmalūnas-sayyiʾāti ḥattāa ʾidhā ḥaḍara ʾaḥada-humul-mawtu qāla ʾinnī tubtul-ʾāna wa lal-ladhīna yamūtūna wa hum kuffārun ʾulāaʾika ʾaʿtadnā lahum ʿadhāban ʾalīmā. (18) Yāa ʾayyuhal-ladhīna ʾāmanū lā yaḥillu lakum ʾañ-tarithun-nisāaʾa karhā. Wa lā taʿḍulūhunna litadhhabū bibaʿḍi māa ʾātaytumūhunna ʾillāa ʾañy-yaʾtīna bifāḥishatim-mubayyinatiñw-wa ʿāshirūhunna bilmaʿrūf. Faʾiñ karihtumūhunna faʿasāa ʾañ-takrahū shayʾañw-wa yajʿalal-lāhu fīhi khayrañ-kathīrā. (19) Wa ʾin ʾarattumus-tibdāla zawjim-makāna zawjiñw-wa ʾātaytum ʾiḥdāhunna qiñṭārañ-falā taʾkhudhū minhu shayʾā.

15 The expression *min qarīb,* which here implies nearness in time, could also be rendered as "soon", i.e., soon after having committed the evil deed; most of the classical commentators, however, hold that in this context it denotes the time before the actual approach of death. This interpretation is borne out by the next verse.

16 Lit., "until, when death approaches one of them, he says".

17 According to one of the interpretations advanced by Zamakhsharī, this refers to a man's forcibly keeping an unloved wife – and thus preventing her from marrying another man – in the hope of inheriting her property under the provisions specified in the first sentence of verse 12 above. Some authorities, however, are of the opinion that the meaning is: "It is not lawful for you to inherit women against their will" – thus expressing a prohibition of the pre-Islamic custom of inheriting the wives of deceased near relatives. But in view of the fact that Islam does not permit the "inheriting" of women under *any* circumstances (and not only "against their will"), the former interpretation is infinitely more plausible.

18 In the event that a wife's immoral conduct has been proved by the direct evidence of four witnesses, as stipulated in verse 15 above, the husband has the right, on divorcing her, to demand the return of the whole or of part of the dower which he gave her at the time when the marriage was contracted. If – as is permissible under Islamic Law – the dower has not been actually handed over to the bride at the time of marriage but has taken the form of a legal obligation on the part of the husband, he is absolved of this obligation in the case of proven immoral conduct on the part of his wife.

19 Lit., "with them".

20 Lit., "and God might place in it".

21 Lit., "if you desire the exchange of a wife in place of a wife, and you have given one of them a treasure (*qinṭār*),

Would you, perchance, take it away by slandering her and thus committing a manifest sin?[22] «20» And how could you take it away after you have given yourselves to one another, and she has[23] received a most solemn pledge from you? «21»

AND DO NOT marry women whom your fathers have previously married – although what is past is past:[24] this, verily, is a shameful deed, and a hateful thing, and an evil way. «22»
Forbidden to you are your mothers, and your daughters, and your sisters, and your aunts paternal and maternal, and a brother's daughters, and a sister's daughters; and your milk-mothers, and your milk-sisters; and the mothers of your wives; and your step-daughters – who are your foster-children – born of your wives with whom you have consummated your marriage; but if you have not consummated your marriage, you will incur no sin [by marrying their daughters]; and [forbidden to you are] the spouses of the sons who have sprung from your loins; and [you are forbidden] to have two sisters [as your wives] at one and the same time – but what is past is past:[25] for, behold, God is indeed much-forgiving, a dispenser of grace. «23»
And [forbidden to you are] all married women other than those whom you rightfully possess [through wedlock]:[26] this is God's ordinance, binding upon you.

أَتَأْخُذُونَهُۥ بُهْتَٰنًا وَإِثْمًا مُّبِينًا ﴿٢٠﴾ وَكَيْفَ تَأْخُذُونَهُۥ وَقَدْ أَفْضَىٰ
بَعْضُكُمْ إِلَىٰ بَعْضٍ وَأَخَذْنَ مِنكُم مِّيثَٰقًا غَلِيظًا ﴿٢١﴾ وَلَا تَنكِحُوا۟ مَا
نَكَحَ ءَابَآؤُكُم مِّنَ ٱلنِّسَآءِ إِلَّا مَا قَدْ سَلَفَ ۚ إِنَّهُۥ كَانَ فَٰحِشَةً وَمَقْتًا
وَسَآءَ سَبِيلًا ﴿٢٢﴾ حُرِّمَتْ عَلَيْكُمْ أُمَّهَٰتُكُمْ وَبَنَاتُكُمْ وَأَخَوَٰتُكُمْ
وَعَمَّٰتُكُمْ وَخَٰلَٰتُكُمْ وَبَنَاتُ ٱلْأَخِ وَبَنَاتُ ٱلْأُخْتِ وَأُمَّهَٰتُكُمُ ٱلَّٰتِىٓ
أَرْضَعْنَكُمْ وَأَخَوَٰتُكُم مِّنَ ٱلرَّضَٰعَةِ وَأُمَّهَٰتُ نِسَآئِكُمْ وَرَبَٰٓئِبُكُمُ
ٱلَّٰتِى فِى حُجُورِكُم مِّن نِّسَآئِكُمُ ٱلَّٰتِى دَخَلْتُم بِهِنَّ فَإِن لَّمْ تَكُونُوا۟ دَخَلْتُم
بِهِنَّ فَلَا جُنَاحَ عَلَيْكُمْ وَحَلَٰٓئِلُ أَبْنَآئِكُمُ ٱلَّذِينَ مِنْ أَصْلَٰبِكُمْ وَأَن
تَجْمَعُوا۟ بَيْنَ ٱلْأُخْتَيْنِ إِلَّا مَا قَدْ سَلَفَ ۗ إِنَّ ٱللَّهَ كَانَ غَفُورًا رَّحِيمًا ﴿٢٣﴾ ۞
وَٱلْمُحْصَنَٰتُ مِنَ ٱلنِّسَآءِ إِلَّا مَا مَلَكَتْ أَيْمَٰنُكُمْ ۖ كِتَٰبَ ٱللَّهِ عَلَيْكُمْ ۚ

حزب 9
جزء 5

ʾAtaʾkhudhūnahū buhtānañw-wa ʾithmam-mubīnā. (20) Wa kayfa taʾkhudhūnahū wa qad ʾafḍā baʿḍukum ʾilā baʿḍiñw-wa ʾakhadhna miñkum-mīthāqan ghalīẓā. (21) Wa lā tañkiḥū mā nakaḥa ʾābāaʾukum-minan-nisāaʾi ʾillā mā qad salaf. ʾInnahū kāna fāḥishatañw-wa maqtañw-wa sāaʾa sabīlā. (22) Ḥurrimat ʿalaykum ʾummahātukum wa banātukum wa ʾakhawātukum wa ʿammātukum wa khālātukum wa banātul-ʾakhi wa banātul-ʾukhti wa ʾummahātu-kumul-lātī ʾarḍaʿnakum wa ʾakhawātukum-minar-raḍāʿati wa ʾummahātu nisāaʾikum wa rabāa-ʾibukumul-lātī fī ḥujūrikum-miñ-nisāaʾikumul-lātī dakhaltum-bihinna faʾil-lam takūnū dakhaltum-bihinna falā junāḥa ʿalaykum wa ḥalāaʾilu ʾabnāaʾikumul-ladhīna min ʾaṣlābikum wa ʾañ-tajmaʿū baynal-ʾukhtayni ʾillā mā qad salaf. ʾInnal-lāha kāna Ghafūrar-Raḥīmā. (23) ۞ Wal-muḥṣanātu minan-nisāaʾi ʾillā mā malakat ʾaymānukum; Kitābal-lāhi ʿalaykum.

do not take away anything thereof". The allusion to the "exchange" of one wife for another is a clear indication of the Qurʾanic view that a monogamous marriage is the desirable norm.

22 I.e., by falsely accusing her of immoral conduct in the hope of regaining her dower (see note 18 above).

23 Lit., "they have" – the reference being to *all* married women.

24 Lit., "except what has come to pass earlier" – i.e., forgiven shall be he who did it before the promulgation of this Qurʾanic ordinance or (in the case of a conversion in later times) before one's acceptance of Islam.

25 See preceding note.

26 The term *muḥṣanah* signifies literally "a woman who is fortified [against unchastity]", and carries three senses: (1) "a married woman", (2) "a chaste woman", and (3) "a free woman". According to almost all the authorities, *al-muḥṣanāt* denotes in the above context "married women". As for the expression *mā malakat aymānukum* ("those whom your right hands possess", i.e., "those whom you *rightfully* possess"), it is often taken to mean female slaves captured in a war in God's cause (see in this connection 8 : 67, and the corresponding note). The commentators who

But lawful to you are all [women] beyond these, for you to seek out, offering them of your possessions,[27] taking them in honest wedlock, and not in fornication. And unto those with whom you desire to enjoy marriage, you shall give the dowers due to them; but you will incur no sin if, after [having agreed upon] this lawful due, you freely agree with one another upon anything [else]:[28] behold, God is indeed all-knowing, wise. «24»

And as for those of you who, owing to circumstances, are not in a position[29] to marry free believing women, [let them marry] believing maidens from among those whom you rightfully possess.[30] And God knows all about your faith; each one of you is an issue of the other.[31] Marry them, then, with their people's leave, and give them their dowers in an equitable manner – they being women who give themselves in honest wedlock, not in fornication, nor as secret love-companions.[32] And when they are married, and thereafter become guilty of immoral conduct, they shall be liable to half the penalty to which free married women are liable.[33]

وَأُحِلَّ لَكُم مَّا وَرَآءَ ذَٰلِكُمْ أَن تَبْتَغُوا۟ بِأَمْوَٰلِكُم مُّحْصِنِينَ غَيْرَ مُسَٰفِحِينَ
فَمَا ٱسْتَمْتَعْتُم بِهِۦ مِنْهُنَّ فَـَٔاتُوهُنَّ أُجُورَهُنَّ فَرِيضَةً وَلَا جُنَاحَ عَلَيْكُمْ فِيمَا
تَرَٰضَيْتُم بِهِۦ مِنۢ بَعْدِ ٱلْفَرِيضَةِ إِنَّ ٱللَّهَ كَانَ عَلِيمًا حَكِيمًا ﴿٢٤﴾ وَمَن لَّمْ
يَسْتَطِعْ مِنكُمْ طَوْلًا أَن يَنكِحَ ٱلْمُحْصَنَٰتِ ٱلْمُؤْمِنَٰتِ فَمِن مَّا
مَلَكَتْ أَيْمَٰنُكُم مِّن فَتَيَٰتِكُمُ ٱلْمُؤْمِنَٰتِ وَٱللَّهُ أَعْلَمُ بِإِيمَٰنِكُم
بَعْضُكُم مِّنۢ بَعْضٍ فَٱنكِحُوهُنَّ بِإِذْنِ أَهْلِهِنَّ وَءَاتُوهُنَّ أُجُورَهُنَّ
بِٱلْمَعْرُوفِ مُحْصَنَٰتٍ غَيْرَ مُسَٰفِحَٰتٍ وَلَا مُتَّخِذَٰتِ أَخْدَانٍ فَإِذَآ
أُحْصِنَّ فَإِنْ أَتَيْنَ بِفَٰحِشَةٍ فَعَلَيْهِنَّ نِصْفُ مَا عَلَى ٱلْمُحْصَنَٰتِ مِنَ ٱلْعَذَابِ

Wa ʾuḥilla lakum-mā warāaʾa dhālikum ʾañ-tabtaghū biʾamwālikum-muḥṣinīna ghayra musāfiḥīn. Famastamtaʿtum-bihī minhunna faʾātūhunna ʾujūrahunna farīḍah. Wa lā junāḥa ʿalaykum fīmā tarāḍaytum-bihī mim-baʿdil-farīḍati ʾinnal-lāha kāna ʿAlīman Ḥakīmā. (24) Wa mal-lam yastaṭiʿ miñkum ṭawlan ʾañy-yañkiḥal-muḥṣanātil-muʾmināti famim-mā malakat ʾaymānukum-miñ-fatayātikumul-muʾmināti wal-lāhu ʾaʿlamu biʾīmānikum. Baʿḍukum mim-baʿḍ. Fañkiḥūhunna biʾidhni ʾahlihinna wa ʾātūhunna ʾujūrahunna bilmaʿrūfi muḥṣanātin ghayra musāfiḥātiñw-wa lā muttakhidhāti ʾakhdān. Faʾidhāa ʾuḥṣinna faʾin ʾatayna bifāḥishatiñ-faʿalayhinna niṣfu ma ʿalal-muḥṣanāti minal-ʿadhāb.

choose this meaning hold that such slave-girls can be taken in marriage irrespective of whether they have husbands in the country of their origin or not. However, quite apart from the fundamental differences of opinion, even among the Companions of the Prophet, regarding the legality of such a marriage, some of the most outstanding commentators hold the view that *mā malakat aymānukum* denotes here "women whom you rightfully possess *through wedlock*"; thus Rāzī in his commentary on this verse, and Ṭabarī in one of his alternative explanations (going back to ʿAbd Allāh ibn ʿAbbās, Mujāhid, and others). Rāzī, in particular, points out that the reference to "all married women" (*al-muḥṣanāt min an-nisāʾ*), coming as it does after the enumeration of prohibited degrees of relationship, is meant to stress the prohibition of sexual relations with any woman other than one's lawful wife.

27 Lit., "with your possessions" – i.e., offering them, as the Law demands, an appropriate dower.

28 Cf. verse 4 of this *sūrah*, and the corresponding note.

29 The phrase *lam yastaṭīʿ ṭawlan* is often taken to mean "he is not in a position to afford", i.e., in the financial sense; but Muḥammad ʿAbduh very convincingly expresses the view that it applies to all manner of preventive circumstances, be they of a material, personal or social nature (*Manār* V, 19).

30 In this context, *mā malakat aymānukum* (lit., "those whom your right hands possess") denotes women who were captured in a holy war and have subsequently embraced Islam. In the above phrase, the pronoun "you" refers to the community as a whole.

31 I.e., since all human beings – whatever their outward "social status" – are members of one and the same human family, and are therefore equal to one another in the sight of God (cf. 3 : 195), it is only the strength or weakness of faith which makes one person superior or inferior to another.

32 Lit., "and not taking unto themselves secret love-companions". This passage lays down in an unequivocal manner that sexual relations with female slaves are permitted only on the basis of *marriage*, and that in this respect there is no difference between them and free women; consequently, concubinage is ruled out.

33 The weaker social status of a slave makes her, obviously, more accessible to temptation than a free married woman is presumed to be.

This [permission to marry slave-girls applies] to those of you who fear lest they stumble into evil.[34] But it is for your own good to persevere in patience [and to abstain from such marriages]: and God is much-forgiving, a dispenser of grace. ‹25› God wants to make [all this] clear unto you, and to guide you onto the [righteous] ways of life of those who preceded you,[35] and to turn unto you in His mercy: for God is all-knowing, wise. ‹26› And God wants to turn unto you in His mercy, whereas those who follow [only] their own lusts want you to drift far away from the right path.[36] ‹27›
God wants to lighten your burdens:[37] for man has been created weak. ‹28›

O YOU who have attained to faith! Do not devour one another's possessions wrongfully – not even by way of trade based on mutual agreement[38] – and do not destroy one another: for, behold, God is indeed a dispenser of grace unto you! ‹29›

ذَٰلِكَ لِمَنْ خَشِيَ ٱلْعَنَتَ مِنكُمْ وَأَن تَصْبِرُوا۟ خَيْرٌ لَّكُمْ وَٱللَّهُ غَفُورٌ
رَّحِيمٌ ﴿٢٥﴾ يُرِيدُ ٱللَّهُ لِيُبَيِّنَ لَكُمْ وَيَهْدِيَكُمْ سُنَنَ ٱلَّذِينَ مِن قَبْلِكُمْ
وَيَتُوبَ عَلَيْكُمْ وَٱللَّهُ عَلِيمٌ حَكِيمٌ ﴿٢٦﴾ وَٱللَّهُ يُرِيدُ أَن يَتُوبَ عَلَيْكُمْ
وَيُرِيدُ ٱلَّذِينَ يَتَّبِعُونَ ٱلشَّهَوَٰتِ أَن تَمِيلُوا۟ مَيْلًا عَظِيمًا ﴿٢٧﴾ يُرِيدُ ٱللَّهُ أَن
يُخَفِّفَ عَنكُمْ وَخُلِقَ ٱلْإِنسَٰنُ ضَعِيفًا ﴿٢٨﴾ يَٰٓأَيُّهَا ٱلَّذِينَ ءَامَنُوا۟ لَا
تَأْكُلُوٓا۟ أَمْوَٰلَكُم بَيْنَكُم بِٱلْبَٰطِلِ إِلَّآ أَن تَكُونَ تِجَٰرَةً عَن تَرَاضٍ
مِّنكُمْ وَلَا تَقْتُلُوٓا۟ أَنفُسَكُمْ إِنَّ ٱللَّهَ كَانَ بِكُمْ رَحِيمًا ﴿٢٩﴾

Dhālika liman khashiyal-ʿanata miñkum. Wa ʾañ-taṣbirū khayruñ-lakum. Wal-lāhu Ghafūrur-Raḥīm. (25) Yurīdul-lāhu liyubayyina lakum wa yahdiyakum sunanal-ladhīna miñ-qablikum wa yatūba ʿalaykum. Wal-lāhu ʿAlīmun Ḥakīm. (26) Wal-lāhu yurīdu ʾañy-yatūba ʿalaykum wa yurīdul-ladhīna yattabiʿūnash-Shahawāti ʾañ-tamīlū maylan ʿaẓīmā. (27) Yurīdul-lāhu ʾañy-yukhaffifa ʿañkum; wa khuliqal-ʾInsānu ḍaʿīfā. (28) Yāa ʾayyuhal-ladhīna ʾāmanū lā taʾkulūu ʾamwālakum-baynakum-bilbāṭili ʾillāa ʾañ-takūna tijāratan ʿañ-tarāḍim-miñkum; wa lā taqtulūu ʾañfusakum; ʾinnal-lāha kāna bikum Raḥīmā. (29)

34 I.e., to those who for one reason or another are unable to marry free women and are, at the same time, not equal to the temptations arising from celibacy. As is made clear in the next sentence, the Qurʾān discourages such marriages – obviously with a view to removing a major attraction from the institution of slavery as such, and thus promoting its abolition.

35 An allusion to the *genuine* religious teachings of the past, which aimed at bringing about a harmony between man's physical nature and the demands of his spirit – a harmony which is destroyed whenever asceticism is postulated as the only possible alternative to licentiousness (see also *sūrah* 2, note 118). This allusion arises from the discussion of sexual morality in the preceding passages devoted to marital relations.

36 Lit., "want you to deviate with a tremendous deviation".

37 I.e., to remove, by means of His guidance, all possibility of conflict between man's spirit and his bodily urges, and to show him a way of life in which these two elements of human nature can be harmonized and brought to full fruition.

38 If the particle *illā* preceding the above clause is given its usual meaning of "except" or "unless it be", the phrase ought to be rendered thus: "unless it be [an act of] trade based on mutual agreement". This formulation, however, has baffled many a commentator: for, if taken literally, it would imply that wrongful profits from trading based on mutual agreement are excepted from the general prohibition, "Devour not one another's possessions wrongfully" – a supposition impossible to maintain in view of the ethics postulated by the Qurʾān. To obviate this difficulty, most of the commentators express the opinion that the particle *illā* has in this context the meaning of "but", and that the clause ought to be understood as follows: "but it is lawful for you to profit from one another's possessions by way of legitimate trade based on mutual agreement". However, quite apart from the fact that this interpretation is highly laboured and artificial, it does not explain why "legitimate trade" should have been singled out here as a sole means of lawfully deriving economic benefits from one another – for, as Rāzī rightly points out in his commentary on this verse, "it is no less lawful to benefit economically through a gift, a bequest, a legal inheritance, alms, a dower, or an indemnity for injuries received: for there are, aside from trade, many ways of acquiring possessions [lawfully.]". Why, then, should trade alone have been stressed? – and, moreover, stressed in a context not particularly devoted to matters of trade? A really satisfactory answer to this puzzle can, in my opinion, be obtained only through a linguistic consideration of the particle *illā*. Apart from its usual connotation of "except" or "unless it be", it has sometimes – as has been pointed out in both *Qāmūs* and *Mughnī* – the meaning of the simple conjunction "and" (*wa*); similarly, if it is

وَمَن يَفْعَلْ ذَٰلِكَ عُدْوَٰنًا وَظُلْمًا فَسَوْفَ نُصْلِيهِ نَارًا ۚ وَكَانَ ذَٰلِكَ عَلَى ٱللَّهِ
يَسِيرًا ﴿٣٠﴾ إِن تَجْتَنِبُوا۟ كَبَآئِرَ مَا تُنْهَوْنَ عَنْهُ نُكَفِّرْ عَنكُمْ سَيِّـَٔاتِكُمْ
وَنُدْخِلْكُم مُّدْخَلًا كَرِيمًا ﴿٣١﴾ وَلَا تَتَمَنَّوْا۟ مَا فَضَّلَ ٱللَّهُ بِهِۦ بَعْضَكُمْ عَلَىٰ
بَعْضٍ ۚ لِّلرِّجَالِ نَصِيبٌ مِّمَّا ٱكْتَسَبُوا۟ ۖ وَلِلنِّسَآءِ نَصِيبٌ مِّمَّا ٱكْتَسَبْنَ ۚ وَسْـَٔلُوا۟
ٱللَّهَ مِن فَضْلِهِۦٓ ۗ إِنَّ ٱللَّهَ كَانَ بِكُلِّ شَىْءٍ عَلِيمًا ﴿٣٢﴾ وَلِكُلٍّ جَعَلْنَا مَوَٰلِىَ مِمَّا
تَرَكَ ٱلْوَٰلِدَانِ وَٱلْأَقْرَبُونَ ۚ وَٱلَّذِينَ عَقَدَتْ أَيْمَٰنُكُمْ فَـَٔاتُوهُمْ نَصِيبَهُمْ ۚ إِنَّ
ٱللَّهَ كَانَ عَلَىٰ كُلِّ شَىْءٍ شَهِيدًا ﴿٣٣﴾ ٱلرِّجَالُ قَوَّٰمُونَ عَلَى ٱلنِّسَآءِ بِمَا فَضَّلَ
ٱللَّهُ بَعْضَهُمْ عَلَىٰ بَعْضٍ وَبِمَآ أَنفَقُوا۟ مِنْ أَمْوَٰلِهِمْ ۚ فَٱلصَّٰلِحَٰتُ قَٰنِتَٰتٌ

And as for him who does this with malicious intent and a will to do wrong[39] – him shall We, in time, cause to endure [suffering through] fire: for this is indeed easy for God. ‹30›

If you avoid the great sins which you have been enjoined to shun, We shall efface your [minor] bad deeds, and shall cause you to enter an abode of glory.[40] ‹31›

Hence, do not covet the bounties which God has bestowed more abundantly on some of you than on others. Men shall have a benefit from what they earn, and women shall have a benefit from what they earn. Ask, therefore, God [to give you] out of His bounty: behold, God has indeed full knowledge of everything. ‹32›

And unto everyone have We appointed heirs to what he may leave behind: parents, and near kinsfolk, and those to whom you have pledged your troth:[41] give them, therefore, their share. Behold, God is indeed a witness unto everything. ‹33›

MEN SHALL take full care of women with the bounties which God has bestowed more abundantly on the former than on the latter,[42] and with what they may spend out of their possessions. And the righteous women are the truly devout ones,

Wa mañy-yafᶜal dhālika ᶜudwānañw-wa ẓulmañ-fasawfa nuṣlīhi nārā. Wa kāna dhālika ᶜalal-lāhi yasīrā. (30) ʾIñ-tajtanibū kabāaʾira mā tunhawna ᶜanhu nukaffir ᶜañkum sayyiʾātikum wa nudkhil-kum-mudkhalañ-karīmā. (31) Wa lā tatamannaw mā faḍḍalal-lāhu bihī baᶜḍakum ᶜalā baᶜḍ. Lirrijāli na-ṣībum-mimmak-tasabū wa linnisāaʾi naṣībum-mim-mak-tasabn. Was-ʾalul-lāha miñ-faḍlih. ʾInnal-lāha kāna bikulli shayʾin ᶜAlīmā. (32) Wa likulliñ-jaᶜalnā mawāliya mimmā tarakal-wālidāni wal-ʾaqrabūn. Wal-ladhīna ᶜaqadat ʾaymānukum faʾātūhum naṣī-bahum. ʾInnal-lāha kāna ᶜalā kulli shayʾiñ-Shahīdā. (33) ʾArrijālu qawwāmūna ᶜalan-nisāaʾi bimā faḍḍalal-lāhu baᶜḍahum ᶜalā baᶜḍiñw-wa bimāa ʾañfaqū min ʾamwālihim. Faṣṣāliḥātu qānitātun

preceded by a negative clause, it can be synonymous with "nor" or "and neither" (*wa-lā*): as, for instance, in 27 : 10-11, "no fear need the message-bearers have in My Presence, and neither (*illā*) need he who . . .", etc. Now if we apply this particular use of *illā* to the passage under consideration, we arrive at the reading, "nor [shall you do it] by means of trade based on mutual agreement", or simply, "not even by way of trade based on mutual agreement" – whereupon the meaning immediately becomes obvious: the believers are prohibited from devouring another person's possessions wrongfully even if that other person – being the weaker party – agrees to such a deprivation or exploitation under the stress of circumstances. The reading adopted by me logically connects, moreover, with verse 32, which admonishes the believers not to covet one another's possessions.

39 Lit., "by way of [deliberate] transgression and wrongdoing" (*ᶜudwānan wa-ẓulman*).

40 I.e., paradise. However, according to some of the commentators, the expression *mudkhal* denotes not the place but the *manner* of "entering" (Rāzī) – in which case the above phrase may be rendered thus: "We shall cause you to enter [upon your afterlife] in a state of glory".

41 I.e., wives and husbands (Abū Muslim, as quoted by Rāzī).

42 Lit., "more on some of them than on the others". – The expression *qawwām* is an intensive form of *qāʾim* ("one who is responsible for" or "takes care of" a thing or a person). Thus, *qāma ᶜala 'l-marʾah* signifies "he undertook the maintenance of the woman" or "he maintained her" (see Lane VIII, 2995). The grammatical form *qawwām* is more comprehensive than *qāʾim*, and combines the concepts of physical maintenance and protection as well as of moral responsibility: and it is because of the last-named factor that I have rendered this phrase as "men *shall* take full care of women".

who guard the intimacy which God has [ordained to be] guarded.[43]
And as for those women whose ill-will[44] you have reason to fear, admonish them [first]; then leave them alone in bed; then beat them;[45] and if thereupon they pay you heed, do not seek to harm them. Behold, God is indeed most high, great! ‹34›
And if you have reason to fear that a breach might occur between a [married] couple, appoint an arbiter from among his people and an arbiter from among her people; if they both want to set things aright, God may bring about their reconciliation. Behold, God is indeed all-knowing, aware. ‹35›

AND WORSHIP God [alone], and do not ascribe divinity, in any way, to aught beside Him.[46]
And do good unto your parents, and near of kin, and unto orphans, and the needy, and the neighbour from among your own people, and the neighbour who is a

حَـٰفِظَـٰتٌ لِّلْغَيْبِ بِمَا حَفِظَ ٱللَّهُ ۚ وَٱلَّـٰتِى تَخَافُونَ نُشُوزَهُنَّ فَعِظُوهُنَّ
وَٱهْجُرُوهُنَّ فِى ٱلْمَضَاجِعِ وَٱضْرِبُوهُنَّ ۖ فَإِنْ أَطَعْنَكُمْ فَلَا تَبْغُوا۟
عَلَيْهِنَّ سَبِيلًا ۗ إِنَّ ٱللَّهَ كَانَ عَلِيًّا كَبِيرًا ﴿٣٤﴾ وَإِنْ خِفْتُمْ شِقَاقَ
بَيْنِهِمَا فَٱبْعَثُوا۟ حَكَمًا مِّنْ أَهْلِهِۦ وَحَكَمًا مِّنْ أَهْلِهَآ إِن يُرِيدَآ
إِصْلَـٰحًا يُوَفِّقِ ٱللَّهُ بَيْنَهُمَآ ۗ إِنَّ ٱللَّهَ كَانَ عَلِيمًا خَبِيرًا ﴿٣٥﴾ ۞
وَٱعْبُدُوا۟ ٱللَّهَ وَلَا تُشْرِكُوا۟ بِهِۦ شَيْـًٔا ۖ وَبِٱلْوَٰلِدَيْنِ إِحْسَـٰنًا وَبِذِى
ٱلْقُرْبَىٰ وَٱلْيَتَـٰمَىٰ وَٱلْمَسَـٰكِينِ وَٱلْجَارِ ذِى ٱلْقُرْبَىٰ وَٱلْجَارِ

ربع الحزب

ḥāfiẓātul-lilghaybi bimā ḥafiẓal-lāh. Wal-lātī takhāfūna nushūzahunna faʿiẓuhunna wah-jurūhunna fil-maḍājiʿi waḍ-ribūhunn. Faʾin ʾaṭaʿnakum falā tabghū ʿalayhinna sabīlā. ʾInnal-lāha kāna ʿAliyyañ-Kabīrā. ﴿34﴾ Wa ʾiñ khiftum shiqāqa baynihimā fabʿathū ḥakamam-min ʾahlihī wa ḥakamam-min ʾahlihā. ʾIñy-yurīdāa ʾiṣlāḥañy-yuwaffiqil-lāhu baynahumā. ʾInnal-lāha kāna ʿAlīman Khabīrā. ﴿35﴾ ۞ Waʿ-budul-lāha wa lā tushrikū bihī shayʾañw-wa bilwālidayni ʾiḥsānañw-wa bidhil-qurbā wal-yatāmā wal-masākīni wal-jāri dhil-qurbā wal-jāril-

43 Lit., "who guard that which cannot be perceived (*al-ghayb*) because God has [willed it to be] guarded".

44 The term *nushūz* (lit., "rebellion" – here rendered as "ill-will") comprises every kind of deliberate bad behaviour of a wife towards her husband or of a husband towards his wife, including what is nowadays described as "mental cruelty"; with reference to the husband, it also denotes "ill-treatment", in the physical sense, of his wife (cf. verse 128 of this *sūrah*). In this context, a wife's "ill-will" implies a deliberate, persistent breach of her marital obligations.

45 It is evident from many authentic Traditions that the Prophet himself intensely detested the idea of beating one's wife, and said on more than one occasion, "Could any of you beat his wife as he would beat a slave, and then lie with her in the evening?" (Bukhārī and Muslim). According to another Tradition, he forbade the beating of *any* woman with the words, "Never beat God's handmaidens" (Abū Dāʾūd, Nasāʾī, Ibn Mājah, Aḥmad ibn Ḥanbal, Ibn Ḥibbān and Ḥākim, on the authority of Iyās ibn ʿAbd Allāh; Ibn Ḥibbān, on the authority of ʿAbd Allāh ibn ʿAbbās; and Bayhaqī, on the authority of Umm Kulthūm). When the above Qurʾān-verse authorizing the beating of a refractory wife was revealed, the Prophet is reported to have said: "I wanted one thing, but God has willed another thing – and what God has willed must be best (see *Manār* V, 74). With all this, he stipulated in his sermon on the occasion of the Farewell Pilgrimage, shortly before his death, that beating should be resorted to only if the wife "has become guilty, in an obvious manner, of immoral conduct", and that it should be done "in such a way as not to cause pain (*ghayr mubarriḥ*)"; authentic Traditions to this effect are found in Muslim, Tirmidhī, Abū Dāʾūd, Nasāʾī and Ibn Mājah. On the basis of these Traditions, all the authorities stress that this "beating", if resorted to at all, should be more or less symbolic – "with a toothbrush, or some such thing" (Ṭabarī, quoting the views of scholars of the earliest times), or even "with a folded handkerchief" (Rāzī); and some of the greatest Muslim scholars (e.g., Ash-Shāfiʿī) are of the opinion that it is just barely permissible, and should preferably be avoided: and they justify this opinion by the Prophet's personal feelings with regard to this problem.

46 The expression *shayʾan* (here rendered as "in any way") makes it clear that *shirk* ("the ascribing of divinity to anything beside God") is not confined to a worship of other "deities", but implies also the attribution of divine or quasi-divine powers to persons or objects not regarded as deities: in other words, it embraces also saint-worship, etc.

stranger,[47] and the friend by your side, and the wayfarer, and those whom you rightfully possess.[48]

Verily, God does not love any of those who, full of self-conceit, act in a boastful manner; ⟨36⟩ [nor] those who are niggardly, and bid others to be niggardly, and conceal whatever God has bestowed upon them out of His bounty; and so We have readied shameful suffering for all who thus deny the truth. ⟨37⟩

And [God does not love] those who spend their possessions on others [only] to be seen and praised by men, the while they believe neither in God nor in the Last Day; and he who has Satan for a soul-mate, how evil a soul-mate has he![49] ⟨38⟩

And what would they have to fear[50] if they would but believe in God and the Last Day, and spend [in His way] out of what God has granted them as sustenance – since God has indeed full knowledge of them? ⟨39⟩

Verily, God does not wrong [anyone] by as much as an atom's weight; and if there be a good deed, He will multiply it, and will bestow out of His grace[51] a mighty reward. ⟨40⟩

How, then, [will the sinners fare on Judgment Day,] when We shall bring forward witnesses from within every

ٱلْجُنُبِ وَٱلصَّاحِبِ بِٱلْجَنۢبِ وَٱبْنِ ٱلسَّبِيلِ وَمَا مَلَكَتْ أَيْمَـٰنُكُمْ ۗ إِنَّ
ٱللَّهَ لَا يُحِبُّ مَن كَانَ مُخْتَالًا فَخُورًا ﴿٣٦﴾ ٱلَّذِينَ يَبْخَلُونَ وَيَأْمُرُونَ
ٱلنَّاسَ بِٱلْبُخْلِ وَيَكْتُمُونَ مَآ ءَاتَىٰهُمُ ٱللَّهُ مِن فَضْلِهِۦ ۗ وَأَعْتَدْنَا لِلْكَـٰفِرِينَ
عَذَابًا مُّهِينًا ﴿٣٧﴾ وَٱلَّذِينَ يُنفِقُونَ أَمْوَٰلَهُمْ رِئَآءَ ٱلنَّاسِ وَلَا يُؤْمِنُونَ
بِٱللَّهِ وَلَا بِٱلْيَوْمِ ٱلْـَٔاخِرِ ۗ وَمَن يَكُنِ ٱلشَّيْطَـٰنُ لَهُۥ قَرِينًا فَسَآءَ قَرِينًا ﴿٣٨﴾
وَمَاذَا عَلَيْهِمْ لَوْ ءَامَنُوا۟ بِٱللَّهِ وَٱلْيَوْمِ ٱلْـَٔاخِرِ وَأَنفَقُوا۟ مِمَّا رَزَقَهُمُ ٱللَّهُ ۚ
وَكَانَ ٱللَّهُ بِهِمْ عَلِيمًا ﴿٣٩﴾ إِنَّ ٱللَّهَ لَا يَظْلِمُ مِثْقَالَ ذَرَّةٍ ۖ وَإِن تَكُ حَسَنَةً
يُضَـٰعِفْهَا وَيُؤْتِ مِن لَّدُنْهُ أَجْرًا عَظِيمًا ﴿٤٠﴾ فَكَيْفَ إِذَا جِئْنَا مِن كُلِّ

junubi waṣ-ṣāḥibi biljambi wab-nis-sabīli wa mā malakat ʾaymānukum. ʾInnal-lāha lā yuḥibbu mañ kāna mukhtālañ-fakhūrā; (36) ʾAlladhīna yabkhalūna wa yaʾmurūnan-nāsa bil-bukhli wa yaktumūna māa ʾātāhumul-lāhu miñ-faḍlih. Wa ʾaʿtadnā lilkāfirīna ʿadhābam-muhīnā. (37) Wal-ladhīna yuñfiqūna ʾamwālahum riʾāaʾan-nāsi wa lā yuʾminūna billāhi wa lā bilYawmil-ʾĀkhir. Wa mañy-yakunish-Shayṭānu lahū qarīnañ-fasāaʾa qarīnā. (38) Wa mādhā ʿalayhim law ʾāmanū billāhi wal-Yawmil-ʾĀkhiri wa ʾañfaqū mimmā razaqahumul-lāh. Wa kānal-lāhu bihim ʿAlīmā. (39) ʾInnal-lāha lā yaẓlimu mithqāla dharratiñw-wa ʾiñ-taku ḥasanatañy-yuḍāʿifhā wa yuʾti mil-ladunhu ʾajran ʿaẓīmā. (40) Fakayfa ʾidhā jiʾnā miñ-kulli

47 I.e., "whether he belongs to your own or to another community". That the expression "your own people" (*dhu 'l-qurbā*) refers to the community and not to one's actual relatives is obvious from the fact that "the near of kin" have already been mentioned earlier in this sentence. The Prophet often stressed a believer's moral obligation towards his neighbours, whatever their faith; and his attitude has been summed up in his words, "Whoever believes in God and the Last Day, let him do good unto his neighbour" (Bukhārī, Muslim, and other compilations).

48 According to ʿAlī ibn Abī Ṭālib, ʿAbd Allāh ibn Masʿūd and other Companions, "the friend by your side" (*aṣ-ṣāḥib bi'l-janb*) is one's wife or husband (Ṭabarī). By "those whom you rightfully possess" (lit., "whom your right hands possess") are meant, in this context, slaves of either sex. Since this verse enjoins the "doing of good" towards all people with whom one is in contact, and since the best that can be done to a slave is to free him, the above passage calls, elliptically, for the freeing of slaves (*Manār* V, 94). See also *sūrah* 2, note 146, as well as 9 : 60, where the freeing of human beings from bondage is explicitly mentioned as one of the objectives to which *zakāh* funds are to be dedicated.

49 An allusion to 2 : 268, where Satan is spoken of as "threatening you with the prospect of poverty and bidding you to be niggardly", the implication being that those who obey him "have Satan for their soul-mate (*qarīn*)". For the derivation of this term, see note 24 on 41 : 25.

50 Lit., "what is it that would be upon them". This seems to be a reference to the oft-repeated Qurʾanic statement that those who believe in God and live righteously "need have no fear" (*lā khawf ʿalayhim* – lit., "no fear [shall be] upon them").

51 Lit., "from Himself" – i.e., far in excess of what the doer of good may have merited.

community,[52] and bring thee [O Prophet] as witness against them? ‹41› Those who were bent on denying the truth and paid no heed to the Apostle will on that Day wish that the earth would swallow them;[53] but they shall not [be able to] conceal from God anything that has happened. ‹42›

O YOU who have attained to faith! Do not attempt to pray while you are in a state of drunkenness,[54] [but wait] until you know what you are saying; nor yet [while you are] in a state requiring total ablution,[55] until you have bathed – except if you are travelling [and are unable to do so]. But if you are ill, or are travelling, or have just satisfied a want of nature,[56] or have cohabited with a woman, and can find no water – then take resort to pure dust, passing [therewith] lightly over your face and your hands.[57] Behold, God is indeed an absolver of sins, much-forgiving. ‹43›

أُمَّةٍ بِشَهِيدٍ وَجِئْنَا بِكَ عَلَىٰ هَٰٓؤُلَآءِ شَهِيدًا ﴿٤١﴾ يَوْمَئِذٍ يَوَدُّ ٱلَّذِينَ كَفَرُوا۟
وَعَصَوُا۟ ٱلرَّسُولَ لَوْ تُسَوَّىٰ بِهِمُ ٱلْأَرْضُ وَلَا يَكْتُمُونَ ٱللَّهَ حَدِيثًا ﴿٤٢﴾ يَٰٓأَيُّهَا
ٱلَّذِينَ ءَامَنُوا۟ لَا تَقْرَبُوا۟ ٱلصَّلَوٰةَ وَأَنتُمْ سُكَٰرَىٰ حَتَّىٰ تَعْلَمُوا۟ مَا تَقُولُونَ وَلَا
جُنُبًا إِلَّا عَابِرِى سَبِيلٍ حَتَّىٰ تَغْتَسِلُوا۟ وَإِن كُنتُم مَّرْضَىٰٓ أَوْ عَلَىٰ سَفَرٍ أَوْ جَآءَ
أَحَدٌ مِّنكُم مِّنَ ٱلْغَآئِطِ أَوْ لَٰمَسْتُمُ ٱلنِّسَآءَ فَلَمْ تَجِدُوا۟ مَآءً فَتَيَمَّمُوا۟ صَعِيدًا
طَيِّبًا فَٱمْسَحُوا۟ بِوُجُوهِكُمْ وَأَيْدِيكُمْ إِنَّ ٱللَّهَ كَانَ عَفُوًّا غَفُورًا ﴿٤٣﴾

ʾummatim-bishahīdiñw-wa jiʾnā bika ʿalā hāaʾulāaʾi shahīdā. ‹41› Yawmaʾidhiñy-yawaddul-ladhīna kafarū wa ʿasawur-Rasūla law tusawwā bihimul-ʾarḍu wa lā yaktumūnal-lāha ḥadīthā. ‹42› Yāa ʾayyuhal-ladhīna ʾāmanū lā taqrabuṣ-Ṣalāta wa ʾañtum sukārā ḥattā taʿlamū mā taqūlūna wa lā junuban ʾillā ʿābirī sabīlin ḥattā taghtasilū. Wa ʾiñ-kuñtum-marḍāa ʾaw ʿalā safarin ʾaw jāaʾa ʾaḥadum-miñkum-minal-ghāaʾiṭi ʾaw lāmastumun-nisāaʾa fa-lam tajidū māaʾañ-fatayammamū ṣaʿīdañ-ṭayyibañ-famsaḥū biwujūhikum wa ʾaydīkum. ʾInnal-lāha kāna ʿAfuwwan Ghafūrā. ‹43›

52 I.e., the earlier apostles, of whom every community or civilization has had a share.

53 Lit., "become level with them". The term "the apostle" is probably used here in its generic sense, and refers to all the apostles who preached God's message at one time or another.

54 The reference to prayer at this place arises from the mention, in the preceding verses, of the Day of Judgment, when man will have to answer before God for what he did during his life in this world: for it is in prayer that man faces God, spiritually, during his earthly life, and reminds himself of his responsibility towards the Creator. As regards the prohibition of attempting to pray "while in a state of drunkenness", some of the commentators assume that this ordinance represented the first stage of the total prohibition of intoxicants, and has been, consequently, "abrogated" by the promulgation of the law of total abstinence from all intoxicants (5 : 90). However, quite apart from the fact that the doctrine of "abrogation" is entirely untenable (see *sūrah* 2, note 87), there is no warrant whatever for regarding the above verse as a "first step" which has become redundant, as it were, after total prohibition was ordained. It is, of course, true that the Qurʾān forbids the use of intoxicants at *all* times, and not merely at the time of prayer; but since "man has been created weak" (4 : 28), his lapse from the way of virtue is always a possibility: and it is to prevent him from adding the sin of praying while in a state of drunkenness to the sin of using intoxicants as such that the above verse was promulgated. Moreover, the expression "while you are in a state of drunkenness (*sukārā*)" does not apply exclusively to alcoholic intoxication, since the term *sukr*, in its wider connotation, signifies any state of mental disequilibrium which prevents man from making full use of his intellectual faculties: that is to say, it can apply also to a temporary clouding of the intellect by drugs or giddiness or passion, as well as to the state metaphorically described as "drunk with sleep" – in brief, to any condition in which normal judgment is confused or suspended. And because the Qurʾān insists throughout on *consciousness* as an indispensable element in every act of worship, prayer is permitted only when man is in full possession of his mental faculties and "knows what he is saying".

55 I.e., after sexual intercourse. The term *junub* (rendered by me as "in a state requiring total ablution") is derived from the verb *janaba*, "he made [a thing] remote", and signifies one's "remoteness" from prayer because of immersion in sexual passion.

56 Lit., "if one of you comes from the place in which one satisfies . . .", etc.

57 This symbolic ablution, called *tayammum*, consists in touching the earth, or anything supposed to contain dust, with the palms of one's hands and then passing them lightly over face and hands. Whenever water is not within reach – or cannot be used because of illness – the *tayammum* takes the place of both the total ablution after sexual intercourse (*ghusl*) and the partial ablution before prayers (*wuḍūʿ*).

ART THOU NOT aware of those who, having been granted their share of the divine writ,[58] now barter it away for error, and want you [too] to lose your way? ‹44›
But God knows best who are your enemies: and none can befriend as God does, and none can give succour as God does. ‹45›
Among those of the Jewish faith there are some who distort the meaning of the [revealed] words, taking them out of their context and saying, [as it were,] "We have heard, but we disobey," and, "Hear without hearkening,"[59] and, "Hearken thou unto us, [O Muḥammad]" – thus making a play with their tongues, and implying that the [true] Faith is false.[60] And had they but said, "We have heard, and we pay heed," and "Hear [us], and have patience with us," it would indeed have been for their own good, and more upright: but God has rejected them because of their refusal to acknowledge the truth – for it is in but few things that they believe.[61] ‹46›
O you who have been granted revelation [aforetime]! Believe in what We have [now] bestowed from on high in confirmation of whatever [of the truth] you already possess, lest We efface your hopes and bring them to an end[62] – or We reject them just as We rejected those people who broke the Sabbath: for God's will is always done.[63] ‹47›

أَلَمْ تَرَ إِلَى ٱلَّذِينَ أُوتُوا۟ نَصِيبًا مِّنَ ٱلْكِتَـٰبِ يَشْتَرُونَ ٱلضَّلَـٰلَةَ وَيُرِيدُونَ
أَن تَضِلُّوا۟ ٱلسَّبِيلَ ﴿٤٤﴾ وَٱللَّهُ أَعْلَمُ بِأَعْدَآئِكُمْ وَكَفَىٰ بِٱللَّهِ وَلِيًّا وَكَفَىٰ
بِٱللَّهِ نَصِيرًا ﴿٤٥﴾ مِّنَ ٱلَّذِينَ هَادُوا۟ يُحَرِّفُونَ ٱلْكَلِمَ عَن مَّوَاضِعِهِۦ
وَيَقُولُونَ سَمِعْنَا وَعَصَيْنَا وَٱسْمَعْ غَيْرَ مُسْمَعٍ وَرَٰعِنَا لَيًّا بِأَلْسِنَتِهِمْ وَطَعْنًا
فِى ٱلدِّينِ وَلَوْ أَنَّهُمْ قَالُوا۟ سَمِعْنَا وَأَطَعْنَا وَٱسْمَعْ وَٱنظُرْنَا لَكَانَ خَيْرًا لَّهُمْ
وَأَقْوَمَ وَلَـٰكِن لَّعَنَهُمُ ٱللَّهُ بِكُفْرِهِمْ فَلَا يُؤْمِنُونَ إِلَّا قَلِيلًا ﴿٤٦﴾ يَـٰٓأَيُّهَا
ٱلَّذِينَ أُوتُوا۟ ٱلْكِتَـٰبَ ءَامِنُوا۟ بِمَا نَزَّلْنَا مُصَدِّقًا لِّمَا مَعَكُم مِّن قَبْلِ أَن
نَّطْمِسَ وُجُوهًا فَنَرُدَّهَا عَلَىٰٓ أَدْبَارِهَآ أَوْ نَلْعَنَهُمْ كَمَا لَعَنَّآ أَصْحَـٰبَ
ٱلسَّبْتِ وَكَانَ أَمْرُ ٱللَّهِ مَفْعُولًا ﴿٤٧﴾

ʾAlam tara ʾilal-ladhīna ʾūtū naṣībam-minal-Kitābi yashtarūnaḍ-ḍalālata wa yurīdūna ʾañ-taḍillus-sabīl. (44) Wal-lāhu ʾaʿlamu biʾaʿdāaʾikum; wa kafā billāhi Waliyyañw-wa kafā billāhi Naṣīrā. (45) Minal-ladhīna hādū yuḥarrifūnal-kalima ʿam-mawāḍiʿihī wa yaqūlūna samiʿnā wa ʿaṣaynā was-maʿ ghayra mus-maʿiñw-wa rāʿinā layyam-biʾalsinatihim wa ṭaʿnañ-fid-dīn. Wa law ʾannahum qālū samiʿnā wa aṭaʿnā was-maʿ wañ-ẓurnā lakāna khayral-lahum wa ʾaqwama wa lākil-laʿanahumul-lāhu bikufrihim falā yuʾminūna ʾillā qalīlā. (46) Yāa ʾayyuhal-ladhīna ʾūtul-Kitāba ʾāminū bimā nazzalnā muṣaddiqal-limā maʿakum-miñ-qabli ʾañ-naṭmisa wujūhañ-fanaruddahā ʿalāa ʾadbārihāa ʾaw nalʿanahum kamā laʿannāa ʾaṣḥābas-sabt. Wa kāna ʾamrul-lāhi mafʿūlā. (47)

58 The people referred to are the followers of the Bible. Thus, after having touched in the preceding verse upon the question of prayer, the Qurʾān resumes its cardinal theme: man's responsibility for his actions and, in particular, for the manner in which he responds to the guidance offered to him through God's revelations.

59 Cf. 2 : 93. The figure of speech "hear without hearkening" addressed, as it were, by the Jews to themselves, describes their attitude towards both their own scriptures and the message of the Qurʾān.

60 Lit., "making a thrust (*ṭaʿn*) against the Faith" – i.e., attributing to it a fundamental defect. The saying "Hearken *thou* unto us" is meant to convey the conviction of the Jews that they had nothing to learn from the teaching propounded by the Prophet Muḥammad, and that he should rather defer to *their* views on religious matters. See, in this connection, their assertion, "Our hearts are already full of knowledge", in 2 : 88.

61 See *sūrah* 2, note 74.

62 Lit., "lest We obliterate the faces" – i.e., that towards which one turns, or that which one faces, with expectation (ʿAbduh in *Manār* V, 144 ff.) – "and bring them back to their ends". It is to be noted that the term *dubur* (of which *adbār* is the plural) does not always signify the "back" of a thing – as most of the translators assume – but often stands for its "last part" or "end" (cf. Lane III, 846).

63 This is an allusion to the story of the Sabbath-breakers (lit., "the people of the Sabbath") referred to in 2 : 65 and fully explained in 7 : 163-166.

إِنَّ ٱللَّهَ لَا يَغْفِرُ أَن يُشْرَكَ بِهِۦ وَيَغْفِرُ مَا دُونَ ذَٰلِكَ لِمَن يَشَآءُ ۚ وَمَن
يُشْرِكْ بِٱللَّهِ فَقَدِ ٱفْتَرَىٰٓ إِثْمًا عَظِيمًا ﴿48﴾ أَلَمْ تَرَ إِلَى ٱلَّذِينَ يُزَكُّونَ
أَنفُسَهُم ۚ بَلِ ٱللَّهُ يُزَكِّى مَن يَشَآءُ وَلَا يُظْلَمُونَ فَتِيلًا ﴿49﴾ ٱنظُرْ كَيْفَ
يَفْتَرُونَ عَلَى ٱللَّهِ ٱلْكَذِبَ ۖ وَكَفَىٰ بِهِۦٓ إِثْمًا مُّبِينًا ﴿50﴾ أَلَمْ تَرَ إِلَى ٱلَّذِينَ
أُوتُوا۟ نَصِيبًا مِّنَ ٱلْكِتَٰبِ يُؤْمِنُونَ بِٱلْجِبْتِ وَٱلطَّٰغُوتِ وَيَقُولُونَ لِلَّذِينَ
كَفَرُوا۟ هَٰٓؤُلَآءِ أَهْدَىٰ مِنَ ٱلَّذِينَ ءَامَنُوا۟ سَبِيلًا ﴿51﴾ أُو۟لَٰٓئِكَ ٱلَّذِينَ

ʾInnal-lāha lā yaghfiru ʾañy-yushraka bihī wa yaghfiru mā dūna dhālika limañy-yashāaʾ. Wa mañy-yushrik billāhi faqadif-tarāa ʾithman ʿaẓīmā. (48) ʾAlam tara ʾilal-ladhīna yuzakkūna ʾañfusahum. Balil-lāhu yuzakkī mañy-yashāaʾu wa lā yuẓlamūna fatīlā. (49) ʾUñẓur kayfa yaftarūna ʿalal-lāhil-kadhib. Wa kafā bihīi ʾithmam-mubīnā. (50) ʾAlam tara ʾilal-ladhīna ʾūtū naṣībam-minal-Kitābi yuʾminūna biljibti waṭ-ṭāghūti wa yaqūlūna lilladhīna kafarū hāaʾulāaʾi ʾahdā minal-ladhīna ʾāmanū sabīlā. (51) ʾUlāaʾikal-ladhīna

VERILY, God does not forgive the ascribing of divinity to aught beside Him, although He forgives any lesser sin[64] unto whomever He wills: for he who ascribes divinity to aught beside God has indeed contrived an awesome sin.[65] ‹48›

Art thou not aware of those who consider themselves pure?[66] Nay, but it is God who causes whomever He wills to grow in purity; and none shall be wronged by as much as a hair's breadth.[67] ‹49›

Behold how they attribute their own lying inventions to God – than which there is no sin more obvious.[68] ‹50›

Art thou not aware of those who, having been granted their share of the divine writ, [now] believe in baseless mysteries and in the powers of evil,[69] and maintain that those who are bent on denying the truth are more surely guided than those who have attained to faith? ‹51› It is they whom

64 Lit., "anything below that".

65 The continuous stress, in the Qurʾān, on God's transcendental oneness and uniqueness aims at freeing man from all sense of dependence on other influences and powers, and thus at elevating him spiritually and bringing about the "purification" alluded to in the next verse. Since this objective is vitiated by the sin of *shirk* ("the ascribing of divine qualities to aught beside God"), the Qurʾān describes it as "unforgivable" so long as it is persisted in, i.e., unless and until the sinner repents (cf. verses 17 and 18 of this *sūrah*).

66 I.e., the Jews, who consider themselves to be "God's chosen people" and, therefore, *a priori* destined for God's grace, and the Christians, who believe in Jesus' "vicarious atonement" for the sins of mankind. There is also an obvious connection between this observation and the reference to *shirk* in the preceding verse, inasmuch as the Jews and the Christians, while not actually believing in the existence of any deity apart from God, ascribe divine or semi-divine qualities, in varying degrees, to certain human beings: the Christians by their elevation of Jesus to the status of a manifestation of God in human form and their open worship of a hierarchy of saints, and the Jews by their attribution of law-giving powers to the great Talmudic scholars, whose legal verdicts are supposed to override, if need be, any ordinance of the scriptures (cf. in this respect 9 : 31). It goes without saying that this condemnation applies also to those Muslims who have fallen into the sin of worshipping saints and according them something of the reverence which is due to God alone. Consequently, the expression "those who consider themselves pure" comprises, in this context, all who think of themselves as believing in the One God (simply because they do not consciously worship a plurality of deities) but are, nevertheless, guilty of the sin of *shirk* in the deeper sense of this term.

67 According to most of the philological authorities (e.g., *Qāmūs*), a *fatīl* is any "slender thread which one rolls between one's fingers" – a term which is also, but by no means exclusively, applied to the tiny fibre adhering to the cleft of the date-stone (cf. Lane VI, 2334). Idiomatically, it is best rendered as "a hair's breadth". The above passage implies, firstly, that spiritual purity is not the privilege of any particular group or community, and, secondly, that one can become or remain pure only by God's grace, for "man has been created weak" (verse 28 above). See also note 27 on the second paragraph of 53 : 32.

68 Lit., "and this is enough as an obvious sin". This passage refers to various theological statements of an arbitrary nature, such as the Jewish assertion that they are "the chosen people" and, thus, immune from God's condemnation; the Christian doctrine of "vicarious atonement"; the definition of God as a "trinity" with Jesus as its "second person"; and so forth.

69 The word *al-jibt* – rendered by me as "baseless mysteries" – is probably, as the *Lisān al-ʿArab* points out, of non-Arabic origin. It denotes, according to some authorities, "something which is worthless in itself" or "something in which there is no good" (*Qāmūs*, Bayḍāwī); according to others, it signifies "enchantment" (ʿUmar ibn al-Khaṭṭāb, Mujāhid and Shaʿbī, as quoted by Ṭabarī; also *Qāmūs*); others, again, interpret it as "anything that is worshipped

God has rejected: and he whom God rejects shall find none to succour him. ⟨52⟩

Have they, perchance, a share in [God's] dominion?[70] But [if they had], lo, they would not give to other people as much as [would fill] the groove of a date-stone! ⟨53⟩

Do they, perchance, envy other people for what God has granted them out of His bounty?[71] But then, We did grant revelation and wisdom unto the House of Abraham, and We did bestow on them a mighty dominion: ⟨54⟩ and among them are such as [truly] believe in him,[72] and among them are such as have turned away from him.

And nothing could be as burning as [the fire of] hell: ⟨55⟩ for, verily, those who are bent on denying the truth of Our messages We shall, in time, cause to endure fire: [and] every time their skins are burnt off, We shall replace them with new skins, so that they may taste suffering [in full].[73] Verily, God is almighty, wise. ⟨56⟩

But those who attain to faith and do righteous deeds We shall bring into gardens through which running waters flow, therein to abide beyond the count of time; there shall they have spouses pure: and [thus] We shall bring them unto happiness abounding.[74] ⟨57⟩

لَعَنَهُمُ ٱللَّهُ وَمَن يَلْعَنِ ٱللَّهُ فَلَن تَجِدَ لَهُۥ نَصِيرًا ﴿٥٢﴾ أَمْ لَهُمْ نَصِيبٌ مِّنَ
ٱلْمُلْكِ فَإِذًا لَّا يُؤْتُونَ ٱلنَّاسَ نَقِيرًا ﴿٥٣﴾ أَمْ يَحْسُدُونَ ٱلنَّاسَ عَلَىٰ مَآ
ءَاتَىٰهُمُ ٱللَّهُ مِن فَضْلِهِۦ فَقَدْ ءَاتَيْنَآ ءَالَ إِبْرَٰهِيمَ ٱلْكِتَٰبَ وَٱلْحِكْمَةَ
وَءَاتَيْنَٰهُم مُّلْكًا عَظِيمًا ﴿٥٤﴾ فَمِنْهُم مَّنْ ءَامَنَ بِهِۦ وَمِنْهُم مَّن صَدَّ عَنْهُ
وَكَفَىٰ بِجَهَنَّمَ سَعِيرًا ﴿٥٥﴾ إِنَّ ٱلَّذِينَ كَفَرُوا۟ بِـَٔايَٰتِنَا سَوْفَ نُصْلِيهِمْ نَارًا
كُلَّمَا نَضِجَتْ جُلُودُهُم بَدَّلْنَٰهُمْ جُلُودًا غَيْرَهَا لِيَذُوقُوا۟ ٱلْعَذَابَ إِنَّ ٱللَّهَ
كَانَ عَزِيزًا حَكِيمًا ﴿٥٦﴾ وَٱلَّذِينَ ءَامَنُوا۟ وَعَمِلُوا۟ ٱلصَّٰلِحَٰتِ
سَنُدْخِلُهُمْ جَنَّٰتٍ تَجْرِى مِن تَحْتِهَا ٱلْأَنْهَٰرُ خَٰلِدِينَ فِيهَآ أَبَدًا لَّهُمْ
فِيهَآ أَزْوَٰجٌ مُّطَهَّرَةٌ وَنُدْخِلُهُمْ ظِلًّا ظَلِيلًا ﴿٥٧﴾

laᶜanahumul-lāh. Wa mañy yalᶜanil-lāhu falañ-tajida lahū naṣīrā. (52) ᵓAm lahum naṣībum-minal-mulki faᵓidhal-lā yuᵓtūnan-nāsa naqīrā. (53) ᵓAm yaḥsudūnan-nāsa ᶜalā māa ᵓātāhumul-lāhu miñ-faḍlih. Faqad ᵓātaynāa ᵓāla ᵓIbrāhīmal-Kitāba wal-ḥikmata wa ᵓātaynāhum-mulkan ᶜaẓīmā. (54) Faminhum-man ᵓāmana bihī wa minhum-mañ-ṣadda ᶜanhu wa kafā bijahannama saᶜīrā. (55) ᵓInnal-ladhīna kafarū biᵓĀyātinā sawfa nuṣlīhim nārā. Kullamā naḍijat julūduhum-baddalnāhum julūdan ghayrahā liyadhūqul-ᶜadhāb. ᵓInnal-lāha kāna ᶜAzīzan Ḥakīmā. (56) Wal-ladhīna ᵓāmanū wa ᶜamiluṣ-ṣāliḥāti sanudkhiluhum jannātiñ-tajrī miñ-taḥtihal-ᵓanhāru khālidīna fīhāa ᵓabadā. Lahum fīhāa ᵓazwājum-muṭahharah; wa nudkhiluhum ẓillañ-ẓalīlā. (57)

instead of God" (Zamakhsharī), and consequently apply it also to idols and idol-worship (*Qāmūs, Lisān al-ᶜArab*) and – according to a Tradition quoted by Abū Dāᵓūd – to all manner of superstitious divination and soothsaying as well. Taking all these interpretations into account, *al-jibt* may be defined as "a combination of confusing ideas (*dijl*), fanciful surmises (*awhām*) and fictitious stories (*khurāfāt*)" (*Manār* V, 157) – in other words, abstruse mysteries without any foundation in fact. – As regards the expression "the powers of evil" (*aṭ-ṭāghūt*), it seems to refer here to superstitious beliefs and practices – like soothsaying, foretelling the future, relying on "good" and "bad" omens, and so forth – all of which are condemned by the Qurᵓān. See also *sūrah* 2, note 250.

70 An allusion to the Jewish belief that they occupy a privileged position in the sight of God.

71 I.e., revelation, which – according to the Jews – has been reserved to them alone.

72 I.e., in Abraham – implying that they are faithful to his message. It is to be borne in mind that the Prophet Muḥammad, too, was a direct-line descendant of Abraham, whose message is confirmed and continued in the Qurᵓān.

73 This awesome allegory of suffering in the life to come is obviously meant to bring out the long-lasting nature of that suffering (Rāzī).

74 The primary meaning of *ẓill* is "shade", and so the expression *ẓill ẓalīl* could be rendered as "most shading shade" – i.e., "dense shade". However, in ancient Arabic usage, the word *ẓill* denotes also "a covering" or "a shelter" and, figuratively, "protection" (Rāghib); and, finally, "a state of ease, pleasure and plenty" (cf. Lane V, 1915 f.), or simply "happiness" – and in the combination of *ẓill ẓalīl*, "abundant happiness" (Rāzī) – which seems to agree best with the allegorical implications of the term "paradise".

BEHOLD, God bids you to deliver all that you have been entrusted with unto those who are entitled thereto, and whenever you judge between people, to judge with justice.[75] Verily, most excellent is what God exhorts you to do: verily, God is all-hearing, all-seeing! ‹58›
O you who have attained to faith! Pay heed unto God, and pay heed unto the Apostle and unto those from among you[76] who have been entrusted with authority; and if you are at variance over any matter, refer it unto God and the Apostle,[77] if you [truly] believe in God and the Last Day. This is the best [for you], and best in the end.[78] ‹59›

ART THOU NOT aware of those who claim that they believe in what has been bestowed from on high upon thee, [O Prophet,] as well as in what was bestowed from on high before thee, [and yet] are willing to defer to the rule of the powers of evil[79] – although they were bidden to deny it, seeing that Satan but wants to lead them far astray? ‹60› And so, whenever they are told, "Come unto that which God has bestowed from on high, and unto the Apostle," thou canst see these hypocrites turn away from thee with aversion.[80] ‹61›

۞ إِنَّ ٱللَّهَ يَأۡمُرُكُمۡ أَن تُؤَدُّواْ ٱلۡأَمَٰنَٰتِ إِلَىٰٓ أَهۡلِهَا وَإِذَا حَكَمۡتُم بَيۡنَ
ٱلنَّاسِ أَن تَحۡكُمُواْ بِٱلۡعَدۡلِۚ إِنَّ ٱللَّهَ نِعِمَّا يَعِظُكُم بِهِۦٓۗ إِنَّ ٱللَّهَ كَانَ سَمِيعَۢا
بَصِيرٗا ﴿٥٨﴾ يَٰٓأَيُّهَا ٱلَّذِينَ ءَامَنُوٓاْ أَطِيعُواْ ٱللَّهَ وَأَطِيعُواْ ٱلرَّسُولَ وَأُوْلِي ٱلۡأَمۡرِ
مِنكُمۡۖ فَإِن تَنَٰزَعۡتُمۡ فِي شَيۡءٖ فَرُدُّوهُ إِلَى ٱللَّهِ وَٱلرَّسُولِ إِن كُنتُمۡ تُؤۡمِنُونَ بِٱللَّهِ
وَٱلۡيَوۡمِ ٱلۡأٓخِرِۚ ذَٰلِكَ خَيۡرٞ وَأَحۡسَنُ تَأۡوِيلًا ﴿٥٩﴾ أَلَمۡ تَرَ إِلَى ٱلَّذِينَ يَزۡعُمُونَ
أَنَّهُمۡ ءَامَنُواْ بِمَآ أُنزِلَ إِلَيۡكَ وَمَآ أُنزِلَ مِن قَبۡلِكَ يُرِيدُونَ أَن يَتَحَاكَمُوٓاْ إِلَى
ٱلطَّٰغُوتِ وَقَدۡ أُمِرُوٓاْ أَن يَكۡفُرُواْ بِهِۦۖ وَيُرِيدُ ٱلشَّيۡطَٰنُ أَن يُضِلَّهُمۡ
ضَلَٰلَۢا بَعِيدٗا ﴿٦٠﴾ وَإِذَا قِيلَ لَهُمۡ تَعَالَوۡاْ إِلَىٰ مَآ أَنزَلَ ٱللَّهُ وَإِلَى
ٱلرَّسُولِ رَأَيۡتَ ٱلۡمُنَٰفِقِينَ يَصُدُّونَ عَنكَ صُدُودٗا ﴿٦١﴾

نصف الحزب

۞ ʾInnal-lāha yaʾmurukum ʾañ-tuʾaddul-ʾamānāti ʾilāa ʾahlihā wa ʾidhā ḥakamtum-baynan-nāsi ʾañ-taḥkumū bilʿadl. ʾInnal-lāha niʿimmā yaʿiẓukum-bih. ʾInnal-lāha kāna Samīʿam-Baṣīrā. (58) Yāa ʾayyuhal-ladhīna ʾāmanūu ʾaṭīʿul-lāha wa ʾaṭīʿur-Rasūla wa ʾulil-ʾamri miñkum. Faʾiñ-tanāzaʿtum fī shayʾiñ-faruddūhu ʾilal-lāhi war-Rasūli ʾiñ-kuñtum tuʾminūna billāhi wal-Yawmil-ʾĀkhir. Dhālika khayruñw-wa ʾaḥsanu taʾwīlā. (59) ʾAlam tara ʾilal-ladhīna yazʿumūna ʾannahum ʾāmanū bimāa ʾuñzila ʾilayka wa māa ʾuñzila miñ-qablika yurīdūna ʾañy-yataḥākamūu ʾilaṭ-ṭāghūti wa qad ʾumirūu ʾañy-yakfurū bihī wa yurīdush-Shayṭānu ʾañy-yuḍillahum ḍalālam-baʿīdā. (60) Wa ʾidhā qīla lahum taʿālaw ʾilā māa ʾañzalal-lāhu wa ʾilar-Rasūli raʾaytal-munāfiqīna yaṣuddūna ʿañka ṣudūdā. (61)

75 I.e., in the judicial sense, as well as in the sense of judging other people's motives, attitudes and behaviour. – The term *amānah* denotes anything one has been entrusted with, be it in the physical or moral sense (Rāzī). If one reads this ordinance in the context of the verses that precede and follow it, it becomes obvious that it relates to the message or – in view of the plural form *amānāt* – to the truths which have been conveyed to the believers by means of the divine writ, and which they must regard as a sacred trust, to be passed on to "those who are entitled thereto" – i.e., to all mankind, for whom the message of the Qurʾān has been intended. This, of course, does not preclude the ordinance from having a wider scope as well – that is, from its being applied to any material object or moral responsibility which may have been entrusted to a believer – and, in particular, to the exercise of worldly power and political sovereignty by the Muslim community or a Muslim state, to which the next verse refers.

76 I.e., from among the believers.

77 I.e., to the Qurʾān and to the *sunnah* (the sayings and the practice) of the Prophet. See also verse 65 of this *sūrah*.

78 Read in conjunction with 3 : 26, which speaks of God as "the Lord of all dominion" – and therefore the ultimate source of all moral and political authority – the above passage lays down a fundamental rule of conduct for the individual believer as well as the conceptual basis for the conduct of the Islamic state. Political power is held in trust (*amānah*) from God; and His will, as manifested in the ordinances comprising the Law of Islam, is the real source of all sovereignty. The stress, in this context, on "those *from among you* who have been entrusted with authority" makes it clear that the holders of authority (*ūlu 'l-amr*) in an Islamic state must be Muslims.

79 Lit., "who summon one another to the judgment [or "rule"] of the powers of evil (*aṭ-ṭāghūt*): an allusion to people like those mentioned in verse 51 above, who, by their deference to what the Qurʾān describes as *aṭ-ṭāghūt* (see *sūrah* 2, note 250), nullify all the good that they could derive from guidance through revelation.

80 The classical commentators see in verses 60-64 a reference to the hypocrites of Medina who, at the time of the

But how [will they fare] when calamity befalls them [on the Day of Judgment] because of what they have wrought in this world[81] – whereupon they will come to thee, swearing by God, "Our aim was but to do good, and to bring about harmony"?[82] ⟨62⟩

As for them – God knows all that is in their hearts; so leave them alone, and admonish them, and speak unto them about themselves in a gravely searching manner: ⟨63⟩ for We have never sent any apostle save that he should be heeded by God's leave.[83] If, then, after having sinned against themselves, they would but come round to thee and ask God to forgive them – with the Apostle, too, praying that they be forgiven – they would assuredly find that God is an acceptor of repentance, a dispenser of grace. ⟨64⟩

But nay, by thy Sustainer! They do not [really] believe unless they make thee [O Prophet] a judge of all on which they disagree among themselves, and then find in their hearts no bar to an acceptance of thy decision and give themselves up [to it] in utter self-surrender.[84] ⟨65⟩

فَكَيْفَ إِذَآ أَصَابَتْهُم مُّصِيبَةٌۢ بِمَا قَدَّمَتْ أَيْدِيهِمْ ثُمَّ جَآءُوكَ يَحْلِفُونَ بِٱللَّهِ إِنْ أَرَدْنَآ إِلَّآ إِحْسَٰنًا وَتَوْفِيقًا ۝ أُو۟لَٰٓئِكَ ٱلَّذِينَ يَعْلَمُ ٱللَّهُ مَا فِى قُلُوبِهِمْ فَأَعْرِضْ عَنْهُمْ وَعِظْهُمْ وَقُل لَّهُمْ فِىٓ أَنفُسِهِمْ قَوْلًۢا بَلِيغًا ۝ وَمَآ أَرْسَلْنَا مِن رَّسُولٍ إِلَّا لِيُطَاعَ بِإِذْنِ ٱللَّهِ وَلَوْ أَنَّهُمْ إِذ ظَّلَمُوٓا۟ أَنفُسَهُمْ جَآءُوكَ فَٱسْتَغْفَرُوا۟ ٱللَّهَ وَٱسْتَغْفَرَ لَهُمُ ٱلرَّسُولُ لَوَجَدُوا۟ ٱللَّهَ تَوَّابًا رَّحِيمًا ۝ فَلَا وَرَبِّكَ لَا يُؤْمِنُونَ حَتَّىٰ يُحَكِّمُوكَ فِيمَا شَجَرَ بَيْنَهُمْ ثُمَّ لَا يَجِدُوا۟ فِىٓ أَنفُسِهِمْ حَرَجًا مِّمَّا قَضَيْتَ وَيُسَلِّمُوا۟ تَسْلِيمًا ۝

Fakayfa ʾidhāa ʾaṣābat-hum-muṣībatum-bimā qaddamat ʾaydīhim thumma jāaʾūka yaḥlifūna billāhi ʾin ʾaradnāa ʾillāa ʾiḥsānanw-wa tawfīqā. ۝ ʾUlāaʾikal-ladhīna yaʿlamul-lāhu mā fī qulūbihim faʾaʿriḍ ʿanhum wa ʿiẓhum wa qul-lahum fīi ʾañfusihim qawlam-balīghā. ۝ Wa māa ʾarsalnā mir-Rasūlin ʾillā liyuṭāʿa biʾidhnil-lāh. Wa law ʾannahum ʾiẓ-ẓalamūu ʾañfusahum jāaʾūka fastagh-farul-lāha was-taghfara lahumur-Rasūlu lawajadul-lāha Tawwābar-Raḥīmā. ۝ Falā wa Rabbika lā yuʾminūna ḥattā yuḥakkimūka fīmā shajara baynahum thumma lā yajidū fīi ʾañfusihim ḥarajam-mimmā qaḍayta wa yusallimū taslīmā. ۝

Prophet, outwardly professed to be his followers but did not really believe in his teachings. It seems to me, however, that this passage goes far beyond the possible historical occasion of its revelation, inasmuch as it touches upon an often-encountered psychological problem of faith. People who are not fully convinced that there exists a reality beyond the reach of human perception (*al-ghayb*, in the sense explained in *sūrah* 2, note 3) find it, as a rule, difficult to dissociate their ethical views from their personal predilections and morally questionable desires – with the result that they are only too often "willing to defer to what the powers of evil tell them". Although they may half-heartedly concede that some of the moral teachings based on revelation (in this case, the Qurʾān) contain "certain verities", they instinctively recoil from those teachings whenever they conflict with what their own idiosyncrasies represent to them as desirable: and so they become guilty of hypocrisy in the deepest, religious connotation of this word.

81 Lit., "what their hands have sent ahead": an allusion to their ambivalent attitude and the confusion which it may have created in others.

82 I.e., they will plead that their aim was no more than a harmonization of the Qurʾanic ethics with a "humanistic" (that is, man-centred) world-view: a plea which the Qurʾān implicitly rejects as being hypocritical and self-deceptive (cf. 2 : 11-12). As regards the phrase "whereupon they will come to thee", see verse 41 of this *sūrah*.

83 The expression "by God's leave" is to be understood, in this context, as "with God's help" or "by God's grace" (Zamakhsharī, Rāzī). As so often in the Qurʾān, the sudden change, within one and the same sentence, from the pronoun "We" or "I" to "He", or from "We" to "God", is meant to impress upon the listener or reader of the Qurʾān the fact that God is not a "person" but an all-embracing Power that cannot be defined or even adequately referred to within the limited range of any human language.

84 This verse lays down in an unequivocal manner the obligation of every Muslim to submit to the ordinances which the Prophet, under divine inspiration, promulgated with a view to exemplifying the message of the Qurʾān and enabling the believers to apply it to actual situations. These ordinances constitute what is described as the *sunnah* (lit., "way") of the Prophet Muḥammad, and have (whenever they are authenticated beyond any possibility of doubt) full legal force side by side with the Qurʾān: see verse 80 of this *sūrah*.

Yet if We were to ordain for them,[85] "Lay down your lives," or, "Forsake your homelands," only a very few of them would do it[86] – although, if they did what they are admonished to do, it would indeed be for their own good and apt to strengthen them greatly [in faith], ‹66› whereupon We should indeed grant them, out of Our grace, a mighty reward, ‹67› and indeed guide them onto a straight way. ‹68›

For, all who pay heed unto God and the Apostle shall be among those upon whom God has bestowed His blessings: the prophets, and those who never deviated from the truth, and those who [with their lives] bore witness to the truth, and the righteous ones: and how goodly a company are these! ‹69›

Such is the bounty of God – and none has the knowledge which God has. ‹70›

O YOU who have attained to faith! Be fully prepared against danger, whether you go to war in small groups or all together.[87] ‹71› And, behold, there are indeed among you such as would lag behind, and then, if calamity befalls you, say, "God has bestowed His favour upon me in that I was not present with them!" ‹72› But if good fortune comes to you from God, such a person[88] is sure to say – just as if there had never been any question of love between you and him: – "Oh, would that I had been with them, and thus had a [share in their] mighty triumph!" ‹73›

وَلَوْ أَنَّا كَتَبْنَا عَلَيْهِمْ أَنِ اقْتُلُوٓا۟ أَنفُسَكُمْ أَوِ اخْرُجُوا۟ مِن دِيَـٰرِكُم مَّا فَعَلُوهُ إِلَّا
قَلِيلٌ مِّنْهُمْ وَلَوْ أَنَّهُمْ فَعَلُوا۟ مَا يُوعَظُونَ بِهِۦ لَكَانَ خَيْرًا لَّهُمْ وَأَشَدَّ تَثْبِيتًا (66) وَإِذًا
لَّـَٔاتَيْنَـٰهُم مِّن لَّدُنَّآ أَجْرًا عَظِيمًا (67) وَلَهَدَيْنَـٰهُمْ صِرَٰطًا مُّسْتَقِيمًا (68) وَمَن
يُطِعِ اللَّهَ وَالرَّسُولَ فَأُو۟لَـٰٓئِكَ مَعَ الَّذِينَ أَنْعَمَ اللَّهُ عَلَيْهِم مِّنَ النَّبِيِّـۧنَ وَالصِّدِّيقِينَ
وَالشُّهَدَآءِ وَالصَّـٰلِحِينَ وَحَسُنَ أُو۟لَـٰٓئِكَ رَفِيقًا (69) ذَٰلِكَ الْفَضْلُ مِنَ اللَّهِ وَكَفَىٰ
بِاللَّهِ عَلِيمًا (70) يَـٰٓأَيُّهَا الَّذِينَ ءَامَنُوا۟ خُذُوا۟ حِذْرَكُمْ فَانفِرُوا۟ ثُبَاتٍ أَوِ انفِرُوا۟
جَمِيعًا (71) وَإِنَّ مِنكُمْ لَمَن لَّيُبَطِّئَنَّ فَإِنْ أَصَـٰبَتْكُم مُّصِيبَةٌ قَالَ قَدْ أَنْعَمَ اللَّهُ
عَلَىَّ إِذْ لَمْ أَكُن مَّعَهُمْ شَهِيدًا (72) وَلَئِنْ أَصَـٰبَكُمْ فَضْلٌ مِّنَ اللَّهِ لَيَقُولَنَّ كَأَن لَّمْ
تَكُنۢ بَيْنَكُمْ وَبَيْنَهُۥ مَوَدَّةٌ يَـٰلَيْتَنِى كُنتُ مَعَهُمْ فَأَفُوزَ فَوْزًا عَظِيمًا (73)

Wa law ʾannā katabnā ʿalayhim ʾaniq-tulūu ʾanfusakum ʾawikh-rujū min-diyārikum-mā faʿalūhu ʾillā qalīlum-minhum; wa law ʾannahum faʿalū mā yūʿaẓūna bihī lakāna khayral-lahum wa ʾashadda tathbītā. (66) Wa ʾidhal-laʾataynāhum-mil-ladunnāa ʾajran ʿaẓīmā. (67) Wa lahadaynāhum ṣirāṭam-mustaqīmā. (68) Wa many-yuṭiʿil-lāha war-Rasūla faʾulāaʾika maʿal-ladhīna ʾanʿamal-lāhu ʿalayhim-minan-Nabiyyīna waṣ-ṣiddīqīna wash-shuhadāaʾi waṣ-ṣāliḥīna wa ḥasuna ʾulāaʾika rafīqā. (69) Dhālikal-faḍlu minal-lāhi wa kafā bil-lāhi ʿAlīmā. (70) Yāa ʾayyuhal-ladhīna ʾāmanū khudhū ḥidhrakum fanfirū thubātin ʾawinfirū jamīʿā. (71) Wa ʾinna minkum la-mal-layubaṭṭiʾanna faʾin ʾaṣābatkum-muṣībatun-qāla qad ʾanʿamal-lāhu ʿalayya ʾidh lam ʾakum-maʿahum shahīdā. (72) Wa laʾin ʾaṣābakum faḍlum-minal-lāhi layaqūlanna kaʾal-lam takum-baynakum wa baynahū mawaddatuny-yālaytanī kuntu maʿahum faʾafūza fawzan ʿaẓīmā. (73)

85 I.e., by means of the God-inspired commands issued by the Prophet (see preceding note).

86 Lit., "they would not do it, save for a few of them": the pronoun obviously relates to the half-hearted, who are not prepared to undergo the sacrifices which their faith demands of them. The reference to laying down one's life in the defence of faith and freedom and, if necessary, abandoning one's homeland, introduces, as it were, the long passage beginning with verse 71, which deals with fighting in God's cause.

87 Lit., "and then go forth, [be it] in small detachments or all together" – the latter expression applying to what nowadays is called "total war". The term *ḥidhr* connotes not merely an effort to guard oneself against imminent danger but also the making of all necessary preparations with regard to (in this context) military organization, equipment, etc. The problem of war as such arises from the principles of ideological statehood postulated in verse 59 of this *sūrah*. Since the Muslims are expected to organize their communal life within the framework of a state based on the ideological premises laid down in the Qurʾān, they must be prepared for hostility on the part of groups or nations opposed to the world-view and the social system of Islam and, conceivably, bent on its destruction: consequently, the concept of a defensive war in God's cause (*jihād*) plays a very prominent role in the socio-political scheme of Islam and is frequently alluded to throughout the Qurʾān.

88 Lit., "he".

ثلاثة ارباع الحزب

۞ فَلْيُقَٰتِلْ فِى سَبِيلِ ٱللَّهِ ٱلَّذِينَ يَشْرُونَ ٱلْحَيَوٰةَ ٱلدُّنْيَا بِٱلْءَاخِرَةِ ۚ وَمَن
يُقَٰتِلْ فِى سَبِيلِ ٱللَّهِ فَيُقْتَلْ أَوْ يَغْلِبْ فَسَوْفَ نُؤْتِيهِ أَجْرًا عَظِيمًا ﴿٧٤﴾
وَمَا لَكُمْ لَا تُقَٰتِلُونَ فِى سَبِيلِ ٱللَّهِ وَٱلْمُسْتَضْعَفِينَ مِنَ ٱلرِّجَالِ
وَٱلنِّسَآءِ وَٱلْوِلْدَٰنِ ٱلَّذِينَ يَقُولُونَ رَبَّنَآ أَخْرِجْنَا مِنْ هَٰذِهِ ٱلْقَرْيَةِ
ٱلظَّالِمِ أَهْلُهَا وَٱجْعَل لَّنَا مِن لَّدُنكَ وَلِيًّا وَٱجْعَل لَّنَا مِن لَّدُنكَ
نَصِيرًا ﴿٧٥﴾ ٱلَّذِينَ ءَامَنُوا۟ يُقَٰتِلُونَ فِى سَبِيلِ ٱللَّهِ ۖ وَٱلَّذِينَ كَفَرُوا۟
يُقَٰتِلُونَ فِى سَبِيلِ ٱلطَّٰغُوتِ فَقَٰتِلُوٓا۟ أَوْلِيَآءَ ٱلشَّيْطَٰنِ ۖ إِنَّ كَيْدَ
ٱلشَّيْطَٰنِ كَانَ ضَعِيفًا ﴿٧٦﴾ أَلَمْ تَرَ إِلَى ٱلَّذِينَ قِيلَ لَهُمْ كُفُّوٓا۟ أَيْدِيَكُمْ
وَأَقِيمُوا۟ ٱلصَّلَوٰةَ وَءَاتُوا۟ ٱلزَّكَوٰةَ فَلَمَّا كُتِبَ عَلَيْهِمُ ٱلْقِتَالُ إِذَا فَرِيقٌ
مِّنْهُمْ يَخْشَوْنَ ٱلنَّاسَ كَخَشْيَةِ ٱللَّهِ أَوْ أَشَدَّ خَشْيَةً ۚ وَقَالُوا۟ رَبَّنَا لِمَ
كَتَبْتَ عَلَيْنَا ٱلْقِتَالَ لَوْلَآ أَخَّرْتَنَآ إِلَىٰٓ أَجَلٍ قَرِيبٍ ۗ قُلْ مَتَٰعُ ٱلدُّنْيَا قَلِيلٌ
وَٱلْءَاخِرَةُ خَيْرٌ لِّمَنِ ٱتَّقَىٰ وَلَا تُظْلَمُونَ فَتِيلًا ﴿٧٧﴾

Hence, let them fight in God's cause – all who are willing to barter the life of this world for the life to come; for unto him who fights in God's cause, whether he be slain or be victorious, We shall in time grant a mighty reward. «74»

And how could you refuse to fight[89] in the cause of God and of the utterly helpless men and women and children who are crying, "O our Sustainer! Lead us forth [to freedom] out of this land whose people are oppressors, and raise for us, out of Thy grace, a protector, and raise for us, out of Thy grace, one who will bring us succour!" «75»

Those who have attained to faith fight in the cause of God, whereas those who are bent on denying the truth fight in the cause of the powers of evil. Fight, then, against those friends of Satan; verily, Satan's guile is weak indeed![90] «76»

ART THOU NOT aware of those who have been told, "Curb your hands,[91] and be constant in prayer, and render the purifying dues"? But as soon as fighting [in God's cause] is ordained for them, lo, some of them stand in awe of men as one should stand in awe of God – or in even greater awe – and say, "O our Sustainer! Why hast Thou ordained fighting for us? If only Thou hadst granted us a delay for a little while!"

Say; "Brief is the enjoyment of this world, whereas the life to come is the best for all who are conscious of God – since none of you shall be wronged by as much as a hair's breadth. «77»

Falyuqātil fī sabīlil-lāhil-ladhīna yashrūnal-ḥayātad-dunyā bilʾĀkhirah. Wa mañy-yuqātil fī sabīlil-lāhi fa-yuqtal ʾaw yaghlib fasawfa nuʾtīhi ʾajran ʿaẓīmā. (74) Wa mā lakum lā tuqātilūna fī sabīlil-lāhi wal-mustaḍʿafīna minar-rijāli wan-nisāaʾi wal-wildānil-ladhīna yaqūlūna Rabbanāa ʾakhrijnā min hādhihil-qaryatiẓ-ẓālimi ʾahluhā waj-ʿal lanā mil-laduñka waliyyañw-waj-ʿal-lanā mil-laduñka naṣīrā. (75) ʾAlladhīna ʾāmanū yuqātilūna fī sabīlil-lāhi wal-ladhīna kafarū yuqātilūna fī sabīliṭ-ṭāghūti faqātilūu ʾawliyāaʾash-Shayṭāni ʾinna kaydash-Shayṭāni kāna ḍaʿīfā. (76) ʾAlam tara ʾilal-ladhīna qīla lahum kuffūu ʾaydiyakum wa ʾaqīmuṣ-Ṣalāta wa ʾātuz-Zakāta fa-lammā kutiba ʿalayhimul-qitālu ʾidhā farīqum-minhum yakhshawnan-nāsa kakhashyatil-lāhi ʾaw ʾashadda khashyah. Wa qālū Rabbanā lima katabta ʿalaynal-qitāla lawlāa ʾakhkhartanāa ʾilāa ʾajaliñ-qarīb. Qul matāʿud-dunyā qalīluñw-wal-ʾĀkhiratu khayrul-limanit-taqā wa lā tuẓlamūna fatīlā. (77)

89 Lit., "what is amiss with you that you do not fight" – implying that they have no moral excuse for such a refusal.

90 Thus the Qurʾān implies that "evil" is not an independent, esoteric factor of life, but rather a result of man's succumbing to the temptations arising from his own moral weakness and thereby "denying the truth". In other words, the "power" of the negative principle symbolized by Satan has no *intrinsic* reality ("Satan's guile is weak indeed"): it becomes real only through man's wilfully choosing a wrong course of action.

91 I.e., from unrighteous violence, to which man so often inclines. The fact that most people have to be *told* to refrain from violence is contrasted, in the next sentence, with the unwillingness on the part of many of them to expose themselves to physical danger in a *righteous* cause.

Wherever you may be, death will overtake you – even though you be in towers raised high."
Yet, when a good thing happens to them, some [people] say, "This is from God," whereas when evil befalls them, they say, "This is from thee [O fellow-man]!"[92]
Say: "All is from God."
What, then, is amiss with these people that they are in no wise near to grasping the truth of what they are told?[93] ‹78›
Whatever good happens to thee is from God; and whatever evil befalls thee is from thyself.[94]

أَيْنَمَا تَكُونُوا يُدْرِككُّمُ ٱلْمَوْتُ وَلَوْ كُنتُمْ فِى بُرُوجٍ مُّشَيَّدَةٍ ۗ وَإِن تُصِبْهُمْ
حَسَنَةٌ يَقُولُوا هَٰذِهِۦ مِنْ عِندِ ٱللَّهِ ۖ وَإِن تُصِبْهُمْ سَيِّئَةٌ يَقُولُوا هَٰذِهِۦ مِنْ
عِندِكَ ۚ قُلْ كُلٌّ مِّنْ عِندِ ٱللَّهِ ۖ فَمَالِ هَٰٓؤُلَآءِ ٱلْقَوْمِ لَا يَكَادُونَ يَفْقَهُونَ
حَدِيثًا ﴿٧٨﴾ مَّآ أَصَابَكَ مِنْ حَسَنَةٍ فَمِنَ ٱللَّهِ ۖ وَمَآ أَصَابَكَ مِن سَيِّئَةٍ فَمِن
نَّفْسِكَ ۚ وَأَرْسَلْنَٰكَ لِلنَّاسِ رَسُولًا ۚ وَكَفَىٰ بِٱللَّهِ شَهِيدًا ﴿٧٩﴾ مَّن يُطِعِ ٱلرَّسُولَ
فَقَدْ أَطَاعَ ٱللَّهَ ۖ وَمَن تَوَلَّىٰ فَمَآ أَرْسَلْنَٰكَ عَلَيْهِمْ حَفِيظًا ﴿٨٠﴾ وَيَقُولُونَ
طَاعَةٌ فَإِذَا بَرَزُوا مِنْ عِندِكَ بَيَّتَ طَآئِفَةٌ مِّنْهُمْ غَيْرَ ٱلَّذِى تَقُولُ ۖ وَٱللَّهُ
يَكْتُبُ مَا يُبَيِّتُونَ ۖ فَأَعْرِضْ عَنْهُمْ وَتَوَكَّلْ عَلَى ٱللَّهِ ۚ وَكَفَىٰ بِٱللَّهِ وَكِيلًا ﴿٨١﴾

AND WE have sent thee [O Muḥammad] as an apostle unto all mankind: and none can bear witness [thereto] as God does. ‹79› Whoever pays heed unto the Apostle pays heed unto God thereby; and as for those who turn away – We have not sent thee to be their keeper. ‹80›
And they say, "We do pay heed unto thee"[95] – but when they leave thy presence, some of them devise, in the dark of night, [beliefs] other than thou art voicing;[96] and all the while God records what they thus devise in the dark of night. Leave them, then, alone, and place thy trust in God: for none is as worthy of trust as God. ‹81›

ʾAynamā takūnū yudrikkumul-mawtu wa law kuñtum fī burūjim-mushayyadah. Wa ʾiñ-tuṣibhum ḥasanatuñy-yaqūlū hādhihī min ʿiñdil-lāh. Wa ʾiñ-tuṣibhum sayyiʾatuñy-yaqūlū hādhihī min ʿiñdik. Qul kullum-min ʿiñdil-lāh. Famāli hāaʾulāaʾil-qawmi lā yakādūna yafqahūna ḥadīthā. (78) Māa ʾaṣābaka min ḥasanatiñ-faminal-lāhi wa māa aṣābaka miñ-sayyiʾatiñ-famiñ-nafsik. Wa ʾarsalnāka linnāsi Rasūlā. Wa kafā billāhi Shahīdā. (79) Mañy-yuṭiʿir-Rasūla faqad aṭāʿal-lāha wa mañ-tawallā famāa ʾarsalnāka ʿalayhim ḥafīẓā. (80) Wa yaqūlūna ṭāʿatuñ-faʾidhā barazū min ʿiñdika bayyata ṭāaʾifatum-minhum ghayral-ladhī taqūl. Wal-lāhu yaktubu mā yubayyitūna faʾaʿriḍ ʿanhum wa tawakkal ʿalal-lāh. Wa kafā billāhi Wakīlā. (81)

92 I.e., they do not realize that the evil happening may possibly be a consequence of their own actions or their own wrong choice between several courses open to them, but are prone to attribute it to the failings of others.

93 Lit., "something [which they are] told" – i.e., a truth which their own reason as well as the teachings of all the prophets should have made obvious to them.

94 There is no contradiction between this statement and the preceding one that "all is from God". In the world-view of the Qurʾān, God is the ultimate source of all happening: consequently, all good that comes to man and all evil that befalls him flows, in the last resort, from God's will. However, not everything that man regards as "evil fortune" is really, in its final effect, evil – for, "it may well be that you hate a thing the while it is good for you, and it may well be that you love a thing the while it is bad for you: and God knows, whereas you do not know" (2 : 216). Thus, many an apparent "evil" may sometimes be no more than a trial and a God-willed means of spiritual growth through suffering, and need not necessarily be the result of a wrong choice or a wrong deed on the part of the person thus afflicted. It is, therefore, obvious that the "evil" or "evil fortune" of which this verse speaks has a restricted connotation, inasmuch as it refers to evil in the *moral* sense of the word: that is to say, to suffering resulting from the actions or the behaviour of the person concerned, and this in accordance with the natural law of cause and effect which God has decreed for all His creation, and which the Qurʾān describes as "the way of God", (*sunnat Allāh*). For all such suffering man has only himself to blame, since "God does not wrong anyone by as much as an atom's weight" (4 : 40).

95 Lit., "And they say, 'Obedience'" – a reference to the hypocrites of Medina, in the time of the Prophet, and – by implication – the hypocritical "admirers" and half-hearted followers of Islam at all times.

96 I.e., they surreptitiously try to corrupt the message of God's Apostle. The verb *bāta* denotes "he spent the night"; in the form *bayyata* it signifies "he meditated by night [upon something, or upon doing something]", or "he devised [something] by night" (*Lisān al-ʿArab*), i.e., in secrecy, which is symbolized by "the dark of night".

أَفَلَا يَتَدَبَّرُونَ ٱلْقُرْءَانَ وَلَوْ كَانَ مِنْ عِندِ غَيْرِ ٱللَّهِ لَوَجَدُوا۟ فِيهِ ٱخْتِلَٰفًا
كَثِيرًا ﴿٨٢﴾ وَإِذَا جَآءَهُمْ أَمْرٌ مِّنَ ٱلْأَمْنِ أَوِ ٱلْخَوْفِ أَذَاعُوا۟ بِهِۦ وَلَوْ
رَدُّوهُ إِلَى ٱلرَّسُولِ وَإِلَىٰٓ أُو۟لِى ٱلْأَمْرِ مِنْهُمْ لَعَلِمَهُ ٱلَّذِينَ يَسْتَنۢبِطُونَهُۥ
مِنْهُمْ وَلَوْلَا فَضْلُ ٱللَّهِ عَلَيْكُمْ وَرَحْمَتُهُۥ لَٱتَّبَعْتُمُ ٱلشَّيْطَٰنَ إِلَّا
قَلِيلًا ﴿٨٣﴾ فَقَٰتِلْ فِى سَبِيلِ ٱللَّهِ لَا تُكَلَّفُ إِلَّا نَفْسَكَ وَحَرِّضِ ٱلْمُؤْمِنِينَ
عَسَى ٱللَّهُ أَن يَكُفَّ بَأْسَ ٱلَّذِينَ كَفَرُوا۟ وَٱللَّهُ أَشَدُّ بَأْسًا وَأَشَدُّ
تَنكِيلًا ﴿٨٤﴾ مَّن يَشْفَعْ شَفَٰعَةً حَسَنَةً يَكُن لَّهُۥ نَصِيبٌ مِّنْهَا وَمَن يَشْفَعْ
شَفَٰعَةً سَيِّئَةً يَكُن لَّهُۥ كِفْلٌ مِّنْهَا وَكَانَ ٱللَّهُ عَلَىٰ كُلِّ شَىْءٍ مُّقِيتًا ﴿٨٥﴾

**ᵓAfalā yatadabbarūnal-Qurᵓān. Wa law kāna min ᶜiñdi ghayril-lāhi lawajadū fīhikh-tilāfañ-kathīrā. ﴿82﴾
Wa ᵓidhā jāaᵓahum ᵓamrum-minal-ᵓamni ᵓawil-khawfi ᵓadhāᶜū bih. Wa law raddūhu ᵓilar-Rasūli wa ᵓilāa ᵓulil-ᵓamri minhum laᶜalimahul-ladhīna yastambiṭūnahū minhum. Wa lawlā faḍlul-lāhi ᶜalaykum wa raḥmatuhū lattabaᶜtumush-Shayṭāna ᵓillā qalīlā. ﴿83﴾
Faqātil fī sabīlil-lāhi lā tukallafu ᵓillā nafsak. Wa ḥarriḍil-muᵓminīna ᶜasal-lāhu ᵓañy-yakuffa baᵓsal-ladhīna kafarū; wal-lāhu ᵓashaddu baᵓsañw-wa ᵓashaddu tañkīlā. ﴿84﴾
Mañy-yashfaᶜ shafāᶜatan ḥasanatañy-yakul-lahū naṣībum-minhā; wa mañy-yashfaᶜ shafāᶜatañ-sayyiᵓatañy-yakul-lahū kiflum-minhā. Wa kānal-lāhu ᶜalā kulli shayᵓim-Muqītā. ﴿85﴾**

Will they not, then, try to understand this Qurᵓān? Had it issued from any but God, they would surely have found in it many an inner contradiction![97] ⟨82⟩

AND IF any [secret] matter pertaining to peace or war comes within their ken, they[98] spread it abroad – whereas, if they would but refer it unto the Apostle and unto those from among the believers[99] who have been entrusted with authority, such of them as are engaged in obtaining intelligence[100] would indeed know [what to do with] it. And but for God's bounty towards you, and His grace, all but a few of you would certainly have followed Satan. ⟨83⟩

Fight thou,[101] then, in God's cause – since thou art but responsible for thine own self – and inspire the believers to overcome all fear of death.[102] God may well curb the might of those who are bent on denying the truth: for God is stronger in might, and stronger in ability to deter. ⟨84⟩

Whoever rallies to a good cause shall have a share in its blessings;[103] and whoever rallies to an evil cause shall be answerable for his part in it: for, indeed, God watches over everything.[104] ⟨85⟩

97 I.e., the fact that it is free of all inner contradictions – in spite of its having been revealed gradually, over a period of twenty-three years – should convince them that it has not been "composed by Muḥammad" (an accusation frequently levelled against him not only by his contemporaries but also by non-believers of later times), but could only have originated from a supra-human source. See also 25 : 32 and 39 : 23.

98 I.e., the half-hearted followers of Islam spoken of in the preceding verses (Zamakhsharī). The above reference to peace or war – lit., "security or danger (*khawf*)" – is connected, firstly, with the basic principles of statecraft mentioned in verse 59 of this *sūrah* and, secondly, with the discourse on fighting in God's cause beginning with verse 71.

99 Lit., "from among them".

100 Lit., "those from among them who elicit [the truth]", i.e., the special organs of the state entrusted with gathering and evaluating political and military intelligence.

101 Although primarily addressed to the Prophet, the "thou" in this sentence relates to every believer. The above exhortation is to be understood in the context of a war already in progress, and not as an *incitement* to war.

102 The term *ḥaraḍ* signifies "corruption of body or mind" or "corruption in one's conduct", as well as "constant disquietude of mind" (*Qāmūs*). According to Rāghib, the verbal form *ḥarraḍahu* means "he rid him of all *ḥaraḍ*" – analogous to the expression *marraḍahu*, "he rid him of illness (*maraḍ*)". In the two instances where this verb occurs in the Qurᵓān (in this verse as well as in 8 : 65), it has the imperative form: "Render the believers free of all disquietude of mind" or, tropically, "of all fear of death" – and may, thus, be suitably expressed as "inspire the believers to overcome all fear of death". The usual rendering of the phrase *ḥarriḍ al-muᵓminīn* as "urge [or "rouse" or "stir up"] the believers" does not convey the full meaning of the verb *ḥarraḍa*, notwithstanding the fact that it has been suggested by some of the classical philologists (cf. Lane II, 548).

103 Lit., "shall have a share (*naṣīb*) therefrom". Since the term *naṣīb* has here a positive meaning, it can be suitably rendered as "a share in its blessings".

104 The noun *kifl* is derived from the root-verb *kafala*, "he made himself responsible [for a thing]". Ṭabarī explains it in this context as denoting "a share in the responsibility and the sin". The expression *minhā* ("out of it") indicates

But when you are greeted with a greeting [of peace], answer with an even better greeting, or [at least] with the like thereof.[105] Verily, God keeps count indeed of all things. ﴾86﴿

God – save whom there is no deity – will surely gather you all together on the Day of Resurrection, [the coming of] which is beyond all doubt: and whose word could be truer than God's? ﴾87﴿

How, then, could you be of two minds[106] about the hypocrites, seeing that God [Himself] has disowned them because of their guilt?[107] Do you, perchance, seek to guide those whom God has let go astray – when for him whom God lets go astray thou canst never find any way? ﴾88﴿ They would love to see you deny the truth even as they have denied it, so that you should be like them. Do not, therefore, take them for your allies until they forsake the domain of evil[108] for the sake of God; and if they revert to [open] enmity, seize them and slay them wherever you may find them.

And do not take any of them[109] for your ally or giver of succour, ﴾89﴿ unless it be such [of them] as have ties with people to whom you yourselves are bound by a covenant, or such as come unto you

وَإِذَا حُيِّيتُم بِتَحِيَّةٍ فَحَيُّوا۟ بِأَحْسَنَ مِنْهَآ أَوْ رُدُّوهَآ ۗ إِنَّ ٱللَّهَ كَانَ عَلَىٰ كُلِّ
شَىْءٍ حَسِيبًا ﴿٨٦﴾ ٱللَّهُ لَآ إِلَـٰهَ إِلَّا هُوَ ۚ لَيَجْمَعَنَّكُمْ إِلَىٰ يَوْمِ ٱلْقِيَـٰمَةِ لَا رَيْبَ
فِيهِ ۗ وَمَنْ أَصْدَقُ مِنَ ٱللَّهِ حَدِيثًا ﴿٨٧﴾ ۞ فَمَا لَكُمْ فِى ٱلْمُنَـٰفِقِينَ فِئَتَيْنِ
وَٱللَّهُ أَرْكَسَهُم بِمَا كَسَبُوٓا۟ ۚ أَتُرِيدُونَ أَن تَهْدُوا۟ مَنْ أَضَلَّ ٱللَّهُ ۖ وَمَن يُضْلِلِ
ٱللَّهُ فَلَن تَجِدَ لَهُۥ سَبِيلًا ﴿٨٨﴾ وَدُّوا۟ لَوْ تَكْفُرُونَ كَمَا كَفَرُوا۟ فَتَكُونُونَ
سَوَآءً ۖ فَلَا تَتَّخِذُوا۟ مِنْهُمْ أَوْلِيَآءَ حَتَّىٰ يُهَاجِرُوا۟ فِى سَبِيلِ ٱللَّهِ ۚ فَإِن تَوَلَّوْا۟
فَخُذُوهُمْ وَٱقْتُلُوهُمْ حَيْثُ وَجَدتُّمُوهُمْ ۖ وَلَا تَتَّخِذُوا۟ مِنْهُمْ وَلِيًّا وَلَا
نَصِيرًا ﴿٨٩﴾ إِلَّا ٱلَّذِينَ يَصِلُونَ إِلَىٰ قَوْمٍۭ بَيْنَكُمْ وَبَيْنَهُم مِّيثَـٰقٌ أَوْ جَآءُوكُمْ حزب 10

Wa ʾidhā ḥuyyītum-bitaḥiyyatiñ-faḥayyū biʾaḥsana minhāa ʾaw ruddūhā. ʾInnal-lāha kāna ʿalā kulli shayʾin Ḥasībā. ﴾86﴿ ʾAllāhu lāa ʾilāha ʾillā Huwa layajmaʿannakum ʾilā Yawmil-Qiyāmati lā rayba fīh. Wa man ʾaṣdaqu minal-lāhi ḥadīthā. ﴾87﴿ ۞ Famā lakum fil-munāfiqīna fiʾatayni wal-lāhu ʾarkasahum-bimā kasabū. ʾAturīdūna ʾañ-tahdū man ʾaḍallal-lāh. Wa mañy-yuḍlilil-lāhu falañ-tajida lahū sabīlā. ﴾88﴿ Waddū law takfurūna kamā kafarū fatakūnūna sawāaʾañ-falā tattakhidhū minhum ʾawliyāaʾa ḥattā yuhājirū fī sabīlil-lāh. Faʾiñ-tawallaw fakhudhūhum waq-tulūhum ḥaythu wajattumūhum; wa lā tattakhidhū minhum waliyyañw-wa lā naṣīrā. ﴾89﴿ ʾIllal-ladhīna yaṣilūna ʾilā qawmim-baynakum wa baynahum-mīthāqun ʾaw jāaʾūkum

the part played by the transgressor in the evil enterprise, to which the pronoun *hā* ("it") refers.

105 Lit., "greet with better than it, or return it". In the above context, this obviously refers to an offer of peace by people with whom the believers are at war as well as to individual persons who, while possibly belonging to the enemy, have, to all outward appearances, peaceful intentions. In accordance with the injunctions, "if they incline to peace, incline thou to it as well" (8 : 61), and "if they desist [from fighting], then all hostility shall cease" (2 : 193), the believers are obliged to make peace with an enemy who makes it clear that he wants to come to an equitable understanding; similarly, they must show every consideration to individual persons from among the enemies who do not actively participate in the hostilities (see also verse 94 of this *sūrah*).

106 Lit., "two parties".

107 Lit., "seeing that God has thrown them back in result of what they have earned". There are various conjectures, almost all of them of a historical nature, as to the identity of these hypocrites. Some of the commentators think that the verse refers to the hypocrites at Medina in the early years after the *hijrah*; others (e.g., Ṭabarī) prefer the view expressed by Ibn ʿAbbās, according to whom this refers to certain people of Mecca who, before the *hijrah*, outwardly accepted Islam but secretly continued to support the pagan Quraysh. It seems to me, however, that there is no need to search after "historical" interpretations of the above verse, since it can easily be understood in general terms. The preceding verse speaks of God, and stresses His oneness and the obvious truth inherent in His revealed message, as well as the certainty of judgment on Resurrection Day. "How, then," continues the argument, "could you be of two minds regarding the moral stature of people who go so far as to pay lip-service to the truth of God's message and are, nevertheless, not willing to make a sincere choice between right and wrong?"

108 See *sūrah* 2, note 203, as well as note 124 of this *sūrah*.

109 I.e., any of those who have not "forsaken the domain of evil" and are wavering between belief and disbelief.

because their hearts shrink from [the thought of] making war either on you or on their own folk – although, if God had willed to make them stronger than you, they would certainly have made war on you.[110] Thus, if they let you be, and do not make war on you, and offer you peace, God does not allow you to harm them.[111] «90»
You will find [that there are] others who would like to be safe from you as well as safe from their own folk, [but who,] whenever they are faced anew with temptation to evil, plunge into it headlong.[112] Hence, if they do not let you be, and do not offer you peace, and do not stay their hands, seize them and slay them whenever you come upon them: for it is against these that We have clearly empowered you [to make war].[113] «91»

AND IT IS not conceivable that a believer should slay another believer, unless it be by mistake.[114]
And upon him who has slain a believer by mistake there is the duty of freeing a believing soul from bondage and paying an indemnity to the victim's relations,[115] unless they forgo it by way of charity.
Now if the slain, while himself a believer, belonged to a people who are at war with you,[116] [the penance shall be confined to] the freeing of a believing soul from bondage; whereas, if he belonged to a people to whom you are bound by a covenant, [it shall consist of] an indemnity

حَصِرَتْ صُدُورُهُمْ أَن يُقَٰتِلُوكُمْ أَوْ يُقَٰتِلُوا۟ قَوْمَهُمْ ۚ وَلَوْ شَآءَ ٱللَّهُ لَسَلَّطَهُمْ
عَلَيْكُمْ فَلَقَٰتَلُوكُمْ ۚ فَإِنِ ٱعْتَزَلُوكُمْ فَلَمْ يُقَٰتِلُوكُمْ وَأَلْقَوْا۟ إِلَيْكُمُ ٱلسَّلَمَ
فَمَا جَعَلَ ٱللَّهُ لَكُمْ عَلَيْهِمْ سَبِيلًا ﴿٩٠﴾ سَتَجِدُونَ ءَاخَرِينَ يُرِيدُونَ أَن
يَأْمَنُوكُمْ وَيَأْمَنُوا۟ قَوْمَهُمْ كُلَّ مَا رُدُّوٓا۟ إِلَى ٱلْفِتْنَةِ أُرْكِسُوا۟ فِيهَا ۚ فَإِن لَّمْ
يَعْتَزِلُوكُمْ وَيُلْقُوٓا۟ إِلَيْكُمُ ٱلسَّلَمَ وَيَكُفُّوٓا۟ أَيْدِيَهُمْ فَخُذُوهُمْ وَٱقْتُلُوهُمْ حَيْثُ
ثَقِفْتُمُوهُمْ ۚ وَأُو۟لَٰٓئِكُمْ جَعَلْنَا لَكُمْ عَلَيْهِمْ سُلْطَٰنًا مُّبِينًا ﴿٩١﴾ وَمَا كَانَ
لِمُؤْمِنٍ أَن يَقْتُلَ مُؤْمِنًا إِلَّا خَطَـًٔا ۚ وَمَن قَتَلَ مُؤْمِنًا خَطَـًٔا فَتَحْرِيرُ رَقَبَةٍ مُّؤْمِنَةٍ
وَدِيَةٌ مُّسَلَّمَةٌ إِلَىٰٓ أَهْلِهِۦٓ إِلَّآ أَن يَصَّدَّقُوا۟ ۚ فَإِن كَانَ مِن قَوْمٍ عَدُوٍّ لَّكُمْ وَهُوَ
مُؤْمِنٌ فَتَحْرِيرُ رَقَبَةٍ مُّؤْمِنَةٍ ۖ وَإِن كَانَ مِن قَوْمٍ بَيْنَكُمْ وَبَيْنَهُم مِّيثَٰقٌ فَدِيَةٌ

ḥaṣirat ṣudūruhum ʾañy-yuqātilūkum ʾaw yuqātilū qawmahum. Wa law shāaʾal-lāhu lasallaṭahum ʿalaykum falaqātalūkum. Faʾiniʿ-tazalūkum falam yuqātilūkum wa ʾalqaw ʾilaykumus-salama famā jaʿalal-lāhu lakum ʿalayhim sabīlā. (90) Satajidūna ʾākharīna yurīdūna ʾañy-yaʾmanūkum wa yaʾmanū qawmahum kulla mā ruddūu ʾilal-fitnati ʾurkisū fīhā; faʾil-lam yaʿtazilūkum wa yulqūu ʾilaykumus-salama wa yakuffūu ʾaydiyahum fakhudhūhum waq-tulūhum ḥaythu thaqiftumūhum; wa ʾulāaʾikum jaʿalnā lakum ʿalayhim sulṭānam-mubīnā. (91) Wa mā kāna limuʾminin ʾañy-yaqtula muʾminan ʾillā khaṭaʾā. Wa mañ-qatala muʾminañ-khaṭaʾañ-fataḥrīru raqabatim-muʾminatiñw-wa diyatum-musallamatun ʾilāa ʾahlihīi ʾillāa ʾañy-yaṣṣaddaqū. Faʾiñ-kāna miñ-qawmin ʿaduwwil-lakum wa huwa muʾminuñ-fataḥrīru raqabatim-muʾminah. Wa ʾiñ-kāna miñ-qawmim-baynakum wa baynahum-mīthāquñ-fadiyatum-

---

110 Lit., "if God had so willed, He would indeed have given them power over you, whereupon . . .", etc. – implying that only the lack of requisite power, and not true good will, causes them to refrain from making war on the believers.

111 Lit., "God has given you no way against them": a reference to the ordinance laid down in verse 86 above.

112 Lit., "whenever they are returned to temptation (*fitnah*), they are thrown back into it", or, "thrown headlong into it".

113 Lit., "that We have given you clear authority (*sulṭān*)" – a solemn reiteration of the ordinance which permits war only in self-defence (cf. 2 : 190 ff. as well as the corresponding notes 167 and 168).

114 On the strength of this verse, read in conjunction with verse 93, some of the Muʿtazilite scholars are of the opinion that a believer who deliberately kills another believer must be considered an unbeliever (*Rāzī*). This does not, of course, apply to the execution of a death sentence passed in due process of law.

115 Lit., "his people" – i.e., the heirs or dependants of the victim. The "freeing of a believing soul from bondage", mentioned three times in this verse, refers in the first instance to persons who have been taken captive in war (cf. *sūrah* 8, note 72). But see also note 5 on 58 : 3.

116 Lit., "who are hostile to you" – implying that they are in an actual state of war.

to be paid to his relations in addition to the freeing of a believing soul from bondage.[117] And he who does not have the wherewithal shall fast [instead] for two consecutive months.[118]
[This is] the atonement ordained by God: and God is indeed all-knowing, wise. ‹92›
But whoever deliberately slays another believer, his requital shall be hell, therein to abide; and God will condemn him, and will reject him, and will prepare for him awesome suffering. ‹93›
[Hence,] O you who have attained to faith, when you go forth [to war] in God's cause, use your discernment, and do not – out of a desire for the fleeting gains of this worldly life – say unto anyone who offers you the greeting of peace, "Thou art not a believer":[119] for with God there are gains abundant. You, too, were once in the same condition[120] – but God has been gracious unto you. Use, therefore, your discernment: verily, God is always aware of what you do. ‹94›

SUCH of the believers as remain passive[121] – other than the disabled – cannot be deemed equal to those who strive hard in God's cause with their possessions and their lives:[122] God has exalted those who

مُّسَلَّمَةٌ إِلَىٰٓ أَهْلِهِۦ وَتَحْرِيرُ رَقَبَةٍ مُّؤْمِنَةٍ ۖ فَمَن لَّمْ يَجِدْ فَصِيَامُ شَهْرَيْنِ مُتَتَابِعَيْنِ
تَوْبَةً مِّنَ ٱللَّهِ ۗ وَكَانَ ٱللَّهُ عَلِيمًا حَكِيمًا ﴿٩٢﴾ وَمَن يَقْتُلْ مُؤْمِنًا مُّتَعَمِّدًا
فَجَزَآؤُهُۥ جَهَنَّمُ خَٰلِدًا فِيهَا وَغَضِبَ ٱللَّهُ عَلَيْهِ وَلَعَنَهُۥ وَأَعَدَّ لَهُۥ عَذَابًا
عَظِيمًا ﴿٩٣﴾ يَٰٓأَيُّهَا ٱلَّذِينَ ءَامَنُوٓا۟ إِذَا ضَرَبْتُمْ فِى سَبِيلِ ٱللَّهِ فَتَبَيَّنُوا۟ وَلَا تَقُولُوا۟
لِمَنْ أَلْقَىٰٓ إِلَيْكُمُ ٱلسَّلَٰمَ لَسْتَ مُؤْمِنًا تَبْتَغُونَ عَرَضَ ٱلْحَيَوٰةِ ٱلدُّنْيَا فَعِندَ
ٱللَّهِ مَغَانِمُ كَثِيرَةٌ ۚ كَذَٰلِكَ كُنتُم مِّن قَبْلُ فَمَنَّ ٱللَّهُ عَلَيْكُمْ فَتَبَيَّنُوٓا۟ ۚ إِنَّ ٱللَّهَ
كَانَ بِمَا تَعْمَلُونَ خَبِيرًا ﴿٩٤﴾ لَّا يَسْتَوِى ٱلْقَٰعِدُونَ مِنَ ٱلْمُؤْمِنِينَ غَيْرُ أُو۟لِى
ٱلضَّرَرِ وَٱلْمُجَٰهِدُونَ فِى سَبِيلِ ٱللَّهِ بِأَمْوَٰلِهِمْ وَأَنفُسِهِمْ ۚ فَضَّلَ ٱللَّهُ

musallamatun ʾilāa ʾahlihī wa taḥrīru raqabatim-muʾminah. Famal-lam yajid faṣiyāmu shahrayni mutatābiʿayn; tawbatam-minal-lāh. Wa kānal-lāhu ʿAlīman Ḥakīmā. (92) Wa mañy-yaqtul-muʾminam-mutaʿammidañ-fajazāaʾuhū jahannamu khālidañ-fīhā wa ghaḍibal-lāhu ʿalayhi wa laʿanahū wa ʾaʿadda lahū ʿadhāban ʿaẓīmā. (93) Yāa ʾayyuhal-ladhīna ʾāmanūu ʾidhā ḍarabtum fī sabīlil-lāhi fatabayyanū wa lā taqūlū liman ʾalqāa ʾilaykumus-salāma lasta muʾminañ-tabtaghūna ʿaraḍal-ḥayātid-dunyā faʿiñdal-lāhi maghānimu kathīrah. Kadhālika kuñtum-miñ-qablu famannal-lāhu ʿalaykum fatabayyanū. ʾInnal-lāha kāna bimā taʿmalūna Khabīrā. (94) Lā yastawil-qāʿidūna minal-muʾminīna ghayru ʾuliḍ-ḍarari wal-mujāhidūna fī sabīlil-lāhi biʾamwālihim wa ʾañfusihim. Faḍḍalal-lāhul-

117 This relates to cases where the victim is a non-Muslim belonging to a people with whom the Muslims have normal, peaceful relations; in such cases the penalty is the same as that imposed for the killing, under similar circumstances, of a fellow-believer.

118 I.e., in the way prescribed for fasting during the month of Ramaḍān (see 2 : 183-187). This alleviation applies to a person who cannot afford to pay the indemnity and/or purchase the freedom of a slave (Rāzī), or cannot find a slave to be freed, as may be the case in our times (*Manār* V, 337).

119 Sc., "and therefore one of the enemies". This verse prohibits the treating of noncombatants as enemies and using their supposed unbelief as a pretext for plundering them. The injunction "use your discernment" (*tabayyanū*) imposes on the believers the duty of making sure, in every case, whether the persons concerned are actively engaged in hostilities or not.

120 Lit., "thus have you [too] been aforetime". Since the preceding injunction refers to the *whole community,* it would seem that the above clause, too, bears the same implication: namely, a reference to the time when the Muslim community was, because of its weakness and numerical insignificance, at the mercy of enemies endowed with greater power. Thus, the believers are told, as it were: "Remember your erstwhile weakness, and treat the peacefully-minded among your enemies with the same consideration with which you yourselves were once hoping to be treated."

121 Lit., "who sit [at home]" – i.e., who do not participate in the struggle in God's cause, be it physical or moral.

122 The term *mujāhid* is derived from the verb *jahada,* which means "he struggled" or "strove hard" or "exerted himself", namely, in a good cause and against evil. Consequently, *jihād* denotes "striving in the cause of God" in the widest sense of this expression: that is to say, it applies not merely to physical warfare (*qitāl*) but to any righteous struggle in the moral sense as well; thus, for instance, the Prophet described man's struggle against his own passions and weaknesses (*jihād an-nafs*) as the "greatest *jihād*" (Bayhaqī, on the authority of Jābir ibn ʿAbd Allāh).

ٱلْمُجَٰهِدِينَ بِأَمْوَٰلِهِمْ وَأَنفُسِهِمْ عَلَى ٱلْقَٰعِدِينَ دَرَجَةً ۚ وَكُلًّا وَعَدَ ٱللَّهُ
ٱلْحُسْنَىٰ ۚ وَفَضَّلَ ٱللَّهُ ٱلْمُجَٰهِدِينَ عَلَى ٱلْقَٰعِدِينَ أَجْرًا عَظِيمًا ﴿٩٥﴾ دَرَجَٰتٍ
مِّنْهُ وَمَغْفِرَةً وَرَحْمَةً ۚ وَكَانَ ٱللَّهُ غَفُورًا رَّحِيمًا ﴿٩٦﴾ إِنَّ ٱلَّذِينَ تَوَفَّىٰهُمُ
ٱلْمَلَٰٓئِكَةُ ظَالِمِىٓ أَنفُسِهِمْ قَالُوا۟ فِيمَ كُنتُمْ ۖ قَالُوا۟ كُنَّا مُسْتَضْعَفِينَ فِى
ٱلْأَرْضِ ۚ قَالُوٓا۟ أَلَمْ تَكُنْ أَرْضُ ٱللَّهِ وَٰسِعَةً فَتُهَاجِرُوا۟ فِيهَا ۚ فَأُو۟لَٰٓئِكَ
مَأْوَىٰهُمْ جَهَنَّمُ ۖ وَسَآءَتْ مَصِيرًا ﴿٩٧﴾ إِلَّا ٱلْمُسْتَضْعَفِينَ مِنَ ٱلرِّجَالِ
وَٱلنِّسَآءِ وَٱلْوِلْدَٰنِ لَا يَسْتَطِيعُونَ حِيلَةً وَلَا يَهْتَدُونَ سَبِيلًا ﴿٩٨﴾ فَأُو۟لَٰٓئِكَ
عَسَى ٱللَّهُ أَن يَعْفُوَ عَنْهُمْ ۚ وَكَانَ ٱللَّهُ عَفُوًّا غَفُورًا ﴿٩٩﴾

strive hard with their possessions and their lives far above those who remain passive. Although God has promised the ultimate good unto all [believers], yet has God exalted those who strive hard above those who remain passive by [promising them] a mighty reward «95» – [many] degrees thereof – and forgiveness of sins, and His grace; for God is indeed much-forgiving, a dispenser of grace. «96»
Behold, those whom the angels gather in death while they are still sinning against themselves, [the angels] will ask, "What was wrong with you?"[123]
They will answer; "We were too weak on earth."
[The angels] will say; "Was, then, God's earth not wide enough for you to forsake the domain of evil?"[124]
For such, then, the goal is hell – and how evil a journey's end! «97» But excepted shall be the truly helpless – be they men or women or children – who cannot bring forth any strength and have not been shown the right way:[125] «98» as for them, God may well efface their sin – for God is indeed an absolver of sins, much-forgiving. «99»

mujāhidīna biʾamwālihim wa ʾañfusihim ᶜalal-qāᶜidīna darajah. Wa kullañw-waᶜadal-lāhul-ḥusnā; wa faḍḍalal-lāhul-mujāhidīna ᶜalal-qāᶜidīna ʾajran ᶜaẓīmā. (95) Darajātim-minhu wa maghfiratañw-wa raḥmah. Wa kānal-lāhu Ghafūrar-Raḥīmā. (96) ʾInnal-ladhīna tawaffāhumul-Malāaʾikatu ẓālimīi ʾañfusihim qālū fīma kuñtum. Qālū kunnā mus-taḍᶜafīna fil-ʾarḍ. Qālūu ʾalam takun ʾarḍul-lāhi wāsiᶜatañ-fatuhājirū fīhā. Faʾulāaʾika maʾwāhum ja-hannamu wa sāaʾat maṣīrā. (97) ʾIllal-mustaḍᶜafīna minar-rijāli wan-nisāaʾi wal-wildāni lā yastaṭīᶜūna ḥīlatañw-wa lā yahtadūna sabīlā. (98) Faʾulāaʾika ᶜasal-lāhu ʾañy-yaᶜfuwa ᶜanhum; wa kānal-lāhu ᶜAfuwwan Ghafūrā. (99)

123 Lit., "in what [condition] were you?" – i.e., while alive. This refers to people who evade, without valid excuse, all struggle in God's cause.

124 Lit., "was not God's earth wide, so that you could migrate therein?" The term *hijrah* (lit., "exodus"), derived from the verb *hajara* ("he migrated"), is used in the Qurʾān in two senses: one of them is historical, denoting the exodus of the Prophet and his Companions from Mecca to Medina, while the other has a moral connotation – namely, man's "exodus" from evil towards God – and does not necessarily imply the leaving of one's homeland in the physical sense. It is this wider, moral and ethical meaning of the term *hijrah* to which the above passage refers – just as the preceding passage (verses 95-96) referred to "striving hard in God's cause" (*jihād*) in the widest sense of the term, embracing both physical and moral efforts and the sacrifice, if need be, of one's possessions and even one's life. While the physical exodus from Mecca to Medina ceased to be obligatory for the believers after the conquest of Mecca in the year 8 H., the spiritual exodus from the domain of evil to that of righteousness continues to be a fundamental demand of Islam; in other words, a person who does not "migrate from evil unto God" cannot be considered a believer – which explains the condemnation, in the next sentence, of all who are remiss in this respect.

125 Or: "cannot find the [right] way" – implying that they are helplessly confused and cannot, therefore, grasp this basic demand of Islam; or, alternatively, that the message relating to this demand has not been adequately conveyed and explained to them.

And he who forsakes the domain of evil for the sake of God shall find on earth many a lonely road,[126] as well as life abundant. And if anyone leaves his home, fleeing from evil unto God and His Apostle, and then death overtakes him – his reward is ready with God: for God is indeed much-forgiving, a dispenser of grace. ‹100›

AND WHEN you go forth [to war] on earth, you will incur no sin by shortening your prayers[127] if you have reason to fear that those who are bent on denying the truth might suddenly fall upon you:[128] for, verily, those who deny the truth are your open foes. ‹101› Thus, when thou art among the believers[129] and about to lead them in prayer, let [only] part of them stand up with thee, retaining their arms. Then, after they have finished their prayer, let them provide you cover[130] while another group, who have not yet prayed, shall come forward and pray with thee, being fully prepared against danger and retaining their arms: [for] those who are bent on denying the truth would love to see you oblivious of your arms

۞ وَمَن يُهَاجِرْ فِي سَبِيلِ ٱللَّهِ يَجِدْ فِي ٱلْأَرْضِ مُرَٰغَمًا كَثِيرًا وَسَعَةً ۚ وَمَن
يَخْرُجْ مِنۢ بَيْتِهِۦ مُهَاجِرًا إِلَى ٱللَّهِ وَرَسُولِهِۦ ثُمَّ يُدْرِكْهُ ٱلْمَوْتُ فَقَدْ وَقَعَ
أَجْرُهُۥ عَلَى ٱللَّهِ ۗ وَكَانَ ٱللَّهُ غَفُورًا رَّحِيمًا ﴿١٠٠﴾ وَإِذَا ضَرَبْتُمْ فِي ٱلْأَرْضِ
فَلَيْسَ عَلَيْكُمْ جُنَاحٌ أَن تَقْصُرُوا۟ مِنَ ٱلصَّلَوٰةِ إِنْ خِفْتُمْ أَن يَفْتِنَكُمُ ٱلَّذِينَ
كَفَرُوٓا۟ ۚ إِنَّ ٱلْكَٰفِرِينَ كَانُوا۟ لَكُمْ عَدُوًّا مُّبِينًا ﴿١٠١﴾ وَإِذَا كُنتَ فِيهِمْ
فَأَقَمْتَ لَهُمُ ٱلصَّلَوٰةَ فَلْتَقُمْ طَآئِفَةٌ مِّنْهُم مَّعَكَ وَلْيَأْخُذُوٓا۟ أَسْلِحَتَهُمْ فَإِذَا
سَجَدُوا۟ فَلْيَكُونُوا۟ مِن وَرَآئِكُمْ وَلْتَأْتِ طَآئِفَةٌ أُخْرَىٰ لَمْ يُصَلُّوا۟ فَلْيُصَلُّوا۟ مَعَكَ
وَلْيَأْخُذُوا۟ حِذْرَهُمْ وَأَسْلِحَتَهُمْ ۗ وَدَّ ٱلَّذِينَ كَفَرُوا۟ لَوْ تَغْفُلُونَ عَنْ أَسْلِحَتِكُمْ

ربع الحزب

**۞ Wa mañy-yuhājir fī sabīlil-lāhi yajid fil-ʾarḍi
murāghamañ-kathīrañw-wa saʿah. Wa mañy-yakhruj
mim-baytihī muhājiran ʾilal-lāhi wa Rasūlihī thumma yudrik-hul-mawtu faqad waqaʿa ʾajruhū ʿalal-
lāh. Wa kānal-lāhu Ghafūrar-Raḥīmā. ﴿١٠٠﴾ Wa ʾidhā
ḍarabtum fil-ʾarḍi falaysa ʿalaykum junāḥun ʾañ-
taqṣurū minaṣ-Ṣalāti ʾin khiftum ʾañy-yaftinakumul-
ladhīna kafarū. ʾInnal-kāfirīna kānū lakum
ʿaduwwam-mubīnā. ﴿١٠١﴾ Wa ʾidhā kuñta fīhim
faʾaqamta lahumuṣ-Ṣalāta faltaqum ṭāaʾifatum-
minhum-maʿaka wal-yaʾkhudhūu ʾasliḥatahum;
faʾidhā sajadū falyakūnū miñw-warāaʾikum wal-
taʾti ṭāaʾifatun ʾukhrā lam yuṣallū falyuṣallū maʿaka
wal-yaʾkhudhū ḥidhrahum wa ʾasliḥatahum. Wad-
dal-ladhīna kafarū law taghfulūna ʿan ʾasliḥatikum**

126 The word *murāgham* is derived from the noun *ragham* ("dust") and is connected with the idiomatic expression *raghima anfuhu*, "his nose was made to cleave to dust", i.e., he became humbled and forced to do something against his will. Thus, *murāgham* denotes "a road by the taking of which one leaves one's people against their will" (Zamakhsharī), it being understood that this separation from one's familiar environment involves what is described as *murāghamah*, the "breaking off [from another]" or the "cutting off from friendly or living communion" (see Lane III, 1113). All this can best be rendered, in the above context, as "a lonely road" – a metaphor of that heartbreaking loneliness which almost always accompanies the first steps of one who sets forth on his "exodus from evil unto God". (Regarding this latter expression, see note 124 above as well as *sūrah* 2, note 203.)

127 Lit., "the prayer": a reference to the five obligatory daily prayers – at dawn, noon, afternoon, after sunset and late in the evening – which may be shortened and combined (the noon prayer with that of the afternoon, and the sunset prayer with that of the late evening) if one is travelling or in actual danger. While the extension of this permission to peaceful travel has been authorized by the Prophet's *sunnah*, the Qurʾān mentions it only in connection with war situations; and this justifies the interpolation, in the opening sentence, of the words "to war". The prayer described in the next verse – with the congregation praying in shifts – is called *ṣalāt al-khawf* ("prayer in danger").

128 Lit., "might cause you an affliction" – implying, according to almost all the commentators, a sudden attack.

129 Lit., "among them". The "thou" in this sentence refers, primarily, to the Prophet and, by implication, to the leader of every group of believers at war with "those who deny the truth".

130 Lit., "when they have prostrated themselves, let them [i.e., that group] be behind you". This idiomatic expression is not to be taken literally: in classical Arabic usage, the phrase *kāna min warāʾika* (lit., "he was behind thee") signifies "he protected thee" or (in military parlance) "he covered thee", and is not meant to describe the *physical* relative position of the two persons or groups.

and your equipment, so that they might fall upon you in a surprise attack.[131] But it shall not be wrong for you to lay down your arms [while you pray] if you are troubled by rain[132] or if you are ill: but [always] be fully prepared against danger. Verily, God has readied shameful suffering for all who deny the truth! ‹102›
And when you have finished your prayer, remember God – standing and sitting and lying down; and when you are once again secure, observe your prayers [fully]. Verily, for all believers prayer is indeed a sacred duty linked to particular times [of day]. ‹103›
And be not faint of heart when you seek out the [enemy] host. If you happen to suffer pain, behold, they suffer pain even as you suffer it; but you are hoping [to receive] from God what they cannot hope for. And God is indeed all-knowing, wise. ‹104›

BEHOLD, We have bestowed upon thee from on high this divine writ, setting forth the truth, so that thou mayest judge between people in accordance with what God has taught thee.[133] Hence, do not contend with those who are false to their trust, ‹105› but pray God to forgive [them]:[134] behold, God is indeed much-forgiving, a dispenser of grace. ‹106›

وَأَمْتِعَتِكُمْ فَيَمِيلُونَ عَلَيْكُم مَّيْلَةً وَاحِدَةً وَلَا جُنَاحَ عَلَيْكُمْ إِن كَانَ
بِكُمْ أَذًى مِّن مَّطَرٍ أَوْ كُنتُم مَّرْضَىٰٓ أَن تَضَعُوٓاْ أَسْلِحَتَكُمْ وَخُذُواْ
حِذْرَكُمْ إِنَّ ٱللَّهَ أَعَدَّ لِلْكَـٰفِرِينَ عَذَابًا مُّهِينًا ﴿١٠٢﴾ فَإِذَا قَضَيْتُمُ ٱلصَّلَوٰةَ
فَٱذْكُرُواْ ٱللَّهَ قِيَـٰمًا وَقُعُودًا وَعَلَىٰ جُنُوبِكُمْ فَإِذَا ٱطْمَأْنَنتُمْ فَأَقِيمُواْ
ٱلصَّلَوٰةَ إِنَّ ٱلصَّلَوٰةَ كَانَتْ عَلَى ٱلْمُؤْمِنِينَ كِتَـٰبًا مَّوْقُوتًا ﴿١٠٣﴾ وَلَا تَهِنُواْ
فِى ٱبْتِغَآءِ ٱلْقَوْمِ إِن تَكُونُواْ تَأْلَمُونَ فَإِنَّهُمْ يَأْلَمُونَ كَمَا تَأْلَمُونَ
وَتَرْجُونَ مِنَ ٱللَّهِ مَا لَا يَرْجُونَ وَكَانَ ٱللَّهُ عَلِيمًا حَكِيمًا ﴿١٠٤﴾ إِنَّآ أَنزَلْنَآ
إِلَيْكَ ٱلْكِتَـٰبَ بِٱلْحَقِّ لِتَحْكُمَ بَيْنَ ٱلنَّاسِ بِمَآ أَرَىٰكَ ٱللَّهُ وَلَا تَكُن
لِّلْخَآئِنِينَ خَصِيمًا ﴿١٠٥﴾ وَٱسْتَغْفِرِ ٱللَّهَ إِنَّ ٱللَّهَ كَانَ غَفُورًا رَّحِيمًا ﴿١٠٦﴾

wa ʾamtiʿatikum fayamīlūna ʿalaykum-maylatañw-wāḥidah. Wa lā junāḥa ʿalaykum ʾiñ kāna bikum ʾadham-mim-maṭarin ʾaw kuñtum-marḍāa ʾañ-taḍaʿūu ʾasliḥatakum; wa khudhū ḥidhrakum. ʾInnal-lāha ʾaʿadda lilkāfirīna ʿadhābam-muhīnā. (102) Faʾidhā qaḍaytumuṣ-Ṣalāta fadhkurul-lāha qiyāmañw-wa quʿūdañw-wa ʿalā junūbikum. Faʾidhaṭ-maʾnañtum faʾaqīmuṣ-Ṣalāh. ʾInnaṣ-Ṣalāta kānat ʿalal-muʾminīna Ktiābam-mawqūtā. (103) Wa lā tahinū fib-tighāaʾil-qawmi ʾiñ-takūnū taʾlamūna faʾinnahum yaʾlamūna kamā taʾlamūna wa tarjūna minal-lāhi mā lā yarjūn. Wa kānal-lāhu ʿAlīman Ḥakīmā. (104) ʾInnā ʾañzalnāa ʾilaykal-Kitāba bilḥaqqi litaḥkuma baynan-nāsi bimāa ʾarākal-lāhu wa lā takul-lilkhāaʾinīna khaṣīmā. (105) Was-taghfiri-lāha ʾinnal-lāha kāna Ghafūrar-Raḥīmā. (106)

131 Lit., "turn upon you in one turning".

132 I.e., if there is a risk of their weapons being damaged by exposure to unfavourable weather conditions, the warriors are exempted from the obligation of keeping their arms with them while praying. This exemption applies, of course, only to such of the soldiers as are in charge of particularly sensitive weapons; and the same applies to the individual cases of illness mentioned in the sequence. It must, however, be remembered that the term *maṭar* (lit., "rain") is often used in the Qurʾān to denote "an affliction": and if we adopt this meaning, the above phrase could be rendered as "if you suffer from an affliction" – thus allowing for a wide range of possible emergencies.

133 The "thou" in this and the following two verses – as well as in verse 113 – refers, on the face of it, to the Prophet; by implication, however, it is addressed to everyone who has accepted the guidance of the Qur'ān: this is evident from the use of the plural "you" in verse 109. Consequently, the attempt on the part of most of the commentators to explain this passage in purely historical terms is not very convincing, the more so as it imposes an unnecessary limitation on an otherwise self-explanatory ethical teaching of general purport.

134 This obviously refers to the hypocrites as well as to the half-hearted followers of the Qurʾān spoken of earlier in this *sūrah*: both are accused of having betrayed the trust reposed in them, inasmuch as they pretend to have accepted the Qurʾanic message but, in reality, are trying to corrupt it (see verse 81). Since they are already aware of what the Qurʾān demands of them and are, nevertheless, bent on evading all real self-surrender to its guidance, there is no use in arguing with them.

Yet do not argue in behalf of those who are false to their own selves:[135] verily, God does not love those who betray their trust and persist in sinful ways. ‹107› They would conceal their doings from men; but from God they cannot conceal them – for He is with them whenever they devise, in the dark of night, all manner of beliefs[136] which He does not approve. And God indeed encompasses [with His knowledge] whatever they do. ‹108›

Oh, you might well argue in their behalf in the life of this world; but who will argue in their behalf with God on the Day of Resurrection, or who will be their defender? ‹109›

Yet he who does evil or [otherwise] sins against himself, and thereafter prays God to forgive him, shall find God much-forgiving, a dispenser of grace: ‹110› for he who commits a sin, commits it only to his own hurt;[137] and God is indeed all-knowing, wise. ‹111› But he who commits a fault or a sin and then throws the blame therefor on an innocent person, burdens himself with the guilt of calumny and [yet another] flagrant sin. ‹112›

And but for God's favour upon thee and His grace, some of those [who are false to themselves] would indeed endeavour to lead thee astray; yet none but themselves do they lead astray. Nor can they harm thee in any way, since God has bestowed upon thee from on high this divine writ and [given thee] wisdom, and has imparted unto thee the knowledge of what thou didst not know. And God's favour upon thee is tremendous indeed. ‹113›

وَلَا تُجَٰدِلْ عَنِ ٱلَّذِينَ يَخْتَانُونَ أَنفُسَهُمْ ۚ إِنَّ ٱللَّهَ لَا يُحِبُّ مَن كَانَ
خَوَّانًا أَثِيمًا ﴿١٠٧﴾ يَسْتَخْفُونَ مِنَ ٱلنَّاسِ وَلَا يَسْتَخْفُونَ مِنَ ٱللَّهِ وَهُوَ مَعَهُمْ
إِذْ يُبَيِّتُونَ مَا لَا يَرْضَىٰ مِنَ ٱلْقَوْلِ ۚ وَكَانَ ٱللَّهُ بِمَا يَعْمَلُونَ مُحِيطًا ﴿١٠٨﴾
هَٰٓأَنتُمْ هَٰٓؤُلَآءِ جَٰدَلْتُمْ عَنْهُمْ فِى ٱلْحَيَوٰةِ ٱلدُّنْيَا فَمَن يُجَٰدِلُ ٱللَّهَ عَنْهُمْ
يَوْمَ ٱلْقِيَٰمَةِ أَم مَّن يَكُونُ عَلَيْهِمْ وَكِيلًا ﴿١٠٩﴾ وَمَن يَعْمَلْ سُوٓءًا أَوْ يَظْلِمْ
نَفْسَهُۥ ثُمَّ يَسْتَغْفِرِ ٱللَّهَ يَجِدِ ٱللَّهَ غَفُورًا رَّحِيمًا ﴿١١٠﴾ وَمَن يَكْسِبْ إِثْمًا
فَإِنَّمَا يَكْسِبُهُۥ عَلَىٰ نَفْسِهِۦ ۚ وَكَانَ ٱللَّهُ عَلِيمًا حَكِيمًا ﴿١١١﴾ وَمَن يَكْسِبْ
خَطِيٓـَٔةً أَوْ إِثْمًا ثُمَّ يَرْمِ بِهِۦ بَرِيٓـًٔا فَقَدِ ٱحْتَمَلَ بُهْتَٰنًا وَإِثْمًا مُّبِينًا ﴿١١٢﴾
وَلَوْلَا فَضْلُ ٱللَّهِ عَلَيْكَ وَرَحْمَتُهُۥ لَهَمَّت طَّآئِفَةٌ مِّنْهُمْ أَن يُضِلُّوكَ وَمَا
يُضِلُّونَ إِلَّآ أَنفُسَهُمْ ۖ وَمَا يَضُرُّونَكَ مِن شَىْءٍ ۚ وَأَنزَلَ ٱللَّهُ عَلَيْكَ ٱلْكِتَٰبَ
وَٱلْحِكْمَةَ وَعَلَّمَكَ مَا لَمْ تَكُن تَعْلَمُ ۚ وَكَانَ فَضْلُ ٱللَّهِ عَلَيْكَ عَظِيمًا ﴿١١٣﴾

Wa lā tujādil ʿanil-ladhīna yakhtānūna ʾañfusahum; ʾinnal-lāha lā yuḥibbu mañ-kāna khawwānan ʾathīmā. (107) Yastakhfūna minan-nāsi wa lā yastakhfūna minal-lāhi wa Huwa maʿahum ʾidh yubayyitūna mā lā yarḍā minal-qawli wa kānal-lāhu bimā yaʿmalūna Muḥīṭā. (108) Hāaʾañtum hāaʾulāaʾi jādaltum ʿanhum fil-ḥayātid-dunyā famañy-yujādilul-lāha ʿanhum Yawmal-Qiyāmati ʾam-mañy-yakūnu ʿalayhim wakīlā. (109) Wa mañy-yaʿmal sūuʾan ʾaw yaẓlim nafsahū thumma yastaghfiril-lāha yajidil-lāha Ghafūrar-Raḥīmā. (110) Wa mañy-yaksib ʾithmañ-faʾinnamā yaksibuhū ʿalā nafsihī wa kānal-lāhu ʿAlīman Ḥakīmā. (111) Wa mañy-yaksib khaṭīiʾatan ʾaw ʾithmañ-thumma yarmi bihī barīiʾañ-faqadiḥ-tamala buhtānañw-wa ʾithmam-mubīnā. (112) Wa lawlā faḍlul-lāhi ʿalayka wa raḥmatuhū lahammaṭ-ṭāaʾifatum-minhum ʾañy-yuḍillūka wa mā yuḍillūna ʾillāa ʾañfusahum wa mā yaḍurrūnaka miñ-shayʾ. Wa ʾañzalal-lāhu ʿalaykal-Kitāba wal-ḥikmata wa ʿallamaka mā lam takuñ-taʿlam. Wa kāna faḍlul-lāhi ʿalayka ʿaẓīmā. (113)

135 I.e., "you may ask God to forgive them, but do not try to find excuses for their behaviour". It is significant that the Qurʾān characterizes a betrayal of trust, whether spiritual or social, as "being false to oneself" – just as it frequently describes a person who deliberately commits a sin or a wrong (*ẓulm*) as "one who sins against *himself*" or "wrongs *himself*" (*ẓalim nafsahu*) – since every deliberate act of sinning damages its author spiritually.

136 Lit., "that of belief" (*min al-qawl*). It is to be remembered that the noun *qawl* does not denote merely "a saying" or "an utterance" (which is its primary significance): it is also employed tropically to denote anything that can be described as a "conceptual statement" – like an opinion, a doctrine, or a belief – and is often used in this sense in the Qurʾān.

137 Lit., "he who earns a sin, earns it only against himself".

نصف الحزب

NO GOOD comes, as a rule, out of secret confabulations – saving such as are devoted to enjoining charity, or equitable dealings, or setting things to rights between people:[138] and unto him who does this out of a longing for God's goodly acceptance We shall in time grant a mighty reward. ‹114›
But as for him who, after guidance has been vouchsafed to him, cuts himself off from the Apostle and follows a path other than that of the believers – him shall We leave unto that which he himself has chosen,[139] and shall cause him to endure hell: and how evil a journey's end! ‹115›

لَّا خَيْرَ فِي كَثِيرٍ مِّن نَّجْوَىٰهُمْ إِلَّا مَنْ أَمَرَ بِصَدَقَةٍ أَوْ مَعْرُوفٍ أَوْ
إِصْلَـٰحٍ بَيْنَ ٱلنَّاسِ وَمَن يَفْعَلْ ذَٰلِكَ ٱبْتِغَآءَ مَرْضَاتِ ٱللَّهِ فَسَوْفَ نُؤْتِيهِ
أَجْرًا عَظِيمًا ﴿114﴾ وَمَن يُشَاقِقِ ٱلرَّسُولَ مِنۢ بَعْدِ مَا تَبَيَّنَ لَهُ ٱلْهُدَىٰ
وَيَتَّبِعْ غَيْرَ سَبِيلِ ٱلْمُؤْمِنِينَ نُوَلِّهِۦ مَا تَوَلَّىٰ وَنُصْلِهِۦ جَهَنَّمَ وَسَآءَتْ
مَصِيرًا ﴿115﴾ إِنَّ ٱللَّهَ لَا يَغْفِرُ أَن يُشْرَكَ بِهِۦ وَيَغْفِرُ مَا دُونَ ذَٰلِكَ لِمَن
يَشَآءُ وَمَن يُشْرِكْ بِٱللَّهِ فَقَدْ ضَلَّ ضَلَـٰلًۢا بَعِيدًا ﴿116﴾ إِن يَدْعُونَ مِن
دُونِهِۦٓ إِلَّآ إِنَـٰثًا وَإِن يَدْعُونَ إِلَّا شَيْطَـٰنًا مَّرِيدًا ﴿117﴾ لَّعَنَهُ ٱللَّهُ وَقَالَ
لَأَتَّخِذَنَّ مِنْ عِبَادِكَ نَصِيبًا مَّفْرُوضًا ﴿118﴾ وَلَأُضِلَّنَّهُمْ وَلَأُمَنِّيَنَّهُمْ
وَلَءَامُرَنَّهُمْ فَلَيُبَتِّكُنَّ ءَاذَانَ ٱلْأَنْعَـٰمِ وَلَءَامُرَنَّهُمْ فَلَيُغَيِّرُنَّ خَلْقَ ٱللَّهِ

VERILY, God does not forgive the ascribing of divinity to aught beside Him, although He forgives any lesser sin unto whomever He wills; for those who ascribe divinity to aught beside God have indeed gone far astray. ‹116› In His stead, they invoke only lifeless symbols[140] – thus invoking none but a rebellious Satan ‹117› whom God has rejected for having said, "Verily, of Thy servants I shall most certainly take my due share, ‹118› and shall lead them astray, and fill them with vain desires; and I shall command them – and they will cut off the ears of cattle [in idolatrous sacrifice]; and I shall command them – and they will corrupt God's creation!"[141]

Lā khayra fī kathīrim-miñ-najwāhum ʾillā man ʾamara biṣadaqatin ʾaw maʿrūfin ʾaw ʾiṣlāḥim-baynan-nās. Wa mañy-yafʿal dhālikab-tighāaʾa marḍātil-lāhi fasawfa nuʾtīhi ʾajran ʿaẓīmā. 114 Wa mañy-yushāqiqir-Rasūla mim-baʿdi mā tabayyana lahul-hudā wa yattabiʿ ghayra sabīlil-muʾminīna nuwallihī mā tawallā wa nuṣlihī jahannama wa sāaʾat maṣīrā. 115 ʾInnal-lāha lā yaghfiru ʾañy-yushraka bihī wa yaghfiru mā dūna dhālika limañy-yashāaʾ. Wa mañy-yushrik billāhi faqad ḍalla ḍalālam-baʿīdā. 116 ʾIñy-yadʿūna miñ-dūnihīi ʾillāa ʾināthañw-wa ʾiñy-yadʿūna ʾillā Shayṭānam-marīdā. 117 Laʿanahul-lāh. Wa qāla laʾattakhidhanna min ʿibādika naṣībam-mafrūḍā. 118 Wa laʾuḍillannahum wa laʾumanniyannahum wa laʾāmurannahum falayubattikunna ʾādhānal-ʾanʿāmi wa laʾāmurannahum falayughayyirunna khalqal-lāh.

138 Lit., "There is no good in much of their secret confabulation (*najwā*) – excepting him who enjoins . . .", etc. Thus, secret talks aiming at positive, beneficial ends – for instance, peace negotiations between states or communities – are excepted from the disapproval of "secret confabulations" because premature publicity may sometimes be prejudicial to the achievement of those ends or may (especially in cases where charity is involved) hurt the feelings of the people concerned.

139 Lit., "him We shall [cause to] turn to that to which he [himself] has turned" – a stress on man's freedom of choice.

140 The term *ināth* (which is the plural of *unthā* "a female being") seems to have been applied by the pre-Islamic Arabs to their idols, probably because most of them were considered to be female. Hence, according to some philologists, the plural form *ināth* signifies "inanimate things" (cf. Lane I, 112). Ibn ʿAbbās, Qatādah and Al-Ḥasan al-Baṣrī explain it as denoting anything that is passive and lifeless (Ṭabarī); this definition has been adopted by Rāghib as well. On the other hand, Ṭabarī mentions a Tradition, on the authority of ʿUrwah, according to which a copy of the Qurʾān in the possession of ʿĀʾishah contained the word *awthān* ("idols") instead of *ināth* (cf. also Zamakhsharī and Ibn Kathīr). The rendering "lifeless symbols" is most appropriate in this context inasmuch as it adequately combines the concept of "idols" with that of "inanimate things".

141 Cf. 7 : 16-17. The pre-Islamic Arabs used to dedicate certain of their cattle to one or another of their idols by cutting off or slitting the ears of the animal, which was thereupon considered sacred (Ṭabarī). In the above context, this reference is used metonymically to describe idolatrous practices, or inclinations, in general. The allusion to

But all who take Satan rather than God for their master do indeed, most clearly, lose all: ‹119› he holds out promises to them, and fills them with vain desires: yet whatever Satan promises them is but meant to delude the mind.[142] ‹120› Such as these have hell for their goal: and they shall find no way to escape therefrom.‹121›

Yet those who attain to faith and do righteous deeds We shall bring into gardens through which running waters flow, therein to abide beyond the count of time: this is, in truth, God's promise – and whose word could be truer than God's? ‹122›

It may not accord with your wishful thinking – nor with the wishful thinking of the followers of earlier revelation[143] – [that] he who does evil shall be requited for it, and shall find none to protect him from God, and none to bring him succour, ‹123› whereas anyone – be it man or woman – who does [whatever he can] of good deeds and is a believer withal, shall enter paradise, and shall not be wronged by as much as [would fill] the groove of a date-stone. ‹124›

And who could be of better faith than he who surrenders his whole being unto God and is a doer of good withal, and follows the creed of Abraham, who turned away from all that is false – seeing that God exalted Abraham with His love?[144] ‹125›

For, unto God belongs all that is in the heavens and all that is on earth; and, indeed, God encompasses everything. ‹126›

وَمَن يَتَّخِذِ ٱلشَّيْطَٰنَ وَلِيًّا مِّن دُونِ ٱللَّهِ فَقَدْ خَسِرَ خُسْرَانًا مُّبِينًا ﴿١١٩﴾
يَعِدُهُمْ وَيُمَنِّيهِمْ ۖ وَمَا يَعِدُهُمُ ٱلشَّيْطَٰنُ إِلَّا غُرُورًا ﴿١٢٠﴾ أُو۟لَٰٓئِكَ مَأْوَىٰهُمْ
جَهَنَّمُ وَلَا يَجِدُونَ عَنْهَا مَحِيصًا ﴿١٢١﴾ وَٱلَّذِينَ ءَامَنُوا۟ وَعَمِلُوا۟ ٱلصَّٰلِحَٰتِ
سَنُدْخِلُهُمْ جَنَّٰتٍ تَجْرِى مِن تَحْتِهَا ٱلْأَنْهَٰرُ خَٰلِدِينَ فِيهَآ أَبَدًا ۖ وَعْدَ
ٱللَّهِ حَقًّا ۚ وَمَنْ أَصْدَقُ مِنَ ٱللَّهِ قِيلًا ﴿١٢٢﴾ لَّيْسَ بِأَمَانِيِّكُمْ وَلَآ أَمَانِىِّ
أَهْلِ ٱلْكِتَٰبِ ۗ مَن يَعْمَلْ سُوٓءًا يُجْزَ بِهِۦ وَلَا يَجِدْ لَهُۥ مِن دُونِ ٱللَّهِ وَلِيًّا
وَلَا نَصِيرًا ﴿١٢٣﴾ وَمَن يَعْمَلْ مِنَ ٱلصَّٰلِحَٰتِ مِن ذَكَرٍ أَوْ أُنثَىٰ وَهُوَ
مُؤْمِنٌ فَأُو۟لَٰٓئِكَ يَدْخُلُونَ ٱلْجَنَّةَ وَلَا يُظْلَمُونَ نَقِيرًا ﴿١٢٤﴾ وَمَنْ أَحْسَنُ
دِينًا مِّمَّنْ أَسْلَمَ وَجْهَهُۥ لِلَّهِ وَهُوَ مُحْسِنٌ وَٱتَّبَعَ مِلَّةَ إِبْرَٰهِيمَ حَنِيفًا ۗ وَٱتَّخَذَ
ٱللَّهُ إِبْرَٰهِيمَ خَلِيلًا ﴿١٢٥﴾ وَلِلَّهِ مَا فِى ٱلسَّمَٰوَٰتِ وَمَا فِى ٱلْأَرْضِ ۚ وَكَانَ
ٱللَّهُ بِكُلِّ شَىْءٍ مُّحِيطًا ﴿١٢٦﴾

Wa mañy-yattakhidhish-Shayṭāna waliyyam-miñ-
dūnil-lāhi faqad khasira khusrānam-mubīnā. ﴾119﴿
Yaᶜiduhum wa yumannīhim; wa mā yaᶜiduhumush-
Shayṭānu ᵓillā ghurūrā. ﴾120﴿ ᵓUlāaᵓika maᵓwāhum ja-
hannamu wa lā yajidūna ᶜanhā maḥīṣā. ﴾121﴿ Wal-
ladhīna ᵓāmanū wa ᶜamiluṣ-ṣāliḥāti sanudkhiluhum
jannātiñ-tajrī miñ-taḥtihal-ᵓanhāru khālidīna fīhāa
ᵓabadā. Waᶜdal-lāhi ḥaqqā. Wa man ᵓaṣdaqu minal-
lāhi qīlā. ﴾122﴿ Laysa biᵓamāniyyikum wa lāa ᵓamāniyyi
ᵓahlil-Kitāb. Mañy-yaᶜmal sūuᵓañy-yujza bihī wa lā
yajid lahū miñ-dūnil-lāhi waliyyañw-wa lā naṣīrā. ﴾123﴿
Wa mañy-yaᶜmal minaṣ-ṣāliḥāti miñ-dhakarin ᵓaw
ᵓuñthā wa huwa muᵓminuñ-faᵓulāaᵓika yadkhulūnal-
jannata wa lā yuẓlamūna naqīrā. ﴾124﴿ Wa man
ᵓaḥsanu dīnam-mimman ᵓaslama wajhahū lillāhi wa
huwa muḥsinuñw-wat-tabaᶜa millata ᵓIbrāhīma
ḥanīfā. Wat-takhadhal-lāhu ᵓIbrāhīma khalīlā. ﴾125﴿ Wa
lillāhi mā fis-samāwāti wa mā fil-ᵓarḍi wa kānal-lāhu
bikulli shayᵓim-Muḥīṭā. ﴾126﴿

Satan's inducing man to "corrupt [lit., "change"] God's creation" has a meaning to which sufficient attention is but seldom paid: Since this creation, and the manner in which it manifests itself, is an expression of God's planning will, any attempt at changing its *intrinsic nature* amounts to corruption. – For the wider meaning of the term *shayṭān* ("Satan" or "satanic force"), see first half of note 16 on 15 : 17.

142 The term *ghurūr* signifies anything by which the mind is beguiled or deceived – for instance, utter self-abandonment to earthly joys, or the absurd belief that there is no limit to man's aims and achievements.

143 An allusion to both the Jewish idea that they are "God's chosen people" and, therefore, assured of His grace in the hereafter, and to the Christian dogma of "vicarious atonement", which promises salvation to all who believe in Jesus as "God's son".

144 Lit., "chose Abraham to be [His] beloved friend (*khalīl*)".

AND THEY will ask thee to enlighten them about the laws concerning women.[145] Say: "God [Himself] enlightens you about the laws concerning them" – for [His will is shown] in what is being conveyed unto you through this divine writ about orphan women [in your charge], to whom – because you yourselves may be desirous of marrying them – you do not give that which has been ordained for them;[146] and about helpless children; and about your duty to treat orphans with equity. And whatever good you may do – behold, God has indeed full knowledge thereof. ‹127›
And if a woman has reason to fear ill-treatment from her husband, or that he might turn away from her, it shall not be wrong for the two to set things peacefully to rights between themselves; for peace is best, and selfishness is ever-present in human souls. But if you do good and are conscious of Him – behold, God is indeed aware of all that you do. ‹128›
And it will not be within your power to treat your wives with equal fairness, however much you may desire it;[147] and so, do not allow yourselves to incline towards one to the exclusion of the other, leaving her in a state, as it were, of having and not having a husband.[148] But if you put things to rights and are conscious of Him – behold,

وَيَسْتَفْتُونَكَ فِي ٱلنِّسَآءِ قُلِ ٱللَّهُ يُفْتِيكُمْ فِيهِنَّ وَمَا يُتْلَىٰ عَلَيْكُمْ فِي
ٱلْكِتَٰبِ فِي يَتَٰمَى ٱلنِّسَآءِ ٱلَّٰتِي لَا تُؤْتُونَهُنَّ مَا كُتِبَ لَهُنَّ وَتَرْغَبُونَ أَن
تَنكِحُوهُنَّ وَٱلْمُسْتَضْعَفِينَ مِنَ ٱلْوِلْدَٰنِ وَأَن تَقُومُوا۟ لِلْيَتَٰمَىٰ بِٱلْقِسْطِ وَمَا
تَفْعَلُوا۟ مِنْ خَيْرٍ فَإِنَّ ٱللَّهَ كَانَ بِهِۦ عَلِيمًا ﴿١٢٧﴾ وَإِنِ ٱمْرَأَةٌ خَافَتْ مِنۢ
بَعْلِهَا نُشُوزًا أَوْ إِعْرَاضًا فَلَا جُنَاحَ عَلَيْهِمَآ أَن يُصْلِحَا بَيْنَهُمَا صُلْحًا
وَٱلصُّلْحُ خَيْرٌ وَأُحْضِرَتِ ٱلْأَنفُسُ ٱلشُّحَّ وَإِن تُحْسِنُوا۟ وَتَتَّقُوا۟ فَإِنَّ ٱللَّهَ
كَانَ بِمَا تَعْمَلُونَ خَبِيرًا ﴿١٢٨﴾ وَلَن تَسْتَطِيعُوٓا۟ أَن تَعْدِلُوا۟ بَيْنَ ٱلنِّسَآءِ وَلَوْ
حَرَصْتُمْ فَلَا تَمِيلُوا۟ كُلَّ ٱلْمَيْلِ فَتَذَرُوهَا كَٱلْمُعَلَّقَةِ وَإِن تُصْلِحُوا۟ وَتَتَّقُوا۟

Wa yastaftūnaka fin-nisāaʾ. Qulil-lāhu yuftīkum fīhinna wa mā yutlā ʿalaykum fil-Kitābi fī yatāman-nisāaʾil-lātī lā tuʾtūnahunna mā kutiba lahunna wa targhabūna ʾañ-tañkiḥūhunna wal-mustaḍʿafīna minal-wildāni wa ʾañ-taqūmū lilyatāmā bilqisṭ. Wa mā tafʿalū min khayriñ-faʾinnal-lāha kāna bihī ʿAlīmā. (127) Wa ʾinim-raʾatun khāfat mim-baʿlihā nushūzan ʾaw ʾiʿrāḍañ-falā junāḥa ʿalayhimāa ʾañy-yuṣliḥā baynahumā ṣulḥañw-waṣ-ṣulḥu khayr. Wa ʾuḥḍiratil-ʾañfusush-shuḥḥ. Wa ʾiñ tuḥsinū wa tat-taqū faʾinnal-lāha kāna bimā taʿmalūna Khabīrā. (128) Wa lañ-tastaṭīʿūu ʾañ-taʿdilū baynan-nisāaʾi wa law ḥaraṣtum falā tamīlū kullal-mayli fatadharūhā kalmuʿallaqah. Wa ʾiñ-tuṣliḥū wa tattaqū

145 I.e., the laws relating to marital relations, women's share in inheritance, etc. A *fatwā* or *iftāʾ* denotes the "clarification of a legal injunction" given in reply to a question; correspondingly, the verb *istaftāhu* means "he asked him to give a legal decision", or "to enlighten him about a [particular] law". Since the laws alluded to in the above passage have already been dealt with early in this *sūrah*, the repeated reference to them is meant to stress the great importance of the problems involved, as well as the responsibility which men bear towards their physiologically weaker counterparts. In accordance with the system prevailing throughout the Qurʾān, a lengthy passage dealing with purely moral or ethical questions is usually – as in the present case – followed by verses relating to social legislation, and this with a view to bringing out the intimate connection between man's spiritual life and his social behaviour.

146 Cf. verse 3 of this *sūrah*, "If you have reason to fear that you might not act equitably towards orphans . . .", and ʿĀʾishah's explanation quoted in the corresponding note 3.

147 This refers to cases where a man has more than one wife – a permission which is conditional upon his determination and ability to "treat them with equal fairness", as laid down in verse 3 of this *sūrah*. Since a man who is fully conscious of his moral responsibility might feel that he is committing a sin if he loves one of his wives more than the other (or others), the above verse provides a "judicial enlightenment" on this point by making it clear that *feelings* are beyond a human being's control: in other words, that the required equality of treatment relates only to outward behaviour towards and practical dealings with one's wives. However, in view of the fact that a man's behaviour towards another person is, in the long run, almost inevitably influenced by what he *feels* about that person, the above passage – read in conjunction with verse 3, and especially its concluding sentence – imposes a *moral* restriction on plural marriages.

148 Lit., "do not incline with all inclination" – i.e., towards one of the wives, implying thereby an exclusion of the

God is indeed much-forgiving, a dispenser of grace. ⟨129⟩
And if husband and wife[149] do separate, God shall provide for each of them out of His abundance: for God is indeed infinite, wise, ⟨130⟩ and unto God belongs all that is in the heavens and all that is on earth.

AND, INDEED, We have enjoined upon those who were granted revelation before your time, as well as upon yourselves, to remain conscious of God. And if you deny Him – behold, unto God belongs all that is in the heavens and all that is on earth, and God is indeed self-sufficient, ever to be praised. ⟨131⟩
And unto God belongs all that is in the heavens and all that is on earth; and none is as worthy of trust as God. ⟨132⟩ If He so wills, He can cause you, O mankind, to disappear, and bring forth other beings [in your stead]: for God has indeed the power to do this. ⟨133⟩
If one desires the rewards of this world, [let him remember that] with God are the rewards of [both] this world and the life to come: and God is indeed all-hearing, all-seeing. ⟨134⟩

O YOU who have attained to faith! Be ever steadfast in upholding equity, bearing witness to the truth for the sake of God, even though it be against your own selves or your parents and kinsfolk. Whether the person concerned be rich or poor, God's claim takes precedence over [the claims of] either of them.[150] Do not, then, follow your own desires, lest you swerve from justice: for if you distort [the truth], or refuse to testify, behold, God is indeed aware of all that you do! ⟨135⟩

فَإِنَّ ٱللَّهَ كَانَ غَفُورًا رَّحِيمًا ﴿١٢٩﴾ وَإِن يَتَفَرَّقَا يُغْنِ ٱللَّهُ كُلًّا مِّن سَعَتِهِۦ
وَكَانَ ٱللَّهُ وَٰسِعًا حَكِيمًا ﴿١٣٠﴾ وَلِلَّهِ مَا فِى ٱلسَّمَٰوَٰتِ وَمَا فِى ٱلْأَرْضِ
وَلَقَدْ وَصَّيْنَا ٱلَّذِينَ أُوتُوا۟ ٱلْكِتَٰبَ مِن قَبْلِكُمْ وَإِيَّاكُمْ أَنِ ٱتَّقُوا۟ ٱللَّهَ
وَإِن تَكْفُرُوا۟ فَإِنَّ لِلَّهِ مَا فِى ٱلسَّمَٰوَٰتِ وَمَا فِى ٱلْأَرْضِ وَكَانَ ٱللَّهُ غَنِيًّا
حَمِيدًا ﴿١٣١﴾ وَلِلَّهِ مَا فِى ٱلسَّمَٰوَٰتِ وَمَا فِى ٱلْأَرْضِ وَكَفَىٰ بِٱللَّهِ وَكِيلًا ﴿١٣٢﴾
إِن يَشَأْ يُذْهِبْكُمْ أَيُّهَا ٱلنَّاسُ وَيَأْتِ بِـَٔاخَرِينَ وَكَانَ ٱللَّهُ عَلَىٰ ذَٰلِكَ
قَدِيرًا ﴿١٣٣﴾ مَّن كَانَ يُرِيدُ ثَوَابَ ٱلدُّنْيَا فَعِندَ ٱللَّهِ ثَوَابُ ٱلدُّنْيَا وَٱلْءَاخِرَةِ
وَكَانَ ٱللَّهُ سَمِيعًۢا بَصِيرًا ﴿١٣٤﴾ ۞ يَٰٓأَيُّهَا ٱلَّذِينَ ءَامَنُوا۟ كُونُوا۟ قَوَّٰمِينَ
بِٱلْقِسْطِ شُهَدَآءَ لِلَّهِ وَلَوْ عَلَىٰٓ أَنفُسِكُمْ أَوِ ٱلْوَٰلِدَيْنِ وَٱلْأَقْرَبِينَ إِن
يَكُنْ غَنِيًّا أَوْ فَقِيرًا فَٱللَّهُ أَوْلَىٰ بِهِمَا فَلَا تَتَّبِعُوا۟ ٱلْهَوَىٰٓ أَن تَعْدِلُوا۟ وَإِن
تَلْوُۥٓا۟ أَوْ تُعْرِضُوا۟ فَإِنَّ ٱللَّهَ كَانَ بِمَا تَعْمَلُونَ خَبِيرًا ﴿١٣٥﴾

ثلاثة ارباع الحزب

faʾinnal-lāha kāna Ghafūrar-Raḥīmā. (129) Wa ʾiñy-yatafarraqā yughnil-lāhu kullam-miñ-saᶜatihī wa kānal-lāhu Wāsiᶜan Ḥakīmā. (130) Wa lil-lāhi mā fis-samāwāti wa mā fil-ʾarḍ. Wa laqad waṣṣaynal-ladhīna ʾūtul-Kitāba miñ-qablikum wa ʾiyyākum ʾanit-taqul-lāh. Wa ʾiñ-takfurū faʾinna lillāhi mā fis-samāwāti wa mā fil-ʾarḍi wa kānal-lāhu Ghaniyyan Ḥamīdā. (131) Wa lillāhi mā fis-samāwāti wa mā fil-ʾarḍi wa kafā billāhi Wakīlā. (132) ʾIñy-yashaʾ yudh-hibkum ʾayyuhan-nāsu wa yaʾti biʾākharīna wa kānal-lāhu ᶜalā dhālika Qadīrā. (133) Mañ-kāna yurīdu thawābad-dunyā faᶜiñdal-lāhi thawābud-dunyā wal-ʾĀkhirati wa kānal-lāhu Samīᶜam-Baṣīrā. (134) ۞ Yāa ʾayyuhal-ladhīna ʾāmanū kūnū qawwāmīna bilqisṭi shuhadāaʾa lillāhi wa law ᶜalāa ʾañfusikum ʾawil-wālidayni wal-ʾaqrabīn. ʾIñy-yakun ghaniyyan ʾaw faqīrañ-fallāhu ʾawlā bihimā. Falā tattabiᶜul-hawāa ʾañ-taᶜdilū wa ʾiñ-talwūu ʾaw tuᶜriḍū faʾinnal-lāha kāna bimā taᶜmalūna Khabīrā. (135)

other from all affection – "leaving her, as it were, in suspense (*ka'l-muᶜallaqah*)". Regarding my rendering of this phrase, see Lane V, 2137.

149 Lit., "the two".

150 I.e., "do not allow the fact that a man is rich to prejudice you in his favour or against him, and do not, out of misplaced compassion, favour the poor man at the expense of the truth".

O you who have attained to faith! Hold fast unto your belief in God and His Apostle, and in the divine writ which He has bestowed from on high upon His Apostle, step by step, as well as in the revelation which He sent down aforetime:[151] for he who denies God, and His angels, and His revelations, and His apostles, and the Last Day, has indeed gone far astray.[152] ‹136›
Behold, as for those who come to believe, and then deny the truth, and again come to believe, and again deny the truth, and thereafter grow stubborn in their denial of the truth[153] – God will not forgive them, nor will He guide them in any way. ‹137›
Announce thou to such hypocrites that grievous suffering awaits them. ‹138›
As for those who take the deniers of the truth for their allies in preference to the believers – do they hope to be honoured by them when, behold, all honour belongs to God [alone]?[154] ‹139›
And, indeed, He has enjoined upon you in this divine writ that whenever you hear people deny the truth of God's messages and mock at them, you shall avoid their company until they begin to talk of other things[155] – or else, verily, you will become like them.
Behold, together with those who deny the truth God will gather in hell the hypocrites, ‹140› who but wait to see what betides you: thus, if triumph comes to you from God, they say, "Were we not on your side?"

يَٰٓأَيُّهَا ٱلَّذِينَ ءَامَنُوٓا۟ ءَامِنُوا۟ بِٱللَّهِ وَرَسُولِهِۦ وَٱلْكِتَٰبِ ٱلَّذِى نَزَّلَ عَلَىٰ رَسُولِهِۦ
وَٱلْكِتَٰبِ ٱلَّذِىٓ أَنزَلَ مِن قَبْلُ ۚ وَمَن يَكْفُرْ بِٱللَّهِ وَمَلَٰٓئِكَتِهِۦ وَكُتُبِهِۦ وَرُسُلِهِۦ
وَٱلْيَوْمِ ٱلْءَاخِرِ فَقَدْ ضَلَّ ضَلَٰلًۢا بَعِيدًا (136) إِنَّ ٱلَّذِينَ ءَامَنُوا۟ ثُمَّ كَفَرُوا۟ ثُمَّ
ءَامَنُوا۟ ثُمَّ كَفَرُوا۟ ثُمَّ ٱزْدَادُوا۟ كُفْرًا لَّمْ يَكُنِ ٱللَّهُ لِيَغْفِرَ لَهُمْ وَلَا لِيَهْدِيَهُمْ
سَبِيلًۢا (137) بَشِّرِ ٱلْمُنَٰفِقِينَ بِأَنَّ لَهُمْ عَذَابًا أَلِيمًا (138) ٱلَّذِينَ يَتَّخِذُونَ
ٱلْكَٰفِرِينَ أَوْلِيَآءَ مِن دُونِ ٱلْمُؤْمِنِينَ ۚ أَيَبْتَغُونَ عِندَهُمُ ٱلْعِزَّةَ فَإِنَّ ٱلْعِزَّةَ لِلَّهِ
جَمِيعًا (139) وَقَدْ نَزَّلَ عَلَيْكُمْ فِى ٱلْكِتَٰبِ أَنْ إِذَا سَمِعْتُمْ ءَايَٰتِ ٱللَّهِ يُكْفَرُ
بِهَا وَيُسْتَهْزَأُ بِهَا فَلَا تَقْعُدُوا۟ مَعَهُمْ حَتَّىٰ يَخُوضُوا۟ فِى حَدِيثٍ غَيْرِهِۦٓ ۚ إِنَّكُمْ إِذًا
مِّثْلُهُمْ ۗ إِنَّ ٱللَّهَ جَامِعُ ٱلْمُنَٰفِقِينَ وَٱلْكَٰفِرِينَ فِى جَهَنَّمَ جَمِيعًا (140)
ٱلَّذِينَ يَتَرَبَّصُونَ بِكُمْ فَإِن كَانَ لَكُمْ فَتْحٌ مِّنَ ٱللَّهِ قَالُوٓا۟ أَلَمْ نَكُن مَّعَكُمْ

Yāa ᵓayyuhal-ladhīna ᵓāmanūu ᵓāminū billāhi wa Rasūlihī wal-Kitābil-ladhī nazzala ᶜalā Rasūlihī wal-Kitābil-ladhīi ᵓañzala miñ-qabl. Wa mañy-yakfur billāhi wa Malāaᵓikatihī wa Kutubihī wa Rusulihī wal-Yawmil-ᵓĀkhiri faqad ḍalla ḍalālam-baᶜīdā. (136) ᵓInnal-ladhīna ᵓāmanū thumma kafarū thumma ᵓāmanū thumma kafarū thummaz-dādū kufral-lam yakunil-lāhu liyaghfira lahum wa lā liyahdiyahum sabīlā. (137) Bashshiril-munāfiqīna biᵓanna lahum ᶜadhāban ᵓalīmā. (138) ᵓAlladhīna yattakhidhūnal-kāfirīna ᵓawliyāaᵓa miñ-dūnil-muᵓminīna ᵓayabtaghuna ᶜiñdahumul-ᶜizzata faᵓin-nal-ᶜizzata lillāhi jamīᶜā. (139) Wa qad nazzala ᶜalaykum fil-Kitābi ᵓan ᵓidhā samiᶜtum ᵓĀyātil-lāhi yukfaru bihā wa yustahzaᵓu bihā falā taqᶜudū maᶜahum ḥattā yakhūḍū fī ḥadīthin ghayrih. ᵓInnakum ᵓidham-mithluhum. ᵓInnal-lāha jā-miᵓul-munāfiqīna wal-kāfirīna fī jahannama jamīᶜā. (140) ᵓAlladhīna yatarabbaṣūna bikum faᵓiñ-kāna lakum fatḥum-minal-lāhi qālūu ᵓalam nakum-maᶜakum

151 What is meant here is belief in the *fact* of earlier revelation, and not in the earlier-revealed scriptures in their present form, which – as repeatedly stated in the Qurᵓān – is the outcome of far-reaching corruption of the original texts.

152 Since it is through the beings or forces described as angels that God conveys His revelations to the prophets, belief in angels is correlated with belief in revelation as such.

153 Lit., "increase in a denial of the truth".

154 See 3 : 28. However, the term "allies" (*awliyāᵓ*, sing. *walī*) does not indicate, in this context, merely *political* alliances. More than anything else, it obviously alludes to a "moral alliance" with the deniers of the truth: that is to say, to an adoption of their way of life in preference to the way of life of the believers, in the hope of being "honoured", or accepted as equals, by the former. Since an imitation of the way of life of confirmed unbelievers must obviously conflict with the moral principles demanded by true faith, it unavoidably leads to a gradual abondonment of those principles.

155 Lit., "you shall not sit with them until they immerse themselves in talk other than this". The injunction referred to is found in 6 : 68, which was revealed at a much earlier period.

– whereas if those who deny the truth are in luck, they say [to them], "Have we not earned your affection by defending you against those believers?"[156]
But God will judge between you all on the Day of Resurrection; and never will God allow those who deny the truth to harm the believers.[157] ‹141›
Behold, the hypocrites seek to deceive God – the while it is He who causes them to be deceived [by themselves].[158] And when they rise to pray, they rise reluctantly, only to be seen and praised by men, remembering God but seldom, ‹142› wavering between this and that, [true] neither to these nor those. But for him whom God lets go astray thou canst never find any way. ‹143›
O you who have attained to faith! Do not take the deniers of the truth for your allies in preference to the believers! Do you want to place before God a manifest proof of your guilt?[159] ‹144›
Verily, the hypocrites shall be in the lowest depth of the fire, and thou wilt find none who could succour them. ‹145› But excepted shall be they who repent, and live righteously, and hold fast unto God, and grow sincere in their faith in God alone: for these shall be one with the believers – and in time God will grant to all believers a mighty reward. ‹146›

وَإِن كَانَ لِلْكَٰفِرِينَ نَصِيبٌ قَالُوٓاْ أَلَمْ نَسْتَحْوِذْ عَلَيْكُمْ وَنَمْنَعْكُم مِّنَ
ٱلْمُؤْمِنِينَ ۚ فَٱللَّهُ يَحْكُمُ بَيْنَكُمْ يَوْمَ ٱلْقِيَٰمَةِ ۗ وَلَن يَجْعَلَ ٱللَّهُ لِلْكَٰفِرِينَ
عَلَى ٱلْمُؤْمِنِينَ سَبِيلًا ﴿١٤١﴾ إِنَّ ٱلْمُنَٰفِقِينَ يُخَٰدِعُونَ ٱللَّهَ وَهُوَ خَٰدِعُهُمْ
وَإِذَا قَامُوٓاْ إِلَى ٱلصَّلَوٰةِ قَامُواْ كُسَالَىٰ يُرَآءُونَ ٱلنَّاسَ وَلَا يَذْكُرُونَ
ٱللَّهَ إِلَّا قَلِيلًا ﴿١٤٢﴾ مُّذَبْذَبِينَ بَيْنَ ذَٰلِكَ لَآ إِلَىٰ هَٰٓؤُلَآءِ وَلَآ إِلَىٰ هَٰٓؤُلَآءِ ۚ
وَمَن يُضْلِلِ ٱللَّهُ فَلَن تَجِدَ لَهُۥ سَبِيلًا ﴿١٤٣﴾ يَٰٓأَيُّهَا ٱلَّذِينَ ءَامَنُواْ لَا
تَتَّخِذُواْ ٱلْكَٰفِرِينَ أَوْلِيَآءَ مِن دُونِ ٱلْمُؤْمِنِينَ ۚ أَتُرِيدُونَ أَن تَجْعَلُواْ لِلَّهِ
عَلَيْكُمْ سُلْطَٰنًا مُّبِينًا ﴿١٤٤﴾ إِنَّ ٱلْمُنَٰفِقِينَ فِى ٱلدَّرْكِ ٱلْأَسْفَلِ مِنَ ٱلنَّارِ
وَلَن تَجِدَ لَهُمْ نَصِيرًا ﴿١٤٥﴾ إِلَّا ٱلَّذِينَ تَابُواْ وَأَصْلَحُواْ وَٱعْتَصَمُواْ بِٱللَّهِ
وَأَخْلَصُواْ دِينَهُمْ لِلَّهِ فَأُوْلَٰٓئِكَ مَعَ ٱلْمُؤْمِنِينَ ۖ وَسَوْفَ يُؤْتِ ٱللَّهُ ٱلْمُؤْمِنِينَ
أَجْرًا عَظِيمًا ﴿١٤٦﴾

wa ʾiñ-kāna lilkāfirīna naṣībuñ-qālūu ʾalam nastaḥwidh ʿalaykum wa namnaʿkum-minal-muʾminīn. Fallāhu yaḥkumu baynakum Yawmal-Qiyāmah. Wa lañy-yajʿalal-lāhu lilkāfirīna ʿalal-muʾminīna sabīlā. (141) ʾInnal-munāfiqīna yukhādiʿūnal-lāha wa Huwa khādiʿuhum wa ʾidhā qāmūu ʾilaṣ-Ṣalāti qāmū kusālā yurāaʾūnan-nāsa wa lā yadhkurūnal-lāha ʾillā qalīlā. (142) Mudhabdhabīna bayna dhālika lāa ʾilā hāaʾulāaʾi wa lāa ʾilā hāaʾulāaʾ. Wa mañy-yuḍlilil-lāhu falañ-tajida lahū sabīlā. (143) Yāa ʾayyuhal-ladhīna ʾāmanū lā tattakhidhul-kāfirīna ʾawliyāaʾa miñ-dūnil-muʾminīn. ʾAturīdūna ʾañ-tajʿalū lillāhi ʿalaykum sulṭānam-mubīnā. (144) ʾInnal-munāfiqīna fid-darkil-ʾasfali minan-nāri wa lañ-tajida lahum naṣīrā. (145) ʾIllal-ladhīna tābū wa ʾaṣlaḥū waʿ-taṣamū billāhi wa ʾakhlaṣū dīnahum lillāhi faʾulāaʾika maʿal-muʾminīn. Wa sawfa yuʾtil-lāhul-muʾminīna ʾajran ʿaẓīmā. (146)

156 Lit., "did we not gain mastery over you [i.e., "over your hearts" – cf. Lane II, 664] and defend you against the believers?" The term "believers" has obviously a sarcastic implication here, which justifies the use of the demonstrative pronoun "those" instead of the definite article "the".

157 This announcement has, of course, a purely spiritual meaning, and does not necessarily apply to the changing fortunes of life – since (as this very verse points out) "those who deny the truth" may on occasion be "in luck", that is to say, may gain temporal supremacy over the believers.

158 Some of the commentators (e.g., Rāzī) interpret the phrase *huwa khādiʿuhum* (lit., "He is their deceiver") as "He will requite them for their deception". However, the rendering adopted by me seems to be more in tune with 2 : 9, where the same type of hypocrisy is spoken of: "They would deceive God and those who have attained to faith – the while they deceive none but themselves, and are not aware of it." See also *Manār* V, 469 f., where both these interpretations are considered to be mutually complementary.

159 Lit., "a manifest proof against yourselves". See note 154 above.

Why would God cause you to suffer [for your past sins] if you are grateful and attain to belief – seeing that God is always responsive to gratitude, all-knowing?[160] ‹147›

God does not like any evil to be mentioned openly, unless it be by him who has been wronged [thereby].[161] And God is indeed all-hearing, all-knowing, ‹148› whether you do good openly or in secret, or pardon others for evil [done unto you]: for, behold, God is indeed an absolver of sins, infinite in His power. ‹149›

حزب 11
جزء 6

VERILY, those who deny God and His apostles by endeavouring to make a distinction between [belief in] God and [belief in] His apostles, and who say "We believe in the one but we deny the other,"[162] and want to pursue a path in- between ‹150› – it is they, they who are truly denying the truth: and for those who deny the truth We have readied shameful suffering. ‹151›

But as for those who believe in God and His apostles and make no distinction between any of them[163] – unto them, in time, will He grant their rewards [in full]. And God is indeed much-forgiving, a dispenser of grace. ‹152›

مَّا يَفْعَلُ ٱللَّهُ بِعَذَابِكُمْ إِن شَكَرْتُمْ وَءَامَنتُمْ ۚ وَكَانَ ٱللَّهُ شَاكِرًا
عَلِيمًا ﴿١٤٧﴾ ۞ لَّا يُحِبُّ ٱللَّهُ ٱلْجَهْرَ بِٱلسُّوٓءِ مِنَ ٱلْقَوْلِ إِلَّا مَن ظُلِمَ ۚ
وَكَانَ ٱللَّهُ سَمِيعًا عَلِيمًا ﴿١٤٨﴾ إِن تُبْدُوا۟ خَيْرًا أَوْ تُخْفُوهُ أَوْ تَعْفُوا۟ عَن سُوٓءٍ
فَإِنَّ ٱللَّهَ كَانَ عَفُوًّا قَدِيرًا ﴿١٤٩﴾ إِنَّ ٱلَّذِينَ يَكْفُرُونَ بِٱللَّهِ وَرُسُلِهِۦ
وَيُرِيدُونَ أَن يُفَرِّقُوا۟ بَيْنَ ٱللَّهِ وَرُسُلِهِۦ وَيَقُولُونَ نُؤْمِنُ بِبَعْضٍ وَنَكْفُرُ
بِبَعْضٍ وَيُرِيدُونَ أَن يَتَّخِذُوا۟ بَيْنَ ذَٰلِكَ سَبِيلًا ﴿١٥٠﴾ أُو۟لَٰٓئِكَ هُمُ
ٱلْكَٰفِرُونَ حَقًّا ۚ وَأَعْتَدْنَا لِلْكَٰفِرِينَ عَذَابًا مُّهِينًا ﴿١٥١﴾ وَٱلَّذِينَ ءَامَنُوا۟
بِٱللَّهِ وَرُسُلِهِۦ وَلَمْ يُفَرِّقُوا۟ بَيْنَ أَحَدٍ مِّنْهُمْ أُو۟لَٰٓئِكَ سَوْفَ يُؤْتِيهِمْ
أُجُورَهُمْ ۗ وَكَانَ ٱللَّهُ غَفُورًا رَّحِيمًا ﴿١٥٢﴾

Mā yafʿalul-lāhu biʿadhābikum ʾiñ-shakartum wa ʾāmañtum. Wa kānal-lāhu Shākiran ʿAlīmā. (147) ۞ Lā yuḥibbul-lāhul-jahra bissūuʾi minal-qawli ʾillā mañ-ẓulima wa kānal-lāhu Samīʿan ʿAlīmā. (148) ʾIñ-tubdū khayran ʾaw tukhfūhu ʾaw taʿfū ʿañ-sūuʾiñ-faʾinnal-lāha kāna ʿAfuwwañ-Qadīrā. (149) ʾInnal-ladhīna yakfurūna billāhi wa Rusulihī wa yurīdūna ʾañy-yufarriqū baynal-lāhi wa Rusulihī wa yaqūlūna nuʾminu bibaʿḍiñw-wa nakfuru bibaʿḍiñw-wa yurīdūna ʾañy-yattakhidhū bayna dhālika sabīlā. (150) ʾUlāaʾika humul-kāfirūna ḥaqqā. Wa ʾaʿtadnā lilkāfirīna ʿadhābam-muhīnā. (151) Wal-ladhīna ʾāmanū billāhi wa Rusulihī wa lam yufarriqū bayna ʾaḥadim-minhum ʾulāaʾika sawfa yuʾtīhim ʾujūrahum. Wa kānal-lāhu Ghafūrar-Raḥīmā. (152)

160 The gratitude spoken of here is of a general nature – a feeling of thankfulness for being alive and endowed with what is described as a "soul": a feeling which often leads man to the realization that this boon of life and consciousness is not accidental, and thus, in a logical process of thought, to belief in God. According to Zamakhsharī, this is the reason why "gratitude" is placed before "belief" in the structure of the above sentence.

161 As some of the commentators (e.g., Rāzī) point out, this may refer to giving currency to earlier sayings or deeds of the repentant sinners – both hypocrites and outright deniers of the truth – mentioned in the preceding two verses: an interpretation which seems to be borne out by the context. However, the above statement has a general import as well: it prohibits the public mention of anybody's evil deeds or sayings, "unless it be by him who has been wronged [thereby]" – which also implies that evil behaviour which affects the society as a whole may be made public if the interests of the wronged party – in this case, the society as such – demand it.

162 Or: "We believe in some and we deny the others" – that is, they believe in God but not in His apostles (Zamakhsharī) or, alternatively, they believe in some of the apostles and deny others (Ṭabarī and Zamakhsharī). To my mind, the first of these two interpretations is preferable inasmuch as it covers not only a rejection of some of the apostles but also a total rejection of the idea that God may have revealed His will through His chosen message-bearers. In Islam, the rejection of any or all of God's apostles constitutes almost as grave a sin as a denial of God Himself.

163 I.e., in point of their being God's message-bearers.

THE FOLLOWERS of the Old Testament[164] demand of thee [O Prophet] that thou cause a revelation to be sent down to *them* from heaven.[165] And an even greater thing than this did they demand of Moses when they said, "Make us see God face to face" – whereupon the thunderbolt of punishment overtook them for this their wickedness.[166] After that, they took to worshipping the [golden] calf – and this after all evidence of the truth had come unto them!
None the less, We effaced this [sin of theirs], and vouchsafed unto Moses a clear proof [of the truth], ‹153› raising Mount Sinai high above them in witness of their solemn pledge. And We said unto them "Enter the gate humbly";[167] and We told them, "Do not break the Sabbath-law"; and We accepted from them a most solemn pledge. ‹154›
And so, [We punished them[168]] for the breaking of their pledge, and their refusal to acknowledge God's messages, and their slaying of prophets against all right, and their boast, "Our hearts are already full of knowledge" – nay, but God has sealed their hearts in result of their denial of the truth, and [now] they believe in but few things;[169] ‹155› – and for their refusal to acknowledge the truth, and the awesome calumny which they utter against Mary,[170] ‹156› and their boast, "Behold, we have slain the Christ Jesus, son of Mary, [who claimed to be] an apostle of God!"
However, they did not slay him, and neither did they crucify him, but it only

يَسْـَٔلُكَ أَهْلُ ٱلْكِتَـٰبِ أَن تُنَزِّلَ عَلَيْهِمْ كِتَـٰبًا مِّنَ ٱلسَّمَآءِ ۚ فَقَدْ سَأَلُوا۟ مُوسَىٰٓ
أَكْبَرَ مِن ذَٰلِكَ فَقَالُوٓا۟ أَرِنَا ٱللَّهَ جَهْرَةً فَأَخَذَتْهُمُ ٱلصَّـٰعِقَةُ بِظُلْمِهِمْ ۚ ثُمَّ
ٱتَّخَذُوا۟ ٱلْعِجْلَ مِنۢ بَعْدِ مَا جَآءَتْهُمُ ٱلْبَيِّنَـٰتُ فَعَفَوْنَا عَن ذَٰلِكَ ۚ وَءَاتَيْنَا مُوسَىٰ
سُلْطَـٰنًا مُّبِينًا ﴿١٥٣﴾ وَرَفَعْنَا فَوْقَهُمُ ٱلطُّورَ بِمِيثَـٰقِهِمْ وَقُلْنَا لَهُمُ ٱدْخُلُوا۟
ٱلْبَابَ سُجَّدًا وَقُلْنَا لَهُمْ لَا تَعْدُوا۟ فِى ٱلسَّبْتِ وَأَخَذْنَا مِنْهُم مِّيثَـٰقًا
غَلِيظًا ﴿١٥٤﴾ فَبِمَا نَقْضِهِم مِّيثَـٰقَهُمْ وَكُفْرِهِم بِـَٔايَـٰتِ ٱللَّهِ وَقَتْلِهِمُ ٱلْأَنۢبِيَآءَ
بِغَيْرِ حَقٍّ وَقَوْلِهِمْ قُلُوبُنَا غُلْفٌۢ ۚ بَلْ طَبَعَ ٱللَّهُ عَلَيْهَا بِكُفْرِهِمْ فَلَا يُؤْمِنُونَ إِلَّا
قَلِيلًا ﴿١٥٥﴾ وَبِكُفْرِهِمْ وَقَوْلِهِمْ عَلَىٰ مَرْيَمَ بُهْتَـٰنًا عَظِيمًا ﴿١٥٦﴾ وَقَوْلِهِمْ إِنَّا قَتَلْنَا
ٱلْمَسِيحَ عِيسَى ٱبْنَ مَرْيَمَ رَسُولَ ٱللَّهِ وَمَا قَتَلُوهُ وَمَا صَلَبُوهُ وَلَـٰكِن

Yasʾaluka ʾahlul-Kitābi ʾañ-tunazzila ʿalayhim Kitābam-minas-samāaʾ. Faqad saʾalū Mūsāa ʾakbara miñ-dhālika faqālūu ʾarinal-lāha jahratañ-faʾakhadhat-humuṣ-ṣāʿiqatu biẓulmihim. Thummat-takhadhul-ʿijla mim-baʿdi mā jāaʾat-humul-bayyinātu faʿafawnā ʿañ-dhālika wa ʾātaynā Mūsā sulṭānam-mubīnā. (153) Wa rafaʿnā fawqahumuṭ-Ṭūra bimīthāqihim wa qulnā lahumud-khulul-bāba sujjadañw-wa qulnā lahum lā taʿdū fis-sabti wa ʾakhadhnā minhum-mīthāqan ghalīẓā. (154) Fabimā naqḍihim-mīthāqahum wa kufrihim-biʾĀyātil-lāhi wa qatlihimul-ʾAmbiyāaʾa bighayri ḥaqqiñw-wa qawlihim qulūbunā ghulf. Bal ṭabaʿal-lāhu ʿalayhā bikufrihim falā yuʾminūna ʾillā qalīlā. (155) Wa bikufrihim wa qawlihim ʿalā Maryama buhtānan ʿaẓīmā. (156) Wa qawlihim ʾinnā qatalnal-Masīḥa ʿĪsab-na Maryama Rasūlal-lāhi wa mā qatalūhu wa mā ṣalabūhu wa lākiñ-

164 As is evident from the sequence, the term *ahl al-kitāb* ("followers of [earlier] revelation") refers here specifically to the Jews, which justifies its rendering as "followers of the Old Testament".

165 Sc., "in proof of thy prophethood". Alternatively, the sentence may be understood thus: "They ask thee to bring down unto them an [actual] book from heaven." In view, however, of the oft-repeated Qurʾanic statement that the Jews were convinced that they alone could be granted divine revelation, it seems to me that the rendering adopted by me is the more appropriate.

166 See 2 : 55 and the corresponding note 40.

167 See 2 : 58-59 and the corresponding notes.

168 The statement relating to their punishment – clearly implied here – is made explicit in verse 160.

169 See 2 : 88 and the corresponding notes.

170 The calumny referred to is the popular Jewish assertion that Jesus was an illegitimate child.

seemed to them [as if it had been] so;[171] and, verily, those who hold conflicting views thereon are indeed confused, having no [real] knowledge thereof, and following mere conjecture. For, of a certainty, they did not slay him: «157» nay, God exalted him unto Himself[172] – and God is indeed almighty, wise. «158» Yet there is not one of the followers of earlier revelation who does not, at the moment of his death, grasp the truth about Jesus;[173] and on the Day of Resurrection he [himself] shall bear witness to the truth against them. «159»
So, then, for the wickedness committed by those who followed the Jewish faith did We deny unto them certain of the good things of life which [aforetime] had been allowed to them;[174] and [We did this] for their having so often turned away from

شُبِّهَ لَهُمْ ۚ وَإِنَّ ٱلَّذِينَ ٱخْتَلَفُوا۟ فِيهِ لَفِى شَكٍّ مِّنْهُ ۚ مَا لَهُم بِهِۦ مِنْ
عِلْمٍ إِلَّا ٱتِّبَاعَ ٱلظَّنِّ ۚ وَمَا قَتَلُوهُ يَقِينًۢا ﴿١٥٧﴾ بَل رَّفَعَهُ ٱللَّهُ إِلَيْهِ ۚ
وَكَانَ ٱللَّهُ عَزِيزًا حَكِيمًا ﴿١٥٨﴾ وَإِن مِّنْ أَهْلِ ٱلْكِتَـٰبِ إِلَّا لَيُؤْمِنَنَّ
بِهِۦ قَبْلَ مَوْتِهِۦ ۖ وَيَوْمَ ٱلْقِيَـٰمَةِ يَكُونُ عَلَيْهِمْ شَهِيدًا ﴿١٥٩﴾ فَبِظُلْمٍ
مِّنَ ٱلَّذِينَ هَادُوا۟ حَرَّمْنَا عَلَيْهِمْ طَيِّبَـٰتٍ أُحِلَّتْ لَهُمْ وَبِصَدِّهِمْ عَن

shubbiha lahum. Wa ʾinnal-ladhīnakh-talafū fīhi lafī shakkim-minh. Mā lahum-bihī min ʿilmin ʾillat-tibāʿaẓ-ẓanni wa mā qatalūhu yaqīnā. (157) Bar-rafaʿahul-lāhu ʾilayhi wa kānal-lāhu ʿAzīzan Ḥakīmā. (158) Wa ʾim-min ʾahlil-Kitābi ʾillā layuʾminanna bihī qabla mawtihī wa Yawmal-Qiyāmati yakūnu ʿalayhim shahīdā. (159) Fabiẓulmim-minal-ladhīna hādū ḥarramnā ʿalayhim ṭayyibātin ʾuḥillat lahum wa biṣaddihim ʿañ-

171 Thus, the Qurʾān categorically denies the story of the crucifixion of Jesus. There exist, among Muslims, many fanciful legends telling us that at the last moment God substituted for Jesus a person closely resembling him (according to some accounts, that person was Judas), who was subsequently crucified in his place. However, none of these legends finds the slightest support in the Qurʾān or in authentic Traditions, and the stories produced in this connection by the classical commentators must be summarily rejected. They represent no more than confused attempts at "harmonizing" the Qurʾanic statement that Jesus was *not* crucified with the graphic description, in the Gospels, of his crucifixion. The story of the crucifixion as such has been succinctly explained in the Qurʾanic phrase *wa-lākin shubbiha lahum,* which I render as "but it only appeared to them as if it had been so" – implying that in the course of time, long after the time of Jesus, a legend had somehow grown up (possibly under the then-powerful influence of Mithraistic beliefs) to the effect that he had died on the cross in order to atone for the "original sin" with which mankind is allegedly burdened; and this legend became so firmly established among the latter-day followers of Jesus that even his enemies, the Jews, began to believe it – albeit in a derogatory sense (for crucifixion was, in those times, a heinous form of death-penalty reserved for the lowest of criminals). This, to my mind, is the only satisfactory explanation of the phrase *wa-lākin shubbiha lahum,* the more so as the expression *shubbiha lī* is idiomatically synonymous with *khuyyila lī,* "[a thing] became a fancied image to me", i.e., "in my mind" – in other words, "[it] seemed to me" (see *Qāmūs,* art. *khayala,* as well as Lane II, 833, and IV, 1500).

172 Cf. 3 : 55, where God says to Jesus, "Verily, I shall cause thee to die, and shall exalt thee unto Me." The verb *rafaʿahu* (lit., "he raised him" or "elevated him") has always, whenever the act of *rafʿ* ("elevating") of a human being is attributed to God, the meaning of "honouring" or "exalting". Nowhere in the Qurʾān is there any warrant for the popular belief that God has "taken up" Jesus bodily, in his lifetime, into heaven. The expression "God exalted him unto Himself" in the above verse denotes the elevation of Jesus to the realm of God's special grace – a blessing in which all prophets partake, as is evident from 19 : 57, where the verb *rafaʿnāhu* ("We exalted him") is used with regard to the Prophet Idrīs. (See also Muḥammad ʿAbduh in *Manār* III, 316 f., and VI, 20 f.) The "nay" (*bal*) at the beginning of the sentence is meant to stress the contrast between the belief of the Jews that they had put Jesus to a shameful death on the cross and the fact of God's having "exalted him unto Himself".

173 Lit., "who does not believe in him before his death". According to this verse, all believing Jews and Christians realize at the moment of their death that Jesus was truly a prophet of God – having been neither an impostor nor "the son of God" (Zamakhsharī).

174 Most of the commentators assume that this refers to the severe dietary restrictions imposed on the Jews, which are alluded to in 3 : 93 and 6 : 146. Since, however, 3 : 93 clearly states that these restrictions and prohibitions were a punishment for evil deeds committed "before the Torah was bestowed from on high", while the verse which we are now discussing relates to their sinful behaviour in later times, we must conclude that the punishment spoken of here has another meaning: namely, the age-long deprivation of the Jewish people of the many "good things of life" which other nations enjoy – in other words, the humiliation and suffering which they have had to undergo throughout most of their recorded history, and particularly after the time of Jesus. It is on the basis of this interpretation that I have rendered the expression *ḥarramnā ʿalayhim* (lit., "We forbade them") as "We denied to them".

the path of God,[175] ‹160› and [for] their taking usury although it had been forbidden to them, and their wrongful devouring of other people's possessions. And for those from among them who [continue to] deny the truth We have readied grievous suffering. ‹161›
But as for those from among them who are deeply rooted in knowledge,[176] and the believers who believe in that which has been bestowed upon thee from on high as well as that which was bestowed from on high before thee, and those who are [especially] constant in prayer,[177] and spend in charity, and all who believe in God and the Last Day – these it is unto whom We shall grant a mighty reward. ‹162›

BEHOLD, We have inspired thee [O Prophet] just as We inspired Noah and all the prophets after him – as We inspired Abraham, and Ismael, and Isaac, and Jacob, and their descendants, including Jesus, and Job, and Jonah, and Aaron, and Solomon; and as We vouchsafed unto David a book of divine wisdom;[178] ‹163› and as [We inspired other] apostles whom We have mentioned to thee ere this,[179] as well as apostles whom We have not mentioned to thee; and as God spoke His word unto Moses: ‹164› [We sent all these] apostles as heralds of glad tidings and as warners, so that men might have no excuse before God after [the coming of] these apostles; and God is indeed almighty, wise. ‹165›

ربع الحزب

سَبِيلِ ٱللَّهِ كَثِيرًا ﴿160﴾ وَأَخْذِهِمُ ٱلرِّبَوٰاْ وَقَدْ نُهُواْ عَنْهُ وَأَكْلِهِمْ أَمْوَٰلَ
ٱلنَّاسِ بِٱلْبَٰطِلِ وَأَعْتَدْنَا لِلْكَٰفِرِينَ مِنْهُمْ عَذَابًا أَلِيمًا ﴿161﴾ لَّٰكِنِ
ٱلرَّٰسِخُونَ فِى ٱلْعِلْمِ مِنْهُمْ وَٱلْمُؤْمِنُونَ يُؤْمِنُونَ بِمَآ أُنزِلَ إِلَيْكَ وَمَآ أُنزِلَ
مِن قَبْلِكَ وَٱلْمُقِيمِينَ ٱلصَّلَوٰةَ وَٱلْمُؤْتُونَ ٱلزَّكَوٰةَ وَٱلْمُؤْمِنُونَ بِٱللَّهِ
وَٱلْيَوْمِ ٱلْـَٔاخِرِ أُوْلَٰٓئِكَ سَنُؤْتِيهِمْ أَجْرًا عَظِيمًا ﴿162﴾ ۞ إِنَّآ أَوْحَيْنَآ إِلَيْكَ
كَمَآ أَوْحَيْنَآ إِلَىٰ نُوحٍ وَٱلنَّبِيِّـۧنَ مِنۢ بَعْدِهِۦ وَأَوْحَيْنَآ إِلَىٰٓ إِبْرَٰهِيمَ
وَإِسْمَٰعِيلَ وَإِسْحَٰقَ وَيَعْقُوبَ وَٱلْأَسْبَاطِ وَعِيسَىٰ وَأَيُّوبَ وَيُونُسَ وَهَٰرُونَ
وَسُلَيْمَٰنَ وَءَاتَيْنَا دَاوُۥدَ زَبُورًا ﴿163﴾ وَرُسُلًا قَدْ قَصَصْنَٰهُمْ عَلَيْكَ مِن
قَبْلُ وَرُسُلًا لَّمْ نَقْصُصْهُمْ عَلَيْكَ وَكَلَّمَ ٱللَّهُ مُوسَىٰ تَكْلِيمًا ﴿164﴾ رُّسُلًا
مُّبَشِّرِينَ وَمُنذِرِينَ لِئَلَّا يَكُونَ لِلنَّاسِ عَلَى ٱللَّهِ حُجَّةٌۢ بَعْدَ ٱلرُّسُلِ وَكَانَ
ٱللَّهُ عَزِيزًا حَكِيمًا ﴿165﴾

sabīlil-lāhi kathīrā. (160) Wa ᵓakhdhihimur-ribā wa qad nuhū ᶜanhu wa ᵓaklihim ᵓamwālan-nāsi bilbāṭili wa ᵓaᶜtadnā lilkāfirīna minhum ᶜadhāban ᵓalīmā. (161) Lākinir-rāsikhūna fil-ᶜilmi minhum wal-muᵓminūna yuᵓminūna bimāa ᵓuñzila ᶜilayka wa māa ᵓuñzila miñ-qablika wal-muqīmīnaṣ-Ṣalāta wal-muᵓtūnaz-Zakāta wal-muᵓminūna billāhi wal-Yawmil-ᵓĀkhiri ᵓulāaᵓika sanuᵓtīhim ᵓajran ᶜaẓīmā. (162) ۞ ᵓInnāa ᵓawḥaynāa ᵓilayka kamāa ᵓawḥaynāa ᵓilā Nūḥiñw-wan-Nabiyyīna mim-baᶜdih. Wa ᵓawḥaynāa ᵓilāa ᵓIbrāhīma wa ᵓIsmāᶜīla wa ᵓIsḥāqa wa Yaᶜqūba wal-ᵓasbāṭi wa ᶜĪsā wa ᵓAyyūba wa Yūnusa wa Hārūna wa Sulaymāna wa ᵓātaynā Dāwūda Zabūrā. (163) Wa Rusulañ-qad qaṣaṣnāhum ᶜalayka miñ-qablu wa Rusulal-lam naqṣuṣhum ᶜalayka wa kallamal-lāhu Mūsā taklīmā. (164) Rusulam-mubashshirīna wa muñdhirīna liᵓallā yakūna linnāsi ᶜalal-lāhi ḥujjatum-baᶜdar-Rusuli wa kānal-lāhu ᶜAzīzan Ḥakīmā. (165)

175 The verb *ṣadda* ("he turned away") can be transitive as well as intransitive, and the same applies to the noun *ṣadd* derived from it. In the former case, the sentence would read, "for their having turned away many [others] from the path of God"; in the latter case, "for their having [so] often turned away from the path of God". In view of the repeated stress, in the Qurᵓān, on the refractory nature of the children of Israel – and the abundant evidence to this effect in the Old Testament – I prefer the intransitive rendering.

176 I.e., those from among the Jews who do not content themselves with a mere observance of rituals, but try to penetrate to the deepest meaning of faith.

177 According to the grammarians of the Baṣrah school, and especially Sībawayh, the use of the accusative (*manṣūb*) case in the expression *al-muqīmīn aṣ-ṣalāh* ("those who are constant in prayer") – instead of the nominative *al-muqīmūn* – is a legitimate grammatical device meant to stress the special, praiseworthy quality attaching to prayer and to those who are devoted to it (see Zamakhsharī and Rāzī); hence my interpolation of "especially" between brackets.

178 I.e., the Psalms (see *sūrah* 21, note 101).

179 I.e., before the revelation of this *sūrah*.

لَٰكِنِ ٱللَّهُ يَشْهَدُ بِمَآ أَنزَلَ إِلَيْكَ أَنزَلَهُۥ بِعِلْمِهِۦ وَٱلْمَلَٰٓئِكَةُ يَشْهَدُونَ وَكَفَىٰ
بِٱللَّهِ شَهِيدًا ﴿١٦٦﴾ إِنَّ ٱلَّذِينَ كَفَرُوا۟ وَصَدُّوا۟ عَن سَبِيلِ ٱللَّهِ قَدْ ضَلُّوا۟ ضَلَٰلًۢا
بَعِيدًا ﴿١٦٧﴾ إِنَّ ٱلَّذِينَ كَفَرُوا۟ وَظَلَمُوا۟ لَمْ يَكُنِ ٱللَّهُ لِيَغْفِرَ لَهُمْ وَلَا لِيَهْدِيَهُمْ
طَرِيقًا ﴿١٦٨﴾ إِلَّا طَرِيقَ جَهَنَّمَ خَٰلِدِينَ فِيهَآ أَبَدًا ۚ وَكَانَ ذَٰلِكَ عَلَى ٱللَّهِ
يَسِيرًا ﴿١٦٩﴾ يَٰٓأَيُّهَا ٱلنَّاسُ قَدْ جَآءَكُمُ ٱلرَّسُولُ بِٱلْحَقِّ مِن رَّبِّكُمْ فَـَٔامِنُوا۟
خَيْرًا لَّكُمْ ۚ وَإِن تَكْفُرُوا۟ فَإِنَّ لِلَّهِ مَا فِى ٱلسَّمَٰوَٰتِ وَٱلْأَرْضِ ۚ وَكَانَ ٱللَّهُ
عَلِيمًا حَكِيمًا ﴿١٧٠﴾ يَٰٓأَهْلَ ٱلْكِتَٰبِ لَا تَغْلُوا۟ فِى دِينِكُمْ وَلَا تَقُولُوا۟
عَلَى ٱللَّهِ إِلَّا ٱلْحَقَّ ۚ إِنَّمَا ٱلْمَسِيحُ عِيسَى ٱبْنُ مَرْيَمَ رَسُولُ ٱللَّهِ وَكَلِمَتُهُۥٓ
أَلْقَىٰهَآ إِلَىٰ مَرْيَمَ وَرُوحٌ مِّنْهُ ۖ فَـَٔامِنُوا۟ بِٱللَّهِ وَرُسُلِهِۦ ۖ وَلَا تَقُولُوا۟ ثَلَٰثَةٌ ۚ ٱنتَهُوا۟

Lākinil-lāhu yashhadu bimāa ᵓañzala ᵓilayka ᵓañza-
lahū biᶜilmihī wal-Malāaᵓikatu yashhadūna wa kafā
billāhi Shahīdā. (166) ᵓInnal-ladhīna kafarū wa ṣaddū
ᶜañ-sabīlil-lāhi qad ḍallū ḍalālam-baᶜīdā. (167) ᵓInnal-
ladhīna kafarū wa ẓalamū lam yakunil-lāhu liyaghfi-
ra lahum wa lā liyahdiyahum ṭarīqā. (168) ᵓIllā ṭarīqa
jahannama khālidīna fīhāa ᵓabadā. Wa kana dhālika
ᶜalal-lāhi yasīrā. (169) Yāa ᵓayyuhan-nāsu qad jāa-
ᵓakumur-Rasūlu bilḥaqqi mir-Rabbikum faᵓāminū
khayral-lakum. Wa ᵓiñ-takfurū faᵓinna lillāhi mā
fis-samāwāti wal-ᵓarḍi wa kānal-lāhu ᶜAlīman
Ḥakīmā. (170) Yāa ᵓAhlal-Kitābi lā taghlū fī dīnikum
wa lā taqūlū ᶜalal-lāhi ᵓilal-ḥaqq. ᵓInnamal-Masīḥu
ᶜĪsab-nu Maryama Rasūlul-lāhi wa Kalimatuhūu
ᵓalqāhāa ᵓilā Maryama wa Rūḥum-minh. Faᵓāminū
billāhi wa Rusulihī wa lā taqūlū thalāthah. ᵓIñtahū

However it be, God [Himself] bears witness to the truth of what He has bestowed from on high upon thee: out of His own wisdom has He bestowed it from on high, with the angels bearing witness thereto – although none can bear witness as God does. ‹166›
Behold, those who are bent on denying the truth and on turning others away from the path of God have indeed gone far astray. ‹167›
Behold, those who are bent on denying the truth and on evildoing – God will indeed not forgive them, nor will He guide them onto any road ‹168› but the road that leads to hell, therein to abide beyond the count of time; and this is indeed easy for God. ‹169›
O mankind! The Apostle has now come unto you with the truth from your Sustainer: believe, then, for your own good! And if you deny the truth – behold, unto God belongs all that is in the heavens and all that is on earth, and God is indeed all-knowing, wise! ‹170›

O FOLLOWERS of the Gospel! Do not overstep the bounds [of truth] in your religious beliefs,[180] and do not say of God anything but the truth. The Christ Jesus, son of Mary, was but God's Apostle – [the fulfilment of] His promise which He had conveyed unto Mary – and a soul created by Him.[181] Believe, then, in God and His apostles, and do not say, "[God is] a trinity". Desist [from this assertion]

180 I.e., by raising Jesus to the rank of divinity. Since here the Christians are addressed specifically, I render the term *kitāb* as "Gospel".

181 Lit., "His word which He conveyed unto Mary and a soul from Him". According to Ṭabarī, the "word" (*kalimah*) was "the announcement (*risālah*) which God bade the angels to convey to Mary, and God's glad tiding to her" (a reference to 3 : 45) – which justifies the rendering of *kalimatuhu* as "[the fulfilment of] His promise". (See also *sūrah* 3, note 28.) As regards the expression. "a soul from Him" or "created by Him", it is to be noted that among the various meanings which the word *rūḥ* bears in the Qurᵓān (e.g., "inspiration" in 2 : 87 and 253), it is also used in its primary significance of "breath of life", "soul", or "spirit": thus, for instance, in 32 : 9, where the ever-recurring evolution of the human embryo is spoken of: "and then He forms him [i.e., man] . . . and breathes into him of His spirit" – that is, endows him with a conscious soul which represents God's supreme gift to man and is, therefore, described as "a breath of His spirit". In the verse under discussion, which stresses the purely human nature of Jesus and refutes the belief in his divinity, the Qurᵓān points out that Jesus, like all other human beings, was "a soul created by Him".

for your own good. God is but One God; utterly remote is He, in His glory, from having a son: unto Him belongs all that is in the heavens and all that is on earth; and none is as worthy of trust as God. ‹171›
Never did the Christ feel too proud to be God's servant, nor do the angels who are near unto Him. And those who feel too proud to serve Him and glory in their arrogance [should know that on Judgment Day] He will gather them all unto Himself; ‹172› whereupon unto those who attained to faith and did good deeds He will grant their just rewards, and give them yet more out of His bounty; whereas those who felt too proud and gloried in their arrogance He will chastise with grievous suffering: and they shall find none to protect them from God, and none to bring them succour. ‹173›

O MANKIND! A manifestation of the truth has now come unto you from your Sustainer, and We have sent down unto you a clear light. ‹174› And as for those who have attained to faith in God and hold fast unto Him – He will enfold them within[182] His grace and bounty, and guide them unto Himself by a straight way. ‹175›

THEY WILL ASK thee to enlighten them.[183] Say: "God enlightens you [thus] about the laws concerning [inheritance from] those who leave no heir in the direct line:

خَيْرًا لَّكُمْ إِنَّمَا ٱللَّهُ إِلَٰهٌ وَٰحِدٌ سُبْحَٰنَهُۥٓ أَن يَكُونَ لَهُۥ وَلَدٌ لَّهُۥ مَا
فِى ٱلسَّمَٰوَٰتِ وَمَا فِى ٱلْأَرْضِ وَكَفَىٰ بِٱللَّهِ وَكِيلًا ﴿١٧١﴾ لَّن يَسْتَنكِفَ
ٱلْمَسِيحُ أَن يَكُونَ عَبْدًا لِّلَّهِ وَلَا ٱلْمَلَٰٓئِكَةُ ٱلْمُقَرَّبُونَ وَمَن
يَسْتَنكِفْ عَنْ عِبَادَتِهِۦ وَيَسْتَكْبِرْ فَسَيَحْشُرُهُمْ إِلَيْهِ جَمِيعًا ﴿١٧٢﴾ فَأَمَّا
ٱلَّذِينَ ءَامَنُوا۟ وَعَمِلُوا۟ ٱلصَّٰلِحَٰتِ فَيُوَفِّيهِمْ أُجُورَهُمْ وَيَزِيدُهُم مِّن
فَضْلِهِۦ وَأَمَّا ٱلَّذِينَ ٱسْتَنكَفُوا۟ وَٱسْتَكْبَرُوا۟ فَيُعَذِّبُهُمْ عَذَابًا أَلِيمًا وَلَا
يَجِدُونَ لَهُم مِّن دُونِ ٱللَّهِ وَلِيًّا وَلَا نَصِيرًا ﴿١٧٣﴾ يَٰٓأَيُّهَا ٱلنَّاسُ قَدْ
جَآءَكُم بُرْهَٰنٌ مِّن رَّبِّكُمْ وَأَنزَلْنَآ إِلَيْكُمْ نُورًا مُّبِينًا ﴿١٧٤﴾ فَأَمَّا ٱلَّذِينَ
ءَامَنُوا۟ بِٱللَّهِ وَٱعْتَصَمُوا۟ بِهِۦ فَسَيُدْخِلُهُمْ فِى رَحْمَةٍ مِّنْهُ وَفَضْلٍ وَيَهْدِيهِمْ
إِلَيْهِ صِرَٰطًا مُّسْتَقِيمًا ﴿١٧٥﴾ يَسْتَفْتُونَكَ قُلِ ٱللَّهُ يُفْتِيكُمْ فِى ٱلْكَلَٰلَةِ

khayral-lakum; ʾinnamal-lāhu ʾIlāhuñw-Waḥid. Subḥānahūu ʾañy-yakūna lahū walad. Lahū mā fis-samāwāti wa mā fil-ʾarḍ. Wa kafā billāhi Wakīlā. (171) Lañy-yastañkifal-Masīḥu ʾañy-yakūna ʿabdal-lillāhi wa lal-Malāaʾikatul-muqarrabūn. Wa mañy-yastañkif ʿan ʿibādatihī wa yastakbir fasayaḥshuruhum ʾilayhi jamīʿā. (172) Faʾammal-ladhīna ʾāmanū wa ʿamiluṣ-ṣāliḥāti fayuwaffīhim ʾujūrahum wa yazīduhum-miñ-faḍlih. Wa ʾammal-ladhīnas-tañkafū was-takbarū fayuʿadhdhibuhum ʿadhāban ʾalīmañw-wa lā yajidūna lahum-miñ-dūnil-lāhi waliyyañw-wa lā naṣīrā. (173) Yāa ʾayyuhan-nāsu qad jāaʾakum-burhānum-mir-Rabbikum wa ʾañzalnāa ʾilaykum Nūram-mubīnā. (174) Faʾammal-ladhīna ʾāmanū billāhi waʿ-taṣamū bihī fasayudkhiluhum fī raḥmatim-minhu wa faḍliñw-wa yahdīhim ʾilayhi ṣirāṭam-mustaqīmā. (175) Yastaftūnaka qulil-lāhu yuftīkum fil-kalālah.

182 Lit., "cause them to enter into".

183 I.e., about the laws of inheritance mentioned in the next sentence. Regarding the meaning of *istiftāʾ* ("a request for enlightenment about a [particular] law"), see note 145 of this *sūrah*. The seemingly abrupt transition from the preceding passages – dealing with questions of theology – to this one is in accord with the Qurʾanic principle of deliberately interweaving moral exhortation with practical legislation: and this in pursuance of the teaching that man's life – spiritual and physical, individual and social – is one integral whole, and therefore requires simultaneous consideration of all its aspects if the concept of "the good life" is to be realized. The above verse completes the series of inheritance laws dealt with early in this *sūrah*.

If a man dies childless and has a sister, she shall inherit one-half of what he has left, just as he shall inherit from her if she dies childless. But if there are two sisters, both [together] shall have two-thirds of what he has left; and if there are brothers and sisters,[184] then the male shall have the equal of two females' share."
God makes [all this] clear unto you, lest you go astray; and God knows everything. ﴿176﴾

إِنِ ٱمْرُؤٌاْ هَلَكَ لَيْسَ لَهُۥ وَلَدٌ وَلَهُۥٓ أُخْتٌ فَلَهَا نِصْفُ مَا تَرَكَ ۚ وَهُوَ يَرِثُهَآ
إِن لَّمْ يَكُن لَّهَا وَلَدٌ ۚ فَإِن كَانَتَا ٱثْنَتَيْنِ فَلَهُمَا ٱلثُّلُثَانِ مِمَّا تَرَكَ ۚ وَإِن
كَانُوٓاْ إِخْوَةً رِّجَالًا وَنِسَآءً فَلِلذَّكَرِ مِثْلُ حَظِّ ٱلْأُنثَيَيْنِ ۗ يُبَيِّنُ ٱللَّهُ لَكُمْ
أَن تَضِلُّواْ ۗ وَٱللَّهُ بِكُلِّ شَىْءٍ عَلِيمٌۢ ﴿١٧٦﴾

ʾInim-ruʾun halaka laysa lahū waladuñw-wa lahūu ʾukhtuñ-falahā niṣfu mā taraka wa huwa yarithuhāa ʾil-lam yakul-lahā walad. Faʾiñ-kānatath-natayni falahumath-thuluthāni mimmā taraka wa ʾiñ-kānūu ʾikhwatar-rijālañw-wa nisāaʾañ-falidhdhakari mithlu ḥaẓẓil-ʾuñthayayn. Yubayyinul-lāhu lakum ʾañ-taḍillū. Wal-lāhu bikulli shayʾin ʿAlīm. ﴿176﴾

184 Lit., "brethren (*ikhwah*), men and women". It is to be noted that the expression *ikhwah* comprises either brothers, or sisters, or brothers *and* sisters.

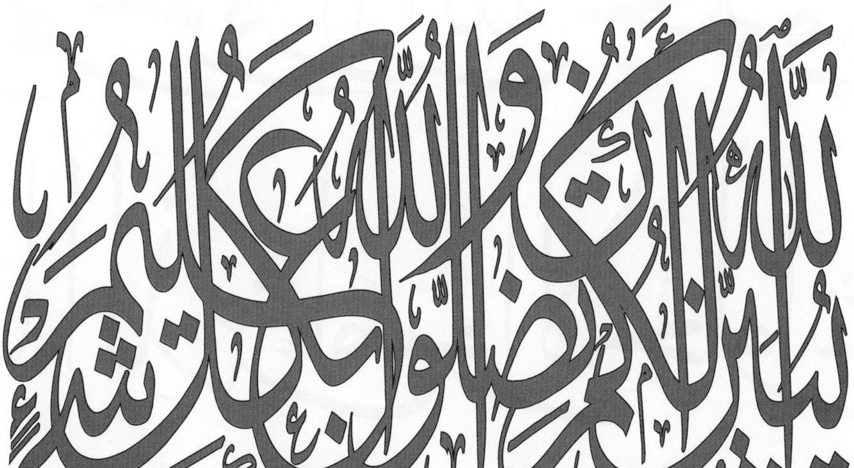

Sūrah 4, verse 176 ... يُبَيِّنُ ٱللَّهُ لَكُمۡ أَن تَضِلُّواْۗ وَٱللَّهُ بِكُلِّ شَيۡءٍ عَلِيمُۢ ١٧٦

مَا يُتْلَىٰ عَلَيْكُمْ غَيْرَ مُحِلِّي الصَّيْدِ
وَأَنتُمْ حُرُمٌ إِنَّ اللَّهَ يَحْكُمُ مَا يُرِيدُ
يَا أَيُّهَا الَّذِينَ آمَنُوا لَا تُحِلُّوا شَعَائِرَ
اللَّهِ وَلَا الشَّهْرَ الْحَرَامَ وَلَا الْهَدْيَ
وَلَا الْقَلَائِدَ وَلَا آمِّينَ الْبَيْتَ

سورة المائدة مدنية

بِسْمِ ٱللَّهِ ٱلرَّحْمَٰنِ ٱلرَّحِيمِ

يَٰٓأَيُّهَا ٱلَّذِينَ ءَامَنُوٓا۟ أَوْفُوا۟ بِٱلْعُقُودِ ۚ

أُحِلَّتْ لَكُم بَهِيمَةُ ٱلْأَنْعَٰمِ إِلَّا

وآياتها عشرون ومائة

The Fifth Sūrah

Al-Māa᾽idah (The Repast)

Medina Period

ACCORDING to all the available evidence, this *sūrah* constitutes one of the last sections of the Qur᾽ān revealed to the Prophet. The consensus of opinion places it in the period of his Farewell Pilgrimage, in the year 10 H. It takes its title from the request for a "repast from heaven" made by the disciples of Jesus (verse 112), and from Jesus' prayer in this connection (verse 114).

The *sūrah* begins with a call to the believers to fulfil their spiritual and social responsibilities, and ends with a reminder of man's utter dependence on God, whose is "the dominion over the heavens and the earth and all that they contain". Being one of the last revelations vouchsafed to the Prophet, it lays down a series of ordinances relating to religious rites and to various social obligations; but, at the same time, it warns the followers of the Qur᾽ān not to enlarge the area of divine ordinances by means of subjective deduction (verse 101), since this might make it difficult for them to act in accordance with God's Law, and might ultimately lead them to denying the truth of revelation as such (verse 102). They are also warned not to take the Jews and the Christians for their "allies" in the moral sense of the word: that is, not to imitate their way of life and their social concepts at the expense of the principles of Islam (verses 51 ff.). This latter warning is necessitated by the fact, repeatedly stressed in this *sūrah*, that both the Jews and the Christians have abandoned and corrupted the truths conveyed to them by their prophets, and thus no longer adhere to the genuine, original message of the Bible (verse 68). In particular, the Jews are taken to task for having become "blind and deaf [of heart]" (verses 70-71, and *passim*), and the Christians, for having deified Jesus in clear contravention of his own God-inspired teachings (verses 72-77 and 116-118).

Addressing the various religious communities, the Qur᾽ān states in verse 48: "Unto every one of you have We appointed a [different] law and way of life. . . . Vie, then, with one another in doing good works!" And once again, all true believers – of whatever persuasion – are assured that "all who believe in God and the Last Day and do righteous deeds – no fear need they have, and neither shall they grieve" (verse 69).

The crowning statement of the whole *sūrah* is found in verse 3, which was revealed to the Prophet shortly before his death: "Today have I perfected your religious law for you, and have bestowed upon you the full measure of My blessings, and willed that self-surrender unto Me (*al-islām*) shall be your religion."

سورة المائدة مدنية

-5-

وآياتها عشرون ومائة

IN THE NAME OF GOD, THE MOST GRACIOUS, THE DISPENSER OF GRACE:

O YOU who have attained to faith! Be true to your covenants![1]

Lawful to you is the [flesh of every] beast that feeds on plants, save what is mentioned to you [hereinafter[2]]: but you are not allowed to hunt while you are in the state of pilgrimage. Behold, God ordains in accordance with His will.[3] ‹1›

O you who have attained to faith! Offend not against the symbols set up by God, nor against the sacred month [of pilgrimage], nor against the garlanded offerings,[4] nor against those who flock to the Inviolable Temple, seeking favour with their Sustainer and His goodly acceptance; and [only] after your pilgrimage is over[5] are you free to hunt.

And never let your hatred of people who would bar you from the Inviolable House of Worship lead you into the sin of aggression:[6] but rather help one another

بِسۡمِ ٱللَّهِ ٱلرَّحۡمَٰنِ ٱلرَّحِيمِ

نصف الحزب

يَٰٓأَيُّهَا ٱلَّذِينَ ءَامَنُوٓاْ أَوۡفُواْ بِٱلۡعُقُودِۚ أُحِلَّتۡ لَكُم بَهِيمَةُ ٱلۡأَنۡعَٰمِ إِلَّا
مَا يُتۡلَىٰ عَلَيۡكُمۡ غَيۡرَ مُحِلِّي ٱلصَّيۡدِ وَأَنتُمۡ حُرُمٌۗ إِنَّ ٱللَّهَ يَحۡكُمُ مَا
يُرِيدُ ١ يَٰٓأَيُّهَا ٱلَّذِينَ ءَامَنُواْ لَا تُحِلُّواْ شَعَٰٓئِرَ ٱللَّهِ وَلَا ٱلشَّهۡرَ
ٱلۡحَرَامَ وَلَا ٱلۡهَدۡيَ وَلَا ٱلۡقَلَٰٓئِدَ وَلَآ ءَآمِّينَ ٱلۡبَيۡتَ ٱلۡحَرَامَ يَبۡتَغُونَ
فَضۡلٗا مِّن رَّبِّهِمۡ وَرِضۡوَٰنٗاۚ وَإِذَا حَلَلۡتُمۡ فَٱصۡطَادُواْۚ وَلَا يَجۡرِمَنَّكُمۡ
شَنَـَٔانُ قَوۡمٍ أَن صَدُّوكُمۡ عَنِ ٱلۡمَسۡجِدِ ٱلۡحَرَامِ أَن تَعۡتَدُواْۘ وَتَعَاوَنُواْ

Bismil-lāhir-Raḥmānir-Raḥīm.

Yāa ʾayyuhal-ladhīna ʾāmanūu ʾawfū bilʿuqūd. ʾUḥillat lakum-bahīmatul-ʾanʿāmi ʾillā mā yutlā ʿalaykum ghayra muḥilliṣ-ṣaydi wa ʾan̄tum ḥurum. ʾInnal-lāha yaḥkumu mā yurīd. ① Yāa ʾayyuhal-ladhīna ʾāmanū lā tuḥillū Shaʿāaʾiral-lāhi wa lash-Shahral-Ḥarāma wa lal-hadya wa lal-qalāaʾida wa lāa ʾāammīnal-Baytal-Ḥarāma yabtaghūna faḍlam-mir-Rabbihim wa riḍwānā. Wa ʾidhā ḥalaltum faṣṭādū. Wa lā yajrimannakum shanaʾānu qawmin ʾan̄-ṣaddūkum ʿanil-Masjidil-Ḥarāmi ʾan̄-taʿtadū. Wa taʿāwanū

---

1 The term *ʿaqd* ("covenant") denotes a solemn undertaking or engagement involving more than one party. According to Rāghib, the covenants referred to in this verse "are of three kinds: the covenants between God and man [i.e., man's obligations towards God], between man and his own soul, and between the individual and his fellow-men" – thus embracing the entire area of man's moral and social responsibilities.

2 I.e., in verse 3. Literally, the expression *bahīmat al-anʿām* could be translated as "a beast of the cattle"; but since this would obviously be a needless tautology, many commentators incline to the view that what is meant here is "any beast which resembles [domesticated] cattle insofar as it feeds on plants and is not a beast of prey" (Rāzī; also *Lisān al-ʿArab*, art. *naʿma*). I have adopted this convincing interpretation in my rendering of the above phrase.

3 Lit., "whatever He wills" or "deems fit": i.e., in accordance with a plan of which He alone has full knowledge. Regarding the prohibition of hunting while on pilgrimage, see verses 94-96 of this *sūrah*.

4 Lit., "nor against the offerings, nor the garlands" – a reference to the animals which are brought to Mecca at the time of pilgrimage, to be sacrificed there in the name of God and most of their flesh distributed among the poor. In order to mark out such animals, and to prevent their being inadvertently used for profane (e.g., commercial) ends, garlands are customarily hung around their necks. See also 2 : 196. – The term *shaʿāʾir Allāh* (lit., "God's symbols"), occurring earlier in this sentence, denotes the places reserved for particular religious rites (e.g., the Kaʿbah) as well as the religious rites themselves. (Cf. 2 : 158, where Aṣ-Ṣafā and Al-Marwah are described as "symbols set up by God"). In the above context, the rites of pilgrimage, in particular, are alluded to.

5 Lit., "when you have become free of the obligations attaching to the state of pilgrimage" (*idhā ḥalaltum*).

6 Inasmuch as this *sūrah* was undoubtedly revealed in the year 10 H. (Ṭabarī, Ibn Kathīr), it is difficult to accept the view of some of the commentators that the above verse alludes to the events culminating in the truce of Ḥudaybiyyah,

عَلَى ٱلْبِرِّ وَٱلتَّقْوَىٰ وَلَا تَعَاوَنُوا۟ عَلَى ٱلْإِثْمِ وَٱلْعُدْوَٰنِ وَٱتَّقُوا۟ ٱللَّهَ إِنَّ ٱللَّهَ
شَدِيدُ ٱلْعِقَابِ ﴿٢﴾ حُرِّمَتْ عَلَيْكُمُ ٱلْمَيْتَةُ وَٱلدَّمُ وَلَحْمُ ٱلْخِنزِيرِ وَمَآ أُهِلَّ
لِغَيْرِ ٱللَّهِ بِهِۦ وَٱلْمُنْخَنِقَةُ وَٱلْمَوْقُوذَةُ وَٱلْمُتَرَدِّيَةُ وَٱلنَّطِيحَةُ وَمَآ أَكَلَ ٱلسَّبُعُ
إِلَّا مَا ذَكَّيْتُمْ وَمَا ذُبِحَ عَلَى ٱلنُّصُبِ وَأَن تَسْتَقْسِمُوا۟ بِٱلْأَزْلَٰمِ ذَٰلِكُمْ
فِسْقٌ ٱلْيَوْمَ يَئِسَ ٱلَّذِينَ كَفَرُوا۟ مِن دِينِكُمْ فَلَا تَخْشَوْهُمْ وَٱخْشَوْنِ ٱلْيَوْمَ
أَكْمَلْتُ لَكُمْ دِينَكُمْ وَأَتْمَمْتُ عَلَيْكُمْ نِعْمَتِى وَرَضِيتُ لَكُمُ ٱلْإِسْلَٰمَ دِينًا

ʿalal-birri wat-taqwā wa lā taʿāwanū ʿalal-ʾithmi wal-ʿudwān. Wat-taqul-lāha ʾinnal-lāha Shadīdul-ʿiqāb. (2) Ḥurrimat ʿalaykumul-maytatu wad-damu wa laḥmul-khinzīri wa māa ʾuhilla lighayril-lāhi bihī wal-munkhaniqatu wal-mawqūdhatu wal-mutaraddiyatu wan-naṭīḥatu wa māa ʾakalas-sabuʿu ʾillā mā dhakkaytum wa mā dhubiḥa ʿalan-nuṣubi wa ʾan-tastaqsimū bilʾazlāmi dhālikum fisq. ʾAlyawma yaʾisal-ladhīna kafarū min-dīnikum falā takhshawhum wakh-shawn. ʾAlyawma ʾakmaltu lakum Dīnakum wa ʾatmamtu ʿalaykum niʿmatī wa raḍītu lakumul-ʾIslāma Dīnā.

in furthering virtue and God-consciousness, and do not help one another in furthering evil and enmity; and remain conscious of God: for, behold, God is severe in retribution! ‹2›

FORBIDDEN to you is carrion, and blood, and the flesh of swine, and that over which any name other than God's has been invoked,[7] and the animal that has been strangled, or beaten to death, or killed by a fall, or gored to death, or savaged by a beast of prey, save that which you [yourselves] may have slaughtered while it was still alive; and [forbidden to you is] all that has been slaughtered on idolatrous altars.[8]

And [you are forbidden] to seek to learn through divination what the future may hold in store for you:[9] this is sinful conduct.

Today, those who are bent on denying the truth have lost all hope of [your ever forsaking] your religion: do not, then, hold them in awe, but stand in awe of Me!

Today have I perfected your religious law for you, and have bestowed upon you the full measure of My blessings, and willed that self-surrender unto Me shall be your religion.[10]

---

in 6 H., when the pagan Quraysh succeeded in preventing the Prophet and his followers from entering Mecca on pilgrimage. At the time of the revelation of this *sūrah* Mecca was already in the possession of the Muslims, and there was no longer any question of their being barred from it by the Quraysh, almost all of whom had by then embraced Islam. We must, therefore, conclude that the above injunction cannot be circumscribed by a historical reference but has a timeless, general import: in other words, that it refers to anybody who might endeavour to bar the believers – physically or metaphorically – from the exercise of their religious duties (symbolized by the "Inviolable House of Worship") and thus to lead them away from their faith. In view of the next sentence, moreover, this interpretation would seem to be the only plausible one.

7 See 2 : 173.

8 The *nuṣub* (sing. *naṣībah*) were the altar-stones set up in pre-Islamic times around the Kaʿbah on which the pagan Quraysh used to sacrifice animals to their idols. However, from the story of Zayd ibn ʿAmr ibn Nufayl (Bukhārī) it appears that not only sacrificial animals but also such as were destined for common consumption were often slaughtered there for the sake of a supposed "blessing" (see *Fatḥ al-Bārī* VII, 113). Some philologists consider the form *nuṣub* a singular, with *anṣāb* as its plural (cf. verse 90 of this *sūrah*). In either case the term denotes an association with all manner of practices which could be described as "idolatrous", and should not be taken merely in its literal sense. Cf. in this respect also verse 90 of this *sūrah*, and the corresponding note 105.

9 Lit., "to aim at divining [the future] by means of arrows". This is a reference to the divining-arrows without a point and without feathers used by the pre-Islamic Arabs to find out what the future might hold in store for them. (A comprehensive description of this practice may be found in Lane III, 1247.) As is usual with such historical allusions in the Qurʾān, this one, too, is used metonymically: it implies a prohibition of *all* manner of attempts at divining or foretelling the future.

10 According to all available Traditions based on the testimony of the Prophet's contemporaries, the above passage – which sets, as it were, a seal on the message of the Qurʾān – was revealed at ʿArafāt in the afternoon of

As for him, however, who is driven [to what is forbidden] by dire necessity[11] and not by an inclination to sinning – behold, God is much-forgiving, a dispenser of grace. ‹3›
They will ask thee as to what is lawful to them. Say: "Lawful to you are all the good things of life."[12]
And as for those hunting animals[13] which you train by imparting to them something of the knowledge that God has imparted to yourselves – eat of what they seize for you, but mention God's name over it, and remain conscious of God: verily, God is swift in reckoning. ‹4›
Today, all the good things of life have been made lawful to you. And the food of those who have been vouchsafed revelation aforetime is lawful to you,[14] and your food is lawful to them. And [lawful to you are], in wedlock, women from among those who believe [in this divine writ], and, in wedlock, women from among those who have been vouchsafed revelation before your time – provided that you give them their dowers, taking them in honest wed-

فَمَنِ ٱضْطُرَّ فِى مَخْمَصَةٍ غَيْرَ مُتَجَانِفٍ لِّإِثْمٍ فَإِنَّ ٱللَّهَ غَفُورٌ رَّحِيمٌ ﴿٣﴾
يَسْـَٔلُونَكَ مَاذَآ أُحِلَّ لَهُمْ قُلْ أُحِلَّ لَكُمُ ٱلطَّيِّبَٰتُ وَمَا عَلَّمْتُم مِّنَ
ٱلْجَوَارِحِ مُكَلِّبِينَ تُعَلِّمُونَهُنَّ مِمَّا عَلَّمَكُمُ ٱللَّهُ فَكُلُوا۟ مِمَّآ أَمْسَكْنَ
عَلَيْكُمْ وَٱذْكُرُوا۟ ٱسْمَ ٱللَّهِ عَلَيْهِ وَٱتَّقُوا۟ ٱللَّهَ إِنَّ ٱللَّهَ سَرِيعُ ٱلْحِسَابِ ﴿٤﴾
ٱلْيَوْمَ أُحِلَّ لَكُمُ ٱلطَّيِّبَٰتُ وَطَعَامُ ٱلَّذِينَ أُوتُوا۟ ٱلْكِتَٰبَ حِلٌّ لَّكُمْ
وَطَعَامُكُمْ حِلٌّ لَّهُمْ وَٱلْمُحْصَنَٰتُ مِنَ ٱلْمُؤْمِنَٰتِ وَٱلْمُحْصَنَٰتُ مِنَ
ٱلَّذِينَ أُوتُوا۟ ٱلْكِتَٰبَ مِن قَبْلِكُمْ إِذَآ ءَاتَيْتُمُوهُنَّ أُجُورَهُنَّ مُحْصِنِينَ

**Famaniḍ-ṭurra fī makhmaṣatin ghayra mutajānifil-
liʾithmiñ-faʾinnal-lāha Ghafūrur-Raḥīm. (3) Yasʾalūnaka mādhāa ʾuḥilla lahum. Qul ʾuḥilla lakumuṭ-
ṭayyibātu wa mā ʿallamtum-minal-jawāriḥi mukal-
libīna tuʿallimūnahunna mimmā ʿallamakumul-lāh.
Fakulū mimmāa ʾamsakna ʿalaykum wadh-kurusmal-
lāhi ʿalayhi wat-taqul-lāh. ʾInnal-lāha Sarīʿul-ḥisāb.
(4) ʾAlyawma ʾuḥilla lakumuṭ-ṭayyibāt. Wa ṭaʿāmul-
ladhīna ʾūtul-Kitāba ḥillul-lakum wa ṭaʿāmukum
ḥillul-lahum. Wal-muḥṣanātu minal-muʾmināti wal-
muḥṣanātu minal-ladhīna ʾūtul-Kitāba miñ-qablikum ʾidhāa ʾātaytumūhunna ʾujūrahunna muḥṣinīna**

Friday, the 9th of Dhu 'l-Ḥijjah, 10 H., eighty-one or eighty-two days before the death of the Prophet. No legal injunction whatsoever was revealed after this verse: and this explains the reference to God's having perfected the Faith and bestowed the full measure of His blessings upon the believers. Man's self-surrender (*islām*) to God is postulated as the basis, or the basic law, of all true religion (*dīn*). This self-surrender expresses itself not only in belief in Him but also in obedience to His commands: and this is the reason why the announcement of the completion of the Qurʾanic message is placed within the context of a verse containing the last legal ordinances ever revealed to the Prophet Muḥammad.

11 Lit., "in [a condition of] emptiness" (*fī makhmaṣah*). This is generally taken to mean "in extreme hunger"; but while this expression does, in the first instance, signify "emptiness caused by hunger", the reference to divination in the above verse points to a metonymical use of the term *makhmaṣah* as well: that is to say, it covers here not merely cases of actual, extreme hunger (which makes the eating of otherwise prohibited categories of meat permissible, as is explicitly stated in 2 : 173) but also other situations in which overwhelming, extraneous forces beyond a person's control may compel him, against his will, to do something that is normally prohibited by Islamic Law – as, for instance, to use intoxicating drugs whenever illness makes their use imperative and unavoidable.

12 The implication is, firstly, that what has been forbidden does *not* belong to the category of "the good things of life" (*aṭ-ṭayyibāt*), and, secondly, that all that has not been expressly forbidden is allowed. It is to be noted that the Qurʾān forbids only those things or actions which are injurious to man physically, morally or socially.

13 Lit., "such of the trained beasts of chase" (*min al-jawāriḥ mukallibīn*). The term *mukallib* signifies "trained like a [hunting] dog", and is applied to every animal used for hunting – a hound, a falcon, a cheetah, etc.

14 This permission to partake of the food of the followers of other revealed religions excludes, of course, the forbidden categories of meat enumerated in verse 3 above. As a matter of fact, the Law of Moses, too, forbids them explicitly; and there is no statement whatsoever in the Gospels to the effect that these prohibitions were cancelled by Jesus: on the contrary, he is reported to have said, "Think not that I have come to destroy the Law [of Moses] . . . : I am not come to destroy, but to fulfil" (Matthew v, 17). Thus, the latitude enjoyed by post-Pauline followers of Jesus in respect of food does not correspond to what he himself practiced and enjoined.

lock not in fornication, nor as secret love-companions.[15]

But as for him who rejects belief [in God] – in vain will be all his works: for in the life to come he shall be among the lost.[16] «5»

O YOU who have attained to faith! When you are about to pray, wash your face, and your hands and arms up to the elbows, and pass your [wet] hands lightly over your head, and [wash] your feet up to the ankles. And if you are in a state requiring total ablution, purify yourselves.[17] But if you are ill, or are travelling, or have just satisfied a want of nature, or have cohabited with a woman, and can find no water – then take resort to pure dust, passing therewith lightly over your face and your hands. God does not want to impose any hardship on you, but wants to make you pure, and to bestow upon you the full measure of His blessings, so that you might have cause to be grateful. «6»

And [always] remember the blessings which God has bestowed upon you, and the solemn pledge by which He bound you to Himself[18] when you said, "We have heard, and we pay heed." Hence, remain conscious of God: verily, God has full knowledge of what is in the hearts [of men]. «7»

غَيْرَ مُسَٰفِحِينَ وَلَا مُتَّخِذِىٓ أَخْدَانٍ ۗ وَمَن يَكْفُرْ بِٱلْإِيمَٰنِ فَقَدْ حَبِطَ
عَمَلُهُۥ وَهُوَ فِى ٱلْءَاخِرَةِ مِنَ ٱلْخَٰسِرِينَ ﴿٥﴾ يَٰٓأَيُّهَا ٱلَّذِينَ ءَامَنُوٓا۟ إِذَا
قُمْتُمْ إِلَى ٱلصَّلَوٰةِ فَٱغْسِلُوا۟ وُجُوهَكُمْ وَأَيْدِيَكُمْ إِلَى ٱلْمَرَافِقِ وَٱمْسَحُوا۟
بِرُءُوسِكُمْ وَأَرْجُلَكُمْ إِلَى ٱلْكَعْبَيْنِ ۚ وَإِن كُنتُمْ جُنُبًا فَٱطَّهَّرُوا۟ ۚ وَإِن
كُنتُم مَّرْضَىٰٓ أَوْ عَلَىٰ سَفَرٍ أَوْ جَآءَ أَحَدٌ مِّنكُم مِّنَ ٱلْغَآئِطِ أَوْ لَٰمَسْتُمُ
ٱلنِّسَآءَ فَلَمْ تَجِدُوا۟ مَآءً فَتَيَمَّمُوا۟ صَعِيدًا طَيِّبًا فَٱمْسَحُوا۟ بِوُجُوهِكُمْ
وَأَيْدِيكُم مِّنْهُ ۚ مَا يُرِيدُ ٱللَّهُ لِيَجْعَلَ عَلَيْكُم مِّنْ حَرَجٍ وَلَٰكِن يُرِيدُ
لِيُطَهِّرَكُمْ وَلِيُتِمَّ نِعْمَتَهُۥ عَلَيْكُمْ لَعَلَّكُمْ تَشْكُرُونَ ﴿٦﴾ وَٱذْكُرُوا۟ نِعْمَةَ
ٱللَّهِ عَلَيْكُمْ وَمِيثَٰقَهُ ٱلَّذِى وَاثَقَكُم بِهِۦٓ إِذْ قُلْتُمْ سَمِعْنَا وَأَطَعْنَا ۖ وَٱتَّقُوا۟
ٱللَّهَ ۚ إِنَّ ٱللَّهَ عَلِيمٌۢ بِذَاتِ ٱلصُّدُورِ ﴿٧﴾

ghayra musāfiḥīna wa lā muttakhidhīi ᾽akhdān. Wa mañy-yakfur bil᾽īmāni faqad ḥabiṭa ᶜamaluhū wa huwa fil-᾽Ākhirati minal-khāsirīn. (5) Yāa ᾽ayyuhal-ladhīna ᾽āmanūu ᾽idhā qumtum ᾽ilaṣ-Ṣalāti faghsilū wujūhakum wa ᾽aydiyakum ᾽ilal-marāfiqi wam-saḥū biru᾽ūsikum wa ᾽arjulakum ᾽ilal-kaᶜbayn. Wa ᾽iñ-kuñtum junubañ-faṭṭahharū. Wa ᾽iñ-kuñtum-marḍāa ᾽aw ᶜalā safarin ᾽aw jāa᾽a ᾽aḥadum-miñkum-minal-ghāa᾽iṭi ᾽aw lāmastumun-nisāa᾽a falam tajidū māa᾽añ-fatayammamū ṣaᶜīdañ-ṭayyibañ-famsaḥū bi-wujūhikum wa ᾽aydīkum-minh. Mā yurīdul-lāhu liya-jᶜala ᶜalaykum-min ḥarajiñw-wa lākiñy-yurīdu liyuṭahhirakum wa liyutimma niᶜmatahū ᶜalaykum laᶜallakum tashkurūn. (6) Wadh-kurū niᶜmatal-lāhi ᶜalaykum wa mīthāqahul-ladhī wāthaqakum-bihīi ᾽idh qultum samiᶜnā wa ᾽aṭaᶜnā; wat-taqul-lāh. ᾽Innal-lāha ᶜAlīmum-bidhātiṣ-ṣudūr. (7)

15 Whereas Muslim men are allowed to marry women from among the followers of another revealed religion, Muslim women may not marry non-Muslims: the reason being that Islam enjoins reverence of *all* the prophets, while the followers of other religions reject some of them – e.g., the Prophet Muḥammad or, as is the case with the Jews, both Muḥammad and Jesus. Thus, while a non-Muslim woman who marries a Muslim can be sure that – despite all doctrinal differences – the prophets of her faith will be mentioned with utmost respect in her Muslim environment, a Muslim woman who would marry a non-Muslim would always be exposed to an abuse of him whom she regards as God's Apostle.

16 The above passage rounds off, as it were, the opening sentences of this *sūrah*, "O you who have attained to faith, be true to your covenants" – of which belief in God and the acceptance of His commandments are the foremost. It is immediately followed by a reference to prayer: for it is in prayer that man's dependence on God finds its most conscious and deliberate expression.

17 For an explanation of this and the following passage, see 4 : 43 and the corresponding notes. Here, the reference to prayer connects with the last sentence of the preceding verse, which speaks of belief in God.

18 Lit., "His solemn pledge by which He bound you". Since this pledge is given by the believers to God and not by Him to them, the possessive adjective in "His pledge" can have only one meaning: namely, God's binding thereby the believers *to Himself.*

O YOU who have attained to faith! Be ever steadfast in your devotion to God, bearing witness to the truth in all equity; and never let hatred of anyone[19] lead you into the sin of deviating from justice. Be just: this is closest to being God-conscious. And remain conscious of God: verily, God is aware of all that you do. ‹8›
God has promised unto those who attain to faith and do good works [that] theirs shall be forgiveness of sins, and a mighty reward; ‹9› whereas they who are bent on denying the truth and giving the lie to Our messages – they are destined for the blazing fire. ‹10›
O you who have attained to faith! Remember the blessings which God bestowed upon you when [hostile] people were about to lay hands on you[20] and He stayed their hands from you. Remain, then, conscious of God: and in God let the believers place their trust. ‹11›

AND, INDEED, God accepted a [similar] solemn pledge[21] from the children of Israel when We caused twelve of their leaders to be sent [to Canaan as spies].[22] And God said: "Behold, I shall be with you! If you are constant in prayer, and spend in charity, and believe in My apostles and aid them, and offer up unto God a goodly loan,[23] I will surely efface your bad deeds and bring you into gardens through which running waters flow. But he from among you who, after this, denies the truth, will indeed have strayed from the right path!" ‹12›

يَٰٓأَيُّهَا ٱلَّذِينَ ءَامَنُوا۟ كُونُوا۟ قَوَّٰمِينَ لِلَّهِ شُهَدَآءَ بِٱلْقِسْطِ ۖ وَلَا يَجْرِمَنَّكُمْ شَنَـَٔانُ قَوْمٍ
عَلَىٰٓ أَلَّا تَعْدِلُوا۟ ۚ ٱعْدِلُوا۟ هُوَ أَقْرَبُ لِلتَّقْوَىٰ ۖ وَٱتَّقُوا۟ ٱللَّهَ ۚ إِنَّ ٱللَّهَ خَبِيرٌۢ بِمَا
تَعْمَلُونَ ﴿8﴾ وَعَدَ ٱللَّهُ ٱلَّذِينَ ءَامَنُوا۟ وَعَمِلُوا۟ ٱلصَّٰلِحَٰتِ ۙ لَهُم مَّغْفِرَةٌ وَأَجْرٌ
عَظِيمٌ ﴿9﴾ وَٱلَّذِينَ كَفَرُوا۟ وَكَذَّبُوا۟ بِـَٔايَٰتِنَآ أُو۟لَٰٓئِكَ أَصْحَٰبُ ٱلْجَحِيمِ ﴿10﴾ يَٰٓأَيُّهَا
ٱلَّذِينَ ءَامَنُوا۟ ٱذْكُرُوا۟ نِعْمَتَ ٱللَّهِ عَلَيْكُمْ إِذْ هَمَّ قَوْمٌ أَن يَبْسُطُوٓا۟ إِلَيْكُمْ أَيْدِيَهُمْ
فَكَفَّ أَيْدِيَهُمْ عَنكُمْ ۖ وَٱتَّقُوا۟ ٱللَّهَ ۚ وَعَلَى ٱللَّهِ فَلْيَتَوَكَّلِ ٱلْمُؤْمِنُونَ ﴿11﴾ ۞ وَلَقَدْ
أَخَذَ ٱللَّهُ مِيثَٰقَ بَنِىٓ إِسْرَٰٓءِيلَ وَبَعَثْنَا مِنْهُمُ ٱثْنَىْ عَشَرَ نَقِيبًا ۖ وَقَالَ ٱللَّهُ إِنِّى مَعَكُمْ ۖ
لَئِنْ أَقَمْتُمُ ٱلصَّلَوٰةَ وَءَاتَيْتُمُ ٱلزَّكَوٰةَ وَءَامَنتُم بِرُسُلِى وَعَزَّرْتُمُوهُمْ وَأَقْرَضْتُمُ ٱللَّهَ
قَرْضًا حَسَنًا لَّأُكَفِّرَنَّ عَنكُمْ سَيِّـَٔاتِكُمْ وَلَأُدْخِلَنَّكُمْ جَنَّٰتٍ تَجْرِى مِن
تَحْتِهَا ٱلْأَنْهَٰرُ ۚ فَمَن كَفَرَ بَعْدَ ذَٰلِكَ مِنكُمْ فَقَدْ ضَلَّ سَوَآءَ ٱلسَّبِيلِ ﴿12﴾

ثلاثة ارباع الحزب

Yāa ʾayyuhal-ladhīna ʾāmanū kūnū qawwāmīna lil-lāhi shuhadāaʾa bilqisṭi wa lā yajrimannakum sha-naʾānu qawmin ʿalāa ʾallā taʿdilū. ʾIʿdilū huwa ʾaqrabu littaqwā; wat-taqul-lāh. ʾInnal-lāha Khabīrum-bimā taʿmalūn. (8) Waʿadal-lāhul-ladhīna ʾāmanū wa ʿamiluṣ-ṣāliḥāti lahum-maghfiratuñw-wa ʾajrun ʿaẓīm. (9) Wal-ladhīna kafarū wa kadhdhabū biʾĀyatināa ʾulāaʾika ʾaṣḥābul-jaḥīm. (10) Yāa ʾayyuhal-ladhīna ʾāmanudh-kurū niʿmatal-lāhi ʿalaykum ʾidh hamma qawmun ʾañy-yabsuṭūu ʾilaykum ʾaydiyahum fakaffa ʾaydiyahum ʿañkum; wat-taqul-lāh. Wa ʿalal-lāhi falyatawakkalil-muʾminūn. (11) ۞ Wa laqad ʾakhadhal-lāhu mīthāqa banīi ʾIsrāaʾīla wa baʿathnā minhumuth-nay ʿashara naqībā. Wa qālal-lāhu ʾinnī maʿakum; laʾin ʾaqamtumuṣ-Ṣalāta wa ʾātaytumuz-Zakāta wa ʾāmañtum-biRusulī wa ʿazzartumūhum wa ʾaqraḍtumul-lāha qarḍan ḥasanal-laʾukaffiranna ʿañkum sayyiʾātikum wa laʾudkhilannakum jan-nātiñ-tajrī miñ-taḥtihal-ʾanhār. Famañ-kafara baʿda dhālika miñkum faqad ḍalla sawāaʾas-sabīl. (12)

19 Lit., "of people".

20 Lit., "to stretch their hands towards you": an allusion to the weakness of the believers at the beginning of the Qurʾanic revelation, and – by implication – to the initial weakness of every religious movement.

21 The interpolation of "similar" is justified by the obvious reference to verse 7 above. The pledge was similar in that it related to obedience to God's commandments.

22 Lit., "when We sent out twelve leaders from among them". This is a reference to the Biblical story (in Numbers xiii), according to which God commanded Moses to send out one leading personality from each of the twelve tribes "to spy out the land of Canaan" before the children of Israel invaded it. (The noun *naqīb*, here rendered as "leader", has also the meaning of "investigator" or "spy" inasmuch as it is derived from the verb *naqaba*, which signifies – among other things – "he scrutinized" or "investigated"). The subsequent near-revolt of the children of Israel – caused by their fear of the powerful tribes which inhabited Canaan (cf. Numbers xiv) – is briefly referred to in the first sentence of verse 13 and more fully described in verses 20-26 of this *sūrah*.

23 I.e., by doing righteous deeds.

Then, for having broken their solemn pledge,[24] We rejected them and caused their hearts to harden – [so that now] they distort the meaning of the [revealed] words, taking them out of their context;[25] and they have forgotten much of what they had been told to bear in mind; and from all but a few of them thou wilt always experience treachery. But pardon them, and forbear: verily, God loves the doers of good. ‹13›

And [likewise,] from those who say, "Behold, we are Christians,"[26] We have accepted a solemn pledge: and they, too, have forgotten much of what they had been told to bear in mind – wherefore We have given rise among them to enmity and hatred, [to last] until Resurrection Day:[27] and in time God will cause them to understand what they have contrived. ‹14›

O followers of the Bible! Now there has come unto you Our Apostle, to make clear unto you much of what you have been concealing [from yourselves] of the Bible,[28] and to pardon much. Now there has come unto you from God a light, and a clear divine writ, ‹15› through which God shows unto all that seek His goodly acceptance the paths leading to salvation[29] and, by His grace, brings them out of the depths of darkness into the light and guides them onto a straight way. ‹16›

فَبِمَا نَقۡضِهِم مِّيثَٰقَهُمۡ لَعَنَّٰهُمۡ وَجَعَلۡنَا قُلُوبَهُمۡ قَٰسِيَةٗۖ يُحَرِّفُونَ ٱلۡكَلِمَ
عَن مَّوَاضِعِهِۦ وَنَسُواْ حَظّٗا مِّمَّا ذُكِّرُواْ بِهِۦۚ وَلَا تَزَالُ تَطَّلِعُ عَلَىٰ خَآئِنَةٖ
مِّنۡهُمۡ إِلَّا قَلِيلٗا مِّنۡهُمۡۖ فَٱعۡفُ عَنۡهُمۡ وَٱصۡفَحۡۚ إِنَّ ٱللَّهَ يُحِبُّ ٱلۡمُحۡسِنِينَ ﴿١٣﴾
وَمِنَ ٱلَّذِينَ قَالُوٓاْ إِنَّا نَصَٰرَىٰٓ أَخَذۡنَا مِيثَٰقَهُمۡ فَنَسُواْ حَظّٗا مِّمَّا ذُكِّرُواْ
بِهِۦ فَأَغۡرَيۡنَا بَيۡنَهُمُ ٱلۡعَدَاوَةَ وَٱلۡبَغۡضَآءَ إِلَىٰ يَوۡمِ ٱلۡقِيَٰمَةِۚ وَسَوۡفَ يُنَبِّئُهُمُ
ٱللَّهُ بِمَا كَانُواْ يَصۡنَعُونَ ﴿١٤﴾ يَٰٓأَهۡلَ ٱلۡكِتَٰبِ قَدۡ جَآءَكُمۡ رَسُولُنَا يُبَيِّنُ
لَكُمۡ كَثِيرٗا مِّمَّا كُنتُمۡ تُخۡفُونَ مِنَ ٱلۡكِتَٰبِ وَيَعۡفُواْ عَن كَثِيرٖۚ قَدۡ
جَآءَكُم مِّنَ ٱللَّهِ نُورٞ وَكِتَٰبٞ مُّبِينٞ ﴿١٥﴾ يَهۡدِي بِهِ ٱللَّهُ مَنِ ٱتَّبَعَ
رِضۡوَٰنَهُۥ سُبُلَ ٱلسَّلَٰمِ وَيُخۡرِجُهُم مِّنَ ٱلظُّلُمَٰتِ إِلَى ٱلنُّورِ بِإِذۡنِهِۦ
وَيَهۡدِيهِمۡ إِلَىٰ صِرَٰطٖ مُّسۡتَقِيمٖ ﴿١٦﴾

Fabimā naqḍihim-mīthāqahum laʿannāhum wa jaʿalnā qulūbahum qāsiyah. Yuḥarrifūnal-kalima ʿam-mawāḍiʿihī wa nasū ḥaẓẓam-mimmā dhukkirū bih. Wa lā tazālu taṭṭaliʿu ʿalā khāaʾinatim-minhum ʾillā qalīlam-minhum faʿfu ʿanhum waṣ-faḥ; ʾinnal-lāha yuḥibbul-muḥsinīn. (13) Wa minal-ladhīna qālūu ʾinnā Naṣārāa ʾakhadhnā mīthāqahum fanasū ḥaẓẓam-mimmā dhukkirū bihī faʾaghraynā baynahumul-ʿadāwata wal-baghḍāaʾa ʾilā Yawmil-Qiyāmah. Wa sawfa yunabbiʾuhumul-lāhu bimā kānū yaṣnaʿūn. (14) Yāa ʾahlal-Kitābi qad jāaʾakum Rasūlunā yubayyinu lakum kathīram-mimmā kuntum tukhfūna minal-Kitābi wa yaʿfū ʿañ-kathīr. Qad jāaʾakum-minal-lāhi Nūruñw-wa Kitābum-mubīn. (15) Yahdī bihil-lāhu manit-tabaʿa riḍwānahū subulas-salāmi wa yukhrijuhum-minaẓ-ẓulumāti ʾilan-nūri biʾidhnihī wa yahdīhim ʾilā ṣirāṭim-mustaqīm. (16)

24 An allusion to their lack of trust in God and their persistent sinning.

25 See 4 : 46, where the same accusation is levelled against the children of Israel.

26 Thus the Qur'ān elliptically rejects their claim of being *true* followers of Jesus: for, by wrongfully elevating him to the status of divinity they have denied the very essence of his message.

27 I.e., their going astray from the genuine teachings of Jesus – and thus from true faith in God – is the innermost cause of the enmity and hatred which has so often set the so-called Christian nations against one another and led to unceasing wars and mutual persecution.

28 Inasmuch as verses 15-19 are addressed to the Jews and the Christians, the term *al-kitāb* may suitably be rendered here as "the Bible". It is to he borne in mind that the primary meaning of the verb *khafiya* is "it became imperceptible" or "not apparent" or "obscure", and that the same significance attaches to the transitive form *akhfā*. There is, of course, no doubt that in its transitive form the verb also denotes "he concealed [something]", i.e., from others: but in view of the preceding phrase, "there has come unto you Our Apostle *to make clear unto you*", it is obvious that what is alluded to in this context is the concealing of something *from oneself*: in other words, it is a reference to the gradual obscuring, by the followers of the Bible, of its original verities which they are now unwilling to admit even to themselves.

29 The word *salām*, here rendered as "salvation", has no proper equivalent in the English language. It denotes inner

لَقَدْ كَفَرَ ٱلَّذِينَ قَالُوٓا۟ إِنَّ ٱللَّهَ هُوَ ٱلْمَسِيحُ ٱبْنُ مَرْيَمَ ۚ قُلْ فَمَن يَمْلِكُ مِنَ
ٱللَّهِ شَيْـًٔا إِنْ أَرَادَ أَن يُهْلِكَ ٱلْمَسِيحَ ٱبْنَ مَرْيَمَ وَأُمَّهُۥ وَمَن فِى ٱلْأَرْضِ
جَمِيعًا ۗ وَلِلَّهِ مُلْكُ ٱلسَّمَٰوَٰتِ وَٱلْأَرْضِ وَمَا بَيْنَهُمَا ۚ يَخْلُقُ مَا يَشَآءُ ۚ وَٱللَّهُ
عَلَىٰ كُلِّ شَىْءٍ قَدِيرٌ ﴿١٧﴾ وَقَالَتِ ٱلْيَهُودُ وَٱلنَّصَٰرَىٰ نَحْنُ أَبْنَٰٓؤُا۟ ٱللَّهِ
وَأَحِبَّٰٓؤُهُۥ ۚ قُلْ فَلِمَ يُعَذِّبُكُم بِذُنُوبِكُم ۖ بَلْ أَنتُم بَشَرٌ مِّمَّنْ خَلَقَ ۚ يَغْفِرُ لِمَن
يَشَآءُ وَيُعَذِّبُ مَن يَشَآءُ ۚ وَلِلَّهِ مُلْكُ ٱلسَّمَٰوَٰتِ وَٱلْأَرْضِ وَمَا بَيْنَهُمَا ۖ
وَإِلَيْهِ ٱلْمَصِيرُ ﴿١٨﴾ يَٰٓأَهْلَ ٱلْكِتَٰبِ قَدْ جَآءَكُمْ رَسُولُنَا يُبَيِّنُ لَكُمْ
عَلَىٰ فَتْرَةٍ مِّنَ ٱلرُّسُلِ أَن تَقُولُوا۟ مَا جَآءَنَا مِنۢ بَشِيرٍ وَلَا نَذِيرٍ ۖ فَقَدْ
جَآءَكُم بَشِيرٌ وَنَذِيرٌ ۗ وَٱللَّهُ عَلَىٰ كُلِّ شَىْءٍ قَدِيرٌ ﴿١٩﴾ وَإِذْ قَالَ مُوسَىٰ
لِقَوْمِهِۦ يَٰقَوْمِ ٱذْكُرُوا۟ نِعْمَةَ ٱللَّهِ عَلَيْكُمْ إِذْ جَعَلَ فِيكُمْ أَنۢبِيَآءَ وَجَعَلَكُم

Laqad kafaral-ladhīna qālūu ʾinnal-lāha Huwal-Masīḥub-nu Maryam. Qul famañy-yamliku minal-lāhi shayʾan ʾin ʾarāda ʾañy-yuhlikal-Masīḥab-na Maryama wa ʾummahū wa mañ-fil-ʾarḍi jamīʿā. Wa lillāhi mulkus-samāwāti wal-ʾarḍi wa mā baynahumā. Yakhluqu mā yashāaʾ. Wal-lāhu ʿalā kulli shayʾiñ-Qadīr. (17) Wa qālatil-Yahūdu wan-Naṣārā naḥnu ʾabnāaʾul-lāhi wa ʾaḥibbāaʾuh. Qul falima yuʿadh-dhibukum-bidhunūbikum. Bal ʾañtum-basharum-mimman khalaq. Yaghfiru limañy-yashāaʾu wa yuʿadhdhibu mañy-yashāaʾ. Wa lillāhi mulkus-samāwāti wal-ʾarḍi wa mā baynahumā wa ʾilayhil-maṣīr. (18) Yāa ʾahlal-Kitābi qad jāaʾakum Rasūlunā yubayyinu lakum ʿalā fatratim-minar-Rusuli ʾañ-taqūlū mā jāaʾanā mim-bashīriñw-wa lā nadhīr. Faqad jāaʾakum-bashīruñw-wa nadhīr. Wal-lāhu ʿalā kulli shayʾiñ-Qadīr. (19) Wa ʾidh qāla Mūsā li-qawmihī yā qawmidh-kurū niʿmatal-lāhi ʿalaykum ʾidh jaʿala fīkum ʾAmbiyāaʾa wa jaʿalakum-

Indeed, the truth deny they who say, "Behold, God is the Christ, son of Mary." Say: "And who could have prevailed with God in any way had it been His will to destroy the Christ, son of Mary, and his mother, and everyone who is on earth – all of them? For, God's is the dominion over the heavens and the earth and all that is between them; He creates what He wills: and God has the power to will anything!" ‹17›

And [both] the Jews and the Christians say, "We are God's children,[30] and His beloved ones." Say: "Why, then, does He cause you to suffer for your sins? Nay, you are but human beings of His creating. He forgives whom He wills, and He causes to suffer whom He wills: for God's is the dominion over the heavens and the earth and all that is between them, and with Him is all journeys' end." ‹18›

O followers of the Bible! Now, after a long time during which no apostles have appeared, there has come unto you [this] Our Apostle to make [the truth] clear to you, lest you say, "No bearer of glad tidings has come unto us, nor any warner": for now there has come unto you a bearer of glad tidings and a warner – since God has the power to will anything. ‹19›

AND, LO, Moses said unto his people:[31] "O my people! Remember the blessings which God bestowed upon you when he raised up prophets among you, and made you

peace, soundness and security from evil of any kind, both physical and spiritual, and the achievement of what, in Christian terminology, is described as "salvation": with the difference, however, that the Christian concept of salvation presupposes the existence of an *a-priori* state of sinfulness, which is justified in Christianity by the doctrine of "original sin", but is not justified in Islam, which does not subscribe to this doctrine. Consequently, the term "salvation" – which I am using here for want of a better word – does not adequately convey the full meaning of *salām*. Its nearest equivalents in Western languages would be the German *Heil* or the French *salut*, both of which express the idea of spiritual peace and fulfilment without being necessarily (i.e., linguistically) connected with the Christian doctrine of salvation.

30 Cf. Exodus iv, 22-23 ("Israel is My son"), Jeremiah xxxi, 9 ("I am a father to Israel"), and the many parallel expressions in the Gospels.

31 With these words the Qurʾān returns to the story of the children of Israel alluded to in verses 12 and 13 – namely, to an illustration of their having "broken their solemn pledge" and gone back on their faith in God. The following story is, moreover, directly connected with the preceding verse inasmuch as Moses appeals here to the children of Israel as "a bearer of glad tidings and a warner".

your own masters,[32] and granted unto you [favours] such as He had not granted to anyone else in the world. ‹20› O my people! Enter the holy land which God has promised you; but do not turn back [on your faith], for then you will be lost!" ‹21›
They answered: "O Moses! Behold, ferocious people dwell in that land,[33] and we will surely not enter it unless they depart therefrom; but if they depart therefrom, then, behold, we will enter it." ‹22›
[Whereupon] two men from among those who feared [God, and] whom God had blessed, said: "Enter upon them through the gate[34] – for as soon as you enter it, behold, you shall be victorious! And in God you must place your trust if you are [truly] believers!" ‹23›
[But] they said: "O Moses! Behold, never shall we enter that [land] so long as those others are in it. Go forth, then, thou and thy Sustainer, and fight, both of you! We, behold, shall remain here!" ‹24›
Prayed [Moses]: "O my Sustainer! Of none am I master but of myself and my brother [Aaron]: draw Thou, then, a dividing line between us and these iniquitous folk!" ‹25›
Answered He: "Then, verily, this [land] shall be forbidden to them for forty years, while they wander on earth, bewildered, to and fro; and sorrow thou not over these iniquitous folk." ‹26›

مُّلُوكًا وَءَاتَىٰكُم مَّا لَمْ يُؤْتِ أَحَدًا مِّنَ ٱلْعَٰلَمِينَ ﴿20﴾ يَٰقَوْمِ ٱدْخُلُوا۟
ٱلْأَرْضَ ٱلْمُقَدَّسَةَ ٱلَّتِى كَتَبَ ٱللَّهُ لَكُمْ وَلَا تَرْتَدُّوا۟ عَلَىٰٓ أَدْبَارِكُمْ
فَتَنقَلِبُوا۟ خَٰسِرِينَ ﴿21﴾ قَالُوا۟ يَٰمُوسَىٰٓ إِنَّ فِيهَا قَوْمًا جَبَّارِينَ وَإِنَّا لَن
نَّدْخُلَهَا حَتَّىٰ يَخْرُجُوا۟ مِنْهَا فَإِن يَخْرُجُوا۟ مِنْهَا فَإِنَّا دَٰخِلُونَ ﴿22﴾ قَالَ
رَجُلَانِ مِنَ ٱلَّذِينَ يَخَافُونَ أَنْعَمَ ٱللَّهُ عَلَيْهِمَا ٱدْخُلُوا۟ عَلَيْهِمُ ٱلْبَابَ فَإِذَا
دَخَلْتُمُوهُ فَإِنَّكُمْ غَٰلِبُونَ ۚ وَعَلَى ٱللَّهِ فَتَوَكَّلُوٓا۟ إِن كُنتُم مُّؤْمِنِينَ ﴿23﴾ قَالُوا۟
يَٰمُوسَىٰٓ إِنَّا لَن نَّدْخُلَهَآ أَبَدًا مَّا دَامُوا۟ فِيهَا ۖ فَٱذْهَبْ أَنتَ وَرَبُّكَ فَقَٰتِلَآ
إِنَّا هَٰهُنَا قَٰعِدُونَ ﴿24﴾ قَالَ رَبِّ إِنِّى لَآ أَمْلِكُ إِلَّا نَفْسِى وَأَخِى ۖ فَٱفْرُقْ
بَيْنَنَا وَبَيْنَ ٱلْقَوْمِ ٱلْفَٰسِقِينَ ﴿25﴾ قَالَ فَإِنَّهَا مُحَرَّمَةٌ عَلَيْهِمْ ۛ أَرْبَعِينَ سَنَةً ۛ
يَتِيهُونَ فِى ٱلْأَرْضِ ۚ فَلَا تَأْسَ عَلَى ٱلْقَوْمِ ٱلْفَٰسِقِينَ ﴿26﴾

mulūkañw-wa ʾātākum-mā lam yuʾti ʾaḥadam-minal-ʿālamīn. ⟨20⟩ Yā qawmid-khulul-ʾarḍal-muqaddasatal-latī katabal-lāhu lakum wa lā tartaddū ʿalāa ʾadbārikum fatañqalibū khāsirīn. ⟨21⟩ Qālū yā Mūsāa ʾinna fīhā qawmañ-jabbārīna wa ʾinnā lañ-nadkhulahā ḥattā yakhrujū minhā; faʾiñy-yakhrujū minhā faʾinnā dākhilūn. ⟨22⟩ Qāla rajulāni minal-ladhīna yakhāfūna ʾanʿamal-lāhu ʿalayhimad-khulū ʿalayhimul-bāba faʾidhā dakhaltumūhu faʾin-nakum ghālibūn. Wa ʿalal-lāhi fatawakkalūu ʾiñ-kuñtum-muʾminīn. ⟨23⟩ Qālū yā Mūsāa ʾinnā lañ-nadkhulahāa ʾabadam-mā dāmū fīhā, fadhhab ʾañta wa Rabbuka faqātilāa ʾinnā hāhunā qāʿidūn. ⟨24⟩ Qāla Rabbi ʾinnī lāa ʾamliku ʾillā nafsī wa ʾakhī fafruq baynanā wa baynal-qawmil-fāsiqīn. ⟨25⟩ Qāla faʾinnahā muḥarramatun ʿalayhim ʾarbaʿīna sanatñy-yatīhūna fil-ʾarḍ. Falā taʾsa ʿalal-qawmil-fāsiqīn. ⟨26⟩

32 Lit., "made you kings". According to most of the commentators (e.g., Ṭabarī, Zamakhsharī, Rāzī), the "kingship" of the Israelites is a metaphorical allusion to their freedom and independence after their Egyptian bondage, the term "king" being equivalent here to "a free man who is master of his own affairs" (*Manār* VI, 323 f.) and can, therefore, adopt any way of life he chooses.

33 Lit., "are in it". See Numbers xiii, 32-33, and also the whole of ch. xiv, which speaks of the terror that overwhelmed the Israelites on hearing the report of the twelve scouts mentioned in verse 12 of this *sūrah*, and of the punishment of their cowardice and lack of faith.

34 I.e., by frontal attack. According to the Bible (Numbers xiv, 6-9, 24, 30, 38), the two God-fearing men were Joshua and Caleb, who had been among the twelve spies sent out to explore Canaan, and who now tried to persuade the terror-stricken children of Israel to place their trust in God. As so often in the Qurʾān, this story of the Israelites serves to illustrate the difference between real, selfless faith and worldly self-love.

AND CONVEY unto them, setting forth the truth, the story of the two sons of Adam[35] – how each offered a sacrifice, and it was accepted from one of them whereas it was not accepted from the other.
[And Cain] said: "I will surely slay thee!"
[Abel] replied: "Behold, God accepts only from those who are conscious of Him. ‹27›
Even if thou lay thy hand on me to slay me, I shall not lay my hand on thee to slay thee: behold, I fear God, the Sustainer of all the worlds. ‹28› I am willing, indeed, for thee to bear [the burden of] all the sins ever done by me as well as of the sin done by thee:[36] [but] then thou wouldst be destined for the fire, since that is the requital of evildoers!" ‹29›
But the other's passion[37] drove him to slaying his brother; and he slew him: and thus he became one of the lost. ‹30›
Thereupon God sent forth a raven which scratched the earth, to show him how he might conceal the nakedness of his brother's body. [And Cain] cried out: "Oh, woe is me! Am I then too weak to do what this raven did,[38] and to conceal the nakedness of my brother's body?" – and was thereupon smitten with remorse.[39] ‹31›
Because of this did We ordain unto the children of Israel that if anyone slays a human being – unless it be [in punishment] for murder or for spreading corruption on earth – it shall be as though he had slain

۞ وَٱتْلُ عَلَيْهِمْ نَبَأَ ٱبْنَىْ ءَادَمَ بِٱلْحَقِّ إِذْ قَرَّبَا قُرْبَانًا فَتُقُبِّلَ مِنْ أَحَدِهِمَا وَلَمْ
يُتَقَبَّلْ مِنَ ٱلْـَٔاخَرِ قَالَ لَأَقْتُلَنَّكَ ۖ قَالَ إِنَّمَا يَتَقَبَّلُ ٱللَّهُ مِنَ ٱلْمُتَّقِينَ ﴿٢٧﴾ لَئِنۢ
بَسَطتَ إِلَىَّ يَدَكَ لِتَقْتُلَنِى مَآ أَنَا۠ بِبَاسِطٍ يَدِىَ إِلَيْكَ لِأَقْتُلَكَ ۖ إِنِّىٓ أَخَافُ ٱللَّهَ
رَبَّ ٱلْعَٰلَمِينَ ﴿٢٨﴾ إِنِّىٓ أُرِيدُ أَن تَبُوٓأَ بِإِثْمِى وَإِثْمِكَ فَتَكُونَ مِنْ أَصْحَٰبِ
ٱلنَّارِ ۚ وَذَٰلِكَ جَزَٰٓؤُا۟ ٱلظَّٰلِمِينَ ﴿٢٩﴾ فَطَوَّعَتْ لَهُۥ نَفْسُهُۥ قَتْلَ أَخِيهِ فَقَتَلَهُۥ
فَأَصْبَحَ مِنَ ٱلْخَٰسِرِينَ ﴿٣٠﴾ فَبَعَثَ ٱللَّهُ غُرَابًا يَبْحَثُ فِى ٱلْأَرْضِ لِيُرِيَهُۥ
كَيْفَ يُوَٰرِى سَوْءَةَ أَخِيهِ ۚ قَالَ يَٰوَيْلَتَىٰٓ أَعَجَزْتُ أَنْ أَكُونَ مِثْلَ هَٰذَا
ٱلْغُرَابِ فَأُوَٰرِىَ سَوْءَةَ أَخِى ۖ فَأَصْبَحَ مِنَ ٱلنَّٰدِمِينَ ﴿٣١﴾ مِنْ أَجْلِ ذَٰلِكَ كَتَبْنَا عَلَىٰ 12 حزب
بَنِىٓ إِسْرَٰٓءِيلَ أَنَّهُۥ مَن قَتَلَ نَفْسًۢا بِغَيْرِ نَفْسٍ أَوْ فَسَادٍ فِى ٱلْأَرْضِ فَكَأَنَّمَا قَتَلَ

۞ Wat-lu ʿalayhim nabaʾab-nay ʾĀdama bilḥaqqi ʾidh qarrabā qurbānañ-fatuqubbila min ʾaḥadihimā wa lam yutaqabbal minal-ʾākhari qāla laʾaqtulan-nak. Qāla ʾinnamā yataqabbalul-lāhu minal-mut-taqīn. (27) Laʾim-basaṭta ʾilayya yadaka litaqtulanī māa ʾana bibāsiṭiñy-yadiya ʾilayka liʾaqtulaka ʾinnīi ʾakhāful-lāha Rabbal-ʿālamīn. (28) ʾInnīi ʾurīdu ʾañ-tabūuʾa biʾithmī wa ʾithmika fatakūna min ʾaṣḥā-bin-nār. Wa dhālika jazāaʾuẓ-ẓālimīn. (29) Faṭawwaʿat lahū nafsuhū qatla ʾakhīhi faqatalahū faʾaṣbaḥa mi-nal-khāsirīn. (30) Fabaʿathal-lāhu ghurābañy-yabḥa-thu fil-ʾarḍi liyuriyahū kayfa yuwārī sawʾata ʾakhīh. Qāla yā waylatāa ʾaʿajaztu ʾan ʾakūna mithla hādhal-ghurābi faʾuwāriya sawʾata ʾakhī faʾaṣbaḥa minan-nādimīn. (31) Min ʾajli dhālika katabnā ʿalā banīi ʾIsrāaʾīla ʾannahū mañ-qatala nafsam-bighayri nafsin ʾaw fasādiñ-fil-ʾarḍi fakaʾannamā qatalan-

35 I.e., the story of Cain and Abel, mentioned in Genesis iv, 1-16. The pronoun in "tell them" refers to the followers of the Bible, and obviously connects with verse 15 of this *sūrah*, "Now there has come unto you Our Apostle, to make clear unto you much of what you have been concealing [from yourselves] of the Bible", the meaning of which has been explained in note 28 above. The moral of this particular Biblical story – a moral which the followers of the Bible have been "concealing from themselves" – is summarized in verse 32.

36 Lit., "my sin as well as thy sin". It is evident from several well-authenticated *aḥādīth* that if a person dies a violent death not caused, directly or indirectly, by his own sinful actions, his previous sins will be forgiven (the reason being, evidently, that he had no time to repent, as he might have done had he been allowed to live). In cases of unprovoked murder, the murderer is burdened – in addition to the sin of murder – with the sins which his innocent victim might have committed in the past and of which he (the victim) is now absolved: this convincing interpretation of the above verse has been advanced by Mujāhid (as quoted by Ṭabarī).

37 Among the many meanings attributable to the noun *nafs* (primarily, "soul", or "mind", or "self"), there is also that of "desire" or "passionate determination" (*Qāmūs*; see also Zamakhsharī's *Asās*); in this context, the best rendering seems to be "passion".

38 Lit., "to be like this raven".

39 Lit., "became of those who feel remorse". The thought of burying his dead brother's body, suggested to Cain by the raven's scratching the earth, brought home to him the enormity of his crime.

all mankind; whereas, if anyone saves a life, it shall be as though he had saved the lives of all mankind.[40]

And, indeed, there came unto them[41] Our apostles with all evidence of the truth: yet, behold, notwithstanding all this, many of them go on committing all manner of excesses on earth.[42] ⟨32⟩

It is but a just recompense for those who make war on God and His apostle,[43] and endeavour to spread corruption on earth, that they are being slain in great numbers, or crucified in great numbers, or have, in result of their perverseness, their hands and feet cut off in great numbers,[44] or are being [entirely] banished from [the face of] the earth: such is their ignominy in this world.[45] But in the life to come [yet more] awesome suffering awaits them ⟨33⟩ –

ٱلنَّاسَ جَمِيعًا وَمَنْ أَحْيَاهَا فَكَأَنَّمَآ أَحْيَا ٱلنَّاسَ جَمِيعًا ۚ وَلَقَدْ
جَآءَتْهُمْ رُسُلُنَا بِٱلْبَيِّنَٰتِ ثُمَّ إِنَّ كَثِيرًا مِّنْهُم بَعْدَ ذَٰلِكَ فِى ٱلْأَرْضِ
لَمُسْرِفُونَ ﴿٣٢﴾ إِنَّمَا جَزَٰٓؤُا۟ ٱلَّذِينَ يُحَارِبُونَ ٱللَّهَ وَرَسُولَهُۥ وَيَسْعَوْنَ فِى
ٱلْأَرْضِ فَسَادًا أَن يُقَتَّلُوٓا۟ أَوْ يُصَلَّبُوٓا۟ أَوْ تُقَطَّعَ أَيْدِيهِمْ وَأَرْجُلُهُم مِّنْ
خِلَٰفٍ أَوْ يُنفَوْا۟ مِنَ ٱلْأَرْضِ ۚ ذَٰلِكَ لَهُمْ خِزْىٌ فِى ٱلدُّنْيَا ۖ وَلَهُمْ فِى
ٱلْءَاخِرَةِ عَذَابٌ عَظِيمٌ ﴿٣٣﴾

nāsa jamīᶜañw-wa man ᵓaḥyāhā fakaᵓannamāa ᵓaḥyan-nāsa jamīᶜā. Wa laqad jāaᵓat-hum Rusulunā bilbayyināti thumma ᵓinna kathīram-minhum-baᶜda dhālika fil-ᵓarḍi lamusrifūn. ⟨32⟩ ᵓInnamā jazāaᵓul-ladhīna yuḥāribūnal-lāha wa Rasūlahū wa yasᶜawna fil-ᵓarḍi fasādan ᵓañy-yuqattalūu ᵓaw yuṣallabūu ᵓaw tuqaṭṭaᶜa ᵓaydīhim wa ᵓarjuluhum-min khilāfin ᵓaw yuñfaw minal-ᵓarḍ. Dhālika lahum khizyuñ-fid-dunyā wa lahum fil-ᵓĀkhirati ᶜadhābun ᶜaẓīm. ⟨33⟩

40 This moral truth is among those to which the first sentence of verse 15 of this *sūrah* alludes, and its succinct formulation fully explains the reason why the story of Cain and Abel is mentioned in this context. The expression "We have ordained unto the children of Israel" does not, of course, detract from the *universal* validity of this moral: it refers merely to its earliest enunciation.

41 I.e., to the followers of the Bible, both the Jews and the Christians.

42 The present participle *la-musrifūn* indicates their "*continuously* committing excesses" (i.e., crimes), and is best rendered as "they go on committing" them. In view of the preceding passages, these "excesses" obviously refer to crimes of violence and, in particular, to the ruthless killing of human beings.

43 The term "apostle" is evidently generic in this context. By "making war on God and His apostle" is meant a hostile opposition to, and wilful disregard of, the ethical precepts ordained by God and explained by all His apostles, combined with the conscious endeavour to destroy or undermine other people's belief in God as well.

44 In classical Arabic idiom, the "cutting off of one's hands and feet" is often synonymous with "destroying one's power", and it is possibly in this sense that the expression has been used here. Alternatively, it might denote "being mutilated", both physically and metaphorically – similar to the (metonymical) use of the expression "being crucified" in the sense of "being tortured". The phrase *min khilāf* – usually rendered as "from opposite sides" – is derived from the verb *khalafahu*, "he disagreed with him", or "opposed him", or "acted contrarily to him": consequently, the primary meaning of *min khilāf* is "in result of contrariness" or "of perverseness".

45 Most of the classical commentators regard this passage as a *legal injunction*, and interpret it, therefore, as follows: "The recompense of those who make war on God and His apostle and spread corruption on earth shall but be that they shall be slain, or crucified, or that their hands and feet be cut off on opposite sides, or that they shall be banished from the earth: such shall be their ignominy in this world." This interpretation is, however, in no way warranted by the text, and this for the following reasons:

(a) The four passive verbs occurring in this sentence – "slain", "crucified", "cut off" and "banished" – are in the present tense and do not, by themselves, indicate the future or, alternatively, the imperative mood.

(b) The form *yuqattalū* does not signify simply "they are being slain" or (as the commentators would have it) "they shall be slain", but denotes – in accordance with a fundamental rule of Arabic grammar – "they are being slain in great numbers"; and the same holds true of the verbal forms *yuṣallabū* ("they are being crucified in great numbers") and *tuqaṭṭaᶜa* ("cut off in great numbers"). Now if we are to believe that these are "ordained punishments", it would imply that great numbers – but not necessarily all – of "those who make war on God and His apostle" should be punished in this way: obviously an inadmissible assumption of arbitrariness on the part of the Divine Law-Giver. Moreover, if the party "waging war on God and His apostle" should happen to consist of one person only, or of a few, how could a command referring to "great numbers" be applied to them or to him?

save for such [of them] as repent ere you [O believers] become more powerful than they:[46] for you must know that God is much-forgiving, a dispenser of grace. ‹34›

O YOU who have attained to faith! Remain conscious of God, and seek to come closer unto Him, and strive hard in His cause, so that you might attain to a happy state. ‹35›

Verily, if those who are bent on denying the truth had all that is on earth, and twice as much,[47] to offer as ransom from suffering on the Day of Resurrection, it would not be accepted from them: for grievous suffering awaits them. ‹36› They will wish to come out of the fire, but they shall not come out of it; and long-lasting suffering awaits them. ‹37›

إِلَّا ٱلَّذِينَ تَابُوا۟ مِن قَبْلِ أَن تَقْدِرُوا۟ عَلَيْهِمْ ۖ فَٱعْلَمُوٓا۟ أَنَّ ٱللَّهَ غَفُورٌ
رَّحِيمٌ ﴿٣٤﴾ يَٰٓأَيُّهَا ٱلَّذِينَ ءَامَنُوا۟ ٱتَّقُوا۟ ٱللَّهَ وَٱبْتَغُوٓا۟ إِلَيْهِ ٱلْوَسِيلَةَ
وَجَٰهِدُوا۟ فِى سَبِيلِهِۦ لَعَلَّكُمْ تُفْلِحُونَ ﴿٣٥﴾ إِنَّ ٱلَّذِينَ كَفَرُوا۟ لَوْ أَنَّ
لَهُم مَّا فِى ٱلْأَرْضِ جَمِيعًا وَمِثْلَهُۥ مَعَهُۥ لِيَفْتَدُوا۟ بِهِۦ مِنْ عَذَابِ يَوْمِ
ٱلْقِيَٰمَةِ مَا تُقُبِّلَ مِنْهُمْ ۖ وَلَهُمْ عَذَابٌ أَلِيمٌ ﴿٣٦﴾ يُرِيدُونَ أَن يَخْرُجُوا۟ مِنَ
ٱلنَّارِ وَمَا هُم بِخَٰرِجِينَ مِنْهَا ۖ وَلَهُمْ عَذَابٌ مُّقِيمٌ ﴿٣٧﴾

ʾIllal-ladhīna tābū miñ-qabli ʾañ-taqdirū ᶜalayhim; faᶜlamūu ʾannal-lāha Ghafūrur-Raḥīm. (34) Yāa ʾayyuhal-ladhīna ʾāmanut-taqul-lāha wab-taghūu ʾilayhil-wasīlata wa jāhidū fī sabīlihī laᶜallakum tufliḥūn. (35) ʾInnal-ladhīna kafaru law ʾanna lahum-mā fil-ʾarḍi jamīᶜañw-wa mithlahū maᶜahū liyaftadū bihī min ᶜadhābi Yawmil-Qiyāmati mā tuqubbila minhum. Wa lahum ᶜadhābun ʾalīm. (36) Yurīdūna ʾañy-yakhrujū minan-nāri wa mā hum-bikhārijīna minhā; wa lahum ᶜadhābum-muqīm. (37)

(c) Furthermore, what would be the meaning of the phrase, "they shall be banished from the earth", if the above verse is to be taken as a legal injunction? This point has, indeed, perplexed the commentators considerably. Some of them assume that the transgressors should be "banished from the land [of Islam]": but there is no instance in the Qurʾān of such a restricted use of the term "earth" (*arḍ*). Others, again, are of the opinion that the guilty ones should be imprisoned in a subterranean dungeon, which would constitute their "banishment from [the face of] the earth"!

(d) Finally – and this is the weightiest objection to an interpretation of the above verse as a "legal injunction" – the Qurʾān places exactly the same expressions referring to mass-crucifixion and mass-mutilation (but this time with a definite *intent* relating to the future) in the mouth of Pharaoh, as a threat to believers (see 7 : 124, 20 : 71 and 26 : 49). Since Pharaoh is invariably described in the Qurʾān as the epitome of evil and godlessness, it is inconceivable that the same Qurʾān would promulgate a divine law in precisely the terms which it attributes elsewhere to a figure characterized as an "enemy of God".

In short, the attempt of the commentators to interpret the above verse as a "legal injunction" must be categorically rejected, however great the names of the persons responsible for it. On the other hand, a really convincing interpretation suggests itself to us at once as soon as we read the verse – as it ought to be read – in the *present tense*: for, read in this way, the verse reveals itself immediately as a *statement of fact* – a declaration of the inescapability of the retribution which "those who make war on God" bring upon themselves. Their hostility to ethical imperatives causes them to lose sight of all moral values; and their consequent mutual discord and "perverseness" gives rise to unending strife among themselves for the sake of worldly gain and power: they kill one another in great numbers, and torture and mutilate one another in great numbers, with the result that whole communities are wiped out or, as the Qurʾān puts it, "banished from [the face of] the earth". It is this interpretation alone that takes full account of all the expressions occurring in this verse – the reference to "great numbers" in connection with deeds of extreme violence, the "banishment from the earth", and, lastly, the fact that these horrors are expressed in the terms used by Pharaoh, the "enemy of God".

46 I.e., before belief in God and in the ethical principles decreed by Him becomes prevalent: for, in that event, repentance on the part of "those who make war on God and His apostle" would be no more than an act of conforming to the dominant trend and, therefore, of no moral value whatever. It is to be noted that the exemption from suffering relates to the *hereafter*.

47 Lit., "and the like with it".

NOW AS FOR the man who steals and the woman who steals, cut off the hand of either of them in requital for what they have wrought, as a deterrent ordained by God:[48] for God is almighty, wise. ⟨38⟩ But as for him who repents after having thus done

وَٱلسَّارِقُ وَٱلسَّارِقَةُ فَٱقْطَعُوٓاْ أَيْدِيَهُمَا جَزَآءًۢ بِمَا كَسَبَا نَكَـٰلًا مِّنَ ٱللَّهِ ۗ وَٱللَّهُ عَزِيزٌ حَكِيمٌ ﴿٣٨﴾ فَمَن تَابَ مِنۢ بَعْدِ ظُلْمِهِۦ

Was-sāriqu was-sāriqatu faqṭaᶜūu ᵓaydiyahumā jazāaᵓam-bimā kasabā nakālam-minal-lāh. Wal-lāhu ᶜAzīzun Ḥakīm. (38) Famañ-tāba mim-baᶜdi ẓulmihī

48 The extreme severity of this Qurᵓanic punishment can be understood only if one bears in mind the fundamental principle of Islamic Law that no duty (*taklīf*) is ever imposed on man without his being granted a corresponding right (*ḥaqq*); and the term "duty" also comprises, in this context, liability to punishment. Now, among the inalienable rights of every member of the Islamic society – Muslim and non-Muslim alike – is the right to *protection* (in every sense of the word) by the community as a whole. As is evident from innumerable Qurᵓanic ordinances as well as the Prophet's injunctions forthcoming from authentic Traditions, every citizen is entitled to a share in the community's economic resources and, thus, to the enjoyment of social security: in other words, he or she must be assured of an equitable standard of living *commensurate with the resources at the disposal of the community.* For, although the Qurᵓān makes it clear that human life cannot be expressed in terms of physical existence alone – the ultimate values of life being spiritual in nature – the believers are not entitled to look upon spiritual truths and values as something that could be divorced from the physical and social factors of human existence. In short, Islam envisages and demands a society that provides not only for the spiritual needs of man, but for his bodily and intellectual needs as well. It follows, therefore, that – in order to be truly Islamic – a society (or state) must be so constituted that every individual, man and woman, may enjoy that minimum of material well-being and security without which there can be no human dignity, no real freedom and, in the last resort, no spiritual progress: for, there can be no real happiness and strength in a society that permits some of its members to suffer undeserved want while others have more than they need. If the whole society suffers privations owing to circumstances beyond its control (as happened, for instance, to the Muslim community in the early days of Islam), such shared privations may become a source of spiritual strength and, through it, of future greatness. But if the available resources of a community are so unevenly distributed that certain groups within it live in affluence while the majority of the people are forced to use up all their energies in search of their daily bread, poverty becomes the most dangerous enemy of spiritual progress, and occasionally drives whole communities away from God-consciousness and into the arms of soul-destroying materialism. It was undoubtedly this that the Prophet had in mind when he uttered the warning words (quoted by As-Suyūṭī in *Al-Jāmiᶜ aṣ-Ṣaghīr*), "Poverty may well turn into a denial of the truth (*kufr*)." Consequently, the social legislation of Islam aims at a state of affairs in which every man, woman and child has (a) enough to eat and wear, (b) an adequate home, (c) equal opportunities and facilities for education, and (d) free medical care in health and in sickness. A corollary of these rights is the right to productive and remunerative work while of working age and in good health, and a provision (by the community or the state) of adequate nourishment, shelter, etc., in cases of disability resulting from illness, widowhood, enforced unemployment, old age, or under-age. As already mentioned, the communal obligation to create such a comprehensive social security scheme has been laid down in many Qurᵓanic verses, and has been amplified and explained by a great number of the Prophet's commandments. It was the second Caliph, ᶜUmar ibn al-Khaṭṭāb, who began to translate these ordinances into a concrete administrative scheme (see Ibn Saᶜd, *Ṭabaqāt* III/1, 213-217); but after his premature death, his successors had neither the vision nor the statesmanship to continue his unfinished work.

It is against the background of this social security scheme envisaged by Islam that the Qurᵓān imposes the severe sentence of hand-cutting as a deterrent punishment for robbery. Since, under the circumstances outlined above, "temptation" cannot be admitted as a justifiable excuse, and since, in the last resort, the entire socio-economic system of Islam is based on the faith of its adherents, its balance is extremely delicate and in need of constant, strictly-enforced protection. In a community in which everyone is assured of full security and social justice, any attempt on the part of an individual to achieve an easy, unjustified gain at the expense of other members of the community must be considered *an attack against the system as a whole,* and must be punished as such: and, therefore, the above ordinance which lays down that the hand of the thief shall be cut off. One must, however, always bear in mind the principle mentioned at the beginning of this note: namely, the absolute interdependence between man's rights and corresponding duties (including liability to punishment). In a community or state which neglects or is unable to provide complete social security for all its members, the temptation to enrich oneself by illegal means often becomes irresistible – and, consequently, theft cannot and should not be punished as severely as it should be punished in a state in which social security is a reality in the full sense of the word. If the society is unable to fulfil its *duties* with regard to every one of its members, it has no *right* to invoke the full sanction of criminal law (*ḥadd*) against the individual transgressor, but must confine itself to milder forms of administrative punishment. (It was in correct appreciation of this principle that the great Caliph ᶜUmar waived the *ḥadd* of hand-cutting in a period of famine which afflicted Arabia during his reign.) To sum up, one may safely conclude that the cutting-off of a hand in punishment for theft is applicable only within the context of an already-existing, fully functioning social security scheme, and in no other circumstances.

wrong, and makes amends,[49] behold, God will accept his repentance: verily, God is much-forgiving, a dispenser of grace. ‹39› Dost thou not know that God's is the dominion over the heavens and the earth? He chastises whom He wills, and He forgives whom He wills: for God has the power to will anything. ‹40›

O APOSTLE! Be not grieved by those who vie with one another in denying the truth: such as those[50] who say with their mouths, "We believe," the while their hearts do not believe; and such of the Jewish faith as eagerly listen to any falsehood, eagerly listen to other people without having come to thee [for enlightenment].[51] They distort the meaning of the [revealed] words, taking them out of their context, saying [to themselves], "If such-and-such [teaching] is vouchsafed unto you, accept it; but if it is not vouchsafed unto you, be on your guard!"[52]
[Be not grieved by them –] for, if God wills anyone to be tempted to evil, thou canst in no wise prevail with God in his behalf.[53] It is they whose hearts God is not willing to cleanse. Theirs shall be ignominy in this world, and awesome suffering in the life to come ‹41› – those who eagerly listen to any falsehood, greedily swallowing all that is evil![54]

وَأَصْلَحَ فَإِنَّ ٱللَّهَ يَتُوبُ عَلَيْهِ ۗ إِنَّ ٱللَّهَ غَفُورٌ رَّحِيمٌ ﴿٣٩﴾ أَلَمْ تَعْلَمْ أَنَّ ٱللَّهَ
لَهُۥ مُلْكُ ٱلسَّمَٰوَٰتِ وَٱلْأَرْضِ يُعَذِّبُ مَن يَشَآءُ وَيَغْفِرُ لِمَن يَشَآءُ ۗ وَٱللَّهُ
عَلَىٰ كُلِّ شَىْءٍ قَدِيرٌ ﴿٤٠﴾ ۞ يَٰٓأَيُّهَا ٱلرَّسُولُ لَا يَحْزُنكَ ٱلَّذِينَ يُسَٰرِعُونَ
فِى ٱلْكُفْرِ مِنَ ٱلَّذِينَ قَالُوٓا۟ ءَامَنَّا بِأَفْوَٰهِهِمْ وَلَمْ تُؤْمِن قُلُوبُهُمْ ۛ وَمِنَ
ٱلَّذِينَ هَادُوا۟ ۛ سَمَّٰعُونَ لِلْكَذِبِ سَمَّٰعُونَ لِقَوْمٍ ءَاخَرِينَ لَمْ يَأْتُوكَ ۖ يُحَرِّفُونَ
ٱلْكَلِمَ مِنۢ بَعْدِ مَوَاضِعِهِۦ ۖ يَقُولُونَ إِنْ أُوتِيتُمْ هَٰذَا فَخُذُوهُ وَإِن لَّمْ
تُؤْتَوْهُ فَٱحْذَرُوا۟ ۚ وَمَن يُرِدِ ٱللَّهُ فِتْنَتَهُۥ فَلَن تَمْلِكَ لَهُۥ مِنَ ٱللَّهِ شَيْـًٔا ۚ
أُو۟لَٰٓئِكَ ٱلَّذِينَ لَمْ يُرِدِ ٱللَّهُ أَن يُطَهِّرَ قُلُوبَهُمْ ۚ لَهُمْ فِى ٱلدُّنْيَا خِزْىٌ ۖ
وَلَهُمْ فِى ٱلْءَاخِرَةِ عَذَابٌ عَظِيمٌ ﴿٤١﴾ سَمَّٰعُونَ لِلْكَذِبِ أَكَّٰلُونَ لِلسُّحْتِ

ربع الحزب

wa ʾaṣlaḥa faʾinnal-lāha yatūbu ʿalayh. ʾInnal-lāha Ghafūrur-Raḥīm. ﴿39﴾ ʾAlam taʿlam ʾannal-lāha lahū mulkus-samāwāti wal-ʾarḍi yuʿadhdhibu mañy-yashāaʾu wa yaghfiru limañy-yashāaʾ. Wal-lāhu ʿalā kulli shayʾiñ-Qadīr. ﴿40﴾ ۞ Yāa ʾayyuhar-Rasūlu lā yaḥzunkal-ladhīna yusāriʿūna fil-kufri minal-ladhīna qālūu ʾāmannā biʾafwāhihim wa lam tuʾmiñ-qulūbuhum. Wa minal-ladhīna hādū sammāʿūna lil-kadhibi sammāʿūna liqawmin ʾākharīna lam yaʾtūk. Yuḥarrifūnal-kalima mim-baʿdi mawāḍiʿih. Yaqūlūna ʾin ʾūtītum hādhā fakhudhūhu wa ʾil-lam tuʾtawhu faḥdharū. Wa mañy-yuridil-lāhu fitnatahū falañ-tamlika lahu minal-lāhi shayʾā. ʾUlāaʾikal-ladhīna lam yuridil-lāhu ʾañy-yuṭahhira qulūbahum. Lahum fid-dunyā khizyuñw-wa lahum fil-ʾĀkhirati ʿadhābun ʿaẓīm. ﴿41﴾ Sammāʿūna lilkadhibi ʾakkālūna lissuḥt.

49 I.e., by restituting the stolen goods before being apprehended by the authorities (*Manār* VI, 382).

50 Lit., "from among those".

51 Although this verse is, in the first instance, addressed to the Prophet, it concerns all followers of the Qurʾān and is, therefore, valid for all times. The same observation applies to the people of whom this verse speaks: although it mentions only the hypocrites and the Jews, it refers, by implication, to all people who are prejudiced against Islam and willingly lend ear to any false statement about its teachings, preferring to listen to unfriendly non-Muslim "experts" rather than to turn to the Qurʾān itself for enlightenment – which is the meaning of the phrase, "without having come to thee [O Muḥammad]".

52 I.e., they are prepared to accept such of the Qurʾanic teachings as might suit their preconceived notions, but are not prepared to accept anything that goes against their own inclinations.

53 This connects with the beginning of this verse; hence my interpolation. For the meaning of *fitnah*, see *sūrah* 8, note 25.

54 The noun *suḥt* is derived from the verb *saḥata*, "he utterly destroyed [a thing]", and signifies, primarily, the "doing of anything that leads to destruction" because it is abominable and, therefore, forbidden (*Lisān al-ʿArab*). Hence, it denotes anything that is evil in itself. In the above context, the intensive expression *akkālūn li' s-suḥt* may denote "those who greedily devour all that is forbidden" (i.e., illicit gain), or, more probably, "those who greedily swallow all that is evil" – i.e., every false statement made about the Qurʾān by its enemies with a view to destroying its impact.

فَإِن جَآءُوكَ فَٱحۡكُم بَيۡنَهُمۡ أَوۡ أَعۡرِضۡ عَنۡهُمۡۖ وَإِن تُعۡرِضۡ عَنۡهُمۡ فَلَن
يَضُرُّوكَ شَيۡـٔٗاۖ وَإِنۡ حَكَمۡتَ فَٱحۡكُم بَيۡنَهُم بِٱلۡقِسۡطِۚ إِنَّ ٱللَّهَ يُحِبُّ
ٱلۡمُقۡسِطِينَ ﴿٤٢﴾ وَكَيۡفَ يُحَكِّمُونَكَ وَعِندَهُمُ ٱلتَّوۡرَىٰةُ فِيهَا حُكۡمُ ٱللَّهِ
ثُمَّ يَتَوَلَّوۡنَ مِنۢ بَعۡدِ ذَٰلِكَۚ وَمَآ أُوْلَٰٓئِكَ بِٱلۡمُؤۡمِنِينَ ﴿٤٣﴾ إِنَّآ أَنزَلۡنَا
ٱلتَّوۡرَىٰةَ فِيهَا هُدٗى وَنُورٞۚ يَحۡكُمُ بِهَا ٱلنَّبِيُّونَ ٱلَّذِينَ أَسۡلَمُواْ لِلَّذِينَ
هَادُواْ وَٱلرَّبَّٰنِيُّونَ وَٱلۡأَحۡبَارُ بِمَا ٱسۡتُحۡفِظُواْ مِن كِتَٰبِ ٱللَّهِ وَكَانُواْ
عَلَيۡهِ شُهَدَآءَۚ فَلَا تَخۡشَوُاْ ٱلنَّاسَ وَٱخۡشَوۡنِ وَلَا تَشۡتَرُواْ بِـَٔايَٰتِي ثَمَنٗا
قَلِيلٗاۚ وَمَن لَّمۡ يَحۡكُم بِمَآ أَنزَلَ ٱللَّهُ فَأُوْلَٰٓئِكَ هُمُ ٱلۡكَٰفِرُونَ ﴿٤٤﴾

Hence, if they come to thee [for judgment],[55] thou mayest either judge between them or leave them alone: for, if thou leave them alone, they cannot harm thee in any way. But if thou dost judge, judge between them with equity:[56] verily, God loves those who act equitably. «42»

But how is it that they ask thee for judgment – seeing that they have the Torah, containing God's injunctions – and thereafter turn away [from thy judgment]? Such as these, then, are no [true] believers.[57] «43»

Verily, it is We who bestowed from on high the Torah, wherein there was guidance and light. On its strength did the prophets, who had surrendered themselves unto God, deliver judgment unto those who followed the Jewish faith;[58] and so did the [early] men of God and the rabbis, inasmuch as some of God's writ had been entrusted to their care:[59] and they [all] bore witness to its truth.

Therefore, [O children of Israel,] hold not men in awe, but stand in awe of Me; and do not barter away My messages for a trifling gain:[60] for they who do not judge in accordance with what God has bestowed from on high are, indeed, deniers of the truth! «44»

Faʾiñ-jāaʾūka faḥkum-baynahum ʾaw ʾaʿriḍ ʿanhum. Wa ʾiñ-tuʿriḍ ʿanhum falañy-yaḍurrūka shayʾā. Wa ʾin ḥakamta faḥkum-baynahum-bilqisṭ. ʾInnal-lāha yuḥibbul-muqsiṭīn. (42) Wa kayfa yuḥakkimūnaka wa ʿiñdahumut-Tawrātu fīhā ḥukmul-lāhi thumma yatawallawna mim-baʿdi dhālik. Wa māa ʾulāaʾika bil-muʾminīn. (43) ʾInnāa ʾañzalnat-Tawrāta fīhā hudañw-wa nūr. Yaḥkumu bihan-Nabiyyūnal-ladhīna ʾaslamū lilladhīna hādū war-rabbāniyyūna wal-ʾaḥbāru bimas-tuḥfiẓū miñ-Kitābil-lāhi wa kānū ʿalayhi shuhadāaʾ. Falā takhshawun-nāsa wakhshawni wa lā tashtarū biʾĀyātī thamanañ-qalīlā. Wa mal-lam yaḥkum-bimāa ʾañzalal-lāhu faʾulāaʾika humul-kāfirūn. (44)

55 I.e., as to what is right and what is wrong in the sight of God. Most of the commentators assume that this passage refers to a specific judicial case, or cases, which the Jews of Medina brought before the Prophet for decision; but in view of the inherent Qurʾanic principle that every historical reference contained in it has also a general import, I rather believe that the "judgment" alluded to in this verse relates to deciding as to whether any of their beliefs – other than those which the Qurʾān explicitly confirms or rejects – is right or wrong.

56 I.e., on the basis of the ethical laws revealed by God, and not in accordance with their personal, arbitrary likes or dislikes.

57 This verse illustrates the strange mentality of the Jews, who – despite the fact that they believe the Torah to contain all of the Divine Law – surreptitiously turn to a religious dispensation in which they do not believe, in the hope that its verdict on certain ethical questions might confirm some of their own wishful beliefs which happen to run counter to the Torah. In other words, they are not *really* prepared to submit to the judgment of the Torah – although they assert their belief in it – nor the judgment of the Qurʾān, which confirms some of the laws of the Torah and abrogates others: for, as soon as they come to realize that the Qurʾān does not agree with their preconceived ideas, they turn away from it.

58 Implying that the Law of Moses (the Torah) was intended only for the children of Israel, and was never meant to have universal validity.

59 The expression "*some* of God's writ (*kitāb*)" implies that the Torah did not exhaust the whole of God's revelation, and that more was yet to be revealed. For an explanation of the term *rabbāniyūn*, see *sūrah* 3, note 62.

60 I.e., for the illusory feeling of superiority based on the spurious belief that the children of Israel are "God's chosen people" and, therefore, the sole recipients of God's grace and revelation. The "messages" referred to in this sentence relate to the Qurʾān as well as to the Biblical prophecies concerning the advent of Muḥammad.

وَكَتَبْنَا عَلَيْهِمْ فِيهَآ أَنَّ ٱلنَّفْسَ بِٱلنَّفْسِ وَٱلْعَيْنَ بِٱلْعَيْنِ وَٱلْأَنفَ بِٱلْأَنفِ
وَٱلْأُذُنَ بِٱلْأُذُنِ وَٱلسِّنَّ بِٱلسِّنِّ وَٱلْجُرُوحَ قِصَاصٌ فَمَن تَصَدَّقَ بِهِۦ فَهُوَ
كَفَّارَةٌ لَّهُۥ وَمَن لَّمْ يَحْكُم بِمَآ أَنزَلَ ٱللَّهُ فَأُوْلَٰٓئِكَ هُمُ ٱلظَّٰلِمُونَ ﴿٤٥﴾
وَقَفَّيْنَا عَلَىٰٓ ءَاثَٰرِهِم بِعِيسَى ٱبْنِ مَرْيَمَ مُصَدِّقًا لِّمَا بَيْنَ يَدَيْهِ مِنَ ٱلتَّوْرَىٰةِ
وَءَاتَيْنَٰهُ ٱلْإِنجِيلَ فِيهِ هُدًى وَنُورٌ وَمُصَدِّقًا لِّمَا بَيْنَ يَدَيْهِ مِنَ ٱلتَّوْرَىٰةِ
وَهُدًى وَمَوْعِظَةً لِّلْمُتَّقِينَ ﴿٤٦﴾ وَلْيَحْكُمْ أَهْلُ ٱلْإِنجِيلِ بِمَآ أَنزَلَ ٱللَّهُ فِيهِ
وَمَن لَّمْ يَحْكُم بِمَآ أَنزَلَ ٱللَّهُ فَأُوْلَٰٓئِكَ هُمُ ٱلْفَٰسِقُونَ ﴿٤٧﴾ وَأَنزَلْنَآ إِلَيْكَ
ٱلْكِتَٰبَ بِٱلْحَقِّ مُصَدِّقًا لِّمَا بَيْنَ يَدَيْهِ مِنَ ٱلْكِتَٰبِ وَمُهَيْمِنًا عَلَيْهِ
فَٱحْكُم بَيْنَهُم بِمَآ أَنزَلَ ٱللَّهُ وَلَا تَتَّبِعْ أَهْوَآءَهُمْ عَمَّا جَآءَكَ مِنَ ٱلْحَقِّ

Wa katabnā ʿalayhim fīhāa ʾannan-nafsa binnafsi wal-ʿayna bil-ʿayni wal-ʾañfa bil-ʾañfi wal-ʾudhuna bilʾudhuni was-sinna bis-sinni wal-jurūḥa qiṣāṣ. Famañ-taṣaddaqa bihī fahuwa kaffāratul-lah. Wa mal-lam yaḥkum-bimāa ʾañzalal-lāhu faʾulāaʾika humuẓ-ẓālimūn. ﴿45﴾ Wa qaffaynā ʿalāa ʾāthārihim-biʿĪsab-ni Maryama muṣaddiqal-limā bayna yadayhi minat-Tawrāh. Wa ʾātaynāhul-ʾIñjīla fīhi hudañw-wa nūruñw-wa muṣaddiqal-limā bayna yadayhi minat-Tawrāti wa hudañw-wa mawʿiẓatal-lil-muttaqīn. ﴿46﴾ Wal-yaḥkum ʾahlul-ʾIñjīli bimāa ʾañzalal-lāhu fīh. Wa mal-lam yaḥkum-bimāa ʾañzalal-lāhu faʾulāa-ʾika humul-fāsiqūn. ﴿47﴾ Wa ʾañzalnāa ʾilaykal-Kitāba bilḥaqqi muṣaddiqal-limā bayna yadayhi minal-Kitābi wa muhayminan ʿalayhi faḥkum-baynahum-bimāa ʾañzalal-lāhu wa lā tattabiʿ ʾahwāaʾahum ʿammā jāaʾaka minal-ḥaqq.

And We ordained for them in that [Torah]: A life for a life, and an eye for an eye, and a nose for a nose, and an ear for an ear, and a tooth for a tooth, and a [similar] retribution for wounds;[61] but he who shall forgo it out of charity will atone thereby for some of his past sins.[62] And they who do not judge in accordance with what God has revealed – they, they are the evildoers! ‹45›
And We caused Jesus, the son of Mary, to follow in the footsteps of those [earlier prophets], confirming the truth of whatever there still remained[63] of the Torah; and We vouchsafed unto him the Gospel, wherein there was guidance and light, confirming the truth of whatever there still remained of the Torah, and as a guidance and admonition unto the God-conscious. ‹46› Let, then, the followers of the Gospel judge in accordance with what God has revealed therein: for they who do not judge in the light of what God has bestowed from on high – it is they, they who are truly iniquitous! ‹47›
And unto thee [O Prophet] have We vouchsafed this divine writ, setting forth the truth, confirming the truth of whatever there still remains of earlier revelations and determining what is true therein.[64] Judge, then, between the followers of earlier revelation in accordance with what God has bestowed from on high,[65] and do not follow their errant views, forsaking the truth that has come unto thee.

61 See Exodus xxi, 23 ff., where details of the extremely harsh penalties provided under Mosaic Law are given.

62 Lit., "it shall be an atonement for him". The Pentateuch does not contain this call to forgiveness which is brought out with great clarity not only in the Qurʾān but also in the teachings of Jesus, especially in the Sermon on the Mount: and this, read in conjunction with the following verses, would seem to be an allusion to the time-bound quality of Mosaic Law. Alternatively, the above admonition may have been part of the original teachings of the Torah which have been subsequently corrupted or deliberately abandoned by its followers, whom the Qurʾān accuses of "distorting the meaning of the revealed words" (see verse 41 above).

63 Regarding the meaning of *mā bayna yadayhi* (lit., "that which was between his [or "its"] hands") occurring twice in this verse, as well as in verse 48, see *sūrah* 3, note 3.

64 The participle *muhaymin* is derived from the quadriliteral verb *haymana*, "he watched [over a thing]" or "controlled [it]", and is used here to describe the Qurʾān as the determinant factor in deciding what is genuine and what is false in the earlier scriptures (see *Manār* VI, 410 ff.).

65 Lit., "judge, then, between them . . .", etc. This apparently applies not merely to judicial cases but also to opinions as to what is right or wrong in the ethical sense (see note 55 above). As is evident from the mention of the "followers of the Gospel" in the preceding verse, and of the Torah in the earlier passages, the people spoken of here are both the Jews and the Christians.

Unto every one of you have We appointed a [different] law and way of life.[66] And if God had so willed, He could surely have made you all one single community: but [He willed it otherwise] in order to test you by means of what He has vouchsafed unto you.[67] Vie, then, with one another in doing good works! Unto God you all must return; and then He will make you truly understand all that on which you were wont to differ.[68] ‹48›

Hence, judge between the followers of earlier revelation[69] in accordance with what God has bestowed from on high, and do not follow their errant views; and beware of them, lest they tempt thee away from aught that God has bestowed from on high upon thee. And if they turn away [from His commandments], then know that it is but God's will [thus] to afflict them for some of their sins:[70] for, behold, a great many people are iniquitous indeed. ‹49›

Do they, perchance, desire [to be ruled by] the law of pagan ignorance?[71] But for people who have inner certainty, who could be a better law-giver than God? ‹50›

لِكُلٍّ جَعَلْنَا مِنكُمْ شِرْعَةً وَمِنْهَاجًا وَلَوْ شَآءَ ٱللَّهُ لَجَعَلَكُمْ أُمَّةً وَٰحِدَةً
وَلَٰكِن لِّيَبْلُوَكُمْ فِى مَآ ءَاتَىٰكُمْ فَٱسْتَبِقُوا۟ ٱلْخَيْرَٰتِ إِلَى ٱللَّهِ مَرْجِعُكُمْ
جَمِيعًا فَيُنَبِّئُكُم بِمَا كُنتُمْ فِيهِ تَخْتَلِفُونَ ﴿٤٨﴾ وَأَنِ ٱحْكُم بَيْنَهُم بِمَآ
أَنزَلَ ٱللَّهُ وَلَا تَتَّبِعْ أَهْوَآءَهُمْ وَٱحْذَرْهُمْ أَن يَفْتِنُوكَ عَنۢ بَعْضِ مَآ أَنزَلَ
ٱللَّهُ إِلَيْكَ فَإِن تَوَلَّوْا۟ فَٱعْلَمْ أَنَّمَا يُرِيدُ ٱللَّهُ أَن يُصِيبَهُم بِبَعْضِ ذُنُوبِهِمْ
وَإِنَّ كَثِيرًا مِّنَ ٱلنَّاسِ لَفَٰسِقُونَ ﴿٤٩﴾ أَفَحُكْمَ ٱلْجَٰهِلِيَّةِ يَبْغُونَ وَمَنْ
أَحْسَنُ مِنَ ٱللَّهِ حُكْمًا لِّقَوْمٍ يُوقِنُونَ ﴿٥٠﴾

Likulliñ-jaʿalnā miñkum shirʿatañw-wa minhājā. Wa law shāaʾal-lāhu lajaʿalakum ʾummatañw-wāḥidatañw-wa lākil-liyabluwakum fī māa ʾātākum fastabiqul-khayrāt. ʾIlal-lāhi marjiʿukum jamīʿañ-fayunabbiʾukum-bimā kuñtum fīhi takhtalifūn. (48) Wa ʾaniḥ-kum-baynahum-bimāa ʾañzalal-lāhu wa lā tattabiʿ ʾahwāaʾahum waḥ-dharhum ʾañy-yaftinūka ʿam-baʿḍi māa ʾañzalal-lāhu ʾilayk. Faʾiñ-tawallaw faʿlam ʾannamā yurīdul-lāhu ʾañy-yuṣībahum-bibaʿḍi dhunūbihim. Wa ʾinna kathīram-minan-nāsi lafāsiqūn. (49) ʾAfaḥukmal-jāhiliyyati yabghūn. Wa man ʾaḥsanu minal-lāhi ḥukmal-liqawmiñy-yūqinūn. (50)

66 The expression "every one of you" denotes the various communities of which mankind is composed. The term *shirʿah* (or *sharīʿah*) signifies, literally, "the way to a watering-place" (from which men and animals derive the element indispensable to their life), and is used in the Qurʾān to denote a system of law necessary for a community's social and spiritual welfare. The term *minhāj*, on the other hand, denotes an "open road", usually in an abstract sense: that is, "a way of life". The terms *shirʿah* and *minhāj* are more restricted in their meaning than the term *dīn*, which comprises not merely the laws relating to a particular religion but also the basic, unchanging spiritual truths which, according to the Qurʾān, have been preached by every one of God's apostles, while the particular body of laws (*shirʿah* or *sharīʿah*) promulgated through them, and the way of life (*minhāj*) recommended by them, varied in accordance with the exigencies of the time and of each community's cultural development. This "unity in diversity" is frequently stressed in the Qurʾān (e.g., in the first sentence of 2 : 148, in 21 : 92-93, or in 23 : 52 ff.). Because of the universal applicability and textual incorruptibility of its teachings – as well as of the fact that the Prophet Muḥammad is "the seal of all prophets", i.e., the last of them (see 33 : 40) – the Qurʾān represents the culminating point of all revelation and offers the final, perfect way to spiritual fulfilment. This uniqueness of the Qurʾanic message does not, however, preclude all adherents of earlier faiths from attaining to God's grace: for – as the Qurʾān so often points out – those among them who believe uncompromisingly in the One God and the Day of Judgment (i.e., in individual moral responsibility) and live righteously "need have no fear, and neither shall they grieve".

67 I.e., "in order to test, by means of the various religious laws imposed on you, your willingness to surrender yourselves to God and to obey Him" (Zamakhsharī, Rāzī), "and thus to enable you to grow, spiritually and socially, in accordance with the God-willed law of evolution" (*Manār* VI, 418 f.).

68 Lit., "inform you of that wherein you used to differ" (cf. *sūrah* 2, note 94). Thus, the Qurʾān impresses upon all who believe in God – Muslims and non-Muslims alike – that the differences in their religious practices should make them "vie with one another in doing good works" rather than lose themselves in mutual hostility.

69 Lit., "between them": see notes 55 and 65 above.

70 The implication is that a conscious disregard of God's commandments brings with it its own punishment: namely, a gradual corruption of the community's moral values and, thus, growing social disruption and internecine conflict.

O YOU who have attained to faith! Do not take the Jews and the Christians for your allies: they are but allies of one another[72] – and whoever of you allies himself with them becomes, verily, one of them; behold, God does not guide such evildoers.[73] ‹51› And yet thou canst see how those in whose hearts there is disease vie with one another for their good will,[74] saying [to themselves], "We fear lest fortune turn against us." But God may well bring about good fortune [for the believers] or any [other] event of His own devising,[75] whereupon those [waverers] will be smitten with remorse for the thoughts which they had secretly harboured within themselves ‹52› – while those who have attained to faith will say [to one another], "Are these the selfsame people who swore by God with their most solemn oaths that they were indeed with you? In vain are all their works, for now they are lost!" ‹53›

۞ يَٰٓأَيُّهَا ٱلَّذِينَ ءَامَنُواْ لَا تَتَّخِذُواْ ٱلْيَهُودَ وَٱلنَّصَٰرَىٰٓ أَوْلِيَآءَ بَعْضُهُمْ
أَوْلِيَآءُ بَعْضٍ وَمَن يَتَوَلَّهُم مِّنكُمْ فَإِنَّهُۥ مِنْهُمْ إِنَّ ٱللَّهَ لَا يَهْدِى ٱلْقَوْمَ
ٱلظَّٰلِمِينَ ﴿٥١﴾ فَتَرَى ٱلَّذِينَ فِى قُلُوبِهِم مَّرَضٌ يُسَٰرِعُونَ فِيهِمْ يَقُولُونَ
نَخْشَىٰٓ أَن تُصِيبَنَا دَآئِرَةٌ فَعَسَى ٱللَّهُ أَن يَأْتِىَ بِٱلْفَتْحِ أَوْ أَمْرٍ مِّنْ عِندِهِۦ
فَيُصْبِحُواْ عَلَىٰ مَآ أَسَرُّواْ فِىٓ أَنفُسِهِمْ نَٰدِمِينَ ﴿٥٢﴾ وَيَقُولُ ٱلَّذِينَ ءَامَنُوٓاْ
أَهَٰٓؤُلَآءِ ٱلَّذِينَ أَقْسَمُواْ بِٱللَّهِ جَهْدَ أَيْمَٰنِهِمْ إِنَّهُمْ لَمَعَكُمْ حَبِطَتْ
أَعْمَٰلُهُمْ فَأَصْبَحُواْ خَٰسِرِينَ ﴿٥٣﴾

نصف الحزب

۞ Yāa ʾayyuhal-ladhīna ʾāmanū lā tattakhidhul-Yahūda wan-Naṣārāa ʾawliyāaʾ. Baᶜḍuhum ʾawliyāaʾu baᶜḍ. Wa mañy-yatawallahum-miñkum faʾinnahū minhum. ʾInnal-lāha lā yahdil-qawmaẓ-ẓālimīn. (51) Fataral-ladhīna fī qulūbihim-maraḍuñy-yusāriᶜūna fīhim yaqūluna nakhshāa ʾañ-tuṣībanā dāaʾirah. Faᶜasal-lāhu ʾañy-yaʾtiya bilfatḥi ʾaw ʾamrim-min ᶜiñdihī fayuṣbiḥū ᶜalā māa ʾasarrū fīi ʾañfusihim nādimīn. (52) Wa yaqūlul-ladhīna ʾāmanūu ʾahāaʾulāaʾil-ladhīna ʾaqsamū billāhi jahda ʾaymānihim ʾinnahum lamaᶜakum. Ḥabiṭat ʾaᶜmāluhum faʾaṣbaḥū khāsirīn. (53)

71 By "pagan ignorance" (*jāhiliyyah*) is meant here not merely the time before the advent of the Prophet Muḥammad but, in general, a state of affairs characterized by a lack of moral perception and a submission of all personal and communal concerns to the criterion of "expediency" alone: that is, exclusively to the consideration as to whether a particular aim or action is useful or damaging (in the short-term, practical sense of these words) to the interests of the person concerned or of the community to which he belongs. Inasmuch as this "law of expediency" is fundamentally opposed to the concepts of morality preached by every higher religion, it is described in the Qurʾān as "the law (*ḥukm*) of pagan ignorance".

72 According to most of the commentators (e.g., Ṭabarī), this means that each of these two communities extends genuine friendship only to its own adherents – i.e., the Jews to the Jews, and the Christians to the Christians – and cannot, therefore, be expected to be really friendly towards the followers of the Qurʾān. See also 8 : 73, and the corresponding note.

73 Lit., "the evildoing folk": i.e., those who deliberately sin in this respect. As regards the meaning of the "alliance" referred to here, see 3 : 28, and more particularly 4 : 139 and the corresponding note, which explains the reference to a believer's loss of his moral identity if he imitates the way of life of, or – in Qurʾanic terminology – "allies himself" with, non-Muslims. However, as has been made abundantly clear in 60 : 7-9 (and implied in verse 57 of this *sūrah*), this prohibition of a "moral alliance" with non-Muslims does *not* constitute an injunction against normal, friendly relations with such of them as are well-disposed towards Muslims. It should be borne in mind that the term *walī* has several shades of meaning: "ally", "friend", "helper", "protector", etc. The choice of the particular term – and sometimes a combination of two terms – is always dependent on the context.

74 Lit., "vie with one another concerning them" – the pronoun referring to the hostile Jews and Christians, for whose good-will the hypocrites within the Muslim community vie with one another by trying to imitate their way of life.

75 Lit., "from Himself". Some of the commentators assume that the word *fatḥ* (lit., "victory" or "triumph") occurring in this sentence is a prophetic reference to the conquest of Mecca by the Muslims. This assumption, however, cannot be correct since Mecca was already in the hands of the Muslims at the time of the revelation of this *sūrah*. Hence, the term *fatḥ* has obviously been used here in its primary significance of "opening" – namely, the opening of good fortune. (Cf. the idiomatic expression *futiḥa ᶜalā fulān*, "so-and-so became fortunate" or "possessed of good fortune", mentioned in Zamakhsharī's *Asās* and in the *Tāj al-ᶜArūs*.) The "other event of God's own devising" may conceivably refer to a divine punishment of the hypocrites apart from the good fortune that might be in store for the true believers.

O you who have attained to faith! If you ever abandon your faith,[76] God will in time bring forth [in your stead] people whom He loves and who love Him – humble towards the believers, proud towards all who deny the truth: [people] who strive hard in God's cause, and do not fear to be censured by anyone who might censure them: such is God's favour, which He grants unto whom He wills. And God is infinite, all-knowing. ‹54›

Behold, your only helper shall be God, and His Apostle, and those who have attained to faith – those that are constant in prayer, and render the purifying dues, and bow down [before God]: ‹55› for, all who ally themselves with God and His Apostle and those who have attained to faith – behold, it is they, the partisans of God, who shall be victorious! ‹56›

O you who have attained to faith! Do not take for your friends such as mock at your faith and make a jest of it – be they from among those who have been vouchsafed revelation before your time, or [from among] those who deny the truth [of revelation as such] – but remain conscious of God, if you are [truly] believers: ‹57› for, when you call to prayer, they mock at it and make a jest of it – simply because they are people who do not use their reason. ‹58›

Say: "O followers of earlier revelation! Do you find fault with us for no other reason than that we believe in God [alone], and in that which He has bestowed from on high upon us as well as that which He has bestowed aforetime? – or [is it only] because most of you are iniquitous?" ‹59›

Say: "Shall I tell you who, in the sight of God, deserves a yet worse retribution than these? They whom God has rejected and whom He has condemned, and whom He has turned into apes and swine

يَٰٓأَيُّهَا ٱلَّذِينَ ءَامَنُواْ مَن يَرۡتَدَّ مِنكُمۡ عَن دِينِهِۦ فَسَوۡفَ يَأۡتِي ٱللَّهُ بِقَوۡمٖ يُحِبُّهُمۡ
وَيُحِبُّونَهُۥٓ أَذِلَّةٍ عَلَى ٱلۡمُؤۡمِنِينَ أَعِزَّةٍ عَلَى ٱلۡكَٰفِرِينَ يُجَٰهِدُونَ فِي سَبِيلِ
ٱللَّهِ وَلَا يَخَافُونَ لَوۡمَةَ لَآئِمٖۚ ذَٰلِكَ فَضۡلُ ٱللَّهِ يُؤۡتِيهِ مَن يَشَآءُۚ وَٱللَّهُ وَٰسِعٌ
عَلِيمٌ ﴿٥٤﴾ إِنَّمَا وَلِيُّكُمُ ٱللَّهُ وَرَسُولُهُۥ وَٱلَّذِينَ ءَامَنُواْ ٱلَّذِينَ يُقِيمُونَ ٱلصَّلَوٰةَ
وَيُؤۡتُونَ ٱلزَّكَوٰةَ وَهُمۡ رَٰكِعُونَ ﴿٥٥﴾ وَمَن يَتَوَلَّ ٱللَّهَ وَرَسُولَهُۥ وَٱلَّذِينَ ءَامَنُواْ
فَإِنَّ حِزۡبَ ٱللَّهِ هُمُ ٱلۡغَٰلِبُونَ ﴿٥٦﴾ يَٰٓأَيُّهَا ٱلَّذِينَ ءَامَنُواْ لَا تَتَّخِذُواْ ٱلَّذِينَ
ٱتَّخَذُواْ دِينَكُمۡ هُزُوٗا وَلَعِبٗا مِّنَ ٱلَّذِينَ أُوتُواْ ٱلۡكِتَٰبَ مِن قَبۡلِكُمۡ وَٱلۡكُفَّارَ
أَوۡلِيَآءَۚ وَٱتَّقُواْ ٱللَّهَ إِن كُنتُم مُّؤۡمِنِينَ ﴿٥٧﴾ وَإِذَا نَادَيۡتُمۡ إِلَى ٱلصَّلَوٰةِ
ٱتَّخَذُوهَا هُزُوٗا وَلَعِبٗاۚ ذَٰلِكَ بِأَنَّهُمۡ قَوۡمٞ لَّا يَعۡقِلُونَ ﴿٥٨﴾ قُلۡ يَٰٓأَهۡلَ
ٱلۡكِتَٰبِ هَلۡ تَنقِمُونَ مِنَّآ إِلَّآ أَنۡ ءَامَنَّا بِٱللَّهِ وَمَآ أُنزِلَ إِلَيۡنَا وَمَآ أُنزِلَ
مِن قَبۡلُ وَأَنَّ أَكۡثَرَكُمۡ فَٰسِقُونَ ﴿٥٩﴾ قُلۡ هَلۡ أُنَبِّئُكُم بِشَرّٖ مِّن ذَٰلِكَ
مَثُوبَةً عِندَ ٱللَّهِۚ مَن لَّعَنَهُ ٱللَّهُ وَغَضِبَ عَلَيۡهِ وَجَعَلَ مِنۡهُمُ ٱلۡقِرَدَةَ وَٱلۡخَنَازِيرَ

Yāa ʾayyuhal-ladhīna ʾāmanū mañy-yartadda miñkum ʿañ-dīnihī fasawfa yaʾtil-lāhu biqawmiñy-yuḥibbuhum wa yuḥibbūnahūu ʾadhillatin ʿalal-muʾminīna ʾaʿizzatin ʿalal-kāfirīna yujāhidūna fī sabīlil-lāhi wa lā yakhāfūna lawmata lāaʾim. Dhālika faḍlul-lāhi yuʾtīhi mañy-yashāaʾ. Wal-lāhu Wāsiʿun ʿAlīm. (54) ʾInnamā Waliyyukumul-lāhu wa Rasūluhū wal-ladhīna ʾāmanul-ladhīna yuqīmūnaṣ-Ṣalāta wa yuʾtūnaz-Zakāta wa hum rākiʿūn. (55) Wa mañy-yatawallal-lāha wa Rasūlahū wal-ladhīna ʾāmanū faʾinna ḥizbal-lāhi humul-ghālibūn. (56) Yāa ʾayyuhal-ladhīna ʾāmanū lā tattakhidhul-ladhīnat-takhadhū dīnakum huzuwañw-wa laʿibam-minal-ladhīna ʾūtul-Kitāba miñ-qablikum wal-kuffāra ʾawliyāaʾ. Wat-taqul-lāha ʾiñ-kuñtum-muʾminīn. (57) Wa ʾidhā nādaytum ʾilaṣ-Ṣalātit-takhadhūhā huzuwañw-wa laʿibā; dhālika biʾannahum qawmul-lā yaʿqilūn. (58) Qul yāa ʾahlal-Kitābi hal tañqimūna minnāa ʾillāa ʾan ʾāmannā billāhi wa māa ʾuñzila ʾilaynā wa māa ʾuñzila miñ-qablu wa ʾanna ʾaktharakum fāsiqūn. (59) Qul hal ʾunabbiʾukum-bisharrim-miñ-dhālika mathūbatan ʿiñdal-lāh. Mal-laʿanahul-lāhu wa ghaḍiba ʿalayhi wa jaʿala minhumul-qiradata wal-khanāzīra

76 Lit., "whosoever from among you abandons his faith" – i.e., in result of having placed his reliance on non-Muslims who are hostile to Islam, and having taken them for his "allies" and spiritual mentors.

because they worshipped the powers of evil:[77] these are yet worse in station, and farther astray from the right path [than the mockers]."[78] ⟨60⟩

For, when they come unto you, they say, "We do believe": whereas, in fact, they come with the resolve to deny the truth, and depart in the same state.[79] But God is fully aware of all that they would conceal. ⟨61⟩ And thou canst see many of them vie with one another in sinning and tyrannical conduct and in their swallowing of all that is evil. Vile indeed is what they do! ⟨62⟩

Why do not their men of God and their rabbis[80] forbid them to make sinful assertions and to swallow all that is evil? Vile indeed is what they contrive! ⟨63⟩

And the Jews say, "God's hand is shackled!" It is their own hands that are shackled; and rejected [by God] are they because of this their assertion.[81] Nay, but wide are His hands stretched out: He dispenses [bounty] as He wills. But all that has been bestowed from on high upon thee [O Prophet] by thy Sustainer is bound to make many of them yet more stubborn in their overweening arrogance and in their denial of the truth.

وَعَبَدَ ٱلطَّـٰغُوتَ أُوْلَـٰٓئِكَ شَرٌّ مَّكَانًا وَأَضَلُّ عَن سَوَآءِ ٱلسَّبِيلِ ﴿٦٠﴾
وَإِذَا جَآءُوكُمْ قَالُوٓاْ ءَامَنَّا وَقَد دَّخَلُواْ بِٱلْكُفْرِ وَهُمْ قَدْ خَرَجُواْ بِهِۦ
وَٱللَّهُ أَعْلَمُ بِمَا كَانُواْ يَكْتُمُونَ ﴿٦١﴾ وَتَرَىٰ كَثِيرًا مِّنْهُمْ يُسَـٰرِعُونَ فِى
ٱلْإِثْمِ وَٱلْعُدْوَٰنِ وَأَكْلِهِمُ ٱلسُّحْتَ لَبِئْسَ مَا كَانُواْ يَعْمَلُونَ ﴿٦٢﴾
لَوْلَا يَنْهَىٰهُمُ ٱلرَّبَّـٰنِيُّونَ وَٱلْأَحْبَارُ عَن قَوْلِهِمُ ٱلْإِثْمَ وَأَكْلِهِمُ ٱلسُّحْتَ
لَبِئْسَ مَا كَانُواْ يَصْنَعُونَ ﴿٦٣﴾ وَقَالَتِ ٱلْيَهُودُ يَدُ ٱللَّهِ مَغْلُولَةٌ غُلَّتْ
أَيْدِيهِمْ وَلُعِنُواْ بِمَا قَالُواْ بَلْ يَدَاهُ مَبْسُوطَتَانِ يُنفِقُ كَيْفَ يَشَآءُ
وَلَيَزِيدَنَّ كَثِيرًا مِّنْهُم مَّآ أُنزِلَ إِلَيْكَ مِن رَّبِّكَ طُغْيَـٰنًا وَكُفْرًا

wa ʿabadaṭ-ṭāghūt. ʾUlāaʾika sharrum-makānañw-wa ʾaḍallu ʿañ-sawāaʾis-sabīl. (60) Wa ʾidhā jāaʾūkum qālūu ʾāmannā wa qad-dakhalū bilkufri wa hum qad kharajū bih. Wal-lāhu ʾaʿlamu bimā kānū yaktumūn. (61) Wa tarā kathīram-minhum yusāriʿūna fil-ʾithmi wal-ʿudwāni wa-ʾaklihimus-suḥt. Labiʾsa mā kānū yaʿmalūn. (62) Lawlā yanhāhumur-rabbāniyyūna wal-ʾaḥbāru ʿañ-qawlihimul-ʾithma wa ʾaklihimus-suḥt. Labiʾsa mā kānū yaṣnaʿūn. (63) Wa qālatil-Yahūdu Yādul-lāhi maghlūlah. Ghullat ʾaydīhim wa luʿinū bimā qālū. Bal Yadāhu mabsūṭatāni yuñfiqu kayfa yashāaʾ. Wa layazīdanna kathīram-minhum-māa ʾuñzila ʾilayka mir-Rabbika ṭughyānañw-wa kufrā.

77 Contrary to many of the commentators who take this reference to "apes and swine" in a literal sense, the famous *tābiʿī* Mujāhid explains it as a metaphorical description (*mathal*) of the moral degradation which such sinners undergo: they become wildly unpredictable like apes, and as abandoned to the pursuit of lusts as swine (*Manār* VI, 448). This interpretation has also been quoted by Ṭabarī in his commentary on 2 : 65. – As regards the expression "powers of evil" (*aṭ-ṭāghūt*), see *sūrah* 2, note 250.

78 As is evident from the following verses, the sinners who are even worse than the mockers are the hypocrites, and particularly those among them who claim to be followers of the Bible: for the obvious reason that, having been enlightened through revelation, they have no excuse for their behaviour. Although in verse 64 the Jews are specifically mentioned, the reference to the Gospel in verse 66 makes it clear that the Christians, too, cannot be exempted from this blame.

79 Lit., "they come in with a denial of the truth and depart with it".

80 According to Baghawī, the *rabbāniyūn* ("men of God" – see *sūrah* 3, note 62) stand, in this context, for the spiritual leaders of the Christians, and the *aḥbār* for the Jewish scholars ("rabbis"). Regarding the "swallowing of evil", see note 54 above.

81 The phrase "one's hand is shackled" is a metaphorical expression denoting niggardliness, just as its opposite – "his hand is stretched out wide" – signifies generosity (Zamakhsharī). However, these two phrases have a wider meaning as well, namely, "lack of power" and "unlimited power", respectively (Rāzī). It would appear that the Jews of Medina, seeing the poverty of the Muslims, derided the latters' conviction that they were struggling in God's cause and that the Qurʾān was divinely revealed. Thus, the "saying" of the Jews mentioned in this verse, "God's hand is shackled", as well as the parallel one in 3 : 181, "God is poor while we are rich", is an elliptical description of their attitude towards Islam and the Muslims – an attitude of disbelief and sarcasm which could be thus paraphrased: "If it were true that you Muslims are doing God's will, He would have bestowed upon you power and riches; but your poverty and your weakness contradict your claim – or else this claim of yours amounts, in effect, to saying that God

ثلاثة ارباع الحزب

And so We have cast enmity and hatred among the followers of the Bible,[82] [to last] until Resurrection Day; every time they light the fires of war, God extinguishes them;[83] and they labour hard to spread corruption on earth: and God does not love the spreaders of corruption. ‹64›
If the followers of the Bible would but attain to [true] faith and God-consciousness, We should indeed efface their [previous] bad deeds, and indeed bring them into gardens of bliss; ‹65› and if they would but truly observe the Torah and the Gospel and all [the revelation] that has been bestowed from on high upon them by their Sustainer, they would indeed partake of all the blessings of heaven and earth. Some of them do pursue a right course; but as for most of them – vile indeed is what they do![84] ‹66›

O APOSTLE! Announce all that has been bestowed from on high upon thee by thy Sustainer: for unless thou doest it fully, thou wilt not have delivered His message [at all]. And God will protect thee from [unbelieving] men: behold, God does not guide people who refuse to acknowledge the truth. ‹67›

وَأَلْقَيْنَا بَيْنَهُمُ ٱلْعَدَٰوَةَ وَٱلْبَغْضَآءَ إِلَىٰ يَوْمِ ٱلْقِيَٰمَةِ ۚ كُلَّمَآ أَوْقَدُوا۟
نَارًا لِّلْحَرْبِ أَطْفَأَهَا ٱللَّهُ ۚ وَيَسْعَوْنَ فِى ٱلْأَرْضِ فَسَادًا ۚ وَٱللَّهُ لَا يُحِبُّ
ٱلْمُفْسِدِينَ ﴿٦٤﴾ وَلَوْ أَنَّ أَهْلَ ٱلْكِتَٰبِ ءَامَنُوا۟ وَٱتَّقَوْا۟ لَكَفَّرْنَا عَنْهُمْ
سَيِّـَٔاتِهِمْ وَلَأَدْخَلْنَٰهُمْ جَنَّٰتِ ٱلنَّعِيمِ ﴿٦٥﴾ وَلَوْ أَنَّهُمْ أَقَامُوا۟ ٱلتَّوْرَىٰةَ
وَٱلْإِنجِيلَ وَمَآ أُنزِلَ إِلَيْهِم مِّن رَّبِّهِمْ لَأَكَلُوا۟ مِن فَوْقِهِمْ وَمِن تَحْتِ
أَرْجُلِهِم ۚ مِّنْهُمْ أُمَّةٌ مُّقْتَصِدَةٌ ۖ وَكَثِيرٌ مِّنْهُمْ سَآءَ مَا يَعْمَلُونَ ﴿٦٦﴾ ۞
يَٰٓأَيُّهَا ٱلرَّسُولُ بَلِّغْ مَآ أُنزِلَ إِلَيْكَ مِن رَّبِّكَ ۖ وَإِن لَّمْ تَفْعَلْ فَمَا
بَلَّغْتَ رِسَالَتَهُۥ ۚ وَٱللَّهُ يَعْصِمُكَ مِنَ ٱلنَّاسِ ۗ إِنَّ ٱللَّهَ لَا يَهْدِى ٱلْقَوْمَ
ٱلْكَٰفِرِينَ ﴿٦٧﴾

Wa ʾalqaynā baynahumul-ʿadāwata wal-baghḍāaʾa ʾilā Yawmil-Qiyāmah. Kullamāa ʾawqadū nāral-lilḥarbi ʾaṭfaʾahal-lāhu wa yasʿawna fil-ʾarḍi fasādā. Wal-lāhu lā yuḥibbul-mufsidīn. (64) Wa law ʾanna ʾahlal-Kitābi ʾāmanū wat-taqaw lakaffarnā ʿanhum sayyiʾātihim wa laʾadkhalnāhum jannātin-naʿīm. (65) Wa law ʾannahum ʾaqāmut-Tawrāta wal-ʾIñjīla wa māa ʾuñzila ʾilayhim-mir-Rabbihim laʾakalū miñ-fawqihim wa miñ-taḥti ʾarjulihim. Minhum ʾummatum-muqtaṣidatuñw-wa kathīrum-minhum sāaʾa mā yaʿmalūn. (66) ۞ Yāa ʾayyuhar-Rasūlu balligh māa ʾuñzila ʾilayka mir-Rabbika wa ʾil-lam tafʿal famā ballaghta risālatah. Wal-lāhu yaʿṣimuka minan-nās. ʾInnal-lāha lā yahdil-qawmal-kāfirīn. (67)

cannot help you." This outstanding example of the elliptic mode of expression (*ījāz*) so often employed in the Qurʾān has, however, a meaning that goes far beyond the historical circumstances to which it refers: it illustrates an attitude of mind which mistakenly identifies worldly riches or power with one's being, spiritually, "on the right way". In the next sentence the Qurʾān takes issue with this attitude and declares, in an equally elliptical manner, that all who see in material success an alleged evidence of God's approval are blind to spiritual truths and, therefore, morally powerless and utterly self-condemned in the sight of God.

82 Lit., "among them". The personal pronoun refers to the hypocritical followers of the Bible – both the Jews and the Christians – spoken of in verses 57-63 (Ṭabarī); cf. verse 14 of this *sūrah*, which makes a similar statement with regard to such of the Christians as "have forgotten much of what they had been told to bear in mind".

83 I.e., He does not allow any of the warring parties to resolve their conflicts through a final victory, with the result that they continue to live in a state of "enmity and hatred".

84 The expression "partake of all the blessings of heaven and earth" (lit., "eat from above them and from beneath their feet") is an allusion to the blessing which accompanies the realization of a spiritual truth, as well as to the social happiness which is bound to follow an observance of the moral principles laid down in the genuine teachings of the Bible. It should be borne in mind that the phrase "if they would but truly observe (*law annahum aqāmū*) the Torah and the Gospel", etc., implies an observance of those scriptures in their genuine spirit, free of the arbitrary distortions due to that "wishful thinking" of which the Qurʾān so often accuses the Jews and the Christians – such as the Jewish concept of "the chosen people", or the Christian doctrines relating to the alleged divinity of Jesus and the "vicarious redemption" of his followers.

Say: "O followers of the Bible! You have no valid ground for your beliefs unless you [truly] observe the Torah and the Gospel, and all that has been bestowed from on high upon you by your Sustainer!"[85]
Yet all that has been bestowed from on high upon thee [O Prophet] by thy Sustainer is bound to make many of them yet more stubborn in their overweening arrogance and in their denial of the truth. But sorrow not over people who deny the truth: «68» for, verily, those who have attained to faith [in this divine writ], as well as those who follow the Jewish faith, and the Sabians,[86] and the Christians – all who believe in God and the Last Day and do righteous deeds – no fear need they have, and neither shall they grieve. «69»

قُلْ يَٰٓأَهْلَ ٱلْكِتَٰبِ لَسْتُمْ عَلَىٰ شَىْءٍ حَتَّىٰ تُقِيمُوا۟ ٱلتَّوْرَىٰةَ وَٱلْإِنجِيلَ وَمَآ
أُنزِلَ إِلَيْكُم مِّن رَّبِّكُمْ ۗ وَلَيَزِيدَنَّ كَثِيرًا مِّنْهُم مَّآ أُنزِلَ إِلَيْكَ مِن رَّبِّكَ
طُغْيَٰنًا وَكُفْرًا ۖ فَلَا تَأْسَ عَلَى ٱلْقَوْمِ ٱلْكَٰفِرِينَ ﴿٦٨﴾ إِنَّ ٱلَّذِينَ ءَامَنُوا۟
وَٱلَّذِينَ هَادُوا۟ وَٱلصَّٰبِـُٔونَ وَٱلنَّصَٰرَىٰ مَنْ ءَامَنَ بِٱللَّهِ وَٱلْيَوْمِ ٱلْءَاخِرِ
وَعَمِلَ صَٰلِحًا فَلَا خَوْفٌ عَلَيْهِمْ وَلَا هُمْ يَحْزَنُونَ ﴿٦٩﴾ لَقَدْ أَخَذْنَا
مِيثَٰقَ بَنِىٓ إِسْرَٰٓءِيلَ وَأَرْسَلْنَآ إِلَيْهِمْ رُسُلًا ۖ كُلَّمَا جَآءَهُمْ رَسُولٌۢ بِمَا لَا تَهْوَىٰٓ
أَنفُسُهُمْ فَرِيقًا كَذَّبُوا۟ وَفَرِيقًا يَقْتُلُونَ ﴿٧٠﴾ وَحَسِبُوٓا۟ أَلَّا تَكُونَ فِتْنَةٌ فَعَمُوا۟
وَصَمُّوا۟ ثُمَّ تَابَ ٱللَّهُ عَلَيْهِمْ ثُمَّ عَمُوا۟ وَصَمُّوا۟ كَثِيرٌ مِّنْهُمْ ۚ وَٱللَّهُ بَصِيرٌۢ بِمَا
يَعْمَلُونَ ﴿٧١﴾ لَقَدْ كَفَرَ ٱلَّذِينَ قَالُوٓا۟ إِنَّ ٱللَّهَ هُوَ ٱلْمَسِيحُ ٱبْنُ مَرْيَمَ ۖ وَقَالَ
ٱلْمَسِيحُ يَٰبَنِىٓ إِسْرَٰٓءِيلَ ٱعْبُدُوا۟ ٱللَّهَ رَبِّى وَرَبَّكُمْ ۖ إِنَّهُۥ مَن يُشْرِكْ بِٱللَّهِ فَقَدْ
حَرَّمَ ٱللَّهُ عَلَيْهِ ٱلْجَنَّةَ وَمَأْوَىٰهُ ٱلنَّارُ ۖ وَمَا لِلظَّٰلِمِينَ مِنْ أَنصَارٍ ﴿٧٢﴾

INDEED, We accepted a solemn pledge from the children of Israel, and We sent apostles unto them; [but] every time an apostle came unto them with anything that was not to their liking, [they rebelled:] to some of them they gave the lie, while others they would slay,[87] «70» thinking that no harm would befall them; and so they became blind and deaf [of heart]. Thereafter God accepted their repentance: and again many of them became blind and deaf. But God sees all that they do. «71»
Indeed, the truth deny they who say, "Behold, God is the Christ, son of Mary" – seeing that the Christ [himself] said, "O children of Israel! Worship God [alone], who is my Sustainer as well as your Sustainer."[88] Behold, whoever ascribes divinity to any being beside God, unto him will God deny paradise, and his goal shall be the fire; and such evildoers will have none to succour them! «72»

Qul yāa ʾahlal-Kitābi lastum ʿalā shayʾin ḥattā tuqīmut-Tawrāta wal-ʾInjīla wa māa ʾunzila ʾilaykum-mir-Rabbikum. Wa layazīdanna kathīram-minhum-māa ʾunzila ʾilayka mir-Rabbika ṭughyānanw-wa kufrā. Falā taʾsa ʿalal-qawmil-kāfirīn. «68» ʾInnal-ladhīna ʾāmanū wal-ladhīna hādū waṣ-Ṣābiʾiūna wan-Naṣārā man ʾāmana billāhi wal-Yawmil-ʾĀkhiri wa ʿamila ṣāliḥan-falā khawfun ʿalayhim wa lā hum yaḥzanūn. «69» Laqad ʾakhadhnā mīthāqa banīi ʾIsrāaʾīla wa ʾarsalnāa ʾilayhim Rusulan-kullamā jāaʾahum Rasūlum-bimā lā tahwāa ʾanfusuhum farīqan-kadhdhabū wa farīqany-yaqtulūn. «70» Wa ḥasibūu ʾal-lā takūna fitnatun-faʿamū wa ṣammū thumma tābal-lāhu ʿalayhim thumma ʿamū wa ṣammū kathīrum-minhum. Wal-lāhu Baṣīrum-bimā yaʿmalūn. «71» Laqad kafaral-ladhīna qālūu ʾinnal-lāha Huwal-Masīḥub-nu Maryam. Wa qālal-Masīḥu yā banīi ʾIsrāaʾīlaʿ-budul-lāha Rabbī wa Rabbakum. ʾInnahū many-yushrik billāhi faqad ḥarramal-lāhu ʿalayhil-jannata wa maʾwāhun-nāru wa mā liẓẓālimīna min ʾanṣār. «72»

85 I.e., all the other God-inspired books of the Old Testament which stress the oneness of God and are full of prophecies relating to the advent of the Prophet Muḥammad (Rāzī). This must be understood in conjunction with the oft-repeated Qurʾanic statement that the Bible, as it exists now, has undergone many textual changes and corruptions.

86 See *sūrah* 2, note 49.

87 Lit., "and some they are slaying". Regarding the significance of the change from the past to the present tense (*yaqtulūn*), see *sūrah* 2, note 72.

88 Cf. Matthew iv, 10; Luke iv, 8; John xx, 17.

لَّقَدۡ كَفَرَ ٱلَّذِينَ قَالُوٓاْ إِنَّ ٱللَّهَ ثَالِثُ ثَلَٰثَةٖۘ وَمَا مِنۡ إِلَٰهٍ إِلَّآ إِلَٰهٞ وَٰحِدٞۚ
وَإِن لَّمۡ يَنتَهُواْ عَمَّا يَقُولُونَ لَيَمَسَّنَّ ٱلَّذِينَ كَفَرُواْ مِنۡهُمۡ عَذَابٌ أَلِيمٌ ﴿٧٣﴾
أَفَلَا يَتُوبُونَ إِلَى ٱللَّهِ وَيَسۡتَغۡفِرُونَهُۥۚ وَٱللَّهُ غَفُورٞ رَّحِيمٞ ﴿٧٤﴾ مَّا ٱلۡمَسِيحُ
ٱبۡنُ مَرۡيَمَ إِلَّا رَسُولٞ قَدۡ خَلَتۡ مِن قَبۡلِهِ ٱلرُّسُلُ وَأُمُّهُۥ صِدِّيقَةٞۖ كَانَا
يَأۡكُلَانِ ٱلطَّعَامَۗ ٱنظُرۡ كَيۡفَ نُبَيِّنُ لَهُمُ ٱلۡأٓيَٰتِ ثُمَّ ٱنظُرۡ أَنَّىٰ
يُؤۡفَكُونَ ﴿٧٥﴾ قُلۡ أَتَعۡبُدُونَ مِن دُونِ ٱللَّهِ مَا لَا يَمۡلِكُ لَكُمۡ ضَرّٗا وَلَا
نَفۡعٗاۚ وَٱللَّهُ هُوَ ٱلسَّمِيعُ ٱلۡعَلِيمُ ﴿٧٦﴾ قُلۡ يَٰٓأَهۡلَ ٱلۡكِتَٰبِ لَا تَغۡلُواْ فِي
دِينِكُمۡ غَيۡرَ ٱلۡحَقِّ وَلَا تَتَّبِعُوٓاْ أَهۡوَآءَ قَوۡمٖ قَدۡ ضَلُّواْ مِن قَبۡلُ وَأَضَلُّواْ
كَثِيرٗا وَضَلُّواْ عَن سَوَآءِ ٱلسَّبِيلِ ﴿٧٧﴾ لُعِنَ ٱلَّذِينَ كَفَرُواْ مِنۢ بَنِيٓ إِسۡرَٰٓءِيلَ
عَلَىٰ لِسَانِ دَاوُۥدَ وَعِيسَى ٱبۡنِ مَرۡيَمَۚ ذَٰلِكَ بِمَا عَصَواْ وَّكَانُواْ يَعۡتَدُونَ ﴿٧٨﴾

Laqad kafaral-ladhīna qālūu ʾinnal-lāha thālithu thalāthah. Wa mā min ʾilāhin ʾillāa ʾilāhuñw-Wāḥid. Wa ʾil-lam yañtahū ʿammā yaqūlūna layamassannal-ladhīna kafarū minhum ʿadhābun ʾalīm. (73) ʾAfalā yatūbūna ʾilal-lāhi wa yastaghfirūnah. Wal-lāhu Ghafūrur-Raḥīm. (74) Mal-Masīḥub-nu Maryama ʾillā Rasūluñ-qad khalat miñ-qablihir-Rusulu wa ʾummuhū ṣiddīqatuñ-kānā yaʾkulāniṭ-ṭaʿām. ʾUñẓur kayfa nubayyinu lahumul-ʾĀyāti thummañ-ẓur ʾannā yuʾfakūn. (75) Qul-ʾataʿbudūna miñ-dūnil-lāhi mā lā yamliku lakum ḍarrañw-wa lā nafʿā. Wal-lāhu Huwas-Samīʿul-ʿAlīm. (76) Qul yāa ʾahlal-Kitābi lā taghlū fī dīnikum ghayral-ḥaqqi wa lā tattabiʿūu ʾahwāaʾa qawmiñ-qad ḍallū miñ-qablu wa ʾaḍallū kathīrañw-wa ḍallū ʿañ-sawāaʾis-sabīl. (77) Luʿinal-ladhīna kafarū mimbanīi ʾIsrāaʾīla ʿalā lisāni Dāwūda wa ʿĪsab-ni Maryam. Dhālika bimā ʿaṣaw-wa kānū yaʿtadūn. (78)

Indeed, the truth deny they who say, "Behold, God is the third of a trinity" – seeing that there is no deity whatever save the One God. And unless they desist from this their assertion, grievous suffering is bound to befall such of them as are bent on denying the truth. ‹73› Will they not, then, turn towards God in repentance, and ask His forgiveness? For God is much-forgiving, a dispenser of grace. ‹74›

The Christ, son of Mary, was but an apostle: all [other] apostles had passed away before him; and his mother was one who never deviated from the truth; and they both ate food [like other mortals].[89]

Behold how clear We make these messages unto them: and then behold how perverted are their minds![90] ‹75› Say: "Would you worship, beside God, aught that has no power either to harm or to benefit you – when God alone is all-hearing, all-knowing?" ‹76›

Say: "O followers of the Gospel! Do not overstep the bounds [of truth] in your religious beliefs;[91] and do not follow the errant views of people who have gone astray aforetime, and have led many [others] astray, and are still straying from the right path."[92] ‹77›

THOSE of the children of Israel who were bent on denying the truth have [already] been cursed by the tongue of David and of Jesus, the son of Mary:[93] this, because they rebelled [against God] and persisted in transgressing the bounds of what is right. ‹78›

89 The purport of this passage is that Jesus was but a mortal like all the other apostles who lived before him, and that Mary never claimed to be "the mother of God".

90 Lit., "how turned away they are [from the truth]". Primarily, the verb *afaka* signifies "he turned [someone or something] away"; in an abstract sense it often denotes "he uttered a lie" (because it implies a turning away from the truth). The passive form *ufika* has frequently the meaning of "he was turned away from his opinion" (or "from his judgment") and, thus, "his mind became perverted" or "deluded". (Cf. *Qāmūs* and *Tāj al-ʿArūs*; also Lane I, 69.)

91 Cf. 4 : 171. This passage, like the preceding ones, is obviously addressed to the Christians, whose love for Jesus has caused them to "overstep the bounds of truth" by elevating him to the rank of divinity; therefore my rendering, in this context, of *ahl al-kitāb* as "followers of the Gospel".

92 Lit., "have gone astray from the right path": i.e., are persisting in this condition until now (Rāzī): an allusion to the many communities who, in the course of time, have come to attribute divinity to their spiritual leaders – a phenomenon frequently encountered in the history of religions.

93 Cf. Psalms lxxviii, 21-22, 31-33, and *passim;* also Matthew xii, 34, and xxiii, 33-35.

They would not prevent one another from doing whatever hateful things they did: vile indeed was what they were wont to do! «79»
[And now] thou canst see many of them allying themselves with those who are bent on denying the truth! [So] vile indeed is what their passions make them do[94] that God has condemned them; and in suffering shall they abide. «80» For, if they [truly] believed in God and their Prophet[95] and all that was bestowed upon him from on high, they would not take those [deniers of the truth] for their allies: but most of them are iniquitous. «81»
Thou wilt surely find that, of all people, the most hostile to those who believe [in this divine writ] are the Jews as well as those who are bent on ascribing divinity to aught beside God; and thou wilt surely find that, of all people,[96] they who say, "Behold, we are Christians," come closest to feeling affection for those who believe [in this divine writ]: this is so because there are priests and monks among them, and because these are not given to arrogance.[97] «82»
For, when they come to understand what has been bestowed from on high upon this Apostle, thou canst see their eyes overflow with tears, because they recognize something of its truth;[98] [and] they say:

كَانُوا۟ لَا يَتَنَاهَوْنَ عَن مُّنكَرٍ فَعَلُوهُ ۚ لَبِئْسَ مَا كَانُوا۟ يَفْعَلُونَ ﴿٧٩﴾ تَرَىٰ
كَثِيرًا مِّنْهُمْ يَتَوَلَّوْنَ ٱلَّذِينَ كَفَرُوا۟ ۚ لَبِئْسَ مَا قَدَّمَتْ لَهُمْ أَنفُسُهُمْ أَن سَخِطَ
ٱللَّهُ عَلَيْهِمْ وَفِى ٱلْعَذَابِ هُمْ خَٰلِدُونَ ﴿٨٠﴾ وَلَوْ كَانُوا۟ يُؤْمِنُونَ بِٱللَّهِ وَٱلنَّبِىِّ
وَمَآ أُنزِلَ إِلَيْهِ مَا ٱتَّخَذُوهُمْ أَوْلِيَآءَ وَلَٰكِنَّ كَثِيرًا مِّنْهُمْ فَٰسِقُونَ ﴿٨١﴾ ۞
لَتَجِدَنَّ أَشَدَّ ٱلنَّاسِ عَدَٰوَةً لِّلَّذِينَ ءَامَنُوا۟ ٱلْيَهُودَ وَٱلَّذِينَ أَشْرَكُوا۟ ۖ
وَلَتَجِدَنَّ أَقْرَبَهُم مَّوَدَّةً لِّلَّذِينَ ءَامَنُوا۟ ٱلَّذِينَ قَالُوٓا۟ إِنَّا نَصَٰرَىٰ ۚ ذَٰلِكَ بِأَنَّ
مِنْهُمْ قِسِّيسِينَ وَرُهْبَانًا وَأَنَّهُمْ لَا يَسْتَكْبِرُونَ ﴿٨٢﴾ وَإِذَا سَمِعُوا۟ مَآ أُنزِلَ
إِلَى ٱلرَّسُولِ تَرَىٰٓ أَعْيُنَهُمْ تَفِيضُ مِنَ ٱلدَّمْعِ مِمَّا عَرَفُوا۟ مِنَ ٱلْحَقِّ ۖ يَقُولُونَ

حزب 13
جزء 7

Kānū lā yatanāhawna ʿam-muñkariñ-faʿalūh. Labiʾsa mā kānū yafʿalūn. (79) Tarā kathīram-minhum yatawallawnal-ladhīna kafarū. Labiʾsa mā qaddamat lahum ʾañfusuhum ʾañ-sakhiṭal-lāhu ʿalayhim wa fil-ʿadhābi hum khālidūn. (80) Wa law kānū yuʾminūna billāhi wan-Nabiyyi wa māa ʾuñzila ʾilayhi mat-takhadhūhum ʾawliyāaʾa wa lākinna kathīram-minhum fāsiqūn. (81) ◆ Latajidanna ʾashaddan-nāsi ʿadāwatal-lilladhīna ʾāmanul-Yahūda wal-ladhīna ʾashrakū; wa latajidanna ʾaqrabahum-mawaddatal-lilladhīna ʾāmanul-ladhīna qālūu ʾinnā Naṣārā; dhālika biʾanna minhum qissīsīna wa ruhbānañw-wa ʾannahum lā yastakbirūn. (82) Wa ʾidhā samiʿū māa ʾuñzila ʾilar-Rasūli tarāa ʾaʿyunahum tafīḍu minad-damʿi mimmā ʿarafū minal-ḥaqqi yaqūlūna

94 Lit., "what their passions (*anfusuhum*) have proffered to them". (Regarding the rendering of *nafs* as "passion", see note 37 on verse 30 of this *sūrah*.) What is alluded to here is their stubborn belief that they are "God's chosen people" and, consequently, their rejection of any revelation that may have been vouchsafed to others.

95 Lit., "the Prophet". According to Zamakhsharī and Rāzī, the prophet referred to is Moses, whom the Jews claim to follow – a claim which the Qurʾān denies by implication.

96 Lit., "of them".

97 I.e., they do not believe, as do the Jews, that revelation is God's exclusive gift to the children of Israel; and their "priests and monks" teach them that humility is the essence of all true faith. – It is noteworthy that the Qurʾān does not *in this context* include the Christians among "those who are bent on ascribing divinity to aught beside God" (*alladhīna ashrakū* – the element of intent being expressed in the use of the past tense, similar to *alladhīna kafarū, alladhīna ẓalamū*, etc.): for although, by their deification of Jesus, they are guilty of the sin of *shirk* ("the ascribing of divinity to anyone or anything beside God"), the Christians do not *consciously* worship a plurality of deities inasmuch as, theoretically, their theology postulates belief in the One God, who is conceived as manifesting Himself in a trinity of aspects, or "persons", of whom Jesus is supposed to be one. However repugnant this doctrine may be to the teachings of the Qurʾān, their *shirk* is not based on conscious intent, but rather flows from their "overstepping the bounds of truth" in their veneration of Jesus (see 4 : 171, 5 : 77). Cf. in this context Rāzī's remarks mentioned in note 16 on 6 : 23.

98 Regarding this rendering of the phrase *mimmā ʿarafū min al-ḥaqq*, see Zamakhsharī and Rāzī; also *Manār* VII, 12. As for my translation of the expression *idhā samiʿū* as "when they come to understand", it is to be noted that beyond its primary significance of "he heard", the verb *samiʿa* has often the meaning of "he understood" or "came to understand" (cf. Lane IV, 1427).

"O our Sustainer! We do believe; make us one, then, with all who bear witness to the truth. ⟪83⟫ And how could we fail to believe in God and in whatever truth has come unto us, when we so fervently desire that our Sustainer count us among the righteous?" ⟪84⟫

And for this their belief[99] God will reward them with gardens through which running waters flow, therein to abide: for such is the requital of the doers of good; ⟪85⟫ whereas they who are bent on denying the truth and giving the lie to Our messages – they are destined for the blazing fire. ⟪86⟫

O YOU who have attained to faith! Do not deprive yourselves of the good things of life which God has made lawful to you,[100] but do not transgress the bounds of what is right: verily, God does not love those who transgress the bounds of what is right. ⟪87⟫ Thus, partake of the lawful, good things which God grants you as sustenance, and be conscious of God, in whom you believe. ⟪88⟫

GOD will not take you to task for oaths which you may have uttered without thought,[101] but He will take you to task for oaths which you have sworn in earnest. Thus, the breaking of an oath must be atoned for by[102] feeding ten needy persons with more or less the same food as you are wont to give to your own families,[103] or by clothing them, or by freeing a human being from bondage;

رَبَّنَآ ءَامَنَّا فَٱكۡتُبۡنَا مَعَ ٱلشَّٰهِدِينَ ﴿٨٣﴾ وَمَا لَنَا لَا نُؤۡمِنُ بِٱللَّهِ وَمَا جَآءَنَا
مِنَ ٱلۡحَقِّ وَنَطۡمَعُ أَن يُدۡخِلَنَا رَبُّنَا مَعَ ٱلۡقَوۡمِ ٱلصَّٰلِحِينَ ﴿٨٤﴾ فَأَثَٰبَهُمُ
ٱللَّهُ بِمَا قَالُواْ جَنَّٰتٖ تَجۡرِي مِن تَحۡتِهَا ٱلۡأَنۡهَٰرُ خَٰلِدِينَ فِيهَاۚ وَذَٰلِكَ
جَزَآءُ ٱلۡمُحۡسِنِينَ ﴿٨٥﴾ وَٱلَّذِينَ كَفَرُواْ وَكَذَّبُواْ بِـَٔايَٰتِنَآ أُوْلَٰٓئِكَ أَصۡحَٰبُ
ٱلۡجَحِيمِ ﴿٨٦﴾ يَٰٓأَيُّهَا ٱلَّذِينَ ءَامَنُواْ لَا تُحَرِّمُواْ طَيِّبَٰتِ مَآ أَحَلَّ ٱللَّهُ لَكُمۡ
وَلَا تَعۡتَدُوٓاْۚ إِنَّ ٱللَّهَ لَا يُحِبُّ ٱلۡمُعۡتَدِينَ ﴿٨٧﴾ وَكُلُواْ مِمَّا رَزَقَكُمُ ٱللَّهُ حَلَٰلٗا
طَيِّبٗاۚ وَٱتَّقُواْ ٱللَّهَ ٱلَّذِيٓ أَنتُم بِهِۦ مُؤۡمِنُونَ ﴿٨٨﴾ لَا يُؤَاخِذُكُمُ ٱللَّهُ بِٱللَّغۡوِ فِيٓ
أَيۡمَٰنِكُمۡ وَلَٰكِن يُؤَاخِذُكُم بِمَا عَقَّدتُّمُ ٱلۡأَيۡمَٰنَۖ فَكَفَّٰرَتُهُۥٓ إِطۡعَامُ عَشَرَةِ
مَسَٰكِينَ مِنۡ أَوۡسَطِ مَا تُطۡعِمُونَ أَهۡلِيكُمۡ أَوۡ كِسۡوَتُهُمۡ أَوۡ تَحۡرِيرُ رَقَبَةٖۖ

Rabbanāa ʾāmannā faktubnā maᶜash-shāhidīn. ⟪83⟫ Wa mā lanā lā nuʾminu billāhi wa mā jāaʾanā minal-ḥaqqi wa naṭmaᶜu ʾañy-yudkhilanā Rabbunā maᶜal-qawmiṣ-ṣāliḥīn. ⟪84⟫ Faʾathābahumul-lāhu bimā qālū jannātiñ-tajrī miñ-taḥtihal-ʾanhāru khālidīna fīhā. Wa dhālika jazāaʾul-muḥsinīn. ⟪85⟫ Wal-ladhīna kafarū wa kadhdhabū biʾĀyātināa ʾulāaʾika ʾaṣḥābul-jaḥīm. ⟪86⟫ Yāa ʾayyuhal-ladhīna ʾāmanū lā tuḥarrimū ṭayyibāti māa ʾaḥallal-lāhu lakum wa lā taᶜtadū; ʾinnal-lāha lā yuḥibbul-muᶜtadīn. ⟪87⟫ Wa kulū mimmā razaqakumul-lāhu ḥalālañ-ṭayyibā. Wat-taqul-lāhal-ladhīi ʾañtum-bihī muʾminūn. ⟪88⟫ Lā yuʾākhidhukumul-lāhu billaghwi fīi ʾaymānikum wa lākiñy-yuʾākhidhukum-bimā ᶜaqqattumul-ʾaymān. Fakaffāratuhūu ʾiṭᶜāmu ᶜasharati masākīna min ʾawsaṭi mā tuṭᶜimūna ʾahlīkum ʾaw kiswatuhum ʾaw taḥrīru raqabah.

99 Lit., "for what they have said" – i.e., expressed as their belief (Zamakhsharī).

100 Most of the commentators – including Ṭabarī, Zamakhsharī and Rāzī – explain the expression *lā tuḥarrimū* (lit., "do not forbid" or "do not declare as forbidden") in the sense given by me above, and take it to refer to the self-mortification practiced, in particular, by Christian priests and monks. The term *aṭ-ṭayyibāt* comprises all that is good and wholesome in life – "the delightful things which human beings desire and towards which their hearts incline" (Ṭabarī): hence my rendering, "the good things of life".

101 Lit., "for a thoughtless word (*laghw*) in your oaths". This refers primarily to oaths aiming at denying to oneself something which the Law of Islam does not prohibit (i.e., "the good things of life"); and, generally, to all oaths uttered without premeditation, e.g., under the influence of anger (cf. 2 : 224-225; also 38 : 44 and the corresponding note 41).

102 Lit., "its atonement shall be" – the pronoun referring to the (implied) sin of breaking an oath. It is obvious from the context that this possibility of atonement relates only to "oaths uttered without thought", and not to deliberate undertakings affecting other persons, which – as has been explicitly stated in the opening sentence of this *sūrah* – a believer is bound to observe faithfully to the best of his ability. Regarding exceptions from this general rule, see *sūrah* 2, note 212.

103 Lit., "the average of what you feed your families with".

فَمَن لَّمْ يَجِدْ فَصِيَامُ ثَلَٰثَةِ أَيَّامٍ ذَٰلِكَ كَفَّٰرَةُ أَيْمَٰنِكُمْ إِذَا حَلَفْتُمْ
وَٱحْفَظُوٓا۟ أَيْمَٰنَكُمْ كَذَٰلِكَ يُبَيِّنُ ٱللَّهُ لَكُمْ ءَايَٰتِهِۦ لَعَلَّكُمْ تَشْكُرُونَ ﴿٨٩﴾
يَٰٓأَيُّهَا ٱلَّذِينَ ءَامَنُوٓا۟ إِنَّمَا ٱلْخَمْرُ وَٱلْمَيْسِرُ وَٱلْأَنصَابُ وَٱلْأَزْلَٰمُ رِجْسٌ
مِّنْ عَمَلِ ٱلشَّيْطَٰنِ فَٱجْتَنِبُوهُ لَعَلَّكُمْ تُفْلِحُونَ ﴿٩٠﴾ إِنَّمَا يُرِيدُ ٱلشَّيْطَٰنُ أَن
يُوقِعَ بَيْنَكُمُ ٱلْعَدَٰوَةَ وَٱلْبَغْضَآءَ فِى ٱلْخَمْرِ وَٱلْمَيْسِرِ وَيَصُدَّكُمْ عَن ذِكْرِ
ٱللَّهِ وَعَنِ ٱلصَّلَوٰةِ فَهَلْ أَنتُم مُّنتَهُونَ ﴿٩١﴾ وَأَطِيعُوا۟ ٱللَّهَ وَأَطِيعُوا۟ ٱلرَّسُولَ
وَٱحْذَرُوا۟ فَإِن تَوَلَّيْتُمْ فَٱعْلَمُوٓا۟ أَنَّمَا عَلَىٰ رَسُولِنَا ٱلْبَلَٰغُ ٱلْمُبِينُ ﴿٩٢﴾
لَيْسَ عَلَى ٱلَّذِينَ ءَامَنُوا۟ وَعَمِلُوا۟ ٱلصَّٰلِحَٰتِ جُنَاحٌ فِيمَا طَعِمُوٓا۟ إِذَا

and he who has not the wherewithal shall fast for three days [instead]. This shall be the atonement for your oaths whenever you have sworn [and broken them]. But be mindful of your oaths![104]
Thus God makes clear unto you His messages, so that you might have cause to be grateful. ‹89›

O YOU who have attained to faith! Intoxicants, and games of chance, and idolatrous practices, and the divining of the future are but a loathsome evil of Satan's doing:[105] shun it, then, so that you might attain to a happy state! ‹90› By means of intoxicants and games of chance Satan seeks only to sow enmity and hatred among you, and to turn you away from the remembrance of God and from prayer. Will you not, then, desist?[106] ‹91›
Hence, pay heed unto God, and pay heed unto the Apostle, and be ever on your guard [against evil]; and if you turn away, then know that Our Apostle's only duty is a clear delivery of the message [entrusted to him].[107] ‹92›
Those who have attained to faith and do righteous deeds incur no sin by partaking of whatever they may,[108] so long as they

Famal-lam yajid faṢiyāmu thalāthati ʾayyām. Dhālika kaffāratu ʾaymānikum ʾidhā ḥalaftum. Waḥ-faẓūu ʾaymānakum. Kadhālika yubayyinul-lāhu lakum ʾĀyātihī laʿallakum tashkurūn. (89) Yāa ʾayyuhal-ladhīna ʾāmanūu ʾinnamal-khamru wal-maysiru wal-ʾañṣābu wal-ʾazlāmu rijsum-min ʿamalish-Shayṭāni fajtanibūhu laʿallakum tufliḥūn. (90) ʾInnamā yurīdush-Shayṭānu ʾañy-yūqiʿa baynakumul-ʿadāwata wal-baghḍāaʾa fil-khamri wal-maysiri wa yaṣuddakum ʿañ-dhikril-lāhi wa ʿaniṣ-Ṣalāti fahal-ʾañtum-muñtahūn. (91) Wa ʾaṭīʿul-lāha wa ʾaṭīʿur-Rasūla waḥ-dharū; faʾiñ-tawallaytum faʿlamūu ʾannamā ʿalā Rasūlinal-balāghul-mubīn. (92) Laysa ʿalal-ladhīna ʾāmanū wa ʿamiluṣ-ṣāliḥāti junāḥuñ-fīmā ṭaʿimūu ʾidhā

104 I.e., "do not make them lightly or often" (Rāzī).

105 According to all the lexicographers, the word *khamr* (derived from the verb *khamara*, "he concealed" or "obscured") denotes every substance the use of which obscures the intellect, i.e., intoxicates. Hence, the prohibition of intoxicants laid down in this verse comprises not merely alcoholic drinks, but also drugs which have a similar effect. The only exception from this total prohibition arises in cases of "dire necessity" (in the strictest sense of these words), as stipulated in the last sentence of verse 3 of this *sūrah*: that is to say, in cases where illness or a bodily accident makes the administration of intoxicating drugs or of alcohol imperative and unavoidable. – As regards the expression "idolatrous practices" (*anṣāb*, lit., "idolatrous altars"), see note 8 of this *sūrah*. This term has, I believe, been used here metaphorically, and is meant to circumscribe all practices of an idolatrous nature – like saint-worship, the attribution of "magic" properties to certain inanimate objects, the observance of all manner of superstitious taboos, and so forth. – For an explanation of the expression rendered by me as "divining of the future" (*al-azlām*, lit., "divining-arrows"), see note 9 on the second paragraph of verse 3 of this *sūrah*.

106 Lit., "Will you, then, desist?" – a rhetorical question implying the *necessity* of desisting, which can be expressed in English only by the use of the negative form.

107 This implies that he cannot *force* people to believe, and cannot, therefore, be held responsible for their failure to do so.

108 Lit., "in whatever they eat" or "taste" (*fī-mā ṭaʿimū*). The verb *ṭaʿima*, which primarily signifies "he ate", applies to eating and drinking as well as – metaphorically – to "partaking of" anything that may be desirable. Most of the commentators assume that this verse relates to the believers who had died before the promulgation of the prohibitions mentioned in verse 90 above. It seems to me, however, that it has a much wider meaning, and relates to the partaking of "the good things of life" – i.e., to those which have *not* been prohibited by God and which, therefore, the believers need not deny themselves (cf. verse 87 above).

مَا ٱتَّقَوا۟ وَّءَامَنُوا۟ وَعَمِلُوا۟ ٱلصَّٰلِحَٰتِ ثُمَّ ٱتَّقَوا۟ وَّءَامَنُوا۟ ثُمَّ ٱتَّقَوا۟ وَّأَحْسَنُوا۟
وَٱللَّهُ يُحِبُّ ٱلْمُحْسِنِينَ ﴿٩٣﴾ يَٰٓأَيُّهَا ٱلَّذِينَ ءَامَنُوا۟ لَيَبْلُوَنَّكُمُ ٱللَّهُ بِشَىْءٍ
مِّنَ ٱلصَّيْدِ تَنَالُهُۥٓ أَيْدِيكُمْ وَرِمَاحُكُمْ لِيَعْلَمَ ٱللَّهُ مَن يَخَافُهُۥ بِٱلْغَيْبِ
فَمَنِ ٱعْتَدَىٰ بَعْدَ ذَٰلِكَ فَلَهُۥ عَذَابٌ أَلِيمٌ ﴿٩٤﴾ يَٰٓأَيُّهَا ٱلَّذِينَ ءَامَنُوا۟ لَا
تَقْتُلُوا۟ ٱلصَّيْدَ وَأَنتُمْ حُرُمٌ وَمَن قَتَلَهُۥ مِنكُم مُّتَعَمِّدًا فَجَزَآءٌ مِّثْلُ مَا قَتَلَ
مِنَ ٱلنَّعَمِ يَحْكُمُ بِهِۦ ذَوَا عَدْلٍ مِّنكُمْ هَدْيًۢا بَٰلِغَ ٱلْكَعْبَةِ أَوْ كَفَّٰرَةٌ
طَعَامُ مَسَٰكِينَ أَوْ عَدْلُ ذَٰلِكَ صِيَامًا لِّيَذُوقَ وَبَالَ أَمْرِهِۦ عَفَا ٱللَّهُ عَمَّا

mat-taqaw-wa ᵓāmanū wa ᶜamiluṣ-ṣāliḥāti thum-mat-taqaw-wa ᵓāmanū thummat-taqaw-wa ᵓaḥsanū. Wal-lāhu yuḥibbul-muḥsinīn. (93) Yāa ᵓayyuhal-ladhīna ᵓāmanū layabluwannakumul-lāhu bi-shayᵓim-minaṣ-ṣaydi tanāluhūu ᵓaydīkum wa rimāḥukum liyaᶜlamal-lāhu mañy-yakhāfuhū bil-ghayb. Famaniᶜ-tadā baᶜda dhālika falahū ᶜadhābun ᵓalīm. (94) Yāa ᵓayyuhal-ladhīna ᵓāmanū lā taqtuluṣ-ṣayda wa ᵓañtum ḥurum. Wa mañ-qatalahū miñkum-mutaᶜammidañ-fajazāaᵓum-mithlu mā qa-tala minan-naᶜami yaḥkumu bihī dhawā ᶜadlim-miñkum hadyam-bālighal-Kaᶜbati ᵓaw kaffāratuñ-ṭaᶜāmu masākīna ᵓaw ᶜadlu dhālika Ṣiyāmal-liyadhūqa wabāla ᵓamrih. ᶜAfal-lāhu ᶜammā

are conscious of God and [truly] believe and do righteous deeds, and continue to be conscious of God and to believe, and grow ever more[109] conscious of God, and persevere in doing good: for God loves the doers of good. ‹93›

O YOU who have attained to faith! Most certainly God will try you by means of the game which may come within the reach of your hands and your weapons[110] [while you are on pilgrimage], so that God might mark out those who fear Him although He is beyond the reach of human perception.[111] And as for him who, after all this, transgresses the bounds of what is right – grievous suffering awaits him! ‹94›

O you who have attained to faith! Kill no game while you are in the state of pilgrimage. And whoever of you kills it intentionally,[112] [shall make] amends in cattle equivalent to what he has killed – with two persons of probity giving their judgment thereon – to be brought as an offering to the Kaᶜbah;[113] or else he may atone for his sin by feeding the needy, or by the equivalent thereof in fasting:[114] [this,] in order that he taste the full gravity of his deed, [while] God shall have effaced

109 Lit., "and then (*thumma*) are . . .": a sequence expressing growth and intensification (Rāzī). Hence, the particle *thumma* – occurring twice in this sentence – has been rendered by me, in the first instance, as "[they] continue to be" and, in the second instance, as "[they] grow ever more [conscious of God]".

110 Lit., "with something of the game which your hands and your lances [may] reach".

111 With this verse, the Qurᵓān returns to the prohibition of hunting during pilgrimage enunciated in verse 1 of this *sūrah*. The "trial" arises from the fact that hunting, although lawful in itself (and therefore included among the things which the believer, according to the preceding verse, may normally partake of), is prohibited in the state of pilgrimage. – As regards the expression *bi'l-ghayb*, rendered by me as "although He is beyond the reach of human perception", see *sūrah* 2, note 3.

112 From the last sentence of this verse it appears that by the "intentional" killing referred to here only an isolated incident (or a first offence) can be meant, and not a wilful, persistent "transgressing of the bounds of what is right", which the preceding verse condemns so severely. It is to be borne in mind that the term "game" (*ṣayd*) relates in this context only to edible animals: for, according to several authentic Traditions, the killing of a dangerous or highly obnoxious animal – for instance, a snake, a scorpion, a rabid dog, etc. – is permitted even in the state of pilgrimage.

113 I.e., for distribution among the poor. In this context, the Kaᶜbah signifies, metonymically, the sacred precincts of Mecca, and not only the sanctuary itself (Rāzī). The "two persons of probity" are supposed to determine the approximate flesh-value of the wild animal which has been killed, and to decide on this basis as to what domestic animal should be offered in compensation.

114 Lit., "or [there shall be] an atonement by way of feeding the needy, or an equivalent by way of fasting". These two alternatives are open to a pilgrim who is too poor to provide a head or heads of cattle corresponding in value to the game which he has killed, or – in the last-named alternative – too poor even to feed other poor people. Since neither the Qurᵓān nor any authentic Tradition specifies the number of poor to be fed or the number of days of fasting, these details are obviously left to the conscience of the person concerned.

the past. But whoever does it again, God will inflict His retribution on him: for God is almighty, an avenger of evil. «95»
Lawful to you is all water-game, and what the sea brings forth,[115] as a provision for you [who are settled] as well as for travellers, although you are forbidden to hunt on land while you are in the state of pilgrimage.[116] And be conscious of God, unto whom you shall be gathered. «96»
God has laid down that the Kaᶜbah, the Inviolable Temple, shall be a symbol for all mankind;[117] and [so, too,] the sacred month [of pilgrimage] and the garlanded offerings [are symbols] meant to make you aware[118] that God is aware of all that is in the heavens and all that is on earth, and that God has full knowledge of everything. «97»
Know that God is severe in retribution – and that God is much-forgiving, a dispenser of grace. «98»
No more is the Apostle bound to do than deliver the message [entrusted to him]: and God knows all that you do openly, and all that you would conceal. «99»

سَلَفَ وَمَنْ عَادَ فَيَنتَقِمُ ٱللَّهُ مِنْهُ وَٱللَّهُ عَزِيزٌ ذُو ٱنتِقَامٍ ﴿٩٥﴾ أُحِلَّ لَكُمْ
صَيْدُ ٱلْبَحْرِ وَطَعَامُهُۥ مَتَٰعًا لَّكُمْ وَلِلسَّيَّارَةِ وَحُرِّمَ عَلَيْكُمْ صَيْدُ ٱلْبَرِّ
مَا دُمْتُمْ حُرُمًا وَٱتَّقُوا۟ ٱللَّهَ ٱلَّذِىٓ إِلَيْهِ تُحْشَرُونَ ﴿٩٦﴾ ۞ جَعَلَ ٱللَّهُ
ٱلْكَعْبَةَ ٱلْبَيْتَ ٱلْحَرَامَ قِيَٰمًا لِّلنَّاسِ وَٱلشَّهْرَ ٱلْحَرَامَ وَٱلْهَدْىَ وَٱلْقَلَٰٓئِدَ
ذَٰلِكَ لِتَعْلَمُوٓا۟ أَنَّ ٱللَّهَ يَعْلَمُ مَا فِى ٱلسَّمَٰوَٰتِ وَمَا فِى ٱلْأَرْضِ وَأَنَّ ٱللَّهَ
بِكُلِّ شَىْءٍ عَلِيمٌ ﴿٩٧﴾ ٱعْلَمُوٓا۟ أَنَّ ٱللَّهَ شَدِيدُ ٱلْعِقَابِ وَأَنَّ ٱللَّهَ غَفُورٌ
رَّحِيمٌ ﴿٩٨﴾ مَّا عَلَى ٱلرَّسُولِ إِلَّا ٱلْبَلَٰغُ وَٱللَّهُ يَعْلَمُ مَا تُبْدُونَ وَمَا
تَكْتُمُونَ ﴿٩٩﴾

ربع الحزب

salaf. Wa man ᶜāda fayañtaqimul-lāhu minh. Wal-lāhu ᶜAzīzuñ-Dhuñ-tiqām. 95 ᵓUḥilla lakum ṣaydul-baḥri wa ṭaᶜāmuhū matāᶜal-lakum wa lissayyārati wa ḥurrima ᶜalaykum ṣaydul-barri mā dumtum ḥurumā. Wat-taqul-lāhal-ladhīi ᵓilayhi tuḥsharūn. 96
Jaᶜalal-lāhul-Kaᶜbatal-Baytal-Ḥarāma qiyāmal-linnāsi wash-Shahral-Ḥarāma wal-hadya wal-qalāaᵓid. Dhālika litaᶜlamūu ᵓannal-lāha yaᶜlamu mā fis-samāwāti wa mā fil-ᵓarḍi wa ᵓannal-lāha bikulli shayᵓin ᶜAlīm. 97 ᵓIᶜlamūu ᵓannal-lāha Shadīdul-ᶜiqābi wa ᵓannal-lāha Ghafūrur-Raḥīm. 98 Mā ᶜalar-Rasūli ᵓillal-balāgh. Wal-lāhu yaᶜlamu mā tubdūna wa mā taktumūn. 99

115 Lit., "the game of the sea and its food". Since the term *baḥr* denotes any large accumulation of water, the classical commentators and jurists agree in that the above ordinance comprises all water-game, whether derived from seas, rivers, lakes or ponds (Ṭabarī). The pronoun in *ṭaᶜāmuhu* (lit., "its food") relates to the word *baḥr*, and thus indicates the fish and other marine animals which may have been cast forth by the waves onto the shore (Ṭabarī, Rāzī). Zamakhsharī, however, regards the pronoun as relating to the object of the game (*ṣayd*) as such, and, consequently, understands the phrase as meaning "the eating thereof". Either of these two readings is agreeable with the text inasmuch as the above verse lays down that all kinds of water-game are lawful to a believer – even if he is in the state of pilgrimage – whereas hunting on land (*ṣayd al-barr*) is forbidden to the pilgrim.

116 According to Al-Ḥasan al-Baṣrī (as quoted by Ṭabarī), the "travellers" are, in this context, synonymous with "pilgrims": in other words, water-game of all descriptions is lawful to the believers irrespective of whether they are on pilgrimage or not.

117 All hunting, whether by pilgrims or non-pilgrims, is prohibited in the vicinity of the Kaᶜbah – i.e., within the precincts of Mecca and its environs – because it is a sanctuary (*amn*, see 2 : 125) for all living beings. For its association with Abraham, see 2 : 125 ff., and the corresponding notes. The noun *kaᶜbah*, by which, owing to its shape, the sanctuary has always been known, denotes any "cubical building". It would seem that he who first built the Kaᶜbah (for, since the time of Abraham, it has been rebuilt several times, always in the same shape) consciously chose the simplest three-dimensional form imaginable – a cube – as a parable of man's humility and awe before the idea of God, whose glory is beyond anything that man could conceive by way of architectural beauty. This symbolism is clearly expressed in the term *qiyām* (lit., "support" or "mainstay"), which – in its abstract sense – signifies "a standard by which [men's] affairs are made sound or improved" (Rāzī): hence my rendering of *qiyām li'n-nās* as "a symbol for all mankind".

118 Lit., "this, so that you may know". The "garlanded offerings" (lit., "offerings and garlands") are a reference to the sacrificial animals (see note 4 of this *sūrah*). Thus, the pilgrimage and the rites connected with it are stated to be symbols of man's self-surrender to God.

Say: "There is no comparison between the bad things and the good things,[119] even though very many of the bad things may please thee greatly. Be, then, conscious of God, O you who are endowed with insight, so that you might attain to a happy state!" ‹100›

O YOU who have attained to faith! Do not ask about matters which, if they were to be made manifest to you [in terms of law], might cause you hardship;[120] for, if you should ask about them while the Qurʾān is being revealed, they might [indeed] be made manifest to you [as laws].[121] God has absolved [you from any obligation] in this respect: for God is much-forgiving, forbearing.[122] ‹101› People before your time have indeed asked such questions – and in result thereof have come to deny the truth.[123] ‹102›

قُل لَّا يَسْتَوِى ٱلْخَبِيثُ وَٱلطَّيِّبُ وَلَوْ أَعْجَبَكَ كَثْرَةُ ٱلْخَبِيثِ ۚ فَٱتَّقُوا۟
ٱللَّهَ يَـٰٓأُو۟لِى ٱلْأَلْبَـٰبِ لَعَلَّكُمْ تُفْلِحُونَ ﴿١٠٠﴾ يَـٰٓأَيُّهَا ٱلَّذِينَ ءَامَنُوا۟ لَا
تَسْـَٔلُوا۟ عَنْ أَشْيَآءَ إِن تُبْدَ لَكُمْ تَسُؤْكُمْ وَإِن تَسْـَٔلُوا۟ عَنْهَا حِينَ يُنَزَّلُ
ٱلْقُرْءَانُ تُبْدَ لَكُمْ عَفَا ٱللَّهُ عَنْهَا ۗ وَٱللَّهُ غَفُورٌ حَلِيمٌ ﴿١٠١﴾ قَدْ سَأَلَهَا قَوْمٌ
مِّن قَبْلِكُمْ ثُمَّ أَصْبَحُوا۟ بِهَا كَـٰفِرِينَ ﴿١٠٢﴾

Qul lā yastawil-khabīthu waṭ-ṭayyibu wa law ʾaʿjabaka kathratul-khabīth. Fattaqul-lāha yāa ʾulil-ʾalbābi laʿallakum tufliḥūn. ﴿100﴾ Yāa ʾayyuhal-ladhīna ʾāmanū lā tasʾalū ʿan ʾashyāaʾaʾiñ-tubda lakum tasuʾkum wa ʾiñ-tasʾalū ʿanhā ḥīna yunazzalul-Qurʾānu tubda lakum ʿafal-lāhu ʿanhā. Wal-lāhu Ghafūrun Ḥalīm. ﴿101﴾ Qad saʾalahā qawmum-miñ-qablikum thumma ʾaṣbaḥū bihā kāfirīn. ﴿102﴾

119 Lit., "the bad things and the good things are not equal".

120 This verse connects directly with verse 99: "No more is the Apostle bound to do than deliver the message." Read in conjunction with the sentence, "Today have I perfected your religious law for you" (occurring in verse 3 of this *sūrah*), the above statement implies that the believers should not try to deduce "additional" laws from the injunctions clearly laid down as such by the Qurʾān or by the Prophet, since this "might cause you hardship" – that is, might (as has indeed happened in the course of the centuries) impose additional burdens on the believers above and beyond anything that has been stipulated in terms of law in the Qurʾān or in the authentic commandments of the Prophet. On the basis of this verse, some of the greatest Muslim scholars have concluded that Islamic Law, in its entirety, consists of no more than the clear-cut injunctions forthcoming from the self-evident (*ẓāhir*) wording of the Qurʾān and the Prophet's commandments, and that, consequently, it is not permissible to extend the scope of such self-evident ordinances by means of subjective methods of deduction. (A most enlightening discussion of this problem is to be found in the Introduction to Ibn Ḥazm's *Muḥallā*, vol. I, 56 ff.) This, of course, does not prevent the Muslim community from evolving, whenever necessary, any amount of additional, temporal legislation in accordance with the spirit of the Qurʾān and the teachings of the Prophet: but it must be clearly understood that such additional legislation cannot be regarded as forming part of Islamic Law (the *sharīʿah*) as such.

121 I.e., with possibly unfortunate consequences. An illustration of this problem has been provided in the following authentic Tradition, quoted by Muslim on the authority of Abū Hurayrah. In one of his sermons, the Prophet said: "O my people! God has ordained the pilgrimage (*al-ḥajj*) for you; therefore perform it." Thereupon somebody asked, "Every year, O Apostle of God?" The Prophet remained silent; and the man repeated his question twice. Then the Prophet said: "Had I answered 'yes', it would have become incumbent on you [to perform the pilgrimage every year]: and, indeed, it would have been beyond your ability to do so. Do not ask me about matters which I leave unspoken: for, behold, there were people before you who went to their doom because they had put too many questions to their prophets and thereupon disagreed [about their teachings]. Therefore, if I command you anything, do of it as much as you are able to do; and if I forbid you anything, abstain from it." Discussing this Tradition, Ibn Ḥazm observes: "It circumscribes all the principles of religious law (*aḥkām ad-dīn*) from the first to the last – namely: what the Prophet has left unspoken – neither ordering nor forbidding it – is allowed (*mubāḥ*), that is, neither forbidden nor obligatory; whatever he ordered is obligatory (*farḍ*), and whatever he forbade is unlawful (*ḥarām*); and whatever he ordered us to do is binding on us to the extent of our ability alone" (*Muḥallā*, I, 64). It should be borne in mind that the term "the Prophet" comprises, in this context, the Qurʾān as well, since it was through the Prophet that the Qurʾanic message was communicated to mankind.

122 I.e., by leaving certain matters unspoken, God has left them to man's discretion, thus enabling him to act in accordance with his conscience and the best interests of the community.

123 Following Ibn Ḥazm's principles of jurisprudence, Rashīd Riḍāʾ thus explains the above verse: "Many of our

IT IS NOT of God's ordaining that certain kinds of cattle should be marked out by superstition and set aside from the use of man;[124] yet those who are bent on denying the truth attribute their own lying inventions to God. And most of them never use their reason: ‹103› for when they are told, "Come unto that which God has bestowed from on high, and unto the Apostle" – they answer, "Enough for us is that which we found our forefathers believing in and doing." Why, even though their forefathers knew nothing, and were devoid of all guidance? ‹104›

O you who have attained to faith! It is [but] for your own selves that you are responsible: those who go astray can do you no harm if you [yourselves] are on the right path. Unto God you all must return: and then He will make you [truly] understand all that you were doing [in life]. ‹105›

O YOU who have attained to faith! Let there be witnesses to what you do when death approaches you and you are about to make bequests:[125] two persons of probity from among your own people, or – if the pangs of death come upon you while you are travelling far from home[126] – two other persons from [among people] other than your own. Take hold of the two after

مَا جَعَلَ ٱللَّهُ مِنۢ بَحِيرَةٍ وَلَا سَآئِبَةٍ وَلَا وَصِيلَةٍ وَلَا حَامٍ وَلَٰكِنَّ ٱلَّذِينَ كَفَرُوا۟
يَفْتَرُونَ عَلَى ٱللَّهِ ٱلْكَذِبَ وَأَكْثَرُهُمْ لَا يَعْقِلُونَ ﴿١٠٣﴾ وَإِذَا قِيلَ لَهُمْ تَعَالَوْا۟ إِلَىٰ
مَآ أَنزَلَ ٱللَّهُ وَإِلَى ٱلرَّسُولِ قَالُوا۟ حَسْبُنَا مَا وَجَدْنَا عَلَيْهِ ءَابَآءَنَآ أَوَلَوْ كَانَ
ءَابَآؤُهُمْ لَا يَعْلَمُونَ شَيْـًٔا وَلَا يَهْتَدُونَ ﴿١٠٤﴾ يَٰٓأَيُّهَا ٱلَّذِينَ ءَامَنُوا۟ عَلَيْكُمْ
أَنفُسَكُمْ لَا يَضُرُّكُم مَّن ضَلَّ إِذَا ٱهْتَدَيْتُمْ إِلَى ٱللَّهِ مَرْجِعُكُمْ جَمِيعًا
فَيُنَبِّئُكُم بِمَا كُنتُمْ تَعْمَلُونَ ﴿١٠٥﴾ يَٰٓأَيُّهَا ٱلَّذِينَ ءَامَنُوا۟ شَهَٰدَةُ بَيْنِكُمْ إِذَا حَضَرَ
أَحَدَكُمُ ٱلْمَوْتُ حِينَ ٱلْوَصِيَّةِ ٱثْنَانِ ذَوَا عَدْلٍ مِّنكُمْ أَوْ ءَاخَرَانِ مِنْ غَيْرِكُمْ
إِنْ أَنتُمْ ضَرَبْتُمْ فِى ٱلْأَرْضِ فَأَصَٰبَتْكُم مُّصِيبَةُ ٱلْمَوْتِ تَحْبِسُونَهُمَا مِنۢ بَعْدِ

Mā jaʿalal-lāhu mim-baḥīratiñw-wa lā sāaʾibatiñw-wa lā waṣīlatiñw-wa lā ḥāmiñw-wa lākinnal-ladhīna kafarū yaftarūna ʿalal-lāhil-kadhiba wa ʾaktharuhum lā yaʿqilūn. ﴿103﴾ Wa ʾidhā qīla lahum taʿālaw ʾilā māa ʾañzalal-lāhu wa ʾilar-Rasūli qālū ḥasbunā mā wajadnā ʿalayhi ʾābāaʾanā. ʾAwa law kāna ʾābāaʾuhum lā yaʿlamūna shayʾañw-wa lā yahtadūn. ﴿104﴾ Yāa ʾayyuhal-ladhīna ʾāmanū ʿalaykum ʾañfusakum; lā yaḍurrukum-mañ-ḍalla ʾidhahtadaytum. ʾIlal-lāhi marjiʿukum jamīʿañ-fayunabbiʾukum-bimā kuñtum taʿmalūn. ﴿105﴾ Yāa ʾayyuhal-ladhīna ʾāmanū shahādatu baynikum ʾidhā ḥaḍara ʾaḥadakumul-mawtu ḥīnal-waṣiyyatith-nāni dhawā ʿadlim-miñkum ʾaw ʾākharāni min ghayrikum ʾin ʾañtum ḍarabtum fil-ʾarḍi faʾaṣābatkum-muṣībatul-mawt. Taḥbisūnahumā mim-baʿdiṣ-

jurists (*fuqahāʾ*) have, by their subjective deductions, unduly widened the range of man's religious obligations (*takālīf*), thus giving rise to the very difficulties and complications which the clear wording [of the Qurʾān] had put an end to; and this has led to the abandonment, by many individual Muslims as well as by their governments, of Islamic Law in its entirety" (*Manār* VII, 138).

124 Lit., "God has not ordained anything [in the nature] of a *baḥīrah*, nor a *sāʾibah*, nor a *waṣīlah*, nor a *ḥām*." These expressions denote certain categories of domestic animals which the pre-Islamic Arabs used to dedicate to their various deities by setting them free to pasture and prohibiting their use or slaughter. They were selected mainly on the basis of the number, sex and sequence of their offspring; but the lexicographers and commentators are by no means unanimous in their attempts at definition. For this reason – as well as because of their inherent complexity – the above four terms cannot be translated into any other language; consequently, I am rendering them in the text as "certain kinds of cattle marked out by superstition and set aside from the use of man": this being, in the consensus of all authorities, the common denominator of the four categories. It is obvious that their mention at this place (as well as, by implication, in 6 : 138-139 and 143-144) serves as an illustration of the arbitrary invention of certain supposedly "religious" obligations and prohibitions alluded to in the preceding two verses and explained in the corresponding notes.

125 Lit., "[let there be] testimony between you" – i.e., between you and your heirs – "when death approaches any of you, at the time of [making a] bequest".

126 Lit., "travelling on earth". According to most of the commentators (cf. Rāzī), the expression *minkum* (lit., "from among you") signifies here "from among *your* own people", i.e., from among the Muslim community.

نصف الحزب

having prayed; and if you have any doubt in your mind, let each of them swear by God "We shall not sell this [our word] for any price, even though it were [for the sake of] a near kinsman; and neither shall we conceal aught of what we have witnessed before God[127] – or else, may we indeed be counted among the sinful." «106»

But if afterwards it should come to light that the two [witnesses] have become guilty of [this very] sin, then two others – from among those whom the two former have deprived of their right[128] – shall take their place and shall swear by God, "Our testimony is indeed truer than the testimony of these two, and we have not transgressed the bounds of what is right – or else, may we indeed be counted among the evil-doers!" «107»

Thus it will be more likely that people will offer testimony in accordance with the truth – or else they will [have cause to] fear that their oaths will be refuted by the oaths of others.[129]

Be, then, conscious of God, and hearken [unto Him]: for God does not bestow His guidance upon iniquitous folk. «108»

ON THE DAY when God shall assemble all the apostles and shall ask, "What response did you receive?" – they will answer, "We have no knowledge; verily, it is Thou alone who fully knowest all the things that are beyond the reach of a created being's perception."[130] «109»

Lo![131] God will say: "O Jesus, son of Mary! Remember the blessings which I bestowed upon thee and thy mother – how I strengthened thee with holy inspiration,[132]

ٱلصَّلَوٰةِ فَيُقْسِمَانِ بِٱللَّهِ إِنِ ٱرْتَبْتُمْ لَا نَشْتَرِى بِهِۦ ثَمَنًا وَلَوْ كَانَ ذَا قُرْبَىٰ
وَلَا نَكْتُمُ شَهَـٰدَةَ ٱللَّهِ إِنَّآ إِذًا لَّمِنَ ٱلْـَٔاثِمِينَ ﴿١٠٦﴾ فَإِنْ عُثِرَ عَلَىٰٓ أَنَّهُمَا
ٱسْتَحَقَّآ إِثْمًا فَـَٔاخَرَانِ يَقُومَانِ مَقَامَهُمَا مِنَ ٱلَّذِينَ ٱسْتَحَقَّ عَلَيْهِمُ ٱلْأَوْلَيَـٰنِ
فَيُقْسِمَانِ بِٱللَّهِ لَشَهَـٰدَتُنَآ أَحَقُّ مِن شَهَـٰدَتِهِمَا وَمَا ٱعْتَدَيْنَآ إِنَّآ إِذًا لَّمِنَ
ٱلظَّـٰلِمِينَ ﴿١٠٧﴾ ذَٰلِكَ أَدْنَىٰٓ أَن يَأْتُوا۟ بِٱلشَّهَـٰدَةِ عَلَىٰ وَجْهِهَآ أَوْ يَخَافُوٓا۟
أَن تُرَدَّ أَيْمَـٰنٌۢ بَعْدَ أَيْمَـٰنِهِمْ ۗ وَٱتَّقُوا۟ ٱللَّهَ وَٱسْمَعُوا۟ ۗ وَٱللَّهُ لَا يَهْدِى ٱلْقَوْمَ
ٱلْفَـٰسِقِينَ ﴿١٠٨﴾ ۞ يَوْمَ يَجْمَعُ ٱللَّهُ ٱلرُّسُلَ فَيَقُولُ مَاذَآ أُجِبْتُمْ ۖ قَالُوا۟
لَا عِلْمَ لَنَآ ۖ إِنَّكَ أَنتَ عَلَّـٰمُ ٱلْغُيُوبِ ﴿١٠٩﴾ إِذْ قَالَ ٱللَّهُ يَـٰعِيسَى ٱبْنَ
مَرْيَمَ ٱذْكُرْ نِعْمَتِى عَلَيْكَ وَعَلَىٰ وَٰلِدَتِكَ إِذْ أَيَّدتُّكَ بِرُوحِ ٱلْقُدُسِ

Ṣalāti fayuqsimāni billāhi 'inir-tabtum lā nashtarī bihī thamanañw-wa law kāna dhā qurbā wa lā naktumu shahādatal-lāhi 'innāa 'idhal-la-minal-'āthimīn. (106) Fa'in ʿuthira ʿalāa 'annahumas-taḥaqqāa 'ithmañ-fa'ākharāni yaqūmāni maqāmahumā minal-ladhīnas-taḥaqqa ʿalayhimul-'awlayāni fayuqsimāni billāhi lashahādatunāa 'aḥaqqu miñ-shahādatihimā wa maʿ-tadaynāa 'innāa 'idhal-laminaẓ-ẓālimīn. (107) Dhālika 'adnāa 'añy-ya'tū bishshahādati ʿalā wajhihāa 'aw yakhāfūu 'añ-turadda 'aymānum-baʿda 'aymānihim; wat-taqul-lāha was-maʿū. Wal-lāhu lā yahdil-qawmal-fāsiqīn. (108) ◈ Yawma yajmaʿul-lāhur-Rusula fayaqūlu mādhāa 'ujibtum. Qālū lā ʿilma lanā; 'innaka 'Añta ʿAllāmul-ghuyūb. (109) 'Idh qālal-lāhu yā ʿĪsab-na Maryamadh-kur niʿmatī ʿalayka wa ʿalā wālidatika 'idh 'ayyattuka birūḥil-qudusi

127 Lit., "we shall not conceal God's testimony".

128 I.e., from among the rightful heirs of the deceased.

129 Lit., "lest [contradictory] oaths be proffered after their oaths".

130 Cf. verse 99 above: "No more is the Apostle bound to do than deliver the message" – for, neither can he force people to follow the right path, nor can he know what is in their hearts. (See also 4 : 41-42.)

131 Regarding my occasional rendering of *idh* (at the beginning of a sentence) as "lo", see *sūrah* 2, note 21. In the above context, this interjection connects with the preceding passage, which states, by implication, that the apostles are not responsible for the reactions of those to whom they communicate the divine message: a connection that is brought out fully in verses 116-117 below.

132 See *sūrah* 2, note 71.

so that thou couldst speak unto men in thy cradle, and as a grown man; and how I imparted unto thee revelation and wisdom, including the Torah and the Gospel;[133] and how by My leave thou didst create out of clay, as it were, the shape of [thy followers'] destiny, and then didst breathe into it, so that it might become, by My leave, [their] destiny;[134] and how thou didst heal the blind and the leper by My leave, and how thou didst raise the dead by My leave;[135] and how I prevented the children of Israel from harming thee when thou camest unto them with all evidence of the truth, and [when] those of them who were bent on denying the truth were saying, 'This is clearly nothing but deception!'" ‹110›

AND [remember the time] when I inspired the white-garbed ones:[136] "Believe in Me and in My Apostle!"
They answered: "We believe; and bear Thou witness that we have surrendered ourselves [unto Thee]." ‹111›
[And,] lo, the white-garbed ones said: "O Jesus, son of Mary! Could thy Sustainer send down unto us a repast from heaven?"[137]
[Jesus] answered: "Be conscious of God, if you are [truly] believers!" ‹112›

تُكَلِّمُ ٱلنَّاسَ فِى ٱلْمَهْدِ وَكَهْلًا ۖ وَإِذْ عَلَّمْتُكَ ٱلْكِتَٰبَ وَٱلْحِكْمَةَ
وَٱلتَّوْرَىٰةَ وَٱلْإِنجِيلَ ۖ وَإِذْ تَخْلُقُ مِنَ ٱلطِّينِ كَهَيْـَٔةِ ٱلطَّيْرِ بِإِذْنِى فَتَنفُخُ
فِيهَا فَتَكُونُ طَيْرًۢا بِإِذْنِى ۖ وَتُبْرِئُ ٱلْأَكْمَهَ وَٱلْأَبْرَصَ بِإِذْنِى ۖ وَإِذْ تُخْرِجُ
ٱلْمَوْتَىٰ بِإِذْنِى ۖ وَإِذْ كَفَفْتُ بَنِىٓ إِسْرَٰٓءِيلَ عَنكَ إِذْ جِئْتَهُم بِٱلْبَيِّنَٰتِ
فَقَالَ ٱلَّذِينَ كَفَرُوا۟ مِنْهُمْ إِنْ هَٰذَآ إِلَّا سِحْرٌ مُّبِينٌ ﴿١١٠﴾ وَإِذْ أَوْحَيْتُ إِلَى
ٱلْحَوَارِيِّۦنَ أَنْ ءَامِنُوا۟ بِى وَبِرَسُولِى قَالُوٓا۟ ءَامَنَّا وَٱشْهَدْ بِأَنَّنَا مُسْلِمُونَ ﴿١١١﴾ إِذْ
قَالَ ٱلْحَوَارِيُّونَ يَٰعِيسَى ٱبْنَ مَرْيَمَ هَلْ يَسْتَطِيعُ رَبُّكَ أَن يُنَزِّلَ عَلَيْنَا
مَآئِدَةً مِّنَ ٱلسَّمَآءِ ۖ قَالَ ٱتَّقُوا۟ ٱللَّهَ إِن كُنتُم مُّؤْمِنِينَ ﴿١١٢﴾

tukallimun-nāsa fil-mahdi wa kahlā. Wa ʾidh ʿallamtukal-Kitāba wal-ḥikmata wat-Tawrāta wal-ʾInjīl. Wa ʾidh takhluqu minaṭ-ṭīni kahayʾatiṭ-ṭayri biʾidhnī fatañfukhu fīhā fatakūnu ṭayram-biʾidhnī. Wa tubriʾul-ʾakmaha wal-ʾabraṣa biʾidhnī. Wa ʾidh tukhrijul-mawtā biʾidhnī. Wa ʾidh kafaftu banīi ʾIsrāaʾīla ʿañka ʾidh jiʾtahum-bilbayyināti faqālal-ladhīna kafarū minhum ʾin hādhāa ʾillā siḥrum-mubīn. (110) Wa ʾidh ʾawḥaytu ʾilal-ḥawāriyyīna ʾan ʾāminū bī wa biRasūlī qālūu ʾāmannā wash-had biʾannanā Muslimūn. (111) ʾIdh qālal-ḥawāriyyūna yā ʿĪsab-na Maryama hal yastaṭīʿu Rabbuka ʾañy-yunazzila ʿalaynā māaʾidatam-minas-samāaʾ. Qālat-taqul-lāha ʾiñ-kuñtum-muʾminīn. (112)

133 Lit., "and the Torah and the Gospel". The conjunction "and" at the beginning of this clause is meant to stress the fact that both the Torah and the Gospel were included in the revelation (*al-kitāb*) vouchsafed to Jesus. Although the Torah was an earlier revelation, it is described as "imparted to Jesus" because his own prophetic mission was based on the Law of Moses, which was only confirmed, and not abrogated, by the Gospel (cf. Matthew v, 17-19). As regards the expression "in thy cradle", see *sūrah* 3, note 33 (first sentence).

134 See 3 : 49, as well as the corresponding note 37.

135 See *sūrah* 3, note 38.

136 I.e., the disciples of Jesus (see *sūrah* 3, note 42).

137 The relevant words, in the generally accepted reading of the Qurʾān, are *hal yastaṭīʿ rabbuka,* meaning "can thy Sustainer", or "could thy Sustainer", or "is thy Sustainer able". Inasmuch as, on the face of it, this reading would imply a fundamental doubt in God's power to do anything that He wills (an imputation which does not agree with the characterization, in the Qurʾān, of Jesus' disciples as firm believers), most of the commentators see in the query of the disciples something similar to one person's asking another, "Could you go with me?" – that is to say, not implying a doubt as to the other's *ability* to go but, rather, an uncertainty as to his *willingness* to do it (cf. in this respect, Ṭabarī, Baghawī, Rāzī, Rāghib; also *Manār* VII, 250 ff.). We have, however, positive evidence of the fact that several of the most outstanding Companions of the Prophet – ʿAlī, Ibn ʿAbbās, ʿĀʾishah and Muʿādh ibn Jabal – read the words in question in the spelling *hal tastaṭīʿ rabbaka,* which might be rendered as "Couldst thou prevail upon thy Sustainer?" (Ṭabarī, Zamakhsharī, Baghawī, Rāzī, Ibn Kathīr): a reading which implies the disciples' uncertainty as to *Jesus'* ability (in the spiritual sense of this word) to make the above request of God. Thus, ʿĀʾishah, refusing to accept

Said they: "We desire to partake thereof, so that our hearts might be set fully at rest, and that we might know that thou hast spoken the truth to us, and that we might be of those who bear witness thereto!" ‹113›
Said Jesus, the son of Mary: "O God, our Sustainer! Send down upon us a repast from heaven: it shall be an ever-recurring feast for us – for the first and the last of us – and a sign from Thee. And provide us our sustenance, for Thou art the best of providers!" ‹114›
God answered: "Verily, I [always] do send it down unto you:[138] and so, if any of you should henceforth deny [this] truth, on him, behold, will I inflict suffering the like of which I have never [yet] inflicted upon anyone in the world!" ‹115›

AND LO! God said:[139] "O Jesus, son of Mary! Didst thou say unto men, 'Worship me and my mother as deities beside God'?"
[Jesus] answered: "Limitless art Thou in Thy glory! It would not have been possible for me to say what I had no right to [say]!

قَالُوا۟ نُرِيدُ أَن نَّأْكُلَ مِنْهَا وَتَطْمَئِنَّ قُلُوبُنَا وَنَعْلَمَ أَن قَدْ صَدَقْتَنَا وَنَكُونَ
عَلَيْهَا مِنَ ٱلشَّٰهِدِينَ ﴿١١٣﴾ قَالَ عِيسَى ٱبْنُ مَرْيَمَ ٱللَّهُمَّ رَبَّنَآ أَنزِلْ عَلَيْنَا
مَآئِدَةً مِّنَ ٱلسَّمَآءِ تَكُونُ لَنَا عِيدًا لِّأَوَّلِنَا وَءَاخِرِنَا وَءَايَةً مِّنكَ ۖ وَٱرْزُقْنَا
وَأَنتَ خَيْرُ ٱلرَّٰزِقِينَ ﴿١١٤﴾ قَالَ ٱللَّهُ إِنِّى مُنَزِّلُهَا عَلَيْكُمْ ۖ فَمَن يَكْفُرْ بَعْدُ
مِنكُمْ فَإِنِّىٓ أُعَذِّبُهُۥ عَذَابًا لَّآ أُعَذِّبُهُۥٓ أَحَدًا مِّنَ ٱلْعَٰلَمِينَ ﴿١١٥﴾ وَإِذْ
قَالَ ٱللَّهُ يَٰعِيسَى ٱبْنَ مَرْيَمَ ءَأَنتَ قُلْتَ لِلنَّاسِ ٱتَّخِذُونِى وَأُمِّىَ إِلَٰهَيْنِ
مِن دُونِ ٱللَّهِ ۖ قَالَ سُبْحَٰنَكَ مَا يَكُونُ لِىٓ أَنْ أَقُولَ مَا لَيْسَ لِى بِحَقٍّ

Qālū nurīdu ʾan-naʾkula minhā wa taṭmaʾinna qulūbunā wa naʿlama ʾañ-qad ṣadaqtanā wa nakūna ʿalayhā minash-shāhidīn. (113) Qāla ʿĪsab-nu Maryamal-lāhumma Rabbanāa ʾañzil ʿalaynā māaʾidatam-minas-samāaʾi takūnu lanā ʿīdal-liʾawwalinā wa ʾākhirinā wa ʾĀyatam-miñka war-zuqnā wa ʾAñta Khayrur-rāziqīn. (114) Qālal-lāhu ʾinnī munazziluhā ʿalaykum. Famañy-yakfur baʿdu miñkum faʾinnīi ʾuʿadhdhibuhū ʿadhābal-lāa ʾuʿadhdhibuhūu ʾaḥadam-minal-ʿālamīn. (115) Wa ʾidh qālal-lāhu yā ʿĪsab-na Maryama ʾaʾañta qulta linnāsit-takhidhūnī wa ʾummiya ʾilāhayni miñ-dūnil-lāh. Qāla subḥānaka mā yakūnu līi ʾan ʾaqūla mā laysa lī biḥaqq.

the more common reading *hal yastaṭīʿ rabbuka* ("can" or "could thy Sustainer"), is reported to have said: "The disciples of Jesus knew better than to ask whether God is able to do anything: they merely asked [of Jesus], 'Art *thou* able to request thy Sustainer?'" (Rāzī). Moreover, according to an authentic Tradition quoted in the *Mustadrak*, Muʿādh ibn Jabal stated unequivocally that the Prophet himself had imparted to him the reading *hal tastaṭīʿ rabbaka* ("Couldst thou prevail upon thy Sustainer?") To my mind, the weight of evidence points to this second alternative; but in view of the more general reading, I have rendered the phrase as above.

As regards the disciples' request – and Jesus' subsequent prayer – for a heavenly "repast" (*māʾidah,* the word which gave the title to this *sūrah*), it might possibly be an echo of the request for daily bread contained in the Lord's Prayer (cf. Matthew vi, 11), since, in religious terminology, every benefit that accrues to man is "sent down from heaven" – that is, by God – even if it comes into being through man's own efforts. But, on the other hand, the manner in which the disciples are said to have asked for the "repast" – and particularly their explanation given in the next verse – rather seems to point to a request for a *miracle* which would assure them of God's "acceptance" of their faith. (See also next note.)

138 The grammatical form *munazzil* in the phrase *innī munazziluhā* (lit., "I am sending it down") implies a continued recurrence of bestowal – a continuity which I have expressed by interpolating the word "always" between brackets. This stress on God's ever-recurrent provision of sustenance, both physical and spiritual, explains the extreme severity of His condemnation of all who – in their arrogant presumption that man is self-sufficient and independent – deny this obvious truth; and, in addition, it implies a condemnation of any demand for a miracle as a "proof" of God's existence.

139 Sc., "after Jesus' death": this is fully evident from Jesus' subsequent reference, in the past tense, to his own death ("since Thou hast caused me to die") in verse 117. On the other hand, the verb *qāla* (lit., "He said") can also have the meaning of "He will say" (see note 141 below).

Had I said this, Thou wouldst indeed have known it! Thou knowest all that is within myself, whereas I know not what is in Thy Self. Verily, it is Thou alone who fully knowest all the things that are beyond the reach of a created being's perception. ⟨116⟩ Nothing did I tell them beyond what Thou didst bid me [to say]: 'Worship God, [who is] my Sustainer as well as your Sustainer.' And I bore witness to what they did as long as I dwelt in their midst; but since Thou hast caused me to die, Thou alone hast been their keeper:[140] for Thou art witness unto everything. ⟨117⟩ If thou cause them to suffer – verily, they are Thy servants; and if Thou forgive them – verily, Thou alone art almighty, truly wise!" ⟨118⟩

[AND on Judgment Day] God will say:[141] "Today, their truthfulness shall benefit all who have been true to their word: theirs shall be gardens through which running waters flow, therein to abide beyond the count of time; well-pleased is God with them, and well-pleased are they with Him: this is the triumph supreme." ⟨119⟩

God's is the dominion over the heavens and the earth and all that they contain; and He has the power to will anything. ⟨120⟩

إِن كُنتُ قُلْتُهُۥ فَقَدْ عَلِمْتَهُۥ تَعْلَمُ مَا فِى نَفْسِى وَلَآ أَعْلَمُ مَا فِى نَفْسِكَ إِنَّكَ أَنتَ عَلَّٰمُ ٱلْغُيُوبِ ۝ مَا قُلْتُ لَهُمْ إِلَّا مَآ أَمَرْتَنِى بِهِۦٓ أَنِ ٱعْبُدُوا۟ ٱللَّهَ رَبِّى وَرَبَّكُمْ وَكُنتُ عَلَيْهِمْ شَهِيدًا مَّا دُمْتُ فِيهِمْ فَلَمَّا تَوَفَّيْتَنِى كُنتَ أَنتَ ٱلرَّقِيبَ عَلَيْهِمْ وَأَنتَ عَلَىٰ كُلِّ شَىْءٍ شَهِيدٌ ۝ إِن تُعَذِّبْهُمْ فَإِنَّهُمْ عِبَادُكَ وَإِن تَغْفِرْ لَهُمْ فَإِنَّكَ أَنتَ ٱلْعَزِيزُ ٱلْحَكِيمُ ۝ قَالَ ٱللَّهُ هَٰذَا يَوْمُ يَنفَعُ ٱلصَّٰدِقِينَ صِدْقُهُمْ لَهُمْ جَنَّٰتٌ تَجْرِى مِن تَحْتِهَا ٱلْأَنْهَٰرُ خَٰلِدِينَ فِيهَآ أَبَدًا رَّضِىَ ٱللَّهُ عَنْهُمْ وَرَضُوا۟ عَنْهُ ذَٰلِكَ ٱلْفَوْزُ ٱلْعَظِيمُ ۝ لِلَّهِ مُلْكُ ٱلسَّمَٰوَٰتِ وَٱلْأَرْضِ وَمَا فِيهِنَّ وَهُوَ عَلَىٰ كُلِّ شَىْءٍ قَدِيرٌ ۝

ʾIñ-kuñtu qultuhū faqad ʿalimtah. Taʿlamu mā fī nafsī wa lāa ʾaʿlamu mā fī nafsik. ʾInnaka ʾAñta ʿAllāmul-ghuyūb. ۝ Mā qultu lahum ʾillā māa ʾamartanī bihī ʾaniʿ-budul-lāha Rabbī wa Rabbakum; wa kuñtu ʿalayhim shahīdam-mā dumtu fīhim. Falammā tawaffaytanī kuñta ʾAñtar-Raqība ʿalayhim; wa ʾAñta ʿalā kulli shayʾiñ-Shahīd. ۝ ʾIñ-tuʿadhdhibhum faʾinnahum ʿibāduka waʾiñ-taghfir lahum faʾinnaka ʾAñtal-ʿAzīzul-Ḥakīm. ۝ Qālal-lāhu hādhā Yawmu yañfaʿuṣ-ṣādiqīna ṣidquhum; lahum jannātuñ-tajrī miñ-taḥtihal-ʾañhāru khālidīna fīhāa ʾabadā. Raḍiyal-lāhu ʿanhum wa raḍū ʿanh. Dhālikal-fawzul-ʿaẓīm. ۝ Lillāhi mulkus-samāwāti wal-ʾarḍi wa mā fīhinn. Wa Huwa ʿalā kulli shayʾiñ-Qadīr. ۝

---

140 The definite article in *anta'r-raqīb* expresses God's exclusiveness in His function as *raqīb* ("keeper"), and can only be rendered by an interpolation of the (elliptically implied) word "alone". Similar expressions relating to God are very often met with in the Qurʾān – e.g., at the end of the next verse.

141 Lit., "said" – but many of the classical commentators understand the verb *qāla* as denoting here the future tense ("He will say"), sc., "on the Day of Judgment".

The Sixth Sūrah

Al-ʾAnʿām (Cattle)

Mecca Period

WITH the possible exception of two or three verses, the whole of this *sūrah* was revealed in one piece, towards the close of the Mecca period – almost certainly in the last year before the Prophet's exodus to Medina. The title *Al-ʾAnʿām* ("Cattle") is derived from several references, in verses 136 ff., to certain pre-Islamic superstitions concerning animals which the Arabs used to dedicate to their various idols. However ephemeral those idolatrous beliefs and practices may appear in the light of later Arabian history, they serve in the Qurʾān as an illustration of man's propensity to attribute divine or semi-divine qualities to created beings or imaginary powers. In fact, most of this *sūrah* can be described as a many-sided argument against this tendency, which is by no means confined to openly polytheistic beliefs. The core of the argument is an exposition of God's oneness and uniqueness. He is the Prime Cause of all that exists, but "no human vision can encompass Him" (verse 103), either physically or conceptually: and, therefore, "He is sublimely exalted above anything that men may devise by way of definition" (verse 100). Consequently, any endeavour to "define" God within the categories of human thought, or to reduce Him to the concept of a "person", constitutes a blasphemous attempt at limiting His infinite existence. (To avoid a conception of God as a "person", the Qurʿān always varies the pronouns relating to Him: He is spoken of – frequently in one and the same sentence – as "He", "I" and "We"; similarly, the possessive pronouns referring to God fluctuate constantly between "His", "My" and "Ours".)

One of the outstanding passages of this *sūrah* is the statement (in verse 50) to the effect that the Prophet is a mere mor tal, like all other human beings, not endowed with any supernatural powers, and "following only what is revealed to him". And, finally, he is commanded to say (in verses 162-163): "Behold, my prayer, and all my acts of worship, and my living and my dying are for God alone . . . in whose divinity none has a share."

سورة الأنعام مكية

-٦-

وآياتها خمس وستون ومائة

IN THE NAME OF GOD, THE MOST GRACIOUS, THE DISPENSER OF GRACE:

ALL PRAISE is due to God, who has created the heavens and the earth, and brought into being deep darkness as well as light:[1] and yet, those who are bent on denying the truth regard other powers as their Sustainer's equals! ‹1›
He it is who has created you out of clay, and then has decreed a term [for you] – a term known [only] to Him.[2] And yet you doubt ‹2› – although He is God in the heavens and on earth, knowing all that you keep secret as well as all that you do openly, and knowing what you deserve. ‹3›
Yet whenever any of their Sustainer's messages comes unto them, they [who are bent on denying the truth] turn their backs upon it:[3] ‹4› and so they give the lie to this truth now that it has come unto them. In time, however, they will come to understand what it was that they were wont to deride.[4] ‹5›

بِسْمِ ٱللَّهِ ٱلرَّحْمَٰنِ ٱلرَّحِيمِ

ٱلْحَمْدُ لِلَّهِ ٱلَّذِى خَلَقَ ٱلسَّمَٰوَٰتِ وَٱلْأَرْضَ وَجَعَلَ ٱلظُّلُمَٰتِ وَٱلنُّورَ
ثُمَّ ٱلَّذِينَ كَفَرُوا۟ بِرَبِّهِمْ يَعْدِلُونَ ﴿١﴾ هُوَ ٱلَّذِى خَلَقَكُم مِّن طِينٍ ثُمَّ
قَضَىٰٓ أَجَلًا ۖ وَأَجَلٌ مُّسَمًّى عِندَهُۥ ۖ ثُمَّ أَنتُمْ تَمْتَرُونَ ﴿٢﴾ وَهُوَ ٱللَّهُ فِى
ٱلسَّمَٰوَٰتِ وَفِى ٱلْأَرْضِ ۖ يَعْلَمُ سِرَّكُمْ وَجَهْرَكُمْ وَيَعْلَمُ مَا تَكْسِبُونَ ﴿٣﴾
وَمَا تَأْتِيهِم مِّنْ ءَايَةٍ مِّنْ ءَايَٰتِ رَبِّهِمْ إِلَّا كَانُوا۟ عَنْهَا مُعْرِضِينَ ﴿٤﴾
فَقَدْ كَذَّبُوا۟ بِٱلْحَقِّ لَمَّا جَآءَهُمْ ۖ فَسَوْفَ يَأْتِيهِمْ أَنۢبَٰٓؤُا۟ مَا كَانُوا۟ بِهِۦ
يَسْتَهْزِءُونَ ﴿٥﴾

Bismil-lāhir-Raḥmānir-Raḥīm.
ʾAlḥamdu lillāhil-ladhī khalaqas-samāwāti wal-ʾarḍa wa jaʿalaẓ-ẓulumāti wan-nūr. Thummal-ladhīna kafarū biRabbihim yaʿdilūn. ‹1› Huwal-ladhī khalaqakum-miñ-ṭīniñ-thumma qaḍāa ʾajalā. Wa ʾajalum-musamman-ʿiñdahū thumma añtum tamtarūn. ‹2› Wa Huwal-lāhu fis-samāwāti wa fil-ʾarḍi yaʿlamu sirrakum wa jahrakum wa yaʿlamu mā taksibūn. ‹3› Wa mā taʾtīhim-min ʾĀyatim-min ʾĀyāti Rabbihim ʾillā kānū ʿanhā muʿriḍīn. ‹4› Faqad kadhdhabū bil-ḥaqqi lammā jāaʾahum; fasawfa yaʾtīhim ʾambāaʾu mā kānū bihī yastahziʾūn. ‹5›

---

1 Both "darkness" and "light" are used here in their spiritual connotation. As always in the Qurʾān, "darkness" is spoken of in the plural (*ẓulumāt*) in order to stress its intensity, and is best translated as "deep darkness" or "depths of darkness".

2 Lit., "and a term is stated with Him" – i.e., known to Him alone (*Manār* VII, 298). Some of the authorities are of the opinion that the "term" refers to the end of the world and the subsequent resurrection, while others relate it to individual human lives. Other commentators, again, see in the *first* mention of this word a reference to individual lives, and in the *second*, to the Day of Resurrection; according to this latter interpretation, the concluding phrase might be rendered thus: "and there is [another] term . . .", etc. However, in view of several other occurrences of the expression *ajal musammā* in the Qurʾān, it is best rendered here as "a term set [by Him]" or "known [to Him]", i.e., relating both to individual lives and to the world as a whole.

3 Lit., "there has not come unto them a message of their Sustainer's messages without that they turned their backs upon it".

4 Lit., "there will come to them information about that which they used to mock at" or "deride" – i.e., the continuation of life after death, in particular, and the Qurʾanic message, in general.

Do they not see how many a generation We have destroyed before their time – [people] whom We had given a [bountiful] place on earth, the like of which We never gave unto you, and upon whom We showered heavenly blessings abundant, and at whose feet We made running waters flow? And yet We destroyed them for their sins, and gave rise to other people in their stead.[5] ‹6›

But even if We had sent down unto thee [O Prophet] a writing on paper, and they had touched it with their own hands – those who are bent on denying the truth would indeed have said, "This is clearly nothing but a deception!" ‹7›

They are saying, too, "Why has not an angel [visibly] been sent down unto him?" But had We sent down an angel, all would indeed have been decided,[6] and they would have been allowed no further respite [for repentance]. ‹8› And [even] if We had appointed an angel as Our message-bearer,[7] We would certainly have made him [appear as] a man – and thus We would only have confused them in the same way as they are now confusing themselves.[8] ‹9›

And, indeed, [even] before thy time have apostles been derided – but those who scoffed at them were [in the end] overwhelmed by the very thing which they were wont to deride.[9] ‹10›

Say: "Go all over the earth, and behold what happened in the end to those who gave the lie to the truth!" ‹11›

أَلَمْ يَرَوْا۟ كَمْ أَهْلَكْنَا مِن قَبْلِهِم مِّن قَرْنٍ مَّكَّنَّـٰهُمْ فِى ٱلْأَرْضِ مَا لَمْ
نُمَكِّن لَّكُمْ وَأَرْسَلْنَا ٱلسَّمَآءَ عَلَيْهِم مِّدْرَارًا وَجَعَلْنَا ٱلْأَنْهَـٰرَ تَجْرِى
مِن تَحْتِهِمْ فَأَهْلَكْنَـٰهُم بِذُنُوبِهِمْ وَأَنشَأْنَا مِنۢ بَعْدِهِمْ قَرْنًا ءَاخَرِينَ ﴿٦﴾
وَلَوْ نَزَّلْنَا عَلَيْكَ كِتَـٰبًا فِى قِرْطَاسٍ فَلَمَسُوهُ بِأَيْدِيهِمْ لَقَالَ ٱلَّذِينَ كَفَرُوٓا۟
إِنْ هَـٰذَآ إِلَّا سِحْرٌ مُّبِينٌ ﴿٧﴾ وَقَالُوا۟ لَوْلَآ أُنزِلَ عَلَيْهِ مَلَكٌ ۖ وَلَوْ أَنزَلْنَا مَلَكًا
لَّقُضِىَ ٱلْأَمْرُ ثُمَّ لَا يُنظَرُونَ ﴿٨﴾ وَلَوْ جَعَلْنَـٰهُ مَلَكًا لَّجَعَلْنَـٰهُ رَجُلًا وَلَلَبَسْنَا
عَلَيْهِم مَّا يَلْبِسُونَ ﴿٩﴾ وَلَقَدِ ٱسْتُهْزِئَ بِرُسُلٍ مِّن قَبْلِكَ فَحَاقَ بِٱلَّذِينَ
سَخِرُوا۟ مِنْهُم مَّا كَانُوا۟ بِهِۦ يَسْتَهْزِءُونَ ﴿١٠﴾ قُلْ سِيرُوا۟ فِى ٱلْأَرْضِ ثُمَّ
ٱنظُرُوا۟ كَيْفَ كَانَ عَـٰقِبَةُ ٱلْمُكَذِّبِينَ ﴿١١﴾

ʾAlam yaraw kam ʾahlaknā miñ-qablihim-miñ-qarnim-makkannāhum fil-ʾarḍi mā lam numakkil-lakum wa ʾarsalnas-samāaʾa ʿalayhim-midrārañw-wa jaʿalnal-ʾanhāra tajrī miñ-taḥtihim faʾahlaknāhum-bidhunūbihim wa ʾañshaʾnā mim-baʿdihim qarnan ʾākharīn. ⟨6⟩ Wa law nazzalnā ʿalayka Kitābañ-fī qirṭāsiñ-falamasūhu biʾaydīhim laqālal-ladhīna kafarūu ʾin hādhāa ʾillā siḥrum-mubīn. ⟨7⟩ Wa qālū lawlāa ʾuñzila ʿalayhi malak. Wa law ʾañzalnā malakal-laquḍiyal-ʾamru thumma lā yuñẓarūn. ⟨8⟩ Wa law jaʿalnāhu malakal-lajaʿalnāhu rajulañw-wa lalabasnā ʿalayhim-mā yalbisūn. ⟨9⟩ Wa laqadis-tuhziʾa biRusulim-miñ-qablika faḥāqa billadhīna sakhirū minhum-mā kānū bihī yastahziʾūn. ⟨10⟩ Qul sīrū fil-ʾarḍi thummañ-ẓurū kayfa kāna ʿāqibatul-mukadhdhibīn. ⟨11⟩

5 Lit.,"a generation of others after them". However, in Qurʾanic usage, the term *qarn* does not always denote "a generation", but – rather more frequently – "an epoch", or "people belonging to one particular epoch", as well as "a civilization" in the historical sense of this word.

6 I.e., Judgment Day would have come – for it is only then that the forces described as angels will manifest themselves to man in their true form and become comprehensible to him. (Cf. a similar passage in 2 : 210.)

7 Lit., "if We had made him an angel" – with the pronoun obviously referring to the bearer of God's message (Zamakhsharī).

8 Lit., "We would have made confusing to them that which they are making confused". Since it is impossible for man to perceive angels as they really are, the hypothetical angelic message-bearer would have to assume the shape of a human being – and so their demand for a direct "verification" of the message would have remained unfulfilled, and their self-caused confusion unresolved.

9 Lit., "that which they were wont to deride enfolded those who scoffed at them" (i.e., at the apostles): the meaning being that a derisive rejection of spiritual truths inexorably rebounds on the scoffers and has not only a disastrous effect on their individual lives after death but also – if persisted in by the majority within a community – destroys the moral basis of their society and, thus, their earthly happiness and sometimes even their physical existence.

Say: "Unto whom belongs all that is in the heavens and on earth?" Say: "Unto God, who has willed upon Himself the law of grace and mercy."[10]
He will assuredly gather you all together on the Day of Resurrection, [the coming of] which is beyond all doubt: yet those who have squandered their own selves – it is they who refuse to believe [in Him], ‹12›
although His is all that dwells in the night and the day, and He alone is all-hearing, all-knowing. ‹13›
Say: "Am I to take for my master anyone but God, the Originator of the heavens and the earth, when it is He who gives nourishment and Himself needs none?"[11]
Say: "I am bidden to be foremost among those who surrender themselves unto God, and not to be[12] among those who ascribe divinity to aught beside Him." ‹14›
Say: "Behold, I would dread, were I [thus] to rebel against my Sustainer, the suffering [which would befall me] on that awesome Day [of Judgment]." ‹15›
Upon him who shall be spared on that Day, He will indeed have bestowed His grace: and this will be a manifest triumph. ‹16›
And if God should touch thee with misfortune, there is none who could remove it but He; and if He should touch thee with good fortune – it is He who has the power to will anything: ‹17› for He alone holds sway over His creatures, and He alone is truly wise, all-aware. ‹18›
Say: "What could most weightily bear witness to the truth?" Say: "God is witness between me and you; and this Qurʾān has been revealed unto me so that on the strength thereof I might warn you and all whom it may reach."

قُل لِّمَن مَّا فِي ٱلسَّمَٰوَٰتِ وَٱلۡأَرۡضِۖ قُل لِّلَّهِۚ كَتَبَ عَلَىٰ نَفۡسِهِ ٱلرَّحۡمَةَۚ
لَيَجۡمَعَنَّكُمۡ إِلَىٰ يَوۡمِ ٱلۡقِيَٰمَةِ لَا رَيۡبَ فِيهِۚ ٱلَّذِينَ خَسِرُوٓاْ أَنفُسَهُمۡ فَهُمۡ
لَا يُؤۡمِنُونَ ﴿١٢﴾ ۞ وَلَهُۥ مَا سَكَنَ فِي ٱلَّيۡلِ وَٱلنَّهَارِۚ وَهُوَ ٱلسَّمِيعُ
ٱلۡعَلِيمُ ﴿١٣﴾ قُلۡ أَغَيۡرَ ٱللَّهِ أَتَّخِذُ وَلِيّٗا فَاطِرِ ٱلسَّمَٰوَٰتِ وَٱلۡأَرۡضِ وَهُوَ
يُطۡعِمُ وَلَا يُطۡعَمُۗ قُلۡ إِنِّيٓ أُمِرۡتُ أَنۡ أَكُونَ أَوَّلَ مَنۡ أَسۡلَمَۖ وَلَا تَكُونَنَّ
مِنَ ٱلۡمُشۡرِكِينَ ﴿١٤﴾ قُلۡ إِنِّيٓ أَخَافُ إِنۡ عَصَيۡتُ رَبِّي عَذَابَ يَوۡمٍ
عَظِيمٖ ﴿١٥﴾ مَّن يُصۡرَفۡ عَنۡهُ يَوۡمَئِذٖ فَقَدۡ رَحِمَهُۥۚ وَذَٰلِكَ ٱلۡفَوۡزُ
ٱلۡمُبِينُ ﴿١٦﴾ وَإِن يَمۡسَسۡكَ ٱللَّهُ بِضُرّٖ فَلَا كَاشِفَ لَهُۥٓ إِلَّا هُوَۖ وَإِن
يَمۡسَسۡكَ بِخَيۡرٖ فَهُوَ عَلَىٰ كُلِّ شَيۡءٖ قَدِيرٞ ﴿١٧﴾ وَهُوَ ٱلۡقَاهِرُ فَوۡقَ عِبَادِهِۦۚ
وَهُوَ ٱلۡحَكِيمُ ٱلۡخَبِيرُ ﴿١٨﴾ قُلۡ أَيُّ شَيۡءٍ أَكۡبَرُ شَهَٰدَةٗۖ قُلِ ٱللَّهُۖ شَهِيدُۢ
بَيۡنِي وَبَيۡنَكُمۡۚ وَأُوحِيَ إِلَيَّ هَٰذَا ٱلۡقُرۡءَانُ لِأُنذِرَكُم بِهِۦ وَمَنۢ بَلَغَۚ

ثلاثة ارباع الحزب

Qul-limam-mā fis-samāwāti wal-ʾarḍi qul-lillāh. Kataba ʿalā Nafsihir-raḥmah. Layajmaʿannakum ʾilā Yawmil-Qiyāmati lā rayba fīh. ʾAlladhīna khasirūu ʾañfusahum fahum lā yuʾminūn. (12) ۞ Wa lahū mā sakana fil-layli wan-nahār. Wa Huwas-Samīʿul-ʿAlīm. (13) Qul ʾaghayral-lāhi ʾattakhidhu waliyyañ-Fāṭiris-samāwāti wal-ʾarḍi wa Huwa yuṭʿimu wa lā yuṭʿam. Qul ʾinnīi ʾumirtu ʾan ʾakūna ʾawwala man ʾaslama wa lā takūnanna minal-mushrikīn. (14) Qul ʾinnīi ʾakhāfu ʾin ʿaṣaytu Rabbī ʿadhāba Yawmin ʿaẓīm. (15) Mañy-yuṣraf ʿanhu Yawmaʾidhiñ-faqad raḥimahū wa dhālikal-fawzul-mubīn. (16) Wa ʾiñy-yamsaskal-lāhu biḍurriñ-falā kāshifa lahūu ʾillā Hū. Wa ʾiñy-yamsaska bikhayriñ-faHuwa ʿalā kulli shayʾiñ-Qadīr. (17) Wa Huwal-Qāhiru fawqa ʿibādihī wa Huwal-Ḥakīmul-Khabīr. (18) Qul ʾayyu shayʾin ʾakbaru shahādah. Qulil-lāhu Shahīdum-baynī wa baynakum. Wa ʾūḥiya ʾilayya hādhal-Qurʾānu li-ʾuñdhirakum-bihī wa mam-balagh.

10 The expression "God has willed upon Himself as a law" (*kataba ʿalā nafsihi*) occurs in the Qurʾān only twice – here and in verse 54 of this *sūrah* – and in both instances with reference to His grace and mercy (*raḥmah*); none of the other divine attributes has been similarly described. This exceptional quality of God's grace and mercy is further stressed in 7 : 156 – "My grace overspreads everything" – and finds an echo in the authentic Tradition in which, according to the Prophet, God says of Himself, "Verily, My grace and mercy outstrips My wrath" (Bukhārī and Muslim).

11 Lit., "when it is He who feeds [others] and is not fed".

12 Lit., "and be thou not" – an elliptic reference to the words in which this commandment has been expressed.

Could you in truth bear witness that there are other deities side by side with God? Say: "I bear no [such] witness!" Say: "He is the One God; and, behold, far be it from me to ascribe divinity, as you do, to aught beside Him!"[13] ‹19›
They unto whom We have vouchsafed revelation aforetime know this[14] as they know their own children; yet those [of them] who have squandered their own selves – it is they who refuse to believe. ‹20› And who could be more wicked than he who attributes his own lying inventions to God or gives the lie to His messages?
Verily, such evildoers will never attain to a happy state: ‹21› for one Day We shall gather them all together, and then We shall say unto those who ascribed divinity to aught beside God: "Where, now, are those beings whom you imagined to have a share in God's divinity?"[15] ‹22›
Whereupon, in their utter confusion, they will only [be able to] say: "By God, our Sustainer, we did not [mean to] ascribe divinity to aught beside Him!"[16] ‹23›
Behold how they have lied to themselves[17] – and [how] their false imagery has forsaken them! ‹24›
And there are among them such as [seem to] listen to thee [O Prophet]: but over their hearts We have laid veils which prevent them from grasping the truth, and into their ears, deafness.[18]

أَئِنَّكُمْ لَتَشْهَدُونَ أَنَّ مَعَ ٱللَّهِ ءَالِهَةً أُخْرَىٰ قُل لَّآ أَشْهَدُ قُلْ إِنَّمَا هُوَ
إِلَٰهٌ وَٰحِدٌ وَإِنَّنِى بَرِىٓءٌ مِّمَّا تُشْرِكُونَ (19) ٱلَّذِينَ ءَاتَيْنَٰهُمُ ٱلْكِتَٰبَ
يَعْرِفُونَهُۥ كَمَا يَعْرِفُونَ أَبْنَآءَهُمُ ٱلَّذِينَ خَسِرُوٓا۟ أَنفُسَهُمْ فَهُمْ لَا
يُؤْمِنُونَ (20) وَمَنْ أَظْلَمُ مِمَّنِ ٱفْتَرَىٰ عَلَى ٱللَّهِ كَذِبًا أَوْ كَذَّبَ بِـَٔايَٰتِهِۦٓ
إِنَّهُۥ لَا يُفْلِحُ ٱلظَّٰلِمُونَ (21) وَيَوْمَ نَحْشُرُهُمْ جَمِيعًا ثُمَّ نَقُولُ لِلَّذِينَ
أَشْرَكُوٓا۟ أَيْنَ شُرَكَآؤُكُمُ ٱلَّذِينَ كُنتُمْ تَزْعُمُونَ (22) ثُمَّ لَمْ تَكُن فِتْنَتُهُمْ
إِلَّآ أَن قَالُوا۟ وَٱللَّهِ رَبِّنَا مَا كُنَّا مُشْرِكِينَ (23) ٱنظُرْ كَيْفَ كَذَبُوا۟
عَلَىٰٓ أَنفُسِهِمْ وَضَلَّ عَنْهُم مَّا كَانُوا۟ يَفْتَرُونَ (24) وَمِنْهُم مَّن يَسْتَمِعُ
إِلَيْكَ وَجَعَلْنَا عَلَىٰ قُلُوبِهِمْ أَكِنَّةً أَن يَفْقَهُوهُ وَفِىٓ ءَاذَانِهِمْ وَقْرًا

ʾAʾinnakum latashhadūna ʾanna maʿal-lāhi ʾālihatan ʾukhrā. Qul lāa ʾashhad. Qul ʾinnamā Huwa ʾIlāhuñw-Wāḥiduñw-wa ʾinnanī barīiʾum-mimmā tushrikūn. (19) ʾAlladhīna ʾātaynāhumul-Kitāba yaʿrifūnahū kamā yaʿrifūna ʾabnāaʾahum. ʾAlladhīna khasirūu ʾañfusahum fahum lā yuʾminūn. (20) Wa man ʾaẓlamu mimmanif-tarā ʿalal-lāhi kadhiban ʾaw kadhdhaba biʾĀyātih. ʾInnahū lā yufliḥuẓ-ẓālimūn. (21) Wa Yawma naḥshuruhum jamīʿañ-thumma naqūlu lilladhīna ʾashrakūu ʾayna shurakāaʾukumul-ladhīna kuñtum tazʿumūn. (22) Thumma lam takuñ-fitnatuhum ʾillāa ʾañ-qālū wal-lāhi Rabbinā mā kunnā mushrikīn. (23) ʾUñẓur kayfa kadhabū ʿalāa ʾañfusihim wa ḍalla ʿanhum-mā kānū yaftarūn. (24) Wa minhum-mañy-yastamiʿu ʾilayka wa jaʿalnā ʿalā qulūbihim ʾakinnatan ʾañy-yafqahūhu wa fīi ʾādhānihim waqrā.

13 Lit., "I am clear of that which you associate [with Him]."

14 I.e., the truth of God's transcendental uniqueness and oneness, which is stressed in all authentic scriptures.

15 Lit., "those [God-]partners of yours whom you supposed [to exist]". Whenever the term *shurakāʾ* (pl. of *sharīk*) is used in the Qurʾān with reference to *beliefs*, it invariably denotes real or imaginary beings or forces to whom one ascribes a share in God's divinity: consequently, this concept – and its utter condemnation in Islam – relates not merely to the worship of false deities but also to the attribution of semi-divine qualities and powers to saints (in the liturgical sense of this word), as well as to abstract notions like wealth, social status, power, nationality, etc., to which men so often ascribe an objective influence on human destinies.

16 This refers to beliefs which undoubtedly imply *shirk* ("the ascribing of divinity or divine qualities to beings or forces other than God") in the objective sense of this concept, but which the person concerned does not subjectively visualize as denying God's oneness (Rāzī): for instance, the mystical dogma of the "Trinity" which, in the Christian view, does not conflict with the principle of God's oneness inasmuch as it is supposed to express a "threefold aspect" of the One Deity, or the attribution of divine or semi-divine qualities to saints as supposed "mediators" between man and God, and so forth. All such beliefs are, of course, emphatically rejected by the Qurʾān.

17 I.e., by allowing themselves to think, in their lifetime, that their beliefs did not offend against the principle of God's oneness (Rāzī). But see also 10 : 28 and the corresponding notes 45 and 46.

18 Regarding the problem of God's "causing" this spiritual blindness and deafness, see 2 : 7 and the corresponding note, as well as note 4 on 14 : 4.

And were they to see every sign [of the truth], they would still not believe in it – so much so that when they come unto thee to contend with thee, those who are bent on denying the truth say, "This is nothing but fables of ancient times!" ‹25› And they bar others therefrom, and go far away from it: but they destroy none but themselves, and perceive it not. ‹26›

If thou couldst but see [them] when they will be made to stand before the fire and will say, "Oh, would that we were brought back [to life]: then we would not give the lie to our Sustainer's messages, but would be among the believers!" ‹27›

But nay – [they will say this only because] the truth which they used to conceal [from themselves] in the past will have become obvious to them; and if they were brought back [to life], they would return to the very thing which was forbidden to them: for, behold, they are indeed liars![19] ‹28›

And some [of the unbelievers] say, "There is nothing beyond our life in this world, for We shall not be raised from the dead." ‹29›

If thou couldst but see [them] when they shall be made to stand before their Sustainer [and] He will say, "Is not this the truth?"

They will answer: "Yea, indeed, by our Sustainer!" [Whereupon] He will say: "Taste, then, the suffering that comes from[20] your having refused to acknowledge the truth!" ‹30›

Lost indeed are they who consider it a lie that they will have to meet God – till the Last Hour suddenly comes upon them, [and] they cry, "Alas for us, that we disregarded it!" – for they shall bear on their backs the burden of their sins:[21] oh, how evil the load with which they shall be burdened! ‹31›

وَإِن يَرَوْا۟ كُلَّ ءَايَةٍ لَّا يُؤْمِنُوا۟ بِهَا ۚ حَتَّىٰٓ إِذَا جَآءُوكَ يُجَـٰدِلُونَكَ يَقُولُ
ٱلَّذِينَ كَفَرُوٓا۟ إِنْ هَـٰذَآ إِلَّآ أَسَـٰطِيرُ ٱلْأَوَّلِينَ ﴿٢٥﴾ وَهُمْ يَنْهَوْنَ عَنْهُ
وَيَنْـَٔوْنَ عَنْهُ ۖ وَإِن يُهْلِكُونَ إِلَّآ أَنفُسَهُمْ وَمَا يَشْعُرُونَ ﴿٢٦﴾ وَلَوْ تَرَىٰٓ إِذْ
وُقِفُوا۟ عَلَى ٱلنَّارِ فَقَالُوا۟ يَـٰلَيْتَنَا نُرَدُّ وَلَا نُكَذِّبَ بِـَٔايَـٰتِ رَبِّنَا وَنَكُونَ
مِنَ ٱلْمُؤْمِنِينَ ﴿٢٧﴾ بَلْ بَدَا لَهُم مَّا كَانُوا۟ يُخْفُونَ مِن قَبْلُ ۖ وَلَوْ رُدُّوا۟
لَعَادُوا۟ لِمَا نُهُوا۟ عَنْهُ وَإِنَّهُمْ لَكَـٰذِبُونَ ﴿٢٨﴾ وَقَالُوٓا۟ إِنْ هِىَ إِلَّا حَيَاتُنَا
ٱلدُّنْيَا وَمَا نَحْنُ بِمَبْعُوثِينَ ﴿٢٩﴾ وَلَوْ تَرَىٰٓ إِذْ وُقِفُوا۟ عَلَىٰ رَبِّهِمْ ۚ قَالَ أَلَيْسَ
هَـٰذَا بِٱلْحَقِّ ۚ قَالُوا۟ بَلَىٰ وَرَبِّنَا ۚ قَالَ فَذُوقُوا۟ ٱلْعَذَابَ بِمَا كُنتُمْ تَكْفُرُونَ ﴿٣٠﴾
قَدْ خَسِرَ ٱلَّذِينَ كَذَّبُوا۟ بِلِقَآءِ ٱللَّهِ ۖ حَتَّىٰٓ إِذَا جَآءَتْهُمُ ٱلسَّاعَةُ بَغْتَةً قَالُوا۟
يَـٰحَسْرَتَنَا عَلَىٰ مَا فَرَّطْنَا فِيهَا وَهُمْ يَحْمِلُونَ أَوْزَارَهُمْ عَلَىٰ ظُهُورِهِمْ ۚ أَلَا
سَآءَ مَا يَزِرُونَ ﴿٣١﴾

Wa ʾiñy-yaraw kulla ʾĀyatil-lā yuʾminū bihā; ḥattāa ʾidhā jāaʾūka yujādilūnaka yaqūlul-ladhīna kafarūu ʾin hādhāa ʾillāa ʾasāṭīrul-ʾawwalīn. (25) Wa hum yanhawna ᶜanhu wa yanʾawna ᶜanhu wa ʾiñy-yuhlikūna ʾillāa ʾañfusahum wa mā yashᶜurūn. (26) Wa law tarāa ʾidh wuqifū ᶜalan-nāri faqālū yā laytanā nuraddu wa lā nukadhdhiba biʾĀyāti Rabbinā wa nakūna minal-muʾminīn. (27) Bal badā lahum-mā kānū yukhfūna miñ-qabl. Wa law ruddū laᶜādū limā nuhū ᶜanhu wa ʾinnahum lakādhibūn. (28) Wa qālūu ʾin hiya ʾillā ḥayātunad-dunyā wa mā naḥnu bimabᶜūthīn. (29) Wa law tarāa ʾidh wuqifū ᶜalā Rabbihim. Qāla ʾalaysa hādhā bilḥaqq. Qālū balā wa Rabbinā. Qāla fadhūqul-ᶜadhāba bimā kuñtum takfurūn. (30) Qad khasiral-ladhīna kadhdhabū biliqāaʾil-lāh. Ḥattāa ʾidhā jāaʾat-humus-Sāᶜatu baghtatañ-qālū yā ḥasratanā ᶜalā mā farraṭnā fīhā wa hum yaḥmilūna ʾawzārahum ᶜalā ẓuhūrihim. ʾAlā sāaʾa mā yazirūn. (31)

19 I.e., their longing for a "second chance" is not dictated by love of truth for its own sake but, rather, by their dread of the evil consequences of their doings; and "faith is useless unless it is desired for its own sake" (Rāzī).

20 Lit., "the suffering [or "chastisement"] because of" or "in consequence of". The particle *bi-mā* expresses here a causal connection between the denial of the truth and the subsequent suffering, and is best rendered as above.

21 Lit., "their burdens". My use of the words "the burden of their sins" rests on the interpretation given by Ibn ᶜAbbās, as quoted by Rāzī.

And nothing is the life of this world but a play and a passing delight; and the life in the hereafter is by far the better for all who are conscious of God. Will you not, then, use your reason? ⟨32⟩

Well do We know that what such people say[22] grieves thee indeed: yet, behold, it is not thee to whom they give the lie, but God's messages do these evildoers deny. ⟨33⟩ And, indeed, [even] before thy time have apostles been given the lie, and they endured with patience all those charges of falsehood, and all the hurt done to them, till succour came unto them from Us: for there is no power that could alter [the outcome of] God's promises. And some of the histories of those apostles have already come within thy ken.[23] ⟨34⟩

And if it distress thee that those who deny the truth[24] turn their backs on thee – why, then, if thou art able to go down deep into the earth or to ascend a ladder unto heaven[25] in order to bring them a [yet more convincing] message, [do so;] but [remember that] had God so willed, He would indeed have gathered them all unto [His] guidance. Do not, therefore, allow thyself to ignore [God's ways].[26] ⟨35⟩ Only they who listen [with their hearts] can respond to a call; and as for the dead [of heart], God [alone] can raise them from the dead, whereupon unto Him they shall return.[27] ⟨36⟩

And they say, "Why has no miraculous sign been bestowed on him[28] from on high by his Sustainer?" Say: Behold, God has the power

حزب 14

وَمَا ٱلْحَيَوٰةُ ٱلدُّنْيَآ إِلَّا لَعِبٌ وَلَهْوٌ وَلَلدَّارُ ٱلْـَٔاخِرَةُ خَيْرٌ لِّلَّذِينَ يَتَّقُونَ أَفَلَا
تَعْقِلُونَ ﴿٣٢﴾ قَدْ نَعْلَمُ إِنَّهُۥ لَيَحْزُنُكَ ٱلَّذِى يَقُولُونَ فَإِنَّهُمْ لَا يُكَذِّبُونَكَ
وَلَٰكِنَّ ٱلظَّٰلِمِينَ بِـَٔايَٰتِ ٱللَّهِ يَجْحَدُونَ ﴿٣٣﴾ وَلَقَدْ كُذِّبَتْ رُسُلٌ مِّن
قَبْلِكَ فَصَبَرُوا۟ عَلَىٰ مَا كُذِّبُوا۟ وَأُوذُوا۟ حَتَّىٰٓ أَتَىٰهُمْ نَصْرُنَا وَلَا مُبَدِّلَ
لِكَلِمَٰتِ ٱللَّهِ وَلَقَدْ جَآءَكَ مِن نَّبَإِى۟ ٱلْمُرْسَلِينَ ﴿٣٤﴾ وَإِن كَانَ كَبُرَ
عَلَيْكَ إِعْرَاضُهُمْ فَإِنِ ٱسْتَطَعْتَ أَن تَبْتَغِىَ نَفَقًا فِى ٱلْأَرْضِ أَوْ سُلَّمًا فِى
ٱلسَّمَآءِ فَتَأْتِيَهُم بِـَٔايَةٍ وَلَوْ شَآءَ ٱللَّهُ لَجَمَعَهُمْ عَلَى ٱلْهُدَىٰ فَلَا تَكُونَنَّ مِنَ
ٱلْجَٰهِلِينَ ﴿٣٥﴾ ۞ إِنَّمَا يَسْتَجِيبُ ٱلَّذِينَ يَسْمَعُونَ وَٱلْمَوْتَىٰ يَبْعَثُهُمُ ٱللَّهُ ثُمَّ
إِلَيْهِ يُرْجَعُونَ ﴿٣٦﴾ وَقَالُوا۟ لَوْلَا نُزِّلَ عَلَيْهِ ءَايَةٌ مِّن رَّبِّهِۦ قُلْ إِنَّ ٱللَّهَ قَادِرٌ

Wa mal-ḥayātud-dunyāa ʾillā laʿibuñw-wa lahw. Wa lad-dārul-ʾĀkhiratu khayrul-lilladhīna yattaqūn. ʾAfalā taʿqilūn. (32) Qad naʿlamu ʾinnahū layaḥzu-nukal-ladhī yaqūlūna faʾinnahum lā yukadhdhibū-naka wa lākinnaẓ-ẓālimīna biʾĀyātil-lāhi yajḥa-dūn. (33) Wa laqad kudhdhibat Rusulum-miñ-qablika faṣabarū ʿalā mā kudhdhibū wa ʾūdhū ḥattāa ʾatāhum naṣrunā. Wa lā mubaddila liKa-limātil-lāh. Wa laqad jāaʾaka miñ-nabaʾil-Mursalīn. (34) Wa ʾiñ-kāna kabura ʿalayka ʾiʿrāḍuhum faʾinis-taṭaʿta ʾañ-tabtaghiya nafaqañ-fil-ʾarḍi ʾaw sulla-mañ-fis-samāaʾi fataʾtiyahum-biʾĀyah. Wa law shāaʾal-lāhu lajamaʿahum ʿalal-hudā falā takūna-nna minal-jāhilīn. (35) ۞ ʾInnamā yastajībul-ladhīna yasmaʿūn. Wal-mawtā yabʿathuhumul-lāhu thumma ʾilayhi yurjaʿūn. (36) Wa qālū law lā nuzzila ʿalayhi ʾĀyatum-mir-Rabbih. Qul ʾinnal-lāha Qādirun

22 Lit., "what they say" – i.e., about life after death (which they regard as a "fable") in particular, and about the Qurʾanic message in general.

23 Lit., "some of the information concerning the apostles has already come to thee": a reference to the fact that only a few of the earlier prophets and their histories have been specifically mentioned in the Qurʾan (always in connection with a particular moral lesson), while the great majority of them are only alluded to in a general manner, in support of the divine statement that no community or civilization has been left without prophetic guidance.

24 Lit., "that they".

25 Lit., "to seek out an opening in the earth or a ladder to heaven".

26 Lit., "be not, therefore, of the ignorant".

27 Lit., "they shall be returned". Most of the classical commentators (e.g., Ṭabarī, Zamakhsharī, Rāzī, as well as the earlier authorities whom they quote) interpret this verse in the metaphorical sense in which it has been rendered by me. As is so often the case with Qurʾanic diction, its elliptical meaning can only be brought out by means of interpolations.

28 I.e., on Muḥammad, to demonstrate that he is really a bearer of God's message.

عَلَىٰٓ أَن يُنَزِّلَ ءَايَةً وَلَٰكِنَّ أَكْثَرَهُمْ لَا يَعْلَمُونَ ﴿٣٧﴾ وَمَا مِن دَآبَّةٍ فِى ٱلْأَرْضِ
وَلَا طَٰٓئِرٍ يَطِيرُ بِجَنَاحَيْهِ إِلَّآ أُمَمٌ أَمْثَالُكُم مَّا فَرَّطْنَا فِى ٱلْكِتَٰبِ مِن شَىْءٍ
ثُمَّ إِلَىٰ رَبِّهِمْ يُحْشَرُونَ ﴿٣٨﴾ وَٱلَّذِينَ كَذَّبُوا۟ بِـَٔايَٰتِنَا صُمٌّ وَبُكْمٌ فِى ٱلظُّلُمَٰتِ
مَن يَشَإِ ٱللَّهُ يُضْلِلْهُ وَمَن يَشَأْ يَجْعَلْهُ عَلَىٰ صِرَٰطٍ مُّسْتَقِيمٍ ﴿٣٩﴾ قُلْ أَرَءَيْتَكُمْ
إِنْ أَتَىٰكُمْ عَذَابُ ٱللَّهِ أَوْ أَتَتْكُمُ ٱلسَّاعَةُ أَغَيْرَ ٱللَّهِ تَدْعُونَ إِن كُنتُمْ
صَٰدِقِينَ ﴿٤٠﴾ بَلْ إِيَّاهُ تَدْعُونَ فَيَكْشِفُ مَا تَدْعُونَ إِلَيْهِ إِن شَآءَ وَتَنسَوْنَ مَا
تُشْرِكُونَ ﴿٤١﴾ وَلَقَدْ أَرْسَلْنَآ إِلَىٰٓ أُمَمٍ مِّن قَبْلِكَ فَأَخَذْنَٰهُم بِٱلْبَأْسَآءِ
وَٱلضَّرَّآءِ لَعَلَّهُمْ يَتَضَرَّعُونَ ﴿٤٢﴾ فَلَوْلَآ إِذْ جَآءَهُم بَأْسُنَا تَضَرَّعُوا۟ وَلَٰكِن
قَسَتْ قُلُوبُهُمْ وَزَيَّنَ لَهُمُ ٱلشَّيْطَٰنُ مَا كَانُوا۟ يَعْمَلُونَ ﴿٤٣﴾ فَلَمَّا نَسُوا۟ مَا

ʿalāa ʾañy-yunazzila ʾĀyatañw-wa lākinna ʾakthara-
hum lā yaʿlamūn. (37) Wa mā miñ-dāabbatiñ-fil-ʾarḍi
wa lā ṭāairiñy-yaṭīru bijanāḥayhi ʾillāa ʾumamun
ʾamthālukum. Mā farraṭnā fil-Kitābi miñ-shayʾiñ-
thumma ʾilā Rabbihim yuḥsharūn. (38) Wal-ladhīna
kadhdhabū biʾĀyātinā ṣummuñw-wa bukmuñ-fiẓ-
ẓulumāt. Mañy-yashaʾil-lāhu yuḍlilhu wa mañy-yashaʾ
yajʿalhu ʿalā ṣirāṭim-mustaqīm. (39) Qul ʾaraʾayta-
kum ʾin ʾatākum ʿadhābul-lāhi ʾaw ʾatatkumus-
Sāʿatu ʾaghayral-lāhi tadʿūn ʾiñ-kuñtum ṣādiqīn. (40)
Bal ʾiyyāhu tadʿūna fayakshifu mā tadʿūna ʾilayhi
ʾiñ-shāaʾa wa tañsawna mā tushrikūn. (41) Wa laqad
ʾarsalnāa ʾilāa ʾumamim-miñ-qablika faʾakhadhnā-
hum-bilbaʾsāaʾi waḍ-ḍarrāaʾi laʿallahum yataḍar-
raʿūn. (42) Falawlāa ʾidh jāaʾahum-baʾsunā taḍarraʿū
wa lākiñ-qasat qulūbuhum wa zayyana lahumush-
Shayṭānu mā kānū yaʿmalūn. (43) Falammā nasū mā

to bestow any sign from on high."
Yet most human beings are unaware of this[29] ‹37› – although there is no beast that walks on earth and no bird that flies on its two wings which is not [God's] creature[30] like yourselves: no single thing have We neglected in Our decree.
And once again:[31] Unto their Sustainer shall they [all] be gathered. ‹38›
And they who give the lie to Our messages are deaf and dumb, in darkness deep. Whomever God wills, He lets go astray; and whomever He wills, He places upon a straight way.[32] ‹39›
Say: "Can you see yourselves invoking any but God when God's chastisement befalls you [in this world], or the Last Hour comes upon you? [Tell me this,] if you are men of truth! ‹40› Nay, but it is Him alone that you will invoke – whereupon He may, if He so wills, remove that [ill] which caused you to call unto Him; and you will have forgotten all that to which you [now] ascribe divinity side by side with Him." ‹41›
And, indeed, We sent Our messages unto people before thy time, [O Prophet,] and visited them with misfortune and hardship so that they might humble themselves: ‹42› yet when the misfortune decreed by Us befell them, they did not humble themselves, but rather their hearts grew hard, for Satan had made all their doings seem goodly to them. ‹43› Then, when they had forgotten all that they had been

---

29 Lit., "most of them do not know", i.e., that God manifests Himself always – as the next verse points out – through the ever-recurring miracle of His creation.

30 Lit., "but they are [God's] creatures (*umam*)". The word *ummah* (of which *umam* is the plural) primarily denotes a group of living beings having certain characteristics or circumstances in common. Thus, it is often synonymous with "community", "people", "nation", "genus", "generation", and so forth. Inasmuch as every such grouping is characterized by the basic fact that its constituents (whether human or animal) are endowed with life, the term *ummah* sometimes signifies "[God's] creatures" (*Lisān al-ʿArab*, with particular reference to this very Qurʾān-verse; also Lane I, 90). Thus, the meaning of the above passage is this: Man can detect God's "signs" or "miracles" in all the life-phenomena that surround him, and should, therefore, try to observe them with a view to better understanding "God's way" (*sunnat Allāh*) – which is the Qurʾanic term for what we call "laws of nature".

31 The particle *thumma* is mostly used as a conjunction indicating a sequence in time or order ("then", "thereafter" or "thereupon"), and occasionally also as a simple conjunction equivalent to "and". But in yet another usage – of which there are frequent instances in the Qurʾān as well as in pre-Islamic Arabian poetry – *thumma* has the significance of a repetitive stress, alluding to something that has already been stated and is now again emphasized. This particular usage of *thumma* is best rendered by the words "and once again", followed by a colon.

32 See note 4 on 14 : 4.

ذُكِّرُوا۟ بِهِۦ فَتَحْنَا عَلَيْهِمْ أَبْوَٰبَ كُلِّ شَىْءٍ حَتَّىٰٓ إِذَا فَرِحُوا۟ بِمَآ أُوتُوٓا۟
أَخَذْنَٰهُم بَغْتَةً فَإِذَا هُم مُّبْلِسُونَ ﴿44﴾ فَقُطِعَ دَابِرُ ٱلْقَوْمِ ٱلَّذِينَ ظَلَمُوا۟ۚ
وَٱلْحَمْدُ لِلَّهِ رَبِّ ٱلْعَٰلَمِينَ ﴿45﴾ قُلْ أَرَءَيْتُمْ إِنْ أَخَذَ ٱللَّهُ سَمْعَكُمْ
وَأَبْصَٰرَكُمْ وَخَتَمَ عَلَىٰ قُلُوبِكُم مَّنْ إِلَٰهٌ غَيْرُ ٱللَّهِ يَأْتِيكُم بِهِۗ ٱنظُرْ
كَيْفَ نُصَرِّفُ ٱلْءَايَٰتِ ثُمَّ هُمْ يَصْدِفُونَ ﴿46﴾ قُلْ أَرَءَيْتَكُمْ إِنْ أَتَىٰكُمْ
عَذَابُ ٱللَّهِ بَغْتَةً أَوْ جَهْرَةً هَلْ يُهْلَكُ إِلَّا ٱلْقَوْمُ ٱلظَّٰلِمُونَ ﴿47﴾ وَمَا
نُرْسِلُ ٱلْمُرْسَلِينَ إِلَّا مُبَشِّرِينَ وَمُنذِرِينَۖ فَمَنْ ءَامَنَ وَأَصْلَحَ فَلَا خَوْفٌ
عَلَيْهِمْ وَلَا هُمْ يَحْزَنُونَ ﴿48﴾ وَٱلَّذِينَ كَذَّبُوا۟ بِـَٔايَٰتِنَا يَمَسُّهُمُ ٱلْعَذَابُ
بِمَا كَانُوا۟ يَفْسُقُونَ ﴿49﴾ قُل لَّآ أَقُولُ لَكُمْ عِندِى خَزَآئِنُ ٱللَّهِ وَلَآ
أَعْلَمُ ٱلْغَيْبَ وَلَآ أَقُولُ لَكُمْ إِنِّى مَلَكٌۖ إِنْ أَتَّبِعُ إِلَّا مَا يُوحَىٰٓ إِلَىَّ

told to take to heart, We threw open to them the gates of all [good] things,[33] until – even as they were rejoicing in what they had been granted – We suddenly took them to task: and lo! they were broken in spirit;[34] «44» and [in the end,] the last remnant of those folk who had been bent on evildoing was wiped out?[35]

For all praise is due to God, the Sustainer of all the worlds. «45»

Say: "What do you think? If God should take away your hearing and your sight and seal your hearts – what deity but God is there that could bring it all back to you?"

Behold how many facets We give to Our messages – and yet they turn away in disdain! «46»

Say: "Can you imagine what your condition will be[36] if God's chastisement befalls you, either suddenly or in a [gradually] perceptible manner? [But then –] will any but evildoing folk [ever] be destroyed?"[37] «47»

And We send [Our] message-bearers only as heralds of glad tidings and as warners: hence, all who believe and live righteously – no fear need they have, and neither shall they grieve; «48» whereas those who give the lie to Our messages – suffering will afflict them in result of all their sinful doings. «49»

Say [O Prophet]: "I do not say unto you, 'God's treasures are with me'; nor [do I say], 'I know the things that are beyond the reach of human perception'; nor do I say unto you, 'Behold, I am an angel': I but follow what is revealed to me."[38]

dhukkirū bihī fataḥnā ᶜalayhim ᵓabwāba kulli shayᵓin ḥattāa ᵓidhā fariḥū bimāa ᵓūtūu ᵓakhadhnāhum-baghtatañ-faᵓidhā hum-mublisūn. (44) Faquṭiᶜa dābirul-qawmil-ladhīna ẓalamū. Wal-ḥamdu lillāhi Rabbil-ᶜālamīn. (45) Qul ᵓaraᵓaytum ᵓin ᵓakhadhal-lāhu samᶜakum wa ᵓabṣārakum wa khatama ᶜalā qulūbikum-man ᵓilāhun-ghayrul-lāhi yaᵓtīkum-bih. ᵓUñẓur kayfa nuṣarriful-ᵓĀyāti thumma hum yaṣdifūn. (46) Qul ᵓaraᵓaytakum ᵓin ᵓatākum ᶜadhābul-lāhi baghtatan ᵓaw jahratan hal yuhlaku ᵓillal-qawmuẓ-ẓālimūn. (47) Wa mā nursilul-Mursalīna ᵓillā mubashshirīna wa muñdhirīn. Faman ᵓāmana wa ᵓaṣlaḥa falā khawfun ᶜalayhim wa lā hum yaḥzanūn. (48) Wal-ladhīna kadhdhabū biᵓĀyātinā yamassuhumul-ᶜadhābu bimā kānū yafsuqūn. (49) Qul lāa ᵓaqūlu lakum ᶜiñdī khazāaᵓinul-lāhi wa lāa ᵓaᶜlamul-ghayba wa lāa ᵓaqūlu lakum ᵓinnī malak. ᵓIn ᵓattabiᶜu ᵓillā mā yūḥāa ᵓilayy.

33 I.e., to test them by happiness after the test by misery.

34 The verb *ablasa* signifies "he despaired of all hope" or "became broken in spirit". (For the linguistic connection of this word with the name of Iblīs, the Fallen Angel, see *sūrah* 7, note 10.)

35 Lit., "cut off". The above passage illustrates a phenomenon well known in history: namely, the inevitable social and moral disintegration of communities which have lost sight of spiritual truths.

36 Lit., "Can you see yourselves".

37 I.e., the righteous will never be really "destroyed" – for, even if they should suffer physical destruction, they are bound to attain to spiritual bliss and cannot, therefore, be said to have been "destroyed" like the evildoers, who, by their actions, lose their happiness both in this world and in the life to come (Rāzī).

38 This denial on the part of the Prophet of any claim to supernatural powers refers, primarily, to the demand of the unbelievers (mentioned in verse 37) that he should prove his prophetic mission by causing a "miraculous sign" to be bestowed on him. Beyond this specific reference, however, the above passage is meant to prevent any deification of the Prophet and to make it clear that he – like all other prophets before him – was but a mortal human being, a servant whom God had chosen to convey His message to mankind. See also 7 : 188.

Say: "Can the blind and the seeing be deemed equal?[39] Will you not, then, take thought?" ⟨50⟩
And warn hereby those who fear lest they be gathered unto their Sustainer with none to protect them from Him or to intercede with Him, so that they might become [fully] conscious of Him.[40] ⟨51⟩
Hence, repulse not [any of] those who at morn and evening invoke their Sustainer, seeking His countenance.[41] Thou art in no wise accountable for them – just as they are in no wise accountable for thee[42] – and thou hast therefore no right to repulse them: for then thou wouldst be among the evildoers.[43] ⟨52⟩
For it is in this way[44] that We try men through one another – to the end that they might ask, "Has God, then, bestowed His favour upon those others in preference to us?"[45] Does not God know best as to who is grateful [to Him]? ⟨53⟩

قُلْ هَلْ يَسْتَوِى ٱلْأَعْمَىٰ وَٱلْبَصِيرُ ۚ أَفَلَا تَتَفَكَّرُونَ ﴿٥٠﴾ وَأَنذِرْ بِهِ ٱلَّذِينَ
يَخَافُونَ أَن يُحْشَرُوٓا۟ إِلَىٰ رَبِّهِمْ ۙ لَيْسَ لَهُم مِّن دُونِهِۦ وَلِىٌّ وَلَا شَفِيعٌ
لَّعَلَّهُمْ يَتَّقُونَ ﴿٥١﴾ وَلَا تَطْرُدِ ٱلَّذِينَ يَدْعُونَ رَبَّهُم بِٱلْغَدَوٰةِ وَٱلْعَشِىِّ
يُرِيدُونَ وَجْهَهُۥ ۖ مَا عَلَيْكَ مِنْ حِسَابِهِم مِّن شَىْءٍ وَمَا مِنْ حِسَابِكَ عَلَيْهِم
مِّن شَىْءٍ فَتَطْرُدَهُمْ فَتَكُونَ مِنَ ٱلظَّـٰلِمِينَ ﴿٥٢﴾ وَكَذَٰلِكَ فَتَنَّا بَعْضَهُم
بِبَعْضٍ لِّيَقُولُوٓا۟ أَهَـٰٓؤُلَآءِ مَنَّ ٱللَّهُ عَلَيْهِم مِّنۢ بَيْنِنَآ ۗ أَلَيْسَ ٱللَّهُ بِأَعْلَمَ
بِٱلشَّـٰكِرِينَ ﴿٥٣﴾

Qul hal yastawil-ᵓaᶜmā wal-baṣīr. ᵓAfalā tatafakkarūn. (50) Wa ᵓañdhir bihil-ladhīna yakhāfūna ᵓañy-yuḥsharūu ᵓilā Rabbihim laysa lahum-miñ-dūnihī waliyyuñw-wa lā shafīᶜul-laᶜallahum yattaqūn. (51) Wa lā taṭrudil-ladhīna yadᶜūna Rabbahum-bilghadāti wal-ᶜashiyyi yurīdūna Wajhah. Mā ᶜalayka min ḥisābihim-miñ-shayᵓiñw-wa mā min ḥisābika ᶜalayhim-miñ-shayᵓiñ-fataṭrudahum fatakūna minaẓ-ẓālimīn. (52) Wa kadhālika fatannā baᶜḍahum-bibaᶜḍil-liyaqūlūu ᵓahāaᵓulāaᵓi mannal-lāhu ᶜalayhim-mim-bayninā. ᵓAlaysal-lāhu biᵓaᶜlama bishshākirīn. (53)

39 I.e., "Can those who remain blind and deaf to God's messages find their way through life equally well as those who have achieved a spiritual vision and guidance through God's revelation?"

40 It is obvious from the context that this verse refers to followers of earlier scriptures – such as the Jews and the Christians – who share with the followers of the Qurᵓān the belief in life after death (Zamakhsharī), as well as to agnostics who, without having definite beliefs on this point, admit the *possibility* of life after death.

41 According to Traditions, this and the next verse were revealed when, several years before the Muslims' exodus to Medina, some of the pagan chieftains at Mecca expressed their willingness to consider accepting Islam on the condition that the Prophet would dissociate himself from the former slaves and other "lowly" persons among his followers – a demand which the Prophet, of course, rejected. This historical reference does not, however, provide a full explanation of the above passage. In accordance with the Qurᵓanic method, allusions to historical events – whether relating to contemporary occurrences or to earlier times – are always made with a view to expressing ethical teachings of a *permanent* nature; and the passage under consideration is no exception in this respect. As the wording shows, it relates not to "lowly" followers of Islam but to people who, while not being Muslims in the current sense of this word, believe in God and are always ("at morn and evening") "seeking His countenance" (i.e., His grace and acceptance): and, thus, verses 52-53 connect logically with verse 51. Although primarily addressed to the Prophet, the exhortation voiced in this passage is directed to all followers of the Qurᵓān: they are enjoined not to repulse anyone who believes in God – even though his beliefs may not fully answer to the demands of the Qurᵓān – but, on the contrary, to try to help him by means of a patient explanation of the Qurᵓanic teachings.

42 I.e., for whatever in their beliefs or actions does not coincide with the teachings of the Qurᵓān, and *vice-versa*. In other words, all are accountable to God alone.

43 Lit., "so that thou shouldst repulse them and thus be of the evildoers".

44 I.e., by endowing man with the power of reasoning and thus, indirectly, giving rise to a multiplicity of faiths.

45 Lit., "Is it those upon whom God has bestowed His favour from among us (*min bayninā*)?" As mentioned by Zamakhsharī, the expression *min bayninā* is here equivalent to *min dūninā*, which, in this context, may suitably be rendered as "in preference to us". This would seem to be an allusion to the sarcastic incredulity with which, as a rule, non-Muslims receive the claim of the Muslims that the Qurᵓān is the final formulation of God's message to man. The "trial" referred to above consists in the unwillingness of people of other faiths to accept this claim as valid, and so to renounce the prejudice against Islam to which their cultural and historical environment has made them, consciously or subconsciously, predisposed.

ربع الحزب

And when those who believe in Our messages come unto thee, say: "Peace be upon you. Your Sustainer has willed upon Himself the law of grace and mercy[46] – so that if any of you does a bad deed out of ignorance, and thereafter repents and lives righteously, He shall be [found] much-forgiving, a dispenser of grace." ‹54›
And thus clearly do We spell out Our messages: and [We do it] so that the path of those who are lost in sin might be distinct [from that of the righteous]. ‹55›

SAY [to the deniers of the truth]: "Behold, I have been forbidden to worship those [beings] whom you invoke instead of God."
Say: "I do not follow your errant views – or else I should have gone astray, and should not be among those who have found the right path." ‹56›
Say: "Behold, I take my stand on a clear evidence from my Sustainer – and [so] it is to Him that you are giving the lie! Not in my power is that which [in your ignorance] you so hastily demand:[47] judgment rests with none but God. He shall declare the truth, since it is He who is the best judge between truth and falsehood." ‹57›
Say: "If that which you so hastily demand were in my power, everything would indeed have been decided between me and you.[48] But God knows best as to who is doing wrong." ‹58›
For, with Him are the keys to the things that are beyond the reach of a created being's perception: none knows them but He.
And He knows all that is on land and in the sea; and not a leaf falls but He knows it; and neither is there a grain in the earth's deep darkness, nor anything living

وَإِذَا جَآءَكَ ٱلَّذِينَ يُؤْمِنُونَ بِـَٔايَـٰتِنَا فَقُلْ سَلَـٰمٌ عَلَيْكُمْ كَتَبَ رَبُّكُمْ عَلَىٰ
نَفْسِهِ ٱلرَّحْمَةَ أَنَّهُۥ مَنْ عَمِلَ مِنكُمْ سُوٓءًۢا بِجَهَـٰلَةٍ ثُمَّ تَابَ مِنۢ بَعْدِهِۦ
وَأَصْلَحَ فَأَنَّهُۥ غَفُورٌ رَّحِيمٌ ﴿٥٤﴾ وَكَذَٰلِكَ نُفَصِّلُ ٱلْـَٔايَـٰتِ وَلِتَسْتَبِينَ
سَبِيلُ ٱلْمُجْرِمِينَ ﴿٥٥﴾ قُلْ إِنِّى نُهِيتُ أَنْ أَعْبُدَ ٱلَّذِينَ تَدْعُونَ مِن دُونِ ٱللَّهِ
قُل لَّآ أَتَّبِعُ أَهْوَآءَكُمْ قَدْ ضَلَلْتُ إِذًا وَمَآ أَنَا۠ مِنَ ٱلْمُهْتَدِينَ ﴿٥٦﴾
قُلْ إِنِّى عَلَىٰ بَيِّنَةٍ مِّن رَّبِّى وَكَذَّبْتُم بِهِۦ مَا عِندِى مَا تَسْتَعْجِلُونَ بِهِۦٓ إِنِ
ٱلْحُكْمُ إِلَّا لِلَّهِ يَقُصُّ ٱلْحَقَّ وَهُوَ خَيْرُ ٱلْفَـٰصِلِينَ ﴿٥٧﴾ قُل لَّوْ أَنَّ عِندِى
مَا تَسْتَعْجِلُونَ بِهِۦ لَقُضِىَ ٱلْأَمْرُ بَيْنِى وَبَيْنَكُمْ وَٱللَّهُ أَعْلَمُ بِٱلظَّـٰلِمِينَ ﴿٥٨﴾
۞ وَعِندَهُۥ مَفَاتِحُ ٱلْغَيْبِ لَا يَعْلَمُهَآ إِلَّا هُوَ وَيَعْلَمُ مَا فِى ٱلْبَرِّ وَٱلْبَحْرِ
وَمَا تَسْقُطُ مِن وَرَقَةٍ إِلَّا يَعْلَمُهَا وَلَا حَبَّةٍ فِى ظُلُمَـٰتِ ٱلْأَرْضِ وَلَا رَطْبٍ

Wa ʾidhā jāaʾakal-ladhīna yuʾminūna biʾĀyātinā faqul salāmun ʿalaykum kataba Rabbukum ʿalā nafsihir-raḥmata ʾannahū man ʿamila miñkum sūuʾam-bijahālatiñ-thumma tāba mim-baʿdihī wa ʾaṣlaḥa faʾannahū Ghafūrur-Raḥīm. (54) Wa kadhālika nufaṣ-ṣilul-ʾĀyāti wa litastabīna sabīlul-mujrimīn. (55) Qul ʾinnī nuhītu ʾan ʾaʿbudal-ladhīna tadʿūna miñ-dūnil-lāh. Qul lāa ʾattabiʿu ʾahwāaʾakum qad ḍalaltu ʾidhañw-wa māa ʾana minal-muhtadīn. (56) Qul ʾinnī ʿalā bayyinatim-mir-Rabbī wa kadhdhabtum-bih. Mā ʿiñdī mā tastaʿjilūna bih. ʾInil-ḥukmu ʾillā lillāhi yaquṣṣul-ḥaqqa wa Huwa Khayrul-fāṣilīn. (57) Qul law ʾanna ʿiñdī mā tastaʿjilūna bihī laquḍiyal-ʾamru baynī wa baynakum. Wal-lāhu ʾaʿlamu biẓẓālimīn. (58) ۞ Wa ʿiñdahū mafātiḥul-ghaybi lā yaʿlamuhāa ʾillā Hū. Wa yaʿlamu mā fil-barri wal-baḥr. Wa mā tasquṭu miñw-waraqatin ʾillā yaʿlamuhā wa lā ḥabbatiñ-fī ẓulumātil-ʾarḍi wa lā raṭbiñw-

46 See note 10 above. Regarding the word *salām*, which has been translated here as "peace", see *sūrah* 5, note 29. The "peace" referred to in the above expression – which occurs many times in the Qurʾān and has become the standard form of Muslim greeting – has a spiritual connotation comprising the concepts of ethical soundness, security from all that is evil and, therefore, freedom from all moral conflict and disquiet.

47 Lit., "not with me is that which you would hasten": a reference to the sarcastic demand of the unbelievers, mentioned in 8 : 32, that God should chastise them forthwith in proof of the Prophet's claim to be His message-bearer.

48 I.e., "you would have been convinced that I am really a bearer of God's message" – the implication being that a conviction based solely on a "miraculous" proof would have no spiritual value.

or dead,[49] but is recorded in [His] clear decree. ‹59›
And He it is who causes you to be [like] dead[50] at night, and knows what you work in daytime; and He brings you back to life each day[51] in order that a term set [by Him] be fulfilled. In the end, unto Him you must return: and then He will make you understand all that you were doing [in life]. ‹60›
And He alone holds sway over His servants. And He sends forth heavenly forces to watch over you[52] until, when death approaches any of you, Our messengers cause him to die: and they do not overlook [anyone]. ‹61› And they [who have died] are thereupon brought before God,[53] their true Lord Supreme. Oh, verily, His alone is all judgment: and He is the swiftest of all reckoners! ‹62›
Say: "Who is it that saves you from the dark dangers[54] of land and sea [when] you call unto Him humbly, and in the secrecy of your hearts, 'If He will but save us from this [distress], we shall most certainly be among the grateful'?" ‹63› Say: "God [alone] can save you from this and from every distress – and still you ascribe divinity to other powers beside Him!" ‹64›
Say: "It is He alone who has the power to let loose upon you suffering from above you or from beneath your feet,[55] or to confound you with mutual discord and let you taste the fear of one another."[56]
Behold how many facets We give to these messages, so that they might understand the truth; ‹65› and yet, to all this thy people[57] have given the lie, although it is the truth.

وَلَا يَابِسٍ إِلَّا فِي كِتَٰبٍ مُّبِينٍ ﴿59﴾ وَهُوَ ٱلَّذِي يَتَوَفَّىٰكُم بِٱلَّيْلِ وَيَعْلَمُ مَا
جَرَحْتُم بِٱلنَّهَارِ ثُمَّ يَبْعَثُكُمْ فِيهِ لِيُقْضَىٰٓ أَجَلٌ مُّسَمًّى ثُمَّ إِلَيْهِ مَرْجِعُكُمْ ثُمَّ
يُنَبِّئُكُم بِمَا كُنتُمْ تَعْمَلُونَ ﴿60﴾ وَهُوَ ٱلْقَاهِرُ فَوْقَ عِبَادِهِۦ وَيُرْسِلُ عَلَيْكُمْ
حَفَظَةً حَتَّىٰٓ إِذَا جَآءَ أَحَدَكُمُ ٱلْمَوْتُ تَوَفَّتْهُ رُسُلُنَا وَهُمْ لَا يُفَرِّطُونَ ﴿61﴾ ثُمَّ
رُدُّوٓاْ إِلَى ٱللَّهِ مَوْلَىٰهُمُ ٱلْحَقِّ أَلَا لَهُ ٱلْحُكْمُ وَهُوَ أَسْرَعُ ٱلْحَٰسِبِينَ ﴿62﴾ قُلْ
مَن يُنَجِّيكُم مِّن ظُلُمَٰتِ ٱلْبَرِّ وَٱلْبَحْرِ تَدْعُونَهُۥ تَضَرُّعًا وَخُفْيَةً لَّئِنْ أَنجَىٰنَا مِنْ
هَٰذِهِۦ لَنَكُونَنَّ مِنَ ٱلشَّٰكِرِينَ ﴿63﴾ قُلِ ٱللَّهُ يُنَجِّيكُم مِّنْهَا وَمِن كُلِّ كَرْبٍ
ثُمَّ أَنتُمْ تُشْرِكُونَ ﴿64﴾ قُلْ هُوَ ٱلْقَادِرُ عَلَىٰٓ أَن يَبْعَثَ عَلَيْكُمْ عَذَابًا مِّن فَوْقِكُمْ
أَوْ مِن تَحْتِ أَرْجُلِكُمْ أَوْ يَلْبِسَكُمْ شِيَعًا وَيُذِيقَ بَعْضَكُم بَأْسَ بَعْضٍ ٱنظُرْ
كَيْفَ نُصَرِّفُ ٱلْءَايَٰتِ لَعَلَّهُمْ يَفْقَهُونَ ﴿65﴾ وَكَذَّبَ بِهِۦ قَوْمُكَ وَهُوَ ٱلْحَقُّ

wa lā yābisin ʾillā fī Kitābim-mubīn. (59) Wa Huwalladhī yatawaffākum-billayli wa yaʿlamu mā jaraḥtum-binnahāri thumma yabʿathukum fīhi liyuqḍāa ʾajalum-musammā. Thumma ʾilayhi marjiʿukum thumma yunabbiʾukum-bimā kuñtum taʿmalūn. (60) Wa Huwal-Qāhiru fawqa ʿibādihī wa yursilu ʿalaykum ḥafaẓatan ḥattāa ʾidhā jāaʾa ʾaḥadakumul-mawtu tawaffat-hu Rusulunā wa hum lā yufarriṭūn. (61) Thumma ruddūu ʾilal-lāhi mawlāhumul-Ḥaqq. ʾAlā lahul-ḥukmu wa Huwa ʾAsraʿul-ḥāsibīn. (62) Qul mañy-yunajjīkum-miñ-ẓulumātil-barri wal-baḥri tadʿūnahū taḍarruʿañw-wa khufyatal-laʾin ʾañjānā miñ-hādhihī lanakūnanna minash-shākirīn. (63) Qulil-lāhu yunajjīkum-minhā wa miñ-kulli karbiñ-thumma ʾañtum tushrikūn. (64) Qul Huwal-Qādiru ʿalāa ʾañy-yabʿatha ʿalaykum ʿadhābam-miñ-fawqikum ʾaw miñ-taḥti ʾarjulikum ʾaw yalbisakum shiyaʿañw-wa yudhīqa baʿḍakum-baʾsa baʿḍ. ʾUñẓur kayfa nuṣarriful-ʾĀyāti laʿallahum yafqahūn. (65) Wa kadhdhaba bihī qawmuka wa huwal-ḥaqq.

49 Lit., "fresh or dry".
50 For a full explanation of the verb *tawaffā* – lit., "he took [something] in full" – see note 44 on 39 : 42, which is the earliest instance of its use in the Qurʾān.
51 Lit., "therein" – referring to the daytime. The polarity of sleep and wakefulness contains an allusion to life and death (cf. 78 : 9-11).
52 Lit., "sends forth guardians over you".
53 Lit., "brought back [or "referred"] to God" – i.e., placed before Him for judgment.
54 Lit., "the darknesses" or "the deep darkness".
55 I.e., from any direction or by any means whatsoever.
56 Or: "the violence of one against another" – inner disintegration, fear, violence and tyranny being the inevitable consequences of a society's departure from spiritual truths.
57 I.e., the unbelieving compatriots of the Prophet and, by implication, all who deny the truth.

Say [then]: "I am not responsible for your conduct. «66» Every tiding [from God] has a term set for its fulfilment: and in time you will come to know [the truth]." «67»

NOW, whenever thou meet such as indulge in [blasphemous] talk about Our messages, turn thy back upon them until they begin to talk of other things;[58] and if Satan should ever cause thee to forget [thyself], remain not, after recollection, in the company of such evildoing folk, «68» for whom those who are conscious of God are in no wise accountable. Theirs, however, is the duty to admonish [the sinners],[59] so that they might become conscious of God. «69»

And leave to themselves all those who, beguiled by the life of this world, have made play and passing delights their religion;[60] but remind [them] herewith that [in the life to come] every human being shall be held in pledge for whatever wrong he has done, and shall have none to protect him from God, and none to intercede for him; and though he offer any conceivable ransom,[61] it shall not be accepted from him. It is [people such as] these that shall be held in pledge for the wrong they have done; for them there is [in the life to come] a draught of burning despair,[62] and grievous suffering awaits them because of their persistent refusal to acknowledge the truth. «70»

قُل لَّسْتُ عَلَيْكُم بِوَكِيلٍ ﴿٦٦﴾ لِّكُلِّ نَبَإٍ مُّسْتَقَرٌّ وَسَوْفَ تَعْلَمُونَ ﴿٦٧﴾
وَإِذَا رَأَيْتَ ٱلَّذِينَ يَخُوضُونَ فِىٓ ءَايَـٰتِنَا فَأَعْرِضْ عَنْهُمْ حَتَّىٰ يَخُوضُوا۟
فِى حَدِيثٍ غَيْرِهِۦ وَإِمَّا يُنسِيَنَّكَ ٱلشَّيْطَـٰنُ فَلَا تَقْعُدْ بَعْدَ ٱلذِّكْرَىٰ مَعَ
ٱلْقَوْمِ ٱلظَّـٰلِمِينَ ﴿٦٨﴾ وَمَا عَلَى ٱلَّذِينَ يَتَّقُونَ مِنْ حِسَابِهِم مِّن شَىْءٍ
وَلَـٰكِن ذِكْرَىٰ لَعَلَّهُمْ يَتَّقُونَ ﴿٦٩﴾ وَذَرِ ٱلَّذِينَ ٱتَّخَذُوا۟ دِينَهُمْ لَعِبًا
وَلَهْوًا وَغَرَّتْهُمُ ٱلْحَيَوٰةُ ٱلدُّنْيَا ۚ وَذَكِّرْ بِهِۦٓ أَن تُبْسَلَ نَفْسٌۢ بِمَا كَسَبَتْ
لَيْسَ لَهَا مِن دُونِ ٱللَّهِ وَلِىٌّ وَلَا شَفِيعٌ وَإِن تَعْدِلْ كُلَّ عَدْلٍ لَّا يُؤْخَذْ
مِنْهَآ ۗ أُو۟لَـٰٓئِكَ ٱلَّذِينَ أُبْسِلُوا۟ بِمَا كَسَبُوا۟ ۖ لَهُمْ شَرَابٌ مِّنْ حَمِيمٍ وَعَذَابٌ
أَلِيمٌۢ بِمَا كَانُوا۟ يَكْفُرُونَ ﴿٧٠﴾

Qul lastu ʿalaykum-biwakīl. (66) Likulli nabaʾim-mustaqarruñw-wa sawfa taʿlamūn. (67) Wa ʾidhā raʾaytal-ladhīna yakhūḍūna fīi ʾĀyātinā faʾaʿriḍ ʿanhum ḥattā yakhūḍū fī ḥadīthin ghayrih. Wa ʾimmā yuñsiyannakash-Shayṭānu falā taqʿud baʿdadh-dhikrā maʿal-qawmiẓ-ẓālimīn. (68) Wa mā ʿalal-ladhīna yattaqūna min ḥisābihim-miñ-shayʾiñw-wa lākiñ-dhikrā laʿallahum yattaqūn. (69) Wa dharil-ladhīnat-takhadhū dīnahum laʿibañw-wa lahwañw-wa gharrat-humul-ḥayātud-dunyā. Wa dhakkir bihīi ʾañ-tubsala nafsum-bimā kasabat laysa lahā miñ-dūnil-lāhi waliyyuñw-wa lā shafīʿuñw-wa ʾiñ-taʿdil kulla ʿadlil-lā yuʾkhadh minhā. ʾUlāaʾikal-ladhīna ʾubsilū bimā kasabū. Lahum sharābum-min ḥamīmiñw-wa ʿadhābun ʾalīmum-bimā kānū yakfurūn. (70)

58 Lit., "until they immerse themselves in talk other than this".

59 This is a paraphrase of the elliptic expression *wa-lākin dhikrā* ("however, an admonition").

60 The phrase *attakhadhū dīnahum laʿiban wa-lahwan* can be understood in either of two ways: (1) "they have made their religion [an object of] play and fun", or (2) "they have made play and fun [or "passing delights"] their religion" – i.e., the main goal of their lives. To my mind, the latter reading is definitely preferable inasmuch as it brings out the fact that many of those who are "beguiled by the life of this world" devote themselves to the pursuit of what the Qurʾān describes as "passing delights" – including the pleasures which money and power can provide – with something akin to religious fervour: an attitude of mind which causes them to lose sight of all spiritual and moral values.

61 Lit., "though he might [try to] ransom himself with all ransom" – i.e., though he might proffer, after resurrection, any atonement whatever for his past sins.

62 Among the various meanings attributable to the word *ḥamīm* are the concepts of intense heat as well as of painful cold (*Qāmūs, Tāj al-ʿArūs*). In the eschatology of the Qurʾān it invariably refers to the suffering of the sinners in the life to come; and since all Qurʾanic references to life after death are, necessarily, allegorical, the term *ḥamīm* may be rendered as "burning despair".

SAY: "Shall we invoke, instead of God, something that can neither benefit us nor harm us, and [thus] turn around on our heels after God has guided us aright? – like one whom the satans have enticed into blundering after earthly lusts, the while his companions, trying to guide him, call out unto him [from afar],[63] 'Come thou to us!'" Say: "Verily, God's guidance is the only guidance: and so we have been bidden to surrender ourselves unto the Sustainer of all the worlds, ‹71› and to be constant in prayer and conscious of Him: for it is He unto whom you all shall be gathered." ‹72›
And He it is who has created the heavens and the earth in accordance with [an inner] truth[64] – and whenever He says, "Be," His word comes true; and His will be the dominion on the Day when the trumpet [of resurrection] is blown.
He knows all that is beyond the reach of a created being's perception, as well as all that can be witnessed by a creature's senses or mind:[65] for He alone is truly wise, all-aware. ‹73›

AND, LO, [thus] spoke Abraham unto his father Āzar:[66] "Takest thou idols for gods? Verily, I see that thou and thy people have obviously gone astray!" ‹74›
And thus We gave Abraham [his first] insight into [God's] mighty dominion over the heavens and the earth – and [this] to the end that he might become one of those who are inwardly sure. ‹75›

قُلْ أَنَدْعُوا۟ مِن دُونِ ٱللَّهِ مَا لَا يَنفَعُنَا وَلَا يَضُرُّنَا وَنُرَدُّ عَلَىٰٓ أَعْقَابِنَا بَعْدَ
إِذْ هَدَىٰنَا ٱللَّهُ كَٱلَّذِى ٱسْتَهْوَتْهُ ٱلشَّيَٰطِينُ فِى ٱلْأَرْضِ حَيْرَانَ لَهُۥٓ
أَصْحَٰبٌ يَدْعُونَهُۥٓ إِلَى ٱلْهُدَى ٱئْتِنَا ۗ قُلْ إِنَّ هُدَى ٱللَّهِ هُوَ ٱلْهُدَىٰ ۖ وَأُمِرْنَا
لِنُسْلِمَ لِرَبِّ ٱلْعَٰلَمِينَ ﴿٧١﴾ وَأَنْ أَقِيمُوا۟ ٱلصَّلَوٰةَ وَٱتَّقُوهُ ۚ وَهُوَ ٱلَّذِىٓ إِلَيْهِ
تُحْشَرُونَ ﴿٧٢﴾ وَهُوَ ٱلَّذِى خَلَقَ ٱلسَّمَٰوَٰتِ وَٱلْأَرْضَ بِٱلْحَقِّ ۖ وَيَوْمَ
يَقُولُ كُن فَيَكُونُ ۚ قَوْلُهُ ٱلْحَقُّ ۚ وَلَهُ ٱلْمُلْكُ يَوْمَ يُنفَخُ فِى ٱلصُّورِ ۚ عَٰلِمُ
ٱلْغَيْبِ وَٱلشَّهَٰدَةِ ۚ وَهُوَ ٱلْحَكِيمُ ٱلْخَبِيرُ ﴿٧٣﴾ ۞ وَإِذْ قَالَ إِبْرَٰهِيمُ
لِأَبِيهِ ءَازَرَ أَتَتَّخِذُ أَصْنَامًا ءَالِهَةً ۖ إِنِّىٓ أَرَىٰكَ وَقَوْمَكَ فِى ضَلَٰلٍ
مُّبِينٍ ﴿٧٤﴾ وَكَذَٰلِكَ نُرِىٓ إِبْرَٰهِيمَ مَلَكُوتَ ٱلسَّمَٰوَٰتِ وَٱلْأَرْضِ
وَلِيَكُونَ مِنَ ٱلْمُوقِنِينَ ﴿٧٥﴾

نصف الحزب

Qul ʾanadʿū miñ-dūnil-lāhi mā lā yañfaʿunā wa lā yaḍurrunā wa nuraddu ʿalāa ʾaʿqābinā baʿda ʾidh hadānal-lāhu kalladhis-tahwat-hush-Shayāṭīnu fil-ʾarḍi ḥayrāna lahūu ʾaṣḥābuñy-yadʿūnahūu ʾilal-hudaʾ-tinā. Qul ʾinna hudal-lāhi huwal-hudā. Wa ʾumirnā linuslima liRabbil-ʿālamīn. (71) Wa ʾan ʾaqīmuṣ-Ṣalāta wat-taqūh. Wa Huwal-ladhīi ʾilayhi tuḥsharūn. (72) Wa Huwal-ladhī khalaqas-samāwāti wal-ʾarḍa bilḥaqq. Wa yawma yaqūlu kuñ-fayakūn. Qawluhul-ḥaqq. Wa lahul-mulku Yawma yuñfakhu fiṣ-ṣūr. ʿĀlimul-ghaybi wash-shahādah. Wa Huwal-Ḥakīmul-Khabīr. (73) ۞ Wa ʾidh qāla ʾIbrāhīmu liʾabīhi ʾĀzara ʾatattakhidhu aṣnāman ʾālihah. ʾInnīi ʾarāka wa qawmaka fī ḍalālim-mubīn. (74) Wa kadhālika nurīi ʾIbrāhīma malakūtas-samāwāti wal-ʾarḍi wa liyakūna minal-mūqinīn. (75)

63 Lit., "whom the satans have enticed with lusts on earth, [rendering him] bewildered, [while] he has companions who call him unto guidance". See in this connection note 10 on 2 : 14, as well as note 31 on 14 : 22 and note 16 on 15 : 17.

64 See *sūrah* 10, note 11.

65 The term *ash-shahādah* (lit., "that which is [or "can be"] witnessed") is used in this and similar contexts as the exact antithesis of *al-ghayb* ("that which is beyond the reach of a created being's perception"). Thus, it circumscribes those aspects of reality which can be sensually or conceptually grasped by a created being.

66 The subsequent passage (verses 74 ff.) continues, by way of narrative, the exposition of God's oneness and uniqueness. – In the Bible, the name of Abraham's father is given not as Āzar but as Tērah (the Tāraḥ or Ṭārakh of the early Muslim genealogists). However, he seems to have been known by other names (or designations) as well, all of them obscure as to origin and meaning. Thus, in various Talmudic stories he is called Zārah, while Eusebius Pamphili (the ecclesiastical historian who lived towards the end of the third and the beginning of the fourth century of the Christian era) gives his name as Athar. Although neither the Talmud nor Eusebius can be regarded as authorities for the purposes of a Qurʾān-commentary, it is not impossible that the designation Āzar (which occurs in the Qurʾān only once) is the pre-Islamic, Arabicized form of Athar or Zārah.

فَلَمَّا جَنَّ عَلَيْهِ ٱلَّيْلُ رَءَا كَوْكَبًا قَالَ هَٰذَا رَبِّى فَلَمَّآ أَفَلَ قَالَ لَآ أُحِبُّ
ٱلْءَافِلِينَ ﴿٧٦﴾ فَلَمَّا رَءَا ٱلْقَمَرَ بَازِغًا قَالَ هَٰذَا رَبِّى فَلَمَّآ أَفَلَ قَالَ لَئِن
لَّمْ يَهْدِنِى رَبِّى لَأَكُونَنَّ مِنَ ٱلْقَوْمِ ٱلضَّآلِّينَ ﴿٧٧﴾ فَلَمَّا رَءَا ٱلشَّمْسَ
بَازِغَةً قَالَ هَٰذَا رَبِّى هَٰذَآ أَكْبَرُ فَلَمَّآ أَفَلَتْ قَالَ يَٰقَوْمِ إِنِّى بَرِىٓءٌ مِّمَّا
تُشْرِكُونَ ﴿٧٨﴾ إِنِّى وَجَّهْتُ وَجْهِىَ لِلَّذِى فَطَرَ ٱلسَّمَٰوَٰتِ وَٱلْأَرْضَ
حَنِيفًا وَمَآ أَنَا۠ مِنَ ٱلْمُشْرِكِينَ ﴿٧٩﴾ وَحَآجَّهُۥ قَوْمُهُۥ قَالَ أَتُحَٰٓجُّوٓنِّى فِى
ٱللَّهِ وَقَدْ هَدَىٰنِ وَلَآ أَخَافُ مَا تُشْرِكُونَ بِهِۦٓ إِلَّآ أَن يَشَآءَ رَبِّى شَيْـًٔا وَسِعَ
رَبِّى كُلَّ شَىْءٍ عِلْمًا أَفَلَا تَتَذَكَّرُونَ ﴿٨٠﴾ وَكَيْفَ أَخَافُ مَآ أَشْرَكْتُمْ وَلَا
تَخَافُونَ أَنَّكُمْ أَشْرَكْتُم بِٱللَّهِ مَا لَمْ يُنَزِّلْ بِهِۦ عَلَيْكُمْ سُلْطَٰنًا فَأَىُّ
ٱلْفَرِيقَيْنِ أَحَقُّ بِٱلْأَمْنِ إِن كُنتُمْ تَعْلَمُونَ ﴿٨١﴾ ٱلَّذِينَ ءَامَنُوا۟ وَلَمْ يَلْبِسُوٓا۟
إِيمَٰنَهُم بِظُلْمٍ أُو۟لَٰٓئِكَ لَهُمُ ٱلْأَمْنُ وَهُم مُّهْتَدُونَ ﴿٨٢﴾ وَتِلْكَ حُجَّتُنَآ

Falammā janna ʿalayhil-laylu raʾā kawkabā. Qāla hādhā Rabbī. Falammāa ʾafala qāla lāa ʾuḥibbul-ʾāfilīn. (76) Falammā raʾal-qamara bāzighañ-qāla hādhā Rabbī. Falammāa ʾafala qāla laʾil-lam yahdinī Rabbī laʾakūnanna minal-qawmiḍ-ḍāallīn. (77) Falammā raʾash-shamsa bāzighatañ-qāla hādhā Rabbī hādhāa ʾakbar. Falammāa ʾafalat qāla yā-qawmi ʾinnī bariiʾum-mimmā tushrikūn. (78) ʾInnī wajjahtu wajhiya lilladhī faṭaras-samāwāti wal-ʾarḍa ḥanīfañw-wa māa ʾana minal-mushrikīn. (79) Wa ḥāajjahū qawmuh. Qāla ʾatuḥāajjūunnī fil-lāhi wa qad hadān. Wa lāa ʾakhāfu mā tushrikūna bihīi ʾillāa ʾañy-yashāaʾa Rabbī shayʾā. Wasiʿa Rabbī kulla shayʾin ʿilmā. ʾAfalā tatadhakkarūn. (80) Wa kayfa ʾakhāfu māa ʾashraktum wa lā takhāfūna ʾannakum ʾashraktum-billāhi mā lam yunazzil bihī ʿalaykum sulṭānā. Faʾayyul-farīqayni ʾaḥaqqu bilʾamni ʾiñ-kuñtum taʿlamūn. (81) ʾAlladhīna ʾāmanū wa lam yalbisūu ʾīmānahum-biẓulmin ʾulāaʾika lahumul-ʾamnu wa hum-muhtadūn. (82) Wa tilka ḥujjatunāa

Then, when the night overshadowed him with its darkness, he beheld a star; [and] he exclaimed, "This is my Sustainer!" – but when it went down, he said, "I love not the things that go down." ‹76›
Then, when he beheld the moon rising, he said, "This is my Sustainer!" – but when it went down, he said, "Indeed, if my Sustainer guide me not, I will most certainly become one of the people who go astray!" ‹77›
Then, when he beheld the sun rising, he said, "This is my Sustainer! This one is the greatest [of all]!" – but when it [too] went down, he exclaimed: "O my people! Behold, far be it from me to ascribe divinity, as you do, to aught beside God! ‹78› Behold, unto Him who brought into being the heavens and the earth have I turned my face, having turned away from all that is false; and I am not of those who ascribe divinity to aught beside Him." ‹79›
And his people argued with him. He said: "Do you argue with me about God, when it is He who has guided me? But I do not fear anything to which you ascribe divinity side by side with Him, [for no evil can befall me] unless my Sustainer So wills.[67] All things does my Sustainer embrace within His knowledge; will you not, then, keep this in mind? ‹80› And why should I fear anything that you worship side by side with Him, seeing that you are not afraid of ascribing divinity to other powers beside God without His ever having bestowed upon you from on high any warrant therefor? [Tell me,] then, which of the two parties has a better right to feel secure – if you happen to know [the answer]? ‹81› Those who have attained to faith, and who have not obscured their faith by wrong-doing – it is they who shall be secure, since it is they who have found the right path!" ‹82›
And this was Our argument[68] which We

67 Lit., "unless my Sustainer wills a thing".

68 The description of Abraham's reasoning as God's *own* argument implies that it was divinely inspired, and is therefore valid for the followers of the Qurʾān as well.

vouchsafed unto Abraham against his people: [for] We do raise by degrees whom We will.[69] Verily, thy Sustainer is wise, all-knowing. ‹83›
And We bestowed upon him Isaac and Jacob; and We guided each of them as We had guided Noah aforetime. And out of his offspring, [We bestowed prophethood upon] David, and Solomon, and Job, and Joseph, and Moses, and Aaron: for thus do We reward the doers of good; ‹84› and [upon] Zachariah, and John, and Jesus, and Elijah: every one of them was of the righteous; ‹85› and [upon] Ishmael, and Elisha, and Jonah, and Lot.[70] And every one of them did We favour above other people; ‹86› and [We exalted likewise] some of their forefathers and their offspring and their brethren: We elected them [all], and guided them onto a straight way. ‹87›
Such is God's guidance: He guides therewith whomever He wills of His servants. And had they ascribed divinity to aught beside Him – in vain, indeed, would have been all [the good] that they ever did: ‹88› [but] it was to them that We vouchsafed revelation, and sound judgment, and prophethood.
And now, although the unbelievers may choose to deny these truths,[71] [know that] We have entrusted them to people who will never refuse to acknowledge them ‹89› – to those whom God has guided. Follow, then, their guidance, [and] say: "No reward do I ask of you for this [truth]: behold, it is but an admonition unto all mankind!" ‹90›

ءَاتَيْنَٰهَآ إِبْرَٰهِيمَ عَلَىٰ قَوْمِهِۦ نَرْفَعُ دَرَجَٰتٍ مَّن نَّشَآءُ إِنَّ رَبَّكَ حَكِيمٌ
عَلِيمٌ ﴿83﴾ وَوَهَبْنَا لَهُۥٓ إِسْحَٰقَ وَيَعْقُوبَ كُلًّا هَدَيْنَا وَنُوحًا هَدَيْنَا مِن
قَبْلُ وَمِن ذُرِّيَّتِهِۦ دَاوُۥدَ وَسُلَيْمَٰنَ وَأَيُّوبَ وَيُوسُفَ وَمُوسَىٰ وَهَٰرُونَ
وَكَذَٰلِكَ نَجْزِى ٱلْمُحْسِنِينَ ﴿84﴾ وَزَكَرِيَّا وَيَحْيَىٰ وَعِيسَىٰ وَإِلْيَاسَ كُلٌّ مِّنَ
ٱلصَّٰلِحِينَ ﴿85﴾ وَإِسْمَٰعِيلَ وَٱلْيَسَعَ وَيُونُسَ وَلُوطًا وَكُلًّا فَضَّلْنَا عَلَى
ٱلْعَٰلَمِينَ ﴿86﴾ وَمِنْ ءَابَآئِهِمْ وَذُرِّيَّٰتِهِمْ وَإِخْوَٰنِهِمْ وَٱجْتَبَيْنَٰهُمْ وَهَدَيْنَٰهُمْ
إِلَىٰ صِرَٰطٍ مُّسْتَقِيمٍ ﴿87﴾ ذَٰلِكَ هُدَى ٱللَّهِ يَهْدِى بِهِۦ مَن يَشَآءُ مِنْ عِبَادِهِۦ
وَلَوْ أَشْرَكُوا۟ لَحَبِطَ عَنْهُم مَّا كَانُوا۟ يَعْمَلُونَ ﴿88﴾ أُو۟لَٰٓئِكَ ٱلَّذِينَ ءَاتَيْنَٰهُمُ
ٱلْكِتَٰبَ وَٱلْحُكْمَ وَٱلنُّبُوَّةَ فَإِن يَكْفُرْ بِهَا هَٰٓؤُلَآءِ فَقَدْ وَكَّلْنَا بِهَا قَوْمًا
لَّيْسُوا۟ بِهَا بِكَٰفِرِينَ ﴿89﴾ أُو۟لَٰٓئِكَ ٱلَّذِينَ هَدَى ٱللَّهُ فَبِهُدَىٰهُمُ ٱقْتَدِهْ قُل
لَّآ أَسْـَٔلُكُمْ عَلَيْهِ أَجْرًا إِنْ هُوَ إِلَّا ذِكْرَىٰ لِلْعَٰلَمِينَ ﴿90﴾

ʾātaynāhāa ʾIbrāhīma ᶜalā qawmih. Narfaᶜu darajātim-mañ-nashāaʾ. ʾInna Rabbaka Ḥakīmun ᶜAlīm. (83) Wa wahabnā lahūu ʾIsḥāqa wa Yaᶜqūb. Kullan hadaynā; wa Nūḥan hadaynā miñ-qablu wa miñ-dhurriyyatihī Dāwūda wa Sulaymāna wa ʾAyyūba wa Yūsufa wa Mūsā wa Hārūn. Wa kadhālika najzil-muḥsinīn. (84) Wa Zakariyyā wa Yaḥyā wa ᶜĪsā wa ʾIlyāsa kullum-minaṣ-ṣāliḥīn. (85) Wa ʾIsmāᶜīla wal-Yasaᶜa wa Yūnusa wa Lūṭā. Wa kullañ-faḍḍalnā ᶜalal-ᶜālamīn. (86) Wa min ʾābāaʾihim wa dhurriyyātihim wa ʾikhwānihim; waj-tabaynāhum wa hadaynāhum ʾilā ṣirāṭim-mustaqīm. (87) Dhālika hudal-lāhi yahdī bihī mañy-yashāaʾu min ᶜibādih. Wa law ʾashrakū laḥabiṭa ᶜanhum-mā kānū yaᶜmalūn. (88) ʾUlāaʾikal-ladhīna ʾātaynāhumul-Kitāba wal-ḥukma wan-Nubuwwah. Faʾiñy-yakfur bihā hāaʾulāaʾi faqad wakkalnā bihā qawmal-laysū bihā bikāfirīn. (89) ʾUlāaʾikal-ladhīna hadal-lāhu fabihudāhumuq-tadih. Qul-lāa ʾasʾalukum ᶜalayhi ajrā. ʾIn huwa ʾillā dhikrā lilᶜālamīn. (90)

69 This is evidently an allusion to Abraham's gradual grasp of the truth, symbolized by his intuitive progress from an adoration of celestial bodies – stars, moon and sun – to a full realization of God's transcendental, all-embracing existence. Alternatively, the expression "by degrees" may be taken to mean "by *many* degrees", signifying the great spiritual dignity to which this forerunner of a long line of prophets was ultimately raised (see 4 : 125).

70 Although Lot was not a "descendant" of Abraham since he was his brother's son, his name is included here for two reasons: firstly, because he followed Abraham from his earliest youth as a son follows his father, and, secondly, because in ancient Arabian usage a paternal uncle is often described as "father" and, conversely, a nephew as "son". – For the Hebrew prophets Elijah (Ilyās) and Elisha (Al-Yasaᶜ), see note 48 on 37 : 123.

71 Lit., "if these deny them" – i.e., the manifestations of God's oneness and of the revelation of His will through the prophets.

For, no true understanding of God have they when they say, "Never has God revealed anything unto man." Say: "Who has bestowed from on high the divine writ which Moses brought unto men as a light and a guidance, [and] which you treat as[72] [mere] leaves of paper, making a show of them the while you conceal [so] much – although you have been taught [by it] what neither you nor your forefathers had ever known?"[73] Say: "God [has revealed that divine writ]!" – and then leave them to play at their vain talk. ‹91›

And this, too, is a divine writ which We have bestowed from on high – blessed, confirming the truth of whatever there still remains [of earlier revelations][74] – and [this] in order that thou mayest warn the foremost of all cities and all who dwell around it.[75] And those who believe in the life to come do believe in this [warning]; and it is they who are ever-mindful of their prayers. ‹92›

And who could be more wicked than he who invents a lie about God,[76] or says, "This has been revealed unto me," the while nothing has been revealed to him? – or he who says, "I, too, can bestow from on high the like of what God has bestowed"?[77]

If thou couldst but see [how it will be] when these evildoers find themselves in the agonies of death, and the angels stretch forth their hands [and call]: "Give up your souls! Today you shall be requited with the suffering of humiliation for having

وَمَا قَدَرُواْ ٱللَّهَ حَقَّ قَدْرِهِۦٓ إِذْ قَالُواْ مَآ أَنزَلَ ٱللَّهُ عَلَىٰ بَشَرٍ مِّن شَىْءٍ قُلْ
مَنْ أَنزَلَ ٱلْكِتَـٰبَ ٱلَّذِى جَآءَ بِهِۦ مُوسَىٰ نُورًا وَهُدًى لِّلنَّاسِ تَجْعَلُونَهُۥ
قَرَاطِيسَ تُبْدُونَهَا وَتُخْفُونَ كَثِيرًا وَعُلِّمْتُم مَّا لَمْ تَعْلَمُوٓاْ أَنتُمْ وَلَآ ءَابَآؤُكُمْ
قُلِ ٱللَّهُ ثُمَّ ذَرْهُمْ فِى خَوْضِهِمْ يَلْعَبُونَ ﴿٩١﴾ وَهَـٰذَا كِتَـٰبٌ أَنزَلْنَـٰهُ مُبَارَكٌ
مُّصَدِّقُ ٱلَّذِى بَيْنَ يَدَيْهِ وَلِتُنذِرَ أُمَّ ٱلْقُرَىٰ وَمَنْ حَوْلَهَا وَٱلَّذِينَ يُؤْمِنُونَ
بِٱلْـَٔاخِرَةِ يُؤْمِنُونَ بِهِۦ وَهُمْ عَلَىٰ صَلَاتِهِمْ يُحَافِظُونَ ﴿٩٢﴾ وَمَنْ أَظْلَمُ مِمَّنِ
ٱفْتَرَىٰ عَلَى ٱللَّهِ كَذِبًا أَوْ قَالَ أُوحِىَ إِلَىَّ وَلَمْ يُوحَ إِلَيْهِ شَىْءٌ وَمَن قَالَ سَأُنزِلُ
مِثْلَ مَآ أَنزَلَ ٱللَّهُ وَلَوْ تَرَىٰٓ إِذِ ٱلظَّـٰلِمُونَ فِى غَمَرَٰتِ ٱلْمَوْتِ وَٱلْمَلَـٰٓئِكَةُ
بَاسِطُوٓاْ أَيْدِيهِمْ أَخْرِجُوٓاْ أَنفُسَكُمُ ٱلْيَوْمَ تُجْزَوْنَ عَذَابَ ٱلْهُونِ بِمَا

Wa mā qadarul-lāha ḥaqqa qadrihī ʾidh qālū māa añzalal-lāhu ʿalā basharim-miñ-shayʾ. Qul man ʾañzalal-Kitābal-ladhī jāaʾa bihī Mūsā nūrañw-wa hudal-linnāsi tajʿalūnahū qarāṭīsa tubdūnahā wa tukhfūna kathīrā. Wa ʿullimtum-mā lam taʿlamū ʾañtum wa lāa ʾābāaʾukum. Qulil-lāhu thumma dharhum fī khawḍihim yalʿabūn. (91) Wa hādhā Kitābun ʾañzalnāhu mubārakum-muṣaddiqul-ladhī bayna yadayhi wa lituñdhira ʾUmmal-qurā wa man ḥawlahā. Wal-ladhīna yuʾminūna bilʾĀkhirati yuʾminūna bihī wa hum ʿalā Ṣalātihim yuḥāfiẓūn. (92) Wa man ʾaẓlamu mimmanif-tarā ʿalal-lāhi kadhiban ʾaw qāla ʾūḥiya ʾilayya wa lam yūḥa ʾilayhi shayʾuñw-wa mañ-qāla saʾuñzilu mithla māa ʾañzalal-lāh. Wa law tarāa ʾidhiẓ-ẓālimūna fī ghamarātil-mawti wal-Malāaʾikatu bāsiṭūu ʾaydīhim ʾakhrijūu ʾañfusakum. ʾAlyawma tujzawna ʿadhābal-hūni bimā

72 Lit., "which you make into": but it should be remembered that the verb *jaʿalahu* has also the abstract meaning of "he considered it to be" or "regarded it as" or "treated it as" (Jawharī, Rāghib, *et al.*): a significance often met with in the Qurʾān.

73 This passage is obviously addressed to those followers of the Bible who pay lip-service to its sacred character as a revealed scripture but, in reality, treat it as "mere leaves of paper" – that is, as something that is of little consequence to their own conduct: for, although they pretend to admire the moral truths which it contains, they conceal from themselves the fact that their own lives have remained empty of those truths.

74 See *sūrah* 3, note 3.

75 "The foremost of all cities" (lit., "the mother of all towns") is an epithet applied in the Qurʾān to Mecca because it is the place where the first temple ever dedicated to the One God was built (cf. 3 : 96) and subsequently became the *qiblah* (direction of prayer) of all believers. The expression "all who dwell around it" denotes all mankind (Ṭabarī, on the authority of Ibn ʿAbbās; Rāzī).

76 In this context, the "lie" would seem to refer to the denial, spoken of in verse 91, of the fact of divine revelation as such.

77 Implying, in a sarcastic manner, that the purported revelation has in reality been composed by a human being and that, therefore, the like of it can be produced by other men.

attributed to God something that is not true, and for having persistently scorned His messages in your arrogance!" ‹93›

[And God shall say:] "And now, indeed, you have come unto Us in a lonely state, even as We created you in the first instance; and you have left behind you all that We bestowed on you [in your lifetime]. And We do not see with you those intercessors of yours whom you supposed to have a share in God's divinity with regard to yourselves![78] Indeed, all the bonds between you [and your earthly life] are now severed, and all your former fancies have forsaken you!"[79] ‹94›

VERILY, God is the One who cleaves the grain and the fruit-kernel asunder, bringing forth the living out of that which is dead, and He is the One who brings forth the dead out of that which is alive. This, then, is God: and yet, how perverted are your minds![80] ‹95›

[He is] the One who causes the dawn to break; and He has made the night to be [a source of] stillness, and the sun and the moon to run their appointed courses:[81] [all] this is laid down by the will of the Almighty, the All-Knowing. ‹96›

And He it is who has set up for you the stars so that you might be guided by them in the midst of the deep darkness of land and sea: clearly, indeed, have We spelled out these messages unto people of [innate] knowledge! ‹97›

And He it is who has brought you [all] into being out of one living entity,[82] and [has appointed for each of you] a time-limit [on earth] and a resting-place [after death]:[83] clearly, indeed, have We spelled out these messages unto people who can grasp the truth! ‹98›

كُنتُمْ تَقُولُونَ عَلَى ٱللَّهِ غَيْرَ ٱلْحَقِّ وَكُنتُمْ عَنْ ءَايَٰتِهِۦ تَسْتَكْبِرُونَ ﴿٩٣﴾
وَلَقَدْ جِئْتُمُونَا فُرَٰدَىٰ كَمَا خَلَقْنَٰكُمْ أَوَّلَ مَرَّةٍ وَتَرَكْتُم مَّا خَوَّلْنَٰكُمْ
وَرَآءَ ظُهُورِكُمْ وَمَا نَرَىٰ مَعَكُمْ شُفَعَآءَكُمُ ٱلَّذِينَ زَعَمْتُمْ أَنَّهُمْ فِيكُمْ
شُرَكَٰٓؤُا۟ لَقَد تَّقَطَّعَ بَيْنَكُمْ وَضَلَّ عَنكُم مَّا كُنتُمْ تَزْعُمُونَ ﴿٩٤﴾ ۞ إِنَّ
ٱللَّهَ فَالِقُ ٱلْحَبِّ وَٱلنَّوَىٰ يُخْرِجُ ٱلْحَىَّ مِنَ ٱلْمَيِّتِ وَمُخْرِجُ ٱلْمَيِّتِ مِنَ
ٱلْحَىِّ ذَٰلِكُمُ ٱللَّهُ فَأَنَّىٰ تُؤْفَكُونَ ﴿٩٥﴾ فَالِقُ ٱلْإِصْبَاحِ وَجَعَلَ ٱلَّيْلَ
سَكَنًا وَٱلشَّمْسَ وَٱلْقَمَرَ حُسْبَانًا ذَٰلِكَ تَقْدِيرُ ٱلْعَزِيزِ ٱلْعَلِيمِ ﴿٩٦﴾ وَهُوَ
ٱلَّذِى جَعَلَ لَكُمُ ٱلنُّجُومَ لِتَهْتَدُوا۟ بِهَا فِى ظُلُمَٰتِ ٱلْبَرِّ وَٱلْبَحْرِ قَدْ
فَصَّلْنَا ٱلْءَايَٰتِ لِقَوْمٍ يَعْلَمُونَ ﴿٩٧﴾ وَهُوَ ٱلَّذِىٓ أَنشَأَكُم مِّن نَّفْسٍ
وَٰحِدَةٍ فَمُسْتَقَرٌّ وَمُسْتَوْدَعٌ قَدْ فَصَّلْنَا ٱلْءَايَٰتِ لِقَوْمٍ يَفْقَهُونَ ﴿٩٨﴾

ثلاثة ارباع الحزب

kuñtum taqūlūna ʿalal-lāhi ghayral-ḥaqqi wa kuñtum ʿan ʾĀyātihī tastakbirūn. (93) Wa laqad jiʾtumūnā furādā kamā khalaqnākum ʾawwala marratiñw-wa taraktum-mā khawwalnākum warāaʾa ẓuhūrikum; wa mā narā maʿakum shufaʿāaʾakumul-ladhīna zaʿamtum ʾannahum fīkum shurakāaʾ. Laqat-taqaṭṭaʿa baynakum wa ḍalla ʿañkum-mā kuñtum tazʿumūn. (94) ۞ ʾInnal-lāha fāliqul-ḥabbi wan-nawā. Yukhrijul-ḥayya minal-mayyiti wa mukhrijul-mayyiti minal-ḥayy. Dhālikumul-lāhu faʾannā tuʾfakūn. (95) Fāliqul-ʾiṣbāḥi wa jaʿalal-layla sakanañw-wash-shamsa wal-qamara ḥusbānā. Dhālika taqdīrul-ʿAzīzil-ʿAlīm. (96) Wa Huwal-ladhī jaʿala lakumun-nujūma litahtadū bihā fī ẓulumātil-barri wal-baḥr. Qad faṣṣalnal-ʾĀyāti liqawmiñy-yaʿlamūn. (97) Wa Huwal-ladhīi ʾañshaʾakum-miñ-nafsiñw-wāḥidatiñ-famustaqarruñw-wa mustawdaʿ. Qad faṣṣalnal-ʾĀyāti liqawmiñy-yafqahūn. (98)

78 Lit., "whom you supposed to be [God's] partners with regard to you" – i.e., being able, in result of their alleged "share in God's divinity", to protect or help you. See note 15 on verse 22 of this *sūrah*.

79 Lit., "all that you were wont to assert [or "to suppose"] has gone away from you" – i.e., all the imaginary intercessors or mediators between man and God.

80 See *sūrah* 5, note 90.

81 Lit., "to be [according to] a definite reckoning".

82 See *sūrah* 4, note 1.

83 The commentators differ widely as to the meaning of the terms *mustaqarr* and *mustawdaʿ* in this context.

And He it is who has caused waters to come down from the sky; and by this means have We brought forth all living growth, and out of this have We brought forth verdure.[84] Out of this do We bring forth close-growing grain; and out of the spathe of the palm tree, dates in thick clusters; and gardens of vines, and the olive tree, and the pomegranate: [all] so alike, and yet so different![85] Behold their fruit when it comes to fruition and ripens! Verily, in all this there are messages indeed for people who will believe! ‹99›

And yet, some [people] have come to attribute to all manner of invisible beings[86] a place side by side with God – although it is He who has created them [all]; and in their ignorance they have invented for Him sons and daughters![87]

Limitless is He in His glory, and sublimely exalted above anything that men may devise by way of definition:[88] ‹100› the Originator of the heavens and the earth! How could it be that He should have a child without there ever having been a mate for Him – since it is He who has created everything, and He alone knows everything? ‹101›

وَهُوَ ٱلَّذِىٓ أَنزَلَ مِنَ ٱلسَّمَآءِ مَآءً فَأَخْرَجْنَا بِهِۦ نَبَاتَ كُلِّ شَىْءٍ فَأَخْرَجْنَا
مِنْهُ خَضِرًا نُّخْرِجُ مِنْهُ حَبًّا مُّتَرَاكِبًا وَمِنَ ٱلنَّخْلِ مِن طَلْعِهَا قِنْوَانٌ دَانِيَةٌ
وَجَنَّٰتٍ مِّنْ أَعْنَابٍ وَٱلزَّيْتُونَ وَٱلرُّمَّانَ مُشْتَبِهًا وَغَيْرَ مُتَشَٰبِهٍ ۗ ٱنظُرُوٓا۟
إِلَىٰ ثَمَرِهِۦٓ إِذَآ أَثْمَرَ وَيَنْعِهِۦٓ ۚ إِنَّ فِى ذَٰلِكُمْ لَءَايَٰتٍ لِّقَوْمٍ يُؤْمِنُونَ ﴿٩٩﴾
وَجَعَلُوا۟ لِلَّهِ شُرَكَآءَ ٱلْجِنَّ وَخَلَقَهُمْ ۖ وَخَرَقُوا۟ لَهُۥ بَنِينَ وَبَنَٰتٍۭ بِغَيْرِ عِلْمٍ ۚ
سُبْحَٰنَهُۥ وَتَعَٰلَىٰ عَمَّا يَصِفُونَ ﴿١٠٠﴾ بَدِيعُ ٱلسَّمَٰوَٰتِ وَٱلْأَرْضِ ۖ أَنَّىٰ
يَكُونُ لَهُۥ وَلَدٌ وَلَمْ تَكُن لَّهُۥ صَٰحِبَةٌ ۖ وَخَلَقَ كُلَّ شَىْءٍ ۖ وَهُوَ بِكُلِّ شَىْءٍ
عَلِيمٌ ﴿١٠١﴾

Wa Huwal-ladhīi ʾañzala minas-samāaʾi māaʾañ-faʾakhrajnā bihī nabāta kulli shayʾiñ-faʾakhrajnā minhu khaḍirañ-nukhriju minhu ḥabbam-mutarākibañw-wa minan-nakhli miñ-ṭalʿihā qinwānuñ-dāniyatuñw-wa jannātim-min ʾaʿnābiñw-waz-zaytūna war-rummāna mushtabihañw-wa ghayra mutashābih. ʾUñẓurūu ʾilā thamarihīi ʾidhāa ʾathmara wa yanʿih. ʾInna fī dhālikum laʾĀyātil-liqawmiñy-yuʾminūn. (99) Wa jaʿalū lillāhi shurakāaʾal-Jinna wa khalaqahum wa kharaqū lahū banīna wa banātim-bighayri ʿilm. Subḥānahū wa taʿālā ʿammā yaṣifūn. (100) Badīʿus-samāwāti wal-ʾarḍ. ʾAnnā yakūnu lahū waladuñw-wa lam takul-lahū ṣāḥibah. Wa khalaqa kulla shayʾiñw-wa Huwa bikulli shayʾiñ-ʿAlīm. (101)

However, taking into account the primary meaning of *mustaqarr* as "the limit of a course" – i.e., the point at which a thing reaches its fulfilment or end – and of *mustawdaʿ* as "a place of consignment" or "repository", we arrive at the rendering adopted by me above. This rendering finds, moreover, strong support in 11 : 6, where God is spoken of as providing sustenance for every living being and knowing "its time-limit [on earth] and its resting-place [after death]" (*mustaqarrahā wa-mustawdaʿahā*), as well as in verse 67 of the present *sūrah*, where *mustaqarr* is used in the sense of "a term set for the fulfilment [of God's tiding]".

84 In contrast with its sequence, which is governed by the present tense, the whole of the above sentence is expressed in the past tense – thus indicating, obliquely, the original, basic aspect of God's creating life "out of water" (cf. 21 : 30 and the corresponding note 39).

85 I.e., all so alike in the basic principles of their life and growth, and yet so different in physiology, appearance and taste.

86 The plural noun *jinn* (popularly, but incorrectly, taken to denote "genii" or "demons") is derived from the verb *janna*, "he was [or "became"] concealed" or "veiled from sight"; thus, the veiling darkness of night is called *jinn* (Jawharī). According to Arab philologists, the term *jinn* signifies, primarily, "beings that are concealed from [man's] senses" (*Qāmūs, Lisān al-ʿArab*, Rāghib), and is thus applicable to all kinds of invisible beings or forces. For a further discussion of this term and of its wider implications, see Appendix III.

87 Lit., "they have invented for Him [or "falsely attributed to Him"] sons and daughters without [having any] knowledge": a reference to the beliefs of the pre-Islamic Arabs who regarded the angels as "God's daughters" (a designation which they also applied to certain of their goddesses), as well as to the Christian view of Jesus as "the son of God". See also 19 : 92 and the corresponding note 77.

88 I.e., utterly remote is He from all imperfection and from the incompleteness which is implied in the concept of having progeny. The very concept of "definition" implies the possibility of a comparison or correlation of an object with other objects; God, however, is unique, there being "nothing like unto Him" (42 : 11) and, therefore, "nothing that could be compared with Him" (112 : 4) – with the result that any attempt at defining Him or His "attributes" is a

ذَٰلِكُمُ ٱللَّهُ رَبُّكُمْ لَآ إِلَٰهَ إِلَّا هُوَ خَٰلِقُ كُلِّ شَيْءٍ فَٱعْبُدُوهُ وَهُوَ عَلَىٰ
كُلِّ شَيْءٍ وَكِيلٌ ﴿102﴾ لَّا تُدْرِكُهُ ٱلْأَبْصَٰرُ وَهُوَ يُدْرِكُ ٱلْأَبْصَٰرَ وَهُوَ
ٱللَّطِيفُ ٱلْخَبِيرُ ﴿103﴾ قَدْ جَآءَكُم بَصَآئِرُ مِن رَّبِّكُمْ فَمَنْ أَبْصَرَ
فَلِنَفْسِهِۦ وَمَنْ عَمِىَ فَعَلَيْهَا وَمَآ أَنَا۠ عَلَيْكُم بِحَفِيظٍ ﴿104﴾ وَكَذَٰلِكَ نُصَرِّفُ
ٱلْءَايَٰتِ وَلِيَقُولُوا۟ دَرَسْتَ وَلِنُبَيِّنَهُۥ لِقَوْمٍ يَعْلَمُونَ ﴿105﴾ ٱتَّبِعْ مَآ أُوحِىَ
إِلَيْكَ مِن رَّبِّكَ لَآ إِلَٰهَ إِلَّا هُوَ وَأَعْرِضْ عَنِ ٱلْمُشْرِكِينَ ﴿106﴾ وَلَوْ شَآءَ
ٱللَّهُ مَآ أَشْرَكُوا۟ وَمَا جَعَلْنَٰكَ عَلَيْهِمْ حَفِيظًا وَمَآ أَنتَ عَلَيْهِم بِوَكِيلٍ ﴿107﴾
وَلَا تَسُبُّوا۟ ٱلَّذِينَ يَدْعُونَ مِن دُونِ ٱللَّهِ فَيَسُبُّوا۟ ٱللَّهَ عَدْوًۢا بِغَيْرِ عِلْمٍ

Dhālikumul-lāhu Rabbukum; lāa ʾilāha ʾillā Huwa Khāliqu kulli shayʾiñ-faʿbudūh. Wa Huwa ʿalā kulli shayʾiñw-Wakīl. (102) Lā tudrikuhul-ʾabṣāru wa Huwa yudrikul-ʾabṣār. Wa Huwal-Laṭīful-Khabīr. (103) Qad jāaʾakum-baṣāaʾiru mir-Rabbikum; faman ʾabṣara falinafsihi wa man ʿamiya faʿalayhā. Wa māa ʾana ʿalaykum-biḥafīẓ. (104) Wa kadhālika nuṣarriful-ʾĀyāti wa liyaqūlū darasta wa linubayyinahū liqawmiñy-yaʿlamūn. (105) ʾIttabiʿ māa ʾūḥiya ʾilayka mir-Rabbik. Lāa ʾilāha ʾillā Huwa wa ʾaʿriḍ ʿanil-mushrikīn. (106) Wa law shāaʾal-lāhu māa ʾashrakū. Wa mā jaʿalnāka ʿalayhim ḥafīẓā, wa māa ʾañta ʿalayhim-biwakīl. (107) Wa lā tasubbul-ladhīna yadʿūna miñ-dūnil-lāhi faya-subbul-lāha ʿadwam-bighayri ʿilm.

Such is God, your Sustainer: there is no deity save Him, the Creator of everything: worship, then, Him alone – for it is He who has everything in His care. ‹102› No human vision can encompass Him, whereas He encompasses all human vision: for He alone is unfathomable, all-aware.[89] ‹103›

Means of insight have now come unto you from your Sustainer [through this divine writ]. Whoever, therefore, chooses to see, does so for his own good; and whoever chooses to remain blind, does so to his own hurt. And [say unto the blind of heart]: "I am not your keeper." ‹104›

And thus do We give many facets to Our messages. And to the end that they might say, "Thou hast taken [all this] well to heart,"[90] and that We might make it clear unto people of [innate] knowledge, ‹105› follow thou what has been revealed unto thee by thy Sustainer – save whom there is no deity – and turn thy back upon all who ascribe divinity to aught beside Him. ‹106›

Yet if God had so willed, they would not have ascribed divinity to aught beside Him;[91] hence, We have not made thee their keeper, and neither art thou responsible for their conduct. ‹107›

But do not revile those [beings] whom they invoke instead of God,[92] lest they revile God out of spite, and in ignorance:

---

logical impossibility and, from the ethical point of view, a sin. The fact that He is undefinable makes it clear that the "attributes" (*ṣifāt*) of God mentioned in the Qurʾān do not circumscribe His reality but, rather, the perceptible *effect of His activity* on and within the universe created by Him.

89 The term *laṭīf* denotes something that is extremely subtle in quality, and therefore intangible and unfathomable. Whenever this term occurs in the Qurʾān with reference to God in conjunction with the adjective *khabīr* ("all-aware"), it is invariably used to express the idea of His inaccessibility to human perception, imagination or comprehension, as contrasted with His Own all-awareness (see, apart from the above verse, also 22 : 63, 31 : 16, 33 : 34 and 67 : 14). In the two instances where the combination of *laṭīf* and *khabīr* carries the definite article *al* (6 : 103 and 67 : 14), the expression *huwa 'l-laṭīf* has the meaning of "He *alone* is unfathomable" – implying that this quality of His is unique and absolute.

90 Lit., "thou hast learned [it well]" – i.e., God's message.

91 I.e., no mortal has it in his power to cause another person to believe unless God graces that person with His guidance.

92 This prohibition of reviling anything that other people hold sacred – even in contravention of the principle of God's oneness – is expressed in the plural and is, therefore, addressed to all believers. Thus, while Muslims are expected to argue against the false beliefs of others, they are not allowed to abuse the objects of those beliefs and to hurt thereby the feelings of their erring fellow-men.

حزب 15
جزء 8

for, goodly indeed have We made their own doings appear unto every community.[93] In time, [however,] unto their Sustainer they must return: and then He will make them [truly] understand all that they were doing. ‹108›
Now they swear by God with their most solemn oaths that if a miracle were shown to them, they would indeed believe in this [divine writ]. Say: "Miracles are in the power of God alone."[94]
And for all you know, even if one should be shown to them, they would not believe ‹109› so long as We keep their hearts and their eyes turned [away from the truth],[95] even as they did not believe in it in the first instance: and [so] We shall leave them in their overweening arrogance, blindly stumbling to and fro. ‹110›
And even if We were to send down angels unto them, and if the dead were to speak unto them,[96] and [even if] We were to assemble before them, face to face, all the things [that can prove the truth], they would still not believe unless God so willed.[97] But [of this] most of them are entirely unaware. ‹111›

كَذَٰلِكَ زَيَّنَّا لِكُلِّ أُمَّةٍ عَمَلَهُمْ ثُمَّ إِلَىٰ رَبِّهِم مَّرْجِعُهُمْ فَيُنَبِّئُهُم بِمَا كَانُوا
يَعْمَلُونَ ﴿١٠٨﴾ وَأَقْسَمُوا بِاللَّهِ جَهْدَ أَيْمَانِهِمْ لَئِن جَاءَتْهُمْ آيَةٌ لَّيُؤْمِنُنَّ
بِهَا ۚ قُلْ إِنَّمَا الْآيَاتُ عِندَ اللَّهِ ۖ وَمَا يُشْعِرُكُمْ أَنَّهَا إِذَا جَاءَتْ لَا
يُؤْمِنُونَ ﴿١٠٩﴾ وَنُقَلِّبُ أَفْئِدَتَهُمْ وَأَبْصَارَهُمْ كَمَا لَمْ يُؤْمِنُوا بِهِ أَوَّلَ مَرَّةٍ
وَنَذَرُهُمْ فِي طُغْيَانِهِمْ يَعْمَهُونَ ﴿١١٠﴾ ۞ وَلَوْ أَنَّنَا نَزَّلْنَا إِلَيْهِمُ الْمَلَائِكَةَ
وَكَلَّمَهُمُ الْمَوْتَىٰ وَحَشَرْنَا عَلَيْهِمْ كُلَّ شَيْءٍ قُبُلًا مَّا كَانُوا لِيُؤْمِنُوا إِلَّا
أَن يَشَاءَ اللَّهُ وَلَٰكِنَّ أَكْثَرَهُمْ يَجْهَلُونَ ﴿١١١﴾

Kadhālika zayyannā likulli ʾummatin ʿamalahum thumma ʾilā Rabbihim-marjiʿuhum fayunabbiʾuhum-bimā kānū yaʿmalūn. (108) Wa ʾaqsamū billāhi jahda ʾaymānihim laʾiñ-jāaʾat-hum ʾĀyatul-layuʾminunna bihā. Qul ʾinnamal-Āyātu ʿiñdal-lāhi wa mā yushʿirukum ʾannahāa ʾidhā jāaʾat lā yuʾminūn. (109) Wa nuqallibu ʾafʾidatahum wa ʾabṣārahum kamā lam yuʾminū bihīi ʾawwala marratiñw-wa nadharuhum fī ṭughyānihim yaʿmahūn. (110) ۞ Wa law ʾannanā nazzalnāa ʾilayhimul-Malāaʾikata wa kallamahumul-mawtā wa ḥasharnā ʿalayhim kulla shayʾiñ-qubulam-mā kānū liyuʾminūu ʾillāa ʾañy-yashāaʾal-lāhu wa lākinna ʾaktharahum yajhalūn. (111)

93 Lit., "thus goodly have We made . . .", etc., implying that it is in the nature of man to regard the beliefs which have been implanted in him from childhood, and which he now shares with his social environment, as the only true and possible ones – with the result that a polemic against those beliefs often tends to provoke a hostile psychological reaction.

94 Lit., "Miracles are only with God." It is to be noted that the Qurʾanic term *āyah* denotes not only a "miracle" (in the sense of a happening that goes beyond the usual – that is, commonly observable – course of nature), but also a "sign" or "message": and the last-mentioned significance is the one which is by far the most frequently met with in the Qurʾān. Thus, what is commonly described as a "miracle" constitutes, in fact, an *unusual message* from God, indicating – sometimes in a symbolic manner – a spiritual truth which would otherwise have remained hidden from man's intellect. But even such extraordinary, "miraculous" messages cannot be regarded as "supernatural": for the so-called "laws of nature" are only a perceptible manifestation of "God's way" (*sunnat Allāh*) in respect of His creation – and, consequently, everything that exists and happens, or could conceivably exist or happen, is "natural" in the innermost sense of this word, irrespective of whether it conforms to the ordinary course of events or goes beyond it. Now since the extraordinary messages referred to manifest themselves, as a rule, through the instrumentality of those specially gifted and divinely elected personalities known as "prophets", these are sometimes spoken of as "performing miracles" – a misconception which the Qurʾān removes by the words, "Miracles are in the power of God alone". (See also 17 : 59 and the corresponding note 71.)

95 I.e., so long as they remain blind to the truth in consequence of their unwillingness to acknowledge it – and this in accordance with the law of cause and effect which God has imposed on His creation (see *sūrah* 2, note 7).

96 Sc., of the fact that there is life after death.

97 See note 95 above.

AND THUS it is that against every prophet We have set up as enemies the evil forces from among humans as well as from among invisible beings that whisper unto one another glittering half-truths meant to delude the mind.[98] But they could not do this unless thy Sustainer had so willed: stand, therefore, aloof from them and from all their false imagery! ‹112›
Yet, to the end that the hearts of those who do not believe in the life to come might incline towards Him, and that in Him they might find contentment, and that they might earn whatever they can earn [of merit] ‹113› – [say thou:] "Am I, then, to look unto anyone but God for judgment[99] [as to what is right and wrong], when it is He who has bestowed upon you from on high this divine writ, clearly spelling out the truth?"[100]
And those unto whom We have vouchsafed revelation aforetime know that this one, too, has been bestowed from on high, setting forth the truth, step by step, by thy Sustainer.[101] Be not, then, among the doubters ‹114› – for, truly and justly has thy Sustainer's promise been fulfilled.[102] There is no power that could alter [the fulfilment of] His promises: and He alone is all-hearing, all-knowing. ‹115›

وَكَذَٰلِكَ جَعَلْنَا لِكُلِّ نَبِيٍّ عَدُوًّا شَيَٰطِينَ ٱلْإِنسِ وَٱلْجِنِّ يُوحِي بَعْضُهُمْ
إِلَىٰ بَعْضٍ زُخْرُفَ ٱلْقَوْلِ غُرُورًا وَلَوْ شَآءَ رَبُّكَ مَا فَعَلُوهُ فَذَرْهُمْ وَمَا
يَفْتَرُونَ ﴿١١٢﴾ وَلِتَصْغَىٰٓ إِلَيْهِ أَفْـِٔدَةُ ٱلَّذِينَ لَا يُؤْمِنُونَ بِٱلْـَٔاخِرَةِ وَلِيَرْضَوْهُ
وَلِيَقْتَرِفُوا۟ مَا هُم مُّقْتَرِفُونَ ﴿١١٣﴾ أَفَغَيْرَ ٱللَّهِ أَبْتَغِي حَكَمًا وَهُوَ ٱلَّذِيٓ أَنزَلَ
إِلَيْكُمُ ٱلْكِتَٰبَ مُفَصَّلًا وَٱلَّذِينَ ءَاتَيْنَٰهُمُ ٱلْكِتَٰبَ يَعْلَمُونَ أَنَّهُۥ
مُنَزَّلٌ مِّن رَّبِّكَ بِٱلْحَقِّ فَلَا تَكُونَنَّ مِنَ ٱلْمُمْتَرِينَ ﴿١١٤﴾ وَتَمَّتْ كَلِمَتُ
رَبِّكَ صِدْقًا وَعَدْلًا لَّا مُبَدِّلَ لِكَلِمَٰتِهِۦ وَهُوَ ٱلسَّمِيعُ ٱلْعَلِيمُ ﴿١١٥﴾

Wa kadhālika jaʿalnā likulli Nabiyyin ʿaduwwañ-Shayāṭīnal-ʾInsi wal-Jinni yūḥī baʿḍuhum ʾilā baʿḍiñ-zukhrufal-qawli ghurūrā. Wa law shāaʾa Rabbuka mā faʿlūhu fadharhum wa mā yaftarūn. ‹112› Wa litaṣghāa ʾilayhi ʾafʾidatul-ladhīna lā yuʾminūna bil-ʾĀkhirati wa liyarḍawhu wa liyaqtarifū mā hum-muqtarifūn. ‹113› ʾAfaghayral-lāhi ʾabtaghī ḥakamañw-wa Huwal-ladhīi ʾañzala ʾilaykumul-Kitāba mufaṣ-ṣalā. Wal-ladhīna ʾātaynāhumul-Kitāba yaʿlamūna ʾannahū munazzalum-mir Rabbika bilḥaqqi falā takūnanna minal-mumtarīn. ‹114› Wa tammat Kalimatu Rabbika ṣidqañw-wa ʿadlā. Lā mubaddila liKalimātihī wa Huwas-Samīʿul-ʿAlīm. ‹115›

98 Lit., "embellished speech" or "varnished falsehood" (Lane III, 1223) "by way of delusion" – i.e., half-truths which entice man by their deceptive attractiveness and cause him to overlook all real spiritual values (see also 25 : 30-31). – Regarding my rendering of *jinn* as "invisible beings", see note 86 above and Appendix III. The term *shayāṭīn* (lit., "satans"), on the other hand, is often used in the Qurʾān in the sense of evil forces inherent in man as well as in the spiritual world (cf. 2 : 14, and the corresponding note). According to several well-authenticated Traditions, quoted by Ṭabarī, the Prophet was asked, "Are there satans from among men?" – and he replied, "Yes, and they are more evil than the satans from among the invisible beings (*al-jinn*)." Thus, the meaning of the above verse is that every prophet has had to contend against the spiritual – and often physical – enmity of the evil ones who, for whatever reason, refuse to listen to the voice of truth and try to lead others astray.

99 Lit., "to seek a judge other than God".

100 The expression *mufaṣṣalan* could also be rendered as "in a manner that brings out the distinction (*faṣl*) between truth and falsehood" (Zamakhsharī). The use of the plural "you" indicates that the divine writ is addressed to all who may come to know it.

101 See 2 : 146, and the corresponding note. The pronoun "it" may refer either to the earlier divine writ – the Bible – and to its prediction of the advent of a prophet descended from Abraham, or, more probably, to the Qurʾān: in which case it must be rendered as "this one, too". In either case, the above phrase seems to allude to the instinctive (perhaps only subconscious) awareness of some of the followers of the Bible that the Qurʾān is, in truth, an outcome of divine revelation.

102 When related to God, the term *kalimah* (lit., "word") is often used in the Qurʾān in the sense of "promise". In this instance it obviously refers to the Biblical promise (Deuteronomy xviii, 15 and 18) that God would raise up a prophet "like unto Moses" among the Arabs (see *sūrah* 2, note 33).

Now if thou pay heed unto the majority of those [who live] on earth, they will but lead thee astray from the path of God: they follow but [other people's] conjectures, and they themselves do nothing but guess.[103] ⟨116⟩
Verily, thy Sustainer knows best as to who strays from His path, and best knows He as to who are the right-guided. ⟨117⟩

EAT, then, of that over which God's name has been pronounced, if you truly believe in His messages.[104] ⟨118⟩ And why should you not eat of that over which God's name has been pronounced, seeing that He has so clearly spelled out to you what He has forbidden you [to eat] unless you are compelled [to do so]? But, behold, [it is precisely in such matters that] many people lead others astray by their own errant views, without [having any real] knowledge. Verily, thy Sustainer is fully aware of those who transgress the bounds of what is right. ⟨119⟩
But abstain from sinning,[105] be it open or secret – for, behold, those who commit sins shall be requited for all that they have earned. ⟨120⟩ Hence, eat not of that over which God's name has not been pronounced: for this would be sinful conduct indeed.
And, verily, the evil impulses [within men's hearts] whisper unto those who have made them their own[106] that they should involve you in argument [as to what is and what is not a sin]; and if you pay heed unto them,

وَإِن تُطِعْ أَكْثَرَ مَن فِي ٱلْأَرْضِ يُضِلُّوكَ عَن سَبِيلِ ٱللَّهِ ۚ إِن يَتَّبِعُونَ إِلَّا
ٱلظَّنَّ وَإِنْ هُمْ إِلَّا يَخْرُصُونَ ﴿116﴾ إِنَّ رَبَّكَ هُوَ أَعْلَمُ مَن يَضِلُّ عَن
سَبِيلِهِۦ ۖ وَهُوَ أَعْلَمُ بِٱلْمُهْتَدِينَ ﴿117﴾ فَكُلُوا۟ مِمَّا ذُكِرَ ٱسْمُ ٱللَّهِ عَلَيْهِ إِن
كُنتُم بِـَٔايَٰتِهِۦ مُؤْمِنِينَ ﴿118﴾ وَمَا لَكُمْ أَلَّا تَأْكُلُوا۟ مِمَّا ذُكِرَ ٱسْمُ ٱللَّهِ
عَلَيْهِ وَقَدْ فَصَّلَ لَكُم مَّا حَرَّمَ عَلَيْكُمْ إِلَّا مَا ٱضْطُرِرْتُمْ إِلَيْهِ ۗ وَإِنَّ
كَثِيرًا لَّيُضِلُّونَ بِأَهْوَآئِهِم بِغَيْرِ عِلْمٍ ۗ إِنَّ رَبَّكَ هُوَ أَعْلَمُ بِٱلْمُعْتَدِينَ ﴿119﴾
وَذَرُوا۟ ظَٰهِرَ ٱلْإِثْمِ وَبَاطِنَهُۥٓ ۚ إِنَّ ٱلَّذِينَ يَكْسِبُونَ ٱلْإِثْمَ سَيُجْزَوْنَ بِمَا
كَانُوا۟ يَقْتَرِفُونَ ﴿120﴾ وَلَا تَأْكُلُوا۟ مِمَّا لَمْ يُذْكَرِ ٱسْمُ ٱللَّهِ عَلَيْهِ وَإِنَّهُۥ لَفِسْقٌ ۗ
وَإِنَّ ٱلشَّيَٰطِينَ لَيُوحُونَ إِلَىٰٓ أَوْلِيَآئِهِمْ لِيُجَٰدِلُوكُمْ ۖ وَإِنْ أَطَعْتُمُوهُمْ

Wa ʾiñ-tuṭiʿ ʾakthara mañ-fil-ʾarḍi yuḍillūka ʿañ-sabīlil-lāh. ʾIñy-yattabiʿūna ʾillaẓ-ẓanna wa ʾin-hum ʾillā yakhruṣūn. (116) ʾInna Rabbaka Huwa ʾaʿlamu mañy-yaḍillu ʿañ-sabīlihī wa Huwa ʾaʿlamu bil-muhtadīn. (117) Fakulū mimmā dhukiras-mul-lāhi ʿalayhi ʾiñ-kuñtum-biʾĀyātihī muʾminīn. (118) Wa mā lakum ʾallā taʾkulū mimmā dhukiras-mul-lāhi ʿalayhi wa qad faṣṣala lakum-mā ḥarrama ʿalaykum ʾillā maḍ-ṭurirtum ʾilayh. Wa ʾinna kathīral-la-yuḍillūna biʾahwāaʾihim-bighayri ʿilm. ʾInna Rabbaka Huwa ʾaʿlamu bilmuʿtadīn. (119) Wa dharū ẓāhiral-ʾithmi wa bāṭinah. ʾInnal-ladhīna yaksibūnal-ʾithma sayujzawna bimā kānū yaqtarifūn. (120) Wa lā taʾkulū mimmā lam yudhkaris-mul-lāhi ʿalayhi wa ʾinnahū lafisq. Wa ʾinnash-Shayāṭīna layūḥūna ʾilāa ʾawliyāaʾihim liyujādilūkum. Wa ʾin ʾaṭaʿtumūhum

103 I.e., regarding the true nature of human life and its ultimate destiny, the problem of revelation, the relationship between God and man, the meaning of good and evil, etc. Apart from leading man astray from spiritual truths, such guesswork gives rise to the arbitrary rules of conduct and self-imposed inhibitions to which the Qurʾān alludes, by way of example, in verses 118 and 119.

104 The purpose of this and the following verse is not, as might appear at first glance, a repetition of already-promulgated food laws but, rather, a reminder that the observance of such laws should not be made an end in itself and an object of *ritual*: and this is the reason why these two verses have been placed in the midst of a discourse on God's transcendental unity and the ways of man's faith. The "errant views" spoken of in verse 119 are such as lay stress on artificial rituals and taboos rather than on spiritual values.

105 This injunction connects with verse 118, thus: 'Eat, then, of that over which God's name has been pronounced . . . , but abstain from sinning" – i.e., "do not go beyond that which God has made lawful to you".

106 Lit., "the satans whisper unto those who are near to them (*ilā awliyāʾihim*)". For my above rendering of *shayāṭīn* as "evil impulses", see note 10 on 2 : 14 and note 31 on 14 : 22.

lo! you will become [like] those who ascribe divinity to other beings or forces beside God.[107] ‹121›

IS THEN HE who was dead [in spirit] and whom We thereupon gave life, and for whom We set up a light whereby he might see his way among men[108] – [is then he] like one [who is lost] in darkness deep, out of which he cannot emerge?
[But] thus it is: goodly seem all their own doings to those who deny the truth. ‹122›
And it is in this way that We cause the great ones in every land to become its [greatest] evildoers,[109] there to weave their schemes: yet it is only against themselves that they scheme – and they perceive it not. ‹123›
And whenever a [divine] message comes to them, they say, "We shall not believe unless we are given the like of what God's apostles were given!"[110]
[But] God knows best upon whom to bestow His message.
Abasement in the sight of God will befall those who have become guilty of evildoing, and suffering severe for all the schemes which they were wont to weave. ‹124›
And whomsoever God wills to guide, his bosom He opens wide with willingness towards self-surrender [unto Him]; and whomsoever He wills to let go astray, his bosom He causes to be tight and constricted, as if he were climbing unto the skies: it is thus that God inflicts horror upon those who will not believe. ‹125› And undeviating is this thy Sustainer's way.[111]

إِنَّكُمْ لَمُشْرِكُونَ ﴿١٢١﴾ أَوَمَن كَانَ مَيْتًا فَأَحْيَيْنَٰهُ وَجَعَلْنَا لَهُۥ نُورًا يَمْشِى
بِهِۦ فِى ٱلنَّاسِ كَمَن مَّثَلُهُۥ فِى ٱلظُّلُمَٰتِ لَيْسَ بِخَارِجٍ مِّنْهَا ۚ كَذَٰلِكَ
زُيِّنَ لِلْكَٰفِرِينَ مَا كَانُوا۟ يَعْمَلُونَ ﴿١٢٢﴾ وَكَذَٰلِكَ جَعَلْنَا فِى كُلِّ قَرْيَةٍ
أَكَٰبِرَ مُجْرِمِيهَا لِيَمْكُرُوا۟ فِيهَا ۖ وَمَا يَمْكُرُونَ إِلَّا بِأَنفُسِهِمْ وَمَا
يَشْعُرُونَ ﴿١٢٣﴾ وَإِذَا جَآءَتْهُمْ ءَايَةٌ قَالُوا۟ لَن نُّؤْمِنَ حَتَّىٰ نُؤْتَىٰ مِثْلَ مَآ
أُوتِىَ رُسُلُ ٱللَّهِ ۘ ٱللَّهُ أَعْلَمُ حَيْثُ يَجْعَلُ رِسَالَتَهُۥ ۗ سَيُصِيبُ ٱلَّذِينَ
أَجْرَمُوا۟ صَغَارٌ عِندَ ٱللَّهِ وَعَذَابٌ شَدِيدٌۢ بِمَا كَانُوا۟ يَمْكُرُونَ ﴿١٢٤﴾
فَمَن يُرِدِ ٱللَّهُ أَن يَهْدِيَهُۥ يَشْرَحْ صَدْرَهُۥ لِلْإِسْلَٰمِ ۖ وَمَن يُرِدْ أَن يُضِلَّهُۥ
يَجْعَلْ صَدْرَهُۥ ضَيِّقًا حَرَجًا كَأَنَّمَا يَصَّعَّدُ فِى ٱلسَّمَآءِ ۚ كَذَٰلِكَ يَجْعَلُ
ٱللَّهُ ٱلرِّجْسَ عَلَى ٱلَّذِينَ لَا يُؤْمِنُونَ ﴿١٢٥﴾ وَهَٰذَا صِرَٰطُ رَبِّكَ مُسْتَقِيمًا ۗ

ʾinnakum lamushrikūn. (121) ʾAwa mañ-kāna maytañ-
faʾaḥyaynāhu wa jaʿalnā lahū nūrañy-yamshī bihī
fin-nāsi kamam-mathaluhū fiẓ-ẓulumāti laysa
bikhārijim-minhā. Kadhālika zuyyina lilkāfirīna mā
kānū yaʿmalūn. (122) Wa kadhālika jaʿalnā fī kulli
qaryatin ʾakābira mujrimīhā liyamkurū fīhā; wa mā
yamkurūna ʾillā biʾañfusihim wa mā yashʿurūn. (123)
Wa ʾidhā jāaʾat-hum ʾĀyatuñ-qālū lañ-nuʾmina
ḥattā nuʾtā mithla māa ʾūtiya Rusulul-lāh. ʾAllāhu
ʾaʿlamu ḥaythu yajʿalu Risālatah. Sayuṣībul-ladhīna
ʾajramū ṣagharun ʿiñdal-lāhi wa ʿadhābuñ-sha-
dīdum-bimā kānū yamkurūn. (124) Fa-mañy-yuridil-
lāhu ʾañy-yahdiyahū yashraḥ ṣadrahū lilʾIslām. Wa
mañy-yurid ʿañy-yuḍillahū yajʿal ṣadrahū ḍayyiqan
ḥarajañ-kaʾannamā yaṣṣaʿʿadu fis-samāaʾ.
Kadhālika yajʿalul-lāhur-rijsa ʿalal-ladhīna lā
yuʾminūn. (125) Wa hādhā ṣirāṭu Rabbika mustaqīmā.

107 I.e., "your own evil impulses are trying to draw you into argument as to what does and what does not constitute a sin in order to make you lose sight of God's clear ordinances in this respect; and if you follow their arbitrary, deceptive reasoning, you will elevate them, as it were, to the position of moral law-givers, and thus ascribe to them a right that belongs to God alone."

108 Lit., "whereby he walks among men". All the commentators agree in that the expression "he who was dead" is metaphorical, and that it refers to people who become spiritually alive through faith and are thereupon able to pursue their way through life unerringly.

109 Because the consciousness of their importance makes them more or less impervious to criticism, the "great ones" are, as a rule, rather less inclined than other people to question the moral aspects of their own behaviour; and the resulting self-righteousness only too often causes them to commit grave misdeeds.

110 I.e., direct revelation.

111 Lit., "and this thy Sustainer's way is straight" – i.e., unchanging in its application of the law of cause and effect to man's inner life as well. – The term *rijs* occurring in the preceding sentence, and rendered by me as "horror", signifies anything that is intrinsically loathsome, horrible or abominable; in this case, it would seem to denote that

قَدْ فَصَّلْنَا ٱلْـَٔايَـٰتِ لِقَوْمٍ يَذَّكَّرُونَ ﴿١٢٦﴾ ۞ لَهُمْ دَارُ ٱلسَّلَـٰمِ عِندَ رَبِّهِمْ
وَهُوَ وَلِيُّهُم بِمَا كَانُوا۟ يَعْمَلُونَ ﴿١٢٧﴾ وَيَوْمَ يَحْشُرُهُمْ جَمِيعًا يَـٰمَعْشَرَ
ٱلْجِنِّ قَدِ ٱسْتَكْثَرْتُم مِّنَ ٱلْإِنسِ ۖ وَقَالَ أَوْلِيَآؤُهُم مِّنَ ٱلْإِنسِ رَبَّنَا ٱسْتَمْتَعَ
بَعْضُنَا بِبَعْضٍ وَبَلَغْنَآ أَجَلَنَا ٱلَّذِىٓ أَجَّلْتَ لَنَا ۚ قَالَ ٱلنَّارُ مَثْوَىٰكُمْ
خَـٰلِدِينَ فِيهَآ إِلَّا مَا شَآءَ ٱللَّهُ ۗ إِنَّ رَبَّكَ حَكِيمٌ عَلِيمٌ ﴿١٢٨﴾ وَكَذَٰلِكَ نُوَلِّى
بَعْضَ ٱلظَّـٰلِمِينَ بَعْضًۢا بِمَا كَانُوا۟ يَكْسِبُونَ ﴿١٢٩﴾

Qad faṣṣalnal-ʾĀyāti liqawmiñy-yadhdhakkarūn. (126)
۞ Lahum dārus-salāmi ᶜiñda Rabbihim wa Huwa
Waliyyuhum-bimā kānū yaᶜmalūn. (127) Wa Yawma
yaḥshuruhum jamīᶜañy-yā maᶜsharal-Jinni qadis-
takthartum-minal-ʾIñs. Wa qāla ʾawliyāaʾuhum-
minal-ʾIñsi Rabbanas-tamtaᶜa baᶜḍunā bibaᶜḍiñw-
wa balaghnāa ʾajalanal-ladhīi ʾajjalta lanā; qālan-nāru
mathwākum khālidīna fīhāa ʾillā mā shāaʾal-lāh.
ʾInna Rabbaka Ḥakīmun ᶜAlīm. (128) Wa kadhālika nu-
wallī baᶜḍaẓ-ẓālimīna baᶜḍam-bimā kānū yaksibūn.
(129)

Clearly, indeed, have We spelled out these messages unto people who [are willing to] take them to heart! «126» Theirs shall be an abode of peace with their Sustainer; and He shall be near unto them in result of what they have been doing. «127»

ربع الحزب

AND ON THE DAY when He shall gather them [all] together, [He will say:] "O you who have lived in close communion with [evil] invisible beings! A great many [other] human beings have you ensnared!"[112]
And those of the humans who were close to them[113] will say: "O our Sustainer! We did enjoy one another's fellowship [in life]; but [now that] we have reached the end of our term – the term which Thou hast laid down for us – [we see the error of our ways]!"
[But] He will say: "The fire shall be your abode, therein to abide – unless God wills it otherwise."[114] Verily, thy Sustainer is wise, all-knowing. «128»
And in this manner do We cause evildoers to seduce one another[115] by means of their [evil] doings. «129»

---

awesome feeling of utter futility which, sooner or later, overcomes everyone who does not believe that life has meaning and purpose.

112 According to most of the commentators, the invisible beings (*al-jinn*) referred to here are the "evil forces" (*shayāṭīn*) among them, such as are spoken of in verse 112 of this *sūrah*. It is generally assumed that these very beings or forces are addressed here; but the primary meaning of the term *maᶜshar* appearing in this context warrants, in my opinion, a different conclusion. It is true that this term is often used to denote a group or community or genus of sentient beings which have certain characteristics in common: a conventional – and undoubtedly justifiable – use based on the verb *ᶜāsharahu*, "he consorted [or "was on intimate terms"] with him" or "lived in close communion with him". But it is precisely this verbal origin of the term *maᶜshar* which gives us a clue as to what is really meant here. Since, in its primary significance, a person's *maᶜshar* denotes those who are on intimate terms or in close communion with him (cf. *Lisān al-ᶜArab*: "A man's *maᶜshar* is his family"), we may well assume that it has a similar significance in the above Qurʾanic phrase. Thus, to my mind, the allocution *yā maᶜshar al-jinn* does not denote, "O you community of [evil] invisible beings" but, rather, "O you who are [or "have lived"] in close communion with [evil] invisible beings": in other words, it is addressed to the misguided *human* beings who have been seduced by "glittering half-truths meant to delude the mind" (verse 112). This interpretation is reinforced by the words, "Have there not come unto you apostles *from among yourselves*", occurring in verse 130 below: for the Qurʾān speaks always only of apostles who belonged to the human race, and never of apostles from among the *jinn*. (As regards the wide significance of this latter term, see Appendix III.)

113 I.e., close to the evil invisible beings. It is to be remembered that the primary meaning of *walī* (of which *awliyāʾ* is the plural) is "one who is close [to another]".

114 I.e., unless He graces them with His mercy (see verse 12 of this *sūrah*, and the corresponding note). Some of the great Muslim theologians conclude from the above and from the similar phrase occurring in 11 : 107 (as well as from several well-authenticated sayings of the Prophet) that – contrary to the bliss of paradise, which will be of unlimited duration – the suffering of the sinners in the life to come will be limited by God's mercy. (See in this connection the *ḥadīth* quoted in note 10 on 40 : 12.)

115 Lit., "to be close to one another", or "get hold of one another". The expression "in this manner" (*kadhālika*),

[And thus will God continue:] "O you who have lived in close communion with [evil] invisible beings and [like-minded] humans! Have there not come unto you apostles from among yourselves, who conveyed unto you My messages and warned you of the coming of this your Day [of Judgment]?"
They will answer: "We do bear witness against ourselves!" – for the life of this world had beguiled them: and so they will bear witness against themselves that they had been denying the truth. ‹130›
And so it is that thy Sustainer would never destroy a community[116] for its wrongdoing so long as its people are still unaware [of the meaning of right and wrong]: ‹131›
for all shall be judged according to their [conscious] deeds[117] – and thy Sustainer is not unaware of what they do. ‹132›
And thy Sustainer alone is self-sufficient, limitless in His grace. If He so wills, He may put an end to you and thereafter cause whom He wills to succeed you – even as He has brought you into being out of other people's seed. ‹133›
Verily, that [reckoning] which you are promised is bound to come, and you cannot elude it! ‹134›
Say: "O my [unbelieving] people! Do yet all that may be within your power, [while] I, behold, shall labour [in God's way]; and in time you will come to know to whom the future belongs.[118] Verily, never will evildoers attain to a happy state!" ‹135›

يَٰمَعۡشَرَ ٱلۡجِنِّ وَٱلۡإِنسِ أَلَمۡ يَأۡتِكُمۡ رُسُلٞ مِّنكُمۡ يَقُصُّونَ عَلَيۡكُمۡ
ءَايَٰتِي وَيُنذِرُونَكُمۡ لِقَآءَ يَوۡمِكُمۡ هَٰذَاۚ قَالُواْ شَهِدۡنَا عَلَىٰٓ أَنفُسِنَاۖ
وَغَرَّتۡهُمُ ٱلۡحَيَوٰةُ ٱلدُّنۡيَا وَشَهِدُواْ عَلَىٰٓ أَنفُسِهِمۡ أَنَّهُمۡ كَانُواْ كَٰفِرِينَ ١٣٠
ذَٰلِكَ أَن لَّمۡ يَكُن رَّبُّكَ مُهۡلِكَ ٱلۡقُرَىٰ بِظُلۡمٖ وَأَهۡلُهَا غَٰفِلُونَ ١٣١
وَلِكُلّٖ دَرَجَٰتٞ مِّمَّا عَمِلُواْۚ وَمَا رَبُّكَ بِغَٰفِلٍ عَمَّا يَعۡمَلُونَ ١٣٢ وَرَبُّكَ
ٱلۡغَنِيُّ ذُو ٱلرَّحۡمَةِۚ إِن يَشَأۡ يُذۡهِبۡكُمۡ وَيَسۡتَخۡلِفۡ مِنۢ بَعۡدِكُم مَّا يَشَآءُ
كَمَآ أَنشَأَكُم مِّن ذُرِّيَّةِ قَوۡمٍ ءَاخَرِينَ ١٣٣ إِنَّ مَا تُوعَدُونَ لَأٓتٖۖ وَمَآ أَنتُم
بِمُعۡجِزِينَ ١٣٤ قُلۡ يَٰقَوۡمِ ٱعۡمَلُواْ عَلَىٰ مَكَانَتِكُمۡ إِنِّي عَامِلٞۖ فَسَوۡفَ
تَعۡلَمُونَ مَن تَكُونُ لَهُۥ عَٰقِبَةُ ٱلدَّارِۚ إِنَّهُۥ لَا يُفۡلِحُ ٱلظَّٰلِمُونَ ١٣٥

Yā maᶜsharal-Jinni wal-ᵓIñsi ᵓalam yaᵓtikum Rusulum-miñkum yaquṣṣūna ᶜalaykum ᵓĀyātī wa yuñdhirūnakum liqāaᵓa Yawmikum hādhā. Qālū shahidnā ᶜalāa ᵓañfusinā wa gharrat-humul-ḥayātud-dunyā wa shahidū ᶜalāa ᵓañfusihim ᵓannahum kānū kāfirīn. (130) Dhālika ᵓal-lam yakur-Rabbuka muhlikal-qurā biẓulmiñw-wa ᵓahluhā ghāfilūn. (131) Wa likulliñ-darajātum-mimmā ᶜamilū; wa mā Rabbuka bighāfilin ᶜammā yaᶜmalūn. (132) Wa Rabbukal-Ghaniyyu Dhur-raḥmah. ᵓIñy-yashaᵓ yudhhibkum wa yastakhlif mim-baᶜdikum-mā yashāaᵓu kamāa ᵓañshaᵓakum-miñ-dhurriyyati qawmin ᵓākharīn. (133) ᵓInna mā tūᶜadūna laᵓātiñw-wa māa ᵓañtum-bimuᶜjizīn. (134) Qul yā qawmiᶜ-malū ᶜalā makānatikum ᵓinnī ᶜāmil. Fasawfa taᶜlamūna mañ-takūnu lahū ᶜāqibatud-dār. ᵓInnahū lā yufliḥuẓ-ẓālimūn. (135)

which introduces the above sentence, is an obvious allusion to the manner in which the evil ones "whisper unto one another glittering half-truths meant to delude the mind" (verse 112 of this *sūrah*).

116 Lit., "communities". The term *qaryah* (lit., "town", "village" or "land") denotes also the *people* of a town or land – in short, a "community" – and it is in this sense that this term is mostly, though not always, used in the Qurᵓān.

117 Lit., "all shall have grades out of what they did", i.e., *consciously* – since God does not take people to task for any wrong they may have committed unless it was done in conscious contravention of a moral law already made clear to them by the prophets.

118 Lit., "to whom the [happy] end of the abode shall belong". The term "abode" (*dār*) is used in the Qurᵓān with reference to both the life of this world (*dār ad-dunyā*) and the life to come (*dār al-ākhirah*). Most of the commentators are of the opinion that it refers here to the life to come; Zamakhsharī, however, relates it to life on earth. Since either of these interpretations is agreeable with the text, I have chosen the above rendering which comprises both.

وَجَعَلُوا۟ لِلَّهِ مِمَّا ذَرَأَ مِنَ ٱلْحَرْثِ وَٱلْأَنْعَٰمِ نَصِيبًا فَقَالُوا۟ هَٰذَا لِلَّهِ بِزَعْمِهِمْ
وَهَٰذَا لِشُرَكَآئِنَا ۖ فَمَا كَانَ لِشُرَكَآئِهِمْ فَلَا يَصِلُ إِلَى ٱللَّهِ ۖ وَمَا كَانَ لِلَّهِ فَهُوَ يَصِلُ
إِلَىٰ شُرَكَآئِهِمْ ۗ سَآءَ مَا يَحْكُمُونَ ﴿١٣٦﴾ وَكَذَٰلِكَ زَيَّنَ لِكَثِيرٍ مِّنَ ٱلْمُشْرِكِينَ قَتْلَ
أَوْلَٰدِهِمْ شُرَكَآؤُهُمْ لِيُرْدُوهُمْ وَلِيَلْبِسُوا۟ عَلَيْهِمْ دِينَهُمْ ۖ وَلَوْ شَآءَ ٱللَّهُ مَا فَعَلُوهُ ۖ فَذَرْهُمْ وَمَا
يَفْتَرُونَ ﴿١٣٧﴾ وَقَالُوا۟ هَٰذِهِۦٓ أَنْعَٰمٌ وَحَرْثٌ حِجْرٌ لَّا يَطْعَمُهَآ إِلَّا مَن نَّشَآءُ بِزَعْمِهِمْ

Wa jaʿalū lillāhi mimmā dharaʾa minal-ḥarthi wal-ʾanʿāmi naṣībañ-faqālū hādhā lillāhi bizaʿmihim wa hādhā lishurakāaʾinā. Famā kāna lishurakāaʾihim falā yaṣilu ʾilal-lāhi wa mā kāna lillāhi fahuwa yaṣilu ʾilā shurakāaʾihim. Sāaʾa mā yaḥkumūn. (136) Wa kadhālika zayyana likathīrim-minal-mushrikīna qatla ʾawlādihim shurakāaʾuhum liyurdūhum wa liyalbisū ʿalayhim dīnahum. Wa law shāaʾal-lāhu mā faʿalūhu fadharhum wa mā yaftarūn. (137) Wa qālū hādhihīi ʾanʿāmuñw-wa ḥarthun ḥijruñ-lā yaṭʿamuhāa ʾillā mañ-nashāaʾu bizaʿmihim

AND OUT OF whatever He has created of the fruits of the field and the cattle, they assign unto God a portion, saying, "This belongs to God" – or so they [falsely] claim[119] – "and this is for those beings who, we are convinced, have a share in God's divinity."[120] But that which is assigned to the beings associated in their minds with God does not bring [them] closer to God – whereas that which is assigned to God brings [them but] closer to those beings to whom they ascribe a share in His divinity.[121] Bad, indeed, is their judgment! ‹136›

And, likewise, their belief in beings or powers that are supposed to have a share in God's divinity makes[122] [even] the slaying of their children seem goodly to many of those who ascribe divinity to aught beside God, thus bringing them to ruin and confusing them in their faith.[123]

Yet, unless God had so willed, they would not be doing all this:[124] stand, therefore, aloof from them and all their false imagery! ‹137›

And they say, "Such-and-such cattle and fruits of the field are sacred; none may eat thereof save those whom we will [to do so]" – so they [falsely] claim;[125] and [they

119 Falsely – because everything that exists belongs, in the last resort, to God alone.

120 Lit., "for our [God-]partners" – i.e., "those whom *we consider* to be associated with God". For an explanation of the term *sharīk*, see note 15 on verse 22 of this *sūrah*. The pre-Islamic Arabs used to dedicate a part of their agricultural produce and cattle to some of their deities, and a part to God, whom they regarded as one – albeit the greatest – of them. In consonance, however, with the method of the Qurʾān, the above verse does not allude merely to this historical aspect of pre-Islamic Arabian life but has a wider, more general implication as well: that is, it refers not only to the apportioning of devotional "shares" between God and the imaginary deities, but also to the attribution of any share in His *creative powers* to anyone or anything beside Him.

121 I.e., the fact that they assign a "share" of their devotions to God does not strengthen their belief in Him but, rather, implies a negation of His transcendental uniqueness and, thus, makes them more and more dependent on imaginary divine or semi-divine "mediators".

122 Lit., "their [God-]partners make". As pointed out by Rāzī, some early commentators were of the opinion that the expression *shurakāʾuhum* (lit., "their associates") denotes here the "evil beings" or "forces" (*shayāṭīn*) from among men and *jinn* referred to in verses 112, 121, 128 and 130 of this *sūrah*. It seems to me, however, that what is meant here – as in the preceding verse – is the *belief in the existence* of anything that could be "associated" with God; hence my rendering of the above phrase as "their belief in beings or powers that are supposed . . .", etc.

123 This is a reference to the custom prevalent among the pre-Islamic Arabs of burying alive some of their unwanted children, mainly girls, and also to the occasional offering of a boy-child in sacrifice to one or another of their idols (Zamakhsharī). Apart from this historical reference, the above Qurʾān-verse seems to point out, by implication, the psychological fact that an attribution of divinity to anyone or anything but God brings with it an ever-growing dependence on all kinds of imaginary powers which must be "propitiated" by formal and often absurd and cruel rites: and this, in turn, leads to the loss of all spiritual freedom and to moral self-destruction.

124 I.e., He allows them to behave as they do because He wants them to make use of their reason and of the free will with which He has endowed man.

125 The pre-Islamic Arabs falsely claimed that these taboos were ordained by God, as is made clear in the last part

declare that] it is forbidden to burden the backs of certain kinds of cattle; and there are cattle over which they do not pronounce God's name[126] – falsely attributing [the origin of these customs] to Him. [But] He will requite them for all their false imagery. ‹138›
And they say, "All that is in the wombs of such-and-such cattle is reserved for our males and forbidden to our women; but if it be stillborn, then both may have their share thereof." [God] will requite them for all that they [falsely] attribute [to Him]: behold, He is wise, all-knowing. ‹139›
Lost, indeed, are they who, in their weak-minded ignorance, slay their children and declare as forbidden that which God has provided for them as sustenance, falsely ascribing [such prohibitions] to God: they have gone astray and have not found the right path. ‹140›
For it is He who has brought into being gardens – [both] the cultivated ones and those growing wild[127] – and the date-palm, and fields bearing multiform produce, and the olive tree, and the pomegranate: [all] resembling one another and yet so different![128] Eat of their fruit when it comes to fruition, and give [unto the poor] their due on harvest day. And do not waste [God's bounties]: verily, He does not love the wasteful! ‹141›
And of the cattle reared for work and for the sake of their flesh, eat whatever God has provided for you as sustenance, and follow not Satan's footsteps:[129] behold, he is your open foe! ‹142›

وَأَنْعَٰمٌ حُرِّمَتْ ظُهُورُهَا وَأَنْعَٰمٌ لَّا يَذْكُرُونَ ٱسْمَ ٱللَّهِ عَلَيْهَا ٱفْتِرَآءً عَلَيْهِ
سَيَجْزِيهِم بِمَا كَانُوا۟ يَفْتَرُونَ ﴿١٣٨﴾ وَقَالُوا۟ مَا فِى بُطُونِ هَٰذِهِ ٱلْأَنْعَٰمِ
خَالِصَةٌ لِّذُكُورِنَا وَمُحَرَّمٌ عَلَىٰٓ أَزْوَٰجِنَا ۖ وَإِن يَكُن مَّيْتَةً فَهُمْ فِيهِ
شُرَكَآءُ ۚ سَيَجْزِيهِمْ وَصْفَهُمْ ۚ إِنَّهُۥ حَكِيمٌ عَلِيمٌ ﴿١٣٩﴾ قَدْ خَسِرَ ٱلَّذِينَ قَتَلُوٓا۟
أَوْلَٰدَهُمْ سَفَهًۢا بِغَيْرِ عِلْمٍ وَحَرَّمُوا۟ مَا رَزَقَهُمُ ٱللَّهُ ٱفْتِرَآءً عَلَى ٱللَّهِ ۚ قَدْ ضَلُّوا۟ نصف الحزب
وَمَا كَانُوا۟ مُهْتَدِينَ ﴿١٤٠﴾ ۞ وَهُوَ ٱلَّذِىٓ أَنشَأَ جَنَّٰتٍ مَّعْرُوشَٰتٍ وَغَيْرَ
مَعْرُوشَٰتٍ وَٱلنَّخْلَ وَٱلزَّرْعَ مُخْتَلِفًا أُكُلُهُۥ وَٱلزَّيْتُونَ وَٱلرُّمَّانَ مُتَشَٰبِهًا وَغَيْرَ
مُتَشَٰبِهٍ ۚ كُلُوا۟ مِن ثَمَرِهِۦٓ إِذَآ أَثْمَرَ وَءَاتُوا۟ حَقَّهُۥ يَوْمَ حَصَادِهِۦ ۖ وَلَا تُسْرِفُوٓا۟ ۚ
إِنَّهُۥ لَا يُحِبُّ ٱلْمُسْرِفِينَ ﴿١٤١﴾ وَمِنَ ٱلْأَنْعَٰمِ حَمُولَةً وَفَرْشًا ۚ كُلُوا۟ مِمَّا
رَزَقَكُمُ ٱللَّهُ وَلَا تَتَّبِعُوا۟ خُطُوَٰتِ ٱلشَّيْطَٰنِ ۚ إِنَّهُۥ لَكُمْ عَدُوٌّ مُّبِينٌ ﴿١٤٢﴾

wa ᵓanᶜāmun ḥurrimat ẓuhūruhā wa ᵓanᶜāmul-lā yadhkurūnas-mal-lāhi ᶜalayhaf-tirāaᵓan ᶜalayh. Saya-jzīhim-bimā kānū yaftarūn. ﴿138﴾ Wa qālū mā fī buṭūni hādhihil-ᵓanᶜāmi khāliṣatul-lidhukūrinā wa muḥarramun ᶜalāa ᵓazwājinā; wa ᵓiñy-yakum-may-tatañ-fahum fīhi shurakāaᵓ. Sayajzīhim waṣfahum; ᵓinnahū Ḥakīmun ᶜAlīm. ﴿139﴾ Qad khasiral-ladhīna qatalūu ᵓawlādahum safaham-bighayri ᶜilmiñw-wa ḥarramū mā razaqahumul-lāhuf-tirāaᵓan ᶜalal-lāh. Qad ḍallū wa mā kānū muhtadīn. ﴿140﴾ ۞ Wa Huwal-ladhīi ᵓañshaᵓa jannātim-maᶜrūshātiñw-wa ghayra maᶜrūshātiñw-wan-nakhla waz-zarᶜa mukhtalifan ᵓukuluhū waz-zaytūna war-rummāna mutashābi-hañw-wa ghayra mutashābih. Kulū miñ-thamarihīi ᵓidhāa ᵓathmara wa ᵓātū ḥaqqahū yawma ḥaṣādih. Wa lā tusrifūu ᵓinnahū lā yuḥibbul-musrifīn. ﴿141﴾ Wa minal-ᵓanᶜāmi ḥamūlatañw-wa farshā. Kulū mimmā razaqakumul-lāhu wa lā tattabiᶜū khuṭuwātish-Shayṭāni ᵓinnahū lakum ᶜaduwwum-mubīn. ﴿142﴾

of this verse. One of these supposed, arbitrary "ordinances" laid down that only the priests of the particular idol and some men belonging to the tribe could eat the flesh of such dedicated animals, while women were not allowed to do so (Zamakhsharī).

126 I.e., while sacrificing them to their idols (see also 5 : 103 and the corresponding note). It would seem from this allusion that, as a rule, the pagan Arabs did pronounce the name of God – whom they regarded as the *supreme* deity – over the animals which they slaughtered; in the above-mentioned exceptional cases, however, they refrained from doing so in the belief that God Himself had forbidden it.

127 This is the generally-accepted explanation of the term *maᶜrūshāt* and *ghayr maᶜrūshāt* (lit., "those which are and those which are not provided with trellises"). The mention of "gardens" serves here to illustrate the doctrine that everything living and growing – like everything else in the universe – owes its existence to God alone, and that it is, therefore, blasphemous to connect it causally or devotionally with any other power, be it real or imaginary.

128 See note 85 on verse 99 of this *sūrah*.

129 I.e., by superstitiously declaring as forbidden what God has made lawful to man. All the references to pre-Islamic taboos given in verses 138-140 as well as 142-144 are meant to stress the lawfulness of any food (and,

[His followers would have it that, in certain cases, any of these] four kinds of cattle of either sex [is unlawful to man]: either of the two sexes of sheep and of goats.[130] Ask [them]: "Is it the two males that He has forbidden, or the two females, or that which the wombs of the two females may contain? Tell me what you know in this respect,[131] if what you say true." ‹143›

And [likewise they declare as unlawful] either of the two sexes of camels and of bovine cattle.[132] Ask [them]: "Is it the two males that He has forbidden, or the two females, or that which the wombs of the two females may contain? Is it, perchance, that you [yourselves] were witnesses when God enjoined [all] this upon you?"

And who could be more wicked than he who, without any [real] knowledge, attributes his own lying inventions to God, and thus leads people astray?[133] Behold, God does not grace [such] evildoing folk with His guidance. ‹144›

Say [O Prophet]: "In all that has been revealed unto me, I do not find anything forbidden to eat, if one wants to eat thereof,[134] unless it be carrion, or blood poured forth, or the flesh of swine – for that, behold, is loathsome – or a sinful offering[135] over which any name other than God's has been invoked. But if one is driven by necessity – neither coveting it nor exceeding his immediate need – then

ثَمَٰنِيَةَ أَزْوَٰجٍ مِّنَ ٱلضَّأْنِ ٱثْنَيْنِ وَمِنَ ٱلْمَعْزِ ٱثْنَيْنِ قُلْ ءَآلذَّكَرَيْنِ حَرَّمَ أَمِ
ٱلْأُنثَيَيْنِ أَمَّا ٱشْتَمَلَتْ عَلَيْهِ أَرْحَامُ ٱلْأُنثَيَيْنِ نَبِّـُٔونِى بِعِلْمٍ إِن كُنتُمْ
صَٰدِقِينَ ﴿١٤٣﴾ وَمِنَ ٱلْإِبِلِ ٱثْنَيْنِ وَمِنَ ٱلْبَقَرِ ٱثْنَيْنِ قُلْ ءَآلذَّكَرَيْنِ حَرَّمَ أَمِ
ٱلْأُنثَيَيْنِ أَمَّا ٱشْتَمَلَتْ عَلَيْهِ أَرْحَامُ ٱلْأُنثَيَيْنِ أَمْ كُنتُمْ شُهَدَآءَ إِذْ وَصَّىٰكُمُ
ٱللَّهُ بِهَٰذَا فَمَنْ أَظْلَمُ مِمَّنِ ٱفْتَرَىٰ عَلَى ٱللَّهِ كَذِبًا لِّيُضِلَّ ٱلنَّاسَ بِغَيْرِ عِلْمٍ إِنَّ
ٱللَّهَ لَا يَهْدِى ٱلْقَوْمَ ٱلظَّٰلِمِينَ ﴿١٤٤﴾ قُل لَّآ أَجِدُ فِى مَآ أُوحِىَ إِلَىَّ مُحَرَّمًا عَلَىٰ
طَاعِمٍ يَطْعَمُهُۥٓ إِلَّآ أَن يَكُونَ مَيْتَةً أَوْ دَمًا مَّسْفُوحًا أَوْ لَحْمَ خِنزِيرٍ فَإِنَّهُۥ
رِجْسٌ أَوْ فِسْقًا أُهِلَّ لِغَيْرِ ٱللَّهِ بِهِۦ فَمَنِ ٱضْطُرَّ غَيْرَ بَاغٍ وَلَا عَادٍ فَإِنَّ

Thamāniyata ᵓazwājim-minaḍ-ḍaᵓnith-nayni wa minal-maᶜzith-nayn. Qul ᵓāadhdhakarayni ḥarrama ᵓamil-ᵓuñthayayni ᵓammash-tamalat ᶜalayhi ᵓarḥāmul-ᵓuñthayayn. Nabbiᵓūnī biᶜilmin ᵓiñ-kuñtum ṣādiqīn. (143) Wa minal-ᵓibilith-nayni wa minal-baqarith-nayn. Qul ᵓāadhdhakarayni ḥarrama ᵓamil-ᵓuñthayayni ᵓammash-tamalat ᶜalayhi ᵓarḥāmul-ᵓuñthayayn. ᵓAm kuñtum shuhadāaᵓa ᵓidh waṣṣākumul-lāhu bihādhā. Faman ᵓaẓlamu mim-manif-tarā ᶜalal-lāhi kadhibal-liyuḍillan-nāsa bighay-ri ᶜilm. ᵓInnal-lāha lā yahdil-qawmaẓ-ẓālimīn. (144) Qul-lāa ᵓajidu fīmāa ᵓūḥiya ᵓilayya muḥarraman ᶜalā ṭāᶜimiñy-yaṭᶜamuhūu ᵓillāa ᵓañy-yakūna maytatan ᵓaw damam-masfūḥan ᵓaw laḥma khinzīriñ-faᵓinnahū rijsun ᵓaw fisqan ᵓuhilla lighayril-lāhi bih. Famaniḍ-ṭurra ghayra bāghiñw-wa lā ᶜādiñ-faᵓinna

by implication, of any other physical enjoyment) which God has not expressly forbidden through revelation.

130 Lit., "eight [in] pairs – of sheep two and of goats two" (the two other pairs are mentioned in the next verse). This is an outstanding example of the ellipticism often employed in the Qurᵓan: a mode of expression which cannot be correctly rendered in any other language without the use of explanatory interpolations. The term *zawj* denotes a pair of things as well as each of the two constituents of a pair: hence my rendering of *thamāniyat azwāj* (lit., "eight [in] pairs") as "four kinds of cattle of either sex". The particular superstition to which this and the next verse refer is probably identical with the one mentioned in 5 : 103.

131 Lit., "tell me with knowledge" – i.e., not on the basis of guesswork but of knowledge acquired through authentic revelation. The preceding and subsequent ironical questions are meant to bring out the vagueness and inconsistency which characterizes all such superstitious, self-ßßimposed prohibitions.

132 Lit., "and of camels two, and of bovine cattle two" – thus completing the enumeration of the "eight kinds [i.e., four pairs] of cattle".

133 Lit., "[thus] to lead people astray". However, the conjunction *li* prefixed to the verb *yuḍill* ("he leads astray") does not denote here – as is usually the case – an intent ("in order that") but, rather, a logical sequel ("and thus . . ."): a use which is described by the grammarians as *lām al-ᶜāqibah*, "the letter *lām* signifying a causal sequence".

134 Lit., "forbidden to an eater to eat thereof".

135 Lit., "a sinful deed" (*fisq*) – here signifying an idolatrous offering.

[know that], behold, thy Sustainer is much-forgiving, a dispenser of grace."[136] ‹145›
And [only] unto those who followed the Jewish faith did We forbid all beasts that have claws;[137] and We forbade unto them the fat of both oxen and sheep, excepting that which is in their backs or entrails or that which is within the bone:[138] thus did We requite them for their evildoing – for, behold, We are true to Our word!"[139] ‹146›
And if they give thee the lie,[140] say: "Limitless is your Sustainer in His grace; but His punishment shall not be averted from people who are lost in sin." ‹147›

THOSE who are bent on ascribing divinity to aught beside God will say, "Had God so willed, we would not have ascribed divinity to aught but Him, nor would our forefathers [have done so]; and neither would we have declared as forbidden anything [that He has allowed]." Even so did those who lived before them give the lie to the truth[141] – until they came to taste Our punishment!
Say: "Have you any [certain] knowledge which you could proffer to us?[142] You follow but [other people's] conjectures, and you yourselves do nothing but guess." ‹148›
Say: "[Know,] then, that the final evidence [of all truth] rests with God alone; and had He so willed, He would have guided you all aright."[143] ‹149›

رَبَّكَ غَفُورٌ رَّحِيمٌ ﴿١٤٥﴾ وَعَلَى ٱلَّذِينَ هَادُواْ حَرَّمْنَا كُلَّ ذِى ظُفُرٍ ۖ وَمِنَ
ٱلْبَقَرِ وَٱلْغَنَمِ حَرَّمْنَا عَلَيْهِمْ شُحُومَهُمَآ إِلَّا مَا حَمَلَتْ ظُهُورُهُمَآ أَوِ
ٱلْحَوَايَآ أَوْ مَا ٱخْتَلَطَ بِعَظْمٍ ۚ ذَٰلِكَ جَزَيْنَٰهُم بِبَغْيِهِمْ ۖ وَإِنَّا
لَصَٰدِقُونَ ﴿١٤٦﴾ فَإِن كَذَّبُوكَ فَقُل رَّبُّكُمْ ذُو رَحْمَةٍ وَٰسِعَةٍ وَلَا يُرَدُّ
بَأْسُهُۥ عَنِ ٱلْقَوْمِ ٱلْمُجْرِمِينَ ﴿١٤٧﴾ سَيَقُولُ ٱلَّذِينَ أَشْرَكُواْ لَوْ شَآءَ ٱللَّهُ مَآ
أَشْرَكْنَا وَلَآ ءَابَآؤُنَا وَلَا حَرَّمْنَا مِن شَىْءٍ ۚ كَذَٰلِكَ كَذَّبَ ٱلَّذِينَ مِن
قَبْلِهِمْ حَتَّىٰ ذَاقُواْ بَأْسَنَا ۗ قُلْ هَلْ عِندَكُم مِّنْ عِلْمٍ فَتُخْرِجُوهُ لَنَآ ۖ إِن
تَتَّبِعُونَ إِلَّا ٱلظَّنَّ وَإِنْ أَنتُمْ إِلَّا تَخْرُصُونَ ﴿١٤٨﴾ قُلْ فَلِلَّهِ ٱلْحُجَّةُ ٱلْبَٰلِغَةُ ۖ
فَلَوْ شَآءَ لَهَدَىٰكُمْ أَجْمَعِينَ ﴿١٤٩﴾

Rabbaka Ghafūrur-Raḥīm. (145) Wa ʿalal-ladhīna hādū ḥarramnā kulla dhī ẓufur. Wa minal-baqari wal-ghanami ḥarramnā ʿalayhim shuḥūmahumāa ʾillā mā ḥamalat ẓuhūruhumāa ʾawil-ḥawāyāa ʾaw makhtalaṭa biʿaẓm. Dhālika jazaynāhum-bibaghyihim; wa ʾinnā laṣādiqūn. (146) Faʾiñ-kadhdhabūka faqur-Rabbukum Dhū raḥmatiñw-wāsiʿatiñw-wa lā yuraddu baʾsuhū ʿanil-qawmil-mujrimīn. (147) Sayaqūlul-ladhīna ʾashrakū law shāaʾal-lāhu māa ʾashraknā wa lāa ʾābāaʾunā wa lā ḥarramnā miñ-shayʾ. Kadhālika kadhdhabal-ladhīna miñ-qablihim ḥattā dhāqū baʾsanā. Qul hal ʿiñdakum-min ʿilmiñ-fatukhrijūhu lanā. ʾIñ-tattabiʿūna ʾillaẓ-ẓanna wa ʾin ʾañtum ʾillā takhruṣūn. (148) Qul falillāhil-ḥujjatul-bālighah. Falaw shāaʾa lahadākum ʾajmaʿīn. (149)

136 Cf. 2 : 173 and 5 : 3.

137 The construction of the above sentence makes it clear that this prohibition was imposed specifically on the Jews, to the exclusion of believers of later times (Rāzī).

138 Cf. Leviticus vii, 23 (where, however, "all manner" of fat of ox, sheep or goat is declared forbidden).

139 See 3 : 93.

140 I.e., regarding the Qurʾanic statement (in verse 145) that God forbids only a few, clearly-defined categories of food. The pronoun "they" refers to the Jews as well as to the pagan Arabs spoken of in the preceding verses – both of whom claim that God has imposed on man various complicated restrictions in the matter of food. According to the Qurʾān, the Jews are wrong in their claim inasmuch as they overlook the fact that the severe Mosaic food laws were a punishment for their past misdeeds (see 3 : 93) and, therefore, intended for them alone; and the pagan Arabs are wrong because their taboos have no divine basis whatsoever and are due to mere superstition.

141 I.e., the truth that God has endowed man with the ability to *choose* between right and wrong. The above verse constitutes a categorical rejection of the doctrine of "predestination" in the commonly-accepted sense of this term.

142 I.e., knowledge regarding "predestination".

143 In other words, the real relationship between God's knowledge of the future (and, therefore, the ineluctability of what is to happen in the future) on the one side, and man's free will, on the other – two propositions which, on the face of it, seem to contradict one another – is beyond man's comprehension; but since both are postulated by God,

ثلاثة ارباع الحزب

Say: "Bring forward your witnesses who could bear witness that God has forbidden [all] this!"[144] – and if they bear witness [falsely], do not bear witness with them; and do not follow the errant views of those who have given the lie to Our messages, nor of those who believe not in the life to come, and who regard other powers as their Sustainer's equals!"[145] ‹150›

Say: "Come, let me convey unto you what God has [really] forbidden to you:

"Do not ascribe divinity, in any way, to aught beside Him; and [do not offend against but, rather,] do good unto your parents;[146] and do not kill your children for fear of poverty – [for] it is We who shall provide sustenance for you as well as for them;[147] and do not commit any shameful deeds, be they open or secret; and do not take any human being's life – [the life] which God has declared to be sacred – otherwise than in [the pursuit of] justice: this has He enjoined upon you so that you might use your reason;[148] ‹151› and do not touch the substance of an orphan – save to improve it – before he comes of age."[149]

And [in all your dealings] give full measure and weight,[150] with equity: [however,] We do not burden any human being with more

قُلْ هَلُمَّ شُهَدَآءَكُمُ ٱلَّذِينَ يَشْهَدُونَ أَنَّ ٱللَّهَ حَرَّمَ هَٰذَا ۖ فَإِن شَهِدُوا۟ فَلَا
تَشْهَدْ مَعَهُمْ ۚ وَلَا تَتَّبِعْ أَهْوَآءَ ٱلَّذِينَ كَذَّبُوا۟ بِـَٔايَٰتِنَا وَٱلَّذِينَ لَا يُؤْمِنُونَ
بِٱلْءَاخِرَةِ وَهُم بِرَبِّهِمْ يَعْدِلُونَ ﴿١٥٠﴾ ۞ قُلْ تَعَالَوْا۟ أَتْلُ مَا حَرَّمَ رَبُّكُمْ
عَلَيْكُمْ ۖ أَلَّا تُشْرِكُوا۟ بِهِۦ شَيْـًٔا ۖ وَبِٱلْوَٰلِدَيْنِ إِحْسَٰنًا ۖ وَلَا تَقْتُلُوٓا۟ أَوْلَٰدَكُم
مِّنْ إِمْلَٰقٍ ۖ نَّحْنُ نَرْزُقُكُمْ وَإِيَّاهُمْ ۖ وَلَا تَقْرَبُوا۟ ٱلْفَوَٰحِشَ مَا ظَهَرَ مِنْهَا
وَمَا بَطَنَ ۖ وَلَا تَقْتُلُوا۟ ٱلنَّفْسَ ٱلَّتِى حَرَّمَ ٱللَّهُ إِلَّا بِٱلْحَقِّ ۚ ذَٰلِكُمْ وَصَّىٰكُم بِهِۦ
لَعَلَّكُمْ تَعْقِلُونَ ﴿١٥١﴾ وَلَا تَقْرَبُوا۟ مَالَ ٱلْيَتِيمِ إِلَّا بِٱلَّتِى هِىَ أَحْسَنُ حَتَّىٰ
يَبْلُغَ أَشُدَّهُۥ ۖ وَأَوْفُوا۟ ٱلْكَيْلَ وَٱلْمِيزَانَ بِٱلْقِسْطِ ۖ لَا نُكَلِّفُ نَفْسًا إِلَّا

**Qul halumma shuhadāaʾakumul-ladhīna yashhadūna ʾannal-lāha ḥarrama hādhā. Faʾin-shahidū falā tashhad maʿahum. Wa lā tattabiʿ ʾahwāaʾal-ladhīna kadhdhabū biʾĀyātinā wal-ladhīna lā yuʾminūna bil-ʾĀkhirati wa hum-biRabbihim yaʿdilūn.
150 ◈ Qul taʿālaw ʾatlu mā ḥarrama Rabbukum ʿalaykum ʾallā tushrikū bihī shayʾañw-wa bil-wālidayni ʾiḥsānā. Wa lā taqtulūu ʾawlādakum-min ʾimlāqiñ-Naḥnu narzuqukum wa ʾiyyāhum; wa lā taqrabul-fawāḥisha mā ẓahara minhā wa mā baṭan. Wa lā taqtulun-nafsal-latī ḥarramal-lāhu ʾillā bilḥaqq. Dhālikum waṣṣākum-bihī laʿallakum taʿqilūn.
151 Wa lā taqrabū mālal-yatīmi ʾillā billatī hiya ʾaḥsanu ḥattā yablugha ʾashuddah. Wa ʾawful-kayla wal-mīzāna bilqisṭ. Lā nukallifu nafsan ʾillā**

both must be true. The very concept of "God" presupposes His omniscience; and the very concept of morality and moral responsibility presupposes free will on man's part. Had God so willed, every human being would have been *forced* to live righteously; but this would have amounted to depriving man of his free will, and morality of all its meaning.

144 A reference to the arbitrary prohibitions mentioned in the preceding passages.

145 Lit., "make [others] equal to their Sustainer": i.e., attribute divine or almost-divine qualities to certain ill-defined natural powers – e.g., believe in "spontaneous" creative evolution, or in a "self-created" universe, or in a mysterious, impersonal *élan vital* that supposedly underlies all existence, etc.

146 In the consensus of all the commentators, the phrase interpolated by me between brackets is clearly implied in the above commandment, since it is mentioned among the things which God has *forbidden* – and being good towards one's parents is not only not forbidden but, on the contrary, enjoined over and over in the Qurʾān.

147 This may possibly refer to abortions dictated by economic considerations.

148 Sc., "and not resort to brute force whenever your private interests are involved". The expression "otherwise than in [the pursuit of] justice" refers to the execution of a legal punishment or to killing in a just – that is, defensive – war, or to individual, legitimate self-defence.

149 I.e., after the orphan in one's charge has come of age, the former guardian may "touch" his property, legally, by borrowing from it or otherwise utilizing it with the owner's consent. The phrase rendered by me as "save to improve it" reads, literally, "in a manner that is best", which implies the intent of bettering it.

150 This refers metonymically to all dealings between men and not only to commercial transactions: hence my interpolation of "in all your dealings".

than he is well able to bear;[151] and when you voice an opinion, be just, even though it be [against] one near of kin.[152]
And [always] observe your bond with God:[153] this has He enjoined upon you, so that you might keep it in mind. ‹152›
And [know] that this is the way leading straight unto Me: follow it, then, and follow not other ways, lest they cause you to deviate[154] from His way.
[All] this has He enjoined upon you, so that you might remain conscious of Him. ‹153›

AND ONCE AGAIN:[155] We vouchsafed the divine writ unto Moses in fulfilment [of Our favour] upon those who persevered in doing good, clearly spelling out everything,[156] and [thus providing] guidance and grace, so that they might have faith in the [final] meeting with their Sustainer. ‹154›
And this, too, is a divine writ which We have bestowed from on high, a blessed one: follow it, then, and be conscious of God, so that you might be graced with His mercy. ‹155› [It has been given to you] lest you say, "Only unto two groups of people, [both of them] before our time, has a divine writ been bestowed from on high[157] – and we were indeed unaware of their teachings"; ‹156› or lest you say, "If a divine writ had been bestowed from on high upon us, we would surely have followed its guidance better than they did."[158]

وُسْعَهَا وَإِذَا قُلْتُمْ فَٱعْدِلُوا۟ وَلَوْ كَانَ ذَا قُرْبَىٰ وَبِعَهْدِ ٱللَّهِ أَوْفُوا۟ ذَٰلِكُمْ
وَصَّىٰكُم بِهِۦ لَعَلَّكُمْ تَذَكَّرُونَ ﴿١٥٢﴾ وَأَنَّ هَٰذَا صِرَٰطِى مُسْتَقِيمًا فَٱتَّبِعُوهُ
وَلَا تَتَّبِعُوا۟ ٱلسُّبُلَ فَتَفَرَّقَ بِكُمْ عَن سَبِيلِهِۦ ذَٰلِكُمْ وَصَّىٰكُم بِهِۦ لَعَلَّكُمْ
تَتَّقُونَ ﴿١٥٣﴾ ثُمَّ ءَاتَيْنَا مُوسَى ٱلْكِتَٰبَ تَمَامًا عَلَى ٱلَّذِىٓ أَحْسَنَ وَتَفْصِيلًا
لِّكُلِّ شَىْءٍ وَهُدًى وَرَحْمَةً لَّعَلَّهُم بِلِقَآءِ رَبِّهِمْ يُؤْمِنُونَ ﴿١٥٤﴾ وَهَٰذَا كِتَٰبٌ
أَنزَلْنَٰهُ مُبَارَكٌ فَٱتَّبِعُوهُ وَٱتَّقُوا۟ لَعَلَّكُمْ تُرْحَمُونَ ﴿١٥٥﴾ أَن تَقُولُوٓا۟ إِنَّمَآ
أُنزِلَ ٱلْكِتَٰبُ عَلَىٰ طَآئِفَتَيْنِ مِن قَبْلِنَا وَإِن كُنَّا عَن دِرَاسَتِهِمْ
لَغَٰفِلِينَ ﴿١٥٦﴾ أَوْ تَقُولُوا۟ لَوْ أَنَّآ أُنزِلَ عَلَيْنَا ٱلْكِتَٰبُ لَكُنَّآ أَهْدَىٰ مِنْهُمْ

wusʿahā; wa ʾidhā qultum faʿdilū wa law kāna dhā qurbā. Wa biʿahdil-lāhi ʾawfū; dhālikum waṣṣākum-bihī laʿallakum tadhakkarūn. (152) Wa ʾanna hādhā ṣirāṭī mustaqīmañ-fattabiʿūh. Wa lā tattabiʿus-subula fatafarraqa bikum ʿañ-sabīlih. Dhālikum waṣṣā-kum-bihī laʿallakum tattaqūn. (153) Thumma ʾātaynā Mūsal-Kitāba tamāman ʿalal-ladhīi ʾaḥsana wa tafṣīlal-likulli shayʾiñw-wa hudañw-wa raḥmatal-laʿallahum-biliqāaʾi Rabbihim yuʾminūn. (154) Wa hādhā Kitābun ʾañzalnāhu mubārakuñ-fattabiʿūhu wattaqū laʿallakum turḥamūn. (155) ʾAñ-taqūlūu ʾinnamāa ʾuñzilal-Kitābu ʿalā ṭāaʾifatayni miñ-qablinā wa ʾiñ-kunnā ʿañ-dirāsatihim laghāfilīn. (156) ʾAw taqūlū law ʾannāa ʾuñzila ʿalaynal-Kitābu lakunnāa ʾahdā minhum.

151 The meaning is that God does not expect man to behave with "mathematical" equity – which, in view of the many intangible factors involved, is rarely attainable in human dealings – but expects him to do his best towards achieving this ideal.

152 According to Rāzī, the phrase "when you voice an opinion" (lit., "when you speak") applies to expressing an opinion on any subject, whether it concerns one personally or not; but the subsequent reference to one's "near of kin" makes it probable that the above injunction relates, in particular, to the giving of evidence in cases under dispute.

153 See *sūrah* 2, note 19.

154 Lit., "to become scattered".

155 See note 31 on the last paragraph of verse 38 of this *sūrah*. In this instance, the stress implied in the use of *thumma* seems to point to verse 91 of this *sūrah*.

156 I.e., everything that they needed by way of laws and injunctions appropriate to their time and the stage of their development (Rāzī). See in this connection the phrase, "Unto every one of you have We appointed a [different] law and way of life", occurring in 5 : 48, and the corresponding note 66.

157 I.e., to the Jews and the Christians, who were the only two communities known to the Arabs as possessing revealed scriptures.

158 Although this passage refers, in the first instance, to the Arabian contemporaries of the Prophet, its message is

فَقَدْ جَآءَكُم بَيِّنَةٌ مِّن رَّبِّكُمْ وَهُدًى وَرَحْمَةٌ ۚ فَمَنْ أَظْلَمُ مِمَّن كَذَّبَ
بِـَٔايَٰتِ ٱللَّهِ وَصَدَفَ عَنْهَا ۗ سَنَجْزِى ٱلَّذِينَ يَصْدِفُونَ عَنْ ءَايَٰتِنَا سُوٓءَ
ٱلْعَذَابِ بِمَا كَانُوا۟ يَصْدِفُونَ ﴿١٥٧﴾ هَلْ يَنظُرُونَ إِلَّآ أَن تَأْتِيَهُمُ
ٱلْمَلَٰٓئِكَةُ أَوْ يَأْتِىَ رَبُّكَ أَوْ يَأْتِىَ بَعْضُ ءَايَٰتِ رَبِّكَ ۗ يَوْمَ يَأْتِى بَعْضُ
ءَايَٰتِ رَبِّكَ لَا يَنفَعُ نَفْسًا إِيمَٰنُهَا لَمْ تَكُنْ ءَامَنَتْ مِن قَبْلُ أَوْ
كَسَبَتْ فِىٓ إِيمَٰنِهَا خَيْرًا ۗ قُلِ ٱنتَظِرُوٓا۟ إِنَّا مُنتَظِرُونَ ﴿١٥٨﴾ إِنَّ ٱلَّذِينَ
فَرَّقُوا۟ دِينَهُمْ وَكَانُوا۟ شِيَعًا لَّسْتَ مِنْهُمْ فِى شَىْءٍ ۚ إِنَّمَآ أَمْرُهُمْ إِلَى ٱللَّهِ ثُمَّ
يُنَبِّئُهُم بِمَا كَانُوا۟ يَفْعَلُونَ ﴿١٥٩﴾ مَن جَآءَ بِٱلْحَسَنَةِ فَلَهُۥ عَشْرُ أَمْثَالِهَا
وَمَن جَآءَ بِٱلسَّيِّئَةِ فَلَا يُجْزَىٰٓ إِلَّا مِثْلَهَا وَهُمْ لَا يُظْلَمُونَ ﴿١٦٠﴾

And so, a clear evidence of the truth has now come unto you from your Sustainer, and guidance, and grace. Who, then, could be more wicked than he who gives the lie to God's messages, and turns away from them in disdain?
We shall requite those who turn away from Our messages in disdain with evil suffering for having thus turned away! ‹157›
Do they, perchance, wait for the angels to appear unto them, or for thy Sustainer [Himself] to appear, or for some of thy Sustainer's [final] portents to appear?[159] [But] on the Day when thy Sustainer's [final] portents do appear, believing will be of no avail to any human being who did not believe before, or who, while believing, did no good works.[160]
Say: "Wait, [then, for the Last Day, O unbelievers:] behold, we [believers] are waiting, too!" ‹158›

VERILY, as for those who have broken the unity of their faith and have become sects – thou hast nothing to do with them.[161] Behold, their case rests with God: and in time He will make them understand what they were doing. ‹159›
Whoever shall come [before God] with a good deed will gain ten times the like thereof; but whoever shall come with an evil deed will be requited with no more than the like thereof; and none shall be wronged.[162] ‹160›

Faqad jāaʾakum-bayyinatum-mir-Rabbikum wa hudañw-wa raḥmah. Faman ʾaẓlamu mimmañ-kadhdhaba biʾĀyātil-lāhi wa ṣadafa ʿanhā. Sanajzil-ladhīna yaṣdifūna ʿan ʾĀyātinā sūuʾal-ʿadhābi bimā kānū yaṣdifūn. (157) Hal yañẓurūna ʾillāa ʾañ-taʾtiyahumul-Malāaʾikatu ʾaw yaʾtiya Rabbuka ʾaw yaʾtiya baʿḍu ʾĀyāti Rabbik. Yawma yaʾtī baʿḍu ʾĀyāti Rabbika lā yañfaʿu nafsan ʾīmānuhā lam takun ʾāmanat miñ-qablu ʾaw kasabat fīi ʾīmānihā khayrā. Quliñ-taẓirūu ʾinnā muñtaẓirūn. (158) ʾInnal-ladhīna farraqū dīnahum wa kānū shiyaʿal-lasta minhum fī shayʾ. ʾInnamāa ʾamruhum ʾilal-lāhi thumma yunabbiʾuhum-bimā kānū yafʿalūn. (159) Mañ-jāaʾa bilḥasanati falahū ʿashru ʾamthālihā; wa mañ-jāaʾa bissayyiʾati falā yujzāa ʾillā mithlahā wa hum lā yuẓlamūn. (160)

not restricted to them but relates to all people, at all times, who refuse to believe in revelation unless they themselves are its direct recipients.

159 I.e., the signs announcing the Day of Judgment.

160 Lit., "or [did not] earn good in his faith": thus, faith without good works is here declared to be equivalent to having no faith at all (Zamakhsharī).

161 A reference, primarily, to the Jews and the Christians, who have departed from the fundamental religious principles which they had originally shared in their entirety, and have gone different ways in respect of doctrine and ethics (cf. 3 : 105). Beyond this "primary" reference, however, the above verse connects logically with verse 153 above, "this is the way leading straight unto Me: follow it, then, and follow not other ways, lest they cause you to deviate from His way" – and thus relates prophetically to the followers of the Qurʾān as well: in other words, it expresses a condemnation of all sectarianism arising out of people's intolerant, mutually-exclusive claims to being "the only true exponents" of the Qurʾanic teachings. Thus, when asked about the implications of this verse, the Prophet's Companion Abū Hurayrah is reported to have answered, "It has been revealed with reference to this [our] community" (Ṭabarī).

162 Lit., "and they shall not be wronged". See in this connection the statement that God "has willed upon Himself

SAY: "Behold, my Sustainer has guided me onto a straight way through an ever-true faith – the way of Abraham, who turned away from all that is false, and was not of those who ascribe divinity to aught beside Him." ‹161›

Say: "Behold, my prayer, and [all] my acts of worship, and my living and my dying are for God [alone], the Sustainer of all the worlds, ‹162› in whose divinity none has a share: for thus have I been bidden – and I shall [always] be foremost among those who surrender themselves unto Him." ‹163›

Say: "Am I, then, to seek a sustainer other than God, when He is the Sustainer of all things?"

And whatever [wrong] any human being commits rests upon himself alone; and no bearer of burdens shall be made to bear another's burden.[163] And, in time, unto your Sustainer you all must return: and then He will make you [truly] understand all that on which you were wont to differ.[164] ‹164›

For, He it is who has made you inherit the earth,[165] and has raised some of you by degrees above others, so that He might try you by means of what He has bestowed upon you.[166]

Verily, thy Sustainer is swift in retribution: yet, behold, He is indeed much-forgiving, a dispenser of grace. ‹165›

قُلْ إِنَّنِى هَدَىٰنِى رَبِّىٓ إِلَىٰ صِرَٰطٍ مُّسْتَقِيمٍ دِينًا قِيَمًا مِّلَّةَ إِبْرَٰهِيمَ حَنِيفًا
وَمَا كَانَ مِنَ ٱلْمُشْرِكِينَ ﴿١٦١﴾ قُلْ إِنَّ صَلَاتِى وَنُسُكِى وَمَحْيَاىَ وَمَمَاتِى لِلَّهِ
رَبِّ ٱلْعَٰلَمِينَ ﴿١٦٢﴾ لَا شَرِيكَ لَهُۥ وَبِذَٰلِكَ أُمِرْتُ وَأَنَا۠ أَوَّلُ
ٱلْمُسْلِمِينَ ﴿١٦٣﴾ قُلْ أَغَيْرَ ٱللَّهِ أَبْغِى رَبًّا وَهُوَ رَبُّ كُلِّ شَىْءٍ وَلَا تَكْسِبُ
كُلُّ نَفْسٍ إِلَّا عَلَيْهَا وَلَا تَزِرُ وَازِرَةٌ وِزْرَ أُخْرَىٰ ثُمَّ إِلَىٰ رَبِّكُم مَّرْجِعُكُمْ
فَيُنَبِّئُكُم بِمَا كُنتُمْ فِيهِ تَخْتَلِفُونَ ﴿١٦٤﴾ وَهُوَ ٱلَّذِى جَعَلَكُمْ خَلَٰٓئِفَ
ٱلْأَرْضِ وَرَفَعَ بَعْضَكُمْ فَوْقَ بَعْضٍ دَرَجَٰتٍ لِّيَبْلُوَكُمْ فِى مَآ ءَاتَىٰكُمْ
إِنَّ رَبَّكَ سَرِيعُ ٱلْعِقَابِ وَإِنَّهُۥ لَغَفُورٌ رَّحِيمٌۢ ﴿١٦٥﴾

Qul ʾinnanī hadānī Rabbīi ʾilā ṣirāṭim-mustaqīmiñ-dīnañ-qiyamam-millata ʾIbrāhima ḥanīfañw-wa mā kāna minal-mushrikīn. (161) Qul ʾinna Ṣalātī wa nusukī wa maḥyāya wa mamātī lil-lāhi Rabbil-ʿālamīn. (162) Lā sharīka lahū wa bidhālika ʾumirtu wa ʾana ʾawwalul-Muslimīn. (163) Qul ʾaghayral-lāhi ʾabghī Rabbañw-wa Huwa Rabbu kulli shayʾ. Wa lā taksibu kullu nafsin ʾillā ʿalayhā; wa lā taziru wāziratuñw-wizra ʾukhrā. Thumma ʾilā Rabbikum-marjiʿukum fayunabbiʾukum-bimā kuñtum fīhi takhtalifūn. (164) Wa Huwal-ladhī jaʿalakum khalāaʾifal-ʾarḍi wa rafaʿa baʿḍakum fawqa baʿḍiñ-darajātil-liyabluwakum fī māa ʾātākum. ʾInna Rabbaka Sarīʿul-ʿiqābi wa ʾinnahū laGhafūrur-Raḥīm. (165)

the law of grace and mercy", occurring in verse 12 of this *sūrah*, and the corresponding note 10.

163 This statement – which is also found in 17 : 15, 35 : 18, 39 : 7 and 53 : 38 – constitutes a categorical rejection of the Christian doctrines of "original sin" and "vicarious atonement". For the wider ethical implications of this statement, see 53 : 38, where it occurs for the first time in the chronological order of revelation.

164 See *sūrah* 2, note 94.

165 See 2 : 30, and the corresponding note 22.

166 I.e., by way of character, strength, knowledge, social position, wealth, etc.

The Seventh Sūrah

Al-ᵓAᶜrāf (The Faculty of Discernment)

Mecca Period

THE TITLE of this *sūrah* is based on an expression which occurs in verses 46 and 48; its meaning is explained in note 37. According to most of the authorities (and particularly Ibn ᶜAbbās), the whole of *Al-ᵓAᶜrāf* was revealed shortly before the preceding *sūrah* – that is, in the last year of the Prophet's stay at Mecca; the assertion of As-Suyūṭī and some other scholars to the effect that verses 163-171 belong to the Medina period is the result of mere conjecture and cannot, therefore, be accepted (*Manār* VIII, 294).

Although, in the chronological order of revelation, *Al-ᵓAᶜrāf* precedes the sixth *sūrah*, it has been placed after the latter because it elaborates the theme outlined therein. After the exposition of God's oneness and uniqueness – which, as I have pointed out in the introductory note to *Al-ᵓAnᶜām*, constitutes the main theme of the sixth *sūrah* – *Al-ᵓAᶜrāf* proceeds with a reference to revelation as a means by which God communicates His will to man: in other words, to the mission of the prophets. The need for continued prophetic guidance arises from the fact of man's weakness and his readiness to follow every temptation that appeals to his appetites, his vanity, or his mistaken sense of self-interest: and this essential aspect of the human condition is illustrated in the allegory of Adam and Eve and their fall from grace (verses 19-25), preceded by the allegory of Iblīs as man's eternal tempter (verses 16-18). Without the guidance which God offers man through His prophets, the right way cannot be found; and, therefore, "unto those who give the lie to Our messages and scorn them in their pride, the gates of heaven shall not be opened" (verse 40). From verse 59 onwards, most of the *sūrah* is devoted to the histories of some of the earlier prophets whose warnings were rejected by their people, beginning with Noah, continuing with Hūd, Ṣāliḥ, Lot and Shuᶜayb, and culminating in a lengthy account of Shuᶜayb's son-in-law, Moses, and his experiences with the children of Israel. With verse 172 the discourse reverts to the complex psychology of man, his instinctive ability to perceive God's existence and oneness, and to "what happens to him to whom God vouchsafes His messages and who then discards them: Satan catches up with him, and he strays, like so many others, into grievous error" (verse 175). This brings us to God's final message, the Qurᵓān, and to the role of the Last Prophet, Muḥammad, who is "nothing but a warner and a herald of glad tidings" (verse 188): a mortal servant of God, having no "supernatural" powers or qualities, and – like all God-conscious men – "never too proud to worship Him" (verse 206).

سورة الأعراف مكية -7-
وآياتها ست ومائتان

IN THE NAME OF GOD, THE MOST GRACIOUS, THE DISPENSER OF GRACE:

Alif. Lām. Mīm. Ṣād.[1] ‹1›
A DIVINE WRIT has been bestowed from on high upon thee – and let there be no doubt about this in thy heart – in order that thou mayest warn [the erring] thereby, and [thus] admonish the believers:[2] ‹2›
"Follow what has been sent down unto you by your Sustainer, and follow no masters other than Him."[3]
How seldom do you keep this in mind! ‹3›
And how many a [rebellious] community have We destroyed, with Our punishment coming upon it by night, or while they were resting at noontide![4] ‹4› And when Our punishment came upon them, they had nothing to say for themselves, and could only cry,[5] "Verily, we were wrongdoers!" ‹5›
Thus, [on Judgment Day] We shall most certainly call to account all those unto whom a [divine] message was sent, and We shall most certainly call to account the message-bearers [themselves];[6] ‹6›

بِسۡمِ ٱللَّهِ ٱلرَّحۡمَٰنِ ٱلرَّحِيمِ

الٓمٓصٓ ﴿١﴾ كِتَٰبٌ أُنزِلَ إِلَيۡكَ فَلَا يَكُن فِي صَدۡرِكَ حَرَجٞ مِّنۡهُ لِتُنذِرَ
بِهِۦ وَذِكۡرَىٰ لِلۡمُؤۡمِنِينَ ﴿٢﴾ ٱتَّبِعُواْ مَآ أُنزِلَ إِلَيۡكُم مِّن رَّبِّكُمۡ وَلَا
تَتَّبِعُواْ مِن دُونِهِۦٓ أَوۡلِيَآءَۗ قَلِيلٗا مَّا تَذَكَّرُونَ ﴿٣﴾ وَكَم مِّن قَرۡيَةٍ
أَهۡلَكۡنَٰهَا فَجَآءَهَا بَأۡسُنَا بَيَٰتًا أَوۡ هُمۡ قَآئِلُونَ ﴿٤﴾ فَمَا كَانَ دَعۡوَىٰهُمۡ إِذۡ
جَآءَهُم بَأۡسُنَآ إِلَّآ أَن قَالُوٓاْ إِنَّا كُنَّا ظَٰلِمِينَ ﴿٥﴾ فَلَنَسۡـَٔلَنَّ ٱلَّذِينَ أُرۡسِلَ
إِلَيۡهِمۡ وَلَنَسۡـَٔلَنَّ ٱلۡمُرۡسَلِينَ ﴿٦﴾

حزب 16

Bismil-lāhir-Raḥmānir-Raḥīm.
ʾAlif-Lāam-Mīim-Ṣāad. (1) Kitābun ʾuñzila ʾilayka falā yakuñ-fī ṣadrika ḥarajum-minhu lituñdhira bihī wa dhikrā lilmuʾminīn. (2) ʾIttabiʿū māa ʾuñzila ʾilaykum-mir-Rabbikum wa la tattabiʿū miñ-dūnihīi ʾawliyāaʾ. Qalīlam-mā tadhakkarūn. (3) Wa kam-miñ-qaryatin ʾahlaknāhā fajāaʾahā baʾsunā bayātan ʾaw hum qāaʾilūn. (4) Famā kāna daʿwāhum ʾidh jāaʾahum-baʾsunāa ʾillāa ʾañ-qālūu ʾinnā kunnā ẓālimīn. (5) Falanasʾalannal-ladhīna ʾursila ʾilayhim wa lanasʾalannal-Mursalīn. (6)

---

1 See Appendix II.

2 The expression *ḥaraj* (lit., "straitness" or "tightness") is often used idiomatically to denote "doubt": and this is, according to Ibn ʿAbbās, Mujāhid and Qatādah, the meaning of the term here (see Ṭabarī, Zamakhsharī, Baghawī, Rāzī, Ibn Kathīr). The construction of the whole sentence makes it clear that the "doubt" does not relate to the *origin* of the divine writ but to its *purpose*: and thus, although ostensibly addressed to the Prophet, the above passage is meant to draw the attention of all whom the Qurʾanic message may reach to the fact that it has a twofold objective – namely, to warn the rejectors of the truth and to guide those who already believe in it. Both the warning and the admonition are summarized in the sequence.

3 Some of the great Muslim thinkers, and particularly Ibn Ḥazm and Ibn Taymiyyah, maintain that the expression *awliyāʾ* (here rendered as "masters") denotes, in this context, "authorities" in the religious sense of the word, implying a prohibition of attributing legal validity – side by side with Qurʾanic ordinances – to the subjective opinions of any person below the Prophet. See in this connection 5 : 101, and the corresponding notes.

4 I.e., suddenly, when the people felt completely secure and at ease. This passage connects with the obligation, laid down in the preceding two verses, to follow God's revealed messages.

5 Lit., "their plea was nothing but that they said".

6 Cf. 5 : 109.

فَلَنَقُصَّنَّ عَلَيْهِم بِعِلْمٍ وَمَا كُنَّا غَآئِبِينَ ﴿٧﴾ وَٱلْوَزْنُ يَوْمَئِذٍ ٱلْحَقُّ فَمَن
ثَقُلَتْ مَوَٰزِينُهُۥ فَأُو۟لَٰٓئِكَ هُمُ ٱلْمُفْلِحُونَ ﴿٨﴾ وَمَنْ خَفَّتْ مَوَٰزِينُهُۥ
فَأُو۟لَٰٓئِكَ ٱلَّذِينَ خَسِرُوٓا۟ أَنفُسَهُم بِمَا كَانُوا۟ بِـَٔايَٰتِنَا يَظْلِمُونَ ﴿٩﴾ وَلَقَدْ
مَكَّنَّٰكُمْ فِى ٱلْأَرْضِ وَجَعَلْنَا لَكُمْ فِيهَا مَعَٰيِشَ قَلِيلًا مَّا تَشْكُرُونَ ﴿١٠﴾
وَلَقَدْ خَلَقْنَٰكُمْ ثُمَّ صَوَّرْنَٰكُمْ ثُمَّ قُلْنَا لِلْمَلَٰٓئِكَةِ ٱسْجُدُوا۟ لِءَادَمَ فَسَجَدُوٓا۟
إِلَّآ إِبْلِيسَ لَمْ يَكُن مِّنَ ٱلسَّٰجِدِينَ ﴿١١﴾ قَالَ مَا مَنَعَكَ أَلَّا تَسْجُدَ إِذْ
أَمَرْتُكَ قَالَ أَنَا۠ خَيْرٌ مِّنْهُ خَلَقْتَنِى مِن نَّارٍ وَخَلَقْتَهُۥ مِن طِينٍ ﴿١٢﴾

and thereupon We shall most certainly reveal unto them Our knowledge [of their doings]:[7] for never have We been absent [from them]. ‹7›

And true will be the weighing on that Day: and those whose weight [of good deeds] is heavy in the balance – it is they, they who shall attain to a happy state; ‹8› whereas those whose weight is light in the balance – it is they who will have squandered their own selves by their wilful rejection of Our messages.[8] ‹9›

Falanaquṣṣanna ᶜalayhim-biᶜilmiñw-wa mā kunnā ghāaᵓibīn. (7) Wal-waznu Yawmaᵓidhinil-ḥaqqu famañ-thaqulat mawāzīnuhū faᵓulāaᵓika humul-mufliḥūn. (8) Wa man khaffat mawāzīnuhū fa-ᵓulāaᵓikal-ladhīna khasirūu ᵓañfusahum-bimā kānū biᵓĀyātinā yaẓlimūn. (9) Wa laqad makkannākum fil-ᵓarḍi wa jaᶜalnā lakum fīhā maᶜāyish. Qalīlam-mā tashkurūn. (10) Wa laqad khalaqnākum thumma ṣawwarnākum thumma qulnā lilMalāaᵓikatis-judū liᵓĀdama fasajadūu ᵓillāa ᵓIblīsa lam yakum-minas-sājidīn. (11) Qāla mā manaᶜaka ᵓallā tasjuda ᵓidh ᵓamartuk. Qāla ᵓana khayrum-minhu khalaqtanī miñ-nāriñw-wa khalaqtahū miñ-ṭīn. (12)

YEA, INDEED, [O men,] We have given you a [bountiful] place on earth, and appointed thereon means of livelihood for you: [yet] how seldom are you grateful! ‹10›

Yea, indeed, We have created you, and then formed you;[9] and then We said unto the angels, "Prostrate yourselves before Adam!" – whereupon they [all] prostrated themselves, save Iblīs: he was not among those who prostrated themselves.[10] ‹11›

[And God] said: "What has kept thee from prostrating thyself when I commanded thee?"

Answered [Iblīs]: "I am better than he: Thou hast created me out of fire, whereas him Thou hast created out of clay." ‹12›

---

7 Lit., "relate to them with knowledge".

8 Lit., "for that they were wont to act wrongfully with regard to Our messages".

9 The sequence of these two statements – "We have created you [i.e., "brought you into being as living organisms"] and then formed you" [or "given you your shape", i.e., as human beings] – is meant to bring out the fact of man's gradual development, in the individual sense, from the embryonic stage to full-fledged existence, as well as of the evolution of the human race as such.

10 As regards God's allegorical command to the angels to "prostrate themselves" before Adam, see 2 : 30-34, and the corresponding notes. The reference to all mankind which precedes the story of Adam in this *sūrah* makes it clear that his name symbolizes, in this context, the whole human race.

Western scholars usually take it for granted that the name "Iblīs" is a corruption of the Greek word *diábolos,* from which the English "devil" is derived. There is, however, not the slightest evidence that the pre-Islamic Arabs borrowed this or any other mythological term from the Greeks – while, on the other hand, it is established that the Greeks derived a good deal of their mythological concepts (including various deities and their functions) from the much earlier South-Arabian civilization (cf. *Encyclopaedia of Islam* I, 379 f.). One may, therefore, assume with something approaching certainty that the Greek *diábolos,* is a Hellenized form of the Arabic name for the Fallen Angel, which, in turn, is derived from the root-verb *ablasa,* "he despaired" or "gave up hope" or "became broken in spirit" (see Lane I, 248). The fact that the noun *diábolos* ("slanderer" – derived from the verb *diaballein,* "to throw [something] across") is of genuinely Greek origin does not, by itself, detract anything from this hypothesis: for it is conceivable that the Greeks, with their well-known tendency to Hellenize foreign names, identified the name "Iblīs" with the, to them, much more familiar term *diábolos.* – As regards Iblīs' statement, in the next verse, that he had been created "out of fire", see *sūrah* 38, note 60.

[God] said: "Down with thee, then, from this [state] – for it is not meet for thee to show arrogance here! Go forth, then: verily, among the humiliated shalt thou be!" ‹13›
Said [Iblīs]: "Grant me a respite till the Day when all shall be raised from the dead." ‹14›
[And God] replied: "Verily, thou shalt be among those who are granted a respite." ‹15›
[Whereupon Iblīs] said: "Now that Thou hast thwarted me,[11] I shall most certainly lie in ambush for them all along Thy straight way, ‹16› and shall most certainly fall upon them openly as well as in a manner beyond their ken,[12] and from their right and from their left: and most of them Thou wilt find ungrateful." ‹17›
[And God] said: "Go forth from here, disgraced and disowned! [And] as for such of them as follow thee – I will most certainly fill hell with you all!" ‹18›
And [as for thee], O Adam, dwell thou and thy wife in this garden, and eat, both of you, whatever you may wish; but do not approach this one tree, lest you become evildoers!"[13] ‹19›
Thereupon Satan whispered unto the two with a view to making them conscious of their nakedness, of which [hitherto] they had been unaware;[14] and he said: "Your Sustainer has but forbidden you this tree lest you two become [as] angels, or lest you live forever."[15] ‹20›

قَالَ فَٱهۡبِطۡ مِنۡهَا فَمَا يَكُونُ لَكَ أَن تَتَكَبَّرَ فِيهَا فَٱخۡرُجۡ إِنَّكَ مِنَ
ٱلصَّٰغِرِينَ ﴿13﴾ قَالَ أَنظِرۡنِيٓ إِلَىٰ يَوۡمِ يُبۡعَثُونَ ﴿14﴾ قَالَ إِنَّكَ مِنَ
ٱلۡمُنظَرِينَ ﴿15﴾ قَالَ فَبِمَآ أَغۡوَيۡتَنِي لَأَقۡعُدَنَّ لَهُمۡ صِرَٰطَكَ ٱلۡمُسۡتَقِيمَ ﴿16﴾
ثُمَّ لَأٓتِيَنَّهُم مِّنۢ بَيۡنِ أَيۡدِيهِمۡ وَمِنۡ خَلۡفِهِمۡ وَعَنۡ أَيۡمَٰنِهِمۡ وَعَن شَمَآئِلِهِمۡۖ
وَلَا تَجِدُ أَكۡثَرَهُمۡ شَٰكِرِينَ ﴿17﴾ قَالَ ٱخۡرُجۡ مِنۡهَا مَذۡءُومٗا مَّدۡحُورٗاۖ لَّمَن
تَبِعَكَ مِنۡهُمۡ لَأَمۡلَأَنَّ جَهَنَّمَ مِنكُمۡ أَجۡمَعِينَ ﴿18﴾ وَيَٰٓـَٔادَمُ ٱسۡكُنۡ أَنتَ
وَزَوۡجُكَ ٱلۡجَنَّةَ فَكُلَا مِنۡ حَيۡثُ شِئۡتُمَا وَلَا تَقۡرَبَا هَٰذِهِ ٱلشَّجَرَةَ
فَتَكُونَا مِنَ ٱلظَّٰلِمِينَ ﴿19﴾ فَوَسۡوَسَ لَهُمَا ٱلشَّيۡطَٰنُ لِيُبۡدِيَ لَهُمَا مَا
وُۥرِيَ عَنۡهُمَا مِن سَوۡءَٰتِهِمَا وَقَالَ مَا نَهَىٰكُمَا رَبُّكُمَا عَنۡ هَٰذِهِ ٱلشَّجَرَةِ
إِلَّآ أَن تَكُونَا مَلَكَيۡنِ أَوۡ تَكُونَا مِنَ ٱلۡخَٰلِدِينَ ﴿20﴾

Qāla fahbiṭ minhā famā yakūnu laka ʾañ-tatakabbara fīhā fakhruj ʾinnaka minaṣ-ṣāghirīn. (13) Qāla ʾañẓirnii ʾillā Yawmi yubʿathūn. (14) Qāla ʾinnaka minal-muñẓarīn. (15) Qāla fabimāa ʾaghwaytanī laʾaqʿudanna lahum ṣirāṭakal-mustaqīm. (16) Thumma laʾātiyannahum-mim-bayni ʾaydīhim wa min khalfihim wa ʿan ʾaymānihim wa ʿañ-shamāaʾilihim; wa lā tajidu ʾaktharahum shākirīn. (17) Qālakh-ruj minhā madhʾūmam-madḥūrā. Lamañ-tabiʿaka minhum laʾamlaʾanna jahannama miñkum ʾajmaʿīn. (18) Wa yāa ʾĀdamus-kun ʾañta wa zawjukal-jannata fakulā min ḥaythu shiʾtumā wa lā taqrabā hādhihish-shajarata fatakūnā minaẓ-ẓālimīn. (19) Fawaswasa lahumash-Shayṭānu liyubdiya lahumā mā wūriya ʿanhumā miñ-sawʾātihimā wa qāla mā nahākumā Rabbukumā ʿan hādhihish-shajarati ʾillāa ʾañ-takūnā Malakayni ʾaw takūnā minal-khālidīn. (20)

11 Or: "allowed me to fall into error". The term *aghwāhu* denotes both "he caused [or "allowed"] him to err" or "he caused him to be disappointed" or "to fail in attaining his desire" (cf. Lane VI, 2304 f.). Since, in this case, the saying of Iblīs refers to the loss of his erstwhile position among the angels, the rendering adopted by me seems to be the most appropriate.

12 Lit., "from between their hands and from behind them". Regarding this idiomatic expression and my rendering of it, see the similar phrase in 2 : 255 ("He knows all that lies open before men and all that is hidden from them"). The subsequent phrase "from their right and from their left" signifies "from all directions and by all possible means".

13 See 2 : 35 and 20 : 120, as well as the corresponding notes.

14 Lit., "so as to make manifest to them that of their nakedness which [hitherto] had been imperceptible to them": an allegory of the state of innocence in which man lived before his fall from grace – that is, before his consciousness made him aware of himself and of the possibility of choosing between alternative courses of action, with all the attending temptations towards evil and the misery which must follow a wrong choice.

15 Lit., "or [lest] you become of those who are enduring": thus instilling in them the *desire* to live forever and to become, in this respect, like God. (See note 106 on 20 : 120.)

And he swore unto them, "Verily I am of those who wish you well indeed!" «21» – and thus he led them on with deluding thoughts.

But as soon as the two had tasted [the fruit] of the tree, they became conscious of their nakedness; and they began to cover themselves with pieced-together leaves from the garden. And their Sustainer called unto them: "Did I not forbid that tree unto you and tell you, 'Verily, Satan is your open foe'?" «22»

The two replied: "O our Sustainer! We have sinned against ourselves – and unless Thou grant us forgiveness and bestow Thy mercy upon us, we shall most certainly be lost!" «23»

Said He: "Down with you,[16] [and be henceforth] enemies unto one another, having on earth your abode and livelihood for a while: «24» there shall you live" – He added – "and there shall you die, and thence shall you be brought forth [on Resurrection Day]!" «25»

O CHILDREN of Adam! Indeed, We have bestowed upon you from on high [the knowledge of making] garments to cover your nakedness, and as a thing of beauty:[17] but the garment of God-consciousness is the best of all. Herein lies a message from God, so that man[18] might take it to heart. «26»

وَقَاسَمَهُمَآ إِنِّى لَكُمَا لَمِنَ ٱلنَّـٰصِحِينَ ﴿٢١﴾ فَدَلَّىٰهُمَا بِغُرُورٍ فَلَمَّا ذَاقَا
ٱلشَّجَرَةَ بَدَتْ لَهُمَا سَوْءَٰتُهُمَا وَطَفِقَا يَخْصِفَانِ عَلَيْهِمَا مِن وَرَقِ
ٱلْجَنَّةِ وَنَادَىٰهُمَا رَبُّهُمَآ أَلَمْ أَنْهَكُمَا عَن تِلْكُمَا ٱلشَّجَرَةِ وَأَقُل لَّكُمَآ
إِنَّ ٱلشَّيْطَـٰنَ لَكُمَا عَدُوٌّ مُّبِينٌ ﴿٢٢﴾ قَالَا رَبَّنَا ظَلَمْنَآ أَنفُسَنَا وَإِن لَّمْ
تَغْفِرْ لَنَا وَتَرْحَمْنَا لَنَكُونَنَّ مِنَ ٱلْخَـٰسِرِينَ ﴿٢٣﴾ قَالَ ٱهْبِطُوا۟ بَعْضُكُمْ
لِبَعْضٍ عَدُوٌّ وَلَكُمْ فِى ٱلْأَرْضِ مُسْتَقَرٌّ وَمَتَـٰعٌ إِلَىٰ حِينٍ ﴿٢٤﴾ قَالَ فِيهَا
تَحْيَوْنَ وَفِيهَا تَمُوتُونَ وَمِنْهَا تُخْرَجُونَ ﴿٢٥﴾ يَـٰبَنِىٓ ءَادَمَ قَدْ أَنزَلْنَا
عَلَيْكُمْ لِبَاسًا يُوَٰرِى سَوْءَٰتِكُمْ وَرِيشًا وَلِبَاسُ ٱلتَّقْوَىٰ ذَٰلِكَ خَيْرٌ
ذَٰلِكَ مِنْ ءَايَـٰتِ ٱللَّهِ لَعَلَّهُمْ يَذَّكَّرُونَ ﴿٢٦﴾

Wa qāsamahumāa ᵓinnī lakumā laminan-nāṣiḥīn. (21) Fadallāhumā bighurūr. Falammā dhāqash-shajarata badat lahumā sawᵓātuhumā wa ṭafiqā yakhṣifāni ᶜalayhimā miñw-waraqil-jannah. Wa nādāhumā Rabbuhumāa ᵓalam ᵓanhakumā ᶜañ-tilkumash-shajarati wa ᵓaqul-lakumā ᵓinnash-Shayṭāna lakumā ᶜaduwwum-mubīn. (22) Qālā Rabbanā ẓalamnāa ᵓañfusanā wa ᵓil-lam taghfir lanā wa tarḥamnā lanakūnanna minal-khāsirīn. (23) Qālah-biṭū baᶜḍukum libaᶜḍin ᶜaduww. Wa lakum fil-ᵓarḍi mustaqarruñw-wa matāᶜun ᵓilā ḥīn. (24) Qāla fīhā taḥyawna wa fīhā tamūtūna wa minha tukhrajūn. (25) Yā banīi ᵓĀdama qad ᵓañzalnā ᶜalaykum libāsañy-yuwārī sawᵓātikum wa rīshā. Wa libāsut-taqwā dhālika khayr. Dhālika min ᵓĀyātil-lāhi laᶜallahum yadhdhakkarūn. (26)

16 Sc., "from this state of blessedness and innocence". As in the parallel account of this parable of the Fall in 2 : 35-36, the dual form of address changes at this stage into the plural, thus connecting once again with verse 10 and the beginning of verse 11 of this *sūrah*, and making it clear that the story of Adam and Eve is, in reality, an allegory of human destiny. In his earlier state of innocence man was unaware of the existence of evil and, therefore, of the ever-present necessity of making a choice between the many possibilities of action and behaviour: in other words, he lived, like all other animals, in the light of his instincts alone. Inasmuch, however, as this innocence was only a condition of his existence and not a virtue, it gave to his life a static quality and thus precluded him from moral and intellectual development. The growth of his consciousness – symbolized by the wilful act of disobedience to God's command – changed all this. It transformed him from a purely instinctive being into a full-fledged human entity as we know it – a human being capable of discerning between right and wrong and thus of *choosing* his way of life. In this deeper sense, the allegory of the Fall does not describe a retrogressive happening but, rather, a new stage of human development: an opening of doors to moral considerations. By forbidding him to "approach this tree", God made it possible for man to act wrongly – and, therefore, to act rightly as well: and so man became endowed with that moral free will which distinguishes him from all other sentient beings. – Regarding the role of Satan – or Iblīs – as the eternal tempter of man, see note 26 on 2 : 34 and note 31 on 15 : 41.

17 Lit., "as plumage" – a metaphorical expression derived from the beauty of birds' plumage.

18 Lit., "this is [one] of God's messages, so that they . . .", etc.

O children of Adam! Do not allow Satan to seduce you in the same way as he caused your ancestors to be driven out of the garden: he deprived them of their garment [of God-consciousness] in order to make them aware of their nakedness. Verily, he and his tribe are lying in wait for you where you cannot perceive them![19]
Verily, We have placed [all manner of] satanic forces near unto those who do not [truly] believe;[20] ‹27› and [so,] whenever they commit a shameful deed, they are wont to say, "We found our forefathers doing it," and, "God has enjoined it upon us".
Say: "Behold, never does God enjoin deeds of abomination. Would you attribute unto God something of which you have no knowledge?" ‹28›
Say: "My Sustainer has [but] enjoined the doing of what is right; and [He desires you to] put your whole being into every act of worship,[21] and to call unto Him, sincere in your faith in Him alone. As it was He who brought you into being in the first instance, so also [unto Him] you will return: ‹29› some [of you] He will have graced with His guidance, whereas for some a straying from the right path will have become unavoidable:[22] for, behold, they will have taken [their own] evil impulses for their masters in preference to God, thinking all the while that they have found the right path!" ‹30›

يَـٰبَنِىٓ ءَادَمَ لَا يَفْتِنَنَّكُمُ ٱلشَّيْطَـٰنُ كَمَآ أَخْرَجَ أَبَوَيْكُم مِّنَ ٱلْجَنَّةِ
يَنزِعُ عَنْهُمَا لِبَاسَهُمَا لِيُرِيَهُمَا سَوْءَٰتِهِمَآ ۗ إِنَّهُۥ يَرَىٰكُمْ هُوَ وَقَبِيلُهُۥ مِنْ
حَيْثُ لَا تَرَوْنَهُمْ ۗ إِنَّا جَعَلْنَا ٱلشَّيَـٰطِينَ أَوْلِيَآءَ لِلَّذِينَ لَا يُؤْمِنُونَ ﴿٢٧﴾
وَإِذَا فَعَلُوا۟ فَـٰحِشَةً قَالُوا۟ وَجَدْنَا عَلَيْهَآ ءَابَآءَنَا وَٱللَّهُ أَمَرَنَا بِهَا ۗ قُلْ إِنَّ
ٱللَّهَ لَا يَأْمُرُ بِٱلْفَحْشَآءِ ۖ أَتَقُولُونَ عَلَى ٱللَّهِ مَا لَا تَعْلَمُونَ ﴿٢٨﴾ قُلْ أَمَرَ
رَبِّى بِٱلْقِسْطِ ۖ وَأَقِيمُوا۟ وُجُوهَكُمْ عِندَ كُلِّ مَسْجِدٍ وَٱدْعُوهُ مُخْلِصِينَ لَهُ
ٱلدِّينَ ۚ كَمَا بَدَأَكُمْ تَعُودُونَ ﴿٢٩﴾ فَرِيقًا هَدَىٰ وَفَرِيقًا حَقَّ عَلَيْهِمُ
ٱلضَّلَـٰلَةُ ۗ إِنَّهُمُ ٱتَّخَذُوا۟ ٱلشَّيَـٰطِينَ أَوْلِيَآءَ مِن دُونِ ٱللَّهِ وَيَحْسَبُونَ أَنَّهُم
مُّهْتَدُونَ ﴿٣٠﴾

Yā banīi ʾĀdama lā yaftinannakumush-Shayṭānu kamāa ʾakhraja ʾabawaykum-minal-jannati yañziʿu ʿanhumā libāsahumā liyuriyahumā sawʾātihimā. ʾInnahū yarākum huwa wa qabīluhū min ḥaythu lā tarawnahum. ʾInnā jaʿalnash-Shayāṭīna ʾawliyāaʾa lilladhīna lā yuʾminūn. ‹27› Wa ʾidhā faʿalū fāḥishatañ-qālū wajadnā ʿalayhāa ʾābāaʾanā wal-lāhu ʾamaranā bihā. Qul ʾinnal-lāha lā yaʾmuru bil-faḥshāaʾ. ʾAtaqūlūna ʿalal-lāhi mā lā taʿlamūn. ‹28› Qul ʾamara Rabbī bilqisṭ. Wa ʾaqīmū wujūhakum ʿiñda kulli masjidiñw-wad-ʿūhu mukhliṣīna lahud-dīn. Kamā badaʾakum taʿūdūn. ‹29› Farīqan hadā wa farīqan ḥaqqa ʿalayhimuḍ-ḍalālah. ʾInnahumut-takhadhush-Shayāṭīna ʾawliyāaʾa miñ-dūnil-lāhi wa yaḥsabūna ʾannahum-muhtadūn. ‹30›

19 Lit., "see you from where you do not see them".

20 The interpolated word "truly" is implied in this phrase in view of the subsequent reference to the *erroneous* beliefs of such people: for, although their beliefs are wrong, some of them are under the impression that the "shameful deeds" subsequently referred to have been enjoined by God. As for the "satanic forces" (*shayāṭīn*), it is to be remembered that this designation is applied in the Qurʾān to all kinds of wicked impulses or propensities that are "near unto" (i.e., in the hearts of) those who do not truly believe in God (see note 31 on 14 : 22): hence, the term *shayāṭīn* occurring in verse 30 below has been rendered as "evil impulses".

21 The term *wajh* (lit., "face") occurring here is often used, in the abstract sense, to denote a person's entire being or entire attention – as, for instance, in the phrase *aslamtu wajhī li'llāhi*, "I have surrendered my whole being unto God" (3 : 20). The word *masjid*, which usually signifies the time or place of prostration in prayer (*sujūd*), evidently stands in this context – as well as in verse 31 below – for any act of worship.

22 Lit., "will have become incumbent upon them (*ḥaqqa ʿalayhim*)", implying that this straying was an inevitable consequence of their own doings and attitudes.

O CHILDREN of Adam! Beautify yourselves[23] for every act of worship, and eat and drink [freely], but do not waste: verily, He does not love the wasteful! ‹31›
Say: "Who is there to forbid the beauty which God has brought forth for His creatures, and the good things from among the means of sustenance?"
Say: "They are [lawful] in the life of this world unto all who have attained to faith – to be theirs alone on Resurrection Day."[24]
Thus clearly do We spell out these messages unto people of [innate] knowledge! ‹32›
Say: "Verily, my Sustainer has forbidden only shameful deeds, be they open or secret, and [every kind of] sinning, and unjustified envy, and the ascribing of divinity to aught beside Him – since He has never bestowed any warrant therefor from on high – and the attributing unto God of aught of which you have no knowledge." ‹33›
And for all people a term has been set:[25] and when [the end of] their term approaches, they can neither delay it by a single moment,[26] nor can they hasten it. ‹34›

O CHILDREN of Adam! Whenever there come unto you apostles of your own, conveying My messages unto you, then all who are conscious of Me and live righteously – no fear need they have, and neither shall they grieve; ‹35› but they who give the lie to Our messages and scorn them in their pride – these are destined for the fire, therein to abide. ‹36›

ربع الحزب

۞ يَٰبَنِيٓ ءَادَمَ خُذُواْ زِينَتَكُمۡ عِندَ كُلِّ مَسۡجِدٖ وَكُلُواْ وَٱشۡرَبُواْ وَلَا
تُسۡرِفُوٓاْۚ إِنَّهُۥ لَا يُحِبُّ ٱلۡمُسۡرِفِينَ ﴿٣١﴾ قُلۡ مَنۡ حَرَّمَ زِينَةَ ٱللَّهِ ٱلَّتِيٓ أَخۡرَجَ
لِعِبَادِهِۦ وَٱلطَّيِّبَٰتِ مِنَ ٱلرِّزۡقِۚ قُلۡ هِيَ لِلَّذِينَ ءَامَنُواْ فِي ٱلۡحَيَوٰةِ ٱلدُّنۡيَا
خَالِصَةٗ يَوۡمَ ٱلۡقِيَٰمَةِۗ كَذَٰلِكَ نُفَصِّلُ ٱلۡأٓيَٰتِ لِقَوۡمٖ يَعۡلَمُونَ ﴿٣٢﴾ قُلۡ إِنَّمَا
حَرَّمَ رَبِّيَ ٱلۡفَوَٰحِشَ مَا ظَهَرَ مِنۡهَا وَمَا بَطَنَ وَٱلۡإِثۡمَ وَٱلۡبَغۡيَ بِغَيۡرِ ٱلۡحَقِّ وَأَن
تُشۡرِكُواْ بِٱللَّهِ مَا لَمۡ يُنَزِّلۡ بِهِۦ سُلۡطَٰنٗا وَأَن تَقُولُواْ عَلَى ٱللَّهِ مَا لَا تَعۡلَمُونَ ﴿٣٣﴾
وَلِكُلِّ أُمَّةٍ أَجَلٞۖ فَإِذَا جَآءَ أَجَلُهُمۡ لَا يَسۡتَأۡخِرُونَ سَاعَةٗ وَلَا يَسۡتَقۡدِمُونَ ﴿٣٤﴾
يَٰبَنِيٓ ءَادَمَ إِمَّا يَأۡتِيَنَّكُمۡ رُسُلٞ مِّنكُمۡ يَقُصُّونَ عَلَيۡكُمۡ ءَايَٰتِي فَمَنِ ٱتَّقَىٰ
وَأَصۡلَحَ فَلَا خَوۡفٌ عَلَيۡهِمۡ وَلَا هُمۡ يَحۡزَنُونَ ﴿٣٥﴾ وَٱلَّذِينَ كَذَّبُواْ بِـَٔايَٰتِنَا
وَٱسۡتَكۡبَرُواْ عَنۡهَآ أُوْلَٰٓئِكَ أَصۡحَٰبُ ٱلنَّارِۖ هُمۡ فِيهَا خَٰلِدُونَ ﴿٣٦﴾

۞ Yā banīi ʾĀdama khudhū zīnatakum ʿiñda kulli masjidiñw-wa kulū wash-rabū wa lā tusrifū. ʾInnahū lā yuḥibbul-musrifīn. (31) Qul man ḥarrama zīnatal-lāhil-latīi ʾakhraja liʿibādihī waṭ-ṭayyibāti minar-rizq. Qul hiya lilladhīna ʾāmanū fil-ḥayātid-dunyā khāliṣatañy-Yawmal-Qiyāmah. Kadhālika nufaṣṣilul-ʾĀyāti liqawmiñy-yaʿlamūn. (32) Qul ʾinnamā ḥarrama Rabbiyal-fawāḥisha mā ẓahara minhā wa mā baṭana wal-ʾithma wal-baghaya bighyril-ḥaqqi wa ʾañ-tushrikū billāhi mā lam yunazzil bihī sulṭānañw-wa ʾañ-taqūlū ʿalal-lāhi mā lā taʿlamūn. (33) Wa likulli ʾummatin ʾajal. Faʾidhā jāaʾa ʾajaluhum lā yastaʾkhirūna sāʿatañw-wa lā yastaqdimūn. (34) Yā banīi ʾĀdama ʾimmā yaʾtiyannakum Rusulum-miñkum yaquṣṣūna ʿalaykum ʾĀyātī famanit-taqā wa ʾaṣlaḥa falā khawfun ʿalayhim wa lā hum yaḥzanūn. (35) Wal-ladhīna kadhdhabū biʾĀyātinā was-takbarū ʿanhāa ʾulāaʾika ʾaṣḥābuñ-nāri hum fīhā khālidūn. (36)

23 Lit., "take to your adornment (*zīnah*)". According to Rāghib (as quoted in Lane III, 1279 f.), the proper meaning of *zīnah* is "a [beautifying] thing that does not disgrace or render unseemly . . . either in the present world or in that which is to come": thus, it signifies anything of beauty in both the physical and moral connotations of the word.

24 By declaring that all good and beautiful things of life – i.e., those which are not expressly prohibited – are lawful to the believers, the Qurʾān condemns, by implication, all forms of life-denying asceticism, world-renunciation and self-mortification. While, in the life of this world, those good things are shared by believers and unbelievers alike, they will be denied to the latter in the hereafter (cf. verses 50-51 of this *sūrah*).

25 Lit., "for every community (*ummah*) there is a term": i.e., all people have a life-term decreed by God, during which they are at liberty to accept or to reject the guidance offered them through revelation. The word *ummah* often denotes "living beings" – in this context, "people".

26 In Arabic usage, the term *sāʿah* (lit., "hour") signifies not merely the astronomical hour – i.e., the twenty-fourth part of a mean solar day – but also "time" in an absolute sense, or any fraction of it, whether large or small. In the above context, it has obviously been used in the sense of "a least fraction of time" or "a single moment".

And who could be more wicked than they who attribute their own lying inventions to God or give the lie to His messages? Whatever has been decreed to be their lot [in life] will be theirs[27] – till there shall come unto them Our messengers to cause them to die, [and] shall say, "Where, now, are those beings whom you were wont to invoke beside God?"
And [those sinners] will reply, "They have forsaken us!" – and [thus] they will bear witness against themselves that they had been denying the truth. ‹37›
[And God] will say: "Join those hosts of invisible beings and humans who have gone before you into the fire!"
[And] every time a host enters [the fire], it will curse its fellow-host – so much so that, when they all shall have passed into it, one after another, the last of them will speak [thus] of the first of them:[28] "O our Sustainer! It is they who have led us astray: give them, therefore, double suffering through fire!"
He will reply: "Every one of you deserves double suffering[29] – but you know it not." ‹38›
And the first of them will say unto the last of them: "So you were in no wise superior to us![30] Taste, then, this suffering for all [the evil] that you were wont to do!" ‹39›

VERILY, unto those who give the lie to Our messages and scorn them in their pride, the gates of heaven shall not be opened;[31]

فَمَنْ أَظْلَمُ مِمَّنِ ٱفْتَرَىٰ عَلَى ٱللَّهِ كَذِبًا أَوْ كَذَّبَ بِـَٔايَـٰتِهِۦٓ ۚ أُو۟لَـٰٓئِكَ
يَنَالُهُمْ نَصِيبُهُم مِّنَ ٱلْكِتَـٰبِ ۖ حَتَّىٰٓ إِذَا جَآءَتْهُمْ رُسُلُنَا يَتَوَفَّوْنَهُمْ
قَالُوٓا۟ أَيْنَ مَا كُنتُمْ تَدْعُونَ مِن دُونِ ٱللَّهِ ۖ قَالُوا۟ ضَلُّوا۟ عَنَّا وَشَهِدُوا۟
عَلَىٰٓ أَنفُسِهِمْ أَنَّهُمْ كَانُوا۟ كَـٰفِرِينَ ﴿٣٧﴾ قَالَ ٱدْخُلُوا۟ فِىٓ أُمَمٍ قَدْ
خَلَتْ مِن قَبْلِكُم مِّنَ ٱلْجِنِّ وَٱلْإِنسِ فِى ٱلنَّارِ ۖ كُلَّمَا دَخَلَتْ أُمَّةٌ
لَّعَنَتْ أُخْتَهَا ۖ حَتَّىٰٓ إِذَا ٱدَّارَكُوا۟ فِيهَا جَمِيعًا قَالَتْ أُخْرَىٰهُمْ لِأُولَىٰهُمْ
رَبَّنَا هَـٰٓؤُلَآءِ أَضَلُّونَا فَـَٔاتِهِمْ عَذَابًا ضِعْفًا مِّنَ ٱلنَّارِ ۖ قَالَ لِكُلٍّ
ضِعْفٌ وَلَـٰكِن لَّا تَعْلَمُونَ ﴿٣٨﴾ وَقَالَتْ أُولَىٰهُمْ لِأُخْرَىٰهُمْ فَمَا كَانَ
لَكُمْ عَلَيْنَا مِن فَضْلٍ فَذُوقُوا۟ ٱلْعَذَابَ بِمَا كُنتُمْ تَكْسِبُونَ ﴿٣٩﴾ إِنَّ
ٱلَّذِينَ كَذَّبُوا۟ بِـَٔايَـٰتِنَا وَٱسْتَكْبَرُوا۟ عَنْهَا لَا تُفَتَّحُ لَهُمْ أَبْوَٰبُ ٱلسَّمَآءِ

Faman ʾaẓlamu mimmanif-tarā ʿalal-lāhi kadhiban
ʾaw kadhdhaba biʾĀyātih. ʾUlāaʾika yanāluhum
naṣībuhum-minal-Kitāb. Ḥattāa ʾidhā jāaʾat-hum
Rusulunā yatawaffawnahum qālūu ʾayna mā kuñtum
tadʿūna miñ-dūnil-lāh. Qālū ḍallū ʿannā wa shahidū
ʿalāa ʾañfusihim ʾannahum kānū kāfirīn. (37) Qālad-
khulū fīi ʾumamiñ-qad khalat miñ-qablikum-minal-
Jinni wal-ʾIñsi fin-nār. Kullamā dakhalat ʾummatul-
laʿanat ʾukhtahā; ḥattāa ʾidhad-dārakū fīhā jamīʿañ-
qālat ʾukhrāhum liʾūlāhum Rabbanā hāaʾulāai
ʾaḍallūnā faʾātihim ʿadhābañ-ḍiʿfam-minan-nār.
Qāla likulliñ-ḍiʿfuñw-wa lākil-lā taʿlamūn. (38) Wa
qālat ʾūlāhum liʾukhrāhum famā kāna lakum ʿalaynā
miñ-faḍliñ-fadhūqul-ʿadhāba bimā kuñtum tak-
sibūn. (39) ʾInnal-ladhīna kadhdhabū biʾĀyātinā was-
takbarū ʿanhā lā tufattaḥu lahum abwābus-samāaʾi

27 Lit., "their share of the [divine] decree (*al-kitāb*) will reach them": i.e., they will have in their lifetime, like all other people, all the good or bad fortune envisaged for them in God's eternal decree. The "messengers" (*rusul*) referred to in the next clause are, apparently, the angels of death.

28 The terms "first" and "last" refer here either to a sequence in time ("those who came earlier" and "those who came later") or in status ("leaders" and "followers"); and in both cases they relate, as the next sentence indicates, to the evil influence which the former exerted on the latter during their lifetime – either directly, as leaders of thought and persons of distinction, or indirectly, as forerunners in time, whose example was followed by later generations.

29 Lit., "to everyone a double [suffering]": i.e., for having gone astray and for having, by his example, led others astray. Cf. 16 : 25 – "on Resurrection Day they shall bear the full weight of their own burdens, as well as some of the burdens of those ignorant ones whom they have led astray".

30 I.e., "You went the wrong way, as we did, out of your own free will, and you bear the same responsibility as we do." Another possible interpretation is: "You are not superior to us because you have learnt nothing from our mistakes".

31 According to Ibn ʿAbbās (as quoted by Rāzī), this metaphor signifies that God will not accept any of the good deeds of such sinners, nor their subsequent supplications.

وَلَا يَدْخُلُونَ ٱلْجَنَّةَ حَتَّىٰ يَلِجَ ٱلْجَمَلُ فِى سَمِّ ٱلْخِيَاطِ ۚ وَكَذَٰلِكَ نَجْزِى
ٱلْمُجْرِمِينَ ﴿٤٠﴾ لَهُم مِّن جَهَنَّمَ مِهَادٌ وَمِن فَوْقِهِمْ غَوَاشٍ ۚ وَكَذَٰلِكَ نَجْزِى
ٱلظَّٰلِمِينَ ﴿٤١﴾ وَٱلَّذِينَ ءَامَنُوا۟ وَعَمِلُوا۟ ٱلصَّٰلِحَٰتِ لَا نُكَلِّفُ نَفْسًا إِلَّا
وُسْعَهَآ أُو۟لَٰٓئِكَ أَصْحَٰبُ ٱلْجَنَّةِ ۖ هُمْ فِيهَا خَٰلِدُونَ ﴿٤٢﴾ وَنَزَعْنَا مَا فِى صُدُورِهِم
مِّنْ غِلٍّ تَجْرِى مِن تَحْتِهِمُ ٱلْأَنْهَٰرُ ۖ وَقَالُوا۟ ٱلْحَمْدُ لِلَّهِ ٱلَّذِى هَدَىٰنَا لِهَٰذَا
وَمَا كُنَّا لِنَهْتَدِىَ لَوْلَآ أَنْ هَدَىٰنَا ٱللَّهُ ۖ لَقَدْ جَآءَتْ رُسُلُ رَبِّنَا بِٱلْحَقِّ ۖ وَنُودُوٓا۟
أَن تِلْكُمُ ٱلْجَنَّةُ أُورِثْتُمُوهَا بِمَا كُنتُمْ تَعْمَلُونَ ﴿٤٣﴾ وَنَادَىٰٓ أَصْحَٰبُ ٱلْجَنَّةِ
أَصْحَٰبَ ٱلنَّارِ أَن قَدْ وَجَدْنَا مَا وَعَدَنَا رَبُّنَا حَقًّا فَهَلْ وَجَدتُّم مَّا وَعَدَ رَبُّكُمْ حَقًّا ۖ

wa lā yadkhulūnal-jannata ḥattā yalijal-jamalu fī sammil-khiyāṭ. Wa kadhālika najzil-mujrimīn. (40) La-hum-miñ-jahannama mihāduñw-wa miñ-fawqihim ghawāsh. Wa kadhālika najziẓ-ẓālimīn. (41) Wal-ladhīna ᵓāmanū wa ᶜamiluṣ-ṣāliḥāti lā nukallifu naf-san ᵓillā wusᶜahāa ᵓulāaᵓika ᵓaṣḥābul-jannati hum fīhā khālidūn. (42) Wa nazaᶜnā mā fī ṣudūrihim-min ghilliñ-tajrī miñ-taḥtihimul-ᵓanhār. Wa qālul-ḥamdu lillāhil-ladhī hadānā lihādhā wa mā kunnā linahta-diya law lāa ᵓañ-hadānal-lāh. Laqad jāaᵓat Rusulu Rabbinā bil-ḥaqq. Wa nūdūu ᵓañ-tilkumul-jannatu ᵓūrithtumūhā bimā kuñtum taᶜmalūn. (43) Wa nādāa ᵓaṣḥābul-jannati ᵓaṣḥāban-nāri ᵓañ-qad wajadnā mā waᶜadanā Rabbunā ḥaqqañ-fahal wajattum-mā waᶜada Rabbukum ḥaqqā.

and they shall not enter paradise any more than a twisted rope can pass through a needle's eye:[32] for thus do We requite such as are lost in sin. «40» Hell will be their resting-place and their covering as well:[33] for thus do We requite the evildoers. «41»
But those who attain to faith and do righteous deeds – [and] We do not burden any human being with more than he is well able to bear – they are destined for paradise, therein to abide, «42» after We shall have removed whatever unworthy thoughts or feelings may have been [lingering] in their bosoms. Running waters will flow at their feet;[34] and they will say: "All praise is due to God, who has guided us unto this; for we would certainly not have found the right path unless God had guided us! Indeed, our Sustainer's apostles have told us the truth!"
And [a voice] will call out unto them: "This is the paradise which you have inherited by virtue of your past deeds!" «43»
And the inmates of paradise will call out to the inmates of the fire: "Now we have found that what our Sustainer promised us has come true; have you, too, found that what your Sustainer promised you has come true?"

32 Lit., "until (*ḥattā*) a twisted rope passes through a needle's eye"; since this phrase is meant to express an impossibility, the rendering of *ḥattā* as "any more than" seems to be appropriate here. As for the word *jamal* occurring in this sentence, there is hardly any doubt that its translation, in this context, as "camel" is erroneous. As pointed out by Zamakhsharī (and confirmed by other classical commentators, including Rāzī), Ibn ᶜAbbās used to read the word in the spelling *jummal*, which signifies "a thick rope" or "a twisted cable"; and the same reading is attributed to ᶜAlī ibn Abī Ṭālib (*Tāj al-ᶜArūs*). It is to be noted that there are also several other dialectical spellings of this word, namely, *jumal*, *juml*, *jumul* and, finally, *jamal* (as in the generally-accepted version of the Qurᵓān) – all of them signifying "a thick, twisted rope" (Jawharī), and all of them used in this sense by some of the Prophet's Companions or their immediate successors (*tābiᶜūn*). Ibn ᶜAbbās is also quoted by Zamakhsharī as having said that God could not have coined so inappropriate a metaphor as "a camel passing through a needle's eye" – meaning that there is no relationship whatsoever between a camel and a needle's eye whereas, on the other hand, there is a definite relationship between the latter and a rope (which, after all, is but an extremely thick thread). On all accounts, therefore, the rendering of *jamal* as "a twisted rope" is, in this context, infinitely preferable to that of "a camel". The fact that the latter rendering occurs in a somewhat similar phrase in the Greek version of the Synoptic Gospels (Matthew xix, 24, Mark x, 25 and Luke xviii, 25) does not affect this contention. One should remember that the Gospels were originally composed in Aramaic, the language of Palestine at the time of Jesus, and that those Aramaic texts are now lost. It is more than probable that, owing to the customary absence of vowel signs in Aramaic writing, the Greek translator misunderstood the consonant spelling *g-m-l* (corresponding to the Arabic *j-m-l*), and took it to mean "a camel": a mistake repeated since, with regard to the above Qurᵓān-verse, by many Muslims and all non-Muslim orientalists as well.

33 Lit., "for them there will be a resting-place of [the fires of] hell and, from above them, coverings [thereof]".

34 Lit., "beneath them": i.e., all blessings will be at their command.

[The others] will answer, "Yes!" – whereupon from their midst a voice[35] will loudly proclaim: "God's rejection is the due of the evildoers ‹44› who turn others away from God's path and try to make it appear crooked, and who refuse to acknowledge the truth of the life to come!"

‹45› And between the two there will be a barrier.[36]

And there will be persons who [in life] were endowed with the faculty of discernment [between right and wrong], recognizing each by its mark.[37] And they will call out unto the inmates of paradise, "Peace be upon you!" – not having entered it themselves, but longing [for it]. ‹46› And whenever their eyes are turned towards the inmates of the fire, they will cry: "O our Sustainer! Place us not among the people who have been guilty of evildoing!" ‹47›

And they who [in life] had possessed this faculty of discernment will call out to those whom they recognize by their marks [as sinners], saying: "What has your amassing [of wealth] availed you, and all the false pride of your past? ‹48› Are those [blessed] ones] the self-same people of whom you once solemnly declared, 'Never will God bestow His grace upon them'?[38]

قَالُوا نَعَمْ فَأَذَّنَ مُؤَذِّنٌ بَيْنَهُمْ أَن لَّعْنَةُ اللَّهِ عَلَى الظَّالِمِينَ ﴿٤٤﴾
الَّذِينَ يَصُدُّونَ عَن سَبِيلِ اللَّهِ وَيَبْغُونَهَا عِوَجًا وَهُم بِالْآخِرَةِ
كَافِرُونَ ﴿٤٥﴾ وَبَيْنَهُمَا حِجَابٌ وَعَلَى الْأَعْرَافِ رِجَالٌ يَعْرِفُونَ
كُلًّا بِسِيمَاهُمْ وَنَادَوْا أَصْحَابَ الْجَنَّةِ أَن سَلَامٌ عَلَيْكُمْ لَمْ يَدْخُلُوهَا
وَهُمْ يَطْمَعُونَ ﴿٤٦﴾ ۞ وَإِذَا صُرِفَتْ أَبْصَارُهُمْ تِلْقَاءَ أَصْحَابِ النَّارِ
قَالُوا رَبَّنَا لَا تَجْعَلْنَا مَعَ الْقَوْمِ الظَّالِمِينَ ﴿٤٧﴾ وَنَادَىٰ أَصْحَابُ
الْأَعْرَافِ رِجَالًا يَعْرِفُونَهُم بِسِيمَاهُمْ قَالُوا مَا أَغْنَىٰ عَنكُمْ جَمْعُكُمْ
وَمَا كُنتُمْ تَسْتَكْبِرُونَ ﴿٤٨﴾ أَهَٰؤُلَاءِ الَّذِينَ أَقْسَمْتُمْ لَا يَنَالُهُمُ اللَّهُ بِرَحْمَةٍ

نصف الحزب

Qālū naʿam. Faʾadhdhana muʾadhdhinum-bayna-hum ʾal-laʿnatul-lāhi ʿalaẓ-ẓālimīn. (44) ʾAlladhīna yaṣuddūna ʿan-sabīlil-lāhi wa yabghunahā ʿiwajanw-wa hum-bilʾĀkhirati kāfirūn. (45) Wa baynahumā ḥijāb. Wa ʿalal-ʾaʿrāfi rijāluny-yaʿrifūna kullam-bisīmāhum. Wa nādaw ʾaṣḥābal-jannati-ʾan-salāmun ʿalaykum; lam yadkhulūhā wa hum yaṭmaʿūn. (46) ۞ Wa ʾidhā ṣurifat ʾabṣāruhum tilqāaʾa ʾaṣḥābin-nāri qālū Rabbanā lā tajʿalnā maʿal-qawmiẓ-ẓālimīn. (47) Wa nādāa ʾaṣḥābul-ʾaʿrāfi rijālany-yaʿrifūnahum-bisīmāhum qālū māa ʾaghnā ʿankum jamʿukum wa mā kuntum tastakbirūn. (48) ʾAhāaʾulāaʾil-ladhīna ʾaqsamtum lā yanāluhumul-lāhu biraḥmah.

35 Lit., "an announcer" (*muʾadhdhin*).

36 The word *ḥijāb* denotes anything that intervenes as an obstacle between things or conceals one thing from another; it is used in both an abstract and a concrete sense.

37 The term *al-aʿrāf* (which gave to this *sūrah* its title) occurs in the Qurʾān only twice – namely, in the above verse and in verse 48. It is the plural of *ʿurf*, which primarily denotes "acknowledgement" or "discernment", and is also used to denote the highest, or most elevated, part of anything (because it is most easily discerned): for instance, the *ʿurf* of a cock is the coxcomb, that of a horse its mane, and so forth. On the basis of this idiomatic usage, many commentators assume that the *aʿrāf* referred to here are "elevated places", like the heights of a wall or its ramparts, and identify it with the "barrier" (*ḥijāb*) mentioned at the end of the preceding sentence. A far more likely interpretation, however, is forthcoming from the *primary* significance of the word *ʿurf* and its plural *aʿrāf*: namely, "discernment" and "the faculty of discernment", respectively. This interpretation has been adopted by some of the great, early commentators of the Qurʾān, like Al-Ḥasan al-Baṣrī and Az-Zajjāj, whose views Rāzī quotes with evident approval. They state emphatically that the expression *ʿala 'l-aʿrāf* is synonymous with *ʿalā maʿrifah*, that is, "possessing knowledge" or "endowed with the faculty of discernment" (i.e., between right and wrong); and that the persons thus described are those who in their lifetime were able to discern between right and wrong ("recognizing each by its mark"), but did not definitely incline to either: in brief, the *indifferent* ones. Their lukewarm attitude has prevented them from doing either much good or much wrong – with the result that, as the next sentence shows, they deserve neither paradise nor hell. (Several Traditions to this effect are quoted by Ṭabarī as well as by Ibn Kathīr in their commentaries on this verse.) – The noun *rijāl* (lit., "men") at the beginning of the next sentence as well as in verse 48 obviously denotes "persons" of both sexes.

38 Implying either that the believers did not deserve God's grace or, alternatively, that God does not exist. The expression "you solemnly declared" (lit., "you said under oath") is a metaphor for the unbelievers' utter conviction in this respect.

[For now they have been told,] 'Enter paradise; no fear need you have, and neither shall you grieve!'" «49»

And the inmates of the fire will call out unto the inmates of paradise: "Pour some water upon us, or some of the sustenance [of paradise] which God has provided for you!" [The inmates of paradise] will reply: "Verily, God has denied both to those who have denied the truth «50» – those who, beguiled by the life of this world, have made play and passing delights their religion!"[39]

[And God will say:] "And so We shall be oblivious of them today as they were oblivious of the coming of this their Day [of Judgment], and as Our messages they did deny: «51» for, indeed, We did convey unto them a divine writ which We clearly, and wisely,[40] spelled out – a guidance and a grace unto people who will believe." «52»

Are [the unbelievers] but waiting for the final meaning of that [Day of Judgment] to unfold?[41] [But] on the Day when its final meaning is unfolded, those who aforetime had been oblivious thereof will say: "Our Sustainer's apostles have indeed told us the truth! Have we, then, any intercessors who could intercede in our behalf? Or could we be brought back [to life] so that we might act otherwise than we were wont to act?"[42]

Indeed, they will have squandered their own selves, and all their false imagery will have forsaken them. «53»

VERILY, your Sustainer is God, who has created the heavens and the earth in six aeons, and is established on the throne of His almightiness.[43] He covers the day with the night in swift pursuit, with the sun and the moon and the stars subservient to His

ٱدْخُلُوا۟ ٱلْجَنَّةَ لَا خَوْفٌ عَلَيْكُمْ وَلَآ أَنتُمْ تَحْزَنُونَ ﴿٤٩﴾ وَنَادَىٰٓ أَصْحَٰبُ
ٱلنَّارِ أَصْحَٰبَ ٱلْجَنَّةِ أَنْ أَفِيضُوا۟ عَلَيْنَا مِنَ ٱلْمَآءِ أَوْ مِمَّا رَزَقَكُمُ ٱللَّهُ
قَالُوٓا۟ إِنَّ ٱللَّهَ حَرَّمَهُمَا عَلَى ٱلْكَٰفِرِينَ ﴿٥٠﴾ ٱلَّذِينَ ٱتَّخَذُوا۟ دِينَهُمْ لَهْوًا وَلَعِبًا
وَغَرَّتْهُمُ ٱلْحَيَوٰةُ ٱلدُّنْيَا ۚ فَٱلْيَوْمَ نَنسَىٰهُمْ كَمَا نَسُوا۟ لِقَآءَ يَوْمِهِمْ هَٰذَا وَمَا
كَانُوا۟ بِـَٔايَٰتِنَا يَجْحَدُونَ ﴿٥١﴾ وَلَقَدْ جِئْنَٰهُم بِكِتَٰبٍ فَصَّلْنَٰهُ عَلَىٰ عِلْمٍ
هُدًى وَرَحْمَةً لِّقَوْمٍ يُؤْمِنُونَ ﴿٥٢﴾ هَلْ يَنظُرُونَ إِلَّا تَأْوِيلَهُۥ ۚ يَوْمَ يَأْتِى
تَأْوِيلُهُۥ يَقُولُ ٱلَّذِينَ نَسُوهُ مِن قَبْلُ قَدْ جَآءَتْ رُسُلُ رَبِّنَا بِٱلْحَقِّ فَهَل لَّنَا
مِن شُفَعَآءَ فَيَشْفَعُوا۟ لَنَآ أَوْ نُرَدُّ فَنَعْمَلَ غَيْرَ ٱلَّذِى كُنَّا نَعْمَلُ ۚ قَدْ خَسِرُوٓا۟
أَنفُسَهُمْ وَضَلَّ عَنْهُم مَّا كَانُوا۟ يَفْتَرُونَ ﴿٥٣﴾ إِنَّ رَبَّكُمُ ٱللَّهُ ٱلَّذِى خَلَقَ
ٱلسَّمَٰوَٰتِ وَٱلْأَرْضَ فِى سِتَّةِ أَيَّامٍ ثُمَّ ٱسْتَوَىٰ عَلَى ٱلْعَرْشِ يُغْشِى ٱلَّيْلَ
ٱلنَّهَارَ يَطْلُبُهُۥ حَثِيثًا وَٱلشَّمْسَ وَٱلْقَمَرَ وَٱلنُّجُومَ مُسَخَّرَٰتٍ بِأَمْرِهِۦٓ ۗ

ʾUdkhulul-jannata lā khawfun ʿalaykum wa lāa ʾañtum taḥzanūn. (49) Wa nādāa ʾaṣḥābun-nāri ʾaṣḥābal-jannatī ʾan ʾafīḍū ʿalaynā minal-māaʾi ʾaw mimmā razaqakumul-lāh. Qālūu ʾinnal-lāha ḥarramahumā ʿalal-kāfirīn. (50) ʾAlladhīnat-takhadhū dīnahum lahwañw-wa laʿibañw-wa gharrat-humul-ḥayātud-dunyā. Falyawma nañsāhum kamā nasū liqāaʾa Yawmihim hādhā wa mā kānū biʾĀyātinā yajḥadūn. (51) Wa laqad jiʾnāhum-biKitābiñ-faṣṣalnāhu ʿalā ʿilmin hudañw-wa raḥmatal-liqawmiñy-yuʾminūn. (52) Hal yañẓurūna ʾillā taʾwīlah. Yawma yaʾtī taʾwīluhū yaqūlul-ladhīna nasūhu miñ-qablu qad jāaʾat Rusulu Rabbinā bil-ḥaqqi fahal lanā miñ-shufaʿāaʾa fayashfaʿū lanāa ʾaw nuraddu fanaʿmala ghayral-ladhī kunnā naʿmal. Qad khasirūu ʾañfusahum wa ḍalla ʿanhum-mā kānū yaftarūn. (53) ʾInna Rabbakumul-lāhul-ladhī khalaqas-samāwāti wal-ʾarḍa fī sittati ʾayyāmiñ-thummas-tawā ʿalal-ʿarshi. Yughshil-laylan-nahāra yaṭlubuhū ḥathīthañw-wash-shamsa wal-qamara wan-nujūma musakhkharātim-biʾamrih.

39 See 6 : 70 and the corresponding note 60.

40 Lit., "with knowledge".

41 In this context, the term *taʾwīl* (which literally means "an endeavour to arrive at the final meaning [of a saying or occurrence]" – cf. 3 : 7) signifies the fulfilment of the warnings contained in the Qurʾān: and in this sense it connotes the "unfolding of its final meaning".

42 Cf. 6 : 27-28.

43 The conjunctive particle *thumma* which precedes this clause does not always denote order in time ("then" or "thereupon"). In cases where it is used to link parallel statements it has often the function of the simple conjunction *wa* ("and") – as, for instance, in 2 : 29 ("*and* has applied His design . . .", etc.). As regards the term *ʿarsh* (lit., "throne"

command: oh, verily, His is all creation and all command. Hallowed is God, the Sustainer of all the worlds! «54»
Call unto your Sustainer humbly, and in the secrecy of your hearts. Verily, He loves not those who transgress the bounds of what is right: «55» hence, do not spread corruption on earth after it has been so well ordered. And call unto Him with fear and longing: verily, God's grace is ever near unto the doers of good! «56»
And He it is who sends forth the winds as a glad tiding of His coming grace – so that, when they have brought heavy clouds, We may drive them towards dead land and cause thereby water to descend; and by this means do We cause all manner of fruit to come forth. Even thus shall We cause the dead to come forth: [and this] you ought to keep in mind.[44] «57» As for the good land, its vegetation comes forth [in abundance] by its Sustainer's leave, whereas from the bad it comes forth but poorly.
Thus do We give many facets to Our messages for [the benefit of] people who are grateful! «58»

INDEED, We sent forth Noah unto his people,[45] and he said: "O my people! Worship God alone: you have no deity other than Him. Verily, I fear lest suffering befall you on an awesome Day!"[46] «59»

أَلَا لَهُ ٱلْخَلْقُ وَٱلْأَمْرُ تَبَارَكَ ٱللَّهُ رَبُّ ٱلْعَٰلَمِينَ ﴿54﴾ ٱدْعُوا۟ رَبَّكُمْ تَضَرُّعًا
وَخُفْيَةً إِنَّهُۥ لَا يُحِبُّ ٱلْمُعْتَدِينَ ﴿55﴾ وَلَا تُفْسِدُوا۟ فِى ٱلْأَرْضِ بَعْدَ
إِصْلَٰحِهَا وَٱدْعُوهُ خَوْفًا وَطَمَعًا إِنَّ رَحْمَتَ ٱللَّهِ قَرِيبٌ مِّنَ ٱلْمُحْسِنِينَ ﴿56﴾
وَهُوَ ٱلَّذِى يُرْسِلُ ٱلرِّيَٰحَ بُشْرًۢا بَيْنَ يَدَىْ رَحْمَتِهِۦ حَتَّىٰٓ إِذَآ أَقَلَّتْ سَحَابًا
ثِقَالًا سُقْنَٰهُ لِبَلَدٍ مَّيِّتٍ فَأَنزَلْنَا بِهِ ٱلْمَآءَ فَأَخْرَجْنَا بِهِۦ مِن كُلِّ ٱلثَّمَرَٰتِ
كَذَٰلِكَ نُخْرِجُ ٱلْمَوْتَىٰ لَعَلَّكُمْ تَذَكَّرُونَ ﴿57﴾ وَٱلْبَلَدُ ٱلطَّيِّبُ يَخْرُجُ نَبَاتُهُۥ
بِإِذْنِ رَبِّهِۦ وَٱلَّذِى خَبُثَ لَا يَخْرُجُ إِلَّا نَكِدًا كَذَٰلِكَ نُصَرِّفُ ٱلْءَايَٰتِ
لِقَوْمٍ يَشْكُرُونَ ﴿58﴾ لَقَدْ أَرْسَلْنَا نُوحًا إِلَىٰ قَوْمِهِۦ فَقَالَ يَٰقَوْمِ ٱعْبُدُوا۟ ٱللَّهَ مَا
لَكُم مِّنْ إِلَٰهٍ غَيْرُهُۥٓ إِنِّىٓ أَخَافُ عَلَيْكُمْ عَذَابَ يَوْمٍ عَظِيمٍ ﴿59﴾

ᵓAlā lahul-khalqu wal-ᵓamr. Tabārakal-lāhu Rabbul-ᶜālamīn. ﴿54﴾ ᵓUdᶜū Rabbakum taḍarruᶜañw-wa khufyah. ᵓInnahū lā yuḥibbul-muᶜtadīn. ﴿55﴾ Wa lā tufsidū fil-ᵓarḍi baᶜda ᵓiṣlāḥihā wad-ᶜūhu khawfañw-wa ṭamaᶜā. ᵓInna raḥmatal-lāhi qarībum-minal-muḥsinīn. ﴿56﴾ Wa Huwal-ladhī yursilur-riyāḥa bushram-bayna yaday raḥmatihī ḥattāa ᵓidhāa ᵓaqallat saḥābañ-thiqālañ-suqnāhu libaladim-mayyitiñ-faᵓañzalnā bihil-māaᵓa faᵓakhrajnā bihī miñ-kullith-thamarāt. Kadhālika nukhrijul-mawtā laᶜallakum tadhakkarūn. ﴿57﴾ Wal-baladuṭ-ṭayyibu yakhruju nabātuhū biᵓidhni Rabbihī wal-ladhī khabutha lā yakhruju ᵓillā nakidā. Kadhālika nuṣarriful-ᵓĀyāti liqawmiñy-yashkurūn. ﴿58﴾ Laqad ᵓarsalnā Nūḥan ᵓilā qawmihī faqāla yā qawmiᶜ-budul-lāha mā lakum-min ᵓilāhiñ-ghayruh. ᵓInnīi ᵓakhāfu ᶜalaykum ᶜadhāba Yawmin ᶜaẓīm. ﴿59﴾

or "seat of power"), all Muslim commentators, classical and modern, are unanimously of the opinion that its metaphorical use in the Qurᵓān is meant to express God's absolute sway over all His creation. It is noteworthy that in all the seven instances where God is spoken of in the Qurᵓān as "established on the throne of His almightiness" (7 : 54, 10 : 3, 13 : 2, 20 : 5, 25 : 59, 32 : 4 and 57 : 4), this expression is connected with a declaration of His having created the universe. – The word *yawm*, commonly translated as "day" – but rendered above as "aeon" – is used in Arabic to denote any period, whether extremely long ("aeon") or extremely short ("moment"): its application to an earthly "day" of twenty-four hours is only one of its many connotations. (Cf. in this respect note 26 above, where the meaning of *sāᶜah* – lit., "hour" – is explained.)

44 This is the key-sentence of the parable set forth in verses 57-58: by the exercise of the same life-giving power by which God causes plants to grow, He will resurrect the dead at the end of time. The next sentence continues the parable by likening those whose hearts are open to the voice of truth to fertile earth, and those who are bent on denying it, to barren earth.

45 In continuation of the stress, in the preceding passages, on God's omnipotence and transcendental oneness, verses 59-93 refer to several of the earlier prophets, who preached the same truth, and whose names were familiar to the Arabs before the revelation of the Qurᵓān. Their stories – beginning with that of Noah, who is considered the first apostle ever sent to mankind – are reduced here to the warnings with which they unsuccessfully tried to persuade their people to worship God alone and to live righteously.

46 This refers either to the Day of Judgment or to the approaching deluge.

ثلاثة ارباع الحزب

The great ones among his people replied. "Verily, we see that thou art obviously lost in error!" ‹60›
Said [Noah]: "O my people! There is no error in me, but I am an apostle from the Sustainer of all the worlds. ‹61› I am delivering unto you my Sustainer's messages and giving you good advice: for I know [through revelation] from God what you do not know. ‹62› Why, do you deem it strange that a tiding from your Sustainer should have come unto you through a man from among yourselves, so that he might warn you, and that you might become conscious of God, and that you might be graced with His mercy?" ‹63›
And yet they gave him the lie! And so We saved him and those who stood by him, in the ark, the while We caused those who had given the lie to Our messages to drown: verily, they were blind folk![47] ‹64›

AND UNTO [the tribe of] ʿAd [We sent] their brother Hūd.[48] He said: "O my people! Worship God alone: you have no deity other than Him. Will you not, then, be conscious of Him?" ‹65›
Said the great ones among his people, who refused to acknowledge the truth: "Verily, we see that thou art weak-minded; and, verily, we think that thou art a liar!"[49] ‹66›

قَالَ ٱلْمَلَأُ مِن قَوْمِهِۦٓ إِنَّا لَنَرَىٰكَ فِى ضَلَـٰلٍ مُّبِينٍ ﴿٦٠﴾ قَالَ يَـٰقَوْمِ لَيْسَ
بِى ضَلَـٰلَةٌ وَلَـٰكِنِّى رَسُولٌ مِّن رَّبِّ ٱلْعَـٰلَمِينَ ﴿٦١﴾ أُبَلِّغُكُمْ رِسَـٰلَـٰتِ
رَبِّى وَأَنصَحُ لَكُمْ وَأَعْلَمُ مِنَ ٱللَّهِ مَا لَا تَعْلَمُونَ ﴿٦٢﴾ أَوَعَجِبْتُمْ أَن
جَآءَكُمْ ذِكْرٌ مِّن رَّبِّكُمْ عَلَىٰ رَجُلٍ مِّنكُمْ لِيُنذِرَكُمْ وَلِتَتَّقُوا۟ وَلَعَلَّكُمْ
تُرْحَمُونَ ﴿٦٣﴾ فَكَذَّبُوهُ فَأَنجَيْنَـٰهُ وَٱلَّذِينَ مَعَهُۥ فِى ٱلْفُلْكِ وَأَغْرَقْنَا ٱلَّذِينَ
كَذَّبُوا۟ بِـَٔايَـٰتِنَآ ۚ إِنَّهُمْ كَانُوا۟ قَوْمًا عَمِينَ ﴿٦٤﴾ ۞ وَإِلَىٰ عَادٍ أَخَاهُمْ هُودًا ۗ قَالَ
يَـٰقَوْمِ ٱعْبُدُوا۟ ٱللَّهَ مَا لَكُم مِّنْ إِلَـٰهٍ غَيْرُهُۥٓ ۚ أَفَلَا تَتَّقُونَ ﴿٦٥﴾ قَالَ ٱلْمَلَأُ ٱلَّذِينَ
كَفَرُوا۟ مِن قَوْمِهِۦٓ إِنَّا لَنَرَىٰكَ فِى سَفَاهَةٍ وَإِنَّا لَنَظُنُّكَ مِنَ ٱلْكَـٰذِبِينَ ﴿٦٦﴾

Qālal-malaʾu miñ-qawmihīi ʾinnā lanarāka fī ḍalālim-
mubīn. (60) Qāla yā qawmi laysa bī ḍalālatuñw-wa
lākinnī Rasūlum-mir-Rabbil-ʿālamīn. (61) ʾUbal-
lighukum risālāti Rabbī wa ʾañṣaḥu lakum wa ʾaʿlamu
minal-lāhi mā lā taʿlamūn. (62) ʾAwaʿajibtum ʾañ-
jāaʾakum dhikrum-mir-Rabbikum ʿalā rajulim-
miñkum liyuñdhirakum wa litattaqū wa laʿallakum
turḥamūn. (63) Fakadhdhabūhu faʾañjaynāhu Wal-
ladhīna maʿahū fil-fulki wa ʾaghraqnal-ladhīna
kadhdhabū biʾĀyātinā. ʾInnahum kānū qawman
ʿamīn. (64) ۞ Wa ʾilā ʿĀdin ʾakhāhum Hūdā. Qāla yā
qawmiʿ-budul-lāha mā lakum-min ʾilāhin ghayruh.
ʾAfalā tattaqūn. (65) Qālal-malaʾul-ladhīna kafarū
miñ-qawmihīi ʾinnā lanarāka fī safāhatiñw-wa ʾinnā
lanaẓunnuka minal-kādhibīn. (66)

47 Explaining this verse in his translation of the Qurʾān, Muḥammad ʿAlī rightly points out that the latter "does not support the theory of a world deluge, for it plainly states . . . that only people to whom Noah had delivered his message called him a liar, and . . . were drowned . . .. Hence the deluge affected the territory of Noah's people, not the whole world, as the Bible would have us believe." To this may be added that the deluge spoken of in the Bible, in the myths of Sumeria and Babylonia, and, finally, in the Qurʾān, most probably represents the inundation, during the Ice Age, of the huge basin which today is covered by the Mediterranean: an inundation which was due to the break-in of the Atlantic through the land-barrier at the modern Gibraltar, and of the Black Sea through what is now the Dardanelles.

48 Hūd is said to have been the first Arabian prophet. He may be identical with the Biblical ʿEbĕr, the ancestor of the Hebrews (*ʿIbrīm*) who – like most of the Semitic tribes – had probably originated in South Arabia. (References to ʿEbĕr are found in Genesis x, 24-25 and xi, 14 ff.) The ancient Arabian name Hūd is still reflected in that of Jacob's son Judah (Yahūdah in Hebrew), which provided the subsequent designation of the Jews. The name ʿEbĕr – both in Hebrew and in its Arabic form ʿĀbir – signifies "one who crosses over" (i.e., from one territory to another), and may be a Biblical echo of the fact that this tribe "crossed over" from Arabia to Mesopotamia in pre-Abrahamic times. – The tribe of ʿĀd, to which Hūd belonged ("their brother Hūd"), inhabited the vast desert region known as Al-Aḥqāf, between ʿUmān and Ḥaḍramawt, and was noted for its great power and influence (see 89 : 8 – "the like of whom has never been reared in all the land"). It disappeared from history many centuries before the advent of Islam, but its memory always remained alive in Arabian tradition.

49 They considered him "weak-minded" because he expected them to give up their traditional beliefs and deities; and a "liar", because he claimed to be a prophet of God.

Said [Hūd]: "O my people! There is no weak-mindedness in me, but I am an apostle from the Sustainer of all the worlds. «67» I am delivering unto you my Sustainer's messages and advising you truly and well.[50] «68» Why, do you deem it strange that a tiding from your Sustainer should have come unto you through a man from among yourselves, so that he might warn you? Do but remember how He made you heirs to Noah's people, and endowed you abundantly with power:[51] remember, then, God's blessings, so that you might attain to a happy state!" «69»

They answered: "Hast thou come to us [with the demand] that we worship God alone, and give up all that our forefathers were wont to worship? Bring upon us, then, that [punishment] with which thou hast threatened us, if thou art a man of truth!" «70»

Said [Hūd]: "You are already beset by loathsome evil[52] and by your Sustainer's condemnation! Do you argue with me about the [empty] names which you have invented[53] – you and your forefathers – for which God has bestowed no warrant from on high? Wait, then, [for what will happen:] verily, I shall wait with you!"[54] «71»

And so, by Our grace, We saved him and those who stood by him, the while We wiped out the last remnant of those who gave the lie to Our messages and would not believe.[55] «72»

قَالَ يَٰقَوْمِ لَيْسَ بِى سَفَاهَةٌ وَلَٰكِنِّى رَسُولٌ مِّن رَّبِّ ٱلْعَٰلَمِينَ ﴿٦٧﴾
أُبَلِّغُكُمْ رِسَٰلَٰتِ رَبِّى وَأَنَا۠ لَكُمْ نَاصِحٌ أَمِينٌ ﴿٦٨﴾ أَوَعَجِبْتُمْ أَن جَآءَكُمْ
ذِكْرٌ مِّن رَّبِّكُمْ عَلَىٰ رَجُلٍ مِّنكُمْ لِيُنذِرَكُمْ وَٱذْكُرُوٓا۟ إِذْ جَعَلَكُمْ
خُلَفَآءَ مِنۢ بَعْدِ قَوْمِ نُوحٍ وَزَادَكُمْ فِى ٱلْخَلْقِ بَصْۜطَةً فَٱذْكُرُوٓا۟ ءَالَآءَ
ٱللَّهِ لَعَلَّكُمْ تُفْلِحُونَ ﴿٦٩﴾ قَالُوٓا۟ أَجِئْتَنَا لِنَعْبُدَ ٱللَّهَ وَحْدَهُۥ وَنَذَرَ مَا كَانَ
يَعْبُدُ ءَابَآؤُنَا فَأْتِنَا بِمَا تَعِدُنَآ إِن كُنتَ مِنَ ٱلصَّٰدِقِينَ ﴿٧٠﴾ قَالَ قَدْ
وَقَعَ عَلَيْكُم مِّن رَّبِّكُمْ رِجْسٌ وَغَضَبٌ أَتُجَٰدِلُونَنِى فِىٓ أَسْمَآءٍ
سَمَّيْتُمُوهَآ أَنتُمْ وَءَابَآؤُكُم مَّا نَزَّلَ ٱللَّهُ بِهَا مِن سُلْطَٰنٍ فَٱنتَظِرُوٓا۟ إِنِّى
مَعَكُم مِّنَ ٱلْمُنتَظِرِينَ ﴿٧١﴾ فَأَنجَيْنَٰهُ وَٱلَّذِينَ مَعَهُۥ بِرَحْمَةٍ مِّنَّا وَقَطَعْنَا
دَابِرَ ٱلَّذِينَ كَذَّبُوا۟ بِـَٔايَٰتِنَا وَمَا كَانُوا۟ مُؤْمِنِينَ ﴿٧٢﴾

Qāla yā qawmi laysa bī safāhatuñw-wa lākinnī Rasūlum-mir-Rabbil-ʿālamīn. (67) ʾUballighukum risālāti Rabbī wa ʾana lakum nāṣiḥun ʾamīn. (68) ʾAwa ʿajibtum ʾañ-jāaʾakum dhikrum-mir-Rabbikum ʿalā rajulim-miñkum liyuñdhirakum. Wadh-kurūu ʾidh jaʿalakum khulafāaʾa mim-baʿdi qawmi Nūḥiñw-wa zādakum fil-khalqi basṭah. Fadhkurūu ʾālāaʾal-lāhi laʿallakum tufliḥūn. (69) Qālūu ʾajiʾtanā linaʿbudal-lāha waḥdahū wa nadhara mā kāna yaʿbudu ʾābāaʾunā. Faʾtinā bimā taʿidunāa ʾiñ-kuñta minaṣ-ṣādiqīn. (70) Qāla qad waqaʿa ʿalay-kum-mir-Rabbikum rijsuñw-wa ghaḍab. ʾAtujādi-lūnanī fīi ʾasmāaʾiñ-sammaytumūhāa ʾañtum wa ʾābāaʾukum-mā nazzalal-lāhu bihā miñ-sulṭān. Fañtaẓirūu ʾinnī maʿakum-minal-muñtaẓirīn. (71) Faʾañjaynāhu wal-ladhīna maʿahū biraḥmatim-minnā wa qaṭaʿnā dābiral-ladhīna kadhdhabū biʾĀyātinā wa mā kānū muʾminīn. (72)

50 Lit., "I am a trustworthy adviser to you".

51 Lit., "successors after Noah's people" – i.e., the most numerous and powerful of all the tribes that descended from Noah – "and increased you abundantly in respect of [your] natural endowment (*khalq*)". The latter term also signifies "power" (Rāzī).

52 A reference to their idolatry and obstinacy.

53 Lit., "names which you have named" – i.e., the false deities, which have no real existence.

54 Lit., "I shall be, together with you, among those who wait."

55 As is shown in 69 : 6-8, this destruction came about through a violent sandstorm raging without a break for seven nights and eight days.

وَإِلَىٰ ثَمُودَ أَخَاهُمۡ صَٰلِحٗاۚ قَالَ يَٰقَوۡمِ ٱعۡبُدُواْ ٱللَّهَ مَا لَكُم مِّنۡ إِلَٰهٍ غَيۡرُهُۥۖ
قَدۡ جَآءَتۡكُم بَيِّنَةٞ مِّن رَّبِّكُمۡۖ هَٰذِهِۦ نَاقَةُ ٱللَّهِ لَكُمۡ ءَايَةٗۖ فَذَرُوهَا تَأۡكُلۡ
فِيٓ أَرۡضِ ٱللَّهِۖ وَلَا تَمَسُّوهَا بِسُوٓءٖ فَيَأۡخُذَكُمۡ عَذَابٌ أَلِيمٞ ﴿٧٣﴾ وَٱذۡكُرُوٓاْ
إِذۡ جَعَلَكُمۡ خُلَفَآءَ مِنۢ بَعۡدِ عَادٖ وَبَوَّأَكُمۡ فِي ٱلۡأَرۡضِ تَتَّخِذُونَ مِن
سُهُولِهَا قُصُورٗا وَتَنۡحِتُونَ ٱلۡجِبَالَ بُيُوتٗاۖ فَٱذۡكُرُوٓاْ ءَالَآءَ ٱللَّهِ وَلَا تَعۡثَوۡاْ
فِي ٱلۡأَرۡضِ مُفۡسِدِينَ ﴿٧٤﴾ قَالَ ٱلۡمَلَأُ ٱلَّذِينَ ٱسۡتَكۡبَرُواْ مِن قَوۡمِهِۦ
لِلَّذِينَ ٱسۡتُضۡعِفُواْ لِمَنۡ ءَامَنَ مِنۡهُمۡ أَتَعۡلَمُونَ أَنَّ صَٰلِحٗا مُّرۡسَلٞ مِّن رَّبِّهِۦۚ

Wa ʾilā Thamūda ʾakhāhum Ṣāliḥā. Qāla yā qawmiʿ-budul-lāha mā lakum-min ʾilāhin ghayruh. Qad jāaʾatkum-bayyinatum-mir-Rabbikum. Hādhihī nāqatul-lāhi lakum ʾĀyatañ-fadharūhā taʾkul fii ʾarḍil-lāhi wa lā tamassūhā bisūuʾiñ-fayaʾ-khudhakum ʿadhābun ʾalīm. (73) Wadh-kurūu ʾidh jaʿalakum khulafāaʾa mim-baʿdi ʿĀdiñw-wa baw-waʾakum fil-ʾarḍi tattakhidhūna miñ-suhūlihā quṣūrañw-wa tanḥitūnal-jibāla buyūtā. Fadhkurūu ʾālāaʾal-lāhi wa lā taʿthaw fil-ʾarḍi mufsidīn. (74) Qālal-malaʾul-ladhīnas-takbarū miñ-qawmihī lil-ladhīnas-tuḍʿifū liman ʾāmana minhum ʾataʿlamūna ʾanna Ṣāliḥam-Mursalum-mir-Rabbih.

AND UNTO [the tribe of] Thamūd [We sent] their brother Ṣāliḥ.[56] He said: "O my people! Worship God alone: you have no deity other than Him. Clear evidence of the truth has now come unto you from your Sustainer.

"This she-camel belonging to God shall be a token for you: so leave her alone to pasture on God's earth, and do her no harm, lest grievous chastisement befall you.[57] «73»

"And remember how He made you heirs to [the tribe of] ʿĀd[58] and settled you firmly on earth, so that you [are able to] build for yourselves castles on its plains and hew out mountains [to serve you] as dwellings:[59] remember, then, God's blessings, and do not act wickedly on earth by spreading corruption." «74»

The great ones among his people, who gloried in their arrogance towards all who were deemed weak, said unto the believers among them: "Do you [really] know that Ṣāliḥ has been sent by his Sustainer?"

---

56 The Nabataean tribe of Thamūd descended from the tribe of ʿĀd mentioned in the preceding passage, and is, therefore, often referred to in pre-Islamic poetry as the "Second ʿĀd". Apart from Arabian sources, "a series of older references, not of Arabian origin, confirm the historical existence of the name and people of Thamūd. Thus the inscription of Sargon of the year 715 B.C. mentions the Thamūd among the people of eastern and central Arabia subjected by the Assyrians. We also find the Thamudaei, Thamudenes mentioned in Aristo, Ptolemy, and Pliny" (*Encyclopaedia of Islam* IV, 736). At the time of which the Qurʾān speaks, the Thamūd were settled in the northernmost Ḥijāz, near the confines of Syria. Rock-inscriptions attributed to them are still extant in the region of Al-Ḥijr. – As in the case of the ʿĀdite prophet Hūd – and the prophet Shuʿayb spoken of in verses 85-93 of this *sūrah* – Ṣāliḥ is called the "brother" of the tribe because he belonged to it.

57 The commentators cite various legends to the effect that this she-camel was of miraculous origin. Since neither the Qurʾān nor any authentic Tradition provides the least support for these legends, we must assume that they are based on the expression *nāqat Allāh* ("God's she-camel"), which has led some pious Muslims to fantastic conjectures. However, as Rashīd Riḍāʾ points out (*Manār* VIII, 502), this expression denotes merely the fact that the animal in question was not owned by any one person, and was therefore to be protected by the whole tribe; a further, analogous expression is found in the words "God's earth" in the same verse: an illustration of the fact that everything belongs to God. The particular stress placed by Ṣāliḥ on good treatment of this ownerless animal – referred to in several places in the Qurʾān – was obviously due to the cruel high-handedness displayed by the tribe, who, as the next two verses show, were wont to "act wickedly on earth by spreading corruption" and "gloried in their arrogance towards all who were deemed weak": in other words, their treatment of the defenceless animal was to be a "token" of their change of heart or (as is made clear in 54 : 27) "a test for them".

58 Cf. the parallel expression in verse 69 above – "heirs to Noah's people" – and the corresponding note. From all the historical references to the Thamūd it is apparent that they were one of the greatest and most powerful Arab tribes of their time.

59 A reference to the elaborate rock-dwellings or tombs – to be seen to this day – which the Thamūd carved out of the cliffs west of Al-Ḥijr, in northern Ḥijāz, and embellished with sculptures of animals as well as many inscriptions attesting to the comparatively high degree of their civilization and power. In popular Arabian parlance, these rock-dwellings are nowadays called *Madāʾin Ṣāliḥ* ("The Towns of Ṣāliḥ").

They answered: "Verily, we believe in the message which he bears."[60] ‹75›
[But] the arrogant ones said: "Behold, what you have come to believe in we refuse to regard as true!" ‹76›
And then they cruelly slaughtered the she-camel,[61] and turned with disdain from their Sustainer's commandment, and said: "O Ṣāliḥ! Bring upon us that [punishment] with which thou hast threatened us, if thou art truly one of God's message-bearers!" ‹77›
Thereupon an earthquake overtook them: and then they lay lifeless, in their very homes, on the ground.[62] ‹78›
And [Ṣāliḥ] turned away from them, and said: "O my people! Indeed, I delivered unto you my Sustainer's message and gave you good advice: but you did not love those who gave [you] good advice." ‹79›

AND [remember] Lot,[63] when he said unto his people: "Will you commit abominations such as none in all the world has ever done before you? ‹80› Verily, with lust you approach men instead of women: nay, but you are people given to excesses!" ‹81›
But his people's only answer was this:[64] "Expel them from your land! Verily, they are folk who make themselves out to be pure!"[65] ‹82›

قَالُوٓاْ إِنَّا بِمَآ أُرْسِلَ بِهِۦ مُؤْمِنُونَ ﴿75﴾ قَالَ ٱلَّذِينَ ٱسْتَكْبَرُوٓاْ إِنَّا بِٱلَّذِىٓ
ءَامَنتُم بِهِۦ كَٰفِرُونَ ﴿76﴾ فَعَقَرُواْ ٱلنَّاقَةَ وَعَتَوْاْ عَنْ أَمْرِ رَبِّهِمْ وَقَالُواْ
يَٰصَٰلِحُ ٱئْتِنَا بِمَا تَعِدُنَآ إِن كُنتَ مِنَ ٱلْمُرْسَلِينَ ﴿77﴾ فَأَخَذَتْهُمُ
ٱلرَّجْفَةُ فَأَصْبَحُواْ فِى دَارِهِمْ جَٰثِمِينَ ﴿78﴾ فَتَوَلَّىٰ عَنْهُمْ وَقَالَ يَٰقَوْمِ لَقَدْ
أَبْلَغْتُكُمْ رِسَالَةَ رَبِّى وَنَصَحْتُ لَكُمْ وَلَٰكِن لَّا تُحِبُّونَ ٱلنَّٰصِحِينَ ﴿79﴾
وَلُوطًا إِذْ قَالَ لِقَوْمِهِۦٓ أَتَأْتُونَ ٱلْفَٰحِشَةَ مَا سَبَقَكُم بِهَا مِنْ أَحَدٍ مِّنَ
ٱلْعَٰلَمِينَ ﴿80﴾ إِنَّكُمْ لَتَأْتُونَ ٱلرِّجَالَ شَهْوَةً مِّن دُونِ ٱلنِّسَآءِ بَلْ أَنتُمْ
قَوْمٌ مُّسْرِفُونَ ﴿81﴾ وَمَا كَانَ جَوَابَ قَوْمِهِۦٓ إِلَّآ أَن قَالُوٓاْ أَخْرِجُوهُم مِّن
قَرْيَتِكُمْ إِنَّهُمْ أُنَاسٌ يَتَطَهَّرُونَ ﴿82﴾

Qālūu ʾinnā bimāa ʾursila bihī muʾminūn. (75) Qālal-ladhīnas-takbarūu ʾinnā billadhīi ʾāmañtum-bihī kāfirūn. (76) Faʿaqarun-nāqata wa ʿataw ʿan ʾamri Rabbihim wa qālū yā Ṣāliḥuʾ-tinā bimā taʿidunāa ʾiñ-kuñta minal-Mursalīn. (77) Faʾakhadhat-humur-rajfatu faʾaṣbaḥū fī dārihim jāthimīn. (78) Fatawallā ʿanhum wa qāla yā qawmi laqad ʾablaghtukum risālata Rabbī wa naṣaḥtu lakum wa lākil-lā tuḥibbūnan-nāṣiḥīn. (79) Wa Lūṭan ʾidh qāla liqawmihīi ʾataʾtūnal-fāḥishata mā sabaqakum-bihā min ʾaḥadim-minal-ʿālamīn. (80) ʾInnakum lataʾtūnar-rijāla shahwatam-miñ-dūnin-nisāaʾ. Bal añtum qawmum-musrifūn. (81) Wa mā kāna jawāba qawmihīi ʾillāa ʾañ-qālūu ʾakhrijūhum-miñ-qaryatikum; ʾinnahum ʾunāsuñy-yataṭahharūn. (82)

60 The *contents* of his message (lit., "that with which he has been sent") appeared to them justification enough to accept it on its merits, without the need of any esoteric "proof" of Ṣāliḥ's mission. In a subtle way, this statement of faith has a meaning which goes far beyond the story of the Thamūd. It is an invitation to the sceptic who is unable to believe in the divine origin of a religious message, to judge it on its intrinsic merits and not to make his acceptance dependent on extraneous, and objectively impossible, proofs of its origin: for only through the *contents* of a message can its truth and validity be established.

61 The verb *ʿaqara* primarily denotes "he hamstrung [an animal]" – i.e., before slaughtering it, so that it might not run away. This barbarous custom was widely practiced in pre-Islamic Arabia, so that *ʿaqr* ("hamstringing") gradually became synonymous with slaughtering in a cruel manner (Rāzī; see also Lane V, 2107 f).

62 Lit., "they became, in their homes, prostrate on the ground". The term *rajfah* which occurs at the beginning of this sentence signifies any violent commotion or trembling, and is often, though not always, applied to an earthquake (*rajfat al-arḍ*). It is possible that the earthquake mentioned here was accompanied by the volcanic eruption which at some time overtook the historical dwelling-places of the Thamūd tribe, and to which the extensive black lava-fields (*ḥarrah*) of northern Ḥijāz, and particularly near Madāʾin Ṣāliḥ (see note 59 above), bear eloquent witness to this day.

63 The story of Lot, Abraham's nephew (Lūṭ in Arabic), is given in greater detail in 11 : 69-83.

64 Lit., "their answer was nothing but that they said".

65 Lit., "who purify themselves"; also, "who keep aloof from unclean things": here obviously used ironically. The plural relates to Lot, his family and his followers (cf. 27 : 56).

فَأَنجَيْنَٰهُ وَأَهْلَهُۥٓ إِلَّا ٱمْرَأَتَهُۥ كَانَتْ مِنَ ٱلْغَٰبِرِينَ ﴿٨٣﴾ وَأَمْطَرْنَا عَلَيْهِم
مَّطَرًا ۖ فَٱنظُرْ كَيْفَ كَانَ عَٰقِبَةُ ٱلْمُجْرِمِينَ ﴿٨٤﴾ وَإِلَىٰ مَدْيَنَ أَخَاهُمْ
شُعَيْبًا ۗ قَالَ يَٰقَوْمِ ٱعْبُدُوا۟ ٱللَّهَ مَا لَكُم مِّنْ إِلَٰهٍ غَيْرُهُۥ ۖ قَدْ جَآءَتْكُم بَيِّنَةٌ
مِّن رَّبِّكُمْ ۖ فَأَوْفُوا۟ ٱلْكَيْلَ وَٱلْمِيزَانَ وَلَا تَبْخَسُوا۟ ٱلنَّاسَ أَشْيَآءَهُمْ وَلَا
تُفْسِدُوا۟ فِى ٱلْأَرْضِ بَعْدَ إِصْلَٰحِهَا ۚ ذَٰلِكُمْ خَيْرٌ لَّكُمْ إِن كُنتُم
مُّؤْمِنِينَ ﴿٨٥﴾ وَلَا تَقْعُدُوا۟ بِكُلِّ صِرَٰطٍ تُوعِدُونَ وَتَصُدُّونَ عَن سَبِيلِ ٱللَّهِ
مَنْ ءَامَنَ بِهِۦ وَتَبْغُونَهَا عِوَجًا ۚ وَٱذْكُرُوٓا۟ إِذْ كُنتُمْ قَلِيلًا فَكَثَّرَكُمْ ۖ
وَٱنظُرُوا۟ كَيْفَ كَانَ عَٰقِبَةُ ٱلْمُفْسِدِينَ ﴿٨٦﴾ وَإِن كَانَ طَآئِفَةٌ مِّنكُمْ
ءَامَنُوا۟ بِٱلَّذِىٓ أُرْسِلْتُ بِهِۦ وَطَآئِفَةٌ لَّمْ يُؤْمِنُوا۟ فَٱصْبِرُوا۟ حَتَّىٰ يَحْكُمَ ٱللَّهُ
بَيْنَنَا ۚ وَهُوَ خَيْرُ ٱلْحَٰكِمِينَ ﴿٨٧﴾

Faʾañjaynāhu wa ʾahlahūu ʾillam-raʾatahū kānat minal-ghābirīn. (83) Wa ʾamṭarnā ʿalayhim-maṭarañ-fañẓur kayfa kāna ʿāqibatul-mujrimīn. (84) Wa ʾilā Madyana ʾakhāhum Shuʿaybā. Qāla yā qawmiʿ-budul-lāha mā lakum-min ʾilāhin ghayruh. Qad jāaʾatkum-bayyinatum-mir-Rabbikum faʾawful-kayla wal-mīzāna wa lā tabkhasun-nāsa ʾashyāaʾahum wa lā tufsidū fil-ʾarḍi baʿda ʾiṣlāḥihā; dhālikum khayrul-lakum ʾiñ-kuñtum-muʾminīn. (85) Wa lā taqʿudū bikulli ṣirāṭiñ-tūʿidūna wa taṣuddūna ʿañ-sabīlil-lāhi man ʾāmana bihī wa tabghūnahā ʿiwajā. Wadhkurūu ʾidh kuñtum qalīlañ-fakaththarakum. Wañẓurū kayfa kāna ʿāqibatul-mufsidīn. (86) Wa ʾiñ-kāna ṭāaʾifatum-miñkum ʾāmanū billadhīi ʾursiltu bihī wa ṭāaʾifatul-lam yuʾminū faṣbirū ḥattā yaḥkumal-lāhu baynanā; wa Huwa Khayrul-ḥākimīn. (87)

Thereupon We saved him and his household – except his wife, who was among those that stayed behind[66] «83» – the while We rained a rain [of destruction] upon the others: and behold what happened in the end to those people lost in sin! «84»

AND UNTO [the people of] Madyan [We sent] their brother Shuʿayb.[67] He said: "O my people! Worship God alone: you have no deity other than Him. Clear evidence of the truth has now come unto you from your Sustainer. Give, therefore, full measure and weight [in all your dealings], and do not deprive people of what is rightfully theirs;[68] and do not spread corruption on earth after it has been so well ordered: [all] this is for your own good, if you would but believe. «85» And do not lie in ambush by every road [that leads to the truth[69]], threatening and trying to turn away from God's path all who believe in Him, and trying to make it appear crooked. And remember [the time] when you were few, and [how] He made you many: and behold what happened in the end to the spreaders of corruption! «86»

"And if there be some among you who have come to believe in the message which I bear, the while the others do not believe, then have patience in adversity till God shall judge between us [and them]: for He is the best of all judges!" «87»

66 Contrary to the Biblical account, according to which Lot's wife only "looked back" inadvertently (Genesis xix, 26), the Qurʾān makes it clear in 11 : 81 and 66 : 10 that she remained behind deliberately, being at heart one with the sinning people of Sodom and having no faith in her husband.

67 Shuʿayb is said to be identical with Jethro, the father-in-law of Moses, also called in the Bible Reú-ēl (Exodus ii, 18), meaning "Faithful to God". The region of Madyan – the Midian of the Bible – extended from the present-day Gulf of Aqabah westwards deep into the Sinai Peninsula and to the mountains of Moab east of the Dead Sea; its inhabitants were Arabs of the Amorite group of tribes.

68 Lit., "do not diminish to people their things" – an expression which applies to physical possessions as well as to moral and social rights. Regarding my interpolation of "in all your dealings", see *sūrah* 6, note 150.

69 Thus Zamakhsharī and Rāzī, stressing the metaphorical meaning of the above phrase. Cf. a similar expression, attributed to Satan, in verse 16 of this *sūrah*.

Said the great ones among his people, who gloried in their arrogance: "Most certainly, O Shuʿayb, we shall expel thee and thy fellow-believers from our land, unless you indeed return to our ways!"

Said [Shuʿayb]: "Why, even though we abhor [them]? ‹88› We should be guilty of blaspheming against God[70] were we to return to your ways after God has saved us from them! It is not conceivable that we should return to them – unless God, our Sustainer, so wills.[71] All things does our Sustainer embrace within His knowledge; in God do we place our trust. O our Sustainer! Lay Thou open the truth between us and our people – for Thou art the best of all to lay open the truth!"[72] ‹89›

But the great ones among his people, who were bent on denying the truth, said [to his followers]: "Indeed, if you follow Shuʿayb, you will, verily, be the losers!" ‹90›

Thereupon an earthquake overtook them: and then they lay lifeless, in their very homes, on the ground[73] ‹91› – they who had given the lie to Shuʿayb – as though they had never lived there: they who had given the lie to Shuʿayb – it was they who were the losers! ‹92›

And he turned away from them, and said: "O my people! Indeed, I delivered unto you my Sustainer's message and gave you good advice: how, then, could I mourn for people who have denied the truth?" ‹93›

AND NEVER YET have We sent a prophet unto any community without trying its people with misfortune and hardship, so that they might humble themselves; ‹94›

۞ قَالَ ٱلۡمَلَأُ ٱلَّذِينَ ٱسۡتَكۡبَرُواْ مِن قَوۡمِهِۦ لَنُخۡرِجَنَّكَ يَٰشُعَيۡبُ وَٱلَّذِينَ
ءَامَنُواْ مَعَكَ مِن قَرۡيَتِنَآ أَوۡ لَتَعُودُنَّ فِي مِلَّتِنَاۚ قَالَ أَوَلَوۡ كُنَّا
كَٰرِهِينَ ﴿٨٨﴾ قَدِ ٱفۡتَرَيۡنَا عَلَى ٱللَّهِ كَذِبًا إِنۡ عُدۡنَا فِي مِلَّتِكُم بَعۡدَ إِذۡ
نَجَّىٰنَا ٱللَّهُ مِنۡهَاۚ وَمَا يَكُونُ لَنَآ أَن نَّعُودَ فِيهَآ إِلَّآ أَن يَشَآءَ ٱللَّهُ رَبُّنَاۚ
وَسِعَ رَبُّنَا كُلَّ شَيۡءٍ عِلۡمًاۚ عَلَى ٱللَّهِ تَوَكَّلۡنَاۚ رَبَّنَا ٱفۡتَحۡ بَيۡنَنَا وَبَيۡنَ قَوۡمِنَا
بِٱلۡحَقِّ وَأَنتَ خَيۡرُ ٱلۡفَٰتِحِينَ ﴿٨٩﴾ وَقَالَ ٱلۡمَلَأُ ٱلَّذِينَ كَفَرُواْ مِن قَوۡمِهِۦ
لَئِنِ ٱتَّبَعۡتُمۡ شُعَيۡبًا إِنَّكُمۡ إِذٗا لَّخَٰسِرُونَ ﴿٩٠﴾ فَأَخَذَتۡهُمُ ٱلرَّجۡفَةُ
فَأَصۡبَحُواْ فِي دَارِهِمۡ جَٰثِمِينَ ﴿٩١﴾ ٱلَّذِينَ كَذَّبُواْ شُعَيۡبٗا كَأَن لَّمۡ يَغۡنَوۡاْ حزب 17
فِيهَاۚ ٱلَّذِينَ كَذَّبُواْ شُعَيۡبٗا كَانُواْ هُمُ ٱلۡخَٰسِرِينَ ﴿٩٢﴾ فَتَوَلَّىٰ عَنۡهُمۡ وَقَالَ جزء 9
يَٰقَوۡمِ لَقَدۡ أَبۡلَغۡتُكُمۡ رِسَٰلَٰتِ رَبِّي وَنَصَحۡتُ لَكُمۡۖ فَكَيۡفَ ءَاسَىٰ عَلَىٰ
قَوۡمٖ كَٰفِرِينَ ﴿٩٣﴾ وَمَآ أَرۡسَلۡنَا فِي قَرۡيَةٖ مِّن نَّبِيٍّ إِلَّآ أَخَذۡنَآ أَهۡلَهَا
بِٱلۡبَأۡسَآءِ وَٱلضَّرَّآءِ لَعَلَّهُمۡ يَضَّرَّعُونَ ﴿٩٤﴾

۞ Qālal-malaʾul-ladhīnas-takbarū miñ-qawmihī lanukhrijannaka yā Shuʿaybu wal-ladhīna ʾāmanūu maʿaka miñ-qaryatināa ʾaw lataʿūdunna fī millatinā. Qāla ʾawa law kunnā kārihīn. (88) Qadif-taraynā ʿalal-lāhi kadhiban ʾin ʿudnā fī millatikum-baʿda ʾidh najjānal-lāhu minhā. Wa mā yakūnu lanāa ʾañ-naʿūda fīhāa ʾillāa ʾañy-yashāaʾal-lāhu Rabbunā. Wasiʿa Rabbunā kulla shayʾin ʿilmā. ʿAlal-lāhi tawakkalnā. Rabbanaf-taḥ baynanā wa bayna qawminā bilḥaqqi wa ʾAñta Khayrul-fātiḥīn. (89) Wa qālal-malaʾul-ladhīna kafarū miñ-qawmihī laʾinit-tabaʿtum Shuʿayban ʾinnakum ʾidhal-lakhāsirūn. (90) Faʾakhadhat-humur-rajfatu faʾaṣbaḥū fī dārihim jāthimīn. (91) ʾAlladhīna kadhdhabū Shuʿaybañ-kaʾal-lam yaghnaw fīha. ʾAlladhīna kadhdhabū Shuʿaybañ-kānū humul-khāsirīn. (92) Fatawallā ʿanhum wa qāla yā qawmi laqad ʾablaghtukum risālāti Rabbī wa naṣaḥtu lakum; fakayfa ʾāsā ʿalā qawmiñ-kāfirīn. (93) Wa māa ʾarsalnā fī qaryatim-miñ-Nabiyyin ʾillāa ʾakhadhnāa ʾahlahā bilbaʾsāaʾi waḍ-ḍarrāaʾi laʿallahum yaḍḍarraʿūn. (94)

70 Lit., "inventing a lie about God".

71 An expression of humility, and not of the idea that God might "will" them to blaspheme.

72 Or: "Thou art the best of all deciders" – since the verb *fataḥa* can also be rendered as "he decided". However, Shuʿayb's prayer could not have implied a request for God's "decision" (for there was no doubt in his mind as to who was right), and therefore the primary significance of *iftaḥ* ("lay open") and *fātiḥ* ("one who lays open", i.e., the truth) is preferable.

73 See note 62 above. Like the *ḥarrah* once inhabited by the Thamūd tribe, the adjoining region of Madyan (the Biblical Midian) shows ample evidence of volcanic eruptions and earthquakes.

ثُمَّ بَدَّلْنَا مَكَانَ ٱلسَّيِّئَةِ ٱلْحَسَنَةَ حَتَّىٰ عَفَوا۟ وَّقَالُوا۟ قَدْ مَسَّ ءَابَآءَنَا
ٱلضَّرَّآءُ وَٱلسَّرَّآءُ فَأَخَذْنَٰهُم بَغْتَةً وَهُمْ لَا يَشْعُرُونَ ﴿٩٥﴾ وَلَوْ أَنَّ أَهْلَ
ٱلْقُرَىٰٓ ءَامَنُوا۟ وَٱتَّقَوْا۟ لَفَتَحْنَا عَلَيْهِم بَرَكَٰتٍ مِّنَ ٱلسَّمَآءِ وَٱلْأَرْضِ
وَلَٰكِن كَذَّبُوا۟ فَأَخَذْنَٰهُم بِمَا كَانُوا۟ يَكْسِبُونَ ﴿٩٦﴾ أَفَأَمِنَ أَهْلُ
ٱلْقُرَىٰٓ أَن يَأْتِيَهُم بَأْسُنَا بَيَٰتًا وَهُمْ نَآئِمُونَ ﴿٩٧﴾ أَوَأَمِنَ أَهْلُ ٱلْقُرَىٰٓ أَن
يَأْتِيَهُم بَأْسُنَا ضُحًى وَهُمْ يَلْعَبُونَ ﴿٩٨﴾ أَفَأَمِنُوا۟ مَكْرَ ٱللَّهِ فَلَا يَأْمَنُ مَكْرَ
ٱللَّهِ إِلَّا ٱلْقَوْمُ ٱلْخَٰسِرُونَ ﴿٩٩﴾ أَوَلَمْ يَهْدِ لِلَّذِينَ يَرِثُونَ ٱلْأَرْضَ مِنۢ بَعْدِ
أَهْلِهَآ أَن لَّوْ نَشَآءُ أَصَبْنَٰهُم بِذُنُوبِهِمْ وَنَطْبَعُ عَلَىٰ قُلُوبِهِمْ فَهُمْ لَا
يَسْمَعُونَ ﴿١٠٠﴾

Thumma baddalnā makānas-sayyiʾatil-ḥasanata ḥattā ʿafaw-wa qālū qad massa ʾābāaʾanaḍ-ḍarrāaʾu was-sarrāaʾu faʾakhadhnāhum-baghtatañw-wa hum lā yashʿurūn. (95) Wa law ʾanna ʾahlal-qurāa ʾāmanū wat-taqaw lafataḥnā ʿalayhim-barakātim-minas-samāaʾi wal-ʾarḍi wa lākiñ-kadhdhabū faʾakhadhnāhum-bimā kānū yaksibūn. (96) ʾAfaʾamina ʾahlul-qurāa ʾañy-yaʾtiyahum-baʾsunā bayātañw-wa hum nāaʾimūn. (97) ʾAwa ʾamina ʾahlul-qurāa ʾañy-yaʾtiyahum-baʾsunā ḍuḥañw-wa hum yalʿabūn. (98) ʾAfaʾaminū makral-lāh. Falā yaʾmanu makral-lāhi ʾillal-qawmul-khāsirūn. (99) ʾAwa lam yahdi lilladhīna yarithūnal-ʾarḍa mim-baʿdi ʾahlihāa ʾal-law nashāaʾu ʾaṣabnāhum-bidhunūbihim wa naṭbaʿu ʿalā qulūbihim fahum lā yasmaʿūn. (100)

then We transformed the affliction into ease of life,[74] so that they throve and said [to themselves], "Misfortune and hardship befell our forefathers as well"[75] – whereupon We took them to task, all of a sudden, without their being aware [of what was coming].[76] ‹95›

Yet if the people of those communities had but attained to faith and been conscious of Us, We would indeed have opened up for them blessings out of heaven and earth: but they gave the lie to the truth – and so We took them to task through what they [themselves] had been doing.[77] ‹96›

Can, then, the people of any community ever feel secure that Our punishment will not come upon them by night, while they are asleep? ‹97› Why, can the people of any community ever feel secure that Our punishment will not come upon them in broad daylight, while they are engaged in [worldly] play?[78] ‹98› Can they, then, ever feel secure from God's deep devising? But none feels secure from God's deep devising save people who are [already] lost.[79] ‹99›

Has it, then, not become obvious unto those who have inherited the earth in the wake of former generations[80] that, if We so willed, We could smite them [too] by means of their sins, sealing their hearts so that they cannot hear [the truth]?[81] ‹100›

---

74 Lit., "then We put good [things] in place of the bad".

75 I.e., they regarded it as a normal course of events and did not draw any lesson from it.

76 Cf. 6 : 42-45.

77 Thus the discourse returns to its starting-point at the beginning of this *sūrah* (verses 4-5): namely, that the destruction which is bound to overtake any community (the proper significance of the term *qaryah* in this context) which lives in opposition to the eternal moral verities amounts, in the last resort, to self-annihilation: for this is the real meaning of God's "taking them to task through what (*bi-mā*) they themselves were doing".

78 I.e., while they enjoy ease and a sense of security, and are unaware of any danger that may threaten them (cf. verse 4 of this *sūrah*).

79 I.e., morally lost and, therefore, destined to perish. The term *makr Allāh* ("God's deep devising") denotes here His unfathomable planning, which is alluded to elsewhere in the Qurʾān by the expression *sunnat Allāh* ("God's [unchangeable] way" – cf., in particular, 33 : 62, 35 : 43 and 48 : 23).

80 Lit., "after its [former] people". The people "who have inherited the earth" are those now living.

81 See *sūrah* 2, note 7. Here, again, we have an affirmation that what the Qurʾān describes as "God's punishment" (as well as "God's reward") is, in reality, *a consequence of man's own doings*, and not an arbitrary act of God: it is "by means of their sins" (*bi-dhunūbihim*) that God "sets a seal" upon the hearts of men. This statement is further elucidated at the end of verse 101.

Unto those [earlier] communities – some of whose stories We [now] relate unto thee – there had indeed come apostles of their own with all evidence of the truth; but they would not believe in anything to which they had once given the lie:[82] thus it is that God seals the hearts of those who deny the truth; ‹101› and in most of them We found no [inner] bond with anything that is right[83] – and most of them We found to be iniquitous indeed. ‹102›

AND AFTER those [early people] We sent Moses with Our messages unto Pharaoh and his great ones, and they wilfully rejected them:[84] and behold what happened in the end to those spreaders of corruption! ‹103›
And Moses said: "O Pharaoh! Verily, I am an apostle from the Sustainer of all the worlds, ‹104› so constituted that I cannot say anything about God but the truth. I have now come unto you with a clear evidence from your Sustainer: let, then, the children of Israel go with me!" ‹105›
Said [Pharaoh]: "If thou hast come with a sign, produce it – if thou art a man of truth!" ‹106›
Thereupon [Moses] threw down his staff and lo! it was a serpent, plainly visible; ‹107› and he drew forth his hand, and lo! it appeared [shining] white to the beholders.[85] ‹108›
The great ones among Pharaoh's people said. "Verily, this is indeed a sorcerer of great knowledge, ‹109› who wants to drive you out of your land!"[86]
[Said Pharaoh:] "What, then, do you advise?" ‹110›

تِلْكَ ٱلْقُرَىٰ نَقُصُّ عَلَيْكَ مِنْ أَنۢبَآئِهَا ۚ وَلَقَدْ جَآءَتْهُمْ رُسُلُهُم بِٱلْبَيِّنَـٰتِ
فَمَا كَانُوا۟ لِيُؤْمِنُوا۟ بِمَا كَذَّبُوا۟ مِن قَبْلُ ۚ كَذَٰلِكَ يَطْبَعُ ٱللَّهُ عَلَىٰ قُلُوبِ
ٱلْكَـٰفِرِينَ ﴿١٠١﴾ وَمَا وَجَدْنَا لِأَكْثَرِهِم مِّنْ عَهْدٍ ۖ وَإِن وَجَدْنَآ أَكْثَرَهُمْ
لَفَـٰسِقِينَ ﴿١٠٢﴾ ثُمَّ بَعَثْنَا مِنۢ بَعْدِهِم مُّوسَىٰ بِـَٔايَـٰتِنَآ إِلَىٰ فِرْعَوْنَ وَمَلَإِي۟هِۦ
فَظَلَمُوا۟ بِهَا ۖ فَٱنظُرْ كَيْفَ كَانَ عَـٰقِبَةُ ٱلْمُفْسِدِينَ ﴿١٠٣﴾ وَقَالَ مُوسَىٰ
يَـٰفِرْعَوْنُ إِنِّى رَسُولٌ مِّن رَّبِّ ٱلْعَـٰلَمِينَ ﴿١٠٤﴾ حَقِيقٌ عَلَىٰٓ أَن لَّآ أَقُولَ عَلَى
ٱللَّهِ إِلَّا ٱلْحَقَّ ۚ قَدْ جِئْتُكُم بِبَيِّنَةٍ مِّن رَّبِّكُمْ فَأَرْسِلْ مَعِىَ بَنِىٓ إِسْرَٰٓءِيلَ ﴿١٠٥﴾
قَالَ إِن كُنتَ جِئْتَ بِـَٔايَةٍ فَأْتِ بِهَآ إِن كُنتَ مِنَ ٱلصَّـٰدِقِينَ ﴿١٠٦﴾
فَأَلْقَىٰ عَصَاهُ فَإِذَا هِىَ ثُعْبَانٌ مُّبِينٌ ﴿١٠٧﴾ وَنَزَعَ يَدَهُۥ فَإِذَا هِىَ بَيْضَآءُ
لِلنَّـٰظِرِينَ ﴿١٠٨﴾ قَالَ ٱلْمَلَأُ مِن قَوْمِ فِرْعَوْنَ إِنَّ هَـٰذَا لَسَـٰحِرٌ عَلِيمٌ ﴿١٠٩﴾
يُرِيدُ أَن يُخْرِجَكُم مِّنْ أَرْضِكُمْ ۖ فَمَاذَا تَأْمُرُونَ ﴿١١٠﴾

Tilkal-qurā naquṣu ʿalayka min ʾambāaʾihā. Wa laqad jāaʾat-hum Rusuluhum-bilbayyināti famā kānū liyuʾminū bimā kadhdhabū miñ-qabl. Kadhālika yaṭbaʿul-lāhu ʿalā qulūbil-kāfirīn. (101) Wa mā wajadnā liʾaktharihim-min ʿahd. Wa ʾiñw-wajadnāa ʾaktharahum lafāsiqīn. (102) Thumma baʿathnā mimbaʿdihim-Mūsā biʾĀyātināa ʾilā Firʿawna wa malaʾihī faẓalamū bihā; fañẓur kayfa kana ʿāqibatul-mufsidīn. (103) Wa qāla Mūsā yā Firʿawnu ʾinnī Rasūlum-mir-Rabbil-ʿālamīn. (104) Ḥaqīqun ʿalāa ʾal-lāa ʾaqūla ʿalal-lāhi ʾillal-ḥaqq. Qad jiʾtukum-bibayyinatim-mir-Rabbikum faʾarsil maʿiya banīi ʾIsrāaʾīl. (105) Qāla ʾiñ-kuñta jiʾta biʾĀyatiñ-faʾti bihāa ʾiñ-kuñta minaṣ-ṣādiqīn. (106) Faʾalqā ʿaṣāhu faʾidhā hiya thuʿbānum-mubīn. (107) Wa nazaʿa yadahū faʾidhā hiya bayḍāaʾu linnāẓirīn. (108) Qālal-malaʾu miñ-qawmi Firʿawna ʾinna hādhā lasāḥirun ʿalīm. (109) Yurīdu ʾañy-yukhrijakum-min ʾarḍikum; famādhā taʾmurūn. (110)

82 Lit., "to which they had given the lie aforetime": an allusion to the instinctive unwillingness of most people to give up the notions – positive or negative – to which they are accustomed.

83 Thus Rāghib explains the term *ʿahd* occurring in this sentence. Its usual rendering as "covenant" or "loyalty to their covenant" is entirely meaningless in this context. Rashīd Riḍāʾ widens Rāghib's interpretation and includes in the above term man's instinctive ability to discern between right and wrong and, thus, to follow the dictates of his own conscience (*Manār* IX, 33 ff.). Regarding the deeper implications of this expression, see *sūrah* 2, note 19.

84 Lit., "they did wrong to them".

85 As is evident from 20 : 22, 27 : 12 and 28 : 32, the hand of Moses was "[shining] white, without blemish", i.e., endowed with transcendent luminosity in token of his prophethood – and not, as stated in the Bible (Exodus iv, 6), "leprous as snow". Regarding the possible mystic significance of the miracle of the staff, see note 14 on 20 : 21.

86 I.e., "deprive you of your rule". The plural "you" relates to Pharaoh and the ruling class.

ربع الحزب

They answered: "Let him and his brother[87] wait awhile, and send unto all cities heralds ‹111› who shall bring before thee every sorcerer of great knowledge." ‹112›
And the sorcerers came unto Pharaoh [and] said: "Verily, we ought to have a great reward[88] if it is we who prevail." ‹113›
Answered [Pharaoh]: "Yes; and, verily, you shall be among those who are near unto me." ‹114›
They said: "O Moses! Either thou shalt throw [thy staff first], or we shall [be the first to] throw." ‹115›
He answered: "You throw [first]."
And when they threw down [their staffs], they cast a spell upon the people's eyes, and struck them with awe, and produced mighty sorcery. ‹116›
And [then] We inspired Moses, "Throw down thy staff!" – and lo! it swallowed up all their deceptions:[89] ‹117› whereupon the truth was established, and vain was proved all that they had been doing. ‹118›
And thus were they vanquished there and then, and became utterly humiliated. ‹119›
And down fell the sorcerers,[90] prostrating themselves ‹120› [and] exclaiming: "We have come to believe in the Sustainer of all the worlds, ‹121› the Sustainer of Moses and Aaron!" ‹122›
Said Pharaoh: "Have you come to believe in him[91] ere I have given you permission? Behold, this is indeed a plot which you have cunningly devised in this [my] city in order to drive out its people hence! But in time you shall come to know [my revenge]: ‹123› most certainly shall I cut

قَالُوٓاْ أَرْجِهْ وَأَخَاهُ وَأَرْسِلْ فِى ٱلْمَدَآئِنِ حَـٰشِرِينَ ﴿١١١﴾ يَأْتُوكَ بِكُلِّ
سَـٰحِرٍ عَلِيمٍ ﴿١١٢﴾ وَجَآءَ ٱلسَّحَرَةُ فِرْعَوْنَ قَالُوٓاْ إِنَّ لَنَا لَأَجْرًا إِن كُنَّا
نَحْنُ ٱلْغَـٰلِبِينَ ﴿١١٣﴾ قَالَ نَعَمْ وَإِنَّكُمْ لَمِنَ ٱلْمُقَرَّبِينَ ﴿١١٤﴾ قَالُواْ
يَـٰمُوسَىٰٓ إِمَّآ أَن تُلْقِىَ وَإِمَّآ أَن نَّكُونَ نَحْنُ ٱلْمُلْقِينَ ﴿١١٥﴾ قَالَ أَلْقُواْ
فَلَمَّآ أَلْقَوْاْ سَحَرُوٓاْ أَعْيُنَ ٱلنَّاسِ وَٱسْتَرْهَبُوهُمْ وَجَآءُو بِسِحْرٍ عَظِيمٍ ﴿١١٦﴾
۞ وَأَوْحَيْنَآ إِلَىٰ مُوسَىٰٓ أَنْ أَلْقِ عَصَاكَ فَإِذَا هِىَ تَلْقَفُ مَا
يَأْفِكُونَ ﴿١١٧﴾ فَوَقَعَ ٱلْحَقُّ وَبَطَلَ مَا كَانُواْ يَعْمَلُونَ ﴿١١٨﴾ فَغُلِبُواْ
هُنَالِكَ وَٱنقَلَبُواْ صَـٰغِرِينَ ﴿١١٩﴾ وَأُلْقِىَ ٱلسَّحَرَةُ سَـٰجِدِينَ ﴿١٢٠﴾ قَالُوٓاْ
ءَامَنَّا بِرَبِّ ٱلْعَـٰلَمِينَ ﴿١٢١﴾ رَبِّ مُوسَىٰ وَهَـٰرُونَ ﴿١٢٢﴾ قَالَ فِرْعَوْنُ
ءَامَنتُم بِهِۦ قَبْلَ أَنْ ءَاذَنَ لَكُمْ إِنَّ هَـٰذَا لَمَكْرٌ مَّكَرْتُمُوهُ فِى
ٱلْمَدِينَةِ لِتُخْرِجُواْ مِنْهَآ أَهْلَهَا فَسَوْفَ تَعْلَمُونَ ﴿١٢٣﴾ لَأُقَطِّعَنَّ

Qālūu ʾarjih wa ʾakhāhu wa ʾarsil fil-madāaʾini ḥāshirīn. ⟨111⟩ Yaʾtūka bikulli sāḥirin ʿalīm. ⟨112⟩ Wa jāaʾas-saḥaratu Firʿawna qālūu ʾinna lanā laʾajran ʾiñ-kunnā naḥnul-ghālibīn. ⟨113⟩ Qāla naʿam wa ʾinnakum laminal-muqarrabīn. ⟨114⟩ Qālū yā Mūsāa ʾimmāa ʾañ-tulqiya wa ʾimmāa ʾañ-nakūna naḥnul-mulqīn. ⟨115⟩ Qāla ʾalqū. Falammāa ʾalqaw saḥarūu ʾaʿyunan-nāsi was-tarhabūhum wa jāaʾū bisiḥrin ʿaẓīm. ⟨116⟩ ۞ Wa ʾawḥaynāa ʾilā Mūsāa ʾan ʾalqi ʿasāka faʾidhā hiya talqafu mā yaʾfikūn. ⟨117⟩ Fawaqaʿal-ḥaqqu wa baṭala mā kānū yaʿmalūn. ⟨118⟩ Faghulibū hunālika wañ-qalabū ṣāghirīn. ⟨119⟩ Wa ʾulqiyas-saḥaratu sājidīn. ⟨120⟩ Qālūu ʾāmannā biRabbil-ʿālamīn. ⟨121⟩ Rabbi Mūsā wa Hārūn. ⟨122⟩ Qāla Firʿawnu ʾāmañtum-bihī qabla ʾan ʾādhana lakum. ʾInna hādhā lamakrum-makartumūhu fil-madīnati litukhrijū minhāa ʾahlahā; fasawfa taʿlamūn. ⟨123⟩ Laʾuqaṭṭiʿanna

87 I.e., Aaron, who – as is mentioned in several other places in the Qurʾān – accompanied Moses on his mission.

88 The particle *la* preceding the noun *ajr* ("reward") indicates an emphasis which gives to this combination the meaning of "*great* reward".

89 Implying that the act of Moses was a genuine miracle, whereas that of the sorcerers was a feat of make-believe (cf. 20 : 66).

90 Lit., "the sorcerers were thrown down" – i.e., they fell to the ground as if thrown by a superior force (Zamakhsharī).

91 This personal pronoun may refer either to God or to Moses; but a similar expression in 20 : 71 and 26 : 49 makes it obvious that it refers here to Moses.

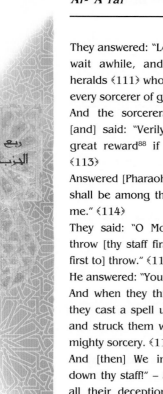

off your hands and your feet in great numbers, because of [your] perverseness, and then I shall most certainly crucify you in great numbers, all together!"[92] ‹124›
They answered: "Verily, unto our Sustainer do we turn ‹125› – for thou takest vengeance on us only because we have come to believe in our Sustainer's messages as soon as they came to us. O our Sustainer! Shower us with patience in adversity, and make us die as men who have surrendered themselves unto Thee!" ‹126›
And the great ones among Pharaoh's people said: "Wilt thou allow Moses and his people to spread corruption on earth, and to [cause thy people to] forsake thee and thy gods?"
[Pharaoh] replied: "We shall slay their sons in great numbers and shall spare [only] their women: for, verily, we hold sway over them!" ‹127›
[And] Moses said unto his people: "Turn unto God for aid, and have patience in adversity. Verily, all the earth belongs to God: He gives it as a heritage to such as He wills of His servants; and the future belongs to the God-conscious! ‹128›
[But the children of Israel] said: "We have suffered hurt ere thou camest to us and since thou hast come to us!"[93]
[Moses] replied: "It may well be that your Sustainer will destroy your foe and make you inherit the earth: and thereupon he will behold how you act."[94] ‹129›

أَيْدِيَكُمْ وَأَرْجُلَكُم مِّنْ خِلَٰفٍ ثُمَّ لَأُصَلِّبَنَّكُمْ أَجْمَعِينَ ﴿١٢٤﴾ قَالُوٓاْ إِنَّآ
إِلَىٰ رَبِّنَا مُنقَلِبُونَ ﴿١٢٥﴾ وَمَا تَنقِمُ مِنَّآ إِلَّآ أَنْ ءَامَنَّا بِـَٔايَٰتِ رَبِّنَا لَمَّا
جَآءَتْنَا رَبَّنَآ أَفْرِغْ عَلَيْنَا صَبْرًا وَتَوَفَّنَا مُسْلِمِينَ ﴿١٢٦﴾ وَقَالَ ٱلْمَلَأُ مِن قَوْمِ
فِرْعَوْنَ أَتَذَرُ مُوسَىٰ وَقَوْمَهُۥ لِيُفْسِدُواْ فِى ٱلْأَرْضِ وَيَذَرَكَ وَءَالِهَتَكَ قَالَ
سَنُقَتِّلُ أَبْنَآءَهُمْ وَنَسْتَحْىِۦ نِسَآءَهُمْ وَإِنَّا فَوْقَهُمْ قَٰهِرُونَ ﴿١٢٧﴾ قَالَ مُوسَىٰ
لِقَوْمِهِ ٱسْتَعِينُواْ بِٱللَّهِ وَٱصْبِرُوٓاْ إِنَّ ٱلْأَرْضَ لِلَّهِ يُورِثُهَا مَن يَشَآءُ مِنْ
عِبَادِهِۦ وَٱلْعَٰقِبَةُ لِلْمُتَّقِينَ ﴿١٢٨﴾ قَالُوٓاْ أُوذِينَا مِن قَبْلِ أَن تَأْتِيَنَا وَمِنۢ بَعْدِ
مَا جِئْتَنَا قَالَ عَسَىٰ رَبُّكُمْ أَن يُهْلِكَ عَدُوَّكُمْ وَيَسْتَخْلِفَكُمْ فِى ٱلْأَرْضِ
فَيَنظُرَ كَيْفَ تَعْمَلُونَ ﴿١٢٩﴾

aydiyakum wa ʾarjulakum-min khilāfiñ-thumma laʾuṣallibannakum ʾajmaᶜīn. (124) Qālūu ʾinnāa ʾilā Rabbinā muñqalibūn. (125) Wa mā tañqimu minnāa ʾillāa ʾan ʾāmannā biʾĀyāti Rabbinā lammā jāaʾatnā. Rabbanāa ʾafrigh ᶜalaynā ṣabrañw-wa tawaffanā Muslimīn. (126) Wa qālal-malaʾu miñ-qawmi Firᶜawna ʾatadharu Mūsā wa qawmahū liyufsidū fil-ʾarḍi wa yadharaka wa ʾālihatak. Qāla sanuqattilu abnāaʾahum wa nastaḥyī nisāaʾahum wa ʾinnā fawqahum qāhirūn. (127) Qāla Mūsā liqawmihis-taᶜīnū billāhi waṣ-birū. ʾInnal-ʾarḍa lillāhi yūrithuhā mañy-yashāaʾu min ᶜibādihī wal-ᶜāqibatu lilmuttaqīn. (128) Qālūu ʾūdhīnā miñ-qabli ʾañ-taʾtiyanā wa mim-baᶜdi mā jiʾtanā. Qāla ᶜasā Rabbukum ʾañy-yuhlika ᶜaduwwakum wa yastakhlifakum fil-ʾarḍi fayañẓura kayfa taᶜmalūn. (129)

92 The grammatical forms *la-uqaṭṭiᶜanna* and *la-uṣallibannakum* must be rendered as "most certainly shall I cut off [your hands and feet] *in great numbers*" and "crucify you *in great numbers*": and this indicates that either the repentant sorcerers thus addressed were many or, alternatively, that they had a large following among the people of Egypt. The latter assumption seems to be corroborated by the Biblical reference to the fact that many Egyptians joined the Israelites in their exodus from Egypt: "And a mixed multitude went up also with them" (Exodus xii, 38). As regards my rendering of *min khilāf* as "because of [your] perverseness", see *sūrah* 5, note 44 (last sentence).

93 This is, in the above context, the first hint of the inconstancy and weakness of faith for which the Qurʾān so often blames the children of Israel: and this, together with what follows in verses 138-140 and 148 ff., is the reason why the story of Moses has been included here among the stories of the earlier prophets whose warnings were neglected by their communities.

94 I.e., "He will judge you by your actions". As is evident from the reference, in verse 137 below, to the "patience in adversity" which the children of Israel subsequently displayed, it would seem that the hope held out to them by Moses helped them, once again, to overcome their moral weakness; but, at the same time, his words "God will behold how you act" imply a distinct warning.

وَلَقَدْ أَخَذْنَآ ءَالَ فِرْعَوْنَ بِٱلسِّنِينَ وَنَقْصٍ مِّنَ ٱلثَّمَرَٰتِ لَعَلَّهُمْ
يَذَّكَّرُونَ ﴿١٣٠﴾ فَإِذَا جَآءَتْهُمُ ٱلْحَسَنَةُ قَالُوا۟ لَنَا هَـٰذِهِۦ ۖ وَإِن تُصِبْهُمْ سَيِّئَةٌ
يَطَّيَّرُوا۟ بِمُوسَىٰ وَمَن مَّعَهُۥٓ ۗ أَلَآ إِنَّمَا طَـٰٓئِرُهُمْ عِندَ ٱللَّهِ وَلَـٰكِنَّ أَكْثَرَهُمْ لَا
يَعْلَمُونَ ﴿١٣١﴾ وَقَالُوا۟ مَهْمَا تَأْتِنَا بِهِۦ مِنْ ءَايَةٍ لِّتَسْحَرَنَا بِهَا فَمَا نَحْنُ لَكَ
بِمُؤْمِنِينَ ﴿١٣٢﴾ فَأَرْسَلْنَا عَلَيْهِمُ ٱلطُّوفَانَ وَٱلْجَرَادَ وَٱلْقُمَّلَ وَٱلضَّفَادِعَ
وَٱلدَّمَ ءَايَـٰتٍ مُّفَصَّلَـٰتٍ فَٱسْتَكْبَرُوا۟ وَكَانُوا۟ قَوْمًا مُّجْرِمِينَ ﴿١٣٣﴾ وَلَمَّا وَقَعَ
عَلَيْهِمُ ٱلرِّجْزُ قَالُوا۟ يَـٰمُوسَى ٱدْعُ لَنَا رَبَّكَ بِمَا عَهِدَ عِندَكَ ۖ لَئِن كَشَفْتَ
عَنَّا ٱلرِّجْزَ لَنُؤْمِنَنَّ لَكَ وَلَنُرْسِلَنَّ مَعَكَ بَنِىٓ إِسْرَٰٓءِيلَ ﴿١٣٤﴾ فَلَمَّا كَشَفْنَا عَنْهُمُ
ٱلرِّجْزَ إِلَىٰٓ أَجَلٍ هُم بَـٰلِغُوهُ إِذَا هُمْ يَنكُثُونَ ﴿١٣٥﴾ فَٱنتَقَمْنَا مِنْهُمْ فَأَغْرَقْنَـٰهُمْ
فِى ٱلْيَمِّ بِأَنَّهُمْ كَذَّبُوا۟ بِـَٔايَـٰتِنَا وَكَانُوا۟ عَنْهَا غَـٰفِلِينَ ﴿١٣٦﴾ وَأَوْرَثْنَا ٱلْقَوْمَ
ٱلَّذِينَ كَانُوا۟ يُسْتَضْعَفُونَ مَشَـٰرِقَ ٱلْأَرْضِ وَمَغَـٰرِبَهَا ٱلَّتِى بَـٰرَكْنَا فِيهَا

Wa laqad ʾakhadhnāa ʾāla Firʿawna bissinīna wa naqṣim-minath-thamarāti laʿallahum yadhdhak-karūn. (130) Fa ʾidhā jāaʾat-humul-ḥasanatu qālū lanā hādhih. Wa ʾiñ-tuṣibhum sayyiʾatuñy-yaṭṭayyarū biMūsā wa mam-maʿah. ʾAlāa ʾinnamā ṭāaʾiruhum ʿiñdal-lāhi wa lākinna ʾaktharahum lā yaʿlamūn. (131) Wa qālū mahmā taʾtinā bihī min ʾĀyatil-litasḥaranā bihā famā naḥnu laka bimuʾminīn. (132) Faʾarsalnā ʿalayhimuṭ-ṭūfāna wal-jarāda wal-qummala waḍ-ḍafādiʿa wad-dama ʾāyātim-mufaṣṣalātiñ-fastakbarū wa kānū qawmam-mujrimīn. (133) Wa lammā waqaʿa ʿalayhimur-rijzu qālū yā Mūsad-ʿu lanā Rabbaka bimā ʿahida ʿiñdaka laʾiñ-kashafta ʿannar-rijza lanuʾminanna laka wa lanursilanna maʿaka banīi ʾIsrāaʾīl. (134) Falammā kashafnā ʿanhumur-rijza ʾilāa ʾajalin hum-bālighūhu ʾidhā hum yañkuthun. (135) Fañtaqamnā minhum faʾaghraqnāhum fil-yammi biʾannahum kadhdhabū biʾĀyatinā wa kānū ʿanhā ghāfilīn. (136) Wa ʾawrathnal-qawmal-ladhīna kānū yustaḍʿafūna mashāriqal-ʾarḍi wa maghāribahal-latī bāraknā fīhā.

And most certainly did We overwhelm Pharaoh's people with drought and scarcity of fruits, so that they might take it to heart. ‹130› But whenever good fortune alighted upon them, they would say, "This is [but] our due"; and whenever affliction befell them, they would blame their evil fortune on Moses and those who followed him.[95] Oh, verily, their [evil] fortune had been decreed by God – but most of them knew it not. ‹131›

And they said [unto Moses]: "Whatever sign thou mayest produce before us in order to cast a spell upon us thereby, we shall not believe thee!" ‹132›

Thereupon We let loose upon them floods, and [plagues of] locusts, and lice, and frogs, and [water turning into] blood[96] – distinct signs [all]: but they gloried in their arrogance, for they were people lost in sin. ‹133›

And whenever a plague struck them, they would cry: "O Moses, pray for us to thy Sustainer on the strength of the covenant [of prophethood] which He has made with thee! If thou remove this plague from us, we will truly believe in thee, and will let the children of Israel go with thee!" ‹134›

But whenever We removed the plague from them, giving them time to make good their promise,[97] lo, they would break their word. ‹135› And so We inflicted Our retribution on them, and caused them to drown in the sea, because they had given the lie to Our messages and had been heedless of them; ‹136› whereas unto the people who [in the past] had been deemed utterly low, We gave as their heritage the eastern and western parts of the land that We had blessed.[98]

95 The phrase *taṭayyara bihi* signifies "he attributed an evil omen to him" or "he augured evil from him". It is based on the pre-Islamic Arab custom of divining the future or establishing an omen from the flight of birds. Thus, the noun *ṭāʾir* (lit., "a flying creature" or "a bird") is often used in classical Arabic to denote "destiny" or "fortune", both good and evil, as in the next sentence of the above verse ("their [evil] fortune had been decreed by [lit., "was with"] God"). Instances of this tropical employment of the expressions *ṭāʾir* and *ṭayr* and their verbal derivations are also found in 3 : 49, 5 : 110, 17 : 13, 27 : 47, 36 : 18-19.

96 For a description of these plagues, see Exodus vii-x.

97 Lit., "until a term which they should reach".

98 Palestine is spoken of as "blessed" because it was the land in which Abraham, Isaac and Jacob had lived, and because so many other prophets were to appear there.

And [thus] thy Sustainer's good promise unto the children of Israel was fulfilled in result of their patience in adversity;[99] whereas We utterly destroyed all that Pharaoh and his people had wrought, and all that they had built.[100] ‹137›

AND WE BROUGHT the children of Israel across the sea; and thereupon they came upon people who were devoted to the worship of some idols of theirs.[101] Said [the children of Israel]: "O Moses, set up for us a god even as they have gods!" He replied: "Verily, you are people without any awareness [of right and wrong]! ‹138› As for these here – verily, their way of life is bound to lead to destruction; and worthless is all that they have ever done!" ‹139› [And] he said: "Am I to seek for you a deity other than God, although it is He who has favoured you above all other people?"[102] ‹140› And [he reminded them of this word of God]: "Lo, We saved you from Pharaoh's people who afflicted you with cruel suffering, slaying your sons in great numbers and sparing [only] your women – which was an awesome trial from your Sustainer."[103] ‹141›

AND [then] We appointed for Moses thirty nights [on Mount Sinai]; and We added to them ten, whereby the term of forty nights set by his Sustainer was fulfilled.[104]

وَتَمَّتْ كَلِمَتُ رَبِّكَ ٱلْحُسْنَىٰ عَلَىٰ بَنِىٓ إِسْرَٰٓءِيلَ بِمَا صَبَرُوا۟ ۖ وَدَمَّرْنَا مَا
كَانَ يَصْنَعُ فِرْعَوْنُ وَقَوْمُهُۥ وَمَا كَانُوا۟ يَعْرِشُونَ ﴿١٣٧﴾ وَجَٰوَزْنَا بِبَنِىٓ
إِسْرَٰٓءِيلَ ٱلْبَحْرَ فَأَتَوْا۟ عَلَىٰ قَوْمٍ يَعْكُفُونَ عَلَىٰٓ أَصْنَامٍ لَّهُمْ ۚ قَالُوا۟
يَٰمُوسَى ٱجْعَل لَّنَآ إِلَٰهًا كَمَا لَهُمْ ءَالِهَةٌ ۚ قَالَ إِنَّكُمْ قَوْمٌ
تَجْهَلُونَ ﴿١٣٨﴾ إِنَّ هَٰٓؤُلَآءِ مُتَبَّرٌ مَّا هُمْ فِيهِ وَبَٰطِلٌ مَّا كَانُوا۟ يَعْمَلُونَ ﴿١٣٩﴾ نصف الحزب
قَالَ أَغَيْرَ ٱللَّهِ أَبْغِيكُمْ إِلَٰهًا وَهُوَ فَضَّلَكُمْ عَلَى ٱلْعَٰلَمِينَ ﴿١٤٠﴾ وَإِذْ
أَنجَيْنَٰكُم مِّنْ ءَالِ فِرْعَوْنَ يَسُومُونَكُمْ سُوٓءَ ٱلْعَذَابِ ۖ يُقَتِّلُونَ أَبْنَآءَكُمْ
وَيَسْتَحْيُونَ نِسَآءَكُمْ ۚ وَفِى ذَٰلِكُم بَلَآءٌ مِّن رَّبِّكُمْ عَظِيمٌ ﴿١٤١﴾ ۞ وَوَٰعَدْنَا
مُوسَىٰ ثَلَٰثِينَ لَيْلَةً وَأَتْمَمْنَٰهَا بِعَشْرٍ فَتَمَّ مِيقَٰتُ رَبِّهِۦٓ أَرْبَعِينَ لَيْلَةً ۚ

Wa tammat Kalimatu Rabbikal-ḥusnā ʿalā banīi ʾIsrāaʾīla bimā ṣabarū; wa dammarnā mā kāna yaṣnaʿu Firʿawnu wa qawmuhū wa mā kānū yaʿrishūn. (137) Wa jāwaznā bibanīi ʾIsrāaʾīlal-baḥra faʾataw ʿalā qawmiñy-yaʿkufūna ʿalāa ʾaṣnāmil-lahum. Qālū yā Mūsaj-ʿal-lanāa ʾilāhañ-kamā lahum ʾālihah. Qāla ʾinnakum qawmuñ-tajhalūn. (138) ʾInna hāaʾulāaʾi mutabbarum-mā hum fīhi wa bāṭilum-mā kānū yaʿmalūn. (139) Qāla ʾaghayral-lāhi ʾabghīkum ʾilāhañw-wa Huwa faḍḍalakum ʿalal-ʿālamīn. (140) Wa ʾidh ʾañjaynākum-min ʾāli Firʿawna yasūmūnakum sūuʾal-ʿadhābi yuqattilūna ʾabnāaʾakum wa yastaḥyūna nisāaʾakum; wa fī dhālikum-balāaʾum-mir-Rabbikum ʿaẓīm. (141) ۞ Wa wāʿadnā Mūsā thalāthīna laylatañw-waʾatmamnāhā biʿashriñ-fatamma mīqātu Rabbihīi ʾarbaʿīna laylah.

99 The promise of God referred to here is the one given to the children of Israel through Moses (see verses 128 and 129).

100 The story of the suffering of the Israelites during their bondage in Egypt, their deliverance through Moses, their crossing of the Red Sea (or, more probably, of what today is known as the Gulf of Suez) and the destruction of Pharaoh and his hosts is narrated in considerable detail in the Bible (Exodus i-xiv). The Qurʾān, on the other hand, does not give us a consecutive narrative: for historical narrative as such is never its purpose. Whenever the Qurʾān refers to past events – whether recorded in the Bible or alive in Arabian tradition – it does so exclusively with a view to bringing out elements that are relevant to the ethical teachings which it propounds.

101 The Qurʾān does not say who those people were. It is, however, probable that they belonged to the group of Arabian tribes described in the Bible as "Amalekites", who inhabited southernmost Palestine, the adjoining regions of the Ḥijāz, and parts of the Sinai Peninsula.

102 I.e., by having raised so many prophets out of their midst.

103 Cf. 2 : 49. It appears that this passage is part of Moses' reminder to his people *(Manār* IX, 115 ff.); I have brought this out by interpolating "he reminded them of this word of God" between brackets.

104 According to several of the Prophet's Companions, and particularly Ibn ʿAbbās, the first thirty nights were to be spent by Moses in spiritual preparation, including fasting, whereupon the Law would be revealed to him in the

And Moses said unto his brother Aaron: "Take thou my place among my people; and act righteously, and follow not the path of the spreaders of corruption." ‹142›
And when Moses came [to Mount Sinai] at the time set by Us, and his Sustainer spoke unto him, he said: "O my Sustainer! Show [Thyself] unto me, so that I might behold Thee!"
Said [God]: "Never canst thou see Me. However, behold this mountain: if it remains firm in its place, then – only then – wilt thou see Me."[105]
And as soon as his Sustainer revealed His glory to the mountain, He caused it to crumble to dust; and Moses fell down in a swoon. And when he came to himself, he said: "Limitless art Thou in Thy glory! Unto Thee do I turn in repentance; and I shall [always] be the first to believe in Thee!"[106] ‹143›
Said [God]: "O Moses! Behold, I have raised thee above all people by virtue of the messages which I have entrusted to thee,[107] and by virtue of My speaking [unto thee]: hold fast, therefore, unto what I have vouchsafed thee, and be among the grateful!" ‹144›
And We ordained for him in the tablets [of the Law] all manner of admonition, clearly spelling out everything.[108] And [We said:] "Hold fast unto them with [all thy] strength, and bid thy people to hold fast to their most goodly rules."
I will show you the way the iniquitous shall go.[109] ‹145› From My messages shall I

وَقَالَ مُوسَىٰ لِأَخِيهِ هَٰرُونَ ٱخْلُفْنِى فِى قَوْمِى وَأَصْلِحْ وَلَا تَتَّبِعْ سَبِيلَ
ٱلْمُفْسِدِينَ ﴿١٤٢﴾ وَلَمَّا جَآءَ مُوسَىٰ لِمِيقَٰتِنَا وَكَلَّمَهُۥ رَبُّهُۥ قَالَ رَبِّ أَرِنِىٓ
أَنظُرْ إِلَيْكَ قَالَ لَن تَرَىٰنِى وَلَٰكِنِ ٱنظُرْ إِلَى ٱلْجَبَلِ فَإِنِ ٱسْتَقَرَّ مَكَانَهُۥ
فَسَوْفَ تَرَىٰنِى فَلَمَّا تَجَلَّىٰ رَبُّهُۥ لِلْجَبَلِ جَعَلَهُۥ دَكًّا وَخَرَّ مُوسَىٰ صَعِقًا
فَلَمَّآ أَفَاقَ قَالَ سُبْحَٰنَكَ تُبْتُ إِلَيْكَ وَأَنَا۠ أَوَّلُ ٱلْمُؤْمِنِينَ ﴿١٤٣﴾ قَالَ
يَٰمُوسَىٰٓ إِنِّى ٱصْطَفَيْتُكَ عَلَى ٱلنَّاسِ بِرِسَٰلَٰتِى وَبِكَلَٰمِى فَخُذْ
مَآ ءَاتَيْتُكَ وَكُن مِّنَ ٱلشَّٰكِرِينَ ﴿١٤٤﴾ وَكَتَبْنَا لَهُۥ فِى ٱلْأَلْوَاحِ مِن كُلِّ
شَىْءٍ مَّوْعِظَةً وَتَفْصِيلًا لِّكُلِّ شَىْءٍ فَخُذْهَا بِقُوَّةٍ وَأْمُرْ قَوْمَكَ يَأْخُذُوا۟
بِأَحْسَنِهَا سَأُو۟رِيكُمْ دَارَ ٱلْفَٰسِقِينَ ﴿١٤٥﴾ سَأَصْرِفُ عَنْ ءَايَٰتِىَ

Wa qāla Mūsā liʾakhīhi Hārūnakh-lufnī fī qawmī wa ʾaṣliḥ wa lā tattabiʿ sabīlal-mufsidīn. (142) Wa lammā jāaʾa Mūsā limīqātinā wa kallamahū Rabbuhū qāla Rabbi ʾarinīi ʾañẓur ʾilayk. Qāla lañ-tarānī wa lākiniñ-ẓur ʾilal-jabali faʾinis-taqarra makānahū fasawfa tarānī. Falammā tajallā Rabbuhū liljabali jaʿalahū dakkañw-wa kharra Mūsā ṣaʿiqā. Falammāa ʾafāqa qāla subḥānaka tubtu ʾilayka wa ʾana ʾawwalul-muʾminīn. (143) Qāla yā Mūsāa ʾinniṣ-ṭafaytuka ʿalan-nāsi biRisālātī wa biKalāmī fakhudh māa ʾātaytuka wa kum-minash-shākirīn. (144) Wa katabnā lahū fil-ʾalwāḥi miñ-kulli shayʾim-mawʿiẓatañw-wa tafṣīlal-likulli shayʾiñ-fakhudhhā biquwwatiñw-waʾ-mur qawmaka yaʾkhudhū biʾaḥsanihā. Saʾurīkum dāral-fāsiqīn. (145) Saʾaṣrifu ʿan ʾĀyātiyal-

remaining ten (Zamakhsharī and Rāzī); see also *Manār* IX, 119 ff.). In Arabic usage, a period of time designated as "nights" comprises the days as well.

105 Lit., "then, in time (*sawfa*) wilt thou see Me". As these words express the *impossibility* of man's seeing God – which is clearly implied in the Arabic construction – a literal rendering would not do justice to it.

106 Since Moses was already a believer, his words do not merely allude to belief in God's existence but, rather, belief in the impossibility of man's *seeing* God (Ibn Kathīr, on the authority of Ibn ʿAbbās).

107 Lit., "by virtue of My messages".

108 See *sūrah* 6, note 156.

109 Lit., "I will show you the abode of the iniquitous". The rendering adopted by me corresponds to the interpretations given by Ṭabarī (on the authority of Mujāhid and Al-Ḥasan al-Baṣrī) and by Ibn Kathīr; regarding the meaning of *dār* ("abode") in this context, see *sūrah* 6, note 118. Some of the commentators are of the opinion that the above sentence concludes God's admonition to Moses, but the plural form of address in "I will show *you*" makes it more probable that it is the beginning of a parenthetic passage connected, no doubt, with the preceding one, but having a general import not confined to Moses.

cause to turn away all those who, without any right, behave haughtily on earth: for, though they may see every sign [of the truth], they do not believe in it, and though they may see the path of rectitude, they do not choose tor follow it – whereas, if they see a path of error, they take it for their own: this, because they have given the lie to Our messages, and have remained heedless of them.[110] ‹146›
Hence, all who give the lie to Our messages, and [thus] to the truth[111] of the life to come – in vain shall be all their doings: [for] are they to be rewarded for aught but what they were wont to do?[112] ‹147›

AND IN his absence the people of Moses took to worshipping the effigy of a calf [made] of their ornaments, which gave forth a lowing sound.[113] Did they not see that it could neither speak unto them nor guide them in any way? [And yet] they took to worshipping it, for they were evildoers: ‹148› although [later,] when they would smite their hands in remorse,[114] having perceived that they had gone astray, they would say, "Indeed, unless our Sustainer have mercy on us and grant us forgiveness, we shall most certainly be among the lost!"[115] ‹149›

ٱلَّذِينَ يَتَكَبَّرُونَ فِى ٱلْأَرْضِ بِغَيْرِ ٱلْحَقِّ وَإِن يَرَوْا۟ كُلَّ ءَايَةٍ لَّا يُؤْمِنُوا۟
بِهَا وَإِن يَرَوْا۟ سَبِيلَ ٱلرُّشْدِ لَا يَتَّخِذُوهُ سَبِيلًا وَإِن يَرَوْا۟ سَبِيلَ ٱلْغَىِّ
يَتَّخِذُوهُ سَبِيلًا ذَٰلِكَ بِأَنَّهُمْ كَذَّبُوا۟ بِـَٔايَٰتِنَا وَكَانُوا۟ عَنْهَا غَٰفِلِينَ ﴿١٤٦﴾
وَٱلَّذِينَ كَذَّبُوا۟ بِـَٔايَٰتِنَا وَلِقَآءِ ٱلْءَاخِرَةِ حَبِطَتْ أَعْمَٰلُهُمْ هَلْ يُجْزَوْنَ
إِلَّا مَا كَانُوا۟ يَعْمَلُونَ ﴿١٤٧﴾ وَٱتَّخَذَ قَوْمُ مُوسَىٰ مِنۢ بَعْدِهِۦ مِنْ حُلِيِّهِمْ
عِجْلًا جَسَدًا لَّهُۥ خُوَارٌ أَلَمْ يَرَوْا۟ أَنَّهُۥ لَا يُكَلِّمُهُمْ وَلَا يَهْدِيهِمْ سَبِيلًا
ٱتَّخَذُوهُ وَكَانُوا۟ ظَٰلِمِينَ ﴿١٤٨﴾ وَلَمَّا سُقِطَ فِىٓ أَيْدِيهِمْ وَرَأَوْا۟ أَنَّهُمْ قَدْ
ضَلُّوا۟ قَالُوا۟ لَئِن لَّمْ يَرْحَمْنَا رَبُّنَا وَيَغْفِرْ لَنَا لَنَكُونَنَّ مِنَ ٱلْخَٰسِرِينَ ﴿١٤٩﴾

ladhīna yatakabbarūna fil-ʾarḍi bighayril-ḥaqqi wa ʾiñy-yaraw kulla ʾĀyatil-lā yuʾminū bihā wa ʾiñy-yaraw-sabīlar-rushdi lā yattakhidhūhu sabilañ-wa ʾiñy-yaraw sabīlal-ghayyi yattakhidhūhu sabīlā. Dhālika biʾannahum kadhdhabū biʾĀyātinā wa kānū ʿanhā ghāfilīn. (146) **Wal-ladhīna kadhdhabū biʾĀyātinā wa liqāaʾil-ʾĀkhirati ḥabiṭat ʾaʿmāluhum. Hal yujzawna ʾillā mā kānū yaʿmalūn.** (147) **Wat-takhadha qawmu Mūsā mim-baʿdihī min ḥuliyyihim ʿijlañ-jasadal-lahū khuwār. ʾAlam yaraw ʾannahu lā yukallimuhum wa lā yahdīhim sabīlā. ʾIttakhadhūhu wa kānū ẓālimīn.** (148) **Wa lammā suqiṭa fīi ʾaydīhim wa raʾaw ʾannahum qad ḍallū qālū laʾil-lam yarḥamnā Rabbunā wa yaghfir lanā lanakūnanna minal-khāsirīn.** (149)

110 As so often in the Qurʾān, God's "causing" the sinners to sin is shown to be a consequence of their own behaviour and the result of their free choice. By "those who, without any right, behave haughtily on earth" are obviously meant people who think that their own judgment as to what constitutes right and wrong is the only valid one, and who therefore refuse to submit their personal concerns to the criterion of absolute (i.e., revealed) moral standards; cf. 96 : 6-7 – "man becomes grossly overweening whenever he believes himself to be self-sufficient".

111 Lit., "to the meeting (*liqāʾ*)" – in the sense of its being a pre-ordained fact.

112 This is the end of the parenthetic passage beginning with the words, "I will show you the way the iniquitous shall go".

113 The golden calf of the Israelites was obviously a result of centuries-old Egyptian influences. The Egyptians worshipped at Memphis the sacred bull, Apis, which they believed to be an incarnation of the god Ptah. A new Apis was supposed always to be born at the moment when the old one died, while the soul of the latter was believed to pass into Osiris in the Realm of the Dead, to be henceforth worshipped as Osiris-Apis (the "Serapis" of the Greco-Egyptian period). The "lowing sound" (*khuwār*) which the golden calf emitted was probably produced by wind effects, as was the case with some of the hollow Egyptian temple effigies.

114 Lit., "when it was made to fall upon their hands" – an idiomatic phrase denoting intense remorse, probably derived from the striking ("falling") of hand upon hand as an expression of grief or regret.

115 The whole of verse 149 is a parenthetic clause (*jumlah muʿtariḍah*) referring to a later time – for the repentance of the Israelites came *after* Moses' return from Mount Sinai, of which the next verse speaks.

And when Moses returned to his people, full of wrath and sorrow, he exclaimed: "Vile is the course which you have followed in my absence! Have you forsaken[116] your Sustainer's commandment?"

And he threw down the tablets [of the Law], and seized his brother's head, dragging him towards himself. Cried Aaron: "O my mother's son! Behold, the people brought me low[117] and almost slew me: so let not mine enemies rejoice at my affliction, and count me not among the evildoing folk!" «150»

Said [Moses]: "O my Sustainer! Grant Thou forgiveness unto me[118] and my brother, and admit us unto Thy grace: for Thou art the most merciful of the merciful!" «151»

[And to Aaron he said:] "Verily, as for those who have taken to worshipping the [golden] calf – their Sustainer's condemnation will overtake them, and ignominy [will be their lot] in the life of this world!"

For thus do We requite all who invent [such] falsehood.[119] «152» But as for those who do bad deeds and afterwards repent and [truly] believe – verily, after such repentance[120] thy Sustainer is indeed much-forgiving, a dispenser of grace! «153»

And when Moses' wrath was stilled, he took up the tablets, in the writing whereof there was guidance and grace for all who stood in awe of their Sustainer.[121] «154»

وَلَمَّا رَجَعَ مُوسَىٰٓ إِلَىٰ قَوْمِهِۦ غَضْبَٰنَ أَسِفًا قَالَ بِئْسَمَا خَلَفْتُمُونِى مِنۢ
بَعْدِىٓ ۖ أَعَجِلْتُمْ أَمْرَ رَبِّكُمْ ۖ وَأَلْقَى ٱلْأَلْوَاحَ وَأَخَذَ بِرَأْسِ أَخِيهِ يَجُرُّهُۥٓ
إِلَيْهِ ۚ قَالَ ٱبْنَ أُمَّ إِنَّ ٱلْقَوْمَ ٱسْتَضْعَفُونِى وَكَادُوا۟ يَقْتُلُونَنِى فَلَا تُشْمِتْ بِىَ
ٱلْأَعْدَآءَ وَلَا تَجْعَلْنِى مَعَ ٱلْقَوْمِ ٱلظَّٰلِمِينَ ﴿150﴾ قَالَ رَبِّ ٱغْفِرْ لِى
وَلِأَخِى وَأَدْخِلْنَا فِى رَحْمَتِكَ ۖ وَأَنتَ أَرْحَمُ ٱلرَّٰحِمِينَ ﴿151﴾ إِنَّ ٱلَّذِينَ
ٱتَّخَذُوا۟ ٱلْعِجْلَ سَيَنَالُهُمْ غَضَبٌ مِّن رَّبِّهِمْ وَذِلَّةٌ فِى ٱلْحَيَوٰةِ ٱلدُّنْيَا ۚ
وَكَذَٰلِكَ نَجْزِى ٱلْمُفْتَرِينَ ﴿152﴾ وَٱلَّذِينَ عَمِلُوا۟ ٱلسَّيِّـَٔاتِ ثُمَّ تَابُوا۟ مِنۢ
بَعْدِهَا وَءَامَنُوٓا۟ إِنَّ رَبَّكَ مِنۢ بَعْدِهَا لَغَفُورٌ رَّحِيمٌ ﴿153﴾ وَلَمَّا سَكَتَ عَن
مُّوسَى ٱلْغَضَبُ أَخَذَ ٱلْأَلْوَاحَ ۖ وَفِى نُسْخَتِهَا هُدًى وَرَحْمَةٌ لِّلَّذِينَ هُمْ
لِرَبِّهِمْ يَرْهَبُونَ ﴿154﴾

**Wa lammā rajaʿa Mūsaa ʾilā qawmihī ghaḍbāna
ʾasifañ-qāla biʾsamā khalaftumūnī mim-baʿdī.
ʾAʿajiltum ʾamra Rabbikum. Wa ʾalqal-ʾalwāḥa wa
ʾakhadha biraʾsi ʾakhīhi yajurruhūu ʾilayh. Qālab-na
ʾumma ʾinnal-qawmas-taḍʿafūnī wa kādū yaq-
tulūnanī falā tushmit biyal-ʾaʿdāaʾa wa lā tajʿalnī
maʿal-qawmiẓ-ẓālimīn. (150) Qāla Rabbigh-fir lī wa
liʾakhī wa ʾadkhilnā fī raḥmatika wa ʾAñta ʾArḥamur-
Rāḥimīn. (151) ʾInnal-ladhīnat-takhadhul-ʿijla saya-
nāluhum ghaḍabum-mir-Rabbihim wa dhillatuñ-fil-
ḥayātid-dunyā. Wa kadhālika najzil-muftarīn. (152)
Wal-ladhīna ʿamilus-sayyiʾāti thumma tābū mim-
baʿdihā wa ʾāmanūu ʾinna Rabbaka mim-baʿdihā
laGhafūrur-Raḥīm. (153) Wa lammā sakata ʿam-Mūsal-
ghaḍabu ʾakhadhal-ʾalwāḥa wa fī nuskhatihā
hudañw-wa raḥmatul-lilladhīna hum liRabbihim
yarhabūn. (154)**

116 Lit., "outrun". The expression "one has outrun a matter" is synonymous with "he has forsaken it" or "left it undone" (Zamakhsharī).

117 Lit., "made me [or "deemed me"] utterly weak". Contrary to the Biblical account (Exodus xxxii, 1-5), the Qurʾān does not accuse Aaron of having actually participated in making or worshipping the golden calf; his guilt consisted in having remained passive in the face of his people's idolatry for fear of causing a split among them (cf. 20 : 92-94).

118 Sc., "for my anger and my harshness" (Rāzī).

119 Throughout the Qurʾān, this expression is used to describe (a) the attribution of divine qualities to any concrete or imaginary object or person, and (b) the making of false statements about God, His attributes, or the contents of His messages. In the above context it refers to any false imagery which deflects man from the worship of the One God.

120 Lit., "after it".

121 According to the Bible (Exodus xxxii, 19), Moses broke the tablets when he threw them down in anger; the Qurʾanic narrative, however, shows them as having remained intact.

وَٱخْتَارَ مُوسَىٰ قَوْمَهُۥ سَبْعِينَ رَجُلًا لِّمِيقَـٰتِنَا ۖ فَلَمَّآ أَخَذَتْهُمُ ٱلرَّجْفَةُ قَالَ رَبِّ لَوْ
شِئْتَ أَهْلَكْتَهُم مِّن قَبْلُ وَإِيَّـٰىَ ۖ أَتُهْلِكُنَا بِمَا فَعَلَ ٱلسُّفَهَآءُ مِنَّآ ۖ إِنْ هِىَ إِلَّا
فِتْنَتُكَ تُضِلُّ بِهَا مَن تَشَآءُ وَتَهْدِى مَن تَشَآءُ ۖ أَنتَ وَلِيُّنَا فَٱغْفِرْ لَنَا وَٱرْحَمْنَا ۖ
وَأَنتَ خَيْرُ ٱلْغَـٰفِرِينَ ﴿١٥٥﴾ ۞ وَٱكْتُبْ لَنَا فِى هَـٰذِهِ ٱلدُّنْيَا حَسَنَةً وَفِى ٱلْـَٔاخِرَةِ
إِنَّا هُدْنَآ إِلَيْكَ ۚ قَالَ عَذَابِىٓ أُصِيبُ بِهِۦ مَنْ أَشَآءُ ۖ وَرَحْمَتِى وَسِعَتْ كُلَّ شَىْءٍ ۚ
فَسَأَكْتُبُهَا لِلَّذِينَ يَتَّقُونَ وَيُؤْتُونَ ٱلزَّكَوٰةَ وَٱلَّذِينَ هُم بِـَٔايَـٰتِنَا يُؤْمِنُونَ ﴿١٥٦﴾
ٱلَّذِينَ يَتَّبِعُونَ ٱلرَّسُولَ ٱلنَّبِىَّ ٱلْأُمِّىَّ ٱلَّذِى يَجِدُونَهُۥ مَكْتُوبًا عِندَهُمْ فِى ٱلتَّوْرَىٰةِ
وَٱلْإِنجِيلِ يَأْمُرُهُم بِٱلْمَعْرُوفِ وَيَنْهَىٰهُمْ عَنِ ٱلْمُنكَرِ وَيُحِلُّ لَهُمُ ٱلطَّيِّبَـٰتِ
وَيُحَرِّمُ عَلَيْهِمُ ٱلْخَبَـٰٓئِثَ وَيَضَعُ عَنْهُمْ إِصْرَهُمْ وَٱلْأَغْلَـٰلَ ٱلَّتِى كَانَتْ عَلَيْهِمْ

ثلاثة ارباع الحزب

And Moses chose out of his people seventy men to come [and pray for forgiveness] at a time set by Us. Then, when violent trembling seized them,[122] he prayed:
"O my Sustainer! Hadst Thou so willed, Thou wouldst have destroyed them ere this, and me [with them]. Wilt Thou destroy us for what the weak-minded among us have done? [All] this is but a trial from Thee, whereby Thou allowest to go astray whom Thou willest, and guidest aright whom Thou willest. Thou art near unto us: grant us, then, forgiveness and have mercy on us – for Thou art the best of all forgivers! «155» And ordain Thou for us what is good in this world as well as in the life to come: behold, unto Thee have we turned in repentance!"
[God] answered: "With My chastisement do I afflict whom I will – but My grace overspreads everything:[123] and so I shall confer it on those who are conscious of Me and spend in charity, and who believe in Our messages «156» – those who shall follow the [last] Apostle, the unlettered Prophet whom they shall find described in the Torah that is with them, and [later on] in the Gospel:[124] [the Prophet] who will enjoin upon them the doing of what is right and forbid them the doing of what is wrong, and make lawful to them the good things of life and forbid them the bad things, and lift from them their burdens and the shackles that were upon them [afore-

Wakh-tāra Mūsā qawmahū sabᶜīna rajulal-limīqātinā. Falammāa ᵓakhadhat-humur-rajfatu qāla Rabbi law shiᵓta ᵓahlaktahum-miñ-qablu wa ᵓiyyāy. ᵓAtuhlikunā bimā faᶜalas-sufahāaᵓu minnā. ᵓIn hiya ᵓillā fitnatuka tuḍillu bihā mañ-tashāaᵓu wa tahdī mañ-tashāaᵓ. ᵓAñta Waliyyunā faghfir lanā war-ḥamnā wa ᵓAñta Khayrul-ghāfirīn. (155) ۞ Wak-tub lanā fī hādhihid-dunyā ḥasanatañw-wa fil-ᵓĀkhirati ᵓinnā hudnāa ᵓilayk. Qāla ᶜadhābīi ᵓuṣību bihī man ᵓashāaᵓu wa raḥmatī wasiᶜat kulla shayᵓ. Fasaᵓaktubuhā lilladhīna yattaqūna wa yuᵓtūnaz-Zakāta wal-ladhīna hum-biᵓĀyātinā yuᵓminūn. (156) ᵓAlladhīna yattabiᶜūnar-Rasūlan-Nabiyyal-ᵓummiyyal-ladhī yajidūnahū maktūban ᶜiñdahum fit-Tawrāti wal-ᵓIñjīli yaᵓmuruhum-bil-maᶜrūfi wa yanhāhum ᶜanil-muñkari wa yuḥillu lahumuṭ-ṭayyibāti wa yuḥarrimu ᶜalayhimul-khabāaᵓitha wa yaḍaᶜu ᶜanhum ᵓiṣrahum wal-ᵓaghlālal-latī kānat ᶜalayhim.

122 Most of the commentators take *rajfah* to mean here "earthquake", as it evidently does in other places in the Qurᵓān (e.g., in verses 78 and 91 of this *sūrah*). However, it should be remembered that this noun denotes any "violent commotion" or "trembling", from whatever cause; and since there is no reason to suppose that in this context an earthquake is meant, we may assume that the violent trembling which seized the seventy elders was caused by their intense regret and fear of God's punishment.

123 Cf. 6 : 12 (and the corresponding note 10), as well as 6 : 54.

124 The interpolation of the words "later on" before the reference to the Gospel is necessitated by the fact that the whole of this passage is addressed to Moses and the children of Israel, that is, long before the Gospel (in the Qurᵓanic sense of this term – cf. *sūrah* 3, note 4) was revealed to Jesus. The stories of some of the earlier prophets given in this *sūrah* – beginning with the story of Noah and ending with that of Moses and the children of Israel – constitute a kind of introduction to this command to follow the "unlettered Prophet", Muḥammad. The stress on his having been "unlettered" (*ummī*), i.e., unable to read and write, serves to bring out the fact that all his knowledge of the earlier prophets and of the messages transmitted by them was due to divine inspiration alone, and not to a familiarity with the Bible as such. For the Old Testament predictions of the advent of the Prophet Muḥammad (especially in Deuteronomy xviii, 15 and 18), see *sūrah* 2, note 33; for the New Testament prophecies to the same effect, see 61 : 6 and the corresponding note 6.

time].[125] Those, therefore, who shall believe in him, and honour him, and succour him, and follow the light that has been bestowed from on high through him – it is they that shall attain to a happy state." ‹157›

Say [O Muḥammad]: "O mankind! Verily, I am an apostle of God to all of you,[126] [sent by Him] unto whom the dominion over the heavens and the earth belongs! There is no deity save Him; He [alone] grants life and deals death!"

Believe, then, in God and His Apostle – the unlettered Prophet who believes in God and His words – and follow him, so that you might find guidance! ‹158›

AND AMONG the folk of Moses there have been people who would guide [others] in the way of the truth and act justly in its light.[127] ‹159›

And We divided them into twelve tribes, [or] communities. And when his people asked Moses for water, We inspired him, "Strike the rock with thy staff!" – whereupon twelve springs gushed forth from it, so that all the people knew whence to drink.

And We caused the clouds to comfort them with their shade, and We sent down unto them manna and quails, [saying:] "Partake of the good things which We have provided for you as sustenance."

فَٱلَّذِينَ ءَامَنُوا۟ بِهِۦ وَعَزَّرُوهُ وَنَصَرُوهُ وَٱتَّبَعُوا۟ ٱلنُّورَ ٱلَّذِىٓ أُنزِلَ مَعَهُۥٓ
أُو۟لَٰٓئِكَ هُمُ ٱلْمُفْلِحُونَ ﴿١٥٧﴾ قُلْ يَٰٓأَيُّهَا ٱلنَّاسُ إِنِّى رَسُولُ ٱللَّهِ إِلَيْكُمْ
جَمِيعًا ٱلَّذِى لَهُۥ مُلْكُ ٱلسَّمَٰوَٰتِ وَٱلْأَرْضِ لَآ إِلَٰهَ إِلَّا هُوَ يُحْىِۦ
وَيُمِيتُ فَـَٔامِنُوا۟ بِٱللَّهِ وَرَسُولِهِ ٱلنَّبِىِّ ٱلْأُمِّىِّ ٱلَّذِى يُؤْمِنُ بِٱللَّهِ وَكَلِمَٰتِهِۦ
وَٱتَّبِعُوهُ لَعَلَّكُمْ تَهْتَدُونَ ﴿١٥٨﴾ وَمِن قَوْمِ مُوسَىٰٓ أُمَّةٌ يَهْدُونَ بِٱلْحَقِّ
وَبِهِۦ يَعْدِلُونَ ﴿١٥٩﴾ وَقَطَّعْنَٰهُمُ ٱثْنَتَىْ عَشْرَةَ أَسْبَاطًا أُمَمًا وَأَوْحَيْنَآ إِلَىٰ
مُوسَىٰٓ إِذِ ٱسْتَسْقَىٰهُ قَوْمُهُۥٓ أَنِ ٱضْرِب بِّعَصَاكَ ٱلْحَجَرَ فَٱنۢبَجَسَتْ
مِنْهُ ٱثْنَتَا عَشْرَةَ عَيْنًا قَدْ عَلِمَ كُلُّ أُنَاسٍ مَّشْرَبَهُمْ وَظَلَّلْنَا عَلَيْهِمُ
ٱلْغَمَٰمَ وَأَنزَلْنَا عَلَيْهِمُ ٱلْمَنَّ وَٱلسَّلْوَىٰ كُلُوا۟ مِن طَيِّبَٰتِ مَا رَزَقْنَٰكُمْ

Falladhīna ʾāmanū bihī wa ʿazzarūhu wa naṣarūhu wat-tabaʿun-Nūral-ladhīi ʾuñzila maʿahūu ʾulāaʾika humul-mufliḥūn. (157) Qul yāa ʾayyuhan-nāsu ʾinnī Rasūlul-lāhi ʾilaykum jamīʿanil-ladhī lahū mulkus-samāwāti wal-ʾarḍ. Lāa ʾilāha ʾillā Huwa yuḥyī wa yumīt. Faʾāminū billāhi wa Rasūlihin-Nabiyyil-ʾummiyyil-ladhī yuʾminu billāhi wa Kalimātihī wat-tabiʿūhu laʿallakum tahtadūn. (158) Wa miñ-qawmi Mūsāa ʾummatuñy-yahdūna bil-ḥaqqi wa bihī yaʿdilūn. (159) Wa qaṭṭaʿnāhumuth-natay ʿashrata ʾasbāṭan ʾumamā. Wa ʾawḥaynāa ʾilā Mūsāa ʾidhis-tasqāhu qawmuhūu ʾaniḍ-rib-biʿaṣākal-ḥajar. Fambajasat minhuth-natā ʿashrata ʿaynā. Qad ʿalima kullu ʾunāsim-mashrabahum. Wa ẓallalnā ʿalayhimul-ghamāma wa ʾañzalnā ʿalayhimul-manna was-salwā; kulū miñ-ṭayyibāti mā razaqnākum.

125 A reference to the many severe rituals and obligations laid down in Mosaic Law, as well as to the tendency towards asceticism evident in the teachings of the Gospels. Thus the Qurʾān implies that those "burdens and shackles", intended as means of spiritual discipline for particular communities and particular stages of man's development, will become unnecessary as soon as God's message to man shall have achieved its final, universal character in the teachings of the Last Prophet, Muḥammad.

126 This verse, placed parenthetically in the midst of the story of Moses and the children of Israel, is meant to elucidate the preceding passage. Each of the earlier prophets was sent to his, and only his, community: thus, the Old Testament addresses itself only to the children of Israel; and even Jesus, whose message had a wider bearing, speaks of himself as "sent only unto the lost sheep of the house of Israel" (Matthew xv, 24). In contrast, the message of the Qurʾān is universal – that is, addressed to mankind as a whole – and is neither time-bound nor confined to any particular cultural environment. It is for this reason that Muḥammad, through whom this message was revealed, is described in the Qurʾān (21 : 107) as an evidence of "[God's] grace towards all the worlds" (i.e., towards all mankind), and as "the Seal of all Prophets" (33 : 40) – in other words, the last of them.

127 I.e., people like those spoken of in 3 : 113-115. With this verse, the discourse returns to the moral history of the children of Israel. The stress on the fact that there have always been righteous people among them is meant to contrast this righteousness with the rebellious sinfulness which most of them displayed throughout their Biblical history. It provides, at the same time, an indication that, although the wrongdoing of some of its members may sometimes plunge whole communities into suffering, God judges men individually, and not in groups.

And [by all their sinning] they did no harm unto Us – but [only] against their own selves did they sin. ‹160›
And [remember] when they were told: "Dwell in this land and eat of its food as you may desire; but say, 'Remove Thou from us the burden of our sins,' and enter the gate humbly – [whereupon] We shall forgive you your sins [and] shall amply reward the doers of good." ‹161›
But those among them who were bent on wrongdoing substituted another saying for that which they had been given: and so We let loose against them a plague from heaven in requital of all their evil doings.[128] ‹162›
And ask them about that town which stood by the sea: how its people would profane the Sabbath whenever their fish came to them, breaking the water's surface, on a day on which they ought to have kept Sabbath – because they would not come to them on other than Sabbath-days![129] Thus did We try them by means of their [own] iniquitous doings. ‹163› And whenever some people[130] among them asked [those who tried to restrain the Sabbath-breakers], "Why do you preach to people whom God is about to destroy or [at least] to chastise with suffering severe?" – the pious ones[131] would answer, "In order to be free from blame before your Sustainer, and that these [transgressors, too,] might become conscious of Him." ‹164›

وَمَا ظَلَمُونَا وَلَٰكِن كَانُوٓا۟ أَنفُسَهُمْ يَظْلِمُونَ ﴿١٦٠﴾ وَإِذْ قِيلَ لَهُمُ
ٱسْكُنُوا۟ هَٰذِهِ ٱلْقَرْيَةَ وَكُلُوا۟ مِنْهَا حَيْثُ شِئْتُمْ وَقُولُوا۟ حِطَّةٌ وَٱدْخُلُوا۟
ٱلْبَابَ سُجَّدًا نَّغْفِرْ لَكُمْ خَطِيٓـَٰٔتِكُمْ ۚ سَنَزِيدُ ٱلْمُحْسِنِينَ ﴿١٦١﴾ فَبَدَّلَ
ٱلَّذِينَ ظَلَمُوا۟ مِنْهُمْ قَوْلًا غَيْرَ ٱلَّذِى قِيلَ لَهُمْ فَأَرْسَلْنَا عَلَيْهِمْ رِجْزًا مِّنَ
ٱلسَّمَآءِ بِمَا كَانُوا۟ يَظْلِمُونَ ﴿١٦٢﴾ وَسْـَٔلْهُمْ عَنِ ٱلْقَرْيَةِ ٱلَّتِى كَانَتْ حَاضِرَةَ
ٱلْبَحْرِ إِذْ يَعْدُونَ فِى ٱلسَّبْتِ إِذْ تَأْتِيهِمْ حِيتَانُهُمْ يَوْمَ سَبْتِهِمْ شُرَّعًا
وَيَوْمَ لَا يَسْبِتُونَ ۙ لَا تَأْتِيهِمْ ۚ كَذَٰلِكَ نَبْلُوهُم بِمَا كَانُوا۟ يَفْسُقُونَ ﴿١٦٣﴾ وَإِذْ
قَالَتْ أُمَّةٌ مِّنْهُمْ لِمَ تَعِظُونَ قَوْمًا ۙ ٱللَّهُ مُهْلِكُهُمْ أَوْ مُعَذِّبُهُمْ عَذَابًا
شَدِيدًا ۖ قَالُوا۟ مَعْذِرَةً إِلَىٰ رَبِّكُمْ وَلَعَلَّهُمْ يَتَّقُونَ ﴿١٦٤﴾

Wa mā ẓalamūnā wa lākiñ-kānūu ᵓañfusahum yaẓlimūn. (160) Wa ᵓidh qīla lahumus-kunū hādhihil-qaryata wa kulū minhā ḥaythu shiᵓtum wa qūlū ḥiṭṭatuñw-wad-khulul-bāba sujjadañ-naghfir lakum khaṭīiᵓātikum; sanazīdul-muḥsinīn. (161) Fabaddalal-ladhīna ẓalamū minhum qawlan ghayral-ladhī qīla lahum faᵓarsalnā ᶜalayhim rijzam-minas-samāaᵓi bimā kānū yaẓlimūn. (162) Was-ᵓalhum ᶜanil-qaryatil-latī kānat ḥāḍiratal-baḥri ᵓidh yaᶜdūna fis-sabti ᵓidh taᵓtīhim ḥītānuhum yawma sabtihim shurraᶜañw-wa yawma lā yasbitūna lā taᵓtīhim. Kadhālika nablūhum-bimā kānū yafsuqūn. (163) Wa ᵓidh qālat ᵓummatum-minhum lima taᶜiẓūna qawmanil-lāhu muhlikuhum ᵓaw muᶜadhdhibuhum ᶜadhābañ-shadīdā. Qālū maᶜdhiratan ᵓilā Rabbikum wa laᶜallahum yattaqūn. (164)

128 For an explanation of this and the preceding verse, see 2 : 58-59, and the corresponding notes.

129 Lit., "on a day when they did not keep Sabbath". Under Mosaic Law, they were obliged to refrain from all work – and, therefore, also from fishing – on Sabbath-days, with the result that the fish were more plentiful and would come closer to the shore on those days: and the inhabitants of the town took this as an excuse to break the Sabbath-law. Since the Qurᵓān does not mention the name of the town nor give any indication as to the historical period in which those offences were committed, it may be assumed that the story of the Sabbath-breakers (alluded to in several places in the Qurᵓān) is a general illustration of the tendency, so often manifested by the children of Israel, to offend against their religious laws in pursuit of their passions or for the sake of worldly gain. Although, according to the teachings of Islam, the Mosaic dispensation has since been abrogated, the Qurᵓān frequently points out its great role in the history of man's monotheistic beliefs, and stresses again and again its (time-bound) importance as a means of enforcing spiritual discipline on the children of Israel. Their repeated, deliberate breaches of the Mosaic Law are shown as evidence of their rebellious attitude towards that discipline and, thus, towards God's commandments in general.

130 Lit., "a community" – obviously people who, while not actively protesting against the impiety of their environment, did not themselves participate in this profanation of the Sabbath.

131 Lit., "they" – an allusion to the really pious among them, such as are described in verse 159 above.

And thereupon, when those [sinners] had forgotten all that they had been told to take to heart, We saved those who had tried to prevent the doing of evil,[132] and overwhelmed those who had been bent on evildoing with dreadful suffering for all their iniquity; ‹165› and then, when they disdainfully persisted in doing what they had been forbidden to do, We said unto them: "Be as apes despicable!"[133] ‹166›

And lo! Thy Sustainer made it known that most certainly He would rouse against them, unto Resurrection Day, people who would afflict them with cruel suffering: verily, thy Sustainer is swift in retribution – yet, verily, He is [also] much-forgiving, a dispenser of grace. ‹167›

And We dispersed them as [separate] communities all over the earth; some of them were righteous, and some of them less than that: and the latter We tried with blessings as well as with afflictions, so that they might mend their ways.[134] ‹168›

And they have been succeeded by [new] generations who – [in spite of] having inherited the divine writ – clutch but at the fleeting good of this lower world and say, "We shall be forgiven,"[135] the while they are ready, if another such fleeting good should come their way, to clutch at it [and sin again]. Have they not been solemnly pledged through the divine writ not to attribute unto God aught but what is true,[136] and [have they not] read again and again all that is therein?

فَلَمَّا نَسُوا۟ مَا ذُكِّرُوا۟ بِهِۦٓ أَنجَيْنَا ٱلَّذِينَ يَنْهَوْنَ عَنِ ٱلسُّوٓءِ وَأَخَذْنَا ٱلَّذِينَ
ظَلَمُوا۟ بِعَذَابٍۭ بَـِٔيسٍۭ بِمَا كَانُوا۟ يَفْسُقُونَ ﴿١٦٥﴾ فَلَمَّا عَتَوْا۟ عَن مَّا نُهُوا۟ عَنْهُ
قُلْنَا لَهُمْ كُونُوا۟ قِرَدَةً خَـٰسِـِٔينَ ﴿١٦٦﴾ وَإِذْ تَأَذَّنَ رَبُّكَ لَيَبْعَثَنَّ عَلَيْهِمْ إِلَىٰ
يَوْمِ ٱلْقِيَـٰمَةِ مَن يَسُومُهُمْ سُوٓءَ ٱلْعَذَابِ ۗ إِنَّ رَبَّكَ لَسَرِيعُ ٱلْعِقَابِ ۖ
وَإِنَّهُۥ لَغَفُورٌ رَّحِيمٌ ﴿١٦٧﴾ وَقَطَّعْنَـٰهُمْ فِى ٱلْأَرْضِ أُمَمًا ۖ مِّنْهُمُ ٱلصَّـٰلِحُونَ
وَمِنْهُمْ دُونَ ذَٰلِكَ ۖ وَبَلَوْنَـٰهُم بِٱلْحَسَنَـٰتِ وَٱلسَّيِّـَٔاتِ لَعَلَّهُمْ يَرْجِعُونَ ﴿١٦٨﴾
فَخَلَفَ مِنۢ بَعْدِهِمْ خَلْفٌ وَرِثُوا۟ ٱلْكِتَـٰبَ يَأْخُذُونَ عَرَضَ هَـٰذَا ٱلْأَدْنَىٰ
وَيَقُولُونَ سَيُغْفَرُ لَنَا وَإِن يَأْتِهِمْ عَرَضٌ مِّثْلُهُۥ يَأْخُذُوهُ ۚ أَلَمْ يُؤْخَذْ عَلَيْهِم
مِّيثَـٰقُ ٱلْكِتَـٰبِ أَن لَّا يَقُولُوا۟ عَلَى ٱللَّهِ إِلَّا ٱلْحَقَّ وَدَرَسُوا۟ مَا فِيهِ ۗ

Falammā nasū mā dhukkirū bihīi ʾañjaynal-ladhīna yanhawna ʿanis-sūuʾi wa ʾakhadhnal-ladhīna ẓalamū biʿadhābim-baʾīsim-bimā kānū yafsuqūn. (165) Falammā ʿataw ʿam-mā nuhū ʿanhu qulnā lahum kūnū qiradatan khāsiʾīn. (166) Wa ʾidh taʾadhdhana Rabbuka layabʿathanna ʿalayhim ʾilā Yawmil-Qiyāmati mañy-yasūmuhum sūuʾal-ʿadhāb. ʾInna Rabbaka laSarīʿul-ʿiqābi wa ʾinnahū laGhafūrur-Raḥīm. (167) Wa qaṭṭaʿnāhum fil-ʾarḍi ʾumamā. Minhumuṣ-ṣāliḥūna wa minhum dūna dhālik. Wa balawnāhum-bilḥasanāti was-sayyiʾāti laʿallahum yarjiʿūn. (168) Fakhalafa mim-baʿdihim khalfuñw-warithul-Kitāba yaʾkhudhūna ʿaraḍa hādhal-ʾadnā wa yaqūlūna sayughfaru lanā wa ʾiñy-yaʾtihim ʿaraḍum-mithluhū yaʾkhudhūh. ʾAlam yuʾkhadh ʿalayhim-mīthāqul-Kitābi ʾal-lā yaqūlū ʿalal-lāhi ʾillal-ḥaqqa wa darasū mā fīh.

132 Lit., "who were forbidding the evil".

133 According to Zamakhsharī and Rāzī, the expression "We said unto them" is here synonymous with "We decreed with regard to them" – God's "saying" being in this case a metonym for a manifestation of His will. As for the substance of God's decree, "Be as apes despicable", the famous *tābiʿī* Mujāhid explains it thus: "[Only] their hearts were transformed, that is, they were not [really] transformed into apes: this is but a metaphor (*mathal*) coined by God with regard to them, similar to the metaphor of 'the ass carrying books' [62 : 5]" (Ṭabarī, in his commentary on 2 : 65; also *Manār* I, 343; VI, 448; and IX, 379). A similar explanation is given by Rāghib. It should be borne in mind that the expression "like an ape" is often used in classical Arabic to describe a person who is unable to restrain his gross appetites or passions.

134 Lit., "so that they might return [to righteousness]".

135 I.e., for breaking God's commandments in their pursuit of worldly gain: an allusion to their persistent belief that they are "God's chosen people" and that, no matter what they do, His forgiveness and grace are assured to them by virtue of their being Abraham's descendants.

136 A reference to their erroneous idea that God's forgiveness could be obtained without sincere repentance. The divine writ mentioned twice in this passage is obviously the Bible.

Since the life in the hereafter is the better [of the two] for all who are conscious of God – will you not, then, use your reason? ‹169› For [We shall requite] all those who hold fast to the divine writ and are constant in prayer: verily, We shall not fail to require those who enjoin the doing of what is right! ‹170›
And [did We not say,] when We caused Mount Sinai to quake above the children of Israel[137] as though it were a [mere] shadow, and they thought that it would fall upon them, "Hold fast with [all your] strength unto what We have vouchsafed you, and bear in mind all that is therein, so that you might remain conscious of God"?[138] ‹171›

وَٱلدَّارُ ٱلْآخِرَةُ خَيْرٌ لِّلَّذِينَ يَتَّقُونَ ۗ أَفَلَا تَعْقِلُونَ ﴿١٦٩﴾ وَٱلَّذِينَ يُمَسِّكُونَ
بِٱلْكِتَٰبِ وَأَقَامُوا۟ ٱلصَّلَوٰةَ إِنَّا لَا نُضِيعُ أَجْرَ ٱلْمُصْلِحِينَ ﴿١٧٠﴾ ۞ وَإِذْ
نَتَقْنَا ٱلْجَبَلَ فَوْقَهُمْ كَأَنَّهُۥ ظُلَّةٌ وَظَنُّوٓا۟ أَنَّهُۥ وَاقِعٌۢ بِهِمْ خُذُوا۟ مَآ
ءَاتَيْنَٰكُم بِقُوَّةٍ وَٱذْكُرُوا۟ مَا فِيهِ لَعَلَّكُمْ تَتَّقُونَ ﴿١٧١﴾ وَإِذْ أَخَذَ رَبُّكَ
مِنۢ بَنِىٓ ءَادَمَ مِن ظُهُورِهِمْ ذُرِّيَّتَهُمْ وَأَشْهَدَهُمْ عَلَىٰٓ أَنفُسِهِمْ أَلَسْتُ
بِرَبِّكُمْ ۖ قَالُوا۟ بَلَىٰ ۛ شَهِدْنَآ ۛ أَن تَقُولُوا۟ يَوْمَ ٱلْقِيَٰمَةِ إِنَّا كُنَّا عَنْ هَٰذَا
غَٰفِلِينَ ﴿١٧٢﴾ أَوْ تَقُولُوٓا۟ إِنَّمَآ أَشْرَكَ ءَابَآؤُنَا مِن قَبْلُ وَكُنَّا ذُرِّيَّةً مِّنۢ
بَعْدِهِمْ ۖ أَفَتُهْلِكُنَا بِمَا فَعَلَ ٱلْمُبْطِلُونَ ﴿١٧٣﴾ وَكَذَٰلِكَ نُفَصِّلُ ٱلْآيَٰتِ حزب 18
وَلَعَلَّهُمْ يَرْجِعُونَ ﴿١٧٤﴾

AND WHENEVER thy Sustainer brings forth their offspring from the loins of the children of Adam, He [thus] calls upon them to bear witness about themselves: "Am I not your Sustainer?" – to which they answer: "Yea, indeed, we do bear witness thereto!"[139]
[Of this We remind you,] lest you say on the Day of Resurrection, "Verily, we were unaware of this"; ‹172› or lest you say, "Verily, it was but our forefathers who, in times gone by, began to ascribe divinity to other beings beside God; and we were but their late offspring: wilt Thou, then, destroy us for the doings of those inventors of falsehoods?" ‹173›
And thus clearly do We spell out these messages; and [We do it] so that they [who have sinned] might return [unto Us]. ‹174›

Wad-dārul-ʾĀkhiratu khayrul-lilladhīna yattaqūn. ʾAfalā taᶜqilūn. (169) Wal-ladhīna yumassikūna bil-Kitābi wa ʾaqāmuṣ-Ṣalāta ʾinnā lā nuḍīᶜu ʾajral-muṣliḥīn. (170) ۞ Wa ʾidh nataqnal-jabala fawqahum kaʾannahū ẓullatuñw-wa ẓannūu ʾannahū wāqiᶜum-bihim khudhū māa ʾātaynākum-biquwwatiñw-wadh-kurū mā fīhi laᶜallakum tattaqūn. (171) Wa ʾidh ʾakhadha Rabbuka mim-banīi ʾĀdama miñ-ẓuhūrihim dhurriyyatahum wa ʾashhadahum ᶜalāa ʾañfusihim ʾalastu biRabbikum. Qālū balā shahidnā. ʾAñ-taqūlū Yawmal-Qiyāmati ʾinnā kunnā ᶜan hādhā ghāfilīn. (172) ʾAw taqūlūu ʾinnamāa ʾashraka ʾābāaʾunā miñ-qablu wa kunnā dhurriyyatam-mim-baᶜdihim; ʾafatuhlikunā bimā faᶜalal-mubṭilūn. (173) Wa kadhālika nufaṣṣilul-ʾĀyāti wa laᶜallahum yar-jiᶜūn. (174)

137 Lit., "when We shook the mountain over them": possibly a reference to an earthquake which took place at the time of the revelation of the Law (the "tablets") to Moses.

138 This is the end, so far as this *sūrah* is concerned, of the story of the children of Israel. In accordance with the method of the Qurʾān, their story is made an object-lesson for all believers in God, of whatever community or time: and, therefore, the next passage speaks of the "children of Adam", that is, of the whole human race.

139 In the original, this passage is in the past tense ("He brought forth", "He asked them", etc.), thus stressing the continuous *recurrence* of the above metaphorical "question" and "answer": a continuity which is more clearly brought out in translation by the use of the present tense. According to the Qurʾān, the ability to perceive the existence of the Supreme Power is inborn in human nature (*fiṭrah*); and it is this instinctive cognition – which may or may not be subsequently blurred by self-indulgence or adverse environmental influences – that makes every sane human being "bear witness about himself" before God. As so often in the Qurʾān, God's "speaking" and man's "answering" is a metonym for the creative act of God and of man's existential response to it.

And tell them what happens to him[140] to whom We vouchsafe Our messages and who then discards them: Satan catches up with him, and he strays, like so many others, into grievous error.[141] ‹175› Now had We so willed, We could indeed have exalted him by means of those [messages]: but he always clung to the earth and followed but his own desires.

Thus, his parable is that of an [excited] dog: if thou approach him threateningly, he will pant with his tongue lolling; and, if thou leave him alone, he will pant with his tongue lolling.[142] Such is the parable of those who are bent on giving the lie to Our messages. Tell [them], then, this story, so that they might take thought. ‹176›

Evil is the example of people who are bent on giving the lie to Our messages: for it is against their own selves that they are sinning! ‹177›

He whom God guides, he alone is truly guided; whereas those whom He lets go astray – it is they, they who are the losers! ‹178›

And most certainly have We destined for hell many of the invisible beings[143] and men who have hearts with which they fail to grasp the truth, and eyes with which they fail to see, and ears with which they fail to hear. They are like cattle – nay, they are even less conscious of the right way:[144] it is they, they who are the [truly] heedless! ‹179›

وَٱتۡلُ عَلَيۡهِمۡ نَبَأَ ٱلَّذِيٓ ءَاتَيۡنَٰهُ ءَايَٰتِنَا فَٱنسَلَخَ مِنۡهَا فَأَتۡبَعَهُ ٱلشَّيۡطَٰنُ
فَكَانَ مِنَ ٱلۡغَاوِينَ ﴿١٧٥﴾ وَلَوۡ شِئۡنَا لَرَفَعۡنَٰهُ بِهَا وَلَٰكِنَّهُۥٓ أَخۡلَدَ إِلَى
ٱلۡأَرۡضِ وَٱتَّبَعَ هَوَىٰهُۚ فَمَثَلُهُۥ كَمَثَلِ ٱلۡكَلۡبِ إِن تَحۡمِلۡ عَلَيۡهِ يَلۡهَثۡ أَوۡ
تَتۡرُكۡهُ يَلۡهَثۚ ذَّٰلِكَ مَثَلُ ٱلۡقَوۡمِ ٱلَّذِينَ كَذَّبُواْ بِـَٔايَٰتِنَاۚ فَٱقۡصُصِ
ٱلۡقَصَصَ لَعَلَّهُمۡ يَتَفَكَّرُونَ ﴿١٧٦﴾ سَآءَ مَثَلًا ٱلۡقَوۡمُ ٱلَّذِينَ كَذَّبُواْ
بِـَٔايَٰتِنَا وَأَنفُسَهُمۡ كَانُواْ يَظۡلِمُونَ ﴿١٧٧﴾ مَن يَهۡدِ ٱللَّهُ فَهُوَ ٱلۡمُهۡتَدِيۖ وَمَن
يُضۡلِلۡ فَأُوْلَٰٓئِكَ هُمُ ٱلۡخَٰسِرُونَ ﴿١٧٨﴾ وَلَقَدۡ ذَرَأۡنَا لِجَهَنَّمَ كَثِيرٗا مِّنَ
ٱلۡجِنِّ وَٱلۡإِنسِۖ لَهُمۡ قُلُوبٞ لَّا يَفۡقَهُونَ بِهَا وَلَهُمۡ أَعۡيُنٞ لَّا يُبۡصِرُونَ بِهَا
وَلَهُمۡ ءَاذَانٞ لَّا يَسۡمَعُونَ بِهَآۚ أُوْلَٰٓئِكَ كَٱلۡأَنۡعَٰمِ بَلۡ هُمۡ أَضَلُّۚ أُوْلَٰٓئِكَ
هُمُ ٱلۡغَٰفِلُونَ ﴿١٧٩﴾

Wat-lu ʿalayhim nabaʾal-ladhīi ʾātaynāhu ʾĀyātinā fañsalakha minhā faʾatbaʿahush-Shayṭānu fakāna minal-ghāwīn. (175) Wa law shiʾnā larafaʿnāhu bihā wa lākinnahūu ʾakhlada ʾilal-ʾarḍi wat-tabaʿa hawāh. Famathaluhū kamathalil-kalbi ʾiñ-taḥmil ʿalayhi yal-hath ʾaw tatruk-hu yalhath. Dhālika mathalul-qawmil-ladhīna kadhdhabū biʾĀyātinā. Faqṣuṣil-qaṣaṣa laʿallahum yatafakkarūn. (176) Sāaʾa mathala-nil-qawmul-ladhīna kadhdhabū biʾĀyātinā wa ʾañfusahum kānū yaẓlimūn. (177) Mañy-yahdil-lāhu fa-huwal-muhtadī wa mañy-yuḍlil faʾulāaʾika humul-khāsirūn. (178) Wa laqad dharaʾnā lijahannama kathīram-minal-Jinni wal-ʾIñsi lahum qulūbul-lā yaf-qahūna bihā wa lahum ʾaʿyunul-lā yubṣirūna bihā wa lahum ʾādhānul-lā yasmaʿūna bihā. ʾUlāaʾika kalʾanʿāmi bal hum ʾaḍall. ʾUlāaʾika humul-ghāfilūn. (179)

140 Lit., "convey to them the tiding of him".

141 Lit., "he became one of those who have strayed into grievous error". In the original, this whole verse is in the past tense; but since its obvious purport is the statement of a general truth (cf. Rāzī, on the authority of Qatādah, ʿIkrimah and Abū Muslim) and not, as some commentators assume, a reference to a particular person, it is best rendered in the present tense. The kind of man spoken of here is one who has understood the divine message but, nevertheless, refuses to admit its truth because – as is pointed out in the next verse – he "clings to the earth", i.e., is dominated by a materialistic, "earthly" outlook on life. (Cf. the allegory of "a creature out of the earth" in 27 : 82.)

142 Because his attitudes are influenced only by what his earth-bound desires represent to him as his immediate "advantages" or "disadvantages", the type of man alluded to in this passage is always – whatever the outward circumstances – a prey to a conflict between his reason and his base urges and, thus, to inner disquiet and imaginary fears, and cannot attain to that peace of mind which a believer achieves through his faith.

143 See Appendix III.

144 Lit., "they are farther astray" – inasmuch as animals follow only their instincts and natural needs and are not conscious of the possibility or necessity of a moral choice.

AND GOD'S [alone] are the attributes of perfection;[145] invoke Him, then, by these, and stand aloof from all who distort the meaning of His attributes:[146] they shall be requited for all that they were wont to do! ‹180›

Now, among those whom We have created there are people who guide [others] in the way of the truth and act justly in its light.[147] ‹181› But as for those who are bent on giving the lie to Our messages – We shall bring them low, step by step, without their perceiving how it came about:[148] ‹182› for, behold, though I may give them rein for a while, My subtle scheme is exceedingly firm! ‹183›

Has it, then, never occurred to them[149] that there is no madness whatever in [this] their fellowman? He is only a plain warner.[150] ‹184›

Have they, then, never considered [God's] mighty dominion over the heavens and the earth, and all the things that God has created, and [asked themselves] whether, perchance, the end of their own term might already have drawn nigh? In what other tiding, then, will they, after this, believe?[151] ‹185›

وَلِلَّهِ ٱلْأَسْمَآءُ ٱلْحُسْنَىٰ فَٱدْعُوهُ بِهَا ۖ وَذَرُوا۟ ٱلَّذِينَ يُلْحِدُونَ فِىٓ أَسْمَٰٓئِهِۦ ۚ
سَيُجْزَوْنَ مَا كَانُوا۟ يَعْمَلُونَ (180) وَمِمَّنْ خَلَقْنَآ أُمَّةٌ يَهْدُونَ بِٱلْحَقِّ وَبِهِۦ
يَعْدِلُونَ (181) وَٱلَّذِينَ كَذَّبُوا۟ بِـَٔايَٰتِنَا سَنَسْتَدْرِجُهُم مِّنْ حَيْثُ لَا
يَعْلَمُونَ (182) وَأُمْلِى لَهُمْ ۚ إِنَّ كَيْدِى مَتِينٌ (183) أَوَلَمْ يَتَفَكَّرُوا۟ ۗ مَا
بِصَاحِبِهِم مِّن جِنَّةٍ ۚ إِنْ هُوَ إِلَّا نَذِيرٌ مُّبِينٌ (184) أَوَلَمْ يَنظُرُوا۟ فِى
مَلَكُوتِ ٱلسَّمَٰوَٰتِ وَٱلْأَرْضِ وَمَا خَلَقَ ٱللَّهُ مِن شَىْءٍ وَأَنْ عَسَىٰٓ أَن
يَكُونَ قَدِ ٱقْتَرَبَ أَجَلُهُمْ ۖ فَبِأَىِّ حَدِيثٍ بَعْدَهُۥ يُؤْمِنُونَ (185)

Wa lillāhil-ʾasmāaʾul-ḥusnā fadʿūhu bihā. Wa dharul-ladhīna yulḥidūna fīi ʾasmāaʾihī sayujzawna mā kānū yaʿmalūn. (180) Wa mimman khalaqnāa ʾummatuñy-yahdūna bilḥaqqi wa bihī yaʿdilūn. (181) Walladhīna kadhdhabū biʾĀyātinā sanastadrijuhum-min ḥaythu lā yaʿlamūn. (182) Wa ʾumlī lahum; ʾinna kaydī matīn. (183) ʾAwa lam yatafakkarū. Mā biṣāḥibihim-miñ-jinnah. ʾIn huwa ʾillā nadhīrum-mubīn. (184) ʾAwa lam yañẓurū fī malakūtis-samāwāti wal-ʾarḍi wa mā khalaqal-lāhu miñ-shayʾiñw-wa ʾan ʿasāa ʾañy-yakūna qadiq-taraba ajaluhum. Fabiʾayyi ḥadīthim-baʿdahū yuʾminūn. (185)

145 This passage connects with the mention, at the end of the preceding verse, of "the heedless ones" who do not use their faculty of discernment in the way intended for it by God, and remain heedless of Him who comprises within Himself all the attributes of perfection and represents, therefore, the Ultimate Reality. As regards the expression *al-asmāʾ al-ḥusnā* (lit., "the most perfect [or "most goodly"] names"), which occurs in the Qurʾān four times – i.e., in the above verse as well as in 17 : 110, 20 : 8 and 59 : 24 – it is to be borne in mind that the term *ism* is, primarily, a word applied to denote the substance or the intrinsic attributes of an object under consideration, while the term *al-ḥusnā* is the plural form of *al-aḥsan* ("that which is best" or "most goodly"). Thus, the combination *al-asmāʾ al-ḥusnā* may be appropriately rendered as "the attributes of perfection" – a term reserved in the Qurʾān for God alone.

146 I.e., by applying them to other beings or objects or, alternatively, by trying to "define" God in anthropomorphic terms and relationships, like "father" or "son" (Rāzī).

147 Sc., "and they will he rewarded accordingly". See verse 159 above, where the righteous "among the folk of Moses" are thus described. In this verse, the reference is broadened to include the righteous of all times and communities – that is, all those who are receptive to God's messages and live up to them by virtue of their conviction that God is the Ultimate Reality.

148 Lit., "without their knowing whence [it comes]". For an explanation of the term *kayd* ("subtle scheme") occurring in the next verse, see note 25 on 68 : 45, where this term appears for the first time in Qurʾānic revelation.

149 Lit., "Have they, then, not reflected".

150 Because he enunciated a message that differed radically from anything to which the Meccans had been accustomed, the Prophet was considered mad by many of his unbelieving contemporaries. The stress on his being "their fellow-man" (*ṣāḥibuhum* – lit., "their companion") is meant to emphasize the fact that he is human, and thus to counteract any possible tendency on the part of his followers to invest him with superhuman qualities: an argument which is more fully developed in verse 188.

151 Apart from a reminder of man's utter dependence on God, the implication of the above passage is this: Since everything in the observable or intellectually conceivable universe is obviously *caused*, it must have had a beginning

ربع الحزب

For those whom God lets go astray, there is no guide; and He shall leave them in their overweening arrogance, blindly stumbling to and fro.[152] ‹186›

THEY WILL ASK thee [O Prophet] about the Last Hour: "When will it come to pass?" Say: "Verily, knowledge thereof rests with my Sustainer alone. None but He will reveal it in its time. Heavily will it weigh on the heavens and the earth; [and] it will not fall upon you otherwise than of a sudden."
They will ask thee – as if thou couldst gain insight into this [mystery] by dint of persistent inquiry![153] Say: "Knowledge thereof rests with my Sustainer alone; but [of this] most people are unaware." ‹187›
Say [O Prophet]: "It is not within my power to bring benefit to, or avert harm from, myself, except as God may please. And if I knew that which is beyond the reach of human perception, abundant good fortune would surely have fallen to my lot, and no evil would ever have touched me. I am nothing but a warner, and a herald of glad tidings unto people who will believe."[154] ‹188›

IT IS HE who has created you [all] out of one living entity, and out of it brought into being its mate, so that man might incline [with love] towards woman.[155]

مَن يُضْلِلِ ٱللَّهُ فَلَا هَادِىَ لَهُۥ ۚ وَيَذَرُهُمْ فِى طُغْيَـٰنِهِمْ يَعْمَهُونَ ﴿١٨٦﴾
يَسْـَٔلُونَكَ عَنِ ٱلسَّاعَةِ أَيَّانَ مُرْسَىٰهَا ۖ قُلْ إِنَّمَا عِلْمُهَا عِندَ رَبِّى ۖ لَا
يُجَلِّيهَا لِوَقْتِهَآ إِلَّا هُوَ ۚ ثَقُلَتْ فِى ٱلسَّمَـٰوَٰتِ وَٱلْأَرْضِ ۚ لَا تَأْتِيكُمْ
إِلَّا بَغْتَةً ۗ يَسْـَٔلُونَكَ كَأَنَّكَ حَفِىٌّ عَنْهَا ۖ قُلْ إِنَّمَا عِلْمُهَا عِندَ ٱللَّهِ وَلَـٰكِنَّ
أَكْثَرَ ٱلنَّاسِ لَا يَعْلَمُونَ ﴿١٨٧﴾ قُل لَّآ أَمْلِكُ لِنَفْسِى نَفْعًا وَلَا ضَرًّا إِلَّا
مَا شَآءَ ٱللَّهُ ۚ وَلَوْ كُنتُ أَعْلَمُ ٱلْغَيْبَ لَٱسْتَكْثَرْتُ مِنَ ٱلْخَيْرِ وَمَا
مَسَّنِىَ ٱلسُّوٓءُ ۚ إِنْ أَنَا۠ إِلَّا نَذِيرٌ وَبَشِيرٌ لِّقَوْمٍ يُؤْمِنُونَ ﴿١٨٨﴾ ۞ هُوَ ٱلَّذِى
خَلَقَكُم مِّن نَّفْسٍ وَٰحِدَةٍ وَجَعَلَ مِنْهَا زَوْجَهَا لِيَسْكُنَ إِلَيْهَا

Mañy-yuḍlilil-lāhu falā hādiya lahu wa yadharuhum fī ṭughyānihim yaʿmahūn. (186) Yasʾalūnaka ʿanis-Sāʿati ʾayyāna mursāhā. Qul ʾinnamā ʿilmuhā ʿiñda Rabbī. Lā yujallīhā liwaqtihāa ʾillā Hū. Thaqulat fis-samāwāti wal-ʾarḍ. Lā taʾtīkum ʾillā baghtah. Yasʾalūnaka kaʾannaka ḥafiyyun ʿanhā. Qul ʾinnamā ʿilmuhā ʿiñdal-lāhi wa lākinna ʾaktharan-nāsi lā yaʿlamūn. (187) Qul lāa ʾamliku linafsī nafʿañw-wa lā ḍarran ʾillā mā shāaʾal-lāh. Wa law kuñtu ʾaʿlamul-ghayba lastakthartu minal-khayri wa mā massaniy-as-sūuʾ. ʾIn ʾana ʾillā nadhīruñw-wa bashīrul-liqawmiñy-yuʾminūn. (188) ۞ Huwal-ladhī khalaqakum-miñ-nafsiñw-wāḥidatiñw-wa jaʿala minhā zawjahā liyaskuna ʾilayhā.

and, therefore, must also have an end. Furthermore, since the universe is not eternal in the sense of having had no beginning, and since it cannot possibly have evolved "by itself" out of nothing, and since "nothingness" is a concept devoid of all reality, we are forced to predicate the existence of a Primary Cause which is beyond the limits of our experience and, hence, beyond the categories of our thought – that is, the existence of God: and this is the meaning of the "tiding" to which this verse refers.

152 As in verse 178 above – and in many other places in the Qurʾān – the expression "he whom God lets [or "causes to"] go astray" indicates the natural law instituted by God (*sunnat Allāh*), whereby a wilful neglect of one's inborn, cognitive faculties unavoidably results in the loss of all ethical orientation: that is, not an act of "predestination" but a result of one's own choice. See also *sūrah* 2, note 7, and *sūrah* 14, note 4.

153 The verb *aḥfā* means "he did [a thing] in an excessive measure" or "he exceeded the usual bounds in doing [something]". In connection with an inquiry, and especially when followed by *ʿanhu* or *ʿanhā* ("about it"), it signifies "he tried hard to gain insight [into something] by persistently inquiring about it". Thus, used as a participle, it means "one who has gained insight [into something] through persistent inquiry". In the above context, the implication is that no amount of inquiry or speculation can reveal to man – the prophets included – the coming of the Last Hour before its actual manifestation.

154 See 6 : 50, as well as the corresponding note. The repeated insistence in the Qurʾān on the *humanness* of the Prophet is in tune with the doctrine that no created being has or could have any share, however small, in any of the Creator's qualities or powers. In logical continuation of this argument, the next passage (verses 189-198) stresses the uniqueness and exclusiveness of God's creative powers.

155 Lit., "so that he might incline towards her". For an explanation of the terms "one living entity" and "its mate",

And so, when he has embraced her, she conceives [what at first is] a light burden, and continues to bear it. Then, when she grows heavy [with child], they both call unto God, their Sustainer, "If Thou indeed grant us a sound [child], we shall most certainly be among the grateful!" ‹189›
And yet, as soon as He has granted them sound [offspring], they begin to ascribe to other powers beside Him a share in bringing about what He has granted them![156] Sublimely exalted, however, is God above anything to which men may ascribe a share in His divinity! ‹190›
Will they, then, ascribe divinity, side by side with Him, unto beings that cannot create anything[157] – since they themselves are created ‹191› – and neither are able to give them succour nor can succour themselves, ‹192› and, if you pray to them for guidance, do not respond to you?[158] As far as you are concerned, it is all one whether you invoke them or keep silent. ‹193›
Verily, all those whom you invoke beside God are but created beings[159] like yourselves: invoke them, then, and let them answer your prayer – if what you claim is true! ‹194›
Have these [images], perchance, feet on which they could walk? Or have they hands with which they could grasp? Or have they eyes with which they could see? Or have they ears with which they could hear?

فَلَمَّا تَغَشَّىٰهَا حَمَلَتْ حَمْلًا خَفِيفًا فَمَرَّتْ بِهِۦ ۖ فَلَمَّآ أَثْقَلَت دَّعَوَا ٱللَّهَ رَبَّهُمَا لَئِنْ
ءَاتَيْتَنَا صَـٰلِحًا لَّنَكُونَنَّ مِنَ ٱلشَّـٰكِرِينَ ﴿189﴾ فَلَمَّآ ءَاتَىٰهُمَا صَـٰلِحًا جَعَلَا لَهُۥ
شُرَكَآءَ فِيمَآ ءَاتَىٰهُمَا ۚ فَتَعَـٰلَى ٱللَّهُ عَمَّا يُشْرِكُونَ ﴿190﴾ أَيُشْرِكُونَ مَا لَا يَخْلُقُ شَيْـًٔا
وَهُمْ يُخْلَقُونَ ﴿191﴾ وَلَا يَسْتَطِيعُونَ لَهُمْ نَصْرًا وَلَآ أَنفُسَهُمْ يَنصُرُونَ ﴿192﴾ وَإِن
تَدْعُوهُمْ إِلَى ٱلْهُدَىٰ لَا يَتَّبِعُوكُمْ ۚ سَوَآءٌ عَلَيْكُمْ أَدَعَوْتُمُوهُمْ أَمْ أَنتُمْ
صَـٰمِتُونَ ﴿193﴾ إِنَّ ٱلَّذِينَ تَدْعُونَ مِن دُونِ ٱللَّهِ عِبَادٌ أَمْثَالُكُمْ ۖ فَٱدْعُوهُمْ
فَلْيَسْتَجِيبُوا۟ لَكُمْ إِن كُنتُمْ صَـٰدِقِينَ ﴿194﴾ أَلَهُمْ أَرْجُلٌ يَمْشُونَ بِهَآ ۖ أَمْ لَهُمْ
أَيْدٍ يَبْطِشُونَ بِهَآ ۖ أَمْ لَهُمْ أَعْيُنٌ يُبْصِرُونَ بِهَآ ۖ أَمْ لَهُمْ ءَاذَانٌ يَسْمَعُونَ بِهَا ۗ

Falammā taghashshāhā ḥamalat ḥamlan khafīfañ-famarrat bih. Falammāa ᵓathqalad-daᶜawal-lāha Rabbahumā laᵓin ᵓātaytanā ṣāliḥal-lanakūnanna mi-nash-shākirīn. (189) Falammāa ᵓātāhumā ṣāliḥañ-ja-ᶜalā lahū shurakāaᵓa fīmāa ᵓātāhumā. Fataᶜālal-lāhu ᶜammā yushrikūn. (190) ᵓAyushrikūna mā lā yakhluqu shayᵓañw-wa hum yukhlaqūn. (191) Wa lā yastaṭīᶜūna lahum naṣrañw-wa lāa ᵓañfusahum yañṣurūn. (192) Wa ᵓiñ-tadᶜūhum ᵓilal-hudā lā yattabiᶜūkum. Sawāaᵓun ᶜalaykum ᵓadaᶜawtumūhum ᵓam ᵓañtum ṣāmitūn. (193) ᵓInnal-ladhīna tadᶜūna miñ-dūnil-lāhi ᶜibādun ᵓamthālukum fadᶜūhum falyastajībū lakum ᵓiñ-kuñtum ṣādiqīn. (194) ᵓAlahum ᵓarjuluñy-yamshūna bihāa ᵓam lahum ᵓaydiñy-yabṭishūna bihāa ᵓam lahum ᵓaᶜyunuñy-yubṣirūna bihāa ᵓam lahum ᵓādhā-nuñy-yasmaᶜūna bihā.

see 4 : 1, and the corresponding note.

156 Lit., "they attribute to Him partners with regard to that which He has granted them": i.e., many of them look upon the contributing factors of sound childbirth (like personal care during pregnancy, medical assistance, eugenics, etc.) as something *independent* of God, forgetting that all these contributing factors are – like the birth of the child itself – but an outcome of God's will and grace: a manifestation of what the Qurᵓān calls "the way of God" (*sunnat Allāh*). Since this kind of mental association of "other" factors with God is not really intentional, it does not amount to the unforgivable sin of *shirk* ("the ascribing of divine qualities to powers other than God"); but it is close enough to it to warrant the subsequent discourse on *shirk* in the real meaning of this term.

157 Lit., "that which does not create anything": a phrase expressed in the singular, but having the plural meaning of "beings" – that is, either animate beings (like saints or supposedly "divine" personalities) or their inanimate representations.

158 Lit., "do not follow you". As regards my translation of *in tadᶜūhum ila 'l-hudā* as "if you pray to them for guidance" (instead of the erroneous – but common – translation "if you invite [or "call"] them to guidance"), see Zamakhsharī, Rāzī and Ibn Kathīr. Cf. also verse 198 below.

159 Lit., "servants" (*ᶜibād*) – i.e., created beings subservient to God's will. This refers to saints, living or dead, as well as to inanimate objects of every description, including idols, fetishes and representational images – physical or mental – of saints or deified persons.

قُلِ ٱدْعُوا۟ شُرَكَآءَكُمْ ثُمَّ كِيدُونِ فَلَا تُنظِرُونِ ﴿١٩٥﴾ إِنَّ وَلِـِّۧىَ ٱللَّهُ ٱلَّذِى نَزَّلَ
ٱلْكِتَـٰبَ ۖ وَهُوَ يَتَوَلَّى ٱلصَّـٰلِحِينَ ﴿١٩٦﴾ وَٱلَّذِينَ تَدْعُونَ مِن دُونِهِۦ لَا
يَسْتَطِيعُونَ نَصْرَكُمْ وَلَآ أَنفُسَهُمْ يَنصُرُونَ ﴿١٩٧﴾ وَإِن تَدْعُوهُمْ إِلَى ٱلْهُدَىٰ لَا
يَسْمَعُوا۟ ۖ وَتَرَىٰهُمْ يَنظُرُونَ إِلَيْكَ وَهُمْ لَا يُبْصِرُونَ ﴿١٩٨﴾ خُذِ ٱلْعَفْوَ وَأْمُرْ بِٱلْعُرْفِ
وَأَعْرِضْ عَنِ ٱلْجَـٰهِلِينَ ﴿١٩٩﴾ وَإِمَّا يَنزَغَنَّكَ مِنَ ٱلشَّيْطَـٰنِ نَزْغٌ فَٱسْتَعِذْ بِٱللَّهِ
إِنَّهُۥ سَمِيعٌ عَلِيمٌ ﴿٢٠٠﴾ إِنَّ ٱلَّذِينَ ٱتَّقَوْا۟ إِذَا مَسَّهُمْ طَـٰٓئِفٌ مِّنَ ٱلشَّيْطَـٰنِ

Qulid-ʿū shurakāaʾakum thumma kīdūni falā tuñẓirūn. (195) ʾInna waliyyiyal-lāhul-ladhī nazzalal-Kitāba wa Huwa yatawallaṣ-ṣāliḥīn. (196) Wal-ladhīna tadʿūna miñ-dūnihī lā yastaṭīʿūna naṣrakum wa lāa ʾañfusahum yañṣurūn. (197) Wa ʾiñ-tadʿūhum ʾilal-hudā lā yasmaʿū wa tarāhum yañẓurūna ʾilayka wa hum lā yubṣirūn. (198) Khudhil-ʿafwa waʾ-mur bil-ʿurfi wa ʾaʿriḍ ʿanil-jāhilīn. (199) Wa ʾimmā yañzaghannaka minash-Shayṭāni nazghuñ-fastaʿidh billāh. ʾInnahū Samīʿun ʿAlīm. (200) ʾInnal-ladhīnat-taqaw ʾidhā massahum ṭāaʾifum-minash-Shayṭāni

Say [O Prophet]: "Summon to your aid all those to whom you ascribe a share in God's divinity,[160] and thereupon contrive [anything you may wish] against me, and give me no respite! ‹195› Verily, my protector is God, who has bestowed this divine writ from on high: for it is He who protects the righteous, ‹196› whereas all those whom you invoke in His stead are neither able to give you succour nor can succour themselves; ‹197› and if you pray unto them for guidance, they do not hear; and though thou mayest imagine that they behold thee,[161] they do not see." ‹198›

MAKE due allowance for man's nature,[162] and enjoin the doing of what is right; and leave alone all those who choose to remain ignorant.[163] ‹199› And if it should happen that a prompting from Satan stirs thee up [to blind anger],[164] seek refuge with God: behold, He is all-hearing, all-knowing. ‹200›

Verily, they who are conscious of God bethink themselves [of Him] whenever any dark suggestion from Satan touches them[165]

160 Lit., "summon your [God-]partners" (see *sūrah* 6, note 15).

161 Lit., "though thou seest them looking at thee" – but since the pronoun "them" in *tarāhum* ("thou seest them") refers to mental images no less than to physical representations, the verb must be understood in its abstract sense of "seeing with the mind", i.e., "considering" or "imagining". In contrast with the preceding passages, which are addressed to those who actually invoke false deities or images, the last sentence is addressed to man in general, sinner and believer alike: and this generalization is brought out by changing the form of address from "you" to "thou".

162 Lit., "accept what is easily forthcoming [from man's nature]". According to Zamakhsharī, *khudh al-ʿafw* means: "Accept what comes easily to thee [or "what is willingly accorded to thee"] of the doings and the nature of men, and make things easy [for them], without causing them undue hardship (*kulfah*); and do not demand of them efforts that may be too difficult for them." This interpretation – which has been adopted by many other classical commentators as well – is based on the identical explanation of the phrase *khudh al-ʿafw* by ʿAbd Allāh ibn az-Zubayr and his brother ʿUrwah (Bukhārī), as well as by ʿĀʾishah and, in the next generation, by Hishām ibn ʿUrwah and Mujāhid (see Ṭabarī, Baghawī and Ibn Kathīr). Thus, in accordance with the Qurʾanic statements that "man has been created weak" (4 : 28) and that "God does not burden any human being with more than he is well able to bear" (2 : 286, 6 : 152, 7 : 42, 23 : 62), the believer is admonished to make due allowance for human nature and not to be too harsh with those who err. This admonition is the more remarkable as it follows immediately upon a discourse on the most unforgivable of all sins – the ascribing of divine powers or qualities to anyone or anything but God.

163 Lit., "the ignorant ones" – i.e., those who *wilfully* remain deaf to moral truths, and not those who are simply unaware of them.

164 I.e., anger at the rejection of the truth by "those who choose to remain ignorant". The words "to blind anger" interpolated between brackets are based on a Tradition according to which the Prophet, after the revelation of the preceding verse calling for forbearance, exclaimed, "And what about [justified] anger, O my Sustainer?" – whereupon the above verse was revealed to him (Ṭabarī, Zamakhsharī, Rāzī, Ibn Kathīr).

165 The noun *ṭāʾif* (also forthcoming in the forms *ṭayf* and *ṭayyif*) denotes any ungraspable phantom, image or suggestion, as in a dream, or "an imperceptible obsession which obscures the mind" (*Tāj al-ʿArūs*). Since, in the above context, it is described as coming from Satan, "a dark suggestion" seems to be an appropriate rendering.

تَذَكَّرُوا۟ فَإِذَا هُم مُّبْصِرُونَ ﴿٢٠١﴾ وَإِخْوَٰنُهُمْ يَمُدُّونَهُمْ فِى ٱلْغَىِّ ثُمَّ لَا
يُقْصِرُونَ ﴿٢٠٢﴾ وَإِذَا لَمْ تَأْتِهِم بِـَٔايَةٍ قَالُوا۟ لَوْلَا ٱجْتَبَيْتَهَا ۚ قُلْ إِنَّمَآ أَتَّبِعُ
مَا يُوحَىٰٓ إِلَىَّ مِن رَّبِّى ۚ هَـٰذَا بَصَآئِرُ مِن رَّبِّكُمْ وَهُدًى وَرَحْمَةٌ لِّقَوْمٍ
يُؤْمِنُونَ ﴿٢٠٣﴾ وَإِذَا قُرِئَ ٱلْقُرْءَانُ فَٱسْتَمِعُوا۟ لَهُۥ وَأَنصِتُوا۟ لَعَلَّكُمْ
تُرْحَمُونَ ﴿٢٠٤﴾ وَٱذْكُر رَّبَّكَ فِى نَفْسِكَ تَضَرُّعًا وَخِيفَةً وَدُونَ ٱلْجَهْرِ
مِنَ ٱلْقَوْلِ بِٱلْغُدُوِّ وَٱلْـَٔاصَالِ وَلَا تَكُن مِّنَ ٱلْغَـٰفِلِينَ ﴿٢٠٥﴾ إِنَّ ٱلَّذِينَ
عِندَ رَبِّكَ لَا يَسْتَكْبِرُونَ عَنْ عِبَادَتِهِۦ وَيُسَبِّحُونَهُۥ وَلَهُۥ يَسْجُدُونَ ۩ ﴿٢٠٦﴾

السجدة

– whereupon, lo! they begin to see [things] clearly, ‹201› even though their [godless] brethren would [like to] draw them into error:[166] and then they cannot fail [to do what is right]. ‹202›

And yet, when thou [O Prophet] dost not produce any miracle for them, some [people] say, "Why dost thou not seek to obtain it [from God]?"[167]

Say: "I only follow whatever is being revealed to me by my Sustainer: this [revelation] is a means of insight from your Sustainer, and a guidance and grace unto people who will believe. ‹203› Hence, when the Qurʾān is voiced, hearken unto it, and listen in silence, so that you might be graced with [God's] mercy." ‹204›

And bethink thyself of thy Sustainer humbly and with awe, and without raising thy voice, at morn and at evening; and do not allow thyself to be heedless. ‹205›

Behold, those who are near unto thy Sustainer[168] are never too proud to worship Him; and they extol His limitless glory, and prostrate themselves before Him [alone]. ‹206›

tadhakkarū faʾidhā hum-mubṣirūn. (201) Wa ʾikhwānuhum yamuddūnahum fil-ghayyi thumma lā yuqṣirūn. (202) Wa ʾidhā lam taʾtihim-biʾĀyatiñ-qālū lawlaj-tabaytahā. Qul ʾinnamāa ʾattabiʿu mā yūḥāa ʾilayya mir-Rabbī. Hādhā baṣāaʾiru mir-Rabbikum wa hudañw-wa raḥmatul-liqawmiñy-yuʾminūn. (203) Wa ʾidhā quriʾal-Qurʾānu fastamiʿū lahū wa ʾañṣitū laʿallakum turḥamūn. (204) Wadh-kur Rabbaka fī nafsika taḍarruʿañw-wa khīfatañw-wa dūnal-jahri minal-qawli bil-ghuduwwi wal-ʾāṣāli wa lā takum-minal-ghāfilīn. (205) ʾInnal-ladhīna ʿiñda Rabbika lā yastakbirūna ʿan ʿibādatihī wa yusabbiḥūnahū wa lahū yasjudūn. (206)

166 I.e., by goading them to anger or trying to engage them in futile argument. "Their brethren" are those who wilfully remain ignorant of the truth (with the pronoun referring to the God-conscious). The conjunctive particle *wa* preceding this clause has here the meaning of "although" or "even though".

167 Sc., "if thou art really His apostle" (cf. 6 : 37 and 109, and the corresponding notes). Some of the commentators assume that the term *āyah* – translated by me as "miracle" – denotes here a verbal "message" which would answer the objections of those who did not believe in the Prophet. Since, however, the continuous revelation of the Qurʾān was full of such messages, the demand of the unbelievers must have related to some *particular* manifestation or "proof" of his divinely-inspired mission: namely, to a concrete miracle which would establish the truth of his claim in a supposedly "objective" manner. In its wider implication, the above verse relates to the primitive mentality of all who regard miracles, and not the message itself, as the only valid "proof " of prophethood.

168 Lit., "those who are with thy Sustainer": a metaphorical description of utter God-consciousness.

The Eighth Sūrah

Al-ʾAnfāl (Spoils of War)

Medina Period

MOST of *Al-ʾAnfāl* (a title taken from the reference to "spoils of war" in verse 1) was revealed during and immediately after the battle of Badr, in the year 2 H.; but some of its verses, and particularly the concluding section, are considered to be of a later date. Since it deals almost entirely with the battle of Badr and the lessons to be derived from it, a historical survey is necessary for a correct understanding of this *sūrah.*

In the month of Shaʿbān, 2 H., the Muslims of Medina learned that a great Meccan trade caravan, which had gone to Syria some months earlier under the leadership of Abū Sufyān, had started on its return journey southwards and would be passing Medina a few weeks later. In view of the fact that ever since the exodus of the Muslims from Mecca to Medina a state of open war had existed between them and the Meccan Quraysh, the Prophet informed his followers that he intended to attack the caravan as soon as it approached Medina; and rumours of this plan reached Abū Sufyān while he and the caravan were still in Syria. The weeks that must elapse before they would reach the area of danger gave Abū Sufyān an opportunity to send a fast-riding courier to Mecca with an urgent request for help (the caravan itself, consisting of about one thousand camels laden with valuable merchandise, was accompanied by only about forty armed men). On receipt of Abū Sufyān's message, the Quraysh assembled a powerful army under the leadership of the Prophet's most bitter opponent, Abū Jahl, and set out northwards to the rescue of the caravan. The latter had, in the meantime, changed its traditional route and veered towards the coastal lowlands in order to put as much distance as possible between itself and Medina.

The fact that the Prophet, contrary to his custom, had on this occasion made his plans known so long in advance suggests that the purported attack on the caravan was no more than a feint, and that from the very outset his real objective had been an encounter with the Quraysh army. As already mentioned, a state of war already existed between the Quraysh of Mecca and the Muslim community at Medina. So far, however, no decisive encounter had taken place, and the Muslims were living under the constant threat of a Quraysh invasion. It is probable that the Prophet wished to put an end to this state of affairs and to inflict, if possible, a decisive defeat on the Quraysh, thus securing a measure of safety for his, as yet weak, community. Had he really intended no more than to attack and plunder Abū Sufyān's caravan, he could have done so by simply waiting until it reached the vicinity of Medina and then swooping down on it; and in that event Abū Sufyān would have had no time to obtain further armed help from Mecca. As it was, the Prophet's announcement, weeks ahead, of the impending attack gave Abū Sufyān time to alert his compatriots in Mecca, and induced the latter to dispatch a considerable force towards Medina.

While Abū Sufyān's caravan was proceeding southwards along the coast, and thus out of reach of the Muslims, the Quraysh army – consisting of about one thousand warriors clad in chain mail, seven hundred camels and over one hundred horses – arrived at the valley of Badr, approximately one hundred miles west-southwest of Medina, expecting to meet Abū Sufyān there, unaware that in the meantime he had taken the coastal route. At the same time the Prophet marched out of Medina at the head of three hundred and odd Muslims, all of them very poorly armed, with only seventy camels and two horses between them. The Prophet's followers had been under the impression that they were going to attack the trade caravan and its weak escort; and when, on the 17th (or, according to some authorities, on the 19th or 21st) of Ramaḍān, they came face to face with a powerful Quraysh force more than thrice their number, they held a council of war. A few of the Muslims were of the opinion that the enemy was too strong for them, and that they should withdraw to Medina. But the overwhelming majority, led by Abū Bakr and ᶜUmar, were in favour of an immediate advance, and their enthusiasm carried the others along with them; and thereupon the Prophet attacked the Quraysh. After a few single combats – held in accordance with time-honoured Arabian custom – the fighting became general; the Meccan forces were completely routed and several of their most prominent chieftains – Abū Jahl among them – were killed.

It was the first open battle between the pagan Quraysh and the young Muslim community of Medina; and its outcome made the Quraysh realize that the movement inaugurated by Muḥammad was not an ephemeral dream but the beginning of a new political power and a new era different from anything that the Arabian past had known. The Meccans' apprehensions, which had already been aroused by the exodus of the Prophet and his Companions to Medina, found a shattering confirmation on the day of Badr. Although the power of Arabian paganism was not finally broken until some years later, its decay became apparent from that historic moment. For the Muslims, too, Badr proved to be a turning-point. It may safely be assumed that until then only a very few of the Prophet's Companions had fully understood the *political* implications of the new order of Islam. To most of them, their exodus to Medina had meant, in those early days, no more than a refuge from the persecutions which they had had to endure in Mecca: after the battle of Badr, however, even the most simple-minded among them became aware that they were on their way towards a new social order. The spirit of passive sacrifice, so characteristic of their earlier days, received its complement in the idea of sacrifice through *action.* The doctrine of action as the most fundamental, creative element of life was, perhaps for the first time in the history of man, consciously realized not only by a few select individuals but by a whole community; and the intense activism which was to distinguish Muslim history in the coming decades and centuries was a direct, immediate consequence of the battle of Badr.

سورة الأنفال مدنية -8- وآياتها خمس وسبعون

نصف الحزب

IN THE NAME OF GOD, THE MOST GRACIOUS, THE DISPENSER OF GRACE:

THEY WILL ASK thee about the spoils of war. Say: "All spoils of war belong to God and the Apostle."[1]
Remain, then, conscious of God, and keep alive the bonds of brotherhood among yourselves,[2] and pay heed unto God and His Apostle, if you are [truly] believers! ‹1›
Believers are only they whose hearts tremble with awe whenever God is mentioned, and whose faith is strengthened whenever His messages are conveyed unto them,[3] and who in their Sustainer place their trust ‹2› – those who are constant in prayer and spend on others out of what We provide for them as sustenance:[4] ‹3› it is they, they who are truly believers! Theirs shall be great dignity in their Sustainer's sight, and forgiveness of sins, and a most excellent sustenance.[5] ‹4›

بِسْمِ ٱللَّهِ ٱلرَّحْمَٰنِ ٱلرَّحِيمِ

يَسْـَٔلُونَكَ عَنِ ٱلْأَنفَالِ ۖ قُلِ ٱلْأَنفَالُ لِلَّهِ وَٱلرَّسُولِ ۖ فَٱتَّقُوا۟ ٱللَّهَ وَأَصْلِحُوا۟
ذَاتَ بَيْنِكُمْ ۖ وَأَطِيعُوا۟ ٱللَّهَ وَرَسُولَهُۥٓ إِن كُنتُم مُّؤْمِنِينَ ﴿١﴾ إِنَّمَا ٱلْمُؤْمِنُونَ
ٱلَّذِينَ إِذَا ذُكِرَ ٱللَّهُ وَجِلَتْ قُلُوبُهُمْ وَإِذَا تُلِيَتْ عَلَيْهِمْ ءَايَٰتُهُۥ زَادَتْهُمْ
إِيمَٰنًا وَعَلَىٰ رَبِّهِمْ يَتَوَكَّلُونَ ﴿٢﴾ ٱلَّذِينَ يُقِيمُونَ ٱلصَّلَوٰةَ وَمِمَّا رَزَقْنَٰهُمْ
يُنفِقُونَ ﴿٣﴾ أُو۟لَٰٓئِكَ هُمُ ٱلْمُؤْمِنُونَ حَقًّا ۚ لَّهُمْ دَرَجَٰتٌ عِندَ رَبِّهِمْ
وَمَغْفِرَةٌ وَرِزْقٌ كَرِيمٌ ﴿٤﴾

Bismil-lāhir-Raḥmānir-Raḥīm.
Yasʾalūnaka ʿanil-ʾañfāl. Qulil-ʾañfālu lillāhi war-Rasūl. Fattaqul-lāha wa ʾaṣliḥū dhāta baynikum wa ʾaṭīʿul-lāha wa Rasūlahūu ʾiñ-kuñtum-muʾminīn. (1) ʾInnamal-muʾminūnal-ladhīna ʾidhā dhukiral-lāhu wajilat qulūbuhum wa ʾidhā tuliyat ʿalayhim ʾĀyātuhū zādat-hum ʾīmānañw-wa ʿalā Rabbihim yatawakkalūn. (2) ʾAlladhīna yuqīmūnaṣ-Ṣalāta wa mimmā razaqnāhum yuñfiqūn. (3) ʾUlāaʾika humul-muʾminūna ḥaqqā. Lahum darajātun ʿiñda Rabbihim wa maghfiratuñw-wa rizquñ-karīm. (4)

---

1 The term *nafl* (of which *anfāl* is the plural) denotes, in its purely linguistic sense, "an accretion or addition received beyond one's due" or "something given in excess of one's obligation" (from which latter meaning the term *ṣalāt an-nafl* – i.e., a "supererogatory prayer" – is derived). In its plural form *anfāl*, which occurs in the Qurʾān only in the above verse, this word signifies "spoils of war", inasmuch as such spoils are an incidental accession above and beyond anything that a *mujāhid* ("a fighter in God's cause") is entitled to expect. The statement that "all spoils of war belong to God and the Apostle" implies that no individual warrior has a *claim* to any war booty: it is public property, to be utilized or distributed by the government of an Islamic state in accordance with the principles laid down in the Qurʾān and the teachings of the Prophet. For further details relating to the division of spoils of war, see verse 41 of this *sūrah*. – The immediate occasion of this revelation was the question of the booty acquired by the Muslims in the battle of Badr (an account of which is given in the introductory note to this *sūrah*); but the principle enunciated above is valid for all times and circumstances.

2 Lit., "set to rights the relationship between yourselves" – i.e., "remain conscious of your brotherhood in faith and banish all discord among yourselves".

3 Lit., "and whenever His messages are conveyed to them, they increase them in faith".

4 See *sūrah* 2, note 4.

5 I.e., in paradise. According to Rāzī, however, the "most excellent sustenance" is a metonym for "the spiritual raptures arising from the knowledge of God, the love of Him, and the self-immersion (*istighrāq*) in worshipping Him". In Rāzī's interpretation, this expression refers to the spiritual reward of faith in *this* world. Some commentators (cf. *Manār* IX, 597) regard the above definition of true believers as the most important passage of this *sūrah*. – The phrase rendered by me as "theirs shall be great dignity" reads, literally, "they shall have degrees", namely, of excellence and dignity.

EVEN AS thy Sustainer brought thee forth from thy home [to fight] in the cause of the truth, although some of the believers were averse to it, ‹5› [so, too,] they would argue with thee about the truth [itself] after it had become manifest[6] – just as if they were being driven towards death and beheld it with their very eyes. ‹6›
And, lo, God gave you the promise that one of the two [enemy] hosts would fall to you: and you would have liked to seize the less powerful one,[7] whereas it was God's will to prove the truth to be true in accordance with His words, and to wipe out the last remnant of those who denied the truth[8] ‹7› – so that He might prove the truth to be true and the false to be false, however hateful this might be to those who were lost in sin.[9] ‹8›
Lo! You were praying unto your Sustainer for aid, whereupon He thus responded to you: "I shall, verily, aid you with a thousand angels following one upon another!" ‹9›
And God ordained this only as a glad tiding, and that your hearts should thereby be set at rest – since no succour can come from any save God: verily, God is almighty, wise![10] ‹10›

كَمَآ أَخۡرَجَكَ رَبُّكَ مِنۢ بَيۡتِكَ بِٱلۡحَقِّ وَإِنَّ فَرِيقٗا مِّنَ ٱلۡمُؤۡمِنِينَ
لَكَٰرِهُونَ ﴿٥﴾ يُجَٰدِلُونَكَ فِي ٱلۡحَقِّ بَعۡدَمَا تَبَيَّنَ كَأَنَّمَا يُسَاقُونَ إِلَى
ٱلۡمَوۡتِ وَهُمۡ يَنظُرُونَ ﴿٦﴾ وَإِذۡ يَعِدُكُمُ ٱللَّهُ إِحۡدَى ٱلطَّآئِفَتَيۡنِ أَنَّهَا لَكُمۡ
وَتَوَدُّونَ أَنَّ غَيۡرَ ذَاتِ ٱلشَّوۡكَةِ تَكُونُ لَكُمۡ وَيُرِيدُ ٱللَّهُ أَن يُحِقَّ ٱلۡحَقَّ
بِكَلِمَٰتِهِۦ وَيَقۡطَعَ دَابِرَ ٱلۡكَٰفِرِينَ ﴿٧﴾ لِيُحِقَّ ٱلۡحَقَّ وَيُبۡطِلَ ٱلۡبَٰطِلَ وَلَوۡ
كَرِهَ ٱلۡمُجۡرِمُونَ ﴿٨﴾ إِذۡ تَسۡتَغِيثُونَ رَبَّكُمۡ فَٱسۡتَجَابَ لَكُمۡ أَنِّي مُمِدُّكُم
بِأَلۡفٖ مِّنَ ٱلۡمَلَٰٓئِكَةِ مُرۡدِفِينَ ﴿٩﴾ وَمَا جَعَلَهُ ٱللَّهُ إِلَّا بُشۡرَىٰ وَلِتَطۡمَئِنَّ بِهِۦ
قُلُوبُكُمۡ وَمَا ٱلنَّصۡرُ إِلَّا مِنۡ عِندِ ٱللَّهِۚ إِنَّ ٱللَّهَ عَزِيزٌ حَكِيمٌ ﴿١٠﴾

Kamāa ᵓakhrajaka Rabbuka mim-baytika bilḥaqqi wa ᵓinna farīqam-minal-muᵓminīna lakārihūn. ‹5›
Yujādilūnaka fil-ḥaqqi baᶜda mā tabayyana kaᵓan-namā yusāqūna ᵓilal-mawti wa hum yañẓurūn. ‹6›
Wa ᵓidh yaᶜidukumul-lāhu ᵓiḥdaṭ-ṭāaᵓifatayni ᵓan-nahā lakum wa tawaddūna ᵓanna ghayra dhātish-shawkati takūnu lakum, wa yurīdul-lāhu ᵓañy-yuḥiqqal-ḥaqqa biKalimātihī wa yaqṭaᶜa dābiral-kāfirīn. ‹7›
Liyuḥiqqal-ḥaqqa wa yubṭilal-bāṭila wa law karihal-mujrimūn. ‹8›
ᵓIdh tastaghīthūna Rabbakum fastajāba lakum ᵓannī mumiddukum-biᵓalfim-minal-Malāaᵓikati murdifīn. ‹9›
Wa mā jaᶜalahul-lāhu ᵓillā bushrā wa litaṭmaᵓinna bihī qulūbukum. Wa man-naṣru ᵓillā min ᶜiñdil-lāh. ᵓInnal-lāha ᶜAzīzun Ḥakīm. ‹10›

---

6 I.e., after it had become clear that it was indeed God's will that the Muslims should give open battle to the Quraysh army. This reference to the antecedents of the battle of Badr (see the introductory note to this *sūrah*) connects with the admonition given in verse 1, "pay heed unto God and His Apostle", as well as with the reminder, in verse 2, that true believers place all their trust in God. A few of the followers of the Prophet disliked the idea of giving battle to the main army of the Quraysh, instead of attacking the Meccan caravan returning from Syria and thus of acquiring easy booty; but the majority of them immediately declared that they would follow God's Apostle wherever he might lead them. – Some of the commentators are inclined to relate the adverbial particle *kamā* ("just as" or "even as"), introducing this sentence, to the preceding passage and, thus, to their duty to follow God's commands. Others, however, regard this interpretation as somewhat laboured, and relate the comparison implied in *kamā* to the first clause of verse 6, explaining the passage thus: "Just as some of the believers were averse to going forth from Medina to give battle to the Quraysh, so, too, they would argue with thee as to whether it was really willed by God." This, in particular, was the view of Mujāhid, whom Ṭabarī quotes with approval in his commentary on this verse.

7 Lit., "while you would have liked the one which was not powerful to be yours" – i.e., the caravan coming from Syria, which was accompanied by only forty armed men and could, therefore, be attacked without great danger.

8 The destruction of the Meccan army at Badr was the prelude to the elimination, in the course of the next few years, of all opposition to Islam in its homeland: and it is to this future fulfilment of God's promise that the above words refer. See also *sūrah* 11, note 103.

9 The implication is that the truth of the Prophet's cause could not have been vindicated by the Muslims' overcoming and plundering the rich caravan which was approaching from the north. Although such an action would have benefited the Muslims materially it would not have lessened the strength of the pagan Quraysh: while, on the other hand, the encounter at Badr with the main, heavily-armed Quraysh force, resulting as it did in a decisive victory of the Muslims, was destined to shatter the self-confidence of the enemy and thus to pave the way for the ultimate triumph of Islam in Arabia.

10 "On the day of the battle of Badr, the Prophet looked at his followers, who were three hundred and odd men, and

[Remember how it was] when He caused inner calm to enfold you,[11] as an assurance from Him, and sent down upon you water from the skies, so that He might purify you thereby and free you from Satan's unclean whisperings[12] and strengthen your hearts and thus make firm your steps. ‹11›
Lo! Thy Sustainer inspired the angels [to convey this His message to the believers]: "I am with you!"[13]
[And He commanded the angels:] "And give firmness unto those who have attained to faith [with these words from Me]:[14] 'I shall cast terror into the hearts of those who are bent on denying the truth; strike, then, their necks, [O believers,] and strike off every one of their finger-tips!'"[15] ‹12›
This, because they have cut themselves off from[16] God and His Apostle: and as for him who cuts himself off from God and His Apostle – verily, God is severe in retribution. ‹13› This [for you, O enemies of God]! Taste it, then, [and know] that suffering through fire awaits those who deny the truth! ‹14›

إِذْ يُغَشِّيكُمُ ٱلنُّعَاسَ أَمَنَةً مِّنْهُ وَيُنَزِّلُ عَلَيْكُم مِّنَ ٱلسَّمَآءِ مَآءً لِّيُطَهِّرَكُم
بِهِۦ وَيُذْهِبَ عَنكُمْ رِجْزَ ٱلشَّيْطَٰنِ وَلِيَرْبِطَ عَلَىٰ قُلُوبِكُمْ وَيُثَبِّتَ بِهِ
ٱلْأَقْدَامَ ﴿١١﴾ إِذْ يُوحِى رَبُّكَ إِلَى ٱلْمَلَٰٓئِكَةِ أَنِّى مَعَكُمْ فَثَبِّتُوا۟ ٱلَّذِينَ
ءَامَنُوا۟ سَأُلْقِى فِى قُلُوبِ ٱلَّذِينَ كَفَرُوا۟ ٱلرُّعْبَ فَٱضْرِبُوا۟ فَوْقَ ٱلْأَعْنَاقِ
وَٱضْرِبُوا۟ مِنْهُمْ كُلَّ بَنَانٍ ﴿١٢﴾ ذَٰلِكَ بِأَنَّهُمْ شَآقُّوا۟ ٱللَّهَ وَرَسُولَهُۥ وَمَن
يُشَاقِقِ ٱللَّهَ وَرَسُولَهُۥ فَإِنَّ ٱللَّهَ شَدِيدُ ٱلْعِقَابِ ﴿١٣﴾ ذَٰلِكُمْ فَذُوقُوهُ وَأَنَّ
لِلْكَٰفِرِينَ عَذَابَ ٱلنَّارِ ﴿١٤﴾

ʾIdh yughashshīkumun-nuʿāsa ʾamanatam-minhu wa yunazzilu ʿalaykum-minas-samāaʾi māaʾal-liyuṭahhirakum-bihī wa yudhhiba ʿañkum rijzash-Shayṭāni wa liyarbiṭa ʿalā qulūbikum wa yuthabbita bihil-ʾaqdām. (11) ʾIdh yūḥī Rabbuka ʾilal-Malāaʾikati ʾannī maʿakum fathabbitul-ladhīna ʾāmanū. Saʾulqī fī qulūbil-ladhīna kafarur-ruʿba faḍribū fawqal-ʾaʿnāqi waḍ-ribū minhum kulla banān. (12) Dhālika biʾannahum shāaqqul-lāha wa Rasūlah. Wa mañy-yushāqiqil-lāha wa Rasūlahū faʾinnal-lāha shadīdul-ʿiqāb. (13) Dhālikum fadhūqūhu wa anna lilkāfirīna ʿadhāban-nār. (14)

---

he looked at those who were ascribing divinity to beings other than God: and lo, they were more than one thousand. Thereupon God's Prophet turned towards the *qiblah*, raised his hands and thus implored his Sustainer: 'O God! Fulfil what Thou hast promised me! O God! If this little band of those who have surrendered themselves unto Thee is destroyed, Thou wilt not be worshipped on earth . . .'." This authentic Tradition, quoted by Muslim, Abū Dāʾūd, Tirmidhī, Aḥmad ibn Ḥanbal, etc., appears also in a very similar version in Bukhārī's *Ṣaḥīḥ*. It is said that the above Qurʾān-verse was revealed in response to the Prophet's prayer – whereupon he recited another, much earlier verse (54 : 45): "The hosts shall be routed, and shall turn their backs [in flight]" (Bukhārī). – As regards the promise of aid through thousands of angels, see 3 : 124-125, where a similar promise – made on the occasion of the battle of Uḥud – is said to have been uttered by the Prophet and thus, by implication, confirmed by God. The *spiritual* nature of this angelic aid is clearly expressed by the words, "and God ordained this only as a glad tiding . . .", etc. (See also *sūrah* 3, notes 93 and 94.)

11 I.e., before the battle of Badr. Regarding the interpretation of *nuʿās* as "inner calm", see *sūrah* 3, note 112. Here it refers to the spiritual quiet and self-confidence of the believers in the face of overwhelming odds.

12 Lit., "take away from you the pollution of Satan". Immediately before the beginning of the battle, the Meccan army invested the wells of Badr, thus depriving the Muslims of water; and, under the influence of thirst, some of the latter fell prey to utter despair (here symbolized by "Satan's unclean whisperings") – when, suddenly, abundant rain fell and enabled them to satisfy their thirst (Ṭabarī, on the authority of Ibn ʿAbbās).

13 The phrase "I am with you" is addressed (through the angels) to the believers – "for, the purport of these words was the removal of fear, since it was the Muslims, and not the angels, who feared the deniers of the truth" (Rāzī).

14 The following is, again, addressed to the believers (Rāzī). Verse 10 of this *sūrah* makes it clear that the aid of the angels was purely spiritual in nature; and there is no evidence anywhere in the Qurʾān that they did, or were meant to, participate in the battle in a physical sense. In his commentary on the above verse, Rāzī stresses this point repeatedly; among modern commentators, Rashīd Riḍāʾ emphatically rejects the legendary notion that angels actually *fought* in this or any other of the Prophet's battles (see *Manār* IX, 612 ff.). It is mainly on the basis of Rāzī's interpretation of this passage that I have interpolated, in several places, explanatory clauses between brackets.

15 I.e., "destroy them utterly".

16 Or: "contended against" (Baghawī). However, since the primary meaning of *shāqqahu* ("he separated himself from him" or "cut himself off from him") comprises the concepts of both estrangement and opposition (Ṭabarī,

O YOU who have attained to faith! When you meet in battle those who are bent on denying the truth, advancing in great force, do not turn your backs on them:[17] ‹15› for, whoever on that day turns his back on them – unless it be in a battle manoeuvre or in an endeavour to join another troop [of the believers] – shall indeed have earned the burden of God's condemnation, and his goal shall be hell: and how vile a journey's end! ‹16›

And yet, [O believers,] it was not you who slew the enemy,[18] but it was God who slew them; and it was not thou who cast [terror into them, O Prophet], when thou didst cast it, but it was God who cast it:[19] and [He did all this] in order that He might test the believers by a goodly test of His Own ordaining.[20] Verily, God is all-hearing, all-knowing! ‹17›

This [was God's purpose] – and also [to show] that God renders vain the artful schemes of those who deny the truth. ‹18›

If you have been praying for victory, [O believers] – victory has now indeed come unto you. And if you abstain [from sinning], it will be for your own good; but if you revert to it, We shall revoke [Our promise of aid] – and never will your community be of any avail to you, however

يَٰٓأَيُّهَا ٱلَّذِينَ ءَامَنُوٓاْ إِذَا لَقِيتُمُ ٱلَّذِينَ كَفَرُواْ زَحۡفٗا فَلَا تُوَلُّوهُمُ
ٱلۡأَدۡبَارَ ١٥ وَمَن يُوَلِّهِمۡ يَوۡمَئِذٖ دُبُرَهُۥٓ إِلَّا مُتَحَرِّفٗا لِّقِتَالٍ أَوۡ مُتَحَيِّزًا إِلَىٰ
فِئَةٖ فَقَدۡ بَآءَ بِغَضَبٖ مِّنَ ٱللَّهِ وَمَأۡوَىٰهُ جَهَنَّمُۖ وَبِئۡسَ ٱلۡمَصِيرُ ١٦ فَلَمۡ
تَقۡتُلُوهُمۡ وَلَٰكِنَّ ٱللَّهَ قَتَلَهُمۡۚ وَمَا رَمَيۡتَ إِذۡ رَمَيۡتَ وَلَٰكِنَّ ٱللَّهَ رَمَىٰ وَلِيُبۡلِيَ
ٱلۡمُؤۡمِنِينَ مِنۡهُ بَلَآءً حَسَنًاۚ إِنَّ ٱللَّهَ سَمِيعٌ عَلِيمٞ ١٧ ذَٰلِكُمۡ وَأَنَّ ٱللَّهَ مُوهِنُ
كَيۡدِ ٱلۡكَٰفِرِينَ ١٨ إِن تَسۡتَفۡتِحُواْ فَقَدۡ جَآءَكُمُ ٱلۡفَتۡحُۖ وَإِن تَنتَهُواْ
فَهُوَ خَيۡرٞ لَّكُمۡۖ وَإِن تَعُودُواْ نَعُدۡ وَلَن تُغۡنِيَ عَنكُمۡ فِئَتُكُمۡ شَيۡـٔٗا وَلَوۡ

Yāa ʾayyuhal-ladhīna ʾamanūu ʾidhā laqītumul-ladhīna kafarū zaḥfañ-falā tuwallūhumul-ʾadbār. (15) Wa mañy-yuwallihim yawmaʾidhiñ-duburahūu ʾillā mutaḥarrifal-liqitālin ʾaw mutaḥayyizan ʾilā fiʾatiñ-faqad bāaʾa bighaḍabim-minal-lāhi wa maʾwāhu jahannama wa biʾsal-maṣīr. (16) Falam taqtulūhum wa lākinnal-lāha qatalahum. Wa mā ramayta ʾidh ramayta wa lākinnal-lāha ramā; wa liyubliyal-muʾminīna minhu balāaʾan ḥasanā. ʾInnal-lāha Samīᶜun ᶜAlīm. (17) Dhālikum wa ʾannal-lāha mūhinu kaydil-kāfirīn. (18) ʾIñ-tastaftiḥū faqad jāaʾakumul-fatḥ. Wa ʾiñ-tañtahū fahuwa khayrul-lakum. Wa ʾiñ-taᶜūdū naᶜud wa lañ-tughniya ᶜañkum fiʾatukum shayʾañw-wa law

Zamakhsharī, Rāzī), the rendering adopted by me seems to be the most suitable in this context.

17 I.e., in flight: the implication being that in view of God's promise of victory no retreat is permissible. Since this verse (like the whole of this *sūrah*) relates predominantly to the battle of Badr, it may well be presumed that the above admonition forms part of the message of encouragement beginning with the words, "I am with you" (verse 12), which God commanded the angels to convey to the believers before the battle. In accordance with the didactic method of the Qurʾān, however, the moral lesson contained in this verse is not confined to the historical occasion to which it refers, but has the validity of a permanent law.

18 Lit., "you did not slay them" – i.e., in the battle of Badr, which ended with a complete victory of the Muslims.

19 According to several Traditions, the Prophet cast, at the beginning of the battle, a handful of pebbles or dust in the direction of the enemy, thus symbolically indicating their approaching defeat. However, none of these accounts attains to the standard of authenticity described as *ṣaḥīḥ*. (i.e., "reliable") by the great exponents of the science of Tradition (*ᶜilm al-ḥadīth*), and cannot, therefore, satisfactorily explain the above Qurʾanic passage (see Ibn Kathīr's commentary on this verse, as well as *Manār* IX, 620 f.). Since the verb *ramā* (lit., "he cast" or "flung") applies also to the act of "shooting an arrow" or "flinging a spear", it might be explained here as a reference to the Prophet's active participation in the battle. Alternatively, it may denote his "casting terror", i.e., into the hearts of his enemies, by his and his followers' extreme valour. Whichever explanation is adopted, the above verse implies that the victory of the Muslims over the much more numerous and much better equipped army of the Quraysh was due to God's grace alone: and, thus, it is a reminder to the faithful, of all times, not to indulge in undue pride in any of their achievements (which is the meaning of the "test" mentioned in the next sentence).

20 Lit., "from Himself".

ثلاثة ارباع الحزب

great its numbers: for, behold, God is [only] with those who believe![21] «19»
[Hence,] O you who have attained to faith, pay heed unto God and His Apostle, and do not turn away from Him now that you hear [His message]; «20» and be not like those who say, " We have heard", the while they do not hearken.[22] «21»
Verily, the vilest of all creatures[23] in the sight of God are those deaf, those dumb ones who do not use their reason. «22»
For, if God had seen any good in them, He would certainly have made them hear: but [as it is,] even if He had made them hear, they would surely have turned away in their obstinacy. «24»
O you who have attained to faith! Respond to the call of God and the Apostle whenever he calls you unto that which will give you life; and know that God intervenes between man and [the desires of] his heart,[24] and that unto Him you shall be gathered. «24»

كَثُرَتْ وَأَنَّ ٱللَّهَ مَعَ ٱلْمُؤْمِنِينَ ﴿١٩﴾ يَٰٓأَيُّهَا ٱلَّذِينَ ءَامَنُوٓا۟ أَطِيعُوا۟ ٱللَّهَ وَرَسُولَهُۥ
وَلَا تَوَلَّوْا۟ عَنْهُ وَأَنتُمْ تَسْمَعُونَ ﴿٢٠﴾ وَلَا تَكُونُوا۟ كَٱلَّذِينَ قَالُوا۟ سَمِعْنَا وَهُمْ
لَا يَسْمَعُونَ ﴿٢١﴾ ۞ إِنَّ شَرَّ ٱلدَّوَآبِّ عِندَ ٱللَّهِ ٱلصُّمُّ ٱلْبُكْمُ ٱلَّذِينَ لَا
يَعْقِلُونَ ﴿٢٢﴾ وَلَوْ عَلِمَ ٱللَّهُ فِيهِمْ خَيْرًا لَّأَسْمَعَهُمْ ۖ وَلَوْ أَسْمَعَهُمْ لَتَوَلَّوا۟ وَّهُم
مُّعْرِضُونَ ﴿٢٣﴾ يَٰٓأَيُّهَا ٱلَّذِينَ ءَامَنُوا۟ ٱسْتَجِيبُوا۟ لِلَّهِ وَلِلرَّسُولِ إِذَا دَعَاكُمْ لِمَا
يُحْيِيكُمْ ۖ وَٱعْلَمُوٓا۟ أَنَّ ٱللَّهَ يَحُولُ بَيْنَ ٱلْمَرْءِ وَقَلْبِهِۦ وَأَنَّهُۥٓ إِلَيْهِ تُحْشَرُونَ ﴿٢٤﴾

kathurat wa ʾannal-lāha maᶜal-muʾminīn. (19) Yāa
ʾayyuhal-ladhīna ʾāmanūu ʾaṭīᶜul-lāha wa Rasūlahū
wa lā tawallaw ᶜanhu wa ʾañtum tasmaᶜūn. (20) Wa lā
takūnū kalladhīna qālū samiᶜnā wa hum lā yas-
maᶜūn. (21) ۞ ʾInna sharrad-dawāabbi ᶜiñdal-lāhiṣ-
ṣummul-bukmul-ladhīna lā yaᶜqilūn. (22) Wa law
ᶜalimal-lāhu fīhim khayral-laʾasmaᶜahum; wa law
ʾasmaᶜahum latawallaw-wa hum-muᶜriḍūn. (23) Yāa
ʾayyuhal-ladhīna ʾāmanus-tajībū lillāhi wa lirRasūli
ʾidhā daᶜākum līmā yuḥyīkum; waᶜ-lamūu ʾannal-
lāha yaḥūlu baynal-marʾi wa qalbihī wa ʾannahūu
ʾilayhi tuḥsharūn. (24)

---

21 There is no unanimity among the commentators as to whether this verse is addressed to the believers or to their opponents at Badr, that is, the pagan Quraysh. While some of the commentators (e.g., Rāzī) are of the opinion that it is an admonition to the believers and understand it in the sense rendered by me above, others maintain that it is a warning addressed to the Quraysh. In order to justify this view, they give to the word *fatḥ* (lit., "opening") occurring in the first sentence the meaning of "judgment" or "decision" (which is undoubtedly permissible from the linguistic point of view), and arrive at the following rendering: "If you have been seeking a decision [O unbelievers] – a decision has now indeed come unto you. And if you abstain [from making war on God and His Apostle], it will be for your own good; but if you revert to it, We shall revert [to defeating you] – and never will your army be of any avail to you, however great its numbers: for, behold, God is with the believers!"

As can be seen from this alternative rendering, the difference in interpretation pivots on the tropical meaning which one gives to the words *fatḥ* ("decision" or "victory") and *fiʾah* ("army" or "community"). As regards the latter, it is to be borne in mind that its primary significance is "a group" or "a congregated body of men" – more or less synonymous with *ṭāʾifah* or *jamāᶜah*; it can, therefore, be used to denote "an army" as well as "a community". Similarly, the expression *naᶜūd* can be understood in either of two ways: namely, as meaning "We shall revert [to defeating you]" – or, as in my rendering, "We shall revoke [Our promise of aid]" – addressed, in the one instance to the unbelievers, and in the other, to the believers. (For the use of the verb *ᶜāda* in the sense of "he revoked", see *Tāj al-ᶜArūs*; also Lane V, 2189.) But while both interpretations of the above verse are linguistically justified, the one adopted by me (and supported, according to Ibn Kathīr, by Ubayy ibn Kaᶜb) is in greater harmony with the context, inasmuch as both the preceding and subsequent passages are unmistakably addressed to the believers. Thus, the verse must be understood as a reminder to the Muslims that God will be with them only so long as they remain firm in faith and righteous in action, and that, however large their community may be in the future, they will be powerless unless they are true believers.

22 See 2 : 93 and 4 : 46, and the corresponding notes. While in the above-mentioned two instances the Jews are alluded to, the present allusion is more general, and relates to all people who have come to know and understand the message of the Qurʾān, but pay no heed to it.

23 Lit., "animals that walk or crawl" (*dawāb*, sing. *dābbah*), including man as well.

24 I.e., between a man's desires and the outward action that may result from those desires: indicating that God can turn man away from what his heart urges him to do (Rāghib). In other words, it is God-consciousness alone that can prevent man from being misled by wrong desires and, thus, from becoming like "those deaf, those dumb ones who do not use their reason" (verse 22 above); and it is God-consciousness alone that can enable man to follow the call "unto that which gives life" – that is, spiritual awareness of right and wrong and the will to act accordingly.

And beware of that temptation to evil which does not befall only those among you who are bent on denying the truth, to the exclusion of others;[25] and know that God is severe in retribution. «25»

And remember the time when you were few [and] helpless on earth, fearful lest people do away with you[26] – whereupon He sheltered you, and strengthened you with His succour, and provided for you sustenance out of the good things of life, so that you might have cause to be grateful. «26»

[Hence,] O you who have attained to faith, do not be false to God and the Apostle, and do not knowingly be false to the trust that has been reposed in you;[27] «27» and know that your worldly goods and your children are but a trial and a temptation, and that with God there is a tremendous reward.[28] «28»

O you who have attained to faith! If you remain conscious of God, He will endow you with a standard by which to discern the true from the false,[29] and will efface your bad deeds, and will forgive you your sins: for God is limitless in His great bounty. «29»

وَٱتَّقُوا۟ فِتْنَةً لَّا تُصِيبَنَّ ٱلَّذِينَ ظَلَمُوا۟ مِنكُمْ خَآصَّةً ۖ وَٱعْلَمُوٓا۟ أَنَّ ٱللَّهَ
شَدِيدُ ٱلْعِقَابِ ﴿٢٥﴾ وَٱذْكُرُوٓا۟ إِذْ أَنتُمْ قَلِيلٌ مُّسْتَضْعَفُونَ فِى ٱلْأَرْضِ
تَخَافُونَ أَن يَتَخَطَّفَكُمُ ٱلنَّاسُ فَـَٔاوَىٰكُمْ وَأَيَّدَكُم بِنَصْرِهِۦ وَرَزَقَكُم
مِّنَ ٱلطَّيِّبَٰتِ لَعَلَّكُمْ تَشْكُرُونَ ﴿٢٦﴾ يَٰٓأَيُّهَا ٱلَّذِينَ ءَامَنُوا۟ لَا تَخُونُوا۟
ٱللَّهَ وَٱلرَّسُولَ وَتَخُونُوٓا۟ أَمَٰنَٰتِكُمْ وَأَنتُمْ تَعْلَمُونَ ﴿٢٧﴾ وَٱعْلَمُوٓا۟ أَنَّمَآ
أَمْوَٰلُكُمْ وَأَوْلَٰدُكُمْ فِتْنَةٌ وَأَنَّ ٱللَّهَ عِندَهُۥٓ أَجْرٌ عَظِيمٌ ﴿٢٨﴾ يَٰٓأَيُّهَا ٱلَّذِينَ
ءَامَنُوٓا۟ إِن تَتَّقُوا۟ ٱللَّهَ يَجْعَل لَّكُمْ فُرْقَانًا وَيُكَفِّرْ عَنكُمْ سَيِّـَٔاتِكُمْ
وَيَغْفِرْ لَكُمْ ۗ وَٱللَّهُ ذُو ٱلْفَضْلِ ٱلْعَظِيمِ ﴿٢٩﴾

Wat-taqū fitnatal-lā tuṣībannal-ladhīna ẓalamū miñkum khāaṣṣah. Waᶜ-lamūu ᵓannal-lāha Shadīdul-ᶜiqāb. (25) Wadh-kurūu ᵓidh ᵓañtum qalīlum-mustaḍᶜafūna fil-ᵓarḍi takhāfūna ᵓañy-yatakhaṭ-ṭafakumun-nāsu faᵓāwākum wa ᵓayyadakum-binaṣrihī wa razaqakum-minaṭ-ṭayyibāti laᶜallakum tashkurūn. (26) Yāa ᵓayyuhal-ladhīna ᵓāmanū lā takhūnul-lāha war-Rasūla wa takhūnūu ᵓamānātikum wa ᵓañtum taᶜlamūn. (27) Waᶜ-lamūu ᵓannamāa ᵓamwālukum wa ᵓawlādukum fitnatuñw-wa ᵓannal-lāha ᶜiñdahūu ᵓajrun ᶜaẓīm. (28) Yāa ᵓayyuhal-ladhīna ᵓāmanūu ᵓiñ-tattaqul-lāha yajᶜal-lakum Furqānañw-wa yukaffir ᶜañkum sayyiᵓātikum wa yaghfir lakum. Wal-lāhu Dhul-faḍlil-ᶜaẓīm. (29)

25 The term *fitnah* – here rendered as "temptation to evil" – comprises a wide range of concepts, e.g., "seduction" or "trial" or "test" or "an affliction whereby one is tried"; hence also "confusion" (as in 3 : 7 and 6 : 23), "discord" or "dissension" (because it constitutes a "trial" of human groups), as well as "persecution" and "oppression" (because it is an affliction which may cause man to go astray and to lose his faith in spiritual values – a meaning in which the word *fitnah* is used in 2 : 191 and 193); and, finally, "sedition" and "civil war" (because it leads whole communities astray). Since the expression "temptation to evil" is applicable to all these meanings, it appears to be the most suitable in the above context: the idea being that it is not merely the deliberate deniers of spiritual truths who are exposed to such a temptation, but that also people who are otherwise righteous may fall prey to it unless they remain always, and consciously, on their guard against anything that might lead them astray from the right course.

26 A reference to the weakness of the believers in the early days of Islam, before their exodus from Mecca to Medina. In its wider meaning, it is a reminder to every community of true believers, at all times, of their initial weakness and numerical insignificance and their subsequent growth in numbers and influence.

27 Lit., "do not be false to your trusts, the while you know". Regarding the deeper meaning of *amānah* ("trust"), see note 87 on 33 : 72.

28 Inasmuch as love of worldly goods and a desire to protect one's family may lead a person to transgression (and, thus, to a betrayal of the moral values postulated in God's message), they are described as *fitnah* – which, in this context, is best rendered by the two words "trial and temptation". This reminder connects with verse 25 above, "beware of that temptation to evil which does not befall only those who are bent on denying the truth," since it is acquisitiveness and a desire to confer benefits on one's own family which often tempt an otherwise good person to offend against the rights of his fellow-men. It is to be borne in mind that, contrary to the New Testament, the Qurᵓān does not postulate a contempt for worldly attachments as a pre-requisite of righteousness: it only demands of man that he should not allow these attachments to deflect him from the pursuit of moral verities.

29 I.e., the faculty of moral valuation (*Manār* IX, 648). See also *sūrah* 2, note 38.

AND [remember, O Prophet,] how those who were bent on denying the truth were scheming against thee, in order to restrain thee [from preaching], or to slay thee, or to drive thee away: thus have they [always] schemed:[30] but God brought their scheming to nought – for God is above all schemers. «30»

And whenever Our messages were conveyed to them, they would say, "We have heard [all this] before; if we wanted, we could certainly compose sayings like these [ourselves]: they are nothing but fables of ancient times!"[31] «31»

And, lo, they would say, "O God! If this be indeed the truth from Thee, then rain down upon us stones from the skies, or inflict [some other] grievous suffering on us!"[32] «32»

But God did not choose thus to chastise them while thou [O Prophet] wert still among them[33] nor would God chastise them when they [might yet] ask for forgiveness. «33» But what have they [now] in their favour that God should not chastise them – seeing that they bar [the believers] from the Inviolable House of Worship, although they are not its [rightful] guardians?[34]

وَإِذْ يَمْكُرُ بِكَ ٱلَّذِينَ كَفَرُوا۟ لِيُثْبِتُوكَ أَوْ يَقْتُلُوكَ أَوْ يُخْرِجُوكَ ۚ
وَيَمْكُرُونَ وَيَمْكُرُ ٱللَّهُ ۖ وَٱللَّهُ خَيْرُ ٱلْمَـٰكِرِينَ ﴿٣٠﴾ وَإِذَا تُتْلَىٰ عَلَيْهِمْ
ءَايَـٰتُنَا قَالُوا۟ قَدْ سَمِعْنَا لَوْ نَشَآءُ لَقُلْنَا مِثْلَ هَـٰذَآ ۙ إِنْ هَـٰذَآ إِلَّآ أَسَـٰطِيرُ
ٱلْأَوَّلِينَ ﴿٣١﴾ وَإِذْ قَالُوا۟ ٱللَّهُمَّ إِن كَانَ هَـٰذَا هُوَ ٱلْحَقَّ مِنْ عِندِكَ
فَأَمْطِرْ عَلَيْنَا حِجَارَةً مِّنَ ٱلسَّمَآءِ أَوِ ٱئْتِنَا بِعَذَابٍ أَلِيمٍ ﴿٣٢﴾ وَمَا كَانَ ٱللَّهُ
لِيُعَذِّبَهُمْ وَأَنتَ فِيهِمْ ۚ وَمَا كَانَ ٱللَّهُ مُعَذِّبَهُمْ وَهُمْ يَسْتَغْفِرُونَ ﴿٣٣﴾ وَمَا لَهُمْ
أَلَّا يُعَذِّبَهُمُ ٱللَّهُ وَهُمْ يَصُدُّونَ عَنِ ٱلْمَسْجِدِ ٱلْحَرَامِ وَمَا كَانُوٓا۟ أَوْلِيَآءَهُۥٓ ۚ

Wa ʾidh yamkuru bikal-ladhīna kafarū liyuthbitūka ʾaw yaqtulūka ʾaw yukhrijūk. Wa yamkurūna wa yamkurul-lāh. Wal-lāhu Khayrul-mākirīn. (30) Wa ʾidhā tutlā ʿalayhim ʾĀyātunā qālū qad samiʿnā law nashāaʾu laqulnā mithla hādhāa ʾin hādhāa ʾillāa ʾasāṭīrul-ʾawwalīn. (31) Wa ʾidh qālul-lāhumma ʾiñ-kāna hādhā huwal-ḥaqqa min ʿiñdika faʾamṭir ʿalaynā ḥijāratam-minas-samāaʾi ʾawiʾ-tinā biʿadhābin ʾalīm. (32) Wa mā kānal-lāhu liyuʿadh-dhibahum wa ʾañta fīhim; wa mā kānal-lāhu muʿadhdhibahum wa hum yastaghfirūn. (33) Wa mā lahum ʾallā yuʿadhdhibahumul-lāhu wa hum yaṣud-dūna ʿanil-Masjidil-Ḥarāmi wa mā kānūu ʾawliyāaʾah.

30 While the first sentence of this verse is a reference to the persecution to which the Prophet and his followers had been exposed in Mecca before their exodus to Medina, this concluding passage points to the ever-recurring fact of man's religious history that those who deny the truth of divine revelation are always intent on rendering its preachers powerless or destroying them, either physically or, figuratively, through ridicule.

31 Cf. 6 : 25. As regards the expression *la-qulnā* – here rendered as "we could certainly [ourselves] compose" – it is to be remembered that the verb *qāla* does not always signify only "he said", but also "he asserted" or "expressed an opinion", as well as – in connection with a literary production – "he composed": thus, *qāla shiʿr* means "he composed a poem". In the above context, this expression alludes to the oft-repeated (but never fulfilled) boast of the pagan Quraysh that they could produce a poetic message comparable in merit to that of the Qurʾān; in its wider sense, it is an allusion to the attitude of many unbelievers towards revealed scriptures in general.

32 This sarcastic appeal of the unbelievers – referred to several times in the Qurʾān – is meant to stress their conviction that the Qurʾān is *not* a divine revelation. According to Anas ibn Mālik, these words were first uttered by Abū Jahl, the Prophet's chief opponent at Mecca, who was killed in the battle of Badr (Bukhārī).

33 I.e., in Mecca, before the exodus to Medina.

34 At the time of the revelation of this *sūrah* (the year 2 H.) Mecca was still in the possession of the hostile Quraysh, and no Muslim was allowed to enter it. Owing to their descent from Abraham, the Quraysh considered themselves entitled to the guardianship of the Kaʿbah ("the Inviolable House of Worship"), which had been built by Abraham as the first temple ever dedicated to the One God (see *sūrah* 2, note 102). The Qurʾān refutes this contention, just as it refutes the claim of the children of Israel to being "the chosen people" by virtue of their descent from Abraham. (Cf. in this connection 2 : 124, and especially the last sentence, "My covenant does not embrace the wrongdoers.") Although they still retained a modicum of belief in God, the Quraysh had entirely forsaken the unitarian faith of Abraham, thus forfeiting any moral claim to the guardianship of the Temple (*al-bayt*) built by him.

None but the God-conscious can be its guardians: but of this most of these [evil-doers] are unaware; ‹34› and their prayers before the Temple are nothing but whistling and clapping of hands.[35]
Taste then, [O unbelievers,] this chastisement as an outcome of your persistent denial of the truth![36] ‹35›
Behold, those who are bent on denying the truth are spending their riches in order to turn others away from the path of God; and they will go on spending them until they become [a source of] intense regret for them; and then they will be overcome!
And those who [until their death] have denied the truth shall be gathered unto hell, ‹36› so that God might separate the bad from the good, and join the bad with one another, and link them all together [within His condemnation], and then place them in hell. They, they are the lost! ‹37›
Tell those who are bent on denying the truth that if they desist,[37] all that is past shall be forgiven them; but if they revert [to their wrongdoing], let them remember what happened to the like of them in times gone by.[38] ‹38› And fight against them until there is no more oppression and all worship is devoted to God alone.[39]
And if they desist – behold, God sees all that they do;[40] ‹39› and if they turn away [from righteousness], know that God is your Lord Supreme: [and] how excellent is this Lord Supreme, and how excellent this Giver of Succour! ‹40›

إِنْ أَوْلِيَآؤُهُۥٓ إِلَّا ٱلْمُتَّقُونَ وَلَـٰكِنَّ أَكْثَرَهُمْ لَا يَعْلَمُونَ ۝٣٤ وَمَا كَانَ
صَلَاتُهُمْ عِندَ ٱلْبَيْتِ إِلَّا مُكَآءً وَتَصْدِيَةً ۚ فَذُوقُوا۟ ٱلْعَذَابَ بِمَا كُنتُمْ
تَكْفُرُونَ ۝٣٥ إِنَّ ٱلَّذِينَ كَفَرُوا۟ يُنفِقُونَ أَمْوَٰلَهُمْ لِيَصُدُّوا۟ عَن سَبِيلِ ٱللَّهِ
فَسَيُنفِقُونَهَا ثُمَّ تَكُونُ عَلَيْهِمْ حَسْرَةً ثُمَّ يُغْلَبُونَ ۗ وَٱلَّذِينَ كَفَرُوٓا۟ إِلَىٰ جَهَنَّمَ
يُحْشَرُونَ ۝٣٦ لِيَمِيزَ ٱللَّهُ ٱلْخَبِيثَ مِنَ ٱلطَّيِّبِ وَيَجْعَلَ ٱلْخَبِيثَ بَعْضَهُۥ
عَلَىٰ بَعْضٍ فَيَرْكُمَهُۥ جَمِيعًا فَيَجْعَلَهُۥ فِى جَهَنَّمَ ۚ أُو۟لَـٰٓئِكَ هُمُ ٱلْخَـٰسِرُونَ ۝٣٧
قُل لِّلَّذِينَ كَفَرُوٓا۟ إِن يَنتَهُوا۟ يُغْفَرْ لَهُم مَّا قَدْ سَلَفَ وَإِن يَعُودُوا۟ فَقَدْ
مَضَتْ سُنَّتُ ٱلْأَوَّلِينَ ۝٣٨ وَقَـٰتِلُوهُمْ حَتَّىٰ لَا تَكُونَ فِتْنَةٌ وَيَكُونَ ٱلدِّينُ
كُلُّهُۥ لِلَّهِ ۚ فَإِنِ ٱنتَهَوْا۟ فَإِنَّ ٱللَّهَ بِمَا يَعْمَلُونَ بَصِيرٌ ۝٣٩ وَإِن تَوَلَّوْا۟ فَٱعْلَمُوٓا۟
أَنَّ ٱللَّهَ مَوْلَىٰكُمْ ۚ نِعْمَ ٱلْمَوْلَىٰ وَنِعْمَ ٱلنَّصِيرُ ۝٤٠

ʾIn ʾawliyāaʾuhūu ʾillal-muttaqūna wa lākinna aktharahum lā yaʿlamūn. (34) Wa mā kāna Ṣalātuhum ʿiñdal-Bayti ʾillā mukāaʾañw-wa taṣdiyah. Fadhūqul-ʿadhāba bimā kuñtum takfurūn. (35) ʾInnal-ladhīna kafarū yuñfiqūna ʾamwālahum liyaṣuddū ʿañ-sabīlil-lāh. Fasayuñfiqūnahā thumma takūnu ʿalayhim ḥasratañ-thumma yughlabūn. Wal-ladhīna kafarūu ʾilā jahannama yuḥsharūn. (36) Liyamīzal-lāhul-khabītha minaṭ-ṭayyibi wa yajʿalal-khabītha baʿḍahū ʿalā baʿḍiñ-fayarkumahū jamīʿañ-fayajʿalahū fī jahannam. ʾUlāaʾika humul-khāsirūn. (37) Qul lilladhīna kafarū ʾiñy-yañtahū yughfar lahum-mā qad salafa wa ʾiñy-yaʿūdū faqad maḍat sunnatul-ʾawwalīn. (38) Wa qātilūhum ḥattā lā takūna fitnatuñw-wa yakūnad-dīnu kulluhū lillāh. Faʾiniñtahaw faʾinnal-lāha bimā yaʿmalūna Baṣīr. (39) Wa ʾiñtawallaw faʿlamūu ʾannal-lāha Mawlākum niʿmal-Mawlā wa niʿman-Naṣīr. (40)

35 I.e., devoid of all spiritual contents. Some of the early authorities maintain that dancing around the Kaʿbah, accompanied by whistling and hand-clapping, was actually a ritual practiced by the pre-Islamic Arabs. Although this explanation is quite plausible, it would appear from the context that the expression "whistling and clapping of hands" is used here metaphorically, to denote the spiritual emptiness of the religious rituals of people who are wont to attribute a quasi-divine efficacy to all manner of circumstantial "forces" – like wealth, power, social status, "luck", etc.

36 The chastisement or suffering referred to here was their crushing defeat at Badr.

37 I.e., from their endeavour to turn others away from the path of God and from waging war against the believers.

38 Lit., "the example (*sunnah*) of the people of old times has already come to pass": an allusion to the disasters that have overtaken, and are bound to overtake, those who persistently deny moral truths.

39 I.e., until man is free to worship God. Cf. the identical phrase in 2 : 193, and the corresponding note. Both these passages stress self-defence – in the widest sense of this word – as the only justification of war.

40 I.e., He knows their motives, and will requite them according to their merits.

AND KNOW that whatever booty you acquire [in war], one-fifth thereof belongs to God and the Apostle, and the near of kin, and the orphans, and the needy, and the wayfarer.[41]
[This you must observe] if you believe in God and in what We bestowed from on high upon Our servant on the day when the true was distinguished from the false – the day when the two hosts met in battle. And God has the power to will anything.[42]
﴿41﴾
19 حزب
10 جزء
[Remember that day] when you were at the near end of the valley [of Badr], and they were at its farthest end, while the caravan was below you.[43] And if you had known that a battle was to take place, you would indeed have refused to accept the challenge:[44] but [the battle was brought about none the less,] so that God might accomplish a thing [which He willed] to be done[45] [and] that he who would perish might perish in clear evidence of the truth, and that he who would remain alive might

۞ وَٱعۡلَمُوٓاْ أَنَّمَا غَنِمۡتُم مِّن شَيۡءٖ فَأَنَّ لِلَّهِ خُمُسَهُۥ وَلِلرَّسُولِ وَلِذِي
ٱلۡقُرۡبَىٰ وَٱلۡيَتَٰمَىٰ وَٱلۡمَسَٰكِينِ وَٱبۡنِ ٱلسَّبِيلِ إِن كُنتُمۡ ءَامَنتُم بِٱللَّهِ وَمَآ
أَنزَلۡنَا عَلَىٰ عَبۡدِنَا يَوۡمَ ٱلۡفُرۡقَانِ يَوۡمَ ٱلۡتَقَى ٱلۡجَمۡعَانِۗ وَٱللَّهُ عَلَىٰ كُلِّ
شَيۡءٖ قَدِيرٌ ﴿٤١﴾ إِذۡ أَنتُم بِٱلۡعُدۡوَةِ ٱلدُّنۡيَا وَهُم بِٱلۡعُدۡوَةِ ٱلۡقُصۡوَىٰ
وَٱلرَّكۡبُ أَسۡفَلَ مِنكُمۡۚ وَلَوۡ تَوَاعَدتُّمۡ لَٱخۡتَلَفۡتُمۡ فِي ٱلۡمِيعَٰدِ وَلَٰكِن
لِّيَقۡضِيَ ٱللَّهُ أَمۡرٗا كَانَ مَفۡعُولٗا لِّيَهۡلِكَ مَنۡ هَلَكَ عَنۢ بَيِّنَةٖ وَيَحۡيَىٰ مَنۡ

۞ Waʿ-lamūu ʾannamā ghanimtum-miñ-shayʾiñ-faʾanna lillāhi khumusahū wa lirRasūli wa lidhil-qurbā wal-yatāmā wal-masākīni wab-nis-sabīli ʾiñ-kuñtum ʾāmañtum-billāhi wa māa ʾañzalnā ʿalā ʿabdinā yawmal-furqāni yawmal-taqal-jamʿān. Wal-lāhu ʿalā kulli shayʾiñ-Qadīr. ﴿41﴾ ʾIdh ʾañtum-bilʿudwatid-dunyā wa hum-bilʿudwatil-quṣwā war-rakbu ʾasfala miñ-kum. Wa law tawāʿattum lakhtalaftum fil-mīʿadi wa lākil-liyaqḍiyal-lāhu ʾamrañ-kāna mafʿūlal-liyahlika man halaka ʿam-bayyinatiñw-wa yaḥyā man

41 According to verse 1 of this *sūrah*, "all spoils of war belong to God and the Apostle", i.e., are to be administered by the authorities of an Islamic state in the interests of the common weal. Most of the great Islamic jurists are of the opinion that whereas four-fifths of all spoils may either be distributed among those who actively took part in the war effort or may be otherwise utilized for the welfare of the community, one-fifth *must* be reserved for the specific purposes enumerated in the above verse, including a share "for God and the Apostle" (which is obviously a metonym for a government that rules in accordance with the laws of the Qurʾān and the teachings of God's Apostle); this latter share is to be used for the exigencies of state administration. Since a full discussion of this complex juridical problem would go far beyond the scope of these explanatory notes, the reader is referred, in particular, to *Manār* X, 4 ff., where the views of the classical exponents of Islamic jurisprudence are summarized. – For the term *ibn as-sabīl* occurring in this verse, see *sūrah* 2, note 145. By "the near of kin and the orphans" apparently the relatives of fallen combatants are meant in this context.

42 I.e., "He can grant you victory or can withhold it from you". The battle of Badr is described here as "the day when the true was distinguished from the false" (*yawm al-furqān*) because on that occasion a small and poorly armed group of believers utterly destroyed an infinitely better equipped army more than three times its number. The revelation referred to in this connection was God's promise of victory, given in verses 12-14 of this *sūrah*. (See also note 38 on 2 : 53.)

43 Before the beginning of the battle, the Prophet and his followers were encamped in the northern part of the valley of Badr, nearest to Medina, while their enemies, having come from Mecca, occupied its southern part. The Meccan trade caravan, coming from Syria under the leadership of Abū Sufyān, was in the meantime proceeding southwards through the coastal lowlands (see introductory note to this *sūrah*).

44 This is a very free rendering of the elliptic phrase which runs, literally, thus: "And if you had mutually made an appointment, you would indeed have failed to keep the appointment" – i.e., for battle. As already mentioned in the introductory note to this *sūrah*, most of the Prophet's followers had been under the impression that their objective was the relatively weak trade caravan, and some of them were dismayed at finding themselves face to face with the powerful Quraysh army advancing from the south.

45 According to all the commentators, the words interpolated by me between brackets are implied in this highly elliptical sentence. Literally translated, its last words might be rendered as "a thing that was [already] done": meaning that if God decrees a thing, it must inevitably come about, and may therefore be described as already done.

live in clear evidence of the truth.[46] And, behold, God is indeed all-hearing, all-knowing. ‹42›
Lo! God showed them to thee in a dream as few:[47] for, had He shown them to you as many, you would surely have lost heart, and would surely have disagreed with one another about what to do.[48] But God saved [you from this]: verily, He has full knowledge of what is the hearts [of men]. ‹43›
And so, when you met in battle, He made them appear as few in your eyes – just as He made you appear as of little account in their eyes – so that God might accomplish a thing [which He willed] to be done:[49] for all things go back to God [as their source]. ‹44›
[Hence] O you who have attained to faith, when you meet a host in battle, be firm, and remember God often, so that you might attain to a happy state! ‹45›
And pay heed unto God and His Apostle, and do not [allow yourselves to] be at variance with one another, lest you lose heart and your moral strength desert you.[50] And be patient in adversity: for, verily, God is with those who are patient in adversity. ‹46›

حَىَّ عَنۢ بَيِّنَةٍ وَإِنَّ ٱللَّهَ لَسَمِيعٌ عَلِيمٌ ﴿٤٢﴾ إِذْ يُرِيكَهُمُ ٱللَّهُ فِى مَنَامِكَ
قَلِيلًا وَلَوْ أَرَىٰكَهُمْ كَثِيرًا لَّفَشِلْتُمْ وَلَتَنَٰزَعْتُمْ فِى ٱلْأَمْرِ وَلَٰكِنَّ ٱللَّهَ سَلَّمَ
إِنَّهُۥ عَلِيمٌۢ بِذَاتِ ٱلصُّدُورِ ﴿٤٣﴾ وَإِذْ يُرِيكُمُوهُمْ إِذِ ٱلْتَقَيْتُمْ فِىٓ أَعْيُنِكُمْ
قَلِيلًا وَيُقَلِّلُكُمْ فِىٓ أَعْيُنِهِمْ لِيَقْضِىَ ٱللَّهُ أَمْرًا كَانَ مَفْعُولًا وَإِلَى ٱللَّهِ
تُرْجَعُ ٱلْأُمُورُ ﴿٤٤﴾ يَٰٓأَيُّهَا ٱلَّذِينَ ءَامَنُوٓا۟ إِذَا لَقِيتُمْ فِئَةً فَٱثْبُتُوا۟ وَٱذْكُرُوا۟ ٱللَّهَ
كَثِيرًا لَّعَلَّكُمْ تُفْلِحُونَ ﴿٤٥﴾ وَأَطِيعُوا۟ ٱللَّهَ وَرَسُولَهُۥ وَلَا تَنَٰزَعُوا۟ فَتَفْشَلُوا۟
وَتَذْهَبَ رِيحُكُمْ وَٱصْبِرُوٓا۟ إِنَّ ٱللَّهَ مَعَ ٱلصَّٰبِرِينَ ﴿٤٦﴾

ḥayya ʿam-bayyinah. Wa ʾinnal-lāha laSamīʿun ʿAlīm. ﴿42﴾ ʾIdh yurīkahumul-lāhu fī manāmika qalīlā. Wa law ʾarākahum kathīral-lafashiltum wa latanāzaʿtum fil-ʾamri wa lākinnal-lāha sallam. ʾInnahū ʿAlīmum-bidhātiṣ-ṣudūr. ﴿43﴾ Wa ʾidh yurīkumūhum ʾidhil-taqaytum fīi ʾaʿyunikum qalīlañw-wa yuqallilukum fīi ʾaʿyunihim liyaqḍiyal-lāhu ʾamrañ-kāna mafʿūlā. Wa ʾilal-lāhi turjaʿul-ʾumūr. ﴿44﴾ Yāa ʾayyuhal-ladhīna ʾāmanūu ʾidhā laqītum fiʾatañ-fathbutū wadh-kurul-lāha kathīral-laʿallakum tufliḥūn. ﴿45﴾ Wa ʾaṭīʿul-lāha wa-Rasūlahū wa lā tanāzaʿū fatafshalū wa tadhhaba rīḥukum waṣ-birū. ʾInnal-lāha maʿaṣ-ṣābirīn. ﴿46﴾

46 Some of the great commentators understand this sentence in a metaphorical sense, with "destruction" signifying persistence in denying the truth (*kufr*), and "life" being synonymous with faith. According to this interpretation, the above sentence would have the following meaning: ". . . so that the denial of the truth on the part of him who has denied it, and the faith of him who has attained to it, might become clearly evident" (Zamakhsharī); or "let him who is bent on denying the truth go on denying it after this clear evidence of God's will, and let him who has attained to belief go on believing" (Ibn Isḥāq, as quoted by Ibn Kathīr). In my opinion, however, it is preferable to interpret the references to death and life in their *prima-facie* (that is, not metaphorical) sense – namely, as applying to the death or survival of all who took part in the battle of Badr, believers and unbelievers alike: the believers who fell in that battle died conscious of being martyrs in God's cause, and those who survived could now clearly discern God's hand in their victory; while the dead among the deniers of the truth had clearly given their lives for nothing, and those of them who survived must now realize that their crushing defeat was due, in the last resort, to something infinitely greater than the valour of the Muslims (cf. verse 17, and the corresponding notes).

47 Lit., "in thy dream" – obviously relating to a dream which the Prophet had had just before the encounter at Badr. We have no authentic Tradition to this effect, but the *tābiʿī* Mujāhid is quoted as having said, "God had shown the enemies to the Prophet, in a dream, as few; he informed his Companions accordingly, and this encouraged them greatly" (Rāzī and Ibn Kathīr, with minor variants).

48 Lit., "about the matter" – i.e., about the advisability of giving battle or retreating.

49 See note 45 above. Since at the time of the actual encounter the Muslims could no longer be in doubt as to the great number of the enemy force, the phrase "He made them appear as few in your eyes" has obviously a metaphorical meaning: it implies that, by that time, the Prophet's followers were so full of courage that the enemy appeared insignificant to them. The Quraysh, on the other hand, were so conscious of their own power and numerical superiority that the Muslims appeared but of little account to *them* – a mistake which ultimately cost them the battle and a great number of lives.

50 The relevant word is *rīḥ*, which literally signifies "wind"; it is used metaphorically to denote "spirit" or "moral strength".

وَلَا تَكُونُوا۟ كَٱلَّذِينَ خَرَجُوا۟ مِن دِيَـٰرِهِم بَطَرًا وَرِئَآءَ ٱلنَّاسِ وَيَصُدُّونَ
عَن سَبِيلِ ٱللَّهِ ۚ وَٱللَّهُ بِمَا يَعْمَلُونَ مُحِيطٌ ﴿٤٧﴾ وَإِذْ زَيَّنَ لَهُمُ ٱلشَّيْطَـٰنُ
أَعْمَـٰلَهُمْ وَقَالَ لَا غَالِبَ لَكُمُ ٱلْيَوْمَ مِنَ ٱلنَّاسِ وَإِنِّى جَارٌ لَّكُمْ ۖ فَلَمَّا
تَرَآءَتِ ٱلْفِئَتَانِ نَكَصَ عَلَىٰ عَقِبَيْهِ وَقَالَ إِنِّى بَرِىٓءٌ مِّنكُمْ إِنِّىٓ أَرَىٰ مَا
لَا تَرَوْنَ إِنِّىٓ أَخَافُ ٱللَّهَ ۚ وَٱللَّهُ شَدِيدُ ٱلْعِقَابِ ﴿٤٨﴾ إِذْ يَقُولُ ٱلْمُنَـٰفِقُونَ
وَٱلَّذِينَ فِى قُلُوبِهِم مَّرَضٌ غَرَّ هَـٰٓؤُلَآءِ دِينُهُمْ ۗ وَمَن يَتَوَكَّلْ عَلَى ٱللَّهِ فَإِنَّ
ٱللَّهَ عَزِيزٌ حَكِيمٌ ﴿٤٩﴾ وَلَوْ تَرَىٰٓ إِذْ يَتَوَفَّى ٱلَّذِينَ كَفَرُوا۟ ۙ ٱلْمَلَـٰٓئِكَةُ
يَضْرِبُونَ وُجُوهَهُمْ وَأَدْبَـٰرَهُمْ وَذُوقُوا۟ عَذَابَ ٱلْحَرِيقِ ﴿٥٠﴾ ذَٰلِكَ بِمَا
قَدَّمَتْ أَيْدِيكُمْ وَأَنَّ ٱللَّهَ لَيْسَ بِظَلَّـٰمٍ لِّلْعَبِيدِ ﴿٥١﴾

Wa lā takūnū kalladhīna kharajū miñ-diyārihim-baṭarañw-wa riʾāaʾan-nāsi wa yaṣuddūna ᶜañ-sabīlil-lāh. Wal-lāhu bimā yaᶜmalūna Muḥīṭ. (47) Wa ʾidh zayyana lahumush-Shayṭānu ʾaᶜmālahum wa qāla lā ghāliba lakumul-yawma minan-nāsi wa ʾinnī jārul-lakum. Falammā tarāaʾatil-fiʾatāni nakaṣa ᶜalā ᶜaqibayhi wa qāla ʾinnī barīiʾum-miñkum ʾinnīi ʾarā mā lā tarawna ʾinnīi ʾakhāful-lāh. Wal-lāhu Shadīdul-ᶜiqāb. (48) ʾIdh yaqūlul-munāfiqūna wal-ladhīna fī qulūbihim-maraḍun gharra hāaʾulāaʾi dīnuhum. Wa mañy-yatawakkal ᶜalal-lāhi faʾinnal-lāha ᶜAzīzun Ḥakīm. (49) Wa law tarāa ʾidh yatawaffal-ladhīna kafarul-Malāaʾikatu yaḍribūna wujūhahum wa ʾadbārahum wa dhūqū ᶜadhābal-ḥarīq. (50) Dhālika bimā qaddamat ʾaydīkum wa ʾannal-lāha laysa biẓallāmil-lilᶜabīd. (51)

And be not like those [unbelievers] who went forth from their homelands full of self-conceit and a desire to be seen and praised by men:[51] for they were trying to turn others away from the path of God – the while God encompassed all their doings [with His might]. ‹47›

And, lo, Satan made all their doings seem goodly to them, and said, "No one can overcome you this day, for, behold, I shall be your protector!"[52] – but as soon as the two hosts came within sight of one another, he turned on his heels and said, "Behold, I am not responsible for you: behold, I see something that you do not see: behold, I fear God – for God is severe in retribution!"[53] ‹48›

At the same time, the hypocrites and those in whose hearts was disease were saying, "Their faith has deluded these [believers]!"[54]

But he who places his trust in God [knows that], verily, God is almighty, wise. ‹49›

AND IF thou couldst but see [how it will be] when He causes those who are bent on denying the truth to die: the angels will strike their faces and their backs,[55] and [will say]: "Taste suffering through fire ‹50› in return for what your own hands have wrought – for, never does God do the least wrong to His creatures!" ‹51›

---

51 A reference to the Quraysh army which set forth from Mecca under the leadership of Abū Jahl in the conviction that they would destroy the Prophet and his followers. These words imply a warning to the believers, of all times, never to go to war boastfully and for the sake of empty glory.

52 Lit., "your neighbour" – an expression derived from the ancient Arabian principle that a man is honour-bound to aid and protect his neighbours.

53 This allegory of Satan's blandishments and of his subsequent abandonment of the sinner occurs, in a more general form, in 59 : 16.

54 I.e., into thinking that in spite of their numerical weakness and lack of arms, they could withstand the powerful Meccan army. The term *dīn*, often denoting "religion", obviously stands here for the *attitude* one has towards his religion: in another word, one's faith. "Those in whose hearts was disease" is a reference to the vacillating and faint-hearted among the Prophet's followers, who were afraid of meeting the Quraysh in battle. – The particle *idh* which introduces this sentence has often the meaning of "when"; in this case, however, it signifies "at the same time".

55 Or: ". . . when the angels gather in death those who were bent on denying the truth, they strike . . .", etc. – depending on whether one attributes the pronoun in *yatawaffā* to the angels, which gives the reading "they gather [them] in death", or to God, in which case it means "He causes [them] to die" (Zamakhsharī and Rāzī). – The beating of the sinners' faces and backs is, according to Rāzī, an allegory of their suffering in the life to come in consequence of their having denied the truth while alive in this world: "They have utter darkness behind them and utter darkness before them – and this is the meaning of the words, '[the angels] strike their faces and their backs'." Most of the commentators assume that this passage refers specifically to the pagan Quraysh who fell in the battle of Badr; but

[To them shall happen] the like of what happened to Pharaoh's people and those who lived before them: they denied the truth of God's messages – and so God took them to task for their sins. Verily, God is powerful, severe in retribution! ‹52›
This, because God would never change[56] the blessings with which He has graced a people unless they change their inner selves:[57] and [know] that God is all-hearing, all-knowing. ‹53›
[To those sinners shall happen] the like of what happened to Pharaoh's people and those who lived before them: they gave the lie to their Sustainer's messages – and so We destroyed them in return for their sins, and caused Pharaoh's people to drown: for they were evildoers all. ‹54›
Verily, the vilest creatures in the sight of God are those who are bent on denying the truth and therefore do not believe.[58] ‹55›

AS FOR THOSE with whom thou hast made a covenant, and who thereupon break their covenant on every occasion,[59] not being conscious of God ‹56› – if thou find them at war [with you], make of them

كَدَأْبِ ءَالِ فِرْعَوْنَ وَٱلَّذِينَ مِن قَبْلِهِمْ كَفَرُوا۟ بِـَٔايَـٰتِ ٱللَّهِ فَأَخَذَهُمُ ٱللَّهُ
بِذُنُوبِهِمْ إِنَّ ٱللَّهَ قَوِىٌّ شَدِيدُ ٱلْعِقَابِ ﴿٥٢﴾ ذَٰلِكَ بِأَنَّ ٱللَّهَ لَمْ يَكُ مُغَيِّرًا
نِّعْمَةً أَنْعَمَهَا عَلَىٰ قَوْمٍ حَتَّىٰ يُغَيِّرُوا۟ مَا بِأَنفُسِهِمْ وَأَنَّ ٱللَّهَ سَمِيعٌ عَلِيمٌ ﴿٥٣﴾
كَدَأْبِ ءَالِ فِرْعَوْنَ وَٱلَّذِينَ مِن قَبْلِهِمْ كَذَّبُوا۟ بِـَٔايَـٰتِ رَبِّهِمْ فَأَهْلَكْنَـٰهُم
بِذُنُوبِهِمْ وَأَغْرَقْنَآ ءَالَ فِرْعَوْنَ وَكُلٌّ كَانُوا۟ ظَـٰلِمِينَ ﴿٥٤﴾ إِنَّ شَرَّ ٱلدَّوَآبِّ عِندَ
ٱللَّهِ ٱلَّذِينَ كَفَرُوا۟ فَهُمْ لَا يُؤْمِنُونَ ﴿٥٥﴾ ٱلَّذِينَ عَـٰهَدتَّ مِنْهُمْ ثُمَّ يَنقُضُونَ
عَهْدَهُمْ فِى كُلِّ مَرَّةٍ وَهُمْ لَا يَتَّقُونَ ﴿٥٦﴾ فَإِمَّا تَثْقَفَنَّهُمْ فِى ٱلْحَرْبِ فَشَرِّدْ

Kadaʾbi ʾāli Firʿawna wal-ladhīna miñ-qablihim; kafarū biʾĀyātil-lāhi faʾakhadhahumul-lāhu bidhunūbihim. ʾInnal-lāha Qawiyyuñ-Shadīdul-ʿiqāb. (52) Dhālika biʾannal-lāha lam yaku mughayyirañ-niʿmatan ʾanʿamahā ʿalā qawmin ḥattā yughayyirū mā biʾañfusihim wa ʾannal-lāha Samīʾun ʿAlīm. (53) Kadaʾbi ʾāli Firʿawna wal-ladhīna miñ-qablihim; kadhdhabū biʾĀyāti Rabbihim faʾahlaknāhum-bidhunūbihim wa ʾaghraqnāa ʾāla Firʿawna wa kulluñ-kānū ẓālimīn. (54) ʾInna sharrad-dawabbi ʿiñdal-lāhil-ladhīna kafarū fahum lā yuʾminūn. (55) ʾAlladhīna ʿāhatta minhum thumma yañquḍūna ʿahdahum fī kulli marratiñw-wa hum lā yattaqūn. (56) Faʾimmā tathqafannahum fil-ḥarbi fasharrid

while it undoubtedly does apply to them, there is no reason, in my opinion, to restrict its import to this particular historical event – especially in view of the subsequent passages (up to and including verse 55), which obviously refer to all who are "bent on denying the truth".

56 I.e., withdraw.

57 For an explanation of the wide implications of this statement in the context of the law of cause and effect which God has decreed on His creation (and which is described elsewhere in the Qurʾān as *sunnat Allāh*, "the way of God"), see my note on the phrase "God does not change men's condition unless they change their inner selves" occurring in 13 : 11,

58 Cf. verse 22 of this *sūrah*, where the same epithet is applied to human beings "who do not use their reason". In the present instance, it should be noted, the particle *fa* at the beginning of the phrase *fa-hum lā yuʾminūn* has the meaning of "and therefore" ("and therefore they do not believe"): thus showing that lack of belief in spiritual verities is a *consequence* of one's being "bent on denying the truth". Expressed in positive terms, this amounts to the statement that belief in any ethical proposition depends on one's readiness to consider it on its merits and to admit the truth of whatever one's mind judges to be in conformity with other – empirically or intuitively established – truths. As regards the expression *alladhīna kafarū*, the use of the past tense is meant here, as so often in the Qurʾān, to stress the element of *intention*, and is, therefore, consistently rendered by me – wherever the context warrants it – as "those who are bent on denying the truth" (see also *sūrah* 2, note 6).

59 Lit., "every time". The covenants referred to are agreements between the Muslim community and non-Muslim political groups. Although this passage is addressed, in the first instance, to the Prophet, the "thou" relates here to every follower of the Qurʾān and, thus, to the Muslim community of all times. With the above verse, the discourse returns to the subject of war with unbelievers to which most of this *sūrah* is devoted. The reference to the unbelievers' "breaking their covenants" has two implications: firstly, that the establishment of covenants (i.e., of peaceful relations) with non-Muslims is not only permissible but, in fact. desirable (cf. verse 61); and, secondly, that the Muslims may resort to war only if and when the other party is openly hostile to them.

ربع
الحزب

a fearsome example for those who follow them,[60] so that they might take it to heart; «57» or, if thou hast reason to fear treachery[61] from people [with whom thou hast made a covenant], cast it back at them in an equitable manner:[62] for, verily, God does not love the treacherous! «58»
And let them not think – those who are bent on denying the truth – that they shall escape[63] [God]: behold, they can never frustrate [His purpose]. «59»
Hence, make ready against them whatever force and war mounts[64] you are able to muster, so that you might deter thereby the enemies of God, who are your enemies as well,[65] and others besides them of whom you may be unaware, [but] of whom God is aware; and whatever you may expend[66] in God's cause shall be repaid to you in full, and you shall not be wronged. «60»
But if they incline to peace, incline thou to it as well, and place thy trust in God: verily, He alone is all-hearing, all-knowing! «61» And should they seek but to deceive thee [by their show of peace] – behold, God is enough for thee![67]
He it is who has strengthened thee with His succour, and by giving thee believing followers[68] «62» whose hearts He has brought together: [for,] if thou hadst

بِهِم مَّنْ خَلْفَهُمْ لَعَلَّهُمْ يَذَّكَّرُونَ ﴿٥٧﴾ وَإِمَّا تَخَافَنَّ مِن قَوْمٍ خِيَانَةً فَانۢبِذْ
إِلَيْهِمْ عَلَىٰ سَوَآءٍ إِنَّ ٱللَّهَ لَا يُحِبُّ ٱلْخَآئِنِينَ ﴿٥٨﴾ وَلَا يَحْسَبَنَّ ٱلَّذِينَ
كَفَرُوا۟ سَبَقُوٓا۟ إِنَّهُمْ لَا يُعْجِزُونَ ﴿٥٩﴾ وَأَعِدُّوا۟ لَهُم مَّا ٱسْتَطَعْتُم مِّن قُوَّةٍ
وَمِن رِّبَاطِ ٱلْخَيْلِ تُرْهِبُونَ بِهِۦ عَدُوَّ ٱللَّهِ وَعَدُوَّكُمْ وَءَاخَرِينَ مِن دُونِهِمْ
لَا تَعْلَمُونَهُمُ ٱللَّهُ يَعْلَمُهُمْ وَمَا تُنفِقُوا۟ مِن شَىْءٍ فِى سَبِيلِ ٱللَّهِ يُوَفَّ إِلَيْكُمْ
وَأَنتُمْ لَا تُظْلَمُونَ ﴿٦٠﴾ ۞ وَإِن جَنَحُوا۟ لِلسَّلْمِ فَٱجْنَحْ لَهَا وَتَوَكَّلْ عَلَى
ٱللَّهِ إِنَّهُۥ هُوَ ٱلسَّمِيعُ ٱلْعَلِيمُ ﴿٦١﴾ وَإِن يُرِيدُوٓا۟ أَن يَخْدَعُوكَ فَإِنَّ حَسْبَكَ
ٱللَّهُ هُوَ ٱلَّذِىٓ أَيَّدَكَ بِنَصْرِهِۦ وَبِٱلْمُؤْمِنِينَ ﴿٦٢﴾ وَأَلَّفَ بَيْنَ قُلُوبِهِمْ لَوْ

bihim-man khalfahum laᶜallahum yadhdhakkarūn.
(57) Wa ʾimmā takhāfanna miñ-qawmin khiyānatañ-
fambidh ʾilayhim ᶜalā sawāaʾ. ʾInnal-lāha lā yuḥib-
bul-khāaʾinīn. (58) Wa lā yaḥsabannal-ladhīna kafarū
sabaqū. ʾInnahum lā yuᶜjizūn. (59) Wa ʾaᶜiddū la-
hum-mas-taṭaᶜtum-miñ-quwwatiñw-wa mir-ribāṭil-
khayli turhibūna bihī ᶜaduwwal-lāhi wa ᶜaduwwakum
wa ʾākharīna miñ-dūnihim lā taᶜlamūnahumul-
lāhu yaᶜlamuhum. Wa mā tuñfiqū miñ-shayʾiñ-fī
sabīlil-lāhi yuwaffa ʾilaykum wa ʾañtum lā tuẓla-
mun. (60) ۞ Wa ʾiñ-janaḥū lissalmi fajnaḥ lahā
wa tawakkal ᶜalal-lāh. ʾInnahū Huwas-Samīᶜul-
ᶜAlīm. (61) Wa ʾiñy-yurīdūu ʾañy-yakhdaᶜūka faʾinna
ḥasbakal-lāh. Huwal-ladhīi ʾayyadaka binaṣrihī wa
bilmuʾminīn. (62) Wa ʾallafa bayna qulūbihim. Law

60 Lit., "put to flight, by means of them, those who come after them"; or "terrify through them those who follow them": i.e., "fight against them and inflict an exemplary punishment on them".

61 The "reason to fear treachery" must not, of course, be based on mere surmise but on clear, objective evidence (Ṭabarī, Baghawī, Rāzī; also *Manār* X, 58).

62 I.e., "renounce the covenant in an equitable manner (*ᶜalā sawāʾ*)". Ṭabarī explains this sentence thus: "Before making war on them, inform them that because of the clear evidence of their treachery thou hast renounced the treaty which existed between thee and them, so that both thou and they should know that thou art at war with them." Baghawī, in his commentary on this verse, gives an almost identical interpretation and adds, "so that they should not be under the false impression that thou hast renounced the treaty *after* having started the war." Thus, the concluding sentence of this verse – "God does not love the treacherous" – is a warning to the believers as well as to their enemies (*Manār* X, 58 f.).

63 Lit., "that they have outstripped".

64 Lit., "tethering of horses" (*ribāṭ al-khayl*): an expression which signifies "holding in readiness mounted troops at all points open to enemy invasion (*thughūr*)"; hence, tropically, the over-all maintenance of military preparedness.

65 Lit., "God's enemy and your enemy" – implying that every "enemy of God" (i.e., everyone who deliberately opposes and seeks to undermine the moral laws laid down by God) is, *eo ipso*, an enemy of those who believe in Him.

66 I.e., of resources, efforts and sacrifice of life.

67 The implication is that "even if they offer peace only with a view to deceiving thee, this [offer of] peace must be accepted, since all judgment [of their intentions] must be based on outward evidence alone" (Rāzī): in other words, mere suspicion cannot be made an excuse for rejecting an offer of peace.

68 Lit., "and by the believers": thus signifying the visible means (*wāsiṭah*) by which God succoured the Prophet.

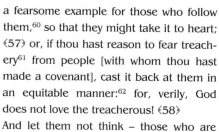

expended all that is on earth, thou couldst not have brought their hearts together [by thyself]: but God did bring them together. Verily, He is almighty, wise. ‹63›
O Prophet! God is enough for thee and those of the believers who follow thee! ‹64›
O Prophet! Inspire the believers to conquer all fear of death when fighting,[69] [so that,] if there be twenty of you who are patient in adversity, they might overcome two hundred; and [that,] if there be one hundred of you, they might overcome one thousand of those who are bent on denying the truth, because they are people who cannot grasp it.[70] ‹65›
For the time being, [however,] God has lightened your burden, for He knows that you are weak: and so, if there be one hundred of you who are patient in adversity, they should [be able to] overcome two hundred; and if there be one thousand of you, they should [be able to] overcome two thousand by God's leave: for God is with those who are patient in adversity.[71] ‹66›

أَنفَقْتَ مَا فِي ٱلْأَرْضِ جَمِيعًا مَّآ أَلَّفْتَ بَيْنَ قُلُوبِهِمْ وَلَـٰكِنَّ ٱللَّهَ أَلَّفَ
بَيْنَهُمْ إِنَّهُۥ عَزِيزٌ حَكِيمٌ ﴿٦٣﴾ يَـٰٓأَيُّهَا ٱلنَّبِيُّ حَسْبُكَ ٱللَّهُ وَمَنِ ٱتَّبَعَكَ مِنَ
ٱلْمُؤْمِنِينَ ﴿٦٤﴾ يَـٰٓأَيُّهَا ٱلنَّبِيُّ حَرِّضِ ٱلْمُؤْمِنِينَ عَلَى ٱلْقِتَالِ إِن يَكُن
مِّنكُمْ عِشْرُونَ صَـٰبِرُونَ يَغْلِبُوا۟ مِا۟ئَتَيْنِ وَإِن يَكُن مِّنكُم مِّا۟ئَةٌ يَغْلِبُوٓا۟ أَلْفًا
مِّنَ ٱلَّذِينَ كَفَرُوا۟ بِأَنَّهُمْ قَوْمٌ لَّا يَفْقَهُونَ ﴿٦٥﴾ ٱلْـَٔـٰنَ خَفَّفَ ٱللَّهُ عَنكُمْ
وَعَلِمَ أَنَّ فِيكُمْ ضَعْفًا فَإِن يَكُن مِّنكُم مِّا۟ئَةٌ صَابِرَةٌ يَغْلِبُوا۟ مِا۟ئَتَيْنِ وَإِن
يَكُن مِّنكُمْ أَلْفٌ يَغْلِبُوٓا۟ أَلْفَيْنِ بِإِذْنِ ٱللَّهِ وَٱللَّهُ مَعَ ٱلصَّـٰبِرِينَ ﴿٦٦﴾

ʾañfaqta mā fil-ʾarḍi jamīʿam-māa ʾallafta bayna qulūbihim wa lākinnal-lāha ʾallafa baynahum. ʾInnahū ʿAzīzun Ḥakīm. (63) Yāa ʾayyuhan-Nabiyyu ḥasbukal-lāhu wa manit-tabaʿaka minal-muʾminīn. (64) Yāa ʾayyuhan-Nabiyyu ḥarriḍil-muʾminīna ʿalal-qitāl. ʾIñy-yakum-miñkum ʿishrūna ṣābirūna yaghlibū miʾatayn. Wa ʾiñy-yakum-miñkum-miʾatuñy-yaghlibū ʾalfam-minal-ladhīna kafarū biʾannahum qawmul-lā yafqahūn. (65) ʾAlʾāna khaffafal-lāhu ʿañkum wa ʿalima ʾanna fīkum ḍaʿfā. Faʾiñy-yakum-miñkum-miʾatun ṣābiratuñy-yaghlibū miʾatayn. Wa ʾiñy-yakum-miñkum ʾalfuñy-yaghlibūu ʾalfayni biʾidhnil-lāh. Wal-lāhu maʿaṣ-ṣābirīn. (66)

69 For an explanation of the phrase *ḥarriḍ al-muʾminīn*, see *sūrah* 4, note 102. Consistently with my interpretation, the words *ʿala 'l-qitāl* can be rendered here in either of two ways: "[with a view] to fighting" or "when fighting". On the basis of the conventional interpretation of the verb *ḥarriḍ* as "urge" or "rouse", the phrase could be translated as "urge the believers to fight": but this, as I have pointed out in the earlier note referred to above, does not convey the true sense of this injunction.

70 Some of the commentators see in this verse a divine *prediction*, thus: "If there be twenty of you . . . , they shall overcome two hundred . . .", etc. Since, however, history shows that the believers, even at the time of the Prophet, were not always victorious against such odds, the above view is not tenable. In order to understand this passage correctly, we must read it in close conjunction with the opening sentence, "Inspire the believers to conquer all fear of death", whereupon we arrive at the meaning given in my rendering: namely, an *exhortation* to the believers to conquer all fear of death and to be so patient in adversity that they might be able to overcome an enemy many times their number (Rāzī; see also *Manār* X, 87). The concluding words of this verse – "because they are people who cannot grasp it [i.e., the truth]" – can be understood in either of two ways: (a) as giving an additional reason of the true believers' superiority over "those who are bent on denying the truth" (*alladhīna kafarū*), inasmuch as the latter, not believing in the eternal verities and in life after death, cannot rise to that enthusiasm and readiness for self-sacrifice which distinguishes the true believers; or (b) as explaining that "those who are bent on denying the truth" deny it simply because their spiritual deafness and blindness prevents them from grasping it. To my mind, the second of these two interpretations is preferable, and particularly so in view of the fact that the Qurʾān often explains in these terms the attitude of "those who deny the truth" (e.g., in 6 : 25, 7 : 179. 9 : 87, etc.).

71 This relates to the time at which the above verse was revealed, namely, immediately after the battle of Badr (2 H.), when the Muslims were extremely weak both in numbers and in equipment, and their community had not yet attained to any significant degree of political organization. Under those circumstances, the Qurʾān says, they could not – nor could any Muslim community of later times, in similar circumstances – be expected to bring forth the effort and the efficiency required of a fully developed community of believers; but even so they should be able to stand up to an enemy twice their number. (The proportions one to two, or – as in the preceding verse, one to ten – are not, of course, to be taken literally; as a matter of fact, the Muslims defeated at Badr a much better-armed force more than

IT DOES NOT behove a prophet to keep captives unless he has battled strenuously on earth.[72] You may desire the fleeting gains of this world – but God desires [for you the good of] the life to come: and God is almighty, wise. ‹67›

Had it not been for a decree from God that had already gone forth, there would indeed have befallen you a tremendous chastisement on account of all [the captives] that you took.[73] ‹68›

Enjoy, then, all that is lawful and good among the things which you have gained in war, and remain conscious of God: verily, God is much-forgiving, a dispenser of grace. ‹69›

[Hence,] O Prophet, say unto the captives who are in your hands: "If God finds any good in your hearts, He will give you something better than all that has been taken from you, and will forgive you your sins: for God is much-forgiving, a dispenser of grace."[74] ‹70›

And should they but seek to play false with thee[75] – well, they were false to God [Himself] ere this: but He gave [the

مَا كَانَ لِنَبِيٍّ أَن يَكُونَ لَهُۥٓ أَسْرَىٰ حَتَّىٰ يُثْخِنَ فِى ٱلْأَرْضِ ۚ تُرِيدُونَ
عَرَضَ ٱلدُّنْيَا وَٱللَّهُ يُرِيدُ ٱلْءَاخِرَةَ ۗ وَٱللَّهُ عَزِيزٌ حَكِيمٌ ﴿٦٧﴾ لَّوْلَا
كِتَٰبٌ مِّنَ ٱللَّهِ سَبَقَ لَمَسَّكُمْ فِيمَآ أَخَذْتُمْ عَذَابٌ عَظِيمٌ ﴿٦٨﴾
فَكُلُوا۟ مِمَّا غَنِمْتُمْ حَلَٰلًا طَيِّبًا ۚ وَٱتَّقُوا۟ ٱللَّهَ ۚ إِنَّ ٱللَّهَ غَفُورٌ رَّحِيمٌ ﴿٦٩﴾
يَٰٓأَيُّهَا ٱلنَّبِىُّ قُل لِّمَن فِىٓ أَيْدِيكُم مِّنَ ٱلْأَسْرَىٰٓ إِن يَعْلَمِ ٱللَّهُ فِى
قُلُوبِكُمْ خَيْرًا يُؤْتِكُمْ خَيْرًا مِّمَّآ أُخِذَ مِنكُمْ وَيَغْفِرْ لَكُمْ ۗ وَٱللَّهُ غَفُورٌ
رَّحِيمٌ ﴿٧٠﴾ وَإِن يُرِيدُوا۟ خِيَانَتَكَ فَقَدْ خَانُوا۟ ٱللَّهَ مِن قَبْلُ فَأَمْكَنَ

Mā kāna liNabiyyin ʾañy-yakūna lahūu ʾasrā ḥattā yuthkhina fil-ʾarḍ. Turīdūna ʿaraḍad-dunyā wal-lāhu yurīdul-ʾĀkhirah. Wal-lāhu ʿAzīzun Ḥakīm. ‹67› Lawlā Kitābum-minal-lāhi sabaqa lamassakum fīmāa ʾakhadhtum ʿadhābun ʿaẓīm. ‹68› Fakulū mimmā ghanimtum ḥalālañ-ṭayyibā. Wat-taqul-lāha ʾinnal-lāha Ghafūrur-Raḥīm. ‹69› Yāa ʾayyuhan-Nabiyyu qul limañ-fīi ʾaydīkum-minal-ʾasrāa ʾiñy-yaʿlamil-lāhu fī qulūbikum khayrañy-yuʾtikum khayram-mimmāa ʾukhidha miñkum wa yaghfir lakum. Wal-lāhu Ghafūrur-Raḥīm. ‹70› Wa ʾiñy-yurīdū khiyānataka faqad khānul-lāha miñ-qablu faʾamkana

thrice their own number.) The reference to God's having "lightened the burden" imposed on the believers in this respect makes it clear that both this and the preceding verse imply a divine command couched in terms of exhortation, and not a prediction of events to come (Rāzī).

72 I.e., as an aftermath of a war in a just cause. As almost always in the Qurʾān, an injunction addressed to the Prophet is, by implication, binding on his followers as well. Consequently, the above verse lays down that no person may be taken, or for any time retained, in captivity unless he was taken prisoner in a *jihād* – that is, a holy war in defence of the Faith or of freedom (regarding which see *sūrah* 2, note 167) – and that, therefore, the acquisition of a slave by "peaceful" means, and the keeping of a slave thus acquired, is entirely prohibited: which, to all practical purposes, amounts to a prohibition of slavery as a "social institution". But even with regard to captives taken in war, the Qurʾān ordains (in 47 : 4) that they should be freed after the war is over.

73 This is apparently a reference to the captives taken by the Muslims at Badr, and the discussions among the Prophet's followers as to what should be done with them. ʿUmar ibn al-Khaṭṭāb was of the opinion that they should be killed in revenge for their past misdeeds, and in particular for their persecution of the Muslims before the latters' exodus to Medina: Abū Bakr, on the other hand, pleaded for forgiveness and a release of the prisoners against ransom, supporting his plea with the argument that such an act of mercy might induce some of them to realize the truth of Islam. The Prophet adopted the course of action advocated by Abū Bakr, and released the captives. (The relevant Traditions are quoted by most of the commentators, and especially – with full indication of the sources – by Ṭabarī and Ibn Kathīr.) The reference in the above verse to the "tremendous chastisement" that might have befallen the Muslims "but for a decree (*kitāb*) from God that had already gone forth" – i.e., a course of action fore-ordained in God's knowledge – makes it clear that the killing of the captives would have been an awesome sin.

74 I.e., "If God finds in your hearts a disposition to realize the truth of His message, He will bestow on you faith and, thus, the good of the life to come: and this will outweigh by far your defeat in war and the loss of so many of your friends and companions." Although these words relate primarily to the pagan Quraysh taken prisoner in the battle of Badr, they circumscribe the Islamic attitude towards all unbelieving enemies who might fall into the believers' hands in the course of war. For a further discussion of the problem of prisoners of war, see 47 : 4.

75 I.e., by falsely pretending to a change of heart and an acceptance of Islam in order to be freed from the obligation of paying ransom.

believers] mastery over them.[76] And God is all-knowing, wise. ‹71›

BEHOLD, as for those who have attained to faith and who have forsaken the domain of evil[77] and are striving hard, with their possessions and their lives, in God's cause, as well as those who shelter and succour [them][78] – these are [truly] the friends and protectors of one another.

But as for those who have come to believe without having migrated [to your country][79] – you are in no wise responsible for their protection until such a time as they migrate [to you]. Yet, if they ask you for succour against religious persecution,[80] it is your duty to give [them] this succour – except against a people between whom and yourselves there is a covenant:[81] for God sees all that you do. ‹72›

With all this, [remember that] those who are bent on denying the truth are allies of one another;[82] and unless you act likewise [among yourselves], oppression will reign on earth, and great corruption. ‹73›

مِنْهُمْ وَٱللَّهُ عَلِيمٌ حَكِيمٌ ﴿٧١﴾ إِنَّ ٱلَّذِينَ ءَامَنُوا۟ وَهَاجَرُوا۟ وَجَٰهَدُوا۟
بِأَمْوَٰلِهِمْ وَأَنفُسِهِمْ فِى سَبِيلِ ٱللَّهِ وَٱلَّذِينَ ءَاوَوا۟ وَّنَصَرُوٓا۟ أُو۟لَٰٓئِكَ
بَعْضُهُمْ أَوْلِيَآءُ بَعْضٍ وَٱلَّذِينَ ءَامَنُوا۟ وَلَمْ يُهَاجِرُوا۟ مَا لَكُم مِّن وَلَٰيَتِهِم
مِّن شَىْءٍ حَتَّىٰ يُهَاجِرُوا۟ وَإِنِ ٱسْتَنصَرُوكُمْ فِى ٱلدِّينِ فَعَلَيْكُمُ ٱلنَّصْرُ
إِلَّا عَلَىٰ قَوْمٍ بَيْنَكُمْ وَبَيْنَهُم مِّيثَٰقٌ وَٱللَّهُ بِمَا تَعْمَلُونَ بَصِيرٌ ﴿٧٢﴾ وَٱلَّذِينَ
كَفَرُوا۟ بَعْضُهُمْ أَوْلِيَآءُ بَعْضٍ إِلَّا تَفْعَلُوهُ تَكُن فِتْنَةٌ فِى ٱلْأَرْضِ وَفَسَادٌ
كَبِيرٌ ﴿٧٣﴾

minhum. Wal-lāhu ʿAlīmun Ḥakīm. ‹71› ʾInnal-ladhīna ʾāmanū wa hājarū wa jāhadū biʾamwālihim wa ʾañfusihim fī sabīlil-lāhi wal-ladhīna ʾāwaw-wa naṣarūu ʾulāaʾika baʿḍuhum ʾawliyāaʾu baʿḍ. Wal-ladhīna ʾāmanū wa lam yuhājirū mā lakum-miñw-walāyatihim-miñ-shayʾin ḥattā yuhājirū. Wa ʾinis-tañṣarūkum fid-dīni faʿalaykumun-naṣru ʾillā ʿalā qawmim-baynakum wa baynahum-mīthāq. Wal-lāhu bimā taʿmalūna Baṣīr. ‹72› Wal-ladhīna kafarū baʿḍuhum ʾawliyāaʾu baʿḍ. ʾIllā tafʿalūhu takuñ-fitnatuñ-fil-ʾarḍi wa fasāduñ-kabīr. ‹73›

76 Sc., "and He can, if He so wills, do it again". Thus, the Muslims are enjoined, by implication, to accept the declarations of the captives at their face value, and not to be swayed by mere suspicion of their motives. The possibility of treachery on the part of those captives, and even a later discovery that some of them had indeed played false, should not induce the Muslims to deviate from the course ordained by God.

77 See *sūrah* 2, note 203. Historically, this expression relates to the Meccan Muslims who migrated with the Prophet to Medina; but the sequence makes it clear that the definitions and injunctions provided by this verse are in the nature of a general law, valid for all times. With all this, it should be noted that the *hijrah* referred to here has a preponderantly *physical* connotation, implying an emigration from a non-Muslim country to a country ruled by the Law of Islam.

78 This refers, in the first instance, to the *anṣār* at Medina – that is, to the newly-converted Muslims of that town, who gave shelter and whole-hearted aid to the *muhājirīn* ("emigrants") from Mecca before and after the Prophet's own migration thither: but, similar to the spiritual meaning attaching to the terms *hijrah* and *muhājir*, the expression *anṣār* transcends its purely historical connotation and applies to all believers who aid and give comfort to "those who flee from evil unto God".

79 I.e., those Muslims who, for some reason or other, remain outside the political jurisdiction of the Islamic state. Since not every non-Muslim country is necessarily a "domain of evil", I am rendering the phrase *wa-lam yuhājirū* as "without having migrated [to your country]".

80 Lit., "to succour them in religion": implying that they are exposed to persecution on account of their religious beliefs.

81 I.e., a treaty of alliance or of non-interference in each other's internal affairs. Since in such cases an armed intervention of the Islamic state on behalf of the Muslim citizens of a non-Muslim state would constitute a breach of treaty obligations, the Islamic state is not allowed to seek redress by force. A solution of the problem could conceivably be brought about by negotiations between the two states or, alternatively, by an emigration of the persecuted Muslims.

82 The fact of their being bent on denying the truth of the divine message constitutes, as it were, a common denominator between them, and precludes the possibility of their ever being real friends to the believers. This refers, of course, to relations between communities, and not necessarily between individuals: hence my rendering of the term *awliyāʾ*, in this context, as "allies".

And they who have attained to faith, and who have forsaken the domain of evil and are striving hard in God's cause, as well as those who shelter and succour [them] – it is they, they who are truly believers! Forgiveness of sins awaits them, and a most excellent sustenance.[83] ‹74›

And as for those who henceforth come to believe[84] and who forsake the domain of evil and strive hard [in God's cause] together with you – these [too] shall belong to you;[85] and they who are [thus] closely related have the highest claim on one another in [accordance with] God's decree.[86]

Verily, God has full knowledge of everything. ‹75›

وَٱلَّذِينَ ءَامَنُواْ وَهَاجَرُواْ وَجَـٰهَدُواْ فِى سَبِيلِ ٱللَّهِ وَٱلَّذِينَ ءَاوَواْ وَّنَصَرُوٓاْ
أُوْلَـٰٓئِكَ هُمُ ٱلْمُؤْمِنُونَ حَقًّاۚ لَّهُم مَّغْفِرَةٌ وَرِزْقٌ كَرِيمٌ ﴿٧٤﴾ وَٱلَّذِينَ
ءَامَنُواْ مِنۢ بَعْدُ وَهَاجَرُواْ وَجَـٰهَدُواْ مَعَكُمْ فَأُوْلَـٰٓئِكَ مِنكُمْۚ وَأُوْلُواْ
ٱلْأَرْحَامِ بَعْضُهُمْ أَوْلَىٰ بِبَعْضٍ فِى كِتَـٰبِ ٱللَّهِۗ إِنَّ ٱللَّهَ بِكُلِّ شَىْءٍ عَلِيمٌۢ ﴿٧٥﴾

Wal-ladhīna ᵓāmanū wa hājarū wa jāhadū fī sabīlil-lāhi wal-ladhīna ᵓāwaw-wa naṣarūu ᵓulāaᵓika humul-muᵓminūna ḥaqqā. Lahum-maghfiratuñw-wa rizquñ-karīm. ‹74› Wal-ladhīna ᵓāmanū mim-baᶜdu wa hājarū wa jāhadū maᶜakum faᵓulāaᵓika miñkum. Wa ᵓulul-arḥāmi baᶜḍuhum ᵓawlā bibaᶜḍiñ-fī Kitābil-lāh. ᵓInnal-lāha bikulli shayᵓin ᶜAlīm. ‹75›

83 See note 5 on verse 4 of this *sūrah*.

84 Although the expression *alladhīna āmanū* (lit., "those who have come to believe") is in the past tense, the words *min baᶜd* ("afterwards" or "henceforth") indicate a future time in relation to the time at which this verse was revealed: hence, the whole sentence beginning with *alladhīna āmanū* must be understood as referring to the future (*Manār* X, 134 f.; see also Rāzī's commentary on this verse).

85 I.e., they, too, shall belong to the brotherhood of Islam, in which the faith held in common supplies the decisive bond between believer and believer.

86 The classical commentators are of the opinion that this last clause refers to actual family relations, as distinct from the spiritual brotherhood based on a community of faith. According to these commentators, the above sentence abolished the custom which was prevalent among the early Muslims, whereby the *anṣār* ("the helpers" – i.e., the newly-converted Muslims of Medina) concluded, individually, symbolic ties of brotherhood with the *muhājirīn* ("the emigrants" from Mecca), who, almost without exception, arrived at Medina in a state of complete destitution: ties of brotherhood, that is, which entitled every *muhājir* to a share in the property of his "brother" from among the *anṣār*, and, in the event of the latter's death, to a share in the inheritance left by him. The above verse is said to have prohibited such arrangements by stipulating that only actual close relations should henceforth have a claim to inheritance. To my mind, however, this interpretation is not convincing. Although the expression *ūlu 'l-arḥām* is derived from the noun *raḥm* (also spelt *riḥm* and *raḥim*), which literally signifies "womb", one should not forget that it is tropically used in the sense of "kinship", "relationship" or "close relationship" *in general* (i.e., not merely blood-relationship). Thus, "in the classical language, *ūlu 'l-arḥām* means *any* relations: and in law, any relations that have no portion [of the inheritances termed *farāᵓiḍ*]" (Lane III, 1056, citing, among other authorities, the *Tāj al-ᶜArūs*). In the present instance, the reference to "close relations" comes at the end of a passage which centres on the injunction that the believers must be "the friends and protectors (*awliyāᵓ*) of one another", and that all later believers shall, similarly, be regarded as members of the Islamic brotherhood. If the reference to "close relations" were meant to be taken in its *literal* sense and conceived as alluding to laws of inheritance, it would be quite out of tune with the rest of the passage, which stresses the bonds of faith among true believers, as well as the moral obligations arising from these bonds.

In my opinion, therefore, the above verse has no bearing on laws of inheritance, but is meant to summarize, as it were, the lesson of the preceding verses: All true believers, of all times, form one single community in the deepest sense of this word; and all who are thus closely related in spirit have the highest claim on one another in accordance with God's decree that "all believers are brethren" (49 : 10).

The Ninth Sūrah

At-Tawbah (Repentance)

Medina Period

IN CONTRAST with every other *sūrah* of the Qurʾān, *At-Tawbah* is not preceded by the invocation "In the name of God, the Most Gracious, the Dispenser of Grace". This undoubtedly deliberate omission is responsible for the view held by many Companions of the Prophet that *At-Tawbah* is in reality a continuation of *Al-ʾAnfāl*, and that the two together constitute one single *sūrah* (Zamakhsharī), notwithstanding the fact that an interval of about seven years separates the revelation of the one from that of the other. Although there is no evidence that the Prophet himself ever made a statement to this effect (Rāzī), the inner relationship between *At-Tawbah* and *Al-ʾAnfāl*, is unmistakable. Both are largely devoted to problems of war between the believers and the deniers of the truth; towards the end of *Al-ʾAnfāl*, there is a mention of treaties and of the possibility that these treaties might be treacherously violated by the unbelievers – a theme that is continued and developed at the beginning of *At-Tawbah*; and both *Al-ʾAnfāl* and *At-Tawbah* dwell, in the main, on the moral distinction between the believers, on the one hand, and their enemies and ill-wishers, on the other.

A very large part of *At-Tawbah* is connected with the conditions prevailing at Medina before the Prophet's expedition to Tabūk in the year 9 H., and the vacillating spirit displayed by some of his nominal followers. There is hardly any doubt that almost the whole of the *sūrah* was revealed shortly before, during and immediately after the campaign, and most of it at the time of the long march from Medina to Tabūk. (Regarding the reasons for this campaign, see notes 59 and 142.)

The title of the *sūrah* is based on the frequent references in it to the repentance (*tawbah*) of the erring ones and to its acceptance by God. Some of the Companions called it *Al-Barāaʾah* ("Disavowal") after the first word occurring in it; and Zamakhsharī mentions also several other titles by which the *sūrah* was designated by the Prophet's Companions and their immediate successors.

At-Tawbah concludes the so-called "seven long sūrahs" (that is, the distinct, almost self-contained group of chapters beginning with *Al-Baqarah* and ending with the combination of *Al-ʾAnfāl* and *At-Tawbah*); and it is significant that some of the last verses of this group (namely, 9 : 124-127) return to the theme which dominates the early part of *Al-Baqarah* (2 : 6-20): the problem of "those in whose hearts is disease" and who cannot attain to faith because they are "bent on denying the truth" whenever it conflicts with their preconceived notions and their personal likes and dislikes: the perennial problem of people whom no spiritual message can convince because they do not *want* to grasp the truth (9 : 127), and who thereby "deceive none but themselves, and perceive it not" (2 : 9).

سورة التوبة -٩- مدنية
وآياتها تسع وعشرون ومائة

نصف الحزب

DISAVOWAL by God and His Apostle [is herewith announced] unto those who ascribe divinity to aught beside God, [and] with whom you [O believers] have made a covenant.[1] ‹1›

[Announce unto them:] "Go, then, [freely] about the earth for four months[2] – but know that you can never elude God, and that, verily, God shall bring disgrace upon all who refuse to acknowledge the truth!" ‹2›

And a proclamation from God and His Apostle [is herewith made] unto all mankind on this day of the Greatest Pilgrimage:[3] "God disavows all who ascribe divinity to aught beside Him, and [so does] His Apostle. Hence, if you repent, it shall be for your own good; and if you turn away, then know that you can never elude God!"

And unto those who are bent on denying the truth give thou [O Prophet] the tiding of grievous chastisement. ‹3›

بَرَآءَةٌ مِّنَ ٱللَّهِ وَرَسُولِهِۦٓ إِلَى ٱلَّذِينَ عَٰهَدتُّم مِّنَ ٱلْمُشْرِكِينَ ﴿١﴾ فَسِيحُوا۟
فِى ٱلْأَرْضِ أَرْبَعَةَ أَشْهُرٍ وَٱعْلَمُوٓا۟ أَنَّكُمْ غَيْرُ مُعْجِزِى ٱللَّهِ ۙ وَأَنَّ ٱللَّهَ
مُخْزِى ٱلْكَٰفِرِينَ ﴿٢﴾ وَأَذَٰنٌ مِّنَ ٱللَّهِ وَرَسُولِهِۦٓ إِلَى ٱلنَّاسِ يَوْمَ ٱلْحَجِّ
ٱلْأَكْبَرِ أَنَّ ٱللَّهَ بَرِىٓءٌ مِّنَ ٱلْمُشْرِكِينَ ۙ وَرَسُولُهُۥ ۚ فَإِن تُبْتُمْ فَهُوَ خَيْرٌ لَّكُمْ ۖ
وَإِن تَوَلَّيْتُمْ فَٱعْلَمُوٓا۟ أَنَّكُمْ غَيْرُ مُعْجِزِى ٱللَّهِ ۗ وَبَشِّرِ ٱلَّذِينَ كَفَرُوا۟
بِعَذَابٍ أَلِيمٍ ﴿٣﴾

Barāaʾatum-minal-lāhi wa Rasūlihīi ʾilal-ladhīna ʿāhattum-minal-mushrikīn. (1) Fasīḥū fil-ʾarḍi ʾarbaʿata ʾashhuriñw-waʿ-lamūu ʾannakum ghayru muʿjizil-lāhi wa ʾannal-lāha mukhzil-kāfirīn. (2) Wa ʾadhānum-minal-lāhi wa Rasūlihīi ʾilan-nāsi yawmal-Ḥajjil-ʿAkbari ʾannal-lāha barīiʾum-minal-mushrikīna wa Rasūluh. Faʾiñ-tubtum fahuwa khayrul-lakum; wa ʾiñ-tawallaytum faʿlamūu ʾannakum ghayru muʿjizil-lāh. Wa bashshiril-ladhīna kafarū biʿadhābin ʾalīm. (3)

---

1 Sc., "which they (the unbelievers) have deliberately broken" (Ṭabarī, Baghawī, Zamakhsharī, Rāzī); see also verse 4, which relates to such of the unbelievers as remain faithful to their treaty obligations towards the believers. The above passage connects with verses 56-58 of the preceding *sūrah* (*Al-Anfāl*). The noun *barāʾah* (derived from the verb *bariʾa*, "he became free [of something]" or "quit of having any part [in something]") signifies a declaration of being free or quit of any bond, moral or contractual, with the person or persons concerned (see Lane I, 178); with reference to God – or the Apostle speaking in God's name – it is best rendered as "disavowal".

2 These words, addressed to the *mushrikīn* ("those who ascribe divinity to aught beside God") who have deliberately broken the treaties in force between them and the believers, indicate a cancellation of all treaty obligations on the latters' part. The period of four months which is to elapse between this announcement and the beginning (or resumption) of hostilities is a further elaboration of the injunction "cast it [i.e., the treaty] back at them in an equitable manner", given in 8 : 58 with reference to a breach of covenant by hostile unbelievers (see also note 62 on verse 58 of *sūrah* 8).

3 There is no unanimity among the commentators as to what is meant by "the day of the Greatest Pilgrimage". Most of them assume that it refers to the pilgrimage in the year 9 H., in which the Prophet himself did not participate, having entrusted Abū Bakr with the office of *amīr al-ḥajj*. This very fact, however, makes it improbable that the designation "the Greatest Pilgrimage" should have been given in the Qurʾān to this particular pilgrimage. On the other hand, there exists a Tradition on the authority of ʿAbd Allāh ibn ʿUmar to the effect that the Prophet described in these very words the last pilgrimage led by himself in 10 H. and known to history as the Farewell Pilgrimage (Zamakhsharī, Rāzī); one may, therefore, assume that it is this which is alluded to here. If this assumption is correct, it would justify the conclusion that verses 3 and 4 of this *sūrah* were revealed during the Farewell Pilgrimage, i.e.,

But excepted shall be[4] – from among those who ascribe divinity to aught beside God – [people] with whom you [O believers] have made a covenant and who thereafter have in no wise failed to fulfil their obligations towards you, and neither have aided anyone against you: observe, then, your covenant with them until the end of the term agreed with them.[5] Verily, God loves those who are conscious of Him. ‹4›
And so, when the sacred months are over,[6] slay those who ascribe divinity to aught beside God wherever you may come upon them,[7] and take them captive, and besiege them, and lie in wait for them at every conceivable place.[8] Yet if they repent, and take to prayer, and render the purifying dues, let them go their way: for, behold, God is much-forgiving, a dispenser of grace.[9] ‹5›

إِلَّا ٱلَّذِينَ عَٰهَدتُّم مِّنَ ٱلْمُشْرِكِينَ ثُمَّ لَمْ يَنقُصُوكُمْ شَيْـًٔا وَلَمْ يُظَٰهِرُوا۟
عَلَيْكُمْ أَحَدًا فَأَتِمُّوٓا۟ إِلَيْهِمْ عَهْدَهُمْ إِلَىٰ مُدَّتِهِمْ ۚ إِنَّ ٱللَّهَ يُحِبُّ
ٱلْمُتَّقِينَ ﴿٤﴾ فَإِذَا ٱنسَلَخَ ٱلْأَشْهُرُ ٱلْحُرُمُ فَٱقْتُلُوا۟ ٱلْمُشْرِكِينَ حَيْثُ
وَجَدتُّمُوهُمْ وَخُذُوهُمْ وَٱحْصُرُوهُمْ وَٱقْعُدُوا۟ لَهُمْ كُلَّ مَرْصَدٍ ۚ فَإِن تَابُوا۟
وَأَقَامُوا۟ ٱلصَّلَوٰةَ وَءَاتَوُا۟ ٱلزَّكَوٰةَ فَخَلُّوا۟ سَبِيلَهُمْ ۚ إِنَّ ٱللَّهَ غَفُورٌ
رَّحِيمٌ ﴿٥﴾

ʾIllal-ladhīna ʿāhattum-minal-mushrikīna thumma lam yañquṣūkum shayʾañw-wa lam yuẓāhirū ʿalaykum ʾaḥadañ-faʾatimmūu ʾilayhim ʿahdahum ʾilā muddatihim. ʾInnal-lāha yuḥibbul-muttaqīn. ﴿4﴾ Faʾidhañ-salakhal-ʾAshhurul-Ḥurumu faqtulul-mushrikīna ḥaythu wajattumūhum wa khudhūhum waḥ-ṣurūhum waq-ʿudū lahum kulla marṣad. Faʾiñ-tābū wa ʾaqāmuṣ-Ṣalāta wa ʾātawuz-Zakāta fakhallū sabīlahum; ʾinnal-lāha Ghafūrur-Raḥīm. ﴿5﴾

shortly before the Prophet's death. This might explain the – otherwise perplexing – statement, reliably attributed to the Prophet's Companion Al-Barāʾ (Bukhārī, *Kitāb at-Tafsīr*), that *At-Tawbah* was the last *sūrah* revealed to the Prophet: for, although it is established beyond any doubt that the *sūrah* as a whole was revealed in 9 H. and was followed by several other parts of the Qurʾān, e.g., *Al-Māʾidah*, it is possible that what Al-Barāʾ had in mind were only these two key-verses (3 and 4) of *At-Tawbah*, which conceivably were revealed during the Farewell Pilgrimage.

4 I.e., from the cancellation, explained in note 2 above, of the treaties which they have concluded with the believers.

5 Lit., "until their term".

6 According to a pre-Islamic custom prevalent in Arabia, the months of Muḥarram, Rajab, Dhu 'l-Qaʿdah and Dhu 'l-Ḥijjah were considered "sacred" in the sense that all tribal warfare had to cease during those months. It was with a view to preserving these periods of truce and thus to promoting peace among the frequently warring tribes that the Qurʾān did not revoke, but rather confirmed, this ancient custom. See also 2 : 194 and 217.

7 Read in conjunction with the two preceding verses, as well as with 2 : 190-194, the above verse relates to warfare *already in progress* with people who have become guilty of a breach of treaty obligations and of aggression.

8 I.e., "do everything that may be necessary and advisable in warfare". The term *marṣad* denotes "any place from which it is possible to perceive the enemy and to observe his movements" (*Manār* X, 199).

9 As I have pointed out on more than one occasion, every verse of the Qurʾān must be read and interpreted against the background of the Qurʾān as a whole. The above verse, which speaks of a possible conversion to Islam on the part of "those who ascribe divinity to aught beside God" with whom the believers are at war, must, therefore, be considered in conjunction with several fundamental Qurʾanic ordinances. One of them, "There shall be no coercion in matters of faith" (2 : 256), lays down categorically that any attempt at a forcible conversion of unbelievers is prohibited – which preclude the possibility of the Muslims' demanding or expecting that a defeated enemy should embrace Islam as the price of immunity. Secondly, the Qurʾān ordains, "Fight in God's cause against those who wage war against you; but do not commit aggression, for, verily, God does not love aggressors" (2 : 190); and, "if they do not let you be, and do not offer you peace, and do not stay their hands, seize them and slay them whenever you come upon them: and it is against these that We have clearly empowered you [to make war]" (4 : 91). Thus, war is permissible only in self-defence (see *sūrah* 2, notes 167 and 168), with the further proviso that "if they desist – behold, God is much-forgiving, a dispenser of grace" (2 : 192), and "if they desist, then all hostility shall cease" (2 : 193). Now the enemy's conversion to Islam – expressed in the words, "if they repent, and take to prayer [lit., "establish prayer"] and render the purifying dues (*zakāh*)" – is no more than one, and by no means the only, way of their "desisting from hostility"; and the reference to it in verses 5 and 11 of this *sūrah* certainly does not imply an alternative of "conversion or death", as some unfriendly critics of Islam choose to assume. Verses 4 and 6 give a further elucidation of the attitude which the believers are enjoined to adopt towards such of the unbelievers as are not hostile to them. (In this connection, see also 60 : 8-9).

وَإِنْ أَحَدٌ مِّنَ ٱلْمُشْرِكِينَ ٱسْتَجَارَكَ فَأَجِرْهُ حَتَّىٰ يَسْمَعَ كَلَـٰمَ ٱللَّهِ ثُمَّ
أَبْلِغْهُ مَأْمَنَهُۥ ۚ ذَٰلِكَ بِأَنَّهُمْ قَوْمٌ لَّا يَعْلَمُونَ ﴿٦﴾ كَيْفَ يَكُونُ
لِلْمُشْرِكِينَ عَهْدٌ عِندَ ٱللَّهِ وَعِندَ رَسُولِهِۦٓ إِلَّا ٱلَّذِينَ عَـٰهَدتُّمْ عِندَ
ٱلْمَسْجِدِ ٱلْحَرَامِ ۖ فَمَا ٱسْتَقَـٰمُوا۟ لَكُمْ فَٱسْتَقِيمُوا۟ لَهُمْ ۚ إِنَّ ٱللَّهَ يُحِبُّ
ٱلْمُتَّقِينَ ﴿٧﴾ كَيْفَ وَإِن يَظْهَرُوا۟ عَلَيْكُمْ لَا يَرْقُبُوا۟ فِيكُمْ إِلًّا وَلَا ذِمَّةً ۚ
يُرْضُونَكُم بِأَفْوَٰهِهِمْ وَتَأْبَىٰ قُلُوبُهُمْ وَأَكْثَرُهُمْ فَـٰسِقُونَ ﴿٨﴾ ٱشْتَرَوْا۟
بِـَٔايَـٰتِ ٱللَّهِ ثَمَنًا قَلِيلًا فَصَدُّوا۟ عَن سَبِيلِهِۦٓ ۚ إِنَّهُمْ سَآءَ مَا كَانُوا۟
يَعْمَلُونَ ﴿٩﴾ لَا يَرْقُبُونَ فِى مُؤْمِنٍ إِلًّا وَلَا ذِمَّةً ۚ وَأُو۟لَـٰٓئِكَ هُمُ ٱلْمُعْتَدُونَ ﴿١٠﴾

Wa ʾin ʾaḥadum-minal-mushrikīnas-tajāraka faʾajirhu ḥattā yasmaʿa Kalāmal-lāhi thumma ʾablighhu maʾmanah. Dhālika biʾannahum qawmul-lā yaʿlamūn. ﴿6﴾ Kayfa yakūnu lilmushrikīna ʿahdun ʿiñdal-lāhi wa ʿiñda Rasūlihīi ʾillal-ladhīna ʿāhattum ʿiñdal-Masjidil-Ḥarām. Famas-taqāmū lakum fas-taqīmū lahum. ʾInnal-lāha yuḥibbul-muttaqīn. ﴿7﴾ Kayfa wa ʾiñy-yaẓharū ʿalaykum lā yarqubū fīkum ʾillañw-wa lā dhimmah. Yurḍūnakum-biʾafwāhihim wa taʾbā qulūbuhum wa ʾaktharuhum fāsiqūn. ﴿8﴾ ʾIshtaraw biʾĀyātil-lāhi thamanañ-qalīlañ-faṣaddū ʿañ-sabīlih. ʾInnahum sāaʾa mā kānū yaʿmalūn. ﴿9﴾ Lā yarqubūna fī muʾminin ʾillañw-wa lā dhimmah. Wa ʾulāaʾika humul-muʿtadūn. ﴿10﴾

And if any of those who ascribe divinity to aught beside God seeks thy protection,[10] grant him protection, so that he might [be able to] hear the word of God [from thee]; and thereupon convey him to a place where he can feel secure:[11] this, because they [may be] people who [sin only because they] do not know [the truth]. ‹6›

HOW COULD they who ascribe divinity to aught beside God be granted a covenant by God and His Apostle,[12] unless it be those [of them] with whom you [O believers] have made a covenant in the vicinity of the Inviolable House of Worship?[13] [As for the latter,] so long as they remain true to you, be true to them: for, verily, God loves those who are conscious of Him. ‹7›
How [else could it be]?[14] – since, if they [who are hostile to you] were to overcome you, they would not respect any tie [with you,] nor any obligation to protect [you].[15] They seek to please you with their mouths, the while their hearts remain averse [to you]; and most of them are iniquitous. ‹8› God's messages have they bartered away for a trifling gain, and have thus turned away from His path: evil, behold, is all that they are wont to do, ‹9› respecting no tie and no protective obligation with regard to a believer; and it is they, they who transgress the bounds of what is right![16] ‹10›

10 Lit., "seeks to become thy neighbour": a metaphorical expression denoting a demand for protection, based on the ancient Arabian custom (strongly affirmed by Islam) of honouring and protecting a neighbour to the best of one's ability.

11 Lit., "his place of security" (*maʾmanahu*) – i.e., "let him rejoin his homeland" (Rāzī), which implies that he is free to accept or not to accept the message of the Qurʾān: a further re-affirmation of the Qurʾanic injunction that "there shall be no coercion in matters of faith" (2 : 256).

12 Lit., "have a covenant before [or "in the sight of"] God and before His Apostle": i.e., be protected by those who believe in God and His Apostle. The specific reference to the latter is meant to stress the fact that he speaks and acts in the name of God.

13 Cf. verse 4 above. The "covenant" alluded to is the truce-agreement concluded in 6 H. at Ḥudaybiyyah, in the vicinity of Mecca, between the Prophet and the pagan Quraysh, which was (and was obviously intended to remain) a model of the self-restraint and the tolerance expected of true believers with regard to such of the unbelievers as are not openly hostile to them.

14 This connects with the opening clause of the preceding verse, and relates to the *hostile* among "those who ascribe divinity to aught beside God".

15 The term *ill* signifies any tie that arises from a compact or from blood-relationship, and which imposes on both parties the obligation to protect each other (cf. Lane I, 75); the latter implication is expressed in the word *dhimmah*, which literally denotes a "covenant of protection".

16 Or: "who are the aggressors" – the two expressions being, in this context, synonymous.

Yet if they repent, and take to prayer, and render the purifying dues, they become your brethren in faith:[17] and clearly do We spell out these messages unto people of [innate] knowledge! ‹11›
But if they break their solemn pledges after having concluded a covenant,[18] and revile your religion, then fight against these archetypes of faithlessness[19] who, behold, have no [regard for their own] pledges, so that they might desist [from aggression]. ‹12› Would you, perchance, fail to fight against people who have broken their solemn pledges, and have done all that they could to drive the Apostle away,[20] and have been first to attack you? Do you hold them in awe? Nay, it is God alone of whom you ought to stand in awe,[21] if you are [truly] believers! ‹13›
Fight against them! God will chastise them by your hands, and will bring disgrace upon them, and will succour you against them; and He will soothe the bosoms of those who believe, ‹14› and will remove the wrath that is in their hearts.
And God will turn in His mercy unto whom He wills:[22] for, God is all-knowing, wise. ‹15›
Do you [O believers] think that you will be spared[23] unless God takes cognizance of your having striven hard [in His cause][24] without seeking help from any but God and His Apostle and those who believe in Him?[25] For, God is aware of all that you do. ‹16›

فَإِن تَابُوا۟ وَأَقَامُوا۟ ٱلصَّلَوٰةَ وَءَاتَوُا۟ ٱلزَّكَوٰةَ فَإِخْوَٰنُكُمْ فِى ٱلدِّينِ ۗ وَنُفَصِّلُ
ٱلْـَٔايَـٰتِ لِقَوْمٍ يَعْلَمُونَ ﴿١١﴾ وَإِن نَّكَثُوٓا۟ أَيْمَـٰنَهُم مِّنۢ بَعْدِ عَهْدِهِمْ وَطَعَنُوا۟ فِى
دِينِكُمْ فَقَـٰتِلُوٓا۟ أَئِمَّةَ ٱلْكُفْرِ ۙ إِنَّهُمْ لَآ أَيْمَـٰنَ لَهُمْ لَعَلَّهُمْ يَنتَهُونَ ﴿١٢﴾ أَلَا
تُقَـٰتِلُونَ قَوْمًا نَّكَثُوٓا۟ أَيْمَـٰنَهُمْ وَهَمُّوا۟ بِإِخْرَاجِ ٱلرَّسُولِ وَهُم بَدَءُوكُمْ أَوَّلَ مَرَّةٍ ۚ
أَتَخْشَوْنَهُمْ ۚ فَٱللَّهُ أَحَقُّ أَن تَخْشَوْهُ إِن كُنتُم مُّؤْمِنِينَ ﴿١٣﴾ قَـٰتِلُوهُمْ يُعَذِّبْهُمُ ٱللَّهُ
بِأَيْدِيكُمْ وَيُخْزِهِمْ وَيَنصُرْكُمْ عَلَيْهِمْ وَيَشْفِ صُدُورَ قَوْمٍ مُّؤْمِنِينَ ﴿١٤﴾
وَيُذْهِبْ غَيْظَ قُلُوبِهِمْ ۗ وَيَتُوبُ ٱللَّهُ عَلَىٰ مَن يَشَآءُ ۗ وَٱللَّهُ عَلِيمٌ حَكِيمٌ ﴿١٥﴾ أَمْ
حَسِبْتُمْ أَن تُتْرَكُوا۟ وَلَمَّا يَعْلَمِ ٱللَّهُ ٱلَّذِينَ جَـٰهَدُوا۟ مِنكُمْ وَلَمْ يَتَّخِذُوا۟ مِن دُونِ
ٱللَّهِ وَلَا رَسُولِهِۦ وَلَا ٱلْمُؤْمِنِينَ وَلِيجَةً ۚ وَٱللَّهُ خَبِيرٌۢ بِمَا تَعْمَلُونَ ﴿١٦﴾

Faʾiñ-tābū wa ʾaqāmuṣ-Ṣalāta wa ʾātawuz-Zakāta faʾikhwānukum fid-dīn. Wa nufaṣṣilul-ʾĀyāti liqawmiñy-yaʿlamūn. (11) Wa ʾin-nakathūu ʾaymānahum-mim-baʿdi ʿahdihim wa ṭaʿanū fī dīnikum faqātilūu ʾaʾimmatal-kufri ʾinnahum lāa ʾaymāna lahum laʿallahum yañtahūn. (12) ʾAlā tuqātilūna qawmañ-nakathūu ʾaymānahum wa hammū biʾikhrājir-Rasūli wa hum-badaʾūkum ʾawwala marrah. ʾAtakhshawnahum. Fallāhu ʾaḥaqqu ʾañ-takhshawhu ʾiñ-kuñtum-muʾminīn. (13) Qātilūhum yuʿadhdhibhumul-lāhu biʾaydīkum wa yukhzihim wa yañṣurkum ʿalayhim wa yashfi ṣudūra qawmim-muʾminīna, (14) wa yudhhib ghayẓa qulūbihim. Wa yatūbul-lāhu ʿalā mañy-yashāaʾ. Wal-lāhu ʿAlīmun Ḥakīm. (15) ʾAm ḥasibtum ʾañ-tutrakū wa lammā yaʿlamil-lāhul-ladhīna jāhadū miñkum wa lam yattakhidhū miñ-dūnil-lāhi wa lā Rasūlihī wa lal-muʾminīna walījah. Wal-lāhu Khabīrum-bimā taʿmalūn. (16)

17 See note 9 above.

18 Lit., "if they break their oaths after their covenant". This obviously refers to unbelievers who, without having renounced their own beliefs, have concluded treaties of friendship with the Muslims. Their subsequent "breaking of the solemn pledges" is an allusion to the breach of the truce of Ḥudaybiyyah by the pagan Quraysh, which, in turn, led to the conquest of Mecca by the Muslims in the year 8 H.

19 The word *imām* (of which *aʾimmah* is the plural) denotes not merely a "leader" but also – and primarily – "a person who is an object of imitation by his followers" (*Tāj al-ʿArūs*): hence, a "model", or "exemplar", or "archetype". The term *kufr*, which usually signifies a "denial of [or "refusal to acknowledge"] the truth", is rendered here as "faithlessness" because it refers, specifically, to a deliberate breaking of solemn engagements.

20 I.e., from Mecca, thus bringing about his and his followers' exodus (*hijrah*) to Medina.

21 Lit., "God is more worthy (*aḥaqq*) that you should stand in awe of Him".

22 This relates to the unbelievers with whom the Muslims are at war: for God may, if He so wills, bring about a change of heart in them and guide them to a realization of the truth (Baghawī and Zamakhsharī; see also *Manār* X, 236).

23 Lit., "left [alone]", i.e., without being tried by means of suffering and hardship.

24 Lit., "while God has not yet taken cognizance of those of you who have striven hard". For an explanation of God's "taking cognizance", see 3 : 142 and the corresponding note.

25 Lit., "without having taken any intimate helper (*walījah*) other than God and His Apostle and the believers".

ثلاثة ارباع الحزب

مَا كَانَ لِلْمُشْرِكِينَ أَن يَعْمُرُواْ مَسَـٰجِدَ ٱللَّهِ شَـٰهِدِينَ عَلَىٰٓ أَنفُسِهِم بِٱلْكُفْرِ
أُوْلَـٰٓئِكَ حَبِطَتْ أَعْمَـٰلُهُمْ وَفِى ٱلنَّارِ هُمْ خَـٰلِدُونَ ﴿١٧﴾ إِنَّمَا يَعْمُرُ مَسَـٰجِدَ
ٱللَّهِ مَنْ ءَامَنَ بِٱللَّهِ وَٱلْيَوْمِ ٱلْـَٔاخِرِ وَأَقَامَ ٱلصَّلَوٰةَ وَءَاتَى ٱلزَّكَوٰةَ وَلَمْ يَخْشَ
إِلَّا ٱللَّهَ فَعَسَىٰٓ أُوْلَـٰٓئِكَ أَن يَكُونُواْ مِنَ ٱلْمُهْتَدِينَ ﴿١٨﴾ ۞ أَجَعَلْتُمْ سِقَايَةَ
ٱلْحَآجِّ وَعِمَارَةَ ٱلْمَسْجِدِ ٱلْحَرَامِ كَمَنْ ءَامَنَ بِٱللَّهِ وَٱلْيَوْمِ ٱلْـَٔاخِرِ وَجَـٰهَدَ
فِى سَبِيلِ ٱللَّهِ لَا يَسْتَوُۥنَ عِندَ ٱللَّهِ وَٱللَّهُ لَا يَهْدِى ٱلْقَوْمَ ٱلظَّـٰلِمِينَ ﴿١٩﴾
ٱلَّذِينَ ءَامَنُواْ وَهَاجَرُواْ وَجَـٰهَدُواْ فِى سَبِيلِ ٱللَّهِ بِأَمْوَٰلِهِمْ وَأَنفُسِهِمْ أَعْظَمُ
دَرَجَةً عِندَ ٱللَّهِ وَأُوْلَـٰٓئِكَ هُمُ ٱلْفَآئِزُونَ ﴿٢٠﴾

Mā kāna lil-mushrikīna añy-yaᶜmurū masājidal-lāhi shāhidīna ᶜalāa ʾañfusihim-bilkufr. ʾUlāaʾika ḥabiṭat ʾaᶜmāluhum wa fin-nāri hum khālidūn. (17) ʾInnamā yaᶜmuru masājidal-lāhi man ʾāmana billāhi wal-Yawmil-ʾĀkhiri wa ʾaqāmaṣ-Ṣalāta wa ʾātaz-Zakāta wa lam yakhsha ʾillal-lāh. Faᶜasāa ʾulāaʾika ʾañy-yakūnū minal-muhtadīn. (18) ۞ ʾAjaᶜaltum siqāyatal-ḥāajji wa ᶜimāratal-Masjidil-Ḥarāmi kaman ʾāmana billāhi wal-Yawmil-ʾĀkhiri wa jāhada fī sabīlil-lāh. Lā yastawūna ᶜiñdal-lāh. Wal-lāhu lā yahdil-qawmaẓ-ẓālimīn. (19) ʾAlladhīna ʾāmanū wa hājarū wa jāhadū fī sabīlil-lāhi biʾamwālihim wa ʾañfusihim ʾaᶜẓamu darajatan ᶜiñdal-lāhi wa ʾulāaʾika humul-fāaʾizūn. (20)

IT IS NOT for those who ascribe divinity to aught beside God to visit or tend[26] God's houses of worship, the while [by their beliefs] they bear witness against themselves that they are denying the truth. It is they whose works shall come to nought, and they who in the fire shall abide![27] ‹17› Only he should visit or tend God's houses of worship who believes in God and the Last Day, and is constant in prayer, and spends in charity, and stands in awe of none but God: for [only such as] these may hope to be among the right-guided![28] ‹18› Do you, perchance, regard the [mere] giving of water to pilgrims, and the tending of the Inviolable House of Worship as being equal to [the works of] one who believes in God and the Last Day and strives hard in God's cause? These [things] are not equal in the sight of God.[29] And God does not grace with His guidance people who [deliberately] do wrong. ‹19› Those who believe, and who have forsaken the domain of evil[30] and have striven hard in God's cause with their possessions and their lives have the highest rank In the sight of God; and it is they, they who shall triumph [in the end]! ‹20›

26 In its transitive form, the verb *ᶜamara* comprises the meanings of both visiting and maintaining a place; hence my rendering of *an yaᶜmurū* as "that they should visit or tend".

27 Some of the commentators conclude from this verse that "those who ascribe divinity to aught beside God" are not *allowed* to enter mosques ("God's houses of worship"). This conclusion, however, is entirely untenable in view of the fact that in 9 H. – that is, after the revelation of this *sūrah* – the Prophet himself lodged a deputation of the pagan Banū Thaqīf in the mosque at Medina (Rāzī). Thus, the above verse expresses no more than the *moral incongruity* of the unbelievers' "visiting or tending God's houses of worship". As regards their exclusion from the central mosque of Islam at Mecca ("the Inviolable House of Worship"), see verse 28 of this *sūrah*.

28 Lit., "it may well be that these will be among the right-guided". However, according to Abū Muslim (as quoted by Rāzī), as well as the great grammarian Sībawayh (see *Manār* X, 253). the word *ᶜasā*, usually signifying "it may well be", is here indicative of the hope which the above-mentioned believers may entertain.

29 Many commentators see in this verse an allusion to the boast of the pagan Quraysh, before the Muslim conquest of Mecca, that they were superior to all other people on account of their guardianship of the Ka'bah and their providing water (*siqāyah*) to pilgrims; and on being taken prisoner by the Muslims in the battle of Badr, Al-ᶜAbbās, the Prophet's uncle, excused on these very grounds his failure to accompany the Muslims on their exodus from Mecca to Medina (Ṭabarī). It is probable, however, that this verse has yet another, deeper import. According to an authentic Tradition quoted by Muslim, Abū Dāʾūd and Ibn Ḥibbān (as well as by Ṭabarī) one of the Prophet's Companions stated in the mosque of Medina, "I would not care, after having accepted Islam, to do any good deed beyond providing water to the pilgrims!" – whereupon another of the Companions declared, "Nay, [I would rather take charge of] the maintenance of the Inviolable House of Worship." But yet another Companion declared, "Nay, struggle (*jihād*) in God's cause is far better than what you have mentioned!" A short time afterwards the above Qurʾān-verse was revealed to the Prophet. It would, therefore, appear that what is meant here is the superior value of faith in God and struggle in His cause as compared with acts which, however meritorious, are concerned only with outward forms: in brief, the immense superiority of real self-surrender to God over mere ritual.

30 See *sūrah* 2, note 203, and *sūrah* 4, note 124.

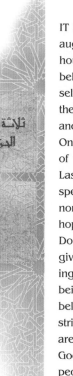

Their Sustainer gives them the glad tiding of the grace [that flows] from Him, and of [His] goodly acceptance, and of the gardens which await them, full of lasting bliss, ‹21› therein to abide beyond the count of time. Verily, with God is a mighty reward! ‹22›

O YOU who have attained to faith! Do not take your fathers and your brothers for allies if a denial of the truth is dearer to them than faith: for those of you who ally themselves with them – it is they, they who are evildoers![31] ‹23›

Say: "If your fathers and your sons and your brothers and your spouses and your clan, and the worldly goods which you have acquired, and the commerce whereof you fear a decline, and the dwellings in which you take pleasure – [if all these] are dearer to you than God and His Apostle and the struggle in His cause, then wait until God makes manifest His will;[32] and [know that] God does not grace iniquitous folk with His guidance." ‹24›

Indeed, God has succoured you on many battlefields, [when you were few;] and [He did so, too,] on the Day of Ḥunayn, when you took pride in your great numbers and they proved of no avail whatever to you – for the earth, despite all its vastness, became [too] narrow for you and you turned back, retreating:[33] ‹25› whereupon God bestowed from on high His [gift of]

يُبَشِّرُهُمْ رَبُّهُم بِرَحْمَةٍ مِّنْهُ وَرِضْوَٰنٍ وَجَنَّٰتٍ لَّهُمْ فِيهَا نَعِيمٌ مُّقِيمٌ ﴿٢١﴾
خَٰلِدِينَ فِيهَآ أَبَدًا ۚ إِنَّ ٱللَّهَ عِندَهُۥٓ أَجْرٌ عَظِيمٌ ﴿٢٢﴾ يَٰٓأَيُّهَا ٱلَّذِينَ ءَامَنُوا۟
لَا تَتَّخِذُوٓا۟ ءَابَآءَكُمْ وَإِخْوَٰنَكُمْ أَوْلِيَآءَ إِنِ ٱسْتَحَبُّوا۟ ٱلْكُفْرَ عَلَى
ٱلْإِيمَٰنِ ۚ وَمَن يَتَوَلَّهُم مِّنكُمْ فَأُو۟لَٰٓئِكَ هُمُ ٱلظَّٰلِمُونَ ﴿٢٣﴾ قُلْ إِن كَانَ
ءَابَآؤُكُمْ وَأَبْنَآؤُكُمْ وَإِخْوَٰنُكُمْ وَأَزْوَٰجُكُمْ وَعَشِيرَتُكُمْ وَأَمْوَٰلٌ
ٱقْتَرَفْتُمُوهَا وَتِجَٰرَةٌ تَخْشَوْنَ كَسَادَهَا وَمَسَٰكِنُ تَرْضَوْنَهَآ أَحَبَّ
إِلَيْكُم مِّنَ ٱللَّهِ وَرَسُولِهِۦ وَجِهَادٍ فِى سَبِيلِهِۦ فَتَرَبَّصُوا۟ حَتَّىٰ يَأْتِىَ ٱللَّهُ
بِأَمْرِهِۦ ۗ وَٱللَّهُ لَا يَهْدِى ٱلْقَوْمَ ٱلْفَٰسِقِينَ ﴿٢٤﴾ لَقَدْ نَصَرَكُمُ ٱللَّهُ فِى
مَوَاطِنَ كَثِيرَةٍ ۙ وَيَوْمَ حُنَيْنٍ ۙ إِذْ أَعْجَبَتْكُمْ كَثْرَتُكُمْ فَلَمْ تُغْنِ عَنكُمْ شَيْـًٔا
وَضَاقَتْ عَلَيْكُمُ ٱلْأَرْضُ بِمَا رَحُبَتْ ثُمَّ وَلَّيْتُم مُّدْبِرِينَ ﴿٢٥﴾ ثُمَّ أَنزَلَ ٱللَّهُ

Yubashshiruhum Rabbuhum-biraḥmatim-minhu wa
riḍwāniñw-wa jannātil-lahum fīhā naᶜīmum-muqīm.
21 Khālidīna fīhāa ᵓabadā. ᵓInnal-lāha ᶜiñdahūu ᵓajrun
ᶜaẓīm. 22 Yāa ᵓayyuhal-ladhīna ᵓāmanū lā tattakhi-
dhūu ᵓābāaᵓakum wa ᵓikhwānakum ᵓawliyāaᵓa ᵓinis-
taḥabbul-kufra ᶜalal-ᵓīmān. Wa mañy-yatawallahum-
miñkum faᵓulāaᵓika humuẓ-ẓālimūn. 23 Qul ᵓiñ-kāna
ᵓābāaᵓukum wa ᵓabnāaᵓukum wa ᵓikhwānukum wa
ᵓazwājukum wa ᶜashīratukum wa ᵓamwāluniq-
taraftumūhā wa tijāratuñ-takhshawna kasādahā wa
masākinu tarḍawnahāa ᵓaḥabba ᵓilaykum-minal-lāhi
wa Rasūlihī wa jihādiñ-fī sabīlihī fatarabbaṣū ḥattā
yaᵓtiyal-lāhu biᵓamrih. Wal-lāhu lā yahdil-qawmal-
fāsiqīn. 24 Laqad naṣarakumul-lāhu fī mawāṭina
kathīrah. Wa yawma Ḥunaynin ᵓidh ᵓaᶜjabatkum
kathratukum falam tughni ᶜañkum shayᵓañw-wa
ḍāqat ᶜalaykumul-ᵓarḍu bimā raḥubat thumma
wallaytum-mudbirīn. 25 Thumma ᵓañzalal-hāhu

31 The term *walāyah* ("alliance" or "friendship") is used in this context in the sense of an alliance against other believers, as in 3 : 28. (Regarding the wider, spiritual implications of this expression, see *sūrah* 4, note 154.) That it does not refer to "friendship" in the sense of normal human affection is obvious from the many exhortations in the Qurᵓān to be good to one's parents and kinsfolk; and, more explicitly, from 60 : 8-9, where the believers are reminded that friendly relations with unbelievers who are not hostile to the Muslim community are permissible, and even desirable. (See also *Manār* X, 269 ff., where a similar interpretation is advanced.)

32 Or: "brings about [the fulfilment of] His command". This may be an allusion to the Day of Judgment or – more probably – to the inevitable degeneration and decline of communities which place narrow self-interest above ethical values. In particular, this passage rejects the tendency to regard ties of kinship and national affiliation (expressed in the term "your clan") as the decisive factors of social behaviour, and postulates *ideology* ("God and His Apostle and the struggle in His cause") as the only valid basis on which a believer's life – individually and socially – should rest.

33 The battle of Ḥunayn, a valley situated on one of the roads leading from Mecca to Ṭāᵓif, took place in the year 8 H., shortly after the conquest of Mecca by the Muslims. The latters' opponents were the pagan tribes of Hawāzin (in whose territory the valley lay) and their allies, the Banū Thaqīf. The Muslim army – reinforced by many newly-

سَكِينَتَهُۥ عَلَىٰ رَسُولِهِۦ وَعَلَى ٱلْمُؤْمِنِينَ وَأَنزَلَ جُنُودًا لَّمْ تَرَوْهَا وَعَذَّبَ
ٱلَّذِينَ كَفَرُوا۟ ۚ وَذَٰلِكَ جَزَآءُ ٱلْكَٰفِرِينَ ﴿٢٦﴾ ثُمَّ يَتُوبُ ٱللَّهُ مِنۢ بَعْدِ
ذَٰلِكَ عَلَىٰ مَن يَشَآءُ ۗ وَٱللَّهُ غَفُورٌ رَّحِيمٌ ﴿٢٧﴾ يَٰٓأَيُّهَا ٱلَّذِينَ ءَامَنُوٓا۟ إِنَّمَا
ٱلْمُشْرِكُونَ نَجَسٌ فَلَا يَقْرَبُوا۟ ٱلْمَسْجِدَ ٱلْحَرَامَ بَعْدَ عَامِهِمْ هَٰذَا ۚ وَإِنْ
خِفْتُمْ عَيْلَةً فَسَوْفَ يُغْنِيكُمُ ٱللَّهُ مِن فَضْلِهِۦٓ إِن شَآءَ ۚ إِنَّ ٱللَّهَ عَلِيمٌ
حَكِيمٌ ﴿٢٨﴾ قَٰتِلُوا۟ ٱلَّذِينَ لَا يُؤْمِنُونَ بِٱللَّهِ وَلَا بِٱلْيَوْمِ ٱلْءَاخِرِ وَلَا

sakīnatahū ᶜalā Rasūlihī wa ᶜalal-muᵓminīna wa ᵓañzala junūdal-lam tarawhā wa ᶜadhdhabal-ladhīna kafarū. Wa dhālika jazāaᵓul-kāfirīn. (26) Thumma yatūbul-lāhu mim-baᶜdi dhālika ᶜalā mañy-yashāaᵓ. Wal-lāhu Ghafūrur-Raḥīm. (27) Yāa ᵓayyuhal-ladhīna ᵓāmanūu ᵓinnamal-mushrikūna najasuñ-falā yaqrabul-Masjidal-Ḥarāma baᶜda ᶜāmihim hādhā. Wa ᵓin khiftum ᶜaylatañ-fasawfa yughnīkumul-lāhu miñ-faḍlihīi ᵓiñ-shāaᵓ. ᵓInnal-lāha ᶜAlīmun Ḥakīm. (28) Qātilul-ladhīna lā yuᵓminūna billāhi wa lā bilYawmil-ᵓĀkhiri wa lā

inner peace upon His Apostle and upon the believers, and bestowed [upon you] from on high forces which you could not see,[34] and chastised those who were bent on denying the truth: for such is the recompense of all who deny the truth! ‹26›
But with all this,[35] God will turn in His mercy unto whom He wills: for God is much-forgiving, a dispenser of grace.[36] ‹27›

O YOU who have attained to faith! Those who ascribe divinity to aught beside God are nothing but impure:[37] and so they shall not approach the Inviolable House of Worship from this year onwards.[38] And should you fear poverty, then [know that] in time God will enrich you out of His bounty, if He so wills:[39] for, verily, God is all-knowing, wise! ‹28›
[And] fight against those who – despite having been vouchsafed revelation [aforetime][40] – do not [truly] believe either in God or the Last Day, and do not consider

converted Meccans – comprised about twelve thousand men, whereas the Hawāzin and Thaqīf had only one-third of that number at their disposal. Relying on their great numerical superiority, the Muslims were over-confident and, apparently, careless. In the narrow defiles beyond the oasis of Ḥunayn they fell into an ambush prepared by the tribesmen and began to retreat in disorder after heavy losses had been inflicted on them by the bedouin archers. It was only the example of the Prophet and his early adherents (the Meccan *muhājirūn* and the *anṣār* from Medina) that saved the day and turned the initial rout of the Muslims into a decisive victory. It is to this battle that verses 25 and 26 refer, pointing out that true succour can come only from God, and that great numbers, ties of kinship and worldly wealth are of no avail if they are "dearer to you than God and His Apostle and the struggle in His cause" (see preceding verse).

34 I.e., spiritual forces. Cf. 3 : 124-125 (relating to the battle of Uḥud) and the corresponding note, as well as 8 : 9 (which refers to the battle of Badr). The *spiritual* nature of this aid is clearly implied in the phrase, "forces which you could not [or "did not"] see".

35 Lit., "then, after this".

36 Most of the commentators (e.g., Ṭabarī, Baghawī, Zamakhsharī, Ibn Kathīr) understand this verse as relating to the unbelievers and having a general import; Rāzī, however, thinks that it refers to the believers who behaved badly at the opening stage of the battle of Ḥunayn. In my opinion, the former interpretation is preferable. (See also last sentence of verse 15 and note 22 above.)

37 The term *najas* ("impure") occurs in the Qurᵓān only in this one instance, and carries an exclusively spiritual meaning (see *Manār* X, 322 ff.). To this day, the bedouin of Central and Eastern Arabia – who, contrary to the modern town-dwellers, have preserved the purity of the Arabic idiom to a high degree – describe a person who is immoral, faithless or wicked as *najas*. "The Inviolable House of Worship" (*al-masjid al-ḥarām*) is, of course, the Kaᶜbah and, by implication, the whole of the territory of Mecca: which explains the next sentence.

38 Lit., "after this their year" – i.e., after the year 9 H., in which this *sūrah* was revealed.

39 This is an allusion to the apprehension on the part of some Muslims (and not only at the time of the revelation of this verse) that an exclusion of unbelievers from living in or visiting Mecca might lead to a loss of its position as a centre of trade and commerce, and thus to an impoverishment of its inhabitants.

40 Lit., "such of those who were vouchsafed revelation [aforetime] as do not believe . . .", etc. In accordance with the fundamental principle – observed throughout my interpretation of the Qurᵓān – that all of its statements and ordinances are mutually complementary and cannot, therefore, be correctly understood unless they are considered as

forbidden that which God and His Apostle have forbidden,[41] and do not follow the religion of truth [which God has enjoined upon them],[42] till they [agree to] pay the exemption tax with a willing hand, after having been humbled [in war].[43] ‹29›

يُحَرِّمُونَ مَا حَرَّمَ ٱللَّهُ وَرَسُولُهُۥ وَلَا يَدِينُونَ دِينَ ٱلْحَقِّ مِنَ ٱلَّذِينَ أُوتُوا۟ ٱلْكِتَٰبَ حَتَّىٰ يُعْطُوا۟ ٱلْجِزْيَةَ عَن يَدٍ وَهُمْ صَٰغِرُونَ ﴿٢٩﴾

yuḥarrimūna mā ḥarramal-lāhu wa Rasūluhū wa lā yadīnūna dīnal-ḥaqqi minal-ladhīna ᵓūtul-Kitāba ḥattā yuᶜṭul-jizyata ᶜañy-yadiñw-wa hum ṣāghirūn. ‹29›

parts of one integral whole, this verse, too, must be read in the context of the clear-cut Qurᵓanic rule that war is permitted only in self-defence (see 2 : 190-194, and the corresponding notes). In other words, the above injunction to fight is relevant only in the event of aggression committed against the Muslim community or state, or in the presence of an unmistakable threat to its security: a view which has been shared by that great Islamic thinker, Muḥammad ᶜAbduh. Commenting on this verse, he declared: "Fighting has been made obligatory in Islam only for the sake of defending the truth and its followers. . . . All the campaigns of the Prophet were defensive in character; and so were the wars undertaken by the Companions in the earliest period [of Islam]" (*Manār* X, 332).

41 This, to my mind, is the key-phrase of the above ordinance. The term "apostle" is obviously used here in its generic sense and applies to all the prophets on whose teachings the beliefs of the Jews and the Christians are supposed to be based – in particular, to Moses and (in the case of the Christians) to Jesus as well (*Manār* X, 333 and 337). Since, earlier in this sentence, the people alluded to are accused of so grave a sin as wilfully refusing to believe in God and the Last Day (i.e., in life after death and man's individual responsibility for his doings on earth), it is inconceivable that they should subsequently be blamed for comparatively minor offences against their religious law: consequently, the stress on their "not forbidding that which God and His apostle have forbidden" must refer to something which is as grave, or almost as grave, as disbelief in God. In the context of an ordinance enjoining war against them, this "something" can mean only, one thing – namely, *unprovoked aggression*: for it is this that has been forbidden by God through *all the apostles* who were entrusted with conveying His message to man. Thus. the above verse must be understood as a call to the believers to fight against such – and only such – of the nominal followers of earlier revelation as deny their own professed beliefs by committing aggression against the followers of the Qurᵓān (cf. *Manār* X, 338).

42 See in this connection the statement (in 5 : 13-14) that the Jews and the Christians "have forgotten much of what they had been told to bear in mind".

43 Sc., "and having become incorporated in the Islamic state". The term *jizyah*, rendered by me as "exemption tax", occurs in the Qurᵓān only once, but its meaning and purpose have been fully explained in many authentic Traditions. It is intimately bound up with the concept of the Islamic state as an *ideological organization:* and this is a point which must always be borne in mind if the real purport of this tax is to be understood. In the Islamic state, every able-bodied Muslim is obliged to take up arms in *jihād* (i.e., in a just war in God's cause) whenever the freedom of his faith or the political safety of his community is imperilled: in other words, every able-bodied Muslim is liable to compulsory military service. Since this is, primarily, a *religious* obligation, non-Muslim citizens, who do not subscribe to the ideology of Islam, cannot in fairness be expected to assume a similar burden. On the other hand, they must be accorded full protection of all their civic rights and of their religious freedom: and it is in order to compensate the Muslim community for this unequal distribution of civic burdens that a special tax is levied on non-Muslim citizens (*ahl adh-dhimmah*, lit., "covenanted [or "protected"] people", i.e., non-Muslims whose safety is statutorily assured by the Muslim community). Thus, *jizyah* is no more and no less than an exemption tax in lieu of military service and in compensation for the "covenant of protection" (*dhimmah*) accorded to such citizens by the Islamic state. (The term itself is derived from the verb *jazā*, "he rendered [something] as a satisfaction", or "as a compensation [in lieu of something else]" – cf. Lane II, 422.) No fixed rate has been set either by the Qurᵓān or by the Prophet for this tax; but from all available Traditions it is evident that it is to be considerably lower than the tax called *zakāh* ("the purifying dues") to which Muslims are liable and which – because it is a specifically *Islamic* religious duty – is naturally not to be levied on non-Muslims. Only such of the non-Muslim citizens who, if they were Muslims, would be expected to serve in the armed forces of the state are liable to the payment of *jizyah*, provided that they can easily afford it. Accordingly, all non-Muslim citizens whose personal status or condition would automatically free them from the obligation to render military service are statutorily – that is, on the basis of clear-cut ordinances promulgated by the Prophet – exempted from the payment of *jizyah*: (a) all women, (b) males who have not yet reached full maturity, (c) old men, (d) all sick or crippled men, (e) priests and monks. All non-Muslim citizens who *volunteer* for military service are obviously exempted from the payment of *jizyah*.

My rendering of the expression *ᶜan yad* (lit., "out of hand") as "with a willing hand", that is, without reluctance, is based on one of several explanations offered by Zamakhsharī in his commentary on the above verse. Rashīd Riḍāᵓ, taking the word *yad* in its metaphorical significance of "power" or "ability", relates the phrase *ᶜan yad* to the financial ability of the person liable to the payment of *jizyah* (see *Manār* X, 342): an interpretation which is undoubtedly

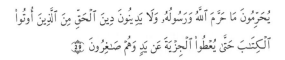

AND THE JEWS say, "Ezra is God's son," while the Christians say, "The Christ is God's son." Such are the sayings which they utter with their mouths, following in spirit assertions made in earlier times by people who denied the truth![44] [They deserve the imprecation:] "May God destroy them!"[45]
How perverted are their minds![46] ‹30›
They have taken their rabbis and their monks – as well as the Christ, son of Mary – for their lords beside God,[47] although they had been bidden to worship none but the One God, save whom there is no deity: the One who is utterly remote, in His limitless glory, from anything to which they may ascribe a share in His divinity! ‹31›
They want to extinguish God's [guiding] light with their utterances:[48] but God will not allow [this to pass], for He has willed to spread His light in all its fullness,[49] however hateful this may be to all who deny the truth. ‹32›

وَقَالَتِ ٱلْيَهُودُ عُزَيْرٌ ٱبْنُ ٱللَّهِ وَقَالَتِ ٱلنَّصَٰرَى ٱلْمَسِيحُ ٱبْنُ ٱللَّهِ ۖ
ذَٰلِكَ قَوْلُهُم بِأَفْوَٰهِهِمْ ۖ يُضَٰهِـُٔونَ قَوْلَ ٱلَّذِينَ كَفَرُوا۟ مِن قَبْلُ ۚ قَٰتَلَهُمُ
ٱللَّهُ ۚ أَنَّىٰ يُؤْفَكُونَ ﴿٣٠﴾ ٱتَّخَذُوٓا۟ أَحْبَارَهُمْ وَرُهْبَٰنَهُمْ أَرْبَابًا مِّن دُونِ ٱللَّهِ
وَٱلْمَسِيحَ ٱبْنَ مَرْيَمَ وَمَآ أُمِرُوٓا۟ إِلَّا لِيَعْبُدُوٓا۟ إِلَٰهًا وَٰحِدًا ۖ لَّآ إِلَٰهَ إِلَّا
هُوَ ۚ سُبْحَٰنَهُۥ عَمَّا يُشْرِكُونَ ﴿٣١﴾ يُرِيدُونَ أَن يُطْفِـُٔوا۟ نُورَ ٱللَّهِ بِأَفْوَٰهِهِمْ
وَيَأْبَى ٱللَّهُ إِلَّآ أَن يُتِمَّ نُورَهُۥ وَلَوْ كَرِهَ ٱلْكَٰفِرُونَ ﴿٣٢﴾

Wa qālatil-Yahūdu ᶜUzayrunib-nul-lāhi wa qālatin-Naṣāral-Masīḥub-nul-lāh. Dhālika qawluhum-biˀafwāhihim; yuḍāhiˀūna qawlal-ladhīna kafarū miñ-qabl. Qātalahumul-lāhu ˀannā yuˀfakūn. ﴿٣٠﴾ ˀIttakhadhūu ˀaḥbārahum wa ruhbānahum ˀarbābam-miñ-dūnil-lāhi wal-Masīḥab-na Maryam wa māa ˀumirūu ˀillā liyaᶜbudūu ˀIlāhañw-Wāḥidā. Lāa ˀilāha ˀillā Huwa subḥānahū ᶜammā yushrikūn. ﴿٣١﴾ Yurīdūna ˀañy-yuṭfiˀū nūral-lāhi biˀafwāhihim wa yaˀbal-lāhu ˀillāa ˀañy-yutimma nūrahū wa law karihal-kāfirūn. ﴿٣٢﴾

justified in view of the accepted definition of this tax.

44 This statement is connected with the preceding verse, which speaks of the erring followers of earlier revelation. The charge of *shirk* ("the ascribing of divinity [or "divine qualities"] to aught beside God") is levelled against both the Jews and the Christians in amplification, as it were, of the statement that they "do not follow the religion of truth [which God has enjoined upon them]".

As regards the belief attributed to the Jews that Ezra (or, in the Arabicized form of this name, ᶜUzayr) was "God's son", it is to be noted that almost all classical commentators of the Qurˀān agree in that only the Jews of Arabia, and not *all* Jews, have been thus accused. (According to a Tradition on the authority of Ibn ᶜAbbās – quoted by Ṭabarī in his commentary on this verse – some of the Jews of Medina once said to Muḥammad, "How could we follow thee when thou hast forsaken our *qiblah* and dost not consider Ezra a son of God?") On the other hand, Ezra occupies a unique position in the esteem of all Jews, and has always been praised by them in the most extravagant terms. It was he who restored and codified the Torah after it had been lost during the Babylonian Exile, and "edited" it in more or less the form which it has today; and thus "he promoted the establishment of an exclusive, legalistic type of religion that became dominant in later Judaism – (*Encyclopaedia Britannica*, 1963. vol. IX, p.15). Ever since then he has been venerated to such a degree that his verdicts on the Law of Moses have come to be regarded by the Talmudists as being practically equivalent to the Law itself: which, in Qurˀanic ideology, amounts to the unforgivable sin of *shirk*, inasmuch as it implies the elevation of a human being to the status of a *quasi*-divine law-giver and the blasphemous attribution to him – albeit metaphorically – of the quality of "sonship" in relation to God. Cf. in this connection Exodus iv, 22-23 ("Israel is My son") or Jeremiah xxxi, 9 ("I am a father to Israel"): expressions to which, because of their idolatrous implications, the Qurˀān takes strong exception.

45 My interpolation, between brackets, of the words "they deserve the imprecation" is based on Zamakhsharī's and Rāzī's convincing interpretation of this phrase. Originally, the Arabs used the expression "may God destroy him" in the sense of a direct imprecation; but already in pre-Qurˀanic Arabic it had assumed the character of an idiomatic device meant to circumscribe anything that is extremely strange or horrifying: and, according to many philologists, "this, rather than its literal meaning, is the purport [of this phrase] here" (*Manār* X. 399).

46 See *sūrah* 5, note 90.

47 Cf. 3 : 64.

48 Lit., "with their mouths" – an allusion to the "sayings" (i.e., beliefs) mentioned in verse 30.

49 Lit., "except (*illā*) that He bring His light to completion" or "to perfection". The expression "for He has willed" (i.e., contrary to what the erring ones want), is here elliptically implied by means of the particle *illā*.

He it is who has sent forth His Apostle with the [task of spreading] guidance and the religion of truth, to the end that He may cause it to prevail over all [false] religion[50] – however hateful this may be to those who ascribe divinity to aught beside God. ‹33› O you who have attained to faith! Behold, many of the rabbis and monks do indeed wrongfully devour men's possessions and turn [others] away, from the path of God. But as for all who lay up treasures of gold and silver and do not spend them for the sake of God[51] – give them the tiding of grieveous suffering [in the life to come]: ‹34› on the Day when that [hoarded wealth] shall be heated in the fire of hell and their foreheads and their sides and their backs branded therewith,[52] [those sinners shall be told:] "These are the treasures which you have laid up for yourselves! Taste, then, [the evil of] your hoarded treasures!" ‹35›

BEHOLD, the number of months, in the sight of God, is twelve months, [laid down] in God's decree on the day when He created the heavens and the earth; [and] out of these, four are sacred:[53] this is the ever-true law [of God]. Do not, then, sin against yourselves with regard to these [months].[54]

هُوَ ٱلَّذِىٓ أَرْسَلَ رَسُولَهُۥ بِٱلْهُدَىٰ وَدِينِ ٱلْحَقِّ لِيُظْهِرَهُۥ عَلَى ٱلدِّينِ كُلِّهِۦ وَلَوْ
كَرِهَ ٱلْمُشْرِكُونَ ﴿٣٣﴾ ۞ يَٰٓأَيُّهَا ٱلَّذِينَ ءَامَنُوٓا۟ إِنَّ كَثِيرًا مِّنَ ٱلْأَحْبَارِ
وَٱلرُّهْبَانِ لَيَأْكُلُونَ أَمْوَٰلَ ٱلنَّاسِ بِٱلْبَٰطِلِ وَيَصُدُّونَ عَن سَبِيلِ ٱللَّهِ ۗ وَٱلَّذِينَ
يَكْنِزُونَ ٱلذَّهَبَ وَٱلْفِضَّةَ وَلَا يُنفِقُونَهَا فِى سَبِيلِ ٱللَّهِ فَبَشِّرْهُم بِعَذَابٍ
أَلِيمٍ ﴿٣٤﴾ يَوْمَ يُحْمَىٰ عَلَيْهَا فِى نَارِ جَهَنَّمَ فَتُكْوَىٰ بِهَا جِبَاهُهُمْ وَجُنُوبُهُمْ
وَظُهُورُهُمْ ۖ هَٰذَا مَا كَنَزْتُمْ لِأَنفُسِكُمْ فَذُوقُوا۟ مَا كُنتُمْ تَكْنِزُونَ ﴿٣٥﴾ إِنَّ عِدَّةَ
ٱلشُّهُورِ عِندَ ٱللَّهِ ٱثْنَا عَشَرَ شَهْرًا فِى كِتَٰبِ ٱللَّهِ يَوْمَ خَلَقَ ٱلسَّمَٰوَٰتِ
وَٱلْأَرْضَ مِنْهَآ أَرْبَعَةٌ حُرُمٌ ۚ ذَٰلِكَ ٱلدِّينُ ٱلْقَيِّمُ ۚ فَلَا تَظْلِمُوا۟ فِيهِنَّ أَنفُسَكُمْ حزب 20

Huwal-ladhīi ʾarsala Rasūlahū bilhudā wa dīnil-ḥaqqi liyuẓhirahū ʿalad-dīni kullihī wa law karihal-mushrikūn. (33) ۞ Yāa ʾayyuhal-ladhīna ʾāmanūu ʾinna kathīram-minal-ʾaḥbāri war-ruhbāni layaʾkulūna ʾamwālan-nāsi bilbāṭili wa yaṣuddūna ʿañ-sabīlil-lāh. Wal-ladhīna yaknizūnadh-dhahaba wal-fiḍḍata wa lā yuñfiqūnahā fī sabīlil-lāhi fabash-shirhum-biʿadhābin ʾalīm. (34) Yawma yuḥmā ʿalayhā fī nāri jahannama fatukwā bihā jibāhuhum wa junūbuhum wa ẓuhūruhum. Hādhā mā kanaztum liʾañfusikum fadhūqū mā kuñtum taknizūn. (35) ʾInna ʿiddatash-shuhūri ʿiñdal-lāhith-nā ʿashara shahrañ-fī Kitābil-lāhi yawma khalaqas-samāwāti wal-arḍa minhāa ʾarbaʿatun ḥurum. Dhālikad-dīnul-qayyim. Falā taẓlimū fīhinna ʾañfusakum.

50 Cf. 3 : 19 – "the only [true] religion in the sight of God is [man's] self-surrender unto Him". See also 61 : 8-9.

51 Most probably this is, in the first instance, an allusion to the wealth of the Jewish and Christian communities, and their misuse of this wealth. Some of the commentators, however, are of the opinion that the reference is wider, comprising all people, including Muslims, who hoard their wealth without spending anything thereof on righteous causes.

52 Cf. the parallel allegory, in 3 : 180, of the suffering which will befall the avaricious and the niggardly in the life to come. Regarding the eschatological implications of this and similar allegories, see Appendix I.

53 This connects with the subsequent reference to fighting against "those who ascribe divinity to aught beside God" (see next note). The months spoken of here are lunar months, progressively rotating through the seasons of the solar year (see *sūrah* 2, note 165). Since reckoning by the easily observable lunar months is more natural than by the arbitrarily fixed months of the solar year, it is described in this passage as "the ever-true law (*dīn*) [of God]". The four "sacred months" during which warfare was considered blasphemous in pre-Islamic Arabia – a view which has been confirmed by Islam (see note 6 above) – are Muḥarram, Rajab, Dhu 'l-Qaʿdah and Dhu 'l-Ḥijjah.

54 In their endeavour to obviate certain disadvantages for their trade caused by the seasonal rotation of the lunar months, the pagan Arabs used to intercalate a thirteenth month in the third, sixth and eighth year of every eight-year period, with a view to making the lunar calendar more or less stationary, and thus roughly corresponding to the solar year. An acceptance of this unwarranted intercalation by the Muslims would have tied the Mecca pilgrimage as well as the fast of Ramaḍān to fixed seasons, and would thus have made, permanently, the performance of these religious duties either too exacting or too easy; and in either case the believers would have been offending against the spiritual purpose underlying these duties – which is the meaning of the words "do not sin against yourselves with regard to

And fight against those who ascribe divinity to aught beside God, all together – just as they fight against you, [O believers,] all together[55] – and know that God is with those who are conscious of Him. ‹36›
The intercalation [of months] is but one more instance of [their] refusal to acknowledge the truth[56] – [a means] by which those who are bent on denying the truth are led astray. They declare this [intercalation] to be permissible in one year and forbidden in [another] year,[57] in order to conform [outwardly] to the number of months which God has hallowed: and thus they make allowable what God has forbidden.[58] Goodly seems unto them the evil of their own doings, since God does not grace with His guidance people who refuse to acknowledge the truth. ‹37›

O YOU who have attained to faith! What is amiss with you that, when you are called upon, "Go forth to war in God's cause," you cling heavily to the earth?[59]

وَقَٰتِلُوا۟ ٱلْمُشْرِكِينَ كَآفَّةً كَمَا يُقَٰتِلُونَكُمْ كَآفَّةً ۚ وَٱعْلَمُوٓا۟ أَنَّ ٱللَّهَ مَعَ
ٱلْمُتَّقِينَ ﴿٣٦﴾ إِنَّمَا ٱلنَّسِىٓءُ زِيَادَةٌ فِى ٱلْكُفْرِ ۖ يُضَلُّ بِهِ ٱلَّذِينَ كَفَرُوا۟ يُحِلُّونَهُۥ
عَامًا وَيُحَرِّمُونَهُۥ عَامًا لِّيُوَاطِـُٔوا۟ عِدَّةَ مَا حَرَّمَ ٱللَّهُ فَيُحِلُّوا۟ مَا حَرَّمَ ٱللَّهُ ۚ زُيِّنَ
لَهُمْ سُوٓءُ أَعْمَٰلِهِمْ ۗ وَٱللَّهُ لَا يَهْدِى ٱلْقَوْمَ ٱلْكَٰفِرِينَ ﴿٣٧﴾ يَٰٓأَيُّهَا ٱلَّذِينَ
ءَامَنُوا۟ مَا لَكُمْ إِذَا قِيلَ لَكُمُ ٱنفِرُوا۟ فِى سَبِيلِ ٱللَّهِ ٱثَّاقَلْتُمْ إِلَى ٱلْأَرْضِ

Wa qātilul-mushrikīna kāaffatañ-kamā yuqātilūnakum kāaffah. Waᶜ-lamūu ᵓannal-lāha maᶜal-muttaqīn. ﴿36﴾ ᵓInna-man-nasīiᵓu ziyādatuñ-fil-kufri yuḍallu bihil-ladhīna kafarū yuḥillūnahū ᶜāmañw-wa yuḥarrimūnahū ᶜāmal-liyuwāṭiᵓū ᶜiddata mā ḥarramal-lāhu fayuḥillū mā ḥarramal-lāh. Zuyyina lahum sūuᵓu ᵓaᶜmālihim. Wal-lāhu lā yahdil-qawmal-kāfirīn. ﴿37﴾ Yāa ᵓayyuhal-ladhīna ᵓāmanū mā lakum ᵓidhā qīla lakumuñ-firū fī sabīlil-lāhith-thāqaltum ᵓilal-ᵓarḍ.

these [months]": i.e., by following, without any warrant from God, a custom devised by "those who ascribe divinity to aught beside Him", to whom the sequence refers.

55 I.e., "just as all of them are, as it were, united against you in their rejection of the truth, be united against them in your readiness for self-sacrifice". As regards the circumstances in which the Muslims are authorized to make war against unbelievers, see the earlier parts of this *sūrah*, and especially verses 12-13, as well as 2 : 190-194, where the general principles relating to war are laid down.

56 Lit., "is but an increase in denying the truth (*kufr*)". The term *nasīᵓ*, rendered by me as "intercalation", may also be translated as "postponement" – i.e., the postponement of lunar months by means of the periodical intercalation of a thirteenth month, as practiced by the pre-Islamic Arabs with a view to bringing the traditional lunar calendar, for purely worldly reasons, into accord with the solar year (see note 54 above). The Qurᵓān describes this practice as an additional instance of *kufr* because it contravenes God's declared will as regards the observance of the lunar calendar in respect of various religious duties (cf. the preceding verse, as well as 2 : 189 and the corresponding note 165).

57 An allusion to the arbitrary manner in which the pre-Islamic Arabs intercalated a thirteenth month in the third, sixth and eighth year of every eight-year period.

58 By means of the intercalation spoken of above, the pagan Arabs did in most years keep the number of months to twelve; but by divorcing the four "sacred months" (Muḥarram, Rajab, Dhu 'l-Qaᶜdah and Dhu 'l-Ḥijjah), from their proper lunar context they obviously profaned and perverted the natural law.

59 I.e., "you are sluggish in your response, clinging to the life of this world". This verse – as well as most of this *sūrah* from here onward – alludes to the campaign of Tabūk, in the year 9 H. The immediate reason for this expedition was the information which the Prophet received to the effect that the Byzantines, made apprehensive by the rapid growth of Islam in Arabia and incited by the Prophet's enemy Abū ᶜĀmir (see note 142 on verse 107 of this *sūrah*), were assembling large forces on the confines of the Peninsula with a view to marching against Medina and overthrowing the Muslims. To guard against such an assault, the Prophet assembled the strongest force the Muslims were capable of, and set out in the month of Rajab, 9 H., towards the frontier. On reaching Tabūk, about half-way between Medina and Damascus, the Prophet ascertained that the Byzantines were either not yet ready to invade Arabia or had entirely given up the idea for the time being; and so – in accordance with the Islamic principle that war may be waged only in self-defence – he returned with his followers to Medina without engaging in hostilities.

Would you content yourselves with [the comforts of] this worldly life in preference to [the good of] the life to come? But the enjoyment of life in this world is but a paltry thing when compared with the life to come! ‹38›
If you do not go forth to war [in God's cause], He will chastise you with grievous chastisement, and will place another people in your stead – whereas you shall in no wise harm Him: for, God has the power to will anything. ‹39›
If you do not succour the Apostle,[60] then [know that God will do so – just as] God succoured him at the time when those who were bent on denying the truth drove him away, [and he was but] one of two:[61] when these two were [hiding] in the cave, [and] the Apostle said to his companion, "Grieve not: verily, God is with us."[62] And thereupon God bestowed upon him from on high His [gift of] inner peace, and aided him with forces which you could not see,[63] and brought utterly low the cause of those who were bent on denying the truth, whereas God's cause remained supreme:[64] for God is almighty, wise. ‹40›
Go forth to war, whether it be easy or difficult [for you],[65] and strive hard in God's cause with your possessions and your lives: this is for your own good – if you but knew it! ‹41›

أَرَضِيتُم بِٱلْحَيَوٰةِ ٱلدُّنْيَا مِنَ ٱلْـَٔاخِرَةِ ۚ فَمَا مَتَٰعُ ٱلْحَيَوٰةِ ٱلدُّنْيَا فِى
ٱلْـَٔاخِرَةِ إِلَّا قَلِيلٌ ﴿٣٨﴾ إِلَّا تَنفِرُوا۟ يُعَذِّبْكُمْ عَذَابًا أَلِيمًا وَيَسْتَبْدِلْ
قَوْمًا غَيْرَكُمْ وَلَا تَضُرُّوهُ شَيْـًٔا ۗ وَٱللَّهُ عَلَىٰ كُلِّ شَىْءٍ قَدِيرٌ ﴿٣٩﴾ إِلَّا
تَنصُرُوهُ فَقَدْ نَصَرَهُ ٱللَّهُ إِذْ أَخْرَجَهُ ٱلَّذِينَ كَفَرُوا۟ ثَانِىَ ٱثْنَيْنِ إِذْ هُمَا فِى
ٱلْغَارِ إِذْ يَقُولُ لِصَٰحِبِهِۦ لَا تَحْزَنْ إِنَّ ٱللَّهَ مَعَنَا ۖ فَأَنزَلَ ٱللَّهُ سَكِينَتَهُۥ
عَلَيْهِ وَأَيَّدَهُۥ بِجُنُودٍ لَّمْ تَرَوْهَا وَجَعَلَ كَلِمَةَ ٱلَّذِينَ كَفَرُوا۟ ٱلسُّفْلَىٰ ۗ وَكَلِمَةُ
ٱللَّهِ هِىَ ٱلْعُلْيَا ۗ وَٱللَّهُ عَزِيزٌ حَكِيمٌ ﴿٤٠﴾ ٱنفِرُوا۟ خِفَافًا وَثِقَالًا وَجَٰهِدُوا۟
بِأَمْوَٰلِكُمْ وَأَنفُسِكُمْ فِى سَبِيلِ ٱللَّهِ ۚ ذَٰلِكُمْ خَيْرٌ لَّكُمْ إِن كُنتُمْ
تَعْلَمُونَ ﴿٤١﴾

ʾAraḍītum-bilḥayātid-dunyā minal-ʾĀkhirah. Famā matāʿul-ḥayātid-dunyā fil-ʾĀkhirati ʾillā qalīl. (38) ʾIllā tañfirū yuʿadhdhibkum ʿadhāban ʾalīmañw-wa yastabdil qawman ghayrakum wa lā taḍurrūhu shayʾā. Wal-lāhu ʿalā kulli shayʾiñ-Qadīr. (39) ʾIllā tañṣurūhu faqad naṣarahul-lāhu ʾidh ʾakhrajahul-ladhīna kafarū thāniyath-nayni ʾidh humā fil-ghāri ʾidh yaqūlu liṣāḥibihī lā taḥzan ʾinnal-lāha maʿanā. Faʾañzalal-lāhu sakīnatahū ʿalayhi wa ʾayyadahū bijunūdil-lam tarawhā wa jaʿala kalimatal-ladhīna ka-farus-suflā. Wa Kalimatul-lāhi hiyal-ʿulyā. Wal-lāhu ʿAzīzun Ḥakīm. (40) ʾIñfirū khifāfañw-wa thiqālañw-wa jāhidū biʾamwālikum wa ʾañfusikum fī sabīlil-lāh. Dhālikum khayrul-lakum ʾiñ-kuñtum taʿlamūn. (41)

At the time of the preparation for this expedition, the hypocrites and a minority among the believers displayed an extreme reluctance (referred to in this and the following verses) to embark on a war with Byzantium: and it is this minority that the above verse reproaches for "clinging heavily to the earth" (*Manār* X, 493).

60 Lit., "him", i.e., Muḥammad.

61 Lit., "the second of two": an allusion to the Prophet's flight, in the company of Abū Bakr, from Mecca to Medina in the year 622 of the Christian era. The expression "the second of two" does not imply any order of precedence but is synonymous with "one of two": cf. the Prophet's saying to Abū Bakr, on that very occasion, "What [could], in thy opinion, [happen] to two [men] who have God as the third with them?" (Bukhārī, in the chapter *Faḍāʾil Aṣḥāb an-Nabī*.)

62 When the Prophet and Abū Bakr left on their *hijrah* to Medina, they first hid for three nights in a cave on Mount Thawr, in the vicinity of Mecca, where they were almost discovered and apprehended by the pagan Quraysh who were pursuing them (Bukhārī, *loc. cit.*).

63 Cf. verse 26 above.

64 Lit., "is the highest". The expression rendered by me as "cause", which occurs twice in this sentence, reads, literally, "word" (*kalimah*).

65 Lit., "lightly or heavily". The rendering adopted by me corresponds to the interpretation given to this expression by most of the classical commentators (e.g., Zamakhsharī and Rāzī).

ربع الحزب

لَوْ كَانَ عَرَضًا قَرِيبًا وَسَفَرًا قَاصِدًا لَّاتَّبَعُوكَ وَلَٰكِنۢ بَعُدَتْ عَلَيْهِمُ
الشُّقَّةُ ۚ وَسَيَحْلِفُونَ بِاللَّهِ لَوِ اسْتَطَعْنَا لَخَرَجْنَا مَعَكُمْ يُهْلِكُونَ أَنفُسَهُمْ
وَاللَّهُ يَعْلَمُ إِنَّهُمْ لَكَاذِبُونَ ﴿42﴾ عَفَا اللَّهُ عَنكَ لِمَ أَذِنتَ لَهُمْ حَتَّىٰ يَتَبَيَّنَ
لَكَ الَّذِينَ صَدَقُوا وَتَعْلَمَ الْكَاذِبِينَ ﴿43﴾ لَا يَسْتَأْذِنُكَ الَّذِينَ يُؤْمِنُونَ
بِاللَّهِ وَالْيَوْمِ الْآخِرِ أَن يُجَاهِدُوا بِأَمْوَالِهِمْ وَأَنفُسِهِمْ ۗ وَاللَّهُ عَلِيمٌ
بِالْمُتَّقِينَ ﴿44﴾ إِنَّمَا يَسْتَأْذِنُكَ الَّذِينَ لَا يُؤْمِنُونَ بِاللَّهِ وَالْيَوْمِ الْآخِرِ
وَارْتَابَتْ قُلُوبُهُمْ فَهُمْ فِي رَيْبِهِمْ يَتَرَدَّدُونَ ﴿45﴾ ۞ وَلَوْ أَرَادُوا الْخُرُوجَ
لَأَعَدُّوا لَهُ عُدَّةً وَلَٰكِن كَرِهَ اللَّهُ انبِعَاثَهُمْ فَثَبَّطَهُمْ وَقِيلَ اقْعُدُوا مَعَ
الْقَاعِدِينَ ﴿46﴾

Law kāna ʿaraḍañ-qarībañw-wa safarañ-qāṣidal-lattabaʿūka wa lākim-baʿudat ʿalayhimush-shuqqah. Wa sayaḥlifūna billāhi lawis-taṭaʿnā lakharajnā maʿakum yuhlikūna ʾañfusahum wal-lāhu yaʿlamu ʾinnahum lakādhibūn. (42) ʿAfal-lāhu ʿañka lima ʾadhiñta lahum ḥattā yatabayyana lakal-ladhīna ṣadaqū wa taʿlamal-kādhibīn. (43) Lā yastaʾdhinukal-ladhīna yuʾminūna billāhi wal-Yawmil-ʾĀkhiri ʾañy-yujāhidū biʾamwālihim wa ʾañfusihim. Wal-lāhu ʿAlīmum-bilmuttaqīn. (44) ʾInnamā yastaʾdhinukal-ladhīna lā yuʾminūna billāhi wal-Yawmil-ʾĀkhiri wartābat qulūbuhum fahum fī raybihim yataraddadūn. (45) ◆ Wa law ʾarādul-khurūja laʾaʿaddū lahū ʿuddatañw-wa lākiñ-karihal-lāhum-biʿāthahum fathabbaṭahum wa qīlaq-ʿudū maʿal-qāʿidīn. (46)

Had there been [a prospect of] immediate gain, and an easy journey, they would certainly have followed thee, [O Prophet:] but the distance was too great for them.[66] And yet, [after your return, O believers,] they will swear by God, "Had we been able to do so, we would certainly have set out with you!" – [and by thus falsely swearing] they will be destroying their own selves: for God knows indeed that they are lying! ‹42›

May God pardon thee [O Prophet]![67] Why didst thou grant them permission [to stay at home] ere it had become obvious to thee as to who was speaking the truth, and [ere] thou camest to know [who were] the liars? ‹43›

Those who [truly] believe in God and the Last Day do not ask thee for exemption from struggling with their possessions and their lives [in God's cause] – and God has full knowledge as to who is conscious of Him:[68] ‹44› – only those ask thee for exemption who do not [truly] believe in God and the Last Day and whose hearts have become a prey to doubt, so that in their doubting they waver between one thing and another. ‹45›

For, had they been [truly] desirous of setting out [with thee], they would surely have made some preparation therefor: but God was averse to their taking the field, and so He caused them to hold back when it was said, "[You may] stay at home with all [the others] who stay at home."[69] ‹46›

66 A reference to the unwillingness of some of the Muslims to follow the Prophet's call and to set out on the expedition to the frontier (see last paragraph of note 59 above). A strenuous march of about fourteen days was needed to reach Tabūk, the goal of this expedition; and the uncertainty of its outcome, as well as the hardships involved, gave rise to all manner of spurious excuses on the part of the half-hearted believers and hypocrites. As the next verse shows, the Prophet accepted these excuses in many cases, and allowed the men concerned to remain at Medina.

67 All the commentators agree in that this phrase, although expressed in the form of an invocation, has the meaning of a *statement* – "God pardons thee" or "has pardoned thee" – absolving the Prophet of any moral responsibility for his mistaken, but humanly understandable, acceptance of equivocal pleas on the part of those who wished to be excused from participating in the campaign. To me it seems that this statement of "absolution" was primarily intended to free the Prophet from any *self-reproach* for his too-great liberality in this respect. (It should be borne in mind that this part of *At-Tawbah* was revealed during or immediately after the expedition.)

68 Lit., "has full knowledge of the God-conscious (*bi'l-muttaqīn*)".

69 This may refer to the permission granted by the Prophet (see verse 43) to certain of his followers who, for apparently legitimate reasons, were unable to take part in the campaign (Ṭabarī, Zamakhsharī, Rāzī) – a permission of which the hypocrites only too readily availed themselves. As regards God's "causing" those hypocrites to sin in this way, see 2 : 7 and the corresponding note 7, as well as *sūrah* 3, note 117

Had these [hypocrites] set out with you, [O believers,] they would have added nothing to you save the evil of corruption, and would surely have scurried to and fro in your midst, seeking to stir up discord among you, seeing that there are in your midst such as would have lent them ear: but God has full knowledge of the evildoers. ‹47›
Indeed, even before this time[70] have they tried to stir up discord and devised all manner of plots against thee, [O Prophet,] until the truth was revealed and God's will became manifest, however hateful this may have been to them. ‹48›
And among them there was [many a one] who said,[71] "Grant me permission [to remain at home], and do not put me to too hard a test!" Oh, verily, [by making such a request] they had [already failed in their test and] succumbed to a temptation to evil:[72] and, behold, hell will indeed encompass all who refuse to acknowledge the truth! ‹49›
Should good fortune alight on thee,[73] [O Prophet,] it will grieve them; and should misfortune befall thee, they will say [to themselves], "We have already taken our precautions beforehand!" – and will turn away, and will rejoice. ‹50›
Say: "Never can anything befall us save what God has decreed! He is our Lord Supreme; and in God let the believers place their trust!" ‹51›
Say: "Are you, perchance, hopefully waiting for something [bad] to happen to us – [the while nothing can happen to us] save one of the two best things?[74] But as far as you

لَوْ خَرَجُوا۟ فِيكُم مَّا زَادُوكُمْ إِلَّا خَبَالًا وَلَأَوْضَعُوا۟ خِلَٰلَكُمْ يَبْغُونَكُمُ
ٱلْفِتْنَةَ وَفِيكُمْ سَمَّٰعُونَ لَهُمْ ۗ وَٱللَّهُ عَلِيمٌۢ بِٱلظَّٰلِمِينَ ﴿٤٧﴾ لَقَدِ ٱبْتَغَوُا۟
ٱلْفِتْنَةَ مِن قَبْلُ وَقَلَّبُوا۟ لَكَ ٱلْأُمُورَ حَتَّىٰ جَآءَ ٱلْحَقُّ وَظَهَرَ أَمْرُ ٱللَّهِ وَهُمْ
كَٰرِهُونَ ﴿٤٨﴾ وَمِنْهُم مَّن يَقُولُ ٱئْذَن لِّى وَلَا تَفْتِنِّىٓ ۚ أَلَا فِى ٱلْفِتْنَةِ سَقَطُوا۟ ۗ
وَإِنَّ جَهَنَّمَ لَمُحِيطَةٌۢ بِٱلْكَٰفِرِينَ ﴿٤٩﴾ إِن تُصِبْكَ حَسَنَةٌ تَسُؤْهُمْ ۖ وَإِن
تُصِبْكَ مُصِيبَةٌ يَقُولُوا۟ قَدْ أَخَذْنَآ أَمْرَنَا مِن قَبْلُ وَيَتَوَلَّوا۟ وَّهُمْ
فَرِحُونَ ﴿٥٠﴾ قُل لَّن يُصِيبَنَآ إِلَّا مَا كَتَبَ ٱللَّهُ لَنَا هُوَ مَوْلَىٰنَا ۚ وَعَلَى ٱللَّهِ
فَلْيَتَوَكَّلِ ٱلْمُؤْمِنُونَ ﴿٥١﴾ قُلْ هَلْ تَرَبَّصُونَ بِنَآ إِلَّآ إِحْدَى ٱلْحُسْنَيَيْنِ ۖ

Law kharajū fīkum-mā zādūkum ʾillā khabālañw-wa laʾawḍaʿū khilālakum yabghūnakumul-fitnata wa fīkum sammāʿūna lahum. Wal-lāhu ʿAlīmum-biẓ-ẓālimīn. (47) Laqadib-taghawul-fitnata miñ-qablu wa qallabū lakal-ʾumūra ḥattā jāaʾal-ḥaqqu wa ẓahara ʾamrul-lāhi wa hum kārihūn. (48) Wa minhum-mañy-yaqūluʾ-dhal-lī wa lā taftinnī. ʾAlā fil-fitnati saqaṭū. Wa ʾinna jahannama lamuḥīṭatum-bilkāfirīn. (49) ʾIñ-tuṣibka ḥasanatuñ-tasuʾhum; wa ʾiñ-tuṣibka muṣībatuñy-yaqūlū qad ʾakhadhnāa ʾamranā miñ-qablu wa yatawallaw-wa hum fariḥūn. (50) Qul lañy-yuṣībanāa ʾillā mā katabal-lāhu lanā. Huwa Mawlānā; wa ʿalal-lāhi falyatawakkalil-muʾminūn. (51) Qul hal tarabbaṣūna bināa ʾillāa ʾiḥdal-ḥusnayayn.

70 I.e., before the expedition to Tabūk, during which these passages were revealed.

71 I.e., at the time when the Prophet was making preparations for the campaign.

72 See verses 44 and 45 above. It is to be noted that both the verbal form *lā taftinnī* (rendered by me as "do not put me to too hard a test") and the noun *fitnah* have the same root, comprising a great complex of meanings: e.g., test, trial, affliction, temptation to evil, seduction, persecution, oppression, discord, civil strife, etc. (cf. *sūrah* 8, note 25). Since it is impossible in any language but Arabic to reproduce all these many shades of meaning in a single expression, the rendering of the term *fitnah* must necessarily vary in accordance with the context in which it is used.

73 I.e., in the course of the expedition to Tabūk, during which most of this *sūrah* was revealed. One should, however, bear in mind that these verses have not merely a historical connotation but, rather, aim at depicting hypocrisy as such.

74 I.e., either victory or martyrdom in God's cause. The verb *tarabbaṣa* has usually the connotation of waiting with *expectancy*, and is, therefore, most suitably rendered as "he hopefully waited".

وَنَحْنُ نَتَرَبَّصُ بِكُمْ أَن يُصِيبَكُمُ ٱللَّهُ بِعَذَابٍ مِّنْ عِندِهِۦٓ أَوْ بِأَيْدِينَا ۖ
فَتَرَبَّصُوٓا۟ إِنَّا مَعَكُم مُّتَرَبِّصُونَ ﴿٥٢﴾ قُلْ أَنفِقُوا۟ طَوْعًا أَوْ كَرْهًا لَّن
يُتَقَبَّلَ مِنكُمْ ۖ إِنَّكُمْ كُنتُمْ قَوْمًا فَٰسِقِينَ ﴿٥٣﴾ وَمَا مَنَعَهُمْ أَن تُقْبَلَ
مِنْهُمْ نَفَقَٰتُهُمْ إِلَّآ أَنَّهُمْ كَفَرُوا۟ بِٱللَّهِ وَبِرَسُولِهِۦ وَلَا يَأْتُونَ ٱلصَّلَوٰةَ إِلَّا
وَهُمْ كُسَالَىٰ وَلَا يُنفِقُونَ إِلَّا وَهُمْ كَٰرِهُونَ ﴿٥٤﴾ فَلَا تُعْجِبْكَ أَمْوَٰلُهُمْ
وَلَآ أَوْلَٰدُهُمْ ۚ إِنَّمَا يُرِيدُ ٱللَّهُ لِيُعَذِّبَهُم بِهَا فِى ٱلْحَيَوٰةِ ٱلدُّنْيَا وَتَزْهَقَ
أَنفُسُهُمْ وَهُمْ كَٰفِرُونَ ﴿٥٥﴾ وَيَحْلِفُونَ بِٱللَّهِ إِنَّهُمْ لَمِنكُمْ وَمَا هُم مِّنكُمْ
وَلَٰكِنَّهُمْ قَوْمٌ يَفْرَقُونَ ﴿٥٦﴾ لَوْ يَجِدُونَ مَلْجَـًٔا أَوْ مَغَٰرَٰتٍ أَوْ مُدَّخَلًا
لَّوَلَّوْا۟ إِلَيْهِ وَهُمْ يَجْمَحُونَ ﴿٥٧﴾ وَمِنْهُم مَّن يَلْمِزُكَ فِى ٱلصَّدَقَٰتِ

Wa naḥnu natarabbaṣu bikum ʾañy-yuṣībakumul-lāhu biʿadhābim-min ʿiñdihīi ʾaw biʾaydīnā. Fatarabbaṣūu ʾinnā maʿakum-mutarabbiṣūn. ﴿52﴾ Qul-ʾañfiqū ṭawʿan ʾaw karhal-lañy-yutaqabbala miñkum; ʾinnakum kuñtum qawmañ-fāsiqīn. ﴿53﴾ Wa mā manaʿahum ʾañ-tuqbala minhūm nafaqātuhum ʾillāa ʾannahum kafarū billāhi wa biRasūlihī wa lā yaʾtūnaṣ-Ṣalāta ʾillā wa hum kusālā wa lā yuñfiqūna ʾillā wa hum kārihūn. ﴿54﴾ Falā tuʿjibka ʾamwāluhum wa lāa ʾawlāduhum. ʾInnamā yurīdul-lāhu liyuʿadhdhibahum-bihā fil-ḥayātid-dunyā wa tazhaqa ʾañfusuhum wa hum kāfirūn. ﴿55﴾ Wa yaḥlifūna billāhi ʾinnahum lamiñkum wa mā hum-miñkum wa lākinnahum qawmuñy-yafraqūn. ﴿56﴾ Law yajidūna maljaʾan ʾaw maghārātin ʾaw muddakhalal-lawallaw ʾilayhi wa hum yajmaḥūn. ﴿57﴾ Wa minhum-mañy-yalmizuka fiṣ-ṣadaqāti

are concerned, we are hopefully waiting for God to inflict chastisement upon you, [either] from Himself[75] or by our hands! Wait, then, hopefully; behold, we shall hopefully wait with you!" ‹52›

Say: "You may spend [anything], willingly or unwillingly, [pretending that you do it for the sake of God:] it shall never be accepted from you[76] – for, verily, you are people bent on iniquity!" ‹53›

For, only this prevents their spending from being accepted from them:[77] they are bent on refusing to acknowledge God and His Apostle, and never pray without reluctance,[78] and never spend [on righteous causes] without resentment. ‹54› Let not, then, their worldly goods or [the happiness which they may derive from] their children excite thy admiration: God but wants to chastise them by these means in this worldly life, and [to cause] their souls to depart while they are [still] denying the truth.[79] ‹55›

And they swear by God that they do indeed belong to you – the while they do not belong to you, but are [only] people ridden by fear: ‹56› if they could but find a place of refuge, or any cavern, or a crevice [in the earth], they would turn towards it in headlong haste.[80] ‹57›

And among them are such as find fault with thee [O Prophet] concerning [the distribution of] the offerings given for the

---

75 Sc., in the life to come.

76 I.e., "it shall never be acceptable to God": an allusion to the readiness on the part of many hypocrites to contribute financially to "good causes", ostensibly for the sake of moral considerations but, in reality, "only to be seen and praised by men" (cf. 2 : 264 and 4 : 38).

77 Lit., "nothing prevents their spending from being accepted from them except that . . .", etc.

78 Lit., "and they do not approach prayer without being reluctant" – i.e., when they participate in acts of worship they do it only for the sake of outward conformity, and not out of inner conviction.

79 Sc., "for which sin they will have to suffer in the life to come". See also 3 : 178 and 8 : 28, and the corresponding notes.

80 Thus the Qurʾān shows that the innermost cause of all hypocrisy is *fear* – fear of a moral commitment and, at the same time, fear of an open breach with one's social environment. In their overriding, immoral desire for social conformity, "the hypocrites seek to deceive God – the while it is He who causes them to be deceived [by themselves]" (4 : 142); and as "they are oblivious of God, so He is oblivious of them" (9 : 67). One should note, in this connection, that the Arabic term *munāfiq* – which, for want of a better word, is rendered as "hypocrite" – applies both to conscious dissemblers bent on deceiving their fellow-men, as well as to people who, out of an inner uncertainty, are deceiving *themselves*. For a fuller discussion of this term, see note 7 on 29 : 11, which probably represents the earliest instance of its use in the Qurʾān.

sake of God:[81] if they are given something thereof, they are well-pleased; but if they are not given anything thereof, lo! they are consumed with anger. ‹58› And yet, [it would be but for their own good] if they were to content themselves with what God has given them and [caused] His Apostle [to give them],[82] and would say, "God is enough for us! God will give us [whatever He wills] out of His bounty, and [will cause] His Apostle [to give us, too]: verily, unto God alone do we turn with hope!" ‹59›

The offerings given for the sake of God[83] are [meant] only for the poor and the needy, and those who are in charge thereof,[84] and those whose hearts are to be won over, and for the freeing of human beings from bondage, and [for] those who are overburdened with debts, and [for every struggle] in God's cause, and [for] the wayfarer: [this is] an ordinance from God – and God is all-knowing, wise.[85] ‹60›

فَإِنْ أُعْطُوا۟ مِنْهَا رَضُوا۟ وَإِن لَّمْ يُعْطَوْا۟ مِنْهَآ إِذَا هُمْ يَسْخَطُونَ ﴿٥٨﴾ وَلَوْ
أَنَّهُمْ رَضُوا۟ مَآ ءَاتَىٰهُمُ ٱللَّهُ وَرَسُولُهُۥ وَقَالُوا۟ حَسْبُنَا ٱللَّهُ سَيُؤْتِينَا ٱللَّهُ مِن
فَضْلِهِۦ وَرَسُولُهُۥٓ إِنَّآ إِلَى ٱللَّهِ رَٰغِبُونَ ﴿٥٩﴾ ۞ إِنَّمَا ٱلصَّدَقَٰتُ لِلْفُقَرَآءِ
وَٱلْمَسَٰكِينِ وَٱلْعَٰمِلِينَ عَلَيْهَا وَٱلْمُؤَلَّفَةِ قُلُوبُهُمْ وَفِى ٱلرِّقَابِ
وَٱلْغَٰرِمِينَ وَفِى سَبِيلِ ٱللَّهِ وَٱبْنِ ٱلسَّبِيلِ ۖ فَرِيضَةً مِّنَ ٱللَّهِ ۗ وَٱللَّهُ عَلِيمٌ
حَكِيمٌ ﴿٦٠﴾

نصف الحزب

faʾin ʾuʿṭū minhā raḍū wa ʾil-lam yuʿṭaw minhāa ʾidhā hum yaskhaṭūn. (58) Wa law ʾannahum raḍū māa ʾātāhumul-lāhu wa Rasūluhū wa qālū ḥasbunal-lāhu sayuʾtīnal-lāhu miñ-faḍlihī wa Rasūluhūu ʾinnāa ʾilal-lāhi rāghibūn. (59) ۞ ʾInnamaṣ-ṣadaqātu lil-fuqarāaʾi wal-masākīni wal-ʿāmilīna ʿalayhā wal-muʾallafati qulūbuhum wa fir-riqābi wal-ghārimīna wa fī sabīlil-lāhi wab-nis-sabīli farīḍatam-minal-lāh. Wal-lāhu ʿAlīmun Ḥakīm. (60)

---

81 Since there is no English equivalent for the term *ṣadaqāt* (sing. *ṣadaqah*), I am rendering it here as "offerings given for the sake of God". This comprises everything that a believer freely gives to another person, out of love or compassion, as well as what he is morally or legally *obliged* to give, without expecting any worldly return: that is, charitable gifts and deeds of every description (which is the primary meaning of *ṣadaqāt* – e.g., in 2 : 263 and 264), as well as the obligatory tax called *zakāh* ("the purifying dues", because its payment purifies, as it were, a person's property from the taint of selfishness). In the context of the above verse, this term refers to the funds thus collected and administered by the Muslim community or state. When these funds are disbursed for the purposes stipulated in verse 60, they assume once more – this time in relation to the recipients – the aspect of "charitable gifts".

82 Lit., "what God has given them, and His Apostle": a typically Qurʾanic construction meant to bring out the fact that the *real* giver is God, and that the Apostle is His instrument. Although this passage relates, primarily, to the hypocrites at Medina and the historical situation obtaining at the time of the expedition to Tabūk, the import of these verses goes beyond the historical occasion of their revelation, describing as it does "the attitude and mentality of hypocrites of all times, and everywhere" (*Manār* X, 567). Consequently, we may assume that the reference, in this context, to "God's Apostle" is not confined to the *person* of the Prophet Muḥammad but implies, metonymically, the Law of Islam as revealed through him – and, thus, to every government that holds authority by virtue of that Law and rules in accordance with it.

83 See note 81 above.

84 I.e., the officials entrusted with the collection and administration of *zakāh* funds.

85 These eight categories circumscribe all the purposes for which *zakāh* funds may be expended. By "those whose hearts are to he won over" are apparently meant such non-Muslims as are close to understanding and, perhaps, accepting Islam, and for whose conversion every effort should be made, either directly or indirectly (i.e., by means of the widest possible propagation of the teachings of Islam). As regards the expression *fi 'r-riqāb* ("for the freeing of human beings from bondage"), which relates both to the ransoming of prisoners of war and to the freeing of slaves, see *sūrah* 2, note 146. The term *al-ghārimūn* describes people who are overburdened with debts contracted in good faith, which – through no fault of their own – they are subsequently unable to redeem. The expression "in God's cause" embraces every kind of struggle in righteous causes, both in war and in peace, including expenditure for the propagation of Islam and for all charitable purposes. Regarding the meaning of *ibn as-sabīl* ("wayfarer"), see *sūrah* 2, note 145.

AND AMONG those [enemies of the truth] there are such as malign the Prophet by saying, "He is all ear."[86]
Say: "[Yes] he is all ear, [listening] to what is good for you![87] He believes in God, and trusts the believers, and is [a manifestation of God's] grace towards such of you as have [truly] attained to faith. And as for those who malign God's Apostle – grievous suffering awaits them [in the life to come]!" ﴾61﴿
[The hypocrites] swear to you by God [that they are acting in good faith], with a view to pleasing you [O believers] – the while it is God and His Apostle whose pleasure they should seek above all else, if indeed they are believers![88] ﴾62﴿
Do they not know that for him who sets himself against God and His Apostle there is in store the fire of hell, therein to abide – that most awesome disgrace? ﴾63﴿
[Some of] the hypocrites dread lest a [new] *sūrah* be revealed [in evidence] against them, making them understand what is [really] in their hearts.[89]

وَمِنْهُمُ ٱلَّذِينَ يُؤْذُونَ ٱلنَّبِىَّ وَيَقُولُونَ هُوَ أُذُنٌ ۚ قُلْ أُذُنُ خَيْرٍ لَّكُمْ يُؤْمِنُ
بِٱللَّهِ وَيُؤْمِنُ لِلْمُؤْمِنِينَ وَرَحْمَةٌ لِّلَّذِينَ ءَامَنُوا۟ مِنكُمْ ۚ وَٱلَّذِينَ يُؤْذُونَ
رَسُولَ ٱللَّهِ لَهُمْ عَذَابٌ أَلِيمٌ ﴿61﴾ يَحْلِفُونَ بِٱللَّهِ لَكُمْ لِيُرْضُوكُمْ وَٱللَّهُ
وَرَسُولُهُۥٓ أَحَقُّ أَن يُرْضُوهُ إِن كَانُوا۟ مُؤْمِنِينَ ﴿62﴾ أَلَمْ يَعْلَمُوٓا۟ أَنَّهُۥ مَن
يُحَادِدِ ٱللَّهَ وَرَسُولَهُۥ فَأَنَّ لَهُۥ نَارَ جَهَنَّمَ خَٰلِدًا فِيهَا ۚ ذَٰلِكَ ٱلْخِزْىُ
ٱلْعَظِيمُ ﴿63﴾ يَحْذَرُ ٱلْمُنَٰفِقُونَ أَن تُنَزَّلَ عَلَيْهِمْ سُورَةٌ تُنَبِّئُهُم بِمَا فِى قُلُوبِهِمْ

Wa minhumul-ladhīna yuʾdhūnan-Nabiyya wa yaqūlūna huwa ʾudhun. Qul ʾudhunu khayril-lakum yuʾminu billāhi wa yuʾminu lilmuʾminīna wa raḥmatul-lilladhīna ʾāmanū miñkum. Wal-ladhīna yuʾdhūna Rasūlal-lāhi lahum ʿadhābun ʾalīm. ﴾61﴿ Yaḥlifūna billāhi lakum liyurḍūkum wal-lāhu wa Rasūluhūu ʾaḥaqqu ʾañy-yurḍūhu ʾiñ-kānū muʾminīn. ﴾62﴿ ʾAlam yaʿlamūu ʾannahū mañy-yuḥādidil-lāha wa Rasūlahū faʾanna lahū nāra jahannama khālidañ-fīhā. Dhālikal-khizyul-ʿaẓīm. ﴾63﴿ Yaḥdharul-munāfiqūna ʾañ-tunazzala ʿalayhim Sūratuñ-tunabbiʾuhum-bimā fī qulūbihim.

86 I.e., "he believes everything that he hears". Most of the commentators assume that the hypocrites were thus alluding to the Prophet's alleged propensity to believe everything – good or bad – that he was told about other people (cf. *Manār* X, 600). Since, however, there is no historical evidence of such a "propensity" on his part, it seems to me that what the hypocrites referred to was the Prophet's readiness to listen to what they – in common with many other unbelievers – regarded as mere hallucinatory sounds, and to interpret them "mistakenly" as revelations. This would explain the statement that "they malign the Prophet" – namely, by attributing to him self-deception – and that this saying of theirs "amounts to a denial of the truth" (see verse 74 of this *sūrah*). – The verb *ādhā* signifies primarily "he molested" or "annoyed [another]", i.e., in a manner not amounting to actual harm (*ḍarar*). Since in the above context this verb is used in the sense of making a derogatory remark, *yuʾdhūn* is best rendered as "they malign".

87 I.e., to divine revelation.

88 Lit., "the while God and His Apostle are most entitled that they should seek His pleasure . . .", etc. As has been pointed out by many of the commentators (and most succinctly by Rashīd Riḍāʾ in *Manār* X, 607 f.), there is no question of any juxtaposition of God and His Apostle in this phrase. This is made clear by the use of the singular pronoun in *an yurḍūhu* ("that they should seek *His* pleasure"), which is meant to bring out – in the inimitable elliptic form so characteristic of the Qurʾān – the idea that God's pleasure is the only worthwhile goal of all human endeavour, and that a believer's duty to surrender to the Prophet's guidance is but an outcome of the fact that he is the bearer of God's message to man. Cf. in this connection, "Whoever pays heed unto the Apostle pays heed unto God thereby" (4 : 80), or, "Say [O Prophet]: 'If you love God, follow me, [and] God will love you'" (3 : 31).

89 This refers to a particular type of hypocrite: namely, to the doubter who, not having any real convictions on this score, leaves the question of God's existence and/or Muḥammad's prophethood open (*Manār* X, 610), but nevertheless, for the sake of worldly advantage, would like to be regarded as a believer. (Since, obviously, not all hypocrites belong to this category, my interpolation of the words "some of" at the beginning of this verse would seem to be justified.) The ambivalent attitude of mind alluded to here implies hypocrisy not merely with regard to one's social environment but also with regard to oneself: an unwillingness – or, rather, fear – on the part of such people to admit to themselves "what is really going on in their hearts" (cf. verses 56-57 and note 80 above), and the dim realization that this ambivalence is only a cover for their desire to escape from all spiritual commitment (cf. 2 : 9 "they would deceive God and those who have attained to faith – the while they deceive none but themselves").

قُلِ ٱسْتَهْزِءُوٓا۟ إِنَّ ٱللَّهَ مُخْرِجٌ مَّا تَحْذَرُونَ ﴿64﴾ وَلَئِن سَأَلْتَهُمْ لَيَقُولُنَّ
إِنَّمَا كُنَّا نَخُوضُ وَنَلْعَبُ ۚ قُلْ أَبِٱللَّهِ وَءَايَٰتِهِۦ وَرَسُولِهِۦ كُنتُمْ
تَسْتَهْزِءُونَ ﴿65﴾ لَا تَعْتَذِرُوا۟ قَدْ كَفَرْتُم بَعْدَ إِيمَٰنِكُمْ ۚ إِن نَّعْفُ عَن
طَآئِفَةٍ مِّنكُمْ نُعَذِّبْ طَآئِفَةًۢ بِأَنَّهُمْ كَانُوا۟ مُجْرِمِينَ ﴿66﴾ ٱلْمُنَٰفِقُونَ
وَٱلْمُنَٰفِقَٰتُ بَعْضُهُم مِّنۢ بَعْضٍ ۚ يَأْمُرُونَ بِٱلْمُنكَرِ وَيَنْهَوْنَ عَنِ
ٱلْمَعْرُوفِ وَيَقْبِضُونَ أَيْدِيَهُمْ ۚ نَسُوا۟ ٱللَّهَ فَنَسِيَهُمْ ۗ إِنَّ ٱلْمُنَٰفِقِينَ هُمُ
ٱلْفَٰسِقُونَ ﴿67﴾ وَعَدَ ٱللَّهُ ٱلْمُنَٰفِقِينَ وَٱلْمُنَٰفِقَٰتِ وَٱلْكُفَّارَ نَارَ جَهَنَّمَ خَٰلِدِينَ
فِيهَا ۚ هِىَ حَسْبُهُمْ ۚ وَلَعَنَهُمُ ٱللَّهُ ۖ وَلَهُمْ عَذَابٌ مُّقِيمٌ ﴿68﴾ كَٱلَّذِينَ مِن قَبْلِكُمْ

Qulis-tahziᵓūu ᵓinnal-lāha mukhrijum-mā taḥdharūn. (64) Wa laᵓiñ-saᵓaltahum layaqūlunna ᵓinnamā kunnā nakhūḍu wa nalᶜab. Qul ᵓabillāhi wa ᵓĀyātihī wa Rasūlihī kuñtum tastahziᵓūn. (65) Lā taᶜtadhirū qad kafartum-baᶜda ᵓimānikum. ᵓIn-naᶜfu ᶜañ-ṭāaᵓifatim-miñkum nuᶜadhdhib ṭāaᵓifatam-biᵓannahum kānū mujrimīn. (66) ᵓAlmunāfiqūna wal-munāfiqātu baᶜḍuhum-mim-baᶜḍ. Yaᵓmurūna bil-muñkari wa yanhawna ᶜanil-maᶜrūfi wa yaqbiḍūna ᵓaydiyahum. Nasul-lāha fanasiyahum. ᵓInnal-munāfiqīna humul-fāsiqūn. (67) Waᶜadal-lāhul-munāfiqīna wal-munāfiqāti wal-kuffāra nāra jahannama khālidīna fīhā. Hiya ḥasbuhum; wa laᶜanahumul-lāhu wa lahum ᶜadhābum-muqīm. (68) Kalladhīna miñ-qablikum

Say: "Go on mocking! Behold, God will bring to light the very thing that you are dreading!"[90] «64»

Yet, indeed, if thou wert to question them, they would surely answer, "We were only indulging in idle talk, and were playing [with words]."[91]

Say: "Were you, then, mocking at God and His messages and His Apostle? «65» Do not offer [empty] excuses! You have indeed denied the truth after [having professed] your belief [in it]!"[92]

Though We may efface the sin of some of you, We shall chastise others – seeing that they were lost in sin.[93] «66»

The hypocrites, both men and women, are all of a kind: they enjoin the doing of what is wrong and forbid the doing of what is right,[94] and withhold their hands [from doing good]. They are oblivious of God, and so He is oblivious of them. Verily, the hypocrites – it is they, they who are truly iniquitous![95] «67»

God has promised the hypocrites, both men and women – as well as the [outright] deniers of the truth – the fire of hell, therein to abide: this shall be their allotted portion. For, God has rejected them, and long-lasting suffering awaits them. «68»

[Say unto them: "You are] like those [hypocrites] who lived before your time.[96]

---

90 Namely, self-knowledge. The accusation of "mocking" refers to their frivolous allusion to the Prophet, "He is all ear" (see verse 61 and note 86 above).

91 Most of the classical commentators assume that this refers to the derisive remarks made by some of the hypocrites about the alleged futility of the expedition to Tabūk. In view of the sequence, however, I am of the opinion that this is a further reference to those who "malign the Prophet by saying, 'He is all ear'" (verse 61) – i.e., accuse him of self-deception – and thus, by implication, "mock at God and His messages" (see next sentence).

92 See note 89 above.

93 I.e., consciously persevered in hypocrisy (Zamakhsharī). The above Qurᵓanic sentence expresses the doctrine that in His final judgment God will take into account all that is in a sinner's heart, and will not indiscriminately condemn everyone who has been sinning out of weakness or out of an inner inability to resolve his doubts, and not out of a conscious inclination to evil (cf. 4 : 98 – "excepted shall be the [truly] helpless – be they men or women or children – who cannot bring forth any strength and have not been shown [or "cannot find"] the right way").

94 I.e., their behaviour is – in its effect, at least – the exact opposite of that expected of the believers (cf. 3 : 104, 110 and 114; 9 : 71 and 112; and 22 : 41).

95 It is to be borne in mind that this and the following verses refer to the *conscious* hypocrites spoken of in the last sentence of the preceding verse, and not to the waverers, whose hypocrisy is an outcome of inner fears and uncertainties.

96 A reference to the statement, in verse 67, that conscious hypocrites are intrinsically "all of a kind" (*baᶜḍuhum min baᶜḍ*).

كَانُوٓاْ أَشَدَّ مِنكُمۡ قُوَّةٗ وَأَكۡثَرَ أَمۡوَٰلٗا وَأَوۡلَٰدٗا فَٱسۡتَمۡتَعُواْ بِخَلَٰقِهِمۡ
فَٱسۡتَمۡتَعۡتُم بِخَلَٰقِكُمۡ كَمَا ٱسۡتَمۡتَعَ ٱلَّذِينَ مِن قَبۡلِكُم بِخَلَٰقِهِمۡ وَخُضۡتُمۡ
كَٱلَّذِي خَاضُوٓاْۚ أُوْلَٰٓئِكَ حَبِطَتۡ أَعۡمَٰلُهُمۡ فِي ٱلدُّنۡيَا وَٱلۡأٓخِرَةِۖ
وَأُوْلَٰٓئِكَ هُمُ ٱلۡخَٰسِرُونَ ٦٩ أَلَمۡ يَأۡتِهِمۡ نَبَأُ ٱلَّذِينَ مِن قَبۡلِهِمۡ قَوۡمِ نُوحٖ
وَعَادٖ وَثَمُودَ وَقَوۡمِ إِبۡرَٰهِيمَ وَأَصۡحَٰبِ مَدۡيَنَ وَٱلۡمُؤۡتَفِكَٰتِۚ أَتَتۡهُمۡ
رُسُلُهُم بِٱلۡبَيِّنَٰتِۖ فَمَا كَانَ ٱللَّهُ لِيَظۡلِمَهُمۡ وَلَٰكِن كَانُوٓاْ أَنفُسَهُمۡ
يَظۡلِمُونَ ٧٠ وَٱلۡمُؤۡمِنُونَ وَٱلۡمُؤۡمِنَٰتُ بَعۡضُهُمۡ أَوۡلِيَآءُ بَعۡضٖۚ يَأۡمُرُونَ
بِٱلۡمَعۡرُوفِ وَيَنۡهَوۡنَ عَنِ ٱلۡمُنكَرِ وَيُقِيمُونَ ٱلصَّلَوٰةَ وَيُؤۡتُونَ ٱلزَّكَوٰةَ
وَيُطِيعُونَ ٱللَّهَ وَرَسُولَهُۥٓۚ أُوْلَٰٓئِكَ سَيَرۡحَمُهُمُ ٱللَّهُۗ إِنَّ ٱللَّهَ عَزِيزٌ
حَكِيمٞ ٧١ وَعَدَ ٱللَّهُ ٱلۡمُؤۡمِنِينَ وَٱلۡمُؤۡمِنَٰتِ جَنَّٰتٖ تَجۡرِي مِن تَحۡتِهَا
ٱلۡأَنۡهَٰرُ خَٰلِدِينَ فِيهَا وَمَسَٰكِنَ طَيِّبَةٗ فِي جَنَّٰتِ عَدۡنٖۚ وَرِضۡوَٰنٞ مِّنَ ٱللَّهِ

kānūu ʾashadda miñkum quwwatañw-wa ʾakthara ʾamwālañw-wa ʾawlādañ-fastamtaᶜū bikhalāqihim fastamtaᶜtum-bikhalāqikum kamas-tamtaᶜal-ladhīna miñ-qablikum-bikhalāqihim wa khuḍtum kalladhī khāḍū. ʾUlāaʾika ḥabiṭat ʾaᶜmāluhum fid-dunyā wal-ʾĀkhirata wa ʾulāaʾika humul-khāsirūn. (69) ʾAlam ya-ʾtihim nabaʾul-ladhīna miñ-qablihim qawmi Nūḥiñw-wa ᶜĀdiñw-wa Thamūda wa qawmi ʾIbrāhīma wa ʾaṣḥābi Madyana wal-muʾtafikāt. ʾAtat-hum Rusulu-hum-bilbayyināt. Famā kānal-lāhu liyaẓlimahum wa lākiñ-kānūu añfusahum yaẓlimūn. (70) Wal-muʾminūna wal-muʾminātu baᶜḍuhum ʾawliyāaʾu baᶜḍ. Yaʾmu-rūna bilmaᶜrūfi wa yanhawna ᶜanil-muñkari wa yuqīmūnaṣ-Ṣalāta wa yuʾtūnaz-Zakāta wa yuṭīᶜūnal-lāha wa Rasūlah. ʾUlāaʾika sayarḥamuhumul-lāh. ʾInnal-lāha ᶜAzīzun Ḥakīm. (71) Waᶜadal-lāhul-muʾminīna wal-muʾmināti jannātiñ-tajrī miñ-taḥtihal-ʾanhāru khālidīna fīhā wa masākina ṭay-yibatañ-fī jannāti ᶜAdn. Wa riḍwānum-minal-lāhi

Greater than you were they in power, and richer in wealth and in children; and they enjoyed their share [of happiness]. And you have been enjoying your share – just as those who preceded you enjoyed their share; and you have been indulging in scurrilous talk – just as they indulged in it. It is they whose works have come to nought in this world and in the life to come – and it is they, they who are the lost!"[97] ‹69›

Have, then, the stories of those who preceded them never come within the ken of these [hypocrites and deniers of the truth]? – [the stories] of Noah's people, and of [the tribes of] ᶜĀd and Thamūd, and of Abraham's people, and of the folk of Madyan, and of the cities that were overthrown?[98] To [all of] them their apostles had come with all evidence of the truth, [but they rejected them:] and so it was not God who wronged them [by His punishment], but it was they who wronged themselves. ‹70›

AND [as for] the believers, both men and women – they are close unto one another:[99] they [all] enjoin the doing of what is right and forbid the doing of what is wrong, and are constant in prayer, and render the purifying dues, and pay heed unto God and His Apostle. It is they upon whom God will bestow His grace: verily, God is almighty, wise! ‹71›

God has promised the believers, both men and women, gardens through which running waters flow, therein to abide, and goodly dwellings in gardens of perpetual bliss:[100] but God's goodly acceptance is

97 Sc., "and the same will happen to you unless you repent".

98 I.e., Sodom and Gomorrah, the cities of Lot's people (see 7 : 80-84 and 11 : 69-83). References to the chastisement meted out to Noah's people as well as to the ᶜĀd and Thamūd and the folk of Madyan (the Biblical Midian) are found in several places in the Qurʾān; see, in particular, 7 : 59-79 and 85-93, and the corresponding notes. The reference to "Abraham's people" seems to point to the Babylonians, who rejected the monotheism preached by him, and to the overthrow of their first empire, at about 1100 B.C., by the Assyrians.

99 Or: "are the protectors [or "friends and protectors"] of one another". Since, however, the believers are here contrasted with the hypocrites, spoken of in verse 67 as being "all of a kind", it is preferable to render the term *walī* (of which *awliyāʾ* is the plural) in its primary meaning of being "near" or "close" to one another.

100 For an explanation of this rendering of *ᶜadn* (akin to the Hebrew *ᶜedēn*, "delight" or "bliss"), see note 45 on 38 : 50, where this expression occurs for the first time in the chronological order of Qurʾanic revelation.

the greatest [bliss of all] – for this, this is the triumph supreme! «72»

O PROPHET! Strive hard against the deniers of the truth and the hypocrites, and be adamant with them.[101] And [if they do not repent,] their goal shall be hell – and how vile a journey's end! «73»

[The hypocrites] swear by God that they have said nothing [wrong]; yet most certainly have they uttered a saying which amounts to a denial of the truth,[102] and have [thus] denied the truth after [having professed] their self-surrender to God: for they were aiming at something which was beyond their reach.[103] And they could find no fault [with the Faith] save that God had enriched them and [caused] His Apostle [to enrich them] out of His bounty![104]

Hence, if they repent, it will be for their own good; but if they turn away, God will cause them to suffer grievous suffering in this world and in the life to come, and they will find no helper on earth, and none to give [them] succour. «74»

And among them are such as vow unto God, "If indeed He grant us [something] out of His bounty, we shall most certainly spend in charity, and shall most certainly be among the righteous!" «75» But as

أَكْبَرُ ۚ ذَٰلِكَ هُوَ ٱلْفَوْزُ ٱلْعَظِيمُ ﴿72﴾ يَٰٓأَيُّهَا ٱلنَّبِيُّ جَٰهِدِ ٱلْكُفَّارَ
وَٱلْمُنَٰفِقِينَ وَٱغْلُظْ عَلَيْهِمْ ۚ وَمَأْوَىٰهُمْ جَهَنَّمُ ۖ وَبِئْسَ ٱلْمَصِيرُ ﴿73﴾ يَحْلِفُونَ
بِٱللَّهِ مَا قَالُوا۟ وَلَقَدْ قَالُوا۟ كَلِمَةَ ٱلْكُفْرِ وَكَفَرُوا۟ بَعْدَ إِسْلَٰمِهِمْ وَهَمُّوا۟ بِمَا
لَمْ يَنَالُوا۟ ۚ وَمَا نَقَمُوٓا۟ إِلَّآ أَنْ أَغْنَىٰهُمُ ٱللَّهُ وَرَسُولُهُۥ مِن فَضْلِهِۦ ۚ فَإِن يَتُوبُوا۟
يَكُ خَيْرًا لَّهُمْ ۖ وَإِن يَتَوَلَّوْا۟ يُعَذِّبْهُمُ ٱللَّهُ عَذَابًا أَلِيمًا فِى ٱلدُّنْيَا وَٱلْءَاخِرَةِ ۚ
وَمَا لَهُمْ فِى ٱلْأَرْضِ مِن وَلِىٍّ وَلَا نَصِيرٍ ﴿74﴾ ۞ وَمِنْهُم مَّنْ عَٰهَدَ ٱللَّهَ
لَئِنْ ءَاتَىٰنَا مِن فَضْلِهِۦ لَنَصَّدَّقَنَّ وَلَنَكُونَنَّ مِنَ ٱلصَّٰلِحِينَ ﴿75﴾ فَلَمَّآ

ثلاثة ارباع الحزب

ʾakbar. Dhālika huwal-fawzul-ʿaẓīm. ﴿72﴾ Yāa ʾayyuhan-Nabiyyu jāhidil-kuffāra wal-munāfiqīna wagh-luẓ ʿalayhim. Wa maʾwāhum jahannamu wa biʾsal-maṣīr. ﴿73﴾ Yaḥlifūna billāhi mā qālū wa laqad qālū kalimatal-kufri wa kafarū baʿda ʾislāmihim wa hammū bimā lam yanālū. Wa mā naqamūu ʾillāa ʾan ʾaghnāhumul-lāhu wa Rasūluhu miñ-faḍlih. Faʾiñy-yatūbū yaku khayral-lahum; wa ʾiñy-yatawallaw yuʿadhdhibhumul-lāhu ʿadhāban ʾalīmañ-fid-dunyā wal-ʾĀkhirah. Wa mā lahum fil-ʾarḍi miñw-waliy-yiñw-wa lā naṣīr. ﴿74﴾ ۞ Wa minhum-man ʿāhadal-lāha laʾin ʾātānā miñ-faḍlihī lanaṣ-ṣaddaqanna wa lanakūnanna minaṣ-ṣāliḥīn. ﴿75﴾ Falammāa

101 I.e., "do not compromise with them in matters of principle". Regarding the meaning of the verb *jahada* ("he strove hard", i.e., in a righteous cause), see *sūrah* 4, note 122. The imperative *jāhid* is obviously used here in its spiritual connotation, implying efforts at convincing both the outspoken unbelievers and the waverers, including the various types of hypocrites spoken of in the preceding passages. Although the imperative is addressed in the first instance to the Prophet, it is considered to be morally binding on all believers.

102 See the first sentence of verse 61 above, and the corresponding note 86. The allegation that the Prophet deceived himself in the matter of revelation is, naturally, equivalent to disbelief in the *outcome* of his revelation, i.e., the Qurʾān.

103 Lit., "which they were unable to attain to". The classical commentators take this as a reference to an abortive plot, on the part of some of the hypocrites, to kill the Prophet during the expedition to Tabūk. However, without contesting the validity of this historical interpretation, I believe that the above allusion has a far deeper meaning – namely, the existential impossibility of one's ever attaining to inner peace without a positive belief that man's life has meaning and purpose, either of which can be glimpsed only through the revelations bestowed on those exceptionally gifted and receptive personalities, the prophets. (An indirect reference to divine revelation as the only source of this kind of cognition appears in 96 : 5, that is, in the earliest Qurʾanic passage revealed to the Prophet.) Thus, torn between their half-hearted desire to "surrender themselves to God" and their unwillingness to accept the divine guidance offered them by the Prophet, the hypocrites "were aiming at something which was beyond their reach".

104 I.e., by means of the spiritual guidance contained in the Qurʾān and the material welfare resulting from an adherence to its moral and social principles. The above phrase implies that the reluctance of the hypocrites to pay heed to the Prophet was not due to their finding fault with the Faith as such but, rather, to their lack of gratitude for the spiritual and material benefits which they had derived from it. (Because of its historical associations, most of this verse is expressed in the past tense, although its moral import is obviously timeless.)

ءَاتَىٰهُم مِّن فَضْلِهِۦ بَخِلُوا۟ بِهِۦ وَتَوَلَّوا۟ وَّهُم مُّعْرِضُونَ ﴿٧٦﴾ فَأَعْقَبَهُمْ نِفَاقًا فِى
قُلُوبِهِمْ إِلَىٰ يَوْمِ يَلْقَوْنَهُۥ بِمَآ أَخْلَفُوا۟ ٱللَّهَ مَا وَعَدُوهُ وَبِمَا كَانُوا۟ يَكْذِبُونَ ﴿٧٧﴾
أَلَمْ يَعْلَمُوٓا۟ أَنَّ ٱللَّهَ يَعْلَمُ سِرَّهُمْ وَنَجْوَىٰهُمْ وَأَنَّ ٱللَّهَ عَلَّـٰمُ ٱلْغُيُوبِ ﴿٧٨﴾ ٱلَّذِينَ
يَلْمِزُونَ ٱلْمُطَّوِّعِينَ مِنَ ٱلْمُؤْمِنِينَ فِى ٱلصَّدَقَـٰتِ وَٱلَّذِينَ لَا يَجِدُونَ إِلَّا
جُهْدَهُمْ فَيَسْخَرُونَ مِنْهُمْ ۙ سَخِرَ ٱللَّهُ مِنْهُمْ وَلَهُمْ عَذَابٌ أَلِيمٌ ﴿٧٩﴾ ٱسْتَغْفِرْ لَهُمْ
أَوْ لَا تَسْتَغْفِرْ لَهُمْ إِن تَسْتَغْفِرْ لَهُمْ سَبْعِينَ مَرَّةً فَلَن يَغْفِرَ ٱللَّهُ لَهُمْ ۚ ذَٰلِكَ بِأَنَّهُمْ

ʾātāhum-miñ-faḍlihī bakhilū bihī wa tawallaw-wa hum-muʿriḍūn. 76 Faʾaʿqabahum nifāqañ-fī qulūbihim ʾilā yawmi yalqawnahū bimāa ʾakhlaful-lāha mā waʿadūhu wa bimā kānū yakdhibūn. 77 ʾAlam yaʿlamūu ʾannal-lāha yaʿlamu sirrahum wa najwāhum wa ʾannal-lāha ʿAllāmul-ghuyūb. 78 ʾAl-ladhīna yalmizūnal-muṭṭawwiʿīna minal-muʾminīna fiṣ-ṣadaqāti wal-ladhīna lā yajidūna ʾillā juhdahum fayaskharūna minhum sakhiral-lāhu minhum wa lahum ʿadhābun ʾalīm. 79 ʾIstaghfir lahum ʾaw lā tastaghfir lahum ʾiñ-tastaghfir lahum sabʿīna marratañ-falañy-yaghfiral-lāhu lahum. Dhālika biʾannahum

soon as He has given them [aught] out of His bounty, they cling to it niggardly, and turn away in their obstinacy [from all that they have vowed]: «76» whereupon He causes hypocrisy to take root in their hearts, [therein to remain] until the Day on which they shall meet Him[105] – because they have failed to fulfil the vow which they had made unto God, and because they were wont to lie.[106] «77»

Do they not know that God knows [all] their hidden thoughts and their secret confabulations, and that God knows fully all the things that are beyond the reach of human perception? «78»

[It is these hypocrites] who find fault with such of the believers as give for the sake of God[107] more than they are duty-bound to give, as well as with such as find nothing [to give] beyond [the meagre fruits of] their toil, and who scoff at them [all].[108]

God will cause their scoffing to rebound on themselves,[109] and grievous suffering awaits them. «79» [And] whether thou dost pray [unto God] that they be forgiven or dost not pray for them – [it will all be the same: for even] if thou wert to pray seventy times[110] that they be forgiven, God will not forgive them, seeing that they are

---

105 Lit., "He has caused hypocrisy to become for them a consequence (*aʿqabahum*) in their hearts until the Day on which they shall meet Him" (i.e., until their resurrection). Thus, the Qurʾān states that it is excessive love of worldly possessions which gives rise, in a certain type of man, to the attitude of mind described as "hypocrisy" – and not *vice versa* (see also 29 : 11 and the corresponding note 7). Cf. in this connection the Prophet's saying, reported by Abū Hurayrah: "The mark (*āyah*) of the hypocrite is threefold: when he speaks, he lies; and when he promises, he breaks his promise; and when he is trusted, he betrays" (Bukhārī, Muslim, Tirmidhī and Nasāʾī; similar Traditions, on the authority of ʿAbd Allāh ibn ʿAmr, are quoted by Bukhārī, Muslim, Abū Dāʾūd, Nasāʾī, Ibn Mājah and Ibn Ḥanbal).

106 I.e., to themselves, trying to find excuses for their breaking their vow.

107 Regarding my rendering of *ṣadaqāt* as "that which is given for the sake of God", see note 81 above.

108 There are many authentic Traditions to the effect that the hypocrites at Medina used to deride the offerings which the believers brought to the Prophet (as head of the community and the state) in response to the Qurʾanic ordinance that they should "give for the sake of God". For instance, the Companion Abū Masʿūd reports: "[When] a man brought an ample offering, they [i.e., the hypocrites] would say, 'He [only] wants to be seen and praised by men'; and when a man brought an offering of a small measure [of dates or grain], they would say, 'God does not stand in need of such an offering'" (Bukhārī and Muslim, and many similar versions in other *ḥadīth* compilations). The above verse, however, does not allude merely to these historical incidents but serves to illustrate the mentality of the hypocrite whose own insincerity colours his view of all other people.

109 Lit., "God will scoff at them": a turn of phrase often occurring in the Qurʾān (e.g., in 2 : 15), indicating God's requital.

110 I.e., many times. In Arabic usage, the number "seventy" often stands for "many", just as "seven" is a synonym for "several" (see *Lisān al-ʿArab* and *Tāj al-ʿArūs*). It is evident from many authentic Traditions (recorded, among others, by Bukhārī and Muslim) that the Prophet often prayed to God that He pardon his enemies.

bent on denying God and His Apostle. And God does not bestow His guidance upon such iniquitous folk.[111] ‹80›

THOSE [hypocrites] who were left behind rejoiced in their staying away [from war][112] after [the departure of] God's Apostle, for they hated the thought of striving with their possessions and their lives in God's cause; and they had [even] said [to the others], "Do not go forth to war in this heat!"
Say: "The fire of hell is hotter by far!"
Had they but grasped this truth! ‹81› Let them, then, laugh a little – for they will weep a lot[113] in return for what they have earned. ‹82›
Hence, [O Prophet,] if God brings thee again face to face with some of them,[114] and then they ask thy leave to go forth [to war with thee], say: "Never shall you go forth with me, nor shall you fight an enemy together with me! Behold, you were well-pleased to stay at home on that first occasion: stay at home, then, with those who [are obliged to] remain behind!"[115] ‹83›
And never shalt thou pray over any of them that has died, and never shalt thou stand by his grave:[116] for, behold, they were

كَفَرُواْ بِٱللَّهِ وَرَسُولِهِۦۗ وَٱللَّهُ لَا يَهۡدِي ٱلۡقَوۡمَ ٱلۡفَٰسِقِينَ ﴿٨٠﴾ فَرِحَ
ٱلۡمُخَلَّفُونَ بِمَقۡعَدِهِمۡ خِلَٰفَ رَسُولِ ٱللَّهِ وَكَرِهُوٓاْ أَن يُجَٰهِدُواْ
بِأَمۡوَٰلِهِمۡ وَأَنفُسِهِمۡ فِي سَبِيلِ ٱللَّهِ وَقَالُواْ لَا تَنفِرُواْ فِي ٱلۡحَرِّۗ قُلۡ نَارُ
جَهَنَّمَ أَشَدُّ حَرّٗاۚ لَّوۡ كَانُواْ يَفۡقَهُونَ ﴿٨١﴾ فَلۡيَضۡحَكُواْ قَلِيلٗا وَلۡيَبۡكُواْ
كَثِيرٗا جَزَآءَۢ بِمَا كَانُواْ يَكۡسِبُونَ ﴿٨٢﴾ فَإِن رَّجَعَكَ ٱللَّهُ إِلَىٰ طَآئِفَةٖ
مِّنۡهُمۡ فَٱسۡتَـٔۡذَنُوكَ لِلۡخُرُوجِ فَقُل لَّن تَخۡرُجُواْ مَعِيَ أَبَدٗا وَلَن تُقَٰتِلُواْ
مَعِيَ عَدُوًّاۖ إِنَّكُمۡ رَضِيتُم بِٱلۡقُعُودِ أَوَّلَ مَرَّةٖ فَٱقۡعُدُواْ مَعَ ٱلۡخَٰلِفِينَ ﴿٨٣﴾
وَلَا تُصَلِّ عَلَىٰٓ أَحَدٖ مِّنۡهُم مَّاتَ أَبَدٗا وَلَا تَقُمۡ عَلَىٰ قَبۡرِهِۦٓۖ إِنَّهُمۡ

kafarū billāhi wa Rasūlih. Wal-lāhu lā yahdil-qawmal-fāsiqīn. (80) Fariḥal-mukhallafūna bimaqʿadihim khilāfa Rasūlil-lāhi wa karihūu ʾañy-yujāhidū biʾamwālihim wa ʾañfusihim fī sabīlil-lāhi wa qālū lā tañfirū fil-ḥarr. Qul nāru jahannama ʾashaddu ḥarrañ-law kānū yafqahūn. (81) Falyaḍḥakū qalīlañw-wal-yabkū kathīrañ-jazāaʾam-bimā kānū yaksibūn. (82) Faʾir-rajaʿakal-lāhu ʾilā ṭāaʾifatim-minhum fastaʾdhanūka lilkhurūji faqul-lañ-takhrujū maʿiya ʾabadañw-wa lañ-tuqātilū maʿiya ʿaduwwā. ʾInnakum raḍītum-bilquʿūdi ʾawwala marratiñ-faqʿudū maʿal-khālifīn. (83) Wa lā tuṣalli ʿalāa ʾaḥadim-minhum-māta ʾabadañw-wa lā taqum ʿalā qabrih. ʾInnahum

111 I.e., "those who are so deeply rooted in their iniquity and in their insolent persistence in evildoing (*tamarrud*) . . . [that] they have lost all disposition for repentance and belief" (*Manār* X, 657).

112 Lit., "rejoiced in their sitting [at home]" – a reference to those who, under one pretext or another, excused themselves from participating in the expedition to Tabūk (see notes 59 and 66 above). As is evident from the sequence – and clearly stated in many authentic Traditions – one of the excuses advanced was the extreme heat of the season.

113 Lit., "and let them weep a lot".

114 Lit., "if God brings thee back [from the campaign] to a group of them" – i.e., to those hypocrites who remained at home under false pretences.

115 I.e., with the old men, the women, the children and the sick, who are not able or not expected to go to war (*Manār* X, 662).

116 I.e., unless he has repented before his death. It is reported that when the life-long opponent of the Prophet and leader of the hypocrites of Medina, ʿAbd Allāh ibn Ubayy, was dying, he sent his son to the Prophet with the request that the latter give him his (the Prophet's) shirt, so that he might be buried in it, and that the Prophet should pray over him after his death. The Prophet took this request as a sign of Ibn Ubayy's repentance, and gave him his shirt and later led the funeral prayers over his body. When ʿUmar ibn al-Khaṭṭāb vehemently protested against this clemency towards the man whom all the believers had regarded as "God's enemy", the Prophet answered, "God has granted me a choice in this matter [a reference to verse 80 of this *sūrah*, "whether thou dost pray that they be forgiven or dost not pray . . .", etc.], and so I shall pray [for him] more than seventy times." Several variants of this Tradition are to be found in Bukhārī, Tirmidhī, Nasāʾī, Ibn Ḥanbal, on the authority of Ibn ʿAbbās; Bukhārī and Muslim, on the authority of Ibn ʿUmar; Muslim, on the authority of Jābir ibn ʿAbd Allāh; and in various other *ḥadīth* compilations. Since ʿAbd Allāh ibn Ubayy died some time *after* the Prophet's return from Tabūk, while verse 84 – like most of this *sūrah* – was revealed *during* the campaign, it is clear that the prohibition expressed in this verse relates only (as the sequence shows) to those who "were bent on denying God and His Apostle, and [who] died in this their iniquity" – that is, to *unrepentant* sinners.

bent on denying God and His Apostle, and they died in this their iniquity.[117] «84»
And let not their worldly goods and [the happiness which they may derive from] their children excite thy admiration: God but wants to chastise them by these means in [the life of] this world, and [to cause] their souls to depart while they are [still] denying the truth.[118] «85»
[They are indeed denying it:] for, when they were called upon through revelation,[119] "Believe in God, and strive hard [in His cause] together with His Apostle," [even] such of them as were well able [to go to war] asked thee for exemption, saying, "Allow us to stay behind with those who remain at home!"[120] «86» They were well-pleased to remain with those who were left behind – wherefor their hearts have been sealed,[121] so that they cannot grasp the truth. «87»
The Apostle, however, and all who share his faith strive hard [in God's cause] with their possessions and their lives: and it is they whom the most excellent things await [in the life to come], and it is they, they who shall attain to a happy state! «88»
God has readied for them gardens through which running waters flow, therein to abide: and this is the triumph supreme! «89»

AND THERE came [unto the Apostle] such of the bedouin as had some excuse to offer, [with the request] that they be granted exemption,[122] whereas those who

كَفَرُواْ بِٱللَّهِ وَرَسُولِهِۦ وَمَاتُواْ وَهُمْ فَٰسِقُونَ ﴿٨٤﴾ وَلَا تُعْجِبْكَ أَمْوَٰلُهُمْ
وَأَوْلَٰدُهُمْ إِنَّمَا يُرِيدُ ٱللَّهُ أَن يُعَذِّبَهُم بِهَا فِى ٱلدُّنْيَا وَتَزْهَقَ أَنفُسُهُمْ وَهُمْ
كَٰفِرُونَ ﴿٨٥﴾ وَإِذَآ أُنزِلَتْ سُورَةٌ أَنْ ءَامِنُواْ بِٱللَّهِ وَجَٰهِدُواْ مَعَ رَسُولِهِ
ٱسْتَـْٔذَنَكَ أُوْلُواْ ٱلطَّوْلِ مِنْهُمْ وَقَالُواْ ذَرْنَا نَكُن مَّعَ ٱلْقَٰعِدِينَ ﴿٨٦﴾
رَضُواْ بِأَن يَكُونُواْ مَعَ ٱلْخَوَالِفِ وَطُبِعَ عَلَىٰ قُلُوبِهِمْ فَهُمْ لَا
يَفْقَهُونَ ﴿٨٧﴾ لَٰكِنِ ٱلرَّسُولُ وَٱلَّذِينَ ءَامَنُواْ مَعَهُۥ جَٰهَدُواْ بِأَمْوَٰلِهِمْ
وَأَنفُسِهِمْ وَأُوْلَٰٓئِكَ لَهُمُ ٱلْخَيْرَٰتُ وَأُوْلَٰٓئِكَ هُمُ ٱلْمُفْلِحُونَ ﴿٨٨﴾ أَعَدَّ
ٱللَّهُ لَهُمْ جَنَّٰتٍ تَجْرِى مِن تَحْتِهَا ٱلْأَنْهَٰرُ خَٰلِدِينَ فِيهَا ذَٰلِكَ ٱلْفَوْزُ
ٱلْعَظِيمُ ﴿٨٩﴾ وَجَآءَ ٱلْمُعَذِّرُونَ مِنَ ٱلْأَعْرَابِ لِيُؤْذَنَ لَهُمْ وَقَعَدَ ٱلَّذِينَ

kafarū billāhi wa Rasūlihī wa mātū wa hum fāsiqūn.
(84) Wa lā tuʿjibka ʾamwāluhum wa ʾawlāduhum.
ʾInnamā yurīdul-lāhu ʾañy-yuʿadh-dhibahum-bihā
fid-dunyā wa tazhaqa ʾañfusuhum wa hum kāfirūn.
(85) Wa ʾidhāa ʾuñzilat Sūratun ʾan ʾāminū billāhi wa
jāhidū maʿa Rasūlihis-taʾdhanaka ʾuluṭ-ṭawli min-
hum wa qālū dharnā nakum-maʿal-qāʿidīn. (86) Raḍū
biʾañy-yakūnū maʿal-khawālifi wa ṭubiʿa ʿalā qulū-
bihim fahum lā yafqahūn. (87) Lākinir-Rasūlu wal-
ladhīna ʾāmanū maʿahu jāhadū biʾamwālihim wa
ʾañfusihim. Wa ʾulāaʾika lahumul-khayrātu wa ʾulāa-
ʾika humul-mufliḥūn. (88) ʾAʿaddal-lāhu lahum
jannātiñ-tajrī miñ-taḥtihal-ʾanhāru khālidīna fīhā;
dhālikal-fawzul-ʿaẓīm. (89) Wa jāaʾal-muʿadhdhirūna
minal-ʾaʿrābi liyuʾdhana lahum wa qaʿadal-ladhīna

117 Lit., "while they were iniquitous".

118 Cf. 3 : 178 and 8 : 28, as well as the corresponding notes. This (almost literal) repetition of verse 55 above is meant to stress the psychological importance of this problem (Zamakhsharī) – namely, the insignificance of worldly happiness as compared with spiritual righteousness or the absence of it.

119 Lit., "when a *sūrah* was bestowed from on high": the word *sūrah* being here synonymous with "revealed message" (see note 25 on 47 : 20).

120 I.e., with those who were either not expected to go to war – like women and children – or were handicapped by old age or illness.

121 Cf. 2 : 7 and the corresponding note, as well as 7 : 100-101.

122 I.e., from participating in the expedition to Tabūk. The term *al-muʿadhdhirūn* connotes both "those having a valid excuse (*ʿudhr*)" and "those offering false excuses"; it is, therefore, best rendered as "such as had some excuse to offer". The specific mention of the *aʿrāb* ("bedouin") in this and the following passages probably arises from the fact that their attitude – positive or negative – towards Islam was of the greatest importance within the context of early Muslim history, inasmuch as the message of Muḥammad could not obtain a real, lasting foothold in Arabia without

were bent on giving the lie to God and His Apostle [simply] remained at home.[123] [And] grievous suffering is bound to befall such of them as are bent on denying the truth! ‹90›

[But] no blame shall attach to the weak,[124] nor to the sick, nor to those who have no means [to equip themselves],[125] provided that they are sincere towards God and His Apostle: there is no cause to reproach the doers of good, for God is much-forgiving, a dispenser of grace. ‹91› Nor [shall blame attach] to those who, when they came unto thee [O Prophet, with the request] that thou provide them with mounts, were told by thee, "I cannot find anything whereon to mount you" – [whereupon] they turned away, their eyes overflowing with tears out of sorrow that they had no means to spend [on their equipment]. ‹92›

Only they may rightly be reproached who asked thee for exemption even though they were fully able [to go to war].[126] They were well-pleased to remain with those who were left behind – wherefore God has sealed their hearts, so that they do not know [what they are doing]. ‹93› [And] they will [still] be offering excuses to you when you return to them [from the campaign]!

Say: "Do not offer [empty] excuses, [for] we shall not believe you: God has already enlightened us about you. And God will behold your [future] deeds, and [so will] His Apostle; and in the end you will be brought

كَذَبُواْ ٱللَّهَ وَرَسُولَهُۥۚ سَيُصِيبُ ٱلَّذِينَ كَفَرُواْ مِنْهُمْ عَذَابٌ أَلِيمٌ ﴿٩٠﴾
لَّيْسَ عَلَى ٱلضُّعَفَآءِ وَلَا عَلَى ٱلْمَرْضَىٰ وَلَا عَلَى ٱلَّذِينَ لَا يَجِدُونَ مَا يُنفِقُونَ
حَرَجٌ إِذَا نَصَحُواْ لِلَّهِ وَرَسُولِهِۦۚ مَا عَلَى ٱلْمُحْسِنِينَ مِن سَبِيلٍۚ وَٱللَّهُ غَفُورٌ
رَّحِيمٌ ﴿٩١﴾ وَلَا عَلَى ٱلَّذِينَ إِذَا مَآ أَتَوْكَ لِتَحْمِلَهُمْ قُلْتَ لَآ أَجِدُ مَآ
أَحْمِلُكُمْ عَلَيْهِ تَوَلَّواْ وَّأَعْيُنُهُمْ تَفِيضُ مِنَ ٱلدَّمْعِ حَزَنًا أَلَّا يَجِدُواْ مَا
يُنفِقُونَ ﴿٩٢﴾ ۞ إِنَّمَا ٱلسَّبِيلُ عَلَى ٱلَّذِينَ يَسْتَـْٔذِنُونَكَ وَهُمْ أَغْنِيَآءُۚ رَضُواْ
بِأَن يَكُونُواْ مَعَ ٱلْخَوَالِفِ وَطَبَعَ ٱللَّهُ عَلَىٰ قُلُوبِهِمْ فَهُمْ لَا يَعْلَمُونَ ﴿٩٣﴾
يَعْتَذِرُونَ إِلَيْكُمْ إِذَا رَجَعْتُمْ إِلَيْهِمْۚ قُل لَّا تَعْتَذِرُواْ لَن نُّؤْمِنَ لَكُمْ قَدْ
نَبَّأَنَا ٱللَّهُ مِنْ أَخْبَارِكُمْۚ وَسَيَرَى ٱللَّهُ عَمَلَكُمْ وَرَسُولُهُۥ ثُمَّ تُرَدُّونَ

حزب 21
جزء 11

kadhabul-lāha wa Rasūlah. Sayuṣībul-ladhīna kafarū minhum ʿadhābun ʾalīm. ﴿٩٠﴾ Laysa ʿalaḍ-ḍuʿafāaʾi wa lā ʿalal-marḍā wa lā ʿalal-ladhīna lā yajidūna mā yuñfiqūna ḥarajun ʾidhā naṣaḥū lillāhi wa Rasūlih. Mā ʿalal-muḥsinīna miñ-sabīl. Wal-lāhu Ghafūrur-Raḥīm. ﴿٩١﴾ Wa lā ʿalal-ladhīna ʾidhā māa ʾatawka litaḥmilahum qulta lāa ʾajidu māa ʾaḥmilukum ʿalayhi tawallaw wa ʾaʿyunuhum tafīḍu minad-damʿi ḥazanan ʾallā yajidū mā yuñfiqūn. ﴿٩٢﴾ ۞ ʾInnamas-sabīlu ʿalal-ladhīna yastaʾdhinūnaka wa hum ʾaghniyāaʾ. Raḍū biʾañy-yakūnū maʿal-khawālifi wa ṭabaʿal-lāhu ʿalā qulūbihim fahum lā yaʿlamūn. ﴿٩٣﴾ Yaʿtadhirūna ʾilaykum ʾidhā rajaʿtum ʾilayhim. Qul lā taʿtadhirū lañ-nuʾmina lakum qad nabbaʾanal-lāhu min ʾakhbārikum. Wa sayaral-lāhu ʿamalakum wa Rasūluhū thumma turaddūna

first securing the allegiance of those warlike nomads and half-nomads, who constituted the great majority of the Peninsula's population. At the time when the Prophet was preparing to set out towards Tabūk, many of the already-converted tribesmen were willing to go to war under his leadership (and, in fact, did so), while others were afraid lest in their absence their encampments, denuded of man-power, be raided by hostile, as yet unconverted tribes (Rāzī); others, again, were simply averse to exposing themselves to the hardships of a campaign in distant lands, which did not seem to them to have any bearing on their own, immediate interests.

123 I.e., without even caring to come to Medina and to excuse themselves.

124 I.e., the old and the infirm.

125 Lit., "who do not find anything to spend", i.e., on their equipment. At the time in question a public treasury did not yet exist, and every participant in a military expedition was expected to provide his own weapons and mounts.

126 Lit., "who ask thee for exemption while they are rich". The term *ghanī* denotes "one who is rich" or "free from want" or "self-sufficient"; in this context it obviously refers to physical competence in addition to financial means: that is, to people who were able-bodied as well as financially in a position to equip themselves (cf. verses 86-87 above).

إِلَىٰ عَٰلِمِ ٱلْغَيْبِ وَٱلشَّهَٰدَةِ فَيُنَبِّئُكُم بِمَا كُنتُمْ تَعْمَلُونَ ﴿٩٤﴾ سَيَحْلِفُونَ
بِٱللَّهِ لَكُمْ إِذَا ٱنقَلَبْتُمْ إِلَيْهِمْ لِتُعْرِضُوا۟ عَنْهُمْ ۖ فَأَعْرِضُوا۟ عَنْهُمْ ۖ إِنَّهُمْ
رِجْسٌ ۖ وَمَأْوَىٰهُمْ جَهَنَّمُ جَزَآءًۢ بِمَا كَانُوا۟ يَكْسِبُونَ ﴿٩٥﴾ يَحْلِفُونَ لَكُمْ
لِتَرْضَوْا۟ عَنْهُمْ ۖ فَإِن تَرْضَوْا۟ عَنْهُمْ فَإِنَّ ٱللَّهَ لَا يَرْضَىٰ عَنِ ٱلْقَوْمِ ٱلْفَٰسِقِينَ ﴿٩٦﴾
ٱلْأَعْرَابُ أَشَدُّ كُفْرًا وَنِفَاقًا وَأَجْدَرُ أَلَّا يَعْلَمُوا۟ حُدُودَ مَآ أَنزَلَ ٱللَّهُ
عَلَىٰ رَسُولِهِۦ ۗ وَٱللَّهُ عَلِيمٌ حَكِيمٌ ﴿٩٧﴾ وَمِنَ ٱلْأَعْرَابِ مَن يَتَّخِذُ مَا يُنفِقُ
مَغْرَمًا وَيَتَرَبَّصُ بِكُمُ ٱلدَّوَآئِرَ ۚ عَلَيْهِمْ دَآئِرَةُ ٱلسَّوْءِ ۗ وَٱللَّهُ سَمِيعٌ
عَلِيمٌ ﴿٩٨﴾ وَمِنَ ٱلْأَعْرَابِ مَن يُؤْمِنُ بِٱللَّهِ وَٱلْيَوْمِ ٱلْءَاخِرِ وَيَتَّخِذُ مَا يُنفِقُ

ʾilā ʿĀlimil-ghaybi wash-shahādati fayunab-bi ʾukum-bimā kuñtum taʿmalūn. (94) Sayaḥlifūna billāhi lakum ʾidhañ-qalabtum ʾilayhim lituʿriḍū ʿanhum. Faʾaʿriḍū ʿanhum; ʾinnahum rijsuñw-wa maʾwāhum jahannamu jazāaʾam-bimā kānū yaksibūn. (95) Yaḥlifūna lakum litarḍaw ʿanhum. Faʾiñ-tarḍaw ʿanhum faʾinnal-lāha lā yarḍā ʿanil-qawmil-fāsiqīn. (96) ʾAlʾaʿrābu ʾashaddu kufrañw-wa nifāqañw-wa ʾajdaru ʾallā yaʿlamū ḥudūda māa ʾañzalal-lāhu ʿalā Rasūlih. Wal-lāhu ʿAlīmun Ḥakīm. (97) Wa minal-ʾaʿrābi mañy-yattakhidhu mā yuñfiqu maghramañw-wa yatarabbaṣu bikumud-dawāaʾira ʿalayhim dāaʾiratus-sawʾ. Wal-lāhu Samīʿun ʿAlīm. (98) Wa minal-ʾaʿrābi mañy-yuʾminu billāhi wal-Yawmil-ʾĀkhiri wa yattakhidhu mā yuñfiqu

before Him[127] who knows all that is beyond the reach of a created being's perception as well as all that can be witnessed by a creature's senses or mind,[128] and then He will make you truly understand what you were doing [in life]." ‹94›

When you will have returned to them, [O believers,] they will swear to you by God, [repeating their excuses,] with a view to your letting them be.[129] Let them be, then: behold, they are loathsome, and hell is their goal in recompense for what they were wont to do. ‹95› They will swear to you with a view to making you pleased with them: but [even] should you be pleased with them, verily, God shall never be pleased with iniquitous folk. ‹96›

[The hypocrites among] the bedouin[130] are more tenacious in [their] refusal to acknowledge the truth and in [their] hypocrisy [than are settled people], and more liable to ignore the ordinances which God has bestowed from on high upon His Apostle – but God is all-knowing, wise.[131] ‹97›

And among the bedouin there are such as regard all that they might spend [in God's cause] as a loss, and wait for misfortune to encompass you, [O believers: but] it is they whom evil fortune shall encompass – for God is all-hearing, all-knowing. ‹98›

However, among the bedouin there are [also] such as believe in God and the Last Day, and regard all that they spend [in God's cause] as a means of drawing them

127 Lit., "and thereafter you will be brought back unto Him".

128 See *sūrah* 6, note 65.

129 Sc., "and not punishing them". As a matter of fact, their fears were unfounded, since, on his return from Tabūk, the Prophet took no punitive action against any of those who had failed to follow him on his campaign.

130 The words interpolated by me between brackets at the beginning of this sentence are based on the interpretation given by Rāzī (see also *Manār* XI, 8), obviously in view of verse 99, which speaks of *believers* among the bedouin.

131 Owing to their nomadic way of life and its inherent hardship and crudity, the bedouin find it more difficult than do settled people to be guided by ethical imperatives unconnected with their immediate tribal interests – a difficulty which is still further enhanced by their physical distance from the centres of higher culture and, consequently, their comparative ignorance of most religious demands. It was for this reason that the Prophet often stressed the superiority of a settled mode of life to a nomadic one: cf. his saying, "He who dwells in the desert (*al-bādiyah*) becomes rough in disposition", recorded by Tirmidhī, Abū Dāʾūd, Nasāʾī and Ibn Ḥanbal, on the authority of Ibn ʿAbbās, and a similar Tradition, on the authority of Abū Hurayrah, by Abū Dāʾūd and Bayhaqī.

nearer to God and of [their being remembered in] the Apostle's prayers. Oh, verily, it shall [indeed] be a means of [God's] nearness to them, [for] God will admit them unto His grace: verily, God is much-forgiving, a dispenser of grace! ‹99›

And as for the first and foremost of those who have forsaken the domain of evil and of those who have sheltered and succoured the Faith,[132] as well as those who follow them in [the way of] righteousness – God is well-pleased with them, and well-pleased are they with Him. And for them has He readied gardens through which running waters flow, therein to abide beyond the count of time: this is the triumph supreme! ‹100›

But among the bedouin who dwell around you there are hypocrites; and among the people of the [Prophet's] City[133] [too] there are such as have grown insolent in [their] hypocrisy. Thou dost not [always] know them, [O Muḥammad – but] We know them. We shall cause them to suffer doubly [in this world];[134] and then they will be given over to awesome suffering [in the life to come]. ‹101›

And [there are] others[135] – [people who] have become conscious of their sinning after having done righteous deeds side by

قُرُبَٰتٍ عِندَ ٱللَّهِ وَصَلَوَٰتِ ٱلرَّسُولِ أَلَآ إِنَّهَا قُرۡبَةٞ لَّهُمۡۚ سَيُدۡخِلُهُمُ ٱللَّهُ فِي
رَحۡمَتِهِۦٓۚ إِنَّ ٱللَّهَ غَفُورٞ رَّحِيمٞ ﴿٩٩﴾ وَٱلسَّٰبِقُونَ ٱلۡأَوَّلُونَ مِنَ ٱلۡمُهَٰجِرِينَ
وَٱلۡأَنصَارِ وَٱلَّذِينَ ٱتَّبَعُوهُم بِإِحۡسَٰنٖ رَّضِيَ ٱللَّهُ عَنۡهُمۡ وَرَضُواْ عَنۡهُ وَأَعَدَّ
لَهُمۡ جَنَّٰتٖ تَجۡرِي تَحۡتَهَا ٱلۡأَنۡهَٰرُ خَٰلِدِينَ فِيهَآ أَبَدٗاۚ ذَٰلِكَ ٱلۡفَوۡزُ
ٱلۡعَظِيمُ ﴿١٠٠﴾ وَمِمَّنۡ حَوۡلَكُم مِّنَ ٱلۡأَعۡرَابِ مُنَٰفِقُونَۖ وَمِنۡ أَهۡلِ ٱلۡمَدِينَةِ
مَرَدُواْ عَلَى ٱلنِّفَاقِ لَا تَعۡلَمُهُمۡۖ نَحۡنُ نَعۡلَمُهُمۡۚ سَنُعَذِّبُهُم مَّرَّتَيۡنِ ثُمَّ يُرَدُّونَ
إِلَىٰ عَذَابٍ عَظِيمٖ ﴿١٠١﴾ وَءَاخَرُونَ ٱعۡتَرَفُواْ بِذُنُوبِهِمۡ خَلَطُواْ عَمَلٗا صَٰلِحٗا

qurubātin ʿiñdal-lāhi wa ṣalawātir-Rasūl. ʾAlāa ʾinnahā qurbatul-lahum. Sayudkhiluhumul-lāhu fī raḥmatih. ʾInnal-lāha Ghafūrur-Raḥīm. (99) Was-sābiqūnal-ʾawwalūna minal-muhājirīna wal-ʾañṣāri wal-ladhīnat-tabaʿūhum-biʾiḥsānir-raḍiyal-lāhu ʿanhum wa raḍū ʿanhu wa ʾaʿadda lahum jannātiñ-tajrī taḥtahal-ʾanhāru khālidīna fīhāa ʾabadā. Dhālikal-fawzul-ʿaẓīm. (100) Wa mimman ḥawlakum-minal-ʾaʿrābi munāfiqūna wa min ʾahlil-madīnati maradū ʿalan-nifāqi lā taʿlamuhum Naḥnu naʿlamuhum. Sanuʿadhdhibuhum marratayni thumma yuraddūna ʾilā ʿadhābin ʿaẓīm. (101) Wa ʾākharūnaʿ-tarafū bidhunūbihim khalaṭū ʿamalañ-ṣāliḥañw-

132 In the above context, the term *muhājirūn* – lit., "emigrants", rendered by me as "those who have forsaken the domain of evil" (see *sūrah* 2, note 203, and *sūrah* 4, note 124) – applies primarily to the Meccan followers of the Prophet who migrated (*hājarū*) from Mecca to Medina – which until then was called Yathrib – at a time when Mecca was still in the possession of the enemies of Islam; the "first and foremost" among them were the earliest emigrants, i.e., those who left Mecca in or before the year 622 of the Christian era (which marks the beginning of the Islamic *hijrī* era) and in the course of the next few years, when the Muslim community at Medina was still in danger of being overrun by the powerful Quraysh of Mecca. Similarly, the term *anṣār* (lit., "helpers") applies here to the early converts from among the people of Medina who sheltered and succoured (*naṣarū*) their brethren in faith – the "first and foremost" among them being those who embraced Islam before and shortly after the Prophet's and his Companions' exodus (*hijrah*) from Mecca, and particularly those who did so on the occasion of the two meetings, at Al-ʿAqabah near Mecca, between the Prophet and deputations of the Yathrib tribes of Al-Aws and Khazraj (a little over a year and a few months, respectively, before the Prophet's *hijrah*). Apart, however, from their purely historical connotations, both the terms *muhājirūn* and *anṣār* bear in the Qurʾān a spiritual meaning as well, and are often used to describe those who morally "forsake the domain of evil" and those who "shelter and succour the Faith" (see *sūrah* 8, note 78).

133 I.e., Medina. Originally, the city bore the name Yathrib; but after the exodus of the Prophet from Mecca it came to be known as *Madīnat an-Nabī* ("the City of the Prophet") and, eventually, as *Al-Madīnah* ("The City" *par excellence*).

134 I.e., first through failure in their worldly concerns, accompanied by pangs of conscience and the resulting spiritual distress, and then through a full realization, at the moment of dying, of the unforgivable nature of their sin (*Manār* XI, 19).

135 I.e., neither believers in the full sense of the word nor hypocrites, but half-hearted, confused waverers between right and wrong, or between truth and falsehood.

side with evil ones;[136] [and] it may well be that God will accept their repentance: for, verily, God is much-forgiving, a dispenser of grace. ‹102› [Hence, O Prophet,] accept that [part] of their possessions which is offered for the sake of God,[137] so that thou mayest cleanse them thereby and cause them to grow in purity, and pray for them: behold, thy prayer will be [a source of] comfort to them – for God is all-hearing, all-knowing. ‹103›

Do they not know that it is God alone who can accept the repentance of His servants[138] and is the [true] recipient of whatever is offered for His sake – and that God alone is an acceptor of repentance, a dispenser of grace? ‹104›

And say [unto them, O Prophet]: "Act![139] And God will behold your deeds, and [so will] His Apostle, and the believers: and [in the end] you will be brought before Him who knows all that is beyond the reach of a created being's perception as well as all that can be witnessed by a creature's senses or mind[140] – and then He will make you understand what you have been doing." ‹105›

And [there are yet] others – [people whose cases are] deferred until God wills to judge them:[141] He will either chastise them or turn again unto them in His mercy – for God is all-knowing, wise. ‹106›

وَءَاخَرَ سَيِّئًا عَسَى ٱللَّهُ أَن يَتُوبَ عَلَيْهِمْ إِنَّ ٱللَّهَ غَفُورٌ رَّحِيمٌ ﴿١٠٢﴾ خُذْ
مِنْ أَمْوَٰلِهِمْ صَدَقَةً تُطَهِّرُهُمْ وَتُزَكِّيهِم بِهَا وَصَلِّ عَلَيْهِمْ إِنَّ صَلَوٰتَكَ
سَكَنٌ لَّهُمْ وَٱللَّهُ سَمِيعٌ عَلِيمٌ ﴿١٠٣﴾ أَلَمْ يَعْلَمُوٓا۟ أَنَّ ٱللَّهَ هُوَ يَقْبَلُ ٱلتَّوْبَةَ
عَنْ عِبَادِهِۦ وَيَأْخُذُ ٱلصَّدَقَٰتِ وَأَنَّ ٱللَّهَ هُوَ ٱلتَّوَّابُ ٱلرَّحِيمُ ﴿١٠٤﴾ وَقُلِ
ٱعْمَلُوا۟ فَسَيَرَى ٱللَّهُ عَمَلَكُمْ وَرَسُولُهُۥ وَٱلْمُؤْمِنُونَ وَسَتُرَدُّونَ إِلَىٰ عَٰلِمِ
ٱلْغَيْبِ وَٱلشَّهَٰدَةِ فَيُنَبِّئُكُم بِمَا كُنتُمْ تَعْمَلُونَ ﴿١٠٥﴾ وَءَاخَرُونَ مُرْجَوْنَ
لِأَمْرِ ٱللَّهِ إِمَّا يُعَذِّبُهُمْ وَإِمَّا يَتُوبُ عَلَيْهِمْ وَٱللَّهُ عَلِيمٌ حَكِيمٌ ﴿١٠٦﴾

wa ʾākhara sayyiʾan ʿasal-lāhu ʾañy-yatūba ʿalayhim; ʾinnal-lāha Ghafūrur-Raḥīm. ﴿102﴾ Khudh min ʾamwālihim ṣadaqatañ-tuṭahhiruhum wa tuzakkīhim-bihā wa ṣalli ʿalayhim. ʾInna ṣalātaka sakanul-lahum. Wal-lāhu Samīʿun ʿAlīm. ﴿103﴾ ʾAlam yaʿlamūu ʾannal-lāha Huwa yaqbalut-tawbata ʿan ʿibādihī wa yaʾkhudhuṣ-ṣadaqāti wa ʾannal-lāha Huwat-Tawwābur-Raḥīm. ﴿104﴾ Wa quliʿ-malū fasayaral-lāhu ʿamalakum wa Rasūluhū wal-muʾminūn. Wa saturaddūna ʾilā ʿĀlimil-ghaybi wash-shahādati fayunabbiʾukum-bimā kuñtum taʿmalūn. ﴿105﴾ Wa ʾākharūna murjawna liʾamril-lāhi ʾimmā yuʿadhdhibuhum wa ʾimmā yatūbu ʿalayhim. Wal-lāhu ʿAlīmun Ḥakīm. ﴿106﴾

136 Lit., "who have acknowledged their sins [after] having mingled a righteous deed with another that was evil". Although it relates primarily to the vacillating Muslims who refused to participate in the expedition to Tabūk, this verse alludes, in its wider meaning, to all sinners who – without external prompting – become conscious of their wrongdoing and repent of it.

137 Lit., "take out of their possessions an offering for the sake of God (*ṣadaqah*)". For the meaning of this term, see note 81 above. In this context, it primarily denotes the tax called *zakāh* ("the purifying dues") incumbent on every Muslim enjoying a certain minimum of property and/or income. Since an acceptance of *zakāh* by the head of state (or of the community) amounts to a recognition of the giver as a "Muslim" in the Qurʾanic sense of this term, the Prophet refused to accept it from all whose behaviour had made it obvious that they were hypocrites; the above verse, however, authorizes him (and, by implication, the authorities of an Islamic state at all times) to accept the payment of *zakāh* from those who express their repentance by deeds as well as by words.

138 Lit., "who accepts repentance from His servants": thus pointing out that no human being, not even the Prophet, has the power to absolve a sinner of his guilt (*Manār* XI, 32). A prophet can do no more than pray to God that He forgive the sinners.

139 This connects with the injunction in verse 103 above, "accept that [part] of their possessions which is offered for the sake of God, . . . and pray for them". The stress on *action* as an integral part of faith is of fundamental importance in the ethics of the Qurʾān: cf. the frequent juxtaposition of the concepts of "believing" and "doing good works", and the condemnation of all "who, while believing, wrought no good works" (see 6 : 158 and the corresponding note 160).

140 See *sūrah* 6, note 65.

141 Lit., "deferred unto God's decree (*amr*)" – i.e., kept in abeyance in anticipation of their future repentance. As in

AND [there are hypocrites] who have established a [separate] house of worship in order to create mischief, and to promote apostasy and disunity among the believers, and to provide an outpost for all who from the outset have been warring against God and His Apostle.[142] And they will surely swear [to you, O believers], "We had but the best of intentions!" – the while God [Himself] bears witness that they are lying.[143] ‹107›
Never set foot in such a place![144] Only a house of worship founded, from the very first day, upon God-consciousness is worthy of thy setting foot therein[145] – [a house of worship] wherein there are men desirous of growing in purity: for God loves all who purify themselves. ‹108›

وَٱلَّذِينَ ٱتَّخَذُوا۟ مَسْجِدًا ضِرَارًا وَكُفْرًا وَتَفْرِيقًۢا بَيْنَ ٱلْمُؤْمِنِينَ وَإِرْصَادًا
لِّمَنْ حَارَبَ ٱللَّهَ وَرَسُولَهُۥ مِن قَبْلُ ۚ وَلَيَحْلِفُنَّ إِنْ أَرَدْنَآ إِلَّا ٱلْحُسْنَىٰ ۖ
وَٱللَّهُ يَشْهَدُ إِنَّهُمْ لَكَٰذِبُونَ ﴿١٠٧﴾ لَا تَقُمْ فِيهِ أَبَدًا ۚ لَّمَسْجِدٌ أُسِّسَ عَلَى
ٱلتَّقْوَىٰ مِنْ أَوَّلِ يَوْمٍ أَحَقُّ أَن تَقُومَ فِيهِ ۚ فِيهِ رِجَالٌ يُحِبُّونَ أَن يَتَطَهَّرُوا۟ ۚ
وَٱللَّهُ يُحِبُّ ٱلْمُطَّهِّرِينَ ﴿١٠٨﴾

Wal-ladhīnat-takhadhū masjidañ-ḍirārañw-wa kufrañw-wa tafrīqam-baynal-muʾminīna wa ʾirṣādal-liman ḥārabal-lāha wa Rasūlahū miñ-qabl. Wa layaḥlifunna ʾin ʾaradnāa ʾillal-ḥusnā; wal-lāhu yashhadu ʾinnahum lakādhibūn. (107) **Lā taqum fīhi ʾabadā. Lamasjidun ʾussisa ʿalat-taqwā min ʾawwali yawmin ʾaḥaqqu ʾañ-taqūma fīh. Fīhi rijāluñy-yuḥibbūna ʾañy-yataṭahharū; wal-lāhu yuḥibbul-muṭṭahhirīn.** (108)

the preceding four verses, the people referred to here are, in the first instance, the waverers who stayed away from the campaign of Tabūk, and, by implication, all half-hearted believers who confusedly hover between right and wrong: with the difference, however, that whereas the repentant sinners spoken of in verses 102-105 are said to have realized their sinfulness spontaneously, the kind of people referred to in verse 106 have not yet reached the stage of moral self-examination and repentance, with the result that their cases are "deferred" until such a time as their impulses sway them entirely one way or another. From a psychological point of view, it is possible to discern a subtle connection between this verse and 7 : 46-47.

142 Lit., "who have been warring against God and His Apostle aforetime" – i.e., before the expedition to Tabūk. The historical occasion to which this verse refers may be thus summarized: Ever since his exodus from Mecca to Medina the Prophet was violently opposed by one Abū ʿĀmir ("The Monk") a prominent member of the Khazraj tribe, who had embraced Christianity many years earlier and enjoyed a considerable reputation among his compatriots and among the Christians of Syria. From the very outset he allied himself with the Prophet's enemies, the Meccan Quraysh, and took part on their side in the battle of Uḥud (3 H.). Shortly thereafter he migrated to Syria and did all that he could to induce the Emperor of Byzantium, Heraclius, to invade Medina and crush the Muslim community once and for all. In Medina itself, Abū ʿĀmir had some secret followers among the members of his tribe, with whom he remained in constant correspondence. In the year 9 H. he informed them that Heraclius had agreed to send out an army against Medina, and that large-scale preparations were being made to this effect (which was apparently the reason for the Prophet's preventive expedition to Tabūk). In order that his followers should have a rallying-place in the event of the expected invasion of Medina, Abū ʿĀmir suggested to his friends that they build a mosque of their own in the village of Qubāʾ, in the immediate vicinity of Medina (which they did), and thus obviate the necessity of congregating in the mosque which the Prophet himself had built in the same village at the time of his arrival at Medina (see note 145 below). It is this "rival" mosque to which the above verse refers. It was demolished at the Prophet's orders immediately after his return from the Tabūk expedition. Abū ʿĀmir himself died in Syria shortly afterwards. (For all the relevant Traditions, see Ṭabarī's and Ibn Kathīr's commentaries on this verse.)

143 Although the whole of this verse relates primarily to the historical occasion explained in the preceding note, it has a definite bearing on all attempts at creating sectarian divisions among Muslims, and is thus a clear amplification of an earlier injunction to this effect (see 6 : 159 and the corresponding note 161).

144 Lit., "in it" – sc., "to pray therein".

145 Lit., "Indeed, a house of worship founded . . . upon God-consciousness (*taqwā*) is most deserving . . .", etc. Some of the commentators believe that this is a reference to the mosque founded by the Prophet at Qubāʾ, a village close to Medina, on his arrival there in the month of Rabīʿ al-Awwal in the year 1 H., since it was the first mosque ever built by him or his followers. There are, however, authentic Traditions to the effect that the Prophet applied the designation of "a house of worship founded on God-consciousness" to his (later-built) mosque at Medina as well (Muslim, Tirmidhī, Nasāʾī, Ibn Ḥanbal. It is, therefore, reasonable to assume that it applies to *every* mosque sincerely dedicated by its founders to the worship of God: a view which is supported by the next verse.

ربع
الحزب

Which, then, is the better: he who has founded his building on God-consciousness and [a desire for] His goodly acceptance – or he who has founded his building on the edge of a water-worn, crumbling river-bank, so that it [is bound to] tumble down with him into the fire of hell?
For, God does not grace with His guidance people who [deliberately] do wrong: «109»
the building which they have built will never cease to be a source of deep disquiet in their hearts until their hearts crumble to pieces.[146] And God is all-knowing, wise. «110»

BEHOLD, God has bought of the believers their lives and their possessions, promising them paradise in return, [and so] they fight in God's cause, and slay, and are slain: a promise which in truth He has willed upon Himself in [the words of] the Torah, and the Gospel, and the Qurʾān. And who could be more faithful to his covenant than God?
Rejoice, then, in the bargain which you have made with Him: for this, this is the triumph supreme! «111»
[It is a triumph of] those who turn [unto God] in repentance [whenever they have sinned], and who worship and praise [Him], and go on and on [seeking His goodly acceptance],[147] and bow down [before Him] and prostrate themselves in adoration, and enjoin the doing of what is right and forbid the doing of what is wrong, and keep to the bounds set by God. And give thou [O Prophet] the glad tiding [of God's promise] to all believers. «112»

أَفَمَنْ أَسَّسَ بُنْيَٰنَهُۥ عَلَىٰ تَقْوَىٰ مِنَ ٱللَّهِ وَرِضْوَٰنٍ خَيْرٌ أَم مَّنْ أَسَّسَ
بُنْيَٰنَهُۥ عَلَىٰ شَفَا جُرُفٍ هَارٍ فَٱنْهَارَ بِهِۦ فِى نَارِ جَهَنَّمَ ۗ وَٱللَّهُ لَا يَهْدِى
ٱلْقَوْمَ ٱلظَّٰلِمِينَ ﴿١٠٩﴾ لَا يَزَالُ بُنْيَٰنُهُمُ ٱلَّذِى بَنَوْا۟ رِيبَةً فِى قُلُوبِهِمْ إِلَّآ
أَن تَقَطَّعَ قُلُوبُهُمْ ۗ وَٱللَّهُ عَلِيمٌ حَكِيمٌ ﴿١١٠﴾ ۞ إِنَّ ٱللَّهَ ٱشْتَرَىٰ مِنَ
ٱلْمُؤْمِنِينَ أَنفُسَهُمْ وَأَمْوَٰلَهُم بِأَنَّ لَهُمُ ٱلْجَنَّةَ ۚ يُقَٰتِلُونَ فِى سَبِيلِ ٱللَّهِ
فَيَقْتُلُونَ وَيُقْتَلُونَ ۖ وَعْدًا عَلَيْهِ حَقًّا فِى ٱلتَّوْرَىٰةِ وَٱلْإِنجِيلِ وَٱلْقُرْءَانِ ۚ وَمَنْ
أَوْفَىٰ بِعَهْدِهِۦ مِنَ ٱللَّهِ ۚ فَٱسْتَبْشِرُوا۟ بِبَيْعِكُمُ ٱلَّذِى بَايَعْتُم بِهِۦ ۚ وَذَٰلِكَ هُوَ
ٱلْفَوْزُ ٱلْعَظِيمُ ﴿١١١﴾ ٱلتَّٰٓئِبُونَ ٱلْعَٰبِدُونَ ٱلْحَٰمِدُونَ ٱلسَّٰٓئِحُونَ
ٱلرَّٰكِعُونَ ٱلسَّٰجِدُونَ ٱلْءَامِرُونَ بِٱلْمَعْرُوفِ وَٱلنَّاهُونَ عَنِ ٱلْمُنكَرِ
وَٱلْحَٰفِظُونَ لِحُدُودِ ٱللَّهِ ۗ وَبَشِّرِ ٱلْمُؤْمِنِينَ ﴿١١٢﴾

ʾAfaman ʾassasa bunyānahū ʿalā taqwā minal-lāhi wa riḍwānin khayrun ʾamman ʾassasa bunyānahū ʿalā shafā jurufin hāriñ-fanhāra bihī fī nāri jahannam. Wal-lāhu lā yahdil-qawmaẓ-ẓālimīn. (109)
Lā yazālu bunyānuhumul-ladhī banaw rībatañ-fī qulūbihim ʾillāa ʾañ-taqaṭṭaʿa qulūbuhum. Wal-lāhu ʿAlīmun Ḥakīm. (110)
۞ ʾInnal-lāhash-tarā minal-muʾminīna ʾañfusahum wa ʾamwālahum-biʾanna lahumul-jannah. Yuqātilūna fī sabīlil-lāhi fayaqtulūna wa yuqtalūna waʿdan ʿalayhi ḥaqqañ-fit-Tawrāti wal-ʾIñjīli wal-Qurʾān. Wa man ʾawfā biʿahdihī minal-lāh. Fastabshirū bibayʿikumul-ladhī bāyaʿtum-bihi wa dhālika huwal-fawzul-ʿaẓīm. (111)
ʾAttāaʾibūnal-ʿābidūnal-ḥāmidūnas-sāaʾiḥūnar-rākiʿūnas-sājidūnal-ʾāmirūna bilmaʿrūfi wan-nāhūna ʿanil-muñkari wal-ḥāfiẓūna liḥudūdil-lāh. Wa bashshiril-muʾminīn. (112)

146 Lit., "unless their hearts are cut into many pieces" – i.e., until they die. In verses 109-110, the reference to "the building which they have built" is, obviously, widened beyond the preceding allusion to houses of worship, and allegorically circumscribes here all the "works" and the behaviour of men.

147 Most of the commentators attribute to the expression *as-sāʾiḥūn* (lit., "those who wander") the meaning of *aṣ-ṣāʾimūn*, i.e., "those who fast", since he who fasts deprives himself, temporarily, of worldly enjoyments similar to one who wanders about the earth (Sufyān ibn ʿUyaynah, as quoted by Rāzī); and they justify this metaphorical equation of *siyāḥah* ("wandering") with *ṣiyām* ("fasting") by the fact that several Companions and some of their successors have thus interpreted the term *as-sāʾiḥūn* in the above context (see Ṭabarī). Other authorities, however, (e.g., Abū Muslim, as quoted by Rāzī) prefer the original significance of this term and explain it as more or less synonymous with *al-muhājirūn* ("those who forsake the domain of evil"). To my mind, the expression *as-sāʾiḥūn* is best rendered as "those who go on and on [seeking God's goodly acceptance]", thus combining the literal and metonymical connotations of the term *siyāḥah*.

IT DOES NOT behove the Prophet and those who have attained to faith to pray that they who ascribed divinity to aught beside God be forgiven [by Him] – even though they happened to be [their] near of kin[148] – after it has been made clear unto them that those [dead sinners] are destined for the blazing fire. ⟨113⟩ And Abraham's prayer that his father be forgiven was but due to a promise which he had given the latter [in his lifetime];[149] but when it was made clear unto him that he had been God's enemy, [Abraham] disavowed him – [although,] behold, Abraham was most tender-hearted, most clement. ⟨114⟩
And God would never – after having invited them to His guidance – condemn people for going astray[150] ere He has made [entirely] clear unto them of what they should beware. Verily, God has full knowledge of everything.[151] ⟨115⟩
Verily, God's alone is the dominion over the heavens and the earth; He [alone] grants life and deals death; and there is none besides God who could protect you or bring you succour. ⟨116⟩

INDEED, God has turned in His mercy unto the Prophet, as well as unto those who have forsaken the domain of evil and those who have sheltered and succoured

مَا كَانَ لِلنَّبِيِّ وَٱلَّذِينَ ءَامَنُوٓاْ أَن يَسۡتَغۡفِرُواْ لِلۡمُشۡرِكِينَ وَلَوۡ كَانُوٓاْ أُوْلِي
قُرۡبَىٰ مِنۢ بَعۡدِ مَا تَبَيَّنَ لَهُمۡ أَنَّهُمۡ أَصۡحَٰبُ ٱلۡجَحِيمِ ﴿١١٣﴾ وَمَا كَانَ ٱسۡتِغۡفَارُ
إِبۡرَٰهِيمَ لِأَبِيهِ إِلَّا عَن مَّوۡعِدَةٖ وَعَدَهَآ إِيَّاهُ فَلَمَّا تَبَيَّنَ لَهُۥٓ أَنَّهُۥ عَدُوّٞ لِّلَّهِ
تَبَرَّأَ مِنۡهُۚ إِنَّ إِبۡرَٰهِيمَ لَأَوَّٰهٌ حَلِيمٞ ﴿١١٤﴾ وَمَا كَانَ ٱللَّهُ لِيُضِلَّ قَوۡمَۢا بَعۡدَ إِذۡ
هَدَىٰهُمۡ حَتَّىٰ يُبَيِّنَ لَهُم مَّا يَتَّقُونَۚ إِنَّ ٱللَّهَ بِكُلِّ شَيۡءٍ عَلِيمٌ ﴿١١٥﴾ إِنَّ ٱللَّهَ لَهُۥ
مُلۡكُ ٱلسَّمَٰوَٰتِ وَٱلۡأَرۡضِۖ يُحۡيِۦ وَيُمِيتُۚ وَمَا لَكُم مِّن دُونِ ٱللَّهِ مِن وَلِيّٖ
وَلَا نَصِيرٖ ﴿١١٦﴾ لَقَد تَّابَ ٱللَّهُ عَلَى ٱلنَّبِيِّ وَٱلۡمُهَٰجِرِينَ وَٱلۡأَنصَارِ

Mā kāna linNabiyyi wal-ladhīna ʾāmanūu ʾañy-yastaghfirū lilmushrikīna wa law kānūu ʾulī qurbā mim-baʿdi mā tabayyana lahum ʾannahum ʾaṣḥābul-jaḥīm. (113) Wa mā kānas-tighfāru ʾIbrāhīma liʾabīhi ʾillā ʿam-mawʿidatiñw-waʿadahāa ʾiyyāhu falammā tabayyana lahūu ʾannahū ʿaduwwul-lillāhi tabarraʾa minh. ʾInna ʾIbrāhīma laʾawwāhun ḥalīm. (114) Wa mā kānal-lāhu liyuḍilla qawmam-baʿda ʾidh hadāhum ḥattā yubayyina lahum-mā yattaqūn. ʾInnal-lāha bikulli shayʾin ʿAlīm. (115) ʾInnal-lāha lahū mulkus-samāwāti wal-ʾarḍi yuḥyī wa yumīt. Wa mā lakum-miñ-dūnil-lāhi miñw-waliyyiñw-wa lā naṣīr. (116) Laqat-tābal-lāhu ʿalan-Nabiyyi wal-muhājirīna wal-ʾañṣāril-

148 As is obvious from the sequence, this prohibition relates to the *dead* among such sinners – i.e., those who have died without repentance (Zamakhsharī, Rāzī) – and not to those who are still living: for "a prayer for forgiveness in respect of a living [sinner] . . . amounts to asking God that He grace him with His guidance . . . and this is permissible" (*Manār* XI, 60).

149 Abraham's promise to his father is mentioned in 19 : 47-48 and 60 : 4; for the actual prayer, see 26 : 86-87.

150 Lit., "it is not for God" – i.e., it is not compatible with God's omniscience and majesty – "that He should cause people to go astray after He has guided them". My rendering of the phrase "that He should cause people to go astray" as "condemn people for going astray" is based on the interpretation given to it by some of the greatest classical commentators (e.g., Ṭabarī, Rāzī). As regards the phrase, "after He has guided them", Rāzī interprets it as meaning "after He has *invited* them to the way of rectitude (*ar-rushd*)".

151 Most of the commentators assume that the people referred to are the believers who, before the revelation of verse 113, used to pray to God that He grant His forgiveness to their relatives and friends who had died in the state of *shirk* ("ascribing divinity to aught beside God"): in other words, the believers need not fear to be taken to task for something which they did *before* the prohibition laid down in verse 113 was revealed (i.e., "ere He has made clear unto them of what they should beware"). However, Rāzī advances also an alternative interpretation of verse 115, suggesting that it is meant to explain the severity with which the whole of this *sūrah* condemns the deniers of the truth and the hypocrites who are going astray *after* God "has made clear unto them of what they should beware". (See in this connection 6 : 131-132 and the corresponding notes.) This interpretation is, to my mind, the more plausible of the two, and particularly so in view of the sequence (verse 116).

the Faith[152] – [all] those who followed him in the hour of distress, when the hearts of some of the other believers had well-nigh swerved from faith.[153]

And once again:[154] He has turned unto them in His mercy – for, behold, He is compassionate towards them, a dispenser of grace. ‹117›

And [He turned in His mercy, too,] towards the three [groups of believers] who had fallen prey to corruption,[155] until in the end – after the earth, despite all its vastness, had become [too] narrow for them and their souls had become [utterly] constricted – they came to know with certainty that there is no refuge from God other than [a return] unto Him; and thereupon He turned again unto them in His mercy, so that they might repent: for, verily, God alone is an acceptor of repentance, a dispenser of grace.[156] ‹118›

O YOU who have attained to faith! Remain conscious of God, and be among those who are true to their word! ‹119›

ٱلَّذِينَ ٱتَّبَعُوهُ فِى سَاعَةِ ٱلْعُسْرَةِ مِنۢ بَعْدِ مَا كَادَ يَزِيغُ قُلُوبُ فَرِيقٍ مِّنْهُمْ
ثُمَّ تَابَ عَلَيْهِمْ إِنَّهُۥ بِهِمْ رَءُوفٌ رَّحِيمٌ ﴿117﴾ وَعَلَى ٱلثَّلَٰثَةِ ٱلَّذِينَ خُلِّفُوا۟
حَتَّىٰٓ إِذَا ضَاقَتْ عَلَيْهِمُ ٱلْأَرْضُ بِمَا رَحُبَتْ وَضَاقَتْ عَلَيْهِمْ أَنفُسُهُمْ
وَظَنُّوٓا۟ أَن لَّا مَلْجَأَ مِنَ ٱللَّهِ إِلَّآ إِلَيْهِ ثُمَّ تَابَ عَلَيْهِمْ لِيَتُوبُوٓا۟ إِنَّ ٱللَّهَ هُوَ
ٱلتَّوَّابُ ٱلرَّحِيمُ ﴿118﴾ يَٰٓأَيُّهَا ٱلَّذِينَ ءَامَنُوا۟ ٱتَّقُوا۟ ٱللَّهَ وَكُونُوا۟ مَعَ
ٱلصَّٰدِقِينَ ﴿119﴾

ladhīnat-taba ͨūhu fī sā ͨatil- ͨusrati mim-ba ͨdi mā
kāda yazīghu qulūbu farīqim-minhum thumma tāba
ͨalayhim. ʾInnahū bihim Ra ʾūfur-Raḥīm. (117) Wa
ͨalath-thalāthatil-ladhīna khullifū ḥattāa ʾidhā ḍāqat
ͨalayhimul-ʾarḍu bimā raḥubat wa ḍāqat ͨalayhim
ʾañfusuhum wa ẓannūu ʾal-lā malja ʾa minal-lāhi
ʾillāa ʾilayhi thumma tāba ͨalayhim liyatūbū. ʾInnal-
lāha Huwat-Tawwābur-Raḥīm. (118) Yāa ʾayyuhal-ladhīna
ʾāmanut-taqul-lāha wa kūnū ma ͨaṣ-ṣādiqīn. (119)

152 See note 132 above.

153 Lit., "after the hearts of a group of them had well-nigh swerved [from faith]": a reference to the believers – who without valid excuse – failed to respond to the Prophet's call when he was setting out on the expedition to Tabūk, and who afterwards repented.

154 See *sūrah* 6, note 31. According to Zamakhsharī and Rāzī, the particle *thumma* has here the meaning given in my rendering, and serves to emphasize the statement that "God has turned in His mercy unto the Prophet . . . and all those who followed him in the hour of distress".

155 Or: "had been left behind", i.e., at the time of the expedition to Tabūk. My rendering of *alladhīna khullifū* as "those who had fallen prey to corruption" is based on the tropical meaning of the verb *khalufa* or *khullifa*, "he was [or "became"] altered [for the worse]", or "he became corrupt" in the moral sense (see *Asās, Nihāyah, Lisān al-ͨArab, Qāmūs, Tāj al-ͨArūs*). This interpretation of *alladhīna khullifū* – applying, in the above context, to those who remained behind under false pretences – has the support of some of the most outstanding Arab philologists, e.g., ͨAbd al-Malik al-Aṣmaͨī (as quoted by Rāzī in his commentary on verse 83 of this *sūrah*). – As regards "the three who had fallen prey to corruption", the classical commentators assume that it is a reference to three *persons* – namely, Kaͨb ibn Mālik, Marārah ibn ar-Rabīͨ and Hilāl ibn Umayyah (all of them from among the *anṣār*) – who abstained from the campaign and were thereafter ostracized by the Prophet and his Companions until the revelation of the above verse. But while it is historically established that these three Companions were indeed among the believers who thus failed in their duty (the relevant Traditions will be found *in extenso* in Ṭabarī's and Ibn Kathīr's commentaries on this verse), it seems to me that the context does not warrant such a restriction of its meaning to three particular persons, and that by "the three" are meant three *groups* of erring believers: (1) those who had advanced equivocal excuses and were thereupon permitted by the Prophet to remain at home (as has been alluded to in verses 43-46 as well as in the first sentence of verse 90); (2) those who absented themselves without permission, but afterwards spontaneously repented their sin (verses 102-105); and (3) those whose cases were at first "deferred" (verse 106), and who repented shortly after the Prophet's return from Tabūk (at which time verse 118 was revealed).

156 In its wider implication – as contrasted with a purely historical allusion – the above verse relates to all believers who temporarily deviate from the right path and then, after having realized – either spontaneously or in consequence of outside reprobation – that they had "fallen prey to corruption", sincerely repent their sin.

It does not behove the people of the [Prophet's] City and the bedouin [who live] around them to hold back from following God's Apostle, or to care for their own selves more than for him[157] – for, whenever they suffer from thirst or weariness or hunger in God's cause, and whenever they take any step which confounds[158] those who deny the truth, and whenever there comes to them from the enemy whatever may be destined for them[159] – [whenever anything thereof comes to pass,] a good deed is recorded in their favour.[160] Verily, God does not fail to requite the doers of good! ‹120›

And whenever they spend anything [for the sake of God], be it little or much, and whenever they move on earth[161] [in God's cause] – it is recorded in their favour, and God will grant them the best reward for all that they have been doing. ‹121›

With all this, it is not desirable that all of the believers take the field [in time of war]. From within every group in their midst, some shall refrain from going forth to war, and shall devote themselves [instead] to acquiring a deeper knowledge of the Faith, and [thus be able to] teach their home-coming brethren, so that these [too] might guard themselves against evil.[162] ‹122›

مَا كَانَ لِأَهْلِ ٱلْمَدِينَةِ وَمَنْ حَوْلَهُم مِّنَ ٱلْأَعْرَابِ أَن يَتَخَلَّفُوا۟ عَن
رَّسُولِ ٱللَّهِ وَلَا يَرْغَبُوا۟ بِأَنفُسِهِمْ عَن نَّفْسِهِۦ ذَٰلِكَ بِأَنَّهُمْ لَا يُصِيبُهُمْ ظَمَأٌ
وَلَا نَصَبٌ وَلَا مَخْمَصَةٌ فِى سَبِيلِ ٱللَّهِ وَلَا يَطَـُٔونَ مَوْطِئًا يَغِيظُ ٱلْكُفَّارَ
وَلَا يَنَالُونَ مِنْ عَدُوٍّ نَّيْلًا إِلَّا كُتِبَ لَهُم بِهِۦ عَمَلٌ صَٰلِحٌ إِنَّ ٱللَّهَ لَا
يُضِيعُ أَجْرَ ٱلْمُحْسِنِينَ ﴿١٢٠﴾ وَلَا يُنفِقُونَ نَفَقَةً صَغِيرَةً وَلَا كَبِيرَةً وَلَا
يَقْطَعُونَ وَادِيًا إِلَّا كُتِبَ لَهُمْ لِيَجْزِيَهُمُ ٱللَّهُ أَحْسَنَ مَا كَانُوا۟
يَعْمَلُونَ ﴿١٢١﴾ ۞ وَمَا كَانَ ٱلْمُؤْمِنُونَ لِيَنفِرُوا۟ كَآفَّةً فَلَوْلَا نَفَرَ مِن كُلِّ
فِرْقَةٍ مِّنْهُمْ طَآئِفَةٌ لِّيَتَفَقَّهُوا۟ فِى ٱلدِّينِ وَلِيُنذِرُوا۟ قَوْمَهُمْ إِذَا رَجَعُوٓا۟
إِلَيْهِمْ لَعَلَّهُمْ يَحْذَرُونَ ﴿١٢٢﴾

نصف الحزب

Mā kāna liʾahlil-madīnati wa man ḥawlahum-minal-ʾaᶜrābi ʾañy-yatakhallafū ᶜar-Rasūlil-lāhi wa lā yarghabū biʾañfusihim ᶜan-nafsih. Dhālika biʾannahum lā yuṣībuhum ẓamaʾuñw-wa lā naṣabuñw-wa lā makhmaṣatuñ-fī sabīlil-lāhi wa lā yaṭaʾūna mawṭiʾañy-yaghīẓul-kuffāra wa lā yanālūna min ᶜaduwwiñ-naylan ʾillā kutiba lahum-bihī ᶜamaluñ-ṣāliḥ. ʾInnal-lāha lā yuḍīᶜu ʾajral-muḥsinīn. (120) Wa lā yuñfiqūna nafaqatañ-ṣaghīratañw-wa lā kabīratañw-wa lā yaqṭaᶜūna wādiyan ʾillā kutiba lahum liyajziya-humul-lāhu ʾaḥsana mā kānū yaᶜmalūn. (121) ۞ Wa mā kānal-muʾminūna liyañfirū kāaffah. Falawlā nafara miñ-kulli firqatim-minhum ṭāaʾifatul-liyatafaqqahū fid-dīni wa liyuñdhirū qawmahum ʾidhā rajaᶜūu ʾilayhim laᶜallahum yaḥdharūn. (122)

157 Although this and the following verses relate, on the face of it, to "the people of the Prophet's City" (see note 133 above) and to "the bedouin who live around them", their purport is obviously general, and applies to all believers at all times. The specific reference to "the Prophet's City" is due to the fact that it was the place where the revelation of the Qurʾān was completed and Islam came to its full fruition under the Prophet's guidance.

158 Lit., "causes wrath to".

159 Lit., "[whenever] they get from the enemy whatever they get" – i.e., victory or death or injury.

160 In its original construction, this sentence reads thus: "and neither thirst afflicts them . . ., nor do they take any step . . ., nor do they get from the enemy . . ., without that a good deed is recorded in their behalf". The same construction is applied to the next verse.

161 Lit., "cross a valley". As Zamakhsharī rightly points out in his commentary on this verse, the term *wādī* ("valley" or "river-bed") is often used in classical Arabic to denote "the earth" – a usage which even in our days is familiar to the bedouin of the Arabian Peninsula, especially when combined with the verb *qaṭaᶜa* (lit., "he cut") in its connotation of "cutting across" or "traversing [a distance]" or "advancing [on a journey]". Thus, the above Qurʾanic phrase may be suitably rendered as "whenever they move on earth". (As regards the construction of this sentence, see preceding note.)

162 Lit., "admonish their people when they come back to them, so that they might be on their guard". Although the above injunction mentions specifically *religious* knowledge, it has a positive bearing on *every* kind of knowledge – and this in view of the fact that the Qurʾān does not draw any dividing-line between the spiritual and the worldly concerns of life but, rather, regards them as different aspects of one and the same reality. In many of its verses, the Qurʾān calls upon the believer to observe all nature and to discern God's creative activity in its manifold phenomena and "laws", as well as to meditate upon the lessons of history with a view to gaining a deeper insight into man's

O you who have attained to faith! Fight against those deniers of the truth who are near you, and let them find you adamant;[163] and know that God is with those who are conscious of Him. «123»

YET WHENEVER a *sūrah* [of this divine writ] is bestowed from on high, some of the deniers of the truth are prone to ask,[164] "Which of you has this [message] strengthened in his faith?"
Now as for those who have attained to faith, it does strengthen them in their faith, and they rejoice in the glad tiding [which God has given them].[165] «124» But as for those in whose hearts is disease, each new message but adds another [element of] disbelief to the disbelief which they already harbour,[166] and they die while [still] refusing to acknowledge the truth. «125»
Are they, then, not aware that they are being tested year-in, year-out?[167] And yet, they do not repent and do not bethink themselves [of God]; «126» and whenever a *sūrah* is bestowed from on high, they look at one another [and say, as it were], "Is there anyone who can see what is in your

يَٰٓأَيُّهَا ٱلَّذِينَ ءَامَنُوا۟ قَٰتِلُوا۟ ٱلَّذِينَ يَلُونَكُم مِّنَ ٱلْكُفَّارِ وَلْيَجِدُوا۟ فِيكُمْ
غِلْظَةً ۚ وَٱعْلَمُوٓا۟ أَنَّ ٱللَّهَ مَعَ ٱلْمُتَّقِينَ ﴿123﴾ وَإِذَا مَآ أُنزِلَتْ سُورَةٌ فَمِنْهُم
مَّن يَقُولُ أَيُّكُمْ زَادَتْهُ هَٰذِهِۦٓ إِيمَٰنًا ۚ فَأَمَّا ٱلَّذِينَ ءَامَنُوا۟ فَزَادَتْهُمْ
إِيمَٰنًا وَهُمْ يَسْتَبْشِرُونَ ﴿124﴾ وَأَمَّا ٱلَّذِينَ فِى قُلُوبِهِم مَّرَضٌ فَزَادَتْهُمْ
رِجْسًا إِلَىٰ رِجْسِهِمْ وَمَاتُوا۟ وَهُمْ كَٰفِرُونَ ﴿125﴾ أَوَلَا يَرَوْنَ أَنَّهُمْ
يُفْتَنُونَ فِى كُلِّ عَامٍ مَّرَّةً أَوْ مَرَّتَيْنِ ثُمَّ لَا يَتُوبُونَ وَلَا هُمْ يَذَّكَّرُونَ ﴿126﴾
وَإِذَا مَآ أُنزِلَتْ سُورَةٌ نَّظَرَ بَعْضُهُمْ إِلَىٰ بَعْضٍ هَلْ يَرَىٰكُم مِّنْ أَحَدٍ

Yāa ʾayyuhal-ladhīna ʾāmanū qātilul-ladhīna yalūnakum-minal-kuffāri wal-yajidū fīkum ghilẓah. Waᶜ-lamūu ʾannal-lāha maᶜal-muttaqīn. ﴿123﴾ Wa ʾidhā māa ʾuñzilat Sūratuñ-faminhum-mañy-yaqūlu ʾayyukum zādat-hu hādhihīi ʾīmānā. Faʾammal-ladhīna ʾāmanū fazādat-hum ʾīmānañw-wa hum yastabshirūn. ﴿124﴾ Wa ʾammal-ladhīna fī qulūbihim-maraḍuñ-fazādat-hum rijsan ʾilā rijsihim wa mātū wa hum kāfirūn. ﴿125﴾ ʾAwa lā yarawna ʾannahum yuftanūna fī kulli ᶜāmim-marratan ʾaw marratayni thumma lā yatūbūna wa lā hum yadhdhakkarūn. ﴿126﴾ Wa ʾidhā māa ʾuñzilat Sūratun-naẓara baᶜḍu-hum ʾilā baᶜḍin hal yarākum-min ʾaḥadiñ-

motivations and the innermost springs of his behaviour; and, thus, the Qurʾān itself is characterized as addressed to "those who think". In short, intellectual activity as such is postulated as a valid way to a better understanding of God's will and – if pursued with moral consciousness – as a valid method of worshipping God. This Qurʾanic principle has been emphasized in many well-authenticated sayings of the Prophet, for instance, "Striving after knowledge is a sacred duty (*farīḍah*) for every man and woman who has surrendered himself or herself to God (*muslim wa-muslimah*)" (Ibn Mājah); or, "The superiority (*faḍl*) of a learned man over a [mere] worshipper [i.e., one who merely prays, fasts, etc.] is like the superiority of the full moon over all the stars" (Tirmidhī, Abū Dāʾūd, Ibn Mājah, Ibn Ḥanbal, Dārimi). Consequently, the obligation of the believers to "devote themselves to acquiring a deeper knowledge of the Faith" (*li-yatafaqqahū fī 'd-dīn*) and to impart its results to their fellow-believers relates to every branch of knowledge as well as to its practical application.

163 I.e., uncompromising with regard to ethical principles. For the general circumstances in which war is permitted, see 2 : 190-194, 22 : 39, 60 : 8-9, and the corresponding notes, as well as notes 7 and 9 on verse 5 of this *sūrah*. The reference to "those deniers of the truth who are near you" may arise from the fact that only "those who are near" can be dangerous in a physical sense or, alternatively, that – having come from afar – they have already approached the Muslim country with an aggressive intent.

164 Lit., "there are among them such as say". The "saying" that follows is perhaps an oblique, sarcastic reference to 8 : 2, which speaks of the believers "whose faith is strengthened whenever His messages are conveyed unto them".

165 A reference to the promise of paradise expressed in verse 111 above.

166 Lit., "it but adds [another] loathsome evil to their loathsome evil" – i.e., makes them more stubborn in their denying the truth of God's messages because they are *a priori* determined to deny everything that is incompatible with their refusal to admit the existence of anything that is beyond the reach of human perception (*al-ghayb* – see *sūrah* 2, note 3).

167 Lit., "every year once or twice" – a figure of speech denoting continuity (*Manār* XI, 83 f.). The "test" consists in the fact that man has been endowed with reason and, therefore, with the ability to choose between right and wrong.

hearts?"[168] – and then they turn away.
God has turned their hearts away [from the truth] for they are people who will not grasp it.[169] ‹127›

INDEED, there has come unto you [O mankind] an Apostle from among yourselves:[170] heavily weighs upon him [the thought] that you might suffer [in the life to come]; full of concern for you [is he, and] full of compassion and mercy towards the believers. ‹128›
But if those [who are bent on denying the truth] turn away, say: "God is enough for me! There is no deity save Him. In Him have I placed my trust, for He is the Sustainer, in awesome almightiness enthroned."[171] ‹129›

ثُمَّ ٱنصَرَفُواْ ۚ صَرَفَ ٱللَّهُ قُلُوبَهُم بِأَنَّهُمْ قَوْمٌ لَّا يَفْقَهُونَ ﴿١٢٧﴾ لَقَدْ جَآءَكُمْ
رَسُولٌ مِّنْ أَنفُسِكُمْ عَزِيزٌ عَلَيْهِ مَا عَنِتُّمْ حَرِيصٌ عَلَيْكُم بِٱلْمُؤْمِنِينَ
رَءُوفٌ رَّحِيمٌ ﴿١٢٨﴾ فَإِن تَوَلَّوْاْ فَقُلْ حَسْبِىَ ٱللَّهُ لَآ إِلَٰهَ إِلَّا هُوَ ۖ عَلَيْهِ
تَوَكَّلْتُ ۖ وَهُوَ رَبُّ ٱلْعَرْشِ ٱلْعَظِيمِ ﴿١٢٩﴾

thummañ-ṣarafū. Ṣarafal-lāhu qulūbahum-biʾannahum qawmul-lā yafqahūn. (127) Laqad jāaʾakum Rasūlum-min ʾañfusikum ᶜazīzun ᶜalayhi mā ᶜanittum ḥarīṣun ᶜalaykum-bilmuʾminīna raʾūfur-raḥīm. (128) Faʾiñ-tawallaw faqul ḥasbiyal-lāhu lāa ʾilāha ʾillā Huwa ᶜalayhi tawakkaltu wa Huwa Rabbul-ᶜArshil-ᶜAẓīm. (129)

168 Lit., "who sees you" – thus implying that God does not exist.

169 Cf. 8 : 55.

170 I.e., "a human being like yourselves, not endowed with any supernatural powers, but only chosen by God to convey His message to you". (See note 2 on 50 : 2.)

171 Lit., "the Sustainer (*rabb*) of the awesome throne of almightiness". For my rendering of *al-ᶜarsh* as "the throne of almightiness", see note 43 on 7 : 54.

إِلَىٰ رَجُلٍ مِّنْهُمْ أَنْ أَنذِرِ النَّاسَ

وَبَشِّرِ الَّذِينَ آمَنُوا أَنَّ لَهُمْ قَدَمَ

صِدْقٍ عِندَ رَبِّهِمْ ۗ قَالَ

الْكَافِرُونَ إِنَّ هَٰذَا لَسَاحِرٌ

مُّبِينٌ إِنَّ رَبَّكُمُ اللَّهُ الَّذِي خَلَقَ

سورة يونس مكية

بسم الله الرحمن الرحيم

الر تلك ءايت الكتب الحكيم

أكان للناس عجبا أن أوحينا

وآياتها تسع ومائة

The Tenth Sūrah

Yūnus (Jonah)

Mecca Period

THIS SŪRAH, which derives its title from the solitary mention of "the people of Jonah" in verse 98, was almost certainly revealed in its entirety at Mecca, and probably not earlier than in the year preceding the Prophet's exodus to Medina. Some authorities are of the opinion that verses 40 and 94-95 belong to the Medina period, but there is no convincing evidence to this effect. On the other hand, there does not seem to be any doubt that, chronologically, this *sūrah* must be placed between *sūrah* 17 (*Al-Isrā*ʾ) and *sūrah* 11 (*Hūd*).

The central theme of *Yūnus* is revelation – in particular, the revelation of the Qurʾān to Muḥammad, and the impossibility of its having been "composed" by the latter and fraudulently attributed by him to God, as the deniers of the truth assert (verses 15-17, 37-38 and 94). Woven around this theme are references to earlier prophets – all of whom were given the lie by the majority of their people – as well as a many-sided exposition of the fundamental tenets of Islam: the oneness, uniqueness and omnipotence of God, the continuity of His revelation to man, the certainty of resurrection and of God's final judgment – culminating in the reminder (in verse 108) that "whoever chooses to follow the right path, follows it but for his own good; and whoever chooses to go astray, goes but astray to his own hurt".

-10-

سورة يونس مكية
وآياتها تسع ومائة

IN THE NAME OF GOD, THE MOST GRACIOUS, THE DISPENSER OF GRACE:

Alif. Lām. Rā.[1]
THESE ARE MESSAGES of the divine writ, full of wisdom.[2] ‹1›
Do people deem it strange that We should have inspired a man from their own midst [with this Our message]:[3] "Warn all mankind, and give unto those who have attained to faith the glad tiding that in their Sustainer's sight they surpass all others in that they are completely sincere"?[4]
[Only] they who deny the truth say, "Behold, he is clearly but a spellbinder!"[5] ‹2›

VERILY, your sustainer is God, who has created the heavens and the earth in six aeons, and is established on the throne of His almightines,[6] governing all that exists. There is none that could intercede with Him unless He grants leave therefor.[7]

بِسۡمِ ٱللَّهِ ٱلرَّحۡمَٰنِ ٱلرَّحِيمِ

الٓرۚ تِلۡكَ ءَايَٰتُ ٱلۡكِتَٰبِ ٱلۡحَكِيمِ ١ أَكَانَ لِلنَّاسِ عَجَبًا أَنۡ
أَوۡحَيۡنَآ إِلَىٰ رَجُلٖ مِّنۡهُمۡ أَنۡ أَنذِرِ ٱلنَّاسَ وَبَشِّرِ ٱلَّذِينَ ءَامَنُوٓاْ أَنَّ لَهُمۡ
قَدَمَ صِدۡقٍ عِندَ رَبِّهِمۡۗ قَالَ ٱلۡكَٰفِرُونَ إِنَّ هَٰذَا لَسَٰحِرٞ مُّبِينٌ ٢
إِنَّ رَبَّكُمُ ٱللَّهُ ٱلَّذِي خَلَقَ ٱلسَّمَٰوَٰتِ وَٱلۡأَرۡضَ فِي سِتَّةِ أَيَّامٖ ثُمَّ
ٱسۡتَوَىٰ عَلَى ٱلۡعَرۡشِۖ يُدَبِّرُ ٱلۡأَمۡرَۖ مَا مِن شَفِيعٍ إِلَّا مِنۢ بَعۡدِ إِذۡنِهِۦۚ

Bismil-lāhir-Raḥmānir-Raḥīm.
ʾAlif-Lāam-Rā. Tilka ʾĀyātul-Kitābil-ḥakīm. ‹1› ʾAkāna linnāsi ʿajaban ʾan ʾawḥaynāa ʾilā rajulim-minhum ʾan ʾañdhirin-nāsa wa bashshiril-ladhīna ʾāmanūu ʾanna lahum qadama ṣidqin ʿiñda Rabbihim. Qālal-kāfirūna ʾinna hādhā lasāḥirum-mubīn. ‹2› ʾInna Rabbakumul-lāhul-ladhī khalaqas-samāwāti wal-ʾarḍa fī sittati ʾayyāmiñ-thummas-tawā ʿalal-ʿarshi yudab-birul-ʾamr. Mā miñ-shafīʿin ʾillā mim-baʿdi ʾidhnih.

---

1 See Appendix II.

2 The term *ḥakīm* – which, when qualifying an animated being, may be translated as "wise" – has here the connotation of a means of *imparting* wisdom. Some of the classical commentators (e.g., Ṭabarī) are of the opinion that the "divine writ" (*kitāb*) mentioned here is the Qurʾān as a whole, while others (e.g., Zamakhsharī) see in it a reference to this particular *sūrah*. In view of the sequence, it seems to me that the former interpretation is preferable.

3 This connects with the end of the preceding *sūrah*, and particularly with the sentence, "There has come unto you [O mankind] an Apostle from among yourselves" (9 : 128; see also note 2 on 50 : 2).

4 Lit., "they have precedence (*qadam*) of truthfulness (*ṣidq*)": the latter term denoting a concord between what a person actually conceives in his mind or feels and what he expresses by word, deed or attitude – in other words, complete sincerity.

5 Lit., "He is indeed an obvious enchanter (*sāḥir*)" – thus implying that the "man from among yourselves" (i.e., Muḥammad) did not really receive any revelation from God, but merely deluded his followers by means of his spellbinding eloquence (which is the meaning of *siḥr* in this context): an accusation levelled by unbelievers of all times not merely against Muḥammad, but – as the Qurʾān frequently states – against most of the earlier prophets as well. The term "those who deny the truth" refers, in this context, specifically to people who *a priori* reject the notion of divine revelation and, thus, of prophethood.

6 See *sūrah* 7, note 43. Since belief in divine revelation naturally presupposes a belief in the existence of God as the self-subsistent fount of all being, the reference to the revelation of the Qurʾān with which this *sūrah* opens is followed by a consideration of God's creative almightiness.

7 Lit., "there is no intercessor whatever, save after His leave [has been granted]". Cf. 2 : 255 – "Who is there that could intercede with Him, unless it be by His leave?" Thus, the Qurʾān rejects the popular belief in unqualified "intercession" by living or dead saints or prophets. As is shown elsewhere in the Qurʾān (e.g., in 20 : 109, 21 : 28 or 34 : 23, God will grant to His prophets on Judgment Day the permission to "intercede", symbolically, for such of the

ذَٰلِكُمُ ٱللَّهُ رَبُّكُمْ فَٱعْبُدُوهُ ۚ أَفَلَا تَذَكَّرُونَ ﴿٣﴾ إِلَيْهِ مَرْجِعُكُمْ جَمِيعًا ۖ
وَعْدَ ٱللَّهِ حَقًّا ۚ إِنَّهُۥ يَبْدَؤُا۟ ٱلْخَلْقَ ثُمَّ يُعِيدُهُۥ لِيَجْزِىَ ٱلَّذِينَ ءَامَنُوا۟
وَعَمِلُوا۟ ٱلصَّٰلِحَٰتِ بِٱلْقِسْطِ ۚ وَٱلَّذِينَ كَفَرُوا۟ لَهُمْ شَرَابٌ مِّنْ حَمِيمٍ
وَعَذَابٌ أَلِيمٌۢ بِمَا كَانُوا۟ يَكْفُرُونَ ﴿٤﴾ هُوَ ٱلَّذِى جَعَلَ ٱلشَّمْسَ ضِيَآءً
وَٱلْقَمَرَ نُورًا وَقَدَّرَهُۥ مَنَازِلَ لِتَعْلَمُوا۟ عَدَدَ ٱلسِّنِينَ وَٱلْحِسَابَ ۚ مَا خَلَقَ
ٱللَّهُ ذَٰلِكَ إِلَّا بِٱلْحَقِّ ۚ يُفَصِّلُ ٱلْءَايَٰتِ لِقَوْمٍ يَعْلَمُونَ ﴿٥﴾ إِنَّ فِى ٱخْتِلَٰفِ
ٱلَّيْلِ وَٱلنَّهَارِ وَمَا خَلَقَ ٱللَّهُ فِى ٱلسَّمَٰوَٰتِ وَٱلْأَرْضِ لَءَايَٰتٍ لِّقَوْمٍ
يَتَّقُونَ ﴿٦﴾

Dhālikumul-lāhu Rabbukum faᶜbudūh. ʾAfalā tadhakkarūn. (3) ʾIlayhi marjiᶜukum jamīᶜañw-waᶜdal-lāhi ḥaqqā. ʾInnahū yabdaʾul-khalqa thumma yuᶜīduhū liyajziyal-ladhīna ʾāmanū wa ᶜamiluṣ-ṣāliḥāti bilqisṭ. Wal-ladhīna kafarū lahum sharābum-min ḥamīmiñw-wa ᶜadhābun ʾalīmum-bimā kānū yakfurūn. (4) Huwal-ladhī jaᶜalash-shamsa ḍiyāaʾañw-wal-qamara nūrañw-wa qaddarahū manāzila litaᶜlamū ᶜadadas-sinīna wal-ḥisāb. Mā khalaqal-lāhu dhālika ʾillā bilḥaqq. Yufaṣṣilul-ʾĀyāti liqawmiñy-yaᶜlamūn. (5) ʾInna fikh-tilāfil-layli wan-nahāri wa mā khalaqal-lāhu fis-samāwāti wal-ʾarḍi laʾĀyātil-liqawmiñy-yattaqūn. (6)

Thus is God, your Sustainer: worship, therefore, Him [alone]: will you not, then, keep this in mind? «3»
Unto Him you all must return: this is, in truth, God's promise – for, behold, He creates [man] in the first instance, and then brings him forth anew[8] to the end that He may reward with equity all who attain to faith and do righteous deeds; whereas for those who are bent on denying the truth there is in store a draught of burning despair and grievous suffering because of their persistent refusal to acknowledge the truth.[9] «4»
He it is who has made the sun a [source of] radiant light and the moon a light [reflected],[10] and has determined for it phases so that you might know how to compute the years and to measure [time]. None of this has God created without [an inner] truth.[11]
Clearly does He spell out these messages unto people of [innate] knowledge: «5» for, verily, in the alternating of night and day, and in all that God has created in the heavens and on earth there are messages indeed for people who are conscious of Him! «6»

sinners as will have *already achieved* His redemptive acceptance (*riḍāʾ*) by virtue of their repentance or basic goodness (see 19 : 87 and the corresponding note 74): in other words, the right of "intercession" thus granted to the prophets will be but an expression of God's approval of the latter. Furthermore, the above denial of the possibility of unqualified intercession stresses, indirectly, not only God's omniscience – which requires no "mediator" – but also the immutability of His will: and thus it connects with the preceding mention of His almightiness. (See also note 27 below.)

8 I.e., He will resurrect him by a new act of creation. That the verb *yuᶜīduhu* ("He brings him forth anew") refers here to the individual resurrection of human beings becomes obvious from the sequence. The noun *khalq* primarily denotes "creation" (i.e., the bringing into being of something that did not exist before); subsequently, it denotes the result or object of creation, i.e., a "created being" (or "beings"); finally, it is used in the sense of "man" in the generic connotation of this word, i.e., "mankind".

9 See *sūrah* 6, note 62 (for my rendering of *ḥamīm* as "burning despair").

10 The nouns *ḍiyāʾ* and *nūr* are often interchangeable, inasmuch as both denote "light"; but many philologists are of the opinion that the term *ḍiyāʾ* (or *ḍawʾ*) has a more intensive connotation, and is used to describe "a light which subsists by itself, as that of the sun and fire" – that is, a *source* of light – while *nūr* signifies "a light that subsists by some other thing" (Lane V, 1809, on the authority of *Tāj al-ᶜArūs*): in other words, light due to an extraneous source or – as in the case of the moon – reflected light.

11 Lit., "God has not created this otherwise than in accordance with truth" – i.e., to fulfil a definite purpose in consonance with His planning wisdom (Zamakhsharī, Baghawī, Rāzī): implying that everything in the universe – whether existent or potential, concrete or abstract – is meaningful, and nothing is "accidental". Cf. 3 : 191 – "O our Sustainer! Thou hast not created [aught of] this without meaning and purpose (*bāṭilan*)"; and 38 : 27 – "We have not created heaven and earth and all that is between them without meaning and purpose, as is the surmise (*ẓann*) of those who are bent on denying the truth".

إِنَّ ٱلَّذِينَ لَا يَرْجُونَ لِقَآءَنَا وَرَضُوا۟ بِٱلْحَيَوٰةِ ٱلدُّنْيَا وَٱطْمَأَنُّوا۟ بِهَا
وَٱلَّذِينَ هُمْ عَنْ ءَايَـٰتِنَا غَـٰفِلُونَ ﴿٧﴾ أُو۟لَـٰٓئِكَ مَأْوَىٰهُمُ ٱلنَّارُ بِمَا كَانُوا۟
يَكْسِبُونَ ﴿٨﴾ إِنَّ ٱلَّذِينَ ءَامَنُوا۟ وَعَمِلُوا۟ ٱلصَّـٰلِحَـٰتِ يَهْدِيهِمْ رَبُّهُم
بِإِيمَـٰنِهِمْ تَجْرِى مِن تَحْتِهِمُ ٱلْأَنْهَـٰرُ فِى جَنَّـٰتِ ٱلنَّعِيمِ ﴿٩﴾ دَعْوَىٰهُمْ
فِيهَا سُبْحَـٰنَكَ ٱللَّهُمَّ وَتَحِيَّتُهُمْ فِيهَا سَلَـٰمٌ وَءَاخِرُ دَعْوَىٰهُمْ أَنِ ٱلْحَمْدُ
لِلَّهِ رَبِّ ٱلْعَـٰلَمِينَ ﴿١٠﴾ ۞ وَلَوْ يُعَجِّلُ ٱللَّهُ لِلنَّاسِ ٱلشَّرَّ ٱسْتِعْجَالَهُم
بِٱلْخَيْرِ لَقُضِىَ إِلَيْهِمْ أَجَلُهُمْ فَنَذَرُ ٱلَّذِينَ لَا يَرْجُونَ لِقَآءَنَا فِى طُغْيَـٰنِهِمْ
يَعْمَهُونَ ﴿١١﴾ وَإِذَا مَسَّ ٱلْإِنسَـٰنَ ٱلضُّرُّ دَعَانَا لِجَنۢبِهِۦٓ أَوْ قَاعِدًا أَوْ قَآئِمًا

ثلاثة ارباع الحزب

Verily, as for those who do not believe that they are destined to meet Us,[12] but content themselves with the life of this world and do not look beyond it,[13] and are heedless of Our messages ⟨7⟩ – their goal is the fire in return for all [the evil] that they were wont to do. ⟨8⟩
[But,] verily, as for those who have attained to faith and do righteous deeds – their Sustainer guides them aright by means of their faith. [In the life to come,] running waters will flow at their feet[14] in gardens of bliss; ⟨9⟩ [and] in that [state of happiness] they will call out,[15] "Limitless art Thou in Thy glory, O God!" – and will be answered with the greeting, "Peace!"[16] And their call will close with [the words], "All praise is due to God, the Sustainer of all the worlds!" ⟨10⟩

NOW IF GOD were to hasten for human beings the ill [which they deserve by their sinning] in the same manner as they [themselves] would hasten [the coming to them of what they consider to be] good, their end would indeed come forthwith![17] But We leave them alone [for a while] – all those who do not believe that they are destined to meet Us:[18] [We leave them alone] in their overweening arrogance, blindly stumbling to and fro. ⟨11⟩
For [thus it is:] when affliction befalls man, he cries out unto Us, whether he be lying on his side or sitting or standing;[19]

ʾInnal-ladhīna lā yarjūna liqāaʾanā wa raḍū bil-ḥayātid-dunyā waṭ-maʾnnū bihā wal-ladhīna hum ʿan ʾĀyātinā ghāfilūna, (7) ʾulāaʾika maʾwāhumun-nāru bimā kānū yaksibūn. (8) ʾInnal-ladhīna ʾāmanū wa ʿamiluṣ-ṣāliḥāti yahdīhim Rabbuhum-biʾīmān-ihim; tajrī miñ-taḥtihimul-ʾanhāru fī jannātin-naʿīm. (9) Daʿwāhum fīhā subḥānakal-lāhumma wa taḥiy-yatuhum fīhā salām. Wa ʾākhiru daʿwāhum ʾanil-ḥamdu lil-lāhi Rabbil-ʿālamīn. (10) ۞ Wa law yuʿaj-jilul-lāhu linnāsish-sharras-tiʿjālahum-bilkhayri laquḍiya ʾilayhim ʾajaluhum. Fanadharul-ladhīna lā yarjūna liqāaʾanā fī ṭughyānihim yaʿmahūn. (11) Wa ʾidhā massal-ʾInsānaḍ-ḍurru daʿānā lijambihīi ʾaw qāʿidan ʾaw qāaʾimañ-

12 Lit., "who do not hope for [i.e., expect] a meeting with Us": implying that they do not believe in a life after death or in God's ultimate judgment.

13 Lit., "are at rest with it" – i.e., regard the life in this world as the only reality, dismissing the idea of resurrection as mere wishful thinking.

14 Lit., "beneath them".

15 Lit., "their invocation (*daʿwā*) therein [will be] . . .", etc.

16 Lit., "their greeting therein [will be], 'Peace'". For an explanation of the term *salām* and its fundamental connotation of inner peace, fulfilment, and security from all that is evil, see *sūrah* 5, note 29.

17 Lit., "[the end of] their term would indeed have been decreed for them": the implication being, firstly, that man is weak (cf. 4 : 28) and therefore prone to sinning; secondly, that God "has willed upon Himself the law of grace and mercy" (see 6 : 12 and the corresponding note) and, consequently, does not punish sinners without taking their circumstances into consideration and giving them time to repent and to mend their ways.

18 See verse 7, with which this verse connects.

19 These three metaphorical expressions are often used in the Qurʾān to describe the various situations in which man may find himself. The "calling unto God" under the stress of misfortune describes the instinctive reaction of many people who consider themselves "agnostics" and in their conscious thinking refuse to believe in God. See also verses 22-23 below, as well as 6 : 40-41.

فَلَمَّا كَشَفْنَا عَنْهُ ضُرَّهُۥ مَرَّ كَأَن لَّمْ يَدْعُنَآ إِلَىٰ ضُرٍّ مَّسَّهُۥ ۚ كَذَٰلِكَ زُيِّنَ
لِلْمُسْرِفِينَ مَا كَانُوا۟ يَعْمَلُونَ ﴿١٢﴾ وَلَقَدْ أَهْلَكْنَا ٱلْقُرُونَ مِن قَبْلِكُمْ لَمَّا
ظَلَمُوا۟ ۙ وَجَآءَتْهُمْ رُسُلُهُم بِٱلْبَيِّنَٰتِ وَمَا كَانُوا۟ لِيُؤْمِنُوا۟ ۚ كَذَٰلِكَ نَجْزِى
ٱلْقَوْمَ ٱلْمُجْرِمِينَ ﴿١٣﴾ ثُمَّ جَعَلْنَٰكُمْ خَلَٰٓئِفَ فِى ٱلْأَرْضِ مِنۢ بَعْدِهِمْ
لِنَنظُرَ كَيْفَ تَعْمَلُونَ ﴿١٤﴾ وَإِذَا تُتْلَىٰ عَلَيْهِمْ ءَايَاتُنَا بَيِّنَٰتٍ ۙ قَالَ ٱلَّذِينَ
لَا يَرْجُونَ لِقَآءَنَا ٱئْتِ بِقُرْءَانٍ غَيْرِ هَٰذَآ أَوْ بَدِّلْهُ ۚ قُلْ مَا يَكُونُ لِىٓ أَنْ
أُبَدِّلَهُۥ مِن تِلْقَآئِ نَفْسِىٓ ۖ إِنْ أَتَّبِعُ إِلَّا مَا يُوحَىٰٓ إِلَىَّ ۖ إِنِّىٓ أَخَافُ إِنْ عَصَيْتُ
رَبِّى عَذَابَ يَوْمٍ عَظِيمٍ ﴿١٥﴾ قُلْ لَّوْ شَآءَ ٱللَّهُ مَا تَلَوْتُهُۥ عَلَيْكُمْ وَلَآ أَدْرَىٰكُم

falammā kashafnā ʿanhu ḍurrahū marra kaʾal-lam yadʿunāa ʾilā ḍurrim-massah. Kadhālika zuyyina lil-musrifīna mā kānū yaʿmalūn. (12) Wa laqad ʾahlaknal-qurūna miñ-qablikum lammā ẓalamū wa jāaʾat-hum Rusuluhum-bilbayyināti wa mā kānū liyuʾminū. Kadhālika najzil-qawmal-mujrimīn. (13) Thumma jaʿalnākum khalāaʾifa fil-ʾarḍi mim-baʿdihim linañẓura kayfa taʿmalūn. (14) Wa ʾidhā tutlā ʿalayhim ʾĀyātunā bayyinātiñ-qālal-ladhīna lā yarjūna liqāa-ʾanaʾ-ti bi-Qurʾānin ghayri hādhāa ʾaw baddilh. Qul mā yakūnu līi ʾan ʾubaddilahū miñ-tilqāaʾi nafsīi ʾin ʾattabiʿu ʾillā mā yūḥāa ʾilayya ʾinnīi ʾakhāfu ʾin ʿaṣaytu Rabbī ʿadhāba yawmin ʿaẓīm. (15) Qul law shāaʾal-lāhu mā talawtuhū ʿalaykum wa lāa ʾadrākum-

but as soon as We have freed him of his affliction, he goes on as though he had never invoked Us to save him from the affliction[20] that befell him! Thus do their own doings seem goodly unto those who waste their own selves.[21] ⟨12⟩
And, indeed, We destroyed before your time [whole] generations when they [persistently] did evil although the apostles sent unto them brought them all evidence of the truth; for they refused to believe [them]. Thus do We requite people who are lost in sin.[22] ⟨13⟩
And thereupon We made you their successors on earth, so that We might behold how you act. ⟨14⟩

AND [thus it is:] whenever Our messages are conveyed unto them in all their clarity, those who do not believe that they are destined to meet Us [are wont to] say, "Bring us a discourse other than this, or alter this one."[23]
Say [O Prophet]: "It is not conceivable that I should alter it of my own volition; I only follow what is revealed to me. Behold, I would dread, were I [thus] to rebel against my Sustainer, the suffering [which would befall me] on that awesome Day [of Judgment]!" ⟨15⟩
Say: "Had God willed it [otherwise], I would not have conveyed this [divine writ] unto you, nor would He have brought it to your

20 Lit., "called out unto Us against (*ilā*) an affliction".

21 The expression *musrif*, which often (e.g., in 5 : 32 or 7 : 81) denotes "one who is given to excesses" or "commits excesses" or (as in 6 : 141) "one who is wasteful", has in the above context the meaning of "one who wastes *his own self*" (Rāzī) – namely, destroys his spiritual potential by following only his base impulses and failing to submit to any moral imperative. (Cf. the very similar expression *alladhīna khasirū anfusahum* occurring in many places and rendered by me as "those who have squandered their own selves".) In the sense in which it is used here, the term *isrāf* (lit., "wastefulness" or "lack of moderation in one's doings") is almost synonymous with the term *tughyān* ("overweening arrogance") occurring in the preceding verse (*Manār* XI 314), and relates to the same type of man. The phrase "goodly seem [to them] their own doings" describes the unthinking complacency with which "those who waste their own selves" go through life.

22 Cf. 6 : 131-132. The phrase rendered by me as "the apostles sent unto them" reads, literally, "their apostles". The sinners' *refusal* to believe is expressed in the text by means of the construction *wa-mā kānū li-yuʾminū*.

23 Sc., "to suit our own views as to what is right and what is wrong". This is an oblique reference to the highly subjective criticism of Qurʾanic ethics and eschatology by many agnostics (both among the contemporaries of the Prophet and in later times), and particularly to their view that the Qurʾān was "composed" by Muḥammad himself and therefore expresses no more than his personal convictions. – Regarding the phrase, "those who do not believe that they are destined to meet Us", see note 12 above.

بِهِۦ فَقَدْ لَبِثْتُ فِيكُمْ عُمُرًا مِّن قَبْلِهِۦٓ أَفَلَا تَعْقِلُونَ ﴿١٦﴾ فَمَنْ أَظْلَمُ مِمَّنِ
ٱفْتَرَىٰ عَلَى ٱللَّهِ كَذِبًا أَوْ كَذَّبَ بِـَٔايَٰتِهِۦٓ إِنَّهُۥ لَا يُفْلِحُ ٱلْمُجْرِمُونَ ﴿١٧﴾
وَيَعْبُدُونَ مِن دُونِ ٱللَّهِ مَا لَا يَضُرُّهُمْ وَلَا يَنفَعُهُمْ وَيَقُولُونَ هَٰٓؤُلَآءِ شُفَعَٰٓؤُنَا
عِندَ ٱللَّهِ قُلْ أَتُنَبِّـُٔونَ ٱللَّهَ بِمَا لَا يَعْلَمُ فِى ٱلسَّمَٰوَٰتِ وَلَا فِى ٱلْأَرْضِ سُبْحَٰنَهُۥ
وَتَعَٰلَىٰ عَمَّا يُشْرِكُونَ ﴿١٨﴾ وَمَا كَانَ ٱلنَّاسُ إِلَّآ أُمَّةً وَٰحِدَةً فَٱخْتَلَفُوا۟

bih. Faqad labiththu fīkum ᶜumuram-miñ-qablihīi ˀafalā taᶜqilūn. (16) Faman ˀaẓlamu mimmanif-tarā ᶜalal-lāhi kadhiban ˀaw kadhdhaba biˀĀyātih. ˀInnahū lā yufliḥul-mujrimūn. (17) Wa yaᶜbudūna miñ-dūnil-lāhi mā lā yaḍurruhum wa lā yañfaᶜuhum wa yaqūlūna hāaˀulāaˀi shufaˀāaˀunā ᶜiñdal-lāh. Qul ˀatunabbiˀūnal-lāha bimā lā yaᶜlamu fis-samāwāti wa lā fil-ˀarḍ. Subḥānahū wa taᶜālā ᶜammā yushrikūn. (18) Wa mā kānan-nāsu ˀillāa ˀummatañw-wāḥidatañ-fakhtalafū.

knowledge. Indeed, a whole lifetime have I dwelt among you ere this [revelation came unto me]: will you not, then, use your reason?"[24] ‹16›
And who could be more wicked than they who attribute their own lying inventions to God or give the lie to His messages? Verily, those who are lost in sin will never attain to a happy state[25] ‹17› – and [neither will] they [who] worship, side by side with God, things or beings that can neither harm nor benefit them, saying [to themselves], "These are our intercessors with God!"[26]
Say: "Do you [think that you could] inform God of anything in the heavens or on earth that He does not know?[27] Limitless is He in His glory, and sublimely exalted above anything to which men may ascribe a share in His divinity!" ‹18›

AND [know that] all mankind were once but one single community, and only later did they begin to hold divergent views.[28]

24 This argument – placed in the mouth of the Prophet – has a twofold implication. Ever since his early youth, Muḥammad had been renowned for his truthfulness and integrity, so much so that his Meccan compatriots applied to him the epithet *Al-Amīn* ("The Trustworthy"). In addition to this, he had never composed a single line of poetry (and this in contrast with a tendency which was widespread among the Arabs of his time), nor had he been distinguished by particular eloquence. "How, then," goes the argument, "can you reconcile your erstwhile conviction – based on the experience of a lifetime – that Muḥammad was incapable of uttering a lie, with your present contention that he himself has composed the Qurˀān and now falsely attributes it to divine revelation? And how could he who, up to the age of forty, has never displayed any poetic or philosophic gifts and is known to be entirely unlettered (*ummī*), have composed a work as perfect in its language, as penetrating in its psychological insight and as compelling in its inner logic as the Qurˀān?"

25 I.e., in the life to come. In this context, the "attributing of one's own lying inventions to God" would seem to apply specifically to the wanton accusation that Muḥammad himself composed the Qurˀān and then attributed it to God; and the "giving the lie to God's messages" refers to the attitude of those who make such an accusation and, consequently, reject the Qurˀān (Rāzī).

26 Thus the discourse returns to the problem of "intercession" touched upon in verse 3 of this *sūrah*. Literally, the beginning of the sentence reads thus: "And they worship that which neither harms them nor benefits them" – an expression alluding to both concrete representations and conceptual images. It should be noted that the "they" elliptically referred to here are not identical with the people spoken of earlier as "those who do not believe that they are destined to meet Us" (in other words, those who deny the reality of resurrection and of the Day of Judgment): for the people of whom the above verse speaks obviously do believe – albeit in a confused manner – in life after death and man's responsibility before God, as is evident from the statement that they worship imaginary "intercessors with God".

27 Thus, belief in the efficacy of anyone's unqualified intercession with God, or mediation between man and Him, is here equated with a denial of God's omniscience, which takes all the circumstances of the sinner and his sinning *a priori* into consideration. (As regards God's symbolic grant of permission to His prophets to "intercede" for their followers on the Day of Judgment, see note 7 above.)

28 Lit., "and then they disagreed [among themselves]". For an explanation of the term "one single community" (*ummah wāḥidah*), see *sūrah* 2, note 197. In the present context, this expression alludes not merely to mankind's one-time homogeneity, but also – by implication – to the fact, repeatedly stressed in the Qurˀān (e.g., in 7 : 172), that the ability to realize God's existence, oneness and omnipotence is *innate* in man, and that all deviation from this basic perception is a consequence of the confusion brought about by man's progressive estrangement from his inborn instincts.

And had it not been for a decree that had already gone forth from thy Sustainer, all their differences would indeed have been settled [from the outset].[29] ‹19›

NOW THEY [who deny the truth] are wont to ask, "Why has no miraculous sign ever been bestowed upon him from on high by his Sustainer?"[30]

Say, then: "God's alone is the knowledge of that which is beyond the reach of human perception.[31] Wait, then, [until His will becomes manifest:] verily, I shall wait with you!" ‹20›

And [thus it is:] whenever We let [such] people[32] taste [some of Our] grace after hardship has visited them – lo! they forthwith turn to devising false arguments against Our messages.[33]

Say: "God is swifter [than you] in His deep devising!"

Behold, Our [heavenly] messengers are recording all that you may devise! ‹21›

He it is who enables you to travel on land and sea. And [behold what happens] when you go to sea in ships:[34] [they go to sea in

وَلَوْلَا كَلِمَةٌ سَبَقَتْ مِن رَّبِّكَ لَقُضِيَ بَيْنَهُمْ فِيمَا فِيهِ يَخْتَلِفُونَ ﴿١٩﴾ وَيَقُولُونَ
لَوْلَآ أُنزِلَ عَلَيْهِ ءَايَةٌ مِّن رَّبِّهِۦ فَقُلْ إِنَّمَا ٱلْغَيْبُ لِلَّهِ فَٱنتَظِرُوٓاْ إِنِّى مَعَكُم
مِّنَ ٱلْمُنتَظِرِينَ ﴿٢٠﴾ وَإِذَآ أَذَقْنَا ٱلنَّاسَ رَحْمَةً مِّنۢ بَعْدِ ضَرَّآءَ مَسَّتْهُمْ
إِذَا لَهُم مَّكْرٌ فِىٓ ءَايَاتِنَا قُلِ ٱللَّهُ أَسْرَعُ مَكْرًا إِنَّ رُسُلَنَا يَكْتُبُونَ مَا
تَمْكُرُونَ ﴿٢١﴾ هُوَ ٱلَّذِى يُسَيِّرُكُمْ فِى ٱلْبَرِّ وَٱلْبَحْرِ حَتَّىٰٓ إِذَا كُنتُمْ فِى ٱلْفُلْكِ

Wa lawlā kalimatuñ-sabaqat mir-Rabbika laquḍiya baynahum fīmā fīhi yakhtalifūn. (19) Wa yaqūlūna lawlāa ʾuñzila ʿalayhi ʾĀyatum-mir-Rabbih. Faqul ʾinnamal-ghaybu lillāhi fañtaẓirūu ʾinnī maʾakum-minal-muñtaẓirīn. (20) Wa ʾidhāa ʾadhaqnan-nāsa raḥmatam-mim-baʿdi ḍarrāaʾa massat-hum ʾidhā lahum-makruñ-fīi ʾĀyātinā. Qu-lil-lāhu ʾasraʿu makrā. ʾInna Rusulanā yaktubūna mā tamkurūn. (21) Huwal-ladhī yusayyirukum fil-barri wal-baḥr. Ḥattāa ʾidhā kuñtum fil-fulki

29 Lit., "it would indeed have been decided between them regarding all that they were differing in": i.e., had it not been for God's decree – which is the meaning, in this context, of the term *kalimah* (lit., "word") – that men should differ in their intellectual approach to the problems touched upon by divine revelation, "they would not have contended with one another after having received all evidence of the truth", but would all have held from the very outset, and would continue to hold, the same views (cf. 2 : 253 and the corresponding note 245). Since, however, such a uniformity would have precluded men's intellectual, moral and social development, God has left it to their *reason*, aided by prophetic guidance, gradually to find their way to the truth. (See also *sūrah* 2, note 198.) The above parenthetic passage must be read in conjunction with 2 : 213.

30 I.e., on Muḥammad, in order to "prove" that he is truly a bearer of God's message (a sceptical objection which resumes the theme enunciated in verses 1-2 and 15-17 above); see also 6 : 37 and 109 and the corresponding notes, especially note 94. The pronoun "they" refers to both categories of deniers of the truth spoken of in the preceding passages: the atheists or agnostics "who do not believe that they are destined to meet God", as well as those who, while believing in God, "ascribe a share in His divinity" to all manner of imaginary intercessors or mediators (see verse 18 above).

31 This answer relates not merely to the question as to why God has not bestowed on Muḥammad a "miraculous sign" of his prophethood, but also to the "why" of his having been chosen for his prophetic mission. See in this connection 2 : 105 ("God singles out for His grace whom He wills") and 3 : 73-74 ("God is infinite, all-knowing, singling out for His grace whom He wills").

32 I.e., the two categories of people referred to in verses 7, 11, 12, 15, 18 and 20.

33 Lit., "they have forthwith a scheme against Our messages". (The particle *idhā* preceding this clause is meant to bring out the element of *immediacy*, and is best rendered as "lo! they forthwith . . .", etc.) Since God's messages are purely conceptual, the "scheming against them" obviously connotes the devising of fallacious arguments meant to cast doubt on the divine origin of these messages or to "disprove" the statements made in them. The above discourse on the psychology of agnosticism and half-belief is continued in the parable of the seafarers set forth in the next two verses.

34 Lit., "until, when you are in the ships . . .", etc. As has been pointed out by Zamakhsharī, the particle "until"

ships,] and they sail on in them in a favourable wind, and they rejoice thereat – until there comes upon them a tempest, and waves surge towards them from all sides, so that they believe themselves to be encompassed [by death; and then] they call unto God, [at that moment] sincere in their faith in Him alone, "If Thou wilt but save us from this, we shall most certainly be among the grateful!" ‹22› Yet as soon as He has saved them from this [danger], lo! they behave outrageously on earth, offending against all right![35]

O men! All your outrageous deeds are bound to fall back upon your own selves![36] [You care only for] the enjoyment of life in this world: [but remember that] in the end unto Us you must return, whereupon We shall make you truly understand all that you were doing [in life]. ‹23›

The parable of the life of this world is but that of rain which We send down from the sky, and which is absorbed by the plants of the earth[37] whereof men and animals draw nourishment, until – when the earth has assumed its artful adornment and has been embellished, and they who dwell on it believe that they have gained mastery over it[38] – there comes down upon it Our judgment, by night or by day, and We cause it to become [like] a field mown down, as if there had been no yesterday.[39] Thus clearly do We spell out these messages unto people who think! ‹24›

وَجَرَيْنَ بِهِم بِرِيحٍ طَيِّبَةٍ وَفَرِحُوا بِهَا جَاءَتْهَا رِيحٌ عَاصِفٌ وَجَاءَهُمُ الْمَوْجُ
مِن كُلِّ مَكَانٍ وَظَنُّوا أَنَّهُمْ أُحِيطَ بِهِمْ دَعَوُا اللَّهَ مُخْلِصِينَ لَهُ الدِّينَ لَئِنْ
أَنجَيْتَنَا مِنْ هَٰذِهِ لَنَكُونَنَّ مِنَ الشَّاكِرِينَ ﴿٢٢﴾ فَلَمَّا أَنجَاهُمْ إِذَا هُمْ يَبْغُونَ
فِي الْأَرْضِ بِغَيْرِ الْحَقِّ يَا أَيُّهَا النَّاسُ إِنَّمَا بَغْيُكُمْ عَلَىٰ أَنفُسِكُم مَّتَاعَ
الْحَيَاةِ الدُّنْيَا ثُمَّ إِلَيْنَا مَرْجِعُكُمْ فَنُنَبِّئُكُم بِمَا كُنتُمْ تَعْمَلُونَ ﴿٢٣﴾ إِنَّمَا مَثَلُ
الْحَيَاةِ الدُّنْيَا كَمَاءٍ أَنزَلْنَاهُ مِنَ السَّمَاءِ فَاخْتَلَطَ بِهِ نَبَاتُ الْأَرْضِ مِمَّا
يَأْكُلُ النَّاسُ وَالْأَنْعَامُ حَتَّىٰ إِذَا أَخَذَتِ الْأَرْضُ زُخْرُفَهَا وَازَّيَّنَتْ وَظَنَّ
أَهْلُهَا أَنَّهُمْ قَادِرُونَ عَلَيْهَا أَتَاهَا أَمْرُنَا لَيْلًا أَوْ نَهَارًا فَجَعَلْنَاهَا حَصِيدًا كَأَن
لَّمْ تَغْنَ بِالْأَمْسِ كَذَٰلِكَ نُفَصِّلُ الْآيَاتِ لِقَوْمٍ يَتَفَكَّرُونَ ﴿٢٤﴾

wa jarayna bihim-birīḥiñ-ṭayyibatiñw-wa fariḥū bihā jāa'at-hā rīḥun ʿāṣifuñw-wa jāa'ahumul-mawju miñ-kulli makāniñw-wa ẓannūu 'annahum 'uḥīṭa bihim daʿawul-lāha mukhliṣīna lahud-dīna la'in 'añjaytanā min hādhihī lanakūnanna minash-shākirīn. ‹22› Fa-lammāa 'añjāhum 'idhā hum yabghūna fil-'arḍi bi-ghayril-ḥaqq. Yāa 'ayyuhan-nāsu 'innamā baghyuk-um ʿalāa 'añfusikum-matāʿal-ḥayātid-dunyā; thum-ma 'ilaynā marjiʿukum fanunabbi'ukum-bimā kuñtum taʿmalūn. ‹23› 'Innamā mathalul-ḥayātid-dunyā kamāa'in 'añzalnāhu minas-samāa'i fakhta-laṭa bihī nabātul-'arḍi mimmā ya'kulun-nāsu wal-'anʿāmu ḥattāa 'idhāa 'akhadhatil-'arḍu zukhrufahā waz-zayyanat wa ẓanna 'ahluhāa'annahum qādirūna ʿalayhāa 'atāhāa 'amrunā laylan 'aw nahārañ-faja-ʿalnāhā ḥaṣīdañ-ka'al-lam taghna bil'ams. Kadhā-lika nufaṣṣilul-'Āyāti liqawmiñy-yatafakkarūn. ‹24›

(*ḥattā*) which precedes this clause refers to the sudden rise of the storm described in the sequence, and not to the "going to sea in ships". It is to be noted that at this point the discourse changes abruptly from the direct address "you" to the third person plural ("they"): a construction which is evidently meant to bring out the allegorical character of the subsequent narrative and to turn it into a lesson of general validity.

35 See verse 12 (of which the above passage is a parabolic illustration) and the corresponding notes.

36 Lit., "your outrageousness (*baghy*) is only against your own selves". Cf. the oft-recurring Qur'anic expression, "they have sinned against themselves" (*ẓalamū anfusahum*, lit., "they have wronged themselves"), indicating the inevitability with which every evil deed damages its perpetrator spiritually.

37 Lit., "with which the plants of the earth mingle".

38 I.e., they come to believe that they have gained "mastery over nature", with no conceivable limits to what they may yet achieve. It is to be borne in mind that the term *zukhruf* bears almost invariably a connotation of artificiality – a connotation which in this case is communicated to the subsequent verb *izzayyanat*. Thus, the whole of the above parabolic sentence may be understood as alluding to the artificial, illusory "adornment" brought about by man's technological efforts, not in *collaboration* with nature but, rather, in hostile "confrontation" with it.

39 Lit., "as if it had not been in existence yesterday": a phrase used in classical Arabic to describe something that has entirely disappeared or perished (*Tāj al-ʿArūs*).

وَٱللَّهُ يَدْعُوٓا۟ إِلَىٰ دَارِ ٱلسَّلَٰمِ وَيَهْدِى مَن يَشَآءُ إِلَىٰ صِرَٰطٍ مُّسْتَقِيمٍ ﴿25﴾
۞ لِّلَّذِينَ أَحْسَنُوا۟ ٱلْحُسْنَىٰ وَزِيَادَةٌ ۖ وَلَا يَرْهَقُ وُجُوهَهُمْ قَتَرٌ وَلَا ذِلَّةٌ ۚ
أُو۟لَٰٓئِكَ أَصْحَٰبُ ٱلْجَنَّةِ ۖ هُمْ فِيهَا خَٰلِدُونَ ﴿26﴾ وَٱلَّذِينَ كَسَبُوا۟ ٱلسَّيِّـَٔاتِ
جَزَآءُ سَيِّئَةٍۭ بِمِثْلِهَا وَتَرْهَقُهُمْ ذِلَّةٌ ۖ مَّا لَهُم مِّنَ ٱللَّهِ مِنْ عَاصِمٍ ۖ كَأَنَّمَآ
أُغْشِيَتْ وُجُوهُهُمْ قِطَعًا مِّنَ ٱلَّيْلِ مُظْلِمًا ۚ أُو۟لَٰٓئِكَ أَصْحَٰبُ ٱلنَّارِ ۖ هُمْ فِيهَا
خَٰلِدُونَ ﴿27﴾ وَيَوْمَ نَحْشُرُهُمْ جَمِيعًا ثُمَّ نَقُولُ لِلَّذِينَ أَشْرَكُوا۟ مَكَانَكُمْ أَنتُمْ
وَشُرَكَآؤُكُمْ ۚ فَزَيَّلْنَا بَيْنَهُمْ ۖ وَقَالَ شُرَكَآؤُهُم مَّا كُنتُمْ إِيَّانَا تَعْبُدُونَ ﴿28﴾

Wal-lāhu yadᶜūu ʾilā dāris-salāmi wa yahdī mañy-yashāaʾu ʾilā ṣirāṭim-mustaqīm. (25) ۞ Lilladhīna ʾaḥsanul-ḥusnā wa ziyādah. Wa lā yarhaqu wujūhahum qataruñw-wa lā dhillah. ʾUlāaʾika ʾaṣḥābul-jannati hum fīhā khālidūn. (26) Wal-ladhīna kasabus-sayyiʾāti jazāaʾu sayyiʾatim-bimithlihā wa tarhaquhum dhillah. Mā lahum-minal-lāhi min ᶜāṣim. Kaʾannamāa ʾughshiyat wujūhuhum qiṭaᶜam-minal-layli muẓlimā. ʾUlāaʾika ʾaṣḥābun-nāri hum fīhā khālidūn. (27) Wa Yawma naḥshuruhum jamīᶜañ-thumma naqūlu lilladhīna ʾashrakū makānakum ʾañtum wa shurakāaʾukum. Fazayyalnā baynahum; wa qāla shurakāaʾuhum-mā kuñtum ʾiyyānā taᶜbudūn. (28)

AND [know that] God invites [man] unto the abode of peace, and guides him that wills [to be guided] onto a straight way.[40] ‹25›
For those who persevere in doing good there is the ultimate good in store, and more [than that].[41] No darkness and no ignominy will overshadow their faces [on Resurrection Day]: it is they who are destined for paradise, therein to abide. ‹26›
حزب 22
But as for those who have done evil deeds – the recompense of an evil deed shall be the like thereof;[42] and – since they will have none to defend them against God – ignominy will overshadow them as though their faces were veiled by the night's own darkness:[43] it is they who are destined for the fire, therein to abide. ‹27›
For, one Day We shall gather them all together, and then We shall say unto those who [in their lifetime] ascribed divinity to aught but God, "Stand where you are, you and those [beings and powers] to whom you were wont to ascribe a share in God's divinity!"[44] – for by then We shall have [visibly] separated them from one another.[45] And the beings to whom they had ascribed a share in God's divinity will say [to those who had worshipped them], "It was not us that you were wont to worship;[46] ‹28›

40 Or: "guides whom He wills onto a straight way". As regards the expression *salām*, rendered here and in many other places as "peace" and elsewhere as "salvation", see *sūrah* 5, note 29. It is obvious that the term *dār as-salām* ("abode of peace") denotes not only the condition of ultimate happiness in the hereafter – alluded to in the allegory of paradise – but also the spiritual condition of a true believer in this world: namely, a state of inner security, of peace with God, with one's natural environment, and within oneself.

41 I.e., more than their actual merits may warrant (cf. 6 : 160 – "Whoever shall come [before God] with a good deed will gain ten times the like thereof"). See also note 79 on 27 : 89.

42 In contrast with the multiple "rewards" for good deeds, the recompense of evil will be only commensurate with the deed itself. (See also note 46 on the last sentence of 41 : 50.)

43 Lit., "by a piece of the night, densely dark".

44 Lit., "you and those [God-]partners of yours"; cf. *sūrah* 6, note 15. The expression *makānakum* (lit., "your place", i.e., "keep to your place") bears a connotation of contempt and an implied threat.

45 I.e., separated those who ascribed divinity to beings other than God from the objects of their one-time adoration (Ṭabarī, Baghawī): a metonymical phrase denoting a realization on the part of the former that there has never been any existential link between them and those false objects of worship (cf. 6 : 24, 10 : 30, 11 : 21, 16 : 87 and 28 : 75 – "and all their false imagery has [or "will have"] forsaken them"). See also the next two notes.

46 I.e., "it was only your own fancies and desires that you worshipped, clothing them in the garb of extraneous beings": in other words, the worship of idols, forces of nature, saints, prophets, angels, etc., is shown here to be nothing but a projection of the worshipper's own subconscious desires. (Cf. also 34 : 41 and the corresponding note 52.)

and none can bear witness between us and you as God does: we were, for certain, unaware of your worshipping [us]."[47] «29»
There and then will every human being clearly apprehend what he has done in the past; and all will be brought back unto God,[48] their true Lord Supreme, and all their false imagery will have forsaken them. «30»

SAY: "Who is it that provides you with sustenance out of heaven and earth,[49] or who is it that has full power over [your] hearing and sight? And who is it that brings forth the living out of that which is dead, and brings forth the dead out of that which is alive? And who is it that governs all that exists?"
And they will [surely] answer: "[It is] God."[50]
Say, then: "Will you not, then, become [fully] conscious of Him «31» – seeing that He is God, your Sustainer, the Ultimate Truth?[51] For, after the truth [has been forsaken], what is there [left] but error? How, then, can you lose sight of the truth?"[52] «32»
Thus is thy Sustainer's word proved true with regard to such as are bent on sinful doings: they will not believe.[53] «33»

فَكَفَىٰ بِٱللَّهِ شَهِيدَۢا بَيۡنَنَا وَبَيۡنَكُمۡ إِن كُنَّا عَنۡ عِبَادَتِكُمۡ لَغَٰفِلِينَ ﴿29﴾
هُنَالِكَ تَبۡلُواْ كُلُّ نَفۡسٖ مَّآ أَسۡلَفَتۡۚ وَرُدُّوٓاْ إِلَى ٱللَّهِ مَوۡلَىٰهُمُ ٱلۡحَقِّۖ وَضَلَّ
عَنۡهُم مَّا كَانُواْ يَفۡتَرُونَ ﴿30﴾ قُلۡ مَن يَرۡزُقُكُم مِّنَ ٱلسَّمَآءِ وَٱلۡأَرۡضِ أَمَّن
يَمۡلِكُ ٱلسَّمۡعَ وَٱلۡأَبۡصَٰرَ وَمَن يُخۡرِجُ ٱلۡحَيَّ مِنَ ٱلۡمَيِّتِ وَيُخۡرِجُ ٱلۡمَيِّتَ
مِنَ ٱلۡحَيِّ وَمَن يُدَبِّرُ ٱلۡأَمۡرَۚ فَسَيَقُولُونَ ٱللَّهُۚ فَقُلۡ أَفَلَا تَتَّقُونَ ﴿31﴾
فَذَٰلِكُمُ ٱللَّهُ رَبُّكُمُ ٱلۡحَقُّۖ فَمَاذَا بَعۡدَ ٱلۡحَقِّ إِلَّا ٱلضَّلَٰلُۖ فَأَنَّىٰ
تُصۡرَفُونَ ﴿32﴾ كَذَٰلِكَ حَقَّتۡ كَلِمَتُ رَبِّكَ عَلَى ٱلَّذِينَ فَسَقُوٓاْ أَنَّهُمۡ لَا
يُؤۡمِنُونَ ﴿33﴾

Fakafā billāhi Shahīdam-baynanā wa baynakum ʾiñ-kunnā ʿan ʿibādatikum laghāfilīn. ﴾29﴿ Hunālika tablū kullu nafsim-māa ʾaslafat wa ruddūu ʾilal-lāhi Mawlāhumul-ḥaqqi wa ḍalla ʿanhum-mā kānū yaftarūn. ﴾30﴿ Qul mañy-yarzuqukum-minas-samāaʾi wal-ʾarḍi ʾammañy-yamlikus-samʿa wal-ʾabṣāra wa mañy-yukhrijul-ḥayya minal-mayyiti wa yukhrijul-mayyita minal-ḥayyi wa mañy-yudabbirul-ʾamr. Fasayaqūlūnal-lāh. Faqul ʾafalā tattaqūn. ﴾31﴿ Fadhālikumul-lāhu Rabbukumul-ḥaqq. Famādhā baʿdal-ḥaqqi ʾillaḍ-ḍalālu faʾannā tuṣrafūn. ﴾32﴿ Kadhālika ḥaqqat Kalimatu Rabbika ʿalal-ladhīna fasaqūu ʾannahum lā yuʾminūn. ﴾33﴿

47 Thus the Qurʾān makes it clear that the saints and prophets who, after their death, have been unwarrantably deified by their followers shall not be held accountable for the blasphemous worship accorded to them (cf. 5 : 116-117); furthermore, even the inanimate objects of false worship will symbolically deny any connection between themselves and their worshippers.

48 I.e., will be brought back to the realization of God's oneness, uniqueness and almightiness – that instinctive cognition which has been implanted in human nature as such (see 7 : 172).

49 The term *rizq* ("provision of sustenance") is used here in both the physical and spiritual connotations of this word, which explains the reference to "heaven and earth" and, subsequently, "[man's] hearing and sight".

50 The people referred to here are those who believe, firstly, that there are beings endowed with certain divine or semi-divine qualities, thus having, as it were, a "share" in God's divinity; and, secondly, that by worshipping such beings men can come closer to God. This idea obviously presupposes belief in God's existence, as is brought out in the "answer" of the people thus addressed (cf. 7 : 172 and the corresponding note 139); but inasmuch as it offends against the concept of God's oneness and uniqueness, it deprives those people's belief in God of its true meaning and spiritual value.

51 Lit., "this [or "such"], then, being God, your Sustainer, the Ultimate Truth" – i.e., "seeing that, on your own admission, He is the One who creates and governs all things and is the Ultimate Reality behind all that exists" (see *sūrah* 20, note 99): which implies a categorical denial of the possibility that any other being could have a share, however small, in His divinity.

52 Lit., "How, then, are you turned away?" – i.e., from the truth.

53 See *sūrah* 2, note 7, as well as 8 : 55 and the corresponding note 58. In this particular context, "the Sustainer's word" seems to be synonymous with "the way of God" (*sunnat Allāh*) concerning deliberate sinners and deniers of the truth (*Manār* XI, 359). The particle *anna* in *annahum* (lit., "that they") is, thus, indicative of the purport of the divine "word" referred to, and is best expressed by a colon.

قُلْ هَلْ مِن شُرَكَآئِكُم مَّن يَبْدَؤُا۟ ٱلْخَلْقَ ثُمَّ يُعِيدُهُۥ ۚ قُلِ ٱللَّهُ يَبْدَؤُا۟ ٱلْخَلْقَ
ثُمَّ يُعِيدُهُۥ ۖ فَأَنَّىٰ تُؤْفَكُونَ ﴿٣٤﴾ قُلْ هَلْ مِن شُرَكَآئِكُم مَّن يَهْدِىٓ إِلَى
ٱلْحَقِّ ۚ قُلِ ٱللَّهُ يَهْدِى لِلْحَقِّ ۗ أَفَمَن يَهْدِىٓ إِلَى ٱلْحَقِّ أَحَقُّ أَن يُتَّبَعَ أَمَّن لَّا
يَهِدِّىٓ إِلَّآ أَن يُهْدَىٰ ۖ فَمَا لَكُمْ كَيْفَ تَحْكُمُونَ ﴿٣٥﴾ وَمَا يَتَّبِعُ أَكْثَرُهُمْ
إِلَّا ظَنًّا ۚ إِنَّ ٱلظَّنَّ لَا يُغْنِى مِنَ ٱلْحَقِّ شَيْـًٔا ۚ إِنَّ ٱللَّهَ عَلِيمٌۢ بِمَا يَفْعَلُونَ ﴿٣٦﴾
وَمَا كَانَ هَٰذَا ٱلْقُرْءَانُ أَن يُفْتَرَىٰ مِن دُونِ ٱللَّهِ وَلَٰكِن تَصْدِيقَ ٱلَّذِى
بَيْنَ يَدَيْهِ وَتَفْصِيلَ ٱلْكِتَٰبِ لَا رَيْبَ فِيهِ مِن رَّبِّ ٱلْعَٰلَمِينَ ﴿٣٧﴾

Qul hal miñ-shurakāaʾikum-mañy-yabdaʾul-khalqa thumma yuʿīduh. Qulil-lāhu yabdaʾul-khalqa thumma yuʿīduhū faʾannā tuʾfakūn. (34) Qul hal miñ-shurakāaʾikum-mañy-yahdīi ʾilal-ḥaqq. Qulil-lāhu yahdī lil-ḥaqq. ʾAfamañy-yahdīi ʾilal-ḥaqqi ʾaḥaqqu ʾañy-yuttabaʿa ʾammal-lā yahiddīi ʾillāa ʾañy-yuhdā. Famā lakum kayfa taḥkumūn. (35) Wa mā yattabiʿu ʾaktharuhum ʾillā ẓannā. ʾInnaẓ-ẓanna lā yughnī minal-ḥaqqi shayʾā. ʾInnal-lāha ʿAlīmum-bimā yafʿalūn. (36) Wa mā kāna hādhal-Qurʾānu ʾañy-yuftarā miñ-dūnil-lāhi wa lākiñ-taṣdīqal-ladhī bayna yadayhi wa tafṣīlal-Kitābi lā rayba fīhi mir-Rabbil-ʿālamīn. (37)

Say: "Can any of those beings to whom you ascribe a share in God's divinity create [life] in the first instance, and then bring it forth anew?"[54]
Say: "It is God [alone] who creates [all life] in the first instance, and then brings it forth anew. How perverted, then, are your minds!"[55] ‹34›
Say: "Does any of those beings to whom you ascribe a share in God's divinity guide unto the truth?"
Say: "It is God [alone] who guides unto the truth. Which, then, is more worthy to be followed – He who guides unto the truth, or he who cannot find the right way unless he is guided?[56] What, then, is amiss with you and your judgment?"[57] ‹35›
For, most of them follow nothing but conjecture: [and,] behold, conjecture can never be a substitute for truth.[58] Verily, God has full knowledge of all that they do. ‹36›
Now this Qurʾān could not possibly have been devised by anyone save God: nay indeed,[59] it confirms the truth of whatever there still remains [of earlier revelations] and clearly spells out the revelation [which comes] – let there be no doubt about it – from the Sustainer of all the worlds.[60] ‹37›

54 This rhetorical question is connected with the false belief that those idolatrously worshipped beings are no more than "intercessors" between their followers and God (see verse 18 above): and so, even their misguided votaries cannot possibly attribute to them the power to create and to resurrect. See also note 8 on verse 4 of this *sūrah*. In its wider sense, this question (and the subsequent answer) relates to the God-willed, cyclic process of birth, death and regeneration evident in all organic nature.

55 See *sūrah* 5, note 90.

56 Since the concept of "finding the right way" cannot apply to lifeless idols and idolatrous images, the above passage obviously relates to animate beings – whether dead or alive – to whom "a share in God's divinity" is falsely attributed: that is, to saintly personalities, prophets or angels whom popular fancy blasphemously endows with some or all of God's qualities, sometimes even to the extent that they are regarded as a manifestation or incarnation of God on earth. As for the act of God's guidance, it is displayed, primarily, in the power of conscious reasoning as well as of instinctive insight with which He has graced man, thus enabling him to follow the divine laws of right conduct (Zamakhsharī).

57 Lit., "[and] how do you judge?"

58 Lit., "conjecture can in no wise make [anyone] independent (*lā yughnī*) of the truth", i.e., of positive insight obtained through authentic revelation (to which the sequence relates). The people referred to here (and apparently also in the first sentence of verse 53 of this *sūrah*) are the agnostics who waver between truth and falsehood. – Some of the great exponents of Islamic Law – foremost among them Ibn Ḥazm – base on this verse their rejection of *qiyās* ("deduction by analogy") as a means of eliciting religious laws which are supposedly "implied" in the wording of the Qurʾān or of the Prophet's teachings, but not clearly laid down in terms of law. In his commentary on this verse, Rāzī thus sums up the above view: "They say that every deduction by analogy is a conjectural process and is, therefore, of necessity, inadmissible [in matters pertaining to religion] – for 'conjecture can never be a substitute for truth'." (See also 5 : 101-102, and the corresponding notes 120-123.)

59 Lit., "but" (*wa-lākin*) – a stress on the impossibility of any assertion to the contrary.

60 The above passage has a twofold significance: firstly, the wisdom inherent in the Qurʾān precludes any

And yet,[61] they [who are bent on denying the truth] assert, "[Muḥammad] has invented it!" Say [unto them]: "Produce, then, a *sūrah* of similar merit; and [to this end] call to your aid whomever you can, other than God, if what you say is true!"[62] ‹38›

Nay, but they are bent on giving the lie to everything the wisdom whereof they do not comprehend, and ere its inner meaning has become clear to them.[63] Even thus did those who lived before their time give the lie to the truth: and behold what happened in the end to those evildoers! ‹39›

And there are among them such as will in time come to believe in this [divine writ], just as there are among them such as will never believe in it;[64] and thy Sustainer is fully aware as to who are the spreaders of corruption. ‹40›

And [so, O Prophet] if they give thee the lie, say: "To me [shall be accounted] my doings, and to you, your doings: you are not accountable for what I am doing, and I am not accountable for whatever you do." ‹41›

And there are among them such as [pretend to] listen to thee: but canst thou cause the deaf to hearken even though they will not use their reason? ‹42› And there are among them such as [pretend to] look towards thee: but canst thou show the right way to the blind even though they cannot see? ‹43›

أَمْ يَقُولُونَ ٱفْتَرَىٰهُ ۖ قُلْ فَأْتُوا۟ بِسُورَةٍ مِّثْلِهِۦ وَٱدْعُوا۟ مَنِ ٱسْتَطَعْتُم مِّن دُونِ
ٱللَّهِ إِن كُنتُمْ صَـٰدِقِينَ ﴿٣٨﴾ بَلْ كَذَّبُوا۟ بِمَا لَمْ يُحِيطُوا۟ بِعِلْمِهِۦ وَلَمَّا
يَأْتِهِمْ تَأْوِيلُهُۥ ۚ كَذَٰلِكَ كَذَّبَ ٱلَّذِينَ مِن قَبْلِهِمْ ۖ فَٱنظُرْ كَيْفَ كَانَ
عَـٰقِبَةُ ٱلظَّـٰلِمِينَ ﴿٣٩﴾ وَمِنْهُم مَّن يُؤْمِنُ بِهِۦ وَمِنْهُم مَّن لَّا يُؤْمِنُ بِهِۦ ۚ
وَرَبُّكَ أَعْلَمُ بِٱلْمُفْسِدِينَ ﴿٤٠﴾ وَإِن كَذَّبُوكَ فَقُل لِّى عَمَلِى وَلَكُمْ
عَمَلُكُمْ ۖ أَنتُم بَرِيٓـُٔونَ مِمَّآ أَعْمَلُ وَأَنَا۠ بَرِىٓءٌ مِّمَّا تَعْمَلُونَ ﴿٤١﴾ وَمِنْهُم مَّن
يَسْتَمِعُونَ إِلَيْكَ ۚ أَفَأَنتَ تُسْمِعُ ٱلصُّمَّ وَلَوْ كَانُوا۟ لَا يَعْقِلُونَ ﴿٤٢﴾ وَمِنْهُم
مَّن يَنظُرُ إِلَيْكَ ۚ أَفَأَنتَ تَهْدِى ٱلْعُمْىَ وَلَوْ كَانُوا۟ لَا يُبْصِرُونَ ﴿٤٣﴾

ʾAm yaqūlūnaf-tarāh. Qul faʾtū bisūratim-mithlihī wad-ʿū manis-taṭaʿtum-miñ-dūnil-lāhi ʾiñ-kuñtum ṣādiqīn. (38) Bal kadhdhabū bimā lam yuḥīṭū biʿilmihī wa lammā yaʾtihim taʾwīluh. Kadhālika kadhdhabal-ladhīna miñ-qablihim fañẓur kayfa kāna ʿāqibatuẓ-ẓālimīn. (39) Wa minhum-mañy-yuʾminu bihī wa minhum-mal-lā yuʾminu bihī wa Rabbuka ʾaʿlamu bilmufsidīn. (40) Wa ʾiñ-kadhdhabūka faqul lī ʿamalī wa lakum ʿamalukum. ʾAñtum-barīiʾūna mimmāa ʾaʿmalu wa ʾana barīiʾum-mimmā taʿmalūn. (41) Wa minhum-mañy-yastamiʿūna ʾilayk. ʾAfaʾañta tusmiʿuṣ-ṣumma wa law kānū lā yaʿqilūn. (42) Wa minhum-mañy-yañẓuru ʾilayk. ʾAfaʾañta tahdil-ʿumya wa law kānū lā yubṣirūn. (43)

possibility of its having been composed by a human being; and, secondly, the Qurʾanic message is meant to confirm, and give a final formulation to, the eternal truths which have been conveyed to man through a long succession of prophets: truths which have subsequently been obscured through wrong interpretation, deliberate omissions or interpolations, or a partial or even total loss of the original texts. For an explanation of the phrase *mā bayna yadayhi*, rendered by me in this context as "whatever there still remains [of earlier revelations]", see *sūrah* 3, note 3.

61 According to the great philologist Abū ʿUbaydah Maʿmar ibn al-Muthannā (as quoted by Baghawī), the particle *am* which introduces this sentence has no interrogative connotation, but is – as in several other places in the Qurʾān – synonymous with the conjunction *wa* ("and"), which in this case can be suitably rendered as above.

62 Cf. 2 : 23 and the corresponding note 15.

63 Lit., "the knowledge whereof they do not encompass, while its inner meaning has not yet come to them". Most of the classical commentators explain this sentence in the way rendered by me; some of them, however (e.g., Ṭabarī and Baghawī), interpret the term *taʾwīl* ("final [or "inner"] meaning") in the sense in which it is used in 7 : 53 (see my translation of that passage and the corresponding note 41).

64 The verb *yuʾminu*, which occurs twice in this verse, can be understood as connoting either the present tense – "[such as] believe", resp. "[such as] do not believe" – or the future tense. The future tense (adopted by me) is the meaning unequivocally attributed to it by Ṭabarī and Ibn Kathīr; some of the other authorities, like Zamakhsharī and Rāzī, prefer the present tense, but nevertheless regard the other interpretation as legitimate. (See also *Manār* XI, 380.)

Verily, God does not do the least wrong unto men, but it is men who wrong themselves. ‹44›
And on the Day when He shall gather them [unto Himself, it will seem to them] as if they had not tarried [on earth] longer than an hour of a day, knowing one another;[65] [and] lost indeed will be they who [in their lifetime] considered it a lie that they were destined to meet God, and [thus] failed to find the right way. ‹45›
And whether We show thee [in this world] something of what We hold in store for those [deniers of the truth],[66] or whether We cause thee to die [before that retribution takes place – know that, in the end], it is unto Us that they must return; and God is witness to all that they do.[67] ‹46›

NOW every community has had an apostle; and only after their apostle has appeared [and delivered his message] is judgment passed on them, in all equity;[68] and never are they wronged. ‹47›
And yet, they [who deny the truth] are wont to ask, "When is that promise [of resurrection and judgment] to be fulfilled? [Answer this, O you who believe in it,] if you are men of truth!" ‹48›

إِنَّ ٱللَّهَ لَا يَظْلِمُ ٱلنَّاسَ شَيْـًٔا وَلَـٰكِنَّ ٱلنَّاسَ أَنفُسَهُمْ يَظْلِمُونَ ﴿٤٤﴾
وَيَوْمَ يَحْشُرُهُمْ كَأَن لَّمْ يَلْبَثُوٓاْ إِلَّا سَاعَةً مِّنَ ٱلنَّهَارِ يَتَعَارَفُونَ بَيْنَهُمْ قَدْ
خَسِرَ ٱلَّذِينَ كَذَّبُواْ بِلِقَآءِ ٱللَّهِ وَمَا كَانُواْ مُهْتَدِينَ ﴿٤٥﴾ وَإِمَّا نُرِيَنَّكَ
بَعْضَ ٱلَّذِى نَعِدُهُمْ أَوْ نَتَوَفَّيَنَّكَ فَإِلَيْنَا مَرْجِعُهُمْ ثُمَّ ٱللَّهُ شَهِيدٌ عَلَىٰ مَا
يَفْعَلُونَ ﴿٤٦﴾ وَلِكُلِّ أُمَّةٍ رَّسُولٌ فَإِذَا جَآءَ رَسُولُهُمْ قُضِىَ بَيْنَهُم بِٱلْقِسْطِ
وَهُمْ لَا يُظْلَمُونَ ﴿٤٧﴾ وَيَقُولُونَ مَتَىٰ هَـٰذَا ٱلْوَعْدُ إِن كُنتُمْ صَـٰدِقِينَ ﴿٤٨﴾

ʾInnal-lāha lā yaẓlimun-nāsa shayʾañw-wa lākinnan-nāsa ʾañfusahum yaẓlimūn. ﴾44﴿ Wa Yawma yaḥshuruhum kaʾal-lam yalbathūu ʾillā sāʿatam-minan-nahāri yataʿārafūna baynahum. Qad khasiral-ladhīna kadhdhabū biliqāaʾil-lāhi wa mā kānū muhtadīn. ﴾45﴿ Wa ʾimma nuriyannaka baʿḍal-ladhī naʿiduhum ʾaw natawaffayannaka faʾilaynā marjiʿuhum thummal-lāhu Shahīdun ʿalā mā yafʿalūn. ﴾46﴿ Wa likulli ʾummatiñ-Rasūl. Faʾidhā jāaʾa Rasūluhum quḍiya baynahum-bilqisṭi wa hum lā yuẓlamūn. ﴾47﴿ Wa yaqūlūna matā hādhal-waʿdu ʾiñ-kuñtum ṣādiqīn. ﴾48﴿

65 I.e., their past sojourn in this world, during which they were bound to one another by various ties of human relationship, will appear to them like a short moment as compared with the timeless duration of the life that awaits them after resurrection (see note 19 on 79 : 46), with all their past relationships cut asunder. See also 6 : 94, which describes the condition of the deniers of the truth on the Day of Resurrection: "And now, indeed, you have come unto Us in a lonely state, even as We created you in the first instance"; and later on, in that same verse: "Indeed, all the bonds between you [and your earthly life] are now severed. . . ."

66 Lit., "of what We promise them" or "of what We threaten them with" – i.e., the inevitable retribution, sometimes even in this world, which a deliberate denial of the truth brings in its wake.

67 The above verse is addressed, in the first instance, to the Prophet, and relates to those of his contemporaries who refused to acknowledge the truth of the Qurʾanic revelation. In its wider sense, however, it is addressed to every believer who might find it incomprehensible that life-long suffering is often the lot of the righteous, while many wrongdoers and deniers of the truth apparently remain unscathed and are allowed to enjoy the good things of life. The Qurʾān solves this apparent paradox by making it clear that, in comparison with the life to come, the life in this world is but a brief moment, and that it is only in the hereafter that man's destiny reveals itself in all its true aspects. Cf. 3 : 185 – "only on the Day of Resurrection will you be requited in full [for whatever you have done] . . . for the life of this world is nothing but an enjoyment of self-delusion".

68 Lit., "and when their apostle has come, a decision is made between them in all equity". This verse stresses (a) the continuity of religious revelation in mankind's history and the fact that in the long run no community, period or civilization (which latter is one of the meanings attributable to the term *ummah*) has been left without prophetic guidance, and (b) the doctrine that God does not punish "a community for its wrongdoing so long as its people are still unaware [of the meaning of right and wrong]: for all shall be judged according to their [conscious] deeds" (6 : 131-132).

Say [O Prophet]: "It is not within my power to avert harm from, or bring benefit to, myself, except as God may please.[69] For all people a term has been set: when the end of their term approaches, they can neither delay it by a single moment, nor hasten it."[70] ‹49›

Say: "Have you ever considered [how you would feel] if His chastisement were to befall you by night or by day? What could there be in that prospect that people lost in sin should wish to hasten?[71] ‹50› Will you, then, believe in it [only] after it has come to pass – [on the Day when you will be asked, 'Do you believe in it] now,[72] after having [contemptuously] called for its speedy advent?' ‹51› – whereupon those who [in their lifetime] were bent on evildoing will be told, 'Taste suffering abiding! Is this requital anything but the just due for what you were wont to do?'"[73] ‹52›

And some people[74] ask thee, "Is all this true?"

Say: "Yea, by my Sustainer! It is most certainly true, and you cannot elude [the final reckoning]!" ‹53›

And all human beings that have been doing evil[75] would surely, if they possessed all that is on earth, offer it as ransom [on Judgment Day];[76] and when they see the suffering [that awaits them], they will be

قُل لَّآ أَمۡلِكُ لِنَفۡسِي ضَرّٗا وَلَا نَفۡعًا إِلَّا مَا شَآءَ ٱللَّهُۗ لِكُلِّ أُمَّةٍ أَجَلٌۚ
إِذَا جَآءَ أَجَلُهُمۡ فَلَا يَسۡتَـٔۡخِرُونَ سَاعَةٗ وَلَا يَسۡتَقۡدِمُونَ ﴿٤٩﴾ قُلۡ
أَرَءَيۡتُمۡ إِنۡ أَتَىٰكُمۡ عَذَابُهُۥ بَيَٰتًا أَوۡ نَهَارٗا مَّاذَا يَسۡتَعۡجِلُ مِنۡهُ
ٱلۡمُجۡرِمُونَ ﴿٥٠﴾ أَثُمَّ إِذَا مَا وَقَعَ ءَامَنتُم بِهِۦٓۚ ءَآلۡـَٰٔنَ وَقَدۡ كُنتُم بِهِۦ
تَسۡتَعۡجِلُونَ ﴿٥١﴾ ثُمَّ قِيلَ لِلَّذِينَ ظَلَمُواْ ذُوقُواْ عَذَابَ ٱلۡخُلۡدِ هَلۡ
تُجۡزَوۡنَ إِلَّا بِمَا كُنتُمۡ تَكۡسِبُونَ ﴿٥٢﴾ ۞ وَيَسۡتَنۢبِـُٔونَكَ أَحَقٌّ هُوَۖ قُلۡ
إِي وَرَبِّيٓ إِنَّهُۥ لَحَقّٞۖ وَمَآ أَنتُم بِمُعۡجِزِينَ ﴿٥٣﴾ وَلَوۡ أَنَّ لِكُلِّ نَفۡسٖ
ظَلَمَتۡ مَا فِي ٱلۡأَرۡضِ لَٱفۡتَدَتۡ بِهِۦۗ وَأَسَرُّواْ ٱلنَّدَامَةَ لَمَّا رَأَوُاْ ٱلۡعَذَابَۖ

ربع الحزب

Qul lāa ʾamliku linafsī ḍarrañw-wa lā nafʿan ʾillā mā shāaʾal-lāh. Likulli ʾummatin ʾajal. ʾIdhā jāaʾa ʾajaluhum falā yastaʾkhirūna sāʿatañw-wa lā yastaqdimūn. (49) Qul ʾaraʾaytum ʾin ʾatākum ʿadhābuhū bayātan ʾaw nahāram-mādhā yastaʿjilu minhul-mujrimūn. (50) ʾAthumma ʾidhā mā waqaʿa ʾāmañtum-bih. ʾĀalʾāna wa qad kuñtum-bihī tastaʿjilūn. (51) Thumma qīla lilladhīna ẓalamū dhūqū ʿadhābal-khuldi hal tujzawna ʾillā bimā kuñtum taksibūn. (52) ۞ Wa yastambiʾūnaka ʾaḥaqqun hū. Qul ʾī wa Rabbīi ʾinnahū laḥaqq. Wa māa ʾañtum-bimuʿjizīn. (53) Wa law ʾanna likulli nafsiñ-ẓalamat mā fil-ʾarḍi laftadat bih. Wa ʾasarrun-nadāmata lammā raʾawul-ʿadhāb.

69 Sc., "and since I do not possess any supernatural powers, I cannot predict that which is beyond the reach of human perception (*al-ghayb*)".

70 See 7 : 34 and the corresponding notes 25 and 26. In the above context, the "end of the term" refers, in particular, to the coming of the Last Hour and the Day of Judgment.

71 Lit., "What [part] thereof might the people lost in sin (*al-mujrimūn*) wish to hasten" – meaning, according to Zamakhsharī, that "all of [God's] chastisement is awful and bitter, and should inspire one with the desire to flee therefrom; . . . and there is nothing in it that ought to make one wish to hasten it". This is an allusion to the incredulous inquiry of the deniers of the truth about the coming of the Last Hour (verse 48 above), as well as to their sarcastic demand that they should be immediately chastised by God in proof of Muḥammad's prophetic mission (cf. 6 : 57-58 and 8 : 32, as well as the corresponding notes). – The expression "by night or by day" occurring in the preceding sentence denotes the suddenness and unexpectedness with which doom is bound to encompass the evildoers on the Day of Judgment.

72 I.e., "when it is too late" (Ṭabarī, Zamakhsharī, Rāzī; my interpolation at the beginning of this sentence is based on these authorities).

73 Lit., "Are you being requited for anything but for what you were wont to earn?"

74 Lit., "they" – i.e., those of the unbelievers who are wavering in their agnosticism and – as mentioned in verse 36 above – "follow nothing but conjecture" (*Manār* XI, 394).

75 In this instance, by deliberately giving the lie to the Prophet and rejecting the message of the Qurʾān.

76 Cf. 3 : 91 and the corresponding note 71.

unable to express their remorse.[77] But
judgment will be passed on them in all
equity; and they will not be wronged. ‹54›
Oh, verily, unto God belongs all that is in
the heavens and on earth! Oh, verily,
God's promise always comes true – but
most of them know it not! ‹55› He alone
grants life and deals death; and unto Him
you all must return.[78] ‹56›

O MANKIND! There has now come unto
you an admonition from your Sustainer,
and a cure for all [the ill] that may be in
men's hearts,[79] and guidance and grace
unto all who believe [in Him]. ‹57›
Say: "In [this] bounty of God and in His
grace – in this, then, let them rejoice: it is
better than all [the worldly wealth] that
they may amass!" ‹58›
Say: "Have you ever considered all the
means of sustenance which God has bestowed upon you from on high[80] – and
which you thereupon divide into 'things
forbidden' and 'things lawful'?"[81]
Say: "Has God given you leave [to do this]
– or do you, perchance, attribute your own
guesswork to God?" ‹59›

وَقُضِيَ بَيْنَهُم بِٱلْقِسْطِ وَهُمْ لَا يُظْلَمُونَ ﴿٥٤﴾ أَلَآ إِنَّ لِلَّهِ مَا فِى ٱلسَّمَٰوَٰتِ
وَٱلْأَرْضِ ۗ أَلَآ إِنَّ وَعْدَ ٱللَّهِ حَقٌّ وَلَٰكِنَّ أَكْثَرَهُمْ لَا يَعْلَمُونَ ﴿٥٥﴾ هُوَ
يُحْىِۦ وَيُمِيتُ وَإِلَيْهِ تُرْجَعُونَ ﴿٥٦﴾ يَٰٓأَيُّهَا ٱلنَّاسُ قَدْ جَآءَتْكُم مَّوْعِظَةٌ
مِّن رَّبِّكُمْ وَشِفَآءٌ لِّمَا فِى ٱلصُّدُورِ وَهُدًى وَرَحْمَةٌ لِّلْمُؤْمِنِينَ ﴿٥٧﴾ قُلْ
بِفَضْلِ ٱللَّهِ وَبِرَحْمَتِهِۦ فَبِذَٰلِكَ فَلْيَفْرَحُوا۟ هُوَ خَيْرٌ مِّمَّا يَجْمَعُونَ ﴿٥٨﴾
قُلْ أَرَءَيْتُم مَّآ أَنزَلَ ٱللَّهُ لَكُم مِّن رِّزْقٍ فَجَعَلْتُم مِّنْهُ حَرَامًا وَحَلَٰلًا قُلْ
ءَآللَّهُ أَذِنَ لَكُمْ ۖ أَمْ عَلَى ٱللَّهِ تَفْتَرُونَ ﴿٥٩﴾

Wa quḍiya baynahum-bilqisṭi wa hum lā yuẓlamūn.
(54) ʾAlāa ʾinna lillāhi mā fis-samāwāti wal-ʾarḍ. ʾAlāa
ʾinna waʿdal-lāhi ḥaqquñw-wa lākinna ʾaktharahum
lā yaʿlamūn. (55) Huwa yuḥyī wa yumītu wa ʾilayhi
turjaʿūn. (56) Yāa ʾayyuhan-nāsu qad jāaʾatkum-
mawʿiẓatum-mir-Rabbikum wa shifāaʾul-limā fiṣ-
ṣudūri wa hudañw-wa raḥmatul-lilmuʾminīn. (57)
Qul bifaḍlil-lāhi wa biraḥmatihī fabidhālika falya-
fraḥū huwa khayrum-mimmā yajmaʿūn. (58) Qul-
ʾaraʾaytum-māa ʾañzalal-lāhu lakum-mir-rizqiñ-
fajaʿaltum-minhu ḥarāmañw-wa ḥalālañ-qul
ʾāallāhu ʾadhina lakum ʾam ʿalal-lāhi taftarūn. (59)

77 The primary meaning of the verb *asarrahu* is "he concealed it" or "he kept it secret"; thus, the phrase *asarru 'n-nadāmah* (expressed in the past tense but in the above context obviously denoting a future event) could be rendered as "they will conceal their remorse". In view, however, of the many statements in the Qurʾān that on the Day of Judgment the sinners will not only not conceal but will, rather, stress their remorse, some of the commentators (e.g., Baghawī, on the authority of Abū ʿUbaydah) are of the opinion that in this particular verse the verb *asarra* denotes the opposite of its primary meaning and, accordingly, interpret the phrase as "they will *manifest* their remorse". But the linguistic validity of this rather forced interpretation has been emphatically contested by many philologists, and particularly by Abū Manṣūr al-Azharī (cf. Lane IV, 1337); and since there is no convincing reason to disregard the original significance of the verb *asarra* with its implication of "concealment", the above Qurʾanic phrase must be understood (as Zamakhsharī understands it), in the metonymical sense of an *involuntary* "concealment", that is, the sinners' inability to express the full depth of their remorse.

78 Lit., "you shall be brought back" – for, "all that exists goes back to Him [as its source]" (11 : 123).

79 I.e., a remedy for all that is contrary to truth and moral good.

80 This connects with the statement, in verse 57, that the Qurʾān offers to man a complete guidance towards the good life and spiritual fulfilment in this world, and happiness in the life to come. As already mentioned in *sūrah* 2, note 4, the term *rizq* connotes all that may be good and useful to man, be it of a physical nature (in the conventional sense of "means of sustenance") or belonging to the realm of the mind (like reason, knowledge, etc.) or of the spirit (like faith, kindness, patience, etc.). Thus, it applies exclusively to positive, beneficial means of sustenance, and never to things or phenomena which are morally reprehensible and/or physically or socially injurious.

81 Lit., "and thereupon you have made some of it forbidden (*ḥarām*) and [some of it] lawful (*ḥalāl*)". The fact that it is God who "has bestowed upon you from on high" (*anzala lakum*) – i.e., has willed that man should make use of – all that can be qualified as *rizq*, automatically makes all its manifestations lawful (Zamakhsharī). In accordance with the doctrine that everything which has not been expressly forbidden by the Qurʾān or the explicit teachings of the Prophet is *eo ipso* lawful, this verse takes a clear-cut stand against all arbitrary prohibitions invented by man or artificially "deduced" from the Qurʾān or the Prophet's *sunnah* (*Manār* XI, 409 f.; see also note 58 on verse 36 of this *sūrah*, as

But what do they think – they who attribute their own lying inventions to God – [what do they think will happen to them] on the Day of Resurrection?
Behold, God is indeed limitless in His bounty unto men – but most of them are ungrateful. ‹60›

AND IN whatever condition thou mayest find thyself, [O Prophet,] and whatever discourse of this [divine writ][82] thou mayest be reciting, and whatever work you [all, O men,] may do – [remember that] We are your witness[83] [from the moment] when you enter upon it: for, not even an atom's weight [of whatever there is] on earth or in heaven escapes thy Sustainer's knowledge; and neither is there anything smaller than that, or larger, but is recorded in [His] clear decree. ‹61›
Oh, verily, they who are close to God[84] – no fear need they have, and neither shall they grieve: ‹62› they who have attained to faith and have always been conscious of Him. ‹63› For them there is the glad tiding [of happiness] in the life of this world[85] and in the life to come; [and since] nothing could ever alter [the outcome of] God's promises, this, this is the triumph supreme! ‹64›
And be not grieved by the sayings of those [who deny the truth]. Behold, all might and glory[86] belong to God alone: He alone is all-hearing, all-knowing. ‹65›

وَمَا ظَنُّ ٱلَّذِينَ يَفۡتَرُونَ عَلَى ٱللَّهِ ٱلۡكَذِبَ يَوۡمَ ٱلۡقِيَٰمَةِۗ إِنَّ ٱللَّهَ لَذُو فَضۡلٍ
عَلَى ٱلنَّاسِ وَلَٰكِنَّ أَكۡثَرَهُمۡ لَا يَشۡكُرُونَ ﴿٦٠﴾ وَمَا تَكُونُ فِي شَأۡنٖ وَمَا
تَتۡلُواْ مِنۡهُ مِن قُرۡءَانٖ وَلَا تَعۡمَلُونَ مِنۡ عَمَلٍ إِلَّا كُنَّا عَلَيۡكُمۡ شُهُودًا إِذۡ
تُفِيضُونَ فِيهِۚ وَمَا يَعۡزُبُ عَن رَّبِّكَ مِن مِّثۡقَالِ ذَرَّةٖ فِي ٱلۡأَرۡضِ وَلَا فِي
ٱلسَّمَآءِ وَلَآ أَصۡغَرَ مِن ذَٰلِكَ وَلَآ أَكۡبَرَ إِلَّا فِي كِتَٰبٖ مُّبِينٍ ﴿٦١﴾ أَلَآ إِنَّ
أَوۡلِيَآءَ ٱللَّهِ لَا خَوۡفٌ عَلَيۡهِمۡ وَلَا هُمۡ يَحۡزَنُونَ ﴿٦٢﴾ ٱلَّذِينَ ءَامَنُواْ وَكَانُواْ
يَتَّقُونَ ﴿٦٣﴾ لَهُمُ ٱلۡبُشۡرَىٰ فِي ٱلۡحَيَوٰةِ ٱلدُّنۡيَا وَفِي ٱلۡأٓخِرَةِۚ لَا تَبۡدِيلَ
لِكَلِمَٰتِ ٱللَّهِۚ ذَٰلِكَ هُوَ ٱلۡفَوۡزُ ٱلۡعَظِيمُ ﴿٦٤﴾ وَلَا يَحۡزُنكَ قَوۡلُهُمۡۘ إِنَّ
ٱلۡعِزَّةَ لِلَّهِ جَمِيعًاۚ هُوَ ٱلسَّمِيعُ ٱلۡعَلِيمُ ﴿٦٥﴾

Wa mā ẓannul-ladhīna yaftarūna ʿalal-lāhil-kadhiba Yawmal-Qiyāmah. ʾInnal-lāha ladhū faḍlin ʿalan-nāsi wa lākinna ʾaktharahum lā yashkurūn. ‹60› Wa mā takūnu fī shaʾniñw-wa mā tatlū minhu miñ-Qurʾāniñw-wa lā taʿmalūna min ʿamalin ʾillā kunnā ʿalaykum shuhūdan ʾidh tufīḍūna fīh. Wa mā yaʿzubu ʿar-Rabbika mim-mithqāli dharratiñ-fil-ʾarḍi wa lā fis-samāaʾi wa lāa ʾaṣghara miñ-dhālika wa lāa ʾakbara ʾillā fī Kitābim-mubīn. ‹61› ʾAlāa ʾinna ʾawliyāaʾal-lāhi lā khawfun ʿalayhim wa lā hum yaḥzanūn. ‹62› ʾAlladhīna ʾāmanū wa kānū yattaqūn. ‹63› Lahumul-bushrā fil-ḥayātid-dunyā wa fil-ʾĀkhirah. Lā tabdīla liKalimātil-lāh. Dhālika huwal-fawzul-ʿaẓīm. ‹64› Wa lā yaḥzuñka qawluhum. ʾInnal-ʿizzata lillāhi jamīʿā. Huwas-Samīʿul-ʿAlīm. ‹65›

well as 5 : 101-102 and the corresponding notes). In its wider sense, the above verse relates to people who refuse to be guided by revelation and prefer to "follow nothing but conjecture" (verse 36).

82 Or: "Whatever discourse (*qurʾān*) from Him".

83 Lit., "witnesses", corresponding to the majestic plural "We". The specific reference to the Prophet and his recitation of the Qurʾān (implied in the singular form of address in the first part of this sentence) is meant to stress the supreme importance of divine revelation in the context of human life.

84 The verb *waliya* (from which the noun *walī*, pl. *awliyāʾ*, is derived) signifies, primarily, the nearness or closeness of one thing to another: thus, God is spoken of in the Qurʾān (e.g., in 2 : 257 and 3 : 68) as being "near unto (*walī*) those who believe". Although the term *walī*, when applied to God, as well as to the relationship between one created being and another, is often used in the Qurʾān in the sense of "helper", "friend", "protector", "guardian", etc., none of these secondary meanings can properly – i.e., without offending against the reverence due to God – describe *man's* attitude to, or relationship with, Him. Consequently, the above reference to the believers as *awliyāʾ* of God is best rendered as "they who are close to God", in the sense of their being always conscious of Him. This rendering has the support of almost all the classical commentators.

85 I.e., the happiness born of the feeling of closeness to God and, hence, of spiritual fulfilment.

86 The noun *ʿizzah* comprises the concepts of superior might as well as of honour and glory. Its rendering into

OH, VERILY, unto God belongs whoever is in the heavens and whoever is on earth: hence, what is it that they follow – those who invoke, beside God, beings to whom they ascribe a share in His divinity?[87] They follow but the conjectures [of others], and themselves do nothing but guess ‹66› – [whereas] it is He who has made the night for you, so that you might have rest therein, and the day, to make [you] see:[88] in this, behold, there are messages indeed for people who [are willing to] listen. ‹67›
[And yet] they assert, "God has taken unto Himself a son!" Limitless is He in His glory![89] Self-sufficient is He: unto Him belongs all that is in the heavens and all that is on earth! No evidence whatever have you for this [assertion]! Would you ascribe unto God something which you cannot know? ‹68›
Say: "Verily, they who attribute their own lying inventions to God will never attain to a happy state!" ‹69› [A brief] enjoyment in this world – and thereafter unto Us they must return: and then We shall let them taste suffering severe as an outcome of their persistent denial of the truth. ‹70›

AND CONVEY unto them the story of Noah – when he said unto his people: "O my people! If my presence [among you] and my announcement of God's messages are repugnant to you[90] – well, in God have I placed my trust. Decide, then, upon what

نصف الحزب

أَلَآ إِنَّ لِلَّهِ مَن فِى ٱلسَّمَٰوَٰتِ وَمَن فِى ٱلْأَرْضِ ۗ وَمَا يَتَّبِعُ ٱلَّذِينَ يَدْعُونَ مِن
دُونِ ٱللَّهِ شُرَكَآءَ ۚ إِن يَتَّبِعُونَ إِلَّا ٱلظَّنَّ وَإِنْ هُمْ إِلَّا يَخْرُصُونَ ﴿٦٦﴾ هُوَ ٱلَّذِى
جَعَلَ لَكُمُ ٱلَّيْلَ لِتَسْكُنُوا۟ فِيهِ وَٱلنَّهَارَ مُبْصِرًا ۚ إِنَّ فِى ذَٰلِكَ لَءَايَٰتٍ لِّقَوْمٍ
يَسْمَعُونَ ﴿٦٧﴾ قَالُوا۟ ٱتَّخَذَ ٱللَّهُ وَلَدًا ۗ سُبْحَٰنَهُۥ ۖ هُوَ ٱلْغَنِىُّ ۖ لَهُۥ مَا فِى
ٱلسَّمَٰوَٰتِ وَمَا فِى ٱلْأَرْضِ ۚ إِنْ عِندَكُم مِّن سُلْطَٰنٍۭ بِهَٰذَآ ۚ أَتَقُولُونَ عَلَى ٱللَّهِ
مَا لَا تَعْلَمُونَ ﴿٦٨﴾ قُلْ إِنَّ ٱلَّذِينَ يَفْتَرُونَ عَلَى ٱللَّهِ ٱلْكَذِبَ لَا يُفْلِحُونَ ﴿٦٩﴾
مَتَٰعٌ فِى ٱلدُّنْيَا ثُمَّ إِلَيْنَا مَرْجِعُهُمْ ثُمَّ نُذِيقُهُمُ ٱلْعَذَابَ ٱلشَّدِيدَ بِمَا كَانُوا۟
يَكْفُرُونَ ﴿٧٠﴾ ۞ وَٱتْلُ عَلَيْهِمْ نَبَأَ نُوحٍ إِذْ قَالَ لِقَوْمِهِۦ يَٰقَوْمِ إِن كَانَ كَبُرَ
عَلَيْكُم مَّقَامِى وَتَذْكِيرِى بِـَٔايَٰتِ ٱللَّهِ فَعَلَى ٱللَّهِ تَوَكَّلْتُ فَأَجْمِعُوٓا۟ أَمْرَكُمْ

ʾAlāa ʾinna lillāhi mañ-fis-samāwāti wa mañ-fil-ʾarḍ. Wa mā yattabiʿul-ladhīna yadʿūna miñ-dūnil-lāhi shurakāaʾ. ʾIñy-yattabiʿūna ʾillaẓ-ẓanna wa ʾin hum ʾillā yakhruṣūn. (66) Huwal-ladhī jaʿala lakumul-layla litaskunū fīhi wan-nahāra mubṣirā. ʾInna fī dhālika laʾĀyātil-liqawmiñy-yasmaʿūn. (67) Qālut-takhadhal-lāhu waladā. Subḥānahū Huwal-Ghaniyy. Lahū mā fis-samāwāti wa mā fil-ʾarḍ. ʾIn ʿiñdakum-miñ-sulṭānim-bihādhā. ʾAtaqūlūna ʿalal-lāhi mā lā taʿlamūn. (68) Qul ʾinnal-ladhīna yaftarūna ʿalal-lāhil-kadhiba lā yufliḥūn. (69) Matāʿuñ-fid-dunyā thumma ʾilaynā marjiʿuhum thumma nudhīquhumul-ʿadhā-bash-shadīda bimā kānū yakfurūn. (70) ۞ Wat-lu ʿalayhim nabaʾa Nūḥin ʾidh qāla liqawmihī yā qawmi ʾiñ-kāna kabura ʿalaykum-maqāmī wa tadhkīrī biʾĀyātil-lāhi faʿalal-lāhi tawakkaltu faʾajmiʿūu ʾamrakum

another language depends on the context, and sometimes – as in this case – necessitates a combination of two terms.

87 Lit., "partners", i.e., of God (see *sūrah* 6, note 15). The substantive pronoun *man* ("whoever") occurring twice in the first part of this verse contains an allusion to rational beings (as distinct from inanimate objects) whom "those who ascribe divinity to aught beside God" consider to be endowed with qualities or powers which, in fact, belong to Him alone. The Qurʾān argues against this idolatrous concept by pointing out that all rational beings, whether men or angels, "belong to God" (i.e., are – like everything else in the universe – wholly dependent on Him for their existence), possessing no divine qualities and, therefore, no reality as objects of worship.

88 See 14 : 32-33 and the corresponding note 46; for the specific significance, in this context, of the reference to "day" and "night", see note 77 on 27 : 86, which belongs to a somewhat earlier revelation than the present *sūrah*.

89 See *sūrah* 2, note 96.

90 Sc., "because they run counter to the idolatrous beliefs which you have inherited from your ancestors". The story of Noah, briefly mentioned in verses 71-73, is told at greater length in 11 : 36-48 (see also 7 : 59-64). Here it connects with verse 47 above, and thus with the main theme of this *sūrah*: the truth of God's revelation of His will through His prophets, and the suffering which in the life to come is bound to befall those who give the lie to His messages.

you are going to do [against me],[91] and [call to your aid] those beings to whom you ascribe a share in God's divinity;[92] and once you have chosen your course of action, let no hesitation deflect you from it;[93] and then carry out against me [whatever you may have decided], and give me no respite! ‹71› But if you turn away [from the message which I bear, remember that] I have asked no reward whatever of you: my reward rests with none but God, for I have been bidden to be among those who have surrendered themselves unto Him." ‹72›
And yet they gave him the lie! And so We saved him and all who stood by him, in the ark, and made them inherit [the earth],[94] the while We caused those who gave the lie to Our messages to drown:[95] behold, then, what happened in the end to those people who had been warned [in vain]! ‹73›

AND THEN, after him, We sent forth [other] apostles – each one unto his own people[96] – and they brought them all evidence of the truth; but they would not believe in anything to which they had once given the lie:[97] thus it is that We seal the hearts of such as [are wont to] transgress the bounds of what is right.[98] ‹74›
And after those [earlier prophets] We sent Moses and Aaron with Our messages unto Pharaoh and his great ones: but they gloried in their arrogance, for they were people lost in sin. ‹75› And so, when the truth came to them from Us, they said, "Behold, this is clearly nothing but sorcery!"[99] ‹76›

وَشُرَكَآءَكُمْ ثُمَّ لَا يَكُنْ أَمْرُكُمْ عَلَيْكُمْ غُمَّةً ثُمَّ ٱقْضُوٓا۟ إِلَىَّ وَلَا تُنظِرُونِ ﴿٧١﴾
فَإِن تَوَلَّيْتُمْ فَمَا سَأَلْتُكُم مِّنْ أَجْرٍ ۖ إِنْ أَجْرِىَ إِلَّا عَلَى ٱللَّهِ ۖ وَأُمِرْتُ أَنْ
أَكُونَ مِنَ ٱلْمُسْلِمِينَ ﴿٧٢﴾ فَكَذَّبُوهُ فَنَجَّيْنَٰهُ وَمَن مَّعَهُۥ فِى ٱلْفُلْكِ
وَجَعَلْنَٰهُمْ خَلَٰٓئِفَ وَأَغْرَقْنَا ٱلَّذِينَ كَذَّبُوا۟ بِـَٔايَٰتِنَا ۖ فَٱنظُرْ كَيْفَ كَانَ
عَٰقِبَةُ ٱلْمُنذَرِينَ ﴿٧٣﴾ ثُمَّ بَعَثْنَا مِنۢ بَعْدِهِۦ رُسُلًا إِلَىٰ قَوْمِهِمْ فَجَآءُوهُم
بِٱلْبَيِّنَٰتِ فَمَا كَانُوا۟ لِيُؤْمِنُوا۟ بِمَا كَذَّبُوا۟ بِهِۦ مِن قَبْلُ ۚ كَذَٰلِكَ نَطْبَعُ عَلَىٰ
قُلُوبِ ٱلْمُعْتَدِينَ ﴿٧٤﴾ ثُمَّ بَعَثْنَا مِنۢ بَعْدِهِم مُّوسَىٰ وَهَٰرُونَ إِلَىٰ فِرْعَوْنَ
وَمَلَإِي۟هِۦ بِـَٔايَٰتِنَا فَٱسْتَكْبَرُوا۟ وَكَانُوا۟ قَوْمًا مُّجْرِمِينَ ﴿٧٥﴾ فَلَمَّا جَآءَهُمُ
ٱلْحَقُّ مِنْ عِندِنَا قَالُوٓا۟ إِنَّ هَٰذَا لَسِحْرٌ مُّبِينٌ ﴿٧٦﴾

wa shurakāaʾakum thumma lā yakun ʾamrukum ʿalaykum ghummatañ-thummaq-ḍūu ʾilayya wa lā tuñẓirūn. (71) Faʾiñ-tawallaytum famā saʾaltukum-min ʾajr. ʾIn ʾajriya ʾillā ʿalal-lāhi wa ʾumirtu ʾan ʾakūna minal-Muslimīn. (72) Fakadhdhabūhu fanajjaynāhu wa mam-maʿahū fil-fulki wa jaʿalnāhum khalāaʾifa wa ʾaghraqnal-ladhīna kadhdhabū biʾĀyātinā. Fañẓur kayfa kāna ʿāqibatul-muñdharīn. (73) Thumma baʿathnā mim-baʿdihī Rusulan ʾilā qawmihim fajāaʾūhum-bilbayyināti famā kānū liyuʾminū bimā kadhdhabū bihī miñ-qabl. Kadhālika naṭbaʿu ʿalā qulūbil-muʿtadīn. (74) Thumma baʿathnā mim-baʿdihim-Mūsā wa Hārūna ʾilā Firʿawna wa malaʾiyhī biʾĀyātinā fastakbarū wa kānū qawmam-mujrimīn. (75) Falammā jāaʾahumul-ḥaqqu min ʿiñdinā qālūu ʾinna hādhā lasiḥrum-mubīn. (76)

91 Lit., "upon your course of action" (which is the meaning of the term *amr* in this context).

92 Lit., "your [God-]partners". For an explanation of this term, see *sūrah* 6, note 15.

93 This is a free rendering of the elliptic phrase, "and let not your course of action (*amrukum*) be an uncertainty to you".

94 I.e., "made them outlive [the others]" (Zamakhsharī). As regards the allegorical rendering of *khalāʾif* (sing. *khalīf* or *khalīfah*) adopted by me, see *sūrah* 2, note 22.

95 See *sūrah* 7, note 47.

96 Lit., "We sent apostles to their [own] people" – an allusion to the fact that each of the apostles before Muḥammad was sent to one particular people or community, and that the Arabian Prophet was the first and the last to bring a universal message addressed to all mankind.

97 Cf. 7 : 101 and the corresponding note 82.

98 See *sūrah* 2, note 7.

99 Lit., "this is indeed obvious sorcery": an accusation which apparently refers to the spellbinding force of the

Said Moses: "Do you speak thus of the truth after it has been brought to you? Can this be sorcery? But sorcerers can never come to a happy end!"[100] ‹77›
[The great ones] replied: "Hast thou come to turn us away from what we found our forefathers believing in and doing, so that the two of you might become supreme in this land? However, we do not believe in you two!"[101] ‹78›
And Pharaoh commanded: "Bring before me every sorcerer of great knowledge!" ‹79›
And when the sorcerers came, Moses said unto them: "Throw whatever you may [wish to] throw!" ‹80›
And when they threw down [their staffs and cast a spell upon the people's eyes[102]], Moses said unto them: "What you have contrived is [but] sorcery which, verily, God will bring to nought! Verily, God does not further the works of spreaders of corruption ‹81› – whereas by His words God proves the truth to be true,[103] however hateful this may be to those who are lost in sin!" ‹82›
But none save a few of his people declared their faith in Moses,[104] [while others held back] for fear of Pharaoh and their great ones, lest they persecute them:[105] for, verily, Pharaoh was mighty on earth and was, verily, of those who are given to excesses. ‹83›

قَالَ مُوسَىٰٓ أَتَقُولُونَ لِلْحَقِّ لَمَّا جَآءَكُمْ أَسِحْرٌ هَٰذَا وَلَا يُفْلِحُ
ٱلسَّٰحِرُونَ ﴿٧٧﴾ قَالُوٓا۟ أَجِئْتَنَا لِتَلْفِتَنَا عَمَّا وَجَدْنَا عَلَيْهِ ءَابَآءَنَا وَتَكُونَ
لَكُمَا ٱلْكِبْرِيَآءُ فِى ٱلْأَرْضِ وَمَا نَحْنُ لَكُمَا بِمُؤْمِنِينَ ﴿٧٨﴾ وَقَالَ فِرْعَوْنُ
ٱئْتُونِى بِكُلِّ سَٰحِرٍ عَلِيمٍ ﴿٧٩﴾ فَلَمَّا جَآءَ ٱلسَّحَرَةُ قَالَ لَهُم مُّوسَىٰٓ أَلْقُوا۟ مَآ
أَنتُم مُّلْقُونَ ﴿٨٠﴾ فَلَمَّآ أَلْقَوْا۟ قَالَ مُوسَىٰ مَا جِئْتُم بِهِ ٱلسِّحْرُ إِنَّ ٱللَّهَ سَيُبْطِلُهُۥٓ
إِنَّ ٱللَّهَ لَا يُصْلِحُ عَمَلَ ٱلْمُفْسِدِينَ ﴿٨١﴾ وَيُحِقُّ ٱللَّهُ ٱلْحَقَّ بِكَلِمَٰتِهِۦ
وَلَوْ كَرِهَ ٱلْمُجْرِمُونَ ﴿٨٢﴾ فَمَآ ءَامَنَ لِمُوسَىٰٓ إِلَّا ذُرِّيَّةٌ مِّن قَوْمِهِۦ عَلَىٰ
خَوْفٍ مِّن فِرْعَوْنَ وَمَلَإِي۟هِمْ أَن يَفْتِنَهُمْ وَإِنَّ فِرْعَوْنَ لَعَالٍ فِى ٱلْأَرْضِ
وَإِنَّهُۥ لَمِنَ ٱلْمُسْرِفِينَ ﴿٨٣﴾

Qāla Mūsāa ʾataqūlūna lilḥaqqi lammā jāaʾakum. ʾAsiḥrun hādhā wa lā yufliḥus-sāḥirūn. ﴿77﴾ Qālūu ʾajiʾtanā litalfitanā ʿammā wajadnā ʿalayhi ʾābāaʾanā wa takūna lakumal-kibriyāaʾu fil-ʾarḍi wa mā naḥnu lakumā bimuʾminīn. ﴿78﴾ Wa qāla Firʿawnuʾ-tūnī bikulli sāḥirin ʿalīm. ﴿79﴾ Falammā jāaʾas-saḥaratu qāla lahum-Mūsāa ʾalqū māa ʾañtum-mulqūn. ﴿80﴾ Falammāa ʾalqaw qāla Mūsā mā jiʾtum-bihis-siḥru ʾinnal-lāha sayubṭiluh. ʾInnal-lāha lā yuṣliḥu ʿamalal-mufsidīn. ﴿81﴾ Wa yuḥiqqul-lāhul-ḥaqqa biKalimātihī wa law karihal-mujrimūn. ﴿82﴾ Famāa ʾāmana liMūsāa ʾillā dhurriyyatum-miñ-qawmihī ʿalā khawfim-miñ-Firʿawna wa malaʾiyhim ʾañy-yaftinahum; wa ʾinna Firʿawna laʿāliñ-fil-ʾarḍi wa ʾinnahū laminal-musrifīn. ﴿83﴾

messages conveyed to them by Moses, similar to the objections raised against the Last Prophet, Muḥammad (See verse 2 of this *sūrah* and the corresponding note 5).

100 The implication is that what is termed "sorcery" cannot achieve more than ephemeral phenomena lacking any spiritual content, and can never prevail against the laws of nature which, in their totality, are described in the Qurʾān as "the way of God". The story of Moses and the sorcerers and the latters' subsequent conversion is told in greater detail in *Al-Aʿrāf* and *Ṭā Hā*, both of which were revealed before the present *sūrah*.

101 The dual address "you two" relates to Moses and his brother Aaron.

102 The above interpolation is based on 7 : 116; see also the second paragraph of 20 : 66.

103 By "God's words" is meant here His creative will, manifested in the laws of nature instituted by Him as well as in the revelations granted by Him to His prophets (*Manār* XI, 468). A similar phrase occurs also in 8 : 7 and 42 : 24.

104 Lit., "believed in Moses"; however, since the sequence shows that not belief as such but its open *profession* is referred to here, I have rendered the above phrase accordingly. As for the term *dhurriyyah* (lit., "offspring"), we have several authoritative statements to the effect that it often denotes "a small group [or "a few"] of one's people" (Ibn ʿAbbās, as quoted by Ṭabarī, Baghawī, Rāzī and Ibn Kathīr, as well as Aḍ-Ḍaḥḥāk and Qatādah, as quoted by Ṭabarī and Ibn Kathīr); hence my rendering. Since the Qurʾān mentions (e.g., in 7 : 120-126) that some Egyptians, too, came to believe in Moses' message and openly proclaimed their belief, it is reasonable to assume that by "his people" are meant not merely the Israelites but, more generally, the people among whom Moses was living: that is, both Israelites and Egyptians. This assumption is strengthened by the reference, in the next clause of this sentence, to "*their* great ones" – an expression obviously relating to the *Egyptian* "great ones".

105 If the expression *ʿalā khawf* is taken to mean "*despite* [their] fear" (referring to those who did declare their

And Moses said: "O my people! If you believe in God, place your trust in Him – if you have [truly] surrendered yourselves unto Him!" ‹84›
Whereupon they answered: "In God have we placed our trust! O our Sustainer, make us not a plaything[106] for evildoing folk, ‹85› and save us, by Thy grace, from people who deny the truth!" ‹86›
And [thus] did We inspire Moses and his brother: "Set aside for your people some houses in the city, and [tell them], 'Turn your houses into places of worship,[107] and be constant in prayer!' And give thou [O Moses] the glad tiding [of God's succour] to all believers." ‹87›
And Moses prayed: "O our Sustainer! Verily, splendour and riches hast Thou vouchsafed, in the life of this world, unto Pharaoh and his great ones – with the result, O our Sustainer, that they are leading [others] astray from Thy path![108] O our Sustainer! Wipe out their riches, and harden their hearts, so that they may not attain to faith ere they see the grievous suffering [that awaits them]!" ‹88›
[God] answered: "Accepted is this your prayer![109] Continue, then, both of you, steadfastly on the right way, and follow not the path of those who have no knowledge [of right and wrong]." ‹89›
And We brought the children of Israel across the sea; and thereupon Pharaoh and his hosts pursued them with vehement insolence and tyranny, until [they were overwhelmed by the waters of the sea. And] when he was about to drown,

وَقَالَ مُوسَىٰ يَٰقَوۡمِ إِن كُنتُمۡ ءَامَنتُم بِٱللَّهِ فَعَلَيۡهِ تَوَكَّلُوٓاْ إِن كُنتُم
مُّسۡلِمِينَ ٨٤ فَقَالُواْ عَلَى ٱللَّهِ تَوَكَّلۡنَا رَبَّنَا لَا تَجۡعَلۡنَا فِتۡنَةٗ لِّلۡقَوۡمِ
ٱلظَّٰلِمِينَ ٨٥ وَنَجِّنَا بِرَحۡمَتِكَ مِنَ ٱلۡقَوۡمِ ٱلۡكَٰفِرِينَ ٨٦ وَأَوۡحَيۡنَآ
إِلَىٰ مُوسَىٰ وَأَخِيهِ أَن تَبَوَّءَا لِقَوۡمِكُمَا بِمِصۡرَ بُيُوتٗا وَٱجۡعَلُواْ بُيُوتَكُمۡ
قِبۡلَةٗ وَأَقِيمُواْ ٱلصَّلَوٰةَۗ وَبَشِّرِ ٱلۡمُؤۡمِنِينَ ٨٧ وَقَالَ مُوسَىٰ رَبَّنَآ إِنَّكَ
ءَاتَيۡتَ فِرۡعَوۡنَ وَمَلَأَهُۥ زِينَةٗ وَأَمۡوَٰلٗا فِي ٱلۡحَيَوٰةِ ٱلدُّنۡيَا رَبَّنَا لِيُضِلُّواْ عَن
سَبِيلِكَۖ رَبَّنَا ٱطۡمِسۡ عَلَىٰٓ أَمۡوَٰلِهِمۡ وَٱشۡدُدۡ عَلَىٰ قُلُوبِهِمۡ فَلَا يُؤۡمِنُواْ حَتَّىٰ
يَرَوُاْ ٱلۡعَذَابَ ٱلۡأَلِيمَ ٨٨ قَالَ قَدۡ أُجِيبَت دَّعۡوَتُكُمَا فَٱسۡتَقِيمَا وَلَا
تَتَّبِعَآنِّ سَبِيلَ ٱلَّذِينَ لَا يَعۡلَمُونَ ٨٩ ۞ وَجَٰوَزۡنَا بِبَنِيٓ إِسۡرَٰٓءِيلَ
ٱلۡبَحۡرَ فَأَتۡبَعَهُمۡ فِرۡعَوۡنُ وَجُنُودُهُۥ بَغۡيٗا وَعَدۡوًاۖ حَتَّىٰٓ إِذَآ أَدۡرَكَهُ ٱلۡغَرَقُ

ثلاثة ارباع الحزب

Wa qāla Mūsā yā qawmi ᵓiṅ-kuṅtum ᵓāmaṅtum
billāhi faᶜalayhi tawakkalūu ᵓiṅ-kuṅtum-Muslimīn. (84)
Faqālū ᶜalal-lāhi tawakkalnā Rabbanā lā tajᶜalnā fit-
natal-lilqawmiẓ-ẓālimīn. (85) Wa najjinā biraḥmatika
minal-qawmil-kāfirīn. (86) Wa ᵓawḥaynāa ᵓilā Mūsā wa
ᵓakhīhi ᵓaṅ-tabawwaᵓā liqawmikumā bimiṣra buyū-
taṅw-waj-ᶜalū buyūtakum qiblataṅw-wa ᵓaqīmuṣ-
Ṣalāta wa bashshiril-muᵓminīn. (87) Wa qāla Mūsā
Rabbanāa ᵓinnaka ᵓātayta Firᶜawna wa malaᵓahū
zīnataṅw-wa ᵓamwālaṅ-fil-ḥayātid-dunyā Rabbanā
liyuḍillū ᶜaṅ-sabīlik. Rabbanaṭ-mis ᶜalāa ᵓamwālihim
wash-dud ᶜalā qulūbihim falā yuᵓminū ḥattā yarawul-ᶜadhābal-ᵓalīm. (88) Qāla qad ᵓujībad-daᶜwatu-
kumā fastaqīmā wa lā tattabiᶜāanni sabīlal-ladhīna
lā yaᶜlamūn. (89) ۞ Wa jāwaznā bibanīi ᵓIsrāaᵓīlal-
baḥra faᵓatbaᶜahum Firᶜawnu wa junūduhū ba-
ghyaṅw-wa ᶜadwā. Ḥattāa ᵓidhāa ᵓadrakahul-gharaqu

faith openly), the above sentence would read thus: ". . . a few of his people declared their faith in Moses despite their fear that Pharaoh and their great ones would persecute them" – implying, as does the rendering adopted by me, that, because of their fear, the majority did *not* declare their faith openly.

106 Lit., "temptation to evil" (*fitnah*).

107 Lit., "a direction of prayer" (*qiblah*) – a metaphor meant to impress upon the children of Israel that their only salvation lay in God-consciousness and unceasing devotion to Him. The primary meaning of *miṣr* – usually rendered as "Egypt" – is "city" or "metropolis".

108 According to most of the classical commentators, the particle *li* prefixed to the verb *yuḍillū* ("they are leading astray") represents in this context the so-called *lām al-ᶜāqibah* ("the [letter] *lām* denoting a consequence") and does not, as in many other instances, express a purpose or an intent ("in order that" or "to the end that"). My rendering of this *li* as "with the result that" is meant to bring out Moses' moral indignation at the perversity of Pharaoh and his great ones who, instead of being grateful to God for His bounty, are using their power to corrupt their own people.

109 Lit., "the prayer of you two", i.e., Moses and Aaron, both of whom are addressed in the next sentence as well.

[Pharaoh] exclaimed:[110] "I have come to believe that there is no deity save Him in whom the children of Israel believe, and I am of those who surrender themselves unto Him!" ‹90›
[But God said:] "Now?[111] – when ever before this thou hast been rebelling [against Us], and hast been among those who spread corruption? ‹91› [Nay,] but today We shall save only thy body,[112] so that thou mayest be a [warning] sign unto those who will come after thee: for, behold, a good many people are heedless of Our messages!" ‹92›
And [thereafter], indeed, We assigned unto the children of Israel a most goodly abode,[113] and provided for them sustenance out of the good things of life. And it was not until knowledge [of God's revelation] was vouchsafed to them that they began to hold divergent views: [but,] verily, thy Sustainer will judge between them on Resurrection Day regarding all on which they were wont to differ.[114] ‹93›

AND SO, [O man,] if thou art in doubt about [the truth of] what We have [now]

قَالَ ءَامَنتُ أَنَّهُۥ لَآ إِلَٰهَ إِلَّا ٱلَّذِىٓ ءَامَنَتْ بِهِۦ بَنُوٓاْ إِسْرَٰٓءِيلَ وَأَنَا۠ مِنَ
ٱلْمُسْلِمِينَ ﴿٩٠﴾ ءَآلْـَٰٔنَ وَقَدْ عَصَيْتَ قَبْلُ وَكُنتَ مِنَ ٱلْمُفْسِدِينَ ﴿٩١﴾
فَٱلْيَوْمَ نُنَجِّيكَ بِبَدَنِكَ لِتَكُونَ لِمَنْ خَلْفَكَ ءَايَةً وَإِنَّ كَثِيرًا مِّنَ ٱلنَّاسِ
عَنْ ءَايَٰتِنَا لَغَٰفِلُونَ ﴿٩٢﴾ وَلَقَدْ بَوَّأْنَا بَنِىٓ إِسْرَٰٓءِيلَ مُبَوَّأَ صِدْقٍ
وَرَزَقْنَٰهُم مِّنَ ٱلطَّيِّبَٰتِ فَمَا ٱخْتَلَفُواْ حَتَّىٰ جَآءَهُمُ ٱلْعِلْمُ إِنَّ رَبَّكَ يَقْضِى
بَيْنَهُمْ يَوْمَ ٱلْقِيَٰمَةِ فِيمَا كَانُواْ فِيهِ يَخْتَلِفُونَ ﴿٩٣﴾ فَإِن كُنتَ فِى شَكٍّ مِّمَّآ

qāla ʾāmañtu ʾannahū lāa ʾilāha ʾillal-ladhīi ʾāmanat bihī banūu ʾIsrāaʾīla wa ʾana minal-Muslimīn. (90) ʾĀalʾāna wa qad ʿaṣayta qablu wa kuñta minal-mufsidīn. (91) Falyawma nunajjīka bi-badanika litakūna limañ-khalfaka ʾāyah. Wa ʾinna kathīram-minan-nāsi ʿan ʾĀyātinā laghāfilūn. (92) Wa laqad bawwaʾnā banīi ʾIsrāaʾīla mubawwaʾa ṣidqiñw-wa razaqnāhum-minaṭ-ṭayyibāti famakh-talafū ḥattā jāaʾahumul-ʿilm. ʾInna Rabbaka yaqḍī baynahum Yawmal-Qiyāmati fīmā kānū fīhi yakhtalifūn. (93) Faʾiñ-kuñta fī shakkim-mimmāa

110 Lit., "until, when drowning overtook him, he said". For the full story of Moses and Pharaoh, the latter's tyrannical oppression of the Israelites and their ultimate deliverance, see Exodus i-xiv, and especially (with reference to the above Qurʾān-verse), ch. xiv, which narrates in great detail the miraculous escape of the Israelites and the doom of Pharaoh and his forces. It should always be remembered that all Qurʾanic references to historical or legendary events – whether described in the Bible or in the oral tradition of pre-Islamic Arabia – are invariably meant to elucidate a particular lesson in ethics and not to narrate a story as such: and this explains the fragmentary character of these references and allusions.

111 I.e., "Dost thou repent now, when it is too late?" Cf. 4 : 18 – "repentance shall not be accepted from those who do evil deeds until their dying hour, and then say, 'Behold, I now repent'."

112 Lit., "We shall save thee in thy body": probably an allusion to the ancient Egyptian custom of embalming the bodies of their kings and nobles and thus preserving them for posterity. Some Egyptologists assume that the "evil Pharaoh" of the Qurʾān and the Bible was Ramses II (about 1324-1258 B.C.), while others identify him with his unlucky predecessor, Tut-ankh-amen, or even with Thotmes (or Thutmosis) III, who lived in the 15th century B.C. However, all these "identifications" are purely speculative and have no definitive historical value. In this connection it should be remembered that the designation "Pharaoh" (*firʿawn* in Arabic) is not a proper name but a title borne by all the kings of ancient Egypt.

113 Lit., "We settled the children of Israel in an abode of excellence" – which latter term, according to almost all commentators, conveys the meaning of *ṣidq* in this context.

114 Commenting on this verse, Rāzī says: "The people of Moses remained of one religious persuasion (*ʿalā millah wāḥidah*) and of one opinion, without any disagreement, until they began to study the Torah: whereupon they became aware of the [various] problems and obligations involved, and disagreements [regarding their interpretation] arose among them. And so God makes it clear [in the above Qurʾān-verse] that this kind of disagreement is inevitable (*lā-budd*) and will always occur in the life of this world." Rāzī's penetrating psychological comment is in tune with the oft-repeated Qurʾanic statement that proneness to intellectual dissension is a permanent characteristic of human nature (see the last sentences of 2 : 213 and 253, respectively, as well as the corresponding notes; also 23 : 53 and note 30).

bestowed upon thee from on high,[115] ask those who read the divine writ [revealed] before thy time:[116] [and thou wilt find that,] surely, the truth has now come unto thee from thy Sustainer. Be not, then, among the doubters ‹94› – and neither be among those who are bent on giving the lie to God's messages, lest thou find thyself among the lost. ‹95›

Verily, they against whom thy Sustainer's word [of judgment] has come true[117] will not attain to faith ‹96› – even though every sign [of the truth] should come within their ken – until they behold the grievous suffering [that awaits them in the life to come].[118] ‹97›

For, alas,[119] there has never yet been any community that attained to faith [in its entirety,] and thereupon benefited by its faith, except the people of Jonah.[120]

أَنزَلْنَآ إِلَيْكَ فَسْـَٔلِ ٱلَّذِينَ يَقْرَءُونَ ٱلْكِتَـٰبَ مِن قَبْلِكَ ۚ لَقَدْ جَآءَكَ
ٱلْحَقُّ مِن رَّبِّكَ فَلَا تَكُونَنَّ مِنَ ٱلْمُمْتَرِينَ ﴿٩٤﴾ وَلَا تَكُونَنَّ مِنَ ٱلَّذِينَ
كَذَّبُوا۟ بِـَٔايَـٰتِ ٱللَّهِ فَتَكُونَ مِنَ ٱلْخَـٰسِرِينَ ﴿٩٥﴾ إِنَّ ٱلَّذِينَ حَقَّتْ عَلَيْهِمْ
كَلِمَتُ رَبِّكَ لَا يُؤْمِنُونَ ﴿٩٦﴾ وَلَوْ جَآءَتْهُمْ كُلُّ ءَايَةٍ حَتَّىٰ يَرَوُا۟ ٱلْعَذَابَ
ٱلْأَلِيمَ ﴿٩٧﴾ فَلَوْلَا كَانَتْ قَرْيَةٌ ءَامَنَتْ فَنَفَعَهَآ إِيمَـٰنُهَآ إِلَّا قَوْمَ يُونُسَ

ʾañzalnāa ʾilayka fasʾalil-ladhīna yaqraʾūnal-Kitāba miñ-qablik. Laqad jāaʾakal-ḥaqqu mir-Rabbika falā takūnanna minal-mumtarīn. (94) Wa lā takūnanna minal-ladhīna kadhdhabū biʾĀyātil-lāhi fatakūna minal-khāsirīn. (95) ʾInnal-ladhīna ḥaqqat ʿalayhim Kalimatu Rabbika lā yuʾminūna, (96) wa law jāaʾat-hum kullu ʾĀyatin ḥattā yarawul-ʿadhābal-ʾalīm. (97) Falawlā kānat qaryatun ʾāmanat fanafaʿahāa ʾīmānuhāa ʾillā qawma Yūnusa

115 Some of the commentators assume that verses 94 and 95 are addressed to the Prophet Muḥammad – an assumption which is highly implausible in view of the admonition (in verse 95), "Be not among those who are bent on giving the lie to God's messages": for it is obvious that God's chosen Prophet was never in danger of falling into such a sin. Consequently, Rāzī interprets these two verses as being addressed to *man in general*, and explains the reference to "what We have bestowed upon thee from on high" in the sense given in my rendering. This interpretation makes it clear, moreover, that the above passage is closely connected with verses 57-58, which speak of the guidance vouchsafed to mankind through the ultimate divine writ, the Qurʾān.

116 I.e., the Jews and the Christians. The "reading" is here a metonym for belief, namely, in the Bible, which – notwithstanding the fact that its text has been corrupted in the course of time – still contains clear references to the advent of the Prophet Muḥammad and thus, by implication, to the truth of the divine message revealed through him. In its wider sense, the above verse alludes to the unbroken continuity of man's religious experience and to the fact, frequently stressed in the Qurʾān, that every one of God's apostles preached one and the same basic truth. (See in this connection the second paragraph of 5 : 48 and the corresponding notes 66 and 67.)

117 See verse 33 and note 53 above; also note 4 on 14 : 4.

118 Sc., "when belief will be of no avail to them": an allusion to verses 90-91, which speak of Pharaoh's "conversion" at the point of death. Cf. also 4 : 17-18.

119 The particle *law-lā* ("were it not that" or "were it not for") is sometimes synonymous with *hal-lā*, and could therefore be translated as "why not" ("why was there not . . .?", etc.). However, neither the interrogative nor the above-mentioned literal rendering would bring out the purport of this passage. Its meaning becomes obvious only if we remember that *law-lā* is – apart from its primary significance – one of the so-called *ḥurūf at-taḥḍīḍ* ("particles denoting insistence"). Whenever it is followed by a verb in the future tense, it expresses an urgent exhortation to do a thing; if followed by a verb in the past tense, as in the above case, it implies reproof for one's not having done something that should have been done. There is no idiomatic equivalent in modern English to convey this meaning. The nearest approach to it would be, I believe, the archaic exclamation "alack", expressive of deep sorrow or reproach; but the use of this expression (probably a compound of "ah! lack!" – i.e., loss or misfortune) is ruled out by its obsoleteness. Consequently, I am constrained to employ the more current interjection "alas", despite the fact that it does not possess the intensity of the ancient "alack". At any rate, the reader must bear in mind that the passage under consideration, although seemingly phrased in a conditional or an interrogatory form, implies a *positive statement*: namely – as has been stressed by several classical commentators, and most explicitly by Ṭabarī – the statement that "there has never yet been . . .", etc.

120 The Qurʾān points out in many places that no prophet has ever been immediately accepted as such and followed *by all* of his people, and that many a community perished in result of the stubborn refusal, by the majority of its members, to listen to the divine message. The only exception in this respect is said to have been the people of Nineveh, who – after having at first rejected their prophet Jonah, so that "he went off in wrath" (cf. 21 : 87) – later

When they came to believe, We removed from them the suffering of disgrace [which otherwise would have befallen them even] in the life of this world, and allowed them to enjoy their life during the time allotted to them.[121] ‹98›
And [thus it is:] had thy Sustainer so willed, all those who live on earth would surely have attained to faith, all of them:[122] dost thou, then, think that thou couldst compel people to believe, ‹99› notwithstanding that no human being can ever attain to faith otherwise than by God's leave,[123] and [that] it is He who lays the loathsome evil [of disbelief] upon those who will not use their reason?[124] ‹100›
Say: "Consider whatever there as in the heavens and on earth!"
But of what avail could all the messages and all the warnings be to people who will not believe? ‹101› Can such, then, expect anything else [to befall them] but the like of the days of [calamity which befell] those [deniers of the truth] who passed away before them?
Say: "Wait, then, [for what will happen:] verily, I shall wait with you!" ‹102›
[For thus it always happens: We seal the doom of all who deny the truth and give the lie to Our messages;] and thereupon We save Our apostles and those who

لَمَّآ ءَامَنُواْ كَشَفۡنَا عَنۡهُمۡ عَذَابَ ٱلۡخِزۡيِ فِي ٱلۡحَيَوٰةِ ٱلدُّنۡيَا وَمَتَّعۡنَٰهُمۡ
إِلَىٰ حِينٖ ﴿٩٨﴾ وَلَوۡ شَآءَ رَبُّكَ لَأٓمَنَ مَن فِي ٱلۡأَرۡضِ كُلُّهُمۡ جَمِيعًاۚ
أَفَأَنتَ تُكۡرِهُ ٱلنَّاسَ حَتَّىٰ يَكُونُواْ مُؤۡمِنِينَ ﴿٩٩﴾ وَمَا كَانَ لِنَفۡسٍ أَن
تُؤۡمِنَ إِلَّا بِإِذۡنِ ٱللَّهِۚ وَيَجۡعَلُ ٱلرِّجۡسَ عَلَى ٱلَّذِينَ لَا يَعۡقِلُونَ ﴿١٠٠﴾ قُلِ
ٱنظُرُواْ مَاذَا فِي ٱلسَّمَٰوَٰتِ وَٱلۡأَرۡضِۚ وَمَا تُغۡنِي ٱلۡأٓيَٰتُ وَٱلنُّذُرُ عَن
قَوۡمٖ لَّا يُؤۡمِنُونَ ﴿١٠١﴾ فَهَلۡ يَنتَظِرُونَ إِلَّا مِثۡلَ أَيَّامِ ٱلَّذِينَ خَلَوۡاْ مِن قَبۡلِهِمۡۚ
قُلۡ فَٱنتَظِرُوٓاْ إِنِّي مَعَكُم مِّنَ ٱلۡمُنتَظِرِينَ ﴿١٠٢﴾ ثُمَّ نُنَجِّي رُسُلَنَا وَٱلَّذِينَ

lammāa ʾāmanū kashafnā ʿanhum ʿadhābal-khizyi fil-ḥayātid-dunyā wa mattaʿnāhum ʾilā ḥīn. ﴿98﴾ Wa law shāaʾa Rabbuka laʾāmana mañ-fil-ʾarḍi kulluhum jamīʿā. ʾAfaʾañta tukrihun-nāsa ḥattā yakūnū muʾminīn. ﴿99﴾ Wa mā kana linafsin ʾañ-tuʾmina ʾillā biʾidhnil-lāhi wa yajʿalur-rijsa ʿalal-ladhīna lā yaʿqilūn. ﴿100﴾ Quliñ-ẓurū mādhā fis-samāwāti wal-ʾarḍ. Wa mā tughnil-ʾĀyātu wan-nudhuru ʿañ-qawmil-lā yuʾminūn. ﴿101﴾ Fahal yañ-taẓirūna ʾillā mithla ʾayyāmil-ladhīna khalaw miñ-qablihim. Qul fañtaẓirūu ʾinnī maʿakum-minal-muñ-taẓirīn. ﴿102﴾ Thumma nunajjī Rusulanā wal-ladhīna

responded to his call in unison, and were saved. For the story of Jonah, see 21 : 87-88 and 37 : 139-148, as well as the corresponding notes; a fuller narrative, which does not conflict with the Qurʾanic references, is forthcoming from the Bible (The Book of Jonah). In the context of the passage which we are now considering, the mention of Jonah's people – who alone among the communities of the past heeded their prophet before it was too late – is meant to warn the hearers and readers of the Qurʾān that a deliberate rejection of its message by "those against whom God's word [of judgment] has come true" (see verse 96) is bound to result in their spiritual doom and, consequently, in grievous suffering in the life to come.

121 Lit., "for a time", i.e., their natural life-span (*Manār* XI, 483).

122 The Qurʾān stresses repeatedly the fact that, "had He so willed, He would have guided you all aright" (6 : 149) – the obvious implication being that He has willed it otherwise: namely, that He has given man the *freedom* to choose between right and wrong, thus raising him to the status of a moral being (in distinction from other animals, which can only follow their instincts). See, in this context, *sūrah* 6, note 143, as well as – in connection with the allegory of the Fall – *sūrah* 7, note 16.

123 I.e., by virtue of God's guidance and within the compass of what He has decreed to be man's nature, comprising the ability to discriminate between right and wrong. Since man's freedom of moral choice expresses itself in his willingness or unwillingness to conform to his true, God-willed nature, it can be said to depend, in the last resort, on God's grace. (Cf. in this respect *sūrah* 2, note 19, as well as *sūrah* 14, note 4.)

124 Cf. 8 : 22 and 55, as well as the corresponding note 58. As in those verses, unbelief is here shown to be the result of a person's *a-priori* unwillingness to use his reason with a view to understanding God's messages, be they

have attained to faith.[125] Thus have We willed it upon Ourselves: We save all who believe [in Us].[126] ‹103›

SAY [O Prophet]: "O mankind! If you are in doubt as to what my faith is, then [know that] I do not worship those beings whom you worship beside God,[127] but [that] I worship God alone, who shall cause you [all] to die:[128] for I have been bidden to be among those who believe [in Him alone]." ‹104›

Hence, [O man,] set thy face steadfastly towards the [true] faith, turning away from all that is false,[129] and be not among those who ascribe divinity to aught beside God. ‹105› Thus, do not invoke, side by side with God, anything that can neither benefit thee nor harm thee: for, behold, if thou do it, thou wilt surely be among the evildoers! ‹106›

And [know that] if God should touch thee with misfortune, there is none who could remove it save Him; and if He intends good for thee, there is none who could turn away His bounty: He causes it to alight upon whomsoever He wills of His servants. And He alone is truly forgiving, truly a dispenser of grace. ‹107›

ءَامَنُوا۟ ۚ كَذَٰلِكَ حَقًّا عَلَيْنَا نُنجِ ٱلْمُؤْمِنِينَ ﴿١٠٣﴾ قُلْ يَٰٓأَيُّهَا ٱلنَّاسُ إِن
كُنتُمْ فِى شَكٍّ مِّن دِينِى فَلَآ أَعْبُدُ ٱلَّذِينَ تَعْبُدُونَ مِن دُونِ ٱللَّهِ وَلَٰكِنْ
أَعْبُدُ ٱللَّهَ ٱلَّذِى يَتَوَفَّىٰكُمْ ۖ وَأُمِرْتُ أَنْ أَكُونَ مِنَ ٱلْمُؤْمِنِينَ ﴿١٠٤﴾ وَأَنْ
أَقِمْ وَجْهَكَ لِلدِّينِ حَنِيفًا وَلَا تَكُونَنَّ مِنَ ٱلْمُشْرِكِينَ ﴿١٠٥﴾ وَلَا تَدْعُ مِن دُونِ
ٱللَّهِ مَا لَا يَنفَعُكَ وَلَا يَضُرُّكَ ۖ فَإِن فَعَلْتَ فَإِنَّكَ إِذًا مِّنَ ٱلظَّٰلِمِينَ ﴿١٠٦﴾
وَإِن يَمْسَسْكَ ٱللَّهُ بِضُرٍّ فَلَا كَاشِفَ لَهُۥٓ إِلَّا هُوَ ۖ وَإِن يُرِدْكَ بِخَيْرٍ فَلَا
رَآدَّ لِفَضْلِهِۦ ۚ يُصِيبُ بِهِۦ مَن يَشَآءُ مِنْ عِبَادِهِۦ ۚ وَهُوَ ٱلْغَفُورُ ٱلرَّحِيمُ ﴿١٠٧﴾

ʾāmanū; kadhālika ḥaqqan ʿalaynā nuñjil-muʾminīn.
103 Qul yāa ʾayyuhan-nāsu ʾiñ-kuñtum fī shakkim-
miñ-dīnī falāa ʾaʿbudul-ladhīna taʿbudūna miñ-dūnil-
lāhi wa lākin ʾaʿbudul-lāhal-ladhī yatawaffākum; wa
ʾumirtu ʾan ʾakūna minal-muʾminīn. 104 Wa ʾan
ʾaqim wajhaka liddīni ḥanīfañw-wa lā takūnanna minal-mushrikīn. 105 Wa lā tadʿu miñ-dūnil-lāhi mā lā
yañfaʿuka wa lā yaḍurruka faʾiñ-faʿalta faʾinnaka
ʾidham-minaẓ-ẓālimīn. 106 Wa ʾiñy-yamsaskal-lāhu
biḍurriñ-falā kāshifa lahūu ʾillā Hū. Wa ʾiñy-yuridka
bikhayriñ-falā rāadda lifaḍlih. Yuṣību bihī mañy-
yashāaʾu min ʿibādihī wa Huwal-Ghafūrur-Raḥīm. 107

directly expressed in the revelations granted to His prophets, or – as the Qurʾān once again stresses in the next verse – open to man's perception in the observable phenomena of His creation.

125 My long interpolation at the beginning of this verse is based, in the main, on Zamakhsharī's interpretation of it. It is necessitated by the fact that the adverbial conjunction *thumma* ("thereupon" or "thereafter") does not relate here to the immediately preceding passage but to a theme repeatedly occurring in the Qurʾān and only indirectly alluded to in verse 102 above: namely, the experiences of the earlier prophets with their recalcitrant communities, the doom of those who gave the lie to their messages and, in every case, a divine deliverance of the prophet concerned and of those who followed him. Rashīd Riḍāʾ describes this passage, rightly, as "one of the most outstanding examples of the elliptic mode of expression (*ījāz*) to be found in the Qurʾān" (*Manār* XI, 487).

126 Rāzī explains the phrase *ḥaqqan ʿalaynā* (lit., "as is incumbent upon Us") as denoting no more than a *logical* necessity, i.e., the unavoidable fulfilment of God's "willing it upon Himself", and not a "duty" on His part: for neither is anything "incumbent" upon Him who has the power to will anything, nor – as Rāzī points out – has man any "right" with regard to his Creator.

127 The use of the pronoun *alladhīna* in the phrase "those whom you worship" shows that it relates here to rational beings – like saints, etc. – and not to inanimate representations. As regards the term *dīn* (rendered here as "faith"), see the first half of note 249 on 2 : 256.

128 Sc., "and call you to account on Judgment Day". The specific reference, in this context, to God as "the One who causes all living beings to die" is meant to impress upon "those who deny the truth" the fact that after their death they will be placed before Him for judgment.

129 In classical Arabic usage, and particularly in the Qurʾān, the word "face" is often employed as a metonym for one's whole being because it is the face, more than any other part of the human body, that expresses man's personality (cf. *sūrah* 2, note 91). – For an explanation of the term *ḥanīf*, see *sūrah* 2, note 110.

SAY [O Prophet]: "O mankind! The truth from your Sustainer has now come unto you. Whoever, therefore, chooses to follow the right path, follows it but for his own good; and whoever chooses to go astray, goes but astray to his own hurt. And I am not responsible for your conduct." ‹108›
And [as for thyself, O Muḥammad,] follow but what is being revealed unto thee, and be patient in adversity, until God shall give His judgment: for He is the best of all judges. ‹109›

قُلْ يَٰٓأَيُّهَا ٱلنَّاسُ قَدْ جَآءَكُمُ ٱلْحَقُّ مِن رَّبِّكُمْ ۖ فَمَنِ ٱهْتَدَىٰ فَإِنَّمَا
يَهْتَدِى لِنَفْسِهِۦ ۖ وَمَن ضَلَّ فَإِنَّمَا يَضِلُّ عَلَيْهَا ۖ وَمَآ أَنَا۠ عَلَيْكُم بِوَكِيلٍ ﴿١٠٨﴾
وَٱتَّبِعْ مَا يُوحَىٰٓ إِلَيْكَ وَٱصْبِرْ حَتَّىٰ يَحْكُمَ ٱللَّهُ ۚ وَهُوَ خَيْرُ ٱلْحَٰكِمِينَ ﴿١٠٩﴾

Qul yāa ʾayyuhan-nāsu qad jāaʾakumul-ḥaqqu mir-Rabbikum. Famanih-tadā faʾinnamā yahtadī linafsihī wa mañ-ḍalla faʾinnamā yaḍillu ʿalayhā; wa māa ʾana ʿalaykum-biwakīl. ﴿108﴾ Wat-tabiʿ mā yūḥāa ʾilayka waṣ-bir ḥattā yaḥkumal-lāhu wa Huwa Khayrul-ḥākimīn. ﴿109﴾

The Eleventh Sūrah

Hūd

Mecca Period

REVEALED very shortly after the tenth *sūrah* (*Yūnus*) – that is, during the last year of the Prophet's sojourn in Mecca – *Hūd* bears a great resemblance to the former, both in method and subject-matter. As in *Yūnus*, the main theme is the revelation of God's will through His prophets and the manifestation of prophethood as such. Some of the stories of earlier prophets mentioned in *Yūnus* are developed in the present *sūrah* in greater detail, and are illuminated from various angles, with a particular stress on just dealings between man and man. Paramount in this connection is verse 117, which states that "never would thy Sustainer destroy a community for wrong [beliefs alone] so long as its people behave righteously [towards one another]". (See in this connection note 149.)

Some of the authorities are of the opinion that verses 12, 17 and 114 were revealed at a later date, in Medina; Rashīd Riḍā᾽, however, rejects this view as unconvincing and holds that the *sūrah* in its entirety was revealed at Mecca (*Manār* XII, 2).

-11-

سورة هود مكية

وآياتها ثلاث وعشرون ومائة

IN THE NAME OF GOD, THE MOST GRACIOUS, THE DISPENSER OF GRACE:

Alif. Lām. Rā.[1]
A DIVINE WRIT [is this], with messages that have been made clear in and by themselves, and have been distinctly spelled out as well[2] – [bestowed upon you] out of the grace of One who is wise, all-aware, ⟨1⟩ so that you may worship none but God. [Say, O Prophet:] "Behold, I come unto you from Him [as] a warner and a bearer of glad tidings:[3] ⟨2⟩ Ask your Sustainer to forgive you your sins, and then turn towards Him in repentance – [whereupon] He will grant you a goodly enjoyment of life [in this world] until a term set [by Him is fulfilled];[4] and [in the life to come] He will bestow upon everyone possessed of merit [a full reward for] his merit.[5] But if you turn away, then, verily, I dread for you

بِسْمِ ٱللَّهِ ٱلرَّحْمَٰنِ ٱلرَّحِيمِ

الٓر كِتَٰبٌ أُحْكِمَتْ ءَايَٰتُهُۥ ثُمَّ فُصِّلَتْ مِن لَّدُنْ حَكِيمٍ خَبِيرٍ ﴿1﴾
أَلَّا تَعْبُدُوٓا۟ إِلَّا ٱللَّهَ إِنَّنِى لَكُم مِّنْهُ نَذِيرٌ وَبَشِيرٌ ﴿2﴾ وَأَنِ ٱسْتَغْفِرُوا۟
رَبَّكُمْ ثُمَّ تُوبُوٓا۟ إِلَيْهِ يُمَتِّعْكُم مَّتَٰعًا حَسَنًا إِلَىٰٓ أَجَلٍ مُّسَمًّى
وَيُؤْتِ كُلَّ ذِى فَضْلٍ فَضْلَهُۥ وَإِن تَوَلَّوْا۟ فَإِنِّىٓ أَخَافُ عَلَيْكُمْ

Bismil-lāhir-Raḥmānir-Raḥīm.
ʾAlif-Lāam-Rā. Kitābun ʾuḥkimat ʾĀyātuhū thumma fuṣṣilat mil-ladun Ḥakīmin-Khabīr. (1) ʾAllā taʿbudūu ʾillal-lāh. ʾInnanī lakum-minhu nadhīruñw-wa bashīr. (2) Wa ʾanis-taghfirū Rabbakum thumma tūbūu ʾilayhi yumattiʿkum-matāʿan ḥasanan ʾilāa ʾajalim-musammañw-wa yuʾti kulla dhī faḍliñ-faḍlah. Wa ʾiñ-tawallaw faʾinnīi ʾakhāfu ʿalaykum

---

1 See Appendix II. In the somewhat strange opinion of Sībawayh (cf. *Manār* XII, 3) and of Rāzī in his commentary on this verse, the letters *Alif-Lām-Rā* represent the *title* of this *sūrah*, and ought therefore to be read in conjunction with the following sentence, thus: "*Alif -Lām-Rā* is a divine writ . . .", etc. However, this opinion conflicts sharply with that of several earlier authorities of great standing, e.g., Az-Zajjāj (quoted by Rāzī), and is, moreover, unacceptable in view of the fact that a number of other *sūrah*s are preceded by such letter-symbols without any syntactic possibility of their being regarded as "titles".

2 According to Zamakhsharī and Rāzī, the conjunction *thumma* at the beginning of the clause *thumma fuṣṣilat* (lit., "and then have been distinctly spelled out") does not denote a sequence in time but, rather, a co-ordination of qualities or conditions; therefore my rendering. As regards my translation of the phrase *uḥkimat āyātuhu* as "messages that have been made clear in and by themselves", see the first sentence of 3 : 7 as well as the corresponding note 5, which explains the expression *āyāt muḥkamāt*. Rashīd Riḍāʾ, interprets this phrase in the same sense (see *Manār* XII, 3 f.).

3 The conjunction *an* ("that") preceding the next sentence ("that you shall . . .", etc.) is in this rendering expressed by means of a colon. The interpolation, between brackets, of the words "Say, O Prophet" is necessitated by the first-person construction of this sentence. The subsequent passage – up to the end of verse 4 – outlines both the "warning" and the "glad tidings" referred to above, and thus circumscribes elliptically the whole of the message entrusted to the Prophet.

4 I.e., "till the end of your lives" (for an explanation of the term *ajal musammā*, see note 2 on 6 : 2). Since God, in His unfathomable wisdom, does not always grant worldly happiness and material benefits to everyone who believes in Him and lives righteously, it is only reasonable to assume – as Rashīd Riḍāʾ does in *Manār* XII, 7 ff. – that the "goodly enjoyment of life" (i.e., in this world) promised in the above sentence relates to the *community* of the believers as a whole, and not necessarily to individuals. (Cf. 3 : 139 – "you are bound to rise high if you are [truly] believers".)

5 The noun *faḍl*, when used with reference to God, invariably denotes "bounty" or "favour"; in its reference to man, it usually signifies "merit" or, occasionally, "eminence". The above verse makes it clear that, in contrast to the partial

عَذَابَ يَوْمٍ كَبِيرٍ ۝٣ إِلَى ٱللَّهِ مَرْجِعُكُمْ ۖ وَهُوَ عَلَىٰ كُلِّ شَىْءٍ قَدِيرٌ ۝٤
أَلَآ إِنَّهُمْ يَثْنُونَ صُدُورَهُمْ لِيَسْتَخْفُوا۟ مِنْهُ ۚ أَلَا حِينَ يَسْتَغْشُونَ ثِيَابَهُمْ يَعْلَمُ
مَا يُسِرُّونَ وَمَا يُعْلِنُونَ ۚ إِنَّهُۥ عَلِيمٌۢ بِذَاتِ ٱلصُّدُورِ ۝٥ ۞ وَمَا مِن دَآبَّةٍ فِى
ٱلْأَرْضِ إِلَّا عَلَى ٱللَّهِ رِزْقُهَا وَيَعْلَمُ مُسْتَقَرَّهَا وَمُسْتَوْدَعَهَا ۚ كُلٌّ فِى كِتَٰبٍ
مُّبِينٍ ۝٦ وَهُوَ ٱلَّذِى خَلَقَ ٱلسَّمَٰوَٰتِ وَٱلْأَرْضَ فِى سِتَّةِ أَيَّامٍ وَكَانَ
عَرْشُهُۥ عَلَى ٱلْمَآءِ لِيَبْلُوَكُمْ أَيُّكُمْ أَحْسَنُ عَمَلًا ۗ وَلَئِن قُلْتَ إِنَّكُم مَّبْعُوثُونَ

ᶜadhāba Yawmiñ-kabīr. ⟨3⟩ ˀIlal-lāhi marjiᶜukum wa Huwa ᶜalā kulli shayˀiñ-Qadīr. ⟨4⟩ ˀAlāa ˀinnahum yathnūna ṣudūrahum liyastakhfū minh. ˀAlā ḥīna yastaghshūna thiyābahum yaᶜlamu mā yusirrūna wa mā yuᶜlinūn. ˀInnahū ᶜAlīmum-bidhātiṣ-ṣudūr. ⟨5⟩ ۞ Wa mā miñ-dāabbatiñ-fil-ˀarḍi ˀillā ᶜalal-lāhi rizquhā wa yaᶜlamu mustaqarrahā wa mustawdaᶜahā. Kulluñ-fī Kitābim-mubīn. ⟨6⟩ Wa Huwal-ladhī khalaqas-samāwāti wal-ˀarḍa fī sittati ˀayyāmiñw-wa kāna ᶜarshuhū ᶜalal-māaˀi liyabluwakum ˀayyukum ˀaḥsanu ᶜamalā. Wa laˀiñ-qulta ˀinnakum-mabᶜūthūna

23 حزب
12 جزء

the suffering [which is bound to befall you] on that awesome Day![6] ⟨3⟩ Unto God you all must return; and He has the power to will anything." ⟨4⟩

Oh, verily, they [who are bent on denying the truth of this divine writ] are enshrouding their hearts in order to hide from Him.[7] Oh, verily, [even] when they cover themselves with their garments [in order not to see or hear],[8] He knows all that they keep secret as well as all that they bring into the open – for, behold, He has full knowledge of what is in the hearts [of men]. ⟨5⟩

And there is no living creature on earth but depends for its sustenance on God; and He knows its time-limit [on earth] and its resting-place [after death]:[9] all [this] is laid down in [His] clear decree. ⟨6⟩

And He it is who has created the heavens and the earth in six aeons; and [ever since He has willed to create life,] the throne of His almightiness has rested upon water.[10] [God reminds you of your dependence on Him] in order to test you [and thus to make manifest] which of you is best in conduct. For thus it is: if[11] thou sayest [unto men], "Behold, you shall be raised

---

and often only moral rewards and punishments in the life of this world, God will, in the life to come, bestow the full measure of His favours upon everyone who has acquired merit by virtue of his faith and his actions. (Cf. 3 : 185 – "only on the Day of Resurrection will you be requited in full for whatever you have done".)

6 Lit., "the suffering of a great Day". See in this connection 9 : 128.

7 Since the people referred to in this verse obviously do *not* believe in the divine origin of Muḥammad's message, their "hiding from God" can have, in this context, only one meaning – namely, that of a metaphor for their unwillingness to listen to the truth which emanates from Him: and this also explains the statement that they are "enshrouding their hearts" (lit., "bosoms", as at the end of this verse), i.e., are allowing their hearts and minds to remain wrapped-up in prejudices, thus making them impervious to spiritual perception. See in this connection 8 : 55 and the corresponding note 58.

8 The above interpolation corresponds to the meaning given to the preceding phrase by most of the lexicographers (cf. Lane VI, 2262).

9 For this rendering of *mustaqarr* and *mustawdaᶜ*, see note 83 on 6 : 98. The above reference to God's all-embracing knowledge connects with the end of the preceding verse ("He has full knowledge of all that is in the hearts of men").

10 As regards my rendering of *ayyām* (lit., "days") as "aeons" and *ᶜarsh* as the "throne of [God's] almightiness", see *sūrah* 7, note 43. The symbolic reference to "the throne of His almightiness resting upon water" would seem to point to the God-willed evolution of all life out of water – a fact clearly brought out by the Qurˀān (see 21 : 30 and the corresponding note 39) and in modern times confirmed by biological research. This tentative interpretation is strengthened by the mention, in the preceding verse, of "living creatures". My interpolation, between brackets, of the phrase "ever since He has willed to create life" is in accordance with the views advanced by Rashīd Riḍāˀ in his lengthy commentary on this verse (*Manār* XII, 16 ff.).

11 The expression *laˀin* (lit., "indeed, if . . .") appearing here as well as in each of the next three verses is meant to stress the typical – i.e., recurrent – character of the situation to which it refers. In my opinion, it is best rendered as "thus it is: if . . .", etc.

مِن بَعْدِ ٱلْمَوْتِ لَيَقُولَنَّ ٱلَّذِينَ كَفَرُوٓا۟ إِنْ هَـٰذَآ إِلَّا سِحْرٌ مُّبِينٌ ﴿٧﴾
وَلَئِنْ أَخَّرْنَا عَنْهُمُ ٱلْعَذَابَ إِلَىٰٓ أُمَّةٍ مَّعْدُودَةٍ لَّيَقُولُنَّ مَا يَحْبِسُهُۥٓ ۗ أَلَا يَوْمَ
يَأْتِيهِمْ لَيْسَ مَصْرُوفًا عَنْهُمْ وَحَاقَ بِهِم مَّا كَانُوا۟ بِهِۦ يَسْتَهْزِءُونَ ﴿٨﴾
وَلَئِنْ أَذَقْنَا ٱلْإِنسَـٰنَ مِنَّا رَحْمَةً ثُمَّ نَزَعْنَـٰهَا مِنْهُ إِنَّهُۥ لَيَـُٔوسٌ كَفُورٌ ﴿٩﴾
وَلَئِنْ أَذَقْنَـٰهُ نَعْمَآءَ بَعْدَ ضَرَّآءَ مَسَّتْهُ لَيَقُولَنَّ ذَهَبَ ٱلسَّيِّـَٔاتُ عَنِّىٓ ۚ إِنَّهُۥ
لَفَرِحٌ فَخُورٌ ﴿١٠﴾

mim-baᶜdil-mawti layaqūlannal-ladhīna kafarūu ʾin hādhāa ʾillā siḥrum-mubīn. (7) Wa laʾin ʾakhkharnā ᶜanhumul-ᶜadhāba ʾilāa ʾummatim-maᶜdūdatil-layaqūlunna mā yaḥbisuh. ʾAlā Yawma yaʾtīhim laysa maṣrūfan ᶜanhum wa ḥāqa bihim-mā kānū bihī yastahziʾūn. (8) Wa laʾin ʾadhaqnal-ʾIñsāna minnā raḥmatañ-thumma nazaᶜnāhā minhu ʾinnahū layaʾūsuñ-kafūr. (9) Wa laʾin ʾadhaqnāhu naᶜmāaʾa baᶜda ḍarrāaʾa massat-hu layaqūlanna dhahabas-sayyiʾātu ᶜannī. ʾInnahū lafariḥuñ-fakhūr. (10)

again after death!" – they who are bent on denying the truth are sure to answer, "This is clearly nothing but an enchanting delusion!"[12] ‹7›

And thus it is: if We defer their suffering until a time-limit set [by Us],[13] they are sure to say, "What is preventing it [from coming now]"?[14]

Oh, verily, on the Day when it befalls them there will be nothing to avert it from them; and they shall be overwhelmed by the very thing which they were wont to deride.[15] ‹8›

And thus it is: if We let man taste some of Our grace,[16] and then take it away from him – behold, he abandons all hope,[17] forgetting all gratitude [for Our past favours]. ‹9› And thus it is: if We let him taste ease and plenty[18] after hardship has visited him, he is sure to say, "Gone is all affliction from me!" – for, behold, he is given to vain exultation, and glories only in himself.[19] ‹10›

---

12 The term *siḥr*, which is often used in the sense of "sorcery" or "magic", denotes, primarily, "the turning of something from its proper [i.e., natural] condition of being into another condition" (*Tāj āl-ᶜArūs*); hence, it signifies any act which causes something that is false or unreal to assume the appearance of reality. Since, however, the Qurʾanic statement that "you shall be raised again after death" is not – as has been pointed out by Rāzī – an "act" in the proper connotation of this word, it would be illogical to assume that this statement could be characterized as "sorcery" even by those who do not believe in it. On the other hand, it is obvious that they dismiss it contemptuously as a mere "enchanting delusion" intended to prevent those who are able to do so from enjoying their worldly life to the full (Rāzī) or, alternatively, to induce the poor and unfortunate to remain passively satisfied with their miserable lot on earth: and this is the meaning of *siḥr* in the above context. (Cf. 10 : 2, where the epithet *sāḥir* – in the sense of "spellbinder" – is applied by unbelievers to the Prophet Muḥammad.)

13 Lit., "a time computed [by Us]", i.e., the Day of Judgment: a reference to the last sentence of verse 3 above, where the Prophet is made to say, "I dread for you the suffering [which is bound to befall you] on that awesome Day!" Among the several meanings which the noun *ummah* comprises, that of "time" or "a period of time" is the most appropriate here (Zamakhsharī, Ibn Kathīr and other classical commentators).

14 For an explanation of this allusion to the attitude of the unbelievers, see 8 : 32 and 10 : 50, as well as the corresponding notes; cf. also 6 : 57-58. The repeated Qur'anic references to the above derisive query are evidently meant to show that the attitude of mind responsible for it is not restricted to an isolated historic incident (see *sūrah* 8, note 32) but is symptomatic of most, if not all, people "who are bent on denying the truth".

15 Lit., "that which they were wont to deride enfolded them (*ḥāqa bihim*)". According to almost all the commentators, the use of the past tense in the verb *ḥāqa*, despite the fact that it refers to the future, has the syntactic value of a stress, implying the inevitability of the happening to which it relates. (See also note 9 on 6 : 10.)

16 The sequence makes it clear that the generic term "man" referred to in this and the next verse applies, primarily, to the agnostics who are either unconvinced of the existence of God or are "bent upon denying the truth"; in its wider implication, however, it applies also to those who, while believing in God, are weak in faith and therefore easily swayed by external circumstances, and particularly by whatever happens to themselves.

17 Lit., "he is [or "becomes"] utterly hopeless" or "despairing" (*yaʾūs*), inasmuch as he attributes his past happy state to a merely accidental chain of causes and effects – in short, to what is commonly regarded as "luck" – and not to God's grace. Hence, the term *yaʾūs*, in its Qurʾanic usage, is indicative of spiritual nihilism.

18 This combination of two words is necessary to bring out the full meaning of the noun *naᶜmāʾ* which occurs in this form in the Qurʾān only once. For my rendering of *laʾin* as "thus it is: if . . .", etc., see note 11 above.

19 Lit., "he is exultant beyond all measure, excessively self-glorifying" – i.e., he usually attributes the turn of fortune to his own good qualities and his supposed "good luck".

[And thus it is with most men –] save those who are patient in adversity and do righteous deeds: it is they whom forgiveness of sins awaits, and a great reward. ⟨11⟩

IS IT, then, conceivable [O Prophet] that thou couldst omit any part of what is being revealed unto thee [because the deniers of the truth dislike it, and] because thy heart is distressed at their saying,[20] "Why has not a treasure been bestowed upon him from on high?" – or, "[Why has not] an angel come [visibly] with him?"[21] [They fail to understand that] thou art only a warner, whereas God has everything in His care;[22] ⟨12⟩ and so they assert, "[Muḥammad himself] has invented this [Qurʾān]!"[23] Say [unto them]: "Produce, then, ten *sūrahs* of similar merit, invented [by yourselves], and [to this end] call to your aid whomever you can, other than God, if what you say is true![24] ⟨13⟩ And if they [whom you have called to your aid] are not able to help you,[25] then know that [this Qurʾān] has been bestowed from on high out of God's wisdom alone[26] and that there is no deity save Him. Will you, then, surrender yourselves unto Him?" ⟨14⟩

إِلَّا ٱلَّذِينَ صَبَرُواْ وَعَمِلُواْ ٱلصَّٰلِحَٰتِ أُوْلَٰٓئِكَ لَهُم مَّغۡفِرَةٞ وَأَجۡرٞ
كَبِيرٞ ﴿١١﴾ فَلَعَلَّكَ تَارِكُۢ بَعۡضَ مَا يُوحَىٰٓ إِلَيۡكَ وَضَآئِقُۢ بِهِۦ صَدۡرُكَ أَن
يَقُولُواْ لَوۡلَآ أُنزِلَ عَلَيۡهِ كَنزٌ أَوۡ جَآءَ مَعَهُۥ مَلَكٌۚ إِنَّمَآ أَنتَ نَذِيرٞۚ وَٱللَّهُ عَلَىٰ
كُلِّ شَيۡءٖ وَكِيلٌ ﴿١٢﴾ أَمۡ يَقُولُونَ ٱفۡتَرَىٰهُۖ قُلۡ فَأۡتُواْ بِعَشۡرِ سُوَرٖ مِّثۡلِهِۦ
مُفۡتَرَيَٰتٖ وَٱدۡعُواْ مَنِ ٱسۡتَطَعۡتُم مِّن دُونِ ٱللَّهِ إِن كُنتُمۡ صَٰدِقِينَ ﴿١٣﴾
فَإِلَّمۡ يَسۡتَجِيبُواْ لَكُمۡ فَٱعۡلَمُوٓاْ أَنَّمَآ أُنزِلَ بِعِلۡمِ ٱللَّهِ وَأَن لَّآ إِلَٰهَ إِلَّا هُوَۖ
فَهَلۡ أَنتُم مُّسۡلِمُونَ ﴿١٤﴾

ʾIllal-ladhīna ṣabarū wa ᶜamiluṣ-ṣāliḥāti ʾulāaʾika la-
hum-maghfiratuñw-wa ʾajruñ-kabīr. (11) Falaᶜallaka
tārikum-baᶜḍa mā yūḥāa ʾilayka wa ḍāaʾiqum-bihī
ṣadruka ʾañy-yaqūlū law lāa ʾuñzila ᶜalayhi kañzun
ʾaw jāaʾa maᶜahū Malak. ʾInnamāa ʾañta nadhīr.
Wal-lāhu ᶜalā kulli shayʾiñw-Wakīl. (12) ʾAm
yaqūlūnaf-tarāh. Qul faʾtū biᶜashri suwarim-mithlihī
muftarayātiñw-wad-ᶜū manis-taṭaᶜtum-miñ-dūnil-
lāhi ʾiñ-kuñtum ṣādiqīn. (13) Faʾil-lam yastajībū la-
kum faᶜlamūu ʾannamāa ʾuñzila biᶜilmil-lāhi wa ʾal-
lāa ʾilāha ʾillā Hū. Fahal ʾañtum-Muslimūn. (14)

20 Lit., "because thy bosom is constricted [for fear] lest they say". According to all available authorities, the expression *laᶜalla* (lit., "it may well be that") at the beginning of the above sentence denotes a *wrong expectation* on the part of the opponents of Muḥammad's message; it is, therefore, best rendered in the form of a query which implies its own denial – thus: "Is it conceivable that . . .", etc. As regards the expectation that the Prophet might omit a part of what was being revealed to him, it has been reported by ᶜAbd Allāh ibn ᶜAbbās and other Companions (see Rāzī's commentary on this verse) that the pagan Quraysh demanded of the Prophet, "Bring us a revelation (*kitāb*) which does not contain a defamation of our deities, so that we could follow thee and believe in thee."

21 Explaining this verse, Ibn ᶜAbbās mentions that some of the pagan chieftains of Mecca said, "O Muḥammad, cause the mountains of Mecca to be turned into gold, if thou art truly an apostle of God", while others exclaimed derisively, "Bring before us angels who would bear witness to thy being a prophet!" – whereupon the above verse was revealed (Rāzī). Cf. 6 : 8 and 17 : 90-93.

22 Sc., "and so it is He who will cause the truth to prevail". Regarding the Prophet's denial of any ability on his part to perform miracles, see 6 : 50 and the corresponding note 38.

23 For my rendering of the particle *am* at the beginning of this sentence as "and", see *sūrah* 10, note 61.

24 I.e., that a divine writ like the Qurʾān could have been "invented" by a human being. Cf. 2 : 23, 10 : 37-38 and 17 : 88, as well as the corresponding notes.

25 Lit., "if they [i.e., your poets and wise men] do not respond to your call". Cf. 2 : 24, where a similar challenge is followed by the words, "And if you cannot do it – and most certainly you cannot do it – then . . .", etc.

26 Lit., "only by God's knowledge".

AS FOR THOSE who care for [no more than] the life of this world and its bounties – We shall repay them in full for all that they did in this [life], and they shall not be deprived of their just due therein: ‹15› [yet] it is they who, in the life to come, shall have nothing but the fire – for in vain shall be all that they wrought in this [world], and worthless all that they ever did![27] ‹16›

Can, then, [he who cares for no more than the life of this world be compared with[28]] one who takes his stand on a clear evidence from his Sustainer, conveyed through [this] testimony from Him,[29] as was the revelation vouchsafed to Moses aforetime – [a divine writ ordained by Him] to be a guidance and grace [unto man]? They [who understand this message – it is they alone who truly] believe in it;[30] whereas for any of those who, leagued together [in common hostility],[31] deny its truth – the fire shall be their appointed state [in the life to come].

And so,[32] be not in doubt about this [revelation]: behold, it is the truth from thy Sustainer, even though[33] most people will not believe in it. ‹17›

And who could be more wicked than they who attribute their own lying inventions to God?[34] [On the Day of Judgment, such as] these shall be arraigned before their Sus-

مَن كَانَ يُرِيدُ ٱلْحَيَوٰةَ ٱلدُّنْيَا وَزِينَتَهَا نُوَفِّ إِلَيْهِمْ أَعْمَٰلَهُمْ فِيهَا وَهُمْ فِيهَا
لَا يُبْخَسُونَ ﴿١٥﴾ أُوْلَٰٓئِكَ ٱلَّذِينَ لَيْسَ لَهُمْ فِى ٱلْءَاخِرَةِ إِلَّا ٱلنَّارُ وَحَبِطَ
مَا صَنَعُواْ فِيهَا وَبَٰطِلٌ مَّا كَانُواْ يَعْمَلُونَ ﴿١٦﴾ أَفَمَن كَانَ عَلَىٰ بَيِّنَةٍ مِّن
رَّبِّهِۦ وَيَتْلُوهُ شَاهِدٌ مِّنْهُ وَمِن قَبْلِهِۦ كِتَٰبُ مُوسَىٰٓ إِمَامًا وَرَحْمَةً أُوْلَٰٓئِكَ
يُؤْمِنُونَ بِهِۦ وَمَن يَكْفُرْ بِهِۦ مِنَ ٱلْأَحْزَابِ فَٱلنَّارُ مَوْعِدُهُۥ فَلَا تَكُ فِى
مِرْيَةٍ مِّنْهُ إِنَّهُ ٱلْحَقُّ مِن رَّبِّكَ وَلَٰكِنَّ أَكْثَرَ ٱلنَّاسِ لَا يُؤْمِنُونَ ﴿١٧﴾
وَمَنْ أَظْلَمُ مِمَّنِ ٱفْتَرَىٰ عَلَى ٱللَّهِ كَذِبًا أُوْلَٰٓئِكَ يُعْرَضُونَ عَلَىٰ رَبِّهِمْ

Mañ-kāna yurīdul-ḥayātad dunyā wa zīnatahā nuwaffi ʾilayhim ʾaʿmālahum fīhā wa hum fīhā lā yubkhasūn. (15) ʾUlāaʾikal-ladhīna laysa lahum fil-ʾĀkhirati ʾillan-nāru wa ḥabiṭa mā ṣanaʿū fīhā wa bāṭilum-mā kānū yaʿmalūn. (16) ʾAfamañ-kāna ʿalā bayyinatim-mir-Rabbihī wa yatlūhu shāhidum-minhu wa miñ-qablihī Kitābu Mūsāa ʾimāmañw-wa raḥmah. ʾUlāaʾika yuʾminūna bih. Wa mañy-yakfur bihī minal-ʾaḥzābi fannāru mawʿiduh. Falā taku fī miryatim-minh. ʾInnahul-ḥaqqu mir-Rabbika wa lākinna ʾaktharan-nāsi lā yuʾminūn. (17) Wa man ʾaẓlamu mimmanif-tarā ʿalal-lāhi kadhibā. ʾUlāaʾika yuʿraḍūna ʿalā Rabbihim

27 I.e., although their good deeds will be taken fully into account on Judgment Day, they will be outweighed by their refusal to believe in resurrection and the life to come.

28 This interpolation is based on the interpretation given by Baghawī, Zamakhsharī and Rāzī.

29 Lit., "which a witness from Him recites", or "announces". According to Zamakhsharī, Rāzī and other classical commentators, this phrase refers to the Qurʾān; hence my rendering of *shāhid* as "testimony". If, as some commentators believe, this term refers to the Prophet or, alternatively, to the Angel Gabriel who transmitted the revelation to him, *shāhid* should be translated as "witness". Whichever interpretation one adopts, the meaning remains the same for – as Ibn Kathīr points out in his commentary on this verse – "the Qurʾān was revealed through Gabriel to Muḥammad, and was conveyed by the latter to the world".

30 Sc., "and shall, therefore, attain to happiness in the hereafter". The *ījāz* (elliptic mode of expression) employed in this passage is comparable in its subtlety to that in 10 : 103

31 I.e., in hostile, *a-priori* opposition to the message of the Qurʾān, without really understanding its purport. The "historical" identification, by some of the commentators, of the *aḥzāb* with the pagan Arabs who leagued together in their hostility to the Prophet is definitely too narrow in this context.

32 Rāzī suggests that the conjunction *fa* ("And so") preceding this sentence (which is obviously addressed to man in general) connects with verses 12-14 above: a suggestion which is most convincing in view of the sequence.

33 Lit., "but" or "nevertheless".

34 This is a refutation of the contention of the unbelievers that the Qurʾān was composed by Muḥammad himself (cf. verse 13 above as well as 10 : 17) and thereupon blasphemously attributed to God.

tainer, and those who are called upon to bear witness [against them][35] shall say, "It is they who uttered lies about their Sustainer!"[36]

Oh, verily, God's rejection is the due of all evildoers[37] ‹18› who turn others away from the path of God and try to make it appear crooked – since it is they, they who refuse to acknowledge the truth of the life to come![38] ‹19› Never can they elude [their final reckoning, even if they remain unscathed] on earth:[39] never will they find anyone who could protect them from God. [In the life to come] double suffering will be imposed on them[40] for having lost the ability to hear [the truth] and having failed to see [it].[41] ‹20›

It is they who have squandered their own selves – for [on the Day of Resurrection] all their false imagery[42] will have forsaken them: ‹21› truly it is they, they who in the life to come shall be the losers! ‹22›

Behold, [only] those who attain to faith and do righteous deeds and humble themselves before their Sustainer – [only] they are destined for paradise, and there shall they abide. ‹23›

وَيَقُولُ ٱلْأَشْهَـٰدُ هَـٰٓؤُلَآءِ ٱلَّذِينَ كَذَبُوا۟ عَلَىٰ رَبِّهِمْ ۚ أَلَا لَعْنَةُ ٱللَّهِ عَلَى
ٱلظَّـٰلِمِينَ ﴿18﴾ ٱلَّذِينَ يَصُدُّونَ عَن سَبِيلِ ٱللَّهِ وَيَبْغُونَهَا عِوَجًا وَهُم
بِٱلْـَٔاخِرَةِ هُمْ كَـٰفِرُونَ ﴿19﴾ أُو۟لَـٰٓئِكَ لَمْ يَكُونُوا۟ مُعْجِزِينَ فِى ٱلْأَرْضِ
وَمَا كَانَ لَهُم مِّن دُونِ ٱللَّهِ مِنْ أَوْلِيَآءَ ۘ يُضَـٰعَفُ لَهُمُ ٱلْعَذَابُ ۚ مَا كَانُوا۟
يَسْتَطِيعُونَ ٱلسَّمْعَ وَمَا كَانُوا۟ يُبْصِرُونَ ﴿20﴾ أُو۟لَـٰٓئِكَ ٱلَّذِينَ خَسِرُوٓا۟
أَنفُسَهُمْ وَضَلَّ عَنْهُم مَّا كَانُوا۟ يَفْتَرُونَ ﴿21﴾ لَا جَرَمَ أَنَّهُمْ فِى ٱلْـَٔاخِرَةِ هُمُ
ٱلْأَخْسَرُونَ ﴿22﴾ إِنَّ ٱلَّذِينَ ءَامَنُوا۟ وَعَمِلُوا۟ ٱلصَّـٰلِحَـٰتِ وَأَخْبَتُوٓا۟ إِلَىٰ
رَبِّهِمْ أُو۟لَـٰٓئِكَ أَصْحَـٰبُ ٱلْجَنَّةِ ۖ هُمْ فِيهَا خَـٰلِدُونَ ﴿23﴾

wa yaqūlul-ᵓashhādu hāaᵓulāaᵓil-ladhīna kadhabū ᶜalā Rabbihim. ᵓAlā laᶜnatul-lāhi ᶜalaẓ-ẓālimīn. (18) ᵓAlladhīna yaṣuddūna ᶜañ-sabīlil-lāhi wa yabghūnahā ᶜiwajañw-wa hum-bilᵓĀkhirati hum kāfirūn. (19) ᵓUlāaᵓika lam yakūnū muᶜjizīna fil-ᵓarḍi wa mā kāna lahum-miñ-dūnil-lāhi min ᵓawliyāaᵓ. Yuḍāᶜafu lahumul-ᶜadhāb. Mā kānū yastaṭīᶜūnas-samᶜa wa mā kānū yubṣirūn. (20) ᵓUlāaᵓikal-ladhīna khasirūu ᵓañfusahum wa ḍalla ᶜanhum-mā kānū yaftarūn. (21) Lā jarama ᵓannahum fil-ᵓĀkhirati humul-ᵓakhsarūn. (22) ᵓInnal-ladhīna ᵓāmanū wa ᶜamiluṣ-ṣāliḥāti wa ᵓakhbatūu ᵓilā Rabbihim ᵓulāaᵓika ᵓaṣḥābul-jannati hum fīhā khālidūn. (23)

35 Lit., "the witnesses". Most of the earliest authorities take this to mean the recording angels, while others (e.g., Ibn ᶜAbbās, as quoted by Baghawī) relate it to the prophets, who, on the Day of Judgment, will be called upon to testify for or against the people to whom they were sent. The latter interpretation is supported by Aḍ-Ḍaḥḥāk (quoted by Ṭabarī and Baghawī) on the basis of 16 : 84, where witnesses "out of every community" are mentioned – an expression which can obviously refer only to human beings.

36 Or: "against their Sustainer".

37 The term *laᶜnah* – which is usually, but inexactly, translated as "curse" – is in its primary meaning synonymous with *ibᶜād* ("alienation", "estrangement" or "banishment") in the moral sense; hence it denotes "rejection from all that is good" (*Lisān al-ᶜArab*) and, with reference to God, the sinner's "exclusion from His grace" (*Manār* II, 50).

38 Cf. 7 : 44-45, with which the above passage is almost identical, with only one difference: whereas in 7 : 45 the pronoun "they" occurs only once (and the phrase is, consequently, rendered as "and who refuse . . .", etc.), in the present verse this pronoun is repeated, to express both stress and causality ("since it is they, they who refuse . . .", etc.) – thus implying that their refusal to believe in a life after death is the ultimate *cause* of their wrongdoing. In other words, belief in resurrection, God's judgment and life in the hereafter is here postulated as the only valid and lasting source of human morality.

39 The above interpolation is, I believe, necessary in view of the highly elliptic character of this phrase. According to Ṭabarī, Zamakhsharī and Ibn Kathīr, the meaning is that whereas God's punishment *may* befall the sinners referred to during their life on earth, it will certainly befall them in the hereafter. Cf. also 3 : 185 – "only on the Day of Resurrection will you be requited in full for whatever you have done."

40 For an explanation of the "double suffering", see *sūrah* 7, note 29.

41 Lit., "they were unable to hear and they did not see": cf. 2 : 7 and the corresponding note 7, as well as 7 : 179.

42 Lit., "all that they were wont to invent": a phrase which implies not merely false imaginings regarding the existence of any real "power" apart from God (i.e., the existence of supposedly divine or semi-divine beings) but also deceptive ideas and "glittering half-truths meant to delude the mind" (see 6: 112 and the corresponding note) – such as "luck", wealth, personal power, nationalism, deterministic materialism, etc. – all of which cause men to lose sight of spiritual values and thus to "squander their own selves".

۞ مَثَلُ ٱلْفَرِيقَيْنِ كَٱلْأَعْمَىٰ وَٱلْأَصَمِّ وَٱلْبَصِيرِ وَٱلسَّمِيعِ هَلْ
يَسْتَوِيَانِ مَثَلًا أَفَلَا تَذَكَّرُونَ ﴿٢٤﴾ وَلَقَدْ أَرْسَلْنَا نُوحًا إِلَىٰ قَوْمِهِۦٓ
إِنِّى لَكُمْ نَذِيرٌ مُّبِينٌ ﴿٢٥﴾ أَن لَّا تَعْبُدُوٓا۟ إِلَّا ٱللَّهَ إِنِّىٓ أَخَافُ عَلَيْكُمْ
عَذَابَ يَوْمٍ أَلِيمٍ ﴿٢٦﴾ فَقَالَ ٱلْمَلَأُ ٱلَّذِينَ كَفَرُوا۟ مِن قَوْمِهِۦ مَا نَرَىٰكَ
إِلَّا بَشَرًا مِّثْلَنَا وَمَا نَرَىٰكَ ٱتَّبَعَكَ إِلَّا ٱلَّذِينَ هُمْ أَرَاذِلُنَا بَادِىَ
ٱلرَّأْىِ وَمَا نَرَىٰ لَكُمْ عَلَيْنَا مِن فَضْلٍۭ بَلْ نَظُنُّكُمْ كَٰذِبِينَ ﴿٢٧﴾
قَالَ يَٰقَوْمِ أَرَءَيْتُمْ إِن كُنتُ عَلَىٰ بَيِّنَةٍ مِّن رَّبِّى وَءَاتَىٰنِى رَحْمَةً مِّنْ
عِندِهِۦ فَعُمِّيَتْ عَلَيْكُمْ أَنُلْزِمُكُمُوهَا وَأَنتُمْ لَهَا كَٰرِهُونَ ﴿٢٨﴾
وَيَٰقَوْمِ لَآ أَسْـَٔلُكُمْ عَلَيْهِ مَالًا إِنْ أَجْرِىَ إِلَّا عَلَى ٱللَّهِ وَمَآ أَنَا۠ بِطَارِدِ

۞ Mathalul-farīqayni kalʾaʿmā wal-ʾaṣammi wal-baṣīri was-samīʿ. Hal yastawiyāni mathalā. ʾAfalā tadhakkarūn. (24) Wa laqad ʾarsalnā Nūḥan ʾilā qawmihīi ʾinnī lakum nadhīrum-mubīn. (25) ʾAl-lā taʿbudūu ʾillal-lāh. ʾInnīi ʾakhāfu ʿalaykum ʿadhāba Yawmin ʾalīm. (26) Faqālal-malaʾul-ladhīna kafarū miñ-qawmihī mā narāka ʾillā basharam-mithlanā wa mā narākat-tabaʿaka ʾillal-ladhīna hum ʾarādhilunā bādiyar-raʾyi wa mā narā lakum ʿalaynā miñ-faḍlim-bal naẓunnukum kādhibīn. (27) Qāla yā qawmi ʾaraʾaytum ʾiñ-kuñtu ʿalā bayyinatim-mir Rabbī wa ʾātānī raḥmatam-min ʿiñdihī faʿummiyat ʿalaykum ʾanulzimukumūhā wa ʾañtum lahā kārihūn. (28) Wa yā qawmi lāa ʾasʾalukum ʿalayhi mālan ʾin ʾajriya ʾillā ʿalal-lāhi wa māa ʾana biṭāridil-

ربع الحزب

These two kinds of man[43] may be likened to the blind and deaf and the seeing and hearing. Can these two be deemed alike in [their] nature?[44]
Will you not, then, keep this in mind? ‹24›

AND INDEED, [it was with the same message that] We sent forth Noah unto his people:[45] "Behold, I come unto you with the plain warning ‹25› that you may worship none but God – for, verily, I fear lest suffering befall you on a grievous Day!"[46] ‹26›
But the great ones among his people, who refused to acknowledge the truth, answered: "We do not see in thee anything but a mortal man like ourselves; and we do not see that any follow thee save those who are quite obviously the most abject among us;[47] and we do not see that you could be in any way superior to us:[48] on the contrary, we think that you are liars!" ‹27›
Said [Noah]: "O my people! What do you think? If [it be true that] I am taking my stand on a clear evidence from my Sustainer, who has vouchsafed unto me grace from Himself – [a revelation] to which you have remained blind: – [if this be true,] can we force it on you even though it be hateful to you?[49] ‹28›
"And, O my people, no benefit do I ask of you for this [message]: my reward rests with none but God. And I shall not repulse

43 Lit., "two groups" – i.e., the believers and those who reject the divine writ.

44 For my rendering, in this context, of *mathal* (lit., "likeness") as "nature", see the first part of note 47 on 3 : 59.

45 The conjunction "and" at the beginning of this sentence apparently connects with the opening verses of this *sūrah*, and stresses the fact that the fundamental message of the Qurʾān is the same as that conveyed to man by the earlier prophets (*Manār* XII, 59 f.); hence my interpolation. See also *sūrah* 7, note 45.

46 As in 7 : 59, this may refer either to the imminent deluge or the Day of Judgment.

47 As is evidenced by the histories of all the prophets – and particularly that of Jesus and, after him, of Muḥammad – most of their early followers belonged to the lowest classes of society – the slaves, the poor and the oppressed – to whom the divine message gave the promise of an equitable social order on earth and the hope of happiness in the hereafter: and it is precisely this revolutionary character of every prophet's mission that has always made it so distasteful to the upholders of the established order and the privileged classes of the society concerned.

48 Lit., "We do not see in you any superiority [or "merit"] over us."

49 A reference to the cardinal Qurʾanic doctrine that "there shall be no coercion in matters of faith" (2 : 256), as well as to the oft-repeated statement that a prophet is no more than "a warner and a bearer of glad tidings", implying that his duty consists only in delivering the message entrusted to him. The plural "we" in this sentence relates to Noah and his followers.

ٱلَّذِينَ ءَامَنُوٓاْ إِنَّهُم مُّلَٰقُواْ رَبِّهِمْ وَلَٰكِنِّىٓ أَرَىٰكُمْ قَوْمًا تَجْهَلُونَ ﴿29﴾
وَيَٰقَوْمِ مَن يَنصُرُنِى مِنَ ٱللَّهِ إِن طَرَدتُّهُمْ أَفَلَا تَذَكَّرُونَ ﴿30﴾ وَلَآ أَقُولُ
لَكُمْ عِندِى خَزَآئِنُ ٱللَّهِ وَلَآ أَعْلَمُ ٱلْغَيْبَ وَلَآ أَقُولُ إِنِّى مَلَكٌ وَلَآ أَقُولُ
لِلَّذِينَ تَزْدَرِىٓ أَعْيُنُكُمْ لَن يُؤْتِيَهُمُ ٱللَّهُ خَيْرًا ٱللَّهُ أَعْلَمُ بِمَا فِىٓ أَنفُسِهِمْ
إِنِّىٓ إِذًا لَّمِنَ ٱلظَّٰلِمِينَ ﴿31﴾ قَالُواْ يَٰنُوحُ قَدْ جَٰدَلْتَنَا فَأَكْثَرْتَ جِدَٰلَنَا
فَأْتِنَا بِمَا تَعِدُنَآ إِن كُنتَ مِنَ ٱلصَّٰدِقِينَ ﴿32﴾ قَالَ إِنَّمَا يَأْتِيكُم بِهِ ٱللَّهُ
إِن شَآءَ وَمَآ أَنتُم بِمُعْجِزِينَ ﴿33﴾ وَلَا يَنفَعُكُمْ نُصْحِىٓ إِنْ أَرَدتُّ أَنْ
أَنصَحَ لَكُمْ إِن كَانَ ٱللَّهُ يُرِيدُ أَن يُغْوِيَكُمْ هُوَ رَبُّكُمْ وَإِلَيْهِ
تُرْجَعُونَ ﴿34﴾

[any of] those who have attained to faith.[50] Verily, they [know that they] are destined to meet their Sustainer, whereas in you I see people without any awareness [of right and wrong]! ‹29› And, O my people, who would shield me from God were I to repulse them? Will you not, then, keep this in mind? ‹30›

"And I do not say unto you, 'God's treasures are with me'; nor [do I say], 'I know the reality which is beyond the reach of human perception'; nor do I say, 'Behold, I am an angel';[51] nor do I say of those whom your eyes hold in contempt,[52] 'Never will God grant them any good' – for God is fully aware of what is in their hearts.[53] [Were I to speak thus,] verily, I would indeed be among the evildoers." ‹31›

[But the great ones] said: "O Noah! Thou hast contended with us in argument, and hast [needlessly] prolonged our controversy:[54] bring upon us, therefore, that with which thou dost threaten us,[55] if thou art a man of truth!" ‹32›

He answered: "Only God can bring it upon you, if He so wills, and you shall not elude it: ‹33› for, my advice will not benefit you – much as I desire to give you good advice – if it be God's will that you shall remain lost in grievous error.[56] He is your Sustainer, and unto Him you must return." ‹34›

ladhīna ʾāmanū. ʾInnahum-mulāqū Rabbihim wa lākinnīi ʾarākum qawmañ-tajhalūn. (29) Wa yā qawmi mañy-yañṣurunī minal-lāhi ʾiñ-ṭarattuhum. ʾAfalā tadhakkarūn. (30) Wa lāa ʾaqūlu lakum ʿiñdī khazāaʾinul-lāhi wa lāa ʾaʿlamul-ghayba wa lāa ʾaqūlu ʾinnī malakuñw-wa lāa ʾaqūlu lilladhīna tazdarīi ʾaʿyunukum lañy-yuʾtiyahumul-lāhu khayrā. ʾAllāhu ʾaʿlamu bimā fīi ʾañfusihim; ʾinnīi ʾidhal-laminaẓ-ẓālimīn. (31) Qālū yā Nūḥu qad jādaltanā faʾaktharta jidālanā faʾtinā bimā taʿidunāa ʾiñ-kuñta minaṣ-ṣādiqīn. (32) Qāla ʾinnamā yaʾtīkum-bihil-lāhu ʾiñ-shāaʾa wa māa ʾañtum-bimuʿjizīn. (33) Wa lā yañfaʿukum nuṣḥīi ʾin ʾarattu ʾan ʾañṣaḥa lakum ʾiñ-kānal-lāhu yurīdu ʾañy-yughwiyakum. Huwa Rabbukum wa ʾilayhi turjaʿūn. (34)

50 This is an allusion to the contemptuous statement of the unbelievers (in verse 27 above) that the followers of Noah were to be found only among the lowest classes of their society – thus indirectly implying that they might perhaps lend ear to Noah if he would but rid himself of those people (cf. 26 : 111). The Prophet Muḥammad had, during the early years of his mission, a similar experience with the leaders of the pagan Quraysh; several Traditions to this effect are quoted by Ibn Kathīr in his commentary on 6 : 52.

51 See 6 : 50 and 7 : 188.

52 I.e., the poor and "abject" followers of Noah spoken of in verse 27 (see also note 47 above).

53 Lit., "all that is within themselves".

54 Sc., "without convincing us" (as is brought out fully in 71 : 5-6). The mounting annoyance with Noah on the part of his unbelieving compatriots has already been alluded to in his saying, "If my presence [among you] and my announcement of God's messages are repugnant to you . . .", etc. (see 10 : 71).

55 See the end of verse 26 above.

56 According to some commentators, the expression an *yughwiyakum* – which literally means "that He shall cause you to err" – is to be understood as "that He shall punish you for your sins" (Al-Ḥasan al-Baṣrī, as quoted by Rāzī), or "that He shall destroy you" (Ṭabarī), or "that He shall deprive you of all good" (Al-Jubbāʾī, as quoted by Rāzī); this last interpretation is similar to the one adopted in my rendering of *aghwaytanī* ("Thou hast thwarted me") in 7 : 16 and explained in the corresponding note 11. However, in the present context I prefer the rendering "if it be God's will that you shall *remain* lost in grievous error", inasmuch as it is in conformity with the Qurʾanic doctrine of "God's way" with regard to those who persistently refuse to acknowledge the truth (see *sūrah* 2, note 7). This interpretation is, moreover, supported by Zamakhsharī in his commentary on the above verse: "When God, knowing the persistence [in

DO SOME, perchance, assert, "[Muhammad] has invented this [story]"?[57]
Say [O Prophet]: "If I have invented it, upon me be this sin; but far be it from me to commit the sin of which you are guilty."[58] ‹35›

AND THIS was revealed unto Noah: "Never will any of thy people believe except those who have already attained to faith. Be not, then, distressed by anything that they may do, ‹36› but build, under Our eyes[59] and according to Our inspiration, the ark [that shall save thee and those who follow thee];[60] and do not appeal to Me in behalf of those who are bent on evildoing – for, behold, they are destined to be drowned!" ‹37›
And [so Noah] set himself to building the ark; and every time the great ones of his people passed by him, they scoffed at him. [Thereupon] he said: "If you are scoffing at us – behold, we are scoffing at you [and your ignorance], just as you are scoffing at us.[61] ‹38› But in time you will come to know who it is that [in this world] shall be visited by suffering which will cover him with ignominy, and upon whom longlasting suffering shall alight [in the life to come]!" ‹39›

أَمْ يَقُولُونَ ٱفْتَرَىٰهُ قُلْ إِنِ ٱفْتَرَيْتُهُۥ فَعَلَىَّ إِجْرَامِى وَأَنَا۠ بَرِىٓءٌ مِّمَّا
تُجْرِمُونَ ﴿٣٥﴾ وَأُوحِىَ إِلَىٰ نُوحٍ أَنَّهُۥ لَن يُؤْمِنَ مِن قَوْمِكَ إِلَّا مَن قَدْ
ءَامَنَ فَلَا تَبْتَئِسْ بِمَا كَانُوا۟ يَفْعَلُونَ ﴿٣٦﴾ وَٱصْنَعِ ٱلْفُلْكَ بِأَعْيُنِنَا وَوَحْيِنَا
وَلَا تُخَٰطِبْنِى فِى ٱلَّذِينَ ظَلَمُوٓا۟ إِنَّهُم مُّغْرَقُونَ ﴿٣٧﴾ وَيَصْنَعُ ٱلْفُلْكَ وَكُلَّمَا
مَرَّ عَلَيْهِ مَلَأٌ مِّن قَوْمِهِۦ سَخِرُوا۟ مِنْهُ قَالَ إِن تَسْخَرُوا۟ مِنَّا فَإِنَّا نَسْخَرُ
مِنكُمْ كَمَا تَسْخَرُونَ ﴿٣٨﴾ فَسَوْفَ تَعْلَمُونَ مَن يَأْتِيهِ عَذَابٌ يُخْزِيهِ
وَيَحِلُّ عَلَيْهِ عَذَابٌ مُّقِيمٌ ﴿٣٩﴾

ʾAm yaqūlūnaf-tarāh. Qul ʾinif-taraytuhū faʿalayya ʾijrāmī wa ʾana barīiʾum-mimmā tujrimūn. (35) Wa ʾūḥiya ʾilā Nūḥin ʾannahū lañy-yuʾmina miñ-qawmika ʾillā mañ-qad ʾāmana falā tabtaʾis bimā kānū yafʿalūn. (36) Waṣ-naʿil-fulka biʾaʿyuninā wa waḥyinā wa lā tukhāṭibnī fil-ladhīna ẓalamūu ʾinnahum-mughraqūn. (37) Wa yaṣnaʿul-fulka wa kullamā marra ʿalayhi malaʾum-miñ-qawmihī sakhirū minh. Qāla ʾiñ-taskharū minnā faʾinnā naskharu miñkum kamā taskharūn. (38) Fasawfa taʿlamūna mañy-yaʾtīhi ʿadhābuñy-yukhzīhi wa yaḥillu ʿalayhi ʿadhābum-muqīm. (39)

sinning] on the part of one who denies the truth (*al-kāfir*), leaves him in this condition and does not compel him [to repent], this [act of God] is described [in the Qurʾān] as 'causing [one] to err' (*ighwāʾ*) and 'causing [one] to go astray' (*iḍlāl*); similarly, when He, knowing that a person will repent, protects him and is kind to him, this [act of God] is described as 'showing the right direction' (*irshād*) or '[offering] guidance' (*hidāyah*)." (See also *sūrah* 14, note 4.)

57 Some of the classical commentators assume that this verse forms part of the story of Noah and his people. This, however, is improbable in view of the sudden change from the past tense employed in the preceding and subsequent verses ("he said", "they said") to the present tense ("do they say"). The only plausible explanation is that given by Ṭabarī, and Ibn Kathīr (and mentioned also by Baghawī on the authority of Muqātil): namely, that the whole of verse 35 is a parenthetic passage addressed to the Prophet Muḥammad, relating in the first instance to the story of Noah as narrated in the Qurʾān and, by implication, to the Qurʾān as such – in other words, a reiteration of the argument mentioned in verse 13 of this *sūrah* and in other places as well. This eminently convincing interpretation has also been adopted by Rashīd Riḍāʾ (*Manār* XII, 71).

58 Or: "I have nothing to do with the sin of which you are guilty" – i.e., the sin of giving the lie to God's messages (cf. 10 : 41) or of inventing lies about God.

59 I.e., "under Our protection".

60 This interpolation is necessitated by the definite article preceding the noun *fulk* (lit., "ship", but rendered by me as "ark" owing to its familiar connotation in European languages).

61 Since it is obviously impossible to attribute to a prophet the levity of scoffing (Baghawī), the meaning of the above phrase seems to be this: "if you consider us ignorant because of what we believe and are doing, we consider you ignorant because of your refusal to acknowledge the truth and your readiness to expose yourselves to God's punishment" (Zamakhsharī and, in a shorter form, Baghawī). Hence my interpolation of the words "and your ignorance".

[And so It went on] till, when Our judgment came to pass, and waters gushed forth in torrents over the face of the earth,[62] We said [unto Noah]: "Place on board of this [ark] one pair of each [kind of animal] of either sex,[63] as well as thy family – except those on whom [Our] sentence has already been passed[64] – and all [others] who have attained to faith!" – for, only a few [of Noah's people] shared his faith. ‹40›
So he said [unto his followers]: "Embark in this [ship]! In the name of God be its run and its riding at anchor! Behold, my Sustainer is indeed much-forgiving, a dispenser of grace!" ‹41›
And it moved on with them into waves that were like mountains.
At that [moment] Noah cried out to a son of his, who had kept himself aloof [from the others]: "O my dear son![65] Embark with us, and remain not with those who deny the truth!" ‹42›
[But the son] answered: "I shall betake myself to a mountain that will protect me from the waters."
Said [Noah]: "Today there is no protection [for anyone] from God's judgment, save [for] those who have earned [His] mercy!"
And a wave rose up between them, and [the son] was among those who were drowned. ‹43›

حَتَّىٰٓ إِذَا جَآءَ أَمْرُنَا وَفَارَ ٱلتَّنُّورُ قُلْنَا ٱحْمِلْ فِيهَا مِن كُلٍّ زَوْجَيْنِ
ٱثْنَيْنِ وَأَهْلَكَ إِلَّا مَن سَبَقَ عَلَيْهِ ٱلْقَوْلُ وَمَنْ ءَامَنَ ۚ وَمَآ ءَامَنَ مَعَهُۥٓ إِلَّا
قَلِيلٌ ﴿٤٠﴾ ۞ وَقَالَ ٱرْكَبُوا۟ فِيهَا بِسْمِ ٱللَّهِ مَجْر۪ىٰهَا وَمُرْسَىٰهَآ ۚ إِنَّ رَبِّى
لَغَفُورٌ رَّحِيمٌ ﴿٤١﴾ وَهِىَ تَجْرِى بِهِمْ فِى مَوْجٍ كَٱلْجِبَالِ وَنَادَىٰ نُوحٌ
ٱبْنَهُۥ وَكَانَ فِى مَعْزِلٍ يَٰبُنَىَّ ٱرْكَب مَّعَنَا وَلَا تَكُن مَّعَ ٱلْكَٰفِرِينَ ﴿٤٢﴾
قَالَ سَـَٔاوِىٓ إِلَىٰ جَبَلٍ يَعْصِمُنِى مِنَ ٱلْمَآءِ ۚ قَالَ لَا عَاصِمَ ٱلْيَوْمَ مِنْ أَمْرِ
ٱللَّهِ إِلَّا مَن رَّحِمَ ۚ وَحَالَ بَيْنَهُمَا ٱلْمَوْجُ فَكَانَ مِنَ ٱلْمُغْرَقِينَ ﴿٤٣﴾

نصف الحزب

Ḥattāa ʾidhā jāaʾa ʾamrunā wa fārat-tannūru qulnaḥ-mil fīhā miñ-kullin zawjaynith-nayni wa ʾahlaka ʾillā mañ-sabaqa ʿalayhil-qawlu wa man ʾāman. Wa māa ʾāmana maʿahūu ʾillā qalīl. (40) ۞ Wa qālar-kabū fīhā bismil-lāhi majraihā wa mursāhā. ʾInna Rabbī laGhafūrur-Raḥīm. (41) Wa hiya tajrī bihim fī mawjiñ-kaljibāli wa nādā Nūḥunib-nahū wa kāna fī maʿziliñy-yā bunayyar-kam-maʿanā wa lā takum-maʿal-kāfirīn. (42) Qāla saʾāwīi ʾilā jabaliñy-yaʿṣimunī minal-māaʾ. Qāla lā ʿāsimal-yawma min ʾamril-lāhi ʾillā mar-raḥim. Wa ḥāla baynahumal-mawju fakāna minal-mughraqīn. (43)

62 Lit., "the face of the earth boiled over" (*fāra 't-tannūr*). This phrase has been subject to several conflicting interpretations, some of which are based on no more than Talmudic legends (*Manār* XII, 75 f.). The most convincing explanation is that given – among others – by Ṭabarī, Baghawī and Ibn Kathīr on the authority of Ibn ʿAbbās and ʿIkrimah: "*At-tannūr* [lit., "oven"] denotes the face of the earth." Rāzī, too, mentions that "the Arabs call the face of the earth *tannūr*", while the *Qāmūs* gives as one of the meanings of *tannūr* – "any place from which water gushes forth". The verb *fāra* – which literally means "it boiled over" – describes the raging torrents of water which "turned the earth into springs" (Ibn Kathīr; see also 54 : 12). This "gushing forth of water over the face of the earth" seems to point to the inundation of the huge valley now covered by the Mediterranean Sea (see *sūrah* 7. note 47) – an inundation which, augmented by continuous, torrential rains (cf. 54 : 11), rapidly spread over the land-mass of present-day Syria and northern ʿIrāq and grew into the immense deluge described in the Bible and in the Qurʾān, and also referred to in the myths of ancient Greece (e.g., in the story of Deukalion and Pyrrhea), as well as in Sumerian and Babylonian legends.

63 The term *zawj* signifies, primarily, each of the two parts of a pair, and is also used in the sense of "a pair". In the present context it obviously has the former meaning; consequently, the expression *min kullin zawjayn ithnayn* is best rendered as above. – As regards the animals which Noah was commanded to take with him in the ark, it is reasonable to assume that this referred to the domesticated animals already in his possession, and not to *all* animals, as the Biblical narrative would have it.

64 I.e., those who stand condemned in the sight of God because of their persistent refusal to acknowledge the truth. See also verses 42-43 and 45-47.

65 The diminutive in *yā bunayya* (lit., "O my little son") is an expression of endearment irrespective of a son's age: for instance, Noah's son appears in the above story as a grown man, while Joseph, similarly addressed by his father in 12 : 5, was a child or, at the most, an adolescent.

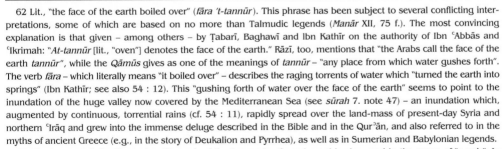

And the word was spoken: "O earth, swallow up thy waters! And, O sky, cease [thy rain]!" And the waters sank into the earth, and the will [of God] was done, and the ark came to rest on Mount Jūdī.[66]
And the word was spoken: "Away with these evildoing folk!" ⟨44⟩
And Noah called out to his Sustainer, and said: "O my Sustainer! Verily, my son was of my family;[67] and, verily, Thy promise always comes true, and Thou art the most just of all judges!" ⟨45⟩
[God] answered: "O Noah, behold, he was not of thy family, for, verily, he was unrighteous in his conduct.[68] And thou shalt not ask of Me anything whereof thou canst not have any knowledge:[69] thus, behold, do I admonish thee lest thou become one of those who are unaware [of what is right]."[70] ⟨46⟩
Said [Noah]: "O my Sustainer! Verily, I seek refuge with Thee from [ever again] asking of Thee anything whereof I cannot have any knowledge! For unless Thou grant me forgiveness and bestow Thy mercy upon me, I shall be among the lost!" ⟨47⟩

وَقِيلَ يَـٰٓأَرْضُ ٱبْلَعِى مَآءَكِ وَيَـٰسَمَآءُ أَقْلِعِى وَغِيضَ ٱلْمَآءُ وَقُضِىَ
ٱلْأَمْرُ وَٱسْتَوَتْ عَلَى ٱلْجُودِىِّ ۖ وَقِيلَ بُعْدًا لِّلْقَوْمِ ٱلظَّـٰلِمِينَ ﴿٤٤﴾
وَنَادَىٰ نُوحٌ رَّبَّهُۥ فَقَالَ رَبِّ إِنَّ ٱبْنِى مِنْ أَهْلِى وَإِنَّ وَعْدَكَ ٱلْحَقُّ
وَأَنتَ أَحْكَمُ ٱلْحَـٰكِمِينَ ﴿٤٥﴾ قَالَ يَـٰنُوحُ إِنَّهُۥ لَيْسَ مِنْ أَهْلِكَ ۖ إِنَّهُۥ
عَمَلٌ غَيْرُ صَـٰلِحٍ ۖ فَلَا تَسْـَٔلْنِ مَا لَيْسَ لَكَ بِهِۦ عِلْمٌ ۖ إِنِّىٓ أَعِظُكَ أَن تَكُونَ
مِنَ ٱلْجَـٰهِلِينَ ﴿٤٦﴾ قَالَ رَبِّ إِنِّىٓ أَعُوذُ بِكَ أَنْ أَسْـَٔلَكَ مَا لَيْسَ لِى بِهِۦ
عِلْمٌ ۖ وَإِلَّا تَغْفِرْ لِى وَتَرْحَمْنِىٓ أَكُن مِّنَ ٱلْخَـٰسِرِينَ ﴿٤٧﴾

Wa qīla yāa ʾarḍub-laʿī māaʾaki wa yā samāaʾu ʾaqliʿī wa ghīḍal-māaʾu wa quḍiyal-ʾamru was-tawat ʿalal-Jūdiyyi wa qīla buʿdal-lilqawmiẓ-ẓālimīn. (44) Wa nādā Nūḥur-Rabbahū faqāla Rabbi ʾinnab-nī min ʾahlī wa ʾinna waʿdakal-ḥaqqu wa ʾAñta ʾaḥkamul-ḥākimīn. (45) Qāla yā Nūḥu ʾinnahū laysa min ʾahlik. ʾInnahū ʿamalun ghayru ṣāliḥ. Falā tasʾalni mā laysa laka bihī ʿilm. ʾInnīi ʾaʿiẓuka ʾañ-takūna minal-jāhilīn. (46) Qāla Rabbi ʾinnīi ʾaʿūdhu bika ʾan ʾasʾalaka mā laysa lī bihī ʿilm. Wa ʾillā taghfir lī wa tarḥamnīi ʾakum-minal-khāsirīn. (47)

66 This mountain, known in ancient Syriac as Qardū, is situated in the region of Lake Van, almost twenty-five miles north-east of the town Jazīrat Ibn ʿUmar, capital of the modern Syrian district of Al-Jazīrah. It "owes its fame to the Mesopotamian tradition which identifies it, and not Mount Ararat, with the mountain on which Noah's ark rested . . . . This localization of the ark's resting-place . . . is certainly based on Babylonian tradition" (*Encyclopaedia of Islam* I, 1059). We should, however, remember that the designation Ararat (the Assyrian Urarṭu) at one time included the *whole area* to the south of Lake Van, in which Jabal Jūdī is situated: this might explain the Biblical statement that "the ark rested . . . upon the mountains of Ararat" (Genesis viii, 4).

67 A reference to the divine command, mentioned in verse 40 – "Place on board this [ark] . . . thy family" – which Noah apparently understood as meaning that the *whole* of his family would be saved, thus overlooking the qualifying clause, "except those on whom sentence has already been passed". – Some of the commentators suppose that verses 45-47 connect with verse 43, and thus precede, in point of time, the events narrated in verse 44 – a supposition which has caused the modern translators of the Qurʾān to render Noah's prayer, erroneously, in the present tense (i.e., in the form of a prayer for his son's rescue from drowning). It is, however, much more plausible to assume – as is done by Ṭabarī, and Ibn Kathīr – that Noah's words were spoken after the ark had come to rest on Mount Jūdī (i.e., long after his son's death) and that they represented "an endeavour on the part of Noah to find out what would be the condition of his drowned son [in the hereafter]" (Ibn Kathīr). Consequently, the sentence relating to this son, both in Noah's prayer and in God's answer, must be rendered in the past tense.

68 According to some commentators (e.g., Ṭabarī and Rāzī), the phrase *innahu ʿamal ghayr ṣāliḥ* relates to Noah's prayer for his son, and constitutes a divine reproach – in which case it should be rendered as "verily, this [prayer] is unrighteous conduct [on thy part]". Others, however (e.g., Zamakhsharī), reject this interpretation and relate the above phrase to the son, in the manner rendered by me. This, I believe, is more in tune with the statement, "he was not of thy family" – i.e., spiritually, inasmuch as he was of, or preferred to remain with, "those who deny the truth".

69 I.e., knowledge of the innermost reasons of God's decrees and of the ultimate destiny of any human being in the hereafter: for, the answers to this "why" and this "how" lie in the realm of things which are beyond the reach of human perception (*al-ghayb*).

70 I.e., "lest thou prove to be one of those ignorant who ask God that He change His decrees in response to their own desires" (*Manār* XII, 85 f.).

[Thereupon] the word was spoken: "O Noah! Disembark in peace from Us,[71] and with [Our] blessings upon thee as well as upon the people [who are with thee, and the righteous ones that will spring from thee and] from those who are with thee.[72] But [as for the unrighteous] folk [that will spring from you] – We shall allow them to enjoy life [for a little while], and then there will befall them grievous suffering from Us." ‹48›

قِيلَ يَٰنُوحُ ٱهْبِطْ بِسَلَٰمٍ مِّنَّا وَبَرَكَٰتٍ عَلَيْكَ وَعَلَىٰٓ أُمَمٍ مِّمَّن مَّعَكَ ۚ وَأُمَمٌ
سَنُمَتِّعُهُمْ ثُمَّ يَمَسُّهُم مِّنَّا عَذَابٌ أَلِيمٌ ﴿٤٨﴾ تِلْكَ مِنْ أَنۢبَآءِ ٱلْغَيْبِ نُوحِيهَآ
إِلَيْكَ ۖ مَا كُنتَ تَعْلَمُهَآ أَنتَ وَلَا قَوْمُكَ مِن قَبْلِ هَٰذَا ۖ فَٱصْبِرْ ۖ إِنَّ ٱلْعَٰقِبَةَ
لِلْمُتَّقِينَ ﴿٤٩﴾ وَإِلَىٰ عَادٍ أَخَاهُمْ هُودًا ۚ قَالَ يَٰقَوْمِ ٱعْبُدُوا۟ ٱللَّهَ مَا لَكُم مِّنْ
إِلَٰهٍ غَيْرُهُۥٓ ۖ إِنْ أَنتُمْ إِلَّا مُفْتَرُونَ ﴿٥٠﴾ يَٰقَوْمِ لَآ أَسْـَٔلُكُمْ عَلَيْهِ أَجْرًا ۖ إِنْ أَجْرِىَ
إِلَّا عَلَى ٱلَّذِى فَطَرَنِىٓ ۚ أَفَلَا تَعْقِلُونَ ﴿٥١﴾

THESE ACCOUNTS of something that was beyond the reach of thy perception We [now] reveal unto thee, [O Muḥammad: for] neither thou nor thy people knew them [fully] ere this.[73] Be, then, [like Noah,] patient in adversity – for, behold, the future belongs to the God-conscious! ‹49›

AND UNTO [the tribe of] ᶜĀd [We sent] their brother Hūd.[74] He said: "O my people! Worship God [alone]: you have no deity other than Him. [As it is,] you are but inventors of falsehood![75] ‹50›

"O my people! No reward do I ask of you for this [message]: my reward rests with none but Him who brought me into being. Will you not, then, use your reason? ‹51›

Qīla yā Nūḥuh-biṭ bisalāmim-minnā wa barakātin ᶜalayka wa ᶜalāa ʾumamim-mimmam-maᶜak. Wa ʾumamuñ-sanumattiᶜuhum thumma yamassuhum-minnā ᶜadhābun ʾalīm. (48) Tilka min ʾambāaʾil-ghaybi nūḥīhāa ʾilayka mā kuñta taᶜlamuhāa ʾañta wa lā qawmuka miñ-qabli hādhā. Faṣbir ʾinnal-ᶜāqibata lilmuttaqīn. (49) Wa ʾilā ᶜĀdin ʾakhāhum Hūdā. Qāla yā qawmiᶜ-budul-lāha mā lakum-min ʾilāhin ghayruh. ʾIn ʾañtum ʾillā muftarūn. (50) Yā qawmi lāa ʾasʾalukum ᶜalayhi ʾajrā. ʾIn ʾajriya ʾillā ᶜalal-ladhī faṭaranī. ʾAfalā taᶜqilūn. (51)

71 The term *salām* – here translated as "peace" – comprises the notions of both external and internal security from all that is evil. For a fuller explanation of the term, see *sūrah* 5, note 29.

72 The above interpolation is based on the consensus of most of the classical commentators. The phrase "the people [or "generations"] *from* those who are with thee" points to generations as yet unborn; but since God's blessing extends to all believers, it *eo ipso* comprises the believers of Noah's generation as well; and since "those who deny the truth" (*al-kāfirūn*) are excluded from God's blessing, only the righteous from among the offspring of these early believers are promised a share in His grace (cf. a similar allusion, relating to Abraham's descendants, in 2 : 124): hence my interpolation of the words "as for the unrighteous that will spring from you" in the next sentence.

73 See verse 35 above. Although the story of Noah had been vaguely known to the Arabs even before the advent of the Prophet Muḥammad, they – and the Prophet with them – were entirely unaware of the details as narrated in the preceding Qurʾānic account (Rāzī). The use of the plural at the beginning of this parenthetic passage ("These accounts") – in contrast with the singular form employed in a similar phrase occurring in 3 : 44, 11 : 100 and 12 : 102 ("This account") – seems, in my opinion, to indicate that it refers not only to the preceding story of Noah but also to the subsequent stories of other prophets. In this connection it should be remembered – and it cannot be stressed too often – that "narrative" as such is never the purpose of the Qurʾān. Whenever it relates the stories of earlier prophets, or alludes to ancient legends or to historical events that took place before the advent of Islam or during the lifetime of the Prophet, the aim is, invariably, a moral lesson; and since one and the same event, or even legend, has usually many facets revealing as many moral implications, the Qurʾān reverts again and again to the same stories, but every time with a slight variation of stress on this or that aspect of the fundamental truths underlying the Qurʾanic revelation as a whole.

74 For particulars relating to the name Hūd as well as the tribe of ᶜĀd, see *sūrah* 7, note 48.

75 I.e., inventors of alleged deities that have no reality in themselves (cf. 7 : 71, which also relates to the story of

"Hence, O my people, ask your Sustainer to forgive you your sins, and then turn towards Him in repentance – [whereupon] He will shower upon you heavenly blessings abundant,[76] and will add strength to your strength: only do not turn away [from me] as people lost in sin!" ‹52›

Said they: "O Hūd! Thou hast brought us no clear evidence [that thou art a prophet]; and we are not going to forsake our gods on thy mere word, the more so as we do not believe thee. ‹53› We can say no more than that one of our gods may have smitten thee with something evil!"[77]

Answered [Hūd]: "Behold, I call God to witness – and you, too, be [my] witnesses – that, verily, it is not in me to ascribe divinity, as you do,[78] to aught ‹54› beside Him! Contrive, then, [anything that you may wish] against me, all of you, and give me no respite.[79] ‹55› Behold, I have placed my trust in God, [who is] my Sustainer as well as your Sustainer: for there is no living creature which He does not hold by its forelock.[80] Verily, straight is my Sustainer's way![81] ‹56›

"But if you choose to turn away, then [know that] I have delivered to you the message with which I was sent unto you, and [that] my Sustainer may cause another people to take your place,[82] whereas you will in no wise harm Him. Verily, my Sustainer watches over all things!" ‹57›

وَيَٰقَوۡمِ ٱسۡتَغۡفِرُواْ رَبَّكُمۡ ثُمَّ تُوبُوٓاْ إِلَيۡهِ يُرۡسِلِ ٱلسَّمَآءَ عَلَيۡكُم مِّدۡرَارٗا
وَيَزِدۡكُمۡ قُوَّةً إِلَىٰ قُوَّتِكُمۡ وَلَا تَتَوَلَّوۡاْ مُجۡرِمِينَ ﴿٥٢﴾ قَالُواْ يَٰهُودُ مَا جِئۡتَنَا
بِبَيِّنَةٖ وَمَا نَحۡنُ بِتَارِكِيٓ ءَالِهَتِنَا عَن قَوۡلِكَ وَمَا نَحۡنُ لَكَ بِمُؤۡمِنِينَ ﴿٥٣﴾ إِن
نَّقُولُ إِلَّا ٱعۡتَرَىٰكَ بَعۡضُ ءَالِهَتِنَا بِسُوٓءٖۗ قَالَ إِنِّيٓ أُشۡهِدُ ٱللَّهَ وَٱشۡهَدُوٓاْ أَنِّي
بَرِيٓءٞ مِّمَّا تُشۡرِكُونَ ﴿٥٤﴾ مِن دُونِهِۦۖ فَكِيدُونِي جَمِيعٗا ثُمَّ لَا تُنظِرُونِ ﴿٥٥﴾
إِنِّي تَوَكَّلۡتُ عَلَى ٱللَّهِ رَبِّي وَرَبِّكُمۚ مَّا مِن دَآبَّةٍ إِلَّا هُوَ ءَاخِذُۢ بِنَاصِيَتِهَآۚ
إِنَّ رَبِّي عَلَىٰ صِرَٰطٖ مُّسۡتَقِيمٖ ﴿٥٦﴾ فَإِن تَوَلَّوۡاْ فَقَدۡ أَبۡلَغۡتُكُم مَّآ أُرۡسِلۡتُ
بِهِۦٓ إِلَيۡكُمۡۚ وَيَسۡتَخۡلِفُ رَبِّي قَوۡمًا غَيۡرَكُمۡ وَلَا تَضُرُّونَهُۥ شَيۡـًٔاۚ إِنَّ رَبِّي عَلَىٰ
كُلِّ شَيۡءٍ حَفِيظٞ ﴿٥٧﴾

Wa yā qawmis-taghfirū Rabbakum thumma tūbūu ʾilayhi yursilis-samāaʾa ʿalaykum-midrārañw-wa yazidkum quwwatan ʾilā quwwatikum wa lā tatawallaw mujrimīn. (52) Qālū yā Hūdu mā jiʾtanā bibayyinatiñw-wa mā naḥnu bitārikīi ʾālihatinā ʿañ-qawlika wa mā naḥnu laka bimuʾminīn. (53) ʾIn-naqūlu ʾillaʿ-tarāka baʿḍu ʾālihatinā bisūuʾ. Qāla ʾinnīi ʾushhidul-lāha wash-hadūu ʾannī barīiʾum-mimmā tushrikūna, (54) miñ-dūnihī fakīdūnī jamīʿañ-thumma lā tuñẓirūn. (55) ʾInnī tawakkaltu ʿalal-lāhi Rabbī wa Rabbikum. Mā miñ-dāabbatin ʾillā Huwa ʾākhidhum-bināṣiyatihā. ʾInna Rabbī ʿalā ṣirāṭim-mustaqīm. (56) Faʾiñ-tawallaw faqad ʾablaghtukum-māa ʾursiltu bihīi ʾilaykum. Wa yastakhlifu Rabbī qawman ghayrakum wa lā taḍurrūnahū shayʾā. ʾInna Rabbī ʿalā kulli shayʾin Ḥafīẓ. (57)

Hūd). Regarding the term *muftarūn*, see *sūrah* 7, note 119.

76 Lit., "He will let loose the sky over you with abundance". The term *samāʾ* – lit., "sky" – is often used in classical Arabic as a metonym for "rain", and scarcity of rains is a characteristic of the desert country called Al-Aḥqāf ("The Sand-Dunes"), the one-time habitat of the – since vanished – tribe of ʿĀd. As would appear from 46 : 24, the time to which the above passage alludes was a period of severe drought, and so it is possible that the "abundant blessings" here denote rains.

77 I.e., with madness.

78 Or: "that, verily, I am guiltless of your ascribing a share in [God's] divinity (*mimmā tushrikūn*) . . .", etc. – thus rejecting the sardonic suggestion of his compatriots that one of their imaginary deities might have stricken him with madness.

79 Cf. a very similar challenge in the last sentence of 7 : 195.

80 I.e., there is no living being over which He has not complete control and which is not entirely dependent on Him (cf. verse 6 of this *sūrah*). When describing a person's humility and subjection to another person, the ancient Arabs used to say, "The forelock of so-and-so is in the hand of so-and-so". See in this connection 96 : 15-16, where this idiomatic expression occurs for the first time in the chronological order of Qurʾanic revelation.

81 Lit., "my Sustainer is on a straight way" – implying that He governs all that exists in accordance with a system of truth and justice in the ultimate, absolute sense of these terms, never allowing the conscious evildoer to escape the consequence of his deeds, and never letting righteousness go unrewarded, either in this world or in the hereafter (since it is only in the combination of these two phases that human life can be considered in its entirety).

82 Lit., "to succeed you"

And so, when Our judgment came to pass,[83] by Our grace We saved Hūd and those who shared his faith; and We saved them [too] from suffering severe [in the life to come].[84] «58»
And that was [the end of the tribe of] ʿĀd, [who] had rejected their Sustainer's messages, and rebelled against His apostles, and followed the bidding of every arrogant enemy of the truth.[85] «59» And they were pursued in this world by [God's] rejection, and [shall finally be overtaken by it] on the Day of Resurrection.[86]
Oh, verily, [the tribe of] ʿĀd denied their Sustainer! Oh, away with the ʿĀd, the people of Hūd! «60»

AND UNTO [the tribe of] Thamūd [We sent] their brother Ṣāliḥ.[87] He said: "O my people! Worship God [alone]: you have no deity other than Him. He brought you into being out of the earth,[88] and made you thrive thereon.[89] Ask Him, therefore, to forgive you your sins, and then turn towards Him in repentance – for, verily, my Sustainer is ever-near, responding [to the call of whoever calls unto Him!"[90] «61»
They answered: "O Ṣāliḥ! Great hopes did we place in thee ere this![91] Wouldst thou forbid us to worship what our forefathers

وَلَمَّا جَآءَ أَمْرُنَا نَجَّيْنَا هُودًا وَٱلَّذِينَ ءَامَنُوا۟ مَعَهُۥ بِرَحْمَةٍ مِّنَّا
وَنَجَّيْنَٰهُم مِّنْ عَذَابٍ غَلِيظٍ ﴿٥٨﴾ وَتِلْكَ عَادٌ جَحَدُوا۟ بِـَٔايَٰتِ رَبِّهِمْ
وَعَصَوْا۟ رُسُلَهُۥ وَٱتَّبَعُوٓا۟ أَمْرَ كُلِّ جَبَّارٍ عَنِيدٍ ﴿٥٩﴾ وَأُتْبِعُوا۟ فِى هَٰذِهِ ٱلدُّنْيَا
لَعْنَةً وَيَوْمَ ٱلْقِيَٰمَةِ أَلَآ إِنَّ عَادًا كَفَرُوا۟ رَبَّهُمْ أَلَا بُعْدًا لِّعَادٍ قَوْمِ
هُودٍ ﴿٦٠﴾ ۞ وَإِلَىٰ ثَمُودَ أَخَاهُمْ صَٰلِحًا قَالَ يَٰقَوْمِ ٱعْبُدُوا۟ ٱللَّهَ مَا
لَكُم مِّنْ إِلَٰهٍ غَيْرُهُۥ هُوَ أَنشَأَكُم مِّنَ ٱلْأَرْضِ وَٱسْتَعْمَرَكُمْ فِيهَا
فَٱسْتَغْفِرُوهُ ثُمَّ تُوبُوٓا۟ إِلَيْهِ إِنَّ رَبِّى قَرِيبٌ مُّجِيبٌ ﴿٦١﴾ قَالُوا۟ يَٰصَٰلِحُ
قَدْ كُنتَ فِينَا مَرْجُوًّا قَبْلَ هَٰذَآ أَتَنْهَىٰنَآ أَن نَّعْبُدَ مَا يَعْبُدُ ءَابَآؤُنَا

ثلاثة ارباع الحزب

Wa lammā jāaʾa ʾamrunā najjaynā Hūdañw-walladhīna ʾāmanū maʿahū biraḥmatim-minnā; wa najjaynāhum-min ʿadhābin ghalīẓ. (58) Wa tilka ʿĀduñ-jaḥadū biʾĀyāti Rabbihim wa ʿaṣaw Rusulahū wat-tabaʿūu ʾamra kulli jabbārin ʿanīd. (59) Wa ʾutbiʿū fī hādhihid-dunyā laʿnatañw-wa Yawmal-Qiyāmah. ʾAlāa ʾinna ʿĀdañ-kafarū Rabbahum. ʾAlā buʿdal-liʿĀdiñ-qawmi Hūd. (60) ۞ Wa ʾilā Thamūda ʾakhāhum Ṣāliḥā. Qāla yā qawmiʿ-budul-lāha mā lakum-min ʾilāhin ghayruh. Huwa ʾañshaʾakum-minal-ʾarḍi was-taʿmarakum fīhā fastaghfirūhu thumma tūbūu ʾilayhi ʾinna Rabbī Qarībum-Mujīb. (61) Qālū yā Ṣāliḥu qad kuñta fīnā marjuwwañ-qabla hādhā. ʾAtanhānāa ʾan-naʿbuda mā yaʿbudu ʾābāaʾunā

83 For the story of the destruction of the tribe of ʿĀd through violent storm-winds, see 54 : 19 and, more particularly, 69 : 6-8.

84 I.e., the suffering which was yet to befall the rest of the tribe of ʿĀd. My addition, between brackets, of the words "in the life to come" is based on the interpretation advanced by Ṭabarī, Zamakhsharī and Rāzī, according to whom the first mention of the saving of Hūd and his followers refers to the destruction of the people of ʿĀd in this world, and the second, to the latters' chastisement in the hereafter.

85 An allusion to "the great ones among them, who refused to acknowledge the truth" (7 : 66). Regarding the above interpretation of the term *jabbār*, see note 58 on 26 : 130.

86 For my rendering of the term *laʿnah* as "[God's] rejection", see note 37 above.

87 A short account of the tribe of Thamūd (the "Second ʿĀd" of pre-Islamic poetry) is found in *sūrah* 7, note 56. Ṣāliḥ is believed to have been the second prophet, after Hūd, sent to the Arabs.

88 I.e., out of organic substances which derive their nourishment – and hence their capability of development, proliferation and evolution – either directly or indirectly from the earth (Rāzī). This is evidently also the meaning of the Qurʾanic references to man as "created out of dust" (cf. 3 : 59, 18 : 37, 22 : 5 and 30 : 20).

89 See 7 : 74 and the corresponding notes.

90 See 2 : 186.

91 Lit., "Thou wert among us one in whom hope was placed ere this": an allusion to Ṣāliḥ's outstanding intellect and strength of character, which had probably caused his tribe to see in him their future leader – until he startled them by his passionate demand that they should abandon their traditional beliefs and devote themselves to the worship of the One God.

وَإِنَّنَا لَفِى شَكٍّ مِّمَّا تَدْعُونَآ إِلَيْهِ مُرِيبٍ ﴿٦٢﴾ قَالَ يَٰقَوْمِ أَرَءَيْتُمْ إِن كُنتُ
عَلَىٰ بَيِّنَةٍ مِّن رَّبِّى وَءَاتَىٰنِى مِنْهُ رَحْمَةً فَمَن يَنصُرُنِى مِنَ ٱللَّهِ إِنْ عَصَيْتُهُۥ
فَمَا تَزِيدُونَنِى غَيْرَ تَخْسِيرٍ ﴿٦٣﴾ وَيَٰقَوْمِ هَٰذِهِۦ نَاقَةُ ٱللَّهِ لَكُمْ ءَايَةً
فَذَرُوهَا تَأْكُلْ فِىٓ أَرْضِ ٱللَّهِ وَلَا تَمَسُّوهَا بِسُوٓءٍ فَيَأْخُذَكُمْ
عَذَابٌ قَرِيبٌ ﴿٦٤﴾ فَعَقَرُوهَا فَقَالَ تَمَتَّعُوا۟ فِى دَارِكُمْ ثَلَٰثَةَ أَيَّامٍ

wa ʾinnanā lafī shakkim-mimmā tadʿūnāa ʾilayhi murīb. (62) Qāla yā qawmi ʾaraʾaytum ʾiñ-kuñtu ʿalā bayyinatim-mir-Rabbī wa ʾātānī minhu raḥmatañ-famañy-yañṣurunī minal-lāhi ʾin ʿaṣaytuh. Famā tazīdūnanī ghayra takhsīir. (63) Wa yā qawmi hādhihī nāqatul-lāhi lakum ʾāyatañ-fadharūhā taʾkul fīi ʾarḍil-lāhi wa lā tamassūhā bisūuʾiñ-fayaʾkhudhakum ʿadhābuñ-qarīb. (64) Faʿaqarūhā faqāla tamattaʿū fī dārikum thalāthata ʾayyām.

were wont to worship? Because [of this], behold, we are in grave doubt, amounting to suspicion, about [the meaning of] thy call to us!"[92] «62»

He retorted: "O my people! What do you think? If [it be true that] I am taking my stand on a clear evidence from my Sustainer, who has vouchsafed unto me grace from Himself – [if this be true,] who would shield me from God were I to rebel against Him?[93] Hence, what you are offering me is no more than perdition!"[94] «63»

And [then he said]: "O my people! This she-camel belonging to God shall be a token for you: so leave her alone to pasture on God's earth, and do her no harm, lest speedy chastisement befall you!"[95] «64»

But they cruelly slaughtered her.[96] And thereupon [Ṣāliḥ] said: "[Only] for three days [more] shall you enjoy life in your homes:

---

92 Lit., "we are indeed in disquieting doubt as to that to which thou invitest us". It is to be borne in mind that the pre-Islamic Arabs regarded their gods, as well as the angels (whom they believed to be "God's daughters"), as legitimate mediators between man and God, whose existence as such they did not deny; consequently, they were greatly disturbed by their prophet's demand that they should abandon the worship of those allegedly divine or semi-divine beings. The above answer of the Thamūd seems to imply that they might consider Ṣāliḥ's claim to be a prophet more favourably if he would but refrain from insisting that "you have no deity other than Him": a suggestion that fully explains Ṣāliḥ's retort in the next verse.

93 I.e., "if I were to suppress – in spite of all the evidence obtained through divine revelation – the fundamental truth that there is no deity save God, and that the ascribing of divinity or divine powers to anyone or anything beside Him is an unforgivable sin" (cf. 4 : 48 and the corresponding note 65).

94 Lit., "you do not add [anything] to me but perdition". Although this dialogue is related in the context of the story of Ṣāliḥ and the leaders of the Thamūd, its implications have – as is always the case with Qurʾanic stories and parables – a universal, timeless import. The stress here is on the intrinsic impossibility of reconciling belief in the One God, whose omniscience and omnipotence embraces all that exists, with an attribution of divine or semi-divine qualities and functions to anyone or anything else. The subtly-veiled suggestion of the Thamūd (see note 92) and its rejection by Ṣāliḥ has a bearing on all religious attitudes based on a desire to "bring God closer to man" through the interposition of alleged "mediators" between Him and man. In primitive religions, this interposition led to the deification of various forces of nature and, subsequently, to the invention of imaginary deities which were thought to act against the background of an undefined, dimly-perceived Supreme Power (for instance, the Moira of the ancient Greeks). In higher religious concepts, this need for mediation assumes the form of personified manifestations of God through subordinate deities (as is the case, in Hinduism, with the personifications of the Absolute Brahma of the Upanishads and the Vedanta in the forms of Vishnu or Shiva), or in His supposed incarnation in human form (as represented in the Christian idea of Jesus as "God's son" and the Second Person of the Trinity). And, lastly, God is supposedly "brought closer to man" by the interposition of a hierarchy of saints, living or dead, whose intercession is sought even by people who consider themselves to be "monotheists" – and this includes many misguided Muslims who do not realize that their belief in saints as "mediators" between men and God conflicts with the very essence of Islam. The ever-recurring Qurʾanic stress on the oneness and uniqueness of God, and the categorical denial of the idea that anyone or anything – whether it be a concrete being or an abstract force – could have the least share in God's qualities or the least influence on the manner in which He governs the universe aims at freeing man from the self-imposed servitude to an imaginary hierarchy of "mediating powers", and at making him realize that "wherever you turn, there is God's countenance" (2 : 115), and that God is "[always] near, responding [to the call of whoever calls unto Him]" (2 : 186; also, in a condensed form, in verse 61 of this *sūrah*).

95 For an explanation of this passage, see *sūrah* 7, note 57.

96 See *sūrah* 7, note 61.

this is a judgment[97] which will not be belied!" ⟨65⟩
And so, when Our judgment came to pass, by Our grace We saved Ṣāliḥ and those who shared his faith; and [We saved them, too,] from the ignominy of [Our rejection on] that Day [of Resurrection].
Verily, thy Sustainer alone is powerful, almighty! ⟨66⟩
And the blast [of God's punishment] overtook those who had been bent on evildoing: and then they lay lifeless, in their very homes, on the ground,[98] ⟨67⟩ as though they had never lived there.
Oh, verily, [the tribe of] Thamūd denied their Sustainer! Oh, away with the Thamūd! ⟨68⟩

AND, INDEED, there came unto Abraham Our [heavenly] messengers, bearing a glad tiding.[99] They bade him peace; [and] he answered, "[And upon you be] peace!" – and made haste to place before them[100] a roasted calf. ⟨69⟩
But when he saw that their hands did not reach out towards it, he deemed their conduct strange and became apprehensive of them.[101] [But] they said: "Fear not! Behold, we are sent to the people of Lot."[102] ⟨70⟩

ذَٰلِكَ وَعْدٌ غَيْرُ مَكْذُوبٍ (65) فَلَمَّا جَآءَ أَمْرُنَا نَجَّيْنَا صَٰلِحًا وَٱلَّذِينَ
ءَامَنُوا۟ مَعَهُۥ بِرَحْمَةٍ مِّنَّا وَمِنْ خِزْىِ يَوْمِئِذٍ ۗ إِنَّ رَبَّكَ هُوَ ٱلْقَوِىُّ
ٱلْعَزِيزُ (66) وَأَخَذَ ٱلَّذِينَ ظَلَمُوا۟ ٱلصَّيْحَةُ فَأَصْبَحُوا۟ فِى دِيَٰرِهِمْ
جَٰثِمِينَ (67) كَأَن لَّمْ يَغْنَوْا۟ فِيهَآ ۗ أَلَآ إِنَّ ثَمُودَا۟ كَفَرُوا۟ رَبَّهُمْ ۗ أَلَا بُعْدًا
لِّثَمُودَ (68) وَلَقَدْ جَآءَتْ رُسُلُنَآ إِبْرَٰهِيمَ بِٱلْبُشْرَىٰ قَالُوا۟ سَلَٰمًا ۖ قَالَ
سَلَٰمٌ ۖ فَمَا لَبِثَ أَن جَآءَ بِعِجْلٍ حَنِيذٍ (69) فَلَمَّا رَءَآ أَيْدِيَهُمْ لَا تَصِلُ
إِلَيْهِ نَكِرَهُمْ وَأَوْجَسَ مِنْهُمْ خِيفَةً ۚ قَالُوا۟ لَا تَخَفْ إِنَّآ أُرْسِلْنَآ إِلَىٰ قَوْمِ
لُوطٍ (70)

Dhālika waʿdun ghayru makdhūb. (65) Falammā jāaʾa ʾamrunā najjaynā Ṣāliḥañw-wal-ladhīna ʾāmanū maʿahū biraḥmatim-minnā wa min khizyi Yawmiʾidh. ʾInna Rabbaka Huwal-Qawiyyul-ʿAzīz. (66) Wa ʾakhadhal-ladhīna ẓalamuṣ-ṣayḥatu faʾaṣbaḥū fī diyārihim jāthimīn. (67) Kaʾal-lam yaghnaw fīhā. ʾAlāa ʾinna Thamūda kafarū Rabbahum. ʾAlā buʿdal-liThamūd. (68) Wa laqad jāaʾat Rusulunāa ʾIbrāhīma bilbushrā qālū salāmañ-qāla salām. Famā labitha ʾañ-jāaʾa biʿijlin ḥanīdh. (69) Falammā raʾāa ʾaydiyahum lā taṣilu ʾilayhi nakirahum wa ʾawjasa minhum khīfah. Qālū lā takhaf ʾinnāa ʾursilnāa ʾilā qawmi Lūṭ. (70)

97 Lit., "promise".

98 Lit., "they became, in their homes, prostrate on the ground". Ibn ʿAbbās – as quoted by Rāzī – explains the term *ṣayḥah* (lit., "vehement cry" or "sound") occurring in this verse as a synonym of *ṣāʿiqah*, a "thunderbolt" or the "sound of thunder". Since the same event is described in 7 : 78 as "violent trembling" (*rajfah*), which in that context apparently denotes an earthquake, it is possible that the "vehement sound" mentioned here and in several other places describes the subterranean rumbling which often precedes and accompanies an earthquake and/or the thunderlike noise of a volcanic eruption (see *sūrah* 7, note 62). However, in view of the repeated use of this expression in varying contexts, we may assume that it has the more general meaning of "blast of punishment" or – as in 50 : 42, where it indicates the Last Hour – of "final blast".

99 The Qurʾān does not state in so many words that these guests of Abraham were angels; but since the term *rusulunā* ("Our messengers") is often used in the sense of *heavenly* messengers, all the classical commentators interpret it thus in the above context. For the contents of the "glad tiding" referred to here, see verse 71 below. – The reason for prefacing the story of Lot with an episode from Abraham's life lies in the latter's subsequent pleading in behalf of the sinful people of Sodom (verses 74-76) and also, possibly, in God's earlier promise to him, "Behold, I shall make thee a leader of men" (see 2 : 124), which must have imbued him with an enhanced sense of moral responsibility not only for his own family but also for the people with whom he was indirectly connected through his nephew Lot (Lūṭ in Arabic).

100 Lit., "and did not delay in bringing". Regarding the deeper implications of the word "peace" (*salām*) as used in this passage, see *sūrah* 5, note 29.

101 Lit., "he did not know [what to make of] them and conceived fear of them". Since they were angels, they did not eat (contrary to the Biblical statement in Genesis xviii, 8); and since, in the Arabian tradition of hospitality, a stranger's refusal to partake of the food offered him is an indication of unfriendly intent, Abraham – who until then had not realized that his guests were angels – became apprehensive of possible hostility on their part.

102 According to the Biblical account (not contradicted by the Qurʾān), Lot, a son of Abraham's brother, lived to

And his wife, standing [nearby], laughed [with happiness][103]; whereupon We gave her the glad tiding of [the birth of] Isaac and, after Isaac, of [his son] Jacob. ‹71›
Said she: "Oh, woe is me![104] Shall I bear a child, now that I am an old woman and this husband of mine is an old man? Verily, that would be a strange thing indeed!" ‹72›
Answered [the messengers]: "Dost thou deem it strange that God should decree what He wills?[105] The grace of God and His blessings be upon you, O people of this house! Verily, ever to be praised, sublime is He!" ‹73›
And when the fear had left Abraham, and the glad tiding had been conveyed to him, he began to plead with Us for Lot's people:[106] ‹74› for, behold, Abraham was most clement, most tender-hearted, intent upon turning to God again and again. ‹75›
[But God's messengers replied:] "O Abraham! Desist from this [pleading]! Behold, thy Sustainer's judgment has already gone forth: and, verily, there shall fall upon them a chastisement which none can avert!" ‹76›

AND WHEN Our messengers came unto Lot, he was sorely grieved on their account, seeing that it was beyond his power to

وَٱمۡرَأَتُهُۥ قَآئِمَةٞ فَضَحِكَتۡ فَبَشَّرۡنَٰهَا بِإِسۡحَٰقَ وَمِن وَرَآءِ إِسۡحَٰقَ
يَعۡقُوبَ ﴿٧١﴾ قَالَتۡ يَٰوَيۡلَتَىٰٓ ءَأَلِدُ وَأَنَا۠ عَجُوزٞ وَهَٰذَا بَعۡلِي شَيۡخًاۖ إِنَّ هَٰذَا
لَشَيۡءٌ عَجِيبٞ ﴿٧٢﴾ قَالُوٓاْ أَتَعۡجَبِينَ مِنۡ أَمۡرِ ٱللَّهِۖ رَحۡمَتُ ٱللَّهِ وَبَرَكَٰتُهُۥ عَلَيۡكُمۡ
أَهۡلَ ٱلۡبَيۡتِۚ إِنَّهُۥ حَمِيدٞ مَّجِيدٞ ﴿٧٣﴾ فَلَمَّا ذَهَبَ عَنۡ إِبۡرَٰهِيمَ ٱلرَّوۡعُ وَجَآءَتۡهُ
ٱلۡبُشۡرَىٰ يُجَٰدِلُنَا فِي قَوۡمِ لُوطٍ ﴿٧٤﴾ إِنَّ إِبۡرَٰهِيمَ لَحَلِيمٌ أَوَّٰهٞ مُّنِيبٞ ﴿٧٥﴾
يَٰٓإِبۡرَٰهِيمُ أَعۡرِضۡ عَنۡ هَٰذَآۖ إِنَّهُۥ قَدۡ جَآءَ أَمۡرُ رَبِّكَۖ وَإِنَّهُمۡ ءَاتِيهِمۡ
عَذَابٌ غَيۡرُ مَرۡدُودٖ ﴿٧٦﴾ وَلَمَّا جَآءَتۡ رُسُلُنَا لُوطٗا سِيٓءَ بِهِمۡ وَضَاقَ بِهِمۡ

Wam-raʾatuhū qāaʾimatuñ-faḍaḥikat fabash-sharnāhā biʾIsḥāqa wa miñw-warāaʾi ʾIsḥāqa Yaʿqūb. (71) Qālat yā waylatāa ʾaʾalidu wa ʾana ʿajūzuñw-wa hādhā baʿlī shaykhā. ʾInna hādhā la-shayʾun ʿajīb. (72) Qālūu ʾataʿjabīna min ʾamril-lāhi raḥmatul-lāhi wa barakātuhū ʿalaykum ʾAhlal-Bayt. ʾInnahū Ḥamīdum-Majīd. (73) Falammā dhahaba ʿan ʾIbrāhīmar-rawʿu wa jāaʾat-hul-bushrā yujādilunā fī qawmi Lūṭ. (74) ʾInna ʾIbrāhīma laḥalīmun ʾaw-wāhum-munīb. (75) Yāa ʾIbrāhīmu ʾaʿriḍ ʿan hādhā. ʾInnahū qad jāaʾa ʾamru Rabbik wa ʾinnahum ʾātīhim ʿadhābun ghayru mardūd. (76) Wa lammā jāaʾat Rusulunā Lūṭañ-sīiʾa bihim wa ḍāqa bihim

the east of the Jordan, in the vicinity of what is today the Dead Sea (called in Arabic *Baḥr Lūṭ*, "Lot's Sea"). The "people of Lot" were not actually the latter's community, for he – like Abraham – was a native of Ur in southern Babylonia, and had migrated thence with his uncle: hence, throughout the Qurʾān, the expression "Lot's people" designates the inhabitants of the town (or country) of Sodom, among whom he had chosen to live, and with regard to whom he was entrusted with a prophetic mission.

103 I.e., on realizing that the strangers were God's messengers, and that she and Abraham had nothing to fear from them (Zamakhsharī): hence the interpolation of the words "with happiness". This differs from the Biblical statement (Genesis xviii, 12-15), according to which Sarah "laughed within herself" at the announcement that she, an old woman, would give birth to a son: for in the above Qurʾanic passage this announcement comes *after* the statement that she laughed, and is introduced by the conjunctive particle *fa*, which in this context denotes "and thereupon" or "whereupon".

104 This expression of grief obviously relates to her past barrenness as well as to her fear that this astonishing announcement might prove illusory.

105 Lit., "Art thou astonished at God's decree?" – or: "Dost thou find God's decree strange?" However, the real meaning of this rhetorical question can only be brought out by paraphrasing it in the manner attempted by me: namely, as an echo of the statement, repeated several times in the Qurʾān: "When God wills a thing to be, He but says unto it, 'Be' – and it is."

106 According to all commentators, this means "he pleaded [lit., "argued"] *with Our messengers*" (who, as is evident from 29 : 31, had announced to him the impending doom of Sodom and Gomorrah), and not with God Himself.

ذَرْعًا وَقَالَ هَٰذَا يَوْمٌ عَصِيبٌ ﴿77﴾ وَجَآءَهُۥ قَوْمُهُۥ يُهْرَعُونَ إِلَيْهِ وَمِن
قَبْلُ كَانُوا۟ يَعْمَلُونَ ٱلسَّيِّـَٔاتِ قَالَ يَٰقَوْمِ هَٰٓؤُلَآءِ بَنَاتِى هُنَّ أَطْهَرُ لَكُمْ
فَٱتَّقُوا۟ ٱللَّهَ وَلَا تُخْزُونِ فِى ضَيْفِىٓ أَلَيْسَ مِنكُمْ رَجُلٌ رَّشِيدٌ ﴿78﴾ قَالُوا۟
لَقَدْ عَلِمْتَ مَا لَنَا فِى بَنَاتِكَ مِنْ حَقٍّ وَإِنَّكَ لَتَعْلَمُ مَا نُرِيدُ ﴿79﴾ قَالَ لَوْ
أَنَّ لِى بِكُمْ قُوَّةً أَوْ ءَاوِىٓ إِلَىٰ رُكْنٍ شَدِيدٍ ﴿80﴾ قَالُوا۟ يَٰلُوطُ إِنَّا رُسُلُ
رَبِّكَ لَن يَصِلُوٓا۟ إِلَيْكَ فَأَسْرِ بِأَهْلِكَ بِقِطْعٍ مِّنَ ٱلَّيْلِ وَلَا يَلْتَفِتْ مِنكُمْ
أَحَدٌ إِلَّا ٱمْرَأَتَكَ إِنَّهُۥ مُصِيبُهَا مَآ أَصَابَهُمْ إِنَّ مَوْعِدَهُمُ ٱلصُّبْحُ أَلَيْسَ
ٱلصُّبْحُ بِقَرِيبٍ ﴿81﴾

dharʿañw-wa qāla hādhā yawmun ʿaṣīb. (77) Wa jāaʾahū qawmuhū yuhraʿūna ʾilayhi wa miñ-qablu kānū yaʿmalūnas-sayyiʾāt. Qāla yā qawmi hāaʾulāaʾi banātī hunna ʾaṭharu lakum fattaqul-lāha wa lā tukhzūni fī ḍayfī. ʾAlaysa miñkum rajulur-rashīd. (78) Qālū laqad ʿalimta mā lanā fī banātika min ḥaqqiñw-wa ʾinnaka lataʿlamu mā nurīd. (79) Qāla law ʾanna lī bikum quwwatan ʾaw ʾāwī ʾilā rukniñ-shadīd. (80) Qālū yā Lūṭu ʾinnā Rusulu Rabbika lañy-yaṣilūu ʾilayk. Faʾasri biʾahlika biqiṭʿim-minal-layli wa lā yaltafit miñkum ʾaḥadun ʾillam-raʾatak. ʾInnahū muṣībuhā māa ʾaṣābahum. ʾInna mawʿidahumuṣ-ṣubḥu ʾalaysaṣ-ṣubḥu biqarīb. (81)

shield them;[107] and he exclaimed: "This is a woeful day!" ⟨77⟩

And his people came running to him, impelled towards his house [by their desire]:[108] for they had ever been wont to commit [such] abominations.

Said [Lot]: "O my people! [Take instead] these daughters of mine: they are purer for you [than men]![109] Be, then, conscious of God, and disgrace me not by [assaulting] my guests. Is there not among you even one right-minded man?" ⟨78⟩

They answered: "Thou hast always known that we have no use whatever for thy daughters;[110] and, verily, well dost thou know what we want!" ⟨79⟩

Exclaimed [Lot]: "Would that I had the strength to defeat you, or that I could lean upon some mightier support!"[111] ⟨80⟩

[Whereupon the angels] said: "O Lot! Behold, we are messengers from thy Sustainer! Never shall [thy enemies] attain to thee! Depart, then, with thy household while it is yet night, and let none of you look back;[112] [and take with thee all thy family] with the exception of thy wife: for, behold, that which is to befall these [people of Sodom] shall befall her [as well].[113] Verily, their appointed time is the morning [and] is not the morning nigh?" ⟨81⟩

---

107 Lit., "he was straitened as regards the reach of his arm in their behalf" – an idiomatic phrase often used in classical Arabic, denoting here Lot's utter inability to afford his guests protection from the people of Sodom, whose homosexual propensities have ever since been commemorated in the term "sodomy". Since Lot thought that the strangers were no more than handsome young men, he felt certain that they would be sexually assaulted by his sinful countrymen.

108 Lit., "towards him" – but since their desire was obviously directed at Lot's guests, and not at himself, my rendering would seem appropriate. It is to be noted that in its passive form, as used here, the verb *yuhraʿūn* does not merely mean "they came running" but, rather, "running as if driven onward by some force" (Zamakhsharī) – in this case, the force of their perverse desire.

109 Most of the commentators are of the opinion that the phrase "these daughters of mine" signifies here "the daughters of my community" (since a prophet is the spiritual father of his people). But whether this is the case, or whether – as is more probable – Lot's words refer to his actual daughters, there is no doubt that in their wider implication they point to the natural relationship between man and woman as contrasted with the perverse desires of the men of Sodom.

110 Lit., "no claim whatever to thy daughters".

111 Lit., "or that I could betake myself to some mighty support". Although some of the commentators are of the opinion that this expression denotes "tribal support" (which was, however, unavailable to Lot inasmuch as he was a stranger in Sodom), we have a number of authentic Traditions (extensively quoted by Ṭabarī) to the effect that what Lot meant was *God's* support: for the Prophet Muḥammad, referring to this Qurʾanic passage, is reported to have said, "God bestowed His grace upon Lot, for he betook himself indeed unto a mighty support!"

112 I.e., in an abstract sense, "to what you are leaving behind" (Rāzī) – evidently meaning the severing of all associations with the sinful city, and not a physical looking-back.

113 Cf. 7 : 83 and the corresponding note, as well as 66 : 10, where it is mentioned that Lot's wife, who was apparently a native of Sodom, had acted faithlessly towards her husband, i.e., had refused to believe in his prophetic

And so, when Our judgment came to pass, We turned those [sinful towns] upside down, and rained down upon them stone-hard blows of chastisement pre-ordained,[114] one upon another, ‹82› marked out in thy Sustainer's sight [for the punishment of such as are lost in sin].
And these [blows of God-willed doom] are never far from evildoers![115] ‹83›

AND UNTO [the people of] Madyan [We sent] their brother Shuʿayb.[116] He said: "O my people! Worship God [alone]: you have no deity other than Him; and do not give short measure and weight [in any of your dealings with men].[117] Behold, I see you [now] in a happy state; but, verily, I dread lest suffering befall you on a Day that will encompass [you with doom]! ‹84› Hence, O my people, [always] give full measure and weight, with equity, and do not deprive people of what is rightfully theirs,[118] and do not act wickedly on earth by spreading corruption. ‹85› That which rests with God[119] is best for you, if you but believe [in Him]! However, I am not your keeper." ‹86›

حزب 24

فَلَمَّا جَآءَ أَمْرُنَا جَعَلْنَا عَـٰلِيَهَا سَافِلَهَا وَأَمْطَرْنَا عَلَيْهَا حِجَارَةً مِّن سِجِّيلٍ
مَّنضُودٍ ﴿82﴾ مُّسَوَّمَةً عِندَ رَبِّكَ وَمَا هِىَ مِنَ ٱلظَّـٰلِمِينَ بِبَعِيدٍ ﴿83﴾ ۞
وَإِلَىٰ مَدْيَنَ أَخَاهُمْ شُعَيْبًا قَالَ يَـٰقَوْمِ ٱعْبُدُوا۟ ٱللَّهَ مَا لَكُم مِّنْ إِلَـٰهٍ غَيْرُهُۥ
وَلَا تَنقُصُوا۟ ٱلْمِكْيَالَ وَٱلْمِيزَانَ إِنِّىٓ أَرَىٰكُم بِخَيْرٍ وَإِنِّىٓ أَخَافُ عَلَيْكُمْ
عَذَابَ يَوْمٍ مُّحِيطٍ ﴿84﴾ وَيَـٰقَوْمِ أَوْفُوا۟ ٱلْمِكْيَالَ وَٱلْمِيزَانَ بِٱلْقِسْطِ وَلَا
تَبْخَسُوا۟ ٱلنَّاسَ أَشْيَآءَهُمْ وَلَا تَعْثَوْا۟ فِى ٱلْأَرْضِ مُفْسِدِينَ ﴿85﴾ بَقِيَّتُ
ٱللَّهِ خَيْرٌ لَّكُمْ إِن كُنتُم مُّؤْمِنِينَ وَمَآ أَنَا۠ عَلَيْكُم بِحَفِيظٍ ﴿86﴾

Falammā jāaʾa ʾamrunā jaʿalnā ʿāliyahā sāfilahā wa ʾamṭarnā ʿalayhā ḥijāratam-miñ-sijjīlim-manḍūd. (82) Musawwamatan ʿiñda Rabbika wa mā hiya minaẓ-ẓālimīna bibaʿīd. (83) ۞ Wa ʾilā Madyana ʾakhāhum Shuʿaybā. Qāla yā qawmiʿ-budul-lāha mā lakum-min ʾilāhin ghayruh. Wa lā tañqusul-mikyāla wal-mīzān. ʾInnīi ʾarākum-bikhayriñw-wa ʾinnīi ʾakhāfu ʿalaykum ʿadhāba Yawmim-muḥīṭ. (84) Wa yā qawmi ʾawful-mikyāla wal-mīzāna bilqisṭi wa lā tabkhasun-nāsa ʾashyāaʾahum wa lā taʿthaw fil-ʾarḍi mufsidīn. (85) Baqiyyatul-lāhi khayrul-lakum ʾiñ-kuñtum-muʾminīn. Wa māa ʾana ʿalaykum-biḥafīẓ. (86)

mission; and her story was thereupon "propounded as a parable of those who are bent on denying the truth".

114 Lit., "stones of *sijjīl*", which latter noun is regarded by some philologists as the Arabicized form of the Persian *sang-i-gil* ("clay-stone" or "petrified clay"): cf. *Qāmūs* and *Tāj al-ʿArūs*. If this supposition is correct, the "stones of petrified clay" would be more or less synonymous with "brimstones", which in its turn would point to a volcanic eruption, probably in conjunction with a severe earthquake (alluded to in the preceding phrase, "We turned those [sinful towns] upside down"). But there is also a strong probability, pointed out by Zamakhsharī and Rāzī, that the term *sijjīl* is of purely Arabic origin – namely, a synonym of *sijill*, which primarily signifies "a writing", and secondarily, "something that has been decreed": in which case the expression *ḥijārah min sijjīl* can be understood in a metaphorical sense, namely, as "stones of all the chastisement laid down in God's decree" (Zamakhsharī and Rāzī, both in conjunction with the above verse and in their commentaries on 105 : 4). It is, I believe, this metaphorical meaning of "stone-hard blows of chastisement pre-ordained", i.e., of God-willed doom, that the concluding sentence of the next verse alludes to.

115 According to some of the earliest Qurʾān-commentators (e.g.. Qatādah and ʿIkrimah, as quoted by Ṭabarī), this threat of ultimate doom applies to evildoers of *all* times – which further supports the assumption that the expression *ḥijārah min sijjīl* has a metaphorical connotation.

116 See *sūrah* 7, note 67.

117 Thus, belief in the One God and justice in all dealings between man and man (see *sūrah* 6, note 150) are here placed together as the twin postulates of all righteousness. Some commentators assume that the people of Madyan were of a particularly commercial bent of mind, and given to fraudulent dealings. It is obvious, however, that the purport of this passage and of its sequence goes far beyond anything that might be construed by a purely "historical" interpretation. What this version of Shuʿayb's story aims at is – as always in the Qurʾān – the enunciation of a generally applicable principle of ethics: namely, the impossibility of one's being righteous with regard to God unless one is righteous – in both the moral and social senses of this word – in the realm of human relationships as well. This explains the insistence with which the above prohibition is re-stated in a positive form, as an injunction, in the next verse.

118 See *sūrah* 7, note 68.

119 I.e., the lasting merit achieved by virtue of good deeds and fair dealings with one's fellow-men (cf. the expression *al-bāqiyāt aṣ-ṣāliḥāt* in 18 : 46 and 19 : 76).

قَالُوا۟ يَـٰشُعَيْبُ أَصَلَوٰتُكَ تَأْمُرُكَ أَن نَّتْرُكَ مَا يَعْبُدُ ءَابَآؤُنَآ أَوْ أَن نَّفْعَلَ
فِىٓ أَمْوَٰلِنَا مَا نَشَـٰٓؤُا۟ ۖ إِنَّكَ لَأَنتَ ٱلْحَلِيمُ ٱلرَّشِيدُ ﴿٨٧﴾ قَالَ يَـٰقَوْمِ أَرَءَيْتُمْ
إِن كُنتُ عَلَىٰ بَيِّنَةٍ مِّن رَّبِّى وَرَزَقَنِى مِنْهُ رِزْقًا حَسَنًا ۚ وَمَآ أُرِيدُ أَنْ أُخَالِفَكُمْ
إِلَىٰ مَآ أَنْهَىٰكُمْ عَنْهُ ۚ إِنْ أُرِيدُ إِلَّا ٱلْإِصْلَـٰحَ مَا ٱسْتَطَعْتُ ۚ وَمَا تَوْفِيقِىٓ إِلَّا
بِٱللَّهِ ۚ عَلَيْهِ تَوَكَّلْتُ وَإِلَيْهِ أُنِيبُ ﴿٨٨﴾ وَيَـٰقَوْمِ لَا يَجْرِمَنَّكُمْ شِقَاقِىٓ أَن
يُصِيبَكُم مِّثْلُ مَآ أَصَابَ قَوْمَ نُوحٍ أَوْ قَوْمَ هُودٍ أَوْ قَوْمَ صَـٰلِحٍ ۚ وَمَا قَوْمُ
لُوطٍ مِّنكُم بِبَعِيدٍ ﴿٨٩﴾ وَٱسْتَغْفِرُوا۟ رَبَّكُمْ ثُمَّ تُوبُوٓا۟ إِلَيْهِ ۚ إِنَّ رَبِّى رَحِيمٌ
وَدُودٌ ﴿٩٠﴾ قَالُوا۟ يَـٰشُعَيْبُ مَا نَفْقَهُ كَثِيرًا مِّمَّا تَقُولُ وَإِنَّا لَنَرَىٰكَ فِينَا ضَعِيفًا

Qālū yā Shuᶜaybu ʾaṣalātuka taʾmuruka ʾañ-natruka mā yaᶜbudu ʾābāaʾunāa ʾaw ʾañ-nafᶜala fīi ʾamwālinā mā nashāaʾ. ʾInnaka la ʾañtal-ḥalīmur-rashīd. (87) Qāla yā qawmi ʾaraʾaytum ʾiñ-kuñtu ᶜalā bayyinatim-mir-Rabbī wa razaqanī minhu rizqan ḥasanā. Wa māa ʾurīdu ʾan ʾukhālifakum ʾilā māa ʾanhākum ᶜanh. ʾIn ʾurīdu ʾillal-ʾiṣlāḥa mas-taṭaᶜtu wa mā tawfīqīi ʾillā billāh. ᶜAlayhi tawakkaltu wa ʾilayhi ʾunīb. (88) Wa yā qawmi lā yajrimannakum shiqāqīi ʾañy-yuṣībakum-mithlu māa ʾaṣāba qawma Nūḥin ʾaw qawma Hūdin ʾaw qawma Ṣāliḥ. Wa mā qawmu Lūṭim-miñkum-bibaᶜīd. (89) Was-taghfirū Rabbakum thumma tūbūu ʾilayhi ʾinna Rabbī Raḥīmuñw-Wadūd. (90) Qālū yā Shuᶜaybu mā nafqahu kathīram-mimmā taqūlu wa ʾinnā lanarāka fīnā ḍaᶜīfā.

Said they: "O Shuᶜayb! Does thy [habit of] praying compel thee to demand of us[120] that we give up all that our forefathers were wont to worship, or that we refrain from doing whatever we please with our possessions?[121] Behold, [thou wouldst have us believe that] thou art indeed the only clement, the only right-minded man!" ‹87›

He answered: "O my people! What do you think? If [it be true that] I am taking my stand on a clear evidence from my Sustainer, who has vouchsafed me goodly sustenance [as a gift] from Himself – [how could I speak to you otherwise than I do]?[122] And yet, I have no desire to do, out of opposition to you, what I am asking *you* not to do:[123] I desire no more than to set things to rights in so far as it lies within my power; but the achievement of my aim depends on God alone. In Him have I placed my trust, and unto Him do I always turn! ‹88›

"And, O my people, let not [your] dissent from me drive you into sin, lest there befall you the like of what befell the people of Noah, or the people of Hūd, or the people of Ṣāliḥ: and [remember that] the people of Lot lived not very far from you![124] ‹89› Hence, ask your Sustainer to forgive you your sins, and then turn towards Him in repentance – for, verily, my Sustainer is a dispenser of grace, a fount of love!" ‹90›

[But his people] said: "O Shuᶜayb! We cannot grasp the purport of much of what thou sayest;[125] on the other hand, behold, we do see clearly how weak thou art in our

120 Lit., "Do thy prayers command thee . . .", etc.

121 I.e., without regard to the rights and needs of others, especially the poor: hence their sarcastic reference, in the next sentence, to Shūᶜayb's clemency and right-mindedness.

122 According to Zamakhsharī, Rāzī and several other commentators, the clause interpolated here between brackets is elliptically implied in Shuᶜayb's answer. His stress on the fact that God has graced him amply with worldly goods is meant to remind his countrymen that it is not self-interest that causes him to ask them to be fair in their dealings with their fellow-men.

123 I.e., "I do not aim at depriving you of what is rightfully yours" – a reference to verse 85 above.

124 As pointed out in *sūrah* 7, note 67, the region inhabited by Shuᶜayb's people extended from what is known today as the Gulf of ᶜAqabah to the mountains of Moab, east of the Dead Sea, in the vicinity of which Sodom and Gomorrah were situated.

125 Cf. 6 : 25. In the present instance, however, the self-confessed lack of understanding on the part of the people of Madyan may have a more subjective meaning, similar to the half-indignant, half-embarrassed retort, "I don't know what you are talking about."

midst:[126] and were it not for thy family, we would have most certainly stoned thee to death, considering that thou hast no power over us!" ‹91›

Said he: "O my people! Do you hold my family in greater esteem than God? – for, Him you regard as something that may be cast behind you and be forgotten![127] Verily, my Sustainer encompasses [with His might] all that you do! ‹92› Hence, O my people, do [to me] anything that may be within your power, [while] I, behold, shall labour [in God's way]; in time you will come to know which [of us] shall be visited by suffering that will cover him with ignominy, and which [of us] is a liar. Watch, then, [for what is coming:] behold, I shall watch with you!" ‹93›

And so, when Our judgment came to pass, by Our grace We saved Shuʿayb and those who shared his faith, whereas the blast [of Our punishment] overtook those who had been bent on evildoing: and then they lay lifeless, in their very homes, on the ground,[128] ‹94› as though they had never lived there.

Oh, away with [the people of] Madyan, even as the Thamūd have been done away with! ‹95›

AND, INDEED, We sent Moses with Our messages and a manifest authority [from Us] ‹96› unto Pharaoh and his great ones: but these followed [only] Pharaoh's bidding – and Pharaoh's bidding led by no means to what is right.[129] ‹97›

وَلَوْلَا رَهْطُكَ لَرَجَمْنَٰكَ وَمَآ أَنتَ عَلَيْنَا بِعَزِيزٍ ﴿٩١﴾ قَالَ يَٰقَوْمِ أَرَهْطِىٓ
أَعَزُّ عَلَيْكُم مِّنَ ٱللَّهِ وَٱتَّخَذْتُمُوهُ وَرَآءَكُمْ ظِهْرِيًّا إِنَّ رَبِّى بِمَا تَعْمَلُونَ
مُحِيطٌ ﴿٩٢﴾ وَيَٰقَوْمِ ٱعْمَلُوا۟ عَلَىٰ مَكَانَتِكُمْ إِنِّى عَٰمِلٌ سَوْفَ تَعْلَمُونَ مَن
يَأْتِيهِ عَذَابٌ يُخْزِيهِ وَمَنْ هُوَ كَٰذِبٌ وَٱرْتَقِبُوٓا۟ إِنِّى مَعَكُمْ رَقِيبٌ ﴿٩٣﴾
وَلَمَّا جَآءَ أَمْرُنَا نَجَّيْنَا شُعَيْبًا وَٱلَّذِينَ ءَامَنُوا۟ مَعَهُۥ بِرَحْمَةٍ مِّنَّا وَأَخَذَتِ
ٱلَّذِينَ ظَلَمُوا۟ ٱلصَّيْحَةُ فَأَصْبَحُوا۟ فِى دِيَٰرِهِمْ جَٰثِمِينَ ﴿٩٤﴾ كَأَن لَّمْ
يَغْنَوْا۟ فِيهَآ أَلَا بُعْدًا لِّمَدْيَنَ كَمَا بَعِدَتْ ثَمُودُ ﴿٩٥﴾ وَلَقَدْ أَرْسَلْنَا مُوسَىٰ
بِـَٔايَٰتِنَا وَسُلْطَٰنٍ مُّبِينٍ ﴿٩٦﴾ إِلَىٰ فِرْعَوْنَ وَمَلَإِي۟هِۦ فَٱتَّبَعُوٓا۟ أَمْرَ فِرْعَوْنَ
وَمَآ أَمْرُ فِرْعَوْنَ بِرَشِيدٍ ﴿٩٧﴾

Wa lawlā rahṭuka larajamnāka wa māa ʾanta ʿalaynā biʿazīz. (91) Qāla yā qawmi ʾarahṭii ʾaʿazzu ʿalaykum-minal-lāh. Wat-takhadhtumūhu warāaʾakum ẓihriyyā. ʾInna Rabbī bimā taʿmalūna Muḥīṭ. (92) Wa yā qawmiʿ-malū ʿalā makānatikum ʾinnī ʿāmil. Sawfa taʿlamūna mañy-yaʾtīhi ʿadhābuñy-yukhzīhi wa man huwa kādhib. War-taqibūu ʾinnī maʿakum raqīb. (93) Wa lammā jāaʾa ʾamrunā najjaynā Shuʿaybañw-wal-ladhīna ʾāmanū maʿahū biraḥmatim-minnā wa ʾakhadhatil-ladhīna ẓalamuṣ-ṣayḥatu faʾaṣbaḥū fī diyārihim jāthimīn. (94) Kaʾal-lam yaghnaw fīhā. ʾAlā buʿdal-liMadyana kamā baʿidat Thamūd. (95) Wa laqad ʾarsalnā Mūsā biʾĀyātinā wa sulṭānim-mubīnin, (96) ʾilā Firʿawna wa malaʾiyhī fattabaʿūu ʾamra Firʿawna wa māa ʾamru Firʿawna birashīd. (97)

126 Lit., "we regard thee indeed as a weak one among us" – i.e., without any appreciable tribal support.

127 In classical Arabic usage, as well as in the speech of certain bedouin tribes to this day, the phrase *ittakhadhahu* (or *jaʿalahu*) *ẓihriyyan* (lit., "he put him behind his back") has the meaning of "he held him in contempt", or "he forgot him", or "regarded him as something that may be forgotten". This last rendering seems to be the most appropriate in the above context.

128 See verse 67 of this *sūrah* and the corresponding note 98; also *sūrah* 7, note 73.

129 Lit., "was not right-guided (*rashīd*)". The short passage dealing with Pharaoh and his followers (verses 96-99) connects with, and amplifies, the reference to the tribe of ʿĀd, who "followed the bidding of every arrogant enemy of the truth" (verse 59 of this *sūrah*). Thus, the main point of this passage is the problem of immoral leadership and, arising from it, the problem of man's individual, moral responsibility for wrongs committed in obedience to a "higher authority". The Qurʾān answers this question emphatically in the affirmative: the leader and the led are equally guilty, and none can be absolved of responsibility on the plea that he was but blindly following orders given by those above him. This indirect allusion to man's relative free will – i.e., his freedom of choice between right and wrong – fittingly concludes the stories of the earlier prophets and their wrongdoing communities as narrated in this *sūrah*.

[And so] he shall go before his people on the Day of Resurrection, having led them [in this world] towards the fire [of the life to come]; and vile was the destination towards which they were led ‹98› – seeing that they were pursued by [God's] rejection in this [world], and [shall be finally overtaken by it] on the Day of Resurrection;[130] [and] vile was the gift which they were given! ‹99›

THIS ACCOUNT[131] of the [fate of those ancient] communities – some of them still remaining, and some [extinct like] a field mown-down – We convey unto thee [as a lesson for mankind]:[132] ‹100› for, no wrong did We do to them, but it was they who wronged themselves. And when thy Sustainer's judgment came to pass, those deities of theirs which they had been wont to invoke instead of God proved of no avail whatever to them, and brought them no more than utter perdition. ‹101›

And such is thy Sustainer's punishing grasp whenever He takes to task any community that is given to evildoing: verily, His punishing grasp is grievous, severe! ‹102›

Herein, behold, lies a message indeed for all who fear the suffering [which may befall them] in the life to come, [and are conscious of the coming of] that Day on which all mankind shall be gathered together – that Day [of Judgment] which shall be witnessed [by all that ever lived], ‹103› which We shall not delay beyond a term set [by Us].[133] ‹104›

When that Day comes, not a soul will speak, unless it be by His leave; and of those [that are gathered together], some will be wretched and some, happy. ‹105›

يَقۡدُمُ قَوۡمَهُۥ يَوۡمَ ٱلۡقِيَٰمَةِ فَأَوۡرَدَهُمُ ٱلنَّارَۖ وَبِئۡسَ ٱلۡوِرۡدُ ٱلۡمَوۡرُودُ (98)
وَأُتۡبِعُواْ فِي هَٰذِهِۦ لَعۡنَةٗ وَيَوۡمَ ٱلۡقِيَٰمَةِۚ بِئۡسَ ٱلرِّفۡدُ ٱلۡمَرۡفُودُ (99) ذَٰلِكَ
مِنۡ أَنۢبَآءِ ٱلۡقُرَىٰ نَقُصُّهُۥ عَلَيۡكَۖ مِنۡهَا قَآئِمٞ وَحَصِيدٞ (100) وَمَا ظَلَمۡنَٰهُمۡ
وَلَٰكِن ظَلَمُوٓاْ أَنفُسَهُمۡۖ فَمَآ أَغۡنَتۡ عَنۡهُمۡ ءَالِهَتُهُمُ ٱلَّتِي يَدۡعُونَ مِن دُونِ
ٱللَّهِ مِن شَيۡءٖ لَّمَّا جَآءَ أَمۡرُ رَبِّكَۖ وَمَا زَادُوهُمۡ غَيۡرَ تَتۡبِيبٖ (101) وَكَذَٰلِكَ
أَخۡذُ رَبِّكَ إِذَآ أَخَذَ ٱلۡقُرَىٰ وَهِيَ ظَٰلِمَةٌۚ إِنَّ أَخۡذَهُۥٓ أَلِيمٞ شَدِيدٌ (102) إِنَّ
فِي ذَٰلِكَ لَأٓيَةٗ لِّمَنۡ خَافَ عَذَابَ ٱلۡأٓخِرَةِۚ ذَٰلِكَ يَوۡمٞ مَّجۡمُوعٞ لَّهُ ٱلنَّاسُ
وَذَٰلِكَ يَوۡمٞ مَّشۡهُودٞ (103) وَمَا نُؤَخِّرُهُۥٓ إِلَّا لِأَجَلٖ مَّعۡدُودٖ (104) يَوۡمَ يَأۡتِ
لَا تَكَلَّمُ نَفۡسٌ إِلَّا بِإِذۡنِهِۦۚ فَمِنۡهُمۡ شَقِيّٞ وَسَعِيدٞ (105)

Yaqdumu qawmahū Yawmal-Qiyāmati faʾawradahumun-nāra wa biʾsal-wirdul-mawrūd. (98) Wa ʾutbiʿū fī hādhihī laʿnatañw-wa Yawmal-Qiyāmati biʾsar-rifdul-marfūd. (99) Dhālika min ʾambāaʾil-qurā naquṣṣuhū ʿalayka minhā qāaʾimuñw-wa ḥaṣīd. (100) Wa mā ẓalamnāhum wa lākiñ-ẓalamūu ʾañfusahum. Famāa ʾaghnat ʿanhum ʾālihatuhumul-latī yadʿūna miñ-dūnil-lāhi miñ-shayʾil-lammā jāaʾa ʾamru Rabbik wa mā zādūhum ghayra tatbīb. (101) Wa kadhālika ʾakhdhu Rabbika ʾidhāa ʾakhadhal-qurā wa hiya ẓālimah. ʾInna ʾakhdhahūu ʾalīmuñ-shadīd. (102) ʾInna fī dhālika laʾāyatal-liman khāfa ʿadhābal-ʾĀkhirah. Dhālika Yawmum-majmūʿul-lahun-nāsu wa dhālika Yawmum-mashhūd. (103) Wa mā nuʾakhkhiruhūu ʾillā liʾajalim-maʿdūd. (104) Yawma yaʾti lā takallamu nafsun ʾillā biʾidhnihī faminhum shaqiyyuñw-wa saʿīd. (105)

130 See note 37 on the last clause of verse 18 of this *sūrah*, as well as verse 60, which refers in identical terms to the destiny of the tribe of ʿĀd .

131 Lit., "This of the accounts" (a construction identical with that employed in 3 : 44, 11 : 49 and 12 : 102), alluding to the fact that only certain aspects of the relevant stories, and not the complete stories as such, are presented here (cf. verse 120 below): the purpose being, as always in the Qurʾān, the illustration of an ethical principle or principles, and of men's varying reactions to the guidance which God offers them directly through His prophets and indirectly through the observable phenomena of His creation. (See in this connection the second part of note 73 on verse 49 of this *sūrah*.)

132 See preceding note.

133 Lit., "except till a term computed [by Us]".

فَأَمَّا ٱلَّذِينَ شَقُواْ فَفِى ٱلنَّارِ لَهُمْ فِيهَا زَفِيرٌ وَشَهِيقٌ ﴿106﴾ خَـٰلِدِينَ فِيهَا مَا دَامَتِ
ٱلسَّمَـٰوَٰتُ وَٱلْأَرْضُ إِلَّا مَا شَآءَ رَبُّكَ ۚ إِنَّ رَبَّكَ فَعَّالٌ لِّمَا يُرِيدُ ﴿107﴾ ۞ وَأَمَّا
ٱلَّذِينَ سُعِدُواْ فَفِى ٱلْجَنَّةِ خَـٰلِدِينَ فِيهَا مَا دَامَتِ ٱلسَّمَـٰوَٰتُ وَٱلْأَرْضُ إِلَّا مَا
شَآءَ رَبُّكَ ۖ عَطَآءً غَيْرَ مَجْذُوذٍ ﴿108﴾ فَلَا تَكُ فِى مِرْيَةٍ مِّمَّا يَعْبُدُ هَـٰٓؤُلَآءِ ۚ مَا
يَعْبُدُونَ إِلَّا كَمَا يَعْبُدُ ءَابَآؤُهُم مِّن قَبْلُ ۚ وَإِنَّا لَمُوَفُّوهُمْ نَصِيبَهُمْ غَيْرَ
مَنقُوصٍ ﴿109﴾ وَلَقَدْ ءَاتَيْنَا مُوسَى ٱلْكِتَـٰبَ فَٱخْتُلِفَ فِيهِ ۚ وَلَوْلَا كَلِمَةٌ سَبَقَتْ

**Faʾammal-ladhīna shaqū fafin-nāri lahum fīhā
zafīruñw-wa shahīq. ﴿106﴾ Khālidīna fīhā mā
dāmatis-samāwātu wal-ʾarḍu ʾillā mā shāaʾa
Rabbuk. ʾInna Rabbaka faᶜᶜālul-limā yurīd. ﴿107﴾ ۞
Wa ʾammal-ladhīna suᶜidū fafil-jannati khālidīna
fīhā mā dāmatis-samāwātu wal-ʾarḍu ʾillā mā
shāaʾa Rabbuka ᶜaṭāaʾan ghayra majdhūdh. ﴿108﴾
Falā taku fī miryatim-mimmā yaᶜbudu hāaʾulāaʾ.
Mā yaᶜbudūna ʾillā kamā yaᶜbudu ʾābāaʾuhum-
miñ-qabl. Wa ʾinnā lamuwaffūhum naṣībahum
ghayra mañqūṣ. ﴿109﴾ Wa laqad ʾātaynā Mūsal-Kitāba
fakhtulifa fīh. Wa lawlā kalimatuñ-sabaqat**

ربع الحزب

Now as for those who [by their deeds] will have brought wretchedness upon themselves, [they shall live] in the fire, where they will have [nothing but] moans and sobs [to relieve their pain], ‹106› therein to abide as long as the heavens and the earth endure – unless thy Sustainer wills it otherwise:[134] for, verily, thy Sustainer is a sovereign doer of whatever He wills. ‹107› But as for those who [by virtue of their past deeds] will have been blest with happiness, [they shall live] in paradise, therein to abide as long as the heavens and the earth endure – unless thy Sustainer wills it otherwise[135] – as a gift unceasing. ‹108›

AND SO, [O Prophet,] be not in doubt about anything that those [misguided people] worship:[136] they but [thoughtlessly] worship as their forefathers worshipped aforetime; and, behold, We shall most certainly give them their full due [for whatever good or evil they have earned], without diminishing aught thereof.[137] ‹109›

And, indeed, [similar was the case when] We vouchsafed the divine writ unto Moses, and some of his people set their own views against it;[138] and had it not been for a decree that had already gone forth

134 I.e., unless God wills to reprieve them (cf. the last paragraph of 6 : 128 and the corresponding note 114, as well as note 10 on 40 : 12). The phrase "as long as the heavens and the earth endure" has caused some perplexity to most of the classical commentators in view of the many Qurʾanic statements to the effect that the world as we know it will come to an end on the Last Day, which is synonymous with the Day of Resurrection. This difficulty, however, can be resolved if we remember – as Ṭabarī points out in his commentary on the above verse – that in ancient Arabic usage the expressions "as long as the heavens and the earth endure", or "as long as night and day alternate", etc., were used metonymically in the sense of "time beyond count" (*abad*). See also 20 : 105-107 and the corresponding note 90, as well as note 63 on 14 : 48.

135 I.e., unless God wills to bestow on them a yet greater reward (Rāzī; also *Manār* XII, 161); or – which to my mind is more probable – unless He opens up to man a new, yet higher stage of evolution.

136 I.e., "do not think that their beliefs are based on reason": a reference, primarily, to the pagan Arabs who – like the wrongdoers spoken of in the preceding passages – rejected God's message on the plea that it conflicted with their ancestral beliefs; and, more generally, to all people who are accustomed to worship (in the widest sense of this word) false values handed down from their ancestors and who, consequently, observe false standards of morality: an attitude which must unavoidably – as the last sentence of this verse shows – result in future suffering, be it in this world or in the hereafter, or in both.

137 Lit., "We shall repay them their portion in full, undiminished". For an explanation of this sentence, see note 27 on verses 15-16 of this *sūrah*.

138 Lit., "and it was disagreed upon", or "discordant views came to be held about it": meaning that, like Muḥammad's early contemporaries, some of Moses' people accepted the divine writ, whereas others refused to submit to its guidance.

from thy Sustainer, judgment would indeed have been passed on them [then and there]:[139] for, behold, they were in grave doubt, amounting to suspicion, about him [who called them unto God].[140] ‹110›

And, verily, unto each and all will thy Sustainer give their full due for whatever [good or evil] they may have done: behold, He is aware of all that they do! ‹111›

Pursue, then, the right course, as thou hast been bidden [by God], together with all who, with thee, have turned unto Him; and let none of you behave in an overweening manner:[141] for, verily, He sees all that you do. ‹112›

And do not incline towards, nor rely upon, those who are bent on evildoing[142] lest the fire [of the hereafter] touch you: for [then] you would have none to protect you from God, nor would you ever be succoured [by Him].[143] ‹113›

And be constant in praying at the beginning and the end[144] of the day, as well as during the early watches of the night:[145] for, verily, good deeds drive away evil deeds: this is a reminder to all who bear [God] in mind. ‹114›

And be patient in adversity: for, verily, God does not fail to requite the doers of good! ‹115›

مِن رَّبِّكَ لَقُضِيَ بَيْنَهُمْ وَإِنَّهُمْ لَفِى شَكٍّ مِّنْهُ مُرِيبٍ ﴿١١٠﴾ وَإِنَّ كُلًّا لَّمَّا
لَيُوَفِّيَنَّهُمْ رَبُّكَ أَعْمَـٰلَهُمْ إِنَّهُۥ بِمَا يَعْمَلُونَ خَبِيرٌ ﴿١١١﴾ فَٱسْتَقِمْ كَمَآ
أُمِرْتَ وَمَن تَابَ مَعَكَ وَلَا تَطْغَوْا۟ إِنَّهُۥ بِمَا تَعْمَلُونَ بَصِيرٌ ﴿١١٢﴾ وَلَا
تَرْكَنُوٓا۟ إِلَى ٱلَّذِينَ ظَلَمُوا۟ فَتَمَسَّكُمُ ٱلنَّارُ وَمَا لَكُم مِّن دُونِ ٱللَّهِ مِنْ
أَوْلِيَآءَ ثُمَّ لَا تُنصَرُونَ ﴿١١٣﴾ وَأَقِمِ ٱلصَّلَوٰةَ طَرَفَىِ ٱلنَّهَارِ وَزُلَفًا مِّنَ
ٱلَّيْلِ إِنَّ ٱلْحَسَنَـٰتِ يُذْهِبْنَ ٱلسَّيِّـَٔاتِ ذَٰلِكَ ذِكْرَىٰ لِلذَّٰكِرِينَ ﴿١١٤﴾
وَٱصْبِرْ فَإِنَّ ٱللَّهَ لَا يُضِيعُ أَجْرَ ٱلْمُحْسِنِينَ ﴿١١٥﴾

mir-Rabbika laquḍiya baynahum. Wa ʾinnahum lafī shakkim-minhu murīb. (110) Wa ʾinna kullal-lammā layuwaffiyannahum Rabbuka ʾaʿmālahum. ʾInnahū bimā yaʿmalūna Khabīr. (111) Fastaqim kamāa ʾumirta wa mañ-tāba maʿaka wa lā taṭghaw. ʾInnahū bimā taʿmalūna Baṣīr. (112) Wa lā tarkanūu ʾilal-ladhīna ẓalamū fatamassakumun-nāru wa mā lakum-miñ-dūnil-lāhi min ʾawliyāaʾa thumma lā tuñṣarūn. (113) Wa ʾaqimiṣ-Ṣalāta ṭarafayin-nahāri wa zulafam-minal-layl. ʾInnal-ḥasanāti yudhhibnas-sayyiʾāt. Dhālika dhikrā lidhdhākirīn. (114) Waṣ-bir faʾinnal-lāha lā yuḍīʿu ʾajral-muḥsinīn. (115)

139 Lit., "it would indeed have been decided between them" – i.e., they would have been punished, like those communities of old, by utter destruction, had it not been for God's decree (*kalimah*, lit., "word") that their punishment should be deferred until the Day of Resurrection (cf. the last sentence of 10 : 93 and the corresponding note 114).

140 Cf. 2 : 55 – "O Moses, indeed we shall not believe thee until we see God face to face!"

141 Explaining this injunction, expressed in the second person plural, Ibn Kathīr points out that it is addressed to all believers, and that it refers to their behaviour towards everyone, be he believer or unbeliever; in this he obviously relies on the interpretation advanced by Ibn ʿAbbās (and quoted by Rāzī): "It means, 'Be humble before God and do not behave with false pride towards anyone'." According to some later commentators (e.g., Ṭabarī, Zamakhsharī, Baghawī, Rāzī), the meaning is wider, namely, "do not overstep the bounds of what God has ordained", or "do not exceed the limits of equity".

142 The verb *rakana* comprises the concepts of inclining (in one's feelings or opinions) towards, as well as of relying on, someone or something, and cannot be translated by a single word; hence my composite rendering of the phrase *lā tarkanū*. The use of the past tense in *alladhīna ẓalamū* indicates – as is often the case in the Qurʾān – deliberate and persistent evildoing; this term is, therefore, suitably rendered as "those who are bent on evildoing".

143 According to Zamakhsharī, the particle *thumma* at the beginning of this last clause does not signify a sequence in time ("and then" or "afterwards") but, rather, a stress on the impossibility (*istibʿād*) of their ever being succoured by God.

144 Lit., "at the two ends".

145 This injunction circumscribes all the obligatory prayers without specifying either their form or the exact times of their performance, both of which are clearly laid down in the *sunnah* (i.e., the authenticated sayings and the practice) of the Prophet: namely, at dawn (*fajr*), shortly after mid-day (*ẓuhr*), in the afternoon (*ʿasr*), immediately

BUT, ALAS, among those generations [whom We destroyed] before your time there were no people endowed with any virtue[146] – [people] who would speak out against the [spread of] corruption on earth – except the few of them whom We saved [because of their righteousness], whereas those who were bent on evildoing only pursued pleasures which corrupted their whole being,[147] and so lost themselves in sinning. ‹116›
For, never would thy Sustainer destroy a community[148] for wrong [beliefs alone] so long as its people behave righteously [towards one another].[149] ‹117›
And had thy Sustainer so willed, He could surely have made all mankind one single community: but [He willed it otherwise, and so] they continue to hold divergent views[150] ‹118› – [all of them,]

فَلَوْلَا كَانَ مِنَ ٱلْقُرُونِ مِن قَبْلِكُمْ أُوْلُواْ بَقِيَّةٍ يَنْهَوْنَ عَنِ ٱلْفَسَادِ فِي
ٱلْأَرْضِ إِلَّا قَلِيلًا مِّمَّنْ أَنجَيْنَا مِنْهُمْ ۗ وَٱتَّبَعَ ٱلَّذِينَ ظَلَمُواْ مَآ أُتْرِفُواْ فِيهِ
وَكَانُواْ مُجْرِمِينَ ﴿١١٦﴾ وَمَا كَانَ رَبُّكَ لِيُهْلِكَ ٱلْقُرَىٰ بِظُلْمٍ وَأَهْلُهَا
مُصْلِحُونَ ﴿١١٧﴾ وَلَوْ شَآءَ رَبُّكَ لَجَعَلَ ٱلنَّاسَ أُمَّةً وَٰحِدَةً ۖ وَلَا يَزَالُونَ
مُخْتَلِفِينَ ﴿١١٨﴾

Falawlā kāna minal-qurūni miñ-qablikum ᵓulū baqiyyatiñy-yanhawna ᶜanil-fasādi fil-ᵓarḍi ᵓillā qalīlam-mimman ᵓañjaynā minhum. Wat-tabaᶜal-ladhīna ẓalamū māa ᵓutrifū fīhi wa kānū mujrimīn. (116) Wa mā kāna Rabbuka liyuhlikal-qurā biẓulmiñw-wa ᵓahluhā muṣliḥūn. (117) Wa law shāaᵓa Rabbuka lajaᶜalan-nāsa ᵓummatañw-wāḥidatañw-wa lā yazālūna mukhtalifīn. (118)

---

after sunset (*maghrib*), and in the first part of the night (*ᶜishāᵓ*). Inasmuch as the above verse stresses the paramount importance of prayer in general, it is safe to assume that it refers not merely to the five obligatory prayers but to a remembrance of God at all times of one's wakeful life.

146 For my rendering of the particle *law-lā*, at the beginning of this sentence, as "alas", see *sūrah* 10, note 119. The present passage connects with the statement in the preceding verse, "God does not fail to requite the doers of good", as well as with verse 111 above, "unto each and all will thy Sustainer give their due for whatever [good or evil] they may have done". – For the wider implications of the term *qarn* ("generation"), see *sūrah* 6, note 5.

147 The verb *tarifa* means "he enjoyed a life of ease and plenty", while the participle *mutraf* denotes "one who enjoys a life of ease and plenty" or "indulges in the pleasures of life", i.e., to the exclusion of moral considerations. The form *mutarraf* has an additional significance, namely, "one whom a life of softness and ease has caused to behave insolently", or "one whom the [exclusive] pursuit of the pleasures of life has corrupted" (*Mughnī*). Hence my above rendering of the phrase *mā utrifū fīhi.*

148 See *sūrah* 6, note 116.

149 This passage connects with the concluding clause of the preceding verse, "and lost themselves in sinning". According to most of the classical commentators, the term *ẓulm* (lit., "wrong" or "evildoing") is in this context synonymous with "wrong beliefs" amounting to a denial of the truths revealed by God through His prophets, a refusal to acknowledge His existence, or the ascribing of divine powers or qualities to anyone or anything beside Him. Explaining the above verse in this sense, Rāzī says: "God's chastisement does not afflict any people merely on account of their holding beliefs amounting to *shirk* and *kufr*, but afflicts them only if they persistently commit evil in their mutual dealings, and deliberately hurt [other human beings] and act tyranically [towards them]. Hence, those who are learned in Islamic Law (*al-fuqahāᵓ*) hold that men's obligations towards God rest on the principle of [His] forgiveness and liberality, whereas the rights of man are of a stringent nature and must always be strictly observed" – the obvious reason being that God is almighty and needs no defender, whereas man is weak and needs protection. (Cf. the last sentence of 28 : 59 and the corresponding note 61.)

150 I.e., about everything, even about the truths revealed to them by God. – For a discussion of the term *ummah wāḥidah* ("one single community") and its wider implications, see *sūrah* 2, notes 197 and 198; the second part of 2 : 253 and the corresponding note 245; and the second part of 5 : 48 and the corresponding notes 66 and 67. Thus, the Qurᵓān stresses once again that the unceasing differentiation in men's views and ideas is not incidental but represents a God-willed, basic factor of human existence. If God had willed that all human beings should be of one persuasion, all intellectual progress would have been ruled out, and "they would have been similar in their social life to the bees and the ants, while in their spiritual life they would have been like the angels, *constrained* by their nature always to believe in what is true and always to obey God" (*Manār* XII, 193) – that is to say, devoid of that relative free will which enables man to choose between right and wrong and thus endows his life – in distinction from all other sentient beings – with a moral meaning and a unique spiritual potential.

save those upon whom thy Sustainer has bestowed His grace.[151]
And to this end has He created them [all].[152]
But [as for those who refuse to avail themselves of divine guidance,] that word of thy Sustainer shall be fulfilled: "Most certainly will I fill hell with invisible beings as well as with humans, all together!"[153] ‹119›

AND [remember:] out of all the accounts relating to the [earlier] apostles We convey unto thee [only] that wherewith We [aim to] make firm thy heart:[154] for through these [accounts] comes the truth unto thee, as well as an admonition and a reminder unto all believers. ‹120›
And say unto those who will not believe: "Do anything that may be within your power, [while] we, behold, shall labour [in God's way]; ‹121› and wait [for what is coming]: behold, we too are waiting!" ‹122›
And God alone comprehends the hidden reality of the heavens and the earth:[155] for, all that exists goes back to Him [as its source].
Worship Him, then, and place thy trust in Him alone: for thy Sustainer is not unaware of what you do. ‹123›

إِلَّا مَن رَّحِمَ رَبُّكَ وَلِذَٰلِكَ خَلَقَهُمْ وَتَمَّتْ كَلِمَةُ رَبِّكَ لَأَمْلَأَنَّ جَهَنَّمَ
مِنَ ٱلْجِنَّةِ وَٱلنَّاسِ أَجْمَعِينَ ﴿119﴾ وَكُلًّا نَّقُصُّ عَلَيْكَ مِنْ أَنۢبَآءِ ٱلرُّسُلِ
مَا نُثَبِّتُ بِهِۦ فُؤَادَكَ وَجَآءَكَ فِى هَٰذِهِ ٱلْحَقُّ وَمَوْعِظَةٌ وَذِكْرَىٰ
لِلْمُؤْمِنِينَ ﴿120﴾ وَقُل لِّلَّذِينَ لَا يُؤْمِنُونَ ٱعْمَلُوا۟ عَلَىٰ مَكَانَتِكُمْ إِنَّا
عَٰمِلُونَ ﴿121﴾ وَٱنتَظِرُوٓا۟ إِنَّا مُنتَظِرُونَ ﴿122﴾ وَلِلَّهِ غَيْبُ ٱلسَّمَٰوَٰتِ
وَٱلْأَرْضِ وَإِلَيْهِ يُرْجَعُ ٱلْأَمْرُ كُلُّهُۥ فَٱعْبُدْهُ وَتَوَكَّلْ عَلَيْهِ وَمَا رَبُّكَ
بِغَٰفِلٍ عَمَّا تَعْمَلُونَ ﴿123﴾

ʾIllā mar-raḥima Rabbuka wa lidhālika khalaqahum. Wa tammat Kalimatu Rabbika laʾamlaʾanna jahannama minal-Jinnati wan-nāsi ʾajmaᶜīn. ﴿119﴾ Wa kullan-naquṣṣu ᶜalayka min ambāaʾir-Rusuli mā nuthabbitu bihī fuʾādak. Wa jāaʾaka fī hādhihil-ḥaqqu wa mawᶜiẓatuñw-wa dhikrā lilmuʾminīn. ﴿120﴾ Wa qul lilladhīna lā yuʾminūnaᶜ-malū ᶜalā makānatikum ʾinnā ᶜāmilūn. ﴿121﴾ Wañ-taẓirūu ʾinnā muñtaẓirūn. ﴿122﴾ Wa lillāhi ghaybus-samāwāti wal-ʾarḍi wa ʾilayhi yurjaul-ʾamru kulluhū faᶜbud-hu wa tawakkal ᶜalayh. Wa mā Rabbuka bighāfilin ᶜammā taᶜmalūn. ﴿123﴾

151 I.e., those who *avail themselves* of His grace, consisting of the God-given ability to realize His existence (cf. 7 : 172 and the corresponding note 139) and the guidance which He offers to mankind through His prophets (Rāzī).

152 Some of the earliest commentators (e.g., Mujāhid and ᶜIkrimah) are of the opinion that the expression *li-dhālika* (rendered by me as "to this end") refers to God's bestowal of His grace upon man, while others (e.g., Al-Ḥasan and ᶜAṭāʾ) relate it to men's ability to differ intellectually from one another. According to Zamakhsharī, it refers to the freedom of moral choice which characterizes man and is spoken of in the preceding passages: and since it is this freedom which constitutes God's special gift to man and raises him above all other created beings (cf. the parable of Adam and the angels in 2 : 30-34), Zamakhsharī's interpretation is, in my opinion, the most comprehensive of all.

153 The "word of God" reiterated here as well as in 32 : 13 has originally been pronounced in 7 : 18 with reference to the "followers of Satan", i.e., those who reject the guidance offered them by God; hence my interpolation at the beginning of the paragraph. As regards the meaning of *jinn* (rendered by me in this and similar instances as "invisible beings"), see Appendix III.

154 I.e., the Qurʾān does not intend to present those stories as such, but uses them (or, rather, relevant parts of them) as illustrations of moral truths and as a means to strengthen the faith of the believer (see the second part of note 73 as well as note 131 above).

155 Lit., "God's is [the knowledge of] the hidden reality of . . .", etc. For this meaning of the term *al-ghayb*, see note 3 on 2 : 3.

The Twelfth Sūrah
Yūsuf (Joseph)
Mecca Period

ACCORDING to all the authoritative sources, this *sūrah* was revealed in its entirety in Mecca, almost immediately after the preceding one. The contention of some of the early commentators that the first three verses were revealed at Medina is, in the words of Suyūṭī, "entirely baseless and cannot be seriously considered".

The story of the Prophet Joseph, as narrated in the Qur᾽ān, agrees in the main, but not completely, with the Biblical version (Genesis xxxvii and xxxix-xlvi); the more important differences between the two accounts are pointed out in my notes. But what distinguishes the Qur᾽anic treatment of the story in a deeper sense is its spiritual tenor: contrary to the Bible, in which the life of Joseph is presented as a romantic account of the envy to which his youthful innocence is first exposed, of the vicissitudes which he subsequently suffers, and, finally, of his worldly triumph over his brothers, the Qur᾽ān uses it primarily as an illustration of God's unfathomable direction of men's affairs – an echo of the statement that "it may well be that you hate a thing the while it is good for you, and it may well be that you love a thing the while it is bad for you: and God knows, whereas you do not know" (2 : 216). The whole of this *sūrah* might be described as a series of variations on the theme "judgment [as to what is to happen] rests with none but God", explicitly enunciated only in verse 67, but running like an unspoken *leitmotif* throughout the story of Joseph.

-12-

سورة يوسف مكية
وآياتها إحدى عشرة ومائة

IN THE NAME OF GOD, THE MOST GRACIOUS, THE DISPENSER OF GRACE:

Alif. Lām. Rā.[1]
THESE ARE MESSAGES of a revelation clear in itself and clearly showing the truth:[2] ‹1› behold, We have bestowed it from on high as a discourse in the Arabic tongue, so that you might encompass it with your reason.[3] ‹2›
In the measure that We reveal[4] this Qurʾān unto thee, [O Prophet,] We explain it to thee in the best possible way,[5] seeing that ere this thou wert indeed among those who are unaware [of what revelation is].[6] ‹3›

بِسۡمِ ٱللَّهِ ٱلرَّحۡمَٰنِ ٱلرَّحِيمِ

الٓرۚ تِلۡكَ ءَايَٰتُ ٱلۡكِتَٰبِ ٱلۡمُبِينِ ١ إِنَّآ أَنزَلۡنَٰهُ قُرۡءَٰنًا عَرَبِيّٗا
لَّعَلَّكُمۡ تَعۡقِلُونَ ٢ نَحۡنُ نَقُصُّ عَلَيۡكَ أَحۡسَنَ ٱلۡقَصَصِ بِمَآ أَوۡحَيۡنَآ
إِلَيۡكَ هَٰذَا ٱلۡقُرۡءَانَ وَإِن كُنتَ مِن قَبۡلِهِۦ لَمِنَ ٱلۡغَٰفِلِينَ ٣

Bismil-lāhir-Raḥmānir-Raḥīm.
ʾAlif-Lāam-Rā. Tilka ʾĀyātul-Kitābil-mubīn. (1) ʾInnāa ʾañzalnāhu Qurʾānan ʿarabiyyal-laʿallakum taʿqilūn. (2) Naḥnu naquṣṣu ʿalayka ʾaḥsanal-qaṣaṣi bimāa ʾawḥaynāa ʾilayka hādhal-Qurʾāna wa ʾiñ-kuñta miñ-qablihī laminal-ghāfilīn. (3)

---

1 See Appendix II.

2 The participial adjective *mubīn* may denote an attribute of the noun which it qualifies ("clear", "manifest", "obvious", etc.) as well as its function ("making clear" or "manifesting", i.e., the truth), either of which meanings is dictated by its context. In the consensus of authoritative opinion, both these meanings are comprised in the above instance; consequently, a compound phrase is necessary in order to render the term appropriately.

3 This, according to Zamakhsharī, is the meaning of *laʿallakum taʿqilūn* in the above context. Although they were in the first instance addressed to the Arabian contemporaries of the Prophet, these two verses apply to all people, whatever their origin, who understand the Arabic language. They are meant to impress upon everyone who listens to or reads the Qurʾān that its appeal is directed, primarily, to man's *reason*, and that "feeling" alone can never provide a sufficient basis of faith. (See also 13 : 37 and 14 : 4, as well as the corresponding notes.)

4 Or: "By Our having revealed".

5 Lit., "with the best explanation (*aḥsan al-qaṣāṣ*)". This rendering is very close to the interpretation given by Zamakhsharī: "We set forth this Qurʾān unto thee in the best way in which it could be set forth." According to Rāzī, it may safely be assumed that the adjective "best" refers not to the *contents* of "that which is set forth" – i.e., the particular story narrated in this *sūrah* – but rather to the *manner* in which the Qurʾān (or this particular *sūrah*) is set forth: and herein he agrees with Zamakhsharī. It should be borne in mind that the verb *qaṣṣa* (the infinitive nouns of which are *qaṣaṣ* and *iqtiṣāṣ*) signifies, primarily, "he followed step by step" or "by degrees", and, subsequently, "he related [a piece of news or a story] as though he followed its traces": hence, "he expounded [it] gradually" or "he explained [it]" (cf. Lane VII, 2526, quoting the *Qāmūs* and the *Tāj al-ʿArūs* with specific reference to the above verse). If, on the other hand, the infinitive noun *qaṣaṣ* is regarded as synonymous, in this context, with *qiṣṣah* ("story" or "narrative"), the above sentence might be rendered as "We narrate unto thee the best of narratives", i.e., the subsequent story of Joseph. In my opinion, however, the rendering "We explain it [i.e., the Qurʾān] in the best possible way" is preferable inasmuch as it fully coincides with the two opening verses of this *sūrah*, which state, in effect, that the Qurʾān is self-explanatory.

6 At this point in his commentary, Rāzī draws the reader's attention to 42 : 52 – "thou didst not know what revelation is, nor what faith [implies]": a passage similar in purport to the closing words of the above verse; hence my addition, between brackets, of the phrase "of what revelation is".

إِذْ قَالَ يُوسُفُ لِأَبِيهِ يَٰٓأَبَتِ إِنِّى رَأَيْتُ أَحَدَ عَشَرَ كَوْكَبًا وَٱلشَّمْسَ
وَٱلْقَمَرَ رَأَيْتُهُمْ لِى سَٰجِدِينَ ﴿٤﴾ قَالَ يَٰبُنَىَّ لَا تَقْصُصْ رُءْيَاكَ عَلَىٰٓ
إِخْوَتِكَ فَيَكِيدُوا۟ لَكَ كَيْدًا ۖ إِنَّ ٱلشَّيْطَٰنَ لِلْإِنسَٰنِ عَدُوٌّ مُّبِينٌ ﴿٥﴾
وَكَذَٰلِكَ يَجْتَبِيكَ رَبُّكَ وَيُعَلِّمُكَ مِن تَأْوِيلِ ٱلْأَحَادِيثِ وَيُتِمُّ نِعْمَتَهُۥ
عَلَيْكَ وَعَلَىٰٓ ءَالِ يَعْقُوبَ كَمَآ أَتَمَّهَا عَلَىٰٓ أَبَوَيْكَ مِن قَبْلُ إِبْرَٰهِيمَ
وَإِسْحَٰقَ ۚ إِنَّ رَبَّكَ عَلِيمٌ حَكِيمٌ ﴿٦﴾ ۞ لَّقَدْ كَانَ فِى يُوسُفَ وَإِخْوَتِهِۦٓ
ءَايَٰتٌ لِّلسَّآئِلِينَ ﴿٧﴾ إِذْ قَالُوا۟ لَيُوسُفُ وَأَخُوهُ أَحَبُّ إِلَىٰٓ أَبِينَا مِنَّا
وَنَحْنُ عُصْبَةٌ إِنَّ أَبَانَا لَفِى ضَلَٰلٍ مُّبِينٍ ﴿٨﴾

نصف الحزب

ʾIdh qāla Yūsufu liʾabīhi yāa ʾabati ʾinnī raʾaytu ʾaḥada ʿashara kawkabañw-wash-shamsa wal-qamara raʾaytuhum lī sājidīn. (4) Qāla yā bunayya lā taqṣuṣ ruʾyāka ʿalāa ʾikhwatika fayakīdū laka kaydā. ʾInnash-Shayṭāna lilʾIñsāni ʿaduwwum-mubīn. (5) Wa kadhālika yajtabīka Rabbuka wa yuʿallimuka miñ-taʾwīlil-ʾaḥādīthi wa yutimmu niʿmatahū ʿalayka wa ʿalā ʾāli Yaʿqūba kamāa ʾatammahā ʿalāa ʾabawayka miñ-qablu ʾIbrāhīma wa ʾIsḥāq. ʾInna Rabbaka ʿAlīmun Ḥakīm. (6) ۞ Laqad kāna fī Yūsufa wa ʾikhwatihīi ʾĀyātul-lissāaʾilīn. (7) ʾIdh qālū laYūsufu wa ʾakhūhu ʾaḥabbu ʾilāa ʾabīnā minnā wa naḥnu ʿuṣbatun ʾinna ʾabānā lafī ḍalālim-mubīn. (8)

LO![7] Thus spoke Joseph unto his father: "O my father! Behold, I saw [in a dream] eleven stars, as well as the sun and the moon: I saw them prostrate themselves before me!" ‹4›

[Jacob] replied: "O my dear son![8] Do not relate thy dream to thy brothers lest [out of envy] they devise an evil scheme against thee; verily, Satan is man's open foe![9] ‹5›

For, [as thou hast been shown in thy dream,] even thus will thy Sustainer elect thee, and will impart unto thee some understanding of the inner meaning of happenings,[10] and will bestow the full measure of His blessings upon thee and upon the House of Jacob – even as, aforetime, He bestowed it in full measure upon thy forefathers Abraham and Isaac. Verily, thy Sustainer is all-knowing, wise!" ‹6›

Indeed, in [the story of] Joseph and his brothers there are messages for all who search [after truth].[11] ‹7›

NOW [Joseph's brothers] spoke [thus to one another:] "Truly, Joseph and his brother [Benjamin] are dearer to our father than we, even though we are so many.[12] Behold, our father is surely suffering from an aberration!"[13] ‹8›

7 The particle *idh* is usually a time-reference, and can in most cases be translated as "when". Occasionally, however, it is used as a corroborative particle meant to draw the reader's (or hearer's) attention to the sudden occurrence of a thing (*Mughnī, Qāmūs, Tāj al-ʿArūs*), or – as is often the case in the Qurʾān – to a turn in the discourse: and in such instances it is suitably rendered as "lo" or "now".

8 See *sūrah* 11, note 65.

9 As in the Biblical account of Joseph's story, the Qurʾān shows that Jacob did not fail to understand the meaning of his son's dream-vision of future greatness, with the eleven stars symbolizing his brothers, and the sun and the moon his parents. But whereas the Bible quotes the father as "rebuking" his son (Genesis xxxvii, 10) in the obvious assumption that the dream was an outcome of wishful thinking, the Qurʾān makes it clear that Jacob – who was himself a prophet – at once realized its prophetic quality and its deeper implications.

10 Lit., "sayings" or "tidings" (*aḥādīth*). Most of the commentators assume that this refers specifically to Joseph's future ability to interpret dreams; but Rāzī points out that in this context the term *ḥadīth* (of which (*aḥādīth* is the plural) may be synonymous with *ḥādith* ("something that newly comes into existence", i.e., "an event" or "a happening"). This is, to my mind, much more convincing than a mere reference to dream-interpretation, the more so as the term *taʾwīl* is often used in the Qurʾān (e.g., in 3 : 7, 10 : 39 or 18 : 78) in the sense of "final meaning", "inner meaning" or "real meaning" of a happening or statement or thing, as distinct from its outward, *prima-facie* appearance. The use of the particle *min* ("of") before the term *taʾwīl* indicates that *absolute* knowledge of what a thing or event implies rests with God alone (cf. 3 : 7 – "none save God knows its final meaning"), and that even God's elect, the prophets – albeit their vision is much wider than that of ordinary men – are granted only a partial insight into the mysteries of God's creation.

11 Lit., "those who inquire".

12 Lit., "a company" or "group". Benjamin was Joseph's full brother – both being sons of Jacob's wife Rachel – whereas the other ten were only his half-brothers.

13 Lit., "is in most obvious error".

[Said one of them:] "Slay Joseph, or else drive him away to some [faraway] land, so that your father's regard may be for you alone: and after this is done, you will be [free to repent and to live once again as] righteous people!"[14] ‹9›
Another of them said: "Do not slay Joseph, but rather – if you must do something – cast him into the dark depths of this well, [whence] some caravan may pick him up."[15] ‹10›
[On this they agreed; and thereupon] they spoke [thus to their father]: "O our father! Wherefore wilt thou not trust us with Joseph, seeing that we are indeed his well-wishers? ‹11› Let him go out with us tomorrow, that he may enjoy himself and play: and, verily, we shall guard him well!" ‹12›
[Jacob] answered: "Behold, it grieves me indeed [to think] that you might take him with you, for I dread lest the wolf devour him at a moment when you are heedless of him!" ‹13›
Said they: "Surely, if the wolf were to devour him notwithstanding that we are so many – then, behold, we ought ourselves to perish!" ‹14›
And so, when they went away with him, they decided to cast him into the dark depths of the well.
And We revealed [this] unto him: "Thou wilt yet remind them of this their deed at a time when they shall not perceive [who thou art]!"[16] ‹15› And at nightfall they came to their father, weeping, ‹16› [and] said: "O our father! Behold, we went off racing with one another, and left Joseph behind with our things; and thereupon the wolf devoured him! But [we know that] thou wouldst not believe us even though we speak the truth" ‹17› –

ٱقْتُلُوا۟ يُوسُفَ أَوِ ٱطْرَحُوهُ أَرْضًا يَخْلُ لَكُمْ وَجْهُ أَبِيكُمْ وَتَكُونُوا۟ مِنۢ
بَعْدِهِۦ قَوْمًا صَٰلِحِينَ ﴿٩﴾ قَالَ قَآئِلٌ مِّنْهُمْ لَا تَقْتُلُوا۟ يُوسُفَ وَأَلْقُوهُ فِى
غَيَٰبَتِ ٱلْجُبِّ يَلْتَقِطْهُ بَعْضُ ٱلسَّيَّارَةِ إِن كُنتُمْ فَٰعِلِينَ ﴿١٠﴾ قَالُوا۟
يَٰٓأَبَانَا مَا لَكَ لَا تَأْمَ۫نَّا عَلَىٰ يُوسُفَ وَإِنَّا لَهُۥ لَنَٰصِحُونَ ﴿١١﴾ أَرْسِلْهُ
مَعَنَا غَدًا يَرْتَعْ وَيَلْعَبْ وَإِنَّا لَهُۥ لَحَٰفِظُونَ ﴿١٢﴾ قَالَ إِنِّى لَيَحْزُنُنِىٓ أَن
تَذْهَبُوا۟ بِهِۦ وَأَخَافُ أَن يَأْكُلَهُ ٱلذِّئْبُ وَأَنتُمْ عَنْهُ غَٰفِلُونَ ﴿١٣﴾ قَالُوا۟ لَئِنْ
أَكَلَهُ ٱلذِّئْبُ وَنَحْنُ عُصْبَةٌ إِنَّآ إِذًا لَّخَٰسِرُونَ ﴿١٤﴾ فَلَمَّا ذَهَبُوا۟ بِهِۦ
وَأَجْمَعُوٓا۟ أَن يَجْعَلُوهُ فِى غَيَٰبَتِ ٱلْجُبِّ وَأَوْحَيْنَآ إِلَيْهِ لَتُنَبِّئَنَّهُم بِأَمْرِهِمْ
هَٰذَا وَهُمْ لَا يَشْعُرُونَ ﴿١٥﴾ وَجَآءُوٓ أَبَاهُمْ عِشَآءً يَبْكُونَ ﴿١٦﴾ قَالُوا۟
يَٰٓأَبَانَآ إِنَّا ذَهَبْنَا نَسْتَبِقُ وَتَرَكْنَا يُوسُفَ عِندَ مَتَٰعِنَا فَأَكَلَهُ ٱلذِّئْبُ وَمَآ
أَنتَ بِمُؤْمِنٍ لَّنَا وَلَوْ كُنَّا صَٰدِقِينَ ﴿١٧﴾

ʾUqtulū Yūsufa ʾawiṭ-raḥūhu ʾarḍañy-yakhlu lakum wajhu ʾabīkum wa takūnū mim-baʿdihī qawmañ-ṣāliḥīn. (9) Qāla qāaʾilum-minhum lā taqtulū Yūsufa wa ʾalqūhu fī ghayābatil-jubbi yaltaqiṭhu baʿḍus-sayyārati ʾiñ-kuñtum fāʿilīn. (10) Qālū yāa ʾabānā mā laka lā taʾmannā ʿalā Yūsufa wa ʾinnā lahū lanāṣiḥūn. (11) ʾArsilhu maʿanā ghadañy-yartaʿ wa yalʿab wa ʾinnā lahū laḥāfiẓūn. (12) Qāla ʾinnī layaḥzununīi ʾañ-tadhhabū bihī wa ʾakhāfu ʾañy-yaʾkulahudh-dhiʾbu wa ʾañtum ʿanhu ghāfilūn. (13) Qālū laʾin ʾakalahudh-dhiʾbu wa naḥnu ʿuṣbatun ʾinnāa ʾidhal-lakhāsirūn. (14) Falammā dhahabū bihī wa ʾajmaʿūu ʾañy-yajʿalūhu fī ghayābatil-jubb. Wa ʾawḥaynāa ʾilayhi latunabbiʾannahum-biʾamrihim hādhā wa hum lā yashʿurūn. (15) Wa jāaʾūu ʾabāhum ʿishāaʾañy-yabkūn. (16) Qālū yāa ʾabānāa ʾinnā dhahabnā nastabiqu wa taraknā Yūsufa ʿiñda matāʿinā faʾakalahudh-dhiʾb. Wa māa ʾañta bimuʾminil-lanā wa law kunnā ṣādiqīn. (17)

14 The phrase interpolated by me within brackets – reflecting the unconscious irony in the attitude of Joseph's brethren – is based on the consensus of most of the classical commentators.

15 Sc., "and take him with them to a faraway land" (cf. the preceding verse). The term *jubb* – rendered by me as "well" – is usually applied to a desert well simply cut through the earth or through rock and not cased with stone: the implication being that this particular well did not contain enough water to drown Joseph, but was deep enough to hide him from sight.

16 See verses 89-90 of this *sūrah*.

وَجَآءُو عَلَىٰ قَمِيصِهِۦ بِدَمٍ كَذِبٍ قَالَ بَلْ سَوَّلَتْ لَكُمْ أَنفُسُكُمْ أَمْرًا
فَصَبْرٌ جَمِيلٌ وَٱللَّهُ ٱلْمُسْتَعَانُ عَلَىٰ مَا تَصِفُونَ ﴿١٨﴾ وَجَآءَتْ سَيَّارَةٌ
فَأَرْسَلُوا۟ وَارِدَهُمْ فَأَدْلَىٰ دَلْوَهُۥ قَالَ يَـٰبُشْرَىٰ هَـٰذَا غُلَـٰمٌ وَأَسَرُّوهُ بِضَـٰعَةً
وَٱللَّهُ عَلِيمٌۢ بِمَا يَعْمَلُونَ ﴿١٩﴾ وَشَرَوْهُ بِثَمَنٍۭ بَخْسٍ دَرَٰهِمَ مَعْدُودَةٍ وَكَانُوا۟
فِيهِ مِنَ ٱلزَّٰهِدِينَ ﴿٢٠﴾ وَقَالَ ٱلَّذِى ٱشْتَرَىٰهُ مِن مِّصْرَ لِٱمْرَأَتِهِۦٓ أَكْرِمِى
مَثْوَىٰهُ عَسَىٰٓ أَن يَنفَعَنَآ أَوْ نَتَّخِذَهُۥ وَلَدًا وَكَذَٰلِكَ مَكَّنَّا لِيُوسُفَ فِى
ٱلْأَرْضِ وَلِنُعَلِّمَهُۥ مِن تَأْوِيلِ ٱلْأَحَادِيثِ وَٱللَّهُ غَالِبٌ عَلَىٰٓ أَمْرِهِۦ
وَلَـٰكِنَّ أَكْثَرَ ٱلنَّاسِ لَا يَعْلَمُونَ ﴿٢١﴾ وَلَمَّا بَلَغَ أَشُدَّهُۥٓ ءَاتَيْنَـٰهُ حُكْمًا
وَعِلْمًا وَكَذَٰلِكَ نَجْزِى ٱلْمُحْسِنِينَ ﴿٢٢﴾

Wa jāaʾū ʿalā qamīṣihī bidamiñ-kadhib. Qāla bal sawwalat lakum ʾañfusukum ʾamrañ-faṣabruñ-jamīl. Wal-lāhul-mustaʿānu ʿalā mā taṣifūn. (18) Wa jāaʾat sayyāratuñ-faʾarsalū wāridahum faʾadlā dalwahū qāla yā bushrā hādhā ghulāmuñw-wa ʾasarrūhu biḍāʿah. Wal-lāhu ʿalīmum-bimā yaʿmalūn. (19) Wa sharawhu bithamanim-bakhsiñ-darāhima maʿdūdatiñw-wa kānū fīhi minaz-zāhidīn. (20) Wa qālal-ladhish-tarāhu mim-miṣra limraʾatihīi ʾakrimī mathwāhu ʿasāa ʾañy-yañfaʿanāa ʾaw nattakhidhahū waladā. Wa kadhālika makkannā liYūsufa fil-ʾarḍi wa linuʿallimahū miñ-taʾwīlil-ʾaḥādīth. Wal-lāhu ghālibun ʿalāa ʾamrihī wa lākinna ʾaktharan-nāsi lā yaʿlamūn. (21) Wa lammā balagha ʾashuddahūu ʾātaynāhu ḥukmañw-wa ʿilmañw-wa kadhālika najzil-muḥsinīn. (22)

and they produced his tunic with false blood upon it.
[But Jacob] exclaimed: "Nay, but it is your [own] minds that have made [so terrible] a happening seem a matter of little account to you![17] But [as for myself,] patience in adversity is most goodly [in the sight of God]; and it is to God [alone] that I pray to give me strength to bear the misfortune which you have described to me."[18] ‹18›

AND THERE CAME a caravan;[19] and they sent forth their drawer of water, and he let down his bucket into the well – [and when he saw Joseph] he exclaimed: "Oh, what a lucky find,[20] this boy!"
And they hid him with a view to selling him: but God had full knowledge of all that they were doing. ‹19›
And they sold him for a paltry price – a mere few silver coins: thus low did they value him. ‹20›
And the man from Egypt who bought him[21] said to his wife: "Make his stay [with us] honourable; he may well be of use to us, or we may adopt him as a son."
And thus We gave unto Joseph a firm place on earth; and [We did this] so that We might impart unto him some understanding of the inner meaning of happenings.[22] For, God always prevails in whatever be His purpose: but most people know it not. ‹21›
And when he reached full manhood, We bestowed upon him the ability to judge [between right and wrong], as well as [innate] knowledge: for thus do We reward the doers of good. ‹22›

17 Apparently Jacob did not believe the tale of the wolf but, knowing his sons' envy of Joseph, at once realized that it was they themselves who had done grievous harm to him. Nevertheless – as is evident from Jacob's expression of hope in verse 83 of this *sūrah* – he was not quite convinced that Joseph was really dead.

18 Lit., "it is to God that I turn for aid against what you are describing".

19 According to the Bible (Genesis xxxvii, 25), they were "Ishmaelites" – i.e., Arabs – who "came from Gilead with their camels bearing spicery and balm and myrrh, going to carry it down to Egypt". (Gilead is the Biblical name for the region east of the Jordan.)

20 Lit., "O good news!"

21 The Qurʾān does not mention his name or position; but a later reference to him (in verse 30 below) as *al-ʿazīz* ("the great [or "mighty"] one") points to his having been a high official or a nobleman.

22 See note 10 above.

And [it so happened that] she in whose house he was living [conceived a passion for him and] sought to make him yield himself unto her; and she bolted the doors and said, "Come thou unto me!"
[But Joseph] answered: "May God preserve me! Behold, goodly has my master made my stay [in this house]! Verily, to no good end come they that do [such] wrong!" ‹23›
And, indeed, she desired him, and he desired her; [and he would have succumbed] had he not seen [in this temptation] an evidence of his Sustainer's truth:[23] thus [We willed it to be] in order that We might avert from him all evil and all deeds of abomination – for, behold, he was truly one of Our servants.[24] ‹24›
And they both rushed to the door; and she [grasped and] rent his tunic from behind – and [lo!] they met her lord at the door!
Said she: "What ought to be the punishment of one who had evil designs on [the virtue of] thy wife – [what] but imprisonment or a [yet more] grievous chastisement? ‹25›
[Joseph] exclaimed: "It was she who sought to make me yield myself unto her!"
Now one of those present, a member of her own household, suggested this:[25] "If his tunic has been torn from the front, then she is telling the truth, and he is a liar; ‹26› but if his tunic has been torn from behind, then she is lying, and he is speaking the truth." ‹27›

وَرَٰوَدَتۡهُ ٱلَّتِي هُوَ فِي بَيۡتِهَا عَن نَّفۡسِهِۦ وَغَلَّقَتِ ٱلۡأَبۡوَٰبَ وَقَالَتۡ هَيۡتَ
لَكَۚ قَالَ مَعَاذَ ٱللَّهِۖ إِنَّهُۥ رَبِّيٓ أَحۡسَنَ مَثۡوَايَۖ إِنَّهُۥ لَا يُفۡلِحُ
ٱلظَّٰلِمُونَ ﴿٢٣﴾ وَلَقَدۡ هَمَّتۡ بِهِۦۖ وَهَمَّ بِهَا لَوۡلَآ أَن رَّءَا بُرۡهَٰنَ رَبِّهِۦۚ
كَذَٰلِكَ لِنَصۡرِفَ عَنۡهُ ٱلسُّوٓءَ وَٱلۡفَحۡشَآءَۚ إِنَّهُۥ مِنۡ عِبَادِنَا
ٱلۡمُخۡلَصِينَ ﴿٢٤﴾ وَٱسۡتَبَقَا ٱلۡبَابَ وَقَدَّتۡ قَمِيصَهُۥ مِن دُبُرٖ وَأَلۡفَيَا
سَيِّدَهَا لَدَا ٱلۡبَابِۚ قَالَتۡ مَا جَزَآءُ مَنۡ أَرَادَ بِأَهۡلِكَ سُوٓءًا إِلَّآ أَن يُسۡجَنَ
أَوۡ عَذَابٌ أَلِيمٞ ﴿٢٥﴾ قَالَ هِيَ رَٰوَدَتۡنِي عَن نَّفۡسِيۚ وَشَهِدَ شَاهِدٞ مِّنۡ أَهۡلِهَآ
إِن كَانَ قَمِيصُهُۥ قُدَّ مِن قُبُلٖ فَصَدَقَتۡ وَهُوَ مِنَ ٱلۡكَٰذِبِينَ ﴿٢٦﴾ وَإِن
كَانَ قَمِيصُهُۥ قُدَّ مِن دُبُرٖ فَكَذَبَتۡ وَهُوَ مِنَ ٱلصَّٰدِقِينَ ﴿٢٧﴾

Wa rāwadat-hul-latī huwa fī baytihā ʿañ-nafsihī wa ghallaqatil-ʾabwāba wa qālat hayta lak. Qāla maʿādhal-lāhi ʾinnahū rabbīi ʾaḥsana mathwāya ʾinnahū lā yufliḥuẓ-ẓālimūn. (23) Wa laqad hammat bihī wa hamma bihā lawlāa ʾar-raʾā burhāna Rabbih. Kadhālika linaṣrifa ʿanhus-sūuʾa wal-faḥshāaʾ. ʾInnahū min ʿibādinal-mukhlaṣīn. (24) Was-tabaqal-bāba wa qaddat qamīṣahū miñ-duburiñw-wa ʾalfayā sayyidahā ladal-bāb. Qālat mā jazāaʾu man ʾarāda biʾahlika sūuʾan ʾillāa ʾañy-yusjana ʾaw ʿadhābun ʾalīm. (25) Qāla hiya rāwadatnī ʿañ-nafsī. Wa shahida shāhidum-min ʾahlihāa ʾiñ-kāna qamīṣuhū qudda miñ-qubuliñ-faṣadaqat wa huwa minal-kādhibīn. (26) Wa ʾiñ-kāna qamīṣuhū qudda miñ-duburiñ-fakadhabat wa huwa minaṣ-ṣādiqīn. (27)

23 The interpolated phrase "and he would have succumbed", is, according to Zamakhsharī, implied in the above sentence. In his commentary on this verse, he further points out that the moral significance of "virtue" consists in one's inner victory over a wrongful desire, and not in the *absence* of such a desire. Cf. the well-known saying of the Prophet, recorded, on the authority of Abū Hurayrah, by Bukhārī and Muslim: "God, exalted be He, says: 'If a servant of Mine [merely] desires to do a good deed, I shall count this [desire] as a good deed; and if he does it, I shall count it tenfold. And if he desires to commit a bad deed, but does not commit it, I shall count this as a good deed, seeing that he refrained from it only for My sake . . .'" – i.e., in consequence of a moral consideration (which, in the present instance, is described as "an evidence of God's truth").

24 Lit., "he was among Our sincere servants".

25 Lit., "a present one (*shāhid*) from her household testified" – i.e., suggested a test on these lines. Here, again, the Qurʾanic narrative differs from the story as told in the Bible, since according to the latter (Genesis xxxix, 19-20), the husband immediately believed the false accusation and cast Joseph into prison; the episodes related in verses 26-34 of this *sūrah* do not appear in the Biblical account.

ثلاثة ارباع الحزب

فَلَمَّا رَءَا قَمِيصَهُۥ قُدَّ مِن دُبُرٍ قَالَ إِنَّهُۥ مِن كَيْدِكُنَّ ۖ إِنَّ كَيْدَكُنَّ
عَظِيمٌ ﴿٢٨﴾ يُوسُفُ أَعْرِضْ عَنْ هَٰذَا ۚ وَٱسْتَغْفِرِى لِذَنۢبِكِ ۖ إِنَّكِ كُنتِ مِنَ
ٱلْخَاطِـِٔينَ ﴿٢٩﴾ ۞ وَقَالَ نِسْوَةٌ فِى ٱلْمَدِينَةِ ٱمْرَأَتُ ٱلْعَزِيزِ تُرَٰوِدُ فَتَىٰهَا
عَن نَّفْسِهِۦ ۖ قَدْ شَغَفَهَا حُبًّا ۖ إِنَّا لَنَرَىٰهَا فِى ضَلَٰلٍ مُّبِينٍ ﴿٣٠﴾ فَلَمَّا سَمِعَتْ
بِمَكْرِهِنَّ أَرْسَلَتْ إِلَيْهِنَّ وَأَعْتَدَتْ لَهُنَّ مُتَّكَـًٔا وَءَاتَتْ كُلَّ وَٰحِدَةٍ
مِّنْهُنَّ سِكِّينًا وَقَالَتِ ٱخْرُجْ عَلَيْهِنَّ ۖ فَلَمَّا رَأَيْنَهُۥٓ أَكْبَرْنَهُۥ وَقَطَّعْنَ أَيْدِيَهُنَّ
وَقُلْنَ حَٰشَ لِلَّهِ مَا هَٰذَا بَشَرًا إِنْ هَٰذَآ إِلَّا مَلَكٌ كَرِيمٌ ﴿٣١﴾ قَالَتْ
فَذَٰلِكُنَّ ٱلَّذِى لُمْتُنَّنِى فِيهِ ۖ وَلَقَدْ رَٰوَدتُّهُۥ عَن نَّفْسِهِۦ فَٱسْتَعْصَمَ ۖ وَلَئِن لَّمْ
يَفْعَلْ مَآ ءَامُرُهُۥ لَيُسْجَنَنَّ وَلَيَكُونًا مِّنَ ٱلصَّٰغِرِينَ ﴿٣٢﴾ قَالَ رَبِّ ٱلسِّجْنُ
أَحَبُّ إِلَىَّ مِمَّا يَدْعُونَنِىٓ إِلَيْهِ ۖ وَإِلَّا تَصْرِفْ عَنِّى كَيْدَهُنَّ أَصْبُ إِلَيْهِنَّ

Falammā ra᾽ā qamīṣahū qudda miñ-duburiñ-qāla ᾽innahū miñ-kaydikunna ᾽inna kaydakunna ᶜaẓīm. (28) Yūsufu ᾽aᶜriḍ ᶜan hādhā. Was-taghfirī lidhambiki ᾽innaki kuñti minal-khāṭi᾽īn. (29) ۞ Wa qāla niswatuñ-fil-madīnatim-ra᾽atul-ᶜazīzi turāwidu fatāhā ᶜañ-nafsihī qad shaghafahā ḥubbā. ᾽Innā lanarāhā fī ḍalālim-mubīn. (30) Falammā samiᶜat bimakrihinna ᾽arsalat ᾽ilayhinna wa ᾽aᶜtadat lahunna mutta-ka᾽añw-wa ᾽ātat kulla wāḥidatim-minhunna sikkīnañw-wa qālatikh-ruj ᶜalayhinn. Falammā ra᾽aynahū ᾽akbarnahū wa qaṭṭaᶜna ᾽aydiyahunna wa qulna ḥāsha lillāhi mā hādhā basharan ᾽in hādhāa ᾽illā malakuñ-karīm. (31) Qālat fadhālikunnal-ladhī lumtunnanī fīh. Wa laqad rāwattuhū ᶜañ-nafsihī fastaᶜṣam. Wa la᾽il-lam yafᶜal-māa ᾽āmuruhū layusjananna wa layakūnam-minaṣ-ṣāghirīn. (32) Qāla Rabbis-sijnu ᾽aḥabbu ᾽ilayya mimmā yadᶜūnanī ᾽ilayh. Wa ᾽illā taṣrif ᶜannī kaydahunna ᾽aṣbu ᾽ilayhinna

And when [her husband] saw that his tunic was torn from behind, he said: "Behold, this is [an instance] of your guile, O womankind! Verily, awesome is your guile! ‹28› [But,] Joseph, let this pass![26] And thou, [O wife,] ask forgiveness for thy sin – for, verily, thou hast been greatly at fault!" ‹29›

NOW the women of the city spoke [thus to one another]: "The wife of this nobleman is trying to induce her slave-boy to yield himself unto her! Her love for him has pierced her heart; verily, we see that she is undoubtedly suffering from an aberration!"[27] ‹30›

Thereupon, when she heard of their malicious talk, she sent for them, and prepared for them a sumptuous repast,[28] and handed each of them a knife and said [to Joseph]: "Come out and show thyself to them!"

And when the women saw him, they were greatly amazed at his beauty,[29] and [so flustered were they that] they cut their hands [with their knives], exclaiming, "God save us! This is no mortal man! This is nought but a noble angel!" ‹31›

Said she: "This, then, is he about whom you have been blaming me! And, indeed, I did try to make him yield himself unto me, but he remained chaste. Now, however, if he does not do what I bid him, he shall most certainly be imprisoned, and shall most certainly find himself among the despised!"[30] ‹32›

Said he: "O my Sustainer! Prison is more desirable to me than [compliance with] what these women invite me to: for, unless Thou turn away their guile from me, I might yet yield to their allure[31] and

26 Lit., "turn aside from this". According to almost all the commentators, the meaning is, "do not mention this to anyone", the implication being that the husband was prepared to forgive and forget.

27 Lit., "we see her indeed in obvious error".

28 The expression *muttaka᾽* – lit., "a place where one reclines [while eating]", i.e., a "cushioned couch" – seems to have been used here tropically to denote a "luxurious [or "sumptuous"] repast".

29 Lit., "they deemed him [i.e., his beauty] great".

30 Lit., "become one of those who are humiliated".

31 Lit., "incline towards them"; it should, however, be borne in mind that the verb *sabā* combines the concepts of inclination, yearning and amorous indulgence (cf. Lane IV, 1649); hence my rendering.

become one of those who are unaware [of right and wrong]." ‹33›
And his Sustainer responded to his prayer, and freed him from the threat of their guile:[32] verily, He alone is all-hearing, all-knowing. ‹34› For, presently it occurred to the nobleman and his household[33] – [even] after they had seen all the signs [of Joseph's innocence] – that they might as well imprison him for a time.[34] ‹35›

NOW two young men happened to go to prison at the same time as Joseph.[35]
One of them said: "Behold, I saw myself [in a dream] pressing wine."
And the other said: "Behold, I saw myself [in a dream] carrying bread on my head, and birds were eating thereof."
[And both entreated Joseph:] "Let us know the real meaning of this! Verily, we see that thou art one of those who know well [how to interpret dreams]."[36] ‹36›
[Joseph] answered: "Ere there comes unto you the meal which you are [daily] fed, I shall have informed you of the real meaning of your dreams,[37] [so that you might know what is to come] before it comes unto you: for this is [part] of the knowledge which my Sustainer has imparted to me.
"Behold, I have left behind me the ways of people who do not believe in God,[38] and who persistently refuse to acknowledge the truth of the life to come; ‹37›

وَأَكُن مِّنَ ٱلۡجَٰهِلِينَ ﴿٣٣﴾ فَٱسۡتَجَابَ لَهُۥ رَبُّهُۥ فَصَرَفَ عَنۡهُ كَيۡدَهُنَّۚ
إِنَّهُۥ هُوَ ٱلسَّمِيعُ ٱلۡعَلِيمُ ﴿٣٤﴾ ثُمَّ بَدَا لَهُم مِّنۢ بَعۡدِ مَا رَأَوُاْ ٱلۡأٓيَٰتِ
لَيَسۡجُنُنَّهُۥ حَتَّىٰ حِينٖ ﴿٣٥﴾ وَدَخَلَ مَعَهُ ٱلسِّجۡنَ فَتَيَانِۖ قَالَ أَحَدُهُمَآ إِنِّيٓ
أَرَىٰنِيٓ أَعۡصِرُ خَمۡرٗاۖ وَقَالَ ٱلۡأٓخَرُ إِنِّيٓ أَرَىٰنِيٓ أَحۡمِلُ فَوۡقَ رَأۡسِي خُبۡزٗا
تَأۡكُلُ ٱلطَّيۡرُ مِنۡهُۖ نَبِّئۡنَا بِتَأۡوِيلِهِۦٓۖ إِنَّا نَرَىٰكَ مِنَ ٱلۡمُحۡسِنِينَ ﴿٣٦﴾ قَالَ لَا
يَأۡتِيكُمَا طَعَامٞ تُرۡزَقَانِهِۦٓ إِلَّا نَبَّأۡتُكُمَا بِتَأۡوِيلِهِۦ قَبۡلَ أَن يَأۡتِيَكُمَاۚ ذَٰلِكُمَا
مِمَّا عَلَّمَنِي رَبِّيٓۚ إِنِّي تَرَكۡتُ مِلَّةَ قَوۡمٖ لَّا يُؤۡمِنُونَ بِٱللَّهِ وَهُم بِٱلۡأٓخِرَةِ هُمۡ
كَٰفِرُونَ ﴿٣٧﴾

wa ᵓakum-minal-jāhilīn. (33) Fastajāba lahū Rabbuhū faṣarafa ᶜanhu kaydahunn. ᵓInnahū Huwas-Samīᶜul-ᶜAlīm. (34) Thumma badā lahum-mim-baᶜdi mā raᵓawul-ᵓĀyāti layasjununnahū ḥattā ḥīn. (35) Wa dakhala maᶜahus-sijna fatayān. Qāla ᵓaḥaduhumāa ᵓinnīi arānīi ᵓaᶜṣiru khamrā. Wa qālal-ᵓākharu ᵓinnīi ᵓarānīi ᵓaḥmilu fawqa raᵓsī khubzañ-taᵓkuluṭ-ṭayru minh. Nabbiᵓnā bitaᵓwīlihīi ᵓinnā narāka minal-muḥsinīn. (36) Qāla lā yaᵓtīkumā ṭaᶜāmuñ-turzaqānihīi ᵓillā nabbaᵓtukumā bitaᵓwīlihī qabla ᵓañy-yaᵓtiyakumā dhālikumā mimmā ᶜallamanī Rabbī. ᵓInnī taraktu millata qawmil-lā yuᵓminūna billāhi wa hum-bilᵓĀkhirati hum kāfirūn. (37)

32 Lit., "turned away their guile from him".

33 Lit., "it occurred to them".

34 Thus, according to the Qurᵓān, Joseph was imprisoned not because his master believed him to be guilty, but because, in his weakness, he wanted to appease his wife, "being entirely submissive to her, and behaving like a riding-camel whose reins she held in her hand" (Zamakhsharī).

35 Lit., "entered the prison with him". According to the Biblical account (not contradicted by the Qurᵓān), they were the King's cup-bearer and baker, both of them imprisoned for unspecified offences.

36 This is the meaning given by Baghawī, Zamakhsharī and Bayḍāwī to the expression *al-muḥsinīn* in the above context, adopting the tropical use of the verb *aḥsana* in the sense of "he knew [something]" or "he knew [it] well". Thus, the Qurᵓān indicates here in its elliptic manner that Joseph's reputation for wisdom and dream-interpretation preceded him to prison.

37 Lit., "the real meaning thereof".

38 Joseph wants to avail himself of this opportunity to guide his two fellow-prisoners towards the true faith; and so, while promising that he would explain their dreams presently, he asks them to listen first to a short discourse on the oneness of God.

and I follow the creed of my forefathers Abraham, Isaac and Jacob. It is not conceivable that we should [be allowed to] ascribe divinity to aught beside God: this is [an outcome] of God's bounty unto us and unto all mankind[39] – but most people are ungrateful. ﴾38﴿

"O my companions in imprisonment! Which is more reasonable:[40] [belief in the existence of numerous divine] lords, each of them different from the other[41] – or [in] the One God, who holds absolute sway over all that exists? ﴾39﴿

"All that you worship instead of God is nothing but [empty] names which you have invented[42] – you and your forefathers – [and] for which God has bestowed no warrant from on high. Judgment [as to what is right and what is wrong] rests with God alone – [and] He has ordained that you should worship nought but Him: this is the [one] ever-true faith; but most people know it not.[43] ﴾40﴿

"[And now,] O my companions in imprisonment, [I shall tell you the meaning of your dreams:] as for one of you two, he will [again] give his lord [the King] wine to drink; but as for the other, he will be crucified, and birds will eat off his head. [But whatever be your future,] the matter on which you have asked me to enlighten you has been decided [by God]." ﴾41﴿

And [thereupon [Joseph] said unto the one of the two whom he considered saved: "Mention me unto thy lord [when thou art free]!"

But Satan caused him to forget to mention [Joseph] to his lord, and so he remained in prison a few [more] years. ﴾42﴿

وَاتَّبَعْتُ مِلَّةَ آبَائِي إِبْرَاهِيمَ وَإِسْحَاقَ وَيَعْقُوبَ ۚ مَا كَانَ لَنَا أَنْ نُشْرِكَ
بِاللَّهِ مِنْ شَيْءٍ ۚ ذَٰلِكَ مِنْ فَضْلِ اللَّهِ عَلَيْنَا وَعَلَى النَّاسِ وَلَٰكِنَّ أَكْثَرَ
النَّاسِ لَا يَشْكُرُونَ ﴿٣٨﴾ يَا صَاحِبَيِ السِّجْنِ أَأَرْبَابٌ مُتَفَرِّقُونَ خَيْرٌ
أَمِ اللَّهُ الْوَاحِدُ الْقَهَّارُ ﴿٣٩﴾ مَا تَعْبُدُونَ مِنْ دُونِهِ إِلَّا أَسْمَاءً سَمَّيْتُمُوهَا
أَنْتُمْ وَآبَاؤُكُمْ مَا أَنْزَلَ اللَّهُ بِهَا مِنْ سُلْطَانٍ ۚ إِنِ الْحُكْمُ إِلَّا لِلَّهِ ۚ أَمَرَ أَلَّا
تَعْبُدُوا إِلَّا إِيَّاهُ ۚ ذَٰلِكَ الدِّينُ الْقَيِّمُ وَلَٰكِنَّ أَكْثَرَ النَّاسِ لَا يَعْلَمُونَ ﴿٤٠﴾
يَا صَاحِبَيِ السِّجْنِ أَمَّا أَحَدُكُمَا فَيَسْقِي رَبَّهُ خَمْرًا ۖ وَأَمَّا الْآخَرُ فَيُصْلَبُ
فَتَأْكُلُ الطَّيْرُ مِنْ رَأْسِهِ ۚ قُضِيَ الْأَمْرُ الَّذِي فِيهِ تَسْتَفْتِيَانِ ﴿٤١﴾ وَقَالَ
لِلَّذِي ظَنَّ أَنَّهُ نَاجٍ مِنْهُمَا اذْكُرْنِي عِنْدَ رَبِّكَ فَأَنْسَاهُ الشَّيْطَانُ ذِكْرَ
رَبِّهِ فَلَبِثَ فِي السِّجْنِ بِضْعَ سِنِينَ ﴿٤٢﴾

Wat-tabaᶜtu millata ʾābāaʾī ʾIbrāhīma wa ʾIsḥāqa wa Yaᶜqūb. Mā kāna lanāa ʾañ-nushrika billāhi miñ-shayʾ. Dhālika miñ-faḍlil-lāhi ᶜalaynā wa ᶜalan-nāsi wa lākinna ʾaktharan-nāsi lā yashkurūn. (38) Yā ṣāḥibayis-sijni ʾaʾarbābum-mutafarriqūna khayrun ʾamil-lāhul-Wāḥidul-Qahhār. (39) Mā taᶜbudūna miñ-dūnihīi ʾillāa ʾasmāaʾañ-sammaytumūhāa ʾañtum wa ʾābāaʾukum-māa ʾañzalal-lāhu bihā miñ-sulṭān. ʾInil-ḥukmu ʾillā lillāh. ʾAmara ʾallā taᶜbudūu ʾillāa ʾiyyāh. Dhālikad-dīnul-qayyimu wa lākinna ʾaktharan-nāsi lā yaᶜlamūn. (40) Yā ṣāḥibayis-sijni ʾammāa ʾaḥadukumā fayasqī rabbahū khamrañw-wa ʾammal-ʾākharu fayuṣlabu fataʾkuluṭ-ṭayru mir-raʾsih. Quḍiyal-ʾamrul-ladhī fīhi tastaftiyān. (41) Wa qāla lilladhī ẓanna ʾannahū nājim-minhumadh-kurnī ᶜiñda rabbik. Faʾañsāhush-Shayṭānu dhikra Rabbihī falabitha fis-sijni biḍᶜa sinīn. (42)

39 Since God is almighty and self-sufficient, it is not for His sake that man is warned not to ascribe divine qualities to aught beside Him: the absolute condemnation of this sin is solely designed to benefit *man* by freeing him from all superstition, and thus enhancing his dignity as a conscious, rational being.

40 Lit., "better", obviously in the sense of "better conforming to the demands of reason".

41 The expression *mutafarriqūn* connotes plurality as well as separateness – in this context, separateness in respect of qualities, functions and degrees.

42 Lit., "names which you have named" – i.e., "figments of your own imagination".

43 Cf. the last sentence of 30 : 30.

وَقَالَ ٱلْمَلِكُ إِنِّىٓ أَرَىٰ سَبْعَ بَقَرَٰتٍ سِمَانٍ يَأْكُلُهُنَّ سَبْعٌ عِجَافٌ وَسَبْعَ
سُنۢبُلَٰتٍ خُضْرٍ وَأُخَرَ يَابِسَٰتٍ يَٰٓأَيُّهَا ٱلْمَلَأُ أَفْتُونِى فِى رُءْيَٰىَ إِن كُنتُمْ
لِلرُّءْيَا تَعْبُرُونَ ﴿٤٣﴾ قَالُوٓا۟ أَضْغَٰثُ أَحْلَٰمٍ وَمَا نَحْنُ بِتَأْوِيلِ ٱلْأَحْلَٰمِ
بِعَٰلِمِينَ ﴿٤٤﴾ وَقَالَ ٱلَّذِى نَجَا مِنْهُمَا وَٱدَّكَرَ بَعْدَ أُمَّةٍ أَنَا۠ أُنَبِّئُكُم بِتَأْوِيلِهِۦ
فَأَرْسِلُونِ ﴿٤٥﴾ يُوسُفُ أَيُّهَا ٱلصِّدِّيقُ أَفْتِنَا فِى سَبْعِ بَقَرَٰتٍ سِمَانٍ يَأْكُلُهُنَّ
سَبْعٌ عِجَافٌ وَسَبْعِ سُنۢبُلَٰتٍ خُضْرٍ وَأُخَرَ يَابِسَٰتٍ لَّعَلِّىٓ أَرْجِعُ إِلَى ٱلنَّاسِ
لَعَلَّهُمْ يَعْلَمُونَ ﴿٤٦﴾ قَالَ تَزْرَعُونَ سَبْعَ سِنِينَ دَأَبًا فَمَا حَصَدتُّمْ فَذَرُوهُ فِى
سُنۢبُلِهِۦٓ إِلَّا قَلِيلًا مِّمَّا تَأْكُلُونَ ﴿٤٧﴾ ثُمَّ يَأْتِى مِنۢ بَعْدِ ذَٰلِكَ سَبْعٌ شِدَادٌ

Wa qālal-maliku ʾinnīi ʾarā sabʿa baqarātiñ-simāniñy-yaʾkuluhunna sabʿun ʿijāfuñw-wa sabʿa sumbulātin khuḍriñw-wa ʾukhara yābisāt. Yāa ʾayyuhal-malaʾu ʾaftūnī fī ruʾyāya ʾiñ-kuñtum lir-ruʾyā taʿburūn. ﴿43﴾ Qālūu ʾaḍghāthu ʾaḥlāmiñw-wa mā naḥnu bitaʾwīlil-ʾaḥlāmi biʿālimīn. ﴿44﴾ Wa qālal-ladhī najā minhumā wad-dakara baʿda ʾummatin ʾana ʾunabbiʾukum-bitaʾwīlihī faʾarsilūn. ﴿45﴾ Yūsufu ʾayyuhaṣ-ṣiddīqu ʾaftinā fī sabʿi baqarātiñ-simāniñy-yaʾkuluhunna sabʿun ʿijāfuñw-wa sabʿi sumbulātin khuḍriñw-wa ʾukhara yābisātil-laʿallīi ʾarjiʿu ʾilan-nāsi laʿallahum yaʿlamūn. ﴿46﴾ Qāla tazraʿūna sabʿa sinīna daʾabañ-famā ḥaṣattum-fadharūhu fī sumbulihīi ʾillā qalīlam-mimmā taʾkulūn. ﴿47﴾ Thumma yaʾtī mim-baʿdi dhālika sabʿuñ-shidāduñy-

AND [one day] the King said:[44] "Behold, I saw [in a dream] seven fat cows being devoured by seven emaciated ones, and seven green ears [of wheat] next to [seven] others that were withered. O you nobles! Enlighten me about [the meaning of] my dream, if you are able to interpret dreams!" ‹43›

They answered: "[This is one of] the most involved and confusing of dreams,[45] and we have no deep knowledge of the real meaning of dreams." ‹44›

At that, the one of the two [erstwhile prisoners] who had been saved, and [who suddenly] remembered [Joseph] after all that time,[46] spoke [thus]: "It is I who can inform you of the real meaning of this [dream]; so let me go [in search of it]."[47] ‹45›

[And he went to see Joseph in the prison and said to him:] – "Joseph, O thou truthful one! Enlighten us about [the meaning of a dream in which] seven fat cows were being devoured by seven emaciated ones, and seven green ears [of wheat appeared] next to [seven] others that were withered – so that I may return [with thy explanation] unto the people [of the court, and] that they may come to know [what manner of man thou art]!" ‹46›

[Joseph] replied: "You shall sow for seven years as usual; but let all [the grain] that you harvest remain [untouched] in its ear, excepting only a little, whereof you may eat: ‹47› for, after that [period of seven good years] there will come seven hard [years]

---

44 This king seems to have been one of the six Hyksos rulers who dominated Egypt from about 1700 to 1580 B.C., after having invaded the country from the east by way of the Sinai Peninsula. The name of this dynasty, which was undoubtedly of foreign origin, is derived from the Egyptian *ḥiq shasu* or *ḥeku shoswet*, meaning "rulers of nomad lands", or – according to the late Egyptian historian Manetho – "shepherd kings": all of which points to their having been Arabs who, despite the fact that before their invasion of Egypt they were already well-established in Syria, had to a large extent preserved their bedouin mode of life. This would explain the confidence which the king mentioned in this story was later to place in Joseph, the Hebrew, and the subsequent settlement of the latter's family (and, thus, of what in due course became the Israelite nation) in Egypt: for it must be borne in mind that the Hebrews, too, descended from one of the many bedouin tribes who some centuries earlier had migrated from the Arabian Peninsula to Mesopotamia and later to Syria (cf. *sūrah* 7, note 48); and that the language of the Hyksos must have been very akin to Hebrew, which, after all, is but an ancient Arabian dialect.

45 Lit., "confusing medleys (*aḍghāth*) of dreams".

46 According to almost all the authorities, the noun *ummah* denotes here "a time" or "a long period of time".

47 The cup-bearer obviously addresses the assembly as a whole, and not the King alone: hence the plural "you".

يَأْكُلْنَ مَا قَدَّمْتُمْ لَهُنَّ إِلَّا قَلِيلًا مِّمَّا تُحْصِنُونَ ﴿٤٨﴾ ثُمَّ يَأْتِي مِنۢ بَعْدِ ذَٰلِكَ
عَامٌ فِيهِ يُغَاثُ ٱلنَّاسُ وَفِيهِ يَعْصِرُونَ ﴿٤٩﴾ وَقَالَ ٱلْمَلِكُ ٱئْتُونِي بِهِۦ
فَلَمَّا جَآءَهُ ٱلرَّسُولُ قَالَ ٱرْجِعْ إِلَىٰ رَبِّكَ فَسْـَٔلْهُ مَا بَالُ ٱلنِّسْوَةِ ٱلَّٰتِي
قَطَّعْنَ أَيْدِيَهُنَّ إِنَّ رَبِّي بِكَيْدِهِنَّ عَلِيمٌ ﴿٥٠﴾ قَالَ مَا خَطْبُكُنَّ إِذْ رَٰوَدتُّنَّ
يُوسُفَ عَن نَّفْسِهِۦ قُلْنَ حَٰشَ لِلَّهِ مَا عَلِمْنَا عَلَيْهِ مِن سُوٓءٍ قَالَتِ ٱمْرَأَتُ
ٱلْعَزِيزِ ٱلْـَٰٔنَ حَصْحَصَ ٱلْحَقُّ أَنَا۠ رَٰوَدتُّهُۥ عَن نَّفْسِهِۦ وَإِنَّهُۥ لَمِنَ
ٱلصَّٰدِقِينَ ﴿٥١﴾ ذَٰلِكَ لِيَعْلَمَ أَنِّي لَمْ أَخُنْهُ بِٱلْغَيْبِ وَأَنَّ ٱللَّهَ لَا يَهْدِي
كَيْدَ ٱلْخَآئِنِينَ ﴿٥٢﴾

which will devour all that you shall have laid up for them, excepting only a little of that which you shall have kept in store. «48»
And after that there will come a year in which the people will be delivered from all distress,[48] and in which they will press [oil and wine as before]." «49»

And [as soon as Joseph's interpretation was conveyed to him,] the King said: "Bring him before me!"

But when the [King's] messenger came unto him, [Joseph] said: "Go back to thy lord and ask him [first to find out the truth] about those women who cut their hands – for, behold, [until now it is] my Sustainer [alone who] has full knowledge of their guile!" «50»

[Thereupon the King sent for those women; and when they came,] he asked: "What was it that you hoped to achieve when you sought to make Joseph yield himself unto you?"[49]

The women answered: "God save us! We did not perceive the least evil [intention] on his part!"

[And] the wife of Joseph's former master[50] exclaimed: "Now has the truth come to light! It was I who sought to make him yield himself unto me – whereas he, behold, was indeed speaking the truth!" «51»

[When Joseph learned what had happened, he said:[51] "I asked for] this, so that [my former master] might know that I did not betray him behind his back,[52] and that God does not bless with His guidance the artful schemes of those who betray their trust. «52»

yaʾkulna mā qaddamtum lahunna ʾillā qalīlam-mimmā tuḥṣinūn. (48) Thumma yaʾtī mim-baʿdi dhālika ʿāmuñ-fīhi yughāthun-nāsu wa fīhi yaʿṣirūn. (49) Wa qālal-malikuʾ-tūnī bih. Falammā jāaʾahur-rasūlu qālar-jiʿ ʾilā rabbika fasʾalhu mā bālun-niswatil-lātī qaṭṭaʿna ʾaydiyahunn. ʾInna Rabbī bikaydihinna ʿAlīm. (50) Qāla mā khaṭbukunna ʾidh rāwattunna Yūsufa ʿañ-nafsih. Qulna ḥāsha lillāhi mā ʿalimnā ʿalayhi miñ-sūuʾ. Qālatim-raʾatul-ʿazīzil-ʾāna ḥaṣḥaṣal-ḥaqqu ʾana rāwattuhū ʿan-nafsihī wa ʾinnahū laminaṣ-ṣādiqīn. (51) Dhālika liyaʿlama ʾannī lam ʾakhunhu bilghaybi wa ʾannal-lāha lā yahdī kaydal-khāaʾinīn. (52)

48 Or: "will be granted rain" – depending on whether one connects the verbal form *yughāth* with either of the infinitive nouns *ghayth* ("rain") or *ghawth* ("deliverance from distress"). Although the crops of Egypt depend entirely on the annual Nile floods, the water-level of the river is, in its turn, contingent upon the quantity of rainfall at its upper reaches.

49 Evidently, the King wanted to find out whether they had previously been encouraged by Joseph, or whether he was truly innocent. The noun *khaṭb* denotes "something that one has in view" or "desires" or "seeks to obtain"; and so the expression *mā khaṭbukunna* (lit., "what was it that you [really] had in view") may be suitably rendered as above.

50 Lit., "the wife of the great one (*al-ʿazīz*)".

51 Some of the commentators (e.g., Ibn Kathīr and, among the moderns, Rashīd Riḍāʾ in *Manār* XII, 323 f.) regard this and the next verse as a continuation of the woman's confession; but the great majority of the classical authorities, including Ṭabarī, Baghawī and Zamakhsharī, attribute the speech that follows unequivocally – and, in my opinion, most convincingly – to Joseph: hence my interpolation at the beginning of this verse.

52 Lit., "in [his] absence" or "in secret" (*bi'l-ghayb*).

And yet, I am not trying to absolve myself: for, verily, man's inner self does incite [him] to evil,[53] and saved are only they upon whom my Sustainer bestows His grace.[54] Behold, my Sustainer is much-forgiving, a dispenser of grace!" ‹53›
And the King said: "Bring him unto me, so that I may attach him to my own person." And when he had spoken with him, [the King] said: "Behold, [from] this day thou shalt be of high standing with us, invested with all trust!" ‹54›
[Joseph] replied: "Place in my charge the store-houses of the land; behold, I shall be a good and knowing keeper."[55] ‹55›
And thus We established Joseph securely in the land [of Egypt]: he had full mastery over it, [doing] whatever he willed.
[Thus do] We cause Our grace to alight upon whomever We will; and We do not fail to requite the doers of good.[56] ‹56›
But in the eyes of those who have attained to faith and have always been conscious of Us, a reward in the life to come is a far greater good [than any reward in this world].[57] ‹57›

AND [after some years,] Joseph's brothers came [to Egypt][58] and presented themselves before him: and he knew them [at once], whereas they did not recognize him. ‹58›

۞ وَمَآ أُبَرِّئُ نَفۡسِيٓۚ إِنَّ ٱلنَّفۡسَ لَأَمَّارَةُۢ بِٱلسُّوٓءِ إِلَّا مَا رَحِمَ رَبِّيٓۚ إِنَّ
رَبِّي غَفُورٞ رَّحِيمٞ ﴿٥٣﴾ وَقَالَ ٱلۡمَلِكُ ٱئۡتُونِي بِهِۦٓ أَسۡتَخۡلِصۡهُ لِنَفۡسِيۖ فَلَمَّا
كَلَّمَهُۥ قَالَ إِنَّكَ ٱلۡيَوۡمَ لَدَيۡنَا مَكِينٌ أَمِينٞ ﴿٥٤﴾ قَالَ ٱجۡعَلۡنِي عَلَىٰ خَزَآئِنِ
ٱلۡأَرۡضِۖ إِنِّي حَفِيظٌ عَلِيمٞ ﴿٥٥﴾ وَكَذَٰلِكَ مَكَّنَّا لِيُوسُفَ فِي ٱلۡأَرۡضِ
يَتَبَوَّأُ مِنۡهَا حَيۡثُ يَشَآءُۚ نُصِيبُ بِرَحۡمَتِنَا مَن نَّشَآءُۖ وَلَا نُضِيعُ أَجۡرَ
ٱلۡمُحۡسِنِينَ ﴿٥٦﴾ وَلَأَجۡرُ ٱلۡأٓخِرَةِ خَيۡرٞ لِّلَّذِينَ ءَامَنُواْ وَكَانُواْ يَتَّقُونَ ﴿٥٧﴾
وَجَآءَ إِخۡوَةُ يُوسُفَ فَدَخَلُواْ عَلَيۡهِ فَعَرَفَهُمۡ وَهُمۡ لَهُۥ مُنكِرُونَ ﴿٥٨﴾

حزب 25
جزء 13

۞ Wa māa ʾubarriʾu nafsī. ʾInnan-nafsa laʾammāratum-bissūuʾi ʾillā mā raḥima Rabbīi ʾinna Rabbī Ghafūrur-Raḥīm. ﴿53﴾ Wa qālal-malikuʾ-tūnī bihīi ʾastakhliṣhu linafsī. Falammā kallamahū qāla ʾinnakal-yawma ladaynā makīnun ʾamīn. ﴿54﴾ Qālaj-ʿalnī ʿalā khazāaʾinil-ʾarḍi ʾinnī ḥafīẓun ʿalīm. ﴿55﴾ Wa kadhālika makkannā liYūsufa fil-ʾarḍi yatabawwaʾu minhā ḥaythu yashāaʾ. Nuṣību biraḥmatinā man-nashāaʾu wa lā nuḍīʿu ʾajral-muḥsinīn. ﴿56﴾ Wa laʾajrul-ʾĀkhirati khayrul-lilladhīna ʾāmanū wa kānū yattaqūn. ﴿57﴾ Wa jāaʾa ʾikhwatu Yūsufa fadakhalū ʿalayhi faʿarafahum wa hum lahū munkirūn. ﴿58﴾

---

53 Lit., "is indeed wont to command [the doing of] evil" – i.e., is filled with impulses which often conflict with what the mind regards as a moral good. This is obviously a reference to the statement in verse 24 above – "she desired him, and he desired her; [and he would have succumbed,] had he not seen [in this temptation] an evidence of his Sustainer's truth" – as well as to Joseph's prayer in verse 33, "unless Thou turn away their guile from me, I might yet yield to their allure". (See also note 23 above.) Joseph's stress on the weakness inherent in human nature is a sublime expression of humility on the part of one who himself had overcome that very weakness: for, as the sequence shows, he attributes his moral victory not to himself but solely to the grace and mercy of God.

54 Lit., "except those upon whom . . .", etc. According to most of the commentators, the pronoun *mā* (lit., "that which") is here synonymous with *man* ("he who" or "those who").

55 By making this request, Joseph wanted to assure an efficient build-up of grain reserves during the coming years of plenty, knowing well that they would be followed by seven years of scarcity. It is obvious from the sequence that his request was granted, and that he was able to fulfil the task which he had set himself.

56 I.e., sometimes in this world as well, but invariably in the hereafter, as the sequence shows.

57 Lit., "for those who have attained to faith . . .", etc.

58 I.e., to buy wheat from the stores which Joseph had accumulated during the seven years of plenty: for all the countries in the vicinity of Egypt were by now affected by the famine which he had predicted, and Egypt alone had a surplus, the distribution of which he supervised personally (cf. Genesis xli, 54-57).

وَلَمَّا جَهَّزَهُم بِجَهَازِهِمْ قَالَ ٱئْتُونِى بِأَخٍ لَّكُم مِّنْ أَبِيكُمْ ۚ أَلَا تَرَوْنَ أَنِّىٓ
أُوفِى ٱلْكَيْلَ وَأَنَا۠ خَيْرُ ٱلْمُنزِلِينَ ﴿٥٩﴾ فَإِن لَّمْ تَأْتُونِى بِهِۦ فَلَا كَيْلَ لَكُمْ
عِندِى وَلَا تَقْرَبُونِ ﴿٦٠﴾ قَالُوا۟ سَنُرَٰوِدُ عَنْهُ أَبَاهُ وَإِنَّا لَفَٰعِلُونَ ﴿٦١﴾ وَقَالَ
لِفِتْيَٰنِهِ ٱجْعَلُوا۟ بِضَٰعَتَهُمْ فِى رِحَالِهِمْ لَعَلَّهُمْ يَعْرِفُونَهَآ إِذَا ٱنقَلَبُوٓا۟ إِلَىٰٓ
أَهْلِهِمْ لَعَلَّهُمْ يَرْجِعُونَ ﴿٦٢﴾ فَلَمَّا رَجَعُوٓا۟ إِلَىٰٓ أَبِيهِمْ قَالُوا۟ يَٰٓأَبَانَا مُنِعَ مِنَّا
ٱلْكَيْلُ فَأَرْسِلْ مَعَنَآ أَخَانَا نَكْتَلْ وَإِنَّا لَهُۥ لَحَٰفِظُونَ ﴿٦٣﴾ قَالَ هَلْ ءَامَنُكُمْ
عَلَيْهِ إِلَّا كَمَآ أَمِنتُكُمْ عَلَىٰٓ أَخِيهِ مِن قَبْلُ ۖ فَٱللَّهُ خَيْرٌ حَٰفِظًا ۖ وَهُوَ أَرْحَمُ
ٱلرَّٰحِمِينَ ﴿٦٤﴾ وَلَمَّا فَتَحُوا۟ مَتَٰعَهُمْ وَجَدُوا۟ بِضَٰعَتَهُمْ رُدَّتْ إِلَيْهِمْ ۖ
قَالُوا۟ يَٰٓأَبَانَا مَا نَبْغِى ۖ هَٰذِهِۦ بِضَٰعَتُنَا رُدَّتْ إِلَيْنَا ۖ وَنَمِيرُ أَهْلَنَا وَنَحْفَظُ

Wa lammā jahhazahum-bijahāzihim qālaʾ-tūnī biʾakhil-lakum-min ʾabīkum. ʾAlā tarawna ʾannīi ūfil-kayla wa ʾana khayrul-muñzilīn. (59) Faʾil-lam taʾtūnī bihī falā kayla lakum ʿiñdī wa lā taqrabūn. (60) Qālū sanurāwidu ʿanhu ʾabāhu wa ʾinnā lafāʿilūn. (61) Wa qāla lifityānihij-ʿalū biḍāʿatahum fī riḥālihim laʿallahum yaʿrifūnahāa ʾidhañ-qalabūu ʾilāa ʾahlihim laʿallahum yarjiʿūn. (62) Falammā rajaʿūu ʾilāa ʾabīhim qālū yāa ʾabānā muniʿa minnal-kaylu faʾarsil maʿanāa ʾakhānā naktal wa ʾinnā lahū laḥāfiẓūn. (63) Qāla hal ʾāmanukum ʿalayhi ʾillā kamāa ʾamiñtukum ʿalāa ʾakhīhi miñ-qabl. Fallāhu Khayrun ḥāfiẓañw-wa Huwa ʾArḥamur-rāḥimīn. (64) Wa lammā fataḥū matāʿahum wajadū biḍāʿatahum ruddat ʾilayhim. Qālū yāa ʾabānā mā nabghī. Hādhihī biḍāʿatunā ruddat ʾilaynā wa namīru ʾahlanā wa naḥfaẓu

And when he had provided them with their provisions, he said: "[When you come here next,] bring unto me that brother of yours from your father's side.[59] Do you not see that I have given [you] full measure and have been the best of hosts? «59» But if you do not bring him unto me, you shall never again receive a single measure [of grain] from me, nor shall you [be allowed to] come near me!" «60»

They answered: "We shall try to persuade his father to part with him, and, verily, we shall do [our utmost]! «61»

And [Joseph] said to his servants: "Place their merchandise[60] in their camel-packs, so that they may find it there when they come home, and hence be the more eager to return."[61] «62»

And so, when they returned to their father, [Joseph's brothers] said: "O our father! All grain[62] is [to be] withheld from us [in the future unless we bring Benjamin with us]: send, therefore, our brother with us, so that we may obtain our measure [of grain]; and, verity, we shall guard him well!" «63»

[Jacob] replied: "Shall I trust you with him in the same way[63] as I trusted you with his brother [Joseph] aforetime? [Nay,] but God's guardianship is better [than yours], for He is the most merciful of the merciful!" «64»

Thereupon, when they opened their packs, they discovered that their merchandise had been returned to them; [and] they said: "O our father! What more could we desire? Here is our merchandise: it has been returned to us! [If thou send Benjamin with us,] we shall [again] be able to bring food for our family, and shall guard

59 Lit., "a brother of yours from your father" – i.e., their half-brother Benjamin, who was Joseph's full brother (their mother having been Rachel, Jacob's favourite wife), whereas the other ten had different mothers. Benjamin, the youngest of Jacob's children, had not accompanied his brothers on their first journey to Egypt, but they had presumably mentioned him in the course of their conversation with Joseph.

60 I.e., the goods which they had bartered for wheat (Ibn Kathīr): a very plausible explanation in view of the fact that barter was the most common form of trade in those ancient times.

61 Lit., "so that they may perceive them when they come back to their family, [and] that they may return".

62 Lit., "measure [of grain]", here used metonymically in an allusion to Joseph's words (verse 60).

63 Lit., "not otherwise than".

our brother [well], and receive in addition another camel-load of grain.[64] That [which we have brought the first time] was but a scanty measure." ‹65›

Said [Jacob] "I will not send him with you until you give me a solemn pledge, before God, that you will indeed bring him back unto me, unless you yourselves be encompassed [by death]!"

And when they had given him their solemn pledge [Jacob] said: "God is witness to all that we say!" ‹66›

And he added: "O my sons! Do not enter [the city all] by one gate, but enter by different gates.[65] Yet [even so,] I can be of no avail whatever to you against [anything that may be willed by] God: judgment [as to what is to happen] rests with none but God. In Him have I placed my trust: for, all who have trust [in His existence] must place their trust in Him alone." ‹67›

But although[66] they entered [Joseph's city] in the way their father had bidden them, this proved of no avail whatever to them against [the plan of] God.[67] [His request] had served only to satisfy Jacob's heartfelt desire [to protect them]:[68] for, behold, thanks to what We had imparted unto him, he was indeed endowed with the knowledge [that God's will must always prevail];[69] but most people know it not. ‹68›

AND WHEN [the sons of [Jacob] presented themselves before Joseph, he drew his brother [Benjamin] unto himself, saying

أَخَانَا وَنَزْدَادُ كَيْلَ بَعِيرٍ ذَٰلِكَ كَيْلٌ يَسِيرٌ ﴿٦٥﴾ قَالَ لَنْ أُرْسِلَهُۥ مَعَكُمْ
حَتَّىٰ تُؤْتُونِ مَوْثِقًا مِّنَ ٱللَّهِ لَتَأْتُنَّنِى بِهِۦٓ إِلَّآ أَن يُحَاطَ بِكُمْ فَلَمَّآ ءَاتَوْهُ
مَوْثِقَهُمْ قَالَ ٱللَّهُ عَلَىٰ مَا نَقُولُ وَكِيلٌ ﴿٦٦﴾ وَقَالَ يَٰبَنِىَّ لَا تَدْخُلُوا۟ مِنۢ
بَابٍ وَٰحِدٍ وَٱدْخُلُوا۟ مِنْ أَبْوَٰبٍ مُّتَفَرِّقَةٍ وَمَآ أُغْنِى عَنكُم مِّنَ ٱللَّهِ مِن
شَىْءٍ إِنِ ٱلْحُكْمُ إِلَّا لِلَّهِ عَلَيْهِ تَوَكَّلْتُ وَعَلَيْهِ فَلْيَتَوَكَّلِ ٱلْمُتَوَكِّلُونَ ﴿٦٧﴾
وَلَمَّا دَخَلُوا۟ مِنْ حَيْثُ أَمَرَهُمْ أَبُوهُم مَّا كَانَ يُغْنِى عَنْهُم مِّنَ ٱللَّهِ مِن شَىْءٍ
إِلَّا حَاجَةً فِى نَفْسِ يَعْقُوبَ قَضَىٰهَا وَإِنَّهُۥ لَذُو عِلْمٍ لِّمَا عَلَّمْنَٰهُ وَلَٰكِنَّ
أَكْثَرَ ٱلنَّاسِ لَا يَعْلَمُونَ ﴿٦٨﴾ وَلَمَّا دَخَلُوا۟ عَلَىٰ يُوسُفَ ءَاوَىٰٓ إِلَيْهِ أَخَاهُ قَالَ

ʾakhānā wa nazdādu kayla baʿīr. Dhālika kayluñy-yasīr. (65) Qāla lan ʾursilahū maʿakum ḥattā tuʾtūni mawthiqam-minal-lāhi lataʾtunnanī bihīi ʾillāa ʾañy-yuḥāṭa bikum. Falammāa ʾātawhu mawthiqahum qālal-lāhu ʿalā mā naqūlu Wakīl. (66) Wa qāla yā baniyya lā tadkhulū mim-bābiñw-wāḥidiñw-wadkhulū min ʾabwābim-mutafarriqah. Wa māa ʾughnī ʿañkum-minal-lāhi miñ-shayʾ. ʾInil-ḥukmu ʾillā lillāhi ʿalayhi tawakkaltu wa ʿalayhi falyatawakkalil-mutawakkilūn. (67) Wa lammā dakhalū min ḥaythu ʾamarahum ʾabūhum mā kāna yughnī ʿanhum-minal-lāhi miñ-shayʾin ʾillā ḥājatañ-fī nafsi Yaʿqūba qaḍāhā. Wa ʾinnahū ladhū ʿilmil-limā ʿallamnāhu wa lākinna ʾaktharan-nāsi lā yaʿlamūn. (68) Wa lammā dakhalū ʿalā Yūsufa ʾāwāa ʾilayhi ʾakhāhu qāla

64 It would seem that Joseph used to allot to foreign buyers of grain one camel-load per person.

65 Probably in order not to attract undue attention in the foreign land and possibly fall prey to intrigues. See in this connection note 68 below.

66 Lit., "when".

67 As is shown in the sequence, they and their father were to suffer severe distress before their adventures came to a happy conclusion.

68 Lit., "it [i.e., his request that they should enter the city by different gates] had been but a desire in Jacob's heart (*nafs*), which he [thus] satisfied". In other words, when he gave his sons this advice, he followed only an instinctive, humanly-understandable urge, and did not really expect that any outward precaution would by itself help them: for, as he himself pointed out on parting, "judgment as to what is to happen rests with none but God". This stress on man's utter dependence on God – a fundamental tenet of Islam – explains why Jacob's advice (which in itself is not relevant to the story) has been mentioned in the above Qurʾanic narrative.

69 This interpolated clause is based on Zamakhsharī's interpretation of the above reference to Jacob's having been "endowed with knowledge".

[to him in secret]: "Behold, I am thy brother! So grieve thou not over their past doings!"[70] ‹69›
And [later,] when he had provided them with their provisions, he placed the [King's] drinking-cup in his brother's camel-pack. And [as they were leaving the city,] a herald[71] called out: "O you people of the caravan! Verily, you are thieves!"[72] ‹70›
Turning towards the herald and his companions, the brothers asked:[73] "What is it that you miss?" ‹71›
They answered: "We miss the King's goblet; and he who produces it shall receive a camel-load [of grain as reward]!"
And [the herald added:] "I pledge myself to this [promise]!" ‹72›
Said [the brothers]: "By God! Well do you know that we have not come to commit deeds of corruption in this land, and that we have not been thieving!" ‹73›
[The Egyptians] said: "But what shall be the requital of this [deed] if you are [proved to be] liars?" ‹74›
[The brothers] replied: "Its requital? He in whose camel-pack [the cup] is found – he shall be [enslaved as] a requital thereof! Thus do we [ourselves] requite the doers of [such] wrong."[74] ‹75›

إِنِّىٓ أَنَا۠ أَخُوكَ فَلَا تَبْتَئِسْ بِمَا كَانُوا۟ يَعْمَلُونَ ﴿٦٩﴾ فَلَمَّا جَهَّزَهُم بِجَهَازِهِمْ
جَعَلَ ٱلسِّقَايَةَ فِى رَحْلِ أَخِيهِ ثُمَّ أَذَّنَ مُؤَذِّنٌ أَيَّتُهَا ٱلْعِيرُ إِنَّكُمْ
لَسَـٰرِقُونَ ﴿٧٠﴾ قَالُوا۟ وَأَقْبَلُوا۟ عَلَيْهِم مَّاذَا تَفْقِدُونَ ﴿٧١﴾ قَالُوا۟ نَفْقِدُ
صُوَاعَ ٱلْمَلِكِ وَلِمَن جَآءَ بِهِۦ حِمْلُ بَعِيرٍ وَأَنَا۠ بِهِۦ زَعِيمٌ ﴿٧٢﴾ قَالُوا۟ تَٱللَّهِ
لَقَدْ عَلِمْتُم مَّا جِئْنَا لِنُفْسِدَ فِى ٱلْأَرْضِ وَمَا كُنَّا سَـٰرِقِينَ ﴿٧٣﴾ قَالُوا۟ فَمَا
جَزَٰٓؤُهُۥٓ إِن كُنتُمْ كَـٰذِبِينَ ﴿٧٤﴾ قَالُوا۟ جَزَٰٓؤُهُۥ مَن وُجِدَ فِى رَحْلِهِۦ فَهُوَ
جَزَٰٓؤُهُۥ ۚ كَذَٰلِكَ نَجْزِى ٱلظَّـٰلِمِينَ ﴿٧٥﴾

ᵓinnī ᵓana ᵓakhūka falā tabtaᵓis bimā kānū yaᶜmalūn. ﴿69﴾ Falammā jahhazahum-bijahāzihim jaᶜalas-siqāyata fī raḥli ᵓakhīhi thumma ᵓadhdhana muᵓadhdhinun ᵓayyatuhal-ᶜīru ᵓinnakum lasāriqūn. ﴿70﴾ Qālū wa ᵓaqbalū ᶜalayhim-mādhā tafqidūn. ﴿71﴾ Qālū nafqidu ṣuwāᶜal-maliki wa limañ-jāaᵓa bihī ḥimlu baᶜīriñw-wa ᵓana bihī zaᶜīm. ﴿72﴾ Qālū tallāhi laqad ᶜalimtum-mā jiᵓnā linufsida fil-ᵓarḍi wa mā kunnā sāriqīn. ﴿73﴾ Qālū famā jazāaᵓuhūu ᵓiñ-kuñtum kādhibīn. ﴿74﴾ Qālū jazāaᵓuhū mañw-wujida fī raḥlihī fahuwa jazāaᵓuh. Kadhālika najziẓ-ẓālimīn. ﴿75﴾

70 Thus, contrary to the Biblical account, Joseph is stated here to have disclosed his identity to Benjamin long before he revealed himself to his ten half-brothers. The words "their past doings" obviously refer to their treacherous behaviour towards himself which Joseph had now presumably disclosed to Benjamin.

71 Lit., "an announcer" (*muᵓadhdhin*) – a noun derived from the verbal form *adhdhana* ("he announced" or "proclaimed" or "called out publicly").

72 Commenting on this verse, Rāzī says: "Nowhere in the Qurᵓān is it stated that they made this accusation on Joseph's orders; the circumstantial evidence shows rather (*al-aqrab ilā ẓāhir al-ḥāl*) that they did this of their own accord: for, when they had missed the drinking-cup, [these servants of Joseph remembered that] nobody had been near it [except the sons of [Jacob] and so it occurred to them that it was they who had taken it." Analogous views are also advanced by Ṭabarī and Zamakhsharī in their comments on the last words of verse 76 below. This extremely plausible explanation contrasts sharply with the Biblical account of this incident (Genesis xliv), according to which the false accusation was part of an inexplicable "stratagem" devised by Joseph. If we discard – as we must – this part of the Biblical version, it is far more logical to assume that Joseph, who had been granted by the King full authority over all that belonged to the latter (see verse 56 above), had placed the royal cup *as a present* in the bag of his favourite brother; and that he did this secretly, without informing his servants, because he did not want anyone, least of all his ten half-brothers, to know his predilection for Benjamin. For a further explanation of this incident and of its ethical relevance within the context of Joseph's story, see note 77 below.

73 Lit., "They said, turning towards them".

74 Most of the commentators (relying, perhaps on Exodus xxii, 2) assume that this was the customary punishment for theft among the ancient Hebrews. Rāzī, however, suggests that this last sentence may not be a part of the brothers' answer but a confirmatory remark made by the *Egyptian herald*, meaning, "[In fact,] thus do we [Egyptians] requite the doers of such wrong".

Thereupon [they were brought before Joseph to be searched; and] he began with the bags of his half-brothers[75] before the bag of his brother [Benjamin]: and in the end he brought forth the drinking cup[76] out of his brother's bag.
In this way did We contrive for Joseph [the attainment of his heart's desire]: under the King's law, he would [otherwise] not have been able to detain his brother, had not God so willed. We do raise to [high] degrees [of knowledge] whomever We will – but above everyone who is endowed with knowledge there is One who knows all.[77] ⟨76⟩
[As soon as the cup came to light out of Benjamin's bag, the brothers] exclaimed: "If he has stolen – well, a brother of his used to steal aforetime!"[78]
Thereupon Joseph said to himself, without revealing his thought to them:[79] "You are far worse in this respect, and God is fully aware of what you are saying."[80] ⟨77⟩
They said: "O thou great one! Behold, he has a father, a very old man: detain, therefore, one of us in his stead. Verily, we see that thou art a doer of good!" ⟨78⟩
He answered: "May God preserve us from [the sin of] detaining any other than him with whom we have found our property –

فَبَدَأَ بِأَوْعِيَتِهِمْ قَبْلَ وِعَاءِ أَخِيهِ ثُمَّ ٱسْتَخْرَجَهَا مِن وِعَاءِ أَخِيهِ ۚ كَذَٰلِكَ
كِدْنَا لِيُوسُفَ ۖ مَا كَانَ لِيَأْخُذَ أَخَاهُ فِي دِينِ ٱلْمَلِكِ إِلَّآ أَن يَشَآءَ ٱللَّهُ ۚ
نَرْفَعُ دَرَجَٰتٍ مَّن نَّشَآءُ ۗ وَفَوْقَ كُلِّ ذِي عِلْمٍ عَلِيمٌ ﴿٧٦﴾ ۞ قَالُوٓاْ إِن
يَسْرِقْ فَقَدْ سَرَقَ أَخٌ لَّهُۥ مِن قَبْلُ ۚ فَأَسَرَّهَا يُوسُفُ فِي نَفْسِهِۦ وَلَمْ يُبْدِهَا
لَهُمْ ۚ قَالَ أَنتُمْ شَرٌّ مَّكَانًا ۖ وَٱللَّهُ أَعْلَمُ بِمَا تَصِفُونَ ﴿٧٧﴾ قَالُواْ يَٰٓأَيُّهَا
ٱلْعَزِيزُ إِنَّ لَهُۥٓ أَبًا شَيْخًا كَبِيرًا فَخُذْ أَحَدَنَا مَكَانَهُۥٓ ۖ إِنَّا نَرَىٰكَ مِنَ
ٱلْمُحْسِنِينَ ﴿٧٨﴾ قَالَ مَعَاذَ ٱللَّهِ أَن نَّأْخُذَ إِلَّا مَن وَجَدْنَا مَتَٰعَنَا عِندَهُۥٓ

ربع الحزب

Fabadaʾa biʾawʿiyatihim qabla wiʿāaʾi ʾakhīhi thummas-takhrajahā miñw-wiʿāaʾi ʾakhīh. Kadhālika kidnā liYūsuf. Mā kāna liyaʾkhudha ʾakhāhu fī dīnil-maliki ʾillāa ʾañy-yashāaʾal-lāh. Narfaʿu darajātim-man-nashāaʾ. Wa fawqa kulli dhī ʿilmin ʿAlīm. ⟨76⟩ ۞ Qālūu ʾiñy-yasriq faqad saraqa ʾakhul-lahū miñ-qabl. Faʾasarrahā Yūsufu fī nafsihī wa lam yubdihā lahum. Qāla ʾañtum sharrum-makānañw-wal-lāhu ʾaʿlamu bimā taṣifūn. ⟨77⟩ Qālū yāa ʾayyuhal-ʿazīzu ʾinna lahūu ʾabañ-shaykhañ-kabīrañ-fakhudh ʾaḥadanā makānah. ʾInnā narāka minal-muḥsinīn. ⟨78⟩ Qāla maʿādhal-lāhi ʾañnaʾkhudha ʾillā mañw-wa jadnā matāʿanā ʿiñdahūu

75 Lit., "with *their* bags".

76 Lit., "he brought it out".

77 The meaning of this story is now clear: it is a further illustration of the basic doctrine that "judgment [as to what is to happen] rests with none but God" (verse 67 above). Joseph had wanted to keep Benjamin with himself, but under the law of Egypt he could not do this without the consent of his half-brothers, who were the legal guardians of their minor brother; and they – bound as they were by the solemn promise given to their father – would certainly not have agreed to Benjamin's remaining behind. The only other alternative open to Joseph was to disclose his identity to them; but since he was not yet prepared to go so far, he was obliged to allow Benjamin to depart with his brothers. The accidental discovery of his gift, entirely unexpected by Joseph (see note 72 above), changed everything: for now Benjamin appeared to be guilty of theft, and under the law of the land Joseph was entitled to claim him as his slave, and thus to keep him in his house. The words, "In this way did We contrive (*kidnā*) for Joseph [the attainment of his heart's desire]", referring to the incident of the cup, indicate that its final outcome was neither planned nor even foreseen by Joseph.

78 The reference is obviously to Benjamin's full brother, Joseph. In the absence of any indication that the latter had ever before been accused of theft, it is reasonable to assume that the brothers, unaware of the fact that they were standing before Joseph, simply wanted to vilify him in order to dissociate themselves more effectively from Benjamin, who now appeared to have been convicted of theft.

79 Lit., "Joseph concealed it within himself and did not reveal it to them; he said . . .", etc. According to almost all the commentators, the pronoun "it" refers to Joseph's subsequent "saying" or, rather, thought, indicated by the verb "he said" (i.e., within himself); hence my free rendering of this phrase.

80 Lit., "of what you attribute", i.e., to Joseph and Benjamin – sc., "since you yourselves have stolen Joseph from his father".

for then, behold, we would indeed be evildoers!" ‹79›
And so, when they lost all hope of [moving] him, they withdrew to take counsel [among themselves].
The eldest of them said: "Do you not remember[81] that your father has bound you by a solemn pledge before God – and how, before that, you had failed with regard to Joseph? Hence, I shall not depart from this land till my father gives me leave or God passes judgment in my favour:[82] for He is the best of all judges. ‹80› [And as for you others,] return to your father and say: 'O our father! Behold, thy son has stolen – but we [can] bear witness to no more than what has become known to us;[83] and [although we gave you our pledge,] we could not guard against something that [lay hidden in the future and, hence,] was beyond the reach of our perception.[84] ‹81› And ask thou in the town in which we were [at the time], and of the people of the caravan with whom we travelled hither, and [thou wilt find that] we are indeed telling the truth!'" ‹82›

[AND WHEN they returned to their father and told him what had happened,] he exclaimed: "Nay, but it is your [own] minds that have made [so terrible] a happening seem a matter of little account to you! But [as for myself,] patience in adversity is most goodly; God may well bring them all [back] unto me:[85] verily, He alone is all-knowing, truly wise!" ‹83›
But he turned away from them and said: "O woe is me for Joseph!" – and his eyes became dim[86] from the grief with which he was filled. ‹84›

إِنَّآ إِذًا لَّظَٰلِمُونَ ﴿٧٩﴾ فَلَمَّا ٱسْتَيْـَٔسُوا۟ مِنْهُ خَلَصُوا۟ نَجِيًّا ۖ قَالَ كَبِيرُهُمْ
أَلَمْ تَعْلَمُوٓا۟ أَنَّ أَبَاكُمْ قَدْ أَخَذَ عَلَيْكُم مَّوْثِقًا مِّنَ ٱللَّهِ وَمِن قَبْلُ مَا
فَرَّطتُمْ فِى يُوسُفَ ۖ فَلَنْ أَبْرَحَ ٱلْأَرْضَ حَتَّىٰ يَأْذَنَ لِىٓ أَبِىٓ أَوْ يَحْكُمَ ٱللَّهُ
لِى ۖ وَهُوَ خَيْرُ ٱلْحَٰكِمِينَ ﴿٨٠﴾ ٱرْجِعُوٓا۟ إِلَىٰٓ أَبِيكُمْ فَقُولُوا۟ يَٰٓأَبَانَآ إِنَّ
ٱبْنَكَ سَرَقَ وَمَا شَهِدْنَآ إِلَّا بِمَا عَلِمْنَا وَمَا كُنَّا لِلْغَيْبِ حَٰفِظِينَ ﴿٨١﴾
وَسْـَٔلِ ٱلْقَرْيَةَ ٱلَّتِى كُنَّا فِيهَا وَٱلْعِيرَ ٱلَّتِىٓ أَقْبَلْنَا فِيهَا ۖ وَإِنَّا
لَصَٰدِقُونَ ﴿٨٢﴾ قَالَ بَلْ سَوَّلَتْ لَكُمْ أَنفُسُكُمْ أَمْرًا ۖ فَصَبْرٌ جَمِيلٌ ۖ
عَسَى ٱللَّهُ أَن يَأْتِيَنِى بِهِمْ جَمِيعًا ۚ إِنَّهُۥ هُوَ ٱلْعَلِيمُ ٱلْحَكِيمُ ﴿٨٣﴾ وَتَوَلَّىٰ
عَنْهُمْ وَقَالَ يَٰٓأَسَفَىٰ عَلَىٰ يُوسُفَ وَٱبْيَضَّتْ عَيْنَاهُ مِنَ ٱلْحُزْنِ فَهُوَ
كَظِيمٌ ﴿٨٤﴾

ᵓinnāa ᵓidhal-laẓālimūn. ﴾79﴿ Falammas-tayᵓasū minhu khalaṣū najiyyā. Qāla kabīruhum ᵓalam taᶜlamūu ᵓanna ᵓabākum qad ᵓakhadha ᶜalaykum-mawthiqam-minal-lāhi wa miñ-qablu mā farraṭtum fī Yūsuf. Falan ᵓabraḥal-ᵓarḍa ḥattā yaᵓdhana līi ᵓabīi ᵓaw yaḥkumal-lāhu lī wa huwa Khayrul-ḥākimīn. ﴾80﴿ ᵓIrjiᶜūu ᵓilāa ᵓabīkum faqūlū yāa ᵓabānāa ᵓinnabnaka saraqa wa mā shahidnāa ᵓillā bimā ᶜalimnā wa mā kunnā lilghaybi ḥāfiẓīn. ﴾81﴿ Was-ᵓalil-qaryatal-latī kunnā fīhā wal-ᶜīral-latīi ᵓaqbalnā fīhā wa ᵓinnā laṣādiqūn. ﴾82﴿ Qāla bal sawwalat lakum ᵓañfusukum ᵓamrañ-faṣabruñ-jamīl. ᶜAsal-lāhu ᵓañy-yaᵓtiyanī bihim jamīᶜā. ᵓInnahū Huwal-ᶜAlīmul-Ḥakīm. ﴾83﴿ Wa tawallā ᶜanhum wa qāla yāa ᵓasafā ᶜalā Yūsufa wabyaḍḍat ᶜaynāhu minal-ḥuzni fahuwa kaẓīm. ﴾84﴿

81 Lit., "know" – but since this expression denotes here remembrance rather than knowledge in the proper sense of the word, it can be suitably translated as above.

82 I.e., "enables me to win back my brother Benjamin".

83 I.e., the finding of the King's cup in Benjamin's bag (Baghawī and Zamakhsharī).

84 Lit., "We were not guardians over that which was beyond the reach of [our] perception": i.e., "at the time when we gave you our pledge regarding Benjamin, we did not know that he would steal" (Zamakhsharī).

85 I.e., Benjamin and the eldest son (who had remained in Egypt) as well as Joseph, of whose alleged death Jacob was never fully convinced (cf. note 17).

86 Lit., "white": i.e., dim with the tears that filled them (Rāzī). Although Jacob was now deprived of three of his

Said [his sons]: "By God! Thou wilt never cease to remember Joseph till thou art broken in body and spirit or art dead!" ‹85›
He answered: "It is only to God that I complain of my deep grief and my sorrow: for I know, from God, something that you do not know.[87] ‹86› [Hence,] O my sons, go forth and try to obtain some tidings of Joseph and his brother; and do not lose hope of God's life-giving mercy:[88] verily, none but people who deny the truth can ever lose hope of God's life-giving mercy." ‹87›

[AND THE SONS of Jacob went back to Egypt and to Joseph;] and when they presented themselves before him, they said: "O thou great one! Hardship has visited us and our folk, and so we have brought but scanty merchandise;[89] but give us a full measure [of grain], and be charitable to us: behold, God rewards those who give in charity!" ‹88›
Replied he: "Do you remember[90] what you did to Joseph and his brother when you were still unaware [of right and wrong]?"[91] ‹89›
They exclaimed: "Why – is it indeed thou who art Joseph?"
He answered: "I am Joseph, and this is my brother. God has indeed been gracious unto us. Verily, if one is[92] conscious of Him and patient in adversity – behold, God does not fail to requite the doers of good!" ‹90›

قَالُواْ تَاللَّهِ تَفۡتَؤُاْ تَذۡكُرُ يُوسُفَ حَتَّىٰ تَكُونَ حَرَضًا أَوۡ تَكُونَ مِنَ
ٱلۡهَٰلِكِينَ ﴿٨٥﴾ قَالَ إِنَّمَآ أَشۡكُواْ بَثِّي وَحُزۡنِيٓ إِلَى ٱللَّهِ وَأَعۡلَمُ مِنَ ٱللَّهِ مَا
لَا تَعۡلَمُونَ ﴿٨٦﴾ يَٰبَنِيَّ ٱذۡهَبُواْ فَتَحَسَّسُواْ مِن يُوسُفَ وَأَخِيهِ وَلَا
تَاْيۡـَٔسُواْ مِن رَّوۡحِ ٱللَّهِۖ إِنَّهُۥ لَا يَاْيۡـَٔسُ مِن رَّوۡحِ ٱللَّهِ إِلَّا ٱلۡقَوۡمُ
ٱلۡكَٰفِرُونَ ﴿٨٧﴾ فَلَمَّا دَخَلُواْ عَلَيۡهِ قَالُواْ يَٰٓأَيُّهَا ٱلۡعَزِيزُ مَسَّنَا وَأَهۡلَنَا
ٱلضُّرُّ وَجِئۡنَا بِبِضَٰعَةٖ مُّزۡجَىٰةٖ فَأَوۡفِ لَنَا ٱلۡكَيۡلَ وَتَصَدَّقۡ عَلَيۡنَآۖ إِنَّ ٱللَّهَ
يَجۡزِي ٱلۡمُتَصَدِّقِينَ ﴿٨٨﴾ قَالَ هَلۡ عَلِمۡتُم مَّا فَعَلۡتُم بِيُوسُفَ وَأَخِيهِ إِذۡ
أَنتُمۡ جَٰهِلُونَ ﴿٨٩﴾ قَالُوٓاْ أَءِنَّكَ لَأَنتَ يُوسُفُۖ قَالَ أَنَا۠ يُوسُفُ وَهَٰذَآ
أَخِيۖ قَدۡ مَنَّ ٱللَّهُ عَلَيۡنَآۖ إِنَّهُۥ مَن يَتَّقِ وَيَصۡبِرۡ فَإِنَّ ٱللَّهَ لَا يُضِيعُ أَجۡرَ
ٱلۡمُحۡسِنِينَ ﴿٩٠﴾

Qālū tallāhi taftaʾu tadhkuru Yūsufa ḥattā takūna ḥaraḍan ʾaw takūna minal-hālikīn. (85) Qāla ʾinnamāa ʾashkū baththī wa ḥuznīi ʾilal-lāhi wa ʾaʿlamu minal-lāhi mā lā taʿlamūn. (86) Yā baniyya-dhhabu fataḥassasū miñy-Yūsufa wa ʾakhīhi wa lā tayʾasū mir-rawḥil-lāh. ʾInnahū lā yayʾasu mir-rawḥil-lāhi ʾillal-qawmul-kāfirūn. (87) Falammā dakhalū ʿalayhi qālū yāa ʾayyuhal-ʿazīzu massanā wa ʾahlanaḍ-ḍurru wa jiʾnā bibiḍāʿatim-muzjātiñ-faʾawfi lanal-kayla wa taṣaddaq ʿalaynāa ʾinnal-lāha yajzil-mutaṣaddiqīn. (88) Qāla hal ʿalimtum-mā faʿaltum-biYūsufa wa ʾakhīhi ʾidh añtum jāhilūn. (89) Qālūu ʾaʾinnaka laʾañta Yūsuf. Qāla ʾana Yūsufu wa hādhāa ʾakhī qad mannal-lāhu ʿalaynā. ʾInnahū mañy-yattaqi wa yaṣbir faʾinnal-lāha lā yuḍīʿu ʾajral-muḥsinīn. (90)

sons, his grief for Joseph was the most acute because he was the only one of the three of whom Jacob did not know whether he was dead or alive.

87 Namely, that "judgment as to what is to happen rests with none but God", and that "all who have trust [in His existence] must place their trust in Him alone" (verse 67): the twin ideas which underlie the whole of this *sūrah*, and which Jacob now seeks to impress upon his sons. In addition to this, his remembrance of Joseph's prophetic dream (verse 4) and his own conviction at the time that his beloved son would be elected by God for His special grace (verse 6), fills Jacob with renewed hope that Joseph is still alive (Rāzī and Ibn Kathīr): and this explains the directives which he gives his sons in the next sentence.

88 According to most of the commentators, especially Ibn ʿAbbās (as quoted by Ṭabarī and others), the term *rawḥ* is here synonymous with *raḥmah* ("grace" or "mercy"). Since it is linguistically related to the noun *rūḥ* ("breath of life" or "spirit"), and has also the metonymic significance of "rest" (*rāḥah*) from grief and sadness (*Tāj al-ʿArūs*), the most appropriate rendering would seem to be "life-giving mercy".

89 I.e., goods which they intended to barter for grain (see note 60 above).

90 Lit., "know" (see note 81).

91 By coupling his own name with that of Benjamin he possibly hinted at his brothers' early envy and hatred of the two sons of Rachel (cf. verse 8 of this *sūrah* and the corresponding note 12); alternatively, the mention of Benjamin may have been due to the readiness with which they accepted the "evidence" of the latter's guilt (verse 77).

92 Lit., "whoever is . . .", etc.

[The brothers] said: "By God! Most certainly has God raised thee high above us, and we were indeed but sinners!" ‹91›
Said he: "No reproach shall be uttered today against you. May God forgive you your sins: for He is the most merciful of the merciful! ‹92› [And now] go and take this tunic of mine and lay it over my father's face, and he will recover his sights.[93] And thereupon come [back] to me with all your family." ‹93›

AND AS SOON as the caravan [with which Jacob's sons were travelling] was on its way,[94] their father said [to the people around him]: "Behold, were it not that you might consider me a dotard, [I would say that] I truly feel the breath of Joseph [in the air]!" ‹94›
They answered: "By God! Thou art indeed still lost in thy old aberration!" ‹95›
But when the bearer of good tidings came [with Joseph's tunic], he laid it over his face; and he regained his sight, [and] exclaimed: "Did I not tell you, 'Verily, I know, from God, something that you do not know'?"[95] ‹96›
[His sons] answered: "O our father! Ask God to forgive us our sins, for, verily, we were sinners." ‹97›
He said: "I shall ask my Sustainer to forgive you: He alone is truly forgiving, a true dispenser of grace!" ‹98›

AND WHEN they [all arrived in Egypt and] presented themselves before Joseph, he drew his parents unto himself,[96] saying, "Enter Egypt! If God so wills, you shall be secure [from all evil]!" ‹99›

قَالُوا۟ تَٱللَّهِ لَقَدْ ءَاثَرَكَ ٱللَّهُ عَلَيْنَا وَإِن كُنَّا لَخَـٰطِـِٔينَ ﴿٩١﴾ قَالَ لَا
تَثْرِيبَ عَلَيْكُمُ ٱلْيَوْمَ يَغْفِرُ ٱللَّهُ لَكُمْ وَهُوَ أَرْحَمُ ٱلرَّٰحِمِينَ ﴿٩٢﴾
ٱذْهَبُوا۟ بِقَمِيصِى هَـٰذَا فَأَلْقُوهُ عَلَىٰ وَجْهِ أَبِى يَأْتِ بَصِيرًا وَأْتُونِى بِأَهْلِكُمْ
أَجْمَعِينَ ﴿٩٣﴾ وَلَمَّا فَصَلَتِ ٱلْعِيرُ قَالَ أَبُوهُمْ إِنِّى لَأَجِدُ رِيحَ يُوسُفَ
لَوْلَآ أَن تُفَنِّدُونِ ﴿٩٤﴾ قَالُوا۟ تَٱللَّهِ إِنَّكَ لَفِى ضَلَـٰلِكَ ٱلْقَدِيمِ ﴿٩٥﴾ فَلَمَّآ أَن
جَآءَ ٱلْبَشِيرُ أَلْقَىٰهُ عَلَىٰ وَجْهِهِۦ فَٱرْتَدَّ بَصِيرًا قَالَ أَلَمْ أَقُل لَّكُمْ إِنِّىٓ
أَعْلَمُ مِنَ ٱللَّهِ مَا لَا تَعْلَمُونَ ﴿٩٦﴾ قَالُوا۟ يَـٰٓأَبَانَا ٱسْتَغْفِرْ لَنَا ذُنُوبَنَآ إِنَّا
كُنَّا خَـٰطِـِٔينَ ﴿٩٧﴾ قَالَ سَوْفَ أَسْتَغْفِرُ لَكُمْ رَبِّىٓ إِنَّهُۥ هُوَ ٱلْغَفُورُ
ٱلرَّحِيمُ ﴿٩٨﴾ فَلَمَّا دَخَلُوا۟ عَلَىٰ يُوسُفَ ءَاوَىٰٓ إِلَيْهِ أَبَوَيْهِ وَقَالَ ٱدْخُلُوا۟
مِصْرَ إِن شَآءَ ٱللَّهُ ءَامِنِينَ ﴿٩٩﴾

Qālū tallāhi laqad ʾātharakal-lāhu ʿalaynā wa ʾiñ-kunnā lakhāṭiʾīn. (91) Qāla lā tathrība ʿalaykumul-yawm. Yaghfirul-lāhu lakum wa Huwa ʾArḥamur-rāḥimīn. (92) ʾIdhhabū biqamīṣī hādhā faʾalqūhu ʿalā wajhi ʾabī yaʾti baṣīrañw-waʾ-tunī biʾahlikum ʾajmaʿīn. (93) Wa lammā faṣalatil-ʿīru qāla ʾabūhum ʾinnī laʾajidu rīḥa Yūsufa lawlāa ʾañ-tufannidūn. (94) Qālū tallāhi ʾinnaka lafī ḍalālikal-qadīm. (95) Falammāa ʾañ-jāaʾal-bashīru ʾalqāhu ʿalā wajhihī fartadda baṣīrā. Qāla ʾalam ʾaqul-lakum ʾinnīi ʾaʿlamu minal-lāhi mā lā taʿlamūn. (96) Qālū yāa ʾabānastaghfir lanā dhunūbanāa ʾinnā kunnā khāṭiʾīn. (97) Qāla sawfa ʾastaghfiru lakum Rabbīi ʾinnahū Huwal-Ghafūrur-Raḥīm. (98) Falammā dakhalū ʿalā Yūsufa ʾāwāa ʾilayhi ʾabawayhi wa qālad-khulū Miṣra ʾiñ-shāaʾal-lāhu ʾāminīn. (99)

93 Lit., "he will become seeing [again]" – i.e., "he will cease to weep for me and the dimness of his sight caused by unhappiness and constant weeping will disappear on learning that I am alive": thus may be summed up Rāzī's explanation of the above sentence. According to him, there is no compelling reason to assume that Jacob had become really blind from grief. – The phrase "lay it over my father's face" could also be rendered as "lay it before my father", since the term *wajh* (lit., "face") is often used in classical Arabic to denote, metonymically, one's whole personality, or whole being.

94 Lit., "had departed", i.e., from Egypt.

95 See verse 86 above.

96 According to the Biblical account – not contradicted by the Qurʾān – Joseph's mother Rachel had died while giving birth to Benjamin. We may, therefore, assume that the "mother" implied in the term "parents" was another of

وَرَفَعَ أَبَوَيْهِ عَلَى ٱلْعَرْشِ وَخَرُّواْ لَهُۥ سُجَّدًاۖ وَقَالَ يَٰٓأَبَتِ هَٰذَا تَأْوِيلُ
رُءْيَٰىَ مِن قَبْلُ قَدْ جَعَلَهَا رَبِّى حَقًّاۖ وَقَدْ أَحْسَنَ بِىٓ إِذْ أَخْرَجَنِى مِنَ
ٱلسِّجْنِ وَجَآءَ بِكُم مِّنَ ٱلْبَدْوِ مِنۢ بَعْدِ أَن نَّزَغَ ٱلشَّيْطَٰنُ بَيْنِى وَبَيْنَ
إِخْوَتِىٓۚ إِنَّ رَبِّى لَطِيفٌ لِّمَا يَشَآءُۚ إِنَّهُۥ هُوَ ٱلْعَلِيمُ ٱلْحَكِيمُ ﴿١٠٠﴾ ۞
رَبِّ قَدْ ءَاتَيْتَنِى مِنَ ٱلْمُلْكِ وَعَلَّمْتَنِى مِن تَأْوِيلِ ٱلْأَحَادِيثِۚ فَاطِرَ
ٱلسَّمَٰوَٰتِ وَٱلْأَرْضِ أَنتَ وَلِىِّۦ فِى ٱلدُّنْيَا وَٱلْءَاخِرَةِۖ تَوَفَّنِى مُسْلِمًا
وَأَلْحِقْنِى بِٱلصَّٰلِحِينَ ﴿١٠١﴾ ذَٰلِكَ مِنْ أَنۢبَآءِ ٱلْغَيْبِ نُوحِيهِ إِلَيْكَۖ وَمَا
كُنتَ لَدَيْهِمْ إِذْ أَجْمَعُوٓاْ أَمْرَهُمْ وَهُمْ يَمْكُرُونَ ﴿١٠٢﴾

نصف الحزب

And he raised his parents to the highest place of honour;[97] and they [all] fell down before Him, prostrating themselves in adoration.[98]
Thereupon [Joseph] said: "O my father! This is the real meaning of my dream of long ago, which my Sustainer has made come true.[99] And He was indeed good to me when He freed me from the prison, and [when] He brought you [all unto me] from the desert after Satan had sown discord between me and my brothers. Verily, my Sustainer is unfathomable in [the way He brings about] whatever He wills:[100] verily, He alone is all-knowing, truly wise! ‹100›
"O my Sustainer! Thou hast indeed bestowed upon me something of power,[101] and hast imparted unto me some knowledge of the inner meaning of happenings.[102] Originator of the heavens and the earth! Thou art near unto me in this world and in the life to come: let me die as one who has surrendered himself unto Thee, and make me one with the righteous!" ‹101›

THIS ACCOUNT of something that was beyond the reach of thy perception We [now] reveal unto thee, [O Prophet:] for thou wert not with Joseph's brothers[103] when they resolved upon what they were going to do and wove their schemes [against him]. ‹102›

Wa rafaʿa ʾabawayhi ʿalal-ʿarshi wa kharrū lahū sujjadā. Wa qāla yāa ʾabati hādhā taʾwīlu ruʾyāya miñ-qablu qad jaʿalahā Rabbī ḥaqqā. Wa qad ʾaḥsana bīi ʾidh ʾakhrajanī minas-sijni wa jāaʾa bikum-minal-badwi mim-baʿdi ʾañ-nazaghash-Shayṭānu baynī wa bayna ʾikhwatī. ʾInna Rabbī Laṭīful-limā yashāaʾ. ʾInnahū Huwal-ʿAlīmul-Ḥakīm. (100) ۞ Rabbi qad ʾātaytanī minal-mulki wa ʿallamtanī miñ-taʾwīlil-ʾaḥādīth. Fāṭiras-samāwāti wal-ʾarḍi ʾAñta waliyyī fid-dunyā wal-ʾĀkhirati tawaffanī muslimañw-wa ʾalḥiqnī biṣṣāliḥīn. (101) Dhālika min ʾambāaʾil-ghaybi nūḥīhi ʾilayka wa mā kuñta ladayhim ʾidh ʾajmaʿūu ʾamrahum wa hum yamkurūn. (102)

Jacob's wives, who had brought up Joseph and Benjamin; this would be in consonance with the ancient Arabian custom of applying the designation "mother" to a foster-mother.

97 Lit., "onto the throne (*al-ʿarsh*)", in the metaphorical sense of this word.

98 According to ʿAbd Allāh ibn ʿAbbās (as quoted by Rāzī), the personal pronoun in "before Him" relates to God, since it is inconceivable that Joseph would have allowed his parents to prostrate themselves before himself.

99 The fulfilment of Joseph's childhood dream consisted in the high dignity with which he was now invested and in the fact that his parents and his brothers had come from Canaan to Egypt for his sake: for "no reasonable person can expect that the fulfilment of a dream should be an exact replica of the dream itself" (Rāzī, alluding to the symbolic prostration of the eleven stars, the sun and the moon mentioned in verse 4 of this *sūrah*).

100 As regards my rendering of *laṭīf* as "unfathomable", see *sūrah* 6, note 89. In the present instance, this term supplies a further accent, as it were, on the theme "judgment as to what is to happen rests with none but God" (verse 67).

101 Lit., "of dominion", indicating that absolute power and absolute dominion belong to God alone.

102 See note 10 on verse 6 of this *sūrah*.

103 Lit., "with them".

Yet – however strongly thou mayest desire it – most people will not believe [in this revelation], ‹103› although thou dost not ask of them any reward for it: it is but [God's] reminder unto all mankind. ‹104›
But [then] – how many a sign is there in the heavens and on earth which they pass by [unthinkingly], and on which they turn their backs! ‹105›
And most of them do not even believe in God without [also] ascribing divine powers to other beings beside Him. ‹106› Do they, then, feel free from the fear that there might fall upon them the overwhelming terror of God's chastisement, or that the Last Hour might come upon them of a sudden, without their being aware [of its approach]? ‹107›
Say [O Prophet]: "This is my way: Resting upon conscious insight accessible to reason, I am calling [you all] unto God[104] – I and they who follow me."
And [say:] "Limitless is God in His glory; and I am not one of those who ascribe divinity to aught beside Him!" ‹108›
And [even] before thy time, We never sent [as Our apostles] any but [mortal] men, whom We inspired, [and whom We always chose] from among the people of the [very] communities [to whom the message was to be brought].[105]
Have, then, they [who reject this divine writ] never journeyed about the earth and beheld what happened in the end to those [deniers of the truth] who lived before them? – and [do they not know that] to those who are conscious of God the life in the hereafter is indeed better [than this

وَمَآ أَكۡثَرُ ٱلنَّاسِ وَلَوۡ حَرَصۡتَ بِمُؤۡمِنِينَ ﴿١٠٣﴾ وَمَا تَسۡـَٔلُهُمۡ عَلَيۡهِ مِنۡ أَجۡرٍۚ إِنۡ
هُوَ إِلَّا ذِكۡرٞ لِّلۡعَٰلَمِينَ ﴿١٠٤﴾ وَكَأَيِّن مِّنۡ ءَايَةٖ فِي ٱلسَّمَٰوَٰتِ وَٱلۡأَرۡضِ
يَمُرُّونَ عَلَيۡهَا وَهُمۡ عَنۡهَا مُعۡرِضُونَ ﴿١٠٥﴾ وَمَا يُؤۡمِنُ أَكۡثَرُهُم بِٱللَّهِ إِلَّا وَهُم
مُّشۡرِكُونَ ﴿١٠٦﴾ أَفَأَمِنُوٓاْ أَن تَأۡتِيَهُمۡ غَٰشِيَةٞ مِّنۡ عَذَابِ ٱللَّهِ أَوۡ تَأۡتِيَهُمُ ٱلسَّاعَةُ
بَغۡتَةٗ وَهُمۡ لَا يَشۡعُرُونَ ﴿١٠٧﴾ قُلۡ هَٰذِهِۦ سَبِيلِيٓ أَدۡعُوٓاْ إِلَى ٱللَّهِۚ عَلَىٰ بَصِيرَةٍ أَنَا۠
وَمَنِ ٱتَّبَعَنِيۖ وَسُبۡحَٰنَ ٱللَّهِ وَمَآ أَنَا۠ مِنَ ٱلۡمُشۡرِكِينَ ﴿١٠٨﴾ وَمَآ أَرۡسَلۡنَا مِن قَبۡلِكَ
إِلَّا رِجَالٗا نُّوحِيٓ إِلَيۡهِم مِّنۡ أَهۡلِ ٱلۡقُرَىٰٓۗ أَفَلَمۡ يَسِيرُواْ فِي ٱلۡأَرۡضِ فَيَنظُرُواْ
كَيۡفَ كَانَ عَٰقِبَةُ ٱلَّذِينَ مِن قَبۡلِهِمۡۗ وَلَدَارُ ٱلۡأٓخِرَةِ خَيۡرٞ لِّلَّذِينَ ٱتَّقَوۡاْۚ

Wa māa ʾaktharun-nāsi wa law ḥaraṣta bimuʾminīn. (103) Wa mā tasʾaluhum ʿalayhi min ʾajrin ʾin huwa ʾillā Dhikrul-lilʿālamīn. (104) Wa kaʾayyim-min ʾāyatiñ-fis-samāwāti wal-ʾarḍi yamurrūna ʿalayhā wa hum ʿanhā muʿriḍūn. (105) Wa mā yuʾminu ʾaktharuhum-billahi ʾillā wa hum-mushrikūn. (106) ʾAfaʾaminūu ʾañ-taʾtiyahum ghāshiyatum-min ʿadhābil-lāhi ʾaw taʾtiyahumus-Sāʿatu baghtatañw-wa hum lā yashʿurūn. (107) Qul hādhihī sabīlīi ʾadʿūu ʾilal-lāhi ʿalā baṣīratin ʾana wa manittabaʿanī. Wa subḥānal-lāhi wa māa ʾana minal-mushrikīn. (108) Wa māa ʾarsalnā miñ-qablika ʾillā rijālañ-nūḥīi ʾilayhim-min ʾahlil-qurā. ʾAfalam yasīrū fil-ʾarḍi fayañẓurū kayfa kāna ʿāqibatul-ladhīna miñ-qablihim. Wa ladārul-ʾĀkhirati khayrul-lilladhīnat-taqaw

104 It is impossible to render the expression *ʿalā baṣīrah* in a more concise manner. Derived from the verb *baṣura* or *baṣira* ("he became seeing" or "he saw"), the noun *baṣīrah* (as also the verb) has the abstract connotation of "seeing with one's mind": and so it signifies "the faculty of understanding based on conscious insight" as well as, tropically, "an evidence accessible to the intellect" or "verifiable by the intellect". Thus, the "call to God" enunciated by the Prophet is described here as the outcome of a conscious insight accessible to, and verifiable by, man's reason: a statement which circumscribes to perfection the Qurʾanic approach to all questions of faith, ethics and morality, and is echoed many times in expressions like "so that you might use your reason" (*laʿallakum taʿqilūn*), or "will you not, then, use your reason?" (*a fa-lā taʿqilūn*), or "so that they might understand [the truth]" (*laʿallahum yafqahūn*), or "so that you might think" (*laʿallakum tatafakkarūn*); and, finally, in the oft-repeated declaration that the message of the Qurʾān as such is meant specifically "for people who think" (*li-qawmin yatafakkarūn*).

105 This is an answer to the objection often raised by unbelievers that a mortal like themselves could not have

world]? Will they not, then, use their reason? ‹109›

[All the earlier apostles had to suffer persecution for a long time;] but at last[106] – when those apostles had lost all hope and saw themselves branded as liars[107] – Our succour attained to them: whereupon everyone whom We willed [to be saved] was saved [and the deniers of the truth were destroyed]. for, never can Our punishment be averted from people who are lost in sin. ‹110›

Indeed, in the stories of these men[108] there is a lesson for those who are endowed with insight.

[As for this revelation,[109]] it could not possibly be a discourse invented [by man]: nay indeed,[110] it is [a divine writ] confirming the truth of whatever there still remains [of earlier revelations], clearly spelling out everything,[111] and [offering] guidance and grace unto people who will believe. ‹111›

أَفَلَا تَعْقِلُونَ ﴿١٠٩﴾ حَتَّىٰٓ إِذَا ٱسْتَيْـَٔسَ ٱلرُّسُلُ وَظَنُّوٓا۟ أَنَّهُمْ قَدْ كُذِبُوا۟
جَآءَهُمْ نَصْرُنَا فَنُجِّىَ مَن نَّشَآءُ ۖ وَلَا يُرَدُّ بَأْسُنَا عَنِ ٱلْقَوْمِ ٱلْمُجْرِمِينَ ﴿١١٠﴾
لَقَدْ كَانَ فِى قَصَصِهِمْ عِبْرَةٌ لِّأُو۟لِى ٱلْأَلْبَـٰبِ ۗ مَا كَانَ حَدِيثًا يُفْتَرَىٰ
وَلَـٰكِن تَصْدِيقَ ٱلَّذِى بَيْنَ يَدَيْهِ وَتَفْصِيلَ كُلِّ شَىْءٍ وَهُدًى وَرَحْمَةً
لِّقَوْمٍ يُؤْمِنُونَ ﴿١١١﴾

ʾafalā taʿqilūn. (109) Ḥattāa ʾidhas-tayʾasar-Rusulu wa ẓannūu ʾannahum qad kudhibū jāaʾahum naṣrunā fanujjiya mañ-nashāaʾ. Wa lā yuraddu baʾsunā ʿanil-qawmil-mujrimīn. (110) Laqad kāna fī qaṣaṣihim ʿibratul-liʾulil-ʾalbāb. Mā kāna ḥadīthañy-yuftarā wa lākiñ-taṣdīqal-ladhī bayna yadayhi wa tafṣīla kulli shayʾiñw-wa hudañw-wa raḥmatal-liqawmiñy-yuʾminūn. (111)

been entrusted with God's message to man.

106 Lit., "until" (*ḥattā*). This connects with the reference to earlier apostles in the first sentence of the preceding verse: the implication being (according to Zamakhsharī) that they used to suffer for a long time before they were vindicated by God.

107 Lit., "thought that they had been given the lie" – i.e., either by their people, who regarded the apostles' expectation of God's succour as mere wishful thinking, or by the harsh reality which seemed to contradict those apostles' own hopes of speedy help from God (Zamakhsharī). Commenting on this verse, ʿAbd Allāh ibn ʿAbbās used to quote 2 : 214 – "so shaken were they that the apostle, and the believers with him, would exclaim, 'When will God's succour come?'" (*ibid.*)

108 Lit., "in their stories" – i.e., the stories of the prophets.

109 I.e., the Qurʾān as a whole (Baghawī and Zamakhsharī). The passage that follows connects with verses 102-105.

110 Lit., "but" – denoting here the *impossibility* of its having been invented by Muḥammad.

111 I.e., everything that man may need for his spiritual welfare. See also 10 : 37 and the corresponding note 60.

The Thirteenth Sūrah

*Ar-Ra*ᶜ*d* (Thunder)

Period Uncertain

THERE ARE considerable differences of opinion regarding the period in which this *sūrah* was revealed. According to one statement attributed to Ibn ᶜAbbās, it is a Meccan *sūrah* (Suyūṭī), while according to other authorities, mentioned by Ṭabarānī, Ibn ᶜAbbās is reported to have described it as belonging to the Medina period (*ibid.*). Suyūṭī himself inclines to the view that it is a Meccan *sūrah* but contains a few verses revealed at Medina; and so do Baghawī and Rāzī. Zamakhsharī, on the other hand, confines himself to the statement that the time of its revelation is uncertain.

Like so many other *sūrahs*, this one, too, takes it's title from the incidental mention of a word which caught the imagination of the earliest generation of Muslims: in this case, the word "thunder" occurring in verse 13, which relates to the evidence of God's creative powers forthcoming from the observable manifestations of nature.

The main theme of this *sūrah* is God's revelation, through His prophets, of certain fundamental moral truths which man may not neglect without suffering the natural consequences of such a neglect (see the last paragraph of verse 31 and note 57) – just as a realization of those moral truths by those "who are endowed with insight . . . [and] are true to their bond with God" (verses 19-20) invariably causes them to "find inner happiness and the most beauteous of all goals" (verse 29): for, "God does not change men's condition unless they change their inner selves" (verse 11).

-13-

سورة الرعد مدنية

وآياتها ثلاث وأربعون

IN THE NAME OF GOD, THE MOST GRACIOUS, THE DISPENSER OF GRACE:

Alif. Lām. Mīm. Rā.[1]

THESE ARE MESSAGES of revelation:[2] and what has been bestowed upon thee from on high by thy Sustainer is the truth – yet most people will not believe [in it].[3] ‹1›

It is God who has raised the heavens without any supports that you could see, and is established on the throne of His almightiness;[4] and He [it is who] has made the sun and the moon subservient [to His laws], each running its course for a term set [by Him].[5] He governs all that exists.

Clearly does He spell out these messages, so that you might be certain in your innermost that you are destined to meet your Sustainer [on Judgment Day].[6] ‹2›

And it is He who has spread the earth wide and placed on it firm mountains and running waters, and created thereon two sexes of every [kind of] plant;[7] [and it is

بِسۡمِ ٱللَّهِ ٱلرَّحۡمَٰنِ ٱلرَّحِيمِ

الٓمٓرٰۚ تِلۡكَ ءَايَٰتُ ٱلۡكِتَٰبِۗ وَٱلَّذِيٓ أُنزِلَ إِلَيۡكَ مِن رَّبِّكَ ٱلۡحَقُّ وَلَٰكِنَّ أَكۡثَرَ
ٱلنَّاسِ لَا يُؤۡمِنُونَ ﴿١﴾ ٱللَّهُ ٱلَّذِي رَفَعَ ٱلسَّمَٰوَٰتِ بِغَيۡرِ عَمَدٖ تَرَوۡنَهَاۖ ثُمَّ
ٱسۡتَوَىٰ عَلَى ٱلۡعَرۡشِۖ وَسَخَّرَ ٱلشَّمۡسَ وَٱلۡقَمَرَۖ كُلّٞ يَجۡرِي لِأَجَلٖ مُّسَمّٗىۚ يُدَبِّرُ
ٱلۡأَمۡرَ يُفَصِّلُ ٱلۡأٓيَٰتِ لَعَلَّكُم بِلِقَآءِ رَبِّكُمۡ تُوقِنُونَ ﴿٢﴾ وَهُوَ ٱلَّذِي مَدَّ
ٱلۡأَرۡضَ وَجَعَلَ فِيهَا رَوَٰسِيَ وَأَنۡهَٰرٗاۖ وَمِن كُلِّ ٱلثَّمَرَٰتِ جَعَلَ فِيهَا زَوۡجَيۡنِ ٱثۡنَيۡنِۖ

Bismil-lāhir-Raḥmānir-Raḥīm.

ʾAlif-Lāam-Mīim-Rā. Tilka ʾĀyātul-Kitāb. Wal-ladhīi ʾuñzila ʾilayka mir-Rabbikal-ḥaqqu wa lākinna ʾaktharan-nāsi lā yuʾminūn. (1) ʾAllāhul-ladhī rafaʿas-samāwāti bighayri ʿamadiñ-tarawnahā thummas-tawā ʿalal-ʿarshi wa sakhkharash-shamsa wal-qamara kulluñy-yajrī liʾajalim-musammā. Yudabbirul-ʾamra yufaṣṣilul-ʾĀyāti laʿallakum-biliqāaʾi Rabbikum tūqinūn. (2) Wa Huwal-ladhī maddal-ʾarḍa wa jaʿala fīhā rawāsiya wa ʾanhārā. Wa miñ-kullith-thamarāti jaʿala fīhā zawjaynith-nayni

---

1 See Appendix II.

2 Although some commentators are of the opinion that the term *kitāb* ("divine writ" or "revelation") refers here to this particular *sūrah*, Ibn ʿAbbās states emphatically that it denotes the Qurʾān as a whole (Baghawī).

3 This passage connects with the concluding verses (102-111) of the preceding *sūrah*, and particularly with verse 103, all of which stress the divine origin of the Qurʾān.

4 For an explanation of this phrase, see *sūrah* 7, note 43. As regards the "raising of the heavens without any supports" visible to man, it should be borne in mind that the noun *samāʾ* denotes, primarily, "something that is above [another thing]", and is used – mostly in its plural form *samāwāt* – to describe (a) the visible skies (as well as, occasionally, the clouds), (b) the cosmic space in which the stars, the solar systems (including our own) and the galaxies pursue their course, and (c) the abstract concept of the forces emanating from God (since He is, in the metonymical sense of this word, "above" all that exists). To my mind, it is the second of these three meanings of *samāwāt* to which the above verse refers: namely, to the spatial universe in which all aggregations of matter – be they planets, stars, nebulae or galaxies – are, as it were, "suspended" in space within a system of unceasing motion determined by centrifugal forces and mutual, gravitational attraction.

5 This may refer either to the end of the world as we know it – thus indicating the finality of all creation – or, according to ʿAbd Allāh ibn ʿAbbās (as quoted by Baghawī and Rāzī), to the "mansions" or stages through which the sun and the moon, like all other celestial bodies, move in time as well as in space.

6 I.e., "so that you might realize that He who has created the universe and governs all that exists is equally able to resurrect the dead, and to judge you in the life to come in accordance with what you did when you were alive on earth".

7 Lit., "and out of all [kinds of] fruits He made thereon [i.e., on earth] pairs (*zawjayn ithnayn*)". The term *zawj*

ثلاثة أرباع الحزب

He who] causes the night to cover the day. Verily, in all this there are messages indeed for people who think! ‹3›

And there are on earth [many] tracts of land close by one another [and yet widely differing from one another[8]]; and [there are on it] vineyards, and fields of grain, and date-palms growing in clusters from one root or standing alone,[9] [all] watered with the same water: and yet, some of them have We favoured above others by way of the food [which they provide for man and beast].[10]

Verily, in all this there are messages indeed for people who use their reason! ‹4›

BUT IF thou art amazed [at the marvels of God's creation], amazing, too, is their saying, "What! After we have become dust, shall we indeed be [restored to life] in a new act of creation?"[11]

It is they who [thus show that they] are bent on denying their Sustainer;[12] and it is they who carry the shackles [of their own making] around their necks;[13] and it is they who are destined for the fire, therein to abide. ‹5›

يُغْشِى ٱلَّيْلَ ٱلنَّهَارَ ۚ إِنَّ فِى ذَٰلِكَ لَءَايَٰتٍ لِّقَوْمٍ يَتَفَكَّرُونَ ﴿٣﴾ وَفِى
ٱلْأَرْضِ قِطَعٌ مُّتَجَٰوِرَٰتٌ وَجَنَّٰتٌ مِّنْ أَعْنَٰبٍ وَزَرْعٌ وَنَخِيلٌ صِنْوَانٌ
وَغَيْرُ صِنْوَانٍ يُسْقَىٰ بِمَآءٍ وَٰحِدٍ وَنُفَضِّلُ بَعْضَهَا عَلَىٰ بَعْضٍ فِى ٱلْأُكُلِ ۚ إِنَّ
فِى ذَٰلِكَ لَءَايَٰتٍ لِّقَوْمٍ يَعْقِلُونَ ﴿٤﴾ ۞ وَإِن تَعْجَبْ فَعَجَبٌ قَوْلُهُمْ
أَءِذَا كُنَّا تُرَٰبًا أَءِنَّا لَفِى خَلْقٍ جَدِيدٍ ۗ أُو۟لَٰٓئِكَ ٱلَّذِينَ كَفَرُوا۟ بِرَبِّهِمْ ۖ
وَأُو۟لَٰٓئِكَ ٱلْأَغْلَٰلُ فِىٓ أَعْنَاقِهِمْ ۖ وَأُو۟لَٰٓئِكَ أَصْحَٰبُ ٱلنَّارِ ۖ هُمْ فِيهَا
خَٰلِدُونَ ﴿٥﴾

yughshil-laylan-nahār. ʾInna fī dhālika laʾĀyātil-liqawmiñy-yatafakkarūn. ﴿3﴾ Wa fil-ʾarḍi qiṭaʿum-mutajāwirātuñw-wa jannātum-min ʾaʿnābiñw-wa zarʿuñw-wa nakhīluñ-ṣinwānuñw-wa ghayru ṣinwāniñy-yusqā bimāaʾiñw-wāḥidiñw-wa nufaḍḍilu baʿḍahā ʿalā baʿḍiñ-fil-ʾukul. ʾInna fī dhālika la-ʾĀyātil-liqawmiñy-yaʿqilūn. ﴿4﴾ ۞ Wa ʾiñ-taʿjab faʿajabuñ-qawluhum ʾaʾidhā kunnā turāban ʾaʾinnā lafī khalqiñ-jadīd. ʾUlāaʾikal-ladhīna kafarū biRabbihim wa ʾulāaʾikal-ʾaghlālu fīi ʾaʿnāqihim wa ʾulāʾika ʾaṣḥābun-nāri hum fīhā khālidūn. ﴿5﴾

denotes, according to the context, either "a pair" or "one of a pair". Whenever the dual form *zawjān* is followed by the additional numerical definition *ithnān* ("two"), it invariably signifies "a pair comprising both sexes". Thus, the above phrase states that there are two sexes to every kind of plant: a statement fully in accord with botanical science. (Usually, the male and female organs of reproduction exist together in one and the same flower of a particular plant, e.g., cotton; alternatively, they are placed in separate flowers of one and the same plant, e.g., in most of the cucurbitaceae; and, in some rare cases, e.g., the date-palm, in entirely separate, uni-sexual plants of the same species.)

8 I.e., regarding the nature of the soil, fertility and kind of vegetation. The necessity of this interpolation – which, in the consensus of all commentators, conveys the meaning of the above phrase – becomes apparent from the subsequent clauses.

9 Lit., "non-clustered" (*ghayr ṣinwān*) – i.e., each tree having separate roots.

10 Cf. 6 : 99 and 141, where a similar stress is laid on the multiformity of plants – and their varying beneficence to man and animal – as some of the signs of God's purposeful, creative activity.

11 I.e., while it is amazing that one can refuse to believe in God despite all the evidence, accessible to human observation, of the existence of a definite purpose in all life-phenomena, and thus of the existence of a conscious Creative Power, it is no less amazing to see people who, while vaguely believing in God, can yet refuse to believe in individual resurrection: for, if God has created the universe and the phenomenon of life as such, He obviously has the power to *re-create* life – and its requisite physical vehicle – in a new act of creation.

12 By denying the possibility of resurrection, they implicitly deny God's almightiness, and thus, in effect, His reality.

13 A metaphor of man's wilful self-abandonment to false values and evil ways, and of the resulting enslavement of the spirit (cf. Zamakhsharī, Rāzī, Bayḍāwī). See also *sūrah* 34, note 44.

And [since, O Prophet, they are bent on denying the truth,] they challenge thee to hasten the coming upon them of evil instead of [hoping for] good[14] – although [they ought to know that] the exemplary punishments [which they now deride] have indeed come to pass before their time.
Now, behold, thy Sustainer is full of forgiveness unto men despite all their evildoing:[15] but, behold, thy Sustainer is [also] truly severe in retribution! ‹6›
However, they who are bent on denying the truth [refuse to believe and] say, "Why has no miraculous sign ever been bestowed on him from on high by his Sustainer?"[16]
[But] thou art only a warner; and [in God] all people have a guide.[17] ‹7›
God knows what any female bears [in her womb], and by how much the wombs may fall short [in gestation], and by how much they may increase [the average period]:[18] for with Him everything is [created] in accordance with its scope and purpose.[19] ‹8›

وَيَسْتَعْجِلُونَكَ بِالسَّيِّئَةِ قَبْلَ الْحَسَنَةِ وَقَدْ خَلَتْ مِن قَبْلِهِمُ الْمَثُلَاتُ ۗ
وَإِنَّ رَبَّكَ لَذُو مَغْفِرَةٍ لِّلنَّاسِ عَلَىٰ ظُلْمِهِمْ ۖ وَإِنَّ رَبَّكَ لَشَدِيدُ الْعِقَابِ ﴿6﴾
وَيَقُولُ الَّذِينَ كَفَرُوا لَوْلَا أُنزِلَ عَلَيْهِ آيَةٌ مِّن رَّبِّهِ ۗ إِنَّمَا أَنتَ مُنذِرٌ ۖ
وَلِكُلِّ قَوْمٍ هَادٍ ﴿7﴾ اللَّهُ يَعْلَمُ مَا تَحْمِلُ كُلُّ أُنثَىٰ وَمَا تَغِيضُ الْأَرْحَامُ
وَمَا تَزْدَادُ ۖ وَكُلُّ شَيْءٍ عِندَهُ بِمِقْدَارٍ ﴿8﴾

Wa yastaʿjilūnaka bissayyiʾati qablal-ḥasanati wa qad khalat miñ-qablihimul-mathulāt. Wa ʾinna Rabbaka ladhū maghfiratil-linnāsi ʿalā ẓulmihim wa ʾinna Rabbaka laShadīdul-ʿiqāb. (6) Wa yaqūlul-ladhīna kafarū lawlāa ʾuñzila ʿalayhi ʾĀyatum-mir-Rabbih. ʾInnamāa ʾañta mundhiruñw-wa likulli qawmin hād. (7) ʾAllāhu yaʿlamu mā taḥmilu kullu ʾuñthā wa mā taghīḍul-ʾarḥāmu wa mā tazdād. Wa kullu shayʾin ʿiñdahū bimiqdār. (8)

14 Lit., "they ask thee to hasten the evil before the good": i.e., instead of willingly accepting the guidance offered them by the Prophet, they mockingly challenge him to bring about the exemplary punishment with which, according to him, God threatens them. (For a fuller explanation of this "challenge", referred to here and in several other places in the Qurʾān, see 6 : 57-58 and 8 : 32, as well as the corresponding notes.)

15 Cf. the first sentence of 10 : 11 and the corresponding note 17.

16 I.e., to prove that he (Muḥammad) is really a prophet inspired by God. But the Qurʾān makes it clear in several places (e.g., 6 : 7 and 111, 10 : 96-97 or 13 : 31) that even a miracle would not convince those who are "bent on denying the truth".

17 According to the classical commentators, this sentence lends itself to several interpretations: (1) "Thou art only a warner; and every nation has had a guide like thee (i.e., a prophet)" – which would be in consonance with the Qurʾanic doctrine of the continuity of prophetic guidance; or (2) "Thou art only a warner – but [at the same time] also a guide unto all people" – which would stress the universality of the Qurʾanic message as contrasted with the time-bound and ethnically limited missions of the earlier prophets; or (3) "Thou art only a warner bound to do no more than deliver the message entrusted to thee, while it is God alone who can truly guide men's hearts towards faith". Since the last of the above three interpretations is the most plausible and has, moreover, the support of ʿAbd Allāh ibn ʿAbbās, Sa ʿīd ibn Jubayr, Mujāhid and Aḍ-Ḍaḥḥāk, I have adopted it in my rendering. According to Zamakhsharī, this interpretation is further strengthened by the subsequent reference to God's omniscience.

18 The term *unthā* denotes any female being, whether human or animal. The "falling short" may refer either to a shortening of the usual period of gestation (e.g., to seven months in human beings) or to a falling short of the completion of pregnancy, i.e., a miscarriage; it is to be noted that the noun *ghayḍ* signifies "an abortive foetus" (*Tāj al-ʿArūs*), i.e., in human beings, a foetus less than seven months old. The "increase", on the other hand, may mean either the completion of gestation or its being in excess of the average period (as, for instance, the occasional lengthening of human pregnancy from the usual period of about 280 days to 305 or, according to some medical authorities, even 307 days). In addition to this, God's knowledge of "what any female bears [in her womb]" obviously relates also to the sex of the unborn embryo as well as to the number of offspring involved in one pregnancy. – As the sequence shows, this reference to the mysteries of gestation, fully known only to God, is meant to bring out the idea that He who knows what is in the wombs knows also the innermost disposition of every human being and the direction in which that human being will develop.

19 Lit., "according to a measure" (*bi-miqdār*) – i.e., in accordance with the particular purpose for which it has been

He knows all that is beyond the reach of a created being's perception as well as all that can be witnessed by a creature's senses or mind[20] – the Great One, the One far above anything that is or could ever be![21] ‹9›
It is all alike [to Him] whether any of you conceals his thought[22] or brings it into the open, and whether he seeks to hide [his evil deeds] under the cover of night or walks [boldly] in the light of day,[23] ‹10›
[thinking that] he has hosts of helpers – both such as can be perceived by him and such as are hidden from him[24] – that could preserve him from whatever God may have willed.[25]
Verily, God does not change men's condition unless they change their inner selves;[26] and when God wills people to

عَٰلِمُ ٱلْغَيْبِ وَٱلشَّهَٰدَةِ ٱلْكَبِيرُ ٱلْمُتَعَالِ ﴿٩﴾ سَوَآءٌ مِّنكُم مَّنْ أَسَرَّ
ٱلْقَوْلَ وَمَن جَهَرَ بِهِۦ وَمَنْ هُوَ مُسْتَخْفٍۭ بِٱلَّيْلِ وَسَارِبٌۢ بِٱلنَّهَارِ ﴿١٠﴾
لَهُۥ مُعَقِّبَٰتٌ مِّنۢ بَيْنِ يَدَيْهِ وَمِنْ خَلْفِهِۦ يَحْفَظُونَهُۥ مِنْ أَمْرِ ٱللَّهِ ۗ إِنَّ
ٱللَّهَ لَا يُغَيِّرُ مَا بِقَوْمٍ حَتَّىٰ يُغَيِّرُوا۟ مَا بِأَنفُسِهِمْ ۗ وَإِذَآ أَرَادَ ٱللَّهُ بِقَوْمٍ

ͨĀlimul-ghaybi wash-shahādatil-Kabīrul-Muta ͨāl. ⟨9⟩
Sawāaʾum-miñkum-man ʾasarral-qawla wa mañ-ja-
hara bihī wa man huwa mustakhfim-billayli wa sāri-
bum-binnahār. ⟨10⟩ Lahū mu ͨaqqibātum-mim-bayni
yadayhi wa min khalfihī yaḥfaẓūnahū min ʾamril-lāh.
ʾInnal-lāha lā yughayyiru mā biqawmin ḥattā yughayy-
irū mā biʾañfusihim. Wa ʾidhāa ʾarādal-lāhu biqawmiñ-

created, the exigencies of its existence and the role which it is destined to play within God's plan of creation.

20 See *sūrah* 6, note 65.

21 God's attribute *al-muta ͨāl*, which occurs in the Qurʾān only in this one instance, denotes His infinite exaltedness above anything existing or potential; also, according to Zamakhsharī, above anything that could be circumscribed by human definitions. (See in this connection the last sentence of 6 : 100 and the corresponding note 88.)

22 The term *qawl* denotes, primarily, "a saying" or "an utterance", but it is also used tropically in the sense of "an idea", irrespective of whether it is expressed in actual words (as a statement, an assertion, a formulated doctrine, etc.) or merely conceived in the mind (e.g., an opinion, a view, or a connected set of ideas). Since in the above verse this term obviously refers to unspoken thoughts, I have rendered it accordingly.

23 Lit., "and goes forth by day" – i.e., commits evil deeds openly (Ibn ͨAbbās, as quoted by Baghawī and Rāzī). In the Arabic construction, the sentence reads thus: "All alike [to Him] is he from among you who conceals his thought (*al-qawl*) and he who brings it into the open, as well as he who . . . ," etc.

24 Lit., "from between his hands and from behind him". As in 2 : 255, the expression "between his hands" denotes "something that is perceivable by him" or "evident to him", while that which is "behind him" is a metonym for something "beyond his ken" or "hidden from him". See also next note.

25 Lit., "from God's command (*amr*)". The rendering of the above passage hinges on the meaning given to the term *mu ͨaqqibāt* – a double plural of *mu ͨaqqib*, which signifies "something that comes immediately after another thing" or "succeeds another thing without interruption". Most of the classical commentators understand by *mu ͨaqqibāt* "hosts of angels", i.e., the recording angels who attend on every human being, succeeding one another without interruption. Consequently, they interpret the phrase *min bayni yadayhi wa-min khalfihi* as meaning "ranged before him and behind him", i.e., surrounding man from all sides; and they explain the words "from God's command" as being here synonymous with "*by* God's command", and take them to refer to the angels or to their function of guardianship. However, this interpretation has by no means the support of all the commentators. Some of the earliest ones assume that the term *mu ͨaqqibāt* refers to all manner of *worldly* forces or concepts on which man so often relies in the mistaken belief that they might help him to achieve his aims independently of God's will: and this is the meaning given to this elliptic passage by the famous commentator Abū Muslim al-Iṣfahānī, as quoted by Rāzī. Explaining verse 10 and the first part of verse 11, he says: "All alike are, in God's knowledge, deeds done secretly or openly, as well as he who hides in the darkness of night and he who walks [boldly] in the light of day . . .: for he that resorts to the [cover of] night can never elude God's will (*amr*), just as he [cannot] that walks in the light of day, surrounded by hosts of helpers (*mu ͨaqqibāt*) – that is, guards and aids – meant to protect him: [for] those guards of his cannot save him from [the will of] God." It is on this convincing interpretation that I have based my rendering. The worldly "guards and aids" on which a sinner relies may be tangible (like wealth, progeny, etc.) or intangible (like personal power, high social standing, or the belief in one's "luck"): and this explains the phrase "both such as can be perceived by him and such as are hidden from him" (see preceding note).

26 Lit., "that which is in themselves". This statement has both a positive and a negative connotation: i.e., God does

suffer evil [in consequence of their own evil deeds], there is none who could avert it: for they have none who could protect them from Him. ‹11›

HE IT IS who displays before you the lightning, to give rise to [both] fear and hope,[27] and calls heavy clouds into being; ‹12› and the thunder extols His limitless glory and praises Him, and [so do] the angels, in awe of Him; and He [it is who] lets loose the thunderbolts and strikes with them whom He wills.
And yet, they stubbornly argue about God,[28] notwithstanding [all evidence] that He alone has the power to contrive whatever His unfathomable wisdom wills![29] ‹13›
Unto Him [alone] is due all prayer aiming at the Ultimate Truth,[30] since those [other beings or powers] whom men invoke instead of God[31] cannot respond to them in any way – [so that he who invokes them is] but like one who stretches his open hands[32] towards water, [hoping] that it will reach his mouth, the while it never reaches him. Hence, the prayer of those who deny the truth amounts to no more than losing oneself in grievous error. ‹14›
And before God prostrate themselves, willingly or unwillingly, all [things and beings]

سُوٓءًا فَلَا مَرَدَّ لَهُۥ ۚ وَمَا لَهُم مِّن دُونِهِۦ مِن وَالٍ ﴿١١﴾ هُوَ ٱلَّذِى يُرِيكُمُ
ٱلْبَرْقَ خَوْفًا وَطَمَعًا وَيُنشِئُ ٱلسَّحَابَ ٱلثِّقَالَ ﴿١٢﴾ وَيُسَبِّحُ ٱلرَّعْدُ
بِحَمْدِهِۦ وَٱلْمَلَٰٓئِكَةُ مِنْ خِيفَتِهِۦ وَيُرْسِلُ ٱلصَّوَٰعِقَ فَيُصِيبُ بِهَا مَن
يَشَآءُ وَهُمْ يُجَٰدِلُونَ فِى ٱللَّهِ وَهُوَ شَدِيدُ ٱلْمِحَالِ ﴿١٣﴾ لَهُۥ دَعْوَةُ ٱلْحَقِّ
وَٱلَّذِينَ يَدْعُونَ مِن دُونِهِۦ لَا يَسْتَجِيبُونَ لَهُم بِشَىْءٍ إِلَّا كَبَٰسِطِ كَفَّيْهِ
إِلَى ٱلْمَآءِ لِيَبْلُغَ فَاهُ وَمَا هُوَ بِبَٰلِغِهِۦ ۚ وَمَا دُعَآءُ ٱلْكَٰفِرِينَ إِلَّا فِى
ضَلَٰلٍ ﴿١٤﴾ وَلِلَّهِ يَسْجُدُ مَن فِى ٱلسَّمَٰوَٰتِ وَٱلْأَرْضِ طَوْعًا وَكَرْهًا

sūu'añ-falā maradda lahū wa mā lahum-miñ-dūnihī
miñw-wāl. (11) Huwal-ladhī yurīkumul-barqa khaw-
fañw-wa ṭa-ma'añw-wa yuñshi'us-saḥābath-thiqāl.
(12) Wa yusabbiḥur-ra'du biḥamdihī wal-Malāa'ikatu
min khīfatihī wa yursiluṣ-ṣawā'iqa fayuṣību bihā
mañy-yashāa'u wa hum yujādilūna fil-lāhi wa
Huwa Shadīdul-miḥāl. (13) Lahū da'watul-ḥaqq. Wal-
ladhīna yad'ūna miñ-dūnihī lā yastajībūna lahum-
bishay'in 'illā kabāsiṭi kaffayhi 'ilal-māa'i liyablu-
gha fāhu wa mā huwa bibālighihī wa mā du'āa'ul-
kāfirīna 'illā fī ḍalāl. (14) Wa lillāhi yasjudu mañ-
fis-samāwāti wal-'arḍi ṭaw'añw-wa karhañw-

not withdraw His blessings from men unless their inner selves become depraved (cf. 8 : 53), just as He does not bestow His blessings upon wilful sinners until they change their inner disposition and become worthy of His grace. In its wider sense, this is an illustration of the divine law of cause and effect (*sunnat Allāh*) which dominates the lives of both individuals and communities, and makes the rise and fall of civilizations dependent on people's moral qualities and the changes in "their inner selves".

27 I.e., hope of rain, which in the Qur'ān frequently symbolizes faith and spiritual life. With this verse, the discourse returns to the theme enunciated at the beginning of this *sūrah* (verses 2-4): namely, to the evidence of a consciously devised plan and purpose inherent in all nature and, thus, of the existence of God.

28 I.e., about His transcendental existence or the quality of His Being.

29 According to Rāghib, the expression *shadīd al-miḥāl* (which occurs in the Qur'ān only in this one place) signifies "powerful in contriving, in a manner hidden from man, that wherein wisdom lies"; hence my rendering.

30 Lit., "His is the call [or "invocation"] of the truth"; or, possibly, "to Him [alone] is due all true invocation". It should, however, be remembered that the term *al-ḥaqq* ("the Truth") is one of the Qur'anic attributes of God, signifying the Ultimate Reality or Primal Cause of all that exists (the *Urgrund* in German philosophical terminology): consequently, the expression *da'wat al-ḥaqq* may be understood in the sense of "prayer directed towards Him who is the Ultimate Reality", implying – as the sequence clearly states – that the invocation of any other being, power or principle is *eo ipso* wrong and futile.

31 Or: "side by side with God".

32 Lit., "his two palms".

that are in the heavens and on earth,[33] as do their shadows in the mornings and the evenings.[34] ‹15›
Say: "Who is the Sustainer of the heavens and the earth?"
Say: "[It is] God."
Say: "[Why] then, do you take for your protectors, instead of Him, such as have it not within their power to bring benefit to, or avert harm from, themselves?"
Say: "Can the blind and the seeing be deemed equal? – or can the depths of darkness and the light be deemed equal?"
Or do they [really] believe that there are, side by side with God, other divine powers[35] that have created the like of what He creates, so that this act of creation appears to them to be similar [to His]?[36]
Say: "God is the Creator of all things; and He is the One who holds absolute sway over all that exists." ‹16›
[Whenever] He sends down water from the sky, and [once-dry] river-beds are running high[37] according to their measure, the stream carries scum on its surface;[38]

السجدة

وَظِلَـٰلُهُم بِٱلْغُدُوِّ وَٱلْـَٔاصَالِ ۩ ﴿١٥﴾ قُلْ مَن رَّبُّ ٱلسَّمَـٰوَٰتِ
وَٱلْأَرْضِ قُلِ ٱللَّهُ قُلْ أَفَٱتَّخَذْتُم مِّن دُونِهِۦٓ أَوْلِيَآءَ لَا يَمْلِكُونَ
لِأَنفُسِهِمْ نَفْعًا وَلَا ضَرًّا قُلْ هَلْ يَسْتَوِى ٱلْأَعْمَىٰ وَٱلْبَصِيرُ أَمْ هَلْ
تَسْتَوِى ٱلظُّلُمَـٰتُ وَٱلنُّورُ أَمْ جَعَلُوا۟ لِلَّهِ شُرَكَآءَ خَلَقُوا۟ كَخَلْقِهِۦ فَتَشَـٰبَهَ
ٱلْخَلْقُ عَلَيْهِمْ قُلِ ٱللَّهُ خَـٰلِقُ كُلِّ شَىْءٍ وَهُوَ ٱلْوَٰحِدُ ٱلْقَهَّـٰرُ ﴿١٦﴾ أَنزَلَ
مِنَ ٱلسَّمَآءِ مَآءً فَسَالَتْ أَوْدِيَةٌۢ بِقَدَرِهَا فَٱحْتَمَلَ ٱلسَّيْلُ زَبَدًا رَّابِيًا

wa ẓilāluhum-bilghuduwwi wal-ʾāṣāl. ۩ ﴿15﴾ Qul mar-Rabbus-samāwāti wal-ʾarḍī qulil-lāh. Qul ʾafattakhadhtum-miñ-dūnihīi ʾawliyāaʾa lā yamlikūna liʾañfusihim nafʿañw-wa lā ḍarrā. Qul hal yastawil-ʾaʿmā wal-baṣīr ʾam hal tastawiẓ-ẓulumātu wan-nūr. ʾAm jaʿalū lillāhi shurakāaʾa khalaqū kakhalqihī fatashābahal-khalqu ʿalayhim. Qulil-lāhu Khāliqu kulli shayʾiñw-wa Huwal-Wāḥidul-Qahhār. ﴿16﴾ ʾAñzala minas-samāʾi māaʾañ-fasālat ʾawdiyatum-biqadarihā faḥtamalas-saylu zabadar-rābiyā.

33 The expression *yasjud* ("prostrates himself" or "prostrate themselves") is a metonym for complete submission to His will (Zamakhsharī), that is, to the natural laws decreed by Him with regard to everything that exists. According to most of the classical commentators, those who submit to God willingly (i.e., consciously) are the angels and the believers, whereas the deniers of the truth, who are "not willing" to submit to Him, are nevertheless, without being conscious of it, subject to His will. However, in view of the subsequent reference to "shadows" it is logical to assume that the relative pronoun *man* relates in this context not merely to conscious beings but also to all other physical objects, whether animate or inanimate – i.e., to "all things and beings that are in the heavens and on earth". (See also 16 : 48-49 and 22 : 18.)

34 I.e., the varying lengths of the shadow projected by any material object depend on the position of the sun in relation to the earth; and since the earth's rotation around the sun is – as everything else in the universe – an outcome of God's creative will, the greater length of a shadow in the morning and evening and its contraction towards noon visibly expresses the shadow's subjection to Him.

35 Lit.,"do they assign to God partners . . .", etc. – i.e., beings that supposedly have a share in God's divinity and/or His creative power. (See also *sūrah* 6, note 15.)

36 Although the term *khalq* ("creation" or "act of creation") is often used metaphorically with reference to *human* achievements, there is an intrinsic difference between the "creation" of an artist, a poet or a philosopher, and the act of creation as attributed to God: for whereas the human "creator" produces his work out of already-existing elements and does no more than bring those elements together in a (possibly) new combination, God alone has the power to create in the true sense of the word – that is, to bring into being something that did not exist, either in its entirety or in its components, before this particular act of creation (cf. 2 : 117 – "when He wills a thing to be, He but says unto it, 'Be' – and it is"). This is the significance of the allusion, in the above verse, to the erroneous belief that any other power or being could ever have "created *the like of* what He creates".

37 The interpolation of the adjective "once-dry" before "river-beds" (*awdiyah*) is necessitated by the absence of the definite article *al* before this noun. According to Zamakhsharī, this indicates that only some of the river-beds are streaming with water while others, not affected by this particular rainfall, remain dry. It is to be borne in mind that the term *wād* (or *wādī* in popular parlance) denotes, primarily, a "water-course" or "river-bed" which is normally dry and carries water only after copious rainfalls; it is only by extension that this term is sometimes applied to an actual river.

38 Sc., "while the water beneath remains clear".

and, likewise, from that [metal] which they smelt in the fire in order to make ornaments or utensils, [there rises] scum.
In this way does God set forth the parable of truth and falsehood: for, as far as the scum is concerned, it passes away as [does all] dross; but that which is of benefit to man abides on earth.
In this way does God set forth the parables ‹17› of those who have responded to their Sustainer with a goodly response, and of those who did not respond to Him.[39] [As for the latter,] if they possessed all that is on earth, and twice as much,[40] they would surely offer it as ransom [on the Day of Judgment]:[41] a most evil reckoning awaits them, and their goal is hell: and how evil a resting-place! ‹18›

CAN, THEN, he who knows that whatever has been bestowed from on high upon thee by thy Sustainer is the truth be deemed equal to one who is blind?
Only they who are endowed with insight keep this in mind: ‹19› they who are true to their bond with God and never break their covenant;[42] ‹20› and who keep together what God has bidden to be joined,[43] and stand in awe of their Sustainer and fear the most evil reckoning [which awaits such as do not respond to Him]; ‹21›

وَمِمَّا يُوقِدُونَ عَلَيْهِ فِي ٱلنَّارِ ٱبْتِغَآءَ حِلْيَةٍ أَوْ مَتَٰعٍ زَبَدٌ مِّثْلُهُۥ ۚ كَذَٰلِكَ
يَضْرِبُ ٱللَّهُ ٱلْحَقَّ وَٱلْبَٰطِلَ ۚ فَأَمَّا ٱلزَّبَدُ فَيَذْهَبُ جُفَآءً ۖ وَأَمَّا مَا يَنفَعُ
ٱلنَّاسَ فَيَمْكُثُ فِي ٱلْأَرْضِ ۚ كَذَٰلِكَ يَضْرِبُ ٱللَّهُ ٱلْأَمْثَالَ ﴿17﴾ لِلَّذِينَ
ٱسْتَجَابُوا۟ لِرَبِّهِمُ ٱلْحُسْنَىٰ ۚ وَٱلَّذِينَ لَمْ يَسْتَجِيبُوا۟ لَهُۥ لَوْ أَنَّ لَهُم مَّا فِي
ٱلْأَرْضِ جَمِيعًا وَمِثْلَهُۥ مَعَهُۥ لَٱفْتَدَوْا۟ بِهِۦٓ ۚ أُو۟لَٰٓئِكَ لَهُمْ سُوٓءُ ٱلْحِسَابِ
وَمَأْوَىٰهُمْ جَهَنَّمُ ۖ وَبِئْسَ ٱلْمِهَادُ ﴿18﴾ ۞ أَفَمَن يَعْلَمُ أَنَّمَآ أُنزِلَ إِلَيْكَ مِن
رَّبِّكَ ٱلْحَقُّ كَمَنْ هُوَ أَعْمَىٰٓ ۚ إِنَّمَا يَتَذَكَّرُ أُو۟لُوا۟ ٱلْأَلْبَٰبِ ﴿19﴾ ٱلَّذِينَ
يُوفُونَ بِعَهْدِ ٱللَّهِ وَلَا يَنقُضُونَ ٱلْمِيثَٰقَ ﴿20﴾ وَٱلَّذِينَ يَصِلُونَ مَآ أَمَرَ ٱللَّهُ حزب 26
بِهِۦٓ أَن يُوصَلَ وَيَخْشَوْنَ رَبَّهُمْ وَيَخَافُونَ سُوٓءَ ٱلْحِسَابِ ﴿21﴾

Wa mimmā yūqidūna ʿalayhi fin-nārib-tighāaʾa
ḥilyatin ʾaw matāʿiñ-zabadum-mithluh. Kadhālika
yaḍribul-lāhul-ḥaqqa wal-bāṭil. Faʾammaz-zabadu
fayadhhabu jufāaʾañw-wa ʾammā mā yañfaʿun-
nāsa fayamkuthu fil-ʾarḍ. Kadhālika yaḍribul-lāhul-
ʾamthāl. 17 Lilladhīnas-tajābū liRabbihimul-ḥusnā.
Wal-ladhīna lam yastajībū lahū law ʾanna lahum-mā
fil-ʾarḍi jamīʿañw-wa mithlahū maʿahū laftadaw
bih. ʾUlāaʾika lahum sūuʾul-ḥisābi wa maʾwāhum
jahannamu wa biʾsal-mihād. 18 ۞ ʾAfamañy-yaʿlamu
ʾannamāa ʾuñzila ʾilayka mir-Rabbikal-ḥaqqu kaman huwa ʾaʿmā. ʾInnamā yatadhakkaru ʾulul-
ʾalbāb. 19 ʾAlladhīna yūfūna biʿahdil-lāhi wa lā
yañquḍūnal-mīthāq. 20 Wal-ladhīna yaṣilūna
māa ʾamaral-lāhu bihīi ʾañy-yūṣala wa yakhshawna Rabbahum wa yakhāfūna sūuʾal-ḥisāb. 21

---

39 This rendering is based on Zamakhsharī's interpretation of the above passage. According to other commentators, the beginning of verse 18 is independent of the last sentence of the preceding verse, and is a new sentence, reading thus: "For those who have responded to their Sustainer there is the ultimate good (*al-ḥusnā*) [in store]; but as for those who did not respond to Him . . .", etc. In my opinion, Zamakhsharī's reading – in which the expression *al-ḥusnā* is regarded as an adjective qualifying the believers' response – is preferable inasmuch as it fully justifies the repetition of the reference to "God's parables".

40 Lit., "and the like of it with it".

41 Cf. 3 : 91 and the corresponding note 71.

42 The "covenant" is, in this context, a general term embracing the spiritual obligations arising from one's faith in God and the moral and social obligations, resulting from that faith, towards one's fellow-men (Zamakhsharī); see in this connection the first sentence of 5 : 1 (where the term *ʿaqd* is used) and the corresponding note 1. As regards my rendering of *ʿahd Allāh* as "bond with God", see *sūrah* 2, note 19.

43 This refers to all ties arising from human relationships – e.g., the bonds of family, responsibility for orphans and the poor, the mutual rights and duties of neighbours – as well as the spiritual and practical bonds which ought to exist between all who belong to the brotherhood of Islam (cf. 8 : 75 and the corresponding notes). In its widest sense, the phrase "what God has bidden to be joined" applies to the spiritual obligation, on the part of man, to remain conscious of the unity of purpose underlying all of God's creation, and hence – according to Rāzī – man's moral duty to treat all living beings with love and compassion.

وَالَّذِينَ صَبَرُوا ابْتِغَاءَ وَجْهِ رَبِّهِمْ وَأَقَامُوا الصَّلَوٰةَ وَأَنفَقُوا مِمَّا
رَزَقْنَٰهُمْ سِرًّا وَعَلَانِيَةً وَيَدْرَءُونَ بِالْحَسَنَةِ السَّيِّئَةَ أُولَٰئِكَ لَهُمْ عُقْبَى
الدَّارِ ﴿٢٢﴾ جَنَّٰتُ عَدْنٍ يَدْخُلُونَهَا وَمَن صَلَحَ مِنْ ءَابَائِهِمْ وَأَزْوَٰجِهِمْ
وَذُرِّيَّٰتِهِمْ وَالْمَلَٰئِكَةُ يَدْخُلُونَ عَلَيْهِم مِّن كُلِّ بَابٍ ﴿٢٣﴾ سَلَٰمٌ عَلَيْكُم بِمَا
صَبَرْتُمْ فَنِعْمَ عُقْبَى الدَّارِ ﴿٢٤﴾ وَالَّذِينَ يَنقُضُونَ عَهْدَ اللَّهِ مِن بَعْدِ مِيثَٰقِهِ
وَيَقْطَعُونَ مَا أَمَرَ اللَّهُ بِهِ أَن يُوصَلَ وَيُفْسِدُونَ فِي الْأَرْضِ أُولَٰئِكَ لَهُمُ
اللَّعْنَةُ وَلَهُمْ سُوءُ الدَّارِ ﴿٢٥﴾ اللَّهُ يَبْسُطُ الرِّزْقَ لِمَن يَشَاءُ وَيَقْدِرُ
وَفَرِحُوا بِالْحَيَوٰةِ الدُّنْيَا وَمَا الْحَيَوٰةُ الدُّنْيَا فِي الْآخِرَةِ إِلَّا مَتَٰعٌ ﴿٢٦﴾

and who are patient in adversity out of a longing for their Sustainer's countenance, and are constant in prayer, and spend on others, secretly and openly, out of what We provide for them as sustenance, and [who] repel evil with good.[44]
It is these that shall find their fulfilment in the hereafter:[45] «22» gardens of perpetual bliss, which they shall enter together with the righteous from among their parents, their spouses, and their offspring;[46] and the angels will come unto them from every gate [and will say]: «23» "Peace be upon you, because you have persevered!" How excellent, then, this fulfilment in the hereafter! «24»
But as for those who break their bond with God after it has been established [in their nature],[47] and cut asunder what God has bidden to be joined, and spread corruption on earth – their due is rejection [by God],[48] and theirs is a most evil fate [in the life to come]. «25»

GOD GRANTS abundant sustenance, or gives it in scant measure, unto whomever He wills; and they [who are given abundance] rejoice in the life of this world – even though, as compared with the life to come, the life of this world is nought but a fleeting pleasure. «26»

Wal-ladhīna ṣabarub-tighāaʾa wajhi Rabbihim wa ʾaqāmuṣ-Ṣalāta wa ʾañfaqū mimmā razaqnāhum sirrañw-wa ᶜalāniyatañw-wa yadraʾūna bilḥasanatis-sayyiʾata ʾulāaʾika lahum ᶜuqbad-dār. (22) Jannātu ᶜadniñy-yadkhulūnahā wa mañ-ṣalaḥa min ʾābāaʾihim wa ʾazwājihim wa dhuriyyātihim wal-Malāaʾikatu yadkhulūna ᶜalayhim-miñ-kulli bāb. (23) Salāmun ᶜalaykum-bimā ṣabartum faniʾma ᶜuqbad-dār. (24) Wal-ladhīna yañquḍūna ᶜahdal-lāhi mim-baᶜdi mīthāqihī wa yaqṭaᶜūna māa ʾamaral-lāhu bihīi ʾañy-yūṣala wa yufsidūna fil-ʾarḍi ʾulāaʾika la-humul-laᶜnatu wa lahum sūuʾud-dār. (25) ʾAllāhu yabsuṭur-rizqa limañy-yashāaʾu wa yaqdir. Wa fariḥū bilḥayātid-dunyā wa mal-ḥayātud-dunyā fil-ʾĀkhirati ʾillā matāᶜ. (26)

44 Some of the commentators take this to mean that "if they have committed a sin, they repel it [i.e., its effect] by repentance" (Ibn Kaysān, as quoted by Zamakhsharī), while others think that the "repelling" connotes the doing of a good deed in atonement of a – presumably unintentional – bad deed (Rāzī), or that it refers to endeavours to set evil situations to rights by word or deed (an alternative interpretation mentioned by Zamakhsharī). But the great majority of the classical commentators hold that the meaning is "they *repay* evil with good"; thus Al-Ḥasan al-Baṣrī (as quoted by Baghawī, Zamakhsharī and Rāzī): "When they are deprived [of anything], they give; and when they are wronged, they forgive." Ṭabarī's explanation is very similar: "They repel the evil done to them by doing good to those who did it"; and "they do not repay evil with evil, but repel it by [doing] good". See also 41 : 34-36.

45 Lit., "For them there will be the end-result [or "fulfilment"] of the [ultimate] abode". The noun *ᶜuqbā* is regarded by almost all the philological authorities as synonymous with *ᶜāqibah* ("consequence" or "end" or "end-result"; hence also "recompense" and, tropically, "destiny" or "fulfilment"). The term *ad-dār* stands for *ad-dār al-ākhirah*, "the ultimate abode", i.e., life in the hereafter.

46 As I have pointed out in several places, the term *zawj* denotes "a pair" or "a couple" as well as each of the components of a couple – i.e., with reference to human couples, "a spouse": hence it signifies either "husband" or "wife". Similarly, the term *abāʾ* (lit., "fathers" or "forefathers") usually denotes both fathers and mothers, i.e., "parents"; and this is, according to Zamakhsharī, the meaning in this instance. – As regards the expression *ᶜadn*, rendered by me as "perpetual bliss", see note on 38 : 50, the earliest instance of the Qurʾanic use of this term.

47 Lit., "after its establishment (*mīthāq*)". For a full explanation of the expression "bond with God" and of my interpolation, between brackets, of the words "in their nature", see *sūrah* 2, note 19.

48 The Qurʾanic term *laᶜnah* – usually but inexactly translated as "curse" (and popularly used in this sense in

NOW THOSE who are bent on denying the truth [of the Prophet's message] say, "Why has no miraculous sign ever been bestowed upon him from on high by his Sustainer?"[49]
Say: "Behold, God lets go astray him who wills [to go astray],[50] just as He guides unto Himself all who turn unto Him ‹27› – those who believe, and whose hearts find their rest in the remembrance of God – for, verily, in the remembrance of God [men's] hearts do find their rest: ‹28› – [and so it is that] they who attain to faith and do righteous deeds are destined for happiness [in this world] and the most beauteous of all goals [in the life to come]!" ‹29›
Thus[51] have We raised thee [O Muḥammad] as Our Apostle amidst a community [of unbelievers] before whose time [similar] communities have come and gone,[52] so that thou might propound to them what We have revealed unto thee: for [in their ignorance] they deny the Most Gracious![53]

وَيَقُولُ ٱلَّذِينَ كَفَرُوا۟ لَوْلَآ أُنزِلَ عَلَيْهِ ءَايَةٌ مِّن رَّبِّهِۦ ۗ قُلْ إِنَّ ٱللَّهَ يُضِلُّ
مَن يَشَآءُ وَيَهْدِىٓ إِلَيْهِ مَنْ أَنَابَ ﴿٢٧﴾ ٱلَّذِينَ ءَامَنُوا۟ وَتَطْمَئِنُّ قُلُوبُهُم بِذِكْرِ
ٱللَّهِ ۗ أَلَا بِذِكْرِ ٱللَّهِ تَطْمَئِنُّ ٱلْقُلُوبُ ﴿٢٨﴾ ٱلَّذِينَ ءَامَنُوا۟ وَعَمِلُوا۟ ٱلصَّٰلِحَٰتِ
طُوبَىٰ لَهُمْ وَحُسْنُ مَـَٔابٍ ﴿٢٩﴾ كَذَٰلِكَ أَرْسَلْنَٰكَ فِىٓ أُمَّةٍ قَدْ خَلَتْ مِن
قَبْلِهَآ أُمَمٌ لِّتَتْلُوَا۟ عَلَيْهِمُ ٱلَّذِىٓ أَوْحَيْنَآ إِلَيْكَ وَهُمْ يَكْفُرُونَ بِٱلرَّحْمَٰنِ

Wa yaqūlul-ladhīna kafarū lawlāa ʾuñzila ʿalayhi ʾĀyatum-mir-Rabbih. Qul ʾinnal-lāha yuḍillu mañy-yashāaʾu wa yahdīi ʾilayhi man ʾanāb. (27) ʾAlladhīna ʾāmanū wa taṭmaʾinnu qulūbuhum-bidhikril-lāh. ʾAlā bidhikril-lāhi taṭmaʾinnul-qulūb. (28) ʾAlladhīna ʾāmanū wa ʿamiluṣ-ṣāliḥāti ṭūbā lahum wa ḥusnu maʾāb. (29) Kadhālika ʾarsalnāka fīi ʾummatiñ-qad khalat miñ-qablihāa ʾumamul-litatluwa ʿalayhimul-ladhīi ʾawḥaynāa ʾilayka wa hum yakfurūna bir-Raḥmān.

post-classical Arabic parlance) – denotes "banishment" or "alienation" (*ibʿād*), i.e., from all that is good (*Lisān al-ʿArab*). Whenever it is attributed in the Qurʾān to God with reference to a sinner, it signifies the latter's "exclusion from God's grace" or his "rejection by God". In the present context, this meaning is reinforced by the subsequent reference to "a most evil fate" (lit., "abode") in afterlife. – For an explanation of the phrase "what God has bidden to be joined", see note 43 above.

49 See verse 7 of this *sūrah* and the corresponding note 16. The repetition of this question at this place points to its connection with the reference to "those who break their bond with God after it has been established [in their nature]" in verse 25 above (elucidated in note 19 on 2 : 27). The abandonment of their original, innate faculty to realize the existence of God and their own dependence on His guidance – caused by their utter immersion in the passing pleasures of this world's life – makes it impossible for "those who are bent on denying the truth" to sense the breath of the divine in the message propounded to them by Muḥammad: and so they refuse to accept it as true unless it is supported by an outward "miracle". (See in this connection note 94 on 6 : 109.)

50 Or: "God lets go astray whomever He wills". Regarding the rendering adopted by me, see *sūrah* 14, note 4.

51 Most of the commentators explain the "thus" or "thus it is" (*kadhālika*) as referring to the earlier prophets, namely, "Thus, [or "in like manner"] as We sent prophets before thee, O Muḥammad, We have now sent thee . . .", etc. It seems to me, however, that this speculative interpolation is unnecessary, and that the adverb "thus" connects directly with the preceding statement that God "guides unto Himself all who turn unto Him": in other words, the "thus" qualifies Muḥammad's mission as an instrument of God's guidance. (This is, apparently, how Ṭabarī understands the above phrase.)

52 Lit., "before whom [other] communities have passed away": an indirect reference to the continuity of prophetic revelation before and up to the time of the Last Prophet, Muḥammad (Zamakhsharī, Rāzī). The interpolation of the words "of unbelievers" is based on Ibn Kathīr's commentary on this verse, whereas my rendering of *arsalnāka* (lit., "We have sent thee") as "We have raised thee as Our Apostle" is necessitated, in English, by the subsequent preposition "amidst".

53 I.e., by refusing to acknowledge His existence, or by rejecting His guidance, or by ascribing divine qualities to other beings or forces side by side with Him.

قُلْ هُوَ رَبِّى لَآ إِلَٰهَ إِلَّا هُوَ عَلَيْهِ تَوَكَّلْتُ وَإِلَيْهِ مَتَابِ ﴿٣٠﴾ وَلَوْ أَنَّ
قُرْءَانًا سُيِّرَتْ بِهِ ٱلْجِبَالُ أَوْ قُطِّعَتْ بِهِ ٱلْأَرْضُ أَوْ كُلِّمَ بِهِ ٱلْمَوْتَىٰ بَل
لِّلَّهِ ٱلْأَمْرُ جَمِيعًا أَفَلَمْ يَا۟يْـَٔسِ ٱلَّذِينَ ءَامَنُوٓا۟ أَن لَّوْ يَشَآءُ ٱللَّهُ لَهَدَى
ٱلنَّاسَ جَمِيعًا وَلَا يَزَالُ ٱلَّذِينَ كَفَرُوا۟ تُصِيبُهُم بِمَا صَنَعُوا۟ قَارِعَةٌ أَوْ
تَحُلُّ قَرِيبًا مِّن دَارِهِمْ حَتَّىٰ يَأْتِىَ وَعْدُ ٱللَّهِ إِنَّ ٱللَّهَ لَا يُخْلِفُ ٱلْمِيعَادَ ﴿٣١﴾
وَلَقَدِ ٱسْتُهْزِئَ بِرُسُلٍ مِّن قَبْلِكَ فَأَمْلَيْتُ لِلَّذِينَ كَفَرُوا۟ ثُمَّ أَخَذْتُهُمْ
فَكَيْفَ كَانَ عِقَابِ ﴿٣٢﴾ أَفَمَنْ هُوَ قَآئِمٌ عَلَىٰ كُلِّ نَفْسٍ بِمَا كَسَبَتْ

Qul Huwa Rabbī lāa ʾilāha ʾillā Huwa ᶜalayhi tawakkaltu wa ʾilayhi matāb. (30) Wa law ʾanna Qurʾānañ-suyyirat bihil-jibālu ʾaw quṭṭiᶜat bihil-ʾarḍu ʾaw kullima bihil-mawtā. Bal lillāhil-ʾamru jamīᶜā. ʾAfalam yayʾasil-ladhīna ʾāmanūu ʾal-law yashāaʾul-lāhu lahadan-nāsa jamīᶜā. Wa lā yazālul-ladhīna kafarū tuṣībuhum-bimā ṣanaᶜū qāriᶜatun ʾaw taḥullu qarībam-miñ-dārihim ḥattā yaʾtiya waᶜdul-lāh. ʾInnal-lāha lā yukhliful-mīᶜād. (31) Wa laqadis-tuhziʾa biRusulim-miñ-qablika faʾamlaytu lilladhīna kafarū thumma ʾakhadhtuhum fakayfa kāna ᶜiqāb. (32) ʾAfaman Huwa qāaʾimun ᶜalā kulli nafsim-bimā kasabat.

Say: "He is my Sustainer. There is no deity save Him. In Him have I placed my trust, and unto Him is my recourse!" ‹30›

Yet even if [they should listen to] a [divine] discourse by which mountains could be moved, or the earth cleft asunder, or the dead made to speak – [they who are bent on denying the truth would still refuse to believe in it]![54]

Nay, but God alone has the power to decide what shall be.[55] Have, then, they who have attained to faith not yet come to know that, had God so willed, He would indeed have guided all mankind aright?[56]

But as for those who are bent on denying the truth – in result of their [evil] deeds, sudden calamities will always befall them or will alight close to their homes;[57] [and this will continue] until God's promise [of resurrection] is fulfilled: verily, God never fails to fulfil His promise! ‹31›

And, indeed, [even] before thy time have [God's] apostles been derided, and for a while I gave rein to those who were [thus] bent on denying the truth: but then I took them to task – and how awesome was My retribution! ‹32›

IS, THEN, HE who has every living being[58] in His almighty care, [dealing with each] according to what it deserves[59] – [is, then,

54 The sentence added by me between brackets corresponds to the interpretation given to the above passage by Ṭabarī and also by Az-Zajjāj (as quoted by Rāzī and – without the mention of Az-Zajjāj by name – by Baghawī and Zamakhsharī as well); cf. 6 : 109-111.

55 Lit., "God's alone is all [power of] command": i.e., no "miraculous sign" can ever convince those whose hearts God has "sealed" in consequence of their "breaking their bond with Him" (see *sūrah* 2, notes 7 and 19).

56 The meaning is that God grants man the freedom to choose between right and wrong: "He guides unto Himself all who turn unto Him (verse 27 above) and "are true to their bond with God" (verse 20); on the other hand, He withholds His guidance from "the iniquitous, who break their bond with God" (2 : 26-27). See also the last sentence of 6 : 149 and the corresponding note 143.

57 Lit., "a sudden calamity (*qāriᶜah*) will not cease (*lā yazāl*) to befall them or to alight close to their home". However, since this phrase connotes repetition and continuity, the singular form of the noun *qāriᶜah* has here obviously a cumulative sense – namely, an unceasing succession of social catastrophes, fratricidal wars and mutual deprivations which, in consequence of their deliberate disregard of all spiritual values, will directly befall "those who are bent on denying the truth" (*alladhīna kafarū*), or will, indirectly, cause them to suffer by affecting their whole organic environment: and this, to my mind, is the meaning of the phrase "or will alight close to their homes". (Cf. in this connection 5 : 33 and the corresponding notes, especially note 45.)

58 The term *nafs* has here apparently the general meaning of "soul" or "living being", applying both to humans and animals.

59 Lit., "what it has acquired" – i.e., according to the exigencies of its life, and – in the case of a human being – according to his or her moral deserts as well.

He like anything else that exists]? And yet, they ascribe to other beings a share in God's divinity!
Say: "Give them any name [you please]:[60] but do you [really think that you could] inform Him of anything on earth that He does not know – or [do you] but play with words?"[61]
Nay, goodly seems their false imagery[62] to those who are bent on denying the truth, and so they are turned away from the [right] path: and he whom God lets go astray can never find any guide.[63] ⟨33⟩ For such, there is suffering in the life of this world;[64] but, truly, [their] suffering in the life to come will be harder still, and they will have none to shield them from God. ⟨34⟩

THE PARABLE of the paradise promised to those who are conscious of God [is that of a garden] through which running waters flow:[65] [but, unlike an earthly garden,] its fruits will be everlasting, and [so will be] its shade.[66]
Such will be the destiny of those who remain conscious of God – just as the destiny

وَجَعَلُواْ لِلَّهِ شُرَكَآءَ قُلْ سَمُّوهُمْ أَمْ تُنَبِّـُٔونَهُۥ بِمَا لَا يَعْلَمُ فِى ٱلْأَرْضِ أَم بِظَٰهِرٍ
مِّنَ ٱلْقَوْلِ بَلْ زُيِّنَ لِلَّذِينَ كَفَرُواْ مَكْرُهُمْ وَصُدُّواْ عَنِ ٱلسَّبِيلِ وَمَن يُضْلِلِ
ٱللَّهُ فَمَا لَهُۥ مِنْ هَادٍ ﴿٣٣﴾ لَّهُمْ عَذَابٌ فِى ٱلْحَيَوٰةِ ٱلدُّنْيَا وَلَعَذَابُ ٱلْـَٔاخِرَةِ
أَشَقُّ وَمَا لَهُم مِّنَ ٱللَّهِ مِن وَاقٍ ﴿٣٤﴾ ۞ مَّثَلُ ٱلْجَنَّةِ ٱلَّتِى وُعِدَ ٱلْمُتَّقُونَ
تَجْرِى مِن تَحْتِهَا ٱلْأَنْهَٰرُ أُكُلُهَا دَآئِمٌ وَظِلُّهَا تِلْكَ عُقْبَى ٱلَّذِينَ ٱتَّقَواْ وَّعُقْبَى

ربع الحزب

Wa jaʿalū lillāhi shurakāaʾa qul sammūhum. ʾAm tunabbiʾūnahū bimā lā yaʿlamu fil-ʾarḍi ʾam-biẓāhirim-minal qawl. Bal zuyyina lilladhīna kafarū makruhum wa ṣuddū ʿanis-sabīl. Wa mañy-yuḍlilil-lāhu famā lahū min hād. ⟨33⟩ Lahum ʿadhābuñ-fil-ḥayātid-dunyā wa laʿadhābul-ʾĀkhirati ʾashaqqu wa mā lahum-minal-lāhi miñw-wāq. ⟨34⟩ ۞ Mathalul-jannatil-latī wuʿidal-mut-taqūna tajrī miñ-taḥtihal-ʾanhāru ʾukuluhā dāaʾimuñw-wa ẓilluhā. Tilka ʿuqbal-ladhīnat-taqaw; wa ʿuqbal-

60 Lit., "Name them!" Most of the commentators explain this phrase as an expression of utter contempt for those allegedly "divine" beings: i.e., "they are so unreal and meaningless as not to deserve even a name". It is also conceivable that we have here an echo of the statement, to be found in 7 : 71, 12 : 40 and 53 : 23, to the effect that those false objects of worship are but "[empty] names which you have invented". However, in view of the next sentence – which refers to God's omniscience and is similar to 10 : 18, where imaginary "intercessors" are explicitly mentioned – it is possible to interpret the above phrase still more precisely, viz., "Call them 'divine intercessors', if you so like: but . . .", etc. (According to Zamakhsharī, the particle *am,* which usually denotes "or", stands here for *bal,* "nay, but" or simply "but".)

61 Lit., "or [do you say this] in the outward appearance (*bi-ẓāhir*) of a saying". Cf. the second part of 10 : 18 (preceded by a reference to deified "intercessors") and the corresponding note 27.

62 Lit., "their cunning [or "artful"] device (*makr*)": but since, as Ṭabarī points out, this term relates here mainly to conscious *shirk* ("the attribution of divine qualities to aught but God") and, hence, to false religious ideas in general, it can be suitably rendered as above.

63 See *sūrah* 7, note 152, and *sūrah* 14, note 4.

64 See the last paragraph of verse 31 and note 57 above.

65 This rendering (and the interpolation of the words "is that of a garden") reproduces literally the interpretation given to the above passage by Az-Zajjāj, as quoted by Zamakhsharī and – in an abbreviated form – by Rāzī; according to Zamakhsharī, this passage serves "as a parabolic illustration, by means of something which we know from our experience, of something that is beyond the reach of our perception" (*tamthīlan li-mā ghāba ʿannā bi-mā nushāhid*). As in the similar (but wider) reference to "the parable of paradise" in 47 : 15, we are here reminded that the Qurʾānic descriptions of what awaits man after resurrection are, of necessity, metaphorical, since the human mind cannot conceive of anything that is – both in its elements and its totality – entirely different from anything that can be experienced in this world. (See in this connection Appendix I.)

66 I.e., its gift of happiness. Regarding this metaphorical meaning of *ẓill* ("shade"), see the last clause of 4 : 57 and the corresponding note 74.

of those who deny the truth will be the fire.[67] ‹35›
Hence, they unto whom We have vouchsafed this revelation[68] rejoice at all that has been bestowed upon thee [O Prophet] from on high;[69] but among the followers of other creeds there are such as deny the validity of some of it.[70]
Say [unto them, O Prophet]: "I have only been bidden to worship God, and not to ascribe divine powers to aught beside Him:[71] unto Him do I call [all mankind], and He is my goal!" ‹36›
Thus, then, have We bestowed from on high this [divine writ] as an ordinance in the Arabic tongue.[72] And, indeed, if thou shouldst defer to men's likes and dislikes[73] after all the [divine] knowledge that has come unto thee, thou wouldst have none to protect thee from God, and none to shield thee [from Him]. ‹37›
And, truly, We sent forth apostles before thee, and We appointed for them wives and offspring;[74] and it was not given to any apostle to produce a miracle save at God's behest.[75]

ٱلْكَـٰفِرِينَ ٱلنَّارُ ﴿٣٥﴾ وَٱلَّذِينَ ءَاتَيْنَـٰهُمُ ٱلْكِتَـٰبَ يَفْرَحُونَ بِمَآ
أُنزِلَ إِلَيْكَ ۖ وَمِنَ ٱلْأَحْزَابِ مَن يُنكِرُ بَعْضَهُۥ ۚ قُلْ إِنَّمَآ أُمِرْتُ أَنْ
أَعْبُدَ ٱللَّهَ وَلَآ أُشْرِكَ بِهِۦٓ ۚ إِلَيْهِ أَدْعُوا۟ وَإِلَيْهِ مَـَٔابِ ﴿٣٦﴾ وَكَذَٰلِكَ
أَنزَلْنَـٰهُ حُكْمًا عَرَبِيًّا ۚ وَلَئِنِ ٱتَّبَعْتَ أَهْوَآءَهُم بَعْدَمَا جَآءَكَ مِنَ ٱلْعِلْمِ مَا
لَكَ مِنَ ٱللَّهِ مِن وَلِىٍّ وَلَا وَاقٍ ﴿٣٧﴾ وَلَقَدْ أَرْسَلْنَا رُسُلًا مِّن قَبْلِكَ وَجَعَلْنَا
لَهُمْ أَزْوَٰجًا وَذُرِّيَّةً ۚ وَمَا كَانَ لِرَسُولٍ أَن يَأْتِىَ بِـَٔايَةٍ إِلَّا بِإِذْنِ ٱللَّهِ ۗ

kāfirīnan-nār. ﴿35﴾ Wal-ladhīna ᵓātaynāhumul-Kitāba yafraḥūna bimāa ᵓuñzila ᵓilayka wa minal-ᵓaḥzābi mañy-yuñkiru baᶜḍah. Qul ᵓinnamāa ᵓumirtu ᵓan ᵓaᶜbudal-lāha wa lāa ᵓushrika bih. ᵓIlayhi ᵓadᶜū wa ᵓilayhi maᵓāb. ﴿36﴾ Wa kadhālika ᵓañzalnāhu ḥukman ᶜarabiyyā. Wa laᵓinit-tabaᶜta ᵓahwāaᵓahum-baᶜda mā jāaᵓaka minal-ᶜilmi mā laka minal-lāhi miñw-waliyyiñw-wa lā wāq. ﴿37﴾ Wa laqad ᵓarsalnā Rusulam-miñ-qablika wa jaᶜalnā lahum ᵓazwājañw-wa dhurriyyah. Wa mā kāna liRasūlin ᵓañy-yaᵓtiya biᵓĀyatin ᵓillā biᵓidhnil-lāh.

67 For my rendering of *ᶜuqbā*, in this context, as "destiny" see note 45 above.

68 Sc., "and who believe in it".

69 I.e., because it offers them guidance in this world and holds out to them the promise of ultimate happiness in the life to come.

70 I.e., while admitting that the Qurᵓān contains much that coincides with the spiritual concepts taught by their own religions. The designation *aḥzāb* (lit., "parties" or "sects", sing. *ḥizb*) connotes here the followers of other religions or creeds (Ṭabarī and Rāzī).

71 The particle "only" (*innamā*) at the beginning of this sentence "clearly shows that there is [in Islam] no obligation, no ordinance and no prohibition that is not connected with this [principle]" (Rāzī).

72 Lit., "as an Arabic ordinance (*ḥukm*)": i.e., so as to enable the Arabian Prophet to propound it to the people of his immediate environment and, through them, to the whole world. Cf. in this connection 14 : 4, where it is stated that every one of God's prophets was entrusted with a message "in his own people's tongue, so that he might make [the truth] clear unto them". That the message of the Qurᵓān is universal, and not restricted to the Arabs alone, is brought out clearly in many places, e.g., in 7 : 158, "Say [O Prophet]: 'O mankind! Verily, I am an apostle of God to all of you'".

73 Lit., "follow their likes and dislikes (*ahwāhum*)" – i.e., by compromising with the followers of other creeds who, while accepting some of the fundamental verities of the Qurᵓān, are unwilling to accept the whole of it.

74 I.e., they were mortals like all other men, and were not endowed with any "supernatural" qualities. This is a rejoinder to those who refuse to accept a divine message as true on the grounds of its having been conveyed to mankind by an "ordinary mortal". (Cf. 25 : 7, where the unbelievers are speaking derisively of Muḥammad as an apostle "who eats food [like all other mortals] and goes about in the market-places", and the many references to their incredulous wondering that God should have chosen as His prophet "a man from among themselves".) In addition to this, the above verse stresses, by implication, the positive value of man's natural, physical life – summarized, as it were, in the expression "wives and offspring" – and the rejection of exaggerated asceticism and self-mortification as an allegedly desirable "way to God".

75 Lit., "by God's leave". Cf. 6 : 109 – "Miracles are in the power of God alone" – and the corresponding note 94. In

Every age has had its revelation:[76] ‹38› God annuls or confirms whatever He wills [of His earlier messages] – for with Him is the source of all revelation.[77] ‹39›

BUT WHETHER We let thee see [in thy lifetime, O Prophet, the fulfilment of] some of what We have promised them,[78] or whether We cause thee to die [before its fulfilment] – thy duty is no more than to deliver the message; and the reckoning is Ours. ‹40›
Have, then, they [who deny the truth] never yet seen how[79] We visit the earth [with Our punishment], gradually depriving it of all that is best thereon?[80]
For, [when] God judges, there is no power that could repel His judgment: and swift in reckoning is He! ‹41›

لِكُلِّ أَجَلٍ كِتَابٌ ﴿٣٨﴾ يَمْحُواْ ٱللَّهُ مَا يَشَآءُ وَيُثْبِتُ وَعِندَهُۥٓ أُمُّ
ٱلْكِتَٰبِ ﴿٣٩﴾ وَإِن مَّا نُرِيَنَّكَ بَعْضَ ٱلَّذِى نَعِدُهُمْ أَوْ نَتَوَفَّيَنَّكَ فَإِنَّمَا
عَلَيْكَ ٱلْبَلَٰغُ وَعَلَيْنَا ٱلْحِسَابُ ﴿٤٠﴾ أَوَلَمْ يَرَوْاْ أَنَّا نَأْتِى ٱلْأَرْضَ
نَنقُصُهَا مِنْ أَطْرَافِهَا وَٱللَّهُ يَحْكُمُ لَا مُعَقِّبَ لِحُكْمِهِۦ وَهُوَ سَرِيعُ
ٱلْحِسَابِ ﴿٤١﴾

Likulli ʾajaliñ-kitāb. (38) Yamḥul-lāhu mā yashāaʾu wa yuthbitu wa ʿiñdahūu ʾUmmul-Kitāb. (39) Wa ʾim-mā nuriyannaka baʿḍal-ladhī naʿiduhum ʾaw natawaffayannaka faʾinnamā ʿalaykal-balāghu wa ʿalaynal-ḥisāb. (40) ʾAwa lam yaraw ʾannā naʾtil-ʾarḍa nañquṣuhā min ʾaṭrāfihā. Wal-lāhu yaḥkumu lā muʿaqqiba liḥukmihi wa Huwa Sarīʿul-ḥisāb. (41)

---

the present context, this is an answer to those who refuse to believe in Muḥammad's message unless "a miraculous sign" is bestowed upon him.

76 Or: "a divine writ" (*kitāb*). See 5 : 48 – "Unto every one of you have We appointed a [different] law and way of life" – and the corresponding note 66, which explains the succession of divine messages culminating in, and ending with, the revelation of the Qurʾān. This interpretation of the above phrase – adopted, among others, by Ibn Kathīr – connects it plausibly with the preceding mention of the apostles who came before Muḥammad and with the subsequent reference to the supersession of the earlier divine messages by that of the Qurʾān. Apart from this, the statement that every age had a revelation suited to the particular needs of the time and the people concerned (Zamakhsharī) constitutes an answer to the objection, often raised by followers of other creeds, that the message of the Qurʾān differs in many respects from the earlier divine revelations (Rāzī).

77 I.e., He *is* the fountainhead or source (*aṣl*) of all revelation. – As regards the preceding reference to the abrogation of earlier divine dispensations and their supersession by later ones – ending with the final revelation, the Qurʾān – see 2 : 106 and the corresponding note 87. (According to Qatādah, as quoted by Ṭabarī and Ibn Kathīr, the passage under consideration has the same purport as 2 : 106.)

78 I.e., the, calamities which, according to the last paragraph of verse 31 above, are in store for "those who are bent on denying the truth" (*alladhīna kafarū*).

79 Lit., "that".

80 Or: "curtailing it from [all] its sides" (*min aṭrāfihā*) – depending on whether one understands by *aṭrāf* the "sides" or "extremities" or "outlying parts" (of a concrete body or land) or, alternatively, the "outstanding men" – i.e., the great leaders, scholars and thinkers (*Tāj al-ʿArūs*) – and "the best of the [earth's] inhabitants and fruits" (*ibid.*). Many commentators, taking the primary meaning of *aṭrāf*, are of the opinion that the above sentence relates to the struggle between the early Muslim community at Medina and the pagans of Mecca, and interpret it thus: "Do they [i.e., the pagans of Mecca] not see that we are visiting [with Our punishment] the land [held by them], gradually curtailing it from [all] its sides?" – which would imply a prophecy of the gradual conquest of all Arabia by the Muslims. Other commentators, however, prefer the secondary meaning of *aṭrāf* and – without denying its relevance to the early history of Islam – interpret this passage in a more general sense, similar to the rendering adopted by me. Thus, for instance, Rāzī: "Have they [i.e., the deniers of the truth] never yet seen the turns of fortune (*ikhtilāfāt*) that take place in this world – destruction after prosperity, death after life, humiliation after glory, deficiency after perfection? . . . Hence, what makes those deniers of the truth so sure that God will not render them abject after they had been mighty, and subjected [by others] after they had been rulers?" Thus, in its widest sense, the phrase "gradually depriving it of all that is best in it" may be taken to relate not merely to physical and social catastrophes but also to the loss of all ethical values – and, thus, to the loss of all worldly power – which "those who are bent on denying the truth" are bound to suffer in the end.

Now those who lived before these [sinners] did, too, devise many a blasphemy[81] – but the most subtle devising is that of God, who knows what each human being deserves:[82] and the deniers of the truth will [in time] come to know to whom the future belongs.[83] ‹42›

And [if] they who are bent on denying the truth say [unto thee, O Prophet], "Thou hast not been sent [by God]", say thou: "None can bear witness between me and you as God does; and [none can bear witness as does] he who truly understands this divine Writ."[84] ‹43›

وَقَدْ مَكَرَ ٱلَّذِينَ مِن قَبْلِهِمْ فَلِلَّهِ ٱلْمَكْرُ جَمِيعًا يَعْلَمُ مَا تَكْسِبُ كُلُّ نَفْسٍ وَسَيَعْلَمُ ٱلْكُفَّٰرُ لِمَنْ عُقْبَى ٱلدَّارِ ﴿٤٢﴾ وَيَقُولُ ٱلَّذِينَ كَفَرُوا۟ لَسْتَ مُرْسَلًا قُلْ كَفَىٰ بِٱللَّهِ شَهِيدًۢا بَيْنِى وَبَيْنَكُمْ وَمَنْ عِندَهُۥ عِلْمُ ٱلْكِتَٰبِ ﴿٤٣﴾

Wa qad makaral-ladhīna miñ-qablihim falillāhil-makru jamīᶜā. Yaᶜlamu mā taksibu kullu nafs. Wa sayaᶜlamul-kuffāru liman ᶜuqbad-dār. (42) Wa yaqūlul-ladhīna kafarū lasta mursalā. Qul kafā billāhi shahīdam-baynī wa baynakum wa man ᶜiñdahū ᶜilmul-Kitāb. (43)

81 Lit., "did scheme" – an expression which in this context apparently refers to blasphemous ideas and attitudes.

82 Lit., "earns" – i.e., of good and evil.

83 For an explanation of this rendering of *ᶜuqba 'd-dār* (which is here synonymous with *ᶜāqibat ad-dār*), see *sūrah* 6, note 118.

84 Lit., "and anyone who possesses (*man ᶜindahu*) knowledge of the revelation" – implying that a true understanding of the Qurᵓān unavoidably leads one to the conviction that it has been revealed by God.

The Fourteenth Sūrah

ᵓIbrāhīm (Abraham)

Mecca Period

ALL AUTHORITIES agree that this *sūrah* belongs to the last group of Meccan revelations; in the *Itqān* it is placed immediately after *sūrah* 71 (*Nūḥ*), and we have no reason to question this chronology. The title is based on Abraham's prayer in verses 35-41; its relevance to the rest of the *sūrah* has been explained in note 48.

As in the preceding *sūrah*, the main theme of *ᵓIbrāhīm* is the revelation of God's word to man, destined to lead him "out of the depths of darkness into the light" (verses 1 and 5) by means of messages expressed in the language of the people to whom it was originally addressed (verse 4; cf. also 13 : 37 and the corresponding note 72): but whereas all earlier instances of the divine writ were meant only for the people thus addressed by their prophet (cf. God's command to Moses, in verse 5, "Lead *thy people* out of the depths of darkness into the light"), the Qurᵓān is, as stated in the first and the last verses of this *sūrah*, a message for all mankind.

سورة إبراهيم مكية
-14-
وآياتها اثنتان وخمسون

IN THE NAME OF GOD, THE MOST GRACIOUS, THE DISPENSER OF GRACE:

بِسْمِ ٱللَّهِ ٱلرَّحْمَٰنِ ٱلرَّحِيمِ

Alif. Lām. Rā.[1]
A DIVINE WRIT [is this – a revelation] which We have bestowed upon thee from on high in order that thou might bring forth all mankind, by their Sustainer's leave, out of the depths of darkness into the light: onto the way that leads to the Almighty, the One to whom all praise is due ‹1› – to God, unto whom all that is in the heavens and all that is on earth belongs.
But woe unto those who deny the truth: for suffering severe ‹2› awaits those who choose the life of this world as the sole object of their love,[2] preferring it to [all thought of] the life to come, and who turn others away from the path of God and try to make it appear crooked. Such as these have indeed gone far astray! ‹3›

AND NEVER have We sent forth any apostle otherwise than [with a message] in his own people's tongue, so that he might make [the truth] clear unto them;[3] but God lets go astray him that wills [to go astray], and guides him that wills [to be guided] – for He alone is almighty, truly wise.[4] ‹4›

الٓر ۚ كِتَٰبٌ أَنزَلْنَٰهُ إِلَيْكَ لِتُخْرِجَ ٱلنَّاسَ مِنَ ٱلظُّلُمَٰتِ إِلَى ٱلنُّورِ بِإِذْنِ
رَبِّهِمْ إِلَىٰ صِرَٰطِ ٱلْعَزِيزِ ٱلْحَمِيدِ ﴿١﴾ ٱللَّهِ ٱلَّذِى لَهُۥ مَا فِى
ٱلسَّمَٰوَٰتِ وَمَا فِى ٱلْأَرْضِ ۗ وَوَيْلٌ لِّلْكَٰفِرِينَ مِنْ عَذَابٍ شَدِيدٍ ﴿٢﴾
ٱلَّذِينَ يَسْتَحِبُّونَ ٱلْحَيَوٰةَ ٱلدُّنْيَا عَلَى ٱلْءَاخِرَةِ وَيَصُدُّونَ عَن سَبِيلِ ٱللَّهِ
وَيَبْغُونَهَا عِوَجًا ۚ أُو۟لَٰٓئِكَ فِى ضَلَٰلٍۭ بَعِيدٍ ﴿٣﴾ وَمَآ أَرْسَلْنَا مِن رَّسُولٍ إِلَّا
بِلِسَانِ قَوْمِهِۦ لِيُبَيِّنَ لَهُمْ ۖ فَيُضِلُّ ٱللَّهُ مَن يَشَآءُ وَيَهْدِى مَن يَشَآءُ ۚ وَهُوَ
ٱلْعَزِيزُ ٱلْحَكِيمُ ﴿٤﴾

Bismil-lāhir-Raḥmānir-Raḥīm.
ᵓAlif-Lāam-Rā. Kitābun ᵓañzalnāhu ᵓilayka litukhrijan-nāsa minaẓ-ẓulumāti ᵓilan-nūri biᵓidhni Rabbihim ᵓilā ṣirāṭil-ᶜAzīzil-Ḥamīd. (1) ᵓAllāhil-ladhī lahū mā fis-samāwāti wa mā fil-ᵓarḍ. Wa waylul-lilkāfirīna min ᶜadhābiñ-shadīd. (2) ᵓAlladhīna yastaḥibbūnal-ḥayātad-dunyā ᶜalal-ᵓĀkhirati wa yaṣuddūna ᶜañ-sabīlil-lāhi wa yabghūnahā ᶜiwajā. ᵓUlāaᵓika fī ḍalālim-baᶜīd. (3) Wa māa ᵓarsalnā mir-Rasūlin ᵓillā bilisāni qawmihī liyubayyina lahum. Fayuḍillul-lāhu mañy-yashāaᵓu wa yahdī mañy-yashāaᵓu wa Huwal-ᶜAzīzul-Ḥakīm. (4)

---

1 See Appendix II: also *sūrah* 11, note 1.

2 According to Zamakhsharī and Rāzī, this is the real meaning of the verbal form *yastaḥibbūn* in the above context – implying that such an all-absorbing, exclusive love of the life of this world leads inevitably to a denial of moral truths.

3 Since every divine writ was meant to be understood by man, it is obvious that each had to be formulated in the language of the people whom the particular prophet was addressing in the first instance; and the Qurᵓān – notwithstanding its universal import (cf. note 126 on 7 : 158) – is no exception in this respect.

4 Or: "God lets go astray whomever He wills, and guides whomever He wills". All Qurᵓanic references to God's "letting man go astray" must be understood against the background of 2 : 26-27 "none does He cause to go astray save the iniquitous, who break their bond with God" (regarding which latter expression, see *sūrah* 2, note 19): that is to say, man's "going astray" is a consequence of his own attitudes and inclinations and not a result of an arbitrary "predestination" in the popular sense of this word (cf. *sūrah* 2, note 7). In his commentary on the above verse,

And [thus], indeed, have We sent forth Moses with Our messages [and this Our command]: "Lead thy people out of the depths of darkness into the light, and remind them of the Days of God!"[5]
Verily, in this [reminder] there are messages indeed for all who are wholly patient in adversity and deeply grateful [to God]. ‹5›
And, lo,[6] Moses spoke [thus] unto his people: "Remember the blessings which God bestowed upon you when He saved you from Pharaoh's people who afflicted you with cruel suffering, and slaughtered your sons, and spared [only] your women[7] – which was an awesome trial from your Sustainer. ‹6› And [remember the time] when your Sustainer made [this promise] known: 'If you are grateful [to Me], I shall most certainly give you more and more;[8] but if you are ungrateful, verily, My chastisement will be severe indeed!'" ‹7›
And Moses added: "If you should [ever] deny the truth – you and whoever else lives on earth, all of you – [know that,] verily, God is indeed self-sufficient, ever to be praised!" ‹8›

وَلَقَدْ أَرْسَلْنَا مُوسَىٰ بِـَٔايَٰتِنَآ أَنْ أَخْرِجْ قَوْمَكَ مِنَ ٱلظُّلُمَٰتِ إِلَى ٱلنُّورِ
وَذَكِّرْهُم بِأَيَّىٰمِ ٱللَّهِ إِنَّ فِى ذَٰلِكَ لَءَايَٰتٍ لِّكُلِّ صَبَّارٍ شَكُورٍ ﴿٥﴾ وَإِذْ
قَالَ مُوسَىٰ لِقَوْمِهِ ٱذْكُرُوا۟ نِعْمَةَ ٱللَّهِ عَلَيْكُمْ إِذْ أَنجَىٰكُم مِّنْ ءَالِ فِرْعَوْنَ
يَسُومُونَكُمْ سُوٓءَ ٱلْعَذَابِ وَيُذَبِّحُونَ أَبْنَآءَكُمْ وَيَسْتَحْيُونَ نِسَآءَكُمْ
وَفِى ذَٰلِكُم بَلَآءٌ مِّن رَّبِّكُمْ عَظِيمٌ ﴿٦﴾ وَإِذْ تَأَذَّنَ رَبُّكُمْ لَئِن شَكَرْتُمْ
لَأَزِيدَنَّكُمْ وَلَئِن كَفَرْتُمْ إِنَّ عَذَابِى لَشَدِيدٌ ﴿٧﴾ وَقَالَ مُوسَىٰٓ إِن تَكْفُرُوٓا۟ أَنتُمْ
وَمَن فِى ٱلْأَرْضِ جَمِيعًا فَإِنَّ ٱللَّهَ لَغَنِىٌّ حَمِيدٌ ﴿٨﴾

Wa laqad ʾarsalnā Mūsā biʾĀyātināa ʾan ʾakhrij qawmaka minaẓ-ẓulumāti ʾilan-nūri wa dhakkirhum-biʾayyāmil-lāh. ʾInna fī dhālika laʾĀyātil-likulli ṣabbāriñ-shakūr. (5) Wa ʾidh qāla Mūsā liqawmi-hidh-kurū niʿmatal-lāhi ʿalaykum ʾidh ʾañjākum-min ʾāli Firʿawna yasūmūnakum sūuʾal-ʿadhābi wa yudhabbiḥūna ʾabnāaʾakum wa yastaḥyūna nisāaʾakum; wa fī dhālikum-balāaʾum-mir-Rabbi-kum ʿaẓīm. (6) Wa ʾidh taʾadhdhana Rabbukum laʾiñ-shakartum laʾazīdannakum wa laʾiñ-kafartum ʾinna ʿadhābī lashadīd. (7) Wa qāla Mūsāa ʾiñ-takfurūu ʾañtum wa mañ-fil-ʾarḍi jamīʿañ-faʾinnal-lāha laGhaniyyun Ḥamīd. (8)

Zamakhsharī stresses this aspect of *free choice* on the part of man and points out that "God does not cause anyone to go astray except one who, as He knows, will never attain to faith; and He does not guide anyone aright except one who, as He knows, will attain to faith. Hence, the [expression] 'causing to go astray' denotes [God's] leaving [one] alone (*takhliyah*) and depriving [him] of all favour, whereas [the expression] 'guidance' denotes [His] grant of fulfilment (*tawfīq*) and favour. . . . Thus, He does not forsake anyone except those who deserve to be forsaken, and does not bestow His favour upon anyone except those who deserve to be favoured." Commenting on the identical phrase occurring in 16 : 93, Zamakhsharī states: "[God] forsakes him who, as He knows, will [consciously] choose to deny the truth and will persevere in this [denial]; and . . . He bestows His favour upon him who, as He knows, will choose faith: which means that He makes the issue dependent on [man's] free choice (*al-ikhtiyār*), and thus on his deserving either [God's] favour or the withdrawal of [His] aid . . . and does not make it dependent on compulsion [i.e., predestination], which would rule out [man's] *deserving* anything of the above."

5 In ancient Arabian tradition, the terms "day" or "days" were often used to describe momentous historical events (e.g., *ayyām al-ʿarab* as a metonym for the inter-tribal wars of pre-Islamic Arabia). However, in view of the frequent Qurʾanic application of the word "day" to eschatological concepts – e.g., the "Last Day", the "Day of Resurrection", the "Day of Reckoning", and so forth – and, particularly, in view of 45 : 14, where the expression "the Days of God" unmistakably points to His judgment at the end of time – it is only logical to assume that in the present context this expression bears the same significance: namely, God' s final judgment of man on the Day of Resurrection. The use of the plural form ("the *Days* of God") is perhaps meant to bring out the idea that the "Day" of which the Qurʾān so often speaks has nothing to do with human time-definitions but, rather, alludes to an ultimate reality in which the concept of "time" has neither place nor meaning.

6 For this rendering of the particle *idh*, see *sūrah* 2, note 21.

7 Cf. 2 : 49; also Exodus i, 15-16 and 22.

8 I.e., "even more than you deserve".

HAVE THE STORIES of those [deniers of the truth] who lived before you never yet come within your ken – [the stories of] the people of Noah, and of [the tribes of] ᶜĀd and Thamūd, and of those who came after them? None knows them [now] save God.[9] There came unto them their apostles with all evidence of the truth – but they covered their mouths with their hands[10] and answered: "Behold, we refuse to regard as true the message with which you [claim to] have been entrusted; and, behold, we are in grave doubt, amounting to suspicion, about [the meaning of] your call to us!"[11] ‹9›

Said the apostles sent unto them:[12] "Can there be any doubt about [the existence and oneness of] God, the Originator of the heavens and the earth? It is He who calls unto you, so that He may forgive you [whatever is past] of your sins and grant you respite until a term [set by Him is fulfilled]."[13]

[But] they replied: "You are nothing but mortal men like ourselves! You want to turn us away from what our forefathers were wont to worship: well, then, bring us a clear proof [of your being God's message-bearers]!" ‹10›

Their apostles answered them: "True, we are nothing but mortal men like yourselves: but God bestows His favour upon whomever He wills of His servants.

نصف الحزب

أَلَمْ يَأْتِكُمْ نَبَؤُا۟ ٱلَّذِينَ مِن قَبْلِكُمْ قَوْمِ نُوحٍ وَعَادٍ وَثَمُودَ وَٱلَّذِينَ
مِنۢ بَعْدِهِمْ لَا يَعْلَمُهُمْ إِلَّا ٱللَّهُ جَآءَتْهُمْ رُسُلُهُم بِٱلْبَيِّنَٰتِ فَرَدُّوٓا۟
أَيْدِيَهُمْ فِىٓ أَفْوَٰهِهِمْ وَقَالُوٓا۟ إِنَّا كَفَرْنَا بِمَآ أُرْسِلْتُم بِهِۦ وَإِنَّا لَفِى شَكٍّ
مِّمَّا تَدْعُونَنَآ إِلَيْهِ مُرِيبٍ ﴿٩﴾ ۞ قَالَتْ رُسُلُهُمْ أَفِى ٱللَّهِ شَكٌّ فَاطِرِ
ٱلسَّمَٰوَٰتِ وَٱلْأَرْضِ يَدْعُوكُمْ لِيَغْفِرَ لَكُم مِّن ذُنُوبِكُمْ وَيُؤَخِّرَكُمْ
إِلَىٰٓ أَجَلٍ مُّسَمًّى قَالُوٓا۟ إِنْ أَنتُمْ إِلَّا بَشَرٌ مِّثْلُنَا تُرِيدُونَ أَن تَصُدُّونَا عَمَّا
كَانَ يَعْبُدُ ءَابَآؤُنَا فَأْتُونَا بِسُلْطَٰنٍ مُّبِينٍ ﴿١٠﴾ قَالَتْ لَهُمْ رُسُلُهُمْ إِن
نَّحْنُ إِلَّا بَشَرٌ مِّثْلُكُمْ وَلَٰكِنَّ ٱللَّهَ يَمُنُّ عَلَىٰ مَن يَشَآءُ مِنْ عِبَادِهِۦ

ᵓAlam yaᵓtikum nabaᵓul-ladhīna miñ-qablikum qawmi Nūḥiñw-wa ᶜĀdiñw-wa Thamūda wal-ladhīna mim-baᶜdihim. Lā yaᶜlamuhum ᵓillal-lāh. Jāaᵓat-hum Rusuluhum-bilbayyināti faraddūu ᵓaydiyahum fīi ᵓafwāhihim wa qālūu ᵓinnā kafarnā bimāa ᵓursiltum-bihī wa ᵓinnā lafī shakkim-mimmā tadᶜūnanāa ᵓilayhi murīb. (9) ۞ Qālat Rusuluhum ᵓafil-lāhi shakkuñ-fāṭiris-samāwāti wal-ᵓarḍ. Yadᶜūkum liyaghfira lakum-miñ-dhunūbikum wa yuᵓakhkhirakum ᵓilāa ᵓajalim-musammā. Qālūu ᵓin ᵓañtum ᵓillā basharum-mithlunā turīdūna ᵓañ-taṣuddūnā ᶜammā kāna yaᶜbudu ᵓābāaᵓunā faᵓtūnā bisulṭānim-mubīn. (10) Qālat lahum Rusuluhum ᵓin-naḥnu ᵓillā basharum-mithlukum wa lākinnal-lāha yamunnu ᶜalā mañy-yashāaᵓu min ᶜibādih.

---

9 I.e., they have disappeared from the face of the earth, and none save God knows today how many they were and how they lived. See verse 14 and note 18 below.

10 Lit., "they put their hands into their mouths" – an idiomatic phrase indicating one's inability to refute a reasonable proposition by cogent, logical counter-arguments: for the out-of-hand rejection of the apostles' message by their recalcitrant compatriots cannot by any means be regarded as an "argument".

11 See *sūrah* 11, note 92. It is to be noted that whereas in 11 : 62 this reply is placed in the mouth of people of one particular community – the Thamūd – and is phrased in the singular ("*thy* call to us"), it appears here in the plural ("*your* call to us") and represents the gist of the answers given by various communities to various prophets. This generalization, underlying the entire subsequent account and containing echos of several Qurᵓanic narratives relating to the experiences of individual apostles of earlier times, is obviously meant to bring out the symptomatic character of the attitude referred to: the stubborn attitude of people who either deny God altogether, or – while not consciously denying His existence – yet feel compelled to interpose all manner of imaginary "mediators" (thought to be divine or semi-divine) between themselves and Him, thus denying, by implication, His omniscience and omnipotence.

12 Lit., "their apostles".

13 I.e., "until the end of your life in this world". This is, I believe, an indirect allusion to the calamities which are bound to befall, even in this world, "those who are bent on denying the truth" (see the last paragraph of 13 : 31 and the corresponding note 57) – implying that they who consciously respond to the call of God, conveyed through His prophets, would be immune to this kind of suffering and would be graced with abiding spiritual happiness (cf. 13 : 29).

Withal, it is not within our power to bring you a proof [of our mission], unless it be by God's leave – and [so] it is in God that all believers must place their trust.[14] «11»
And how could we not place our trust in God, seeing that it is He who has shown us the path which we are to follow?[15]
"Hence, we shall certainly bear with patience whatever hurt you may do us: for, all who have trust [in His existence] must place their trust in God [alone]!" «12»
But they who denied the truth spoke [thus] unto their apostles: "We shall most certainly expel you from our land, unless you return forthwith to our ways!"[16]
Whereupon their Sustainer revealed this to His apostles:[17] "Most certainly shall We destroy these evildoers, «13» and most certainly shall We cause you to dwell on earth [long] after they have passed away:[18] this is [My promise] unto all who stand in awe of My presence, and stand in awe of My warning!"[19] «14»
And they prayed [to God] that the truth be made to triumph.[20]
And [thus it is:] every arrogant enemy of the truth shall be undone [in the life to come], «15» with hell awaiting him;[21] and he shall be made to drink of the water of most bitter distress[22] «16» gulping it

وَمَا كَانَ لَنَآ أَن نَّأْتِيَكُم بِسُلْطَٰنٍ إِلَّا بِإِذْنِ ٱللَّهِ ۚ وَعَلَى ٱللَّهِ فَلْيَتَوَكَّلِ
ٱلْمُؤْمِنُونَ ﴿١١﴾ وَمَا لَنَآ أَلَّا نَتَوَكَّلَ عَلَى ٱللَّهِ وَقَدْ هَدَىٰنَا سُبُلَنَا ۚ وَلَنَصْبِرَنَّ
عَلَىٰ مَآ ءَاذَيْتُمُونَا ۚ وَعَلَى ٱللَّهِ فَلْيَتَوَكَّلِ ٱلْمُتَوَكِّلُونَ ﴿١٢﴾ وَقَالَ ٱلَّذِينَ
كَفَرُوا۟ لِرُسُلِهِمْ لَنُخْرِجَنَّكُم مِّنْ أَرْضِنَآ أَوْ لَتَعُودُنَّ فِى مِلَّتِنَا ۖ فَأَوْحَىٰٓ
إِلَيْهِمْ رَبُّهُمْ لَنُهْلِكَنَّ ٱلظَّٰلِمِينَ ﴿١٣﴾ وَلَنُسْكِنَنَّكُمُ ٱلْأَرْضَ مِنۢ بَعْدِهِمْ ۚ
ذَٰلِكَ لِمَنْ خَافَ مَقَامِى وَخَافَ وَعِيدِ ﴿١٤﴾ وَٱسْتَفْتَحُوا۟ وَخَابَ كُلُّ
جَبَّارٍ عَنِيدٍ ﴿١٥﴾ مِّن وَرَآئِهِۦ جَهَنَّمُ وَيُسْقَىٰ مِن مَّآءٍ صَدِيدٍ ﴿١٦﴾ يَتَجَرَّعُهُۥ

Wa mā kāna lanāa ᵓan-naᵓtiyakum-bisulṭānin ᵓillā biᵓidhnil-lāh. Wa ᶜalal-lāhi falyatawakkalil-muᵓminūn. (11) Wa mā lanāa ᵓallā natawakkala ᶜalal-lāhi wa qad hadānā subulanā. Wa lanaṣbiranna ᶜalā māa ᵓādhaytumūnā. Wa ᶜalal-lāhi falyatawakkalil-mutawakkilūn. (12) Wa qālal-ladhīna kafarū liRusulihim lanukhrijannakum-min ᵓarḍināa ᵓaw lataᶜūdunna fī millatinā. Faᵓawḥāa ᵓilayhim Rabbuhum lanuhlikannaẓ-ẓālimīn. (13) Wa lanuskinannakumul-ᵓarḍa mim-baᶜdihim. Dhālika liman khāfa maqāmī wa khāfa waᶜīd. (14) Was-taftaḥū wa khāba kullu jabbārin ᶜanīd. (15) Minw-warāaᵓihī jahannamu wa yusqā mim-māaᵓiñ-ṣadīd. (16) Yatajarraᶜuhū

14 I.e., it is to the *contents* of the divine message propounded to them that all seekers after truth must turn for illumination (see 7 : 75 and 13 : 43, as well as the corresponding notes). The Qurᵓān dwells in many places (e.g., in 6 : 109-111 or 13 : 31) on the futility – moral as well as intellectual – of the demand that the divine origin of a prophetic message should be proved by tangible, extraneous means: for, a morally valid and intellectually justifiable conviction of the intrinsic truth of such a message can be gained only through "conscious insight accessible to reason" (12 : 108).

15 Lit., "guided us on our paths" – a plural indicating (as does the whole of the passage beginning with verse 9) the fundamental identity of the message preached by all the prophets.

16 Cf. 7 : 88-89, where this alternative is placed before Shuᶜayb.

17 Lit., "to them".

18 Lit., "after them": implying a divine promise that the truth preached by the apostles would outlive its detractors (cf. verse 9 above, "None knows them [now] save God"), and would triumph in the end.

19 As Zamakhsharī points out, the divine promise expressed in the above verse is equivalent to the statement in 7 : 128 that "the future (*al-ᶜāqibah*) belongs to the God-conscious".

20 Or: "they [i.e., the apostles] prayed for victory" or "for [God's] aid" – both these meanings being contained in the noun *fatḥ*, with which the verbal form *istaftaḥū*, used here, is connected. It should be borne in mind that the primary significance of *fataḥa* is "he opened", and of *istaftaḥa*, "he sought to open [something]" or "he desired that it be opened". Thus, the above passage echoes, in a generalized form, Shuᶜayb's prayer in 7 : 89, "Lay Thou open (*iftaḥ*) the truth between us and our people".

21 Lit., "[with] hell beyond him", i.e., as his destiny. For my rendering of *jabbār*, in this context, as "enemy of the truth", see the first part of note 58 on 26 : 130.

22 The word *ṣadīd* is an infinitive noun of *ṣadda*, which in its primary meaning denotes "he turned away" or "was

[unceasingly,] little by little, and yet hardly able to swallow it.[23] And death will beset him from every quarter – but he shall not die: for [yet more] severe suffering lies ahead of him. ‹17›

[This, then, is] the parable of those who are bent on denying their Sustainer: all their works[24] are as ashes which the wind blows about fiercely on a stormy day: [in the life to come,] they cannot achieve any benefit whatever from all [the good] that they may have wrought: for this [denial of God] is indeed the farthest one can go astray.[25] ‹18›

ART THOU NOT aware that God has created the heavens and the earth in accordance with [an inner] truth?[26] He can, if He so wills, do away with you and bring forth a new mankind [in your stead]:[27] ‹19› nor is this difficult for God. ‹20›

And all [mankind] will appear before God [on the Day of Judgment]; and then the weak[28] will say unto those who had gloried in their arrogance: "Behold, we were but your followers: can you, then, relieve us of something of God's chastisement?"

وَلَا يَكَادُ يُسِيغُهُۥ وَيَأْتِيهِ ٱلْمَوْتُ مِن كُلِّ مَكَانٍ وَمَا هُوَ بِمَيِّتٍ وَمِن
وَرَآئِهِۦ عَذَابٌ غَلِيظٌ ﴿١٧﴾ مَّثَلُ ٱلَّذِينَ كَفَرُوا۟ بِرَبِّهِمْ أَعْمَـٰلُهُمْ كَرَمَادٍ
ٱشْتَدَّتْ بِهِ ٱلرِّيحُ فِى يَوْمٍ عَاصِفٍ لَّا يَقْدِرُونَ مِمَّا كَسَبُوا۟ عَلَىٰ شَىْءٍ
ذَٰلِكَ هُوَ ٱلضَّلَـٰلُ ٱلْبَعِيدُ ﴿١٨﴾ أَلَمْ تَرَ أَنَّ ٱللَّهَ خَلَقَ ٱلسَّمَـٰوَٰتِ
وَٱلْأَرْضَ بِٱلْحَقِّ إِن يَشَأْ يُذْهِبْكُمْ وَيَأْتِ بِخَلْقٍ جَدِيدٍ ﴿١٩﴾ وَمَا ذَٰلِكَ
عَلَى ٱللَّهِ بِعَزِيزٍ ﴿٢٠﴾ وَبَرَزُوا۟ لِلَّهِ جَمِيعًا فَقَالَ ٱلضُّعَفَـٰٓؤُا۟ لِلَّذِينَ ٱسْتَكْبَرُوٓا۟
إِنَّا كُنَّا لَكُمْ تَبَعًا فَهَلْ أَنتُم مُّغْنُونَ عَنَّا مِنْ عَذَابِ ٱللَّهِ مِن شَىْءٍ

wa lā yakādu yusīghuhū wa yaʾtīhil-mawtu miñ-kulli makāniñw-wa mā huwa bimayyitiñw-wa miñw-warāaʾihī ʿadhābun ghalīẓ. (17) Mathalul-ladhīna kafarū biRabbihim ʾaʿmāluhum karamādinish-taddat bihir-rīḥu fī yawmin ʿāṣifil-lā yaqdirūna mimmā kasabū ʿalā shayʾ. Dhālika huwaḍ-ḍalālul-baʿīd. (18) ʾAlam tara ʾannal-lāha khalaqas-samāwāti wal-ʾarḍa bilḥaqq. ʾIñy-yashaʾ yudhhibkum wa yaʾti bikhalqiñ-jadīd. (19) Wa mā dhālika ʿalal-lāhi biʿazīz. (20) Wa barazū lillāhi jamīʿañ-faqālaḍ-ḍuʿafāaʾu lilladhīnas-takbarūu ʾinnā kunnā lakum tabaʿañ-fahal ʾañtum-mughnūna ʿannā min ʿadhābil-lāhi miñ-shayʾ.

averse [from something]"; also – as noted in the *Qāmūs* and the *Asās* – "he cried out loudly" (i.e., by reason of his aversion to something). Since *ṣadīd* signifies anything that is repulsive, it is also used tropically to describe the pus that flows from wounds or the viscous liquid that oozes from corpses. In his commentary on this verse, Rāzī suggests that the expression *māʾ ṣadīd* is here purely metaphorical, and should be understood as "water like [what is described as] *ṣadīd*". It is in pursuance of this interpretation that I have rendered the above expression as "waters of most bitter distress" – a metaphor of the boundless suffering and bitter frustration which, in the life to come, awaits those who during their life in this world were bent on denying all spiritual truths. (Cf. the expression *sharāb min ḥamīm* – rendered by me as "a draught of burning despair" – occurring in several places and elucidated in note 62 on 6 : 70.)

23 I.e., to reconcile himself to this suffering.

24 I.e., even the good ones (Rāzī).

25 Lit., "this, this is the straying far-away". The definite article in the expression *aḍ-ḍalāl al-baʿīd*, preceded by the pronouns *dhālika huwa*, is meant to stress the extreme degree of this "straying far-away" or "going astray": a construction that can be rendered in English only by a paraphrase, as above. It is to be noted that this phrase occurs in the Qurʾān only twice – namely, in the above passage and in 22 : 12 – and refers in both cases to a denial, conscious or implied, of God's oneness and uniqueness.

26 See note 11 on 10 : 5.

27 Lit., "bring forth a new creation" or "new people", for it should be remembered that the term *khalq* denotes not merely "creation" or "act of creation" but also "people" or "mankind", which seems to be its meaning here (Ibn ʿAbbās, as quoted by Rāzī).

28 I.e., those who had sinned out of moral weakness and self-indulgence, relying on the supposedly superior wisdom of the so-called "leaders of thought", who are described in the sequence as having "gloried in their arrogance" (*astakbarū*) inasmuch as they refused to pay heed to God's messages (Ṭabarī, on the authority of Ibn ʿAbbās).

[And the others] will answer: "If God would but show us the way [to salvation], we would indeed guide you [towards it].[29] It is [now] all one, as far as we are concerned, whether we grieve impatiently or endure [our lot] with patience: there is no escape for us!" ‹21›

And when everything will have been decided, Satan will say: "Behold, God promised you something that was bound to come true![30] I, too, held out [all manner of] promises to you – but I deceived you. Yet I had no power at all over you: I but called you – and you responded unto me. Hence, blame not me, but blame yourselves.[31] It is not for me to respond to your cries, nor for you to respond to mine:[32] for, behold, I have [always] refused to admit that there was any truth in your erstwhile belief that I had a share in God's divinity."[33]

Verily, for all evildoers[34] there is grievous suffering in store. ‹22›

قَالُوا۟ لَوْ هَدَىٰنَا ٱللَّهُ لَهَدَيْنَـٰكُمْ سَوَآءٌ عَلَيْنَآ أَجَزِعْنَآ أَمْ صَبَرْنَا مَا لَنَا مِن
مَّحِيصٍ ﴿٢١﴾ وَقَالَ ٱلشَّيْطَـٰنُ لَمَّا قُضِىَ ٱلْأَمْرُ إِنَّ ٱللَّهَ وَعَدَكُمْ وَعْدَ
ٱلْحَقِّ وَوَعَدتُّكُمْ فَأَخْلَفْتُكُمْ وَمَا كَانَ لِىَ عَلَيْكُم مِّن سُلْطَـٰنٍ إِلَّآ أَن
دَعَوْتُكُمْ فَٱسْتَجَبْتُمْ لِى فَلَا تَلُومُونِى وَلُومُوٓا۟ أَنفُسَكُم مَّآ أَنَا۠ بِمُصْرِخِكُمْ
وَمَآ أَنتُم بِمُصْرِخِىَّ إِنِّى كَفَرْتُ بِمَآ أَشْرَكْتُمُونِ مِن قَبْلُ إِنَّ ٱلظَّـٰلِمِينَ
لَهُمْ عَذَابٌ أَلِيمٌ ﴿٢٢﴾

Qālū law hadānal-lāhu lahadaynākum. Sawāaʾun ʿalaynāa ʾajaziʿnāa ʾam ṣabarnā mā lanā mim-maḥīṣ. (21) Wa qālash-Shayṭānu lammā quḍiyal-ʾamru ʾinnal-lāha waʿadakum waʿdal-ḥaqqi wa waʿattukum faʾakhlaftukum. Wa mā kāna liya ʿalaykum-miñ-sulṭānin ʾillāa ʾañ-daʿawtukum fastajabtum lī; falā talūmūnī wa lūmūu ʾañfusakum. Māa ʾana bimuṣrikhikum wa māa ʾañtum-bimuṣrikhiyy. ʾInnī kafartu bimāa ʾashraktumūni miñ-qabl. ʾInnaẓ-ẓālimīna lahum ʿadhābun ʾalīm. (22)

29 Sc., "but now it is too late for repentance". According to Ṭabarī and Rāzī, this is the meaning of the above passage. Zamakhsharī, however, prefers another interpretation, implying a reference not to the present but to the past, thus: "If God had guided us aright, we would have guided you [too] aright": in other words, he understands the phrase as an attempt on the part of the doomed to divest themselves of all responsibility, and to attribute their past sinning to God's "not having willed" to guide them aright. To my mind, the interpretation offered by Ṭabarī and Rāzī is preferable because – all other considerations apart – it provides a logical connection between the request of "the weak" (see preceding note) and the reply of those who in their earthly life had "gloried in their arrogance", as well as with the latters' subsequent, despairing utterance, which can be summed up in the words, "too late!"

30 Lit., "God promised you a promise of truth" – i.e., the promise of resurrection and last judgment.

31 In his commentary on this passage, Rāzī remarks: "This verse shows that the real Satan (*ash-shayṭān al-aṣlī*) is [man's own] complex of desires (*an-nafs*): for, Satan makes it clear [in the above] that it was only by means of insinuations (*waswasah*) that he was able to reach [the sinner's soul]; and had it not been for an already-existing [evil] disposition due to lusts, anger, superstition or fanciful ideas, these [satanic] insinuations would have had no effect whatsoever."

32 I.e., "I cannot respond to your call for help, just as you should not have, in your lifetime, responded to my call." The above sentence is often interpreted in another sense, namely, "I cannot succour you, just as you cannot succour me". However, in view of Satan's allegorical reference – in the preceding passages as well as in the next sentence – to the sinners' earthly past, the rendering adopted by me seems to be more suitable; moreover, it is closer to the primary meaning of the verb *ṣarakha* ("he cried out"), from which the form *muṣrikh* ("one who responds to a cry") is derived (Jawharī).

33 This is, to my mind, the meaning of the highly elliptical phrase *kafartu bi-mā ashraktumūnī min qabl*, which could be literally – but most inadequately – translated thus: "I have refused to admit the truth of that whereby you associated me aforetime [with God]." The implication is that Satan, while endeavouring to lead men astray, never claims to be God's "equal" (cf. 7 : 20, where he speaks of God, to Adam and Eve, as "your Sustainer", or 15 : 36 and 39, where he addresses Him as "my Sustainer", or 8 : 48 and 59 : 16, where he says, "behold, I fear God") but, rather, tries to make men's sinful doings "seem goodly to them" (cf. 6 : 43, 8 : 48, 16 : 63, 27 : 24, 29 : 38), i.e., persuades them that it is morally justifiable to follow one's fancies and selfish desires without any restraint. But while Satan himself does not make any claim to equality with God, the sinner who submits to Satan's blandishments attributes to him thereby, as it were, "a share in God's divinity". – It must be stressed, in this connection, that the Qurʾanic expression *shayṭān* is often used as a metaphor for every human impulse that is intrinsically immoral and, therefore, contrary to man's best – i.e., spiritual – interests.

34 I.e., all those who had consciously – either from intellectual arrogance or from moral weakness – responded to "Satan's call".

ثلاثة ارباع الحزب

But those who shall have attained to faith and done righteous deeds will be brought into gardens through which running waters flow, therein to abide by their Sustainer's leave, and will be welcomed with the greeting, "Peace!"[35] ‹23›

ART THOU NOT aware how God sets forth the parable of a good word?[36] [It is] like a good tree, firmly rooted, [reaching out] with its branches towards the sky, ‹24› yielding its fruit at all times by its Sustainer's leave.
And [thus it is that] God propounds parables unto men, so that they might bethink themselves [of the truth].[37] ‹25›
And the parable of a corrupt word is that of a corrupt tree, torn up [from its roots] onto the face of the earth, wholly unable to endure.[38] ‹26›
[Thus,] God grants firmness unto those who have attained to faith through the word that is unshakably true[39] in the life of this world as well as in the life to come; but the wrongdoers He lets go astray:[40] for God does whatever He wills. ‹27›

ART THOU NOT aware of those who have preferred a denial of the truth to God's blessings,[41] and [thereby] invited

وَأُدْخِلَ ٱلَّذِينَ ءَامَنُوا۟ وَعَمِلُوا۟ ٱلصَّٰلِحَٰتِ جَنَّٰتٍ تَجْرِى مِن تَحْتِهَا
ٱلْأَنْهَٰرُ خَٰلِدِينَ فِيهَا بِإِذْنِ رَبِّهِمْ ۖ تَحِيَّتُهُمْ فِيهَا سَلَٰمٌ ﴿٢٣﴾ أَلَمْ تَرَ كَيْفَ
ضَرَبَ ٱللَّهُ مَثَلًا كَلِمَةً طَيِّبَةً كَشَجَرَةٍ طَيِّبَةٍ أَصْلُهَا ثَابِتٌ وَفَرْعُهَا فِى
ٱلسَّمَآءِ ﴿٢٤﴾ تُؤْتِىٓ أُكُلَهَا كُلَّ حِينٍۭ بِإِذْنِ رَبِّهَا ۗ وَيَضْرِبُ ٱللَّهُ ٱلْأَمْثَالَ
لِلنَّاسِ لَعَلَّهُمْ يَتَذَكَّرُونَ ﴿٢٥﴾ وَمَثَلُ كَلِمَةٍ خَبِيثَةٍ كَشَجَرَةٍ خَبِيثَةٍ ٱجْتُثَّتْ
مِن فَوْقِ ٱلْأَرْضِ مَا لَهَا مِن قَرَارٍ ﴿٢٦﴾ يُثَبِّتُ ٱللَّهُ ٱلَّذِينَ ءَامَنُوا۟ بِٱلْقَوْلِ
ٱلثَّابِتِ فِى ٱلْحَيَوٰةِ ٱلدُّنْيَا وَفِى ٱلْءَاخِرَةِ ۖ وَيُضِلُّ ٱللَّهُ ٱلظَّٰلِمِينَ ۚ وَيَفْعَلُ
ٱللَّهُ مَا يَشَآءُ ﴿٢٧﴾ ۞ أَلَمْ تَرَ إِلَى ٱلَّذِينَ بَدَّلُوا۟ نِعْمَتَ ٱللَّهِ كُفْرًا وَأَحَلُّوا۟

Wa ʾudkhilal-ladhīna ʾāmanū wa ʿamiluṣ-ṣāliḥāti jannātiñ-tajrī miñ-taḥtihal-ʾanhāru khālidīna fīhā biʾidhni Rabbihim taḥiyyatuhum fīhā salām. (23) ʾAlam tara kayfa ḍarabal-lāhu mathalañ-kalimatañ-ṭayyibatañ-kashajaratiñ-ṭayyibatin ʾaṣluhā thābituñw-wa farʿuhā fis-samāaʾ. (24) Tuʾtīi ʾukulahā kulla ḥīnim-biʾidhni Rabbihā. Wa yaḍribul-lāhul-ʾamthāla linnāsi laʿallahum yatadhakkarūn. (25) Wa mathalu kalimatiñ-khabīthatin kashajaratin khabīthatinij-tuththat miñ-fawqil-ʾarḍi mā lahā miñ-qarār. (26) Yuthabbitul-lāhul-ladhīna ʾāmanū bilqawlith-thābiti fil-ḥayātid-dunyā wa fil-ʾĀkhirati wa yuḍillul-lāhuẓ-ẓālimīn. Wa yafʿalul-lāhu mā yashāaʾ. (27) ۞ ʾAlam tara ʾilal-ladhīna baddalū niʿmatal-lāhi kufrañw-wa ʾaḥallū

35 As in 10 : 10, this phrase reads literally, "their greeting therein [will be], 'Peace!' (*salām*)" – a term which has been explained in *sūrah* 5, note 29.

36 In its wider meaning, the term *kalimah* ("word") denotes any conceptual statement or proposition. Thus, a "good word" circumscribes any proposition (or idea) that is intrinsically true and – because it implies a call to what is good in the moral sense – is ultimately beneficent and enduring; and since a call to moral righteousness is the innermost purport of every one of God's messages, the term "good word" applies to them as well. Similarly, the "corrupt word" mentioned in verse 26 applies to the opposite of what a divine message aims at: namely, to every idea that is intrinsically false or morally evil and, therefore, spiritually harmful.

37 See note 33 on the first clause of 39 : 27.

38 Lit., "having no permanence (*qarār*) whatever": i.e., the "corrupt word" (see note 36 above) is ephemeral in its effect, however strong its original impact on the minds of people who fall prey to it.

39 Lit., "firm" (*thābit*). The term *qawl* – similar to the term *kalimah* (see note 36 above) – denotes, beyond its primary meaning of "saying" or "utterance", also anything that can be defined as a statement of belief or opinion, namely, "concept", "tenet", "assertion of faith", and so on. In this context it expresses the concept that there is no deity save God, and that Muḥammad is His Apostle: which is an interpretation of the above phrase given by the Prophet himself, as quoted by Bukhārī in a Tradition on the authority of Al-Barāʾ ibn ʿĀzib (*Kitāb at-Tafsīr*), and by other Traditionists, including Muslim, on the authority of Shuʿbah. The adjective *thābit* connotes the "firmness" – that is, the unshakable truth – of the "word" (or "concept") which it qualifies, thus connecting it with the preceding parable of the "good word" and the "good tree".

40 See note 4 on verse 4 of this *sūrah*.

41 Lit., "who have exchanged God's blessings for a denial of the truth". The expression "God's blessings (*niʿmah*)" obviously refers here to the messages revealed through His apostles.

their people to alight in that abode of utter desolation «28» – hell – which they [themselves] will have to endure?[42] And how vile a state to settle in! «29»

For, they claimed that there are powers that could rival God,[43] and so they strayed from His path.

Say: "Enjoy yourselves [in this world], but, verily, the fire will be your journey's end!" «30»

[And] tell [those of] My servants who have attained to faith that they should be constant in prayer and spend [in Our way], secretly and openly, out of what We provide for them as sustenance,[44] ere there come a Day when there will be no bargaining, and no mutual befriending.[45] «31»

[And remember that] it is God who has created the heavens and the earth, and who sends down water from the sky and thereby brings forth [all manner] of fruits for your sustenance; and who has made ships subservient to you, so that they may sail through the sea at His behest; and has made the rivers subservient [to His laws, so that they be of use] to you; «32» and has made the sun and the moon, both of them constant upon their courses, subservient [to His laws, so that they be of use] to you; and has made the night and the day subservient [to His laws, so that they be of use] to you.[46] «33»

قَوۡمَهُمۡ دَارَ ٱلۡبَوَارِ ﴿٢٨﴾ جَهَنَّمَ يَصۡلَوۡنَهَاۖ وَبِئۡسَ ٱلۡقَرَارُ ﴿٢٩﴾ وَجَعَلُواْ لِلَّهِ
أَندَادٗا لِّيُضِلُّواْ عَن سَبِيلِهِۦۗ قُلۡ تَمَتَّعُواْ فَإِنَّ مَصِيرَكُمۡ إِلَى ٱلنَّارِ ﴿٣٠﴾ قُل
لِّعِبَادِيَ ٱلَّذِينَ ءَامَنُواْ يُقِيمُواْ ٱلصَّلَوٰةَ وَيُنفِقُواْ مِمَّا رَزَقۡنَٰهُمۡ سِرّٗا
وَعَلَانِيَةٗ مِّن قَبۡلِ أَن يَأۡتِيَ يَوۡمٞ لَّا بَيۡعٞ فِيهِ وَلَا خِلَٰلٌ ﴿٣١﴾ ٱللَّهُ ٱلَّذِي
خَلَقَ ٱلسَّمَٰوَٰتِ وَٱلۡأَرۡضَ وَأَنزَلَ مِنَ ٱلسَّمَآءِ مَآءٗ فَأَخۡرَجَ بِهِۦ مِنَ
ٱلثَّمَرَٰتِ رِزۡقٗا لَّكُمۡۖ وَسَخَّرَ لَكُمُ ٱلۡفُلۡكَ لِتَجۡرِيَ فِي ٱلۡبَحۡرِ بِأَمۡرِهِۦۖ
وَسَخَّرَ لَكُمُ ٱلۡأَنۡهَٰرَ ﴿٣٢﴾ وَسَخَّرَ لَكُمُ ٱلشَّمۡسَ وَٱلۡقَمَرَ دَآئِبَيۡنِۖ وَسَخَّرَ
لَكُمُ ٱلَّيۡلَ وَٱلنَّهَارَ ﴿٣٣﴾

qawmahum dāral-bawār. (28) Jahannama yaṣlawnahā wa bi'sal-qarār. (29) Wa jaᶜalū lillāhi 'añdādal-liyuḍillū ᶜañ-sabīlih. Qul tamattaᶜū fa'inna maṣīr-akum 'ilan-nār. (30) Qul liᶜibādiyal-ladhīna 'āmanū yuqīmuṣ-Ṣalāta wa yuñfiqū mimmā razaqnāhum sir-rañw-wa ᶜalāniyatam-miñ-qabli 'añy-ya'tiya yaw-mul-lā bayᶜuñ-fīhi wa lā khilāl. (31) 'Allāhul-ladhī khalaqas-samāwāti wal-'arḍa wa 'añzala minas-samāa'i māa'añ-fa'akhraja bihī minath-thamarāti rizqal-lakum; wa sakhkhara lakumul-fulka litajriya fil-baḥri bi'amrihi wa sakhkhara lakumul-'anhār. (32) Wa sakhkhara lakumush-shamsa wal-qamara dāa-'ibayni wa sakhkhara lakumul-layla wan-nahār. (33)

42 This is evidently an allusion to the relationship between the arrogant leaders of thought and their weak followers spoken of in verse 21 above.

43 Lit., "they gave God compeers (*andād*)". For an explanation of my paraphrase of this sentence (fully justified by Rāzī), see *sūrah* 2, note 13. – The particle *li* prefixed to the subsequent verb *li-yuḍillu* does not denote intent but is a so-called *lām al-ᶜāqibah*, i.e., "the [letter] *lām* indicating a consequence" or "a result" (Rāzī), and is in this case suitably rendered as "and so".

44 See *sūrah* 2, note 4.

45 Cf. 2 : 254. According to the philologist Abū ᶜUbaydah, as quoted by Rāzī, the expression *bayᶜ* ("selling and buying" or "bargaining") denotes here the metaphorical "[giving and taking] ransom" which, as the Qur'ān repeatedly stresses, will be inadmissible on the Day of Judgment (cf. 3 : 91 and the corresponding note 71, as well as 5 : 36, 10 : 54, 13 : 18, 39 : 47 and 70 : 11-15); similarly, the denial of *khilāl* – which Abū ᶜUbaydah regards as synonymous, in this context, with *mukhālah* ("mutual befriending") – expresses the impossibility of "ransom" through intercession on Judgment Day, for "now, indeed, you have come unto Us in a lonely state, even as We created you in the first instance" (6 : 94).

46 Almost all classical commentators agree that God's having made the natural phenomena "subservient" to man is a metaphor (*majāz*) for His having enabled man to derive lasting benefit from them: hence my explanatory interpolations. In the same sense, the night and the day are spoken of in 10 : 67, 27 : 86 or 40 : 61 as having been "made for you" (resp. "for them").

And [always] does He give you something out of what you may be asking of Him;[47] and should you try to count God's blessings, you could never compute them. [And yet,] behold, man is indeed most persistent in wrongdoing, stubbornly ingrate! ‹34›

AND [remember the time] when Abraham spoke [thus]:[48] "O my Sustainer! Make this land secure,[49] and preserve me and my children from ever worshipping idols[50] ‹35› – for, verily, O my Sustainer, these [false objects of worship] have led many people astray!

"Hence, [only] he who follows me [in this my faith] is truly of me;[51] and as for him who disobeys me – Thou art, verily, much-forgiving, a dispenser of grace! ‹36›

"O our Sustainer! Behold, I have settled some of my offspring in a valley in which there is no arable land,[52] close to Thy sanctified Temple, so that, O our Sustainer, they might devote themselves to prayer: cause Thou, therefore, people's hearts to incline towards them,[53] and grant them fruitful sustenance, so that they might have cause to be grateful. ‹37›

وَءَاتَىٰكُم مِّن كُلِّ مَا سَأَلْتُمُوهُ ۚ وَإِن تَعُدُّوا۟ نِعْمَتَ ٱللَّهِ لَا تُحْصُوهَآ ۗ إِنَّ
ٱلْإِنسَـٰنَ لَظَلُومٌ كَفَّارٌ ﴿٣٤﴾ وَإِذْ قَالَ إِبْرَٰهِيمُ رَبِّ ٱجْعَلْ هَـٰذَا ٱلْبَلَدَ
ءَامِنًا وَٱجْنُبْنِى وَبَنِىَّ أَن نَّعْبُدَ ٱلْأَصْنَامَ ﴿٣٥﴾ رَبِّ إِنَّهُنَّ أَضْلَلْنَ كَثِيرًا
مِّنَ ٱلنَّاسِ ۖ فَمَن تَبِعَنِى فَإِنَّهُۥ مِنِّى ۖ وَمَنْ عَصَانِى فَإِنَّكَ غَفُورٌ رَّحِيمٌ ﴿٣٦﴾
رَّبَّنَآ إِنِّىٓ أَسْكَنتُ مِن ذُرِّيَّتِى بِوَادٍ غَيْرِ ذِى زَرْعٍ عِندَ بَيْتِكَ ٱلْمُحَرَّمِ
رَبَّنَا لِيُقِيمُوا۟ ٱلصَّلَوٰةَ فَٱجْعَلْ أَفْـِٔدَةً مِّنَ ٱلنَّاسِ تَهْوِىٓ إِلَيْهِمْ وَٱرْزُقْهُم
مِّنَ ٱلثَّمَرَٰتِ لَعَلَّهُمْ يَشْكُرُونَ ﴿٣٧﴾

Wa ʾātākum-miñ-kulli mā saʾaltumūh. Wa ʾiñ-taʿuddū niʿmatal-lāhi lā tuḥṣūhā. ʾInnal-ʾIñsāna laẓalūmuñ-kaffār. (34) Wa ʾidh qāla ʾIbrāhīmu Rabbij-ʿal hādhal-balada ʾāminañw-waj-nubnī wa baniyya ʾañ-naʿbudal-ʾaṣnām. (35) Rabbi ʾinnahunna ʾaḍlalna kathīram-minan-nās. Famañ-tabiʿanī faʾinnahū minnī; wa man ʿaṣānī faʾinnaka Ghafūrur-Raḥīm. (36) Rabbanāa ʾinnīi ʾaskañtu miñ-dhurriyyatī biwādin ghayri dhī zarʿin ʿiñda Baytikal-Muḥarrami Rabbanā liyuqīmuṣ-Ṣalāta fajʿal ʾafʾidatam-minan-nāsi tahwīi ʾilayhim war-zuqhum-minath-thamarāti laʿallahum yashkurūn. (37)

47 I.e., God satisfies every one of man's desires, provided that His unfathomable wisdom regards its satisfaction as ultimately beneficial to the human being concerned: this is the meaning of the preposition *min* (lit., "out of", but in this context, "*something* out of") preceding the phrase "what you may be asking".

48 The whole of this passage (verses 35-41) – from which the title of this *sūrah* is derived – represents a parenthetic reminder, in the form of Abraham's prayer, of the only way to righteousness, in the deepest sense of the word, open to man: namely, a recognition of God's existence, oneness and uniqueness and, hence, a rejection of all belief in "other powers" supposedly co-existent with Him (cf. verse 30 above). Inasmuch as this prayer implies a realization of, and gratitude for, God's infinite bounty, it connects directly with the preceding verse 34 and the subsequent verse 42.

49 I.e., the land in which the Kaʿbah is situated (see *sūrah* 2, note 102) and, more specifically, Mecca.

50 The term "idols" (*aṣnām*, sing. *ṣanam*) does not apply exclusively to actual, concrete representations of false "deities": for *shirk* – that is, an attribution of divine powers or qualities to anyone or anything beside God – may consist also, as Rāzī points out, in a worshipful devotion to all manner of "causative agencies and outward means to an end" – an obvious allusion to wealth, power, luck, people's favour or disfavour, and so forth – "whereas genuine faith in the oneness and uniqueness of God (*at-tawḥīd al-maḥḍ*) consists in divesting oneself of all inner attachment to [such] causative agencies and in being convinced that there exists no real directing power apart from God".

51 Thus, Abraham accepts God's verdict (given in 2 : 124) regarding the sinners from among his descendants.

52 I.e., the narrow desert valley of Mecca, which is enclosed by barren, rocky hills. By "some of my offspring" Abraham refers to Ishmael and his descendants who settled at Mecca.

53 I.e., to be desirous of visiting them – namely, on pilgrimage to Mecca – and thus help them to maintain themselves in the holy but barren land. The phrase *afʾidah min an-nās* lends itself also to the rendering "the hearts of some people", in which case it could be taken to mean "the hearts of the believers" (Baghawī, Rāzī, Ibn Kathīr).

"O our Sustainer! Thou truly knowest all that we may hide [in our hearts] as well as all that we bring into the open: for nothing whatever, be it on earth or in heaven, remains hidden from God. ‹38›
"All praise is due to God, who has bestowed upon me, in my old age, Ishmael and Isaac! Behold, my Sustainer hears indeed all prayer: ‹39› [hence,] O my Sustainer, cause me and [some] of my offspring to remain constant in prayer![54]
"And, O our Sustainer, accept this my prayer: ‹40› O our Sustainer, grant Thy forgiveness unto me, and my parents, and all the believers, on the Day on which the [last] reckoning will come to pass!" ‹41›

رَبَّنَآ إِنَّكَ تَعۡلَمُ مَا نُخۡفِي وَمَا نُعۡلِنُۗ وَمَا يَخۡفَىٰ عَلَى ٱللَّهِ مِن شَيۡءٖ فِي ٱلۡأَرۡضِ
وَلَا فِي ٱلسَّمَآءِ ﴿٣٨﴾ ٱلۡحَمۡدُ لِلَّهِ ٱلَّذِي وَهَبَ لِي عَلَى ٱلۡكِبَرِ إِسۡمَٰعِيلَ وَإِسۡحَٰقَۚ
إِنَّ رَبِّي لَسَمِيعُ ٱلدُّعَآءِ ﴿٣٩﴾ رَبِّ ٱجۡعَلۡنِي مُقِيمَ ٱلصَّلَوٰةِ وَمِن ذُرِّيَّتِيۚ رَبَّنَا
وَتَقَبَّلۡ دُعَآءِ ﴿٤٠﴾ رَبَّنَا ٱغۡفِرۡ لِي وَلِوَٰلِدَيَّ وَلِلۡمُؤۡمِنِينَ يَوۡمَ يَقُومُ
ٱلۡحِسَابُ ﴿٤١﴾ وَلَا تَحۡسَبَنَّ ٱللَّهَ غَٰفِلًا عَمَّا يَعۡمَلُ ٱلظَّٰلِمُونَۚ إِنَّمَا يُؤَخِّرُهُمۡ
لِيَوۡمٖ تَشۡخَصُ فِيهِ ٱلۡأَبۡصَٰرُ ﴿٤٢﴾ مُهۡطِعِينَ مُقۡنِعِي رُءُوسِهِمۡ لَا يَرۡتَدُّ إِلَيۡهِمۡ
طَرۡفُهُمۡۖ وَأَفۡـِٔدَتُهُمۡ هَوَآءٞ ﴿٤٣﴾ وَأَنذِرِ ٱلنَّاسَ يَوۡمَ يَأۡتِيهِمُ ٱلۡعَذَابُ فَيَقُولُ
ٱلَّذِينَ ظَلَمُواْ رَبَّنَآ أَخِّرۡنَآ إِلَىٰٓ أَجَلٖ قَرِيبٖ نُّجِبۡ دَعۡوَتَكَ وَنَتَّبِعِ ٱلرُّسُلَۗ
أَوَلَمۡ تَكُونُوٓاْ أَقۡسَمۡتُم مِّن قَبۡلُ مَا لَكُم مِّن زَوَالٖ ﴿٤٤﴾ وَسَكَنتُمۡ فِي

AND DO NOT think that God is unaware of what the evildoers are doing: He but grants them respite until the Day when their eyes will stare in horror,[55] ‹42› the while they will be running confusedly to and fro, with their heads upraised [in supplication], unable to look away from what they shall behold,[56] and their hearts an abysmal void. ‹43›
Hence, warn men of the Day when this suffering may befall them, and when those who did wrong [in their lifetime] will exclaim: "O our Sustainer! Grant us respite for a short while, so that we might respond to Thy call and follow the apostles!"[57]
[But God will answer:] "Why – were you not aforetime wont to swear that no kind of resurrection and retribution awaited you?[58] ‹44› And yet, you dwelt in the

Rabbanāa ʾinnaka taʿlamu mā nukhfī wa mā nuʿlin. Wa mā yakhfā ʿalal-lāhi miñ-shayʾiñ-fil-ʾarḍi wa lā fis-samāaʾ. (38) ʾAlḥamdu lillāhil-ladhī wahaba lī ʿalal-kibari ʾIsmāʿīla wa ʾIsḥāq. ʾInna Rabbī laSamīʿud-duʿāaʾ. (39) Rabbij-ʿalnī muqīmaṣ-Ṣalāti wa miñ-dhurriyyatī. Rabbanā wa taqabbal duʿāaʾ. (40) Rabbanagh-fir lī wa liwālidayya wa lil muʾminīna Yawma yaqūmul-ḥisāb. (41) Wa lā taḥsabannal-lāha ghāfilan ʿamma yaʿmaluẓ-ẓālimūn. ʾInnamā yuʾakhkhiruhum liYawmiñ-tash-khaṣu fīhil-ʾabṣār. (42) Muhṭiʿīna muqniʿī ruʾūsihim lā yartaddu ʾilayhim ṭarfuhum; wa ʾafʾidatuhum hawāaʾ. (43) Wa añdhirin-nāsa Yawma yaʾtīhimul-ʿadhābu fayaqūlul-ladhīna ẓalamū Rabbanāa ʾakhkhirnāa ʾilāa ʾajaliñ-qarībiñ-nujib daʿwataka wa nattabiʿir-Rusul. ʾAwalam takūnūu ʾaqsamtum-miñ-qablu mā lakum-miñ-zawāl. (44) Wa sakañtum fī

54 I.e., metonymically, "to remain utterly devoted to Thee". The particle *min* ("[some] of") preceding the word *dhurriyatī* ("my offspring") is obviously an allusion to 2 : 124 where God says in answer to Abraham's question about his descendants: "My covenant does not embrace the evildoers." Thus, Abraham has been given to understand that not all of his posterity would be righteous and that none can claim to belong to a "chosen people" by virtue of his or her descent from an apostle of God: a statement which relates not only to the Israelites, who descended from Abraham through Isaac, but also to the Arabian (Ishmaelite) branch of the Abrahamic peoples, from whom the Quraysh were to spring: hence, by implication, even to the unrighteous among the descendants of the Last Prophet, Muḥammad, who belonged to the tribe of Quraysh.

55 This verse connects with the last sentence of Abraham's prayer, namely, his reference to "the Day on which the [last] reckoning will come to pass". The wrongdoers mentioned here are those who indulge in the belief "that there are other powers that can rival God" (cf. verse 30 above), and thus commit the unforgivable sin of *shirk*. As regards the "respite" granted to them, see the first clause of 11 : 20 and the corresponding note 39.

56 Lit., "their gaze will not revert to them".

57 Cf. 6 : 27.

58 Lit.,"that there would be no going down [or "no removal"] whatever for you" – i.e., no passing-over from earthly

dwelling-places of those who had sinned against their own selves [before your time],[59] and it was made obvious to you how We had dealt with them: for We have set forth unto you many a parable [of sin, resurrection and divine retribution]."[60] ‹45›
And [this retribution will befall all evildoers because] they devise that false imagery of theirs[61] – and all their false imagery is within God's knowledge.
[And never can the blasphemers prevail against the truth – not] even if their false imagery were so [well-devised and so powerful] that mountains could be moved thereby. ‹46›

HENCE, do not think that God will fail to fulfil the promise which He gave to His apostles:[62] verily, God is almighty, an avenger of evil! ‹47›
[His promise will be fulfilled] on the Day when the earth shall be changed into another earth, as shall be the heavens,[63] and when [all men] shall appear before God, the One who holds absolute sway over all that exists. ‹48› For on that Day thou wilt see all who were lost in sin linked together in fetters,[64] ‹49› clothed in

مَسَٰكِنِ ٱلَّذِينَ ظَلَمُوٓاْ أَنفُسَهُمۡ وَتَبَيَّنَ لَكُمۡ كَيۡفَ فَعَلۡنَا بِهِمۡ وَضَرَبۡنَا لَكُمُ
ٱلۡأَمۡثَالَ ﴿٤٥﴾ وَقَدۡ مَكَرُواْ مَكۡرَهُمۡ وَعِندَ ٱللَّهِ مَكۡرُهُمۡ وَإِن كَانَ مَكۡرُهُمۡ
لِتَزُولَ مِنۡهُ ٱلۡجِبَالُ ﴿٤٦﴾ فَلَا تَحۡسَبَنَّ ٱللَّهَ مُخۡلِفَ وَعۡدِهِۦ رُسُلَهُۥٓۚ إِنَّ ٱللَّهَ عَزِيزٞ ذُو
ٱنتِقَامٖ ﴿٤٧﴾ يَوۡمَ تُبَدَّلُ ٱلۡأَرۡضُ غَيۡرَ ٱلۡأَرۡضِ وَٱلسَّمَٰوَٰتُۖ وَبَرَزُواْ لِلَّهِ ٱلۡوَٰحِدِ
ٱلۡقَهَّارِ ﴿٤٨﴾ وَتَرَى ٱلۡمُجۡرِمِينَ يَوۡمَئِذٖ مُّقَرَّنِينَ فِي ٱلۡأَصۡفَادِ ﴿٤٩﴾ سَرَابِيلُهُم

masākinil-ladhīna ẓalamūu ʾañfusahum wa tabayyana lakum kayfa faʿalnā bihim wa ḍarabnā lakumul-ʾamthāl. ﴿45﴾ Wa qad makarū makrahum wa ʿiñdal-lāhi makruhum wa ʾiñ-kāna makruhum litazūla minhul-jibāl. ﴿46﴾ Falā taḥsabannal-lāha mukhlifa waʿdihī Rusulah. ʾInnal-lāha ʿAzīzun Dhuñ-tiqām. ﴿47﴾ Yawma tubaddalul-ʾarḍu ghayr al-ʾarḍi was-samāwātu wa barazū lillāhil-Wāḥidil-Qahhār. ﴿48﴾ Wa taral-mujrimīna Yawmaʾidhim-muqarranīna fil-ʾaṣfād. ﴿49﴾ Sarābīluhum-

life to a life in the hereafter, attended by God's retribution of sins: a reference to many people's refusal, often mentioned in the Qurʾān, to believe in life after death and, hence, in God's ultimate judgment.

59 I.e., "you lived on the same earth, and in basically the same human environment, as those earlier generations who offended against all ethical values and thereby brought destruction upon themselves: hence, their tragic fate should have been a warning to you".

60 Lit., "the parables", i.e., the parables in the Qurʾān which illuminate the idea of resurrection and of God's final judgment (Rāzī). See also note 37 above.

61 Lit., "they devised their devising", i.e., their blasphemous belief in the existence of other "divine powers" side by side with God: this is the interpretation given by Ṭabarī towards the end of his long commentary on this verse. For my rendering of the term *makr*, in this context, as "false imagery", see *sūrah* 13, note 62.

62 I.e., the promise of resurrection and recompense on the Day of Judgment. This relates specifically to the "respite" occasionally granted to evildoers for the duration of their lifetime (cf. verse 42 above).

63 This is an allusion to the total, cataclysmic change, on the Last Day, of all natural phenomena, and thus of the universe as known to man (cf. 20 : 105-107 and the corresponding note 90). Since that change will be beyond anything that man has ever experienced or what the human mind can conceive, all the Qurʾanic descriptions – in the next two verses as well as in many other places – of what is to happen on that Last Day are, of necessity, expressed in allegorical terms: and this applies also to all descriptions of man's condition, good or bad, in the life to come. (Cf. note 37 above, relating to the term "parable" often used in the Qurʾān.)

64 In his commentary on this passage, Rāzī expresses the view that the reference to the sinners' being "linked together in fetters" is a metaphor of their own evil deeds and inclinations and, consequently, of the utter despair which will be common to all of them in the hereafter. To my mind, it may also be an allusion to the chain-reaction which every evil deed is bound to set in motion on earth, one evil unavoidably begetting another.

garments of black pitch, with fire veiling their faces.[65] ‹50›
[And all shall be judged on that Day,] so that God may requite every human being for all that he has earned [in life]: verily, God is swift in reckoning! ‹51›

مِّن قَطِرَانٍ وَتَغْشَىٰ وُجُوهَهُمُ ٱلنَّارُ ﴿٥٠﴾ لِيَجْزِىَ ٱللَّهُ كُلَّ نَفْسٍ مَّا
كَسَبَتْ إِنَّ ٱللَّهَ سَرِيعُ ٱلْحِسَابِ ﴿٥١﴾ هَـٰذَا بَلَـٰغٌ لِّلنَّاسِ وَلِيُنذَرُوا۟ بِهِۦ
وَلِيَعْلَمُوٓا۟ أَنَّمَا هُوَ إِلَـٰهٌ وَٰحِدٌ وَلِيَذَّكَّرَ أُو۟لُوا۟ ٱلْأَلْبَـٰبِ ﴿٥٢﴾

THIS IS A MESSAGE unto all mankind. Hence, let them be warned thereby, and let them know that He is the One and Only God; and let those who are endowed with insight take this to heart! ‹52›

miñ-qaṭirāniñw-wa taghshā wujūhahumun-nār. (50) Liyajziyal-lāhu kulla nafsim-mā kasabat; ʾinnal-lāha Sarīʿul-ḥisāb. (51) Hādhā balāghul-linnāsi wa liyuñdharū bihī wa liyaʿlamūu ʾannamā Huwa ʾIlāhuñw-Wāḥiduñw-wa liyadhdhakkara ʾulul-ʾalbāb. (52)

65 According to Rāzī, the "garments of black pitch (*qaṭirān*)" and the "fire veiling their faces" are metaphors of the inexpressible suffering and loathsome horror which will enwrap the sinners' souls on the Day of Judgment. (See also *sūrah* 73, note 7.)

The Fifteenth Sūrah

Al-Ḥijr

Mecca Period

ACCORDING to Suyūṭī, this *sūrah* was revealed very shortly after *sūrah* 12 (*Yūsuf*): in other words, during the last year before the Prophet's exodus to Medina. The supposition (mentioned by Rāzī) that verse 87 was revealed at Medina lacks any factual corroboration and may, therefore, be safely dismissed.

As in most *sūrahs* of this period, the main theme of *Al-Ḥijr* is the evidence of God's creative activity and of the guidance vouchsafed by Him to man through revelation – especially the revelation of the Qurʾān, which, as verse 9 predicts, will for all times remain impervious to corruption.

The title, derived from the mention in verse 80 of the Arabian region known as Al-Ḥijr, obviously suggested itself to the Prophet's Companions because of the many legends attached to that place-name since time immemorial. That it is a place-name and not a description ("rocky tract" or, according to some, "forbidden tract") is evident from the fact that an ancient township of that name, long since non-existent, is mentioned by Ptolemy as "Hegra" and by Pliny as "Egra". Consequently, I have left this title untranslated.

سورة الحجر مكية

وآياتها تسع وتسعون

IN THE NAME OF GOD, THE MOST GRACIOUS, THE DISPENSER OF GRACE:

Alif. Lām. Rā.[1]

THESE ARE MESSAGES of revelation – of a discourse clear in itself and clearly showing the truth.[2] ‹1› And it will come to pass that those who are [now] bent on denying this truth will wish that they had surrendered themselves to God [in their lifetime].[3] ‹2›

Leave them alone; let them eat and enjoy themselves the while the hope [of vain delights] beguiles them: for in time they will come to know [the truth]. ‹3›

And never have We destroyed any community [for its wrongdoing] unless a divine writ had [previously] been made known to it;[4] ‹4› [but remember that] no community can ever forestall [the end of] its term – and neither can they delay [it].[5] ‹5›

And yet, they [who deny the truth] say: "O thou unto whom this reminder has [allegedly] been bestowed from on high:

بِسْمِ ٱللَّهِ ٱلرَّحْمَٰنِ ٱلرَّحِيمِ

الٓر تِلْكَ ءَايَٰتُ ٱلْكِتَٰبِ وَقُرْءَانٍ مُّبِينٍ ﴿١﴾ رُّبَمَا يَوَدُّ ٱلَّذِينَ كَفَرُوا۟
لَوْ كَانُوا۟ مُسْلِمِينَ ﴿٢﴾ ذَرْهُمْ يَأْكُلُوا۟ وَيَتَمَتَّعُوا۟ وَيُلْهِهِمُ ٱلْأَمَلُ فَسَوْفَ
يَعْلَمُونَ ﴿٣﴾ وَمَآ أَهْلَكْنَا مِن قَرْيَةٍ إِلَّا وَلَهَا كِتَابٌ مَّعْلُومٌ ﴿٤﴾ مَّا تَسْبِقُ
مِنْ أُمَّةٍ أَجَلَهَا وَمَا يَسْتَـْٔخِرُونَ ﴿٥﴾ وَقَالُوا۟ يَٰٓأَيُّهَا ٱلَّذِى نُزِّلَ عَلَيْهِ ٱلذِّكْرُ

Bismil-lāhir-Raḥmānir-Raḥīm.

ᵓAlif-Lāam-Rā. Tilka ᵓĀyātul-Kitābi wa Qurᵓānim-mu-
bīn. (1) Rubamā yawaddul-ladhīna kafarū law kānū
Muslimīn. (2) Dharhum yaᵓkulū wa yatamattaᶜū wa yul-
hihimul-ᵓamalu fasawfa yaᶜlamūn. (3) Wa māa ᵓahlak-
nā miñ-qaryatin ᵓillā wa lahā Kitābum-maᶜlūm. (4) Mā
tasbiqu min ᵓummatin ᵓajalahā wa mā yastaᵓkhirūn.
(5) Wa qālū yāa ᵓayyuhal-ladhī nuzzila ᶜalayhidh-Dhikru

حزب 27
جزء 14

1 See Appendix II.

2 Regarding this lengthy rendering of the participial adjective *mubīn,* see *sūrah* 12, note 2. In the above context, the term *qurᵓān* (which, whenever it appears without the definite article *al,* denotes a solemn "recital" or "discourse") is preceded by the conjunction *wa,* which, in its simplest connotation, signifies "and"; but since it is used here to stress the present, particular instance of the divine writ (*al-kitāb*), it can be omitted in the translation without affecting the meaning of the sentence.

3 Since this revelation – i.e., the Qurᵓān – is clear in itself and clearly shows the truth, those who deliberately reject it now will have no excuse on Resurrection Day. As so often in the Qurᵓān, the past tense in the expression *alladhīna kafarū* is indicative of conscious intent (see *sūrah* 2, note 6).

4 Lit., "unless it [the community] had a known divine writ (*kitāb maᶜlūm*)" – i.e., unless the people in question had been shown through a divine writ the meaning of right and wrong, and had deliberately rejected this divine guidance: cf. the statement, in 26 : 208, that "never have We destroyed any community unless it had had its warners", or in 6 : 131, that God "would never destroy a community for its wrongdoing so long as its people are still unaware [of the meaning of right and wrong]".

5 I.e., every community – and, in the widest sense of this term, every civilization – has a God-willed, organic span of life resembling in this respect all other living organisms, destined to grow, to reach maturity and ultimately to decay. For the ethical implications of this law of nature and its bearing on the passage that follows, see 7 : 34 and the corresponding note 25.

verily, thou art mad! ‹6› Why dost thou not bring before us angels, if thou art a man of truth?"[6] ‹7›

[Yet] We never send down angels otherwise than in accordance with the [demands of] truth;[7] and [were the angels to appear now,] lo! they [who reject this divine writ] would have no further respite![8] ‹8›

Behold, it is We Ourselves who have bestowed from on high, step by step, this reminder:[9] and, behold, it is We who shall truly guard it [from all corruption].[10] ‹9›

AND, INDEED, [O Prophet,] even before thy time did We send [Our apostles] unto communities[11] of old ‹10› – and never yet came an apostle to them without their deriding him. ‹11› Even so do We [now] cause this [scorn of Our message] to pervade the hearts of those who are lost in sin, ‹12› who do not believe in it,[12] although the way which those [evildoers] of olden times had to go has long been within their ken.[13] ‹13›

إِنَّكَ لَمَجْنُونٌ ﴿٦﴾ لَّوْ مَا تَأْتِينَا بِالْمَلَٰٓئِكَةِ إِن كُنتَ مِنَ
الصَّٰدِقِينَ ﴿٧﴾ مَا نُنَزِّلُ الْمَلَٰٓئِكَةَ إِلَّا بِالْحَقِّ وَمَا كَانُوٓا۟ إِذًا
مُّنظَرِينَ ﴿٨﴾ إِنَّا نَحْنُ نَزَّلْنَا الذِّكْرَ وَإِنَّا لَهُۥ لَحَٰفِظُونَ ﴿٩﴾ وَلَقَدْ
أَرْسَلْنَا مِن قَبْلِكَ فِى شِيَعِ الْأَوَّلِينَ ﴿١٠﴾ وَمَا يَأْتِيهِم مِّن رَّسُولٍ إِلَّا
كَانُوا۟ بِهِۦ يَسْتَهْزِءُونَ ﴿١١﴾ كَذَٰلِكَ نَسْلُكُهُۥ فِى قُلُوبِ الْمُجْرِمِينَ ﴿١٢﴾
لَا يُؤْمِنُونَ بِهِۦ ۖ وَقَدْ خَلَتْ سُنَّةُ الْأَوَّلِينَ ﴿١٣﴾

ʾinnaka lamajnūn. (6) **Law mā taʾtīnā bilMalāaʾikati ʾiñ-kuñta minaṣ-ṣādiqīn.** (7) **Mā nunazzilul-Malāaʾikata ʾillā bilḥaqqi wa mā kānūu ʾidham-muñẓarīn.** (8) **ʾInnā Naḥnu nazzalnadh-Dhikra wa ʾinnā lahū laḤāfiẓūn.** (9) **Wa laqad ʾarsalnā miñ-qablika fī shiyaʿil-ʾawwalīn.** (10) **Wa mā yaʾtīhim-mir-Rasūlin ʾillā kānū bihī yastahziʾūn.** (11) **Kadhālika naslukuhū fī qulūbil-mujrimīn** (12) **Lā yuʾminūna bihī wa qad khalat sunnatul-ʾawwalīn.** (13)

6 Cf. 6 : 8-9. The reference of the unbelievers to the Prophet's revelation is obviously sarcastic (Zamakhsharī); hence my interpolation of the word "allegedly". Although these verses relate primarily to the pagan contemporaries of the Prophet, they broadly describe the negative attitude of unbelievers of all times.

7 Sc., "and not just to satisfy a frivolous demand of people who refuse to consider a prophetic message on its merits". Moreover – as is evident from the next clause – an actual appearance of the angels to ordinary men would but presage the Day of Judgment (described in 78 : 39 as "the Day of Ultimate Truth") and, thus, the doom of the deniers of the truth spoken of here.

8 Cf. 6 : 8 – "had We sent down an angel, all would indeed have been decided", i.e., the Day of Judgment would have come.

9 I.e., the Qurʾān. The grammatical form *nazzalnā* implies a gradual revelation ("step by step") over a period of time, as has been pointed out by Zamakhsharī in his commentary on 2 : 23 (see the last sentence of my corresponding note 14).

10 This prophecy has been strikingly confirmed by the fact that the text of the Qurʾān has remained free from all alterations, additions or deletions ever since it was enunciated by the Prophet in the seventh century of the Christian era; and there is no other instance of any book, of whatever description, which has been similarly preserved over such a length of time. The early-noted variants in the reading of certain words of the Qurʾān, occasionally referred to by the classical commentators, represent no more than differences in respect of diacritical marks or of vocalisation, and, as a rule, do not affect the meaning of the passage in question. (See also note 11 on 85 : 22, explaining the expression *lawḥ maḥfūẓ*.)

11 The term *shīʿah* denotes a distinct group of people having in common the same persuasion or adhering to the same principles of behaviour, and is sometimes (though not here) used in the sense of "sect".

12 Cf. 6 : 10 and the corresponding note 9. My interpolation of the words "scorn of Our message" is based on Ṭabarī's and Zamakhsharī's interpretations of the above passage. Regarding God's "causing" the deniers of the truth to sin, see *sūrah* 2, note 7, as well as *sūrah* 14, note 4.

13 Lit., "although the way of life (*sunnah*) of those of olden times has already passed" – i.e., although the manner in which God has dealt with them has long since become a matter of common knowledge (Ibn Kathīr).

Yet even had We opened to them a gateway to heaven and they had ascended, on and on, up to it, ‹14› they would surely have said, "It is only our eyes that are spellbound! Nay, we have been bewitched!"[14] ‹15›

AND, INDEED, We have set up in the heavens great constellations,[15] and endowed them with beauty for all to behold; ‹16› and We have made them secure against every satanic force accursed[16] ‹17› – so that anyone who seeks to learn [the unknowable] by stealth is pursued by a flame clear to see.[17] ‹18›

And the earth – We have spread it out wide, and placed on it mountains firm, and caused [life] of every kind to grow on it in a balanced manner, ‹19› and provided thereon means of livelihood for you [O men] as well as for all [living beings] whose sustenance does not depend on you.[18] ‹20›

For, no single thing exists that does not have its source with Us;[19] and nought do We bestow from on high unless it be in

وَلَوْ فَتَحْنَا عَلَيْهِم بَابًا مِّنَ ٱلسَّمَآءِ فَظَلُّواْ فِيهِ يَعْرُجُونَ ﴿١٤﴾ لَقَالُوٓاْ إِنَّمَا سُكِّرَتْ
أَبْصَٰرُنَا بَلْ نَحْنُ قَوْمٌ مَّسْحُورُونَ ﴿١٥﴾ وَلَقَدْ جَعَلْنَا فِى ٱلسَّمَآءِ بُرُوجًا وَزَيَّنَّٰهَا
لِلنَّٰظِرِينَ ﴿١٦﴾ وَحَفِظْنَٰهَا مِن كُلِّ شَيْطَٰنٍ رَّجِيمٍ ﴿١٧﴾ إِلَّا مَنِ ٱسْتَرَقَ
ٱلسَّمْعَ فَأَتْبَعَهُۥ شِهَابٌ مُّبِينٌ ﴿١٨﴾ وَٱلْأَرْضَ مَدَدْنَٰهَا وَأَلْقَيْنَا فِيهَا رَوَٰسِىَ
وَأَنۢبَتْنَا فِيهَا مِن كُلِّ شَىْءٍ مَّوْزُونٍ ﴿١٩﴾ وَجَعَلْنَا لَكُمْ فِيهَا مَعَٰيِشَ وَمَن
لَّسْتُمْ لَهُۥ بِرَٰزِقِينَ ﴿٢٠﴾ وَإِن مِّن شَىْءٍ إِلَّا عِندَنَا خَزَآئِنُهُۥ وَمَا نُنَزِّلُهُۥٓ إِلَّا

Wa law fataḥnā ᶜalayhim-bābam-minas-samāaᵓi faẓ**allū fīhi yaᶜrujūna, ‹14› laqālūu ᵓinnamā sukkirat ᵓabṣārunā bal naḥnu qawmum-masḥūrūn. ‹15› Wa laqad jaᶜalnā fis-samāaᵓi burūjañw-wa zayyannāhā linnāẓirīn. ‹16› Wa ḥafiẓnāhā miñ-kulli Shayṭānir-rajīm. ‹17› ᵓIllā manis-taraqas-samᶜa faᵓatbaᶜahū shihābum-mubīn. ‹18› Wal-ᵓarḍa madadnāhā wa ᵓalqaynā fīhā rawāsiya wa ᵓambatnā fīhā miñ-kulli shayᵓim-mawzūn. ‹19› Wa jaᶜalnā lakum fīhā maᶜāyisha wa mal-lastum lahū birāziqīn. ‹20› Wa ᵓim-miñ-shayᵓin ᵓillā ᶜiñdanā khazāaᵓinuhū wa mā nunazziluhūu ᵓillā**

14 Lit., "we are people bewitched". Cf. 6 : 7, as well as the last paragraph of 10 : 2 and the corresponding note 5. The confusing of revealed truths with illusory "enchantment" or "sorcery" is often pointed out in the Qurᵓān as characteristic of the attitude of people who *a priori* refuse to accept the idea of revelation and, thus, of prophethood. The above two verses, implying that not even a direct insight into the wonders of heaven could convince "those who are bent on denying the truth", are a prelude to the subsequent passage, which once again draws our attention to the wonders of nature as an evidence of God's creative activity.

15 My rendering of *burūj* as "great constellations" is based on the *Tāj al-ᶜArūs*; among the classical commentators, Baghawī, Bayḍāwī and Ibn Kathīr give the same interpretation, while Ṭabarī (on the authority of Mujāhid and Qatādah) explains this term as signifying "the stars" in general.

16 The term *shayṭān* ("satan") – derived from the verb *shaṭana* ("he was [or "became"] remote") – often denotes in the Qurᵓān a force or influence remote from, and opposed to, all that is true and good (*Tāj al-ᶜArūs*, Rāghib): thus, for instance, in 2 : 14 it is used to describe the evil impulses (*shayāṭīn*) within the hearts of "those who are bent on denying the truth". In its widest, abstract sense it denotes every "satanic force", i.e., every impulsion directed towards ends which are contrary to valid ethical postulates. In the present context, the phrase "every satanic force accursed (*rajīm*)" – like the phrase "every rebellious (*mārid*) satanic force" in a similar context in 37 : 7 – apparently refers to endeavours, strongly condemned in Islam, to divine the future by means of astrological speculations: hence the preceding reference to the skies and the stars. The statement that God has made the heavens "secure" against such satanic forces obviously implies that He has made it impossible for the latter to obtain, through astrology or what is popularly described as "occult sciences", any real knowledge of "that which is beyond the reach of human perception" (*al-ghayb*).

17 Lit., "excepting [or "except that"] anyone who seeks to hear by stealth . . .", etc. The implication seems to be that any attempt at fathoming the mysteries of the unknowable by such illicit means ("by stealth") is inevitably followed by "a flame clear to see", i.e., by burning, self-evident frustration. (Cf. also 37 : 10.)

18 Lit., "whose providers you are not"; i.e., all living organisms – whether plants or animals – which are not tended by man but are nevertheless provided for. In its wider sense, this phrase stresses the notion that all living beings – man included – are provided for by God, and by Him alone (cf. 11 : 6).

19 Lit., "but with Us are its storehouses".

accordance with a measure well-defined.[20] ‹21›

And We let loose the winds to fertilize [plants],[21] and We send down water from the skies and let you drink thereof: and it is not you who dispose of its source ‹22› – for, behold, it is We – We alone – who grant life and deal death, and it is We alone who shall remain after all else will have passed away![22] ‹23›

And well do We know [the hearts and deeds of all human beings – both] those who lived before you and those who will come after you;[23] ‹24› and, behold, it is thy Sustainer who will gather them all together [on Judgment Day]: verily, He is wise, all-knowing! ‹25›

AND, INDEED, We have created man out of sounding clay, out of dark slime transmuted[24] ‹26› – whereas the invisible beings We had created, [long] before that, out of the fire of scorching winds.[25] ‹27›

بِقَدَرٍ مَّعْلُومٍ ﴿٢١﴾ وَأَرْسَلْنَا ٱلرِّيَٰحَ لَوَٰقِحَ فَأَنزَلْنَا مِنَ ٱلسَّمَآءِ مَآءً
فَأَسْقَيْنَٰكُمُوهُ وَمَآ أَنتُمْ لَهُۥ بِخَٰزِنِينَ ﴿٢٢﴾ وَإِنَّا لَنَحْنُ نُحْيِۦ وَنُمِيتُ
وَنَحْنُ ٱلْوَٰرِثُونَ ﴿٢٣﴾ وَلَقَدْ عَلِمْنَا ٱلْمُسْتَقْدِمِينَ مِنكُمْ وَلَقَدْ عَلِمْنَا
ٱلْمُسْتَـْٔخِرِينَ ﴿٢٤﴾ وَإِنَّ رَبَّكَ هُوَ يَحْشُرُهُمْ إِنَّهُۥ حَكِيمٌ عَلِيمٌ ﴿٢٥﴾ وَلَقَدْ
خَلَقْنَا ٱلْإِنسَٰنَ مِن صَلْصَٰلٍ مِّنْ حَمَإٍ مَّسْنُونٍ ﴿٢٦﴾ وَٱلْجَآنَّ خَلَقْنَٰهُ مِن
قَبْلُ مِن نَّارِ ٱلسَّمُومِ ﴿٢٧﴾

biqadarim-maᶜlūm. (21) Wa ᵓarsalnar-riyāḥa lawāqiḥa faᵓañzalnā minas-samāaᵓi māaᵓañ-faᵓasqaynā-kumūh wa māa ᵓañtum lahū bikhāzinīn. (22) Wa ᵓinnā laNaḥnu nuḥyī wa numītu wa Naḥnul-wārithun. (23) Wa laqad ᶜalimnal-mustaqdimīna miñkum wa laqad ᶜalimnal-mustaᵓkhirīn. (24) Wa ᵓinna Rabbaka Huwa yaḥshuruhum; ᵓinnahū Ḥakīmun ᶜAlīm. (25) Wa laqad khalaqnal-ᵓIñsāna miñ-ṣalṣālim-min ḥamaᵓim-masnūn. (26) Wal-Jāanna khalaqnāhu miñ-qablu min-nāris-samūm. (27)

20 Lit., "and We do not send it down [i.e., "create it"] otherwise than according to a measure known [to Us]": that is, in accordance with the exigencies of God's plan as such and with the function which any particular thing or phenomenon is to have within that plan.

21 I.e., by pollination as well as by bringing rain-clouds.

22 Lit., "We are [or "shall be"] the inheritors (*al-wārithūn*)": an idiomatic metaphor based, according to the consensus of all classical commentators, on the use of the term "inheritor" or "heir" in the sense of "one who remains after his predecessor has passed away" – in this case, after all creation has perished. (Cf. the expression "the heritage of the heavens and of the earth" used, with reference to God, in 3 : 180 and 57 : 10.)

23 Or: "those of you who hasten forward [towards Us], and those who lag behind". Both these interpretations are considered equally legitimate by the early commentators.

24 There are many references in the Qurᵓān to man's having been "created out of clay (*ṭīn*)" or "out of dust (*turāb*)", both these terms signifying man's lowly biological origins as well as the fact that his body is composed of various organic and inorganic substances existing – in other combinations or in their elementary forms – on or in the earth. The term *ṣalṣāl*, occurring in three verses of this *sūrah* as well as in 55 : 14, adds a further dimension to this concept. According to most of the philological authorities, it denotes "dried clay that emits a sound" (i.e., when it is struck); and since it is used in the Qurᵓān exclusively with reference to the creation of man, it seems to contain an allusion to the power of *articulate speech* which distinguishes man from all other animal species, as well as to the brittleness of his existence (cf. the expression "like pottery" in 55 : 14). As the construction of the sentence shows, this *ṣalṣāl*, is stated to have *evolved* (Rāzī) out of *ḥamaᵓ* – which, according to some authorities, is the plural of *ḥamᵓah*, signifying "dark, fetid mud" or "dark slime" – while the participial adjective *masnūn* which qualifies this noun denotes, as Rāzī points out, both "altered" (i.e., in its composition) and "brought into shape": hence my rendering of this expression as "transmuted", which to some extent combines both of the above meanings. To my mind, we have here a description of the primeval biological environment out of which the "sounding clay" – the matrix, as it were – of man's physical body has evolved in accordance with God's plan of creation.

25 Cf. 55 : 15 – "out of the confusing flame of fire (*mārij min nār*)": i.e., of non-corporeal elements. The noun *al-jānn*, rendered by me as "the invisible beings", is in reality a singular, denoting here the *kind* of these particular beings or forces, similar to the use of the singular noun "man" (*al-insān*) which describes the collective entity "mankind". The etymology of the word *jānn* (the plural of which is *jinn*) has been briefly touched upon in note 86 on 6 : 100; a more detailed discussion of its meaning is found in Appendix III.

And lo! Thy Sustainer said unto the angels: "Behold, I am about to create mortal man out of sounding clay, out of dark slime transmuted; ‹28› and when I have formed him fully and breathed into him of My spirit, fall down before him in prostration!"[26] ‹29›
Thereupon the angels prostrated themselves, all of them together, ‹30› save Iblīs: he refused to be among those who prostrated themselves.[27] ‹31›
Said He: "O Iblīs! What is thy reason for not being among those who have prostrated themselves?" ‹32›
[Iblīs] replied: "It is not for me to prostrate myself before mortal man whom Thou hast created out of sounding clay, out of dark slime transmuted!" ‹33›
Said He: "Go forth, then, from this [angelic state]: for, behold, thou art [henceforth] accursed, ‹34› and [My] rejection shall be thy due[28] until the Day of Judgment!" ‹35›
Said [Iblīs]: "Then, O my Sustainer, grant me a respite till the Day when all shall be raised from the dead!" ‹36›
Answered He: "Verily, so be it: thou shalt be among those who are granted respite ‹37› till the Day the time whereof is known [to Me alone]." ‹38›
[Whereupon] Iblīs: said: "O my Sustainer! Since Thou hast thwarted me,[29] I shall indeed make [all that is evil] on earth seem goodly to them, and shall most certainly beguile them into grievous error - ‹39› [all] save such of them as are truly Thy servants!"[30] ‹40›

وَإِذْ قَالَ رَبُّكَ لِلْمَلَٰٓئِكَةِ إِنِّى خَٰلِقٌۢ بَشَرًا مِّن صَلْصَٰلٍ مِّنْ حَمَإٍ
مَّسْنُونٍ (28) فَإِذَا سَوَّيْتُهُۥ وَنَفَخْتُ فِيهِ مِن رُّوحِى فَقَعُوا۟ لَهُۥ
سَٰجِدِينَ (29) فَسَجَدَ ٱلْمَلَٰٓئِكَةُ كُلُّهُمْ أَجْمَعُونَ (30) إِلَّآ إِبْلِيسَ أَبَىٰٓ
أَن يَكُونَ مَعَ ٱلسَّٰجِدِينَ (31) قَالَ يَٰٓإِبْلِيسُ مَا لَكَ أَلَّا تَكُونَ مَعَ
ٱلسَّٰجِدِينَ (32) قَالَ لَمْ أَكُن لِّأَسْجُدَ لِبَشَرٍ خَلَقْتَهُۥ مِن صَلْصَٰلٍ مِّنْ
حَمَإٍ مَّسْنُونٍ (33) قَالَ فَٱخْرُجْ مِنْهَا فَإِنَّكَ رَجِيمٌ (34) وَإِنَّ عَلَيْكَ ٱللَّعْنَةَ
إِلَىٰ يَوْمِ ٱلدِّينِ (35) قَالَ رَبِّ فَأَنظِرْنِىٓ إِلَىٰ يَوْمِ يُبْعَثُونَ (36) قَالَ فَإِنَّكَ
مِنَ ٱلْمُنظَرِينَ (37) إِلَىٰ يَوْمِ ٱلْوَقْتِ ٱلْمَعْلُومِ (38) قَالَ رَبِّ بِمَآ
أَغْوَيْتَنِى لَأُزَيِّنَنَّ لَهُمْ فِى ٱلْأَرْضِ وَلَأُغْوِيَنَّهُمْ أَجْمَعِينَ (39) إِلَّا عِبَادَكَ
مِنْهُمُ ٱلْمُخْلَصِينَ (40)

Wa ʾidh qāla Rabbuka lilMalāaʾikati ʾinnī khāliqum-basharam-miñ-ṣalṣālim-min ḥamaʾim-masnūn. (28) Faʾidhā sawwaytuhū wa nafakhtu fīhi mir-Rūḥī faqaʿū lahū sājidīn. (29) Fasajadal-Malāaʾikatu kulluhum ʾajmaʿūn. (30) ʾIllāa ʾIblīsa ʾabāa ʾañy-yakūna maʿas-sājidīn. (31) Qāla yāa ʾIblīsu mā laka ʾallā takūna maʿas-sājidīn. (32) Qāla lam ʾakul-liʾasjuda libasharin khalaqtahū miñ-ṣalṣālim-min ḥamaʾim-masnūn. (33) Qāla fakhruj minhā faʾinnaka rajīm. (34) Wa ʾinna ʿalaykal-laʿnata ʾilā Yawmid-Dīn. (35) Qāla Rabbi faʾañẓirnīi ʾilā Yawmi yubʿathūn. (36) Qāla faʾinnaka minal-muñẓarīna, (37) ʾilā Yawmil-waqtil-maʿlūm. (38) Qāla Rabbi bimāa ʾaghwaytanī laʾuzayyinanna lahum fil-ʾarḍi wa laʾughwiyannahum ʾajmaʿīna, (39) ʾillā ʿibādaka minhumul-mukhlaṣīn. (40)

26 Cf. 2 : 30-34 and the corresponding notes, as well as 7 : 11-18. The allegorical character of all the passages bearing on the creation of man and on God's command to the angels to prostrate themselves before him is brought out clearly in God's saying, "I am about to create mortal man . . .; and when I have formed him fully . . .", etc.: for it is obvious that, in reality, no lapse of time is required for God's completing His creation – since, "when He wills a thing to be, He but says unto it, 'Be' – and it is" (cf. 2 : 117, 3 : 47 and 59, 6 : 73, 16 : 40, 19 : 35, 36 : 82 and 40 : 68). God's "breathing of His spirit" into man is obviously a metaphor for His endowing him with life and consciousness: that is, with a soul.

27 See note 10 on 7 : 11. For the deeper meaning of this "rebellion", see note 31 below.

28 Lit., "is upon thee".

29 See *sūrah* 7, note 11.

30 Lit., "Thy sincere servants": i.e., those who are so deeply conscious of God that no "blandishment of Satan" can lead them astray. (See also note 32 below.)

ربع الحزب

Said He: "This is, with Me, a straight way:[31] ‹41› verily, thou shalt have no power over My creatures – unless it be such as are [already] lost in grievous error and follow thee [of their own will]:[32] ‹42› and for all such, behold, hell is the promised goal, ‹43› with seven gates leading into it, each gate receiving its allotted share of sinners."[33] ‹44›

VERILY, those who are conscious of God [shall find themselves in the hereafter] amidst gardens and springs, ‹45› [having been received with the greeting,] "Enter here in peace, secure!" ‹46›

And [by then] We shall have removed whatever unworthy thoughts or feelings may have been [lingering] in their breasts, [and they shall rest] as brethren, facing one another [in love] upon thrones of happiness.[34] ‹47› No weariness shall ever touch them in this [state of bliss], and never shall they have to forgo it.[35] ‹48›

Tell My servants that I – I alone – am truly forgiving, a true dispenser of grace; ‹49›

قَالَ هَٰذَا صِرَٰطٌ عَلَيَّ مُسْتَقِيمٌ (41) إِنَّ عِبَادِى لَيْسَ لَكَ عَلَيْهِمْ سُلْطَٰنٌ
إِلَّا مَنِ ٱتَّبَعَكَ مِنَ ٱلْغَاوِينَ (42) وَإِنَّ جَهَنَّمَ لَمَوْعِدُهُمْ أَجْمَعِينَ (43)
لَهَا سَبْعَةُ أَبْوَٰبٍ لِّكُلِّ بَابٍ مِّنْهُمْ جُزْءٌ مَّقْسُومٌ (44) إِنَّ ٱلْمُتَّقِينَ فِى
جَنَّٰتٍ وَعُيُونٍ (45) ٱدْخُلُوهَا بِسَلَٰمٍ ءَامِنِينَ (46) وَنَزَعْنَا مَا فِى صُدُورِهِم
مِّنْ غِلٍّ إِخْوَٰنًا عَلَىٰ سُرُرٍ مُّتَقَٰبِلِينَ (47) لَا يَمَسُّهُمْ فِيهَا نَصَبٌ وَمَا هُم
مِّنْهَا بِمُخْرَجِينَ (48) ۞ نَبِّئْ عِبَادِىٓ أَنِّىٓ أَنَا ٱلْغَفُورُ ٱلرَّحِيمُ (49)

**Qāla hādhā ṣirāṭun ʿalayya mustaqīm. (41) ʾInna
ʿibādī laysa laka ʿalayhim sulṭānun ʾillā manit-
tabaʿaka minal-ghāwīn. (42) Wa ʾinna jahannama la-
mawʿiduhum ʾajmaʿīn. (43) Lahā sabʿatu ʾabwābil-
likulli bābim-minhum juzʾum-maqsūm. (44) ʾInnal-
muttaqīna fī jannātiñw-wa ʿuyūn. (45) ʾUdkhulūhā bi-
salāmin ʾāminīn. (46) Wa nazaʿnā mā fī ṣudūrihim-
min ghillin ʾikhwānan ʿalā sururim-mutaqābilīn. (47)
Lā yamassuhum fīhā naṣabuñw-wa mā hum-minhā
bimukhrajīn. (48) ۞ Nabbiʾ ʿibādīi ʾannīi ʾAnal-Ghafū-
rur-Raḥīm. (49)**

31 I.e., "this is what I have willed" – namely, that Iblīs (or Satan) should tempt man, but should have no power to seduce those who are truly conscious of God. Thus, the Qurʾān makes it clear that despite his ostensible "rebellion" against his Creator, Satan fulfils a definite *function* in God's plan: he is the eternal tempter who enables man to exercise his God-given freedom of choice between good and evil and, thus, to become a being endowed with moral free will. (See in this connection 19 : 83, as well as note 26 on 2 : 34 and note 16 on 7 : 24.)

32 Lit., "except him who shall follow thee from among those who are lost in grievous error". (Cf. 14 : 22, according to which Satan will thus address his erstwhile followers on Judgment Day: "I had no power at all over you: I but called you – and you responded unto me.") This phrase constitutes the essential difference between the above passage and the similar one in 7 : 11-18.

33 Lit., "it has seven gates, [with] an allotted share of them for each gate". This probably means "seven degrees" of hell, i.e., of the suffering which, in the life to come, awaits the "followers of Satan" in accordance with the gravity of their sins (Rāzī; a similar explanation is given by Qatādah, as quoted by Ṭabarī). It should also be remembered that the concept of "hell" as such is referred to in the Qurʾān under seven different names, all of them metaphorical (necessarily so, because they relate to what the Qurʾān describes as *al-ghayb*, "something that is beyond the reach of human perception"): namely *nār* ("fire", which is the general term), *jahannam* ("hell"), *jaḥīm* ("blazing fire"), *saʿīr* ("blazing flame"), *saqar* ("hell-fire"), *laẓā* ("raging flame"), and *ḥuṭamah* ("crushing torment"). Since, as I have mentioned, these designations of other-worldly suffering are obviously allegorical, we may also assume that the "seven gates of hell" have the same character, and signify "seven approaches [or "ways"] to hell". Furthermore, it is well known that in the Semitic languages – and most particularly in classical Arabic – the number "seven" is often used in the sense of "several" or "various" (cf. *Lisān al-ʿArab, Tāj al-ʿArūs*, etc.): and so the above Qurʾanic phrase may well have the meaning of "various ways leading to hell" – in other words, many ways of sinning.

34 I.e., all being equal in dignity, and therefore free from envy. As Rāzī points out, the plural noun *surur* (sing. *sarīr*), which literally denotes "couches" or, occasionally, "thrones", signifies also "seats [or "thrones"] of eminence" or "of happiness (*surūr*)", from which latter word the noun *sarīr* and its plural *surur* may be derived. The sublime quality of these "thrones of happiness" is in some instances further symbolized by expressions like "gold-encrusted" (56 : 15) or "raised high" (88 : 13).

35 Lit., "never shall they be caused to depart from it".

and [also,] that the suffering which I shall impose [on sinners] will indeed be a suffering most grievous.[36] ‹50›

AND TELL THEM [once again] about Abraham's guests[37] ‹51› – [how,] when they presented themselves before him and bade him peace, he answered: "Behold, we are afraid of you!"[38] ‹52›

Said they: "Fear not! Behold, we bring thee the glad tiding of [the birth of] a son who will be endowed with deep knowledge."[39] ‹53›

Said he: "Do you give me this glad tiding despite the fact that old age has overtaken me? Of what [strange thing], then, are you giving me a tiding!" ‹54›

They answered: "We have given thee the glad tiding of something that is bound to come true:[40] so be not of those who abandon hope!" ‹55›

[Abraham] exclaimed: "And who – other than those who have utterly lost their way – could ever abandon the hope of his Sustainer's grace?" ‹56›

He added: "And what [else] may you have in view, O you [heavenly] messengers?" ‹57›

They answered: "We are sent to people lost in sin[41] [who are to be destroyed], ‹58› barring Lot's household, all of whom, behold, we shall save ‹59› – excepting only his wife, [of whom God says,] 'We

وَأَنَّ عَذَابِى هُوَ ٱلْعَذَابُ ٱلْأَلِيمُ ﴿٥٠﴾ وَنَبِّئْهُمْ عَن ضَيْفِ إِبْرَٰهِيمَ ﴿٥١﴾
إِذْ دَخَلُوا۟ عَلَيْهِ فَقَالُوا۟ سَلَٰمًا قَالَ إِنَّا مِنكُمْ وَجِلُونَ ﴿٥٢﴾ قَالُوا۟ لَا
تَوْجَلْ إِنَّا نُبَشِّرُكَ بِغُلَٰمٍ عَلِيمٍ ﴿٥٣﴾ قَالَ أَبَشَّرْتُمُونِى عَلَىٰٓ أَن مَّسَّنِىَ
ٱلْكِبَرُ فَبِمَ تُبَشِّرُونَ ﴿٥٤﴾ قَالُوا۟ بَشَّرْنَٰكَ بِٱلْحَقِّ فَلَا تَكُن مِّنَ
ٱلْقَٰنِطِينَ ﴿٥٥﴾ قَالَ وَمَن يَقْنَطُ مِن رَّحْمَةِ رَبِّهِۦٓ إِلَّا ٱلضَّآلُّونَ ﴿٥٦﴾ قَالَ
فَمَا خَطْبُكُمْ أَيُّهَا ٱلْمُرْسَلُونَ ﴿٥٧﴾ قَالُوٓا۟ إِنَّآ أُرْسِلْنَآ إِلَىٰ قَوْمٍ
مُّجْرِمِينَ ﴿٥٨﴾ إِلَّآ ءَالَ لُوطٍ إِنَّا لَمُنَجُّوهُمْ أَجْمَعِينَ ﴿٥٩﴾ إِلَّا ٱمْرَأَتَهُۥ

Wa ʾanna ʿadhābī huwal-ʿadhābul-ʾalīm. (50) Wa nab-
biʾhum ʿañ-ḍayfi ʾIbrāhīm. (51) ʾIdh dakhalū ʿalayhi
faqālū salāmañ-qāla ʾinnā miñkum wajilūn. (52)
Qālū lā tawjal ʾinnā nubashshiruka bighulāmin ʿalīm.
(53) Qāla ʾabashshartumūnī ʿalāa ʾam-massaniyal-
kibaru fabima tubashshirūn. (54) Qālū bashsharnāka
bilḥaqqi falā takum-minal-qāniṭīn. (55) Qāla wa mañy-
yaqnaṭu mir-raḥmati Rabbihīi ʾillaḍ-ḍaallūn. (56) Qāla
famā khaṭbukum ʾayyuhal-Mursalūna, (57) qālūu ʾinnāa
ʾursilnāa ʾilā qawmim-mujrimīna. (58) ʾIllāa ʾāla Lūṭin
ʾinnā lamunajjūhum ʾajmaʿīn. (59) ʾIllam-raʾatahū

36 In his commentary on the above two verses, Rāzī notes that the statement relating to God's forgiveness and grace contains a threefold emphasis – expressed by the repetition of the personal pronoun *anā* relating to God, and the definite article *al* before each of the two participial adjectives – whereas there is no such stress in the mention of His chastisement of recalcitrant sinners. (Cf. 6 : 12 – and the corresponding note 10 – as well as 6 : 54, both of which verses state that God "has willed upon Himself the law of grace and mercy".)

37 For a more detailed story of Abraham and the heavenly messengers, see verses 69-76 of *sūrah* 11 (*Hūd*), which was revealed shortly before the present one. The connection between this story and the preceding stress on God's grace arises from Abraham's saying (in verse 56), "And who – other than those who have utterly lost their way – could ever lose the hope of his Sustainer's grace?" Similarly, the subsequent references (in verses 58-84) to the sinful communities that were destroyed because they refused to heed the warnings of their prophets are, obviously, meant to illustrate the reverse of God's grace, namely, His inevitable chastisement of deliberate, unrepented sinning (verse 50 above).

38 For the reason of Abraham's and Sarah's apprehension, see 11 : 70.

39 I.e., will be a prophet.

40 Lit., "We have given thee the glad tiding of the truth" – i.e., of the truth willed by God (Ibn ʿAbbās, as quoted by Rāzī).

41 I.e., to the people of Sodom (see also 7: 80-84 and 11 : 77-83).

have ordained [that], behold, she should be among those who stay behind!'"[42] «60»

AND WHEN the messengers [of God] came to the house of Lot, «61» he said: "Behold, you are people unknown [here]!"[43] «62»
They answered: "Nay, but we have come unto thee with [the announcement of] something that they [who are given to evil] have always been wont to call in question,[44] «63» and we are bringing thee the certainty [of its fulfilment]:[45] for, behold, we are speaking the truth indeed. «64» Go, then, with thy household while it is yet night, with thyself following them in the rear; and let none of you look back,[46] but proceed whither you are bidden." «65»
And [through Our messengers] We revealed unto him this decree: "The last remnant of those [sinners] shall be wiped out[47] in the morn." «66»
And the people of the city came [unto Lot], rejoicing at the glad tiding.[48] «67»
Exclaimed [Lot]: "Behold, these are my guests: so put me not to shame, «68» but be conscious of God and disgrace me not!" «69»
They answered: "Have we not forbidden thee [to offer protection] to any kind of people?"[49] «70»

قَدَّرْنَآ إِنَّهَا لَمِنَ ٱلْغَٰبِرِينَ ﴿٦٠﴾ فَلَمَّا جَآءَ ءَالَ لُوطٍ ٱلْمُرْسَلُونَ ﴿٦١﴾
قَالَ إِنَّكُمْ قَوْمٌ مُّنكَرُونَ ﴿٦٢﴾ قَالُوا۟ بَلْ جِئْنَٰكَ بِمَا كَانُوا۟ فِيهِ
يَمْتَرُونَ ﴿٦٣﴾ وَأَتَيْنَٰكَ بِٱلْحَقِّ وَإِنَّا لَصَٰدِقُونَ ﴿٦٤﴾ فَأَسْرِ بِأَهْلِكَ بِقِطْعٍ
مِّنَ ٱلَّيْلِ وَٱتَّبِعْ أَدْبَٰرَهُمْ وَلَا يَلْتَفِتْ مِنكُمْ أَحَدٌ وَٱمْضُوا۟ حَيْثُ
تُؤْمَرُونَ ﴿٦٥﴾ وَقَضَيْنَآ إِلَيْهِ ذَٰلِكَ ٱلْأَمْرَ أَنَّ دَابِرَ هَٰٓؤُلَآءِ مَقْطُوعٌ
مُّصْبِحِينَ ﴿٦٦﴾ وَجَآءَ أَهْلُ ٱلْمَدِينَةِ يَسْتَبْشِرُونَ ﴿٦٧﴾ قَالَ إِنَّ هَٰٓؤُلَآءِ
ضَيْفِى فَلَا تَفْضَحُونِ ﴿٦٨﴾ وَٱتَّقُوا۟ ٱللَّهَ وَلَا تُخْزُونِ ﴿٦٩﴾ قَالُوٓا۟ أَوَلَمْ نَنْهَكَ
عَنِ ٱلْعَٰلَمِينَ ﴿٧٠﴾

qaddarnāa ᵓinnahā laminal-ghābirīn. (60) Falammā jāaᵓa ᵓāla Lūṭinil-Mursalūn. (61) Qāla ᵓinnakum qawmum-muñkarūn. (62) Qālū bal jiᵓnāka bimā kānū fīhi yamtarūn. (63) Wa ᵓataynāka bilḥaqqi wa ᵓinnā laṣādiqūn. (64) Faᵓasri biᵓahlika biqiṭᶜim-minal-layli wattabiᶜ adbārahum wa lā yaltafit miñkum ᵓaḥaduñw-wam-ḍū ḥaythu tuᵓmarūn. (65) Wa qaḍaynāa ᵓilayhi dhālikal-ᵓamra ᵓanna dābira hāaᵓulāaᵓi maqṭūᶜum-muṣbiḥīn. (66) Wa jāaᵓa ᵓahlul-madīnati yastabshirūn. (67) Qāla ᵓinna hāaᵓulāaᵓi ḍayfī falā tafḍaḥūn. (68) Wat-taqul-lāha wa lā tukhzūn. (69) Qālūu ᵓawalam nanhaka ᶜanil-ᶜālamīn. (70)

42 See 7 : 83 and the corresponding note 66, as well as 11 : 81 and 66 : 10. My interpolation of the words "of whom God says" is necessitated by the elliptic use of the verb *qaddarnā* – which, in the sense of "We have ordained" or "decreed", is an act attributed in the Qurᵓān invariably, and exclusively, to God. As I have repeatedly pointed out in my notes, God's "ordaining" a sinner to commit a sin or His "decreeing" that he should remain deaf to the voice of truth is a metonym for the natural law instituted by Him, which has been explained in *sūrah* 2, note 7; it refers also, generally speaking, to God's absolute fore-knowledge of how any of His creatures will act in a given situation (Zamakhsharī). See also note 56 on 11 : 34 and note 4 on 14 : 4.

43 Implying that they might be assaulted by the sinful people of his town: cf. 11 : 77 and the corresponding note 107.

44 Lit., "that about which they have persistently been (*kānū*) in doubt" – i.e., the doom which, in this world or in the hereafter, is the inevitable consequence of deliberate sinning: a prediction which the sinners themselves so often deride (cf. 6 : 57-58, 8 : 32, 11 : 8, and the corresponding notes). To my mind, this sentence constitutes the reason for the repetition, in this *sūrah*, of the stories of Lot's people and the other sinful communities of old that were punished for their persistent transgressions against all moral laws.

45 Lit., "We have brought thee [or "come to thee with"] the truth".

46 For an explanation of this metaphorical "looking back", see *sūrah* 11, note 112.

47 Lit., "cut off".

48 Sc., "of the arrival of handsome strangers". See also 7 : 80-81 and 11 : 77-79, as well as the relevant notes.

49 Lit., "all people" (*al-ᶜālamīn*): obviously, because Lot was a stranger in Sodom – having come there from Mesopotamia, his and Abraham's country of origin (see *sūrah* 11, note 102) – and had previously aroused the ire of the Sodomites by his moral reproaches (cf. 7 : 80-82).

[Lot] said: "[Take instead] these daughters of mine,[50] if you must do [whatever you intend to do]!" ‹71›
[But the angels spoke thus:] "As thou livest, [O Lot, they will not listen to thee:][51] behold, in their delirium [of lust] they are but blindly stumbling to and fro!" ‹72›
And thereupon the blast [of Our punishment] overtook them[52] at the time of sunrise, ‹73› and We turned those [sinful towns] upside down, and rained down upon them stone-hard blows of chastisement pre-ordained.[53] ‹74›
Verily, in all this there are messages indeed for those who can read the signs:[54] ‹75› for, behold, those [towns] stood by a road that still exists.[55] ‹76›
Verily, herein lies a message indeed for all who believe [in God]. ‹77›

AND THE DWELLERS of the wooded dales [of Madyan, too,] were inveterate evildoers,[56] ‹78› and so We inflicted Our retribution on them.
And, behold, both these [sinful communities] lived by a highway, [to this day] plain to see.[57] ‹79›

AND, [likewise,] indeed, the people of Al-Ḥijr[58] gave the lie to [Our] message-bearers: ‹80› for We did vouchsafe them

قَالَ هَٰٓؤُلَآءِ بَنَاتِىٓ إِن كُنتُمْ فَٰعِلِينَ ﴿71﴾ لَعَمْرُكَ إِنَّهُمْ لَفِى سَكْرَتِهِمْ
يَعْمَهُونَ ﴿72﴾ فَأَخَذَتْهُمُ ٱلصَّيْحَةُ مُشْرِقِينَ ﴿73﴾ فَجَعَلْنَا عَٰلِيَهَا سَافِلَهَا
وَأَمْطَرْنَا عَلَيْهِمْ حِجَارَةً مِّن سِجِّيلٍ ﴿74﴾ إِنَّ فِى ذَٰلِكَ لَأَيَٰتٍ
لِّلْمُتَوَسِّمِينَ ﴿75﴾ وَإِنَّهَا لَبِسَبِيلٍ مُّقِيمٍ ﴿76﴾ إِنَّ فِى ذَٰلِكَ لَأَيَةً لِّلْمُؤْمِنِينَ ﴿77﴾
وَإِن كَانَ أَصْحَٰبُ ٱلْأَيْكَةِ لَظَٰلِمِينَ ﴿78﴾ فَٱنتَقَمْنَا مِنْهُمْ وَإِنَّهُمَا لَبِإِمَامٍ
مُّبِينٍ ﴿79﴾ وَلَقَدْ كَذَّبَ أَصْحَٰبُ ٱلْحِجْرِ ٱلْمُرْسَلِينَ ﴿80﴾ وَءَاتَيْنَٰهُمْ

Qāla hāaʾulāaʾi banātīi ʾiñ-kuñtum fāᶜilīn. (71)
Laᶜamruka ʾinnahum lafī sakratihim yaᶜmahūn. (72)
Faʾakhadhat-humuṣ-ṣayḥatu mushriqīn. (73) Fajaᶜalnā
ᶜāliyahā sāfilahā wa ʾamṭarnā ᶜalayhim ḥijāratam-
miñ-sijjīl. (74) ʾInna fī dhālika laʾĀyātil-lilmutawas-
simīn. (75) Wa ʾinnahā labisabīlim-muqīm. (76) ʾInna fī
dhālika laʾāyatal-lilmuʾminīn. (77) Wa ʾiñ-kāna ʾaṣḥābul-ʾaykati laẓālimīn. (78) Fañtaqamnā minhum wa
ʾinnahumā labiʾimāmim-mubīn. (79) Wa laqad kadhdhaba ʾaṣḥābul-Ḥijril-mursalīn. (80) Wa ʾātaynāhum

50 See *sūrah* 11, note 109.

51 The above two interpolations are based on Zamakhsharī's commentary on this verse. The oath "As thou livest" reads, literally, "By thy life".

52 Regarding the meaning of the term *ṣayḥah*, rendered by me as "blast of [God's] punishment", see *sūrah* 11, note 98.

53 See *sūrah* 11, note 114.

54 In its full significance, the term *mutawassim* denotes "one who applies his mind to the study of the outward appearance of a thing with a view to understanding its real nature and its inner characteristics" (Zamakhsharī and Rāzī).

55 The existence of that road, which led from northern Ḥijāz to Syria, skirting the Dead Sea – to the north-east of which Sodom and Gomorrah were situated – has received startling confirmation through aerial photographs recently published by the American School of Oriental Research (New Haven, Connecticut). These photographs clearly show the ancient road as a dark streak winding northwards, more or less parallel with the eastern shores of the Dead Sea.

56 As is evident from 26 : 176 ff., the "dwellers of the wooded dales (*al-aykah*)" were the people of Madyan, who refused to pay heed to their prophet, Shuᶜayb, and were thereupon destroyed, apparently by an earthquake and/or a volcanic eruption (cf. 7 : 85-93 and 11 : 84-95).

57 I.e., the people of Lot and those of Shuᶜayb, who inhabited adjacent regions (see *sūrah* 7, note 67), and whose fate should be an example as plain to see as the highway which passes through the regions once inhabited by them.

58 I.e., the tribe of Thamūd (see *sūrah* 7, note 56), who in pre-Islamic times inhabited the region of Al-Ḥijr in northernmost Ḥijāz, south of the oasis of Taymah. The story of the Thamūd is found in 7 : 73-79.

Our messages, but they obstinately turned their backs upon them ‹81› – notwithstanding that they had been wont [to enjoy Our blessings and] to hew out dwellings from the mountains, [wherein they could live] in security:[59] ‹82› – and so the blast [of Our punishment] overtook them at early morn, ‹83› and of no avail to them was all [the power] that they had acquired. ‹84›

AND [remember:] We have not created the heavens and the earth and all that is between them without [an inner] truth;[60] but, behold, the Hour [when this will become clear to all] is indeed yet to come. Hence, forgive [men's failings] with fair forbearance: ‹85› verily, thy Sustainer is the all-knowing Creator of all things![61] ‹86›

AND, INDEED, We have bestowed upon thee seven of the oft-repeated [verses], and [have, thus, laid open before thee] this sublime Qurʾān:[62] ‹87› [so] turn not thine eyes [longingly] towards the worldly benefits which We have granted unto some[63] of those [that deny the truth]. And neither grieve over those [who refuse to heed thee], but spread the wings of thy tenderness over the believers,[64] ‹88› and say: "Behold, I am indeed the plain warner [promised by God]!"[65] ‹89›

ءَايَـٰتِنَا فَكَانُوا۟ عَنْهَا مُعْرِضِينَ (81) وَكَانُوا۟ يَنْحِتُونَ مِنَ ٱلْجِبَالِ بُيُوتًا
ءَامِنِينَ (82) فَأَخَذَتْهُمُ ٱلصَّيْحَةُ مُصْبِحِينَ (83) فَمَآ أَغْنَىٰ عَنْهُم مَّا كَانُوا۟
يَكْسِبُونَ (84) وَمَا خَلَقْنَا ٱلسَّمَـٰوَٰتِ وَٱلْأَرْضَ وَمَا بَيْنَهُمَآ إِلَّا بِٱلْحَقِّ
وَإِنَّ ٱلسَّاعَةَ لَـَٔاتِيَةٌ فَٱصْفَحِ ٱلصَّفْحَ ٱلْجَمِيلَ (85) إِنَّ رَبَّكَ هُوَ
ٱلْخَلَّـٰقُ ٱلْعَلِيمُ (86) وَلَقَدْ ءَاتَيْنَـٰكَ سَبْعًا مِّنَ ٱلْمَثَانِى وَٱلْقُرْءَانَ
ٱلْعَظِيمَ (87) لَا تَمُدَّنَّ عَيْنَيْكَ إِلَىٰ مَا مَتَّعْنَا بِهِۦٓ أَزْوَٰجًا مِّنْهُمْ وَلَا تَحْزَنْ
عَلَيْهِمْ وَٱخْفِضْ جَنَاحَكَ لِلْمُؤْمِنِينَ (88) وَقُلْ إِنِّىٓ أَنَا ٱلنَّذِيرُ
ٱلْمُبِينُ (89)

ʾĀyātinā fakānū ʿanhā muʿriḍīn. (81) Wa kānū yanḥitūna minal-jibāli buyūtan ʾāminīn. (82) Faʾakhadhat-humuṣ-ṣayḥatu muṣbiḥīn. (83) Famā ʾaghnā ʿanhum-mā kānū yaksibūn. (84) Wa mā khalaqnas-samāwāti wal-ʾarḍa wa mā baynahumāa ʾillā bilḥaqq. Wa ʾinnas-Sāʿata laʾātiyatuñ-faṣfaḥiṣ-ṣafḥal-jamīl. (85) ʾInna Rabbaka Huwal-Khallāqul-ʿAlīm. (86) Wa laqad ʾātaynāka sabʿam-minal-mathānī wal-Qurʾānal-ʿaẓīm. (87) Lā tamuddanna ʿaynayka ʾilā mā mattaʿnā bihīi ʾazwājam-minhum wa lā taḥzan ʿalayhim wakh-fiḍ janāḥaka lilmuʾminīn. (88) Wa qul ʾinnīi ʾanan-nadhīrul-mubīn. (89)

59 See 7 : 74 and the corresponding notes (particularly note 59).

60 For an explanation of this rendering of *illā bi'l-ḥaqq* (lit., "otherwise than with [or "in"] truth"), see *sūrah* 10, note 11.

61 I.e., "He has created all human beings with full knowledge of their natural differentiation and the disparity in their respective conditions" (Rāzī) – and this, of course, includes their failings and errors. (Cf. 7 : 199 – "Make due allowance for man's nature" – and the corresponding note 162.)

62 With these words, the discourse returns to the theme enunciated at the beginning of this *sūrah* and indirectly alluded to in verse 85 as well: namely, the revelation of the divine writ, destined to serve as a moral guidance to man, who cannot, as yet, discern the meaning and purpose of God's creation. – According to most of the authorities, including some of the foremost Companions of the Prophet, "The Seven Oft-Repeated [Verses]" is a designation given by Muḥammad himself to the first *sūrah* of the Qurʾān, which has also been described by him as "The Essence of the Divine Writ" (*Umm al-Kitāb*) inasmuch as it alludes to all the ethical and metaphysical principles set forth in the Qurʾān (Bukhārī, *Kitāb at-Tafsīr*). See also my introductory note to *Al-Fātiḥah* ("The Opening").

63 The philological authorities are unanimous in that the plural noun *azwāj* denotes here "kinds" of people, or "some" of them, and not – as certain modern translators of the Qurʾān have assumed – "pairs".

64 Lit., "lower thy wing for the believers": an idiomatic metaphor for loving tenderness and humility (see 17 : 24 and the corresponding note 28).

65 The above interpolated phrase offers, to my mind, the only satisfactory explanation of the definite articles

[For, thou art the bearer of a divine writ[66]] such as We have bestowed from on high upon those who [afterwards] broke it up into parts,[67] ‹90› [and] who [now] declare this Qurʾān to be [a tissue of] falsehoods![68] ‹91›

But, by thy Sustainer! [On the Day of Judgment] We shall indeed call them to account, one and all, ‹92› for whatever they have done! ‹93›

Hence, proclaim openly all that thou hast been bidden [to say], and leave alone all those who ascribe divinity to aught beside God: ‹94› verily, We shall suffice thee against all who [now] deride [this message – all] ‹95› who assert that there are, side by side with God, other divine powers as well:[69] for in time they will come to know [the truth]. ‹96›

And well do We know that thy bosom is constricted by the [blasphemous] things that they say: ‹97› but extol thou thy Sustainer's limitless glory and praise Him, and be of those who prostrate themselves [before Him] in adoration, ‹98› and worship thy Sustainer till death comes to thee.[70] ‹99›

كَمَآ أَنزَلْنَا عَلَى ٱلْمُقْتَسِمِينَ ﴿٩٠﴾ ٱلَّذِينَ جَعَلُوا۟ ٱلْقُرْءَانَ عِضِينَ ﴿٩١﴾
فَوَرَبِّكَ لَنَسْـَٔلَنَّهُمْ أَجْمَعِينَ ﴿٩٢﴾ عَمَّا كَانُوا۟ يَعْمَلُونَ ﴿٩٣﴾ فَٱصْدَعْ بِمَا
تُؤْمَرُ وَأَعْرِضْ عَنِ ٱلْمُشْرِكِينَ ﴿٩٤﴾ إِنَّا كَفَيْنَـٰكَ ٱلْمُسْتَهْزِءِينَ ﴿٩٥﴾
ٱلَّذِينَ يَجْعَلُونَ مَعَ ٱللَّهِ إِلَـٰهًا ءَاخَرَ فَسَوْفَ يَعْلَمُونَ ﴿٩٦﴾ وَلَقَدْ نَعْلَمُ
أَنَّكَ يَضِيقُ صَدْرُكَ بِمَا يَقُولُونَ ﴿٩٧﴾ فَسَبِّحْ بِحَمْدِ رَبِّكَ وَكُن مِّنَ
ٱلسَّـٰجِدِينَ ﴿٩٨﴾ وَٱعْبُدْ رَبَّكَ حَتَّىٰ يَأْتِيَكَ ٱلْيَقِينُ ﴿٩٩﴾

Kamāa ʾañzalnā ʿalal-muqtasimīn. (90) ʾAlladhīna jaʿalul-Qurʾāna ʿiḍīn. (91) FawaRabbika lanasʾalannahum ʾajmaʿīna, (92) ʿammā kānū yaʿmalūn. (93) Faṣdaʿ bimā tuʾmaru wa ʾaʿriḍ ʿanil-mushrikīn. (94) ʾInnā kafaynākal-mustahziʾīn. (95) ʾAlladhīna yajʿalūna maʿal-lāhi ʾilahan ʾākhara fasawfa yaʿlamūn. (96) Wa laqad naʿlamu ʾannaka yaḍīqu ṣadruka bimā yaqūlūn. (97) Fasabbiḥ biḥamdi Rabbika wa kum-minas-sājidīn. (98) Waʿ-bud Rabbaka ḥattā yaʾtiyakal-yaqīn. (99)

prefixed to the words *an-nadhīr al-mubīn* ("*the* plain warner"). This construction possibly alludes to the Biblical prediction of the advent of the Prophet Muḥammad appearing in Deuteronomy xviii, 15 and 18, which has been discussed by me in *sūrah* 2, note 33.

66 Thus Zamakhsharī, explaining the elliptic beginning of this sentence and its logical connection with the preceding verse as well as with verse 87.

67 This is apparently a reference to the followers of the Bible, who "believe in some parts of the divine writ and deny the truth of other parts" (cf. 2 : 85) – i.e., who act in accordance with those principles of the Bible which suit their inclinations and the prevailing social trends, and disregard the others, thus denying, by implication, their validity.

68 This, according to the *Tāj al-ʿArūs* (art. *ʿaḍiha* and *ʿaḍawa*) is the meaning of *ʿiḍīn* in the above context: an interpretation also advanced by Ṭabarī and Rāzī (in the last paragraph of the latter's commentary on this verse). Another interpretation – equally acceptable from the purely linguistic point of view – is "[those] who cut up the Qurʾān into separate parts": i.e., accept (on the analogy of the Jews and the Christians) some of it as true and regard the rest as Muḥammad's invention. But since – as Ṭabarī points out – those who refuse to believe in the divine origin of the Qurʾān do not accept *any* of it as true, the first interpretation is by far the preferable.

69 Lit., "who postulate (*yajʿalūn*), side by side with God, another deity (*ilāh*)" – a term which is obviously used here in its generic sense, embracing anything that could be visualized as a "divine power": hence my use of the plural.

70 Lit., "till there comes unto thee that which is certain (*al-yaqīn*)" – a term which in the Qurʾān is often used as a metonym for "death" (Bukhārī, *Kitāb-at-Tafsīr*). However, see also the earliest occurrence of this term in 74 : 47.

The Sixteenth Sūrah

An-Naḥl (The Bee)

Mecca Period

ACCORDING to almost all the authorities (including the *Itqān*), this *sūrah* was revealed a few months before the Prophet's emigration to Medina. Although some commentators maintain that the last three verses belong to the Medina period, there is no evidence for this more or less speculative view.

The title – or, rather, the key-word by which this *sūrah* has been identified ever since the time of the Prophet – is based on the reference, in verses 68-69, to the marvellous instance of God's creativeness manifested in the instincts with which He has endowed the bee. Indeed, it is the evidence of the Creator's purposeful activity that provides the subject-matter of most of this *sūrah* – an activity that culminates in the guidance which He offers man through His revealed messages, summed up, as it were, in verse 90: "Behold, God enjoins justice, and the doing of good, and generosity towards [one's] fellow-men; and He forbids all that is shameful and all that runs counter to reason, as well as envy."

-16-

سورة النحل مكية

وآياتها ثمان وعشرون ومائة

IN THE NAME OF GOD, THE MOST GRACIOUS, THE DISPENSER OF GRACE:

GOD'S JUDGMENT is [bound to] come: do not, therefore, call for its speedy advent![1] Limitless is He in His glory and sublimely exalted above anything to which men may ascribe a share in His divinity! ‹1›

He causes the angels to descend with this divine inspiration,[2] [bestowed] at His behest upon whomever He wills of His servants: "Warn [all human beings] that there is no deity save Me: be, therefore, conscious of Me!" ‹2›

He has created the heavens and the earth in accordance with [an inner] truth;[3] sublimely exalted is He above anything to which men may ascribe a share in His divinity![4] ‹3›

He creates man out of a [mere] drop of sperm: and lo! this same being shows himself endowed with the power to think and to argue![5] ‹4›

بِسْمِ ٱللَّهِ ٱلرَّحْمَـٰنِ ٱلرَّحِيمِ

أَتَىٰٓ أَمْرُ ٱللَّهِ فَلَا تَسْتَعْجِلُوهُ ۚ سُبْحَـٰنَهُۥ وَتَعَـٰلَىٰ عَمَّا يُشْرِكُونَ ﴿١﴾ يُنَزِّلُ
ٱلْمَلَـٰٓئِكَةَ بِٱلرُّوحِ مِنْ أَمْرِهِۦ عَلَىٰ مَن يَشَآءُ مِنْ عِبَادِهِۦٓ أَنْ أَنذِرُوٓا۟ أَنَّهُۥ
لَآ إِلَـٰهَ إِلَّآ أَنَا۠ فَٱتَّقُونِ ﴿٢﴾ خَلَقَ ٱلسَّمَـٰوَٰتِ وَٱلْأَرْضَ بِٱلْحَقِّ ۚ تَعَـٰلَىٰ
عَمَّا يُشْرِكُونَ ﴿٣﴾ خَلَقَ ٱلْإِنسَـٰنَ مِن نُّطْفَةٍ فَإِذَا هُوَ خَصِيمٌ مُّبِينٌ ﴿٤﴾

نصف الحزب

Bismil-lāhir-Raḥmānir-Raḥīm.

ʾAtāa ʾamrul-lāhi falā tastaʿjilūh. Subḥānahū wa taʿālā ʿammā yushrikūn. (1) Yunazzilul-Malāaʾikata birrūḥi min ʾamrihī ʿalā mañy-yashāaʾu min ʿibādihīi ʾan ʾañdhirūu ʾannahū lāa ʾilāha ʾillāa ʾAna fattaqūn. (2) Khalaqas-samāwāti walʾarḍa bilḥaqq. Taʿālā ʿammā yushrikūn. (3) Khalaqal-ʾIñsāna miñ-nuṭfatiñ-faʾidhā huwa khaṣīmum-mubīn. (4)

---

1 Regarding this allusion to the incredulous inquiry of the unbelievers, see 6 : 57-58, 8 : 32 and 10 : 50-51, as well as the corresponding notes.

2 The term *rūḥ* (lit., "spirit", "soul" or "breath of life") is often used in the Qurʾān in the sense of "inspiration" – and, more particularly, "divine inspiration" – since, as Zamakhsharī points out in connection with the above verse as well as with the first sentence of 42 : 52, "it gives life to hearts that were [as] dead in their ignorance, and has in religion the same function as a soul has in a body". A very similar explanation is given by Rāzī in the same context. The earliest instance in which the term *rūḥ* has been used in this particular sense is 97 : 4.

3 I.e., in accordance with a meaning and a purpose known only to Him. See also 10 : 5 and, in particular, the corresponding note 11.

4 This repetition of part of verse 1 is meant to stress the uniqueness of God's creative powers.

5 Lit., "he becomes an open contender in argument (*khaṣīm*)". According to Zamakhsharī and Rāzī, the above phrase is liable to two interpretations. In the words of Zamakhsharī, "one interpretation is that after having been a [mere] drop of sperm, a particle of matter without consciousness or motion, man becomes highly articulate (*minṭīq*), able to argue on his own [for or against a proposition], courageously facing disputes, and clearly formulating his arguments: [and herein lies] an indication of God's creative power. The other [interpretation] is that man is [prone to become] a contender in argument against his Sustainer, refusing to acknowledge his [very] Creator." Rāzī, on his part, gives his unqualified support to the first of these two interpretations, "because the above verses are meant to stress the evidence of the existence of a wise Creator, and not the fact of men's insolence and their proneness to blasphemy and ingratitude". However, in view of 36 : 77-78 (revealed at a considerably earlier period), I am of the opinion that the above two interpretations are not mutually exclusive but, rather, complementary, inasmuch as this passage is meant to bring out man's unique quality as a rational being – a quality that may lead him to great heights

وَٱلْأَنْعَٰمَ خَلَقَهَا ۗ لَكُمْ فِيهَا دِفْءٌ وَمَنَٰفِعُ وَمِنْهَا تَأْكُلُونَ ﴿٥﴾ وَلَكُمْ
فِيهَا جَمَالٌ حِينَ تُرِيحُونَ وَحِينَ تَسْرَحُونَ ﴿٦﴾ وَتَحْمِلُ أَثْقَالَكُمْ إِلَىٰ
بَلَدٍ لَّمْ تَكُونُوا۟ بَٰلِغِيهِ إِلَّا بِشِقِّ ٱلْأَنفُسِ ۚ إِنَّ رَبَّكُمْ لَرَءُوفٌ رَّحِيمٌ ﴿٧﴾
وَٱلْخَيْلَ وَٱلْبِغَالَ وَٱلْحَمِيرَ لِتَرْكَبُوهَا وَزِينَةً ۚ وَيَخْلُقُ مَا لَا تَعْلَمُونَ ﴿٨﴾
وَعَلَى ٱللَّهِ قَصْدُ ٱلسَّبِيلِ وَمِنْهَا جَآئِرٌ ۚ وَلَوْ شَآءَ لَهَدَىٰكُمْ أَجْمَعِينَ ﴿٩﴾
هُوَ ٱلَّذِىٓ أَنزَلَ مِنَ ٱلسَّمَآءِ مَآءً ۖ لَّكُم مِّنْهُ شَرَابٌ وَمِنْهُ شَجَرٌ فِيهِ
تُسِيمُونَ ﴿١٠﴾ يُنۢبِتُ لَكُم بِهِ ٱلزَّرْعَ وَٱلزَّيْتُونَ وَٱلنَّخِيلَ وَٱلْأَعْنَٰبَ وَمِن
كُلِّ ٱلثَّمَرَٰتِ ۗ إِنَّ فِى ذَٰلِكَ لَءَايَةً لِّقَوْمٍ يَتَفَكَّرُونَ ﴿١١﴾

Wal-ʾanʿāma khalaqahā lakum fīhā difʾuñw-wa manāfiʿu wa minhā taʾkulūn. (5) Wa lakum fīhā jamālun ḥīna turīḥūna wa ḥīna tasraḥūn. (6) Wa taḥmilu ʾathqālakum ʾilā baladil-lam takūnū bālighīhi ʾillā bishiqqil-ʾañfusi ʾinna Rabbakum laRaʾūfur-Raḥīm. (7) Wal-khayla wal-bighāla wal-ḥamīra litarkabūhā wa zīnah. Wa yakhluqu mā lā taʿlamūn. (8) Wa ʿalal-lāhi qaṣdus-sabīli wa minhā jāaʾir. Wa law shāaʾa lahadākum ʾajmaʿīn. (9) Huwal-ladhīi ʾañzala minas-samāaʾi māaʾal-lakum-minhu sharābuñw-wa minhu shajaruñ-fīhi tusīmūn. (10) Yumbitu lakum-bihiz-zarʿa waz-zaytūna wan-nakhīla wal-ʾaʿnāba wa miñ-kullith-thamarāt. ʾInna fī dhālika laʾĀyatal-liqawmiñy-yatafakkarūn. (11)

And He creates cattle: you derive warmth from them, and [various other] uses; and from them you obtain food; ‹5› and you find beauty in them when you drive them home in the evenings and when you take them out to pasture in the mornings. ‹6› And they carry your loads to [many] a place which [otherwise] you would be unable to reach without great hardship to yourselves.
Verily, your Sustainer is most compassionate, a dispenser of grace! ‹7›
And [it is He who creates] horses and mules and asses for you to ride, as well as for [their] beauty: and He will yet create things of which [today] you have no knowledge.[6] ‹8›
And [because He is your Creator,] it rests with God alone to show you the right path:[7] yet there is [many a one] who swerves from it. However, had He so willed, He would have guided you all aright.[8] ‹9›
It is He who sends down water from the skies; you drink thereof, and thereof [drink] the plants upon which you pasture your beasts; ‹10› [and] by virtue thereof He causes crops to grow for you, and olive trees, and date-palms, and grapes, and all [other] kinds of fruit: in this, behold, there is a message indeed for people who think! ‹11›

---

of achievement, but may equally well lead him utterly astray: hence my free rendering of this profound, elliptic phrase.

6 The use, in this context, of the aorist *yakhluqu* implies the future tense ("He will create") in contrast with the past tense *khalaqa* employed in the preceding passages. Since this reference to God's continuing creation comes immediately after a mention of primitive means of transport (i.e., of animals domesticated by man to this end), it obviously relates to other – as yet unknown – things of the same category: that is to say, to new means of transport which God unceasingly creates through the instrumentality of the inventiveness with which He has endowed man's mind (cf. 36 : 42). Inasmuch as every successive stage of human development bears witness to new, previously undreamt-of inventions in the realm of transport, the Qurʾanic statement that "He will yet create things of which [today] you have no knowledge" is valid for every period – past, present and future – of man's history.

7 Lit., "upon God rests the [showing of the] goal of the path" – i.e., the establishing of the goals of ethics and morality implied in the concept of the "right path". In further analysis of this phrase, the expression "it rests upon God" (*ʿala 'llāh*) is similar in intent to the statement in 6 : 12 and 54 that He "has willed upon Himself the law of grace and mercy": in other words, God invariably shows the right path to everyone who is *willing* to follow it.

8 Since the concept of morality is linked with man's God-given freedom of choice between good and evil, God does not "impose" His guidance upon man but leaves it to him to accept or reject it.

And He has made the night and the day and the sun and the moon subservient [to His laws, so that they be of use] to you;[9] and all the stars are subservient to His command: in this, behold, there are messages indeed for people who use their reason! ‹12›
And all the [beauty of] many hues which He has created for you on earth: in this, behold, there is a message for people who [are willing to] take it to heart! ‹13›
And He it is who has made the sea subservient [to His laws], so that you might eat fresh meat from it, and take from it gems which you may wear.
And on that [very sea] one sees[10] ships ploughing through the waves, so that you might [be able to] go forth in quest of some of His bounty, and thus have cause to be grateful [to Him]. ‹14›
And He has placed firm mountains on earth, lest it sway with you,[11] and rivers and paths, so that you might find your way, ‹15› as well as [various other] means of orientation: for [it is] by the stars that men find their way.[12] ‹16›

IS, THEN, HE who creates comparable to any [being] that cannot create?
Will you not, then, bethink yourselves? ‹17›

وَسَخَّرَ لَكُمُ ٱلَّيْلَ وَٱلنَّهَارَ وَٱلشَّمْسَ وَٱلْقَمَرَ ۖ وَٱلنُّجُومُ مُسَخَّرَٰتٌۢ
بِأَمْرِهِۦٓ ۗ إِنَّ فِى ذَٰلِكَ لَءَايَٰتٍ لِّقَوْمٍ يَعْقِلُونَ ﴿12﴾ وَمَا ذَرَأَ لَكُمْ فِى ٱلْأَرْضِ
مُخْتَلِفًا أَلْوَٰنُهُۥٓ ۗ إِنَّ فِى ذَٰلِكَ لَءَايَةً لِّقَوْمٍ يَذَّكَّرُونَ ﴿13﴾ وَهُوَ ٱلَّذِى سَخَّرَ
ٱلْبَحْرَ لِتَأْكُلُوا۟ مِنْهُ لَحْمًا طَرِيًّا وَتَسْتَخْرِجُوا۟ مِنْهُ حِلْيَةً تَلْبَسُونَهَا وَتَرَى
ٱلْفُلْكَ مَوَاخِرَ فِيهِ وَلِتَبْتَغُوا۟ مِن فَضْلِهِۦ وَلَعَلَّكُمْ تَشْكُرُونَ ﴿14﴾ وَأَلْقَىٰ فِى
ٱلْأَرْضِ رَوَٰسِىَ أَن تَمِيدَ بِكُمْ وَأَنْهَٰرًا وَسُبُلًا لَّعَلَّكُمْ تَهْتَدُونَ ﴿15﴾
وَعَلَٰمَٰتٍ ۚ وَبِٱلنَّجْمِ هُمْ يَهْتَدُونَ ﴿16﴾ أَفَمَن يَخْلُقُ كَمَن لَّا يَخْلُقُ ۗ أَفَلَا
تَذَكَّرُونَ ﴿17﴾

Wa sakhkhara lakumul-layla wan-nahāra wash-shamsa wal-qamar. Wan-nujūmu musakhkharātum-biʾamrih. ʾInna fī dhālika laʾĀyātil-liqawmiñy-yaʿqilūn. (12) Wa mā dharaʾa lakum fil-ʾarḍi mukhtalifan ʾalwānuh. ʾInna fī dhālika laʾāyatal-liqawmiñy-yadhdhakkarūn. (13) Wa Huwal-ladhī sakhkharal-baḥra litaʾkulū minhu laḥmañ-ṭariy-yañw-wa tastakhrijū minhu ḥilyatañ-talbasūnahā wa taral-fulka mawākhira fīhi wa litabtaghū miñ-faḍlihī wa laʿallakum tashkurūn. (14) Wa ʾalqā fil-ʾarḍi rawāsiya ʾañ-tamīda bikum wa ʾanhārañw-wa subulal-laʿallakum tahtadūn. (15) Wa ʿalāmātiñw- wa binnajmi hum yahtadūn. (16) ʾAfamañy-yakhluqu kamal-lā yakhluq. ʾAfalā tadhakkarūn. (17)

9 See 14 : 33 and the corresponding note 46.

10 Lit., "thou seest".

11 This is apparently an allusion to the fact that the mountains owe their rise to the gradual balancing process to which the solid crust of the earth is subject – a process which, in its turn, is the result of stresses and disturbances due to the cooling and hardening, progressing from the surface towards the centre, of the presumably molten or perhaps even gaseous matter of which the earth's interior seems to be composed. It appears that part of this interior is kept solid only by the enormous pressure of the overlaying material, of which the mountains are the most vivid evidence: and this explains the Qurʾanic reference (in 78 : 7) to mountains as "pegs" (*awtād*), i.e., symbols of the firmness and relative equilibrium which the surface of the earth has gradually achieved in the course of its geological history. Notwithstanding the fact that this equilibrium is not absolute (as is evidenced by earthquakes and volcanic eruptions), it is the solidity of the earth's crust – as contrasted with its possibly fluid but certainly very unstable interior – which makes life on earth possible: and this, to my mind, is the meaning of the phrase "lest it sway with you" (or "with them") occurring in the above verse as well as in 21 : 31 and 31 : 10.

12 Lit., "they find their way". This passage rounds off the preceding description of God's favours to man by returning, in a subtle manner, to the theme introduced in verse 4 and alluded to, indirectly, in the last sentence of verse 8 as well as in verse 14: namely, the consideration of man's intellectual potential – the greatest of all the gifts bestowed upon him by God. (See in this connection note 5 above, as well as the allegory of the creation of man enunciated in 2 : 30-33.)

For, should you try to count God's blessings, you could never compute them! Behold, God is indeed much-forgiving, a dispenser of grace; ‹18› and God knows all that you keep secret as well as all that you bring into the open. ‹19›

Now those beings that some people invoke[13] beside God cannot create anything, since they themselves are but created: ‹20› they are dead, not living,[14] and they do not [even] know when they will be raised from the dead! ‹21›

Your God is the One God: but because of their false pride, the hearts of those who do not believe in the life to come refuse to admit this [truth].[15] ‹22›

Truly, God knows all that they keep secret as well as all that they bring into the open – [and,] behold, He does not love those who are given to arrogance, ‹23› and [who], whenever they are asked, "What is it that your Sustainer has bestowed from on high?" – are wont to answer, "Fables of ancient times!"[16] ‹24›

Hence,[17] on Resurrection Day they shall bear the full weight of their own burdens, as well as some of the burdens of those ignorant ones whom they have led astray:[18] oh, how evil the load with which they shall be burdened! ‹25›

Those who lived before them did, too, devise many a blasphemy[19] – whereupon God visited with destruction all that they had ever built,[20] [striking] at its very foundations, so that the roof fell in upon

وَإِن تَعُدُّواْ نِعْمَةَ ٱللَّهِ لَا تُحْصُوهَآ ۗ إِنَّ ٱللَّهَ لَغَفُورٌ رَّحِيمٌ (18) وَٱللَّهُ يَعْلَمُ
مَا تُسِرُّونَ وَمَا تُعْلِنُونَ (19) وَٱلَّذِينَ يَدْعُونَ مِن دُونِ ٱللَّهِ لَا يَخْلُقُونَ
شَيْـًٔا وَهُمْ يُخْلَقُونَ (20) أَمْوَٰتٌ غَيْرُ أَحْيَآءٍ ۖ وَمَا يَشْعُرُونَ أَيَّانَ
يُبْعَثُونَ (21) إِلَٰهُكُمْ إِلَٰهٌ وَٰحِدٌ ۚ فَٱلَّذِينَ لَا يُؤْمِنُونَ بِٱلْءَاخِرَةِ قُلُوبُهُم
مُّنكِرَةٌ وَهُم مُّسْتَكْبِرُونَ (22) لَا جَرَمَ أَنَّ ٱللَّهَ يَعْلَمُ مَا يُسِرُّونَ وَمَا يُعْلِنُونَ
إِنَّهُۥ لَا يُحِبُّ ٱلْمُسْتَكْبِرِينَ (23) وَإِذَا قِيلَ لَهُم مَّاذَآ أَنزَلَ رَبُّكُمْ
قَالُوٓاْ أَسَٰطِيرُ ٱلْأَوَّلِينَ (24) لِيَحْمِلُوٓاْ أَوْزَارَهُمْ كَامِلَةً يَوْمَ ٱلْقِيَٰمَةِ وَمِنْ
أَوْزَارِ ٱلَّذِينَ يُضِلُّونَهُم بِغَيْرِ عِلْمٍ ۗ أَلَا سَآءَ مَا يَزِرُونَ (25) قَدْ مَكَرَ
ٱلَّذِينَ مِن قَبْلِهِمْ فَأَتَى ٱللَّهُ بُنْيَٰنَهُم مِّنَ ٱلْقَوَاعِدِ فَخَرَّ عَلَيْهِمُ ٱلسَّقْفُ

Wa ʾiñ-taᶜuddū niᶜmatal-lāhi lā tuḥṣūhā. ʾInnal-lāha laGhafūrur-Raḥīm. (18) Wal-lāhu yaᶜlamu mā tusirrūna wa mā tuᶜlinūn. (19) Wal-ladhīna yadᶜūna miñ-dūnil-lāhi lā yakhluqūna shayʾañw-wa hum yukhlaqūn. (20) ʾAmwātun ghayru ʾaḥyāaʾiñw-wa mā yashᶜurūna ʾayyāna yubᶜathūn. (21) ʾIlāhukum ʾIlāhuñw-Wāḥid. Falladhīna lā yuʾminūna bilʾĀkhirati qulūbuhum muñkiratuñw-wa hum-mustakbirūn. (22) Lā jarama ʾannal-lāha yaᶜlamu mā yusirrūna wa mā yuᶜlinūn. ʾInnahū lā yuḥibbul-mustakbirīn. (23) Wa ʾidhā qīla lahum mādhāa ʾañzala Rabbukum qālūu ʾasāṭīrul-ʾawwalīn. (24) Liyaḥmilūu ʾawzārahum kāmilatañy-Yawmal-Qiyāmati wa min ʾawzāril-ladhīna yuḍillūnahum bighayri ᶜilm. ʾAlā sāaʾa mā yazirūn. (25) Qad makar al-ladhīna miñ-qablihim faʾatal-lāhu bunyānahum minal-qawāᶜidi fakharra ᶜalayhimus-saqfu

13 Lit., "those whom they invoke": this refers – as is obvious from verse 21 below – to dead saints invested by their followers with divine or semi-divine qualities.

14 Cf. 7 : 191-194.

15 I.e., they are too arrogant to accept the idea of man's utter dependence on, and responsibility to, a Supreme Being.

16 Sc., "and not divine revelations" (cf. 8 : 31).

17 The conjunction *li* prefixed to the verb *yaḥmilū* ("they shall carry") has here obviously – as pointed out by Rāzī – the function of what the grammarians call a *lām al-ᶜāqibah*, indicating no more than a causal sequence (*ᶜāqibah*); it may be appropriately rendered by means of the conjunctive particle "and" or – as in this context – by the adverb "hence".

18 Lit., "those whom they are leading astray without knowledge" – i.e., without knowledge or understanding on the latters' part (Zamakhsharī).

19 Lit., "schemed" (*makara*): i.e., they blasphemed by describing the divine revelations as "fables of ancient times" and by refusing to admit the truth of God's existence or of His oneness and uniqueness.

20 Lit., "their building" (see next note).

them from above,[21] and suffering befell them without their having perceived whence it came. ‹26›

And then, on Resurrection Day, He will cover them [all] with ignominy,[22] and will say: "Where, now, are those beings to whom you ascribed a share in My divinity,[23] [and] for whose sake you cut yourselves off [from My guidance]?"[24]

[Whereupon] those who [in their lifetime] were endowed with knowledge[25] will say: "Verily, ignominy and misery [have fallen] this day upon those who have been denying the truth ‹27› – those whom the angels have gathered in death while they were still sinning against themselves!"

Then will they [who are thus arraigned] proffer their submission, [saying:] "We did not [mean to] do any evil!"[26]

[But they will be answered:] "Yea, verily, God has full knowledge of all that you were doing![27] ‹28› Hence, enter the gates of hell, therein to abide!"

And evil, indeed, shall be the state of all who are given to false pride! ‹29›

But [when] those who are conscious of God are asked, "What is it that your Sustainer has bestowed from on high?" – they answer, "Goodness supreme!"

Good fortune awaits, in this world, all who persevere in doing good;[28] but their ultimate state will be far better still: for, how excellent indeed will be the state of the God-conscious [in the life to come]! ‹30›

مِن فَوْقِهِمْ وَأَتَىٰهُمُ ٱلْعَذَابُ مِنْ حَيْثُ لَا يَشْعُرُونَ ﴿26﴾ ثُمَّ يَوْمَ ٱلْقِيَـٰمَةِ
يُخْزِيهِمْ وَيَقُولُ أَيْنَ شُرَكَآءِىَ ٱلَّذِينَ كُنتُمْ تُشَـٰٓقُّونَ فِيهِمْ ۚ قَالَ ٱلَّذِينَ
أُوتُوا۟ ٱلْعِلْمَ إِنَّ ٱلْخِزْىَ ٱلْيَوْمَ وَٱلسُّوٓءَ عَلَى ٱلْكَـٰفِرِينَ ﴿27﴾ ٱلَّذِينَ
تَتَوَفَّىٰهُمُ ٱلْمَلَـٰٓئِكَةُ ظَالِمِىٓ أَنفُسِهِمْ ۖ فَأَلْقَوُا۟ ٱلسَّلَمَ مَا كُنَّا نَعْمَلُ مِن سُوٓءٍۭ ۚ
بَلَىٰٓ إِنَّ ٱللَّهَ عَلِيمٌۢ بِمَا كُنتُمْ تَعْمَلُونَ ﴿28﴾ فَٱدْخُلُوٓا۟ أَبْوَٰبَ جَهَنَّمَ خَـٰلِدِينَ
فِيهَا ۖ فَلَبِئْسَ مَثْوَى ٱلْمُتَكَبِّرِينَ ﴿29﴾ ۞ وَقِيلَ لِلَّذِينَ ٱتَّقَوْا۟ مَاذَآ أَنزَلَ
رَبُّكُمْ ۚ قَالُوا۟ خَيْرًا ۗ لِّلَّذِينَ أَحْسَنُوا۟ فِى هَـٰذِهِ ٱلدُّنْيَا حَسَنَةٌ ۚ وَلَدَارُ ٱلْـَٔاخِرَةِ
خَيْرٌ ۚ وَلَنِعْمَ دَارُ ٱلْمُتَّقِينَ ﴿30﴾

ثلاثة ارباع الحزب

miñ-fawqihim wa ʾatāhumul-ᶜadhābu min ḥaythu lā yashᶜurūn. (26) Thumma Yawmal-Qiyāmati yukhzīhim wa yaqūlu ʾayna shurakāaʾiyal-ladhīna kuñtum tushāaqqūna fīhim. Qālal-ladhīna ʾūtul-ᶜilma ʾinnal-khizyal-Yawma was-sūuʾa ᶜalal-kāfirīn. (27) ʾAlladhīna tatawaffāhumul-Malāaʾikatu ẓālimīi ʾañfusihim. Faʾalqawus-salama mā kunnā naᶜmalu miñ-sūuʾ. Balāa ʾinnal-lāha ᶜAlīmum-bimā kuñtum taᶜmalun. (28) Fadkhulūu ʾabwāba jahannama khālidīna fīhā falabiʾsa mathwal-mutakabbirīn. (29) ۞ Wa qīla lil-ladhīnat-taqaw mādhāa ʾañzala Rabbukum. Qālū khayrā. Lilladhīna ʾaḥsanū fī hādhihid-dunyā ḥasanah. Wa ladārul-ʾĀkhirati khayr. Wa laniᶜma dārul-muttaqīn. (30)

21 This is obviously a metaphor (Rāzī) describing the utter collapse of all endeavours – both individual and social – rooted in godlessness and false pride.

22 I.e., finally and utterly – for, "only on the Day of Resurrection will you be requited in full for whatever you have done" (3 : 185). Since the pronoun "them" refers not only to the earlier sinners mentioned parenthetically in the preceding verse but also to those spoken of in verses 22-25, I have interpolated the word "all".

23 Lit., "those [alleged] partners of Mine". Regarding the Qurʾanic use of the term *sharīk* (pl. *shurakāʾ*) in connection with religious beliefs, see *sūrah* 6, note 15.

24 Or: "you were wont to contend [against My guidance]". See in this connection *sūrah* 8, note 16.

25 I.e., those who had *availed themselves* of the knowledge of good and evil which God offers to mankind through His prophets.

26 Cf. 6 : 23 and the corresponding note, as well as 2 : 11.

27 Sc., "and He will judge you on the basis of your motivation" – implying that their plea of ignorance is rejected in view of the fact that they were offered God's guidance through His revealed messages, which they deliberately scorned in their false pride and dismissed out of hand as "fables of ancient times" (see verses 22-24 above).

28 This "good fortune" (*ḥasanah*) does not necessarily signify, in this context, material benefits but refers, rather, to the spiritual satisfaction and the feeling of inner security resulting from genuine God-consciousness.

جَنَّـٰتُ عَدۡنٍ يَدۡخُلُونَهَا تَجۡرِي مِن تَحۡتِهَا ٱلۡأَنۡهَـٰرُ لَهُمۡ فِيهَا مَا يَشَآءُونَ
كَذَٰلِكَ يَجۡزِي ٱللَّهُ ٱلۡمُتَّقِينَ ﴿٣١﴾ ٱلَّذِينَ تَتَوَفَّىٰهُمُ ٱلۡمَلَـٰٓئِكَةُ طَيِّبِينَ
يَقُولُونَ سَلَـٰمٌ عَلَيۡكُمُ ٱدۡخُلُواْ ٱلۡجَنَّةَ بِمَا كُنتُمۡ تَعۡمَلُونَ ﴿٣٢﴾ هَلۡ
يَنظُرُونَ إِلَّآ أَن تَأۡتِيَهُمُ ٱلۡمَلَـٰٓئِكَةُ أَوۡ يَأۡتِيَ أَمۡرُ رَبِّكَ كَذَٰلِكَ فَعَلَ
ٱلَّذِينَ مِن قَبۡلِهِمۡ وَمَا ظَلَمَهُمُ ٱللَّهُ وَلَـٰكِن كَانُوٓاْ أَنفُسَهُمۡ يَظۡلِمُونَ ﴿٣٣﴾
فَأَصَابَهُمۡ سَيِّـَٔاتُ مَا عَمِلُواْ وَحَاقَ بِهِم مَّا كَانُواْ بِهِۦ يَسۡتَهۡزِءُونَ ﴿٣٤﴾
وَقَالَ ٱلَّذِينَ أَشۡرَكُواْ لَوۡ شَآءَ ٱللَّهُ مَا عَبَدۡنَا مِن دُونِهِۦ مِن شَيۡءٖ نَّحۡنُ وَلَآ
ءَابَآؤُنَا وَلَا حَرَّمۡنَا مِن دُونِهِۦ مِن شَيۡءٖۚ كَذَٰلِكَ فَعَلَ ٱلَّذِينَ مِن قَبۡلِهِمۡۚ
فَهَلۡ عَلَى ٱلرُّسُلِ إِلَّا ٱلۡبَلَـٰغُ ٱلۡمُبِينُ ﴿٣٥﴾

Gardens of perpetual bliss will they enter – [gardens] through which running waters flow – having therein all that they might desire. Thus will God reward those who are conscious of Him ‹31› – those whom the angels gather in death while they are in a state of inner purity, greeting them thus: "Peace be upon you! Enter paradise by virtue of what you were doing [in life]!" ‹32›

ARE THEY [who deny the truth] but waiting for the angels to appear unto them, or for your Sustainer's judgment to become manifest?[29]

Even thus did behave those [stubborn sinners] who lived before their time; and [when they were destroyed,] it was not God who wronged them, but it was they who had wronged themselves: ‹33› for all the evil that they had done fell [back] upon them, and they were overwhelmed by the very thing which they had been wont to deride.[30] ‹34›

Now they who ascribe divinity to aught beside God say, "Had God so willed, we would not have worshipped aught but Him – neither we nor our forefathers; nor would we have declared aught as forbidden without a commandment from Him."[31]

Even thus did speak those [sinners] who lived before their time; but, then, are the apostles bound to do more than clearly deliver the message [entrusted to them]?[32] ‹35›

Jannātu ᶜadniñy-yadkhulūnahā tajrī miñ-taḥtihal-ᵓanhāru lahum fīhā mā yashāaᵓūn. Kadhālika yajzil-lāhul-muttaqīn. (31) ᵓAlladhīna tatawaffāhumul-Malāaᵓikatu ṭayyibīna yaqūlūna salāmun ᶜalaykumud-khulul-jannata bimā kuñtum taᶜmalūn. (32) Hal yañẓurūna ᵓillāa ᵓañ-taᵓtiyahumul-Malāaᵓikatu ᵓaw yaᵓtiya ᵓamru Rabbik. Kadhālika faᶜalal-ladhīna miñ-qablihim. Wa mā ẓalamahumul-lāhu wa lākiñ-kānūu ᵓañfusahum yaẓlimūn. (33) Faᵓaṣābahum sayyiᵓātu mā ᶜamilū wa ḥāqa bihim-mā kānū bihī yastahziᵓūn. (34) Wa qālal-ladhīna ᵓashrakū law shāaᵓal-lāhu mā ᶜabadnā miñ-dūnihī miñ-shayᵓiñ-naḥnu wa lāa ᵓābāaᵓunā wa lā ḥarramnā miñ-dūnihī miñ-shayᵓ. Kadhālika faᶜalal-ladhīna miñ-qablihim. Fahal ᶜalar-Rusuli ᵓillal-balāghul-mubīn. (35)

29 Lit., "for the angels to come to them, or for your Sustainer's judgment (*amr*) to come" – i.e., for the Day of Resurrection. The full meaning of this passage is forthcoming from 6 : 158, revealed at the same period as the present *sūrah*.

30 See 6 : 10 and the corresponding note. Similar phrases occur in many places in the Qurᵓān, always with reference to a derision of divine messages and, particularly, of predictions relating to God's chastisement of reprobate sinners. As so often, the Qurᵓān points out here that this "chastisement" or "suffering" (*ᶜadhāb*) is but a natural, unavoidable *consequence* of deliberate wrongdoing: hence, he who becomes guilty of it is, in reality, "doing wrong to himself" or "sinning against himself" inasmuch as he destroys his own spiritual integrity and must subsequently suffer for it.

31 Lit., "apart from Him". See in this connection 6 : 148 and the corresponding note 141. (The arbitrary, unwarranted prohibitions and taboos alluded to in that verse as well as in the present one are discussed in 6 : 136-153 and explained in my notes.) The derision of God's messages by the deniers of the truth is implied in their questioning His grant of free will to man – that is to say, the ability to choose between right and wrong, which is the basis of all morality.

32 I.e., the apostles could not *force* anyone to make the right choice.

And indeed, within every community[33] have We raised up an apostle [entrusted with this message]: "Worship God, and shun the powers of evil!"[34]
And among those [past generations] were people whom God graced with His guidance,[35] just as there was among them [many a one] who inevitably fell prey to grievous error:[36] go, then, about the earth and behold what happened in the end to those who gave the lie to the truth! ⟨36⟩
[As for those who are bent on denying the truth –] though thou be ever so eager to show them the right way, [know that,] verily, God does not bestow His guidance upon any whom He judges to have gone astray;[37] and such shall have none to succour them [on Resurrection Day]. ⟨37⟩
As it is,[38] they swear by God with their most solemn oaths, "Never will God raise from the dead anyone who has died!"[39]
Yea indeed! [This very thing has God promised] by a promise which He has willed upon Himself; but most people know it not. ⟨38⟩ [He will resurrect them] to the end that He might make clear unto them all whereon they [now] hold divergent views,[40] and that they who are bent on denying the truth [of resurrection] might come to know that they were liars. ⟨39⟩

وَلَقَدۡ بَعَثۡنَا فِي كُلِّ أُمَّةٖ رَّسُولًا أَنِ ٱعۡبُدُواْ ٱللَّهَ وَٱجۡتَنِبُواْ ٱلطَّٰغُوتَۖ
فَمِنۡهُم مَّنۡ هَدَى ٱللَّهُ وَمِنۡهُم مَّنۡ حَقَّتۡ عَلَيۡهِ ٱلضَّلَٰلَةُۚ فَسِيرُواْ فِي
ٱلۡأَرۡضِ فَٱنظُرُواْ كَيۡفَ كَانَ عَٰقِبَةُ ٱلۡمُكَذِّبِينَ ٣٦ إِن تَحۡرِصۡ عَلَىٰ
هُدَىٰهُمۡ فَإِنَّ ٱللَّهَ لَا يَهۡدِي مَن يُضِلُّۖ وَمَا لَهُم مِّن نَّٰصِرِينَ ٣٧ وَأَقۡسَمُواْ
بِٱللَّهِ جَهۡدَ أَيۡمَٰنِهِمۡ لَا يَبۡعَثُ ٱللَّهُ مَن يَمُوتُۚ بَلَىٰ وَعۡدًا عَلَيۡهِ حَقّٗا
وَلَٰكِنَّ أَكۡثَرَ ٱلنَّاسِ لَا يَعۡلَمُونَ ٣٨ لِيُبَيِّنَ لَهُمُ ٱلَّذِي يَخۡتَلِفُونَ فِيهِ
وَلِيَعۡلَمَ ٱلَّذِينَ كَفَرُوٓاْ أَنَّهُمۡ كَانُواْ كَٰذِبِينَ ٣٩

Wa laqad baᶜathnā fī kulli ᵓummatir-Rasūlan ᵓaniᶜ-budul-lāha waj-tanibuṭ-ṭāghut. Faminhum-man hadal-lāhu wa minhum-man ḥaqqat ᶜalayhiḍ-ḍalālah. Fasīrū fil-ᵓarḍi fañẓurū kayfa kāna ᶜāqibatul-mukadhdhibīn. (36) ᵓIñ-taḥriṣ ᶜalā hudāhum faᵓinnal-lāha lā yahdī mañy-yuḍillu wa mā lahum miñ-nāṣirīn. (37) Wa ᵓaqsamu billāhi jahda ᵓaymānihim lā yabᶜathul-lāhu mañy-yamūt. Balā waᶜdan ᶜalayhi ḥaqqañw-wa lākinna ᵓaktharan-nāsi lā yaᶜlamūn. (38) Liyubayyina lahumul-ladhī yakhtalifūna fīhi wa liya-ᶜlamal-ladhīna kafarūu ᵓannahum kānū kādhibīn. (39)

33 Or "at every period", since the term *ummah* has this significance as well. In its wider sense, it may also be taken here to denote "civilization", thus comprising a human groupment as well as a period of time.

34 For this rendering of the term *aṭ-ṭāghūt*, see *sūrah* 2, note 250. It is to be borne in mind that, in Qurᵓanic terminology, "worship of God" invariably implies the concept of man's sense of responsibility before Him: hence, the above commandment comprises, in the most concise formulation imaginable, the sum-total of all ethical injunctions and prohibitions, and is the basis and source of all morality as well as the one unchanging message inherent in every true religion.

35 I.e., who *availed themselves* of the guidance offered by Him to all human beings.

36 Lit., "upon whom error came to be inevitably established (*ḥaqqa ᶜalayhi*)" or "against whom [a verdict of] error became inevitable": i.e., one whose heart "God has sealed" in consequence of his persistent, conscious refusal to submit to His guidance (see *sūrah* 2, note 7, as well as *sūrah* 14, note 4).

37 See preceding note; also 8 : 55 and the corresponding note 58.

38 Lit., "And" – but since this conjunction is obviously meant to elaborate the preceding statement, it is best rendered as above.

39 This categorical denial of resurrection – implying as it does a denial of God's ultimate judgment of good and evil – is characteristic of a mental attitude which refuses to admit the reality, or even possibility, of anything that lies beyond the range of man's actual or potential observation. Since such an attitude is an outcome of an intrinsically materialistic outlook on life and the "false pride" referred to in verses 22-23 above, it is anti-religious in the deepest sense of this word even if it is accompanied by a vague – because non-consequential – belief in the existence of God.

40 I.e., in the first instance, the truth of resurrection and judgment as such, and, in general, the final answers to all the metaphysical problems which perplex man during his life on earth.

Whenever We will anything to be, We but say unto it Our word "Be" – and it is. ‹40›

NOW as for those who forsake the domain of evil[41] in the cause of God, after having suffered wrong [on account of their faith] – We shall most certainly grant them a station of good fortune in this world:[42] but their reward in the life to come will be far greater yet.
If they [who deny the truth] could but understand[43] ‹41› those who, having attained to patience in adversity, in their Sustainer place their trust![44] ‹42›

AND [even] before thy time, [O Muḥammad,] We never sent [as Our apostles] any but [mortal] men, whom We inspired:[45] and if you have not [yet] realized this, ask the followers of [earlier] revelation,[46] ‹43› [and they will tell you that their prophets, too, were but mortal men whom We had endowed] with all evidence of the truth and with books of divine wisdom.[47]
And upon thee [too] have We bestowed from on high this reminder, so that thou might make clear unto mankind all that

إِنَّمَا قَوْلُنَا لِشَيْءٍ إِذَآ أَرَدْنَٰهُ أَن نَّقُولَ لَهُۥ كُن فَيَكُونُ ﴿٤٠﴾ وَٱلَّذِينَ
هَاجَرُواْ فِى ٱللَّهِ مِنۢ بَعْدِ مَا ظُلِمُواْ لَنُبَوِّئَنَّهُمْ فِى ٱلدُّنْيَا حَسَنَةً وَلَأَجْرُ ٱلْءَاخِرَةِ
أَكْبَرُ لَوْ كَانُواْ يَعْلَمُونَ ﴿٤١﴾ ٱلَّذِينَ صَبَرُواْ وَعَلَىٰ رَبِّهِمْ يَتَوَكَّلُونَ ﴿٤٢﴾ وَمَآ
أَرْسَلْنَا مِن قَبْلِكَ إِلَّا رِجَالًا نُّوحِىٓ إِلَيْهِمْ فَسْـَٔلُوٓاْ أَهْلَ ٱلذِّكْرِ إِن كُنتُمْ
لَا تَعْلَمُونَ ﴿٤٣﴾ بِٱلْبَيِّنَٰتِ وَٱلزُّبُرِ وَأَنزَلْنَآ إِلَيْكَ ٱلذِّكْرَ لِتُبَيِّنَ لِلنَّاسِ مَا

ᵓInnamā qawlunā lishayᵓin ᵓidhāa ᵓaradnāhu ᵓañ-naqūla lahū kuñ-fayakūn. (40) Wal-ladhīna hājarū fil-lāhi mim-baᶜdi mā ẓulimū lanubawwiᵓannahum fid-dunyā ḥasanatañw-wa laᵓajrul-ᵓĀkhirati ᵓakbaru law kānū yaᶜlamūn. (41) ᵓAlladhīna ṣabarū wa ᶜalā Rabbi-him yatawakkalūn. (42) Wa māa ᵓarsalnā miñ-qablika ᵓillā rijālañ-nūḥīi ᵓilayhim fasᵓalūu ᵓahladh-Dhikri ᵓiñ-kuñtum lā taᶜlamūna, (43) bilbayyināti waz-Zubur. Wa ᵓañzalnāa ᵓilaykadh-Dhikra litubayyina linnāsi mā

41 For an explanation of this rendering of *alladhīna hājarū*, see *sūrah* 2, note 203, and *sūrah* 4, note 124. That the "forsaking of the domain of evil" has here a purely spiritual connotation is obvious from its juxtaposition with the "denial of the truth" referred to in the preceding verses.

42 See note 28 above.

43 The verb *ᶜalima*, which primarily denotes "he knew", has also the meaning of "he came to know", i.e., "he understood"; and since – as pointed out by Baghawī, Zamakhsharī and Rāzī – the pronoun "they" in the phrase *law kānū yaᶜlamūn* relates to the deniers of the truth spoken of in the preceding passages, the rendering "if they could but understand" is here clearly indicated – the more so as it provides a self-evident connection with the subsequent, objective clause.

44 I.e., if they could really understand the spiritual motivation of the believers, they (the deniers of the truth) would themselves begin to believe.

45 This passage has a double purport: firstly, it connects with the statement enunciated in verse 36 to the effect that God's apostles have appeared, at one time or another, within every civilization, and that, consequently, no substantial human groupment has ever been left without divine guidance; secondly, it answers the objection frequently raised by unbelievers that Muḥammad could not be God's message-bearer since he was "a mere mortal man". (As regards the Qurᵓanic doctrine that no created being, not even a prophet, has ever been endowed with "supernatural" powers or qualities, see 6 : 50 and 7 : 188, as well as the notes relating to those verses; also note 94 on 6 : 109.)

46 Lit., "reminder" – because every divine message is meant to remind one of the truth. The people to be asked for enlightenment in this respect are apparently the Jews and the Christians (Ṭabarī, Zamakhsharī).

47 The above sentence is addressed, parenthetically, to all who question the divine origin of the Qurᵓān on the grounds mentioned in note 45 above. For an explanation of the term *zubur* ("books of divine wisdom"), see *sūrah* 21, note 101.

has ever been thus bestowed upon them,[48] and that they might take thought. ‹44›
Can, then, they who devise evil schemes[49] ever feel sure that God will not cause the earth to swallow them,[50] or that suffering will not befall them without their perceiving whence [it came]? ‹45› – or that He will not take them to task [suddenly] in the midst of their comings and goings,[51] without their being able to elude [Him], ‹46› or take them to task through slow decay?[52] And yet, behold, your Sustainer is most compassionate, a dispenser of grace![53] ‹47›

HAVE, THEN, they [who deny the truth] never considered any of the things that God has created[54] – [how] their shadows turn right and left, prostrating themselves before God and utterly submissive [to His will]?[55] ‹48›
For, before God prostrates itself all that is in the heavens and all that is on earth – every beast that moves, and the angels:[56] [even] these do not bear themselves with false pride: ‹49› they fear their Sustainer high above them, and do whatever they are bidden to do.[57] ‹50›

نُزِّلَ إِلَيْهِمْ وَلَعَلَّهُمْ يَتَفَكَّرُونَ ﴿٤٤﴾ أَفَأَمِنَ ٱلَّذِينَ مَكَرُوا۟ ٱلسَّيِّـَٔاتِ أَن
يَخْسِفَ ٱللَّهُ بِهِمُ ٱلْأَرْضَ أَوْ يَأْتِيَهُمُ ٱلْعَذَابُ مِنْ حَيْثُ لَا
يَشْعُرُونَ ﴿٤٥﴾ أَوْ يَأْخُذَهُمْ فِى تَقَلُّبِهِمْ فَمَا هُم بِمُعْجِزِينَ ﴿٤٦﴾ أَوْ يَأْخُذَهُمْ
عَلَىٰ تَخَوُّفٍ فَإِنَّ رَبَّكُمْ لَرَءُوفٌ رَّحِيمٌ ﴿٤٧﴾ أَوَلَمْ يَرَوْا۟ إِلَىٰ مَا خَلَقَ ٱللَّهُ
مِن شَىْءٍ يَتَفَيَّؤُا۟ ظِلَٰلُهُۥ عَنِ ٱلْيَمِينِ وَٱلشَّمَآئِلِ سُجَّدًا لِّلَّهِ وَهُمْ دَٰخِرُونَ ﴿٤٨﴾
وَلِلَّهِ يَسْجُدُ مَا فِى ٱلسَّمَٰوَٰتِ وَمَا فِى ٱلْأَرْضِ مِن دَآبَّةٍ وَٱلْمَلَٰٓئِكَةُ وَهُمْ لَا
يَسْتَكْبِرُونَ ﴿٤٩﴾ يَخَافُونَ رَبَّهُم مِّن فَوْقِهِمْ وَيَفْعَلُونَ مَا يُؤْمَرُونَ ۩ ﴿٥٠﴾

السجدة

**nuzzila ʾilayhim wa laʿallahum yatafakkarūn. (44)
ʾAfaʾaminal-ladhīna makarus-sayyiʾāti ʾañy-yakh-
sifal-lāhu bihimul-ʾarḍa ʾaw yaʾtiyahumul-ʿadhābu
min ḥaythu lā yashʿurūn. (45) ʾAw yaʾkhudhahum fī
taqallubihim famā hum bimuʿjizīn. (46) ʾAw
yaʾkhudhahum ʿalā takhawwufiñ-faʾinna Rabbakum
laRaʾūfur-Raḥīm. (47) ʾAwa lam yaraw ʾilā mā khalaqal-lāhu miñ-shayʾiñy-yatafayyaʾū ẓilāluhū ʿanil-
yamīni wash-shamāaʾili sujjadal-lillāhi wa hum
dākhirūn. (48) Wa lillāhi yasjudu mā fis-samāwāti wa
mā fil-ʾarḍi miñ-dāabbatiñw-wal-Malāaʾikatu wa
hum lā yastakbirūn. (49) Yakhāfūna Rabbahum miñ-
fawqihim wa yafʿalūna mā yuʾmarūn. ۩ (50)**

48 Sc., "through revelation" – implying that moral values are independent of all time-bound changes and must, therefore, be regarded as permanent.

49 To my mind, by "evil schemes" are meant here systems of God-denying philosophy and of perverted morality.

50 I.e., destroy them utterly.

51 I.e., in the midst of their habitual occupations. My interpolation of the word "suddenly" is warranted by the reference, in the next verse, to the alternative of *gradual* decay.

52 One of the meanings of *takhawwuf* is "gradual diminution" or "decay" or "slow destruction" (*Lisān al-ʿArab*, art. *khawafa*; thus also Ṭabarī and Zamakhsharī); in the above context, the term has obviously both a social and a moral connotation: a gradual disintegration of all ethical values, of power, of civic cohesion, of happiness and, finally, of life itself.

53 Sc., "seeing that He offers you guidance through His prophets, and gives you time to reflect and mend your ways before you do irreparable harm to yourselves".

54 In view of the separate mention, in the next verse, of animals and angels, the "things" referred to here apparently denote inanimate objects and perhaps also living organisms like plants.

55 Lit., "and they are utterly lowly" or "submissive". The "prostration" referred to in this and the next verse is obviously a symbolism expressing the intrinsic subjection of all created beings and things to God's will. See also 13 : 15 and the corresponding notes 33 and 34.

56 I.e., the lowest as well as the highest. The term *dābbah* denotes any sentient, corporeal being capable of spontaneous movement, and is contrasted here with the non-corporeal, spiritual beings designated as "angels" (Rāzī).

57 I.e., they must, by virtue of their nature, obey the impulses implanted in them by God and are, therefore, incapable of what is described as "sinning". Man, however, is fundamentally different in this respect. In contrast with the natural sinlessness of "every beast that moves, and the angels", man is endowed with free will in the moral sense of this term: he can *choose* between right and wrong – and therefore he can, and often does, sin. But even while he sins he is subject to the universal law of cause and effect instituted by God and referred to in the Qurʾān as *sunnat Allāh* ("God's way"): hence the Qurʾanic statement that "before God prostrate themselves, *willingly or unwillingly*, all [things and beings] that are in the heavens and on earth" (13 : 15).

وَقَالَ ٱللَّهُ لَا تَتَّخِذُوٓا۟ إِلَـٰهَيْنِ ٱثْنَيْنِ ۖ إِنَّمَا هُوَ إِلَـٰهٌ وَٰحِدٌ ۖ فَإِيَّـٰىَ
فَٱرْهَبُونِ ﴿٥١﴾ وَلَهُۥ مَا فِى ٱلسَّمَـٰوَٰتِ وَٱلْأَرْضِ وَلَهُ ٱلدِّينُ وَاصِبًا ۚ أَفَغَيْرَ ٱللَّهِ
تَتَّقُونَ ﴿٥٢﴾ وَمَا بِكُم مِّن نِّعْمَةٍ فَمِنَ ٱللَّهِ ۖ ثُمَّ إِذَا مَسَّكُمُ ٱلضُّرُّ فَإِلَيْهِ
تَجْـَٔرُونَ ﴿٥٣﴾ ثُمَّ إِذَا كَشَفَ ٱلضُّرَّ عَنكُمْ إِذَا فَرِيقٌ مِّنكُم بِرَبِّهِمْ
يُشْرِكُونَ ﴿٥٤﴾ لِيَكْفُرُوا۟ بِمَآ ءَاتَيْنَـٰهُمْ ۚ فَتَمَتَّعُوا۟ ۖ فَسَوْفَ تَعْلَمُونَ ﴿٥٥﴾ وَيَجْعَلُونَ
لِمَا لَا يَعْلَمُونَ نَصِيبًا مِّمَّا رَزَقْنَـٰهُمْ ۗ تَٱللَّهِ لَتُسْـَٔلُنَّ عَمَّا كُنتُمْ تَفْتَرُونَ ﴿٥٦﴾
وَيَجْعَلُونَ لِلَّهِ ٱلْبَنَـٰتِ سُبْحَـٰنَهُۥ ۙ وَلَهُم مَّا يَشْتَهُونَ ﴿٥٧﴾ وَإِذَا بُشِّرَ أَحَدُهُمْ

Wa qālal-lāhu lā tattakhidhūu ʾilāhaynith-nayni ʾinnamā Huwa ʾIlāhuñw-Wāḥiduñ-faʾIyyāya farhabūn. (51) Wa lahū mā fis-samāwāti wal-ʾarḍi wa lahud-dīnu wāṣiban ʾafaghayral-lāhi tattaqūn. (52) Wa mā bikum-miñ-niʿmatiñ-faminal-lāhi thumma ʾidhā massakumuḍ-ḍurru faʾilayhi tajʾarūn. (53) Thumma ʾidhā kashafaḍ-ḍurra ʿañkum ʾidhā farīqum-miñkum-biRabbihim yushrikūn. (54) Liyakfurū bimāa ʾātaynāhum; fatamattaʿū fasawfa taʿlamūn. (55) Wa yajʿalūna limā lā yaʿlamūna naṣībam-mimmā razaqnāhum. Tallāhi latusʾalunna ʿammā kuñtum taftarūn. (56) Wa yajʿalūna lillāhil-banāti subḥānahu wa lahum-mā yashtahūn. (57) Wa ʾidhā bushshira ʾaḥaduhum-

And God has said: "Do not take to worshipping two [or more] deities.[58] He is the One and Only God: hence, of Me, of Me alone stand in awe!"[59] ‹51›

And His is all that is in the heavens and on earth, and to Him [alone] obedience is always due: will you, then, pay reverence to aught but God? ‹52›

For, whatever good thing comes to you, comes from God; and whenever harm befalls you, it is unto Him that you cry for help[60] ‹53› – yet as soon as He has removed the harm from you, lo! some of you [begin to] ascribe to other powers a share in their Sustainer's divinity,[61] ‹54› [as if] to prove their ingratitude for all that We have granted them!

حزب 28

Enjoy, then, your [brief] life: but in time you will come to know [the truth]! ‹55›

As it is, they ascribe – out of what We provide for them as sustenance – a share unto things of which they know nothing.[62] By God, you shall most certainly be called to account for all your false imagery! ‹56›

And [thus, too,] they ascribe daughters unto God, who is limitless in His glory[63] – whereas for themselves [they would choose, if they could, only] what they desire:[64] ‹57› for, whenever any of them is given the glad

58 The double dual in *ilāhayn ithnayn* ("two deities") serves to emphasize the prohibition of worshipping "more than one deity" – i.e., anything but the One God.

59 This is a striking example of the fluctuation to which personal pronouns are subjected in the Qurʾān whenever they refer to God. As already pointed out in my Foreword, note 2, as well as in other places, such abrupt changes of pronoun ("He", "I", "We", "Us", "Me", etc.) indicate that God is limitless and, therefore, beyond the range of definition implied in the use of "personal" pronouns.

60 Cf. 6 : 40-41.

61 Lit., "associate [other powers] with their Sustainer": i.e., by attributing the change in their "luck" to what they regard as "extraneous" factors and influences, they invest the latter, as it were, with divine qualities and powers.

62 According to most of the classical commentators, this relates to the custom of the pagan Arabs – mentioned in 6 : 136 – of dedicating a part of their agricultural produce and cattle to their deities; and because those deities were mere figments of imagination, they are described here as "things of which they know nothing". However, as I have pointed out in note 120 on 6 : 136, the above statement bears a much wider, more general meaning: it connects directly with the three preceding verses of this *sūrah* – namely, with the attribution of a share (*naṣīb*) in God's creativeness – and thus of a decisive influence on one's life – to "causes" or "powers" other than Him. This view has also been advanced by Rāzī (with a specific reference to astrological speculations) in the concluding sentence of his commentary on the above verse.

63 The pre-Islamic Arabs believed that the goddesses Al-Lāt, Al-ʿUzzā and Manāt (see note 13 on 53 : 19-20), as well as the angels, whom they conceived as females, were "God's daughters". As against this, the Qurʾān states that God is utterly remote from every imperfection (*subḥānahu*), complete in Himself, and therefore free from the incompleteness inherent in the concept of "progeny" as an extension of one's own being (cf. 6 : 100 and the corresponding notes 87 and 88). – This parenthetic passage, comprising verses 57-59, is explained in note 66 below.

64 Namely, only male issue, because the pre-Islamic Arabs regarded daughters as no more than a necessary evil.

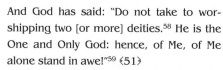

tiding of [the birth of] a girl,[65] his face darkens, and he is filled with suppressed anger, ⟨58⟩ avoiding all people because of the [alleged] evil of the glad tiding which he has received, [and debating within himself:] Shall he keep this [child] despite the contempt [which he feels for it] – or shall he bury it in the dust? Oh, evil indeed is whatever they decide![66] ⟨59⟩
[Thus it is that] the attribute of evil applies to all who do not believe in the life to come[67] – whereas unto God applies the attribute of all that is most sublime: for He alone is almighty, truly wise! ⟨60⟩
Now if God were to take men [immediately] to task for all the evil that they do [on earth], He would not leave a single living creature upon its face. However, He grants them respite until a term set [by Him]:[68] but when the end of their term approaches, they can neither delay it by a single moment, nor can they hasten it.[69] ⟨61⟩
As it is, they ascribe to God something that they [themselves] dislike[70] – and [all the while] their tongues utter the lie that [by doing so] they earn supreme merit![71]

بِٱلْأُنثَىٰ ظَلَّ وَجْهُهُۥ مُسْوَدًّا وَهُوَ كَظِيمٌ ﴿٥٨﴾ يَتَوَٰرَىٰ مِنَ ٱلْقَوْمِ مِن
سُوٓءِ مَا بُشِّرَ بِهِۦٓ ۚ أَيُمْسِكُهُۥ عَلَىٰ هُونٍ أَمْ يَدُسُّهُۥ فِى ٱلتُّرَابِ ۗ أَلَا سَآءَ
مَا يَحْكُمُونَ ﴿٥٩﴾ لِلَّذِينَ لَا يُؤْمِنُونَ بِٱلْءَاخِرَةِ مَثَلُ ٱلسَّوْءِ ۖ وَلِلَّهِ
ٱلْمَثَلُ ٱلْأَعْلَىٰ ۚ وَهُوَ ٱلْعَزِيزُ ٱلْحَكِيمُ ﴿٦٠﴾ وَلَوْ يُؤَاخِذُ ٱللَّهُ ٱلنَّاسَ
بِظُلْمِهِم مَّا تَرَكَ عَلَيْهَا مِن دَآبَّةٍ وَلَٰكِن يُؤَخِّرُهُمْ إِلَىٰٓ أَجَلٍ مُّسَمًّى ۖ
فَإِذَا جَآءَ أَجَلُهُمْ لَا يَسْتَـْٔخِرُونَ سَاعَةً ۖ وَلَا يَسْتَقْدِمُونَ ﴿٦١﴾
وَيَجْعَلُونَ لِلَّهِ مَا يَكْرَهُونَ وَتَصِفُ أَلْسِنَتُهُمُ ٱلْكَذِبَ أَنَّ لَهُمُ ٱلْحُسْنَىٰ ۖ

bilʾuñthā ẓalla wajhuhū muswaddañw-wa huwa kaẓīm. ⟨58⟩ Yatawārā minal-qawmi miñ-sūuʾi mā bushshira bih. ʾAyumsikuhū ʿalā hūnin ʾam yadus-suhū fit-turāb. ʾAlā sāaʾa mā yaḥkumūn. ⟨59⟩ Lil-ladhīna lā yuʾminūna bilʾĀkhirati mathalus-sawʾi wa lillāhil-mathalul-ʾaʿlā; wa Huwal-ʿAzīzul-Ḥakīm. ⟨60⟩ Wa law yuʾākhidhul-lāhun-nāsa biẓulmihim-mā taraka ʿalayhā miñ-dāabbatiñw-wa lākiñy-yuʾakh-khiruhum ʾilāa ʾajalim-musammā. Faʾidhā jāaʾa ʾajaluhum lā yastaʾkhirūna sāʿatañw-wa lā yastaq-dimūn. ⟨61⟩ Wa yajʿalūna lillāhi mā yakrahūna wa taṣifu ʾalsinatuhumul-kadhiba ʾanna lahumul-ḥusnā.

65 I.e., a tiding that *should* have been regarded as a happy one, since the sex of the child ought to make no difference to parental love.

66 I.e., either of these alternatives is evil: to keep the child as an object of perpetual contempt, or to bury it alive, as was frequently done by the pagan Arabs. – This passage, containing as it does an utter condemnation of men's attitude towards women in pre-Islamic Arabia, has – as is always the case with Qurʾanic references to historical events or customs – a meaning that goes far beyond this specific social phenomenon and the resulting infanticide. It would seem that the pivotal point of the whole passage is the sentence, "for themselves [they would choose, if they could, only] what they desire": that is to say, while they are only too ready to associate with God ideas which are repugnant to *themselves* (for instance, female progeny, which they themselves despise), they are unwilling to accept the concept of man's ultimate responsibility to Him, because such a concept militates against their own hedonistic inclinations by obliging them to impose a moral discipline on themselves. And because they rebel against the idea of ultimate moral responsibility, they instinctively reject the idea of resurrection and of life after bodily death; and since they deny, by implication, God's power to resurrect the dead, they deny His omnipotence and, consequently, begin to "ascribe divinity" – i.e., a *genuinely* causative function – to all manner of imaginary forces, beings or influences: and so, by means of a parenthetic reference to pre-Islamic Arabian beliefs and customs, the discourse returns full circle to the concept of God's oneness, uniqueness and omnipotence, around which the whole of the Qurʾān revolves.

67 I.e., inasmuch as they deny, by implication, man's ultimate responsibility before God. According to Zamakhsharī and Rāzī, the term *mathal* (lit., "example" or "parable") has here and in the next clause the connotation of *ṣifah* ("attribute").

68 Or: "known [only to Him]" – i.e., the period of their lives on earth, during which they may reflect and repent.

69 For my rendering of *sāʿah* as "a single moment", see *sūrah* 7, note 26.

70 I.e., "daughters" (see verses 57-59 above): but this alludes also, as Zamakhsharī points out, to the association with God of imaginary beings which allegedly have a share in His power and thus nullify the concept of His uniqueness: in other words, while the people spoken of here would hate to see their own legitimate spheres of influence encroached upon and curtailed by rivals, they do not extend the same consideration to their idea of God.

71 Lit., "that theirs is the supreme good (*al-ḥusnā*)" – i.e., in the sight of God – because they regard their own religious or anti-religious views, in spite of their absurdity, as good and true. This interpretation of *al-ḥusnā* in the

لَا جَرَمَ أَنَّ لَهُمُ ٱلنَّارَ وَأَنَّهُم مُّفْرَطُونَ ﴿٦٢﴾ تَٱللَّهِ لَقَدْ أَرْسَلْنَآ إِلَىٰٓ أُمَمٍ مِّن
قَبْلِكَ فَزَيَّنَ لَهُمُ ٱلشَّيْطَٰنُ أَعْمَٰلَهُمْ فَهُوَ وَلِيُّهُمُ ٱلْيَوْمَ وَلَهُمْ عَذَابٌ
أَلِيمٌ ﴿٦٣﴾ وَمَآ أَنزَلْنَا عَلَيْكَ ٱلْكِتَٰبَ إِلَّا لِتُبَيِّنَ لَهُمُ ٱلَّذِى ٱخْتَلَفُوا۟ فِيهِ
وَهُدًى وَرَحْمَةً لِّقَوْمٍ يُؤْمِنُونَ ﴿٦٤﴾ وَٱللَّهُ أَنزَلَ مِنَ ٱلسَّمَآءِ مَآءً فَأَحْيَا بِهِ
ٱلْأَرْضَ بَعْدَ مَوْتِهَآ إِنَّ فِى ذَٰلِكَ لَءَايَةً لِّقَوْمٍ يَسْمَعُونَ ﴿٦٥﴾ وَإِنَّ لَكُمْ فِى
ٱلْأَنْعَٰمِ لَعِبْرَةً نُّسْقِيكُم مِّمَّا فِى بُطُونِهِۦ مِنۢ بَيْنِ فَرْثٍ وَدَمٍ لَّبَنًا خَالِصًا
سَآئِغًا لِّلشَّٰرِبِينَ ﴿٦٦﴾

Lā jarama ʾanna lahumun-nāra wa ʾannahum-mufraṭūn. (62) Tallāhi laqad ʾarsalnāa ʾilāa ʾumamim-miñ-qablika fazayyana lahumush-Shayṭānu ʾaʿmālahum fahuwa waliyyuhumul-Yawma wa lahum ʿadhābun ʾalīm. (63) Wa māa ʾañzalnā ʿalaykal-Kitāba ʾillā litubayyina lahumul-ladhikh-talafū fīhi wa hudañw-wa raḥmatal-liqawmiñy-yuʾminūn. (64) Wallāhu ʾañzala minas-samāaʾi māaʾañ-faʾaḥyā bihil-ʾarḍa baʿda mawtihā; ʾinna fī dhālika laʾāyatal-liqawmiñy-yasmaʿūn. (65) Wa ʾinna lakum fil-ʾanʿāmi laʿibrah. Nusqīkum-mimmā fī buṭūnihī mim-bayni farthiñw-wa damil-labanan khāliṣañ-sāaʾighal-lishshāribīn. (66)

Truly, they earn but the fire, and will be left out [of God's grace]![72] «62»

By God, [O Prophet,] even before thy time have We sent apostles unto [various] communities: but [those who were bent on denying the truth have always refused to listen to Our messages because] Satan has made all their own doings seem goodly to them: and he is [as] close to them today[73] [as he was to the sinners of yore]; hence, grievous suffering awaits them. «63»

And upon thee [too] have We bestowed from on high this divine writ for no other reason than that thou might make clear unto them all [questions of faith] on which they have come to hold divergent views, and [thus offer] guidance and grace unto people who will believe. «64»

AND GOD sends down water from the skies, giving life thereby to the earth after it had been lifeless:[74] in this, behold, there is a message indeed for people who [are willing to] listen. «65»

And, behold, in the cattle [too] there is indeed a lesson for you: We give you to drink of that [fluid] which is [secreted from] within their bellies between that which is to be eliminated [from the animal's body] and [its] life-blood: milk pure and pleasant to those who drink it.[75] «66»

---

above context (mentioned, among others, by Zamakhsharī and Rāzī) connects logically with the statement in the next verse that "Satan had made their own doings seem goodly to them".

72 Lit., "theirs [or "their portion"] will be the fire, and they will be abandoned".

73 Or: "He is their patron [or "master"] today". It should be borne in mind that the noun *walī* is derived from the verb *waliya*, which primarily signifies "he was [or "became"] close [or "near", i.e., to someone or something]". It is in this sense that the term *walī* is used in the Qurʾān with reference to God's nearness to the believers (e.g., in 2 : 257 or 3 : 68), or their nearness to God (see 10 : 62 and the corresponding note 84). Similarly, the "powers of evil" (*aṭ-ṭāghūt*) are spoken of in 2 : 257 as being "near unto those who are bent on denying the truth (*alladhīna kafarū*)".

74 As so often in the Qurʾān, a reference to the spiritual life engendered by divine revelation is followed here by a reference to the miracle of organic life as another indication of God's creative activity.

75 Milk – in itself a glandular secretion – is not necessary for the mother-animal's life (or, as it is here metonymically described, its "blood"); on the other hand, it is not just something that the body eliminates as being of no further use to its metabolism: hence it is referred to as a substance "*between* that which is to be eliminated [from the animal's body] and [its] life-blood".

And [We grant you nourishment] from the fruit of date-palms and vines: from it you derive intoxicants as well as wholesome sustenance – in this, behold, there is a message indeed for people who use their reason![76] ‹67›
And [consider how] thy Sustainer has inspired the bee:[77] "Prepare for thyself dwellings in mountains and in trees, and in what [men] may build [for thee by way of hives]; ‹68› and then eat of all manner of fruit, and follow humbly the paths ordained for thee by thy Sustainer.[78]
[And lo!] there issues from within these [bees] a fluid of many hues, wherein there is health for man.
In all this, behold, there is a message indeed for people who think! ‹69›

AND GOD has created you, and in time will cause you to die; and many a one of you is reduced in old age to a most abject state, ceasing to know anything of what he once knew so well.[79]
Verily, God is all-knowing, infinite in His power! ‹70›
And on some of you God has bestowed more abundant means of sustenance than on others: and yet, they who are more abundantly favoured are [often] unwilling to share their sustenance with those whom their right hands possess, so that they [all] might be equal in this respect.[80] Will they, then, God's blessings [thus] deny? ‹71›

وَمِن ثَمَرَٰتِ ٱلنَّخِيلِ وَٱلْأَعْنَٰبِ تَتَّخِذُونَ مِنْهُ سَكَرًا وَرِزْقًا حَسَنًا ۗ إِنَّ
فِى ذَٰلِكَ لَءَايَةً لِّقَوْمٍ يَعْقِلُونَ ﴿٦٧﴾ وَأَوْحَىٰ رَبُّكَ إِلَى ٱلنَّحْلِ أَنِ ٱتَّخِذِى
مِنَ ٱلْجِبَالِ بُيُوتًا وَمِنَ ٱلشَّجَرِ وَمِمَّا يَعْرِشُونَ ﴿٦٨﴾ ثُمَّ كُلِى مِن كُلِّ
ٱلثَّمَرَٰتِ فَٱسْلُكِى سُبُلَ رَبِّكِ ذُلُلًا ۚ يَخْرُجُ مِنۢ بُطُونِهَا شَرَابٌ مُّخْتَلِفٌ
أَلْوَٰنُهُۥ فِيهِ شِفَآءٌ لِّلنَّاسِ ۗ إِنَّ فِى ذَٰلِكَ لَءَايَةً لِّقَوْمٍ يَتَفَكَّرُونَ ﴿٦٩﴾ وَٱللَّهُ
خَلَقَكُمْ ثُمَّ يَتَوَفَّىٰكُمْ ۚ وَمِنكُم مَّن يُرَدُّ إِلَىٰٓ أَرْذَلِ ٱلْعُمُرِ لِكَىْ لَا يَعْلَمَ بَعْدَ
عِلْمٍ شَيْـًٔا ۚ إِنَّ ٱللَّهَ عَلِيمٌ قَدِيرٌ ﴿٧٠﴾ وَٱللَّهُ فَضَّلَ بَعْضَكُمْ عَلَىٰ بَعْضٍ فِى
ٱلرِّزْقِ ۚ فَمَا ٱلَّذِينَ فُضِّلُوا۟ بِرَآدِّى رِزْقِهِمْ عَلَىٰ مَا مَلَكَتْ أَيْمَٰنُهُمْ فَهُمْ
فِيهِ سَوَآءٌ ۚ أَفَبِنِعْمَةِ ٱللَّهِ يَجْحَدُونَ ﴿٧١﴾

Wa miñ-thamarātin-nakhīli wal-ʾaᶜnābi tattakhidhūna minhu sakarañw-wa rizqan ḥasanā. ʾInna fī dhālika laʾāyatal-liqawmiñy-yaᶜqilūn. (67) Wa ʾawḥā Rabbuka ʾilan-naḥli ʾanit-takhidhī minal-jibāli buyūtañw-wa minash-shajari wa mimmā yaᶜrishūn. (68) Thumma kulī miñ-kullith-thamarāti fasluki subula Rabbiki dhululā. Yakhruju mim-buṭūnihā sharābum-mukhtalifun ʾalwānuhū fīhi shifāaʾul-linnās. ʾInna fī dhālika laʾāyatal-liqawmiñy-yatafakkarūn. (69) Wal-lāhu khalaqakum thumma yatawaffākum wa miñkum-mañy-yuraddu ʾilāa ʾardhalil-ᶜumuri likay lā yaᶜlama baᶜda ᶜilmiñ-shayʾā. ʾInnal-lāha ᶜAlīmuñ-Qadīr. (70) Wal-lāhu faḍḍala baᶜḍakum ᶜalā baᶜḍiñ-fir-rizq. Famal-ladhīna fuḍḍilū birāaddī rizqihim ᶜalā mā malakat ʾaymānuhum fahum fīhi sawāaʾ. ʾAfabiniᶜmatil-lāhi yajḥadūn. (71)

---

76 The term *sakar* (lit., "wine" or, generically, "intoxicants") is contrasted here with *rizq ḥasan* ("wholesome sustenance"), thus circumscribing both the positive and the negative properties and effects of alcohol. Although this *sūrah*. was revealed about ten years before the Qurʾanic prohibition of intoxicants in 5 : 90-91, there is no doubt that their *moral* condemnation is already implied in the above verse (Ibn ᶜAbbās, as quoted by Ṭabarī; also Rāzī).

77 The expression "He has inspired" (*awḥā*) is meant to bring out the wonderful quality of the instinct which enables the lowly insect to construct the geometrical masterpiece of a honeycomb out of perfectly-proportioned hexagonal, prismatic wax cells – a structure which is most economical, and therefore most rational, as regards space and material. Together with the subsequently mentioned transmutation, in the bee's body, of plant juices into honey, this provides a striking evidence of "God's ways" manifested in all nature.

78 Lit., "thy Sustainer's paths".

79 Lit., "is reduced to a most abject age, so that he knows nothing after [having had] knowledge": alluding to the organic curve of man's growth, his acquisition of bodily strength, intelligence and experience, followed by gradual decay and, in some cases, the utter helplessness of senility, comparable to the helplessness of a new-born child.

80 The phrase "to share their sustenance with . . .", etc., reads, literally, "to turn over their sustenance to". The expression "those whom their right hands possess" (i.e., "those whom they rightfully possess") may relate either to

ربع الحزب

And God has given you mates of your own kind[81] and has given you, through your mates, children and children's children, and has provided for you sustenance out of the good things of life.

Will men,[82] then, [continue to] believe in things false and vain, and thus blaspheme against God's blessings? ‹72› – and will they [continue to] worship, instead of God, something that has it not within its power to provide for them any sustenance whatever from the heavens or the earth,[83] and can do nothing at all? ‹73›

Hence, do not coin any similitudes for God![84] Verily, God knows [all], whereas you have no [real] knowledge. ‹74›

God propounds [to you] the parable of [two men –] a man enslaved, unable to do anything of his own accord, and a [free] man upon whom We have bestowed goodly sustenance [as a gift] from Ourselves, so that he can spend thereof [at will, both] secretly and openly. Can these [two] be deemed equal?[85]

All praise is due to God [alone]: but most of them do not understand it. ‹75›

وَٱللَّهُ جَعَلَ لَكُم مِّنْ أَنفُسِكُمْ أَزْوَٰجًا وَجَعَلَ لَكُم مِّنْ أَزْوَٰجِكُم
بَنِينَ وَحَفَدَةً وَرَزَقَكُم مِّنَ ٱلطَّيِّبَٰتِ ۚ أَفَبِٱلْبَٰطِلِ يُؤْمِنُونَ وَبِنِعْمَتِ ٱللَّهِ
هُمْ يَكْفُرُونَ ﴿٧٢﴾ وَيَعْبُدُونَ مِن دُونِ ٱللَّهِ مَا لَا يَمْلِكُ لَهُمْ رِزْقًا مِّنَ
ٱلسَّمَٰوَٰتِ وَٱلْأَرْضِ شَيْـًٔا وَلَا يَسْتَطِيعُونَ ﴿٧٣﴾ فَلَا تَضْرِبُوا۟ لِلَّهِ
ٱلْأَمْثَالَ ۚ إِنَّ ٱللَّهَ يَعْلَمُ وَأَنتُمْ لَا تَعْلَمُونَ ﴿٧٤﴾ ۞ ضَرَبَ ٱللَّهُ مَثَلًا عَبْدًا
مَّمْلُوكًا لَّا يَقْدِرُ عَلَىٰ شَىْءٍ وَمَن رَّزَقْنَٰهُ مِنَّا رِزْقًا حَسَنًا فَهُوَ يُنفِقُ مِنْهُ
سِرًّا وَجَهْرًا ۖ هَلْ يَسْتَوُۥنَ ۚ ٱلْحَمْدُ لِلَّهِ ۚ بَلْ أَكْثَرُهُمْ لَا يَعْلَمُونَ ﴿٧٥﴾

Wal-lāhu jaᶜala lakum-min ᵓañfusikum ᵓazwājañw-wa jaᶜala lakum-min ᵓazwājikum-banīna wa ḥafadatañw-wa razaqakum-minaṭ-ṭayyibāt. ᵓAfabilbāṭili yuᵓminūna wa biniᶜmatil-lāhi hum yakfurūn. (72) Wa yaᶜbudūna miñ-dūnil-lāhi mā lā yamliku lahum rizqam-minas-samāwāti wal-ᵓarḍi shayᵓañw-wa lā yastaṭīᶜūn. (73) Falā taḍribū lillāhil-ᵓamthāla ᵓinnal-lāha yaᶜlamu wa ᵓañtum lā taᶜlamūn. (74) ۞ Ḍarabal-lāhu mathalan ᶜabdam-mamlūkal-lā yaqdiru ᶜalā shayᵓiñw-wa mar-razaqnāhu minnā rizqan ḥasanañ-fahuwa yuñfiqu minhu sirrañw-wa jahran hal yastawūn. ᵓAlḥamdu lillāhi bal ᵓaktharuhum lā yaᶜlamūn. (75)

slaves taken captive in a war in God's cause (see *sūrah* 2, notes 167 and 168, and *sūrah* 8, note 72) or, metonymically, to all who are dependent on others for their livelihood and thus become the latters' responsibility. The placing of one's dependants on an equal footing with oneself with regard to the basic necessities of life is a categorical demand of Islam; thus, the Prophet said: "They are your brethren, these dependants of yours (*khawalukum*) whom God has placed under your authority [lit., "under your hand"]. Hence, whoso has his brother under his authority shall give him to eat of what he eats himself, and shall clothe him with what he clothes himself. And do not burden them with anything that may be beyond their strength; but if you [must] burden them, help them yourselves." (This authentic Tradition, recorded by Bukhārī in several variants in his *Ṣaḥīḥ*, appears in the compilations of Muslim, Tirmidhī and Ibn Ḥanbal as well.) However, men often fail to live up to this consciousness of moral responsibility: and this failure amounts, as the sequence shows, to a denial of God's blessings and of His unceasing care for all His creatures.

81 Lit., "has made [or "provided"] for you mates out of yourselves". The term *zawj* denotes not only "a pair" or "a couple" but also – as in this instance – "one of a pair" or "a mate" of the opposite sex; hence, with reference to human beings, the plural *azwāj* signifies both "husbands" and "wives".

82 Lit., "they", i.e., those who deny the truth of God's existence and/or oneness.

83 For the comprehensive meaning embodied in the term *rizq*, see the first sentence of note 4 on 2 : 3.

84 I.e., "do not blaspheme against God by regarding anyone or anything as comparable with Him, or by trying to *define* Him in any terms whatsoever" – since "definition" is, in the last resort, equivalent to a delimitation of the qualities of the object thus to be defined in relation to, or in comparison with, another object or objects: God, however, is "sublimely exalted above anything that men may devise by way of definition" (see last sentence of 6 : 100, and the corresponding note 88).

85 The obvious answer is that they cannot. The implication is equally clear: if even these two kinds of *man* cannot be deemed equal, how could any created being, with its intrinsic, utter dependence on other created beings, or any force of nature conceivable or imaginable by man, be thought of as possessing powers comparable with those of God, who is almighty, limitless, inconceivable – the self-sufficient fount of all that exists? (This argument is continued and further elaborated in the subsequent parable.)

And God propounds [to you] the parable of two [other] men – one of them dumb,[86] unable to do anything of his own accord, and a sheer burden on his master: to whichever task the latter directs him,[87] he accomplishes no good. Can such a one be considered the equal of [a wise man] who enjoins the doing of what is right and himself follows a straight way?[88] ‹76›

And[89] God's [alone] is the knowledge of the hidden reality of the heavens and the earth.[90] And so, the advent of the Last Hour will but manifest itself [in a single moment,] like the twinkling of an eye, or closer still:[91] for, behold, God has the power to will anything. ‹77›

And God has brought you forth from your mothers' wombs knowing nothing – but He has endowed you with hearing, and sight, and minds, so that you might have cause to be grateful. ‹78›

Have, then, they [who deny the truth] never considered the birds, enabled [by God] to fly in mid-air,[92] with none but God holding them aloft? In this, behold, there are messages indeed for people who will believe! ‹79›

And God has given you [the ability to build] your houses as places of rest, and has endowed you with [the skill to make] dwellings out of the skins of animals[93] –

وَضَرَبَ ٱللَّهُ مَثَلًا رَّجُلَيْنِ أَحَدُهُمَآ أَبْكَمُ لَا يَقْدِرُ عَلَىٰ شَىْءٍ وَهُوَ كَلٌّ عَلَىٰ
مَوْلَىٰهُ أَيْنَمَا يُوَجِّههُّ لَا يَأْتِ بِخَيْرٍ هَلْ يَسْتَوِى هُوَ وَمَن يَأْمُرُ بِٱلْعَدْلِ وَهُوَ
عَلَىٰ صِرَٰطٍ مُّسْتَقِيمٍ ﴿٧٦﴾ وَلِلَّهِ غَيْبُ ٱلسَّمَٰوَٰتِ وَٱلْأَرْضِ وَمَآ أَمْرُ ٱلسَّاعَةِ
إِلَّا كَلَمْحِ ٱلْبَصَرِ أَوْ هُوَ أَقْرَبُ إِنَّ ٱللَّهَ عَلَىٰ كُلِّ شَىْءٍ قَدِيرٌ ﴿٧٧﴾ وَٱللَّهُ
أَخْرَجَكُم مِّنۢ بُطُونِ أُمَّهَٰتِكُمْ لَا تَعْلَمُونَ شَيْـًٔا وَجَعَلَ لَكُمُ ٱلسَّمْعَ
وَٱلْأَبْصَٰرَ وَٱلْأَفْـِٔدَةَ لَعَلَّكُمْ تَشْكُرُونَ ﴿٧٨﴾ أَلَمْ يَرَوْا۟ إِلَى ٱلطَّيْرِ مُسَخَّرَٰتٍ
فِى جَوِّ ٱلسَّمَآءِ مَا يُمْسِكُهُنَّ إِلَّا ٱللَّهُ إِنَّ فِى ذَٰلِكَ لَءَايَٰتٍ لِّقَوْمٍ يُؤْمِنُونَ ﴿٧٩﴾
وَٱللَّهُ جَعَلَ لَكُم مِّنۢ بُيُوتِكُمْ سَكَنًا وَجَعَلَ لَكُم مِّن جُلُودِ ٱلْأَنْعَٰمِ بُيُوتًا

Wa ḍarabal-lāhu mathalar-rajulayni ʾaḥaduhumāa ʾabkamu lā yaqdiru ʿalā shayʾiñw-wa huwa kallun ʿalā mawlāhu ʾaynamā yuwajjihhu lā yaʾti bikhayrin hal yastawī huwa wa mañy-yaʾmuru bilʿadli wa huwa ʿalā ṣirāṭim-mustaqīm. (76) Wa lillāhi ghaybus-samāwāti wal-ʾarḍ. Wa māa ʾamrus-Sāʿati ʾillā kalamḥil-baṣari ʾaw huwa ʾaqrab. ʾInnal-lāha ʿalā kulli shayʾiñ-Qadīr. (77) Wal-lāhu ʾakhrajakum-mim-buṭūni ʾummahātikum lā taʿlamūna shayʾañw-wa jaʿala lakumus-samʿa wal-ʾabṣāra wal-ʾafʾidata laʿallakum tashkurūn. (78) ʾAlam yaraw ʾilaṭ-ṭayri musakhkharātiñ-fī jawwis-samāaʾi mā yumsikuhunna ʾillal-lāh. ʾInna fī dhālika laʾĀyātil-liqawmiñy-yuʾminūn. (79) Wal-lāhu jaʿala lakum-mim-buyūtikum sakanañw-wa jaʿala lakum-miñ julūdil-ʾanʿāmi buyūtañ-

86 The term *abkam* signifies "dumb" both in the literal, physiological sense and (as in colloquial English) in the sense of being "unable to speak properly" on account of intellectual weakness: i.e., "dull-witted" or "stupid". Both these meanings are contained in the above Qurʾanic description.

87 Or: "wherever he sends him".

88 I.e., who is not only wise and righteous but also has the strength and authority to enjoin a righteous way of living upon others. Thus, while in the first parable the main issue is the contrast between freedom and bondage or – more generally – between dependence and independence, in the second parable we are given the antithesis of dumbness and incompetence, on the one hand, and wisdom, justice and competence, on the other; and in both parables the implication is the same (see note 85 above).

89 This passage connects with the second sentence of verse 74 – "Verily, God knows [all], whereas you have no [real] knowledge."

90 As may be inferred from the sequence, the term *ghayb* – rendered here as the "hidden reality" – alludes in this context to the coming of the Last Hour, the time whereof is known to God alone (Zamakhsharī). Parallel with this, it may also relate to God's Own existence, which cannot be directly established by the testimony of our senses (Bayḍāwī) but, as the Qurʾān consistently points out, may be inferred from the observable effects of His creativeness.

91 Lit., "the case [i.e., the manifestation] of the [Last] Hour will be like . . .", etc. – implying that it will be characterized by utter suddenness and unpredictability, both of them an outcome of the absence of any time-interval between God's decreeing it and its materialization: and this explains the phrase "or closer still" at the end of the above sentence.

92 Lit., "subservient [to God's laws] in the air of the sky".

93 The term *julūd* (sing. *jild*) denotes, literally, "skins", but apparently comprises here also the wool which grows

easy for you to handle when you travel and when you camp – and [to make] furnishings and goods for temporary use of their [rough] wool and their soft, furry wool[94] and their hair. ‹80›
And among the many objects of His creation,[95] God has appointed for you [various] means of protection:[96] thus, He has given you in the mountains places of shelter, and has endowed you with [the ability to make] garments to protect you from heat [and cold],[97] as well as such garments as might protect you from your [mutual] violence.[98]
In this way does He bestow the full measure of His blessings on you, so that you might surrender yourselves unto Him. ‹81›

BUT IF they turn away [from thee, O Prophet, remember that] thy only duty is a clear delivery of the message [entrusted to thee]. ‹82› They [who turn away from it] are fully aware of God's blessings, but none the less they refuse to acknowledge them [as such], since most of them are given to denying the truth.[99] ‹83›
But one Day We shall raise up a witness out of every community,[100] whereupon

تَسْتَخِفُّونَهَا يَوْمَ ظَعْنِكُمْ وَيَوْمَ إِقَامَتِكُمْ وَمِنْ أَصْوَافِهَا وَأَوْبَارِهَا
وَأَشْعَارِهَآ أَثَٰثًا وَمَتَٰعًا إِلَىٰ حِينٍ ﴿٨٠﴾ وَٱللَّهُ جَعَلَ لَكُم مِّمَّا خَلَقَ ظِلَٰلًا
وَجَعَلَ لَكُم مِّنَ ٱلْجِبَالِ أَكْنَٰنًا وَجَعَلَ لَكُمْ سَرَٰبِيلَ تَقِيكُمُ ٱلْحَرَّ
وَسَرَٰبِيلَ تَقِيكُم بَأْسَكُمْ كَذَٰلِكَ يُتِمُّ نِعْمَتَهُۥ عَلَيْكُمْ لَعَلَّكُمْ تُسْلِمُونَ ﴿٨١﴾
فَإِن تَوَلَّوْا۟ فَإِنَّمَا عَلَيْكَ ٱلْبَلَٰغُ ٱلْمُبِينُ ﴿٨٢﴾ يَعْرِفُونَ نِعْمَتَ ٱللَّهِ ثُمَّ
يُنكِرُونَهَا وَأَكْثَرُهُمُ ٱلْكَٰفِرُونَ ﴿٨٣﴾ وَيَوْمَ نَبْعَثُ مِن كُلِّ أُمَّةٍ شَهِيدًا

tastakhiffūnahā yawma ẓaᶜnikum wa yawma ᵓiqāmatikum wa min ᵓaṣwāfihā wa ᵓawbārihā wa ᵓashᶜārihāa ᵓathāthañw-wa matāᶜan ᵓilā ḥīn. ‹80› Wallāhu jaᶜala lakum mimmā khalaqa ẓilālañw-wa jaᶜala la-kum-minal-jibāli ᵓaknānañw-wa jaᶜala lakum sarābīla taqīkumul-ḥarra wa sarābīla taqīkum baᵓsakum. Kadhalika yutimmu niᶜmatahū ᶜalaykum laᶜallakum tuslimūn. ‹81› Faᵓiñ-tawallaw faᵓinnamā ᶜalaykal-balāghul-mubīn. ‹82› Yaᶜrifūna niᶜmatal-lāhi thumma yuñkirūnahā wa ᵓaktharuhumul-kāfirūn. ‹83› Wa Yawma nabᶜathu miñ-kulli ᵓummatiñ-shahīdañ-

on the skins of domesticated animals. It is to be noted that in Arabian usage the noun *bayt* ("house") signifies not only a solid building but also a "tent" – in brief, every kind of dwelling, whether permanent or temporary.

94 *Wabar* (here given in its plural, *awbār*) is the soft wool growing on the shoulders of camels ("camel-hair"), used in the weaving of fine cloths and sometimes also of bedouin tents.

95 Lit., "out of that which He has created".

96 Lit., "shades" (*ẓilāl,* sing. *ẓill*). Metonymically, this term is occasionally used to describe anything that "shades" one in the sense of protecting him; and since the sequence clearly refers to means of protection, I believe that this derivative meaning of *ẓilāl* is here preferable to the literal.

97 According to almost all the classical commentators, the mention of "heat" implies here its opposite as well, namely "cold"; hence my interpolation.

98 According to most of the commentators, the second incidence of the term "garments" (*sarābīl*) in this verse is to be understood as "coats of mail" or "armour", in which case it would allude to wars and other instances of mutual violence. But although this interpretation cannot be ruled out, it seems to me that the second mention of "garments" can be understood in a much wider sense, perhaps metonymically denoting *all* manner of "coverings" (i.e., devices meant to protect the body) which man may be constrained to use in dangerous situations of his own making: hence the stress on "*your* violence" (*baᵓsakum*).

99 I.e., although they are aware of the many blessings which man enjoys, they refuse to attribute them to God's creative activity, thus implicitly denying the truth of His existence. My rendering of *al-kāfirūn* as "[such as] are *given to denying* the truth" is conditioned by the definite article *al* which, in the above construction, is meant to stress the quality of deliberate intent.

100 An allusion to the Day of Judgment, when the prophets whom God has called forth within every community – or, in the wider sense of the term *ummah*, within every civilization or cultural period – will symbolically bear witness

they who were bent on denying the truth will not be allowed to plead [ignorance],[101] and neither will they be allowed to make amends. «84»
And when they who were bent on evil-doing behold the suffering [that awaits them, they will realize that] it will not be lightened for them [by virtue of their pleading]; and neither will they be granted respite. «85»
And when they who were wont to ascribe divinity to beings other than God behold [on Judgment Day] those beings to whom they were wont to ascribe a share in His divinity,[102] they will exclaim: "O our Sustainer! These are the beings to whom we ascribed a share in Thy divinity, and whom we were wont to invoke instead of Thee!"[103] – whereupon [those beings] will fling at them the retort: "Behold, you have indeed been lying [to yourselves]!"[104] «86»
And on that Day will they [who had thus been sinning, belatedly] proffer their surrender to God; and all their false imagery will have forsaken them. «87»
Upon all who were bent on denying the truth and who turned others away from the path of God will We heap suffering upon suffering in return for all the corruption that they wrought: «88» for one Day We shall raise up within every community a witness against them from among themselves.[105]
And thee [too, O Prophet,] have We brought forth to bear witness regarding those

ثُمَّ لَا يُؤْذَنُ لِلَّذِينَ كَفَرُوا۟ وَلَا هُمْ يُسْتَعْتَبُونَ ﴿٨٤﴾ وَإِذَا رَءَا ٱلَّذِينَ ظَلَمُوا۟
ٱلْعَذَابَ فَلَا يُخَفَّفُ عَنْهُمْ وَلَا هُمْ يُنظَرُونَ ﴿٨٥﴾ وَإِذَا رَءَا ٱلَّذِينَ أَشْرَكُوا۟
شُرَكَآءَهُمْ قَالُوا۟ رَبَّنَا هَٰٓؤُلَآءِ شُرَكَآؤُنَا ٱلَّذِينَ كُنَّا نَدْعُوا۟ مِن دُونِكَ ۖ
فَأَلْقَوْا۟ إِلَيْهِمُ ٱلْقَوْلَ إِنَّكُمْ لَكَٰذِبُونَ ﴿٨٦﴾ وَأَلْقَوْا۟ إِلَى ٱللَّهِ يَوْمَئِذٍ ٱلسَّلَمَ ۖ
وَضَلَّ عَنْهُم مَّا كَانُوا۟ يَفْتَرُونَ ﴿٨٧﴾ ٱلَّذِينَ كَفَرُوا۟ وَصَدُّوا۟ عَن سَبِيلِ ٱللَّهِ
زِدْنَٰهُمْ عَذَابًا فَوْقَ ٱلْعَذَابِ بِمَا كَانُوا۟ يُفْسِدُونَ ﴿٨٨﴾ وَيَوْمَ نَبْعَثُ
فِى كُلِّ أُمَّةٍ شَهِيدًا عَلَيْهِم مِّنْ أَنفُسِهِمْ ۖ وَجِئْنَا بِكَ شَهِيدًا عَلَىٰ هَٰٓؤُلَآءِ ۚ

thumma lā yuʾdhanu lilladhīna kafarū wa lā hum yustaᶜtabūn. (84) Wa ʾidhā raʾal-ladhīna ẓalamul-ᶜadhāba falā yukhaffafu ᶜanhum wa lā hum yuñẓarūn. (85) Wa ʾidhā raʾal-ladhīna ʾashrakū shurakāaʾahum qālū Rabbanā hāaʾulāaʾi shurakāaʾunal-ladhīna kunnā nadᶜū miñ-dūnik. Faʾalqaw ʾilayhimul-qawla ʾinnakum lakādhibūn. (86) Wa ʾalqaw ʾilal-lāhi Yawmaʾidhinis-salama wa ḍalla ᶜanhum-mā kānū yaftarūn. (87) ʾAlladhīna kafarū wa ṣaddū ᶜañ-sabīlil-lāhi zidnāhum ᶜadhābañ-fawqal-ᶜadhābi bimā kānū yufsidūn. (88) Wa Yawma nabᶜathu fī kulli ʾummatiñ-shahīdan ᶜalayhim-min ʾañfusihim wa jiʾnā bika shahīdan ᶜalā hāaʾulāaʾ.

to the fact that they had delivered God's message to their people and explained to them the meaning of right and wrong, thus depriving them of any subsequent excuse.

101 According to Zamakhsharī, their being "refused permission" to plead is a metonym for their having no valid argument or excuse to proffer. (Cf. also 77 : 35-36.)

102 Cf. 6 : 22 and the corresponding note 15.

103 The Qurʾān states in many places that every sinner who dies without repentance will be endowed on Judgment Day with a clear, objectified vision of his sins, every one of which will have assumed for him the status of an independent reality bearing witness against him and forcing him to acknowledge his now irremediable guilt. It is to be remembered in this connection that the Qurʾān describes every act of sinning – whether it be an offence against the concept of God's oneness and uniqueness or a wrong done to any of His creatures – as, primarily, one's "wronging oneself" or "sinning against oneself".

104 Cf. 6 : 23-24 and the corresponding notes 16 and 17.

105 See note 100 above.

نصف الحزب

[whom thy message may have reached],[106] inasmuch as We have bestowed from on high upon thee, step by step, this divine writ, to make everything clear,[107] and to provide guidance and grace and a glad tiding unto all who have surrendered themselves to God. ﴾89﴿

BEHOLD, God enjoins justice, and the doing of good, and generosity towards [one's] fellow-men;[108] and He forbids all that is shameful and all that runs counter to reason,[109] as well as envy; [and] He exhorts you [repeatedly] so that you might bear [all this] in mind. ﴾90﴿

And be true to your bond with God whenever you bind yourselves by a pledge,[110] and do not break [your] oaths after having [freely] confirmed them[111] and having called upon God to be witness to your good faith:[112] behold, God knows all that you do. ﴾91﴿

Hence, be not like her who breaks and completely untwists the yarn which she [herself] has spun and made strong –

وَنَزَّلْنَا عَلَيْكَ ٱلْكِتَٰبَ تِبْيَٰنًا لِّكُلِّ شَىْءٍ وَهُدًى وَرَحْمَةً وَبُشْرَىٰ
لِلْمُسْلِمِينَ ﴿٨٩﴾ إِنَّ ٱللَّهَ يَأْمُرُ بِٱلْعَدْلِ وَٱلْإِحْسَٰنِ وَإِيتَآئِ ذِى
ٱلْقُرْبَىٰ وَيَنْهَىٰ عَنِ ٱلْفَحْشَآءِ وَٱلْمُنكَرِ وَٱلْبَغْىِ يَعِظُكُمْ لَعَلَّكُمْ
تَذَكَّرُونَ ﴿٩٠﴾ وَأَوْفُوا۟ بِعَهْدِ ٱللَّهِ إِذَا عَٰهَدتُّمْ وَلَا تَنقُضُوا۟ ٱلْأَيْمَٰنَ
بَعْدَ تَوْكِيدِهَا وَقَدْ جَعَلْتُمُ ٱللَّهَ عَلَيْكُمْ كَفِيلًا ۚ إِنَّ ٱللَّهَ يَعْلَمُ مَا
تَفْعَلُونَ ﴿٩١﴾ وَلَا تَكُونُوا۟ كَٱلَّتِى نَقَضَتْ غَزْلَهَا مِنۢ بَعْدِ قُوَّةٍ أَنكَٰثًا

Wa nazzalnā ᶜalaykal-Kitāba tibyānal-likulli shayᵓiñw-wa hudañw-wa raḥmatañw-wa bushrā lilmuslimīn. ﴾89﴿ ᵓInnal-lāha yaᵓmuru bilᶜadli wal-ᵓiḥsāni wa ᵓītāaᵓi dhil-qurbā wa yanhā ᶜanil-faḥshāaᵓi wal-muñkari wal-baghy. Yaᶜiẓukum laᶜallakum tadhakkarūn. ﴾90﴿ Wa ᵓawfū biᶜahdil-lāhi ᵓidhā ᶜāhattum wa lā tañquḍul-ᵓaymāna baᶜda tawkīdihā wa qad jaᶜaltumul-lāha ᶜalaykum kafīlā. ᵓInnal-lāha yaᶜlamu mā tafᶜalūn. ﴾91﴿ Wa lā takūnū kallatī naqaḍat ghazlahā mim-baᶜdi quwwatin ᵓañkāthañ-

106 Although the Arabian contemporaries of the Prophet were, naturally, the first to whom his revelation was conveyed – a fact that gave a particular weight to the manner in which they responded to it – the Qurᵓanic message as such is addressed to all mankind (see in this connection, in particular, 7 : 158 and 21 : 107, as well as the corresponding notes).

107 I.e., everything that pertains to the knowledge of good and evil, in both the individual and social senses of these terms. – Regarding my rendering of *nazzalnā*, it should be borne in mind that this particular grammatical form is often used in the Qurᵓān to bring out the fact that it was revealed gradually ("step by step") over a considerable period of time, and not in one piece.

108 Lit., "the giving to [one's] kinsfolk (*dhu 'l-qurbā*)". The latter term usually denotes "relatives", either by blood or by marriage; but since it occurs here in the context of a comprehensive ethical exhortation, it obviously alludes to man's "kinsfolk" in the widest sense of the term, namely, to his "fellow-men".

109 The term *al-munkar* (rendered by me in other places as "that which is wrong") has here its original meaning of "that which the mind [or the moral sense] rejects", respectively "ought to reject". Zamakhsharī is more specific, and explains this term as signifying in the above context "that which [men's] intellects disown" or "declare to be untrue" (*mā tunkiruhu al-ᶜuqūl*): in other words, all that runs counter to reason and good sense (which, obviously, must not be confused with that which is *beyond* man's comprehension). This eminently convincing explanation relates not merely to intellectually unacceptable propositions (in the abstract sense of the term) but also to grossly unreasonable and, therefore, reprehensible actions or attitudes and is, thus, fully in tune with the rational approach of the Qurᵓān to questions of ethics as well as with its insistence on reasonableness and moderation in man's behaviour. Hence my rendering of *al-munkar*, in this and in similar instances, as "all that runs counter to reason".

110 Regarding the expression "bond with God" (*ᶜahd Allāh*), see *sūrah* 2, note 19. The clause "whenever you bind yourselves by a pledge" has a twofold meaning: in the first instance (as in 13 : 20) it refers to the spiritual, moral and social obligations arising from one's faith in God; and, secondly, it applies to all pledges or promises given by one person to another – for, as Rāzī points out, every pledge given by man to man represents, in its essence, a pledge to God. It is to this second aspect of man's "bond with God" that the sequence refers.

111 I.e., as distinct from oaths "uttered without thought" (see 2 : 225).

112 Lit., "and having made God [or "named God as"] your guarantor (*kafīl*)".

[be not like this by] using your oaths as a means of deceiving one another,[113] simply because some of you may be more powerful than others.[114]
By all this, God but puts you to a test – and [He does it] so that on Resurrection Day He might make clear unto you all that on which you were wont to differ.[115] ⟨92⟩
For, had God so willed, He could surely have made you all one single community;[116] however, He lets go astray him that wills [to go astray], and guides aright him that wills [to be guided];[117] and you will surely be called to account for all that you ever did![118] ⟨93⟩
And do not use your oaths as a means of deceiving one another – or else [your] foot will slip after having been firm,[119] and then you will have to taste the evil [consequences][120] of your having turned away from the path of God, with tremendous suffering awaiting you [in the life to come]. ⟨94⟩
Hence, do not barter away your bond with God for a trifling gain!
Verily, that which is with God is by far the best for you, if you but knew it: ⟨95⟩ all that is with you is bound to come to an end, whereas that which is with God is everlasting.

تَتَّخِذُونَ أَيْمَٰنَكُمْ دَخَلًۢا بَيْنَكُمْ أَن تَكُونَ أُمَّةٌ هِىَ أَرْبَىٰ مِنْ أُمَّةٍ ۚ إِنَّمَا
يَبْلُوكُمُ ٱللَّهُ بِهِۦ ۚ وَلَيُبَيِّنَنَّ لَكُمْ يَوْمَ ٱلْقِيَٰمَةِ مَا كُنتُمْ فِيهِ تَخْتَلِفُونَ ﴿٩٢﴾
وَلَوْ شَآءَ ٱللَّهُ لَجَعَلَكُمْ أُمَّةً وَٰحِدَةً وَلَٰكِن يُضِلُّ مَن يَشَآءُ وَيَهْدِى مَن
يَشَآءُ ۚ وَلَتُسْـَٔلُنَّ عَمَّا كُنتُمْ تَعْمَلُونَ ﴿٩٣﴾ وَلَا تَتَّخِذُوٓا۟ أَيْمَٰنَكُمْ دَخَلًۢا
بَيْنَكُمْ فَتَزِلَّ قَدَمٌۢ بَعْدَ ثُبُوتِهَا وَتَذُوقُوا۟ ٱلسُّوٓءَ بِمَا صَدَدتُّمْ عَن سَبِيلِ ٱللَّهِ ۖ
وَلَكُمْ عَذَابٌ عَظِيمٌ ﴿٩٤﴾ وَلَا تَشْتَرُوا۟ بِعَهْدِ ٱللَّهِ ثَمَنًا قَلِيلًا ۚ إِنَّمَا عِندَ ٱللَّهِ
هُوَ خَيْرٌ لَّكُمْ إِن كُنتُمْ تَعْلَمُونَ ﴿٩٥﴾ مَا عِندَكُمْ يَنفَدُ ۖ وَمَا عِندَ ٱللَّهِ بَاقٍ ۗ

tattakhidhūna ʾaymānakum dakhalam-baynakum ʾañ-takūna ʾummatun hiya ʾarbā min ʾummah. ʾInnamā yablūkumul-lāhu bihī wa layubayyinanna lakum Yawmal-Qiyāmati mā kuñtum fīhi takhtalifūn. (92) Wa law shāaʾal-lāhu lajaʿalakum ʾummatañw-wāḥidatañw-wa lākiñy-yuḍillu mañy-yashāaʾu wa yahdī mañy-yashāaʾu wa latusʾalunna ʿammā kuñtum taʿmalūn. (93) Wa lā tattakhidhūu ʾaymānakum dakhalam-baynakum fatazilla qadamum-baʿda thubūtihā wa tadhūqus-sūuʾa bimā ṣadattum ʿañ-sabīlil-lāhi wa lakum ʿadhābun ʿaẓīm. (94) Wa lā tashtarū biʿahdil-lāhi thamanañ-qalīlā. ʾInnamā ʿiñdal-lāhi huwa khayrul-lakum ʾiñ-kuñtum taʿlamūn. (95) Mā ʿiñdakum yañfadu wa mā ʿiñdal-lāhi bāq.

113 Lit., "as a [means of] deception (*dakhalan*) among yourselves".

114 Lit., "because there are people (*ummah*) more powerful than [other] people": relating to declarations and false promises made out of fear.

115 As is evident from the preceding passage as well as from the sequence, the differences alluded to here relate to ethical and moral values, regarding the truth and relevance of which people of various communities and persuasions hold most divergent views. See also *sūrah* 2, note 94.

116 I.e., bound by mutually agreed-upon moral values. See in this connection 10 : 19 and the corresponding notes, especially note 29. For an elucidation of the concept of *ummah wāḥidah* ("one single community") and its further implications, see *sūrah* 2, notes 197 and 198.

117 Or: "He lets go astray whomever He wills, and guides aright whomever He wills". Regarding the problem of free will *versus* predestination, seemingly implied in the concept of God's "letting man go [or "causing him to go"] astray" or, alternatively, "guiding him aright", see *sūrah* 14, note 4.

118 Alluding to the erroneous idea that man's good or evil actions – and therefore also his propensities and resulting attitudes – are "predetermined" by God and not really an outcome of free choice, Zamakhsharī rounds off his views on this problem (quoted by me in *sūrah* 14, note 4) in these words: "If [it were true that] God *compels* [men] to go astray or, alternatively, to follow His guidance – why should He have postulated their deeds as something for which they will be held responsible?"

119 I.e., "you will offend against God after having attained to faith", seeing that – as has been pointed out in note 110 above – every pledge given by man to man is synonymous with a pledge to God.

120 I.e., in this world (Ṭabarī, Zamakhsharī, Bayḍāwī), inasmuch as the breaking of pledges unavoidably leads to a gradual disappearance of all mutual trust and, thus, to the decomposition of the social fabric.

And most certainly shall We grant unto those who are patient in adversity their reward in accordance with the best that they ever did. «96»
As for anyone – be it man or woman – who does righteous deeds, and is a believer withal – him shall We most certainly cause to live a good life;[121] and most certainly shall We grant unto such as these their reward in accordance with the best that they ever did. «97»

وَلَنَجۡزِيَنَّ ٱلَّذِينَ صَبَرُوٓاْ أَجۡرَهُم بِأَحۡسَنِ مَا كَانُواْ يَعۡمَلُونَ ﴿٩٦﴾ مَنۡ عَمِلَ
صَٰلِحٗا مِّن ذَكَرٍ أَوۡ أُنثَىٰ وَهُوَ مُؤۡمِنٞ فَلَنُحۡيِيَنَّهُۥ حَيَوٰةٗ طَيِّبَةٗۖ وَلَنَجۡزِيَنَّهُمۡ
أَجۡرَهُم بِأَحۡسَنِ مَا كَانُواْ يَعۡمَلُونَ ﴿٩٧﴾ فَإِذَا قَرَأۡتَ ٱلۡقُرۡءَانَ فَٱسۡتَعِذۡ
بِٱللَّهِ مِنَ ٱلشَّيۡطَٰنِ ٱلرَّجِيمِ ﴿٩٨﴾ إِنَّهُۥ لَيۡسَ لَهُۥ سُلۡطَٰنٌ عَلَى ٱلَّذِينَ
ءَامَنُواْ وَعَلَىٰ رَبِّهِمۡ يَتَوَكَّلُونَ ﴿٩٩﴾ إِنَّمَا سُلۡطَٰنُهُۥ عَلَى ٱلَّذِينَ يَتَوَلَّوۡنَهُۥ
وَٱلَّذِينَ هُم بِهِۦ مُشۡرِكُونَ ﴿١٠٠﴾ وَإِذَا بَدَّلۡنَآ ءَايَةٗ مَّكَانَ ءَايَةٖ وَٱللَّهُ أَعۡلَمُ
بِمَا يُنَزِّلُ قَالُوٓاْ إِنَّمَآ أَنتَ مُفۡتَرِۭۚ بَلۡ أَكۡثَرُهُمۡ لَا يَعۡلَمُونَ ﴿١٠١﴾

NOW whenever thou happen to read this Qurʾān, seek refuge with God from Satan, the accursed.[122] «98» Behold, he has no power over those who have attained to faith and in their Sustainer place their trust: «99» he has power only over those who are willing to follow him,[123] and who [thus] ascribe to him a share in God's divinity.[124] «100»
And now that We replace one message by another[125] – since God is fully aware of what He bestows from on high, step by step[126] – they [who deny the truth] are wont to say, "Thou but inventest it!" Nay, but most of them do not understand it![127] «101»

Wa lanajziyannal-ladhīna ṣabarūu ʾajrahum biʾaḥsani mā kānū yaʿmalūn. (96) Man ʿamila ṣāliḥam-miñ-dhakarin ʾaw ʾuñthā wa huwa muʾminuñ-falanuḥyiyannahū ḥayātañ-ṭayyibah. Wa lanajziyannahum ʾajrahum biʾaḥsani mā kānū yaʿmalūn. (97) Faʾidhā qaraʾtal-Qurʾāna fastaʿidh billāhi minash-Shayṭānir-rajīm. (98) ʾInnahū laysa lahū sulṭānun ʿalal-ladhīna ʾāmanū wa ʿalā Rabbihim yatawakkalūn. (99) ʾInnamā sulṭānuhū ʿalal-ladhīna yatawallawnahū wal-ladhīna hum-bihī mushrikūn. (100) Wa ʾidhā baddalnāa ʾāyatam-makāna ʾāyatiñw-wal-lāhu ʾaʿlamu bimā yunazzilu qālūu ʾinnamāa ʾañta muftarim-bal ʾaktharuhum lā yaʿlamūn. (101)

121 This may relate either to life in this world – inasmuch as a true believer invariably finds happiness in his God-consciousness – or to the happiness which awaits him in the hereafter, or to both.

122 The present passage (verses 98-105) evidently connects with the broad ethical exhortation given in verse 90 above and, thus, with the statement (in verse 89) that the Qurʾān is meant "to make everything clear and to provide guidance and grace and a glad tiding unto all who have surrendered themselves to God" – which, in its turn, implies that the Qurʾān is the ultimate source of all God-willed ethical and moral values, and thus an unchanging criterion of good and evil. But since man is always, by virtue of his nature, prone to question the very *validity* of the moral standards established through revelation, the believer is now called upon to seek, whenever he reads or meditates on this divine writ, God's spiritual aid against the whisperings of what the Qurʾān describes as "Satan, the accursed" – that is, all the evil forces, both within man's own soul and within his social environment, which tend to undermine his moral convictions and to lead him away from God.

123 Or: "who make him their master". Cf. in this connection 14 : 22 and the corresponding note 31.

124 I.e., inasmuch as they pay an almost worshipful reverence to such blandishments as wealth, power, social position, etc.

125 I.e., by substituting the message of the Qurʾān for the earlier dispensations – and not, as some Muslim scholars maintain, "abrogating" one Qurʾanic verse and replacing it by another. (Regarding the untenable "doctrine of abrogation", in the latter sense, see 2 : 106 and the corresponding note 87; see also note 35 on 41 : 42.)

126 I.e., the gradualness of revelation (implied in the verbal form *yunazzil*) corresponds to God's plan, according to which He has gradually unfolded His will to man, substituting one dispensation for another in the measure of mankind's intellectual and social development, bringing it to its culmination in the message of the Qurʾān.

127 I.e., they do not understand the *necessity* of a new dispensation and, therefore, do not really understand the Qurʾān.

Say: "Holy inspiration[128] has brought it down from thy Sustainer by stages, setting forth the truth, so that it might give firmness unto those who have attained to faith, and provide guidance and a glad tiding unto all who have surrendered themselves to God." ‹102›
And, indeed, full well do We know that they say, "It is but a human being that imparts [all] this to him!"[129] – [notwithstanding that] the tongue of him to whom they so maliciously point is wholly outlandish,[130] whereas this is Arabic speech, clear [in itself] and clearly showing the truth [of its source].[131] ‹103›
Verily, as for those who will not believe in God's messages, God does not guide them aright; and grievous suffering will be their lot [in the life to come]. ‹104› It is but they who will not believe in God's messages that invent this falsehood;[132] and it is they, they who are lying! ‹105›
As for anyone who denies God after having once attained to faith – and this, to be sure, does not apply to[133] one who does it under duress, the while his heart remains true to his faith,[134] but [only to]

قُلْ نَزَّلَهُۥ رُوحُ ٱلْقُدُسِ مِن رَّبِّكَ بِٱلْحَقِّ لِيُثَبِّتَ ٱلَّذِينَ ءَامَنُوا۟ وَهُدًى
وَبُشْرَىٰ لِلْمُسْلِمِينَ ﴿102﴾ وَلَقَدْ نَعْلَمُ أَنَّهُمْ يَقُولُونَ إِنَّمَا يُعَلِّمُهُۥ بَشَرٌ ۗ لِّسَانُ
ٱلَّذِى يُلْحِدُونَ إِلَيْهِ أَعْجَمِىٌّ وَهَٰذَا لِسَانٌ عَرَبِىٌّ مُّبِينٌ ﴿103﴾ إِنَّ ٱلَّذِينَ لَا
يُؤْمِنُونَ بِـَٔايَٰتِ ٱللَّهِ لَا يَهْدِيهِمُ ٱللَّهُ وَلَهُمْ عَذَابٌ أَلِيمٌ ﴿104﴾ إِنَّمَا يَفْتَرِى
ٱلْكَذِبَ ٱلَّذِينَ لَا يُؤْمِنُونَ بِـَٔايَٰتِ ٱللَّهِ ۖ وَأُو۟لَٰٓئِكَ هُمُ ٱلْكَٰذِبُونَ ﴿105﴾ مَن
كَفَرَ بِٱللَّهِ مِنۢ بَعْدِ إِيمَٰنِهِۦٓ إِلَّا مَنْ أُكْرِهَ وَقَلْبُهُۥ مُطْمَئِنٌّ بِٱلْإِيمَٰنِ وَلَٰكِن

Qul nazzalahū Rūḥul-Qudusi mir-Rabbika bilḥaqqi liyuthabbital-ladhīna ʾāmanū wa hudañw-wa bushrā lilmuslimīn. ﴾102﴿ Wa laqad naʿlamu ʾannahum yaqūlūna ʾinnamā yuʿallimuhū bashar. Lisānul-ladhī yulḥidūna ʾilayhi ʾaʿjamiyyuñw-wa hādhā lisānun ʿarabiyyum-mubīn. ﴾103﴿ ʾInnal-ladhīna lā yuʾminūna biʾĀyātil-lāhi lā yahdīhimul-lāhu wa lahum ʿadhābun ʾalīm. ﴾104﴿ ʾInnamā yaftaril-kadhibal-ladhīna lā yuʾminūna biʾĀyātil-lāhi wa ʾulāaʾika humul-kādhibūn. ﴾105﴿ Mañ-kafara billāhi mim-baʿdi ʾīmānihīi ʾillā man ʾukriha wa qalbuhū muṭmaʾinnum-bilʾīmāni wa lākim-

128 As in the three other places in which the expression *rūḥ al-qudus* occurs (2 : 87 and 253, and 5 : 110), I am rendering it here, too, as "holy inspiration" (see *sūrah* 2, note 71), a term which, to my mind, is a Qurʾanic synonym for "divine revelation". However, a literal rendering – "spirit of holiness" – is also possible if one applies this term to the angel who communicates God's revelations to the prophets. (See also verse 2 of this *sūrah* and the corresponding note 2.)

129 I.e., to Muḥammad – thus insinuating that his claim to divine revelation was false.

130 Whereas some of the pagan Quraysh regarded the ideas expressed in the Qurʾān as "invented" by Muḥammad, others thought that they must have been imparted to him by a foreigner – perhaps a Christian – who lived in Mecca at that time, or whom the Prophet was supposed to have encountered at an earlier period of his life. Various conjectures have been advanced – both by early Muslim commentators and by modern orientalists – as to the "identity" of the person or persons whom the suspicious Meccans might have had in mind in this connection; but all these conjectures are purely speculative and, therefore, of no historical value whatever. The suspicion of the pagan Meccans implies no more than the historical fact that those of the Prophet's opponents who were unwilling to pay him the compliment of having "invented" the Qurʾān (the profundity of which they were unable to deny) conveniently attributed its authorship – or at least its inspiration – to a mythical non-Arab "teacher" of the Prophet.

131 For an explanation of this composite rendering of the descriptive term *mubīn*, see *sūrah* 12, note 2. The term is used here to stress the fact that no human being – and certainly no non-Arab – could ever have produced the flawless, exalted Arabic diction in which the Qurʾān is expressed.

132 I.e., the scurrilous allegation referred to in verse 103. Although this statement alludes, in the first instance, to the hostile contemporaries of the Prophet, it extends, by obvious implication, to people of all times who refuse to believe in the *reality* of Muḥammad's revelations, and try to explain them away as obsessive illusions or even as deliberate fabrications.

133 Lit., "except" – but the Arabic construction of the sentence that follows makes it necessary to render the simple particle *illā* in the manner adopted by me ("and this, to be sure, does not apply to . . .", etc.).

134 Lit., "one who is coerced, the while his heart is at rest in [his] faith". This relates to believers who, under torture or threat of death, ostensibly "recant" in order to save themselves. Although the Qurʾān makes it clear in several

ثلاثة ارباع الحزب

him who willingly opens up his heart to a denial of the truth: – upon all such [falls] God's condemnation, and tremendous suffering awaits them: ‹106› all this, because they hold this world's life in greater esteem than the life to come, and because God does not bestow His guidance upon people who deny the truth. ‹107›

They whose hearts and whose hearing and whose sight God has sealed – it is they, they who are heedless![135] ‹108› Truly it is they, they who in the life to come shall be the losers! ‹109›

And yet, behold, thy Sustainer [grants His forgiveness] unto those who forsake the domain of evil after having succumbed to its temptation,[136] and who thenceforth strive hard [in God's cause] and are patient in adversity: behold, after such [repentance] thy Sustainer is indeed much-forgiving, a dispenser of grace! ‹110›

[Be conscious, then, of] the Day when every human being shall come to plead for himself [alone], and every human being shall be repaid in full for whatever he has done, and none shall be wronged. ‹111›

AND GOD propounds [to you] a parable: [Imagine] a town which was [once] secure and at ease, with its sustenance coming to it abundantly from all quarters, and which thereupon blasphemously refused to show gratitude for God's blessings: and therefore God caused it to taste the all-embracing misery[137] of hunger and fear in result of all [the evil] that its people had so persistently wrought.[138] ‹112›

مَّن شَرَحَ بِٱلۡكُفۡرِ صَدۡرٗا فَعَلَيۡهِمۡ غَضَبٞ مِّنَ ٱللَّهِ وَلَهُمۡ عَذَابٌ
عَظِيمٞ ﴿١٠٦﴾ ذَٰلِكَ بِأَنَّهُمُ ٱسۡتَحَبُّواْ ٱلۡحَيَوٰةَ ٱلدُّنۡيَا عَلَى ٱلۡأٓخِرَةِ وَأَنَّ ٱللَّهَ
لَا يَهۡدِي ٱلۡقَوۡمَ ٱلۡكَٰفِرِينَ ﴿١٠٧﴾ أُوْلَٰٓئِكَ ٱلَّذِينَ طَبَعَ ٱللَّهُ عَلَىٰ قُلُوبِهِمۡ
وَسَمۡعِهِمۡ وَأَبۡصَٰرِهِمۡۖ وَأُوْلَٰٓئِكَ هُمُ ٱلۡغَٰفِلُونَ ﴿١٠٨﴾ لَا جَرَمَ أَنَّهُمۡ فِي
ٱلۡأٓخِرَةِ هُمُ ٱلۡخَٰسِرُونَ ﴿١٠٩﴾ ثُمَّ إِنَّ رَبَّكَ لِلَّذِينَ هَاجَرُواْ مِنۢ بَعۡدِ مَا
فُتِنُواْ ثُمَّ جَٰهَدُواْ وَصَبَرُوٓاْ إِنَّ رَبَّكَ مِنۢ بَعۡدِهَا لَغَفُورٞ رَّحِيمٞ ﴿١١٠﴾ ۞ يَوۡمَ
تَأۡتِي كُلُّ نَفۡسٖ تُجَٰدِلُ عَن نَّفۡسِهَا وَتُوَفَّىٰ كُلُّ نَفۡسٖ مَّا عَمِلَتۡ وَهُمۡ لَا
يُظۡلَمُونَ ﴿١١١﴾ وَضَرَبَ ٱللَّهُ مَثَلٗا قَرۡيَةٗ كَانَتۡ ءَامِنَةٗ مُّطۡمَئِنَّةٗ يَأۡتِيهَا
رِزۡقُهَا رَغَدٗا مِّن كُلِّ مَكَانٖ فَكَفَرَتۡ بِأَنۡعُمِ ٱللَّهِ فَأَذَٰقَهَا ٱللَّهُ لِبَاسَ
ٱلۡجُوعِ وَٱلۡخَوۡفِ بِمَا كَانُواْ يَصۡنَعُونَ ﴿١١٢﴾

mañ-sharaḥa bilkufri ṣadrañ-faᶜalayhim ghaḍabum-minal-lāhi wa lahum ᶜadhābun ᶜaẓīm. (106) Dhālika biˀannahumus-taḥabbul-ḥayātad-dunyā ᶜalal-ˀĀkhirati wa ˀannal-lāha lā yahdil-qawmal-kāfirīn. (107) ˀUlāaˀikal-ladhīna ṭabaᶜal-lāhu ᶜalā qulūbihim wa samᶜihim wa ˀabṣārihim wa ˀulāaˀika humul-ghāfilūn. (108) Lā jarama ˀannahum fil-ˀĀkhirati humul-khāsirūn. (109) Thumma ˀinna Rabbaka lilladhīna hājarū mim-baᶜdi mā futinū thumma jāhadū wa ṣabarūu ˀinna Rabbaka mim-baᶜdihā laGhafūrur-Raḥīm. (110) ۞ Yawma taˀtī kullu nafsiñ-tujādilu ᶜan-nafsihā wa tuwaffā kullu nafsim-mā ᶜamilat wa hum lā yuẓlamūn. (111) Wa ḍarabal-lāhu mathalañ-qaryatañ-kānat ˀāminatam-muṭmaˀinnatañy-yaˀtīhā rizquhā raghadam-miñ-kulli makāniñ-fakafarat biˀanᶜumil-lāhi faˀadhāqahal-lāhu libāsal-jūᶜi wal-khawfi bimā kānū yaṣnaᶜūn. (112)

places that martyrdom in the cause of faith is highly meritorious, "God does not burden any human being with more than he is well able to bear" (cf. 2 : 233 and 286, 6 : 152, 7 : 42, 23 : 62, and many other Qurˀanic statements to the same effect).

135 Sc., "of what is good and what is bad for them". – For an explanation of God's "sealing" the hearts of those who are bent on denying the truth, see 2 : 7 and the corresponding note.

136 For an explanation of the concept of *fitnah* (appearing here in the verbal form *futinū*) and of my rendering it as "temptation to evil", see *sūrah* 8, note 25. As regards the expression *alladhīna hājarū* in its spiritual connotation, see *sūrah* 2, note 203 and *sūrah* 4, note 124.

137 Lit., "the garment" (*libās*) – idiomatically used in classical Arabic to describe the utmost degree of misfortune which "envelops man like a garment" (*Tāj al-ᶜArūs*, with specific reference to the above verse).

138 This parable is meant to show that deliberate ingratitude for the manifold blessings which God bestows upon man – in other words, a deliberate refusal to submit to His guidance – is bound, in the long run and in the context of

And indeed, there had come unto them an apostle from among themselves – but they gave him the lie; and therefore suffering overwhelmed them while they were thus doing wrong [to themselves]. «113»

AND SO, partake of all the lawful, good things which God has provided for you as sustenance, and render thanks unto God for His blessings, if it is [truly] Him that you worship.[139] «114»
He has forbidden to you only carrion, and blood, and the flesh of swine, and that over which any name other than God's has been invoked; but if one is driven [to it] by necessity – neither coveting it nor exceeding his immediate need – verily, God is much-forgiving, a dispenser of grace.[140] «115»
Hence, do not utter falsehoods by letting your tongues determine [at your own discretion], "This is lawful and that is forbidden", thus attributing your own lying inventions to God:[141] for, behold, they who attribute their own lying inventions to God will never attain to a happy state! «116» A brief enjoyment [may be theirs in this world] – but grievous suffering awaits them [in the life to come]! «117»
And [only] unto those who followed the Jewish faith did We forbid all that We have mentioned to thee ere this;[142] and no wrong did We do to them, but it was they who persistently wronged themselves. «118»

وَلَقَدْ جَآءَهُمْ رَسُولٌ مِّنْهُمْ فَكَذَّبُوهُ فَأَخَذَهُمُ ٱلْعَذَابُ وَهُمْ ظَٰلِمُونَ ﴿١١٣﴾
فَكُلُوا۟ مِمَّا رَزَقَكُمُ ٱللَّهُ حَلَٰلًا طَيِّبًا وَٱشْكُرُوا۟ نِعْمَتَ ٱللَّهِ إِن كُنتُمْ
إِيَّاهُ تَعْبُدُونَ ﴿١١٤﴾ إِنَّمَا حَرَّمَ عَلَيْكُمُ ٱلْمَيْتَةَ وَٱلدَّمَ وَلَحْمَ ٱلْخِنزِيرِ وَمَآ
أُهِلَّ لِغَيْرِ ٱللَّهِ بِهِۦ ۖ فَمَنِ ٱضْطُرَّ غَيْرَ بَاغٍ وَلَا عَادٍ فَإِنَّ ٱللَّهَ غَفُورٌ رَّحِيمٌ ﴿١١٥﴾
وَلَا تَقُولُوا۟ لِمَا تَصِفُ أَلْسِنَتُكُمُ ٱلْكَذِبَ هَٰذَا حَلَٰلٌ وَهَٰذَا حَرَامٌ
لِّتَفْتَرُوا۟ عَلَى ٱللَّهِ ٱلْكَذِبَ ۚ إِنَّ ٱلَّذِينَ يَفْتَرُونَ عَلَى ٱللَّهِ ٱلْكَذِبَ لَا
يُفْلِحُونَ ﴿١١٦﴾ مَتَٰعٌ قَلِيلٌ وَلَهُمْ عَذَابٌ أَلِيمٌ ﴿١١٧﴾ وَعَلَى ٱلَّذِينَ هَادُوا۟
حَرَّمْنَا مَا قَصَصْنَا عَلَيْكَ مِن قَبْلُ ۖ وَمَا ظَلَمْنَٰهُمْ وَلَٰكِن كَانُوٓا۟ أَنفُسَهُمْ
يَظْلِمُونَ ﴿١١٨﴾

Wa laqad jāaʾahum Rasūlum-minhum fakadhdhabūhu faʾakhadhahumul-ᶜadhābu wa hum ẓālimūn. (113) Fakulū mimmā razaqakumul-lāhu ḥalālañ-ṭayyibañw-wash-kurū niᶜmatal-lāhi ʾiñ-kuñtum ʾIyyāhu taᶜbudūn. (114) ʾInnamā ḥarrama ᶜalaykumul-maytata wad-dama wa laḥmal-khiñzīri wa māa ʾuhilla lighayril-lāhi bih. Famaniḍ-ṭurra ghayra bāghiñw-wa lā ᶜādiñ-faʾinnal-lāha Ghafūrur-Raḥīm. (115) Wa lā taqūlū limā taṣifu ʾalsinatukumul-kadhiba hādhā ḥalāluñw-wa hādhā ḥarāmul-litaftarū ᶜalal-lāhil-kadhib. ʾInnal-ladhīna yaftarūna ᶜalal-lāhil-kadhiba lā yufliḥūn. (116) Matāᶜuñ-qalīluñw-wa lahum ᶜadhābun ʾalīm. (117) Wa ᶜalal-ladhīna hādū ḥarramnā mā qaṣaṣnā ᶜalayka miñ-qablu wa mā ẓalamnāhum wa lākiñ-kānūu ʾañfusahum yaẓlimūn. (118)

aggregate social life, to have disastrous consequences not only in the hereafter but in this world as well, inasmuch as no society may expect to live in security and ease unless it conforms to the ethical and social standards inherent in the concept of man's "bond with God" (as explained in *sūrah* 2, note 19).

139 It is this call to *gratitude* that provides a connection between the present passage and the foregoing parable of the ungrateful town and, thus, with the opening passages (verses 1-15) of this *sūrah*.

140 It is to be noted that the above two verses are almost identical with 2 : 172-173, and ought, therefore, to be read in conjunction with the whole passage of which those two verses form a part – namely, 2 : 168-173. Cf. also 6 : 145.

141 Regarding the very important problem of an arbitrary determination, based on subjective preferences, of what is to be considered ethically right or wrong, see *sūrah* 2, note 137.

142 I.e., in 6 : 146, revealed shortly before the present *sūrah*. The conjunctive particle "And" at the beginning of this sentence establishes a connection with the precept laid down in verse 114 above, "partake of all the lawful, good things which God has provided for you as sustenance": the implication being (as in 6 : 145) that none of the really good and wholesome things have been forbidden to the believer, and that the many dietary prohibitions and restrictions imposed on the Jews were imposed *on them alone* in punishment of their persistent sinning (cf. 3 : 93).

ثُمَّ إِنَّ رَبَّكَ لِلَّذِينَ عَمِلُوا۟ ٱلسُّوٓءَ بِجَهَٰلَةٍ ثُمَّ تَابُوا۟ مِنۢ بَعْدِ ذَٰلِكَ
وَأَصْلَحُوٓا۟ إِنَّ رَبَّكَ مِنۢ بَعْدِهَا لَغَفُورٌ رَّحِيمٌ ﴿١١٩﴾ إِنَّ إِبْرَٰهِيمَ كَانَ أُمَّةً
قَانِتًا لِّلَّهِ حَنِيفًا وَلَمْ يَكُ مِنَ ٱلْمُشْرِكِينَ ﴿١٢٠﴾ شَاكِرًا لِّأَنْعُمِهِ ٱجْتَبَىٰهُ
وَهَدَىٰهُ إِلَىٰ صِرَٰطٍ مُّسْتَقِيمٍ ﴿١٢١﴾ وَءَاتَيْنَٰهُ فِى ٱلدُّنْيَا حَسَنَةً وَإِنَّهُۥ فِى
ٱلْءَاخِرَةِ لَمِنَ ٱلصَّٰلِحِينَ ﴿١٢٢﴾ ثُمَّ أَوْحَيْنَآ إِلَيْكَ أَنِ ٱتَّبِعْ مِلَّةَ إِبْرَٰهِيمَ
حَنِيفًا وَمَا كَانَ مِنَ ٱلْمُشْرِكِينَ ﴿١٢٣﴾ إِنَّمَا جُعِلَ ٱلسَّبْتُ عَلَى ٱلَّذِينَ
ٱخْتَلَفُوا۟ فِيهِ وَإِنَّ رَبَّكَ لَيَحْكُمُ بَيْنَهُمْ يَوْمَ ٱلْقِيَٰمَةِ فِيمَا كَانُوا۟ فِيهِ
يَخْتَلِفُونَ ﴿١٢٤﴾

Thumma ᵓinna Rabbaka lilladhīna ᶜamilus-sūūᵓa bi-jahālatiñ-thumma tābū mim-baᶜdi dhālika wa ᵓaṣlaḥūu ᵓinna Rabbaka mim-baᶜdihā laGhafūrur-Raḥīm. (119)
ᵓInna ᵓIbrāhīma kāna ᵓummatañ-qānital-lillāhi ḥanīfañw-wa lam yaku minal-mushrikīn. (120)
Shākiral-liᵓanᶜumihij-tabāhu wa hadāhu ᵓilā ṣirāṭim-mustaqīm. (121)
Wa ᵓātaynāhu fid-dunyā ḥasanatañw-wa ᵓinnahū fil-ᵓĀkhirati laminaṣ-ṣāliḥīn. (122)
Thumma ᵓawḥaynāa ᵓilayka ᵓanit-tabiᶜ millata ᵓIbrāhīma ḥanīfañw-wa mā kāna minal-mushrikīn. (123)
ᵓInnamā juᶜilas-Sabtu ᶜalal-ladhīnakh-talafū fīhi wa ᵓinna Rabbaka layaḥkumu baynahum Yawmal-Qiyāmati fīmā kānū fīhi yakhtalifūn. (124)

And once again:[143] Behold, thy Sustainer [shows mercy] to those who do evil out of ignorance and afterwards repent and live righteously: behold, after such [repentance] thy Sustainer is indeed much-forgiving, a dispenser of grace. ‹119›

VERILY, Abraham was a man who combined within himself all virtues,[144] devoutly obeying God's will, turning away from all that is false,[145] and not being of those who ascribe divinity to aught beside God: ‹120› [for he was always] grateful for the blessings granted by Him who had elected him and guided him onto a straight way. ‹121›

And so We vouchsafed him good in this world; and, verily, in the life to come [too] he shall find himself among the righteous. ‹122›

And lastly,[146] We have inspired thee, [O Muḥammad, with this message:] "Follow the creed of Abraham, who turned away from all that is false, and was not of those who ascribe divinity to aught beside God; ‹123› [and know that the observance of] the Sabbath was ordained only for those who came to hold divergent views about him;[147] but, verily, thy Sustainer will judge between them on Resurrection Day with regard to all on which they were wont to differ."[148] ‹124›

---

143 For this rendering of *thumma*, see *sūrah* 6, note 31.

144 This is one of the many meanings of the term *ummah* and, to my mind, the one most appropriate in the above context. – The mention of Abraham at this place contains a subtle allusion to verse 118, where the Jews are spoken of: for the latter claim to be "the chosen people" on account of their descent from Abraham, whereas the Qurᵓān consistently rejects all claims to a special status by virtue of one's descent. Moreover, the Qurᵓān states in many places that whereas this particular ancestor of the Hebrews – and, by the way, of most of the Arab tribes as well – was a personification of all that is good and upright, so that "God exalted him with His love" (4 : 125), his Jewish descendants always tended to rebel against God and, thus, "persistently wronged themselves".

145 For an explanation of this rendering of the term *ḥanīf*, see *sūrah* 2, note 110.

146 Lit., "thereafter" or "afterwards" (*thumma*): but since this particle evidently alludes here to the climax of all revelation as manifested in the Qurᵓān, the above rendering seems to be suitable.

147 I.e., about Abraham. The implication is that the majority of the Jews had deviated from the true creed of Abraham (which is the meaning of the phrase, "those who came to hold divergent views about him") inasmuch as most of them became convinced that they were "God's chosen people" simply because of their physical descent from that great Prophet: an assumption which obviously runs counter to every truly religious principle. As the Qurᵓān repeatedly points out, this spiritual arrogance was punished by God's imposition on the children of Israel – and on them alone – of all manner of severe restrictions and rituals, of which the obligation to refrain from all work and even travel on the Sabbath was one. In its widest implication, this passage is meant to stress the fact that all God-imposed rituals are only a means towards the achievement of spiritual discipline, and never a religious goal in themselves.

148 I.e., He will judge between those who are convinced of their ultimate salvation on the basis of their alleged

CALL THOU [all mankind] unto thy Sustainer's path with wisdom and goodly exhortation, and argue with them in the most kindly manner:[149] for, behold, thy Sustainer knows best as to who strays from His path, and best knows He as to who are the right-guided. ‹125›
Hence, if you have to respond to an attack [in argument], respond only to the extent of the attack levelled against you;[150] but to bear yourselves with patience is indeed far better for [you, since God is with] those who are patient in adversity. ‹126›
Endure, then, with patience [all that they who deny the truth may say] – always remembering that it is none but God who gives thee the strength to endure adversity[151] – and do not grieve over them, and neither be distressed by the false arguments which they devise:[152] ‹127›
for, verily, God is with those who are conscious of Him and are doers of good withal! ‹128›

ٱدْعُ إِلَىٰ سَبِيلِ رَبِّكَ بِٱلْحِكْمَةِ وَٱلْمَوْعِظَةِ ٱلْحَسَنَةِ ۖ وَجَٰدِلْهُم بِٱلَّتِى
هِىَ أَحْسَنُ ۚ إِنَّ رَبَّكَ هُوَ أَعْلَمُ بِمَن ضَلَّ عَن سَبِيلِهِۦ ۖ وَهُوَ أَعْلَمُ
بِٱلْمُهْتَدِينَ ﴿125﴾ وَإِنْ عَاقَبْتُمْ فَعَاقِبُوا۟ بِمِثْلِ مَا عُوقِبْتُم بِهِۦ ۖ وَلَئِن صَبَرْتُمْ
لَهُوَ خَيْرٌ لِّلصَّٰبِرِينَ ﴿126﴾ وَٱصْبِرْ وَمَا صَبْرُكَ إِلَّا بِٱللَّهِ ۚ وَلَا تَحْزَنْ عَلَيْهِمْ
وَلَا تَكُ فِى ضَيْقٍ مِّمَّا يَمْكُرُونَ ﴿127﴾ إِنَّ ٱللَّهَ مَعَ ٱلَّذِينَ ٱتَّقَوا۟ وَّٱلَّذِينَ هُم
مُّحْسِنُونَ ﴿128﴾

ᵓUdᶜu ᵓilā sabbīli Rabbika bilḥikmati wal-mawᶜiẓatil-ḥasanati wa jādilhum billatī hiya ᵓaḥsan. ᵓInna Rabbaka Huwa ᵓaᶜlamu bimañ-ḍalla ᶜañ-sabīlihī wa Huwa ᵓaᶜlamu bilmuhtadīn. (125) Wa ᵓin ᶜāqabtum faᶜāqibū bimithli mā ᶜūqibtum-bihī wa laᵓiñ-ṣabartum lahuwa khayrul-liṣṣābirīn. (126) Waṣ-bir wa mā ṣabruka ᵓillā billāhi wa lā taḥzan ᶜalayhim wa lā taku fī ḍayqim-mimmā yamkurūn. (127) ᵓInnal-lāha maᶜal-ladhīnat-taqaw wal-ladhīna hum-muḥsinūn. (128)

status of "God's chosen people", and those who believe in man's *individual* responsibility before God: and thus the discourse returns to the problem of God-consciousness and righteous living.

149 Cf. 29 : 46 – "And do not argue with the followers of earlier revelation otherwise than in the most kindly manner". This stress on kindness and tact and, hence, on the use of reason alone in all religious discussions with adherents of other creeds is fully in tune with the basic, categorical injunction, "There shall be no coercion in matters of faith" (2 : 256).

150 Lit., "retaliate [or "respond"] with the like of what you have been afflicted with": thus, the believers are admonished to observe self-restraint while arguing with people of another persuasion, and never to offend against decency and intellectual equity. Although retaliation in argument is permissible if one's integrity is impeached by an opponent, the sequence makes it clear that it is morally preferable to renounce it altogether and to bear the unjust attack with patience.

151 Lit., "and thy patience in adversity (*ṣabr*) is due to [or "rests with"] none but God" – i.e., it must never be allowed to become a source of spiritual arrogance and false self-righteousness.

152 Lit., "all that they are scheming", i.e., by inventing false and irrelevant arguments against God's messages.

The Seventeenth Sūrah

Al-ʾIsrāaʾ (The Night Journey)

Mecca Period

THE REFERENCE to the mystic Night Journey in the first verse of this *sūrah* (see Appendix IV) shows that it cannot have been revealed earlier than in the last year before the *hijrah*; Suyūṭī places it chronologically between *sūrah* 28 and the group of *sūrahs* 10-12. The assumption of some authorities that certain of its verses belong to a much later time – namely, the Medina period – is purely conjectural and may, therefore, be disregarded.

Because of the mention of the children of Israel in verses 2-8 and 101-104, some of the contemporaries of the Prophet used to designate this *sūrah* by the title of *Banū ʾIsrāʾīl* ("The Children of Israel"); most of the classical commentators, however, prefer the title *Al-ʾIsrāaʾ*.

According to ʿĀʾishah, the Prophet used to recite this *sūrah* every night in his prayer (Tirmidhī, Nasāʾī and Ibn Ḥanbal).

سورة الإسراء مكية -17-
وآياتها إحدى عشرة ومائة

IN THE NAME OF GOD, THE MOST GRACIOUS, THE DISPENSER OF GRACE:

LIMITLESS in His glory is He who transported His servant by night from the Inviolable House of Worship [at Mecca] to the Remote House of Worship [at Jerusalem] – the environs of which We had blessed[1] – so that We might show him some of Our symbols: for, verily, He alone is all-hearing, all-seeing.[2] ‹1›
And [thus, too,] We vouchsafed revelation unto Moses,[3] and made it a [source of] guidance for the children of Israel, [commanding them:] "Do not ascribe to any but Me the power to determine your fate,[4] ‹2›

بِسْمِ ٱللَّهِ ٱلرَّحْمَٰنِ ٱلرَّحِيمِ

سُبْحَٰنَ ٱلَّذِىٓ أَسْرَىٰ بِعَبْدِهِۦ لَيْلًا مِّنَ ٱلْمَسْجِدِ ٱلْحَرَامِ إِلَى ٱلْمَسْجِدِ
ٱلْأَقْصَا ٱلَّذِى بَٰرَكْنَا حَوْلَهُۥ لِنُرِيَهُۥ مِنْ ءَايَٰتِنَآ إِنَّهُۥ هُوَ ٱلسَّمِيعُ
ٱلْبَصِيرُ ﴿1﴾ وَءَاتَيْنَا مُوسَى ٱلْكِتَٰبَ وَجَعَلْنَٰهُ هُدًى لِّبَنِىٓ إِسْرَٰٓءِيلَ
أَلَّا تَتَّخِذُواْ مِن دُونِى وَكِيلًا ﴿2﴾

Bismil-lāhir-Raḥmānir-Raḥīm.
Subḥānal-ladhīi ʾasrā biʿabdihī laylam-minal-Masjidil-Ḥarāmi ʾilal-Masjidil-ʾAqṣal-ladhī bāraknā ḥawlahū linuriyahū min ʾĀyātināa ʾinnahū Huwas-Samīʿul-Baṣīr. ⟨1⟩ Wa ʾātaynā Mūsal-Kitāba wa jaʿalnāhu hudal-libanīi ʾIsrāaʾīla ʾallā tattakhidhū miñ-dūnī wakīlā. ⟨2⟩

29 حزب
15 جزء

---

1 The above short reference to the Prophet's mystic experience of the "Night Journey" (*al-isrāʾ*) to Jerusalem and the subsequent "Ascension" (*miʿrāj*) to heaven is fully discussed in Appendix IV at the end of this work. – "The Inviolable House of Worship" (*al-masjid al-ḥarām*) is one of the designations given in the Qurʾān to the Temple of the Kaʿbah, the prototype of which owed its origin to Abraham (see *sūrah* 2, note 102) and was "the first Temple set up for mankind" (3 : 96), i.e., the first ever built for the worship of the One God. "The Remote [lit., "farthest"] House of Worship", on the other hand, denotes the ancient Temple of Solomon – or, rather, its site – which symbolizes here the long line of Hebrew prophets who preceded the advent of Muḥammad and are alluded to by the phrase "the environs of which We had blessed". The juxtaposition of these two sacred temples is meant to show that the Qurʾān does not inaugurate a "new" religion but represents a continuation and the ultimate development of the same divine message which was preached by the prophets of old.

2 Although the term *āyah* is most frequently used in the Qurʾān in the sense of "[divine] message", we must remember that, primarily, it denotes "a sign [or "token"] by which a thing is known" (*Qāmūs*). As defined by Rāghib, it signifies any perceivable phenomenon (irrespective of whether it is apparent to the senses or only to the intellect) connected with a thing that is not, by itself, similarly perceivable: in brief, a "symbol". Hence, the expression *min āyātinā* may be suitably rendered as "some of Our symbols", i.e., insight, through symbols, into some of the ultimate truths.

3 The conjunctive particle "And" which introduces this verse is meant to show that the mystic Night Journey – and, by implication, the subsequent Ascension as well – were experiences of the same high order of divine grace as the revelation bestowed upon Moses. The Qurʾān mentions in 4 : 164 that "God spoke His word unto Moses", i.e., directly (*taklīman*); see also 7 : 143-144, and especially verse 144, in which God says to Moses, "I have raised thee above all people . . . by virtue of My speaking [unto thee]". A similar directness of experience is alluded to in the opening words of this *sūrah*, "Limitless in His glory is He who transported His servant [Muḥammad] by night . . . so that We might show him some of Our symbols" (see note 2 above; also, Appendix IV). Apart from this, the reference, in this and many other places in the Qurʾān, to the religious history of the Hebrews is due to the fact that the revelations granted to their prophets represent the earliest formulation of monotheism, which makes it ideologically important for its later development.

4 The term *wakīl* denotes "one who is entrusted with the management of [another person's] affairs", or "is responsible for [another person's] conduct". When applied to God, it is sometimes used in the sense of "guardian" (e.g., in 3 : 173), or "defender" (e.g., in 4 : 109), or – in combination with the phrase *ʿalā kulli shayʾin* (as, e.g.,

ذُرِّيَّةَ مَنْ حَمَلْنَا مَعَ نُوحٍ إِنَّهُۥ كَانَ عَبْدًا شَكُورًا ﴿٣﴾ وَقَضَيْنَآ إِلَىٰ
بَنِىٓ إِسْرَٰٓءِيلَ فِى ٱلْكِتَٰبِ لَتُفْسِدُنَّ فِى ٱلْأَرْضِ مَرَّتَيْنِ وَلَتَعْلُنَّ عُلُوًّا
كَبِيرًا ﴿٤﴾ فَإِذَا جَآءَ وَعْدُ أُولَىٰهُمَا بَعَثْنَا عَلَيْكُمْ عِبَادًا لَّنَآ أُو۟لِى بَأْسٍ
شَدِيدٍ فَجَاسُوا۟ خِلَٰلَ ٱلدِّيَارِ ۚ وَكَانَ وَعْدًا مَّفْعُولًا ﴿٥﴾ ثُمَّ رَدَدْنَا لَكُمُ
ٱلْكَرَّةَ عَلَيْهِمْ وَأَمْدَدْنَٰكُم بِأَمْوَٰلٍ وَبَنِينَ وَجَعَلْنَٰكُمْ أَكْثَرَ نَفِيرًا ﴿٦﴾
إِنْ أَحْسَنتُمْ أَحْسَنتُمْ لِأَنفُسِكُمْ ۖ وَإِنْ أَسَأْتُمْ فَلَهَا ۚ فَإِذَا جَآءَ وَعْدُ ٱلْءَاخِرَةِ
لِيَسُـۥٓـُٔوا۟ وُجُوهَكُمْ وَلِيَدْخُلُوا۟ ٱلْمَسْجِدَ كَمَا دَخَلُوهُ أَوَّلَ مَرَّةٍ وَلِيُتَبِّرُوا۟
مَا عَلَوْا۟ تَتْبِيرًا ﴿٧﴾

Dhurriyyata man ḥamalnā maʿa Nūḥin ʾinnahū kāna ʿabdañ-shakūrā. ﴾3﴿ Wa qaḍaynāa ʾilā banīi ʾIsrāaʾīla fil-Kitābi latufsidunna fil-ʾarḍi marratayni wa lataʿlunna ʿuluwwañ-kabīrā. ﴾4﴿ Faʾidhā jāaʾa waʿdu ʾūlāhumā baʿathnā ʿalaykum ʿibādal-lanāa ʾulī baʾsiñ-shadīdiñ-fajāsū khilālad-diyāri wa kāna waʿdam-mafʿūlā. ﴾5﴿ Thumma radadnā lakumul-karrata ʿalayhim wa ʾamdadnākum biʾamwāliñw-wa banīna wa jaʿalnākum ʾakthara nafīrā. ﴾6﴿ ʾIn ʾaḥsañtum ʾaḥsañtum liʾañfusikum; wa ʾin ʾasaʾtum falahā. Faʾidhā jāaʾa waʿdul-ʾākhirati liyasūʾū wujūhakum wa liyadkhulul-Masjida kamā dakhalūhu ʾawwala marratiñw-wa liyutabbirū mā ʿalaw tatbīrā. ﴾7﴿

O you descendants of those whom We caused to be borne [in the ark] with Noah! Behold, he was a most grateful servant [of Ours]!" ﴾3﴿

And we made [this] known to the children of Israel through revelation:[5] "Twice, indeed, will you spread corruption on earth and will indeed become grossly overbearing!"[6] ﴾4﴿

Hence, when the prediction of the first of those two [periods of iniquity] came true, We sent against you some of Our bondmen of terrible prowess in war, and they wrought havoc throughout the land: and so the prediction was fulfilled.[7] ﴾5﴿

And after a time We allowed you to prevail against them once again,[8] and aided you with wealth and offspring, and made you more numerous [than ever]. ﴾6﴿

[And We said:] "If you persevere in doing good, you will but be doing good to yourselves; and if you do evil, it will be [done] to yourselves."

And so, when the prediction of the second [period of your iniquity] came true, [We raised new enemies against you, and allowed them] to disgrace you utterly,[9] and to enter the Temple as [their forerunners] had entered it once before, and to destroy with utter destruction all that they had conquered. ﴾7﴿

---

in 6 : 102 or 11 : 12) – in the sense of "the One who has everything in His care". In the present instance (as well as in 39 : 62) the term evidently alludes to God's exclusive power to *determine the fate* of any created being or thing.

5 Lit., "in the revelation" – here evidently used in the generic sense of the word, and probably applying to predictions contained in the Torah (Leviticus xxvi, 14-39 and Deuteronomy xxviii, 15-68) as well as the prophecies of Isaiah, Jeremiah, John and Jesus.

6 Since both the Bible and the Qurʾān mention that the children of Israel rebelled against the law of God on *many* occasions, there is every reason to assume that the expression "twice" (*marratayn*) does not refer to two single instances but, rather, to two distinct, extended *periods* of their history.

7 The term *ʿibād*, rendered by me above as "bondmen", denotes every kind of "created beings" (in this case, obviously human beings) inasmuch as all of them are, willingly or unwillingly, subservient to God's will (cf. 13 : 15 and the corresponding note 33). It is probable that the phrase "Our bondmen of terrible prowess in war" relates to the Assyrians who overran Palestine in the seventh century B.C. and caused the disappearance of the greater part of the Hebrew nation (the ten "lost tribes"), and to the Babylonians who, about one hundred years later, destroyed Solomon's Temple and carried off the remainder of the children of Israel into captivity, or to both, thus comprising all these events within one "period" (see foregoing note). – God's "sending" tribulations upon reprobate sinners is here, as elsewhere in the Qurʾān, a metonym for the natural law of cause and effect to which, in the long run, the life of man – and particularly the corporate life of nations and communities – is subject.

8 Lit., "We gave back to you the turn against them" – apparently a reference to the return of the Jews from the Babylonian captivity in the last quarter of the sixth century B.C., the partial re-establishment of their state, and the building of a new temple in the place of the one that had been destroyed.

9 Lit., "to bring evil to your faces". Inasmuch as the face is the most prominent and expressive part of the human

Your Sustainer may well show mercy unto you; but if you revert [to sinning], We shall revert [to chastising you]. And [remember this:] We have ordained that [in the hereafter] hell shall close upon all who deny the truth. «8»

VERILY, this Qurʾān shows the way to all that is most upright,[10] and gives the believers who do good deeds the glad tiding that theirs will be a great reward; «9» and [it announces, too,] that We have readied grievous suffering for those who will not believe in the life to come. «10»
As it is,[11] man [often] prays for things that are bad as if he were praying for something that is good:[12] for man is prone to be hasty [in his judgments]. «11»
And We have established the night and the day as two symbols;[13] and thereupon We have effaced the symbol of night and set up [in its place] the light-giving symbol of day,[14] so that you might seek to obtain your Sustainer's bounty and be aware of the passing years[15] and of the reckoning [that is bound to come]. For clearly, most clearly, have We spelt out everything![16] «12»

عَسَىٰ رَبُّكُمْ أَن يَرْحَمَكُمْ وَإِنْ عُدتُّمْ عُدْنَا وَجَعَلْنَا جَهَنَّمَ لِلْكَٰفِرِينَ
حَصِيرًا ﴿٨﴾ إِنَّ هَٰذَا ٱلْقُرْءَانَ يَهْدِى لِلَّتِى هِىَ أَقْوَمُ وَيُبَشِّرُ ٱلْمُؤْمِنِينَ
ٱلَّذِينَ يَعْمَلُونَ ٱلصَّٰلِحَٰتِ أَنَّ لَهُمْ أَجْرًا كَبِيرًا ﴿٩﴾ وَأَنَّ ٱلَّذِينَ لَا
يُؤْمِنُونَ بِٱلْءَاخِرَةِ أَعْتَدْنَا لَهُمْ عَذَابًا أَلِيمًا ﴿١٠﴾ وَيَدْعُ ٱلْإِنسَٰنُ بِٱلشَّرِّ
دُعَآءَهُۥ بِٱلْخَيْرِ ۖ وَكَانَ ٱلْإِنسَٰنُ عَجُولًا ﴿١١﴾ وَجَعَلْنَا ٱلَّيْلَ وَٱلنَّهَارَ
ءَايَتَيْنِ ۖ فَمَحَوْنَآ ءَايَةَ ٱلَّيْلِ وَجَعَلْنَآ ءَايَةَ ٱلنَّهَارِ مُبْصِرَةً لِّتَبْتَغُوا۟ فَضْلًا
مِّن رَّبِّكُمْ وَلِتَعْلَمُوا۟ عَدَدَ ٱلسِّنِينَ وَٱلْحِسَابَ ۚ وَكُلَّ شَىْءٍ فَصَّلْنَٰهُ
تَفْصِيلًا ﴿١٢﴾

ʿAsā Rabbukum ʾañy-yarḥamakum; wa ʾin ʿuttum ʿudnā. Wa jaʿalnā jahannama lilkāfirīna ḥaṣīrā. (8) ʾInna hādhal-Qurʾāna yahdī lillatī hiya ʾaqwamu wa yubashshirul-muʾminīnal-ladhīna yaʿmalūnaṣ-ṣāliḥāti ʾanna lahum ʾajrañ-kabīrā. (9) Wa ʾannal-ladhīna lā yuʾminūna bilʾĀkhirati ʾaʿtadnā lahum ʿadhāban ʾalīmā. (10) Wa yadʿul-ʾIñsānu bishsharri duʿāaʾahū bilkhayri wa kānal-ʾIñsānu ʿajūlā. (11) Wa jaʿalnal-layla wan-nahāra ʾāyatayni famaḥawnāa ʾāyatal-layli wa jaʿalnāa ʾāyatan-nahāri mubṣiratal-litabtaghū faḍlam-mir-Rabbikum wa litaʿlamū ʿadadas-sinīna wal-ḥisāb. Wa kulla shayʾiñ-faṣṣalnāhu tafṣīlā. (12)

---

body, it is often used as a metonym for one's whole being; hence, the "evil done to one's face" is synonymous with "utter disgrace". Most probably, this passage relates to the destruction of the Second Temple and of Jewish statehood by Titus in the year 70 of the Christian era.

10 I.e., conformable to ethical rectitude and beneficial to man's individual and social life. Thus, after showing that sinning is synonymous with denying the truth, the discourse returns to the fundamental theme of the Qurʾān, already alluded to in verse 2 of this *sūrah*: namely, the statement that God always offers guidance to man through the revelations which He bestows upon His prophets.

11 This, to my mind, is the meaning of the conjunctive particle *wa* in the above context.

12 Cf. 2 : 216 – "it may well be that you hate a thing the while it is good for you, and it may well be that you love a thing the while it is bad for you: and God knows, whereas you do not know": in other words, divine guidance is the only objective criterion as to what is good and what is bad.

13 Regarding the primary meaning of the term *āyah*, see note 2 above. In the present context, the expression *āyatayn* ("two symbols") refers – as the subsequent clause shows – to the symbols of spiritual darkness and light.

14 I.e., the message of the Qurʾān, which is meant to lead man out of spiritual ignorance and error into the light of faith and reason.

15 Lit., "the count (*ʿadad*) of years". Since, as the *Qāmūs* points out, this phrase denotes also "the years of [a person's] life, which he counts", it obviously implies here a call to spiritual self-criticism in view of the ephemeral nature of one's worldly life.

16 I.e., everything that man may be in need of in the domain of ethics and religion.

وَكُلَّ إِنسَـٰنٍ أَلْزَمْنَـٰهُ طَـٰٓئِرَهُۥ فِى عُنُقِهِۦ ۖ وَنُخْرِجُ لَهُۥ يَوْمَ ٱلْقِيَـٰمَةِ كِتَـٰبًا
يَلْقَىٰهُ مَنشُورًا ﴿١٣﴾ ٱقْرَأْ كِتَـٰبَكَ كَفَىٰ بِنَفْسِكَ ٱلْيَوْمَ عَلَيْكَ حَسِيبًا ﴿١٤﴾
مَّنِ ٱهْتَدَىٰ فَإِنَّمَا يَهْتَدِى لِنَفْسِهِۦ ۖ وَمَن ضَلَّ فَإِنَّمَا يَضِلُّ عَلَيْهَا ۚ وَلَا تَزِرُ
وَازِرَةٌ وِزْرَ أُخْرَىٰ ۗ وَمَا كُنَّا مُعَذِّبِينَ حَتَّىٰ نَبْعَثَ رَسُولًا ﴿١٥﴾ وَإِذَآ
أَرَدْنَآ أَن نُّهْلِكَ قَرْيَةً أَمَرْنَا مُتْرَفِيهَا فَفَسَقُوا۟ فِيهَا فَحَقَّ عَلَيْهَا ٱلْقَوْلُ
فَدَمَّرْنَـٰهَا تَدْمِيرًا ﴿١٦﴾ وَكَمْ أَهْلَكْنَا مِنَ ٱلْقُرُونِ مِنۢ بَعْدِ نُوحٍ ۗ وَكَفَىٰ
بِرَبِّكَ بِذُنُوبِ عِبَادِهِۦ خَبِيرًۢا بَصِيرًا ﴿١٧﴾

Wa kulla ʾIñsānin ʾalzamnāhu ṭāaʾirahū fī ʿunuqih. Wa nukhriju lahū Yawmal-Qiyāmati kitābañy-yalqāhu mañshūrā. ⟨13⟩ ʾIqraʾ kitābaka kafā binafsikal-Yawma ʿalayka ḥasībā. ⟨14⟩ Manih-tadā faʾinnamā yahtadī li-nafsihi wa mañ-ḍalla faʾinnamā yaḍillu ʿalayhā. Wa lā taziru wāziratuñw-wizra ʾukhrā. Wa mā kunnā muʿadhdhibīna ḥattā nabʿatha Rasūlā. ⟨15⟩ Wa ʾidhāa ʾaradnāa ʾañ-nuhlika qaryatan ʾamarnā mutrafīhā fafasaqū fīhā faḥaqqa ʿalayhal-qawlu fadammarnāhā tadmīrā. ⟨16⟩ Wa kam ʾahlaknā minal-qurūni mim-baʿdi Nūḥ. Wa kafā biRabbika bidhunūbi ʿibādihī Khabiram-Baṣīrā. ⟨17⟩

And every human being's destiny have We tied to his neck;[17] and on the Day of Resurrection We shall bring forth for him a record which he will find wide open; «13» [and he will be told:] "Read this thy record! Sufficient is thine own self today to make out thine account!"[18] «14»

Whoever chooses to follow the right path, follows it but for his own good; and whoever goes astray, goes but astray to his own hurt; and no bearer of burdens shall be made to bear another's burden.[19] Moreover, We would never chastise [any community for the wrong they may do] ere We have sent an apostle [to them].[20] «15»

But when [this has been done, and] it is Our will to destroy a community, We convey Our last warning[21] to those of its people who have lost themselves entirely in the pursuit of pleasures;[22] and [if] they [continue to] act sinfully, the sentence [of doom] passed on the community takes effect, and We break it to smithereens. «16»

And how many a generation have We [thus] destroyed after [the time of] Noah! For, none has the like of thy Sustainer's awareness and insight into His creatures' sins. «17»

---

17 The word *ṭāʾir* literally signifies a "bird" or, more properly, a "flying creature". Since the pre-Islamic Arabs often endeavoured to establish a good or bad omen and, in general, to foretell the future from the manner and direction in which birds would fly, the term *ṭāʾir* came to be tropically used in the sense of "fortune", both good and evil, or "destiny". (See in this connection *sūrah* 3, note 37, and *sūrah* 7, note 95.) It should, however, be borne in mind that the Qurʾanic concept of "destiny" relates not so much to the external circumstances of and events in man's life as, rather, to the *direction* which this life takes in result of one's moral choices: in other words, it relates to man's *spiritual* fate – and this, in its turn, depends – as the Qurʾān so often points out – on a person's inclinations, attitudes and conscious actions (including self-restraint from morally bad actions or, alternatively, a deliberate omission of good actions). Hence, man's spiritual fate depends on *himself* and is inseparably linked with the whole tenor of his personality; and since it is God who has made man responsible for his behaviour on earth, He speaks of Himself as having "tied every human being's destiny to his neck".

18 The "record" and the subsequent "account" represent man's total comprehension, on Judgment Day, of all his past life (Rāzī). This allegory occurs in the Qurʾān in many formulations, e.g., in 37 : 19 or 39 : 68, and perhaps most incisively in 50 : 22 – "now We have lifted from thee thy veil, and sharp is thy sight today!"

19 See 6 : 164, 35 : 18 and 39 : 7, as well as the corresponding notes; also 53 : 38, which represents the earliest Qurʾanic statement of this fundamental principle of ethics.

20 Sc., "so that they might fully understand the meaning of right and wrong": cf. 6 : 131-132 and the corresponding note 117, as well as 28 : 59 (which, in the chronology of revelation, immediately precedes the present *sūrah*).

21 Lit., "Our command", i.e., to mend their ways. The term *qaryah* (lit., "town") denotes usually – though not always – a "community" or "people of a community".

22 I.e., to the exclusion of all moral considerations. (For the above rendering of the expression *mutraf*, see *sūrah* 11, note 147.) The people referred to here are those who, by virtue of their wealth and social position, embody the real leadership of their community and are, therefore, morally responsible for the behaviour of their followers.

مَّن كَانَ يُرِيدُ ٱلۡعَاجِلَةَ عَجَّلۡنَا لَهُۥ فِيهَا مَا نَشَآءُ لِمَن نُّرِيدُ ثُمَّ جَعَلۡنَا لَهُۥ
جَهَنَّمَ يَصۡلَىٰهَا مَذۡمُومٗا مَّدۡحُورٗا ﴿١٨﴾ وَمَنۡ أَرَادَ ٱلۡأٓخِرَةَ وَسَعَىٰ لَهَا
سَعۡيَهَا وَهُوَ مُؤۡمِنٞ فَأُوْلَٰٓئِكَ كَانَ سَعۡيُهُم مَّشۡكُورٗا ﴿١٩﴾ كُلّٗا نُّمِدُّ
هَٰٓؤُلَآءِ وَهَٰٓؤُلَآءِ مِنۡ عَطَآءِ رَبِّكَۚ وَمَا كَانَ عَطَآءُ رَبِّكَ مَحۡظُورًا ﴿٢٠﴾
ٱنظُرۡ كَيۡفَ فَضَّلۡنَا بَعۡضَهُمۡ عَلَىٰ بَعۡضٖۚ وَلَلۡأٓخِرَةُ أَكۡبَرُ دَرَجَٰتٖ وَأَكۡبَرُ
تَفۡضِيلٗا ﴿٢١﴾ لَّا تَجۡعَلۡ مَعَ ٱللَّهِ إِلَٰهًا ءَاخَرَ فَتَقۡعُدَ مَذۡمُومٗا مَّخۡذُولٗا ﴿٢٢﴾
۞ وَقَضَىٰ رَبُّكَ أَلَّا تَعۡبُدُوٓاْ إِلَّآ إِيَّاهُ وَبِٱلۡوَٰلِدَيۡنِ إِحۡسَٰنًاۚ إِمَّا يَبۡلُغَنَّ
عِندَكَ ٱلۡكِبَرَ أَحَدُهُمَآ أَوۡ كِلَاهُمَا فَلَا تَقُل لَّهُمَآ أُفّٖ وَلَا تَنۡهَرۡهُمَا وَقُل
لَّهُمَا قَوۡلٗا كَرِيمٗا ﴿٢٣﴾ وَٱخۡفِضۡ لَهُمَا جَنَاحَ ٱلذُّلِّ مِنَ ٱلرَّحۡمَةِ وَقُل رَّبِّ

ربع الحزب

Mañ-kāna yurīdul-ᶜājilata ᶜajjalnā lahū fīhā mā nashāaᵓu limañ-nurīdu thumma jaᶜalnā lahū jahannama yaṣlāhā madhmūmam-madḥūrā. (18) Wa man ᵓarādal-ᵓĀkhirata wa saᶜā lahā saᶜyahā wa huwa muᵓminuñ-faᵓulāaᵓika kāna saᶜyuhum-mashkūrā. (19) Kullañ-numiddu hāaᵓulāaᵓi wa hāaᵓulāaᵓi min ᶜaṭāaᵓi Rabbik. Wa mā kāna ᶜaṭāaᵓu Rabbika maḥẓūrā. (20) ᵓUñẓur kayfa faḍḍalnā baᶜḍahum ᶜalā baᶜḍ. Wa lalᵓĀkhiratu ᵓakbaru darajātiñw-wa ᵓakbaru tafḍīlā. (21) Lā tajᶜal maᶜal-lāhi ᵓilāhan ᵓākhara fataqᶜuda madhmūmam-makhdhūlā. (22) ۞ Wa qaḍā Rabbuka ᵓallā taᶜbudūu ᵓillāa ᵓIyyāhu wa bilwālidayni ᵓiḥsānā. ᵓImmā yablughanna ᶜiñdakal-kibara ᵓaḥaduhumāa ᵓaw kilāhumā falā taqul-lahumāa ᵓuffiñw-wa lā tanharhumā wa qul-lahumā qawlañ-karīmā. (23) Wakh-fiḍ lahumā janāḥadh-dhulli minar-raḥmati wa qur-Rabbir-

Unto him who cares for [no more than the enjoyment of] this fleeting life We readily grant thereof as much as We please, [giving] to whomever it is Our will [to give]; but in the end We consign him to [the suffering of] hell,[23] which he will have to endure disgraced and disowned! ‹18›
But as for those who care for the [good of the] life to come, and strive for it as it ought to be striven for, and are [true] believers withal[24] – they are the ones whose striving finds favour [with God]! ‹19›
All [of them] – these as well as those – do We freely endow with some of thy Sustainer's gifts, since thy Sustainer's giving is never confined [to one kind of man]. ‹20› Behold how We bestow [on earth] more bounty on some of them than on others: but [remember that] the life to come will be far higher in degree and far greater in merit and bounty.[25] ‹21›

DO NOT set up any other deity side by side with God lest thou find thyself disgraced and forsaken: ‹22› for thy Sustainer has ordained that you shall worship none but Him.
And do good unto [thy] parents.[26] Should one of them, or both, attain to old age in thy care, never say "Ugh"[27] to them or scold them, but [always] speak unto them with reverent speech, ‹23› and spread over them humbly the wings of thy tenderness,[28] and say: "O my Sustainer!

23 Lit., "We assign [or "shall assign"] hell to him".

24 Since caring and striving for the good of the hereafter *presupposes* belief in God and in man's responsibility before Him, it is obvious that the term "believer" relates, in this context, to a cognition of God's absolute oneness and uniqueness as well as to a willing acceptance of the guidance offered to man through prophetic revelation. – In the original, the whole preceding sentence has the singular form ("he who cares . . . and strives . . . and is a believer"); but in view of the next clause, which is expressed in the plural, it is preferable to render these pronouns, agreeably with Arabic usage, uniformly in the plural.

25 Lit., "greater in degrees and greater in the bestowal of bounty (*tafḍīlan*)" – but since the latter term obviously comprises, in this instance, the concept of "merit" as well, a composite rendering would seem to be indicated.

26 Whereas God is the real, ultimate cause of man's coming to life, his parents are its outward, immediate cause: and so the preceding call to God is followed by the injunction to honour and cherish one's parents. Beyond this, the whole of the present passage – up to and including verse 39 – is meant to show that kindness and just dealings between man and man are an integral part of the concept of "striving for the good of the life to come".

27 In Arabic, *uff* – a word or sound indicative of contempt, dislike or disgust.

28 Lit., "lower for them the wing of humility, out of tenderness (*raḥmah*)" – a metonymical expression evocative of a bird that lovingly spreads its wings over its offspring in the nest.

Bestow Thy grace upon them, even as they cherished and reared me when I was a child!" «24»
Your Sustainer is fully aware of what is in your hearts. If you are righteous, [He will forgive you your errors]:[29] for, behold, He is much-forgiving to those who turn unto Him again and again. «25»
And give his due to the near of kin,[30] as well as to the needy and the wayfarer,[31] but do not squander [thy substance] senselessly.[32] «26» Behold, the squanderers are, indeed, of the ilk of the satans – inasmuch as Satan has indeed proved most ungrateful to his Sustainer.[33] «27»
And if thou [must] turn aside from those [that are in want, because thou thyself art] seeking to obtain thy Sustainer's grace and hoping for it,[34] at least speak unto them with gentle speech. «28»
And neither allow thy hand to remain shackled to thy neck,[35] nor stretch it forth to the utmost limit [of thy capacity], lest thou find thyself blamed [by thy dependants], or even destitute. «29» Behold, thy Sustainer grants abundant sustenance, or gives it in scant measure, unto whomever He wills: verily, fully aware is He of [the needs of] His creatures, and sees them all. «30»
Hence, do not kill your children for fear of poverty:[36] it is We who shall provide sustenance for them as well as for you. Verily, killing them is a great sin. «31»

ٱرْحَمْهُمَا كَمَا رَبَّيَانِى صَغِيرًا ﴿٢٤﴾ رَّبُّكُمْ أَعْلَمُ بِمَا فِى نُفُوسِكُمْ إِن
تَكُونُوا۟ صَٰلِحِينَ فَإِنَّهُۥ كَانَ لِلْأَوَّٰبِينَ غَفُورًا ﴿٢٥﴾ وَءَاتِ ذَا ٱلْقُرْبَىٰ
حَقَّهُۥ وَٱلْمِسْكِينَ وَٱبْنَ ٱلسَّبِيلِ وَلَا تُبَذِّرْ تَبْذِيرًا ﴿٢٦﴾ إِنَّ ٱلْمُبَذِّرِينَ
كَانُوٓا۟ إِخْوَٰنَ ٱلشَّيَٰطِينِ وَكَانَ ٱلشَّيْطَٰنُ لِرَبِّهِۦ كَفُورًا ﴿٢٧﴾ وَإِمَّا
تُعْرِضَنَّ عَنْهُمُ ٱبْتِغَآءَ رَحْمَةٍ مِّن رَّبِّكَ تَرْجُوهَا فَقُل لَّهُمْ قَوْلًا
مَّيْسُورًا ﴿٢٨﴾ وَلَا تَجْعَلْ يَدَكَ مَغْلُولَةً إِلَىٰ عُنُقِكَ وَلَا تَبْسُطْهَا كُلَّ
ٱلْبَسْطِ فَتَقْعُدَ مَلُومًا مَّحْسُورًا ﴿٢٩﴾ إِنَّ رَبَّكَ يَبْسُطُ ٱلرِّزْقَ لِمَن يَشَآءُ
وَيَقْدِرُ إِنَّهُۥ كَانَ بِعِبَادِهِۦ خَبِيرًۢا بَصِيرًا ﴿٣٠﴾ وَلَا تَقْتُلُوٓا۟ أَوْلَٰدَكُمْ
خَشْيَةَ إِمْلَٰقٍ نَّحْنُ نَرْزُقُهُمْ وَإِيَّاكُمْ إِنَّ قَتْلَهُمْ كَانَ خِطْـًٔا كَبِيرًا ﴿٣١﴾

ḥamhumā kamā rabbayānī ṣaghīrā. (24) Rabbukum ʾaʿlamu bimā fī nufūsikum. ʾIñ-takūnū ṣāliḥīna faʾinnahū kāna lilʾawwābīna Ghafūrā. (25) Wa ʾāti dhal-qurbā ḥaqqahū wal-miskīna wab-nas-sabīli wa lā tubadhdhir tabdhīrā. (26) ʾInnal-mubadhdhirīna kānūu ʾikhwānash-Shayāṭīni wa kānash-Shayṭānu li-Rabbihī kafūrā. (27) Wa ʾimmā tuʿriḍanna ʿanhumub-tighāaʾa raḥmatim-mir-Rabbika tarjūhā faqul-lahum qawlam-maysūrā. (28) Wa lā tajʿal yadaka maghlūlatan ʾilā ʿunuqika wa lā tabsuṭhā kullal-basṭi fataqʿuda malūmam-maḥsūrā. (29) ʾInna Rabbaka yabsuṭur-rizqa limañy-yashāaʾu wa yaqdir. ʾInnahū kāna biʿibādihī Khabīram-Baṣīrā. (30) Wa lā taqtulūu ʾawlādakum khashyata ʾimlāqiñ-Naḥnu narzuquhum wa ʾiyyākum. ʾInna qatlahum kāna khiṭʾañ-kabīrā. (31)

29 This interpolation gives the meaning of the above elliptic sentence (Ṭabarī, Baghawī, Zamakhsharī, Rāzī).

30 In this instance, "his due" evidently refers to the loving consideration due to one's relatives (Zamakhsharī and Rāzī); those of them who are in a state of want are included in the subsequent mention of "the needy" (*al-miskīn*).

31 Regarding this expression, see *sūrah* 2, note 145.

32 Lit., "with [utter] squandering" (*tabdhīran*), i.e., senselessly and to no good purpose. It is to be borne in mind that the term *tabdhīr* does not relate to the quantity but, rather, to the purpose of one's spending. Thus, Ibn ʿAbbās and Ibn Masʿūd (both of them quoted by Ṭabarī) defined *tabdhīr* as "spending without a righteous purpose" or "in a frivolous (*bāṭil*) cause": and Mujāhid is reported (*ibid.*) to have said, "if a man were to spend all that he possesses in a righteous cause, it could not be termed squandering; but if he spends even a small amount in a frivolous cause, it is squandering."

33 Since squandering – in the sense explained in the preceding note – implies an utter lack of gratitude for the gift of sustenance bestowed by God upon man, the squanderers are described as being "of the ilk [lit., "brethren"] of the satans". Regarding the deeper meaning of the terms "satans" and "satanic", see *sūrah* 15, note 16.

34 I.e., "because thou art thyself in want, and therefore unable to help others".

35 A metaphor signifying miserliness and, in particular, unwillingness to help others (cf. a similar expression in 5 : 64).

36 Historically, this may be a reference to the pre-Islamic Arabian custom of burying unwanted female children alive (see note 4 on 81 : 8-9), as well as to the occasional – though much rarer – sacrifices of male children to some

And do not commit adultery[37] – for, behold, it is an abomination and an evil way. «32»

And do not take any human being's life – [the life] which God has willed to be sacred – otherwise than in [the pursuit of] justice.[38] Hence, if anyone has been slain wrongfully, We have empowered the defender of his rights [to exact a just retribution];[39] but even so, let him not exceed the bounds of equity in [retributive] killing.[40] [And as for him who has been slain wrongfully –] behold, he is indeed succoured [by God]![41] «33»

And do not touch the substance of an orphan, save to improve it, before he comes of age.[42]

And be true to every promise – for, verily, [on Judgment Day] you will be called to account for every promise which you have made![43] «34»

And give full measure whenever you measure, and weigh with a balance that is true:[44] this will be [for your own] good, and best in the end. «35»

وَلَا تَقْرَبُوا۟ ٱلزِّنَىٰٓ ۖ إِنَّهُۥ كَانَ فَٰحِشَةً وَسَآءَ سَبِيلًا ﴿٣٢﴾ وَلَا تَقْتُلُوا۟
ٱلنَّفْسَ ٱلَّتِى حَرَّمَ ٱللَّهُ إِلَّا بِٱلْحَقِّ ۗ وَمَن قُتِلَ مَظْلُومًا فَقَدْ جَعَلْنَا لِوَلِيِّهِۦ
سُلْطَٰنًا فَلَا يُسْرِف فِّى ٱلْقَتْلِ ۖ إِنَّهُۥ كَانَ مَنصُورًا ﴿٣٣﴾ وَلَا تَقْرَبُوا۟ مَالَ
ٱلْيَتِيمِ إِلَّا بِٱلَّتِى هِىَ أَحْسَنُ حَتَّىٰ يَبْلُغَ أَشُدَّهُۥ ۚ وَأَوْفُوا۟ بِٱلْعَهْدِ ۖ إِنَّ ٱلْعَهْدَ
كَانَ مَسْـُٔولًا ﴿٣٤﴾ وَأَوْفُوا۟ ٱلْكَيْلَ إِذَا كِلْتُمْ وَزِنُوا۟ بِٱلْقِسْطَاسِ ٱلْمُسْتَقِيمِ ۚ
ذَٰلِكَ خَيْرٌ وَأَحْسَنُ تَأْوِيلًا ﴿٣٥﴾

Wa lā taqrabuz-zināa ʾinnahū kāna fāḥishatañw-wa sāaʾa sabīlā. (32) Wa lā taqtulun-nafsal-latī ḥarramal-lāhu ʾillā bilḥaqq. Wa mañ-qutila maẓlūmañ-faqad jaʿalnā liwaliyyihī sulṭānañ-falā yusrif-fil-qatli ʾinnahū kāna mañṣūrā. (33) Wa lā taqrabū mālal-yatīmi ʾillā billatī hiya ʾaḥsanu ḥattā yablugha ʾashuddah. Wa ʾawfū bilʿahdi ʾinnal-ʿahda kāna masʾūlā. (34) Wa ʾawful-kayla ʾidhā kiltum wa zinū bilqisṭāsil-mustaqīmi dhālika khayruñw-wa ʾaḥsanu taʾwīlā. (35)

of their gods (see Zamakhsharī's comments on 6 : 137). Beyond this, however, the above prohibition has a timeless validity inasmuch as it relates also to abortions undertaken "for fear of poverty", i.e., on purely economic grounds.

37 Lit., "do not come near adultery", thus intensifying the prohibition. It is to be noted that the term *zinā* signifies all sexual intercourse between a man and a woman who are not husband and wife, irrespective of whether either of them is married to another partner or not; hence, it denotes both "adultery" and "fornication" in the English senses of these terms.

38 I.e., in the execution of a legal sentence or in a just war (see 2 : 190 and the corresponding note 167), or in individual, legitimate self-defence.

39 This refers to the legal punishment for homicide, termed *qiṣāṣ* ("just retribution") and explained in 2 : 178 and the corresponding notes. In the present context, the term *walī* ("protector" or "defender of [one's] rights") is usually taken to mean the heir or next of kin of the victim; Zamakhsharī, however, observes that it may also apply to the government (*as-sulṭān*): an interpretation which is obviously based on the concept of the government as the "protector" or "defender of the rights" of all its citizens. As regards the expression *qutila maẓlūman* ("slain wrongfully"), it is obvious that it refers only to cases of wilful homicide, since the concept of *ẓulm* applies in the Qurʾān exclusively to intentional and never to accidental wrongdoing.

40 Thus, the defender of the victim's rights (in this case, a court of justice) is not only not entitled to impose a capital sentence on any but the *actual* murderer or murderers, but may also, if the case warrants it, concede mitigating circumstances and refrain from capital punishment altogether.

41 I.e., he is avenged in this world by the retribution exacted from his murderer, and in the life to come, blessed by the special grace which God bestows on all who have been slain without any legal or moral justification (Rāzī). Some of the commentators, however, relate the pronoun "he" to the defender of the victim's rights, respectively, to the latter's heir or next of kin, and explain the above phrase as meaning "he is sufficiently helped by the law of just retribution (*qiṣāṣ*) and should not, therefore, demand any punishment in excess of what is equitable".

42 See *sūrah* 6, note 149.

43 Lit., "every promise shall be asked about" or "investigated".

44 Lit., "straight" (*mustaqīm*) – a term which in the Qurʾān has invariably a spiritual or moral connotation. Hence, as in the similar phrase in 6 : 152, the above injunction applies not merely to commercial transactions but to all dealings between man and man.

And never concern thyself with anything of which thou hast no knowledge:[45] verily, [thy] hearing and sight and heart – all of them – will be called to account for it [on Judgment Day]! ‹36›

And walk not on earth with haughty self-conceit: for, verily, thou canst never rend the earth asunder, nor canst thou ever grow as tall as the mountains! ‹37›

The evil of all this is odious in thy Sustainer's sight:[46] ‹38› this is part of that knowledge of right and wrong with which thy Sustainer has inspired thee.[47]

Hence, do not set up any other deity side by side with God,[48] lest thou be cast into hell, blamed [by thyself] and rejected [by Him]! ‹39›

HAS, THEN, your Sustainer distinguished you by [giving you] sons, and taken unto Himself daughters in the guise of angels?[49] Verily, you are uttering a dreadful saying! ‹40›

And, indeed, many facets have We given [to Our message] in this Qurʾān, so that they [who deny the truth] might take it to heart: but all this only increases their aversion. ‹41›

وَلَا تَقْفُ مَا لَيْسَ لَكَ بِهِۦ عِلْمٌ ۚ إِنَّ ٱلسَّمْعَ وَٱلْبَصَرَ وَٱلْفُؤَادَ كُلُّ
أُو۟لَـٰٓئِكَ كَانَ عَنْهُ مَسْـُٔولًا ﴿٣٦﴾ وَلَا تَمْشِ فِى ٱلْأَرْضِ مَرَحًا ۖ إِنَّكَ لَن
تَخْرِقَ ٱلْأَرْضَ وَلَن تَبْلُغَ ٱلْجِبَالَ طُولًا ﴿٣٧﴾ كُلُّ ذَٰلِكَ كَانَ سَيِّئُهُۥ
عِندَ رَبِّكَ مَكْرُوهًا ﴿٣٨﴾ ذَٰلِكَ مِمَّآ أَوْحَىٰٓ إِلَيْكَ رَبُّكَ مِنَ ٱلْحِكْمَةِ ۗ
وَلَا تَجْعَلْ مَعَ ٱللَّهِ إِلَـٰهًا ءَاخَرَ فَتُلْقَىٰ فِى جَهَنَّمَ مَلُومًا مَّدْحُورًا ﴿٣٩﴾
أَفَأَصْفَىٰكُمْ رَبُّكُم بِٱلْبَنِينَ وَٱتَّخَذَ مِنَ ٱلْمَلَـٰٓئِكَةِ إِنَـٰثًا ۚ إِنَّكُمْ لَتَقُولُونَ
قَوْلًا عَظِيمًا ﴿٤٠﴾ وَلَقَدْ صَرَّفْنَا فِى هَـٰذَا ٱلْقُرْءَانِ لِيَذَّكَّرُوا۟ وَمَا يَزِيدُهُمْ
إِلَّا نُفُورًا ﴿٤١﴾

Wa lā taqfu mā laysa laka bihī ʿilm. ʾInnas-samʿa wal-baṣara wal-fuʾāda kullu ʾulāaʾika kāna ʿanhu masʾūlā. (36) Wa lā tamshi fil-ʾarḍi maraḥan ʾinnaka lañ-takhriqal-ʾarḍa wa lañ-tablughal-jibāla ṭūlā. (37) Kullu dhālika kāna sayyiʾuhū ʿiñda Rabbika makrūhā. (38) Dhālika mimmāa ʾawḥāa ʾilayka Rabbuka minal-ḥikmah. Wa lā tajʿal maʿal-lāhi ʾilāhan ʾākhara fatulqā fī jahannama malūmam-madḥūrā. (39) ʾAfaʾaṣfākum Rabbukum-bilbanīna wat-takhadha minal-Malāaʾikati ʾināthā. ʾInnakum lataqūlūna qawlan ʿaẓīmā. (40) Wa laqad ṣarrafnā fī hādhal-Qurʾāni liyadhdhakkarū wa mā yazīduhum ʾillā nufūrā. (41)

45 Or: "do not follow [or "pursue"] anything . . .", etc. This would seem to relate to groundless assertions about events or people (and hence to slander or false testimony), to statements based on guesswork unsupported by evidence, or to interfering in social situations which one is unable to evaluate correctly.

46 According to some commentators, this condemnation refers to what has been mentioned in the preceding two verses; more probably, however, it extends to the subject-matter of all the prohibitions – whether enunciated as such or merely implied – in verses 22-37.

47 Or: "which thy Sustainer has revealed to thee". It is to be noted that the noun *ḥikmah*, usually signifying "wisdom", is derived from the verb *ḥakama* ("he prevented or "restrained [him or it]", i.e., from acting in an undesirable manner). Hence, the primary meaning of *ḥikmah*, is "that which prevents one from evil or ignorant behaviour" (cf. Lane II, 617); in its positive sense, it signifies "[conscious] insight into that which is most excellent" (*Lisān al-ʿArab, Tāj al-ʿArūs*). Inasmuch as this term refers here, in particular, to what is "odious in God's sight", it implies moral discrimination (or "the knowledge of right and wrong") on the part of men; and this, in its turn, presupposes the existence of an absolute, God-willed standard of moral values.

48 Since there is no basis for an acceptance of absolute moral values – i.e., values that are independent of time and social circumstances – without a belief in God and His ultimate judgment, the passage ends, as it began, with a call to a cognition of God's oneness and uniqueness.

49 Lit., "and taken unto Himself, out of the angels, females": an allusion to the pre-Islamic Arabian belief that the angels – conceived of as a kind of female sub-deities – were God's "daughters", and this despite the pagan Arabs' contempt for female offspring (cf. 16 : 57-59 and the corresponding notes). In its wider implication, this rhetorical question is meant to bring out the absurdity of the supposition that God's divinity could be projected into, or shared by, any other being (cf. 6 : 100-101).

Say: "If there were – as some people assert – [other] deities side by side with Him, surely [even] they would have to strive to find a way unto Him who is enthroned on His almightiness?"[50] ‹42›
Limitless is He in His glory, and sublimely, immeasurably exalted above anything that men may say [about Him]![51] ‹43›
The seven heavens[52] extol His limitless glory, and the earth, and all that they contain; and there is not a single thing but extols His limitless glory and praise: but you [O men] fail to grasp the manner of their glorifying Him![53] Verily, He is forbearing, much-forgiving! ‹44›
But [thus it is:][54] whenever thou recitest the Qurʾān, We place an invisible barrier between thee and those who will not believe in the life to come: ‹45› for, over their hearts We have laid veils which prevent them from grasping its purport, and into their ears, deafness.[55] And so, whenever thou dost mention, while reciting the Qurʾān, thy Sustainer as the one and only Divine Being,[56] they turn their backs [upon thee] in aversion. ‹46›

قُل لَّوْ كَانَ مَعَهُۥٓ ءَالِهَةٌ كَمَا يَقُولُونَ إِذًا لَّٱبْتَغَوْا۟ إِلَىٰ ذِى ٱلْعَرْشِ
سَبِيلًا ﴿٤٢﴾ سُبْحَٰنَهُۥ وَتَعَٰلَىٰ عَمَّا يَقُولُونَ عُلُوًّا كَبِيرًا ﴿٤٣﴾ تُسَبِّحُ لَهُ
ٱلسَّمَٰوَٰتُ ٱلسَّبْعُ وَٱلْأَرْضُ وَمَن فِيهِنَّ ۚ وَإِن مِّن شَىْءٍ إِلَّا يُسَبِّحُ
بِحَمْدِهِۦ وَلَٰكِن لَّا تَفْقَهُونَ تَسْبِيحَهُمْ ۗ إِنَّهُۥ كَانَ حَلِيمًا غَفُورًا ﴿٤٤﴾
وَإِذَا قَرَأْتَ ٱلْقُرْءَانَ جَعَلْنَا بَيْنَكَ وَبَيْنَ ٱلَّذِينَ لَا يُؤْمِنُونَ بِٱلْءَاخِرَةِ
حِجَابًا مَّسْتُورًا ﴿٤٥﴾ وَجَعَلْنَا عَلَىٰ قُلُوبِهِمْ أَكِنَّةً أَن يَفْقَهُوهُ وَفِىٓ ءَاذَانِهِمْ
وَقْرًا ۚ وَإِذَا ذَكَرْتَ رَبَّكَ فِى ٱلْقُرْءَانِ وَحْدَهُۥ وَلَّوْا۟ عَلَىٰٓ أَدْبَٰرِهِمْ
نُفُورًا ﴿٤٦﴾

Qul-law kāna maʿahūu ʾālihatuñ-kamā yaqūlūna ʾidhal-labtaghaw ʾilā Dhil-ʿarshi sabīlā. ⟨42⟩ Subḥānahū wa taʿālā ʿammā yaqūlūna ʿuluwwañ-kabīrā. ⟨43⟩ Tusabbiḥu lahus-samāwātus-sabʿu wal-ʾarḍu wa mañ-fīhinn. Wa ʾim-miñ-shayʾin ʾillā yusabbiḥu biḥamdihī wa lākil-lā tafqahūna tasbīḥahum; ʾinnahū kāna Ḥalīman Ghafūrā. ⟨44⟩ Wa ʾidhā qaraʾtal-Qurʾāna jaʿalnā baynaka wa baynal-ladhīna lā yuʾminūna bilʾĀkhirati ḥijābam-mastūrā. ⟨45⟩ Wa jaʿalnā ʿalā qulūbihim ʾakinnatan ʾañy-yafqahūhu wa fīi ʾādhānihim waqrā. Wa ʾidhā dhakarta Rabbaka fil-Qurʾāni Waḥdahū wallaw ʿalāa ʾadbārihim nufūrā. ⟨46⟩

50 The term *ʿarsh* (lit., "throne" or, more properly, "seat of power") is used in the Qurʾān to denote God's absolute sway over all that exists; hence, the expression *dhu 'l-ʿarsh* may be suitably rendered as "He who is enthroned in His almightiness". Beyond this, the commentators are not entirely agreed as to the purport of the above sentence. Some take it to mean that "had there been other deities apart from God, they would endeavour to deprive Him of some or all of His power, and would thus create chaos in the universe". Others – and most prominently among them Ṭabarī and Ibn Kathīr – have a far better, though somewhat more complicated explanation to offer. Starting from the legitimate assumption that those who believe in the existence of other deities or divine powers apart from God regard them as no more than *mediators* between man and Him, the argument runs thus: If those alleged divine or semi-divine "mediators" would really exist, then it is obvious that, being no more than mediators, even they would have to recognize Him as the Supreme Being – which would amount to admitting that they have no power of their own but are, in the last resort, entirely dependent on and subject to Him: and this unavoidable conclusion implies a negation of any divinity in those imaginary "mediators". This being so, is it not far more reasonable for man to turn *directly* to God, who is almighty, all-seeing, all-hearing, and has therefore no need of any mediator?

51 See *sūrah* 6, note 88.

52 For an explanation of this expression, see *sūrah* 2, note 20.

53 I.e., although everything in creation bears witness to the existence of a conscious Creative Will, man is only too often blind and deaf to this overwhelming evidence of God's ever-present almightiness.

54 This passage connects with verse 41 above.

55 Cf. 6 : 25. See also 2 : 7 and the corresponding note.

56 Lit., "whenever thou dost mention in the Qurʾān thy Sustainer alone".

نصف الحزب

We are fully aware of what they are listening for when they listen to thee:[57] for when they are secluded among themselves, lo! these wrongdoers say [unto one another], "If you were to follow Muḥammad, you would follow] only a man bewitched"' ‹47›

See to what they liken thee, [O Prophet, simply] because they have gone astray and are now unable to find a way [to the truth]! ‹48›

And [thus, too,] they say, "After we will have become bones and dust, shall we, forsooth, be raised from the dead in a new act of creation?" ‹49›

Say: "[You will be raised from the dead even though] you be stones or iron ‹50› or any [other] substance which, to your minds, appears yet farther removed [from life]!"[58]

And [if] thereupon they ask, "Who is it that will bring us back [to life]?" – say thou: "He who has brought you into being in the first instance."

And [if] thereupon they shake their heads at thee [in disbelief] and ask, "When shall this be?" – say thou: "It may well be soon, ‹51› on a Day when He will call you, and you will answer by praising Him, thinking all the while that you have tarried [on earth] but a little while."[59] ‹52›

AND TELL My servants that they should speak in the most kindly manner [unto those who do not share their beliefs]:[60] verily, Satan is always ready to stir up discord between men[61] – for, verily, Satan is man's open foe! ‹53›

نَّحْنُ أَعْلَمُ بِمَا يَسْتَمِعُونَ بِهِۦٓ إِذْ يَسْتَمِعُونَ إِلَيْكَ وَإِذْ هُمْ نَجْوَىٰٓ إِذْ
يَقُولُ ٱلظَّٰلِمُونَ إِن تَتَّبِعُونَ إِلَّا رَجُلًا مَّسْحُورًا ﴿٤٧﴾ ٱنظُرْ كَيْفَ
ضَرَبُوا۟ لَكَ ٱلْأَمْثَالَ فَضَلُّوا۟ فَلَا يَسْتَطِيعُونَ سَبِيلًا ﴿٤٨﴾ وَقَالُوٓا۟ أَءِذَا
كُنَّا عِظَٰمًا وَرُفَٰتًا أَءِنَّا لَمَبْعُوثُونَ خَلْقًا جَدِيدًا ﴿٤٩﴾ ۞ قُل كُونُوا۟
حِجَارَةً أَوْ حَدِيدًا ﴿٥٠﴾ أَوْ خَلْقًا مِّمَّا يَكْبُرُ فِى صُدُورِكُمْ ۚ فَسَيَقُولُونَ مَن
يُعِيدُنَا ۖ قُلِ ٱلَّذِى فَطَرَكُمْ أَوَّلَ مَرَّةٍ ۚ فَسَيُنْغِضُونَ إِلَيْكَ رُءُوسَهُمْ وَيَقُولُونَ
مَتَىٰ هُوَ ۖ قُلْ عَسَىٰٓ أَن يَكُونَ قَرِيبًا ﴿٥١﴾ يَوْمَ يَدْعُوكُمْ فَتَسْتَجِيبُونَ
بِحَمْدِهِۦ وَتَظُنُّونَ إِن لَّبِثْتُمْ إِلَّا قَلِيلًا ﴿٥٢﴾ وَقُل لِّعِبَادِى يَقُولُوا۟ ٱلَّتِى
هِىَ أَحْسَنُ ۚ إِنَّ ٱلشَّيْطَٰنَ يَنزَغُ بَيْنَهُمْ ۚ إِنَّ ٱلشَّيْطَٰنَ كَانَ لِلْإِنسَٰنِ عَدُوًّا
مُّبِينًا ﴿٥٣﴾

Naḥnu ʾaʿlamu bimā yastamiʿūna bihīi ʾidh yastamiʿūna ʾilayka wa ʾidh hum najwāa ʾidh yaqūluẓ-ẓālimūna ʾiñ-tattabiʿūna ʾillā rajulam-masḥūrā. (47) ʾUñẓur kayfa ḍarabū lakal-ʾamthāla faḍallū falā yastaṭīʿūna sabīlā. (48) Wa qālūu ʾaʾidhā kunnā ʿiẓāmañw-wa rufātan ʾaʾinnā lamabʿūthūna khalqañ-jadīdā. (49) ۞ Qul kūnū ḥijāratan ʾaw ḥadīdā. (50) ʾAw khalqam-mimmā yakburu fī ṣudūrikum. Fasayaqūlūna mañy-yuʿīdunā. Qulil-ladhī faṭarakum ʾawwala marrah. Fasayunghiḍūna ʾilayka ruʾūsahum wa yaqūlūna matā hū. Qul ʿasāa ʾañy-yakūna qarībā. (51) Yawma yadʿūkum fatastajībūna biḥamdihī wa taẓunnūna ʾil-labiththum ʾillā qalīlā. (52) Wa qul-liʿibādī yaqūlul-latī hiya ʾaḥsan. ʾInnash-Shayṭāna yañzaghu baynahum; ʾinnash-Shayṭāna kāna lilʾIñsāni ʿaduwwam-mubīnā. (53)

57 I.e., to find fault with the message of the Qurʾān.

58 Lit., "or any created matter which, in your hearts, appears yet more difficult" – i.e., even less susceptible of having or receiving life.

59 Man's life on earth will appear to him "but as a little while" in comparison with the unlimited duration of the life in the hereafter (Ṭabarī, Zamakhsharī). A further implication is that man's concept of "time" is earthbound and, hence, has no meaning in the context of ultimate reality. The preceding reference to the erstwhile deniers of the possibility of resurrection as "answering God's call by praising Him" implies that as soon as they are resurrected they will become fully aware of His existence and almightiness.

60 Cf. 16 : 125 (and the corresponding note 149) as well as 29 : 46.

61 Lit., "Satan stirs up discord between them".

Your Sustainer is fully aware of what you are [and what you deserve]: if He so wills, he will bestow [His] grace upon you; and if He so wills, He will chastise you.
Hence, We have not sent thee [unto men, O Prophet,] with the power to determine their fate,[62] «54» seeing that thy Sustainer is fully aware of [what is in the minds of] all beings that are in the heavens and on earth. But, indeed, We did endow some of the prophets more highly than others[63] – just as We bestowed upon David a book of divine wisdom [in token of Our grace].[64] «55»

رَّبُّكُمْ أَعْلَمُ بِكُمْ إِن يَشَأْ يَرْحَمْكُمْ أَوْ إِن يَشَأْ يُعَذِّبْكُمْ وَمَآ أَرْسَلْنَٰكَ
عَلَيْهِمْ وَكِيلًا ﴿٥٤﴾ وَرَبُّكَ أَعْلَمُ بِمَن فِى ٱلسَّمَٰوَٰتِ وَٱلْأَرْضِ وَلَقَدْ
فَضَّلْنَا بَعْضَ ٱلنَّبِيِّۦنَ عَلَىٰ بَعْضٍ وَءَاتَيْنَا دَاوُۥدَ زَبُورًا ﴿٥٥﴾ قُلِ ٱدْعُوا۟
ٱلَّذِينَ زَعَمْتُم مِّن دُونِهِۦ فَلَا يَمْلِكُونَ كَشْفَ ٱلضُّرِّ عَنكُمْ وَلَا
تَحْوِيلًا ﴿٥٦﴾ أُو۟لَٰٓئِكَ ٱلَّذِينَ يَدْعُونَ يَبْتَغُونَ إِلَىٰ رَبِّهِمُ ٱلْوَسِيلَةَ أَيُّهُمْ
أَقْرَبُ وَيَرْجُونَ رَحْمَتَهُۥ وَيَخَافُونَ عَذَابَهُۥٓ إِنَّ عَذَابَ رَبِّكَ كَانَ
مَحْذُورًا ﴿٥٧﴾ وَإِن مِّن قَرْيَةٍ إِلَّا نَحْنُ مُهْلِكُوهَا قَبْلَ يَوْمِ ٱلْقِيَٰمَةِ أَوْ
مُعَذِّبُوهَا عَذَابًا شَدِيدًا كَانَ ذَٰلِكَ فِى ٱلْكِتَٰبِ مَسْطُورًا ﴿٥٨﴾

SAY:[65] "Call upon those [beings] whom you imagine [to be endowed with divine powers] beside Him[66] – and [you will find that] they have it not in their power to remove any affliction from you, or to shift it [elsewhere]."[67] «56»
Those [saintly beings] whom they invoke are themselves striving to obtain their Sustainer's favour – [even] those among them who are closest [to Him][68] – hoping for His grace and dreading His chastisement: for, verily, thy Sustainer's chastisement is something to beware of! «57»
And [bear in mind:] there is no community which We will not destroy before the Day of Resurrection,[69] or chastise [even earlier, if it proves sinful,] with suffering severe: all this is laid down in Our decree.[70] «58»

Rabbukum ʾaʿlamu bikum; ʾiñy-yashaʾ yarḥamkum ʾaw ʾiñy-yashaʾ yuʿadhdhibkum. Wa māa ʾarsalnāka ʿalayhim wakīlā. (54) Wa Rabbuka ʾaʿlamu bimañ-fis-samāwāti wal-ʾarḍi wa laqad faḍḍalnā baʿḍan-Nabiyyīna ʿallā baʿḍiñw-wa ʾātaynā Dāwūda Zabūrā. (55) Qulid-ʿul-ladhīna zaʿamtum-miñ-dūnihī falā yamlikūna kashfaḍ-ḍurri ʿañkum wa lā taḥwīlā. (56) ʾUlāaʾikal-ladhīna yadʿūna yabtaghūna ʾilā Rabbihimul-wasīlata ʾayyuhum ʾaqrabu wa yarjūna raḥmatahū wa yakhāfūna ʿadhābah. ʾInna ʿadhāba Rabbika kāna maḥdhūrā. (57) Wa ʾim-miñ-qaryatin ʾillā Naḥnu muhlikūhā qabla Yawmil-Qiyāmati ʾaw muʿadhdhibūhā ʿadhābañ-shadīdā. Kāna dhālika fil-Kitābi masṭūrā. (58)

62 For my rendering of the term *wakīl*, in this context, as "one who has the power to determine the fate [of another being]", see note 4 on verse 2 of this *sūrah* . An alternative, equally acceptable rendering of the above phrase would be, "We have not sent thee charged with responsibility for their conduct".

63 This seems to be an allusion to the role of Muḥammad as the Last Prophet (Zamakhsharī, Bayḍāwī): despite his personal inability to "determine the fate" of the people to whom he conveyed God's message, that message is destined to remain alive forever.

64 I.e., just as David's "book of divine wisdom" (the Psalms) had outlived the glory of his earthly kingdom, so will Muḥammad's message, the Qurʾān, outlive all the changing fortunes of his followers.

65 Sc., "to those who believe in the existence of any divine power apart from God".

66 As the sequence shows, this relates to the worship of saints or angels.

67 I.e., to transfer it onto themselves: obviously an allusion to the Christian doctrine of "vicarious atonement".

68 I.e., the greatest of the prophets, as well as the angels.

69 I.e., since everything in this world is ephemeral and bound to perish, man ought to be conscious of the life to come.

70 Lit., "in the decree" – i.e., in accordance with the immutable laws which God has laid down for His creation.

وَمَا مَنَعَنَآ أَن نُّرۡسِلَ بِٱلۡأٓيَٰتِ إِلَّآ أَن كَذَّبَ بِهَا ٱلۡأَوَّلُونَۚ وَءَاتَيۡنَا
ثَمُودَ ٱلنَّاقَةَ مُبۡصِرَةٗ فَظَلَمُواْ بِهَاۚ وَمَا نُرۡسِلُ بِٱلۡأٓيَٰتِ إِلَّا تَخۡوِيفٗا ﴿٥٩﴾
وَإِذۡ قُلۡنَا لَكَ إِنَّ رَبَّكَ أَحَاطَ بِٱلنَّاسِۚ وَمَا جَعَلۡنَا ٱلرُّءۡيَا ٱلَّتِيٓ أَرَيۡنَٰكَ
إِلَّا فِتۡنَةٗ لِّلنَّاسِ وَٱلشَّجَرَةَ ٱلۡمَلۡعُونَةَ فِي ٱلۡقُرۡءَانِۚ وَنُخَوِّفُهُمۡ فَمَا يَزِيدُهُمۡ
إِلَّا طُغۡيَٰنٗا كَبِيرٗا ﴿٦٠﴾

And nothing has prevented Us from sending [this message, like the earlier ones,] with miraculous signs [in its wake], save [Our knowledge] that the people of olden times [only too often] gave the lie to them:[71] thus, We provided for [the tribe of] Thamūd the she-camel as a light-giving portent, and they sinned against it.[72] And never did We send those signs for any other purpose than to convey a warning. ‹59›
And lo! We said unto thee, [O Prophet:] "Behold, thy Sustainer encompasses all mankind [within His knowledge and might]: and so We have ordained that the vision which We have shown thee[73] – as also the tree [of hell,] cursed in this Qurʾān – shall be but a trial for men.[74] Now [by Our mentioning hell] We convey a warning to them: but [if they are bent on denying the truth,] this [warning] only increases their gross, overweening arrogance." ‹60›

Wa mā manaʿanāa ʾañ-nursila bilʾĀyāti ʾillāa ʾañ-kadhdhaba bihal-ʾawwalūn. Wa ʾātaynā Thamūdan-nāqata mubṣiratañ-faẓalamū bihā; wa mā nursilu bilʾĀyāti ʾillā takhwīfā. (59) Wa ʾidh qulnā laka ʾinna Rabbaka ʾaḥāṭa binnās. Wa mā jaʿalnar-ruʾyal-latīi ʾaraynāka ʾillā fitnatal-linnāsi wash-shajaratal-malʿūnata fil-Qurʾān. Wa nukhawwifuhum famā yazīduhum ʾillā ṭughyānañ-kabīrā. (60)

71 This highly elliptic sentence has a fundamental bearing on the purport of the Qurʾān as a whole. In many places the Qurʾān stresses the fact that the Prophet Muḥammad, despite his being the last and greatest of God's apostles, was not empowered to perform miracles similar to those with which the earlier prophets are said to have reinforced their verbal messages. His only miracle was and is the Qurʾān itself – a message perfect in its lucidity and ethical comprehensiveness, destined for all times and all stages of human development, addressed not merely to the feelings but also to the minds of men, open to everyone, whatever his race or social environment, and bound to remain unchanged forever. Since the earlier prophets invariably appealed to their own community and their own time alone, their teachings were, of necessity, circumscribed by the social and intellectual conditions of that particular community and time; and since the people to whom they addressed themselves had not yet reached the stage of independent thinking, those prophets stood in need of symbolic portents or miracles (see *sūrah* 6, note 94) in order to make the people concerned realize the inner truth of their mission. The message of the Qurʾān, on the other hand, was revealed at a time when mankind (and, in particular, that part of it which inhabited the regions marked by the earlier, Judaeo-Christian religious development) had reached a degree of maturity which henceforth enabled it to grasp an *ideology* as such without the aid of those persuasive portents and miraculous demonstrations which in the past, as the above verse points out, only too often gave rise to new, grave misconceptions.

72 See the second paragraph of 7 : 73 and the corresponding note 57. Although there is absolutely no indication in the Qurʾān that the she-camel referred to was of miraculous origin, it was meant to be a test for the people of Thamūd (cf. 54 : 27), and thus a "light-giving portent" (*mubṣirah*).

73 The vision (*ruʾyā*) mentioned here is the Prophet's experience of the Ascension, preceded by the Night Journey (see Appendix IV). Inasmuch as this experience was and is open to most conflicting interpretations and, hence, may give rise to doubts regarding its objective reality, it becomes – as stated in the sequence – "a trial for men": the weak of faith and the superficial are shaken in their belief in Muḥammad's veracity and, thus, in his prophethood; whereas those who firmly believe in God see in it an extraordinary evidence of the spiritual grace which He bestows on His chosen ones, and are, therefore, strengthened in their faith in the message of the Qurʾān.

74 As regards "the tree cursed in this Qurʾān", there is no doubt that it is the "tree of deadly fruit" (*shajarat az-zaqqūm*) spoken of in 37 : 62 ff. and 44 : 43 ff. as one of the manifestations of hell (see 37 : 62-63 and the corresponding notes 22 and 23, the latter of which explains why this "tree" has become "a trial for men"). In the above context it is described as "cursed" because it obviously symbolizes hell itself. The reason why only "hell" – and no other manifestation of the hereafter – is specifically alluded to here becomes evident in the subsequent statement that it is meant to convey a *warning*.

AND LO! We said unto the angels, "Prostrate yourselves before Adam" – whereupon they all prostrated themselves, save Iblīs.[75]

Said he: "Shall I prostrate myself before one whom Thou hast created out of clay?" «61» [And] he added: "Tell me, is this [foolish being] the one whom Thou hast exalted above me? Indeed, if Thou wilt but allow me a respite till the Day of Resurrection, I shall most certainly cause his descendants – all but a few – to obey me blindly!"[76] «62»

[God] answered: "Go [the way thou hast chosen]! But as for such of them as shall follow thee – behold, hell will be the recompense of you [all], a recompense most ample! «63» Entice, then, with thy voice such of them as thou canst, and bear upon them with all thy horses and all thy men,[77] and be their partner in [all sins relating to] worldly goods and children,[78] and hold out [all manner of] promises to them: and [they will not know that] whatever Satan promises them is but meant to delude the mind.[79] «64»

"[And yet,] behold, thou shalt have no power over [such of] My servants [as place their trust in Me]:[80] for none is as worthy of trust as thy Sustainer." «65»

YOUR SUSTAINER is He who causes ships to move onward for you through the sea, so that you might go about in quest of some of His bounty: verily, a dispenser of grace is He unto you. «66»

وَإِذْ قُلْنَا لِلْمَلَٰٓئِكَةِ ٱسْجُدُوا۟ لِءَادَمَ فَسَجَدُوٓا۟ إِلَّآ إِبْلِيسَ قَالَ ءَأَسْجُدُ لِمَنْ
خَلَقْتَ طِينًا ﴿61﴾ قَالَ أَرَءَيْتَكَ هَٰذَا ٱلَّذِى كَرَّمْتَ عَلَىَّ لَئِنْ أَخَّرْتَنِ
إِلَىٰ يَوْمِ ٱلْقِيَٰمَةِ لَأَحْتَنِكَنَّ ذُرِّيَّتَهُۥٓ إِلَّا قَلِيلًا ﴿62﴾ قَالَ ٱذْهَبْ فَمَن
تَبِعَكَ مِنْهُمْ فَإِنَّ جَهَنَّمَ جَزَآؤُكُمْ جَزَآءً مَّوْفُورًا ﴿63﴾ وَٱسْتَفْزِزْ مَنِ
ٱسْتَطَعْتَ مِنْهُم بِصَوْتِكَ وَأَجْلِبْ عَلَيْهِم بِخَيْلِكَ وَرَجِلِكَ وَشَارِكْهُمْ فِى
ٱلْأَمْوَٰلِ وَٱلْأَوْلَٰدِ وَعِدْهُمْ ۚ وَمَا يَعِدُهُمُ ٱلشَّيْطَٰنُ إِلَّا غُرُورًا ﴿64﴾ إِنَّ
عِبَادِى لَيْسَ لَكَ عَلَيْهِمْ سُلْطَٰنٌ ۚ وَكَفَىٰ بِرَبِّكَ وَكِيلًا ﴿65﴾ رَّبُّكُمُ ٱلَّذِى
يُزْجِى لَكُمُ ٱلْفُلْكَ فِى ٱلْبَحْرِ لِتَبْتَغُوا۟ مِن فَضْلِهِۦٓ ۚ إِنَّهُۥ كَانَ بِكُمْ
رَحِيمًا ﴿66﴾

Wa ʾidh qulnā lilMalāaʾikatis-judū liʾĀdama fasajadūu ʾillāa ʾIblīsa qāla ʾaʾasjudu liman khalaqta ṭīnā. (61) Qāla ʾaraʾaytaka hādhal-ladhī karramta ʿalayya laʾin ʾakhkhartani ʾilā Yawmil-Qiyāmati laʾaḥtanikanna dhurriyyatahūu ʾillā qalīlā. (62) Qāladh-hab famañ-tabiʿaka minhum faʾinna jahannama jazāaʾukum jazāaʾam-mawfūrā. (63) Was-tafziz manis-taṭaʿta minhum biṣawtika wa ʾajlib ʿalayhim bikhaylika wa rajilika wa shārik-hum fil-ʾamwāli wal-ʾawlādi wa ʿid-hum. Wa mā yaʿiduhumush-Shayṭānu ʾillā ghurūrā. (64) ʾInna ʿibādī laysa laka ʿalayhim sulṭānuñw-wa kafā biRabbika Wakīlā. (65) Rabbukumul-ladhī yuzjī lakumul-fulka fil-baḥri litabtaghū miñ-faḍlih. ʾInnahū kana bikum Raḥīmā. (66)

75 For an explanation of the allegory of Adam and the angels, see 2 : 30-34, 7 : 11-18 and 15 : 26-41, as well as the corresponding notes. In the present instance, as in *Al-Aʿrāf* and *Al-Ḥijr*, the accent is on the contempt of Iblīs for Adam (which is obviously a metonym for the whole human race): hence, this passage apparently connects with the end of verse 53 above – "verily, Satan is man's open foe!" The stress on man's dignity – expressed in God's commandment to the angels to "prostrate themselves before Adam" – links this allegory with verses 70-72.

76 Cf. 7 : 16-17. The verb *ḥanaka* denotes, literally, "he put a rope around the lower jaw (*ḥanak*) [of a horse]", i.e., in order to lead it; hence, the form *iḥtanaka* means "he made [another being] follow him submissively" or "obey him blindly".

77 This is an idiomatically established metaphor, signifying "with all thy might".

78 An allusion to possessions acquired by sinful means or spent on sinful purposes, and to the begetting of children through fornication or adultery. (It must, however, be pointed out that in the ethics and the canon law of Islam no moral stigma and no legal disability whatever attaches to the *child* thus begotten.)

79 Cf. 4 : 120 and the corresponding note 142.

80 I.e., "thou shalt have no *real* power over them", as brought out in 14 : 22 and 15 : 42.

ثلاثة ارباع الحزب

And whenever danger befalls you at sea, all those [powers] that you are wont to invoke forsake you, [and nothing remains for you] save Him: but as soon as He has brought you safe ashore, you turn aside [and forget Him] – for, indeed, bereft of all gratitude is man! «67»

Can you, then, ever feel sure that He will not cause a tract of dry land to swallow you up, or let loose upon you a deadly stormwind,[81] whereupon you would find none to be your protector? «68»

Or can you, perchance, feel sure that He will not make you put back to sea[82] once again, and then let loose upon you a raging tempest and cause you to drown in requital of your ingratitude – whereupon you would find none to uphold you against Us? «69»

NOW, INDEED, We have conferred dignity on the children of Adam,[83] and borne them over land and sea, and provided for them sustenance out of the good things of life, and favoured them far above most of Our creation: «70» [but] one Day We shall summon all human beings [and judge them] according to the conscious disposition which governed their deeds [in life]:[84] whereupon they whose record shall be placed in their right hand[85] – it is they who will read their record [with happiness]. Yet none shall be wronged by as much as a hair's breadth:[86] «71»

وَإِذَا مَسَّكُمُ ٱلضُّرُّ فِى ٱلْبَحْرِ ضَلَّ مَن تَدْعُونَ إِلَّآ إِيَّاهُ فَلَمَّا نَجَّىٰكُمْ
إِلَى ٱلْبَرِّ أَعْرَضْتُمْ وَكَانَ ٱلْإِنسَـٰنُ كَفُورًا ﴿٦٧﴾ أَفَأَمِنتُمْ أَن يَخْسِفَ بِكُمْ
جَانِبَ ٱلْبَرِّ أَوْ يُرْسِلَ عَلَيْكُمْ حَاصِبًا ثُمَّ لَا تَجِدُوا۟ لَكُمْ وَكِيلًا ﴿٦٨﴾ أَمْ
أَمِنتُمْ أَن يُعِيدَكُمْ فِيهِ تَارَةً أُخْرَىٰ فَيُرْسِلَ عَلَيْكُمْ قَاصِفًا مِّنَ ٱلرِّيحِ
فَيُغْرِقَكُم بِمَا كَفَرْتُمْ ثُمَّ لَا تَجِدُوا۟ لَكُمْ عَلَيْنَا بِهِۦ تَبِيعًا ﴿٦٩﴾ ۞ وَلَقَدْ
كَرَّمْنَا بَنِىٓ ءَادَمَ وَحَمَلْنَـٰهُمْ فِى ٱلْبَرِّ وَٱلْبَحْرِ وَرَزَقْنَـٰهُم مِّنَ ٱلطَّيِّبَـٰتِ
وَفَضَّلْنَـٰهُمْ عَلَىٰ كَثِيرٍ مِّمَّنْ خَلَقْنَا تَفْضِيلًا ﴿٧٠﴾ يَوْمَ نَدْعُوا۟ كُلَّ أُنَاسٍ
بِإِمَـٰمِهِمْ فَمَنْ أُوتِىَ كِتَـٰبَهُۥ بِيَمِينِهِۦ فَأُو۟لَـٰٓئِكَ يَقْرَءُونَ كِتَـٰبَهُمْ وَلَا
يُظْلَمُونَ فَتِيلًا ﴿٧١﴾

Wa ʾidhā massakumuḍ-ḍurru fil-baḥri ḍalla mañ-tadʿūna ʾillāa ʾIyyāhu falammā najjākum ʾilal-barri ʾaʿraḍtum. Wa kānal-ʾIñsānu kafūrā. (67) ʾAfaʾamiñtum ʾañy-yakhsifa bikum jānibal-barri ʾaw yursila ʿalaykum ḥāṣibañ-thumma lā tajidū lakum wakīlā. (68) ʾAm ʾamiñtum ʾañy-yuʿīdakum fīhi tāratan ʾukhrā fayursila ʿalaykum qāṣifam-minar-rīḥi fayughriqakum bimā kafartum thumma lā tajidū lakum ʿalaynā bihī tabīʿā. (69) ۞ Wa laqad karramnā banīi ʾĀdama wa ḥamalnāhum fil-barri wal-baḥri wa razaqnāhum-minaṭ-ṭayyibāti wa faḍalnāhum ʿalā kathīrim-mimman khalaqnā tafḍīlā. (70) Yawma nadʿū kulla ʾunāsim-biʾimāmihim; faman ʾūtiya kitābahū biyamīnihī faʾulāaʾika yaqraʾūna kitābahum wa lā yuẓlamūna fatīlā. (71)

81 Lit., "a stormwind that raises stones" (*Tāj al-ʿArūs,* art. *ḥaṣaba*).

82 Lit., "therein".

83 I.e., by bestowing upon them the faculty of conceptual thinking (cf. 2 : 31 and the corresponding note 23), which makes them superior in this respect to all other animate beings, and even to the angels. By stressing here this unique distinction of man, the present passage connects with, and continues the theme of, verse 61 above.

84 Thus Rāzī interprets the phrase *nadʿū kulla unāsin bi-imāmihim* (lit., "We shall summon all human beings by [mentioning] their leaders" or "guides"). In his opinion, the expression *imām* (lit., "leader" or "guide") has in this context an abstract connotation, signifying the conscious disposition, good or bad, which governs a person's behaviour and provides the motives for his deeds. This interpretation is most convincing, and particularly so in view of the fundamental *ḥadīth* quoted in my note 32 on 53 : 39.

85 A symbolic image, often used in the Qurʾān, denoting an acknowledgement of righteousness in the spiritual sense, just as the "left hand" indicates its opposite (cf. 69 : 19 and 25, as well as 84 : 7).

86 This last clause obviously applies to both the righteous and the unrighteous. (For my above rendering of *fatīl,* see *sūrah* 4, note 67.)

for whoever is blind [of heart] in this [world] will be blind in the life to come [as well], and still farther astray from the path [of truth].[87] ‹72›

AND, behold, they [who have gone astray] endeavour to tempt thee away from all [the truth] with which We have inspired thee, [O Prophet:] with a view to making thee invent something else in Our name – in which case they would surely have made thee their friend![88] ‹73› And had We not made thee firm [in faith], thou might have inclined to them a little[89] ‹74› – in which case We would indeed have made thee taste double [chastisement] in life and double [chastisement] after death,[90] and thou wouldst have found none to succour thee against Us! ‹75›

And [since they see that they cannot persuade thee,] they endeavour to estrange thee from the land [of thy birth][91] with a view to driving thee away from it – but, then, after thou wilt have left,[92] they themselves will not remain [in it] for more than a little while:[93] ‹76› [such has been Our] way with all of Our apostles whom We sent before thy time;[94] and no change wilt thou find in Our ways. ‹77›

وَمَن كَانَ فِي هَٰذِهِۦٓ أَعْمَىٰ فَهُوَ فِي ٱلْـَٔاخِرَةِ أَعْمَىٰ وَأَضَلُّ سَبِيلًا ﴿٧٢﴾ وَإِن
كَادُوا۟ لَيَفْتِنُونَكَ عَنِ ٱلَّذِىٓ أَوْحَيْنَآ إِلَيْكَ لِتَفْتَرِىَ عَلَيْنَا غَيْرَهُۥ ۖ وَإِذًا
لَّٱتَّخَذُوكَ خَلِيلًا ﴿٧٣﴾ وَلَوْلَآ أَن ثَبَّتْنَٰكَ لَقَدْ كِدتَّ تَرْكَنُ إِلَيْهِمْ شَيْـًٔا
قَلِيلًا ﴿٧٤﴾ إِذًا لَّأَذَقْنَٰكَ ضِعْفَ ٱلْحَيَوٰةِ وَضِعْفَ ٱلْمَمَاتِ ثُمَّ لَا تَجِدُ
لَكَ عَلَيْنَا نَصِيرًا ﴿٧٥﴾ وَإِن كَادُوا۟ لَيَسْتَفِزُّونَكَ مِنَ ٱلْأَرْضِ لِيُخْرِجُوكَ
مِنْهَا ۖ وَإِذًا لَّا يَلْبَثُونَ خِلَٰفَكَ إِلَّا قَلِيلًا ﴿٧٦﴾ سُنَّةَ مَن قَدْ أَرْسَلْنَا قَبْلَكَ
مِن رُّسُلِنَا ۖ وَلَا تَجِدُ لِسُنَّتِنَا تَحْوِيلًا ﴿٧٧﴾

Wa mañ-kāna fī hādhihīi ʾaʿmā fahuwa fil-ʾĀkhirati ʾaʿmā wa ʾaḍallu sabīlā. (72) Wa ʾiñ-kādū layaftinūnaka ʿanil-ladhīi ʾawḥaynāa ʾilayka litaftariya ʿalaynā ghayrahu wa ʾidhal-lattakhadhūka khalīlā. (73) Wa lawlāa ʾañ-thabbatnāka laqad kitta tarkanu ʾilayhim shayʾañ-qalīlā. (74) ʾIdhal-laʾadhaqnāka ḍiʿfal-ḥayāti wa ḍiʿfal-mamāti thumma lā tajidu laka ʿalaynā naṣīrā. (75) Wa ʾiñ-kādū layastafizzūnaka minal-ʾarḍi liyukhrijūka minhā wa ʾidhal-lā yalbathūna khilāfaka ʾillā qalīlā. (76) Sunnata mañ-qad ʾarsalnā qablaka mir-Rusulinā wa lā tajidu lisunnatinā taḥwīlā. (77)

87 Cf. 20 : 124-125. This passage shows that man's life in the hereafter is not merely *conditioned* by the manner of his life on earth, but is also an organic *extension* of the latter, manifested in a natural development and intensification of previously-existing tendencies.

88 This relates to an offer of "compromise" made by the pagan Quraysh: they demanded of the Prophet that he give some sort of recognition to their tribal deities and attribute this recognition to God; in return, they promised to recognize him as a prophet and to make him their leader. Naturally, the Prophet rejected this offer.

89 The implication is that the Prophet's deep faith made it *impossible* for him to consider anything of this kind.

90 I.e., "for having gone astray despite the revelation bestowed on thee by God, and for having, by thy example, led thy followers astray as well". The purport of the above passage goes, however, beyond the historical event or events to which it relates: it expresses the idea that any *conscious* offence against a fundamental truth is an unforgivable sin.

91 It must be borne in mind that this is a Meccan *sūrah,* revealed at a time when the persecution, both physical and moral, which the Prophet and his followers had to suffer at the hands of the pagan Quraysh reached the peak of its intensity.

92 Lit., "after thee".

93 This prophecy was fulfilled a little over two years later, in the month of Ramaḍān, 2 H., when those same leaders of the Quraysh were killed in the battle of Badr.

94 I.e., the people who drove them away were invariably punished with destruction.

BE CONSTANT in [thy] prayer from the time when the sun has passed its zenith till the darkness of night, and [be ever mindful of its] recitation at dawn:[95] for, behold, the recitation [of prayer] at dawn is indeed witnessed [by all that is holy].[96] ‹78›
And rise from thy sleep and pray during part of the night [as well], as a free offering from thee,[97] and thy Sustainer may well raise thee to a glorious station [in the life to come]. ‹79›
And say [in thy prayer]: "O my Sustainer! Cause me to enter [upon whatever I may do] in a manner true and sincere, and cause me to leave [it] in a manner true and sincere, and grant me, out of Thy grace, sustaining strength!" ‹80›
And say: "The truth has now come [to light], and falsehood has withered away: for, behold, all falsehood is bound to wither away!" ‹81›

THUS, step by step, We bestow from on high through this Qurʾān all that gives health [to the spirit] and is a grace unto those who believe [in Us], the while it only adds to the ruin of evildoers:[98] ‹82› for [it often happens that] when We bestow Our blessings upon man, he turns away and arrogantly keeps aloof [from any thought of Us]; and when evil fortune touches him, he abandons all hope.[99] ‹83›

أَقِمِ ٱلصَّلَوٰةَ لِدُلُوكِ ٱلشَّمْسِ إِلَىٰ غَسَقِ ٱلَّيْلِ وَقُرْءَانَ ٱلْفَجْرِ إِنَّ قُرْءَانَ
ٱلْفَجْرِ كَانَ مَشْهُودًا ﴿٧٨﴾ وَمِنَ ٱلَّيْلِ فَتَهَجَّدْ بِهِۦ نَافِلَةً لَّكَ عَسَىٰٓ أَن
يَبْعَثَكَ رَبُّكَ مَقَامًا مَّحْمُودًا ﴿٧٩﴾ وَقُل رَّبِّ أَدْخِلْنِى مُدْخَلَ صِدْقٍ
وَأَخْرِجْنِى مُخْرَجَ صِدْقٍ وَٱجْعَل لِّى مِن لَّدُنكَ سُلْطَـٰنًا نَّصِيرًا ﴿٨٠﴾ وَقُلْ
جَآءَ ٱلْحَقُّ وَزَهَقَ ٱلْبَـٰطِلُ ۚ إِنَّ ٱلْبَـٰطِلَ كَانَ زَهُوقًا ﴿٨١﴾ وَنُنَزِّلُ مِنَ
ٱلْقُرْءَانِ مَا هُوَ شِفَآءٌ وَرَحْمَةٌ لِّلْمُؤْمِنِينَ ۙ وَلَا يَزِيدُ ٱلظَّـٰلِمِينَ إِلَّا
خَسَارًا ﴿٨٢﴾ وَإِذَآ أَنْعَمْنَا عَلَى ٱلْإِنسَـٰنِ أَعْرَضَ وَنَـَٔا بِجَانِبِهِۦ ۖ وَإِذَا مَسَّهُ
ٱلشَّرُّ كَانَ يَـُٔوسًا ﴿٨٣﴾

ʾAqimiṣ-Ṣalāta lidulūkish-shamsi ʾilā ghasaqil-layli wa Qurʾānal-fajri ʾinna Qurʾānal-fajri kāna mashhūdā. (78) Wa minal-layli fatahajjad bihī nāfilatal-laka ʿasāa ʾañy-yabʿathaka Rabbuka maqāmam-maḥmūdā. (79) Wa qur-Rabbi ʾadkhilnī mudkhala ṣidqiñw-wa ʾakhrijnī mukhraja ṣidqiñw-waj-ʿal-lī mil-laduñka sulṭānañ-naṣīrā. (80) Wa qul jāaʾal-ḥaqqu wa zahaqal-bāṭilu ʾinnal-bāṭila kāna zahūqā. (81) Wa nunazzilu minal-Qurʾāni mā huwa shifāaʾuñw-wa raḥmatul-lilmuʾminīna wa lā yazīduẓ-ẓālimīna ʾillā khasārā. (82) Wa ʾidhāa ʾanʿamnā ʿalal-ʾIñsāni ʾaʿraḍa wa naʾā bijānibihī wa ʾidhā massa-hush-sharru kāna yaʾūsā. (83)

95 As is evidenced by the practice (*sunnah*) of the Prophet, this verse fully circumscribes the five daily prayers laid down in Islam as obligatory for every adult man and woman: at dawn (*fajr*), shortly after the sun passes its zenith (*ẓuhr*), in the middle of the afternoon (*ʿaṣr*), immediately after sunset (*maghrib*), and after the night has fully set in (*ʿishāʾ*). Although parts of the Qurʾān should be recited in every prayer, the early morning prayer is metonymically singled out as the "recitation (*qurʾān*) at dawn" because the Prophet, under divine inspiration, used to lengthen his recitation while praying at that time, thus stressing the special significance of this particular prayer. (See next note.)

96 Most of the classical commentators take this to mean "witnessed by the angels of night as well as those of day", since dawn is the time between night and day. Rāzī, however, is of the opinion that the "witness" to which the Qurʾān refers here is the spark of God-given illumination in man's own soul – the heightening of his inner perception at the time when the darkness and stillness of night begins to give way to the life-giving light of day, so that prayer becomes a means of attaining to deeper insight into the realm of spiritual truths and, thus, of achieving communion with all that is holy.

97 Lit., "as a deed beyond that which is incumbent on thee" (*nāfilatan laka*) – i.e., in addition to the five obligatory prayers. Hence, the above is not an injunction, but a *recommendation*, although the Prophet himself invariably spent the greater part of the night in prayer.

98 By "evildoers" are meant people who, out of self-conceit or an excessive "love of this world", reject out of hand any suggestion of divine guidance – and, with it, any belief in the existence of absolute moral values – and in the end, as the sequence shows, fall prey to spiritual nihilism.

99 Cf. 11 : 9-10 and the corresponding notes.

Say: "Everyone acts in a manner peculiar to himself – and your Sustainer is fully aware as to who has chosen the best path.[100] ‹84›

AND THEY will ask thee about [the nature of] divine inspiration.[101] Say: "This inspiration [comes] at my Sustainer's behest; and [you cannot understand its nature, O men, since] you have been granted very little of [real] knowledge." ‹85›

And if We so willed, We could indeed take away whatever We have revealed unto thee, and in that [state of need] thou wouldst find none to plead in thy behalf before Us.[102] ‹86› [Thou art spared] only by thy Sustainer's grace: behold, His favour towards thee is great indeed! ‹87›

Say: "If all mankind and all invisible beings[103] would come together with a view to producing the like of this Qurʾān, they could not produce its like even though they were to exert all their strength in aiding one another!" ‹88›

For, indeed, many facets have We given in this Qurʾān to every kind of lesson [designed] for [the benefit of] mankind![104] However, most men are unwilling to accept anything but blasphemy[105] ‹89› – and so they say: "[O Muḥammad,] we shall not believe thee till thou cause a spring to gush forth for us from the earth,[106] ‹90› or thou have a garden of date-palms and vines and cause rivers to gush forth in their midst in a sudden rush,[107] ‹91›

قُلْ كُلٌّ يَعْمَلُ عَلَىٰ شَاكِلَتِهِۦ فَرَبُّكُمْ أَعْلَمُ بِمَنْ هُوَ أَهْدَىٰ سَبِيلًا ﴿٨٤﴾
وَيَسْـَٔلُونَكَ عَنِ ٱلرُّوحِ ۖ قُلِ ٱلرُّوحُ مِنْ أَمْرِ رَبِّى وَمَآ أُوتِيتُم مِّنَ ٱلْعِلْمِ إِلَّا
قَلِيلًا ﴿٨٥﴾ وَلَئِن شِئْنَا لَنَذْهَبَنَّ بِٱلَّذِىٓ أَوْحَيْنَآ إِلَيْكَ ثُمَّ لَا تَجِدُ لَكَ بِهِۦ
عَلَيْنَا وَكِيلًا ﴿٨٦﴾ إِلَّا رَحْمَةً مِّن رَّبِّكَ ۚ إِنَّ فَضْلَهُۥ كَانَ عَلَيْكَ كَبِيرًا ﴿٨٧﴾
قُل لَّئِنِ ٱجْتَمَعَتِ ٱلْإِنسُ وَٱلْجِنُّ عَلَىٰٓ أَن يَأْتُوا۟ بِمِثْلِ هَـٰذَا ٱلْقُرْءَانِ لَا
يَأْتُونَ بِمِثْلِهِۦ وَلَوْ كَانَ بَعْضُهُمْ لِبَعْضٍ ظَهِيرًا ﴿٨٨﴾ وَلَقَدْ صَرَّفْنَا لِلنَّاسِ
فِى هَـٰذَا ٱلْقُرْءَانِ مِن كُلِّ مَثَلٍ فَأَبَىٰٓ أَكْثَرُ ٱلنَّاسِ إِلَّا كُفُورًا ﴿٨٩﴾
وَقَالُوا۟ لَن نُّؤْمِنَ لَكَ حَتَّىٰ تَفْجُرَ لَنَا مِنَ ٱلْأَرْضِ يَنۢبُوعًا ﴿٩٠﴾ أَوْ تَكُونَ
لَكَ جَنَّةٌ مِّن نَّخِيلٍ وَعِنَبٍ فَتُفَجِّرَ ٱلْأَنْهَـٰرَ خِلَـٰلَهَا تَفْجِيرًا ﴿٩١﴾

Qul kulluñy-yaʿmalu ʿalā shākilatihī faRabbukum ʾaʿlamu biman huwa ʾahdā sabīlā. (84) Wa yasʾalūnaka ʿanir-rūḥ. Qulir-rūḥu min ʾamri Rabbī wa māa ʾūtītum-minal-ʿilmi ʾillā qalīlā. (85) Wa laʾiñ-shiʾnā lanadhhabanna billadhīi ʾawḥaynāa ʾilayka thumma lā tajidu laka bihī ʿalaynā wakīlā. (86) ʾIllā raḥmatam-mir-Rabbik. ʾInna faḍlahū kāna ʿalayka kabīrā. (87) Qul-laʾinij-tamaʿatil-ʾIñsu wal-Jinnu ʿalāa ʾañy-yaʾtū bimithli hādhal-Qurʾāni lā yaʾtūna bimithlihī wa law kāna baʿḍuhum libaʿḍiñ-ẓahīrā. (88) Wa laqad ṣarrafnā linnāsi fī hādhal-Qurʾāni miñ-kulli mathaliñ-faʾabāa ʾaktharun-nāsi ʾillā kufūrā. (89) Wa qālū lañ-nuʾmina laka ḥattā tafjura lanā minal-ʾarḍi yambūʿā. (90) ʾAw takūna laka jannatum-miñ-nakhīliñw-wa ʿinabiñ-fatufajjiral-ʾanhāra khilālahā tafjīrā. (91)

100 Lit., "as to who is best guided on a path".

101 For this interpretation of the term *rūḥ*, see *sūrah* 16, note 2. Some commentators are of the opinion that it refers here, specifically, to the revelation of the Qurʾān; others understand by it the "soul", in particular the soul of man. This latter interpretation is, however, unconvincing inasmuch as the preceding as well as the subsequent verses relate explicitly to the Qurʾān and, hence, to the phenomenon of divine revelation.

102 Lit., "to be thy guardian against [or "before"] Us" – i.e., "to provide thee with other means of guidance": an allusion to the fact that divine guidance is the only source of ethics in the absolute sense of this word. The "taking away" of revelation denotes its alienation from the hearts and the memory of men, as well as its disappearance in written form.

103 See Appendix III.

104 According to Rāghib, the noun *mathal* (lit., "similitude", "parable" or "example") is here more or less synonymous with *waṣf* ("description by means of a comparison", i.e., "definition"). In its broadest sense, this term signifies "a lesson".

105 I.e., they are unwilling to accept any idea which runs counter to their own, blasphemous inclinations.

106 I.e., like Moses (cf. 2 : 60).

107 This seems to be a derisory allusion to the allegory of paradise so often mentioned in the Qurʾān.

or thou cause the skies to fall down upon us in smithereens, as thou hast threatened,[108] or [till] thou bring God and the angels face to face before us, ‹92› or thou have a house [made] of gold, or thou ascend to heaven – but nay, we would not [even] believe in thy ascension unless thou bring down to us [from heaven] a writing which we [ourselves] could read!"[109]
Say thou, [O Prophet:] "Limitless in His glory is my Sustainer!"[110] Am I, then, aught but a mortal man, an apostle?" ‹93›
Yet whenever [God's] guidance came to them [through a prophet:] nothing has ever kept people from believing [in him] save this their objection:[111] "Would God have sent a [mere] mortal man as His apostle?" ‹94›
Say: "If angels were walking about on earth as their natural abode, We would indeed have sent down unto them an angel out of heaven as Our apostle." ‹95›
Say: "None can bear witness between me and you as God does: verily, fully aware is He of His creatures, and He sees all [that is in their hearts]." ‹96›
And he whom God guides, he alone has found the right way; whereas for those whom He lets go astray thou canst never find anyone to protect them from Him: and [so, when] We shall gather them together on the Day of Resurrection, [they will lie] prone upon their faces, blind and dumb and deaf, with hell as their goal; [and] every time [the fire] abates, We shall increase for them [its] blazing flame.[112] ‹97›

أَوْ تُسْقِطَ ٱلسَّمَآءَ كَمَا زَعَمْتَ عَلَيْنَا كِسَفًا أَوْ تَأْتِىَ بِٱللَّهِ وَٱلْمَلَٰٓئِكَةِ
قَبِيلًا ﴿٩٢﴾ أَوْ يَكُونَ لَكَ بَيْتٌ مِّن زُخْرُفٍ أَوْ تَرْقَىٰ فِى ٱلسَّمَآءِ وَلَن نُّؤْمِنَ
لِرُقِيِّكَ حَتَّىٰ تُنَزِّلَ عَلَيْنَا كِتَٰبًا نَّقْرَؤُهُۥ ۗ قُلْ سُبْحَانَ رَبِّى هَلْ كُنتُ إِلَّا
بَشَرًا رَّسُولًا ﴿٩٣﴾ وَمَا مَنَعَ ٱلنَّاسَ أَن يُؤْمِنُوٓا۟ إِذْ جَآءَهُمُ ٱلْهُدَىٰٓ إِلَّآ أَن
قَالُوٓا۟ أَبَعَثَ ٱللَّهُ بَشَرًا رَّسُولًا ﴿٩٤﴾ قُل لَّوْ كَانَ فِى ٱلْأَرْضِ مَلَٰٓئِكَةٌ
يَمْشُونَ مُطْمَئِنِّينَ لَنَزَّلْنَا عَلَيْهِم مِّنَ ٱلسَّمَآءِ مَلَكًا رَّسُولًا ﴿٩٥﴾ قُلْ كَفَىٰ
بِٱللَّهِ شَهِيدًۢا بَيْنِى وَبَيْنَكُمْ ۚ إِنَّهُۥ كَانَ بِعِبَادِهِۦ خَبِيرًۢا بَصِيرًا ﴿٩٦﴾ وَمَن
يَهْدِ ٱللَّهُ فَهُوَ ٱلْمُهْتَدِ ۖ وَمَن يُضْلِلْ فَلَن تَجِدَ لَهُمْ أَوْلِيَآءَ مِن دُونِهِۦ ۖ
وَنَحْشُرُهُمْ يَوْمَ ٱلْقِيَٰمَةِ عَلَىٰ وُجُوهِهِمْ عُمْيًا وَبُكْمًا وَصُمًّا ۖ مَّأْوَىٰهُمْ جَهَنَّمُ ۖ
كُلَّمَا خَبَتْ زِدْنَٰهُمْ سَعِيرًا ﴿٩٧﴾

ʾAw tusqiṭas-samāaʾa kamā zaʿamta ʿalaynā kisafan ʾaw taʾtiya billāhi wal-Malāaʾikati qabīlā. (92) ʾAw yakūna laka baytum-miñ-zukhrufin ʾaw tarqā fis-samāaʾi wa lañ-nuʾmina liruqiyyika ḥattā tunazzila ʿalaynā kitābañ-naqraʾuh. Qul subḥāna Rabbī hal kuñtu ʾillā basharar-Rasūlā. (93) Wa mā manaʿan-nāsa ʾañy-yuʾminūu ʾidh jāaʾahumul-hudāa ʾillāa ʾañ-qālūu ʾabaʿathal-lāhu basharar-Rasūlā. (94) Qul-law kāna fil-ʾarḍi Malāaʾikatuñy-yamshūna muṭmaʾinnīna lanazzalnā ʿalayhim-minas-samāaʾi Malakar-Rasūlā. (95) Qul kafā billāhi Shahīdam-baynī wa baynakum. ʾInnahū kāna biʿibādihī Khabīram-Baṣīrā. (96) Wa mañy-yahdil-lāhu fahuwal-muhtadi wa mañy-yuḍlil falañ-tajida lahum ʾawliyāaʾa miñ-dūnih. Wa naḥshuruhum Yawmal-Qiyāmati ʿalā wujūhihim ʿumyañw-wa bukmañw-wa ṣummam-maʾwāhum jahannamu kullamā khabat zidnāhum saʿīrā. (97)

108 Lit., "claimed": possibly a reference to the warning expressed in 34 : 9, which was revealed somewhat earlier than the present *sūrah*.

109 A reply to this demand of the unbelievers is found in verse 7 of *Al-Anʿām*, revealed – according to Suyūṭī – shortly after the present *sūrah*. But the allusion to this and the preceding "conditions" is not merely historical: it illustrates a widely prevalent, psychologically contradictory attitude of mind – a strange mixture of *prima-facie* scepticism and primitive credulity which makes belief in a prophetic message dependent on the prophet's "performing miracles" (cf. 6 : 37 and 109 and 7 : 203). Since the only miracle granted by God to Muḥammad is the Qurʾān itself (see the first part of verse 59 of this *sūrah* as well as note 71 above), he is bidden, in the next passage, to declare that these demands are irrelevant and, by implication, frivolous.

110 I.e., "miracles are in the power of God alone" (cf. 6 : 109 and the corresponding note 94).

111 Lit., "save that they said". The verb *qāla* (as also the noun *qawl*) is often used tropically in the sense of holding or asserting an opinion or a belief; in the above case it obviously implies a conceptual *objection*.

112 The phrase "for them" is meant, I believe, to stress the *individual* character of the suffering allegorized in the

Such will be their requital for having rejected Our messages and having said, "After we will have become bones and dust, shall we, forsooth, be raised from the dead in a new act of creation?"[113] ‹98›
Are they, then, not aware that God, who has created the heavens and the earth, has the power to create them anew in their own likeness,[114] having, beyond any doubt, set a term for their resurrection?[115] However, all [such] evildoers are unwilling to accept anything but blasphemy![116] ‹99›
Say: "If you were to own all the treasure-houses of my Sustainer's bounty,[117] lo! you would still try to hold on [to them] tightly for fear of spending [too much]: for man has always been avaricious [whereas God is limitless in His bounty]."[118] ‹100›

AND, INDEED, We gave unto Moses nine clear messages.[119]
Ask, then, the children of Israel[120] [to tell thee what happened] when he came unto them, [and appealed to Pharaoh,[121]] and Pharaoh said unto him, "Verily, O Moses, I think that thou art full of sorcery!"[122] ‹101›

ذَٰلِكَ جَزَآؤُهُم بِأَنَّهُمْ كَفَرُواْ بِـَٔايَـٰتِنَا وَقَالُوٓاْ أَءِذَا كُنَّا عِظَـٰمًا وَرُفَـٰتًا
أَءِنَّا لَمَبْعُوثُونَ خَلْقًا جَدِيدًا ﴿٩٨﴾ ۞ أَوَلَمْ يَرَوْاْ أَنَّ ٱللَّهَ ٱلَّذِى خَلَقَ
ٱلسَّمَـٰوَٰتِ وَٱلْأَرْضَ قَادِرٌ عَلَىٰٓ أَن يَخْلُقَ مِثْلَهُمْ وَجَعَلَ لَهُمْ أَجَلًا لَّا
رَيْبَ فِيهِ فَأَبَى ٱلظَّـٰلِمُونَ إِلَّا كُفُورًا ﴿٩٩﴾ قُل لَّوْ أَنتُمْ تَمْلِكُونَ خَزَآئِنَ
رَحْمَةِ رَبِّىٓ إِذًا لَّأَمْسَكْتُمْ خَشْيَةَ ٱلْإِنفَاقِ ۚ وَكَانَ ٱلْإِنسَـٰنُ قَتُورًا ﴿١٠٠﴾
وَلَقَدْ ءَاتَيْنَا مُوسَىٰ تِسْعَ ءَايَـٰتٍۭ بَيِّنَـٰتٍ ۖ فَسْـَٔلْ بَنِىٓ إِسْرَٰٓءِيلَ إِذْ جَآءَهُمْ
فَقَالَ لَهُۥ فِرْعَوْنُ إِنِّى لَأَظُنُّكَ يَـٰمُوسَىٰ مَسْحُورًا ﴿١٠١﴾

30 حزب

Dhālika jazāaʾuhum biʾannahum kafarū biʾĀyātinā wa qālūu ʾaʾidhā kunnā ʿiẓāmañw-wa rufātan ʾaʾinnā lamabʿūthūna khalqañ-jadīdā. (98) ۞ ʾAwa lam yaraw ʾannal-lāhal-ladhī khalaqas-samāwāti wal-ʾarḍa Qādirun ʿalāa ʾañy-yakhluqa mithlahum wa jaʿala lahum ʾajalal-lā rayba fīhi faʾabaẓ-ẓālimūna ʾillā kufūrā. (99) Qul-law ʾañtum tamlikūna khazāaʾina raḥmati Rabbīi ʾidhal-laʾamsaktum khashyatal-ʾiñfāqi wa kānal-ʾIñsānu qatūrā. (100) Wa laqad ʾātaynā Mūsā tisʿa ʾĀyātim-bayyinātiñ-fasʾal banīi-ʾIsrāaʾīla ʾidh jāaʾahum faqāla lahū Firʿawnu ʾinnī laʾaẓunnuka yā Mūsā masḥūrā. (101)

Qurʾān as a "blazing flame" (*saʿīr*). For a further discussion of this terminology and its philosophical implications, see Appendix I.

113 Implying that this denial of God's power to resurrect the dead (mentioned in exactly the same phrasing in verse 49 of this *sūrah*) is equivalent to a denial of His almightiness and, hence, of His Being – all of which is characterized by the words "blind and deaf and dumb" in the preceding verse.

114 Lit., "to create the like of them" – i.e., to resurrect them individually, each of them having the same identity (or "likeness") which he or she had before death.

115 Lit., "a term (*ajal*) for them". Since *ajal* denotes, primarily, "a specified term [at which something falls due]", it obviously relates here to the inescapable fact of resurrection.

116 See notes 98 and 105 above.

117 Lit., "grace" (*raḥmah*)"

118 I.e., since man is, by his very nature, dependent on material possessions, he instinctively tries to hold on to them; God, on the other hand, is self-sufficient and, therefore, above all need of placing any limits on His bestowal of bounty (hence my interpolation). This *implied* reference to God's grace and bounty is necessitated by the emphasis, in the preceding as well as in the subsequent passages, on the fact that He has never ceased to guide man, through His prophets, towards the good life.

119 Some of the commentators assume that this is an allusion to the miracles performed by Moses, while others (relying on a Tradition quoted in the compilations of Nasāʾī, Ibn Ḥanbal). Bayhaqī, Ibn Mājah and Ṭabarānī) see in it a reference to nine specific commandments or ethical principles, the foremost of them being a stress on God's oneness and uniqueness. In my opinion, however, the number "nine" may be no more than a metonym for "several", just as the numbers "seven" and "seventy" are often used in classical Arabic to denote "several" or "many".

120 I.e., of the present time. The whole phrase has this meaning: "Ask them about what the Qurʾān tells us in this respect, and they will be bound to confirm it on the basis of their own scriptures." This "confirmation" apparently relates to what is said in verse 104, explaining why the story of Moses and Pharaoh has been mentioned in the present context. (The story as such appears in greater detail in 7 : 103-137 and 20 : 49-79.)

121 Cf. 7 : 105 – "let the children of Israel go with me!"

122 Or: "that thou art bewitched". However, my rendering is based on Ṭabarī's interpretation of the passive

قَالَ لَقَدْ عَلِمْتَ مَآ أَنزَلَ هَٰٓؤُلَآءِ إِلَّا رَبُّ ٱلسَّمَٰوَٰتِ وَٱلْأَرْضِ
بَصَآئِرَ وَإِنِّى لَأَظُنُّكَ يَٰفِرْعَوْنُ مَثْبُورًا ﴿102﴾ فَأَرَادَ أَن يَسْتَفِزَّهُم مِّنَ
ٱلْأَرْضِ فَأَغْرَقْنَٰهُ وَمَن مَّعَهُۥ جَمِيعًا ﴿103﴾ وَقُلْنَا مِنۢ بَعْدِهِۦ لِبَنِىٓ
إِسْرَٰٓءِيلَ ٱسْكُنُوا۟ ٱلْأَرْضَ فَإِذَا جَآءَ وَعْدُ ٱلْءَاخِرَةِ جِئْنَا بِكُمْ
لَفِيفًا ﴿104﴾ وَبِٱلْحَقِّ أَنزَلْنَٰهُ وَبِٱلْحَقِّ نَزَلَ وَمَآ أَرْسَلْنَٰكَ إِلَّا مُبَشِّرًا
وَنَذِيرًا ﴿105﴾ وَقُرْءَانًا فَرَقْنَٰهُ لِتَقْرَأَهُۥ عَلَى ٱلنَّاسِ عَلَىٰ مُكْثٍ وَنَزَّلْنَٰهُ
تَنزِيلًا ﴿106﴾

Qāla laqad ʿalimta māa ʾaṅzala hāaʾulāaʾi ʾillā Rabbus-samāwāti wal-ʾarḍi baṣāaʾira wa ʾinnī laʾaẓunnuka yā Firʿawnu mathbūrā. (102) Faʾarāda ʾaṅy-yastafizzahum-minal-ʾarḍi faʾaghraqnāhu wa mam-maʿahū jamīʿā. (103) Wa qulnā mim-baʿdihī libanīi ʾIsrāaʾīlas-kunul-ʾarḍaa faʾidhā jāaʾa waʿdul-ʾĀkhirati jiʾnā bikum lafīfā. (104) Wa bilḥaqqi ʾaṅzalnāhu wa bilḥaqqi nazal. Wa māa ʾarsalnāka ʾillā mubashshiraṅw-wa nadhīrā. (105) Wa Qurʾānaṅ-faraqnāhu litaqraʾahū ʿalan-nāsi ʿalā mukthiṅw-wa nazzalnāhu taṅzīlā. (106)

Answered [Moses]: "Thou knowest well that none but the Sustainer of the heavens and the earth has bestowed these [miraculous signs] from on high, as a means of insight [for thee];[123] and, verily, O Pharaoh, [since thou hast chosen to reject them,] I think that thou art utterly lost!" ‹102›

And then [Pharaoh] resolved to wipe them off [the face of] the earth – whereupon We caused him and all who were with him to drown [in the sea].[124] ‹103›

And after that We said unto the children of Israel: "Dwell now securely on earth – but [remember that] when the promise of the Last Day shall come to pass, We will bring you forth as [parts of] a motley crowd!"[125] ‹104›

AND AS a guide towards the truth[126] have We bestowed this [revelation] from on high; with this [very] truth has it come down [unto thee, O Prophet]:[127] for We have sent thee but as a herald of glad tidings and a warner, ‹105› [bearing] a discourse which We have gradually unfolded,[128] so that thou might read it out to mankind by stages, seeing that We have bestowed it from on high step by step, as [one] revelation.[129] ‹106›

---

participle *masḥūr*, which I consider preferable in view of the subsequent reference to the miraculous signs granted by God to Moses.

123 See *sūrah* 6, note 94.

124 See *sūrah* 7, note 100.

125 According to Rāzī, the expression *lafīf* denotes a human crowd composed of innumerable heterogeneous elements, good and bad, strong and weak, fortunate and unfortunate: in short, it characterizes mankind in all its aspects. It is obviously used here to refute, once again, the idea that the children of Israel are a "chosen people" by virtue of their Abrahamic descent and, therefore, *a priori* and invariably destined for God's grace. The Qurʾān rejects this claim by stating that on Resurrection Day *all* mankind will be judged, and none will have a privileged position.

126 Lit., "with truth" or "in truth".

127 I.e., it has come down to man, through the Prophet, without any alteration, omission or addition.

128 Lit., "which We have divided into [consecutive] parts" or, according to some authorities (quoted by Rāzī), "set forth with clarity". The rendering adopted by me allows for both these meanings.

129 The above verse alludes both to the historical fact that the process of the revelation of the Qurʾān was gradual, extending over the twenty-three years of the Prophet's ministry, and to the fact that it is nevertheless one integral whole and can, therefore, be properly understood only if it is considered *in its entirety* – that is to say, if each of its passages is read in the light of all the other passages which it contains. (See also 20 : 114 and the corresponding note 101.)

قُلْ ءَامِنُوا۟ بِهِۦٓ أَوْ لَا تُؤْمِنُوٓا۟ ۚ إِنَّ ٱلَّذِينَ أُوتُوا۟ ٱلْعِلْمَ مِن قَبْلِهِۦٓ إِذَا يُتْلَىٰ
عَلَيْهِمْ يَخِرُّونَ لِلْأَذْقَانِ سُجَّدًا ﴿١٠٧﴾ وَيَقُولُونَ سُبْحَـٰنَ رَبِّنَآ إِن كَانَ
وَعْدُ رَبِّنَا لَمَفْعُولًا ﴿١٠٨﴾ وَيَخِرُّونَ لِلْأَذْقَانِ يَبْكُونَ وَيَزِيدُهُمْ خُشُوعًا
۩ ﴿١٠٩﴾ قُلِ ٱدْعُوا۟ ٱللَّهَ أَوِ ٱدْعُوا۟ ٱلرَّحْمَـٰنَ ۖ أَيًّا مَّا تَدْعُوا۟ فَلَهُ ٱلْأَسْمَآءُ
ٱلْحُسْنَىٰ ۚ وَلَا تَجْهَرْ بِصَلَاتِكَ وَلَا تُخَافِتْ بِهَا وَٱبْتَغِ بَيْنَ ذَٰلِكَ سَبِيلًا ﴿١١٠﴾
وَقُلِ ٱلْحَمْدُ لِلَّهِ ٱلَّذِى لَمْ يَتَّخِذْ وَلَدًا وَلَمْ يَكُن لَّهُۥ شَرِيكٌ فِى ٱلْمُلْكِ
وَلَمْ يَكُن لَّهُۥ وَلِىٌّ مِّنَ ٱلذُّلِّ ۖ وَكَبِّرْهُ تَكْبِيرًۢا ﴿١١١﴾

السجدة

Qul ᵓāminū bihīi ᵓaw lā tuᵓminū. ᵓInnal-ladhīna ᵓūtul-ᶜilma miñ-qablihīi ᵓidhā yutlā ᶜalayhim yakhirrūna lilᵓadhqāni sujjadā. ﴿107﴾ Wa yaqūlūna subḥāna Rabbināa ᵓiñ-kāna waᶜdu Rabbinā lamafᶜūlā. ﴿108﴾ Wa yakhirrūna lilᵓadhqāni yabkūna wa yazīduhum khushūᶜā. ۩ ﴿109﴾ Qulid-ᶜul-lāha ᵓawid-ᶜur-Raḥmāna ᵓayyam-mā tadᶜū falahul-ᵓAsmāaᵓul-Ḥusnā. Wa lā tajhar biṢalātika wa lā tukhāfit bihā wab-taghi bayna dhālika sabīlā. ﴿110﴾ Wa qulil-ḥamdu lillāhil-ladhī lam yattakhidh waladañw-wa lam yakul-lahū sharīkuñ-fil-mulki wa lam yakul-lahū waliyyum-minadh-dhulli wa kabbirhu takbīrā. ﴿111﴾

Say: "Believe in it or do not believe." Behold, those who are already[130] endowed with [innate] knowledge fall down upon their faces in prostration as soon as this [divine writ] is conveyed unto them, ‹107› and say, "Limitless in His glory is our Sustainer! Verily, our Sustainer's promise has been fulfilled!"[131] ‹108›

And so they fall down upon their faces, weeping, and [their consciousness of God's grace] increases their humility. ‹109›

Say: "Invoke God, or invoke the Most Gracious: by whichever name you invoke Him, [He is always the One – for] His are all the attributes of perfection."[132]

And [pray unto Him; yet] be not too loud in thy prayer nor speak it in too low a voice, but follow a way in-between; ‹110› and say: "All praise is due to God, who begets no offspring,[133] and has no partner in His dominion, and has no weakness, and therefore no need of any aid"[134] – and [thus] extol His limitless greatness. ‹111›

---

130 Lit., "before it" – i.e., before the Qurᵓān as such has come within their ken.

131 This may be an allusion to the many Biblical predictions of the advent of the Prophet Muḥammad, especially to Deuteronomy xviii, 15 and 18 (cf. *sūrah* 2, note 33). In its wider sense, however, the "fulfilment of God's promise" relates to His bestowal of a definitive revelation, the Qurᵓān, henceforth destined to guide man at all stages of his spiritual, cultural and social development.

132 For an explanation of the expression *al-asmāᵓ al-ḥusnā* (lit., "the most perfect [or "most goodly"] names"), see *sūrah* 7, note 145. The epithet *ar-rahman* – rendered by me throughout as "the Most Gracious" – has an intensive significance, denoting the unconditional, all-embracing quality and exercise of grace and mercy, and is applied exclusively to God, "who has willed upon Himself the law of grace and mercy" (6 : 12 and 54).

133 Lit., "who has not taken unto Himself [or "begotten"] a son" – i.e., who is free of the imperfection inherent in the concept of begetting a child as an extension of one's own being. Since this statement not merely refutes the Christian doctrine of Jesus as "the son of God" but, beyond that, stresses the *logical impossibility* of connecting such a concept with God, the clause is best rendered in the present tense, and the noun *walad* in its primary sense of "offspring", which applies to a child of either sex.

134 Lit., "and has no protector [to aid Him] on account of any [supposed] weakness [on His part]".

The Eighteenth Sūrah

Al-kahf (The Cave)

Mecca Period

THIS SŪRAH – revealed immediately before *An-Naḥl* ("The Bee"), i.e., in the last year of the Mecca period – is almost entirely devoted to a series of parables or allegories built around the theme of faith in God *versus* an undue attachment to the life of this world; and the key-phrase of the whole *sūrah* is the statement in verse 7, "We have willed that all beauty on earth be a means by which we put men to a test" – an idea that is most clearly formulated in the parable of the rich man and the poor man (verses 32-44).

The story of the Men of the Cave – from which the *sūrah* takes its title – illustrates (in verses 13-20) the principle of world-abandonment for the sake of faith, and is deepened into an allegory of death, resurrection and spiritual awakening. In the story of Moses and the unnamed sage (verses 60-82) the theme of spiritual awakening undergoes a significant variation: it is shifted to the plane of man's *intellectual* life and his search after ultimate truths. Appearance and reality are shown to be intrinsically different – so different that only mystic insight can reveal to us what is apparent and what is real. And, finally, the allegory of *Dhu 'l-Qarnayn*, "the Two-Horned One", tells us that world-renunciation is not, in itself, a necessary complement of one's faith in God: in other words, that worldly life and power need not conflict with spiritual righteousness so long as we remain conscious of the ephemeral nature of all works of man and of our ultimate responsibility to Him who is above all limitations of time and appearance. And so the *sūrah* ends with the words: "Hence, whoever looks forward to meeting his Sustainer, let him do righteous deeds, and let him not ascribe unto anyone or anything a share in the worship due to his Sustainer."

سورة الكهف مكية -18-
وآياتها عشر ومائة

IN THE NAME OF GOD, THE MOST GRACIOUS, THE DISPENSER OF GRACE:

ALL PRAISE is due to God, who has bestowed this divine writ from on high upon His servant, and has not allowed any deviousness to obscure its meaning:[1] ‹1› [a divine writ] unerringly straight, meant to warn [the godless] of a severe punishment from Him, and to give unto the believers who do good works the glad tiding that theirs shall be a goodly reward ‹2› – [a state of bliss] in which they shall dwell beyond the count of time. ‹3›

Furthermore, [this divine writ is meant] to warn all those who assert, "God has taken unto Himself a son." ‹4› No knowledge whatever have they of Him,[2] and neither had their forefathers: dreadful is this saying that comes out of their mouths, [and] nothing but falsehood do they utter! ‹5›

But wouldst thou, perhaps,[3] torment thyself to death with grief over them if they are not willing to believe in this message?[4] ‹6›

بِسْمِ ٱللَّهِ ٱلرَّحْمَٰنِ ٱلرَّحِيمِ

ٱلْحَمْدُ لِلَّهِ ٱلَّذِىٓ أَنزَلَ عَلَىٰ عَبْدِهِ ٱلْكِتَٰبَ وَلَمْ يَجْعَل لَّهُۥ عِوَجَا ﴿١﴾
قَيِّمًا لِّيُنذِرَ بَأْسًا شَدِيدًا مِّن لَّدُنْهُ وَيُبَشِّرَ ٱلْمُؤْمِنِينَ ٱلَّذِينَ يَعْمَلُونَ
ٱلصَّٰلِحَٰتِ أَنَّ لَهُمْ أَجْرًا حَسَنًا ﴿٢﴾ مَّٰكِثِينَ فِيهِ أَبَدًا ﴿٣﴾ وَيُنذِرَ
ٱلَّذِينَ قَالُوا۟ ٱتَّخَذَ ٱللَّهُ وَلَدًا ﴿٤﴾ مَّا لَهُم بِهِۦ مِنْ عِلْمٍ وَلَا لِءَابَآئِهِمْ
كَبُرَتْ كَلِمَةً تَخْرُجُ مِنْ أَفْوَٰهِهِمْ إِن يَقُولُونَ إِلَّا كَذِبًا ﴿٥﴾ فَلَعَلَّكَ
بَٰخِعٌ نَّفْسَكَ عَلَىٰٓ ءَاثَٰرِهِمْ إِن لَّمْ يُؤْمِنُوا۟ بِهَٰذَا ٱلْحَدِيثِ أَسَفًا ﴿٦﴾

سكتة لطيفة على الف عوجا

Bismil-lāhir-Raḥmānir-Raḥīm.
ʾAlḥamdu lillāhil-ladhīi ʾañzala ʿalā ʿabdihil-Kitāba wa lam yajʿal-lahū ʿiwajā. (1) Qayyimal-liyuñdhira baʾsañ-shadīdam-mil-ladunhu wa yubashshiral-muʾminīnal-ladhīna yaʿmalūnaṣ-ṣāliḥāti ʾanna lahum ʾajran ḥasanā. (2) Mākithīna fīhi ʾabadā. (3) Wa yuñdhiral-ladhīna qālut-takhadhal-lāhu waladā. (4) Mā lahum-bihī min ʿilmiñw-wa lā liʾābāaʾihim. Kaburat kalimatañ-takhruju min ʾafwāhihim; ʾiñy-yaqūlūna ʾillā kadhibā. (5) Falaʿallaka bākhiʿuñ-nafsaka ʿalāa ʾāthārihim ʾil-lam yuʾminū bihādhal-ḥadīthi ʾasafā. (6)

---

1 Lit., "and has not given it any deviousness". The term *ʿiwaj* signifies "crookedness", "tortuousness" or "deviation" (e.g., from a path), as well as "distortion" or "deviousness" in the abstract sense of these words. The above phrase is meant to establish the direct, unambiguous character of the Qurʾān and to stress its freedom from all obscurities and internal contradictions: cf. 4 : 82 – "Had it issued from any but God, they would surely have found in it many an inner contradiction!"

2 Most of the classical commentators (and, as far as I am aware, all the earlier translators of the Qurʾān) relate the pronoun in *bihi* to the assertion that "God has taken unto Himself a son", and hence take the phrase to mean, "They have no knowledge of it", i.e., no knowledge of such a happening. However, this interpretation is weak inasmuch as absence of knowledge does not necessarily imply an objective negation of the fact to which it relates. It is, therefore, obvious that *bihi* cannot signify "of it": it signifies "of *Him*", and relates to God. Hence, the phrase must be rendered as above – meaning that they who make such a preposterous claim have no real knowledge of Him, since they attribute to the Supreme Being something that is attributable only to created, imperfect beings. This interpretation is supported, in an unequivocal manner, by Ṭabarī and, as an alternative, by Bayḍāwī.

3 Lit., "it may well be that thou wilt . . .", etc. However, the particle *laʿalla* does not, in this context, indicate a *possibility* but, rather, a rhetorical question implying a reproach for the attitude referred to (Marāghī XIII, 116).

4 This rhetorical question is addressed, in the first instance, to the Prophet, who was deeply distressed by the hostility which his message aroused among the pagan Meccans, and suffered agonies of apprehension regarding

Behold, We have willed that all beauty on earth be a means by which We put men to a test,[5] [showing] which of them are best in conduct; ‹7› and, verily, [in time] We shall reduce all that is on it to barren dust! ‹8›

إِنَّا جَعَلْنَا مَا عَلَى ٱلْأَرْضِ زِينَةً لَّهَا لِنَبْلُوَهُمْ أَيُّهُمْ أَحْسَنُ عَمَلًا ﴿٧﴾
وَإِنَّا لَجَٰعِلُونَ مَا عَلَيْهَا صَعِيدًا جُرُزًا ﴿٨﴾ أَمْ حَسِبْتَ أَنَّ أَصْحَٰبَ
ٱلْكَهْفِ وَٱلرَّقِيمِ كَانُوا۟ مِنْ ءَايَٰتِنَا عَجَبًا ﴿٩﴾

[AND SINCE the life of this world is but a test,][6] dost thou [really] think that [the parable of] the Men of the Cave and of [their devotion to] the scriptures could be deemed more wondrous than any [other] of Our messages?[7] ‹9›

ʾInnā jaʿalnā mā ʿalal-ʾarḍi zīnatal-lahā linabluwahum ʾayyuhum ʾaḥsanu ʿamalā. (7) Wa ʾinnā lajāʿilūna mā ʿalayhā ṣaʿīdañ-juruzā. (8) ʾAm ḥasibta ʾanna ʾaṣḥābal-kahfi war-raqīmi kānū min ʾĀyātinā ʿajabā. (9)

their spiritual fate. Beyond that, however, it applies to everyone who, having become convinced of the truth of an ethical proposition, is dismayed at the indifference with which his social environment reacts to it.

5 Lit., "We have made all that exists on earth as its adornment in order that We might put them [i.e., all human beings] to a test": meaning that God lets them reveal their real characters in their respective attitudes – moral or immoral - towards the material goods and benefits which the world offers them. In further analysis, this passage implies that the real motive underlying men's refusal to believe in God's spiritual message (see preceding verse) is almost always their excessive, blind attachment to the good of this world, combined with a false pride in what they regard as their own achievements (cf. 16 : 22 and the corresponding note 15).

6 This interpolation establishes the elliptically implied connection between the long passage that follows and the preceding two verses.

7 Lit., "that the Men of the Cave . . . were more wondrous . . .", etc. – the implication being that the allegory or parable based on this story is entirely in tune with the ethical doctrine propounded in the Qurʾān as a whole, and therefore not "more wondrous" than any other of its statements. – As regards the story of the Men of the Cave as such, most of the commentators incline to the view that it relates to a phase in early Christian history – namely, the persecution of the Christians by Emperor Decius in the third century. Legend has it that some young Christians of Ephesus, accompanied by their dog, withdrew into a secluded cave in order to be able to live in accordance with their faith, and remained there, miraculously asleep, for a great length of time (according to some accounts, referred to in verse 25 of this *sūrah*, for about three centuries). When they finally awoke – unaware of the long time during which they had lain asleep – they sent one of their company to the town to purchase some food. In the meantime the situation had changed entirely: Christianity was no longer persecuted and had even become the official religion of the Roman Empire. The ancient coin (dating from the reign of Decius) with which the young man wanted to pay for his purchases immediately aroused curiosity; people began to question the stranger, and the story of the Men of the Cave and their miraculous sleep came to light.

As already mentioned, the majority of the classical commentators rely on this Christian legend in their endeavour to interpret the Qurʾanic reference (in verses 9-26) to the Men of the Cave. It seems, however, that the Christian formulation of this theme is a later development of a much older oral tradition – a tradition which, in fact, goes back to pre-Christian, Jewish sources. This is evident from several well-authenticated *aḥādīth* (mentioned by all the classical commentators), according to which it was the Jewish rabbis (*aḥbār*) of Medina who induced the Meccan opponents of Muḥammad to "test his veracity" by asking him to explain, among other problems, the story of the Men of the Cave. Referring to these *aḥādīth*, Ibn Kathīr remarks in his commentary on verse 13 of this *sūrah* : "It has been said that they were followers of Jesus the son of Mary, but God knows it better: it is obvious that they lived much earlier than the Christian period – for, had they been Christians, why should the Jewish rabbis have been intent on preserving their story, seeing that the Jews had cut themselves off from all friendly communion with them [i.e., the Christians]?" We may, therefore, safely assume that the legend of the Men of the Cave – stripped of its Christian garb and the superimposed Christian background – is, substantially, of Jewish origin. If we discard the later syncretic additions and reduce the story to its fundamentals – voluntary withdrawal from the world, agelong "sleep" in a secluded cave and a miraculous "awakening" after an indeterminate period of time – we have before us a striking allegory relating to a movement which played an important role in Jewish religious history during the centuries immediately preceding and following the advent of Jesus: namely, the ascetic Essene Brotherhood (to which, as I have pointed out in note 42 on 3 : 52, Jesus himself may have belonged), and particularly that of its branches which lived in self-imposed solitude in the vicinity of the Dead Sea and has recently, after the discovery of the Dead Sea Scrolls, come to be known as the "Qumran community". The expression *ar-raqīm* occurring in the above Qurʾān-verse (and rendered by me as "scriptures") lends strong support to this theory. As recorded by Ṭabarī, some

When those youths took refuge in the cave, they prayed: "O our Sustainer! Bestow on us grace from Thyself, and endow us, whatever our [outward] condition, with consciousness of what is right!"[8] ‹10›

And thereupon We veiled their ears in the cave[9] for many a year, ‹11› and then We awakened them:[10] [and We did all this] so that We might mark out [to the world][11] which of the two points of view showed a better comprehension of the time-span during which they had remained in this state.[12] ‹12›

[And now] We shall truly relate to thee their story:[13]

Behold, they were young men who had attained to faith in their Sustainer: and [so] We deepened their consciousness of the right way[14] ‹13› and endowed their hearts

إِذْ أَوَى ٱلْفِتْيَةُ إِلَى ٱلْكَهْفِ فَقَالُوا۟ رَبَّنَآ ءَاتِنَا مِن لَّدُنكَ رَحْمَةً وَهَيِّئْ لَنَا مِنْ
أَمْرِنَا رَشَدًا ﴿10﴾ فَضَرَبْنَا عَلَىٰٓ ءَاذَانِهِمْ فِى ٱلْكَهْفِ سِنِينَ عَدَدًا ﴿11﴾ ثُمَّ
بَعَثْنَٰهُمْ لِنَعْلَمَ أَىُّ ٱلْحِزْبَيْنِ أَحْصَىٰ لِمَا لَبِثُوٓا۟ أَمَدًا ﴿12﴾ نَّحْنُ نَقُصُّ عَلَيْكَ
نَبَأَهُم بِٱلْحَقِّ ۚ إِنَّهُمْ فِتْيَةٌ ءَامَنُوا۟ بِرَبِّهِمْ وَزِدْنَٰهُمْ هُدًى ﴿13﴾ وَرَبَطْنَا عَلَىٰ قُلُوبِهِمْ

ʾIdh ʾawal-fityatu ʾilal-kahfi faqālū Rabbanāa ʾātinā mil-laduñka raḥmatañw-wa hayyiʾ lanā min ʾamrinā rashadā. (10) Faḍarabnā ʿalāa ʾādhānihim fil-kahfi sinīna ʿadadā. (11) Thumma baʿathnāhum linaʿlama ʾayyul-ḥizbayni ʾaḥṣā limā labithūu ʾamadā. (12) Naḥnu naquṣṣu ʿalayka nabaʾahum bilḥaqq. ʾInnahum fityatun ʾāmanū biRabbihim wa zidnāhum hudā. (13) Wa rabaṭnā ʿalā qulūbihim

of the earliest authorities – and particularly Ibn ʿAbbās – regarded this expression as synonymous with *marqūm* ("something that is written") and hence with *kitāb* ("a writ" or "a scripture"); and Rāzī adds that "all rhetoricians and Arabic philologists assert that *ar-raqīm* signifies [the same as] *al-kitāb*". Since it is historically established that the members of the Qumran community – the strictest group among the Essenes – devoted themselves entirely to the study, the copying and the preservation of the sacred scriptures, and since they lived in complete seclusion from the rest of the world and were highly admired for their piety and moral purity, it is more than probable that their mode of life made so strong an impression on the imagination of their more worldly co-religionists that it became gradually allegorized in the story of the Men of the Cave who "slept" – that is, were cut off from the outside world – for countless years, destined to be "awakened" after their spiritual task was done.

But whatever the source of this legend, and irrespective of whether it is of Jewish or Christian origin, the fact remains that it is used in the Qurʾān in a purely parabolic sense: namely, as an illustration of God's power to bring about death (or "sleep") and resurrection (or "awakening"); and, secondly, as an allegory of the piety that induces men to abandon a wicked or frivolous world in order to keep their faith unsullied, and of God's recognition of that faith by His bestowal of a spiritual awakening which transcends time and death.

8 Lit., "and provide for us, out of our condition (*min amrinā*), consciousness of what is right" – which latter phrase gives the meaning of the term *rushd* in this context. This passage is a kind of introduction to the allegory of the Men of the Cave, giving a broad outline of what is expounded more fully in verses 13 ff.

9 I.e., God caused them to remain cut off – physically or metaphorically – from the sounds and the bustle of the outside world. The classical commentators take the above phrase to mean that God "veiled their ears with sleep".

10 Or: "sent them forth" – which may indicate a return to the active life of this world.

11 Lit., "so that We might take cognizance of": but since God embraces all past, present and future with His knowledge, His "taking cognizance" of an event denotes His *causing it to come into being* and, thus, allowing it to become known by His creatures: hence, "marking it out" to the world.

12 Lit., "which of the two parties" – alluding, metonymically, to the two viewpoints mentioned in verse 19 below – "was better at computing the time-span . . .", etc.: it should, however, be borne in mind that the verb *aḥṣā* does not merely signify "he computed" or "reckoned", but also "he understood" or "comprehended" (*Tāj al-ʿArūs*). Since a "computing" of the time which those seekers after truth had spent in the cave could have no particular bearing on the ethical implications of this parable, *aḥṣā* has here obviously the meaning of "better at comprehending" or "showing a better comprehension" – namely, of the spiritual meaning of the time-lapse between their "falling asleep" and their "awakening" (see note 25 below).

13 I.e., without the many legendary embellishments which, in times past, have obscured the purport of this story or parable.

14 Lit., "We increased [or "advanced"] them in guidance".

إِذْ قَامُوا۟ فَقَالُوا۟ رَبُّنَا رَبُّ ٱلسَّمَٰوَٰتِ وَٱلْأَرْضِ لَن نَّدْعُوَا۟ مِن دُونِهِۦٓ
إِلَٰهًا ۖ لَّقَدْ قُلْنَآ إِذًا شَطَطًا ﴿١٤﴾ هَٰٓؤُلَآءِ قَوْمُنَا ٱتَّخَذُوا۟ مِن دُونِهِۦٓ ءَالِهَةً ۖ
لَّوْلَا يَأْتُونَ عَلَيْهِم بِسُلْطَٰنٍۭ بَيِّنٍ ۖ فَمَنْ أَظْلَمُ مِمَّنِ ٱفْتَرَىٰ عَلَى ٱللَّهِ
كَذِبًا ﴿١٥﴾ وَإِذِ ٱعْتَزَلْتُمُوهُمْ وَمَا يَعْبُدُونَ إِلَّا ٱللَّهَ فَأْوُۥٓا۟ إِلَى ٱلْكَهْفِ
يَنشُرْ لَكُمْ رَبُّكُم مِّن رَّحْمَتِهِۦ وَيُهَيِّئْ لَكُم مِّنْ أَمْرِكُم مِّرْفَقًا ﴿١٦﴾ ۞
وَتَرَى ٱلشَّمْسَ إِذَا طَلَعَت تَّزَٰوَرُ عَن كَهْفِهِمْ ذَاتَ ٱلْيَمِينِ وَإِذَا غَرَبَت
تَّقْرِضُهُمْ ذَاتَ ٱلشِّمَالِ وَهُمْ فِى فَجْوَةٍ مِّنْهُ ۚ ذَٰلِكَ مِنْ ءَايَٰتِ ٱللَّهِ ۗ مَن يَهْدِ ٱللَّهُ
فَهُوَ ٱلْمُهْتَدِ ۖ وَمَن يُضْلِلْ فَلَن تَجِدَ لَهُۥ وَلِيًّا مُّرْشِدًا ﴿١٧﴾ وَتَحْسَبُهُمْ أَيْقَاظًا
وَهُمْ رُقُودٌ ۚ وَنُقَلِّبُهُمْ ذَاتَ ٱلْيَمِينِ وَذَاتَ ٱلشِّمَالِ ۖ وَكَلْبُهُم بَٰسِطٌ ذِرَاعَيْهِ

ربع الحزب

with strength, so that they stood up[15] and said [to one another]: "Our Sustainer is the Sustainer of the heavens and the earth. Never shall we invoke any deity other than Him: [if we did,] we should indeed have uttered an enormity! ‹14› These people of ours have taken to worshipping [other] deities instead of Him, without being able to[16] adduce any reasonable evidence in support of their beliefs;[17] and who could be more wicked than he who invents a lie about God?[18] ‹15› Hence, now that you have withdrawn from them and from all that they worship instead of God, take refuge in that cave: God will spread His grace over you, and will endow you – whatever your [outward] condition – with all that your souls may need!"[19] ‹16›

And [for many a year] thou might have seen the sun, on its rising, incline away from their cave on the right, and, on its setting, turn aside from them on the left, while they lived on in that spacious chamber,[20] [bearing witness to] this of God's messages: He whom God guides, he alone has found the right way; whereas for him whom He lets go astray thou canst never find any protector who would point out the right way. ‹17›

And thou wouldst have thought that they were awake, whereas they lay asleep. And We caused them to turn over repeatedly, now to the right, now to the left; and their dog [lay] on the threshold, its forepaws

ʾidh qāmū faqālū Rabbunā Rabbus-samāwāti wal-ʾarḍi lañ-nadʿuwa miñ-dūnihīi ʾilāhal-laqad qulnāa ʾidhañ-shaṭaṭā. (14) Hāaʾulāaʾi qawmunat-takhadhū miñ-dūnihīi ʾālihah. Lawlā yaʾtūna ʿalayhim-bisulṭānim-bayyin. Faman ʾaẓlamu mim-manif-tarā ʿalal-lāhi kadhibā. (15) Wa ʾidhiʿ-tazaltumūhum wa mā yaʿbudūna ʾillal-lāha faʾwūu ʾilal-kahfi yañshur lakum Rabbukum-mir-raḥmatihī wa yuhayyiʾ lakum-min ʾamrikum-mirfaqā. (16) ۞ Wa tarash-shamsa ʾidhā ṭalaʿat-tazāwaru ʿañ-kahfihim dhātal-yamīni wa ʾidhā gharabat-taqriḍuhum zātash-shimāli wa hum fī fajwatim-minh. Dhālika min ʾĀyātil-lāh. Mañy-yahdil-lāhu fahuwal-muhtadi wa mañy-yuḍlil falañ-tajida lahū waliyyam-murshidā. (17) Wa taḥsabuhum ʾayqāẓañw-wa hum ruqūd. Wa nuqallibuhum dhātal-yamīni wa dhātash-shimāli wa kalbuhum bāsiṭuñ-dhirāʿayhi

15 Lit., "*when* they stood up" – i.e., stood up to their misguided fellow-men, or to the rulers who persecuted the believers (see note 7).

16 Lit., "Why do they not . . .", etc., in the form of a rhetorical query introducing a new sentence.

17 Lit., "any clear evidence [or "authority"] in their support". The adjective *bayyin* ("clear", "obvious", "manifest") implies an evidence accessible to reason.

18 I.e., invents imaginary deities and thus gives the lie to the truth of His oneness and uniqueness, or even denies His existence altogether.

19 The term *mirfaq* signifies "anything by which one benefits", whether concrete or abstract; in this context it has obviously a spiritual connotation, marking the young men's abandonment of the world and withdrawal into utter seclusion.

20 Lit., "while they were in a broad cleft thereof". The cave evidently opened to the north, so that the heat of the sun never disturbed them: and this, I believe is an echo of the many Qurʾanic allusions to the happiness of the righteous in paradise, symbolized by its "everlasting shade" (see, in particular, *sūrah* 4, note 74, on the metaphorical use of the term *ẓill* in the sense of "happiness").

outstretched. Hadst thou come upon them [unprepared], thou wouldst surely have turned away from them in flight, and wouldst surely have been filled with awe of them.[21] ‹18›

And so, [in the course of time,] We awakened them;[22] and they began to ask one another [as to what had happened to them].[23]

One of them asked: "How long have you remained thus?"

[The others] answered: "We have remained thus a day, or part of a day."[24]

Said they [who were endowed with deeper insight]: "Your Sustainer knows best how long you have thus remained.[25] Let, then, one of you go with these silver coins to the town, and let him find out what food is purest there, and bring you thereof [some] provisions. But let him behave with great care and by no means make anyone aware of you: ‹19› for, behold, if they should come to know of you, they might stone you to death or force you back to their faith – in which case you would never attain to any good!"[26] ‹20›

بِٱلْوَصِيدِ لَوِ ٱطَّلَعْتَ عَلَيْهِمْ لَوَلَّيْتَ مِنْهُمْ فِرَارًا وَلَمُلِئْتَ مِنْهُمْ
رُعْبًا ﴿١٨﴾ وَكَذَٰلِكَ بَعَثْنَٰهُمْ لِيَتَسَآءَلُوا۟ بَيْنَهُمْ ۚ قَالَ قَآئِلٌ مِّنْهُمْ كَمْ
لَبِثْتُمْ ۖ قَالُوا۟ لَبِثْنَا يَوْمًا أَوْ بَعْضَ يَوْمٍ ۚ قَالُوا۟ رَبُّكُمْ أَعْلَمُ بِمَا لَبِثْتُمْ فَٱبْعَثُوٓا۟
أَحَدَكُم بِوَرِقِكُمْ هَٰذِهِۦٓ إِلَى ٱلْمَدِينَةِ فَلْيَنظُرْ أَيُّهَآ أَزْكَىٰ طَعَامًا فَلْيَأْتِكُم
بِرِزْقٍ مِّنْهُ وَلْيَتَلَطَّفْ وَلَا يُشْعِرَنَّ بِكُمْ أَحَدًا ﴿١٩﴾ إِنَّهُمْ إِن يَظْهَرُوا۟
عَلَيْكُمْ يَرْجُمُوكُمْ أَوْ يُعِيدُوكُمْ فِى مِلَّتِهِمْ وَلَن تُفْلِحُوٓا۟ إِذًا أَبَدًا ﴿٢٠﴾

bilwaṣīd. Lawiṭ-ṭalaʿta ʿalayhim lawallayta minhum firārañw-wa lamuliʾta minhum ruʿbā. (18) Wa kadhālika baʿathnāhum liyatasāaʾalū baynahum. Qāla qāaʾilum-minhum kam labithtum. Qālū labithnā yawman ʾaw baʿḍa yawm. Qālū Rabbukum ʾaʿlamu bimā labithtum fabʿathūu ʾaḥadakum biwariqikum hādhihīi ʾilal-madīnati falyañẓur ʾayyuhāa ʾazkā ṭaʿāmañ-falyaʾtikum-birizqim-minhu wal-yatalaṭṭaf wa lā yushʿiranna bikum ʾaḥadā. (19) ʾInnahum ʾiñy-yaẓharū ʿalaykum yarjumūkum ʾaw yuʿīdūkum fī millatihim wa lañ-tufliḥūu ʾidhan ʾabadā. (20)

21 I.e., an accidental onlooker would immediately have felt the mystic, awe-inspiring aura that surrounded the Men of the Cave, and would have become conscious that he stood before God's elect (Ṭabarī, Rāzī, Ibn Kathīr, Bayḍāwī).

22 See note 10 above.

23 It seems to me that the prefix *li* in *li-yatasāʾalū* (which most commentators take to mean "so that they might ask one another") is not a particle denoting a purpose ("so that") but, rather, a *lām al-ʿāqibah* – that is, a particle indicating no more than a causal sequence – which in this context may be brought out by the phrase "and they began . . .", etc.

24 Cf. 2 : 259, where exactly the same question is asked and exactly the same wondering answer is given in the parable of the man whom God caused to be dead for a hundred years and thereupon brought back to life. The striking verbal identity of question and answer in the two passages is obviously not accidental: it points, in a deliberately revealing manner, to the identity of the *idea* underlying these two allegories: namely, God's power to "bring forth the living out of that which is dead, and the dead out of that which is alive" (3 : 27, 6 : 95, 10 : 31, 30 : 19), i.e., to create life, to cause it to disappear and then to resurrect it. Beyond this, the above verse alludes to the deceptive, purely earthbound character of the human concept of "time".

25 I.e., they understood – in contrast to their companions, who were merely concerned about what had "actually" happened to them – that the lapse of time between their "falling asleep" and their "awakening" had no reality of its own and no meaning, just as it has no reality or meaning in connection with a human being's death and subsequent resurrection (cf. 17 : 52 and the corresponding note 59): and this explains the reference to the "two viewpoints" (lit., "two parties") in verse 12 above.

26 During their "sleep", time had stood still for the Men of the Cave, and so they assumed that the outside world had remained unchanged and was, as before, hostile to them. – At this point, the story as such ends abruptly (for, as we know, the Qurʾān is never concerned with narratives for their own sake) and is revealed in the sequence as an allegory of death and resurrection and of the relativity of "time" as manifested in man's consciousness.

وَكَذَٰلِكَ أَعْثَرْنَا عَلَيْهِمْ لِيَعْلَمُوٓاْ أَنَّ وَعْدَ ٱللَّهِ حَقٌّ وَأَنَّ ٱلسَّاعَةَ لَا رَيْبَ
فِيهَآ إِذْ يَتَنَٰزَعُونَ بَيْنَهُمْ أَمْرَهُمْ ۖ فَقَالُواْ ٱبْنُواْ عَلَيْهِم بُنْيَٰنًا ۖ رَّبُّهُمْ أَعْلَمُ
بِهِمْ ۚ قَالَ ٱلَّذِينَ غَلَبُواْ عَلَىٰٓ أَمْرِهِمْ لَنَتَّخِذَنَّ عَلَيْهِم مَّسْجِدًا ﴿21﴾ سَيَقُولُونَ
ثَلَٰثَةٌ رَّابِعُهُمْ كَلْبُهُمْ وَيَقُولُونَ خَمْسَةٌ سَادِسُهُمْ كَلْبُهُمْ رَجْمًا بِٱلْغَيْبِ ۖ
وَيَقُولُونَ سَبْعَةٌ وَثَامِنُهُمْ كَلْبُهُمْ ۚ قُل رَّبِّىٓ أَعْلَمُ بِعِدَّتِهِم مَّا يَعْلَمُهُمْ إِلَّا
قَلِيلٌ ۗ فَلَا تُمَارِ فِيهِمْ إِلَّا مِرَآءً ظَٰهِرًا وَلَا تَسْتَفْتِ فِيهِم مِّنْهُمْ أَحَدًا ﴿22﴾
وَلَا تَقُولَنَّ لِشَاْىْءٍ إِنِّى فَاعِلٌ ذَٰلِكَ غَدًا ﴿23﴾ إِلَّآ أَن يَشَآءَ ٱللَّهُ ۚ وَٱذْكُر رَّبَّكَ

AND IN THIS way[27] have We drawn [people's] attention to their story,[28] so that they might know – whenever they debate among themselves as to what happened to those [Men of the Cave][29] – that God's promise [of resurrection] is true, and that there can be no doubt as to [the coming of] the Last Hour.

And so, some [people] said: "Erect a building in their memory;[30] their Sustainer knows best what happened to them." Said they whose opinion prevailed in the end: "Indeed, we must surely raise a house of worship in their memory!" ‹21›

[And in times to come] some will say,[31] "[They were] three, the fourth of them being their dog," while others will say, "Five, with their dog as the sixth of them" – idly guessing at something of which they can have no knowledge – and [so on, until] some will say, "[They were] seven, the eighth of them being their dog."

Say: "My Sustainer knows best how many they were. None but a few have any [real] knowledge of them. Hence, do not argue about them otherwise than by way of an obvious argument,[32] and do not ask any of those [story-tellers] to enlighten thee about them." ‹22›

AND NEVER say about anything, "Behold, I shall do this tomorrow," ‹23› without [adding], "if God so wills."[33] And if thou shouldst forget [thyself at the time, and become aware of it later], call thy Sustainer

Wa kadhālika ʾaʿtharnā ʿalayhim liyaʿlamūu ʾanna waʿdal-lāhi ḥaqquñw-wa ʾannas-Sāʿata lā rayba fīhāa ʾidh yatanāzaʿūna baynahum ʾamrahum. Faqālub-nū ʿalayhim bunyānañ-Rabbuhum ʾaʿlamu bihim; qālal-ladhīna ghalabū ʿalāa ʾamrihim lanat-takhidhanna ʿalayhim-masjidā. (21) Sayaqūlūna thalāthatur-rābiʿuhum kalbuhum wa yaqūlūna khamsatuñ-sādisuhum kalbuhum rajmam-bilghaybi wa yaqūlūna sabʿatuñw-wa thāminuhum kalbuhum. Qur-Rabbīi ʾaʿlamu biʿiddatihim-mā yaʿlamuhum ʾillā qalīl. Falā tumāri fīhim ʾillā mirāaʾañ-ẓāhirañw-wa lā tastafti fīhim-minhum ʾaḥadā. (22) Wa lā taqūlanna lishayʾin ʾinnī fāʿiluñ-dhālika ghadan, (23) ʾillāa ʾañy-yashāaʾal-lāh. Wadh-kur-Rabbaka

27 I.e., by means of the legend which has grown up around the Men of the Cave and, more particularly, by means of the allegoric use which the Qurʾān makes of this legend.

28 Lit., "given knowledge about them [to others]".

29 Lit., "debate their case (*amrahum*) among themselves": an indication of the fact that the legend of the Men of the Cave occupied men's minds for a long time, leading to many discussions and conflicting interpretations. The next sentence explains why God has "drawn [people's] attention" to this story in the context of the Qurʾān.

30 This, to my mind, is the meaning of the expression *ʿalayhim* (lit., "over them") occurring here as well as in the subsequent reference to the building of a *house of worship* at the suggestion of those "whose opinion prevailed in the end" (*alladhīna ghalabū ʿalā amrihim*).

31 The future tense in *sayaqūlūn* points once again to the legendary character of the story as such, and implies that all speculation about its details is irrelevant to its parabolic, ethical purport.

32 I.e., for the sake of the self-evident ethical lesson to be derived from their story: an allusion to the first paragraph of verse 21 above.

33 According to almost all of the commentators, this parenthetic passage (verses 23-24) is primarily addressed to

to mind and say: "I pray that my Sustainer guide me, even closer than this, to a consciousness of what is right!" ‹24›

AND [some people assert], "They remained in their cave three hundred years"; and some have added nine [to that number].[34] ‹25›
Say: "God knows best how long they remained [there]. His [alone] is the knowledge of the hidden reality of the heavens and the earth: how well does He see and hear! No guardian have they apart from Him, since He allots to no one a share in His rule!" ‹26›

إِذَا نَسِيتَ وَقُلْ عَسَىٰٓ أَن يَهْدِيَنِ رَبِّي لِأَقْرَبَ مِنْ هَٰذَا رَشَدًا ﴿٢٤﴾
وَلَبِثُواْ فِي كَهْفِهِمْ ثَلَٰثَ مِاْئَةٍ سِنِينَ وَٱزْدَادُواْ تِسْعًا ﴿٢٥﴾ قُلِ ٱللَّهُ أَعْلَمُ
بِمَا لَبِثُواْ لَهُۥ غَيْبُ ٱلسَّمَٰوَٰتِ وَٱلْأَرْضِ أَبْصِرْ بِهِۦ وَأَسْمِعْ مَا لَهُم مِّن
دُونِهِۦ مِن وَلِيٍّ وَلَا يُشْرِكُ فِي حُكْمِهِۦٓ أَحَدًا ﴿٢٦﴾ وَٱتْلُ مَآ أُوحِيَ إِلَيْكَ
مِن كِتَابِ رَبِّكَ لَا مُبَدِّلَ لِكَلِمَٰتِهِۦ وَلَن تَجِدَ مِن دُونِهِۦ مُلْتَحَدًا ﴿٢٧﴾
وَٱصْبِرْ نَفْسَكَ مَعَ ٱلَّذِينَ يَدْعُونَ رَبَّهُم بِٱلْغَدَوٰةِ وَٱلْعَشِيِّ يُرِيدُونَ وَجْهَهُۥ
وَلَا تَعْدُ عَيْنَاكَ عَنْهُمْ تُرِيدُ زِينَةَ ٱلْحَيَوٰةِ ٱلدُّنْيَا وَلَا تُطِعْ مَنْ أَغْفَلْنَا
قَلْبَهُۥ عَن ذِكْرِنَا وَٱتَّبَعَ هَوَىٰهُ وَكَانَ أَمْرُهُۥ فُرُطًا ﴿٢٨﴾

AND CONVEY [to the world] whatever has been revealed to thee of thy Sustainer's writ. There is nothing that could alter His words;[35] and thou canst find no refuge other than with Him. ‹27›
And contain thyself in patience by the side of all who at morn and at evening invoke their Sustainer, seeking His countenance, and let not thine eyes pass beyond them in quest of the beauties of this world's life;[36] and pay no heed to any whose heart We have rendered heedless of all remembrance of Us[37] because he had always followed [only] his own desires, abandoning all that is good and true.[38] ‹28›

ʾidhā nasīta wa qul ʿasāa ʾañy-yahdiyani Rabbī liʾaqraba min hādhā rashadā. (24) Wa labithū fī kahfihim thalātha miʾatiñ-sinīna waz-dādū tisʿā. (25) Qulil-lāhu ʾaʿlamu bimā labithū; lahū ghaybus-samāwāti wal-ʾarḍi ʾabṣir bihī wa ʾasmiʿ. Mā lahum-miñ-dūnihī miñw-waliyyiñw-wa lā yushriku fī ḥukmihīi ʾaḥadā. (26) Wat-lu māa ʾūḥiya ʾilayka miñ-Kitābi Rabbika lā mubaddila liKalimātihī wa lañ-tajida miñ-dūnihī multaḥadā. (27) Waṣ-bir nafsaka maʿal-ladhīna yadʿūna Rabbahum bilghadāti wal-ʿashiyyi yurīdūna Wajhahū wa lā taʿdu ʿaynāka ʿanhum turīdu zīnatal-ḥayātid-dunyā; wa lā tuṭiʿ man ʾaghfalnā qalbahū ʿañ-dhikrinā wat-tabaʿa hawāhu wa kāna ʾamruhū furuṭā. (28)

---

the Prophet, who, on being asked by some of the pagan Quraysh as to what "really" happened to the Men of the Cave, is said to have replied, "I shall give you my answer tomorrow" – whereupon revelation was temporarily withheld from him in token of God's disapproval; in the second instance, this exhortation expresses a general principle addressed to all believers.

34 This obviously connects with the "idle guesses" mentioned in the first paragraph of verse 22 above – guesses refuted by the subsequent statements, "My Sustainer knows best how many they were" in verse 22, and "God knows best how long they remained [there]" in verse 26. This was, in particular, the view of ʿAbd Allāh ibn Masʿūd, whose copy of the Qurʾān is said to have contained the words, "And *they* [i.e., some people] said, 'They remained . . .'," etc. (which was probably a marginal, explanatory remark added by Ibn Masʿūd), as well as of Qatādah and of Maṭar al-Warrāq (Ṭabarī, Zamakhsharī and Ibn Kathīr). My interpolation, at the beginning of the verse, of the words "some people asserted" is based on the word *qālū* ("they said") used by Ibn Masʿūd in his marginal note.

35 According to Rāzī, it is on this passage, among others, that the great Qurʾān-commentator Abū Muslim al-Iṣfahānī based his rejection of the so-called "doctrine of abrogation" discussed in my note 87 on 2 : 106.

36 For an explanation of this verse, see 6 : 52 and the corresponding note 41.

37 See *sūrah* 2, note 7. Zamakhsharī and Rāzī explain the verb *aghfalnā* – agreeably with Qurʾanic doctrine – as meaning "whom We have *found to be* heedless". (See also my note 4 on the second part of 14 : 4.)

38 Lit., "and whose case (*amr*) was one of abandonment of [or "transgression against"] all bounds [of what is right]".

And say: "The truth [has now come] from your Sustainer: let, then, him who wills, believe in it, and let him who wills, reject it."

Verily, for all who sin against themselves [by rejecting Our truth][39] We have readied a fire whose billowing folds will encompass them from all sides;[40] and if they beg for water, they will be given water [hot] like molten lead, which will scald their faces: how dreadful a drink, and how evil a place to rest! ‹29›

[But,] behold, as for those who attain to faith and do righteous deeds – verily, We do not fail to requite any who persevere in doing good: ‹30› theirs shall be gardens of perpetual bliss – [gardens] through which running waters flow – wherein they will be adorned with bracelets of gold and will wear green garments of silk and brocade, [and] wherein upon couches they will recline:[41] how excellent a recompense, and how goodly a place to rest! ‹31›

AND PROPOUND unto them the parable of two men, upon one of whom We had bestowed two vineyards, and surrounded them with date-palms, and placed a field of grain in-between.[42] ‹32› Each of the two gardens yielded its produce and never failed therein in any way, for We had caused a stream to gush forth in the midst of each of them. ‹33›

نصف الحزب

وَقُلِ ٱلْحَقُّ مِن رَّبِّكُمْ فَمَن شَآءَ فَلْيُؤْمِن وَمَن شَآءَ فَلْيَكْفُرْ إِنَّآ أَعْتَدْنَا
لِلظَّٰلِمِينَ نَارًا أَحَاطَ بِهِمْ سُرَادِقُهَا وَإِن يَسْتَغِيثُوا۟ يُغَاثُوا۟ بِمَآءٍ
كَٱلْمُهْلِ يَشْوِى ٱلْوُجُوهَ بِئْسَ ٱلشَّرَابُ وَسَآءَتْ مُرْتَفَقًا ﴿٢٩﴾ إِنَّ
ٱلَّذِينَ ءَامَنُوا۟ وَعَمِلُوا۟ ٱلصَّٰلِحَٰتِ إِنَّا لَا نُضِيعُ أَجْرَ مَنْ أَحْسَنَ
عَمَلًا ﴿٣٠﴾ أُو۟لَٰٓئِكَ لَهُمْ جَنَّٰتُ عَدْنٍ تَجْرِى مِن تَحْتِهِمُ ٱلْأَنْهَٰرُ
يُحَلَّوْنَ فِيهَا مِنْ أَسَاوِرَ مِن ذَهَبٍ وَيَلْبَسُونَ ثِيَابًا خُضْرًا مِّن سُندُسٍ
وَإِسْتَبْرَقٍ مُّتَّكِـِٔينَ فِيهَا عَلَى ٱلْأَرَآئِكِ نِعْمَ ٱلثَّوَابُ وَحَسُنَتْ
مُرْتَفَقًا ﴿٣١﴾ ۞ وَٱضْرِبْ لَهُم مَّثَلًا رَّجُلَيْنِ جَعَلْنَا لِأَحَدِهِمَا جَنَّتَيْنِ مِنْ
أَعْنَٰبٍ وَحَفَفْنَٰهُمَا بِنَخْلٍ وَجَعَلْنَا بَيْنَهُمَا زَرْعًا ﴿٣٢﴾ كِلْتَا ٱلْجَنَّتَيْنِ
ءَاتَتْ أُكُلَهَا وَلَمْ تَظْلِم مِّنْهُ شَيْـًٔا وَفَجَّرْنَا خِلَٰلَهُمَا نَهَرًا ﴿٣٣﴾

Wa qulil-ḥaqqu mir-Rabbikum; famañ-shāaʾa fal-yuʾmiñw-wa mañ-shāaʾa falyakfur. ʾInnāa ʾaᶜtadnā lizẓālimīna nāran ʾaḥāṭa bihim surādiquhā; wa ʾiñy-yastaghīthū yughāthū bimāaʾiñ-kalmuhli yashwil-wujūh. Biʾsash-sharābu wa sāaʾat murtafaqā. (29) ʾInnal-ladhīna ʾāmanū wa ᶜamiluṣ-ṣāliḥāti ʾinnā lā nuḍīᶜu ʾajra man ʾaḥsana ᶜamalā. (30) ʾUlāaʾika lahum jannātu ᶜadniñ-tajrī miñ-taḥtihimul-ʾanhāru yuḥallawna fīhā min ʾasāwira miñ-dhahabiñw-wa yalbasūna thiyaban khuḍram-miñ-suñdusiñw-wa ʾistabraqim-muttakiʾīna fīhā ᶜalal-ʾarāaʾik. Niᶜmath-thawābu wa ḥasunat murtafaqā. (31) ۞ Waḍ-rib lahum-mathalar-rajulayni jaᶜalnā liʾaḥadihimā jannatayni min ʾaᶜnābiñw-wa ḥafafnāhumā binakhliñw-wa jaᶜalnā baynahumā zarᶜā. (32) Kiltal-jannatayni ʾātat ukulahā wa lam taẓlim-minhu shayʾañw-wa fajjarnā khilālahumā naharā. (33)

39 Thus Rāzī explains the expression *aẓ-ẓālimūn* (lit., "the evildoers") in the above context.

40 The expression *surādiq* – rendered by me as "billowing folds" – literally denotes an awning or the outer covering of a tent, and alludes here to the billowing "walls of smoke" that will surround the sinners (Zamakhsharī): a symbolism meant to stress the inescapability of their suffering in the hereafter (Rāzī).

41 Like all other Qurʾanic descriptions of happenings in the hereafter, the above reference to the "adornment" of the believers with gold and jewels and silk (cf. similar passages in 22 : 23, 35 : 33 and 76 : 21) and their "reclining upon couches (*arāʾik*)" is obviously an allegory – in this case, an allegory of the splendour, the ever-fresh life (symbolized by "*green* garments"), and the restful fulfilment that awaits them in result of the many acts of self-denial which their faith had imposed on them during their earthly life. – Referring to the symbolism of these joys of paradise, Rāzī draws our attention to the difference in the construction of the two parts of this clause: the first part is in the passive form ("they will be adorned . . .") and the second, in the active ("they will wear . . ."). In his opinion, the active form alludes to what the righteous will have earned by virtue of their deeds, whereas the passive form denotes all that will be bestowed on them by God above and beyond their deserts.

42 This parable connects with verses 7-8 of this *sūrah*, and serves as an illustration of the statement that "all beauty on earth is a means by which God puts men to a test".

And so [the man] had fruit in abundance. And [one day] he said to his friend, bandying words with him, "More wealth have I than thou, and mightier am I as regards [the number and power of my] followers!" ‹34›
And having [thus] sinned against himself, he entered his garden, saying, "I do not think that this will ever perish! ‹35› And neither do I think that the Last Hour will ever come. But even if [it should come, and] I am brought before my Sustainer,[43] I will surely find something even better than this as [my last] resort!" ‹36›
And his friend answered him in the course of their argument: "Wilt thou blaspheme against Him who has created thee out of dust,[44] and then out of a drop of sperm, and in the end has fashioned thee into a [complete] man? ‹37› But as for myself, [I know that] He is God, my Sustainer; and I cannot attribute divine powers to any but my Sustainer."[45] ‹38›
And [he continued:] "Alas,[46] if thou hadst but said, on entering thy garden, 'Whatever God wills [shall come to pass, for] there is no power save with God!' Although, as thou seest, I have less wealth and offspring than thou, ‹39› yet it may well be that my Sustainer will give me something better than thy garden – just as He may let loose a calamity out of heaven upon this [thy garden], so that it becomes a heap of barren dust ‹40› or its water sinks deep into the ground, so that thou wilt never be able to find it again!" ‹41›
And [thus it happened:] his fruitful gardens were encompassed [by ruin], and there he was, wringing his hands over all that he had spent on that which now lay waste, with its trellises caved in; and he could but say, "Oh, would that I had not attributed divine powers to any but my Sustainer!" ‹42›

وَكَانَ لَهُۥ ثَمَرٌ فَقَالَ لِصَٰحِبِهِۦ وَهُوَ يُحَاوِرُهُۥٓ أَنَا۠ أَكۡثَرُ مِنكَ مَالٗا وَأَعَزُّ
نَفَرٗا ﴿٣٤﴾ وَدَخَلَ جَنَّتَهُۥ وَهُوَ ظَالِمٞ لِّنَفۡسِهِۦ قَالَ مَآ أَظُنُّ أَن تَبِيدَ هَٰذِهِۦٓ
أَبَدٗا ﴿٣٥﴾ وَمَآ أَظُنُّ ٱلسَّاعَةَ قَآئِمَةٗ وَلَئِن رُّدِدتُّ إِلَىٰ رَبِّي لَأَجِدَنَّ خَيۡرٗا
مِّنۡهَا مُنقَلَبٗا ﴿٣٦﴾ قَالَ لَهُۥ صَاحِبُهُۥ وَهُوَ يُحَاوِرُهُۥٓ أَكَفَرۡتَ بِٱلَّذِي
خَلَقَكَ مِن تُرَابٖ ثُمَّ مِن نُّطۡفَةٖ ثُمَّ سَوَّىٰكَ رَجُلٗا ﴿٣٧﴾ لَّٰكِنَّا۠ هُوَ ٱللَّهُ رَبِّي
وَلَآ أُشۡرِكُ بِرَبِّيٓ أَحَدٗا ﴿٣٨﴾ وَلَوۡلَآ إِذۡ دَخَلۡتَ جَنَّتَكَ قُلۡتَ مَا شَآءَ ٱللَّهُ
لَا قُوَّةَ إِلَّا بِٱللَّهِۚ إِن تَرَنِ أَنَا۠ أَقَلَّ مِنكَ مَالٗا وَوَلَدٗا ﴿٣٩﴾ فَعَسَىٰ رَبِّيٓ أَن
يُؤۡتِيَنِ خَيۡرٗا مِّن جَنَّتِكَ وَيُرۡسِلَ عَلَيۡهَا حُسۡبَانٗا مِّنَ ٱلسَّمَآءِ فَتُصۡبِحَ صَعِيدٗا
زَلَقًا ﴿٤٠﴾ أَوۡ يُصۡبِحَ مَآؤُهَا غَوۡرٗا فَلَن تَسۡتَطِيعَ لَهُۥ طَلَبٗا ﴿٤١﴾ وَأُحِيطَ
بِثَمَرِهِۦ فَأَصۡبَحَ يُقَلِّبُ كَفَّيۡهِ عَلَىٰ مَآ أَنفَقَ فِيهَا وَهِيَ خَاوِيَةٌ عَلَىٰ
عُرُوشِهَا وَيَقُولُ يَٰلَيۡتَنِي لَمۡ أُشۡرِكۡ بِرَبِّيٓ أَحَدٗا ﴿٤٢﴾

Wa kana lahū thamaruñ-faqāla liṣāḥibihī wa huwa yuḥāwiruhūu ʾana ʾaktharu miñka mālañw-wa ʾaʿazzu nafarā. (34) Wa dakhala jannatahū wa huwa ẓālimul-linafsihī qāla māa ʾaẓunnu ʾañ-tabīda hādhihīi ʾabadā. (35) Wa māa ʾaẓunnus-Sāʿata qāaʾimatañw-wa laʾir-rudittu ʾilā Rabbī laʾajidanna khayram-minhā muñqalabā. (36) Qāla lahū ṣāḥibuhū wa huwa yuḥāwiruhūu ʾakafarta billadhī khalaqaka miñ-turābiñ-thumma miñ-nuṭfatiñ-thumma sawwāka rajulā. (37) Lākinna Huwal-lāhu Rabbī wa lāa ʾushriku biRabbīi ʾaḥadā. (38) Wa lawlāa ʾidh dakhalta jannataka qulta mā shāaʾal-lāhu lā quwwata ʾillā billāh. ʾIñ-tarani ʾana ʾaqalla miñka mālañw-wa waladā. (39) Faʿasā Rabbīi ʾañy-yuʾtiyani khayram-miñ-jannatika wa yursila ʿalayhā ḥusbānam-minas-samāaʾi fatuṣbiḥa ṣaʿīdañ-zalaqā. (40) ʾAw yuṣbiḥa māaʾuhā ghawrañ-falañ-tastaṭīʿa lahū ṭalabā. (41) Wa ʾuḥīṭa bithamarihī faʾaṣbaḥa yuqallibu kaffayhi ʿalā māa ʾañfaqa fīhā wa hiya khāwiyatun ʿalā ʿurūshihā wa yaqūlu yā laytanī lam ʾushrik biRabbīi ʾaḥadā. (42)

43 Lit., "brought back [or "referred"] to my Sustainer" – i.e., for judgment.

44 See second half of note 47 on 3 : 59, and note 4 on 23 : 12.

45 Lit., "I shall not [or "do not"] associate anyone [or "anything"] with my Sustainer" – i.e., "I cannot associate in my mind wealth or poverty with any power or creative cause other than Him" (Qiffāl, as quoted by Rāzī).

46 For an explanation of my rendering of *law-lā* as "alas", see note 119 on 10 : 98.

– for now he had nought[47] to succour him in God's stead, nor could he succour himself. ‹43›

For thus it is: all protective power belongs to God alone, the True One. He is the best to grant recompense, and the best to determine what is to be.[48] ‹44›

AND PROPOUND unto them the parable of the life of this world: [it is] like the water which We send down from the skies, and which is absorbed by the plants of the earth: but [in time] they turn into dry stubble which the winds blow freely about. And it is God [alone] who determines all things. ‹45›

Wealth and children are an adornment of this world's life: but good deeds, the fruit whereof endures forever, are of far greater merit in thy Sustainer's sight, and a far better source of hope.[49] ‹46›

Hence, [bear in mind] the Day on which We shall cause the mountains to disappear and thou shalt behold the earth void and bare: for [on that Day] We will [resurrect the dead and] gather them all together, leaving out none of them. ‹47› And they will be lined up before thy Sustainer, [and He will say:[50]] "Now, indeed, you have come unto Us [in a lonely state], even as We created you in the first instance[51] – although you were wont to assert that We would never appoint for you a meeting [with Us]! ‹48›

And the record [of everyone's deeds] will be laid open; and thou wilt behold the guilty filled with dread at what [they see] therein; and they will exclaim: "Oh, woe unto us! What a record is this! It leaves out nothing, be it small or great, but takes everything into account!"

وَلَمْ تَكُن لَّهُۥ فِئَةٌ يَنصُرُونَهُۥ مِن دُونِ ٱللَّهِ وَمَا كَانَ مُنتَصِرًا ﴿٤٣﴾ هُنَالِكَ
ٱلْوَلَٰيَةُ لِلَّهِ ٱلْحَقِّ ۚ هُوَ خَيْرٌ ثَوَابًا وَخَيْرٌ عُقْبًا ﴿٤٤﴾ وَٱضْرِبْ لَهُم مَّثَلَ
ٱلْحَيَوٰةِ ٱلدُّنْيَا كَمَآءٍ أَنزَلْنَٰهُ مِنَ ٱلسَّمَآءِ فَٱخْتَلَطَ بِهِۦ نَبَاتُ ٱلْأَرْضِ
فَأَصْبَحَ هَشِيمًا تَذْرُوهُ ٱلرِّيَٰحُ ۗ وَكَانَ ٱللَّهُ عَلَىٰ كُلِّ شَىْءٍ مُّقْتَدِرًا ﴿٤٥﴾
ٱلْمَالُ وَٱلْبَنُونَ زِينَةُ ٱلْحَيَوٰةِ ٱلدُّنْيَا ۖ وَٱلْبَٰقِيَٰتُ ٱلصَّٰلِحَٰتُ خَيْرٌ عِندَ
رَبِّكَ ثَوَابًا وَخَيْرٌ أَمَلًا ﴿٤٦﴾ وَيَوْمَ نُسَيِّرُ ٱلْجِبَالَ وَتَرَى ٱلْأَرْضَ بَارِزَةً
وَحَشَرْنَٰهُمْ فَلَمْ نُغَادِرْ مِنْهُمْ أَحَدًا ﴿٤٧﴾ وَعُرِضُوا۟ عَلَىٰ رَبِّكَ صَفًّا لَّقَدْ
جِئْتُمُونَا كَمَا خَلَقْنَٰكُمْ أَوَّلَ مَرَّةٍۭ ۚ بَلْ زَعَمْتُمْ أَلَّن نَّجْعَلَ لَكُم
مَّوْعِدًا ﴿٤٨﴾ وَوُضِعَ ٱلْكِتَٰبُ فَتَرَى ٱلْمُجْرِمِينَ مُشْفِقِينَ مِمَّا فِيهِ وَيَقُولُونَ
يَٰوَيْلَتَنَا مَالِ هَٰذَا ٱلْكِتَٰبِ لَا يُغَادِرُ صَغِيرَةً وَلَا كَبِيرَةً إِلَّآ أَحْصَىٰهَا ۚ

Wa lam takul-lahū fiʾatuñy-yañṣurūnahū miñ-dūnil-lāhi wa mā kāna muñtaṣirā. (43) Hunālikal-walāyatu lillāhil-Ḥaqq. Huwa khayruñ-thawābañw-wa khayrun ʿuqbā. (44) Waḍ-rib lahum-mathalal-ḥayātid-dunyā kamāaʾin ʾañzalnāhu minas-samāaʾi fakh-talaṭa bihī nabātul-ʾarḍi faʾaṣbaḥa hashīmañ-tadhrūhur-riyāḥ. Wa kānal-lāhu ʿalā kulli shayʾim-Muqtadirā. (45) ʾAlmālu wal-banūna zīnatul-ḥayātid-dunyā; wal-bāqiyātuṣ-ṣāliḥātu khayrun ʿiñda Rabbi-ka thawābañw-wa khayrun ʾamalā. (46) Wa Yawma nusayyirul-jibāla wa taral-ʾarḍa bārizatañw-wa ḥasharnāhum falam nughādir minhum ʾaḥadā. (47) Wa ʿuriḍū ʿalā Rabbika ṣaffal-laqad jiʾtumūnā kamā khalaqnākum ʾawwala marratim-bal zaʿamtum ʾallañ-najʿala lakum-mawʿidā. (48) Wa wuḍiʿal-Kitābu fataral-mujrimīna mushfiqīna mimmā fīhi wa yaqūlūna yā waylatanā māli hādhal-Kitābi lā yughādiru ṣaghīratañw-wa lā kabīratan ʾillāa ʾaḥṣāhā.

47 Lit., "he had no host whatever".

48 Lit., "the best as regards the consequence".

49 Lit., "are better in thy Sustainer's sight as regards merit, and better as regards hope". The expression *al-bāqiyāt aṣ-ṣāliḥāt* ("good deeds, the fruit whereof endures forever") occurs in the Qurʾān twice – in the above verse as well as in 19 : 76.

50 I.e., to those who in their lifetime denied the truth of resurrection.

51 Cf. 6 : 94.

وَوَجَدُواْ مَا عَمِلُواْ حَاضِرًا ۗ وَلَا يَظۡلِمُ رَبُّكَ أَحَدًا ﴿٤٩﴾ وَإِذۡ قُلۡنَا
لِلۡمَلَٰٓئِكَةِ ٱسۡجُدُواْ لِأٓدَمَ فَسَجَدُوٓاْ إِلَّآ إِبۡلِيسَ كَانَ مِنَ ٱلۡجِنِّ فَفَسَقَ عَنۡ
أَمۡرِ رَبِّهِۦٓۗ أَفَتَتَّخِذُونَهُۥ وَذُرِّيَّتَهُۥٓ أَوۡلِيَآءَ مِن دُونِي وَهُمۡ لَكُمۡ عَدُوُّۢۚ بِئۡسَ
لِلظَّٰلِمِينَ بَدَلٗا ﴿٥٠﴾ ۞ مَّآ أَشۡهَدتُّهُمۡ خَلۡقَ ٱلسَّمَٰوَٰتِ وَٱلۡأَرۡضِ وَلَا
خَلۡقَ أَنفُسِهِمۡ وَمَا كُنتُ مُتَّخِذَ ٱلۡمُضِلِّينَ عَضُدٗا ﴿٥١﴾ وَيَوۡمَ يَقُولُ نَادُواْ
شُرَكَآءِيَ ٱلَّذِينَ زَعَمۡتُمۡ فَدَعَوۡهُمۡ فَلَمۡ يَسۡتَجِيبُواْ لَهُمۡ وَجَعَلۡنَا بَيۡنَهُم
مَّوۡبِقٗا ﴿٥٢﴾ وَرَءَا ٱلۡمُجۡرِمُونَ ٱلنَّارَ فَظَنُّوٓاْ أَنَّهُم مُّوَاقِعُوهَا وَلَمۡ يَجِدُواْ
عَنۡهَا مَصۡرِفٗا ﴿٥٣﴾

ثلاثة ارباع الحزب

Wa wajadū mā ʿamilū ḥāḍirā. Wa lā yaẓlimu Rabbu-ka ʾaḥadā. (49) Wa ʾidh qulnā lilMalāaʾikatis-judū liʾĀdama fasajadūu ʾillāa ʾIblīsa kāna minal-Jinni fafasaqa ʿan ʾamri Rabbih. ʾAfatattakhidhūnahū wa dhurriyyatahūu ʾawliyāaʾa miñ-dūnī wa hum lakum ʿaduww. Biʾsa liẓẓālimīna badalā. (50) ۞ Māa ʾash-hattuhum khalqas-samāwāti wal-ʾarḍi wa lā khalqa ʾañfusihim wa mā kuñtu muttakhidhal-muḍillīna ʿaḍudā. (51) Wa Yawma yaqūlu nādū shurakāaʾiyal-ladhīna zaʿamtum fadaʿawhum falam yastajībū la-hum wa jaʿalnā baynahum-mawbiqā. (52) Wa raʾal-mujrimūnan-nāra faẓannūu ʾannahum-muwāqiʿūhā wa lam yajidū ʿanhā maṣrifā. (53)

For they will find all that they ever wrought [now] facing them, and [will know that] thy Sustainer does not wrong anyone. ‹49›

AND [remember that] when We told the angels, "Prostrate yourselves before Adam,"[52] they all prostrated themselves, save Iblīs: he [too] was one of those invisible beings,[53] but then he turned away from his Sustainer's command. Will you, then, take him and his cohorts[54] for [your] masters instead of Me, although they are your foes? How vile an exchange on the evildoers' part![55] ‹50›

I did not make them witnesses of the creation of the heavens and the earth, nor of the creation of their own selves;[56] and neither do I [have any need to] take as My helpers those [beings] that lead [men] astray.[57] ‹51›

Hence, [bear in mind] the Day on which He will say, "Call [now] unto those beings whom you imagined to have a share in My divinity!"[58] whereupon they will invoke them, but those [beings] will not respond to them: for We shall have placed between them an unbridgeable gulf.[59] ‹52›

And those who were lost in sin will behold the fire, and will know that they are bound to fall into it, and will find no way of escape therefrom. ‹53›

---

52 This short reference to the oft-repeated allegory of God's command to the angels to "prostrate themselves before Adam" is meant, in the above context, to stress man's inborn faculty of conceptual thinking (see 2 : 31-34 and the corresponding notes) and, thus, his ability and obligation to discern between right and wrong. Since man's deliberate choice of a morally wrong course – of which the preceding passages speak – is almost invariably due to his exaggerated attachment to the allurements of worldly life, attention is drawn here to the fact that this attachment is the means by which Satan (or Iblīs) induces man to forgo all moral considerations and thus brings about his spiritual ruin.

53 Denoting, in this instance, the angels (see Appendix III).

54 Lit., "his offspring" – a metonym for all who follow him.

55 Lit., "for the evildoers". As regards Satan's symbolic "rebellion" against God, see note 26 on 2 : 34 and note 31 on 15 : 41.

56 I.e., "since they are but created beings, and not co-existent with Me, how can you take them for your masters?" – an allusion to the beings, real or imaginary, to which men ascribe divine qualities, either consciously or (as in the case of one's submission to the "whisperings of Satan") by subconscious implication.

57 Since God is almighty, all-knowing and self-sufficient, the belief that any being or power could have a "helping" share in His divinity, or could "mediate" between Him and man, causes the latter to go utterly astray.

58 Lit., "those partners of Mine whom you supposed [to exist]": see note 15 on 6 : 22.

59 Or: "a gulf [or "a barrier"] of perdition": an allusion to the wide gulf of unreality that separates those sinners from the blasphemous figments of their imagination or, more probably, the gulf that separates them from the saintly persons whom they were wont to worship despite the fact that the latter had never made any claim to divine status (Zamakhsharī and Rāzī in one of their alternative interpretations, with specific mention of Jesus and Mary).

THUS, INDEED, have We given in this Qurʾān many facets to every kind of lesson [designed] for [the benefit of] mankind.[60]

However, man is, above all else, always given to contention: ⟨54⟩ for, what is there to keep people from attaining to faith now that guidance has come unto them, and from asking their Sustainer to forgive them their sins – unless it be [their wish] that the fate of the [sinful] people of ancient times should befall them [as well], or that the [ultimate] suffering should befall them in the hereafter?[61] ⟨55⟩

But We send [Our] message-bearers only as heralds of glad tidings and as warners – whereas those who are bent on denying the truth contend [against them] with fallacious arguments, so as to render void the truth thereby, and to make My messages and warnings a target of their mockery. ⟨56⟩

And who could be more wicked than he to whom his Sustainer's messages are conveyed and who thereupon turns away from them, forgetting all [the evil] that his hands may have wrought?[62]

Behold, over their hearts have We laid veils which prevent them from grasping the truth, and into their ears, deafness; and though thou call them onto the right path,[63] they will never allow themselves to be guided. ⟨57⟩

Yet, [withal,] thy Sustainer is the Truly-Forgiving One, limitless in His grace. Were He to take them [at once] to task for whatever [wrong] they commit, He would indeed bring about their speedy punishment [then and there]:[64] but nay, they have a time-limit beyond which they shall find no

وَلَقَدْ صَرَّفْنَا فِى هَٰذَا ٱلْقُرْءَانِ لِلنَّاسِ مِن كُلِّ مَثَلٍ وَكَانَ ٱلْإِنسَٰنُ أَكْثَرَ
شَىْءٍ جَدَلًا ﴿٥٤﴾ وَمَا مَنَعَ ٱلنَّاسَ أَن يُؤْمِنُوٓا۟ إِذْ جَآءَهُمُ ٱلْهُدَىٰ وَيَسْتَغْفِرُوا۟
رَبَّهُمْ إِلَّآ أَن تَأْتِيَهُمْ سُنَّةُ ٱلْأَوَّلِينَ أَوْ يَأْتِيَهُمُ ٱلْعَذَابُ قُبُلًا ﴿٥٥﴾ وَمَا
نُرْسِلُ ٱلْمُرْسَلِينَ إِلَّا مُبَشِّرِينَ وَمُنذِرِينَ وَيُجَٰدِلُ ٱلَّذِينَ كَفَرُوا۟ بِٱلْبَٰطِلِ
لِيُدْحِضُوا۟ بِهِ ٱلْحَقَّ وَٱتَّخَذُوٓا۟ ءَايَٰتِى وَمَآ أُنذِرُوا۟ هُزُوًا ﴿٥٦﴾ وَمَنْ أَظْلَمُ مِمَّن
ذُكِّرَ بِـَٔايَٰتِ رَبِّهِۦ فَأَعْرَضَ عَنْهَا وَنَسِىَ مَا قَدَّمَتْ يَدَاهُ إِنَّا جَعَلْنَا عَلَىٰ
قُلُوبِهِمْ أَكِنَّةً أَن يَفْقَهُوهُ وَفِىٓ ءَاذَانِهِمْ وَقْرًا وَإِن تَدْعُهُمْ إِلَى ٱلْهُدَىٰ
فَلَن يَهْتَدُوٓا۟ إِذًا أَبَدًا ﴿٥٧﴾ وَرَبُّكَ ٱلْغَفُورُ ذُو ٱلرَّحْمَةِ لَوْ يُؤَاخِذُهُم بِمَا
كَسَبُوا۟ لَعَجَّلَ لَهُمُ ٱلْعَذَابَ بَل لَّهُم مَّوْعِدٌ لَّن يَجِدُوا۟ مِن دُونِهِۦ

Wa laqad ṣarrafnā fī hādhal-Qurʾāni linnāsi miñ-kulli mathaliñw-wa kānal-ʾIñsānu ʾakthara shayʾiñ-jadalā. (54) Wa mā manaʿan-nāsa ʾañy-yuʾminūu ʾidh jāaʾahumul-hudā wa yastaghfirū Rabbahum ʾillāa ʾañ-taʾtiyahum sunnatul-ʾawwalīna ʾaw yaʾtiyahumul-ʿadhābu qubulā. (55) Wa mā nursilul-Mursalīna ʾillā mubashshirīna wa muñẕirīn. Wa yujādilul-ladhīna kafarū bilbāṭili liyudḥiḍū bihil-ḥaqqa wat-takhadhūu ʾĀyātī wa māa ʾuñdhirū huzuwā. (56) Wa man ʾaẓlamu mimmañ-dhukkira biʾĀyāti Rabbihī faʾaʿraḍa ʿanhā wa nasiya mā qaddamat yadāh. ʾInnā jaʿalnā ʿalā qulūbihim ʾakinnatan ʾañy-yafqahūhu wa fīi ʾādhāni-him waqrā. Wa ʾiñ-tadʿuhum ʾilal-hudā falañy-yahtadūu ʾidhan ʾabadā. (57) Wa Rabbukal-Ghafūru Dhur-raḥmah. Law yuʾākhidhuhum-bimā kasabū laʿajjala lahumul-ʿadhāb. Bal-lahum-mawʿidul-lañy-yajidū miñ-dūnihī

60 Cf. note 104 on 17 : 89, explaining my translation of *mathal*, in this context, as "lesson".

61 Lit., "face to face" or "in the future" (Zamakhsharī) – both these meanings of *qubulan* being comprised in the concept of "the hereafter" or "the life to come".

62 I.e., persevering in his unrighteous behaviour (Rāzī).

63 Lit., "to guidance".

64 Lit., "He would indeed hasten the punishment for them" – the implication being that He invariably allows them time to repent and mend their ways.

redemption[65] ⟨58⟩ – as [was the case with all] those communities that We destroyed when they went on and on doing wrong:[66] for We had set a time-limit for their destruction. ⟨59⟩

AND LO![67] [In the course of his wanderings,] Moses said to his servant:[68] "I shall not give up until I reach the junction of the two seas, even if I [have to] spend untold years [in my quest]!" ⟨60⟩
But when they reached the junction between the two [seas], they forgot all about their fish, and it took its way into the sea and disappeared from sight.[69] ⟨61⟩
And after the two had walked some distance, [Moses] said to his servant: "Bring us our mid-day meal; we have indeed suffered hardship on this [day of] our journey!" ⟨62⟩

مَوْئِلًا ﴿58﴾ وَتِلْكَ ٱلْقُرَىٰٓ أَهْلَكْنَٰهُمْ لَمَّا ظَلَمُوا۟ وَجَعَلْنَا لِمَهْلِكِهِم
مَّوْعِدًا ﴿59﴾ وَإِذْ قَالَ مُوسَىٰ لِفَتَىٰهُ لَآ أَبْرَحُ حَتَّىٰٓ أَبْلُغَ مَجْمَعَ ٱلْبَحْرَيْنِ
أَوْ أَمْضِىَ حُقُبًا ﴿60﴾ فَلَمَّا بَلَغَا مَجْمَعَ بَيْنِهِمَا نَسِيَا حُوتَهُمَا فَٱتَّخَذَ سَبِيلَهُۥ
فِى ٱلْبَحْرِ سَرَبًا ﴿61﴾ فَلَمَّا جَاوَزَا قَالَ لِفَتَىٰهُ ءَاتِنَا غَدَآءَنَا لَقَدْ لَقِينَا
مِن سَفَرِنَا هَٰذَا نَصَبًا ﴿62﴾

mawʾilā. (58) Wa tilkal-qurāa ʾahlaknāhum lammā ẓalamū wa jaᶜalnā limahlikihim-mawᶜidā. (59) Wa ʾidh qāla Mūsā lifatāhu lāa ʾabraḥu ḥattāa ʾablugha majmaᶜal-baḥrayni ʾaw ʾamḍiya ḥuqubā. (60) Falammā balaghā majmaᶜa baynihimā nasiyā ḥūtahumā fattakhadha sabīlahū fil-baḥri sarabā. (61) Falammā jāwazā qāla lifatāhu ʾātinā ghadāaʾanā laqad laqīnā miñ-safarinā hādhā naṣabā. (62)

65 Cf. somewhat similar passages in 16 : 61 and 35 : 45. The "time-limit" (*mawᶜid*) signifies, in this context, the end of the sinners' life on earth or – as in the next verse – the "point of no return" beyond which God does not allow them to sin with impunity.

66 Lit., "when [or "after"] they had been doing wrong" – i.e., persistently and for a long time.

67 The particle *idh* (which usually signifies "when", but is, I believe, properly rendered here as "lo!") often serves in the Qurʾān to draw attention to a sudden turn in the discourse, without, however, involving a break in the continuity of thought. In this instance, it evidently marks a connection with verse 54 above ("many facets have We given in this Qurʾān to every kind of lesson [designed] for [the benefit of] mankind"), and introduces an allegory meant to illustrate the fact that knowledge, and particularly spiritual knowledge, is inexhaustible, so that no human being – not even a prophet – can ever claim to possess answers to all the questions that perplex man throughout his life. (This idea is brought out fully in the last two verses of this *sūrah*.)

The subsequent parable of Moses and his quest for knowledge (verses 60-82) has become, in the course of time, the nucleus of innumerable legends with which we are not concerned here. We have, however, a Tradition on the authority of Ubayy ibn Kaᶜb (recorded in several versions by Bukhārī, Muslim and Tirmidhī), according to which Moses was rebuked by God for having once asserted that he was the wisest of all men, and was subsequently told through revelation that a "servant of God" who lived at the "Junction of the two seas" was far superior to him in wisdom. When Moses expressed his eagerness to find that man, God commanded him to "take a fish in a basket" and to go on and on until the fish would disappear: and its disappearance was to be a sign that the goal had been reached. – There is no doubt that this Tradition is a kind of allegorical introduction to our Qurʾanic parable. The "fish" mentioned in the latter as well as in the above-mentioned *ḥadīth* is an ancient religious symbol, possibly signifying divine knowledge or life eternal. As for the "junction of the two seas", which many of the early commentators endeavoured to "identify" in geographical terms (ranging from the meeting of the Red Sea and the Indian Ocean at the Bab al-Mandab to that of the Mediterranean Sea and the Atlantic Ocean at the Straits of Gibraltar), Bayḍāwī offers, in his commentary on verse 60, a purely allegorical explanation: the "two seas" represent the two sources or streams of knowledge – the one obtainable through the observation and intellectual coordination of outward phenomena (*ᶜilm aẓ-ẓāhir*), and the other through intuitive, mystic insight (*ᶜilm al-bāṭin*) – the meeting of which is the real goal of Moses' quest.

68 Lit., "young man" (*fatā*) – a term applied, in early Arabic usage, to one's servant (irrespective of his age). According to tradition, it was Joshua, who was to become the leader of the Israelites after the death of Moses.

69 Lit., "burrowing [into it]". Their forgetting the symbolic "fish" (see last third of note 67) is perhaps an allusion to man's frequently forgetting that God is the ultimate source of all knowledge and life.

Said [the servant]: "Wouldst thou believe it?[70] When we betook ourselves to that rock for a rest, behold, I forgot about the fish – and none but Satan made me thus forget it![71] – and it took its way into the sea! How strange!" ‹63›
[Moses] exclaimed: "That [was the place] which we were seeking!"[72]
And the two turned back, retracing their footsteps, ‹64› and found one of Our servants, on whom We had bestowed grace from Ourselves and unto whom We had imparted knowledge [issuing] from Ourselves.[73] ‹65›
Moses said unto him: "May I follow thee on the understanding that thou wilt impart to me something of that consciousness of what is right which has been imparted to thee?" ‹66›
[The other] answered: "Behold, thou wilt never be able to have patience with me ‹67› – for how couldst thou be patient about something that thou canst not comprehend within the compass of [thy] experience?"[74] ‹68›
Replied [Moses]: "Thou wilt find me patient, if God so wills; and I shall not disobey thee in anything!" ‹69›
Said [the sage]: "Well, then, if thou art to follow me, do not question me about aught [that I may do] until I myself give thee an account thereof." ‹70›

قَالَ أَرَءَيْتَ إِذْ أَوَيْنَآ إِلَى ٱلصَّخْرَةِ فَإِنِّى نَسِيتُ ٱلْحُوتَ وَمَآ أَنسَىٰنِيهُ
إِلَّا ٱلشَّيْطَٰنُ أَنْ أَذْكُرَهُۥ ۚ وَٱتَّخَذَ سَبِيلَهُۥ فِى ٱلْبَحْرِ عَجَبًا ﴿٦٣﴾ قَالَ
ذَٰلِكَ مَا كُنَّا نَبْغِ ۚ فَٱرْتَدَّا عَلَىٰٓ ءَاثَارِهِمَا قَصَصًا ﴿٦٤﴾ فَوَجَدَا عَبْدًا مِّنْ
عِبَادِنَآ ءَاتَيْنَٰهُ رَحْمَةً مِّنْ عِندِنَا وَعَلَّمْنَٰهُ مِن لَّدُنَّا عِلْمًا ﴿٦٥﴾ قَالَ لَهُۥ
مُوسَىٰ هَلْ أَتَّبِعُكَ عَلَىٰٓ أَن تُعَلِّمَنِ مِمَّا عُلِّمْتَ رُشْدًا ﴿٦٦﴾ قَالَ إِنَّكَ لَن
تَسْتَطِيعَ مَعِىَ صَبْرًا ﴿٦٧﴾ وَكَيْفَ تَصْبِرُ عَلَىٰ مَا لَمْ تُحِطْ بِهِۦ خُبْرًا ﴿٦٨﴾
قَالَ سَتَجِدُنِىٓ إِن شَآءَ ٱللَّهُ صَابِرًا وَلَآ أَعْصِى لَكَ أَمْرًا ﴿٦٩﴾ قَالَ فَإِنِ
ٱتَّبَعْتَنِى فَلَا تَسْـَٔلْنِى عَن شَىْءٍ حَتَّىٰٓ أُحْدِثَ لَكَ مِنْهُ ذِكْرًا ﴿٧٠﴾

Qāla ʾaraʾayta ʾidh ʾawaynāa ʾilaṣ-ṣakhrati faʾinnī nasītul-ḥūta wa māa ʾañsānīhu ʾillash-Shayṭānu ʾan ʾadhkurahū wat-takhadha sabīlahū fil-baḥri ʿajabā. (63) Qāla dhālika mā kunnā nabghi fartaddā ʿalāa ʾāthārihimā qaṣaṣā. (64) Fawajadā ʿabdam-min ʿibādināa ʾātaynāhu raḥmatam-min ʿiñdinā wa ʿallamnāhu mil-ladunnā ʿilmā. (65) Qāla lahū Mūsā hal ʾattabiʿuka ʿalāa ʾañ-tuʿallimani mimmā ʿullimta rushdā. (66) Qāla ʾinnaka lañ-tastaṭīʿa maʿiya ṣabrā. (67) Wa kayfa taṣbiru ʿalā mā lam tuḥiṭ bihī khubrā. (68) Qāla satajidunīi ʾiñ-shāaʾal-lāhu ṣābirañw-wa lāa ʾaʿṣī laka ʾamrā. (69) Qāla faʾinit-tabaʿtanī falā tasʾalnī ʿañ-shayʾin ḥattāa ʾuḥditha laka minhu dhikrā. (70)

70 Lit., "Didst thou see?" Although formulated as a question, this idiomatic phrase often expresses – as does its modern equivalent, "Would you believe it?" – no more than a sudden remembrance of, or surprise at, an unusual or absurd happening.

71 Lit., "made me forget it lest I remember it".

72 I.e., the disappearance of the fish indicated the point at which their quest was to end (see note 67).

73 In the Tradition on the authority of Ubayy ibn Kaʿb (referred to in note 67) this mysterious sage is spoken of as Al-Khaḍir or Al-Khiḍr, meaning "the Green One". Apparently this is an epithet rather than a name, implying (according to popular legend) that his wisdom was ever-fresh ("green") and imperishable: a notion which bears out the assumption that we have here an allegoric figure symbolizing the utmost depth of mystic insight accessible to man.

74 Lit., "that thou dost not encompass with [thy] experience (*khubran*)": according to Rāzī, an allusion to the fact that even a prophet like Moses did not fully comprehend the inner reality of things (*ḥaqāʾiq al-ashyāʾ kamā hiya*); and, more generally, to man's lack of equanimity whenever he is faced with something that he has never yet experienced or cannot immediately comprehend. In the last analysis, the above verse implies – as is brought out fully in Moses' subsequent experiences – that appearance and reality do not always coincide; beyond that, it touches in a subtle manner upon the profound truth that man cannot really comprehend or even visualize anything that has no counterpart – at least in its component elements – in his own intellectual experience: and this is the reason for the Qurʾānic use of metaphor and allegory with regard to "all that is beyond the reach of a created being's perception" (*al-ghayb*).

And so the two went on their way, till [they reached the seashore; and] when they disembarked from the boat [that had ferried them a cross], the sage[75] made a hole in it – [whereupon Moses] exclaimed: "Hast thou made a hole in it in order to drown the people who may be [travelling] in it? Indeed, thou hast done a grievous thing!" ‹71›

He replied: "Did I not tell thee that thou wilt never be able to have patience with me?" ‹72›

Said [Moses]: "Take me not to task for my having forgotten [myself], and be not hard on me on account of what I have done!" ‹73›

And so the two went on, till, when they met a young man, [the sage] slew him – [whereupon Moses] exclaimed: "Hast thou slain an innocent human being without [his having taken] another man's life? Indeed, thou hast done a terrible thing!" ‹74›

He replied: "Did I not tell thee that thou wilt never be able to have patience with me?" ‹75›

Said [Moses]: "If, after this, I should ever question thee, keep me not in thy company: [for by] now thou hast heard enough excuses from me." ‹76›

And so the two went on, till, when they came upon some village people, they asked them[76] for food; but those [people] refused them all hospitality. And they saw in that [village] a wall which was on the point of tumbling down, and [the sage] rebuilt it – [whereupon Moses] said: "Hadst thou so wished, surely thou couldst [at least] have obtained some payment for it." ‹77›

[The sage] replied: "This is the parting of ways between me and thee. [And now] I shall let thee know the real meaning of all [those events] that thou wert unable to bear with patience: ‹78›

فَٱنطَلَقَا حَتَّىٰٓ إِذَا رَكِبَا فِى ٱلسَّفِينَةِ خَرَقَهَا قَالَ أَخَرَقْتَهَا لِتُغْرِقَ أَهْلَهَا
لَقَدْ جِئْتَ شَيْـًٔا إِمْرًا ﴿٧١﴾ قَالَ أَلَمْ أَقُلْ إِنَّكَ لَن تَسْتَطِيعَ مَعِىَ صَبْرًا ﴿٧٢﴾
قَالَ لَا تُؤَاخِذْنِى بِمَا نَسِيتُ وَلَا تُرْهِقْنِى مِنْ أَمْرِى عُسْرًا ﴿٧٣﴾ فَٱنطَلَقَا
حَتَّىٰٓ إِذَا لَقِيَا غُلَٰمًا فَقَتَلَهُۥ قَالَ أَقَتَلْتَ نَفْسًا زَكِيَّةًۢ بِغَيْرِ نَفْسٍ لَّقَدْ
جِئْتَ شَيْـًٔا نُّكْرًا ﴿٧٤﴾ ۞ قَالَ أَلَمْ أَقُل لَّكَ إِنَّكَ لَن تَسْتَطِيعَ مَعِىَ
صَبْرًا ﴿٧٥﴾ قَالَ إِن سَأَلْتُكَ عَن شَىْءٍۭ بَعْدَهَا فَلَا تُصَٰحِبْنِى قَدْ بَلَغْتَ
مِن لَّدُنِّى عُذْرًا ﴿٧٦﴾ فَٱنطَلَقَا حَتَّىٰٓ إِذَآ أَتَيَآ أَهْلَ قَرْيَةٍ ٱسْتَطْعَمَآ أَهْلَهَا
فَأَبَوْا۟ أَن يُضَيِّفُوهُمَا فَوَجَدَا فِيهَا جِدَارًا يُرِيدُ أَن يَنقَضَّ فَأَقَامَهُۥ قَالَ
لَوْ شِئْتَ لَتَّخَذْتَ عَلَيْهِ أَجْرًا ﴿٧٧﴾ قَالَ هَٰذَا فِرَاقُ بَيْنِى وَبَيْنِكَ
سَأُنَبِّئُكَ بِتَأْوِيلِ مَا لَمْ تَسْتَطِع عَّلَيْهِ صَبْرًا ﴿٧٨﴾

حزب 31
جزء 16

Fañṭalaqā ḥattāa ʾidhā rakibā fis-safīnati kharaqahā. Qāla ʾakharaqtahā litughriqa ʾahlahā laqad jiʾta shayʾan ʾimrā. (71) Qāla ʾalam ʾaqul ʾinnaka lañ-tastaṭīʿa maʿiya ṣabrā. (72) Qāla lā tuʾākhidhnī bimā nasītu wa lā turhiqnī min ʾamrī ʿusrā. (73) Fañṭalaqā ḥattāa ʾidhā laqiyā ghulāmañ-faqatalahū qāla ʾaqatalta nafsañ-zakiyyatam-bighayri nafsiñ-laqad jiʾta shayʾañ-nukrā. (74) ۞ Qāla ʾalam ʾaqul-laka ʾinnaka lañ-tastaṭīʿa maʿiya ṣabrā. (75) Qāla ʾiñ-saʾaltuka ʿañ-shayʾim-baʿdahā falā tuṣāḥibnī; qad balaghta mil-ladunnī ʿudhrā. (76) Fañṭalaqā ḥattāa ʾidhāa ʾatayāa ʾahla qaryatinis-taṭʿamāa ʾahlahā faʾabaw ʾañy-yuḍayyifūhumā fawajadā fīhā jidārañy-yurīdu ʾañy-yañqaḍḍa faʾaqāmah. Qāla law shiʾta lattakhadhta ʿalayhi ʾajrā. (77) Qāla hādhā firāqu baynī wa baynik. Saʾunabbiʾuka bitaʾwīli mā lam tastaṭiʿ ʿalayhi ṣabrā. (78)

75 Lit., "he".

76 Lit., "asked its people".

"As for that boat, it belonged to some needy people who toiled upon the sea – and I desired to damage it[77] because [I knew that] behind them was a king who is wont to seize every boat by brute force. ‹79›

"And as for that young man, his parents were [true] believers – whereas we had every reason to fear[78] that he would bring bitter grief upon them by [his] overweening wickedness and denial of all truth: ‹80› and so we desired that their Sustainer grant them in his stead [a child] of greater purity than him, and closer [to them] in loving tenderness. ‹81›

"And as for that wall, it belonged to two orphan boys [living] in the town, and beneath it was [buried] a treasure belonging to them [by right].[79] Now their father had been a righteous man, and so thy Sustainer willed it that when they come of age they should bring forth their treasure by thy Sustainer's grace.

"And I did not do [any of] this of my own accord:[80] this is the real meaning of all [those events] that thou wert unable to bear with patience." ‹82›

AND THEY will ask thee about the Two-Horned One. Say: "I will convey unto you something by which he ought to be remembered."[81] ‹83›

أَمَّا ٱلسَّفِينَةُ فَكَانَتۡ لِمَسَٰكِينَ يَعۡمَلُونَ فِي ٱلۡبَحۡرِ فَأَرَدتُّ أَنۡ أَعِيبَهَا
وَكَانَ وَرَآءَهُم مَّلِكٞ يَأۡخُذُ كُلَّ سَفِينَةٍ غَصۡبٗا ﴿٧٩﴾ وَأَمَّا ٱلۡغُلَٰمُ فَكَانَ
أَبَوَاهُ مُؤۡمِنَيۡنِ فَخَشِينَآ أَن يُرۡهِقَهُمَا طُغۡيَٰنٗا وَكُفۡرٗا ﴿٨٠﴾ فَأَرَدۡنَآ أَن
يُبۡدِلَهُمَا رَبُّهُمَا خَيۡرٗا مِّنۡهُ زَكَوٰةٗ وَأَقۡرَبَ رُحۡمٗا ﴿٨١﴾ وَأَمَّا ٱلۡجِدَارُ فَكَانَ
لِغُلَٰمَيۡنِ يَتِيمَيۡنِ فِي ٱلۡمَدِينَةِ وَكَانَ تَحۡتَهُۥ كَنزٞ لَّهُمَا وَكَانَ أَبُوهُمَا
صَٰلِحٗا فَأَرَادَ رَبُّكَ أَن يَبۡلُغَآ أَشُدَّهُمَا وَيَسۡتَخۡرِجَا كَنزَهُمَا رَحۡمَةٗ مِّن
رَّبِّكَۚ وَمَا فَعَلۡتُهُۥ عَنۡ أَمۡرِيۚ ذَٰلِكَ تَأۡوِيلُ مَا لَمۡ تَسۡطِع عَّلَيۡهِ صَبۡرٗا ﴿٨٢﴾
وَيَسۡـَٔلُونَكَ عَن ذِي ٱلۡقَرۡنَيۡنِۖ قُلۡ سَأَتۡلُواْ عَلَيۡكُم مِّنۡهُ ذِكۡرًا ﴿٨٣﴾

ʾAmmas-safīnatu fakānat limasākīna yaʿmalūna fil-baḥri faʾarattu ʾan ʾaʿībahā wa kāna warāaʾahum-malikuñy-yaʾkhudhu kulla safīnatin ghaṣbā. (79) Wa ʾammal-ghulāmu fakāna ʾabawāhu muʾminayni fakhashīnāa ʾañy-yurhiqahumā ṭughyānañw-wa kufrā. (80) Faʾaradnāa ʾañy-yubdilahumā Rabbuhumā khayram-minhu zakātañw-wa ʾaqraba ruḥmā. (81) Wa ʾammal-jidāru fakāna lighulāmayni yatīmayni fil-madīnati wa kāna taḥtahū kañzul-lahumā wa kāna ʾabūhumā ṣāliḥañ-faʾarāda Rabbuka ʾañy-yablughāa ʾashuddahumā wa yastakhrijā kañzahumā raḥmatam-mir-Rabbik. Wa mā faʿaltuhū ʿan ʾamrī. Dhālika taʾwīlu mā lam tasṭiʿ ʿalayhi ṣabrā. (82) Wa yasʾalūnaka ʿañ-Dhil-qarnayni qul saʾatlū ʿalaykum-minhu dhikrā. (83)

77 Lit., "to cause a fault in it" – i.e., to make it temporarily unserviceable.

78 Lit., "we feared" – but it should be borne in mind that, beyond this primary meaning, the verb *khashiya* sometimes denotes "he had reason to fear" and, consequently, "he knew", i.e., that something bad would happen (*Tāj al-ʿArūs*, with specific reference to the above verse): and so we may assume that the sage's expression of "fear" was synonymous with positive "knowledge" gained through outward evidence or through mystic insight (the latter being more probable, as indicated by his statement in the second paragraph of the next verse, "I did not do [any of] this of my own accord").

79 I.e., left to them as an inheritance. Presumably that treasure would have been exposed to view if the wall had been allowed to tumble down, and would have been stolen by the avaricious village folk, who had shown their true character by refusing all hospitality to weary travellers.

80 Implying that whatever he had done was done under the impulsion of a higher truth – the mystic insight which revealed to him the reality behind the outward appearance of things and made him a *conscious* particle in God's unfathomable plan: and this explains the use of the plural "we" in verses 80-81, as well as the direct attribution, in the first paragraph of verse 82, of a concrete human action to God's will (Rāzī).

81 Lit., "I will convey unto you a remembrance [or "mention"] of him" – i.e., something that is *worthy* of remembrance and mention: which, I believe, is an allusion to the parabolic character of the subsequent story and the fact that it is confined, like the preceding parable of Moses and the unknown sage, to a few fundamental, spiritual truths. – The epithet *Dhu 'l-Qarnayn* signifies "the Two-Horned One" or "He of the Two Epochs", since the noun *qarn* has the meaning

Behold, We established him securely on earth, and endowed him with [the knowledge of] the right means to achieve anything[82] [that he might set out to achieve]; ‹84› and so he chose the right means [in whatever he did].[83] ‹84›
[And he marched westwards] till, when he came to the setting of the sun,[84] it appeared to him that it was setting in a dark, turbid sea;[85] and nearby he found a people [given to every kind of wrongdoing].
We said: "O thou Two-Horned One! Thou mayest either cause [them] to suffer or treat them with kindness!"[86] ‹86›
He answered: "As for him who does wrong [unto others[87]] – him shall we, in time, cause to suffer; and thereupon he shall be referred to his Sustainer,

إِنَّا مَكَّنَّا لَهُۥ فِى ٱلْأَرْضِ وَءَاتَيْنَٰهُ مِن كُلِّ شَىْءٍ سَبَبًا ﴿٨٤﴾ فَأَتْبَعَ
سَبَبًا ﴿٨٥﴾ حَتَّىٰٓ إِذَا بَلَغَ مَغْرِبَ ٱلشَّمْسِ وَجَدَهَا تَغْرُبُ فِى عَيْنٍ حَمِئَةٍ
وَوَجَدَ عِندَهَا قَوْمًا ۗ قُلْنَا يَٰذَا ٱلْقَرْنَيْنِ إِمَّآ أَن تُعَذِّبَ وَإِمَّآ أَن تَتَّخِذَ
فِيهِمْ حُسْنًا ﴿٨٦﴾ قَالَ أَمَّا مَن ظَلَمَ فَسَوْفَ نُعَذِّبُهُۥ ثُمَّ يُرَدُّ إِلَىٰ رَبِّهِۦ

ʾInnā makkannā lahū fil-ʾarḍi wa ʾātaynāhu miñ-kulli shayʾiñ-sababā. (84) Faʾatbaʿa sababā. (85) Ḥattāa ʾidhā balagha maghribash-shamsi wajadahā taghrubu fī ʿaynin ḥamiʾatiñw-wa wajada ʿiñdahā qawmā. Qulnā yā Dhal-qarnayni ʾimmāa ʾañ-tuʿadhdhiba wa ʾimmāa ʾañ-tattakhidha fīhim ḥusnā. (86) Qāla ʾammā mañ-ẓalama fasawfa nuʿadhdhibuhū thumma yuraddu ʾilā Rabbihī

of "horn" as well as of "generation" or "epoch" or "age" or "century". The classical commentators incline to the first of these meanings ("the Two-Horned"); and in this they appear to have been influenced by the ancient Middle-Eastern imagery of "horns" as symbols of power and greatness, although the Qurʾān itself does not offer any warrant for this interpretation. In fact, the term *qarn* (and its plural *qurūn*) occurs in the Qurʾān – apart from the combination *Dhu 'l-Qarnayn* appearing in verses 83, 86 and 94 of this *sūrah* – twenty times: and each time it has the meaning of "generation" in the sense of people belonging to one particular epoch or civilization. However, since the allegory of *Dhu 'l-Qarnayn* is meant to illustrate the qualities of a powerful and just ruler, it is possible to assume that this designation is an echo of the above-mentioned ancient symbolism, which – being familiar to the Arabs from very early times – had acquired idiomatic currency in their language long before the advent of Islam. Within the context of our Qurʾanic allegory, the "two horns" may be taken to denote the *two sources of power* with which *Dhu 'l-Qarnayn* is said to have been endowed: namely, the worldly might and prestige of kingship as well as the spiritual strength resulting from his faith in God. This last point is extremely important – for it is precisely the Qurʾanic stress on his faith in God that makes it impossible to identify *Dhu 'l-Qarnayn*, as most of the commentators do, with Alexander the Great (who is represented on some of his coins with two horns on his head) or with one or another of the pre-Islamic, Ḥimyaritic kings of Yemen. All those historic personages were pagans and worshipped a plurality of deities as a matter of course, whereas our *Dhu 'l-Qarnayn* is depicted as a firm believer in the One God: indeed, it is this aspect of his personality that provides the innermost reason of the Qurʾanic allegory. We must, therefore, conclude that the latter has nothing to do with history or even legend, and that its sole purport is a parabolic discourse on faith and ethics, with specific reference to the problem of worldly power (see the concluding passage in the introductory note to this *sūrah*).

82 According to Ibn ʿAbbās, Mujāhid, Saʿīd ibn Jubayr, ʿIkrimah, Qatādah and Aḍ-Ḍaḥḥāk (all of them quoted by Ibn Kathīr), the term *sabab* – lit., "a means to achieve [anything]" – denotes, in this context, the *knowledge* of the right means for the achievement of a particular end.

83 Lit., "he followed [the right] means": i.e., he never employed wrong means to achieve even a righteous goal.

84 I.e., the westernmost point of his expedition (Rāzī).

85 Or: "abundance of water" – which, according to many philologists (cf. *Tāj al-ʿArūs*), is one of the meanings of *ʿayn* (primarily denoting a "spring"). As for my rendering of the phrase "he found it (*wajadahā*) setting . . .", etc., as "it *appeared to him* that it was setting", see Rāzī and Ibn Kathīr, both of whom point out that we have here a metaphor based on the common optical illusion of the sun's "disappearing into the sea"; and Rāzī explains this, correctly, by the fact that the earth is spherical. (It is interesting to note that, according to him, this explanation was already advanced in the – now lost – Qurʾān-commentary of Abū ʿAlī al-Jubbāʾī, the famous Muʿtazilī scholar who died in 303 H., which corresponds to 915 or 916 of the Christian era.)

86 This divine permission to choose between two possible courses of action is not only a metonymic statement of the freedom of will accorded by God to man, but establishes also the important legal principle of *istiḥsān* (social or moral preference) open to a ruler or government in deciding as to what might be conducive to the greatest good (*maṣlaḥah*) of the community as a whole: and this is the first "lesson" of the parable of *Dhu 'l-Qarnayn*.

87 Cf. 11 : 117 and the corresponding note 149.

فَيُعَذِّبُهُۥ عَذَابًا نُّكْرًا ﴿87﴾ وَأَمَّا مَنْ ءَامَنَ وَعَمِلَ صَـٰلِحًا فَلَهُۥ جَزَآءً
ٱلْحُسْنَىٰ ۖ وَسَنَقُولُ لَهُۥ مِنْ أَمْرِنَا يُسْرًا ﴿88﴾ ثُمَّ أَتْبَعَ سَبَبًا ﴿89﴾ حَتَّىٰٓ إِذَا
بَلَغَ مَطْلِعَ ٱلشَّمْسِ وَجَدَهَا تَطْلُعُ عَلَىٰ قَوْمٍ لَّمْ نَجْعَل لَّهُم مِّن دُونِهَا
سِتْرًا ﴿90﴾ كَذَٰلِكَ وَقَدْ أَحَطْنَا بِمَا لَدَيْهِ خُبْرًا ﴿91﴾ ثُمَّ أَتْبَعَ سَبَبًا ﴿92﴾
حَتَّىٰٓ إِذَا بَلَغَ بَيْنَ ٱلسَّدَّيْنِ وَجَدَ مِن دُونِهِمَا قَوْمًا لَّا يَكَادُونَ يَفْقَهُونَ
قَوْلًا ﴿93﴾ قَالُوا۟ يَـٰذَا ٱلْقَرْنَيْنِ إِنَّ يَأْجُوجَ وَمَأْجُوجَ مُفْسِدُونَ فِى
ٱلْأَرْضِ فَهَلْ نَجْعَلُ لَكَ خَرْجًا عَلَىٰٓ أَن تَجْعَلَ بَيْنَنَا وَبَيْنَهُمْ سَدًّا ﴿94﴾

fayuʿadhdhibuhū ʿadhābañ-nukrā. ﴿87﴾ Wa ʾammā man ʾāmana wa ʿamila ṣāliḥañ-falahū jazāaʾanil-ḥusnā wa sanaqūlu lahū min ʾamrinā yusrā. ﴿88﴾ Thumma ʾatbaʿa sababā. ﴿89﴾ Ḥattāa ʾidhā balagha maṭliʿash-shamsi wajadahā taṭluʿu ʿalā qawmil-lam najʿal-lahum-miñ-dūnihā sitrā. ﴿90﴾ Kadhālika wa qad ʾaḥaṭnā bimā ladayhi khubrā. ﴿91﴾ Thumma ʾatbaʿa sababā. ﴿92﴾ Ḥattāa ʾidhā balagha baynas-saddayni wajada miñ-dūnihimā qawmal-lā yakādūna yafqahūna qawlā. ﴿93﴾ Qālū yā-Dhal-qarnayni ʾinna Yaʾjūja wa Maʾjūja mufsidūna fil-ʾarḍi fahal najʿalu laka kharjan ʿalāa ʾañ-tajʿala baynanā wa baynahum saddā. ﴿94﴾

and He will cause him to suffer with unnameable suffering.[88] «87» But as for him who believes and does righteous deeds – he will have the ultimate good [of the life to come] as his reward; and [as for us,] we shall make binding on him [only] that which is easy to fulfill."[89] «88»

And once again[90] he chose the right means [to achieve a right end]. «89»

[And then he marched eastwards] till, when he came to the rising of the sun,[91] he found that it was rising on a people for whom We had provided no coverings against it: «90» thus [We had made them, and thus he left them[92]]; and We did encompass with Our knowledge all that he had in mind.[93] «91»

And once again he chose the right means [to achieve a right end]. «92»

[And he marched on] till, when he reached [a place] between the two mountain-barriers,[94] he found beneath them a people who could scarcely understand a word [of his language]. «93»

They said: "O thou Two-Horned One! Behold, Gog and Magog[95] are spoiling this land. May we, then, pay unto thee a tribute on the understanding that thou wilt erect a barrier between us and them?" «94»

---

88 I.e., in the hereafter – implying that nothing that pertains to the life to come could ever be imagined or defined in terms of human experience.

89 Since righteous behaviour is the *norm* expected of man, the laws relating thereto must not be too demanding – which is another lesson to be drawn from this parable.

90 For this rendering of the particle *thumma*, see *sūrah* 6, note 31.

91 I.e., the easternmost point of his expedition (similar to the expression "the setting of the sun" in verse 86).

92 This is Rāzī's interpretation of the isolated expression *kadhālika* ("thus" or "thus it was") occurring here. It obviously relates to the primitive, natural state of those people who needed no clothes to protect them from the sun, and to the (implied) fact that *Dhu 'l-Qarnayn* left them as he had found them, being mindful not to upset their mode of life and thus to cause them misery.

93 Lit., "all that was with him" – i.e., his resolve not to "corrupt [or "change"] God's creation" (cf. the second half of my note 141 on 4 : 119) – which, I believe, is a further ethical lesson to be derived from this parable.

94 This is generally assumed to be the Caucasus. However, since neither the Qurʾān nor any authentic Tradition says anything about the location of these "two mountain-barriers" or the people who lived there, we can safely dismiss all the speculations advanced by the commentators on this score as irrelevant, the more so as the story of *Dhu 'l-Qarnayn* aims at no more than the illustration of certain ethical principles in a parabolic manner.

95 This is the form in which these names (in Arabic, *Yājūj* and *Mājūj*) have achieved currency in all European languages on the basis of certain vague references to them in the Bible (Genesis x, 2, I Chronicles i, 5, Ezekiel xxxviii, 2 and xxxix, 6, Revelation of St. John xx, 8). Most of the post-classical commentators identify these tribes with the Mongols and Tatars (see note 100 below).

He answered: "That wherein my Sustainer has so securely established me is better [than anything that you could give me];[96] hence, do but help me with [your labour's] strength, [and] I shall erect a rampart between you and them! ‹95› Bring me ingots of iron!"

Then, after he had [piled up the iron and] filled the gap between the two mountain-sides, he said: "[Light a fire and] ply your bellows!"[97]

At length, when he had made it [glow like] fire, he commanded: "Bring me molten copper which I may pour upon it." ‹96›

And thus [the rampart was built, and] their enemies[98] were unable to scale it, and neither were they able to pierce it. ‹97›

Said [the King]: "This is a mercy from my Sustainer! Yet when the time appointed by my Sustainer[99] shall come, He will make this [rampart] level with the ground: and my Sustainer's promise always comes true!"[100] ‹98›

قَالَ مَا مَكَّنِّى فِيهِ رَبِّى خَيْرٌ فَأَعِينُونِى بِقُوَّةٍ أَجْعَلْ بَيْنَكُمْ وَبَيْنَهُمْ
رَدْمًا ﴿٩٥﴾ ءَاتُونِى زُبَرَ ٱلْحَدِيدِ حَتَّىٰٓ إِذَا سَاوَىٰ بَيْنَ ٱلصَّدَفَيْنِ قَالَ
ٱنفُخُوا۟ حَتَّىٰٓ إِذَا جَعَلَهُۥ نَارًا قَالَ ءَاتُونِىٓ أُفْرِغْ عَلَيْهِ قِطْرًا ﴿٩٦﴾ فَمَا
ٱسْطَٰعُوٓا۟ أَن يَظْهَرُوهُ وَمَا ٱسْتَطَٰعُوا۟ لَهُۥ نَقْبًا ﴿٩٧﴾ قَالَ هَٰذَا رَحْمَةٌ مِّن
رَّبِّى فَإِذَا جَآءَ وَعْدُ رَبِّى جَعَلَهُۥ دَكَّآءَ وَكَانَ وَعْدُ رَبِّى حَقًّا ﴿٩٨﴾

Qāla mā makkannī fīhi Rabbī khayruñ-faʾaʿīnūnī biquwwatin ʾajʿal baynakum wa baynahum radmā. (95) ʾĀtūnī zubaral-ḥadīdi ḥattāa ʾidhā sāwā baynaṣ-ṣadafayni qālañ-fukhū; ḥattāa ʾidhā jaʿalahū nārañ-qāla ʾātūnīi ʾufrigh ʿalayhi qiṭrā. (96) Famas-ṭāʿūu ʾañy-yaẓharūhu wa mas-taṭāʿū lahū naqbā. (97) Qāla hādhā raḥmatum-mir-Rabbī. Faʾidhā jāaʾa waʿdu Rabbī jaʿalahū dakkāaʾa wa kāna waʿdu Rabbī ḥaqqā. (98)

96 It is generally assumed that the phrase "that wherein my Sustainer has so securely established me (*makkannī*)" refers to the power and wealth bestowed on him; but it is much more probable – and certainly more consistent with the ethical tenor of the whole parable of *Dhu 'l-Qarnayn* – that it refers to God's *guidance* rather than to worldly possessions.

97 Lit., "Blow!"

98 Lit., "they".

99 Lit., "my Sustainer's promise".

100 Some of the classical commentators (e.g., Ṭabarī) regard this as a prediction of a definite, historic event: namely, the future break-through of the savage tribes of "Gog and Magog", who are conceived of as identical with the Mongols and Tatars (see note 95 above). This "identification" is mainly based on a well-authenticated Tradition – recorded by Ibn Ḥanbal, Bukhārī and Muslim – which tells us that the Apostle of God had a prophetic dream to which he referred, on awakening, with an exclamation of distress: "There is no deity save God! Woe unto the Arabs from a misfortune that is approaching: a little gap has been opened today in the rampart of Gog and Magog!" Ever since the late Middle Ages, Muslims have been inclined to discern in this dream a prediction of the great Mongol invasion in the thirteenth century, which destroyed the Abbasid Empire and, thus, the political power of the Arabs. However, the mention, in verses 99-101 of this *sūrah*, of "the Day" – i.e., the Day of Judgment – in connection with "Gog and Magog" shows that "the time appointed by my Sustainer" relates to the coming of the Last Hour, when all works of man will be destroyed. But since none of the Qurʾanic references to the "approach" or the "nearness" of the Last Hour has anything to do with the *human* concept of time, it is possible to accept both of the above interpretations as equally valid in the sense that the "coming of the Last Hour" comprises an indefinite – and, in human terms, perhaps even immensely long – span of time, and that the break-through of the godless forces of "Gog and Magog" was to be one of the signs of its approach. And, finally, it is most logical to assume (especially on the basis of 21 : 96-97) that the terms *Yājūj* and *Mājūj* are purely allegorical, applying not to any specific tribes or beings but to a series of social catastrophes which would cause a complete destruction of man's civilization before the coming of the Last Hour.

ربع الحزب

۞ وَتَرَكْنَا بَعْضَهُمْ يَوْمَئِذٍ يَمُوجُ فِي بَعْضٍ وَنُفِخَ فِي الصُّورِ فَجَمَعْنَاهُمْ
جَمْعًا ﴿٩٩﴾ وَعَرَضْنَا جَهَنَّمَ يَوْمَئِذٍ لِلْكَافِرِينَ عَرْضًا ﴿١٠٠﴾ الَّذِينَ كَانَتْ
أَعْيُنُهُمْ فِي غِطَاءٍ عَنْ ذِكْرِي وَكَانُوا لَا يَسْتَطِيعُونَ سَمْعًا ﴿١٠١﴾ أَفَحَسِبَ
الَّذِينَ كَفَرُوا أَنْ يَتَّخِذُوا عِبَادِي مِنْ دُونِي أَوْلِيَاءَ إِنَّا أَعْتَدْنَا جَهَنَّمَ
لِلْكَافِرِينَ نُزُلًا ﴿١٠٢﴾ قُلْ هَلْ نُنَبِّئُكُمْ بِالْأَخْسَرِينَ أَعْمَالًا ﴿١٠٣﴾ الَّذِينَ
ضَلَّ سَعْيُهُمْ فِي الْحَيَاةِ الدُّنْيَا وَهُمْ يَحْسَبُونَ أَنَّهُمْ يُحْسِنُونَ صُنْعًا ﴿١٠٤﴾
أُولَٰئِكَ الَّذِينَ كَفَرُوا بِآيَاتِ رَبِّهِمْ وَلِقَائِهِ فَحَبِطَتْ أَعْمَالُهُمْ فَلَا
نُقِيمُ لَهُمْ يَوْمَ الْقِيَامَةِ وَزْنًا ﴿١٠٥﴾ ذَٰلِكَ جَزَاؤُهُمْ جَهَنَّمُ بِمَا كَفَرُوا وَاتَّخَذُوا
آيَاتِي وَرُسُلِي هُزُوًا ﴿١٠٦﴾ إِنَّ الَّذِينَ آمَنُوا وَعَمِلُوا الصَّالِحَاتِ كَانَتْ
لَهُمْ جَنَّاتُ الْفِرْدَوْسِ نُزُلًا ﴿١٠٧﴾ خَالِدِينَ فِيهَا لَا يَبْغُونَ عَنْهَا
حِوَلًا ﴿١٠٨﴾

◆ Wa taraknā baᶜḍahum Yawma᾽idhiñy-yamūju fī
baᶜḍiñw-wa nufikha fiṣ-ṣūri fajamaᶜnāhum jamᶜā.
99 Wa ᶜaraḍnā jahannama Yawma᾽idhil-lilkāfirīna
ᶜarḍā. 100 ᾽Alladhīna kānat ᾽aᶜyunuhum fī ghiṭāa᾽in
ᶜañ-dhikrī wa kānū lā yastaṭīᶜūna samᶜā. 101
᾽Afaḥasibal-ladhīna kafarūu ᾽añy-yattakhidhū ᶜibādī
miñ-dūnii ᾽awliyāa᾽. ᾽Innāa ᾽aᶜtadnā jahannama
lilkāfirīna nuzulā. 102 Qul hal nunabbi᾽ukum
bil᾽akhsarīna ᾽aᶜmālā. 103 ᾽Alladhīna ḍalla saᶜyuhum
fil-ḥayātid-dunyā wa hum yaḥsabūna ᾽annahum
yuḥsinūna ṣunᶜā. 104 ᾽Ulāa᾽ikal-ladhīna kafarū
bi᾽Āyāti Rabbihim wa liqāa᾽ihī faḥabiṭat
᾽aᶜmāluhum falā nuqīmu lahum Yawmal-Qiyāmati
waznā. 105 Dhālika jazāa᾽uhum jahannamu bimā ka-
farū wat-takhadhūu ᾽Āyātī wa Rusulī huzuwā. 106
᾽Innal-ladhīna ᾽āmanū wa ᶜamiluṣ-ṣāliḥāti kānat la-
hum jannātul-firdawsi nuzulā. 107 Khālidīna fīhā lā
yabghūna ᶜanhā ḥiwalā. 108

AND ON that Day[101] We shall [call forth all mankind and] leave them to surge like waves [that dash] against one another; and the trumpet [of judgment] will be blown, and We shall gather them all together. ‹99›

And on that Day We shall place hell, for all to see, before those who denied the truth ‹100› – those whose eyes had been veiled against any remembrance of Me because they could not bear to listen [to the voice of truth]! ‹101›

Do they who are bent on denying the truth think, perchance, that they could take [any of] My creatures for protectors against Me?[102] Verily, We have readied hell to welcome all who [thus] deny the truth![103] ‹102›

Say: "Shall we tell you who are the greatest losers in whatever they may do? ‹103›

"[It is] they whose labour has gone astray in [the pursuit of no more than] this world's life, and who none the less think that they are doing good works: ‹104› it is they who have chosen to deny their Sustainer's messages and the truth that they are destined to meet Him."

Hence, all their [good] deeds come to nought, and no weight shall We assign to them on Resurrection Day.[104] ‹105› That will be their recompense – [their] hell – for having denied the truth and made My messages and My apostles a target of their mockery. ‹106›

[But,] verily, as for those who attain to faith and do righteous deeds – the gardens of paradise will be there to welcome them; ‹107› therein will they abide, [and] never will they desire any change therefrom. ‹108›

---

101 I.e., on the Day of Judgment alluded to in the preceding verse.

102 This is an allusion not only to the worship of created beings or forces of nature, but also to the popular belief that saints, whether alive or dead, could effectively "intercede" with God in behalf of anyone whom He has rejected.

103 I.e., of God's oneness and uniqueness, and hence of the fact that no created being can have any "influence" on God's judgment.

104 Although each of their good actions will be taken into account on Judgment Day in accordance with the Qur᾽anic statement that "he who shall have done an atom's weight of good, shall behold it" (99 : 7), the above verse implies that whatever good such sinners may do is far outweighed by their godlessness (Al-Qāḍī ᶜIyāḍ, as quoted by Rāzī).

SAY: "If all the sea were ink for my Sustainer's words, the sea would indeed be exhausted ere my Sustainer's words are exhausted! And [thus it would be] if We were to add to it sea upon sea."[105] ‹109›

Say [O Prophet]: "I am but a mortal man like all of you. It has been revealed unto me that your God is the One and Only God. Hence, whoever looks forward [with hope and awe] to meeting his Sustainer [on Judgment Day], let him do righteous deeds, and let him not ascribe unto anyone or anything a share in the worship due to his Sustainer!" ‹110›

قُل لَّوْ كَانَ ٱلْبَحْرُ مِدَادًا لِّكَلِمَٰتِ رَبِّى لَنَفِدَ ٱلْبَحْرُ قَبْلَ أَن تَنفَدَ
كَلِمَٰتُ رَبِّى وَلَوْ جِئْنَا بِمِثْلِهِۦ مَدَدًا ﴿١٠٩﴾ قُلْ إِنَّمَآ أَنَا۠ بَشَرٌ مِّثْلُكُمْ يُوحَىٰٓ
إِلَىَّ أَنَّمَآ إِلَٰهُكُمْ إِلَٰهٌ وَٰحِدٌ ۖ فَمَن كَانَ يَرْجُوا۟ لِقَآءَ رَبِّهِۦ فَلْيَعْمَلْ عَمَلًا
صَٰلِحًا وَلَا يُشْرِكْ بِعِبَادَةِ رَبِّهِۦٓ أَحَدًۢا ﴿١١٠﴾

Qul-law kānal-baḥru midādal-liKalimāti Rabbī la-nafidal-baḥru qabla ʾañ-tañfada Kalimātu Rabbī wa law jiʾnā bimithlihī madadā. (109) Qul ʾinnamāa ʾana basharum-mithlukum yūḥāa ʾilayya ʾannamāa ʾIlāhukum ʾIlāhuñw-Wāḥid. Famañ-kāna yarjū liqāaʾa Rabbihī falyaʿmal ʿamalañ-ṣāliḥañw-wa lā yushrik biʿibādati Rabbihīi ʾaḥadā. (110)

105 Lit., "if We were to produce the like of it [i.e., of the sea] in addition". It is to be noted that, as pointed out by Zamakhsharī, the term *al-baḥr* ("the sea") is used here in a generic sense, comprising all the seas that exist: hence, the expression "the like of it" has been rendered by me as "sea upon sea". (See also 31 : 27.)

نِدَآءً خَفِيًّا قَالَ رَبِّ إِنِّي وَهَنَ

ٱلْعَظْمُ مِنِّي وَٱشْتَعَلَ

ٱلرَّأْسُ شَيْبًا وَلَمْ أَكُنۢ بِدُعَآئِكَ

رَبِّ شَقِيًّا وَإِنِّي خِفْتُ ٱلْمَوَٰلِيَ

مِن وَرَآءِى وَكَانَتِ ٱمْرَأَتِى

سورة مريم مكية

بِسْمِ ٱللَّهِ ٱلرَّحْمَٰنِ ٱلرَّحِيمِ

كٓهيعٓصٓ ذِكْرُ رَحْمَتِ رَبِّكَ عَبْدَهُۥ زَكَرِيَّآ إِذْ نَادَىٰ رَبَّهُۥ

وآياتها ثمان وتسعون

The Nineteenth Sūrah

Maryam (Mary)

Mecca Period

ALL THE AUTHORITIES agree in that this *sūrah* belongs to the Mecca period; but whereas some of them (e.g., Suyūṭī) place it chronologically towards the end of that period, there is uncontrovertible historical evidence that it was revealed not later than the sixth and possibly even as early as the fifth year of the Prophet's mission, i.e., about seven or eight years before his *hijrah* to Medina. The Companions who at about that time took part in the second emigration of Muslims from Mecca to Abyssinia were already acquainted with this *sūrah*: thus, for instance, it is recorded that Jaᶜfar ibn Abī Ṭālib – the Prophet's cousin and leader of the first group of those emigrants – recited it before the Negus (i.e., King) of Abyssinia in order to explain the Islamic attitude towards Jesus (Ibn Hishām).

The title by which this *sūrah* is commonly known is based on the story of Mary and Jesus, which (together with the story of Zachariah and his son John, the precursor of Jesus) occupies about one-third of the whole *sūrah* and is re-echoed towards its end in verses 88-91.

-19-

سورة مريم مكية

وآياتها ثمان وتسعون

IN THE NAME OF GOD, THE MOST GRACIOUS, THE DISPENSER OF GRACE:

Kāf. Hā. Yā. ᶜAyn. Ṣād.[1] ‹1›
AN ACCOUNT of the grace which thy Sustainer bestowed upon His servant Zachariah:[2] ‹2›
When he called out to his Sustainer in the secrecy of his heart,[3] ‹3› he prayed: "O my Sustainer! Feeble have become my bones, and my head glistens with grey hair. But never yet, O my Lord, has my prayer unto Thee remained unanswered.[4] ‹4›
"Now, behold, I am afraid of [what] my kinsfolk [will do] after I am gone,[5] for my wife has always been barren. Bestow, then, upon me, out of Thy grace, the gift of a successor ‹5› who will be my heir as well as an heir [to the dignity] of the House of Jacob; and make him, O my Sustainer, well-pleasing to Thee! ‹6›
[Thereupon the angels called out unto him:[6]] "O Zachariah! We bring thee the glad tiding of [the birth of] a son whose name shall be John. [And God says,] 'Never have We given this name to anyone before him.'"[7] ‹7›
[Zachariah] exclaimed: "O my Sustainer! How can I have a son when my wife has always been barren and I have become utterly infirm through old age?" ‹8›

بِسْمِ ٱللَّهِ ٱلرَّحْمَٰنِ ٱلرَّحِيمِ

كهيعص ﴿١﴾ ذِكْرُ رَحْمَتِ رَبِّكَ عَبْدَهُۥ زَكَرِيَّآ ﴿٢﴾ إِذْ نَادَىٰ رَبَّهُۥ
نِدَآءً خَفِيًّا ﴿٣﴾ قَالَ رَبِّ إِنِّى وَهَنَ ٱلْعَظْمُ مِنِّى وَٱشْتَعَلَ ٱلرَّأْسُ شَيْبًا
وَلَمْ أَكُنۢ بِدُعَآئِكَ رَبِّ شَقِيًّا ﴿٤﴾ وَإِنِّى خِفْتُ ٱلْمَوَٰلِىَ مِن وَرَآءِى
وَكَانَتِ ٱمْرَأَتِى عَاقِرًا فَهَبْ لِى مِن لَّدُنكَ وَلِيًّا ﴿٥﴾ يَرِثُنِى وَيَرِثُ مِنْ ءَالِ
يَعْقُوبَ ۖ وَٱجْعَلْهُ رَبِّ رَضِيًّا ﴿٦﴾ يَٰزَكَرِيَّآ إِنَّا نُبَشِّرُكَ بِغُلَٰمٍ ٱسْمُهُۥ
يَحْيَىٰ لَمْ نَجْعَل لَّهُۥ مِن قَبْلُ سَمِيًّا ﴿٧﴾ قَالَ رَبِّ أَنَّىٰ يَكُونُ لِى غُلَٰمٌ
وَكَانَتِ ٱمْرَأَتِى عَاقِرًا وَقَدْ بَلَغْتُ مِنَ ٱلْكِبَرِ عِتِيًّا ﴿٨﴾

Bismil-lāhir-Raḥmānir-Raḥīm.
Kāaf-Hā-Yā-ᶜAyyñ-Ṣāad. (1) **Dhikru raḥmati Rabbika ᶜabdahū Zakariyyā.** (2) **ʾIdh nādā Rabbahū nidāaʾan khafiyyā.** (3) **Qāla Rabbi ʾinnī wahanal-ᶜaẓmu minnī wash-taᶜalar-raʾsu shaybañw-wa lam ʾakum-biduᶜāaʾika Rabbi shaqiyyā.** (4) **Wa ʾinnī khiftul-mawāliya miñw-warāaʾī wa kānatim-raʾatī ᶜāqirañ-fahab lī mil-laduñka waliyyā.** (5) **Yarithunī wa yarithu min ʾāli Yaᶜqūba waj-ᶜalhu Rabbi raḍiyyā.** (6) **Yā Zakariyyāa ʾinnā nubashshiruka bighulāminis-muhū Yaḥyā lam najᶜal-lahū miñ-qablu samiyyā.** (7) **Qāla Rabbi ʾannā yakūnu lī ghulāmuñw-wa kānatim-raʾatī ᶜāqirañw-wa qad balaghtu minal-kibari ᶜitiyyā.** (8)

---

1 See Appendix II.ỹ

2 Lit., "An account of thy Sustainer's grace upon . . .", etc. According to the account in the Gospels, not contradicted by the Qurʾān, Zachariah's wife Elisabeth was a cousin of Mary, the mother of Jesus (Cf. Luke i, 36).

3 Lit., "with secret calling".

4 Lit., "never have I been unfortunate in my prayer to Thee".

5 Lit., "after me". He evidently anticipated that his kinsfolk – who, like himself, were priests attached to the Temple – would be morally too weak to fulfil their duties with dignity and conviction (Rāzī), and thus, perhaps, unable to safeguard the future of Mary, whose guardian he was (cf. the first paragraph of 3 : 37).

6 See 3 : 39.

7 Lit., "Never before have We made a namesake for him". The name *Yaḥyā* (John) signifies "he shall live", i.e., he will be spiritually alive and will be remembered forever; and the fact that God Himself had chosen this name for him was a singular distinction, equivalent to a divine promise (*kalimah*, cf. note 28 on 3 : 39).

Answered [the angel]: "Thus it is; [but] thy Sustainer says, 'This is easy for Me – even as I have created *thee* aforetime out of nothing.'"[8] ‹9›
[Zachariah] prayed: "O my Sustainer! Appoint a sign for me!"
Said [the angel]: "Thy sign shall be that for full three nights [and days] thou wilt not speak unto men."[9] ‹10›
Thereupon he came out of the sanctuary unto his people and signified to them [by gestures]: "Extol His limitless glory by day and by night!" ‹11›
[And when the son was born and grew up,[10] he was told,] "O John! Hold fast unto the divine writ with [all thy] strength!" – for We granted him wisdom while he was yet a little boy, ‹12› as well as, by Our grace, [the gift of] compassion[11] and purity; and he was [always] conscious of Us ‹13› and full of piety towards his parents; and never was he haughty or rebellious. ‹14›
Hence, [God's] peace was upon him on the day when he was born, and on the day of his death, and will be [upon him] on the day when he shall be raised to life [again]. ‹15›

AND CALL to mind, through this divine writ,[12] Mary. Lo! She withdrew from her family to an eastern place ‹16› and kept herself in seclusion from them,[13] whereupon We sent unto her Our angel of revelation, who appeared to her in the shape of a well-made human being.[14] ‹17›

قَالَ كَذَٰلِكَ قَالَ رَبُّكَ هُوَ عَلَيَّ هَيِّنٌ وَقَدْ خَلَقْتُكَ مِن قَبْلُ وَلَمْ تَكُ
شَيْـًٔا ﴿٩﴾ قَالَ رَبِّ ٱجْعَل لِّيٓ ءَايَةً قَالَ ءَايَتُكَ أَلَّا تُكَلِّمَ ٱلنَّاسَ
ثَلَٰثَ لَيَالٍ سَوِيًّا ﴿١٠﴾ فَخَرَجَ عَلَىٰ قَوْمِهِۦ مِنَ ٱلْمِحْرَابِ فَأَوْحَىٰٓ إِلَيْهِمْ
أَن سَبِّحُوا۟ بُكْرَةً وَعَشِيًّا ﴿١١﴾ يَٰيَحْيَىٰ خُذِ ٱلْكِتَٰبَ بِقُوَّةٍ وَءَاتَيْنَٰهُ
ٱلْحُكْمَ صَبِيًّا ﴿١٢﴾ وَحَنَانًا مِّن لَّدُنَّا وَزَكَوٰةً وَكَانَ تَقِيًّا ﴿١٣﴾ وَبَرًّۢا
بِوَٰلِدَيْهِ وَلَمْ يَكُن جَبَّارًا عَصِيًّا ﴿١٤﴾ وَسَلَٰمٌ عَلَيْهِ يَوْمَ وُلِدَ وَيَوْمَ يَمُوتُ
وَيَوْمَ يُبْعَثُ حَيًّا ﴿١٥﴾ وَٱذْكُرْ فِى ٱلْكِتَٰبِ مَرْيَمَ إِذِ ٱنتَبَذَتْ مِنْ أَهْلِهَا
مَكَانًا شَرْقِيًّا ﴿١٦﴾ فَٱتَّخَذَتْ مِن دُونِهِمْ حِجَابًا فَأَرْسَلْنَآ إِلَيْهَا رُوحَنَا
فَتَمَثَّلَ لَهَا بَشَرًا سَوِيًّا ﴿١٧﴾

Qāla kadhālika qāla Rabbuka huwa ᶜalayya hayyinuñw-wa qad khalaqtuka miñ-qablu wa lam taku shayʾā. (9) Qāla Rabbij-ᶜal-lī ʾāyah. Qāla ʾāyatuka ʾallā tukalliman-nāsa thalātha layāliñ-sawiyyā. (10) Fakharaja ᶜalā qawmihī minal-miḥrābi faʾawḥāa ʾilayhim ʾañ-sabbiḥū bukratañw-wa ᶜashiyyā. (11) Yā Yaḥyā khudhil-Kitāba biquwwahtiñw-wa ʾātaynāhul-ḥukma ṣabiyyā. (12) Wa ḥanānam-mil-ladunnā wa zakātañ-wa kāna taqiyyā. (13) Wa barram-biwālidayhi wa lam yakuñ-jabbāran ᶜaṣiyyā. (14) Wa salāmun ᶜalayhi yawma wulida wa yawma yamūtu wa yawma yubᶜathu ḥayyā. (15) Wadh-kur fil-Kitābi Maryama ʾidhiñ-tabadhat min ʾahlihā makānañ-sharqiyyā. (16) Fattakhadhat miñ-dūnihim ḥijābañ-faʾarsalnāa ʾilayhā rūḥanā fatamaththala lahā basharañ-sawiyyā. (17)

8 Lit., "when [or "although"] thou wert nothing". This stress on God's unlimited power to bring into being a new chain of causes and effects forms here, as in *Āl ᶜImrān*, a preamble to the announcement, expressed in very similar terms, of the birth of Jesus (see verses 19 ff.).

9 See 3 : 41 and the corresponding note 29.

10 According to Rāzī, this is clearly implied inasmuch as the sequence presupposes that John had in the meantime reached an age which enabled him to receive and understand God's commandment.

11 Lit., "compassion from Us" – i.e., as a special divine gift.

12 Lit., "in the divine writ". In this *sūrah* as well as in *Āl ᶜImrān* the story of the birth of John is followed by that of Jesus – firstly, because John (called "the Baptist" in the Bible) was to be a precursor of Jesus, and, secondly, because of the obvious parallelism in the form of the announcements of these two births.

13 Apparently, in order to devote herself undisturbed to prayer and meditation. The "eastern place" may possibly, as Ibn Kathīr suggests, signify an eastern chamber of the Temple, to the service of which Mary had been dedicated by her mother (cf. 3 : 35-37).

14 As pointed out in *sūrah* 2, note 71, and *sūrah* 16, note 2, the term *rūḥ* often denotes "divine inspiration". Occasionally, however, it is used to describe the *medium* through which such inspiration is imparted to God's elect: in

She exclaimed: "Verily, I seek refuge from thee with the Most Gracious! [Approach me not] if thou art conscious of Him!" «18»
[The angel] answered: "I am but a messenger of thy Sustainer, [who says,] 'I shall bestow upon thee the gift of a son endowed with purity.'" «19»
Said she: "How can I have a son when no man has ever touched me? – for, never have I been a loose woman!" «20»
[The angel] answered: "Thus it is; [but] thy Sustainer says, 'This is easy for Me;[15] and [thou shalt have a son,] so that We might make him a symbol unto mankind and an act of grace from Us.'"[16]
And it was a thing decreed [by God]: «21»
and in time she conceived him, and then she withdrew with him to a far-off place. «22»
And [when] the throes of childbirth drove her to the trunk of a palm-tree,[17] she exclaimed: "Oh, would that I had died ere this, and had become a thing forgotten, utterly forgotten!" «23»
Thereupon [a voice] called out to her from beneath that [palm-tree]:[18] "Grieve not! Thy Sustainer has provided a rivulet [running] beneath thee; «24» and shake the trunk of the palm-tree towards thee: it will drop fresh, ripe dates upon thee. «25»

قَالَتْ إِنِّىٓ أَعُوذُ بِٱلرَّحْمَٰنِ مِنكَ إِن كُنتَ تَقِيًّا (18) قَالَ إِنَّمَآ أَنَا۠
رَسُولُ رَبِّكِ لِأَهَبَ لَكِ غُلَٰمًا زَكِيًّا (19) قَالَتْ أَنَّىٰ يَكُونُ لِى غُلَٰمٌ
وَلَمْ يَمْسَسْنِى بَشَرٌ وَلَمْ أَكُ بَغِيًّا (20) قَالَ كَذَٰلِكِ قَالَ رَبُّكِ هُوَ عَلَىَّ
هَيِّنٌ وَلِنَجْعَلَهُۥٓ ءَايَةً لِّلنَّاسِ وَرَحْمَةً مِّنَّا وَكَانَ أَمْرًا مَّقْضِيًّا (21) ۞
فَحَمَلَتْهُ فَٱنتَبَذَتْ بِهِۦ مَكَانًا قَصِيًّا (22) فَأَجَآءَهَا ٱلْمَخَاضُ إِلَىٰ جِذْعِ
ٱلنَّخْلَةِ قَالَتْ يَٰلَيْتَنِى مِتُّ قَبْلَ هَٰذَا وَكُنتُ نَسْيًا مَّنسِيًّا (23) فَنَادَىٰهَا
مِن تَحْتِهَآ أَلَّا تَحْزَنِى قَدْ جَعَلَ رَبُّكِ تَحْتَكِ سَرِيًّا (24) وَهُزِّىٓ إِلَيْكِ
بِجِذْعِ ٱلنَّخْلَةِ تُسَٰقِطْ عَلَيْكِ رُطَبًا جَنِيًّا (25)

نصف الحزب

Qālat ʾinnī ʾaʿūdhu birRaḥmāni miñka ʾiñ-kuñta taqiyyā. (18) Qāla ʾinnamāa ʾana Rasūlu Rabbiki liʾahaba laki ghulāmañ-zakiyyā. (19) Qālat ʾannā yakūnu lī ghulāmuñw-wa lam yamsasnī basharuñw-wa lam ʾaku baghiyyā. (20) Qāla kadhāliki qāla Rabbuki huwa ʿalayya hayyin. Wa linajʿalahūu ʾāyatal-linnāsi wa raḥmatam-minnā; wa kāna ʾamram-maqḍiyyā. (21) ۞ Faḥamalat-hu fañtabadhat bihī makānañ-qaṣiyyā. (22) Faʾajāaʾahal-makhāḍu ʾilā jidhʿin-nakhlati qālat yā laytanī mittu qabla hādhā wa kuñtu nasyam-mañsiyyā. (23) Fanādāhā miñ-taḥtihāa ʾallā taḥzanī qad jaʿala Rabbuki taḥtaki sariyyā. (24) Wa huzzīi ʾilayki bijidhʿin-nakhlati tusāqiṭ ʿalayki ruṭabañ-janiyyā. (25)

other words, the angel (or angelic force) of revelation. Since – as is implied in 6 : 9 – mortals cannot perceive an angel in his true manifestation, God caused him to appear to Mary "in the shape of a well-made human being", i.e., in a shape accessible to her perception. According to Rāzī, the designation of the angel as *rūḥ* ("spirit" or "soul") indicates that this category of beings is purely spiritual, without any physical element.

15 Cf. the identical phrase in verse 9 above, relating to the announcement of John's birth to Zachariah. In both these cases, the implication is that God can and does bring about events which may be utterly unexpected or even inconceivable before they materialize. In connection with the announcement of a son to Mary, the Qurʾān states in 3 : 47 that "when He wills a thing to be, He but says unto it, 'Be' – and it is": but since neither the Qurʾān nor any authentic Tradition tells us anything about the chain of causes and effects (*asbāb*) which God's decree "Be" was to bring into being, all speculation as to the "how" of this event must remain beyond the scope of a Qurʾān-commentary. (But see also note 87 on (21 : 91.)

16 One of the several meanings of the term *āyah* is "a sign" or, as elaborately defined by Rāghib, "a symbol" (cf. *sūrah* 17, note 2). However, the sense in which it is most frequently used in the Qurʾān is "a [divine] message": hence, its metonymic application to Jesus may mean that he was destined to become a vehicle of God's message to man – i.e., a prophet – and, thus, a symbol of God's grace. – As regards the words "thou shalt have a son" interpolated by me between brackets, a statement to this effect is implied in the subsequent phrase beginning with "so that" (Zamakhsharī and Rāzī).

17 I.e., compelling her to cling to it for support: thus stressing the natural, normal circumstances of this childbirth, attended – as is the case with all women – by severe labour pains.

18 Or: "from beneath her". However, Qatādah (as quoted by Zamakhsharī) interprets this as meaning "from beneath the palm-tree".

Eat, then, and drink, and let thine eye be gladdened! And if thou shouldst see any human being, convey this unto him:[19] 'Behold, abstinence from speech have I vowed unto the Most Gracious; hence, I may not speak today to any mortal.'"[20] ‹26›
And in time she returned to her people, carrying the child with her.[21]
They said: "O Mary! Thou hast indeed done an amazing thing! ‹27› O sister of Aaron![22] Thy father was not a wicked man, nor was thy mother a loose woman!" ‹28›
Thereupon she pointed to him.
They exclaimed: "How can we talk to one who [as yet] is a little boy in the cradle?" ‹29›
[But] he said:[23] "Behold, I am a servant of God. He has vouchsafed unto me revelation and made me a prophet,[24] ‹30› and made me blessed wherever I may be; and He has enjoined upon me prayer and charity as long as I live, ‹31› and [has endowed me with] piety towards my mother; and He has not made me haughty or bereft of grace.‹32›
"Hence, peace was upon me on the day when I was born, and [will be upon me] on the day of my death, and on the day when I shall be raised to life [again]!" ‹33›

فَكُلِي وَٱشْرَبِي وَقَرِّي عَيْنًا فَإِمَّا تَرَيِنَّ مِنَ ٱلْبَشَرِ أَحَدًا فَقُولِيٓ إِنِّي نَذَرْتُ
لِلرَّحْمَٰنِ صَوْمًا فَلَنْ أُكَلِّمَ ٱلْيَوْمَ إِنسِيًّا ﴿٢٦﴾ فَأَتَتْ بِهِۦ قَوْمَهَا تَحْمِلُهُۥ
قَالُوا۟ يَٰمَرْيَمُ لَقَدْ جِئْتِ شَيْـًٔا فَرِيًّا ﴿٢٧﴾ يَٰٓأُخْتَ هَٰرُونَ مَا كَانَ أَبُوكِ
ٱمْرَأَ سَوْءٍ وَمَا كَانَتْ أُمُّكِ بَغِيًّا ﴿٢٨﴾ فَأَشَارَتْ إِلَيْهِ قَالُوا۟ كَيْفَ نُكَلِّمُ
مَن كَانَ فِي ٱلْمَهْدِ صَبِيًّا ﴿٢٩﴾ قَالَ إِنِّي عَبْدُ ٱللَّهِ ءَاتَىٰنِيَ ٱلْكِتَٰبَ
وَجَعَلَنِي نَبِيًّا ﴿٣٠﴾ وَجَعَلَنِي مُبَارَكًا أَيْنَ مَا كُنتُ وَأَوْصَٰنِي بِٱلصَّلَوٰةِ
وَٱلزَّكَوٰةِ مَا دُمْتُ حَيًّا ﴿٣١﴾ وَبَرًّۢا بِوَٰلِدَتِي وَلَمْ يَجْعَلْنِي جَبَّارًا
شَقِيًّا ﴿٣٢﴾ وَٱلسَّلَٰمُ عَلَيَّ يَوْمَ وُلِدتُّ وَيَوْمَ أَمُوتُ وَيَوْمَ أُبْعَثُ حَيًّا ﴿٣٣﴾

Fakulī wash-rabī wa qarrī ᶜaynā. Faᵓimmā tarayinna minal-bashari ᵓaḥadañ-faqūlīi ᵓinnī nadhartu lir-Raḥmāni ṣawmañ-falan ᵓukallimal-yawma ᵓIñsiyyā. ﴿26﴾ Faᵓatat bihī qawmahā taḥmiluh. Qālū yā Maryamu laqad jiᵓti shayᵓañ-fariyyā. ﴿27﴾ Yāa ᵓukhta Hārūna mā kāna ᵓabūkim-raᵓa sawᵓiñw-wa mā kānat ᵓummuki baghiyyā. ﴿28﴾ Faᵓashārat ᵓilayhi qālū kayfa nukallimu mañ-kāna fil-mahdi ṣabiyyā. ﴿29﴾ Qāla ᵓinnī ᶜabdul-lāhi ᵓātāniyal-Kitāba wa jaᶜalanī Nabiyyā. ﴿30﴾ Wa jaᶜalanī mubārakan ᵓaynamā kuñtu wa ᵓawṣānī biṣ-Ṣalāti waz-Zakāti mā dumtu ḥayyā. ﴿31﴾ Wa barram-biwālidatī wa lam yajᶜalnī jabbārañ-shaqiyyā. ﴿32﴾ Was-salāmu ᶜalayya yawma wulittu wa yawma ᵓamūtu wa yawma ᵓubᶜathu ḥayyā. ﴿33﴾

19 Lit., "say" – but since actual speech would contradict what follows, the "saying" implies here a communication by gestures.

20 In its primary sense, the term *ṣawm* denotes "abstinence" or "self-denial"; in the present context it is synonymous with *ṣamt* ("abstinence from speech"); in fact – as pointed out by Zamakhsharī – the latter term is said to have figured in the Qurᵓān-copy belonging to ᶜAbd Allāh ibn Masᶜūd (possibly as a marginal, explanatory notation).

(21) Lit., "she came with him to her people, carrying him".

22 In ancient Semitic usage, a person's name was often linked with that of a renowned ancestor or founder of the tribal line. Thus, for instance, a man of the tribe of Banū Tamīm was sometimes addressed as "son of Tamīm" or "brother of Tamīm". Since Mary belonged to the priestly caste, and hence descended from Aaron, the brother of Moses, she was called a "sister of Aaron" (in the same way as her cousin Elisabeth, the wife of Zachariah, is spoken of in Luke i, 5, as one "of the daughters of Aaron").

23 Although the Qurᵓān mentions in 3 : 46 that Jesus would "speak unto men [while yet] in his cradle" – i.e., would be imbued with wisdom from his early childhood – verses 30-33 seem to be in the nature of a trope, projecting the shape of things to come by using, for the sake of emphasis, the past tense to describe something that was to become real in the future. (See also next note.)

24 Since it is not conceivable that anyone could be granted divine revelation and made a prophet *before* attaining to full maturity of intellect and experience, ᶜIkrimah and Aḍ-Ḍaḥḥāk – as quoted by Ṭabarī – interpret this passage as meaning, "God has decreed (*qaḍā*) that He would vouchsafe unto me revelation . . .", etc., thus regarding it as an allusion to the future. Ṭabarī himself applies the same interpretation to the next verse, explaining it thus: "He has decreed that He would enjoin upon me prayer and charity". However, the whole of this passage (verses 30-33) may also be understood as having been uttered by Jesus at a much later time – namely, *after* he had reached maturity and

SUCH WAS, in the words of truth, Jesus the son of Mary, about whose nature they so deeply disagree.[25] ‹34›
It is not conceivable that God should have taken unto Himself a son: limitless is He in His glory![26] When He wills a thing to be, He but says unto it "Be" – and it is! ‹35›
And [thus it was that Jesus always said]. "Verily, God is my Sustainer as well as your Sustainer; so worship [none but] Him: this [alone] is a straight way."[27] ‹36›
And yet, the sects [that follow the Bible] are at variance among themselves [about the nature of Jesus]![28]
Woe, then, unto all who deny the truth when that awesome Day will appear![29] ‹37› How well will they hear and see [the truth] on the Day when they come before Us!
Today, however, these evildoers are obviously lost in error: ‹38› hence, warn them of [the coming of] the Day of Regrets, when everything will have been decided – for as yet they are heedless, and they do not believe [in it]. ‹39›
Behold, We alone shall remain after the earth and all who live on it have passed away,[30] and [when] unto Us all will have been brought back. ‹40›

AND CALL to mind, through this divine writ, Abraham.[31] Behold, he was a man of truth, [already] a prophet ‹41› when he spoke [thus] unto his father: "O my father!

ذَٰلِكَ عِيسَى ٱبْنُ مَرْيَمَ ۚ قَوْلَ ٱلْحَقِّ ٱلَّذِى فِيهِ يَمْتَرُونَ ﴿٣٤﴾ مَا كَانَ لِلَّهِ أَن
يَتَّخِذَ مِن وَلَدٍ ۖ سُبْحَٰنَهُۥٓ ۚ إِذَا قَضَىٰٓ أَمْرًا فَإِنَّمَا يَقُولُ لَهُۥ كُن فَيَكُونُ ﴿٣٥﴾
وَإِنَّ ٱللَّهَ رَبِّى وَرَبُّكُمْ فَٱعْبُدُوهُ ۚ هَٰذَا صِرَٰطٌ مُّسْتَقِيمٌ ﴿٣٦﴾ فَٱخْتَلَفَ
ٱلْأَحْزَابُ مِنۢ بَيْنِهِمْ ۖ فَوَيْلٌ لِّلَّذِينَ كَفَرُوا۟ مِن مَّشْهَدِ يَوْمٍ عَظِيمٍ ﴿٣٧﴾ أَسْمِعْ
بِهِمْ وَأَبْصِرْ يَوْمَ يَأْتُونَنَا ۖ لَٰكِنِ ٱلظَّٰلِمُونَ ٱلْيَوْمَ فِى ضَلَٰلٍ مُّبِينٍ ﴿٣٨﴾
وَأَنذِرْهُمْ يَوْمَ ٱلْحَسْرَةِ إِذْ قُضِىَ ٱلْأَمْرُ وَهُمْ فِى غَفْلَةٍ وَهُمْ لَا يُؤْمِنُونَ ﴿٣٩﴾
إِنَّا نَحْنُ نَرِثُ ٱلْأَرْضَ وَمَنْ عَلَيْهَا وَإِلَيْنَا يُرْجَعُونَ ﴿٤٠﴾ وَٱذْكُرْ فِى
ٱلْكِتَٰبِ إِبْرَٰهِيمَ ۚ إِنَّهُۥ كَانَ صِدِّيقًا نَّبِيًّا ﴿٤١﴾ إِذْ قَالَ لِأَبِيهِ يَٰٓأَبَتِ

Dhālika ᶜĪsab-nu Maryama qawlal-ḥaqqil-ladhī fīhi yamtarūn. (34) Mā kāna lillāhi ʾañy-yattakhidha miñw-waladiñ-subḥānah. ʾIdhā qaḍāa ʾamrañ-faʾinnamā yaqūlu lahū kuñ-fayakūn. (35) Wa ʾinnal-lāha Rabbī wa Rabbukum faᶜbudūh. Hādhā ṣirāṭum-mustaqīm. (36) Fakhtalafal-ʾaḥzābu mim-baynihim; fawaylul-lilladhīna kafarū mim-mashhadi Yawmin ᶜaẓīm. (37) ʾAsmiᶜ bihim wa ʾabṣir yawma yaʾtūnanā; lākiniẓ-ẓālimūnal-yawma fī ḍalālim-mubīn. (38) Wa ʾañdhirhum Yawmal-Ḥasrati ʾidh quḍiyal-ʾamru wa hum fī ghaflatiñw-wa hum lā yuʾminūn. (39) ʾInnā Naḥnu narithul-ʾarḍa wa man ᶜalayhā wa ʾilaynā yurjaᶜūn. (40) Wadh-kur fil-Kitābi ʾIbrāhīma ʾinnahū kāna ṣiddīqañ-Nabiyyā. (41) ʾIdh qāla liʾabīhi yāa ʾabati

been actually entrusted with his prophetic mission: that is to say, it may be understood as an anticipatory description of the ethical and moral principles which were to dominate the adult life of Jesus and particularly his deep consciousness of being only "a servant of God".

25 Lit., "about whom they are in doubt", or "about whom they [vainly] dispute": an allusion to the many conflicting views about the nature of Jesus and his origins, ranging from the blasphemous Jewish assertion that he was a "false prophet" and the product of a shameful, illicit union (cf. 4 : 156), to the Christian belief that he was "the son of God" and, therefore, God incarnate. In this connection, see also 3 : 59 and the corresponding note 47.

26 See note 96 on 2 : 116

27 Cf. 3 : 51 and 43 : 64.

28 I.e., either rejecting him entirely, as do the Jews, or – as is the case with the Christians – deifying him.

29 Lit., "from the manifestation (*mashhad*) of an awesome Day", i.e., the Day of Judgment.

30 Lit., "We alone shall inherit the earth and all who are on it". For an explanation of this metaphoric use of the concept of "inheritance", see *sūrah* 15, note 22.

31 The mention of Abraham and his subsequent, unavailing plea to his father to recognize God's oneness and uniqueness connects with the preceding discourse, under the same aspect, on the true nature of Jesus as a mortal human being and a mere servant of the One and Only God.

Why dost thou worship something that neither hears nor sees and can be of no avail whatever to thee? ﴾42﴿
"O my father! Behold, there has indeed come to me a [ray of] knowledge such as has never yet come unto thee:[32] follow me, then; I shall guide thee onto a perfect way. ﴾43﴿
"O my father! Do not worship Satan – for, verily, Satan is a rebel against the Most Gracious![33] ﴾44﴿ O my father! I dread lest a chastisement from the Most Gracious befall thee, and then thou wilt become [aware of having been] close unto Satan!"[34] ﴾45﴿
He answered: "Dost thou dislike my gods, O Abraham? Indeed, if thou desist not, I shall most certainly cause thee to be stoned to death! Now begone from me for good!" ﴾46﴿
[Abraham] replied: "Peace be upon thee! I shall ask my Sustainer to forgive thee: for, behold, He has always been kind unto me. ﴾47﴿ But I shall withdraw from you all and from whatever you invoke instead of God, and shall invoke my Sustainer [alone]: it may well be that my prayer [for thee] will not remain unanswered by my Sustainer."[35] ﴾48﴿
And after he had withdrawn from them and from all that they were worshipping instead of God, We bestowed upon him Isaac and Jacob, and made each of them a prophet; ﴾49﴿ and We bestowed upon them [manifold] gifts out of Our grace, and granted them a lofty power to convey the truth [unto others].[36] ﴾50﴿

لِمَ تَعْبُدُ مَا لَا يَسْمَعُ وَلَا يُبْصِرُ وَلَا يُغْنِى عَنكَ شَيْـًٔا ﴿42﴾ يَـٰٓأَبَتِ إِنِّى قَدْ
جَآءَنِى مِنَ ٱلْعِلْمِ مَا لَمْ يَأْتِكَ فَٱتَّبِعْنِىٓ أَهْدِكَ صِرَٰطًا سَوِيًّا ﴿43﴾ يَـٰٓأَبَتِ
لَا تَعْبُدِ ٱلشَّيْطَـٰنَ إِنَّ ٱلشَّيْطَـٰنَ كَانَ لِلرَّحْمَـٰنِ عَصِيًّا ﴿44﴾ يَـٰٓأَبَتِ إِنِّىٓ
أَخَافُ أَن يَمَسَّكَ عَذَابٌ مِّنَ ٱلرَّحْمَـٰنِ فَتَكُونَ لِلشَّيْطَـٰنِ وَلِيًّا ﴿45﴾
قَالَ أَرَاغِبٌ أَنتَ عَنْ ءَالِهَتِى يَـٰٓإِبْرَٰهِيمُ لَئِن لَّمْ تَنتَهِ لَأَرْجُمَنَّكَ
وَٱهْجُرْنِى مَلِيًّا ﴿46﴾ قَالَ سَلَـٰمٌ عَلَيْكَ سَأَسْتَغْفِرُ لَكَ رَبِّىٓ إِنَّهُۥ كَانَ بِى
حَفِيًّا ﴿47﴾ وَأَعْتَزِلُكُمْ وَمَا تَدْعُونَ مِن دُونِ ٱللَّهِ وَأَدْعُوا۟ رَبِّى عَسَىٰٓ أَلَّآ
أَكُونَ بِدُعَآءِ رَبِّى شَقِيًّا ﴿48﴾ فَلَمَّا ٱعْتَزَلَهُمْ وَمَا يَعْبُدُونَ مِن دُونِ ٱللَّهِ
وَهَبْنَا لَهُۥٓ إِسْحَـٰقَ وَيَعْقُوبَ وَكُلًّا جَعَلْنَا نَبِيًّا ﴿49﴾ وَوَهَبْنَا لَهُم مِّن
رَّحْمَتِنَا وَجَعَلْنَا لَهُمْ لِسَانَ صِدْقٍ عَلِيًّا ﴿50﴾

lima taʿbudu mā lā yasmaʿu wa lā yubṣiru wa lā yughnī ʿanka shayʾā. ﴾42﴿ Yāa ʾabati ʾinnī qad jāaʾanī minal-ʿilmi mā lam yaʾtika fattabiʿnīi ʾahdika ṣirāṭañ-sawiyyā. ﴾43﴿ Yāa ʾabati lā taʿbudish-Shayṭāna ʾinnash-Shayṭāna kana lirRaḥmāni ʿaṣiyyā. ﴾44﴿ Yāa ʾabati ʾinnīi ʾakhāfu ʾañy-yamassaka ʿadhābum-minar-Raḥmāni fatakūna lish-Shayṭāni waliyyā. ﴾45﴿ Qāla ʾarāghibun ʾañta ʿan ʾālihatī yāa ʾIbrāhīm. Laʾil-lam tañtahi laʾarjumannaka wah-jurnī maliyyā. ﴾46﴿ Qāla salāmun ʿalayka saʾastaghfiru laka Rabbīi ʾinnahū kana bī ḥafiyyā. ﴾47﴿ Wa ʾaʿtazilukum wa mā tadʿūna miñ-dūnil-lāhi wa ʾadʿū Rabbī ʿasāa ʾallāa ʾakūna biduʿāaʾi Rabbī shaqiyyā. ﴾48﴿ Falammaʿ-tazalahum wa mā yaʿbudūna miñ-dūnil-lāhi wa-habnā lahūu ʾIsḥāqa wa Yaʿqūba wa kullañ-jaʿalnā Nabiyyā. ﴾49﴿ Wa wahabnā lahum-mir-Raḥmatinā wa jaʿalnā lahum lisāna ṣidqin ʿaliyyā. ﴾50﴿

32 I.e., a cognition of God's existence and uniqueness through *intellectual insight* (cf. 6 : 74-82).

33 The absurdity inherent in the attribution of divine qualities to anything or anyone but God is here declared, by implication, to be equivalent to "worshipping" the epitome of unreason and ingratitude symbolized in Satan's rebellion against his Creator. In this connection it should be noted that the term *shayṭān* is derived from the verb *shaṭana*, signifying "he was [or "became"] remote [from the truth]" (*Lisān al-ʿArab, Tāj al-ʿArūs*); hence, the Qurʾān describes every impulse that inherently offends against truth, reason and morality as "satanic", and every conscious act of submission to such satanic influences as a "worship of Satan".

34 According to Zamakhsharī and Rāzī, the construction of this clause (beginning with "and then") is meant to bring out the idea that one's belated realization, in the hereafter, of having been "close unto Satan" is the most terrible consequence of deliberate sinning.

35 Lit., "that I will not be unfortunate in the prayer to my Sustainer".

36 Lit., "a lofty language of truth" or "of truthfulness" – the term *lisān* ("language" or "tongue") being used here metonymically for what may be pronounced *by* the tongue (Zamakhsharī). An alternative interpretation of the phrase,

AND CALL to mind, through this divine writ, Moses. Behold, he was a chosen one, and was an apostle [of God], a prophet.[37] ⟨51⟩ And [remember how] We called upon him from the right-hand slope of Mount Sinai[38] and drew him near [unto Us] in mystic communion, ⟨52⟩ and [how], out of Our grace, We granted unto him his brother Aaron, to be a prophet [by his side]. ⟨53⟩

AND CALL to mind, through this divine writ, Ishmael.[39] Behold, he was always true to his promise, and was an apostle [of God], a prophet, ⟨54⟩ who used to enjoin upon his people prayer and charity,[40] and found favour in his Sustainer's sight. ⟨55⟩

AND CALL to mind, through this divine writ, Idrīs.[41] Behold, he was a man of truth, a prophet, ⟨56⟩ whom We exalted onto a lofty station.[42] ⟨57⟩

THESE WERE some of the prophets upon whom God bestowed His blessings – [prophets] of the seed of Adam and of those whom We caused to be borne [in the

وَٱذۡكُرۡ فِى ٱلۡكِتَٰبِ مُوسَىٰٓ إِنَّهُۥ كَانَ مُخۡلَصٗا وَكَانَ رَسُولٗا نَّبِيّٗا ﴿٥١﴾ وَنَٰدَيۡنَٰهُ مِن جَانِبِ ٱلطُّورِ ٱلۡأَيۡمَنِ وَقَرَّبۡنَٰهُ نَجِيّٗا ﴿٥٢﴾ وَوَهَبۡنَا لَهُۥ مِن رَّحۡمَتِنَآ أَخَاهُ هَٰرُونَ نَبِيّٗا ﴿٥٣﴾ وَٱذۡكُرۡ فِى ٱلۡكِتَٰبِ إِسۡمَٰعِيلَ إِنَّهُۥ كَانَ صَادِقَ ٱلۡوَعۡدِ وَكَانَ رَسُولٗا نَّبِيّٗا ﴿٥٤﴾ وَكَانَ يَأۡمُرُ أَهۡلَهُۥ بِٱلصَّلَوٰةِ وَٱلزَّكَوٰةِ وَكَانَ عِندَ رَبِّهِۦ مَرۡضِيّٗا ﴿٥٥﴾ وَٱذۡكُرۡ فِى ٱلۡكِتَٰبِ إِدۡرِيسَ إِنَّهُۥ كَانَ صِدِّيقٗا نَّبِيّٗا ﴿٥٦﴾ وَرَفَعۡنَٰهُ مَكَانًا عَلِيّٗا ﴿٥٧﴾ أُوْلَٰٓئِكَ ٱلَّذِينَ أَنۡعَمَ ٱللَّهُ عَلَيۡهِم مِّنَ ٱلنَّبِيِّـۧنَ مِن ذُرِّيَّةِ ءَادَمَ وَمِمَّنۡ حَمَلۡنَا

Wadh-kur fil-Kitābi Mūsā. ʾInnahū kāna mukh-laṣañw-wa kāna Rasulañ-Nabiyyā. ⟨51⟩ Wa nādaynāhu miñ-jānibiṭ-Ṭūril-ʾaymani wa qarrabnāhu najiyyā. ⟨52⟩ Wa wahabnā lahū mir-raḥmatināa ʾakhāhu Hārūna Nabiyyā. ⟨53⟩ Wadh-kur fil-Kitābi ʾIsmāʿīla ʾinnahū kana ṣādiqal-waʿdi wa kāna Rasūlañ-Nabiyyā. ⟨54⟩ Wa kāna yaʾmuru ʾahlahū biṣṢalāti waz-Zakāti wa kana ʿiñda Rabbihī marḍiyyā. ⟨55⟩ Wadh-kur fil-Kitābi ʾIdrīsa ʾinnahū kāna ṣiddīqañ-Nabiyyā. ⟨56⟩ Wa rafaʿnāhu makānan ʿaliyyā. ⟨57⟩ ʾUlāaʾikal-ladhīna ʾanʿamal-lāhu ʿalayhim-minan-Nabiyyīna miñ-dhurriyyati ʾĀdama wa mimman-ḥamalnā

---

advanced by many commentators, is "granted them a lofty renown for truth" or "truthfulness", or simply "a most goodly renown".

37 The mention of Moses and other prophets in this context serves to reinforce the statement that all of them – like Jesus – were but mortal servants of God whom He had inspired with His message to man (cf. verse 30 above). As regards the distinction between the terms "prophet" (nabī) and "apostle" (rasūl), see the opening clause of 22 : 52 and the corresponding note 65.

38 I.e., to the right side from the standpoint of Moses, as he was facing Mount Sinai (Ṭabarī). However, it is much more probable that the term "right side" has here, as elsewhere in the Qurʾān, the abstract connotation of "blessedness" (cf. note 25 on 74 : 39). For a fuller account of God's calling Moses to prophethood, see 20 : 9 ff.

39 After the mention of Moses, who descended from Abraham through Isaac, we are reminded of Ishmael, Abraham's first-born son and the progenitor of the "northern" group of Arab tribes, and thus of the Prophet Muḥammad, who descended in direct line, through the tribe of Quraysh, from Ishmael.

40 This may perhaps mean that Ishmael was the first among the prophets to establish prayer and charity as obligatory forms of worship.

41 The majority of the classical commentators identify the Prophet Idrīs – who is mentioned in the Qurʾān once again, namely in 21 : 85 – with the Biblical Enoch (Genesis v, 18-19 and 21-24), without, however, being able to adduce any authority for this purely conjectural identification. Some modern Qurʾān-commentators suggest that the name Idrīs may be the Arabicized form of Osiris (which, in its turn, was the ancient Greek version of the Egyptian name As-ar or Us-ar), said to have been a wise king and/or prophet whom the Egyptians subsequently deified (cf. Marāghī XVI, 64, and Sayyid Quṭb, Fī Ẓilāl al-Qurʾān, Cairo, n.d., vol. XVI, 44); but this assumption is too far-fetched to deserve any serious consideration. Finally, some of the earliest Qurʾān-commentators (ʿAbd Allāh ibn Masʿūd, Qatādah, ʿIkrimah and Aḍ-Ḍaḥḥāk) assert – with, to my mind, great plausibility – that "Idrīs" is but another name for Ilyās, the Biblical Elijah (regarding whom see note 48 on 37 : 123).

42 As regards my rendering of rafaʿnāhu as "whom We exalted", see 3 : 55 and 4 : 158, where the same expression is used with reference to Jesus, as well as note 172 on the last-named verse.

ثلاثة ارباع الحزب

السجدة

ark] with Noah, and of the seed of Abraham and Israel[43]: and [all of them were] among those whom We had guided and elected; [and] whenever the messages of the Most Gracious were conveyed unto them, they would fall down [before Him], prostrating themselves and weeping.[44] «58»
Yet they were succeeded by generations [of people] who lost all [thought of] prayer and followed [but] their own lusts; and these will, in time, meet with utter disillusion.[45] «59»
Excepted, however, shall be those who repent and attain to faith and do righteous deeds: for it is they who will enter paradise and will not be wronged in any way:[46] «60» [theirs will be the] gardens of perpetual bliss which the Most Gracious has promised unto His servants, in a realm which is beyond the reach of human perception:[47] [and,] verily, His promise is ever sure of fulfilment! «61»
No empty talk will they hear there – nothing but [tidings of] inner soundness and peace;[48] and there will they have their sustenance by day and by night:[49] «62» this is the paradise which We grant as a heritage unto such of Our servants as are conscious of Us. «63»

AND [the angels say]: "We do not descend [with revelation], again and again, other than by thy Sustainer's command: unto Him belongs all that lies open before us

مَعَ نُوحٍ وَمِن ذُرِّيَّةِ إِبْرَٰهِيمَ وَإِسْرَٰٓءِيلَ وَمِمَّنْ هَدَيْنَا وَٱجْتَبَيْنَآ إِذَا تُتْلَىٰ
عَلَيْهِمْ ءَايَٰتُ ٱلرَّحْمَٰنِ خَرُّوا۟ سُجَّدًا وَبُكِيًّا ۩ ﴿٥٨﴾ ۞ فَخَلَفَ مِنۢ
بَعْدِهِمْ خَلْفٌ أَضَاعُوا۟ ٱلصَّلَوٰةَ وَٱتَّبَعُوا۟ ٱلشَّهَوَٰتِ فَسَوْفَ يَلْقَوْنَ
غَيًّا ﴿٥٩﴾ إِلَّا مَن تَابَ وَءَامَنَ وَعَمِلَ صَٰلِحًا فَأُو۟لَٰٓئِكَ يَدْخُلُونَ ٱلْجَنَّةَ
وَلَا يُظْلَمُونَ شَيْـًٔا ﴿٦٠﴾ جَنَّٰتِ عَدْنٍ ٱلَّتِى وَعَدَ ٱلرَّحْمَٰنُ عِبَادَهُۥ
بِٱلْغَيْبِ إِنَّهُۥ كَانَ وَعْدُهُۥ مَأْتِيًّا ﴿٦١﴾ لَّا يَسْمَعُونَ فِيهَا لَغْوًا إِلَّا سَلَٰمًا
وَلَهُمْ رِزْقُهُمْ فِيهَا بُكْرَةً وَعَشِيًّا ﴿٦٢﴾ تِلْكَ ٱلْجَنَّةُ ٱلَّتِى نُورِثُ مِنْ
عِبَادِنَا مَن كَانَ تَقِيًّا ﴿٦٣﴾ وَمَا نَتَنَزَّلُ إِلَّا بِأَمْرِ رَبِّكَ لَهُۥ مَا بَيْنَ أَيْدِينَا

maᶜa Nūḥiñw-wa miñ-dhurriyyati ᵓIbrāhīma wa ᵓIsrāaᵓīla wa mimman hadaynā waj-tabaynā. ᵓIdhā tutlā ᶜalayhim ᵓĀyātur-Raḥmāni kharrū sujjadañw-wa bukiyyā. ۩ (58) ۞ Fakhalafa mim-baᶜdihim khalfun ᵓaḍāᶜuṣ-Ṣalāta wat-tabaᶜush-shahawāti fasawfa yalqawna ghayyā. (59) ᵓIllā mañ-tāba wa ᵓāmana wa ᶜamila ṣāliḥañ-faᵓulāaᵓika yadkhulūnal-jannata wa lā yuẓlamūna shayᵓā. (60) Jannāti ᶜadninil-latī waᶜadar-Raḥmānu ᶜibādahū bilghaybi ᵓinnahū kāna waᶜduhū maᵓtiyyā. (61) Lā yasmaᶜūna fīhā laghwan ᵓillā salāmañw-wa lahum rizquhum fīhā bukratañw-wa ᶜashiyyā. (62) Tilkal-jannatul-latī nūrithu min ᶜibādinā mañ-kāna taqiyyā. (63) Wa mā natanazzalu ᵓillā biᵓamri Rabbika lahū ma bayna ᵓaydīnā

43 Whereas the Hebrew prophets, whose line ended with Jesus, descended from Abraham through Isaac and Israel (Jacob), Muḥammad traced his descent from the same patriarch through the latter's first-born son, Ishmael.

44 I.e., all of the prophets were conscious of being no more than mortal, humble servants of God. (See also 32 : 15.)

45 I.e., they will realize in the hereafter the full extent of the self-deception which has led to their spiritual ruin.

46 I.e., they will not only not be deprived of reward for the least of their good deeds, but will be granted blessings far beyond their actual deserts (cf. 4 : 40).

47 This lengthy paraphrase of the expression *bi'l-ghayb* gives, I think, the closest possible interpretation of the idea underlying it: namely, the prospect of a reality which is inconceivable by man in terms of his worldly experiences, and which can, therefore, only be hinted at by means of allegorical allusions. (See also the first clause of 2 : 3 and the corresponding note 3.)

48 The term *salām* comprises the concepts of spiritual soundness and peace, freedom from faults and evils of any kind, and inner contentment. As I have pointed out in note 29 on 5 : 16 (where this term has been rendered, in a different context, as "salvation"), its closest – though by no means perfect – equivalent would be the French *salut*, in the abstract sense of that word, or the German *Heil*.

49 I.e., always. It is to be noted that the term *rizq* ("sustenance") applies to all that might be of benefit to a living being, spiritually as well as physically.

and all that is hidden from us and all that is in-between.[50] And never does thy Sustainer forget [anything] ‹64› – the Sustainer of the heavens and the earth and all that is between them! Worship, then, Him alone, and remain steadfast in His worship! Dost thou know any whose name is worthy to be mentioned side by side with His?" ‹65›

WITH ALL THIS, man [often] says, "What! Once I am dead, shall I again be brought forth alive?" ‹66›

But does man not bear in mind that We have created him aforetime out of nothing?[51] ‹67›

And so, by thy Sustainer, [on Judgment Day] We shall most certainly bring them forth together with the satanic forces [which impelled them in life],[52] and then We shall most certainly gather them, on their knees, around hell; ‹68› and thereupon We shall, indeed, draw forth from every group [of sinners] the ones that had been most determined in their disdainful rebellion against the Most Gracious:[53] ‹69›

for, indeed, We know best as to which of them is most deserving of the fires of hell.[54] ‹70›

And every one of you will come within sight of it:[55] this is, with thy Sustainer, a decree that must be fulfilled. ‹71›

وَمَا خَلْفَنَا وَمَا بَيْنَ ذَٰلِكَ ۚ وَمَا كَانَ رَبُّكَ نَسِيًّا ﴿٦٤﴾ رَّبُّ ٱلسَّمَٰوَٰتِ
وَٱلْأَرْضِ وَمَا بَيْنَهُمَا فَٱعْبُدْهُ وَٱصْطَبِرْ لِعِبَٰدَتِهِۦ ۚ هَلْ تَعْلَمُ لَهُۥ
سَمِيًّا ﴿٦٥﴾ وَيَقُولُ ٱلْإِنسَٰنُ أَءِذَا مَا مِتُّ لَسَوْفَ أُخْرَجُ حَيًّا ﴿٦٦﴾ أَوَلَا
يَذْكُرُ ٱلْإِنسَٰنُ أَنَّا خَلَقْنَٰهُ مِن قَبْلُ وَلَمْ يَكُ شَيْـًٔا ﴿٦٧﴾ فَوَرَبِّكَ
لَنَحْشُرَنَّهُمْ وَٱلشَّيَٰطِينَ ثُمَّ لَنُحْضِرَنَّهُمْ حَوْلَ جَهَنَّمَ جِثِيًّا ﴿٦٨﴾ ثُمَّ لَنَنزِعَنَّ
مِن كُلِّ شِيعَةٍ أَيُّهُمْ أَشَدُّ عَلَى ٱلرَّحْمَٰنِ عِتِيًّا ﴿٦٩﴾ ثُمَّ لَنَحْنُ أَعْلَمُ بِٱلَّذِينَ
هُمْ أَوْلَىٰ بِهَا صِلِيًّا ﴿٧٠﴾ وَإِن مِّنكُمْ إِلَّا وَارِدُهَا ۚ كَانَ عَلَىٰ رَبِّكَ حَتْمًا
مَّقْضِيًّا ﴿٧١﴾

wa mā khalfanā wa mā bayna dhālik. Wa mā kāna
Rabbuka nasiyyā. (64) Rabbus-samāwāti wal-ᵓarḍi wa
mā baynahumā faᶜbud-hu waṣ-ṭabir liᶜibādatih. Hal
taᶜlamu lahū samiyyā. (65) Wa yaqūlul-ᵓIñsānu
ᵓaᵓidhā mā mittu lasawfa ᵓukhraju ḥayyā. (66) ᵓAwalā
yadhkurul-ᵓIñsānu ᵓannā khalaqnāhu miñ-qablu wa
lam yaku shayᵓā. (67) FawaRabbika lanaḥshuran-
nahum wash-Shayāṭīna thumma lanuḥḍirannahum
ḥawla jahannama jithiyyā. (68) Thumma lanañziᶜan-
na miñ-kulli shīᶜatin ᵓayyuhum ᵓashaddu ᶜalar-
Raḥmāni ᶜitiyyā. (69) Thumma laNaḥnu ᵓaᶜlamu bil-
ladhīna hum ᵓawlā bihā ṣiliyyā. (70) Wa ᵓim-miñkum
ᵓillā wāriduhā; kana ᶜalā Rabbika ḥatmam-
maqḍiyyā. (71)

50 I.e., that which even the angels can only glimpse but not fully understand. Literally, the above phrase reads, "that which is between our hands and that which is behind us and that which is between these". Regarding this idiomatic expression, see 2 : 255 – "He knows all that lies open before men and all that is hidden from them" – and the corresponding note 247. The reference to the angels connects with the preceding mention of some of the earlier prophets who, like Muḥammad, were recipients of divine revelation.

51 Lit., "when [or "although"] he was nothing".

52 See *sūrah* 15, first half of note 16; cf. also the reference to the "worship of Satan" in verses 44-45 of the present *sūrah*, as well as the corresponding notes 33 and 34. The symbolism of the sinners being linked on Judgment Day "with the satanic forces which impelled them in life" is easily understood if we remember – as has been pointed out in note 10 on 2 : 14 – that the term *shayṭān* ("satan" or "satanic force") is often used in the Qurᵓān to describe every evil propensity in man's own self. The personal pronoun relates to those who reject the concept of resurrection and life after death.

53 I.e., those who have consciously and deliberately rejected the idea of man's responsibility before God and have thus led their weaker, less conscious fellow-men astray will be consigned to the deepest suffering in the hereafter.

54 Lit., "of burning therein": an allusion to the fact that not every one of the sinners will be irrevocably consigned to the suffering described in the Qurᵓān as hell. (The particle *thumma* which introduces this clause has here the function of an explanatory conjunction with the preceding statement and is, therefore, best rendered as "for".)

55 Lit., "none of you but will reach it". According to some of the classical authorities, the pronoun "you" relates to the sinners spoken of in the preceding passages, and particularly to those who refuse to believe in resurrection; the

And once again:[56] We shall save [from hell] those who have been conscious of Us; but We shall leave in it the evildoers, on their knees.[57] ﴾72﴿

AS IT IS, whenever Our messages are conveyed to them in all their clarity, those who are bent on denying the truth are wont to say unto those who have attained to faith: "Which of the two kinds of man[58] is in a stronger position and superior as a community?"[59] ﴾73﴿

And yet, how many a generation have We destroyed before their time – [people] who surpassed them in material power[60] and in outward show! ﴾74﴿

Say: "As for him who lives in error, may the Most Gracious lengthen the span of his life!"[61]

[And let them say whatever they say[62]] until the time when they behold that [doom] of which they were forewarned –

ثُمَّ نُنَجِّى ٱلَّذِينَ ٱتَّقَوا۟ وَّنَذَرُ ٱلظَّـٰلِمِينَ فِيهَا جِثِيًّا ﴿٧٢﴾ وَإِذَا تُتْلَىٰ عَلَيْهِمْ
ءَايَـٰتُنَا بَيِّنَـٰتٍ قَالَ ٱلَّذِينَ كَفَرُوا۟ لِلَّذِينَ ءَامَنُوٓا۟ أَىُّ ٱلْفَرِيقَيْنِ خَيْرٌ مَّقَامًا
وَأَحْسَنُ نَدِيًّا ﴿٧٣﴾ وَكَمْ أَهْلَكْنَا قَبْلَهُم مِّن قَرْنٍ هُمْ أَحْسَنُ أَثَـٰثًا وَرِءْيًا ﴿٧٤﴾
قُلْ مَن كَانَ فِى ٱلضَّلَـٰلَةِ فَلْيَمْدُدْ لَهُ ٱلرَّحْمَـٰنُ مَدًّا ۚ حَتَّىٰٓ إِذَا رَأَوْا۟ مَا يُوعَدُونَ

**Thumma nunajjil-ladhīnat-taqaw-wa nadharuẓ-
ẓālimīna fīhā jithiyyā. ﴾72﴿ Wa ᵓidhā tutlā ᶜalayhim
ᵓĀyātunā bayyinātiñ-qālal-ladhīna kafarū lilladhīna ᵓāmanūu ᵓayyul-farīqayni khayrum-maqāmañw-wa
ᵓaḥsanu nadiyyā. ﴾73﴿ Wa kam ᵓahlaknā qablahum-
miñ-qarnin hum ᵓaḥsanu ᵓathāthañw-wa riᵓyā. ﴾74﴿
Qul mañ-kāna fiḍ-ḍalālati falyamdud lahur-Raḥmānu maddā. Ḥattāa ᵓidhā raᵓaw mā yūᶜadūna**

---

majority of the commentators, however, are of the opinion that *all* human beings, sinners and righteous alike, are comprised within this address in the sense that all "will come within sight of it": hence my rendering.

56 For this particular rendering of *thumma*, see *sūrah* 6, note 31.

57 I.e., utterly humbled and crushed by their belated realization of God's judgment and of the ethical truths which they had arrogantly neglected in life.

58 Lit., "two groups" or "parties": an allusion to two kinds or types of human society characterized by their fundamentally different approach to problems of faith and morality. (See next note.)

59 Lit., "better in assembly". This parabolic "saying" of the unbelievers implies, in the garb of a rhetorical question, a superficially plausible but intrinsically fallacious argument in favour of a society which refuses to submit to any absolute moral imperatives and is determined to obey the dictates of expediency alone. In such a social order, material success and power are usually seen as consequences of a more or less conscious rejection of all metaphysical considerations – and, in particular, of all that is comprised in the concept of God-willed standards of morality – on the assumption that they are but an obstacle in the path of man's free, unlimited "development". It goes without saying that this attitude (which has reached its epitome in the modern statement that "religion is opium for the people") is diametrically opposed to the demand, voiced by every higher religion, that man's social life, if it is to be a truly "good" life, must be subordinated to definite ethical principles and restraints. By their very nature, these restraints inhibit the unprincipled power-drive which dominates the more materialistic societies and enables them to achieve – without regard to the damage done to others and, spiritually, to themselves – outward comforts and positions of strength in the shortest possible time: but precisely because they do act as a brake on man's selfishness and power-hunger, it is these moral considerations and restraints – and they alone – that can free a community from the interminable, self-destructive inner tensions and frustrations to which materialistic societies are subject, and thus bring about a more enduring, because more organic, state of social well-being. This, in short, is the elliptically implied answer of the Qurᵓān to a rhetorical question placed in the mouths of "those who are bent on denying the truth".

60 Lit., "in property" or "abundance of property". In this context – as in the last verse of this *sūrah* – the term *qarn* apparently signifies "people of one and the same epoch", i.e., a "civilization".

61 Or: "grant him a respite", so that he might have a chance to realize the error of his ways and to repent: thus, every believer is enjoined to pray for those who are sinning.

62 This interpolation refers to, and connects with, the "saying" of the deniers of the truth mentioned in verse 73 above (Zamakhsharī).

whether it be suffering [in this world] or [at the coming of] the Last Hour: – for then they will understand which [of the two kinds of man] was worse in station and weaker in resources![63] ‹75›

And God endows those who avail themselves of [His] guidance with an ever-deeper consciousness of the right way;[64] and good deeds, the fruit whereof endures forever, are, in thy Sustainer's sight, of far greater merit [than any worldly goods], and yield far better returns.[65] ‹76›

And hast thou ever considered [the kind of man] who is bent on denying the truth of Our messages and says, "I will surely be given wealth and children"?[66] ‹77›

Has he, perchance, attained to a realm which is beyond the reach of a created being's perception?[67] – or has he concluded a covenant with the Most Gracious? ‹78›

Nay! We shall record what he says, and We shall lengthen the length of his suffering [in the hereafter], ‹79› and divest him of[68] all that he is [now] speaking of: for [on Judgment Day] he will appear before Us in a lonely state.[69] ‹80›

For [such as] these have taken to worshipping deities other than God, hoping that they would be a [source of] strength for them.[70] ‹81› But nay! [On Judgment Day] these [very objects of adoration] will disavow the worship that was paid to them, and will turn against those [who had worshipped them]! ‹82›

إِمَّا ٱلْعَذَابَ وَإِمَّا ٱلسَّاعَةَ فَسَيَعْلَمُونَ مَنْ هُوَ شَرٌّ مَّكَانًا وَأَضْعَفُ
جُندًا ﴿٧٥﴾ وَيَزِيدُ ٱللَّهُ ٱلَّذِينَ ٱهْتَدَوْا۟ هُدًى ۗ وَٱلْبَٰقِيَٰتُ ٱلصَّٰلِحَٰتُ
خَيْرٌ عِندَ رَبِّكَ ثَوَابًا وَخَيْرٌ مَّرَدًّا ﴿٧٦﴾ أَفَرَءَيْتَ ٱلَّذِى كَفَرَ بِـَٔايَٰتِنَا
وَقَالَ لَأُوتَيَنَّ مَالًا وَوَلَدًا ﴿٧٧﴾ أَطَّلَعَ ٱلْغَيْبَ أَمِ ٱتَّخَذَ عِندَ ٱلرَّحْمَٰنِ
عَهْدًا ﴿٧٨﴾ كَلَّا ۚ سَنَكْتُبُ مَا يَقُولُ وَنَمُدُّ لَهُۥ مِنَ ٱلْعَذَابِ مَدًّا ﴿٧٩﴾
وَنَرِثُهُۥ مَا يَقُولُ وَيَأْتِينَا فَرْدًا ﴿٨٠﴾ وَٱتَّخَذُوا۟ مِن دُونِ ٱللَّهِ ءَالِهَةً
لِّيَكُونُوا۟ لَهُمْ عِزًّا ﴿٨١﴾ كَلَّا ۚ سَيَكْفُرُونَ بِعِبَادَتِهِمْ وَيَكُونُونَ عَلَيْهِمْ
ضِدًّا ﴿٨٢﴾

**ʾimmal-ʿadhāba wa ʾimmas-Sāʿata fasayaʿlamūna
man huwa sharrum-makānañw-wa ʾaḍʿafu juñdā.
‹75› Wa yazīdul-lāhul-ladhīnah-tadaw hudā. Wal-
bāqiyātuṣ-ṣāliḥātu khayrun ʿiñda Rabbika
thawābañw-wa khayrum-maraddā. ‹76› ʾAfaraʾaytal-
ladhī kafara biʾĀyātinā wa qāla laʾūtayanna mālañw-
wa waladā. ‹77› ʾAṭṭalaʿal-ghayba ʾamit-takhadha
ʿiñdar-Raḥmāni ʿahdā. ‹78› Kallā; sanaktubu mā
yaqūlu wa namuddu lahū minal-ʿadhābi maddā. ‹79›
Wa narithuhū mā yaqūlu wa yaʾtīnā fardā. ‹80› Wat-
takhadhū miñ-dūnil-lāhi ʾālihatal-liyakūnū lahum
ʿizzā. ‹81› Kallā; sayakfurūna biʿibādatihim wa
yakūnūna ʿalayhim ḍiddā. ‹82›**

63 Lit., "in respect of support" or "of forces" (*jundan*) – an expression which, in this context, denotes both material resources and the ability to utilize them towards good ends.

64 Lit., "God increases in guidance those who . . .", etc.

65 Lit., "which are better in thy Sustainer's sight as regards merit, and better as regards returns" (cf. 18 : 46).

66 This is a further illustration of the attitude described in verses 73-75 (and referred to in note 59): namely, the insistence on material values to the exclusion of all moral considerations, and the conviction that worldly "success" is the only thing that really counts in life. As in many other places in the Qurʾān, this materialistic concept of "success" is metonymically equated with one's absorption in the idea of "wealth and children".

67 In this context, the term *al-ghayb* denotes the unknowable future.

68 Lit., "inherit from him" – a metaphor based on the concept of one person's taking over what once belonged to, or was vested in, another.

69 I.e., bereft of any extraneous support, and thus depending on God's grace and mercy alone (cf. 6 : 94 as well as verse 95 of the present *sūrah*).

70 This refers to the type of man spoken of in the preceding passage as well as in verses 73-75: people who "worship" wealth and power with an almost religious devotion, attributing to these manifestations of worldly success the status of divine forces.

ART THOU NOT aware that We have let loose all [manner of] satanic forces[71] upon those who deny the truth – [forces] that impel them [towards sin] with strong impulsion?[72] ⟨83⟩
Hence, be not in haste [to call down God's punishment] upon them: for We but number the number of their days.[73] ⟨84⟩
On the Day when We shall gather the God-conscious unto [Us,] the Most Gracious, as honoured guests, ⟨85⟩ and drive those who were lost in sin unto hell as a thirsty herd is driven to a well ⟨86⟩ – [on that Day] none will have [the benefit of] intercession unless he has [in his lifetime] entered into a bond with the Most Gracious.[74] ⟨87⟩
As it is,[75] some assert, "The Most Gracious has taken unto Himself a son"![76] ⟨88⟩
Indeed, [by this assertion] you have brought forth something monstrous, ⟨89⟩ whereat the heavens might well-nigh be rent into fragments, and the earth be split asunder, and the mountains fall down in ruins! ⟨90⟩
That men should ascribe a son to the Most Gracious, ⟨91⟩ although it is inconceivable that the Most Gracious should take unto Himself a son![77] ⟨92⟩

أَلَمْ تَرَ أَنَّآ أَرْسَلْنَا ٱلشَّيَٰطِينَ عَلَى ٱلْكَٰفِرِينَ تَؤُزُّهُمْ أَزًّا ﴿٨٣﴾ فَلَا
تَعْجَلْ عَلَيْهِمْ ۖ إِنَّمَا نَعُدُّ لَهُمْ عَدًّا ﴿٨٤﴾ يَوْمَ نَحْشُرُ ٱلْمُتَّقِينَ إِلَى
ٱلرَّحْمَٰنِ وَفْدًا ﴿٨٥﴾ وَنَسُوقُ ٱلْمُجْرِمِينَ إِلَىٰ جَهَنَّمَ وِرْدًا ﴿٨٦﴾ لَّا
يَمْلِكُونَ ٱلشَّفَٰعَةَ إِلَّا مَنِ ٱتَّخَذَ عِندَ ٱلرَّحْمَٰنِ عَهْدًا ﴿٨٧﴾ وَقَالُوا۟ ٱتَّخَذَ
ٱلرَّحْمَٰنُ وَلَدًا ﴿٨٨﴾ لَّقَدْ جِئْتُمْ شَيْـًٔا إِدًّا ﴿٨٩﴾ تَكَادُ ٱلسَّمَٰوَٰتُ يَتَفَطَّرْنَ
مِنْهُ وَتَنشَقُّ ٱلْأَرْضُ وَتَخِرُّ ٱلْجِبَالُ هَدًّا ﴿٩٠﴾ أَن دَعَوْا۟ لِلرَّحْمَٰنِ
وَلَدًا ﴿٩١﴾ وَمَا يَنۢبَغِى لِلرَّحْمَٰنِ أَن يَتَّخِذَ وَلَدًا ﴿٩٢﴾

ᵓAlam tara ᵓannāa ᵓarsalnash-Shayāṭīna ᶜalal-kāfirīna taᵓuzzuhum ᵓazzā. (83) Falā taᶜjal ᶜalayhim; ᵓinnamā naᶜuddu lahum ᶜaddā. (84) Yawma naḥshurul-muttaqīna ᵓilar-Raḥmāni wafdā. (85) Wa nasūqul-mujrimīna ᵓilā jahannama wirdā. (86) Lā yamlikūnash-shafāᶜata ᵓillā manit-takhadha ᶜiñdar-Raḥmāni ᶜahdā. (87) Wa qālut-takhadhar-Raḥmānu waladā. (88) Laqad jiᵓtum shayᵓan ᵓiddā. (89) Takādus-samāwātu yatafaṭṭarna minhu wa tañshaqqul-ᵓarḍu wa takhirrul-jibālu haddā. (90) ᵓAñ-daᶜaw lirRaḥmāni waladā. (91) Wa mā yambaghī lirRaḥmāni ᵓañy-yat-takhidha waladā. (92)

71 Lit., "the satans", by which term the Qurᵓān often describes all that is intrinsically evil, especially the immoral impulses in man's own soul (cf. note 10 on 2 : 14 and note 33 on verse 44 of the present *sūrah*).

72 See note 31 on 15 : 41. According to Zamakhsharī and Rāzī, the expression "We have let loose (*arsalnā*) all [manner of] satanic forces (*shayāṭīn*) upon those who deny the truth" has here the meaning of "We have allowed them to be active (*khallaynā*) among them", leaving it to man's free will to accept or to reject those evil influences or impulses. Rāzī, in particular, points in this context to *sūrah* 14, verse 22, according to which Satan will thus address the sinners on Resurrection Day: "I had no power at all over you: I but called you – and you responded to me. Hence, blame not me, but blame yourselves." See also note 31 on 14 :22, in which Rāzī's comment is quoted *verbatim*.

73 Lit., "We number for them but a number". Cf. also the first sentence of verse 75 above.

74 Lit., "except him who has . . .", etc. According to the classical commentators – including some of the most outstanding Companions of the Prophet – the "bond with God" denotes, in this context, the realization of His oneness and uniqueness; for the wider implications of this term, see *sūrah* 2, note 19. Consequently, as pointed out by Rāzī, even great sinners may hope for God's forgiveness – symbolically expressed by the right of "intercession" which will be granted to the prophets on Judgment Day (see note 7 on 10 : 3) – provided that, during their life on earth, they were aware of God's existence and oneness.

75 Lit., "And" (*wa*), connecting the present passage with verse 81.

76 This allusion to the Christian belief in Jesus as "the son of God" – and, in general, to every belief in God's "incarnation" in a created being – takes up the theme broached in verse 81 above: namely, the deification of powers or beings other than God "with a view to their being a source of strength" to those who turn to them. But whereas verse 81 refers specifically to the godless who accord a *quasi*-divine status to material wealth and power and abandon themselves entirely to the pursuit of worldly success, the present passage refers to people who, while believing in God, deify prophets and saints, too, in the subconscious hope that they might act as "mediators" between them and the Almighty. Since this deification offends against the principle of God's transcendent oneness and uniqueness, it implies a breach of man's "bond with God" and, if consciously persisted in, constitutes an unforgivable sin (cf. 4 : 48 and 116).

77 The idea that God might have a "son" – either in the real or in the metaphorical sense of this term – would

Not one of all [the beings] that are in the heavens or on earth appears before the Most Gracious other than as a servant:[78] ‹93› indeed, He has full cognizance of them, and has numbered them with [unfailing] numbering; ‹94› and every one of them will appear before Him on Resurrection Day in a lonely state.[79] ‹95›

VERILY, those who attain to faith and do righteous deeds will the Most Gracious endow with love:[80] ‹96› and only to this end have We made this [divine writ] easy to understand, in thine own tongue, [O Prophet,][81] so that thou might convey thereby a glad tiding to the God-conscious, and warn thereby those who are given to [futile] contention: ‹97› for, how many a generation[82] have We destroyed before their time – [and] canst thou perceive any one of them [now], or hear any whisper of them? ‹98›

إِن كُلُّ مَن فِي ٱلسَّمَٰوَٰتِ وَٱلۡأَرۡضِ إِلَّآ ءَاتِي ٱلرَّحۡمَٰنِ عَبۡدٗا ﴿٩٣﴾ لَّقَدۡ
أَحۡصَىٰهُمۡ وَعَدَّهُمۡ عَدّٗا ﴿٩٤﴾ وَكُلُّهُمۡ ءَاتِيهِ يَوۡمَ ٱلۡقِيَٰمَةِ فَرۡدًا ﴿٩٥﴾ إِنَّ
ٱلَّذِينَ ءَامَنُواْ وَعَمِلُواْ ٱلصَّٰلِحَٰتِ سَيَجۡعَلُ لَهُمُ ٱلرَّحۡمَٰنُ وُدّٗا ﴿٩٦﴾
فَإِنَّمَا يَسَّرۡنَٰهُ بِلِسَانِكَ لِتُبَشِّرَ بِهِ ٱلۡمُتَّقِينَ وَتُنذِرَ بِهِۦ قَوۡمٗا لُّدّٗا ﴿٩٧﴾ وَكَمۡ
أَهۡلَكۡنَا قَبۡلَهُم مِّن قَرۡنٍ هَلۡ تُحِسُّ مِنۡهُم مِّنۡ أَحَدٍ أَوۡ تَسۡمَعُ لَهُمۡ
رِكۡزَۢا ﴿٩٨﴾

ʾIñ-kullu mañ-fis-samāwāti wal-ʾarḍi ʾillāa ʾātir-Raḥmāni ʿabdā. (93) Laqad ʾaḥṣāhum wa ʿaddahum ʿaddā. (94) Wa kulluhum ʾātīhi Yawmal-Qiyāmati fardā. (95) ʾInnal-ladhīna ʾāmanū wa ʿamiluṣ-ṣāliḥāti sayajʿalu lahumur-Raḥmānu wuddā. (96) Faʾinnamā yassarnāhu bilisānika litubashshira bihil-muttaqīna wa tuñdhira bihī qawmal-luddā. (97) Wa kam ʾahlaknā qablahum-miñ-qarnin hal tuḥissu min-hum-min ʾaḥadin ʾaw tasmaʿu lahum rikzā. (98)

presuppose a degree of innate *likeness* between "the father" and "the son": but God is in every respect unique, so that "there is nothing like unto Him" (42 : 11) and "nothing that could be compared with Him" (112 : 4). Moreover, the concept of "progeny" implies an organic continuation of the progenitor, or of part of him, in another being and, therefore, presupposes a degree of incompleteness *before* the act of procreation (or incarnation, if the term "sonship" is used metaphorically): and the idea of incompleteness, in whatever sense, negates the very concept of God. But even if the idea of "sonship" is meant to express no more than one of the different "aspects" of the One Deity (as is claimed in the Christian dogma of the "Trinity"), it is described in the Qurʾān as blasphemous inasmuch as it amounts to an attempt at *defining* Him who is "sublimely exalted above anything that men may devise by way of definition" (see last sentence of 6 : 100).

78 I.e., all of them – whether men or angels – are but created beings, having no share whatever in His divinity, and all of them submit, consciously or unconsciously, to His will (cf. 13 : 15 and 16 : 48-49).

79 See note 69 above.

80 I.e., bestow on them His love and endow them with the capability to love His creation, as well as cause them to be loved by their fellow-men. As is shown in the next verse, this gift of love is inherent in the guidance offered to man through divine revelation.

81 Since man is incapable of understanding the "word" of God as such, it has always been revealed to him in his own, human tongue (cf. 14 : 4 – "never have We sent forth any apostle otherwise than [with a message] in his own people's tongue"), and has always been expounded in concepts accessible to the human mind: hence the reference to the Prophet's revelations as "brought down *upon thy heart*" (2 : 97), or "[divine inspiration] has alighted with it *upon thy heart*" (26 : 193 – 194).

82 I.e., civilization – a meaning which the term *qarn* has also in the identical phrase in verse 74.

The Twentieth Sūrah

Ṭā Hā (O Man)

Mecca Period

FOR THE RENDERING of the title of this *sūrah* as "O Man", see note 1 below. As is the case with the preceding *sūrah,* its position in the chronology of Qur᾿anic revelation is not difficult to establish. Despite the vague assertions of some of the later authorities that it was revealed during the last phase (or even in the last year) of the Prophet's sojourn in Mecca, we know for certain that it was fully known to his Companions as early as the sixth year of his mission (that is, at least seven years before he left Mecca for Medina): for it was this very *sūrah* which at that period accidentally fell into the hands of ᶜUmar ibn al-Khaṭṭāb – who until than had been a bitter opponent of the Prophet – and caused his conversion to Islam (Ibn Saᶜd III/1, 191 ff.).

The main theme of *Ṭā Hā* is the guidance which God offers man through His prophets, and the fact that the fundamental truths inherent in all revealed religions are identical: hence the long story of Moses in verses 9-98, and the reference to the "clear evidence [of the truth of this divine writ]", i.e., of the Qur᾿ān, forthcoming from "what is [to be found] in the earlier scriptures" (verse 133).

-20- سورة طه مكية
وآياتها خمس وثلاثون ومائة

IN THE NAME OF GOD, THE MOST GRACIOUS, THE DISPENSER OF GRACE:

O MAN![1] ⟨1⟩ We did not bestow the Qur᾿ān on thee from on high to make thee unhappy,[2] ⟨2⟩ but only as an exhortation to all who stand in awe [of God]: ⟨3⟩ a revelation from Him who has created the earth and the high heavens ⟨4⟩ – the Most Gracious, established on the throne of His almightiness.[3] ⟨5⟩
Unto Him belongs all that is in the heavens and all that is on earth, as well as all that is between them and all that is beneath the sod. ⟨6⟩
And if thou say anything aloud, [He hears it –] since, behold, He knows [even] the secret [thoughts of man] as well as all that is yet more hidden [within him].[4] ⟨7⟩
God – there is no deity save Him; His [alone] are the attributes of perfection![5] ⟨8⟩

AND HAS the story of Moses ever come within thy ken?[6] ⟨9⟩

بِسۡمِ ٱللَّهِ ٱلرَّحۡمَٰنِ ٱلرَّحِيمِ

طه ۝١ مَآ أَنزَلۡنَا عَلَيۡكَ ٱلۡقُرۡءَانَ لِتَشۡقَىٰٓ ۝٢ إِلَّا تَذۡكِرَةٗ لِّمَن
يَخۡشَىٰ ۝٣ تَنزِيلٗا مِّمَّنۡ خَلَقَ ٱلۡأَرۡضَ وَٱلسَّمَٰوَٰتِ ٱلۡعُلَى ۝٤
ٱلرَّحۡمَٰنُ عَلَى ٱلۡعَرۡشِ ٱسۡتَوَىٰ ۝٥ لَهُۥ مَا فِي ٱلسَّمَٰوَٰتِ وَمَا فِي
ٱلۡأَرۡضِ وَمَا بَيۡنَهُمَا وَمَا تَحۡتَ ٱلثَّرَىٰ ۝٦ وَإِن تَجۡهَرۡ بِٱلۡقَوۡلِ فَإِنَّهُۥ
يَعۡلَمُ ٱلسِّرَّ وَأَخۡفَى ۝٧ ٱللَّهُ لَآ إِلَٰهَ إِلَّا هُوَۖ لَهُ ٱلۡأَسۡمَآءُ ٱلۡحُسۡنَىٰ ۝٨
وَهَلۡ أَتَىٰكَ حَدِيثُ مُوسَىٰٓ ۝٩

حزب 32

Bismil-lāhir-Raḥmānir-Raḥīm.
Ṭā-Hā. ⟨1⟩ Māa ᵓañzalnā ᶜalaykal-Qurᵓāna litashqā.
⟨2⟩ ᵓIllā tadhkiratal-limañy-yakhshā. ⟨3⟩ Tañzīlam-
mimman khalaqal-ᵓarḍa was-samāwātil-ᶜulā. ⟨4⟩ ᵓAr-
Raḥmānī ᶜalal-ᶜarshis-tawā. ⟨5⟩ Lahū mā fis-
samāwāti wa mā fil-ᵓarḍi wa mā baynahumā wa mā
taḥtath-tharā. ⟨6⟩ Wa ᵓiñ-tajhar bilqawli faᵓinnahū
yaᶜlamus-sirra wa ᵓakhfā. ⟨7⟩ ᵓAllāhu lāa ᵓilāha ᵓillā
Huwa lahul-ᵓAsmāaᵓul-Ḥusnā. ⟨8⟩ Wa hal ᵓatāka
ḥadīthu Mūsā. ⟨9⟩

---

1 According to some commentators, the letters *ṭ* and *h* (pronounced *ṭā hā*) which introduce this *sūrah* belong to the group of *al-muqaṭṭaᶜāt* – the "single [or "disjointed"] letters" – which are prefixed to a number of the Qurᵓanic *sūrahs* (see Appendix II). However, in the opinion of some of the Prophet's Companions (e.g., ᶜAbd Allāh ibn ᶜAbbās) and a number of outstanding personalities of the next generation (like Saᶜīd ibn Jubayr, Mujāhid, Qatādah, Al-Ḥasan al-Baṣrī, ᶜIkrimah, Aḍ-Ḍaḥḥāk, Al-Kalbī, etc.), *ṭā hā* is not just a combination of two single letters but a meaningful expression of its own, signifying "O man" (synonymous with *yā rajul*) in both the Nabataean and Syriac branches of the Arabic language (Ṭabarī, Rāzī, Ibn Kathīr), as well as in the – purely Arabian – dialect of the Yemenite tribe of ᶜAkk, as is evident from certain fragments of their pre-Islamic poetry (quoted by Ṭabarī and Zamakhsharī). Ṭabarī, in particular, gives his unqualified support to the rendering of *ṭā hā* as "O man".

2 I.e., the ethical discipline imposed upon man by the teachings of the Qurᵓān is not meant to narrow down his feel of life, but, on the contrary, to enhance it by deepening his consciousness of right and wrong.

3 For my rendering of the metaphorical term *al-ᶜarsh* as "the throne of His almightiness", see note 43 on 7 : 54.

4 I.e., He knows not only man's unspoken, conscious thoughts but also all that goes on within his subconscious self.

5 For an explanation of this rendering of *al-asmāᵓ al-ḥusnā*, see *sūrah* 7, note 145.

6 Apart from two short references to Moses in earlier *sūrahs* (53 : 36 and 87 : 19), the narrative appearing in verses 9-98 is undoubtedly the earliest Qurᵓanic exposition of the *story* of Moses as such. Its mention at this stage is connected with the reference to revelation at the beginning of this *sūrah*, (verses 2-4) and, generally, with the Qurᵓanic doctrine of the basic ideological unity of all revealed religions.

Lo! he saw a fire [in the desert];[7] and so he said to his family: "Wait here! Behold, I perceive a fire [far away]: perhaps I can bring you a brand therefrom, or find at the fire some guidance." ‹10›

But when he came close to it, a voice called out:[8] "O Moses! ‹11› Verily, I am thy Sustainer! Take off, then, thy sandals! Behold, thou art in the twice-hallowed valley,[9] ‹12› and I have chosen thee [to be My apostle]: listen, then, to what is being revealed [unto thee]. ‹13›

"Verily, I – I alone – am God; there is no deity save Me. Hence, worship Me alone, and be constant in prayer, so as to remember Me![10] ‹14›

"Behold, [although] I have willed to keep it[11] hidden, the Last Hour is bound to come, so that every human being may be recompensed in accordance with what he strove for [in life].[12] ‹15› Hence, let not anyone who does not believe in its coming[13] and follows [but] his own desires divert thee from [belief in] it, lest thou perish! ‹16›

"Now, what is this in thy right hand, O Moses?" ‹17›

He answered: "It is my staff; I lean on it; and with it I beat down leaves for my sheep; and [many] other uses have I for it." ‹18›

إِذْ رَءَا نَارًا فَقَالَ لِأَهْلِهِ ٱمْكُثُوٓا۟ إِنِّىٓ ءَانَسْتُ نَارًا لَّعَلِّىٓ ءَاتِيكُم مِّنْهَا
بِقَبَسٍ أَوْ أَجِدُ عَلَى ٱلنَّارِ هُدًى ﴿10﴾ فَلَمَّآ أَتَىٰهَا نُودِىَ يَٰمُوسَىٰٓ ﴿11﴾ إِنِّىٓ
أَنَا۠ رَبُّكَ فَٱخْلَعْ نَعْلَيْكَ ۖ إِنَّكَ بِٱلْوَادِ ٱلْمُقَدَّسِ طُوًى ﴿12﴾ وَأَنَا
ٱخْتَرْتُكَ فَٱسْتَمِعْ لِمَا يُوحَىٰٓ ﴿13﴾ إِنَّنِىٓ أَنَا ٱللَّهُ لَآ إِلَٰهَ إِلَّآ أَنَا۠ فَٱعْبُدْنِى
وَأَقِمِ ٱلصَّلَوٰةَ لِذِكْرِىٓ ﴿14﴾ إِنَّ ٱلسَّاعَةَ ءَاتِيَةٌ أَكَادُ أُخْفِيهَا لِتُجْزَىٰ
كُلُّ نَفْسٍۭ بِمَا تَسْعَىٰ ﴿15﴾ فَلَا يَصُدَّنَّكَ عَنْهَا مَن لَّا يُؤْمِنُ بِهَا وَٱتَّبَعَ
هَوَىٰهُ فَتَرْدَىٰ ﴿16﴾ وَمَا تِلْكَ بِيَمِينِكَ يَٰمُوسَىٰ ﴿17﴾ قَالَ هِىَ عَصَاىَ
أَتَوَكَّؤُا۟ عَلَيْهَا وَأَهُشُّ بِهَا عَلَىٰ غَنَمِى وَلِىَ فِيهَا مَـَٔارِبُ أُخْرَىٰ ﴿18﴾

ᵓIdh raᵓā nāraṅ-faqāla liᵓahlihim-kuthūu ᵓinnīi ᵓānastu nāral-laᶜallīi ᵓātīkum-minhā biqabasin ᵓaw ᵓajidu ᶜalan-nāri hudā. ﴿10﴾ Falammāa ᵓatāhā nūdiya yā Mūsā. ﴿11﴾ ᵓInnīi ᵓAna Rabbuka fakhlaᶜ naᶜlayka ᵓinnaka bilwādil-muqaddasi Ṭuwā. ﴿12﴾ Wa ᵓAnakh-tartuka fastamiᶜ limā yūḥā. ﴿13﴾ ᵓInnanīi ᵓAnal-lāhu lāa ᵓilāha ᵓillāa ᵓAna faᶜbudnī wa ᵓaqimiṣ-Ṣalāta lidhikrī. ﴿14﴾ ᵓInnas-Sāᶜata ᵓātiyatun ᵓakādu ᵓukhfīhā litujzā kullu nafsim-bimā tasᶜā. ﴿15﴾ Falā yaṣud-dannaka ᶜanhā mal-lā yuᵓminu bihā wat-tabaᶜa hawāhu fatardā. ﴿16﴾ Wa mā tilka biyamīnika yā Mūsā. ﴿17﴾ Qāla hiya ᶜaṣāya ᵓatawakkaᵓu ᶜalayhā wa ᵓahushshu bihā ᶜalā ghanamī wa liya fīhā maᵓāribu ᵓukhrā. ﴿18﴾

7 From the sequence (here as well as in 27 : 7 and 28 : 29) it appears that Moses had lost his way in the desert: probably a symbolic allusion to his dawning awareness that he was in need of spiritual guidance. This part of the story relates to the period of his wanderings subsequent to his flight from Egypt (see 28 : 14 ff.). Regarding the allegory of the "fire" – the "burning bush" of the Bible – see note 7 on 27 : 7-8.

8 Lit., "he was called".

9 Whereas some commentators assume that the word *ṭuwan* (or *ṭuwā*) is the *name* of the "hallowed valley", Zamakhsharī explains it, more convincingly, as meaning "twice" (from *ṭuwan* or *ṭiwan*, "twice done") – i.e., "twice-hallowed" – apparently because God's voice was heard in it and because Moses was raised there to prophethood.

10 Thus, conscious remembrance of God and of His oneness and uniqueness is declared to be the innermost purpose, as well as the intellectual justification, of all true prayer.

11 I.e., the time of its coming.

12 The expression "what he strove for" implies consciousness of endeavour, and thus excludes *involuntary actions* (in the widest sense of the latter term, comprising everything that is manifested in word or actual deed), as well as *involuntary omissions*, irrespective of whether the relevant action or omission is morally good or bad. By enunciating the above principle within the context of the story of Moses, the Qurᵓān stresses the essential identity of the ethical concepts underlying all true religions. (See also 53 : 39 and the corresponding note 32.)

13 Lit., "in it".

قَالَ أَلْقِهَا يَـٰمُوسَىٰ ﴿١٩﴾ فَأَلْقَىٰهَا فَإِذَا هِىَ حَيَّةٌ تَسْعَىٰ ﴿٢٠﴾ قَالَ خُذْهَا
وَلَا تَخَفْ سَنُعِيدُهَا سِيرَتَهَا ٱلْأُولَىٰ ﴿٢١﴾ وَٱضْمُمْ يَدَكَ إِلَىٰ جَنَاحِكَ
تَخْرُجْ بَيْضَآءَ مِنْ غَيْرِ سُوٓءٍ ءَايَةً أُخْرَىٰ ﴿٢٢﴾ لِنُرِيَكَ مِنْ ءَايَـٰتِنَا
ٱلْكُبْرَى ﴿٢٣﴾ ٱذْهَبْ إِلَىٰ فِرْعَوْنَ إِنَّهُۥ طَغَىٰ ﴿٢٤﴾ قَالَ رَبِّ ٱشْرَحْ لِى
صَدْرِى ﴿٢٥﴾ وَيَسِّرْ لِىٓ أَمْرِى ﴿٢٦﴾ وَٱحْلُلْ عُقْدَةً مِّن لِّسَانِى ﴿٢٧﴾
يَفْقَهُوا۟ قَوْلِى ﴿٢٨﴾ وَٱجْعَل لِّى وَزِيرًا مِّنْ أَهْلِى ﴿٢٩﴾ هَـٰرُونَ أَخِى ﴿٣٠﴾
ٱشْدُدْ بِهِۦٓ أَزْرِى ﴿٣١﴾ وَأَشْرِكْهُ فِىٓ أَمْرِى ﴿٣٢﴾ كَىْ نُسَبِّحَكَ كَثِيرًا ﴿٣٣﴾
وَنَذْكُرَكَ كَثِيرًا ﴿٣٤﴾ إِنَّكَ كُنتَ بِنَا بَصِيرًا ﴿٣٥﴾ قَالَ قَدْ أُوتِيتَ سُؤْلَكَ
يَـٰمُوسَىٰ ﴿٣٦﴾ وَلَقَدْ مَنَنَّا عَلَيْكَ مَرَّةً أُخْرَىٰ ﴿٣٧﴾

Said He: "Throw it down, O Moses!" ‹19›
So he threw it – and lo! it was a snake, moving rapidly. ‹20›
Said He: "Take hold of it, and fear not: We shall restore it to its former state.[14] ‹21›
"Now place thy hand within thy armpit: it will come forth [shining] white, without blemish,[15] as another sign [of Our grace], ‹22› so that We might make thee aware of some of Our greatest wonders. ‹23›
"[And now] go thou unto Pharaoh: for, verily, he has transgressed all bounds of equity."[16] ‹24›
Said [Moses]: "O my Sustainer! Open up my heart [to Thy light], ‹25› and make my task easy for me, ‹26› and loosen the knot from my tongue ‹27› so that they might fully understand my speech,[17] ‹28› and appoint for me, out of my kinsfolk, one who will help me to bear my burden:[18] ‹29› Aaron, my brother. ‹30› Add Thou through him to my strength, ‹31› and let him share my task, ‹32› so that [together] we might abundantly extol Thy limitless glory ‹33› and remember Thee without cease![19] ‹34› Verily, Thou seest all that is within us!" ‹35›
Said He: "Thou art granted all that thou hast asked for, O Moses! ‹36›
"And, indeed, We bestowed Our favour upon thee at a time long since past,[20] ‹37›

Qāla ʾalqihā yā Mūsā. (19) Faʾalqāhā faʾidhā hiya ḥayyatuñ-tasʿā. (20) Qāla khudhhā wa lā takhaf; sanuʿīduhā sīratahal-ʾūlā. (21) Waḍ-mum yadaka ʾilā janāḥika takhruj bayḍāaʾa min ghayri sūuʾin ʾāyatan ʾukhrā. (22) Linuriyaka min ʾĀyātinal-kubrā. (23) ʾIdhhab ʾilā Firʿawna ʾinnahū ṭaghā. (24) Qāla Rabbish-raḥ lī ṣadrī. (25) Wa yassir lii ʾamrī. (26) Waḥ-lul ʿuqdatam-mil-lisānī, (27) yafqahū qawlī. (28) Waj-ʿal-lī wazīram-min ʾahlī. (29) Hārūna ʾakhī. (30) ʾUshdud bihii ʾazrī. (31) Wa ʾashrik-hu fii ʾamrī. (32) Kay nusabbiḥaka kathīrā. (33) Wa nadhkuraka kathīrā. (34) ʾInnaka kuñta binā Baṣīrā. (35) Qāla qad ʾūtīta suʾlaka yā Mūsā. (36) Wa laqad manannā ʿalayka marratan ʾukhrā. (37)

14 The miraculous transformation of the staff into a serpent has, I believe, a mystic significance: it seems to be an allusion to the intrinsic difference between appearance and reality, and, consequently, to the spiritual insight into this difference bestowed by God on His chosen servants (cf. the experience of Moses with the unnamed sage described in 18 : 66-82). This interpretation finds strong support in 27 : 10 and 28 : 31, in both of which places it is said that Moses saw the staff "move rapidly, *as if it were* a serpent (*kaʾannahā jānn*)".

15 I.e., strangely luminescent by virtue of the prophethood to which he had been raised. (See also note 85 on 7 : 108.)

16 This seems to be a reference to Pharaoh's greatest sin, namely, his claim to divine status (cf. 28 : 38 and 79 : 24).

17 I.e., "remove all impediment from my speech" (cf. Exodus iv, 10, "I am slow of speech, and of a slow tongue"), which would imply that he was not gifted with natural eloquence.

18 This is the primary meaning of the term *wazīr* (lit., "burden-carrier", derived from *wizr*, "a burden"); hence its later – post-classical – application to government ministers.

19 Lit., "much" or "abundantly".

20 Lit., "at another time", i.e., the time of Moses' childhood and youth, which is recalled in verses 38-40. For a fuller explanation of the subsequent references to that period – the Pharaonic persecution of the children of Israel and the killing of their new-born males, the rescue of the infant Moses and his adoption by Pharaoh's family, his killing of the Egyptian, and his subsequent flight from Egypt – see 28 : 3-21, where the story is narrated in greater detail.

إِذْ أَوْحَيْنَآ إِلَىٰٓ أُمِّكَ مَا يُوحَىٰٓ ﴿٣٨﴾ أَنِ ٱقْذِفِيهِ فِى ٱلتَّابُوتِ فَٱقْذِفِيهِ فِى
ٱلْيَمِّ فَلْيُلْقِهِ ٱلْيَمُّ بِٱلسَّاحِلِ يَأْخُذْهُ عَدُوٌّ لِّى وَعَدُوٌّ لَّهُۥ ۚ وَأَلْقَيْتُ عَلَيْكَ
مَحَبَّةً مِّنِّى وَلِتُصْنَعَ عَلَىٰ عَيْنِىٓ ﴿٣٩﴾ إِذْ تَمْشِىٓ أُخْتُكَ فَتَقُولُ هَلْ أَدُلُّكُمْ
عَلَىٰ مَن يَكْفُلُهُۥ ۖ فَرَجَعْنَٰكَ إِلَىٰٓ أُمِّكَ كَىْ تَقَرَّ عَيْنُهَا وَلَا تَحْزَنَ ۚ وَقَتَلْتَ
نَفْسًا فَنَجَّيْنَٰكَ مِنَ ٱلْغَمِّ وَفَتَنَّٰكَ فُتُونًا ۚ فَلَبِثْتَ سِنِينَ فِىٓ أَهْلِ مَدْيَنَ ثُمَّ
جِئْتَ عَلَىٰ قَدَرٍ يَٰمُوسَىٰ ﴿٤٠﴾ وَٱصْطَنَعْتُكَ لِنَفْسِى ﴿٤١﴾ ٱذْهَبْ أَنتَ
وَأَخُوكَ بِـَٔايَٰتِى وَلَا تَنِيَا فِى ذِكْرِى ﴿٤٢﴾ ٱذْهَبَآ إِلَىٰ فِرْعَوْنَ إِنَّهُۥ طَغَىٰ ﴿٤٣﴾
فَقُولَا لَهُۥ قَوْلًا لَّيِّنًا لَّعَلَّهُۥ يَتَذَكَّرُ أَوْ يَخْشَىٰ ﴿٤٤﴾

ʾIdh ʾawḥaynāa ʾilāa ʾummika mā yūḥā. (38) ʾAniqdhifīhi fit-tābūti faqdhifīhi fil-yammi falyulqihil-yammu bissāḥili yaʾkhudhhu ᶜaduwwul-lī wa ᶜaduwwul-lah. Wa ʾalqaytu ᶜalayka maḥabbatam-minnī wa lituṣnaᶜa ᶜalā ᶜaynī. (39) ʾIdh tamshīi ʾukhtuka fataqūlu hal ʾadullukum ᶜalā mañy-yakfuluh. Farajaᶜnāka ʾilāa ʾummika kay taqarra ᶜaynuhā wa lā taḥzan. Wa qatalta nafsañ-fanajjaynāka minal-ghammi wa fatannāka futūnā. Falabithta sinīna fīi ʾahli Madyana thumma jiʾta ᶜalā qadariñy-yā Mūsā. (40) Waṣ-ṭanaᶜtuka liNafsī. (41) ʾIdhhab ʾañta wa ʾakhūka biʾĀyātī wa lā taniyā fī dhikrī. (42) ʾIdhhabāa ʾilā Firᶜawna ʾinnahū ṭaghā. (43) Faqūlā lahū qawlal-layyinal-laᶜallahū yatadhakkaru ʾaw yakhshā. (44)

when We inspired thy mother with this inspiration: ‹38› 'Place him in a chest and throw it into the river, and thereupon the river will cast him ashore, [and] one who is an enemy unto Me and an enemy unto him will adopt him.'[21]

"And [thus early] I spread Mine Own love over thee – and [this] in order that thou might be formed under Mine eye.[22] ‹39›

"[And thou wert under Mine eye] when thy sister went forth and said [to Pharaoh's people], 'Shall I guide you unto [a woman] who might take charge of him?'[23] And so We returned thee unto thy mother, so that her eye be gladdened, and that she might not sorrow [any longer].[24]

"And [when thou camest of age,[25]] thou didst slay a man: but We did save thee from all grief, although We tried thee with various trials.[26]

"And then thou didst sojourn for years among the people of Madyan;[27] and now thou hast come [here] as ordained [by Me], O Moses: ‹40› for I have chosen thee for Mine Own service. ‹41›

"Go forth, [then,] thou and thy brother, with My messages, and never tire of remembering Me: ‹42› go forth, both of you, unto Pharaoh: for, verily, he has transgressed all bounds of equity! ‹43› But speak unto him in a mild manner, so that he might bethink himself or [at least] be filled with apprehension."[28] ‹44›

---

21 Lit., "take him" (cf. 28 : 9). Pharaoh is described as an enemy of God because of his overweening arrogance and cruelty as well as his claim to the status of divinity (see 79 : 24); and he was, unknowingly, an enemy of the infant Moses inasmuch as he hated and feared the people to whom the latter belonged.

22 I.e., "under My protection and in accordance with the destiny which I have decreed for thee": possibly a reference to Moses' upbringing within the cultural environment of the royal palace and his subsequent acquisition of the ancient wisdom of Egypt – circumstances which were to qualify him for his future leadership and the special mission that God had in view for him.

23 For a fuller account, see 28 : 12.

24 As is implied here and in 28 : 12-13, his own mother became his wet-nurse.

25 Cf. 28 : 14.

26 For the details of this particular incident, which proved a turning-point in the life of Moses, see 28 : 15-21.

27 See 28 : 22-28.

28 Lit., "or [that he might] fear" – i.e., that there is some truth in the words of Moses. Since God knows the future, the tentative form in the above phrase – "so that he might (*laᶜallahu*) bethink himself", etc., – obviously does not imply any "doubt" on God's part as to Pharoah's future reaction: it implies no more than His command to the bearer of His message to address the sinner *with a view* to the latter's bethinking himself: in other words, it relates to the

قَالَا رَبَّنَآ إِنَّنَا نَخَافُ أَن يَفْرُطَ عَلَيْنَآ أَوْ أَن يَطْغَىٰ ﴿٤٥﴾ قَالَ لَا تَخَافَآ
إِنَّنِى مَعَكُمَآ أَسْمَعُ وَأَرَىٰ ﴿٤٦﴾ فَأْتِيَاهُ فَقُولَآ إِنَّا رَسُولَا رَبِّكَ فَأَرْسِلْ
مَعَنَا بَنِىٓ إِسْرَٰٓءِيلَ وَلَا تُعَذِّبْهُمْ قَدْ جِئْنَٰكَ بِـَٔايَةٍ مِّن رَّبِّكَ وَٱلسَّلَٰمُ
عَلَىٰ مَنِ ٱتَّبَعَ ٱلْهُدَىٰٓ ﴿٤٧﴾ إِنَّا قَدْ أُوحِىَ إِلَيْنَآ أَنَّ ٱلْعَذَابَ عَلَىٰ مَن
كَذَّبَ وَتَوَلَّىٰ ﴿٤٨﴾ قَالَ فَمَن رَّبُّكُمَا يَٰمُوسَىٰ ﴿٤٩﴾ قَالَ رَبُّنَا ٱلَّذِىٓ
أَعْطَىٰ كُلَّ شَىْءٍ خَلْقَهُۥ ثُمَّ هَدَىٰ ﴿٥٠﴾ قَالَ فَمَا بَالُ ٱلْقُرُونِ ٱلْأُولَىٰ ﴿٥١﴾
قَالَ عِلْمُهَا عِندَ رَبِّى فِى كِتَٰبٍ لَّا يَضِلُّ رَبِّى وَلَا يَنسَى ﴿٥٢﴾

Qālā Rabbanāa ʾinnanā nakhāfu ʾañy-yafruṭa ʿalaynāa ʾaw ʾañy-yaṭghā. (45) Qāla lā takhāfāa ʾinnanī maʿakumāa ʾasmaʿu wa ʾarā. (46) Faʾtiyāhu faqūlāa ʾinnā Rasūlā Rabbika faʾarsil maʿanā banīi ʾIsrāaʾīla wa lā tuʿadhdhibhum. Qad jiʾnāka biʾāyatim-mir-Rabbik. Was-salāmu ʿalā manit-tabaʿal-hudā. (47) ʾInnā qad ʾūḥiya ʾilaynāa ʾannal-ʿadhāba ʿalā mañ-kadhdhaba wa tawallā. (48) Qāla famar-Rabbukumā yā Mūsā. (49) Qāla Rabbunal-ladhīi ʾaʿṭā kulla shayʾin khalqahū thumma hadā. (50) Qāla famā bālul-qurūnil-ʾūlā. (51) Qāla ʿilmuhā ʿiñda Rabbī fī Kitābil-lā yaḍillu Rabbī wa lā yañsā. (52)

The two [brothers] said: "O our Sustainer! Verily, we fear lest he act hastily with regard to us,[29] or lest he [continue to] transgress all bounds of equity." ‹45›

Answered He: "Fear not! Verily, I shall be with you two, hearing and seeing [all]. ‹46› Go, then, you two unto him and say, 'Behold, we are apostles sent by thy Sustainer: let, then, the children of Israel go with us, and cause them not to suffer [any longer].[30] We have now come unto thee with a message from thy Sustainer; and [know that His] peace shall be [only] on those who follow [His] guidance: ‹47› for, behold, it has been revealed to us that [in the life to come] suffering shall befall all who give the lie to the truth and turn away [from it]!'" ‹48›

[But when God's message was conveyed unto Pharaoh,] he said: "Who, now, is this Sustainer of you two, O Moses?" ‹49›

He replied: "Our Sustainer is He who gives unto every thing [that exists] its true nature and form, and thereupon guides it [towards its fulfilment]."[31] ‹50›

Said [Pharaoh]: "And what of all the past generations?"[32] ‹51›

[Moses] answered: "Knowledge thereof rests with my Sustainer [alone, and is laid down] in His decree;[33] my Sustainer does not err, and neither does He forget."[34] ‹52›

---

intention or hope with which the message-bearer should approach his task (Rāzī). And since every Qurʾanic narrative aims at bringing out an eternal truth or truths or at elucidating a universal principle of human behaviour, it is evident that God's command to Moses to speak to one particular sinner "in a mild manner, so that he might [have a chance to] bethink himself" retains its validity for all times and all such attempts at conversion.

29 I.e., "lest he prevent us, by banishing or killing us outright, from delivering Thy message fully".

30 Cf. 2 : 49, 7 : 141 and 14 : 6. For a more detailed description of this Pharaonic oppression of the Israelites, see Exodus i, 8-22.

31 In the original, this sentence appears in the past tense ("has given" and "has guided"); but as it obviously relates to the continuous process of God's creation, it is independent of the concept of time and denotes, as in so many other places in the Qurʾān, an unceasing present. The term *khalq* signifies in this context not merely the inner nature of a created thing or being but also the outward *form* in which this nature manifests itself; hence my composite rendering of *khalqahu* as "its true nature and form". The idea underlying the above sentence is expressed for the first time in 87 : 2-3, i.e., in a *sūrah* which belongs to the earliest period of Qurʾanic revelation.

32 Sc., "who used to worship a plurality of deities: are they, in thy view, irretrievably doomed?"

33 I.e., He alone decrees their destiny in the life to come, for He alone knows their motives and understands the cause of their errors, and He alone can appreciate their spiritual merits and demerits.

34 According to Rāzī, the dialogue between Moses and Pharaoh ends here for the time being, with verses 53-55 representing a direct Qurʾanic discourse addressed to man in general.

HE IT IS who has made the earth a cradle for you, and has traced out for you ways [of livelihood] thereon,[35] and [who] sends down waters from the sky: and by this means We bring forth various kinds[36] of plants. ‹53› Eat, [then, of this produce of the soil,] and pasture your cattle [thereon]. In all this, behold, there are messages indeed for those who are endowed with reason: ‹54› out of this [earth] have We created you, and into it shall We return you, and out of it shall We bring you forth once again.[37] ‹55›

ربع الحزب

AND, INDEED, We made Pharaoh aware of[38] all Our messages – but he gave them the lie and refused [to heed them].[39] ‹56› He said: "Hast thou come to drive us out of our land[40] by thy sorcery, O Moses? ‹57› In that case, we shall most certainly produce before thee sorcery the like thereof! Appoint, then, a tryst between us and thee – which we shall not fail to keep, nor [mayest] thou – at a suitable place!" ‹58› Answered [Moses]: "Your tryst shall be the day of the Festival;[41] and let the people assemble when the sun is risen high." ‹59›
Thereupon Pharaoh withdrew [with his counsellors] and decided upon the scheme which he would pursue;[42] and then he came [to the tryst]. ‹60›

ٱلَّذِى جَعَلَ لَكُمُ ٱلْأَرْضَ مَهْدًا وَسَلَكَ لَكُمْ فِيهَا سُبُلًا وَأَنزَلَ مِنَ
ٱلسَّمَآءِ مَآءً فَأَخْرَجْنَا بِهِۦٓ أَزْوَٰجًا مِّن نَّبَاتٍ شَتَّىٰ ﴿٥٣﴾ كُلُوا۟ وَٱرْعَوْا۟
أَنْعَـٰمَكُمْ ۗ إِنَّ فِى ذَٰلِكَ لَـَٔايَـٰتٍ لِّأُو۟لِى ٱلنُّهَىٰ ﴿٥٤﴾ ۞ مِنْهَا خَلَقْنَـٰكُمْ
وَفِيهَا نُعِيدُكُمْ وَمِنْهَا نُخْرِجُكُمْ تَارَةً أُخْرَىٰ ﴿٥٥﴾ وَلَقَدْ أَرَيْنَـٰهُ ءَايَـٰتِنَا
كُلَّهَا فَكَذَّبَ وَأَبَىٰ ﴿٥٦﴾ قَالَ أَجِئْتَنَا لِتُخْرِجَنَا مِنْ أَرْضِنَا بِسِحْرِكَ
يَـٰمُوسَىٰ ﴿٥٧﴾ فَلَنَأْتِيَنَّكَ بِسِحْرٍ مِّثْلِهِۦ فَٱجْعَلْ بَيْنَنَا وَبَيْنَكَ مَوْعِدًا لَّا
نُخْلِفُهُۥ نَحْنُ وَلَآ أَنتَ مَكَانًا سُوًى ﴿٥٨﴾ قَالَ مَوْعِدُكُمْ يَوْمُ ٱلزِّينَةِ وَأَن
يُحْشَرَ ٱلنَّاسُ ضُحًى ﴿٥٩﴾ فَتَوَلَّىٰ فِرْعَوْنُ فَجَمَعَ كَيْدَهُۥ ثُمَّ أَتَىٰ ﴿٦٠﴾

ʾAlladhī jaʿala lakumul-ʾarḍa mahdañw-wa salaka lakum fīhā subulañw-wa ʾañzala minas-samāaʾi māaʾañ-faʾakhrajnā bihīi ʾazwājam-miñ-nabātiñ-shattā. (53) Kulū war-ʿaw ʾanʿāmakum; ʾinna fī dhālika laʾĀyātil-liʾulin-nuhā. (54) ۞ Minhā khalaqnākum wa fīhā nuʿīdukum wa minhā nukhrijukum tāratan ʾukhrā. (55) Wa laqad ʾaraynāhu ʾĀyātinā kullahā fakadhdhaba wa ʾabā. (56) Qāla ʾajiʾtanā litukhrijanā min ʾarḍinā bisiḥrika yā Mūsā. (57) Falanaʾtiyannaka bisiḥrim-mithlihī fajʿal baynanā wa baynaka mawʿidal-lā nukhlifuhū naḥnu wa lāa ʾañta makānañ-suwā. (58) Qāla mawʿidukum yawmuz-zīnati wa ʾañy-yuḥsharan-nāsu ḍuḥā. (59) Fatawallā Firʿawnu fajamaʿa kaydahū thumma ʾatā. (60)

35 I.e., "has provided you with ways and means – both material and intellectual – to gain your livelihood on earth and from it".

36 Lit., "pairs" (*azwāj*), a term which in this context apparently denotes "kinds"; but see also 13 : 3 and the corresponding note 7.

37 Regarding the creation of man's body "out of the earth", see the second half of note 47 on 3 : 59, as well as note 24 on 15 : 26; its "return into it" signifies the dissolution of this body, after death, into the elementary organic and inorganic substances of which it was composed; and all these facts – creation, subsistence and dissolution – contain the message of God's almightiness, of the ephemeral nature of man's life on earth, and of his future resurrection.

38 Lit., "We showed him" (*araynāhu*), i.e., Pharaoh. According to Zamakhsharī, Rāzī and Bayḍāwī, this verb has here the meaning of "We made him acquainted with" or "aware of".

39 The messages alluded to here are both those entrusted directly to Moses and the intangible "messages" forthcoming from God's creation and referred to in the preceding passage.

40 I.e., "deprive us of our rule" (cf. 7 : 110).

41 Lit., "the day of adornment" – possibly the Egyptian New Year's Day. The expression "*your* tryst" has the connotation of "the tryst proposed by you".

42 Lit., "he decided upon his artful scheme" (*jamaʿa kaydahu*): evidently an allusion to his summoning all the greatest sorcerers of Egypt (cf. 7 : 111-114).

قَالَ لَهُم مُّوسَىٰ وَيْلَكُمْ لَا تَفْتَرُوا۟ عَلَى ٱللَّهِ كَذِبًا فَيُسْحِتَكُم بِعَذَابٍ ۖ
وَقَدْ خَابَ مَنِ ٱفْتَرَىٰ ﴿٦١﴾ فَتَنَٰزَعُوٓا۟ أَمْرَهُم بَيْنَهُمْ وَأَسَرُّوا۟ ٱلنَّجْوَىٰ ﴿٦٢﴾
قَالُوٓا۟ إِنْ هَٰذَٰنِ لَسَٰحِرَٰنِ يُرِيدَانِ أَن يُخْرِجَاكُم مِّنْ أَرْضِكُم
بِسِحْرِهِمَا وَيَذْهَبَا بِطَرِيقَتِكُمُ ٱلْمُثْلَىٰ ﴿٦٣﴾ فَأَجْمِعُوا۟ كَيْدَكُمْ ثُمَّ ٱئْتُوا۟
صَفًّا ۚ وَقَدْ أَفْلَحَ ٱلْيَوْمَ مَنِ ٱسْتَعْلَىٰ ﴿٦٤﴾ قَالُوا۟ يَٰمُوسَىٰٓ إِمَّآ أَن تُلْقِىَ وَإِمَّآ
أَن نَّكُونَ أَوَّلَ مَنْ أَلْقَىٰ ﴿٦٥﴾ قَالَ بَلْ أَلْقُوا۟ ۖ فَإِذَا حِبَالُهُمْ وَعِصِيُّهُمْ
يُخَيَّلُ إِلَيْهِ مِن سِحْرِهِمْ أَنَّهَا تَسْعَىٰ ﴿٦٦﴾ فَأَوْجَسَ فِى نَفْسِهِۦ خِيفَةً
مُّوسَىٰ ﴿٦٧﴾ قُلْنَا لَا تَخَفْ إِنَّكَ أَنتَ ٱلْأَعْلَىٰ ﴿٦٨﴾ وَأَلْقِ مَا فِى يَمِينِكَ
تَلْقَفْ مَا صَنَعُوٓا۟ ۖ إِنَّمَا صَنَعُوا۟ كَيْدُ سَٰحِرٍ ۖ وَلَا يُفْلِحُ ٱلسَّاحِرُ حَيْثُ
أَتَىٰ ﴿٦٩﴾ فَأُلْقِىَ ٱلسَّحَرَةُ سُجَّدًا قَالُوٓا۟ ءَامَنَّا بِرَبِّ هَٰرُونَ وَمُوسَىٰ ﴿٧٠﴾

Said Moses to them: "Woe unto you! Do not invent lies against God,[43] lest He afflict you with most grievous suffering: for He who contrives [such] a lie is already undone!" «61»

So they debated among themselves as to what to do; but they kept their counsel secret, «62» saying [to one another]: "These two are surely sorcerers intent on driving you from your land[44] by their sorcery, and on doing away with your time-honoured way of life.[45] «63» Hence, [O sorcerers of Egypt,] decide upon the scheme which you will pursue, and then come forward in one single body:[46] for, indeed, he who prevails today shall prosper indeed!"[47] «64»

Said [the sorcerers]: "O Moses! Either thou throw [thy staff first], or we shall be the first to throw." «65»

He answered: "Nay, you throw [first]."

And lo! by virtue of their sorcery, their [magic] ropes and staffs seemed to him to be moving rapidly: «66» and in his heart Moses became apprehensive.[48] «67»

[But] We said: "Fear not! Verily, it is thou who shalt prevail! «68» And [now] throw that [staff] which is in thy right hand – it shall swallow up all that they have wrought: [for] they have wrought only a sorcerer's artifice, and the sorcerer can never come to any good, whatever he may aim at!"[49] «69»

[And so it happened[50] –] and down fell the sorcerers, prostrating themselves in adoration,[51] [and] exclaimed: "We have come to believe in the Sustainer of Moses and Aaron!" «70»

Qāla lahum-Mūsā waylakum lā taftarū ᶜalal-lāhi kadhibañ-fayusḥitakum biᶜadhābiñw-wa qad khāba manif-tarā. (61) Fatanāzaᶜūu ᵓamrahum-baynahum wa ᵓasarrun-najwā. (62) Qālūu ᵓin hādhāni lasāḥirāni yurīdāni ᵓañy-yukhrijākum-min ᵓarḍikum-bisiḥrihimā wa yadhhabā biṭarīqatikumul-muthlā. (63) Faᵓajmiᶜū kaydakum thummaᵓ-tū ṣaffañw-wa qad ᵓaflaḥal-yawma manis-taᶜlā. (64) Qālū yā Mūsāa ᵓimmāa ᵓañ-tulqiya wa ᵓimmāa ᵓan-nakūna ᵓawwala man ᵓalqā. (65) Qāla bal ᵓalqū. Faᵓidhā ḥibāluhum wa ᶜiṣiyyuhum yukhayyalu ᵓilayhi miñ-siḥrihim ᵓannahā tasᶜā. (66) Faᵓawjasa fī nafsihī khīfatam-Mūsā. (67) Qulnā lā takhaf ᵓinnaka ᵓañtal-ᵓaᶜlā. (68) Wa ᵓalqi mā fī yamīnika talqaf mā ṣanaᶜūu ᵓinnamā ṣanaᶜū kaydu sāḥiriñw-wa lā yufliḥus-sāḥiru ḥaythu ᵓatā. (69) Faᵓulqiyas-saḥaratu sujjadañ-qālūu ᵓāmannā biRabbi Hārūna wa Mūsā. (70)

43 I.e., by deliberately denying the truth of His messages.

44 See note 40 above. The dual form refers to Moses and Aaron.

45 Lit., "your exemplary [or "ideal"] way of life (*ṭarīqah*)".

46 Lit., "in one [single] line", i.e., in unison.

47 Cf. 7 : 113-114.

48 Lit., "conceived fear within himself". The implication is that the feat of the sorcerers was based on mass-hallucination (cf. 7 : 116 – "they cast a spell upon the people's eyes"), a hallucination to which even Moses succumbed for a while.

49 Lit., "wherever he may come" – i.e., irrespective of whether he aims at a good or at an evil end (Rāzī). The above statement implies a categorical condemnation of all endeavours which fall under the heading of "magic", whatever the intention of the person who devotes himself to it. (In this connection, see also *sūrah* 2, note 84.)

50 Cf. 7 : 117-119.

51 See note 90 on 7 : 120.

Said [Pharaoh]: "Have you come to believe in him[52] ere I have given you permission? Verily, he must be your master who has taught you magic! But I shall most certainly cut off your hands and feet in great numbers, because of [your] perverseness, and I shall most certainly crucify you in great numbers on trunks of palm-trees:[53] and [I shall do this] so that you might come to know for certain as to which of us [two][54] can inflict a more severe chastisement, and [which] is the more abiding!" ‹71›

They answered: "Never shall we prefer thee to all the evidence of the truth that has come unto us, nor to Him who has brought us into being! Decree, then, whatever thou art going to decree: thou canst decree only [something that pertains to] this worldly life![55] ‹72› As for us, behold, we have come to believe in our Sustainer, [hoping] that He may forgive us our faults and all that magic unto which thou hast forced us:[56] for God is the best [to look forward to], and the One who is truly abiding."[57] ‹73›

VERILY, as for him who shall appear before his Sustainer [on Judgment Day] lost in sin – his [portion], behold, shall be hell: he will neither die therein nor live;[58] ‹74› whereas he who shall appear before Him as a believer who has done righteous deeds[59] – it is such that shall have lofty stations [in the life to come]: ‹75›

قَالَ ءَامَنتُمْ لَهُۥ قَبْلَ أَنْ ءَاذَنَ لَكُمْ ۖ إِنَّهُۥ لَكَبِيرُكُمُ ٱلَّذِى عَلَّمَكُمُ
ٱلسِّحْرَ ۖ فَلَأُقَطِّعَنَّ أَيْدِيَكُمْ وَأَرْجُلَكُم مِّنْ خِلَـٰفٍ وَلَأُصَلِّبَنَّكُمْ فِى
جُذُوعِ ٱلنَّخْلِ وَلَتَعْلَمُنَّ أَيُّنَآ أَشَدُّ عَذَابًا وَأَبْقَىٰ ﴿٧١﴾ قَالُوا۟ لَن نُّؤْثِرَكَ
عَلَىٰ مَا جَآءَنَا مِنَ ٱلْبَيِّنَـٰتِ وَٱلَّذِى فَطَرَنَا ۖ فَٱقْضِ مَآ أَنتَ قَاضٍ ۖ إِنَّمَا
تَقْضِى هَـٰذِهِ ٱلْحَيَوٰةَ ٱلدُّنْيَآ ﴿٧٢﴾ إِنَّآ ءَامَنَّا بِرَبِّنَا لِيَغْفِرَ لَنَا خَطَـٰيَـٰنَا
وَمَآ أَكْرَهْتَنَا عَلَيْهِ مِنَ ٱلسِّحْرِ ۗ وَٱللَّهُ خَيْرٌ وَأَبْقَىٰٓ ﴿٧٣﴾ إِنَّهُۥ مَن يَأْتِ
رَبَّهُۥ مُجْرِمًا فَإِنَّ لَهُۥ جَهَنَّمَ لَا يَمُوتُ فِيهَا وَلَا يَحْيَىٰ ﴿٧٤﴾ وَمَن يَأْتِهِۦ
مُؤْمِنًا قَدْ عَمِلَ ٱلصَّـٰلِحَـٰتِ فَأُو۟لَـٰٓئِكَ لَهُمُ ٱلدَّرَجَـٰتُ ٱلْعُلَىٰ ﴿٧٥﴾

Qāla ʾāmañtum lahū qabla ʾan ʾādhana lakum. ʾInnahū lakabīrukumul-ladhī ʿallamakumus-siḥr. Falaʾuqaṭṭiʿanna ʾaydiyakum wa ʾarjulakum-min khilāfiñw-wa laʾuṣallibannakum fī judhūʿin-nakhli wa lataʿlamunna ʾayyunāa ʾashaddu ʿadhābañw-wa ʾabqā. (71) Qālū lañ-nuʾthiraka ʿalā mā jāaʾanā minal-bayyināti wal-ladhī faṭaranā faqḍi māa ʾañta qāḍin ʾinnamā taqḍī hādhihil-ḥayātad-dunyā. (72) ʾInnāa ʾāmannā biRabbinā liyaghfira lanā khaṭāyānā wa māa ʾakrahtanā ʿalayhi minas-siḥr. Wal-lāhu khayruñw-wa ʾabqā. (73) ʾInnahū mañy-yaʾti Rabbahū mujrimañ-faʾinna lahū jahannama lā yamūtu fīhā wa lā yaḥyā. (74) Wa mañy-yaʾtihī muʾminañ-qad ʿamilaṣ-ṣāliḥāti faʾulāaʾika lahumud-darajātul-ʿulā. (75)

52 I.e., Moses (cf. note 91 on 7 : 123).

53 Regarding the meaning of the stress on "great numbers", forthcoming from the grammatical form of the verbs employed by Pharaoh, see *sūrah* 7, note 92.

54 Sc., "I or the God in whom you now believe".

55 Or: "thou canst end [for us] only this worldly life". It is to be noted that the verb *qaḍā* signifies, among other meanings, "he decreed" as well as "he ended [something]".

56 Pharaoh (a title borne by every indigenous ruler of Egypt) was considered to be a "god-king" and, thus, the embodiment of the Egyptian religion, in which occult practices and magic played a very important role; hence, every one of his subjects was duty-bound to accept magic as an integral part of the scheme of life.

57 Lit., "and the most abiding", i.e., eternal: cf. 55 : 26-27.

58 I.e., he will neither be reborn spiritually nor find peace through extinction (Baghawī, Bayḍāwī). As is apparent from the juxtaposition, in the next verse, of the term *mujrim* (rendered by me as "one who is lost in sin") with that of *muʾmin* ("believer"), the former term is here applied to one who, in his lifetime, has consciously and persistently denied God (Bayḍāwī).

59 Thus the Qurʾān implies – here as well as in many other places – that the spiritual value of a person's faith

gardens of perpetual bliss, through which running waters flow, therein to abide: for that shall be the recompense of all who attain to purity. «76»

AND, INDEED, [a time came[60] when] We thus inspired Moses: "Go forth with My servants by night, and strike out for them a dry path through the sea; [and] fear not of being overtaken, and dread not [the sea]."[61] «77»

And Pharaoh pursued them with his hosts: and they were overwhelmed by the sea which was destined to overwhelm them[62] «78» because Pharaoh had led his people astray and had not guided [them] aright. «79»

O children of Israel! [Thus] We saved you from your enemy, and [then] We made a covenant with you on the right-hand slope of Mount Sinai,[63] and repeatedly sent down manna and quails unto you, [saying,] «80» "Partake of the good things which We have provided for you as sustenance,[64] but do not transgress therein the bounds of equity[65] lest My condemnation fall upon you: for, he upon whom My condemnation falls has indeed thrown himself into utter ruin!"[66] «81»

جَنَّٰتُ عَدْنٍ تَجْرِى مِن تَحْتِهَا ٱلْأَنْهَٰرُ خَٰلِدِينَ فِيهَا وَذَٰلِكَ جَزَآءُ مَن
تَزَكَّىٰ ﴿٧٦﴾ وَلَقَدْ أَوْحَيْنَآ إِلَىٰ مُوسَىٰٓ أَنْ أَسْرِ بِعِبَادِى فَٱضْرِبْ لَهُمْ
طَرِيقًا فِى ٱلْبَحْرِ يَبَسًا لَّا تَخَٰفُ دَرَكًا وَلَا تَخْشَىٰ ﴿٧٧﴾ فَأَتْبَعَهُمْ فِرْعَوْنُ
بِجُنُودِهِۦ فَغَشِيَهُم مِّنَ ٱلْيَمِّ مَا غَشِيَهُمْ ﴿٧٨﴾ وَأَضَلَّ فِرْعَوْنُ قَوْمَهُۥ وَمَا
هَدَىٰ ﴿٧٩﴾ يَٰبَنِىٓ إِسْرَٰٓءِيلَ قَدْ أَنجَيْنَٰكُم مِّنْ عَدُوِّكُمْ وَوَٰعَدْنَٰكُمْ
جَانِبَ ٱلطُّورِ ٱلْأَيْمَنَ وَنَزَّلْنَا عَلَيْكُمُ ٱلْمَنَّ وَٱلسَّلْوَىٰ ﴿٨٠﴾ كُلُوا۟ مِن
طَيِّبَٰتِ مَا رَزَقْنَٰكُمْ وَلَا تَطْغَوْا۟ فِيهِ فَيَحِلَّ عَلَيْكُمْ غَضَبِى وَمَن يَحْلِلْ
عَلَيْهِ غَضَبِى فَقَدْ هَوَىٰ ﴿٨١﴾

Jannātu ʿadniñ-tajrī miñ-taḥtihal-ʾanhāru khālidīna fīhā; wa dhālika jazāaʾu mañ-tazakkā. (76) Wa laqad ʾawḥaynāa ʾilā Mūsāa ʾan ʾasri biʿibādī faḍrib lahum ṭarīqañ-fil-baḥri yabasal-lā takhāfu darakañw-wa lā takhshā. (77) Faʾatbaʿahum Firʿawnu bijunūdihī faghashiyahum-minal-yammi mā ghashiyahum. (78) Wa ʾaḍalla Firʿawnu qawmahū wa mā hadā. (79) Yā banīi ʾIsrāaʾīla qad ʾañjaynākum-min ʿaduwwikum wa wāʿadnākum jānibaṭ-Ṭūril-ʾaymana wa nazzalnā ʿalaykumul-manna was-salwā. (80) Kulū miñ-ṭayyibāti mā razaqnākum wa lā taṭghaw fīhi fayaḥilla ʿalaykum ghaḍabī; wa mañy-yaḥlil ʿalayhi ghaḍabī faqad hawā. (81)

depends on his *doing righteous deeds* as well: cf. the statement in 6 : 158 that on Judgment Day "believing will be of no avail to any human being . . . who, while believing, did no good works".

60 I.e., after all the trials which the Israelites had to undergo in Egypt, and after the plagues with which Pharaoh and his followers were afflicted (cf. 7 : 130 ff.).

61 Referring to the phrase "strike out (*iḍrib*) for them a dry path through the sea", Ṭabarī explains it as meaning "choose (*ittakhidh*) for them a dry path". See also 26 : 63-66 and the corresponding notes 33 and 35.

62 Lit., "there overwhelmed them [that] of the sea which overwhelmed them" – expressing the inevitability of the doom which encompassed them.

63 See note 38 on 19 : 52. As regards God's "covenant" with the children of Israel, see 2 : 63 and 83.

64 The reference to God's bestowal of "manna (*mann*) and quails (*salwā*)" upon the Israelites during their wanderings in the Sinai Desert after their exodus from Egypt is found in the Qurʾān in two other places as well (namely, in 2 : 57 and 7 : 160). According to Arab philologists, the term *mann* denotes not only the sweet, resinous substance exuded by certain plants of the desert, but also everything that is "bestowed as a favour", i.e., without any effort on the part of the recipient. Similarly, the term *salwā* signifies not merely "a quail" or "quails", but also "all that makes man content and happy after privation" (*Qāmūs*). Hence the combination of these two terms denotes, metonymically, the gift of sustenance freely bestowed by God upon the followers of Moses.

65 Or: "do not behave in an overweening manner" – i.e., "do not attribute these favours to your own supposed excellence on account of your descent from Abraham".

66 There is almost complete unanimity among the classical commentators in that God's "condemnation" (*ghaḍab*, lit., "wrath") is a metonym for the inescapable retribution which man brings upon himself if he deliberately rejects God's guidance and "transgresses the bounds of equity".

وَإِنِّي لَغَفَّارٌ لِّمَن تَابَ وَءَامَنَ وَعَمِلَ صَٰلِحًا ثُمَّ ٱهْتَدَىٰ ﴿٨٢﴾ ۞ وَمَآ
أَعْجَلَكَ عَن قَوْمِكَ يَٰمُوسَىٰ ﴿٨٣﴾ قَالَ هُمْ أُوْلَآءِ عَلَىٰٓ أَثَرِى وَعَجِلْتُ
إِلَيْكَ رَبِّ لِتَرْضَىٰ ﴿٨٤﴾ قَالَ فَإِنَّا قَدْ فَتَنَّا قَوْمَكَ مِنۢ بَعْدِكَ وَأَضَلَّهُمُ
ٱلسَّامِرِىُّ ﴿٨٥﴾ فَرَجَعَ مُوسَىٰٓ إِلَىٰ قَوْمِهِۦ غَضْبَٰنَ أَسِفًا ۚ قَالَ يَٰقَوْمِ أَلَمْ
يَعِدْكُمْ رَبُّكُمْ وَعْدًا حَسَنًا ۚ أَفَطَالَ عَلَيْكُمُ ٱلْعَهْدُ أَمْ أَرَدتُّمْ أَن يَحِلَّ
عَلَيْكُمْ غَضَبٌ مِّن رَّبِّكُمْ فَأَخْلَفْتُم مَّوْعِدِى ﴿٨٦﴾

Wa ʾinnī laGhaffārul-limañ-tāba wa ʾāmana wa ʿamila ṣāliḥañ-thummah-tadā. (82) **◈ Wa māa ʾaʿjalaka ʿañ-qawmika yā Mūsā.** (83) **Qāla hum ʾulāaʾi ʿalāa ʾatharī wa ʿajiltu ʾilayka Rabbi litarḍā.** (84) **Qāla faʾinnā qad fatannā qawmaka mim-baʿdika wa ʾaḍallahumus-Sāmiriyy.** (85) **Farajaʿa Mūsāa ʾilā qawmihī ghaḍbāna ʾasifā. Qāla yā qawmi ʾalam yaʿidkum Rabbukum waʿdan ḥasanā. ʾAfaṭāla ʿalaykumul-ʿahdu ʾam ʾarattum ʾañy-yaḥilla ʿalaykum ghaḍabum-mir Rabbikum faʾakhlaftum-mawʿidī.** (86)

نصف الحزب

Yet withal, behold, I forgive all sins unto any who repents and attains to faith and does righteous deeds, and thereafter keeps to the right path. ‹82›

[AND GOD SAID:[67]] "Now what has caused thee, O Moses, to leave thy people behind in so great a haste?"[68] ‹83›

He answered: "They are treading in my footsteps[69] while I have hastened unto Thee, O my Sustainer, so that Thou might be well-pleased [with me]." ‹84›

Said He: "Then [know that], verily, in thy absence We have put thy people to a test, and the Samaritan has led them astray."[70] ‹85›

Thereupon Moses returned to his people full of wrath and sorrow, [and] exclaimed: "O my people! Did not your Sustainer hold out [many] a goodly promise to you? Did, then, [the fulfilment of] this promise seem to you too long in coming?[71] Or are you, perchance, determined to see your Sustainer's condemnation fall upon you,[72] and so you broke your promise to me?" ‹86›

67 This passage relates to the time of Moses' ascent of Mount Sinai, mentioned in 2 : 51 and 7 : 142.

68 Lit., "what has hastened thee ahead of thy people?" – implying that he should not have left them alone, without his personal guidance, at so early a stage in their freedom. In this inimitable elliptic manner the Qurʾān alludes to the psychological fact that a community which attains to political and social freedom after centuries of bondage remains for a long time subject to the demoralizing influences of its past, and cannot all at once develop a spiritual and social discipline of its own.

69 The classical commentators understand this phrase in its physical sense, i.e., "they are coming up behind me and are now close by". Since, however, Moses was obviously meant to be alone on his ascent of Mount Sinai, I am of the opinion that his answer has a tropical sense, expressing his assumption that the children of Israel would *follow his guidance* even in his absence: an assumption which proved erroneous, as shown in the sequence.

70 The designation *as-sāmirī* is undoubtedly an adjectival noun denoting the person's descent or origin. According to one of the explanations advanced by Ṭabarī and Zamakhsharī, it signifies "a man of the Jewish clan of the Sāmirah", i.e., the ethnic and religious group designated in later times as the Samaritans (a small remnant of whom is still living in Nablus, in Palestine). Since that sect as such did not yet exist at the time of Moses, it is possible that – as Ibn ʿAbbas maintained (Rāzī) – the person in question was one of the many Egyptians who had been converted to the faith of Moses and joined the Israelites on their exodus from Egypt (cf. note 92 on 7 : 124): in which case the designation *sāmirī* might be connected with the ancient Egyptian *shemer*, "a foreigner" or "stranger". This surmise is strengthened by his introduction of the worship of the golden calf, undoubtedly an echo of the Egyptian cult of Apis (see note 113 on 7 : 148). In any case, it is not impossible that the latter-day Samaritans descended – or were reputed to descend – from this personality, whether of Hebrew or of Egyptian origin; this might partly explain the persistent antagonism between them and the rest of the Israelite community.

71 Or, according to Zamakhsharī: "Did, then, the time [of my absence] seem too long to you?" (It is to be noted that the term *ʿahd* signifies a "time" or "period" as well as a "covenant" or "promise".)

72 Lit., "Or have you decided that condemnation by your Sustainer should fall due upon you?" – i.e., "are you determined to disregard the consequences of your doings?"

They answered: "We did not break our promise to thee of our own free will, but [this is what happened:] we were loaded with the [sinful] burdens of the [Egyptian] people's ornaments, and so we threw them [into the fire],[73] and likewise did this Samaritan cast [his into it]." ‹87›
But then, [so they told Moses,[74] the Samaritan] had produced for them [out of the molten gold] the effigy of a calf, which made a lowing sound;[75] and thereupon they said [to one another], "This is your deity, and the deity of Moses – but he has forgotten [his past]!"[76] ‹88›
Why – did they not see that [the thing] could not give them any response, and had no power to harm or to benefit them? ‹89›
And, indeed, even before [the return of Moses] had Aaron said unto them: "O my people! You are but being tempted to evil by this [idol] – for, behold, your [only] Sustainer is the Most Gracious! Follow me, then, and obey my bidding!"[77] ‹90›
[But] they answered: "By no means shall we cease to worship it until Moses comes back to us!" ‹91›
[And now that he had come back, Moses] said: "O Aaron! What has prevented thee, when thou didst see that they had gone astray, ‹92› from [abandoning them and] following me? Hast thou, then, [deliberately] disobeyed my commandment?"[78] ‹93›

قَالُواْ مَآ أَخْلَفْنَا مَوْعِدَكَ بِمَلْكِنَا وَلَـٰكِنَّا حُمِّلْنَآ أَوْزَارًا مِّن زِينَةِ ٱلْقَوْمِ
فَقَذَفْنَـٰهَا فَكَذَٰلِكَ أَلْقَى ٱلسَّامِرِىُّ ﴿87﴾ فَأَخْرَجَ لَهُمْ عِجْلًا جَسَدًا لَّهُۥ
خُوَارٌ فَقَالُواْ هَـٰذَآ إِلَـٰهُكُمْ وَإِلَـٰهُ مُوسَىٰ فَنَسِىَ ﴿88﴾ أَفَلَا يَرَوْنَ أَلَّا
يَرْجِعُ إِلَيْهِمْ قَوْلًا وَلَا يَمْلِكُ لَهُمْ ضَرًّا وَلَا نَفْعًا ﴿89﴾ وَلَقَدْ قَالَ لَهُمْ
هَـٰرُونُ مِن قَبْلُ يَـٰقَوْمِ إِنَّمَا فُتِنتُم بِهِۦ وَإِنَّ رَبَّكُمُ ٱلرَّحْمَـٰنُ فَٱتَّبِعُونِى
وَأَطِيعُوٓاْ أَمْرِى ﴿90﴾ قَالُواْ لَن نَّبْرَحَ عَلَيْهِ عَـٰكِفِينَ حَتَّىٰ يَرْجِعَ إِلَيْنَا
مُوسَىٰ ﴿91﴾ قَالَ يَـٰهَـٰرُونُ مَا مَنَعَكَ إِذْ رَأَيْتَهُمْ ضَلُّوٓاْ ﴿92﴾ أَلَّا تَتَّبِعَنِ
أَفَعَصَيْتَ أَمْرِى ﴿93﴾

Qālū māa ʾakhlafnā mawᶜidaka bimalkinā wa lākinnā ḥummilnāa ʾawzāram-miñ-zīnatil-qawmi faqadhafnāhā fakadhālika ʾalqas-Sāmiriyy. (87) Faʾakhraja lahum ᶜijlañ-jasadal-lahū khuwāruñ-faqālū hādhāa ʾilāhukum wa ʾilāhu Mūsā fanasī. (88) ʾAfalā yarawna ʾallā yarjiᶜu ʾilayhim qawlañw-wa lā yamliku lahum ḍarrañw-wa lā nafᶜā. (89) Wa laqad qāla lahum Hārūnu miñ-qablu yā qawmi ʾinnamā futiñtum bihī wa ʾinna Rabbakumur-Raḥmānu fattabiᶜūnī wa ʾaṭīᶜūu ʾamrī. (90) Qālū lañ-nabraḥa ᶜalayhi ᶜākifīna ḥattā yarjiᶜa ʾilaynā Mūsā. (91) Qāla yā Hārūnu mā manaᶜaka ʾidh raʾaytahum ḍallūu, (92) ʾallā tattabiᶜani ʾafaᶜaṣayta ʾamrī. (93)

73 It is mentioned in Exodus xii, 35 that, immediately before their departure from Egypt, the Israelites "borrowed of the Egyptians jewels of silver and jewels of gold". This "borrowing" was obviously done under false pretences, without any intention on the part of the Israelites to return the jewellery to its rightful owners: for, according to the Biblical statement (*ibid.*, verse 36), "they spoiled [i.e., robbed] the Egyptians" by doing so. While it is noteworthy that the Old Testament, in its present, corrupted form, does not condemn this behaviour, its iniquity seems to have gradually dawned upon the Israelites, and so they decided to get rid of those sinfully acquired ornaments (Baghawī, Zamakhsharī and – in one of his alternative interpretations – Rāzī).

74 This interpolation is necessary in view of the change from the direct speech in the preceding verse to the indirect in this one and in the sequence.

75 See *sūrah* 7, note 113.

76 An allusion to the fact that Moses had been brought up – obviously as an Egyptian – at Pharaoh's court.

77 Sc., "and do not follow the Samaritan". This is in sharp contrast to the Bible (Exodus xxxii, 1-5), which declares Aaron guilty of making and worshipping the golden calf.

78 Cf. the last sentence of 7 : 142, where Moses, before leaving for Mount Sinai, exhorts Aaron to "*act* righteously" (*iṣliḥ*). In this connection see also Aaron's reply to Moses in 7 : 150, as well as the corresponding note 117.

Answered [Aaron]: "O my mother's son! Seize me not by my beard, nor by my head![79] Behold, I was afraid lest [on thy return] thou say, 'Thou hast caused a split among the children of Israel, and hast paid no heed to my bidding!'"[80] ‹94›
Said [Moses]: "What, then, didst *thou* have in view, O Samaritan?" ‹95›
He answered: "I have gained insight into something which they were unable to see:[81] and so I took hold of a handful of the Apostle's teachings and cast it away: for thus has my mind prompted me [to act]."[82] ‹96›
Said [Moses]: "Begone, then! And, behold, it shall be thy lot to say throughout [thy] life, 'Touch me not!'[83] But, verily, [in the life to come] thou shalt be faced with a destiny from which there will be no escape![84] And [now] look at this deity of thine to whose worship thou hast become so devoted: we shall most certainly burn it, and then scatter [whatever remains of] it far and wide over the sea! ‹97› Your only deity is God – He save whom there is no deity, [and who] embraces all things within His knowledge!" ‹98›

قَالَ يَبْنَؤُمَّ لَا تَأْخُذْ بِلِحْيَتِي وَلَا بِرَأْسِيٓ إِنِّي خَشِيتُ أَن تَقُولَ فَرَّقْتَ بَيْنَ بَنِيٓ إِسْرَٰٓءِيلَ وَلَمْ تَرْقُبْ قَوْلِي ﴿٩٤﴾ قَالَ فَمَا خَطْبُكَ يَٰسَٰمِرِيُّ ﴿٩٥﴾ قَالَ بَصُرْتُ بِمَا لَمْ يَبْصُرُواْ بِهِۦ فَقَبَضْتُ قَبْضَةً مِّنْ أَثَرِ ٱلرَّسُولِ فَنَبَذْتُهَا وَكَذَٰلِكَ سَوَّلَتْ لِي نَفْسِي ﴿٩٦﴾ قَالَ فَٱذْهَبْ فَإِنَّ لَكَ فِي ٱلْحَيَوٰةِ أَن تَقُولَ لَا مِسَاسَ وَإِنَّ لَكَ مَوْعِدًا لَّن تُخْلَفَهُۥ وَٱنظُرْ إِلَىٰٓ إِلَٰهِكَ ٱلَّذِي ظَلْتَ عَلَيْهِ عَاكِفًا لَّنُحَرِّقَنَّهُۥ ثُمَّ لَنَنسِفَنَّهُۥ فِي ٱلْيَمِّ نَسْفًا ﴿٩٧﴾ إِنَّمَآ إِلَٰهُكُمُ ٱللَّهُ ٱلَّذِي لَآ إِلَٰهَ إِلَّا هُوَ وَسِعَ كُلَّ شَيْءٍ عِلْمًا ﴿٩٨﴾

Qāla yab-na ʾumma lā taʾkhudh biliḥyatī wa lā biraʾsīi ʾinnī khashītu añ-taqūla farraqta bayna banīi ʾIsrāaʾīla wa lam tarqub qawlī. ﴿94﴾ Qāla famā khaṭbuka yā Sāmiriyy. ﴿95﴾ Qāla baṣurtu bimā lam yabṣurū bihī faqabaḍtu qabḍatam-min ʾatharir-Rasūli fanabadhtuhā wa kadhālika sawwalat lī nafsī. ﴿96﴾ Qāla fadhhab faʾinna laka fil-ḥayāti ʾañ-taqūla lā misās. Wa ʾinna laka mawʿidal-lañ-tukhlafah. Wañ-ẓur ʾilāa ʾilāhikal-ladhī ẓalta ʿalayhi ʿākifā. Lanuḥarriqannahū thumma lanañsifannahū fil-yammi nasfā. ﴿97﴾ ʾInnamāa ʾIlāhukumul-lāhul-ladhī lāa ʾilāha ʾillā Huwa wasiʿa kulla shayʾin ʿilmā. ﴿98﴾

79 See 7 : 150.

80 Lit., "to my word" or "to what I had said" – evidently, about the importance of keeping the people united (Zamakhsharī).

81 It is to be noted that the verb *baṣura* (lit., "he became seeing") has the tropical significance of "he perceived [something] mentally" or "he gained insight" or "he understood". Hence, Abū Muslim al-Iṣfahānī (whose interpretation of the whole of this verse Rāzī analyzes and finds most convincing) explains the above phrase as meaning, "I realized what they [i.e., the rest of the people] did not realize – namely, that some of thy beliefs, O Moses, were wrong". It would seem that the Samaritan objected to the idea of a transcendental, imperceivable God, and thought that the people ought to have something more "tangible" to believe in. (See also next note.)

82 Contrary to the fanciful interpretations advanced by some of the other commentators, Abū Muslim (as quoted by Rāzī) explains the term *athar* (lit., "vestige" or "trace") in its tropical sense of the "practices and sayings" or – collectively – the "teachings" of any person, and particularly of a prophet; thus, he makes it clear that the phrase *qabaḍtu qabḍatan min athari 'r-rasūl fa-nabadhtuhā* signifies "I took hold of a handful [i.e., "something"] of the teachings of the Apostle, and discarded it": it being understood that "the Apostle" referred to by the Samaritan in the third person is Moses himself. (As already mentioned in the preceding note, Rāzī unreservedly subscribes to Abū Muslim's interpretation of this passage.) In my opinion, the Samaritan's rejection of a part of Moses' teachings is meant to explain the subconscious tendency underlying all forms of idolatry and of the attribution of divine qualities to things or beings other than God: a futile, self-deceiving hope of bringing the Unperceivable closer to one's limited perception by creating a tangible "image" of the Divine Being or, at least, of something that could be conceived as His "emanation". Inasmuch as all such endeavours obscure rather than illuminate man's understanding of God, they defeat their own purpose and destroy the misguided devotee's spiritual potential: and this is undoubtedly the purport of the story of the golden calf as given in the Qurʾān.

83 Lit., "no touching" – a metaphorical description of the loneliness and the social ostracism in which he would henceforth find himself.

84 Lit., "there is for thee an appointment which thou canst not fail to keep".

THUS DO WE relate unto thee some of the stories of what happened in the past; and [thus] have We vouchsafed unto thee, out of Our grace, a reminder.[85] ‹99›
All who shall turn away from it will, verily, bear a [heavy] burden on the Day of Resurrection: ‹100› they will abide in this [state], and grievous for them will be the weight [of that burden] on the Day of Resurrection ‹101› – on the Day when the trumpet is blown: for on that Day We will assemble all such as had been lost in sin, their eyes dimmed[86] [by terror], ‹102› whispering unto one another, "You have spent but ten [days on earth]. . . ."[87] ‹103›
[But] We know best[88] what they will be saying when the most perceptive of them shall say, "You have spent [there] but one day!" ‹104›

AND THEY WILL ask thee about [what will happen to] the mountains [when this world comes to an end].
Say, then: "My Sustainer will scatter them far and wide, ‹105› and leave the earth[89] level and bare, ‹106› [so that] thou wilt see no curve thereon, and no ruggedness."[90] ‹107›
On that Day, all will follow the Summoning Voice from which there will be no escape;[91] and all sounds will be hushed before the Most Gracious, and thou wilt hear nothing but a faint sough in the air. ‹108›

كَذَٰلِكَ نَقُصُّ عَلَيْكَ مِنْ أَنۢبَآءِ مَا قَدْ سَبَقَ ۚ وَقَدْ ءَاتَيْنَٰكَ مِن لَّدُنَّا
ذِكْرًا ﴿99﴾ مَّنْ أَعْرَضَ عَنْهُ فَإِنَّهُۥ يَحْمِلُ يَوْمَ ٱلْقِيَٰمَةِ وِزْرًا ﴿100﴾
خَٰلِدِينَ فِيهِ ۖ وَسَآءَ لَهُمْ يَوْمَ ٱلْقِيَٰمَةِ حِمْلًا ﴿101﴾ يَوْمَ يُنفَخُ فِى ٱلصُّورِ ۚ
وَنَحْشُرُ ٱلْمُجْرِمِينَ يَوْمَئِذٍ زُرْقًا ﴿102﴾ يَتَخَٰفَتُونَ بَيْنَهُمْ إِن لَّبِثْتُمْ إِلَّا
عَشْرًا ﴿103﴾ نَّحْنُ أَعْلَمُ بِمَا يَقُولُونَ إِذْ يَقُولُ أَمْثَلُهُمْ طَرِيقَةً إِن لَّبِثْتُمْ إِلَّا
يَوْمًا ﴿104﴾ وَيَسْـَٔلُونَكَ عَنِ ٱلْجِبَالِ فَقُلْ يَنسِفُهَا رَبِّى نَسْفًا ﴿105﴾ فَيَذَرُهَا
قَاعًا صَفْصَفًا ﴿106﴾ لَّا تَرَىٰ فِيهَا عِوَجًا وَلَآ أَمْتًا ﴿107﴾ يَوْمَئِذٍ يَتَّبِعُونَ
ٱلدَّاعِىَ لَا عِوَجَ لَهُۥ ۖ وَخَشَعَتِ ٱلْأَصْوَاتُ لِلرَّحْمَٰنِ فَلَا تَسْمَعُ إِلَّا
هَمْسًا ﴿108﴾

Kadhālika naquṣṣu ᶜalayka min ʾambāaʾi mā qad sabaqa wa qad ʾātaynāka mil-ladunnā Dhikrā. (99) Man ʾaᶜraḍa ᶜanhu faʾinnahū yaḥmilu Yawmal-Qiyāmati wizrā. (100) Khālidīna fīhi wa sāaʾa lahum Yawmal-Qiyāmati ḥimlā. (101) Yawma yuñfakhu fiṣ-ṣūri wa naḥshurul-mujrimīna yawmaʾidhiñ-zurqā. (102) Yatakhāfatūna baynahum ʾil-labithtum ʾillā ᶜashrā. (103) Naḥnu ʾaᶜlamu bimā yaqūlūna ʾidh yaqūlu ʾamthaluhum ṭarīqatan ʾil-labithtum ʾillā yawmā. (104) Wa yasʾalūnaka ᶜanil-jibāli faqul yañsifuhā Rabbī nasfā. (105) Fayadharuhā qāᶜañ-ṣafṣafā. (106) Lā tarā fīhā ᶜiwajañw-wa lāa ʾamtā. (107) Yawmaʾidhiñy-yattabiᶜūnad-dāᶜiya lā ᶜiwaja lahū wa khashaᶜatil-ʾaṣwātu lirRaḥmāni falā tasmaᶜu ʾillā hamsā. (108)

---

85 The adverb *kadhālika* ("thus") which introduces this verse is meant to stress the *purpose* of all Qurʾanic references to past events – be they historical or legendary – as well as the *manner* in which the relevant stories are treated. Since the purpose underlying every Qurʾanic narrative is, invariably, the illustration of certain fundamental truths, the narrative as such is often condensed and elliptic, omitting all that has no direct bearing on the point or points which the Qurʾān means to bring out. The term "reminder" alludes to the unceasing guidance which God offers to man through His revelations.

86 Lit., "blue [of eye]" – i.e., as if their eyes were covered with a bluish, opaque film.

87 As in several other places in the Qurʾān (e.g., in 2 : 259, 17 : 52, 18 : 19, 23 : 112-113, 30 : 55, 79 : 46, etc.), this and the next verse touch upon the illusory character of man's consciousness of "time" and, thus, upon the relativity of the *concept* of "time" as such. The number "ten" is often used in Arabic to denote "a few" (Rāzī).

88 Signifying, in this context, "We *alone* understand fully".

89 Lit., "leave it" – the pronoun relating, by implication, to the earth (Zamakhsharī and Rāzī).

90 In the eschatology of the Qurʾān, the "end of the world" does not signify an annihilation – i.e., reduction to nothingness – of the physical universe but, rather, its fundamental, cataclysmic transformation into something that men cannot now visualize. This is brought out in many allegorical allusions to the Last Day, e.g., in 14 : 48, which speaks of "the Day when the earth shall be changed into another earth, as shall be the heavens".

91 Lit., "the caller in whom there will be no deviation (*lā ᶜiwaja lahu*)" – i.e., the summons to the Last Judgment.

On that Day, intercession shall be of no avail [to any] save him in whose case the Most Gracious will have granted leave therefor, and whose word [of faith] He will have accepted:[92] ‹109› [for] He knows all that lies open before men and all that is hidden from them,[93] whereas they cannot encompass Him with their knowledge. ‹110›

And [on that Day] all faces will be humbled before the Ever-Living, the Self-Subsistent Fount of All Being; and undone shall be he who bears [a burden of] evildoing[94] ‹111› – whereas anyone who will have done [whatever he could] of righteous deeds, and was a believer withal, need have no fear of being wronged or deprived [of aught of his merit].[95] ‹112›

AND THUS[96] have We bestowed from on high this [divine writ] as a discourse in the Arabic tongue,[97] and have given therein many facets to all manner of warnings, so that men might remain conscious of Us, or that it give rise to a new awareness in them.[98] ‹113›

[Know,] then, [that] God is sublimely exalted, the Ultimate Sovereign, the Ultimate Truth:[99] and [knowing this,] do not ap-

يَوۡمَئِذٖ لَّا تَنفَعُ ٱلشَّفَٰعَةُ إِلَّا مَنۡ أَذِنَ لَهُ ٱلرَّحۡمَٰنُ وَرَضِيَ لَهُۥ قَوۡلٗا ١٠٩
يَعۡلَمُ مَا بَيۡنَ أَيۡدِيهِمۡ وَمَا خَلۡفَهُمۡ وَلَا يُحِيطُونَ بِهِۦ عِلۡمٗا ١١٠ ۞
وَعَنَتِ ٱلۡوُجُوهُ لِلۡحَيِّ ٱلۡقَيُّومِۖ وَقَدۡ خَابَ مَنۡ حَمَلَ ظُلۡمٗا ١١١ وَمَن
يَعۡمَلۡ مِنَ ٱلصَّٰلِحَٰتِ وَهُوَ مُؤۡمِنٞ فَلَا يَخَافُ ظُلۡمٗا وَلَا هَضۡمٗا ١١٢
وَكَذَٰلِكَ أَنزَلۡنَٰهُ قُرۡءَانًا عَرَبِيّٗا وَصَرَّفۡنَا فِيهِ مِنَ ٱلۡوَعِيدِ لَعَلَّهُمۡ
يَتَّقُونَ أَوۡ يُحۡدِثُ لَهُمۡ ذِكۡرٗا ١١٣ فَتَعَٰلَى ٱللَّهُ ٱلۡمَلِكُ ٱلۡحَقُّۗ وَلَا تَعۡجَلۡ

Yawmaʾidhil-lā tañfaʿush-shafāʿatu ʾillā man ʾadhina lahur-Raḥmānu wa raḍiya lahū qawlā. (109) Yaʿlamu mā bayna ʾaydīhim wa mā khalfahum wa lā yuḥīṭūna bihī ʿilmā. (110) ◈ Wa ʿanatil-wujūhu lilḤayyil-Qayyūmi wa qad khāba man ḥamala ẓulmā. (111) Wa mañy-yaʿmal minaṣ-ṣāliḥāti wa huwa muʾminuñ-falā yakhāfu ẓulmañw-wa lā haḍmā. (112) Wa kadhālika ʾañzalnāhu Qurʾānan ʿarabiyyañw-wa ṣarrafnā fīhi minal-waʿīdi laʿallahum yattaqūna ʾaw yuḥdithu lahum dhikrā. (113) Fataʿālal-lāhul-Malikul-Ḥaqq. Wa lā taʿjal

92 Regarding the Qurʾanic concept of "intercession" on the Day of Judgment, see note 7 on 10 : 3. The "word [of faith]" referred to towards the end of the above verse is – according to Ibn ʿAbbās (as quoted by Baghawī) – a metonym for the belief that "there is no deity save God", i.e., the realization of His oneness and uniqueness. See also 19 : 87 and the corresponding note 74.

93 For an explanation of this phrase – which occurs in exactly the same wording in 2 : 255, 21 : 28 and 22 : 76 as well – see *sūrah* 2, note 247.

94 I.e., evildoing which has not been atoned for by repentance before death (Rāzī). In this particular context, it may be an allusion to the rejection of God's guidance – His "reminder" – spoken of in verses 99-101.

95 Lit., "no fear of [any] wrong" – i.e., punishment for any sin which he may have contemplated but not committed – "and neither of a diminution", i.e., of his merit: cf. the twice-repeated statement in 16 : 96-97 that the righteous shall be recompensed in the hereafter "in accordance with the *best* that they ever did".

96 As in verse 99 above – with which this passage connects – the adverb *kadhālika* ("thus") refers to the method and purpose of the Qurʾān.

97 Lit., "as an Arabic discourse (*qurʾān*)". See, in particular, 12 : 2, 13 : 37, 14 : 4 and 19 : 97, as well as the corresponding notes.

98 Lit., "so that they might be [or "remain"] God-conscious, or that it create for them a remembrance", i.e., of God. The verb *aḥdatha* signifies "he brought [something] into existence", i.e., newly or for the first time, while the noun *dhikr* denotes "remembrance" as well as the "presence [of something] in the mind" (Rāghib), i.e., awareness.

99 Whenever the noun *al-ḥaqq* is used as a designation of God, it signifies "the Truth" in the absolute, intrinsic sense, eternally and immutably existing beyond the ephemeral, changing phenomena of His creation: hence, "the Ultimate Truth". God's attribute of *al-malik*, on the other hand, denotes His absolute sway over all that exists and can, therefore, be suitably rendered as "the Ultimate Sovereign".

proach the Qurʾān in haste,[100] ere it has been revealed unto thee in full, but [always] say: "O my Sustainer, cause me to grow in knowledge!"[101] ‹114›

AND, INDEED, long ago did We impose Our commandment on Adam;[102] but he forgot it, and We found no firmness of purpose in him. ‹115›

For [thus it was:] when We told the angels, "Prostrate yourselves before Adam!" – they all prostrated themselves, save Iblīs, who refused [to do it];[103] ‹116› and thereupon We said: "O Adam! Verily, this is a foe unto thee and thy wife: so let him not drive the two of you out of this garden and render thee unhappy.[104] ‹117› Behold, it is provided for thee that thou shalt not hunger here or feel naked,[105] ‹118› and that thou shalt not thirst here or suffer from the heat of the sun." ‹119›

But Satan whispered unto him, saying: "O Adam! Shall I lead thee to the tree of life eternal, and [thus] to a kingdom that will never decay?"[106] ‹120›

بِٱلْقُرْءَانِ مِن قَبْلِ أَن يُقْضَىٰٓ إِلَيْكَ وَحْيُهُۥ ۖ وَقُل رَّبِّ زِدْنِى عِلْمًا ﴿١١٤﴾
وَلَقَدْ عَهِدْنَآ إِلَىٰٓ ءَادَمَ مِن قَبْلُ فَنَسِىَ وَلَمْ نَجِدْ لَهُۥ عَزْمًا ﴿١١٥﴾ وَإِذْ قُلْنَا
لِلْمَلَٰٓئِكَةِ ٱسْجُدُوا۟ لِءَادَمَ فَسَجَدُوٓا۟ إِلَّآ إِبْلِيسَ أَبَىٰ ﴿١١٦﴾ فَقُلْنَا يَٰٓـَٔادَمُ إِنَّ
هَٰذَا عَدُوٌّ لَّكَ وَلِزَوْجِكَ فَلَا يُخْرِجَنَّكُمَا مِنَ ٱلْجَنَّةِ فَتَشْقَىٰٓ ﴿١١٧﴾ إِنَّ لَكَ
أَلَّا تَجُوعَ فِيهَا وَلَا تَعْرَىٰ ﴿١١٨﴾ وَأَنَّكَ لَا تَظْمَؤُا۟ فِيهَا وَلَا تَضْحَىٰ ﴿١١٩﴾
فَوَسْوَسَ إِلَيْهِ ٱلشَّيْطَٰنُ قَالَ يَٰٓـَٔادَمُ هَلْ أَدُلُّكَ عَلَىٰ شَجَرَةِ ٱلْخُلْدِ وَمُلْكٍ
لَّا يَبْلَىٰ ﴿١٢٠﴾

bilQurʾāni miñ-qabli ʾañy-yuqḍāa ʾilayka waḥyuhū wa qur-Rabbi zidnī ʿilmā. (114) Wa laqad ʿahidnāa ʾilāa ʾĀdama miñ-qablu fanasiya wa lam najid lahū ʿazmā. (115) Wa ʾidh qulnā lilMalāaʾikatis-judū liʾĀdama fasajadūu ʾillāa ʾIblīsa ʾabā. (116) Faqulnā yāa ʾĀdamu ʾinna hādhā ʿaduwwul-laka wa lizawjika falā yukhrijannakumā minal-jannati fatashqā. (117) ʾInna laka ʾallā tajūʿa fīhā wa lā taʿrā. (118) Wa ʾannaka lā taẓmaʾu fīhā wa lā taḍḥā. (119) Fawaswasa ʾilayhish-Shayṭānu qāla yāa ʾĀdamu hal ʾadulluka ʿalā shajaratil-khuldi wa mulkil-lā yablā. (120)

100 Lit., "be not hasty with the Qurʾān" (see next note).

101 Although it is very probable that – as most of the classical commentators point out – this exhortation was in the first instance addressed to the Prophet Muḥammad, there is no doubt that it applies to every person, at all times, who reads the Qurʾān. The idea underlying the above verse may be summed up thus: Since the Qurʾān is the Word of God, all its component parts – phrases, sentences, verses and *sūrahs* – form one integral, coordinated whole (cf. the last sentence of 25 : 32 and the corresponding note 27). Hence, if one is really intent on understanding the Qurʾanic message, one must beware of a "hasty approach" – that is to say, of drawing hasty conclusions from isolated verses or sentences taken out of their context – but should, rather, allow *the whole* of the Qurʾān to be revealed to one's mind before attempting to interpret single aspects of its message. (See also 75 : 16-19 and the corresponding notes.)

102 The relevant divine commandment – or, rather, warning – is spelled out in verse 117. The present passage connects with the statement in verse 99, "Thus do We relate unto thee some of the stories of what happened in the past", and is meant to show that negligence of spiritual truths is one of the recurrent characteristics of the human race (Rāzī), which is symbolized here – as in many other places in the Qurʾān – by Adam.

103 See 2 : 30-34 and the corresponding notes, especially 23, 25 and 26, as well as note 31 on 15 : 41. Since – as I have shown in those notes – the faculty of conceptual thinking is man's outstanding endowment, his "forgetting" God's commandment – resulting from a lack of all "firmness of purpose" in the domain of ethics – is an evidence of the moral weakness characteristic of the human race (cf. 4 : 28 – "man has been created weak"): and this, in its turn, explains man's dependence on unceasing divine guidance, as pointed out in verse 113 above.

104 Lit., "so that thou wilt become unhappy". Regarding the significance of "the garden" spoken of here, see *sūrah* 2, note 27.

105 Lit., "*be naked*": but in view of the statement in verse 121 (as well as in 7 : 22) to the effect that only after their fall from grace did Adam and Eve become "conscious of their nakedness", it is but logical to assume that the words "that thou shalt not . . . be naked" have a spiritual significance, implying that man, in his original state of innocence, would not *feel* naked despite all absence of clothing. (For the deeper implications of this allegory, see note 14 on 7 : 20.)

106 This symbolic tree is designated in the Bible as "the tree of life" and "the tree of knowledge of good and evil" (Genesis ii, 9), while in the above Qurʾanic account Satan speaks of it as "the tree of life eternal (*al-khuld*)". Seeing that Adam and Eve did not achieve immortality despite their tasting the forbidden fruit, it is obvious that Satan's

فَأَكَلَا مِنْهَا فَبَدَتْ لَهُمَا سَوْءَٰتُهُمَا وَطَفِقَا يَخْصِفَانِ عَلَيْهِمَا مِن
وَرَقِ ٱلْجَنَّةِ وَعَصَىٰٓ ءَادَمُ رَبَّهُۥ فَغَوَىٰ ﴿١٢١﴾ ثُمَّ ٱجْتَبَٰهُ رَبُّهُۥ فَتَابَ
عَلَيْهِ وَهَدَىٰ ﴿١٢٢﴾ قَالَ ٱهْبِطَا مِنْهَا جَمِيعًۢا بَعْضُكُمْ لِبَعْضٍ عَدُوٌّ
فَإِمَّا يَأْتِيَنَّكُم مِّنِّى هُدًى فَمَنِ ٱتَّبَعَ هُدَاىَ فَلَا يَضِلُّ وَلَا يَشْقَىٰ ﴿١٢٣﴾
وَمَنْ أَعْرَضَ عَن ذِكْرِى فَإِنَّ لَهُۥ مَعِيشَةً ضَنكًا وَنَحْشُرُهُۥ يَوْمَ
ٱلْقِيَٰمَةِ أَعْمَىٰ ﴿١٢٤﴾ قَالَ رَبِّ لِمَ حَشَرْتَنِىٓ أَعْمَىٰ وَقَدْ كُنتُ
بَصِيرًا ﴿١٢٥﴾ قَالَ كَذَٰلِكَ أَتَتْكَ ءَايَٰتُنَا فَنَسِيتَهَا ۖ وَكَذَٰلِكَ ٱلْيَوْمَ
تُنسَىٰ ﴿١٢٦﴾ وَكَذَٰلِكَ نَجْزِى مَنْ أَسْرَفَ وَلَمْ يُؤْمِنۢ بِـَٔايَٰتِ رَبِّهِۦ

And so the two ate [of the fruit] thereof: and thereupon they became conscious of their nakedness and began to cover themselves with pieced-together leaves from the garden. And [thus] did Adam disobey his Sustainer, and thus did he fall into grievous error.[107] «121»
Thereafter, [however,] his Sustainer elected him [for His grace], and accepted his repentance, and bestowed His guidance upon him, «122» saying: "Down with you all[108] from this [state of innocence, and be henceforth] enemies unto one another! None the less, there shall most certainly come unto you guidance from Me: and he who follows My guidance will not go astray, and neither will he be unhappy. «123» But as for him who shall turn away from remembering Me – his shall be a life of narrow scope;[109] and on the Day of Resurrection We shall raise him up blind." «124»
[And so, on Resurrection Day, the sinner] will ask: "O my Sustainer! Why hast Thou raised me up blind, whereas [on earth] I was endowed with sight?" «125»
[God] will reply: "Thus it is: there came unto thee Our messages, but thou wert oblivious of them; and thus shalt thou be today consigned to oblivion!" «126»
For, thus shall We recompense him who wastes his own self[110] and does not believe in his Sustainer's messages:

Faʾakalā minhā fabadat lahumā sawʾātuhumā wa ṭafiqā yakhṣifāni ʿalayhimā miñw-waraqil-jannah. Wa ʿaṣāa ʾĀdamu Rabbahū faghawā. (121) Thummaj-tabāhu Rabbuhū fatāba ʿalayhi wa hadā. (122) Qālah-biṭā minhā jamīʿam-baʿḍukum libaʿḍin ʿaduww. Faʾimmā yaʾtiyannakum-minnī hudañ-famanit-tabaʿa hudāya falā yaḍillu wa lā yashqā. (123) Wa man ʾaʿraḍa ʿañ-Dhikrī faʾinna lahū maʿīshatañ-ḍañkañw-wa naḥshuruhū Yawmal-Qiyāmati ʾaʿmā. (124) Qāla Rabbi lima ḥashartanīi ʾaʿmā wa qad kuñtu baṣīrā. (125) Qāla kadhālika ʾatatka ʾĀyātunā fanasītahā; wa kadhālikal-Yawma tuñsā. (126) Wa kadhālika najzī man ʾasrafa wa lam yuʾmim-biʾĀyāti Rabbih.

suggestion was, as it always is, deceptive. On the other hand, the Qurʾān tells us nothing about the real nature of that "tree" beyond pointing out that it was *Satan* who described it – falsely – as "the tree of immortality": and so we may assume that the forbidden tree is simply an allegory of the limits which the Creator has set to man's desires and actions: limits beyond which he may not go without offending against his own, God-willed nature. Man's desire for immortality *on earth* implies a wishful denial of death and resurrection, and thus of the ultimate reality of what the Qurʾān describes as "the hereafter" or "the life to come" (*al-ākhirah*). This desire is intimately connected with Satan's insinuation that it is within man's reach to become the master of "a kingdom that will never decay": in other words, to become "free" of all limitations and thus, in the last resort, of the very concept of God – the only concept which endows human life with real meaning and purpose.

107 Regarding the symbolism of Adam and Eve's becoming "conscious of their nakedness", see note 105 above as well as the reference, in 7 : 26-27, to "the garment of God-consciousness", the loss of which made man's ancestors "aware of their nakedness", i.e., of their utter helplessness and, hence, their dependence on God.

108 See *sūrah* 7, note 16.

109 I.e., sterile and spiritually narrow, without any real meaning or purpose: and this, as is indicated in the subsequent clause, will be a source of their suffering in the hereafter.

110 Regarding this rendering of the phrase *man asrafa,* see *sūrah* 10, note 21, in which I have discussed the meaning of the participial noun *musrif,* derived from the same verbal root.

وَلَعَذَابُ ٱلْـَٔاخِرَةِ أَشَدُّ وَأَبْقَىٰٓ ﴿127﴾ أَفَلَمْ يَهْدِ لَهُمْ كَمْ أَهْلَكْنَا قَبْلَهُم
مِّنَ ٱلْقُرُونِ يَمْشُونَ فِى مَسَٰكِنِهِمْ ۗ إِنَّ فِى ذَٰلِكَ لَءَايَٰتٍ لِّأُو۟لِى ٱلنُّهَىٰ ﴿128﴾
وَلَوْلَا كَلِمَةٌ سَبَقَتْ مِن رَّبِّكَ لَكَانَ لِزَامًا وَأَجَلٌ مُّسَمًّى ﴿129﴾ فَٱصْبِرْ عَلَىٰ
مَا يَقُولُونَ وَسَبِّحْ بِحَمْدِ رَبِّكَ قَبْلَ طُلُوعِ ٱلشَّمْسِ وَقَبْلَ غُرُوبِهَا ۖ وَمِنْ
ءَانَآئِ ٱلَّيْلِ فَسَبِّحْ وَأَطْرَافَ ٱلنَّهَارِ لَعَلَّكَ تَرْضَىٰ ﴿130﴾ وَلَا تَمُدَّنَّ
عَيْنَيْكَ إِلَىٰ مَا مَتَّعْنَا بِهِۦٓ أَزْوَٰجًا مِّنْهُمْ زَهْرَةَ ٱلْحَيَوٰةِ ٱلدُّنْيَا لِنَفْتِنَهُمْ
فِيهِ ۚ وَرِزْقُ رَبِّكَ خَيْرٌ وَأَبْقَىٰ ﴿131﴾

wa laᶜadhābul-ᵓĀkhirati ᵓashaddu wa ᵓabqā. (127)
ᵓAfalam yahdi lahum kam ᵓahlaknā qablahum-minal-qurūni yamshūna fī masākinihim. ᵓInna fī dhālika laᵓĀyātil-liᵓulin-nuhā. (128)
Wa lawlā Kalimatuñ-sabaqat mir-Rabbika lakāna lizāmañw-wa ᵓajalum-musammā. (129)
Faṣbir ᶜalā mā yaqūlūna wa sabbiḥ biḥamdi Rabbika qabla ṭulūᶜish-shamsi wa qabla ghurūbihā; wa min ᵓānāaᵓil-layli fasabbiḥ wa ᵓaṭrāfan-nahāri laᶜallaka tarḍā. (130)
Wa lā tamuddanna ᶜaynayka ᵓilā mā mattaᶜnā bihīi ᵓazwājam-minhum zahratal-ḥayātid-dunyā linaftinahum fīh. Wa rizqu Rabbika khayruñw-wa ᵓabqā. (131)

and, indeed, the suffering [of such sinners] in the life to come shall be most severe and most enduring! ‹127›

CAN, THEN, they [who reject the truth] learn no lesson by recalling how many a generation We have destroyed before their time,[111] – [people] in whose dwelling-places they [themselves now] walk about? In this, behold, there are messages indeed for those who are endowed with reason! ‹128›

Now were it not for a decree that has already gone forth from thy Sustainer, setting a term[112] [for each sinner's repentance], it would inescapably follow [that all who sin must be doomed at once].[113] ‹129›

Hence, bear with patience whatever they [who deny the truth] may say, and extol thy Sustainer's limitless glory and praise Him before the rising of the sun and before its setting; and extol His glory, too, during some of the hours of the night as well as during the hours of the day,[114] so that thou might attain to happiness. ‹130›

And never turn thine eyes [with longing] towards whatever splendour of this world's life We may have allowed so many others[115] to enjoy in order that We might test them thereby: for the sustenance which thy Sustainer provides [for thee] is better and more enduring.[116] ‹131›

---

111 Lit., "Is it, then, no guidance for them how many a generation . . .", etc. It is to be borne in mind that, in Qurᵓanic usage, the noun *qarn* signifies not only "a generation", but also – and rather more often – "people belonging to one particular epoch", i.e., "a civilization" in the historical sense of this term.

112 Lit., "and a term set [by Him]". This phrase, placed in the original at the end of the sentence, connects – as most of the classical commentators point out – with the *opening clause* of this verse, and has been rendered accordingly.

113 Cf. 10 : 11 and 16 : 61.

114 Lit., "at the sides [or "extremities"] of the day". See in this connection also 11 : 114 and the corresponding note 145.

115 Lit., "groups [or "kinds"] of them" (*azwājan minhum*). According to most of the commentators, this relates to the deniers of the truth spoken of in the preceding passages; but since the above injunction has obviously a wider purport, condemning envy in general, I have rendered this expression as "so many others".

116 Implying that whatever God grants a person is an outcome of divine wisdom and, therefore, truly appropriate to the destiny which God has decreed for that person. Alternatively, the phrase may be understood as referring to the life to come and the spiritual sustenance which God bestows upon the righteous.

And bid thy people to pray, and persevere therein. [But remember:] We do not ask thee to provide sustenance [for Us]:[117] it is We who provide sustenance for thee. And the future belongs to the God-conscious.[118] ⟨132⟩

NOW THEY [who are blind to the truth] are wont to say, "If [Muḥammad] would but produce for us a miracle from his Sustainer!"[119] [But] has there not come unto them a clear evidence [of the truth of this divine writ] in what is [to be found] in the earlier scriptures?[120] ⟨133⟩

For [thus it is:] had We destroyed them by means of a chastisement ere this [divine writ was revealed], they would indeed [be justified to] say [on Judgment Day]: "O our Sustainer! If only Thou hadst sent an apostle unto us, we would have followed Thy messages rather than be humiliated and disgraced [in the hereafter]!"[121] ⟨134⟩

Say: "Every one is hopefully waiting [for what the future may bring]: [122] wait, then, [for the Day of Judgment –] for then you will come to know as to who has followed the even path, and who has found guidance!" ⟨135⟩

وَأْمُرْ أَهْلَكَ بِالصَّلَوٰةِ وَاصْطَبِرْ عَلَيْهَا ۖ لَا نَسْـَٔلُكَ رِزْقًا ۖ نَّحْنُ نَرْزُقُكَ ۗ
وَالْعَٰقِبَةُ لِلتَّقْوَىٰ ﴿١٣٢﴾ وَقَالُوا لَوْلَا يَأْتِينَا بِـَٔايَةٍ مِّن رَّبِّهِۦٓ ۚ أَوَلَمْ تَأْتِهِم
بَيِّنَةُ مَا فِى الصُّحُفِ الْأُولَىٰ ﴿١٣٣﴾ وَلَوْ أَنَّآ أَهْلَكْنَٰهُم بِعَذَابٍ مِّن قَبْلِهِۦ
لَقَالُوا رَبَّنَا لَوْلَآ أَرْسَلْتَ إِلَيْنَا رَسُولًا فَنَتَّبِعَ ءَايَٰتِكَ مِن قَبْلِ أَن نَّذِلَّ
وَنَخْزَىٰ ﴿١٣٤﴾ قُلْ كُلٌّ مُّتَرَبِّصٌ فَتَرَبَّصُوا ۖ فَسَتَعْلَمُونَ مَنْ أَصْحَٰبُ
الصِّرَٰطِ السَّوِىِّ وَمَنِ اهْتَدَىٰ ﴿١٣٥﴾

Waʾ-mur ʾahlaka bisṢalāti waṣ-ṭabir ʿalayhā. Lā nasʾaluka rizqañ-Naḥnu narzuquk. Wal-ʿāqibatu lit-taqwā. (132) Wa qālū lawlā yaʾtīnā biʾĀyatim-mir-Rabbih. ʾAwalam taʾtihim bayyinatu mā fiṣ-Ṣuḥufil-ʾūlā. (133) Wa law ʾannāa ʾahlaknāhum biʿadhābim-miñ-qablihī laqālū Rabbanā lawlāa ʾarsalta ʾilaynā Rasūlañ-fanattabiʿa ʾĀyātika miñ-qabli ʾañ-nadhilla wa nakhzā. (134) Qul kullum-mutarabbiṣuñ-fatarabbaṣū; fasataʿlamūna man ʾaṣḥābuṣ-ṣirāṭis-sawiyyi wa manih-tadā. (135)

117 My interpolation of the words "for Us" is based on Rāzī's interpretation of the above sentence: "God makes it clear that He has enjoined this [i.e., prayer] upon men for their own benefit alone, inasmuch as He Himself is sublimely exalted above any [need of] benefits." In other words, prayer must *not* be conceived as a kind of tribute to a "jealous God" – as the Old Testament, in its present corrupted form, frequently describes Him – but solely as a spiritual benefit for the person who prays.

118 Lit., "to God-consciousness".

119 I.e.. in proof of his prophetic mission: cf. 6 : 109 and many other instances in which the deniers of the truth are spoken of as making their belief in the Qurʾanic message dependent on tangible "miracles".

120 I.e., "Does not the Qurʾān express the same fundamental truths as were expressed in the revelations granted to the earlier prophets?" Beyond this, the above rhetorical question contains an allusion to the predictions of the advent of Muḥammad, to be found in the earlier scriptures. e.g., in Deuteronomy xviii, 15 and 18 (discussed in my note 33 on 2 : 42) or in John xiv, 16, xv, 26 and xvi, 7, where Jesus speaks of the "Comforter" who is to come after him. (Regarding this latter prediction, see my note on 61 : 6.)

121 Cf. 6 : 131, 15 : 4 or 26 : 208-209, where it is stressed that God never punishes man for any wrong committed in ignorance of what constitutes right and wrong in the moral sense – i.e., before making it possible for him to avail himself of divine guidance.

122 I.e., human nature is such that no man, whatever his persuasion or condition, can ever cease to hope that the way of life chosen by him will prove to have been the right way.

The Twenty-First Sūrah

Al-ʾAmbiyāaʾ (The Prophets)

Mecca Period

THE MAIN theme of this *sūrah* – which according to the *ʿItqān* belongs to the last group of the Meccan revelations – is the stress on the oneness, uniqueness and transcendence of God and on the fact that this truth has always been the core of all prophetic revelation, the essence of "all that you ought to bear in mind" (verse 10), and which man only too often forgets: for "the deaf [of heart] will not hearken to this call, however often they are warned" (verse 45), and "but listen to it with playful amusement, their hearts set on passing delights" (verses 2-3).

The repeated allusions to some of the prophets of old, all of whom preached the same fundamental truth, provide the title of this *sūrah*. The stories of those prophets are meant to illustrate the continuity and intrinsic unity of all divine revelation and of man's religious experience: hence, addressing all who believe in Him, God says, "Verily, this community of yours is one single community, since I am the Sustainer of you all" (verse 92), thus postulating the brotherhood of all true believers, whatever their outward designation, as a logical corollary of their belief in Him – the belief that "your God is the One and Only God" (verse 108).

سورة الأنبياء مكية -21-
وآياتها اثنتا عشرة ومائة

IN THE NAME OF GOD, THE MOST GRACIOUS, THE DISPENSER OF GRACE:

CLOSER DRAWS unto men their reckoning: and yet they remain stubbornly heedless [of its approach].[1] ‹1›
Whenever there comes unto them any new reminder from their Sustainer, they but listen to it with playful amusement,[2] ‹2›
their hearts set on passing delights; yet they who are [thus] bent on wrongdoing conceal their innermost thoughts[3] [when they say to one another], "Is this [Muḥammad] anything but a mortal like yourselves? Will you, then, yield to [his] spellbinding eloquence with your eyes open?"[4] ‹3›
Say:[5] "My Sustainer knows whatever is spoken in heaven and on earth; and He alone is all-hearing, all-knowing." ‹4›
"Nay," they say, "[Muḥammad propounds] the most involved and confusing of dreams!"[6] – "Nay, but he has invented [all] this!" – "Nay, but he is [only] a poet!" – [and,] "Let him, then, come unto us with a miracle, just as those [prophets] of old were sent [with miracles]!" ‹5›

حزب 33
جزء 17

بِسۡمِ ٱللَّهِ ٱلرَّحۡمَٰنِ ٱلرَّحِيمِ

ٱقۡتَرَبَ لِلنَّاسِ حِسَابُهُمۡ وَهُمۡ فِي غَفۡلَةٖ مُّعۡرِضُونَ ١ مَا يَأۡتِيهِم مِّن ذِكۡرٖ
مِّن رَّبِّهِم مُّحۡدَثٍ إِلَّا ٱسۡتَمَعُوهُ وَهُمۡ يَلۡعَبُونَ ٢ لَاهِيَةٗ قُلُوبُهُمۡۗ وَأَسَرُّواْ
ٱلنَّجۡوَى ٱلَّذِينَ ظَلَمُواْ هَلۡ هَٰذَآ إِلَّا بَشَرٞ مِّثۡلُكُمۡۖ أَفَتَأۡتُونَ ٱلسِّحۡرَ
وَأَنتُمۡ تُبۡصِرُونَ ٣ قَالَ رَبِّي يَعۡلَمُ ٱلۡقَوۡلَ فِي ٱلسَّمَآءِ وَٱلۡأَرۡضِۖ وَهُوَ
ٱلسَّمِيعُ ٱلۡعَلِيمُ ٤ بَلۡ قَالُوٓاْ أَضۡغَٰثُ أَحۡلَٰمِۭ بَلِ ٱفۡتَرَىٰهُ بَلۡ هُوَ شَاعِرٞ
فَلۡيَأۡتِنَا بِـَٔايَةٖ كَمَآ أُرۡسِلَ ٱلۡأَوَّلُونَ ٥

Bismil-lāhir-Raḥmānir-Raḥīm.
ᵓIqtaraba linnāsi ḥisābuhum wa hum fī ghaflatim-muᶜriḍūn. (1) Mā yaᵓtīhim-miñ-Dhikrim-mir-Rabbihim-muḥdathin ᵓillas-tamaᶜūhu wa hum yalᶜabūn. (2) Lāhiyatañ-qulūbuhum. Wa ᵓasarrun-najwal-ladhīna ẓalamū hal hādhāa ᵓillā basharum-mithlukum. ᵓAfataᵓtūnas-siḥra wa ᵓañtum tubṣirūn. (3) Qāla Rabbī yaᶜlamul-qawla fis-samāaᵓi wal-ᵓarḍi wa Huwas-Samīᶜul-ᶜAlīm. (4) Bal qālūu ᵓaḍghāthu ᵓaḥlāmim-balif-tarāhu bal huwa shāᶜiruñ-falyaᵓtinā biᵓĀyatiñ-kamāa ᵓursilal-ᵓawwalūn. (5)

---

1 Lit., "and yet in [their] heedlessness they are obstinate (*muᶜriḍūn*)".

2 Lit., "while they are playing".

3 See next note.

4 As regards my occasional rendering of *siḥr* (lit., "sorcery" or "magic") as "spellbinding eloquence", see 74 : 24, where this term occurs for the first time in the chronology of Qurᵓanic revelation. – By rejecting the message of the Qurᵓān on the specious plea that Muḥammad is but a human being endowed with "spellbinding eloquence", the opponents of the Qurᵓanic doctrine in reality "conceal their innermost thoughts": for, their rejection is due not so much to any pertinent criticism of this doctrine as, rather, to their instinctive, deep-set unwillingness to submit to the moral and spiritual discipline which an acceptance of the Prophet's call would entail.

5 According to the earliest scholars of Medina and Baṣrah, as well as some of the scholars of Kūfah, this word is spelt *qul*, as an imperative ("Say"), whereas some of the Meccan scholars and the majority of those of Kūfah read it as *qāla* ("He [i.e., the Prophet] said"). In the earliest copies of the Qurᵓān the spelling was apparently confined, in this instance, to the consonants *q–l*: hence the possibility of reading it either as *qul* or as *qāla*. However, as Ṭabarī points out, both these readings have the same meaning and are, therefore, equally valid, "for, when God bade Muḥammad to say this, he [undoubtedly] said it. . . . Hence, in whichever way this word is read, the reader is correct (*muṣīb aṣ-ṣawāb*) in his reading." Among the classical commentators, Baghawī and Bayḍāwī explicitly use the spelling *qul*, while Zamakhsharī's short remark that "it has also been read as *qāla*" seems to indicate his own preference for the imperative *qul*.

6 Lit., "confusing medleys (*aḍghāth*) of dreams".

Not one of the communities that We destroyed in bygone times[7] would ever believe [their prophets]: will these, then, [be more willing to] believe?[8] ⟨6⟩
For [even] before thy time, [O Muḥammad,] We never sent [as Our apostles] any but [mortal] men, whom We inspired – hence, [tell the deniers of the truth,] "If you do not know this, ask the followers of earlier revelation"[9] ⟨7⟩ – and neither did We endow them with bodies that could dispense with food,[10] nor were they immortal. ⟨8⟩
In the end, We made good unto them Our promise, and We saved them and all whom We willed [to save],[11] and We destroyed those who had wasted their own selves.[12] ⟨9⟩

[O MEN!] We have now bestowed upon you from on high a divine writ containing all that you ought to bear in mind:[13] will you not, then, use your reason? ⟨10⟩
For, how many a community that persisted in evildoing have We dashed into fragments, and raised another people in its stead![14] ⟨11⟩
And [every time,] as soon as they began to feel Our punishing might, lo! they tried to flee from it ⟨12⟩ – [and at the same time

مَآ ءَامَنَتْ قَبْلَهُم مِّن قَرْيَةٍ أَهْلَكْنَٰهَآ أَفَهُمْ يُؤْمِنُونَ (6) وَمَآ أَرْسَلْنَا
قَبْلَكَ إِلَّا رِجَالًا نُّوحِىٓ إِلَيْهِمْ فَسْـَٔلُوٓا۟ أَهْلَ ٱلذِّكْرِ إِن كُنتُمْ لَا تَعْلَمُونَ (7)
وَمَا جَعَلْنَٰهُمْ جَسَدًا لَّا يَأْكُلُونَ ٱلطَّعَامَ وَمَا كَانُوا۟ خَٰلِدِينَ (8) ثُمَّ
صَدَقْنَٰهُمُ ٱلْوَعْدَ فَأَنجَيْنَٰهُمْ وَمَن نَّشَآءُ وَأَهْلَكْنَا ٱلْمُسْرِفِينَ (9) لَقَدْ
أَنزَلْنَآ إِلَيْكُمْ كِتَٰبًا فِيهِ ذِكْرُكُمْ ۚ أَفَلَا تَعْقِلُونَ (10) وَكَمْ قَصَمْنَا مِن
قَرْيَةٍ كَانَتْ ظَالِمَةً وَأَنشَأْنَا بَعْدَهَا قَوْمًا ءَاخَرِينَ (11) فَلَمَّآ أَحَسُّوا۟
بَأْسَنَآ إِذَا هُم مِّنْهَا يَرْكُضُونَ (12)

Māa ʾāmanat qablahum-miñ-qaryatin ʾahlaknāhāa
ʾafahum yuʾminūn. (6) Wa māa ʾarsalnā qablaka
ʾillā rijālañ-nūḥīi ʾilayhim fasʾalūu ʾahladh-Dhikri
ʾiñ-kuñtum lā taʿlamūn. (7) Wa mā jaʿalnāhum jasa-
dal-lā yaʾkulūnaṭ-ṭaʿāma wa mā kānū khālidīn. (8)
Thumma ṣadaqnāhumul-waʿda faʾañjaynāhum wa
mañ-nashāaʾu wa ʾahlaknal-musrifīn. (9) Laqad
ʾañzalnāa ʾilaykum Kitābañ-fīhi dhikrukum; ʾafalā
taʿqilūn. (10) Wa kam qaṣamnā miñ-qaryatiñ-kānat
ẓālimatañw-wa ʾañshaʾnā baʿdahā qawman
ʾākharīn. (11) Falammāa ʾaḥassū baʾsanāa ʾidhā
hum-minhā yarkuḍūn. (12)

7 Lit., "before them".

8 The downfall of those communities of old – frequently referred to in the Qurʾān – was invariably due to the fact that they had been resolved to ignore all spiritual truths which militated against their own, materialistic concept of life: is it, then (so the Qurʾanic argument goes), reasonable to expect that the opponents of the Prophet Muḥammad, who are similarly motivated, would be more willing to consider his message on its merits?

9 Lit., "followers of the reminder" – i.e., of the Bible, which in its original, uncorrupted form represented one of God's "reminders" to man.

10 Lit., "neither did We fashion them [i.e., those apostles] as bodies that ate no food", implying a denial of any supernatural quality in the prophets entrusted with God's message (cf. 5 : 75, 13 : 38 and 25 : 20, as well as the corresponding notes). The above is an answer to the unbelievers' objection to Muḥammad's prophethood expressed in verse 3 of this *sūrah*.

11 I.e., their believing followers.

12 As regards my rendering of *al-musrifūn* as "those who had wasted their own selves", see note 21 on the last sentence of 10 : 12.

13 The term *dhikr*, which primarily denotes a "reminder" or a "remembrance", or, as Rāghib defines it, the "presence [of something] in the mind", has also the meaning of "that *by which* one is remembered", i.e., with praise – in other words, "renown" or "fame" – and, tropically, "honour", "eminence" or "dignity". Hence, the above phrase contains, apart from the concept of a "reminder", an indirect allusion to the dignity and happiness to which man may attain by following the spiritual and social precepts laid down in the Qurʾān. By rendering the expression *dhikrukum* as "all that you ought to bear in mind", I have tried to bring out all these meanings.

14 Lit., "after it".

they seemed to hear a scornful voice]: "Do not try to flee, but return to all that [once] gave you pleasure and corrupted your whole being,[15] and [return] to your homes, so that you might be called to account [for what you have done]!"[16] ‹13›
And they could only cry:[17] "Oh, woe unto us! Verily, we were wrongdoers!" ‹14›
And that cry of theirs did not cease until We caused them to become [like] a field mown down, still and silent as ashes. ‹15›

AND [know that] We have not created the heavens and the earth and all that is between them in mere idle play:[18] ‹16›
[for,] had We willed to indulge in a pastime, We would indeed have produced it from within Ourselves – if such had been Our will at all![19] ‹17›
Nay, but [by the very act of creation] We hurl the truth against falsehood,[20] and it crushes the latter: and lo! it withers away.[21]
But woe unto you for all your [attempts at] defining [God][22] ‹18› – for, unto Him belong all [beings] that are in the heavens and on earth; and those that are with Him[23] are never too proud to worship Him and never grow weary [thereof]: ‹19›
they extol His limitless glory by night and by day, never flagging [therein]. ‹20›

لَا تَرْكُضُوا۟ وَٱرْجِعُوٓا۟ إِلَىٰ مَآ أُتْرِفْتُمْ فِيهِ وَمَسَـٰكِنِكُمْ لَعَلَّكُمْ تُسْـَٔلُونَ ﴿١٣﴾
قَالُوا۟ يَـٰوَيْلَنَآ إِنَّا كُنَّا ظَـٰلِمِينَ ﴿١٤﴾ فَمَا زَالَت تِّلْكَ دَعْوَىٰهُمْ حَتَّىٰ
جَعَلْنَـٰهُمْ حَصِيدًا خَـٰمِدِينَ ﴿١٥﴾ وَمَا خَلَقْنَا ٱلسَّمَآءَ وَٱلْأَرْضَ وَمَا
بَيْنَهُمَا لَـٰعِبِينَ ﴿١٦﴾ لَوْ أَرَدْنَآ أَن نَّتَّخِذَ لَهْوًا لَّٱتَّخَذْنَـٰهُ مِن لَّدُنَّآ إِن كُنَّا
فَـٰعِلِينَ ﴿١٧﴾ بَلْ نَقْذِفُ بِٱلْحَقِّ عَلَى ٱلْبَـٰطِلِ فَيَدْمَغُهُۥ فَإِذَا هُوَ زَاهِقٌ
وَلَكُمُ ٱلْوَيْلُ مِمَّا تَصِفُونَ ﴿١٨﴾ وَلَهُۥ مَن فِى ٱلسَّمَـٰوَٰتِ وَٱلْأَرْضِ وَمَنْ
عِندَهُۥ لَا يَسْتَكْبِرُونَ عَنْ عِبَادَتِهِۦ وَلَا يَسْتَحْسِرُونَ ﴿١٩﴾ يُسَبِّحُونَ ٱلَّيْلَ
وَٱلنَّهَارَ لَا يَفْتُرُونَ ﴿٢٠﴾

Lā tarkuḍū war-jiᶜūu ᵓilā māa ᵓutriftum fīhi wa masākinikum laᶜallakum tusᵓalūn. (13) **Qālū yā waylanāa ᵓinnā kunnā ẓālimīn.** (14) **Famā zālat tilka daᶜwāhum ḥattā jaᶜalnāhum ḥaṣīdan khāmidīn.** (15) **Wa mā khalaqnas-samāaᵓa wal-ᵓarḍa wa mā baynahumā lāᶜibīn.** (16) **Law ᵓaradnāa ᵓañ-nattakhidha lahwal-lattakhadhnāhu mil-ladunnāa ᵓiñ-kunnā fāᶜilīn.** (17) **Bal naqdhifu bil-ḥaqqi ᶜalal-bāṭili fayadmaghuhū faᵓidhā huwa zāhiq. Wa lakumul-waylu mimmā taṣifūn.** (18) **Wa lahū mañ-fis-samāwāti wal-ᵓarḍi wa man ᶜiñdahū lā yastakbirūna ᶜan ᶜibādatihī wa lā yastaḥsirūn.** (19) **Yusabbiḥūnal-layla wan-nahāra lā yafturūn.** (20)

15 For an explanation of the phrase *mā utriftum fīhi*, see *sūrah* 11, note 147.

16 The Qurᵓān does not say whose words these are, but the tenor of this passage indicates, I believe, that it is the scornful, self-accusing voice of the sinners' own conscience: hence my interpolation, between brackets, at the beginning of this verse.

17 Lit., "They said".

18 Lit., "playing" or "playfully", i.e., without meaning and purpose: see note 11 on 10 : 5.

19 Lit., "if We had [ever] willed to do so": meaning that, had God ever willed to "indulge in a pastime" (which, being almighty and self-sufficient, He has no need to do), He could have found it within His Own Self, without any necessity to create a universe which would embody His hypothetical – and logically inconceivable – will to "please Himself", and would thus represent a "projection", as it were, of His Own Being. In the elliptic manner of the Qurᵓān, the above passage amounts to a statement of God's transcendence.

20 I.e., the truth of God's transcendence against the false idea of His existential immanence in, or co-existence with, the created universe.

21 The obvious fact that everything in the created universe is finite and perishable effectively refutes the claim that it could be a "projection" of the Creator, who is infinite and eternal.

22 Lit., "for all that you attribute [to God] by way of description" or "of definition" (cf. the last sentence of 6 : 100 and the corresponding note 88) – implying that the idea of God's "immanence" in His creation is equivalent to an attempt to define His Being.

23 According to the classical commentators, this refers to the angels; but it is possible to understand the expression "those who are with Him" in a wider sense, comprising not only the angels but also all human beings who are truly God-conscious and wholly dedicated to Him. In either case, their "being with Him" is a metaphorical

أَمِ ٱتَّخَذُوٓا۟ ءَالِهَةً مِّنَ ٱلْأَرْضِ هُمْ يُنشِرُونَ ﴿21﴾ لَوْ كَانَ فِيهِمَآ ءَالِهَةٌ
إِلَّا ٱللَّهُ لَفَسَدَتَا ۚ فَسُبْحَـٰنَ ٱللَّهِ رَبِّ ٱلْعَرْشِ عَمَّا يَصِفُونَ ﴿22﴾ لَا يُسْـَٔلُ
عَمَّا يَفْعَلُ وَهُمْ يُسْـَٔلُونَ ﴿23﴾ أَمِ ٱتَّخَذُوا۟ مِن دُونِهِۦٓ ءَالِهَةً ۖ قُلْ هَاتُوا۟
بُرْهَـٰنَكُمْ ۖ هَـٰذَا ذِكْرُ مَن مَّعِىَ وَذِكْرُ مَن قَبْلِى ۗ بَلْ أَكْثَرُهُمْ لَا يَعْلَمُونَ
ٱلْحَقَّ ۖ فَهُم مُّعْرِضُونَ ﴿24﴾ وَمَآ أَرْسَلْنَا مِن قَبْلِكَ مِن رَّسُولٍ إِلَّا نُوحِىٓ
إِلَيْهِ أَنَّهُۥ لَآ إِلَـٰهَ إِلَّآ أَنَا۠ فَٱعْبُدُونِ ﴿25﴾ وَقَالُوا۟ ٱتَّخَذَ ٱلرَّحْمَـٰنُ وَلَدًا

ʾAmit-takhadhūu ʾālihatam-minal-ʾarḍi hum yuñshirūn. (21) Law kāna fīhimāa ʾālihatun ʾillal-lāhu la-fasadatā. Fasubḥānal-lāhi Rabbil-ʿarshi ʿammā yaṣifūn. (22) Lā yusʾalu ʿammā yafʿalu wa hum yusʾalūn. (23) ʾAmit-takhadhū miñ-dūnihīi ʾālihah. Qul hātū burhānakum; hādhā Dhikru mam-maʿiya wa Dhikru mañ-qablī. Bal ʾaktharuhum lā yaʿla-mūnal-ḥaqqa fahum-muʿriḍūn. (24) Wa māa ʾarsalnā miñ-qablika mir-Rasūlin ʾillā nūḥīi ʾilayhi ʾannahū lāa ʾilāha ʾillāa ʾAna faʿbudūn. (25) Wa qālut-takhadhar-Raḥmānu waladā.

And yet,[24] some people choose to worship certain earthly things or beings as deities[25] that [are supposed to] resurrect [the dead; and they fail to realize that], ‹21› had there been in heaven or on earth[26] any deities other than God, both [those realms] would surely have fallen into ruin!

But limitless in His glory is God, enthroned in His awesome almightiness[27] [far] above anything that men may devise by way of definition![28] ‹22›

He cannot be called to account for whatever He does, whereas they will be called to account: ‹23› and yet,[29] they choose to worship [imaginary] deities instead of Him!

Say [O Prophet]: "Produce an evidence for what you are claiming:[30] this is a reminder [unceasingly voiced] by those who are with me, just as it was a reminder [voiced] by those who came before me."[31]

But nay, most of them do not know the truth, and so they stubbornly turn away [from it][32] ‹24› – and [this despite the fact that even] before thy time We never sent any apostle without having revealed to him that there is no deity save Me, [and that,] therefore, you shall worship Me [alone]! ‹25›

And [yet,] some say, "The Most Gracious has taken unto Himself a son"!

---

indication of their spiritual eminence and place of honour in God's sight, and does not bear any *spatial* connotation of "nearness" (Zamakhsharī and Rāzī): obviously so, because God is limitless in space as well as in time. (See also 40 : 7 and the corresponding note 4.)

24 As stressed by Zamakhsharī, the particle *am* which introduces this sentence has not, as is so often the case, an interrogative sense ("is it that . . ."), but is used here in the sense of *bal*, which in this instance may be rendered as "and yet".

25 Lit., "they have taken unto themselves deities from the earth", i.e., from among the things or beings found on earth: an expression which alludes to all manner of false objects of worship – idols of every description, forces of nature, deified human beings, and, finally, abstract concepts such as wealth, power, etc.

26 Lit., "in those two [realms]", alluding to the first clause of verse 19 above.

27 Lit., "the Sustainer (*rabb*) of the awesome throne of almightiness". (For this rendering of *al-ʿarsh*, see note 43 on 7 : 54.

28 Cf. last sentence of verse 18 and the corresponding note 22, as well as note 88 on 6 : 100.

29 See note 24 above.

30 Lit., "produce your evidence", i.e., for the existence of deities other than God, as well as for the intellectual and moral justification of worshipping anything but Him.

31 I.e., the earlier prophets, the purport of whose messages was always the stress on the oneness of God.

32 In other words, most people's obstinate refusal to consider a reasonable proposition on its merits is often due to no more than the simple fact that it is not familiar to them.

ربع الحزب

Limitless is He in His glory![33] Nay, [those whom they regard as God's "offspring"[34] are but His] honoured servants: ‹26› they speak not until He has spoken unto them,[35] and [whenever they act,] they act at His behest. ‹27›

He knows all that lies open before them and all that is hidden from them:[36] hence, they cannot intercede for any but those whom He has [already] graced with His goodly acceptance,[37] since they themselves stand in reverent awe of Him. ‹28›

And if any of them were to say, "Behold, I am a deity beside Him" – that one We should requite with hell: thus do We requite all [such] evildoers. ‹29›

ARE, THEN, they who are bent on denying the truth not aware that the heavens and the earth were [once] one single entity, which We then parted asunder?[38] – and [that] We made out of water every living thing? Will they not, then, [begin to] believe?[39] ‹30›

سُبۡحَٰنَهُۥۚ بَلۡ عِبَادٞ مُّكۡرَمُونَ ٢٦ لَا يَسۡبِقُونَهُۥ بِٱلۡقَوۡلِ وَهُم بِأَمۡرِهِۦ
يَعۡمَلُونَ ٢٧ يَعۡلَمُ مَا بَيۡنَ أَيۡدِيهِمۡ وَمَا خَلۡفَهُمۡ وَلَا يَشۡفَعُونَ إِلَّا لِمَنِ
ٱرۡتَضَىٰ وَهُم مِّنۡ خَشۡيَتِهِۦ مُشۡفِقُونَ ٢٨ ۞ وَمَن يَقُلۡ مِنۡهُمۡ إِنِّيٓ إِلَٰهٞ مِّن
دُونِهِۦ فَذَٰلِكَ نَجۡزِيهِ جَهَنَّمَۚ كَذَٰلِكَ نَجۡزِي ٱلظَّٰلِمِينَ ٢٩ أَوَلَمۡ يَرَ
ٱلَّذِينَ كَفَرُوٓاْ أَنَّ ٱلسَّمَٰوَٰتِ وَٱلۡأَرۡضَ كَانَتَا رَتۡقٗا فَفَتَقۡنَٰهُمَاۖ وَجَعَلۡنَا
مِنَ ٱلۡمَآءِ كُلَّ شَيۡءٍ حَيٍّۚ أَفَلَا يُؤۡمِنُونَ ٣٠

Subḥānahū bal ʿibādum-mukramūn. (26) Lā yas-
biqūnahū bilqawli wa hum-biʾamrihī yaʿmalūn. (27)
Yaʿlamu mā bayna ʾaydīhim wa mā khalfahum wa
lā yashfaʿūna ʾillā limanir-taḍā wa hum-min kha-
shyatihī mushfiqūn. (28) ۞ Wa mañy-yaqul minhum
ʾinnīi ʾilāhum-miñ-dūnihī fadhālika najzīhi jahan-
nam. Kadhālika najziẓ-ẓālimīn. (29) ʾAwa lam yaral-
ladhīna kafarūu ʾannas-samāwāti wal-ʾarḍa kānatā
ratqañ-fafataqnāhumā. Wa jaʿalnā minal-māaʾi
kulla shayʾin ḥayyin ʾafalā yuʾminūn. (30)

33 I.e., utterly remote from the imperfection implied in the concept of "offspring": see note 77 on 19 : 92.

34 This alludes to prophets like Jesus, whom the Christians regard as "the son of God", as well as to the angels, whom the pre-Islamic Arabs considered to be "God's daughters" (since they were conceived of as females).

35 Lit., "they do not precede Him in speech" – meaning that they proclaim only what He has revealed to them and bidden them to proclaim.

36 See note 247 on 2 : 255.

37 Cf. 19 : 87 and 20 : 109. Regarding the problem of "intercession" as such, see note 7 on 10 : 3.

38 It is, as a rule, futile to make an explanation of the Qurʾān dependent on "scientific findings" which may appear true today, but may equally well be disproved tomorrow by new findings. Nevertheless, the above unmistakable reference to the unitary origin of the universe – metonymically described in the Qurʾān as "the heavens and the earth" – strikingly anticipates the view of almost all modern astrophysicists that this universe has originated as one entity from one single element, namely, hydrogen, which became subsequently consolidated through gravity and then separated into individual nebulae, galaxies and solar systems, with further individual parts progressively breaking away to form new entities in the shape of stars, planets and the latters' satellites. (Regarding the Qurʾanic reference to the phenomenon described by the term "expanding universe", see 51 : 47 and the corresponding note 31.)

39 The statement that God "made out of water every living thing" expresses most concisely a truth that is nowadays universally accepted by science. It has a threefold meaning: (1) Water – and, specifically, the sea – was the environment within which the prototype of all living matter originated; (2) among all the innumerable – existing or conceivable – liquids, only water has the peculiar properties necessary for the emergence and development of life; and (3) the protoplasm, which is the physical basis of every living cell – whether in plants or in animals – and represents the only form of matter in which the phenomena of life are manifested, consists overwhelmingly of water and is, thus, utterly dependent on it. Read together with the preceding statement, which alludes to the unitary origin of the physical universe, the emergence of life from and within an equally unitary element points to the existence of a unitary *plan* underlying all creation and, hence, to the existence and oneness of the Creator. This accent on the oneness of God and the unity of His creation is taken up again in verse 92 below.

And [are they not aware that] We have set up firm mountains on earth, lest it sway with them,[40] and [that] We have appointed thereon broad paths, so that they might find their way, ⟨31⟩ and [that] We have set up the sky as a canopy well-secured?[41]
And yet, they stubbornly turn away from fail] the signs of this [creation], ⟨32⟩ and [fail to see that] it is He who has created the night and the day and the sun and the moon – all of them floating through space! ⟨33⟩

AND [remind those who deny thee, O Prophet,[42] that] never have We granted life everlasting to any mortal before thee:[43] but do they, perchance, hope that although thou must die, they will live forever?[44] ⟨34⟩
Every human being is bound to taste death; and We test you [all] through the bad and the good [things of life] by way of trial: and unto Us you all must return.[45] ⟨35⟩
But [thus it is:] whenever they who are bent on denying the truth consider thee,[46] they make thee but a target of their mockery, [saying to one another,] "Is this the one who speaks [so contemptuously] of your gods?"[47]
And yet, it is they themselves who, at [every] mention of the Most Gracious, are wont to deny the truth![48] ⟨36⟩
Man is a creature of haste;[49] [but in time]

وَجَعَلْنَا فِى ٱلْأَرْضِ رَوَٰسِىَ أَن تَمِيدَ بِهِمْ وَجَعَلْنَا فِيهَا فِجَاجًا سُبُلًا لَّعَلَّهُمْ
يَهْتَدُونَ ﴿31﴾ وَجَعَلْنَا ٱلسَّمَآءَ سَقْفًا مَّحْفُوظًا ۖ وَهُمْ عَنْ ءَايَٰتِهَا مُعْرِضُونَ ﴿32﴾
وَهُوَ ٱلَّذِى خَلَقَ ٱلَّيْلَ وَٱلنَّهَارَ وَٱلشَّمْسَ وَٱلْقَمَرَ ۖ كُلٌّ فِى فَلَكٍ يَسْبَحُونَ ﴿33﴾
وَمَا جَعَلْنَا لِبَشَرٍ مِّن قَبْلِكَ ٱلْخُلْدَ ۖ أَفَإِي۟ن مِّتَّ فَهُمُ ٱلْخَٰلِدُونَ ﴿34﴾ كُلُّ
نَفْسٍ ذَآئِقَةُ ٱلْمَوْتِ ۗ وَنَبْلُوكُم بِٱلشَّرِّ وَٱلْخَيْرِ فِتْنَةً ۖ وَإِلَيْنَا تُرْجَعُونَ ﴿35﴾
وَإِذَا رَءَاكَ ٱلَّذِينَ كَفَرُوٓا۟ إِن يَتَّخِذُونَكَ إِلَّا هُزُوًا أَهَٰذَا ٱلَّذِى يَذْكُرُ
ءَالِهَتَكُمْ وَهُم بِذِكْرِ ٱلرَّحْمَٰنِ هُمْ كَٰفِرُونَ ﴿36﴾ خُلِقَ ٱلْإِنسَٰنُ مِنْ عَجَلٍ

Wa jaᶜalnā fil-ᵓarḍi rawāsiya ᵓañ-tamīda bihim wa jaᶜalnā fīhā fijājañ-subulal-laᶜallahum yahtadūn. (31)
Wa jaᶜalnas-samāaᵓa saqfam-maḥfūẓañw-wa hum ᶜan ᵓĀyātihā muᶜriḍūn. (32) **Wa Huwal-ladhī khalaqal-layla wañ-nahāra wash-shamsa wal-qamara kulluñ-fī falakiñy-yasbaḥūn. (33)** **Wa mā jaᶜalnā libasharim-miñ-qablikal-khulda ᵓafaᵓim-mitta fahumul-khālidūn. (34)** **Kullu nafsiñ-dhāaᵓiqatul-mawt. Wa nablūkum-bishsharri wal-khayri fitnatañw-wa ᵓilaynā turjaᶜūn. (35)** **Wa ᵓidhā raᵓākal-ladhīna kafarūu ᵓiñy-yattakhidhūnaka ᵓillā huzuwan ᵓahādhal-ladhī yadhkuru ᵓālihatakum wa hum-bidhikrir-Raḥmāni hum kāfirūn. (36)** **Khuliqal-ᵓIñsānu min ᶜajal.**

40 See 16 : 15 and the corresponding note 11.

41 See note 4 on the first sentence of 13 : 2, which seems to have a similar meaning.

42 This relates to the objection of the unbelievers, mentioned in verse 3 of this *sūrah*, that Muḥammad is "but a mortal like yourselves", and connects also with verses 7-8, which stress that *all* of God's apostles were but mortal men (cf. 3 : 144).

43 The obvious implication is, "and so We shall not grant it unto thee, either". Cf. 39 : 30 – "thou art bound to die".

44 Lit., "but if, then, thou shouldst die, will they live forever?" – implying an assumption on their part that they would not be called to account on death and resurrection.

45 Lit., "you shall be brought back", i.e., for judgment.

46 Lit., "see thee": but since this verb has here obviously an abstract meaning, relating to the *message* propounded by the Prophet, it is best rendered as above.

47 Sc., "and dares to deny their reality although he is a mere mortal like ourselves?"

48 I.e., although they resent any aspersion cast on whatever things or forces they unthinkingly worship, they refuse to acknowledge God's planning will be manifested in every aspect of His creation.

49 Lit., "is created out of haste" – i.e., he is by nature imbued with impatience: cf. last sentence of 17 : 11. In the present context this refers to man's impatience regarding things to come: in this case – as is obvious from the sequence – his hasty refusal to believe in God's coming judgment.

I shall make obvious to you [the truth of] My messages: do not, then, ask Me to hasten [it]![50] «37»
But they [who reject My messages are wont to] ask, "When is that promise [of God's judgment] to be fulfilled? [Answer this, O you who believe in it,] if you are men of truth!"[51] «38»
If they but knew – they who are bent on denying the truth – [that there will come] a time when they will not be able to ward off the fire from their faces, nor from their backs, and will not find any succour! «39»
Nay, but [the Last Hour] will come upon them of a sudden, and will stupefy them: and they will be unable to avert it, and neither will they be allowed any respite. «40»
And, indeed, [O Muḥammad, even] before thy time have [God's] apostles been derided – but those who scoffed at them were [in the end] overwhelmed by the very thing which they had been wont to deride.[52] «41»
Say: "Who could protect you, by night or by day, from the Most Gracious?"[53] And yet, from a remembrance of their Sustainer do they stubbornly turn away! «42»
Do they [really think that they] have deities that could shield them from Us? Those [alleged deities] are not [even] able to succour themselves: hence, neither can they [who worship them hope to] be aided [by them] against Us. «43»
Nay, We have allowed these [sinners] – as [We allowed] their forebears – to enjoy the good things of life for a great length of time:[54] but then – have they never yet seen how We visit the earth [with Our punishment], gradually depriving it of all that is best thereon?[55] Can they, then, [hope to] be the winners? «44»

سَأُوْرِيكُمْ ءَايَٰتِى فَلَا تَسْتَعْجِلُونِ ﴿٣٧﴾ وَيَقُولُونَ مَتَىٰ هَٰذَا ٱلْوَعْدُ إِن كُنتُمْ
صَٰدِقِينَ ﴿٣٨﴾ لَوْ يَعْلَمُ ٱلَّذِينَ كَفَرُوا۟ حِينَ لَا يَكُفُّونَ عَن وُجُوهِهِمُ
ٱلنَّارَ وَلَا عَن ظُهُورِهِمْ وَلَا هُمْ يُنصَرُونَ ﴿٣٩﴾ بَلْ تَأْتِيهِم بَغْتَةً فَتَبْهَتُهُمْ
فَلَا يَسْتَطِيعُونَ رَدَّهَا وَلَا هُمْ يُنظَرُونَ ﴿٤٠﴾ وَلَقَدِ ٱسْتُهْزِئَ بِرُسُلٍ مِّن
قَبْلِكَ فَحَاقَ بِٱلَّذِينَ سَخِرُوا۟ مِنْهُم مَّا كَانُوا۟ بِهِۦ يَسْتَهْزِءُونَ ﴿٤١﴾ قُلْ مَن
يَكْلَؤُكُم بِٱلَّيْلِ وَٱلنَّهَارِ مِنَ ٱلرَّحْمَٰنِ ۗ بَلْ هُمْ عَن ذِكْرِ رَبِّهِم
مُّعْرِضُونَ ﴿٤٢﴾ أَمْ لَهُمْ ءَالِهَةٌ تَمْنَعُهُم مِّن دُونِنَا ۚ لَا يَسْتَطِيعُونَ نَصْرَ
أَنفُسِهِمْ وَلَا هُم مِّنَّا يُصْحَبُونَ ﴿٤٣﴾ بَلْ مَتَّعْنَا هَٰٓؤُلَآءِ وَءَابَآءَهُمْ حَتَّىٰ
طَالَ عَلَيْهِمُ ٱلْعُمُرُ ۗ أَفَلَا يَرَوْنَ أَنَّا نَأْتِى ٱلْأَرْضَ نَنقُصُهَا مِنْ أَطْرَافِهَآ ۚ
أَفَهُمُ ٱلْغَٰلِبُونَ ﴿٤٤﴾

Saʾurīkum ʾĀyātī falā tastaᶜjilūn. (37) Wa yaqūlūna matā hādhal-waᶜdu ʾiñ-kuñtum ṣādiqīn. (38) Law yaᶜlamul-ladhīna kafarū ḥina lā yakuffūna ᶜañw-wujūhihimuñ-nāra wa lā ᶜañ-ẓuhūrihim wa lā hum yuñṣarūn. (39) Bal taʾtīhim-baghtatañ-fatabhatuhum falā yastaṭīᶜūna raddahā wa lā hum yuñẓarūn. (40) Wa laqadis-tuhziʾa biRusulim-miñ-qablika faḥāqa billadhīna sakhirū minhum-mā kānū bihī yastahziʾūn. (41) Qul mañy-yaklaʾukum-billayli wan-nahāri minar-Raḥmān. Bal hum ᶜañ-dhikri Rabbihim-muᶜriḍūn. (42) ʾAm lahum ʾālihatuñ-tamnaᶜuhum-miñ-dūninā. Lā yastaṭīᶜūna naṣra ʾañfusihim wa lā hum-minnā yuṣḥabūn. (43) Bal mattaᶜnā hāaʾulāaʾi wa ʾābāaʾahum ḥattā ṭāla ᶜalayhimul-ᶜumur. ʾAfalā yarawna ʾannā naʾtil-ʾarḍa nañquṣuhā min ʾaṭrāfihāa ʾafahumul-ghālibūn. (44)

50 Cf. 16 : 1 – "God's judgment is [bound to] come: do not, then, call for its speedy advent!"

51 The Qurʾanic answer to this question is given in 7 : 187.

52 See 6 : 10 (which has exactly the same wording) and the corresponding note 9.

53 The reference to God, in this context, as "the Most Gracious" (*ar-raḥmān*) is meant to bring out the fact that He – and He alone – is the protector of all creation.

54 Lit., "until their lives (*ᶜumur*) grew long" – i.e., until they grew accustomed to the thought that their prosperity would last forever (Zamakhsharī).

55 For an explanation, see the identical phrase in 13 : 41 and the corresponding notes 79 and 80.

SAY [unto all men]: "I but warn you on the strength of divine revelation!"
But the deaf [of heart] will not hearken to this call, however often they are warned.[56] ‹45›
And yet, if but a breath of thy Sustainer's chastisement touches them, they are sure to cry, "Oh, woe unto us! Verily, we were evildoers!" ‹46›
But We shall set up just balance-scales on Resurrection Day, and no human being shall be wronged in the least: for though there be [in him but] the weight of a mustard-seed [of good or evil], We shall bring it forth; and none can take count as We do! ‹47›

AND, INDEED, We vouchsafed unto Moses and Aaron [Our revelation as] the standard by which to discern the true from the false,[57] and as a [guiding] light and a reminder for the God-conscious ‹48› who stand in awe of their Sustainer although He is beyond the reach of human perception,[58] and who tremble at the thought of the Last Hour. ‹49›
And [like those earlier revelations,] this one, too, is a blessed reminder which We have bestowed from on high: will you, then, disavow it? ‹50›

AND, INDEED, long before [the time of Moses] We vouchsafed unto Abraham his consciousness of what is right;[59] and We were aware of [what moved] him ‹51› when he said unto his father and his people, "What are these images to which you are so intensely devoted?" ‹52›

قُلْ إِنَّمَآ أُنذِرُكُم بِٱلْوَحْيِ ۚ وَلَا يَسْمَعُ ٱلصُّمُّ ٱلدُّعَآءَ إِذَا مَا يُنذَرُونَ ﴿٤٥﴾
وَلَئِن مَّسَّتْهُمْ نَفْحَةٌ مِّنْ عَذَابِ رَبِّكَ لَيَقُولُنَّ يَٰوَيْلَنَآ إِنَّا كُنَّا ظَٰلِمِينَ ﴿٤٦﴾
وَنَضَعُ ٱلْمَوَٰزِينَ ٱلْقِسْطَ لِيَوْمِ ٱلْقِيَٰمَةِ فَلَا تُظْلَمُ نَفْسٌ شَيْـًٔا ۖ وَإِن كَانَ
مِثْقَالَ حَبَّةٍ مِّنْ خَرْدَلٍ أَتَيْنَا بِهَا ۗ وَكَفَىٰ بِنَا حَٰسِبِينَ ﴿٤٧﴾ وَلَقَدْ ءَاتَيْنَا
مُوسَىٰ وَهَٰرُونَ ٱلْفُرْقَانَ وَضِيَآءً وَذِكْرًا لِّلْمُتَّقِينَ ﴿٤٨﴾ ٱلَّذِينَ يَخْشَوْنَ
رَبَّهُم بِٱلْغَيْبِ وَهُم مِّنَ ٱلسَّاعَةِ مُشْفِقُونَ ﴿٤٩﴾ وَهَٰذَا ذِكْرٌ مُّبَارَكٌ
أَنزَلْنَٰهُ ۚ أَفَأَنتُمْ لَهُۥ مُنكِرُونَ ﴿٥٠﴾ ۞ وَلَقَدْ ءَاتَيْنَآ إِبْرَٰهِيمَ رُشْدَهُۥ مِن
قَبْلُ وَكُنَّا بِهِۦ عَٰلِمِينَ ﴿٥١﴾ إِذْ قَالَ لِأَبِيهِ وَقَوْمِهِۦ مَا هَٰذِهِ ٱلتَّمَاثِيلُ
ٱلَّتِىٓ أَنتُمْ لَهَا عَٰكِفُونَ ﴿٥٢﴾

نصف الحزب

Qul ʾinnamāa ʾuñdhirukum-bilwaḥyi wa lā yasmaʿuṣ-ṣummud-duʿāaʾa ʾidhā mā yuñdharūn. (45) Wa laʾim-massat-hum nafḥatum-min ʿadhābi Rabbika layaqūlunna yā waylanāa ʾinnā kunnā ẓālimīn. (46) Wa naḍaʿul-mawāzīnal-qisṭa liYawmil-Qiyāmati falā tuẓlamu nafsuñ-shayʾā. Wa ʾiñ-kāna mithqāla ḥabbatim-min khardalin ʾataynā bihā. Wa kafā binā ḥāsibīn. (47) Wa laqad ʾātaynā Mūsā wa Hārūnal-Furqāna wa Ḍiyāaʾañw-wa Dhikral-lilmuttaqīn. (48) ʾAlladhīna yakhshawna Rabbahum-bilghaybi wa hum-minas-Sāʿati mushfiqūn. (49) Wa hādhā Dhikrum-mubārakun ʾañzalnāhu ʾafaʾañtum lahū muñkirūn. (50) ۞ Wa laqad ʾātaynāa ʾIbrāhīma rushdahū miñ-qablu wa kunnā bihī ʿālimīn. (51) ʾIdh qāla liʾabīhi wa qawmihī mā hādhihit-tamāthīlul-latīi ʾañtum lahā ʿākifūn. (52)

56 Lit., "whenever they are warned".

57 See note 38 on 2 : 53. The reference to the revelation bestowed on the earlier prophets as "the standard by which to discern the true from the false" (*al-furqān*) has here a twofold implication: firstly, it alludes to the Qurʾanic doctrine – explained in note 5 on 2 : 4 – of the historical continuity in all divine revelation, and, secondly, it stresses the fact that revelation – and revelation alone – provides an *absolute* criterion of all moral valuation. Since the Mosaic dispensation as such was binding on the children of Israel alone and remained valid only within a particular historical and cultural context, the term *al-furqān* relates here not to the Mosaic Law as such, but to the fundamental ethical truths contained in the Torah and common to all divine revelations.

58 For an explanation of the above rendering of the expression *bi'l-ghayb*, see note 3 on 2 : 3.

59 The possessive pronoun "his" affixed to the noun *rushd* (which, in this context, has the meaning of "consciousness of what is right") emphasizes the highly personal, intellectual quality of Abraham's progressive realization of God's almightiness and uniqueness (cf. 6 : 74-79 as well as note 69 on 6 : 83)., while the expression *min qabl* – rendered by me as "long before [the time of Moses]" – stresses, once again, the element of continuity in man's religious insight and experience.

They answered: "We found our forefathers worshipping them." ‹53›
Said he: "Indeed, you and your forefathers have obviously gone astray!" ‹54›
They asked: "Hast thou come unto us [with this claim] in all earnest – or art thou one of those jesters?" ‹55›
He answered: "Nay, but your [true] Sustainer is the Sustainer of the heavens and the earth – He who has brought them into being: and I am one of those who bear witness to this [truth]!" ‹56›
And [he added to himself,] "By God, I shall most certainly bring about the downfall of your idols as soon as you have turned your backs and gone away!" ‹57›
And then he broke those [idols] to pieces, [all] save the biggest of them, so that they might [be able to] turn to it.[60] ‹58›
[When they saw what had happened,] they said: "Who has done this to our gods? Verily, one of the worst wrongdoers is he!" ‹59›
Said some [of them]: "We heard a youth speak of these [gods with scorn]: he is called Abraham." ‹60›
[The others] said: "Then bring him before the people's eyes, so that they might bear witness [against him]!" ‹61›
[And when he came,] they asked: "Hast thou done this to our gods, O Abraham?" ‹62›
He answered: "Nay, it was this one, the biggest of them, that did it: but ask them [yourselves] – provided they can speak!" ‹63›
And so they turned upon one another,[61] saying, "Behold, it is you who are doing wrong."[62] ‹64›
But then they relapsed into their former way of thinking[63] [and said]: "Thou knowest very well that these [idols] cannot speak!" ‹65›

قَالُواْ وَجَدْنَآ ءَابَآءَنَا لَهَا عَٰبِدِينَ ﴿٥٣﴾ قَالَ لَقَدْ كُنتُمْ أَنتُمْ وَءَابَآؤُكُمْ
فِى ضَلَٰلٍ مُّبِينٍ ﴿٥٤﴾ قَالُوٓاْ أَجِئْتَنَا بِٱلْحَقِّ أَمْ أَنتَ مِنَ ٱللَّٰعِبِينَ ﴿٥٥﴾
قَالَ بَل رَّبُّكُمْ رَبُّ ٱلسَّمَٰوَٰتِ وَٱلْأَرْضِ ٱلَّذِى فَطَرَهُنَّ وَأَنَا۠ عَلَىٰ
ذَٰلِكُم مِّنَ ٱلشَّٰهِدِينَ ﴿٥٦﴾ وَتَٱللَّهِ لَأَكِيدَنَّ أَصْنَٰمَكُم بَعْدَ أَن تُوَلُّواْ
مُدْبِرِينَ ﴿٥٧﴾ فَجَعَلَهُمْ جُذَٰذًا إِلَّا كَبِيرًا لَّهُمْ لَعَلَّهُمْ إِلَيْهِ يَرْجِعُونَ ﴿٥٨﴾
قَالُواْ مَن فَعَلَ هَٰذَا بِـَٔالِهَتِنَآ إِنَّهُۥ لَمِنَ ٱلظَّٰلِمِينَ ﴿٥٩﴾ قَالُواْ سَمِعْنَا فَتًى
يَذْكُرُهُمْ يُقَالُ لَهُۥٓ إِبْرَٰهِيمُ ﴿٦٠﴾ قَالُواْ فَأْتُواْ بِهِۦ عَلَىٰٓ أَعْيُنِ ٱلنَّاسِ لَعَلَّهُمْ
يَشْهَدُونَ ﴿٦١﴾ قَالُوٓاْ ءَأَنتَ فَعَلْتَ هَٰذَا بِـَٔالِهَتِنَا يَٰٓإِبْرَٰهِيمُ ﴿٦٢﴾ قَالَ بَلْ
فَعَلَهُۥ كَبِيرُهُمْ هَٰذَا فَسْـَٔلُوهُمْ إِن كَانُواْ يَنطِقُونَ ﴿٦٣﴾ فَرَجَعُوٓاْ إِلَىٰٓ
أَنفُسِهِمْ فَقَالُوٓاْ إِنَّكُمْ أَنتُمُ ٱلظَّٰلِمُونَ ﴿٦٤﴾ ثُمَّ نُكِسُواْ عَلَىٰ رُءُوسِهِمْ لَقَدْ
عَلِمْتَ مَا هَٰٓؤُلَآءِ يَنطِقُونَ ﴿٦٥﴾

Qālū wajadnāa ʾābāaʾanā lahā ʿābidīn. (53) Qāla laqad kuñtum ʾañtum wa ʾābāaʾukum fī ḍalālim-mubīn. (54) Qālūu ʾajiʾtanā bilḥaqqi ʾam ʾañta minal-lāʿibīn. (55) Qāla bar-Rabbukum Rabbus-samāwāti wal-ʾarḍil-ladhī faṭarahunna wa ʾana ʿalā dhālikum-minash-shāhidīn. (56) Wa tallāhi laʾakīdanna ʾaṣnāmakum-baʿda ʾañ-tuwallū mudbirīn. (57) Faja-ʿalahum judhādhan ʾillā kabīral-lahum laʿallahum ʾilayhi yarjiʿūn. (58) Qālū mañ-faʿala hādhā biʾālihatināa ʾinnahū laminaẓ-ẓālimīn. (59) Qālū samiʿnā fatañy-yadhkuruhum yuqālu lahūu ʾIbrāhīm. (60) Qālū faʾtū bihī ʿalāa ʾaʿyunin-nāsi laʿallahum yashhadūn. (61) Qālūu ʾaʾañta faʿalta hādhā biʾālihatinā yāa ʾIbrāhīm. (62) Qāla bal faʿalahū kabīruhum hādhā fasʾalūhum ʾiñ-kānū yañṭiqūn. (63) Farajaʿūu ʾilāa ʾañfusihim faqālūu ʾinnakum ʾañtumuẓ-ẓālimūn. (64) Thumma nukisū ʿalā ruʾūsihim laqad ʿalimta mā hāaʾulāaʾi yañṭiqūn. (65)

60 Sc., "for an explanation of what had happened".
61 Lit., "they turned to [or "upon"] themselves", i.e., blaming one another.
62 I.e., "you are doing wrong to Abraham by rashly suspecting him" (Ṭabarī).
63 Lit., "they were turned upside down upon their heads": an idiomatic phrase denoting a "mental somersault" – in this case, a sudden reversal of their readiness to exonerate Abraham and a return to their former suspicion.

Said [Abraham]: "Do you then worship, instead of God, something that cannot benefit you in any way, nor harm you? ‹66› Fie upon you and upon all that you worship instead of God! Will you not, then, use your reason?" ‹67›

They exclaimed: "Burn him, and [thereby] succour your gods, if you are going to do [anything]!" ‹68›

[But] We said: "O fire! Be thou cool, and [a source of] inner peace for Abraham!"[64] ‹69› – and whereas they sought to do evil unto him, We caused *them* to suffer the greatest loss:[65] ‹70› for We saved him and Lot, [his brother's son, by guiding them] to the land which We have blessed for all times to come.[66] ‹71›

And We bestowed upon him Isaac and [Isaac's son] Jacob as an additional gift,[67] and caused all of them to be righteous men, ‹72› and made them leaders who would guide [others] in accordance with Our behest: for We inspired them [with a will] to do good works, and to be constant in prayer, and to dispense charity: and Us [alone] did they worship. ‹73›

AND UNTO Lot, too, We vouchsafed sound judgment and knowledge [of right and wrong], and saved him from that community which was given to deeds of abomination.[68] [We destroyed those people – for,] verily, they were people lost in evil, depraved ‹74› – whereas him We admitted unto Our grace: for, behold, he was among the righteous. ‹75›

قَالَ أَفَتَعْبُدُونَ مِن دُونِ ٱللَّهِ مَا لَا يَنفَعُكُمْ شَيْـًٔا وَلَا يَضُرُّكُمْ ﴿66﴾ أُفٍّ
لَّكُمْ وَلِمَا تَعْبُدُونَ مِن دُونِ ٱللَّهِ ۖ أَفَلَا تَعْقِلُونَ ﴿67﴾ قَالُوا۟ حَرِّقُوهُ
وَٱنصُرُوٓا۟ ءَالِهَتَكُمْ إِن كُنتُمْ فَـٰعِلِينَ ﴿68﴾ قُلْنَا يَـٰنَارُ كُونِى بَرْدًا
وَسَلَـٰمًا عَلَىٰٓ إِبْرَٰهِيمَ ﴿69﴾ وَأَرَادُوا۟ بِهِۦ كَيْدًا فَجَعَلْنَـٰهُمُ ٱلْأَخْسَرِينَ ﴿70﴾
وَنَجَّيْنَـٰهُ وَلُوطًا إِلَى ٱلْأَرْضِ ٱلَّتِى بَـٰرَكْنَا فِيهَا لِلْعَـٰلَمِينَ ﴿71﴾ وَوَهَبْنَا
لَهُۥٓ إِسْحَـٰقَ وَيَعْقُوبَ نَافِلَةً ۖ وَكُلًّا جَعَلْنَا صَـٰلِحِينَ ﴿72﴾ وَجَعَلْنَـٰهُمْ أَئِمَّةً
يَهْدُونَ بِأَمْرِنَا وَأَوْحَيْنَآ إِلَيْهِمْ فِعْلَ ٱلْخَيْرَٰتِ وَإِقَامَ ٱلصَّلَوٰةِ وَإِيتَآءَ
ٱلزَّكَوٰةِ ۖ وَكَانُوا۟ لَنَا عَـٰبِدِينَ ﴿73﴾ وَلُوطًا ءَاتَيْنَـٰهُ حُكْمًا وَعِلْمًا وَنَجَّيْنَـٰهُ مِنَ
ٱلْقَرْيَةِ ٱلَّتِى كَانَت تَّعْمَلُ ٱلْخَبَـٰٓئِثَ ۗ إِنَّهُمْ كَانُوا۟ قَوْمَ سَوْءٍ فَـٰسِقِينَ ﴿74﴾
وَأَدْخَلْنَـٰهُ فِى رَحْمَتِنَآ ۖ إِنَّهُۥ مِنَ ٱلصَّـٰلِحِينَ ﴿75﴾

Qāla ʾafataʿbudūna miñ-dūnil-lāhi mā lā
yañfaʿukum shayʾañw-wa lā yaḍurrukum. (66) ʾUffil-
lakum wa limā taʿbudūna miñ-dūnil-lāhi ʾafalā
taʿqilūn. (67) Qālū ḥarriqūhu wañ-ṣurūu ʾālihatakum
ʾiñ-kuñtum fāʿilīn. (68) Qulnā yā nāru kūnī bardañw-
wa salāman ʿalāa ʾIbrāhīm. (69) Wa ʾarādū bihī kay-
dañ-fajaʿalnāhumul-ʾakhsarīn. (70) Wa najjaynāhu wa
Lūṭan ʾilal-ʾarḍil-latī bāraknā fīhā lilʿālamīn. (71) Wa
wahabnā lahūu ʾIsḥāqa wa Yaʿqūba nāfilatañw-wa
kullañ-jaʿalnā ṣāliḥīn. (72) Wa jaʿalnāhum ʾaʾim-
matañy-yahdūna biʾamrinā wa ʾawḥaynāa ʾilayhim
fiʿlal-khayrāti wa ʾiqāmaṣ-Ṣalāti wa ʾītāaʾaz-Zakāti
wa kānū lanā ʿābidīn. (73) Wa Lūṭan ʾātaynāhu
ḥukmañw-wa ʿilmañw-wa najjaynāhu minal-qaryatil-
latī kānat taʿmalul-khabāaʾith. ʾInnahum kānū qaw-
ma sawʾiñ-fāsiqīn. (74) Wa ʾadkhalnāhu fī raḥmatināa
ʾinnahū minaṣ-ṣāliḥīn. (75)

64 Nowhere does the Qurʾān state that Abraham was actually, bodily thrown into the fire and miraculously kept alive in it: on the contrary, the phrase "God saved him from the fire" occurring in 29 : 24 points, rather, to the fact of his *not* having been thrown into it. On the other hand, the many elaborate (and conflicting) stories with which the classical commentators have embroidered their interpretation of the above verse can invariably be traced back to Talmudic legends and may, therefore, be disregarded. What the Qurʾān gives us here, as well as in 29 : 24 and 37 : 97, is apparently an allegorical allusion to the fire of persecution which Abraham had to suffer and which, by dint of its intensity, was to become in his later life a source of spiritual strength and inner peace (*salām*). Regarding the deeper implications of the term *salām*, see note 29 on 5 : 16.

65 Inasmuch as Abraham forsook – as shown in the next verse – his homeland, and thus abandoned his people to their spiritual ignorance.

66 Lit., "for all the worlds" or "for all people": i.e., Palestine, which subsequently became the homeland of a long line of prophets. (Abraham's native place – and the scene of his early struggles against polytheism – was Ur in Mesopotamia.)

67 I.e., in addition (*nāfilatan*) to his eldest son Ishmael (*Ismāʿīl*) who had been born years before Isaac.

68 For the story of Lot, see 7 : 80-84, 11 : 77-83 and 15 : 58-76.

AND [remember] Noah – [how,] when He called out [unto Us], long before [the time of Abraham and Lot], We responded to him and saved him and his household from that awesome calamity;[69] ‹76› and [how] We succoured him against the people who had given the lie to Our messages: verily, they were people lost in evil – and [so] We caused them all to drown. ‹77›

AND [remember] David and Solomon – [how it was] when both of them gave judgment concerning the field into which some people's sheep had strayed by night and pastured therein, and [how] We bore witness to their judgment:[70] ‹78› for, [though] We made Solomon understand the case [more profoundly], yet We vouchsafed unto both of them sound judgment and knowledge [of right and wrong].[71]
And We caused[72] the mountains to join David in extolling Our limitless glory, and likewise the birds:[73] for We are able to do [all things]. ‹79›

وَنُوحًا إِذْ نَادَىٰ مِن قَبْلُ فَٱسْتَجَبْنَا لَهُۥ فَنَجَّيْنَٰهُ وَأَهْلَهُۥ مِنَ ٱلْكَرْبِ
ٱلْعَظِيمِ ﴿76﴾ وَنَصَرْنَٰهُ مِنَ ٱلْقَوْمِ ٱلَّذِينَ كَذَّبُوا۟ بِـَٔايَٰتِنَآ ۚ إِنَّهُمْ كَانُوا۟ قَوْمَ
سَوْءٍ فَأَغْرَقْنَٰهُمْ أَجْمَعِينَ ﴿77﴾ وَدَاوُۥدَ وَسُلَيْمَٰنَ إِذْ يَحْكُمَانِ فِى
ٱلْحَرْثِ إِذْ نَفَشَتْ فِيهِ غَنَمُ ٱلْقَوْمِ وَكُنَّا لِحُكْمِهِمْ شَٰهِدِينَ ﴿78﴾
فَفَهَّمْنَٰهَا سُلَيْمَٰنَ ۚ وَكُلًّا ءَاتَيْنَا حُكْمًا وَعِلْمًا ۚ وَسَخَّرْنَا مَعَ دَاوُۥدَ
ٱلْجِبَالَ يُسَبِّحْنَ وَٱلطَّيْرَ ۚ وَكُنَّا فَٰعِلِينَ ﴿79﴾

Wa Nūḥan ʾidh nādā miñ-qablu fastajabnā lahū fa-najjaynāhu wa ʾahlahū minal-karbil-ʿaẓīm. (76) Wa naṣarnāhu minal-qawmil-ladhīna kadhdhabū biʾĀyātinā. ʾInnahum kānū qawma sawʾiñ-faʾaghraq-nāhum ʾajmaʿīn. (77) Wa Dāwūda wa Sulaymāna ʾidh yaḥkumāni fil-ḥarthi ʾidh nafashat fīhi ghanamul-qawmi wa kunnā liḥukmihim shāhidīn. (78) Fafah-hamnāhā Sulaymāna wa kullan ʾātaynā ḥukmañw-wa ʿilmā. Wa sakhkharnā maʿa Dāwūdal-jibāla yu-sabbiḥna waṭ-ṭayra wa kunnā fāʿilīn. (79)

69 I.e., the Deluge. The story of Noah is mentioned several times in the Qurʾān, and particularly in 11 : 25-48. Regarding the Deluge itself, see *sūrah* 7, note 47.

70 For an elucidation of the story – or, rather, legend – to which the above verse alludes, we must rely exclusively on the Companions of the Prophet, since neither the Qurʾān nor any authentic saying of the Prophet spells it out to us. However, the fact that a good many Companions and their immediate successors (*tābiʿūn*) fully agreed on the substance of the story, differing only in one or two insignificant details, seems to indicate that at that period it was already well-established in ancient Arabian tradition (cf. note 77 below). According to this story, a flock of sheep strayed at night into a neighbouring field and destroyed its crop. The case was brought before King David for judicial decision. On finding that the incident was due to the negligence of the owner of the sheep, David awarded the whole flock – the value of which corresponded roughly to the extent of the damage – as an indemnity to the owner of the field. David's young son, Solomon, regarded this judgment as too severe, inasmuch as the sheep represented the defendant's *capital*, whereas the damage was of a transitory nature, involving no more than the loss of one year's crop, i.e., of *income*. He therefore suggested to his father that the judgment should be altered: the owner of the field should have the temporary possession and usufruct of the sheep (milk, wool, new-born lambs, etc.), while their owner should tend the damaged field until it was restored to its former productivity, whereupon both the field and the flock of sheep should revert to their erstwhile owners; in this way the plaintiff would be fully compensated for his loss without depriving the defendant of his substance. David realized that his son's solution of the case was better than his own, and passed judgment accordingly; but since he, no less than Solomon, had been inspired by a deep sense of justice, God – in the words of the Qurʾān – "bore witness to their judgment".

71 I.e., the fact that Solomon's judgment was more profound did not disprove the intrinsic justice of David's original judgment or deprive it of its merit.

72 Lit., "We compelled".

73 A reference to the Psalms of David, which call upon all nature to extol the glory of God – similar to the Qurʾanic verses, "The seven heavens extol His limitless glory, and the earth, and all that they contain" (17 : 44), or "All that is in the heavens and on earth extols God's limitless glory" (57 : 1).

And We taught him how to make garments [of God-consciousness] for you, [O men,] so that they might fortify you against all that may cause you fear: but are you grateful [for this boon]?[74] ‹80›
And unto Solomon [We made subservient] the stormy wind, so that it sped at his behest towards the land which We had blessed:[75] for it is We who have knowledge of everything. ‹81› And among the rebellious forces [which We made subservient to him][76] there were some that dived for him [into the sea] and performed other works besides: but it was We who kept watch over them.[77] ‹82›

AND [remember] Job, when he cried out to his Sustainer, "Affliction has befallen me: but Thou art the most merciful of the merciful!"[78] ‹83› – whereupon We responded

وَعَلَّمۡنَٰهُ صَنۡعَةَ لَبُوسٖ لَّكُمۡ لِتُحۡصِنَكُم مِّنۢ بَأۡسِكُمۡۖ فَهَلۡ أَنتُمۡ
شَٰكِرُونَ ﴿٨٠﴾ وَلِسُلَيۡمَٰنَ ٱلرِّيحَ عَاصِفَةٗ تَجۡرِي بِأَمۡرِهِۦٓ إِلَى ٱلۡأَرۡضِ
ٱلَّتِي بَٰرَكۡنَا فِيهَاۚ وَكُنَّا بِكُلِّ شَيۡءٍ عَٰلِمِينَ ﴿٨١﴾ وَمِنَ ٱلشَّيَٰطِينِ مَن يَغُوصُونَ
لَهُۥ وَيَعۡمَلُونَ عَمَلٗا دُونَ ذَٰلِكَۖ وَكُنَّا لَهُمۡ حَٰفِظِينَ ﴿٨٢﴾ ۞ وَأَيُّوبَ إِذۡ
نَادَىٰ رَبَّهُۥٓ أَنِّي مَسَّنِيَ ٱلضُّرُّ وَأَنتَ أَرۡحَمُ ٱلرَّٰحِمِينَ ﴿٨٣﴾ فَٱسۡتَجَبۡنَا

ثلاثة ارباع الحزب

Wa ʿallamnāhu ṣanʿata labūsil-lakum lituḥṣinakum-mim-baʾsikum; fahal ʾañtum shākirūn. ﴿80﴾ Wa liSulaymānar-rīḥa ʿāṣifatañ-tajrī biʾamrihīi ʾilal-ʾarḍil-latī bāraknā fīhā; wa kunnā bikulli shayʾin ʿālimīn. ﴿81﴾ Wa minash-Shayāṭīni mañy-yaghūṣūna lahū wa yaʿmalūna ʿamalañ-dūna dhālika wa kunnā lahum ḥāfiẓīn. ﴿82﴾ ۞ Wa ʾAyyūba ʾidh nādā Rabbahūu ʾannī massaniyaḍ-ḍurru wa ʾAñta ʾArḥamur-rāḥimīn. ﴿83﴾ Fastajabnā

74 The noun *labūs* is synonymous with *libās* or *libs*, signifying "a garment" or "garments" (*Qāmūs, Lisān al-ʿArab*). But since this term has occasionally been used by pre-Islamic Arabs in the sense of "mail" or "coats of mail" (*ibid.*), the classical commentators assume that it has this meaning in the above context as well; and in this they rely on the – otherwise unsupported – statement of the *tābiʿī* Qatādah to the effect that "David was the first to make chain mail" (Ṭabarī). Accordingly, they understand the term *baʾs* which occurs at the end of the sentence in its secondary sense of "war" or "warlike violence", and interpret the relevant part of the verse thus: "We taught him how to make coats of mail for you, so that they might fortify you against your [mutual acts of] violence", or "against [the effects of] your warlike violence". One should, however, bear in mind that *baʾs* signifies also "harm", "misfortune", "distress", etc., as well as "danger"; hence it denotes, it its widest sense, anything that *causes* distress or fear (*Tāj al-ʿArūs*). If we adopt this last meaning, the term *labūs* may be understood in its primary significance of "garment" – in this case, the metaphorical "garment of God-consciousness" (*libās at-taqwā*) of which the Qurʾān speaks in 7 : 26. Rendered in this sense, the above verse expresses the idea that the Almighty taught David how to imbue his followers with that deep God-consciousness which frees men from all spiritual distress and all fears, whether it be fear of one another or the subconscious fear of the Unknown. The concluding rhetorical question, "but are you grateful [for this boon]?" implies that, as a rule, man does not fully realize – and, hence, is not really grateful for – the spiritual bounty thus offered him by God.

75 This is apparently an allusion to the fleets of sailing ships which brought untold riches to Palestine ("the land which We had blessed") and made Solomon's wealth proverbial.

76 My rendering, in this particular context, of *shayāṭīn* (lit., "satans") as "rebellious forces" is based on the tropical use of the term *shayṭān* in the sense of anything "rebellious", "inordinately proud" or "insolent" (cf. Lane IV, 1552) – in this case, possibly a reference to subdued and enslaved enemies or, more probably, to "rebellious" forces of nature which Solomon was able to tame and utilize; however, see also next note.

77 In this as well as in several other passages relating to Solomon, the Qurʾān alludes to the many poetic legends which were associated with his name since early antiquity and had become part and parcel of Judaeo-Christian and Arabian lore long before the advent of Islam. Although it is undoubtedly possible to interpret such passages in a "rationalistic" manner, I do not think that this is really necessary. Because they were so deeply ingrained in the imagination of the people to whom the Qurʾān addressed itself in the first instance, these legendary accounts of Solomon's wisdom and magic powers had acquired a cultural reality of their own and were, therefore, eminently suited to serve as a medium for the parabolic exposition of certain ethical truths with which this book is concerned: and so, without denying or confirming their mythical character, the Qurʾān uses them as a foil for the idea that God is the ultimate source of all human power and glory. and that all achievements of human ingenuity, even though they may sometimes border on the miraculous, are but an expression of His transcendental creativity.

78 The story of Job (Ayyūb in Arabic), describing his erstwhile happiness and prosperity, his subsequent trials and

لَهُۥ فَكَشَفْنَا مَا بِهِۦ مِن ضُرٍّ ۖ وَءَاتَيْنَٰهُ أَهْلَهُۥ وَمِثْلَهُم مَّعَهُمْ رَحْمَةً مِّنْ
عِندِنَا وَذِكْرَىٰ لِلْعَٰبِدِينَ ﴿٨٤﴾ وَإِسْمَٰعِيلَ وَإِدْرِيسَ وَذَا ٱلْكِفْلِ ۖ كُلٌّ
مِّنَ ٱلصَّٰبِرِينَ ﴿٨٥﴾ وَأَدْخَلْنَٰهُمْ فِى رَحْمَتِنَآ ۖ إِنَّهُم مِّنَ ٱلصَّٰلِحِينَ ﴿٨٦﴾
وَذَا ٱلنُّونِ إِذ ذَّهَبَ مُغَٰضِبًا فَظَنَّ أَن لَّن نَّقْدِرَ عَلَيْهِ فَنَادَىٰ فِى
ٱلظُّلُمَٰتِ أَن لَّآ إِلَٰهَ إِلَّآ أَنتَ سُبْحَٰنَكَ إِنِّى كُنتُ مِنَ ٱلظَّٰلِمِينَ ﴿٨٧﴾
فَٱسْتَجَبْنَا لَهُۥ وَنَجَّيْنَٰهُ مِنَ ٱلْغَمِّ ۚ وَكَذَٰلِكَ نُۨجِى ٱلْمُؤْمِنِينَ ﴿٨٨﴾

lahū fakashafnā mā bihī miñ-ḍurriñw-wa ᵓātaynāhu ᵓahlahū wa mithlahum-maᶜahum raḥmatam-min ᶜiñdinā wa dhikrā lilᶜābidīn. (84) Wa ᵓIsmāᶜīla wa ᵓIdrīsa wa Dhal-kifli kullum-minaṣ-ṣābirīn. (85) Wa ᵓadkhalnāhum fī raḥmatināa ᵓinnahum-minaṣ-ṣāliḥīn. (86) Wa Dhan-nūni ᵓidh dhahaba mughāḍibañ-faẓanna ᵓal-lañ-naqdira ᶜalayhi fanādā fiẓ-ẓulumāti ᵓal-lāa ᵓilāha ᵓillāa ᵓAñta subḥānaka ᵓinnī kuñtu minaẓ-ẓālimīn. (87) Fastajabnā lahū wa najjaynāhu minal-ghammi wa kadhālika nuñjil-muᵓminīn. (88)

unto him and removed all the affliction from which he suffered; and We gave him new offspring,[79] doubling their number as an act of grace from Us, and as a reminder unto all who worship Us. ‹84›

AND [remember] Ishmael and Idrīs,[80] and every one who [like them] has pledged himself [unto God]:[81] they all were among those who are patient in adversity, ‹85› and so We admitted them unto Our grace: behold, they were among the righteous! ‹86›

AND [remember] him of the great fish[82] – when he went off in wrath, thinking that We had no power over him![83] But then he cried out in the deep darkness [of his distress]: "There is no deity save Thee! Limitless art Thou in Thy glory! Verily, I have done wrong!"[84] ‹87›
And so We responded unto him and delivered him from [his] distress: for thus do We deliver all who have faith. ‹88›

---

tribulations, the loss of all his children and his property, his own loathsome illness and utter despair and, finally, God's reward of his patience in adversity, is given in full in the Old Testament (The Book of Job). This Biblical, highly philosophical epic is most probably a Hebrew translation or paraphrase – still evident in the language employed – of an ancient Nabataean (i.e., North-Arabian) poem, for "Job, the author of the finest piece of poetry that the ancient Semitic world produced, was an Arab, not a Jew, as the form of his name (*Iyyōb*) and the scene of his book, North Arabia, indicate" (Philip K. Hitti, *History of the Arabs*, London 1937, pp. 42-43). Since God "spoke" to him, Job ranks in the Qurᵓān among the prophets, personifying the supreme virtue of patience in adversity (*ṣabr*).

79 Lit., "his family" – i.e., new children in place of those who had died.

80 See *sūrah* 19, note 41.

81 Lit., "and him of the pledge". The expression *dhu 'l-kifl* is derived from the verb *kafala* – and especially the form *takaffala* – which signifies "he became responsible [for something or someone]" or "pledged himself [to do something]". Although the classical commentators consider *dhu 'l-kifl* to be the epithet or the proper name of a particular prophet – whom they variously, more or less at random, identify with Elijah or Joshua or Zachariah or Ezekiel – I fail to see any reason whatever for such attempts at "identification", the more so since we have not a single authentic *ḥadīth* which would mention, or even distantly allude to, a prophet by this name. I am, therefore, of the opinion that we have here (as in the identical expression in 38 : 48) a *generic term* applying to every one of the prophets, inasmuch as each of them pledged himself unreservedly to God and accepted the responsibility for delivering His message to man.

82 I.e., the Prophet Jonah, who is said to have been swallowed by a "great fish", as mentioned in 37 : 139 ff. and more fully narrated in the Old Testament (The Book of Jonah).

83 According to the Biblical account (which more or less agrees with the Qurᵓanic references to his story), Jonah was a prophet sent to the people of Nineveh, the capital of Assyria. At first his preaching was disregarded by his people, and he left them in anger, thus abandoning the mission entrusted to him by God; in the words of the Qurᵓān (37 : 140), "he fled like a runaway slave". The allegory of his temporary punishment and his subsequent rescue and redemption is referred to elsewhere in the Qurᵓān (i.e., in 37 : 139 – 148) and explained in the corresponding notes. It is to that punishment, repentance and salvation that the present and the next verse allude. (The redemption of Jonah's people is mentioned in 10 : 98 and 37 : 147-148.)

84 Lit., "I was among the wrongdoers!"

AND [thus did We deliver] Zachariah when he cried out unto his Sustainer: "O my Sustainer! Leave me not childless! But [even if Thou grant me no bodily heir, I know that] Thou wilt remain when all else has ceased to be!"[85] ‹89›

And so We responded unto him, and bestowed upon him the gift of John, having made his wife fit to bear him a child:[86] [and,] verily, these [three] would vie with one another in doing good works, and would call unto Us in yearning and awe; and they were always humble before Us. ‹90›

AND [remember] her who guarded her chastity, whereupon We breathed into her of Our spirit[87] and caused her, together with her son, to become a symbol [of Our grace] unto all people.[88] ‹91›

VERILY, [O you who believe in Me,] this community of yours is one single community, since I am the Sustainer of you all: worship, then, Me [alone]![89] ‹92›

وَزَكَرِيَّآ إِذْ نَادَىٰ رَبَّهُۥ رَبِّ لَا تَذَرْنِى فَرْدًا وَأَنتَ خَيْرُ ٱلْوَٰرِثِينَ ﴿٨٩﴾
فَٱسْتَجَبْنَا لَهُۥ وَوَهَبْنَا لَهُۥ يَحْيَىٰ وَأَصْلَحْنَا لَهُۥ زَوْجَهُۥٓ ۚ إِنَّهُمْ كَانُوا۟
يُسَٰرِعُونَ فِى ٱلْخَيْرَٰتِ وَيَدْعُونَنَا رَغَبًا وَرَهَبًا ۖ وَكَانُوا۟ لَنَا خَٰشِعِينَ ﴿٩٠﴾
وَٱلَّتِىٓ أَحْصَنَتْ فَرْجَهَا فَنَفَخْنَا فِيهَا مِن رُّوحِنَا وَجَعَلْنَٰهَا وَٱبْنَهَآ ءَايَةً
لِّلْعَٰلَمِينَ ﴿٩١﴾ إِنَّ هَٰذِهِۦٓ أُمَّتُكُمْ أُمَّةً وَٰحِدَةً وَأَنَا۠ رَبُّكُمْ فَٱعْبُدُونِ ﴿٩٢﴾

Wa Zakariyyāa ʾidh nādā Rabbahū Rabbi lā tadharnī fardañw-wa ʾAñta Khayrul-wārithīn. (89) Fastajabnā lahū wa wahabnā lahū Yaḥyā wa ʾaṣlaḥnā lahū zawjah. ʾInnahum kānū yusāriʿūna fil-khayrāti wa yadʿūnanā raghabañw-wa rahabañw-wa kānū lanā khāshiʿīn. (90) Wal-latīi ʾaḥṣanat farjahā fanafakhnā fīhā mir-rūḥinā wa jaʿalnāhā wab-nahāa ʾĀyatal-lilʿālamīn. (91) ʾInna hādhihīi ʾummatukum ʾummatañw-wāḥidatañw-wa ʾAna Rabbukum faʿbudūn. (92)

85 Lit., "Thou art the best of inheritors" – a phrase explained in note 22 on 15 : 23. The words interpolated by me between brackets correspond to Zamakhsharī's and Rāzī's interpretation of this phrase. For more detailed references to Zachariah, father of John the Baptist, see 3 : 37 ff. and 19 : 2 ff.

86 Lit., "for We had made his wife fit for him", i.e., after her previous barrenness.

87 This allegorical expression, used here with reference to Mary's conception of Jesus, has been widely – and erroneously – interpreted as relating specifically to *his* birth. As a matter of fact, the Qurʾān uses the same expression in three other places with reference to the creation of *man in general* – namely in 15 : 29 and 38 : 72, "when I have formed him . . . and breathed into him of My spirit"; and in 32 : 9, "and thereupon He forms [lit., "formed"] him fully and breathes [lit., "breathed"] into him of His spirit". In particular, the passage of which the last-quoted phrase is a part (i.e., 32 : 7-9) makes it abundantly and explicitly clear that God "breathes of His spirit" into *every* human being. Commenting on the verse under consideration, Zamakhsharī states that "the breathing of the spirit [of God] into a body signifies the endowing it with life": an explanation with which Rāzī concurs. (In this connection, see also note 181 on 4 : 171.) As for the description of Mary as *allatī aḥṣanat farjahā*, idiomatically denoting "one who guarded her chastity" (lit., "her private parts"), it is to be borne in mind that the term *iḥṣān* – lit., "[one's] being fortified [against any danger or evil]" – has the tropical meaning of "abstinence from what is unlawful or reprehensible" (*Tāj al-ʿArūs*), and especially from illicit sexual intercourse, and is applied to a man as well as a woman: thus, for instance, the terms *muḥṣan* and *muḥṣanah* are used elsewhere in the Qurʾān to describe, respectively, a man or a woman who is "fortified [by marriage] against unchastity". Hence, the expression *allatī aḥṣanat farjahā*, occurring in the above verse as well as in 66 : 12 with reference to Mary, is but meant to stress her outstanding chastity and complete abstinence, in thought as well as in deed, from anything unlawful or morally reprehensible: in other words, a rejection of the calumny (referred to in 4 : 156 and obliquely alluded to in 19 : 27-28) that the birth of Jesus was the result of an "illicit union".

88 For my rendering of the term *āyah* as "symbol", see *sūrah* 17, note 2, and *sūrah* 19, note 16.

89 After calling to mind, in verses 48-91, some of the earlier prophets, all of whom stressed the oneness and uniqueness of God, the discourse returns to that principle of oneness as it ought to be reflected in the unity of all who believe in Him. (See 23 : 51 ff.)

But men have torn their unity wide asunder,[90] [forgetting that] unto Us they all are bound to return. ‹93›
And yet, whoever does [the least] of righteous deeds and is a believer withal, his endeavour shall not be disowned: for, behold, We shall record it in his favour.[91] ‹94›
Hence, it has been unfailingly true of[92] any community whom We have ever destroyed that they [were people who] would never turn back [from their sinful ways][93] ‹95› until such a time as Gog and Magog are let loose [upon the world] and swarm down from every corner [of the earth],[94] ‹96› the while the true promise [of resurrection] draws close [to its fulfilment].
But then, lo! the eyes of those who [in their lifetime] were bent on denying the truth will stare in horror, [and they will exclaim:] "Oh, woe unto us! We were indeed heedless of this [promise of resurrection]! – nay, we were [bent on] doing evil!"[95] ‹97›
[Then they will be told:] "Verily, you and all that you [were wont to] worship instead of God are but the fuel of hell: that is what you are destined for.[96] ‹98›

وَتَقَطَّعُوٓاْ أَمۡرَهُم بَيۡنَهُمۡۖ كُلٌّ إِلَيۡنَا رَٰجِعُونَ ﴿٩٣﴾ فَمَن يَعۡمَلۡ مِنَ ٱلصَّٰلِحَٰتِ
وَهُوَ مُؤۡمِنٌ فَلَا كُفۡرَانَ لِسَعۡيِهِۦ وَإِنَّا لَهُۥ كَٰتِبُونَ ﴿٩٤﴾ وَحَرَٰمٌ عَلَىٰ قَرۡيَةٍ
أَهۡلَكۡنَٰهَآ أَنَّهُمۡ لَا يَرۡجِعُونَ ﴿٩٥﴾ حَتَّىٰٓ إِذَا فُتِحَتۡ يَأۡجُوجُ وَمَأۡجُوجُ
وَهُم مِّن كُلِّ حَدَبٖ يَنسِلُونَ ﴿٩٦﴾ وَٱقۡتَرَبَ ٱلۡوَعۡدُ ٱلۡحَقُّ فَإِذَا هِيَ
شَٰخِصَةٌ أَبۡصَٰرُ ٱلَّذِينَ كَفَرُواْ يَٰوَيۡلَنَا قَدۡ كُنَّا فِي غَفۡلَةٖ مِّنۡ هَٰذَا بَلۡ
كُنَّا ظَٰلِمِينَ ﴿٩٧﴾ إِنَّكُمۡ وَمَا تَعۡبُدُونَ مِن دُونِ ٱللَّهِ حَصَبُ جَهَنَّمَ أَنتُمۡ
لَهَا وَٰرِدُونَ ﴿٩٨﴾

Wa taqaṭṭaʿūu ʾamrahum-baynahum; kullun ʾilaynā rājiʿūn. ﴿٩٣﴾ Famañy-yaʿmal minaṣ-ṣāliḥāti wa huwa muʾminuñ-falā kufrāna lisaʿyihī wa ʾinnā lahū kātibūn. ﴿٩٤﴾ Wa ḥarāmun ʿalā qaryatin ʾahlaknāhāa ʾannahum lā yarjiʿūn. ﴿٩٥﴾ Ḥattāa ʾidhā futiḥat Yaʾjūju wa Maʾjūju wa hum-miñ-kulli ḥadabiñy-yañsilūn. ﴿٩٦﴾ Waq-tarabal-waʿdul-ḥaqqu faʾidhā hiya shākhiṣatun ʾabṣārul-ladhīna kafarū yā waylanā qad kunnā fī ghaflatim-min hādhā bal kunnā ẓālimīn. ﴿٩٧﴾ ʾInnakum wa mā taʿbudūna miñ-dūnil-lāhi ḥaṣabu jahannama ʾañtum lahā wāridūn. ﴿٩٨﴾

90 This is the meaning of the idiomatic phrase, *taqaṭṭaʿū amrahum baynahum*. As Zamakhsharī points out, the sudden turn of the discourse from the second person plural to the third person is indicative of God's severe disapproval – His "turning away", as it were, from those who are or were guilty of breaking the believers' unity. (See also 23 : 53 and the corresponding note 30.)

91 I.e., even a breach of religious unity may not be unforgivable so long as it does not involve a worship of false deities or false moral values (cf. verses 98-99 below): this is the meaning of the stress, in this context, on man's being "a believer withal" – an echo of the principle clearly spelt out in 2 : 62 and several other Qurʾanic passages.

92 Lit., "an inviolable law (*ḥarām*) upon . . .", expressing the impossibility of conceiving anything to the contrary (Zamakhsharī).

93 I.e., whenever God consigns a community to destruction, He does it not because of its people's occasional lapses but only because of their irremediable, conscious unwillingness to forsake their sinful ways.

94 I.e., until the Day of Resurrection, heralded by the allegorical break-through of "Gog and Magog" (see *sūrah* 18, note 100, especially the last sentence): for it is on that Day that even the most hardened sinner will at last realize his guilt and be filled with belated remorse. – The term *ḥadab* literally denotes "raised ground" or "elevation", but the expression *min kulli ḥadabin* is used here idiomatically, signifying "from all directions" or "from every corner [of the earth]": an allusion to the irresistible nature of the social and cultural catastrophes which will overwhelm mankind before the coming of the Last Hour.

95 I.e., deliberately and without any excuse, since all the prophets had warned man of the Day of Resurrection and Judgment: cf. 14 : 44-45. The words "bent on" interpolated by me within brackets indicate intent, similar to the preceding expression *alladhīna kafarū*, "those who were *bent on* denying the truth" (see also note 6 on 2 : 6).

96 Lit., "you are bound to reach it". The expression "all that you have worshipped instead of God" comprises not merely all false religious imagery but also all false ethical values endowed with *quasi*-divine sanctity, all of which are but "the fuel of hell".

If those [false objects of your worship] had truly been divine, they would not have been destined for it: but [as it is, you] all shall abide therein!" ‹99›
Moaning will be their lot therein, and nothing [else] will they hear therein.[97] ‹100›
[But,] behold, as for those for whom [the decree of] ultimate good has already gone forth from Us[98] – these will be kept far away from that [hell]: ‹101› no sound thereof will they hear; and they will abide in all that their souls have ever desired. ‹102›
The supreme awesomeness [of the Day of Resurrection] will cause them no grief, since the angels will receive them with the greeting, "This is your Day [of triumph – the Day] which you were promised!" ‹103›
On that Day We shall roll up the skies as written scrolls are rolled up; [and] as We brought into being the first creation, so We shall bring it forth anew[99] – a promise which We have willed upon Ourselves: for, behold, We are able to do [all things]! ‹104›

AND, INDEED, after having exhorted [man],[100] We laid it down in all the books of divine wisdom that My righteous servants shall inherit the earth:[101] ‹105› herein, behold, there is a message for people who [truly] worship God. ‹106›
And [thus, O Prophet,] We have sent thee as [an evidence of Our] grace towards all the worlds.[102] ‹107›

لَوْ كَانَ هَٰٓؤُلَآءِ ءَالِهَةً مَّا وَرَدُوهَا ۖ وَكُلٌّ فِيهَا خَٰلِدُونَ ﴿٩٩﴾ لَهُمْ فِيهَا
زَفِيرٌ وَهُمْ فِيهَا لَا يَسْمَعُونَ ﴿١٠٠﴾ إِنَّ ٱلَّذِينَ سَبَقَتْ لَهُم مِّنَّا ٱلْحُسْنَىٰٓ
أُو۟لَٰٓئِكَ عَنْهَا مُبْعَدُونَ ﴿١٠١﴾ لَا يَسْمَعُونَ حَسِيسَهَا ۖ وَهُمْ فِى مَا ٱشْتَهَتْ
أَنفُسُهُمْ خَٰلِدُونَ ﴿١٠٢﴾ لَا يَحْزُنُهُمُ ٱلْفَزَعُ ٱلْأَكْبَرُ وَتَتَلَقَّىٰهُمُ ٱلْمَلَٰٓئِكَةُ
هَٰذَا يَوْمُكُمُ ٱلَّذِى كُنتُمْ تُوعَدُونَ ﴿١٠٣﴾ يَوْمَ نَطْوِى ٱلسَّمَآءَ كَطَىِّ
ٱلسِّجِلِّ لِلْكُتُبِ ۚ كَمَا بَدَأْنَآ أَوَّلَ خَلْقٍ نُّعِيدُهُۥ ۚ وَعْدًا عَلَيْنَآ ۚ إِنَّا كُنَّا
فَٰعِلِينَ ﴿١٠٤﴾ وَلَقَدْ كَتَبْنَا فِى ٱلزَّبُورِ مِنۢ بَعْدِ ٱلذِّكْرِ أَنَّ ٱلْأَرْضَ يَرِثُهَا
عِبَادِىَ ٱلصَّٰلِحُونَ ﴿١٠٥﴾ إِنَّ فِى هَٰذَا لَبَلَٰغًا لِّقَوْمٍ عَٰبِدِينَ ﴿١٠٦﴾ وَمَآ
أَرْسَلْنَٰكَ إِلَّا رَحْمَةً لِّلْعَٰلَمِينَ ﴿١٠٧﴾

Law kāna hāaʾulāaʾi ʾālihatam-mā waradūhā; wa
kulluñ-fīhā khālidūn. (99) Lahum fīhā zafīruñw-wa
hum fīhā lā yasmaʿūn. (100) ʾInnal-ladhīna sabaqat la-
hum-minnal-ḥusnāa ʾulāaʾika ʿanhā mubʿadūn. (101)
Lā yasmaʿūna ḥasīsahā; wa hum fī mash-tahat
ʾañfusuhum khālidūn. (102) Lā yaḥzunuhumul-fazaʿul-
ʾakbaru wa tatalaqqāhumul-Malāaʾikatu hādhā Yaw-
mukumul-ladhī kuñtum tūʿadūn. (103) Yawma naṭwis-
samāaʾa kaṭayyis-sijilli lilkutub. Kamā badaʾnāa
ʾawwala khalqiñ-nuʿīduhū waʿdan ʿalaynāa ʾinnā
kunnā fāʿilīn. (104) Wa laqad katabnā fiz-Zabūri mim-
baʿdidh-Dhikri ʾannal-ʾarḍa yarithuhā ʿibādiyaṣ-
ṣāliḥūn. (105) ʾInna fī hādhā labalāghal-liqawmin
ʿābidīn. (106) Wa māa ʾarsalnāka ʾillā raḥmatal-
lilʿālamīn. (107)

97 Thus, spiritual "deafness" in the life to come will be the inexorable consequence of one's having remained deaf, in this world, to the voice of truth, just as "blindness" and oblivion will be part of the suffering of all who have been spiritually blind to the truth (cf. 20 : 124-126).

98 I.e., those who have been promised paradise on account of their faith and their good deeds.

99 See in this connection 14 : 48 and the corresponding note 63.

100 Lit., "after the reminder (*adh-dhikr*)". For the deeper implications of the Qurʾanic term *dhikr*, see note 13 on verse 10 of this *sūrah*.

101 *Zabūr* (lit., "scripture" or "book") is a generic term denoting any "book of wisdom": hence, any and all of the divine scriptures revealed by God to the prophets (Ṭabarī). The statement that "My righteous servants shall inherit the earth" is obviously an echo of the promise, "You are bound to rise high if you are [truly] believers" (3 : 139) – the implication being that it is only through faith in God and righteous behaviour on earth that man can reach the heights envisaged for him by his Creator's grace.

102 I.e., towards all mankind. For an elucidation of this fundamental principle underlying the message of the Qurʾān, see 7 : 158 and the corresponding note 126. The universality of the Qurʾanic revelation arises from three factors: firstly, its appeal to all mankind irrespective of descent, race or cultural environment; secondly, the fact that it appeals exclusively to man's *reason* and, hence, does not postulate any dogma that could be accepted on the basis of

Say: "It has but been revealed unto me[103] that your God is the One and Only God: will you, then, surrender yourselves unto Him?" ‹108›
But if they turn away, say: "I have proclaimed this in equity unto all of you alike;[104] but I do not know whether that [judgment] which you are promised [by God] is near or far [in time]. ‹109›
"Verily, He knows all that is said openly, just as He [alone] knows all that you would conceal. ‹110› But [as for me,] I do not know whether, perchance, this [delay in God's judgment] is but a trial for you, and a [merciful] respite for a while."[105] ‹111›

Say:[106] "O my Sustainer! Judge Thou in truth!" – and [say]: "Our Sustainer is the Most Gracious, the One whose aid is ever to be sought against all your [attempts at] defining [Him]!"[107] ‹112›

قُلْ إِنَّمَا يُوحَىٰٓ إِلَيَّ أَنَّمَآ إِلَٰهُكُمْ إِلَٰهٌ وَٰحِدٌ فَهَلْ أَنتُم مُّسْلِمُونَ ﴿108﴾
فَإِن تَوَلَّوْا۟ فَقُلْ ءَاذَنتُكُمْ عَلَىٰ سَوَآءٍ وَإِنْ أَدْرِىٓ أَقَرِيبٌ أَم بَعِيدٌ مَّا
تُوعَدُونَ ﴿109﴾ إِنَّهُۥ يَعْلَمُ ٱلْجَهْرَ مِنَ ٱلْقَوْلِ وَيَعْلَمُ مَا تَكْتُمُونَ ﴿110﴾
وَإِنْ أَدْرِى لَعَلَّهُۥ فِتْنَةٌ لَّكُمْ وَمَتَٰعٌ إِلَىٰ حِينٍ ﴿111﴾ قَٰلَ رَبِّ ٱحْكُم
بِٱلْحَقِّ وَرَبُّنَا ٱلرَّحْمَٰنُ ٱلْمُسْتَعَانُ عَلَىٰ مَا تَصِفُونَ ﴿112﴾

Qul ʾinnamā yūḥāa ʾilayya ʾannamāa ʾIlāhukum
ʾIlāhuñw-Wāḥiduñ-fahal-ʾañtum-Muslimūn. (108) Faʾiñ-
tawallaw faqul ʾādhañtukum ʿalā sawāaʾiñw-wa ʾin
ʾadrīi ʾaqarībun ʾam-baʿīdum-mā tūʿadūn. (109)
ʾInnahū yaʿlamul-jahra minal-qawli wa yaʿlamu mā
taktumūn. (110) Wa ʾin ʾadrī laʿallahū fitnatul-lakum
wa matāʿun ʾilā ḥīn. (111) Qāla Rabbiḥ-kum-bil-
ḥaqq. Wa Rabbunar-Raḥmānul-Mustaʿānu ʿalā mā
taṣifūn. (112)

---

blind faith alone; and, finally, the fact that – contrary to all other sacred scriptures known to history – the Qurʾān has remained entirely unchanged in its wording ever since its revelation fourteen centuries ago and will, because it is so widely recorded, forever remain so in accordance with the divine promise, "it is We who shall truly guard it [from all corruption]" (cf. 15 : 9 and the corresponding note 10). It is by virtue of these three factors that the Qurʾān represents the final stage of all divine revelation, and that the Prophet through whom it has been conveyed to mankind is stated to have been the last (in Qurʾanic terminology, "the seal") of all prophets (cf. 33 : 40).

103 Cf. the first sentence of verse 45 of this *sūrah*. This stress on divine revelation as the *only* source of the Prophet's knowledge referred to in the sequence is expressed, in Arabic, by means of the restrictive particle *innamā*.

104 The expression *ʿalā sawā* (lit., "in an equitable manner") comprises in this context two distinct concepts: that of *fairness* as regards the clarity and unambiguity of the above announcement, as well as of *equality*, implying that it is being made to all human beings alike; hence my composite rendering of this phrase.

105 Lit., "enjoyment [of life] for a while": i.e., a chance, mercifully granted by God, to attain to faith.

106 See note 5 on verse 4 of this *sūrah*.

107 Lit., "against (*ʿalā*) all that you attribute [to Him] by way of description" or "of definition" (see note 88 on the last sentence of 6 : 100): implying that only God's grace can save man from the blasphemous attempts – prompted by his inherent weakness – to bring God "closer" to his own, human understanding by means of humanly-conceived "definitions" of Him who is transcendent, infinite and unfathomable.

The Twenty-Second Sūrah

Al-Ḥajj (The Pilgrimage)

Period Uncertain

SUYŪṬĪ places most of this *sūrah* chronologically in the middle of the Medina period, excepting verses 39-40 – which (according to Ibn ᶜAbbās, as quoted by Ṭabarī) were revealed during the Prophet's exodus from Mecca to Medina – as well as some other verses said to have been revealed at the time of the battle of Badr (in the year 2 H.). As against this, however, most of the classical Qur'ān-commentators (e.g., Baghawī, Zamakhsharī, Rāzī, Bayḍāwī) describe it unequivocally as a Meccan revelation, with the possible exception of six verses (19-24) which, according to some authorities, may belong to the Medina period. On the whole, it is most probable that by far the largest part of the *sūrah* is Meccan, while the rest was revealed shortly after the Prophet's arrival at Medina.

The title is derived from the reference, in verses 25 ff., to the Mecca pilgrimage (*al-ḥajj*) and some of the rituals connected therewith.

-22-

سورة الحج مدنية

وآياتها ثمان وسبعون

IN THE NAME OF GOD, THE MOST GRACIOUS, THE DISPENSER OF GRACE:

O MEN! Be conscious of your Sustainer: for, verily, the violent convulsion of the Last Hour will be an awesome thing! ⟨1⟩ On the Day when you behold it, every woman that feeds a child at her breast will utterly forget her nursling, and every woman heavy with child will bring forth her burden [before her time]; and it will seem to thee that all mankind is drunk,[1] although they will not be drunk – but vehement will be [their dread of] God's chastisement.[2] ⟨2⟩

حزب 34

And yet, among men there is many a one who argues about God without having any knowledge [of Him], and follows every rebellious satanic force[3] ⟨3⟩ about which it has been decreed that whoever entrusts himself to it, him will it lead astray and guide towards the suffering of the blazing flame! ⟨4⟩

O MEN! If you are in doubt as to the [truth of] resurrection, [remember that,] verily, We have created [every one of] you out of dust, then out of a drop of sperm, then out of a germ-cell, then out of an embryonic lump complete [in itself] and yet incomplete,[4] so that We might make [your origin] clear unto you.

بِسۡمِ ٱللَّهِ ٱلرَّحۡمَٰنِ ٱلرَّحِيمِ

يَٰٓأَيُّهَا ٱلنَّاسُ ٱتَّقُواْ رَبَّكُمۡۚ إِنَّ زَلۡزَلَةَ ٱلسَّاعَةِ شَيۡءٌ عَظِيمٞ ﴿١﴾ يَوۡمَ
تَرَوۡنَهَا تَذۡهَلُ كُلُّ مُرۡضِعَةٍ عَمَّآ أَرۡضَعَتۡ وَتَضَعُ كُلُّ ذَاتِ حَمۡلٍ حَمۡلَهَا
وَتَرَى ٱلنَّاسَ سُكَٰرَىٰ وَمَا هُم بِسُكَٰرَىٰ وَلَٰكِنَّ عَذَابَ ٱللَّهِ شَدِيدٞ ﴿٢﴾
وَمِنَ ٱلنَّاسِ مَن يُجَٰدِلُ فِي ٱللَّهِ بِغَيۡرِ عِلۡمٖ وَيَتَّبِعُ كُلَّ شَيۡطَٰنٖ مَّرِيدٖ ﴿٣﴾
كُتِبَ عَلَيۡهِ أَنَّهُۥ مَن تَوَلَّاهُ فَأَنَّهُۥ يُضِلُّهُۥ وَيَهۡدِيهِ إِلَىٰ عَذَابِ ٱلسَّعِيرِ ﴿٤﴾
يَٰٓأَيُّهَا ٱلنَّاسُ إِن كُنتُمۡ فِي رَيۡبٖ مِّنَ ٱلۡبَعۡثِ فَإِنَّا خَلَقۡنَٰكُم مِّن تُرَابٖ ثُمَّ
مِن نُّطۡفَةٖ ثُمَّ مِنۡ عَلَقَةٖ ثُمَّ مِن مُّضۡغَةٖ مُّخَلَّقَةٖ وَغَيۡرِ مُخَلَّقَةٖ لِّنُبَيِّنَ لَكُمۡۚ

Bismil-lāhir-Raḥmānir-Raḥīm.
Yāa ᵓayyuhan-nāsut-taqū Rabbakum; ᵓinna zalzala-
tas-Sāᶜati shayᵓun ᶜaẓīm. (1) Yawma tarawnahā
tadhhalu kullu murḍiᶜatin ᶜammāa ᵓarḍaᶜat wa
taḍaᶜu kullu dhāti ḥamlin ḥamlahā wa taran-nāsa
sukārā wa mā hum-bisukārā wa lākinna ᶜadhābal-
lāhi shadīd. (2) Wa minan-nāsi mañy-yujādilu fil-
lāhi bighayri ᶜilmiñw-wa yattabiᶜu kulla Shayṭānim-
marīd. (3) Kutiba ᶜalayhi ᵓannahū mañ-tawallāhu
faᵓannahū yuḍilluhū wa yahdīhi ᵓilā ᶜadhābis-saᶜīr.
(4) Yāa ᵓayyuhan-nāsu ᵓiñ-kuñtum fī raybim-minal-
baᶜthi faᵓinnā khalaqnākum-miñ-turābiñ-thumma
miñ-nuṭfatiñ-thumma min ᶜalaqatiñ-thumma mim-
muḍghatim-mukhallaqatiñw-wa ghayri mukhallaqa-
til-linubayyina lakum.

---

1 Lit., "thou shalt see [or "behold"] mankind drunk", i.e., behaving *as if* they were drunk. The illusory, purely subjective character of this "seeing" – implied in the use of the singular form *tarā* ("*thou* shalt see") after the plural "you" employed in the first clause of this verse – justifies the rendering "it will seem to thee that . . .", etc.

2 My interpolation of the words "their dread of" is based on the statement in 21 : 103 that, as far as the *righteous* are concerned, "the supreme awesomeness [of the Day of Resurrection] will cause them no grief" despite the dread with which it will overwhelm every human being.

3 See first half of note 16 on 15 : 17.

4 This rendering conforms with the interpretation of the phrase *mukhallaqah wa-ghayr mukhallaqah* by Ibn ᶜAbbās and Qatādah (the latter quoted by Ṭabarī and the former by Baghawī), alluding to the various stages of embryonic

And whatever We will [to be born] We cause to rest in the [mother's] wombs for a term set [by Us], and then We bring you forth as infants and [allow you to live] so that [some of] you might attain to maturity: for among you are such as are caused to die [in childhood], just as many a one of you is reduced in old age to a most abject state, ceasing to know anything of what he once knew so well.[5]
And [if, O man, thou art still in doubt as to resurrection, consider this:] thou canst see the earth dry and lifeless – and [suddenly,] when We send down waters upon it, it stirs and swells and puts forth every kind of lovely plant! ‹5›
All this [happens] because God alone is the Ultimate Truth,[6] and because He alone brings the dead to life, and because He has the power to will anything. ‹6›
And [know, O man,] that the Last Hour is bound to come, beyond any doubt, and that God will [indeed] resurrect all who are in their graves. ‹7›
And yet, among men there is many a one that argues about God without having any knowledge [of Him], without any guidance, and without any light-giving revelation ‹8› – scornfully turning aside [from the truth] so as to lead [others] astray from the path of God.
Disgrace [of the spirit] is in store for him in this world;[7] and on the Day of Resurrection We shall make him taste suffering through fire; ‹9› [and he shall he told:] "This is an outcome of what thine own hands have wrought – for, never does God do the least wrong to His creatures! ‹10›

وَنُقِرُّ فِي ٱلۡأَرۡحَامِ مَا نَشَآءُ إِلَىٰٓ أَجَلٖ مُّسَمّٗى ثُمَّ نُخۡرِجُكُمۡ طِفۡلٗا ثُمَّ
لِتَبۡلُغُوٓاْ أَشُدَّكُمۡۖ وَمِنكُم مَّن يُتَوَفَّىٰ وَمِنكُم مَّن يُرَدُّ إِلَىٰٓ أَرۡذَلِ ٱلۡعُمُرِ
لِكَيۡلَا يَعۡلَمَ مِنۢ بَعۡدِ عِلۡمٖ شَيۡـٔٗاۚ وَتَرَى ٱلۡأَرۡضَ هَامِدَةٗ فَإِذَآ أَنزَلۡنَا
عَلَيۡهَا ٱلۡمَآءَ ٱهۡتَزَّتۡ وَرَبَتۡ وَأَنۢبَتَتۡ مِن كُلِّ زَوۡجِۢ بَهِيجٖ ﴿٥﴾ ذَٰلِكَ بِأَنَّ
ٱللَّهَ هُوَ ٱلۡحَقُّ وَأَنَّهُۥ يُحۡيِ ٱلۡمَوۡتَىٰ وَأَنَّهُۥ عَلَىٰ كُلِّ شَيۡءٖ قَدِيرٞ ﴿٦﴾ وَأَنَّ
ٱلسَّاعَةَ ءَاتِيَةٞ لَّا رَيۡبَ فِيهَا وَأَنَّ ٱللَّهَ يَبۡعَثُ مَن فِي ٱلۡقُبُورِ ﴿٧﴾ وَمِنَ
ٱلنَّاسِ مَن يُجَٰدِلُ فِي ٱللَّهِ بِغَيۡرِ عِلۡمٖ وَلَا هُدٗى وَلَا كِتَٰبٖ مُّنِيرٖ ﴿٨﴾
ثَانِيَ عِطۡفِهِۦ لِيُضِلَّ عَن سَبِيلِ ٱللَّهِۖ لَهُۥ فِي ٱلدُّنۡيَا خِزۡيٞۖ وَنُذِيقُهُۥ يَوۡمَ
ٱلۡقِيَٰمَةِ عَذَابَ ٱلۡحَرِيقِ ﴿٩﴾ ذَٰلِكَ بِمَا قَدَّمَتۡ يَدَاكَ وَأَنَّ ٱللَّهَ لَيۡسَ
بِظَلَّٰمٖ لِّلۡعَبِيدِ ﴿١٠﴾

Wa nuqirru fil-ʾarḥāmi mā nashāaʾu ʾilāa ʾajalim-musammañ-thumma nukhrijukum ṭiflañ-thumma litablughūu ʾashuddakum. Wa miñkum-mañy-yutawaffā wa miñkum-mañy-yuraddu ʾilāa ʾardhalil-ʿumuri likaylā yaʿlama mim-baʿdi ʿilmiñ-shayʾā. Wa taral-ʾarḍa hāmidatañ-faʾidhāa ʾañzalnā ʿalayhal-māaʾah-tazzat wa rabat wa ʾambatat miñ-kulli zawjim-bahīj. (5) Dhālika biʾannal-lāha Huwal-Ḥaqqu wa ʾannahū yuḥyil-mawtā wa ʾannahū ʿalā kulli shayʾiñ-Qadīr. (6) Wa ʾannas-Sāʿata ʾātiyatul-lā rayba fīhā wa ʾannal-lāha yabʿathu mañ-fil-qubūr. (7) Wa minan-nāsi mañy-yujādilu fil-lāhi bighayri ʿilmiñw-wa lā hudañw-wa lā Kitābim-munīr. (8) Thāniya ʿiṭfihī liyuḍilla ʿañ-sabīlil-lāh. Lahū fid-dunyā khizyuñw-wa nudhīquhū Yawmal-Qiyāmati ʿadhābal-ḥarīq. (9) Dhālika bimā qaddamat yadāka wa ʾannal-lāha laysa biẓallāmil-lilʿabīd. (10)

development. In addition, Ṭabarī explains the expression *ghayr mukhallaqah* as denoting the stage at which the embryonic lump (*muḍghah*) has as yet no individual life – or, in his words, "when no soul has as yet been breathed into it" (*lā yunfakh fīhā ar-rūḥ*). – As regards the expression "created out of dust", it is meant to indicate man's lowly biological origin and his affinity with other "earthy" substances; see in this connection the second half of note 47 on 3 : 59, and note 4 on 23 : 12.

5 See note 79 on 16 : 70.

6 See *sūrah* 20, note 99.

7 Since many unrighteous people apparently "prosper" in this world, it is clear that the disgrace of which the above verse speaks is of a moral nature – namely, a gradual coarsening of all moral perceptions and, thus, a degradation of the spirit.

وَمِنَ ٱلنَّاسِ مَن يَعْبُدُ ٱللَّهَ عَلَىٰ حَرْفٍ ۖ فَإِنْ أَصَابَهُۥ خَيْرٌ ٱطْمَأَنَّ بِهِۦ ۖ وَإِنْ
أَصَابَتْهُ فِتْنَةٌ ٱنقَلَبَ عَلَىٰ وَجْهِهِۦ خَسِرَ ٱلدُّنْيَا وَٱلْءَاخِرَةَ ۚ ذَٰلِكَ هُوَ
ٱلْخُسْرَانُ ٱلْمُبِينُ ﴿١١﴾ يَدْعُوا۟ مِن دُونِ ٱللَّهِ مَا لَا يَضُرُّهُۥ وَمَا لَا يَنفَعُهُۥ ۚ
ذَٰلِكَ هُوَ ٱلضَّلَٰلُ ٱلْبَعِيدُ ﴿١٢﴾ يَدْعُوا۟ لَمَن ضَرُّهُۥٓ أَقْرَبُ مِن نَّفْعِهِۦ ۚ
لَبِئْسَ ٱلْمَوْلَىٰ وَلَبِئْسَ ٱلْعَشِيرُ ﴿١٣﴾ إِنَّ ٱللَّهَ يُدْخِلُ ٱلَّذِينَ ءَامَنُوا۟
وَعَمِلُوا۟ ٱلصَّٰلِحَٰتِ جَنَّٰتٍ تَجْرِى مِن تَحْتِهَا ٱلْأَنْهَٰرُ ۚ إِنَّ ٱللَّهَ يَفْعَلُ
مَا يُرِيدُ ﴿١٤﴾ مَن كَانَ يَظُنُّ أَن لَّن يَنصُرَهُ ٱللَّهُ فِى ٱلدُّنْيَا وَٱلْءَاخِرَةِ فَلْيَمْدُدْ
بِسَبَبٍ إِلَى ٱلسَّمَآءِ ثُمَّ لْيَقْطَعْ فَلْيَنظُرْ هَلْ يُذْهِبَنَّ كَيْدُهُۥ مَا يَغِيظُ ﴿١٥﴾

And there is, too, among men many a one who worships God on the borderline [of faith]:[8] thus, if good befalls him, he is satisfied with Him; but if a trial assails him, he turns away utterly,[9] losing [thereby both] this world and the life to come: [and] this, indeed, is a loss beyond compare![10] ‹11›
[By behaving thus,] he invokes, instead of God, something that can neither harm nor benefit him:[11] [and] this is indeed the utmost one can go astray.[12] ‹12›
[And sometimes] he invokes [another human being –] one that is far more likely to cause harm than benefit: vile, indeed, is such a patron, and vile the follower![13] ‹13›

VERILY, God will admit those who have attained to faith and have done righteous deeds into gardens through which running waters flow: for, behold, God does whatever He wills. ‹14›
If anyone thinks that God will not succour him[14] in this world and in the life to come, let him reach out unto heaven by any [other] means and [thus try to] make headway:[15] and then let him see whether this scheme of his will indeed do away with the cause of his anguish.[16] ‹15›

Wa minan-nāsi mañy-yaʿbudul-lāha ʿalā ḥarf. Faʾin ʾaṣābahū khayruniṭ-maʾanna bihī wa ʾin ʾaṣābat-hu fitnatuniñ-qalaba ʿalā wajhihī khasirad-dunyā wal-ʾĀkhirah. Dhālika huwal-khusrānul-mubīn. (11) Yadʿū miñ-dūnil-lāhi mā lā yaḍurruhū wa mā lā yañfaʿuh. Dhālika huwaḍ-ḍalālul-baʿīd. (12) Yadʿū lamañ-ḍarruhūu ʾaqrabu miñ-nafʿih. Labiʾsal-mawlā wa labiʾsal-ʿashīr. (13) ʾInnal-lāha yudkhilul-ladhīna ʾāmanū wa ʿamiluṣ-ṣāliḥāti jannātiñ-tajrī miñ-taḥtihal-ʾanhār. ʾInnal-lāha yafʿalu mā yurīd. (14) Mañ-kāna yaẓunnu ʾal-lañy-yañṣurahul-lāhu fid-dunyā wal-ʾĀkhirati falyamdud bisababin ʾilas-samāaʾi thumma lyaqṭaʿ falyañẓur hal yudhhibanna kayduhū mā yaghīẓ. (15)

8 I.e., wavering between belief and disbelief, and not really committed to either.

9 Lit., "he turns about on his face" – the "face" (*wajh*) of man signifying metonymically his whole being.

10 Lit., "the [most] obvious loss".

11 By failing to commit himself unreservedly to the faith which he professes, man is often inclined to attribute to all manner of extraneous forces, be they real or imaginary, a decisive "influence" on his own destiny, and thus invests them, as it were, with divine qualities.

12 Lit., "this, this (*dhālika huwa*) is the straying far-away". For an explanation of my paraphrase, see note 25 on the last sentence of 14 : 18.

13 The interpolation of "another human being" in the opening clause of this verse is necessitated by the relative pronoun *man* ("one that" or "who"), which almost always relates to an animate person – in this case, a human being who, by allowing himself to be idolized by those who "worship God on the borderline of faith", causes infinite spiritual harm to himself and to his followers.

14 I.e., that God is not *enough* to succour him: obviously an allusion to the type of man who "worships God on the borderline of faith" (verse 11 above) and therefore doubts His power to guide men towards happiness in this world and in the hereafter. The assumption of the majority of the commentators that the personal pronoun "him" relates to the Prophet Muḥammad is, to my mind, very far-fetched and certainly not warranted by the context.

15 The rendering of *la-yaqṭaʿ* as "let him [try to] make headway" is based on the accepted, tropical use of the verb *qaṭaʿa* (lit., "he cut") in the sense of "traversing a distance": and this is the interpretation of *yaqṭaʿ* by Abū Muslim (as quoted by Rāzī). The expression "by any [other] means" (*bi-sabab*) relates to what has been said in verses 12-13 above.

16 Lit., "that which causes anger" or "exasperation", i.e., anguish at finding himself helpless and abandoned.

And thus have We bestowed from on high this [divine writ] in the shape of clear messages: for [thus it is] that God guides him who wills [to be guided].[17] ‹16›
Verily, as for those who have attained to faith [in this divine writ], and those who follow the Jewish faith, and the Sabians,[18] and the Christians, and the Magians,[19] [on the one hand,] and those who are bent on ascribing divinity to aught but God, [on the other,][20] – verily, God will decide between them on Resurrection Day: for, behold, God is witness unto everything. ‹17›

وَكَذَٰلِكَ أَنزَلْنَٰهُ ءَايَٰتٍۭ بَيِّنَٰتٍ وَأَنَّ ٱللَّهَ يَهْدِى مَن يُرِيدُ ﴿16﴾ إِنَّ
ٱلَّذِينَ ءَامَنُوا۟ وَٱلَّذِينَ هَادُوا۟ وَٱلصَّٰبِـِٔينَ وَٱلنَّصَٰرَىٰ وَٱلْمَجُوسَ وَٱلَّذِينَ
أَشْرَكُوٓا۟ إِنَّ ٱللَّهَ يَفْصِلُ بَيْنَهُمْ يَوْمَ ٱلْقِيَٰمَةِ ۚ إِنَّ ٱللَّهَ عَلَىٰ كُلِّ شَىْءٍ
شَهِيدٌ ﴿17﴾ أَلَمْ تَرَ أَنَّ ٱللَّهَ يَسْجُدُ لَهُۥ مَن فِى ٱلسَّمَٰوَٰتِ وَمَن فِى ٱلْأَرْضِ
وَٱلشَّمْسُ وَٱلْقَمَرُ وَٱلنُّجُومُ وَٱلْجِبَالُ وَٱلشَّجَرُ وَٱلدَّوَآبُّ وَكَثِيرٌ مِّنَ
ٱلنَّاسِ ۖ وَكَثِيرٌ حَقَّ عَلَيْهِ ٱلْعَذَابُ ۗ وَمَن يُهِنِ ٱللَّهُ فَمَا لَهُۥ مِن مُّكْرِمٍ ۚ إِنَّ
ٱللَّهَ يَفْعَلُ مَا يَشَآءُ ۩ ﴿18﴾ ۞ هَٰذَانِ خَصْمَانِ ٱخْتَصَمُوا۟ فِى رَبِّهِمْ ۖ

ربع الحزب

السجدة

ART THOU NOT aware that before God prostrate themselves all [things and beings] that are in the heavens and all that are on earth[21] – the sun, and the moon, and the stars, and the mountains, and the trees, and the beasts?
And many human beings [submit to God consciously],[22] whereas many [others, having defied Him,] will inevitably have to suffer [in the life to come];[23] and he whom God shall scorn [on Resurrection Day] will have none who could bestow honour on him: for, verily, God does what He wills. ‹18›
These two contrary kinds of man[24] have become engrossed in contention about their Sustainer!

Wa kadhālika ʾañzalnāhu ʾĀyātim-bayyinātiñw-wa ʾannal-lāha yahdī mañy-yurīd. (16) ʾInnal-ladhīna ʾāmanū wal-ladhīna hādū waṣ-Ṣābiʾīna wan-Naṣārā wal-Majūsa wal-ladhīna ʾashrakūu ʾinnal-lāha yafṣilu baynahum Yawmal-Qiyāmah. ʾInnal-lāha ʿalā kulli shayʾiñ-Shahīd. (17) ʾAlam tara ʾannal-lāha yasjudu lahū mañ-fis-samāwāti wa mañ-fil-ʾarḍi wash-shamsu wal-qamaru wan-nujūmu wal-jibālu wash-shajaru wad-dawāabbu wa kathīrum-minan-nāsi wa kathīrun ḥaqqa ʿalayhil-ʿadhāb. Wa mañy-yuhinil-lāhu famā lahū mim-mukrimin ʾinnal-lāha yafʿalu mā yashāaʾ. (18) Hādhāni khaṣmānikh-taṣamū fī Rabbihim.

17 Or: "God guides aright whomever He wills". For an explanation of the rendering adopted by me, see note 4 on 14 : 4.

18 See *sūrah* 2, note 49.

19 *Al-majūs*: the followers of Zoroaster or Zarathustra (Zardusht), the Iranian prophet who lived about the middle of the last millenium B.C. and whose teachings are laid down in the *Zend-Avesta*. They are represented today by the Gabrs of Iran and, more prominently, by the Parsis of India and Pakistan. Their religion, though dualistic in philosophy, is based on belief in God as the Creator of the universe.

20 The Christians and the Magians (Zoroastrians) are included in the first category, for although they do ascribe divine qualities to other beings beside God, they regard those beings, fundamentally, as no more than manifestations – or incarnations – of the One God, thus persuading themselves that they are worshipping Him alone; whereas "those who are *bent on* ascribing divinity to beings other than God" (*alladhīna ashrakū*) by obvious implication reject the principle of His oneness and uniqueness.

21 For the meaning of this "prostration", see 13 : 15 and 16 : 48-49, and the corresponding notes. My rendering of the relative pronoun *man*, in this context, as "all [things and beings] that . . ." is explained in note 33 on 13 : 15.

22 According to Zamakhsharī and Rāzī, this interpolated phrase – with its stress on "consciously" – is an elliptically implied predicate (*khabar*) linked with the preceding nominal subject (*mubtadaʾ*): the purport being that although *everything* in creation "prostrates itself" before God, willingly or unwillingly (cf. 13 : 15), not all human beings do so consciously.

23 Lit., "whereas upon many a one the suffering [in the life to come] has become unavoidably incumbent (*ḥaqqa ʿalayhi*)", i.e., as a necessary consequence and corollary of his attitude in this world, and not as an arbitrary "punishment" in the conventional sense of this term.

24 Lit., "these two adversaries" or "antagonists", i.e., those who believe in God's oneness and uniqueness, and those who ascribe divine qualities to beings other than Him, or even deny His existence altogether.

But [thus it is:] as for those who are bent on denying the truth[25] – garments of fire shall be cut out for them [in the life to come]; burning despair[26] will be poured over their heads, ‹19› causing all that is within their bodies, as well as the skins, to melt away.[27] ‹20› And they shall be held [in this state as if] by iron grips;[28] ‹21› and every time they try in their anguish to come out of it, they shall be returned thereto and [be told]: "Taste suffering through fire [to the full]!" ‹22›

[As against this,] behold, God will admit those who attain to faith and do righteous deeds into gardens through which running waters flow, wherein they will be adorned with bracelets of gold and pearls, and where silk will be their raiment:[29] ‹23› for they were [willing to be] guided towards the best of all tenets,[30] and so they were guided onto the way that leads to the One unto whom all praise is due. ‹24›

BEHOLD, as for those who are bent on denying the truth and bar [others] from the path of God[31] and from the Inviolable House of Worship which We have set up for all people alike – [both] those who dwell there and those who come from abroad – and all who seek to profane it[32] by [deliberate] evildoing: [all] such shall We cause to taste grievous suffering [in the life to come.][33] ‹25›

فَٱلَّذِينَ كَفَرُواْ قُطِّعَتۡ لَهُمۡ ثِيَابٞ مِّن نَّارٖ يُصَبُّ مِن فَوۡقِ رُءُوسِهِمُ
ٱلۡحَمِيمُ ﴿١٩﴾ يُصۡهَرُ بِهِۦ مَا فِي بُطُونِهِمۡ وَٱلۡجُلُودُ ﴿٢٠﴾ وَلَهُم مَّقَٰمِعُ مِنۡ
حَدِيدٖ ﴿٢١﴾ كُلَّمَآ أَرَادُوٓاْ أَن يَخۡرُجُواْ مِنۡهَا مِنۡ غَمٍّ أُعِيدُواْ فِيهَا وَذُوقُواْ
عَذَابَ ٱلۡحَرِيقِ ﴿٢٢﴾ إِنَّ ٱللَّهَ يُدۡخِلُ ٱلَّذِينَ ءَامَنُواْ وَعَمِلُواْ ٱلصَّٰلِحَٰتِ
جَنَّٰتٖ تَجۡرِي مِن تَحۡتِهَا ٱلۡأَنۡهَٰرُ يُحَلَّوۡنَ فِيهَا مِنۡ أَسَاوِرَ مِن ذَهَبٖ
وَلُؤۡلُؤٗاۖ وَلِبَاسُهُمۡ فِيهَا حَرِيرٞ ﴿٢٣﴾ وَهُدُوٓاْ إِلَى ٱلطَّيِّبِ مِنَ ٱلۡقَوۡلِ وَهُدُوٓاْ
إِلَىٰ صِرَٰطِ ٱلۡحَمِيدِ ﴿٢٤﴾ إِنَّ ٱلَّذِينَ كَفَرُواْ وَيَصُدُّونَ عَن سَبِيلِ ٱللَّهِ
وَٱلۡمَسۡجِدِ ٱلۡحَرَامِ ٱلَّذِي جَعَلۡنَٰهُ لِلنَّاسِ سَوَآءً ٱلۡعَٰكِفُ فِيهِ وَٱلۡبَادِۚ
وَمَن يُرِدۡ فِيهِ بِإِلۡحَادِۭ بِظُلۡمٖ نُّذِقۡهُ مِنۡ عَذَابٍ أَلِيمٖ ﴿٢٥﴾

Falladhīna kafarū quṭṭiᶜat lahum thiyābum-miñ-nāriñy-yuṣabbu miñ-fawqi ruᵓūsihimul-ḥamīm. (19) Yuṣharu bihī mā fī buṭūnihim wal-julūd. (20) Wa lahum-maqāmiᶜu min ḥadīd. (21) Kullamāa ᵓarādūu ᵓañy-yakhrujū minhā min ghammin ᵓuᶜīdū fīhā wa dhūqū ᶜadhābal-ḥarīq. (22) ᵓInnal-lāha yudkhilul-ladhīna ᵓāmanū wa ᶜamiluṣ-ṣāliḥāti jannātiñ-tajrī miñ-taḥtihal-ᵓanhāru yuḥallawna fīhā min ᵓasāwira miñ-dhahabiñw-wa luᵓluᵓañw-wa libāsuhum fīhā ḥarīr. (23) Wa hudūu ᵓilaṭ-ṭayyibi minal-qawli wa hudūu ᵓilā ṣirāṭil-Ḥamīd. (24) ᵓInnal-ladhīna kafarū wa yaṣuddūna ᶜañ-sabīlil-lāhi wal-Masjidil-Ḥarāmil-ladhī jaᶜalnāhu linnāsi sawāaᵓanil-ᶜākifu fīhi wal-bād. Wa mañy-yurid fīhi biᵓilḥādim-biẓulmiñ-nudhiqhu min ᶜadhābin ᵓalīm. (25)

25 I.e., in distinction from those who err out of ignorance.

26 For this rendering of *ḥamīm*, see note 62 on the concluding sentence of 6 : 70, as well as note 65 on 14 : 50 and note 7 on 73 : 12-13, which mention Rāzī's interpretations of similar allegorical descriptions of the suffering that will befall the sinners in the hereafter.

27 I.e., causing their inner and outer personality utterly to disintegrate.

28 Lit., "for them will be grips (*maqāmiᶜ*) of iron". The noun *miqmaᶜah* – of which *maqāmiᶜ* is the plural – is derived from the verb *qamaᶜa*, signifying "he curbed" or "restrained" or "held in subjection" (*Lisān al-ᶜArab*). Hence, the "iron grips" mentioned in the above verse denote the inescapability of the suffering in the hereafter to which "they who are bent on denying the truth" condemn themselves.

29 See 18 : 31 and the corresponding note 41.

30 I.e., that there is no deity save God. (One must bear in mind that the term *qawl* denotes not merely a "saying" but also an intellectually formulated "opinion" or "tenet".)

31 This connects with the allusion, in the preceding verse, to "the way that leads to the One unto whom all praise is due".

32 Lit., "who aim therein at a deviation from the right course (*ilḥād*)" – a term which circumscribes every perversion of religious tenets.

33 According to Ibn ᶜAbbās, as quoted by Ibn Hishām, this verse was revealed towards the end of the year 6 H, when the pagan Quraysh refused the Prophet and his followers, who had come on pilgrimage from Medina, the right

For, when We assigned unto Abraham the site of this Temple,[34] [We said unto him:] "Do not ascribe divinity to aught beside Me!"[35] – and: "Purify My Temple for those who will walk around it,[36] and those who will stand before it [in meditation], and those who will bow down and prostrate themselves [in prayer]." ‹26›
Hence, [O Muḥammad,] proclaim thou unto all people the [duty of] pilgrimage:[37] they will come unto thee on foot and on every [kind of] fast mount,[38] coming from every far-away point [on earth], ‹27› so that they might experience much that shall be of benefit to them,[39] and that they might extol the name of God on the days appointed [for sacrifice], over whatever heads of cattle He may have provided for them[40] [to this end]: eat, then, thereof, and feed the unfortunate poor.[41] ‹28›

وَإِذْ بَوَّأْنَا لِإِبْرَٰهِيمَ مَكَانَ ٱلْبَيْتِ أَن لَّا تُشْرِكْ بِى شَيْـًٔا وَطَهِّرْ بَيْتِىَ
لِلطَّآئِفِينَ وَٱلْقَآئِمِينَ وَٱلرُّكَّعِ ٱلسُّجُودِ ﴿٢٦﴾ وَأَذِّن فِى ٱلنَّاسِ بِٱلْحَجِّ
يَأْتُوكَ رِجَالًا وَعَلَىٰ كُلِّ ضَامِرٍ يَأْتِينَ مِن كُلِّ فَجٍّ عَمِيقٍ ﴿٢٧﴾ لِّيَشْهَدُوا۟
مَنَٰفِعَ لَهُمْ وَيَذْكُرُوا۟ ٱسْمَ ٱللَّهِ فِىٓ أَيَّامٍ مَّعْلُومَٰتٍ عَلَىٰ مَا رَزَقَهُم مِّنۢ
بَهِيمَةِ ٱلْأَنْعَٰمِ ۖ فَكُلُوا۟ مِنْهَا وَأَطْعِمُوا۟ ٱلْبَآئِسَ ٱلْفَقِيرَ ﴿٢٨﴾

Wa ʾidh bawwaʾnā liʾIbrāhīma makānal-Bayti ʾal-lā tushrik bī shayʾañw-wa ṭahhir Baytiya liṭ ṭāaʾifīna wal-qāaʾimīna war-rukkaʿis-sujūd. ﴿26﴾ Wa ʾadhdhiñ-fin-nāsi bilḤajji yaʾtūka rijālañw-wa ʿalā kulli ḍāmiriñy-yaʾtīna miñ-kulli fajjin ʿamīq. ﴿27﴾ Liyash-hadū manāfiʿa lahum wa yadhkurus-mal-lāhi fīi ʾayyāmim-maʿlūmātin ʿalā mā razaqahum-mim-bahīmatil-ʾanʿāmi fakulū minhā wa ʾaṭʿimul-bāaʾisal-faqīr. ﴿28﴾

of entry into Mecca, and thus into the sanctuary of the Kaʿbah (the "Inviolable House of Worship"). But whether or not this claim is correct – and we have no definite historical evidence in either sense – the purport of the above verse is not restricted to any historical situation but relates to every attempt at preventing believers, be it physically or through intellectual seduction, from going on pilgrimage to this symbolic centre of their faith, or at destroying its sanctity in their eyes.

34 I.e., the Kaʿbah: see note 102 on 2 : 125.

35 In view of the oft-repeated Qurʾanic statement that Abraham was beyond all temptation to ascribe divinity to anything but God, it seems to me that the above injunction has a specific import, namely, "Do not allow *this Temple* to become an object of worship, but make it clear that it is holy only by virtue of its being the first temple ever dedicated to the worship of the One God" (cf. 3 : 96). Apart from that, it refers to "those who are bent on denying the truth" spoken of at the beginning of the preceding verse.

36 See *sūrah* 2, note 104.

37 Lit., "proclaim thou the pilgrimage among the people", i.e., the believers (Ṭabarī). Most of the commentators assume that this passage is a continuation of God's command to Abraham; but some of them – in particular, Al-Ḥasan al-Baṣrī – consider it to have been addressed to the Prophet Muḥammad. (Regarding the annual pilgrimage to Mecca, as instituted in Islam, see 2 : 196-203 and the corresponding notes.)

38 Lit., "lean mount" – an expression which has induced some of the commentators to assume that it denotes "a camel that has become lean on account of a long and fatiguing journey". However, the verb *ḍammarahu* or *aḍmarahu* relates in classical Arabic not only to camels but also to horses, and has the meaning of "he made it [i.e., the mount] lean and fit [for racing or war]"; thus, the noun *miḍmār* signifies "a training-ground where horses are prepared for racing or war", as well as "a race-course" (Jawharī, *Asās*, etc.; cf. also Lane V, 1803 f.). Hence, the adjectival noun *ḍāmir* – especially when contrasted, as above, with the expression *rijālan* ("on foot") – has the connotation of "fleetness" or, more properly, "fitness for speed", and may by inference be applied to every kind of "fast conveyance".

39 Lit., "that they might witness benefits [accruing] to them" – i.e., increased consciousness of God through facing the first temple ever dedicated to Him, as well as the consciousness of being part of a brotherhood embracing all believers. Apart from these spiritual benefits, the annual pilgrimage to Mecca provides an opportunity for believers from all parts of the world to become acquainted with the many social and political problems that confront the various geographically separated sectors of the community.

40 The repeated Qur'anic insistence on pronouncing the name of God whenever one slaughters an animal is meant to make the believers "realize the awfulness of taking life, and the solemn nature of the trust which God has conferred upon them in the permission to eat the flesh of animals" (Marmaduke Pickthall, *The Meaning of the Glorious Koran*, London 1930, p. 342, footnote 2). As regards the "days appointed" (*ayyām maʿlūmāt*) spoken of above, they apparently denote the Festival of Sacrifices, which falls on the 10th of the lunar month of Dhu 'l-Ḥijjah, as well as the next two days, marking the end of the pilgrimage (Ibn ʿAbbās, as quoted by Rāzī).

41 Whereas the pilgrims are merely *permitted* to eat some of the flesh of the animals which they have sacrificed, the feeding of the poor is *mandatory* (Ṭabari and Zamakhsharī) and constitutes, thus, the primary objective of these

ثُمَّ لْيَقْضُوا۟ تَفَثَهُمْ وَلْيُوفُوا۟ نُذُورَهُمْ وَلْيَطَّوَّفُوا۟ بِٱلْبَيْتِ ٱلْعَتِيقِ ﴿٢٩﴾ ذَٰلِكَ
وَمَن يُعَظِّمْ حُرُمَٰتِ ٱللَّهِ فَهُوَ خَيْرٌ لَّهُۥ عِندَ رَبِّهِۦ ۗ وَأُحِلَّتْ لَكُمُ ٱلْأَنْعَٰمُ
إِلَّا مَا يُتْلَىٰ عَلَيْكُمْ ۖ فَٱجْتَنِبُوا۟ ٱلرِّجْسَ مِنَ ٱلْأَوْثَٰنِ وَٱجْتَنِبُوا۟ قَوْلَ
ٱلزُّورِ ﴿٣٠﴾ حُنَفَآءَ لِلَّهِ غَيْرَ مُشْرِكِينَ بِهِۦ ۚ وَمَن يُشْرِكْ بِٱللَّهِ فَكَأَنَّمَا خَرَّ مِنَ
ٱلسَّمَآءِ فَتَخْطَفُهُ ٱلطَّيْرُ أَوْ تَهْوِى بِهِ ٱلرِّيحُ فِى مَكَانٍ سَحِيقٍ ﴿٣١﴾ ذَٰلِكَ
وَمَن يُعَظِّمْ شَعَٰٓئِرَ ٱللَّهِ فَإِنَّهَا مِن تَقْوَى ٱلْقُلُوبِ ﴿٣٢﴾

Thummal-yaqḍū tafathahum wal-yūfū nudhūrahum wal-yaṭṭawwafū bilBaytil-ᶜAtīq. (29) Dhālika wa mañy-yuᶜaẓẓim ḥurumātil-lāhi fahuwa khayrul-lahū ᶜiñda Rabbih. Wa ʾuḥillat lakumul-ʾanᶜāmu ʾillā mā yutlā ᶜalaykum fajtanibur-rijsa minal-ʾawthāni waj-tanibū qawlaz-zūr. (30) Ḥunafāaʾa lillāhi ghayra mushrikīna bih. Wa mañy-yushrik billāhi fakaʾannamā kharra minas-samāaʾi fatakhṭafuhuṭ-ṭayru ʾaw tahwī bihir-rīḥu fī makāniñ-saḥīq. (31) Dhālika wa mañy-yuᶜaẓẓim Shaᶜāaʾiral-lāhi faʾinnahā miñ-taqwal-qulūb. (32)

Thereafter let them bring to an end their state of self-denial,[42] and let them fulfil the vows which they [may] have made, and let them walk [once again] around the Most Ancient Temple.[43] ‹29›

All this [is ordained by God]; and if one honours God's sacred commandments, it will redound to his own good in his Sustainer's sight.

And all [kinds of] cattle have been made lawful to you [for sacrifice and food], save what is mentioned to you [as forbidden].[44]

Shun, then, [all that God has forbidden and, most of all,] the loathsome evil of idolatrous beliefs and practices;[45] and shun every word that is untrue, ‹30› [inclining] towards God, [and] turning away from all that is false,[46] without ascribing divine qualities to aught beside Him: for he who ascribes divinity to aught but God is like one who is hurtling down from the skies – whereupon the birds carry him off, or the wind blows him away onto a far-off place. ‹31›

This is [to be borne in mind]. And anyone who honours the symbols set up by God[47] [shall know that,] verily, these [symbols derive their value] from the God-consciousness in the [believers'] hearts. ‹32›

---

sacrifices. Apart from this, they are meant to commemorate Abraham's readiness to sacrifice his first-born son after he dreamt that God demanded of him this supreme sacrifice (see 37 : 102-107 and the corresponding notes); furthermore, they are a reminder that God is the Provider of all sustenance and the One who gives life and deals death, and that all must return to Him; and, lastly (as stressed by Rāzī), they are to be symbols of each believer's readiness to sacrifice *himself* in the cause of truth.

42 In Ṭabarī's opinion, the phrase *thumma 'l-yaqḍū tafathahum* signifies "then let them complete the acts of worship (*manāsik*) incumbent on them by virtue of their pilgrimage". Other commentators, however, understand by the (extremely rare) expression *tafath* the prohibition of enjoying, while in the actual state of pilgrimage, certain bodily comforts like cutting or shaving one's hair (see 2 : 196), wearing any clothing but the simple, unsewn pilgrim's garb *(iḥrām)*, indulging in sexual intercourse (2 : 197), etc. Consequently, they explain the above phrase as meaning "let them bring to an end the [condition of self-denial described as] *tafath* which was incumbent on them during pilgrimage".

43 I.e., around the Kaᶜbah (see *sūrah* 2, notes 102 and 104), thus completing the pilgrimage.

44 See the first paragraph of 5 : 3. Once again, the Qurʾān stresses the principle that everything that has not been explicitly forbidden is *per se* lawful.

45 The term *awthān* (lit., "idols") denotes not merely actual, concrete images of false deities but also, in its widest sense, everything that is associated with false beliefs and practices or with a tendency to "worship" false values: hence the subsequent injunction to shun "every word that is untrue".

46 For an explanation of the term *ḥunafāʾ* (sing. *ḥanīf*), see note 110 on 2 : 135.

47 Lit., "God's symbols (*shaᶜāʾir*)" – an expression which in this context refers to the rites of pilgrimage (see the second half of note 4 on 5 : 2). This stress on the *symbolic* character of all the rites connected with the pilgrimage is meant to draw the believer's attention to the spiritual meaning of those rites, and thus to warn him against making, unthinkingly, a sort of fetish of them. – The assumption of some of the commentators that the "symbols" referred to here relate specifically to the sacrificial animals, resp. their sacrifice as such, is not warranted by the text. As Ṭabarī

لَكُمْ فِيهَا مَنَٰفِعُ إِلَىٰٓ أَجَلٍ مُّسَمًّى ثُمَّ مَحِلُّهَآ إِلَى ٱلْبَيْتِ ٱلْعَتِيقِ ﴿٣٣﴾
وَلِكُلِّ أُمَّةٍ جَعَلْنَا مَنسَكًا لِّيَذْكُرُوا۟ ٱسْمَ ٱللَّهِ عَلَىٰ مَا رَزَقَهُم مِّنۢ بَهِيمَةِ
ٱلْأَنْعَٰمِ ۗ فَإِلَٰهُكُمْ إِلَٰهٌ وَٰحِدٌ فَلَهُۥٓ أَسْلِمُوا۟ ۗ وَبَشِّرِ ٱلْمُخْبِتِينَ ﴿٣٤﴾
ٱلَّذِينَ إِذَا ذُكِرَ ٱللَّهُ وَجِلَتْ قُلُوبُهُمْ وَٱلصَّٰبِرِينَ عَلَىٰ مَآ أَصَابَهُمْ
وَٱلْمُقِيمِى ٱلصَّلَوٰةِ وَمِمَّا رَزَقْنَٰهُمْ يُنفِقُونَ ﴿٣٥﴾ وَٱلْبُدْنَ جَعَلْنَٰهَا لَكُم
مِّن شَعَٰٓئِرِ ٱللَّهِ لَكُمْ فِيهَا خَيْرٌ ۖ فَٱذْكُرُوا۟ ٱسْمَ ٱللَّهِ عَلَيْهَا صَوَآفَّ ۖ فَإِذَا
وَجَبَتْ جُنُوبُهَا فَكُلُوا۟ مِنْهَا وَأَطْعِمُوا۟ ٱلْقَانِعَ وَٱلْمُعْتَرَّ ۚ كَذَٰلِكَ سَخَّرْنَٰهَا
لَكُمْ لَعَلَّكُمْ تَشْكُرُونَ ﴿٣٦﴾

Lakum fīhā manāfiʿu ʾilāa ʾajalim-musammañ-thumma maḥilluhāa ʾilal-Baytil-ʿAtīq. ﴿33﴾ Wa likulli ʾummatiñ-jaʿalnā mañsakal-liyadhkurus-mal-lāhi ʿalā mā razaqahum-mim-bahīmatil-ʾanʿām. Faʾilāhukum ʾIlāhuñw-Wāḥiduñ-falahūu ʾaslimū. Wa bashshiril-mukhbitīn. ﴿34﴾ ʾAlladhīna ʾidhā dhukiral-lāhu wajilat qulūbuhum waṣ-ṣābirīna ʿalā māa ʾaṣābahum wal-muqīmiṣ-Ṣalāti wa mimmā razaqnāhum yuñfiqūn. ﴿35﴾ Wal-budna jaʿalnāhā lakum-miñ-Shaʿāaʾiril-lāhi lakum fīhā khayruñ fadhkurus-mal-lāhi ʿalayhā ṣawāaff. Faʾidhā wajabat junūbuhā fakulū minhā wa ʾaṭiʿmul-qāniʿa wal-muʿtarr. Kadhālika sakhkharnāhā lakum laʿallakum tashkurūn. ﴿36﴾

In that [God-consciousness] you shall find benefits until a term set [by Him is fulfilled],[48] and [you shall know that] its goal and end is the Most Ancient[49] Temple. 《33》 And [thus it is:] unto every community [that has ever believed in Us] have We appointed [sacrifice as] an act of worship, so that they might extol the name of God over whatever heads of cattle He may have provided for them [to this end].[50] And [always bear in mind:] your God is the One and Only God: hence, surrender yourselves unto Him.

And give thou the glad tiding [of God's acceptance] unto all who are humble 《34》 – all whose hearts tremble with awe whenever God is mentioned, and all who patiently bear whatever ill befalls them, and all who are constant in prayer and spend on others out of what We provide for them as sustenance.[51] 《35》

And as for the sacrifice of cattle, We have ordained it for you as one of the symbols set up by God,[52] in which there is [much] good for you. Hence, extol the name of God over them when they are lined up [for sacrifice]; and after they have fallen lifeless to the ground, eat of their flesh,[53] and feed the poor who is contented with his lot [and does not beg], as well as him who is forced to beg. It is to this end[54] that We have made them[55] subservient to your needs, so that you might have cause to be grateful. 《36》

---

explains in his commentary on this and the next verse, the term *shaʿāʾir* comprises all the rites, actions and places connected with the pilgrimage (all of which have a symbolic meaning), and cannot be restricted to any one of them.

48 I.e., "until the end of your lives" (Bayḍāwī).

49 The noun *maḥill*, derived from the verb *ḥalla* (lit., "he untied" or "undid" [e.g., a knot]", or "he loosened [a load]", or "he alighted"), denotes primarily a "destination", as well as "the time or place at which an obligation [e.g., a debt] falls due" (*Tāj al-ʿArūs*). In the above context, in which this term obviously relates to the "God-consciousness" (*taqwā*) unequivocally mentioned in the preceding verse, it has the tropical meaning of "goal and end", implying that the realization of God's oneness and uniqueness – symbolized by the Kaʿbah (the "Most Ancient Temple") – is the goal and end of all true God-consciousness.

50 I.e., as a conscious, selfless offering in His name of something that one cherishes as necessary and valuable, and not as an attempt to "propitiate" Him who is far above anything that resembles human emotion. (See also verse 36 below.)

51 See *sūrah* 2, note 4.

52 See note 47 above.

53 Lit.,"of them".

54 Lit., "thus".

55 I.e., the sacrificial animals.

نصف الحزب

لَن يَنَالَ ٱللَّهَ لُحُومُهَا وَلَا دِمَآؤُهَا وَلَـٰكِن يَنَالُهُ ٱلتَّقْوَىٰ مِنكُمْ كَذَٰلِكَ
سَخَّرَهَا لَكُمْ لِتُكَبِّرُواْ ٱللَّهَ عَلَىٰ مَا هَدَىٰكُمْ وَبَشِّرِ ٱلْمُحْسِنِينَ ﴿٣٧﴾ إِنَّ
ٱللَّهَ يُدَٰفِعُ عَنِ ٱلَّذِينَ ءَامَنُوٓاْ إِنَّ ٱللَّهَ لَا يُحِبُّ كُلَّ خَوَّانٍ كَفُورٍ ﴿٣٨﴾
أُذِنَ لِلَّذِينَ يُقَـٰتَلُونَ بِأَنَّهُمْ ظُلِمُواْ وَإِنَّ ٱللَّهَ عَلَىٰ نَصْرِهِمْ لَقَدِيرٌ ﴿٣٩﴾
ٱلَّذِينَ أُخْرِجُواْ مِن دِيَـٰرِهِم بِغَيْرِ حَقٍّ إِلَّآ أَن يَقُولُواْ رَبُّنَا ٱللَّهُ وَلَوْلَا دَفْعُ
ٱللَّهِ ٱلنَّاسَ بَعْضَهُم بِبَعْضٍ لَّهُدِّمَتْ صَوَٰمِعُ وَبِيَعٌ وَصَلَوَٰتٌ وَمَسَـٰجِدُ
يُذْكَرُ فِيهَا ٱسْمُ ٱللَّهِ كَثِيرًا وَلَيَنصُرَنَّ ٱللَّهُ مَن يَنصُرُهُۥٓ إِنَّ ٱللَّهَ لَقَوِىٌّ
عَزِيزٌ ﴿٤٠﴾ ٱلَّذِينَ إِن مَّكَّنَّـٰهُمْ فِى ٱلْأَرْضِ أَقَامُواْ ٱلصَّلَوٰةَ وَءَاتَوُاْ
ٱلزَّكَوٰةَ وَأَمَرُواْ بِٱلْمَعْرُوفِ وَنَهَوْاْ عَنِ ٱلْمُنكَرِ وَلِلَّهِ عَـٰقِبَةُ ٱلْأُمُورِ ﴿٤١﴾

Lañy-yanālal-lāha luḥūmuhā wa lā dimāaᵓuhā wa lākiñy-yanāluhut-taqwā miñkum. Kadhālika sakh-kharahā lakum litukabbirul-lāha ᶜalā mā hadākum. Wa bashshiril-muḥsinīn. (37) ᵓInnal-lāha yudāfiᶜu ᶜanil-ladhīna ᵓāmanū. ᵓInnal-lāha lā yuḥibbu kulla khawwāniñ-kafūr. (38) ᵓUdhina lilladhīna yuqātalūna biᵓannahum ẓulimū; wa ᵓinnal-lāha ᶜalā naṣrihim laQadīr. (39) ᵓAlladhīna ᵓukhrijū miñ-diyārihim-bighayri ḥaqqin ᵓillāa ᵓañy-yaqūlū Rabbunal-lāh. Wa lawlā dafᶜul-lāhin-nāsa baᶜḍahum-bibaᶜḍil-lahuddimat ṣawāmiᶜu wa biyaᶜuñw-wa Ṣalawātuñw-wa Masājidu yudhkaru fīhas-mul-lāhi kathīrā. Wa layañṣurannal-lāhu mañy-yañṣuruh. ᵓInnal-lāha la-Qawiyyun ᶜAzīz. (40) ᵓAlladhīna ᵓim-makkannāhum fil-ᵓarḍi ᵓaqāmuṣ-Ṣalāta wa ᵓātawuz-Zakāta wa ᵓamarū bilmaᶜrūfi wa nahaw ᶜanil-muñkar. Wa lillāhi ᶜāqibatul-ᵓumūr. (41)

[But bear in mind:] never does their flesh reach God, and neither their blood: it is only your God-consciousness that reaches Him. It is to this end that We have made them subservient to your needs, so that you might glorify God for all the guidance with which He has graced you.

And give thou this glad tiding unto the doers of good: ‹37› Verily, God will ward off [all evil] from those who attain to faith; [and,] verily, God does not love anyone who betrays his trust and is bereft of gratitude.[56] ‹38›

PERMISSION [to fight] is given to those against whom war is being wrongfully waged[57] – and, verily, God has indeed the power to succour them: ‹39› – those who have been driven from their homelands against all right for no other reason than their saying, "Our Sustainer is God!"

For, if God had not enabled people to defend themselves against one another,[58] [all] monasteries and churches and synagogues and mosques – in [all of] which God's name is abundantly extolled – would surely have been destroyed [ere now].[59]

And God will most certainly succour him who succours His cause: for, verily, God is most powerful, almighty, ‹40› [well aware of] those who, [even] if We firmly establish them on earth, remain constant in prayer, and give in charity, and enjoin the doing of what is right and forbid the doing of what is wrong; but with God rests the final outcome of all events. ‹41›

56 See *sūrah* 4, note 134.

57 Lit., "inasmuch as they have been wronged". Connecting with the promise, in the preceding verse, that "God will ward off [all evil] from those who attain to faith", the present verse enunciates the permission to fight physically in self-defence. All relevant Traditions (quoted, in particular, by Ṭabarī and Ibn Kathīr) show that this is the earliest Qurᵓanic reference to the problem of war as such. According to ᶜAbd Allāh ibn ᶜAbbās, it was revealed immediately after the Prophet left Mecca for Medina, i.e., at the beginning of the year 1 H The principle of war in self-defence – and only in self-defence – has been further elaborated in *Al-Baqarah*, which was revealed about a year later (see 2 : 190-193 and the corresponding notes).

58 Lit., "were it not that God repels some people by means of others" (cf. the identical phrase in the second paragraph of 2 : 251).

59 The implication is that the defence of religious freedom is the foremost cause for which arms may – and, indeed, must – be taken up (see 2 : 193 and the corresponding note 170), or else, as stressed in the concluding clause of 2 : 251, "corruption would surely overwhelm the earth".

AND IF THEY [who are bent on denying the truth] give thee the lie, [O Muḥammad, remember that, long] before their time, the people of Noah and [the tribes of] ᶜĀd and Thamūd gave the lie [to their prophets], ‹42› as did the people of Abraham, and the people of Lot, ‹43› and the dwellers of Madyan; and [so, too,] Moses was given the lie [by Pharaoh].[60]

And [in every case] I gave rein, for a while, to the deniers of the truth: but then I took them to task – and how awesome was My denial [of them]! ‹44›

And how many a township have We destroyed because it had been immersed in evildoing – and now they [all] lie deserted, with their roofs caved in! And how many a well lies abandoned, and how many a castle that [once] stood high! ‹45›

Have they, then, never journeyed about the earth, letting their hearts gain wisdom, and causing their ears to hear?[61] Yet, verily, it is not their eyes that have become blind – but blind have become the hearts that are in their breasts! ‹46›

And [so, O Muḥammad,] they challenge thee to hasten the coming upon them of [God's] chastisement:[62] but God never fails to fulfil His promise – and, behold, in thy Sustainer's sight a day is like a thousand years of your reckoning.[63] ‹47›

And to how many a community that was immersed in evildoing have I given rein for a while! But then I took it to task: for with Me is all journeys' end! ‹48›

SAY [O Muḥammad]: "O men! I am but a plain warner [sent by God] unto you!" ‹49›

وَإِن يُكَذِّبُوكَ فَقَدْ كَذَّبَتْ قَبْلَهُمْ قَوْمُ نُوحٍ وَعَادٌ وَثَمُودُ ﴿42﴾ وَقَوْمُ
إِبْرَٰهِيمَ وَقَوْمُ لُوطٍ ﴿43﴾ وَأَصْحَٰبُ مَدْيَنَ وَكُذِّبَ مُوسَىٰ فَأَمْلَيْتُ
لِلْكَٰفِرِينَ ثُمَّ أَخَذْتُهُمْ فَكَيْفَ كَانَ نَكِيرِ ﴿44﴾ فَكَأَيِّن مِّن قَرْيَةٍ
أَهْلَكْنَٰهَا وَهِىَ ظَالِمَةٌ فَهِىَ خَاوِيَةٌ عَلَىٰ عُرُوشِهَا وَبِئْرٍ مُّعَطَّلَةٍ وَقَصْرٍ
مَّشِيدٍ ﴿45﴾ أَفَلَمْ يَسِيرُوا۟ فِى ٱلْأَرْضِ فَتَكُونَ لَهُمْ قُلُوبٌ يَعْقِلُونَ بِهَآ أَوْ
ءَاذَانٌ يَسْمَعُونَ بِهَا فَإِنَّهَا لَا تَعْمَى ٱلْأَبْصَٰرُ وَلَٰكِن تَعْمَى ٱلْقُلُوبُ
ٱلَّتِى فِى ٱلصُّدُورِ ﴿46﴾ وَيَسْتَعْجِلُونَكَ بِٱلْعَذَابِ وَلَن يُخْلِفَ ٱللَّهُ وَعْدَهُۥ
وَإِنَّ يَوْمًا عِندَ رَبِّكَ كَأَلْفِ سَنَةٍ مِّمَّا تَعُدُّونَ ﴿47﴾ وَكَأَيِّن مِّن قَرْيَةٍ أَمْلَيْتُ
لَهَا وَهِىَ ظَالِمَةٌ ثُمَّ أَخَذْتُهَا وَإِلَىَّ ٱلْمَصِيرُ ﴿48﴾ قُلْ يَٰٓأَيُّهَا ٱلنَّاسُ إِنَّمَآ
أَنَا۠ لَكُمْ نَذِيرٌ مُّبِينٌ ﴿49﴾

Wa ᵓiñy-yukadhdhibūka faqad kadhdhabat qablahum qawmu Nūḥiñw-wa ᶜĀduñw-wa Thamūd. (42) Wa qawmu ᵓIbrāhīma wa qawmu Lūṭ. (43) Wa ᵓaṣḥābu Madyana wa kudhdhiba Mūsā faᵓamlaytu lilkāfirīna thumma ᵓakhadhtuhum; fakayfa kāna nakīr. (44) Fakaᵓayyim-miñ-qaryatin ᵓahlaknāhā wa hiya ẓālimatuñ-fahiya khāwiyatun ᶜalā ᶜurūshihā wa biᵓrim-muᶜaṭṭalatiñw-wa qaṣrim-mashīd. (45) ᵓAfalam yasīrū fil-ᵓarḍi fatakūna lahum qulūbuñy-yaᶜqilūna bihāa ᵓaw ᵓādhānuñy-yasmaᶜūna bihā. Faᵓinnahā lā taᶜmal-ᵓabṣāru wa lākiñ-taᶜmal-qulūbul-latī fiṣ-ṣudūr. (46) Wa yastaᶜjilūnaka bilᶜadhābi wa lañy-yukhlifal-lāhu waᶜdah. Wa ᵓinna yawman ᶜiñda Rabbika kaᵓalfi sanatim-mimmā taᶜuddūn. (47) Wa kaᵓayyim-miñ-qaryatin ᵓamlaytu lahā wa hiya ẓālimatuñ-thumma ᵓakhadhtuhā wa ᵓilayyal-maṣīr. (48) Qul yāa ᵓayyuhan-nāsu ᵓinnamāa ᵓana lakum nadhīrum-mubīn. (49)

60 I.e., not by *his own people,* since these, despite their sinning, had accepted him as God's prophet (Ṭabarī). References to the tribes of ᶜĀd and Thamūd and the people of Madyan are given in *sūrah* 7, notes 48, 56 and 67.

61 Lit., "whereupon they would have hearts wherewith they might understand, or ears whereby they might hear".

62 For an explanation, see 6 : 57, 8 : 32 and 13 : 6, as well as the corresponding notes.

63 I.e., what men conceive of as "time" has no meaning with regard to God, because He is timeless, without beginning and without end, so that "in relation to Him, one day and a thousand years are alike" (Rāzī). Cf. 70 : 4, where in the same sense, a "day" is said to be equal to "fifty thousand years", or the well-authenticated saying of the Prophet, "God says, 'I am Time Absolute (*ad-dahr*)'."

فَالَّذِينَ ءَامَنُوا وَعَمِلُوا الصَّالِحَاتِ لَهُم مَّغْفِرَةٌ وَرِزْقٌ كَرِيمٌ ﴿٥٠﴾
وَالَّذِينَ سَعَوْا فِي ءَايَاتِنَا مُعَاجِزِينَ أُولَٰئِكَ أَصْحَابُ الْجَحِيمِ ﴿٥١﴾ وَمَا
أَرْسَلْنَا مِن قَبْلِكَ مِن رَّسُولٍ وَلَا نَبِيٍّ إِلَّا إِذَا تَمَنَّىٰ أَلْقَى الشَّيْطَانُ فِي
أُمْنِيَّتِهِ فَيَنسَخُ اللَّهُ مَا يُلْقِي الشَّيْطَانُ ثُمَّ يُحْكِمُ اللَّهُ ءَايَاتِهِ وَاللَّهُ
عَلِيمٌ حَكِيمٌ ﴿٥٢﴾ لِّيَجْعَلَ مَا يُلْقِي الشَّيْطَانُ فِتْنَةً لِّلَّذِينَ فِي قُلُوبِهِم مَّرَضٌ
وَالْقَاسِيَةِ قُلُوبُهُمْ وَإِنَّ الظَّالِمِينَ لَفِي شِقَاقٍ بَعِيدٍ ﴿٥٣﴾ وَلِيَعْلَمَ الَّذِينَ
أُوتُوا الْعِلْمَ أَنَّهُ الْحَقُّ مِن رَّبِّكَ فَيُؤْمِنُوا بِهِ فَتُخْبِتَ لَهُ قُلُوبُهُمْ وَإِنَّ
اللَّهَ لَهَادِ الَّذِينَ ءَامَنُوا إِلَىٰ صِرَاطٍ مُّسْتَقِيمٍ ﴿٥٤﴾

Falladhīna ᵓāmanū wa ᶜamiluṣ-ṣāliḥāti lahum-maghfiratuñw-wa rizquñ-karīm. (50) Wal-ladhīna saᶜaw fīi ᵓĀyātinā muᶜājizīna ᵓulāaᵓika ᵓaṣḥābul-jaḥīm. (51) Wa māa ᵓarsalnā miñ-qablika mir-Rasūliñw-wa lā Nabiyyin ᵓillāa ᵓidhā tamannāa ᵓalqash-Shayṭānu fīi ᵓumniyyatihī fayañsakhul-lāhu mā yulqish-Shayṭānu thumma yuḥkimul-lāhu ᵓĀyātih. Wal-lāhu ᶜAlīmun Ḥakīm. (52) Liyajᶜala mā yulqish-Shayṭānu fitnatal-lilladhīna fī qulūbihim-maraḍuñw-wal-qāsiyati qulūbuhum. Wa ᵓinnaẓ-ẓālimīna lafī shiqāqim-baᶜīd. (53) Wa liyaᶜlamal-ladhīna ᵓūtul-ᶜilma ᵓannahul-ḥaqqu mir-Rabbika fayuᵓminū bihī fatukhbita lahū qulūbuhum. Wa ᵓinnal-lāha lahādil-ladhīna ᵓāmanūu ᵓilā ṣirāṭim-mustaqīm. (54)

And [know that] those who attain to faith and do righteous deeds shall be granted forgiveness of sins and a most excellent sustenance;[64] ‹50› whereas those who strive against Our messages, seeking to defeat their purpose – they are destined for the blazing fire. ‹51›

Yet whenever We sent forth any apostle or prophet before thee, and he was hoping[65] [that his warnings would be heeded], Satan would cast an aspersion on his innermost aims:[66] but God renders null and void whatever aspersion Satan may cast; and God makes His messages clear in and by themselves[67] – for God is all-knowing, wise. ‹52›

[And He allows doubts to arise] so that He might cause whatever aspersion Satan may cast [against His prophets] to become a trial for all in whose hearts is disease[68] and all whose hearts are hardened: for, verily, all who are [thus] sinning [against themselves][69] are most deeply in the wrong. ‹53›

And [God renders Satan's aspersions null and void] so that they who are endowed with [innate] knowledge might know that this [divine writ] is the truth from thy Sustainer, and that they might believe in it, and that their hearts might humbly submit unto Him.

For, behold, God does guide onto a straight way those who have attained to faith ‹54›

64 See 8 : 4 and the corresponding note 5.

65 Lit., "We never sent any apostle or prophet before thee without that, when he was hoping (*tamannā*) . . .", etc. According to most of the commentators, the designation "apostle" (*rasūl*) is applied to bearers of divine revelations which comprise a new doctrinal system or dispensation; a "prophet" (*nabī*), on the other hand, is said to be one whom God has entrusted with the enunciation of ethical principles on the basis of an already-existing dispensation, or of principles common to all divine dispensations. Hence, every apostle is a prophet as well, but not every prophet is an apostle.

66 I.e., insinuating that the innermost aim (*umniyyah*, lit., "longing" or "hope") of the message-bearer in question was not the spiritual improvement of his community but, rather, the attainment of personal power and influence: cf. 6 : 112 – "against every prophet We have set up as enemies the evil forces (*shayāṭīn*) from among humans as well as from among invisible beings (*al-jinn*)" – a statement which is explained in *sūrah* 6, note 98.

67 Lit., "and God makes His messages clear in and by themselves". This is the meaning of the phrase *yuḥkimu āyātahu* (cf. the expression *uḥkimat āyātuhu* in 11 : 1): i.e., God causes His messages to speak for themselves, so that any insinuation as to the prophet's "hidden motives" is automatically disproved. The conjunction *thumma* at the beginning of this clause does not connote a sequence in time but a coordination of activities, and is best rendered by the simple conjunction "and".

68 See 2 : 10 and the corresponding note.

69 Lit., "all [such] evildoers".

– whereas those who are bent on denying the truth will not cease to be in doubt about Him until the Last Hour comes suddenly upon them and [supreme] suffering befalls them on a Day void of all hope.[70] ‹55›
On that Day, all dominion shall [visibly] belong to God. He shall judge [all men and make a distinction] between them: thus, all who had attained to faith and did righteous deeds shall find themselves in gardens of bliss, ‹56› whereas for those who were bent on denying the truth and gave the lie to Our messages, there shall be shameful suffering in store. ‹57›

AND AS FOR those who forsake the domain of evil[71] [and strive] in God's cause, and then are slain or die – God will most certainly provide for them a goodly sustenance [in the life to come]: for, verily, God – He alone – is the best of providers; ‹58› [and] He will most certainly cause them to enter upon a state [of being] that shall please them well:[72] for, verily, God is all-knowing, most forbearing. ‹59› Thus shall it be.
And as for him who responds to aggression only to the extent of the attack levelled against him,[73] and is thereupon [again] treacherously attacked – God will most certainly succour him: for, behold, God is indeed an absolver of sins, much-forgiving.[74] ‹60›

وَلَا يَزَالُ ٱلَّذِينَ كَفَرُوا۟ فِى مِرْيَةٍ مِّنْهُ حَتَّىٰ تَأْتِيَهُمُ ٱلسَّاعَةُ بَغْتَةً أَوْ يَأْتِيَهُمْ
عَذَابُ يَوْمٍ عَقِيمٍ ﴿٥٥﴾ ٱلْمُلْكُ يَوْمَئِذٍ لِّلَّهِ يَحْكُمُ بَيْنَهُمْ ۚ فَٱلَّذِينَ ءَامَنُوا۟
وَعَمِلُوا۟ ٱلصَّٰلِحَٰتِ فِى جَنَّٰتِ ٱلنَّعِيمِ ﴿٥٦﴾ وَٱلَّذِينَ كَفَرُوا۟ وَكَذَّبُوا۟
بِـَٔايَٰتِنَا فَأُو۟لَٰٓئِكَ لَهُمْ عَذَابٌ مُّهِينٌ ﴿٥٧﴾ وَٱلَّذِينَ هَاجَرُوا۟ فِى سَبِيلِ ٱللَّهِ ثُمَّ
قُتِلُوٓا۟ أَوْ مَاتُوا۟ لَيَرْزُقَنَّهُمُ ٱللَّهُ رِزْقًا حَسَنًا ۚ وَإِنَّ ٱللَّهَ لَهُوَ خَيْرُ
ٱلرَّٰزِقِينَ ﴿٥٨﴾ لَيُدْخِلَنَّهُم مُّدْخَلًا يَرْضَوْنَهُۥ ۗ وَإِنَّ ٱللَّهَ لَعَلِيمٌ حَلِيمٌ ﴿٥٩﴾ ۞
ذَٰلِكَ وَمَنْ عَاقَبَ بِمِثْلِ مَا عُوقِبَ بِهِۦ ثُمَّ بُغِىَ عَلَيْهِ لَيَنصُرَنَّهُ ٱللَّهُ ۗ إِنَّ ٱللَّهَ
لَعَفُوٌّ غَفُورٌ ﴿٦٠﴾

ثلاثة ارباع الحزب

Wa lā yazālul-ladhīna kafarū fī miryatim-minhu ḥattā taʾtiyahumus-Sāʿatu baghtatan ʾaw yaʾtiyahum ʿadhābu Yawmin ʿaqīm. (55) ʾAlmulku Yawmaʾidhil-lillāhi yaḥkumu baynahum; falladhīna ʾāmanū wa ʿamiluṣ-ṣāliḥāti fī jannātin-naʿīm. (56) Wal-ladhīna kafarū wa kadhdhabū biʾĀyātinā faʾulāaʾika lahum ʿadhābum-muhīn. (57) Wal-ladhīna hājarū fī sabīlil-lāhi thumma qutilūu ʾaw mātū layarzuqannahumul-lāhu rizqan ḥasanā. Wa ʾinnal-lāha laHuwa Khayrur-rāziqīn. (58) Layudkhilannahum-mudkhalañy-yarḍawnah. Wa ʾinnal-lāha laʿAlīmun Ḥalīm. (59) ۞ Dhālika wa man ʿāqaba bimithli mā ʿūqiba bihī thumma bughiya ʿalayhi layañṣurannahul-lāh. ʾInnal-lāha laʿAfuwwuñ-Ghafūr. (60)

70 Lit., "or [until] there comes upon them the chastisement [or "suffering] of a barren Day", i.e., the Day of Judgment, which will offer no hope to those who, until their death, failed to realize the existence of God or to submit to His guidance.

71 For this rendering of the phrase *alladhīna hājarū*, see note 203 on 2 : 218. The subsequent mention of "those who strive in God's cause, and then are slain or die" connects with the reference, in verses 39-40, to God's permission to the believers to fight in defence of their faith and liberty. The extreme merit of the self-sacrifice involved is stressed in several Qurʾanic passages, and particularly in 4 : 95-96; hence, it has also a bearing on the Day of Judgment spoken of in the preceding passage.

72 Or: "cause them to enter [upon their life after death] in a manner that will please them well" (cf. note 40 on the last clause of 4 : 31) – thus implying that by sacrificing their lives in God's cause they will have obtained His forgiveness of whatever sins they may have previously committed.

73 Lit., "who has retaliated with the like of what he had been afflicted with" – i.e., has acted only in self-defence and done to his enemy no more than the enemy had done to him. (A similar phrase, relating to retaliation in argument, is found in 16 : 126 and explained in the corresponding note 150.)

74 While the opening sentence of this verse stresses the principle of self-defence as the only justification of war (cf. 2 : 190 and 192-193) – with the proviso that retaliation must not exceed the injury initially suffered – the concluding

Thus it is, because God [is almighty[75] – the One who] makes the night grow longer by shortening the day, and makes the day grow longer by shortening the night; and because God is all-hearing, all-seeing.[76] ‹61›
Thus it is, because God alone is the Ultimate Truth,[77] so that all that men invoke beside Him is sheer falsehood, and because God alone is exalted, great! ‹62›
Art thou not aware that it is God who sends down water from the skies, whereupon the earth becomes green? Verily, God is unfathomable [in His wisdom], all-aware.[78] ‹63›
Unto Him belongs all that is in the heavens and all that is on earth; and, verily, God – He alone – is self-sufficient, the One to whom all praise is due. ‹64›
Art thou not aware that it is God who has made subservient to you all that is on earth,[79] and the ships that sail through the sea at His behest – and [that it is He who] holds the celestial bodies[80] [in their orbits], so that they may not fall upon the earth otherwise than by His leave?[81]
Verily, God is most compassionate towards men, a dispenser of grace ‹65› – seeing that it is He who gave you life, and then will cause you to die, and then will bring you back to life: [but,] verily, bereft of all gratitude is man! ‹66›

ذَٰلِكَ بِأَنَّ ٱللَّهَ يُولِجُ ٱلَّيۡلَ فِي ٱلنَّهَارِ وَيُولِجُ ٱلنَّهَارَ فِي ٱلَّيۡلِ وَأَنَّ ٱللَّهَ
سَمِيعُۢ بَصِيرٞ ﴿61﴾ ذَٰلِكَ بِأَنَّ ٱللَّهَ هُوَ ٱلۡحَقُّ وَأَنَّ مَا يَدۡعُونَ مِن دُونِهِۦ هُوَ
ٱلۡبَٰطِلُ وَأَنَّ ٱللَّهَ هُوَ ٱلۡعَلِيُّ ٱلۡكَبِيرُ ﴿62﴾ أَلَمۡ تَرَ أَنَّ ٱللَّهَ أَنزَلَ مِنَ ٱلسَّمَآءِ
مَآءٗ فَتُصۡبِحُ ٱلۡأَرۡضُ مُخۡضَرَّةًۚ إِنَّ ٱللَّهَ لَطِيفٌ خَبِيرٞ ﴿63﴾ لَّهُۥ مَا فِي
ٱلسَّمَٰوَٰتِ وَمَا فِي ٱلۡأَرۡضِۗ وَإِنَّ ٱللَّهَ لَهُوَ ٱلۡغَنِيُّ ٱلۡحَمِيدُ ﴿64﴾ أَلَمۡ تَرَ
أَنَّ ٱللَّهَ سَخَّرَ لَكُم مَّا فِي ٱلۡأَرۡضِ وَٱلۡفُلۡكَ تَجۡرِي فِي ٱلۡبَحۡرِ بِأَمۡرِهِۦ
وَيُمۡسِكُ ٱلسَّمَآءَ أَن تَقَعَ عَلَى ٱلۡأَرۡضِ إِلَّا بِإِذۡنِهِۦٓۚ إِنَّ ٱللَّهَ بِٱلنَّاسِ
لَرَءُوفٞ رَّحِيمٞ ﴿65﴾ وَهُوَ ٱلَّذِيٓ أَحۡيَاكُمۡ ثُمَّ يُمِيتُكُمۡ ثُمَّ يُحۡيِيكُمۡۗ إِنَّ
ٱلۡإِنسَٰنَ لَكَفُورٞ ﴿66﴾

Dhālika biᵓannal-lāha yūlijul-layla fin-nahāri wa yūlijun-nahāra fil-layli wa ᵓannal-lāha Samīᶜum-Baṣīr. (61) Dhālika biᵓannal-lāha Huwal-Ḥaqqu wa ᵓanna mā yadᶜūna miñ-dūnihī huwal-bāṭilu wa ᵓannal-lāha Huwal-ᶜAliyyul-Kabīr. (62) ᵓAlam tara ᵓannal-lāha ᵓañzala minas-samāaᵓi māaᵓañ-fatuṣbiḥul-ᵓarḍu mukhḍarrah. ᵓInnal-lāha Laṭīfun-Khabīr. (63) Lahū mā fis-samāwāti wa mā fil-ᵓarḍi wa ᵓinnal-lāha laHuwal-Ghaniyyul-Ḥamīd. (64) ᵓAlam tara ᵓannal-lāha sakhkhara lakum-mā fil-ᵓarḍi wal-fulka tajrī fil-baḥri biᵓamrihī wa yumsikus-samāaᵓa ᵓañ-taqaᶜa ᶜalal-ᵓarḍi ᵓillā biᵓidhnih. ᵓInnal-lāha binnāsi laRaᵓūfur-Raḥīm. (65) Wa Huwal-ladhīi ᵓaḥyākum thumma yumītukum thumma yuḥyīkum. ᵓInnal-ᵓIñsāna lakafūr. (66)

part of the verse implies that in case of repeated, unprovoked aggression the believers are allowed to wage an all-out war with a view to destroying completely the enemy's military power. Since such an all-out war might seem to conflict with the principle of limited retaliation alluded to above, the Qurᵓān states that God absolves the believers of what otherwise might have been a sin, since it is they "against whom war is being wrongfully waged" (verse 39) by repeated acts of aggression.

75 Sc., "and therefore has the power to succour the believers who have been wronged".

76 I.e., it is He who knows what is in the hearts of men, and nevertheless, in His unfathomable wisdom, allows the darkness of oppression to grow at the expense of the light of freedom, and then causes the light to overcome the darkness: an eternal, cyclical recurrence which dominates the life of mankind. (As Ibn Kathīr points out, the above passage contains a direct allusion to 3 : 26-27 – "Say: O God, Lord of all dominion! Thou grantest dominion unto whom Thou willest, and takest away dominion from whom Thou willest. . . . Thou hast the power to will anything: Thou makest the night grow longer by shortening the day, and Thou makest the day grow longer by shortening the night. . . ."

77 See *sūrah* 20, note 99.

78 For an explanation of the term *laṭīf* ("unfathomable"), see *sūrah* 6, note 89.

79 I.e., "has enabled you to benefit from all . . .", etc. (cf. *sūrah* 14, note 46).

80 Lit., "the sky" – used here as a metonym for the stars and planets, which are held on their courses by the God-willed laws of cosmic movement (Maraghī XVII, 137).

81 I.e., at the Last Hour, which – as the Qurᵓān so often states – will manifest itself in a universal cosmic catastrophe.

UNTO every community have We appointed [different] ways of worship,[82] which they ought to observe. Hence, [O believer,] do not let those [who follow ways other than thine] draw thee into disputes on this score,[83] but summon [them all] unto thy Sustainer: for, behold, thou art indeed on the right way. ‹67› And if they [try to] argue with thee, say [only]: "God knows best what you are doing."[84] ‹68›
[For, indeed,] God will judge between you [all] on Resurrection Day with regard to all on which you were wont to differ.[85] ‹69›
Dost thou not know that God knows all that occurs in heaven as well as on earth? All this, behold, is in [God's] record: verily, [to know] all this is easy for God. ‹70›
And yet,[86] they [who claim to believe in Him often] worship [other beings or forces] beside God – something for which He has never bestowed any warrant from on high,[87] and [of the reality] whereof they cannot have any knowledge:[88] and such evildoers shall have none to succour them [on Judgment Day]. ‹71›
As it is, whenever Our messages are conveyed unto them in all their clarity, thou canst perceive utter repugnance on the faces of those who are bent on denying the truth: they would almost assault those who convey Our messages unto them!
Say: "Shall I, then, tell you of something worse than what you feel at present?[89] It is the fire [of the hereafter] that God has promised to those who are bent on denying the truth: and how vile a journey's end!" ‹72›

لِكُلِّ أُمَّةٍ جَعَلْنَا مَنسَكًا هُمْ نَاسِكُوهُ فَلَا يُنَٰزِعُنَّكَ فِي ٱلْأَمْرِ وَٱدْعُ إِلَىٰ
رَبِّكَ إِنَّكَ لَعَلَىٰ هُدًى مُّسْتَقِيمٍ ﴿٦٧﴾ وَإِن جَٰدَلُوكَ فَقُلِ ٱللَّهُ أَعْلَمُ بِمَا
تَعْمَلُونَ ﴿٦٨﴾ ٱللَّهُ يَحْكُمُ بَيْنَكُمْ يَوْمَ ٱلْقِيَٰمَةِ فِيمَا كُنتُمْ فِيهِ
تَخْتَلِفُونَ ﴿٦٩﴾ أَلَمْ تَعْلَمْ أَنَّ ٱللَّهَ يَعْلَمُ مَا فِي ٱلسَّمَآءِ وَٱلْأَرْضِ إِنَّ ذَٰلِكَ
فِي كِتَٰبٍ إِنَّ ذَٰلِكَ عَلَى ٱللَّهِ يَسِيرٌ ﴿٧٠﴾ وَيَعْبُدُونَ مِن دُونِ ٱللَّهِ مَا لَمْ
يُنَزِّلْ بِهِۦ سُلْطَٰنًا وَمَا لَيْسَ لَهُم بِهِۦ عِلْمٌ وَمَا لِلظَّٰلِمِينَ مِن نَّصِيرٍ ﴿٧١﴾
وَإِذَا تُتْلَىٰ عَلَيْهِمْ ءَايَٰتُنَا بَيِّنَٰتٍ تَعْرِفُ فِي وُجُوهِ ٱلَّذِينَ كَفَرُوا۟ ٱلْمُنكَرَ
يَكَادُونَ يَسْطُونَ بِٱلَّذِينَ يَتْلُونَ عَلَيْهِمْ ءَايَٰتِنَا قُلْ أَفَأُنَبِّئُكُم بِشَرٍّ مِّن
ذَٰلِكُمُ ٱلنَّارُ وَعَدَهَا ٱللَّهُ ٱلَّذِينَ كَفَرُوا۟ وَبِئْسَ ٱلْمَصِيرُ ﴿٧٢﴾

Likulli ʾummatiñ-jaʿalnā mañsakan hum nāsikūhu falā yunāziʿunnaka fil-ʾamr. Wad-ʿu ʾilā Rabbika ʾinnaka laʿalā hudam-mustaqīm. ⁽⁶⁷⁾ Wa ʾiñ-jādalūka faqulil-lāhu ʾaʿlamu bimā taʿmalūn. ⁽⁶⁸⁾ ʾAllāhu yaḥkumu baynakum Yawmal-Qiyāmati fīmā kuñtum fīhi takhtalifūn. ⁽⁶⁹⁾ ʾAlam taʿlam ʾannal-lāha yaʿlamu mā fis-samāaʾi wal-ʾarḍ. ʾInna dhālika fī Kitābin ʾinna dhālika ʿalal-lāhi yasīr. ⁽⁷⁰⁾ Wa yaʿbudūna miñ-dūnil-lāhi mā lam yunazzil bihī sulṭānañw-wa mā laysa lahum-bihī ʿilm. Wa mā liẓẓālimīna miñ-naṣīr. ⁽⁷¹⁾ Wa ʾidhā tutlā ʿalayhim ʾĀyātunā bayyinātiñ-taʿrifu fī wujūhil-ladhīna kafarul-muñkara yakādūna yasṭūna billadhīna yatlūna ʿalayhim ʾĀyātinā. Qul ʾafaʾunabbiʾukum-bisharrim-miñ-dhālikum. ʾAnnāru waʿadahal-lāhul-ladhīna kafarū; wa biʾsal-maṣīr. ⁽⁷²⁾

82 Lit., "a way of worship" (*mansak*, which sometimes denotes also "an *act* of worship"). For a fuller explanation of this passage, see the second paragraph of 5 : 48 – "Unto every one of you have We appointed a [different] law and way of life" – and the corresponding notes 66-68.

83 I.e., "do not *allow thyself* to be drawn into disputes" (Zamakhsharī and Baghawī).

84 Cf. 10 : 41 – "To me [shall be accounted] my doings, and to you, your doings: you are not accountable for what I am doing, and I am not accountable for whatever you do".

85 See *sūrah* 2, note 94.

86 I.e., despite their awareness that God *alone* knows all and is, therefore, unique in His all-embracing Presence.

87 See *sūrah* 3, note 106.

88 I.e., through independent reasoning or observation.

89 Lit., "worse than this" – i.e., "more painful than the repugnance which you feel with regard to God's messages".

O MEN! A parable is set forth [herewith]; hearken, then, to it! Behold, those beings whom you invoke instead of God cannot create [as much as] a fly, even were they to join all their forces to that end! And if a fly robs them of anything, they cannot [even] rescue it from him! Weak indeed is the seeker, and [weak] the sought! ‹73›

No true understanding of God have they [who err in this way]: for, verily, God is most powerful, almighty! ‹74›

[In His almightiness,] God chooses message-bearers from among the angels as well as from among men. But, behold, God [alone] is all-hearing, all-seeing:[90] ‹75› [whereas their knowledge is limited,] He knows all that lies open before them and all that is hidden from them[91] – for all things go back to God [as their source]. ‹76›

السجدة

O YOU who have attained to faith! Bow down and prostrate yourselves, and worship your Sustainer [alone], and do good, so that you might attain to a happy state! ‹77›

And strive hard in God's cause with all the striving that is due to Him: it is He who has elected you [to carry His message], and has laid no hardship on you in [anything that pertains to] religion,[92] [and made you follow] the creed of your forefather Abraham.[93]

يَٰٓأَيُّهَا ٱلنَّاسُ ضُرِبَ مَثَلٌ فَٱسْتَمِعُوا۟ لَهُۥٓ ۚ إِنَّ ٱلَّذِينَ تَدْعُونَ مِن دُونِ ٱللَّهِ لَن
يَخْلُقُوا۟ ذُبَابًا وَلَوِ ٱجْتَمَعُوا۟ لَهُۥ ۖ وَإِن يَسْلُبْهُمُ ٱلذُّبَابُ شَيْـًٔا لَّا يَسْتَنقِذُوهُ مِنْهُ ۚ
ضَعُفَ ٱلطَّالِبُ وَٱلْمَطْلُوبُ ﴿73﴾ مَا قَدَرُوا۟ ٱللَّهَ حَقَّ قَدْرِهِۦٓ ۗ إِنَّ ٱللَّهَ لَقَوِىٌّ
عَزِيزٌ ﴿74﴾ ٱللَّهُ يَصْطَفِى مِنَ ٱلْمَلَٰٓئِكَةِ رُسُلًا وَمِنَ ٱلنَّاسِ ۚ إِنَّ ٱللَّهَ سَمِيعٌۢ
بَصِيرٌ ﴿75﴾ يَعْلَمُ مَا بَيْنَ أَيْدِيهِمْ وَمَا خَلْفَهُمْ ۗ وَإِلَى ٱللَّهِ تُرْجَعُ ٱلْأُمُورُ ﴿76﴾
يَٰٓأَيُّهَا ٱلَّذِينَ ءَامَنُوا۟ ٱرْكَعُوا۟ وَٱسْجُدُوا۟ وَٱعْبُدُوا۟ رَبَّكُمْ وَٱفْعَلُوا۟
ٱلْخَيْرَ لَعَلَّكُمْ تُفْلِحُونَ ۩ ﴿77﴾ وَجَٰهِدُوا۟ فِى ٱللَّهِ حَقَّ جِهَادِهِۦ ۚ هُوَ
ٱجْتَبَىٰكُمْ وَمَا جَعَلَ عَلَيْكُمْ فِى ٱلدِّينِ مِنْ حَرَجٍ ۚ مِّلَّةَ أَبِيكُمْ إِبْرَٰهِيمَ ۚ

Yāa ᵓayyuhan-nāsu ḍuriba mathaluñ-fastamiᶜū lah. ᵓInnal-ladhīna tadᶜūna miñ-dūnil-lāhi lañy-yakhluqū dhubābañw-wa lawij-tamaᶜū lah. Wa ᵓiñy-yaslubhumudh-dhubābu shayᵓal-lā yastañqidhūhu minh. Ḍaᶜufaṭ-ṭālibu wal-maṭlūb. (73) Mā qadarul-lāha ḥaqqa qadrih. ᵓInnal-lāha laQawiyyun ᶜAzīz. (74) ᵓAllāhu yaṣṭafī minal-Malāaᵓikati Rusulañw-wa minan-nās. ᵓInnal-lāha Samīᶜum-Baṣīr. (75) Yaᶜlamu mā bayna ᵓaydīhim wa mā khalfahum. Wa ᵓilal-lāhi turjaᶜul-ᵓumūr. (76) Yāa ᵓayyuhal-ladhīna ᵓāmanur-kaᶜū was-judū waᶜ-budū Rabbakum waf-ᶜalul-khayra laᶜallakum tufliḥūn. ۩ (77) Wa jāhidū fil-lāhi ḥaqqa jihādih. Huwaj-tabākum wa mā jaᶜala ᶜalaykum fid-dīni min ḥaraj. Millata ᵓabīkum ᵓIbrāhīm.

90 I.e., the prophets and the angels are but created beings having no share whatever in His omniscience and, hence, no claim to being worshipped.

91 For an explanation of this rendering of the phrase *mā bayna aydīhim wa-mā khalfahum*, see *sūrah* 2, note 247.

92 The absence of any "hardship" in the religion of Islam is due to several factors: (1) it is free of any dogma or mystical proposition which might make the Qurᵓanic doctrine difficult to understand or might even conflict with man's innate reason; (2) it avoids all complicated ritual or system of taboos which would impose undue restrictions on man's everyday life; (3) it rejects all self-mortification and exaggerated asceticism, which must unavoidably conflict with man's true nature (cf. in this connection note 118 on the first sentence of 2 : 143); and (4) it takes fully into account the fact that "man has been created weak" (4 : 28).

93 Abraham is designated here as "your forefather" not only because he was, in fact, an ancestor of the Prophet Muḥammad – to whose followers this passage is addressed – but also because he is the prototype (and thus, the *spiritual* "forefather") of all who consciously "surrender themselves to God" (see next note).

It is He who has named you – in bygone times as well as in this [divine writ] – "those who have surrendered themselves to God",[94] so that the Apostle might bear witness to the truth before you, and that you might bear witness to it before all mankind.
Thus, be constant in prayer, and render the purifying dues, and hold fast unto God. He is your Lord Supreme: and how excellent is this Lord Supreme, and how excellent this Giver of Succour! ‹78›

هُوَ سَمَّىٰكُمُ ٱلْمُسْلِمِينَ مِن قَبْلُ وَفِي هَٰذَا لِيَكُونَ ٱلرَّسُولُ شَهِيدًا
عَلَيْكُمْ وَتَكُونُوا۟ شُهَدَآءَ عَلَى ٱلنَّاسِ فَأَقِيمُوا۟ ٱلصَّلَوٰةَ وَءَاتُوا۟ ٱلزَّكَوٰةَ
وَٱعْتَصِمُوا۟ بِٱللَّهِ هُوَ مَوْلَىٰكُمْ فَنِعْمَ ٱلْمَوْلَىٰ وَنِعْمَ ٱلنَّصِيرُ ﴿٧٨﴾

Huwa sammākumul-Muslimīna miñ-qablu wa fī hādhā liyakūnar-Rasūlu shahīdan ᶜalaykum wa takūnū shuhadāaʾa ᶜalan-nās. Faʾaqīmuṣ-Ṣalāta wa ʾātuz-Zakāta waᶜ-taṣimū billāhi Huwa Mawlākum faniᶜmal-Mawlā wa niᶜman-Naṣīr. (78)

94 The term *muslim* signifies "one who surrenders himself to God"; correspondingly, *islām* denotes "self-surrender to God". Both these terms are applied in the Qurʾān to all who believe in the One God and affirm this belief by an unequivocal acceptance of His revealed messages. Since the Qurʾān represents the final and most universal of these divine revelations, the believers are called upon, in the sequence, to follow the guidance of its Apostle and thus to become an example for all mankind (cf. 2 : 143 and the corresponding note 119).

The Twenty-Third Sūrah

Al-Mu'minūn (The Believers)

Mecca Period

MOST of the classical commentators agree in that this *sūrah* was revealed towards the end of the Mecca period; some authorities (quoted by Suyūṭī) are even of the opinion that it is the very last Meccan revelation, but we have no conclusive evidence to that effect.

From the first to the last verse, the discourse centres – as the title of the *sūrah* indicates – on the problem of true faith, the overwhelming evidence which points to the existence of an almighty Creator, and on man's ultimate responsibility before Him. Stress is laid on the fact of unceasing divine guidance manifested in a long succession of God-inspired prophets; and since all of them propounded one and the same truth, all who believe in God are reminded – as in 21 : 92-93 – that "this community of yours is one single community" (verse 52), and that this unity has been torn asunder by man's egotism, greed and striving after power (verses 53 ff.). But the main theme of the *sūrah* is the reminder, expressed in a variety of arguments, that it is *logically impossible* to believe in God as a conscious Creative Power without believing in the reality of a life after death as well.

-23-

سورة المؤمنون مكية

وآياتها ثماني عشرة ومائة

IN THE NAME OF GOD, THE MOST GRACIOUS, THE DISPENSER OF GRACE:

TRULY, to a happy state shall attain the
believers: ‹1› those who humble themselves in their prayer, ‹2› and who turn
away from all that is frivolous, ‹3› and
who are intent on inner purity;[1] ‹4›
and who are mindful of their chastity,[2] ‹5›
[not giving way to their desires] with any
but their spouses – that is, those whom
they rightfully possess [through wedlock]:[3]
– for then, behold, they are free of all
blame, ‹6› whereas such as seek to go
beyond that [limit] are truly transgressors;
‹7›
and who are faithful to their trusts and to
their pledges, ‹8›
and who guard their prayers [from all
worldly intent]. ‹9›
It is they, they who shall be the inheritors
‹10› that will inherit the paradise; [and]
therein shall they abide. ‹11›

بِسْمِ ٱللَّهِ ٱلرَّحْمَٰنِ ٱلرَّحِيمِ

قَدْ أَفْلَحَ ٱلْمُؤْمِنُونَ ﴿١﴾ ٱلَّذِينَ هُمْ فِى صَلَاتِهِمْ خَٰشِعُونَ ﴿٢﴾ وَٱلَّذِينَ
هُمْ عَنِ ٱللَّغْوِ مُعْرِضُونَ ﴿٣﴾ وَٱلَّذِينَ هُمْ لِلزَّكَوٰةِ فَٰعِلُونَ ﴿٤﴾ وَٱلَّذِينَ هُمْ
لِفُرُوجِهِمْ حَٰفِظُونَ ﴿٥﴾ إِلَّا عَلَىٰٓ أَزْوَٰجِهِمْ أَوْ مَا مَلَكَتْ أَيْمَٰنُهُمْ
فَإِنَّهُمْ غَيْرُ مَلُومِينَ ﴿٦﴾ فَمَنِ ٱبْتَغَىٰ وَرَآءَ ذَٰلِكَ فَأُو۟لَٰٓئِكَ هُمُ ٱلْعَادُونَ ﴿٧﴾
وَٱلَّذِينَ هُمْ لِأَمَٰنَٰتِهِمْ وَعَهْدِهِمْ رَٰعُونَ ﴿٨﴾ وَٱلَّذِينَ هُمْ عَلَىٰ صَلَوَٰتِهِمْ
يُحَافِظُونَ ﴿٩﴾ أُو۟لَٰٓئِكَ هُمُ ٱلْوَٰرِثُونَ ﴿١٠﴾ ٱلَّذِينَ يَرِثُونَ ٱلْفِرْدَوْسَ هُمْ
فِيهَا خَٰلِدُونَ ﴿١١﴾

حزب 35
جزء 18

Bismil-lāhir-Raḥmānir-Raḥīm.
Qad ʾaflaḥal-muʾminūn. (1) ʾAlladhīna hum fī
Ṣalātihim khāshiʿūn. (2) Wal-ladhīna hum ʿanil-
laghwi muʿriḍūn. (3) Wal-ladhīna hum liz-Zakāti
fāʿilūn. (4) Wal-ladhīna hum lifurūjihim ḥāfiẓūna, (5)
ʾillā ʿalāa ʾazwājihim ʾaw mā malakat ʾaymānuhum
faʾinnahum ghayru malūmīn. (6) Famanib-taghā
warāaʾa dhālika faʾulāaʾika humul-ʿādūn. (7) Wal-
ladhīna hum liʾamānātihim wa ʿahdihim rāʿūn. (8)
Wal-ladhīna hum ʿalā Ṣalawātihim yuḥāfiẓūn. (9)
ʾUlāaʾika humul-wārithūn. (10) ʾAlladhīna yarithūnal-
firdawsa hum fīhā khālidūn. (11)

---

1 Lit., "working for" or "active in behalf of [inner] purity", which is the meaning of *zakāh* in this context (Zamakhsharī; the same interpretation has been advanced by Abū Muslim).

2 Lit., "who guard their private parts".

3 Lit., "*or* those whom their right hands possess" (*aw mā malakat aymānuhum*). Most of the commentators assume unquestioningly that this relates to female slaves, and that the particle *aw* ("or") denotes a permissible alternative. This conventional interpretation is, in my opinion, inadmissible inasmuch as it is based on the assumption that sexual intercourse with one's female slave is permitted *without* marriage: an assumption which is contradicted by the Qurʾān itself (see 4 : 3, 24, 25 and 24 : 32, with the corresponding notes). Nor is this the only objection to the above-mentioned interpretation. Since the Qurʾān applies the term "believers" to men and women alike, and since the term *azwāj* ("spouses"), too, denotes both the male and the female partners in marriage, there is no reason for attributing to the phrase *mā malakat aymānuhum* the meaning of "their *female* slaves"; and since, on the other hand, it is out of the question that female *and* male slaves could have been referred to here, it is obvious that this phrase does not relate to slaves at all, but has the same meaning as in 4 : 24 – namely, "those whom they rightfully possess *through wedlock*" (see note 26 on 4 : 24) – with the significant difference that in the present context this expression relates to

NOW, INDEED, We create man out of the essence of clay,[4] ‹12› and then We cause him to remain as a drop of sperm in [the womb's] firm keeping, ‹13› and then We create out of the drop of sperm a germ-cell, and then We create out of the germ-cell an embryonic lump, and then We create within the embryonic lump bones, and then We clothe the bones with flesh – and then We bring [all] this into being as a new creation:[5] hallowed, therefore, is God, the best of artisans![6] ‹14›
And then, behold! after all this, you are destined to die; ‹15› and then, behold! you shall be raised from the dead on Resurrection Day. ‹16›
And, indeed, We have created above you seven [celestial] orbits;[7] and never are We unmindful of [any aspect of Our] creation. ‹17›
And We send down water from the skies in accordance with a measure [set by Us], and then We cause it to lodge in the earth: but, behold, We are most certainly able to withdraw this [blessing]! ‹18›
And by means of this [water] We bring forth for you gardens of date-palms and vines, wherein you have fruit abundant and whereof you eat, ‹19›

وَلَقَدْ خَلَقْنَا ٱلْإِنسَـٰنَ مِن سُلَـٰلَةٍ مِّن طِينٍ ﴿12﴾ ثُمَّ جَعَلْنَـٰهُ نُطْفَةً فِى قَرَارٍ
مَّكِينٍ ﴿13﴾ ثُمَّ خَلَقْنَا ٱلنُّطْفَةَ عَلَقَةً فَخَلَقْنَا ٱلْعَلَقَةَ مُضْغَةً فَخَلَقْنَا
ٱلْمُضْغَةَ عِظَـٰمًا فَكَسَوْنَا ٱلْعِظَـٰمَ لَحْمًا ثُمَّ أَنشَأْنَـٰهُ خَلْقًا ءَاخَرَ فَتَبَارَكَ
ٱللَّهُ أَحْسَنُ ٱلْخَـٰلِقِينَ ﴿14﴾ ثُمَّ إِنَّكُم بَعْدَ ذَٰلِكَ لَمَيِّتُونَ ﴿15﴾ ثُمَّ إِنَّكُمْ
يَوْمَ ٱلْقِيَـٰمَةِ تُبْعَثُونَ ﴿16﴾ وَلَقَدْ خَلَقْنَا فَوْقَكُمْ سَبْعَ طَرَآئِقَ وَمَا كُنَّا عَنِ
ٱلْخَلْقِ غَـٰفِلِينَ ﴿17﴾ وَأَنزَلْنَا مِنَ ٱلسَّمَآءِ مَآءًۢ بِقَدَرٍ فَأَسْكَنَّـٰهُ فِى
ٱلْأَرْضِ وَإِنَّا عَلَىٰ ذَهَابٍۭ بِهِۦ لَقَـٰدِرُونَ ﴿18﴾ فَأَنشَأْنَا لَكُم بِهِۦ جَنَّـٰتٍ
مِّن نَّخِيلٍ وَأَعْنَـٰبٍ لَّكُمْ فِيهَا فَوَٰكِهُ كَثِيرَةٌ وَمِنْهَا تَأْكُلُونَ ﴿19﴾

Wa laqad khalaqnal-᾿Iñsāna miñ-sulālatim-miñ-ṭīn. (12) Thumma jaᶜalnāhu nuṭfatañ-fī qarārim-makīn. (13) Thumma khalaqnan-nuṭfata ᶜalaqatañ-fakhalaqnal-ᶜalaqata muḍghatañ-fakhalaqnal-muḍghata ᶜiẓāmañ-fakasawnal-ᶜiẓāma laḥmañ-thumma ᾿añsha᾿nāhu khalqan ᾿ākhar. Fatabārakal lāhu ᾿Aḥsanul-khāliqīn. (14) Thumma ᾿innakum-baᶜda dhālik lamayyitūn. (15) Thumma ᾿innakum Yawmal-Qiyāmati tubᶜathūn. (16) Wa laqad khalaqnā fawqakum sabᶜa ṭarāa᾿iqa wa mā kunnā ᶜanil-khalqi ghāfilīn. (17) Wa ᾿añzalnā minas-samāa᾿i māa᾿am-biqadariñ-fa᾿askannāhu fil-᾿arḍi wa ᾿innā ᶜalā dhahābim-bihī laqādirūn. (18) Fa᾿añsha᾿nā lakum-bihī jannātim-miñ-nakhīliñw-wa ᾿aᶜnābil-lakum fīhā fawākihu kathīratuñw-wa minhā ta᾿kulūn. (19)

both husbands and wives, who "rightfully possess" one another by virtue of marriage. On the basis of this interpretation, the particle *aw* which precedes this clause does not denote an alternative ("or") but is, rather, in the nature of an explanatory amplification, more or less analogous to the phrase "in other words" or "that is", thus giving to the whole sentence the meaning, ". . . save with their spouses – that is, those whom they rightfully possess [through wedlock] . . .", etc. (Cf. a similar construction in 25 : 62 – "for him who has the will to take thought – that is [lit., "or"], has the will to be grateful".)

4 The frequent Qur᾿anic references to man's being "created out of clay" or "out of dust" or (as in this instance) "out of the essence (*sulālah*) of clay" point to the fact that his body is composed of various organic and inorganic substances existing on or in the earth, as well as to the continuous transmutation of those substances, through the intake of earth-grown food, into reproductive cells (Rāzī) – thus stressing man's humble origin, and hence the debt of gratitude which he owes to God for having endowed him with a conscious soul. The past tense in verses 12-14 (lit., "We have created", "We have caused him to remain", etc.) emphasizes the fact that all this has been ordained by God and has been happening again and again ever since man was brought into being by Him; in the above context, this recurrence is brought out best by the use of the present tense.

5 Lit., "as another creature", i.e., existing independently of the mother's body.

6 Lit., "the best of creators". As Ṭabarī points out, the Arabs apply the designation "creator" to every artisan (*ṣāniᶜ*) – a usage also current in European languages with reference to the "creation" of works of art and imagination. Since God is the *only* Creator in the real, primary sense of this word, the phrase *aḥsan al-khāliqīn* must be understood in this secondary sense of the term *khāliq* (cf. *Tāj al-ᶜArūs*, art. *khalaqa*).

7 Lit., "seven paths", which may signify the orbits of the visible planets or – as the classical commentators assume

as well as a tree that issues from [the lands adjoining] Mount Sinai,[8] yielding oil and relish for all to eat. ‹20›
And, behold, in the cattle [too] there is indeed a lesson for you: We give you to drink of that [milk] which is within their bellies; and you derive many [other] uses from them: for, you eat of their flesh,[9] ‹21› and by them – as by the ships [over the sea] – you are borne [overland]. ‹22›

AND, INDEED, We sent forth Noah unto his people,[10] and he said: "O my people! Worship God [alone]: you have no deity other than Him. Will you not, then, become conscious of Him?" ‹23›
But the great ones among his people, who refused to acknowledge the truth, replied: "This [man] is nothing but a mortal like yourselves who wants to make himself superior to you! For, if God had willed [to convey a message unto us], He would surely have sent down angels; [moreover,] we have never heard [anything like] this from our forebears of old![11] ‹24› He is nothing but a madman: so bear with him for a while." ‹25›
Said [Noah]: "O my Sustainer! Succour me against their accusation of lying!" ‹26›
Thereupon We inspired him thus: "Build, under Our eyes[12] and according to Our inspiration, the ark [that shall save thee and those who follow thee].[13]

وَشَجَرَةً تَخْرُجُ مِن طُورِ سَيْنَآءَ تَنۢبُتُ بِٱلدُّهْنِ وَصِبْغٍ لِّلْـَٔاكِلِينَ ﴿٢٠﴾ وَإِنَّ لَكُمْ
فِى ٱلْأَنْعَٰمِ لَعِبْرَةً ۖ نُّسْقِيكُم مِّمَّا فِى بُطُونِهَا وَلَكُمْ فِيهَا مَنَٰفِعُ كَثِيرَةٌ وَمِنْهَا
تَأْكُلُونَ ﴿٢١﴾ وَعَلَيْهَا وَعَلَى ٱلْفُلْكِ تُحْمَلُونَ ﴿٢٢﴾ وَلَقَدْ أَرْسَلْنَا نُوحًا إِلَىٰ
قَوْمِهِۦ فَقَالَ يَٰقَوْمِ ٱعْبُدُوا۟ ٱللَّهَ مَا لَكُم مِّنْ إِلَٰهٍ غَيْرُهُۥٓ ۖ أَفَلَا تَتَّقُونَ ﴿٢٣﴾ فَقَالَ
ٱلْمَلَؤُا۟ ٱلَّذِينَ كَفَرُوا۟ مِن قَوْمِهِۦ مَا هَٰذَآ إِلَّا بَشَرٌ مِّثْلُكُمْ يُرِيدُ أَن يَتَفَضَّلَ
عَلَيْكُمْ وَلَوْ شَآءَ ٱللَّهُ لَأَنزَلَ مَلَٰٓئِكَةً مَّا سَمِعْنَا بِهَٰذَا فِىٓ ءَابَآئِنَا ٱلْأَوَّلِينَ ﴿٢٤﴾
إِنْ هُوَ إِلَّا رَجُلٌۢ بِهِۦ جِنَّةٌ فَتَرَبَّصُوا۟ بِهِۦ حَتَّىٰ حِينٍ ﴿٢٥﴾ قَالَ رَبِّ
ٱنصُرْنِى بِمَا كَذَّبُونِ ﴿٢٦﴾ فَأَوْحَيْنَآ إِلَيْهِ أَنِ ٱصْنَعِ ٱلْفُلْكَ بِأَعْيُنِنَا وَوَحْيِنَا

Wa shajaratañ-takhruju miñ-Ṭūri Saynāaʾa tambutu bidduhni wa ṣibghil-lilʾākilīn. ﴿20﴾ Wa ʾinna lakum fil-ʾanᶜāmi laᶜibratañ-nusqīkum mimmā fī buṭūnihā wa lakum fīhā manāfiᶜu kathīratuñw-wa minhā taʾkulūn. ﴿21﴾ Wa ᶜalayhā wa ᶜalal-fulki tuḥmalūn. ﴿22﴾ Wa laqad ʾarsalnā Nūḥan ʾilā qawmihī faqāla yā qawmiᶜ-budul-lāha mā lakum-min ʾilāhin ghayruhūu ʾafalā tattaqūn. ﴿23﴾ Faqālal-malaʾul-ladhīna kafarū miñ-qawmihī mā hādhāa ʾillā basharum-mithlukum yurīdu ʾañy-yatafaḍḍala ᶜalaykum wa law shāaʾal-lāhu laʾañzala Malāaʾikatam-mā samiᶜnā bihādhā fīi ʾābāaʾinal-ʾawwalīn. ﴿24﴾ ʾIn huwa ʾillā rajulum-bihī jinnatuñ-fatarabbaṣū bihī ḥattā ḥīn. ﴿25﴾ Qāla Rabbiñ-ṣurnī bimā kadhdhabūn. ﴿26﴾ Faʾawḥaynāa ʾilayhi ʾaniṣ-naᶜil-fulka biʾaᶜyuninā wa waḥyinā

– the "seven heavens" (i.e., cosmic systems) repeatedly spoken of in the Qurʾān. In either case, the number "seven" is used metonymically, indicating multiplicity. See in this connection note 20 on 2 : 29.

8 I.e., the olive-tree, native to the lands around the eastern Mediterranean, where so many pre-Qurʾanic prophets (here symbolized – because of its sacred associations – by Mount Sinai) lived and preached.

9 Lit., "of them".

10 Sc., "who had lost sight of all the multiform evidence of the Creator's uniqueness and, thus, all gratitude for the innumerable blessings which He bestows upon man".

11 Lit., "in connection with (*fī*) our early forebears" – a Qurʾanic allusion to the fact that people often reject a new ethical proposition on no better grounds than that it conflicts with their "inherited" habits of thought and ways of life. Indirectly, this allusion implies a condemnation of all blind *taqlīd*, i.e., an unthinking acceptance of religious doctrines or assertions which are not unequivocally supported by divine revelation, the explicit teachings of a prophet, or the evidence of unprejudiced reason.

12 I.e., "under Our protection".

13 Regarding this interpolation, see *sūrah* 11, note 60. For an explanation of the passage that follows, see 11 : 40 and the corresponding notes 62-64. The reason for the (abbreviated) repetition of Noah's story – given in much greater detail in 11 : 25-48 – becomes evident from verse 29.

فَإِذَا جَآءَ أَمْرُنَا وَفَارَ ٱلتَّنُّورُ فَٱسْلُكْ فِيهَا مِن كُلٍّ زَوْجَيْنِ ٱثْنَيْنِ
وَأَهْلَكَ إِلَّا مَن سَبَقَ عَلَيْهِ ٱلْقَوْلُ مِنْهُمْ وَلَا تُخَٰطِبْنِى فِى ٱلَّذِينَ ظَلَمُوٓا۟
إِنَّهُم مُّغْرَقُونَ ﴿27﴾ فَإِذَا ٱسْتَوَيْتَ أَنتَ وَمَن مَّعَكَ عَلَى ٱلْفُلْكِ فَقُلِ
ٱلْحَمْدُ لِلَّهِ ٱلَّذِى نَجَّىٰنَا مِنَ ٱلْقَوْمِ ٱلظَّٰلِمِينَ ﴿28﴾ وَقُل رَّبِّ أَنزِلْنِى
مُنزَلًا مُّبَارَكًا وَأَنتَ خَيْرُ ٱلْمُنزِلِينَ ﴿29﴾ إِنَّ فِى ذَٰلِكَ لَءَايَٰتٍ وَإِن كُنَّا
لَمُبْتَلِينَ ﴿30﴾ ثُمَّ أَنشَأْنَا مِنۢ بَعْدِهِمْ قَرْنًا ءَاخَرِينَ ﴿31﴾ فَأَرْسَلْنَا فِيهِمْ رَسُولًا
مِّنْهُمْ أَنِ ٱعْبُدُوا۟ ٱللَّهَ مَا لَكُم مِّنْ إِلَٰهٍ غَيْرُهُۥٓ أَفَلَا تَتَّقُونَ ﴿32﴾ وَقَالَ ٱلْمَلَأُ
مِن قَوْمِهِ ٱلَّذِينَ كَفَرُوا۟ وَكَذَّبُوا۟ بِلِقَآءِ ٱلْـَٔاخِرَةِ وَأَتْرَفْنَٰهُمْ فِى ٱلْحَيَوٰةِ ٱلدُّنْيَا

faʾidhā jāaʾa ʾamrunā wa fārat-tannūru fasluk fīhā miñ-kulliñ-zawjaynith-nayni wa ʾahlaka ʾillā mañ-sabaqa ʿalayhil-qawlu minhum; wa lā tukhāṭibnī fil-ladhīna ẓalamūu ʾinnahum-mughraqūn. (27) Faʾidhas-tawayta ʾañta wa mam-maʿaka ʿalal-fulki faqulil-ḥamdu lillāhil-ladhī najjānā minal-qawmiẓ-ẓālimīn. (28) Wa qur-Rabbi ʾañzilnī muñzalam-mubārakañw-wa ʾAñta Khayrul-muñzilīn. (29) ʾInna fī dhālika laʾĀyātiñw-wa ʾiñ-kunnā lamubtalīn. (30) Thumma ʾañshaʾnā mim-baʿdihim qarnan ʾākharīn. (31) Faʾarsalnā fīhim Rasūlam-minhum ʾaniʿ-budul-lāha mā lakum-min ʾilāhin ghayruhūu ʾafalā tattaqūn. (32) Wa qālal-malaʾu miñ-qawmihil-ladhīna kafarū wa kadhdhabū biliqāaʾil-ʾĀkhirati wa ʾatrafnāhum fil-ḥayātid-dunyā

And when Our judgment comes to pass, and waters gush forth in torrents over the face of the earth, place on board of this [ark] one pair of each [kind of animal] of either sex, as well as thy family – excepting those on whom sentence has already been passed – and do not appeal to Me [any more] in behalf of those who are bent on evildoing – for, behold, they are destined to be drowned! ‹27›

"And as soon as thou and those who are with thee are settled in the ark, say: 'All praise is due to God, who has saved us from those evildoing folk!' ‹28›

"And say: 'O my Sustainer! Cause me to reach a destination blessed [by Thee][14] – for Thou art the best to show man how to reach his [true] destination!'"[15] ‹29›

In this [story], behold, there are messages indeed [for those who think]: for, verily, We always put [man] to a test. ‹30›

AND AFTER those [people of old] We gave rise to new generations;[16] ‹31› and [every time] We sent unto them an apostle from among themselves, [he told them:] "Worship God [alone]: you have no deity other than Him. Will you not, then, become conscious of Him?"[17] ‹32›

And [every time] the great ones among his people, who refused to acknowledge the truth and gave the lie to the announcement of a life to come [simply] because We had granted them ease and plenty in [their] worldly life, and they had become corrupted by it[18] – [every time] they would say:

14 Lit., "Cause me to alight with a blessed alighting" – i.e., in a blessed *condition* of alighting, or at a blessed *place* of alighting (Ṭabarī); both these meanings are implied in the word "destination".

15 Lit., "the best of all who cause [man] to alight". i.e., at his true destination. In this prayer enjoined upon Noah – and, by implication, on every believer – the story of the ark is raised to symbolic significance: it reveals itself as a parable of the human soul's longing for divine illumination, which alone can show man how to save himself and to reach his true destination in the realm of the spirit as well as in worldly life.

16 Lit., "a generation (*qarn*) of others". For a wider meaning of the term *qarn*, see *sūrah* 6, note 5.

17 Most of the classical commentators assume that the apostle referred to in verses 32-41 is Hūd, the prophet of the tribe of ʿĀd (see *sūrah* 7, note 48). Since, however, this passage contains elements appearing in the stories of many prophets – including that of the Prophet Muḥammad – I am of the opinion that it has a general import: namely, an allusion to *all* of God's apostles and to the ever-recurring similarity of their experiences.

18 Thus Ṭabarī interprets the concise but meaningful phrase *atrafnāhum fī 'l-ḥayāti 'd-dunyā*. For a fuller explanation of the verb *tarifa*, see note 147 on 11 : 116.

مَا هَٰذَآ إِلَّا بَشَرٌ مِّثْلُكُمْ يَأْكُلُ مِمَّا تَأْكُلُونَ مِنْهُ وَيَشْرَبُ مِمَّا
تَشْرَبُونَ ﴿33﴾ وَلَئِنْ أَطَعْتُم بَشَرًا مِّثْلَكُمْ إِنَّكُمْ إِذًا لَّخَٰسِرُونَ ﴿34﴾
أَيَعِدُكُمْ أَنَّكُمْ إِذَا مِتُّمْ وَكُنتُمْ تُرَابًا وَعِظَٰمًا أَنَّكُم مُّخْرَجُونَ ﴿35﴾ ۞
هَيْهَاتَ هَيْهَاتَ لِمَا تُوعَدُونَ ﴿36﴾ إِنْ هِىَ إِلَّا حَيَاتُنَا ٱلدُّنْيَا نَمُوتُ
وَنَحْيَا وَمَا نَحْنُ بِمَبْعُوثِينَ ﴿37﴾ إِنْ هُوَ إِلَّا رَجُلٌ ٱفْتَرَىٰ عَلَى ٱللَّهِ كَذِبًا
وَمَا نَحْنُ لَهُۥ بِمُؤْمِنِينَ ﴿38﴾ قَالَ رَبِّ ٱنصُرْنِى بِمَا كَذَّبُونِ ﴿39﴾ قَالَ
عَمَّا قَلِيلٍ لَّيُصْبِحُنَّ نَٰدِمِينَ ﴿40﴾ فَأَخَذَتْهُمُ ٱلصَّيْحَةُ بِٱلْحَقِّ فَجَعَلْنَٰهُمْ
غُثَآءً فَبُعْدًا لِّلْقَوْمِ ٱلظَّٰلِمِينَ ﴿41﴾ ثُمَّ أَنشَأْنَا مِنۢ بَعْدِهِمْ قُرُونًا ءَاخَرِينَ ﴿42﴾
مَا تَسْبِقُ مِنْ أُمَّةٍ أَجَلَهَا وَمَا يَسْتَـْٔخِرُونَ ﴿43﴾ ثُمَّ أَرْسَلْنَا رُسُلَنَا تَتْرَا كُلَّ
مَا جَآءَ أُمَّةً رَّسُولُهَا كَذَّبُوهُ فَأَتْبَعْنَا بَعْضَهُم بَعْضًا وَجَعَلْنَٰهُمْ أَحَادِيثَ
فَبُعْدًا لِّقَوْمٍ لَّا يُؤْمِنُونَ ﴿44﴾

ربع الحزب

"This [man] is nothing but a mortal like yourselves, eating of what you eat, and drinking of what you drink: ‹33› and, indeed, if you pay heed to a mortal like yourselves, you will surely be the losers! ‹34› Does he promise you that, after you have died and become [mere] dust and bones, you shall be brought forth [to a new life]? ‹35› Far-fetched, far-fetched indeed is what you are promised! ‹36› There is no life beyond our life in this world: we die and we live [but once], and we shall never be raised from the dead! ‹37› He is nothing but a man who attributes his own lying inventions to God, and we are not going to believe him!" ‹38›

[Whereupon the prophet] would say: "O my Sustainer! Succour me against their accusation of lying!" ‹39›

[And God] would say: "After a little while they will surely be smitten with remorse!"[19] ‹40›

And then the blast [of Our punishment] overtook them, justly and unavoidably,[20] and We caused them to become as the flotsam of dead leaves and the scum borne on the surface of a torrent: and so – away with those evildoing folk! ‹41›

AND AFTER them We gave rise to new generations:[21] ‹42› [for,] no community can ever forestall [the end of] its term – and neither can they delay [its coming].[22] ‹43› And We sent forth Our apostles, one after another: [and] every time their apostle came to a community, they gave him the lie: and so We caused them to follow one another [into the grave], and let them become [mere] tales: and so – away with the folk who would not believe! ‹44›

mā hādhaa ʾillā basharum-mithlukum yaʾkulu mimmā taʾkulūna minhu wa yashrabu mimmā tashrabūn. ﴿33﴾ Wa laʾin ʾaṭaʿtum-basharam-mithlakum ʾinnakum ʾidhal-lakhāsirūn. ﴿34﴾ ʾAyaʿidukum ʾannakum ʾidhā mittum wa kuñtum turābañw-wa ʿiẓāman ʾannakum-mukhrajūn. ﴿35﴾ ۞ Hayhāta hayhāta limā tūʿadūn. ﴿36﴾ ʾIn hiya ʾillā ḥayātunad-dunyā namūtu wa naḥyā wa mā naḥnu bimabʿūthīn. ﴿37﴾ ʾIn huwa ʾillā rajulunif-tarā ʿalal-lāhi kadhibañw-wa mā naḥnu lahū bimuʾminīn. ﴿38﴾ Qāla Rabbiñ-ṣurnī bimā kadhdhabūn. ﴿39﴾ Qāla ʿammā qalīlil-layuṣbiḥunna nādimīn. ﴿40﴾ Faʾakhadhat-humuṣ-ṣayḥatu bil-ḥaqqi fajaʿalnāhum ghuthāaʾañ-fabuʿdal-lilqawmiẓ-ẓālimīn. ﴿41﴾ Thumma ʾañshaʾnā mim-baʿdihim qurūnan ʾākharīn. ﴿42﴾ Mā tasbiqu min ʾummatin ʾajalahā wa mā yastaʾkhirūn. ﴿43﴾ Thumma ʾarsalnā Rusulanā tatrā kulla mā jāaʾa ʾummatar-Rasūluhā kadhdhabūh. Faʾatbaʿnā baʿḍahum-baʿḍañw-wa jaʿalnāhum ʾaḥādīth. Fabuʿdal-liqawmil-lā yuʾminūn. ﴿44﴾

19 Lit., "they will surely become of those who feel remorse".

20 The expression *bi'l-ḥaqq* (lit., "in accordance with truth" or "with justice") combines in this instance the concepts of justice, wisdom, reality, inescapability, and consonance with the exigencies of the case under consideration (Rāghib), and can be only approximately rendered in translation.

21 Lit., "generations of others", i.e., new civilizations.

22 See note 5 on the identical phrase in 15 : 5.

AND THEN We sent forth Moses and his brother Aaron with Our messages and a manifest authority [from Us] ‹45› unto Pharaoh and his great ones;[23] but these behaved with arrogance, for they were people wont to glorify [only] themselves. ‹46›

And so they said: "Shall we believe [them –] two mortals like ourselves – although their people are our slaves?" ‹47›

Thus, they gave the lie to those two, and earned [thereby] their place among the doomed:[24] ‹48› for, indeed, We had vouchsafed revelation unto Moses in order that they might find the right way. ‹49›

And [as We exalted Moses, so, too,] We made the son of Mary and his mother a symbol [of Our grace],[25] and provided for both an abode in a lofty place of lasting restfulness and unsullied springs.[26] ‹50›

O YOU APOSTLES! Partake of the good things of life,[27] and do righteous deeds: verily, I have full knowledge of all that you do. ‹51›

And, verily, this community of yours is one single community, since I am the Sustainer of you all: remain, then, conscious of Me![28] ‹52›

But they [who claim to follow you] have torn their unity wide asunder,[29] piece by piece,

ثُمَّ أَرْسَلْنَا مُوسَىٰ وَأَخَاهُ هَٰرُونَ بِـَٔايَٰتِنَا وَسُلْطَٰنٍ مُّبِينٍ ﴿٤٥﴾ إِلَىٰ فِرْعَوْنَ
وَمَلَإِيْهِۦ فَٱسْتَكْبَرُوا۟ وَكَانُوا۟ قَوْمًا عَالِينَ ﴿٤٦﴾ فَقَالُوٓا۟ أَنُؤْمِنُ لِبَشَرَيْنِ
مِثْلِنَا وَقَوْمُهُمَا لَنَا عَٰبِدُونَ ﴿٤٧﴾ فَكَذَّبُوهُمَا فَكَانُوا۟ مِنَ ٱلْمُهْلَكِينَ ﴿٤٨﴾
وَلَقَدْ ءَاتَيْنَا مُوسَى ٱلْكِتَٰبَ لَعَلَّهُمْ يَهْتَدُونَ ﴿٤٩﴾ وَجَعَلْنَا ٱبْنَ مَرْيَمَ
وَأُمَّهُۥٓ ءَايَةً وَءَاوَيْنَٰهُمَآ إِلَىٰ رَبْوَةٍ ذَاتِ قَرَارٍ وَمَعِينٍ ﴿٥٠﴾ يَٰٓأَيُّهَا ٱلرُّسُلُ
كُلُوا۟ مِنَ ٱلطَّيِّبَٰتِ وَٱعْمَلُوا۟ صَٰلِحًا إِنِّى بِمَا تَعْمَلُونَ عَلِيمٌ ﴿٥١﴾ وَإِنَّ هَٰذِهِۦٓ
أُمَّتُكُمْ أُمَّةً وَٰحِدَةً وَأَنَا۠ رَبُّكُمْ فَٱتَّقُونِ ﴿٥٢﴾ فَتَقَطَّعُوٓا۟ أَمْرَهُم بَيْنَهُمْ زُبُرًا

Thumma 'arsalnā Mūsā wa 'akhāhu Hārūna
bi'Āyātinā wa sulṭānim-mubīnin, (45) 'ilā Fir'awna
wa mala'ihī fastakbarū wa kānū qawman 'ālīn. (46)
Faqālūu 'anu'minu libasharayni mithlinā wa qaw-
muhumā lanā 'ābidūn. (47) Fakadhdhabūhumā
fakānū minal-muhlakīn. (48) Wa laqad 'ātaynā
Mūsal-Kitāba la'allahum yahtadūn. (49) Wa
ja'alnab-na Maryama wa 'ummahūu 'Āyatañw-wa
'āwaynāhumāa 'ilā rabwatiñ-dhāti qarāriñw-wa
ma'īn. (50) Yāa 'ayyuhar-Rusulu kulū minaṭ-
ṭayyibāti wa'-malū ṣāliḥā. 'Innī bimā ta'malūna
'Alīm. (51) Wa 'inna hādhihīi 'ummatukum
'ummatañw-wāḥidatañw-wa 'Ana Rabbukum fattaqūn.
(52) Fataqaṭṭa'ūu 'amrahum-baynahum zuburañ-

23 Moses and Aaron are mentioned here by name because their case was different from that of all other prophets: they were rejected not by *their own* community but by their community's oppressors.

24 Lit., "became of those who were destroyed".

25 For my rendering of *āyah*, in this instance, as "symbol", see *sūrah* 19, note 16. Jesus and his mother Mary are mentioned here specifically because they, too, had to suffer persecution and slander at the hands of "those who were bent on denying the truth".

26 I.e., in paradise. The expression *ma'īn* signifies "unsullied springs" or "running waters" (Ibn 'Abbās, as quoted by Ṭabarī; also *Lisān al-'Arab* and *Tāj al-'Arūs*), and thus symbolizes the spiritual purity associated with the concept of paradise, the "gardens through which running waters flow".

27 This rhetorical apostrophe to all of God's apostles is meant to stress their humanness and mortality, and thus to refute the argument of the unbelievers that God could not have chosen "a mortal like ourselves" to be His message-bearer: an argument which overlooks the fact that only human beings who themselves "partake of the good things of life" are able to understand the needs and motives of their fellow-men and, thus, to guide them in their spiritual and social concerns.

28 As in 21 : 92, the above verse is addressed to all who truly believe in God, whatever their historical denomination. By the preceding reference to *all* of God's apostles the Qur'ān clearly implies that all of them were inspired by, and preached, the same fundamental truths, notwithstanding all the differences in the ritual or the specific laws which they propounded in accordance with the exigencies of the time and the social development of their followers. (See notes 66-68 on the second paragraph of 5 : 48.)

29 Cf. 21 : 93.

each group delighting in [but] what they themselves possess [by way of tenets].[30] «53»
But leave them alone, lost in their ignorance, until a [future] time.[31] «54»
Do they think that by all the wealth and offspring with which We provide them «55» We [but want to] make them vie with one another in doing [what *they* consider] good works?[32] Nay, but they do not perceive [their error]! «56»
Verily, [only] they who stand in reverent awe of their Sustainer, «57» and who believe in their Sustainer's messages, «58» and who do not ascribe divinity to aught but their Sustainer, «59» and who give whatever they [have to] give[33] with their hearts trembling at the thought that unto their Sustainer they must return: «60» it is they who vie with one another in doing good works, and it is they who outrun [all others] in attaining to them! «61»
And [withal,] We do not burden any human being with more than he is well able to bear: for with Us is a record that speaks the truth [about what men do and can do]; and none shall be wronged. «62»

كُلُّ حِزْبٍۭ بِمَا لَدَيْهِمْ فَرِحُونَ ﴿53﴾ فَذَرْهُمْ فِى غَمْرَتِهِمْ حَتَّىٰ حِينٍ ﴿54﴾
أَيَحْسَبُونَ أَنَّمَا نُمِدُّهُم بِهِۦ مِن مَّالٍ وَبَنِينَ ﴿55﴾ نُسَارِعُ لَهُمْ فِى ٱلْخَيْرَٰتِ ۚ
بَل لَّا يَشْعُرُونَ ﴿56﴾ إِنَّ ٱلَّذِينَ هُم مِّنْ خَشْيَةِ رَبِّهِم مُّشْفِقُونَ ﴿57﴾ وَٱلَّذِينَ هُم
بِـَٔايَٰتِ رَبِّهِمْ يُؤْمِنُونَ ﴿58﴾ وَٱلَّذِينَ هُم بِرَبِّهِمْ لَا يُشْرِكُونَ ﴿59﴾ وَٱلَّذِينَ
يُؤْتُونَ مَآ ءَاتَوا۟ وَّقُلُوبُهُمْ وَجِلَةٌ أَنَّهُمْ إِلَىٰ رَبِّهِمْ رَٰجِعُونَ ﴿60﴾ أُو۟لَٰٓئِكَ
يُسَٰرِعُونَ فِى ٱلْخَيْرَٰتِ وَهُمْ لَهَا سَٰبِقُونَ ﴿61﴾ وَلَا نُكَلِّفُ نَفْسًا إِلَّا
وُسْعَهَا ۖ وَلَدَيْنَا كِتَٰبٌ يَنطِقُ بِٱلْحَقِّ ۚ وَهُمْ لَا يُظْلَمُونَ ﴿62﴾

kullu ḥizbim-bimā ladayhim fariḥūn. (53) Fadharhum fī ghamratihim ḥattā ḥīn. (54) ʾAyaḥsabūna ʾannamā numidduhum-bihī mim-māliñw-wa banīna, (55) nusāriʿu lahum fil-khayrāt. Bal lā yashʿurūn. (56) ʾInnal-ladhīna hum-miñ-khashyati Rabbihim-mushfiqūn. (57) Wal-ladhīna hum-biʾĀyāti Rabbihim yuʾminūn. (58) Wal-ladhīna hum-biRabbihim lā yushrikūn. (59) Wal-ladhīna yuʾtūna māa ʾātaw wa qulūbuhum wajilatun ʾannahum ʾilā Rabbihim rājiʿūn. (60) ʾUlāaʾika yusāriʿūna fil-khayrāti wa hum lahā sābiqūn. (61) Wa lā nukallifu nafsan ʾillā wusʿahā wa ladaynā Kitābuñy-yañṭiqu bil-ḥaqqi wa hum lā yuẓlamūn. (62)

30 Lit." "in what they have [themselves]". In the first instance, this verse refers to the various religious groups as such: that is to say, to the followers of one or another of the earlier revelations who, in the course of time, consolidated themselves within different "denominations", each of them jealously guarding its own set of tenets, dogmas and rituals and intensely intolerant of all other ways of worship (*manāsik*, see 22 : 67). In the second instance, however, the above condemnation applies to the breach of unity *within* each of the established religious groups; and since it applies to the followers of *all* the prophets, it includes the latter-day followers of Muḥammad as well, and thus constitutes a prediction and condemnation of the doctrinal disunity prevailing in the world of Islam in our times – cf. the well-authenticated saying of the Prophet quoted by Ibn Ḥanbal, Abū Dāʾūd, Tirmidhī and Dārimī: "The Jews have been split up into seventy-one sects, the Christians into seventy-two sects, whereas my community will be split up into seventy-three sects." (It should be remembered that in classical Arabic usage the number "seventy" often stands for "many" – just as "seven" stands for "several" or "various" – and does not necessarily denote an actual figure; hence, what the Prophet meant to say was that the sects and divisions among the Muslims of later days would become many, and even more numerous than those among the Jews and the Christians.)

31 I.e., until they themselves realize their error. This sentence is evidently addressed to the last of the apostles, Muḥammad, and thus to all who truly follow him.

32 I.e., "Do they think that by bestowing on them worldly prosperity God but wants them to vie with one another in their race after material goods and comforts, which they mistakenly identify with 'doing good works'?" Another – linguistically permissible – rendering of the above two verses would be: "Do they think that by all the wealth and offspring with which We provide them We [but] hasten on [the coming] to them of all that is good?" Either of these two renderings implies, firstly, that worldly prosperity is *not* the ultimate good, and, secondly, that the breach of the unity spoken of in the preceding passage was, more often than not, an outcome of mere worldly greed and of factional striving after power.

33 This is an allusion to the giving of what one is *morally* obliged to give, whether it be in charity or in satisfaction of rightful claims on the part of one's fellow-men, including such intangible "gifts" as the dispensing of justice.

NAY, [as for those who have torn asunder the unity of faith –] their hearts are lost in ignorance of all this![34]
But apart from that [breach of unity] they have [on their conscience even worse] deeds;[35] and they will [continue to] commit them ‹63› until – after We shall have taken to task, through suffering, those from among them who [now] are lost in the pursuit of pleasure[36] – they cry out in [belated] supplication. ‹64›
[But they will be told:] "Cry not in supplication today: for, behold, you shall not be succoured by Us! ‹65› Time and again[37] were My messages conveyed unto you, but [every time] you would turn about on your heels ‹66› [and,] impelled by your arrogance, you would talk senselessly far into the night."[38] ‹67›
Have they, then, never tried to understand this word [of God]? Or has there [now] come to them something that never came to their forefathers of old?[39] ‹68›
Or is it, perchance, that they have not recognized their Apostle, and so they disavow him? ‹69›
Or do they say, "There is madness in him"? Nay, he has brought them the truth – and the truth do most of them detest![40] ‹70›

بَلۡ قُلُوبُهُمۡ فِي غَمۡرَةٖ مِّنۡ هَٰذَا وَلَهُمۡ أَعۡمَٰلٞ مِّن دُونِ ذَٰلِكَ هُمۡ لَهَا
عَٰمِلُونَ ﴿٦٣﴾ حَتَّىٰٓ إِذَآ أَخَذۡنَا مُتۡرَفِيهِم بِٱلۡعَذَابِ إِذَا هُمۡ يَجۡـَٔرُونَ ﴿٦٤﴾
لَا تَجۡـَٔرُواْ ٱلۡيَوۡمَۖ إِنَّكُم مِّنَّا لَا تُنصَرُونَ ﴿٦٥﴾ قَدۡ كَانَتۡ ءَايَٰتِي تُتۡلَىٰ
عَلَيۡكُمۡ فَكُنتُمۡ عَلَىٰٓ أَعۡقَٰبِكُمۡ تَنكِصُونَ ﴿٦٦﴾ مُسۡتَكۡبِرِينَ بِهِۦ سَٰمِرٗا
تَهۡجُرُونَ ﴿٦٧﴾ أَفَلَمۡ يَدَّبَّرُواْ ٱلۡقَوۡلَ أَمۡ جَآءَهُم مَّا لَمۡ يَأۡتِ ءَابَآءَهُمُ
ٱلۡأَوَّلِينَ ﴿٦٨﴾ أَمۡ لَمۡ يَعۡرِفُواْ رَسُولَهُمۡ فَهُمۡ لَهُۥ مُنكِرُونَ ﴿٦٩﴾ أَمۡ يَقُولُونَ
بِهِۦ جِنَّةُۢۚ بَلۡ جَآءَهُم بِٱلۡحَقِّ وَأَكۡثَرُهُمۡ لِلۡحَقِّ كَٰرِهُونَ ﴿٧٠﴾

Bal qulūbuhum fī ghamratim-min hādhā wa lahum 'a'mālum-miñ-dūni dhālika hum lahā 'āmilūn. (63) Ḥattāa 'idhāa 'akhadhnā mutrafīhim-bil'adhābi 'idhā hum yaj'arūn. (64) Lā taj'arul-yawma 'innakum-minnā lā tuñṣarūn. (65) Qad kānat 'Āyātī tutlā 'alaykum fakuñtum 'alāa 'a'qābikum tañkiṣūn. (66) Mustakbirīna bihī sāmirañ-tahjurūn. (67) 'Afalam yaddabbarul-qawla 'am jāa'ahum-mā lam ya'ti 'ābāa'ahumul-'awwalīn. (68) 'Am lam ya'rifū Rasūlahum fahum lahū muñkirūn. (69) 'Am yaqūlūna bihī jinnah. Bal jāa'ahum-bil-ḥaqqi wa 'aktharuhum lilḥaqqi kārihūn. (70)

34 This passage obviously connects with the last sentence of verse 56 – "Nay, but they do not perceive [their error]!" – and, hence, refers to the people spoken of in verse 54 as being "lost in their ignorance" (*fī ghamratihim*).

35 Namely, actions and dogmatic assertions which utterly contradict the teachings of the very apostles whom they claim to follow, like ascribing divine qualities to beings other than God, worshipping saints, or rejecting divine revelations which do not accord with their own likes and dislikes or with their customary mode of thinking.

36 See *sūrah* 17, note 22. The particular reference, in this context, to people "who [at present] are lost in the pursuit of pleasures" contains an allusion to verse 55 above (see my explanation in note 32, especially the last sentence). The "taking to task through suffering" spoken of here may refer to the Day of Judgment or – as in 17 : 16 – to the inevitable social ruin which, in the long run, wrong beliefs and actions bring with themselves in *this* world.

37 This is the meaning implied in the auxiliary verb *kānat* preceded by the particle *qad*.

38 Lit., "as one who keeps awake at night" (*sāmiran*). In combination with the phrase *kuntum . . . tahjurūn*, this expression indicates the pursuit of endless, fruitless discussions divorced from all reality, or a mere play with words leading nowhere. (See also 31 : 6 and the corresponding note 4.)

39 Implying that the message of the Qur'ān is but a continuation of all the divine messages ever revealed to man.

40 I.e., they hate *to admit* the truth: the reason being – as the sequence shows – that the world-view propounded by the Qur'ān is not in accord with their own likes and dislikes or preconceived notions.

But if the truth[41] were in accord with their own likes and dislikes, the heavens and the earth would surely have fallen into ruin, and all that lives in them [would long ago have perished]![42]
Nay, [in this divine writ] We have conveyed unto them all that they ought to bear in mind:[43] and from this their reminder they [heedlessly] turn away! ‹71›
Or dost thou [O Muḥammad] ask of them any worldly recompense? But [they ought to know that] a recompense from thy Sustainer is best, since He is the best of providers![44] ‹72›
And, verily, thou callest them onto a straight way ‹73› – but, behold, those who will not believe in the life to come are bound to deviate from that way. ‹74›
And even were We to show them mercy and remove whatever distress might befall them [in this life],[45] they would still persist in their overweening arrogance, blindly stumbling to and fro. ‹75›
And, indeed, We tested them[46] through suffering, but they did not abase themselves before their Sustainer; and they will never humble themselves ‹76› until We open before them a gate of [truly] severe suffering [in the life to come]: and then, lo! they will be broken in spirit.[47] ‹77›

[O MEN! Pay heed to God's messages,] for it is He who has endowed you with hearing, and sight, and minds: [yet] how seldom are you grateful! ‹78›

وَلَوِ ٱتَّبَعَ ٱلْحَقُّ أَهْوَآءَهُمْ لَفَسَدَتِ ٱلسَّمَٰوَٰتُ وَٱلْأَرْضُ وَمَن فِيهِنَّ
بَلْ أَتَيْنَٰهُم بِذِكْرِهِمْ فَهُمْ عَن ذِكْرِهِم مُّعْرِضُونَ ﴿٧١﴾ أَمْ تَسْـَٔلُهُمْ خَرْجًا
فَخَرَاجُ رَبِّكَ خَيْرٌ ۖ وَهُوَ خَيْرُ ٱلرَّٰزِقِينَ ﴿٧٢﴾ وَإِنَّكَ لَتَدْعُوهُمْ إِلَىٰ صِرَٰطٍ
مُّسْتَقِيمٍ ﴿٧٣﴾ وَإِنَّ ٱلَّذِينَ لَا يُؤْمِنُونَ بِٱلْءَاخِرَةِ عَنِ ٱلصِّرَٰطِ
لَنَٰكِبُونَ ﴿٧٤﴾ ۞ وَلَوْ رَحِمْنَٰهُمْ وَكَشَفْنَا مَا بِهِم مِّن ضُرٍّ لَّلَجُّوا۟ فِى
طُغْيَٰنِهِمْ يَعْمَهُونَ ﴿٧٥﴾ وَلَقَدْ أَخَذْنَٰهُم بِٱلْعَذَابِ فَمَا ٱسْتَكَانُوا۟ لِرَبِّهِمْ
وَمَا يَتَضَرَّعُونَ ﴿٧٦﴾ حَتَّىٰٓ إِذَا فَتَحْنَا عَلَيْهِم بَابًا ذَا عَذَابٍ شَدِيدٍ إِذَا هُمْ
فِيهِ مُبْلِسُونَ ﴿٧٧﴾ وَهُوَ ٱلَّذِىٓ أَنشَأَ لَكُمُ ٱلسَّمْعَ وَٱلْأَبْصَٰرَ وَٱلْأَفْـِٔدَةَ
قَلِيلًا مَّا تَشْكُرُونَ ﴿٧٨﴾

نصف الحزب

Wa lawit-tabaʿal-ḥaqqu ʾahwāaʾahum lafasadatis-samāwātu wal-ʾarḍu wa mañ-fīhinn. Bal-ʾataynāhum-bidhikrihim fahum ʿañ-dhikrihim-muʿriḍūn. (71) ʾAm tasʾaluhum kharjañ-fakharāju Rabbika khayruñw-wa Huwa Khayrur-rāziqīn. (72) Wa ʾinnaka latadʿūhum ʾilā ṣirāṭim-mustaqīm. (73) Wa ʾinnal-ladhīna lā yuʾminūna bil-ʾĀkhirati ʿaniṣ-ṣirāṭi lanākibūn. (74) ۞ Wa law raḥimnāhum wa kashafnā mā bihim-miñ-ḍurril-lalajjū fī ṭughyānihim yaʿmahūn. (75) Wa laqad ʾakhadhnāhum-bilʿadhābi famas-takānū liRabbihim wa mā yataḍarraʿūn. (76) Ḥattāa ʾidhā fataḥnā ʿalayhim-bābañ-dhā ʿadhābiñ-shadīdin ʾidhā hum fīhi mublisūn. (77) Wa Huwal-ladhī ʾañshaʾa lakumus-samʿa wal-ʾabṣāra wal-ʾafʾidah. Qalīlam-mā tashkurūn. (78)

41 I.e., the reality of all creation.

42 I.e., if the universe – and, especially, human life – had been as devoid of meaning and purpose as they imagine, nothing could have endured, and everything would have long since perished in chaos.

43 For this rendering of the term *dhikr*, see note 13 on 21 : 10.

44 The terms *kharj* and *kharāj* which occur in the above verse are more or less synonymous, both of them denoting "recompense". According to Zamakhsharī, however, there is a slight difference between these two expressions, *kharj* being more restricted in its meaning than *kharāj*: hence, the first has been rendered as "*worldly* recompense" and the second as "recompense" without any restrictive definition, implying that a recompense from God is unlimited, relating both to this world and the hereafter.

45 Sc., "as it inevitably befalls all human beings": an oblique allusion to the fact that human life is never free from distress.

46 Lit., "We took them to task".

47 Or: "they will despair of all hope".

وَهُوَ ٱلَّذِى ذَرَأَكُمْ فِى ٱلْأَرْضِ وَإِلَيْهِ تُحْشَرُونَ ﴿79﴾ وَهُوَ ٱلَّذِى يُحْىِۦ
وَيُمِيتُ وَلَهُ ٱخْتِلَٰفُ ٱلَّيْلِ وَٱلنَّهَارِ أَفَلَا تَعْقِلُونَ ﴿80﴾ بَلْ قَالُوا۟ مِثْلَ
مَا قَالَ ٱلْأَوَّلُونَ ﴿81﴾ قَالُوٓا۟ أَءِذَا مِتْنَا وَكُنَّا تُرَابًا وَعِظَٰمًا أَءِنَّا
لَمَبْعُوثُونَ ﴿82﴾ لَقَدْ وُعِدْنَا نَحْنُ وَءَابَآؤُنَا هَٰذَا مِن قَبْلُ إِنْ هَٰذَآ إِلَّآ
أَسَٰطِيرُ ٱلْأَوَّلِينَ ﴿83﴾ قُل لِّمَنِ ٱلْأَرْضُ وَمَن فِيهَآ إِن كُنتُمْ
تَعْلَمُونَ ﴿84﴾ سَيَقُولُونَ لِلَّهِ قُلْ أَفَلَا تَذَكَّرُونَ ﴿85﴾ قُلْ مَن رَّبُّ
ٱلسَّمَٰوَٰتِ ٱلسَّبْعِ وَرَبُّ ٱلْعَرْشِ ٱلْعَظِيمِ ﴿86﴾ سَيَقُولُونَ لِلَّهِ قُلْ أَفَلَا
تَتَّقُونَ ﴿87﴾ قُلْ مَنۢ بِيَدِهِۦ مَلَكُوتُ كُلِّ شَىْءٍ وَهُوَ يُجِيرُ وَلَا يُجَارُ عَلَيْهِ
إِن كُنتُمْ تَعْلَمُونَ ﴿88﴾ سَيَقُولُونَ لِلَّهِ قُلْ فَأَنَّىٰ تُسْحَرُونَ ﴿89﴾ بَلْ أَتَيْنَٰهُم
بِٱلْحَقِّ وَإِنَّهُمْ لَكَٰذِبُونَ ﴿90﴾

And He it is who has caused you to multiply on earth; and unto Him you shall be gathered. ‹79›

And He it is who grants life and deals death; and to Him is due the alternation of night and day.

Will you not, then, use your reason? ‹80›

But nay, they speak as the people of olden times did speak: ‹81› they say: "What! After we have died and become mere dust and bones, shall we, forsooth, be raised from the dead? ‹82› Indeed, this [very thing] we have been promised – we and our forefathers – long ago! This is nothing but fables of ancient times!" ‹83›

Say: "Unto whom belongs the earth and all that lives thereon?[48] [Tell me this] if you happen to know [the answer]!" ‹84›

[And] they will reply: "Unto God."

Say: "Will you not, then, bethink yourselves [of Him]?" ‹85›

Say: "Who is it that sustains the seven heavens and is enthroned in His awesome almightiness?"[49] ‹86›

[And] they will reply: "[All this power belongs] to God."

Say: "Will you not, then, remain conscious of Him?" ‹87›

Say: "In whose hand rests the mighty dominion over all things, and who is it that protects, the while there is no protection against Him? [Tell me this] if you happen to know [the answer]!" ‹88›

[And] they will reply: "[All this power belongs] to God."

Say: "How, then, can you be so deluded?"[50] ‹89›

Nay, We have conveyed unto them the truth: and yet, behold, they are intent on lying [to themselves]![51] ‹90›

**Wa Huwal-ladhī dhara'akum fil-'arḍi wa 'ilayhi
tuḥsharūn. (79) Wa Huwal-ladhī yuḥyī wa yumītu wa
lahukh-tilāful-layli wan-nahāri 'afalā ta'qilūn. (80) Bal
qālū mithla mā qālal-'awwalūn. (81) Qālūu 'a'idhā
mitnā wa kunnā turābañw-wa 'iẓāman 'a'innā lam-
ab'ūthūn. (82) Laqad wu'idnā naḥnu wa 'ābāa'unā
hādhā miñ-qablu 'in hādhāa 'illāa 'asāṭīrul-
'awwalīn. (83) Qul limanil-'arḍu wa mañ-fīhāa 'iñ-
kuñtum ta'lamūn. (84) Sayaqūlūna lillāh. Qul 'afalā
tadhakkarūn. (85) Qul mar-Rabbus-samāwātis-sab'i
wa Rabbul-'arshil-'aẓīm. (86) Sayaqūlūna lillāh. Qul
'afalā tattaqūn. (87) Qul mam-biyadihī malakūtu kulli
shay'iñw-wa Huwa yujīru wa lā yujāru 'alayhi 'iñ-
kuñtum ta'lamūn. (88) Sayaqūlūna lillāh. Qul fa'annā
tusḥarūn. (89) Bal 'ataynāhum-bilḥaqqi wa 'innahum
lakādhibūn. (90)**

48 Lit., "and all who are on it".

49 Lit., "who is the Sustainer (*rabb*) of the seven heavens" – see note 20 on 2 : 29 – "and the Sustainer of the awesome throne of almightiness": cf. 9 : 129 as well as note 43 on 7 : 54.

50 Sc., "as to deny the prospect of resurrection".

51 Lit., "they are indeed liars" – i.e., they deceive *themselves* by asserting that they believe in God and, at the same time, rejecting the idea of a life after death, which – in view of the fact that many wrongdoers prosper in this world while many righteous lead a life of suffering – is insolubly bound up with the concept of divine *justice*. Apart from this, a denial of the possibility of resurrection implies a doubt as to God's unlimited power and, thus, of His Godhead in

Never did God take unto Himself any offspring,[52] nor has there ever been any deity side by side with Him: [for, had there been any,] lo! each deity would surely have stood apart [from the others] in whatever it had created,[53] and they would surely have [tried to] overcome one another!
Limitless in His glory is God, [far] above anything that men may devise by way of definition,[54] ‹91› knowing all that is beyond the reach of a created being's perception as well as all that can be witnessed by a creature's senses or mind[55] – and, hence, sublimely exalted is He above anything to which they may ascribe a share in His divinity! ‹92›

SAY: "O my Sustainer! If it be Thy will to let me witness[56] [the fulfilment of] whatever they [who blaspheme against Thee] have been promised [to suffer] ‹93› – do not, O my Sustainer, let me be one of those evildoing folk!" ‹94›
[Pray thus –] for, behold, We are most certainly able to let thee witness [the fulfilment, even in this world, of] whatever We promise them! ‹95›
[But whatever they may say or do,] repel the evil [which they commit] with something that is better:[57] We are fully aware of what they attribute [to Us]. ‹96›

مَا ٱتَّخَذَ ٱللَّهُ مِن وَلَدٍ وَمَا كَانَ مَعَهُۥ مِنْ إِلَٰهٍ ۚ إِذًا لَّذَهَبَ كُلُّ إِلَٰهٍۭ بِمَا
خَلَقَ وَلَعَلَا بَعْضُهُمْ عَلَىٰ بَعْضٍ ۚ سُبْحَٰنَ ٱللَّهِ عَمَّا يَصِفُونَ ﴿٩١﴾ عَٰلِمِ
ٱلْغَيْبِ وَٱلشَّهَٰدَةِ فَتَعَٰلَىٰ عَمَّا يُشْرِكُونَ ﴿٩٢﴾ قُل رَّبِّ إِمَّا تُرِيَنِّى مَا
يُوعَدُونَ ﴿٩٣﴾ رَبِّ فَلَا تَجْعَلْنِى فِى ٱلْقَوْمِ ٱلظَّٰلِمِينَ ﴿٩٤﴾ وَإِنَّا عَلَىٰٓ أَن
نُّرِيَكَ مَا نَعِدُهُمْ لَقَٰدِرُونَ ﴿٩٥﴾ ٱدْفَعْ بِٱلَّتِى هِىَ أَحْسَنُ ٱلسَّيِّئَةَ ۚ نَحْنُ
أَعْلَمُ بِمَا يَصِفُونَ ﴿٩٦﴾

Mat-takhadhal-lāhu miñw-waladiñw-wa mā kāna maʿahū min ʾilāhin ʾidhal-ladhahaba kullu ʾilāhim-bimā khalaqa wa laʿalā baʿḍuhum ʿalā baʿḍ. Subḥānal-lāhi ʿammā yaṣifūn. ﴿91﴾ ʿĀlimil-ghaybi wash-shahādati fataʿālā ʿammā yushrikūn. ﴿92﴾ Qur-Rabbi ʾimmā turiyannī mā yūʿadūn. ﴿93﴾ Rabbi falā tajʿalnī fil-qawmiẓ-ẓālimīn. ﴿94﴾ Wa ʾInnā ʿalāa ʾañ-nuriyaka mā naʿiduhum laqādirūn. ﴿95﴾ ʾIdfaʿ bil-latī hiya ʾaḥsanus-sayyiʾah. Naḥnu ʾaʿlamu bimā yaṣifūn. ﴿96﴾

the true sense of this concept. This latter doubt often finds its expression in the mystic belief in a multiplicity of divine powers: and it is to this erroneous belief that the next verse alludes.

52 This allusion to the pre-Islamic Arabian belief in angels as "God's daughters" and the Christian dogma of Jesus' "sonship of God" connects with the statement "they are intent on lying [to themselves]", which has been explained in the preceding note.

53 This is how almost all the classical commentators explain the phrase *la-dhahaba bi-mā khalaqa* (lit., "would surely have taken away whatever he had created"), implying that in such a hypothetical case each of the gods would have been concerned only with *his own* sector of creation, thus causing complete confusion in the universe.

54 See note 88 on 6 : 100.

55 See *sūrah* 6, note 65.

56 Lit., "to show me" [sc., "in my lifetime"]. According to Zamakhsharī, the combination of the conditional particle *in* ("if") with *mā* ("that which" or "whatever") – spelt and pronounced *immā* – endows the verb *turīnī* (lit., "Thou wilt show me") with the quality of intrinsic necessity – thus: "If it is inevitable (*lā budd*) that Thou show me [or "let me witness"] . . .", etc. In translation, this particular phrasing is best rendered as above, since anything that is God's will becomes *eo ipso* inevitable.

57 See *sūrah* 13, note 44. In the present context, the evil referred to consists – as the next clause shows – in blasphemous attempts at "defining" God (cf. verse 91); but the ethical principle implied in the above injunction is the same as that expressed in the last clause of 13 : 22 as well as in 41 : 34 – namely, that evil must not be countered with another evil but, rather, *repelled* by an act of goodness.

وَقُل رَّبِّ أَعُوذُ بِكَ مِنْ هَمَزَٰتِ ٱلشَّيَٰطِينِ ﴿٩٧﴾ وَأَعُوذُ بِكَ رَبِّ أَن
يَحْضُرُونِ ﴿٩٨﴾ حَتَّىٰٓ إِذَا جَآءَ أَحَدَهُمُ ٱلْمَوْتُ قَالَ رَبِّ
ٱرْجِعُونِ ﴿٩٩﴾ لَعَلِّىٓ أَعْمَلُ صَٰلِحًا فِيمَا تَرَكْتُ كَلَّآ إِنَّهَا كَلِمَةٌ هُوَ
قَآئِلُهَا وَمِن وَرَآئِهِم بَرْزَخٌ إِلَىٰ يَوْمِ يُبْعَثُونَ ﴿١٠٠﴾ فَإِذَا نُفِخَ فِى ٱلصُّورِ
فَلَآ أَنسَابَ بَيْنَهُمْ يَوْمَئِذٍ وَلَا يَتَسَآءَلُونَ ﴿١٠١﴾ فَمَن ثَقُلَتْ مَوَٰزِينُهُۥ
فَأُوْلَٰٓئِكَ هُمُ ٱلْمُفْلِحُونَ ﴿١٠٢﴾ وَمَنْ خَفَّتْ مَوَٰزِينُهُۥ فَأُوْلَٰٓئِكَ ٱلَّذِينَ
خَسِرُوٓا۟ أَنفُسَهُمْ فِى جَهَنَّمَ خَٰلِدُونَ ﴿١٠٣﴾ تَلْفَحُ وُجُوهَهُمُ ٱلنَّارُ وَهُمْ فِيهَا
كَٰلِحُونَ ﴿١٠٤﴾ أَلَمْ تَكُنْ ءَايَٰتِى تُتْلَىٰ عَلَيْكُمْ فَكُنتُم بِهَا تُكَذِّبُونَ ﴿١٠٥﴾
قَالُوا۟ رَبَّنَا غَلَبَتْ عَلَيْنَا شِقْوَتُنَا وَكُنَّا قَوْمًا ضَآلِّينَ ﴿١٠٦﴾ رَبَّنَآ

**Wa qur-Rabbi ʾaʿūdhu bika min hamazātish-
Shayāṭīn. (97) Wa ʾaʿūdhu bika Rabbi ʾañy-yaḥḍurūn.
(98) Ḥattāa ʾidhā jāaʾa ʾaḥadahumul-mawtu qāla
Rabbir-jiʿūn. (99) Laʿallīi ʾaʿmalu ṣāliḥañ-fīmā tarakt.
Kallāa ʾinnahā kalimatun huwa qāaʾiluhā; wa miñw-
warāaʾihim-barzakhun ʾilā Yawmi yubʿathūn. (100)
Faʾidhā nufikha fiṣ-ṣūri falāa ʾañsāba baynahum
Yawmaʾidhiñw-wa lā yatasāaʾalūn. (101) Famañ-thaqulat
mawāzīnuhū faʾulāaʾika humul-mufliḥūn. (102) Wa
man khaffat mawāzīnuhū faʾulāaʾikal-ladhīna khasirūu ʾañfusahum fī jahannama khālidūn. (103) Talfaḥu
wujūhahumun-nāru wa hum fīhā kāliḥūn. (104) ʾAlam
takun ʾĀyātī tutlā ʿalaykum fakuñtum-bihā tukadhdhibūn. (105) Qālū Rabbanā ghalabat ʿalaynā shiqwa-
tunā wa kunnā qawmañ-ḍāallīn. (106) Rabbanāa**

And say: "O my Sustainer! I seek refuge with Thee from the promptings of all evil impulses;[58] ‹97› and I seek refuge with Thee, O my Sustainer, lest they come near unto me!" ‹98›

[AS FOR THOSE who will not believe in the life to come, they go on lying to themselves[59]] until, when death approaches any of them, he prays: "O my Sustainer! Let me return, let me return[60] [to life], ‹99› so that I might act righteously in whatever I have failed [aforetime]!"[61]

Nay, it is indeed but a [meaningless] word that he utters: for behind those [who leave the world] there is a barrier [of death] until the Day when all will be raised from the dead! ‹100›

Then, when the trumpet [of resurrection] is blown, no ties of kinship will on that Day prevail among them, and neither will they ask about one another. ‹101›

And they whose weight [of righteousness] is heavy in the balance – it is they, they who will have attained to a happy state; ‹102› whereas they whose weight is light in the balance – it is they who will have squandered their own selves, [destined] to abide in hell: ‹103› the fire will scorch their faces, and they will abide therein with their lips distorted in pain. ‹104›

[And God will say:] "Were not My messages conveyed unto you, and were you [not] wont to give them the lie?" ‹105›

They will exclaim: "O our Sustainer! Our bad luck has overwhelmed us, and so we went astray![62] ‹106› O our Sustainer!

58 Lit., "of the satans" or "satanic forces": see note 10 on 2 : 14.

59 Cf. verses 74 and 90 above, with which the present passage connects.

60 Most of the commentators regard the plural form of address in the verb *irjiʿūnī* ("let me return") as an expression of reverence. Since, however, the Qurʾān offers no other instance of God's being *addressed* in the plural (in contrast with the frequent use of the plural in His speaking of Himself), Bayḍāwī suggests – on the strength of examples from pre-Islamic poetry – that this plural form of address is equivalent to an *emphatic repetition* of the singular form *irjiʿnī*: hence the repetition of this phrase in my rendering.

61 Lit., "in respect of that which (*fī-mā*) I have left", comprising both the omission of good and the commission of bad deeds.

62 Lit., "we became people who go astray". This allegorical "dialogue" is meant to bring out the futile excuse characteristic of so many sinners who attribute their failings to an abstract "bad luck" (which is the meaning of

Cause us to come out of this [suffering] – and then, if ever We revert [to sinning], may we truly be [deemed] evildoers!" ‹107›

[But] He will say: "Away with you into this [ignominy]![63] And speak no more unto Me! ‹108›

"Behold, there were among My servants such as would pray, 'O our Sustainer! We have come to believe [in Thee]; forgive, then, our sins and bestow Thy mercy on us: for Thou art the truest bestower of mercy!'[64] ‹109› – but you made them a target of your derision to the point where it made you forget[65] all remembrance of Me; and you went on and on laughing at them. ‹110› [But,] behold, today I have rewarded them for their patience in adversity: verily, it is they, they who have achieved a triumph!" ‹111›

[And] He will ask [the doomed]: "What number of years have you spent on earth?" ‹112›

They will answer: "We have spent there a day, or part of a day; but ask those who [are able to] count [time]. . . ."[66] ‹113›

[Whereupon] He will say: "You have spent there but a short while: had you but known [how short it was to be]! ‹114› Did you, then, think that We created you in mere idle play, and that you would not have to return to Us?"[67] ‹115›

أَخۡرِجۡنَا مِنۡهَا فَإِنۡ عُدۡنَا فَإِنَّا ظَٰلِمُونَ ١٠٧ قَالَ ٱخۡسَـُٔواْ فِيهَا وَلَا
تُكَلِّمُونِ ١٠٨ إِنَّهُۥ كَانَ فَرِيقٞ مِّنۡ عِبَادِي يَقُولُونَ رَبَّنَآ ءَامَنَّا فَٱغۡفِرۡ لَنَا
وَٱرۡحَمۡنَا وَأَنتَ خَيۡرُ ٱلرَّٰحِمِينَ ١٠٩ فَٱتَّخَذۡتُمُوهُمۡ سِخۡرِيًّا حَتَّىٰٓ أَنسَوۡكُمۡ
ذِكۡرِي وَكُنتُم مِّنۡهُمۡ تَضۡحَكُونَ ١١٠ إِنِّي جَزَيۡتُهُمُ ٱلۡيَوۡمَ بِمَا صَبَرُوٓاْ أَنَّهُمۡ
هُمُ ٱلۡفَآئِزُونَ ١١١ قَٰلَ كَمۡ لَبِثۡتُمۡ فِي ٱلۡأَرۡضِ عَدَدَ سِنِينَ ١١٢ قَالُواْ
لَبِثۡنَا يَوۡمًا أَوۡ بَعۡضَ يَوۡمٖ فَسۡـَٔلِ ٱلۡعَآدِّينَ ١١٣ قَٰلَ إِن لَّبِثۡتُمۡ إِلَّا قَلِيلٗاۖ لَّوۡ
أَنَّكُمۡ كُنتُمۡ تَعۡلَمُونَ ١١٤ أَفَحَسِبۡتُمۡ أَنَّمَا خَلَقۡنَٰكُمۡ عَبَثٗا وَأَنَّكُمۡ إِلَيۡنَا لَا
تُرۡجَعُونَ ١١٥

**ʾakhrijnā minhā faʾin ʿudnā faʾinnā ẓālimūn. (107)
Qālakh-saʾū fīhā wa lā tukallimūn. (108) ʾInnahū kāna
farīqum-min ʿibādī yaqūlūna Rabbanāa ʾāmannā
faghfir lanā war-ḥamnā wa ʾAñta Khayrur-rāḥimīn.
(109) Fattakhadhtumūhum sikhriyyan ḥattāa ʾañsaw-
kum dhikrī wa kuñtum-minhum taḍḥakūn. (110)
ʾInnī jazaytuhumul-Yawma bimā ṣabarūu ʾannahum
humul-fāaʾizūn. (111) Qāla kam labiththum fil-ʾarḍi
ʿadada sinīn. (112) Qālū labithnā yawman ʾaw baʿḍa
yawmiñ-fasʾalil-ʿāaddīn. (113) Qāla ʾil-labiththum ʾillā
qalīlal-law ʾannakum kuñtum taʿlamūn. (114)
ʾAfaḥasibtum ʾannamā khalaqnākum ʿabathañw-wa
ʾannakum ʾilaynā lā turjaʿūn. (115)**

shiqwah in this context); and thus, indirectly, it stresses the element of free will – and, therefore, of responsibility – in man's actions and behaviour.

63 My interpolation of the word "ignominy" is based on the fact that this concept is inherent in the verb *khasaʾa* (lit., "he drove [someone or something] scornfully away"), and is, therefore, forcefully expressed in the imperative *ikhsaʾū*.

64 Lit., "the best of those [or "of all"] who show mercy". The same expression is found in the concluding verse of this *sūrah*.

65 Lit., "until *they* made you forget": i.e., "your scoffing at them became the cause of your forgetting".

66 This part of the allegorical "dialogue" between God and the doomed sinners touches (as do several other verses of the Qurʾān) upon the illusory, problematical character of "time" as conceived by man, and the comparative irrelevancy of the life of this world within the context of the ultimate – perhaps timeless – reality known only to God. The disappearance, upon resurrection, of man's earth-bound concept of time is indicated by the helpless answer, "ask those who are able to count time".

67 Lit., "that you would not be brought back to Us", i.e., for judgment.

[KNOW,] then, [that] God is sublimely exalted, the Ultimate Sovereign, the Ultimate Truth:[68] there is no deity save Him, the Sustainer, in bountiful almightiness enthroned![69] ‹116›
Hence, he who invokes, side by side with God, any other deity [– a deity] for whose existence he has no evidence – shall but find his reckoning with his Sustainer: [and,] verily, such deniers of the truth will never attain to a happy state! ‹117›
Hence, [O believer,] say: "O my Sustainer! Grant [me] forgiveness and bestow Thy mercy [upon me]: for Thou art the truest bestower of mercy!" ‹118›

فَتَعَـٰلَى ٱللَّهُ ٱلۡمَلِكُ ٱلۡحَقُّۖ لَآ إِلَـٰهَ إِلَّا هُوَ رَبُّ ٱلۡعَرۡشِ ٱلۡكَرِيمِ ﴿١١٦﴾
وَمَن يَدۡعُ مَعَ ٱللَّهِ إِلَـٰهًا ءَاخَرَ لَا بُرۡهَـٰنَ لَهُۥ بِهِۦ فَإِنَّمَا حِسَابُهُۥ عِندَ
رَبِّهِۦٓۚ إِنَّهُۥ لَا يُفۡلِحُ ٱلۡكَـٰفِرُونَ ﴿١١٧﴾ وَقُل رَّبِّ ٱغۡفِرۡ وَٱرۡحَمۡ وَأَنتَ خَيۡرُ
ٱلرَّٰحِمِينَ ﴿١١٨﴾

Fataʿālal-lāhul-Malikul-Ḥaqqu lāa ʾIlāha ʾillā Huwa Rabbul-ʿarshil-karīm. (116) Wa mañy-yadʿu maʿal-lāhi ʾilāhan ʾākhara lā burhāna lahū bihī faʾinnamā ḥisābuhū ʿiñda Rabbih. ʾInnahū lā yufliḥul-kāfirūn. (117) Wa qur-Rabbigh-fir war-ḥam wa ʾAñta Khayrur-rāḥimīn. (118)

68 See *sūrah* 20, note 99.

69 Lit., "the Sustainer (*rabb*) of the bountiful throne of almightiness (*al-ʿarsh al-karīm*)". See also *sūrah* 7, note 43, for an explanation of my rendering of *al-ʿarsh* as "the throne of [His] almightiness".

The Twenty-Fourth Sūrah

An-Nūr (The Light)

Medina Period

FROM various allusions (particularly in verses 11-20) to historical incidents connected with the Prophet's campaign against the tribe of Muṣṭaliq, it is evident that this *sūrah* was revealed towards the end of the fifth or the beginning of the sixth year after the *hijrah*.

A large part of it deals with the mutual relations of the sexes and with certain ethical rules to be observed in the context of this relationship. Verses 2-9, in particular, lay down definite legal injunctions concerning illicit sexual intercourse, while verses 27-29 and 58-59 stress each individual's right to privacy.

The title is derived from the mystic parable of the "light of God" in verse 35 and its echo in verse 40: "he to whom God gives no light, no light whatever has he!"

سورة النور مدنية -24-

وآياتها أربع وستون

IN THE NAME OF GOD, THE MOST GRACIOUS, THE DISPENSER OF GRACE:

بِسۡمِ ٱللَّهِ ٱلرَّحۡمَٰنِ ٱلرَّحِيمِ

ثلاثة ارباع الحزب

A *SŪRAH* [is this] which We have bestowed from on high, and which We have laid down in plain terms;[1] and in it have We bestowed from on high messages which are clear [in themselves], so that you might keep [them] in mind. ⟨1⟩

AS FOR the adulteress and the adulterer[2] – flog each of them with a hundred stripes, and let not compassion with them keep you from [carrying out] this law of God, if you [truly] believe in God and the Last Day; and let a group of the believers witness their chastisement.[3] ⟨2⟩

[Both are equally guilty:] the adulterer couples with none other than an adulteress – that is, a woman who accords [to her own lust] a place side by side with God;[4] and with the adulteress couples none other than an adulterer – that is, a man who accords [to his own lust] a place side by side with God: and this is forbid-

سُورَةٌ أَنزَلۡنَٰهَا وَفَرَضۡنَٰهَا وَأَنزَلۡنَا فِيهَآ ءَايَٰتِۭ بَيِّنَٰتٖ لَّعَلَّكُمۡ
تَذَكَّرُونَ ﴿١﴾ ٱلزَّانِيَةُ وَٱلزَّانِي فَٱجۡلِدُواْ كُلَّ وَٰحِدٖ مِّنۡهُمَا مِاْئَةَ جَلۡدَةٖۖ
وَلَا تَأۡخُذۡكُم بِهِمَا رَأۡفَةٞ فِي دِينِ ٱللَّهِ إِن كُنتُمۡ تُؤۡمِنُونَ بِٱللَّهِ وَٱلۡيَوۡمِ
ٱلۡأٓخِرِۖ وَلۡيَشۡهَدۡ عَذَابَهُمَا طَآئِفَةٞ مِّنَ ٱلۡمُؤۡمِنِينَ ﴿٢﴾ ٱلزَّانِي لَا يَنكِحُ إِلَّا
زَانِيَةً أَوۡ مُشۡرِكَةٗ وَٱلزَّانِيَةُ لَا يَنكِحُهَآ إِلَّا زَانٍ أَوۡ مُشۡرِكٞۚ وَحُرِّمَ ذَٰلِكَ

Bismil-lāhir-Raḥmānir-Raḥīm.
Sūratun ʾañzalnāhā wa faraḍnāhā wa ʾañzalnā fīhāa ʾĀyātim-bayyinātil-laʿallakum tadhakkarūn. (1) ʾAzzāniyatu waz-zānī fajlidū kulla wāḥidim-minhumā miʾata jaldah. Wa lā taʾkhudhkum-bihimā raʾfatuñ-fī dīnil-lāhi ʾiñ-kuñtum tuʾminūna billāhi wal-Yawmil-ʾĀkhir. Wal-yashhad ʿadhābahumā ṭāaʾifatum-minal-muʾminīn. (2) ʾAzzānī lā yañkiḥu ʾillā zāniyatan ʾaw mushrikatañw-waz-zāniyatu lā yañkiḥuhāa ʾillā zānin ʾaw mushrik. Wa ḥurrima dhālika

---

1 I.e., "the injunctions whereof We have made self-evident by virtue of their wording": thus, according to Bukhārī (*Kitāb at-Tafsīr*), ʿAbd Allāh ibn ʿAbbās explains the expression *faraḍnāhā* in this context (cf. *Fatḥ al-Bārī* VIII, 361). The same explanation, also on the authority of Ibn ʿAbbās, is advanced by Ṭabarī. It would seem that the special stress on God's having laid down this *sūrah* "in plain terms" is connected with the gravity of the injunctions spelt out in the sequence: in other words, it implies a solemn warning against any attempt at widening or re-defining those injunctions by means of deductions, inferences or any other considerations unconnected with the plain wording of the Qurʾān.

2 The term *zinā* signifies voluntary sexual intercourse between a man and a woman not married to one another, irrespective of whether one or both of them are married to other persons or not: hence, it does not – in contrast with the usage prevalent in most Western languages – differentiate between the concepts of "adultery" (i.e., sexual intercourse of a married man with a woman other than his wife, or of a married woman with a man other than her husband) and "fornication" (i.e., sexual intercourse between two unmarried persons). For the sake of simplicity I am rendering *zinā* throughout as "adultery", and the person guilty of it as "adulterer" or "adulteress", respectively.

3 The number of those to be present has been deliberately left unspecified, thus indicating that while the punishment must be given publicity, it need not be made a "public spectacle".

4 The term *mushrik* (fem. *mushrikah*), which normally signifies a person who associates in his or her mind all manner of imaginary deities or forces with God, or who believes that any created being has a share in His qualities or powers, is here evidently used in the widest metaphorical sense of this term, denoting one who accords to his or her desires a supremacy which is due to God alone, and thus blasphemes against the principles of ethics and morality

den unto the believers.[5] ‹3›

And as for those who accuse chaste women [of adultery],[6] and then are unable to produce four witnesses [in support of their accusation], flog them with eighty stripes;[7] and ever after refuse to accept from them any testimony – since it is they, they that are truly depraved! ‹4› – excepting [from this interdict] only those who afterwards repent and made amends:[8] for, behold, God is much-forgiving, a dispenser of grace. ‹5›

And as for those who accuse their own wives [of adultery], but have no witnesses except themselves, let each of these [accusers] call God four times to witness[9] that he is indeed telling the truth, ‹6›

عَلَى ٱلْمُؤْمِنِينَ ﴿٣﴾ وَٱلَّذِينَ يَرْمُونَ ٱلْمُحْصَنَـٰتِ ثُمَّ لَمْ يَأْتُوا۟ بِأَرْبَعَةِ
شُهَدَآءَ فَٱجْلِدُوهُمْ ثَمَـٰنِينَ جَلْدَةً وَلَا تَقْبَلُوا۟ لَهُمْ شَهَـٰدَةً أَبَدًا ۚ وَأُو۟لَـٰٓئِكَ هُمُ
ٱلْفَـٰسِقُونَ ﴿٤﴾ إِلَّا ٱلَّذِينَ تَابُوا۟ مِنۢ بَعْدِ ذَٰلِكَ وَأَصْلَحُوا۟ فَإِنَّ ٱللَّهَ غَفُورٌ
رَّحِيمٌ ﴿٥﴾ وَٱلَّذِينَ يَرْمُونَ أَزْوَٰجَهُمْ وَلَمْ يَكُن لَّهُمْ شُهَدَآءُ إِلَّآ أَنفُسُهُمْ
فَشَهَـٰدَةُ أَحَدِهِمْ أَرْبَعُ شَهَـٰدَٰتٍۭ بِٱللَّهِ ۙ إِنَّهُۥ لَمِنَ ٱلصَّـٰدِقِينَ ﴿٦﴾

ʿalal-muʾminīn. (3) Wal-ladhīna yarmūnal-muḥṣanāti thumma lam yaʾtū biʾarbaʿati shuhadāaʾa fajlidūhum thamānīna jaldatañw-wa lā taqbalū lahum shahādatan ʾabadañw-wa ʾulāaʾika humul-fāsiqūn.
(4) ʾIllal-ladhīna tābū mim-baʿdi dhālika wa ʾaṣlaḥū faʾinnal-lāha Ghafūrur-Raḥīm. (5) Wal-ladhīna yarmūna ʾazwājahum wa lam yakul-lahum shuhadāaʾu ʾillāa ʾañfusuhum fashahādatu ʾaḥadihim ʾarbaʿu shahādātim-billāhi ʾinnahū laminaṣ-ṣādiqīn. (6)

enjoined by Him. The particle *aw* (lit., "*or*") which connects the word *mushrikah* with the preceding word *zāniyah* ("adulteress") has in this context – as well as in the next clause, where both these terms appear in their masculine form – an amplifying, explanatory value equivalent to the expression "in other words" or "that is", similar to the use of this particle in 23 : 6. For a further elucidation of the above passage, see next note.

5 Some of the commentators understand this passage in the sense of an injunction: "The adulterer shall not marry any but an adulteress or a *mushrikah*; and as for the adulteress, none shall marry her but an adulterer or a *mushrik*." This interpretation is objectionable on several counts: firstly, the Qurʾān does not ever countenance the marriage of a believer, however great a sin he or she may have committed, with an unbeliever (in the most pejorative sense of this term); secondly, it is a fundamental principle of Islamic Law that once a crime has been expiated by the transgressor's undergoing the ordained legal punishment (in this case, a hundred stripes), it must be regarded, insofar as the society is concerned, as atoned for and done with; and, lastly, the construction of the above passage is clearly that of a *statement of fact* (Rāzī), and cannot be interpreted as an injunction. On the other hand, since adultery is an illicit sexual union, the verb *yankiḥu*, which appears twice in this passage, cannot have the customary, specific meaning of "he marries" but must, rather, be understood in its general sense – applicable to both lawful and unlawful sexual intercourse – namely, "he couples with". It is in this sense that the great commentator Abū Muslim (as quoted by Rāzī) explains the above verse, which stresses the fact that both partners are equally guilty inasmuch as they commit their sin consciously – implying that neither of them can excuse himself or herself on the ground of having been merely "seduced".

6 The term *muḥṣanāt* denotes literally "women who are fortified [against unchastity]", i.e., by marriage and/or faith and self-respect, implying that, from a legal point of view, every woman must be considered chaste unless a conclusive proof to the contrary is produced. (This passage relates to women other than the accuser's own wife, for in the latter case – as shown in verses 6-9 – the law of evidence and the consequences are different.)

7 By obvious implication, this injunction applies also to cases where a woman accuses a man of illicit sexual intercourse, and is subsequently unable to prove her accusation legally. The severity of the punishment to be meted out in such cases, as well as the requirement of *four* witnesses – instead of the two that Islamic Law regards as sufficient in all other criminal and civil suits – is based on the imperative necessity of preventing slander and off-hand accusations. As laid down in several authentic sayings of the Prophet, the evidence of the four witnesses must be direct, and not merely circumstantial: in other words, it is not sufficient for them to have witnessed a *situation* which made it evident that sexual intercourse was taking or had taken place: they must have witnessed the sexual *act* as such, and must be able to prove this to the entire satisfaction of the judicial authority (Rāzī, summing up the views of the greatest exponents of Islamic Law). Since such a complete evidence is extremely difficult, if not impossible, to obtain, it is obvious that the purpose of the above Qurʾanic injunction is to preclude, in practice, all third-party accusations relating to illicit sexual intercourse – for, "man has been created weak" (4 : 28) – and to make a proof of adultery dependent on a voluntary, faith-inspired confession of the guilty parties themselves.

8 I.e., who publicly withdraw their accusation after having suffered the punishment of flogging – which, being a legal right of the wrongly accused person, cannot be obviated by mere repentance and admission of guilt. Thus, the above-mentioned exemption relates only to the interdict on giving testimony and not to the punishment by flogging.

9 Lit., "then the testimony of any of these shall be four testimonies [or "solemn affirmations"] before God".

وَٱلْخَٰمِسَةُ أَنَّ لَعْنَتَ ٱللَّهِ عَلَيْهِ إِن كَانَ مِنَ ٱلْكَٰذِبِينَ ﴿7﴾ وَيَدْرَؤُا۟ عَنْهَا
ٱلْعَذَابَ أَن تَشْهَدَ أَرْبَعَ شَهَٰدَٰتٍۭ بِٱللَّهِ إِنَّهُۥ لَمِنَ ٱلْكَٰذِبِينَ ﴿8﴾
وَٱلْخَٰمِسَةَ أَنَّ غَضَبَ ٱللَّهِ عَلَيْهَآ إِن كَانَ مِنَ ٱلصَّٰدِقِينَ ﴿9﴾ وَلَوْلَا
فَضْلُ ٱللَّهِ عَلَيْكُمْ وَرَحْمَتُهُۥ وَأَنَّ ٱللَّهَ تَوَّابٌ حَكِيمٌ ﴿10﴾ إِنَّ ٱلَّذِينَ جَآءُو
بِٱلْإِفْكِ عُصْبَةٌ مِّنكُمْ لَا تَحْسَبُوهُ شَرًّا لَّكُم بَلْ هُوَ خَيْرٌ لَّكُمْ لِكُلِّ ٱمْرِئٍ
مِّنْهُم مَّا ٱكْتَسَبَ مِنَ ٱلْإِثْمِ وَٱلَّذِى تَوَلَّىٰ كِبْرَهُۥ مِنْهُمْ لَهُۥ عَذَابٌ عَظِيمٌ ﴿11﴾

Wal-khāmisatu ʾanna laʿnatal-lāhi ʿalayhi ʾiñ-kāna minal-kādhibīn. (7) Wa yadraʾū ʿanhal-ʿadhāba ʾañ-tashhada ʾarbaʿa shahādātim-billāhi ʾinnahū laminal-kādhibīn. (8) Wal-khāmisata ʾanna ghaḍabal-lāhi ʿalayhāa ʾiñ-kāna minaṣ-ṣādiqīn. (9) Wa lawlā faḍlul-lāhi ʿalaykum wa raḥmatuhū wa ʾannal-lāha Tawwābun Ḥakīm. (10) ʾInnal-ladhīna jāaʾū bilʾifki ʿuṣbatum-miñkum; lā taḥsabūhu sharral-lakum; bal huwa khayrul-lakum. Likullim-riʾim-minhum-maktasaba minal-ʾithm. Wal-ladhī tawallā kibrahū minhum lahū ʿadhābun ʿaẓīm. (11)

and the fifth time, that God's curse be upon him if he is telling a lie. ‹7›
But [as for the wife, all] chastisement shall be averted from her by her calling God four times to witness that he is indeed telling a lie, ‹8› and the fifth [time], that God's curse be upon her if he is telling the truth.[10] ‹9›

AND WERE it not for God's favour upon you, [O man,] and His grace, and that God is a wise acceptor of repentance . . .![11] ‹10›
Verily, numerous among you are those who would falsely accuse others of unchastity:[12] [but, O you who are thus wronged,] deem it not a bad thing for you: nay, it is good for you![13]
[As for the slanderers,] unto every one of them [will be accounted] all that he has earned by [thus] sinning; and awesome suffering awaits any of them who takes it upon himself to enhance this [sin]![14] ‹11›

10 Thus, the husband's accusation is to be regarded as proven if the wife refuses to take an oath to the contrary, and disproved if she solemnly sets her word against his. Inasmuch as this procedure, which is called *liʿān* ("oath of condemnation"), leaves the question of guilt legally undecided, both parties are absolved of all the legal consequences otherwise attending upon adultery – resp. an unproven accusation of adultery – the only consequence being a mandatory divorce.

11 This sentence, which introduces the section dealing with the condemnation of all unfounded or unproven accusations of unchastity – as well as the similar sentence which closes it in verse 20 – is deliberately left incomplete, leaving it to man to imagine what would have happened to individual lives and to society if God had not ordained all the above-mentioned legal and moral safeguards against possibly false accusations, or if He had made a proof of adultery dependent on mere circumstantial evidence. This idea is further elaborated in verses 14-15.

12 Lit., "those who brought forth the lie (*al-ifk*, here denoting a false accusation of unchastity) are a numerous group (*ʿuṣbah*) among you". The term *ʿuṣbah* signifies any group of people, of indeterminate number, banded together for a particular purpose (*Tāj al-ʿArūs*). – According to all the commentators, the passage comprising verses 11-20 relates to an incident which occurred on the Prophet's return from the campaign against the tribe of Muṣṭaliq, in the year 5 H. The Prophet's wife ʿĀʾishah, who had accompanied him on that expedition, was inadvertently left behind when the Muslims struck camp before dawn. After having spent several hours alone, she was found by one of the Prophet's Companions, who led her to the next halting-place of the army. This incident gave rise to malicious insinuations of misconduct on the part of ʿĀʾishah; but these rumours were short-lived, and her innocence was established beyond all doubt. – As is the case with all Qurʾanic allusions to historical events, this one, too, is primarily meant to bring out an ethical proposition valid for all times and all social circumstances: and this is the reason why the grammatical construction of the above passage is such that the past-tense verbs occurring in verses 11-16 can be – and, I believe, should be – understood as denoting the present tense.

13 I.e., in the sight of God: for, the unhappiness caused by unjust persecution confers – as does every undeserved and patiently borne suffering – a spiritual merit on the person thus afflicted. Cf. the saying of the Prophet, quoted by Bukhārī and Muslim: "Whenever a believer is stricken with any hardship, or pain, or anxiety, or sorrow, or harm, or distress – even if it be a thorn that has hurt him – God redeems thereby some of his failings."

14 I.e., by stressing, in a legally and morally inadmissible manner, certain "circumstantial" details or aspects of the case in order to make the slanderous, unfounded allegation more believable.

Why do not the believing men and women, whenever such [a rumour] is heard,[15] think the best of one another and say, "This is an obvious falsehood"? ‹12›
Why do they not [demand of the accusers[16] that they] produce four witnesses to prove their allegation?[17] – for, if they do not produce such witnesses, it is those [accusers] who, in the sight of God, are liars indeed! ‹13›
And were it not for God's favour upon you, [O men,] and His grace in this world and in the life to come, awesome suffering would indeed have afflicted you[18] in result of all [the calumny] in which you indulge ‹14› when you take it up with your tongues, uttering with your mouths something of which you have no knowledge, and deeming it a light matter whereas in the sight of God it is an awful thing! ‹15›
And [once again]: Why do you not say, whenever you hear such [a rumour], "It does not behove us to speak of this, O Thou who art limitless in Thy glory: this is an awesome calumny"?[19] ‹16›
God admonishes you [hereby] lest you ever revert to the like of this [sin], if you are [truly] believers; ‹17› for God makes [His] messages clear unto you – and God is all-knowing, wise! ‹18›
Verily, as for those who like [to hear] foul slander[20] spread against [any of] those who have attained to faith – grievous suffering awaits them in this world[21]

لَّوۡلَآ إِذۡ سَمِعۡتُمُوهُ ظَنَّ ٱلۡمُؤۡمِنُونَ وَٱلۡمُؤۡمِنَٰتُ بِأَنفُسِهِمۡ خَيۡرٗا وَقَالُواْ هَٰذَآ
إِفۡكٞ مُّبِينٞ ﴿١٢﴾ لَّوۡلَا جَآءُو عَلَيۡهِ بِأَرۡبَعَةِ شُهَدَآءَۚ فَإِذۡ لَمۡ يَأۡتُواْ بِٱلشُّهَدَآءِ
فَأُوْلَٰٓئِكَ عِندَ ٱللَّهِ هُمُ ٱلۡكَٰذِبُونَ ﴿١٣﴾ وَلَوۡلَا فَضۡلُ ٱللَّهِ عَلَيۡكُمۡ وَرَحۡمَتُهُۥ
فِي ٱلدُّنۡيَا وَٱلۡأٓخِرَةِ لَمَسَّكُمۡ فِي مَآ أَفَضۡتُمۡ فِيهِ عَذَابٌ عَظِيمٌ ﴿١٤﴾ إِذۡ
تَلَقَّوۡنَهُۥ بِأَلۡسِنَتِكُمۡ وَتَقُولُونَ بِأَفۡوَاهِكُم مَّا لَيۡسَ لَكُم بِهِۦ عِلۡمٞ
وَتَحۡسَبُونَهُۥ هَيِّنٗا وَهُوَ عِندَ ٱللَّهِ عَظِيمٞ ﴿١٥﴾ وَلَوۡلَآ إِذۡ سَمِعۡتُمُوهُ قُلۡتُم مَّا
يَكُونُ لَنَآ أَن نَّتَكَلَّمَ بِهَٰذَا سُبۡحَٰنَكَ هَٰذَا بُهۡتَٰنٌ عَظِيمٞ ﴿١٦﴾
يَعِظُكُمُ ٱللَّهُ أَن تَعُودُواْ لِمِثۡلِهِۦٓ أَبَدًا إِن كُنتُم مُّؤۡمِنِينَ ﴿١٧﴾
وَيُبَيِّنُ ٱللَّهُ لَكُمُ ٱلۡأٓيَٰتِۚ وَٱللَّهُ عَلِيمٌ حَكِيمٌ ﴿١٨﴾ إِنَّ ٱلَّذِينَ يُحِبُّونَ
أَن تَشِيعَ ٱلۡفَٰحِشَةُ فِي ٱلَّذِينَ ءَامَنُواْ لَهُمۡ عَذَابٌ أَلِيمٞ فِي ٱلدُّنۡيَا

Lawlāa ʾidh samiʿtumūhu ẓannal-muʾminūna wal-muʾminātu biʾañfusihim khayrañw-wa qālū hādhāa ʾifkum-mubīn. (12) **Lawlā jāaʾū ʿalayhi biʾarbaʿati shuhadāaʾ. Faʾidh lam yaʾtū bishshuhadāaʾi faʾulāaʾika ʿiñdal-lāhi humul-kādhibūn.** (13) **Wa lawlā faḍlul-lāhi ʿalaykum wa raḥmatuhū fid-dunyā wal-ʾĀkhirati lamassakum fī māa ʾafaḍtum fīhi ʿadhābun ʿaẓīm.** (14) **ʾIdh talaqqawnahū biʾalsinatikum wa taqūlūna biʾafwāhikum-mā laysa lakum-bihī ʿilmuñw-wa taḥsabūnahū hayyinañw-wa huwa ʿiñdal-lāhi ʿaẓīm.** (15) **Wa lawlāa ʾidh samiʿtumūhu qultum-mā yakūnu lanāa ʾañ-natakallama bihādhā subḥānaka hādhā buhtānun ʿaẓīm.** (16) **Yaʿiẓukumul-lāhu ʾañ-taʿūdū limithlihīi ʾabadan ʾiñ-kuñtum-muʾminīn.** (17) **Wa yubayyinul-lāhu lakumul-ʾĀyāti wal-lāhu ʿAlīmun Ḥakīm.** (18) **ʾInnal-ladhīna yuḥibbūna ʾañ-tashīʿal-fāḥishatu fil-ladhīna ʾāmanū lahum ʿadhābun ʾalīmuñ-fid-dunyā**

15 Lit., "whenever *you* hear it" – the pronoun "you" indicating here the community as a whole.

16 This interpolation is necessary in view of the fact that the believers spoken of in the preceding verse are blamed, not for *making* the false accusation, but for not giving it the lie.

17 Lit.. "in support thereof" (*ʿalayhi*).

18 Sc., "yourselves and your whole society". With this and the next verse the discourse returns to, and elaborates, the idea touched upon in verse 10 and explained in note 11.

19 The interjection *subḥānaka* ("O Thou who art limitless in Thy glory") stresses here the believer's moral duty to bethink himself of God whenever he is tempted to listen to, or to repeat, a calumny (since every such rumour must be considered a calumny unless its truth is legally proved).

20 The term *fāḥishah* signifies anything that is morally reprehensible or abominable: hence, "immoral conduct" in the widest sense of this expression. In the above context it refers to unfounded or unproven *allegations* of immoral conduct, in other words, "foul slander".

21 I.e., the legal punishment as stipulated in verse 4 of this *sūrah*

and in the life to come: for God knows [the full truth], whereas you know [it] not.[22] ‹19›

And were it not for God's favour upon you and His grace, and that God is compassionate, a dispenser of grace . . . ![23] ‹20›

O YOU who have attained to faith! Follow not Satan's footsteps: for he who follows Satan's footsteps [will find that], behold,
36 حزب
he enjoins but deeds of abomination and all that runs counter to reason.[24]

And were it not for God's favour upon you and His grace, not one of you would ever have remained pure. For [thus it is:] it is God who causes whomever He wills to grow in purity: for God is all-hearing, all-knowing. ‹21›

Hence, [even if they have been wronged by slander,] let not those of you who have been graced with [God's] favour and ease of life ever become remiss in helping[25] [the erring ones among] their near of kin, and the needy, and those who have forsaken the domain of evil for the sake of God,[26] but let them pardon and forbear.

وَٱلْءَاخِرَةِ ۚ وَٱللَّهُ يَعْلَمُ وَأَنتُمْ لَا تَعْلَمُونَ ﴿١٩﴾ وَلَوْلَا فَضْلُ ٱللَّهِ عَلَيْكُمْ
وَرَحْمَتُهُۥ وَأَنَّ ٱللَّهَ رَءُوفٌ رَّحِيمٌ ﴿٢٠﴾ ۞ يَـٰٓأَيُّهَا ٱلَّذِينَ ءَامَنُوا۟ لَا
تَتَّبِعُوا۟ خُطُوَٰتِ ٱلشَّيْطَـٰنِ ۚ وَمَن يَتَّبِعْ خُطُوَٰتِ ٱلشَّيْطَـٰنِ فَإِنَّهُۥ
يَأْمُرُ بِٱلْفَحْشَآءِ وَٱلْمُنكَرِ ۚ وَلَوْلَا فَضْلُ ٱللَّهِ عَلَيْكُمْ وَرَحْمَتُهُۥ مَا
زَكَىٰ مِنكُم مِّنْ أَحَدٍ أَبَدًا وَلَـٰكِنَّ ٱللَّهَ يُزَكِّى مَن يَشَآءُ ۗ وَٱللَّهُ سَمِيعٌ
عَلِيمٌ ﴿٢١﴾ وَلَا يَأْتَلِ أُو۟لُوا۟ ٱلْفَضْلِ مِنكُمْ وَٱلسَّعَةِ أَن يُؤْتُوٓا۟ أُو۟لِى
ٱلْقُرْبَىٰ وَٱلْمَسَـٰكِينَ وَٱلْمُهَـٰجِرِينَ فِى سَبِيلِ ٱللَّهِ ۖ وَلْيَعْفُوا۟ وَلْيَصْفَحُوٓا۟ ۗ

wal-ʾĀkhirati wal-lāhu yaʿlamu wa ʾañtum lā taʿlamūn. (19) Wa lawlā faḍlul-lāhi ʿalaykum wa raḥmatuhū wa ʾannal-lāha Raʾūfur-Raḥīm. (20) ۞ Yāa ʾayyuhal-ladhīna ʾāmanū lā tattabiʿū khuṭuwātish-Shayṭān. Wa mañy-yattabiʿ khuṭuwātish-Shayṭāni faʾinnahū yaʾmuru bilfaḥshāaʾi wal-muñkar. Wa lawlā faḍlul-lāhi ʿalaykum wa raḥmatuhū mā zakā miñkum-min ʾaḥadin ʾabadañw-wa lākinnal-lāha yuzakkī mañy-yashāaʾ. Wal-lāhu Samīʿun ʿAlīm. (21) Wa lā yaʾtali ʾulul-faḍli miñkum was-saʿati ʾañy-yuʾtūu ʾulil-qurbā wal-masākīna wal-muhājirīna fī sabīlil-lāhi wal-yaʿfū wal-yaṣfaḥū.

22 This Qurʾanic warning against slander and, by obvious implication, against any attempt at *seeking out* other people's faults finds a clear echo in several well-authenticated sayings of the Prophet: "Beware of all guesswork [about one another], for, behold, all [such] guesswork is most deceptive (*akdhab al-ḥadīth*); and do not spy upon one another, and do not try to bare [other people's] failings" (*Muwaṭṭaʾ*; almost identical versions of this Tradition have been quoted by Bukhārī, Muslim and Abū Dāʾūd); "Do not hurt those who have surrendered themselves to God (*al-muslimīn*), and do not impute evil to them, and do not try to uncover their nakedness [i.e., their faults]: for, behold, if anyone tries to uncover his brother's nakedness, God will uncover his own nakedness [on the Day of Judgment]" (Tirmidhī); and, "Never does a believer draw a veil over the nakedness of another believer without God's drawing a veil over his own nakedness on Resurrection Day" (Bukhārī). All these injunctions have received their seal, as it were, in the Qurʾanic exhortation: "Avoid most guesswork [about one another] – for, behold, some of [such] guesswork is [in itself] a sin" (49 : 12).

23 See verse 10 of this *sūrah* and the corresponding note 11.

24 In this context, the term *al-munkar* has apparently the same meaning as in 16 : 90 (explained in the corresponding note 109) since, as the sequence shows, it clearly relates to the unreasonable self-righteousness of so many people who "follow Satan's footsteps" by imputing moral failings to others and forgetting that it is only due to God's grace that man, in his inborn weakness, can ever remain pure.

25 Or: "Swear that [henceforth] they would not help [lit., "give to"] . . .", etc. Both these meanings – "he swore [that]" and "he became remiss [in]" – are attributable to the verb *alā*, which appears in the above sentence in the form *yaʾtal*. My rendering is based on the interpretation given to this verb by the great philologist Abu ʿUbayd al-Qāsim al-Harawī (cf. Lane I, 84).

26 For an explanation of this rendering of the designation *al-muhājirūn* (or, in other places, *alladhīna hājarū*), see *sūrah* 2, note 203.

[For,] do you not desire that God should forgive you *your* sins, seeing that God is much-forgiving, a dispenser of grace?[27]
⟪22⟫
[But,] verily, those who [falsely, and without repentance,[28]] accuse chaste women who may have been unthinkingly careless but have remained true to their faith,[29] shall be rejected [from God's grace] in this world as well as in the life to come: and awesome suffering awaits them ⟪23⟫ on the Day when their own tongues and hands and feet will bear witness against them by [recalling] all that they did! ⟪24⟫
On that day will God pay them in full their just due, and they will come to know that God alone is the Ultimate Truth, manifest, and manifesting [the true nature of all that has ever been done].[30] ⟪25⟫
[In the nature of things,] corrupt women are for corrupt men, and corrupt men, for corrupt women – just as good women are for good men, and good men, for good women. [Since God is aware that] these are innocent of all that evil tongues may impute to them,[31] forgiveness of sins shall be theirs, and a most excellent sustenance![32] ⟪26⟫

أَلَا تُحِبُّونَ أَن يَغْفِرَ ٱللَّهُ لَكُمْ ۗ وَٱللَّهُ غَفُورٌ رَّحِيمٌ ﴿٢٢﴾ إِنَّ ٱلَّذِينَ يَرْمُونَ
ٱلْمُحْصَنَٰتِ ٱلْغَٰفِلَٰتِ ٱلْمُؤْمِنَٰتِ لُعِنُوا۟ فِى ٱلدُّنْيَا وَٱلْءَاخِرَةِ وَلَهُمْ
عَذَابٌ عَظِيمٌ ﴿٢٣﴾ يَوْمَ تَشْهَدُ عَلَيْهِمْ أَلْسِنَتُهُمْ وَأَيْدِيهِمْ وَأَرْجُلُهُم بِمَا
كَانُوا۟ يَعْمَلُونَ ﴿٢٤﴾ يَوْمَئِذٍ يُوَفِّيهِمُ ٱللَّهُ دِينَهُمُ ٱلْحَقَّ وَيَعْلَمُونَ أَنَّ ٱللَّهَ هُوَ
ٱلْحَقُّ ٱلْمُبِينُ ﴿٢٥﴾ ٱلْخَبِيثَٰتُ لِلْخَبِيثِينَ وَٱلْخَبِيثُونَ لِلْخَبِيثَٰتِ ۖ
وَٱلطَّيِّبَٰتُ لِلطَّيِّبِينَ وَٱلطَّيِّبُونَ لِلطَّيِّبَٰتِ ۚ أُو۟لَٰٓئِكَ مُبَرَّءُونَ مِمَّا يَقُولُونَ ۖ
لَهُم مَّغْفِرَةٌ وَرِزْقٌ كَرِيمٌ ﴿٢٦﴾

ʾAlā tuḥibbūna ʾañy-yaghfiral-lāhu lakum. Wal-lāhu Ghafūrur-Raḥīm. (22) ʾInnal-ladhīna yarmūnal-muḥṣanātil-ghāfilātil-muʾmināti luʿinū fid-dunyā wal-ʾĀkhirati wa lahum ʿadhābun ʿaẓīm. (23) Yawma tashhadu ʿalayhim ʾalsinatuhum wa ʾaydīhim wa ʾarjuluhum-bimā kānū yaʿmalūn. (24) Yawmaʾidhiñy-yuwaffīhimul-lāhu dīnahumul-ḥaqqa wa yaʿlamūna ʾannal-lāha Huwal-Ḥaqqul-Mubīn. (25) ʾAlkhabīthātu lilkhabīthīna wal-khabīthūna lilkhabīthāti waṭ-ṭayyibātu liṭṭayyibīna waṭ-ṭayyibūna liṭṭayyibāt. ʾUlāaʾika mubarraʾūna mimmā yaqūlūna lahum-maghfiratuñw-wa rizquñ-karīm. (26)

27 It is generally assumed that this verse refers to Abū Bakr, who swore that he would never again help his poor relative, the *muhājir* Misṭaḥ (whom he used to support until then) after the latter had taken part in slandering Abū Bakr's daughter, ʿĀʾishah (see note 12 above). There is no doubt that this assumption of the commentators is well-founded; but there is also no doubt that the ethical purport of the above verse is timeless and, therefore, independent of the fact or facts with which it appears to be historically linked. (This view finds additional support in the use of the *plural form* throughout the above passage.) The call to "pardon and forbear" is fully consonant with the Qurʾanic principle of countering evil with good (see 13 : 22 and the corresponding note 44).

28 According to Rāzi, the *absence of repentance* is incontrovertibly implied in the condemnation expressed in the sequence, since the Qurʾān makes it clear in many places that God always accepts a sinner's sincere repentance.

29 Lit., "chaste, unmindful [or "careless"] believing women", i.e., virtuous women who thoughtlessly expose themselves to situations on which a slanderous construction may be put.

30 Regarding the double meaning ("manifest" and "manifesting") inherent in the adjective *mubīn*, see note 2 on 12 : 1; for my rendering of God's attribute *al-ḥaqq* as "the Ultimate Truth", see note 99 on 20 : 114. In this particular instance, the active form of *mubīn* ("manifesting") apparently relates to God's revelation, on Judgment Day, of the true nature of man's actions and, thus, of the enormity of the sin to which this passage refers.

31 Lit., "innocent of all that they [i.e., the slanderers] may say".

32 See note 5 on 8 : 4. The reference, in this context, to God's "forgiveness of sins" (*maghfirah*) is obviously meant to stress the innate weakness of man's nature, which makes him prone to sinning, however good and pure he may be (cf. 4 : 28).

O YOU who have attained to faith! Do not enter houses other than your own unless you have obtained permission and greeted their inmates. This is [enjoined upon you] for your own good, so that you might bear [your mutual rights] in mind.[33] ‹27›
Hence, [even] if you find no one within [the house], do not enter it until you are given leave;[34] and if you are told, "Turn back," then turn back. This will be most conducive to your purity; and God has full knowledge of all that you do. ‹28›
[On the other hand,] you will incur no sin if you [freely] enter houses not intended for living in but serving a purpose useful to you:[35] but [always remember that] God knows all that you do openly, and all that you would conceal. ‹29›

TELL the believing men to lower their gaze and to be mindful of their chastity:[36] this will be most conducive to their purity – [and,] verily, God is aware of all that they do. ‹30›
And tell the believing women to lower their gaze and to be mindful of their chastity, and not to display their charms [in public] beyond what may [decently] be apparent thereof;[37] hence, let them draw

يَـٰٓأَيُّهَا ٱلَّذِينَ ءَامَنُواْ لَا تَدْخُلُواْ بُيُوتًا غَيْرَ بُيُوتِكُمْ حَتَّىٰ تَسْتَأْنِسُواْ وَتُسَلِّمُواْ
عَلَىٰٓ أَهْلِهَا ۚ ذَٰلِكُمْ خَيْرٌ لَّكُمْ لَعَلَّكُمْ تَذَكَّرُونَ ﴿٢٧﴾ فَإِن لَّمْ تَجِدُواْ فِيهَآ
أَحَدًا فَلَا تَدْخُلُوهَا حَتَّىٰ يُؤْذَنَ لَكُمْ ۖ وَإِن قِيلَ لَكُمُ ٱرْجِعُواْ فَٱرْجِعُواْ ۖ هُوَ
أَزْكَىٰ لَكُمْ ۚ وَٱللَّهُ بِمَا تَعْمَلُونَ عَلِيمٌ ﴿٢٨﴾ لَّيْسَ عَلَيْكُمْ جُنَاحٌ أَن تَدْخُلُواْ
بُيُوتًا غَيْرَ مَسْكُونَةٍ فِيهَا مَتَـٰعٌ لَّكُمْ ۚ وَٱللَّهُ يَعْلَمُ مَا تُبْدُونَ وَمَا تَكْتُمُونَ ﴿٢٩﴾
قُل لِّلْمُؤْمِنِينَ يَغُضُّواْ مِنْ أَبْصَـٰرِهِمْ وَيَحْفَظُواْ فُرُوجَهُمْ ۚ ذَٰلِكَ أَزْكَىٰ لَهُمْ ۗ إِنَّ
ٱللَّهَ خَبِيرٌۢ بِمَا يَصْنَعُونَ ﴿٣٠﴾ وَقُل لِّلْمُؤْمِنَـٰتِ يَغْضُضْنَ مِنْ أَبْصَـٰرِهِنَّ
وَيَحْفَظْنَ فُرُوجَهُنَّ وَلَا يُبْدِينَ زِينَتَهُنَّ إِلَّا مَا ظَهَرَ مِنْهَا ۖ وَلْيَضْرِبْنَ

Yāa ʾayyuhal-ladhīna ʾāmanū lā tadkhulū buyūtan ghayra buyūtikum ḥattā tastaʾnisū wa tusallimū ᶜalāa ʾahlihā; dhālikum khayrul-lakum laᶜallakum tadhakkarūn. (27) Faʾil-lam tajidū fīhāa ʾaḥadañ-falā tadkhulūhā ḥattā yuʾdhana lakum; wa ʾiñ-qīla lakumur-jiᶜū farjiᶜū huwa ʾazkā lakum; wal-lāhu bimā taᶜmalūna ᶜAlīm. (28) Laysa ᶜalaykum junāḥun ʾañ-tadkhulū buyūtan ghayra maskūnatiñ-fīhā matāᶜul-lakum; wal-lāhu yaᶜlamu mā tubdūna wa mā taktumūn. (29) Qul lilmuʾminīna yaghuḍḍū min ʾabṣārihim wa yaḥfaẓū furūjahum. Dhālika ʾazkā lahum. ʾInnal-lāha Khabīrum-bimā yaṣnaᶜūn. (30) Wa qul lilmuʾmināti yaghḍuḍna min ʾabṣārihinna wa yaḥfaẓna furūjahunna wa lā yubdīna zīnata-hunna ʾillā mā ẓahara minhā; wal-yaḍribna

33 This categorical prohibition connects with the preceding passages inasmuch as it serves as an additional protection of individuals against possible slander. In its wider purport, it postulates the inviolability of each person's home and private life. (For the socio-political implications of this principle, see *State and Government in Islam*, pp. 84 ff.)

34 I.e., by the rightful owner or caretaker.

35 Lit., "uninhabited houses wherein there are things of use (*matāᶜ*) for you". In the consensus of all the authorities, including the Companions of the Prophet, this relates to buildings or premises of a more or less public nature, like inns, shops, administrative offices, public baths, etc., as well as to ancient ruins.

36 Lit., "to restrain [something] of their gaze and to guard their private parts". The latter expression may be understood both in the literal sense of "covering one's private parts" – i.e., modesty in dress – as well as in the metonymical sense of "restraining one's sexual urges", i.e., restricting them to what is lawful, namely, marital intercourse (cf. 23 : 5-6). The rendering adopted by me in this instance allows for both interpretations. The "lowering of one's gaze", too, relates both to physical and to emotional modesty (Rāzī).

37 My interpolation of the word "decently" reflects the interpretation of the phrase *illā mā ẓahara minhā* by several of the earliest Islamic scholars, and particularly by Al-Qiffāl (quoted by Rāzī), as "that which a human being may openly show in accordance with prevailing custom (*al-ᶜādah al-jāriyah*)". Although the traditional exponents of Islamic Law have for centuries been inclined to restrict the definition of "what may [decently] be apparent" to a woman's face, hands and feet – and sometimes even less than that – we may safely assume that the meaning of *illā mā ẓahara minhā* is much wider, and that the deliberate vagueness of this phrase is meant to allow for all the time-bound changes that are necessary for man's moral and social growth. The pivotal clause in the above injunction is the demand, addressed in identical terms to men as well as to women, to "lower their gaze and be mindful of their chastity": and this determines the extent of what, at any given time, may legitimately – i.e., in consonance with the Qurʾanic principles of social morality – be considered "decent" or "indecent" in a person's outward appearance.

their head-coverings over their bosoms.[38] And let them not display [more of] their charms to any but their husbands, or their fathers, or their husbands' fathers, or their sons, or their husbands' sons, or their brothers, or their brothers' sons, or their sisters' sons, or their womenfolk, or those whom they rightfully possess, or such male attendants as are beyond all sexual desire,[39] or children that are as yet unaware of women's nakedness; and let them not swing their legs [in walking] so as to draw attention to their hidden charms.[40]
And [always], O you believers – all of you – turn unto God in repentance, so that you might attain to a happy state![41] ‹31›

AND [you ought to] marry the single from among you[42] as well as such of your male and female slaves as are fit [for marriage].[43]

بِخُمُرِهِنَّ عَلَىٰ جُيُوبِهِنَّ ۖ وَلَا يُبْدِينَ زِينَتَهُنَّ إِلَّا لِبُعُولَتِهِنَّ أَوْ ءَابَآئِهِنَّ
أَوْ ءَابَآءِ بُعُولَتِهِنَّ أَوْ أَبْنَآئِهِنَّ أَوْ أَبْنَآءِ بُعُولَتِهِنَّ أَوْ إِخْوَٰنِهِنَّ أَوْ بَنِىٓ
إِخْوَٰنِهِنَّ أَوْ بَنِىٓ أَخَوَٰتِهِنَّ أَوْ نِسَآئِهِنَّ أَوْ مَا مَلَكَتْ أَيْمَـٰنُهُنَّ أَوِ
ٱلتَّـٰبِعِينَ غَيْرِ أُو۟لِى ٱلْإِرْبَةِ مِنَ ٱلرِّجَالِ أَوِ ٱلطِّفْلِ ٱلَّذِينَ لَمْ يَظْهَرُوا۟
عَلَىٰ عَوْرَٰتِ ٱلنِّسَآءِ ۖ وَلَا يَضْرِبْنَ بِأَرْجُلِهِنَّ لِيُعْلَمَ مَا يُخْفِينَ مِن
زِينَتِهِنَّ ۚ وَتُوبُوٓا۟ إِلَى ٱللَّهِ جَمِيعًا أَيُّهَ ٱلْمُؤْمِنُونَ لَعَلَّكُمْ تُفْلِحُونَ ﴿٣١﴾
وَأَنكِحُوا۟ ٱلْأَيَـٰمَىٰ مِنكُمْ وَٱلصَّـٰلِحِينَ مِنْ عِبَادِكُمْ وَإِمَآئِكُمْ

bikhumurihinna ᶜalā juyūbihinn. Wa lā yubdīna zīnatahunna ᵓillā libuᶜūlatihinna ᵓaw ᵓābāaᵓihinna ᵓaw ᵓābāaᵓi buᶜūlatihinna ᵓaw ᵓabnāaᵓihinna ᵓaw ᵓabnāaᵓi buᶜūlatihinna ᵓaw ᵓikhwānihinna ᵓaw banīi ᵓikhwānihinna ᵓaw banīi ᵓakhawātihinna ᵓaw nisāaᵓihinna ᵓaw mā malakat ᵓaymānuhunna ᵓawit-tābiᶜīna ghayri ᵓulil-ᵓirbati minar-rijāli ᵓawiṭ-ṭiflil-ladhīna lam yaẓharū ᶜalā ᶜawrātin-nisāaᵓ. Wa lā yaḍribna biᵓarjulihinna liyuᶜlama mā yukhfīna miñ-zīnatihinn. Wa tūbūu ᵓilal-lāhi jamīᶜan ᵓayyuhal-muᵓminūna laᶜallakum tufliḥūn. ﴿31﴾ **Wa ᵓañkiḥul-ᵓayāmā miñkum waṣ-ṣāliḥīna min ᶜibādikum wa ᵓimāaᵓikum;**

38 The noun *khimār* (of which *khumur* is the plural) denotes the head-covering customarily used by Arabian women before and after the advent of Islam. According to most of the classical commentators, it was worn in pre-Islamic times more or less as an ornament and was let down loosely over the wearer's back; and since, in accordance with the fashion prevalent at the time, the upper part of a woman's tunic had a wide opening in the front, her breasts were left bare. Hence. the injunction to cover the bosom by means of a *khimār* (a term so familiar to the contemporaries of the Prophet) does not necessarily relate to the use of a *khimār* as such but is, rather, meant to make it clear that a woman's breasts are *not* included in the concept of "what may decently be apparent" of her body and should not, therefore, be displayed.

39 I.e., very old men. The preceding phrase "those whom they rightfully possess" (lit., "whom their right hands possess") denotes slaves; but see also note 78.

40 Lit., "so that those of their charms which they keep hidden may become known". The phrase *yaḍribna bi-arjulihinna* is idiomatically similar to the phrase *ḍaraba bi-yadayhi fī mishyatihi*, "he swung his arms in walking" (quoted in this context in *Tāj al-ᶜArūs*), and alludes to a deliberately provocative gait.

41 The implication of this general call to repentance is that since "man has been created weak" (4 : 28), no one is ever free of faults and temptations – so much so that even the Prophet used to say, "Verily, I turn unto Him in repentance a hundred times every day" (Ibn Ḥanbal, Bukhārī and Bayhaqī, all of them on the authority of ᶜAbd Allāh ibn ᶜUmar).

42 I.e., from among the free members of the community, as is evident from the subsequent juxtaposition with slaves. (As most of the classical commentators point out, this is not an injunction but a *recommendation* to the community as a whole: hence my interpolation of the words "you ought to".) The term *ayyim* – of which *ayāmā* is the plural – signifies a person of either sex who has no spouse, irrespective of whether he or she has never been married or is divorced or widowed. Thus, the above verse expresses the idea – reiterated in many authentic sayings of the Prophet – that, from both the ethical and the social points of view, the married state is infinitely preferable to celibacy.

43 The term *aṣ-ṣāliḥīn* connotes here both moral and physical fitness for marriage: i.e., the attainment of bodily and mental maturity as well as mutual affection between the man and the woman concerned. As in 4 : 25, the above verse rules out all forms of concubinage and postulates *marriage* as the only basis of lawful sexual relations between a man and his female slave.

If they [whom you intend to marry] are poor, [let this not deter you;] God will grant them sufficiency out of His bounty – for God is infinite [in His mercy], all-knowing. ‹32› And as for those who are unable to marry,[44] let them live in continence until God grants them sufficiency out of His bounty.

And if any of those whom you rightfully possess[45] desire [to obtain] a deed of freedom, write it out for them if you are aware of any good in them:[46] and give them [their share] of the wealth of God which He has given you.[47]

And do not, in order to gain[48] some of the fleeting pleasures of this worldly life, coerce your [slave] maidens into whoredom if they happen to be desirous of marriage;[49] and if anyone should coerce them, then, verily, after they have been compelled [to submit in their helplessness], God will be much-forgiving, a dispenser of grace! ‹33›

إِن يَكُونُوا۟ فُقَرَآءَ يُغْنِهِمُ ٱللَّهُ مِن فَضْلِهِۦ ۗ وَٱللَّهُ وَٰسِعٌ عَلِيمٌ ﴿٣٢﴾
وَلْيَسْتَعْفِفِ ٱلَّذِينَ لَا يَجِدُونَ نِكَاحًا حَتَّىٰ يُغْنِيَهُمُ ٱللَّهُ مِن فَضْلِهِۦ ۗ
وَٱلَّذِينَ يَبْتَغُونَ ٱلْكِتَٰبَ مِمَّا مَلَكَتْ أَيْمَٰنُكُمْ فَكَاتِبُوهُمْ إِنْ عَلِمْتُمْ
فِيهِمْ خَيْرًا ۖ وَءَاتُوهُم مِّن مَّالِ ٱللَّهِ ٱلَّذِىٓ ءَاتَىٰكُمْ ۚ وَلَا تُكْرِهُوا۟ فَتَيَٰتِكُمْ
عَلَى ٱلْبِغَآءِ إِنْ أَرَدْنَ تَحَصُّنًا لِّتَبْتَغُوا۟ عَرَضَ ٱلْحَيَوٰةِ ٱلدُّنْيَا ۚ وَمَن
يُكْرِههُّنَّ فَإِنَّ ٱللَّهَ مِنۢ بَعْدِ إِكْرَٰهِهِنَّ غَفُورٌ رَّحِيمٌ ﴿٣٣﴾

ʾiñy-yakūnū fuqarāaʾa yughnihimul-lāhu miñ-faḍlih. Wal-lāhu Wāsiʿun ʿAlīm. ‹32› Wal-yastaʿfifil-ladhīna lā yajidūna nikāḥan ḥattā yughniyahumul-lāhu miñ-faḍlih. Wal-ladhīna yabtaghūnal-Kitāba mimmā ma-lakat ʾaymānukum fakātibūhum ʾin ʿalimtum fīhim khayrañw-wa ʾātūhum-mim-mālil-lāhil-ladhīi ʾātā-kum. Wa lā tukrihū fatayātikum ʿalal-bighāaʾi ʾin ʾaradna taḥaṣṣunal-litabtaghū ʿaraḍal-ḥayātid-dunyā. Wa mañy-yukrihhunna faʾinnal-lāha mim-baʿdi ʾikrāhihinna Ghafūrur-Raḥīm. ‹33›

44 I.e., because of poverty, or because they cannot find a suitable mate, or for any other personal reason.

45 Lit., "whom your right hands possess", i.e., male or female slaves.

46 The noun *kitāb* is, in this context, an equivalent of *kitābah* or *mukātabah* (lit., "mutual agreement in writing"), a juridical term signifying a "deed of freedom" or "of manumission" executed on the basis of an agreement between a slave and his or her owner, to the effect that the slave undertakes to purchase his or her freedom for an equitable sum of money payable in instalments before or after the manumission, or, alternatively, by rendering a clearly specified service or services to his or her owner. With this end in view, the slave is legally entitled to engage in any legitimate, gainful work or to obtain the necessary sum of money by any other lawful means (e.g., through a loan or a gift from a third person). In view of the imperative form of the verb *kātibūhum* ("write it out for them"), the deed of manumission cannot he refused by the owner, the only pre-condition being an evidence – to be established, if necessary, by an unbiassed arbiter or arbiters – of the slave's good character and ability to fulfil his or her contractual obligations. The stipulation that such a deed of manumission may not be refused, and the establishment of precise juridical directives to this end, clearly indicates that Islamic Law has from its very beginning aimed at an abolition of slavery as a social institution, and that its prohibition in modern times constitutes no more than a final implementation of that aim. (See also next note, as well as note 146 on 2 : 177.)

47 According to all the authorities, this relates (a) to a moral obligation on the part of the owner to promote the slave's efforts to obtain the necessary revenues by helping him or her to achieve an independent economic status and/or by remitting part of the agreed-upon compensation, and (b) to the obligation of the state treasury (*bayt al-māl*) to finance the freeing of slaves in accordance with the Qurʾanic principle – enunciated in 9 : 60 – that the revenues obtained through the obligatory tax called *zakāh* are to be utilized, among other purposes, "for the freeing of human beings from bondage" (*fī 'r-riqāb*, an expression explained in *sūrah* 2, note 146). Hence, Zamakhsharī holds that the above clause is addressed not merely to persons owning slaves but to the community as a whole. – The expression "the wealth of God" contains an allusion to the principle that "God has bought of the believers their lives and their possessions, promising them paradise in return" (9 : 111) implying that all of man's possessions are vested in God, and that man is entitled to no more than their usufruct.

48 Lit., "so that you might seek out" or "endeavour to attain to".

49 Lit., "if they desire protection against unchastity (*taḥaṣṣun*)", i.e., through marriage (cf. the expression *muḥṣanāt* as used in 4 : 24). Most of the classical commentators are of the opinion that the term *fatayāt* ("maidens") denotes here "slave-girls": an assumption which is fully warranted by the context. Hence, the above verse reiterates the prohibition of concubinage by explicitly describing it as "whoredom" (*bighāʾ*).

AND, INDEED, from on high have We bestowed upon you messages clearly showing the truth, and [many] a lesson from [the stories of] those who have passed away before you, and [many] an admonition to the God-conscious. ﴾34﴿
God is the Light of the heavens and the earth. The parable of His light is, as it were,[50] that of a niche containing a lamp; the lamp is [enclosed] in glass, the glass [shining] like a radiant star:[51] [a lamp] lit from a blessed tree – an olive-tree that is neither of the east nor of the west[52] – the oil whereof [is so bright that it] would well-nigh give light [of itself] even though fire had not touched it: light upon light![53] God guides unto His light him that wills [to be guided];[54] and [to this end] God propounds parables unto men, since God [alone] has full knowledge of all things.[55] ﴾35﴿

وَلَقَدْ أَنزَلْنَآ إِلَيْكُمْ ءَايَٰتٍ مُّبَيِّنَٰتٍ وَمَثَلًا مِّنَ ٱلَّذِينَ خَلَوْا۟ مِن قَبْلِكُمْ
وَمَوْعِظَةً لِّلْمُتَّقِينَ ﴿٣٤﴾ ۞ ٱللَّهُ نُورُ ٱلسَّمَٰوَٰتِ وَٱلْأَرْضِ ۚ مَثَلُ نُورِهِۦ
كَمِشْكَوٰةٍ فِيهَا مِصْبَاحٌ ۖ ٱلْمِصْبَاحُ فِى زُجَاجَةٍ ۖ ٱلزُّجَاجَةُ كَأَنَّهَا كَوْكَبٌ
دُرِّىٌّ يُوقَدُ مِن شَجَرَةٍ مُّبَٰرَكَةٍ زَيْتُونَةٍ لَّا شَرْقِيَّةٍ وَلَا غَرْبِيَّةٍ يَكَادُ زَيْتُهَا
يُضِىٓءُ وَلَوْ لَمْ تَمْسَسْهُ نَارٌ ۚ نُّورٌ عَلَىٰ نُورٍ ۗ يَهْدِى ٱللَّهُ لِنُورِهِۦ مَن يَشَآءُ ۚ
وَيَضْرِبُ ٱللَّهُ ٱلْأَمْثَٰلَ لِلنَّاسِ ۗ وَٱللَّهُ بِكُلِّ شَىْءٍ عَلِيمٌ ﴿٣٥﴾

ربع الحزب

Wa laqad ʾañzalnāa ʾilaykum ʾĀyātim-mubayyinātiñw-wa mathalam-minal-ladhīna khalaw miñ-qablikum wa mawʿiẓatal-lilmuttaqīn. ﴾34﴿ ۞ ʾAllāhu nūrus-samāwāti wal-ʾarḍ. Mathalu nūrihī ka-mishkātiñ-fīhā miṣbāḥ. ʾAlmiṣbāḥu fī zujājah. ʾAzzujājatu kaʾannahā kawkabuñ-durriyyuñy-yūqadu miñ-shajaratim-mubārakatiñ-zaytūnatil-lā sharqiyyatiñw-wa lā gharbiyyatiñy-yakādu zaytuhā yuḍīʾu wa law lam tamsas-hu nār. Nūrun ʿalā nūr. Yahdil-lāhu linūrihī mañy-yashāaʾ. Wa yaḍribul-lāhul-ʾamthāla linnās. Wal-lāhu bikulli shayʾin ʿAlīm. ﴾35﴿

50 The particle *ka* ("as if" or "as it were") prefixed to a noun is called *kāf at-tashbīh* ("the letter *kāf* pointing to a resemblance [of one thing to another]" or "indicating a metaphor"). In the above context it alludes to the *impossibility* of defining God even by means of a metaphor or a parable – for, since "there is nothing like unto Him" (42 : 11), there is also "nothing that could he compared with Him" (112 : 4). Hence, the parable of "the light of God" is not meant to express His reality – which is inconceivable to any created being and, therefore, inexpressible in any human language – but only to allude to the illumination which He, who is the Ultimate Truth, bestows upon the mind and the feelings of all who are willing to be guided. Ṭabarī, Baghawī and Ibn Kathīr quote Ibn ʿAbbās and Ibn Masʿūd as saying in this context: "It is the parable of His light *in the heart* of a believer."

51 The "lamp" is the revelation which God grants to His prophets and which is reflected in the believer's heart – the "niche" of the above parable (Ubayy ibn Kaʿb, as quoted by Ṭabarī) – after being received and consciously grasped by his reason ("the glass [shining brightly] like a radiant star"): for it is through reason alone that true faith can find its way into the heart of man.

52 It would seem that this is an allusion to the organic continuity of all divine revelation which, starting like a tree from one "root" or proposition – the statement of God's existence and uniqueness – grows steadily throughout man's spiritual history, branching out into a splendid variety of religious experience, thus endlessly widening the range of man's perception of the truth. The association of this concept with the *olive-tree* apparently arises from the fact that this particular kind of tree is characteristic of the lands in which most of the prophetic precursors of the Qurʾanic message lived, namely, the lands to the east of the Mediterranean: but since all true revelation flows from the Infinite Being, it is "neither of the east nor of the west" – and especially so the revelation of the Qur'an, which, being addressed to all mankind, is universal in its goal as well.

53 The essence of the Qurʾanic message is described elsewhere as "clear [in itself] and clearly showing the truth" (cf. note 2 on 12 : 1); and it is, I believe, this aspect of the Qurʾān that the above sentence alludes to. Its message gives light because it proceeds from God; but it "would well-nigh give light [of itself] even though fire had not touched it" i.e., even though one may be unaware that it has been "touched by the fire" of divine revelation, its inner consistency, truth and wisdom ought to be self-evident to anyone who approaches it in the light of his reason and without prejudice.

54 Although most of the commentators read the above phrase in the sense of "God guides unto His light *whomever He wills*", Zamakhsharī gives it the sense adopted in my rendering (both being syntactically permissible).

55 I.e., because of their complexity, certain truths can be conveyed to man only by means of parables or allegories: see notes 5 and 8 on 3 : 7.

فِي بُيُوتٍ أَذِنَ ٱللَّهُ أَن تُرْفَعَ وَيُذْكَرَ فِيهَا ٱسْمُهُۥ يُسَبِّحُ لَهُۥ فِيهَا بِٱلْغُدُوِّ
وَٱلْآصَالِ ﴿٣٦﴾ رِجَالٌ لَّا تُلْهِيهِمْ تِجَٰرَةٌ وَلَا بَيْعٌ عَن ذِكْرِ ٱللَّهِ وَإِقَامِ
ٱلصَّلَوٰةِ وَإِيتَآءِ ٱلزَّكَوٰةِ يَخَافُونَ يَوْمًا تَتَقَلَّبُ فِيهِ ٱلْقُلُوبُ
وَٱلْأَبْصَٰرُ ﴿٣٧﴾ لِيَجْزِيَهُمُ ٱللَّهُ أَحْسَنَ مَا عَمِلُوا۟ وَيَزِيدَهُم مِّن فَضْلِهِۦ
وَٱللَّهُ يَرْزُقُ مَن يَشَآءُ بِغَيْرِ حِسَابٍ ﴿٣٨﴾ وَٱلَّذِينَ كَفَرُوٓا۟ أَعْمَٰلُهُمْ
كَسَرَابٍۭ بِقِيعَةٍ يَحْسَبُهُ ٱلظَّمْـَٔانُ مَآءً حَتَّىٰٓ إِذَا جَآءَهُۥ لَمْ يَجِدْهُ شَيْـًٔا
وَوَجَدَ ٱللَّهَ عِندَهُۥ فَوَفَّىٰهُ حِسَابَهُۥ ۗ وَٱللَّهُ سَرِيعُ ٱلْحِسَابِ ﴿٣٩﴾ أَوْ
كَظُلُمَٰتٍ فِي بَحْرٍ لُّجِّيٍّ يَغْشَىٰهُ مَوْجٌ مِّن فَوْقِهِۦ مَوْجٌ مِّن فَوْقِهِۦ سَحَابٌ
ظُلُمَٰتٌۢ بَعْضُهَا فَوْقَ بَعْضٍ إِذَآ أَخْرَجَ يَدَهُۥ لَمْ يَكَدْ يَرَىٰهَا ۗ وَمَن لَّمْ يَجْعَلِ
ٱللَّهُ لَهُۥ نُورًا فَمَا لَهُۥ مِن نُّورٍ ﴿٤٠﴾

IN THE HOUSES [of worship] which God has allowed to be raised so that His name be remembered in them,[56] there [are such as] extol His limitless glory at morn and evening ‹36› – people whom neither [worldly] commerce nor striving after gain[57] can divert from the remembrance of God, and from constancy in prayer, and from charity:[58] [people] who are filled with fear [at the thought] of the Day on which all hearts and eyes will be convulsed, ‹37› [and who only hope] that God may reward them in accordance with the best that they ever did, and give them, out of His bounty, more [than they deserve]: for, God grants sustenance unto whom He wills, beyond all reckoning. ‹38›

But as for those who are bent on denying the truth, their [good] deeds are like a mirage in the desert, which the thirsty supposes to be water – until, when he approaches it, he finds that it was nothing:[59] instead, he finds [that] God [has always been present] with him, and [that] He will pay him his account in full – for God is swift in reckoning! ‹39›

Or [else, their deeds[60] are] like the depths of darkness upon an abysmal sea, made yet more dark by wave billowing over wave, with [black] clouds above it all: depths of darkness, layer upon layer,[61] [so that] when one holds up his hand, he can hardly see it: for he to whom God gives no light, no light whatever has he! ‹40›

Fī buyūtin ᵓadhinal-lāhu ᵓañ-turfaᶜa wa yudhkara fīhas-muhū yusabbiḥu lahū fīhā bilghuduwwi wal-ᶜāṣāli, (36) rijālul-lā tulhīhim tijāratuñw-wa lā bayᶜun ᶜañ-dhikril-lāhi wa ᵓiqāmiṣ-Ṣalāti wa ᵓītāaᵓiz-Zakāti yakhāfūna Yawmañ-tataqallabu fīhil-qulūbu wal-ᵓabṣār. (37) Liyajziyahumul-lāhu ᵓaḥsana mā ᶜamilū wa yazīdahum-miñ-faḍlih. Wal-lāhu yarzuqu mañy-yashāaᵓu bighayri ḥisāb. (38) Wal-ladhīna kafarūu ᵓaᶜmāluhum kasarābim-biqīᶜatiñy-yaḥsabuhuẓ-ẓamᵓānu māaᵓan ḥattāa ᵓidhā jāaᵓahū lam yajid-hu shayᵓañw-wa wajadal-lāha ᶜiñdahū fawaffāhu ḥisābah. Wal-lāhu sarīᶜul-ḥisāb. (39) ᵓAw kaẓulumātiñ-fī baḥril-lujjiyyiñy-yaghshāhu mawjum-miñ-fawqihī mawjum-miñ-fawqihī saḥāb. Ẓulumātum-baᶜḍuhā fawqa baᶜḍin ᵓidhāa ᵓakhraja yadahū lam yakad yarāhā. Wa mal-lam yajᶜalil-lāhu lahū nūrañ-famā lahū miñ-nūr. (40)

56 Lit., "and [ordained] that His name . . .", etc.: implying, as the sequence shows, that the spiritual purpose of those houses of worship is fulfilled only by some, and not all, of the people who are wont to congregate in them out of habit.

57 Lit., "bargaining" or "selling" or "buying and selling" (*bayᶜ*) – a metonym for anything that might bring worldly gain.

58 For this rendering of the term *zakāh*, see *sūrah* 2, note 34.

59 I.e., he is bound to realize on Judgment Day that all his supposedly "good" deeds have been rendered worthless by his deliberate refusal to listen to the voice of truth (Zamakhsharī and Rāzī).

60 I.e., their *bad* deeds, as contrasted with their good deeds, which in the preceding verse have been likened to a mirage.

61 Lit., "one above another".

ART THOU NOT aware that it is God whose limitless glory all [creatures] that are in the heavens and on earth extol, even the birds as they spread out their wings?[62] Each [of them] knows indeed how to pray unto Him and to glorify Him; and God has full knowledge of all that they do: «41» for, God's is the dominion over the heavens and the earth, and with God is all journeys' end. «42»

Art thou not aware that it is God who causes the clouds to move onward, then joins them together, then piles them up in masses, until thou canst see rain come forth from their midst?

And He it is who sends down from the skies, by degrees, mountainous masses [of clouds] charged with hail, striking therewith whomever He wills and averting it from whomever He wills, [the while] the flash of His lightning well-nigh deprives [men of their] sight! «43»

It is God who causes night and day to alternate: in this [too], behold, there is surely a lesson for all who have eyes to see! «44»

And it is God who has created all animals out of water;[63] and [He has willed that] among them are such as crawl on their bellies, and such as walk on two legs, and such as walk on four.

God creates what He wills: for, verily, God has the power to will anything. «45»

INDEED, from on high have We bestowed messages clearly showing the truth; but God guides onto a straight way [only] him that wills [to be guided].[64] «46»

أَلَمْ تَرَ أَنَّ ٱللَّهَ يُسَبِّحُ لَهُۥ مَن فِى ٱلسَّمَٰوَٰتِ وَٱلْأَرْضِ وَٱلطَّيْرُ صَٰٓفَّٰتٍۢ ۖ
كُلٌّ قَدْ عَلِمَ صَلَاتَهُۥ وَتَسْبِيحَهُۥ ۗ وَٱللَّهُ عَلِيمٌۢ بِمَا يَفْعَلُونَ ﴿٤١﴾ وَلِلَّهِ مُلْكُ
ٱلسَّمَٰوَٰتِ وَٱلْأَرْضِ ۖ وَإِلَى ٱللَّهِ ٱلْمَصِيرُ ﴿٤٢﴾ أَلَمْ تَرَ أَنَّ ٱللَّهَ يُزْجِى
سَحَابًا ثُمَّ يُؤَلِّفُ بَيْنَهُۥ ثُمَّ يَجْعَلُهُۥ رُكَامًا فَتَرَى ٱلْوَدْقَ يَخْرُجُ مِنْ خِلَٰلِهِۦ
وَيُنَزِّلُ مِنَ ٱلسَّمَآءِ مِن جِبَالٍ فِيهَا مِنۢ بَرَدٍ فَيُصِيبُ بِهِۦ مَن يَشَآءُ
وَيَصْرِفُهُۥ عَن مَّن يَشَآءُ ۖ يَكَادُ سَنَا بَرْقِهِۦ يَذْهَبُ بِٱلْأَبْصَٰرِ ﴿٤٣﴾ يُقَلِّبُ
ٱللَّهُ ٱلَّيْلَ وَٱلنَّهَارَ ۚ إِنَّ فِى ذَٰلِكَ لَعِبْرَةً لِّأُو۟لِى ٱلْأَبْصَٰرِ ﴿٤٤﴾ وَٱللَّهُ خَلَقَ
كُلَّ دَآبَّةٍ مِّن مَّآءٍ ۖ فَمِنْهُم مَّن يَمْشِى عَلَىٰ بَطْنِهِۦ وَمِنْهُم مَّن يَمْشِى عَلَىٰ
رِجْلَيْنِ وَمِنْهُم مَّن يَمْشِى عَلَىٰٓ أَرْبَعٍ ۚ يَخْلُقُ ٱللَّهُ مَا يَشَآءُ ۚ إِنَّ ٱللَّهَ عَلَىٰ كُلِّ
شَىْءٍ قَدِيرٌ ﴿٤٥﴾ لَّقَدْ أَنزَلْنَآ ءَايَٰتٍ مُّبَيِّنَٰتٍ ۚ وَٱللَّهُ يَهْدِى مَن يَشَآءُ إِلَىٰ
صِرَٰطٍ مُّسْتَقِيمٍ ﴿٤٦﴾

ʾAlam tara ʾannal-lāha yusabbiḥu lahū mañ-fis-samāwāti wal-ʾarḍi waṭ-ṭayru ṣāaffātiñ-kulluñ-qad ᶜalima ṣalātahū wa tasbīḥah. Wal-lāhu ᶜAlīmum-bimā yafᶜalūn. ﴿41﴾ Wa lillāhi mulkus-samāwāti wal-ʾarḍi wa ʾilal-lāhil-maṣīr. ﴿42﴾ ʾAlam tara ʾannal-lāha yuzjī saḥābañ-thumma yuʾallifu baynahū thumma yajᶜaluhū rukāmañ-fataral-wadqa yakhruju min khilālihī wa yunazzilu minas-samāaʾi miñ-jibāliñ-fīhā mim-baradiñ-fayuṣību bihī mañy-yashāaʾu wa yaṣrifuhū ᶜam-mañy-yashāaʾ. Yakādu sanā barqihī yadhhabu bilʾabṣār. ﴿43﴾ Yuqallibul-lāhul-layla wan-nahār. ʾInna fī dhālika laᶜibratal-liʾulil-ʾabṣār. ﴿44﴾ Wal-lāhu khalaqa kulla dāabbatim-mim-māaʾ. Faminhum-mañy-yamshī ᶜalā baṭnihī wa minhum-mañy yamshī ᶜalā rijlayni wa minhum-mañy-yamshī ᶜalāa ʾarbaᶜ. Yakhluqul-lāhu mā yashāaʾ. ʾInnal-lāha ᶜalā kulli shayʾiñ-Qadīr. ﴿45﴾ Laqad ʾañzalnāa ʾĀyātim-mubayyinātiñw-wal-lāhu yahdī mañy-yashāaʾu ʾilā ṣirāṭim-mustaqīm. ﴿46﴾

62 Cf. 17 : 44 and the corresponding note 53.

63 See note 39 on 21 : 30. The term *dābbah* denotes every corporeal being endowed with both life and spontaneous movement; hence, in its widest sense, it comprises the entire animal world, including man.

64 Or: "God guides whomever He wills onto a straight way". The rendering adopted by me in this instance seems preferable in view of the preceding, intensive stress on the evidence, forthcoming from all nature, of God's creative, planning activity and the appeal to "all who have eyes to see" to let themselves be guided by this overwhelming evidence.

نصف الحزب

For, [many are] they [who] say, "We believe in God and in the Apostle, and we pay heed!" – but then, some of them turn away after this [assertion]: and these are by no means [true] believers. ‹47› And [so it is that] whenever they are summoned unto God and His Apostle in order that [the divine writ] might judge between them,[65] lo! some of them turn away; ‹48› but if the truth happens to be to their liking, they are quite willing to accept it![66] ‹49›
Is there disease in their hearts? Or have they begun to doubt [that this is a divine writ]? Or do they fear that God and His Apostle might deal unjustly with them?[67]
Nay, it is [but] they, they who are doing wrong [to themselves]! ‹50›
The only response of believers, whenever they are summoned unto God and His Apostle in order that [the divine writ] might judge between them, can be no other than,[68] "We have heard, and we pay heed!" – and it is they, they who shall attain to a happy state: ‹51› for, they who pay heed unto God and His Apostle, and stand in awe of God and are conscious of Him, it is they, they who shall triumph [in the end]! ‹52›
Now [as for those half-hearted ones,] they do swear by God with their most solemn oaths that if thou [O Apostle] shouldst ever bid them to do so, they would most certainly go forth [and sacrifice themselves].[69]

وَيَقُولُونَ ءَامَنَّا بِٱللَّهِ وَبِٱلرَّسُولِ وَأَطَعْنَا ثُمَّ يَتَوَلَّىٰ فَرِيقٌ مِّنْهُم مِّنۢ بَعْدِ
ذَٰلِكَ وَمَآ أُو۟لَٰٓئِكَ بِٱلْمُؤْمِنِينَ ﴿٤٧﴾ وَإِذَا دُعُوٓا۟ إِلَى ٱللَّهِ وَرَسُولِهِۦ لِيَحْكُمَ
بَيْنَهُمْ إِذَا فَرِيقٌ مِّنْهُم مُّعْرِضُونَ ﴿٤٨﴾ وَإِن يَكُن لَّهُمُ ٱلْحَقُّ يَأْتُوٓا۟ إِلَيْهِ
مُذْعِنِينَ ﴿٤٩﴾ أَفِى قُلُوبِهِم مَّرَضٌ أَمِ ٱرْتَابُوٓا۟ أَمْ يَخَافُونَ أَن يَحِيفَ ٱللَّهُ عَلَيْهِمْ
وَرَسُولُهُۥ بَلْ أُو۟لَٰٓئِكَ هُمُ ٱلظَّٰلِمُونَ ﴿٥٠﴾ إِنَّمَا كَانَ قَوْلَ ٱلْمُؤْمِنِينَ إِذَا
دُعُوٓا۟ إِلَى ٱللَّهِ وَرَسُولِهِۦ لِيَحْكُمَ بَيْنَهُمْ أَن يَقُولُوا۟ سَمِعْنَا وَأَطَعْنَا وَأُو۟لَٰٓئِكَ
هُمُ ٱلْمُفْلِحُونَ ﴿٥١﴾ وَمَن يُطِعِ ٱللَّهَ وَرَسُولَهُۥ وَيَخْشَ ٱللَّهَ وَيَتَّقْهِ فَأُو۟لَٰٓئِكَ
هُمُ ٱلْفَآئِزُونَ ﴿٥٢﴾ ۞ وَأَقْسَمُوا۟ بِٱللَّهِ جَهْدَ أَيْمَٰنِهِمْ لَئِنْ أَمَرْتَهُمْ لَيَخْرُجُنَّ

Wa yaqūlūna ʾāmannā billāhi wa birRasūli wa ʾaṭaʿnā thumma yatawallā farīqum-minhum-mim-baʿdi dhālika wa māa ʾulāaʾika bilmuʾminīn. (47) Wa ʾidhā duʿūu ʾilal-lāhi wa Rasulihī liyaḥkuma baynahum ʾidhā farīqum-minhum-muʿriḍūn. (48) Wa ʾiñy-yakul-lahumul-ḥaqqu yaʾtūu ʾilayhi mudhʿinīn. (49) ʾAfī qulūbihim-maraḍun ʾamir-tābūu ʾam yakhāfūna ʾañy-yaḥīfal-lāhu ʿalayhim wa Rasūluh. Bal ʾulāaʾika humuẓ-ẓālimūn. (50) ʾInnamā kāna qawlal-muʾminīna ʾidhā duʿūu ʾilal-lāhi wa Rasūlihī liyaḥkuma baynahum ʾañy-yaqūlū samiʿnā wa ʾaṭaʿnā; wa ʾulāaʾika humul-mufliḥūn. (51) Wa mañy-yuṭiʿil-lāha wa Rasūlahū wa yakhshal-lāha wa yattaqhi faʾulāaʾika humul-fāaʾizūn. (52) ۞ Wa ʾaqsamū billāhi jahda ʾaymānihim laʾin ʾamartahum layakhrujunn.

65 I.e., in order that the divine writ – which is implied in the preceding expression "God and His Apostle" – might determine their ethical values and, consequently, their social behaviour.

66 Lit., "if the truth happens to be with them, they come to it willingly": cf. 4 : 60-61 and the corresponding notes, especially note 80.

67 I.e., by depriving them of what they choose to regard as "legitimate" liberties and enjoyments, or by supposedly preventing them from "keeping up with the times". As in verses 47 and 48 (as well as in verse 51 below) the expression "God and His Apostle" is here a synonym for the divine writ revealed to the Apostle.

68 Lit., "The only saying of the believers . . . is that they say" – i.e., without any mental reservation. The term *qawl* (lit., "saying") has here the sense of a genuine spiritual "response" in contrast to the mere lip-service alluded to in verse 47 above.

69 This is an allusion to the ephemeral, self-deceiving enthusiasms of the half-hearted and their supposed readiness for "self-sacrifice", contrasting with their obvious reluctance to live up to the message of the Qurʾān in their day-to-day concerns.

Say: "Swear not! Reasonable compliance [with God's message is all that is required of you].[70] Verily, God is aware of all that you do!" ‹53›
Say: "pay heed unto God, and pay heed unto the Apostle."
And if you turn away [from the Apostle, know that] he will have to answer only for whatever he has been charged with, and you, for what you have been charged with; but if you pay heed unto him, you will be on the right way. Withal, the Apostle is not bound to do more than clearly deliver the message [entrusted to him]. ‹54›
God has promised those of you who have attained to faith and do righteous deeds that, of a certainty, He will cause them to accede to power on earth,[71] even as He caused [some of] those who lived before them to accede to it; and that, of a certainty, He will firmly establish for them the religion which He has been pleased to bestow on them;[72] and that, of a certainty, He will cause their erstwhile state of fear to be replaced by a sense of security[73] – [seeing that] they worship Me [alone], not ascribing divine powers to aught beside Me.[74]
But all who, after [having understood] this, choose to deny the truth – it is they, they who are truly iniquitous! ‹55›
Hence, [O believers,] be constant in prayer, and render the purifying dues,[75]

قُلْ لَّا تُقْسِمُوا۟ ۖ طَاعَةٌ مَّعْرُوفَةٌ ۚ إِنَّ ٱللَّهَ خَبِيرٌۢ بِمَا تَعْمَلُونَ ﴿٥٣﴾ قُلْ أَطِيعُوا۟
ٱللَّهَ وَأَطِيعُوا۟ ٱلرَّسُولَ ۖ فَإِن تَوَلَّوْا۟ فَإِنَّمَا عَلَيْهِ مَا حُمِّلَ وَعَلَيْكُم مَّا حُمِّلْتُمْ ۖ
وَإِن تُطِيعُوهُ تَهْتَدُوا۟ ۚ وَمَا عَلَى ٱلرَّسُولِ إِلَّا ٱلْبَلَٰغُ ٱلْمُبِينُ ﴿٥٤﴾ وَعَدَ ٱللَّهُ
ٱلَّذِينَ ءَامَنُوا۟ مِنكُمْ وَعَمِلُوا۟ ٱلصَّٰلِحَٰتِ لَيَسْتَخْلِفَنَّهُمْ فِى ٱلْأَرْضِ كَمَا
ٱسْتَخْلَفَ ٱلَّذِينَ مِن قَبْلِهِمْ وَلَيُمَكِّنَنَّ لَهُمْ دِينَهُمُ ٱلَّذِى ٱرْتَضَىٰ لَهُمْ
وَلَيُبَدِّلَنَّهُم مِّنۢ بَعْدِ خَوْفِهِمْ أَمْنًا ۚ يَعْبُدُونَنِى لَا يُشْرِكُونَ بِى شَيْـًٔا ۚ وَمَن كَفَرَ
بَعْدَ ذَٰلِكَ فَأُو۟لَٰٓئِكَ هُمُ ٱلْفَٰسِقُونَ ﴿٥٥﴾ وَأَقِيمُوا۟ ٱلصَّلَوٰةَ وَءَاتُوا۟ ٱلزَّكَوٰةَ

Qul lā tuqsimū; ṭāᶜatum-maᶜrūfah. ᵓInnal-lāha Khabīrum-bimā taᶜmalūn. (53) Qulᵓaṭīᶜul-lāha wa ᵓaṭīᶜur-Rasūla faᵓiñ-tawallaw faᵓinnamā ᶜalayhi mā ḥummila wa ᶜalaykum-mā ḥummiltum wa ᵓiñ-tuṭīᶜūhu tahtadū. Wa mā ᶜalar-Rasūli ᵓillal-balāghul-mubīn. (54) Waᶜadal-lāhul-ladhīna ᵓāmanū miñkum wa ᶜamiluṣ-ṣāliḥāti layastakhlifannahum fil-ᵓarḍi kamas-takhlafal-ladhīna miñ-qablihim wa layumakkinanna lahum dīnahumul-ladhir-taḍā lahum wa layubaddilannahum-mim-baᶜdi khawfihim ᵓamnā. Yaᶜbudūnanī lā yushrikūna bī shayᵓā. Wa mañ-kafara baᶜda dhālika faᵓulāaᵓika humul-fāsiqūn. (55) Wa ᵓaqīmuṣ-Ṣalāta wa ᵓātuz-Zakāta

70 This elliptic phrase alludes to the principle – repeatedly stressed in the Qurᵓān – that God does not burden man with more than he can easily bear.

71 Lit., "cause them to be successors on earth" – i.e., enable them to achieve, in their turn, power and security and, thus, the capability to satisfy their worldly needs. This Qurᵓanic reference to God's "promise" contains an oblique allusion to the God-willed natural law which invariably makes the rise and fall of nations dependent on their moral qualities.

72 Cf. 5 : 3 – "I have willed that self-surrender unto Me (*al-islām*) shall be your religion". Its "firm establishment" (*tamkīn*) relates to the strengthening of the believers' faith as well as to the growth of its moral influence in the world.

73 Lit., "exchange for them, after their fear [or "danger"], security". It is to be noted that the term *amn* signifies not merely outward, physical security but also – and, indeed, originally – "freedom from fear" (*Tāj al-ᶜArūs*). Hence, the above clause implies not only a promise of communal security after an initial period of weakness and danger (which, as history tells us, overshadows the beginnings of every genuine religious movement), but also the promise of an *individual* sense of inner security – that absence of all fear of the Unknown which characterizes a true believer. (See next note.)

74 I.e., the believer's freedom from fear is a direct outcome of his intellectual and emotional refusal to attribute to anyone or anything but God the power to shape his destiny.

75 The specific mention of the "purifying dues" (*az-zakāh*) in this context is meant to stress the element of

and pay heed unto the Apostle, so that you might be graced with God's mercy. «56»
[And] think not that those who are bent on denying the truth can elude [their final reckoning even if they remain unscathed] on earth:[76] the fire is their goal [in the life to come] – and vile indeed is such a journey's end! «57»

O YOU who have attained to faith![77] At three times [of day], let [even] those whom you rightfully possess,[78] as well as those from among you who have not yet attained to puberty,[79] ask leave of you [before intruding upon your privacy]: before the prayer of daybreak, and whenever you lay aside your garments in the middle of the day, and after the prayer of nightfall:[80] the three occasions on which your nakedness is likely to be bared.[81] Beyond these [occasions], neither you nor they will incur any sin if they move [freely] about you, attending to [the needs of] one another.
In this way God makes clear unto you His messages: for God is all-knowing, wise! «58»

وَأَطِيعُوا۟ ٱلرَّسُولَ لَعَلَّكُمْ تُرْحَمُونَ ﴿٥٦﴾ لَا تَحْسَبَنَّ ٱلَّذِينَ كَفَرُوا۟ مُعْجِزِينَ
فِى ٱلْأَرْضِ وَمَأْوَىٰهُمُ ٱلنَّارُ وَلَبِئْسَ ٱلْمَصِيرُ ﴿٥٧﴾ يَٰٓأَيُّهَا ٱلَّذِينَ ءَامَنُوا۟
لِيَسْتَـْٔذِنكُمُ ٱلَّذِينَ مَلَكَتْ أَيْمَٰنُكُمْ وَٱلَّذِينَ لَمْ يَبْلُغُوا۟ ٱلْحُلُمَ مِنكُمْ
ثَلَٰثَ مَرَّٰتٍ مِّن قَبْلِ صَلَوٰةِ ٱلْفَجْرِ وَحِينَ تَضَعُونَ ثِيَابَكُم مِّنَ
ٱلظَّهِيرَةِ وَمِنۢ بَعْدِ صَلَوٰةِ ٱلْعِشَآءِ ثَلَٰثُ عَوْرَٰتٍ لَّكُمْ لَيْسَ عَلَيْكُمْ
وَلَا عَلَيْهِمْ جُنَاحٌۢ بَعْدَهُنَّ طَوَّٰفُونَ عَلَيْكُم بَعْضُكُمْ عَلَىٰ بَعْضٍ كَذَٰلِكَ
يُبَيِّنُ ٱللَّهُ لَكُمُ ٱلْءَايَٰتِ وَٱللَّهُ عَلِيمٌ حَكِيمٌ ﴿٥٨﴾

wa ʾaṭīʿur-Rasūla laʿallakum turḥamūn. (56) Lā taḥsabannal-ladhīna kafarū muʿjizīna fil-ʾarḍi wa maʾwāhumun-nāru wa labiʾsal-maṣīr. (57) Yāa ʾayyuhal-ladhīna ʾāmanū liyastaʾdhiñkumul-ladhīna malakat ʾaymānukum wal-ladhīna lam yablughul-ḥuluma miñkum thalātha marrāt. Miñ-qabli Ṣalātil-fajri wa ḥīna taḍaʿūna thiyābakum-minaẓ-ẓahīrati wa mim-baʿdi Ṣalātil-ʿishāaʾ. Thalāthu ʿawrātil-lakum; laysa ʿalaykum wa lā ʿalayhim junāḥum-baʿdahunna ṭawwāfūna ʿalaykum-baʿḍukum ʿalā baʿḍ. Kadhālika yubayyinul-lāhu lakumul-ʾĀyāt. Wal-lāhu ʿAlīmun Ḥakīm. (58)

unselfishness as an integral aspect of true faith. According to Zamakhsharī, the above verse connects with, and concludes, verse 54.

76 For an explanation of the above sentence and the words interpolated by me, see note 39 on a similar phrase in 11 : 20.

77 In pursuance of the Qurʾanic principle that the social and individual – as well as the spiritual and material – aspects of human life form one indivisible whole and cannot, therefore, be dealt with independently of one another, the discourse returns to the consideration of some of the rules of healthy social behaviour enunciated in the earlier parts of this *sūrah*. The following passage takes up and elaborates the theme of the individual's right to privacy, already touched upon in verses 27-29 above.

78 Lit., "whom your right hands possess" – a phrase which, primarily and as a rule, denotes male and female slaves. Since, however, the institution of slavery is envisaged in the Qurʾān as a mere historic phenomenon that must in time be abolished (cf. notes 46 and 47 on verse 33 of this *sūrah*, as well as note 146 on 2 : 177), the above expression may also be understood as referring, in general, to one's close dependants and to domestic servants of either sex. Alternatively, the phrase *mā malakat aymānukum* may denote, in this context, "those whom you rightfully possess *through wedlock*", i.e., wives and husbands (cf. 4 : 24 and the corresponding note 26).

79 I.e., *all* children, irrespective of whether they are related to one or not.

80 The term *ẓahīrah* (lit., "midday" or, occasionally, "heat of midday"), which occurs in the Qurʾān only in this one instance, may have been used metonymically in the sense of "day-time" as contrasted with the time after the prayer of nightfall and before the prayer of daybreak: hence my tentative rendering as "middle of the day".

81 Lit., "three [periods] of nakedness (*thalāth ʿawrāt*) for you". This phrase is to be understood both literally and figuratively. Primarily, the term *ʿawrah* signifies those parts of a mature person's body which cannot in decency be exposed to any but one's wife or husband or, in case of illness, one's physician. In its tropical sense, it is also used to denote spiritual "nakedness", as well as situations and circumstances in which a person is entitled to absolute privacy. The number "three" used twice in this context is not, of course, enumerative or exclusive, but is obviously meant to stress the *recurrent* nature of the occasions on which even the most familiar members of the household, including husbands, wives and children, must respect that privacy.

Yet when the children among you attain to puberty, let them ask leave of you [at all times], even as those [who have reached maturity] before them have been enjoined to ask it.[82]
In this way God makes clear unto you His messages: for God is all-knowing, wise! «59»

AND[83] [know that] women advanced in years, who no longer feel any sexual desire,[84] incur no sin if they discard their [outer] garments, provided they do not aim at a showy display of [their] charms. But [even so,] it is better for them to abstain [from this]: and God is all-hearing, all-knowing. «60»

[ALL OF YOU, O believers, are brethren:[85] hence,] no blame attaches to the blind, nor does blame attach to the lame, nor does blame attach to the sick [for accepting charity from the hale], and neither to yourselves for eating [whatever is offered to you by others, whether it be food obtained] from your [children's] houses,[86] or your fathers' houses, or your mothers' houses, or your brothers' houses, or your sisters' houses, or your paternal uncles' houses, or your paternal aunts' houses,

وَإِذَا بَلَغَ ٱلْأَطْفَٰلُ مِنكُمُ ٱلْحُلُمَ فَلْيَسْتَـْٔذِنُوا۟ كَمَا ٱسْتَـْٔذَنَ ٱلَّذِينَ مِن قَبْلِهِمْ
كَذَٰلِكَ يُبَيِّنُ ٱللَّهُ لَكُمْ ءَايَٰتِهِۦ ۗ وَٱللَّهُ عَلِيمٌ حَكِيمٌ ﴿٥٩﴾ وَٱلْقَوَٰعِدُ مِنَ ٱلنِّسَآءِ
ٱلَّٰتِى لَا يَرْجُونَ نِكَاحًا فَلَيْسَ عَلَيْهِنَّ جُنَاحٌ أَن يَضَعْنَ ثِيَابَهُنَّ غَيْرَ مُتَبَرِّجَٰتٍۭ
بِزِينَةٍ ۖ وَأَن يَسْتَعْفِفْنَ خَيْرٌ لَّهُنَّ ۗ وَٱللَّهُ سَمِيعٌ عَلِيمٌ ﴿٦٠﴾ لَّيْسَ عَلَى ٱلْأَعْمَىٰ
حَرَجٌ وَلَا عَلَى ٱلْأَعْرَجِ حَرَجٌ وَلَا عَلَى ٱلْمَرِيضِ حَرَجٌ وَلَا عَلَىٰٓ أَنفُسِكُمْ
أَن تَأْكُلُوا۟ مِنۢ بُيُوتِكُمْ أَوْ بُيُوتِ ءَابَآئِكُمْ أَوْ بُيُوتِ أُمَّهَٰتِكُمْ أَوْ بُيُوتِ
إِخْوَٰنِكُمْ أَوْ بُيُوتِ أَخَوَٰتِكُمْ أَوْ بُيُوتِ أَعْمَٰمِكُمْ أَوْ بُيُوتِ عَمَّٰتِكُمْ

Wa ʾidhā balaghal-ʾaṭfālu miñkumul-ḥuluma falyasta ʾdhinū kamas-taʾdhanal-ladhīna miñ-qablihim; kadhālika yubayyinul-lāhu lakum ʾĀyātih. Wal-lāhu ʿAlīmun Ḥakīm. (59) Wal-qawāʿidu minan-nisāaʾil-lātī lā yarjūna nikāḥañ-falaysa ʿalayhinna junāḥun ʾañy-yaḍaʿna thiyābahunna ghayra mutabarrijātim-bizīnatiñw-wa ʾañy-yastaʿfifna khayrul-lahunn. Wal-lāhu Samīʿun ʿAlīm. (60) Laysa ʿalal-ʾaʿmā ḥarajuñw-wa lā ʿalal-ʾaʿraji ḥarajuñw-wa lā ʿalal-marīḍi ḥarajuñw-wa lā ʿalāa ʾañfusikum ʾañ-taʾkulū mim-buyūtikum ʾaw buyūti ʾābāaʾikum ʾaw buyūti ʾummahātikum ʾaw buyūti ʾikhwānikum ʾaw buyūti ʾakhawātikum ʾaw buyūti ʾaʿmāmikum ʾaw buyūti ʿammātikum

82 Lit., "have asked it": a reference to the injunction laid down in verses 27-28 above. My interpolation, between brackets, of the phrase "who have reached maturity" is based on Zamakhsharī's interpretation of the words "those before them".

83 This conjunction is, I believe, meant to indicate that the verse which it introduces is connected with certain previously revealed passages, namely, verse 31 above and 33 : 59, both of which allude to the principle of modesty to be observed by Muslim women in the matter of dress: hence, it must be regarded as a separate "section".

84 Lit., "who do not desire [or "hope for"] sexual intercourse" – the latter evidently being the meaning of *nikāḥ* in this context. Although this noun, as well as the verb from which it is derived, is almost always used in the Qurʾān in the sense of "marriage" or "marrying", there are undoubtedly exceptions from this general rule: for instance, the manner in which the verbal form *yankiḥu* is used in verse 3 of this *sūrah* (see the corresponding note 5 above). These exceptions confirm the view held by some philologists of great renown, e.g., Al-Jawharī or Al-Azharī (the latter quoted in the *Lisān al-ʿArab*), to the effect that "in the speech of the Arabs, the original meaning of *nikāḥ* is sexual intercourse (*al-waṭʾ*)".

85 The whole of verse 61 is construed in so highly elliptic a form that disagreements as to its purport have always been unavoidable. However, if all the explanations offered by the early commentators are taken into consideration, we find that their common denominator is the view that the innermost purport of this passage is a stress on the brotherhood of all believers, expressed in a call to mutual charity, compassion and good-fellowship and, hence, the avoidance of all unnecessary formalities in their mutual relations.

86 In the consensus of all the authorities, the expression "your houses" implies in this context also "your *children's* houses", since all that belongs to a person may be said to belong, morally, to his parents as well.

or your maternal uncles' houses, or your maternal aunts' houses, or [houses] the keys whereof are in your charge,[87] or [the house] of any of your friends; nor will you incur any sin by eating in company or separately. But whenever you enter [any of these] houses, greet one another with a blessed, goodly greeting, as enjoined by God.
In this way God makes clear unto you His messages, so that you might [learn to] use your reason. «61»

[TRUE] BELIEVERS are only they who have attained to faith in God and His Apostle, and who, whenever they are [engaged] with him upon a matter of concern to the whole community,[88] do not depart [from whatever has been decided upon] unless they have sought [and obtained] his leave.[89]
Verily, those who [do not abstain from the agreed-upon action unless they] ask leave of thee – it is [only] they who [truly] believe in God and His Apostle!
Hence, when they ask leave of thee for some [valid] reason of their own, grant thou this leave to whomsoever of them thou choose [to grant it],[90] and ask God to forgive them: for, behold, God is much-forgiving, a dispenser of grace![91] «62»

أَوْ بُيُوتِ أَخْوَٰلِكُمْ أَوْ بُيُوتِ خَـٰلَـٰتِكُمْ أَوْ مَا مَلَكْتُم مَّفَاتِحَهُۥٓ أَوْ
صَدِيقِكُمْ ۚ لَيْسَ عَلَيْكُمْ جُنَاحٌ أَن تَأْكُلُوا۟ جَمِيعًا أَوْ أَشْتَاتًا ۚ فَإِذَا
دَخَلْتُم بُيُوتًا فَسَلِّمُوا۟ عَلَىٰٓ أَنفُسِكُمْ تَحِيَّةً مِّنْ عِندِ ٱللَّهِ مُبَـٰرَكَةً طَيِّبَةً ۚ
كَذَٰلِكَ يُبَيِّنُ ٱللَّهُ لَكُمُ ٱلْـَٔايَـٰتِ لَعَلَّكُمْ تَعْقِلُونَ ﴿٦١﴾ إِنَّمَا ٱلْمُؤْمِنُونَ
ٱلَّذِينَ ءَامَنُوا۟ بِٱللَّهِ وَرَسُولِهِۦ وَإِذَا كَانُوا۟ مَعَهُۥ عَلَىٰٓ أَمْرٍ جَامِعٍ لَّمْ يَذْهَبُوا۟
حَتَّىٰ يَسْتَـْٔذِنُوهُ ۚ إِنَّ ٱلَّذِينَ يَسْتَـْٔذِنُونَكَ أُو۟لَـٰٓئِكَ ٱلَّذِينَ يُؤْمِنُونَ بِٱللَّهِ
وَرَسُولِهِۦ ۚ فَإِذَا ٱسْتَـْٔذَنُوكَ لِبَعْضِ شَأْنِهِمْ فَأْذَن لِّمَن شِئْتَ مِنْهُمْ
وَٱسْتَغْفِرْ لَهُمُ ٱللَّهَ ۚ إِنَّ ٱللَّهَ غَفُورٌ رَّحِيمٌ ﴿٦٢﴾

ʾaw buyūti ʾakhwālikum ʾaw buyūti khālātikum ʾaw mā malaktum-mafātiḥahūu ʾaw ṣadīqikum. Laysa ᶜalaykum junāḥun ʾañ-taʾkulū jamīᶜan ʾaw ʾashtātā. Faʾidhā dakhaltum-buyūtañ-fasallimū ᶜalāa ʾañfusikum taḥiyyatam-min ᶜiñdil-lāhi mubārakatañ-ṭayyibah. Kadhālika yubayyinul-lāhu lakumul-ʾĀyāti laᶜallakum taᶜqilūn. (61) ʾInnamal-muʾminūnal-ladhīna ʾāmanū billāhi wa Rasulihī wa ʾidhā kānū maᶜahū ᶜalāa ʾamriñ-jāmiᶜil-lam yadhhabū ḥattā yastaʾdhinūh. ʾInnal-ladhīna yastaʾdhinūnaka ʾulāaʾikal-ladhīna yuʾminūna billāhi wa Rasūlih. Faʾidhas-taʾdhanūka libaᶜḍi shaʾnihim faʾdhal-limañ-shiʾta minhum was-taghfir lahumul-lāha ʾinnal-lāha Ghafūrur-Raḥīm. (62)

87 I.e., "for which you are responsible".

88 Lit., "a uniting [or "collective"] matter" (*amr jāmiᶜ*). The personal pronoun in "with him" relates to the Apostle and, by analogy, to every legitimate leader (*imām*) of the Muslim community acting in accordance with the spirit of the Qurʾān and the Prophet's life-example.

89 I.e., his permission to abstain, for valid reasons, from participating in a course of action or a policy agreed upon by the majority of the community (*ᶜammā ijtamaᶜū lahu min al-amr*: Ṭabarī). In a logical development of this principle we arrive at something like the concept of a "loyal opposition", which implies the possibility of dissent on a particular point of communal or state policy combined with absolute loyalty to the common cause. (But see also note 91.)

90 I.e., after weighing the reasons advanced by the individual or the individuals concerned against the interests of the society as a whole.

91 The statement that "God is much-forgiving" obviously implies that an *avoidance* of "asking leave" to abstain from participation in an agreed-upon course of action is, under all circumstances, morally preferable (Zamakhsharī).

DO NOT regard the Apostle's summons to you[92] [in the same light] as a summons of one of you to another: God is indeed aware of those of you who would withdraw surreptitiously: so let those who would go against His bidding beware, lest a [bitter] trial befall them [in this world] or grievous suffering befall them [in the life to come]. ⟨63⟩
Oh, verily, unto God belongs all that is in the heavens and on earth: well does He know where you stand and at what you aim![93]
And one Day, all [who have ever lived] will be brought back unto Him, and then He will make them [truly] understand all that they were doing [in life]: for, God has full knowledge of everything. ⟨64⟩

لَّا تَجۡعَلُواْ دُعَآءَ ٱلرَّسُولِ بَيۡنَكُمۡ كَدُعَآءِ بَعۡضِكُم بَعۡضٗاۚ قَدۡ يَعۡلَمُ ٱللَّهُ
ٱلَّذِينَ يَتَسَلَّلُونَ مِنكُمۡ لِوَاذٗاۚ فَلۡيَحۡذَرِ ٱلَّذِينَ يُخَالِفُونَ عَنۡ أَمۡرِهِۦٓ أَن
تُصِيبَهُمۡ فِتۡنَةٌ أَوۡ يُصِيبَهُمۡ عَذَابٌ أَلِيمٌ ﴿٦٣﴾ أَلَآ إِنَّ لِلَّهِ مَا فِي
ٱلسَّمَٰوَٰتِ وَٱلۡأَرۡضِۖ قَدۡ يَعۡلَمُ مَآ أَنتُمۡ عَلَيۡهِ وَيَوۡمَ يُرۡجَعُونَ إِلَيۡهِ
فَيُنَبِّئُهُم بِمَا عَمِلُواْۗ وَٱللَّهُ بِكُلِّ شَيۡءٍ عَلِيمُۢ ﴿٦٤﴾

Lā tajᶜalū duᶜaaʾar-Rasūli baynakum kaduᶜaaʾi baᶜḍikum-baᶜḍā. Qad yaᶜlamul-lāhul-ladhīna yatasallalūna miñkum liwādhā. Falyaḥdharil-ladhīna yukhālifūna ᶜan ʾamrihīi ʾañ-tuṣībahum fitnatun ʾaw yuṣībahum ᶜadhābun ʾalīm. (63) ʾAlāa ʾinna lillāhi mā fis-samāwāti wal-ʾarḍ. Qad yaᶜlamu māa ʾañtum ᶜalayhi wa Yawma yurjaᶜūna ʾilayhi fayunabbiʾuhum-bimā ᶜamilū. Wal-lāhu bikulli shayʾin ᶜAlīm. (64)

92 I.e., his summons to God's message in general, spoken of in verses 46-54 above, as well as to a particular course of communal action, referred to in verse 62. Alternatively, "the Apostle's summons" may, in this context, be synonymous with the Qurʾān itself.

93 Lit., "well does He know upon what you are": i.e., "what your beliefs are and what moral principles govern your attitudes and actions".

The Twenty-Fifth Sūrah

Al-Furqān (The Standard of True and False)

Mecca Period

THERE IS little doubt that this *sūrah* belongs to the middle group of Meccan revelations, and is almost contemporaneous with *Maryam* (which can be placed chronologically in the fifth or the beginning of the sixth year of the Prophet's mission).

The title by which it has always been known – *Al-Furqān* – pithily circumscribes the main theme of this *sūrah*: namely, the statement that it is the innermost purport of every divine revelation to provide man with a stable criterion of true and false or right and wrong and, thus, with a standard of moral valuation binding on the individual and on the society. Consequent upon this proposition is the stress on the *humanness* of every apostle sent by God to man (verse 20), in rebuttal of the false argument that the Qur᾽ān could not have been God-inspired inasmuch as Muḥammad was but a mortal human being who shared the physical needs of all other mortals and took part in all normal human activities (verses 7-8).

By implication, the revelation of the divine writ is shown as belonging to the same majestic order of God's creative activity as all the visible phenomena of nature (see, e.g., verses 2, 45-54, 61-62, etc.). But men do not easily submit to this divine guidance; hence, on the Day of Judgment the Prophet himself will point out that many of his own followers had "come to regard this Qur᾽ān as something [that ought to be] discarded" (verse 30): a statement of particular significance for our time.

سورة الفرقان مكية -25- وآياتها سبع وسبعون

IN THE NAME OF GOD, THE MOST GRACIOUS, THE DISPENSER OF GRACE:

HALLOWED is He who from on high, step by step, has bestowed upon His servant the standard by which to discern the true from the false,[1] so that to all the world it might be a warning: ‹1› He to whom the dominion over the heavens and the earth belongs, and who begets no offspring,[2] and has no partner in His dominion: for it is He who creates every thing and determines its nature in accordance with [His own] design.[3] ‹2›

And yet, some choose to worship, instead of Him, [imaginary] deities that cannot create anything but are themselves created,[4] and have it not within their power to avert harm from, or bring benefit to, themselves, and have no power over death, nor over life, nor over resurrection! ‹3›

Moreover, those who are bent on denying the truth are wont to say, "This [Qur᾽ān] is nothing but a lie which he [himself] has devised with the help of other people,[5] who thereupon have perverted the truth and brought a falsehood into being."[6] ‹4›

بِسْمِ ٱللَّهِ ٱلرَّحْمَـٰنِ ٱلرَّحِيمِ

تَبَارَكَ ٱلَّذِى نَزَّلَ ٱلْفُرْقَانَ عَلَىٰ عَبْدِهِۦ لِيَكُونَ لِلْعَـٰلَمِينَ نَذِيرًا ﴿١﴾ ٱلَّذِى
لَهُۥ مُلْكُ ٱلسَّمَـٰوَٰتِ وَٱلْأَرْضِ وَلَمْ يَتَّخِذْ وَلَدًا وَلَمْ يَكُن لَّهُۥ شَرِيكٌ
فِى ٱلْمُلْكِ وَخَلَقَ كُلَّ شَىْءٍ فَقَدَّرَهُۥ تَقْدِيرًا ﴿٢﴾ وَٱتَّخَذُوا۟ مِن دُونِهِۦٓ
ءَالِهَةً لَّا يَخْلُقُونَ شَيْـًٔا وَهُمْ يُخْلَقُونَ وَلَا يَمْلِكُونَ لِأَنفُسِهِمْ ضَرًّا وَلَا
نَفْعًا وَلَا يَمْلِكُونَ مَوْتًا وَلَا حَيَوٰةً وَلَا نُشُورًا ﴿٣﴾ وَقَالَ ٱلَّذِينَ كَفَرُوٓا۟
إِنْ هَـٰذَآ إِلَّآ إِفْكٌ ٱفْتَرَىٰهُ وَأَعَانَهُۥ عَلَيْهِ قَوْمٌ ءَاخَرُونَ ۖ فَقَدْ جَآءُو ظُلْمًا
وَزُورًا ﴿٤﴾

ثلاثة أرباع الحزب

Bismil-lāhir-Raḥmānir-Raḥīm.
Tabārakal-ladhī nazzalal-Furqāna ᶜalā ᶜabdihī liyakūna lilᶜālamīna nadhīrā. ‹1› ᵓAlladhī lahū mulkus-samāwāti wal-ᵓarḍi wa lam yattakhidh waladañw-wa lam yakul-lahū sharīkuñ-fil-mulki wa khalaqa kulla shayᵓiñ-faqaddarahū taqdīrā. ‹2› Wat-takhadhū miñ-dūnihīi ᵓālihatal-lā yakhluqūna shayᵓañw-wa hum yukhlaqūna wa lā yamlikūna liᵓañfusihim ḍarrañw-wa lā nafᶜañw-wa lā yamlikūna mawtañw-wa lā ḥayātañw-wa lā nushūrā. ‹3› Wa qālal-ladhīna kafarūu ᵓin hādhāa ᵓillāa ᵓifkunif-tarāhu wa ᵓaᶜānahū ᶜalayhi qawmun ᵓākharūna faqad jāaᵓū ẓulmañw-wa zūrā. ‹4›

---

1 Almost all the commentators give this meaning to the term *al-furqān*. In the above context it denotes the Qur᾽ān as well as the phenomenon of divine revelation as such. (For an amplified interpretation of this term by Muḥammad ᶜAbduh, see note 38 on 2 : 53.) The verbal form *nazzala* implies gradualness both in time ("successively") and in method ("step by step").

2 See note 133 on 17 : 111.

3 I.e., in accordance with the function assigned by Him to each individlual thing or phenomenon: cf. the oldest formulation of this idea in 87 : 2-3.

4 I.e., whether they be inanimate "representations" of imaginary deities, or personified forces of nature, or deified human beings, or simply figments of the imagination.

5 Implying that the Qur᾽ān, or most of it, is based on Judaeo-Christian teachings allegedly communicated to Muḥammad by some unnamed foreigners (cf. 16 : 103 and the corresponding notes, especially note 130) or, alternatively, by various Arab converts to Judaism or Christianity; furthermore, that Muḥammad had either deceived himself into believing that the Qur᾽ān was a divine revelation, or had deliberately – knowing that it was not so – attributed it to God.

6 Lit., "and thus, indeed, have they come with [or "brought"] a perversion of the truth" [which obviously is the

And they say, "Fables of ancient times which he has caused to be written down,[7] so that they might be read out to him at morn and evening!" ‹5›
Say [O Muḥammad]: "He who knows all the mysteries of the heavens and the earth has bestowed from on high this [Qurʾān upon me]! Verily, He is much-forgiving, a dispenser of grace!" ‹6›
Yet they say: "What sort of apostle is this [man] who eats food [like all other mortals] and goes about in the market-places? Why has not an angel [visibly] been sent down unto him, to act as a warner together with him?" ‹7› Or: "[Why has not] a treasure been granted to him [by God]?" Or: "He should [at least] have a [bountiful] garden, so that he could eat thereof [without effort]!"[8]
And so these evildoers say [unto one another], "If you were to follow [Muḥammad you would follow] but a man bewitched!" ‹8›
See to what they liken thee, [O Prophet, simply] because they have gone astray and are now unable to find a way [to the truth]! ‹9›
Hallowed is He who, if it be His will, shall give thee something better than that [whereof they speak] – gardens through which running waters flow – and shall assign to thee mansions [of bliss in the life to come]. ‹10›
But nay! It is [the very coming of] the Last Hour to which they give the lie!
However, for such as give the lie to [the announcement of] the Last Hour We have readied a blazing flame: ‹11› when it shall face them from afar,[9] they will hear its angry roar and its hiss; ‹12›

وَقَالُوٓاْ أَسَٰطِيرُ ٱلۡأَوَّلِينَ ٱكۡتَتَبَهَا فَهِيَ تُمۡلَىٰ عَلَيۡهِ بُكۡرَةٗ وَأَصِيلٗا ﴿5﴾
قُلۡ أَنزَلَهُ ٱلَّذِي يَعۡلَمُ ٱلسِّرَّ فِي ٱلسَّمَٰوَٰتِ وَٱلۡأَرۡضِۚ إِنَّهُۥ كَانَ غَفُورٗا
رَّحِيمٗا ﴿6﴾ وَقَالُواْ مَالِ هَٰذَا ٱلرَّسُولِ يَأۡكُلُ ٱلطَّعَامَ وَيَمۡشِي فِي
ٱلۡأَسۡوَاقِ لَوۡلَآ أُنزِلَ إِلَيۡهِ مَلَكٞ فَيَكُونَ مَعَهُۥ نَذِيرًا ﴿7﴾ أَوۡ يُلۡقَىٰٓ إِلَيۡهِ
كَنزٌ أَوۡ تَكُونُ لَهُۥ جَنَّةٞ يَأۡكُلُ مِنۡهَاۚ وَقَالَ ٱلظَّٰلِمُونَ إِن تَتَّبِعُونَ إِلَّا
رَجُلٗا مَّسۡحُورًا ﴿8﴾ ٱنظُرۡ كَيۡفَ ضَرَبُواْ لَكَ ٱلۡأَمۡثَٰلَ فَضَلُّواْ فَلَا
يَسۡتَطِيعُونَ سَبِيلٗا ﴿9﴾ تَبَارَكَ ٱلَّذِيٓ إِن شَآءَ جَعَلَ لَكَ خَيۡرٗا مِّن ذَٰلِكَ
جَنَّٰتٖ تَجۡرِي مِن تَحۡتِهَا ٱلۡأَنۡهَٰرُ وَيَجۡعَل لَّكَ قُصُورَۢا ﴿10﴾ بَلۡ كَذَّبُواْ
بِٱلسَّاعَةِۖ وَأَعۡتَدۡنَا لِمَن كَذَّبَ بِٱلسَّاعَةِ سَعِيرًا ﴿11﴾ إِذَا رَأَتۡهُم مِّن مَّكَانِۭ
بَعِيدٖ سَمِعُواْ لَهَا تَغَيُّظٗا وَزَفِيرٗا ﴿12﴾

Wa qālūu ʾasāṭīrul-ʾawwalīnak-tatabahā fahiya tumlā ʿalayhi bukratañw-wa aṣīlā. ⑤ Qul-ʾañzalahul-ladhī yaʿlamus-sirra fis-samāwāti wal-ʾarḍi ʾinnahū kāna Ghafūrar-Raḥīmā. ⑥ Wa qālū mā lihādhar-Rasūli yaʾkuluṭ-ṭaʿāma wa yamshī fil-ʾaswāqi lawlāa ʾuñzila ʾilayhi malakuñ-fayakūna maʿahū nadhīrā. ⑦ ʾAw yulqāa ʾilayhi kañzun ʾaw takūnu lahū jannatuñy-yaʾkulu minhā. Wa qālaẓ-ẓālimūna ʾiñ-tattabiʿūna ʾillā rajulam-masḥūrā. ⑧ ʾUñẓur kayfa ḍarabū lakal-ʾamthāla faḍallū falā yastaṭīʿūna sabīlā. ⑨ Tabārakal-ladhīi ʾiñ-shāaʾa jaʿala laka khayram-miñ-dhālika jannātiñ-tajrī miñ-taḥtihal-ʾanhāru wa yajʿal laka quṣūrā. ⑩ Bal kadhdhabū bisSāʿati wa ʾaʿtadnā limañ-kadhdhaba bisSāʿati saʿīrā. ⑪ ʾIdhā raʾat-hum-mim-makānim-baʿīdiñ-samiʿū lahā taghayyuẓañw-wa zafīrā. ⑫

meaning of *ẓulm* in this context] "and a falsehood". Whereas it is generally assumed that this clause constitutes a Qurʾanic rebuttal of the malicious allegation expressed in the preceding clause, I am of the opinion that *it forms part of that allegation*, making the mythical "helpers" of Muḥammad co-responsible, as it were, for the "invention" of the Qurʾān.

7 Because it was known to his contemporaries that he was unlettered (*ummī*) and could not read and write.

8 A sarcastic allusion to the "gardens of paradise" of which the Qurʾān so often speaks. (Cf. 13 : 38 and the corresponding notes 74 and 75; also 5 : 75 and 21 : 7-8)

9 Lit., "When it shall see them from a far-off place": a metaphorical allusion, it would seem, to the moment of their

and when they are flung, linked [all] together, into a tight space within, they will pray for extinction there and then![10] ‹13›
[But they will be told:] "Pray not today for one single extinction, but pray for many extinctions!"[11] ‹14›
Say: "Which is better – that, or the paradise of life abiding which has been promised to the God-conscious as their reward and their journey's end ‹15› – on that [paradise] they shall have whatever they may desire, therein to abide – a promise given by thy Sustainer, [always] to be prayed for?" ‹16›

وَإِذَآ أُلۡقُواْ مِنۡهَا مَكَانٗا ضَيِّقٗا مُّقَرَّنِينَ دَعَوۡاْ هُنَالِكَ ثُبُورٗا ﴿13﴾ لَّا تَدۡعُواْ
ٱلۡيَوۡمَ ثُبُورٗا وَٰحِدٗا وَٱدۡعُواْ ثُبُورٗا كَثِيرٗا ﴿14﴾ قُلۡ أَذَٰلِكَ خَيۡرٌ أَمۡ جَنَّةُ
ٱلۡخُلۡدِ ٱلَّتِي وُعِدَ ٱلۡمُتَّقُونَۚ كَانَتۡ لَهُمۡ جَزَآءٗ وَمَصِيرٗا ﴿15﴾ لَّهُمۡ فِيهَا مَا
يَشَآءُونَ خَٰلِدِينَۚ كَانَ عَلَىٰ رَبِّكَ وَعۡدٗا مَّسۡـُٔولٗا ﴿16﴾ وَيَوۡمَ يَحۡشُرُهُمۡ وَمَا
يَعۡبُدُونَ مِن دُونِ ٱللَّهِ فَيَقُولُ ءَأَنتُمۡ أَضۡلَلۡتُمۡ عِبَادِي هَٰٓؤُلَآءِ أَمۡ هُمۡ ضَلُّواْ
ٱلسَّبِيلَ ﴿17﴾ قَالُواْ سُبۡحَٰنَكَ مَا كَانَ يَنۢبَغِي لَنَآ أَن نَّتَّخِذَ مِن دُونِكَ مِنۡ
أَوۡلِيَآءَ وَلَٰكِن مَّتَّعۡتَهُمۡ وَءَابَآءَهُمۡ حَتَّىٰ نَسُواْ ٱلذِّكۡرَ وَكَانُواْ قَوۡمَۢا
بُورٗا ﴿18﴾

BUT [as for people who are oblivious of thy Sustainer's oneness[12] –] one Day He will gather them together with all that they [now] worship instead of God, and will ask [those to whom divinity was falsely ascribed[13]]: "Was it you who led these My creatures astray, or did they by themselves stray from the right path?" ‹17›
They will answer: "Limitless art Thou in Thy glory! It was inconceivable for us to take for our masters anyone but Thyself![14] But [as for them –] Thou didst allow them and their forefathers to enjoy [the pleasures of] life to such an extent that[15] they forgot all remembrance [of Thee]: for they were people devoid of all good." ‹18›

Wa ʾidhāa ʾulqū minhā makānañ-ḍayyiqam-muqarranīna daʿaw hunālika thubūrā. (13) Lā tadʿul-yawma thubūrañw-wāḥidañw-wadʿū thubūrañ-kathīrā. (14) Qul ʾadhālika khayrun ʾam jannatul-khuldil-latī wuʿidal-muttaqūn. Kānat lahum jazāaʾañw-wa maṣīrā. (15) Lahum fīhā mā yashāaʾūna khālidīna kāna ʿalā Rabbika waʿdam-masʾūlā. (16) Wa Yawma yaḥshuruhum wa mā yaʿbudūna miñ-dūnil-lāhi fayaqūlu ʾaʾañtum ʾaḍlaltum ʿibādī hāaʾulāaʾi ʾam hum ḍallus-sabīl. (17) Qālū subḥānaka mā kāna yambaghī lanāa ʾañ-nattakhidha miñ-dūnika min ʾawliyāaʾa wa lākim-mattaʿtahum wa ʾābāaʾahum ḥattā nasudh-Dhikra wa kānū qawmam-būrā. (18)

death on earth. As in many other instances, we are given here a subtle verbal hint of the allegorical nature of the Qurʾanic descriptions of conditions in the life to come by a rhetorical "transfer" of man's faculty of seeing to the *object* of his seeing: a usage which Zamakhsharī explicitly characterizes as metaphorical (*ʿalā sabīl al-majāz*).

10 For a tentative explanation of the allegory of the sinners' being "linked together" in hell, see my note 64 on 14 : 49. As regards the "tight space" into which they will be flung, Zamakhsharī remarks: "Distress is accompanied by [a feeling of] constriction, just as happiness is accompanied by [a feeling of] spaciousness; and because of this, God has described paradise as being 'as vast as the heavens and the earth' [3 : 133]."

11 Although the concept of "extinction" (*thubūr*) implies finality and is, therefore, unrepeatable, the sinners' praying for "many extinctions" is used here as a metonym for their indescribable suffering and a corresponding, indescribable desire for a final escape.

12 This passage connects elliptically with verse 3 above.

13 The rhetorical "question" which follows is obviously addressed to wrongfully deified rational beings – i.e., prophets or saints – and not, as some commentators assume, to lifeless idols which, as it were, "will be made to speak".

14 Sc., "and so it would have been morally impossible for us to ask others to worship *us*". On the other hand, Ibn Kathīr understands the expression "for us" (*lanā*) as denoting "us human beings" in general, and not merely the speakers – in which case the sentence could be rendered thus: "It is not right for us [human beings] to take . . .", etc. In either case, the above allegorical "question-and-answer" – repeated in many variations throughout the Qurʾān – is meant to stress, in a dramatic manner, the moral odiousness and intellectual futility of attributing divine qualities to any being other than God.

15 This is the meaning of *ḥattā* (lit., "till" or "until") in the present context.

[Thereupon God will say:] "And now, they [whom you regarded as divine] have given the lie to all your [past] assertions, and you can neither ward off [your punishment] nor obtain any succour! For, whoever of you has committed [such] evil, him shall We cause to taste great suffering!" ‹19›

حزب 37
جزء 19

AND [even] before thee, [O Muḥammad,] We never sent as Our message-bearers any but [mortal men,] who indeed ate food [like other human beings] and went about in the market-places: for [it is thus that] We cause you [human beings] to be a means of testing one another.[16]
Are you[17] able to endure [this test] with patience? For [remember, O man,] thy Sustainer is truly all-seeing! ‹20›
But those who do not believe that they are destined to meet Us[18] are wont to say, "Why have no angels been sent down to us?" – or, "Why do we not see our Sustainer?
Indeed, they are far too proud of themselves, having rebelled [against God's truth] with utter disdain! ‹21›
[Yet] on that Day – the Day on which they shall see the angels[19] – there will be no glad tiding for those who were lost in sin; and they will exclaim, "By a forbidding ban [are we from God's grace debarred]!" ‹22› – for We shall have turned towards all the [supposedly good] deeds they ever wrought, and shall have transformed them into scattered dust ‹23› –

فَقَدْ كَذَّبُوكُم بِمَا تَقُولُونَ فَمَا تَسْتَطِيعُونَ صَرْفًا وَلَا نَصْرًا ۚ وَمَن يَظْلِم
مِّنكُمْ نُذِقْهُ عَذَابًا كَبِيرًا ﴿19﴾ وَمَآ أَرْسَلْنَا قَبْلَكَ مِنَ ٱلْمُرْسَلِينَ إِلَّآ
إِنَّهُمْ لَيَأْكُلُونَ ٱلطَّعَامَ وَيَمْشُونَ فِى ٱلْأَسْوَاقِ ۗ وَجَعَلْنَا بَعْضَكُمْ لِبَعْضٍ
فِتْنَةً أَتَصْبِرُونَ ۗ وَكَانَ رَبُّكَ بَصِيرًا ﴿20﴾ ۞ وَقَالَ ٱلَّذِينَ لَا يَرْجُونَ
لِقَآءَنَا لَوْلَآ أُنزِلَ عَلَيْنَا ٱلْمَلَٰٓئِكَةُ أَوْ نَرَىٰ رَبَّنَا ۗ لَقَدِ ٱسْتَكْبَرُوا۟ فِىٓ
أَنفُسِهِمْ وَعَتَوْ عُتُوًّا كَبِيرًا ﴿21﴾ يَوْمَ يَرَوْنَ ٱلْمَلَٰٓئِكَةَ لَا بُشْرَىٰ يَوْمَئِذٍ
لِّلْمُجْرِمِينَ وَيَقُولُونَ حِجْرًا مَّحْجُورًا ﴿22﴾ وَقَدِمْنَآ إِلَىٰ مَا عَمِلُوا۟ مِنْ عَمَلٍ
فَجَعَلْنَٰهُ هَبَآءً مَّنثُورًا ﴿23﴾

Faqad kadhdhabūkum-bimā taqūlūna famā tas-
taṭīᶜūna ṣarfañw-wa lā naṣrā. Wa mañy-yaẓlim-
miñkum nudhiqhu ᶜadhābañ-kabīrā. (19) Wa māa
ᵓarsalnā qablaka minal-Mursalīna ᵓillāa ᵓinnahum
layaᵓkulūnaṭ-ṭaᶜāma wa yamshūna fil-ᵓaswāq. Wa
jaᶜalnā baᶜḍakum libaᶜḍiñ-fitnatan ᵓataṣbirūn. Wa
kāna Rabbuka Baṣīrā. (20) ۞ Wa qālal-ladhīna lā
yarjūna liqāaᵓanā lawlāa ᵓuñzila ᶜalaynal-
Malāaᵓikatu ᵓaw narā Rabbanā. Laqadis-takbarū fīi
ᵓañfusihim wa ᶜataw ᶜutuwwañ-kabīrā. (21) Yawma
yarawnal-Malāaᵓikata lā bushrā Yawmaᵓidhil-
lilmujrimīna wa yaqūlūna ḥijram-maḥjūrā. (22) Wa
qadimnāa ᵓilā mā ᶜamilū min ᶜamaliñ-fajaᶜalnāhu
habāaᵓam-mañthūrā. (23)

16 This elliptic passage undoubtedly alludes to the fact that the appearance of each new prophet had, as a rule, a twofold purpose: firstly, to convey a divinely-inspired ethical message to man, and thus to establish a criterion of right and wrong or a standard by which to discern the true from the false (*al-furqān*, as stated in the first verse of this *sūrah*); and, secondly, to be a means of testing men's moral perceptions and dispositions as manifested in their reactions to the prophet's message – that is, their willingness or unwillingness to accept it on the basis of its intrinsic merit, without demanding or even expecting any "supernatural" proof of its divine origin. Indirectly, in its deepest sense, this passage implies that not only a prophet but every human being is, by virtue of his social existence, a means whereby the moral qualities of his fellow-men are put to a test: hence, some of the earliest commentators (among them Ṭabarī) give to the above phrase the connotation of "We caused you *human beings* to be a means of testing one another".

17 I.e., "you men" or, more specifically, "you whom the message of the Qurᵓān has reached".

18 Lit., "who do not hope for [i.e., expect] a meeting with Us": the implication being that they do not believe in resurrection and, consequently, do not expect to be judged by God in after-life.

19 I.e., on Judgment Day, when "all will have been decided" (cf. 6 : 8).

[whereas] on that same Day those who are destined for paradise will be graced with the best of abodes and the fairest place of repose.[20] ‹24›
And on the Day on which the skies, together with the clouds, shall burst asunder, and the angels are made to descend in a mighty descent ‹25› – on that Day [it will become obvious to all that] true sovereignty belongs to the Most Gracious [alone]: hence, a Day of distress will it be for all who deny the truth, ‹26› and a Day on which the evildoer will bite his hands [in despair], exclaiming: "Oh, would that I had followed the path shown to me by the apostle![21] ‹27› Oh, woe is me! Would that I had not taken so-and-so for a friend! ‹28› Indeed, he led me astray from the remembrance [of God] after it had come unto me!"
For [thus it is:] Satan is ever a betrayer of man.[22] ‹29›

AND [on that Day] the Apostle will say:[23] "O my Sustainer! Behold, [some of] my people have come to regard this Qur'ān as something [that ought to be] discarded!"[24] ‹30›
For so it is that against every prophet We have set up enemies from among those who are lost in sin:[25] yet none can guide and give succour as thy Sustainer does! ‹31›

أَصْحَٰبُ ٱلْجَنَّةِ يَوْمَئِذٍ خَيْرٌ مُّسْتَقَرًّا وَأَحْسَنُ مَقِيلًا ﴿٢٤﴾ وَيَوْمَ تَشَقَّقُ
ٱلسَّمَآءُ بِٱلْغَمَٰمِ وَنُزِّلَ ٱلْمَلَٰٓئِكَةُ تَنزِيلًا ﴿٢٥﴾ ٱلْمُلْكُ يَوْمَئِذٍ ٱلْحَقُّ
لِلرَّحْمَٰنِ وَكَانَ يَوْمًا عَلَى ٱلْكَٰفِرِينَ عَسِيرًا ﴿٢٦﴾ وَيَوْمَ يَعَضُّ ٱلظَّالِمُ
عَلَىٰ يَدَيْهِ يَقُولُ يَٰلَيْتَنِى ٱتَّخَذْتُ مَعَ ٱلرَّسُولِ سَبِيلًا ﴿٢٧﴾ يَٰوَيْلَتَىٰ لَيْتَنِى
لَمْ أَتَّخِذْ فُلَانًا خَلِيلًا ﴿٢٨﴾ لَّقَدْ أَضَلَّنِى عَنِ ٱلذِّكْرِ بَعْدَ إِذْ جَآءَنِى ۗ وَكَانَ
ٱلشَّيْطَٰنُ لِلْإِنسَٰنِ خَذُولًا ﴿٢٩﴾ وَقَالَ ٱلرَّسُولُ يَٰرَبِّ إِنَّ قَوْمِى ٱتَّخَذُوا۟
هَٰذَا ٱلْقُرْءَانَ مَهْجُورًا ﴿٣٠﴾ وَكَذَٰلِكَ جَعَلْنَا لِكُلِّ نَبِىٍّ عَدُوًّا مِّنَ
ٱلْمُجْرِمِينَ ۗ وَكَفَىٰ بِرَبِّكَ هَادِيًا وَنَصِيرًا ﴿٣١﴾

'Aṣḥābul-jannati Yawma'idhin khayrum-mustaqarrañw-wa 'aḥsanu maqīlā. (24) Wa Yawma tashaqqaqus-samāa'u bilghamāmi wa nuzzilal-Malāa'ikatu tañzīlā. (25) 'Almulku Yawma'idhinil-ḥaqqu lir-Raḥmāni wa kāna yawman ʿalal-kāfirīna ʿasīrā. (26) Wa Yawma yaʿaḍḍuẓ-ẓālimu ʿalā yadayhi yaqūlu yālaytanit-takhadhtu maʿar-Rasūli sabīlā. (27) Yā waylatā laytanī lam 'attakhidh fulānan khalīlā. (28) Laqad 'aḍallanī ʿanidh-Dhikri baʿda 'idh jāa'anī. Wa kānash-Shayṭānu lil'Iñsāni khadhūlā. (29) Wa qālar-Rasūlu yā Rabbi 'inna qawmit-takhadhū hādhal-Qur'āna mahjūrā. (30) Wa kadhālika jaʿalnā likulli Nabiyyin ʿaduwwam-minal-mujrimīn. Wa kafā biRabbika Hādiyañw-wa Naṣīrā. (31)

20 Lit., "will be happiest as regards their abode, and best as regards their place of repose".

21 Lit., "taken a path with the apostle". The terms "the apostle" and "the evildoer" are here obviously used in their generic sense, applying to all of God's apostles and all who consciously reject their guidance. Similarly, the expression "so-and-so" (*fulān*) occurring in the next verse circumscribes any person or personified influence responsible for leading a human being astray.

22 For the implication of the term "Satan" as used here, see note 10 on 2 : 14, first half of note 16 on 15 : 17, as well as note 31 on 14 : 22.

23 My interpolation of the words "on that Day" and the (linguistically permissible) attribution of futurity to the past-tense verb *qāla* is based on the identical interpretation of the above phrase by great commentators like Abū Muslim (as quoted by Rāzī) or Baghawī.

24 I.e., as mere wishful thinking and, therefore, of no account, or as something that in the course of time has "ceased to be relevant". Since many of those whom the message of the Qur'ān has reached did and do regard it as a divine revelation and therefore as most "relevant" in every sense of the word, it is obvious that the expression "my people" cannot possibly denote here *all* of the Prophet's community (either in the national or in the ideological sense of this word), but signifies only such of his nominal followers as have lost all real faith in the Qur'anic message: hence the necessity of interpolating the (elliptically implied) words "some of" before "my people".

25 Cf. 6 : 112, which refers in very similar terms to the evil forces (*shayāṭīn*) against which every prophet has had to contend. The "glittering half-truths meant to delude the mind" spoken of in that verse are exemplified in the present

Now they who are bent on denying the truth are wont to ask, "Why has not the Qurʾān been bestowed on him from on high in one single revelation?"[26]
[It has been revealed] in this manner so that We might strengthen thy heart thereby – for We have so arranged its component parts that they form one consistent whole[27] ‹32› – and [that] they [who deny the truth] might never taunt thee with any deceptive half-truth[28] without Our conveying to thee the [full] truth and [providing thee] with the best explanation.[29] ‹33›
[And so, tell those who are bent on denying the truth that] they who shall be gathered unto hell upon their faces[30] – it is they who [in the life to come] will be worst in station and still farther astray from the path [of truth]![31] ‹34›

AND, INDEED, [long before Muḥammad] We vouchsafed revelation unto Moses, and appointed his brother Aaron to help him to bear his burden;[32] ‹35› and We said, "Go you both unto the people who have given the lie to Our messages!" – and thereupon We broke those [sinners] to smithereens. ‹36›

وَقَالَ ٱلَّذِينَ كَفَرُوا۟ لَوْلَا نُزِّلَ عَلَيْهِ ٱلْقُرْءَانُ جُمْلَةً وَٰحِدَةً ۚ كَذَٰلِكَ
لِنُثَبِّتَ بِهِۦ فُؤَادَكَ ۖ وَرَتَّلْنَٰهُ تَرْتِيلًا ﴿٣٢﴾ وَلَا يَأْتُونَكَ بِمَثَلٍ إِلَّا جِئْنَٰكَ
بِٱلْحَقِّ وَأَحْسَنَ تَفْسِيرًا ﴿٣٣﴾ ٱلَّذِينَ يُحْشَرُونَ عَلَىٰ وُجُوهِهِمْ إِلَىٰ جَهَنَّمَ
أُو۟لَٰٓئِكَ شَرٌّ مَّكَانًا وَأَضَلُّ سَبِيلًا ﴿٣٤﴾ وَلَقَدْ ءَاتَيْنَا مُوسَى ٱلْكِتَٰبَ
وَجَعَلْنَا مَعَهُۥٓ أَخَاهُ هَٰرُونَ وَزِيرًا ﴿٣٥﴾ فَقُلْنَا ٱذْهَبَآ إِلَى ٱلْقَوْمِ ٱلَّذِينَ
كَذَّبُوا۟ بِـَٔايَٰتِنَا فَدَمَّرْنَٰهُمْ تَدْمِيرًا ﴿٣٦﴾

Wa qālal-ladhīna kafarū lawlā nuzzila ʿalayhil-Qurʾānu jumlatañw-wāḥidah. Kadhālika linuthabbita bihī fuʾādaka wa rattalnāhu tartīlā. (32) Wa lā yaʾtūnaka bimathalin ʾillā jiʾnāka bil-ḥaqqi wa ʾaḥsana tafsīrā. (33) ʾAlladhīna yuḥsharūna ʿalā wujūhihim ʾilā jahannama ʾulāaʾika sharrum-makānañw-wa ʾaḍallu sabīlā. (34) Wa laqad ʾātaynā Mūsal-Kitāba wa jaʿalnā maʿahūu ʾakhāhu Hārūna wazīrā. (35) Faqulnadh-habāa ʾilal-qawmil-ladhīna kadhdhabū biʾĀyātinā fadammarnāhum tadmīrā. (36)

passage, prophetically, by the deceptive argument that the Qurʾān, having been enunciated fourteen centuries ago, must now be considered "obsolete".

26 Lit., "in one piece" or "as one statement" (*jumlatan wāḥidatan*) – implying, in the view of the opponents of Islam, that the gradual, step-by-step revelation of the Qurʾān points to its having been "composed" by Muḥammad to suit his changing personal and political requirements.

27 I.e., free of all inner contradictions (cf. 4 : 82). See also 39 : 23, where the Qurʾān is spoken of as "fully consistent within itself". The concise phrase *rattalnāhu tartīlan* comprises the parallel concepts of "putting the component parts [of a thing] together and arranging them well" as well as "endowing it with inner consistency". Inasmuch as full consistency and freedom from contradictions in a message spread over twenty-three years of a life as full of movement and drama as that of the Prophet does give a clear indication of its God-inspired quality, it is bound to strengthen the faith of every thinking believer: and herein lies, according to the Qurʾān itself, the deepest reason for its slow, gradual revelation. (When applied to the *reciting* of the Qurʾān – as in 73 : 4 – the term *tartīl* refers to the measured diction and the thoughtful manner in which it ought to be enunciated.)

28 Lit., "come to thee with a parable (*mathal*)" – i.e., with all manner of seemingly plausible parabolic objections (exemplified in verses 7-8, 21 and 32 of this *sūrah* as well as in many other places in the Qur'ān) meant to throw doubt on Muḥammad's claim to prophethood and, hence, on the God-inspired character of the Qurʾanic message.

29 Sc., "of the problem or problems involved": an allusion to the self-explanatory character of the Qurʾān. Throughout this section (verses 30-34) the personal pronoun "thou" (in the forms "thy" and "thee") relates not only to the Prophet but also to every one of his followers at all times.

30 I.e., in utter spiritual abasement (Rāzī, mentioning some other commentators as well).

31 Cf. 17 : 72 and the corresponding note 87.

32 For this rendering of the term *wazīr*, see note 18 on 20 : 29. The mention, at this place, of Moses and Aaron – and of Noah, etc., in the following verses – is intended to remind us of the statement in verse 31 above that "against every prophet We have set up enemies from among those who are lost in sin".

And [think of] the people of Noah: when they gave the lie to [one of] the apostles, We caused them to drown, and made them a symbol for all mankind: for, grievous suffering have We readied for all who [knowingly] do wrong! ‹37›

And [remember how We punished the tribes of] ᶜĀd and Thamūd, and the people of Ar-Rass,[33] and many generations [of sinners] in-between: ‹38› and unto each of them did We proffer lessons,[34] and each of them did We destroy with utter destruction. ‹39›

And they [who now deny Our messages] must surely have come across that town which was rained upon by a rain of evil:[35] have they, then, never beheld it [with their mind's eye]? But nay, they would not believe in resurrection![36] ‹40›

Hence, whenever they consider thee, [O Muḥammad,] they but make thee a target of their mockery, [saying:] "Is this the one whom God has sent as an apostle? ‹41› Indeed, he would well-nigh have led us astray from our deities, had we not been [so] steadfastly attached to them!"

But in time, when they see the suffering [that awaits them], they will come to know who it was that went farthest astray from the path [of truth]! ‹42›

Hast thou ever considered [the kind of man] who makes his own desires his deity? Couldst thou, then, [O Prophet,] be held responsible for him? ‹43› Or dost thou think that most of them listen [to thy

وَقَوْمَ نُوحٍ لَّمَّا كَذَّبُوا۟ ٱلرُّسُلَ أَغْرَقْنَـٰهُمْ وَجَعَلْنَـٰهُمْ لِلنَّاسِ ءَايَةً ۖ وَأَعْتَدْنَا
لِلظَّـٰلِمِينَ عَذَابًا أَلِيمًا (37) وَعَادًا وَثَمُودَا۟ وَأَصْحَـٰبَ ٱلرَّسِّ وَقُرُونًۢا بَيْنَ
ذَٰلِكَ كَثِيرًا (38) وَكُلًّا ضَرَبْنَا لَهُ ٱلْأَمْثَـٰلَ ۖ وَكُلًّا تَبَّرْنَا تَتْبِيرًا (39) وَلَقَدْ
أَتَوْا۟ عَلَى ٱلْقَرْيَةِ ٱلَّتِىٓ أُمْطِرَتْ مَطَرَ ٱلسَّوْءِ ۚ أَفَلَمْ يَكُونُوا۟ يَرَوْنَهَا ۚ بَلْ كَانُوا۟
لَا يَرْجُونَ نُشُورًا (40) وَإِذَا رَأَوْكَ إِن يَتَّخِذُونَكَ إِلَّا هُزُوًا أَهَـٰذَا ٱلَّذِى
بَعَثَ ٱللَّهُ رَسُولًا (41) إِن كَادَ لَيُضِلُّنَا عَنْ ءَالِهَتِنَا لَوْلَآ أَن صَبَرْنَا عَلَيْهَا
وَسَوْفَ يَعْلَمُونَ حِينَ يَرَوْنَ ٱلْعَذَابَ مَنْ أَضَلُّ سَبِيلًا (42) أَرَءَيْتَ مَنِ ٱتَّخَذَ
إِلَـٰهَهُۥ هَوَىٰهُ أَفَأَنتَ تَكُونُ عَلَيْهِ وَكِيلًا (43) أَمْ تَحْسَبُ أَنَّ أَكْثَرَهُمْ يَسْمَعُونَ

Wa qawma Nūḥil-lammā kadhdhabur-Rusula ʾaghraqnāhum wa jaᶜalnāhum linnāsi ʾĀyatañw-wa ʾaᶜtadnā liẓẓālimīna ᶜadhāban ʾalīmā. (37) Wa ᶜĀdañw-wa Thamūda wa ʾAṣḥābar-Rassi wa qurūnam-bayna dhālika kathīrā. (38) Wa kullañ-ḍarabnā lahul-ʾamthāla wa kullañ-tabbarnā tatbīrā. (39) Wa laqad ʾataw ᶜalal-qaryatil-latīi ʾumṭirat maṭaras-sawʾi ʾafalam yakūnū yarawnahā. Bal kānū lā yarjūna nushūrā. (40) Wa ʾidhā raʾawka ʾiñy-yattakhidhūnaka ʾillā huzuwan ʾahādhal-ladhī baᶜathal-lāhu Rasūlā. (41) ʾIñ-kāda layuḍillunā ᶜan ʾālihatinā lawlāa ʾañ-ṣabarnā ᶜalayhā. Wa sawfa yaᶜlamūna ḥīna yarawnal-ᶜadhāba man ʾaḍallu sabīlā. (42) ʾAraʾayta manit-takhadha ʾilāhahū hawāhu ʾafaʾañta takūnu ᶜalayhi wakīlā. (43) ʾAm taḥsabu ʾanna ʾaktharahum yasmaᶜūna

33 Regarding the tribes of ᶜĀd and Thamūd, see *sūrah* 7, notes 48 and 56. As for Ar-Rass, a town of that name exists to this day in the Central-Arabian province of Al-Qaṣīm; in the ancient times referred to it seems to have been inhabited by descendants of the Nabataean tribe of Thamūd (Ṭabarī). There is, however, no agreement among the commentators as to the real meaning of this name or designation; Rāzī cites several of the current, conflicting interpretations and rejects all of them as purely conjectural.

34 Sc., "which they failed to heed". For my rendering of *mathal*, in this context, as "lesson", see note 104 on 17 : 89.

35 A reference to Sodom and its destruction by a rain of "stone-hard blows of chastisement pre-ordained" (see 11 : 82 and the corresponding note 114). The phrase "they have come across" may be understood in either of two ways: (a) in its literal sense of "chancing upon" or "passing by", in which case it applies to the Prophet's contemporaries and opponents, the pagan Meccans, whose customary caravan route to Syria passed close by the Dead Sea and the probable site of Sodom and Gomorrah; or (b) in the tropical sense of "becoming aware [of something]" through reading or hearsay – in which case it may be taken to refer to people of all times, and to the fact that the story of Sodom and Gomorrah is part and parcel of mankind's moral heritage.

36 Lit., "they were wont not to look forward to [i.e., to expect or believe in] resurrection".

message] and use their reason? Nay, they are but like cattle – nay, they are even less conscious of the right way![37] ‹44›

ART THOU NOT aware of thy Sustainer [through His works]? – how He causes the shadow to lengthen [towards the night] when, had He so willed, He could indeed have made it stand still: but then, We have made the sun its guide; ‹45› and then, [after having caused it to lengthen,] We draw it in towards Ourselves[38] with a gradual drawing-in. ‹46›

And He it is who makes the night a garment for you, and [your] sleep a rest, and causes every [new] day to be a resurrection. ‹47›

And He it is who sends forth the winds as a glad tiding of His coming grace; and [thus, too,] We cause pure water to descend from the skies, ‹48› so that We may bring dead land to life thereby, and give to drink thereof to many [beings] of Our creation, beasts as well as humans. ‹49›

And, indeed, many times have We repeated [all] this unto men,[39] so that they might take it to heart: but most men refuse to be aught but ingrate. ‹50›

Now had We so willed, We could have [continued as before and] raised up a [separate] warner in every single community:[40] ‹51› hence, do not defer to [the likes and dislikes of] those who deny the truth, but strive hard against them, by means of this [divine writ], with utmost striving. ‹52›

أَوْ يَعْقِلُونَ ۚ إِنْ هُمْ إِلَّا كَٱلْأَنْعَٰمِ ۖ بَلْ هُمْ أَضَلُّ سَبِيلًا ﴿٤٤﴾ أَلَمْ تَرَ إِلَىٰ
رَبِّكَ كَيْفَ مَدَّ ٱلظِّلَّ وَلَوْ شَآءَ لَجَعَلَهُۥ سَاكِنًا ثُمَّ جَعَلْنَا ٱلشَّمْسَ عَلَيْهِ
دَلِيلًا ﴿٤٥﴾ ثُمَّ قَبَضْنَٰهُ إِلَيْنَا قَبْضًا يَسِيرًا ﴿٤٦﴾ وَهُوَ ٱلَّذِى جَعَلَ لَكُمُ
ٱلَّيْلَ لِبَاسًا وَٱلنَّوْمَ سُبَاتًا وَجَعَلَ ٱلنَّهَارَ نُشُورًا ﴿٤٧﴾ وَهُوَ ٱلَّذِىٓ أَرْسَلَ
ٱلرِّيَٰحَ بُشْرًۢا بَيْنَ يَدَىْ رَحْمَتِهِۦ ۚ وَأَنزَلْنَا مِنَ ٱلسَّمَآءِ مَآءً طَهُورًا ﴿٤٨﴾
لِّنُحْـِۧىَ بِهِۦ بَلْدَةً مَّيْتًا وَنُسْقِيَهُۥ مِمَّا خَلَقْنَآ أَنْعَٰمًا وَأَنَاسِىَّ كَثِيرًا ﴿٤٩﴾
وَلَقَدْ صَرَّفْنَٰهُ بَيْنَهُمْ لِيَذَّكَّرُوا۟ فَأَبَىٰٓ أَكْثَرُ ٱلنَّاسِ إِلَّا كُفُورًا ﴿٥٠﴾ وَلَوْ
شِئْنَا لَبَعَثْنَا فِى كُلِّ قَرْيَةٍ نَّذِيرًا ﴿٥١﴾ فَلَا تُطِعِ ٱلْكَٰفِرِينَ وَجَٰهِدْهُم بِهِۦ
جِهَادًا كَبِيرًا ﴿٥٢﴾

ʾaw yaʿqilūn. ʾIn hum ʾillā kalʾanʿāmi bal hum ʾaḍallu sabīlā. (44) ʾAlam tara ʾilā Rabbika kayfa maddaẓ-ẓilla wa law shāaʾa lajaʿalahū sākinañ-thumma jaʿalnash-shamsa ʿalayhi dalīlā. (45) Thumma qabaḍ-nāhu ʾilaynā qabḍañy-yasīrā. (46) Wa Huwal-ladhī jaʿala lakumul-layla libāsañw-wan-nawma subātañw-wa jaʿalan-nahāra nushūrā. (47) Wa Huwal-ladhīi ʾarsalar-riyāḥa bushram-bayna yaday raḥmatihī wa ʾañzalnā minas-samāaʾi māaʾañ-ṭahūrā. (48) Linuḥyiya bihī baldatam-maytañw-wa nusqiyahū mimmā khalaqnāa ʾanʿāmañw-wa ʾanāsiyya kathīrā. (49) Wa laqad ṣarrafnāhu baynahum liyadhdhakkarū faʾabāa ʾaktharun-nāsi ʾillā kufūrā. (50) Wa law shiʾnā laba-ʿathnā fī kulli qaryatiñ-nadhīrā. (51) Falā tuṭiʿil-kā-firīna wa jāhid-hum-bihī jihādañ-kabīrā. (52)

37 Lit., "they are farther astray from the path [of truth]": see note 144 on 7 : 179.

38 I.e., "We cause it to contract in accordance with the 'laws of nature' which We Ourselves have instituted." As in so many other instances in the Qurʾān, the abrupt change from the third-person pronoun "He" to "We" is meant to illustrate the fact that God is undefinable, and that it is only the inadequacy of human speech – and, hence, of the human mind – that makes it necessary to refer to the Supreme Being by pronouns which in reality are applicable only to finite, created "persons" (cf. Foreword, note 2).

39 Lit., "have We turned it over (*ṣarrafnāhu*) among them": a reference to the frequent, many-faceted reiteration, in the Qurʾān as well as in earlier revelations, of all the evidence unmistakably pointing to the existence of a conscious Creator (Zamakhsharī).

40 Sc., "but We have willed instead that Muḥammad be Our last prophet and, hence, a warner unto all people for all times to come".

AND HE it is who has given freedom of movement to the two great bodies of water[41] – the one sweet and thirst-allaying, and the other salty and bitter – and yet has wrought between them a barrier and a forbidding ban.[42] ‹53›
And He it is who out of this [very] water has created man,[43] and has endowed him with [the consciousness of] descent and marriage-tie:[44] for thy Sustainer is ever infinite in His power. ‹54›
And yet, some people[45] worship, instead of God, things that can neither benefit them nor harm them: thus, he who denies the truth does indeed turn his back on his Sustainer! ‹55›
Yet [withal, O Prophet,] We have sent thee only as a herald of glad tidings and a warner. ‹56› Say: "For this, no reward do I ask of you [– no reward] other than that he who so wills may unto his Sustainer find a way!" ‹57›
Hence, place thy trust in the Living One who dies not, and extol His limitless glory and praise: for none is as aware of His creatures' sins as He ‹58› – He who has created the heavens and the earth and all that is between them in six aeons, and is established on the throne of His almightiness:[46] the Most Gracious! Ask, then, about Him, [the] One who is [truly] aware.[47] ‹59›
Yet when they [who are bent on denying the truth] are told, "Prostrate yourselves before the Most Gracious," they are wont to ask,

۞ وَهُوَ ٱلَّذِى مَرَجَ ٱلْبَحْرَيْنِ هَٰذَا عَذْبٌ فُرَاتٌ وَهَٰذَا مِلْحٌ أُجَاجٌ
وَجَعَلَ بَيْنَهُمَا بَرْزَخًا وَحِجْرًا مَّحْجُورًا ﴿٥٣﴾ وَهُوَ ٱلَّذِى خَلَقَ مِنَ ٱلْمَآءِ
بَشَرًا فَجَعَلَهُۥ نَسَبًا وَصِهْرًا ۗ وَكَانَ رَبُّكَ قَدِيرًا ﴿٥٤﴾ وَيَعْبُدُونَ مِن دُونِ
ٱللَّهِ مَا لَا يَنفَعُهُمْ وَلَا يَضُرُّهُمْ ۗ وَكَانَ ٱلْكَافِرُ عَلَىٰ رَبِّهِۦ ظَهِيرًا ﴿٥٥﴾ وَمَآ
أَرْسَلْنَٰكَ إِلَّا مُبَشِّرًا وَنَذِيرًا ﴿٥٦﴾ قُلْ مَآ أَسْـَٔلُكُمْ عَلَيْهِ مِنْ أَجْرٍ إِلَّا مَن
شَآءَ أَن يَتَّخِذَ إِلَىٰ رَبِّهِۦ سَبِيلًا ﴿٥٧﴾ وَتَوَكَّلْ عَلَى ٱلْحَىِّ ٱلَّذِى لَا يَمُوتُ
وَسَبِّحْ بِحَمْدِهِۦ ۚ وَكَفَىٰ بِهِۦ بِذُنُوبِ عِبَادِهِۦ خَبِيرًا ﴿٥٨﴾ ٱلَّذِى خَلَقَ
ٱلسَّمَٰوَٰتِ وَٱلْأَرْضَ وَمَا بَيْنَهُمَا فِى سِتَّةِ أَيَّامٍ ثُمَّ ٱسْتَوَىٰ عَلَى ٱلْعَرْشِ ۚ
ٱلرَّحْمَٰنُ فَسْـَٔلْ بِهِۦ خَبِيرًا ﴿٥٩﴾ وَإِذَا قِيلَ لَهُمُ ٱسْجُدُوا۟ لِلرَّحْمَٰنِ قَالُوا۟

ربع الحزب

۞ Wa Huwal-ladhī marajal-baḥrayni hādhā ʿadhbuñ-furātuñw-wa hādhā milḥun ʾujājuñ-wa jaʿala baynahumā barzakhañw-wa ḥijram-maḥjūrā. (53) Wa Huwal-ladhī khalaqa minal-māaʾi basharañ-fajaʿalahū nasabañw-wa ṣihrā. Wa kāna Rabbuka Qadīrā. (54) Wa yaʿbudūna miñ-dūnil-lāhi mā lā yañfaʿuhum wa lā yaḍurruhum. Wa kānal-kāfiru ʿalā Rabbihī ẓahīrā. (55) Wa māa ʾarsalnāka ʾillā mubashshirañw-wa nadhīrā. (56) Qul māa ʾasʾalukum ʿalayhi min ʾajrin ʾillā mañ-shāaʾa ʾañy-yattakhidha ʾilā Rabbihī sabīlā. (57) Wa tawakkal ʿalal-Ḥayyil-ladhī lā yamūtu wa sabbiḥ biḥamdihī wa kafā bihī bidhunūbi ʿibādihī Khabīrā. (58) ʾAlladhī khalaqas-samāwāti wal-ʾarḍa wa mā baynahumā fī sittati ʾayyāmiñ-thummas-tawā ʿalal-ʿarsh. ʾArRaḥmanu fasʾal bihī Khabīrā. (59) Wa ʾidhā qīla lahumus-judū lirRaḥmāni qālū

41 The noun *baḥr*, usually signifying "sea", is also applied to large agglomerations of sweet water, like rivers, lakes, etc.; in the above context, the dual *al-baḥrayn* denotes "the two great bodies [or "kinds"] of water" – the salty and the sweet – existing side by side on earth.

42 I.e., has caused them – as if by an invisible barrier – to remain distinct in kind despite their continuous meeting and mingling in the oceans: an indirect reminder of God's planning creativeness inherent in the cyclic transformation of water – its evaporation from the salty seas, followed by a formation of clouds, their condensation into rain and snow which feed springs and rivers, and its return to the seas. Some Muslim mystics see in this stress on the two kinds of water an allegory of the gulf – and, at the same time, interaction – between man's spiritual perceptions, on the one hand, and his worldly needs and passions, on the other.

43 See second half of 21 : 30 where the creation of "every living thing out of water" is spoken of, as well as 24 : 45, which mentions in this connection the entire animal world (including, of course, man).

44 I.e., has enabled him to attribute spiritual value to, and to derive strength from, his organic and social relationships.

45 Lit., "they".

46 See note 43 on the first sentence of 7 : 54.

47 I.e., "ask God Himself": since He alone holds the keys to the mysteries of the universe, it is only by observing His creation and listening to His revealed messages that man can obtain a glimpse, however distant, of God's Own reality.

وَمَا ٱلرَّحْمَـٰنُ أَنَسْجُدُ لِمَا تَأْمُرُنَا وَزَادَهُمْ نُفُورًا ۩ ﴿٦٠﴾ تَبَارَكَ ٱلَّذِى
جَعَلَ فِى ٱلسَّمَآءِ بُرُوجًا وَجَعَلَ فِيهَا سِرَٰجًا وَقَمَرًا مُّنِيرًا ﴿٦١﴾ وَهُوَ ٱلَّذِى
جَعَلَ ٱلَّيْلَ وَٱلنَّهَارَ خِلْفَةً لِّمَنْ أَرَادَ أَن يَذَّكَّرَ أَوْ أَرَادَ شُكُورًا ﴿٦٢﴾
وَعِبَادُ ٱلرَّحْمَـٰنِ ٱلَّذِينَ يَمْشُونَ عَلَى ٱلْأَرْضِ هَوْنًا وَإِذَا خَاطَبَهُمُ
ٱلْجَـٰهِلُونَ قَالُوا۟ سَلَـٰمًا ﴿٦٣﴾ وَٱلَّذِينَ يَبِيتُونَ لِرَبِّهِمْ سُجَّدًا وَقِيَـٰمًا ﴿٦٤﴾
وَٱلَّذِينَ يَقُولُونَ رَبَّنَا ٱصْرِفْ عَنَّا عَذَابَ جَهَنَّمَ إِنَّ عَذَابَهَا كَانَ
غَرَامًا ﴿٦٥﴾ إِنَّهَا سَآءَتْ مُسْتَقَرًّا وَمُقَامًا ﴿٦٦﴾ وَٱلَّذِينَ إِذَآ أَنفَقُوا۟ لَمْ
يُسْرِفُوا۟ وَلَمْ يَقْتُرُوا۟ وَكَانَ بَيْنَ ذَٰلِكَ قَوَامًا ﴿٦٧﴾ وَٱلَّذِينَ لَا يَدْعُونَ
مَعَ ٱللَّهِ إِلَـٰهًا ءَاخَرَ وَلَا يَقْتُلُونَ ٱلنَّفْسَ ٱلَّتِى حَرَّمَ ٱللَّهُ إِلَّا بِٱلْحَقِّ
وَلَا يَزْنُونَ وَمَن يَفْعَلْ ذَٰلِكَ يَلْقَ أَثَامًا ﴿٦٨﴾ يُضَـٰعَفْ لَهُ ٱلْعَذَابُ

wa mar-Raḥmānu ʾanasjudu limā taʾmurunā wa zādahum nufūrā. (60) Tabārakal-ladhī jaʿala fis-samāaʾi burūjañw-wa jaʿala fīhā sirājañw-wa qamaram-munīrā. (61) Wa Huwal-ladhī jaʿalal-layla wan-nahāra khilfatal-liman ʾarāda ʾañy-yadhdhakkara ʾaw ʾarāda shukūrā. (62) Wa ʿibādur-Raḥmānil-ladhīna yamshūna ʿalal-ʾarḍi hawnañw-wa ʾidhā khāṭabahumul-jāhilūna qālū salāmā. (63) Wal-ladhīna yabītūna liRabbihim sujjadañw-wa qiyāmā. (64) Wal-ladhīna yaqūlūna Rabbanaṣ-rif ʿannā ʿadhāba jahannama ʾinna ʿadhābahā kana gharāmā. (65) ʾInnahā sāaʾat mustaqarrañw-wa muqāmā. (66) Wal-ladhīna ʾidhāa ʾañfaqū lam yusrifū wa lam yaqturū wa kāna bayna dhālika qawāmā. (67) Wal-ladhīna lā yadʿūna maʿal-lāhi ʾilāhan ʾākhara wa lā yaqtulūnan-nafsal-latī ḥarramal-lāhu ʾillā bilḥaqqi wa lā yaznūna wa mañy-yafʿal dhālika yalqa ʾathāmā. (68) Yuḍāʿaf lahul-ʿadhābu

"And [who and] what is the Most Gracious? Are we to prostrate ourselves before whatever thou biddest us [to worship]?" – and so [thy call] but increases their aversion. ‹60›

السجدة

HALLOWED is He who has set up in the skies great constellations, and has placed among them a [radiant] lamp and a light-giving moon.[48] ‹61›

And He it is who causes the night and the day to succeed one another, [revealing Himself in His works] unto him who has the will to take thought – that is,[49] has the will to be grateful. ‹62›

For, [true] servants of the Most Gracious are [only] they who walk gently on earth, and who, whenever the foolish address them,[50] reply with [words of] peace; ‹63›

and who remember their Sustainer far into the night, prostrating themselves and standing; ‹64›

and who pray: "O our Sustainer, avert from us the suffering of hell – for, verily, the suffering caused by it is bound to be a torment dire: ‹65› verily, how evil an abode and a station!"; ‹66›

– and who, whenever they spend on others,[51] are neither wasteful nor niggardly but [remember that] there is always a just mean between those [two extremes]; ‹67›

and who never invoke any [imaginary] deity side by side with God, and do not take any human being's life – [the life] which God has willed to be sacred – otherwise than in [the pursuit of] justice,[52] and do not commit adultery.

And [know that] he who commits aught thereof[53] shall [not only] meet with a full requital ‹68› [but] shall have his suffering

48 See 10 : 5, where the sun is spoken of as "a [source of] radiant light", explained in the corresponding note 10. For my rendering of *burūj* as "great constellations", see note 15 on 15 : 16.

49 Lit., "or" (*aw*) – a particle which obviously does not denote here an alternative but, rather, an explanatory amplification, similar to the expression "in other words".

50 Sc., "with the aim to ridicule them or to argue against their beliefs".

51 In the Qurʾān, the verb *anfaqa* (and the corresponding noun *nafaqah*) has usually this connotation.

52 See *sūrah* 6, note 148.

53 Lit., "he who does that (*dhālika*)", i.e., any of the three sins referred to in this verse. (For my translation of *zinā* as "adultery", see *sūrah* 24, note 2.)

doubled on Resurrection Day: for on that [Day] he shall abide in ignominy. ‹69›
Excepted, however, shall be they who repent and attain to faith and do righteous deeds: for it is they whose [erstwhile] bad deeds God will transform into good ones – seeing that God is indeed much-forgiving, a dispenser of grace, ‹70› and seeing that he who repents and [thenceforth] does what is right has truly turned unto God by [this very act of] repentance. ‹71›
And [know that true servants of God are only] those who never bear witness to what is false,[54] and [who], whenever they pass by [people engaged in] frivolity, pass on with dignity; ‹72›
and who, whenever they are reminded of their Sustainer's messages, do not throw themselves upon them [as if] deaf and blind;[55] ‹73›
and who pray: "O our Sustainer! Grant that our spouses and our offspring be a joy to our eyes,[56] and cause us to be foremost among those who are conscious of Thee! ‹74›
[Such as] these will be rewarded for all their patient endurance [in life] with a high station [in paradise], and will be met therein with a greeting of welcome and peace, ‹75› therein to abide: [and] how goodly an abode and [how high] a station! ‹76›

SAY [unto those who believe]: "No weight or value would my Sustainer attach to you were it not for your faith [in Him]!"[57]
[And say unto those who deny the truth:] "You have indeed given the lie [to God's message], and in time this [sin] will cleave unto you!"[58] ‹77›

يَوْمَ ٱلْقِيَـٰمَةِ وَيَخْلُدْ فِيهِۦ مُهَانًا ﴿69﴾ إِلَّا مَن تَابَ وَءَامَنَ وَعَمِلَ عَمَلًا
صَـٰلِحًا فَأُو۟لَـٰٓئِكَ يُبَدِّلُ ٱللَّهُ سَيِّـَٔاتِهِمْ حَسَنَـٰتٍ ۗ وَكَانَ ٱللَّهُ غَفُورًا
رَّحِيمًا ﴿70﴾ وَمَن تَابَ وَعَمِلَ صَـٰلِحًا فَإِنَّهُۥ يَتُوبُ إِلَى ٱللَّهِ مَتَابًا ﴿71﴾
وَٱلَّذِينَ لَا يَشْهَدُونَ ٱلزُّورَ وَإِذَا مَرُّوا۟ بِٱللَّغْوِ مَرُّوا۟ كِرَامًا ﴿72﴾ وَٱلَّذِينَ
إِذَا ذُكِّرُوا۟ بِـَٔايَـٰتِ رَبِّهِمْ لَمْ يَخِرُّوا۟ عَلَيْهَا صُمًّا وَعُمْيَانًا ﴿73﴾ وَٱلَّذِينَ
يَقُولُونَ رَبَّنَا هَبْ لَنَا مِنْ أَزْوَٰجِنَا وَذُرِّيَّـٰتِنَا قُرَّةَ أَعْيُنٍ وَٱجْعَلْنَا
لِلْمُتَّقِينَ إِمَامًا ﴿74﴾ أُو۟لَـٰٓئِكَ يُجْزَوْنَ ٱلْغُرْفَةَ بِمَا صَبَرُوا۟ وَيُلَقَّوْنَ فِيهَا
تَحِيَّةً وَسَلَـٰمًا ﴿75﴾ خَـٰلِدِينَ فِيهَا ۚ حَسُنَتْ مُسْتَقَرًّا وَمُقَامًا ﴿76﴾ قُلْ مَا
يَعْبَؤُا۟ بِكُمْ رَبِّى لَوْلَا دُعَآؤُكُمْ ۖ فَقَدْ كَذَّبْتُمْ فَسَوْفَ يَكُونُ لِزَامًۢا ﴿77﴾

Yawmal-Qiyāmati wa yakhlud fīhī muhānan, (69) ᵓillā mañ-tāba wa ᵓāmana wa ᶜamila ᶜamalañ-ṣāliḥañ-faᵓulāaᵓika yubaddilul-lāhu sayyiᵓātihim ḥasanāt. Wa kānal-lāhu Ghafūrar-Raḥīmā. (70) Wa mañ-tāba wa ᶜamila ṣāliḥañ-faᵓinnahū yatūbu ᵓilal-lāhi matābā. (71) Wal-ladhīna lā yashhadūnaz-zūra wa ᵓidhā marrū billaghwi marrū kirāmā. (72) Wal-ladhīna ᵓidhā dhukkirū biᵓĀyāti Rabbihim lam yakhirrū ᶜalayhā ṣummañw-wa ᶜumyānā. (73) Wal-ladhīna yaqūlūna Rabbanā hab lanā min ᵓazwājinā wa dhurriyyātinā qurrata ᵓaᶜyuniñw-waj-ᶜalnā lilmuttaqīna ᵓimāmā. (74) ᵓUlāaᵓika yujzawnal-ghurfata bimā ṣabarū wa yulaqqawna fīhā taḥiyyatañw-wa salāmā. (75) Khālidīna fīhā ḥasunat mustaqarrañw-wa muqāmā. (76) Qul mā yaᶜbaᵓu bikum Rabbī lawlā duᶜāaᵓukum. Faqad kadhdhabtum fasawfa yakūnu lizāmā. (77)

54 Implying that neither do they themselves ever bear false witness (i.e., in the widest sense of this expression, tell any lie), nor do they knowingly take part in anything that is based on falsehood (Rāzī).

55 Explaining this verse, Zamakhsharī remarks that whereas the average run of people approach the divine writ with a mere outward show of eagerness, "throwing themselves upon it" for the sake of appearances but, in reality, not making the least attempt to understand the message as such and, hence, remaining deaf and blind to its contents – the truly God-conscious are deeply desirous of *understanding* it, and therefore "listen to it with wide-awake ears and look into it with seeing eyes".

56 I.e., by living a righteous life.

57 Lit., "were it not for your prayer", which term Ibn ᶜAbbās (as quoted by Ṭabarī) equates in this context with "faith".

58 I.e., "unless you repent, this sin will determine your spiritual destiny in the life to come".

The Twenty-Sixth Sūrah

Ash-Shuʿarāa' (The Poets)

Mecca Period

THE WORD which suggested to the Companions of the Prophet the "title" of this *sūrah* is found in verse 224. Some of the commentators are of the opinion that the last four verses (beginning with this very key-word) were revealed at Medina, but all the available evidence shows that the entire *sūrah* belongs to the middle Mecca period, having been revealed about six or seven years before the Prophet's *hijrah*. Similarly, there is no cogent reason to assume, as Suyūṭī does, that verse 197 belongs to the Medina period simply because it mentions the "learned men from among the children of Israel", since references to the latter abound in many Meccan revelations.

The main purport of this *sūrah* lies in its stress on the unchanging character of man's weakness and proneness to self-deception, which explains why the great majority of people, at all times and in all communities, so readily reject the truth – whether it be the truth of God's messages or of self-evident moral values – and, in consequence, lose themselves in a worship of power, wealth or what is commonly described as "glory", as well as in a mindless acceptance of slogans and prevailing fashions of thought.

سورة الشعراء مكية -26-
وآياتها سبع وعشرون ومائتان

IN THE NAME OF GOD, THE MOST GRACIOUS, THE DISPENSER OF GRACE:

بِسْمِ ٱللَّهِ ٱلرَّحْمَٰنِ ٱلرَّحِيمِ

Ṭā. Sīn. Mīm.[1] ‹1›
THESE ARE MESSAGES of the divine writ, clear in itself and clearly showing the truth.[2] ‹2›
Wouldst thou, perhaps, torment thyself to death [with grief] because they [who live around thee] refuse to believe [in it]?[3] ‹3›
Had We so willed, We could have sent down unto them a message from the skies, so that their necks would [be forced to] bown down before it in humility.[4] ‹4›
[But We have not willed it:] and so, whenever there comes unto them any fresh reminder from the Most Gracious, they [who are blind of heart] always turn their backs upon it: ‹5› thus, indeed, have they given the lie [to this message as well]. But [in time] they will come to understand what it was that they were wont to deride![5] ‹6›
Have they, then, never considered the earth – how much of every noble kind [of life] We have caused to grow thereon? ‹7›
In this, behold, there is a message [unto men], even though most of them will not believe [in it]. ‹8› But, verily, thy Sustainer – He alone – is almighty, a dispenser of grace![6] ‹9›

نصف الحزب

طسٓمٓ ﴿١﴾ تِلْكَ ءَايَٰتُ ٱلْكِتَٰبِ ٱلْمُبِينِ ﴿٢﴾ لَعَلَّكَ بَٰخِعٌ نَّفْسَكَ أَلَّا
يَكُونُوا۟ مُؤْمِنِينَ ﴿٣﴾ إِن نَّشَأْ نُنَزِّلْ عَلَيْهِم مِّنَ ٱلسَّمَآءِ ءَايَةً فَظَلَّتْ
أَعْنَٰقُهُمْ لَهَا خَٰضِعِينَ ﴿٤﴾ وَمَا يَأْتِيهِم مِّن ذِكْرٍ مِّنَ ٱلرَّحْمَٰنِ مُحْدَثٍ
إِلَّا كَانُوا۟ عَنْهُ مُعْرِضِينَ ﴿٥﴾ فَقَدْ كَذَّبُوا۟ فَسَيَأْتِيهِمْ أَنۢبَٰٓؤُا۟ مَا كَانُوا۟ بِهِۦ
يَسْتَهْزِءُونَ ﴿٦﴾ أَوَلَمْ يَرَوْا۟ إِلَى ٱلْأَرْضِ كَمْ أَنۢبَتْنَا فِيهَا مِن كُلِّ زَوْجٍ
كَرِيمٍ ﴿٧﴾ إِنَّ فِى ذَٰلِكَ لَءَايَةً ۖ وَمَا كَانَ أَكْثَرُهُم مُّؤْمِنِينَ ﴿٨﴾ وَإِنَّ رَبَّكَ
لَهُوَ ٱلْعَزِيزُ ٱلرَّحِيمُ ﴿٩﴾

Bismil-lāhir-Raḥmānir-Raḥīm.
Ṭā-Sīim-Mīim. (1) Tilka ʾĀyātul-Kitābil-mubīn. (2)
Laʿallaka bākhiʿuñ-nafsaka ʾallā yakūnū muʾminīn.
(3) ʾIñ-nashaʾ nunazzil ʿalayhim-minas-samāaʾi
ʾĀyatañ-faẓallat ʾaʿnāquhum lahā khāḍiʿīn. (4) Wa
mā yaʾtīhim-miñ-dhikrim-minar-Raḥmāni muḥ-
dathin ʾillā kānū ʿanhu muʿriḍīn. (5) Faqad kadh-
dhabū fasayaʾtīhim ʾambāaʾu mā kānū bihī yastah-
ziʾūn. (6) ʾAwa lam yaraw ʾilal-ʾarḍi kam ʾambatnā
fīhā miñ-kulli zawjiñ-karīm. (7) ʾInna fī dhālika la-
ʾĀyatañw-wa mā kāna ʾaktharuhum-muʾminīn. (8)
Wa ʾinna Rabbaka laHuwal-ʿAzīzur-Raḥīm. (9)

---

1 The letters *ṭā, sīn* and *mīm* are among the mysterious, disjointed letter-symbols (*al-muqaṭṭaʿāt*) preceding some of the chapters of the Qurʾān (see Appendix II).

2 See *sūrah* 12, note 2.

3 See notes 3 and 4 on 18 : 6.

4 Inasmuch as the spiritual value of man's faith depends on its being an outcome of free choice and not of compulsion, the visible or audible appearance of a "message from the skies" would, by its very obviousness, nullify the element of free choice and, therefore, deprive man's faith in that message of all its moral significance.

5 See 6 : 4-5 and the corresponding note 4.

6 The above two verses appear eight times in this *sūrah*. Apart from the present instance, they conclude, like a refrain, each of the subsequent seven stories of earlier prophets, which – by means of their, in places, almost identical phrasing – are meant to stress the essential identity of the ethical teachings of all the prophets, as well as to

HENCE, [remember how it was] when thy Sustainer summoned Moses: "Go unto those evildoing people, ‹10› the people of Pharaoh, who refuse to be conscious of Me!"[7] ‹11›

He answered: "O my Sustainer! Behold, I fear that they will give me the lie, ‹12› and then my breast will be straitened and my tongue will not be free: send, then, [this Thy command] to Aaron.[8] ‹13› Moreover, they keep a grave charge [pending] against me, and I fear that they will slay me."[9] ‹14›

Said He: "Not so, indeed! Go forth, then, both of you, with Our messages: verily, We shall be with you, listening [to your call]! ‹15› And go, both of you, unto Pharaoh and say, 'Behold, we bear a message from the Sustainer of all the worlds: ‹16› Let the children of Israel go with us!'" ‹17›

[But when Moses had delivered his message, Pharaoh] said: "Did we not bring thee up among us when thou wert a child? And didst thou not spend among us years of thy [later] life? ‹18› And yet thou didst commit that [heinous] deed of thine,[10] and [hast thus shown that] thou art one of the ingrate!" ‹19›

Replied [Moses]: "I committed it while I was still going astray; ‹20› and I fled from you because I feared you. But [since] then my Sustainer has endowed me with the ability to judge [between right and wrong],[11] and has made me one of [His] message-bearers. ‹21›

وَإِذْ نَادَىٰ رَبُّكَ مُوسَىٰٓ أَنِ ٱئْتِ ٱلْقَوْمَ ٱلظَّٰلِمِينَ ﴿10﴾ قَوْمَ فِرْعَوْنَ ۚ أَلَا
يَتَّقُونَ ﴿11﴾ قَالَ رَبِّ إِنِّىٓ أَخَافُ أَن يُكَذِّبُونِ ﴿12﴾ وَيَضِيقُ صَدْرِى
وَلَا يَنطَلِقُ لِسَانِى فَأَرْسِلْ إِلَىٰ هَٰرُونَ ﴿13﴾ وَلَهُمْ عَلَىَّ ذَنۢبٌ فَأَخَافُ أَن
يَقْتُلُونِ ﴿14﴾ قَالَ كَلَّا ۖ فَٱذْهَبَا بِـَٔايَٰتِنَآ ۖ إِنَّا مَعَكُم مُّسْتَمِعُونَ ﴿15﴾ فَأْتِيَا
فِرْعَوْنَ فَقُولَآ إِنَّا رَسُولُ رَبِّ ٱلْعَٰلَمِينَ ﴿16﴾ أَنْ أَرْسِلْ مَعَنَا بَنِىٓ
إِسْرَٰٓءِيلَ ﴿17﴾ قَالَ أَلَمْ نُرَبِّكَ فِينَا وَلِيدًا وَلَبِثْتَ فِينَا مِنْ عُمُرِكَ
سِنِينَ ﴿18﴾ وَفَعَلْتَ فَعْلَتَكَ ٱلَّتِى فَعَلْتَ وَأَنتَ مِنَ ٱلْكَٰفِرِينَ ﴿19﴾ قَالَ
فَعَلْتُهَآ إِذًا وَأَنَا۠ مِنَ ٱلضَّآلِّينَ ﴿20﴾ فَفَرَرْتُ مِنكُمْ لَمَّا خِفْتُكُمْ فَوَهَبَ
لِى رَبِّى حُكْمًا وَجَعَلَنِى مِنَ ٱلْمُرْسَلِينَ ﴿21﴾

Wa ʾidh nādā Rabbuka Mūsāa ʾani-ʾtil-qawmaẓ-
ẓālimīn. (10) Qawma Firʿawna ʾalā yattaqūn. (11)
Qāla Rabbi ʾinnīi ʾakhāfu ʾañy-yukadhdhibūn. (12)
Wa yaḍīqu ṣadrī wa lā yañṭaliqu lisānī faʾarsil ʾilā
Hārūn. (13) Wa lahum ʿalayya dhambuñ-faʾakhāfu
ʾañy-yaqtulūn. (14) Qāla kallā; fadhhabā biʾĀyātināa
ʾinnā maʿakum-mustamiʿūn. (15) Faʾtiyā Firʿawna
faqūlāa ʾinnā Rasūlu Rabbil-ʿālamīn. (16) ʾAn ʾarsil
maʿanā banīi ʾIsrāaʾīl. (17) Qāla ʾalam nurabbika fīnā
walīdañw-wa labithta fīnā min ʿumurika sinīn. (18)
Wa faʿalta faʿlatakal-latī faʿalta wa ʾañta minal-
kāfirīn. (19) Qāla faʿaltuhāa ʾidhañw-wa ʾana minaḍ-
ḍāallīn. (20) Fafarartu miñkum lammā khiftukum
fawahaba lī Rabbī ḥukmañw-wa jaʿalanī minal-
Mursalīn. (21)

illustrate the statement, in verse 5, that a rejection of God's messages is a recurrent phenomenon in the history of mankind despite the fact that His existence is clearly manifested in all living creation.

7 Lit., "Will they not be [or "become"] conscious [of Me]?" Zamakhsharī and Rāzī understand this rhetorical question in the sense apparent in my rendering, namely, as a statement of fact.

8 Cf. 20 : 25-34 and the corresponding notes. In the present context, stress is laid on the deep humility of Moses, who considered himself incapable of fulfilling the task for which he had been chosen, and asked God to entrust it to Aaron instead.

9 Sc., "and thus frustrate my mission". This is a reference to Moses' killing of the Egyptian, which was the cause of his subsequent flight from his native land (cf. 28 : 15 ff.)

10 Lit., "thou didst commit thy deed which thou hast committed" – a construction meant to express the speaker's utter condemnation of the deed referred to: hence, my interpolation of the word "heinous". As regards the above allusions to Moses' childhood and youth at Pharaoh's court, the manslaughter committed by him, and his flight from Egypt, see 28 : 4-22.

11 As is shown in 28 : 15-16, after having killed the Egyptian, Moses suddenly realized that he had committed a grievous sin (see also note 15 on the last two sentences of 28 : 15).

And [as for] that favour of which thou so tauntingly remindest me – [was it not] due to thy having enslaved the children of Israel?"[12] ‹22›
Said Pharaoh: "And what [and who] is that 'Sustainer of all the worlds'?"[13] ‹23›
[Moses] answered: "[He is] the Sustainer of the heavens and the earth and all that is between them: if you would but [allow yourselves to] be convinced!"[14] ‹24›
Said [Pharaoh] unto those around him: "Did you hear [what he said]?"[15] ‹25›
[And Moses] continued: "[He is] your Sustainer, [too] as well as the Sustainer of your forefathers of old!" ‹26›
[Pharaoh] exclaimed: "Behold, [this] your 'apostle' who [claims that he] has been sent unto you is mad indeed!" ‹27›
[But Moses] went on: "[He of whom I speak is] the Sustainer of the east and the west and of all that is between the two[16] – [as you would know] if you would but use your reason!" ‹28›
Said [Pharaoh]: "Indeed, if thou choose to worship any deity other than me, I shall most certainly throw thee into prison!"[17] ‹29›
Said he: "Even if I should bring about before thee something that clearly shows the truth?"[18] ‹30›
[Pharaoh] answered: "Produce it, then, if thou art a man of truth!" ‹31›
Thereupon [Moses] threw down his staff – and lo! it was a serpent, plainly visible; ‹32› and he drew forth his hand – and lo! it appeared [shining] white to the beholders.[19] ‹33›

وَتِلْكَ نِعْمَةٌ تَمُنُّهَا عَلَيَّ أَنْ عَبَّدتَّ بَنِىٓ إِسْرَٰٓءِيلَ ﴿٢٢﴾ قَالَ فِرْعَوْنُ وَمَا رَبُّ
ٱلْعَٰلَمِينَ ﴿٢٣﴾ قَالَ رَبُّ ٱلسَّمَٰوَٰتِ وَٱلْأَرْضِ وَمَا بَيْنَهُمَآ إِن كُنتُم
مُّوقِنِينَ ﴿٢٤﴾ قَالَ لِمَنْ حَوْلَهُۥٓ أَلَا تَسْتَمِعُونَ ﴿٢٥﴾ قَالَ رَبُّكُمْ وَرَبُّ
ءَابَآئِكُمُ ٱلْأَوَّلِينَ ﴿٢٦﴾ قَالَ إِنَّ رَسُولَكُمُ ٱلَّذِىٓ أُرْسِلَ إِلَيْكُمْ
لَمَجْنُونٌ ﴿٢٧﴾ قَالَ رَبُّ ٱلْمَشْرِقِ وَٱلْمَغْرِبِ وَمَا بَيْنَهُمَآ إِن كُنتُمْ
تَعْقِلُونَ ﴿٢٨﴾ قَالَ لَئِنِ ٱتَّخَذْتَ إِلَٰهًا غَيْرِى لَأَجْعَلَنَّكَ مِنَ
ٱلْمَسْجُونِينَ ﴿٢٩﴾ قَالَ أَوَلَوْ جِئْتُكَ بِشَىْءٍ مُّبِينٍ ﴿٣٠﴾ قَالَ فَأْتِ بِهِۦٓ إِن
كُنتَ مِنَ ٱلصَّٰدِقِينَ ﴿٣١﴾ فَأَلْقَىٰ عَصَاهُ فَإِذَا هِىَ ثُعْبَانٌ مُّبِينٌ ﴿٣٢﴾ وَنَزَعَ
يَدَهُۥ فَإِذَا هِىَ بَيْضَآءُ لِلنَّٰظِرِينَ ﴿٣٣﴾

Wa tilka niʿmatuñ-tamunnuhā ʿalayya ʾan ʿabbatta banīi ʾIsrāaʾīl. (22) Qāla Firʿawnu wa mā Rabbul-ʿālamīn. (23) Qāla Rabbus-samāwāti wal-ʾarḍi wa mā baynahumāa ʾiñ-kuñtum-mūqinīn. (24) Qāla liman ḥawlahūu ʾalā tastamiʿūn. (25) Qāla Rabbukum wa Rabbu ʾābāaʾikumul-ʾawwalīn. (26) Qāla ʾinna Rasūlakumul-ladhīi ʾursila ʾilaykum lamajnūn. (27) Qāla Rabbul-mashriqi wal-maghribi wa mā baynahumāa ʾiñ-kuñtum taʿqilūn. (28) Qāla laʾinit-takhadhta ʾilāhan ghayrī laʾajʿalannaka minal-masjūnīn. (29) Qāla ʾawa law jiʾtuka bishayʾim-mubīn. (30) Qāla faʾti bihīi ʾiñ-kuñta minaṣ-ṣādiqīn. (31) Faʾalqā ʿaṣāhu faʾidhā hiya thuʿbānum-mubīn. (32) Wa nazaʿa yadahū faʾidhā hiya bayḍāaʾu linnāẓirīn. (33)

12 See 28 : 4-5.

13 A reference to the terms in which Moses was to – and apparently did – announce his mission (see verse 16 above).

14 Sc., "by the evidence of His creative will in all that exists": this proposition being, I believe, the main reason for a repetition of the story of Moses in the present *sūrah*. (Cf. also verse 28 above.)

15 Lit., "Do you not hear?" – a rhetorical question meant to convey astonishment, indignation or derision, which may be idiomatically rendered in translation as above.

16 Cf. 2 : 115.

17 In the religion of ancient Egypt, the king (or "Pharaoh", as each of the rulers was styled) represented an incarnation of the divine principle, and was considered to be a god in his own right. Hence, a challenge to his divinity implied a challenge to the prevalent religious system as a whole.

18 For this rendering of the term *mubīn*, see note 2 on 12 : 1.

19 See 7 : 107-108 and the corresponding note 85, as well as 20 : 22, 27 : 12 and 28 : 32.

قَالَ لِلْمَلَإِ حَوْلَهُۥٓ إِنَّ هَٰذَا لَسَٰحِرٌ عَلِيمٌ ﴿٣٤﴾ يُرِيدُ أَن يُخْرِجَكُم مِّنْ
أَرْضِكُم بِسِحْرِهِۦ فَمَاذَا تَأْمُرُونَ ﴿٣٥﴾ قَالُوٓا۟ أَرْجِهْ وَأَخَاهُ وَٱبْعَثْ فِى
ٱلْمَدَآئِنِ حَٰشِرِينَ ﴿٣٦﴾ يَأْتُوكَ بِكُلِّ سَحَّارٍ عَلِيمٍ ﴿٣٧﴾ فَجُمِعَ ٱلسَّحَرَةُ
لِمِيقَٰتِ يَوْمٍ مَّعْلُومٍ ﴿٣٨﴾ وَقِيلَ لِلنَّاسِ هَلْ أَنتُم مُّجْتَمِعُونَ ﴿٣٩﴾ لَعَلَّنَا نَتَّبِعُ
ٱلسَّحَرَةَ إِن كَانُوا۟ هُمُ ٱلْغَٰلِبِينَ ﴿٤٠﴾ فَلَمَّا جَآءَ ٱلسَّحَرَةُ قَالُوا۟ لِفِرْعَوْنَ
أَئِنَّ لَنَا لَأَجْرًا إِن كُنَّا نَحْنُ ٱلْغَٰلِبِينَ ﴿٤١﴾ قَالَ نَعَمْ وَإِنَّكُمْ إِذًا لَّمِنَ
ٱلْمُقَرَّبِينَ ﴿٤٢﴾ قَالَ لَهُم مُّوسَىٰٓ أَلْقُوا۟ مَآ أَنتُم مُّلْقُونَ ﴿٤٣﴾ فَأَلْقَوْا۟ حِبَالَهُمْ
وَعِصِيَّهُمْ وَقَالُوا۟ بِعِزَّةِ فِرْعَوْنَ إِنَّا لَنَحْنُ ٱلْغَٰلِبُونَ ﴿٤٤﴾ فَأَلْقَىٰ مُوسَىٰ عَصَاهُ
فَإِذَا هِىَ تَلْقَفُ مَا يَأْفِكُونَ ﴿٤٥﴾ فَأُلْقِىَ ٱلسَّحَرَةُ سَٰجِدِينَ ﴿٤٦﴾ قَالُوٓا۟
ءَامَنَّا بِرَبِّ ٱلْعَٰلَمِينَ ﴿٤٧﴾ رَبِّ مُوسَىٰ وَهَٰرُونَ ﴿٤٨﴾ قَالَ ءَامَنتُمْ لَهُۥ قَبْلَ
أَنْ ءَاذَنَ لَكُمْ ۖ إِنَّهُۥ لَكَبِيرُكُمُ ٱلَّذِى عَلَّمَكُمُ ٱلسِّحْرَ فَلَسَوْفَ

Qāla lilmalaʾi ḥawlahūu ʾinna hādhā lasāḥirun ʿalīm. (34) Yurīdu ʾañy-yukhrijakum-min ʾarḍikum-bisiḥrihī famādhā taʾmurūn. (35) Qālūu ʾarjih wa ʾakhāhu wab-ʿath fil-madāaʾini ḥāshirīna, (36) yaʾtūka bikulli saḥḥārin ʿalīm. (37) Fajumiʿas-saḥaratu limīqāti yawmim-maʿlūm. (38) Wa qīla linnāsi hal-ʾañtum-mujtamiʿūn. (39) Laʿallanā nattabiʿus-saḥarata ʾiñ-kānū humul-ghālibīn. (40) Falammā jāaʾas-saḥaratu qālū liFirʿawna ʾaʾinna lanā laʾajran ʾiñ-kunnā naḥnul-ghālibīn. (41) Qāla naʿam wa ʾinnakum ʾidhal-laminal-muqarrabīn. (42) Qāla lahum-Mūsāa ʾalqū māa ʾañtum-mulqūn. (43) Faʾalqaw ḥibālahum wa ʿiṣiyyahum wa qālū biʿizzati Firʿawna ʾinnā lanaḥnul-ghālibūn. (44) Faʾalqā Mūsā ʿaṣāhu faʾidhā hiya talqafu mā yaʾfikūn. (45) Faʾulqiyas-saḥaratu sājidīn. (46) Qālūu ʾāmannā biRabbil-ʿālamīn. (47) Rabbi Mūsā wa Hārūn. (48) Qāla ʾāmañtum lahū qabla ʾan ʾādhana lakum. ʾInnahū lakabīrukumul-ladhī ʿallamakumus-siḥra falasawfa

Said [Pharaoh] unto the great ones around him: "Verily, this is indeed a sorcerer of great knowledge ‹34› who wants to drive you out of your land by his sorcery.[20] What, then, do you advise?" ‹35›

They answered: "Let him and his brother wait a while, and send unto all cities heralds ‹36› who shall assemble before thee all sorcerers of great knowledge." ‹37›

And so the sorcerers were assembled at a set time on a certain day, ‹38› and the people were asked: "Are you all present, ‹39› so that we might follow [in the footsteps of] the sorcerers if it is they who prevail?"[21] ‹40›

Now when the sorcerers came, they said unto Pharaoh: "Verily, we ought to have a great reward if it is we who prevail."[22] ‹41›

Answered he: "Yea – and, verily, in that case you shall be among those who are near unto me." ‹42›

[And] Moses said unto them: "Throw whatever you are going to throw!" ‹43›

Thereupon they threw their [magic] ropes and their staffs, and said: "By Pharaoh's might, behold, it is we indeed who have prevailed!"[23] ‹44›

[But] then Moses threw his staff – and lo! it swallowed up all their deceptions.[24] ‹45›

And down fell the sorcerers, prostrating themselves in adoration, ‹46› [and] exclaimed: "We have come to believe in the Sustainer of all the worlds, ‹47› the Sustainer of Moses and Aaron!" ‹48›

Said [Pharaoh]: "Have you come to believe in him[25] ere I have given you permission? Verily, he must be your master who has taught you magic![26] But in time you shall

20 Cf. 7 : 109-110 and the corresponding note 86.

21 There is no doubt that these "sorcerers" were priests of the official Amon cult, in which magic played an important role. Thus, their victory over Moses would constitute a public vindication of the state religion.

22 See note 88 on 7 : 113.

23 The reason for their premature sense of triumph is given in 7 : 116 ("they cast a spell upon the people's eyes, and struck them with awe") and 20 : 66-67 ("by virtue of their sorcery, their [magic] ropes and staffs seemed to him to be moving rapidly; and in his heart, Moses became apprehensive").

24 See note 89 on 7 : 117.

25 See note 91 on 7 : 123.

26 I.e., "he is so superior a sorcerer that he could be your teacher".

come to know [my revenge]: most certainly shall I cut off your hands and your feet in great numbers, because of [your] perverseness, and shall most certainly crucify you in great numbers, all together!"[27] «49»
They answered: "No harm [canst thou do to us]: verily, unto our Sustainer do we turn! «50» Behold, we [but] ardently desire that our Sustainer forgive us our faults in return for our having been foremost among the believers!" «51»

AND [there came a time[28] when] We inspired Moses thus: "Go forth with My servants by night: for, behold, you will be pursued!" «52»
And Pharaoh sent heralds unto all cities, «53» [bidding them to call out his troops and to proclaim:] "Behold, these [children of Israel] are but a contemptible band;[29] «54» but they are indeed filled with hatred of us «55» seeing that we are, verily, a nation united, fully prepared against danger[30] «56» – and so we have [rightly] driven them out of [their] gardens and springs, «57» and [deprived them of their erstwhile] treasures and station of honour!"[31] «58»
Thus it was: but [in the course of time] We were to bestow all these [things] as a heritage on the children of Israel.[32] «59»
And so [the Egyptians] caught up with them at sunrise; «60» and as soon as the two hosts came in sight of one another,

تَعْلَمُونَ لَأُقَطِّعَنَّ أَيْدِيَكُمْ وَأَرْجُلَكُم مِّنْ خِلَٰفٍ وَلَأُصَلِّبَنَّكُمْ أَجْمَعِينَ (49)
قَالُوا۟ لَا ضَيْرَ إِنَّآ إِلَىٰ رَبِّنَا مُنقَلِبُونَ (50) إِنَّا نَطْمَعُ أَن يَغْفِرَ لَنَا رَبُّنَا خَطَٰيَٰنَآ
أَن كُنَّآ أَوَّلَ ٱلْمُؤْمِنِينَ (51) ۞ وَأَوْحَيْنَآ إِلَىٰ مُوسَىٰٓ أَنْ أَسْرِ بِعِبَادِىٓ إِنَّكُم
مُّتَّبَعُونَ (52) فَأَرْسَلَ فِرْعَوْنُ فِى ٱلْمَدَآئِنِ حَٰشِرِينَ (53) إِنَّ هَٰٓؤُلَآءِ لَشِرْذِمَةٌ
قَلِيلُونَ (54) وَإِنَّهُمْ لَنَا لَغَآئِظُونَ (55) وَإِنَّا لَجَمِيعٌ حَٰذِرُونَ (56)
فَأَخْرَجْنَٰهُم مِّن جَنَّٰتٍ وَعُيُونٍ (57) وَكُنُوزٍ وَمَقَامٍ كَرِيمٍ (58) كَذَٰلِكَ
وَأَوْرَثْنَٰهَا بَنِىٓ إِسْرَٰٓءِيلَ (59) فَأَتْبَعُوهُم مُّشْرِقِينَ (60) فَلَمَّا تَرَٰٓءَا ٱلْجَمْعَانِ

ثلاثة ارباع الحزب

taʿlamūn. Laʾuqaṭṭiʿanna ʾaydiyakum wa ʾarjulakum-min khilāfiñw-wa laʾuṣallibannakum ʾajmaʿīn. (49)
Qālū lā ḍayra ʾinnāa ʾilā Rabbinā muñqalibūn. (50)
ʾInnā naṭmaʿu ʾañy-yaghfira lanā Rabbunā khaṭāyānāa ʾañ-kunnāa ʾawwalal-muʾminīn. (51) ۞ Wa ʾawḥaynāa ʾilā Mūsāa ʾan ʾasri biʿibādīi ʾinnakum-muttabaʿūn. (52) Faʾarsala Firʿawnu fil-madāaʾini ḥāshirīn. (53) ʾInna hāaʾulāaʾi lashirdhimatuñ-qalīlūn. (54) Wa ʾinnahum lanā laghāaʾiẓūn. (55) Wa ʾinnā lajamīʿun ḥādhirūn. (56) Faʾakhrajnāhum-miñ-jannātiñw-wa ʿuyūn. (57) Wa kunūziñw-wa maqāmiñ-karīm. (58) Kadhālika wa ʾawrathnāhā banīi ʾIsrāaʾīl. (59) Fa-ʾatbaʿūhum-mushriqīn. (60) Falammā tarāaʾal-jamʿāni

27 See notes 44 and 45 on 5 : 33, and note 92 on 7 : 124, which explain the repeated stress on "great numbers" in the above sentence.

28 I.e., after the period of plagues with which the Egyptians were visited (cf. 7 : 130 ff.).

29 Lit., "a small band": Zamakhsharī, however, suggests that in this context the adjective *qalīlūn* is expressive of contempt, and does not necessarily denote "few in numbers".

30 Thus the Qurʾān illustrates the psychological truth that, as a rule, a dominant nation is unable really to understand the desire for liberty on the part of the group or groups which it oppresses, and therefore attributes their rebelliousness to no more than unreasonable hatred and blind envy of the strong.

31 This is apparently an allusion to the honourable state and the prosperity which the children of Israel had enjoyed in Egypt for a few generations after the time of Joseph – i.e., before a new Egyptian dynasty dispossessed them of their wealth and reduced them to the bondage from which Moses was to free them. In the above passage, Pharaoh seeks to justify his persecution of the Israelites by emphasizing their dislike (real or alleged) of the Egyptians.

32 This parenthetical sentence echoes the allusion, in 7 : 137, to the period of prosperity and honour which the children of Israel were to enjoy in Palestine after their sufferings in Egypt. The reference to "heritage" is, in this and in similar contexts, a metonym for God's bestowal on the oppressed of a life of well-being and dignity.

قَالَ أَصۡحَٰبُ مُوسَىٰٓ إِنَّا لَمُدۡرَكُونَ ﴿٦١﴾ قَالَ كَلَّآۖ إِنَّ مَعِيَ رَبِّي
سَيَهۡدِينِ ﴿٦٢﴾ فَأَوۡحَيۡنَآ إِلَىٰ مُوسَىٰٓ أَنِ ٱضۡرِب بِّعَصَاكَ ٱلۡبَحۡرَۖ فَٱنفَلَقَ
فَكَانَ كُلُّ فِرۡقٖ كَٱلطَّوۡدِ ٱلۡعَظِيمِ ﴿٦٣﴾ وَأَزۡلَفۡنَا ثَمَّ ٱلۡأٓخَرِينَ ﴿٦٤﴾ وَأَنجَيۡنَا
مُوسَىٰ وَمَن مَّعَهُۥٓ أَجۡمَعِينَ ﴿٦٥﴾ ثُمَّ أَغۡرَقۡنَا ٱلۡأٓخَرِينَ ﴿٦٦﴾ إِنَّ فِي ذَٰلِكَ
لَأٓيَةٗۖ وَمَا كَانَ أَكۡثَرُهُم مُّؤۡمِنِينَ ﴿٦٧﴾ وَإِنَّ رَبَّكَ لَهُوَ ٱلۡعَزِيزُ ٱلرَّحِيمُ ﴿٦٨﴾
وَٱتۡلُ عَلَيۡهِمۡ نَبَأَ إِبۡرَٰهِيمَ ﴿٦٩﴾ إِذۡ قَالَ لِأَبِيهِ وَقَوۡمِهِۦ مَا تَعۡبُدُونَ ﴿٧٠﴾
قَالُواْ نَعۡبُدُ أَصۡنَامٗا فَنَظَلُّ لَهَا عَٰكِفِينَ ﴿٧١﴾ قَالَ هَلۡ يَسۡمَعُونَكُمۡ إِذۡ
تَدۡعُونَ ﴿٧٢﴾ أَوۡ يَنفَعُونَكُمۡ أَوۡ يَضُرُّونَ ﴿٧٣﴾ قَالُواْ بَلۡ وَجَدۡنَآ ءَابَآءَنَا
كَذَٰلِكَ يَفۡعَلُونَ ﴿٧٤﴾ قَالَ أَفَرَءَيۡتُم مَّا كُنتُمۡ تَعۡبُدُونَ ﴿٧٥﴾ أَنتُمۡ وَءَابَآؤُكُمُ
ٱلۡأَقۡدَمُونَ ﴿٧٦﴾

qāla ^ɔ^aṣḥābu Mūsāa ^ɔ^innā lamudrakūn. (61) Qāla kallāa ^ɔ^inna ma^c^iya Rabbī sayahdīn. (62) Fa^ɔ^awḥaynāa ^ɔ^ilā Mūsāa ^ɔ^aniḍ-rib bi^c^aṣākal-baḥra faṅfalaqa fakāna kullu firqiṅ-kaṭṭawdil-^c^aẓīm. (63) Wa ^ɔ^azlafnā thammal-^ɔ^ākharīn. (64) Wa ^ɔ^aṅjaynā Mūsā wa mamma^c^ahūu ^ɔ^ajma^c^īn. (65) Thumma ^ɔ^aghraqnal-^ɔ^ākharīn. (66) ^ɔ^Inna fī dhālika la^ɔ^Āyataṅw-wa mā kāna ^ɔ^aktharuhum-mu^ɔ^minīn. (67) Wa ^ɔ^inna Rabbaka laHuwal-^c^Azīzur-Raḥīm. (68) Wat-lu ^c^alayhim naba^ɔ^a ^ɔ^Ibrāhīm. (69) ^ɔ^Idh qāla li^ɔ^abīhi wa qawmihī mā ta^c^budūn. (70) Qālū na^c^budu ^ɔ^aṣnāmaṅ-fanaẓallu lahā ^c^ākifīn. (71) Qāla hal yasma^c^ūnakum ^ɔ^idh tad^c^ūn. (72) ^ɔ^Aw yaṅfa^c^ūnakum ^ɔ^aw yaḍurrūn. (73) Qālū bal wajadnāa ^ɔ^ābāa^ɔ^anā kadhālika yaf^c^alūn. (74) Qāla ^ɔ^afara^ɔ^aytum-mā kuṅtum ta^c^budūn. (75) ^ɔ^Aṅtum wa ^ɔ^ābāa^ɔ^ukumul-^ɔ^aqdamūn. (76)

the followers of Moses exclaimed: "Behold, we shall certainly be overtaken [and defeated]!" ‹61›
He replied: "Nay indeed! My Sustainer is with me, [and] He will guide me!" ‹62›
Thereupon We inspired Moses thus: "Strike the sea with thy staff!" – whereupon it parted, and each part appeared like a mountain vast.[33] ‹63›
And We caused the pursuers[34] to draw near unto that place: ‹64› and We saved Moses and all who were with him, ‹65› and then We caused the others to drown.[35] ‹66›
In this [story], behold, there is a message [unto all men], even though most of them will not believe [in it]. ‹67› And yet, verily, thy Sustainer – He alone – is almighty, a dispenser of grace![36] ‹68›

AND CONVEY unto them[37] the story of Abraham ‹69› – [how it was] when he asked his father and his people, "What is it that you worship?" ‹70›
They answered: "We worship idols, and we remain ever devoted to them." ‹71›
Said he: "Do [you really think that] they hear you when you invoke them, ‹72› or benefit you or do you harm?" ‹73›
They exclaimed: "But we found our forefathers doing the same!"[38] ‹74›
Said [Abraham]: "Have you, then, ever considered what it is that you have been worshipping ‹75›
– you and those ancient forebears of yours? ‹76›

33 See 20 : 77 and the corresponding note 61. Cf. also the Biblical account (Exodus xiv, 21), according to which "the Lord caused the sea to go back by a strong east wind all that night, and made the sea dry land, and the waters were divided".

34 Lit., "the others".

35 From various indications in the Bible (in particular, Exodus xiv, 2 and 9), it appears that the miracle of the crossing of the Red Sea took place at the north-western extremity of what is known today as the Gulf of Suez. In those ancient times it was not as deep as it is now, and in some respects may have resembled the shallow part of the North Sea between the mainland and the Frisian Islands, with its total ebbs which lay bare the sandbanks and make them temporarily passable, followed by sudden, violent tides which submerge them entirely.

36 See note 6 on verses 8-9.

37 I.e., to the kind of people spoken of in verses 3-8 of this *sūrah*.

38 The particle *bal* at the beginning of the sentence expresses astonishment. Thus, evading a direct answer to Abraham's criticism of idol-worship, his people merely stress its antiquity, forgetting – as Zamakhsharī points out – that "ancient usage and precedence in time are no proof of [a concept's] soundness". Rāzī, for his part, states that the above verse represents "one of the strongest [Qur^ɔ^anic] indications of the immorality (*fasād*) inherent in [the principle of] *taqlīd*", i.e., the blind, unquestioning adoption of religious concepts or practices on the basis of one's uncritical faith in no more than the "authority" of a scholar or religious leader.

"Now [as for me, I know that,] verily, these [false deities] are my enemies, [and that none is my helper] save the Sustainer of all the worlds, ‹77› who has created me and is the One who guides me, ‹78› and is the One who gives me to eat and to drink, ‹79› and when I fall ill, is the One who restores me to health, ‹80› and who will cause me to die and then will bring me back to life ‹81› – and who, I hope, will forgive me my faults on Judgment Day! ‹82›

"O my Sustainer! Endow me with the ability to judge [between right and wrong], and make me one with the righteous, ‹83› and grant me the power to convey the truth unto those who will come after me,[39] ‹84› and place me among those who shall inherit the garden of bliss! ‹85›

"And forgive my father – for, verily, he is among those who have gone astray[40] ‹86› – and do not put me to shame on the Day when all shall be raised from the dead:[41] ‹87› the Day on which neither wealth will be of any use, nor children, ‹88› [and when] only he [will be happy] who comes before God with a heart free of evil!" ‹89›

For, [on that Day,] paradise will be brought within sight of the God-conscious, ‹90› whereas the blazing fire will be laid open before those who had been lost in grievous error; ‹91› and they will be asked: "Where now is all that you were wont to worship ‹92› instead of God?[42] Can these [things and beings] be of any help to you or to themselves?" ‹93›

Thereupon they will be hurled into hell[43] – they as well as all [others] who had been lost in grievous error, ‹94› and the hosts of Iblīs – all together.[44] ‹95›

فَإِنَّهُمْ عَدُوٌّ لِّىٓ إِلَّا رَبَّ ٱلْعَٰلَمِينَ ﴿٧٧﴾ ٱلَّذِى خَلَقَنِى فَهُوَ يَهْدِينِ ﴿٧٨﴾ وَٱلَّذِى
هُوَ يُطْعِمُنِى وَيَسْقِينِ ﴿٧٩﴾ وَإِذَا مَرِضْتُ فَهُوَ يَشْفِينِ ﴿٨٠﴾ وَٱلَّذِى يُمِيتُنِى
ثُمَّ يُحْيِينِ ﴿٨١﴾ وَٱلَّذِىٓ أَطْمَعُ أَن يَغْفِرَ لِى خَطِيٓـَٔتِى يَوْمَ ٱلدِّينِ ﴿٨٢﴾ رَبِّ
هَبْ لِى حُكْمًا وَأَلْحِقْنِى بِٱلصَّٰلِحِينَ ﴿٨٣﴾ وَٱجْعَل لِّى لِسَانَ صِدْقٍ فِى
ٱلْءَاخِرِينَ ﴿٨٤﴾ وَٱجْعَلْنِى مِن وَرَثَةِ جَنَّةِ ٱلنَّعِيمِ ﴿٨٥﴾ وَٱغْفِرْ لِأَبِىٓ إِنَّهُۥ
كَانَ مِنَ ٱلضَّآلِّينَ ﴿٨٦﴾ وَلَا تُخْزِنِى يَوْمَ يُبْعَثُونَ ﴿٨٧﴾ يَوْمَ لَا يَنفَعُ مَالٌ وَلَا
بَنُونَ ﴿٨٨﴾ إِلَّا مَنْ أَتَى ٱللَّهَ بِقَلْبٍ سَلِيمٍ ﴿٨٩﴾ وَأُزْلِفَتِ ٱلْجَنَّةُ لِلْمُتَّقِينَ ﴿٩٠﴾
وَبُرِّزَتِ ٱلْجَحِيمُ لِلْغَاوِينَ ﴿٩١﴾ وَقِيلَ لَهُمْ أَيْنَ مَا كُنتُمْ تَعْبُدُونَ ﴿٩٢﴾
مِن دُونِ ٱللَّهِ هَلْ يَنصُرُونَكُمْ أَوْ يَنتَصِرُونَ ﴿٩٣﴾ فَكُبْكِبُوا۟ فِيهَا هُمْ
وَٱلْغَاوُۥنَ ﴿٩٤﴾ وَجُنُودُ إِبْلِيسَ أَجْمَعُونَ ﴿٩٥﴾

Faʾinnahum ʿaduwwul-līi ʾillā Rabbal-ʿālamīn. (77) ʾAlladhī khalaqanī faHuwa yahdīn. (78) Wal-ladhī Huwa yuṭʿimunī wa yasqīn. (79) Wa ʾidhā mariḍtu fa-Huwa yashfīn. (80) Wal-ladhī yumītunī thumma yuḥyīn. (81) Wal-ladhīi ʾaṭmaʿu ʾañy-yaghfira lī khaṭīiʾatī Yawmad-dīn. (82) Rabbi hab lī ḥukmañw-wa ʾalḥiqnī biṣ-ṣāliḥīn. (83) Waj-ʿal-lī lisāna ṣidqiñ-fil-ʾākhirīn. (84) Waj-ʿalnī miñw-warathati jannatiñ-naʿīm. (85) Wagh-fir liʾabīi ʾinnahū kana minaḍ-ḍāallīin. (86) Wa lā tukhzinī Yawma yubʿathūn. (87) Yawma lā yañfaʿu māluñw-wa lā banūn. (88) ʾIllā man ʾatal-lāha biqalbiñ-salīm. (89) Wa ʾuzlifatil-jannatu lil-muttaqīn. (90) Wa burrizatil-jaḥīmu lilghāwīn. (91) Wa qīla lahum ʾayna mā kuñtum taʿbudūna, (92) miñ-dūnil-lāhi hal yañṣurūnakum ʾaw yañtaṣirūn. (93) Fa-kubkibū fīhā hum wal-ghāwūn. (94) Wa junūdu ʾIblīsa ʾajmaʿūn. (95)

39 Lit., "grant me a language of truth among the others" or "the later ones". For alternative interpretations of this phrase, see note 36 on 19 : 50.

40 Cf. 19 : 47-48.

41 Sc., "by letting me see my father among the damned" (Zamakhsharī).

42 Or: "beside God". Whenever the relative pronoun *mā* ("that which" or "all that which") is used in the Qurʾān with reference to false objects of worship, it indicates not merely inanimate things (like idols, fetishes, supposedly "holy" relics, etc.) or falsely deified saints, dead or alive, but also forces of nature, real or imaginary, as well as man's "worship" of wealth, power, social position, etc. (See also 10 : 28-29 and the corresponding notes.)

43 Lit., "into it".

44 Cf. 2 : 24 – "the fire whose fuel is human beings and stones" – and the corresponding note 16. The "hosts of

قَالُوا۟ وَهُمْ فِيهَا يَخْتَصِمُونَ ﴿96﴾ تَٱللَّهِ إِن كُنَّا لَفِى ضَلَـٰلٍ مُّبِينٍ ﴿97﴾ إِذْ
نُسَوِّيكُم بِرَبِّ ٱلْعَـٰلَمِينَ ﴿98﴾ وَمَآ أَضَلَّنَآ إِلَّا ٱلْمُجْرِمُونَ ﴿99﴾ فَمَا لَنَا
مِن شَـٰفِعِينَ ﴿100﴾ وَلَا صَدِيقٍ حَمِيمٍ ﴿101﴾ فَلَوْ أَنَّ لَنَا كَرَّةً فَنَكُونَ مِنَ
ٱلْمُؤْمِنِينَ ﴿102﴾ إِنَّ فِى ذَٰلِكَ لَـَٔايَةً ۖ وَمَا كَانَ أَكْثَرُهُم مُّؤْمِنِينَ ﴿103﴾ وَإِنَّ
رَبَّكَ لَهُوَ ٱلْعَزِيزُ ٱلرَّحِيمُ ﴿104﴾ كَذَّبَتْ قَوْمُ نُوحٍ ٱلْمُرْسَلِينَ ﴿105﴾ إِذْ
قَالَ لَهُمْ أَخُوهُمْ نُوحٌ أَلَا تَتَّقُونَ ﴿106﴾ إِنِّى لَكُمْ رَسُولٌ أَمِينٌ ﴿107﴾ فَٱتَّقُوا۟
ٱللَّهَ وَأَطِيعُونِ ﴿108﴾ وَمَآ أَسْـَٔلُكُمْ عَلَيْهِ مِنْ أَجْرٍ ۖ إِنْ أَجْرِىَ إِلَّا عَلَىٰ رَبِّ
ٱلْعَـٰلَمِينَ ﴿109﴾ فَٱتَّقُوا۟ ٱللَّهَ وَأَطِيعُونِ ﴿110﴾ ۞ قَالُوٓا۟ أَنُؤْمِنُ لَكَ وَٱتَّبَعَكَ
ٱلْأَرْذَلُونَ ﴿111﴾ قَالَ وَمَا عِلْمِى بِمَا كَانُوا۟ يَعْمَلُونَ ﴿112﴾ إِنْ حِسَابُهُمْ إِلَّا
عَلَىٰ رَبِّى ۖ لَوْ تَشْعُرُونَ ﴿113﴾

And there and then, blaming one another,[45] they [who had grievously sinned in life] will exclaim. ‹96› "By God, we were most obviously astray ‹97› when we deemed you [false deities] equal to the Sustainer of all the worlds ‹98› – yet they who have seduced us [into believing in you] are the truly guilty ones![46] ‹99› And now we have none to intercede for us, ‹100› nor any loving friend. ‹101› Would that we had a second chance [in life],[47] so that we could be among the believers!" ‹102›

حزب 38 In all this, behold, there is a message [unto men], even though most of them will not believe [in it]. ‹103› But, verily, thy Sustainer – He alone – is almighty, a dispenser of grace![48] ‹104›

THE PEOPLE of Noah [too] gave the lie to [one of God's] message-bearers ‹105› when their brother Noah said unto them: "Will you not be conscious of God? ‹106› Behold, I am an apostle [sent by Him] to you, [and therefore] worthy of your trust: ‹107› be, then, conscious of God, and pay heed unto me! ‹108›

"And no reward whatever do I ask of you for it: my reward rests with none but the Sustainer of all the worlds. ‹109› Hence, remain conscious of God, and pay heed unto me!" ‹110›

They answered: "Shall we place our faith in thee, even though [only] the most abject [of people] follow thee?"[49] ‹111›

Said he: "And what knowledge could I have as to what they were doing [before they came to me]? ‹112› Their reckoning rests with none but my Sustainer: if you could but understand [this]![50] ‹113›

Qālū wa hum fīhā yakhtaṣimūna, ﴿96﴾ tallāhi ɔiñ-
kunnā lafī ḍalālim-mubīn. ﴿97﴾ ɔIdh nusawwīkum-
biRabbil-ᶜālamīn. ﴿98﴾ Wa māa ɔaḍallanāa ɔillal-
mujrimūn. ﴿99﴾ Famā lanā miñ-shāfiᶜīn. ﴿100﴾ Wa lā
ṣadīqin ḥamīm. ﴿101﴾ Falaw ɔanna lanā karratañ-
fanakūna minal-muɔminīn. ﴿102﴾ ɔInna fī dhālika
laɔĀyatañw-wa mā kāna ɔaktharuhum-muɔminīn. ﴿103﴾
Wa ɔinna Rabbaka laHuwal-ᶜAzīzur-Raḥīm. ﴿104﴾ Kadh-
dhabat qawmu Nūḥinil-Mursalīn. ﴿105﴾ ɔIdh qāla lahum
ɔakhuhum Nūḥun ɔalā tattaqūn. ﴿106﴾ ɔInnī lakum
Rasūlun ɔamīn. ﴿107﴾ Fattaqul-lāha wa ɔaṭīᶜūn. ﴿108﴾
Wa māa ɔasɔalukum ᶜalayhi min ɔajrin ɔin ɔajriya ɔillā
ᶜalā Rabbil-ᶜālamīn. ﴿109﴾ Fattaqul-lāha wa ɔaṭīᶜūn. ﴿110﴾
۞ Qālūu ɔanuɔminu laka wat-tabaᶜakal-ɔardhalūn.
﴿111﴾ Qāla wa mā ᶜilmī bimā kānū yaᶜmalūn. ﴿112﴾ ɔIn
ḥisābuhum ɔillā ᶜalā Rabbī law tashᶜurūn. ﴿113﴾

Iblīs" are the forces of evil ("satans") frequently mentioned in the Qurɔān in connection with man's sinning (see note 10 on 2 : 14, the first half of note 16 on 15 : 17, as well as note 52 on 19 : 68; also cf. 19 : 83 and the corresponding note 72).

45 Lit., "while they quarrel with one another".

46 Lit., "yet none but those guilty ones (*al-mujrimūn*) have led us astray": cf. 7 : 38, 33 : 67-68, 38 : 60-61 and the corresponding notes.

47 Lit., "would that there were a return for us". See also 6 : 27-28 and the corresponding note.

48 Sc., "and He may grant forgiveness to whomever He wills".

49 See note 47 on 11 : 27.

50 This is obviously a retort to the unbelievers' suggestion (elliptically implied here) that those "abject" followers of

Hence, I shall not drive away [any of] those [who profess to be] believers; ‹114› I am nothing but a plain warner." ‹115›
Said they: "Indeed, if thou desist not, O Noah, thou wilt surely be stoned to death!"[51] ‹116›
[Whereupon] he prayed: "O my Sustainer! Behold, my people have given me the lie: ‹117› hence, lay Thou wide open the truth between me and them,[52] and save me and those of the believers who are with me!" ‹118›
And so We saved him and those [who were] with him in the fully-laden ark, ‹119› and then We caused those who stayed behind to drown.[53] ‹120›
In this [story], behold, there is a message [unto men],[54] even though most of them will not believe [in it]. ‹121› But, verily, thy Sustainer – He alone – is almighty, a dispenser of grace! ‹122›

[AND the tribe of] ᶜĀd gave the lie to [one of God's] message-bearers ‹123› when their brother Hūd[55] said unto them: "Will you not be conscious of God? ‹124› Behold, I am an apostle [sent by Him] to you, [and therefore] worthy of your trust: ‹125› be, then, conscious of God, and pay heed unto me! ‹126›
"And no reward whatever do I ask of you for it: my reward rests with none but the Sustainer of all the worlds. ‹127›
"Will you, in your wanton folly, build [idolatrous] altars on every height,[56] ‹128›

وَمَآ أَنَا۠ بِطَارِدِ ٱلْمُؤْمِنِينَ ﴿114﴾ إِنْ أَنَا۠ إِلَّا نَذِيرٌ مُّبِينٌ ﴿115﴾ قَالُوا۟ لَئِن لَّمْ تَنتَهِ
يَٰنُوحُ لَتَكُونَنَّ مِنَ ٱلْمَرْجُومِينَ ﴿116﴾ قَالَ رَبِّ إِنَّ قَوْمِى كَذَّبُونِ ﴿117﴾
فَٱفْتَحْ بَيْنِى وَبَيْنَهُمْ فَتْحًا وَنَجِّنِى وَمَن مَّعِىَ مِنَ ٱلْمُؤْمِنِينَ ﴿118﴾ فَأَنجَيْنَٰهُ
وَمَن مَّعَهُۥ فِى ٱلْفُلْكِ ٱلْمَشْحُونِ ﴿119﴾ ثُمَّ أَغْرَقْنَا بَعْدُ ٱلْبَاقِينَ ﴿120﴾ إِنَّ فِى
ذَٰلِكَ لَءَايَةً ۖ وَمَا كَانَ أَكْثَرُهُم مُّؤْمِنِينَ ﴿121﴾ وَإِنَّ رَبَّكَ لَهُوَ ٱلْعَزِيزُ
ٱلرَّحِيمُ ﴿122﴾ كَذَّبَتْ عَادٌ ٱلْمُرْسَلِينَ ﴿123﴾ إِذْ قَالَ لَهُمْ أَخُوهُمْ هُودٌ أَلَا
تَتَّقُونَ ﴿124﴾ إِنِّى لَكُمْ رَسُولٌ أَمِينٌ ﴿125﴾ فَٱتَّقُوا۟ ٱللَّهَ وَأَطِيعُونِ ﴿126﴾ وَمَآ
أَسْـَٔلُكُمْ عَلَيْهِ مِنْ أَجْرٍ ۖ إِنْ أَجْرِىَ إِلَّا عَلَىٰ رَبِّ ٱلْعَٰلَمِينَ ﴿127﴾ أَتَبْنُونَ
بِكُلِّ رِيعٍ ءَايَةً تَعْبَثُونَ ﴿128﴾

Wa māa ᵓana biṭāridil-muᵓminīn. ﴿114﴾ ᵓIn ᵓana ᵓillā nadhīrum-mubīn. ﴿115﴾ Qālū laᵓillam tañtahi yā Nūḥu latakūnanna minal-marjūmīn. ﴿116﴾ Qāla Rabbi ᵓinna qawmī kadhdhabūn. ﴿117﴾ Faftaḥ baynī wa baynahum fatḥañw-wa najjinī wa mam-maᶜiya minal-muᵓminīn. ﴿118﴾ Faᵓañjaynāhu wa mam-maᶜahū fil-fulkil-mashḥūn. ﴿119﴾ Thumma ᵓaghraqnā baᶜdul-bāqīn. ﴿120﴾ ᵓInna fī dhālika laᵓĀyatañw-wa mā kāna aktharuhum-muᵓminīn. ﴿121﴾ Wa ᵓinna Rabbaka laHuwal-ᶜAzīzur-Raḥīm. ﴿122﴾ Kadhdhabat ᶜĀdunil-Mursalīn. ﴿123﴾ ᵓIdh qāla lahum ᵓakhūhum Hūdun ᵓalā tattaqūn. ﴿124﴾ ᵓInnī lakum Rasūlun ᵓamīn. ﴿125﴾ Fattaqul-lāha wa ᵓaṭīᶜūn. ﴿126﴾ Wa māa ᵓasᵓalukum ᶜalayhi min ᵓajrin ᵓin ᵓajriya ᵓillā ᶜalā Rabbil-ᶜālamīn. ﴿127﴾ ᵓAtabnūna bikulli rīᶜin ᵓāyatañ-taᶜbathūn. ﴿128﴾

Noah had declared their faith in him, not out of conviction, but only in order to gain some material advantages. Noah's answer embodies a cardinal principle of Qurᵓanic ethics and, hence, of Islamic Law: No human being has the right to sit in judgment on another person's faith or hidden motives; whereas God knows what is in the hearts of men, society may judge only by external evidence (*aẓ-ẓāhir*), which comprises a person's words as well as deeds. Thus, if anyone says, "I am a believer", and does not act or speak in a manner contradicting his professed faith, the community must consider him a believer.

51 Lit., "thou wilt surely be among those who are stoned [to death]".

52 Or: "decide Thou with a [clear] decision between me and them". My choice of the primary significance of *iftaḥ* ("lay open", i.e., the truth) has been explained in note 72 on the last sentence of 7 : 89.

53 The story of Noah and his people, as well as of the Deluge, is given in greater detail in 11 : 25-48.

54 For the message specifically alluded to here, see verses 111-115, as well as note 50 above.

55 See 7 : 65 and the corresponding note 48.

56 The noun *āyah*, which primarily denotes "a sign" or "a token", evidently refers here to the ancient Semitic

and make for yourselves mighty castles, [hoping] that you might become immortal?[57] ‹129› And will you [always], whenever you lay hand [on others], lay hand [on them] cruelly, without any restraint?[58] ‹130›

"Be, then, conscious of God and pay heed unto me: ‹131› and [thus] be conscious of Him who has [so] amply provided you with all [the good] that you might think of[59] ‹132› – amply provided you with flocks, and children, ‹133› and gardens, and springs: ‹134› – for, verily, I fear lest suffering befall you on an awesome day!" ‹135›

[But] they answered: "It is all one to us whether thou preachest [something new] or art not of those who [like to] preach. ‹136› This [religion of ours] is none other than that to which our forebears clung,[60] ‹137› and we are not going to be chastised [for adhering to it]!" ‹138›

And so they gave him the lie: and thereupon We destroyed them.

In this [story], behold, there is a message [unto men], even though most of them will not believe [in it].[61] ‹139› But, verily, thy Sustainer – He alone – is almighty, a dispenser of grace! ‹140›

[AND the tribe of] Thamūd gave the lie to [one of God's] message-bearers ‹141›

وَتَتَّخِذُونَ مَصَانِعَ لَعَلَّكُمْ تَخْلُدُونَ ﴿١٢٩﴾ وَإِذَا بَطَشْتُم بَطَشْتُمْ جَبَّارِينَ ﴿١٣٠﴾
فَاتَّقُوا اللَّهَ وَأَطِيعُونِ ﴿١٣١﴾ وَاتَّقُوا الَّذِي أَمَدَّكُم بِمَا تَعْلَمُونَ ﴿١٣٢﴾
أَمَدَّكُم بِأَنْعَامٍ وَبَنِينَ ﴿١٣٣﴾ وَجَنَّاتٍ وَعُيُونٍ ﴿١٣٤﴾ إِنِّي أَخَافُ عَلَيْكُمْ
عَذَابَ يَوْمٍ عَظِيمٍ ﴿١٣٥﴾ قَالُوا سَوَاءٌ عَلَيْنَا أَوَعَظْتَ أَمْ لَمْ تَكُن مِّنَ
الْوَاعِظِينَ ﴿١٣٦﴾ إِنْ هَٰذَا إِلَّا خُلُقُ الْأَوَّلِينَ ﴿١٣٧﴾ وَمَا نَحْنُ بِمُعَذَّبِينَ ﴿١٣٨﴾
فَكَذَّبُوهُ فَأَهْلَكْنَاهُمْ إِنَّ فِي ذَٰلِكَ لَآيَةً وَمَا كَانَ أَكْثَرُهُم مُّؤْمِنِينَ ﴿١٣٩﴾
وَإِنَّ رَبَّكَ لَهُوَ الْعَزِيزُ الرَّحِيمُ ﴿١٤٠﴾ كَذَّبَتْ ثَمُودُ الْمُرْسَلِينَ ﴿١٤١﴾

Wa tattakhidhūna maṣāniʿa laʿallakum takhludūn. (129) Wa ʾidhā baṭashtum-baṭashtum jabbārīn. (130) Fattaqul-lāha wa ʾaṭīʿūn. (131) Wat-taqul-ladhīi ʾamaddakum-bimā taʿlamūn. (132) ʾAmaddakum-biʾanʿāmiñw-wa banīn. (133) Wa jannātiñw-wa ʿuyūn. (134) ʾInnīi ʾakhāfu ʿalaykum ʿadhāba Yawmin ʿaẓīm. (135) Qālū sawāaʾun ʿalaynāa ʾawaʿaẓta ʾam lam takum-minal-wāʿiẓīn. (136) ʾIn hādhāa ʾillā khuluqul-ʾawwalīn. (137) Wa mā naḥnu bimuʿadhdhabīn. (138) Fakadhdhabūhu faʾahlaknāhum. ʾInna fī dhālika laʾĀyatañw-wa mā kāna ʾaktharuhum-muʾminīn. (139) Wa inna Rabbaka laHuwal-ʾAzīzur-Raḥīm. (140) Kadhdhabat Thamūdul-Mursalīn. (141)

custom of worshipping the tribal gods on hilltops, which were crowned to this end by sacrificial altars or monuments, each of them devoted to a particular deity: hence my rendering of *āyah*, in this particular context, as "altars" (in the plural).

57 The meaning could be either "hoping that you might live in them forever", or "that you might gain immortal renown for having built them".

58 The term *jabbār*, when applied to man, as a rule denotes one who is haughty, overbearing, exorbitant and cruel, and does not submit to any moral restraints in his dealings with those who are weaker than himself. Sometimes (as, e.g., in 11 : 59 or 14 : 15) this term is used to describe a person's negative *ethical attitude*, and in that case it may be rendered as "enemy of the truth". In the present instance, however, stress is laid on the tyrannical *behaviour* of the tribe of ʿĀd, evidently relating to their warlike conflicts with other people: and in this sense it expresses a Qurʾanic prohibition, valid for all times, of all unnecessary cruelty in warfare, coupled with the positive, clearly-implied injunction to subordinate every act of war – as well as the decision to wage war as such – to moral considerations and restraints.

59 Lit., "with all that you know" or "that you are [or "might be"] aware of".

60 Lit., "the innate habit of the earlier people (*al-awwalīn*)". The noun *khuluq* denotes one's "nature" in the sense of "innate disposition" (*tabīʿah*) or "moral character" (*Tāj al-ʿArūs*); hence the use of this term to describe "that to which one clings", i.e., one's "innate habit" or "custom", and, in a specific sense, one's religion (*ibid.*).

61 The message referred to here is contained in verses 128-130, which point out the three cardinal sins resulting from man's inordinate striving for power: worship of anything apart from God, self-admiring search for "glory", and cruelty or harshness towards one's fellow-men.

when their brother Ṣāliḥ[62] said unto them: "Will you not be conscious of God? ‹142› Behold, I am an apostle [sent by Him] to you, [and therefore] worthy of your trust: ‹143› be, then, conscious of God, and pay heed unto me! ‹144›

"And no reward whatever do I ask of you for it: my reward rests with none but the Sustainer of all the worlds. ‹145›

"Do you think that you will be left secure [forever] in the midst of what you have here and now?[63] ‹146› – amidst [these] gardens and springs ‹147› and fields, and [these] palm-trees with slender spathes? ‹148› – and that you will [always be able to] hew dwellings out of the mountains with [the same] great skill?[64] ‹149›

"Be, then, conscious of God, and pay heed unto me, ‹150› and pay no heed to the counsel of those who are given to excesses ‹151› – those who spread corruption on earth instead of setting things to rights!" ‹152›

Said they: "Thou art but one of the bewitched! ‹153› Thou art nothing but a mortal like ourselves! Come, then, forward with a token [of thy mission][65] if thou art a man of truth!" ‹154›

Replied he: "This she-camel[66] shall have a share of water, and you shall have a share of water, on the days appointed [therefore];[67] ‹155› and do her no harm, lest suffering befall you on an awesome day!" ‹156›

إِذْ قَالَ لَهُمْ أَخُوهُمْ صَٰلِحٌ أَلَا تَتَّقُونَ ﴿١٤٢﴾ إِنِّي لَكُمْ رَسُولٌ أَمِينٌ ﴿١٤٣﴾
فَٱتَّقُوا۟ ٱللَّهَ وَأَطِيعُونِ ﴿١٤٤﴾ وَمَآ أَسْـَٔلُكُمْ عَلَيْهِ مِنْ أَجْرٍ إِنْ أَجْرِىَ إِلَّا
عَلَىٰ رَبِّ ٱلْعَٰلَمِينَ ﴿١٤٥﴾ أَتُتْرَكُونَ فِى مَا هَٰهُنَآ ءَامِنِينَ ﴿١٤٦﴾ فِى جَنَّٰتٍ
وَعُيُونٍ ﴿١٤٧﴾ وَزُرُوعٍ وَنَخْلٍ طَلْعُهَا هَضِيمٌ ﴿١٤٨﴾ وَتَنْحِتُونَ مِنَ ٱلْجِبَالِ
بُيُوتًا فَٰرِهِينَ ﴿١٤٩﴾ فَٱتَّقُوا۟ ٱللَّهَ وَأَطِيعُونِ ﴿١٥٠﴾ وَلَا تُطِيعُوٓا۟ أَمْرَ
ٱلْمُسْرِفِينَ ﴿١٥١﴾ ٱلَّذِينَ يُفْسِدُونَ فِى ٱلْأَرْضِ وَلَا يُصْلِحُونَ ﴿١٥٢﴾ قَالُوٓا۟
إِنَّمَآ أَنتَ مِنَ ٱلْمُسَحَّرِينَ ﴿١٥٣﴾ مَآ أَنتَ إِلَّا بَشَرٌ مِّثْلُنَا فَأْتِ بِـَٔايَةٍ إِن
كُنتَ مِنَ ٱلصَّٰدِقِينَ ﴿١٥٤﴾ قَالَ هَٰذِهِۦ نَاقَةٌ لَّهَا شِرْبٌ وَلَكُمْ شِرْبُ
يَوْمٍ مَّعْلُومٍ ﴿١٥٥﴾ وَلَا تَمَسُّوهَا بِسُوٓءٍ فَيَأْخُذَكُمْ عَذَابُ يَوْمٍ عَظِيمٍ ﴿١٥٦﴾

ʾIdh qāla lahum ʾakhūhum Ṣāliḥun ʾalā tattaqūn. ﴿142﴾ ʾInnī lakum Rasūlun ʾamīn. ﴿143﴾ Fattaqul-lāha wa ʾaṭīʿūn. ﴿144﴾ Wa māa ʾasʾalukum ʿalayhi min ʾajrin ʾin ʾajriya ʾillā ʿalā Rabbil-ʿālamīn. ﴿145﴾ ʾAtutrakūna fī mā hāhunāa ʾāminīn. ﴿146﴾ Fī jannātiñw-wa ʿuyūn. ﴿147﴾ Wa zurūʿiñw-wa nakhliñ-ṭalʿuhā haḍīm. ﴿148﴾ Wa tanḥitūna minal-jibāli buyūtañ-fārihīn. ﴿149﴾ Fattaqul-lāha wa ʾaṭīʿūn. ﴿150﴾ Wa lā tuṭīʿūu ʾamral-musrifīn. ﴿151﴾ ʾAlladhīna yufsidūna fil-ʾarḍi wa lā yuṣliḥūn. ﴿152﴾ Qālūu ʾinnamāa ʾañta minal-musaḥḥarīn. ﴿153﴾ Māa ʾañta ʾillā basharum-mithlunā faʾti biʾĀyatin ʾiñ-kuñta minaṣ-ṣādiqīn. ﴿154﴾ Qāla hādhihī nāqatul-lahā shirbuñw-wa lakum shirbu yawmim-maʿlūm. ﴿155﴾ Wa lā tamassūhā bisūuʾiñ-fayaʾkhudhakum ʿadhābu Yawmin ʿaẓīm. ﴿156﴾

---

62 For the story of Ṣāliḥ and the tribe of Thamūd, see 7 : 73 and the corresponding note 56; also, the version appearing in 11 : 61-68.

63 Lit., "of what is here", i.e., on earth. In the original, this question has a direct form, thus: "Will you be left secure . . . ?", etc. (See also note 69 below.)

64 See note 59 on 7 : 74.

65 Ṭabarī: ". . . that is to say, 'with an indication (*dalālah*) and a proof that thou art to be trusted as regards thy claim that thou hast been sent to us by God'."

66 Cf. the second paragraph of 7 : 73 – "This she-camel belonging to God shall be a token for you" – and the corresponding note 57, which explains that the "token" spoken of by Ṣāliḥ was to consist in the manner in which the tribe would treat the animal.

67 Lit., "on a day appointed", which may mean either "*each* on a day appointed" (i.e., by turns), or, more probably – because more in consonance with the tribal customs of ancient Arabia – "on the days appointed for the watering of camels": implying that on those days the ownerless she-camel should receive a full share of water side by side with the herds and flocks belonging to the tribe.

But they cruelly slaughtered her – and then they had cause to regret it:[68] ‹157› for the suffering [predicted by Ṣāliḥ] befell them [then and there].
In this [story], behold, there is a message [unto men], even though most of them will not believe [in it].[69] ‹158› But, verily, thy Sustainer – He alone – is almighty, a dispenser of grace! ‹159›

[AND] the people of Lot[70] gave the lie to [one of God's] message-bearers ‹160› when their brother Lot said unto them: "Will you not be conscious of God? ‹161› Behold, I am an apostle [sent by Him] to you, [and therefore] worthy of your trust: ‹162› be, then, conscious of God, and pay heed unto me! ‹163›
"And no reward whatever do I ask of you for it: my reward rests with none but the Sustainer of all the worlds. ‹164›
"Must you, of all people, [lustfully] approach men, ‹165› keeping yourselves aloof from all the [lawful] spouses whom your Sustainer has created for you? Nay, but you are people who transgress all bounds of what is right!" ‹166›
Said they: "Indeed, if thou desist not, O Lot, thou wilt most certainly be expelled [from this township]!" ‹167›
[Lot] exclaimed: "Behold, I am one of those who utterly abhor your doings!" ‹168›
[And then he prayed:] "O my Sustainer! Save me and my household from all that they are doing!" ‹169›
Thereupon We saved him and all his household ‹170› – all but an old woman, who was among those that stayed behind;[71] ‹171› and then We utterly

فَعَقَرُوهَا فَأَصْبَحُوا۟ نَـٰدِمِينَ ﴿157﴾ فَأَخَذَهُمُ ٱلْعَذَابُ ۗ إِنَّ فِى ذَٰلِكَ لَـَٔايَةً ۖ وَمَا
كَانَ أَكْثَرُهُم مُّؤْمِنِينَ ﴿158﴾ وَإِنَّ رَبَّكَ لَهُوَ ٱلْعَزِيزُ ٱلرَّحِيمُ ﴿159﴾ كَذَّبَتْ
قَوْمُ لُوطٍ ٱلْمُرْسَلِينَ ﴿160﴾ إِذْ قَالَ لَهُمْ أَخُوهُمْ لُوطٌ أَلَا تَتَّقُونَ ﴿161﴾ إِنِّى
لَكُمْ رَسُولٌ أَمِينٌ ﴿162﴾ فَٱتَّقُوا۟ ٱللَّهَ وَأَطِيعُونِ ﴿163﴾ وَمَآ أَسْـَٔلُكُمْ عَلَيْهِ مِنْ
أَجْرٍ ۖ إِنْ أَجْرِىَ إِلَّا عَلَىٰ رَبِّ ٱلْعَـٰلَمِينَ ﴿164﴾ أَتَأْتُونَ ٱلذُّكْرَانَ مِنَ
ٱلْعَـٰلَمِينَ ﴿165﴾ وَتَذَرُونَ مَا خَلَقَ لَكُمْ رَبُّكُم مِّنْ أَزْوَٰجِكُم ۚ بَلْ أَنتُمْ
قَوْمٌ عَادُونَ ﴿166﴾ قَالُوا۟ لَئِن لَّمْ تَنتَهِ يَـٰلُوطُ لَتَكُونَنَّ مِنَ ٱلْمُخْرَجِينَ ﴿167﴾
قَالَ إِنِّى لِعَمَلِكُم مِّنَ ٱلْقَالِينَ ﴿168﴾ رَبِّ نَجِّنِى وَأَهْلِى مِمَّا يَعْمَلُونَ ﴿169﴾
فَنَجَّيْنَـٰهُ وَأَهْلَهُۥٓ أَجْمَعِينَ ﴿170﴾ إِلَّا عَجُوزًا فِى ٱلْغَـٰبِرِينَ ﴿171﴾ ثُمَّ

Faʿaqarūhā faʾaṣbaḥū nādimīn. (157) Faʾakhadhahumul-ʿadhāb. ʾInna fī dhālika laʾĀyatañw-wa mā kāna ʾaktharuhum-muʾminīn. (158) Wa ʾinna Rabbaka laHuwal-ʿAzīzur-Rahīm. (159) Kadhdhabat qawmu Lūṭinil-Mursalīn. (160) ʾIdh qāla lahum ʾakhūhum Lūṭun ʾalā tattaqūn. (161) ʾInnī lakum Rasūlun ʾamīn. (162) Fatta-qul-lāha wa ʾaṭīʿūn. (163) Wa māa ʾasʾalukum ʿalayhi min ʾajrin ʾin ʾajriya illā ʿalā Rabbil-ʿālamīn. (164) ʾAtaʾtūnadh-dhukrāna minal-ʿālamīn. (165) Wa tadharūna mā khalaqa lakum Rabbukum-min ʾazwājikum. Bal ʾañtum qawmun ʿādūn. (166) Qālū laʾil-lam tañtahi yā Lūṭu latakūnanna minal-mukhrajīn. (167) Qāla ʾInnī liʿamalikum-minal-qālīn. (168) Rabbi najjinī wa ʾahlī mimmā yaʿmalūn. (169) Fanajjaynāhu wa ʾahla-hūu ʾajmaʿīna, (170) ʾillā ʿajūzañ-fil-ghābirīn. (171) Thumma

68 Lit., "they became regretful". For my rendering of *ʿaqarūhā* as "they cruelly slaughtered her", see note 61 on 7 : 77.

69 In my opinion, the specific message alluded to here relates, in the first instance, to the individual person's emotional reluctance to visualize the limited, transitory character of his own life on earth (hinted at in verses 146-149 above) and, hence, the judgment that awaits everyone in the life to come; and, secondly, to the element of compassion for all other living beings as a basis of true morality.

70 The story of Lot and the sinful people among whom he lived is narrated in greater detail in 11 : 69-83.

71 As is evident from 7 : 83, 11 : 81, 27 : 57 and 29 : 32-33, the old woman was Lots' wife – a native of Sodom – who chose to remain with her own people instead of accompanying her husband, whom she thus betrayed (cf. also 66 : 10).

destroyed the others, ‹172› and rained down upon them a rain [of destruction]:[72] and dire is such rain upon all who let themselves be warned [to no avail]![73] ‹173›
In this [story], behold, there is a message [unto men], even though most of them will not believe [in it]. ‹174› But, verily, thy Sustainer – He alone – is almighty, a dispenser of grace! ‹175›

[AND] the dwellers of the wooded dales [of Madyan] gave the lie to [one of God's] message-bearers ‹176› when their brother Shuʿayb[74] said unto them: "Will you not be conscious of God? ‹177› Behold, I am an apostle [sent by Him] to you, [and therefore] worthy of your trust: ‹178› be, then, conscious of God, and pay heed unto me! ‹179›
"And no reward whatever do I ask of you for it: my reward rests with none but the Sustainer of all the worlds. ‹180›
"[Always] give full measure, and be not among those who [unjustly] cause loss [to others]; ‹181› and [in all your dealings] weigh with a true balance, ‹182› and do not deprive people of what is rightfully theirs;[75] and do not act wickedly on earth by spreading corruption, ‹183› but be conscious of Him who has created you, just as [He created] those countless generations of old!"[76] ‹184›
Said they: "Thou art but one of the bewitched, ‹185› for thou art nothing but a mortal like ourselves! And, behold, we think that thou art a consummate liar![77] ‹186› Cause, then, fragments of the sky to fall down upon us, if thou art a man of truth!" ‹187›

دَمَّرْنَا ٱلْـَٔاخَرِينَ ﴿١٧٢﴾ وَأَمْطَرْنَا عَلَيْهِم مَّطَرًا فَسَآءَ مَطَرُ ٱلْمُنذَرِينَ ﴿١٧٣﴾
إِنَّ فِى ذَٰلِكَ لَـَٔايَةً وَمَا كَانَ أَكْثَرُهُم مُّؤْمِنِينَ ﴿١٧٤﴾ وَإِنَّ رَبَّكَ لَهُوَ ٱلْعَزِيزُ
ٱلرَّحِيمُ ﴿١٧٥﴾ كَذَّبَ أَصْحَٰبُ لْـَٔيْكَةِ ٱلْمُرْسَلِينَ ﴿١٧٦﴾ إِذْ قَالَ لَهُمْ شُعَيْبٌ
أَلَا تَتَّقُونَ ﴿١٧٧﴾ إِنِّى لَكُمْ رَسُولٌ أَمِينٌ ﴿١٧٨﴾ فَٱتَّقُوا۟ ٱللَّهَ وَأَطِيعُونِ ﴿١٧٩﴾ وَمَآ
أَسْـَٔلُكُمْ عَلَيْهِ مِنْ أَجْرٍ إِنْ أَجْرِىَ إِلَّا عَلَىٰ رَبِّ ٱلْعَٰلَمِينَ ﴿١٨٠﴾ ۞ أَوْفُوا۟
ٱلْكَيْلَ وَلَا تَكُونُوا۟ مِنَ ٱلْمُخْسِرِينَ ﴿١٨١﴾ وَزِنُوا۟ بِٱلْقِسْطَاسِ
ٱلْمُسْتَقِيمِ ﴿١٨٢﴾ وَلَا تَبْخَسُوا۟ ٱلنَّاسَ أَشْيَآءَهُمْ وَلَا تَعْثَوْا۟ فِى ٱلْأَرْضِ
مُفْسِدِينَ ﴿١٨٣﴾ وَٱتَّقُوا۟ ٱلَّذِى خَلَقَكُمْ وَٱلْجِبِلَّةَ ٱلْأَوَّلِينَ ﴿١٨٤﴾ قَالُوٓا۟ إِنَّمَآ
أَنتَ مِنَ ٱلْمُسَحَّرِينَ ﴿١٨٥﴾ وَمَآ أَنتَ إِلَّا بَشَرٌ مِّثْلُنَا وَإِن نَّظُنُّكَ لَمِنَ
ٱلْكَٰذِبِينَ ﴿١٨٦﴾ فَأَسْقِطْ عَلَيْنَا كِسَفًا مِّنَ ٱلسَّمَآءِ إِن كُنتَ مِنَ
ٱلصَّٰدِقِينَ ﴿١٨٧﴾

ربع الحزب

dammarnal-ʾākharīn. ﴿١٧٢﴾ Wa ʾamṭarnā ʿalayhim-maṭarañ-fasāaʾa maṭarul-muñdharīn. ﴿١٧٣﴾ ʾInna fī dhālika laʾĀyatañw-wa mā kāna ʾaktharuhum-muʾminīn. ﴿١٧٤﴾ Wa ʾinna Rabbaka laHuwal-ʿAzīzur-Raḥīm. ﴿١٧٥﴾ Kadhdhaba ʾaṣḥābul-ʾaykatil-Mursalīn. ﴿١٧٦﴾ ʾIdh qāla lahum Shuʿaybun ʾalā tattaqūn. ﴿١٧٧﴾ ʾInnī lakum Rasūlun ʾamīn. ﴿١٧٨﴾ Fattaqul-lāha wa ʾaṭīʿūn. ﴿١٧٩﴾ Wa māa ʾasʾalukum ʿalayhi min ʾajrin ʾin ʾajriya ʾillā ʿalā Rabbil-ʿālamīn. ﴿١٨٠﴾ ۞ ʾAwful-kayla wa lā takūnū minal-mukhsirīn. ﴿١٨١﴾ Wa zinū bil-qisṭāsil-mustaqīm. ﴿١٨٢﴾ Wa lā tabkhasun-nāsa ʾashyāaʾahum wa lā taʿthaw fil-ʾarḍi mufsidīn. ﴿١٨٣﴾ Wat-taqul-ladhī khalaqakum wal-jibillatal-ʾawwalīn. ﴿١٨٤﴾ Qālūu ʾinnamāa ʾañta minal-musaḥḥarīn. ﴿١٨٥﴾ Wa māa ʾañta ʾillā basharum-mithlunā wa ʾiñ-naẓunnuka laminal-kādhibīn. ﴿١٨٦﴾ Faʾasqiṭ ʿalaynā kisafam-minas-samāaʾi ʾiñ-kuñta minaṣ-ṣādiqīn. ﴿١٨٧﴾

72 See 11 : 82 and the corresponding note 114.

73 Or, in the past tense: "dire was the rain upon those who had been warned" – in which case this sentence would refer specifically to the sinful people of Sodom and Gomorrah. However, it is much more probable that its purport is general (see note 115 on the last sentence of 11 : 83). Zamakhsharī's interpretation of the above sentence is analogous to mine.

74 See note 67 on the first sentence of 7 : 85. The story of Shuʿayb and the people of Madyan (the "wooded dales") is given in greater detail in 11 : 84-95.

75 Cf. *sūrah* 7, note 68.

76 An allusion to the ephemeral character of man's life on earth and, by implication, to God's judgment.

77 Lit., "that thou art indeed one of the liars".

Answered [Shuᶜayb]: "My Sustainer knows fully well what you are doing." ‹188›
But they gave him the lie. And thereupon suffering overtook them on a day dark with shadows:[78] and, verily, it was the suffering of an awesome day! ‹189›
In this [story], behold, there is a message [unto men], even though most of them will not believe [in it]. ‹190› But, verily, thy Sustainer – He alone – is almighty, a dispenser of grace![79] ‹191›

NOW, BEHOLD, this [divine writ] has indeed been bestowed from on high by the Sustainer of all the worlds:[80] ‹192› trustworthy divine inspiration has alighted with it from on high ‹193› upon thy heart, [O Muḥammad,][81] so that thou mayest be among those who preach ‹194› in the clear Arabic tongue.[82] ‹195›
And, verily, [the essence of] this [revelation] is indeed found in the ancient books of divine wisdom [as well].[83] ‹196›

قَالَ رَبِّيٓ أَعۡلَمُ بِمَا تَعۡمَلُونَ ١٨٨ فَكَذَّبُوهُ فَأَخَذَهُمۡ عَذَابُ يَوۡمِ ٱلظُّلَّةِۚ
إِنَّهُۥ كَانَ عَذَابَ يَوۡمٍ عَظِيمٍ ١٨٩ إِنَّ فِي ذَٰلِكَ لَأٓيَةٗۖ وَمَا كَانَ أَكۡثَرُهُم
مُّؤۡمِنِينَ ١٩٠ وَإِنَّ رَبَّكَ لَهُوَ ٱلۡعَزِيزُ ٱلرَّحِيمُ ١٩١ وَإِنَّهُۥ لَتَنزِيلُ رَبِّ
ٱلۡعَٰلَمِينَ ١٩٢ نَزَلَ بِهِ ٱلرُّوحُ ٱلۡأَمِينُ ١٩٣ عَلَىٰ قَلۡبِكَ لِتَكُونَ مِنَ
ٱلۡمُنذِرِينَ ١٩٤ بِلِسَانٍ عَرَبِيّٖ مُّبِينٖ ١٩٥ وَإِنَّهُۥ لَفِي زُبُرِ ٱلۡأَوَّلِينَ ١٩٦

Qāla Rabbīi ᵓaᶜlamu bimā taᶜmalūn. 188 Fakadh-dhabūhu faᵓakhadhahum ᶜadhābu yawmiẓ-ẓullah. ᵓInnahū kāna ᶜadhāba yawmin ᶜaẓīm. 189 ᵓInna fī dhālika laᵓĀyatañw-wa mā kāna ᵓaktharuhum-muᵓminīn. 190 Wa ᵓinna Rabbaka laHuwal-ᶜAzīzur-Rahīm. 191 Wa ᵓinnahū latañzīlu Rabbil-ᶜālamīn. 192 Nazala bihir-Rūhul-ᵓamīnu, 193 ᶜalā qalbika litakūna minal-muñdhirīna, 194 bilisānin ᶜarabiyyim-mubīn. 195 Wa ᵓinnahū lafī Zuburil-ᵓawwalīn. 196

---

78 This may refer either to the physical darkness which often accompanies volcanic eruptions and earthquakes (which, as shown in 7 : 91, overtook the people of Madyan), or to the spiritual darkness and gloom which comes in the wake of belated regrets.

79 With this refrain ends the cycle of seven stories showing that spiritual truth in all its manifestations – whether it relates to an intellectual realization of God's existence, to a refusal to regard power, wealth or fame as real values, or to the virtues of compassion and kindness towards all that lives on earth – has at all times been unacceptable to the overwhelming majority of mankind, and has always been submerged under the average man's blindness and deafness of heart. The very repetition of phrases, sentences and situations in all of the above stories – or, rather, in the above versions of these oft-narrated stories – tends to bring home to us the fact that the human situation as such never really changes, and that, in consequence, those who preach the truth must always struggle against human greed, power-hunger and proneness to self-adulation.

80 Thus the discourse returns to the theme enunciated at the beginning of this *sūrah*, namely, the phenomenon of divine revelation as exemplified in the Qurᵓān, and men's reactions to it.

81 According to almost all the classical commentators, the expression *ar-rūḥ al-amīn* (lit., "the faithful [or "trustworthy"] spirit") is a designation of Gabriel, the Angel of Revelation, who, by virtue of his purely spiritual, functional nature, is incapable of sinning and cannot, therefore, be other than utterly faithful to the trust reposed in him by God (cf. 16 : 50). On the other hand, since the term *rūḥ* is often used in the Qurᵓān in the sense of "divine inspiration" (see *sūrah* 2, note 71, and *sūrah* 16, note 2), it may have this latter meaning in the above context as well, especially in view of the statement that it had "alighted from on high *upon the heart*" of the Prophet.

82 See 14 : 4 – "never have We sent forth any apostle otherwise than [with a message] in his own people's tongue" – and the corresponding note 3. That the message of the Qurᵓān is, nevertheless, universal has been stressed in many of its verses (e.g., in 7 : 158 or 25 : 1). The other prophets mentioned in the Qurᵓān who "preached in the Arabic tongue" were Ishmael, Hūd, Ṣāliḥ and Shuᶜayb, all of them Arabians. In addition, if we bear in mind that Hebrew and Aramaic are but ancient Arabic dialects, all the Hebrew prophets may be included among "those who preached in the Arabic tongue".

83 Lit., "in the scriptures (*zubur*, sing. *zabūr*) of the ancients" (see *sūrah* 21, note 101). This interpretation of the above verse – advanced among others by Zamakhsharī and Bayḍāwī (and, according to the former, attributed to Imām Abū Ḥanīfah as well) – is in full consonance with the oft-repeated Qurᵓanic doctrine that the basic teachings

Is it not evidence enough for them[84] that [so many] learned men from among the children of Israel have recognized this [as true]?[85] ‹197›
But [even] had We bestowed it from on high upon any of the non-Arabs, ‹198› and had he recited it unto them [in his own tongue], they would not have believed in it.[86] ‹199›
Thus have We caused this [message] to pass [unheeded] through the hearts of those who are lost in sin:[87] ‹200› they will not believe in it till they behold the grievous suffering ‹201› that will come upon them [on resurrection,] all of a sudden, without their being aware [of its approach]; ‹202› and then they will exclaim, "Could we have a respite?"[88] ‹203›
Do they, then, [really] wish that Our chastisement be hastened on?[89] ‹204›
But hast thou ever considered [this]: If We do allow them to enjoy [this life] for some years, ‹205› and thereupon that [chastisement] which they were promised befalls them ‹206› – of what avail to them will be all their past enjoyments? ‹207›

أَوَلَمْ يَكُن لَّهُمْ ءَايَةً أَن يَعْلَمَهُۥ عُلَمَٰٓؤُا۟ بَنِىٓ إِسْرَٰٓءِيلَ ﴿١٩٧﴾ وَلَوْ نَزَّلْنَٰهُ
عَلَىٰ بَعْضِ ٱلْأَعْجَمِينَ ﴿١٩٨﴾ فَقَرَأَهُۥ عَلَيْهِم مَّا كَانُوا۟ بِهِۦ مُؤْمِنِينَ ﴿١٩٩﴾
كَذَٰلِكَ سَلَكْنَٰهُ فِى قُلُوبِ ٱلْمُجْرِمِينَ ﴿٢٠٠﴾ لَا يُؤْمِنُونَ بِهِۦ حَتَّىٰ يَرَوُا۟
ٱلْعَذَابَ ٱلْأَلِيمَ ﴿٢٠١﴾ فَيَأْتِيَهُم بَغْتَةً وَهُمْ لَا يَشْعُرُونَ ﴿٢٠٢﴾ فَيَقُولُوا۟ هَلْ
نَحْنُ مُنظَرُونَ ﴿٢٠٣﴾ أَفَبِعَذَابِنَا يَسْتَعْجِلُونَ ﴿٢٠٤﴾ أَفَرَءَيْتَ إِن مَّتَّعْنَٰهُمْ
سِنِينَ ﴿٢٠٥﴾ ثُمَّ جَآءَهُم مَّا كَانُوا۟ يُوعَدُونَ ﴿٢٠٦﴾ مَآ أَغْنَىٰ عَنْهُم مَّا كَانُوا۟
يُمَتَّعُونَ ﴿٢٠٧﴾

ᵓAwa lam yakul-lahum ᵓĀyatan ᵓañy-yaᶜlamahū ᶜulamāaᵓu banīi ᵓIsrāaᵓīl. 197 Wa law nazzalnāhu ᶜalā baᶜḍil-ᵓaᶜjamīna, 198 faqaraᵓahū ᶜalayhim-mā kānū bihī muᵓminīn. 199 Kadhālika salaknāhu fī qulūbil-mujrimīn. 200 Lā yuᵓminūna bihī ḥattā yarawul-ᶜadhābal-ᵓalīm. 201 Fayaᵓtiyahum-baghtatañw-wa hum lā yashᶜurūn. 202 Fayaqūlū hal naḥnu muñẓarūn. 203 ᵓAfabiᶜadhābinā yastaᶜjilūn. 204 ᵓAfaraᵓayta ᵓim-mattaᶜnāhum sinīn. 205 Thumma jāaᵓahum-mā kānū yūᶜadūn. 206 Māa ᵓaghnā ᶜanhum-mā kānū yumattaᶜūn. 207

revealed to Muḥammad are in their purport (*maᶜānī*) identical with those preached by the earlier prophets. Another, more popular interpretation is, ". . . this [Qurᵓān] has been mentioned [or "foretold"] in the earlier scriptures" (see in this connection note 33 on 2 : 42 and – with particular reference to a prediction made by Jesus – note 6 on 61 : 6).

84 I.e., for those who disbelieve in the prophethood of Muḥammad.

85 Sc., "and in consequence have become Muslims": for instance, ᶜAbd Allāh ibn Salām, Kaᶜb ibn Mālik and other learned Jews of Medina in the lifetime of the Prophet, Kaᶜb al-Aḥbār the Yemenite and a number of his compatriots during the reign of ᶜUmar, and countless others throughout the world who embraced Islam in the course of centuries. The reason why only learned Jews and not learned Christians as well are spoken of in this context lies in the fact that – contrary to the Torah, which still exists, albeit in a corrupted form – the original revelation granted to Jesus has been lost (see *sūrah* 3, note 4) and cannot, therefore, be cited in evidence of the basic identity of his teachings with those of the Qurᵓān.

86 As the Qurᵓān points out in many places, most of the Meccan contemporaries of Muḥammad refused in the beginning to believe in his prophethood on the ground that God could not have entrusted "a man from among themselves" with His message: and this in spite of the fact that the Qurᵓān was expressed "in the clear Arabic tongue", which they could fully understand: but (so the argument goes) if the Prophet had been a foreigner, and his message expressed in a non-Arabic tongue, they would have been even less prepared to accept it – for then they would have had the legitimate excuse that they were unable to understand it (cf. 41 : 44).

87 I.e., not to take root in their hearts, but to "go into one ear and out of the other". As regards God's "causing" this to happen, see *sūrah* 2, note 7, and *sūrah* 14, note 4.

88 I.e., a second chance in life.

89 For this sarcastic demand of the unbelievers, see 6 : 57 and 8 : 32, as well as the corresponding notes; also verse 187 of the present *sūrah*.

And withal, never have We destroyed any community unless it had been warned ‹208› and reminded:[90] for, never do We wrong [anyone]. ‹209›

And [this divine writ is such a reminder:] no evil spirits have brought it down:[91] ‹210› for, neither does it suit their ends, nor is it in their power [to impart it to man]: ‹211› verily, [even] from hearing it are they utterly debarred! ‹212›

Hence, [O man,] do not invoke any other deity side by side with God, lest thou find thyself among those who are made to suffer [on Judgment Day].[92] ‹213›

And warn [whomever thou canst reach, beginning with] thy kinsfolk,[93] ‹214› and spread the wings of thy tenderness over all of the believers who may follow thee;[94] ‹215› but if they disobey thee, say, "I am free of responsibility for aught that you may do!" ‹216› – and place thy trust in the Almighty, the Dispenser of Grace, ‹217› who sees thee when thou standest [alone],[95] ‹218› and [sees] thy behaviour among those who prostrate themselves [before Him]:[96] ‹219› for, verily, He alone is all-hearing, all-knowing! ‹220›

[And] shall I tell you upon whom it is that those evil spirits descend? ‹221›

وَمَآ أَهْلَكْنَا مِن قَرْيَةٍ إِلَّا لَهَا مُنذِرُونَ ﴿208﴾ ذِكْرَىٰ وَمَا كُنَّا
ظَٰلِمِينَ ﴿209﴾ وَمَا تَنَزَّلَتْ بِهِ ٱلشَّيَٰطِينُ ﴿210﴾ وَمَا يَنۢبَغِى لَهُمْ وَمَا
يَسْتَطِيعُونَ ﴿211﴾ إِنَّهُمْ عَنِ ٱلسَّمْعِ لَمَعْزُولُونَ ﴿212﴾ فَلَا تَدْعُ مَعَ ٱللَّهِ
إِلَٰهًا ءَاخَرَ فَتَكُونَ مِنَ ٱلْمُعَذَّبِينَ ﴿213﴾ وَأَنذِرْ عَشِيرَتَكَ ٱلْأَقْرَبِينَ ﴿214﴾
وَٱخْفِضْ جَنَاحَكَ لِمَنِ ٱتَّبَعَكَ مِنَ ٱلْمُؤْمِنِينَ ﴿215﴾ فَإِنْ عَصَوْكَ فَقُلْ
إِنِّى بَرِىٓءٌ مِّمَّا تَعْمَلُونَ ﴿216﴾ وَتَوَكَّلْ عَلَى ٱلْعَزِيزِ ٱلرَّحِيمِ ﴿217﴾ ٱلَّذِى
يَرَىٰكَ حِينَ تَقُومُ ﴿218﴾ وَتَقَلُّبَكَ فِى ٱلسَّٰجِدِينَ ﴿219﴾ إِنَّهُۥ هُوَ ٱلسَّمِيعُ
ٱلْعَلِيمُ ﴿220﴾ هَلْ أُنَبِّئُكُمْ عَلَىٰ مَن تَنَزَّلُ ٱلشَّيَٰطِينُ ﴿221﴾

Wa māa ʾahlaknā miñ-qaryatin ʾillā lahā muñdhirūn.
208 Dhikrā wa mā kunnā ẓālimīn. 209 Wa mā tanazza-
lat bihish-Shayāṭīn. 210 Wa mā yambaghī lahum wa
mā yastaṭīʿūn. 211 ʾInnahum ʿanis-samʿi lamaʿzūlūn.
212 Falā tadʿu maʿal-lāhi ʾilahan ʾākhara fatakūna
minal-muʿadhdhabīn. 213 Wa ʾañdhir ʿashīratakal-
ʾaqrabīn. 214 Wakh-fiḍ janāḥaka limanit-tabaʿaka
minal-muʾminīn. 215 Faʾin ʿaṣawka faqul ʾinnī
barīiʾum-mimmā taʿmalūn. 216 Wa tawakkal ʿalal-
ʿAzīzir-Raḥīm. 217 ʾAlladhī yarāka ḥīna taqūm. 218
Wa taqallubaka fis-sājidīn. 219 ʾInnahū Huwas-
Samīʿul-ʿAlīm. 220 Hal ʾunabbiʾukum ʿalā mañ-
tanazzalush-Shayāṭīn. 221

90 Lit., "unless it had its warners by way of a reminder": see 6 : 131, 15 : 4, 20 : 134, and the corresponding notes.

91 During the early years of his prophetic mission, some of Muḥammad's Meccan opponents tried to explain the rhetorical beauty and persuasiveness of the Qurʾān by insinuating that he was a soothsayer (*kāhin*) in communion with all manner of dark forces and evil spirits (*shayāṭīn*).

92 The conjunctive particle *fa* at the beginning of this sentence (rendered here as "hence") evidently connects with verse 208 above. As shown in note 94 below, the whole of the present passage is addressed to man in general.

93 A believer is morally obliged to preach the truth to *all* whom he can reach, but obviously he must begin with those who are nearest to him, and especially those who recognize his authority.

94 For an explanation of the metaphorical expression "lower thy wing" – rendered by me as "spread the wings of thy tenderness" – see 17 : 24 and the corresponding note 28. The phrase "all of the believers *who follow thee*" shows that (contrary to the assumption of most of the commentators) the above passage is not addressed to the Prophet – since all who believe in him are, by definition, his followers, and *vice versa* – but to everyone who chooses to be guided by the Qurʾān, and who is herewith called upon to extend his loving kindness and care to all believers who may "follow" him, i.e., who may regard him as spiritually or intellectually superior or more experienced. This interpretation also explains verse 213 above: for whereas the exhortation contained in that verse is meaningful with regard to all who may listen to or read the Qurʾān, it would be meaningless with reference to its Prophet, for whom the principle of God's oneness and uniqueness was the unquestionable beginning and end of all truth.

95 According to Mujāhid (as quoted by Ṭabarī), this means "wherever thou mayest be". Other commentators take it to mean "when thou standest up for prayer", but this seems to be too narrow an interpretation.

96 I.e., among the believers, as contrasted with those who "disobey thee" (see verse 216 above).

They descend upon all sinful self-deceivers[97] ‹222› who readily lend ear [to every falsehood], and most of whom lie to others as well.[98] ‹223›

And as for the poets[99] – [they, too, are prone to deceive themselves: and so, only] those who are lost in grievous error would follow them. ‹224› Art thou not aware that they roam confusedly through all the valleys [of words and thoughts],[100] ‹225› and that they [so often] say what they do not do [or feel]? ‹226›

[Most of them are of this kind –] save those who have attained to faith, and do righteous deeds, and remember God unceasingly, and defend themselves [only] after having been wronged,[101] and [trust in God's promise that] those who are bent on wrongdoing will in time come to know how evil a turn their destinies are bound to take![102] ‹227›

تَنَزَّلُ عَلَىٰ كُلِّ أَفَّاكٍ أَثِيمٍ ﴿222﴾ يُلْقُونَ ٱلسَّمْعَ وَأَكْثَرُهُمْ كَـٰذِبُونَ ﴿223﴾
وَٱلشُّعَرَآءُ يَتَّبِعُهُمُ ٱلْغَاوُۥنَ ﴿224﴾ أَلَمْ تَرَ أَنَّهُمْ فِى كُلِّ وَادٍ يَهِيمُونَ ﴿225﴾
وَأَنَّهُمْ يَقُولُونَ مَا لَا يَفْعَلُونَ ﴿226﴾ إِلَّا ٱلَّذِينَ ءَامَنُوا۟ وَعَمِلُوا۟ ٱلصَّـٰلِحَـٰتِ
وَذَكَرُوا۟ ٱللَّهَ كَثِيرًا وَٱنتَصَرُوا۟ مِنۢ بَعْدِ مَا ظُلِمُوا۟ ۗ وَسَيَعْلَمُ ٱلَّذِينَ ظَلَمُوٓا۟
أَىَّ مُنقَلَبٍ يَنقَلِبُونَ ﴿227﴾

Tanazzalu ʿalā kulli ʾaffākin ʾathīm. (222) Yulqūnas-samʿa wa ʾaktharuhum kādhibūn. (223) Wash-shuʿarāaʾu yattabiʿuhumul-ghāwūn. (224) ʾAlam tara ʾannahum fī kulli wādiñy-yahīmūn. (225) Wa ʾannahum yaqūluna mā lā yafʿalūn. (226) ʾIllal-ladhīna ʾāmanū wa ʿamiluṣ-ṣāliḥāti wa dhakarul-lāha kathīrañw-wañ-taṣarū mim-baʿdi mā ẓulimu. Wa sayaʿlamul-ladhīna ẓalamūu ʾayya muñqalabiñy-yañqalibūn. (227)

97 The term *affāk*, which literally denotes "a great [or "habitual"] liar", has here the meaning of "one who lies to *himself*": this is brought out in the next verse, which stresses the psychological fact that most of such self-deceivers readily lie to others as well.

98 Lit., "most of them are lying".

99 An allusion to the fact that some of the pagan Arabs regarded the Qurʾān as a product of Muḥammad's supposedly poetic mind. (See also 36 : 69 and the corresponding notes 38 and 39.)

100 The idiomatic phrase *hāma fī widyān* (lit., "he wandered [or "roamed"] through valleys") is used, as most of the commentators point out, to describe a confused or aimless – and often self-contradictory – play with words and thoughts. In this context it is meant to stress the difference between the precision of the Qurʾān, which is free from all inner contradictions (cf. note 97 on 4 : 82), and the vagueness often inherent in poetry.

101 Thus the Qurʾān makes it clear that a true believer may fight only in self-defence: cf. 22 : 39-40, the earliest reference to war as such, and 2 : 190-194, where the circumstances making war fully justified are further elaborated.

102 Lit., "by what [kind of] turning they will turn".

The Twenty-Seventh Sūrah

An-Naml (The Ants)

Mecca Period

THE PROPHET and most of his close Companions used to refer to this *sūrah* as *Ṭā-Sīn* (the letter-symbols which precede its first verse). In later times, however, it came to be known as *An-Naml* after a word occurring in verse 18, which, because of its association with Solomonic legends, caught and held the imagination of countless Muslims who listened to or read the Qur'ān. As pointed out in my note 77 on 21 : 82, the Qur'ān often employs such legends as a vehicle for allegories expressing certain universal ethical truths; and it employs them for the simple reason that even before the advent of Islam they had become so firmly embedded in the poetic memories of the Arabs – the people in whose language the Qur'ān was expressed and to whom it was addressed in the first instance – that most of these legends had acquired, as it were, a cultural reality of their own, which made a denial or a confirmation of their mythical origin utterly irrelevant. Within the context of the Qur'ān, the only thing that is relevant in this respect is the spiritual truth underlying each one of these legends: a many-sided, many-layered truth which the Qur'ān invariably brings out, sometimes explicitly, sometimes elliptically, often allegorically, but always with a definite bearing on some of the hidden depths and conflicts within our own, human psyche.

In the consensus of most of the authorities, *An-Naml* belongs to the middle Mecca period, having been revealed shortly after the preceding *sūrah*.

سورة النمل مكية -27- وآياتها ثلاث وتسعون

IN THE NAME OF GOD, THE MOST GRACIOUS, THE DISPENSER OF GRACE:

بِسۡمِ ٱللَّهِ ٱلرَّحۡمَٰنِ ٱلرَّحِيمِ

Ṭā. Sīn.[1]
THESE ARE MESSAGES of the Qur'ān – a divine writ clear in itself and clearly showing the truth:[2] ‹1› a guidance and a glad tiding to the believers ‹2› who are constant in prayer and spend in charity:[3] for it is they, they who in their innermost are certain of the life to come! ‹3›
As for those who will not believe in the life to come – behold, goodly have We made their own doings appear unto them, and so they stumble blindly to and fro.[4] ‹4› It is they whom the worst of suffering awaits: for it is they, they who in the life to come shall be the greatest losers! ‹5›
But [as for thee, O believer,] verily, thou hast received this Qur'ān out of the grace of One who is wise, all-knowing.[5] ‹6›

LO! [While lost in the desert,[6]] Moses said to his family: "Behold, I perceive a fire [far away]; I may bring you from there some tiding [as to which way we are to pursue], or bring you [at least] a burning brand so that you might warm yourselves." ‹7›

طسٓۚ تِلۡكَ ءَايَٰتُ ٱلۡقُرۡءَانِ وَكِتَابٖ مُّبِينٍ ﴿١﴾ هُدٗى وَبُشۡرَىٰ
لِلۡمُؤۡمِنِينَ ﴿٢﴾ ٱلَّذِينَ يُقِيمُونَ ٱلصَّلَوٰةَ وَيُؤۡتُونَ ٱلزَّكَوٰةَ وَهُم بِٱلۡأٓخِرَةِ
هُمۡ يُوقِنُونَ ﴿٣﴾ إِنَّ ٱلَّذِينَ لَا يُؤۡمِنُونَ بِٱلۡأٓخِرَةِ زَيَّنَّا لَهُمۡ أَعۡمَٰلَهُمۡ فَهُمۡ
يَعۡمَهُونَ ﴿٤﴾ أُوْلَٰٓئِكَ ٱلَّذِينَ لَهُمۡ سُوٓءُ ٱلۡعَذَابِ وَهُمۡ فِي ٱلۡأٓخِرَةِ هُمُ
ٱلۡأَخۡسَرُونَ ﴿٥﴾ وَإِنَّكَ لَتُلَقَّى ٱلۡقُرۡءَانَ مِن لَّدُنۡ حَكِيمٍ عَلِيمٍ ﴿٦﴾ إِذۡ
قَالَ مُوسَىٰ لِأَهۡلِهِۦٓ إِنِّيٓ ءَانَسۡتُ نَارٗا سَـَٔاتِيكُم مِّنۡهَا بِخَبَرٍ أَوۡ ءَاتِيكُم
بِشِهَابٖ قَبَسٖ لَّعَلَّكُمۡ تَصۡطَلُونَ ﴿٧﴾

نصف الحزب

Bismil-lāhir-Raḥmānir-Raḥīm.
Ṭā-Sīin. Tilka 'Āyātul-Qur'āni wa Kitābim-mubīn. (1) Hudañw-wa bushrā lilmu'minīn. (2) 'Alladhīna yuqīmūnaṣ-Ṣalāta wa yu'tūnaz-Zakāta wa hum-bil'Ākhirati hum yūqinūn. (3) 'Innal-ladhīna lā yu'-minūna bil'Ākhirati zayyannā lahum 'a'mālahum fa-hum ya'mahūn. (4) 'Ulāa'ikal-ladhīna lahum sūu'ul-'adhābi wa hum fil-'Ākhirati humul-'akhsarūn. (5) Wa 'innaka latulaqqal-Qur'āna mil-ladun Ḥakīmin 'Alīm. (6) 'Idh qāla Mūsā li'ahlihīi 'innīi 'ānastu nārañ-sa'ātīkum-minhā bikhabarin 'aw 'ātīkum-bishihābiñ-qabasil-la'allakum taṣṭalūn. (7)

---

1 See Appendix II.

2 For an explanation of this composite rendering of the adjective *mubīn*, see note 2 on 12 : 1. In the present instance, the term *kitāb* ("divine writ") is preceded by the conjunction *wa*, which primarily signifies "and", but in this case has a function more or less similar to the expression "namely"; hence, it may be replaced in translation by a dash without affecting the meaning of the sentence.

3 This is obviously the meaning of the term *zakāh* in the above context, since at the time of the revelation of this *sūrah* it had not yet received its later, specific connotation of a tax incumbent upon Muslims (cf. *sūrah* 2, note 34).

4 The implication is that people who do not believe in life after death concentrate all their endeavours, as a rule, on material gains alone, and cannot think of anything worthwhile beyond "their own doings". See also note 7 on 2 : 7, which explains why the "causing" of this spiritual blindness and confusion – in itself but a consequence of man's own behaviour – is attributed to God.

5 This stress on the spiritual illumination offered to man through divine revelation not only connects with the opening verses of this *sūrah*, but also forms a link between this passage and the following one, which calls to mind the sudden illumination of Moses, symbolized by the vision of the burning bush.

6 Cf. 20 : 9 ff., and particularly note 7 on verse 10 of that *sūrah*.

But when he came close to it, a call was sounded: "Blessed are all who are within [reach of] this fire, and all who are near it![7] And limitless in His glory is God, the Sustainer of all the worlds!" ‹8›
[And God spoke thus:] "O Moses! Verily I alone am God, the Almighty, the Wise!" ‹9›
[And then He said:] "Now throw down thy staff!"[8]
But when he saw it move rapidly, as if it were a serpent, he drew back [in terror], and did not [dare to] return.[9]
[And God spoke to him again:] "O Moses! Fear not – for, behold, no fear need the message-bearers have in My Presence, ‹10› and neither[10] need anyone who has done wrong and then has replaced the wrong with good:[11] for, verily, I am much-forgiving, a dispenser of grace! ‹11›
"Now place thy hand into thy bosom: it will come forth [shining] white, without blemish![12]
"[And thou shalt go] with nine [of My] messages unto Pharaoh and his people[13] – for, verily, they are people depraved!" ‹12›
But when Our light-giving messages came unto them, they said, "This is clearly [but] spellbinding deception!"[14] ‹13› – and in their wickedness and self-exaltation they rejected them, although their minds were convinced of their truth: and behold what happened in the end to those spreaders of corruption! ‹14›

فَلَمَّا جَآءَهَا نُودِيَ أَنۢ بُورِكَ مَن فِي ٱلنَّارِ وَمَنْ حَوْلَهَا وَسُبْحَٰنَ ٱللَّهِ
رَبِّ ٱلْعَٰلَمِينَ ﴿٨﴾ يَٰمُوسَىٰٓ إِنَّهُۥٓ أَنَا ٱللَّهُ ٱلْعَزِيزُ ٱلْحَكِيمُ ﴿٩﴾ وَأَلْقِ
عَصَاكَ فَلَمَّا رَءَاهَا تَهْتَزُّ كَأَنَّهَا جَآنٌّ وَلَّىٰ مُدْبِرًا وَلَمْ يُعَقِّبْ يَٰمُوسَىٰ
لَا تَخَفْ إِنِّي لَا يَخَافُ لَدَيَّ ٱلْمُرْسَلُونَ ﴿١٠﴾ إِلَّا مَن ظَلَمَ ثُمَّ بَدَّلَ
حُسْنًۢا بَعْدَ سُوٓءٍ فَإِنِّي غَفُورٌ رَّحِيمٌ ﴿١١﴾ وَأَدْخِلْ يَدَكَ فِي جَيْبِكَ تَخْرُجْ
بَيْضَآءَ مِنْ غَيْرِ سُوٓءٍ فِي تِسْعِ ءَايَٰتٍ إِلَىٰ فِرْعَوْنَ وَقَوْمِهِۦٓ إِنَّهُمْ كَانُوا۟ قَوْمًا
فَٰسِقِينَ ﴿١٢﴾ فَلَمَّا جَآءَتْهُمْ ءَايَٰتُنَا مُبْصِرَةً قَالُوا۟ هَٰذَا سِحْرٌ مُّبِينٌ ﴿١٣﴾
وَجَحَدُوا۟ بِهَا وَٱسْتَيْقَنَتْهَآ أَنفُسُهُمْ ظُلْمًا وَعُلُوًّا فَٱنظُرْ كَيْفَ كَانَ عَٰقِبَةُ
ٱلْمُفْسِدِينَ ﴿١٤﴾

Falammā jāaʾahā nūdiya ʾam-būrika mañ-fin-nāri wa man ḥawlahā wa subḥānal-lāhi Rabbil-ʿālamīn. (8) Yā Mūsāa ʾinnahūu ʾAnal-lāhul-ʿAzīzul-Ḥakīm. (9) Wa ʾalqi ʿaṣāk. Falammā raʾāhā tahtazzu kaʾannahā jāannuñw-wallā mudbirañw-wa lam yuʿaqqib. Yā Mūsā lā takhaf ʾinnī lā yakhāfu ladayyal-Mursalūn. (10) ʾIllā mañ-ẓalama thumma baddala ḥusnam-baʿda sūuʾiñ-faʾinnī Ghafūrur-Raḥīm. (11) Wa ʾadkhil yadaka fī jaybika takhruj bayḍāaʾa min ghayri sūuʾiñ-fī tisʿi ʾĀyātin ʾilā Firʿawna wa qawmih. ʾInnahum kānū qawmañ-fāsiqīn. (12) Falammā jāaʾat-hum ʾĀyātunā mubṣiratañ-qālū hādhā siḥrum-mubīn. (13) Wa jaḥadū bihā was-tayqanat-hāa ʾañfusuhum ẓulmañw-wa ʿuluwwā. Fañẓur kayfa kāna ʿāqibatul-mufsidīn. (14)

7 Thus Zamakhsharī explains the expression *ḥawlahā* (lit., "around it"). According to some of the earliest commentators, quoted by Ṭabarī, the "fire" (*nār*) is in this context synonymous with "light" (*nūr*), namely, the illumination which God bestows on His prophets, who – one may presume – are *a priori* "near it" by virtue of their inborn spiritual sensitivity. Alternatively, the phrase *man fi 'n-nār wa-man ḥawlahā* may be understood as referring to God's Own light, which encompasses, and is the core of, all spiritual illumination.

8 Cf. 20 : 17-20.

9 For a tentative explanation of the symbolism underlying the miracle of the staff, see note 14 on 20 : 20-21.

10 For my rendering of *illā*, in this context, as "and neither", see note 38 on 4 : 29.

11 I.e., by sincere repentance. Apart from its general significance, this may also be an allusion to the crime which Moses had committed in his youth by slaying the Egyptian (see 28 : 15-17).

12 See note 85 on 7 : 108.

13 Cf. 17 : 101 – "We gave unto Moses nine clear messages" – and the corresponding note 119.

14 See note 99 on 10 : 76. The people referred to as "they" are Pharaoh and his nobles.

AND, INDEED, We granted [true] knowledge[15] unto David and Solomon [as well]; and both were wont to say: "All praise is due to God, who has [thus] favoured us above many of His believing servants!" «15»

And [in this insight] Solomon was [truly] David's heir; and he would say: "O you people! We have been taught the speech of birds, and have been given [in abundance] of all [good] things: this, behold, is indeed a manifest favour [from God]!" «16»

And [one day] there were assembled before Solomon his hosts of invisible beings,[16] and of men, and of birds; and then they were led forth in orderly ranks, «17» till, when they came upon a valley [full] of ants, an ant exclaimed: "O you ants! Get into your dwellings, lest Solomon and his hosts crush you without [even] being aware [of you]!" «18»

Thereupon [Solomon] smiled joyously at her words, and said: "O my Sustainer! Inspire me so that I may forever be grateful for those blessings of Thine with which Thou hast graced me and my parents,[17] and that I may do what is right [in a manner] that will please Thee; and include me, by Thy grace, among Thy righteous servants!" «19»

And [one day] he looked in vain for [a particular one of] the birds; and so he said: "How is it that I do not see the hoopoe? Or could he be among the absent? «20» [If so,] I will punish him most severely or will kill him unless he bring me a convincing excuse!"[18] «21»

وَلَقَدْ ءَاتَيْنَا دَاوُۥدَ وَسُلَيْمَـٰنَ عِلْمًا ۖ وَقَالَا ٱلْحَمْدُ لِلَّهِ ٱلَّذِى فَضَّلَنَا عَلَىٰ
كَثِيرٍ مِّنْ عِبَادِهِ ٱلْمُؤْمِنِينَ ﴿١٥﴾ وَوَرِثَ سُلَيْمَـٰنُ دَاوُۥدَ ۖ وَقَالَ يَـٰٓأَيُّهَا
ٱلنَّاسُ عُلِّمْنَا مَنطِقَ ٱلطَّيْرِ وَأُوتِينَا مِن كُلِّ شَىْءٍ ۖ إِنَّ هَـٰذَا لَهُوَ ٱلْفَضْلُ
ٱلْمُبِينُ ﴿١٦﴾ وَحُشِرَ لِسُلَيْمَـٰنَ جُنُودُهُۥ مِنَ ٱلْجِنِّ وَٱلْإِنسِ وَٱلطَّيْرِ فَهُمْ
يُوزَعُونَ ﴿١٧﴾ حَتَّىٰٓ إِذَآ أَتَوْا۟ عَلَىٰ وَادِ ٱلنَّمْلِ قَالَتْ نَمْلَةٌ يَـٰٓأَيُّهَا ٱلنَّمْلُ
ٱدْخُلُوا۟ مَسَـٰكِنَكُمْ لَا يَحْطِمَنَّكُمْ سُلَيْمَـٰنُ وَجُنُودُهُۥ وَهُمْ لَا
يَشْعُرُونَ ﴿١٨﴾ فَتَبَسَّمَ ضَاحِكًا مِّن قَوْلِهَا وَقَالَ رَبِّ أَوْزِعْنِىٓ أَنْ أَشْكُرَ
نِعْمَتَكَ ٱلَّتِىٓ أَنْعَمْتَ عَلَىَّ وَعَلَىٰ وَٰلِدَىَّ وَأَنْ أَعْمَلَ صَـٰلِحًا تَرْضَىٰهُ وَأَدْخِلْنِى
بِرَحْمَتِكَ فِى عِبَادِكَ ٱلصَّـٰلِحِينَ ﴿١٩﴾ وَتَفَقَّدَ ٱلطَّيْرَ فَقَالَ مَا لِىَ لَآ أَرَى
ٱلْهُدْهُدَ أَمْ كَانَ مِنَ ٱلْغَآئِبِينَ ﴿٢٠﴾ لَأُعَذِّبَنَّهُۥ عَذَابًا شَدِيدًا أَوْ
لَأَا۟ذْبَحَنَّهُۥٓ أَوْ لَيَأْتِيَنِّى بِسُلْطَـٰنٍ مُّبِينٍ ﴿٢١﴾

**Wa laqad ʾātaynā Dāwūda wa Sulaymāna ʿilmā. Wa
qālāl-ḥamdu lillāhil-ladhī faḍḍalanā ʿalā kathīrim-
min ʿibādihil-muʾminīn. (15) Wa waritha Sulaymānu
Dāwūda wa qāla yāa ʾayyuhan-nāsu ʿullimnā
mañṭiqaṭ-ṭayri wa ʾūtīnā miñ-kulli shayʾ. ʾInna
hādhā lahuwal-faḍlul-mubīn. (16) Wa ḥushira liSu-
laymāna junūduhū minal-Jinni wal-ʾIñsi waṭ-ṭayri fahum yūzaʿūn. (17) Ḥattāa ʾidhāa ʾataw ʿalā wādin-
namli qālat namlatuñy-yāa ʾayyuhan-namlud-khulū
masākinakum lā yaḥṭimannakum Sulaymānu wa
junūduhū wa hum lā yashʿurūn. (18) Fatabassama
ḍāḥikam-miñ-qawlihā wa qāla Rabbi ʾawziʿnīi ʾan
ʾashkura niʿmatakal-latīi ʾanʿamta ʿalayya wa ʿalā
wālidayya wa ʾan ʾaʿmala ṣāliḥañ-tarḍāhu wa
ʾadkhilnī biraḥmatika fī ʿibādikaṣ-ṣāliḥīn. (19) Wa ta-
faqqadaṭ-ṭayra faqāla mā liya lāa ʾaral-Hud-huda
ʾam kāna minal-ghāaʾibīn. (20) Laʾuʿadhdhibannahū
ʿadhābañ-shadīdan ʾaw laʾadhbaḥannahūu ʾaw la-
yaʾtiyannī bisulṭānim-mubīn. (21)**

15 I.e., spiritual insight.

16 Apart from 114 : 6, which contains the earliest Qurʾanic reference to the concept of *jinn*, the above is apparently the oldest instance where this concept occurs in the personalized form of "invisible beings". (For a fuller discussion, see Appendix III.)

17 In this instance, Solomon evidently refers to his own understanding and admiration of nature (cf. 38 : 31-33 and the corresponding notes) as well as to his loving compassion for the humblest of God's creatures, as a great divine blessing: and this is the Qurʾanic moral of the legendary story of the ant.

18 Lit., "a clear evidence". The threat of "killing" the hoopoe is, of course, purely idiomatic, and not to be taken literally.

ثلاثة ارباع الحزب

السجدة

But [the hoopoe] tarried but a short while; and [when it came] it said: "I have encompassed [with my knowledge] something that thou hast never yet encompassed [with thine] – for I have come to thee from Sheba with a tiding sure![19] ⟨22⟩

"Behold, I found there a woman ruling over them; and she has been given [abundance] of all [good] things, and hers is a mighty throne. ⟨23⟩ And I found her and her people adoring the sun instead of God; and Satan has made these doings of theirs seem goodly to them, and [thus] has barred them from the path [of God], so that they cannot find the right way: ⟨24⟩ [for they have come to believe] that they *ought not* to adore God[20] – [although it is He] who brings forth all that is hidden in the heavens and on earth,[21] and knows all that you would conceal as well as all that you bring into the open: ⟨25⟩ God, save whom there is no deity – the Sustainer, in awesome almightiness enthroned!"[22] ⟨26⟩

Said [Solomon]: "We shall see whether thou hast told the truth or art one of the liars! ⟨27⟩ Go with this my letter and convey it to them; and thereafter withdraw from them and see what [answer] they return." ⟨28⟩

[When the Queen had read Solomon's letter,] she said: "O you nobles! A truly distinguished letter has been conveyed unto me. ⟨29⟩ Behold, it is from Solomon, and it says, 'In the name of God, the Most Gracious, the Dispenser of Grace: ⟨30⟩ [God says:] Exalt not yourselves against Me, but come unto Me in willing surrender!'"[23] ⟨31⟩

فَمَكَثَ غَيْرَ بَعِيدٍ فَقَالَ أَحَطتُ بِمَا لَمْ تُحِطْ بِهِۦ وَجِئْتُكَ مِن سَبَإٍۭ بِنَبَإٍ
يَقِينٍ ﴿٢٢﴾ إِنِّى وَجَدتُّ ٱمْرَأَةً تَمْلِكُهُمْ وَأُوتِيَتْ مِن كُلِّ شَىْءٍ وَلَهَا عَرْشٌ
عَظِيمٌ ﴿٢٣﴾ وَجَدتُّهَا وَقَوْمَهَا يَسْجُدُونَ لِلشَّمْسِ مِن دُونِ ٱللَّهِ وَزَيَّنَ لَهُمُ
ٱلشَّيْطَٰنُ أَعْمَٰلَهُمْ فَصَدَّهُمْ عَنِ ٱلسَّبِيلِ فَهُمْ لَا يَهْتَدُونَ ﴿٢٤﴾ أَلَّا يَسْجُدُوا۟ لِلَّهِ
ٱلَّذِى يُخْرِجُ ٱلْخَبْءَ فِى ٱلسَّمَٰوَٰتِ وَٱلْأَرْضِ وَيَعْلَمُ مَا تُخْفُونَ وَمَا
تُعْلِنُونَ ﴿٢٥﴾ ٱللَّهُ لَآ إِلَٰهَ إِلَّا هُوَ رَبُّ ٱلْعَرْشِ ٱلْعَظِيمِ ۩ ﴿٢٦﴾ ۞ قَالَ
سَنَنظُرُ أَصَدَقْتَ أَمْ كُنتَ مِنَ ٱلْكَٰذِبِينَ ﴿٢٧﴾ ٱذْهَب بِّكِتَٰبِى هَٰذَا
فَأَلْقِهْ إِلَيْهِمْ ثُمَّ تَوَلَّ عَنْهُمْ فَٱنظُرْ مَاذَا يَرْجِعُونَ ﴿٢٨﴾ قَالَتْ يَٰٓأَيُّهَا ٱلْمَلَؤُا۟
إِنِّىٓ أُلْقِىَ إِلَىَّ كِتَٰبٌ كَرِيمٌ ﴿٢٩﴾ إِنَّهُۥ مِن سُلَيْمَٰنَ وَإِنَّهُۥ بِسْمِ ٱللَّهِ
ٱلرَّحْمَٰنِ ٱلرَّحِيمِ ﴿٣٠﴾ أَلَّا تَعْلُوا۟ عَلَىَّ وَأْتُونِى مُسْلِمِينَ ﴿٣١﴾

Famakatha ghayra baᶜīdiñ-faqāla aḥaṭtu bimā lam tuḥiṭ bihī wa jiᵓtuka miñ-Sabaᵓim-binabaᵓiñy-yaqīn. ⟨22⟩ ᵓInnī wajattum-raᵓatañ-tamlikuhum wa ᵓūtiyat miñ-kulli shayᵓiñw-wa lahā ᶜarshun ᶜaẓīm. ⟨23⟩ Wajattuhā wa qawmahā yasjudūna lishshamsi miñ-dūnillāhi wa zayyana lahumush-Shayṭānu ᵓaᶜmālahum faṣaddahum ᶜanis-sabīli fahum lā yahtadūn. ⟨24⟩ ᵓAllā yasjudū lillāhil-ladhī yukhrijul-khabᵓa fis-samāwāti wal-ᵓarḍi wa yaᶜlamu mā tukhfūna wa mā tuᶜlinūn. ⟨25⟩ ᵓAllāhu lā ᵓilāha ᵓillā Huwa Rabbul-ᶜArshil-ᶜaẓīm. ⟨26⟩ Qāla sanañẓuru ᵓaṣadaqta ᵓam kuñta minal-kādhibīn. ⟨27⟩ ᵓIdhhab-bikitābī hādhā faᵓalqih ᵓilayhim thumma tawalla ᶜanhum fañẓur mādhā yarjiᶜūn. ⟨28⟩ Qālat yāa ᵓayyuhal-malaᵓu ᵓinnii ᵓulqiya ᵓilayya kitābuñ-karīm. ⟨29⟩ ᵓInnahū miñ-Sulaymāna wa ᵓinnahū bismil-lāhir-Raḥmānir-Raḥīm. ⟨30⟩ ᵓAllā taᶜlū ᶜalayya waᵓ-tūnī Muslimīn. ⟨31⟩

19 Thus, we are parabolically reminded that even the most lowly being can – and on occasion does – have knowledge of things of which even a Solomon in all his wisdom may be ignorant (Rāzī) – a reminder which ought to counteract the ever-present danger (*fitnah*) of self-conceit to which learned men, more than anyone else, are exposed (Zamakhsharī). – As regards the kingdom of Sheba, see note 23 on 34 : 15.

20 I.e., their own immoral impulses (which is the meaning of *ash-shayṭān* in this context) had persuaded them that they should not submit to the idea of man's responsibility to a Supreme Being who, by definition, is "beyond the reach of human perception", but should worship certain perceivable natural phenomena instead.

21 An allusion to the appearance and disappearance of the sun and other celestial bodies which the Sabaeans – in common with almost all the Semites of antiquity – used to worship. (Cf. the story of Abraham's search for God in 6 : 74 ff.)

22 See *sūrah* 9, note 171.

23 My interpolation, at the beginning of this verse, of the words "God says" is based on the fact that, within the

She added: "O you nobles! Give me your opinion on the problem with which I am now faced;[24] I would never make a [weighty] decision unless you are present with me." ‹32›
They answered: "We are endowed with power and with mighty prowess in war – but the command is thine; consider, then, what thou wouldst command." ‹33›
Said she: "Verily, whenever kings enter a country they corrupt it,[25] and turn the noblest of its people into the most abject. And this is the way they [always] behave.[26] ‹34› Hence, behold, I am going to send a gift to those [people], and await whatever [answer] the envoys bring back." ‹35›
Now when [the Queen's messenger] came unto Solomon, he said: "Do you people mean to add to my wealth? But that which God has given me[27] is [so much] better than all that He has given you! Nay, it is [only such as] you[28] that would rejoice in this gift of yours! ‹36›
"Go thou back unto them [that have sent thee]! For, [God says:] 'We shall most certainly come upon them with forces which they will never be able to withstand, and shall most certainly cause them to be driven from that [land of theirs], despicable and humbled!'"[29] ‹37›

قَالَتْ يَٰٓأَيُّهَا ٱلْمَلَؤُا۟ أَفْتُونِى فِىٓ أَمْرِى مَا كُنتُ قَاطِعَةً أَمْرًا حَتَّىٰ
تَشْهَدُونِ ﴿٣٢﴾ قَالُوا۟ نَحْنُ أُو۟لُوا۟ قُوَّةٍ وَأُو۟لُوا۟ بَأْسٍ شَدِيدٍ وَٱلْأَمْرُ إِلَيْكِ
فَٱنظُرِى مَاذَا تَأْمُرِينَ ﴿٣٣﴾ قَالَتْ إِنَّ ٱلْمُلُوكَ إِذَا دَخَلُوا۟ قَرْيَةً
أَفْسَدُوهَا وَجَعَلُوٓا۟ أَعِزَّةَ أَهْلِهَآ أَذِلَّةً ۖ وَكَذَٰلِكَ يَفْعَلُونَ ﴿٣٤﴾ وَإِنِّى مُرْسِلَةٌ
إِلَيْهِم بِهَدِيَّةٍ فَنَاظِرَةٌۢ بِمَ يَرْجِعُ ٱلْمُرْسَلُونَ ﴿٣٥﴾ فَلَمَّا جَآءَ سُلَيْمَٰنَ قَالَ
أَتُمِدُّونَنِ بِمَالٍ فَمَآ ءَاتَىٰنِۦَ ٱللَّهُ خَيْرٌ مِّمَّآ ءَاتَىٰكُم بَلْ أَنتُم بِهَدِيَّتِكُمْ
تَفْرَحُونَ ﴿٣٦﴾ ٱرْجِعْ إِلَيْهِمْ فَلَنَأْتِيَنَّهُم بِجُنُودٍ لَّا قِبَلَ لَهُم بِهَا
وَلَنُخْرِجَنَّهُم مِّنْهَآ أَذِلَّةً وَهُمْ صَٰغِرُونَ ﴿٣٧﴾

Qālat yāa ʾayyuhal-malaʾu ʾaftūnī fīi ʾamrī mā kuñtu qāṭiᶜatan ʾamran ḥattā tashhadūn. (32) Qālū naḥnu ʾulū quwwatiñw-wa ʾulū baʾsiñ-shadīdiñw-wal-ʾamru ʾilayki fañẓurī mādhā taʾmurīn. (33) Qālat ʾinnal-mulūka ʾidhā dakhalū qaryatan ʾafsadūhā wa jaᶜalūu ʾaᶜizzata ʾahlihā ʾadhillah. Wa kadhālika yafᶜalūn. (34) Wa ʾinnī mursilatun ʾilayhim-bihadiy-yatiñ-fanāẓiratum-bima yarjiᶜul-mursalūn. (35) Fa-lammā jāaʾa Sulaymāna qāla ʾatumiddūnani bimāliñ-famāa ʾātāniyal-lāhu khayrum-mimmāa ʾātākum; bal ʾañtum-bihadiyyatikum tafraḥūn. (36) ʾIrjiᶜ ʾilayhim falanaʾtiyannahum-bijunūdil-lā qibala lahum-bihā wa lanukhrijannahum minhāa ʾadhil-latañw-wa hum ṣāghirūn. (37)

context of the above legend, the information brought by the hoopoe is the very first link between the kingdoms of Sheba and of Solomon. In the absence of any previous contact, hostile or otherwise, there would have been no point whatever in Solomon's telling the people of Sheba that they should not "exalt themselves" against or above himself. On the other hand, the narrative of the hoopoe makes it clear that the Sabaeans did "exalt themselves" against God by worshipping the sun and by being convinced "that they *ought not* to worship God" (verses 24-25 above). Hence, Solomon, being a prophet, is justified in calling upon them, in the name of God, to abandon this blasphemy and to surrender themselves to Him. (Cf. the almost identical phrase, "Exalt not yourselves against God", in 44 : 19.)

24 Lit., "on this case [or "problem"] of mine".

25 In this context – as pointed out by all classical commentators – the term *dukhūl* undoubtedly connotes "entering by force (*ᶜanwatan*)", whether it be by armed invasion or by usurpation of political power from within the country. (The term *mulūk*, lit., "kings", may be understood to denote also persons who, while not being "kings" in the conventional sense of this word, wrongfully seize and forcibly hold absolute power over their "subjects".)

26 Thus, the Queen of Sheba rules out force as a suitable method for dealing with Solomon. Implied in her statement is the Qurʾanic condemnation of all political power obtained through violence (*ᶜanwatan*) inasmuch as it is bound to give rise to oppression, suffering and moral corruption.

27 I.e., not only worldly wealth but also faith, wisdom and an insight into realities normally hidden from other men.

28 I.e., people who prize only material things and have no inkling of spiritual values.

29 Lit., "and they will be humbled". Since the Qurʾān explicitly prohibits all wars of aggression (see 2 : 190-194 and the corresponding notes), it is not plausible that this same Qurʾān should place a crude threat of warlike aggression in the mouth of a prophet. We must, therefore, assume that here again, as in verse 31 above, it is God who, through His prophet, warns the people of Sheba of *His* "coming upon them" – i.e., punishing them – unless they abandon

قَالَ يَٰٓأَيُّهَا ٱلْمَلَؤُا۟ أَيُّكُمْ يَأْتِينِى بِعَرْشِهَا قَبْلَ أَن يَأْتُونِى مُسْلِمِينَ ﴿٣٨﴾
قَالَ عِفْرِيتٌ مِّنَ ٱلْجِنِّ أَنَا۠ ءَاتِيكَ بِهِۦ قَبْلَ أَن تَقُومَ مِن مَّقَامِكَ ۖ وَإِنِّى
عَلَيْهِ لَقَوِىٌّ أَمِينٌ ﴿٣٩﴾ قَالَ ٱلَّذِى عِندَهُۥ عِلْمٌ مِّنَ ٱلْكِتَٰبِ أَنَا۠ ءَاتِيكَ
بِهِۦ قَبْلَ أَن يَرْتَدَّ إِلَيْكَ طَرْفُكَ ۚ فَلَمَّا رَءَاهُ مُسْتَقِرًّا عِندَهُۥ قَالَ هَٰذَا مِن
فَضْلِ رَبِّى لِيَبْلُوَنِىٓ ءَأَشْكُرُ أَمْ أَكْفُرُ ۖ وَمَن شَكَرَ فَإِنَّمَا يَشْكُرُ لِنَفْسِهِۦ ۖ
وَمَن كَفَرَ فَإِنَّ رَبِّى غَنِىٌّ كَرِيمٌ ﴿٤٠﴾ قَالَ نَكِّرُوا۟ لَهَا عَرْشَهَا نَنظُرْ أَتَهْتَدِىٓ
أَمْ تَكُونُ مِنَ ٱلَّذِينَ لَا يَهْتَدُونَ ﴿٤١﴾

Qāla yāa ʾayyuhal-malaʾu ʾayyukum yaʾtīnī biʿarshihā qabla ʾañy-yaʾtūnī Muslimīn. (38) Qāla ʿIfrītum-minal-Jinni ʾana ʾātīka bihī qabla ʾañ-taqūma mim-maqāmika wa ʾinnī ʿalayhi laqawiyyun ʾamīn. (39) Qālal-ladhī ʿiñdahū ʿilmum-minal-Kitābi ʾana ʾātīka bihī qabla ʾañy-yartadda ʾilayka ṭarfuk. Falammā raʾāhu mustaqirran ʿiñdahū qāla hādhā miñ-faḍli Rabbī liyabluwanīi ʾaʾashkuru ʾam ʾakfur. Wa mañ-shakara faʾinnamā yashkuru linafsihī wa mañ-kafara faʾinna Rabbī Ghaniyyuñ-Karīm. (40) Qāla nakkirū lahā ʿarshahā nañẓur ʾatahtadīi ʾam takūnu minal-ladhīna lā yahtadūn. (41)

[WHEN SOLOMON learned that the Queen of Sheba was coming,[30]] he said [to his council]: "O you nobles! Which of you can bring me her throne ere she and her followers come unto me in willing surrender to God?"[31] ‹38›

Said a bold one of the invisible beings [subject to Solomon]: "I shall bring it to thee ere thou rise from thy council-seat – for, behold, I am powerful enough to do it, [and] worthy of trust!" ‹39›

Answered he who was illumined by revelation:[32] "[Nay,] as for me – I shall bring it to thee ere the twinkling of thy eye ceases!"[33]

And when he saw it truly before him,[34] he exclaimed: "This is [an outcome] of my Sustainer's bounty, to test me as to whether I am grateful or ungrateful![35] However, he who is grateful [to God] is but grateful for his own good; and he who is ungrateful [should know that], verily, my Sustainer is self-sufficient, most generous in giving!" ‹40›

[And] he continued: "Alter her throne so that she may not know it as hers: let us see whether she allows herself to be guided [to the truth] or remains one of those who will not be guided."[36] ‹41›

---

their blasphemous belief that they "ought not" to worship God. This interpretation finds considerable support in the sudden change from the singular in which Solomon speaks of himself in the preceding (as well as in the subsequent) verses, to the majestic plural "We" appearing in the above sentence.

30 I.e., evidently in response to his message (Rāzī, Ibn Kathīr).

31 Lit., "before they come unto me as people who surrender themselves (*muslimīn*)" i.e., to God (see verse 31 above). The term "throne" (*ʿarsh*) is used here and in the sequence – as well as at the end of verse 23 – in its metonymic sense of "dominion" or "regal power" (Rāghib). It appears that Solomon intends to confront his guest with an image of her worldly power, and thus to convince her that her "throne" is as nothing when compared with the awesome almightiness of God.

32 Lit., "he who had knowledge out of [or "through"] revelation (*al-kitāb*)" – i.e., Solomon himself (Rāzī).

33 I.e., faster than any magic could achieve: thus alluding to the symbolic nature of the forthcoming appearance of the "throne". Here, as in the whole of the story of Solomon and the Queen of Sheba, symbolism and legendary "fact" are subtly intertwined, evolving into an allegory of the human soul's awakening to a gradual realization of spiritual values.

34 Lit., "established before him". Since the verbal form *istaqarra* and its participle *mustaqirr* often indicate no more than that something "has being" or "exists" (cf. Lane VII, 2500), the phrase *raʾāhu mustaqirran ʿindahu* may be understood as "he saw it *being* [i.e., actually] before him": hence my rendering.

35 I.e., "whether I attribute my spiritual powers to God or, vaingloriously, to myself".

36 I.e., whether she remains satisfied with perceiving only the outward appearance of things and happenings, or endeavours to fathom their spiritual reality. Seeing that the people of Sheba were, until then, motivated by love of luxury and worldly power, Solomon intends to show the Queen her "throne", or the image of her dominion, as it *could* be if it were inspired by faith in God and, hence, by a consciousness of moral responsibility.

And so, as soon as she arrived, she was asked: "Is thy throne like this?"
She answered: "It is as though it were the same!"[37]
[And Solomon said to his nobles: "She has arrived at the truth without any help from us,[38]] although it is *we* who have been given [divine] knowledge before her, and have [long ago] surrendered ourselves unto God! ‹42› [And she has recognized the truth] although that which she has been wont to worship instead of God[39] had kept her away [from the right path]: for, behold, she is descended of people who deny the truth!"[40] ‹43›
[After a while] she was told: "Enter this court!" – but when she saw it, she thought that it was a fathomless expanse of water, and she bared her legs.[41]
Said he: "Behold, it is [but] a court smoothly paved with glass!"[42]
Cried she: "O my Sustainer! I have been sinning against myself [by worshipping aught but Thee]: but [now] I have surrendered myself, with Solomon, unto the Sustainer of all the worlds!" ‹44›

AND [likewise], indeed, We sent unto [the tribe of] Thamūd their brother Ṣāliḥ [with this message]: "Worship God alone!"[43] –

فَلَمَّا جَآءَتۡ قِيلَ أَهَٰكَذَا عَرۡشُكِۖ قَالَتۡ كَأَنَّهُۥ هُوَۚ وَأُوتِينَا ٱلۡعِلۡمَ
مِن قَبۡلِهَا وَكُنَّا مُسۡلِمِينَ ﴿٤٢﴾ وَصَدَّهَا مَا كَانَت تَّعۡبُدُ مِن دُونِ ٱللَّهِۖ
إِنَّهَا كَانَتۡ مِن قَوۡمٖ كَٰفِرِينَ ﴿٤٣﴾ قِيلَ لَهَا ٱدۡخُلِي ٱلصَّرۡحَۖ فَلَمَّا
رَأَتۡهُ حَسِبَتۡهُ لُجَّةٗ وَكَشَفَتۡ عَن سَاقَيۡهَاۚ قَالَ إِنَّهُۥ صَرۡحٞ مُّمَرَّدٞ مِّن
قَوَارِيرَۗ قَالَتۡ رَبِّ إِنِّي ظَلَمۡتُ نَفۡسِي وَأَسۡلَمۡتُ مَعَ سُلَيۡمَٰنَ لِلَّهِ رَبِّ
ٱلۡعَٰلَمِينَ ﴿٤٤﴾ وَلَقَدۡ أَرۡسَلۡنَآ إِلَىٰ ثَمُودَ أَخَاهُمۡ صَٰلِحًا أَنِ ٱعۡبُدُواْ ٱللَّهَ

Falammā jāaʾat qīla ʾahākadhā ʿarshuk. Qālat kaʾannahū hū. Wa ʾūtīnal-ʿilma miñ-qablihā wa kunnā Muslimīn. ﴿42﴾ Wa ṣaddahā mā kānat-taʿbudu miñ-dūnil-lāhi ʾinnahā kānat miñ-qawmiñ-kāfirīn. ﴿43﴾ Qīla lahad-khuliṣ-ṣarḥa falammā raʾat-hu ḥasibat-hu lujjatañw-wa kashafat ʿañ-sāqayhā. Qāla ʾinnahū ṣarḥum-mumarradum-miñ-qawārīr. Qālat Rabbi ʾinnī ẓalamtu nafsī wa ʾaslamtu maʿa Sulaymāna lillāhi Rabbil-ʿālamīn. ﴿44﴾ Wa laqad ʾarsalnāa ʾilā Thamūda ʾakhāhum Ṣāliḥan ʾaniʿ-budul-lāha

37 Sc., "and yet not quite the same": thus, she expresses doubt – and doubt is the first step in all spiritual progress. She realizes that the "altered throne" is outwardly the same as that which she has left behind; but she perceives intuitively that it is imbued with a spiritual quality which the other did not possess, and which she cannot yet quite understand.

38 Thus Ṭabarī, Zamakhsharī and Ibn Kathīr, on whose interpretation of this passage my rendering and the above interpolation are based.

39 An allusion to her and her people's worship of celestial bodies (cf. verses 24-25 and the corresponding notes 20 and 21).

40 Lit., "she was [sc., "born"] of people . . .", etc. – thus stressing the role of the idolatrous tradition in which she had grown up, and which in the past had made it difficult for her to find the right path. Considering this cultural background, Solomon points out, her awakening at the very moment of her leaving her ancestral environment must be deemed most remarkable and praiseworthy.

41 I.e., in order to wade into it, or perhaps to swim through it, thus braving the seemingly fathomless deep: possibly a symbolic indication of the fear which a human being may feel when his own search after truth forces him to abandon the warm, soothing security of his erstwhile social and mental environment, and to venture into the – as yet – unknown realm of the spirit.

42 I.e., not a dangerous, bottomless deep, as it appeared at first glance, but, rather, the firm, glass-clear light of truth: and with her perception of the ever-existing difference between appearance and reality, the Queen of Sheba comes to the end of her spiritual journey.

43 For the story of the Thamūd and their prophet Ṣāliḥ, see notes 56 and 57 on 7 : 73. My interpolation of the word "likewise" at the beginning of this verse is based on the fact that Ṣāliḥ's message to the tribe of Thamūd is

and, behold, they were [split into] two factions contending with one another. ‹45›
Said [Ṣāliḥ to the erring ones]: "O my people! Why do you seek to hasten the coming upon you of evil instead of hoping for the good?[44] Why do you not, rather, ask God to forgive you your sins, so that you might be graced with His mercy?" ‹46›
They answered: "We augur evil from thee and those that follow thee!"[45]
Said he: "Your destiny, good or evil, rests with God:[46] yea, you are people undergoing a test!" ‹47›
Now there were in the city nine men[47] who were wont to commit deeds of depravity all over the land, and would not reform; ‹48› [and] after having bound one another by an oath in God's name,[48] they said: "Indeed, we shall suddenly fall upon him and his household by night [and slay them all]; and then we shall boldly say to his next of kin, 'We did not witness the destruction of his household – and, behold, we are indeed men of truth!'" ‹49›
And so they devised an evil scheme; but We devised a subtle scheme [of Our own], and they perceived it not. ‹50›
Behold, then, what all their scheming came to in the end: We utterly destroyed them and their people, all of them; ‹51› and [now] those dwellings of theirs are empty, [ruined] as an outcome of their evil deeds.
In this, behold, there is a message indeed for people of [innate] knowledge ‹52› – seeing that We saved those who had attained to faith and were conscious of Us. ‹53›

فَإِذَا هُمْ فَرِيقَانِ يَخْتَصِمُونَ ﴿٤٥﴾ قَالَ يَٰقَوْمِ لِمَ تَسْتَعْجِلُونَ بِٱلسَّيِّئَةِ قَبْلَ
ٱلْحَسَنَةِ لَوْلَا تَسْتَغْفِرُونَ ٱللَّهَ لَعَلَّكُمْ تُرْحَمُونَ ﴿٤٦﴾ قَالُوا۟ ٱطَّيَّرْنَا بِكَ
وَبِمَن مَّعَكَ قَالَ طَٰٓئِرُكُمْ عِندَ ٱللَّهِ بَلْ أَنتُمْ قَوْمٌ تُفْتَنُونَ ﴿٤٧﴾ وَكَانَ فِى
ٱلْمَدِينَةِ تِسْعَةُ رَهْطٍ يُفْسِدُونَ فِى ٱلْأَرْضِ وَلَا يُصْلِحُونَ ﴿٤٨﴾ قَالُوا۟
تَقَاسَمُوا۟ بِٱللَّهِ لَنُبَيِّتَنَّهُۥ وَأَهْلَهُۥ ثُمَّ لَنَقُولَنَّ لِوَلِيِّهِۦ مَا شَهِدْنَا مَهْلِكَ أَهْلِهِۦ
وَإِنَّا لَصَٰدِقُونَ ﴿٤٩﴾ وَمَكَرُوا۟ مَكْرًا وَمَكَرْنَا مَكْرًا وَهُمْ لَا
يَشْعُرُونَ ﴿٥٠﴾ فَٱنظُرْ كَيْفَ كَانَ عَٰقِبَةُ مَكْرِهِمْ أَنَّا دَمَّرْنَٰهُمْ وَقَوْمَهُمْ
أَجْمَعِينَ ﴿٥١﴾ فَتِلْكَ بُيُوتُهُمْ خَاوِيَةًۢ بِمَا ظَلَمُوٓا۟ إِنَّ فِى ذَٰلِكَ لَءَايَةً لِّقَوْمٍ
يَعْلَمُونَ ﴿٥٢﴾ وَأَنجَيْنَا ٱلَّذِينَ ءَامَنُوا۟ وَكَانُوا۟ يَتَّقُونَ ﴿٥٣﴾

fa'idhā hum farīqāni yakhtaṣimūn. (45) Qāla yā qawmi lima tasta'jilūna bissayyi'ati qablal-ḥasanati law-lā tastaghfirūnal-lāha la'allakum turḥamūn. (46) Qāluṭ-ṭayyarnā bika wa bimam-ma'ak. Qāla ṭāa'irukum 'indal-lāhi bal 'antum qawmuñ-tuftanūn. (47) Wa kāna fil-madīnati tis'atu rahṭiñy-yufsidūna fil-'arḍi wa lā yuṣliḥūn. (48) Qālū taqāsamū billāhi lanubayyitannahū wa 'ahlahū thumma la-naqūlanna liwaliyyihī mā shahidnā mahlika 'ahlihī wa 'innā laṣādiqūn. (49) Wa makarū makrañw-wa makarnā makrañw-wa hum lā yash'urūn. (50) Fañẓur kayfa kāna 'āqibatu makrihim 'annā dammarnāhum wa qawmahum 'ajma'īn. (51) Fatilka buyūtuhum khāwiyatam-bimā ẓalamū. 'Inna fī dhālika la'āyatal-liqawmiñy-ya'lamūn. (52) Wa 'añjaynal-ladhīna 'āmanū wa kānū yattaqūn. (53)

---

identical with that of Solomon to the Queen of Sheba – which, in itself, is an indication of the sameness of the fundamental truths underlying all revealed religions.

44 Lit., "hasten the evil before the good": cf. 13 : 6 and the corresponding note 14; also the second sentence of 10 : 50 and note 71.

45 See *sūrah* 7, note 95.

46 Sc., "who has tied every human being's destiny (*ṭā'ir*) to his neck": see 17 : 13 and the corresponding note 17.

47 Or "nine clans", since, in the above context, the term *rahṭ* is liable to either of these two interpretations. The "city" referred to is evidently the region known as Al-Ḥijr, in northern Hijāz (cf. *sūrah* 7, notes 56 and 59). – In contrast with the preceding story of the Queen of Sheba's eager way to faith, the stories of the tribe of Thamūd and (in verses 54-58) of Lot's people are meant to call attention to the hostility which a call to righteousness so often evokes in people who are strong but vain, or, alternatively, weak and addicted to senseless passions.

48 Lit., "by God". As is evident from 7 : 73 ff. and from the above allusion, the Thamūd did have a vague notion of God, but their erstwhile faith had been overlaid by their excessive arrogance and thus deprived of all spiritual value.

AND [thus, too, did We save] Lot, when he said unto his people:[49] "Would you commit this abomination with your eyes open [to its being against all nature[50]]? ‹54› Must you really approach men with lust instead of women? Nay, but you are people without any awareness [of right and wrong]!" ‹55›

But his people's only answer was this: "Expel [Lot and] Lot's followers from your township! Verily, they are folk who make themselves out to be pure!"[51] ‹56›

Thereupon We saved him and his household – all but his wife, whom We willed to be among those that stayed behind[52] ‹57› – the while We rained a rain [of destruction] upon the others: and dire is such rain upon all who let themselves be warned [to no avail]![53] ‹58›

SAY: "All praise is due to God, and peace be upon those servants of His whom He chose [to be His message-bearers]!"

Is not God far better than anything to which men [falsely] ascribe a share in His divinity?[54] ‹59›

Nay – who is it that has created the heavens and the earth, and sends down for you [life-giving] water from the skies? For it is by this means that We cause gardens of shining beauty to grow – [whereas] it is not in your power to cause [even one single of] its trees to grow!

Could there be any divine power besides God? Nay, they [who think so] are people who swerve [from the path of reason]! ‹60›

وَلُوطًا إِذۡ قَالَ لِقَوۡمِهِۦٓ أَتَأۡتُونَ ٱلۡفَٰحِشَةَ وَأَنتُمۡ تُبۡصِرُونَ ﴿٥٤﴾ أَئِنَّكُمۡ
لَتَأۡتُونَ ٱلرِّجَالَ شَهۡوَةً مِّن دُونِ ٱلنِّسَآءِۚ بَلۡ أَنتُمۡ قَوۡمٞ تَجۡهَلُونَ ﴿٥٥﴾ ۞
فَمَا كَانَ جَوَابَ قَوۡمِهِۦٓ إِلَّآ أَن قَالُوٓاْ أَخۡرِجُوٓاْ ءَالَ لُوطٖ مِّن قَرۡيَتِكُمۡۖ
إِنَّهُمۡ أُنَاسٞ يَتَطَهَّرُونَ ﴿٥٦﴾ فَأَنجَيۡنَٰهُ وَأَهۡلَهُۥٓ إِلَّا ٱمۡرَأَتَهُۥ قَدَّرۡنَٰهَا مِنَ
ٱلۡغَٰبِرِينَ ﴿٥٧﴾ وَأَمۡطَرۡنَا عَلَيۡهِم مَّطَرٗاۖ فَسَآءَ مَطَرُ ٱلۡمُنذَرِينَ ﴿٥٨﴾ قُلِ
ٱلۡحَمۡدُ لِلَّهِ وَسَلَٰمٌ عَلَىٰ عِبَادِهِ ٱلَّذِينَ ٱصۡطَفَىٰٓۗ ءَآللَّهُ خَيۡرٌ أَمَّا يُشۡرِكُونَ ﴿٥٩﴾
أَمَّنۡ خَلَقَ ٱلسَّمَٰوَٰتِ وَٱلۡأَرۡضَ وَأَنزَلَ لَكُم مِّنَ ٱلسَّمَآءِ مَآءٗ فَأَنۢبَتۡنَا
بِهِۦ حَدَآئِقَ ذَاتَ بَهۡجَةٖ مَّا كَانَ لَكُمۡ أَن تُنۢبِتُواْ شَجَرَهَآۗ أَءِلَٰهٞ مَّعَ ٱللَّهِۚ 39 حزب / 20 جزء
بَلۡ هُمۡ قَوۡمٞ يَعۡدِلُونَ ﴿٦٠﴾

Wa Lūṭan ʾidh qāla liqawmihīi ʾataʾtūnal-fāḥishata wa ʾañtum tubṣirūn. (54) ʾAʾinnakum lataʾtūnar-rijāla shahwatam-miñ-dūnin-nisāaʾ. Bal ʾañtum qawmuñ-tajhalūn. (55) ◈ Famā kāna jawāba qawmihīi ʾillāa ʾañ-qālūu ʾakhrijūu ʾāla Lūṭim-miñ-qaryatikum; ʾinnahum ʾunāsuñy-yataṭahharūn. (56) Faʾañjaynāhu wa ʾahlahūu ʾillam-raʾatahū qaddarnāhā minal-ghābirīn. (57) Wa ʾamṭarnā ʿalayhim-maṭarañ-fasāaʾa maṭarul-muñdharīn. (58) Qulil-ḥamdu lillāhi wa salāmun ʿalā ʿibādihil-ladhīnaṣ-ṭafā. ʾĀallāhu khayrun ʾammā yushrikūn. (59) ʾAmman khalaqas-samāwāti wal-ʾarḍa wa ʾañzala lakum-minas-samāaʾi māaʾañ-faʾambatnā bihī ḥadāaʾiqa dhāta bahjatim-mā kāna lakum ʾañ-tumbitū shajarahā. ʾAʾilāhum-maʿal-lāh. Bal hum qawmuñy-yaʿdilūn. (60)

49 The story of Lot and the perverted people of Sodom is mentioned in several places, particularly in 7 : 80-84, 11 : 69-83 and 26 : 160-173.

50 Thus Zamakhsharī and Rāzī, stressing the principle that a revolt against the God-willed nature of heterosexuality is a revolt against God Himself.

51 See note 65 on 7 : 82.

52 See note 66 on 7 : 83; also 11 : 81 and 66 : 10, and the corresponding notes.

53 Cf. 26 : 173 and the corresponding note 73.

54 Lit., "Is God better, or that to which they ascribe . . .", etc.: thus including, by implication, not only deified beings or forces of nature, but also false social and moral values to which custom and ancestral tradition have lent an almost "religious" sanction.

Nay – who is it that has made the earth a fitting abode[55] [for living things], and has caused running waters [to flow] in its midst, and has set upon it mouintains firm, and has placed a barrier between the two great bodies of water?[56]
Could there be any divine power besides God? Nay, most of those [who think so] do not know [what they are saying]! ‹61›
Nay – who is it that responds to the distressed when he calls out to Him, and who removes the ill [that caused the distress], and has made you inherit the earth?[57]
Could there be any divine power besides God? How seldom do you keep this in mind! ‹62›
Nay – who is it that guides you in the midst of the deep darkness of land and sea,[58] and sends forth the winds as a glad tiding of His coming grace?[59]
Could there be any divine power besides God? Sublimely exalted is God above anything to which men may ascribe a share in His divinity! ‹63›
Nay – who is it that creates [all life] in the first instance, and then brings it forth anew?[60] And who is it that provides you with sustenance out of heaven and earth?[61]
Could there be any divine power besides God?
Say: "[If you think so,] produce your evidence – if you truly believe in your claim!"[62] ‹64›

أَمَّن جَعَلَ ٱلْأَرْضَ قَرَارًا وَجَعَلَ خِلَٰلَهَآ أَنْهَٰرًا وَجَعَلَ لَهَا رَوَٰسِىَ
وَجَعَلَ بَيْنَ ٱلْبَحْرَيْنِ حَاجِزًا ۗ أَءِلَٰهٌ مَّعَ ٱللَّهِ ۚ بَلْ أَكْثَرُهُمْ لَا يَعْلَمُونَ (61)
أَمَّن يُجِيبُ ٱلْمُضْطَرَّ إِذَا دَعَاهُ وَيَكْشِفُ ٱلسُّوٓءَ وَيَجْعَلُكُمْ خُلَفَآءَ
ٱلْأَرْضِ ۗ أَءِلَٰهٌ مَّعَ ٱللَّهِ ۚ قَلِيلًا مَّا تَذَكَّرُونَ (62) أَمَّن يَهْدِيكُمْ فِى
ظُلُمَٰتِ ٱلْبَرِّ وَٱلْبَحْرِ وَمَن يُرْسِلُ ٱلرِّيَٰحَ بُشْرًۢا بَيْنَ يَدَىْ رَحْمَتِهِۦٓ ۗ أَءِلَٰهٌ
مَّعَ ٱللَّهِ ۚ تَعَٰلَى ٱللَّهُ عَمَّا يُشْرِكُونَ (63) أَمَّن يَبْدَؤُا۟ ٱلْخَلْقَ ثُمَّ يُعِيدُهُۥ وَمَن
يَرْزُقُكُم مِّنَ ٱلسَّمَآءِ وَٱلْأَرْضِ ۗ أَءِلَٰهٌ مَّعَ ٱللَّهِ ۚ قُلْ هَاتُوا۟ بُرْهَٰنَكُمْ إِن
كُنتُمْ صَٰدِقِينَ (64)

ʾAmmañ-jaʿalal-ʾarḍa qarārañw-wa jaʿala khilālahāa ʾanhārañw-wa jaʿala lahā rawāsiya wa jaʿala baynal-baḥrayni ḥājizā. ʾAʾilāhum-maʿal-lāh. Bal ʾaktharuhum lā yaʿlamūn. (61) ʾAmmañy-yujībul-muḍṭarra ʾidhā daʿāhu wa yakshifus-sūuʾa wa yajʿalukum khulafāaʾal-ʾarḍ. ʾAʾilāhum-maʿal-lāh. Qalīlam-mā tadhakkarūn. (62) ʾAmmañy-yahdīkum fī ẓulumātil-barri wal-baḥri wa mañy-yursilur-riyāḥa bushram-bayna yaday raḥmatih. ʾAʾilāhum-maʿal-lāh. Taʿālal-lāhu ʿammā yushrikūn. (63) ʾAmmañy-yabdaʾul-khalqa thumma yuʿīduhū wa mañy-yarzuqukum-minas-samāaʾi wal-ʾarḍ. ʾAʾilāhum-maʿal-lāh. Qul hātū burhānakum ʾiñ-kuñtum ṣādiqīn. (64)

55 Lit., "place of rest" (*qarār*). But see also 77 : 25-26 and the corresponding note 9.

56 See 25 : 53 and the corresponding notes 41 and 42.

57 Cf. 2 : 30 and the corresponding note 22. In the present instance the accent is on God's having *caused* man to "inherit the earth" by endowing him with specific faculties and abilities – an implicit denial of man's claim that he is independent and "master of his fate".

58 I.e., metonymically, through all the seemingly insoluble complexities of human life.

59 See 7 : 57 and the corresponding note 44.

60 This relates to man's life on earth and his resurrection after bodily death as well as to the this-worldly cycle of birth, death and regeneration manifested in all organic nature.

61 As in 10 : 31, the term "sustenance" (*rizq*) has here both a physical and a spiritual connotation; hence the phrase, "out of heaven and earth".

62 Lit., "if you are truthful" – the implication being that most people who profess a belief in a multiplicity of divine powers, or even in the possibility of the One God's "incarnation" in a created being, do so blindly, sometimes only under the influence of inherited cultural traditions and habits of thought, and not out of a reasoned conviction.

Say: "None in the heavens or on earth knows the hidden reality [of anything that exists: none knows it] save God."[63]
And neither can they [who are living] perceive when they shall be raised from the dead: ‹65› nay, their knowledge of the life to come stops short of the truth:[64] nay, they are [often] in doubt as to its reality: nay, they are blind to it.[65] ‹66›
And so, they who are bent on denying the truth are saying: "What! After we have become dust – we and our forefathers – shall we [all], forsooth, be brought forth [from the dead]? ‹67› Indeed, we were promised this – we and our forefathers – in the past as well; it is nothing but fables of ancient times!" ‹68›
Say: "Go all over the earth and behold what happened in the end to those [who were thus] lost in sin!"[66] ‹69›
But do not grieve over them, and neither be distressed by the false arguments which they devise [against God's messages].[67] ‹70›
And [when] they ask, "When is this promise [of resurrection] to be fulfilled? [Answer this, O you who believe in it,] if you are men of truth!" ‹71› – say thou: "It may well be that something of that which [in your ignorance] you so hastily demand[68] has already drawn close unto you. . . ." ‹72›

قُل لَّا يَعْلَمُ مَن فِي ٱلسَّمَٰوَٰتِ وَٱلْأَرْضِ ٱلْغَيْبَ إِلَّا ٱللَّهُ وَمَا يَشْعُرُونَ
أَيَّانَ يُبْعَثُونَ ﴿65﴾ بَلِ ٱدَّٰرَكَ عِلْمُهُمْ فِي ٱلْءَاخِرَةِ بَلْ هُمْ فِي شَكٍّ مِّنْهَا
بَلْ هُم مِّنْهَا عَمُونَ ﴿66﴾ وَقَالَ ٱلَّذِينَ كَفَرُوٓاْ أَءِذَا كُنَّا تُرَٰبًا وَءَابَآؤُنَآ
أَئِنَّا لَمُخْرَجُونَ ﴿67﴾ لَقَدْ وُعِدْنَا هَٰذَا نَحْنُ وَءَابَآؤُنَا مِن قَبْلُ إِنْ هَٰذَآ
إِلَّآ أَسَٰطِيرُ ٱلْأَوَّلِينَ ﴿68﴾ قُلْ سِيرُواْ فِي ٱلْأَرْضِ فَٱنظُرُواْ كَيْفَ كَانَ
عَٰقِبَةُ ٱلْمُجْرِمِينَ ﴿69﴾ وَلَا تَحْزَنْ عَلَيْهِمْ وَلَا تَكُن فِي ضَيْقٍ مِّمَّا
يَمْكُرُونَ ﴿70﴾ وَيَقُولُونَ مَتَىٰ هَٰذَا ٱلْوَعْدُ إِن كُنتُمْ صَٰدِقِينَ ﴿71﴾ قُلْ
عَسَىٰٓ أَن يَكُونَ رَدِفَ لَكُم بَعْضُ ٱلَّذِي تَسْتَعْجِلُونَ ﴿72﴾

Qul lā yaᶜlamu mañ-fis-samāwāti wal-ᵓarḍil-ghayba ᵓillal-lāhu wa mā yashᶜurūna ᵓayyāna yubᶜathūn. (65) Balid-dāraka ᶜilmuhum fil-ᵓĀkhirah. Bal hum fī shakkim-minhā bal hum-minhā ᶜamūn. (66) Wa qālal-ladhīna kafarūu ᵓaᵓidhā kunnā turābañw-wa ᵓābāaᵓunāa ᵓaᵓinnā lamukhrajūn. (67) Laqad wuᶜidnā hādhā naḥnu wa ᵓābāaᵓunā miñ-qablu ᵓin hādhāa ᵓillāa ᵓasāṭīrul-ᵓawwalīn. (68) Qul sīrū fil-ᵓarḍi fañẓurū kayfa kāna ᶜāqibatul-mujrimīn. (69) Wa lā taḥzan ᶜalayhim wa lā takuñ-fī ḍayqim-mimmā yamkurūn. (70) Wa yaqūluna matā hādhal-waᶜdu ᵓiñ-kuñtum ṣādiqīn. (71) Qul ᶜasāa ᵓañy-yakūna radifa lakum-baᶜḍul-ladhī tastaᶜjilūn. (72)

63 In this context, the term *al-ghayb* – rendered by me here as "the hidden reality" – apparently relates to the "how" of God's Being, the ultimate reality underlying the observable aspects of the universe, and the meaning and purpose inherent in its creation. My repetition, within brackets, of the words "none knows it", i.e., save God, is necessitated by the fact that He is infinite, unlimited as to space, and cannot, therefore, be included among the beings "in the heavens or on earth", who have all been created by Him.

64 I.e., they cannot truly visualize the hereafter because its reality is beyond anything that man may experience in this world: and this, it cannot be stressed often enough, is an indirect explanation of the reason why all Qurᵓanic references to the conditions, good or bad, of man's life after death are of necessity expressed in purely allegorical terms.

65 I.e., blind to its *logical necessity* within God's plan of creation. For it is only on the premise of a life after death that the concept of man's moral responsibility and, hence, of God's ultimate judgment can have any meaning; and if there is no moral responsibility, there can be no question of a preceding moral *choice*; and if the absence of choice is taken for granted, all differentiation between right and wrong becomes utterly meaningless as well.

66 I.e., those who denied the reality of a life after death and, hence, of man's ultimate responsibility for his conscious doings. As pointed out in the preceding note, the unavoidable consequence of this denial is the loss of all sense of right and wrong: and this, in its turn, leads to spiritual and social chaos, and so to the downfall of communities and civilizations.

67 Lit., "by their scheming". For the Qurᵓanic use of the term *makr* in the sense of "devising false arguments [against something]", see 10 : 21 and the corresponding note 33.

68 I.e., the end of their own life, which must precede their resurrection.

وَإِنَّ رَبَّكَ لَذُو فَضْلٍ عَلَى ٱلنَّاسِ وَلَـٰكِنَّ أَكْثَرَهُمْ لَا يَشْكُرُونَ ﴿٧٣﴾
وَإِنَّ رَبَّكَ لَيَعْلَمُ مَا تُكِنُّ صُدُورُهُمْ وَمَا يُعْلِنُونَ ﴿٧٤﴾ وَمَا مِنْ غَآئِبَةٍ
فِى ٱلسَّمَآءِ وَٱلْأَرْضِ إِلَّا فِى كِتَـٰبٍ مُّبِينٍ ﴿٧٥﴾ إِنَّ هَـٰذَا ٱلْقُرْءَانَ
يَقُصُّ عَلَىٰ بَنِىٓ إِسْرَٰٓءِيلَ أَكْثَرَ ٱلَّذِى هُمْ فِيهِ يَخْتَلِفُونَ ﴿٧٦﴾ وَإِنَّهُۥ
لَهُدًى وَرَحْمَةٌ لِّلْمُؤْمِنِينَ ﴿٧٧﴾ إِنَّ رَبَّكَ يَقْضِى بَيْنَهُم بِحُكْمِهِۦ ۚ وَهُوَ
ٱلْعَزِيزُ ٱلْعَلِيمُ ﴿٧٨﴾ فَتَوَكَّلْ عَلَى ٱللَّهِ ۖ إِنَّكَ عَلَى ٱلْحَقِّ ٱلْمُبِينِ ﴿٧٩﴾
إِنَّكَ لَا تُسْمِعُ ٱلْمَوْتَىٰ وَلَا تُسْمِعُ ٱلصُّمَّ ٱلدُّعَآءَ إِذَا وَلَّوْا۟ مُدْبِرِينَ ﴿٨٠﴾
وَمَآ أَنتَ بِهَـٰدِى ٱلْعُمْىِ عَن ضَلَـٰلَتِهِمْ ۖ إِن تُسْمِعُ إِلَّا مَن يُؤْمِنُ
بِـَٔايَـٰتِنَا فَهُم مُّسْلِمُونَ ﴿٨١﴾ ۞ وَإِذَا وَقَعَ ٱلْقَوْلُ عَلَيْهِمْ أَخْرَجْنَا

Wa ʾinna Rabbaka ladhū faḍlin ʿalan-nāsi wa lākinna aktharahum lā yashkurūn. (73) Wa inna Rabbaka layaʿlamu mā tukinnu ṣudūruhum wa mā yuʿlinūn. (74) Wa mā min ghāaʾibatiñ-fis-samāaʾi wal-ʾarḍi ʾillā fī kitābim-mubīn. (75) ʾInna hādhal-Qurʾāna yaquṣṣu ʿalā banīi-ʾIsrāaʾīla aktharal-ladhī hum fīhi yakhtalifūn. (76) Wa ʾinnahū lahudañw-wa rahmatul-lilmuʾminīn. (77) ʾInna Rabbaka yaqḍī baynahum-biḥukmihī wa Huwal-ʿAzīzul-ʿAlīm. (78) Fa-tawakkal ʿalal-lāhi ʾinnaka ʿalal-ḥaqqil-mubīn. (79) ʾInnaka lā tusmiʿul-mawtā wa lā tusmiʿuṣ-ṣum-mad-duʿāaʾa ʾidhā wallaw mudbirīn. (80) Wa māa ʾañta bihādil-ʿumyi ʿañ-ḍalālatihim ʾiñ-tusmiʿu ʾillā mañy-yuʾminu biʾĀyātinā fahum-Muslimūn. (81) ۞ Wa ʾidhā waqaʿal-qawlu ʿalayhim ʾakhrajnā

ربع الحزب

Now, verily, thy Sustainer is indeed limitless in His bounty unto men – but most of them are bereft of gratitude. «73»
But, verily, thy Sustainer knows all that their hearts conceal as well as all that they bring into the open: «74» for there is nothing [so deeply] hidden in the heavens or on earth but is recorded in [His] clear decree. «75»

BEHOLD, this Qurʾān explains[69] to the children of Israel most [of that] whereon they hold divergent views;[70] «76» and, verily, it is a guidance and a grace unto all who believe [in it]. «77»
Verily, [O believer,] thy Sustainer will judge between them in His wisdom – for He alone is almighty, all-knowing. «78»
Hence, place thy trust in God [alone] – for, behold, that in which thou believest is truth self-evident.[71] «79»
[But,] verily, thou canst not make the dead hear: and [so, too,] thou canst not make the deaf [of heart] hear this call when they turn their backs [on thee] and go away, «80» just as thou canst not lead the blind [of heart] out of their error; none canst thou make hear save such as [are willing to] believe in Our messages, and thus surrender themselves unto Us.[72] «81»
Now, [as for the deaf and blind of heart –] when the word [of truth] stands revealed against them,[73] We shall bring forth unto

69 For this rendering of the verb *yaquṣṣu*, see note 5 on 12 : 3.

70 I.e., where they differ from the truth made evident to them in their scriptures. The term "children of Israel" comprises here both the Jews and the Christians (Zamakhsharī) inasmuch as both follow the Old Testament, albeit in a corrupted form. It is precisely because of this corruption, and because of the great influence which Jewish and Christian ideas exert over a large segment of mankind, that the Qurʾān sets out to *explain* certain ethical truths to both these communities. The above reference to "most" (and not all) of the problems alluded to in this context shows that the present passage bears only on man's moral outlook and social life in this world, and not on ultimate, metaphysical questions which – as the Qurʾān so often repeats – will be answered only in the hereafter.

71 Lit., "thou art [or "standest"] upon the obvious [or "self-evident"] truth".

72 This passage corresponds to the oft-repeated Qurʾanic statement that "God guides him that wills [to be guided] (*yahdī man yashāʾ*)".

73 Lit., "comes to pass against them" – i.e., when the truth becomes obvious to them against all their expectations, and thus confounds them utterly: an allusion to the approach of the Last Hour, Resurrection and God's Judgment, all of which they were wont to regard as "fables of ancient times" (cf. verses 67-68 above). Alternatively, the phrase *idhā waqaʿa al-qawl ʿalayhim* may be understood as "when the sentence [of doom] is passed on them", i.e., at the approach of the Last Hour, when it will be too late for repentance.

them out of the earth a creature which will tell them that mankind had no real faith in Our messages.[74] ‹82›
And on that Day We shall gather from within every community a host of those who gave the lie to Our messages; and they will be grouped [according to the gravity of their sins] ‹83› until such a time as they shall come [to be judged. And] He will say: "Did you give the lie to My messages even though you failed to encompass them with [your] knowledge?[75] Or what was it that [you thought] you were doing?" ‹84›
And the word [of truth] will stand revealed against them in the face of[76] all the wrong which they had committed, and they will not [be able to] utter a single word [of excuse]: ‹85› for, were they not aware that it is We who had made the night for them, so that they might rest therein, and the day, to make [them] see?[77]
In this, behold, there are messages indeed for people who will believe! ‹86›
And on that Day the trumpet [of judgment] will be sounded, and all [creatures] that are in the heavens and all that are on earth will be stricken with terror, except such as God wills [to exempt]: and in utter lowliness all will come unto Him. ‹87›
And thou wilt see the mountains, which [now] thou deemest so firm, pass away as clouds pass away: a work of God, who has ordered all things to perfection![78]
Verily, He is fully aware of all that you do! ‹88›

لَهُمْ دَآبَّةً مِّنَ ٱلْأَرْضِ تُكَلِّمُهُمْ أَنَّ ٱلنَّاسَ كَانُوا۟ بِـَٔايَـٰتِنَا لَا
يُوقِنُونَ ﴿٨٢﴾ وَيَوْمَ نَحْشُرُ مِن كُلِّ أُمَّةٍ فَوْجًا مِّمَّن يُكَذِّبُ بِـَٔايَـٰتِنَا فَهُمْ
يُوزَعُونَ ﴿٨٣﴾ حَتَّىٰٓ إِذَا جَآءُو قَالَ أَكَذَّبْتُم بِـَٔايَـٰتِى وَلَمْ تُحِيطُوا۟ بِهَا
عِلْمًا أَمَّاذَا كُنتُمْ تَعْمَلُونَ ﴿٨٤﴾ وَوَقَعَ ٱلْقَوْلُ عَلَيْهِم بِمَا ظَلَمُوا۟ فَهُمْ لَا
يَنطِقُونَ ﴿٨٥﴾ أَلَمْ يَرَوْا۟ أَنَّا جَعَلْنَا ٱلَّيْلَ لِيَسْكُنُوا۟ فِيهِ وَٱلنَّهَارَ مُبْصِرًا
إِنَّ فِى ذَٰلِكَ لَـَٔايَـٰتٍ لِّقَوْمٍ يُؤْمِنُونَ ﴿٨٦﴾ وَيَوْمَ يُنفَخُ فِى ٱلصُّورِ فَفَزِعَ مَن فِى
ٱلسَّمَـٰوَٰتِ وَمَن فِى ٱلْأَرْضِ إِلَّا مَن شَآءَ ٱللَّهُ وَكُلٌّ أَتَوْهُ دَٰخِرِينَ ﴿٨٧﴾
وَتَرَى ٱلْجِبَالَ تَحْسَبُهَا جَامِدَةً وَهِىَ تَمُرُّ مَرَّ ٱلسَّحَابِ صُنْعَ ٱللَّهِ ٱلَّذِىٓ
أَتْقَنَ كُلَّ شَىْءٍ إِنَّهُۥ خَبِيرٌۢ بِمَا تَفْعَلُونَ ﴿٨٨﴾

lahum dāabbatam-minal-ʾarḍi tukallimuhum ʾannan-nāsa kānū biʾĀyātinā lā yūqinūn. (82) Wa Yawma naḥshuru miñ-kulli ʾummatiñ-fawjam-mimmañy-yukadhdhibu biʾĀyātinā fahum yūzaʿūn. (83) Ḥattāa ʾidhā jāaʾū qāla ʾakadhdhabtum-biʾĀyātī wa lam tuḥīṭū bihā ʿilman ʾammādhā kuñtum taʿmalūn. (84) Wa waqaʿal-qawlu ʿalayhim-bimā ẓalamū fahum lā yañṭiqūn. (85) ʾAlam yaraw ʾannā jaʿalnal-layla liyaskunū fīhi wan-nahāra mubṣirā. ʾInna fī dhālika laʾĀyātil-liqawmiñy-yuʾminūn. (86) Wa Yawma yuñfakhu fiṣ-ṣūri fafaziʿa mañ-fis-samāwāti wa mañ-fil-ʾarḍi ʾillā mañ-shāaʾal-lāhu wa kullun ʾatawhu dākhirīn. (87) Wa taral-jibāla taḥsabuhā jāmidatañw-wa hiya tamurru marras-saḥāb. Ṣunʿal-lāhil-ladhīi ʾatqana kulla shayʾin ʾinnahū khabīrum-bimā tafʿalūn. (88)

74 The "creature brought forth out of the earth" is apparently an allegory of man's "earthly" outlook on life – in other words, the soul-destroying materialism characteristic of the time preceding the Last Hour. This "creature" parabolically "tells" men that their submergence in exclusively materialistic values – and, hence, their approaching self-destruction – is an outcome of their lack of belief in God. (See also 7 : 175-176 and the corresponding note 141.)

75 I.e., without having understood them or made any attempt to understand them (Zamakhsharī).

76 Or: "the sentence [of doom] will have been passed on them in recompense of . . .", etc. (see note 73 above).

77 In the present context (as in 10 : 67 or 40 : 61) the reference to "night" and "day" has a symbolic significance: namely, man's God-given ability to gain insight through conscious reasoning ("the day that makes them see") as well as through the intuition that comes from a restful surrender to the voice of one's own heart ("the night made for rest") – both of which tell us that the existence of God is a logical necessity, and that a rejection of His messages is a sin against ourselves.

78 I.e., in perfect consonance with the purpose for which He has created them: which is the approximate meaning of the verb *atqana*. In this particular instance, stress is laid on the God-willed transitory nature of the world as we know it (cf. 14 : 48 and 20 : 105-107, and the corresponding notes) in contrast with the lasting reality of the life to come.

Whoever shall come [before Him] with a good deed will gain [further] good therefrom;[79] and they will be secure from the terror of that Day. ‹89›

But they who shall come with evil deeds[80] – their faces will be thrust into the fire, [and they will be asked:] "Is this aught but a just requital[81] for what you were doing [in life]?" ‹90›

[SAY, O Muḥammad:] "I have been bidden to worship the Sustainer of this City[82] – Him who has made it sacred, and unto whom all things belong; and I have been bidden to be of those who surrender themselves to Him, ‹91› and to convey this Qurʾān [to the world]."

Whoever, therefore, chooses to follow the right path, follows it but for his own good; and if any wills to go astray, say [unto him]: "I am only a warner!" ‹92›

And say: "All praise is due to God! In time He will make you see [the truth of] His messages, and then you shall know them [for what they are]."

And thy Sustainer is not unmindful of whatever you all may do. ‹93›

مَن جَآءَ بِٱلۡحَسَنَةِ فَلَهُۥ خَيۡرٞ مِّنۡهَا وَهُم مِّن فَزَعٖ يَوۡمَئِذٍ ءَامِنُونَ ﴿٨٩﴾ وَمَن
جَآءَ بِٱلسَّيِّئَةِ فَكُبَّتۡ وُجُوهُهُمۡ فِي ٱلنَّارِ هَلۡ تُجۡزَوۡنَ إِلَّا مَا كُنتُمۡ
تَعۡمَلُونَ ﴿٩٠﴾ إِنَّمَآ أُمِرۡتُ أَنۡ أَعۡبُدَ رَبَّ هَٰذِهِ ٱلۡبَلۡدَةِ ٱلَّذِي حَرَّمَهَا
وَلَهُۥ كُلُّ شَيۡءٖۖ وَأُمِرۡتُ أَنۡ أَكُونَ مِنَ ٱلۡمُسۡلِمِينَ ﴿٩١﴾ وَأَنۡ أَتۡلُوَاْ
ٱلۡقُرۡءَانَۖ فَمَنِ ٱهۡتَدَىٰ فَإِنَّمَا يَهۡتَدِي لِنَفۡسِهِۦۖ وَمَن ضَلَّ فَقُلۡ إِنَّمَآ أَنَا۠ مِنَ
ٱلۡمُنذِرِينَ ﴿٩٢﴾ وَقُلِ ٱلۡحَمۡدُ لِلَّهِ سَيُرِيكُمۡ ءَايَٰتِهِۦ فَتَعۡرِفُونَهَاۚ وَمَا رَبُّكَ
بِغَٰفِلٍ عَمَّا تَعۡمَلُونَ ﴿٩٣﴾

Mañ-jāaʾa bilḥasanati falahū khayrum-minhā wa hum-miñ-fazaʿiñy-Yawmaʾidhin ʾāminūn. ﴿89﴾ Wa mañ-jāaʾa bissayyiʾati fakubbat wujūhuhum fin-nāri hal tujzawna ʾillā mā kuñtum taʿmalūn. ﴿90﴾ ʾInnamāa ʾumirtu ʾan ʾaʿbuda Rabba hādhihil-baldatil-ladhī harramahā wa lahū kullu shayʾiñw-wa ʾumirtu ʾan ʾakūna minal-Muslimīn. ﴿91﴾ Wa ʾan ʾatluwal-Qurʾāna famanih-tadā faʾinnamā yahtadī linafsihī wa mañ-ḍalla faqul ʾinnamāa ʾana minal-muñdhirīn. ﴿92﴾ Wa qulil-ḥamdu lillāhi sayurīkum ʾĀyātihī fataʿrifūnahā; wa mā Rabbuka bighāfilin ʿammā taʿmalūm. ﴿93﴾

79 Lit., "good shall be his from it", i.e., in consequence or in result of it (Ibn ʿAbbās, Al-Ḥasan, Qatādah, Ibn Jurayj, all of them quoted by Ṭabarī) – thus stressing the Qurʾanic doctrine that what is metaphorically described as "rewards" and "punishments" in the life to come are but the natural *consequences*, good or bad, of man's attitudes and doings in this world. On a different level, the above phrase may also be understood thus: "Whoever shall come with a good deed will gain something better than [or "through"] it" – an allusion to the fact that whereas the deed itself may be transitory, its merit is enduring (Zamakhsharī).

80 I.e., those who did *only* evil, or whose evil deeds greatly outweigh their good deeds (Ibn Kathīr).

81 Lit., "Are you requited for anything else than . . .", etc.

82 I.e., Mecca, where the first temple dedicated to the One God was built (cf. 3 : 96).

The Twenty-Eighth Sūrah

Al-Qaṣaṣ (The Story)

Mecca Period

THERE is hardly any doubt that this *sūrah* as a whole was revealed in the late part of the Mecca period, immediately preceding *sūrah* 17 (*Al-Isrāʾ*); but according to some authorities, verse 85 was revealed at a place called Juḥfah during the Prophet's flight from Mecca to Medina.

The conventional "title" appears to have been taken at random from the word *al-qaṣaṣ* occurring in the second part of verse 25 – a choice that may have been influenced by the fact that about one-half of the *sūrah* is devoted to the story of Moses. It is noteworthy that most of this story depicts the purely *human* aspects of his life – that is to say, the impulses, perplexities and errors which are part of the human condition as such: aspects which the Qurʾān stresses in order to counteract any possible tendency on the part of the pious to attribute "superhuman" or, in the last resort, semi-divine qualities to God's apostles. Appropriately, the *sūrah* ends with a sonorous evocation of the truth that "there is no deity save God", and that "everything is bound to perish, save His [eternal] Self".

-28-

سورة القصص مكية

وآياتها ثمان وثمانون

IN THE NAME OF GOD, THE MOST GRACIOUS, THE DISPENSER OF GRACE:

Ṭā. Sīn. Mīm.[1] ‹1›

THESE ARE MESSAGES of a divine writ clear in itself and clearly showing the truth.[2] ‹2›

We [now] convey unto thee some of the story of Moses and Pharaoh, setting forth the truth for [the benefit of] people who will believe. ‹3›

Behold, Pharaoh exalted himself in the land and divided its people into castes.[3] One group of them he deemed utterly low; he would slaughter their sons and spare [only] their women:[4] for, behold, he was one of those who spread corruption [on earth]. ‹4›

But it was Our will to bestow Our favour upon those [very people] who were deemed [so] utterly low in the land, and to make them forerunners in faith,[5] and to make them heirs [to Pharaoh's glory], ‹5› and to establish them securely on earth, and to let Pharaoh and Hāmān[6] and their hosts

بِسۡمِ ٱللَّهِ ٱلرَّحۡمَٰنِ ٱلرَّحِيمِ

طسٓمٓ ﴿١﴾ تِلۡكَ ءَايَٰتُ ٱلۡكِتَٰبِ ٱلۡمُبِينِ ﴿٢﴾ نَتۡلُواْ عَلَيۡكَ مِن نَّبَإِ
مُوسَىٰ وَفِرۡعَوۡنَ بِٱلۡحَقِّ لِقَوۡمٖ يُؤۡمِنُونَ ﴿٣﴾ إِنَّ فِرۡعَوۡنَ عَلَا فِي ٱلۡأَرۡضِ
وَجَعَلَ أَهۡلَهَا شِيَعٗا يَسۡتَضۡعِفُ طَآئِفَةٗ مِّنۡهُمۡ يُذَبِّحُ أَبۡنَآءَهُمۡ وَيَسۡتَحۡيِۦ
نِسَآءَهُمۡۚ إِنَّهُۥ كَانَ مِنَ ٱلۡمُفۡسِدِينَ ﴿٤﴾ وَنُرِيدُ أَن نَّمُنَّ عَلَى ٱلَّذِينَ
ٱسۡتُضۡعِفُواْ فِي ٱلۡأَرۡضِ وَنَجۡعَلَهُمۡ أَئِمَّةٗ وَنَجۡعَلَهُمُ ٱلۡوَٰرِثِينَ ﴿٥﴾
وَنُمَكِّنَ لَهُمۡ فِي ٱلۡأَرۡضِ وَنُرِيَ فِرۡعَوۡنَ وَهَٰمَٰنَ وَجُنُودَهُمَا

Bismil-lāhir-Raḥmānir-Raḥīm.

Ṭā-Sīim-Mīim. (1) Tilka ᵓĀyātul-Kitābil-mubīn. (2) Natlū ᶜalayka miñ-nabaᵓi Mūsā wa Firᶜawna bil-ḥaqqi liqawmiñ-yuᵓminūn. (3) ᵓInna Firᶜawna ᶜalā fil-ᵓarḍi wa jaᶜala ᵓahlahā shiyaᶜañy-yastaḍᶜifu ṭāaᵓifatam-minhum yudhabbiḥu ᵓabnāaᵓahum wa yastaḥyī nisāaᵓahum. ᵓInnahū kāna minal-mufsidīn. (4) Wa nurīdu ᵓañ-namunna ᶜalal-ladhīnas-tuḍᶜifū fil-ᵓarḍi wa najᶜalahum ᵓaᵓimmatañw-wa najᶜala-humul-wārithīn. (5) Wa numakkina lahum fil-ᵓarḍi wa nuriya Firᶜawna wa Hāmāna wa junūdahumā

---

1 See Appendix II.

2 For an explanation of the above rendering of the adjective *mubīn*, see note 2 on 12 : 1.

3 Lit., "parties" or "sects" – here undoubtedly referring to the division of people into "high" and "low-born": a division which the Qurᵓān utterly condemns. The group which, as mentioned in the next sentence, Pharaoh "deemed utterly low" were the Israelites, who had been placed on the lowest rung of the Egyptian social scale and were deprived of almost all human rights.

4 See note 7.

5 Lit., "leaders" or "exemplars" (*aᵓimmah,* sing. *imām*) – an allusion to the historical fact that the Hebrews were the first to accept a monotheistic creed in a clear, unequivocal formulation, and thus became the forerunners of both Christianity and Islam.

6 This Hāmān, who is mentioned several times in the Qurᵓān as Pharaoh's chief adviser, is not to be confused with the Persian Haman of the Old Testament (The Book of Esther iii ff.). Most probably, the word "Hāmān" as used in the Qurᵓān is not a proper name at all but the Arabicized echo of the compound designation *Hā-Amen* given to every high priest of the Egyptian god Amon. Since at the time in question the cult of Amon was paramount in Egypt, his high priest held a rank second only to that of the reigning Pharaoh. The assumption that the person spoken of in the Qurᵓān as Hāmān was indeed the high priest of the cult of Amon is strengthened by Pharaoh's demand (mentioned in verse 38 of this *sūrah* as well as in 40 : 36-37) that Hāmān erect for him "a lofty tower" from which he could "have a

مِنْهُم مَّا كَانُوا۟ يَحْذَرُونَ ﴿٦﴾ وَأَوْحَيْنَآ إِلَىٰٓ أُمِّ مُوسَىٰٓ أَنْ أَرْضِعِيهِ ۖ فَإِذَا
خِفْتِ عَلَيْهِ فَأَلْقِيهِ فِى ٱلْيَمِّ وَلَا تَخَافِى وَلَا تَحْزَنِىٓ ۖ إِنَّا رَآدُّوهُ إِلَيْكِ
وَجَاعِلُوهُ مِنَ ٱلْمُرْسَلِينَ ﴿٧﴾ فَٱلْتَقَطَهُۥٓ ءَالُ فِرْعَوْنَ لِيَكُونَ لَهُمْ عَدُوًّا
وَحَزَنًا ۗ إِنَّ فِرْعَوْنَ وَهَٰمَٰنَ وَجُنُودَهُمَا كَانُوا۟ خَٰطِـِٔينَ ﴿٨﴾ وَقَالَتِ
ٱمْرَأَتُ فِرْعَوْنَ قُرَّتُ عَيْنٍ لِّى وَلَكَ ۖ لَا تَقْتُلُوهُ عَسَىٰٓ أَن يَنفَعَنَآ أَوْ نَتَّخِذَهُۥ
وَلَدًا وَهُمْ لَا يَشْعُرُونَ ﴿٩﴾ وَأَصْبَحَ فُؤَادُ أُمِّ مُوسَىٰ فَٰرِغًا ۖ إِن كَادَتْ
لَتُبْدِى بِهِۦ لَوْلَآ أَن رَّبَطْنَا عَلَىٰ قَلْبِهَا لِتَكُونَ مِنَ ٱلْمُؤْمِنِينَ ﴿١٠﴾
وَقَالَتْ لِأُخْتِهِۦ قُصِّيهِ ۖ فَبَصُرَتْ بِهِۦ عَن جُنُبٍ وَهُمْ لَا يَشْعُرُونَ ﴿١١﴾ ۞
وَحَرَّمْنَا عَلَيْهِ ٱلْمَرَاضِعَ مِن قَبْلُ فَقَالَتْ هَلْ أَدُلُّكُمْ عَلَىٰٓ أَهْلِ بَيْتٍ
يَكْفُلُونَهُۥ لَكُمْ وَهُمْ لَهُۥ نَٰصِحُونَ ﴿١٢﴾

نصف الحزب

experience through those [children of Israel] the very thing against which they sought to protect themselves.[7] ‹6›

And so, [when he was born,] We inspired [thus] the mother of Moses: "Suckle him [for a time], and then, when thou hast cause to fear for him, cast him into the river,[8] and have no fear and do not grieve – for We shall restore him to thee, and shall make him one of Our message-bearers!" ‹7›

And [some of] Pharaoh's household[9] found [and spared] him: for [We had willed] that he become an enemy unto them and [a source of] grief, seeing that Pharaoh and Hāmān and their hosts were sinners indeed! ‹8›

Now the wife of Pharaoh said: "A joy to the eye [could this child be] for me and thee! Slay him not: he may well be of use to us, or we may adopt him as a son!" And they had no presentiment [of what he was to become]. ‹9›

On the morrow, however, an aching void grew up in the heart of the mother of Moses, and she would indeed have disclosed all about him[10] had We not endowed her heart with enough strength to keep alive her faith [in Our promise].[11] ‹10› And so she said to his sister, "Follow him" – and [the girl] watched him from afar, while they [who had taken him in] were not aware of it. ‹11›

Now from the very beginning We caused him to refuse the breast of [Egyptian] nurses; and [when his sister came to know this,] she said: "Shall I guide you to a family that might rear him for you, and look after him with good will?" ‹12›

minhum-mā kānū yaḥdharūn. (6) Wa ʾawḥaynāa
ʾilāa ʾummi Mūsāa ʾan ʾarḍiʿīh. Faʾidhā khifti
ʿalayhi faʾalqīhi fil-yammi wa lā takhāfī wa lā
taḥzanīi ʾinnā rāaddūhu ʾilayki wa jāʿilūhu minal-
Mursalīn. (7) Faltaqaṭahūu ʾālu Firʿawna liyakūna
lahum ʿaduwwañw-wa ḥazanā. ʾInna Firʿawna wa
Hāmāna wa junūdahumā kānū khāṭiʾīn. (8) Wa
qālatim-raʾatu Firʿawna qurratu ʿaynil-lī wa lak. Lā
taqtulūhu ʿasāa ʾañy-yañfaʿanāa ʾaw nattakhidhahū
waladañw-wa hum lā yashʿurūn. (9) Wa ʾaṣbaḥa
fuʾādu ʾummi Mūsā fārighā. ʾIñ-kādat latubdī bihī
lawlāa ʾar-rabaṭnā ʿalā qalbihā litakūna minal-
muʾminīn. (10) Wa qālat liʾukhtihī quṣṣīhi fabaṣurat
bihī ʿañ-junubiñw-wa hum lā yashʿurūn. (11) ۞ Wa
ḥarramnā ʿalayhil-marāḍiʿa miñ-qablu faqālat hal
ʾadullukum ʿalāa ʾahli baytiñy-yakfulūnahū lakum
wa hum lahū nāṣiḥūn. (12)

look at [or "ascend to"] the god of Moses": which may be, among other things, an allusion to the hieratic purpose of the great pyramids of Egypt and to the function of the high priest as their chief architect. (But see also note 37.)

7 The Egyptians – obviously remembering the earlier, alien Hyksos dynasty that had invaded Egypt and subsequently allied itself with the Hebrews (see *sūrah* 12, note 44) – feared that the latter might in the future, too, make common cause with foreign invaders (cf. Exodus i, 10): and to protect themselves against this danger, they decided – as mentioned in several places in the Qurʾān as well as in the Bible – to have every male Hebrew child killed.

8 Sc., "and he will be saved": cf. 20 : 39.

9 As is evident from the next verse as well as from 66 : 11, it was Pharaoh's own wife.

10 I.e., disclose his true identity in the hope that he would be returned to her.

11 Lit., "so that she might be of those who have faith".

And thus We restored him to his mother, so that her eye might be gladdened, and that she might grieve no longer, and that she might know that God's promise always comes true – even though most of them know it not! ‹13›

NOW WHEN [Moses] reached full manhood and had become mature [of mind], We bestowed upon him the ability to judge [between right and wrong] as well as [innate] knowledge: for thus do We reward the doers of good.[12] ‹14›

And [one day] he entered the city at a time when [most of] its people were [resting in their houses,] unaware of what was going on [in the streets];[13] and there he encountered two men fighting with one another – one of his own people,[14] and the other of his enemies. And the one who belonged to his own people cried out to him for help against him who was of his enemies – whereupon Moses struck him down with his fist, and [thus] brought about his end. ‹15›

[But then] he said [to himself]: "This is of Satan's doing! Verily, he is an open foe, leading [man] astray!"[15]

[And] he prayed: O my Sustainer! Verily, I have sinned against myself! Grant me, then, Thy forgiveness!"

And He forgave him – for, verily, He alone is truly-forgiving, a dispenser of grace. ‹16›

فَرَدَدْنَٰهُ إِلَىٰٓ أُمِّهِۦ كَىْ تَقَرَّ عَيْنُهَا وَلَا تَحْزَنَ وَلِتَعْلَمَ أَنَّ وَعْدَ ٱللَّهِ حَقٌّ
وَلَٰكِنَّ أَكْثَرَهُمْ لَا يَعْلَمُونَ ﴿١٣﴾ وَلَمَّا بَلَغَ أَشُدَّهُۥ وَٱسْتَوَىٰٓ ءَاتَيْنَٰهُ
حُكْمًا وَعِلْمًا ۚ وَكَذَٰلِكَ نَجْزِى ٱلْمُحْسِنِينَ ﴿١٤﴾ وَدَخَلَ ٱلْمَدِينَةَ عَلَىٰ
حِينِ غَفْلَةٍ مِّنْ أَهْلِهَا فَوَجَدَ فِيهَا رَجُلَيْنِ يَقْتَتِلَانِ هَٰذَا مِن شِيعَتِهِۦ
وَهَٰذَا مِنْ عَدُوِّهِۦ ۖ فَٱسْتَغَٰثَهُ ٱلَّذِى مِن شِيعَتِهِۦ عَلَى ٱلَّذِى مِنْ عَدُوِّهِۦ
فَوَكَزَهُۥ مُوسَىٰ فَقَضَىٰ عَلَيْهِ ۖ قَالَ هَٰذَا مِنْ عَمَلِ ٱلشَّيْطَٰنِ ۖ إِنَّهُۥ عَدُوٌّ
مُّضِلٌّ مُّبِينٌ ﴿١٥﴾ قَالَ رَبِّ إِنِّى ظَلَمْتُ نَفْسِى فَٱغْفِرْ لِى فَغَفَرَ لَهُۥٓ ۚ إِنَّهُۥ
هُوَ ٱلْغَفُورُ ٱلرَّحِيمُ ﴿١٦﴾

Faradadnāhu ʾilāa ʾummihī kay taqarra ʿaynuhā wa lā taḥzana wa litaʿlama ʾanna waʿdal-lāhi ḥaqquñw-wa lākinna ʾaktharahum lā yaʿlamūn. (13) Wa lammā balagha ʾashuddahū was-tawāa ʾātaynāhu ḥukmañw-wa ʿilmañw-wa kadhālika najzil-muḥsinīn. (14) Wa dakhalal-madīnata ʿalā ḥīni ghaflatim-min ʾahlihā fawajada fīhā rajulayni yaqtatilāni hādhā miñ-shīʿatihī wa hādhā min ʿaduwwihī fas-taghāthahul-ladhī miñ-shīʿatihī ʿalal-ladhī min ʿaduwwihī fawakazahū Mūsā faqaḍā ʿalayh. Qāla hādhā min ʿamalish-Shayṭāni ʾinnahū ʿaduwwum-muḍillum-mubīn. (15) Qāla Rabbi ʾinnī ẓalamtu nafsī faghfir lī faghafara lah. ʾInnahū Huwal-Ghafūrur-Raḥīm. (16)

12 This statement, almost entirely identical with 12 : 22 (where it refers to Joseph), stresses the supreme divine blessing of spiritual consciousness (*ʿilm* in its deepest significance) combined with rational thought, as expressed in the concept of *ḥukm,* the "ability to judge [between right and wrong]". As is evident from 26 : 20, Moses reached this spiritual maturity *after* the events described in verses 15 ff.

13 Lit., "at a time of its people's unawareness".

14 I.e., of the Hebrews.

15 Regarding the reference to "Satan's doing", see first half of note 16 on 15 : 17. In the present instance, verses 16-17 seem to indicate that it was the Israelite, and not the Egyptian, who had been in the wrong (cf. next note). Apparently, Moses had come to the assistance of the Israelite out of an instinctive sense of racial kinship without regard to the rights and wrongs of the case; but immediately afterwards he realized that he had committed a grave sin not only by killing, however inadvertently, an innocent person, but also by basing his action on a mere tribal – or, as we would describe it today, racial or national – prejudice. Evidently, this is the purport of the above Qurʾanic segment of the story of Moses. Its moral has been stressed and explained by the Prophet on many occasions: cf. his famous saying, "He is not of us who proclaims the cause of tribal partisanship (*ʿaṣabiyyah*); and he is not of us who fights in the cause of tribal partisanship; and he is not of us who dies in the cause of tribal partisanship" (Abū Daʾūd,

Said he: "O my Sustainer! [I vow] by all the blessings which Thou hast bestowed on me: Nevermore shall I aid such as are lost in sin!"[16] ‹17›

And next morning he found himself in the city, looking fearfully about him, when lo! the one who had sought his help the day before [once again] cried out to him [for help[17] – whereupon] Moses said unto him: "Behold, thou art indeed, most clearly, deeply in the wrong!"[18] ‹18›

But then,[19] as soon as he was about to lay violent hands on the man who was their [common] enemy, the latter exclaimed: "O Moses, dost thou intend to slay me as thou didst slay another man yesterday? Thy sole aim is to become a tyrant in this land, for thou dost not care to be of those who would set things to rights!" ‹19›

And [then and there] a man came running from the farthermost end of the city, and said: "O Moses! Behold, the great ones [of the kingdom] are deliberating upon thy case with a view to killing thee! Begone, then: verily, I am of those who wish thee well!" ‹20›

So he went forth from thence, looking fearfully about him, and prayed: "O my Sustainer! Save me from all evildoing folk!" ‹21›

And as he turned his face towards Madyan, he said [to himself]: "It may well be that my Sustainer will [thus] guide me onto the right path !"[20] ‹22›

قَالَ رَبِّ بِمَآ أَنْعَمْتَ عَلَىَّ فَلَنْ أَكُونَ ظَهِيرًا لِّلْمُجْرِمِينَ ﴿١٧﴾ فَأَصْبَحَ فِى
ٱلْمَدِينَةِ خَآئِفًا يَتَرَقَّبُ فَإِذَا ٱلَّذِى ٱسْتَنصَرَهُۥ بِٱلْأَمْسِ يَسْتَصْرِخُهُۥ قَالَ
لَهُۥ مُوسَىٰٓ إِنَّكَ لَغَوِىٌّ مُّبِينٌ ﴿١٨﴾ فَلَمَّآ أَنْ أَرَادَ أَن يَبْطِشَ بِٱلَّذِى هُوَ
عَدُوٌّ لَّهُمَا قَالَ يَٰمُوسَىٰٓ أَتُرِيدُ أَن تَقْتُلَنِى كَمَا قَتَلْتَ نَفْسًۢا بِٱلْأَمْسِ إِن
تُرِيدُ إِلَّآ أَن تَكُونَ جَبَّارًا فِى ٱلْأَرْضِ وَمَا تُرِيدُ أَن تَكُونَ مِنَ
ٱلْمُصْلِحِينَ ﴿١٩﴾ وَجَآءَ رَجُلٌ مِّنْ أَقْصَا ٱلْمَدِينَةِ يَسْعَىٰ قَالَ يَٰمُوسَىٰٓ إِنَّ
ٱلْمَلَأَ يَأْتَمِرُونَ بِكَ لِيَقْتُلُوكَ فَٱخْرُجْ إِنِّى لَكَ مِنَ ٱلنَّٰصِحِينَ ﴿٢٠﴾
فَخَرَجَ مِنْهَا خَآئِفًا يَتَرَقَّبُ قَالَ رَبِّ نَجِّنِى مِنَ ٱلْقَوْمِ ٱلظَّٰلِمِينَ ﴿٢١﴾
وَلَمَّا تَوَجَّهَ تِلْقَآءَ مَدْيَنَ قَالَ عَسَىٰ رَبِّىٓ أَن يَهْدِيَنِى سَوَآءَ ٱلسَّبِيلِ ﴿٢٢﴾

Qāla Rabbi bimāa ʾanᶜamta ᶜalayya falan ʾakūna ẓahīral-lilmujrimīn. (17) Faʾaṣbaḥa fil-madīnati khāaʾifañy-yataraqqabu faʾidhal-ladhis-tañṣarahū bil-ʾamsi yastaṣrikhuh. Qāla lahū Mūsāa ʾinnaka laghawiyyum-mubīn. (18) Falammāa ʾan ʾarāda ʾañy-yabṭisha billadhī huwa ᶜaduwwul- lahumā qāla yā Mūsāa ʾaturīdu ʾañ-taqtulanī kamā qatalta nafsam-bilʾams. ʾIñ-turīdu ʾillāa ʾañ-takūna jabbārañ-fil-ʾarḍi wa mā turīdu ʾañ-takūna minal-muṣliḥīn. (19) Wa jāaʾa rajulum-min ʾaqṣal-madīnati yasᶜā qāla yā Mūsāa ʾinnal-malaʾa yaʾtamirūna bika liyaqtulūka fakhruj ʾinnī laka minan-nāṣiḥīn. (20) Fakharaja minhā khāaʾifañy-yataraqqabu qāla Rabbi najjinī minal-qawmiẓ-ẓālimīn. (21) Wa lammā tawajjaha tilqāaʾa Madyana qāla ᶜasā Rabbīi ʾañy-yahdiyanī sawāaʾas-sabīl. (22)

on the authority of Jubayr ibn Muṭᶜim). When he was asked to explain the meaning of "tribal partisanship", the Prophet answered, "It means helping thine own people in an unjust cause" (*ibid.*, on the authority of Wāthilah ibn al-Asqaᶜ).

16 According to Ibn ᶜAbbās and Muqātil (both of them quoted by Baghawī), "this is an indication that the Israelite whom Moses had helped was a denier of the truth (*kāfir*)" – i.e., in the moral sense of this definition. (See also last sentence of verse 86 of this *sūrah*.)

17 Sc., "against another Egyptian".

18 Lit., "lost in grievous error" or "deviating from what is right".

19 Sc., "swayed once again by his feeling of kinship with the Israelite", as indicated in the subsequent reference to the Egyptian as "their [common] enemy".

20 The inhabitants of Madyan (called Midian in the Bible) were Arabs of the Amorite group. Since they were racially and linguistically closely related to the Hebrews, they could be counted upon to help Moses in his plight. For the geographical location of the region of Madyan, see *sūrah* 7, note 67.

NOW WHEN he arrived at the wells[21] of Madyan, he found there a large group of men who were watering [their herds and flocks]; and at some distance from them he came upon two women who were keeping back their flock.
He asked [them]: "What is the matter with you?"
They answered: "We cannot water [our animals] until the herdsmen drive [theirs] home – for [we are weak and] our father is a very old man." ‹23›
So he watered [their flock] for them; and then he withdrew into the shade and prayed: "O my Sustainer! Verily, in dire need am I of any good which Thou mayest bestow upon me!" ‹24›
[Shortly] afterwards, one of the two [maidens] approached him, walking shyly, and said: "Behold, my father invites thee, so that he might duly reward thee for thy having watered [our flock] for us."
And as soon as [Moses] came unto him and told him the story [of his life], he said: "Have no fear! Thou art now safe from those evildoing folk!" ‹25›
Said one of the two [daughters]: "O my father! Hire him: for, behold, the best [man] that thou couldst hire is one who is [as] strong and worthy of trust [as he]!" ‹26›
[After some time, the father] said: "Behold, I am willing to let thee wed one of these two daughters of mine on the understanding that thou wilt remain eight years in my service; and if thou shouldst complete ten [years], that would be [an act of grace] from thee, for I do not want to impose any hardship on thee: [on the contrary,] thou wilt find me, if God so wills, righteous in all my dealings."[22] ‹27›
Answered [Moses]: "Thus shall it be between me and thee! Whichever of the two terms I fulfil, let there be no ill-will against me. And God be witness to all that we say!" ‹28›

وَلَمَّا وَرَدَ مَآءَ مَدْيَنَ وَجَدَ عَلَيْهِ أُمَّةً مِّنَ ٱلنَّاسِ يَسْقُونَ وَوَجَدَ مِن دُونِهِمُ
ٱمْرَأَتَيْنِ تَذُودَانِ قَالَ مَا خَطْبُكُمَا قَالَتَا لَا نَسْقِى حَتَّىٰ يُصْدِرَ ٱلرِّعَآءُ
وَأَبُونَا شَيْخٌ كَبِيرٌ ﴿٢٣﴾ فَسَقَىٰ لَهُمَا ثُمَّ تَوَلَّىٰٓ إِلَى ٱلظِّلِّ فَقَالَ رَبِّ إِنِّى لِمَآ
أَنزَلْتَ إِلَىَّ مِنْ خَيْرٍ فَقِيرٌ ﴿٢٤﴾ فَجَآءَتْهُ إِحْدَىٰهُمَا تَمْشِى عَلَى ٱسْتِحْيَآءٍ
قَالَتْ إِنَّ أَبِى يَدْعُوكَ لِيَجْزِيَكَ أَجْرَ مَا سَقَيْتَ لَنَا فَلَمَّا جَآءَهُۥ وَقَصَّ
عَلَيْهِ ٱلْقَصَصَ قَالَ لَا تَخَفْ نَجَوْتَ مِنَ ٱلْقَوْمِ ٱلظَّٰلِمِينَ ﴿٢٥﴾ قَالَتْ
إِحْدَىٰهُمَا يَٰٓأَبَتِ ٱسْتَـْٔجِرْهُ إِنَّ خَيْرَ مَنِ ٱسْتَـْٔجَرْتَ ٱلْقَوِىُّ ٱلْأَمِينُ ﴿٢٦﴾
قَالَ إِنِّىٓ أُرِيدُ أَنْ أُنكِحَكَ إِحْدَى ٱبْنَتَىَّ هَٰتَيْنِ عَلَىٰٓ أَن تَأْجُرَنِى ثَمَٰنِىَ
حِجَجٍ فَإِنْ أَتْمَمْتَ عَشْرًا فَمِنْ عِندِكَ وَمَآ أُرِيدُ أَنْ أَشُقَّ عَلَيْكَ
سَتَجِدُنِىٓ إِن شَآءَ ٱللَّهُ مِنَ ٱلصَّٰلِحِينَ ﴿٢٧﴾ قَالَ ذَٰلِكَ بَيْنِى وَبَيْنَكَ أَيَّمَا
ٱلْأَجَلَيْنِ قَضَيْتُ فَلَا عُدْوَٰنَ عَلَىَّ وَٱللَّهُ عَلَىٰ مَا نَقُولُ وَكِيلٌ ﴿٢٨﴾

Wa lammā warada māaʾa Madyana wajada ʿalayhi ʾummatam-minan-nāsi yasqūna wa wajada miñ-dūnihimum-raʾatayni tadhūdāni qāla mā khaṭbukumā. Qālatā lā nasqī ḥattā yuṣdirar-riʿāaʾu wa ʾabūnā shaykhuñ-kabīr. (23) Fasaqā lahumā thumma tawallāa ʾilaẓ-ẓilli faqāla Rabbi ʾinnī limāa ʾañzalta ʾilayya min khayriñ-faqīr. (24) Fajāaʾat-hu ʾiḥdāhumā tamshī ʿalas-tiḥyāaʾiñ-qālat ʾinna ʾabī yadʿūka liyajziyaka ʾajra mā saqayta lanā. Falammā jāaʾahū wa qaṣṣa ʿalayhil-qaṣaṣa qāla lā takhaf; najawta minal-qawmiẓ-ẓālimīn. (25) Qālat ʾiḥdāhumā yāa ʾabatis-taʾjirhu ʾinna khayra manis-taʾjartal-qawiyyul-ʾamīn. (26) Qāla ʾinnīi ʾurīdu ʾan ʾuñkiḥaka ʾiḥdabnatayya hātayni ʿalāa ʾañ-taʾjuranī thamāniya ḥijaj. Faʾin ʾatmamta ʿashrañ-famin ʿiñdik. Wa māa ʾurīdu ʾan ʾashuqqa ʿalayka satajidunīi ʾiñ-shāaʾal-lāhu minaṣ-ṣāliḥīn. (27) Qāla dhālika baynī wa baynaka ʾayyamal-ʾajalayni qaḍaytu falā ʿudwāna ʿalayy. Wal-lāhu ʿalā mā naqūlu Wakīl. (28)

21 Lit., "water" or "waters".
22 Lit., "one of the righteous".

ثلاثة ارباع الحزب

۞ فَلَمَّا قَضَىٰ مُوسَى ٱلْأَجَلَ وَسَارَ بِأَهْلِهِۦٓ ءَانَسَ مِن جَانِبِ ٱلطُّورِ نَارًا
قَالَ لِأَهْلِهِ ٱمْكُثُوٓا۟ إِنِّىٓ ءَانَسْتُ نَارًا لَّعَلِّىٓ ءَاتِيكُم مِّنْهَا بِخَبَرٍ أَوْ
جَذْوَةٍ مِّنَ ٱلنَّارِ لَعَلَّكُمْ تَصْطَلُونَ ﴿٢٩﴾ فَلَمَّآ أَتَىٰهَا نُودِىَ مِن شَٰطِئِ
ٱلْوَادِ ٱلْأَيْمَنِ فِى ٱلْبُقْعَةِ ٱلْمُبَٰرَكَةِ مِنَ ٱلشَّجَرَةِ أَن يَٰمُوسَىٰٓ إِنِّىٓ أَنَا
ٱللَّهُ رَبُّ ٱلْعَٰلَمِينَ ﴿٣٠﴾ وَأَنْ أَلْقِ عَصَاكَ فَلَمَّا رَءَاهَا تَهْتَزُّ كَأَنَّهَا جَآنٌّ
وَلَّىٰ مُدْبِرًا وَلَمْ يُعَقِّبْ يَٰمُوسَىٰٓ أَقْبِلْ وَلَا تَخَفْ إِنَّكَ مِنَ ٱلْءَامِنِينَ ﴿٣١﴾
ٱسْلُكْ يَدَكَ فِى جَيْبِكَ تَخْرُجْ بَيْضَآءَ مِنْ غَيْرِ سُوٓءٍ وَٱضْمُمْ إِلَيْكَ
جَنَاحَكَ مِنَ ٱلرَّهْبِ فَذَٰنِكَ بُرْهَٰنَانِ مِن رَّبِّكَ إِلَىٰ فِرْعَوْنَ وَمَلَإِي۟هِۦٓ
إِنَّهُمْ كَانُوا۟ قَوْمًا فَٰسِقِينَ ﴿٣٢﴾

AND WHEN Moses had fulfilled his term, and was wandering with his family [in the desert], he perceived a fire on the slope of Mount Sinai;[23] [and so] he said to his family: "Wait here. Behold, I perceive a fire [far away]; perhaps I may bring you from there some tiding,[24] or [at least] a burning brand from the fire, so that you might warm yourselves." ‹29›

But when he came close to it, a call was sounded from the right-side bank of the valley, out of the tree [burning] on blessed ground:[25] "O Moses! Verily, I am God, the Sustainer of all the worlds!" ‹30›

And [then He said]: "Throw down thy staff!" But as soon as [Moses] saw it move rapidly, as if it were a snake, he drew back [in terror], and did not [dare to] return.[26] [And God spoke to him again:] "O Moses! Draw near, and have no fear – for, behold, thou art of those who are secure [in this world and in the next]![27] ‹31›

"[And now] put thy hand into thy bosom: it will come forth [shining] white, without blemish.[28] And [henceforth] hold thine arm close to thyself, free of all fear.[29] "These, then, shall be the two signs [of thy bearing a message] from thy Sustainer[30] unto Pharaoh and his great ones – for, behold, they are people depraved!" ‹32›

۞ Falammā qaḍā Mūsal-ʾajala wa sāra biʾahlihīi ʾānasa miñ-jānibiṭ-Ṭūri nārā. Qāla liʾahlihim-kuthūu ʾinnīi ʾānastu nāral-laʿallīi ʾātīkum-minhā bikhabarin ʾaw jadhwatim-minan-nāri laʿallakum taṣṭalūn. (29) Falammāa ʾatāhā nūdiya miñ-shāṭiʾil-wādil-ʾaymani fil-buqʿatil-mubārakati minash-shajarati ʾañy-yā Mūsāa ʾinnīi ʾAnal-lāhu Rabbul-ʿālamīn. (30) Wa ʾan ʾalqi ʿaṣāk. Falammā raʾāhā tahtazzu kaʾannahā Jāannuñw-wallā mudbirañw-wa lam yuʿaqqib. Yā Mūsāa ʾaqbil wa lā takhaf. ʾInnaka minal-ʾāminīn. (31) ʾUsluk yadaka fī jaybika takhruj bayḍāaʾa min ghayri sūuʾiñw-waḍ-mum ʾilayka janāḥaka minar-rahbi fadhānika burhānāni mir-Rabbika ʾilā Firʿawna wa malaʾiyhīi ʾinnahum kānū qawmañ-fāsiqīn. (32)

23 For an explanation of Moses' wanderings in the desert, see note 7 on 20 : 10; for that of the allegory of the "fire", note 7 on 27 : 7-8. – Throughout this work, the noun *aṭ-ṭūr* ("the mountain") is being rendered as "Mount Sinai", for it is to this and to no other mountain that the Qurʾān invariably refers in the above term.

24 Se., "as to which way we are to pursue".

25 As in 19 : 52 and 20 : 80, the reference to the "right" side has a connotation of "blessedness": see in this respect note 25 on 74 : 39. As regards the "blessed ground", see note 9 on the expression "twice-hallowed valley" in 20 : 12. The "tree" referred to in the above verse is obviously identical with the "burning bush" of the Bible (Exodus iii, 2).

26 The miracle of the staff has, possibly, a symbolic significance: see *sūrah* 20, note 14.

27 Cf. 27 : 10 – "no fear need the message-bearers have in My Presence".

28 See note 85 on 7 : 108.

29 As pointed out by Zamakhsharī, the above idiomatic sentence is a metonym recalling a well-known gesture of terror – the involuntary stretching-forth of one's hands or arms when suddenly faced with something terrifying; conversely, the "holding of one's arm [lit., "wing"] close to oneself" is expressive of freedom from fear. In the present instance, the phrase echoes the concluding words of verse 31 – "behold, thou art of those who are secure [in this world and in the next]".

30 The "two signs" (*burhānān*) may be understood as Moses' ability to remain, by virtue of his certainty of God's omnipresence, forever free of all physical or moral fear, as well as his ability to show that appearance and reality are not always identical.

Said [Moses]: "O my Sustainer! I have slain one of them, and so I fear that they will slay me. . . .[31] ‹33› And my brother Aaron – he is far better in speech than I am.[32] Send him with me, therefore, as a helper, so that he might [more eloquently] bear witness to my speaking the truth: for I fear indeed that they will give me the lie." ‹34›
Said He: "We shall strengthen thine arm through thy brother, and endow both of you with power, so that they will not be able to touch you:[33] by virtue of Our messages shall you two, and all who follow you, prevail!" ‹35›

BUT AS SOON as Moses came unto them with Our clear messages [Pharaoh and his great ones] said: "All this is nothing but spellbinding eloquence devised [by man]:[34] and never did we hear [the like of] this, [nor has it ever been heard of] in the time of our forebears of old!" ‹36›
And Moses replied: "My Sustainer knows best as to who comes with guidance from Him, and to whom the future belongs![35] Verily, never will evildoers attain to a happy state!" ‹37›
Whereupon Pharaoh said: "O you nobles! I did not know that you could have any deity other than myself![36] Well, then, O Hāmān, kindle me a fire for [baking bricks of] clay, and then build me a lofty tower, that haply I may have a look at the god of Moses[37] – although, behold, I am convinced that he is of those who [always] tell lies!" ‹38›

قَالَ رَبِّ إِنِّي قَتَلْتُ مِنْهُمْ نَفْسًا فَأَخَافُ أَن يَقْتُلُونِ ﴿٣٣﴾ وَأَخِي هَٰرُونُ
هُوَ أَفْصَحُ مِنِّي لِسَانًا فَأَرْسِلْهُ مَعِيَ رِدْءًا يُصَدِّقُنِيٓ إِنِّيٓ أَخَافُ أَن
يُكَذِّبُونِ ﴿٣٤﴾ قَالَ سَنَشُدُّ عَضُدَكَ بِأَخِيكَ وَنَجْعَلُ لَكُمَا سُلْطَٰنًا فَلَا
يَصِلُونَ إِلَيْكُمَا بِـَٔايَٰتِنَآ أَنتُمَا وَمَنِ ٱتَّبَعَكُمَا ٱلْغَٰلِبُونَ ﴿٣٥﴾ فَلَمَّا
جَآءَهُم مُّوسَىٰ بِـَٔايَٰتِنَا بَيِّنَٰتٍ قَالُوا۟ مَا هَٰذَآ إِلَّا سِحْرٌ مُّفْتَرًى وَمَا سَمِعْنَا
بِهَٰذَا فِيٓ ءَابَآئِنَا ٱلْأَوَّلِينَ ﴿٣٦﴾ وَقَالَ مُوسَىٰ رَبِّيٓ أَعْلَمُ بِمَن جَآءَ
بِٱلْهُدَىٰ مِنْ عِندِهِۦ وَمَن تَكُونُ لَهُۥ عَٰقِبَةُ ٱلدَّارِ إِنَّهُۥ لَا يُفْلِحُ
ٱلظَّٰلِمُونَ ﴿٣٧﴾ وَقَالَ فِرْعَوْنُ يَٰٓأَيُّهَا ٱلْمَلَأُ مَا عَلِمْتُ لَكُم مِّنْ إِلَٰهٍ
غَيْرِى فَأَوْقِدْ لِى يَٰهَٰمَٰنُ عَلَى ٱلطِّينِ فَٱجْعَل لِّى صَرْحًا لَّعَلِّىٓ أَطَّلِعُ إِلَىٰٓ
إِلَٰهِ مُوسَىٰ وَإِنِّى لَأَظُنُّهُۥ مِنَ ٱلْكَٰذِبِينَ ﴿٣٨﴾

Qāla Rabbi ʾinnī qataltu minhum nafsañ-faʾakhāfu ʾañy-yaqtulūn. (33) Wa ʾakhī Hārūnu huwa ʾafṣaḥu minnī lisānañ-faʾarsilhu maᶜiya ridʾañy-yuṣaddiqunīi ʾinnīi ʾakhāfu ʾañy-yukadhdhibūn. (34) Qāla sanashuddu ᶜaḍudaka biʾakhīka wa najᶜalu lakumā sulṭānañ-falā yaṣilūna ʾilaykumā; biʾĀyātinā ʾañtumā wa manit-tabaᶜakumal-ghālibūn. (35) Falammā jāaʾahum-Mūsā biʾĀyātinā bayyinātiñ-qālū mā hādhāa ʾillā siḥrum-muftarañw-wa mā samiᶜnā bihādhā fīi ʾābāaʾinal-ʾawwalīn. (36) Wa qāla Mūsā Rabbīi ʾaᶜlamu bimañ-jāaʾa bilhudā min ᶜiñdihī wa mañ-takūnu lahū ᶜāqibatud-dāri ʾinnahū lā yufliḥuẓ-ẓālimūn. (37) Wa qāla Firᶜawnu yāa ʾayyuhal-malaʾu mā ᶜalimtu lakum-min ʾilāhin ghayrī faʾawqid lī yā Hāmānu ᶜalaṭ-ṭīni fajᶜal lī ṣarḥal-laᶜallīi ʾaṭṭaliᶜu ʾilāa ʾilāhi Mūsā wa ʾinnī laʾaẓunnuhū minal-kādhibīn. (38)

31 Sc., "and thus make it impossible for me to accomplish my mission": for, as regards himself, Moses was henceforth free of fear.

32 Cf. 20 : 27-28 and 26 : 12-13, as well as the corresponding notes.

33 Lit., "so that they will not reach you".

34 See note 12 on 74 : 24, which is the earliest Qurʾanic instance of the term *siḥr* in the above connotation.

35 For an explanation of the above phrase, see *sūrah* 6, note 118.

36 In view of the fact that the ancient Egyptians worshipped many gods, this observation is not to be taken literally; but since each of the Pharaohs was regarded as an incarnation of the divine principle as such, he claimed – and received – his people's adoration as their "Lord All-Highest" (cf. 79 : 24), combining within himself, as it were, all the qualities attributable to gods.

37 Or: "ascend to the god of Moses". Whichever of the two meanings is given to the verb *iṭṭaliᶜu*, Pharaoh's demand for a "lofty tower" is not only an allusion to the building of one of the great pyramids (see note 6 above), but also a derisory, contemptuous reference to Moses' concept of God as an all-embracing Power, inconceivably high above all that exists.

Thus arrogantly, without the least good sense,[38] did he and his hosts behave on earth – just as if they thought that they would never have to appear before Us [for judgment]![39] ‹39›
And so We seized him and his hosts and cast them into the sea: and behold what happened in the end to those evildoers: ‹40› [We destroyed them,] and We set them up as archetypes [of evil] that show the way to the fire [of hell];[40] and [whereas] no succour will come to them on Resurrection Day, ‹41› We have caused a curse to follow them in this world as well;[41] and on Resurrection Day they will find themselves among those who are bereft of all good.[42] ‹42›
And [then,] indeed, after We had destroyed those earlier generations [of sinners], We vouchsafed unto Moses [Our] revelation as a means of insight for men,[43] and as a guidance and grace, so that they might bethink themselves [of Us]. ‹43›

NOW [as for thee, O Muḥammad,] thou wert not present on the sunset slope [of Mount Sinai] when We imposed the Law upon Moses, nor wert thou among those who witnessed [his times]:[44] ‹44›

وَٱسْتَكْبَرَ هُوَ وَجُنُودُهُۥ فِى ٱلْأَرْضِ بِغَيْرِ ٱلْحَقِّ وَظَنُّوٓا۟ أَنَّهُمْ إِلَيْنَا لَا
يُرْجَعُونَ ﴿٣٩﴾ فَأَخَذْنَٰهُ وَجُنُودَهُۥ فَنَبَذْنَٰهُمْ فِى ٱلْيَمِّ ۖ فَٱنظُرْ كَيْفَ كَانَ
عَٰقِبَةُ ٱلظَّٰلِمِينَ ﴿٤٠﴾ وَجَعَلْنَٰهُمْ أَئِمَّةً يَدْعُونَ إِلَى ٱلنَّارِ ۖ وَيَوْمَ ٱلْقِيَٰمَةِ
لَا يُنصَرُونَ ﴿٤١﴾ وَأَتْبَعْنَٰهُمْ فِى هَٰذِهِ ٱلدُّنْيَا لَعْنَةً ۖ وَيَوْمَ ٱلْقِيَٰمَةِ هُم مِّنَ
ٱلْمَقْبُوحِينَ ﴿٤٢﴾ وَلَقَدْ ءَاتَيْنَا مُوسَى ٱلْكِتَٰبَ مِنۢ بَعْدِ مَآ أَهْلَكْنَا
ٱلْقُرُونَ ٱلْأُولَىٰ بَصَآئِرَ لِلنَّاسِ وَهُدًى وَرَحْمَةً لَّعَلَّهُمْ يَتَذَكَّرُونَ ﴿٤٣﴾
وَمَا كُنتَ بِجَانِبِ ٱلْغَرْبِىِّ إِذْ قَضَيْنَآ إِلَىٰ مُوسَى ٱلْأَمْرَ وَمَا كُنتَ مِنَ
ٱلشَّٰهِدِينَ ﴿٤٤﴾

Was-takbara huwa wa junūduhū fil-ʾarḍi bighayril-ḥaqqi wa ẓannūu ʾannahum ʾilaynā lā yurjaʿūn. (39) Faʾakhadhnāhu wa junūdahū fanabadhnāhum fil-yammi fañẓur kayfa kāna ʿāqibatuẓ-ẓālimīn. (40) Wa jaʿalnāhum ʾaʾimmatañy-yadʿūna ʾilan-nāri wa Yawmal-Qiyāmati lā yuñṣarūn. (41) Wa ʾatbaʿnāhum fī hādhihid-dunyā laʿnatañ-wa Yawmal-Qiyāmati humminal-maqbūḥīn. (42) Wa laqad ʾātaynā Mūsal-Kitāba mim-baʿdi māa ʾahlaknal-qurūnal-ʾūlā baṣāaʾira linnāsi wa hudañw-wa raḥmatal-laʿallahum yatadhakkarūn. (43) Wa mā kuñta bijānibil-gharbiyyi ʾidh qaḍaynāa ʾilā Mūsal-ʾamra wa mā kuñta minash-shāhidīn. (44)

38 Lit., "without [any] truth" or "justification" (*bi-ghayr al-ḥaqq*).

39 Lit., "and they thought that they would not be brought back to Us". There is no doubt that the ancient Egyptians did believe in a life after death, and that this belief included the concept of a divine judgment as well. Since, however, the particular Pharaoh whom Moses confronted is said to have behaved with an arrogance opposed to all good sense, the Qurʾān – by implication – likens his attitude to that of a person who does *not* believe in resurrection and in man's ultimate responsibility before God: hence my rendering of the conjunctive particle *wa* at the beginning of the above clause as "just as if".

40 Lit., "archetypes (*aʾimmah*) inviting to the fire". This is the pivotal sentence of the above fragment of the story of Moses. Just as verses 15-16 are meant to draw our attention to the sin of tribal or racial prejudice (see note 15), the present reference to Pharaoh as an "archetype [of evil]" points to the fact that false pride (*takabbur*) and arrogance (*istikbār*) are truly "satanic" attitudes of mind, repeatedly exemplified in the Qurʾān by Iblīs's symbolic "revolt" against God (for the meaning of which see note 26 on 2 : 34 and note 31 on 15 : 41). Inasmuch as they are intrinsically evil, these "satanic" impulses lead to evil actions and, consequently, to a weakening or even a total destruction of man's spiritual potential: which, in its turn, is bound to cause suffering in the hereafter.

41 I.e., in the pejorative connotation universally given to the adjective "pharaonic". It is to be noted that the term *laʿnah,* here rendered as "curse", primarily denotes "estrangement" (*ibʿād*), i.e., from all that is good and, hence, really desirable.

42 I.e., among those who by their own actions will have removed themselves from God's grace: a meaning given to the term *maqbūḥ,* in this context, by most of the classical commentators and philologists (cf. *Lisān al-ʿArab, Tāj al-ʿArūs,* etc.).

43 By virtue of its being the first instance of a divinely-inspired Law, the Torah inaugurated a new phase in mankind's religious history (cf. the reference to the children of Israel as "forerunners in faith" in verse 5 of this *sūrah*).

44 Implying that the story of Moses as narrated in the Qurʾān could not have come to Muḥammad's knowledge

nay, but [between them and thee] We brought into being [many] generations, and long was their span of life.

And neither didst thou dwell among the people of Madyan, conveying Our messages unto them:[45] nay, but We have [always] been sending [Our message-bearers unto man]. ‹45›

And neither wert thou present on the slope of Mount Sinai when We called out [to Moses]:[46] but [thou, too, art sent] as an act of thy Sustainer's grace, to warn people to whom no warner has come before thee, so that they might bethink themselves [of Us]; ‹46› and [We have sent thee] lest they say [on Judgment Day], when disaster befalls them as an outcome of what their own hands have wrought, "O our Sustainer, if only Thou hadst sent an apostle unto us, we would have followed Thy messages, and would have been among those who believe!" ‹47›

And yet, now that the truth has come unto them from Us, they say, "Why has he not been vouchsafed the like of what Moses was vouchsafed?"[47]

But did they not also, before this, deny the truth of what Moses was vouchsafed?

وَلَٰكِنَّآ أَنشَأْنَا قُرُونًا فَتَطَاوَلَ عَلَيْهِمُ ٱلْعُمُرُ ۚ وَمَا كُنتَ ثَاوِيًا فِىٓ أَهْلِ
مَدْيَنَ تَتْلُوا۟ عَلَيْهِمْ ءَايَٰتِنَا وَلَٰكِنَّا كُنَّا مُرْسِلِينَ ﴿٤٥﴾ وَمَا كُنتَ
بِجَانِبِ ٱلطُّورِ إِذْ نَادَيْنَا وَلَٰكِن رَّحْمَةً مِّن رَّبِّكَ لِتُنذِرَ قَوْمًا مَّآ أَتَىٰهُم
مِّن نَّذِيرٍ مِّن قَبْلِكَ لَعَلَّهُمْ يَتَذَكَّرُونَ ﴿٤٦﴾ وَلَوْلَآ أَن تُصِيبَهُم مُّصِيبَةٌۢ
بِمَا قَدَّمَتْ أَيْدِيهِمْ فَيَقُولُوا۟ رَبَّنَا لَوْلَآ أَرْسَلْتَ إِلَيْنَا رَسُولًا فَنَتَّبِعَ
ءَايَٰتِكَ وَنَكُونَ مِنَ ٱلْمُؤْمِنِينَ ﴿٤٧﴾ فَلَمَّا جَآءَهُمُ ٱلْحَقُّ مِنْ عِندِنَا قَالُوا۟
لَوْلَآ أُوتِىَ مِثْلَ مَآ أُوتِىَ مُوسَىٰٓ ۚ أَوَلَمْ يَكْفُرُوا۟ بِمَآ أُوتِىَ مُوسَىٰ مِن قَبْلُ

Wa lākinnāa ᵓañshaᵓnā qurūnañ-fataṭāwala ᶜalayhimul-ᶜumur. Wa mā kuñta thāwiyañ-fīi ᵓahli Madyana tatlū ᶜalayhim ᵓĀyātinā wa lākinnā kunnā mursilīn. ﴿45﴾ Wa mā kuñta bijānibiṭ-Ṭūri ᵓidh nādaynā wa lākir-raḥmatam-mir Rabbika lituñdhira qawmam-māa ᵓatāhum-miñ-Nadhīrim-miñ-qablika laᶜallahum yatadhakkarūn. ﴿46﴾ Wa lawlāa ᵓañ-tuṣībahum-muṣībatum-bimā qaddamat ᵓaydīhim fayaqūlū Rabbanā lawlāa ᵓarsalta ᵓilaynā Rasūlañ-fanattabiᶜa ᵓĀyātika wa nakūna minal-muᵓminīn. ﴿47﴾ Falammā jāaᵓahumul-ḥaqqu min ᶜiñdinā qālū lawlāa ᵓūtiya mithla māa ᵓūtiya Mūsā. ᵓAwalam yakfurū bimāa ᵓūtiya Mūsā miñ-qabl.

otherwise than through revelation: consequently, the Qurᵓān as such must obviously be a result of divine revelation. – The term *al-amr*, rendered above as "the Law", is the Arabic equivalent of the Hebrew word *torah* ("law" or "precept"), the commonly-accepted title of the revelation granted to Moses.

45 I.e., "thou art not the first of Our apostles, O Muḥammad: We have sent thee to the people of thy time just as We sent Shuᶜayb to the people of Madyan" (Aḍ-Ḍaḥḥāk, as quoted by Rāzī).

46 According to some of the classical commentators, this second reference to "the slope of Mount Sinai" contains an allusion to the divine assurance mentioned in 7 : 156: "My grace overspreads everything . . ." (Ṭabarī, Rāzī). This interpretation is most plausible in view of the subsequent reference to Muḥammad's mission as "an act of thy Sustainer's grace (*raḥmah*)".

47 As the Qurᵓān frequently points out, the basic ethical truths enunciated in it are the same as those of earlier revelations. It is this very statement which induced the opponents of Muḥammad – in his own time as well as in later times – to question the *authenticity* of the Qurᵓān: "If it had really been revealed by God," they argue, "would so many of its propositions, especially its social laws, differ so radically from the laws promulgated in that earlier divine writ, the Torah?" By advancing this argument (and quite apart from the question of whether the text of the Bible as we know it today has or has not been corrupted in the course of time), the opponents of Muḥammad's message deliberately overlook the fact, repeatedly stressed in the Qurᵓān, that the earlier systems of law were conditioned by the spiritual level of a particular people and the exigencies of a particular chapter of human history, and therefore *had* to be superseded by new laws at a higher stage of human development (see in this connection the second paragraph of 5 : 48 and the corresponding note 66). However, as is evident from the immediate sequence – and especially from the last sentence of this verse – the above specious argument is not meant to uphold the authenticity of the Bible as against that of the Qurᵓān, but, rather, aims at discrediting both – and, through them, the basic religious principle against which the irreligious mind always revolts: namely, the idea of divine revelation and of man's absolute dependence on and responsibility to God, the Ultimate Cause of all that exists.

[For] they do say, "Two examples of delusion, [seemingly] supporting each other!"[48] And they add, "Behold, we refuse to accept either of them as true!" ‹48›
Say: "Produce, then, [another] revelation from God which would offer better guidance than either of these two[49] – [and] I shall follow it, if you speak the truth!" ‹49›
And since they cannot respond to this thy challenge,[50] know that they are following only their own likes and dislikes: and who could be more astray than he who follows [but] his own likes and dislikes without any guidance from God?
Verily, God does not grace with His guidance people who are given to evildoing! ‹50›

NOW, INDEED, We have caused this word [of Ours] to reach mankind step by step,[51] so that they might [learn to] keep it in mind. ‹51›
As for those unto whom We have vouchsafed revelation aforetime – they [are bound to] believe in this one [as well];[52] ‹52› and whenever it is [clearly] conveyed unto them, they [are bound to] profess, "We have come to believe in it, for, behold, it is the truth from our Sustainer – and, verily, even before this have we surrendered ourselves unto Him!" ‹53›
These it is that shall receive a twofold reward for having been patient in adversity, and having repelled evil with good,[53]

قَالُوا سِحْرَانِ تَظَـٰهَرَا وَقَالُوٓا إِنَّا بِكُلٍّ كَـٰفِرُونَ ﴿٤٨﴾ قُلْ فَأْتُوا بِكِتَـٰبٍ
مِّنْ عِندِ ٱللَّهِ هُوَ أَهْدَىٰ مِنْهُمَآ أَتَّبِعْهُ إِن كُنتُمْ صَـٰدِقِينَ ﴿٤٩﴾ فَإِن لَّمْ
يَسْتَجِيبُوا لَكَ فَٱعْلَمْ أَنَّمَا يَتَّبِعُونَ أَهْوَآءَهُمْ وَمَنْ أَضَلُّ مِمَّنِ ٱتَّبَعَ
هَوَىٰهُ بِغَيْرِ هُدًى مِّنَ ٱللَّهِ إِنَّ ٱللَّهَ لَا يَهْدِى ٱلْقَوْمَ ٱلظَّـٰلِمِينَ ﴿٥٠﴾ ۞
وَلَقَدْ وَصَّلْنَا لَهُمُ ٱلْقَوْلَ لَعَلَّهُمْ يَتَذَكَّرُونَ ﴿٥١﴾ ٱلَّذِينَ ءَاتَيْنَـٰهُمُ
ٱلْكِتَـٰبَ مِن قَبْلِهِۦ هُم بِهِۦ يُؤْمِنُونَ ﴿٥٢﴾ وَإِذَا يُتْلَىٰ عَلَيْهِمْ قَالُوٓا
ءَامَنَّا بِهِۦٓ إِنَّهُ ٱلْحَقُّ مِن رَّبِّنَآ إِنَّا كُنَّا مِن قَبْلِهِۦ مُسْلِمِينَ ﴿٥٣﴾
أُولَـٰٓئِكَ يُؤْتَوْنَ أَجْرَهُم مَّرَّتَيْنِ بِمَا صَبَرُوا وَيَدْرَءُونَ بِٱلْحَسَنَةِ ٱلسَّيِّئَةَ حزب ٤٠

Qālū siḥrāni taẓāharā wa qālūu ʾinnā bikulliñ-kāfirūn. (48) Qul faʾtū biKitābim-min ʿiñdil-lāhi huwa ʾahdā minhumāa ʾattabiʿhu ʾiñ-kuñtum ṣādiqīn. (49) Faʾil-lam yastajībū laka faʿlam ʾannamā yattabiʿūna ʾahwāaʾahum; wa man ʾaḍallu mimmanit-tabaʿa hawāhu bighayri hudam-minal-lāh. ʾInnal-lāha lā yahdil-qawmaẓ-ẓālimīn. (50) ۞ Wa laqad waṣṣalnā lahumul-qawla laʿallahum yatadhakkarūn. (51) ʾAlladhīna ʾātaynāhumul-Kitāba miñ-qablihī hum-bihī yuʾminūn. (52) Wa ʾidhā yutlā ʿalayhim qālūu ʾāmannā bihīi ʾinnahul-ḥaqqu mir-Rabbināa ʾinnā kunnā miñ-qablihī Muslimīn. (53) ʾUlāaʾika yuʾtawna ʾajrahum-marratayni bimā ṣabarū wa yadraʾūna bilḥasanatis-sayyiʾata

48 A contemptuous allusion, on the one hand, to Old-Testament predictions of the coming of the Prophet Muḥammad: (cf. *sūrah* 2, note 33), and, on the other, to the oft-repeated Qurʾanic statement that this divine writ had been revealed to "confirm the truth of earlier revelations". As regards my rendering of the term *siḥr* (lit., "magic" or "sorcery") as "delusion" – and occasionally as "spellbinding eloquence" – see note 12 on 74 : 24.

49 I.e., the Torah and the Qurʾān. The Gospel is not mentioned in this context because, as Jesus himself had stressed, his message was based on the Law of Moses, and was not meant to displace the latter.

50 Lit., "if they do not respond to thee", implying that they are *unable* to accept the above challenge.

51 Lit., "We have caused this word to reach them gradually": this meaning is implied in the verbal form *waṣṣalnā*, which – like the grammatically identical form *nazzalnā* – points to the gradual, step-by-step revelation of the Qurʾān during the twenty-three years of Muḥammad's prophetic ministry.

52 This is both a statement of historical fact – alluding to conversions of Jews and Christians in Muḥammad's lifetime – and a prophecy. It must, however, be understood that, in the above context, God's "vouchsafing" revelation implies a conscious, sincere *acceptance of its teachings* by those to whom it has been conveyed: for it is this sincerity that has enabled them – or will enable them – to realize that the Qurʾān preaches the same ethical truths as those forthcoming from earlier revelations. (Cf. 26 : 196-197 and the corresponding notes 83-85.)

53 See note 44 on the identical phrase in 13 : 22. In the present context, the reference to "patience in adversity"

and having spent on others out of what We provided for them as sustenance, ⟨54⟩ and, whenever they heard frivolous talk,[54] having turned away from it and said: "Unto us shall be accounted our deeds, and unto you, your deeds. Peace be upon you – [but] we do not seek out such as are ignorant [of the meaning of right and wrong]." ⟨55⟩

وَمِمَّا رَزَقۡنَٰهُمۡ يُنفِقُونَ ﴿٥٤﴾ وَإِذَا سَمِعُواْ ٱللَّغۡوَ أَعۡرَضُواْ عَنۡهُ وَقَالُواْ لَنَآ
أَعۡمَٰلُنَا وَلَكُمۡ أَعۡمَٰلُكُمۡ سَلَٰمٌ عَلَيۡكُمۡ لَا نَبۡتَغِي ٱلۡجَٰهِلِينَ ﴿٥٥﴾ إِنَّكَ
لَا تَهۡدِي مَنۡ أَحۡبَبۡتَ وَلَٰكِنَّ ٱللَّهَ يَهۡدِي مَن يَشَآءُۚ وَهُوَ أَعۡلَمُ
بِٱلۡمُهۡتَدِينَ ﴿٥٦﴾ وَقَالُوٓاْ إِن نَّتَّبِعِ ٱلۡهُدَىٰ مَعَكَ نُتَخَطَّفۡ مِنۡ أَرۡضِنَآۚ
أَوَلَمۡ نُمَكِّن لَّهُمۡ حَرَمًا ءَامِنٗا يُجۡبَىٰٓ إِلَيۡهِ ثَمَرَٰتُ كُلِّ شَيۡءٖ رِّزۡقٗا مِّن لَّدُنَّا

VERILY, thou canst not guide aright everyone whom thou lovest: but it is God who guides him that wills [to be guided];[55] and He is fully aware of all who would let themselves be guided.[56] ⟨56⟩

Now some say, "If we were to follow the guidance to which thou invitest us, we would be torn away from our very soil!"[57]

Why – have We not established for them a sanctuary secure, to which, as a provision from Us, shall be gathered the fruits of all [good] things?[58]

wa mimmā razaqnāhum yuñfiqūn. (54) Wa ʾidhā
samiʿul-laghwa ʾaʿraḍū ʿanhu wa qālū lanāa
ʾaʿmālunā wa lakum ʾaʿmālukum salāmun
ʿalaykum lā nabtaghil-jāhilīn. (55) ʾInnaka lā tahdī
man ʾaḥbabta wa lākinnal-lāha yahdī mañy-yashāaʾu
wa Huwa ʾaʿlamu bilmuhtadīn. (56) Wa qālūu ʾin-
nattabiʿil-hudā maʿaka nutakhaṭṭaf min ʾarḍinā.
ʾAwalam numakkil-lahum Ḥaraman ʾāminañy-yujbāa
ʾilayhi thamarātu kulli shayʾir-rizqam-mil-ladunnā

---

and "repelling evil with good" evidently relates to the loss of erstwhile communal links, social ostracism, and all manner of physical or moral persecution which is so often the lot of persons who accept religious tenets different from those of their own community.

54 This obviously refers to attempts, based on prejudice, at deriding the spiritual re-orientation of the person concerned.

55 Or: "God guides whomever He wills" – either of these two renderings being syntactically correct. According to several extremely well-authenticated Traditions, the above verse relates to the Prophet's inability to induce his dying uncle Abū Ṭālib, whom he loved dearly and who had loved and protected him throughout his life, to renounce the pagan beliefs of his ancestors and to profess faith in God's oneness. Influenced by Abū Jahl and other Meccan chieftains, Abū Ṭālib, died professing, in his own words, "the creed of ʿAbd al-Muṭṭalib" (Bukhārī) or, according to another version (quoted by Ṭabarī), "the creed of my ancestors (*al-ashyākh*)". However, the Qurʾanic statement "thou canst not guide aright everyone whom thou lovest" has undoubtedly a timeless import as well: it stresses the inadequacy of all human endeavours to "convert" any other person, however loving and loved, to one's own beliefs, or to prevent him from falling into what one regards as error, unless that person *wills* to be so guided.

56 The above rendering of the expression *al-muhtadīn* conforms to the interpretations offered in this context by many classical commentators – e.g., "those who accept guidance" (Zamakhsharī), "everyone who in time would find the right way" (Rāzī), "those who are prepared (*mustaʿiddīn*) for it" (Bayḍāwī), "all who deserve guidance" (Ibn Kathīr), and so forth. Thus, God's guidance is but the final act of His grace with which He rewards all who *desire* to be guided. For a further consideration of this problem, the reader is referred to Zamakhsharī's illuminating remarks quoted in note 4 on 14 : 4.

57 Lit., "If we were to follow the guidance together with thee, we would be snatched away from our land" (or "our soil"). This passage has obviously a twofold connotation. On the historical plane, it echoes an objection voiced by many pagan Meccans to Muḥammad's preaching: "If we were to accept thy call, most of the other tribes would regard this as a betrayal of our common ancestral beliefs, and would drive us away from our land." In a more general, timeless sense it reflects the hesitation of so many people – of whatever period, environment or religious persuasion – who, while realizing the truth of a new spiritual call, are yet fearful of acknowledging it as true lest this acknowledgment cause a total breach between them and their community and thus, as it were, cut the ground from under their feet.

58 Like the preceding expression of fear, this Qurʾanic answer, too, can be understood in two senses. In the limited, historical sense it is an allusion to Abraham's prayer that the land around the Kaʿbah be made secure for all

But most of them are unaware [of this truth]. «57»
And how many a community that [once] exulted in its wanton wealth and ease of life have We destroyed, so that those dwelling-places of theirs – all but a few – have never been dwelt-in after them: for it is indeed We alone who shall remain when all else will have passed away![59] «58»
Yet, withal, thy Sustainer would never destroy a community without having [first] raised in its midst an apostle who would convey unto them Our messages;[60] and never would We destroy a community unless its people are wont to do wrong [to one another].[61] «59»
And [remember:] whatever you are given [now] is but for the [passing] enjoyment of life in this world, and for its embellishment – whereas that which is with God is [so much] better and more enduring. Will you not, then, use your reason? «60»
Is, then, he to whom We have given that goodly promise which he shall see fulfilled [on his resurrection][62] comparable to one on whom We have bestowed [all] the enjoyments of this worldly life but who, on Resurrection Day, will find himself among those that shall be arraigned [before Us]?[63] «61»

وَلَٰكِنَّ أَكْثَرَهُمْ لَا يَعْلَمُونَ ﴿57﴾ وَكَمْ أَهْلَكْنَا مِن قَرْيَةٍۭ بَطِرَتْ
مَعِيشَتَهَا ۖ فَتِلْكَ مَسَٰكِنُهُمْ لَمْ تُسْكَن مِّنۢ بَعْدِهِمْ إِلَّا قَلِيلًا ۖ وَكُنَّا نَحْنُ
ٱلْوَٰرِثِينَ ﴿58﴾ وَمَا كَانَ رَبُّكَ مُهْلِكَ ٱلْقُرَىٰ حَتَّىٰ يَبْعَثَ فِىٓ أُمِّهَا رَسُولًا
يَتْلُوا۟ عَلَيْهِمْ ءَايَٰتِنَا ۚ وَمَا كُنَّا مُهْلِكِى ٱلْقُرَىٰٓ إِلَّا وَأَهْلُهَا ظَٰلِمُونَ ﴿59﴾
وَمَآ أُوتِيتُم مِّن شَىْءٍ فَمَتَٰعُ ٱلْحَيَوٰةِ ٱلدُّنْيَا وَزِينَتُهَا ۚ وَمَا عِندَ ٱللَّهِ خَيْرٌ
وَأَبْقَىٰٓ ۚ أَفَلَا تَعْقِلُونَ ﴿60﴾ أَفَمَن وَعَدْنَٰهُ وَعْدًا حَسَنًا فَهُوَ لَٰقِيهِ كَمَن
مَّتَّعْنَٰهُ مَتَٰعَ ٱلْحَيَوٰةِ ٱلدُّنْيَا ثُمَّ هُوَ يَوْمَ ٱلْقِيَٰمَةِ مِنَ ٱلْمُحْضَرِينَ ﴿61﴾

wa lākinna ʾaktharahum lā yaᶜlamūn. (57) Wa kam ʾahlaknā miñ-qaryatim-baṭirat maᶜīshatahā; fatilka masākinuhum lam tuskam-mim-baᶜdihim ʾillā qalīlañw-wa kunnā Naḥnul-Wārithīn. (58) Wa mā kāna Rabbuka muhlikal-qurā ḥattā yabᶜatha fīi ʾummihā Rasūlañy-yatlū ᶜalayhim ʾĀyātinā; wa mā kunnā muhlikil-qurāa ʾillā wa ʾahluhā ẓālimūn. (59) Wa māa ʾūtītum-miñ-shayʾiñ-famatāᶜul-ḥayātid-dunyā wa zīnatuhā; wa mā ᶜindal-lāhi khayruñw-wa ʾabqāa ʾafalā taᶜqilūn. (60) ʾAfamañw-waᶜadnāhu waᶜdan ḥasanañ-fahuwa lāqīhi kamam-mattaᶜnāhu matāᶜal-ḥayātid-dunyā thumma huwa Yawmal-Qiyāmati minal-muḥḍarīn. (61)

times and its natural barrenness be compensated by fruitful help from outside (cf. 14 : 35-41; also 2 : 126), and to God's acceptance of this prayer: thus, the Prophet's Meccan contemporaries are reminded that they need not fear to be dispossessed of this holy land so long as they remain righteous and trust in God. In its purely spiritual connotation, on the other hand, the "sanctuary secure" is God's promise – referred to in verse 61 below – that all who have faith in Him and are conscious of their responsibility to Him shall be graced with a sense of inner peace in this world and with enduring bliss in the life to come; and since they are thus to be rewarded with the "fruits" of all their good deeds, "no fear need they have, and neither shall they grieve" (cf. 2 : 62, 3 : 170, 5 : 69, 6 : 48, 7 : 35, 10 : 62, 46 : 13). See also note 59 on 29 : 67.

59 Lit., "We are indeed (*kunnā*) the inheritors". For an explanation of my rendering of this phrase, see note 22 on 15 : 23. The above passage stresses the insignificance and brittleness of all worldly "advantages" as compared with the imperishable good of divine guidance.

60 Sc., "and thus make them aware of the meaning of right and wrong": cf. 6 : 130-132 and the corresponding notes 116 and 117.

61 Cf. in this connection 11 : 117 and note 149. All the three passages referred to in this as well as the preceding note (i.e., 6 : 130-132, 11 : 117 and 28 : 59) are interdependent and must, therefore, be read side by side. The present passage connects with verse 58 above and its reference to "wanton wealth and ease of life", for the sake of which people so often wrong one another.

62 See second half of note 58.

63 Sc., "for having misused Our gifts and attributed them to powers other than Us".

For, on that Day He will call unto them, and will ask: "Where, now, are those [beings or powers] whom you imagined to have a share in My divinity?"[64] «62» – [whereupon] they against whom the word [of truth] shall thus stand revealed[65] will exclaim: "O our Sustainer! Those whom we caused to err so grievously, we but caused to err as we ourselves had been erring.[66] We [now] disavow them before Thee: it was not us that they worshipped!"[67] «63»
And [they] will be told: "Call [now] unto those [beings or powers] to whom you were wont to ascribe a share in God's divinity !"[68] – and they will call unto them [for help], but those [false objects of worship] will not respond to them: whereupon they will see the suffering [that awaits them – the suffering which could have been avoided] if only they had allowed themselves to be guided![69] «64»
And on that Day He will call unto them, and will ask: "How did you respond to My message-bearers?"[70] «65» – but all arguments and excuses will by then have been erased from their minds,[71] and they will not [be able to] obtain any [helpful] answer from one another.[72] «66»

وَيَوْمَ يُنَادِيهِمْ فَيَقُولُ أَيْنَ شُرَكَآءِيَ ٱلَّذِينَ كُنتُمْ تَزْعُمُونَ ﴿٦٢﴾ قَالَ ٱلَّذِينَ
حَقَّ عَلَيْهِمُ ٱلْقَوْلُ رَبَّنَا هَٰٓؤُلَآءِ ٱلَّذِينَ أَغْوَيْنَآ أَغْوَيْنَٰهُمْ كَمَا غَوَيْنَا
تَبَرَّأْنَآ إِلَيْكَ مَا كَانُوٓاْ إِيَّانَا يَعْبُدُونَ ﴿٦٣﴾ وَقِيلَ ٱدْعُواْ شُرَكَآءَكُمْ
فَدَعَوْهُمْ فَلَمْ يَسْتَجِيبُواْ لَهُمْ وَرَأَوُاْ ٱلْعَذَابَ لَوْ أَنَّهُمْ كَانُواْ يَهْتَدُونَ ﴿٦٤﴾
وَيَوْمَ يُنَادِيهِمْ فَيَقُولُ مَاذَآ أَجَبْتُمُ ٱلْمُرْسَلِينَ ﴿٦٥﴾ فَعَمِيَتْ عَلَيْهِمُ
ٱلْأَنۢبَآءُ يَوْمَئِذٍ فَهُمْ لَا يَتَسَآءَلُونَ ﴿٦٦﴾

Wa Yawma yunādīhim fayaqūlu ᵓayna shurakāaᵓiyal-ladhīna kuñtum tazᶜumūn. (62) Qālal-ladhīna ḥaqqa ᶜalayhimul-qawlu Rabbanā hāaᵓulāaᵓil-ladhīna ᵓaghwaynāa ᵓaghwaynāhum kamā ghawaynā. Tabarraᵓnāa ᵓilayka mā kānūu ᵓiyyānā yaᶜbudūn. (63) Wa qīlad-ᶜū shurakāaᵓakum fadaᶜawhum falam yastajībū lahum wa raᵓawul-ᶜadhāba law ᵓannahum kānū yahtadūn. (64) Wa Yawma yunādīhim fayaqūlu mādhāa ᵓajabtumul-Mursalīn. (65) Faᶜamiyat ᶜalayhimul-ᵓambāaᵓu Yawmaᵓidhiñ-fahum lā yatasāaᵓalūn. (66)

64 Lit., "those partners of Mine whom you supposed [to exist]": see notes 15 and 16 on 6 : 22-23.

65 I.e., in the very fact of God's calling them to account (cf. 27 : 82 and the corresponding note 73). As the sequence shows, the persons thus addressed are the "leaders of thought" supposed to have set the community's faulty standards of social behaviour and moral valuation; and since they are primarily responsible for the wrong direction which their followers have taken, they will be the first to suffer in the life to come.

66 I.e., "we did not lead them astray out of malice, but simply because we ourselves had been led astray by our predecessors". This "answer" is, of course, evasive, but it is quoted here to show that man's attachment to false – but, nevertheless, almost deified – values and concepts based on stark materialism is, more often than not, a matter of "social continuity": in other words, the validity of those materialistic pseudo-values is taken for granted simply because they are time-honoured, with every generation blindly subscribing to the views held by their forebears. In its deepest sense, this passage – as so many similar ones throughout the Qurᵓān – points to the moral inadmissibility of accepting an ethical or intellectual proposition as true on no other grounds than that it was held to be true by earlier generations.

67 In other words, they were but wont to worship their own passions and desires projected onto extraneous beings. See in this connection 10 : 28 and the corresponding notes, especially note 46; also 34 : 41 and note 52.

68 Lit., "those [God-]partners of yours": see note 64 above.

69 For this rendering of the phrase law *kānū yahtadūn*, see note 56 above.

70 This connects with the first sentence of verse 59, which has been explained in the corresponding note 60. The present verse clearly implies that those sinners had *not* responded to the guidance offered them by God's apostles. As in many other instances in the Qurᵓān, God's "question" is but meant to stress a moral failure which by now has become obvious to man's self-accusing conscience.

71 Lit., "will on that Day have become obscured to them". The operative noun *anbāᵓ*, which literally denotes "tidings", has here the compound meaning of "arguments and excuses" (Ṭabarī).

72 I.e., they will all be equally confused. For the above rendering of *lā yatasāᵓalūn* (lit., "they will not [be able to] ask one another"), see the explanations of this phrase advanced by Baghawī, Zamakhsharī and Bayḍāwī.

But as against this – anyone who repents[73] and attains to faith and does righteous deeds may well [hope to] find himself among those who achieve a happy state [in the life to come]. ‹67›

AND [thus it is:] thy Sustainer creates whatever He wills; and He chooses [for mankind] whatever is best for them.[74] Limitless is God in His glory, and sublimely exalted above anything to which they may ascribe a share in His divinity! ‹68›
And thy Sustainer knows all that their hearts conceal as well as all that they bring into the open: ‹69› for He is God, save whom there is no deity. Unto Him all praise is due, at the beginning and at the end [of time];[75] and with Him rests all judgment; and unto Him shall you all be brought back. ‹70›
Say: "Have you ever considered [this]: If God had willed that there should always be night about you, without break, until the Day of Resurrection – is there any deity other than God that could bring you light?[76] Will you not, then, listen [to the truth]?" ‹71›
Say: "Have you ever considered [this]: If God had willed that there should always be daylight about you, without break, until the Day of Resurrection – is there any deity other than God that could bring you

فَأَمَّا مَن تَابَ وَءَامَنَ وَعَمِلَ صَٰلِحًا فَعَسَىٰٓ أَن يَكُونَ مِنَ ٱلْمُفْلِحِينَ ﴿٦٧﴾
وَرَبُّكَ يَخْلُقُ مَا يَشَآءُ وَيَخْتَارُ ۗ مَا كَانَ لَهُمُ ٱلْخِيَرَةُ ۚ سُبْحَٰنَ ٱللَّهِ وَتَعَٰلَىٰ
عَمَّا يُشْرِكُونَ ﴿٦٨﴾ وَرَبُّكَ يَعْلَمُ مَا تُكِنُّ صُدُورُهُمْ وَمَا يُعْلِنُونَ ﴿٦٩﴾ وَهُوَ
ٱللَّهُ لَآ إِلَٰهَ إِلَّا هُوَ ۖ لَهُ ٱلْحَمْدُ فِى ٱلْأُولَىٰ وَٱلْءَاخِرَةِ ۖ وَلَهُ ٱلْحُكْمُ وَإِلَيْهِ
تُرْجَعُونَ ﴿٧٠﴾ قُلْ أَرَءَيْتُمْ إِن جَعَلَ ٱللَّهُ عَلَيْكُمُ ٱلَّيْلَ سَرْمَدًا إِلَىٰ يَوْمِ ٱلْقِيَٰمَةِ
مَنْ إِلَٰهٌ غَيْرُ ٱللَّهِ يَأْتِيكُم بِضِيَآءٍ ۖ أَفَلَا تَسْمَعُونَ ﴿٧١﴾ قُلْ أَرَءَيْتُمْ إِن جَعَلَ
ٱللَّهُ عَلَيْكُمُ ٱلنَّهَارَ سَرْمَدًا إِلَىٰ يَوْمِ ٱلْقِيَٰمَةِ مَنْ إِلَٰهٌ غَيْرُ ٱللَّهِ يَأْتِيكُم

Faʾammā mañ-tāba wa ʾāmana wa ʿamila ṣāliḥañ-faʿasāa ʾañy-yakūna minal-mufliḥīn. (67) Wa Rabbuka yakhluqu mā yashāaʾu wa yakhtāru mā kāna lahumul-khiyarah. Subḥānal-lāhi wa taʿālā ʿammā yushrikūn. (68) Wa Rabbuka yaʿlamu mā tukinnu ṣudūruhum wa mā yuʿlinūn. (69) Wa Huwal-lāhu lāa ʾilāha ʾillā Huwa lahul-ḥamdu fil-ʾūlā wal-ʾĀkhirati wa lahul-ḥukmu wa ʾilayhi turjaʿūn. (70) Qul ʾaraʾaytum ʾiñ-jaʿalal-lāhu ʿalaykumul-layla sarmadan ʾilā Yawmil-Qiyāmati man ʾilāhun ghayrul-lāhi yaʾtikum-biḍiyāaʾ. ʾAfalā tasmaʿūn. (71) Qul-ʾaraʾaytum ʾiñ-jaʿalal-lāhu ʿalaykumun-nahāra sarmadan ʾilā Yawmil-Qiyāmati man ʾilāhun ghayrul-lāhi yaʾtīkum-

73 I.e., during his life in this world. For an explanation of this stress on repentance – which flows from one's realization of moral failure – see *sūrah* 24, note 41.

74 Some of the classical commentators incline to interpret the *mā* in the phrase *mā kāna lahum al-khiyarah* as a particle of negation and the noun *khiyarah* as "choice" or "freedom of choice", thus giving to this phrase the meaning of "He chooses, [but] they [i.e., human beings] have no freedom of choice". To my mind, however, this interpretation conflicts not only with the immediately preceding passages but with the tenor of the Qurʾān as a whole, which insists throughout on man's responsibility for (and, hence, on relative freedom in) choosing between right and wrong – and this side by side with its stress on God's unlimited power to determine the *factual* course of events. Hence, I prefer to base my rendering on the interpretation advanced and convincingly argued by Ṭabarī, who regards the crucial particle *mā* not as a negation but as a relative pronoun synonymous with *alladhī* ("that which" or "whatever"), and understands the noun *khiyarah* in its primary significance of "that which is chosen" or "preferred", i.e., because it is considered to be *the best*: in another word, as a synonym of *khayr*. Zamakhsharī refers to this interpretation with evident approval (without, however, mentioning Ṭabarī, specifically), and enlarges upon it thus: "God chooses for mankind whatever is best (*mā huwa khayr*) and most beneficial (*aṣlaḥ*) for them, for He knows better than they themselves do what is good for them."

75 Or: "in this first [i.e., present life] as well as in the life to come".

76 Lit., "who [i.e., "where"] is a deity . . .", etc., obviously implying that no such "deity" exists.

ربع
الحزب

[the darkness of] night, wherein you might rest? Will you not, then, see [the truth]?"[77] ‹72›

For it is out of His grace that He has made for you the night and the day, so that you might rest therein as well as seek to obtain [what you need] of His bounty: and [He gave you all this] so that you might have cause to be grateful. ‹73›

AND ON THAT DAY[78] He will call unto those [that shall have been arraigned before His judgment seat], and will ask: "Where, now, are those [beings or powers] whom you imagined to have a share in My divinity?"[79] ‹74›

And [they will remain silent: for by then] We will have called forth witnesses from within every community,[80] and will have said [unto the sinners]: "Produce an evidence for what you have been claiming!"[81]

And so they will come to understand that all truth is God's [alone];[82] and all their false imagery will have forsaken them.[83] ‹75›

[NOW,] BEHOLD, Qārūn was one of the people of Moses;[84] but he arrogantly exalted himself above them – simply because We had granted him such riches

بِلَيْلٍ تَسْكُنُونَ فِيهِ أَفَلَا تُبْصِرُونَ ﴿٧٢﴾ وَمِن رَّحْمَتِهِۦ جَعَلَ لَكُمُ
ٱلَّيْلَ وَٱلنَّهَارَ لِتَسْكُنُوا۟ فِيهِ وَلِتَبْتَغُوا۟ مِن فَضْلِهِۦ وَلَعَلَّكُمْ
تَشْكُرُونَ ﴿٧٣﴾ وَيَوْمَ يُنَادِيهِمْ فَيَقُولُ أَيْنَ شُرَكَآءِىَ ٱلَّذِينَ كُنتُمْ
تَزْعُمُونَ ﴿٧٤﴾ وَنَزَعْنَا مِن كُلِّ أُمَّةٍ شَهِيدًا فَقُلْنَا هَاتُوا۟ بُرْهَٰنَكُمْ
فَعَلِمُوٓا۟ أَنَّ ٱلْحَقَّ لِلَّهِ وَضَلَّ عَنْهُم مَّا كَانُوا۟ يَفْتَرُونَ ﴿٧٥﴾ ۞ إِنَّ
قَٰرُونَ كَانَ مِن قَوْمِ مُوسَىٰ فَبَغَىٰ عَلَيْهِمْ وَءَاتَيْنَٰهُ مِنَ ٱلْكُنُوزِ

bilayliñ-taskunūna fīh. ˀAfalā tubṣirūn. ⟨72⟩ Wa mir-raḥmatihī jaᶜala lakumul-layla wan-nahāra litaskunū fīhi wa litabtaghū miñ-faḍlihī wa laᶜallakum tashkurūn. ⟨73⟩ Wa Yawma yunādīhim fa-yaqūlu ˀayna shurakāaˀiyal-ladhīna kuñtum tazᶜumūn. ⟨74⟩ Wa nazaᶜnā miñ-kulli ˀummatiñ-shahīdañ-faqulnā hātū burhānakum faᶜalimūu ˀannal-ḥaqqa lillāhi wa ḍalla ᶜanhum-mā kānū yaftarūn. ⟨75⟩ ۞ ˀInna Qārūna kāna miñ-qawmi Mūsā fabaghā ᶜalayhim; wa ˀātaynāhu minal-kunūzi

77 I.e., "Will you not recognize the miracle of planned and purposeful creation?"

78 I.e., the Day of Resurrection – thus reverting to the theme enunciated in verses 62-66 above.

79 This repetition of God's "question", already mentioned in verse 62 above, is meant to stress the utter inability of the sinners concerned to justify their erstwhile attitude rationally; hence my interpolation at the beginning of the next verse.

80 I.e., the prophets who had appeared at various stages of man's history, and who will now bear witness that they had duly conveyed God's message to the people for whom it was meant.

81 Lit., "Produce your evidence" – i.e., for the possibility of anyone or anything having a share in God's divinity.

82 I.e., that He is the Ultimate Reality, and that whatever is or could be is an outcome of His will alone.

83 For the meaning of the phrase *mā kānu yaftarūn* (lit., "all that they were wont to invent" – rendered by me here as well as in 6 : 24, 7 : 53, 10 : 30, 11 : 21 and 16 : 87 as "all their false imagery"), see *sūrah* 11, note 42; also note 15 on 6 : 22. A specific instance of such "false imagery" – the futility of man's relying on his own wealth and worldly power – is illustrated in the immediately following legend of Qārūn (see next note).

84 The structure of the above sentence is meant to show that even a person who had been a follower of one of the greatest of God's apostles was not above the possibility of sinning under the influence of false pride and self-exaltation – a particular example of the "false imagery" referred to in the preceding passage. The conventional "identification" of Qārūn with the Korah of the Old Testament (Numbers xvi) is neither relevant nor warranted by the Qurˀanic text, the more so as the purport of this legend is a moral lesson and not a historical narrative. This, by the way, explains also the juxtaposition, elsewhere in the Qurˀān (29 : 39 and 40 : 24), of Qārūn with Pharaoh, the arch-sinner.

that his treasure-chests alone would surely have been too heavy a burden for a troop of ten strong men or even more.[85]
When [they perceived his arrogance,] his people said unto him: "Exult not [in thy wealth], for, verily, God does not love those who exult [in things vain]! «76» Seek instead, by means of what God has granted thee, [the good of] the life to come,[86] without forgetting, withal, thine own [rightful] share in this world;[87] and do good [unto others] as God has done good unto thee; and seek not to spread corruption on earth: for, verily, God does not love the spreaders of corruption!" «77»
Answered he: "This [wealth] has been given to me only by virtue of the knowledge that is in me!"[88]
Did he not know that God had destroyed [the arrogant of] many a generation that preceded him – people who were greater than he in power, and richer in what they had amassed?
But such as are lost in sin may not be asked about their sins. . . .[89] «78»
And so he went forth before his people in all his pomp; [and] those who cared only for the life of this world would say, "Oh, if we but had the like of what Qārūn has been given! Verily, with tremendous good fortune is he endowed!" «79»
But those who had been granted true knowledge said: "Woe unto you! Merit in the sight of God[90] is by far the best for any who attains to faith and does what is right: but none save the patient in adversity can ever achieve this [blessing]." «80»

مَآ إِنَّ مَفَاتِحَهُۥ لَتَنُوٓأُ بِٱلْعُصْبَةِ أُو۟لِى ٱلْقُوَّةِ إِذْ قَالَ لَهُۥ قَوْمُهُۥ لَا تَفْرَحْ ۖ
إِنَّ ٱللَّهَ لَا يُحِبُّ ٱلْفَرِحِينَ ﴿٧٦﴾ وَٱبْتَغِ فِيمَآ ءَاتَىٰكَ ٱللَّهُ ٱلدَّارَ ٱلْـَٔاخِرَةَ ۖ
وَلَا تَنسَ نَصِيبَكَ مِنَ ٱلدُّنْيَا ۖ وَأَحْسِن كَمَآ أَحْسَنَ ٱللَّهُ إِلَيْكَ ۖ وَلَا تَبْغِ
ٱلْفَسَادَ فِى ٱلْأَرْضِ ۖ إِنَّ ٱللَّهَ لَا يُحِبُّ ٱلْمُفْسِدِينَ ﴿٧٧﴾ قَالَ إِنَّمَآ أُوتِيتُهُۥ
عَلَىٰ عِلْمٍ عِندِىٓ ۚ أَوَلَمْ يَعْلَمْ أَنَّ ٱللَّهَ قَدْ أَهْلَكَ مِن قَبْلِهِۦ مِنَ ٱلْقُرُونِ مَنْ
هُوَ أَشَدُّ مِنْهُ قُوَّةً وَأَكْثَرُ جَمْعًا ۚ وَلَا يُسْـَٔلُ عَن ذُنُوبِهِمُ ٱلْمُجْرِمُونَ ﴿٧٨﴾
فَخَرَجَ عَلَىٰ قَوْمِهِۦ فِى زِينَتِهِۦ ۖ قَالَ ٱلَّذِينَ يُرِيدُونَ ٱلْحَيَوٰةَ ٱلدُّنْيَا يَٰلَيْتَ
لَنَا مِثْلَ مَآ أُوتِىَ قَٰرُونُ إِنَّهُۥ لَذُو حَظٍّ عَظِيمٍ ﴿٧٩﴾ وَقَالَ ٱلَّذِينَ أُوتُوا۟
ٱلْعِلْمَ وَيْلَكُمْ ثَوَابُ ٱللَّهِ خَيْرٌ لِّمَنْ ءَامَنَ وَعَمِلَ صَٰلِحًا وَلَا يُلَقَّىٰهَآ إِلَّا
ٱلصَّٰبِرُونَ ﴿٨٠﴾

māa ʾinna mafātiḥahū latanūuʾu bilʿuṣbati ʾulil-quwwati ʾidh qāla lahū qawmuhū lā tafraḥ. ʾInnal-lāha lā yuḥibbul-fariḥīn. (76) Wab-taghi fīmāa ʾātākal-lāhud-dāral-ʾĀkhirata wa lā tañsa naṣībaka minad-dunyā. Wa ʾaḥsiñ-kamāa ʾaḥsanal-lāhu ʾilayka wa lā tabghil-fasāda fil-ʾarḍi ʾinnal-lāha lā yuḥibbul-mufsidīn. (77) Qāla ʾinnamāa ʾūtītuhū ʿalā ʿilmin ʿiñdī. ʾAwalam yaʿlam ʾannal-lāha qad ʾahlaka miñ-qablihī minal-qurūni man huwa ʾashaddu minhu quwwatañw-wa ʾaktharu jamʿā. Wa lā yusʾalu ʿañ-dhunūbihimul-mujrimūn. (78) Fakharaja ʿalā qawmihī fī zīnatih. Qālal-ladhīna yurīdūnal-ḥayātad-dunyā yā layta lanā mithla māa ʾūtiya Qārūnu ʾinnahū ladhū ḥaẓẓin ʿaẓīm. (79) Wa qālal-ladhīna ʾūtul-ʿilma way-lakum thawābul-lāhi khayrul-liman ʾāmana wa ʿamila ṣāliḥā. Wa lā yulaqqāhāa ʾillaṣ-ṣābirūn. (80)

85 The term *ʿuṣbah* denotes a company of ten or more (up to forty) persons; since it is used here metonymically, pointing to the great weight involved, it is best rendered as above. – The noun *mafātiḥ* is a plural of both *miftaḥ* or *miftāḥ* ("key") and *maftaḥ* ("that which is under lock and key", i.e., a "hoard of wealth" or "treasure chest"), which latter meaning is obviously the one intended in the present context.

86 I.e., by spending in charity and on good causes.

87 Lit., "and do not forget . . .", etc.: a call to generosity and, at the same time, to moderation (cf. 2 : 143 – "We have willed you to be a community of the middle way").

88 I.e., "as a result of my own experience, shrewdness and ability" (cf. 39 : 49 and the corresponding note 55).

89 Obviously implying that "such as are lost in sin" (*al-mujrimūn*) are, as a rule, blind to their own failings and, therefore, not responsive to admonition.

90 Lit., "God's reward", sc., "of spiritual merit".

And thereupon We caused the earth to swallow him and his dwelling; and he had none and nothing to succour him against God, nor was he of those who could succour themselves.[91] ‹81›

And on the morrow, those who but yesterday had longed to be in his place exclaimed: "Alas [for our not having been aware] that it is indeed God [alone] who grants abundant sustenance, or gives it in scant measure, unto whichever He wills of His creatures! Had not God been gracious to us, He might have caused [the earth] to swallow us, too! Alas [for our having forgotten] that those who deny the truth can never attain to a happy state!" ‹82›

As for that [happy] life in the hereafter, We grant it [only] to those who do not seek to exalt themselves on earth, nor yet to spread corruption: for the future belongs to the God-conscious.[92] ‹83›

Whosoever shall come [before God] with a good deed will gain [further] good therefrom;[93] but as for any who shall come with an evil deed – [know that] they who do evil deeds will not be requited with more than [the like of] what they have done.[94] ‹84›

VERILY, [O believer,] He who has laid down this Qur'ān in plain terms, making it binding on thee,[95] will assuredly bring thee back [from death] to a life renewed.[96]

فَخَسَفْنَا بِهِۦ وَبِدَارِهِ ٱلْأَرْضَ فَمَا كَانَ لَهُۥ مِن فِئَةٍ يَنصُرُونَهُۥ مِن دُونِ
ٱللَّهِ وَمَا كَانَ مِنَ ٱلْمُنتَصِرِينَ ﴿٨١﴾ وَأَصْبَحَ ٱلَّذِينَ تَمَنَّوْا۟ مَكَانَهُۥ
بِٱلْأَمْسِ يَقُولُونَ وَيْكَأَنَّ ٱللَّهَ يَبْسُطُ ٱلرِّزْقَ لِمَن يَشَآءُ مِنْ عِبَادِهِۦ
وَيَقْدِرُ لَوْلَآ أَن مَّنَّ ٱللَّهُ عَلَيْنَا لَخَسَفَ بِنَا وَيْكَأَنَّهُۥ لَا يُفْلِحُ
ٱلْكَٰفِرُونَ ﴿٨٢﴾ تِلْكَ ٱلدَّارُ ٱلْءَاخِرَةُ نَجْعَلُهَا لِلَّذِينَ لَا يُرِيدُونَ عُلُوًّا فِى
ٱلْأَرْضِ وَلَا فَسَادًا وَٱلْعَٰقِبَةُ لِلْمُتَّقِينَ ﴿٨٣﴾ مَن جَآءَ بِٱلْحَسَنَةِ فَلَهُۥ خَيْرٌ
مِّنْهَا وَمَن جَآءَ بِٱلسَّيِّئَةِ فَلَا يُجْزَى ٱلَّذِينَ عَمِلُوا۟ ٱلسَّيِّـَٔاتِ إِلَّا مَا كَانُوا۟
يَعْمَلُونَ ﴿٨٤﴾ إِنَّ ٱلَّذِى فَرَضَ عَلَيْكَ ٱلْقُرْءَانَ لَرَآدُّكَ إِلَىٰ مَعَادٍ

Fakhasafnā bihī wa bidārihil-'arḍa famā kāna lahū miñ-fi'atiñy-yañṣurūnahū miñ-dūnil-lāhi wa mā kana minal-muñtaṣirīn. (81) Wa 'aṣbaḥal-ladhīna tamannaw makānahū bil'amsi yaqūlūna wayka'annal-lāha yabsuṭur-rizqa limañy-yashāa'u min 'ibādihī wa yaqdir. Lawlāa 'am-mannal-lāhu 'alaynā lakhasafa binā. Wayka'annahū lā yufliḥul-kāfirūn. (82) Tilkad-dārul-'Ākhiratu naj'aluhā lilladhīna lā yurīdūna 'uluwwañ-fil-'arḍi wa lā fasādañw-wal-'āqibatu lil-muttaqīn. (83) Mañ-jāa'a bilḥasanati falahū khayrum-minhā; wa mañ-jāa'a bissayyi'ati falā yujzal-ladhīna 'amilus-sayyi'āti 'illā mā kānū ya'malūn. (84) 'Innal-ladhī faraḍa 'alaykal-Qur'āna larāadduka 'ilā ma'ād.

91 Lit., "he had no host whatever to succour him . . .", etc. Qārūn's being "swallowed by the earth" may possibly be a metaphor of a catastrophic, unforeseen loss – from whatever cause – of all his worldly goods and, thus, of his erstwhile grandeur.

92 This last clause makes it clear that, in order to have spiritual value, man's "not seeking" worldly grandeur or self-indulgence in things depraved must be an outcome, not of indifference or of a lack of opportunity, but solely of a conscious moral *choice*.

93 See note 79 on the identical phrase in 27 : 89.

94 Cf. 6 : 160 and the corresponding note 162.

95 According to Mujāhid (as quoted by Ṭabarī), the phrase *faraḍa 'alayka* is almost synonymous with *a'ṭāka*, "He gave [it] to thee". This, however, elucidates only *one* part of the above complex expression, which, I believe, has here a meaning similar to that of *faraḍnāhā* ("We laid it down in plain terms") occurring in the first verse of *sūrah* 24 (*An-Nūr*) and explained in the corresponding note 1. In the present context, the particle *'alayka* ("upon thee"), with its pronominal suffix, gives to the above clause the additional meaning of a moral *obligation* on the part of the recipient of the Qur'anic message to conform his or her way of life to its teachings; hence my compound rendering of the phrase.

96 The term *ma'ād* denotes, literally, "a place [or "a state"] to which one returns", and, tropically, one's "ultimate destination" or "ultimate condition"; in the present context, it is obviously synonymous with "life in the hereafter". This

Say [unto those who reject the truth]: "My Sustainer knows best as to who is right-guided[97] and who is obviously lost in error!" ‹85›
Now [as for thyself, O believer,] thou couldst never foresee[98] that this divine writ would [one day] be offered to thee: but [It did come to thee] by thy Sustainer's grace.
Hence, never uphold those who deny the truth [of divine guidance], ‹86› and never let them turn thee away from God's messages after they have been bestowed upon thee from on high: instead,[99] summon [all men] to thy Sustainer.
And never be of those who ascribe divinity to aught but Him, ‹87› and never call upon any other deity side by side with God.
There is no deity save Him. Everything is bound to perish, save His [eternal] Self.[100]
With Him rests all judgment; and unto Him shall you all be brought back. ‹88›

قُل رَّبِّيٓ أَعۡلَمُ مَن جَآءَ بِٱلۡهُدَىٰ وَمَنۡ هُوَ فِي ضَلَٰلٖ مُّبِينٖ ﴿٨٥﴾ وَمَا
كُنتَ تَرۡجُوٓاْ أَن يُلۡقَىٰٓ إِلَيۡكَ ٱلۡكِتَٰبُ إِلَّا رَحۡمَةٗ مِّن رَّبِّكَۖ فَلَا تَكُونَنَّ
ظَهِيرٗا لِّلۡكَٰفِرِينَ ﴿٨٦﴾ وَلَا يَصُدُّنَّكَ عَنۡ ءَايَٰتِ ٱللَّهِ بَعۡدَ إِذۡ أُنزِلَتۡ
إِلَيۡكَۖ وَٱدۡعُ إِلَىٰ رَبِّكَۖ وَلَا تَكُونَنَّ مِنَ ٱلۡمُشۡرِكِينَ ﴿٨٧﴾ وَلَا تَدۡعُ مَعَ ٱللَّهِ
إِلَٰهًا ءَاخَرَۘ لَآ إِلَٰهَ إِلَّا هُوَۚ كُلُّ شَيۡءٍ هَالِكٌ إِلَّا وَجۡهَهُۥۚ لَهُ ٱلۡحُكۡمُ
وَإِلَيۡهِ تُرۡجَعُونَ ﴿٨٨﴾

Qur-Rabbīi ᵓaᶜlamu mañ-jāaᵓa bilhudā wa man huwa fī ḍalālim-mubīn. (85) Wa mā kuñta tarjūu ᵓañy-yulqāa ᵓilaykal-Kitābu ᵓillā raḥmatam-mir-Rabbika falā takūnanna ẓahīral-lilkāfirīn. (86) Wa lā yaṣud-dunnaka ᶜan ᵓĀyātil-lāhi baᶜda ᵓidh ᵓuñzilat ᵓilayka wad-ᶜu ᵓilā Rabbika wa lā takūnanna minal-mushrikīn. (87) Wa lā tadᶜu maᶜal-lāhi ᵓilāhan ᵓākhar. Lāa ᵓilāha ᵓillā Hū. Kullu shayᵓin hālikun ᵓillā Wajhah. Lahul-ḥukmu wa ᵓilayhi turjaᶜūn. (88)

---

is how most of the classical authorities interpret the above phrase. But on the vague assumption that this passage is addressed exclusively to the Prophet, some commentators incline to the view that the noun has here a specific, purely physical connotation – "*a place* of return" – allegedly referring to God's promise to His Apostle (given during or after the latter's exodus from Mecca to Medina) that one day he would return victoriously to the city of his birth. To my mind, however, the passage has a much deeper meaning, unconnected with any place or specific point in history: it is addressed to every believer, and promises not only a continuation of life after bodily death but also a spiritual rebirth, in this world, to anyone who opens his heart to the message of the Qurᵓān and comes to regard it as binding on himself.

97 Lit., "as to who comes with guidance".

98 Lit., "hope" or "expect".

99 Lit., "and".

100 See 55 : 26-27 and the corresponding note 11.

The Twenty-Ninth Sūrah

Al-ʿAñkabūt (The Spider)

Period Uncertain

MOST of the authorities are of the opinion that this *sūrah* is one of the last to have been revealed in Mecca, while some maintain that it is one of the earliest Medina revelations. Others, again, assert that while the main body of the *sūrah* is Meccan, the first ten or eleven verses were revealed at Medina. And, finally, there are some scholars who hold the opposite view, ascribing the first nine verses to Mecca, and the rest to Medina. On the whole, it would seem that, historically, the *sūrah* marks the transition between the Mecca and Medina periods.

The title has been derived from the parable of "the spider's house" in verse 41, a symbol of false beliefs and false values, which in the long run are bound to be blown away by the winds of truth.

سورة العنكبوت مكية
-29-
وآياتها تسع وستون

IN THE NAME OF GOD, THE MOST GRACIOUS, THE DISPENSER OF GRACE:

Alif. Lām. Mīm.[1] ‹1›
DO MEN THINK that on their [mere] saying, "We have attained to faith", they will be left to themselves, and will not be put to a test? ‹2›
Yea, indeed, We did test those who lived before them; and so, [too, shall be tested the people now living: and] most certainly will God mark out those who prove themselves true, and most certainly will He mark out those who are lying.[2] ‹3›
Or do they think – they who do evil deeds [while claiming to have attained to faith] – that they can escape Us? Bad, indeed, is their judgment! ‹4›
Whoever looks forward [with hope and awe] to meeting God [on Resurrection Day, let him be ready for it]: for, behold, the end set by God [for everyone's life] is bound to come – and He alone is all-hearing, all-knowing! ‹5›
Hence, whoever strives hard [in God's cause] does so only for his own good: for, verily, God does not stand in need of anything in all the worlds! ‹6› And as for those who attain to faith and do righteous deeds, We shall most certainly efface their [previous] bad deeds, and shall most certainly reward them in accordance with the best that they ever did. ‹7›
Now [among the best of righteous deeds which] We have enjoined upon man [is] goodness towards his parents;[3]

بِسۡمِ ٱللَّهِ ٱلرَّحۡمَٰنِ ٱلرَّحِيمِ

الٓمٓ ﴿1﴾ أَحَسِبَ ٱلنَّاسُ أَن يُتۡرَكُوٓاْ أَن يَقُولُوٓاْ ءَامَنَّا وَهُمۡ لَا يُفۡتَنُونَ ﴿2﴾
وَلَقَدۡ فَتَنَّا ٱلَّذِينَ مِن قَبۡلِهِمۡۖ فَلَيَعۡلَمَنَّ ٱللَّهُ ٱلَّذِينَ صَدَقُواْ وَلَيَعۡلَمَنَّ
ٱلۡكَٰذِبِينَ ﴿3﴾ أَمۡ حَسِبَ ٱلَّذِينَ يَعۡمَلُونَ ٱلسَّيِّـَٔاتِ أَن يَسۡبِقُونَاۚ سَآءَ مَا
يَحۡكُمُونَ ﴿4﴾ مَن كَانَ يَرۡجُواْ لِقَآءَ ٱللَّهِ فَإِنَّ أَجَلَ ٱللَّهِ لَأٓتٖۚ وَهُوَ ٱلسَّمِيعُ
ٱلۡعَلِيمُ ﴿5﴾ وَمَن جَٰهَدَ فَإِنَّمَا يُجَٰهِدُ لِنَفۡسِهِۦٓۚ إِنَّ ٱللَّهَ لَغَنِيٌّ عَنِ ٱلۡعَٰلَمِينَ ﴿6﴾
وَٱلَّذِينَ ءَامَنُواْ وَعَمِلُواْ ٱلصَّٰلِحَٰتِ لَنُكَفِّرَنَّ عَنۡهُمۡ سَيِّـَٔاتِهِمۡ وَلَنَجۡزِيَنَّهُمۡ
أَحۡسَنَ ٱلَّذِي كَانُواْ يَعۡمَلُونَ ﴿7﴾ وَوَصَّيۡنَا ٱلۡإِنسَٰنَ بِوَٰلِدَيۡهِ حُسۡنٗاۖ

نصف الحزب

Bismil-lāhir-Raḥmānir-Raḥīm.
ʾAlif-Lāam-Mīim. (1) ʾAḥasiban-nāsu ʾañy-yutrakūu ʾañy-yaqūlūu ʾāmannā wa hum lā yuftanūn. (2) Wa laqad fatannal-ladhīna miñ-qablihim falayaʿlamannal-lāhul-ladhīna ṣadaqū wa layaʿlamannal-kādhibīn. (3) ʾAm ḥasibal-ladhīna yaʿmalūnas-sayyiʾāti ʾañy-yasbiqūnā. Sāaʾa mā yaḥkumūn. (4) Mañ-kāna yarjū liqāaʾal-lāhi faʾinna ʾajalal-lāhi laʾāt. Wa Huwas-Samīʿul-ʿAlīm. (5) Wa mañ-jāhada faʾinnamā yujāhidu linafsih. ʾInnal-lāha laGhaniyyun ʿanil-ʿālamīn. (6) Wal-ladhīna ʾāmanū wa ʿamiluṣ-ṣāliḥāti lanukaffiranna ʿanhum sayyiʾātihim wa lanajziyannahum ʾaḥsanal-ladhī kānū yaʿmalūn. (7) Wa waṣṣaynal-ʾIñsāna biwālidayhi ḥusnā.

---

1 See Appendix II.
2 I.e., to others and/or to themselves (see note 7).
3 Cf. 31 : 14-15 and, particularly, the corresponding note 15.

yet [even so,] should they endeavour to make thee ascribe divinity, side by side with Me, to something which thy mind cannot accept [as divine],[4] obey them not: [for] it is unto Me that you all must return, whereupon I shall make you [truly] understand [the right and wrong of] all that you were doing [in life]. ‹8›
But as for those who have attained to faith and have done righteous deeds, We shall most certainly cause them to join the righteous [in the hereafter as well]. ‹9›

وَإِن جَٰهَدَاكَ لِتُشْرِكَ بِى مَا لَيْسَ لَكَ بِهِۦ عِلْمٌ فَلَا تُطِعْهُمَآ إِلَىَّ
مَرْجِعُكُمْ فَأُنَبِّئُكُم بِمَا كُنتُمْ تَعْمَلُونَ ﴿8﴾ وَٱلَّذِينَ ءَامَنُوا۟ وَعَمِلُوا۟
ٱلصَّٰلِحَٰتِ لَنُدْخِلَنَّهُمْ فِى ٱلصَّٰلِحِينَ ﴿9﴾ وَمِنَ ٱلنَّاسِ مَن يَقُولُ
ءَامَنَّا بِٱللَّهِ فَإِذَآ أُوذِىَ فِى ٱللَّهِ جَعَلَ فِتْنَةَ ٱلنَّاسِ كَعَذَابِ ٱللَّهِ وَلَئِن
جَآءَ نَصْرٌ مِّن رَّبِّكَ لَيَقُولُنَّ إِنَّا كُنَّا مَعَكُمْ أَوَلَيْسَ ٱللَّهُ بِأَعْلَمَ بِمَا فِى
صُدُورِ ٱلْعَٰلَمِينَ ﴿10﴾ وَلَيَعْلَمَنَّ ٱللَّهُ ٱلَّذِينَ ءَامَنُوا۟ وَلَيَعْلَمَنَّ
ٱلْمُنَٰفِقِينَ ﴿11﴾

NOW THERE IS among men many a one who says [of himself and of others like him], "We do believe in God" – but whenever he is made to suffer in God's cause, he thinks that persecution at the hands of man is as [much to be feared, or even more than,] God's chastisement;[5] whereas, if succour from thy Sustainer comes [to those who truly believe],[6] he is sure to say, "Behold, we have always been with you!"
Is not God fully aware of what is in the hearts of all creatures? ‹10›
[Yea –] and most certainly will God mark out those who have [truly] attained to faith, and most certainly will He mark out the hypocrites.[7] ‹11›

Wa ʾiñ-jāhadāka litushrika bī mā laysa laka bihī ʿilmuñ-falā tuṭiʿhumā. ʾIlayya marjiʿukum faʾunabbiʾukum-bimā kuñtum taʿmalūn. ﴿8﴾ Wal-ladhīna ʾāmanū wa ʿamiluṣ-ṣāliḥāti lanudkhilannahum fiṣ-ṣāliḥīn. ﴿9﴾ Wa minan-nāsi mañy-yaqūlu ʾāmannā billāhi faʾidhāa ʾūdhiya fil-lāhi jaʿala fitnatan-nāsi kaʿadhābil-lāh wa laʾiñ-jāaʾa naṣrum-mir-Rabbika layaqūlunna ʾinnā kunnā maʿakum. ʾAwa laysal-lāhu biʾaʿlama bimā fī ṣudūril-ʿālamīn. ﴿10﴾ Wa layaʿlamannal-lāhul-ladhīna ʾāmanū wa layaʿlamannal-munāfiqīn. ﴿11﴾

4 Lit., "something of which thou hast no knowledge": i.e., in this particular case, "something which conflicts with thy knowledge that none and nothing can have any share in God's qualities or powers". According to Rāzī, this phrase may also allude to concepts not evolved through personal knowledge but, rather, acquired through a blind, uncritical acceptance of other people's views (*taqlīd*).

5 I.e., the suffering which is bound to befall in the hereafter all who abandon their faith for fear of being persecuted in this world. (It is to be borne in mind that a mere *outward* renunciation of faith under torture or threat of death is not considered a sin in Islam, although martyrdom for the sake of one's faith is the highest degree of merit to which man can attain.)

6 I.e., when it is no longer risky to be counted as one of them.

7 This is probably the earliest occurrence of the term *munāfiq* in the chronology of Qurʾanic revelation. Idiomatically, the term is derived from the noun *nafaq*, which denotes an "underground passage" having an outlet different from the entry, and signifying, specifically, the complicated burrow of a field-mouse, a lizard, etc., from which the animal can easily escape or in which it can outwit a pursuer. Tropically, the term *munāfiq* describes a person who is "two-faced", inasmuch as he always tries to find an easy way out of any real commitment, be it spiritual or social, by adapting his course of action to what promises to be of *practical* advantage to him in the situation in which he happens to find himself. Since a person thus characterized usually pretends to be morally better than he really is, the epithet *munāfiq* may roughly be rendered as "hypocrite". It should, however, be noted that whereas this Western term invariably implies conscious dissembling with the intent to deceive others, the Arabic term *munāfiq* may also be applied – and occasionally is applied in the Qurʾān – to a person who, being weak or uncertain in his beliefs or moral convictions, merely deceives *himself*. Hence, while using in my rendering of the Qurʾanic text the conventional expression "hypocrite", I have endeavoured to point out the above differentiation, whenever possible and necessary, in my explanatory notes.

And [He is aware, too, that] they who are bent on denying the truth speak [thus, as it were,] to those who have attained to faith: "Follow our way [of life], and we shall indeed take your sins upon ourselves!"[8] But never could they take upon themselves[9] aught of the sins of those [whom they would thus mislead]: behold, they are liars indeed! ‹12›

Yet most certainly will they have to bear their own burdens, and other burdens besides their own;[10] and most certainly will they be called to account on Resurrection Day for all their false assertions! ‹13›

AND, INDEED, [in times long past] We sent forth Noah unto his people,[11] and he dwelt among them a thousand years bar fifty;[12] and then the floods overwhelmed them while they were still lost in evildoing: ‹14› but We saved him, together with all who were in the ark, which We then set up as a symbol [of Our grace] for all people [to remember]. ‹15›

AND ABRAHAM, [too, was inspired by Us] when he said unto his people: "Worship God, and be conscious of Him: this is the best for you, if you but knew it! ‹16›

وَقَالَ ٱلَّذِينَ كَفَرُواْ لِلَّذِينَ ءَامَنُواْ ٱتَّبِعُواْ سَبِيلَنَا وَلۡنَحۡمِلۡ خَطَـٰيَـٰكُمۡ
وَمَا هُم بِحَـٰمِلِينَ مِنۡ خَطَـٰيَـٰهُم مِّن شَيۡءٍۖ إِنَّهُمۡ لَكَـٰذِبُونَ ﴿١٢﴾ وَلَيَحۡمِلُنَّ
أَثۡقَالَهُمۡ وَأَثۡقَالٗا مَّعَ أَثۡقَالِهِمۡۖ وَلَيُسۡـَٔلُنَّ يَوۡمَ ٱلۡقِيَٰمَةِ عَمَّا كَانُواْ يَفۡتَرُونَ ﴿١٣﴾
وَلَقَدۡ أَرۡسَلۡنَا نُوحًا إِلَىٰ قَوۡمِهِۦ فَلَبِثَ فِيهِمۡ أَلۡفَ سَنَةٍ إِلَّا خَمۡسِينَ عَامٗا
فَأَخَذَهُمُ ٱلطُّوفَانُ وَهُمۡ ظَـٰلِمُونَ ﴿١٤﴾ فَأَنجَيۡنَـٰهُ وَأَصۡحَـٰبَ ٱلسَّفِينَةِ
وَجَعَلۡنَـٰهَآ ءَايَةٗ لِّلۡعَـٰلَمِينَ ﴿١٥﴾ وَإِبۡرَٰهِيمَ إِذۡ قَالَ لِقَوۡمِهِ ٱعۡبُدُواْ ٱللَّهَ
وَٱتَّقُوهُۖ ذَٰلِكُمۡ خَيۡرٞ لَّكُمۡ إِن كُنتُمۡ تَعۡلَمُونَ ﴿١٦﴾

Wa qālal-ladhīna kafarū lilladhīna ʾāmanut-tabiʿū sabīlanā wal-naḥmil khaṭāyākum wa mā hum-biḥāmilīna min khaṭāyāhum-miñ-shayʾ. ʾInnahum lakādhibūn. (12) Wa layaḥmilunna ʾathqālahum wa ʾathqālam-maʿa ʾathqālihim wa layusʾalunna Yawmal-Qiyāmati ʿammā kānū yaftarūn. (13) Wa laqad ʾarsalnā Nūḥan ʾilā qawmihī falabitha fīhim ʾalfa sanatin ʾillā khamsīna ʿāmañ-faʾakhadhahumuṭ-ṭūfānu wa hum ẓālimūn. (14) Faʾañjaynāhu wa ʾaṣḥābas-safīnati wa jaʿalnāhāa ʾĀyatal-lilʿālamīn. (15) Wa ʾIbrāhīma ʾidh qāla liqawmihiʿ-budul-lāha wat-taqūh. Dhālikum khayrul-lakum ʾiñ-kuñtum taʿlamūn. (16)

8 The above "saying" of the deniers of the truth is, of course, but a metonym for their *attitude* towards the believers; hence my interpolation, between brackets, of the words "as it were". The implication is that people who deny the validity of any spiritual commitment arising out of one's faith in "something that is beyond the reach of human perception" (*al-ghayb*) – in this case, the existence of God – are, as a rule, unwilling to tolerate such a faith and such a commitment in others as well: and so they endeavour to bring the believers to their way of thinking by a sarcastic, contemptuous reference to the alleged irrelevance of the concept of "sin" as such.

9 Lit., "bear" – implying a *reduction* of the burden which the others would have to bear (Rāzī). See also next note.

10 Cf. the Prophet's saying: "Whoever calls [others] unto the right way shall have a reward equal to the [combined] rewards of all who may follow him until Resurrection Day, without anything being lessened of *their* rewards; and whoever calls unto the way of error will have to bear a sin equal to the [combined] sins of all who may follow him until Resurrection Day, without anything being lessened of *their* sins" (Bukhārī).

11 This passage connects with verse 2 above, "We did test those who lived before them". The story of Noah and of his failure to convert his people occurs in the Qurʾān several times, and most extensively in 11 : 25-48. In the present instance it is meant to illustrate the truth that no one – not even a prophet – can bestow faith on another person (cf. 28 : 56 – "thou canst not guide aright everyone whom thou lovest"). The same purport underlies the subsequent references, in verses 16-40, to other prophets.

12 Sc., "and despite this great length of time was unable to convince them of the truth of his mission". The identical figure – 950 years – is given in the Bible (Genesis ix, 29) as Noah's life-span. By repeating this element of the Biblical legend, the Qurʾān merely stresses the fact that the *duration* of a prophet's mission has nothing to do with its success or failure, since "all true guidance is God's guidance" (3 : 73) – and, as we are so often told in the Qurʾān, "God guides [only] him that wills [to be guided]". Thus, the reference to Noah is meant to reassure the believer who may be distressed at seeing the majority of his fellow-men refuse to accept, all at once, a truth which appears self-evident to him.

You worship only [lifeless] idols instead of God, and [thus] you give visible shape to a lie![13] Behold, those [things and beings] that you worship instead of God have it not in their power to provide sustenance for you: seek, then, all [your] sustenance from God, and worship Him [alone] and be grateful to Him: [for] unto Him you shall be brought back! ‹17›

"And if you give [me] the lie – well, [other] communities have given the lie [to God's prophets] before your time: but no more is an apostle bound to do than clearly deliver the message [entrusted to him]." ‹18›

ARE, THEN, they [who deny the truth] not aware of how God creates [life] in the first instance, and then brings it forth anew'?[14] This, verily, is easy for God! ‹19›

Say: "Go all over the earth and behold how [wondrously] He has created [man] in the first instance:[15] and thus, too, will God bring into being your second life – for, verily. God has the power to will anything! ‹20›

"He causes to suffer whomever He wills, and bestows His mercy on whomever He wills; and unto Him you shall be made to return: ‹21› and never – not on earth and not in the skies – can you [hope to] elude Him; and you have none to protect you from God, and none to bring you succour." ‹22›

And [thus it is:] they who are bent on denying the truth of God's messages and of their [ultimate] meeting with Him – it is they who abandon all hope of My grace and mercy: and it is they whom grievous suffering awaits [in the life to come].[16] ‹23›

إِنَّمَا تَعْبُدُونَ مِن دُونِ ٱللَّهِ أَوْثَـٰنًا وَتَخْلُقُونَ إِفْكًا ۚ إِنَّ ٱلَّذِينَ تَعْبُدُونَ مِن
دُونِ ٱللَّهِ لَا يَمْلِكُونَ لَكُمْ رِزْقًا فَٱبْتَغُوا۟ عِندَ ٱللَّهِ ٱلرِّزْقَ وَٱعْبُدُوهُ
وَٱشْكُرُوا۟ لَهُۥٓ ۖ إِلَيْهِ تُرْجَعُونَ ﴿١٧﴾ وَإِن تُكَذِّبُوا۟ فَقَدْ كَذَّبَ أُمَمٌ مِّن
قَبْلِكُمْ ۖ وَمَا عَلَى ٱلرَّسُولِ إِلَّا ٱلْبَلَـٰغُ ٱلْمُبِينُ ﴿١٨﴾ أَوَلَمْ يَرَوْا۟ كَيْفَ
يُبْدِئُ ٱللَّهُ ٱلْخَلْقَ ثُمَّ يُعِيدُهُۥٓ ۚ إِنَّ ذَٰلِكَ عَلَى ٱللَّهِ يَسِيرٌ ﴿١٩﴾ قُلْ سِيرُوا۟ فِى
ٱلْأَرْضِ فَٱنظُرُوا۟ كَيْفَ بَدَأَ ٱلْخَلْقَ ۚ ثُمَّ ٱللَّهُ يُنشِئُ ٱلنَّشْأَةَ ٱلْـَٔاخِرَةَ ۚ إِنَّ
ٱللَّهَ عَلَىٰ كُلِّ شَىْءٍ قَدِيرٌ ﴿٢٠﴾ يُعَذِّبُ مَن يَشَآءُ وَيَرْحَمُ مَن يَشَآءُ ۖ وَإِلَيْهِ
تُقْلَبُونَ ﴿٢١﴾ وَمَآ أَنتُم بِمُعْجِزِينَ فِى ٱلْأَرْضِ وَلَا فِى ٱلسَّمَآءِ ۖ وَمَا لَكُم
مِّن دُونِ ٱللَّهِ مِن وَلِىٍّ وَلَا نَصِيرٍ ﴿٢٢﴾ وَٱلَّذِينَ كَفَرُوا۟ بِـَٔايَـٰتِ ٱللَّهِ وَلِقَآئِهِۦٓ
أُو۟لَـٰٓئِكَ يَئِسُوا۟ مِن رَّحْمَتِى وَأُو۟لَـٰٓئِكَ لَهُمْ عَذَابٌ أَلِيمٌ ﴿٢٣﴾

ʾInnamā taʿbudūna miñ-dūnil-lāhi ʾawthānañw-wa takhluqūna ʾifkā. ʾInnal-ladhīna taʿbudūna miñ-dūnil-lāhi lā yamlikūna lakum rizqañ-fabtaghū ʿiñdal-lāhir-rizqa waʿ-budūhu wash-kurū lahūu ʾilayhi turjaʿūn. (17) Wa ʾiñ-tukadhdhibū faqad kadhdhaba ʾumamum-miñ-qablikum. Wa mā ʿalar-Rasūli ʾillal-balāghul-mubīn. (18) ʾAwa lam yaraw kayfa yubdiʾul-lāhul-khalqa thumma yuʿīduh. ʾInna dhālika ʿalal-lāhi yasīr. (19) Qul sīrū fil-ʾarḍi fañẓurū kayfa badaʾal-khalqa thummal-lāhu yuñshiʾun-nashʾatal-ʾākhirah. ʾInnal-lāha ʿalā kulli shayʾiñ-Qadīr. (20) Yuʿadhdhibu mañy-yashāaʾu wa yarḥamu mañy-yashāaʾu wa ʾilayhi tuqlabūn. (21) Wa māa ʾañtum-bimuʿjizīna fil-ʾarḍi wa lā fis-samāaʾi wa mā lakum-miñ-dūnil-lāhi miñw-waliyyiñw-wa lā naṣīr. (22) Wal-ladhīna kafarū biʾĀyātil-lāhi wa liqāaʾihīi ʾulāaʾika yaʾisū mir-raḥmatī wa ʾulāaʾika lahum ʿadhābun ʾalīm. (23)

13 Lit., "you create a lie".

14 This passage – consisting of verses 19-23 – is parenthetically placed in the midst of the story of Abraham, connecting with the latter's reference to resurrection at the end of verse 17 ("unto Him you shall be brought back"). The ever-recurring emergence, decay and re-emergence of life, so vividly exemplified in all organic nature, is often cited in the Qurʾān not merely in support of the doctrine of resurrection, but also as evidence of a consciously-devised plan underlying creation as such – and, thus, of the existence of the Creator.

15 Cf., for example, 23 : 12-14, which alludes to man's coming into existence out of most primitive elements, and gradually evolving into a highly complex being endowed not only with a physical body but also with a mind, with feelings, and instincts.

16 Implying that such people *deprive themselves* of God's grace and mercy (which is the twofold significance of the term *raḥmah* in this context) by rejecting all belief in His existence: in other words, belief in God – or one's readiness

NOW [as for Abraham,] his people's only answer was,[17] "Slay him, or burn him!" – but God saved him from the fire.[18] Behold, in this [story] there are messages indeed for people who will believe! ‹24›
And [Abraham] said: "You have chosen to worship idols instead of God for no other reason than to have a bond of love,[19] in the life of this world, between yourselves [and your forebears]:[20] but then, on Resurrection Day, you shall disown one another and curse one another – for the goal of you all will be the fire, and you will have none to succour you." ‹25›
Thereupon [his brother's son] Lot came to believe in him and said: "Verily, I [too] shall forsake the domain of evil [and turn] to my Sustainer:[21] for, verily, He alone is almighty, truly wise!" ‹26›
And [as for Abraham,] We bestowed upon him Isaac and [Isaac's son] Jacob,[22] and caused prophethood and revelation to continue among his offspring. And We vouchsafed him his reward in this world;[23] and, verily, in the life to come [too] he shall find himself among the righteous. ‹27›

AND LOT, [too, was inspired by Us] when he said unto his people: "Verily, you commit abominations such as none in all the world has ever committed before you! ‹28›

فَمَا كَانَ جَوَابَ قَوْمِهِۦٓ إِلَّآ أَن قَالُوا۟ ٱقْتُلُوهُ أَوْ حَرِّقُوهُ فَأَنجَىٰهُ ٱللَّهُ مِنَ
ٱلنَّارِ ۚ إِنَّ فِى ذَٰلِكَ لَءَايَٰتٍ لِّقَوْمٍ يُؤْمِنُونَ ﴿٢٤﴾ وَقَالَ إِنَّمَا ٱتَّخَذْتُم مِّن
دُونِ ٱللَّهِ أَوْثَٰنًا مَّوَدَّةَ بَيْنِكُمْ فِى ٱلْحَيَوٰةِ ٱلدُّنْيَا ۖ ثُمَّ يَوْمَ ٱلْقِيَٰمَةِ يَكْفُرُ
بَعْضُكُم بِبَعْضٍ وَيَلْعَنُ بَعْضُكُم بَعْضًا وَمَأْوَىٰكُمُ ٱلنَّارُ وَمَا لَكُم مِّن
نَّٰصِرِينَ ﴿٢٥﴾ ۞ فَـَٔامَنَ لَهُۥ لُوطٌ ۘ وَقَالَ إِنِّى مُهَاجِرٌ إِلَىٰ رَبِّىٓ ۖ إِنَّهُۥ هُوَ
ٱلْعَزِيزُ ٱلْحَكِيمُ ﴿٢٦﴾ وَوَهَبْنَا لَهُۥٓ إِسْحَٰقَ وَيَعْقُوبَ وَجَعَلْنَا فِى ذُرِّيَّتِهِ
ٱلنُّبُوَّةَ وَٱلْكِتَٰبَ وَءَاتَيْنَٰهُ أَجْرَهُۥ فِى ٱلدُّنْيَا ۖ وَإِنَّهُۥ فِى ٱلْءَاخِرَةِ لَمِنَ
ٱلصَّٰلِحِينَ ﴿٢٧﴾ وَلُوطًا إِذْ قَالَ لِقَوْمِهِۦٓ إِنَّكُمْ لَتَأْتُونَ ٱلْفَٰحِشَةَ مَا
سَبَقَكُم بِهَا مِنْ أَحَدٍ مِّنَ ٱلْعَٰلَمِينَ ﴿٢٨﴾

ثلاثة ارباع الحزب

Famā kāna jawāba qawmihīi ʾillāa ʾañ-qāluq-tulūhu ʾaw ḥārriqūhu faʾañjāhul-lāhu minan-nār. ʾInna fī dhālika laʾĀyātil-liqawmiñy-yuʾminūn. (24) Wa qāla ʾinnamat-takhadhtum-miñ-dūnil-lāhi ʾawthānam-mawaddata baynikum fil-ḥayātid-dunyā; thumma Yawmal-Qiyāmati yakfuru baʿḍukum-bibaʿḍiñw-wa yalʿanu baʿḍukum-baʿḍañw-wa maʾwākumun-nāru wa mā lakum-miñ-nāṣirīn. (25) ۞ Faʾāmana lahū Lūṭ. Wa qāla ʾinnī muhājirun ʾilā Rabbīi ʾinnahū Huwal-ʿAzīzul-Ḥakīm. (26) Wa wahabnā lahūu ʾIsḥāqa wa Yaʿqūba wa jaʿalnā fī dhurriyyatihin-Nubuwwata wal-Kitāba wa ʾātaynāhu ʾajrahū fid-dunyā wa ʾinnahū fil-ʾĀkhirati laminaṣ-ṣāliḥīn. (27) Wa Lūṭan ʾidh qāla liqawmihīi ʾinnakum lataʾtūnal-fāḥishata mā sabqa-kum-bihā min ʾaḥadim-minal-ʿālamīn. (28)

to believe in Him – is, in and by itself, already an *outcome* of His grace and mercy, just as suffering in the hereafter is an *outcome* of one's being "bent on denying the truth".

17 Lit., "the answer of his people was nothing but that they said" – thus connecting with the passage ending with verse 18.

18 See note 64 on 21 : 69.

19 Lit., "solely out of love".

20 Thus Rāzī, explaining this idol-worship as a result of a mere blind imitation (*taqlīd*) of attitudes inherited from past generations.

21 For an explanation of the concept of *hijrah* and of my above rendering of the term *muhājir*, see *sūrah* 2, note 203, and *sūrah* 4, note 124. In the present instance this term is obviously used in both its physical and spiritual senses, analogous to the earlier allusion (in 19 : 48-49) to Abraham's "withdrawal" (*iʿtizāl*) from his evil, native environment and to his physical migration to Ḥarrān (in northern Mesopotamia), and thence to Syria and Palestine. The story of Lot (Lūṭ) is mentioned in the Qurʾān several times, and particularly in 11 : 69-83.

22 I.e., in addition to Ishmael (Ismāʿīl), who had been born some years earlier (cf. 21 : 72).

23 Among other things, by making him "a leader of men" (2 : 124).

Must you indeed approach men [with lust], and thus cut across the way [of nature]?[24] – and must you commit these shameful deeds in your [open] assemblies'?"
But his people's only answer was, "Bring down upon us God's chastisement, if thou art a man of truth!" ‹29›
[And] he prayed: "O my Sustainer! Succour Thou me against these people who spread corruption!" ‹30›
And so, when Our [heavenly] messengers came to Abraham with the glad tiding [of the birth of Isaac],[25] they [also] said, "Behold, we are about to destroy the people of that land,[26] for its people are truly evildoers!" ‹31›
[And when Abraham] exclaimed, "But Lot lives there!" – they answered: "We know fully well who is there; most certainly we shall save him and his household – all but his wife: she will indeed be among those that stay behind."[27] ‹32›
And when Our messengers came unto Lot, he was sorely grieved on their account, seeing that it was beyond his power to shield them;[28] but they said: "Fear not, and grieve not! Behold, we shall save thee and thy household – all but thy wife: she will indeed be among those that stay behind. ‹33› Verily, we shall bring down upon the people of this land a horror from heaven in requital of all their iniquitous doings!" ‹34›
And [so it happened; and] thereof, indeed, We have left a clear sign for people who use their reason.[29] ‹35›

أَئِنَّكُمْ لَتَأْتُونَ ٱلرِّجَالَ وَتَقْطَعُونَ ٱلسَّبِيلَ وَتَأْتُونَ فِى نَادِيكُمُ ٱلْمُنكَرَ ۖ
فَمَا كَانَ جَوَابَ قَوْمِهِۦٓ إِلَّآ أَن قَالُوا۟ ٱئْتِنَا بِعَذَابِ ٱللَّهِ إِن كُنتَ مِنَ
ٱلصَّـٰدِقِينَ ﴿٢٩﴾ قَالَ رَبِّ ٱنصُرْنِى عَلَى ٱلْقَوْمِ ٱلْمُفْسِدِينَ ﴿٣٠﴾ وَلَمَّا
جَآءَتْ رُسُلُنَآ إِبْرَٰهِيمَ بِٱلْبُشْرَىٰ قَالُوٓا۟ إِنَّا مُهْلِكُوٓا۟ أَهْلِ هَـٰذِهِ ٱلْقَرْيَةِ ۖ
إِنَّ أَهْلَهَا كَانُوا۟ ظَـٰلِمِينَ ﴿٣١﴾ قَالَ إِنَّ فِيهَا لُوطًا ۚ قَالُوا۟ نَحْنُ أَعْلَمُ بِمَن
فِيهَا ۖ لَنُنَجِّيَنَّهُۥ وَأَهْلَهُۥٓ إِلَّا ٱمْرَأَتَهُۥ كَانَتْ مِنَ ٱلْغَـٰبِرِينَ ﴿٣٢﴾ وَلَمَّآ أَن
جَآءَتْ رُسُلُنَا لُوطًا سِىٓءَ بِهِمْ وَضَاقَ بِهِمْ ذَرْعًا وَقَالُوا۟ لَا تَخَفْ وَلَا
تَحْزَنْ ۖ إِنَّا مُنَجُّوكَ وَأَهْلَكَ إِلَّا ٱمْرَأَتَكَ كَانَتْ مِنَ ٱلْغَـٰبِرِينَ ﴿٣٣﴾ إِنَّا
مُنزِلُونَ عَلَىٰٓ أَهْلِ هَـٰذِهِ ٱلْقَرْيَةِ رِجْزًا مِّنَ ٱلسَّمَآءِ بِمَا كَانُوا۟
يَفْسُقُونَ ﴿٣٤﴾ وَلَقَد تَّرَكْنَا مِنْهَآ ءَايَةًۢ بَيِّنَةً لِّقَوْمٍ يَعْقِلُونَ ﴿٣٥﴾

ʾAʾinnakum lataʾtūnar-rijāla wa taqṭaʿūnas-sabīla
wa taʾtūna fī nādīkumul-muñkar. Famā kāna jawāba
qawmihīi ʾillāa ʾañ-qāluʾ-tinā biʿadhābil-lāhi ʾiñ-
kuñta minaṣ-ṣādiqīn. (29) Qāla Rabbiñ-ṣurnī ʿalal-
qawmil-mufsidīn. (30) Wa lammā jāaʾat Rusulunāa
ʾIbrāhīma bilbushrā qālūu ʾinnā muhlikūu ʾahli
hādhihil-qaryati ʾinna ʾahlahā kānū ẓālimīn. (31) Qāla
ʾinna fīhā Lūṭā. Qālū naḥnu ʾaʿlamu bimañ-fīhā.
Lanunajjiyannahū wa ʾahlahūu ʾillam-raʾatahū
kānat minal-ghābirīn. (32) Wa lammāa ʾañ-jāaʾat Rusulunā Lūṭañ-sīiʾa bihim wa ḍāqa bihim dharʿañw-
wa qālū lā takhaf wa lā taḥzan. ʾInnā munajjūka wa
ʾahlaka ʾillam-raʾataka kānat minal-ghābirīn. (33)
ʾInnā muñzilūna ʿalāa ʾahli hādhihil-qaryati rijzam-
minas-samāaʾi bimā kānū yafsuqūn. (34) Wa laqat-
taraknā minhāa ʾĀyatam-bayyinatal-liqawmiñy-
yaʿqilūn. (35)

24 This particular interpretation of the phrase *taqṭaʿūn as-sabīl* is advanced by Baghawī and (on the authority of Al-Ḥasan) by Zamakhsharī; Rāzī adopts it exclusively and without reservation.

25 See 11 : 69 ff., as well as the first half of the corresponding note 99.

26 The term *qaryah* has here, as so often in classical Arabic, the connotation of "land", in this instance comprising the towns of Sodom and Gomorrah.

27 See note 66 on 7 : 83 and note 113 on 11 : 81. In the present instance, as well as in the next verse, the past-tense auxiliary verb *kānat* is meant to stress the inevitability of the future event referred to; hence, "she will indeed be . . .", etc.

28 See note 107 on 11 : 77.

29 This is an allusion to the Dead Sea – known to this day as *Baḥr Lūṭ* ("The Sea of Lot") – which covers most of the region in which Sodom and Gomorrah were once situated. Its waters contain so high a percentage of sulphur and potash that no fish or plants can live in them.

AND UNTO [the people of] Madyan [We sent] their brother Shuʿayb,[30] who thereupon said: "O my people! Worship God [alone], and look forward to the Last Day, and do not act wickedly on earth by spreading corruption!" «36»
But they gave him the lie. Thereupon an earthquake overtook them: and then they lay lifeless, in their very homes, on the ground.[31] «37»

AND [the tribes of] ʿĀd and Thamūd,[32] [too, did We destroy –] as should have become obvious to you from [whatever there remains of] their dwellings.[33]
[They perished] because Satan had made their [sinful] doings seem goodly to them, and thus had barred them from the path [of God] despite their having been endowed with the ability to perceive the truth.[34] «38»
And [thus, too, did We deal with] Qārūn and Pharaoh, and Hāmān:[35] to them had come Moses with all evidence of the truth, but they behaved arrogantly on earth [and rejected him]; and withal, they could not escape [Us]. «39»
For, every one of them did We take to task for his sin: and so, upon some of them We let loose a deadly stormwind; and some of them were overtaken by a [sudden] blast;[36] and some of them We caused to be swallowed by the earth; and some of them We caused to drown. And it was not God who wronged them, but it was they who had wronged themselves. «40»

وَإِلَىٰ مَدْيَنَ أَخَاهُمْ شُعَيْبًا فَقَالَ يَٰقَوْمِ ٱعْبُدُوا۟ ٱللَّهَ وَٱرْجُوا۟ ٱلْيَوْمَ ٱلْءَاخِرَ
وَلَا تَعْثَوْا۟ فِى ٱلْأَرْضِ مُفْسِدِينَ ﴿٣٦﴾ فَكَذَّبُوهُ فَأَخَذَتْهُمُ ٱلرَّجْفَةُ فَأَصْبَحُوا۟
فِى دَارِهِمْ جَٰثِمِينَ ﴿٣٧﴾ وَعَادًا وَثَمُودَا۟ وَقَد تَّبَيَّنَ لَكُم مِّن مَّسَٰكِنِهِمْ
وَزَيَّنَ لَهُمُ ٱلشَّيْطَٰنُ أَعْمَٰلَهُمْ فَصَدَّهُمْ عَنِ ٱلسَّبِيلِ وَكَانُوا۟
مُسْتَبْصِرِينَ ﴿٣٨﴾ وَقَٰرُونَ وَفِرْعَوْنَ وَهَٰمَٰنَ وَلَقَدْ جَآءَهُم مُّوسَىٰ
بِٱلْبَيِّنَٰتِ فَٱسْتَكْبَرُوا۟ فِى ٱلْأَرْضِ وَمَا كَانُوا۟ سَٰبِقِينَ ﴿٣٩﴾ فَكُلًّا أَخَذْنَا
بِذَنۢبِهِۦ فَمِنْهُم مَّنْ أَرْسَلْنَا عَلَيْهِ حَاصِبًا وَمِنْهُم مَّنْ أَخَذَتْهُ ٱلصَّيْحَةُ
وَمِنْهُم مَّنْ خَسَفْنَا بِهِ ٱلْأَرْضَ وَمِنْهُم مَّنْ أَغْرَقْنَا وَمَا كَانَ ٱللَّهُ لِيَظْلِمَهُمْ
وَلَٰكِن كَانُوٓا۟ أَنفُسَهُمْ يَظْلِمُونَ ﴿٤٠﴾

Wa ʾilā Madyana ʾakhāhum Shuʿaybañ-faqāla yā qawmiʿ-budul-lāha war-jul-Yawmal-ʾĀkhira wa lā taʿthaw fil-ʾarḍi mufsidīn. ﴿٣٦﴾ Fakadhdhabūhu faʾakhadhat-humur-rajfatu faʾaṣbaḥū fī dārihim jāthimīn. ﴿٣٧﴾ Wa ʿĀdañw-wa Thamūda wa qat-tabayyana lakum-mim-masākinihim. Wa zayyana lahumush-Shayṭānu ʾaʿmālahum faṣaddahum ʿanis-sabīli wa kānū mustabṣirīn. ﴿٣٨﴾ Wa Qārūna wa Firʿawna wa Hāmāna wa laqad jāaʾahum-Mūsā bil-bayyināti fastakbarū fil-ʾarḍi wa mā kānū sābiqīn. ﴿٣٩﴾ Fakullan ʾakhadhnā bidhambih. Faminhum-man ʾarsalnā ʿalayhi ḥāṣibañw-wa minhum-man ʾakhadhat-huṣ-ṣayḥatu wa minhum-man khasafnā bihil-ʾarḍa wa minhum-man ʾaghraqnā. Wa mā kānal-lāhu liyaẓlimahum wa lākiñ-kānū ʾañfusahum yaẓlimūn. ﴿٤٠﴾

30 See note 67 on 7 : 85. The story of Shuʿayb and his people appears in greater detail in 11 : 84-95.

31 See note 62 on 7 : 78 (a passage which relates to the tribe of Thamūd), and note 73 on 7 : 91.

32 See *sūrah* 7, second half of note 48, and note 56.

33 As regards the tribe of ʿĀd, the above seems to be an allusion to their one-time capital, the legendary "Iram the many-pillared" (mentioned in the Qurʾān only once, namely, in 89 : 7). It has since been buried by the moving sand-dunes of Al-Aḥqāf (a region between ʿUmān and Ḥaḍramawt, within the great South-Arabian desert of Rubʿ al-Khālī); it is said, however, that its traces are occasionally uncovered by strong winds. For an explanation of the reference to the dwellings of the Thamūd, see note 59 on 7 : 74.

34 Thus, the Qurʾān implies that it is man's "ability to perceive the truth" (*istibṣār*) that makes him morally responsible for his doings and, hence, for his failure to resist his own evil impulses – which is evidently the meaning of "Satan" in this context. See in this connection 14 : 22 and the corresponding notes 31 and 33.

35 As regards Qārūn, see 28 : 76 ff. and, in particular, the corresponding note 84; for Hāmān, note 6 on 28 : 6. The common denominator between these two and Pharaoh is their false pride (*takabbur*) and arrogance (*istikbār*), which cause them to become "archetypes of evil" (cf. 28 : 41 and the corresponding note 40). A similar attitude of mind is said to have been characteristic of the tribes of ʿĀd and Thamūd, mentioned in the preceding verse.

36 Sc., "of God's punishment": cf. note 98 on 11 : 67.

THE PARABLE of those who take [beings or forces] other than God for their protectors is that of the spider which makes for itself a house: for, behold, the frailest of all houses is the spider's house. Could they but understand this! ⟨41⟩
Verily, God knows whatever it is that men invoke instead of Him[37] – for He alone is almighty, truly wise. ⟨42⟩
And so We propound these parables unto man: but none can grasp their innermost meaning save those who [of Us] are aware,[38] ⟨43⟩ [and hence are certain that] God has created the heavens and the earth in accordance with an inner] truth:[39] for, behold, in this [very creation] there is a message indeed for all who believe [in Him]. ⟨44⟩

حزب 41
جزء 21

CONVEY [unto others] whatever of this divine writ has been revealed unto thee,[40] and be constant in prayer: for, behold, prayer restrains [man] from loathsome deeds and from all that runs counter to reason;[41] and remembrance of God is indeed the greatest [good]. And God knows all that you do. ⟨45⟩
And do not argue with the followers of earlier revelation otherwise than in a most kindly manner – unless it be such of them as are bent on evildoing[42] – and say: "We believe in that which has been bestowed from on high upon us, as well as that

مَثَلُ ٱلَّذِينَ ٱتَّخَذُواْ مِن دُونِ ٱللَّهِ أَوْلِيَآءَ كَمَثَلِ ٱلْعَنكَبُوتِ ٱتَّخَذَتْ بَيْتًا
وَإِنَّ أَوْهَنَ ٱلْبُيُوتِ لَبَيْتُ ٱلْعَنكَبُوتِ لَوْ كَانُواْ يَعْلَمُونَ ﴿٤١﴾ إِنَّ ٱللَّهَ يَعْلَمُ
مَا يَدْعُونَ مِن دُونِهِۦ مِن شَىْءٍ وَهُوَ ٱلْعَزِيزُ ٱلْحَكِيمُ ﴿٤٢﴾ وَتِلْكَ ٱلْأَمْثَـٰلُ
نَضْرِبُهَا لِلنَّاسِ وَمَا يَعْقِلُهَآ إِلَّا ٱلْعَـٰلِمُونَ ﴿٤٣﴾ خَلَقَ ٱللَّهُ ٱلسَّمَـٰوَٰتِ
وَٱلْأَرْضَ بِٱلْحَقِّ إِنَّ فِى ذَٰلِكَ لَءَايَةً لِّلْمُؤْمِنِينَ ﴿٤٤﴾ ٱتْلُ مَآ أُوحِىَ إِلَيْكَ مِنَ
ٱلْكِتَـٰبِ وَأَقِمِ ٱلصَّلَوٰةَ إِنَّ ٱلصَّلَوٰةَ تَنْهَىٰ عَنِ ٱلْفَحْشَآءِ وَٱلْمُنكَرِ وَلَذِكْرُ
ٱللَّهِ أَكْبَرُ وَٱللَّهُ يَعْلَمُ مَا تَصْنَعُونَ ﴿٤٥﴾ ۞ وَلَا تُجَـٰدِلُوٓاْ أَهْلَ ٱلْكِتَـٰبِ إِلَّا
بِٱلَّتِى هِىَ أَحْسَنُ إِلَّا ٱلَّذِينَ ظَلَمُواْ مِنْهُمْ وَقُولُوٓاْ ءَامَنَّا بِٱلَّذِىٓ أُنزِلَ إِلَيْنَا وَأُنزِلَ

Mathalul-ladhīnat-takhadhū miñ dūnil-lāhi ʾawliyāaʾa kamathalil-ʿAñkabūtit-takhadhat baytā. Wa ʾinna ʾawhanal-buyūti labaytul-ʿAñkabūti law kānū yaʿlamūn. ⟨41⟩ ʾInnal-lāha yaʿlamu mā yadʿūna miñ-dūnihī miñ-shayʾ. Wa Huwal-ʿAzīzul-Ḥakīm. ⟨42⟩ Wa tilkal-ʾAmthālu naḍribuhā linanāsi wa mā yaʿqiluhāa ʾillal-ʿālimūn. ⟨43⟩ Khalaqal-lāhus-samāwāti wal-ʾarḍa bil-ḥaqq. ʾInna fī dhālika laʾĀyatal-lilmuʾminīn. ⟨44⟩ ʾUtlu māa ʾūḥiya ʾilayka minal-Kitābi wa ʾaqimiṣ-Ṣalāh. ʾInnaṣ-Ṣalāta tanhā ʿanil-faḥshāaʾi wal-muñkar. Wa ladhikrul-lāhi ʾakbar. Wal-lāhu yaʿlamu mā taṣnaʿūn. ⟨45⟩ ۞ Wa lā tujādilūu ʾahlal-Kitābi ʾillā billatī hiya ʾaḥsanu ʾillal-ladhīna ẓalamū minhum wa qūlūu ʾāmannā billadhīi ʾuñzila ʾilaynā wa ʾuñzila

37 Lit., "whatever thing they invoke instead of Him": i.e., He knows the nothingness of those false objects of worship (Zamakhsharī), irrespective of whether they be imaginary deities, or deified saints, or forces of nature, or even false concepts or ideas; but He also knows the weakness of the human heart and mind and, hence, the hidden motivation of all such irrational worship.

38 Inasmuch as awareness of the existence of God is here postulated as a prerequisite of a full understanding of the Qurʾanic parables (and, by implication, allegories as well), the above verse should be read side by side with the statement that the Qurʾān is meant to be "a guidance for all the God-conscious, who believe in [the existence of] a reality which is beyond the reach of human perception" (see 2 : 2-3 and the corresponding note 3).

39 I.e., endowed with meaning and purpose: see *sūrah* 10, note 11. In other words, belief in the existence of a meaning and a purpose underlying the creation of the universe is a logical corollary of one's belief in God.

40 If we assume that verses 45-46 are addressed not merely to the Prophet but to believers in general (an assumption which is strengthened by the plural form of address in the last clause of verse 45 and throughout verse 46), the above phrase may be taken to mean "whatever of the divine writ has *revealed itself to thy understanding*".

41 For an explanation of this rendering of the term and concept of *al-munkar*, see *sūrah* 16, note 109.

42 Sc., "and are therefore not accessible to friendly argument": the implication being that in such cases all disputes should *a priori* be avoided. As regards religious discussions in general, see note 149 on 16 : 125.

which has been bestowed upon you: for our God and your God is one and the same, and it is unto Him that we [all] surrender ourselves." ‹46›

For it is thus[43] that We have bestowed this divine writ from on high upon thee [O Muḥammad]. And they to whom we have vouchsafed this divine writ[44] believe in it – just as among those [followers of earlier revelation] there are some who believe in it. And none could knowingly reject Our messages[45] unless it be such as would deny [an obvious] truth: ‹47› for, [O Muḥammad,] thou hast never been able to recite any divine writ ere this one [was revealed], nor didst thou ever transcribe one with thine own hand[46] – or else, they who try to disprove the truth [of thy revelation][47] might indeed have had cause to doubt [it]. ‹48›

Nay, but this [divine writ] consists of messages clear to the hearts of all who are gifted with [innate] knowledge[48] – and none could knowingly reject Our messages unless it be such as would do wrong [to themselves]. ‹49›

And yet they say, "Why have no miraculous signs ever been bestowed upon him from on high by his Sustainer?"

Say: "Miracles are in the power of God alone;[49] and as for me – I am but a plain warner." ‹50›

إِلَيْكُمْ وَإِلَٰهُنَا وَإِلَٰهُكُمْ وَٰحِدٌ وَنَحْنُ لَهُۥ مُسْلِمُونَ ﴿٤٦﴾ وَكَذَٰلِكَ
أَنزَلْنَآ إِلَيْكَ ٱلْكِتَٰبَ ۚ فَٱلَّذِينَ ءَاتَيْنَٰهُمُ ٱلْكِتَٰبَ يُؤْمِنُونَ بِهِۦ ۖ وَمِنْ
هَٰٓؤُلَآءِ مَن يُؤْمِنُ بِهِۦ ۚ وَمَا يَجْحَدُ بِـَٔايَٰتِنَآ إِلَّا ٱلْكَٰفِرُونَ ﴿٤٧﴾ وَمَا
كُنتَ تَتْلُوا۟ مِن قَبْلِهِۦ مِن كِتَٰبٍ وَلَا تَخُطُّهُۥ بِيَمِينِكَ ۖ إِذًا لَّٱرْتَابَ
ٱلْمُبْطِلُونَ ﴿٤٨﴾ بَلْ هُوَ ءَايَٰتٌۢ بَيِّنَٰتٌ فِى صُدُورِ ٱلَّذِينَ أُوتُوا۟ ٱلْعِلْمَ ۚ
وَمَا يَجْحَدُ بِـَٔايَٰتِنَآ إِلَّا ٱلظَّٰلِمُونَ ﴿٤٩﴾ وَقَالُوا۟ لَوْلَآ أُنزِلَ عَلَيْهِ ءَايَٰتٌ
مِّن رَّبِّهِۦ ۖ قُلْ إِنَّمَا ٱلْءَايَٰتُ عِندَ ٱللَّهِ وَإِنَّمَآ أَنَا۠ نَذِيرٌ مُّبِينٌ ﴿٥٠﴾

ʾilaykum wa ʾIlāhunā wa ʾIlāhukum Wāḥiduñw-wa naḥnu lahū Muslimūn. (46) Wa kadhālika ʾañzalnāa ʾilaykal-Kitāb. Falladhīna ʾātaynāhumul-Kitāba yuʾminūna bihī wa min hāaʾulāaʾi mañy-yuʾminu bihī wa mā yajḥadu biʾĀyātināa ʾillal-kāfirūn. (47) Wa mā kuñta tatlū miñ-qablihī miñ-Kitābiñw-wa lā takhuṭṭuhū biyamīnika ʾidhal-lartābal-mubṭilūn. (48) Bal huwa ʾĀyātum-bayyinātuñ-fī ṣudūril-ladhīna ʾutul-ʿilma wa mā yajḥadu biʾAyātināa ʾillaẓ-ẓālimūn. (49) Wa qālū lawlāa ʾuñzila ʿalayhi ʾĀyātum-mir-Rabbih. Qul-ʾinnamal-ʾĀyātu ʿiñdal-lāhi wa ʾinnamāa ʾana Nadhīrum-mubīn. (50)

43 I.e., "in this spirit": a reference to the sameness of the fundamental truths in all revealed religions.

44 I.e., "they to whom We grant the ability to *understand* this divine writ".

45 This rendering of the verb *jaḥada* – in the present instance and in verse 49 below (as well as in 31 : 32, 40 : 63 or 41 : 28) – in the sense of a person's denying or rejecting something which he *knows* to be true is based on the authority of Zamakhsharī's *Asās*.

46 Lit., "with thy right hand" – the term *yamīn* being used here metonymically, denoting no more than one's "*own* hand". – It is historically established that Muḥammad, the "unlettered prophet" (cf. 7 : 157 and 158), could neither read nor write, and could not, therefore, have derived his extensive knowledge of the contents of earlier revelations from the Bible or other scriptures: which – as the Qurʾān points out – ought to convince any unprejudiced person that this knowledge must have come to him through divine revelation.

47 The participial noun *mubṭil* is derived from the verb *abṭala*, "he made a false [or "vain"] claim", or "tried to disprove the truth [of something]", or "to reduce [something] to nothing", or "to prove [it] to be of no account", or "null and void", or "unfounded", "false", "spurious", etc., irrespective of whether the object is true or false, authentic or spurious, valid or unfounded (*Lisān al-ʿArab* and *Tāj al-ʿArūs*).

48 Lit., "self-evident (*bayyināt*) in the breasts of those who have been given knowledge" – the term *ʿilm* having here the connotation of intuitive, spiritual perception.

49 See note 94 on 6 : 109.

Why – is it not enough for them that We have bestowed this divine writ on thee from on high, to be conveyed [by thee] to them?[50] For, verily, in it is [manifested Our] grace, and a reminder to people who will believe. ‹51›
Say [unto those who will not believe]: "God is witness enough between me and you! He knows all that is in the heavens and on earth; and they who are bent on believing in what is false and vain, and thus on denying God – it is they, they who shall be the losers!" ‹52›
Now they challenge thee to hasten the coming upon them of [God's] chastisement:[51] and indeed, had not a term been set [for it by God], that suffering would already have come upon them! But indeed, it will most certainly come upon them of a sudden, and they will be taken unawares. ‹53›
They challenge thee to hasten the coming upon them of [God's] chastisement: but, verily, hell is bound to encompass all who deny the truth ‹54› – [encompass them] on the Day when suffering will overwhelm them from above them and from beneath their feet,[52] whereupon He shall say: "Taste [now the fruit of] your own doings!" ‹55›

O YOU servants of Mine who have attained to faith! Behold, wide is Mine earth: worship Me, then, Me alone![53] ‹56›
Every human being is bound to taste death, [and] in the end unto Us shall all be brought back: ‹57› whereupon unto those who have attained to faith and wrought good works We shall most certainly assign mansions in that paradise through which running waters flow, therein to abide: how excellent a reward for those who labour ‹58› –

أَوَلَمْ يَكْفِهِمْ أَنَّآ أَنزَلْنَا عَلَيْكَ ٱلْكِتَٰبَ يُتْلَىٰ عَلَيْهِمْ إِنَّ فِى ذَٰلِكَ
لَرَحْمَةً وَذِكْرَىٰ لِقَوْمٍ يُؤْمِنُونَ ﴿٥١﴾ قُلْ كَفَىٰ بِٱللَّهِ بَيْنِى وَبَيْنَكُمْ شَهِيدًا
يَعْلَمُ مَا فِى ٱلسَّمَٰوَٰتِ وَٱلْأَرْضِ وَٱلَّذِينَ ءَامَنُوا۟ بِٱلْبَٰطِلِ وَكَفَرُوا۟ بِٱللَّهِ
أُو۟لَٰٓئِكَ هُمُ ٱلْخَٰسِرُونَ ﴿٥٢﴾ وَيَسْتَعْجِلُونَكَ بِٱلْعَذَابِ وَلَوْلَآ أَجَلٌ
مُّسَمًّى لَّجَآءَهُمُ ٱلْعَذَابُ وَلَيَأْتِيَنَّهُم بَغْتَةً وَهُمْ لَا يَشْعُرُونَ ﴿٥٣﴾
يَسْتَعْجِلُونَكَ بِٱلْعَذَابِ وَإِنَّ جَهَنَّمَ لَمُحِيطَةٌۢ بِٱلْكَٰفِرِينَ ﴿٥٤﴾ يَوْمَ
يَغْشَىٰهُمُ ٱلْعَذَابُ مِن فَوْقِهِمْ وَمِن تَحْتِ أَرْجُلِهِمْ وَيَقُولُ ذُوقُوا۟ مَا كُنتُمْ
تَعْمَلُونَ ﴿٥٥﴾ يَٰعِبَادِىَ ٱلَّذِينَ ءَامَنُوٓا۟ إِنَّ أَرْضِى وَٰسِعَةٌ فَإِيَّٰىَ
فَٱعْبُدُونِ ﴿٥٦﴾ كُلُّ نَفْسٍ ذَآئِقَةُ ٱلْمَوْتِ ثُمَّ إِلَيْنَا تُرْجَعُونَ ﴿٥٧﴾ وَٱلَّذِينَ
ءَامَنُوا۟ وَعَمِلُوا۟ ٱلصَّٰلِحَٰتِ لَنُبَوِّئَنَّهُم مِّنَ ٱلْجَنَّةِ غُرَفًا تَجْرِى مِن
تَحْتِهَا ٱلْأَنْهَٰرُ خَٰلِدِينَ فِيهَا نِعْمَ أَجْرُ ٱلْعَٰمِلِينَ ﴿٥٨﴾

ʾAwa lam yakfihim ʾannāa ʾañzalnā ʿalaykal-Kitāba yutlā ʿalayhim. ʾInna fī dhālika laraḥmatañw-wa dhikrā liqawmiñy-yuʾminūn. (51) Qul kafā billāhi baynī wa baynakum shahīdā. Yaʿlamu mā fis-samāwāti wal-ʾarḍ. Wal-ladhīna ʾāmanū bilbāṭili wa kafarū billāhi ʾulāaʾika humul-khāsirūn. (52) Wa yastaʿjilūnaka bilʿadhābi wa lawlāa ʾajalum-musammal-lajāaʾahumul-ʿadhābu wa layaʾtiyannahum-baghtatañw-wa hum lā yashʿurūn. (53) Yastaʿjilūnaka bilʿadhābi wa ʾinna jahannama lamuḥīṭatum-bilkāfirīn. (54) Yawma yaghshāhumul-ʿadhābu miñ-fawqihim wa miñ-taḥti ʾarjulihim wa yaqūlu dhūqū mā kuñtum taʿmalūn. (55) Yāa ʿibādiyal-ladhīna ʾāmanūu ʾinna ʾarḍī wāsiʿatuñ-faʾIyyāya faʿbudūn. (56) Kullu nafsiñ-dhāaʾiqatul-mawti thumma ʾilaynā turjaʿūn. (57) Wal-ladhīna ʾāmanū wa ʿamiluṣ-ṣāliḥāti lanubawwiʾannahum-minal-jannati ghurafañ-tajrī miñ-taḥtihal-ʾanhāru khālidīna fīhā niʿmā ʾajrul-ʿāmilīn. (58)

50 I.e., "are the *contents* of this revelation not enough for them to make them grasp its intrinsic truth without the help of 'miraculous proofs' of its divine origin?" (Cf. note 60 on the last sentence of 7 : 75.)

51 See note 32 on 8 : 32.

52 I.e., from all directions and from many causes.

53 Implying that since the earth offers innumerable, multiform facilities to human life, there is no excuse for forgetting God "owing to the pressure of adverse circumstances". Whenever or wherever the worship of God – in its

ٱلَّذِينَ صَبَرُوا۟ وَعَلَىٰ رَبِّهِمْ يَتَوَكَّلُونَ ﴿٥٩﴾ وَكَأَيِّن مِّن دَآبَّةٍ لَّا تَحْمِلُ رِزْقَهَا
ٱللَّهُ يَرْزُقُهَا وَإِيَّاكُمْ وَهُوَ ٱلسَّمِيعُ ٱلْعَلِيمُ ﴿٦٠﴾ وَلَئِن سَأَلْتَهُم مَّنْ خَلَقَ
ٱلسَّمَٰوَٰتِ وَٱلْأَرْضَ وَسَخَّرَ ٱلشَّمْسَ وَٱلْقَمَرَ لَيَقُولُنَّ ٱللَّهُ فَأَنَّىٰ يُؤْفَكُونَ ﴿٦١﴾
ٱللَّهُ يَبْسُطُ ٱلرِّزْقَ لِمَن يَشَآءُ مِنْ عِبَادِهِۦ وَيَقْدِرُ لَهُۥٓ إِنَّ ٱللَّهَ بِكُلِّ شَىْءٍ
عَلِيمٌ ﴿٦٢﴾ وَلَئِن سَأَلْتَهُم مَّن نَّزَّلَ مِنَ ٱلسَّمَآءِ مَآءً فَأَحْيَا بِهِ ٱلْأَرْضَ مِنۢ بَعْدِ
مَوْتِهَا لَيَقُولُنَّ ٱللَّهُ قُلِ ٱلْحَمْدُ لِلَّهِ بَلْ أَكْثَرُهُمْ لَا يَعْقِلُونَ ﴿٦٣﴾ وَمَا هَٰذِهِ
ٱلْحَيَوٰةُ ٱلدُّنْيَآ إِلَّا لَهْوٌ وَلَعِبٌ وَإِنَّ ٱلدَّارَ ٱلْءَاخِرَةَ لَهِىَ ٱلْحَيَوَانُ لَوْ
كَانُوا۟ يَعْلَمُونَ ﴿٦٤﴾ فَإِذَا رَكِبُوا۟ فِى ٱلْفُلْكِ دَعَوُا۟ ٱللَّهَ مُخْلِصِينَ لَهُ ٱلدِّينَ

those who are patient in adversity and in their Sustainer place their trust! ‹59›
And how many a living creature is there that takes no thought of its own sustenance,[54] [the while] God provides for it as [He provides] for you – since He alone is all-hearing, all-knowing. ‹60›
And thus it is [with most people]: if[55] thou ask them, "Who is it that has created the heavens and the earth, and made the sun and the moon subservient [to His laws]?" – they will surely answer, "God."
How perverted, then, are their minds![56] ‹61›
God grants abundant sustenance, or gives it in scant measure, to whichever He wills of His creatures: for, behold, God has full knowledge of everything.[57] ‹62›
And thus it is: if thou ask them, "Who is it that sends down water from the skies, giving life thereby to the earth after it had been lifeless?" – they will surely answer, "God."
Say thou: "[Since this is so,] all praise is due to God [alone]!"
But most of them will not use their reason: ‹63› for, [if they did, they would know that] the life of this world is nothing but a passing delight and a play – whereas, behold, the life in the hereafter is indeed the only [true] life: if they but knew this! ‹64›
And so, when they embark on a ship [and find themselves in danger], they call unto God, [at that moment] sincere in their faith

ʾAlladhīna ṣabarū wa ʿalā Rabbihim yatawakkalūn. (59) Wa kaʾayyim-miñ-dāabbatil-lā taḥmilu rizqahal-lāhu yarzuquhā wa ʾiyyākum wa Huwas-Samīʿul-ʿAlīm. (60) Wa laʾiñ-saʾaltahum-man khalaqas-samāwāti wal-ʾarḍa wa sakhkharash-shamsa wal-qamara layaqūlunnal-lāh. Faʾannā yuʾfakūn. (61) ʾAllāhu yabsuṭur-rizqa limañy-yashāaʾu min ʿibādihī wa yaqdiru lah. ʾInnal-lāha bikulli shayʾin ʿAlīm. (62) Wa laʾiñ-saʾaltahum-mañ-nazzala minas-samāaʾi māaʾañ-faʾaḥyā bihil-ʾarḍa mim-baʿdi mawtihā laya-yaqūlunnal-lāh. Qulil-ḥamdu lillāh. Bal ʾaktharuhum lā yaʿqilūn. (63) Wa mā hādhihil-ḥayātud-dunyāa ʾillā lahwuñw-wa laʿib. Wa ʾinnad-dāral-ʾĀkhirata lahiyal-ḥayawānu law kānū yaʿlamūn. (64) Faʾidhā rakibū fil-fulki daʿawul-lāha mukhliṣīna lahud-dīn.

essential, and not merely liturgical sense – becomes impossible, the believer is obliged to "forsake the domain of evil" (which, as explained in note 124 on 4 : 97, is the innermost meaning of the concept of *hijrah*) and to "migrate unto God", that is, to a place where it is possible to live in accordance with one's faith.

54 Lit., "that does not bear [or "assume responsibility for"] its sustenance" – i.e., is either too weak to fend for itself or (according to Al-Ḥasan, as quoted by Zamakhsharī) does not store up provisions for the morrow. This passage connects with the reference at the end of the preceding verse to "those who in their Sustainer place their trust".

55 Regarding my rendering of *laʾin* as "thus it is: if . . .", etc., see *sūrah* 30, note 45. The people spoken of in the sequence are such as do acknowledge the existence of God but have only a vague idea as to what this acknowledgment implies or should imply.

56 See *sūrah* 5, note 90. The perversion consists in their thinking that they really "believe in God" and nevertheless worshipping false values and allegedly "divine" powers side by side with Him: all of which amounts to a virtual denial of His almightiness and uniqueness.

57 Sc., "and, hence, knows what is really good and, from the viewpoint of His unfathomable plan, necessary for each living being".

فَلَمَّا نَجَّىٰهُمْ إِلَى ٱلْبَرِّ إِذَا هُمْ يُشْرِكُونَ ﴿٦٥﴾ لِيَكْفُرُوا۟ بِمَآ ءَاتَيْنَٰهُمْ
وَلِيَتَمَتَّعُوا۟ ۖ فَسَوْفَ يَعْلَمُونَ ﴿٦٦﴾ أَوَلَمْ يَرَوْا۟ أَنَّا جَعَلْنَا حَرَمًا ءَامِنًا
وَيُتَخَطَّفُ ٱلنَّاسُ مِنْ حَوْلِهِمْ ۚ أَفَبِٱلْبَٰطِلِ يُؤْمِنُونَ وَبِنِعْمَةِ ٱللَّهِ
يَكْفُرُونَ ﴿٦٧﴾ وَمَنْ أَظْلَمُ مِمَّنِ ٱفْتَرَىٰ عَلَى ٱللَّهِ كَذِبًا أَوْ كَذَّبَ بِٱلْحَقِّ
لَمَّا جَآءَهُۥٓ ۚ أَلَيْسَ فِى جَهَنَّمَ مَثْوًى لِّلْكَٰفِرِينَ ﴿٦٨﴾ وَٱلَّذِينَ جَٰهَدُوا۟
فِينَا لَنَهْدِيَنَّهُمْ سُبُلَنَا ۚ وَإِنَّ ٱللَّهَ لَمَعَ ٱلْمُحْسِنِينَ ﴿٦٩﴾

Falammā najjāhum ʾilal-barri ʾidhā hum yushrikūn.
(65) Liyakfurū bimāa ʾātaynāhum wa liyatamattaᶜū;
fasawfa yaᶜlamūn. (66) ʾAwa lam yaraw ʾannā jaᶜalnā
Ḥaraman ʾāminañw-wa yutakhaṭṭafun-nāsu min
ḥawlihim. ʾAfabilbāṭili yuʾminūna wa biniᶜmatil-lāhi
yakfurūn. (67) Wa man ʾaẓlamu mimmanif-tarā ᶜalal-
lāhi kadhiban ʾaw kadhdhaba bil-ḥaqqi lammā
jāaʾah. ʾAlaysa fī jahannama mathwal-lilkāfirīn. (68)
Wal-ladhīna jāhadū fīnā lanahdiyannahum subulanā;
wa ʾinnal-lāha lamaᶜal-muḥsinīn. (69)

in Him alone; but as soon as He has brought them safe ashore, they [begin to] ascribe to imaginary powers a share in His divinity: ‹65› and thus[58] they show utter ingratitude for all that We have vouchsafed them, and go on [thoughtlessly] enjoying their worldly life. But in time they will come to know [the truth]. ‹66›

Are they, then, not aware that We have set up a sanctuary secure [for those who believe in Us], the while all around them men are being carried away [by fear and despair]?[59] Will they, then, [continue to] believe in things false and vain, and thus God's blessings deny? ‹67›

And who could be more wicked than he who attributes his own lying inventions to God,[60] or gives the lie to the truth when it comes unto him [through revelation]? Is not hell the [proper] abode for all who [thus] deny the truth? ‹68›

But as for those who strive hard in Our cause – We shall most certainly guide them onto paths that lead unto Us:[61] for, behold, God is indeed with the doers of good. ‹69›

58 The particle *li* prefixed to the subsequent verbs *yakfurū* ("they show [utter] ingratitude") and *yatamattaᶜū* ("they enjoy [or "go on enjoying"] their worldly life") is not an indication of intent ("so that" or "in order that") but merely of a *causal sequence*; in the above context, it may be appropriately rendered as "and thus".

59 See note 58 on the second paragraph of 28 : 57. In contrast to the "sanctuary secure" – the inner peace and sense of spiritual fulfilment which God bestows on those who truly believe in Him – the atheist or agnostic is more often than not exposed to fear of the Unknown and a despair born of the uncertainty as to what will happen to him after death.

60 I.e., by persuading himself that there is, side by side with God or even independently of Him, any "power" that could govern men's destinies.

61 Lit., "Our paths". The plural used here is obviously meant to stress the fact – alluded to often in the Qurʾān – that there are many paths which lead to a cognizance (*maᶜrifah*) of God.

Sūrah 29, *verse* 69 وَٱلَّذِينَ جَٰهَدُواْ فِينَا لَنَهۡدِيَنَّهُمۡ سُبُلَنَاۚ وَإِنَّ ٱللَّهَ لَمَعَ ٱلۡمُحۡسِنِينَ ﴿٦٩﴾

سَيَغْلِبُونَ فِي بِضْعِ سِنِينَ

لِلَّهِ الْأَمْرُ مِنْ قَبْلُ وَمِنْ بَعْدُ

وَيَوْمَئِذٍ يَفْرَحُ الْمُؤْمِنُونَ

بِنَصْرِ اللَّهِ يَنْصُرُ مَنْ يَشَاءُ

وَهُوَ الْعَزِيزُ الرَّحِيمُ وَعْدَ اللَّهِ

سورة الروم مكية

بِسْمِ اللَّهِ الرَّحْمَٰنِ الرَّحِيمِ

الٓمٓ غُلِبَتِ الرُّومُ فِىٓ أَدْنَى

الْأَرْضِ وَهُم مِّنۢ بَعْدِ غَلَبِهِمْ

وآياتها ستون

The Thirtieth Sūrah

Ar-Rūm (The Byzantines)

Mecca Period

THIS *SŪRAH*, revealed about six or seven years before the *hijrah*, takes its designation from the prophetic reference to the Byzantines in the opening verses. (For the historical background of this prophecy, see notes 2 and 3 below.) From this unequivocal prediction of events which at the time of its revelation were still shrouded in the mists of the future, the *sūrah* proceeds rapidly to its central theme: the wonder of God's creation of all that exists, His constant "bringing forth the living out of that which is dead", and thus His ability, and promise, to resurrect the dead at the end of time. But this, the Qur'ān says, most people are "determined not to know" (verse 56), because "they know but the outer surface of this world's life, whereas of the ultimate things they are utterly unaware" (verse 7); and because of their oblivion of those ultimate things, "corruption has appeared on land and in the sea as an outcome of what men's hands have wrought" (verse 41): a most incisive prediction of what is happening in the world of our days.

-30- سورة الروم مكية
وآياتها ستون

IN THE NAME OF GOD, THE MOST GRACIOUS, THE DISPENSER OF GRACE:

Alif. Lām. Mīm.[1] ‹1›
DEFEATED have been the Byzantines ‹2› in the lands close-by; yet it is they who, notwithstanding this their defeat, shall be victorious ‹3› within a few years: [for] with God rests all power of decision, first and last.[2]
And on that day will the believers [too, have cause to] rejoice ‹4› in God's succour:[3] [for] He gives succour to whomever He wills, since He alone is almighty, a dispenser of grace. ‹5›
[This is] God's promise. Never does God fail to fulfil His promise – but most people know [it] not: ‹6› they know but the outer surface of this world's life, whereas of the ultimate things they are utterly unaware.[4] ‹7›

بِسۡمِ ٱللَّهِ ٱلرَّحۡمَٰنِ ٱلرَّحِيمِ

الٓمٓ ﴿١﴾ غُلِبَتِ ٱلرُّومُ ﴿٢﴾ فِيٓ أَدۡنَى ٱلۡأَرۡضِ وَهُم مِّنۢ بَعۡدِ غَلَبِهِمۡ
سَيَغۡلِبُونَ ﴿٣﴾ فِي بِضۡعِ سِنِينَۗ لِلَّهِ ٱلۡأَمۡرُ مِن قَبۡلُ وَمِنۢ بَعۡدُۚ وَيَوۡمَئِذٖ يَفۡرَحُ
ٱلۡمُؤۡمِنُونَ ﴿٤﴾ بِنَصۡرِ ٱللَّهِۚ يَنصُرُ مَن يَشَآءُۖ وَهُوَ ٱلۡعَزِيزُ ٱلرَّحِيمُ ﴿٥﴾
وَعۡدَ ٱللَّهِۖ لَا يُخۡلِفُ ٱللَّهُ وَعۡدَهُۥ وَلَٰكِنَّ أَكۡثَرَ ٱلنَّاسِ لَا يَعۡلَمُونَ ﴿٦﴾
يَعۡلَمُونَ ظَٰهِرٗا مِّنَ ٱلۡحَيَوٰةِ ٱلدُّنۡيَا وَهُمۡ عَنِ ٱلۡأٓخِرَةِ هُمۡ غَٰفِلُونَ ﴿٧﴾

ربع الحزب

Bismil-lāhir-Raḥmānir-Raḥīm.
ʾAlif-Lāam-Mīim. (1) **Ghulibatir-Rūmu,** (2) **fīi ʾadnal-**
ʾarḍi wa hum-mim-baᶜdi ghalabihim sayaghlibūna,
(3) **fī biḍᶜi sinīn. Lillāhil-ʾamru miñ-qablu wa mim-**
baᶜd. Wa yawmaʾidhiñy-yafraḥul-muʾminūna, (4)
binaṣril-lāh. Yañṣuru mañy-yashāaʾu wa Huwal-
ᶜAzīzur-Raḥīm. (5) **Waᶜdal-lāhi lā yukhliful-lāhu**
waᶜdahū wa lākinna ʾaktharan-nāsi lā yaᶜlamūn.
(6) **Yaᶜlamūna ẓāhiram-minal-ḥayātid-dunyā wa hum**
ᶜanil-ʾĀkhirati hum ghāfilūn. (7)

---

1 See Appendix II.

2 Lit., "before and after". The defeats and victories spoken of above relate to the last phases of the centuries-long struggle between the Byzantine and Persian Empires. During the early years of the seventh century the Persians conquered parts of Syria and Anatolia, "the lands close-by", i.e., near the heartland of the Byzantine Empire; in 613 they took Damascus, and in 614, Jerusalem; Egypt fell to them in 615–16, and at the same time they laid siege to Constantinople itself. At the time of the revelation of this *sūrah* – about the seventh year before the *hijrah*, corresponding to 615 or 616 of the Christian era – the total destruction of the Byzantine Empire seemed imminent. The few Muslims around the Prophet were despondent on hearing the news of the utter discomfiture of the Byzantines, who were Christians and, as such, believed in the One God. The pagan Quraysh, on the other hand, sympathized with the Persians who, they thought, would vindicate their own opposition to the One-God idea. When Muḥammad enunciated the above Qurʾān-verses predicting a Byzantine victory "within a few years", this prophecy was received with derision by the Quraysh. Now the term *biḍᶜ* (commonly rendered as "a few") denotes any number between three and ten; and, as it happened, in 622 – i.e., six or seven years after the Qurʾanic prediction – the tide turned in favour of the Byzantines. In that year, Emperor Heraclius succeeded in defeating the Persians at Issus, south of the Taurus Mountains, and subsequently drove them out of Asia Minor. By 624, he carried the war into Persian territory and thus put the enemy on the defensive; and in the beginning of December, 626, the Persian armies were completely routed by the Byzantines.

3 This is a prediction of the battle of Badr, which was to take place eight or nine years later, in the month of Ramaḍān, 2 H. (corresponding to January, 624, of the Christian era), when the Muslims decisively defeated a very much superior force of pagan Quraysh (see introductory note to *sūrah* 8). The expression "on that day" has in this context the meaning of "at the same time", for although the battle of Badr began and ended on one day, the victories of Heraclius over the Persians took some years to materialize.

4 The term *al-ākhirah* circumscribes, in this context, both the inner reality of this world's life and the ultimate

أَوَلَمۡ يَتَفَكَّرُواْ فِيٓ أَنفُسِهِمۗ مَّا خَلَقَ ٱللَّهُ ٱلسَّمَٰوَٰتِ وَٱلۡأَرۡضَ وَمَا
بَيۡنَهُمَآ إِلَّا بِٱلۡحَقِّ وَأَجَلٖ مُّسَمّٗىۗ وَإِنَّ كَثِيرٗا مِّنَ ٱلنَّاسِ بِلِقَآيِٕ رَبِّهِمۡ
لَكَٰفِرُونَ ﴿٨﴾ أَوَلَمۡ يَسِيرُواْ فِي ٱلۡأَرۡضِ فَيَنظُرُواْ كَيۡفَ كَانَ عَٰقِبَةُ
ٱلَّذِينَ مِن قَبۡلِهِمۡۚ كَانُوٓاْ أَشَدَّ مِنۡهُمۡ قُوَّةٗ وَأَثَارُواْ ٱلۡأَرۡضَ وَعَمَرُوهَآ أَكۡثَرَ
مِمَّا عَمَرُوهَا وَجَآءَتۡهُمۡ رُسُلُهُم بِٱلۡبَيِّنَٰتِۖ فَمَا كَانَ ٱللَّهُ لِيَظۡلِمَهُمۡ وَلَٰكِن
كَانُوٓاْ أَنفُسَهُمۡ يَظۡلِمُونَ ﴿٩﴾ ثُمَّ كَانَ عَٰقِبَةَ ٱلَّذِينَ أَسَٰٓـُٔواْ ٱلسُّوٓأَىٰٓ أَن
كَذَّبُواْ بِـَٔايَٰتِ ٱللَّهِ وَكَانُواْ بِهَا يَسۡتَهۡزِءُونَ ﴿١٠﴾ ٱللَّهُ يَبۡدَؤُاْ ٱلۡخَلۡقَ ثُمَّ
يُعِيدُهُۥ ثُمَّ إِلَيۡهِ تُرۡجَعُونَ ﴿١١﴾ وَيَوۡمَ تَقُومُ ٱلسَّاعَةُ يُبۡلِسُ ٱلۡمُجۡرِمُونَ ﴿١٢﴾
وَلَمۡ يَكُن لَّهُم مِّن شُرَكَآئِهِمۡ شُفَعَٰٓؤُاْ وَكَانُواْ بِشُرَكَآئِهِمۡ كَٰفِرِينَ ﴿١٣﴾

ʾAwalam yatafakkarū fii ʾañfusihim. Mā khalaqal-lāhus-samāwāti wal-ʾarḍa wa mā baynahumāa ʾillā bilḥaqqi wa ʾajalim-musammā. Wa ʾinna kathīram-minan-nāsi biliqāaʾi Rabbihim lakāfirūn. (8) ʾAwalam yasīrū filʾarḍi fayañẓurū kayfa kāna ʿāqibatul-ladhīna miñ-qablihim. Kānūu ʾashadda minhum quwwatañw-wa ʾathārul-ʾarḍa wa ʿamarūhāa ʾakthara mimmā ʿamarūhā wa jāaʾat-hum Rusuluhum-bilbayyināti famā kānal-lāhu liyaẓlimahum wa lākiñ-kānūu ʾañfusahum yaẓlimūn. (9) Thumma kāna ʿāqibatal-ladhīna ʾasāaʾus-sūuʾāa ʾañ-kadhdhabū biʾĀyātil-lāhi wa kānū bihā yastahziʾūn. (10) ʾAllāhu yabdaʾul-khalqa thumma yuʿīduhū thumma ʾilayhi turjaʿūn. (11) Wa yawma taqūmus-Sāʿatu yublisul-mujrimūn. (12) Wa lam yakul-lahum-miñ-shurakāaʾihim shufaʿāaʾu wa kānū bishurakāaʾihim kāfirīn. (13)

Have they never learned to think for themselves?[5]
God has not created the heavens and the earth and all that is between them without [an inner] truth and a term set [by Him]:[6] and yet, behold, there are many people who stubbornly deny the truth that they are destined to meet their Sustainer! ‹8›
Have they, then, never journeyed about the earth and beheld what happened in the end to those [deniers of the truth] who lived before their time? Greater were they in power than they are; and they left a stronger impact on the earth, and built it up even better[7] than these [are doing]; and to them [too] came their apostles with all evidence of the truth: and so, [when they rejected the truth and thereupon perished,] it was not God who wronged them, but it was they who had wronged themselves. ‹9›
And once again:[8] evil is bound to be the end of those who do evil by giving the lie to God's messages and deriding them. ‹10›

GOD CREATES [man] in the first instance, and then brings him forth anew:[9] and, in the end, unto Him you all will be brought back. ‹11›
And when the Last Hour dawns, those who were lost in sin will be broken in spirit: ‹12› for they will have no intercessors in the beings to whom they were wont to ascribe a share in God's divinity,[10] seeing that [by then] they themselves will have ceased to believe in their erstwhile blasphemous fancies.[11] ‹13›

---

reality of the hereafter.

5 Lit., "Have they never thought within themselves?"

6 I.e., in contrast to God, who is eternal and unlimited, everything created is limited and subject to change and termination. As regards my rendering of *illā bi'l-ḥaqq* (lit., "otherwise than with [or "in"] truth") as "without [an inner] truth", see note 11 on the second sentence of 10 : 5.

7 Lit., "more". The phrase can also be rendered as "peopled it [or "dwelt in it"] in greater numbers".

8 For this particular rendering of *thumma*, see *sūrah* 6, note 31.

9 I.e., He *will* bring him forth anew: cf. 10 : 4 and the corresponding note 8. (A more general formulation of the same statement is found in verse 27 of this *sūrah*.)

10 Lit., "among their [God-]partners" (see *sūrah* 6, note 15).

11 Lit., "they will have rejected those [God-]partners of theirs".

And when the Last Hour dawns – on that Day will all [men] be sorted out: ‹14› as for those who attained to faith and did righteous deeds, they shall be made happy in a garden of delight; ‹15› but as for those who refused to acknowledge the truth and gave the lie to Our messages – and [thus] to the announcement[12] of a life to come – they will be given over to suffering. ‹16›

EXTOL, then, God's limitless glory when you enter upon the evening hours, and when you rise at morn; ‹17› and [seeing that] unto Him is due all praise in the heavens and on earth, [glorify Him] in the afternoon as well, and when you enter upon the hour of noon.[13] ‹18›

He [it is who] brings forth the living out of that which is dead, and brings forth the dead out of that which is alive, and gives life to the earth after it had been lifeless: and even thus will you be brought forth [from death to life]. ‹19›

And among His wonders is this: He creates you out of dust[14] – and then, lo! you become human beings ranging far and wide! ‹20›

And among His wonders is this: He creates for you mates out of your own kind,[15] so that you might incline towards them, and He engenders love and tenderness between you: in this, behold, there are messages indeed for people who think! ‹21›

And among his wonders is the creation of the heavens and the earth, and the diversity of your tongues and colours: for in this, behold, there are messages indeed for all who are possessed of [innate] knowledge! ‹22›

وَيَوْمَ تَقُومُ ٱلسَّاعَةُ يَوْمَئِذٍ يَتَفَرَّقُونَ ﴿١٤﴾ فَأَمَّا ٱلَّذِينَ ءَامَنُوا۟ وَعَمِلُوا۟
ٱلصَّٰلِحَٰتِ فَهُمْ فِى رَوْضَةٍ يُحْبَرُونَ ﴿١٥﴾ وَأَمَّا ٱلَّذِينَ كَفَرُوا۟ وَكَذَّبُوا۟
بِـَٔايَٰتِنَا وَلِقَآئِ ٱلْـَٔاخِرَةِ فَأُو۟لَٰٓئِكَ فِى ٱلْعَذَابِ مُحْضَرُونَ ﴿١٦﴾ فَسُبْحَٰنَ
ٱللَّهِ حِينَ تُمْسُونَ وَحِينَ تُصْبِحُونَ ﴿١٧﴾ وَلَهُ ٱلْحَمْدُ فِى ٱلسَّمَٰوَٰتِ
وَٱلْأَرْضِ وَعَشِيًّا وَحِينَ تُظْهِرُونَ ﴿١٨﴾ يُخْرِجُ ٱلْحَىَّ مِنَ ٱلْمَيِّتِ
وَيُخْرِجُ ٱلْمَيِّتَ مِنَ ٱلْحَىِّ وَيُحْىِ ٱلْأَرْضَ بَعْدَ مَوْتِهَا وَكَذَٰلِكَ
تُخْرَجُونَ ﴿١٩﴾ وَمِنْ ءَايَٰتِهِۦٓ أَنْ خَلَقَكُم مِّن تُرَابٍ ثُمَّ إِذَآ أَنتُم بَشَرٌ
تَنتَشِرُونَ ﴿٢٠﴾ وَمِنْ ءَايَٰتِهِۦٓ أَنْ خَلَقَ لَكُم مِّنْ أَنفُسِكُمْ أَزْوَٰجًا
لِّتَسْكُنُوٓا۟ إِلَيْهَا وَجَعَلَ بَيْنَكُم مَّوَدَّةً وَرَحْمَةً إِنَّ فِى ذَٰلِكَ لَـَٔايَٰتٍ لِّقَوْمٍ
يَتَفَكَّرُونَ ﴿٢١﴾ وَمِنْ ءَايَٰتِهِۦ خَلْقُ ٱلسَّمَٰوَٰتِ وَٱلْأَرْضِ وَٱخْتِلَٰفُ
أَلْسِنَتِكُمْ وَأَلْوَٰنِكُمْ إِنَّ فِى ذَٰلِكَ لَـَٔايَٰتٍ لِّلْعَٰلِمِينَ ﴿٢٢﴾

Wa yawma taqūmus-Sāʿatu Yawmaʾidhiñy-yatafarraqūn. (14) Faʾammal-ladhīna ʾāmanū wa ʿamiluṣ-ṣāliḥāti fahum fī rawḍatiñy-yuḥbarūn. (15) Wa ʾammal-ladhīna kafarū wa kadhdhabū biʾĀyātinā wa liqāaʾil-ʾĀkhirati faʾulāaʾika fil-ʿadhābi muḥḍarūn. (16) Fasubḥānal-lāhi ḥīna tumsūna wa ḥīna tuṣbiḥūn. (17) Wa lahul-ḥamdu fis-samāwāti wal-ʾarḍi wa ʿashiyyañw-wa ḥīna tuẓhirūn. (18) Yukhrijul-ḥayya minal-mayyiti wa yukhrijul-mayyita minal-ḥayyi wa yuḥyil-ʾarḍa baʿda mawtihā; wa kadhālika tukhrajūn. (19) Wa min ʾĀyātihīi ʾan khalaqakum-miñ-turābiñ-thumma ʾidhāa ʾañtum-basharuñ-tañtashirūn. (20) Wa min ʾĀyātihīi ʾan khalaqa lakum-min ʾañfusikum ʾazwājal-litaskunūu ʾilayhā wa jaʿala baynakum-mawaddatañw-wa raḥmah. ʾInna fī dhālika laʾĀyātil-liqawmiñy-yatafakkarūn. (21) Wa min ʾĀyātihī khalqus-samāwāti wal-ʾarḍi wakh-tilāfu ʾalsinatikum wa ʾalwānikum; ʾinna fī dhālika laʾĀyātil-lilʿālimīn. (22)

12 See note 111 on 7 : 147.

13 I.e., "remember God at all times". Apart from this general exhortation, the hours mentioned above circumscribe the times of the five daily prayers incumbent upon a Muslim. The "evening hours" indicate the prayer after sunset (*maghrib*) as well as that after nightfall (*ʿishāʾ*).

14 See second half of note 47 on 3 : 59, and note 4 on 23 : 12.

15 Lit., "from among yourselves" (see *sūrah* 4, note 1).

وَمِنْ ءَايَٰتِهِۦ مَنَامُكُم بِٱلَّيْلِ وَٱلنَّهَارِ وَٱبْتِغَآؤُكُم مِّن فَضْلِهِۦٓ ۚ إِنَّ فِى
ذَٰلِكَ لَءَايَٰتٍ لِّقَوْمٍ يَسْمَعُونَ ﴿23﴾ وَمِنْ ءَايَٰتِهِۦ يُرِيكُمُ ٱلْبَرْقَ خَوْفًا
وَطَمَعًا وَيُنَزِّلُ مِنَ ٱلسَّمَآءِ مَآءً فَيُحْىِۦ بِهِ ٱلْأَرْضَ بَعْدَ مَوْتِهَآ ۚ إِنَّ فِى
ذَٰلِكَ لَءَايَٰتٍ لِّقَوْمٍ يَعْقِلُونَ ﴿24﴾ وَمِنْ ءَايَٰتِهِۦٓ أَن تَقُومَ ٱلسَّمَآءُ
وَٱلْأَرْضُ بِأَمْرِهِۦ ۚ ثُمَّ إِذَا دَعَاكُمْ دَعْوَةً مِّنَ ٱلْأَرْضِ إِذَآ أَنتُمْ
تَخْرُجُونَ ﴿25﴾ وَلَهُۥ مَن فِى ٱلسَّمَٰوَٰتِ وَٱلْأَرْضِ ۖ كُلٌّ لَّهُۥ قَٰنِتُونَ ﴿26﴾
وَهُوَ ٱلَّذِى يَبْدَؤُا۟ ٱلْخَلْقَ ثُمَّ يُعِيدُهُۥ وَهُوَ أَهْوَنُ عَلَيْهِ ۚ وَلَهُ ٱلْمَثَلُ
ٱلْأَعْلَىٰ فِى ٱلسَّمَٰوَٰتِ وَٱلْأَرْضِ ۚ وَهُوَ ٱلْعَزِيزُ ٱلْحَكِيمُ ﴿27﴾ ضَرَبَ
لَكُم مَّثَلًا مِّنْ أَنفُسِكُمْ ۖ هَل لَّكُم مِّن مَّا مَلَكَتْ أَيْمَٰنُكُم مِّن شُرَكَآءَ

Wa min ʾĀyātihī manāmukum-billayli wan-nahāri wab-tighāaʾukum-miñ-faḍlih. ʾInna fī dhālika laʾĀyātil-liqawmiñy-yasmaʿūn. (23) Wa min ʾĀyātihī yurīkumul-barqa khawfañw-wa ṭamaʿañw-wa yunazzilu minas-samāaʾi māaʾañ-fayuḥyī bihil-ʾarḍa baʿda mawtihāa ʾinna fī dhālika laʾĀyātil-liqawmiñy-yaʿqilūn. (24) Wa min ʾĀyātihīi ʾañ-taqūmas-samāaʾu wal-ʾarḍu biʾamrihī thumma ʾidhā daʿākum daʿwatam-minal-ʾarḍi ʾidhāa ʾañtum takhrujūn. (25) Wa lahū mañ-fis-samāwāti wal-ʾarḍi kullul-lahū qānitūn. (26) Wa Huwal-ladhī yabdaʾul-khalqa thumma yuʿīduhū wa huwa ʾahwanu ʿalayh. Wa lahul-mathalul-ʾaʿlā fis-samāwāti wal-ʾarḍi wa Huwal-ʿAzīzul-Ḥakīm. (27) Ḍaraba lakum-mathalam-min ʾañfusikum; hal-lakum-mim-mā malakat ʾaymānukum-miñ-shurakāaʾa

And among His wonders is your sleep, at night or in daytime, as well as your [ability to go about in] quest of some of His bounties: in this, behold, there are messages indeed for people who [are willing to] listen! ‹23›

And among His wonders is this: He displays before you the lightning, giving rise to [both] fear and hope,[16] and sends down water from the skies, giving life thereby to the earth after it had been lifeless: in this, behold, there are messages indeed for people who use their reason! ‹24›

And among His wonders is this: the skies and the earth stand firm at His behest.[17] [Remember all this: for] in the end, when He will call you forth from the earth with a single call – lo! you will [all] emerge [for judgment]. ‹25›

For, unto Him belongs every being that is in the heavens and on earth; all things devoutly obey His will. ‹26›

And He it is who creates [all life] in the first instance, and then brings it forth anew:[18] and most easy is this for Him, since His is the essence of all that is most sublime in the heavens and on earth,[19] and He alone is almighty, truly wise. ‹27›

He propounds unto you a parable drawn from your own life:[20] Would you [agree to] have some of those whom your right hands possess[21] as [full-fledged] partners

---

16 I.e., hope of rain – an oft-recurring Qurʾanic symbol of faith and spiritual life (cf. 13 : 12).

17 Cf. 13 : 2, where God is spoken of as having "raised the skies without any supports that you could see" – a phrase explained in the corresponding note 4.

18 Although this statement is phrased in almost exactly the same words as in verse 11 above (as well as in 10 : 4), it evidently has here a more general purport, relating not only to man and man's individual resurrection but to the creation and constant re-creation of *all* life.

19 Primarily, the term *mathal* denotes a "likeness" or "similitude", and hence is often used in the Qurʾān (e.g., in the next verse) in the sense of "parable". Occasionally, however, it is synonymous with *ṣifah*, which signifies the intrinsic "attribute", "quality" or "nature" of a thing, concept or living being (cf. the reference to "the nature of Jesus" and "the nature of Adam" in 3 : 59). With reference to God, who is "sublimely exalted above anything that men may devise by way of definition" (see 6 : 100 and the corresponding note 88), the expression *mathal* clearly points to a *quality of being* entirely different from all other categories of existence, inasmuch as there is "nothing like unto Him" (42 : 11) and "nothing that could be compared with Him" (112 : 4): hence, the rendering of *mathal* as "essence" is most appropriate in this context.

20 Lit., "a parable (*mathal*) from yourselves".

21 I.e., slaves or persons otherwise subject to one's authority.

in whatever We may have bestowed upon you as sustenance, so that you [and they] would have equal shares in it, and you would fear [to make use of it without consulting] them, just as you might fear [the more powerful of] your equals?[22] Thus clearly do We spell out these messages unto people who use their reason. ‹28› But nay – they who are bent on evildoing follow but their own desires, without having any knowledge [of the truth].[23] And who could guide those whom God has [thus] let go astray, and who [thereupon] have none to succour them?[24] ‹29›

AND SO, set thy face[25] steadfastly towards the [one ever-true] faith, turning away from all that is false,[26] in accordance with the natural disposition which God has instilled into man:[27] [for,] not to allow any change to corrupt what God has thus created[28] – this is the [purpose of the one] ever-true faith; but most people know it not. ‹30› [Turn, then, away from all that is false,] turning unto Him [alone]; and remain conscious of Him, and be constant in prayer, and be not among those who ascribe divinity to aught beside Him, ‹31›

فِي مَا رَزَقْنَٰكُمْ فَأَنتُمْ فِيهِ سَوَآءٌ تَخَافُونَهُمْ كَخِيفَتِكُمْ أَنفُسَكُمْ
كَذَٰلِكَ نُفَصِّلُ ٱلْءَايَٰتِ لِقَوْمٍ يَعْقِلُونَ ﴿٢٨﴾ بَلِ ٱتَّبَعَ ٱلَّذِينَ ظَلَمُوٓا۟
أَهْوَآءَهُم بِغَيْرِ عِلْمٍ فَمَن يَهْدِى مَنْ أَضَلَّ ٱللَّهُ وَمَا لَهُم مِّن نَّٰصِرِينَ ﴿٢٩﴾
فَأَقِمْ وَجْهَكَ لِلدِّينِ حَنِيفًا فِطْرَتَ ٱللَّهِ ٱلَّتِى فَطَرَ ٱلنَّاسَ عَلَيْهَا لَا
تَبْدِيلَ لِخَلْقِ ٱللَّهِ ذَٰلِكَ ٱلدِّينُ ٱلْقَيِّمُ وَلَٰكِنَّ أَكْثَرَ ٱلنَّاسِ لَا يَعْلَمُونَ ﴿٣٠﴾
۞ مُنِيبِينَ إِلَيْهِ وَٱتَّقُوهُ وَأَقِيمُوا۟ ٱلصَّلَوٰةَ وَلَا تَكُونُوا۟ مِنَ ٱلْمُشْرِكِينَ ﴿٣١﴾

نصف الحزب

fī mā razaqnākum faʾañtum fīhi sawāaʾuñ-takhāfūnahum kakhīfatikum ʾañfusakum. Kadhālika nufaṣṣilul-ʾĀyāti liqawmiñy-yaʿqilūn. ﴿28﴾ Balit-tabaʿal-ladhīna ẓalamūu ʾahwāaʾahum-bighayri ʿilm. Famañy-yahdī man ʾaḍallal-lāh. Wa mā lahum-miñ-nāṣirīn. ﴿29﴾ Faʾaqim wajhaka liddīni ḥanīfā. Fiṭratal-lāhil-latī faṭaran-nāsa ʿalayhā; lā tabdīla likhalqil-lāhi dhālikad-dīnul-qayyimu wa lākinna ʾaktharan-nāsi lā yaʿlamūn. ﴿30﴾ ۞ Munībīna ʾilayhi wat-taqūhu wa ʾaqīmuṣ-Ṣalāta wa lā takūnū minal-mushrikīn. ﴿31﴾

22 Lit., "yourselves" – i.e., "those who are equal to you in status". The question is, of course, rhetorical, and must be answered in the negative. But if (so the implied argument goes) a human master would not willingly accept his slaves as full-fledged partners – even though master and slave are essentially equal by virtue of the humanness common to both of them (Zamakhsharī) – how can man regard any created beings or things as equal to Him who is their absolute Lord and Master, and is beyond comparison with anything that exists or could ever exist? (Parables with a similar purport are found in 16 : 75-76.)

23 In this instance, the phrase *alladhīna ẓalamū* ("they who are bent on evildoing") relates to those who deliberately ascribe divinity or divine powers to anyone or anything beside God, thus yielding to a desire for divine or semi-divine "mediators" between themselves and Him. Inasmuch as such a desire offends against the concept of God's omniscience and omnipresence, its very existence shows that the person concerned does not really believe in Him and, therefore, does not have the least knowledge of the truth.

24 For an explanation of God's "letting man go astray", see note 4 on the second sentence of 14 : 4, as well as note 7 on 2 : 7.

25 I.e., "surrender thy whole being"; the term "face" is often used metonymically in the sense of one's "whole being".

26 For this rendering of *ḥanīf*, see note 110 on 2 : 135.

27 See 7 : 172 and the corresponding note 139. The term *fiṭrah*, rendered by me as "natural disposition", connotes in this context man's inborn, intuitive ability to discern between right and wrong, true and false, and, thus, to sense God's existence and oneness. Cf. the famous saying of the Prophet, quoted by Bukhārī and Muslim: "Every child is born in this natural disposition; it is only his parents that later turn him into a 'Jew', a 'Christian', or a 'Magian'." These three religious formulations, best known to the contemporaries of the Prophet, are thus contrasted with the "natural disposition" which, by definition, consists in man's instinctive cognition of God and self-surrender (*islām*) to Him. (The term "parents" has here the wider meaning of "social influences" or "environment").

28 Lit., "no change shall there be [or "shall be made"] in God's creation (*khalq*)", i.e., in the natural disposition referred to above (Zamakhsharī). In this context, the term *tabdīl* ("change") obviously comprises the concept of "corruption".

[or] among those who have broken the unity of their faith and have become sects, each group delighting in but what they themselves hold [by way of tenets].[29] «32»

NOW [thus it is:] when affliction befalls men, they cry out unto their Sustainer, turning unto Him [for help]; but as soon as He lets them taste of His grace, lo! some of them [begin to] ascribe to other powers a share in their Sustainer's divinity,[30] «33» [as if] to prove their ingratitude for all that We have granted them!
Enjoy, then, your [brief] life: but in time you will come to know [the truth]! «34»
Have We ever bestowed upon them from on high a divine writ[31] which would speak [with approval] of their worshipping aught beside Us?[32] «35»
And [thus it is:] when we let men taste [Our] grace, they rejoice in it; but if evil befalls them as an outcome of what their own hands have wrought[33] – lo! they lose all hope! «36»
Are they, then, not aware that it is God who grants abundant sustenance, or gives it in scant measure, unto whomever He wills?
In this, behold, there are messages indeed for people who will believe! «37»
Hence, give his due to the near of kin, as well as to the needy and the wayfarer;[34] this is best for all who seek God's countenance: for it is they, they that shall attain to a happy state! «38»
And [remember:] whatever you may give out in usury so that it might increase through [other] people's possessions will bring [you] no increase in the sight of God[35] –

مِنَ ٱلَّذِينَ فَرَّقُوا۟ دِينَهُمْ وَكَانُوا۟ شِيَعًا ۖ كُلُّ حِزْبٍۭ بِمَا لَدَيْهِمْ فَرِحُونَ ﴿٣٢﴾ وَإِذَا
مَسَّ ٱلنَّاسَ ضُرٌّ دَعَوْا۟ رَبَّهُم مُّنِيبِينَ إِلَيْهِ ثُمَّ إِذَآ أَذَاقَهُم مِّنْهُ رَحْمَةً إِذَا فَرِيقٌ
مِّنْهُم بِرَبِّهِمْ يُشْرِكُونَ ﴿٣٣﴾ لِيَكْفُرُوا۟ بِمَآ ءَاتَيْنَٰهُمْ ۚ فَتَمَتَّعُوا۟ فَسَوْفَ
تَعْلَمُونَ ﴿٣٤﴾ أَمْ أَنزَلْنَا عَلَيْهِمْ سُلْطَٰنًا فَهُوَ يَتَكَلَّمُ بِمَا كَانُوا۟ بِهِۦ
يُشْرِكُونَ ﴿٣٥﴾ وَإِذَآ أَذَقْنَا ٱلنَّاسَ رَحْمَةً فَرِحُوا۟ بِهَا ۖ وَإِن تُصِبْهُمْ سَيِّئَةٌۢ بِمَا
قَدَّمَتْ أَيْدِيهِمْ إِذَا هُمْ يَقْنَطُونَ ﴿٣٦﴾ أَوَلَمْ يَرَوْا۟ أَنَّ ٱللَّهَ يَبْسُطُ ٱلرِّزْقَ لِمَن
يَشَآءُ وَيَقْدِرُ ۚ إِنَّ فِى ذَٰلِكَ لَءَايَٰتٍ لِّقَوْمٍ يُؤْمِنُونَ ﴿٣٧﴾ فَـَٔاتِ ذَا ٱلْقُرْبَىٰ حَقَّهُۥ
وَٱلْمِسْكِينَ وَٱبْنَ ٱلسَّبِيلِ ۚ ذَٰلِكَ خَيْرٌ لِّلَّذِينَ يُرِيدُونَ وَجْهَ ٱللَّهِ ۖ وَأُو۟لَٰٓئِكَ هُمُ
ٱلْمُفْلِحُونَ ﴿٣٨﴾ وَمَآ ءَاتَيْتُم مِّن رِّبًا لِّيَرْبُوَا۟ فِىٓ أَمْوَٰلِ ٱلنَّاسِ فَلَا يَرْبُوا۟ عِندَ ٱللَّهِ ۖ

Minal-ladhīna farraqū dīnahum wa kānū shiyaᶜā. Kullu ḥizbim-bimā ladayhim fariḥūn. ﴿32﴾ Wa ᵓidhā massan-nāsa ḍurruñ-daᶜaw Rabbahum-munībīna ᵓilayhi thumma ᵓidhāa ᵓadhāqahum-minhu raḥmatan ᵓidhā farīqum-minhum-biRabbihim yushrikūn. ﴿33﴾ Liyakfurū bimāa ᵓātaynāhum. Fatamattaᶜū fasawfa taᶜlamūn. ﴿34﴾ ᵓAm ᵓañzalnā ᶜalayhim sulṭānañ-fahuwa yatakallamu bimā kānū bihī yushrikūn. ﴿35﴾ Wa ᵓidhāa ᵓadhaqnan-nāsa raḥmatañ-fariḥū bihā. Wa ᵓiñ-tuṣibhum sayyiᵓatum-bimā qaddamat ᵓaydīhim ᵓidhā hum yaqnaṭūn. ﴿36﴾ ᵓAwalam yaraw ᵓannal-lāha yabsuṭur-rizqa limañy-yashāaᵓu wa yaqdir. ᵓInna fī dhālika laᵓĀyātil-liqawmiñy-yuᵓminūn. ﴿37﴾ Faᵓāti dhal-qurbā ḥaqqahū wal-miskīna wabnas-sabīl. Dhālika khayrul-lilladhīna yurīdūna Wajhal-lāhi wa ᵓulāaᵓika humul-mufliḥūn. ﴿38﴾ Wa māa ᵓātaytum-mir-ribal-liyarbuwa fīi ᵓamwālin-nāsi falā yarbū ᶜiñdal-lāh.

---

29 See 6 : 159, 21 : 92-93 and 23 : 52-53, as well as the corresponding notes.

30 See note 61 on 16 : 54.

31 Lit., "a warrant" or "authority" (*sulṭān*), in this context obviously denoting a revelation.

32 Lit., "of that which they were wont to associate [with Us]". Cf. second paragraph of 35 : 40 and the corresponding note 27.

33 See 4 : 79 and the corresponding note 94.

34 Cf. 17 : 26.

35 This is the earliest mention of the term and concept of *ribā* in the chronology of Qurᵓanic revelation. In its general, linguistic sense, this term denotes an "addition" to or an "increase" of a thing over and above its original size or amount; in the terminology of the Qurᵓān, it signifies any unlawful addition, by way of interest, to a sum of money

وَمَآ ءَاتَيْتُم مِّن زَكَوٰةٍ تُرِيدُونَ وَجْهَ ٱللَّهِ فَأُوْلَٰٓئِكَ هُمُ ٱلْمُضْعِفُونَ ﴿٣٩﴾
ٱللَّهُ ٱلَّذِى خَلَقَكُمْ ثُمَّ رَزَقَكُمْ ثُمَّ يُمِيتُكُمْ ثُمَّ يُحْيِيكُمْ هَلْ مِن
شُرَكَآئِكُم مَّن يَفْعَلُ مِن ذَٰلِكُم مِّن شَىْءٍ سُبْحَٰنَهُۥ وَتَعَٰلَىٰ عَمَّا
يُشْرِكُونَ ﴿٤٠﴾ ظَهَرَ ٱلْفَسَادُ فِى ٱلْبَرِّ وَٱلْبَحْرِ بِمَا كَسَبَتْ أَيْدِى ٱلنَّاسِ

Wa māa ʾātaytum-miñ-Zakātiñ-turīdūna Wajhal-lāhi faʾulāaʾika humul-muḍʿifūn. (39) ʾAllāhul-ladhī khalaqakum thumma razaqakum thumma yumītukum thumma yuḥyīkum. Hal miñ-shurakāaʾikum-mañy-yafʿalu miñ-dhālikum-miñ-shayʾ. Subḥānahū wa taʿālā ʿammā yushrikūn. (40) Ẓaharal-fasādu fil-barri wal-baḥri bimā kasabat ʾaydin-nāsi

whereas all that you give out in charity, seeking God's countenance, [will be blessed by Him:[36]] for it is they, they [who thus seek His countenance] that shall have their recompense multiplied! ‹39›

IT IS GOD who has created you, and then has provided you with sustenance, and then will cause you to die, and then will bring you to life again. Can any of those beings or powers to whom you ascribe a share in His divinity[37] do any of these things? Limitless is He in His glory, and sublimely exalted above anything to which men may ascribe a share in His divinity! ‹40›

[Since they have become oblivious of God,] corruption has appeared on land and in the sea as an outcome of what men's hands have wrought: and so He will let

or goods lent by one person or body of persons to another. Considering the problem in terms of the economic conditions prevailing at or before their time, most of the early Muslim jurists identified this "unlawful addition" with profits obtained through any kind of interest-bearing loans irrespective of the rate of interest and the economic motivation involved. With all this – as is evidenced by the voluminous juridical literature on this subject – Islamic scholars have not yet been able to reach an absolute agreement on the definition of *ribā*: a definition, that is, which would cover all conceivable legal situations and positively respond to all the exigencies of a variable economic environment. In the words of Ibn Kathīr (in his commentary on 2 : 275), "the subject of *ribā* is one of the most difficult subjects for many of the scholars (*ahl al-ʿilm*)". It should be borne in mind that the passage condemning and prohibiting *ribā* in legal terms (2 : 275 – 281) was the last revelation received by the Prophet, who died a few days later (cf. note 268 on 2 : 281); hence, the Companions had no opportunity to ask him about the *sharʿī* implications of the relevant injunction – so much so that even ʿUmar ibn al-Khaṭṭāb is reliably reported to have said: "The last [of the Qurʾān] that was revealed was the passage [lit., "the verse"] on *ribā*; and, behold, the Apostle of God passed away without [lit., "before"] having explained its meaning to us" (Ibn Ḥanbal, on the authority of Saʿīd ibn al-Musayyab). Nevertheless, the severity with which the Qurʾān condemns *ribā* and those who practice it furnishes – especially when viewed against the background of mankind's economic experiences during the intervening centuries – a sufficiently clear indication of its nature and its social as well as moral implications. Roughly speaking, the opprobrium of *ribā* (in the sense in which this term is used in the Qurʾān and in many sayings of the Prophet) attaches to profits obtained through interest-bearing loans involving an *exploitation of the economically weak by the strong and resourceful*: an exploitation characterized by the fact that the lender, while retaining full ownership of the capital loaned and having no legal concern with the purpose for which it is to be used or with the manner of its use, remains *contractually* assured of gain irrespective of any losses which the borrower may suffer in consequence of this transaction. With this definition in mind, we realize that the question as to what kinds of financial transactions fall within the category of *ribā* is, in the last resort, a moral one, closely connected with the socio-economic motivation underlying the mutual relationship of borrower and lender; and, stated in purely economic terms, it is a question as to how profits and risks may be equitably shared by *both* partners to a loan transaction. It is, of course, impossible to answer this double question in a rigid, once-for-all manner: our answers must necessarily vary in accordance with the changes to which man's social and technological development – and, thus, his economic environment – is subject. Hence, while the Qurʾanic condemnation of the concept and practice of *ribā* is unequivocal and final, every successive Muslim generation is faced with the challenge of giving new dimensions and a fresh economic meaning to this term which, for want of a better word, may be rendered as "usury". – In the present instance (which, as I have mentioned, is the earliest in the history of the Qurʾān), no clear-cut prohibition is as yet laid down; but the prohibition appearing in 2 : 275 ff. is already foreshadowed by the reference to the immoral hope of increasing one's own substance "through [other] people's possessions", i.e., through the exploitation of others.

36 Cf. 2 : 276.

37 Lit., "any of your [God-]partners". Cf. note 15 on 6 : 22.

them taste[38] [the evil of] some of their doings, so that they might return [to the right path].[39] «41»
Say: "Go all over the earth, and behold what happened in the end to those [sinners] who lived before [you]: most of them were wont to ascribe divine qualities to things or beings other than God."[40] «42»
Set, then, thy face steadfastly towards the one ever-true faith,[41] ere there come from God a Day [of reckoning – the Day] which cannot be averted.
On that Day all will be sundered: «43» he who has denied the truth will have to bear [the burden of] his denial, whereas all who did what is right and just will have made goodly provision for themselves, «44» so that He might reward, out of His bounty, those who have attained to faith and done righteous deeds.
Verily, He does not love those who refuse to acknowledge the truth «45» – for among His wonders is this: He sends forth [His messages as He sends forth] the winds that bear glad tidings,[42] so that He might give you a taste of His grace [through life-giving rains], and that ships might sail at His behest, and that you might go about in quest of some of His bounties, and that you might have cause to be grateful. «46»

لِيُذِيقَهُم بَعْضَ ٱلَّذِى عَمِلُوا۟ لَعَلَّهُمْ يَرْجِعُونَ ﴿41﴾ قُلْ سِيرُوا۟ فِى
ٱلْأَرْضِ فَٱنظُرُوا۟ كَيْفَ كَانَ عَٰقِبَةُ ٱلَّذِينَ مِن قَبْلُ ۚ كَانَ أَكْثَرُهُم
مُّشْرِكِينَ ﴿42﴾ فَأَقِمْ وَجْهَكَ لِلدِّينِ ٱلْقَيِّمِ مِن قَبْلِ أَن يَأْتِىَ يَوْمٌ لَّا مَرَدَّ
لَهُۥ مِنَ ٱللَّهِ ۖ يَوْمَئِذٍ يَصَّدَّعُونَ ﴿43﴾ مَن كَفَرَ فَعَلَيْهِ كُفْرُهُۥ ۖ وَمَنْ عَمِلَ
صَٰلِحًا فَلِأَنفُسِهِمْ يَمْهَدُونَ ﴿44﴾ لِيَجْزِىَ ٱلَّذِينَ ءَامَنُوا۟ وَعَمِلُوا۟
ٱلصَّٰلِحَٰتِ مِن فَضْلِهِۦٓ ۚ إِنَّهُۥ لَا يُحِبُّ ٱلْكَٰفِرِينَ ﴿45﴾ وَمِنْ ءَايَٰتِهِۦٓ أَن
يُرْسِلَ ٱلرِّيَاحَ مُبَشِّرَٰتٍ وَلِيُذِيقَكُم مِّن رَّحْمَتِهِۦ وَلِتَجْرِىَ ٱلْفُلْكُ
بِأَمْرِهِۦ وَلِتَبْتَغُوا۟ مِن فَضْلِهِۦ وَلَعَلَّكُمْ تَشْكُرُونَ ﴿46﴾

liyudhīqahum-baʿḍal-ladhī ʿamilū laʿallahum yarjiʿūn. (41) Qul sīrū fil-ʾarḍi fañẓurū kayfa kāna ʿāqibatul-ladhīna miñ-qabl. Kāna ʾaktharuhum-mushrikīn. (42) Faʾaqim wajhaka liddīnil-qayyimi miñ-qabli ʾañy-yaʾtiya Yawmul-lā maradda lahū minal-lāhi Yawmaʾidhiñy-yaṣṣaddaʿūn. (43) Mañ-kafara faʿalayhi kufruhū wa man ʿamila ṣāliḥañ-falīʾañfusihim yamhadūn. (44) Liyajziyal-ladhīna ʾāmanū wa ʿamiluṣ-ṣāliḥati miñ-faḍlih. ʾInnahū lā yuḥibbul-kāfirīn. (45) Wa min ʾĀyātihīi ʾañy-yursilar-riyāḥa mubashshirātiñw-wa liyudhīqakum-mir-raḥmatihī wa litajriyal-fulku biʾamrihī wa litabtaghū miñ-faḍlihī wa laʿallakum tashkurūn. (46)

38 The prefix *li* in *li-yudhīqahum* does not indicate here a purport or intent ("so that" or "in order that"), but is a *lām al-ʿāqibah*, i.e., a prefix expressing a factual consequence (best rendered as "thereupon" or "and so").

39 Thus, the growing corruption and destruction of our natural environment, so awesomely – if as yet only partially – demonstrated in our time, is here predicted as "an outcome of what men's hands have wrought", i.e., of that self-destructive – because utterly materialistic – inventiveness and frenzied activity which now threatens mankind with previously unimaginable ecological disasters: an unbridled pollution of land, air and water through industrial and urban waste, a progressive poisoning of plant and marine life, all manner of genetic malformations in men's own bodies through an ever-widening use of drugs and seemingly "beneficial" chemicals, and the gradual extinction of many animal species essential to human well-being. To all this may be added the rapid deterioration and decomposition of man's social life, the all-round increase in sexual perversion, crime and violence, with, perhaps, nuclear annihilation as the ultimate stage: all of which is, in the last resort, an outcome of man's oblivion of God and, hence, of all absolute moral values, and their supersession by the belief that material "progress" is the only thing that matters.

40 I.e., they worshipped material comfort and power, and thus lost sight of all spiritual values and, in the end, destroyed themselves.

41 See verse 30 above, as well as the corresponding notes; also 3 : 19 – "the only [true] religion in the sight of God is [man's] self-surrender unto Him".

42 The mention of God's messages, interpolated by me between brackets, is justified by the verses which precede and follow this passage. Moreover, it is only by means of such an interpolation that the symbolic purport of the above reference to "the winds that bear glad tidings" can be made fully obvious.

And indeed, [O Muḥammad, even] before thee did We send forth apostles – each one unto his own people[43] – and they brought them all evidence of the truth: and then, [by causing the believers to triumph,] We inflicted Our retribution upon those who [deliberately] did evil: for We had willed it upon Ourselves to succour the believers. «47»
It is God who sends forth the winds [of hope],[44] so that they raise a cloud – whereupon He spreads it over the skies as He wills, and causes it to break up so that thou seest rain issue from within it: and as soon as He causes it to fall upon whomever He wills of His servants – lo! they rejoice, «48» even though a short while ago, [just] before it was sent down upon them, they had abandoned all hope! «49»
Behold, then, [O man,] these signs of God's grace – how He gives life to the earth after it had been lifeless! Verily, this Selfsame [God] is indeed the One that can bring the dead back to life: for He has the power to will anything! «50»
But thus it is: if[45] We send a wind [that scorches their land], and they see it turn yellow, they begin, after that [erstwhile joy], to deny the truth [of Our almightiness and grace]![46] «51»
And, verily, thou canst not make the dead hear: and [so, too,] thou canst not make the deaf [of heart] hear this call when they turn their backs [on thee] and go away, «52» just as thou canst not lead the blind [of heart] out of their error: none canst thou make hear [thy call] save such as [are willing to] believe in Our messages, and thus surrender themselves unto Us.[47] «53»

وَلَقَدْ أَرْسَلْنَا مِن قَبْلِكَ رُسُلًا إِلَىٰ قَوْمِهِمْ فَجَآءُوهُم بِٱلْبَيِّنَٰتِ فَٱنتَقَمْنَا
مِنَ ٱلَّذِينَ أَجْرَمُوا۟ ۖ وَكَانَ حَقًّا عَلَيْنَا نَصْرُ ٱلْمُؤْمِنِينَ ﴿47﴾ ٱللَّهُ ٱلَّذِى
يُرْسِلُ ٱلرِّيَٰحَ فَتُثِيرُ سَحَابًا فَيَبْسُطُهُۥ فِى ٱلسَّمَآءِ كَيْفَ يَشَآءُ وَيَجْعَلُهُۥ
كِسَفًا فَتَرَى ٱلْوَدْقَ يَخْرُجُ مِنْ خِلَٰلِهِۦ ۖ فَإِذَآ أَصَابَ بِهِۦ مَن يَشَآءُ مِنْ
عِبَادِهِۦٓ إِذَا هُمْ يَسْتَبْشِرُونَ ﴿48﴾ وَإِن كَانُوا۟ مِن قَبْلِ أَن يُنَزَّلَ عَلَيْهِم مِّن
قَبْلِهِۦ لَمُبْلِسِينَ ﴿49﴾ فَٱنظُرْ إِلَىٰٓ ءَاثَٰرِ رَحْمَتِ ٱللَّهِ كَيْفَ يُحْىِ ٱلْأَرْضَ
بَعْدَ مَوْتِهَآ ۚ إِنَّ ذَٰلِكَ لَمُحْىِ ٱلْمَوْتَىٰ ۖ وَهُوَ عَلَىٰ كُلِّ شَىْءٍ قَدِيرٌ ﴿50﴾ وَلَئِنْ
أَرْسَلْنَا رِيحًا فَرَأَوْهُ مُصْفَرًّا لَّظَلُّوا۟ مِنۢ بَعْدِهِۦ يَكْفُرُونَ ﴿51﴾ فَإِنَّكَ لَا
تُسْمِعُ ٱلْمَوْتَىٰ وَلَا تُسْمِعُ ٱلصُّمَّ ٱلدُّعَآءَ إِذَا وَلَّوْا۟ مُدْبِرِينَ ﴿52﴾ وَمَآ أَنتَ
بِهَٰدِ ٱلْعُمْىِ عَن ضَلَٰلَتِهِمْ ۖ إِن تُسْمِعُ إِلَّا مَن يُؤْمِنُ بِـَٔايَٰتِنَا فَهُم
مُّسْلِمُونَ ﴿53﴾

Wa laqad ʾarsalnā miñ-qablika Rusulan ʾilā qawmihim fajāaʾūhum-bilbayyināti fañtaqamnā minal-ladhīna ʾajramū; wa kāna ḥaqqan ʿalaynā naṣrul-muʾminīn. (47) ʾAllāhul-ladhī yursilur-riyāḥa fatuthīru saḥābañ-fayabsuṭuhū fis-samāaʾi kayfa yashāaʾu wa yajʿaluhū kisafañ-fataral-wadqa yakhruju min khilālihī faʾidhāa ʾaṣāba bihī mañy-yashāaʾu min ʿibādihīi ʾidhā hum yastabshirūn. (48) Wa ʾiñ-kānū miñ-qabli añy-yunazzala ʿalayhim-miñ-qablihī lamublisīn. (49) Fañẓur ʾilāa ʾāthāri raḥmatil-lāhi kayfa yuḥyil-ʾarḍa baʿda mawtihā. ʾInna dhālika laMuḥyil-mawtā; wa Huwa ʿalā kulli shayʾiñ-Qadīr. (50) Wa laʾin ʾarsalnā rīḥañ-faraʾawhu muṣfarral-laẓallū mim-baʿdihī yakfurūn. (51) Faʾinnaka lā tusmiʿul-mawtā wa lā tusmiʿuṣ-ṣummad-duʿāaʾa ʾidhā wallaw mudbirīn. (52) Wa māa ʾañta bihādil-ʿumyi ʿañ-ḍalālatihim; ʾiñ-tusmiʿu ʾillā mañy-yuʾminu biʾĀyātinā fahum-Muslimūn. (53)

43 Lit., "did We send apostles to their [own] people": see note 96 on 10 : 74.

44 As in verse 46 above, the reference to "the winds" has here a symbolic significance, namely, spiritual life and hope; hence my interpolation.

45 The particle *laʾin* (lit., "indeed, if . . .") is often used in the Qurʾān to express the recurrent, typical character of the attitude or situation referred to in the sequence; in all such cases it may be suitably rendered as "thus it is: if . . .", etc.

46 For a full explanation of this verse, see 11 : 9 and the corresponding notes 16-19.

47 Cf. the identical passage in 27 : 80-81 and the corresponding note 72.

ثلاثة ارباع الحزب

IT IS GOD who creates you [all in a state] of weakness, and then, after weakness, ordains strength [for you], and then, after [a period of] strength, ordains [old-age] weakness and grey hair.[48] He creates what He wills; and He alone is all-knowing, infinite in His power. ‹54›

[He it is who will cause you to die, and in time will resurrect you.][49] And when the Last Hour dawns, those who had been lost in sin will swear that they had not tarried [on earth] longer than an hour: thus were they wont to delude themselves [all their lives]![50] ‹55›

But those who [in their lifetime] were endowed with knowledge[51] and faith will say: "Indeed, you have been tardy in [accepting as true] what God has revealed,[52] [and you have waited] until the Day of Resurrection: this, then, is the Day of Resurrection: but you – you were determined not to know it!"[53] ‹56›

And so, on that Day their excuse will be of no avail to those who were bent on evil-doing, nor will they be allowed to make amends. ‹57›

AND, INDEED, We have propounded unto men all kinds of parables in this Qurʾān.[54] But thus it is: if thou approach them with any [such] message, those who are bent on denying the truth are sure to say "You are but making false claims!" ‹58›

۞ ٱللَّهُ ٱلَّذِى خَلَقَكُم مِّن ضَعْفٍ ثُمَّ جَعَلَ مِنۢ بَعْدِ ضَعْفٍ قُوَّةً ثُمَّ جَعَلَ
مِنۢ بَعْدِ قُوَّةٍ ضَعْفًا وَشَيْبَةً ۚ يَخْلُقُ مَا يَشَآءُ ۖ وَهُوَ ٱلْعَلِيمُ ٱلْقَدِيرُ ﴿٥٤﴾ وَيَوْمَ
تَقُومُ ٱلسَّاعَةُ يُقْسِمُ ٱلْمُجْرِمُونَ مَا لَبِثُوا۟ غَيْرَ سَاعَةٍ ۚ كَذَٰلِكَ كَانُوا۟
يُؤْفَكُونَ ﴿٥٥﴾ وَقَالَ ٱلَّذِينَ أُوتُوا۟ ٱلْعِلْمَ وَٱلْإِيمَٰنَ لَقَدْ لَبِثْتُمْ فِى كِتَٰبِ
ٱللَّهِ إِلَىٰ يَوْمِ ٱلْبَعْثِ ۖ فَهَٰذَا يَوْمُ ٱلْبَعْثِ وَلَٰكِنَّكُمْ كُنتُمْ لَا تَعْلَمُونَ ﴿٥٦﴾
فَيَوْمَئِذٍ لَّا يَنفَعُ ٱلَّذِينَ ظَلَمُوا۟ مَعْذِرَتُهُمْ وَلَا هُمْ يُسْتَعْتَبُونَ ﴿٥٧﴾ وَلَقَدْ
ضَرَبْنَا لِلنَّاسِ فِى هَٰذَا ٱلْقُرْءَانِ مِن كُلِّ مَثَلٍ ۚ وَلَئِن جِئْتَهُم بِـَٔايَةٍ
لَّيَقُولَنَّ ٱلَّذِينَ كَفَرُوٓا۟ إِنْ أَنتُمْ إِلَّا مُبْطِلُونَ ﴿٥٨﴾

۞ ʾAllāhul-ladhī khalaqakum-miñ-ḍaʿfiñ-thumma jaʿala mim-baʿdi ḍaʿfiñ-quwwatiñ-thumma jaʿala mim-baʿdi quwwatiñ-ḍaʿfañw-wa shaybah. Yakhluqu mā yashāaʾu wa Huwal-ʿAlīmul-Qadīr. (54) Wa yawma taqūmus-sāʿatu yuqsimul-mujrimūna mā labithū ghayra Sāʿatiñ-kadhālika kānū yuʾfakūn. (55) Wa qālal-ladhīna ʾūtul-ʿilma wal-ʾīmāna laqad labithtum fī Kitābil-lāhi ʾilā Yawmil-Baʿthi fahādhā Yawmul-Baʿthi wa lākinnakum kuñtum lā taʿlamūn. (56) FaYawmaʾidhil-lā yañfaʿul-ladhīna ẓalamū maʿdhiratuhum wa lā hum yustaʿtabūn. (57) Wa laqad ḍarabnā linnāsi fī hādhal-Qurʾāni miñ-kulli mathal. Wa laʾiñ-jiʾtahum-biʾĀyatil-layaqūlannal-ladhīna kafarūu ʾin ʾañtum ʾillā mubṭilūn. (58)

48 In the original, this sentence is formulated in the past tense ("has created you" and "has ordained"), stressing the recurrent character of man's life-phases. In translation, this recurrence can he suitably expressed by using the present tense.

49 This interpolation – the meaning of which is elliptically implied here – shows the connection of the present passage with the preceding one, as well as with verses 11-16 and 27.

50 The illusory character of man's earthbound concept of "time" is brought out in the Qurʾān in several places. In the above context stress is laid, firstly, on the *relativity* of this concept – i.e., on the infinitesimal shortness of our life on earth as compared with the timeless duration of life in the hereafter (cf., for instance, 10 : 45 or 17 : 52) – and, secondly, on the resurrected sinners' self-deluding excuse that their life on earth had been too short to allow them to realize their errors and mend their ways. It is to this second aspect of the problem that the Qurʾān alludes in the words, "thus were they wont to delude themselves" (lit., "to be turned away", i.e., from the truth). For an explanation of the verb *yuʾfikūn*, see *sūrah* 5, note 90.

51 See *sūrah* 16, note 25.

52 Lit., "with regard to (*fī*) God's revelation (*kitāb*)", i.e., that the dead shall be resurrected and judged by Him. It is to be noted that the verb *labitha* signifies "he waited [for something]" or "he was tardy [with regard to something]" as well as "he stayed [in a place]" or "he remained". Evidently, in verse 55 *mā labithū* has the meaning of "they had not stayed" or "remained", while in verse 56 *labithtum* denotes "you have been tardy" or "you have waited".

53 Lit., "you were wont not to know" – i.e., "you persistently closed your mind to this promise".

54 See note 33 on the first clause of 39 : 27.

In this way does God seal the hearts of those who do not [want to] know [the truth].[55] ‹59›
Remain, then, patient in adversity: verily, God's promise [of resurrection] is true indeed – so let not those who are devoid of all inner certainty disquiet thy mind! ‹60›

كَذَٰلِكَ يَطۡبَعُ ٱللَّهُ عَلَىٰ قُلُوبِ ٱلَّذِينَ لَا يَعۡلَمُونَ ﴿٥٩﴾ فَٱصۡبِرۡ إِنَّ وَعۡدَ ٱللَّهِ حَقّٞۖ وَلَا يَسۡتَخِفَّنَّكَ ٱلَّذِينَ لَا يُوقِنُونَ ﴿٦٠﴾

Kadhālika yaṭbaᶜul-lāhu ᶜalā qulūbil-ladhīna lā yaᶜlamūn. (59) Faṣbir ᵓinna waᶜdal-lāhi ḥaqquñw-wa lā yastakhiffannakal-ladhīna lā yūqinūn. (60)

55 For an explanation of God's "sealing" the hearts of such people, see note 7 on 2 : 7.

The Thirty-First Sūrah

Luqmān

Mecca Period

REVEALED, like the preceding *sūrah,* in the middle of the Mecca period, *Luqmān* owes its title to verses 12-19, where this legendary sage (see note 12) is spoken of as counselling his son.

There is no cogent reason to ascribe, as some commentators do, certain verses of this *sūrah* to the Medina period.

سورة لقمان مكية -31-
وآياتها أربع وثلاثون

IN THE NAME OF GOD, THE MOST GRACIOUS, THE DISPENSER OF GRACE:

بِسۡمِ ٱللَّهِ ٱلرَّحۡمَٰنِ ٱلرَّحِيمِ

Alif. Lām. Mīm.[1] ‹1›
THESE ARE MESSAGES of the divine writ,
full of wisdom,[2] ‹2› providing guidance and
grace unto the doers of good ‹3› who are
constant in prayer and dispense charity:[3]
for it is they, they who in their innermost
are certain of the life to come! ‹4›
It is they who follow the guidance [that
comes to them] from their Sustainer; and
it is they, they who shall attain to a happy
state! ‹5›
But among men there is many a one that
prefers a mere play with words [to divine
guidance],[4] so as to lead [those] without
knowledge astray from the path of God,
and to turn it to ridicule: for such there is
shameful suffering in store. ‹6›
For, whenever Our messages are conveyed
to such a one, he turns away in his
arrogance[5] as though he had not heard
them – as though there were deafness in
his ears: give him, then, the tiding of
grievous suffering [in the life to come].
‹7›
[As against this,] verily, those who attain
to faith and do righteous deeds shall have

الٓمٓ ﴿١﴾ تِلۡكَ ءَايَٰتُ ٱلۡكِتَٰبِ ٱلۡحَكِيمِ ﴿٢﴾ هُدٗى وَرَحۡمَةٗ
لِّلۡمُحۡسِنِينَ ﴿٣﴾ ٱلَّذِينَ يُقِيمُونَ ٱلصَّلَوٰةَ وَيُؤۡتُونَ ٱلزَّكَوٰةَ وَهُم
بِٱلۡأٓخِرَةِ هُمۡ يُوقِنُونَ ﴿٤﴾ أُوْلَٰٓئِكَ عَلَىٰ هُدٗى مِّن رَّبِّهِمۡۖ وَأُوْلَٰٓئِكَ هُمُ
ٱلۡمُفۡلِحُونَ ﴿٥﴾ وَمِنَ ٱلنَّاسِ مَن يَشۡتَرِي لَهۡوَ ٱلۡحَدِيثِ لِيُضِلَّ عَن
سَبِيلِ ٱللَّهِ بِغَيۡرِ عِلۡمٖ وَيَتَّخِذَهَا هُزُوًاۚ أُوْلَٰٓئِكَ لَهُمۡ عَذَابٞ مُّهِينٞ ﴿٦﴾
وَإِذَا تُتۡلَىٰ عَلَيۡهِ ءَايَٰتُنَا وَلَّىٰ مُسۡتَكۡبِرٗا كَأَن لَّمۡ يَسۡمَعۡهَا كَأَنَّ فِيٓ أُذُنَيۡهِ
وَقۡرٗاۖ فَبَشِّرۡهُ بِعَذَابٍ أَلِيمٍ ﴿٧﴾ إِنَّ ٱلَّذِينَ ءَامَنُواْ وَعَمِلُواْ ٱلصَّٰلِحَٰتِ لَهُمۡ

Bismil-lāhir-Raḥmānir-Raḥīm.
ᵓAlif-Lāam-Mīim. (1) Tilka ᵓĀyātul-Kitābil-ḥakīm. (2)
Hudañw-wa raḥmatal-lilmuḥsinīn. (3) ᵓAlladhīna
yuqīmūnaṣ-Ṣalāta wa yuᵓtūnaz-Zakāta wa hum-
bilᵓĀkhirati hum yūqinūn. (4) ᵓUlāaᵓika ᶜalā hudam-
mir-Rabbihim wa ᵓulāaᵓika humul-mufliḥūn. (5)
Wa minan-nāsi mañy-yashtarī lahwal-ḥadīthi
liyuḍilla ᶜañ-sabīlil-lāhi bighayri ᶜilmiñw-wa yatta-
khidhahā huzuwā. ᵓUlāaᵓika lahum ᶜadhābum-
muhīn. (6) Wa ᵓidhā tutlā ᶜalayhi ᵓĀyātunā wallā
mustakbirañ-kaᵓal-lam yasmaᶜhā kaᵓanna fīi
ᵓudhunayhi waqrā. Fabashshirhu biᶜadhābin ᵓalīm.
(7) ᵓInnal-ladhīna ᵓāmanū wa ᶜamiluṣ-ṣāliḥāti lahum

---

1 See Appendix II.

2 See note 2 on 10 : 1.

3 The term *az-zakāh* seems to have here its more general meaning of "charity" rather than the legal connotation of "purifying dues" (see note 34 on 2 : 43), the more so as the above passage has a close inner resemblance to 2 : 2-4, where "spending on others out of what We provide as sustenance" is described as one of the characteristics of the God-conscious.

4 Lit., "among the people there is he who [or "such as"] takes playful [or "idle"] talk in exchange", i.e., for divine guidance: apparently an allusion to a pseudo-philosophical play with words and metaphysical speculations without any real meaning behind them (cf. note 38 on 23 : 67). Contrary to what some of the commentators assume, the above statement does not refer to any one person (allegedly a contemporary of the Prophet) but describes a *type* of mentality and has, therefore, a general import.

5 Cf. 23 : 66-67.

gardens of bliss, ‹8› to abide therein in accordance with God's true promise: for He alone is almighty, truly wise.[6] ‹9›

He [it is who] has created the skies without any supports that you could see,[7] and has placed firm mountains upon the earth, lest it sway with you,[8] and has caused all manner of living creatures to multiply thereon.

And We[9] send down water from the skies, and thus We cause every noble kind [of life] to grow on earth.[10] ‹10›

[All] this is God's creation: show Me, then, what others than He may have created! Nay, but the evildoers[11] are obviously lost in error! ‹11›

AND, INDEED, We granted this wisdom unto Luqmān:[12] "Be grateful unto God – for he who is grateful [unto Him] is but grateful for the good of his own self; whereas he who chooses to be ungrateful [ought to know that], verily, God is self-sufficient, ever to be praised!" ‹12›

And, lo, Luqmān spoke thus unto his son, admonishing him: "O my dear son![13] Do not ascribe divine powers to aught beside God: for, behold, such [a false] ascribing of divinity is indeed an awesome wrong! ‹13›

جَنَّٰتُ ٱلنَّعِيمِ (8) خَٰلِدِينَ فِيهَا وَعْدَ ٱللَّهِ حَقًّا وَهُوَ ٱلْعَزِيزُ
ٱلْحَكِيمُ (9) خَلَقَ ٱلسَّمَٰوَٰتِ بِغَيْرِ عَمَدٍ تَرَوْنَهَا وَأَلْقَىٰ فِى ٱلْأَرْضِ
رَوَٰسِىَ أَن تَمِيدَ بِكُمْ وَبَثَّ فِيهَا مِن كُلِّ دَآبَّةٍ وَأَنزَلْنَا مِنَ ٱلسَّمَآءِ مَآءً
فَأَنۢبَتْنَا فِيهَا مِن كُلِّ زَوْجٍ كَرِيمٍ (10) هَٰذَا خَلْقُ ٱللَّهِ فَأَرُونِى مَاذَا خَلَقَ
ٱلَّذِينَ مِن دُونِهِۦ بَلِ ٱلظَّٰلِمُونَ فِى ضَلَٰلٍ مُّبِينٍ (11) وَلَقَدْ ءَاتَيْنَا
لُقْمَٰنَ ٱلْحِكْمَةَ أَنِ ٱشْكُرْ لِلَّهِ وَمَن يَشْكُرْ فَإِنَّمَا يَشْكُرُ لِنَفْسِهِۦ وَمَن
كَفَرَ فَإِنَّ ٱللَّهَ غَنِىٌّ حَمِيدٌ (12) وَإِذْ قَالَ لُقْمَٰنُ لِٱبْنِهِۦ وَهُوَ يَعِظُهُۥ يَٰبُنَىَّ
لَا تُشْرِكْ بِٱللَّهِ إِنَّ ٱلشِّرْكَ لَظُلْمٌ عَظِيمٌ (13)

jannātun-naʿīm. (8) Khālidīna fīhā waʿdal-lāhi ḥaqqañw-wa Huwal-ʿAzīzul-Ḥakīm. (9) Khalaqas-samāwāti bighayri ʿamadiñ-tarawnahā wa ʾalqā fil-ʾarḍi rawāsiya ʾañ-tamīda bikum wa baththa fīhā miñ-kulli dāabbah. Wa ʾañzalnā minas-samāaʾi māaʾañ-faʾambatnā fīhā miñ-kulli zawjiñ-karīm. (10) Hādhā khalqul-lāhi faʾarūnī mādhā khalaqal-ladhīna miñ-dūnih. Baliẓ-ẓālimūna fī ḍalālim-mubīn. (11) Wa laqad ʾātaynā Luqmānal-ḥikmata ʾanish-kur lillāh. Wa mañy-yashkur faʾinnamā yashkuru linafsihī wa mañ-kafara faʾinnal-lāha Ghaniyyun Ḥamīd. (12) Wa ʾidh qāla Luqmānu libnihī wa huwa yaʿiẓuhū yā bunayya lā tushrik billāh. ʾInnash-shirka laẓulmun ʿaẓīm. (13)

6 Commenting on the above three verses, Rāzī points out, firstly, that the deliberate contrast between the plural in the promise of "gardens (*jannāt*) of bliss" and the singular in that of "suffering" (*ʿadhāb*) is meant to show that God's grace surpasses His wrath (cf. note 10 on 6 : 12); and, secondly, that the use of the expression "to abide therein" in connection with the mention of paradise only, and not with that of otherworldly suffering (or hell), is an indication that whereas the enjoyment of the former will be unlimited in duration, suffering in what is described as "hell" will be limited.

7 See note 4 on 13 : 2.

8 See note 11 on 16 : 15.

9 This is another of the many Qurʾanic instances where the personal pronoun relating to God is suddenly changed – in this instance, from "He" to "We" – in order to indicate that God, being infinite, cannot be circumscribed by any pronoun applicable to created, finite beings, and that the use of such pronouns with reference to Him is no more than a concession to the limited nature of every human language.

10 Lit., "thereon". As in 26 : 7, the term *zawj* has here the significance of "a kind".

11 Sc., "who ascribe divine powers to beings or things other than God".

12 Popularly (though without sufficient justification) identified with Aesop, Luqmān is a legendary figure firmly established in ancient Arabian tradition as a prototype of the sage who disdains worldly honours or benefits and strives for inner perfection. Celebrated in a poem by Ziyād ibn Muʿāwiyah (better known under his pen-name Nābighah adh-Dhubyānī), who lived in the sixth century of the Christian era, the person of Luqmān had become, long before the advent of Islam, a focal point of innumerable legends, stories and parables expressive of wisdom and spiritual maturity: and it is for this reason that the Qurʾān uses this mythical figure – as it uses the equally mythical figure of Al-Khiḍr in *sūrah* 18 – as a vehicle for some of its admonitions bearing upon the manner in which man ought to behave.

13 Lit., "O my little son" – a diminutive idiomatically expressive of endearment irrespective of whether the son is a child or a grown man.

وَوَصَّيْنَا ٱلْإِنسَٰنَ بِوَٰلِدَيْهِ حَمَلَتْهُ أُمُّهُۥ وَهْنًا عَلَىٰ وَهْنٍ وَفِصَٰلُهُۥ فِى
عَامَيْنِ أَنِ ٱشْكُرْ لِى وَلِوَٰلِدَيْكَ إِلَىَّ ٱلْمَصِيرُ ﴿14﴾ وَإِن جَٰهَدَاكَ عَلَىٰٓ
أَن تُشْرِكَ بِى مَا لَيْسَ لَكَ بِهِۦ عِلْمٌ فَلَا تُطِعْهُمَا وَصَاحِبْهُمَا فِى ٱلدُّنْيَا
مَعْرُوفًا وَٱتَّبِعْ سَبِيلَ مَنْ أَنَابَ إِلَىَّ ثُمَّ إِلَىَّ مَرْجِعُكُمْ فَأُنَبِّئُكُم بِمَا كُنتُمْ
تَعْمَلُونَ ﴿15﴾ يَٰبُنَىَّ إِنَّهَآ إِن تَكُ مِثْقَالَ حَبَّةٍ مِّنْ خَرْدَلٍ فَتَكُن فِى
صَخْرَةٍ أَوْ فِى ٱلسَّمَٰوَٰتِ أَوْ فِى ٱلْأَرْضِ يَأْتِ بِهَا ٱللَّهُ إِنَّ ٱللَّهَ لَطِيفٌ
خَبِيرٌ ﴿16﴾ يَٰبُنَىَّ أَقِمِ ٱلصَّلَوٰةَ وَأْمُرْ بِٱلْمَعْرُوفِ وَٱنْهَ عَنِ ٱلْمُنكَرِ
وَٱصْبِرْ عَلَىٰ مَآ أَصَابَكَ إِنَّ ذَٰلِكَ مِنْ عَزْمِ ٱلْأُمُورِ ﴿17﴾ وَلَا تُصَعِّرْ
خَدَّكَ لِلنَّاسِ وَلَا تَمْشِ فِى ٱلْأَرْضِ مَرَحًا إِنَّ ٱللَّهَ لَا يُحِبُّ كُلَّ مُخْتَالٍ
فَخُورٍ ﴿18﴾ وَٱقْصِدْ فِى مَشْيِكَ وَٱغْضُضْ مِن صَوْتِكَ إِنَّ أَنكَرَ ٱلْأَصْوَٰتِ
لَصَوْتُ ٱلْحَمِيرِ ﴿19﴾

Wa waṣṣaynal-ʾInsāna biwālidayhi ḥamalat-hu ʾummuhū wahnan ʿalā wahniñw-wa fiṣāluhū fī ʿāmayni ʾanish-kur lī wa liwālidayka ʾilayyal-maṣīr. ﴿14﴾ Wa ʾiñ-jāhadāka ʿalāa ʾañ-tushrika bī mā laysa laka bihī ʿilmuñ-falā tuṭiʿhumā wa ṣāḥibhumā fid-dunyā maʿrūfañw-wat-tabiʿ sabīla man ʾanāba ʾilayy. Thumma ʾilayya marjiʿukum faʾunabbiʾukum bimā kuñtum taʿmalūn. ﴿15﴾ Yā bunayya ʾinnahāa ʾiñ-taku mithqāla ḥabbatim-min khardaliñ-fatakuñ-fī ṣakhratin ʾaw fis-samāwāti ʾaw fil-ʾarḍi yaʾti bihal-lāh. ʾInnal-lāha Laṭīfun Khabīr. ﴿16﴾ Yā bunayya ʾaqimiṣ-Ṣalāta waʾ-mur bilmaʿrūfi wan-ha ʿanil-muñkari waṣ-bir ʿalā māa ʾaṣābaka ʾinna dhālika min ʿazmil-ʾumūr. ﴿17﴾ Wa lā tuṣaʿʿir khaddaka linnāsi wa lā tamshi fil-ʾarḍi maraḥā. ʾInnal-lāha lā yuḥibbu kulla mukhtāliñ-fakhūr. ﴿18﴾ Waq-ṣid fī mashyika wagh-ḍuḍ miñ-ṣawtik. ʾInna ʾañkaral-ʾaṣwāti laṣawtul-ḥamīr. ﴿19﴾

"And [God says:] 'We have enjoined upon man goodness towards his parents: his mother bore him by bearing strain upon strain, and his utter dependence on her lasted two years:[14] [hence, O man,] be grateful towards Me and towards thy parents, [and remember that] with Me is all journeys' end.[15] ‹14›

"'[Revere thy parents;] yet should they endeavour to make thee ascribe divinity, side by side with Me, to something which thy mind cannot accept [as divine],[16] obey them not; but [even then] bear them company in this world's life with kindness, and follow the path of those who turn towards Me. In the end, unto Me you all must return; and thereupon I shall make you [truly] understand all that you were doing [in life].' ‹15›

"O my dear son," [continued Luqmān,] "verily, though there be aught of but the weight of a mustard-seed, and though it be [hidden] in a rock, or in the skies, or in the earth, God will bring it to light: for, behold, God is unfathomable [in His wisdom], all-aware.[17] ‹16›

"O my dear son! Be constant in prayer, and enjoin the doing of what is right and forbid the doing of what is wrong, and bear in patience whatever [ill] may befall thee: this, behold, is something to set one's heart upon! ‹17›

"And turn not thy cheek away from people in [false] pride, and walk not haughtily on earth: for, behold, God does not love anyone who, out of self-conceit, acts in a boastful manner. ‹18›

"Hence, be modest in thy bearing, and lower thy voice: for, behold, the ugliest of all voices is the [loud] voice of asses . . ." ‹19›

---

14 Lit., "his weaning is [or "takes place"] within two years". According to some philologists, the term *fiṣāl* circumscribes the entire period of conception, gestation, birth and earliest infancy (*Tāj al-ʿArūs*): in brief, the period of a child's utter dependence on its mother.

15 Thus, gratitude towards parents, who were instrumental in one's coming to life, is here stipulated as a concomitant to man's gratitude towards God, who is the ultimate cause and source of his existence (cf. 17 : 23-24).

16 Lit., "something of which thou hast no knowledge", i.e., "something which is contrary to thy knowledge that divine qualities are God's alone" (cf. 29 : 8).

17 For my rendering of *laṭīf* as "unfathomable", see *sūrah* 6, note 89.

ARE YOU NOT aware that God has made subservient to you all[18] that is in the heavens and all that is on earth, and has lavished upon you His blessings, both outward and inward?[19]
And yet, among men there is many a one that argues about God without having any knowledge [of Him], without any guidance, and without any light-giving revelation; ‹20› and when such [people] are told to follow that which God has bestowed from on high, they answer, "Nay, we shall follow
حزب 42 that which we found our forefathers believing in and doing!"
Why – [would you follow your forefathers] even if Satan had invited them unto the suffering of the blazing flame?[20] ‹21›
Now whoever surrenders his whole being unto God,[21] and is a doer of good withal, has indeed taken hold of a support most unfailing: for with God rests the final outcome of all events. ‹22›
But as for him who is bent on denying the truth – let not his denial grieve thee: unto Us they must return, and then We shall make them [truly] understand all that they were doing [in life]: for, verily, God has full knowledge of what is in the hearts [of men]. ‹23› We will let them enjoy themselves for a short while – but in the end We shall drive them into suffering severe. ‹24›

AND THUS it is [with most people]: if[22] thou ask them, "Who is it that has created the heavens and the earth?" – they will surely answer, "God."
Say: "[Then you ought to know that] all praise is due to God!" – for most of them do not know [what this implies].[23] ‹25›

أَلَمْ تَرَوْاْ أَنَّ ٱللَّهَ سَخَّرَ لَكُم مَّا فِى ٱلسَّمَٰوَٰتِ وَمَا فِى ٱلْأَرْضِ وَأَسْبَغَ
عَلَيْكُمْ نِعَمَهُۥ ظَٰهِرَةً وَبَاطِنَةً ۗ وَمِنَ ٱلنَّاسِ مَن يُجَٰدِلُ فِى ٱللَّهِ بِغَيْرِ عِلْمٍ
وَلَا هُدًى وَلَا كِتَٰبٍ مُّنِيرٍ ﴿٢٠﴾ وَإِذَا قِيلَ لَهُمُ ٱتَّبِعُواْ مَآ أَنزَلَ ٱللَّهُ
قَالُواْ بَلْ نَتَّبِعُ مَا وَجَدْنَا عَلَيْهِ ءَابَآءَنَآ ۚ أَوَلَوْ كَانَ ٱلشَّيْطَٰنُ يَدْعُوهُمْ إِلَىٰ
عَذَابِ ٱلسَّعِيرِ ﴿٢١﴾ ۞ وَمَن يُسْلِمْ وَجْهَهُۥٓ إِلَى ٱللَّهِ وَهُوَ مُحْسِنٌ فَقَدِ
ٱسْتَمْسَكَ بِٱلْعُرْوَةِ ٱلْوُثْقَىٰ ۗ وَإِلَى ٱللَّهِ عَٰقِبَةُ ٱلْأُمُورِ ﴿٢٢﴾ وَمَن كَفَرَ فَلَا
يَحْزُنكَ كُفْرُهُۥٓ ۚ إِلَيْنَا مَرْجِعُهُمْ فَنُنَبِّئُهُم بِمَا عَمِلُوٓاْ ۚ إِنَّ ٱللَّهَ عَلِيمٌۢ بِذَاتِ
ٱلصُّدُورِ ﴿٢٣﴾ نُمَتِّعُهُمْ قَلِيلًا ثُمَّ نَضْطَرُّهُمْ إِلَىٰ عَذَابٍ غَلِيظٍ ﴿٢٤﴾ وَلَئِن
سَأَلْتَهُم مَّنْ خَلَقَ ٱلسَّمَٰوَٰتِ وَٱلْأَرْضَ لَيَقُولُنَّ ٱللَّهُ ۚ قُلِ ٱلْحَمْدُ لِلَّهِ ۚ بَلْ
أَكْثَرُهُمْ لَا يَعْلَمُونَ ﴿٢٥﴾

ʾAlam taraw ʾannal-lāha sakhkhara lakum-mā fis-samāwāti wa mā fil-ʾarḍi wa asbagha ʿalaykum niʿamahū ẓāhiratañw-wa bāṭinah. Wa minan-nāsi mañy-yujādilu fil-lāhi bighayri ʿilmiñw-wa lā hudañw-wa lā Kitābim-munīr. ⟨20⟩ Wa ʾidhā qīla lahumut-tabiʿū māa ʾañzalal-lāhu qālū bal nattabiʿu mā wajadnā ʿalayhi ʾābāaʾanā. ʾAwalaw kānash-Shayṭānu yadʿūhum ʾilā ʿadhābis-saʿīr. ⟨21⟩ ۞ Wa mañy-yuslim wajhahūu ʾilal-lāhi wa huwa muḥisnuñ-faqadis-tamsaka bilʿurwatil-wuthqā. Wa ʾilal-lāhi ʿāqibatul-ʾumūr. ⟨22⟩ Wa mañ-kafara falā yaḥzuñka kufruh. ʾIlaynā marjiʿuhum fanunabbiʾuhum-bimā ʿamilū. ʾInnal-lāha ʿAlīmum-bidhātiṣ-ṣudūr. ⟨23⟩ Numattiʿuhum qalīlañ-thumma naḍṭarruhum ʾilā ʿadhābin ghalīẓ. ⟨24⟩ Wa laʾiñ-saʾaltahum-man khalaqas-samāwāti wal-ʾarḍa layaqūlunnal-lāh. Qulil-ḥamdu lillāh. Bal ʾaktharuhum lā yaʿlamūn. ⟨25⟩

18 I.e., "has enabled you to derive benefit from all . . .", etc. (Cf. note 46 on 14 : 32-33.)

19 I.e., both visible and invisible benefits, as well as both physical and intellectual (or spiritual) endowments.

20 Regarding the implications of the term "Satan" in this context, see note 10 on 2 : 14 and note 16 on 15 : 17. As in many other places in the Qurʾān, the above verse expresses an oblique condemnation of the principle and practice of *taqlīd* (see Rāzī's observations quoted in note 38 on 26 : 74).

21 See note 91 on 2 : 112.

22 For the above rendering of *laʾin*, see *sūrah* 30, note 45.

23 I.e., they give the above answer unthinkingly, following a vague habit of thought, without realizing that a cognition

Unto God belongs all that is in the heavens and on earth. Verily, God alone is self-sufficient, the One to whom all praise is due! ⟨26⟩

And if all the trees on earth were pens, and the sea [were ink], with seven [more] seas yet[24] added to it, the words of God would not be exhausted: for, verily, God is almighty, wise.[25] ⟨27⟩

[For Him,] the creation of you all and the resurrection of you all is but like [the creation and resurrection of] a single soul:[26] for, verily, God is all-hearing, all-seeing. ⟨28⟩

Art thou not aware that it is God who makes the night grow longer by shortening the day, and makes the day grow longer by shortening the night, and that He has made the sun and the moon subservient [to His laws], each running its course for a term set [by Him][27] – and that God is fully aware of all that you do? ⟨29⟩

Thus it is, because God alone is the Ultimate Truth,[28] so that all that men invoke instead of Him is sheer falsehood; and because God alone is exalted, truly great! ⟨30⟩

Art thou not aware how the ships speed through the sea by God's favour, so that He might show you some of His wonders?

Herein, behold, there are messages indeed for all who are wholly patient in adversity and deeply grateful [to God]. ⟨31⟩

For [thus it is with most men:] when the waves engulf them like shadows [of death], they call unto God, sincere [at that moment] in their faith in Him alone: but as soon as He has brought them safe ashore, some of them stop half-way [between belief and unbelief].[29]

لِلَّهِ مَا فِى ٱلسَّمَٰوَٰتِ وَٱلْأَرْضِ إِنَّ ٱللَّهَ هُوَ ٱلْغَنِىُّ ٱلْحَمِيدُ ۝ وَلَوْ أَنَّمَا فِى ٱلْأَرْضِ مِن شَجَرَةٍ أَقْلَٰمٌ وَٱلْبَحْرُ يَمُدُّهُۥ مِنۢ بَعْدِهِۦ سَبْعَةُ أَبْحُرٍ مَّا نَفِدَتْ كَلِمَٰتُ ٱللَّهِ إِنَّ ٱللَّهَ عَزِيزٌ حَكِيمٌ ۝ مَّا خَلْقُكُمْ وَلَا بَعْثُكُمْ إِلَّا كَنَفْسٍ وَٰحِدَةٍ إِنَّ ٱللَّهَ سَمِيعٌۢ بَصِيرٌ ۝ أَلَمْ تَرَ أَنَّ ٱللَّهَ يُولِجُ ٱلَّيْلَ فِى ٱلنَّهَارِ وَيُولِجُ ٱلنَّهَارَ فِى ٱلَّيْلِ وَسَخَّرَ ٱلشَّمْسَ وَٱلْقَمَرَ كُلٌّ يَجْرِىٓ إِلَىٰٓ أَجَلٍ مُّسَمًّى وَأَنَّ ٱللَّهَ بِمَا تَعْمَلُونَ خَبِيرٌ ۝ ذَٰلِكَ بِأَنَّ ٱللَّهَ هُوَ ٱلْحَقُّ وَأَنَّ مَا يَدْعُونَ مِن دُونِهِ ٱلْبَٰطِلُ وَأَنَّ ٱللَّهَ هُوَ ٱلْعَلِىُّ ٱلْكَبِيرُ ۝ أَلَمْ تَرَ أَنَّ ٱلْفُلْكَ تَجْرِى فِى ٱلْبَحْرِ بِنِعْمَتِ ٱللَّهِ لِيُرِيَكُم مِّنْ ءَايَٰتِهِۦٓ إِنَّ فِى ذَٰلِكَ لَءَايَٰتٍ لِّكُلِّ صَبَّارٍ شَكُورٍ ۝ وَإِذَا غَشِيَهُم مَّوْجٌ كَٱلظُّلَلِ دَعَوُا۟ ٱللَّهَ مُخْلِصِينَ لَهُ ٱلدِّينَ فَلَمَّا نَجَّىٰهُمْ إِلَى ٱلْبَرِّ فَمِنْهُم مُّقْتَصِدٌ

Lillāhi mā fis-samāwāti wal-ʾarḍ. ʾInnal-lāha Huwal-Ghaniyyul-Ḥamīd. ⟨26⟩ Wa law ʾanna mā fil-ʾarḍi miñ-shajaratin ʾaqlāmuñw-wal-baḥru yamudduhū mim-baʿdihī sabʿatu ʾabḥurim-mā nafidat Kalimātul-lāh. ʾInnal-lāha ʿAzīzun Ḥakīm. ⟨27⟩ Mā khalqukum wa lā baʿthukum ʾillā kanafsiñw-wāḥidah. ʾInnal-lāha Samīʿum-Baṣīr. ⟨28⟩ ʾAlam tara ʾannal-lāha yūlijul-layla fin-nahāri wa yūlijun-nahāra fil-layli wa sakh-kharash-shamsa wal-qamara kulluñy-yajrī ʾilā ʾajalim-musammañw-wa ʾannal-lāha bimā taʿmalūna Khabīr. ⟨29⟩ Dhālika biʾannal-lāha Huwal-Ḥaqqu wa ʾanna mā yadʿūna miñ-dūnihil-bāṭilu wa ʾannal-lāha Huwal-ʿAliyyul-Kabīr. ⟨30⟩ ʾAlam tara ʾannal-fulka tajrī fil-baḥri biniʿmatil-lāhi liyuriyakum-min ʾĀyātih. ʾInna fī dhālika la-ʾĀyātil-likulli ṣabbārin-shakūr. ⟨31⟩ Wa ʾidhā ghashiyahum-mawjuñ-kaẓẓulali daʿawul-lāha mukhliṣīna lahud-dīn falammā najjāhum ʾilal-barri faminhum-muqtaṣid.

---

of God as the Ultimate Cause of all existence logically postulates one's full surrender to Him, and to Him alone.

24 Lit., "after that".

25 Cf. a similar passage in 18 : 109.

26 I.e., in view of His almightiness, there is no difference between the creation and resurrection of many and of one, just as every single soul is as much within His ken as is all mankind.

27 See note 5 on 13 : 2.

28 See *sūrah* 20, note 99.

29 Cf. 17 : 67, as well as 29 : 65, which says – in a similar context – that "they [begin to] ascribe to imaginary

Yet none could knowingly reject Our messages unless he be utterly perfidious, ingrate. ⟨32⟩

O MEN! Be conscious of your Sustainer, and stand in awe of the Day on which no parent will be of any avail to his child, nor a child will in the least avail his parent! Verily, God's promise [of resurrection] is true indeed: let not, then, the life of this world delude you, and let not [your own] deceptive thoughts about God delude you![30] ⟨33⟩

Verily, with God alone rests the knowledge of when the Last Hour will come; and He [it is who] sends down rain; and He [alone] knows what is in the wombs:[31] whereas no one knows what he will reap tomorrow, and no one knows in what land he will die. Verily, God [alone] is all-knowing, all-aware. ⟨34⟩

وَمَا يَجْحَدُ بِـَٔايَـٰتِنَآ إِلَّا كُلُّ خَتَّارٍ كَفُورٍ ﴿٣٢﴾ يَـٰٓأَيُّهَا ٱلنَّاسُ ٱتَّقُوا۟
رَبَّكُمْ وَٱخْشَوْا۟ يَوْمًا لَّا يَجْزِى وَالِدٌ عَن وَلَدِهِۦ وَلَا مَوْلُودٌ هُوَ جَازٍ عَن
وَالِدِهِۦ شَيْـًٔا ۚ إِنَّ وَعْدَ ٱللَّهِ حَقٌّ ۖ فَلَا تَغُرَّنَّكُمُ ٱلْحَيَوٰةُ ٱلدُّنْيَا وَلَا يَغُرَّنَّكُم
بِٱللَّهِ ٱلْغَرُورُ ﴿٣٣﴾ إِنَّ ٱللَّهَ عِندَهُۥ عِلْمُ ٱلسَّاعَةِ وَيُنَزِّلُ ٱلْغَيْثَ وَيَعْلَمُ مَا
فِى ٱلْأَرْحَامِ ۖ وَمَا تَدْرِى نَفْسٌ مَّاذَا تَكْسِبُ غَدًا ۖ وَمَا تَدْرِى نَفْسٌۢ بِأَىِّ
أَرْضٍ تَمُوتُ ۚ إِنَّ ٱللَّهَ عَلِيمٌ خَبِيرٌۢ ﴿٣٤﴾

Wa mā yajḥadu biʾĀyātinaa ʾillā kullu khattāriñ-kafūr. (32) Yaa ʾayyuhan-nāsut-taqū Rabbakum wakhshaw Yawmal-lā yajzī wālidun ʿañw-waladihī wa lā mawlūdun huwa jāzin ʿañw-wālidihī shayʾā. ʾInna waʿdal-lāhi ḥaqquñ-falā taghurrannakumul ḥayātud-dunyā wa lā yaghurrannakum-billāhil-gharūr. (33) ʾInnal-lāha ʿiñdahū ʿilmus-Sāʿati wa yunazzilul-ghaytha wa yaʿlamu mā fil-ʾarḥām. Wa mā tadrī nafsum-mādhā taksibu ghadañw-wa mā tadrī nafsum-biʾayyi ʾarḍiñ-tamūt. ʾInnal-lāha ʿAlīmun Khabīr. (34)

powers a share in His divinity" (*yushrikūn*). The parable of a storm at sea is, of course, a metonym applying to every kind of danger that may beset man in life.

30 For instance, the self-deluding expectation, while deliberately committing a sin, that God will forgive it (Saʿīd ibn Jubayr, as quoted by Ṭabarī, Baghawī, Zamakhsharī). According to Ṭabarī, the term *gharūr* denotes "anything that deludes" (*mā gharra*) a person in the moral sense, whether it be Satan, or another human being, or an abstract concept, or (as in 57 : 14) "wishful thinking".

31 This relates not merely to the problem of the sex of the as yet unborn embryo, but also to the question of whether it will be born at all, and if so, what its natural endowments and its character will be, as well as what role it will be able to play in life; and life itself is symbolized by the preceding mention of rain, and the end of all life in this world, by the mention of the Last Hour.

The Thirty-Second Sūrah

As-Sajdah (Prostration)

Mecca Period

ALMOST all the authorities agree in that this *sūrah* belongs to the late Mecca period, and that it was revealed immediately after *sūrah* 23 ("The Believers"). The view advanced by some commentators that verses 16-20 were revealed at Medina is purely speculative and does not deserve serious consideration.

The key-word which came to be accepted as the "title" of this *sūrah* is found in verse 15.

سورة السجدة مكية -32-
وآياتها ثلاثون

IN THE NAME OF GOD, THE MOST GRACIOUS, THE DISPENSER OF GRACE:

Alif. Lām. Mīm.[1] ‹1›
THE BESTOWAL from on high of this divine writ issues, beyond any doubt, from the Sustainer of all the worlds: ‹2› and yet,[2] they [who are bent on denying the truth] assert, "[Muḥammad] has invented it!"
Nay, but it is the truth from thy Sustainer, enabling thee to warn [this] people to whom no warner has come before thee, so that they might follow the right path. ‹3›

IT IS GOD who has created the heavens and the earth and all that is between them in six aeons, and is established on the throne of His almightiness.[3] You have none to protect you from God, and none to intercede for you [on Judgment Day]: will you not, then, bethink yourselves? ‹4›

بِسْمِ ٱللَّهِ ٱلرَّحْمَٰنِ ٱلرَّحِيمِ

الٓمٓ ﴿١﴾ تَنزِيلُ ٱلْكِتَٰبِ لَا رَيْبَ فِيهِ مِن رَّبِّ ٱلْعَٰلَمِينَ ﴿٢﴾ أَمْ
يَقُولُونَ ٱفْتَرَىٰهُ ۚ بَلْ هُوَ ٱلْحَقُّ مِن رَّبِّكَ لِتُنذِرَ قَوْمًا مَّآ أَتَىٰهُم مِّن نَّذِيرٍ مِّن
قَبْلِكَ لَعَلَّهُمْ يَهْتَدُونَ ﴿٣﴾ ٱللَّهُ ٱلَّذِى خَلَقَ ٱلسَّمَٰوَٰتِ وَٱلْأَرْضَ وَمَا
بَيْنَهُمَا فِى سِتَّةِ أَيَّامٍ ثُمَّ ٱسْتَوَىٰ عَلَى ٱلْعَرْشِ ۖ مَا لَكُم مِّن دُونِهِۦ مِن وَلِىٍّ
وَلَا شَفِيعٍ ۚ أَفَلَا تَتَذَكَّرُونَ ﴿٤﴾

Bismil-lāhir-Raḥmānir-Raḥīm.
ʾAlif-Lāam-Mīim. (1) Tańzīlul-Kitābi lā rayba fīhi mir-Rabbil-ᶜālamīn. (2) ʾAm yaqūlūnaf-tarāh. Bal huwal-ḥaqqu mir-Rabbika lituńdhira qawmam-māa ʾatāhum-min Nadhīrim-miń-qablika laᶜallahum yahtadūn. (3) ʾAllāhul-ladhī khalaqas-samāwāti wal-ʾarḍa wa mā baynahumā fī sittati ʾayyāmiń-thum-mas-tawā ᶜalal-ᶜarsh. Mā lakum-miń-dūnihī mińw-waliyyińw-wa lā shafīᶜin ʾafalā tatadhakkarūn. (4)

---

1 See Appendix II.
2 Cf. note 61 on 10 : 38.
3 See note 43 on 7 : 54.

ربع الحزب

He governs all that exists, from the celestial space to the earth; and in the end all shall ascend unto Him [for judgment] on a Day the length whereof will be [like] a thousand years of your reckoning.[4] ‹5›
Such is He who knows all that is beyond the reach of a created being's perception, as well as all that can be witnessed by a creature's senses or mind:[5] the Almighty, the Dispenser of Grace, ‹6› who makes most excellent everything that He creates.[6]
Thus, He begins the creation of man out of clay;[7] ‹7› then He causes him to be begotten[8] out of the essence of a humble fluid; ‹8› and then He forms him in accordance with what he is meant to be, and breathes into him of His spirit:[9] and [thus, O men,] He endows you with hearing, and sight, and feelings as well as minds:[10] [yet] how seldom are you grateful! ‹9›
For, [many are] they [who] say, "What! After we have been [dead and] lost in the earth, shall we indeed be [restored to life] in a new act of creation?"
Nay, but [by saying this] they deny the truth that they are destined to meet their Sustainer![11] ‹10›
Say: "[One day,] the angel of death who has been given charge of you will gather you, and then unto your Sustainer you will be brought back." ‹11›

يُدَبِّرُ ٱلْأَمْرَ مِنَ ٱلسَّمَآءِ إِلَى ٱلْأَرْضِ ثُمَّ يَعْرُجُ إِلَيْهِ فِى يَوْمٍ كَانَ مِقْدَارُهُۥٓ
أَلْفَ سَنَةٍ مِّمَّا تَعُدُّونَ ﴿٥﴾ ذَٰلِكَ عَٰلِمُ ٱلْغَيْبِ وَٱلشَّهَٰدَةِ ٱلْعَزِيزُ
ٱلرَّحِيمُ ﴿٦﴾ ٱلَّذِىٓ أَحْسَنَ كُلَّ شَىْءٍ خَلَقَهُۥ ۖ وَبَدَأَ خَلْقَ ٱلْإِنسَٰنِ مِن
طِينٍ ﴿٧﴾ ثُمَّ جَعَلَ نَسْلَهُۥ مِن سُلَٰلَةٍ مِّن مَّآءٍ مَّهِينٍ ﴿٨﴾ ثُمَّ سَوَّىٰهُ وَنَفَخَ فِيهِ
مِن رُّوحِهِۦ ۖ وَجَعَلَ لَكُمُ ٱلسَّمْعَ وَٱلْأَبْصَٰرَ وَٱلْأَفْـِٔدَةَ ۚ قَلِيلًا مَّا
تَشْكُرُونَ ﴿٩﴾ وَقَالُوٓا۟ أَءِذَا ضَلَلْنَا فِى ٱلْأَرْضِ أَءِنَّا لَفِى خَلْقٍ جَدِيدٍۭ ۚ بَلْ
هُم بِلِقَآءِ رَبِّهِمْ كَٰفِرُونَ ﴿١٠﴾ ۞ قُلْ يَتَوَفَّىٰكُم مَّلَكُ ٱلْمَوْتِ ٱلَّذِى وُكِّلَ
بِكُمْ ثُمَّ إِلَىٰ رَبِّكُمْ تُرْجَعُونَ ﴿١١﴾

Yudabbirul-ʾamra minas-samāaʾi ʾilal-ʾarḍi thumma yaʿruju ʾilayhi fī yawmiñ-kāna miqdāruhūu ʾalfa sanatim-mimmā taʿuddūn. ﴿5﴾ Dhālika ʿĀlimul-ghaybi wash-shahādatil-ʿAzīzur-Raḥīm. ﴿6﴾ ʾAlladhīi ʾaḥsana kulla shayʾin khalaqah. Wa badaʾa khalqal-ʾIñsāni miñ-ṭīn. ﴿7﴾ Thumma jaʿala naslahū miñ-sulālatim-mim-māaʾim-mahīn. ﴿8﴾ Thumma sawwāhu wa nafakha fīhi mir-Rūḥihī wa jaʿala lakumus-samʿa wal-ʾabṣāra wal-ʾafʾidata qalīlam-mā tashkurūn. ﴿9﴾ Wa qālūu ʾaʾidhā ḍalalnā fil-ʾarḍi ʾaʾinnā lafī khalqiñ-jadīd. Bal hum-biliqāaʾi Rabbihim kāfirūn. ﴿10﴾ ۞ Qul yatawaffākum-Malakul-mawtil-ladhī wukkila bikum thumma ʾilā Rabbikum turjaʿūn. ﴿11﴾

---

4 I.e., the Day of Judgment will seem to be endless to those who are judged. In the ancient Arabic idiom, a day that is trying or painful is described as "long", just as a happy day is spoken of as "short" (Marāghī XXI, 105).

5 See *sūrah* 6, note 65.

6 I.e., He fashions every detail of His creation in accordance with the functions intended for it, irrespective of whether those functions can be understood by us or are beyond the reach of our perception. In the text, the passage comprising verses 7-9 is in the past tense; but since it relates to a *continuous* act of creation, it signifies the present and the future as well as the past, and may, therefore, be suitably rendered in the present tense.

7 Cf. note 4 on 23 : 12. In view of the next verse, this "beginning" of man's creation seems to allude to the basic composition of the human body as such, as well as to each individual's pre-natal existence in the separate bodies of his parents.

8 Lit., "He caused [i.e., as pointed out in note 6 above, "He causes"] his procreation [or "his begetting"] to be out of . . .", etc.

9 As in 15 : 29 and 38 : 72, God's "breathing of His spirit into man" is a metaphor for the divine gift of life and consciousness, or of a "soul" (which, as pointed out in *sūrah* 4, note 181, is one of the meanings of the term *rūḥ*). Consequently, "the soul of every human being is of the spirit of God" (Rāzī). Regarding the verb *sawwāhu* – rendered by me as "He forms him in accordance with what he is meant to be" – see note 1 on 87 : 2 and note 5 on 91 : 7.

10 Lit., "hearts" (*afʾidah*), which in classical Arabic is a metonym for both "feelings" and "minds"; hence my composite rendering of this term.

11 Sc., "and thus, by implication, they deny His existence". (Cf. notes 11 and 12 on 13 : 5.)

If thou couldst but see [how it will be on Judgment Day,] when those who are lost in sin will hang their heads before their Sustainer, [saying:] "O our Sustainer! [Now] we have seen, and we have heard! Return us, then, [to our earthly life] that we may do good deeds: for [now], behold, we are certain [of the truth]!" ‹12›
Yet had We so willed, We could indeed have imposed Our guidance upon every human being:[12] but [We have not willed it thus – and so] that word of Mine has come true: "Most certainly will I fill hell with invisible beings as well as with humans, all together!"[13] ‹13›
[And He will say unto the sinners:] "Taste, then, [the recompense] for your having been oblivious of the coming of this your Day [of Judgment] – for, verily, We are [now] oblivious of you: taste, then, [this] abiding suffering for all [the evil] that you were wont to do!" ‹14›

ONLY THEY [truly] believe in Our messages who, whenever they are conveyed to them, fall down, prostrating themselves in adoration, and extol their Sustainer's limitless glory and praise; and who are never filled with false pride; ‹15› [and] who are impelled to rise[14] from their beds [at night] to call out to their Sustainer in fear and hope; and who spend on others out of what We provide for them as sustenance. ‹16›
And [as for all such believers,] no human being can imagine what blissful delights, as yet hidden, await them [in the life to come][15] as a reward for all that they did. ‹17›

وَلَوْ تَرَىٰٓ إِذِ ٱلْمُجْرِمُونَ نَاكِسُوا۟ رُءُوسِهِمْ عِندَ رَبِّهِمْ رَبَّنَآ أَبْصَرْنَا
وَسَمِعْنَا فَٱرْجِعْنَا نَعْمَلْ صَٰلِحًا إِنَّا مُوقِنُونَ ﴿١٢﴾ وَلَوْ شِئْنَا لَءَاتَيْنَا كُلَّ
نَفْسٍ هُدَىٰهَا وَلَٰكِنْ حَقَّ ٱلْقَوْلُ مِنِّى لَأَمْلَأَنَّ جَهَنَّمَ مِنَ ٱلْجِنَّةِ وَٱلنَّاسِ
أَجْمَعِينَ ﴿١٣﴾ فَذُوقُوا۟ بِمَا نَسِيتُمْ لِقَآءَ يَوْمِكُمْ هَٰذَآ إِنَّا نَسِينَٰكُمْ
وَذُوقُوا۟ عَذَابَ ٱلْخُلْدِ بِمَا كُنتُمْ تَعْمَلُونَ ﴿١٤﴾ إِنَّمَا يُؤْمِنُ بِـَٔايَٰتِنَا ٱلَّذِينَ السجدة
إِذَا ذُكِّرُوا۟ بِهَا خَرُّوا۟ سُجَّدًا وَسَبَّحُوا۟ بِحَمْدِ رَبِّهِمْ وَهُمْ لَا يَسْتَكْبِرُونَ
۩ ﴿١٥﴾ تَتَجَافَىٰ جُنُوبُهُمْ عَنِ ٱلْمَضَاجِعِ يَدْعُونَ رَبَّهُمْ خَوْفًا وَطَمَعًا
وَمِمَّا رَزَقْنَٰهُمْ يُنفِقُونَ ﴿١٦﴾ فَلَا تَعْلَمُ نَفْسٌ مَّآ أُخْفِىَ لَهُم مِّن قُرَّةِ أَعْيُنٍ
جَزَآءًۢ بِمَا كَانُوا۟ يَعْمَلُونَ ﴿١٧﴾

Wa law taraa ʾidhil-mujrimūna nākisū ruʾūsihim ʿiñda Rabbihim Rabbanāa ʾabṣarnā wa samiʿnā farjiʿnā naʿmal ṣāliḥan ʾinnā mūqinūn. (12) Wa law shiʾnā laʾātaynā kulla nafsin hudāhā wa lākin ḥaqqal-qawlu minnī laʾamlaʾanna jahannama minal-Jinnati wan-nāsi ʾajmaʿīn. (13) Fadhūqū bimā nasītum liqāaʾa Yawmikum hādhāa ʾinnā nasīnākum wa dhūqū ʿadhābal-khuldi bimā kuñtum taʿmalūn. (14) ʾInnamā yuʾminu biʾĀyātinal-ladhīna ʾidhā dhukkirū bihā kharrū sujjadañw-wa sabbaḥū biḥamdi Rabbihim wa hum lā yastakbirūn. ۩ (15) Tatajāfā junūbuhum ʿanil-maḍājiʿi yadʿūna Rabbahum khawfañw-wa ṭamaʿañw-wa mimmā razaqnāhum yuñfiqūn. (16) Falā taʿlamu nafsum-māa ʾukhfiya lahum-miñ-qurrati ʾaʿyuniñ-jazāaʾam-bimā kānū yaʿmalūn. (17)

12 Lit., "We could indeed have given unto every human being (*nafs*) his guidance", i.e., forcibly: but since this would have deprived man of his ability to choose between right and wrong – and, thus, of all moral responsibility – God does not "impose" His guidance upon anyone (cf. 26 : 4 and the corresponding note).

13 See 7 : 18 as well as the last paragraph of 11 : 119. As regards the "invisible beings" (*jinn*), see Appendix III.

14 Lit., "whose sides [i.e., bodies] restlessly rise".

15 Lit., "what is kept hidden for them [by way] of a joy of the eyes", i.e., of blissful delights, irrespective of whether seen, heard or felt. The expression "what is kept hidden for them" clearly alludes to the unknowable – and, therefore, only allegorically describable – quality of life in the hereafter. The impossibility of man's really "imagining" paradise has been summed up by the Prophet in the well-authenticated *ḥadīth*: "God says: 'I have readied for My righteous servants what no eye has ever seen, and no ear has ever heard, and no heart of man has ever conceived'" (Bukhārī and Muslim, on the authority of Abū Hurayrah; also Tirmidhī). This *ḥadīth* has always been regarded by the Companions as the Prophet's own comment on the above verse (cf. *Fatḥ al-Bārī* VIII, 418 f.).

Is, then, he who [in his earthly life] was a believer to be compared with one who was iniquitous? [Nay,] these two are not equal! ‹18›
As for those who attain to faith and do righteous deeds – gardens of rest await them, as a welcome [from God], in result of what they did; ‹19› but as for those who are lost in iniquity – their goal is the fire: as oft as they will try to come out of it, they will be thrown back into it; and they will be told, "Taste [now] this suffering through fire which you were wont to call a lie!" ‹20›
However, ere [We condemn them to] that supreme suffering, We shall most certainly let them taste of a suffering closer at hand,[16] so that they might [repent and] mend their ways.[17] ‹21›
And who could be more wicked than he to whom his Sustainer's messages are conveyed and who thereupon turns away from them? Verily, We shall inflict Our retribution on those who are [thus] lost in sin! ‹22›

AND, INDEED, [O Muḥammad,] We did vouchsafe revelation unto Moses [as well]: so be not in doubt of [thy] having met with the same [truth in the revelation vouchsafed to thee].[18]
And [just as] We caused that [earlier revelation] to be a guidance for the children of Israel, ‹23› and [as] We raised among them leaders who, so long as they bore themselves with patience and had sure faith in Our messages, guided [their

أَفَمَن كَانَ مُؤْمِنًا كَمَن كَانَ فَاسِقًا لَّا يَسْتَوُۥنَ ﴿18﴾ أَمَّا ٱلَّذِينَ ءَامَنُوا۟
وَعَمِلُوا۟ ٱلصَّٰلِحَٰتِ فَلَهُمْ جَنَّٰتُ ٱلْمَأْوَىٰ نُزُلًۢا بِمَا كَانُوا۟ يَعْمَلُونَ ﴿19﴾
وَأَمَّا ٱلَّذِينَ فَسَقُوا۟ فَمَأْوَىٰهُمُ ٱلنَّارُ ۖ كُلَّمَآ أَرَادُوٓا۟ أَن يَخْرُجُوا۟ مِنْهَآ أُعِيدُوا۟
فِيهَا وَقِيلَ لَهُمْ ذُوقُوا۟ عَذَابَ ٱلنَّارِ ٱلَّذِى كُنتُم بِهِۦ تُكَذِّبُونَ ﴿20﴾
وَلَنُذِيقَنَّهُم مِّنَ ٱلْعَذَابِ ٱلْأَدْنَىٰ دُونَ ٱلْعَذَابِ ٱلْأَكْبَرِ لَعَلَّهُمْ يَرْجِعُونَ ﴿21﴾
وَمَنْ أَظْلَمُ مِمَّن ذُكِّرَ بِـَٔايَٰتِ رَبِّهِۦ ثُمَّ أَعْرَضَ عَنْهَآ ۚ إِنَّا مِنَ ٱلْمُجْرِمِينَ
مُنتَقِمُونَ ﴿22﴾ وَلَقَدْ ءَاتَيْنَا مُوسَى ٱلْكِتَٰبَ فَلَا تَكُن فِى مِرْيَةٍ مِّن
لِّقَآئِهِۦ ۖ وَجَعَلْنَٰهُ هُدًى لِّبَنِىٓ إِسْرَٰٓءِيلَ ﴿23﴾ وَجَعَلْنَا مِنْهُمْ أَئِمَّةً يَهْدُونَ

ʾAfamañ-kāna muʾminañ-kamañ-kāna fāsiqā. Lā yastawūn. (18) ʾAmmal-ladhīna ʾāmanū wa ʿamiluṣ-ṣāliḥāti falahum jannātul-maʾwā nuzulam-bimā kānū yaʿmalūn. (19) Wa ʾammal-ladhīna fasaqū famaʾwā-humun-nār. Kullamāa ʾarādūu ʾañy-yakhrujū minhāa ʾuʿīdū fīhā wa qīla lahum dhūqū ʿadhāban-nāril-ladhī kuñtum-bihī tukadhdhibūn. (20) Wa lanudhīqan-nahum-minal-ʿadhābil-ʾadnā dūnal-ʿadhābil-ʾakbari laʿallahum yarjiʿūn. (21) Wa man ʾaẓlamu mimman-dhukkira biʾĀyāti Rabbihī thumma ʾaʿraḍa ʿanhā. ʾInnā minal-mujrimīna muñtaqimūn. (22) Wa laqad ʾātaynā Mūsal-Kitāba fala takuñ-fī miryatim-mil-liqāaʾihī wa jaʿalnāhu hudal-libanīi ʾIsrāaʾīl. (23) Wa jaʿalnā minhum ʾaʾimmatañy-yahdūna

16 Lit., "nearer", i.e., in this world: for an explanation, see note 27 on 52 : 47.
17 Lit., "so that they might return [to righteousness]".
18 With this passage the discourse returns to the theme enunciated at the beginning of this *sūrah* – namely, the divine origin of the revelation granted to Muḥammad, which, as the present passage points out, proceeds from the same source as that granted to Moses (the last of the great apostles of God accepted as such by all the three monotheistic religions, Judaism, Christianity and Islam). Furthermore, the identity of the fundamental truths in *all* divine revelations, stressed in the above verse, implies an identity of the moral demands made of the followers of those revelations irrespective of period, race or social environment.

people] in accordance with Our behest[19] – [so, too, shall it be with the divine writ revealed unto thee, O Muḥammad.][20] ‹24›

VERILY, it is your Sustainer alone who will decide between men[21] on Resurrection Day with regard to all on which they were wont to differ.[22] ‹25› [But] can, then, they [who deny the truth] learn no lesson by recalling how many a generation We have destroyed before their time,[23] – [people] in whose dwelling-places they [themselves now] walk about?
In this, behold, there are messages indeed: will they not, then, listen? ‹26›
Are they not aware that it is We who drive the rain onto dry land devoid of herbage, and thereby bring forth herbage of which their cattle and they themselves do eat? Can they not, then, see [the truth of resurrection]? ‹27›
But they answer: "When will that final decision take place, if what you [believers] say is true?"[24] ‹28›
Say: "On the Day of the Final Decision, their [newly-found] faith will be of no use to those who [in their lifetime] were bent on denying the truth, nor will they be granted respite!" ‹29› – and then leave them alone, and wait [for the truth to unfold as] they, behold, are waiting. . . . ‹30›

بِأَمْرِنَا لَمَّا صَبَرُواْ وَكَانُواْ بِـَٔايَـٰتِنَا يُوقِنُونَ ﴿٢٤﴾ إِنَّ رَبَّكَ هُوَ يَفْصِلُ
بَيْنَهُمْ يَوْمَ ٱلْقِيَـٰمَةِ فِيمَا كَانُواْ فِيهِ يَخْتَلِفُونَ ﴿٢٥﴾ أَوَلَمْ يَهْدِ لَهُمْ كَمْ
أَهْلَكْنَا مِن قَبْلِهِم مِّنَ ٱلْقُرُونِ يَمْشُونَ فِى مَسَـٰكِنِهِمْ إِنَّ فِى ذَٰلِكَ
لَـَٔايَـٰتٍ أَفَلَا يَسْمَعُونَ ﴿٢٦﴾ أَوَلَمْ يَرَوْاْ أَنَّا نَسُوقُ ٱلْمَآءَ إِلَى ٱلْأَرْضِ
ٱلْجُرُزِ فَنُخْرِجُ بِهِۦ زَرْعًا تَأْكُلُ مِنْهُ أَنْعَـٰمُهُمْ وَأَنفُسُهُمْ أَفَلَا
يُبْصِرُونَ ﴿٢٧﴾ وَيَقُولُونَ مَتَىٰ هَـٰذَا ٱلْفَتْحُ إِن كُنتُمْ صَـٰدِقِينَ ﴿٢٨﴾ قُلْ
يَوْمَ ٱلْفَتْحِ لَا يَنفَعُ ٱلَّذِينَ كَفَرُوٓاْ إِيمَـٰنُهُمْ وَلَا هُمْ يُنظَرُونَ ﴿٢٩﴾ فَأَعْرِضْ
عَنْهُمْ وَٱنتَظِرْ إِنَّهُم مُّنتَظِرُونَ ﴿٣٠﴾

biʾamrinā lammā ṣabarū; wa kānū biʾĀyātinā
yūqinūn. (24) ʾInna Rabbaka Huwa yafṣilu bayna-
hum Yawmal-Qiyāmati fīmā kānū fīhi yakhtalifūn.
(25) ʾAwalam yahdi lahum kam ʾahlaknā miñ-
qablihim-minal qurūni yamshūna fī masākinihim.
ʾInna fī dhālika laʾĀyātin ʾafalā yasmaʿūn. (26)
ʾAwalam yaraw ʾannā nasūqul-māaʾa ʾilal-ʾarḍil-
juruzi fanukhriju bihī zarʿañ-taʾkulu minhu
ʾanʿāmuhum wa ʾañfusuhum; ʾafalā yubṣirūn. (27)
Wa yaqūlūna matā hādhal-fatḥu ʾiñ-kuñtum ṣādiqīn.
(28) Qul Yawmal-Fatḥi lā yañfaʿul-ladhīna kafarūu
ʾīmānuhum wa lā hum yuñẓarūn. (29) Faʾaʿriḍ ʿan-
hum wañ-taẓir ʾinnahum-muñtaẓirūn. (30)

19 I.e., in accordance with the divine ordinances enunciated in and for their time in the Torah: an allusion to the decline of faith, frequently mentioned in the Qurʾān, among the children of Israel of later times, and to the tendency among many of their leaders and learned men to corrupt the text of the Torah and, thus, to "overlay the truth with falsehood" (see, e.g., 2 : 42, 75, 79, and the corresponding notes).

20 This interpolation reflects Zamakhsharī's commentary on the above passage, to the effect that the Qurʾān is destined to provide guidance and light so long as the community's religious leaders are patient in adversity and steadfast in their faith: an interpretation which implies that the Qurʾān will cease to be of benefit to people who have lost their moral virtues and their faith.

21 Lit., "between them".

22 See *sūrah* 2, note 94; also 22 : 67-69. In the present instance, this difference of opinion relates to belief in resurrection, on the one hand, and its denial, on the other.

23 For the wider meaning of the term *qarn* (lit., "generation"), see note 111 on 20 : 128.

24 A reference to the statement in verse 25.

The Thirty-Third Sūrah

Al-ʾAḥzāb (The Confederates)

Medina Period

THE DESIGNATION of this *sūrah* is derived from the references in verses 9-27 to the War of the Confederates, which took place in the year 5 H. (see note 13 below). The tone of these references, and especially of verse 20, shows that this part of the *sūrah* was revealed immediately after that war, i.e., towards the end of 5 H. Verses 37-40, which deal with the Prophet's marriage to Zaynab bint Jaḥsh, were revealed in the same year, probably a few months earlier; the same can be said of verses 4-5, which apparently contain an indirect allusion to the Prophet's adoptive relationship with Zaynab's first husband, Zayd ibn Ḥārithah (see in this connection note 42 below). On the other hand, verses 28-29 and 52 cannot have been revealed earlier than the year 7 H., and may even belong to a later period (cf. note 65 on verse 52). There is no clear evidence as to the date of the rest of this *sūrah*, although some authorities (e.g., Suyūṭī) maintain that much – if not most – of it was revealed after *sūrah* 3 ("The House of ʿImrān") and before *sūrah* 4 ("Women"), which would place it towards the end of 3 H. or in the early part of 4 H. In brief, it can be stated with certainty that the *sūrah* was revealed in small segments at various times between the end of the first and the middle of the last third of the Medina period. This, together with the fact that a considerable portion of it deals with the personal history of the Prophet, the relationship between him and his contemporaries – in particular, his family – and certain rules of behaviour which applied explicitly, and specifically, to his wives alone, explains why this *sūrah* is so complex in its structure and so diversified in its modes of expression.

سورة الأحزاب مدنية
-33-
وآياتها ثلاث وسبعون

IN THE NAME OF GOD, THE MOST GRACIOUS, THE DISPENSER OF GRACE:

O PROPHET! Remain conscious of God, and defer not to the deniers of the truth and the hypocrites: for God is truly all-knowing, wise. ⟨1⟩ And follow [but] that which comes unto thee through revelation from thy Sustainer:[1] for God is truly aware of all that you do, [O men]. ⟨2⟩ And place thy trust in God [alone]: for none is as worthy of trust as God. ⟨3⟩

NEVER has God endowed any man with two hearts in one body:[2] and [just as] He has never made your wives whom you may have declared to be "as unlawful to you as your mothers' bodies" [truly] your mothers,[3] so, too, has He never made your adopted sons [truly] your sons:[4] these are but [figures of] speech uttered by your mouths – whereas God speaks the [absolute] truth:[5] and it is He alone who can show [you] the right path. ⟨4⟩

بِسْمِ ٱللَّهِ ٱلرَّحْمَٰنِ ٱلرَّحِيمِ

يَٰٓأَيُّهَا ٱلنَّبِيُّ ٱتَّقِ ٱللَّهَ وَلَا تُطِعِ ٱلْكَٰفِرِينَ وَٱلْمُنَٰفِقِينَ ۗ إِنَّ ٱللَّهَ كَانَ
عَلِيمًا حَكِيمًا ﴿١﴾ وَٱتَّبِعْ مَا يُوحَىٰٓ إِلَيْكَ مِن رَّبِّكَ ۚ إِنَّ ٱللَّهَ كَانَ بِمَا
تَعْمَلُونَ خَبِيرًا ﴿٢﴾ وَتَوَكَّلْ عَلَى ٱللَّهِ ۚ وَكَفَىٰ بِٱللَّهِ وَكِيلًا ﴿٣﴾ مَّا جَعَلَ ٱللَّهُ
لِرَجُلٍ مِّن قَلْبَيْنِ فِى جَوْفِهِۦ ۚ وَمَا جَعَلَ أَزْوَٰجَكُمُ ٱلَّٰٓـِٔى تُظَٰهِرُونَ مِنْهُنَّ
أُمَّهَٰتِكُمْ ۚ وَمَا جَعَلَ أَدْعِيَآءَكُمْ أَبْنَآءَكُمْ ۚ ذَٰلِكُمْ قَوْلُكُم بِأَفْوَٰهِكُمْ ۖ
وَٱللَّهُ يَقُولُ ٱلْحَقَّ وَهُوَ يَهْدِى ٱلسَّبِيلَ ﴿٤﴾

نصف الحزب

Bismil-lāhir-Raḥmānir-Raḥīm.
Yāa ʾayyuhan-Nabiyyut-taqil-lāha wa lā tuṭiʿil-kāfirīna wal-munāfiqīn. ʾInnal-lāha kāna ʿAlīman Ḥakīmā. (1) Wat-tabiʿ mā yūḥāa ʾilayka mir-Rabbik. ʾInnal-lāha kāna bimā taʿmalūna khabīrā. (2) Wa tawakkal ʿalal-lāhi wa kafā billāhi Wakīlā. (3) Mā jaʿalal-lāhu lirajulim-miñ-qalbayni fī jawfih. Wa mā jaʿala ʾazwājakumul-lāaʾī tuẓāhirūna minhunna ʾummahātikum. Wa mā jaʿala adʿiyāaʿakum ʾabnāa-ʾakum. Dhālikum qawlukum-biʾafwāhikum; wal-lāhu yaqūlul-ḥaqqa wa Huwa yahdis-sabīl. (4)

---

1 Lit., "what is revealed to thee from thy Sustainer" – indicating that He is the *source* of all revelation.

2 Lit., "within him". In the first instance, this connects with the preceding passage, implying that man cannot be truly conscious of God and at the same time defer to the views of "the deniers of the truth and the hypocrites" (Rāzī). Beyond this, however, the above sentence forms a conceptual link with the sequence, which states that it is against the God-willed laws of nature – and, therefore, unreasonable and morally inadmissible – to attribute to one and the same person two mutually incompatible roles within the framework of human relationships (Zamakhsharī).

3 This is a reference to the pre-Islamic Arabian custom called *ẓihār*, whereby a husband could divorce his wife by simply declaring, "Thou art [henceforth as unlawful] to me as my mother's back", the term *ẓahr* ("back") being in this case a metonym for "body". In pagan Arab society, this mode of divorce was considered final and irrevocable; but a woman thus divorced was not allowed to remarry, and had to remain forever in her former husband's custody. As is evident from the first four verses of *sūrah* 58 (*Al-Mujādalah*) – which was revealed somewhat earlier than the present *sūrah* – this cruel pagan custom had already been abolished by the time of the revelation of the above verse, and is mentioned here only as an illustration of the subsequent dictum that the "figures of speech [lit., "your sayings"] which you utter with your mouths" do not necessarily coincide with the reality of human relations.

4 I.e., in the sense of blood relationship: hence, the marriage restrictions applying to real sons – and, by obvious implication, daughters as well – do not apply to adoptive children. This statement has a definite bearing on verses 37 ff. below.

5 Sc., by bringing into being the factual, biological relationship of parent and child in distinction from all

[As for your adopted children,] call them by their [real] fathers' names: this is more equitable in the sight of God; and if you know not who their fathers were, [call them] your brethren in faith and your friends.[6] However, you will incur no sin if you err in this respect:[7] [what really matters is] but what your hearts intend – for God is indeed much-forgiving, a dispenser of grace! ‹5›
The Prophet has a higher claim on the believers than [they have on] their own selves, [seeing that he is as a father to them] and his wives are their mothers:[8] and they who are [thus] closely related have, in accordance with God's decree, a higher claim upon one another than [was even the case between] the believers [of Yathrib] and those who had migrated [there for the sake of God].[9] None the less, you are to act with utmost goodness towards your [other] close friends as well:[10] this [too] is written down in God's decree. ‹6›

ٱدْعُوهُمْ لِءَابَآئِهِمْ هُوَ أَقْسَطُ عِندَ ٱللَّهِ ۚ فَإِن لَّمْ تَعْلَمُوٓا۟ ءَابَآءَهُمْ
فَإِخْوَٰنُكُمْ فِى ٱلدِّينِ وَمَوَٰلِيكُمْ ۚ وَلَيْسَ عَلَيْكُمْ جُنَاحٌ فِيمَآ أَخْطَأْتُم
بِهِۦ وَلَٰكِن مَّا تَعَمَّدَتْ قُلُوبُكُمْ ۚ وَكَانَ ٱللَّهُ غَفُورًا رَّحِيمًا ﴿٥﴾ ٱلنَّبِىُّ
أَوْلَىٰ بِٱلْمُؤْمِنِينَ مِنْ أَنفُسِهِمْ ۖ وَأَزْوَٰجُهُۥٓ أُمَّهَٰتُهُمْ ۗ وَأُو۟لُوا۟ ٱلْأَرْحَامِ
بَعْضُهُمْ أَوْلَىٰ بِبَعْضٍ فِى كِتَٰبِ ٱللَّهِ مِنَ ٱلْمُؤْمِنِينَ وَٱلْمُهَٰجِرِينَ إِلَّآ أَن
تَفْعَلُوٓا۟ إِلَىٰٓ أَوْلِيَآئِكُم مَّعْرُوفًا ۚ كَانَ ذَٰلِكَ فِى ٱلْكِتَٰبِ مَسْطُورًا ﴿٦﴾

ʾUdʿūhum liʾābāaʾihim huwa ʾaqsaṭu ʿiñdal-lāh. Faʾil-lam taʿlamūu ʾābāaʾahum faʾikhwānukum fid-dīni wa mawālīkum. Wa laysa ʿalaykum junāḥuñ-fīmāa ʾakhṭaʾtum-bihī wa lākim-mā taʿammadat qulūbukum. Wa kānal-lāhu Ghafūrar-Raḥīmā. ‹5› ʾAn-Nabiyyu ʾawlā bilmuʾminīna min ʾañfusihim wa ʾazwājuhūu ʾummahātuhum. Wa ʾulul-ʾarḥāmi baʿḍuhum ʾawlā bibaʿḍiñ-fī Kitābil-lāhi minal-muʾminīna wal-muhājirīna ʾillāa ʾañ-tafʿalūu ʾilāa ʾawliyāaʾikum-maʿrūfā. Kāna dhālika fil-Kitābi masṭūrā. ‹6›

man-made, social relationships like husband and wife, or foster-parent and adoptive child. In this connection it should be borne in mind that the Qurʾān frequently uses the metaphor of God's "speech" to express His creative activity.

6 I.e., "make it clear that your relationship is an adoptive one, and do not create the impression that they are your real children" – thus safeguarding their true identity.

7 I.e., by making a mistake in the attribution of the child's parentage, or by calling him or her, out of love, "my son" or "my daughter".

8 Thus, connecting with the preceding mention of voluntary, elective relationships (as contrasted with those by blood), this verse points to the highest manifestation of an elective, spiritual relationship: that of the God-inspired Prophet and the person who freely chooses to follow him. The Prophet himself is reported to have said: "None of you has real faith unless I am dearer unto him than his father, and his child, and all mankind" (Bukhārī and Muslim, on the authority of Anas, with several almost identical versions in other compilations). The Companions invariably regarded the Prophet as the spiritual father of his community. Some of them – e.g., Ibn Masʿūd (as quoted by Zamakhsharī) or Ubayy ibn Kaʿb, Ibn ʿAbbās and Muʿāwiyah (as quoted by Ibn Kathīr) – hardly ever recited the above verse without adding, by way of explanation, "seeing that he is [as] a father to them"; and many of the *tābiʿīn* – including Mujāhid, Qatādah, ʿIkrimah and Al-Ḥasan (cf. Ṭabarī and Ibn Kathīr) – did the same: hence my interpolation, between brackets, of this phrase. (However, see also verse 40 of this *sūrah* and the corresponding note 50.) As regards the status of the Prophet's wives as the "mothers of the believers", this arises primarily from the fact of their having shared the life of God's Apostle in its most intimate aspect. Consequently, they could not remarry after his death (see verse 53 below), since all the believers were, spiritually, their "children".

9 See note 86 on the last but one sentence of 8 : 75. As explained in that note, neither of these two passages (8 : 75 and 33 : 6) can be satisfactorily interpreted as bearing on the laws of inheritance: all endeavours to interpret them in that sense only do violence to the logical build-up and inner cohesion of the Qurʾanic discourse. On the other hand, it is obvious that both passages have basically a similar (namely, spiritual) import – with the difference only that whereas the concluding sentences of *Al-Anfāl* refer to the brotherhood of all believers in general, the present passage lays stress on the yet deeper, special relationship between every true believer and God's Apostle.

10 I.e., towards all other believers, as stressed so often in the Qurʾān, and particularly in 8 : 75 (see preceding note): in other words, a believer's exalted love for the Prophet should not blind him to the fact that "*all* believers are brethren" (49 : 10). The extremely complex term *maʿrūf,* rendered by me in this context as "utmost goodness", may be defined as "any act [or attitude] the goodness whereof is evident to reason" (Rāghib).

AND LO! We did accept a solemn pledge from all the prophets[11] – from thee, [O Muḥammad,] as well as from Noah, and Abraham, and Moses, and Jesus the son of Mary: – for We accepted a most weighty, solemn pledge from [all of] them, ‹7› so that [at the end of time] He might ask those men of truth as to [what response] their truthfulness [had received on earth].[12] And grievous suffering has He readied for all who deny the truth! ‹8›

O YOU who have attained to faith! Call to mind the blessings which God bestowed on you [at the time] when [enemy] hosts came down upon you, whereupon We let loose against them a stormwind and [heavenly] hosts that you could not see:[13] yet God saw all that you did. ‹9›
[Remember what you felt] when they came upon you from above you and from below you,[14] and when [your] eyes became dim and [your] hearts came up to [your] throats, and [when] most conflicting thoughts about God passed through your minds:[15] ‹10›

وَإِذْ أَخَذْنَا مِنَ ٱلنَّبِيِّـۧنَ مِيثَـٰقَهُمْ وَمِنكَ وَمِن نُّوحٍ وَإِبْرَٰهِيمَ وَمُوسَىٰ
وَعِيسَى ٱبْنِ مَرْيَمَ ۖ وَأَخَذْنَا مِنْهُم مِّيثَـٰقًا غَلِيظًا ﴿7﴾ لِّيَسْـَٔلَ ٱلصَّـٰدِقِينَ
عَن صِدْقِهِمْ ۚ وَأَعَدَّ لِلْكَـٰفِرِينَ عَذَابًا أَلِيمًا ﴿8﴾ يَـٰٓأَيُّهَا ٱلَّذِينَ ءَامَنُوا۟
ٱذْكُرُوا۟ نِعْمَةَ ٱللَّهِ عَلَيْكُمْ إِذْ جَآءَتْكُمْ جُنُودٌ فَأَرْسَلْنَا عَلَيْهِمْ رِيحًا
وَجُنُودًا لَّمْ تَرَوْهَا ۚ وَكَانَ ٱللَّهُ بِمَا تَعْمَلُونَ بَصِيرًا ﴿9﴾ إِذْ جَآءُوكُم مِّن
فَوْقِكُمْ وَمِنْ أَسْفَلَ مِنكُمْ وَإِذْ زَاغَتِ ٱلْأَبْصَـٰرُ وَبَلَغَتِ ٱلْقُلُوبُ
ٱلْحَنَاجِرَ وَتَظُنُّونَ بِٱللَّهِ ٱلظُّنُونَا۠ ﴿10﴾

Wa ʾidh ʾakhadhnā minan-Nabiyyīna mīthāqahum wa miñka wa miñ-Nūḥiñw-wa ʾIbrāhīma wa Mūsā wa ʿĪsab-ni Maryama wa ʾakhadhnā minhum-mīthāqan ghalīẓā. (7) Liyasʾalaṣ-ṣādiqīna ʿañ-ṣidqihim; wa ʾaʿadda lilkāfirīna ʿadhāban ʾalīmā. (8) Yāa ʾayyuhal-ladhīna ʾāmanudh-kurū niʿmatal-lāhi ʿalaykum ʾidh jāaʾatkum junūduñ-faʾarsalnā ʿalayhim rīḥañw-wa junūdal-lam tarawhā; wa kānal-lāhu bimā taʿmalūna Baṣīrā. (9) ʾIdh jāaʾūkum-miñ-fawqikum wa min ʾasfala miñkum wa ʾidh zāghatil-ʾabṣāru wa balaghatil-qulūbul-ḥanājira wa taẓunnūna billāhiẓ-ẓunūnā. (10)

11 This parenthetic passage connects with verses 1-3 above, and relates to every prophet's "pledge" – i.e., sacred duty – to convey God's message to man, and thus to act as "a bearer of glad tidings and a warner". (For my rendering of *idh*, in this context, as "lo", see *sūrah* 2, note 21.)

12 Cf. 5 : 109 and, more particularly, 7 : 6 – "We shall most certainly call to account all those unto whom a [divine] message was sent, and We shall most certainly call to account the message-bearers [themselves]".

13 Cf. 3 : 124-125 and the corresponding note 93. The present passage (verses 9-27) relates to the War of the Confederates (*al-aḥzāb*) – also called the War of the Trench (*al-khandaq*) – which took place in 5 H. At the instigation of the Jewish tribe of Banu 'n-Naḍīr, who had been expelled from Yathrib (Medina) after they had broken the treaty binding them to the Muslims, several of the most powerful Abrabian tribes formed a confederacy with a view to overcoming, once and for all, the threat posed by Islam to the beliefs and many of the customs of pagan Arabia. In the month of Shawwāl, 5 H., a force of well over 12,000 men, composed of the Quraysh and their allies – the Banū Kinānah, Banū Asad and the people of the coastlands (the Tihāmah), as well as the great Najdī tribe of Ghaṭafān and its allies, the Hawāzin (or Banū ʿĀmir) and Banū Sulaym – converged upon Medina. Forewarned of their coming, the Prophet had ordered a deep trench to be dug around the town – a defensive measure unknown in pre-Islamic Arabia – and thus brought the assault of the Confederates to a halt. At that point, however, another danger arose for the Muslims: the Jewish tribe of Banū Qurayẓah, who lived in the outskirts of Medina and until then had been allied with the Muslims, broke the treaty of alliance and openly joined the Confederates. Nevertheless, during a siege lasting several weeks all the attempts of the latter to cross the trench – manned by the numerically much weaker and less well-armed Muslims – were repulsed with heavy losses to the attackers; dissensions, based on mutual distrust, gradually undermined the much-vaunted alliance between the Jewish and the pagan Arab tribes; in the month of Dhu 'l-Qaʿdah their frustration became complete when a bitterly-cold stormwind raged for several days, making life unbearable even for hardened warriors. And so, finally, the siege was raised and the Confederates dispersed, thus ending the last attempt of the pagans to destroy the Prophet and his community.

14 The Ghaṭafān group tried to take the trench by assault from the upper, eastern part of the Medina plain, while the Quraysh and their allies launched an attack from its lower, i.e., western part (Zamakhsharī), and this obviously in consonance with their original lines of approach – the Ghaṭafān having come from the highlands (Najd), and the Quraysh from the coastal lowlands (the Tihāmah).

15 Lit., "[when] you thought all [manner of] thoughts about God": i.e., "whether He would save you or allow your

[for] there and then were the believers tried, and shaken with a shock severe. ‹11›
And [remember how it was] when the hypocrites and those with hearts diseased[16] said [to one another], "God and His Apostle have promised us nothing but delusions!"[17] ‹12› – and when some of them said, "O you people of Yathrib! You cannot withstand [the enemy] here:[18] hence, go back [to your homes]!" – whereupon a party from among them asked leave of the Prophet, saying, "Behold, our houses are exposed [to attack]!" – the while they were not [really] exposed: they wanted nothing but to flee. ‹13›
Now if their town had been stormed,[19] and they had been asked [by the enemy] to commit apostasy, [the hypocrites] would have done so without much delay[20] ‹14› – although ere that they had vowed before God that they would never turn their backs [on His message]: and a vow made to God must surely be answered for! ‹15›
Say: "Whether you flee from [natural] death or from being slain [in battle], flight will not profit you – for, however you fare,[21] you are not [allowed] to enjoy life for more than a little while!" ‹16›
Say: "Who is there that could keep you away from God if it be His will to harm you, or if it be His will to show you mercy?"
For, [do they not know that] besides God they can find none to protect them, and none to bring them succour? ‹17›

هُنَالِكَ ٱبْتُلِىَ ٱلْمُؤْمِنُونَ وَزُلْزِلُوا۟ زِلْزَالًا شَدِيدًا ﴿11﴾ وَإِذْ يَقُولُ
ٱلْمُنَٰفِقُونَ وَٱلَّذِينَ فِى قُلُوبِهِم مَّرَضٌ مَّا وَعَدَنَا ٱللَّهُ وَرَسُولُهُۥٓ إِلَّا غُرُورًا ﴿12﴾
وَإِذْ قَالَت طَّآئِفَةٌ مِّنْهُمْ يَٰٓأَهْلَ يَثْرِبَ لَا مُقَامَ لَكُمْ فَٱرْجِعُوا۟ ۚ وَيَسْتَـْٔذِنُ
فَرِيقٌ مِّنْهُمُ ٱلنَّبِىَّ يَقُولُونَ إِنَّ بُيُوتَنَا عَوْرَةٌ وَمَا هِىَ بِعَوْرَةٍ ۖ إِن يُرِيدُونَ
إِلَّا فِرَارًا ﴿13﴾ وَلَوْ دُخِلَتْ عَلَيْهِم مِّنْ أَقْطَارِهَا ثُمَّ سُئِلُوا۟ ٱلْفِتْنَةَ لَءَاتَوْهَا
وَمَا تَلَبَّثُوا۟ بِهَآ إِلَّا يَسِيرًا ﴿14﴾ وَلَقَدْ كَانُوا۟ عَٰهَدُوا۟ ٱللَّهَ مِن قَبْلُ لَا يُوَلُّونَ
ٱلْأَدْبَٰرَ ۚ وَكَانَ عَهْدُ ٱللَّهِ مَسْـُٔولًا ﴿15﴾ قُل لَّن يَنفَعَكُمُ ٱلْفِرَارُ إِن فَرَرْتُم
مِّنَ ٱلْمَوْتِ أَوِ ٱلْقَتْلِ وَإِذًا لَّا تُمَتَّعُونَ إِلَّا قَلِيلًا ﴿16﴾ قُلْ مَن ذَا ٱلَّذِى
يَعْصِمُكُم مِّنَ ٱللَّهِ إِنْ أَرَادَ بِكُمْ سُوٓءًا أَوْ أَرَادَ بِكُمْ رَحْمَةً ۚ وَلَا
يَجِدُونَ لَهُم مِّن دُونِ ٱللَّهِ وَلِيًّا وَلَا نَصِيرًا ﴿17﴾

Hunālikab-tuliyal-muʾminūna wa zulzilū zilzālañ-shadīdā. (11) Wa ʾidh yaqūlul-munāfiqūna wal-ladhīna fī qulūbihim-maraḍum-mā waʿadanal-lāhu wa Rasūluhūu ʾillā ghurūrā. (12) Wa ʾidh qālaṭ-ṭāaʾifatum-minhum yāa ʾahla Yathriba lā muqāma lakum farjiʿū; wa yastaʾdhinu farīqum-minhumun-Nabiyya yaqūlūna ʾinna buyūtanā ʿawratuñw-wa mā hiya biʿawratin ʾiñy-yurīdūna ʾillā firārā. (13) Wa law dukhilat ʿalayhim-min ʾaqṭārihā thumma suʾilul-fitnata laʾatawhā wa mā talabbathū bihāa ʾillā yasīrā. (14) Wa laqad kānū ʿāhadul-lāha miñ-qablu lā yuwallūnal-ʾadbāra wa kāna ʿahdul-lāhi masʾūlā. (15) Qul-lañy-yañfaʿakumul-firāru ʾiñ-farartum-minal-mawti ʾawil-qatli wa ʾidhal-lā tumattaʿūna ʾillā qalīlā. (16) Qul mañ-dhal-ladhī yaʿṣimukum-minal-lāhi ʾin ʾarāda bikum sūuʾan ʾaw ʾarāda bikum raḥmah. Wa lā yajidūna lahum-miñ-dūnil-lāhi wa-liyyañw-wa lā naṣīrā. (17)

enemies to triumph".

16 This phrase obviously denotes here the weak of faith among the believers.

17 This is a reference to Muḥammad's prophetic vision, at the time of digging the trench, of the future Muslim conquest of the whole Arabian Peninsula as well as of the Persian and Byzantine Empires (Ṭabarī). Several authentic Traditions testify to the Prophet's announcement of this vision at the time in question.

18 I.e., outside the city, defending the trench.

19 Lit., "if entry to them had been forced".

20 Lit., "and would not have tarried more than a little [while]".

21 Lit., "for then" or "in that case" (*idhan*), signifying here "however it may be".

God is indeed aware of those of you who would divert others [from fighting in His cause], as well as of those who say to their brethren, "Come hither to us [and face the enemy]!" – the while they [themselves] join battle but seldom, ‹18› begrudging you all help. But then, when danger threatens, thou canst see them looking to thee [for help, O Prophet], their eyes rolling [in terror] like [the eyes of] one who is overshadowed by death: yet as soon as the danger has passed, they will assail you [believers] with sharp tongues, begrudging you all that is good!
[People like] these have never known faith – and therefore God will cause all their works to come to nought: for this is indeed easy for God. ‹19›
They think that the Confederates have not [really] withdrawn;[22] and should the Confederates return, these [hypocrites] would prefer to be in the desert, among the bedouin, asking for news about you, [O believers, from far away;] and even were they to find themselves in your midst, they would but make a pretence at fighting [by your side].[23] ‹20›

VERILY, in the Apostle of God you have a good example for everyone who looks forward [with hope and awe] to God and the Last Day, and remembers God unceasingly.[24] ‹21›
And [so,] when the believers saw the Confederates [advancing against them], they said, "This is what God and His Apostle have promised us!" – and, "Truly spoke God

۞ قَدْ يَعْلَمُ ٱللَّهُ ٱلْمُعَوِّقِينَ مِنكُمْ وَٱلْقَآئِلِينَ لِإِخْوَٰنِهِمْ هَلُمَّ إِلَيْنَا ۖ وَلَا
يَأْتُونَ ٱلْبَأْسَ إِلَّا قَلِيلًا ﴿١٨﴾ أَشِحَّةً عَلَيْكُمْ ۖ فَإِذَا جَآءَ ٱلْخَوْفُ
رَأَيْتَهُمْ يَنظُرُونَ إِلَيْكَ تَدُورُ أَعْيُنُهُمْ كَٱلَّذِى يُغْشَىٰ عَلَيْهِ مِنَ ٱلْمَوْتِ ۖ
فَإِذَا ذَهَبَ ٱلْخَوْفُ سَلَقُوكُم بِأَلْسِنَةٍ حِدَادٍ أَشِحَّةً عَلَى ٱلْخَيْرِ ۚ أُو۟لَٰٓئِكَ
لَمْ يُؤْمِنُوا۟ فَأَحْبَطَ ٱللَّهُ أَعْمَٰلَهُمْ ۚ وَكَانَ ذَٰلِكَ عَلَى ٱللَّهِ يَسِيرًا ﴿١٩﴾
يَحْسَبُونَ ٱلْأَحْزَابَ لَمْ يَذْهَبُوا۟ ۖ وَإِن يَأْتِ ٱلْأَحْزَابُ يَوَدُّوا۟ لَوْ أَنَّهُم
بَادُونَ فِى ٱلْأَعْرَابِ يَسْـَٔلُونَ عَنْ أَنۢبَآئِكُمْ ۖ وَلَوْ كَانُوا۟ فِيكُم مَّا قَٰتَلُوٓا۟
إِلَّا قَلِيلًا ﴿٢٠﴾ لَّقَدْ كَانَ لَكُمْ فِى رَسُولِ ٱللَّهِ أُسْوَةٌ حَسَنَةٌ لِّمَن كَانَ
يَرْجُوا۟ ٱللَّهَ وَٱلْيَوْمَ ٱلْءَاخِرَ وَذَكَرَ ٱللَّهَ كَثِيرًا ﴿٢١﴾ وَلَمَّا رَءَا
ٱلْمُؤْمِنُونَ ٱلْأَحْزَابَ قَالُوا۟ هَٰذَا مَا وَعَدَنَا ٱللَّهُ وَرَسُولُهُۥ وَصَدَقَ ٱللَّهُ

ثلاثة ارباع الحزب

◈ Qad yaᶜlamul-lāhul-muᶜawwiqīna miñkum wal-qāaʾilīna liʾikhwānihim halumma ʾilaynā wa lā yaʾtūnal-baʾsa ʾillā qalīlā. (18) ʾAshiḥḥatan ᶜalaykum. Faʾidhā jāaʾal-khawfu raʾaytahum yañẓurūna ʾilayka tadūru ʾaᶜyunuhum kalladhī yughshā ᶜalayhi minal-mawt. Faʾidhā dhahabal-khawfu salaqūkum-biʾalsinatin ḥidādin ʾashiḥḥatan ᶜalal-khayr. ʾUlāaʾika lam yuʾminū faʾaḥbaṭal-lāhu ʾaᶜmālahum; wa kana dhālika ᶜalal-lāhi yasīrā. (19) Yaḥsabūnal-ʾAḥzāba lam yadhhabū; wa ʾiñy-yaʾtil-ʾAḥzābu yawaddū law ʾannahum-bādūna fil-ʾaᶜrābi yasʾalūna ᶜan ʾambāaʾikum; wa law kānū fīkum-mā qātalūu ʾillā qalīlā. (20) Laqad kāna lakum fī Rasūlil-lāhi ʾuswatun ḥasanatul-limañ-kāna yarjul-lāha wal-Yawmal-ʾĀkhira wa dhakaral-lāha kathīrā. (21) Wa lammā raʾal-muʾminūnal-ʾAḥzāba qālū hādhā mā waᶜadanal-lāhu wa Rasūluhū wa ṣadaqal-lāhu

22 Sc., "but would come back in force and resume the siege".
23 Lit., "they would not fight except a little".
24 This verse (and the passage that follows) connects with verses 9-11 above, and especially with verse 11 – "there and then were the believers tried, and shaken with a shock severe" – which summarizes, as it were, their experiences during the critical days and weeks of the War of the Trench. Although it is addressed, in the first instance, to those early defenders of Medina who were thus exhorted to emulate the Prophet's faith, courage and steadfastness, the above verse is timeless in its import and its validity for all situations and conditions. – Since the verb *rajawa*, as well as the noun-forms *rajw*, *rujuww* and *rajāʾ* derived from it, carry the connotation of both "hope" and "fear" (or "awe"), I have rendered *yarjū* accordingly.

and His Apostle!"[25] – and all this but increased their faith and their readiness to surrender themselves unto God. ‹22›
Among the believers are men who have [always] been true to what they have vowed before God;[26] and among them are such as have [already] redeemed their pledge by death, and such as yet await [its fulfilment] without having changed [their resolve] in the least. ‹23›
[Such trials are imposed upon man] so that God may reward the truthful for having been true to their word, and cause the hypocrites to suffer – if that be His will – or [if they repent,] accept their repentance:[27] for, verily, God is indeed much-forgiving, a dispenser of grace! ‹24›
Thus, for all their fury, God repulsed those who were bent on denying the truth;[28] no advantage did they gain, since God was enough to [protect] the believers in battle – seeing that God is most powerful, almighty; ‹25› – and He brought down from their strongholds those of the followers of earlier revelation who had aided the aggressors,[29] and cast terror into their hearts: some you slew, and some you made captive; ‹26› and He made you heirs to their lands, and their houses, and their goods – and [promised you] lands on which you had never yet set foot:[30] for God has indeed the power to will anything. ‹27›

وَرَسُولُهُۥ ۚ وَمَا زَادَهُمْ إِلَّآ إِيمَٰنًا وَتَسْلِيمًا (22) مِّنَ ٱلْمُؤْمِنِينَ رِجَالٌ
صَدَقُوا۟ مَا عَٰهَدُوا۟ ٱللَّهَ عَلَيْهِ ۖ فَمِنْهُم مَّن قَضَىٰ نَحْبَهُۥ وَمِنْهُم مَّن يَنتَظِرُ ۖ
وَمَا بَدَّلُوا۟ تَبْدِيلًا (23) لِّيَجْزِىَ ٱللَّهُ ٱلصَّٰدِقِينَ بِصِدْقِهِمْ وَيُعَذِّبَ
ٱلْمُنَٰفِقِينَ إِن شَآءَ أَوْ يَتُوبَ عَلَيْهِمْ ۚ إِنَّ ٱللَّهَ كَانَ غَفُورًا رَّحِيمًا (24)
وَرَدَّ ٱللَّهُ ٱلَّذِينَ كَفَرُوا۟ بِغَيْظِهِمْ لَمْ يَنَالُوا۟ خَيْرًا ۚ وَكَفَى ٱللَّهُ ٱلْمُؤْمِنِينَ
ٱلْقِتَالَ ۚ وَكَانَ ٱللَّهُ قَوِيًّا عَزِيزًا (25) وَأَنزَلَ ٱلَّذِينَ ظَٰهَرُوهُم مِّنْ أَهْلِ
ٱلْكِتَٰبِ مِن صَيَاصِيهِمْ وَقَذَفَ فِى قُلُوبِهِمُ ٱلرُّعْبَ فَرِيقًا تَقْتُلُونَ
وَتَأْسِرُونَ فَرِيقًا (26) وَأَوْرَثَكُمْ أَرْضَهُمْ وَدِيَٰرَهُمْ وَأَمْوَٰلَهُمْ وَأَرْضًا لَّمْ
تَطَـُٔوهَا ۚ وَكَانَ ٱللَّهُ عَلَىٰ كُلِّ شَىْءٍ قَدِيرًا (27)

wa Rasūluhū wa mā zādahum ʾillāa ʾīmānañw-wa taslīmā. (22) Minal-muʾminīna rijāluñ-ṣadaqū mā ʿāhadul-lāha ʿalayhi faminhum-mañ-qaḍā naḥbahū wa minhum-mañy-yañtaẓiru wa mā baddalū tabdīlā. (23) Liyajziyal-lāhuṣ-ṣādiqīna biṣidqihim wa yuʿadhdhibal-munāfiqīna ʾiñ-shāaʾa ʾaw yatūba ʿalayhim. ʾInnal-lāha kāna Ghafūrar-Raḥīmā. (24) Wa raddal-lāhul-ladhīna kafarū bighayẓihim lam yanālū khayrā. Wa kafal-lāhul-muʾminīnal-qitāla wa kānal-lāhu Qawiyyan ʿAzīzā. (25) Wa ʾañzalal-ladhīna ẓāharūhum-min ʾahlil-Kitābi miñ-ṣayāṣīhim wa qadhafa fī qulūbihimur-ruʿba farīqañ-taqtulūna wa taʾsirūna farīqā. (26) Wa ʾawrathakum ʾarḍahum wa diyārahum wa ʾamwālahum wa ʾarḍal-lam taṭaʾūhā; wa kānal-lāhu ʿalā kulli shayʾiñ-Qadīrā. (27)

25 These seem to be allusions to 29 : 2 (which may have been one of the last Meccan revelations) as well as to 2 : 155 and 214 (i.e., verses of the first *sūrah* of the Medina period).

26 Specifically, this verse is said to apply to certain of the Companions who vowed, at the time of the early campaigns, that they would fight until death at the Prophet's side (Zamakhsharī); in its wider sense, however, it relates to all efforts involving a supreme sacrifice in God's cause.

27 Cf. 6 : 12 – "God, who has willed upon Himself the law of grace and mercy" – and the corresponding note 10.

28 I.e., the pagans among the Confederates (see note 13 above); their Jewish allies are mentioned separately in the next verse.

29 Lit., "them", i.e., the tribes allied against Muḥammad and his community. The "followers of earlier revelation" (*ahl al-kitāb*) referred to here were the Jews of the tribe of Banū Qurayẓah, who despite their monotheistic faith had betrayed the Muslims and made common cause with the pagan Confederates. After the dismal rout of the latter, the Banū Qurayẓah, anticipating the vengeance of the community which they had betrayed, withdrew to their fortresses in the vicinity of Medina. After a siege lasting twenty-five days they surrendered to the Muslims, forfeiting all that they possessed.

30 I.e., lands which the Muslims were to conquer and hold in the future. This clause – with its allusion to yet more prosperous times to come – provides a connection between the present passage and the next.

O PROPHET! Say unto thy wives: "If you desire [but] the life of this world and its charms – well, then, I shall provide for you and release you in a becoming manner;[31] ⟨28⟩ but if you desire God and His Apostle, and [thus the good of] the life in the hereafter, then [know that], verily, for the doers of good among you God has readied a mighty reward!"[32] ⟨29⟩

O wives of the Prophet! If any of you were to become guilty of manifestly immoral conduct,[33] double [that of other sinners] would be her suffering [in the hereafter]: for that is indeed easy for God. ⟨30⟩ But if any of you devoutly obeys God and His Apostle and does good deeds, on her shall We bestow her reward twice-over: for We shall have readied for her a most excellent sustenance [in the life to come].[34] ⟨31⟩

O wives of the Prophet! You are not like any of the [other] women, provided that you remain [truly] conscious of God.[35] Hence, be not over-soft in your speech, lest any whose heart is diseased should be moved to desire [you]: but, withal, speak in a kindly way. ⟨32⟩ And abide quietly in your homes, and do not flaunt your charms as they used to flaunt them in the old days of pagan ignorance;[36] and be constant in prayer,

يَٰٓأَيُّهَا ٱلنَّبِيُّ قُل لِّأَزْوَٰجِكَ إِن كُنتُنَّ تُرِدْنَ ٱلْحَيَوٰةَ ٱلدُّنْيَا وَزِينَتَهَا
فَتَعَالَيْنَ أُمَتِّعْكُنَّ وَأُسَرِّحْكُنَّ سَرَاحًا جَمِيلًا ﴿٢٨﴾ وَإِن كُنتُنَّ تُرِدْنَ
ٱللَّهَ وَرَسُولَهُۥ وَٱلدَّارَ ٱلْءَاخِرَةَ فَإِنَّ ٱللَّهَ أَعَدَّ لِلْمُحْسِنَٰتِ مِنكُنَّ أَجْرًا
عَظِيمًا ﴿٢٩﴾ يَٰنِسَآءَ ٱلنَّبِيِّ مَن يَأْتِ مِنكُنَّ بِفَٰحِشَةٍ مُّبَيِّنَةٍ يُضَٰعَفْ لَهَا
ٱلْعَذَابُ ضِعْفَيْنِ وَكَانَ ذَٰلِكَ عَلَى ٱللَّهِ يَسِيرًا ﴿٣٠﴾ ۞ وَمَن يَقْنُتْ مِنكُنَّ
لِلَّهِ وَرَسُولِهِۦ وَتَعْمَلْ صَٰلِحًا نُّؤْتِهَآ أَجْرَهَا مَرَّتَيْنِ وَأَعْتَدْنَا لَهَا رِزْقًا
كَرِيمًا ﴿٣١﴾ يَٰنِسَآءَ ٱلنَّبِيِّ لَسْتُنَّ كَأَحَدٍ مِّنَ ٱلنِّسَآءِ إِنِ ٱتَّقَيْتُنَّ فَلَا
تَخْضَعْنَ بِٱلْقَوْلِ فَيَطْمَعَ ٱلَّذِى فِى قَلْبِهِۦ مَرَضٌ وَقُلْنَ قَوْلًا مَّعْرُوفًا ﴿٣٢﴾ حزب 43
وَقَرْنَ فِى بُيُوتِكُنَّ وَلَا تَبَرَّجْنَ تَبَرُّجَ ٱلْجَٰهِلِيَّةِ ٱلْأُولَىٰ وَأَقِمْنَ ٱلصَّلَوٰةَ جزء 22

Yāa ᵓayyuhan-Nabiyyu qul-liᵓazwājika ᵓiñ-kuñtunna turidnal-ḥayātad-dunyā wa zīnatahā fataᶜālayna ᵓumattiᶜkunna wa ᵓusarriḥkunna sarāḥañ-jamīlā. (28) Wa ᵓiñ-kuñtunna turidnal-lāha wa Rasūlahū wad-dāral-ᵓĀkhirata faᵓinnal-lāha ᵓaᶜadda lilmuḥsināti miñkunna ᵓajran ᶜaẓīmā. (29) Yā nisāaᵓan-Nabiyyi mañy-yaᵓti miñkunna bifāḥishatim-mubayyinatiñy-yuḍāᶜaf lahal-ᶜadhābu ḍiᶜfayni wa kāna dhālika ᶜalal-lāhi yasīrā. (30) ۞ Wa mañy-yaqnut miñkunna lillāhi wa Rasūlihī wa taᶜmal ṣāliḥañ-nuᵓtihāa ajrahā marratayni wa ᵓaᶜtadnā lahā rizqañ-karīmā. (31) Yā nisāaᵓan-Nabiyyi lastunna kaᵓaḥadim-minan-nisāaᵓi ᵓinit-taqaytunna falā takhḍaᶜna bilqawli fayaṭmaᶜal-ladhī fī qalbihī maraḍuñw-wa qulna qawlam-maᶜrūfā. (32) Wa qarna fī buyūtikunna wa lā tabar-rajna tabarrujal-jāhiliyyatil-ᵓūlā wa ᵓaqimnaṣ-Ṣalāta

31 By the time this verse was revealed (see note 65 on verse 52 of this *sūrah*) the Muslims had conquered the rich agricultural region of Khaybar, and the community had grown more prosperous. But while life was becoming easier for most of its members, this ease was not reflected in the household of the Prophet who, as before, allowed himself and his family only the absolute minimum necessary for the most simple living. In view of the changed circumstances, it was no more than natural that his wives were longing for a share in the comparative luxuries which other Muslim women could now enjoy: but an acquiescence by Muḥammad to their demand would have conflicted with the principle, observed by him throughout his life, that the standard of living of God's Apostle and his family should not be higher than that of the poorest of the believers.

32 When, immediately after their revelation, the Prophet recited the above two verses to his wives, all of them emphatically rejected all thought of separation and declared that they had chosen "God and His Apostle and the [good of the] hereafter" (recorded in several compilations of *aḥādīth*, among them Bukhārī and Muslim). Some of the earliest Islamic scholars (e.g., Qatādah and Al-Ḥasan as quoted by Ṭabarī) held that the subsequent revelation of verse 52 of this *sūrah* constituted God's reward, as it were, for this attitude.

33 Regarding this connotation of the term *fāḥishah*, see *sūrah* 4, note 14. According to Zamakhsharī, in his commentary on the present verse, this term comprises all that may be described as a "gross sin" (*kabīrah*).

34 See note 5 on 8 : 4.

35 Sc., "and, thus, conscious of your special position as the consorts of God's Apostle and mothers of the believers".

36 The term *jāhiliyyah* denotes the period of a people's – or civilization's – moral ignorance between the

and render the purifying dues, and pay heed unto God and His Apostle: for God only wants to remove from you all that might be loathsome, O you members of the [Prophet's] household, and to purify you to utmost purity. «33»
And bear in mind all that is recited in your homes of God's messages and [His] wisdom: for God is unfathomable [in His wisdom], all-aware.[37] «34»

VERILY, for all men and women who have surrendered themselves unto God, and all believing men and believing women, and all truly devout men and truly devout women, and all men and women who are true to their word, and all men and women who are patient in adversity, and all men and women who humble themselves [before God], and all men and women who give in charity, and all self-denying men and self-denying women,[38] and all men and women who are mindful of their chastity,[39] and all men and women who remember God unceasingly: for [all of] them has God readied forgiveness of sins and a mighty reward. «35»
Now whenever God and His Apostle have decided a matter,[40] it is not for a believing man or a believing woman to claim freedom of choice insofar as they themselves are concerned:[41] for he who [thus] rebels against God and His Apostle has already, most obviously, gone astray. «36»

وَءَاتِينَ ٱلزَّكَوٰةَ وَأَطِعْنَ ٱللَّهَ وَرَسُولَهُۥٓ ۚ إِنَّمَا يُرِيدُ ٱللَّهُ لِيُذْهِبَ عَنكُمُ
ٱلرِّجْسَ أَهْلَ ٱلْبَيْتِ وَيُطَهِّرَكُمْ تَطْهِيرًا ﴿٣٣﴾ وَٱذْكُرْنَ مَا يُتْلَىٰ فِى
بُيُوتِكُنَّ مِنْ ءَايَٰتِ ٱللَّهِ وَٱلْحِكْمَةِ ۚ إِنَّ ٱللَّهَ كَانَ لَطِيفًا خَبِيرًا ﴿٣٤﴾ إِنَّ
ٱلْمُسْلِمِينَ وَٱلْمُسْلِمَٰتِ وَٱلْمُؤْمِنِينَ وَٱلْمُؤْمِنَٰتِ وَٱلْقَٰنِتِينَ وَٱلْقَٰنِتَٰتِ
وَٱلصَّٰدِقِينَ وَٱلصَّٰدِقَٰتِ وَٱلصَّٰبِرِينَ وَٱلصَّٰبِرَٰتِ وَٱلْخَٰشِعِينَ
وَٱلْخَٰشِعَٰتِ وَٱلْمُتَصَدِّقِينَ وَٱلْمُتَصَدِّقَٰتِ وَٱلصَّٰٓئِمِينَ وَٱلصَّٰٓئِمَٰتِ
وَٱلْحَٰفِظِينَ فُرُوجَهُمْ وَٱلْحَٰفِظَٰتِ وَٱلذَّٰكِرِينَ ٱللَّهَ كَثِيرًا
وَٱلذَّٰكِرَٰتِ أَعَدَّ ٱللَّهُ لَهُم مَّغْفِرَةً وَأَجْرًا عَظِيمًا ﴿٣٥﴾ وَمَا كَانَ لِمُؤْمِنٍ
وَلَا مُؤْمِنَةٍ إِذَا قَضَى ٱللَّهُ وَرَسُولُهُۥٓ أَمْرًا أَن يَكُونَ لَهُمُ ٱلْخِيَرَةُ مِنْ
أَمْرِهِمْ ۗ وَمَن يَعْصِ ٱللَّهَ وَرَسُولَهُۥ فَقَدْ ضَلَّ ضَلَٰلًا مُّبِينًا ﴿٣٦﴾

wa ʾātīnaz-Zakāta wa ʾaṭiʿnal-lāha wa Rasūlah. ʾInnamā yurīdul-lāhu liyudhhiba ʿañkumur-rijsa ʾAhlal-Bayti wa yuṭahhirakum taṭhīrā. (33) Wadhkurna mā yutlā fī buyūtikunna min ʾĀyātil-lāhi wal-Ḥikmah. ʾInnal-lāha kāna Laṭīfan Khabīrā. (34) ʾInnal-Muslimīna wal-Muslimāti wal-muʾminīna wal-muʾmināti wal-qānitīna wal-qānitāti waṣ-ṣādiqīna waṣ-ṣādiqāti waṣ-ṣābirīna waṣ-ṣābirāti wal-khāshiʿīna wal-khāshiʿāti wal-mutaṣaddiqīna wal-mutaṣaddiqāti waṣ-ṣāaʾimīna waṣ-ṣāaʾimāti wal-ḥāfiẓīna furūjahum wal-ḥāfiẓāti wadh-dhākirīnal-lāha kathīrañw-wadh-dhākirāti ʾaʿaddal-lāhu lahum-maghfiratañw-wa ajran ʿaẓīmā. (35) Wa mā kāna limuʾminiñw-wa lā muʾminatin ʾidhā qaḍal-lāhu wa Rasūluhūu ʾamran ʾañy-yakūna lahumul-khiyaratu miñ ʾamrihim. Wa mañy-yaʿṣil-lāha wa Rasūlahū faqad ḍalla ḍalālam-mubīnā. (36)

---

obliteration of one prophetic teaching and the emergence of another; and, more specifically, the period of Arabian paganism before the advent of Muḥammad. Apart from these historical connotations, however, the term describes the state of moral ignorance or unconsciousness in its general sense, irrespective of time or social environment. (See also note 71 on 5 : 50.)

37 For the meaning of the term *laṭīf* as applied to God, especially in combination with the term *khabīr*, see note 89 on 6 : 103.

38 The term *ṣāʾim*, usually rendered as "fasting", has here its primary connotation of "one who abstains [from anything]" or "denies to himself [anything]": cf. 19 : 26, where the noun *ṣawm* denotes "abstinence from speech".

39 Lit., "the men who guard their private parts and the women who guard [them]": see note 36 on 24 : 30.

40 I.e., whenever a specific law has been *formulated as such* in the Qurʾān or in an injunction promulgated by the Prophet.

41 Lit., "to have a choice in their concern (*min amrihim*)" – i.e., to let their attitude or course of action be determined, not by the relevant law, but by their personal interests or predilections.

AND LO,[42] [O Muḥammad,] thou didst say unto the one to whom God had shown favour and to whom thou hadst shown favour,[43] "Hold on to thy wife, and remain conscious of God!" And [thus] wouldst thou hide within thyself something that God was about to bring to light[44] – for thou didst stand in awe of [what] people [might think], whereas it was God alone of whom thou shouldst have stood in awe![45]
[But] then, when Zayd had come to the end of his union with her,[46] We gave her to thee in marriage, so that [in future] no blame should attach to the believers for [marrying] the spouses of their adopted children when the latter have come to the end of their union with them.[47] And [thus] God's will was done. ⟨37⟩
[Hence,] no blame whatever attaches to the Prophet for [having done] what God has ordained for him.[48] [Indeed, such was]

وَإِذْ تَقُولُ لِلَّذِىٓ أَنْعَمَ ٱللَّهُ عَلَيْهِ وَأَنْعَمْتَ عَلَيْهِ أَمْسِكْ عَلَيْكَ زَوْجَكَ
وَٱتَّقِ ٱللَّهَ وَتُخْفِى فِى نَفْسِكَ مَا ٱللَّهُ مُبْدِيهِ وَتَخْشَى ٱلنَّاسَ وَٱللَّهُ أَحَقُّ أَن
تَخْشَىٰهُ فَلَمَّا قَضَىٰ زَيْدٌ مِّنْهَا وَطَرًا زَوَّجْنَٰكَهَا لِكَىْ لَا يَكُونَ عَلَى
ٱلْمُؤْمِنِينَ حَرَجٌ فِىٓ أَزْوَٰجِ أَدْعِيَآئِهِمْ إِذَا قَضَوْا۟ مِنْهُنَّ وَطَرًا وَكَانَ
أَمْرُ ٱللَّهِ مَفْعُولًا ﴿٣٧﴾ مَّا كَانَ عَلَى ٱلنَّبِىِّ مِنْ حَرَجٍ فِيمَا فَرَضَ ٱللَّهُ لَهُۥ

Wa ʾidh taqūlu lilladhīi ʾanʿamal-lāhu ʿalayhi wa ʾanʿamta ʿalayhi ʾamsik ʿalayka zawjaka wat-taqil-lāha wa tukhfī fī nafsika mal-lāhu mubdīhi wa takhshan-nasa wal-lāhu ʾaḥaqqu ʾañ-takhshāh. Falammā qaḍā Zaydum-minhā waṭarañ-zawwajnākahā likay lā yakūna ʿalal-muʾminīna ḥarajuñ-fīi ʾazwāji ʾadʿiyāaʾihim ʾidhā qaḍaw minhunna waṭarā. Wa kāna ʾamrul-lāhi mafʿūlā. ﴿37﴾ Mā kāna ʿalan-Nabiyyi min ḥarajiñ-fīmā faraḍal-lāhu lah.

42 For this rendering of the particle *idh*, see *sūrah* 2, note 21. – With the above verse, the discourse returns to the problem of "elective" relationships touched upon in verses 4 ff.

Several years before Muḥammad's call to prophethood, his wife Khadījah made him a present of a young slave, Zayd ibn Ḥārithah, a descendant of the North-Arabian tribe of Banū Kalb, who had been taken captive as a child in the course of one of the many tribal wars and then sold into slavery at Mecca. As soon as he became the boy's owner, Muḥammad freed him, and shortly afterwards adopted him as his son; and Zayd, in his turn, was among the first to embrace Islam. Years later, impelled by the desire to break down the ancient Arabian prejudice against a slave's or even a freedman's marrying a "free-born" woman, the Prophet persuaded Zayd to marry his (Muḥammad's) own cousin, Zaynab bint Jaḥsh, who, without his being aware of it, had been in love with Muḥammad ever since her childhood. Hence, she consented to the proposed marriage with great reluctance, and only in deference to the authority of the Prophet. Since Zayd, too, was not at all keen on this alliance (being already happily married to another freed slave, Umm Ayman, the mother of his son Usāmah), it was not surprising that the marriage did not bring happiness to either Zaynab or Zayd. On several occasions the latter was about to divorce his new wife who, on her part, did not make any secret of her dislike of Zayd; and each time they were persuaded by the Prophet to persevere in patience and not to separate. In the end, however, the marriage proved untenable, and Zayd divorced Zaynab in the year 5 H. Shortly afterwards the Prophet married her in order to redeem what he considered to be his moral responsibility for her past unhappiness.

43 I.e., Zayd ibn Ḥārithah whom God had caused to become one of the earliest believers, and whom the Prophet had adopted as his son.

44 Namely, that the marriage of Zayd and Zaynab, which had been sponsored by Muḥammad himself, and on which he had so strongly insisted, was a total failure and could only end in divorce (see also next note).

45 Lit., "whereas God was more worthy (*aḥaqq*) that thou shouldst stand in awe of Him". Referring to this divine reprimand (which, in itself, disproves the allegation that the Qurʾān was "composed by Muḥammad), ʿĀʾishah is reliably quoted as having said, "Had the Apostle of God been inclined to suppress anything of what was revealed to him, he would surely have suppressed this verse" (Bukhārī and Muslim).

46 Lit., "ended his want of [or "claim on"] her", Sc., by divorcing her (Zamakhsharī).

47 Thus, apart from the Prophet's desire to make amends for Zaynab's past unhappiness, the divine purpose in causing him to marry the former wife of his adopted son (stressed in the phrase, "*We* gave her to thee in marriage") was to show that – contrary to what the pagan Arabs believed – an adoptive relationship does not involve any of the marriage-restrictions which result from actual, biological parent-and-child relations (cf. note 3 on verse 4 of this *sūrah*).

48 I.e., his marriage with Zaynab, which was meant to exemplify a point of canon law as well as to satisfy what the Prophet regarded as his personal moral duty.

سُنَّةَ ٱللَّهِ فِى ٱلَّذِينَ خَلَوْا۟ مِن قَبْلُ ۚ وَكَانَ أَمْرُ ٱللَّهِ قَدَرًا مَّقْدُورًا ﴿٣٨﴾
ٱلَّذِينَ يُبَلِّغُونَ رِسَـٰلَـٰتِ ٱللَّهِ وَيَخْشَوْنَهُۥ وَلَا يَخْشَوْنَ أَحَدًا إِلَّا ٱللَّهَ ۗ
وَكَفَىٰ بِٱللَّهِ حَسِيبًا ﴿٣٩﴾ مَّا كَانَ مُحَمَّدٌ أَبَآ أَحَدٍ مِّن رِّجَالِكُمْ وَلَـٰكِن
رَّسُولَ ٱللَّهِ وَخَاتَمَ ٱلنَّبِيِّـۧنَ ۗ وَكَانَ ٱللَّهُ بِكُلِّ شَىْءٍ عَلِيمًا ﴿٤٠﴾ يَـٰٓأَيُّهَا ٱلَّذِينَ
ءَامَنُوا۟ ٱذْكُرُوا۟ ٱللَّهَ ذِكْرًا كَثِيرًا ﴿٤١﴾ وَسَبِّحُوهُ بُكْرَةً وَأَصِيلًا ﴿٤٢﴾ هُوَ
ٱلَّذِى يُصَلِّى عَلَيْكُمْ وَمَلَـٰٓئِكَتُهُۥ لِيُخْرِجَكُم مِّنَ ٱلظُّلُمَـٰتِ إِلَى ٱلنُّورِ ۚ
وَكَانَ بِٱلْمُؤْمِنِينَ رَحِيمًا ﴿٤٣﴾ تَحِيَّتُهُمْ يَوْمَ يَلْقَوْنَهُۥ سَلَـٰمٌ ۚ وَأَعَدَّ لَهُمْ
أَجْرًا كَرِيمًا ﴿٤٤﴾ يَـٰٓأَيُّهَا ٱلنَّبِىُّ إِنَّآ أَرْسَلْنَـٰكَ شَـٰهِدًا وَمُبَشِّرًا وَنَذِيرًا ﴿٤٥﴾
وَدَاعِيًا إِلَى ٱللَّهِ بِإِذْنِهِۦ وَسِرَاجًا مُّنِيرًا ﴿٤٦﴾

Sunnatal-lāhi fil-ladhīna khalaw miñ-qabl. Wa kāna ʾamrul-lāhi qadaram-maqdūrā. (38) ʾAlladhīna yuballighūna Risālātil-lāhi wa yakhshawnahū wa lā yakhshawna ʾaḥadan ʾillal-lāh. Wa kafā billāhi Ḥasībā. (39) Mā kana Muḥammadun ʾabāa ʾaḥadim-mir-rijālikum wa lākir-Rasūlal-lāhi wa khātaman-Nabiyyīn. Wa kānal-lāhu bikulli shayʾin ʿAlīmā. (40) Yāa ʾayyuhal-ladhīna ʾāmanudh-kurul-lāha dhikrañ-kathīrā. (41) Wa sabbiḥūhu bukratañw-wa ʾaṣīlā. (42) Huwal-ladhī yuṣallī ʿalaykum wa Malāaʾikatuhū liyukhrijakum-minaẓ-ẓulumāti ʾilan-nūri wa kāna bilmuʾminīna Raḥīmā. (43) Taḥiyyatuhum Yawma yalqawnahū salām. Wa ʾaʿadda lahum ʾajrañ-karīmā. (44) Yāa ʾayyuhan-Nabiyyu ʾinnāa ʾarsalnāka Shāhidañw-wa Mubashshirañw-wa Nadhīrā. (45) Wa Dāʿiyan ʾilal-lāhi biʾidhnihī wa Sirājam-munīrā. (46)

God's way with those that have passed away aforetime[49] – and [remember that] God's will is always destiny absolute; ‹38› – [and such will always be His way with] those who convey God's messages [to the world], and stand in awe of Him, and hold none but God in awe: for none can take count [of man's doings] as God does! ‹39› [And know, O believers, that] Muḥammad is not the father of any one of your men,[50] but is God's Apostle and the Seal of all Prophets.[51] And God has indeed full knowledge of everything. ‹40›

O YOU who have attained to faith! Remember God with unceasing remembrance, ‹41› and extol His limitless glory from morn to evening.[52] ‹42›

He it is who bestows His blessings upon you, with His angels [echoing Him], so that He might take you out of the depths of darkness into the light.

And, indeed, a dispenser of grace is He unto the believers. ‹43› On the Day when they meet Him, they will be welcomed with the greeting, "Peace"; and He will have readied for them a most excellent reward. ‹44›

[And as for thee,] O Prophet – behold, We have sent thee as a witness [to the truth], and as a herald of glad tidings and a warner, ‹45› and as one who summons [all men] to God by His leave,[53] and as a light-giving beacon. ‹46›

---

49 I.e., the prophets who preceded Muḥammad, in all of whom, as in him, all personal desires coincided with their willingness to surrender themselves to God: an inborn, harmonious disposition of the spirit which characterizes God's elect and – as the subsequent, parenthetic clause declares – is their "destiny absolute" (*qadar maqdūr*).

50 I.e., he is the spiritual "father" of the whole community (cf. note 8 on verse 6 of this *sūrah*), and not of any one person or particular persons – thus, incidentally, refuting the erroneous idea that physical descent from a prophet confers, by itself, any merit on the persons concerned.

51 I.e., the last of the prophets, just as a seal (*khātam*) marks the end of a document; apart from this, the term *khātam* is also synonymous with *khitām*, the "end" or "conclusion" of a thing: from which it follows that the message revealed through Muḥammad – the Qurʾān – must be regarded as the culmination and the end of all prophetic revelation (cf. note 66 on the first sentence of the second paragraph of 5 : 48, and note 126 on 7 : 158). See also note 102 on 21 : 107.

52 Lit., "at morn and evening", i.e., at all times.

53 I.e., at His behest (Ṭabarī).

And [so,] convey to the believers the glad tiding that a great bounty from God awaits them; ‹47› and defer not to [the likes and dislikes of] the deniers of the truth and the hypocrites, and disregard their hurtful talk,[54] and place thy trust in God: for none is as worthy of trust as God. ‹48›

O YOU who have attained to faith! If you marry believing women and then divorce them ere you have touched them, you have no reason to expect, and to calculate, any waiting-period on their part:[55] hence, make [at once] provision for them, and release them in a becoming manner.[56] ‹49›

O PROPHET! Behold, We have made lawful to thee thy wives unto whom thou hast paid their dowers,[57] as well as those whom thy right hand has come to possess from among the captives of war whom God has bestowed upon thee.[58] And [We have made lawful to thee] the daughters of thy paternal uncles and aunts, and the daughters of thy maternal uncles and aunts, who have migrated with thee [to Yathrib];[59]

وَبَشِّرِ ٱلْمُؤْمِنِينَ بِأَنَّ لَهُم مِّنَ ٱللَّهِ فَضْلًا كَبِيرًا ﴿٤٧﴾ وَلَا تُطِعِ ٱلْكَٰفِرِينَ
وَٱلْمُنَٰفِقِينَ وَدَعْ أَذَىٰهُمْ وَتَوَكَّلْ عَلَى ٱللَّهِ وَكَفَىٰ بِٱللَّهِ وَكِيلًا ﴿٤٨﴾ يَٰٓأَيُّهَا
ٱلَّذِينَ ءَامَنُوٓا۟ إِذَا نَكَحْتُمُ ٱلْمُؤْمِنَٰتِ ثُمَّ طَلَّقْتُمُوهُنَّ مِن قَبْلِ أَن
تَمَسُّوهُنَّ فَمَا لَكُمْ عَلَيْهِنَّ مِنْ عِدَّةٍ تَعْتَدُّونَهَا فَمَتِّعُوهُنَّ وَسَرِّحُوهُنَّ
سَرَاحًا جَمِيلًا ﴿٤٩﴾ يَٰٓأَيُّهَا ٱلنَّبِىُّ إِنَّآ أَحْلَلْنَا لَكَ أَزْوَٰجَكَ ٱلَّٰتِىٓ ءَاتَيْتَ
أُجُورَهُنَّ وَمَا مَلَكَتْ يَمِينُكَ مِمَّآ أَفَآءَ ٱللَّهُ عَلَيْكَ وَبَنَاتِ عَمِّكَ
وَبَنَاتِ عَمَّٰتِكَ وَبَنَاتِ خَالِكَ وَبَنَاتِ خَٰلَٰتِكَ ٱلَّٰتِى هَاجَرْنَ مَعَكَ

Wa bashshiril-muʾminīna biʾanna lahum-minal-lāhi faḍlañ-kabīrā. ﴿47﴾ Wa lā tuṭiᶜil-kāfirīna wal-munāfiqīna wa daᶜ ʾadhāhum wa tawakkal ᶜalal-lāhi wa kafā billāhi Wakīlā. ﴿48﴾ Yāa ʾayyuhal-ladhīna ʾāmanūu ʾidhā nakaḥtumul-muʾmināti thumma ṭallaqtumūhunna miñ-qabli ʾañ-tamassūhunna famā lakum ᶜalayhinna min ᶜiddatiñ-taᶜtaddūnahā famat-tiᶜūhunna wa sarriḥūhunna sarāḥañ-jamīlā. ﴿49﴾ Yāa ʾayyuhan-Nabiyyu ʾinnāa ʾaḥlalnā laka ʾazwājakal-lātīi ʾātayta ʾujūrahunna wa mā mala-kat yamīnuka mimmāa ʾafāaʾal-lāhu ᶜalayka wa banāti ᶜammika wa banāti ᶜammātika wa banāti khālika wa banāti khālātikal-lāti hājarna maᶜaka

54 Or: "yet [withal,] abstain from injuring them" (Zamakhsharī) – depending on whether *adhāhum* is taken to mean "the hurt caused *by* them" or "done *to* them".

55 Lit., "you have no waiting-period whatever upon them which you should count" – i.e., "which either of you should take into account as an obligation": cf. the first part of 2 : 228, and the corresponding note 215. Since the question of pregnancy does not arise if the marriage has not been consummated, a waiting-period on the part of the divorced wife would be meaningless and of no benefit either to her or to her former husband.

56 This injunction, relating to certain marital problems which affect the believers in general, forms an introduction, as it were, to a resumption, in the next verse, of the discourse on the marital laws applying exclusively to the Prophet: thus, it connects with the passage beginning with the words, "O wives of the Prophet! You are not like any of the [other] women" (verse 32), as well as with the subsequent reference to his marriage with Zaynab (verses 37 f.).

57 The term *ajr* is in this context synonymous with *farīḍah* in its specific sense of "dower" (*mahr*): see *sūrah* 2, note 224.

58 As pointed out in several places (see, in particular, note 32 on 4 : 25), Islam does not countenance any form of concubinage, and categorically prohibits sexual relations between a man and a woman unless they are lawfully *married* to one another. In this respect, the only difference between a "free" woman and a slave is that whereas the former must receive a dower from her husband, no such obligation is imposed on a man who marries his rightfully owned slave (lit., "one whom his right hand possesses") – that is, a woman taken captive in a "holy war" (*jihād*) waged in defence of the Faith or of liberty (note 167 on 2 : 190 and note 72 on 8 : 67) – : for, in such a case, the freedom conferred upon the bride by the very act of marriage is considered to be equivalent to a dower.

59 This was – in addition to his not being allowed to divorce any of his wives (see verse 52 below) – a further restriction imposed on the Prophet in the matter of marriage: whereas all other Muslims are free to marry any of their paternal or maternal cousins, the Prophet was allowed to marry only such from among them as had proved their strong, early attachment to Islam by having accompanied him on his exodus (the *hijrah*) from Mecca to Medina. In the opinion of Baghawī – an opinion obviously based on the corresponding, ancient Arabian usage – the term "daughters

ربع الحزب

وَٱمْرَأَةً مُّؤْمِنَةً إِن وَهَبَتْ نَفْسَهَا لِلنَّبِيِّ إِنْ أَرَادَ ٱلنَّبِيُّ أَن يَسْتَنكِحَهَا
خَالِصَةً لَّكَ مِن دُونِ ٱلْمُؤْمِنِينَ قَدْ عَلِمْنَا مَا فَرَضْنَا عَلَيْهِمْ فِىٓ
أَزْوَٰجِهِمْ وَمَا مَلَكَتْ أَيْمَٰنُهُمْ لِكَيْلَا يَكُونَ عَلَيْكَ حَرَجٌ وَكَانَ ٱللَّهُ
غَفُورًا رَّحِيمًا ﴿٥٠﴾ ۞ تُرْجِى مَن تَشَآءُ مِنْهُنَّ وَتُـْٔوِىٓ إِلَيْكَ مَن تَشَآءُ
وَمَنِ ٱبْتَغَيْتَ مِمَّنْ عَزَلْتَ فَلَا جُنَاحَ عَلَيْكَ ذَٰلِكَ أَدْنَىٰٓ أَن تَقَرَّ أَعْيُنُهُنَّ
وَلَا يَحْزَنَّ وَيَرْضَيْنَ بِمَآ ءَاتَيْتَهُنَّ كُلُّهُنَّ وَٱللَّهُ يَعْلَمُ مَا فِى قُلُوبِكُمْ
وَكَانَ ٱللَّهُ عَلِيمًا حَلِيمًا ﴿٥١﴾ لَّا يَحِلُّ لَكَ ٱلنِّسَآءُ مِنۢ بَعْدُ وَلَآ أَن تَبَدَّلَ

wam-raʾatam-muʾminatan ʾiñw-wahabat nafsahā lin-Nabiyyi ʾin ʾarādan-Nabiyyu ʾañy-yastañkiḥahā khāliṣatal-laka miñ-dūnil-muʾminīn. Qad ʿalimnā mā faraḍnā ʿalayhim fīi ʾazwājihim wa mā malakat ʾaymānuhum likaylā yakūna ʿalayka ḥaraj. Wa kānal-lāhu Ghafūrar-Raḥīmā. (50) ۞ Turjī mañ-tashāaʾu minhunna wa tuʾwīi ʾilayka mañ-tashāaʾ. Wa manib-taghayta mimman ʿazalta falā junāḥa ʿalayk. Dhālika ʾadnā ʾañ-taqarra ʾaʿyunuhunna wa lā yaḥzanna wa yarḍayna bimāa ʾātaytahunna kulluhunn. Wal-lāhu yaʿlamu mā fī qulūbikum; wa kānal-lāhu ʿAlīman Ḥalīmā. (51) Lā yaḥillu lakan-nisāaʾu mim-baʿdu wa lāa ʾañ-tabaddala

and any believing woman who offers herself freely to the Prophet and whom the Prophet might be willing to wed:[60] [this latter being but] a privilege for thee, and not for other believers – [seeing that] We have already made known what We have enjoined upon them with regard to their wives and those whom their right hands may possess.[61]

[And] in order that thou be not burdened with [undue] anxiety – for God is indeed much-forgiving, a dispenser of grace ‹50› – [know that] thou mayest put off for a time whichever of them thou pleasest, and mayest take unto thee whichever thou pleasest; and [that,] if thou seek out any from whom thou hast kept away [for a time], thou wilt incur no sin [thereby]:[62] this will make it more likely that their eyes are gladdened [whenever they see thee],[63] and that they do not grieve [whenever they are overlooked], and that all of them may find contentment in whatever thou hast to give them: for God [alone] knows what is in your hearts – and God is indeed all-knowing, forbearing.[64] ‹51›

No [other] women shall henceforth be lawful to thee[65] – nor art thou [allowed] to supplant

---

of thy paternal uncles and aunts" comprises in this context not only the actual paternal cousins but, in general, all women of the tribe of Quraysh, to which Muḥammad's father belonged, while the term "daughters of thy maternal uncles and aunts" comprises all women of his mother's tribe, the Banū Zuhrah.

60 The relevant clause reads, literally, "if she offered herself as a gift (*in wahabat nafsahā*) to the Prophet". Most of the classical commentators take this to mean "without demanding or expecting a dower (*mahr*)", which, as far as ordinary Muslims are concerned, is an essential item in a marriage agreement (cf. 4 : 4 and 24, and the corresponding notes; also *sūrah* 2, note 224).

61 The above parenthetic sentence refers to the previously revealed, general laws relating to marriage (see 2 : 221, 4 : 3-4 and 19-25, as well as the corresponding notes), and particularly the laws bearing on the question of dower.

62 Thus, the Prophet was told that he need not observe a strict "rotation" in the conjugal attentions due to his wives, although he himself, impelled by an inborn sense of fairness, always endeavoured to give them a feeling of absolute equality.

63 I.e., by the inner certainty that whenever he turned to any of them, he did so on impulse, out of genuine affection, and not out of a sense of marital "obligation".

64 According to a *ḥadīth* on the authority of ʿĀʾishah, recorded in the *Musnad* of Ibn Ḥanbal, the Prophet "used to divide his attentions equitably among his wives, and then would pray: 'O God! I am doing whatever is in my power: do not, then, blame me for [failing in] something which is in Thy power [alone], and not in mine!' – thus alluding to his heart, and to loving some [of his wives] more than others."

65 Some commentators (e.g., Ṭabarī) assume that this restriction relates to the four categories of women enumerated in verse 50 above: it is, however, much more probable that it is a prohibition barring the Prophet from marrying any woman *in addition* to those to whom he was already married (Baghawī, Zamakhsharī). Some of the earliest, most outstanding authorities on the Qurʾān, like Ibn ʿAbbās, Mujāhid, Aḍ-Ḍaḥḥāk, Qatādah, Ibn Zayd (all of them cited by Ibn Kathīr), or Al-Ḥasan al-Baṣrī (quoted by Ṭabarī in his commentary on verses 28-29), link this prohibition of further marriages with the choice between the charms of worldly life and the good of the hereafter with

[any of] them by other wives,[66] even though their beauty should please thee greatly: – [none shall be lawful to thee] beyond those whom thou [already] hast come to possess.[67] And God keeps watch over everything. ‹52›

O YOU who have attained to faith! Do not enter the Prophet's dwellings unless you are given leave; [and when invited] to a meal, do not come [so early as] to wait for it to be readied: but whenever you are invited, enter [at the proper time]; and when you have partaken of the meal, disperse without lingering for the sake of mere talk: that, behold, might give offence to the Prophet, and yet he might feel shy of [asking] you [to leave]: but God is not shy of [teaching you] what is right.[68]
And [as for the Prophet's wives,] whenever you ask them for anything that you need, ask them from behind a screen:[69] this will but deepen the purity of your hearts and theirs.

بِهِنَّ مِنْ أَزْوَٰجٍ وَلَوْ أَعْجَبَكَ حُسْنُهُنَّ إِلَّا مَا مَلَكَتْ يَمِينُكَ ۗ وَكَانَ ٱللَّهُ
عَلَىٰ كُلِّ شَىْءٍ رَّقِيبًا ﴿٥٢﴾ يَٰٓأَيُّهَا ٱلَّذِينَ ءَامَنُوا۟ لَا تَدْخُلُوا۟ بُيُوتَ ٱلنَّبِىِّ
إِلَّآ أَن يُؤْذَنَ لَكُمْ إِلَىٰ طَعَامٍ غَيْرَ نَٰظِرِينَ إِنَىٰهُ وَلَٰكِنْ إِذَا دُعِيتُمْ
فَٱدْخُلُوا۟ فَإِذَا طَعِمْتُمْ فَٱنتَشِرُوا۟ وَلَا مُسْتَـْٔنِسِينَ لِحَدِيثٍ ۚ إِنَّ ذَٰلِكُمْ كَانَ
يُؤْذِى ٱلنَّبِىَّ فَيَسْتَحْىِۦ مِنكُمْ ۖ وَٱللَّهُ لَا يَسْتَحْىِۦ مِنَ ٱلْحَقِّ ۚ وَإِذَا سَأَلْتُمُوهُنَّ
مَتَٰعًا فَسْـَٔلُوهُنَّ مِن وَرَآءِ حِجَابٍ ۚ ذَٰلِكُمْ أَطْهَرُ لِقُلُوبِكُمْ وَقُلُوبِهِنَّ ۚ

bihinna min ʾazwājiñw-wa law ʾaʿjabaka ḥusnuhunna ʾillā mā malakat yamīnuk; wa kānal-lāhu ʿalā kulli shayʾir-Raqībā. (52) Yāa ʾayyuhal-ladhīna ʾāmanū lā tadkhulū buyūtan-Nabiyyi ʾillāa añy-yuʾdhana lakum ʾilā ṭaʿāmin ghayra nāẓirīna ʾināhu wa lākin ʾidhā duʿītum fadkhulū faʾidhā ṭaʿimtum fañtashirū wa lā mustaʾnisīna liḥadīth. ʾInna dhālikum kāna yuʾdhin-Nabiyya fayastaḥyī miñkum; wal-lāhu lā yastaḥyī minal-ḥaqq. Wa ʾidhā saʾaltumūhunna matāʿañ-fasʾalūhunna miñw-warāaʾi ḥijāb; dhālikum ʾaṭharu liqulūbikum wa qulūbihinn.

which the wives of the Prophet were confronted on the strength of verses 28-29, and their emphatic option for "God and His Apostle" (cf. note 32 above). All those early authorities describe the revelation of verse 52 – and the assurance which it was meant to convey to the wives of the Prophet – as God's reward, in this world, of their faith and fidelity. Since it is inconceivable that the Prophet could have disregarded the categorical injunction, "No [other] women shall henceforth be lawful to thee", the passage in question cannot have been revealed earlier than the year 7 H., that is, the year in which the conquest of Khaybar and the Prophet's marriage with Ṣafiyyah – his last marriage – took place. Consequently, verses 28-29 (with which, as we have seen, verse 52 is closely connected) must have been revealed at that later period, and not, as some commentators think, in the year 5 H. (i.e., at the time of the Prophet's marriage with Zaynab).

66 I.e., to divorce any of them with a view to taking another wife in her stead (with the prohibitive accent on the "supplanting" – i.e., divorcing – of any of his wives).

67 In my opinion, the expression *ma malakat yamīnuka* (lit., "what thy right hand possesses", or "has come to possess") has here the same meaning as in 4 : 24, namely, "those whom thou hast come to possess *through wedlock*" (see *sūrah* 4, note 26); thus, the above verse is to be understood as limiting the Prophet's marriages to those already contracted.

68 Connecting with the reference, in verses 45-48, to the Prophet's mission, the above passage is meant to stress his unique position among his contemporaries; but as is so often the case with Qurʾanic references to historical events and situations, the ethical principle enunciated here is not restricted to a particular time or environment. By exhorting the Prophet's Companions to revere his person, the Qurʾān reminds all believers, at all times, of his exalted status (cf. note 85 on 2 : 104); beyond that, it teaches them certain rules of behaviour bearing on the life of the community as such: rules which, however insignificant they may appear at first glance, are of psychological value in a society that is to be governed by a genuine feeling of brotherhood, mutual consideration, and respect for the sanctity of each other's personality and privacy.

69 The term *ḥijāb* denotes anything that intervenes between two things, or conceals, shelters or protects the one from the other; it may be rendered, according to the context, as "barrier", "obstacle", "partition", "screen", "curtain", "veil", etc., in both the concrete and abstract connotations of these words. The prohibition to approach the Prophet's wives otherwise than "from behind a screen" or "curtain" may be taken literally – as indeed it was taken by most of the Companions of the Prophet – or metaphorically, indicating the exceptional reverence due to these "mothers of the faithful".

وَمَا كَانَ لَكُمْ أَن تُؤْذُوا۟ رَسُولَ ٱللَّهِ وَلَآ أَن تَنكِحُوٓا۟ أَزْوَٰجَهُۥ مِنۢ بَعْدِهِۦٓ أَبَدًا
إِنَّ ذَٰلِكُمْ كَانَ عِندَ ٱللَّهِ عَظِيمًا ﴿٥٣﴾ إِن تُبْدُوا۟ شَيْـًٔا أَوْ تُخْفُوهُ فَإِنَّ ٱللَّهَ كَانَ
بِكُلِّ شَىْءٍ عَلِيمًا ﴿٥٤﴾ لَّا جُنَاحَ عَلَيْهِنَّ فِىٓ ءَابَآئِهِنَّ وَلَآ أَبْنَآئِهِنَّ وَلَآ إِخْوَٰنِهِنَّ
وَلَآ أَبْنَآءِ إِخْوَٰنِهِنَّ وَلَآ أَبْنَآءِ أَخَوَٰتِهِنَّ وَلَا نِسَآئِهِنَّ وَلَا مَا مَلَكَتْ أَيْمَٰنُهُنَّ
وَٱتَّقِينَ ٱللَّهَ إِنَّ ٱللَّهَ كَانَ عَلَىٰ كُلِّ شَىْءٍ شَهِيدًا ﴿٥٥﴾ إِنَّ ٱللَّهَ وَمَلَٰٓئِكَتَهُۥ
يُصَلُّونَ عَلَى ٱلنَّبِىِّ يَٰٓأَيُّهَا ٱلَّذِينَ ءَامَنُوا۟ صَلُّوا۟ عَلَيْهِ وَسَلِّمُوا۟ تَسْلِيمًا ﴿٥٦﴾ إِنَّ
ٱلَّذِينَ يُؤْذُونَ ٱللَّهَ وَرَسُولَهُۥ لَعَنَهُمُ ٱللَّهُ فِى ٱلدُّنْيَا وَٱلْءَاخِرَةِ وَأَعَدَّ لَهُمْ عَذَابًا
مُّهِينًا ﴿٥٧﴾ وَٱلَّذِينَ يُؤْذُونَ ٱلْمُؤْمِنِينَ وَٱلْمُؤْمِنَٰتِ بِغَيْرِ مَا ٱكْتَسَبُوا۟ فَقَدِ
ٱحْتَمَلُوا۟ بُهْتَٰنًا وَإِثْمًا مُّبِينًا ﴿٥٨﴾ يَٰٓأَيُّهَا ٱلنَّبِىُّ قُل لِّأَزْوَٰجِكَ وَبَنَاتِكَ وَنِسَآءِ
ٱلْمُؤْمِنِينَ يُدْنِينَ عَلَيْهِنَّ مِن جَلَٰبِيبِهِنَّ ذَٰلِكَ أَدْنَىٰٓ أَن يُعْرَفْنَ فَلَا يُؤْذَيْنَ

Wa mā kāna lakum ʾañ-tuʾdhū Rasūlal-lāhi wa lāa ʾañ-tañkiḥūu ʾazwājahū mim-baʿdihīi ʾabadā. ʾInna dhālikum kāna ʿiñdal-lāhi ʿaẓīmā. (53) ʾIñ-tubdū shayʾan ʾaw tukhfūhu faʾinnal-lāha kāna bikulli shayʾin ʿAlīmā. (54) Lā junāḥa ʿalayhinna fīi ʾābāaʾihinna wa lāa ʾabnāaʾihinna wa lāa ʾikhwānihinna wa lāa ʾabnāaʾi ʾikhwānihinna wa lāa ʾabnāaʾi ʾakhawātihinna wa lā nisāaʾihinna wa lā mā malakat ʾaymānuhunn. Wat-taqīnal-lāh. ʾInnal-lāha kāna ʿalā kulli shayʾiñ-Shahīdā. (55) ʾInnal-lāha wa Malāaʾikatahū yuṣallūna ʿalan-Nabiyy. Yāa ʾayyuhal-ladhīna ʾāmanū ṣallū ʿalayhi wa sallimū taslīmā. (56) ʾInnal-ladhīna yuʾdhūnal-lāha wa Rasūlahū laʿanahumul-lāhu fid-dunyā wal-ʾĀkhirati wa ʾaʿadda lahum ʿadhābam-muhīnā. (57) Wal-ladhīna yuʾdhūnal-muʾminīna wal-muʾmināti bighayri maktasabū faqadiḥ-tamalū buhtānañw-wa ʾithmam-mubīnā. (58) Yāa ʾayyuhan-Nabiyyu qul liʾazwājika wa banātika wa nisāaʾil-muʾminīna yudnīna ʿalayhinna miñ-jalābībihinna dhālika ʾadnāa ʾañy-yuʿrafna falā yuʾdhayn.

Moreover, it does not behove you to give offence to God's Apostle – just as it would not behove you ever to marry his widows after he has passed away:[70] that, verily, would be an enormity in the sight of God. ‹53›

Whether you do anything openly or in secret, [remember that,] verily, God has full knowledge of everything. ‹54›

[However,] it is no sin for them[71] [to appear freely] before their fathers, or their sons, or their brothers, or their brothers' sons, or their sisters' sons, or their womenfolk, or such [male slaves] as their right hands may possess.

But [always, O wives of the Prophet,[72]] remain conscious of God – for, behold, God is witness unto everything. ‹55›

Verily, God and His angels bless the Prophet: [hence,] O you who have attained to faith, bless him and give yourselves up [to his guidance] in utter self-surrender! ‹56›

Verily, as for those who [knowingly] affront God and His Apostle – God will reject them[73] in this world and in the life to come; and shameful suffering will He ready for them. ‹57›

And as for those who malign believing men and believing women without their having done any wrong – they surely burden themselves with the guilt of calumny, and [thus] with a flagrant sin! ‹58›

O Prophet! Tell thy wives and thy daughters, as well as all [other] believing women, that they should draw over themselves some of their outer garments [when in public]: this will be more conducive to their being recognized [as decent women] and not annoyed.[74]

---

70 Lit., "to marry his wives after him".

71 I.e., the wives of the Prophet (connecting with the injunction, in verse 53 above, that they should be spoken to "from behind a screen").

72 This interpolation is conditioned by the feminine gender of the subsequent plural imperative *ittaqīna*.

73 In classical Arabic, the term *laʿnah* is more or less synonymous with *ibʿād* ("removal into distance" or "banishment"); hence, God's *laʿnah* denotes "His rejection of a sinner from all that is good" (*Lisān al-ʿArab*) or "exclusion from His grace" (*Manār* II, 50). The term *malʿūn* which occurs in verse 61 below signifies, therefore, "one who is bereft of God's grace".

74 Cf. the first two sentences of 24 : 31 and the corresponding notes 37 and 38.

But [withal,] God is indeed much-forgiving, a dispenser of grace![75] ‹59›

THUS IT IS: if[76] the hypocrites, and they in whose hearts is disease,[77] and they who, by spreading false rumours, would cause disturbances[78] in the City [of the Prophet] desist not [from their hostile doings], We shall indeed give thee mastery over them, [O Muḥammad] – and then they will not remain thy neighbours in this [city] for more than a little while:[79] ‹60› bereft of God's grace, they shall be seized wherever they may be found, and slain one and all.[80] ‹61› Such has been God's way with those who [sinned in like manner and] passed away aforetime – and never wilt thou find any change in God's way![81] ‹62›

PEOPLE will ask thee about the Last Hour. Say: "Knowledge thereof rests with God alone; yet for all thou knowest, the Last Hour may well be near!"[82] ‹63›
Verily, God has rejected the deniers of the truth, and has readied for them a blazing fire, ‹64› therein to abide beyond the count of time: no protector will they find, and none to bring them succour. ‹65›
On the Day when their faces shall be tossed about in the fire,[83] they will exclaim, "Oh, would that we had paid heed unto God, and paid heed unto the Apostle!" ‹66›

وَكَانَ ٱللَّهُ غَفُورًا رَّحِيمًا ﴿٥٩﴾ ۞ لَّئِن لَّمْ يَنتَهِ ٱلْمُنَـٰفِقُونَ وَٱلَّذِينَ فِى
قُلُوبِهِم مَّرَضٌ وَٱلْمُرْجِفُونَ فِى ٱلْمَدِينَةِ لَنُغْرِيَنَّكَ بِهِمْ ثُمَّ لَا يُجَاوِرُونَكَ
فِيهَآ إِلَّا قَلِيلًا ﴿٦٠﴾ مَّلْعُونِينَ ۖ أَيْنَمَا ثُقِفُوٓا۟ أُخِذُوا۟ وَقُتِّلُوا۟ تَقْتِيلًا ﴿٦١﴾
سُنَّةَ ٱللَّهِ فِى ٱلَّذِينَ خَلَوْا۟ مِن قَبْلُ ۖ وَلَن تَجِدَ لِسُنَّةِ ٱللَّهِ تَبْدِيلًا ﴿٦٢﴾
يَسْـَٔلُكَ ٱلنَّاسُ عَنِ ٱلسَّاعَةِ ۖ قُلْ إِنَّمَا عِلْمُهَا عِندَ ٱللَّهِ ۚ وَمَا يُدْرِيكَ لَعَلَّ نصف الحزب
ٱلسَّاعَةَ تَكُونُ قَرِيبًا ﴿٦٣﴾ إِنَّ ٱللَّهَ لَعَنَ ٱلْكَـٰفِرِينَ وَأَعَدَّ لَهُمْ سَعِيرًا ﴿٦٤﴾
خَـٰلِدِينَ فِيهَآ أَبَدًا ۖ لَّا يَجِدُونَ وَلِيًّا وَلَا نَصِيرًا ﴿٦٥﴾ يَوْمَ تُقَلَّبُ وُجُوهُهُمْ
فِى ٱلنَّارِ يَقُولُونَ يَـٰلَيْتَنَآ أَطَعْنَا ٱللَّهَ وَأَطَعْنَا ٱلرَّسُولَا۠ ﴿٦٦﴾

Wa kānal-lāhu Ghafūrar-Raḥīmā. (59) ۞ Laᵓil-lam yañtahil-munāfiqūna wal-ladhīna fī qulūbihim-maraḍuñw-wal-murjifūna fil-Madīnati lanughriyanna-ka bihim thumma lā yujāwirūnaka fīhāa ᵓillā qalīlā. (60) Malᶜūnīna ᵓaynamā thuqifūu ᵓukhidhū wa quttilū taqtīlā. (61) Sunnatal-lāhi fil-ladhīna khalaw miñ-qablu wa lañ-tajida lisunnatil-lāhi tabdīlā. (62) Yasᵓalukan-nāsu ᶜanis-Sāᶜati qul ᵓinnamā ᶜilmuhā ᶜiñdal-lāh. Wa mā yudrīka laᶜallas-Sāᶜata takūnu qarībā. (63) ᵓInnal-lāha laᶜanal-kāfirīna wa ᵓaᶜadda la-hum saᶜīrā. (64) Khālidīna fīhāa ᵓabadañ-lā yajidūna waliyyañw-wa lā naṣīrā. (65) Yawma tuqallabu wujūhuhum fin-nāri yaqūlūna yā laytanāa ᵓaṭaᶜnal-lāha wa ᵓaṭaᶜnar-Rasūlā. (66)

75 The specific, time-bound formulation of the above verse (evident in the reference to the wives and daughters of the Prophet), as well as the deliberate vagueness of the recommendation that women "should draw upon themselves some of their outer garments (*min jalābībihinna*)" when in public, makes it clear that this verse was not meant to be an injunction (*ḥukm*) in the general, timeless sense of this term but, rather, a moral guideline to be observed against the ever-changing background of time and social environment. This finding is reinforced by the concluding reference to God's forgiveness and grace.

76 For my above rendering of *laᵓin*, see *sūrah* 30, note 45. With this passage, the discourse returns to the theme touched upon in verse 1 and more fully dealt with in verses 9-27: namely, the opposition with which the Prophet and his followers were faced in their early years at Yathrib (which by that time had come to be known as *Madīnat an-Nabī*, "the City of the Prophet").

77 See note 16 above.

78 Thus Zamakhsharī, explaining the term *al-murjifūn* in the above context.

79 I.e., "there will be open warfare between thee and them", which will result in their expulsion from Medina: a prediction which was fulfilled in the course of time.

80 Lit., "slain with [a great] slaying". See in this connection note 168 on 2 : 191. For my rendering of *malᶜūnīn* as "bereft of God's grace", see note 73 above.

81 Cf. 35 : 42-44, and particularly the last paragraph of verse 43.

82 See 7 : 187.

83 As in several other instances in the Qurᵓān, the "face", being the noblest and most expressive part of a human

And they will say: "O our Sustainer! Behold, we paid heed unto our leaders, and our great men, and it is they who have led us astray from the right path! ‹67› O our Sustainer! Give them double suffering, and banish them utterly from Thy grace!"[84] ‹68›

O YOU who have attained to faith! Be not like those [children of Israel] who gave offence to Moses, and [remember that] God showed him to be innocent of whatever they alleged [against him or demanded of him]:[85] for of great honour was he in the sight of God. ‹69›

O you who have attained to faith! Remain conscious of God, and [always] speak with a will to bring out [only] what is just and true[86] ‹70› – [whereupon] He will cause your deeds to be virtuous, and will forgive you your sins. And [know that] whoever pays heed unto God and His Apostle has already attained to a mighty triumph. ‹71› Verily, We did offer the trust [of reason and volition] to the heavens, and the earth, and the mountains:[87] but they refused to bear it because they were afraid of it. Yet man took it up[88] – for, verily, he has always been prone to be most wicked, most foolish. ‹72›

وَقَالُوا۟ رَبَّنَآ إِنَّآ أَطَعْنَا سَادَتَنَا وَكُبَرَآءَنَا فَأَضَلُّونَا ٱلسَّبِيلَا۠ ﴿٦٧﴾ رَبَّنَآ
ءَاتِهِمْ ضِعْفَيْنِ مِنَ ٱلْعَذَابِ وَٱلْعَنْهُمْ لَعْنًا كَبِيرًا ﴿٦٨﴾ يَٰٓأَيُّهَا ٱلَّذِينَ
ءَامَنُوا۟ لَا تَكُونُوا۟ كَٱلَّذِينَ ءَاذَوْا۟ مُوسَىٰ فَبَرَّأَهُ ٱللَّهُ مِمَّا قَالُوا۟ ۚ وَكَانَ عِندَ
ٱللَّهِ وَجِيهًا ﴿٦٩﴾ يَٰٓأَيُّهَا ٱلَّذِينَ ءَامَنُوا۟ ٱتَّقُوا۟ ٱللَّهَ وَقُولُوا۟ قَوْلًا
سَدِيدًا ﴿٧٠﴾ يُصْلِحْ لَكُمْ أَعْمَٰلَكُمْ وَيَغْفِرْ لَكُمْ ذُنُوبَكُمْ ۗ وَمَن يُطِعِ
ٱللَّهَ وَرَسُولَهُۥ فَقَدْ فَازَ فَوْزًا عَظِيمًا ﴿٧١﴾ إِنَّا عَرَضْنَا ٱلْأَمَانَةَ عَلَى
ٱلسَّمَٰوَٰتِ وَٱلْأَرْضِ وَٱلْجِبَالِ فَأَبَيْنَ أَن يَحْمِلْنَهَا وَأَشْفَقْنَ مِنْهَا
وَحَمَلَهَا ٱلْإِنسَٰنُ ۖ إِنَّهُۥ كَانَ ظَلُومًا جَهُولًا ﴿٧٢﴾

Wa qālū Rabbanāa ʾinnāa ʾaṭaʿnā sādatanā wa kubarāaʾanā faʾaḍallūnas-sabīlā. (67) Rabbanāa ʾātihim ḍiʿfayni minal-ʿadhābi wal-ʿanhum laʿnañ-kabīrā. (68) Yāa ʾayyuhal-ladhīna ʾāmanū lā takūnū kalladhīna ʾādhaw Mūsā fabarraʾahul-lāhu mimmā qālū; wa kāna ʿiñdal-lāhi wajīhā. (69) Yāa ʾayyuhal-lādhīna ʾāmanut-taqul-lāha wa qūlū qawlañ-sadīdā. (70) Yuṣliḥ lakum ʾaʿmālakum wa yaghfir lakum dhunūbakum. Wa mañy-yuṭiʿil-lāha wa Rasūlahū faqad fāza fawzan ʿaẓīmā. (71) ʾInnā ʿaraḍnal-ʾamānata ʿalas-samāwāti wal-ʾarḍi wal-jibāli faʾabayna ʾañy-yaḥmilnahā wa ʾashfaqna minhā wa ḥamalahal-ʾIñsānu ʾinnahū kāna ẓalūmañ-jahūlā. (72)

person, represents here man's "personality" in its entirety; and its being "tossed about in the fire" is symbolic of the annihilation of the sinner's will and his reduction to utter passivity.

84 Lit., "reject them (*ilʿanhum*) with a great rejection", i.e., "from Thy grace".

85 This is an allusion to the aspersions occasionally cast upon Moses by some of his followers and mentioned in the Old Testament (e.g., Numbers xii, 1-13), as well as to the blasphemous demands of which the Qur'ān speaks – e.g., "O Moses, indeed we shall not believe thee until we see God face to face" (2 : 55) or, "Go forth, thou and thy Sustainer, and fight, both of you!" (5 : 24). These instances are paralleled here with the frequently cited accusations that Muḥammad had "invented" the Qurʾān and then falsely attributed it to God, that he was a madman, and so forth, as well as with frivolous demands to prove his prophethood by bringing about miracles or – as is re-stated in verse 63 of this *sūrah* – by predicting the date of the Last Hour.

86 The expression *qawl sadīd* signifies, literally, "a saying that hits the mark", i.e., is truthful, relevant and to the point. In the only other instance where this expression is used in the Qurʾān (at the end of 4 : 9) it may be appropriately rendered as "speaking in a just manner"; in the present instance, however, it obviously relates to speaking *of others* in a manner devoid of all hidden meanings, insinuations and frivolous suspicions, aiming at no more and no less than the truth.

87 The classical commentators give all kinds of laborious explanations to the term *amānah* ("trust") occurring in this parable, but the most convincing of them (mentioned in Lane I, 102, with reference to the above verse) are "reason", or "intellect", and "the faculty of volition" – i.e., the ability to choose between two or more possible courses of action or modes of behaviour, and thus between good and evil.

88 Sc., "and then failed to measure up to the moral responsibility arising from the reason and the comparative free

[And so it is] that God imposes suffering on the hypocrites, both men and women, as well as on the men and women who ascribe divinity to aught beside Him.[89] And [so, too, it is] that God turns in His mercy unto the believing men and believing women: for God is indeed much-forgiving, a dispenser of grace! ‹73›

لِّيُعَذِّبَ ٱللَّهُ ٱلْمُنَـٰفِقِينَ وَٱلْمُنَـٰفِقَـٰتِ وَٱلْمُشْرِكِينَ وَٱلْمُشْرِكَـٰتِ
وَيَتُوبَ ٱللَّهُ عَلَى ٱلْمُؤْمِنِينَ وَٱلْمُؤْمِنَـٰتِ ۗ وَكَانَ ٱللَّهُ غَفُورًا رَّحِيمًۢا ﴿٧٣﴾

Liyuᶜadhdhibal-lāhul-munāfiqīna wal-munāfiqāti wal-mushrikīna wal-mushrikāti wa yatūbal-lāhu ᶜalal-muᵓminīna wal-muᵓmināt. Wa kānal-lāhu Ghafūrar-Raḥīmā. ﴿٧٣﴾

will with which he has been endowed" (Zamakhsharī). This obviously applies to the human race as such, and not necessarily to all of its individuals.

89 In other words, on those who offend against what their own reason and conscience would have them do. This suffering, whether in this world or in the hereafter, is but a causal consequence – as the *lām al-ᶜāqibah* at the beginning of this sentence shows – of man's moral failure, and not an arbitrary act of God. (Cf. in this connection note 7 on 2 : 7, which speaks of God's "sealing" the hearts of those who are bent on denying the truth.)

The Thirty-Fourth Sūrah

*Saba*ʾ (Sheba)

Mecca Period

ALMOST certainly, this *sūrah* was revealed in the second half of the Mecca period, probably a short time before *sūrah* 17 ("The Night Journey"). The title is based on the reference, in verses 15-20, to the people of Sabaʾ (the Biblical Sheba), who are cited as an example of the impermanence of all human power, wealth and glory.

The pivotal ideas of the whole *sūrah* may be summed up in the question, addressed to all human beings, in verse 9: "Are they, then, not aware of how little of the sky and the earth lies open before them, and how much is hidden from them?" – and in the call to moral responsibility sounded in verse 46: "Say: 'I counsel you one thing only: Be ever conscious of standing before God, whether you are in the company of others or alone.'"

-34-

سورة سبإ مكية
وآياتها أربع وخمسون

IN THE NAME OF GOD, THE MOST GRACIOUS, THE DISPENSER OF GRACE:

ALL PRAISE is due to God, to whom all that is in the heavens and all that is on earth belongs; and to Him will be due all praise in the life to come.
For He alone is truly wise, all-aware: ‹1›
He knows all that enters the earth, and all that comes out of it, as well as all that descends from the skies, and all that ascends to them.[1] And He alone is a dispenser of grace, truly-forgiving. ‹2›
And yet, they who are bent on denying the truth assert, "Never will the Last Hour come upon Us!"[2]
Say: "Nay, by my Sustainer! By Him who knows all that is beyond the reach of a created being's perception: it will most certainly come upon you!"
Not an atom's weight [of whatever there is] in the heavens or on earth escapes His knowledge; and neither is there anything smaller than that, or larger, but is recorded in [His] clear decree, ‹3› to the end that He may reward those who believe and do righteous deeds: [for] it is they whom forgiveness of sins awaits, and a most excellent sustenance[3] ‹4› –

بِسْمِ ٱللَّهِ ٱلرَّحْمَٰنِ ٱلرَّحِيمِ

ٱلْحَمْدُ لِلَّهِ ٱلَّذِى لَهُۥ مَا فِى ٱلسَّمَٰوَٰتِ وَمَا فِى ٱلْأَرْضِ وَلَهُ ٱلْحَمْدُ فِى
ٱلْءَاخِرَةِ وَهُوَ ٱلْحَكِيمُ ٱلْخَبِيرُ (1) يَعْلَمُ مَا يَلِجُ فِى ٱلْأَرْضِ وَمَا يَخْرُجُ
مِنْهَا وَمَا يَنزِلُ مِنَ ٱلسَّمَآءِ وَمَا يَعْرُجُ فِيهَا وَهُوَ ٱلرَّحِيمُ ٱلْغَفُورُ (2)
وَقَالَ ٱلَّذِينَ كَفَرُوا۟ لَا تَأْتِينَا ٱلسَّاعَةُ قُلْ بَلَىٰ وَرَبِّى لَتَأْتِيَنَّكُمْ عَٰلِمِ
ٱلْغَيْبِ لَا يَعْزُبُ عَنْهُ مِثْقَالُ ذَرَّةٍ فِى ٱلسَّمَٰوَٰتِ وَلَا فِى ٱلْأَرْضِ وَلَآ
أَصْغَرُ مِن ذَٰلِكَ وَلَآ أَكْبَرُ إِلَّا فِى كِتَٰبٍ مُّبِينٍ (3) لِّيَجْزِىَ ٱلَّذِينَ ءَامَنُوا۟
وَعَمِلُوا۟ ٱلصَّٰلِحَٰتِ أُو۟لَٰٓئِكَ لَهُم مَّغْفِرَةٌ وَرِزْقٌ كَرِيمٌ (4)

Bismil-lāhir-Raḥmānir-Raḥīm.
ʾAlḥamdu-lillāhil-ladhī lahū mā fis-samāwāti wa mā fil-ʾarḍi wa lahul-ḥamdu fil-ʾĀkhirati wa Huwal-Ḥakīmul-Khabīr. (1) Yaᶜlamu mā yaliju fil-ʾarḍi wa mā yakhruju minhā wa mā yañzilu minas-samāaʾi wa mā yaᶜruju fīhā; wa Huwar-Raḥīmul-Ghafūr. (2) Wa qālal-ladhīna kafarū lā taʾtīnas-Sāᶜah. Qul balā wa Rabbī lataʾtiyannakum ᶜĀlimil-ghayb. Lā yaᶜzubu ᶜanhu mithqālu dharratiñ-fis-samāwāti wa lā fil-ʾarḍi wa lāa ʾaṣgharu miñ-dhalika wa lāa ʾakbaru ʾillā fī Kitābim-mubīn. (3) Liyajziyal-ladhīna ʾāmanū wa ᶜamiluṣ-ṣāliḥāti ʾulāaʾika lahum-maghfiratuñw-wa rizquñ-karīm. (4)

---

1 This definition comprises things physical and spiritual: waters disappearing underground and reappearing; the metamorphosis of seed into plant, and of decaying plant into oil and coal; traces of old artifacts and entire civilizations buried in the earth and then reappearing within the sight and consciousness of later generations of men; the transformation of dead bodies of animals and men into elements of nourishment for new life; the ascent of earthy vapours towards the skies, and their descent as rain, snow or hail; the ascent towards the heavens of men's longings, hopes and ambitions, and the descent of divine inspiration into the minds of men, and thus a revival of faith and thought and, with it, the growth of new artifacts, new skills and new hopes: in short, the endless recurrence of birth, death and re-birth which characterizes all of God's creation.

2 This assertion of the godless has a twofold meaning: (1) "The universe is without beginning and without end; it can only change, but can never cease to exist" – which amounts to a denial of the fact that God alone is eternal; and (2) "There is no resurrection and divine judgment as symbolized by the Last Hour" – which amounts to a denial of life after death and, hence, of all significance and purpose attaching to human life as such.

3 See note 5 on 8 : 4.

whereas for those who strive against Our messages, seeking to defeat their purpose, there is grievous suffering in store as an outcome of [their] vileness.[4] ⟨5⟩

NOW THEY who are endowed with [innate] knowledge are well aware that whatever has been bestowed upon thee from on high by thy Sustainer is indeed the truth, and that it guides onto the way that leads to the Almighty, the One to whom all praise is due! ⟨6⟩

As against this, they who are bent on denying the truth say [unto all who are of like mind]: "Shall we point out to you a man who will tell you that [after your death,] when you will have been scattered in countless fragments, you shall – lo and behold! – be [restored to life] in a new act of creation? ⟨7⟩ Does he [knowingly] attribute his own lying inventions to God – or is he a madman?"

Nay, [there is no madness in this Prophet –] but they who will not believe in the life to come are [bound to lose themselves] in suffering and in a profound aberration.[5] ⟨8⟩

Are they, then, not aware of how little of the sky and the earth lies open before them, and how much is hidden from them?[6] – [or that,] if We so willed, We could cause the earth to swallow them,[7] or cause fragments of the sky to fall down upon them?[8]

وَالَّذِينَ سَعَوْ فِي آيَاتِنَا مُعَاجِزِينَ أُولَٰئِكَ لَهُمْ عَذَابٌ مِّن رِّجْزٍ أَلِيمٌ ﴿٥﴾
وَيَرَى الَّذِينَ أُوتُوا الْعِلْمَ الَّذِي أُنزِلَ إِلَيْكَ مِن رَّبِّكَ هُوَ الْحَقَّ وَيَهْدِي إِلَىٰ
صِرَاطِ الْعَزِيزِ الْحَمِيدِ ﴿٦﴾ وَقَالَ الَّذِينَ كَفَرُوا هَلْ نَدُلُّكُمْ عَلَىٰ رَجُلٍ
يُنَبِّئُكُمْ إِذَا مُزِّقْتُمْ كُلَّ مُمَزَّقٍ إِنَّكُمْ لَفِي خَلْقٍ جَدِيدٍ ﴿٧﴾ أَفْتَرَىٰ عَلَى اللَّهِ
كَذِبًا أَم بِهِ جِنَّةٌ ۗ بَلِ الَّذِينَ لَا يُؤْمِنُونَ بِالْآخِرَةِ فِي الْعَذَابِ وَالضَّلَالِ
الْبَعِيدِ ﴿٨﴾ أَفَلَمْ يَرَوْا إِلَىٰ مَا بَيْنَ أَيْدِيهِمْ وَمَا خَلْفَهُم مِّنَ السَّمَاءِ
وَالْأَرْضِ ۚ إِن نَّشَأْ نَخْسِفْ بِهِمُ الْأَرْضَ أَوْ نُسْقِطْ عَلَيْهِمْ كِسَفًا مِّنَ السَّمَاءِ

Wal-ladhīna saᶜaw fīi ᵓĀyātinā muᶜājizīna ᵓulāaᵓika lahum ᶜadhābum-mir-rijzin ᵓalīm. ⟨5⟩ Wa yaral-ladhīna ᵓūtul-ᶜilmal-ladhīi ᵓuñzila ᵓilayka mir Rabbika huwal-ḥaqqa wa yahdīi ᵓilā ṣirāṭil-ᶜAzīzil-Ḥamīd. ⟨6⟩ Wa qālal-ladhīna kafarū hal nadullukum ᶜalā rajuliñy-yunabbiᵓukum ᵓidhā muzziqtum kulla mumazzaqin ᵓinnakum lafī khalqiñ-jadīd. ⟨7⟩ ᵓAftarā ᶜalal-lāhi kadhiban ᵓam-bihī jinnah. Balil-ladhīna lā yuᵓminūna bilᵓĀkhirati fil-ᶜadhābi waḍ-ḍalālil-baᶜīd. ⟨8⟩ ᵓAfalam yaraw ᵓilā mā bayna ᵓaydīhim wa mā khalfahum-minas-samāaᵓi wal-ᵓarḍ. ᵓIñ-nashaᵓ nakhsif bihimul-ᵓarḍa ᵓaw nusqiṭ ᶜalayhim kisafam-minas-samāaᵓ.

4 The particle *min* (lit., "out of") which precedes the noun *rijz* ("vileness" or "vile conduct") indicates that the suffering which awaits such sinners in the life to come is an organic *consequence* of their deliberately evil conduct in this world.

5 Lit., "remote aberration". (For the Qurᵓanic use of the term *ḍalāl* – lit., "error" or "going astray" – in the sense of "aberration", see 12 : 8 and 95.) The construction of this phrase points definitely to suffering in *this* world (in contrast with the suffering in the hereafter spoken of in verse 5 above): for whereas the concept of "aberration" is meaningless in the context of the life to come, it has an obvious meaning in the context of the moral and social confusion – and, hence, of the individual and social suffering – which is the unavoidable consequence of people's loss of belief in the existence of absolute moral values and, thus, in an ultimate divine judgment on the basis of those values.

6 Lit., ". . . not aware of what of the sky and the earth is between their hands, and what is behind them": an idiomatic phrase explained in *sūrah* 2, note 247. In the present context – as well as in 2 : 255 – the above phrase stresses the insignificance of the knowledge attained to by man, or accessible to him; hence, so the argument goes, how can anyone be so presumptuous as to *deny* the reality of resurrection and life after death, seeing that it is a phenomenon beyond man's experience, while, on the other hand, everything within the universe points to God's unlimited creative power?

7 I.e., in an earthquake.

8 This allusion to unpredictable geological and cosmic occurrences – earthquakes, the fall of meteors and meteorites, cosmic rays, and so forth – reinforces the statement about "how little of the sky and the earth lies open

In all this, behold, there is a message indeed for every servant [of God] who is wont to turn unto Him [in repentance].[9] ‹9›

AND [thus], indeed, did We grace David with Our favour:[10] "O you mountains! Sing with him the praise of God! And [likewise] you birds!"[11]
And We softened all sharpness in him,[12] ‹10› [and inspired him thus:] "Do good deeds lavishly, without stint, and give deep thought to their steady flow."[13]
And [thus should you all, O believers,] do righteous deeds: for, verily, I see all that you do! ‹11›

AND UNTO Solomon [We made subservient] the wind: its morning course [covered the distance of] a month's journey, and its evening course, a month's journey.[14]
And We caused a fountain of molten copper to flow at his behest;[15] and [even] among the invisible beings there were some that had [been constrained] to labour for him[16] by his Sustainer's leave –

إِنَّ فِى ذَٰلِكَ لَأٓيَةً لِّكُلِّ عَبْدٍ مُّنِيبٍ ﴿٩﴾ ۞ وَلَقَدْ ءَاتَيْنَا دَاوُۥدَ مِنَّا فَضْلًا ۖ يَٰجِبَالُ
أَوِّبِى مَعَهُۥ وَٱلطَّيْرَ ۖ وَأَلَنَّا لَهُ ٱلْحَدِيدَ ﴿١٠﴾ أَنِ ٱعْمَلْ سَٰبِغَٰتٍ وَقَدِّرْ فِى ٱلسَّرْدِ ۖ
وَٱعْمَلُوا۟ صَٰلِحًا ۖ إِنِّى بِمَا تَعْمَلُونَ بَصِيرٌ ﴿١١﴾ وَلِسُلَيْمَٰنَ ٱلرِّيحَ غُدُوُّهَا شَهْرٌ
وَرَوَاحُهَا شَهْرٌ ۖ وَأَسَلْنَا لَهُۥ عَيْنَ ٱلْقِطْرِ ۖ وَمِنَ ٱلْجِنِّ مَن يَعْمَلُ بَيْنَ يَدَيْهِ بِإِذْنِ رَبِّهِۦ ۖ

ثلاثة ارباع الحزب

ʾInna fī dhalika laʾĀyatal-likulli ʿabdim-munīb. ‹9›
۞ Wa laqad ʾātaynā Dāwūda minnā faḍlā. Yā jibālu
ʾawwibī maʿahū waṭ-ṭayra wa ʾalannā lahul-ḥadīd.
‹10› ʾAniʿ-mal sābighātiñw-wa qaddir fis-sardi waʿ-
malū ṣāliḥā. ʾInnī bimā taʿmalūna Baṣīr. ‹11› Wa li-
Sulaymānar-rīḥa ghuduwwuhā shahruñw-wa rawā-
ḥuhā shahr. Wa ʾasalnā lahū ʿaynal-qiṭri wa minal-
jinni mañy-yaʿmalu bayna yadayhi biʾidhni Rabbih.

before them, and how much is hidden from them", and contrasts man's insignificance with God's omniscience and almightiness.

9 See last sentence of 24 : 31 and the corresponding note 41.

10 Lit., "did We bestow upon David a favour from Ourselves". This connects with the elliptic reference to repentance in the preceding verse: David is singled out for special mention in view of the allusion, in *sūrah* 38, to his having suddenly become aware that he had committed a sin, whereupon "he asked his Sustainer to forgive him his sin . . . and *turned unto Him in repentance*" (38 : 24).

11 Cf. 21 : 79 and the corresponding note 73.

12 Lit., "for him". The term *ḥadīd* denotes, primarily, something that is "sharp" in both the concrete and abstract senses of the word: for the latter sense, cf. the Qurʾanic phrase "sharp (*ḥadīd*) is thy sight today" (50 : 22), or the many idiomatic expressions like *rajul ḥadīd*, "a man of sharp intellect", *ḥadīd an-naẓar*, "one who looks boldly [at others]", *rāʾiḥah ḥadīdah*, "a sharp odour", etc. (*Lisān al-ʿArab*). As a noun with a definite article (*al-ḥadīd*), it signifies "all that is sharp", or "sharpness", as well as "iron". God's having "softened all sharpness" in David is evidently an allusion to his exalted sense of beauty (expressed in the poetry of his Psalms) as well as to his goodness and humility. – An alternative rendering of the above phrase would be: "We caused iron to become soft for him", which might be an allusion to his outstanding abilities as poet, warrior and ruler.

13 The adjective *sābigh* (fem. *sābighah*) signifies anything that is "ample", "abundant" and "complete" (in the sense of being perfect). In its plural form *sābighāt* it assumes the function of the noun which it is meant to qualify, and denotes, literally, "things [or "deeds"] ample and complete" or "perfect" – i.e., good deeds done abundantly and without stint: cf. the only other Qurʾanic instance of the same stem in 31 : 20 – "[God] has lavished (*asbagha*) upon you His blessings". The noun *sard*, on the other hand, denotes something "carried on consecutively", or something the parts (or stages) whereof are "following one another steadily", i.e., are continued or repeated.

14 Cf. 21 : 81 and the corresponding note 75. For a more general explanation of the legends connected with the person of Solomon, see note 77 on 21 : 82.

15 Lit., "for him": probably a reference to the many furnishings of copper and brass which, according to the Bible (cf. II Chronicles iv), Solomon caused to be made for his newly-built temple.

16 Lit., "between his hands", i.e., subject to his will: see 21 : 82 and the corresponding notes 76 and 77. For my rendering of *jinn* as "invisible beings", see Appendix III.

وَمَن يَزِغْ مِنْهُمْ عَنْ أَمْرِنَا نُذِقْهُ مِنْ عَذَابِ ٱلسَّعِيرِ ﴿١٢﴾ يَعْمَلُونَ
لَهُۥ مَا يَشَآءُ مِن مَّحَٰرِيبَ وَتَمَٰثِيلَ وَجِفَانٍ كَٱلْجَوَابِ وَقُدُورٍ
رَّاسِيَٰتٍ ٱعْمَلُوٓا۟ ءَالَ دَاوُۥدَ شُكْرًا وَقَلِيلٌ مِّنْ عِبَادِىَ ٱلشَّكُورُ ﴿١٣﴾
فَلَمَّا قَضَيْنَا عَلَيْهِ ٱلْمَوْتَ مَا دَلَّهُمْ عَلَىٰ مَوْتِهِۦٓ إِلَّا دَآبَّةُ ٱلْأَرْضِ
تَأْكُلُ مِنسَأَتَهُۥ ۖ فَلَمَّا خَرَّ تَبَيَّنَتِ ٱلْجِنُّ أَن لَّوْ كَانُوا۟ يَعْلَمُونَ ٱلْغَيْبَ
مَا لَبِثُوا۟ فِى ٱلْعَذَابِ ٱلْمُهِينِ ﴿١٤﴾

Wa mañy-yazigh minhum ᶜan ʾamrinā nudhiqhu min ᶜadhābis-saᶜīr. (12) Yaᶜmalūna lahū mā yashāaʾu mim-maḥārība wa tamāthīla wa jifāniñ-kaljawābi wa qudūrir-rāsiyāt. ʾIᶜmalūu ʾāla Dāwūda shukrañw-wa qalīlum-min ᶜibādiyash-shakūr. (13) Falammā qaḍaynā ᶜalayhil-mawta mā dallahum ᶜalā mawtihīi ʾillā dāabbatul-ʾarḍi taʾkulu miñsaʾatah. Falammā kharra tabayyanatil-Jinnu ʾal-law kānū yaᶜlamūnal-ghayba mā labithū fil-ᶜadhābil-muhīn. (14)

and whichever of them deviated from Our command, him would We let taste suffering through a blazing flame: ‹12› – they made for him whatever he wished of sanctuaries, and statues, and basins as [large as] great watering-troughs, and cauldrons firmly anchored.[17]
[And We said:] "Labour, O David's people, in gratitude [towards Me][18] – and [remember that] few are the truly grateful [even] among My servants!"[19] ‹13›
Yet [even Solomon had to die; but] when We decreed that he should die, nothing showed them that he was dead except an earthworm that gnawed away his staff.[20] And when he fell to the ground, those invisible beings [subservient to him] saw clearly that, had they but understood the reality which was beyond the reach of [their] perception,[21] they would not have continued [to toil] in the shameful suffering [of servitude].[22] ‹14›

17 I.e., because of their enormous size. Cf. II Chronicles iii, 10-13, where statues ("images") of cherubim are mentioned, as well as iv, 2-5, describing "a molten sea" (i.e., basin) of huge dimensions, resting upon twelve statues of oxen, and meant to contain water "for the priests to wash in" (*ibid.*, iv, 6). The "sanctuaries" were apparently the various halls of the new temple.

18 These words, ostensibly addressed to "the people" or "the family" of David, are in reality an admonition to all believers, at all times, since all of them are, spiritually, "David's people".

19 I.e., even among those who *consider* themselves God's servants – for "truly grateful [to God] is only he who realizes his *inability* to render adequate thanks to Him" (Zamakhsharī).

20 This is yet another of the many Solomonic legends which had become an inalienable part of ancient Arabian tradition, and which the Qurʾān uses as a vehicle for the allegorical illustration of some of its teachings. According to the legend alluded to above, Solomon died on his throne, leaning forward on his staff, and for a length of time nobody became aware of his death: with the result that the *jinn*, who had been constrained to work for him, went on labouring at the heavy tasks assigned to them. Gradually, however, a termite ate away Solomon's staff, and his body, deprived of support, fell to the ground. This story – only hinted at in its outline – is apparently used here as an allegory of the insignificance and inherent brittleness of human life and of the perishable nature and emptiness of all worldly might and glory.

21 *Al-ghayb*, "that which is beyond the reach of [a created being's] perception", either in an absolute or – as in this instance – in a relative, temporary sense.

22 I.e., because they would have known that Solomon's sway over them had ended. In the elliptic manner so characteristic of the Qurʾān, stress is laid here, firstly, on the limited nature of all empirical knowledge, including the result of deductions and inferences based on no more than observable or calculable phenomena, and, secondly, on the impossibility to determine correctly, on the basis of such limited fragments of knowledge alone, what course of action would be right in a given situation. Although the story as such relates to "invisible beings", its moral lesson (which may be summed up in the statement that empirical knowledge cannot provide any ethical guideline unless it is accompanied, and completed, by divine guidance) is obviously addressed to human beings as well.

INDEED, in [the luxuriant beauty of] their homeland, the people of Sheba had an evidence [of God's grace][23] – two [vast expanses of] gardens, to the right and to the left, [calling out to them, as it were:] "Eat of what your Sustainer has provided for you, and render thanks unto Him: a land most goodly, and a Sustainer much-forgiving!" ‹15›

But they turned away [from Us], and so We let loose upon them a flood that overwhelmed the dams,[24] and changed their two [expanses of luxuriant] gardens into a couple of gardens yielding bitter fruit, and tamarisks, and some few [wild] lote-trees: ‹16› thus We requited them for their having denied the truth. But do We ever requite [thus] any but the utterly ingrate?[25] ‹17›

Now [before their downfall,] We had placed between them and the cities which We had blessed[26] [many] towns within sight of one another; and thus We had made travelling easy [for them, as if to say]: "Travel safely in this [land], by night or by day!" ‹18›

لَقَدْ كَانَ لِسَبَإٍ فِي مَسْكَنِهِمْ آيَةٌ جَنَّتَانِ عَنْ يَمِينٍ وَشِمَالٍ كُلُوا مِنْ
رِزْقِ رَبِّكُمْ وَاشْكُرُوا لَهُ بَلْدَةٌ طَيِّبَةٌ وَرَبٌّ غَفُورٌ ﴿١٥﴾ فَأَعْرَضُوا
فَأَرْسَلْنَا عَلَيْهِمْ سَيْلَ الْعَرِمِ وَبَدَّلْنَاهُمْ بِجَنَّتَيْهِمْ جَنَّتَيْنِ ذَوَاتَيْ أُكُلٍ
خَمْطٍ وَأَثْلٍ وَشَيْءٍ مِنْ سِدْرٍ قَلِيلٍ ﴿١٦﴾ ذَٰلِكَ جَزَيْنَاهُمْ بِمَا كَفَرُوا وَهَلْ
نُجَازِي إِلَّا الْكَفُورَ ﴿١٧﴾ وَجَعَلْنَا بَيْنَهُمْ وَبَيْنَ الْقُرَى الَّتِي بَارَكْنَا فِيهَا
قُرًى ظَاهِرَةً وَقَدَّرْنَا فِيهَا السَّيْرَ سِيرُوا فِيهَا لَيَالِيَ وَأَيَّامًا آمِنِينَ ﴿١٨﴾

Laqad kāna liSaba'iñ-fī maskanihim 'Āyah. Jannatāni 'añy-yamīniñw-wa shimāl. Kulū mir-rizqi Rabbikum wash-kurū lah. Baldatuñ-ṭayyibatuñw-wa Rabbun Ghafūr. (15) Fa'a'raḍū fa'arsalnā 'alayhim saylal-'arimi wa baddalnāhum-bijannatayhim jannatayni dhawātay 'ukulin khamṭiñw-wa 'athliñw-wa shay'im-miñ-sidriñ-qalīl. (16) Dhālika jazaynāhum-bimā kafarū; wa hal nujāzīi 'illal-kafūr. (17) Wa ja'alnā baynahum wa baynal-quralatī bāraknā fīhā qurañ-ẓāhiratañw-wa qaddarnā fīhas-sayr. Sīrū fīhā layāliya wa 'ayyāman 'āminīn. (18)

23 This connects with the call to gratitude towards God in the preceding passage, and the mention, at the end of verse 13, that "few are the truly grateful" even among those who think of themselves as "God's servants" (see note 19 above). – The kingdom of Sheba (Sabā' in Arabic) was situated in south-western Arabia, and at the time of its greatest prosperity (i.e., in the first millenium B.C.) comprised not only the Yemen but also a large part of Ḥaḍramawt and the Mahrah country, and probably also much of present-day Ethiopia. In the vicinity of its capital Ma'rib – sometimes also spelled Mārib – the Sabaeans had built in the course of centuries an extraordinary system of dams, dykes and sluices, which became famous in history, with astonishing remnants extant to this day. It was to this great dam that the whole country of Sheba owed its outstanding prosperity, which became proverbial throughout Arabia. (According to the geographer Al-Hamdānī, who died in 334 H., the area irrigated by this system of dams stretched eastward to the desert of Ṣayhad on the confines of the Rub' al-Khālī.) The flourishing state of the country was reflected in its people's intense trading activities and their control of the "incense road" which led from Ma'rib northwards to Mecca, Yathrib and Syria, and eastwards to Ḍufār on the shores of the Arabian Sea, thus connecting with the maritime routes from India and China. – The period to which the above Qur'anic passage refers is evidently much later than that spoken of in 27 : 22-44.

24 Lit., "the flooding of the dams" (*sayl al-'arim*). The date of that catastrophe cannot be established with any certainty, but the most probable period of the *first* bursting of the Dam of Ma'rib seems to have been the second century of the Christian era. The kingdom of Sheba was largely devastated, and this led to the migration of many southern (Qaḥṭān) tribes towards the north of the Peninsula. Subsequently, it appears, the system of dams and dykes was to some extent repaired, but the country never regained its earlier prosperity; and a few decades before the advent of Islam the great dam collapsed completely and finally.

25 Neither the Qur'ān nor any authentic *ḥadīth* tells us anything definite about the way in which the people of Sheba had sinned at the time immediately preceding the final collapse of the Dam of Ma'rib (i.e., in the sixth century of the Christian era). This omission, however, seems to be deliberate. In view of the fact that the story of Sheba's prosperity and subsequent catastrophic downfall had become a byword in ancient Arabia, it is most probable that its mention in the Qur'ān has a purely moral purport similar to that of the immediately preceding legend of Solomon's death, inasmuch as both these legends, in their Qur'anic presentation, are allegories of the ephemeral nature of all human might and achievement. As mentioned at the beginning of note 23 above, the story of Sheba's downfall is closely linked with the phenomenon of men's recurrent ingratitude towards God. (See also verse 20 and the corresponding note 29.)

26 I.e., Mecca and Jerusalem, both of which lay on the caravan route much used by the people of Sheba.

But now they would say, "Long has our Sustainer made the distance between our journey-stages!"[27] – for they had sinned against themselves. And in the end We caused them to become [one of those] tales [of things long past], and scattered them in countless fragments.[28]
Herein, behold, there are messages indeed for all who are wholly patient in adversity and deeply grateful [to God]. ‹19›
Now, indeed, Iblīs did prove that his opinion of them had been right:[29] for [when he called them,] they followed him – all but some of the believers [among them]. ‹20›
And yet, he had no power at all over them:[30] [for if We allow him to tempt man,] it is only to the end that We might make a clear distinction between those who [truly] believe in the life to come and those who are in doubt thereof:[31] for thy Sustainer watches over all things. ‹21›

SAY: "Call upon those [beings] whom you imagine [to be endowed with divine powers] beside God: they have not an atom's weight of power either in the heavens or on earth, nor have they any share in [governing] either, nor does He [choose to] have any helper from among them."[32] ‹22›

فَقَالُوا۟ رَبَّنَا بَٰعِدْ بَيْنَ أَسْفَارِنَا وَظَلَمُوٓا۟ أَنفُسَهُمْ فَجَعَلْنَٰهُمْ أَحَادِيثَ
وَمَزَّقْنَٰهُمْ كُلَّ مُمَزَّقٍ ۚ إِنَّ فِى ذَٰلِكَ لَءَايَٰتٍ لِّكُلِّ صَبَّارٍ شَكُورٍ ﴿١٩﴾ وَلَقَدْ
صَدَّقَ عَلَيْهِمْ إِبْلِيسُ ظَنَّهُۥ فَٱتَّبَعُوهُ إِلَّا فَرِيقًا مِّنَ ٱلْمُؤْمِنِينَ ﴿٢٠﴾ وَمَا
كَانَ لَهُۥ عَلَيْهِم مِّن سُلْطَٰنٍ إِلَّا لِنَعْلَمَ مَن يُؤْمِنُ بِٱلْءَاخِرَةِ مِمَّنْ هُوَ مِنْهَا
فِى شَكٍّ ۗ وَرَبُّكَ عَلَىٰ كُلِّ شَىْءٍ حَفِيظٌ ﴿٢١﴾ قُلِ ٱدْعُوا۟ ٱلَّذِينَ زَعَمْتُم مِّن
دُونِ ٱللَّهِ ۖ لَا يَمْلِكُونَ مِثْقَالَ ذَرَّةٍ فِى ٱلسَّمَٰوَٰتِ وَلَا فِى ٱلْأَرْضِ وَمَا
لَهُمْ فِيهِمَا مِن شِرْكٍ وَمَا لَهُۥ مِنْهُم مِّن ظَهِيرٍ ﴿٢٢﴾

Faqālū Rabbanā bāᶜid bayna ᵓasfārinā wa ẓalamūu ᵓan̄fusahum fajaᶜalnāhum ᵓaḥādītha wa mazzaqnāhum kulla mumazzaq. ᵓInna fī dhālika laᵓĀyātil-likulli ṣabbārin̄-shakūr. ⟨19⟩ Wa laqad ṣaddaqa ᶜalayhim ᵓIblīsu ẓannahū fattabaᶜūhu ᵓillā farīqam-minal-muᵓminīn. ⟨20⟩ Wa mā kāna lahū ᶜalayhim-min̄-sulṭānin ᵓillā linaᶜlama man̄y-yuᵓminu bilᵓĀkhirati mimman huwa minhā fī shakk. Wa Rabbuka ᶜalā kulli shayᵓin Ḥafīẓ. ⟨21⟩ Qulid-ᶜulladhīna zaᶜamtum-min̄-dūnil-lāh. Lā yamlikūna mithqāla dharratin̄-fis-samāwāti wa lā fil-ᵓarḍi wa mā lahum fīhimā min̄-shirkin̄w-wa mā lahū minhum-min̄-ẓahīr. ⟨22⟩

27 In its generally-accepted spelling – based on the reading adopted by most of the early scholars of Medina and Kūfah – the above phrase reads in the vocative *rabbanā* and the imperative *bāᶜid* ("Our Sustainer! Make long the distances . . .", etc.), which, however, cannot be convincingly explained. On the other hand, Ṭabarī, Baghawī and Zamakhsharī mention, on the authority of some of the earliest Qurᵓān-commentators, another legitimate reading of the relevant words, namely, *rabbunā* (in the nominative) and *baᶜada* (in the indicative), which gives the meaning adopted by me: "Long has our Sustainer made the distances . . .", etc. To my mind, this reading is much more appropriate since (as pointed out by Zamakhsharī) it expresses the belated regrets and the sorrow of the people of Sheba at the devastation of their country, the exodus of large groups of the population, and the resultant abandonment of many towns and villages on the great caravan routes.

28 An allusion to the mass-migration of South-Arabian tribes in all directions – particularly towards central and northern Arabia – subsequent to the destruction of the Dam of Maᵓrib.

29 See 17 : 62, as well as the last sentence of 7 : 17, in which Iblīs (i.e., Satan) says of the human race, "most of them wilt Thou find ungrateful".

30 Cf. a similar phrase placed in the mouth of Satan in 14 : 22 ("I had no power at all over you: I but called you – and you responded unto me"), and the corresponding note 31; also, see note 30 on 15 : 39-40. – Although, on the face of it, verses 20-21 of the present *sūrah* refer to the people of Sheba, their import is (as the sequence shows) much wider, applying to the human race as such.

31 See 15 : 41 and the corresponding note 31.

32 I.e., anybody who would "mediate" between Him and any of His creatures. As is evident from the sequence (as well as from 17 : 56-57), this passage relates, in particular, to the attribution of divine or semi-divine qualities to

And, before Him, intercession can be of no avail [to any] save one in whose case He may have granted leave [therefore]:[33] so much so that when the terror [of the Last Hour] is lifted from their hearts, they [who have been resurrected] will ask [one another], "What has your Sustainer decreed [for you]?" – [to which] the others will answer, "Whatever is true and deserved[34] – for He alone is exalted, great!" ‹23›
Say: "Who is it that provides for you sustenance out of the heavens and the earth?"[35]
Say: "It is God. And, behold, either we [who believe in Him] or you [who deny His oneness] are on the right path, or have clearly gone astray!" ‹24›
Say: "Neither shall you be called to account for whatever we may have become guilty of, nor shall we be called to account for whatever you are doing." ‹25› Say: "Our Sustainer will bring us all together [on Judgment Day], and then He will lay open the truth between us, in justice – for He alone is the One who opens all truth, the All-Knowing!" ‹26›
Say: "Point out to me those [beings] that you have joined with Him [in your minds] as partners [in His divinity]! Nay – nay, but He [alone] is God, the Almighty, the Wise!" ‹27›

NOW [as for thee, O Muḥammad,] We have not sent thee otherwise than to mankind at large, to be a herald of glad tidings and a warner; but most people do not understand [this], ‹28› and so they ask, "When is this promise [of resurrection and judgment] to be fulfilled? [Answer this, O you who believe in it,] if you are men of truth!"[36] ‹29›

وَلَا تَنفَعُ ٱلشَّفَٰعَةُ عِندَهُۥٓ إِلَّا لِمَنْ أَذِنَ لَهُۥ حَتَّىٰٓ إِذَا فُزِّعَ عَن قُلُوبِهِمْ
قَالُوا۟ مَاذَا قَالَ رَبُّكُمْ قَالُوا۟ ٱلْحَقَّ وَهُوَ ٱلْعَلِىُّ ٱلْكَبِيرُ ﴿٢٣﴾ ۞ قُلْ مَن
يَرْزُقُكُم مِّنَ ٱلسَّمَٰوَٰتِ وَٱلْأَرْضِ قُلِ ٱللَّهُ وَإِنَّآ أَوْ إِيَّاكُمْ لَعَلَىٰ هُدًى
أَوْ فِى ضَلَٰلٍ مُّبِينٍ ﴿٢٤﴾ قُل لَّا تُسْـَٔلُونَ عَمَّآ أَجْرَمْنَا وَلَا نُسْـَٔلُ عَمَّا
تَعْمَلُونَ ﴿٢٥﴾ قُلْ يَجْمَعُ بَيْنَنَا رَبُّنَا ثُمَّ يَفْتَحُ بَيْنَنَا بِٱلْحَقِّ وَهُوَ ٱلْفَتَّاحُ
ٱلْعَلِيمُ ﴿٢٦﴾ قُلْ أَرُونِىَ ٱلَّذِينَ أَلْحَقْتُم بِهِۦ شُرَكَآءَ كَلَّا بَلْ هُوَ ٱللَّهُ
ٱلْعَزِيزُ ٱلْحَكِيمُ ﴿٢٧﴾ وَمَآ أَرْسَلْنَٰكَ إِلَّا كَآفَّةً لِّلنَّاسِ بَشِيرًا وَنَذِيرًا
وَلَٰكِنَّ أَكْثَرَ ٱلنَّاسِ لَا يَعْلَمُونَ ﴿٢٨﴾ وَيَقُولُونَ مَتَىٰ هَٰذَا ٱلْوَعْدُ إِن حزب 44
كُنتُمْ صَٰدِقِينَ ﴿٢٩﴾

Wa lā tañfaʿush-shafāʿatu ʿiñdahūu ʾillā liman adhina lah. Ḥattāa ʾidhā fuzziʿa ʿañ-qulūbihim qālū mādhā qāla Rabbukum. Qālul-ḥaqqa wa Huwal-ʿAliyyul-Kabīr. (23) ۞ Qul mañy-yarzuqukum-minas-samāwāti wal-ʾarḍ. Qulil-lāh. Wa ʾinnāa ʾaw ʾiyyākum laʿalā hudan ʾaw fī ḍalālim-mubīn. (24) Qul-lā tusʾalūna ʿammāa ʾajramnā wa lā nusʾalu ʿammā taʿmalūn. (25) Qul yajmaʿu baynanā Rabbunā thumma yaftaḥu baynanā bil-ḥaqqi wa Huwal-Fattāḥul-ʿAlīm. (26) Qul ʾarūniyal-ladhīna ʾalḥaqtum-bihī shurakāaʾa kallā; bal Huwal-lāhul-ʿAzīzul-Ḥakīm. (27) Wa māa ʾarsalnāka ʾillā kāaffatal-linnāsi Bashīrañw-wa Nadhīrañw-wa lākinna ʾaktharan-nāsi lā yaʿlamūn. (28) Wa yaqūlūna matā hādhal-waʿdu ʾiñ-kuñtum ṣādiqīn. (29)

saints and angels and to the problem of their "intercession" with God.

33 Regarding the Qurʾanic concept of "intercession", see note 7 on 10 : 3. Cf. also 19 : 87 and 20 : 109.

34 Lit., "the truth" – i.e., whatever God decides regarding His grant or refusal of leave for intercession (which is synonymous with His redemptive acceptance or His rejection of the human being concerned) will conform with the requirements of absolute truth and justice (see note 74 on 19 : 87).

35 See note 49 on the first sentence of 10 : 31.

36 The Qurʾanic answer to this ironic question is found in 7 : 187.

Say: "There has been appointed for you a Day which you can neither delay nor advance by a single moment."[37] ‹30›

And [yet,] those who are bent on denying the truth do say, "We shall never believe in this Qur'ān, and neither in whatever there still remains of earlier revelations!"[38]

But if thou couldst only see [how it will be on Judgment Day,] when these evildoers shall be made to stand before their Sustainer, hurling reproaches back and forth at one another!

Those [of them] who had been weak [on earth] will say unto those who had gloried in their arrogance:[39] "Had it not been for you, we would certainly have been believers!" ‹31›

[And] those who were wont to glory in their arrogance will say unto those who had been weak: "Why – did we keep you [forcibly] from following the right path after it had become obvious to you?[40] Nay, it was but you [yourselves] who were guilty!" ‹32›

But those who had been weak will say unto those who had gloried in their arrogance: "Nay, [what kept us away was your] devising of false arguments, night and day,[41] [against God's messages – as you did] when you persuaded us to blaspheme against God and to claim that there are powers that could rival Him!"[42]

And when they see the suffering [that awaits them], they will [all] be unable to express [the full depth of] their remorse:[43] for We shall have put shackles around the

قُل لَّكُم مِّيعَادُ يَوۡمٖ لَّا تَسۡتَـٔۡخِرُونَ عَنۡهُ سَاعَةٗ وَلَا تَسۡتَقۡدِمُونَ ٣٠ وَقَالَ
ٱلَّذِينَ كَفَرُواْ لَن نُّؤۡمِنَ بِهَٰذَا ٱلۡقُرۡءَانِ وَلَا بِٱلَّذِي بَيۡنَ يَدَيۡهِۗ وَلَوۡ تَرَىٰٓ إِذِ
ٱلظَّٰلِمُونَ مَوۡقُوفُونَ عِندَ رَبِّهِمۡ يَرۡجِعُ بَعۡضُهُمۡ إِلَىٰ بَعۡضٍ ٱلۡقَوۡلَ يَقُولُ
ٱلَّذِينَ ٱسۡتُضۡعِفُواْ لِلَّذِينَ ٱسۡتَكۡبَرُواْ لَوۡلَآ أَنتُمۡ لَكُنَّا مُؤۡمِنِينَ ٣١ قَالَ
ٱلَّذِينَ ٱسۡتَكۡبَرُواْ لِلَّذِينَ ٱسۡتُضۡعِفُوٓاْ أَنَحۡنُ صَدَدۡنَٰكُمۡ عَنِ ٱلۡهُدَىٰ بَعۡدَ
إِذۡ جَآءَكُمۖ بَلۡ كُنتُم مُّجۡرِمِينَ ٣٢ وَقَالَ ٱلَّذِينَ ٱسۡتُضۡعِفُواْ لِلَّذِينَ
ٱسۡتَكۡبَرُواْ بَلۡ مَكۡرُ ٱلَّيۡلِ وَٱلنَّهَارِ إِذۡ تَأۡمُرُونَنَآ أَن نَّكۡفُرَ بِٱللَّهِ وَنَجۡعَلَ
لَهُۥٓ أَندَادٗاۚ وَأَسَرُّواْ ٱلنَّدَامَةَ لَمَّا رَأَوُاْ ٱلۡعَذَابَ وَجَعَلۡنَا ٱلۡأَغۡلَٰلَ فِيٓ

Qul-lakum-mīʿādu Yawmil-lā tastaʾkhirūna ʿanhu sāʿatañw-wa lā tastaqdimūn. (30) Wa qālal-ladhīna kafarū lañ-nuʾmina bihādhal-Qurʾāni wa lā billadhī bayna yadayh. Wa law tarāa ʾidhiẓ-ẓālimūna mawqūfūna ʿiñda Rabbihim yarjiʿu baʿḍuhum ʾilā baʿḍinil-qawla yaqūlul-ladhīnas-tuḍʿifū lilladhīnas-takbarū lawlāa ʾañtum lakunnā muʾminīn. (31) Qālal-ladhīnas-takbarū lilladhīnas-tuḍʿifūu ʾanaḥnu ṣadadnākum ʿanil-hudā baʿda ʾidh jāaʾakum-bal kuñtum-mujrimīn. (32) Wa qālal-ladhīnas-tuḍʿifū lilladhīnas-takbarū bal-makrul-layli wan-nahāri ʾidh taʾmurūnanāa ʾañ-nakfura billāhi wa najʿala lahūu ʾañdādā. Wa ʾasarrun-nadāmata lammā raʾawul-ʿadhāba wa jaʿalnal-ʾaghlāla fīi

37 For my rendering of *sāʿah* (lit., "hour") as "a single moment", see *sūrah* 7, note 26.

38 For the rendering of *mā bayna yadayhi*, in relation to the Qur'ān, as "whatever there still remains of earlier revelations", see *sūrah* 3, note 3. As is evident from the preceding and subsequent verses, the rejection by "those who are bent on denying the truth" of *all* revelation is motivated by their refusal to believe in resurrection and God's judgment, and, hence, to admit the validity of absolute moral standards as postulated by every higher religion.

39 I.e., as the "intellectual leaders" of their community.

40 Lit., "did we keep you away from guidance after it had come to you?"

41 I.e., always. The term *makr* (lit., "a scheme" or "scheming") has here the connotation of "devising false arguments" against something that is true: in this case, as is shown in the first paragraph of verse 31 above, against God's messages (cf. a similar use of this term in 10 : 21 and 35 : 43; see also 86 : 15).

42 Lit., "[that we should] give Him compeers (*andād*)". For an explanation of this phrase and my rendering of it, see *sūrah* 2, note 13.

43 For a justification of this rendering of the phrase *asarru 'n-nadāmah*, see *sūrah* 10, note 77.

necks of those who had been bent on denying the truth:[44] [and] will this be aught but a [just] requital for what they were doing? ‹33›

For [thus it is:] whenever We sent a warner to any community, those of its people who had lost themselves entirely in the pursuit of pleasures[45] would declare, "Behold, we deny that there is any truth in [what you claim to be] your message!" ‹34› – and they would add, "Richer [than you] are we in wealth and in children, and [so] we are not going to be made to suffer!"[46] ‹35›

Say: "Behold, my Sustainer grants abundant sustenance, or gives it in scant measure, unto whomever He wills: but most men do not understand [God's ways]."[47] ‹36›

For, it is neither your riches nor your children that can bring you nearer to Us: only he who attains to faith and does what is right and just [comes near unto Us]; and it is [such as] these whom multiple recompense awaits for all that they have done; and it is they who shall dwell secure in the mansions [of paradise] ‹37› – whereas all who strive against Our messages, seeking to defeat their purpose, shall be given over to suffering. ‹38›

Say: "Behold, my Sustainer grants abundant sustenance, or gives it in scant measure, unto whomever He wills of His servants;[48] and whatever it be that you spend on others, He [always] replaces it:[49] for He is the best of providers." ‹39›

أَعۡنَاقِ ٱلَّذِينَ كَفَرُواْۚ هَلۡ يُجۡزَوۡنَ إِلَّا مَا كَانُواْ يَعۡمَلُونَ ﴿٣٣﴾ وَمَآ أَرۡسَلۡنَا فِي
قَرۡيَةٖ مِّن نَّذِيرٍ إِلَّا قَالَ مُتۡرَفُوهَآ إِنَّا بِمَآ أُرۡسِلۡتُم بِهِۦ كَٰفِرُونَ ﴿٣٤﴾ وَقَالُواْ
نَحۡنُ أَكۡثَرُ أَمۡوَٰلٗا وَأَوۡلَٰدٗا وَمَا نَحۡنُ بِمُعَذَّبِينَ ﴿٣٥﴾ قُلۡ إِنَّ رَبِّي يَبۡسُطُ
ٱلرِّزۡقَ لِمَن يَشَآءُ وَيَقۡدِرُ وَلَٰكِنَّ أَكۡثَرَ ٱلنَّاسِ لَا يَعۡلَمُونَ ﴿٣٦﴾ وَمَآ
أَمۡوَٰلُكُمۡ وَلَآ أَوۡلَٰدُكُم بِٱلَّتِي تُقَرِّبُكُمۡ عِندَنَا زُلۡفَىٰٓ إِلَّا مَنۡ ءَامَنَ
وَعَمِلَ صَٰلِحٗا فَأُوْلَٰٓئِكَ لَهُمۡ جَزَآءُ ٱلضِّعۡفِ بِمَا عَمِلُواْ وَهُمۡ فِي
ٱلۡغُرُفَٰتِ ءَامِنُونَ ﴿٣٧﴾ وَٱلَّذِينَ يَسۡعَوۡنَ فِيٓ ءَايَٰتِنَا مُعَٰجِزِينَ أُوْلَٰٓئِكَ فِي
ٱلۡعَذَابِ مُحۡضَرُونَ ﴿٣٨﴾ قُلۡ إِنَّ رَبِّي يَبۡسُطُ ٱلرِّزۡقَ لِمَن يَشَآءُ مِنۡ
عِبَادِهِۦ وَيَقۡدِرُ لَهُۥۚ وَمَآ أَنفَقۡتُم مِّن شَيۡءٖ فَهُوَ يُخۡلِفُهُۥۖ وَهُوَ خَيۡرُ
ٱلرَّٰزِقِينَ ﴿٣٩﴾

ʾaʿnāqil-ladhīna kafarū; hal yujzawna ʾillā mā kānū yaʿmalūn. (33) Wa māa ʾarsalnā fī qaryatim-miñ-Nadhīrin ʾillā qāla mutrafūhāa ʾinnā bimāa ʾursiltum-bihī kāfirūn. (34) Wa qālū naḥnu ʾaktharu amwālañw-wa ʾawlādañw-wa mā naḥnu bimuʿadhdhabīn. (35) Qul ʾinna Rabbī yabsuṭur-rizqa limañy-yashāaʾu wa yaqdiru wa lākinna ʾaktharan-nāsi lā yaʿlamūn. (36) Wa māa ʾamwālukum wa lāa awlādukum-billatī tuqarribukum ʿiñdanā zulfāa ʾilla man ʾāmana wa ʿamila ṣāliḥañ-faʾulāaʾika lahum jazāaʾuḍ-ḍiʿfi bimā ʿamilū wa hum fil-ghurufāti ʾāminūn. (37) Wal-ladhīna yasʿawna fīi ʾĀyātinā muʿājizīna ʾulāaʾika fil-ʿadhābi muḥḍarūn. (38) Qul ʾinna Rabbī yabsuṭur-rizqa limañy-yashāaʾu min ʿibādihī wa yaqdiru lah. Wa māa ʾañfaqtum-miñ-shayʾiñ-faHuwa yukhlifuhū wa Huwa Khayrur-rāziqīn. (39)

44 As pointed out by several of the classical commentators (e.g., Zamakhsharī, Rāzī and Bayḍāwī) in their explanations of similar phrases occurring in 13 : 5 and 36 : 8, the "shackles" (*aghlāl*) which these sinners carry, as it were, "around their necks" in life, and will carry on Judgment Day, are a metaphor of the enslavement of their souls to the false values to which they had surrendered, and of the suffering which will be caused by that surrender.

45 The term *mutraf* denotes "one who indulges in the pursuit of pleasures", i.e., to the exclusion of all moral considerations: cf. note 147 on 11 : 116.

46 Implying, firstly, that the only thing that really counts in life is the enjoyment of material benefits; and, secondly, that a materially successful life is, by itself, an evidence of one's being "on the right way".

47 Sc., "and foolishly regard riches and poverty as indications of God's favour or disfavour". Indirectly, this statement refutes the belief held by many people in the present as well as in the past that material prosperity is a justification of all human endeavour.

48 I.e., God's promise to the righteous that they would attain to happiness in the life to come neither precludes nor implies their being wealthy or poor in this world.

49 I.e., either with worldly goods, or with inner contentment, or with spiritual merit (Zamakhsharī).

And [as for those who now deny the truth,] one Day He will gather them all together, and will ask the angels, "Was it you that they were wont to worship?"[50] ‹40›
They will answer: "Limitless art Thou in Thy glory! Thou [alone] art close unto us, not they![51] Nay, [when they thought that they were worshipping us,] they were but [blindly] worshipping forces concealed from their senses; most of them believed in them."[52] ‹41›
And [on that Day God will say]: "None of you [created beings] has today any power to benefit or to harm another!"
And [then] We shall say unto those who had been bent on evildoing: "Taste [now] that suffering through fire which you were wont to call a lie!" ‹42›
For [thus it is:] whenever Our messages are conveyed unto them in all their clarity, they [who are bent on denying the truth] say [to one another], "This [Muḥammad] is nothing but a man who wants to turn you away from what your forefathers were wont to worship!"
And they say, "This [Qurʾān] is nothing but a falsehood invented [by man]!"
And [finally,] they who are bent on denying the truth speak thus of the truth when it comes to them: "This is clearly nothing but spellbinding eloquence!"[53] ‹43›
And yet, [O Muḥammad,] never have We vouchsafed them any revelations which they could quote,[54] and neither have We sent unto them any warner before thee. ‹44›

وَيَوْمَ يَحْشُرُهُمْ جَمِيعًا ثُمَّ يَقُولُ لِلْمَلَٰٓئِكَةِ أَهَٰٓؤُلَآءِ إِيَّاكُمْ كَانُوا۟
يَعْبُدُونَ ﴿٤٠﴾ قَالُوا۟ سُبْحَٰنَكَ أَنتَ وَلِيُّنَا مِن دُونِهِم ۖ بَلْ كَانُوا۟ يَعْبُدُونَ
ٱلْجِنَّ ۖ أَكْثَرُهُم بِهِم مُّؤْمِنُونَ ﴿٤١﴾ فَٱلْيَوْمَ لَا يَمْلِكُ بَعْضُكُمْ لِبَعْضٍ نَّفْعًا
وَلَا ضَرًّا وَنَقُولُ لِلَّذِينَ ظَلَمُوا۟ ذُوقُوا۟ عَذَابَ ٱلنَّارِ ٱلَّتِى كُنتُم بِهَا
تُكَذِّبُونَ ﴿٤٢﴾ وَإِذَا تُتْلَىٰ عَلَيْهِمْ ءَايَٰتُنَا بَيِّنَٰتٍ قَالُوا۟ مَا هَٰذَآ إِلَّا رَجُلٌ
يُرِيدُ أَن يَصُدَّكُمْ عَمَّا كَانَ يَعْبُدُ ءَابَآؤُكُمْ وَقَالُوا۟ مَا هَٰذَآ إِلَّآ إِفْكٌ
مُّفْتَرًى ۚ وَقَالَ ٱلَّذِينَ كَفَرُوا۟ لِلْحَقِّ لَمَّا جَآءَهُمْ إِنْ هَٰذَآ إِلَّا سِحْرٌ
مُّبِينٌ ﴿٤٣﴾ وَمَآ ءَاتَيْنَٰهُم مِّن كُتُبٍ يَدْرُسُونَهَا ۖ وَمَآ أَرْسَلْنَآ إِلَيْهِمْ قَبْلَكَ
مِن نَّذِيرٍ ﴿٤٤﴾

Wa Yawma yaḥshuruhum jamīʿañ-thumma yaqūlu lilMalāaʾikati ʾahāaʾulāaʾi ʾiyyākum kānū yaʿbudūn. (40) Qālū subḥānaka ʾAñta Waliyyunā miñ-dūnihim bal kānū yaʿbudūnal-Jinna ʾaktharuhum-bihim-muʾminūn. (41) FalYawma lā yamliku baʿḍukum libaʿḍiñ-nafʿañw-wa lā ḍarrañw-wa naqūlu lilladhīna ẓalamū dhūqū ʿadhāban-nāril-latī kuñtum-bihā tukadhdhibūn. (42) Wa ʾidhā tutlā ʿalayhim ʾĀyātunā bayyinātiñ-qālū mā hādhāa ʾillā rajuluñy-yurīdu ʾañy-yaṣuddakum ʿammā kana yaʿbudu ʾābāaʾukum wa qālū mā hādhāa ʾillāa ʾifkum-muftarā. Wa qālal-ladhīna kafarū lilḥaqqi lammā jāaʾahum ʾin hādhāa ʾillā siḥrum-mubīn. (43) Wa māa ʾātaynāhum-miñ-Kutubiñy-yadrusūnahā wa māa ʾarsalnāa ʾilayhim qablaka miñ-Nadhīr. (44)

50 This allegorical "question" – allegorical, because God is omniscient and has no need to "ask" – implies that many of "those who deny the truth" of God's messages delude themselves into believing that they are, nevertheless, worshipping spiritual forces, here comprised in the term "angels".

51 Implying that they (the angels) would never have accepted that worship which is due to God alone.

52 In this instance, I believe, the term *jinn* has its primary meaning of "that which is concealed from [man's] senses" (see Appendix III), thus including all manner of unknown forces, both real and imaginary, believed to be inherent in what we describe as "nature". Hence, the answer of the angels implies that the sinners' alleged worship of *them* had never been more than a subconscious screen for their fear of the invisible forces of nature and, ultimately, of the yet deeper fear of the Unknown – that fear which sooner or later engulfs all who refuse to believe in the existence of God and, hence, cannot see any meaning or purpose in human life. (See also the last sentence of 10 : 28 and the corresponding note 46.)

53 Lit., "sorcery" or "magic" – a term frequently used in the sense of "spellbinding eloquence" (cf. 74 : 24, the earliest instance in the chronology of Qurʾanic revelation).

54 Lit., "which they could study", i.e., in support of the blasphemous beliefs and practices inherited from their ancestors. Cf. 30 : 35, which expresses a similar idea.

Thus, too, gave the lie to the truth [many of] those who lived before them; and although those [earlier people] had not attained to even a tenth of [the evidence of the truth] which We have vouchsafed unto these [late successors of theirs], yet when they gave the lie to My apostles, how awesome was My rejection![55] ‹45›

Say: "I counsel you one thing only: Be [ever-conscious of] standing before God, whether you are in the company of others or alone;[56] and then bethink yourselves [that] there is no madness in [this prophet,] your fellow-man:[57] he is only a warner to you of suffering severe to come." ‹46›

Say: "No reward have I ever asked of you [out of anything] that is yours:[58] my reward rests with none but God, and He is witness unto everything!" ‹47›

Say: "Verily, my Sustainer hurls the truth [against all that is false][59] – He who fully knows all the things that are beyond the reach of a created being's perception!" ‹48›

Say: "The truth has now come [to light, and falsehood is bound to wither away[60]]: for, falsehood cannot bring forth anything new, nor can it bring back [what has passed away]."[61] ‹49›

Say: "Were I to go astray, I would but go astray [due to my own self, and] to the hurt of myself;[62] but if I am on the right path, it is but by virtue of what my Sustainer reveals unto me: for, verily, He is all-hearing, ever-near!" ‹50›

وَكَذَّبَ ٱلَّذِينَ مِن قَبْلِهِمْ وَمَا بَلَغُوا۟ مِعْشَارَ مَآ ءَاتَيْنَٰهُمْ فَكَذَّبُوا۟ رُسُلِى
فَكَيْفَ كَانَ نَكِيرِ ﴿٤٥﴾ ۞ قُلْ إِنَّمَآ أَعِظُكُم بِوَٰحِدَةٍ أَن تَقُومُوا۟ لِلَّهِ
مَثْنَىٰ وَفُرَٰدَىٰ ثُمَّ تَتَفَكَّرُوا۟ مَا بِصَاحِبِكُم مِّن جِنَّةٍ إِنْ هُوَ إِلَّا نَذِيرٌ
لَّكُم بَيْنَ يَدَىْ عَذَابٍ شَدِيدٍ ﴿٤٦﴾ قُلْ مَا سَأَلْتُكُم مِّنْ أَجْرٍ فَهُوَ لَكُمْ
إِنْ أَجْرِىَ إِلَّا عَلَى ٱللَّهِ وَهُوَ عَلَىٰ كُلِّ شَىْءٍ شَهِيدٌ ﴿٤٧﴾ قُلْ إِنَّ رَبِّى يَقْذِفُ
بِٱلْحَقِّ عَلَّٰمُ ٱلْغُيُوبِ ﴿٤٨﴾ قُلْ جَآءَ ٱلْحَقُّ وَمَا يُبْدِئُ ٱلْبَٰطِلُ وَمَا
يُعِيدُ ﴿٤٩﴾ قُلْ إِن ضَلَلْتُ فَإِنَّمَآ أَضِلُّ عَلَىٰ نَفْسِى وَإِنِ ٱهْتَدَيْتُ فَبِمَا
يُوحِىٓ إِلَىَّ رَبِّىٓ إِنَّهُۥ سَمِيعٌ قَرِيبٌ ﴿٥٠﴾

ربع الحزب

Wa kadhdhabal-ladhīna miñ-qablihim wa mā balaghū miʿshāra māa ʾātaynāhum fakadhdhabū Rusulī; fakayfa kāna nakīr. ﴿45﴾ ۞ Qul ʾinnamāa ʾaʿiẓukum-biwāḥidatin ʾañ-taqūmū lillāhi mathnā wa furādā thumma tatafakkarū; mā biṣāḥibikum-miñ-jinnah. ʾIn huwa ʾillā Nadhīrul-lakum-bayna yaday ʿadhābiñ-shadīd. ﴿46﴾ Qul mā saʾaltukum-min ʾajriñ-fahuwa lakum; ʾin ʾajriya ʾillā ʿalal-lāhi wa Huwa ʿalā kulli shayʾiñ-Shahīd. ﴿47﴾ Qul ʾinna Rabbī yaqdhifu bil-ḥaqqi ʿAllāmul-ghuyūb. ﴿48﴾ Qul jāaʾal-ḥaqqu wa mā yubdiʾul-bāṭilu wa mā yuʿīd. ﴿49﴾ Qul ʾiñ-ḍalaltu faʾinnamāa ʾaḍillu ʿalā nafsī wa ʾinihtadaytu fabimā yūḥīi ʾilayya Rabbī. ʾInnahū Samīʿuñ-Qarīb. ﴿50﴾

---

55 Sc., "And how much worse will fare the deniers of the truth to whom so explicit and so comprehensive a divine writ as the Qurʾān has been conveyed!" My rendering of the whole of this verse is based on Rāzī's interpretation, which differs from that of most of the other commentators.

56 Lit., "two by two (*mathnā*) and singly (*furādā*)". According to Rāzī, the expression *mathnā* denotes, in this context, "together with another person" or "other persons": hence, the above phrase may be understood to refer to man's social behaviour – i.e., his actions concerning others – as well as to his inner, personal attitude in all situations requiring a moral choice.

57 See note 150 on 7 : 184.

58 I.e., no reward of a material nature: cf. 25 : 57 – "no reward other than that he who so wills may unto his Sustainer find a way".

59 Cf. 21 : 18.

60 Cf. 17 : 81.

61 I.e., in contrast to the creativeness inherent in every true idea, falsehood – being in itself an illusion – cannot really create anything or revive any values that may have been alive in the past.

62 According to Zamakhsharī, the idea expressed by the interpolated words "due to my own self" is implied in the above, inasmuch as "everything that goes against [the spiritual interests of] oneself is *caused* by oneself". (See note 4 on 14 : 4.)

IF THOU couldst but see [how the deniers of the truth will fare on Resurrection Day,] when they will shrink in terror, with nowhere to escape – since they will have been seized from so close nearby[63] ⟨51⟩ – and will cry, "We do [now] believe in it!"
But how can they [hope to] attain [to salvation] from so far away,[64] ⟨52⟩ seeing that aforetime they had been bent on denying the truth, and had been wont to cast scorn, from far away, on something that was beyond the reach of human perception?[65] ⟨53⟩
And so, a barrier will be set between them and all that they had [ever] desired,[66] as will be done to such of their kind as lived before their time: for, behold, they [too] were lost in doubt amounting to suspicion.[67] ⟨54⟩

وَلَوْ تَرَىٰٓ إِذْ فَزِعُوا۟ فَلَا فَوْتَ وَأُخِذُوا۟ مِن مَّكَانٍ قَرِيبٍ ﴿٥١﴾ وَقَالُوٓا۟
ءَامَنَّا بِهِۦ وَأَنَّىٰ لَهُمُ ٱلتَّنَاوُشُ مِن مَّكَانٍۭ بَعِيدٍ ﴿٥٢﴾ وَقَدْ كَفَرُوا۟ بِهِۦ مِن
قَبْلُ ۖ وَيَقْذِفُونَ بِٱلْغَيْبِ مِن مَّكَانٍۭ بَعِيدٍ ﴿٥٣﴾ وَحِيلَ بَيْنَهُمْ وَبَيْنَ مَا
يَشْتَهُونَ كَمَا فُعِلَ بِأَشْيَاعِهِم مِّن قَبْلُ ۚ إِنَّهُمْ كَانُوا۟ فِى شَكٍّ مُّرِيبٍۭ ﴿٥٤﴾

Wa law taräa ᵓidh faziᶜū falā fawta wa ᵓukhidhū mim-makāniñ-qarīb. (51) Wa qālūu ᵓāmannā bihī wa ᵓannā lahumut-tanāwushu mim-makānim-baᶜīd. (52) Wa qad kafarū bihī miñ-qablu wa yaqdhifūna bil-ghaybi mim-makānim-baᶜīd. (53) Wa ḥīla baynahum wa bayna mā yashtahūna kamā fuᶜila biᵓashyāᶜihim-miñ-qablu ᵓinnahum kānū fī shakkim-murīb. (54)

63 Lit., "from a place nearby" – i.e., from within their own selves: cf. 17 : 13 ("every human being's destiny have We tied to his neck") and the corresponding note 17. The same idea is expressed in 13 : 5 ("it is they who carry the shackles [of their own making] around their necks"), as well as in the second part of verse 33 of the present *sūrah* ("We shall have put shackles around the necks of those who had been bent on denying the truth"). See also 50 : 41 and the corresponding note 33.

64 Lit., "from a place far-away" – i.e., from their utterly different past life on earth.

65 The obvious implication is that man's fate in the hereafter will be a consequence of, and invariably conditioned by, his spiritual attitude and the manner of his life during the first, earthly stage of his existence. In this instance, the expression "from far away" is apparently used in a sense similar to sayings like "far off the mark" or "without rhyme or reason", and is meant to qualify as groundless and futile all negative speculations about what the Qurᵓān describes as *al-ghayb* ("that which is beyond the reach of human [or "a created being's"] perception"): in this case, life after death.

66 Thus, the impossibility of attaining to the fulfilment of any of their desires – whether positive or negative – sums up, as it were, the suffering of the damned in the life to come.

67 I.e., a suspicion that all moral postulates were but meant to deprive them of what they considered to be the "legitimate advantages" of life in this world.

قُلْ إِنَّ رَبِّي يَبْسُطُ الرِّزْقَ لِمَن يَشَاءُ

مِنْ عِبَادِهِ وَيَقْدِرُ لَهُ وَمَا أَنفَقْتُم مِّن شَيْءٍ

فَهُوَ يُخْلِفُهُ وَهُوَ خَيْرُ الرَّازِقِينَ

وَيَوْمَ يَحْشُرُهُمْ جَمِيعًا ثُمَّ يَقُولُ

لِلْمَلَائِكَةِ أَهَٰؤُلَاءِ إِيَّاكُمْ كَانُوا يَعْبُدُونَ

The Thirty-Fifth Sūrah

Fāṭir (The Originator)

Mecca Period

MOST of the authorities place this *sūrah* – which derives its title from God's attribute of "Originator of the heavens and the earth" in its first verse – chronologically between *sūrahs* 25 (*Al-Furqān*) and 19 (*Maryam*): that is, about seven or eight years before the Prophet's exodus from Mecca to Medina. Another title given to it by some of the Companions and several classical commentators is *Al-Malā'ikah* ("The Angels"), also based on verse 1.

Almost the whole of *Fāṭir* deals with God's unique power to create and to resurrect, as well as with His having revealed His will through the medium of His prophets – but "only such as are endowed with [innate] knowledge stand [truly] in awe of God: [for they alone comprehend that,] verily, God is almighty, much-forgiving" (second paragraph of verse 28).

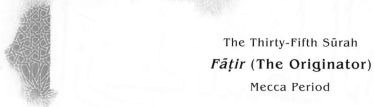

-35-

سورة فاطر مكية

وآياتها خمس وأربعون

IN THE NAME OF GOD, THE MOST GRACIOUS, THE DISPENSER OF GRACE:

ALL PRAISE is due to God, Originator of the heavens and the earth, who causes the angels to be [His] message-bearers, endowed with wings, two, or three, or four.[1]

[Unceasingly] He adds to His creation whatever He wills:[2] for, verily, God has the power to will anything. ‹1›

Whatever grace God opens up to man, none can withhold it; and whatever He withholds, none can henceforth release: for He alone is almighty, truly wise. ‹2›

O men! Call to mind the blessings which God has bestowed upon you! Is there any creator, other than God, that could provide for you sustenance out of heaven and earth?[3] There is no deity save Him: and yet, how perverted are your minds![4] ‹3›

But if they [whose minds are perverted] give thee the lie, [O Prophet, remember that] even so, before thy time, have [other] apostles been given the lie: for [the unbelievers always refuse to admit that] all things go back to God [as their source]. ‹4›

بِسْمِ ٱللَّهِ ٱلرَّحْمَٰنِ ٱلرَّحِيمِ

ٱلْحَمْدُ لِلَّهِ فَاطِرِ ٱلسَّمَٰوَٰتِ وَٱلْأَرْضِ جَاعِلِ ٱلْمَلَٰٓئِكَةِ رُسُلًا أُوْلِيٓ
أَجْنِحَةٍ مَّثْنَىٰ وَثُلَٰثَ وَرُبَٰعَ يَزِيدُ فِي ٱلْخَلْقِ مَا يَشَآءُ إِنَّ ٱللَّهَ عَلَىٰ كُلِّ
شَيْءٍ قَدِيرٌ ﴿١﴾ مَّا يَفْتَحِ ٱللَّهُ لِلنَّاسِ مِن رَّحْمَةٍ فَلَا مُمْسِكَ لَهَا وَمَا
يُمْسِكْ فَلَا مُرْسِلَ لَهُۥ مِنۢ بَعْدِهِۦ وَهُوَ ٱلْعَزِيزُ ٱلْحَكِيمُ ﴿٢﴾ يَٰٓأَيُّهَا
ٱلنَّاسُ ٱذْكُرُواْ نِعْمَتَ ٱللَّهِ عَلَيْكُمْ هَلْ مِنْ خَٰلِقٍ غَيْرُ ٱللَّهِ يَرْزُقُكُم
مِّنَ ٱلسَّمَآءِ وَٱلْأَرْضِ لَآ إِلَٰهَ إِلَّا هُوَ فَأَنَّىٰ تُؤْفَكُونَ ﴿٣﴾ وَإِن يُكَذِّبُوكَ
فَقَدْ كُذِّبَتْ رُسُلٌ مِّن قَبْلِكَ وَإِلَى ٱللَّهِ تُرْجَعُ ٱلْأُمُورُ ﴿٤﴾

Bismil-lāhir-Raḥmānir-Raḥīm.

ʾAlḥamdu lillāhi Fāṭiris-samāwāti wal-ʾarḍi jāᶜilil-Malāaʾikati Rusulan ʾulīi ʾajniḥatim-mathnā wa thulātha wa rubāᶜ. Yazīdu fil-khalqi mā yashāaʾ. ʾInnal-lāha ᶜalā kulli shayʾiñ-Qadīr. (1) Mā yaftaḥil-lāhu linnāsi mir-raḥmatiñ-falā mumsika lahā wa mā yumsik falā mursila lahū mim-baᶜdihi wa Huwal-ᶜAzīzul-Ḥakīm. (2) Yāa ʾayyuhan-nāsudh-kurū niᶜmatal-lāhi ᶜalaykum. Hal min khāliqin ghayrul-lāhi yarzuqukum-minas-samāaʾi wal-ʾarḍ. Lāa ʾilaha ʾillā Huwa faʾannā tuʾfakūn. (3) Wa ʾiñy-yukadh-dhibūka faqad kudhdhibat Rusulum-miñ-qablika wa ʾilal-lāhi turjaᶜul-ʾumūr. (4)

---

1 The "wings" of the spiritual beings or forces comprised within the designation of angels are, obviously, a metaphor for the speed and power with which God's revelations are conveyed to His prophets. Their multiplicity ("two, or three, or four") is perhaps meant to stress the countless ways in which He causes His commands to materialize within the universe created by Him: an assumption which, to my mind, is supported by an authentic *ḥadīth* to the effect that on the night of his Ascension (see Appendix IV) the Prophet saw Gabriel "endowed with six hundred wings" (Bukhārī and Muslim, on the authority of Ibn Masᶜūd).

2 I.e., the process of creation is continuous, constantly expanding in scope, range and variety.

3 See 10 : 31 and the corresponding note 49.

4 Sc., "inasmuch as you attribute divine qualities or powers to anyone or anything beside Him". For an explanation of the phrase *annā tuʾfakūn* (lit., "how turned-away you are", i.e., from the truth), see *sūrah* 5, note 90.

O MEN! Verily, God's promise [of resurrection] is true indeed: let not, then, the life of this world delude you, and let not [your own] deceptive thoughts about God delude you![5] ‹5›

Behold, Satan is a foe unto you: so treat him as a foe. He but calls on his followers to the end that they might find themselves among such as are destined for the blazing flame ‹6› – [seeing that] for those who are bent on denying the truth there is suffering severe in store, just as for those who have attained to faith and do righteous deeds there is forgiveness of sins, and a great reward. ‹7›

Is, then, he to whom the evil of his own doings is [so] alluring that [in the end] he regards it as good [anything but a follower of Satan]?

For, verily, God lets go astray him that wills [to go astray], just as He guides him that wills [to be guided].[6] Hence, [O believer,] do not waste thyself in sorrowing over them: verily, God has full knowledge of all that they do! ‹8›

AND [remember:] it is God who sends forth the winds, so that they raise a cloud, whereupon We drive it towards dead land and thereby give life to the earth after it had been lifeless: even thus shall resurrection be! ‹9›

He who desires might and glory [ought to know that] all might and glory belong to God [alone]. Unto Him ascend all good words, and the righteous deed does He exalt. But as for those who cunningly devise evil deeds – suffering severe awaits them; and all their devising is bound to come to nought.[7] ‹10›

يَٰٓأَيُّهَا ٱلنَّاسُ إِنَّ وَعۡدَ ٱللَّهِ حَقّٞۖ فَلَا تَغُرَّنَّكُمُ ٱلۡحَيَوٰةُ ٱلدُّنۡيَاۖ وَلَا
يَغُرَّنَّكُم بِٱللَّهِ ٱلۡغَرُورُ ٥ إِنَّ ٱلشَّيۡطَٰنَ لَكُمۡ عَدُوّٞ فَٱتَّخِذُوهُ عَدُوًّاۚ
إِنَّمَا يَدۡعُواْ حِزۡبَهُۥ لِيَكُونُواْ مِنۡ أَصۡحَٰبِ ٱلسَّعِيرِ ٦ ٱلَّذِينَ كَفَرُواْ لَهُمۡ
عَذَابٞ شَدِيدٞۖ وَٱلَّذِينَ ءَامَنُواْ وَعَمِلُواْ ٱلصَّٰلِحَٰتِ لَهُم مَّغۡفِرَةٞ وَأَجۡرٞ
كَبِيرٌ ٧ أَفَمَن زُيِّنَ لَهُۥ سُوٓءُ عَمَلِهِۦ فَرَءَاهُ حَسَنٗاۖ فَإِنَّ ٱللَّهَ يُضِلُّ مَن
يَشَآءُ وَيَهۡدِي مَن يَشَآءُۖ فَلَا تَذۡهَبۡ نَفۡسُكَ عَلَيۡهِمۡ حَسَرَٰتٍۚ إِنَّ ٱللَّهَ
عَلِيمُۢ بِمَا يَصۡنَعُونَ ٨ وَٱللَّهُ ٱلَّذِيٓ أَرۡسَلَ ٱلرِّيَٰحَ فَتُثِيرُ سَحَابٗا فَسُقۡنَٰهُ
إِلَىٰ بَلَدٖ مَّيِّتٖ فَأَحۡيَيۡنَا بِهِ ٱلۡأَرۡضَ بَعۡدَ مَوۡتِهَاۚ كَذَٰلِكَ ٱلنُّشُورُ ٩ مَن
كَانَ يُرِيدُ ٱلۡعِزَّةَ فَلِلَّهِ ٱلۡعِزَّةُ جَمِيعًاۚ إِلَيۡهِ يَصۡعَدُ ٱلۡكَلِمُ ٱلطَّيِّبُ وَٱلۡعَمَلُ
ٱلصَّٰلِحُ يَرۡفَعُهُۥۚ وَٱلَّذِينَ يَمۡكُرُونَ ٱلسَّيِّـَٔاتِ لَهُمۡ عَذَابٞ شَدِيدٞۖ وَمَكۡرُ
أُوْلَٰٓئِكَ هُوَ يَبُورُ ١٠

Yāa ʾayyuhan-nāsu ʾinna waᶜdal-lāhi ḥaqquñ-falā taghurrannakumul-ḥayātud-dunyā; wa lā yaghurrannakum-billāhil-gharūr. (5) ʾInnash-Shayṭāna lakum ᶜaduwwuñ-fattakhidhūhu ᶜaduwwā. ʾInnamā yadᶜū ḥizbahū liyakūnū min ʾaṣḥābis-saᶜīr. (6) ʾAlladhīna kafarū lahum ᶜadhābuñ-shadīd. Wal-ladhīna ʾāmanū wa ᶜamiluṣ-ṣāliḥāti lahum-maghfiratuñw-wa ʾajruñ-kabīr. (7) ʾAfamañ-zuyyina lahū sūuʾu ᶜamalihī faraʾāhu ḥasanā. Faʾinnal-lāha yuḍillu mañy-yashāaʾu wa yahdī mañy-yashāaʾu falā tadhhab nafsuka ᶜalayhim ḥasarāt. ʾInnal-lāha ᶜAlīmum-bimā yaṣnaᶜūn. (8) Wal-lāhul-ladhīi ʾarsalar-riyāḥa fatuthīru saḥābañ-fasuqnāhu ʾilā baladim-mayyitiñ-faʾaḥyaynā bihil-ʾarḍa baᶜda mawtihā. Kadhālikan-nushūr. (9) Mañ-kāna yurīdul-ᶜizzata falillāhil-ᶜizzatu jamīᶜā. ʾIlayhi yaṣᶜadul-kalimuṭ-ṭayyibu wal-ᶜamaluṣ-ṣāliḥu yarfaᶜuh. Wal-ladhīna yamkurūnas-sayyiʾāti lahum ᶜadhābuñ-shadīduñw-wa makru ʾulāaʾika huwa yabūr. (10)

5 See 31 : 33 (which is phrased in exactly the same way) and the corresponding note 30. – As regards the explicit reference to Satan in the next verse of the present *sūrah*, see Rāzī's remarks quoted in note 31 on 14 : 22, as well as note 16 on 15 : 17.

6 See *sūrah*, 14, note 4, which explains my rendering of this sentence.

7 It appears that in this context – as in the first paragraph of 10 : 21 or in 34 : 33 – both the noun *makr* (lit., "a scheme", or "scheming" or "plotting") and the verb *yamkurūn* (lit., "they scheme" or "plot") have the connotation of "devising false [or "fallacious"] arguments" against something that is true. Since the preceding passages refer to God's creativeness and, in particular, to His power to create life and resurrect the dead (verse 9), the "evil deeds"

And [remember:] God creates [every one of] you out of dust,[8] then out of a drop of sperm; and then He fashions you into either of the two sexes.[9] And no female conceives or gives birth unless it be with His knowledge; and none that is long-lived has his days lengthened – and neither is aught lessened of his days – unless it be thus laid down in [God's] decree: for, behold, all this is easy for God. ‹11›

[Easy is it for Him to create likeness and variety:[10]] thus, the two great bodies of water [on earth][11] are not alike – the one sweet, thirst-allaying, pleasant to drink, and the other salty and bitter: and yet, from either of them do you eat fresh meat, and [from either] you take gems which you may wear; and on either thou canst see ships ploughing through the waves, so that you might [be able to] go forth in quest of some of His bounty, and thus have cause to be grateful. ‹12›

He makes the night grow longer by shortening the day, and He makes the day grow longer by shortening the night; and He has made the sun and the moon subservient [to His laws], each running its course for a term set [by Him].[12]

Thus is God, your Sustainer: unto Him belongs all dominion – whereas those whom you invoke instead of Him do not own so much as the husk of a date-stone! ‹13› If you invoke them, they do not hear your call; and even if they could hear, they would not [be able to] respond to you. And [withal,] on the Day of Resurrection they will utterly disown your having associated them with God.[13]

وَٱللَّهُ خَلَقَكُم مِّن تُرَابٍ ثُمَّ مِن نُّطْفَةٍ ثُمَّ جَعَلَكُمْ أَزْوَٰجًا ۚ وَمَا تَحْمِلُ مِنْ
أُنثَىٰ وَلَا تَضَعُ إِلَّا بِعِلْمِهِۦ ۚ وَمَا يُعَمَّرُ مِن مُّعَمَّرٍ وَلَا يُنقَصُ مِنْ عُمُرِهِۦٓ إِلَّا فِى
كِتَٰبٍ ۚ إِنَّ ذَٰلِكَ عَلَى ٱللَّهِ يَسِيرٌ ﴿١١﴾ وَمَا يَسْتَوِى ٱلْبَحْرَانِ هَٰذَا عَذْبٌ
فُرَاتٌ سَآئِغٌ شَرَابُهُۥ وَهَٰذَا مِلْحٌ أُجَاجٌ ۖ وَمِن كُلٍّ تَأْكُلُونَ لَحْمًا طَرِيًّا
وَتَسْتَخْرِجُونَ حِلْيَةً تَلْبَسُونَهَا ۖ وَتَرَى ٱلْفُلْكَ فِيهِ مَوَاخِرَ لِتَبْتَغُوا۟ مِن فَضْلِهِۦ
وَلَعَلَّكُمْ تَشْكُرُونَ ﴿١٢﴾ يُولِجُ ٱلَّيْلَ فِى ٱلنَّهَارِ وَيُولِجُ ٱلنَّهَارَ فِى ٱلَّيْلِ وَسَخَّرَ
ٱلشَّمْسَ وَٱلْقَمَرَ كُلٌّ يَجْرِى لِأَجَلٍ مُّسَمًّى ۚ ذَٰلِكُمُ ٱللَّهُ رَبُّكُمْ لَهُ ٱلْمُلْكُ ۚ
وَٱلَّذِينَ تَدْعُونَ مِن دُونِهِۦ مَا يَمْلِكُونَ مِن قِطْمِيرٍ ﴿١٣﴾ إِن تَدْعُوهُمْ لَا يَسْمَعُوا۟
دُعَآءَكُمْ وَلَوْ سَمِعُوا۟ مَا ٱسْتَجَابُوا۟ لَكُمْ ۖ وَيَوْمَ ٱلْقِيَٰمَةِ يَكْفُرُونَ بِشِرْكِكُمْ ۚ

Wal-lāhu khalaqakum-miñ-turābiñ-thumma miñ-nuṭfatiñ-thumma jaᶜalakum ᵓazwājā. Wa mā taḥmilu min ᵓuñthā wa lā taḍaᶜu ᵓillā biᶜilmih. Wa mā yuᶜammaru mim-muᶜammariñw-wa lā yuñqaṣu min ᶜumurihīi ᵓillā fī Kitāb. ᵓInna dhālika ᶜalal-lāhi yasīr. (11) Wa mā yastawil-baḥrāni hādhā ᶜadhbuñ-furātuñ-sāaᵓighuñ-sharābuhū wa hādhā milḥun ᵓujāj. Wa miñ-kulliñ-taᵓkulūna laḥmañ-ṭariyyañw-wa tastakh-rijūna ḥilyatañ-talbasūnahā; wa taral-fulka fīhi mawākhira litabtaghū miñ-faḍlihī wa laᶜallakum tashkurūn. (12) Yūlijul-layla fin-nahāri wa yūlijun-nahāra fil-layli wa sakhkharash-shamsa wal-qamara kulluñy-yajrī liᵓajalim-musammā. Dhālikumul-lāhu Rabbukum lahul-mulk. Wal-ladhīna tadᶜūna miñ-dūnihī mā yamlikūna miñ-qiṭmīr. (13) ᵓIñ-tadᶜūhum lā yasmaᶜū duᶜāaᵓakum wa law samiᶜū mas-tajābū lakum; wa Yawmal-Qiyāmati yakfurūna bishirkikum.

spoken of above are, presumably, specious arguments meant to "disprove" the announcement of resurrection.

8 See second half of note 47 on 3 : 59, and note 4 on 23 : 12.

9 Lit., "makes you pairs" or "mates [of one another]".

10 This interpolated sentence reflects Rāzī's convincing explanation of the passage that follows here, and its connection with the preceding one.

11 For this rendering of *al-baḥrān*, see note 41 on 25 : 53.

12 See *sūrah* 13, note 5.

13 The Qurᵓān states in many places that all false objects of worship – whether saints, angels, relics, fetishes, or deified forces of nature – will "bear witness" against their one-time worshippers on Resurrection Day, and will "disown" them: a symbolic allusion to man's perception, at the end of time, of the ultimate reality.

وَلَا يُنَبِّئُكَ مِثْلُ خَبِيرٍ ﴿١٤﴾ ۞ يَٰٓأَيُّهَا ٱلنَّاسُ أَنتُمُ ٱلْفُقَرَآءُ إِلَى ٱللَّهِ ۖ وَٱللَّهُ هُوَ
ٱلْغَنِىُّ ٱلْحَمِيدُ ﴿١٥﴾ إِن يَشَأْ يُذْهِبْكُمْ وَيَأْتِ بِخَلْقٍ جَدِيدٍ ﴿١٦﴾ وَمَا ذَٰلِكَ
عَلَى ٱللَّهِ بِعَزِيزٍ ﴿١٧﴾ وَلَا تَزِرُ وَازِرَةٌ وِزْرَ أُخْرَىٰ ۚ وَإِن تَدْعُ مُثْقَلَةٌ
إِلَىٰ حِمْلِهَا لَا يُحْمَلْ مِنْهُ شَىْءٌ وَلَوْ كَانَ ذَا قُرْبَىٰٓ ۗ إِنَّمَا تُنذِرُ ٱلَّذِينَ يَخْشَوْنَ
رَبَّهُم بِٱلْغَيْبِ وَأَقَامُوا۟ ٱلصَّلَوٰةَ ۚ وَمَن تَزَكَّىٰ فَإِنَّمَا يَتَزَكَّىٰ لِنَفْسِهِۦ ۚ وَإِلَى ٱللَّهِ
ٱلْمَصِيرُ ﴿١٨﴾ وَمَا يَسْتَوِى ٱلْأَعْمَىٰ وَٱلْبَصِيرُ ﴿١٩﴾ وَلَا ٱلظُّلُمَٰتُ وَلَا
ٱلنُّورُ ﴿٢٠﴾ وَلَا ٱلظِّلُّ وَلَا ٱلْحَرُورُ ﴿٢١﴾ وَمَا يَسْتَوِى ٱلْأَحْيَآءُ وَلَا
ٱلْأَمْوَٰتُ ۚ إِنَّ ٱللَّهَ يُسْمِعُ مَن يَشَآءُ ۖ وَمَآ أَنتَ بِمُسْمِعٍ مَّن فِى ٱلْقُبُورِ ﴿٢٢﴾ إِنْ
أَنتَ إِلَّا نَذِيرٌ ﴿٢٣﴾ إِنَّآ أَرْسَلْنَٰكَ بِٱلْحَقِّ بَشِيرًا وَنَذِيرًا ۚ وَإِن مِّنْ أُمَّةٍ إِلَّا

Wa lā yunabbiʾuka mithlu Khabīr. (14) ۞ Yāa ʾayyuhan-nāsu ʾañtumul-fuqarāaʾu ʾilal-lāh. Wal-lāhu Huwal-Ghaniyyul-Ḥamīd. (15) ʾIñy-yashaʾ yudhhibkum wa yaʾti bikhalqiñ-jadīd. (16) Wa mā dhālika ʿalal-lāhi biʿazīz. (17) Wa lā taziru wāziratuñw-wizra ʾukhrā. Wa ʾiñ-tadʿu muthqalatun ʾilā ḥimlihā lā yuḥmal minhu shayʾuñw-wa law kāna dhā qurbā. ʾInnamā tuñdhirul-ladhīna yakhshawna Rabbahum-bilghaybi wa ʾaqāmuṣ-Ṣalāh. Wa mañ-tazakkā faʾinnamā yatazakkā linafsihī wa ʾilal-lāhil-maṣīr. (18) Wa mā yastawil-ʾaʿmā wal-baṣīr. (19) Wa laẓ-ẓulumātu wa lan-nūr. (20) Wa laẓ-ẓillu wa lal-ḥarūr. (21) Wa mā yastawil-ʾaḥyāaʾu wa lal-ʾamwāt. ʾInnal-lāha yusmiʿu mañy-yashāaʾu wa māa ʾañta bimusmiʿim-mañ-fil-qubūr. (22) ʾIn ʾañta ʾillā Nadhīr. (23) ʾInnāa ʾarsalnāka bil-ḥaqqi Bashīrañw-wa Nadhīrā. Wa ʾim-min ʾummatin ʾillā

نصف الحزب

And none can make thee understand [the truth] like the One who is all-aware. ‹14›
O men! It is you who stand in need of God, whereas He alone is self-sufficient, the One to whom all praise is due. ‹15›
If He so wills, He can do away with you and bring forth a new mankind [in your stead]:[14] ‹16› nor is this difficult for God. ‹17›

AND NO BEARER of burdens shall be made to bear another's burden;[15] and if one weighed down by his load calls upon [another] to help him carry it, nothing thereof may be carried [by that other], even if it be one's near of kin.[16]
Hence, thou canst [truly] warn only those who stand in awe of their Sustainer although He is beyond the reach of their perception,[17] and are constant in prayer, and [know that] whoever grows in purity, attains to purity but for the good of his own self, and [that] with God is all journeys' end. ‹18›
For [thus it is:] the blind and the seeing are not equal; ‹19› nor are the depths of darkness and the light; ‹20› nor the [cooling] shade and the scorching heat: ‹21› and neither are equal the living and the dead [of heart].
Behold, [O Muḥammad,] God can make hear whomever He wills, whereas thou canst not make hear such as are [dead of heart like the dead] in their graves: ‹22› thou art nothing but a warner. ‹23›
Verily, We have sent thee with the truth, as a bearer of glad tidings and a warner: for there never was any community but

14 See note 27 on 14 : 19.

15 I.e., on Judgment Day – for "whatever [wrong] any human being commits rests upon him alone" (6 : 164, which is followed by a sentence identical with the one above).

16 Thus, any transfer of moral responsibility from one person to another is shown to be impossible. Whereas the first part of the above statement implies a negation of the Christian doctrine of "original sin" with which mankind is supposedly burdened, the second part categorically refutes the doctrine of the "vicarious atonement" of that sin by Jesus. (See also 53 : 38 and the corresponding note 31.)

17 For an explanation of this rendering of *bi'l-ghayb*, see *sūrah* 2, note 3. The meaning is that only those "who believe in the existence of that which is beyond the reach of human perception" can really benefit by the "warning" inherent in the preceding statement. (See also 27 : 80-81 and 30 : 52-53.)

a warner has [lived and] passed away in its midst.[18] ‹24› And if they give thee the lie – even so gave the lie to the truth [many of] those who lived before their time, [when] there came unto them their apostles with all evidence of the truth, and with books of divine wisdom, and with light-giving revelation; ‹25› [but] in the end I took to task all those who were bent on denying the truth: and how awesome was My rejection! ‹26›

ART THOU NOT aware that God sends down water from the skies, whereby We bring forth fruits of many hues – just as in the mountains there are streaks of white and red of various shades, as well as [others] raven-black, ‹27› and [as] there are in men, and in crawling beasts, and in cattle, too, many hues?[19]

Of all His servants, only such as are endowed with [innate] knowledge[20] stand [truly] in awe of God: [for they alone comprehend that,] verily, God is almighty, much-forgiving. ‹28›

[It is] they who [truly] follow God's revelation, and are constant in prayer, and spend on others, secretly and openly, out of what We provide for them as sustenance – it is they who may look forward to a bargain that can never fail, ‹29› since He will grant them their just rewards, and give them yet more out of His bounty: for, verily, He is much-forgiving, ever-responsive to gratitude. ‹30›

خَلَا فِيهَا نَذِيرٌ ﴿24﴾ وَإِن يُكَذِّبُوكَ فَقَدْ كَذَّبَ ٱلَّذِينَ مِن قَبْلِهِمْ
جَآءَتْهُمْ رُسُلُهُم بِٱلْبَيِّنَٰتِ وَبِٱلزُّبُرِ وَبِٱلْكِتَٰبِ ٱلْمُنِيرِ ﴿25﴾ ثُمَّ أَخَذْتُ
ٱلَّذِينَ كَفَرُوا۟ ۖ فَكَيْفَ كَانَ نَكِيرِ ﴿26﴾ أَلَمْ تَرَ أَنَّ ٱللَّهَ أَنزَلَ مِنَ ٱلسَّمَآءِ
مَآءً فَأَخْرَجْنَا بِهِۦ ثَمَرَٰتٍ مُّخْتَلِفًا أَلْوَٰنُهَا ۚ وَمِنَ ٱلْجِبَالِ جُدَدٌۢ بِيضٌ
وَحُمْرٌ مُّخْتَلِفٌ أَلْوَٰنُهَا وَغَرَابِيبُ سُودٌ ﴿27﴾ وَمِنَ ٱلنَّاسِ وَٱلدَّوَآبِّ
وَٱلْأَنْعَٰمِ مُخْتَلِفٌ أَلْوَٰنُهُۥ كَذَٰلِكَ ۗ إِنَّمَا يَخْشَى ٱللَّهَ مِنْ عِبَادِهِ ٱلْعُلَمَٰٓؤُا۟ ۗ
إِنَّ ٱللَّهَ عَزِيزٌ غَفُورٌ ﴿28﴾ إِنَّ ٱلَّذِينَ يَتْلُونَ كِتَٰبَ ٱللَّهِ وَأَقَامُوا۟ ٱلصَّلَوٰةَ
وَأَنفَقُوا۟ مِمَّا رَزَقْنَٰهُمْ سِرًّا وَعَلَانِيَةً يَرْجُونَ تِجَٰرَةً لَّن تَبُورَ ﴿29﴾
لِيُوَفِّيَهُمْ أُجُورَهُمْ وَيَزِيدَهُم مِّن فَضْلِهِۦٓ ۚ إِنَّهُۥ غَفُورٌ شَكُورٌ ﴿30﴾

khalā fīhā Nadhīr. ﴿24﴾ Wa ˀiñy-yukadhdhibūka faqad kadhdhabal-ladhīna miñ-qablihim jāaˀat-hum Rusuluhum-bilbayyināti wa bizZuburi wa bilKitābil-munīr. ﴿25﴾ Thumma ˀakhadhtul-ladhīna kafarū fakayfa kāna nakīr. ﴿26﴾ ˀAlam tara ˀannal-lāha ˀañzala minas-samāaˀi māaˀañ-faˀakhrajnā bihī thamarātim-mukhtalifan ˀalwānuhā. Wa minal-jibāli judadum-bīḍuñw-wa ḥumrum-mukhtalifun ˀalwānuhā wa gharābību sūd. ﴿27﴾ Wa minan-nāsi wad-dawāabbi wal-ˀanᶜāmi mukhtalifun ˀalwānuhū kadhālik. ˀInnamā yakhshal-lāha min ᶜibādihil-ᶜulamāaˀ. ˀInnal-lāha ᶜAzīzun Ghafūr. ﴿28﴾ ˀInnal-ladhīna yatlūna Kitābal-lāhi wa ˀaqāmuṣ-Ṣalāta wa ˀañfaqū mimmā razaqnāhum sirrañw-wa ᶜalāniyatañy-yarjūna tijāratal-lañ-tabūr. ﴿29﴾ Liyuwaffiyahum ˀujūrahum wa yazīdahum-miñ-faḍlihīi ˀinnahū Ghafūruñ-Shakūr. ﴿30﴾

---

18 One of the meanings of the term *ummah* (preferred by Zamakhsharī in his commentary on the above verse) is "people of one time" or "age"; another, "people of one kind", i.e., "a nation" or "a community" (which is adopted by me in this context). Taking into consideration a third, well-established meaning, namely, "a [particular] way of life" or "of behaviour" (Jawharī), the term "community" comes, in this instance, close to the modern concept of "civilization" in its historical sense. – The stress on the warners' (i.e., prophets) having "passed away" is meant to emphasize the humanness and mortality of each and all of them.

19 Cf. 16 : 13, where the splendour of nature ("the beauty of many hues") is spoken of as an evidence of God's creative power.

20 I.e., spiritual knowledge, born of the realization that the phenomena which can be observed do not comprise the whole of reality, inasmuch as there is "a realm beyond the reach of a created being's perception" (cf. *sūrah* 2, note 3).

وَٱلَّذِىٓ أَوْحَيْنَآ إِلَيْكَ مِنَ ٱلْكِتَٰبِ هُوَ ٱلْحَقُّ مُصَدِّقًا لِّمَا بَيْنَ يَدَيْهِ ۗ إِنَّ
ٱللَّهَ بِعِبَادِهِۦ لَخَبِيرٌۢ بَصِيرٌ ﴿٣١﴾ ثُمَّ أَوْرَثْنَا ٱلْكِتَٰبَ ٱلَّذِينَ ٱصْطَفَيْنَا مِنْ
عِبَادِنَا ۖ فَمِنْهُمْ ظَالِمٌ لِّنَفْسِهِۦ وَمِنْهُم مُّقْتَصِدٌ وَمِنْهُمْ سَابِقٌۢ بِٱلْخَيْرَٰتِ
بِإِذْنِ ٱللَّهِ ۚ ذَٰلِكَ هُوَ ٱلْفَضْلُ ٱلْكَبِيرُ ﴿٣٢﴾ جَنَّٰتُ عَدْنٍ يَدْخُلُونَهَا
يُحَلَّوْنَ فِيهَا مِنْ أَسَاوِرَ مِن ذَهَبٍ وَلُؤْلُؤًا ۖ وَلِبَاسُهُمْ فِيهَا حَرِيرٌ ﴿٣٣﴾
وَقَالُوا۟ ٱلْحَمْدُ لِلَّهِ ٱلَّذِىٓ أَذْهَبَ عَنَّا ٱلْحَزَنَ ۖ إِنَّ رَبَّنَا لَغَفُورٌ
شَكُورٌ ﴿٣٤﴾ ٱلَّذِىٓ أَحَلَّنَا دَارَ ٱلْمُقَامَةِ مِن فَضْلِهِۦ لَا يَمَسُّنَا فِيهَا
نَصَبٌ وَلَا يَمَسُّنَا فِيهَا لُغُوبٌ ﴿٣٥﴾ وَٱلَّذِينَ كَفَرُوا۟ لَهُمْ نَارُ جَهَنَّمَ لَا
يُقْضَىٰ عَلَيْهِمْ فَيَمُوتُوا۟ وَلَا يُخَفَّفُ عَنْهُم مِّنْ عَذَابِهَا ۚ كَذَٰلِكَ نَجْزِى
كُلَّ كَفُورٍ ﴿٣٦﴾ وَهُمْ يَصْطَرِخُونَ فِيهَا رَبَّنَآ أَخْرِجْنَا نَعْمَلْ صَٰلِحًا غَيْرَ
ٱلَّذِى كُنَّا نَعْمَلُ ۚ أَوَلَمْ نُعَمِّرْكُم مَّا يَتَذَكَّرُ فِيهِ مَن تَذَكَّرَ وَجَآءَكُمُ
ٱلنَّذِيرُ ۖ فَذُوقُوا۟ فَمَا لِلظَّٰلِمِينَ مِن نَّصِيرٍ ﴿٣٧﴾

Wal-ladhīi ʾawḥaynāa ʾilayka minal-Kitābi huwal-ḥaqqu muṣaddiqal-limā bayna yadayh. ʾInnal-lāha biʿibādihī laKhabīrum-Baṣīr. (31) Thumma ʾawrathnal-Kitābal-ladhīnaṣ-ṭafaynā min ʿibādinā. Faminhum ẓālimul-linafsihī wa minhum-muqtaṣiduñw-wa minhum sābiqum-bilkhayrāti biʾidhnil-lāh. Dhālika huwal-faḍlul-kabīr. (32) Jannātu ʿadniñy-yadkhulūnahā yuḥallawna fīhā min ʾasāwira miñ-dhahabiñw-wa luʾluʾañw-wa libāsuhum fīhā ḥarīr. (33) Wa qālul-ḥamdu lillāhil-ladhīi ʾadhhaba ʿannal-ḥazana ʾinna Rabbanā laGhafūruñ-Shakūr. (34) ʾAlladhīi ʾaḥallanā dāral-muqāmati miñ-faḍlihī lā yamassunā fīhā naṣabuñw-wa lā yamassunā fīhā lughūb. (35) Wal-ladhīna kafarū lahum nāru jahannama lā yuqḍā ʿalayhim fayamūtū wa lā yukhaffafu ʿanhum-min ʿadhābihā. Kadhālika najzī kulla kafūr. (36) Wa hum yaṣṭarikhūna fīhā Rabbanāa ʾakhrijnā naʿmal ṣāliḥan ghayral-ladhī kunnā naʿmal. ʾAwa lam nuʿammirkum-mā yatadhakkaru fīhi mañ-tadhakkara wa jāaʾakumun-Nadhīru fadhūqū famā liẓ-ẓalimīna miñ-naṣīr. (37)

And [know that] all of the divine writ with which We have inspired thee is the very truth, confirming the truth of whatever there still remains of earlier revelations[21] – for, behold, of [the needs of] His servants God is fully aware, all-seeing. ‹31›

And so, We have bestowed this divine writ as a heritage unto such of Our servants as We chose: and among them are some who sin against themselves; and some who keep half-way [between right and wrong];[22] and some who, by God's leave, are foremost in deeds of goodness: [and] this, indeed, is a merit most high! ‹32›

[Hence,] gardens of perpetual bliss will they enter, therein to be adorned with bracelets of gold and pearls, and therein to be clad in raiments of silk;[23] ‹33› and they will say: "All praise is due to God, who has caused all sorrow to leave us: for, verily, our Sustainer is indeed much-forgiving, ever-responsive to gratitude ‹34› – He who, out of His bounty, has made us alight in this abode of life enduring, wherein no struggle can assail us, and wherein no weariness can touch us!" ‹35›

But as for those who are bent on denying the truth – the fire of hell awaits them: no end shall be put to their lives so that they could die, nor shall aught of the suffering caused by that [fire] be lightened for them: thus shall We requite all who are bereft of gratitude. ‹36›

And in that [hell] they will cry aloud: "O our Sustainer! Cause us to come out [of this suffering]! We shall [henceforth] do good deeds, not such as we were wont to do [aforetime]!"

[But We shall answer] "Did We not grant you a life long enough so that whoever was willing to take thought could bethink himself? And [withal,] a warner had come unto you! Taste, then, [the fruit of your evil deeds]: for evildoers shall have none to succour them!" ‹37›

21 For this explanatory rendering of the phrase *mā bayna yadayhi,* see note 3 on 3 : 3.

22 See 7 : 46 and the corresponding note 37.

23 Regarding this symbolic "adornment" of the blessed in paradise, see note 41 on 18 : 31.

VERILY, God knows the hidden reality of the heavens and the earth: [and,] behold, He has full knowledge of what is in the hearts [of men]. ‹38›
He it is who has made you inherit the earth.[24] Hence, he who is bent on denying the truth [of God's oneness and uniqueness ought to know that] this denial of his will fall back upon him: for their [persistent] denial of this truth does but add to the deniers' loathsomeness in their Sustainer's sight and, thus, their denial of this truth does but add to the deniers' loss. ‹39›
Say: "Have you ever [really] considered those beings and forces to whom you ascribe a share in God's divinity,[25] [and] whom you invoke beside God? Show me what it is that they have created on earth – or do [you claim that] they have a share in [governing] the heavens?"
Have We ever vouchsafed them[26] a divine writ on which they could rely as evidence [in support of their views]?[27] Nay, [the hope which] the evildoers hold out to one another [is] nothing but a delusion.[28] ‹40›
Verily, it is God [alone] who upholds the celestial bodies[29] and the earth, lest they deviate [from their orbits] – for if they should ever deviate, there is none that could uphold them after He will have ceased to do so.[30]

إِنَّ ٱللَّهَ عَـٰلِمُ غَيْبِ ٱلسَّمَـٰوَٰتِ وَٱلْأَرْضِ إِنَّهُۥ عَلِيمٌۢ بِذَاتِ
ٱلصُّدُورِ ﴿٣٨﴾ هُوَ ٱلَّذِى جَعَلَكُمْ خَلَـٰٓئِفَ فِى ٱلْأَرْضِ فَمَن كَفَرَ فَعَلَيْهِ
كُفْرُهُۥ وَلَا يَزِيدُ ٱلْكَـٰفِرِينَ كُفْرُهُمْ عِندَ رَبِّهِمْ إِلَّا مَقْتًا وَلَا يَزِيدُ
ٱلْكَـٰفِرِينَ كُفْرُهُمْ إِلَّا خَسَارًا ﴿٣٩﴾ قُلْ أَرَءَيْتُمْ شُرَكَآءَكُمُ ٱلَّذِينَ
تَدْعُونَ مِن دُونِ ٱللَّهِ أَرُونِى مَاذَا خَلَقُوا۟ مِنَ ٱلْأَرْضِ أَمْ لَهُمْ شِرْكٌ فِى
ٱلسَّمَـٰوَٰتِ أَمْ ءَاتَيْنَـٰهُمْ كِتَـٰبًا فَهُمْ عَلَىٰ بَيِّنَتٍ مِّنْهُ بَلْ إِن يَعِدُ
ٱلظَّـٰلِمُونَ بَعْضُهُم بَعْضًا إِلَّا غُرُورًا ﴿٤٠﴾ ۞ إِنَّ ٱللَّهَ يُمْسِكُ ٱلسَّمَـٰوَٰتِ
وَٱلْأَرْضَ أَن تَزُولَا وَلَئِن زَالَتَآ إِنْ أَمْسَكَهُمَا مِنْ أَحَدٍ مِّنۢ بَعْدِهِۦٓ

ثلاثة ارباع الحزب

ʾInnal-lāha ʿĀlimu ghaybis-samāwāti wal-ʾarḍ. ʾInnahū ʿAlīmum-bidhātiṣ-ṣudūr. (38) Huwal-ladhī jaʿalakum khalāaʾifa fil-ʾarḍi famañ-kafara faʿalayhi kufruh. Wa lā yazīdul-kāfirīna kufruhum ʿiñda Rabbihim ʾillā maqtā. Wa lā yazīdul-kāfirīna kufruhum ʾillā khasārā. (39) Qul ʾaraʾaytum shurakāaʾakumul-ladhīna tadʿūna miñ-dūnil-lāhi ʾarūnī mādhā khalaqū minal-ʾarḍi ʾam lahum shirkuñ-fis-samāwāti ʾam ʾātaynāhum Kitābañ-fahum ʿalā bayyinatim-minh. Bal ʾiñy-yaʿiduẓ-ẓālimūna baʿḍuhum-baʿḍan ʾillā ghurūrā. (40) ۞ ʾInnal-lāha yumsikus-samāwāti wal-ʾarḍa ʾañ-tazūlā; wa laʾiñ-zālatāa ʾin ʾamsakahumā min ʾaḥadim-mim-baʿdih.

24 See note 22 on 2 : 30. In this instance, God's having made man "inherit the earth" implies the grant to him of the ability to discern between right and wrong as well as between truth and falsehood.

25 Lit., "those [God-] partners of yours": see note 15 on 6 : 22.

26 I.e., to those who ascribe divinity to beings or forces other than God.

27 Cf. 30 : 35 – "Have We ever bestowed upon them from on high a divine writ which would speak [with approval] of their worshipping aught beside Us?" The reference to a "divine writ" makes it clear that the people spoken of here are the erring followers of earlier revelation, and not atheists.

28 I.e., their expectation that the saints whom they invest with divine or semi-divine qualities will "mediate" between them and God, or "intercede" for them before Him, is based on nothing but wishful thinking.

29 Lit., "the heavens" – in this case apparently a metonym for all the stars, galaxies, nebulae, etc., which traverse the cosmic spaces in obedience to a most intricate system of God-willed laws, of which the law of gravity, perhaps most obvious to man, is but one.

30 Lit., "after Him". This seems to be an allusion to the Last Hour, which, according to the Qurʾān, will be heralded by a cosmic catastrophe.

إِنَّهُۥ كَانَ حَلِيمًا غَفُورًا ﴿٤١﴾ وَأَقْسَمُوا۟ بِٱللَّهِ جَهْدَ أَيْمَـٰنِهِمْ لَئِن جَآءَهُمْ
نَذِيرٌ لَّيَكُونُنَّ أَهْدَىٰ مِنْ إِحْدَى ٱلْأُمَمِ ۖ فَلَمَّا جَآءَهُمْ نَذِيرٌ مَّا زَادَهُمْ إِلَّا
نُفُورًا ﴿٤٢﴾ ٱسْتِكْبَارًا فِى ٱلْأَرْضِ وَمَكْرَ ٱلسَّيِّئِ ۚ وَلَا يَحِيقُ ٱلْمَكْرُ
ٱلسَّيِّئُ إِلَّا بِأَهْلِهِۦ ۚ فَهَلْ يَنظُرُونَ إِلَّا سُنَّتَ ٱلْأَوَّلِينَ ۚ فَلَن تَجِدَ لِسُنَّتِ
ٱللَّهِ تَبْدِيلًا ۖ وَلَن تَجِدَ لِسُنَّتِ ٱللَّهِ تَحْوِيلًا ﴿٤٣﴾ أَوَلَمْ يَسِيرُوا۟ فِى ٱلْأَرْضِ
فَيَنظُرُوا۟ كَيْفَ كَانَ عَـٰقِبَةُ ٱلَّذِينَ مِن قَبْلِهِمْ وَكَانُوٓا۟ أَشَدَّ مِنْهُمْ قُوَّةً ۚ وَمَا
كَانَ ٱللَّهُ لِيُعْجِزَهُۥ مِن شَىْءٍ فِى ٱلسَّمَـٰوَٰتِ وَلَا فِى ٱلْأَرْضِ ۚ إِنَّهُۥ كَانَ
عَلِيمًا قَدِيرًا ﴿٤٤﴾ وَلَوْ يُؤَاخِذُ ٱللَّهُ ٱلنَّاسَ بِمَا كَسَبُوا۟ مَا تَرَكَ عَلَىٰ
ظَهْرِهَا مِن دَآبَّةٍ وَلَـٰكِن يُؤَخِّرُهُمْ إِلَىٰٓ أَجَلٍ مُّسَمًّى ۖ فَإِذَا جَآءَ أَجَلُهُمْ فَإِنَّ
ٱللَّهَ كَانَ بِعِبَادِهِۦ بَصِيرًۢا ﴿٤٥﴾

[But,] verily, He is ever-forbearing, much-forgiving![31] ‹41›

As it is, they [who are averse to the truth often] swear by God with their most solemn oaths that if a warner should ever come to them, they would follow his guidance better than any of the communities [of old had followed the warner sent to them]:[32] but now that a warner has come unto them, [his call] but increases their aversion, ‹42› their arrogant behaviour on earth, and their devising of evil [arguments against God's messages].[33]

Yet [in the end,] such evil scheming will engulf none but its authors; and can they expect anything but [to be made to go] the way of those [sinners] of olden times?[34]

Thus [it is]: no change wilt thou ever find in God's way; yea, no deviation wilt thou ever find in God's way! ‹43›

Have they never journeyed about the earth and beheld what happened in the end to those [deniers of the truth] who lived before their time and were [so much] greater than they in power? And [do they not see that the will of] God can never be foiled by anything whatever in the heavens or on earth, since, verily, He is all-knowing, infinite in His power? ‹44›

Now if God were to take men [at once] to task for whatever [wrong] they commit [on earth], He would not leave a single living creature upon its surface. However, He grants them respite for a term set [by Him]:[35] but when their term comes to an end – then, verily, [they come to know that] God sees all that is in [the hearts of] His servants. ‹45›

ʾInnahū kāna Ḥalīman Ghafūrā. (41) Wa ʾaqsamū billāhi jahda ʾaymānihim laʾiñ-jāaʾahum Nadhīrul-layakūnunna ʾahdā min ʾiḥdal-ʾumami falammā jāaʾahum Nadhīrum-mā zādahum ʾillā nufūrā. (42) ʾIstikbārañ-fil-ʾarḍi wa makras-sayyiʾ. Wa lā yaḥīqul-makrus-sayyiʾu ʾillā biʾahlih. Fahal yañẓurūna ʾillā sunnatal-ʾawwalīn. Falañ-tajida lisunnatil-lāhi tabdīlañw-wa lañ-tajida lisunnatil-lāhi taḥwīlā. (43) ʾAwa lam yasīrū fil-ʾarḍi fayañẓurū kayfa kāna ʿāqibatul-ladhīna miñ-qablihim wa kānūu ʾashadda minhum quwwah. Wa mā kānal-lāhu liyuʿjizahū miñ-shayʾiñ-fis-samāwāti wa lā fil-ʾarḍ. ʾInnahū kāna ʿAlīmañ-Qadīrā. (44) Wa law yuʾākhidhul-lāhun-nāsa bimā kasabū mā taraka ʿalā ẓahrihā miñ-dāabbatiñw-wa lākiñy-yuʾakhkhiruhum ʾilāa ʾajalim-musammā. Faʾidhā jāaʾa ʾajaluhum faʾinnal-lāha kāna biʿibādihī Baṣīrā. (45)

31 I.e., inasmuch as He does not speed up the end of the world despite the sinfulness of most of its inhabitants, and neither punishes without giving the sinner time to reflect and to repent (cf. verse 45),

32 Cf. 6 : 157 and the corresponding note 158.

33 I.e., fallacious arguments meant to disparage those messages and to "disprove" their divine origin (cf. 10 : 21 or 34 : 33 and the corresponding notes on the Qurʾanic use of the term *makr* in this sense).

34 I.e., the way (*sunnah*) in which God has punished them.

35 Or: "known [to Him alone]" – i.e., the end of their lives on earth,

The Thirty-Sixth Sūrah

Yā Sīn (O Thou Human Being)

Mecca Period

FOR an explanation of my rendering of the title *Yā Sīn* as "O Thou Human Being", see note 1 on following page.

Revealed in the early part of what is termed the "middle" Mecca period (probably just before *Al-Furqān*), this *sūrah* is almost entirely devoted to the problem of man's moral responsibility and, hence, to the certainty of resurrection and God's judgment: and it is for this reason that the Prophet called upon his followers to recite it over the dying and in prayers for the dead (cf. several Traditions to this effect quoted by Ibn Kathīr at the beginning of his commentary on this *sūrah*).

-36-
سورة يس مكية
وآياتها ثلاث وثمانون

IN THE NAME OF GOD, THE MOST GRACIOUS, THE DISPENSER OF GRACE:

O THOU human being![1] ‹1› Consider this Qurʾān full of wisdom: ‹2› verily, thou art indeed one of God's message-bearers,[2] ‹3› pursuing a straight way ‹4› by [virtue of] what is being bestowed from on high by the Almighty, the Dispenser of Grace,[3] ‹5› [bestowed upon thee] so that thou mayest warn people whose forefathers had not been warned, and who therefore are unaware [of the meaning of right and wrong].[4] ‹6›

Indeed, the word [of God's condemnation] is bound to come true[5] against most of them: for they will not believe. ‹7›

Behold, around their necks We have put shackles,[6] reaching up to their chins, so that their heads are forced up;[7] ‹8›

بِسۡمِ ٱللَّهِ ٱلرَّحۡمَٰنِ ٱلرَّحِيمِ

يسٓ ﴿١﴾ وَٱلۡقُرۡءَانِ ٱلۡحَكِيمِ ﴿٢﴾ إِنَّكَ لَمِنَ ٱلۡمُرۡسَلِينَ ﴿٣﴾ عَلَىٰ
صِرَٰطٖ مُّسۡتَقِيمٖ ﴿٤﴾ تَنزِيلَ ٱلۡعَزِيزِ ٱلرَّحِيمِ ﴿٥﴾ لِتُنذِرَ قَوۡمٗا مَّآ أُنذِرَ
ءَابَآؤُهُمۡ فَهُمۡ غَٰفِلُونَ ﴿٦﴾ لَقَدۡ حَقَّ ٱلۡقَوۡلُ عَلَىٰٓ أَكۡثَرِهِمۡ فَهُمۡ لَا
يُؤۡمِنُونَ ﴿٧﴾ إِنَّا جَعَلۡنَا فِيٓ أَعۡنَٰقِهِمۡ أَغۡلَٰلٗا فَهِيَ إِلَى ٱلۡأَذۡقَانِ فَهُم
مُّقۡمَحُونَ ﴿٨﴾

Bismil-lāhir-Raḥmānir-Raḥīm.
Yā-Sīin. (1) **Wal-Qurʾānil-ḥakīm.** (2) **ʾInnaka laminal-Mursalīn.** (3) **ʿAlā ṣirāṭim-mustaqīm.** (4) **Tañzīlal-ʿAzīzir-Raḥīm.** (5) **Lituñdhira qawmam-māa ʾuñdhira ʾābāaʾuhum fahum ghāfilūn.** (6) **Laqad ḥaqqal-qawlu ʿalāa ʾaktharihim fahum lā yuʾminūn.** (7) **ʾInnā jaʿalnā fīi ʾaʿnāqihim ʾaghlālañ-fahiya ʾilal-ʾadhqāni fahum-muqmaḥūn.** (8)

---

1 Whereas some of the classical commentators incline to the view that the letters *y-s* (pronounced *yā sīn*) with which this *sūrah* opens belong to the category of the mysterious letter-symbols (*al-muqaṭṭaʿāt*) introducing a number of Qurʾanic chapters (see Appendix II), ʿAbd Allāh ibn ʿAbbās states that they actually represent two distinct *words*, namely the exclamatory particle *yā* ("O") and *sīn*, which in the dialect of the tribe of Ṭayyʾ is synonymous with *insān* ("human being" or "man"): hence, similar to the two syllables *ṭā hā* in *sūrah* 20, *yā sīn* denotes "O thou human being!" This interpretation has been accepted by ʿIkrimah, Aḍ-Ḍaḥḥāk, Al-Ḥasan al-Baṣrī, Saʿīd ibn Jubayr, and other early Qurʾān-commentators (see Ṭabarī, Baghawī, Zamakhsharī, Bayḍāwī, Ibn Kathīr, etc.). According to Zamakhsharī, it would seem that the syllable *sīn* is an abbreviation of *unaysīn*, the diminutive form of *insān* used by the Ṭayyʾ in exclamations. (It is to be borne in mind that in classical Arabic a diminutive is often expressive of no more than endearment: e.g., *yā bunayya*, which does not necessarily signify "O my little son" but, rather, "my dear son" irrespective of the son's age.) On the whole, we may safely assume that the words *yā sīn* apostrophize the Prophet Muḥammad, who is explicitly addressed in the sequence, and are meant to stress – as the Qurʾān so often does – the fact of his and all other apostles' humanness.

2 This statement explains the adjurative particle *wa* (rendered by me as "Consider") at the beginning of the preceding verse – namely: "Let the wisdom apparent in the Qurʾān serve as an evidence of the fact that thou art an apostle of God". As regards my rendering of *al-qurʾān al-ḥakīm* as "this Qurʾān full of wisdom", see note 2 on 10 : 1.

3 Cf. 34 : 50 – "if I am on the right path, it is but by virtue of what my Sustainer reveals unto me".

4 Cf. 6 : 131-132. In the wider sense of this expression, the "forefathers" may be a metonym for a community's cultural past: hence, the reference to those "forefathers" not having been "warned" (i.e., against evil) evidently alludes to the defectiveness of the ethical heritage of people who have become estranged from true moral values.

5 Lit., "has come true", the past tense indicating the inevitability of its "coming true" – i.e., taking effect.

6 Zamakhsharī: "[This is] an allegory of their deliberate denial of the truth." See note 13 on 13 : 5 and note 44 on 34 : 33.

7 Sc., "and they cannot see the right way" (Rāzī); their "forced-up heads" symbolize also their arrogance. On the

and We have set a barrier before them and a barrier behind them,[8] and We have enshrouded them in veils so that they cannot see: ‹9› thus, it is all one to them whether thou warnest them or dost not warn them: they will not believe. ‹10›
Thou canst [truly] warn only him who is willing to take the reminder to heart,[9] and who stands in awe of the Most Gracious although He is beyond the reach of human perception: unto such, then, give the glad tiding of [God's] forgiveness and of a most excellent reward! ‹11›
Verily, We shall indeed bring the dead back to life; and We shall record whatever [deeds] they have sent ahead, and the traces [of good and evil] which they have left behind: for of all things do We take account in a record clear. ‹12›

AND SET FORTH unto them a parable – [the story of how] the people of a township [behaved] when [Our] message-bearers came unto them. ‹13›
Lo! We sent unto them two [apostles], and they gave the lie to both; and so We strengthened [the two] with a third; and thereupon they said: "Behold, we have been sent unto you [by God]!"[10] ‹14›
[The others] answered: "You are nothing but mortal men like ourselves; moreover, the Most Gracious has never bestowed aught [of revelation] from on high. You do nothing but lie!"[11] ‹15›

وَجَعَلْنَا مِنۢ بَيْنِ أَيْدِيهِمْ سَدًّا وَمِنْ خَلْفِهِمْ سَدًّا فَأَغْشَيْنَٰهُمْ فَهُمْ لَا
يُبْصِرُونَ ﴿٩﴾ وَسَوَآءٌ عَلَيْهِمْ ءَأَنذَرْتَهُمْ أَمْ لَمْ تُنذِرْهُمْ لَا يُؤْمِنُونَ ﴿١٠﴾
إِنَّمَا تُنذِرُ مَنِ ٱتَّبَعَ ٱلذِّكْرَ وَخَشِىَ ٱلرَّحْمَٰنَ بِٱلْغَيْبِ فَبَشِّرْهُ بِمَغْفِرَةٍ
وَأَجْرٍ كَرِيمٍ ﴿١١﴾ إِنَّا نَحْنُ نُحْىِ ٱلْمَوْتَىٰ وَنَكْتُبُ مَا قَدَّمُوا۟ وَءَاثَٰرَهُمْ
وَكُلَّ شَىْءٍ أَحْصَيْنَٰهُ فِىٓ إِمَامٍ مُّبِينٍ ﴿١٢﴾ وَٱضْرِبْ لَهُم مَّثَلًا أَصْحَٰبَ
ٱلْقَرْيَةِ إِذْ جَآءَهَا ٱلْمُرْسَلُونَ ﴿١٣﴾ إِذْ أَرْسَلْنَآ إِلَيْهِمُ ٱثْنَيْنِ فَكَذَّبُوهُمَا
فَعَزَّزْنَا بِثَالِثٍ فَقَالُوٓا۟ إِنَّآ إِلَيْكُم مُّرْسَلُونَ ﴿١٤﴾ قَالُوا۟ مَآ أَنتُمْ إِلَّا بَشَرٌ
مِّثْلُنَا وَمَآ أَنزَلَ ٱلرَّحْمَٰنُ مِن شَىْءٍ إِنْ أَنتُمْ إِلَّا تَكْذِبُونَ ﴿١٥﴾

Wa jaʿalnā mim-bayni ʾaydīhim saddañw-wa min khalfihim saddañ-faʾaghshaynāhum fahum lā yubṣirūn. ﴿9﴾ Wa sawāaʾun ʿalayhim ʾaʾañdhartahum ʾam lam tuñdhirhum lā yuʾminūn. ﴿10﴾ ʾInnamā tuñdhiru manit-tabaʿadh-Dhikra wa khashiyar-Raḥmāna bilghaybi fabashshirhu bimaghfiratiñw-wa ʾajriñ-karīm. ﴿11﴾ ʾInnā Naḥnu nuḥyil-mawtā wa naktubu mā qaddamū wa ʾāthārahum wa kulla shayʾin ʾaḥṣaynāhu fīi ʾImāmim-mubīn. ﴿12﴾ Waḍ-rib lahum-mathalan ʾaṣḥābal-qaryati ʾidh jāaʾahal-Mursalūn. ﴿13﴾ ʾIdh ʾarsalnāa ʾilayhimuth-nayni fa-kadhdhabūhumā faʿazzaznā bithālithiñ-faqālūu ʾinnāa ʾilaykum-Mursalūn. ﴿14﴾ Qālū māa ʾañtum ʾillā basharum-mithlunā wa māa ʾañzalar-Raḥmānu miñ-shayʾin ʾin ʾañtum ʾillā takdhibūn. ﴿15﴾

---

other hand, *God's* "placing shackles" around the sinners' necks is a metaphor similar to His "sealing their hearts and their hearing", spoken of in 2 : 7 and explained in the corresponding note 7. The same applies to the metaphor of the "barriers" and the "veiling" mentioned in the next verse.

8 Sc., "so that they can neither advance nor go back": a metaphor of utter spiritual stagnation.

9 Lit., "who is following the reminder".

10 As is usual with such passages, the commentators advance various speculations as to the "identity" of the town and the apostles. Since, however, the story is clearly described as a parable, it must be understood as such and not as an historical narrative. It seems to me that we have here an allegory of the three great monotheistic religions, successively propounded by Moses, Jesus and Muḥammad, and embodying, essentially, the same spiritual truths. The "township" (*qaryah*) mentioned in the parable represents, I think, the common cultural environment within which these three religions appeared. The apostles of the first two are said to have been sent "together", implying that the teachings of both were – and are – anchored in one and the same scripture, the Old Testament of the Bible. When, in the course of time, their impact proved insufficient to mould the ethical attitude of the people or peoples concerned, God "strengthened" them by means of His final message, conveyed to the world by the third and last of the apostles, Muḥammad.

11 Cf. 6 : 91 – "no true understanding of God have they when they say, 'Never has God revealed anything unto

Said [the apostles]: "Our Sustainer knows that we have indeed been sent unto you; ‹16› but we are not bound to do more than clearly deliver the message [entrusted to us]." ‹17›

Said [the others]: "Truly, we augur evil from you![12] Indeed, if you desist not, we will surely stone you, and grievous suffering is bound to befall you at our hands!" ‹18›

[The apostles] replied: "Your destiny, good or evil, is [bound up] with yourselves![13] [Does it seem evil to you] if you are told to take [the truth] to heart? Nay, but you are people who have wasted their own selves!"[14] ‹19›

At that, a man came running from the farthest end of the city, [and] exclaimed: "O my people! Follow these message-bearers! ‹20› Follow those who ask no reward of you, and themselves are rightly guided! ‹21›

"[As for me,] why should I not worship Him who has brought me into being, and to whom you all will be brought back? ‹22› Should I take to worshipping [other] deities beside Him? [But then,] if the Most Gracious should will that harm befall me, their intercession could not in the least avail me, nor could they save me: ‹23› and so, behold, I would have indeed, most obviously, lost myself in error! ‹24›

"Verily, [O my people,] in the Sustainer of you all have I come to believe: listen, then, to me!" ‹25›

[And] he was told,[15] "[Thou shalt] enter paradise!" – [whereupon] he exclaimed: "Would that my people knew ‹26› how my Sustainer has forgiven me [the sins of my past], and has placed me among the honoured ones!" ‹27›

قَالُوا۟ رَبُّنَا يَعْلَمُ إِنَّآ إِلَيْكُمْ لَمُرْسَلُونَ ﴿١٦﴾ وَمَا عَلَيْنَآ إِلَّا ٱلْبَلَٰغُ
ٱلْمُبِينُ ﴿١٧﴾ قَالُوٓا۟ إِنَّا تَطَيَّرْنَا بِكُمْ لَئِن لَّمْ تَنتَهُوا۟ لَنَرْجُمَنَّكُمْ
وَلَيَمَسَّنَّكُم مِّنَّا عَذَابٌ أَلِيمٌ ﴿١٨﴾ قَالُوا۟ طَٰٓئِرُكُم مَّعَكُمْ أَئِن ذُكِّرْتُم بَلْ
أَنتُمْ قَوْمٌ مُّسْرِفُونَ ﴿١٩﴾ وَجَآءَ مِنْ أَقْصَا ٱلْمَدِينَةِ رَجُلٌ يَسْعَىٰ قَالَ يَٰقَوْمِ
ٱتَّبِعُوا۟ ٱلْمُرْسَلِينَ ﴿٢٠﴾ ٱتَّبِعُوا۟ مَن لَّا يَسْـَٔلُكُمْ أَجْرًا وَهُم مُّهْتَدُونَ ﴿٢١﴾
وَمَا لِىَ لَآ أَعْبُدُ ٱلَّذِى فَطَرَنِى وَإِلَيْهِ تُرْجَعُونَ ﴿٢٢﴾ ءَأَتَّخِذُ مِن دُونِهِۦٓ ءَالِهَةً
إِن يُرِدْنِ ٱلرَّحْمَٰنُ بِضُرٍّ لَّا تُغْنِ عَنِّى شَفَٰعَتُهُمْ شَيْـًٔا وَلَا يُنقِذُونِ ﴿٢٣﴾
إِنِّىٓ إِذًا لَّفِى ضَلَٰلٍ مُّبِينٍ ﴿٢٤﴾ إِنِّىٓ ءَامَنتُ بِرَبِّكُمْ فَٱسْمَعُونِ ﴿٢٥﴾ قِيلَ
ٱدْخُلِ ٱلْجَنَّةَ قَالَ يَٰلَيْتَ قَوْمِى يَعْلَمُونَ ﴿٢٦﴾ بِمَا غَفَرَ لِى رَبِّى وَجَعَلَنِى
مِنَ ٱلْمُكْرَمِينَ ﴿٢٧﴾

Qlālū Rabbunā yaʿlamu ʾinnāa ʾilaykum laMursalūn. (16) Wa mā ʿalaynāa ʾillal-balāghul-mubīn. (17) Qālūu ʾinnā taṭayyarnā bikum laʾil-lam tañtahū lanarjumannakum wa layamassannakum minnā ʿadhābun ʾalīm. (18) Qālū ṭāaʾirukum maʿakum; ʾaʾiñ-dhukkirtum bal ʾañtum qawmum-musrifūn. (19) Wa jāaʾa min ʾaqṣal-madīnati rajuluñy-yasʿā qāla yā qawmit-tabiʿul-Mursalīn. (20) ʾIttabiʿū mal-lā yasʾalukum ʾajrañw-wa hum muhtadūn. (21) Wa mā liya lāa ʾaʿbudul-ladhī faṭaranī wa ʾilayhi turjaʿūn. (22) ʾAʾattakhidhu miñ-dūnihīi ʾālihatan ʾiñy-yuridnir-Raḥmānu biḍurril-lā tughni ʿannī shafāʿatuhum shayʾañw-wa lā yuñqidhūn. (23) ʾInnīi ʾidhal-lafī ḍalālim-mubīn. (24) ʾInnīi ʾāmañtu biRabbikum fasmaʿūn. (25) Qīlad-khulil-jannata qāla yā layta qawmī yaʿlamūna, (26) bimā ghafara lī Rabbī wa jaʿalanī minal-mukramīn. (27)

man."' See also 34 : 31 and the corresponding note 38. Both these passages, as well as the one above, allude to people who like to think of themselves as "believing" in God without, however, allowing their "belief" to interfere in the practical concerns of their lives: and this they justify by conceding to religion no more than a vaguely emotional role, and by refusing to admit the fact of objective revelation – for the concept of revelation invariably implies a promulgation, by God, of absolute moral values and, thus, a demand for one's self-surrender to them.

12 For an explanation of the phrase *taṭayyarnā bikum*, see *sūrah* 7, note 95.

13 Cf. 17 : 13 – "every human being's destiny (*ṭāʾir*) have We tied to his neck" – and the corresponding note 17.

14 For this rendering of *musrifūn* (sing. *musrif*), see note 21 on the last sentence of 10 : 12.

15 I.e., by the apostles or, more probably (in view of the allegorical character of this story), by his own insight. The

۞ وَمَآ أَنزَلْنَا عَلَىٰ قَوْمِهِۦ مِنۢ بَعْدِهِۦ مِن جُندٍ مِّنَ ٱلسَّمَآءِ وَمَا كُنَّا
مُنزِلِينَ ﴿٢٨﴾ إِن كَانَتْ إِلَّا صَيْحَةً وَٰحِدَةً فَإِذَا هُمْ خَـٰمِدُونَ ﴿٢٩﴾ يَـٰحَسْرَةً
عَلَى ٱلْعِبَادِ مَا يَأْتِيهِم مِّن رَّسُولٍ إِلَّا كَانُوا۟ بِهِۦ يَسْتَهْزِءُونَ ﴿٣٠﴾ أَلَمْ
يَرَوْا۟ كَمْ أَهْلَكْنَا قَبْلَهُم مِّنَ ٱلْقُرُونِ أَنَّهُمْ إِلَيْهِمْ لَا يَرْجِعُونَ ﴿٣١﴾ وَإِن كُلٌّ
لَّمَّا جَمِيعٌ لَّدَيْنَا مُحْضَرُونَ ﴿٣٢﴾ وَءَايَةٌ لَّهُمُ ٱلْأَرْضُ ٱلْمَيْتَةُ أَحْيَيْنَـٰهَا
وَأَخْرَجْنَا مِنْهَا حَبًّا فَمِنْهُ يَأْكُلُونَ ﴿٣٣﴾ وَجَعَلْنَا فِيهَا جَنَّـٰتٍ مِّن نَّخِيلٍ
وَأَعْنَـٰبٍ وَفَجَّرْنَا فِيهَا مِنَ ٱلْعُيُونِ ﴿٣٤﴾ لِيَأْكُلُوا۟ مِن ثَمَرِهِۦ وَمَا عَمِلَتْهُ
أَيْدِيهِمْ أَفَلَا يَشْكُرُونَ ﴿٣٥﴾ سُبْحَـٰنَ ٱلَّذِى خَلَقَ ٱلْأَزْوَٰجَ كُلَّهَا مِمَّا
تُنۢبِتُ ٱلْأَرْضُ وَمِنْ أَنفُسِهِمْ وَمِمَّا لَا يَعْلَمُونَ ﴿٣٦﴾

حزب 45
جزء 23

And after that, no host out of heaven did We send down against his people, nor did We need to send down any: «28» nothing was [needed] but one single blast [of Our punishment] – and lo! they became as still and silent as ashes. «29»

OH, THE REGRETS that [most] human beings will have to bear![16] Never has an apostle come to them without their deriding him! «30
Are they not aware of how many a generation We have destroyed before their time, [and] that those [that have perished] will never return to them,[17] «31» and [that] all of them, all together, will [in the end] before Us be arraigned? «32»
And [yet,] they have a sign [of Our power to create and to resurrect] in the lifeless earth which We make alive, and out of which We bring forth grain, whereof they may eat; «33» and [how] We make gardens of date-palms and vines [grow] thereon, and cause springs to gush [forth] within it, «34» so that they may eat of the fruit thereof, though it was not their hands that made it.
Will they not, then, be grateful? «35»
Limitless in His glory is He who has created opposites in whatever the earth produces, and in men's own selves, and in that of which [as yet] they have no knowledge.[18] «36»

۞ **Wa māa ʾañzalnā ʿalā qawmihī mim-baʿdihī miñ-juñdim-minas-samāaʾi wa mā kunnā muñzilīn.** ﴿28﴾
ʾIñ-kānat ʾillā ṣayḥatañw-wāḥidatañ-faʾidhā hum khāmidūn. ﴿29﴾ **Yā ḥasratan ʿalal-ʿibādi mā yaʾtīhim-mir-Rasūlin ʾillā kānū bihī yastahziʾūn.** ﴿30﴾ **ʾAlam yaraw kam ʾahlaknā qablahum minal-qurūni ʾannahum ʾilayhim lā yarjiʿūn.** ﴿31﴾ **Wa ʾiñ-kullul-lammā jamīʿul-ladaynā muḥḍarūn.** ﴿32﴾ **Wa ʾĀyatul-lahumul-ʾarḍul-maytatu ʾaḥyaynāhā wa ʾakhrajnā minhā ḥabbañ-faminhu yaʾkulūn.** ﴿33﴾ **Wa jaʿalnā fīhā jannātim-miñ-nakhīliñw-wa ʾaʿnābiñw-wa fajjarnā fīhā minal-ʿuyūn.** ﴿34﴾ **Liyaʾkulū miñ-thamarihī wa mā ʿamilat-hu ʾaydīhim; ʾafalā yashkurūn.** ﴿35﴾ **Subḥānal-ladhī khalaqal-ʾazwāja kullahā mimmā tumbitul-ʾarḍu wa min ʾañfusihim wa mimmā lā yaʿlamūn.** ﴿36﴾

---

intervention of the man who "came running from the farthest end of the city" is evidently a parable of the truly believing minority in every religion, and of their desperate, mostly unavailing endeavours to convince their erring fellow-men that God-consciousness alone can save human life from futility.

16 Lit., "Oh, the regrets upon the bondmen" (*al-ʿibād*) – since all human beings, good or bad, are God's "bondmen". This phrase alludes to the Day of Judgment – which is described in 19 : 39 as "the Day of Regrets" – as well as to the fact, repeatedly stressed in the Qurʾān, that most human beings choose to remain deaf to the voice of truth, and thus condemn themselves to spiritual death.

17 I.e., to the people now living. As in many other Qurʾanic passages, the term *qarn,* which literally signifies a "generation" or "people living at the same period", has in this context the wider meaning of "society" or "civilization" in the historical connotation of these terms. Thus, the downfall and utter disappearance of past societies and civilizations is here linked to their spiritual frivolity and consequent moral failure. A further lesson to be drawn from this parable is the implied conclusion that the majority of people in every society, at all times (our own included), refuse to be guided by moral considerations, regarding them as opposed to their conventional mode of life and their pursuit of materialistic values – with the result that "never has an apostle come to them without their deriding him".

18 Lit., "who has created all the pairs out of whatever the earth produces, and out of themselves, and out of that of which they have no knowledge": a reference to the polarity evident in all creation, both animate and inanimate, which

And [of Our sway over all that exists] they have a sign in the night: We withdraw from it the [light of] day – and lo! they are in darkness. ⟨37⟩
And [they have a sign in] the sun: it runs in an orbit of its own[19] – [and] that is laid down by the will of the Almighty, the All-Knowing; ⟨38⟩ and [in] the moon, for which We have determined phases [which it must traverse] till it becomes like an old date-stalk, dried-up and curved:[20] ⟨39⟩ [and] neither may the sun overtake the moon, nor can the night usurp the time of day,[21] since all of them float through space [in accordance with Our laws]. ⟨40⟩
And [it ought to be] a sign for them that We bear their offspring [over the seas] in laden ships,[22] ⟨41⟩ and [that] We create for them things of a similar kind, on which they may embark [in their travels];[23] ⟨42⟩ and [that,] if such be Our will, We may cause them to drown, with none to respond to their cry for help: and [then] they cannot be saved, ⟨43⟩ unless it be by an act of mercy from Us and a grant of life for a [further span of] time. ⟨44⟩
And [yet,] when they are told, "Beware of [God's insight into] all that lies open before you and all that is hidden from you,[24] so that you might be graced with His mercy," [most men choose to remain deaf;] ⟨45⟩

وَءَايَةٞ لَّهُمُ ٱلَّيۡلُ نَسۡلَخُ مِنۡهُ ٱلنَّهَارَ فَإِذَا هُم مُّظۡلِمُونَ ﴿٣٧﴾ وَٱلشَّمۡسُ
تَجۡرِي لِمُسۡتَقَرّٖ لَّهَاۚ ذَٰلِكَ تَقۡدِيرُ ٱلۡعَزِيزِ ٱلۡعَلِيمِ ﴿٣٨﴾ وَٱلۡقَمَرَ قَدَّرۡنَٰهُ
مَنَازِلَ حَتَّىٰ عَادَ كَٱلۡعُرۡجُونِ ٱلۡقَدِيمِ ﴿٣٩﴾ لَا ٱلشَّمۡسُ يَنۢبَغِي لَهَآ أَن
تُدۡرِكَ ٱلۡقَمَرَ وَلَا ٱلَّيۡلُ سَابِقُ ٱلنَّهَارِۚ وَكُلّٞ فِي فَلَكٖ يَسۡبَحُونَ ﴿٤٠﴾ وَءَايَةٞ
لَّهُمۡ أَنَّا حَمَلۡنَا ذُرِّيَّتَهُمۡ فِي ٱلۡفُلۡكِ ٱلۡمَشۡحُونِ ﴿٤١﴾ وَخَلَقۡنَا لَهُم مِّن
مِّثۡلِهِۦ مَا يَرۡكَبُونَ ﴿٤٢﴾ وَإِن نَّشَأۡ نُغۡرِقۡهُمۡ فَلَا صَرِيخَ لَهُمۡ وَلَا هُمۡ
يُنقَذُونَ ﴿٤٣﴾ إِلَّا رَحۡمَةٗ مِّنَّا وَمَتَٰعًا إِلَىٰ حِينٖ ﴿٤٤﴾ وَإِذَا قِيلَ لَهُمُ ٱتَّقُواْ
مَا بَيۡنَ أَيۡدِيكُمۡ وَمَا خَلۡفَكُمۡ لَعَلَّكُمۡ تُرۡحَمُونَ ﴿٤٥﴾

Wa ᵓāyatul-lahumul-laylu naslakhu minhun-nahāra faᵓidhā hum muẓlimūn. (37) Wash-shamsu tajrī limustaqarril-lahā; dhālika taqdīrul-ᶜAzīzil-ᶜAlīm. (38) Wal-qamara qaddarnāhu manāzila ḥattā ᶜāda kal-ᶜurjūnil-qadīm. (39) Lash-shamsu yambaghī lahāa ᵓañ-tudrikal-qamara wa lal-laylu sābiqun-nahār wa kulluñ-fī falakiñy-yasbaḥūn. (40) Wa ᵓĀyatul-lahum ᵓannā ḥamalnā dhurriyyatahum fil-fulkil-mashḥūn. (41) Wa khalaqnā lahum-mim-mithlihī mā yarkabūn. (42) Wa ᵓiñ-nashaᵓ nughriqhum falā ṣarīkha lahum wa lā hum yuñqadhūna, (43) ᵓillā raḥmatam-minnā wa matāᶜan ᵓilā ḥīn. (44) Wa ᵓidhā qīla lahumut-taqū mā bayna ᵓaydīkum wa mā khalfakum laᶜallakum turḥamūn. (45)

expresses itself in the existence of antithetic and yet complementary forces, like the sexuality in human beings, animals and plants, light and darkness, heat and cold, positive and negative magnetism and electricity, the positive and negative charges (protons and electrons) in the structure of the atom, and so forth. (It is to be borne in mind that the noun *zawj* denotes both "a pair" and "one of a pair", as explained in note 7 on 13 : 3.) The mention of "that of which they have no knowledge" evidently relates to things or phenomena not yet understood by man but potentially within the range of his comprehension: hence my interpolation, between brackets, of the words "as yet".

19 In the generally-accepted reading, this phrase is spelled *li-mustaqarrin lahā*, which may be rendered as above or, more conventionally, as "to its point of rest", i.e., the time (or point) of the daily sunset (Rāzī). However, ᶜAbd Allāh ibn Masᶜūd is reliably reported to have read these words as *lā mustaqarra lahā* (Zamakhsharī), which gives us the meaning of "it runs [on its course] without having any rest", i.e., unceasingly.

20 This is, in a condensed form, the meaning of the noun *ᶜurjūn* – the raceme of the date-palm, which, when old and dry, becomes slender and curves like a crescent (cf. Lane V, 1997).

21 Lit., "nor does the night outrun [or "outstrip"] the day".

22 Lit., "in the laden ship": a generic singular with a plural significance. The term "offspring" denotes here the human race as a whole (cf. the recurring expression "children of Adam").

23 Cf. 16 : 8 and the corresponding note 6. In both of these passages man's ingenuity is shown to be a direct manifestation of God's creativeness.

24 For an explanation of this rendering of the above phrase, see *sūrah* 2, note 247. In the present instance it apparently denotes men's conscious doings as well as their unconscious or half-conscious motivations.

and no message of their Sustainer's messages[25] ever reaches them without their turning away from it. ‹46›
Thus, when they are told, "Spend on others out of what God has provided for you as sustenance,"[26] those who are bent on denying the truth say unto those who believe, "Shall we feed anyone whom, if [your] God had so willed, He could have fed [Himself]? Clearly, you are but lost in error!" ‹47› And they add, "When is this promise [of resurrection] to be fulfilled? [Answer this] if you are men of truth!" ‹48›
[And they are unaware that] nothing awaits them beyond a single blast [of God's punishment],[27] which will overtake them while they are still arguing [against resurrection]: ‹49› and so [sudden will be their end that] no testament will they be able to make, nor to their own people will they return! ‹50›
And [then] the trumpet [of resurrection] will be blown – and lo! out of their graves towards their Sustainer will they all rush forth! ‹51›
They will say: "Oh, woe unto us! Who has roused us from our sleep [of death]?"
[Whereupon they will be told:] "This is what the Most Gracious has promised! And His message-bearers spoke the truth!" ‹52›
Nothing will there have been but one single blast – and lo! before Us will all of them be arraigned [and be told]: ‹53› "Today, then, no human being shall be wronged in the least, nor shall you be requited for aught but what you were doing [on earth]. ‹54›
"Behold, those who are destined for paradise shall today have joy in whatever they do: ‹55› in happiness will they and their spouses on couches recline;[28] ‹56›

وَمَا تَأْتِيهِم مِّنْ ءَايَةٍ مِّنْ ءَايَٰتِ رَبِّهِمْ إِلَّا كَانُوا۟ عَنْهَا مُعْرِضِينَ ﴿٤٦﴾
وَإِذَا قِيلَ لَهُمْ أَنفِقُوا۟ مِمَّا رَزَقَكُمُ ٱللَّهُ قَالَ ٱلَّذِينَ كَفَرُوا۟ لِلَّذِينَ ءَامَنُوٓا۟
أَنُطْعِمُ مَن لَّوْ يَشَآءُ ٱللَّهُ أَطْعَمَهُۥٓ إِنْ أَنتُمْ إِلَّا فِى ضَلَٰلٍ مُّبِينٍ ﴿٤٧﴾
وَيَقُولُونَ مَتَىٰ هَٰذَا ٱلْوَعْدُ إِن كُنتُمْ صَٰدِقِينَ ﴿٤٨﴾ مَا يَنظُرُونَ إِلَّا
صَيْحَةً وَٰحِدَةً تَأْخُذُهُمْ وَهُمْ يَخِصِّمُونَ ﴿٤٩﴾ فَلَا يَسْتَطِيعُونَ تَوْصِيَةً وَلَآ
إِلَىٰٓ أَهْلِهِمْ يَرْجِعُونَ ﴿٥٠﴾ وَنُفِخَ فِى ٱلصُّورِ فَإِذَا هُم مِّنَ ٱلْأَجْدَاثِ إِلَىٰ
رَبِّهِمْ يَنسِلُونَ ﴿٥١﴾ قَالُوا۟ يَٰوَيْلَنَا مَنۢ بَعَثَنَا مِن مَّرْقَدِنَا ۜ هَٰذَا مَا وَعَدَ
ٱلرَّحْمَٰنُ وَصَدَقَ ٱلْمُرْسَلُونَ ﴿٥٢﴾ إِن كَانَتْ إِلَّا صَيْحَةً وَٰحِدَةً فَإِذَا
هُمْ جَمِيعٌ لَّدَيْنَا مُحْضَرُونَ ﴿٥٣﴾ فَٱلْيَوْمَ لَا تُظْلَمُ نَفْسٌ شَيْـًٔا وَلَا تُجْزَوْنَ
إِلَّا مَا كُنتُمْ تَعْمَلُونَ ﴿٥٤﴾ إِنَّ أَصْحَٰبَ ٱلْجَنَّةِ ٱلْيَوْمَ فِى شُغُلٍ فَٰكِهُونَ ﴿٥٥﴾
هُمْ وَأَزْوَٰجُهُمْ فِى ظِلَٰلٍ عَلَى ٱلْأَرَآئِكِ مُتَّكِـُٔونَ ﴿٥٦﴾

سكتة لطيفة على الألف

Wa mā taʾtīhim-min ʾĀyatim-min ʾĀyāti Rabbihim ʾillā kānū ᶜanhā muᶜriḍīn. (46) Wa ʾidhā qīla lahum ʾañfiqū mimmā razaqakumul-lāhu qālal-ladhīna kafarū lilladhīna ʾāmanūu ʾanuṭᶜimu mal-law yashāaʾul-lāhu ʾaṭᶜamahūu ʾin ʾañtum ʾillā fī ḍalālim-mubīn. (47) Wa yaqūlūna matā hādhal-waᶜdu ʾiñ-kuñtum ṣādiqīn. (48) Mā yañẓurūna ʾillā ṣayḥatañw-wāḥidatañ taʾkhudhuhum wa hum yakhiṣ-ṣimūn. (49) Falā yastaṭīᶜūna tawṣiyatañw-wa lāa ʾilāa ʾahlihim yarjiᶜūn. (50) Wa nufikha fiṣ-ṣūri faʾidhā hum minal-ʾajdāthi ʾilā Rabbihim yañsilūn. (51) Qālū yā waylanā mam-baᶜathanā mim-marqadinā. Hādhā mā waᶜadar-Raḥmānu wa ṣadaqal-Mursalūn. (52) ʾIñ-kānat ʾillā ṣayḥatañw-wāḥidatañ faʾidhā hum jamīᶜul-ladaynā muḥḍarūn. (53) FalYawma lā tuẓlamu nafsuñ-shayʾañw-wa lā tujzawna ʾillā mā kuñtum taᶜmalūn. (54) ʾInna ʾaṣḥābal-jannatil-Yawma fī shughuliñ-fākihūn. (55) Hum wa ʾazwājuhum fī ẓilālin ᶜalal-ʾarāaʾiki muttakiʾūn. (56)

25 Or: "no sign of their Sustainer's signs" – since the noun *āyah*, repeated several times in the preceding passage, denotes "a message" as well as "a sign".

26 In Qurʾanic usage, the verb *anfaqa* (lit., "he spent") invariably signifies one's spending on others, or for the good of others, whatever the motive. The ethical importance of this "spending on others" is frequently stressed in the Qurʾān, and is embodied in the concept of *zakāh*, which denotes "purifying dues" or, in its broader sense, "charity" (see note 34 on 2 : 43).

27 Lit., "they wait for nothing but a single blast . . .", etc.

28 In the Qur'anic descriptions of paradise, the term *ẓill* ("shade") and its plural *ẓilāl* is often used as a metaphor

ربع الحزب

لَهُمْ فِيهَا فَـٰكِهَةٌ وَلَهُم مَّا يَدَّعُونَ ﴿٥٧﴾ سَلَـٰمٌ قَوْلًا مِّن رَّبٍّ رَّحِيمٍ ﴿٥٨﴾
وَٱمْتَـٰزُوا۟ ٱلْيَوْمَ أَيُّهَا ٱلْمُجْرِمُونَ ﴿٥٩﴾ ۞ أَلَمْ أَعْهَدْ إِلَيْكُمْ يَـٰبَنِىٓ
ءَادَمَ أَن لَّا تَعْبُدُوا۟ ٱلشَّيْطَـٰنَ ۖ إِنَّهُۥ لَكُمْ عَدُوٌّ مُّبِينٌ ﴿٦٠﴾ وَأَنِ ٱعْبُدُونِى
هَـٰذَا صِرَٰطٌ مُّسْتَقِيمٌ ﴿٦١﴾ وَلَقَدْ أَضَلَّ مِنكُمْ جِبِلًّا كَثِيرًا ۖ أَفَلَمْ
تَكُونُوا۟ تَعْقِلُونَ ﴿٦٢﴾ هَـٰذِهِۦ جَهَنَّمُ ٱلَّتِى كُنتُمْ تُوعَدُونَ ﴿٦٣﴾ ٱصْلَوْهَا
ٱلْيَوْمَ بِمَا كُنتُمْ تَكْفُرُونَ ﴿٦٤﴾ ٱلْيَوْمَ نَخْتِمُ عَلَىٰٓ أَفْوَٰهِهِمْ وَتُكَلِّمُنَآ
أَيْدِيهِمْ وَتَشْهَدُ أَرْجُلُهُم بِمَا كَانُوا۟ يَكْسِبُونَ ﴿٦٥﴾ وَلَوْ نَشَآءُ لَطَمَسْنَا
عَلَىٰٓ أَعْيُنِهِمْ فَٱسْتَبَقُوا۟ ٱلصِّرَٰطَ فَأَنَّىٰ يُبْصِرُونَ ﴿٦٦﴾ وَلَوْ نَشَآءُ

Lahum fīhā fākihatuñw-wa lahum-mā yaddaᶜūn.
(57) Salāmuñ-qawlam-mir-Rabbir-Raḥīm. (58) Wam-
tāzul-Yawma ᵓayyuhal-mujrimūn. (59) ۞ ᵓAlam ᵓaᶜhad
ᵓilaykum yā banīi ᵓĀdama ᵓallā taᶜbudush-Shayṭāna
ᵓinnahū lakum ᶜaduwwum-mubīn. (60) Wa ᵓaniᶜ-
budūnī hādhā ṣirāṭum-mustaqīm. (61) Wa laqad
ᵓaḍalla miñkum jibillañ-kathīran ᵓafalam takūnū
taᶜqilūn. (62) Hādhihī jahannamul-latī kuñtum
tūᶜadūn. (63) ᵓIṣlawhal-yawma bimā kuñtum tak-
furūn. (64) ᵓAlYawma nakhtimu ᶜalāa ᵓafwāhihim
wa tukallimunāa aydīhim wa tashhadu
ᵓarjuluhum-bimā kānū yaksibūn. (65) Wa law
nashāaᵓu laṭamasnā ᶜalāa ᵓaᶜyunihim fastabaquṣ-
ṣirāṭa faᵓannā yubṣirūn. (66) Wa law nashāaᵓu

[only] delight will there be for them, and theirs shall be all that they could ask for: «57» peace and fulfilment[29] through the word of a Sustainer who dispenses all grace. «58»

"But stand aside today, O you who were lost in sin! «59» Did I not enjoin on you, O you children of Adam, that you should not worship Satan – since, verily, he is your open foe[30] «60» – and that you should worship Me [alone]? This would have been a straight way! «61» And [as for Satan –] he had already led astray a great many of you: could you not, then, use your reason? «62»

"This, then, is the hell of which you were warned again and again:[31] «63» endure it today as an outcome of your persistent denial of the truth!" «64»

On that Day We shall set a seal on their mouths[32] – but their hands will speak unto Us, and their feet will bear witness to whatever they have earned [in life]. «65»

NOW HAD IT BEEN Our will [that men should not be able to discern between right and wrong], We could surely have deprived them of their sight,[33] so that they would stray forever from the [right] way: for how could they have had insight [into what is true]?[34] «66»

And had it been Our will [that they should not be free to choose between right and

for "happiness" – thus, for instance, in 4 : 57, where *ẓill ẓalīl* signifies "happiness abounding" (see *sūrah* 4, note 74) – while the "couches" on which the blessed are to recline are obviously a symbol of inner fulfilment and peace of mind, as pointed out by Rāzī in his comments on 18 : 31 and 55 : 54.

29 This composite expression is, I believe, the nearest approach in English to the concept of *salām* in the above context. For a further explanation of this term, see note 29 on 5 : 16, where *salām* is rendered as "salvation".

30 For the meaning of what the Qurᵓān describes as "worship of Satan", see note 33 on 19 : 44.

31 The phrase "This, then, is the hell" points to the fact that the sinners' realization of their having gone astray despite repeated warnings by the prophets will, in itself, be a source of intense suffering (*ᶜadhāb*) in the life to come. The element of repetition or persistence is implied in the use of the auxiliary verb *kuntum* both here and in the next verse.

32 A metaphor for their being unable really to excuse or defend their past actions and attitudes.

33 Lit., "We could surely have effaced their eyes": a metaphor for "We could have created them morally blind" and, thus, devoid of all sense of moral responsibility – which, in its turn, would constitute a negation of all spiritual value in human life as such. (Cf. 2 : 20 – "if God so willed, He could indeed take away their hearing and their sight".)

34 In this instance – as, e.g., in 20 : 96 – the verb *baṣura* ("he became seeing" or "he saw") is obviously used in its tropical sense of "perceiving [something] mentally". According to Ibn ᶜAbbās, as quoted by Ṭabarī, the phrase *annā yubṣirūn* signifies "how could they perceive the truth".

لَمَسَخْنَٰهُمْ عَلَىٰ مَكَانَتِهِمْ فَمَا ٱسْتَطَٰعُوا۟ مُضِيًّا وَلَا يَرْجِعُونَ ﴿٦٧﴾ وَمَن
نُّعَمِّرْهُ نُنَكِّسْهُ فِى ٱلْخَلْقِ ۖ أَفَلَا يَعْقِلُونَ ﴿٦٨﴾ وَمَا عَلَّمْنَٰهُ ٱلشِّعْرَ وَمَا
يَنۢبَغِى لَهُۥٓ ۚ إِنْ هُوَ إِلَّا ذِكْرٌ وَقُرْءَانٌ مُّبِينٌ ﴿٦٩﴾ لِّيُنذِرَ مَن كَانَ حَيًّا
وَيَحِقَّ ٱلْقَوْلُ عَلَى ٱلْكَٰفِرِينَ ﴿٧٠﴾ أَوَلَمْ يَرَوْا۟ أَنَّا خَلَقْنَا لَهُم مِّمَّا
عَمِلَتْ أَيْدِينَآ أَنْعَٰمًا فَهُمْ لَهَا مَٰلِكُونَ ﴿٧١﴾ وَذَلَّلْنَٰهَا لَهُمْ فَمِنْهَا
رَكُوبُهُمْ وَمِنْهَا يَأْكُلُونَ ﴿٧٢﴾

lamasakhnāhum ʿalā makānatihim famas-taṭāʿū muḍiyyañw-wa lā yarjiʿūn. (67) Wa mañ-nuʿammirhu nunakkis-hu fil-khalqi ʾafalā yaʿqilūn. (68) Wa mā ʿallamnāhush-shiʿra wa mā yambaghī lah. ʾIn huwa ʾillā Dhikruñw-wa Qurʾānum-mubīn. (69) Liyuñdhira mañ-kāna ḥayyañw-wa yaḥiqqal-qawlu ʿalal-kāfirīn. (70) ʾAwa lam yaraw ʾannā khalaqnā lahum-mimmā ʿamilat ʾaydīnaa ʾanʿāmañ-fahum lahā mālikūn. (71) Wa dhallalnāhā lahum faminhā rakūbuhum wa minhā yaʾkulūn. (72)

wrong], We could surely have given them a different nature[35] [and created them as beings rooted] in their places, so that they would not be able to move forward, and could not turn back.[36] ‹67›

But [let them always remember that] if We lengthen a human being's days, We also cause him to decline in his powers [when he grows old]: will they not, then, use their reason?[37] ‹68›

AND [thus it is:] We have not imparted to this [Prophet the gift of] poetry, nor would [poetry] have suited this [message]:[38] it is but a reminder and a [divine] discourse, clear in itself and clearly showing the truth,[39] ‹69› to the end that it may warn everyone who is alive [of heart], and that the word [of God] may bear witness[40] against all who deny the truth. ‹70›

Are they, then, not aware that it is for them that We have created, among all the things which Our hands have wrought,[41] the domestic animals of which they are [now] masters? ‹71› – and that We have subjected them to men's will,[42] so that some of them they may use for riding and of some they may eat, ‹72›

35 Lit., "transformed [or "transmuted"] them".

36 I.e., if it had been God's will that men should have no freedom of will or moral choice, He would have endowed them from the very beginning with a spiritually and morally stationary nature, entirely rooted in their instincts ("in their places"), devoid of all urge to advance, and incapable either of positive development or of retreat from a wrong course.

37 I.e., man should never *postpone* his exercise of moral choice – for if human beings are superior creatures inasmuch as they have been endowed with the faculty of discernment and a wide measure of free will, let them also remember that "man has been created weak" (4 : 28) and liable to decline still further in old age, so that the time at his disposal is short.

38 This passage resumes the theme enunciated in the opening verses of this *sūrah*, namely, the revelation of the Qurʾān. As in 26 : 224, we have here an allusion to the allegation of Muḥammad's opponents, in his own as well as in later times, that what he described as divine revelation was in reality an outcome of his own poetic invention. This the Qurʾān refutes by alluding to the fundamental difference between poetry – especially Arabic poetry – and divine revelation as exemplified by the Qurʾān: whereas in the former the meaning is often subordinated to the rhythm and the melody of language, in the Qurʾān the exact opposite is the case, inasmuch as here the choice of words, their sound and their position in the sentence – and, hence, its rhythm and melody – are always subordinated to the meaning intended. (Cf. also 26 : 225 and the corresponding note 100.)

39 For this composite rendering of the adjective *mubīn*, see *sūrah* 12, note 2. Literally, the above phrase reads, "a reminder *and* a [divine] discourse . . .", etc., with the conjunctive particle *wa* ("and") being used here, as in 15 : 1, to point out that the Qurʾān is an integral element in the process of divine revelation.

40 Lit., "may come [or "be proved"] true", i.e., on the Day of Judgment (cf. verse 7 of this *sūrah*).

41 I.e., "which We alone have or could have created" (Zamakhsharī and Rāzī). The above metaphorical expression is based on the concept of "handiwork" in its widest sense, abstract as well as concrete.

42 Lit., "made them submissive (*dhallalnāhā*) to them": implying also that man is morally responsible for the manner in which he uses or misuses them.

and may have [yet other] benefits from them, and [milk] to drink?
Will they not, then, be grateful? ‹73›
But [nay,] they take to worshipping deities other than God,[43] [hoping] to be succoured [by them, and not knowing that] ‹74› they are unable to succour their devotees,[44] even though to them they may [appear to] be hosts drawn up [for succour]. ‹75›
However, be not grieved by the sayings of those [who deny the truth]: verily, We know all that they keep secret as well as all that they bring into the open. ‹76›

IS MAN, then, not aware that it is We who create him out of a [mere] drop of sperm – whereupon, lo! he shows himself endowed with the power to think and to argue?[45] ‹77›
And [now] he [argues about Us, and] thinks of Us in terms of comparison,[46] and is oblivious of how he himself was created! [And so] he says, "Who could give life to bones that have crumbled to dust?" ‹78›
Say: "He who brought them into being in the first instance will give them life [once again], seeing that He has full knowledge of every act of creation: ‹79› He who produces for you fire out of the green tree, so that, lo! you kindle [your fires] therewith."[47] ‹80›

وَلَهُمْ فِيهَا مَنَٰفِعُ وَمَشَارِبُ ۖ أَفَلَا يَشْكُرُونَ ﴿73﴾ وَٱتَّخَذُوا۟ مِن دُونِ ٱللَّهِ
ءَالِهَةً لَّعَلَّهُمْ يُنصَرُونَ ﴿74﴾ لَا يَسْتَطِيعُونَ نَصْرَهُمْ وَهُمْ لَهُمْ جُندٌ
مُّحْضَرُونَ ﴿75﴾ فَلَا يَحْزُنكَ قَوْلُهُمْ ۘ إِنَّا نَعْلَمُ مَا يُسِرُّونَ وَمَا يُعْلِنُونَ ﴿76﴾
أَوَلَمْ يَرَ ٱلْإِنسَٰنُ أَنَّا خَلَقْنَٰهُ مِن نُّطْفَةٍ فَإِذَا هُوَ خَصِيمٌ مُّبِينٌ ﴿77﴾
وَضَرَبَ لَنَا مَثَلًا وَنَسِىَ خَلْقَهُۥ ۖ قَالَ مَن يُحْىِ ٱلْعِظَٰمَ وَهِىَ رَمِيمٌ ﴿78﴾
قُلْ يُحْيِيهَا ٱلَّذِىٓ أَنشَأَهَآ أَوَّلَ مَرَّةٍ ۖ وَهُوَ بِكُلِّ خَلْقٍ عَلِيمٌ ﴿79﴾ ٱلَّذِى
جَعَلَ لَكُم مِّنَ ٱلشَّجَرِ ٱلْأَخْضَرِ نَارًا فَإِذَآ أَنتُم مِّنْهُ تُوقِدُونَ ﴿80﴾

Wa lahum fīhā manāfiᶜu wa mashāribu ᵓafalā yashkurūn. (73) Wat-takhadhū miñ-dūnil-lāhi ᵓālihatal-laᶜallahum yuñṣarūn. (74) Lā yastaṭīᶜūna naṣrahum wa hum lahum juñdum-muḥḍarūn. (75) Falā yaḥzuñka qawluhum. ᵓInnā naᶜlamu mā yusirrūna wa mā yuᶜlinūn. (76) ᵓAwalam yaral-ᵓIñsānu ᵓannā khalaqnāhu miñ-nuṭfatiñ-faᵓidhā huwa khaṣīmum-mubīn. (77) Wa ḍaraba lanā mathalañw-wa nasiya khalqahū qāla mañy-yuḥyil-ᶜiẓāma wa hiya ramīm. (78) Qul yuḥyīhal-ladhīi ᵓañshaᵓahāa ᵓawwala marratiñw-wa Huwa bikulli khalqin ᶜAlīm. (79) ᵓAlladhī jaᶜala lakum-minash-shajaril-ᵓakhḍari nārañ-faᵓidhāa ᵓañtum minhu tūqidūn. (80)

43 Or: "other deities beside God" – alluding, in either case, to objects of worship consciously conceived as such – i.e., idols, imaginary deities, deified persons, saints, etc. – as well as to abstract concepts like power, wealth or "luck", which may not be consciously "worshipped" but are nevertheless often revered in an almost idolatrous fashion. The verb *ittakhadhū* (lit., "they took [or "have taken"] for themselves"), used in the Qurᵓan in this and in similar contexts, is particularly suited for the wide range of meanings alluded to inasmuch as it bears the connotation of *adopting* something – whether it be concrete or abstract – for one's own use or adoration.

44 Lit., "them".

45 See similar passage in 16 : 4, as well as the corresponding note 5. Completing the interpretation advanced in his (and Zamakhsharī's) commentary on the above-mentioned verse, Rāzī equates here the term *khaṣīm* (lit., "contender in argument") with the highest manifestation of what is described as *nāṭiq* ("articulate [or "rational"] being").

46 Lit., "he coins for Us a simile (*mathal*)" – an elliptic allusion to the unwillingness of "those who deny the truth" to conceive of a transcendental Being, fundamentally different from all that is graspable by man's senses or imagination, and having powers beyond all comparison with those which are available to any of the created beings. (Cf. 42 : 11, "there is nothing like unto Him", and 112 : 4, "there is nothing that could be compared with Him".) Since they are enmeshed in a materialistic outlook on life, such people deny – as the sequence shows – all possibility of resurrection, which amounts to a denial of God's creative powers and, in the final analysis, of His existence.

47 Cf. the ancient Arabian proverb, "In every tree there is a fire" (Zamakhsharī): evidently an allusion to the metamorphosis of green – i.e., water-containing – plants into fuel, be it through desiccation or man-made

Is, then, He who has created the heavens and the earth not able to create [anew] the like of those [who have died]?
Yea, indeed – for He alone is the all-knowing Creator: ‹81› His Being alone[48] is such that when He wills a thing to be, He but says unto it, "Be" – and it is. ‹82›
Limitless, then, in His glory is He in whose hand rests the mighty dominion over all things; and unto Him you all will be brought back! ‹83›

أَوَلَيْسَ ٱلَّذِى خَلَقَ ٱلسَّمَٰوَٰتِ وَٱلْأَرْضَ بِقَٰدِرٍ عَلَىٰٓ أَن يَخْلُقَ مِثْلَهُمۚ
بَلَىٰ وَهُوَ ٱلْخَلَّٰقُ ٱلْعَلِيمُ ﴿81﴾ إِنَّمَآ أَمْرُهُۥٓ إِذَآ أَرَادَ شَيْـًٔا أَن يَقُولَ لَهُۥ
كُن فَيَكُونُ ﴿82﴾ فَسُبْحَٰنَ ٱلَّذِى بِيَدِهِۦ مَلَكُوتُ كُلِّ شَىْءٍ وَإِلَيْهِ
تُرْجَعُونَ ﴿83﴾

ʾAwalaysal-ladhī khalaqas-samāwāti wal-ʾarḍa biqādirin ʿalāa ʾañy-yakhluqa mithlahum. Balā wa Huwal-Khallāqul-ʿAlīm. (81) ʾInnamāa ʾamruhūu ʾidhāa ʾarāda shayʾan ʾañy-yaqūla lahū Kuñ-fayakūn. (82) Fasubḥānal-ladhī biyadihī malakūtu kulli shayʾiñw-wa ʾilayhi turjaʿūn. (83)

carbonization (charcoal), or by a millenial, subterranean process of decomposition into oil or coal. In a spiritual sense, this "fire" seems also to symbolize the God-given warmth and light of human reason spoken of in verse 77 above.

48 This is the meaning of the phrase *innamā amruhu* – the term *amr* being synonymous, in this instance, with *shaʾn* ("state [or "manner"] of being"). The exclusiveness of God's creative Being is stressed by the restrictive particle *innamā*.

The Thirty-Seventh Sūrah

Aṣ-Ṣāaffāt (Those Ranged in Ranks)

Mecca Period

ALL authorities agree in that this *sūrah* was revealed in its entirety in Mecca, most probably about the middle of that period.

Like the preceding *sūrah*, this one deals mainly with the prospect of resurrection and, hence, the certainty that all human beings will have to answer before God for what they have done on earth. Since man is apt to err (cf. verse 71 – "most of the people of old went astray"), he is in constant need of prophetic guidance: and this explains the renewed reference (in verses 75-148) to the stories of some of the earlier prophets, as well as the frequent allusions to the message of the Qur'ān itself, which centres in the tenet that "your God is One" (verse 4), "above anything that men may devise by way of definition" (verses 159 and 180).

سورة الصافات مكية

-37-

وآياتها اثنتان وثمانون ومائة

IN THE NAME OF GOD, THE MOST GRACIOUS, THE DISPENSER OF GRACE:

CONSIDER these [messages] ranged in serried ranks,[1] ‹1›
and restraining [from evil] by a call to restraint, ‹2›
and conveying [to all the world] a reminder: ‹3›
Verily, most surely, your God is One ‹4› – the Sustainer of the heavens and the earth and of all that is between them, and the Sustainer of all the points of sunrise![2] ‹5›
Behold, We have adorned the skies nearest to the earth with the beauty of stars, ‹6› and have made them secure against every rebellious, satanic force,[3] ‹7› [so that] they [who seek to learn the unknowable] should not be able to overhear the host on high,[4] but shall be repelled from all sides, ‹8› cast out [from all grace], with lasting suffering in store for them [in the life to come]; ‹9› but if anyone[5] does

بِسۡمِ ٱللَّهِ ٱلرَّحۡمَٰنِ ٱلرَّحِيمِ

وَٱلصَّٰٓفَّٰتِ صَفّٗا ﴿١﴾ فَٱلزَّٰجِرَٰتِ زَجۡرٗا ﴿٢﴾ فَٱلتَّٰلِيَٰتِ ذِكۡرًا ﴿٣﴾
إِنَّ إِلَٰهَكُمۡ لَوَٰحِدٞ ﴿٤﴾ رَّبُّ ٱلسَّمَٰوَٰتِ وَٱلۡأَرۡضِ وَمَا بَيۡنَهُمَا وَرَبُّ
ٱلۡمَشَٰرِقِ ﴿٥﴾ إِنَّا زَيَّنَّا ٱلسَّمَآءَ ٱلدُّنۡيَا بِزِينَةٍ ٱلۡكَوَاكِبِ ﴿٦﴾ وَحِفۡظٗا
مِّن كُلِّ شَيۡطَٰنٖ مَّارِدٖ ﴿٧﴾ لَّا يَسَّمَّعُونَ إِلَى ٱلۡمَلَإِ ٱلۡأَعۡلَىٰ وَيُقۡذَفُونَ
مِن كُلِّ جَانِبٖ ﴿٨﴾ دُحُورٗاۖ وَلَهُمۡ عَذَابٞ وَاصِبٌ ﴿٩﴾ إِلَّا مَنۡ

Bismil-lāhir-Raḥmānir-Raḥīm.
Waṣ-ṣāaffāti ṣaffā. (1) Fazzājirāti zajrā. (2) Fattāliyāti dhikrā. (3) ʾInna ʾIlāhakum laWāḥid. (4) Rabbus-samāwāti wal-ʾarḍi wa mā baynahumā wa Rabbul-mashāriq. (5) ʾInnā zayyannas-samāaʾad-dunyā bizīnatinil-kawākib. (6) Wa ḥifẓam-miñ-kulli Shayṭānim-mārid. (7) Lā yassammaʿunna ʾilal-malaʾil-ʾaʿlā wa yuqdhafūna miñ-kulli jānib. (8) Duḥūrañw-wa lahum ʿadhābuñw-wāṣib. (9) ʾIllā man-

---

1 Regarding the adjurative particle *wa* and my rendering it as "Consider", see first half of note 23 on 74 : 32. – Most of the classical commentators assume that verses 1-3 refer to angels – an assumption which Abū Muslim al-Iṣfahānī (as quoted by Rāzī) rejects, stating that the passage refers to the true believers among human beings. However, Rāzī advances yet another (and, to my mind, most convincing) interpretation, suggesting that what is meant here are the messages (*āyāt*) of the Qurʾān, which – in the commentator's words – "deal with various subjects, some speaking of the evidence of God's oneness or of the evidence of His omniscience, omnipotence and wisdom, and some setting forth the evidence of [the truth of] prophetic revelation or of resurrection, while some deal with man's duties and the laws [relating thereto], and yet others are devoted to the teaching of high moral principles; and these messages are arranged in accordance with a coherent system above all [need of] change or alteration, so that they resemble beings or things standing 'in serried ranks'."

2 Sc., "and of sunset" (cf. 55 : 17 and the corresponding note 7). The stress on the *various* "points of sunrise" (*al-mashāriq*) brings out the endless variety of all created phenomena as contrasted with the oneness and uniqueness of their Creator. The mention of "the points of sunrise" and omission of "the points of sunset" in the wording (though not in the meaning) of the above phrase alludes, I believe, to the light-giving quality of the Qurʾān spoken of in verses 1-3.

3 For an explanation of this passage, see note 16 on 15 : 17.

4 I.e., the angelic forces, whose "speech" is a metonym for God's decrees.

5 Lit., "excepting [or "except that"] anyone who . . .", etc. However, as pointed out by some authorities (e.g., *Mughnī*), the particle *illā* is occasionally synonymous with the simple conjunction *wa*, which in this case has the significance of "but".

نصف الحزب

خَطِفَ ٱلْخَطْفَةَ فَأَتْبَعَهُۥ شِهَابٌ ثَاقِبٌ ﴿10﴾ فَٱسْتَفْتِهِمْ أَهُمْ أَشَدُّ
خَلْقًا أَم مَّنْ خَلَقْنَآ ۚ إِنَّا خَلَقْنَٰهُم مِّن طِينٍ لَّازِبٍ ﴿11﴾ بَلْ عَجِبْتَ
وَيَسْخَرُونَ ﴿12﴾ وَإِذَا ذُكِّرُوا۟ لَا يَذْكُرُونَ ﴿13﴾ وَإِذَا رَأَوْا۟ ءَايَةً
يَسْتَسْخِرُونَ ﴿14﴾ وَقَالُوٓا۟ إِنْ هَٰذَآ إِلَّا سِحْرٌ مُّبِينٌ ﴿15﴾ أَءِذَا مِتْنَا وَكُنَّا
تُرَابًا وَعِظَٰمًا أَءِنَّا لَمَبْعُوثُونَ ﴿16﴾ أَوَءَابَآؤُنَا ٱلْأَوَّلُونَ ﴿17﴾ قُلْ نَعَمْ وَأَنتُمْ
دَٰخِرُونَ ﴿18﴾ فَإِنَّمَا هِىَ زَجْرَةٌ وَٰحِدَةٌ فَإِذَا هُمْ يَنظُرُونَ ﴿19﴾ وَقَالُوا۟
يَٰوَيْلَنَا هَٰذَا يَوْمُ ٱلدِّينِ ﴿20﴾ هَٰذَا يَوْمُ ٱلْفَصْلِ ٱلَّذِى كُنتُم بِهِۦ
تُكَذِّبُونَ ﴿21﴾ ۞ ٱحْشُرُوا۟ ٱلَّذِينَ ظَلَمُوا۟ وَأَزْوَٰجَهُمْ وَمَا كَانُوا۟
يَعْبُدُونَ ﴿22﴾ مِن دُونِ ٱللَّهِ فَٱهْدُوهُمْ إِلَىٰ صِرَٰطِ ٱلْجَحِيمِ ﴿23﴾

khaṭifal-khaṭfata faʾatbaᶜahū shihābuñ-thāqib. (10)
Fastaftihim ʾahum ʾashaddu khalqan ʾam-man khalaqnā. ʾInnā khalaqnāhum-miñ-ṭīnil-lāzib. (11) Bal
ᶜajibta wa yaskharūn. (12) Wa ʾidhā dhukkirū lā yadh-
kurūn. (13) Wa ʾidhā raʾaw ʾāyatañy-yastaskhirūn. (14)
Wa qālūu ʾin hādhāa ʾillā siḥrum-mubīn. (15) ʾAʾidhā
mitnā wa kunnā turābañw-wa ᶜiẓaman ʾaʾinnā lam-
ab-ᶜūthūn. (16) ʾAwa ʾābāaʾunal-ʾawwalūn. (17) Qul
naᶜam wa ʾañtum dākhirūn. (18) Faʾinnamā hiya zaj-
ratuñw-wāḥidatuñ-faʾidhā hum yañẓurūn. (19) Wa
qālū yā waylanā hādhā Yawmud-Dīn. (20) Hādhā Yaw-
mul-Faṣlil-ladhī kuñtum bihī tukadhdhibūn. (21) ۞
ʾUḥshurul-ladhīna ẓalamū wa ʾazwājahum wa mā
kānū yaᶜbudūna, (22) miñ-dūnil-lāhi fahdūhum ʾilā
ṣirāṭil-jaḥīm. (23)

succeed in snatching a glimpse [of such knowledge], he is [henceforth] pursued by a piercing flame.[6] ‹10›

AND NOW ask those [who deny the truth] to enlighten thee: Were they more difficult to create than all those [untold marvels] that We have created? – for, behold, them have We created out of [mere] clay commingled with water![7] ‹11›

Nay, but whereas thou dost marvel,[8] they [only] scoff; ‹12› and when they are reminded [of the truth], they refuse to take it to heart; ‹13› and when they become aware of a [divine] message, they turn it to ridicule ‹14› and say: "This is clearly nothing but [a mortal's] spellbinding eloquence! ‹15› Why – after we have died and become mere dust and bones, shall we, forsooth, be raised from the dead? ‹16› – and perhaps also our forebears of old?" ‹17›

Say: "Yea, indeed – and most abject will you then be!" ‹18› – for that [resurrection which they deride] will be [upon them of a sudden, as if it were] but a single accusing cry – and then, lo! they will begin to see [the truth] ‹19› and will say: "Oh, woe unto us! This is the Day of Judgment!" ‹20›

[And they will be told:] "This is the Day of Distinction [between the true and the false[9] – the Day] which you were wont to call a lie!" ‹21›

[And God will thus command:] "Assemble all those who were bent on evildoing, together with others of their ilk[10] and [with] all that they were wont to worship ‹22› instead of God, and lead them all onto the way to the blazing fire, ‹23›

---

6 For the meaning of this phrase, see note 17 on 15 : 18. After the stress on God's oneness in verses 4-5, the passage comprising verses 6-l0 points to the fact that human beings are precluded from really grasping the variety and depth of the universe created by Him. We have here an echo of 34 : 9 – "Are they, then, not aware of how little of the sky and the earth lies open before them, and how much is hidden from them?" – and, thus, a new, oblique approach to the theme of resurrection, which is taken up in the sequence in the form of an indirect question.

7 I.e., out of primitive substances existing in their elementary forms in and on the earth (see *sūrah* 23, note 4) – substances which are as nothing when compared with the complexity of "the heavens and the earth and all that is between them": hence, man's individual resurrection is as nothing when compared with the creation of the multiform universe.

8 I.e., at God's creative power as well as at the blind arrogance of those who deny it.

9 See note 6 on 77 : 13.

10 According to almost all of the earliest authorities – including ᶜUmar ibn al-Khaṭṭāb, ᶜAbd Allāh ibn ᶜAbbās,

and halt them [there]!"
[And then,] behold, they shall be asked, ‹24› "How is it that [now] you cannot succour one another?" ‹25›
Nay, but on that Day they would willingly surrender [to God]; ‹26› but [since it will be too late,] they will turn upon one another, demanding of each other [to relieve them of the burden of their past sins].[11] ‹27›
Some [of them] will say: "Behold, you were wont to approach us [deceptively] from the right!"[12] ‹28›
[To which] the others will reply: "Nay, you yourselves were bereft of all faith! ‹29› Moreover, we had no power at all over you: nay, you were people filled with overweening arrogance! ‹30› But now our Sustainer's word has come true against us [as well]: verily, we are bound to taste [the fruit of our sins]. ‹31› So then, [if it be true that] we have caused you to err grievously – behold, we ourselves had been lost in grievous error!"[13] ‹32›
And, verily, on that Day they all will share in their common suffering. ‹33›
Verily, thus shall We deal with all who were lost in sin: ‹34› for, behold, whenever they were told, "There is no deity save God," they would glory in their arrogance ‹35› and would say, "Shall we, then, give up our deities at the bidding of a mad poet?"[14] ‹36›

وَقِفُوهُمْۖ إِنَّهُم مَّسْـُٔولُونَ ﴿24﴾ مَا لَكُمْ لَا تَنَاصَرُونَ ﴿25﴾ بَلْ هُمُ ٱلْيَوْمَ
مُسْتَسْلِمُونَ ﴿26﴾ وَأَقْبَلَ بَعْضُهُمْ عَلَىٰ بَعْضٍ يَتَسَآءَلُونَ ﴿27﴾ قَالُوٓا۟ إِنَّكُمْ
كُنتُمْ تَأْتُونَنَا عَنِ ٱلْيَمِينِ ﴿28﴾ قَالُوا۟ بَل لَّمْ تَكُونُوا۟ مُؤْمِنِينَ ﴿29﴾ وَمَا
كَانَ لَنَا عَلَيْكُم مِّن سُلْطَٰنٍۭ ۖ بَلْ كُنتُمْ قَوْمًا طَٰغِينَ ﴿30﴾ فَحَقَّ عَلَيْنَا قَوْلُ
رَبِّنَآ ۖ إِنَّا لَذَآئِقُونَ ﴿31﴾ فَأَغْوَيْنَٰكُمْ إِنَّا كُنَّا غَٰوِينَ ﴿32﴾ فَإِنَّهُمْ يَوْمَئِذٍ فِى
ٱلْعَذَابِ مُشْتَرِكُونَ ﴿33﴾ إِنَّا كَذَٰلِكَ نَفْعَلُ بِٱلْمُجْرِمِينَ ﴿34﴾ إِنَّهُمْ كَانُوٓا۟
إِذَا قِيلَ لَهُمْ لَآ إِلَٰهَ إِلَّا ٱللَّهُ يَسْتَكْبِرُونَ ﴿35﴾ وَيَقُولُونَ أَئِنَّا لَتَارِكُوٓا۟
ءَالِهَتِنَا لِشَاعِرٍ مَّجْنُونٍۭ ﴿36﴾

Wa qifūhum ʾinnahum masʾūlūn. (24) Mā lakum lā tanāṣarūn. (25) Bal humul-Yawma mustaslimūn. (26) Wa ʾaqbala baᶜḍuhum ᶜalā baᶜḍiñy-yatasāaʾalūn. (27) Qālūu ʾinnakum kuñtum taʾtūnanā ᶜanil-yamīn. (28) Qālū bal-lam takūnū muʾminīn. (29) Wa mā kāna lanā ᶜalaykum-miñ-sulṭānim-bal kuñtum qawmañ-ṭāghīn. (30) Faḥaqqa ᶜalaynā qawlu Rabbināa ʾinnā ladhāaʾiqūn. (31) Faʾaghwaynākum ʾinnā kunnā ghāwīn. (32) Faʾinnahum Yawmaʾidhiñ-fil-ᶜadhābi mushtarikūn. (33) ʾInnā kadhālika nafᶜalu bilmujrimīn. (34) ʾInnahum kānūu ʾidhā qīla lahum lāa ʾilāha ʾillal-lāhu yastakbirūn. (35) Wa yaqūlūna ʾaʾinnā latārikūu ʾālihatinā lishāᶜirim-majnūn. (36)

Qatādah, Mujāhid, As-Suddī, Saᶜīd ibn Jubayr, Al-Ḥasan al-Baṣrī, etc., – the expression *azwāj* denotes here "people resembling one another [in their dispositions]", or "people of the same kind" or "of the same ilk".

11 Cf. the contrasting – though verbally identical – passage in verses 50 ff. of the present *sūrah*. Whereas in the latter instance the verb *yatasāʾalūn* has its primary connotation of "asking one another [about something]", it signifies here "demanding [something] of one another" – as the sequence shows, to assume responsibility for their erstwhile denial of the truth.

12 I.e., "claiming that what you were asking us to do was right and good". The idiomatic phrase "approaching one from the right" is more or less synonymous with "pretending to give a morally good advice", as well as "approaching another person from a position of power and influence" (Zamakhsharī).

13 For an explanation see 28 : 62-64 and the corresponding notes.

14 Lit., "for [or "for the sake of"] a mad poet" – thus alluding to the allegation that the Qurʾān is a product of Muḥammad's mind (see note 38 on 36 : 69). The reference to "deities" comprises, in this context, everything that man may "worship" in both the literal and the metaphorical senses of this word.

Nay, but he [whom you call a mad poet] has brought the truth; and he confirms the truth of [what the earlier of God's] message-bearers [have taught].[15] ‹37›
Behold, you will indeed taste grievous suffering [in the life to come], ‹38› although you shall not be requited for aught but what you were wont to do. ‹39›
Not so, however, God's true servants:[16] ‹40› [in the hereafter,] theirs shall be a sustenance which they will recognize[17] ‹41› as the fruits [of their life on earth]; and honoured shall they be ‹42› in gardens of bliss, ‹43› facing one another [in love] upon thrones of happiness.[18] ‹44›
A cup will be passed round among them [with a drink] from unsullied springs, ‹45› clear, delightful to those who drink it: ‹46› no headiness will be in it, and they will not get drunk thereon. ‹47›
And with them will be mates of modest gaze,[19] most beautiful of eye, ‹48› [as free of faults] as if they were hidden [ostrich] eggs.[20] ‹49›
And they will all turn to one another, asking each other [about their past lives].[21] ‹50›
One of them speaks thus: "Behold, I had [on earth] a close companion ‹51› who was wont to ask [me], 'Why – art thou really one of those who believe it to be true ‹52› [that] after we have died and become mere dust and bones we shall, forsooth, be brought to judgment?'" ‹53›

بَلْ جَآءَ بِٱلْحَقِّ وَصَدَّقَ ٱلْمُرْسَلِينَ ﴿٣٧﴾ إِنَّكُمْ لَذَآئِقُواْ ٱلْعَذَابِ
ٱلْأَلِيمِ ﴿٣٨﴾ وَمَا تُجْزَوْنَ إِلَّا مَا كُنتُمْ تَعْمَلُونَ ﴿٣٩﴾ إِلَّا عِبَادَ ٱللَّهِ
ٱلْمُخْلَصِينَ ﴿٤٠﴾ أُوْلَٰٓئِكَ لَهُمْ رِزْقٌ مَّعْلُومٌ ﴿٤١﴾ فَوَٰكِهُ وَهُم
مُّكْرَمُونَ ﴿٤٢﴾ فِى جَنَّٰتِ ٱلنَّعِيمِ ﴿٤٣﴾ عَلَىٰ سُرُرٍ مُّتَقَٰبِلِينَ ﴿٤٤﴾ يُطَافُ
عَلَيْهِم بِكَأْسٍ مِّن مَّعِينٍ ﴿٤٥﴾ بَيْضَآءَ لَذَّةٍ لِّلشَّٰرِبِينَ ﴿٤٦﴾ لَا فِيهَا غَوْلٌ
وَلَا هُمْ عَنْهَا يُنزَفُونَ ﴿٤٧﴾ وَعِندَهُمْ قَٰصِرَٰتُ ٱلطَّرْفِ عِينٌ ﴿٤٨﴾ كَأَنَّهُنَّ
بَيْضٌ مَّكْنُونٌ ﴿٤٩﴾ فَأَقْبَلَ بَعْضُهُمْ عَلَىٰ بَعْضٍ يَتَسَآءَلُونَ ﴿٥٠﴾ قَالَ قَآئِلٌ
مِّنْهُمْ إِنِّى كَانَ لِى قَرِينٌ ﴿٥١﴾ يَقُولُ أَءِنَّكَ لَمِنَ ٱلْمُصَدِّقِينَ ﴿٥٢﴾ أَءِذَا
مِتْنَا وَكُنَّا تُرَابًا وَعِظَٰمًا أَءِنَّا لَمَدِينُونَ ﴿٥٣﴾

Bal jāaʾa bil-ḥaqqi wa ṣaddaqal-Mursalīn. (37) ʾInnakum ladhāaʾiqul-ʿadhābil-ʾalīm. (38) Wa mā tujzawna ʾillā mā kuñtum taʿmalūn. (39) ʾIllā ʿibādal-lāhil-mukhlaṣīn. (40) ʾUlāaʾika lahum rizqum-maʿlūm. (41) Fawākihu wa hum-mukramūn. (42) Fī jannātin-naʿīm. (43) ʿAlā sururim-mutaqābilīn. (44) Yuṭāfu ʿalayhim-bikaʾsim-mim-maʿīn. (45) Bayḍāaʾa ladhdhatil-lishshāribīn. (46) Lā fīhā ghawluñw-wa lā hum ʿanhā yuñzafūn. (47) Wa ʿiñdahum qāṣirātuṭ-ṭarfi ʿīn. (48) Kaʾannahunna bayḍum-maknūn. (49) Faʾaqbala baʿḍuhum ʿalā baʿḍiñy-yatasāaʾalūn. (50) Qāla qāaʾilum-minhum ʾinnī kāna lī qarīn. (51) Yaqūlu ʾaʾinnaka laminal-muṣaddiqīn. (52) ʾAʾidhā mitnā wa kunnā turābañw-wa ʿiẓāman ʾaʾinnā lamadīnūn. (53)

15 See *sūrah* 2, note 5. It is to be borne in mind that this refers to the fundamental teachings, which have always been the same in every true religion, and not to the many time-bound laws evident in the earlier religious codes.

16 Lit., "sincere servants". In contrast to the principle that "a bad deed will be requited with no more than the like thereof", implied in the preceding verse, the Qurʾān states here that he who "shall come [before God] with a good deed will receive ten times the like thereof" (see 6 : 160).

17 Lit., "a known sustenance". For a tentative explanation of this phrase, see note 17 on 2 : 25.

18 For my occasional rendering of the plural noun *surur* as "thrones of happiness", see note 34 on 15 : 47.

19 See note 46 on 38 : 52, where the expression *qāṣirāt aṭ-ṭarf* (lit., "such as restrain their gaze") appears for the first time in the chronology of Qurʾanic revelation.

20 This is an ancient Arabian figure of speech derived from the habit of the female ostrich, which buries its eggs in the sand for protection (Zamakhsharī). Its particular application to the women who attain to paradise becomes clear from 56 : 34 ff., which states that all righteous women, irrespective of their age and condition at the time of death, will be resurrected as beautiful maidens.

21 Cf. verse 27 above and the corresponding note 11. Like the mutual reproaches of the sinners in that passage, the "conversation" of the blessed which follows here is, of course, allegorical, and is meant to stress the continuity of individual consciousness in the hereafter.

[And] he adds: "Would you like to look [and see him]?" ‹54› – and then he looks and sees that [companion of his] in the midst of the blazing fire, ‹55› and says: "By God! Verily, thou hast almost destroyed me [too, O my erstwhile companion] ‹56› – for had it not been for my Sustainer's favour, I would surely be [now] among those who are given over [to suffering]! ‹57› But then, [O my friends in paradise,] is it [really] so that we are not to die ‹58› [again,] beyond our previous death, and that we shall never [again] be made to suffer? ‹59› Verily, this – this indeed – is the triumph supreme!" ‹60›
For the like of this, then, let them labour, those who labour [in God's way]! ‹61›
Is such [a paradise] the better welcome – or the [hellish] tree of deadly fruit?[22] ‹62› Verily, We have caused it to be a trial for evildoers:[23] ‹63› for, behold, it is a tree that grows in the very heart of the blazing fire [of hell], ‹64› its fruit [as repulsive] as satans' heads;[24] ‹65› and they [who are lost in evil] are indeed bound to eat thereof, and to fill their bellies therewith. ‹66› And, behold, above all this they will be confounded with burning despair![25] ‹67›
And once again:[26] Verily, the blazing fire is their ultimate goal ‹68› – for, behold, they found their forebears on a wrong way, ‹69›

قَالَ هَلۡ أَنتُم مُّطَّلِعُونَ ﴿٥٤﴾ فَٱطَّلَعَ فَرَءَاهُ فِي سَوَآءِ ٱلۡجَحِيمِ ﴿٥٥﴾ قَالَ
تَٱللَّهِ إِن كِدتَّ لَتُرۡدِينِ ﴿٥٦﴾ وَلَوۡلَا نِعۡمَةُ رَبِّي لَكُنتُ مِنَ ٱلۡمُحۡضَرِينَ ﴿٥٧﴾
أَفَمَا نَحۡنُ بِمَيِّتِينَ ﴿٥٨﴾ إِلَّا مَوۡتَتَنَا ٱلۡأُولَىٰ وَمَا نَحۡنُ بِمُعَذَّبِينَ ﴿٥٩﴾ إِنَّ
هَٰذَا لَهُوَ ٱلۡفَوۡزُ ٱلۡعَظِيمُ ﴿٦٠﴾ لِمِثۡلِ هَٰذَا فَلۡيَعۡمَلِ ٱلۡعَٰمِلُونَ ﴿٦١﴾
أَذَٰلِكَ خَيۡرٞ نُّزُلًا أَمۡ شَجَرَةُ ٱلزَّقُّومِ ﴿٦٢﴾ إِنَّا جَعَلۡنَٰهَا فِتۡنَةٗ
لِّلظَّٰلِمِينَ ﴿٦٣﴾ إِنَّهَا شَجَرَةٞ تَخۡرُجُ فِيٓ أَصۡلِ ٱلۡجَحِيمِ ﴿٦٤﴾ طَلۡعُهَا كَأَنَّهُۥ
رُءُوسُ ٱلشَّيَٰطِينِ ﴿٦٥﴾ فَإِنَّهُمۡ لَأٓكِلُونَ مِنۡهَا فَمَالِـُٔونَ مِنۡهَا ٱلۡبُطُونَ ﴿٦٦﴾
ثُمَّ إِنَّ لَهُمۡ عَلَيۡهَا لَشَوۡبٗا مِّنۡ حَمِيمٖ ﴿٦٧﴾ ثُمَّ إِنَّ مَرۡجِعَهُمۡ لَإِلَى ٱلۡجَحِيمِ ﴿٦٨﴾
إِنَّهُمۡ أَلۡفَوۡاْ ءَابَآءَهُمۡ ضَآلِّينَ ﴿٦٩﴾

Qāla hal ʾantum-muṭṭaliʿūn. (54) Faṭṭalaʿa faraʾāhu fī sawāaʾil-jaḥīm. (55) Qāla tallāhi ʾin-kitta laturdīn. (56) Wa lawlā niʿmatu Rabbī lakuntu minal-muḥḍarīn. (57) ʾAfamā naḥnu bimayyitīna, (58) ʾillā mawtatanal-ʾūlā wa mā naḥnu bimuʿadhdhabīn. (59) ʾInna hādhā lahuwal-fawzul-ʿaẓīm. (60) Limithli hādhā falyaʿmalil-ʿāmilūn. (61) ʾAdhālika khayrun-nuzulan ʾam shajaratuz-zaqqūm. (62) ʾInnā jaʿalnāhā fitnatal-liẓẓālimīn. (63) ʾInnahā shajaratun-takhruju fīi ʾaṣlil-jaḥīm. (64) Ṭalʿuhā kaʾannahū ruʾūsush-Shayāṭīn. (65) Faʾinnahum laʾākilūna minhā famāliʾūna minhal-buṭūn. (66) Thumma ʾinna lahum ʿalayhā lashawbam-min ḥamīm. (67) Thumma ʾinna marjiʿahum laʾilal-jaḥīm. (68) ʾInnahum ʾalfaw ʾābāaʾahum ḍāallīn. (69)

22 According to the lexicographers, the noun *zaqqūm* (which occurs, apart from the present instance, in 44 : 43 and in 56 : 52 as well) denotes any "deadly food"; hence, the expression *shajarat az-zaqqūm*, a symbol of hell, may be appropriately rendered as "the tree of deadly fruit" (undoubtedly identical with "the tree cursed in this Qurʾān", mentioned in 17 : 60), symbolizing the fact that the otherworldly sufferings which the Qurʾān describes as "hell" are but the fruit – i.e., organic consequence – of one's evil deeds done on earth.

23 It cannot be often enough repeated that all Qurʾanic references to hell and paradise – and, for that matter, all descriptions of men's conditions in the hereafter – are, of necessity, highly allegorical (see Appendix I) and therefore liable to be grossly misunderstood if one takes them in their literal sense or, conversely, interprets them in an arbitrary manner (cf. 3 : 7 and the corresponding notes 5, 7 and 8): and this, to my mind, explains why the symbol of the "tree of deadly fruit" – one of the metonyms for the suffering of the sinners in the hereafter – has become "a trial (*fitnah*) for evildoers" (or "for men" in 17 : 60). See in this connection 74 : 31, which is the earliest Qurʾanic instance of this concept of "trial".

24 According to Zamakhsharī, "this purely verbal metaphor (*istiʿārah lafẓiyyah*) is meant to express the ultimate in repulsiveness and ugliness . . . inasmuch as Satan is considered to be the epitome of all that is evil".

25 Lit., "and upon it, behold, they will have an admixture [or "confusion"] of *ḥamīm*". (For my rendering of the last term as "burning despair", see *sūrah* 6, note 62.)

26 See *sūrah*. 6, note 31.

and [now] they make haste to follow in their footsteps![27] ‹70›
Thus, indeed, most of the people of old went astray before them, ‹71› although, verily, We had sent warners unto them: ‹72› and behold what happened in the end to those that had been warned [to no avail]! ‹73›

ثلاثة ارباع الحزب

EXCEPT for God's true servants, [most people are apt to go astray.][28] ‹74›
And, indeed, [it was for this reason that] Noah cried unto Us – and how excellent was Our response: ‹75› for We saved him and his household from that awesome calamity,[29] ‹76› and caused his offspring to endure [on earth]; ‹77› and We left him thus to be remembered[30] among later generations: ‹78› "Peace be upon Noah throughout all the worlds!" ‹79›
Verily, thus do We reward the doers of good ‹80› – for he was truly one of Our believing servants: ‹81› [and so We saved him and those who followed him] and then We caused the others to drown. ‹82›

AND, BEHOLD, of his persuasion was Abraham, too, ‹83› when he turned to his Sustainer with a heart free of evil, ‹84› and [thus] spoke to his father and his people: "What is it that you worship? ‹85› Do you want [to bow down before] a lie – [before] deities other than God? ‹86› What, then, do you think of the Sustainer of all the worlds?"[31] ‹87›
Then he cast a glance at the stars,[32] ‹88›

فَهُمْ عَلَىٰٓ ءَاثَٰرِهِمْ يُهْرَعُونَ ﴿٧٠﴾ وَلَقَدْ ضَلَّ قَبْلَهُمْ أَكْثَرُ ٱلْأَوَّلِينَ ﴿٧١﴾ وَلَقَدْ
أَرْسَلْنَا فِيهِم مُّنذِرِينَ ﴿٧٢﴾ فَٱنظُرْ كَيْفَ كَانَ عَٰقِبَةُ ٱلْمُنذَرِينَ ﴿٧٣﴾ إِلَّا
عِبَادَ ٱللَّهِ ٱلْمُخْلَصِينَ ﴿٧٤﴾ وَلَقَدْ نَادَىٰنَا نُوحٌ فَلَنِعْمَ ٱلْمُجِيبُونَ ﴿٧٥﴾
وَنَجَّيْنَٰهُ وَأَهْلَهُۥ مِنَ ٱلْكَرْبِ ٱلْعَظِيمِ ﴿٧٦﴾ وَجَعَلْنَا ذُرِّيَّتَهُۥ هُمُ ٱلْبَاقِينَ ﴿٧٧﴾
وَتَرَكْنَا عَلَيْهِ فِى ٱلْءَاخِرِينَ ﴿٧٨﴾ سَلَٰمٌ عَلَىٰ نُوحٍ فِى ٱلْعَٰلَمِينَ ﴿٧٩﴾ إِنَّا
كَذَٰلِكَ نَجْزِى ٱلْمُحْسِنِينَ ﴿٨٠﴾ إِنَّهُۥ مِنْ عِبَادِنَا ٱلْمُؤْمِنِينَ ﴿٨١﴾ ثُمَّ
أَغْرَقْنَا ٱلْءَاخَرِينَ ﴿٨٢﴾ ۞ وَإِنَّ مِن شِيعَتِهِۦ لَإِبْرَٰهِيمَ ﴿٨٣﴾ إِذْ جَآءَ رَبَّهُۥ
بِقَلْبٍ سَلِيمٍ ﴿٨٤﴾ إِذْ قَالَ لِأَبِيهِ وَقَوْمِهِۦ مَاذَا تَعْبُدُونَ ﴿٨٥﴾ أَئِفْكًا ءَالِهَةً
دُونَ ٱللَّهِ تُرِيدُونَ ﴿٨٦﴾ فَمَا ظَنُّكُم بِرَبِّ ٱلْعَٰلَمِينَ ﴿٨٧﴾ فَنَظَرَ نَظْرَةً فِى
ٱلنُّجُومِ ﴿٨٨﴾

Fahum ʿalāa ʾāthārihim yuhraʿūn. 70 **Wa laqad ḍalla**
qablahum ʾaktharul-ʾawwalīn. 71 **Wa laqad ʾarsalnā**
fīhim-Muñdhirīn. 72 **Fañẓur kayfa kāna ʿāqibatul-**
muñdharīn. 73 **ʾIllā ʿibādal-lāhil-mukhlaṣīn.** 74 **Wa**
laqad nādānā Nūḥuñ-falaniʿmal-Mujībūn. 75 **Wa**
najjaynāhu wa ʾahlahū minal-karbil-ʿaẓīm. 76 **Wa**
jaʿalnā dhurriyyatahū humul-bāqīn. 77 **Wa ta-**
raknā ʿalayhi fil-ʾākhirīn. 78 **Salāmun ʿalā Nūḥiñ-fil-**
ʿālamīn. 79 **ʾInnā kadhālika najzil-muḥsinīn.** 80
ʾInnahū min ʿibādinal-muʾminīn. 81 **Thumma**
ʾaghraqnal-ʾākharīn. 82 ۞ **Wa ʾinna miñ-shīʿatihī la-**
ʾIbrāhīm. 83 **ʾIdh jāaʾa Rabbahū biqalbiñ-salīm.** 84
ʾIdh qāla liʾabīhi wa qawmihī mādhā taʿbudūn. 85
ʾAʾifkan ʾālihatañ-dūnal-lāhi turīdūn. 86 **Famā ẓan-**
nukum biRabbil-ʿālamīn. 87 **Fanaẓara naẓratañ-fin-**
nujūm. 88

27 I.e., blind imitation (*taqlīd*) of the – obviously absurd – beliefs, valuations and customs of one's erring predecessors, and disregard of all evidence of the truth supplied by both reason and divine revelation, is here shown to be the principal cause of the suffering referred to in the preceding passage (Zamakhsharī).

28 Sc., "and are, therefore, in need of prophetic guidance": which explains the subsequent mention of stories relating to several of the prophets. The story of Noah, which is briefly referred to here, appears in greater detail in 11 : 25-48.

29 I.e., the Deluge.

30 Lit., "and We left upon him", sc., "this praise" or "remembrance", expressed in the salutation which follows.

31 Abraham's argument goes thus: "Do you believe in the existence of a Creator and Lord of the universe?" – a question which his people were bound to answer in the affirmative, since belief in a Supreme Deity was an integral part of their religion. The next stage of the argument would be: "How, then, can you worship idols – the work of your own hands – side by side with the idea of a Creator of the universe?"

32 Obviously an allusion to his early, futile attempts at identifying God with the stars, the sun or the moon (see 6 : 76-78).

and said, "Verily, I am sick [at heart]!"[33] ‹89› – and at that they turned their backs on him and went away. ‹90›

Thereupon he approached their gods stealthily and said, "What! You do not eat [of the offerings placed before you]? ‹91› What is amiss with you that you do not speak?" ‹92›

And then he fell upon them, smiting them with his right hand.[34] ‹93›

[But] then the others came towards him hurriedly [and accused him of his deed]. ‹94›

He answered: "Do you worship something that you [yourselves] have carved, ‹95› the while it is God who has created you and all your handiwork?" ‹96›

They exclaimed: "Build a pyre[35] for him, and cast him into the blazing fire!" ‹97›

But whereas they sought to do evil unto him, We [frustrated their designs, and thus] brought them low.[36] ‹98›

And [Abraham] said: "Verily, I shall [leave this land and] go wherever my Sustainer will guide me!"[37] ‹99›

[And he prayed:] "O my Sustainer! Bestow upon me the gift of [a son who shall be] one of the righteous!" ‹100› – whereupon We gave him the glad tiding of a boy-child gentle [like himself].[38] ‹101›

And [one day,] when [the child] had become old enough to share in his [father's] endeavours,[39] the latter said: "O my dear son! I have seen in a dream that I should sacrifice thee: consider, then, what would be thy view!"

[Ishmael] answered: "O my father! Do as thou art bidden: thou wilt find me, if God so wills, among those who are patient in adversity!" ‹102›

فَقَالَ إِنِّى سَقِيمٌ ﴿٨٩﴾ فَتَوَلَّوْا۟ عَنْهُ مُدْبِرِينَ ﴿٩٠﴾ فَرَاغَ إِلَىٰٓ ءَالِهَتِهِمْ فَقَالَ
أَلَا تَأْكُلُونَ ﴿٩١﴾ مَا لَكُمْ لَا تَنطِقُونَ ﴿٩٢﴾ فَرَاغَ عَلَيْهِمْ ضَرْبًۢا بِٱلْيَمِينِ ﴿٩٣﴾
فَأَقْبَلُوٓا۟ إِلَيْهِ يَزِفُّونَ ﴿٩٤﴾ قَالَ أَتَعْبُدُونَ مَا تَنْحِتُونَ ﴿٩٥﴾ وَٱللَّهُ خَلَقَكُمْ
وَمَا تَعْمَلُونَ ﴿٩٦﴾ قَالُوا۟ ٱبْنُوا۟ لَهُۥ بُنْيَٰنًا فَأَلْقُوهُ فِى ٱلْجَحِيمِ ﴿٩٧﴾
فَأَرَادُوا۟ بِهِۦ كَيْدًا فَجَعَلْنَٰهُمُ ٱلْأَسْفَلِينَ ﴿٩٨﴾ وَقَالَ إِنِّى ذَاهِبٌ إِلَىٰ
رَبِّى سَيَهْدِينِ ﴿٩٩﴾ رَبِّ هَبْ لِى مِنَ ٱلصَّٰلِحِينَ ﴿١٠٠﴾ فَبَشَّرْنَٰهُ بِغُلَٰمٍ
حَلِيمٍ ﴿١٠١﴾ فَلَمَّا بَلَغَ مَعَهُ ٱلسَّعْىَ قَالَ يَٰبُنَىَّ إِنِّىٓ أَرَىٰ فِى ٱلْمَنَامِ أَنِّىٓ
أَذْبَحُكَ فَٱنظُرْ مَاذَا تَرَىٰ قَالَ يَٰٓأَبَتِ ٱفْعَلْ مَا تُؤْمَرُ سَتَجِدُنِىٓ إِن شَآءَ
ٱللَّهُ مِنَ ٱلصَّٰبِرِينَ ﴿١٠٢﴾

Faqāla ᵓinnī saqīm. (89) Fatawallaw ᶜanhu mudbirīn.
(90) Farāgha ᵓilāa ᵓālihatihim faqāla ᵓalā taᵓkulūn.
(91) Mā lakum lā tanṭiqūn. (92) Farāgha ᶜalayhim
ḍarbam-bilyamīn. (93) Faᵓaqbalūu ᵓilayhi yaziffūn. (94)
Qāla ᵓataᶜbudūna mā tanḥitūn. (95) Wal-lāhu khalaqakum wa mā taᶜmalūn. (96) Qālub-nū lahū bunyānañ-
faᵓalqūhu fil-jaḥīm. (97) Faᵓarādū bihī kaydañ-faja-
ᶜalnāhumul-ᵓasfalīn. (98) Wa qāla ᵓinnī dhāhibun ᵓilā
Rabbī sayahdīn. (99) Rabbi hab lī minaṣ-ṣāliḥīn. (100)
Fabashsharnāhu bighulāmin ḥalīm. (101) Falammā balagha maᶜahus-saᶜya qāla yā bunayya ᵓinnīi ᵓarā fil-
manāmi ᵓannīi ᵓadhbaḥuka fañẓur mādhā tarā. Qāla
yāa ᵓabatif-ᶜal mā tuᵓmaru satajidunīi ᵓiñ-shāaᵓal-
lāhu minaṣ-ṣābirīn. (102)

33 Sc., "at your worshipping idols instead of God" (Ibn Kathīr; cf. also Lane IV, 1384).

34 A metonym for "with all his strength". For what happened afterwards, see 21 : 58 ff.

35 Lit., "a building" or "a structure".

36 See *sūrah* 21, note 64.

37 Lit., "I shall go to my Sustainer: He will guide me."

38 I.e., Abraham's first-born son, Ishmael (Ismāᶜīl).

39 Lit., "attained to [the age of] walking [or "striving"] with him": evidently a metonym for the child's attaining to an age when he could understand, and share in, his father's faith and aims.

But as soon as the two had surrendered themselves to [what they thought to be] the will of God,[40] and [Abraham] had laid him down on his face, ‹103› We called out to him: "O Abraham, ‹104› thou hast already fulfilled [the purpose of] that dream-vision!"[41]

Thus, verily, do We reward the doers of good: ‹105› for, behold, all this was indeed a trial, clear in itself.[42] ‹106›

And We ransomed him with a tremendous sacrifice,[43] ‹107› and left him thus to be remembered among later generations:[44] ‹108› "Peace be upon Abraham! ‹109›

Thus do We reward the doers of good ‹110› – for he was truly one of Our believing servants. ‹111›

And [in time] We gave him the glad tiding of Isaac, [who, too, would be] a prophet, one of the righteous; ‹112› and We blessed him and Isaac: but among the offspring of these two there were [destined] to be both doers of good and such as would glaringly sin against themselves.[45] ‹113›

THUS, INDEED, did We bestow Our favour upon Moses and Aaron;[46] ‹114› and We saved them and their people from the awesome calamity [of bondage], ‹115›

فَلَمَّآ أَسْلَمَا وَتَلَّهُۥ لِلْجَبِينِ ﴿١٠٣﴾ وَنَٰدَيْنَٰهُ أَن يَٰٓإِبْرَٰهِيمُ ﴿١٠٤﴾ قَدْ
صَدَّقْتَ ٱلرُّءْيَآ ۚ إِنَّا كَذَٰلِكَ نَجْزِى ٱلْمُحْسِنِينَ ﴿١٠٥﴾ إِنَّ هَٰذَا لَهُوَ
ٱلْبَلَٰٓؤُا۟ ٱلْمُبِينُ ﴿١٠٦﴾ وَفَدَيْنَٰهُ بِذِبْحٍ عَظِيمٍ ﴿١٠٧﴾ وَتَرَكْنَا عَلَيْهِ فِى
ٱلْءَاخِرِينَ ﴿١٠٨﴾ سَلَٰمٌ عَلَىٰٓ إِبْرَٰهِيمَ ﴿١٠٩﴾ كَذَٰلِكَ نَجْزِى
ٱلْمُحْسِنِينَ ﴿١١٠﴾ إِنَّهُۥ مِنْ عِبَادِنَا ٱلْمُؤْمِنِينَ ﴿١١١﴾ وَبَشَّرْنَٰهُ بِإِسْحَٰقَ نَبِيًّا
مِّنَ ٱلصَّٰلِحِينَ ﴿١١٢﴾ وَبَٰرَكْنَا عَلَيْهِ وَعَلَىٰٓ إِسْحَٰقَ ۚ وَمِن ذُرِّيَّتِهِمَا مُحْسِنٌ
وَظَالِمٌ لِّنَفْسِهِۦ مُبِينٌ ﴿١١٣﴾ وَلَقَدْ مَنَنَّا عَلَىٰ مُوسَىٰ وَهَٰرُونَ ﴿١١٤﴾
وَنَجَّيْنَٰهُمَا وَقَوْمَهُمَا مِنَ ٱلْكَرْبِ ٱلْعَظِيمِ ﴿١١٥﴾

Falammāa ᵓaslamā wa tallahū liljabīn. (103) Wa nādaynāhu ᵓañy-yāa ᵓIbrāhīm. (104) Qad ṣaddaqtar-ruᵓyā.
ᵓInnā kadhālika najzil-muḥsinīn. (105) ᵓInna hādhā la-
huwal-balāaᵓul-mubīn. (106) Wa fadaynāhu bidhibḥin
ᶜaẓīm. (107) Wa taraknā ᶜalayhi fil-ᵓākhirīn. (108) Salāmun
ᶜalāa ᵓIbrāhīm. (109) Kadhālika najzil-muḥsinīn. (110)
ᵓInnahū min ᶜibādinal-muᵓminīn. (111) Wa bash-
sharnāhu biᵓIsḥāqa nabiyyam-minaṣ-ṣāliḥīn. (112)
Wa bāraknā ᶜalayhi wa ᶜalāa ᵓIsḥāqa wa miñ-
dhurriyyatihimā muḥsinuñw-wa ẓālimul-linafsihī
mubīn. (113) Wa laqad manannā ᶜalā Mūsā wa Hārūn.
(114) Wa najjaynāhumā wa qawmahumā minal-karbil-
ᶜaẓīm. (115)

40 The above interpolation is, I believe, absolutely necessary for a proper understanding of this passage. As pointed out repeatedly in these notes, the verb *aslama* signifies, in Qurᵓanic usage, "he surrendered himself to God", or "to God's will", even if there is no express mention of God; hence, the dual form *aslamā* occurring in the above verse might, on the face of it, have this meaning as well. Since, however, the sequence clearly shows that it was *not* God's will that Ishmael should be sacrificed, his and his father's "self-surrender to God's will" can have in this context only a purely subjective meaning – namely "to what they *thought* to be the will of God".

41 I.e., the moral significance of Abraham's dream-vision consisted in a test of his readiness to sacrifice, at what he thought to be God's behest (see preceding note), all that was dearest to him in life.

42 I.e., a trial of this severity clearly implied that Abraham would be capable to bear it, and thus constituted a high moral distinction – in itself a reward from God.

43 The epithet *ᶜaẓīm* ("tremendous" or "mighty") renders it improbable that this sacrifice refers to nothing but the ram which Abraham subsequently found and slaughtered in Ishmael's stead (Genesis xxii, 13). To my mind, the sacrifice spoken of here is the one repeated every year by countless believers in connection with the pilgrimage to Mecca (*al-ḥajj*), which, in itself, commemorates the experience of Abraham and Ishmael and constitutes one of the "five pillars" of Islam. (See 22 : 27-37, as well as 2 : 196-203.)

44 See note 30 on verse 78.

45 I.e., commit evil. With this prediction the Qurᵓān refutes, as in so many other places, the spurious contention of the Jews that they are "the chosen people" by virtue of their descent from Abraham, Isaac and Jacob, and therefore *a priori* "assured", as it were, of God's acceptance. In other words, God's blessing a prophet or a saint does not, by itself, imply the conferment of any special status on his descendants.

46 I.e., in consideration of their own merit, and not because of their descent from Abraham and Isaac (see preceding verse and note).

and succoured them, so that [in the end] it was they who achieved victory. ‹116›
And We gave them the divine writ that made [right and wrong] distinct,[47] ‹117› and guided them the straight way, ‹118› and left them thus to be remembered among later generations: ‹119› "Peace be upon Moses and Aaron!" ‹120›
Thus do We reward the doers of good ‹121› – for those two were truly among Our believing servants. ‹122›

AND, BEHOLD, Elijah [too] was indeed one of Our message-bearers[48] ‹123› when he spoke [thus] to his people: "Will you not remain conscious of God? ‹124› Will you invoke Baal and forsake [God,] the best of artisans[49] ‹125› – God, your Sustainer and the Sustainer of your forebears of old?" ‹126›
But they gave him the lie: and therefore they will most surely be arraigned [on Judgment Day], ‹127› excepting only [those who were] God's true servants; ‹128› and him We left thus to be remembered among later generations: ‹129› "Peace be upon Elijah and his followers!"[50] ‹130›
Verily, thus do We reward the doers of good ‹131› – for he was truly one of Our believing servants! ‹132›

وَنَصَرْنَٰهُمْ فَكَانُوا۟ هُمُ ٱلْغَٰلِبِينَ (116) وَءَاتَيْنَٰهُمَا ٱلْكِتَٰبَ ٱلْمُسْتَبِينَ (117)
وَهَدَيْنَٰهُمَا ٱلصِّرَٰطَ ٱلْمُسْتَقِيمَ (118) وَتَرَكْنَا عَلَيْهِمَا فِى ٱلْـَٔاخِرِينَ (119)
سَلَٰمٌ عَلَىٰ مُوسَىٰ وَهَٰرُونَ (120) إِنَّا كَذَٰلِكَ نَجْزِى ٱلْمُحْسِنِينَ (121)
إِنَّهُمَا مِنْ عِبَادِنَا ٱلْمُؤْمِنِينَ (122) وَإِنَّ إِلْيَاسَ لَمِنَ ٱلْمُرْسَلِينَ (123) إِذْ
قَالَ لِقَوْمِهِۦٓ أَلَا تَتَّقُونَ (124) أَتَدْعُونَ بَعْلًا وَتَذَرُونَ أَحْسَنَ ٱلْخَٰلِقِينَ (125)
ٱللَّهَ رَبَّكُمْ وَرَبَّ ءَابَآئِكُمُ ٱلْأَوَّلِينَ (126) فَكَذَّبُوهُ فَإِنَّهُمْ لَمُحْضَرُونَ (127)
إِلَّا عِبَادَ ٱللَّهِ ٱلْمُخْلَصِينَ (128) وَتَرَكْنَا عَلَيْهِ فِى ٱلْـَٔاخِرِينَ (129) سَلَٰمٌ
عَلَىٰٓ إِلْ يَاسِينَ (130) إِنَّا كَذَٰلِكَ نَجْزِى ٱلْمُحْسِنِينَ (131) إِنَّهُۥ مِنْ
عِبَادِنَا ٱلْمُؤْمِنِينَ (132)

Wa naṣarnāhum fakānū humul-ghālibīn. (116) Wa ʾātaynāhumal-Kitābal-mustabīn. (117) Wa hadaynāhumaṣ-ṣirāṭal-mustaqīm. (118) Wa taraknā ʿalayhimā fil-ʾākhirīn. (119) Salāmun ʿalā Mūsā wa Hārūn. (120) ʾInnā kadhālika najzil-muḥsinīn. (121) ʾInnahumā min ʿibādinal-muʾminīn. (122) Wa ʾinna ʾIlyāsa laminal-Mursalīn. (123) ʾIdh qāla liqawmihīi ʾalā tattaqūn. (124) ʾAtadʿūna baʿlanw-wa tadharūna ʾAḥsanal-Khāliqīn. (125) ʾAllāha Rabbakum wa Rabba ʾābāaʾikumul-ʾawwalīn. (126) Fakadhdhabūhu faʾinnahum lamuḥḍarūna, (127) ʾillā ʿibādal-lāhil-mukhlaṣīn. (128) Wa taraknā ʿalayhi fil-ʾākhirīn. (129) Salāmun ʿalāa ʾIlyāsīn. (130) ʾInnā kadhālika najzil-muḥsinīn. (131) ʾInnahū min ʿibādinal-muʾminīn. (132)

47 I.e., "the Torah, wherein there was guidance and light . . . unto those who followed the Jewish faith" (5 : 44).

48 The Hebrew prophet Elijah (Ilyās in Arabic) is mentioned in the Bible (I Kings xvii ff. and II Kings i-ii) as having lived in the Northern Kingdom of Israel during the reigns of Ahab and Ahazīah – i.e., in the ninth century B.C. – and having been succeeded by Elisha (Al-Yasaʿ in Arabic). The above stress on his, too, having been "one of the message-bearers" (*min al-mursalīn*) recalls the Qurʾanic principle that God makes "no distinction between any of His apostles" (cf. 2 : 136 and 285, 3 : 84, 4 : 152, and the corresponding notes).

49 As regards this rendering of *aḥsan al-khāliqīn*, see *sūrah* 23, note 6. – The term *baʿl* (conventionally spelt *Baal* in European languages) signified "lord" or "master" in all branches of ancient Arabic, including Hebrew and Phoenician; it was an honorific applied to every one of the many "male" deities worshipped by the ancient Semites, especially in Syria and Palestine. In the Old Testament this designation has sometimes the generic connotation of "idol-worship" – a sin into which, according to the Bible, the early Israelites often relapsed.

50 The form *Il-Yāsīn* in which this name appears in the above verse is either a variant of Ilyās (Elijah) or, more probably, a plural – "the Elijahs" – meaning "Elijah and his followers" (Ṭabarī, Zamakhsharī, *et al.*). According to Ṭabarī, ʿAbd Allāh ibn Masʿūd used to read this verse as "Peace be upon *Idrāsīn*", which, apart from giving us a variant or a plural of Idrīs ("Idrīs and his followers"), lends support to the view that Idrīs and Ilyās are but two designations of one and the same person, the Biblical Elijah. (See also note 41 on 19 : 56.)

AND, BEHOLD, Lot was indeed one of Our message-bearers; ‹133› [and so,] when [We decreed the doom of his sinful town,[51]] We saved him and his household, ‹134› except an old woman who was among those that stayed behind;[52] ‹135› and then We utterly destroyed the others: ‹136› and, verily, [to this day] you pass by the remnants of their dwellings[53] at morning-time ‹137› and by night.
Will you not, then, use your reason? ‹138›

AND, BEHOLD, Jonah was indeed one of Our message-bearers ‹139› when he fled like a runaway slave onto a laden ship.[54] ‹140›
And then they cast lots, and he was the one who lost;[55] ‹141› [and they cast him into the sea,] whereupon the great fish swallowed him, for he had been blameworthy.[56] ‹142› And had he not been of those who [even in the deep darkness of their distress are able to] extol God's limitless glory,[57] ‹143› he would indeed have remained in its belly till the Day when all shall be raised from the dead: ‹144›

وَإِنَّ لُوطًا لَّمِنَ ٱلْمُرْسَلِينَ ﴿١٣٣﴾ إِذْ نَجَّيْنَٰهُ وَأَهْلَهُۥٓ أَجْمَعِينَ ﴿١٣٤﴾
إِلَّا عَجُوزًا فِى ٱلْغَٰبِرِينَ ﴿١٣٥﴾ ثُمَّ دَمَّرْنَا ٱلْءَاخَرِينَ ﴿١٣٦﴾ وَإِنَّكُمْ
لَتَمُرُّونَ عَلَيْهِم مُّصْبِحِينَ ﴿١٣٧﴾ وَبِٱلَّيْلِ أَفَلَا تَعْقِلُونَ ﴿١٣٨﴾ وَإِنَّ يُونُسَ
لَمِنَ ٱلْمُرْسَلِينَ ﴿١٣٩﴾ إِذْ أَبَقَ إِلَى ٱلْفُلْكِ ٱلْمَشْحُونِ ﴿١٤٠﴾ فَسَاهَمَ فَكَانَ
مِنَ ٱلْمُدْحَضِينَ ﴿١٤١﴾ فَٱلْتَقَمَهُ ٱلْحُوتُ وَهُوَ مُلِيمٌ ﴿١٤٢﴾ فَلَوْلَآ أَنَّهُۥ كَانَ
مِنَ ٱلْمُسَبِّحِينَ ﴿١٤٣﴾ لَلَبِثَ فِى بَطْنِهِۦٓ إِلَىٰ يَوْمِ يُبْعَثُونَ ﴿١٤٤﴾

Wa ʾinna Lūṭal-laminal-Mursalīn. (133) ʾIdh najjaynāhu wa ʾahlahūu ʾajmaʿīna, (134) ʾillā ʿajūzañ-fil-ghābirīn. (135) Thumma dammarnal-ʾākharīn. (136) Wa ʾinnakum latamurrūna ʿalayhim-muṣbiḥīna, (137) wa billayli ʾafalā taʿqilūn. (138) Wa ʾinna Yūnusa laminal-Mursalīn. (139) ʾIdh ʾabaqa ʾilal-fulkil-mashḥūn. (140) Fasāhama fakāna minal-mudḥaḍīn. (141) Faltaqamhul-ḥūtu wa huwa mulīm. (142) Falawlāa ʾannahū kāna minal-musabbiḥīna, (143) lalabitha fī baṭnihīi ʾilā Yawmi yubʿathūn. (144)

51 See 7 : 80-84 and 11 : 69-83.

52 As is evident from 7 : 83 and 11 : 81, that woman was Lot's wife, who had *chosen* to stay behind (cf. note 66 on 7 : 83).

53 Lit., "you pass by them", i.e., by the places where they lived (see 15 : 76 and the corresponding note 55).

54 I.e., when he abandoned the mission with which he had been entrusted by God (see *sūrah* 21, note 83, which gives the first part of Jonah's story), and thus, in the words of the Bible (The Book of Jonah i, 3 and 10), committed the sin of "fleeing from the presence of the Lord". In its primary significance, the infinitive noun *ibāq* (derived from the verb *abaqa*) denotes "a slave's running-away from his master"; and Jonah is spoken of as having "fled like a runaway slave" because – although he was God's message-bearer – he abandoned his task under the stress of violent anger. The subsequent mention of "the laden ship" alludes to the central, allegorical part of Jonah's story. The ship ran into a storm and was about to founder; and the mariners "said everyone to his fellow, Come and let us cast lots, that we may know for whose cause this evil is upon us" (The Book of Jonah i, 7) – a procedure to which Jonah agreed.

55 Lit., "he cast lots [with the mariners], and was among the losers". According to the Biblical account (The Book of Jonah i, 10-15), Jonah told them that he had "fled from the presence of the Lord", and that it was because of this sin of his that they all were now in danger of drowning. "And he said unto them, Take me up, and cast me forth into the sea; so shall the sea be calm unto you: for I know that for my sake this tempest is upon you. . . . So they took up Jonah, and cast him forth into the sea: and the sea ceased from her raging."

56 In all the three instances where Jonah's "great fish" is explicitly mentioned in the Qurʾān (as *al-ḥūt* in the above verse and in 68 : 48, and *an-nūn* in 21 : 87), it carries the definite article *al*. This may possibly be due to the fact that the legend of Jonah was and is so widely known that every reference to the allegory of "the great fish" is presumed to be self-explanatory. The inside of the fish that "swallowed" Jonah apparently symbolizes the deep darkness of spiritual distress of which 21 : 87 speaks: the distress at having "fled like a runaway slave" from his prophetic mission and, thus, "from the presence of the Lord". Parenthetically, the story is meant to show that, since "man has been created weak" (4 : 28), even prophets are not immune against all the failings inherent in human nature.

57 I.e., to remember God and to repent: see 21 : 87, which reveals in its very formulation the universal purport of Jonah's story.

but We caused him to be cast forth on a desert shore, sick [at heart] as he was, ‹145› and caused a creeping plant to grow over him [out of the barren soil].[58] ‹146›

And [then] We sent him [once again] to [his people,] a hundred thousand [souls] or more: ‹147› and [this time] they believed [in him][59] – and so We allowed them to enjoy their life during the time allotted to them.[60] ‹148›

AND NOW ask them[61] to enlighten thee: Has thy Sustainer daughters, whereas they would have [only] sons?[62] ‹149› – or is it that We have created the angels female, and they [who believe them to be divine] have witnessed [that act of creation]? ‹150›

Oh, verily, it is out of their own [inclination to] falsehood that some people[63] assert, ‹151› "God has begotten [a son]"; and, verily, they are lying [too, when they say], ‹152› "He has chosen daughters in preference to sons"![64] ‹153›

What is amiss with you and your judgment?[65] ‹154›

Will you not, then, bethink yourselves? ‹155›

Or have you, perchance, a clear evidence [for your assertions]? ‹156› Produce, then, that divine writ of yours, if you are speaking the truth! ‹157›

And some people[66] have invented a kinship between Him and all manner of

۞ فَنَبَذْنَـٰهُ بِٱلْعَرَآءِ وَهُوَ سَقِيمٌ ١٤٥ وَأَنۢبَتْنَا عَلَيْهِ شَجَرَةً مِّن يَقْطِينٍ ١٤٦
وَأَرْسَلْنَـٰهُ إِلَىٰ مِاْئَةِ أَلْفٍ أَوْ يَزِيدُونَ ١٤٧ فَـَٔامَنُوا۟ فَمَتَّعْنَـٰهُمْ إِلَىٰ
حِينٍ ١٤٨ فَٱسْتَفْتِهِمْ أَلِرَبِّكَ ٱلْبَنَاتُ وَلَهُمُ ٱلْبَنُونَ ١٤٩ أَمْ خَلَقْنَا
ٱلْمَلَـٰٓئِكَةَ إِنَـٰثًا وَهُمْ شَـٰهِدُونَ ١٥٠ أَلَآ إِنَّهُم مِّنْ إِفْكِهِمْ لَيَقُولُونَ ١٥١
وَلَدَ ٱللَّهُ وَإِنَّهُمْ لَكَـٰذِبُونَ ١٥٢ أَصْطَفَى ٱلْبَنَاتِ عَلَى ٱلْبَنِينَ ١٥٣ مَا
لَكُمْ كَيْفَ تَحْكُمُونَ ١٥٤ أَفَلَا تَذَكَّرُونَ ١٥٥ أَمْ لَكُمْ سُلْطَـٰنٌ
مُّبِينٌ ١٥٦ فَأْتُوا۟ بِكِتَـٰبِكُمْ إِن كُنتُمْ صَـٰدِقِينَ ١٥٧ وَجَعَلُوا۟ بَيْنَهُۥ وَبَيْنَ

حزب 46

۞ **Fanabadhnāhu bilʿarāaʾi wa huwa saqīm. 145**
Wa ʾambatnā ʿalayhi shajaratam-miñy-yaqṭīn. 146
Wa ʾarsalnāhu ʾilā miʾati ʾalfin ʾaw yazīdūn. 147
Faʾāmanū famattaʿnāhum ʾilā ḥīn. 148 Fastaftihim
ʾaliRabbikal-banātu wa lahumul-banūn. 149 ʾAm
khalaqnal-Malāaʾikata ʾināthañw-wa hum shā-
hidūn. 150 ʾAlāa ʾinnahum-min ʾifkihim layaqūlūna,
151 waladal-lāhu wa ʾinnahum lakādhibūn. 152
ʾAṣṭafal-banāti ʿalal-banīn. 153 Mā lakum kayfa
taḥkumūn. 154 ʾAfalā tadhakkarūn. 155 ʾAm lakum
sulṭānum-mubīn. 156 Faʾtū bikitābikum ʾiñ-kuñ-
tum ṣādiqīn. 157 Wa jaʿalū baynahū wa baynal-

58 I.e., to shade and comfort him. Thus, rounding off the allegory of Jonah and the fish, the Qurʾān points out in the figurative manner so characteristic of its style that God, who can cause a plant to grow out of the most arid and barren soil, can equally well cause a heart lost in darkness to come back to light and spiritual life.

59 Cf. the reference to the people of Jonah in 10 : 98. For the Biblical version of this story, see The Book of Jonah iii.

60 Lit., "for a time": i.e., for the duration of their natural lives (Rāzī; also *Manār* XI, 483).

61 This reference to people who ascribe divinity to beings other than God connects with verse 4 ("verily, most surely, your God is One") as well as with verses 69-70 ("behold, they found their forebears on a wrong way, and [now] they make haste to follow in their footsteps").

62 For an explanation of this passage, see 16 : 57-59 and the corresponding notes.

63 Lit., "they".

64 Cf. 6 : 100 ("they have invented for Him sons and daughters") and the corresponding notes 87 and 88. See also note 49 on 17 : 40, as well as 53 : 19-22 and the corresponding notes.

65 Lit., "how do you judge?"

66 Lit., "they".

invisible forces[67] – although [even] these invisible forces know well that, verily, they [who thus blaspheme against God] shall indeed be arraigned [before Him on Judgment Day:[68] for] ‹158› limitless is God in His glory, above anything that men may devise by way of definition![69] ‹159›

Not thus, however, [behave] God's true servants: ‹160› for, verily, neither you [blasphemers] nor the objects of your worship ‹161› can cause anyone to fall prey to your temptation ‹162› unless it be such as rushes towards the blazing fire [of his own accord]![70] ‹163›

[All forces of nature praise God and say:[71]] "Among us, too, there is none but has a place assigned to it [by Him]; ‹164› and, verily, we too are ranged [before Him in worship]; ‹165› and, verily, we too extol His limitless glory!" ‹166›

AND, INDEED, they [who deny the truth] have always been wont to say, ‹167› "If only we had a tradition [to this effect] from our forebears,[72] ‹168› we would certainly be true servants of God." ‹169› And yet, [now that this divine writ has been placed before them,] they refuse to acknowledge it as true!

In time, however, they will come to know [what it was that they had rejected]: ‹170›

ٱلْجِنَّةِ نَسَبًا ۚ وَلَقَدْ عَلِمَتِ ٱلْجِنَّةُ إِنَّهُمْ لَمُحْضَرُونَ ﴿158﴾ سُبْحَـٰنَ ٱللَّهِ عَمَّا
يَصِفُونَ ﴿159﴾ إِلَّا عِبَادَ ٱللَّهِ ٱلْمُخْلَصِينَ ﴿160﴾ فَإِنَّكُمْ وَمَا تَعْبُدُونَ ﴿161﴾ مَآ
أَنتُمْ عَلَيْهِ بِفَـٰتِنِينَ ﴿162﴾ إِلَّا مَنْ هُوَ صَالِ ٱلْجَحِيمِ ﴿163﴾ وَمَا مِنَّآ إِلَّا لَهُۥ
مَقَامٌ مَّعْلُومٌ ﴿164﴾ وَإِنَّا لَنَحْنُ ٱلصَّآفُّونَ ﴿165﴾ وَإِنَّا لَنَحْنُ ٱلْمُسَبِّحُونَ ﴿166﴾
وَإِن كَانُوا۟ لَيَقُولُونَ ﴿167﴾ لَوْ أَنَّ عِندَنَا ذِكْرًا مِّنَ ٱلْأَوَّلِينَ ﴿168﴾ لَكُنَّا
عِبَادَ ٱللَّهِ ٱلْمُخْلَصِينَ ﴿169﴾ فَكَفَرُوا۟ بِهِۦ ۖ فَسَوْفَ يَعْلَمُونَ ﴿170﴾

**Jinnati nasabā. Wa laqad ᶜalimatil-Jinnatu
ᵓinnahum lamuḥḍarūn. ⑮⑧ Subḥānal-lāhi ᶜammā
yaṣifūn. ⑮⑨ ᵓIllā ᶜibādal-lāhil-mukhlaṣīn. ⑯⓪ Faᵓin-
nakum wa mā taᶜbudūn. ⑯① Māa ᵓañtum ᶜalayhi
bifātinīna, ⑯② ᵓillā man huwa ṣālil-jaḥīm. ⑯③ Wa mā
minnāa ᵓillā lahū maqāmum-maᶜlūm. ⑯④ Wa ᵓinnā
lanaḥnuṣ-ṣāaffūn. ⑯⑤ Wa ᵓinnā lanaḥnul-musab-
biḥūn. ⑯⑥ Wa ᵓiñ-kānū layaqūlūna, ⑯⑦ law ᵓanna
ᶜiñdanā dhikram-minal-ᵓawwalīna, ⑯⑧ lakunnā ᶜibādal-lāhil-mukhlaṣīn. ⑯⑨ Fakafarū bihī fasawfa yaᶜlamūn. ⑰⓪**

67 See Appendix III. Whereas most of the classical commentators are of the opinion that the term *al-jinnah* denotes here the angels, since they – like all beings of this category – are imperceptible to man's senses, I believe that the above verse refers to those intangible forces of nature which elude all direct observation and manifest themselves only in their effects: hence their designation, in this context, by the plural noun *al-jinnah*, which primarily denotes "that which is concealed from [man's] senses". Inasmuch as people who refuse to believe in God often tend to regard those elemental forces as mysteriously endowed with a purposeful creative power (cf. Bergson's concept of the *élan vital*), the Qur'ān states that their votaries invent a "kinship" between them and God, i.e., attribute to them qualities and powers similar to His.

68 For this metaphorical attribution of "knowledge" to the elemental forces of nature, see verses 164-166 and the corresponding note 71.

69 See note 88 on the last sentence of 6 : 100.

70 True belief in God precludes all temptation to define Him who is undefinable, or to associate, conceptually, anyone or anything with Him; conversely, the blasphemy inherent in such attempts destroys the potential value of one's belief in God and, thus, brings about the spiritual ruin of the person concerned.

71 The metaphorical "saying" that follows is in tune with many other Qurᵓanic passages which speak of even inanimate objects as "praising God", e.g., "The seven heavens extol His limitless glory, and the earth, and all that they contain" (17 : 44), or "We caused the mountains to join David in extolling Our glory" (21 : 79), or "O you mountains! Sing with him the praise of God!" (34 : 10); similarly, even the shadows of material things are spoken of as "prostrating themselves before God", (16 : 48).

72 Lit., "a reminder (*dhikr*) from those of old": see note 27 on verses 69-70 above. Most of the commentators

for, long ago has Our word gone forth unto Our servants, the message-bearers, ‹171› that, verily, they – they indeed – would be succoured, ‹172› and that, verily, Our hosts – they indeed – would [in the end] be victorious! ‹173›

Hence, turn thou aside for a while from those [who deny the truth], ‹174› and see them [for what they are];[73] and in time they [too] will come to see [what they do not see now].[74] ‹175›

Do they, then, [really] wish that Our chastisement be hastened on?[75] ‹176› But then, once it alights upon them, hapless will be the awakening of those who were warned [to no avail]![76] ‹177›

Hence, turn thou aside for a while from them, ‹178› and see [them for what they are]; and in time they [too] will come to see [what they do not see now]. ‹179›

LIMITLESS in His glory is thy Sustainer, the Lord of almightiness, [exalted] above anything that men may devise by way of definition! ‹180›

And peace be upon all His message-bearers! ‹181›

And all praise is due to God alone, the Sustainer of all the worlds! ‹182›

وَلَقَدْ سَبَقَتْ كَلِمَتُنَا لِعِبَادِنَا ٱلْمُرْسَلِينَ ﴿171﴾ إِنَّهُمْ لَهُمُ ٱلْمَنصُورُونَ ﴿172﴾ وَإِنَّ جُندَنَا لَهُمُ ٱلْغَٰلِبُونَ ﴿173﴾ فَتَوَلَّ عَنْهُمْ حَتَّىٰ حِينٍ ﴿174﴾ وَأَبْصِرْهُمْ فَسَوْفَ يُبْصِرُونَ ﴿175﴾ أَفَبِعَذَابِنَا يَسْتَعْجِلُونَ ﴿176﴾ فَإِذَا نَزَلَ بِسَاحَتِهِمْ فَسَآءَ صَبَاحُ ٱلْمُنذَرِينَ ﴿177﴾ وَتَوَلَّ عَنْهُمْ حَتَّىٰ حِينٍ ﴿178﴾ وَأَبْصِرْ فَسَوْفَ يُبْصِرُونَ ﴿179﴾ سُبْحَٰنَ رَبِّكَ رَبِّ ٱلْعِزَّةِ عَمَّا يَصِفُونَ ﴿180﴾ وَسَلَٰمٌ عَلَى ٱلْمُرْسَلِينَ ﴿181﴾ وَٱلْحَمْدُ لِلَّهِ رَبِّ ٱلْعَٰلَمِينَ ﴿182﴾

Wa laqad sabaqat kalimatunā liᶜibādinal-Mursalīn. (171) ʾInnahum lahumul-mañṣūrūn. (172) Wa ʾinna juñdanā lahumul-ghālibūn. (173) Fatawalla ᶜanhum ḥattā ḥīn. (174) Wa ʾabṣirhum fasawfa yubṣirūn. (175) ʾAfabiᶜadhābinā yastaᶜjilūn. (176) Faʾidhā nazala bisāḥatihim fasāaʾa ṣabāḥul-muñdharīn. (177) Wa tawalla ᶜanhum ḥattā ḥīn. (178) Wa ʾabṣir fasawfa yubṣirūn. (179) Subḥāna Rabbika Rabbil-ᶜizzati ᶜammā yaṣifūn. (180) Wa salāmun ᶜalal-Mursalīn. (181) Wal-ḥamdu lillāhi Rabbil-ᶜālamīn. (182)

---

assume that the term *dhikr* connotes here, as so often in the Qurʾān, a "divine writ". In my opinion, however, it is far more probable – because more in tune with the context – that in this case it signifies an ancestral tradition bearing on the (to them astonishing) message of God's oneness and uniqueness as promulgated by the Qurʾān.

73 I.e., as people who are bent on deceiving themselves. In this context, the verb *baṣura* (lit., "he saw" or "became seeing") is used tropically, in the sense of "seeing mentally" or "gaining insight".

74 I.e., they will realize the truth as well as the suffering which its rejection entails: obviously a reference to the Day of Judgment.

75 This is an allusion to the sarcastic demand of the people who refused to regard the Qurʾān as a divine revelation, to be punished forthwith "if this be indeed the truth from God" (see 8 : 32 and the corresponding note).

76 Lit., "when it alights in their courtyard, evil [or "hapless"] is the morning of those . . .", etc. In ancient Arabic usage, the idiomatic phrase "chastisement [or "suffering"] has alighted (*nazala*) in so-and-so's courtyard" denotes its coming-down upon, or befalling, the person or persons concerned (Ṭabarī). Similarly, the "morning" (*ṣabāḥ*) is a metonym for "awakening".

The Thirty-Eighth Sūrah

Ṣād

Mecca Period

REVEALED comparatively early – probably towards the end of the fourth or the beginning of the fifth year of the Prophet's mission – this *sūrah* is devoted almost entirely to the problem of divine guidance and its rejection by those who are "lost in false pride, and [hence] deeply in the wrong" (verse 2).

The only "title" – or, rather, key-word – applied to this *sūrah* since the earliest times is the letter *ṣ* (*ṣād*) which introduces the first verse.

-38-

سورة ص مكية

وآياتها ثمان وثمانون

IN THE NAME OF GOD, THE MOST GRACIOUS, THE DISPENSER OF GRACE:

Ṣād.[1]
CONSIDER[2] this Qur'ān, endowed with all that one ought to remember![3] ‹1›
But nay – they who are bent on denying the truth are lost in [false] pride, and [hence] deeply in the wrong.[4] ‹2›
How many a generation[5] have We destroyed before their time [for this very sin]! And [how] they called [unto Us] when it was too late to escape![6] ‹3›
Now these [people] deem it strange that a warner should have come unto them from their own midst – and [so] the deniers of the truth are saying: "A [mere] spellbinder is he, a liar![7] ‹4› Does he claim that all the deities are [but] one God? Verily, a most strange thing is this!"[8] ‹5›

بِسْمِ ٱللَّهِ ٱلرَّحْمَٰنِ ٱلرَّحِيمِ

صٓ وَٱلْقُرْءَانِ ذِى ٱلذِّكْرِ ﴿1﴾ بَلِ ٱلَّذِينَ كَفَرُواْ فِى عِزَّةٍ وَشِقَاقٍ ﴿2﴾
كَمْ أَهْلَكْنَا مِن قَبْلِهِم مِّن قَرْنٍ فَنَادَواْ وَّلَاتَ حِينَ مَنَاصٍ ﴿3﴾
وَعَجِبُوٓاْ أَن جَآءَهُم مُّنذِرٌ مِّنْهُمْ وَقَالَ ٱلْكَٰفِرُونَ هَٰذَا سَٰحِرٌ
كَذَّابٌ ﴿4﴾ أَجَعَلَ ٱلْـَٔالِهَةَ إِلَٰهًا وَٰحِدًا إِنَّ هَٰذَا لَشَىْءٌ عُجَابٌ ﴿5﴾

Bismil-lāhir-Raḥmānir-Raḥīm.
Ṣāad. Wal-Qurʾāni dhidh-Dhikr. ‹1› Balil-ladhīna kafarū fī ʿizzatiñw-wa shiqāq. ‹2› Kam ʾahlaknā miñ-qablihim-miñ-qarniñ-fanādaw-wa lāta ḥīna manāṣ. ‹3› Wa ʿajibūu ʾañ-jāaʾahum-Muñdhirum-minhum; wa qālal-kāfirūna hādhā sāḥiruñ-kadh-dhāb. ‹4› ʾAjaʿalal-ʾālihata ʾIlāhañw-Wāḥidā. ʾInna hādhā lashayʾun ʿujāb. ‹5›

---

1 See Appendix II.

2 For an explanation of this rendering of the adjurative particle *wa*, see first half of note 23 on 74 : 32.

3 Or: "endowed with eminence" (Zamakhsharī), since the term *dhikr* (lit., "reminder" or "remembrance") has also the connotation of "that which is remembered", i.e., "renown", "fame" and, tropically, "eminence". As regards the rendering preferred by me, see 21 : 10, where the phrase *fīhi dhikrukum* (relating, as above, to the Qurʾān) has been translated as "wherein is found all that you ought to bear in mind", i.e., in order to attain to dignity and happiness.

4 I.e., they refuse to acknowledge the fact of divine revelation because such an acknowledgment would imply an admission of man's responsibility to God – and this their false pride, manifested in their arrogant belief in man's "self-sufficiency", does not allow them to do. The same idea is expressed in 16 : 22 and, in a more general way, in 2 : 206. Cf. also 96 : 6-7.

5 It is to be noted that the term *qarn* signifies not merely a "generation" but also – and quite frequently in the Qurʾān – "people belonging to a particular period and environment", i.e., a "civilization" in the historical connotation of this word.

6 Lit., "while there was no time for escaping".

7 Although this passage describes, in the first instance, the attitude of the pagan Quraysh towards the Prophet, it touches upon the reluctance of most people, at all times, to recognize "a man from their own midst" – i.e., a human being like themselves – as God-inspired. (See note 2 on 50 : 2.)

8 Divorced from its purely historical background, this criticism acquires a timeless significance, and may be thus paraphrased: "Does he claim that all creative powers and qualities are inherent exclusively in what he conceives as 'one God'?" – a paraphrase which illustrates the tendency of many people to attribute a decisive influence on human life – and, hence, a *quasi*-divine status – to a variety of fortuitous phenomena or circumstances (like wealth, "luck", social position, etc.) rather than to acknowledge the overwhelming evidence, in all observable nature, of God's unique existence.

وَانطَلَقَ الْمَلَأُ مِنْهُمْ أَنِ امْشُوا وَاصْبِرُوا عَلَىٰ آلِهَتِكُمْ ۖ إِنَّ هَٰذَا لَشَيْءٌ
يُرَادُ ﴿6﴾ مَا سَمِعْنَا بِهَٰذَا فِي الْمِلَّةِ الْآخِرَةِ إِنْ هَٰذَا إِلَّا اخْتِلَاقٌ ﴿7﴾
أَأُنزِلَ عَلَيْهِ الذِّكْرُ مِن بَيْنِنَا ۚ بَلْ هُمْ فِي شَكٍّ مِّن ذِكْرِي ۖ بَل لَّمَّا يَذُوقُوا
عَذَابِ ﴿8﴾ أَمْ عِندَهُمْ خَزَائِنُ رَحْمَةِ رَبِّكَ الْعَزِيزِ الْوَهَّابِ ﴿9﴾ أَمْ
لَهُم مُّلْكُ السَّمَاوَاتِ وَالْأَرْضِ وَمَا بَيْنَهُمَا ۖ فَلْيَرْتَقُوا فِي الْأَسْبَابِ ﴿10﴾
جُندٌ مَّا هُنَالِكَ مَهْزُومٌ مِّنَ الْأَحْزَابِ ﴿11﴾ كَذَّبَتْ قَبْلَهُمْ قَوْمُ نُوحٍ
وَعَادٌ وَفِرْعَوْنُ ذُو الْأَوْتَادِ ﴿12﴾

And their leaders launch forth [thus]: "Go ahead, and hold steadfastly onto your deities: this, behold, is the only thing to do![9] «6» Never did we hear of [a claim like] this in any faith of latter days![10] It is nothing but [a mortal man's] invention! «7» What! Upon him alone from among all of us should a [divine] reminder have been bestowed from on high?"

Nay, but it is My Own reminder that they distrust![11]

Nay, they have not yet tasted the suffering which I do impose![12] «8»

Or do they [think that they] own the treasures of thy Sustainer's grace – [the grace] of the Almighty, the Giver of Gifts?[13] «9» Or [that] the dominion over the heavens and the earth and all that is between them is theirs? Why, then, let them try to ascend [to God-like power] by all [conceivable] means![14] «10»

[But] there it is: any and all human beings, however [strongly] leagued together,[15] are bound to suffer defeat [whenever they refuse to accept the truth]. «11»

To the truth gave the lie aforetime[16] Noah's people, and [the tribe of] ʿĀd, and Pharaoh of the [many] tent-poles,[17] «12»

Wañ-ṭalaqal-malaʾu minhum ʾanim-shū waṣ-birū ʿalāa ʾālihatikum; ʾinna hādhā lashayʾuñy-yurād. (6) Mā samiʿnā bihādhā fil-millatil-ʾākhirati ʾin hādhāa ʾillakh-tilāq. (7) ʾAʾuñzila ʿalayhidh-Dhikru mim-bayninā. Bal hum fī shakkim-miñ-Dhikrī, bal-lammā yadhūqū ʿadhāb. (8) ʾAm ʿiñdahum khazāaʾinu raḥmati Rabbikal-ʿAzīzil-Wahhāb. (9) ʾAm lahum-mulkus-samāwāti wal-ʾarḍi wa mā baynahumā; falyartaqū fil-ʾasbāb. (10) Juñdum-mā hunālika mah-zūmum-minal-ʾaḥzāb. (11) Kadhdhabat qablahum qawmu Nūḥiñw-wa ʿĀduñw-wa Firʿawnu dhul-ʾawtād. (12)

9 Lit., "a thing desired" or "to be desired", i.e., a sensible course of action.

10 I.e., "in any of the faiths prevalent in our days": an oblique reference to Christianity and its dogma of the Trinity, which contrasts with the Qurʾanic concept of God's oneness and uniqueness, as well as to any other faith based on the belief in a multiplicity or multiform incarnation of divine powers (e.g., Hinduism with its triad of Brahma, Vishnu and Shiva).

11 Lit., "that they are in doubt of": i.e., it is not the personality of the Prophet that fills them with distrust, but, rather, the *substance* of the message proclaimed by him – and, in particular, his insistence on God's absolute oneness and uniqueness, which runs counter to their habits of thought and social traditions.

12 Sc., "on people who refuse to accept the truth".

13 I.e., "Do they think that it is for them to decide as to who should and who should not be graced with divine revelation?"

14 I.e., "Do they think that human beings are so highly endowed that they are bound to attain, some day, to mastery over the universe and all nature, and thus to God-like power?" Cf. in this connection 96 : 6-8 and the corresponding note 4. – As regards my rendering of *al-asbāb* as "all [conceivable] means", see note 82 on 18 : 84.

15 The collective noun *jund*, which primarily denotes "a host" or "an army", has also the meaning of "created beings", in this context obviously *human* beings; in combination with the particle *mā*, "any number of human beings". The term *ḥizb* (of which *aḥzāb* is the plural), on the other hand, denotes "a party" or "a group of people of the same mind" or "people leagued together", i.e., for a definite purpose.

16 Lit., "before them", i.e., before the people who opposed or oppose Muḥammad's message.

17 In classical Arabic, this ancient bedouin term is used idiomatically as a metonym for "mighty dominion" or "firmness of power" (Zamakhsharī). The number of poles supporting a bedouin tent is determined by its size, and the latter has always depended on the status and power of its owner: thus, a mighty chieftain is often alluded to as "he of many tent-poles".

وَثَمُودُ وَقَوْمُ لُوطٍ وَأَصْحَٰبُ لْـَٔيْكَةِ ۚ أُو۟لَٰٓئِكَ ٱلْأَحْزَابُ ﴿١٣﴾ إِن كُلٌّ إِلَّا
كَذَّبَ ٱلرُّسُلَ فَحَقَّ عِقَابِ ﴿١٤﴾ وَمَا يَنظُرُ هَٰٓؤُلَآءِ إِلَّا صَيْحَةً وَٰحِدَةً مَّا
لَهَا مِن فَوَاقٍ ﴿١٥﴾ وَقَالُوا۟ رَبَّنَا عَجِّل لَّنَا قِطَّنَا قَبْلَ يَوْمِ ٱلْحِسَابِ ﴿١٦﴾
ٱصْبِرْ عَلَىٰ مَا يَقُولُونَ وَٱذْكُرْ عَبْدَنَا دَاوُۥدَ ذَا ٱلْأَيْدِ ۖ إِنَّهُۥٓ أَوَّابٌ ﴿١٧﴾
إِنَّا سَخَّرْنَا ٱلْجِبَالَ مَعَهُۥ يُسَبِّحْنَ بِٱلْعَشِىِّ وَٱلْإِشْرَاقِ ﴿١٨﴾ وَٱلطَّيْرَ
مَحْشُورَةً ۖ كُلٌّ لَّهُۥٓ أَوَّابٌ ﴿١٩﴾ وَشَدَدْنَا مُلْكَهُۥ وَءَاتَيْنَٰهُ ٱلْحِكْمَةَ وَفَصْلَ
ٱلْخِطَابِ ﴿٢٠﴾ ۞ وَهَلْ أَتَىٰكَ نَبَؤُا۟ ٱلْخَصْمِ إِذْ تَسَوَّرُوا۟ ٱلْمِحْرَابَ ﴿٢١﴾

ربع الحزب

Wa Thamūdu wa qawmu Lūṭiñw-wa ʾaṣḥābul-ʾaykati ʾulāaʾikal-ʾaḥzāb. (13) ʾIñ-kullun ʾillā kadhdhabar-Rusula faḥaqqa ʿiqāb. (14) Wa mā yañẓuru hāaʾulāaʾi ʾillā ṣayḥatañw-wāḥidatam-mā lahā miñ-fawāq. (15) Wa qālū Rabbanā ʿajjil-lanā qiṭṭanā qabla Yawmil-Ḥisāb. (16) ʾIṣbir ʿalā mā yaqūlūna wadh-kur ʿabdanā Dāwūda dhal-ʾaydi ʾinnahūu ʾawwāb. (17) ʾInnā sakhkharnal-jibāla maʿahū yusabbiḥna bilʿashiyyi wal-ʾishrāq. (18) Waṭ-ṭayra maḥshūratañ-kullul-lahūu ʾawwāb. (19) Wa shadadnā mulkahū wa ʾātaynāhul-ḥikmata wa faṣlal-khiṭāb. (20) ۞ Wa hal ʾatāka nabaʾul-khaṣmi ʾidh tasawwarul-miḥrāb. (21)

and [the tribe of] Thamūd, and the people of Lot, and the dwellers of the wooded dales [of Madyan]: they all were leagued together, [as it were, in their unbelief:] ‹13› not one [was there] but gave the lie to the apostles – and thereupon My retribution fell due. ‹14›

And they [who now deny the truth – they, too,] have but to wait for one single blast [of punishment to overtake them]: it shall not be delayed a whit.[18] ‹15›

As it is, they say [mockingly]: "O our Sustainer! Hasten on to us our share [of punishment even] before the Day of Reckoning!"[19] ‹16›

[But] bear thou with patience whatever they may say, and remember Our servant David, him who was endowed with [so much] inner strength! He, verily, would always turn unto Us: ‹17› [and for this,] behold, We caused[20] the mountains to join him in extolling Our limitless glory at eventide and at sunrise, ‹18› and [likewise] the birds in their assemblies:[21] [together] they all would turn again and again unto Him [who had created them]. ‹19› And We strengthened his dominion, and bestowed upon him wisdom and sagacity in judgment. ‹20›

AND YET, has the story of the litigants come within thy ken – [the story of the two] who surmounted the walls of the sanctuary [in which David prayed]?[22] ‹21›

---

18 Sc., "beyond the term set for it by God".

19 Cf. 8 : 32. This mocking "demand" of the unbelievers is mentioned in several other places in the Qurʾān.

20 Lit., "We compelled" or "constrained".

21 See *sūrah* 21, note 73.

22 The story which, according to the oldest sources at our disposal, is alluded to in verses 21-26 affects the question as to whether God's elect, the prophets – all of whom were endowed, like David, with "wisdom and sagacity in judgment" – could or could not ever commit a sin: in other words, whether they, too, were originally subject to the weaknesses inherent in human nature as such or were *a priori* endowed with an essential purity of character which rendered each of them "incapable of sinning" (*maʿṣūm*). In the form in which it has been handed down from the earliest authorities (including, according to Ṭabarī and Baghawī, Companions like ʿAbd Allāh ibn ʿAbbās and Anas ibn Mālik, as well as several of the most prominent of their immediate successors), the story contradicts the doctrine – somewhat arbitrarily developed by Muslim theologians in the course of the centuries – that prophets *cannot* sin by virtue of their very nature, and tends to show that their purity and subsequent sinlessness is a result of inner struggles and trials and, thus, represents in each case a *moral achievement* rather than an inborn quality.

As they came upon David, and he shrank back in fear from them, they said: "Fear not! [We are but] two litigants. One of us has wronged the other: so judge thou between us with justice, and deviate not from what is right, and show [both of] us the way to rectitude. ‹22›

"Behold, this is my brother: he has ninety-nine ewes, whereas I have [only] one ewe – and yet he said, 'Make her over to me,' and forcibly prevailed against me in this [our] dispute." ‹23›

Said [David]: "He has certainly wronged thee by demanding that thy ewe be added to his ewes! Thus, behold, do many kinsmen[23] wrong one another – [all] save those who believe [in God] and do righteous deeds: but how few are they!"

And [suddenly] David understood that We had tried him:[24] and so he asked his Sustainer to forgive him his sin, and fell down in prostration, and turned unto Him in repentance. ‹24›

And thereupon We forgave him that [sin]: and, verily, nearness to Us awaits him [in the life to come], and the most beauteous of all goals! ‹25›

[And We said:] "O David! Behold, We have made thee a [prophet and, thus, Our] vicegerent on earth: judge, then, between men with justice, and do not follow vain desire,

إِذْ دَخَلُوا۟ عَلَىٰ دَاوُۥدَ فَفَزِعَ مِنْهُمْ ۖ قَالُوا۟ لَا تَخَفْ ۖ خَصْمَانِ بَغَىٰ بَعْضُنَا
عَلَىٰ بَعْضٍ فَٱحْكُم بَيْنَنَا بِٱلْحَقِّ وَلَا تُشْطِطْ وَٱهْدِنَآ إِلَىٰ سَوَآءِ
ٱلصِّرَٰطِ ﴿٢٢﴾ إِنَّ هَٰذَآ أَخِى لَهُۥ تِسْعٌ وَتِسْعُونَ نَعْجَةً وَلِىَ نَعْجَةٌ وَٰحِدَةٌ
فَقَالَ أَكْفِلْنِيهَا وَعَزَّنِى فِى ٱلْخِطَابِ ﴿٢٣﴾ قَالَ لَقَدْ ظَلَمَكَ بِسُؤَالِ
نَعْجَتِكَ إِلَىٰ نِعَاجِهِۦ ۖ وَإِنَّ كَثِيرًا مِّنَ ٱلْخُلَطَآءِ لَيَبْغِى بَعْضُهُمْ عَلَىٰ
بَعْضٍ إِلَّا ٱلَّذِينَ ءَامَنُوا۟ وَعَمِلُوا۟ ٱلصَّٰلِحَٰتِ وَقَلِيلٌ مَّا هُمْ ۗ وَظَنَّ دَاوُۥدُ
أَنَّمَا فَتَنَّٰهُ فَٱسْتَغْفَرَ رَبَّهُۥ وَخَرَّ رَاكِعًا وَأَنَابَ ۩ ﴿٢٤﴾ فَغَفَرْنَا لَهُۥ
السجدة
ذَٰلِكَ ۖ وَإِنَّ لَهُۥ عِندَنَا لَزُلْفَىٰ وَحُسْنَ مَـَٔابٍ ﴿٢٥﴾ يَٰدَاوُۥدُ إِنَّا جَعَلْنَٰكَ
خَلِيفَةً فِى ٱلْأَرْضِ فَٱحْكُم بَيْنَ ٱلنَّاسِ بِٱلْحَقِّ وَلَا تَتَّبِعِ ٱلْهَوَىٰ

ʾIdh dakhalū ʿalā Dāwūda fafaziʿa minhum qālū lā takhaf; khaṣmāni baghā baʿḍunā ʿalā baʿḍiñ-faḥkum baynanā bil-ḥaqqi wa lā tushṭiṭ wah-dināa ʾilā sawāaʾiṣ-ṣirāṭ. ﴿22﴾ ʾInna hādhāa ʾakhī lahū tisʿuñw-wa tisʿūna naʿjatañw-wa liya naʿjatuñw-wāḥidatuñ-faqāla ʾakfilnīhā wa ʿazzanī fil-khiṭāb. ﴿23﴾ Qāla laqad ẓalamaka bisuʾāli naʿjatika ʾilā niʿājih. Wa ʾinna kathīram-minal-khulaṭāaʾi layabghī baʿḍuhum ʿalā baʿḍin ʾillal-ladhīna ʾāmanū wa ʿamiluṣ-ṣāliḥāti wa qalīlum-mā hum. Wa ẓanna Dāwūdu ʾannamā fatannāhu fastaghfara Rabbahū wa kharra rākiʿañw-wa ʾanāb. ۩ ﴿24﴾ Faghafarnā lahū dhālika wa ʾinna lahū ʿiñdanā lazulfā wa ḥusna maʾāb. ﴿25﴾ Yā Dāwūdu ʾinnā jaʿalnāka khalīfatañ-fil-ʾarḍi faḥkum baynan-nāsi bil-ḥaqqi wa lā tattabiʿil-hawā

As narrated in some detail by Ṭabarī and other early commentators, David fell in love with a beautiful woman whom he accidentally observed from his roof terrace. On inquiring, he was told that she was the wife of one of his officers, named Uriah. Impelled by his passion, David ordered his field-commander to place Uriah in a particularly exposed battle position, where he would be certain to be killed; and as soon as his order was fulfilled and Uriah died, David married the widow (who subsequently became the mother of Solomon). This story agrees more or less with the Old Testament, which gives the woman's name as Bath-Sheba (II Samuel xi), barring the Biblical allegation that David committed adultery with her before Uriah's death (*ibid.* xi, 4-5) – an allegation which has always been rejected by Muslims as highly offensive and slanderous: cf. the saying of the fourth Caliph, ʿAlī ibn Abī Ṭālib (quoted by Zamakhsharī on the authority of Saʿīd ibn al-Musayyab): "If anyone should narrate the story of David in the manner in which the story-tellers narrate it, I will have him flogged with one hundred and sixty stripes – for this is a [suitable] punishment for slandering prophets" (thus indirectly recalling the Qurʾanic ordinance, in 24 : 4, which stipulates flogging with eighty stripes for accusing *ordinary* persons of adultery without legal proof).

According to most of the commentators, the two "litigants" who suddenly appeared before David were angels sent to bring home to him his sin. It is possible, however, to see in their appearance an allegory of David's *own* realization of having sinned: voices of his own conscience which at last "surmounted the walls" of the passion that had blinded him for a time.

23 The term *khulaṭāʾ* (sing. *khalīṭ*) denotes, literally, "people who mix [i.e., are familiar or intimate] with others" or "with one another". In the present instance it evidently alludes to the "brotherhood" between the two mysterious litigants, and is therefore best rendered as "kinsmen".

24 Sc., "and that he had failed" (in the matter of Bath-Sheba).

lest it lead thee astray from the path of God: verily, for those who go astray from the path of God there is suffering severe in store for having forgotten the Day of Reckoning!" ‹26›

AND [thus it is:] We have not created heaven and earth and all that is between them without meaning and purpose, as is the surmise of those who are bent on denying the truth:[25] but then, woe from the fire [of hell] unto all who are bent on denying the truth![26] ‹27›
[For,] would We treat those who have attained to faith and do righteous deeds in the same manner as [We shall treat] those who spread corruption on earth? Would We treat the God-conscious in the same manner as the wicked?[27] ‹28›
[All this have We expounded in this] blessed divine writ which We have revealed unto thee, [O Muḥammad,] so that men may ponder over its messages, and that those who are endowed with insight may take them to heart. ‹29›

AND UNTO DAVID We granted Solomon [as a son – and] how excellent a servant [of Ours he grew up to be]!
Behold, he would always turn unto Us[28] ‹30› – [and even] when, towards the close of day, nobly-bred, swift-footed steeds were brought before him, ‹31› he would say, "Verily, I have come to love the love

فَيُضِلَّكَ عَن سَبِيلِ ٱللَّهِ إِنَّ ٱلَّذِينَ يَضِلُّونَ عَن سَبِيلِ ٱللَّهِ لَهُمْ عَذَابٌ شَدِيدٌۢ
بِمَا نَسُوا۟ يَوْمَ ٱلْحِسَابِ ﴿٢٦﴾ وَمَا خَلَقْنَا ٱلسَّمَآءَ وَٱلْأَرْضَ وَمَا بَيْنَهُمَا بَـٰطِلًا
ذَٰلِكَ ظَنُّ ٱلَّذِينَ كَفَرُوا۟ فَوَيْلٌ لِّلَّذِينَ كَفَرُوا۟ مِنَ ٱلنَّارِ ﴿٢٧﴾ أَمْ نَجْعَلُ ٱلَّذِينَ
ءَامَنُوا۟ وَعَمِلُوا۟ ٱلصَّـٰلِحَـٰتِ كَٱلْمُفْسِدِينَ فِى ٱلْأَرْضِ أَمْ نَجْعَلُ ٱلْمُتَّقِينَ
كَٱلْفُجَّارِ ﴿٢٨﴾ كِتَـٰبٌ أَنزَلْنَـٰهُ إِلَيْكَ مُبَـٰرَكٌ لِّيَدَّبَّرُوٓا۟ ءَايَـٰتِهِۦ وَلِيَتَذَكَّرَ
أُو۟لُوا۟ ٱلْأَلْبَـٰبِ ﴿٢٩﴾ وَوَهَبْنَا لِدَاوُۥدَ سُلَيْمَـٰنَ نِعْمَ ٱلْعَبْدُ إِنَّهُۥٓ أَوَّابٌ ﴿٣٠﴾
إِذْ عُرِضَ عَلَيْهِ بِٱلْعَشِىِّ ٱلصَّـٰفِنَـٰتُ ٱلْجِيَادُ ﴿٣١﴾ فَقَالَ إِنِّىٓ أَحْبَبْتُ حُبَّ

fayuḍillaka ᶜañ-sabīlil-lāh. ᵓInnal-ladhīna yaḍillūna ᶜañ-sabīlil-lāhi lahum ᶜadhābuñ-shadīdum-bimā nasū Yawmal-Ḥisāb. (26) Wa mā khalaqnas-samāaᵓa wal-ᵓarḍa wa mā baynahumā bāṭilā. Dhālika ẓannul-ladhīna kafarū; fawaylul-lilladhīna kafarū minan-nār. (27) ᵓAm najᶜalul-ladhīna ᵓāmanū wa ᶜamiluṣ-ṣāliḥāti kalmufsidīna fil-ᵓarḍi ᵓam najᶜalul-muttaqīna kal-fujjār. (28) Kitābun ᵓañzalnāhu ᵓilayka mubārakul-liyad-dabbarūu ᵓĀyātihī wa liyatadhakkara ᵓulul-ᵓalbāb. (29) Wa wahabnā liDāwūda Sulaymān. Niᶜmal-ᶜabdu ᵓinnahūu ᵓawwāb. (30) ᵓIdh ᶜuriḍa ᶜalayhi bilᶜashiyyiṣ-ṣāfinātul-jiyād. (31) Faqāla ᵓinnii ᵓaḥbabtu-ḥubbal-

25 Cf. 3 : 191. The above statement appears in the Qurᵓān in several formulations; see, in particular, note 11 on 10 : 5. In the present instance it connects with the mention of the Day of Reckoning in the preceding verse, thus leading organically from a specific aspect of David's story to a moral teaching of wider import.

26 I.e., a deliberate rejection of the belief that the universe – and, in particular, human life – is imbued with meaning and purpose leads unavoidably – though sometimes imperceptibly – to a rejection of all moral imperatives, to spiritual blindness and, hence, to suffering in the life to come.

27 By implication, belief in resurrection, judgment and life after death is postulated in this passage (verses 27-28) as a logical corollary – almost a premise – of all belief in God: for, since we see that many righteous people suffer all manner of misery and deprivations in this world, while, on the other hand, many of the wicked and depraved enjoy their lives in peace and affluence, we must either assume that God does not exist (because the concept of injustice is incompatible with that of Godhead), or – alternatively – that there is a hereafter in which both the righteous and the unrighteous will harvest in full what they had morally sown during their lives on earth.

28 I.e., he would always *think* of God, as illustrated by the example given in the sequence.

of all that is good because I bear my Sustainer in mind!"[29] – [repeating these words as the steeds raced away,] until they were hidden by the veil [of distance[30] – whereupon he would command], ⟨32⟩ "Bring them back unto me!" – and would [lovingly] stroke their legs and their necks.[31] ⟨33⟩

But [ere this], indeed, We had tried Solomon by placing upon his throne a [lifeless] body;[32] and thereupon he turned [towards Us; and] ⟨34⟩ he prayed: "O my Sustainer! Forgive me my sins, and bestow upon me the gift of a kingdom which may not suit anyone after me:[33] verily, Thou alone art a giver of gifts!" ⟨35⟩

And so[34] We made subservient to him the wind, so that it gently sped at his behest whithersoever he willed,[35] ⟨36⟩ as well as all the rebellious forces [that We made to work for him] – every kind of builder and diver ⟨37⟩ – and others linked together in fetters.[36] ⟨38⟩

[And We told him:] "This is Our gift, for thee to bestow freely on others, or to withhold, without [having to render] account!" ⟨39⟩

And, verily, nearness to Us awaits him [in the life to come], and the most beauteous of all goals! ⟨40⟩

ٱلْخَيْرِ عَن ذِكْرِ رَبِّى حَتَّىٰ تَوَارَتْ بِٱلْحِجَابِ ﴿٣٢﴾ رُدُّوهَا عَلَىَّ فَطَفِقَ
مَسْحًۢا بِٱلسُّوقِ وَٱلْأَعْنَاقِ ﴿٣٣﴾ وَلَقَدْ فَتَنَّا سُلَيْمَـٰنَ وَأَلْقَيْنَا عَلَىٰ كُرْسِيِّهِۦ
جَسَدًا ثُمَّ أَنَابَ ﴿٣٤﴾ قَالَ رَبِّ ٱغْفِرْ لِى وَهَبْ لِى مُلْكًا لَّا يَنۢبَغِى لِأَحَدٍ
مِّنۢ بَعْدِىٓ ۖ إِنَّكَ أَنتَ ٱلْوَهَّابُ ﴿٣٥﴾ فَسَخَّرْنَا لَهُ ٱلرِّيحَ تَجْرِى بِأَمْرِهِۦ
رُخَآءً حَيْثُ أَصَابَ ﴿٣٦﴾ وَٱلشَّيَـٰطِينَ كُلَّ بَنَّآءٍ وَغَوَّاصٍ ﴿٣٧﴾ وَءَاخَرِينَ
مُقَرَّنِينَ فِى ٱلْأَصْفَادِ ﴿٣٨﴾ هَـٰذَا عَطَآؤُنَا فَٱمْنُنْ أَوْ أَمْسِكْ بِغَيْرِ
حِسَابٍ ﴿٣٩﴾ وَإِنَّ لَهُۥ عِندَنَا لَزُلْفَىٰ وَحُسْنَ مَـَٔابٍ ﴿٤٠﴾

khayri ʿañ-dhikri Rabbī ḥattā tawārat bilḥijāb. (32) Ruddūhā ʿalayya faṭafiqa masḥam-bissūqi wal-ʾaʿnāq. (33) Wa laqad fatannā Sulaymāna wa ʾalqaynā ʿalā kursiyyihī jasadañ-thumma ʾanāb. (34) Qāla Rabbigh-fir lī wa hab lī mulkal-lā yambaghī liʾaḥadim-mim baʿdīi ʾinnaka ʾAñtal-Wahhāb. (35) Fasakhkharnā lahur-riḥa tajrī biʾamrihī rukhāaʾan ḥaythu ʾaṣāb. (36) Wash-Shayāṭīna kulla bannāaʾiñw-wa ghawwāṣ. (37) Wa ʾākharīna muqarranīna fil-ʾaṣfād. (38) Hādhā ʿAṭāaʾunā famnun ʾaw ʾamsik bighayri ḥisāb. (39) Wa ʾinna lahū ʿiñdanā lazulfā wa ḥusna maʾāb. (40)

29 Lit., "because of [or "out of"] (*ʿan*) the remembrance of my Sustainer".

30 This and the preceding interpolation are based on Rāzī's interpretation of this passage.

31 The story of Solomon's love of beautiful horses is meant to show that all true love of God is bound to be reflected in one's realization of, and reverence for, the beauty created by Him.

32 To explain this verse, some of the commentators advance the most fantastic stories, almost all of them going back to Talmudic sources. Rāzī rejects them all, maintaining that they are unworthy of serious consideration. Instead, he plausibly suggests that the "body" (*jasad*) upon Solomon's throne is an allusion to *his own* body, and – metonymically – to his kingly power, which was bound to remain "lifeless" so long as it was not inspired by God-willed ethical values. (It is to be borne in mind that in classical Arabic a person utterly weakened by illness, worry or fear, or devoid of moral values, is often described as "a body without a soul".) In other words, Solomon's early trial consisted in his inheriting no more than a kingly position, and it rested upon him to endow that position with spiritual essence and meaning.

33 I.e., a spiritual kingdom, which could not be inherited by anyone and, hence, would not be exposed to envy or worldly intrigue.

34 I.e., as a reward for his humility and turning-away from worldly ambitions, implied in the prayer, "Forgive me my sins".

35 Cf. 21 : 81 and the corresponding note 75. For the meaning, in general, of the many legends surrounding the person of Solomon, see note 77 on 21 : 82.

36 I.e., subdued and, as it were, tamed by him: see note 76 on 21 : 82, which explains my rendering, in this context, of *shayāṭīn* as "rebellious forces".

AND CALL to mind Our servant Job,[37] [how it was] when he cried out to his Sustainer, "Behold, Satan has afflicted me with [utter] weariness and suffering!"[38] ‹41› – [and thereupon was told:] "Strike [the ground] with thy foot: here is cool water to wash with and to drink!"[39] ‹42›

And We bestowed upon him new offspring,[40] doubling their number as an act of grace from Us, and as a reminder unto all who are endowed with insight. ‹43›

[And finally We told him:] "Now take in thy hand a small bunch of grass, and strike therewith, and thou wilt not break thine oath!"[41] – for, verily, We found him full of patience in adversity: how excellent a servant [of Ours], who, behold, would always turn unto Us! ‹44›

AND CALL to mind Our servants Abraham and Isaac and Jacob, [all of them] endowed with inner strength and vision: ‹45› for, verily, We purified them by means of a thought most pure: the remembrance of the life to come.[42] ‹46› And, behold, in Our sight they were indeed among the elect, the truly good! ‹47›

And call to mind Ishmael and Elisha,[43] and every one who [like them] has pledged himself [unto Us]:[44] for, each of them was of the truly good! ‹48›

وَٱذْكُرْ عَبْدَنَآ أَيُّوبَ إِذْ نَادَىٰ رَبَّهُۥٓ أَنِّى مَسَّنِىَ ٱلشَّيْطَٰنُ بِنُصْبٍ
وَعَذَابٍ ﴿٤١﴾ ٱرْكُضْ بِرِجْلِكَ ۖ هَٰذَا مُغْتَسَلٌۢ بَارِدٌ وَشَرَابٌ ﴿٤٢﴾ وَوَهَبْنَا
لَهُۥٓ أَهْلَهُۥ وَمِثْلَهُم مَّعَهُمْ رَحْمَةً مِّنَّا وَذِكْرَىٰ لِأُو۟لِى ٱلْأَلْبَٰبِ ﴿٤٣﴾ وَخُذْ
بِيَدِكَ ضِغْثًا فَٱضْرِب بِّهِۦ وَلَا تَحْنَثْ ۗ إِنَّا وَجَدْنَٰهُ صَابِرًا ۚ نِّعْمَ ٱلْعَبْدُ ۖ
إِنَّهُۥٓ أَوَّابٌ ﴿٤٤﴾ وَٱذْكُرْ عِبَٰدَنَآ إِبْرَٰهِيمَ وَإِسْحَٰقَ وَيَعْقُوبَ أُو۟لِى
ٱلْأَيْدِى وَٱلْأَبْصَٰرِ ﴿٤٥﴾ إِنَّآ أَخْلَصْنَٰهُم بِخَالِصَةٍ ذِكْرَى ٱلدَّارِ ﴿٤٦﴾
وَإِنَّهُمْ عِندَنَا لَمِنَ ٱلْمُصْطَفَيْنَ ٱلْأَخْيَارِ ﴿٤٧﴾ وَٱذْكُرْ إِسْمَٰعِيلَ وَٱلْيَسَعَ
وَذَا ٱلْكِفْلِ ۖ وَكُلٌّ مِّنَ ٱلْأَخْيَارِ ﴿٤٨﴾

Wadh-kur ᶜabdanāa ᵓAyyūba ᵓidh nādā Rabbahūu ᵓannī massaniyash-Shayṭānu binuṣbiñw-wa ᶜadhāb. (41) ᵓUrkuḍ birijlika hādhā mughtasalum-bāriduñw-wa sharāb. (42) Wa wahabnā lahūu ahlahū wa mithlahum-maᶜahum raḥmatam-minnā wa dhikrā liᵓulil-ᵓalbāb. (43) Wa khudh biyadika ḍighthañ-faḍrib-bihī wa lā taḥnath. ᵓInnā wajadnāhu ṣābirā. Niᶜmal-ᶜabdu ᵓinnahūu ᵓawwāb. (44) Wadh-kur ᶜibādanāa ᵓIbrāhīma wa ᵓIsḥāqa wa Yaᶜqūba ᵓulil-ᵓaydī wal-ᵓabṣār. (45) ᵓInnāa ᵓakhlaṣnāhum-bikhāliṣatiñ-dhikrad-dār. (46) Wa ᵓinnahum ᶜiñdanā laminal-muṣṭafaynal-ᵓakhyār. (47) Wadh-kur ᵓIsmāᶜīla wal-Yasaᶜa wa Dhalkifli wa kullum-minal-ᵓakhyār. (48)

---

37 See note 78 on 21 : 83.

38 I.e., with life-weariness *in consequence of* suffering. As soon as he realizes that God has been testing him, Job perceives that his utter despondency and weariness of life – eloquently described in the Old Testament (The Book of Job iii) – was but due to what is described as "Satan's whisperings": this is the moral to be drawn from the above evocation of Job's story.

39 According to the classical commentators, the miraculous appearance of a healing spring heralded the end of Job's suffering, both physical and mental.

40 Lit., "his family" (cf. 21 : 84 and the corresponding note 79).

41 In the words of the Bible (The Book of Job ii, 9), at the time of his seemingly hopeless suffering Job's wife reproached her husband for persevering in his faith: "Dost thou still retain thine integrity? Curse God, and die." According to the classical Qurᵓān-commentators, Job swore that, if God would restore him to health, he would punish her blasphemy with a hundred stripes. But when he did recover, he bitterly regretted his hasty oath, for he realized that his wife's "blasphemy" had been an outcome of her love and pity for him; and thereupon he was told in a revelation that he could fulfil his vow in a symbolic manner by striking her *once* with "a bunch of grass containing a hundred blades or more". (Cf. 5 : 89 – "God will not take you to task for oaths which you may have uttered without thought.")

42 Lit., "of the [final] abode".

43 Al-Yasaᶜ in Arabic – the Biblical prophet who succeeded Elijah (see *sūrah* 37, note 48).

44 For an explanation of this rendering of *dhu 'l-kifl*, see *sūrah* 21, note 81.

نصف
الحزب

LET [all] this be a reminder [to those who believe in God] – for, verily, the most beauteous of all goals awaits the God-conscious: ‹49› gardens of perpetual bliss,[45] with gates wide-open to them, ‹50› wherein they will recline, [and] wherein they may [freely] call for many a fruit and drink, ‹51› having beside them well-matched mates of modest gaze.[46] ‹52›

This is what you are promised for the Day of Reckoning: ‹53› this, verily, shall be Our provision [for you], with no end to it! ‹54›

All this [for the righteous]: but, verily, the most evil of all goals awaits those who are wont to transgress the bounds of what is right: ‹55› hell will they have to endure – and how vile a resting-place! ‹56›

This, [then, for them –] so let them taste it: burning despair and ice-cold darkness ‹57› and, coupled with it, further [suffering] of a similar nature.[47] ‹58›

[And they will say to one another: "Do you see] this crowd of people who rushed

هَٰذَا ذِكْرٌ وَإِنَّ لِلْمُتَّقِينَ لَحُسْنَ مَـَٔابٍ ﴿٤٩﴾ جَنَّٰتِ عَدْنٍ مُّفَتَّحَةً لَّهُمُ
ٱلْأَبْوَٰبُ ﴿٥٠﴾ مُتَّكِـِٔينَ فِيهَا يَدْعُونَ فِيهَا بِفَٰكِهَةٍ كَثِيرَةٍ وَشَرَابٍ ﴿٥١﴾
۞ وَعِندَهُمْ قَٰصِرَٰتُ ٱلطَّرْفِ أَتْرَابٌ ﴿٥٢﴾ هَٰذَا مَا تُوعَدُونَ لِيَوْمِ
ٱلْحِسَابِ ﴿٥٣﴾ إِنَّ هَٰذَا لَرِزْقُنَا مَا لَهُۥ مِن نَّفَادٍ ﴿٥٤﴾ هَٰذَا ۚ وَإِنَّ لِلطَّٰغِينَ
لَشَرَّ مَـَٔابٍ ﴿٥٥﴾ جَهَنَّمَ يَصْلَوْنَهَا فَبِئْسَ ٱلْمِهَادُ ﴿٥٦﴾ هَٰذَا فَلْيَذُوقُوهُ
حَمِيمٌ وَغَسَّاقٌ ﴿٥٧﴾ وَءَاخَرُ مِن شَكْلِهِۦٓ أَزْوَٰجٌ ﴿٥٨﴾ هَٰذَا فَوْجٌ مُّقْتَحِمٌ

Hādhā dhikruñw-wa ᵓinna lilmuttaqīna laḥusna maᵓāb. (49) Jannāti ᶜadnim-mufattaḥatal-lahumul-ᵓabwāb. (50) Muttakiᵓīna fīhā yadᶜūna fīhā bifākihatiñ-kathīratiñw-wa sharāb. (51) ۞ Wa ᶜiñdahum qāṣirātuṭ-ṭarfi ᵓatrāb. (52) Hādhā mā tūᶜadūna liYawmil-Ḥisāb. (53) ᵓInna hādhā larizqunā mā lahū miñ-nafād. (54) Hādhā wa ᵓinna liṭṭāghīna lasharra maᵓāb. (55) Jahannam yaṣlawnahā fabiᵓsal-mihād. (56) Hādhā falyadhūqūhu ḥamīmuñw-wa ghassāq. (57) Wa ᵓākharu miñ-shaklihīi ᵓazwāj. (58) Hādhā fawjum-muqtaḥimum-

45 In all the eleven instances in which the noun *ᶜadn* occurs in the Qurᵓān – and of which the present is the oldest – it is used as a qualifying term for the "gardens" (*jannāt*) of paradise. This noun is derived from the verb *ᶜadana*, which primarily denotes "he remained [somewhere]" or "he kept [to something]", i.e., permanently: cf. the phrase *ᶜadantu 'l-balad* ("I remained for good [or "settled"] in the country"). In Biblical Hebrew – which, after all, is but a very ancient Arabian dialect – the closely related noun *ᶜedēn* has also the additional connotation of "delight", "pleasure" or "bliss". Hence the combination of the two concepts in my rendering of *ᶜadn* as "perpetual bliss". As in many other places in the Qurᵓān, this bliss is here allegorized – and thus brought closer to man's imagination – by means of descriptions recalling earthly joys.

46 Lit., "such as restrain their gaze", i.e., are of modest bearing and have eyes only for their mates (Rāzī). This allegorical reference to the delights of paradise occurs in the Qurᵓān three times (apart from the above instance, which is chronologically the earliest, in 37 : 48 and 55 : 56 as well). As an allegory, this phrase evidently applies to the righteous of both sexes, who in the life to come will be rejoined with those whom they loved and by whom they were loved in this world: for, "God has promised the believers, both men and women, gardens through which running waters flow, therein to abide, and goodly dwellings in gardens of perpetual bliss" (9 : 72); and, "anyone – be it man or woman – who does [whatever he can] of good deeds and is a believer withal, shall enter paradise" (4 : 124, with similar statements in 16 : 97 and 40 : 40). Finally, we are told in 36 : 56 that in this paradise "will they *and their spouses* on couches recline" – i.e., will find peace and inner fulfilment with and in one another. (For an explanation of the term *atrāb*, rendered by me as "well-matched", see note 15 on 56 : 38.)

47 Lit., "of its kind": i.e., corresponding in intensity to what the Qurᵓān describes as *ḥamīm* and *ghassāq*. For my rendering of *ḥamīm* as "burning despair", see *sūrah* 6, note 62. The term *ghassāq*, on the other hand, is derived from the verb *ghasaqa*, "it became dark" or "intensely dark" (*Tāj al-ᶜArūs*); thus, *al-ghāsiq* denotes "black darkness" and, tropically, "the night" or, rather, "the black night". According to some authorities, the form *ghassāq* signifies "intense [or "icy"] cold". A combination of these two meanings gives us the concept of the "ice-cold darkness" of the spirit which, together with "burning despair" (*ḥamīm*), will characterize the suffering of inveterate sinners in the life to come. All other interpretations of the term *ghassāq* are purely speculative and, therefore, irrelevant.

headlong [into sin] with you?[48] No welcome to them! Verily, they [too] shall have to endure the fire!"[49] ‹59›
[And] they [who had been seduced] will exclaim: "Nay, but it is you! No welcome to you! It is you who have prepared this for us: and how vile a state to abide in!" ‹60›
[And] they will pray: "O our Sustainer! Whoever has prepared this for us, double Thou his suffering in the fire!"[50] ‹61›
And they will add: "How is it that we do not see [here any of the] men whom we were wont to count among the wicked, ‹62› [and] whom we made the target of our derision?[51] Or is it that [they are here, and] our eyes have missed them?" ‹63›
Such, behold, will in truth be the [confusion and] mutual wrangling of the people of the fire! ‹64›

SAY [O Muḥammad]: "I am only a warner; and there is no deity whatever save God, the One, who holds absolute sway over all that exists, ‹65› the Sustainer of the heavens and the earth and all that is between them, the Almighty, the All-Forgiving! ‹66›
Say: "This is a message tremendous: ‹67› [how can] you turn away from it?" ‹68›
[Say, O Muḥammad:] "No knowledge would I have had of [what passed among] the host on high when they argued [against the creation of man],[52] ‹69›

مَعَكُمْ لَا مَرْحَبًۢا بِهِمْ إِنَّهُمْ صَالُوا۟ ٱلنَّارِ ﴿٥٩﴾ قَالُوا۟ بَلْ أَنتُمْ لَا مَرْحَبًۢا
بِكُمْ أَنتُمْ قَدَّمْتُمُوهُ لَنَا فَبِئْسَ ٱلْقَرَارُ ﴿٦٠﴾ قَالُوا۟ رَبَّنَا مَن قَدَّمَ لَنَا هَٰذَا
فَزِدْهُ عَذَابًا ضِعْفًا فِى ٱلنَّارِ ﴿٦١﴾ وَقَالُوا۟ مَا لَنَا لَا نَرَىٰ رِجَالًا كُنَّا
نَعُدُّهُم مِّنَ ٱلْأَشْرَارِ ﴿٦٢﴾ أَتَّخَذْنَٰهُمْ سِخْرِيًّا أَمْ زَاغَتْ عَنْهُمُ
ٱلْأَبْصَٰرُ ﴿٦٣﴾ إِنَّ ذَٰلِكَ لَحَقٌّ تَخَاصُمُ أَهْلِ ٱلنَّارِ ﴿٦٤﴾ قُلْ إِنَّمَآ أَنَا۠
مُنذِرٌ وَمَا مِنْ إِلَٰهٍ إِلَّا ٱللَّهُ ٱلْوَٰحِدُ ٱلْقَهَّارُ ﴿٦٥﴾ رَبُّ ٱلسَّمَٰوَٰتِ
وَٱلْأَرْضِ وَمَا بَيْنَهُمَا ٱلْعَزِيزُ ٱلْغَفَّٰرُ ﴿٦٦﴾ قُلْ هُوَ نَبَؤٌا۟ عَظِيمٌ ﴿٦٧﴾ أَنتُمْ
عَنْهُ مُعْرِضُونَ ﴿٦٨﴾ مَا كَانَ لِىَ مِنْ عِلْمٍۭ بِٱلْمَلَإِ ٱلْأَعْلَىٰٓ إِذْ
يَخْتَصِمُونَ ﴿٦٩﴾

maᶜakum lā marḥabam-bihim; ᵓinnahum ṣālun-nār. (59) Qālū bal ᵓañtum lā marḥabam-bikum ᵓañtum qaddamtumūhu lanā fabiᵓsal-qarār. (60) Qālū Rabbanā mañ-qaddama lanā hādhā fazid-hu ᶜadhābañ-ḍiᶜfañ-fin-nār. (61) Wa qālū mā lanā lā narā rijālañ-kunnā naᶜudduhum-minal-ᵓashrār. (62) ᵓAttakhadhnāhum sikhriyyan ᵓam zāghat ᶜanhumul-abṣār. (63) ᵓInna dhālika laḥaqquñ-takhāṣumu ᵓahlin-nār. (64) Qul ᵓinnamāa ᵓana Muñdhiruñw-wa mā min ᵓilāhin ᵓillal-lāhul-Wāḥidul-Qahhār. (65) Rabbus-samāwāti wal-ᵓarḍi wa mā baynahumal-ᶜAzīzul-Ghaffār. (66) Qul huwa nabaᵓun ᶜaẓīm. (67) ᵓAñtum ᶜanhu muᶜriḍūn. (68) Mā kāna liya min ᶜilmim-bilmalaᵓil-ᵓaᶜlāa ᵓidh yakhtaṣimūn. (69)

48 I.e., "people whom you had seduced, and who thereupon blindly followed you": an apostrophe stressing the double responsibility of the seducers.

49 In Arabic usage, the phrase "no welcome to them" or "to you" (*lā marḥaban bihim*, resp. *bikum*) is equivalent to a curse. In this context – carried on into the next verse – it expresses a mutual disavowal of the seducers and the seduced.

50 Cf. 7 : 38 (and the corresponding notes 28 and 29) as well as 33 : 67-68.

51 I.e., the prophets and the righteous, who – as the Qurᵓān points out in many places – have always been derided by people enamoured of the life of this world and, therefore, averse to all moral exhortation.

52 For the allegorical contention of the angels ("the host on high") against the creation of man, see 2 : 30 ff. and the corresponding notes 22-24. The allegory of man's creation, of God's command to the angels to "prostrate themselves" before the new creature, and of Iblīs' refusal to do so appears in the Qurᵓān six times (2 : 30-34, 7 : 11 ff., 15 : 28-44, 17 : 61-65, 18 : 50, and 38 : 69-85), each time with an accent on a different aspect of this allegory. In the present instance (which is undoubtedly the earliest in the chronology of revelation) it is connected with the statement, in 2 : 31, that God "imparted unto Adam the names of all things", i.e., endowed man with the faculty of conceptual thinking (see note 23 on 2 : 31) and, thus, with the ability to discern between what is true and what false. Since he possesses this faculty, man has no excuse for not realizing God's existence and oneness – the "message tremendous" referred to in the preceding passage.

had it not been revealed unto me [by God] – to no other end than that I might convey [unto you] a plain warning."[53] ‹70› [For,] lo,[54] thy Sustainer said unto the angels: "Behold, I am about to create a human being out of clay;[55] ‹71› and when I have formed him fully and breathed into him of My spirit, fall you down before him in prostration!"[56] ‹72›

Thereupon the angels prostrated themselves, all of them together, ‹73› save Iblīs: he gloried in his arrogance, and [thus] became one of those who deny the truth.[57] ‹74›

Said He: "O Iblīs! What has kept thee from prostrating thyself before that [being] which I have created with My hands?[58] Art thou too proud [to bow down before another created being], or art thou of those who think [only] of themselves as high?"[59] ‹75›

Answered [Iblīs]: "I am better than he: Thou hast created me out of fire,[60] whereas him Thou hast created out of clay." ‹76›

Said He: "Go forth, then, from this [angelic state] – for, behold, thou art henceforth accursed, ‹77› and My rejection shall be thy due until the Day of Judgment!" ‹78›

Said [Iblīs]: "Then, O my Sustainer, grant me a respite till the Day when all shall be raised from the dead!" ‹79›

إِن يُوحَىٰٓ إِلَىَّ إِلَّآ أَنَّمَآ أَنَا۠ نَذِيرٌ مُّبِينٌ ﴿٧٠﴾ إِذْ قَالَ رَبُّكَ لِلْمَلَٰٓئِكَةِ إِنِّى
خَٰلِقٌۢ بَشَرًا مِّن طِينٍ ﴿٧١﴾ فَإِذَا سَوَّيْتُهُۥ وَنَفَخْتُ فِيهِ مِن رُّوحِى فَقَعُوا۟
لَهُۥ سَٰجِدِينَ ﴿٧٢﴾ فَسَجَدَ ٱلْمَلَٰٓئِكَةُ كُلُّهُمْ أَجْمَعُونَ ﴿٧٣﴾ إِلَّآ إِبْلِيسَ
ٱسْتَكْبَرَ وَكَانَ مِنَ ٱلْكَٰفِرِينَ ﴿٧٤﴾ قَالَ يَٰٓإِبْلِيسُ مَا مَنَعَكَ أَن تَسْجُدَ
لِمَا خَلَقْتُ بِيَدَىَّ ۖ أَسْتَكْبَرْتَ أَمْ كُنتَ مِنَ ٱلْعَالِينَ ﴿٧٥﴾ قَالَ أَنَا۠ خَيْرٌ
مِّنْهُ ۖ خَلَقْتَنِى مِن نَّارٍ وَخَلَقْتَهُۥ مِن طِينٍ ﴿٧٦﴾ قَالَ فَٱخْرُجْ مِنْهَا فَإِنَّكَ
رَجِيمٌ ﴿٧٧﴾ وَإِنَّ عَلَيْكَ لَعْنَتِىٓ إِلَىٰ يَوْمِ ٱلدِّينِ ﴿٧٨﴾ قَالَ رَبِّ فَأَنظِرْنِىٓ
إِلَىٰ يَوْمِ يُبْعَثُونَ ﴿٧٩﴾

ʾIñy-yūḥāa ʾilayya ʾillāa ʾannamāa ʾana Nadhīrum-mubīn. (70) ʾIdh qāla Rabbuka lilMalāaʾikati ʾinnī khāliqum-basharam-miñ-ṭīn. (71) Faʾidhā sawwaytuhū wa nafakhtu fīhi mir-Rūḥī faqaʿū lahū sājidīn. (72) Fasajadal-Malāaʾikatu kulluhum ʾajmaʿūn. (73) ʾIllāa ʾIblīsas-takbara wa kāna minal-kāfirīn. (74) Qāla yāa ʾIblīsu mā manaʿaka ʾañ-tasjuda limā khalaqtu biyadayy. ʾAstakbarta ʾam kuñta minal-ʿālīn. (75) Qāla ʾana khayrum-minhu khalaqtanī miñ-nāriñw-wa khalaqtahū miñ-ṭīn. (76) Qāla fakhruj minhā faʾinnaka rajīm. (77) Wa ʾinna ʿalayka laʿnatīi ʾilā Yawmid-Dīn. (78) Qāla Rabbi faʾañẓirnīi ʾilā Yawmi yubʿathūn. (79)

53 Lit., "otherwise than that I be (*illā annamā anā*) a plain warner" – i.e., of the prospect of spiritual self-destruction inherent in a wilful disregard of the fact of God's existence and oneness, which is the core of all religious cognition and, hence, of all true prophethood.

54 For this rendering of *idh*, see *sūrah* 2, note 21.

55 See note 24 on 15 : 26.

56 See 15 : 29 and the corresponding note 26.

57 See note 26 on 2 : 34 and note 31 on 15 : 41.

58 Cf. the metaphorical phrase "the things which Our hands have wrought" in 36 : 71, explained in the corresponding note 41. In the present instance, the stress lies on the God-willed superiority of man's intellect – which, like everything else in the universe, is God's "handiwork" – over the rest of creation (see note 25 on 2 : 34).

59 This "question" is, of course, only rhetorical, since God is omniscient. The phrase interpolated by me ("to bow down before another created being") reflects Zamakhsharī's interpretation of this passage.

60 I.e., out of something non-corporeal and, therefore (in the view of Iblīs), superior to the "clay" out of which man has been created. Inasmuch as "fire" is a symbol of passion, the above "saying" of Iblīs contains, I believe, a subtle allusion to the Qurʾanic concept of the "satanic forces" (*shayāṭīn*) active within man's own heart: forces engendered by uncontrolled passions and love of self, symbolized by the preceding characterization of Iblīs, the foremost of the *shayāṭīn* as "one of those who think only of themselves as high" (*min al-ʿālīn*).

Answered He: "Verily, so [be it:] thou shalt be among those who are granted respite ‹80› till the Day the time whereof is known [only to Me]."[61] ‹81›
[Whereupon Iblīs] said: "Then [I swear] by Thy very might: I shall most certainly beguile them all into grievous error ‹82› – [all] save such of them as are truly Thy servants!" ‹83›
[And God] said: "This, then, is the truth![62] And this truth do I state: ‹84› Most certainly will I fill hell with thee and such of them as shall follow thee, all together!" ‹85›

SAY [O Prophet]: "No reward whatever do I ask of you for this [message]; and I am not one of those who claim to be what they are not.[63] ‹86› This [divine writ], behold, is no less than a reminder to all the worlds ‹87› – and you will most certainly grasp its purport after a lapse of time!" ‹88›

قَالَ فَإِنَّكَ مِنَ ٱلۡمُنظَرِينَ ﴿٨٠﴾ إِلَىٰ يَوۡمِ ٱلۡوَقۡتِ ٱلۡمَعۡلُومِ ﴿٨١﴾ قَالَ
فَبِعِزَّتِكَ لَأُغۡوِيَنَّهُمۡ أَجۡمَعِينَ ﴿٨٢﴾ إِلَّا عِبَادَكَ مِنۡهُمُ ٱلۡمُخۡلَصِينَ ﴿٨٣﴾
قَالَ فَٱلۡحَقُّ وَٱلۡحَقَّ أَقُولُ ﴿٨٤﴾ لَأَمۡلَأَنَّ جَهَنَّمَ مِنكَ وَمِمَّن تَبِعَكَ مِنۡهُمۡ
أَجۡمَعِينَ ﴿٨٥﴾ قُلۡ مَآ أَسۡـَٔلُكُمۡ عَلَيۡهِ مِنۡ أَجۡرٖ وَمَآ أَنَا۠ مِنَ
ٱلۡمُتَكَلِّفِينَ ﴿٨٦﴾ إِنۡ هُوَ إِلَّا ذِكۡرٞ لِّلۡعَٰلَمِينَ ﴿٨٧﴾ وَلَتَعۡلَمُنَّ نَبَأَهُۥ بَعۡدَ
حِينِۭ ﴿٨٨﴾

Qāla faʾinnaka minal-muñẓarīna, (80) ʾilā Yawmil-waqtil-maʿlūm. (81) Qāla fabiʿizzatika laʾughwiyannahum ʾajmaʿīna, (82) ʾillā ʿibādaka minhumul-mukhlaṣīn. (83) Qāla falḥaqqu wal-ḥaqqa ʾaqūl. (84) Laʾamlaʾanna jahannama miñka wa mimmañtabiʿaka minhum ʾajmaʿīn. (85) Qul māa ʾasʾalukum ʿalayhi min ʾajriñw-wa māa ʾana minal-mutakallifīn. (86) ʾIn huwa ʾillā Dhikrul-lilʿālamīn. (87) Wa lataʿlamunna nabaʾahū baʿda ḥīn. (88)

61 The grant of "respite" to Iblīs implies that he would have the power to tempt man until the end of time.
62 Cf. 15 : 41 – "This is, with Me, a straight way" – and the corresponding note 31.
63 The expression *mutakallif* denotes, primarily, "a person who takes too much upon himself", be it in action or in feeling; hence, a person who pretends to be more than he really is, or to feel what he does not really feel. In this instance, it indicates the Prophet's disclaimer of any "supernatural" status.

The Thirty-Ninth Sūrah

Az-Zumar (The Throngs)

Mecca Period

REVEALED in the middle of the Mecca period, this *sūrah* derives its title from the incidental mention of the word *zumaran* ("in throngs") in verses 71 and 73. Its central theme is the evidence, in all manifestations of nature, of God's existence and oneness – from which it follows that He alone can determine man's fate, and that it is to Him that man is ultimately responsible. A pivotal idea is expressed in verse 53 – "O you servants of Mine who have transgressed against your own selves! Despair not of God's mercy: behold, God forgives all sins", i.e., to him who repents before his death. Hence, a large part of the *sūrah* consists of allegories of the Last Hour and the Day of Judgment – for "in this way does God imbue His servants with fear" (verse 16), just as He promises the righteous that "all that they have ever yearned for awaits them with their Sustainer" (verse 34).

-39-
سورة الزمر مكية
وآياتها خمس وسبعون

IN THE NAME OF GOD, THE MOST GRACIOUS, THE DISPENSER OF GRACE:

THE BESTOWAL from on high of this divine writ issues from God, the Almighty, the Wise: ‹1› for, behold, it is We who have bestowed this revelation upon thee from on high, setting forth the truth: so worship Him, sincere in thy faith in God alone! ‹2›

Is it not to God alone that all sincere faith is due?

And yet, they who take for their protectors aught beside Him [are wont to say], "We worship them for no other reason than that they bring us nearer to God."[1]

Behold, God will judge between them[2] [on Resurrection Day] with regard to all wherein they differ [from the truth]: for, verily, God does not grace with His guidance anyone who is bent on lying [to himself[3] and is] stubbornly ingrate! ‹3›

Had God willed to take unto Himself a son, He could have chosen anyone that He wanted out of whatever He has created – [but] limitless is He in His glory![4] He is the One God, the One who holds absolute sway over all that exists! ‹4›

بِسْمِ ٱللَّهِ ٱلرَّحْمَٰنِ ٱلرَّحِيمِ

تَنزِيلُ ٱلْكِتَٰبِ مِنَ ٱللَّهِ ٱلْعَزِيزِ ٱلْحَكِيمِ ﴿١﴾ إِنَّآ أَنزَلْنَآ إِلَيْكَ
ٱلْكِتَٰبَ بِٱلْحَقِّ فَٱعْبُدِ ٱللَّهَ مُخْلِصًا لَّهُ ٱلدِّينَ ﴿٢﴾ أَلَا لِلَّهِ ٱلدِّينُ
ٱلْخَالِصُ وَٱلَّذِينَ ٱتَّخَذُوا۟ مِن دُونِهِۦٓ أَوْلِيَآءَ مَا نَعْبُدُهُمْ إِلَّا لِيُقَرِّبُونَآ إِلَى
ٱللَّهِ زُلْفَىٰٓ إِنَّ ٱللَّهَ يَحْكُمُ بَيْنَهُمْ فِى مَا هُمْ فِيهِ يَخْتَلِفُونَ إِنَّ ٱللَّهَ لَا يَهْدِى
مَنْ هُوَ كَٰذِبٌ كَفَّارٌ ﴿٣﴾ لَّوْ أَرَادَ ٱللَّهُ أَن يَتَّخِذَ وَلَدًا لَّٱصْطَفَىٰ مِمَّا
يَخْلُقُ مَا يَشَآءُ سُبْحَٰنَهُۥ هُوَ ٱللَّهُ ٱلْوَٰحِدُ ٱلْقَهَّارُ ﴿٤﴾

Bismil-lāhir-Raḥmānir-Raḥīm.

Tañzīlul-Kitābi minal-lāhil-ᶜAzīzil-Ḥakīm. (1) ᵓInnāa ᵓañzalnāa ᵓilaykal-Kitāba bil-ḥaqqi faᶜbudil-lāha mukhliṣal-lahud-dīn. (2) ᵓAlā lillāhid-dīnul-khāliṣ. Wal-ladhīnat-takhadhū miñ-dūnihīi ᵓawliyāaᵓa mā naᶜbuduhum ᵓillā liyuqarribūnāa ᵓilal-lāhi zulfāa ᵓinnal-lāha yaḥkumu baynahum fī mā hum fīhi yakhtalifūn. ᵓInnal-lāha lā yahdī man huwa kādhibuñ-kaffār. (3) Law ᵓarādal-lāhu ᵓañy-yattakhidha waladal-laṣṭafā mimmā yakhluqu mā yashāaᵓ. Subḥānahū Huwal-lāhul-Wāḥidul-Qahhār. (4)

---

1 This relates not only to the worship of saints, angels and "deified" persons as such, but also to that of their symbolic representations (statues, pictures, relics, etc.) and, in the case of defunct human personalities, of their real or reputed tombs. Since all such practices are based on the worshipper's hope of "mediation" between himself and God, they obviously conflict with the concept of His omniscience and justice, and are, therefore – notwithstanding their widespread occurrence – utterly rejected by the Qurᵓān.

2 I.e., between those worshippers and the spiritual leaders who have led them astray (cf. 34 : 31-33).

3 Cf. 6 : 22-24 and the corresponding notes.

4 The implication is this: Since God is almighty, He can have or do anything that He wills; and so, if He wanted, He could "take unto Himself a son" (which is an allusion to the Christian doctrine of Jesus as "the son of God"). Since, however, He is "limitless in His glory" – i.e., complete in His excellence and utterly remote from all imperfection – He is *ipso facto* remote from the incompleteness inherent in the need of, or desire for, progeny, which logically precludes the possibility of His having a "son". (Cf. the last sentence of 6 : 100 and the corresponding note 88.)

خَلَقَ ٱلسَّمَٰوَٰتِ وَٱلْأَرْضَ بِٱلْحَقِّ ۖ يُكَوِّرُ ٱلَّيْلَ عَلَى ٱلنَّهَارِ وَيُكَوِّرُ
ٱلنَّهَارَ عَلَى ٱلَّيْلِ ۖ وَسَخَّرَ ٱلشَّمْسَ وَٱلْقَمَرَ ۖ كُلٌّ يَجْرِى لِأَجَلٍ مُّسَمًّى ۗ أَلَا
هُوَ ٱلْعَزِيزُ ٱلْغَفَّٰرُ ﴿٥﴾ خَلَقَكُم مِّن نَّفْسٍ وَٰحِدَةٍ ثُمَّ جَعَلَ مِنْهَا
زَوْجَهَا وَأَنزَلَ لَكُم مِّنَ ٱلْأَنْعَٰمِ ثَمَٰنِيَةَ أَزْوَٰجٍ ۚ يَخْلُقُكُمْ فِى بُطُونِ
أُمَّهَٰتِكُمْ خَلْقًا مِّنۢ بَعْدِ خَلْقٍ فِى ظُلُمَٰتٍ ثَلَٰثٍ ۚ ذَٰلِكُمُ ٱللَّهُ رَبُّكُمْ لَهُ
ٱلْمُلْكُ ۖ لَآ إِلَٰهَ إِلَّا هُوَ ۖ فَأَنَّىٰ تُصْرَفُونَ ﴿٦﴾ إِن تَكْفُرُوا۟ فَإِنَّ ٱللَّهَ غَنِىٌّ
عَنكُمْ ۖ وَلَا يَرْضَىٰ لِعِبَادِهِ ٱلْكُفْرَ ۖ وَإِن تَشْكُرُوا۟ يَرْضَهُ لَكُمْ ۗ وَلَا تَزِرُ
وَازِرَةٌ وِزْرَ أُخْرَىٰ ۗ ثُمَّ إِلَىٰ رَبِّكُم مَّرْجِعُكُمْ فَيُنَبِّئُكُم بِمَا كُنتُمْ تَعْمَلُونَ
إِنَّهُۥ عَلِيمٌۢ بِذَاتِ ٱلصُّدُورِ ﴿٧﴾

Khalaqas-samāwāti wal-ʾarḍa bil-ḥaqq. Yukawwirul-layla ʿalan-nahāri wa yukawwirun-nahāra ʿalal-layli wa sakhkharash-shamsa wal-qamara kulluñy-yajrī liʾajalim-musammā. ʾAlā Huwal-ʿAzīzul-Ghaffār. (5) Khalaqakum-miñ-nafsiñw-wāḥidatiñ-thumma jaʿala minhā zawjahā wa ʾañzala lakum-minal-ʾanʿāmi thamāniyata ʾazwāj. Yakhluqukum fī buṭūni ʾummahātikum khalqam-mim-baʿdi khalqiñ-fī ẓulumātiñ-thalāth. Dhālikumul-lāhu Rabbukum lahul-mulku lāa ʾilāha ʾillā Huwa faʾannā tuṣrafūn. (6) ʾIñ-takfurū faʾinnal-lāha Ghaniyyun ʿañkum; wa lā yarḍā liʿibādihil-kufra wa ʾiñ-tashkurū yarḍahu lakum. Wa lā taziru wāziratuñw-wizra ʾukhrā. Thumma ʾilā Rabbikum-marjiʿukum fayunabbiʾukum-bimā kuñtum taʿmalūn. ʾInnahū ʿAlīmum-bidhātiṣ-ṣudūr. (7)

He it is who has created the heavens and the earth in accordance with [an inner] truth.[5] He causes the night to flow into the day, and causes the day to flow into the night; and He has made the sun and the moon subservient [to His laws], each running its course for a term set [by Him].[6]

Is not He the Almighty, the All-Forgiving? «5»

He has created you [all] out of one living entity, and out of it fashioned its mate;[7] and he has bestowed upon you four kinds of cattle of either sex;[8] [and] He creates you in your mothers' wombs, one act of creation after another, in threefold depths of darkness.[9]

Thus is God, your Sustainer: unto Him belongs all dominion: there is no deity save Him: how, then, can you lose sight of the truth?[10] «6»

If you are ingrate[11] – behold, God has no need of you; none the less, He does not approve of ingratitude in His servants: whereas, if you show gratitude, He approves it in you.

And no bearer of burdens shall be made to bear another's burden.[12]

In time, unto your Sustainer you all must return, and then He will make you [truly] understand all that you were doing [in life]: for, verily, He has full knowledge of what is in the hearts [of men]. «7»

5 See note 11 on the last but one sentence of 10 : 5.

6 See note 5 on 13 : 2.

7 See 4 : 1 and the corresponding note 1.

8 Lit., "eight [in] pairs", i.e., the male and the female of four kinds of cattle (sheep, goats, camels and bovine cattle). For an explanation of my rendering, see note 130 on 6 : 143-144, where the same kinds of domesticated cattle are spoken of in connection with certain meaningless, superstitious taboos of pre-Islamic times, whereas here they are mentioned as "bestowed upon you" by God, and therefore lawful. Beyond this, the mention of cattle in this context is meant to remind man that it is God who provides his sustenance and that, therefore, man is utterly dependent on Him.

9 Lit., "by creation after creation, in three darknesses": an allusion to the successive stages of embryonic development, repeatedly spoken of in the Qurʾān (cf. 22 : 5 and 23 : 12-14), and to the darkness of the womb, the membrane enveloping the embryo, and its pre-natal blindness.

10 Lit., "how, then, are you turned away?" – i.e., from the truth.

11 Or: "If you deny the truth".

12 This statement occurs in the Qurʾān five times in exactly the same formulation (apart from the above instance, in 6 : 164, 17 : 15, 35 : 18 and 53 : 38 – this last being the earliest in the chronology of revelation). In the present instance, it contains an allusion to (and rejection of) the Christian doctrine of "vicarious atonement" and, indirectly, to the worship of saints, etc., spoken of in verse 3 above and referred to in note 1. (See also note 31 on 53 : 38.)

NOW [thus it is:] when affliction befalls man, he is likely to cry out[13] to his Sustainer, turning unto Him [for help]; but as soon as He has bestowed upon him a boon by His grace, he forgets Him whom he invoked before, and claims that there are other powers that could rival God[14] – and thus leads [others] astray from His path.

Say [unto him who sins in this way]: "Enjoy thyself for a while in this thy denial of the truth; [yet,] verily, thou art of those who are destined for the fire! ‹8› Or [dost thou deem thyself equal to] one who devoutly worships [God] throughout the night, prostrating himself or standing [in prayer], evermindful of the life to come, and hoping for his Sustainer's grace?"[15]

Say: "Can they who know and they who do not know be deemed equal?"

[But] only they who are endowed with insight keep this in mind! ‹9›

Say: "[Thus speaks God:[16]] 'O you servants of Mine who have attained to faith! Be conscious of your Sustainer! Ultimate good awaits those who persevere in doing good in this world. And [remember:] wide is God's earth,[17] [and,] verily, they who are patient in adversity will be given their reward in full, beyond all reckoning!" ‹10›

Say [O Muḥammad]: "Behold, I am bidden to worship God, sincere in my faith in Him alone; ‹11› and I am bidden to be foremost among those who surrender themselves unto God." ‹12›

Say: "Behold, I would dread, were I to rebel against my Sustainer, the suffering [which would befall me] on that awesome Day [of Judgment]." ‹13›

۞ وَإِذَا مَسَّ ٱلْإِنسَٰنَ ضُرٌّ دَعَا رَبَّهُۥ مُنِيبًا إِلَيْهِ ثُمَّ إِذَا خَوَّلَهُۥ نِعْمَةً مِّنْهُ
نَسِىَ مَا كَانَ يَدْعُوٓا۟ إِلَيْهِ مِن قَبْلُ وَجَعَلَ لِلَّهِ أَندَادًا لِّيُضِلَّ عَن سَبِيلِهِۦ ۚ قُلْ
تَمَتَّعْ بِكُفْرِكَ قَلِيلًا ۖ إِنَّكَ مِنْ أَصْحَٰبِ ٱلنَّارِ ﴿٨﴾ أَمَّنْ هُوَ قَٰنِتٌ ءَانَآءَ
ٱلَّيْلِ سَاجِدًا وَقَآئِمًا يَحْذَرُ ٱلْءَاخِرَةَ وَيَرْجُوا۟ رَحْمَةَ رَبِّهِۦ ۗ قُلْ هَلْ يَسْتَوِى
ٱلَّذِينَ يَعْلَمُونَ وَٱلَّذِينَ لَا يَعْلَمُونَ ۗ إِنَّمَا يَتَذَكَّرُ أُو۟لُوا۟ ٱلْأَلْبَٰبِ ﴿٩﴾ قُلْ
يَٰعِبَادِ ٱلَّذِينَ ءَامَنُوا۟ ٱتَّقُوا۟ رَبَّكُمْ ۚ لِلَّذِينَ أَحْسَنُوا۟ فِى هَٰذِهِ ٱلدُّنْيَا حَسَنَةٌ ۗ
وَأَرْضُ ٱللَّهِ وَٰسِعَةٌ ۗ إِنَّمَا يُوَفَّى ٱلصَّٰبِرُونَ أَجْرَهُم بِغَيْرِ حِسَابٍ ﴿١٠﴾ قُلْ
إِنِّىٓ أُمِرْتُ أَنْ أَعْبُدَ ٱللَّهَ مُخْلِصًا لَّهُ ٱلدِّينَ ﴿١١﴾ وَأُمِرْتُ لِأَنْ أَكُونَ أَوَّلَ
ٱلْمُسْلِمِينَ ﴿١٢﴾ قُلْ إِنِّىٓ أَخَافُ إِنْ عَصَيْتُ رَبِّى عَذَابَ يَوْمٍ عَظِيمٍ ﴿١٣﴾

ثلاثة ارباع الحزب

۞ Wa ʾidhā massal-ʾInsāna ḍurruñ-daʿā Rabbahū munīban ʾilayhi thumma ʾidhā khawwalahū niʿmatam-minhu nasiya mā kāna yadʿūu ʾilayhi miñ-qablu wa jaʿala lillāhi ʾañdādal-liyuḍilla ʿañ-sabīlih. Qul tamattaʿ bikufrika qalīlan ʾinnaka min ʾaṣḥābin-nār. (8) ʾAmman huwa qānitun ʾānāaʾal-layli sājidañw-wa qāaʾimañy-yaḥdharul-ʾĀkhirata wa yarjū raḥmata Rabbih. Qul hal yastawil-ladhīna yaʿlamūna wal-ladhīna lā yaʿlamūn. ʾInnamā yatadhakkaru ʾulul-ʾalbāb. (9) Qul yā ʿibādil-ladhīna ʾāmanut-taqū Rabbakum; lilladhīna ʾaḥsanū fī hādhihid-dunyā ḥasanah. Wa ʾarḍul-lāhi wāsiʿah. ʾInnamā yuwaffaṣ-ṣābirūna ʾajrahum bighayri ḥisāb. (10) Qul ʾinnīi ʾumirtu ʾan ʾaʿbudal-lāha mukhliṣal-lahud-dīn. (11) Wa ʾumirtu liʾan ʾakūna ʾawwalal-Muslimīn. (12) Qul ʾinnīi ʾakhāfu ʾin ʿaṣaytu Rabbī ʿadhāba Yawmin ʿaẓīm. (13)

13 Lit., "he cries out", i.e., instinctively, and as a rule.

14 Lit., "and gives God compeers (*andād*, sing. *nidd*)". Cf. the last sentence of 2 : 22 and the corresponding note 13.

15 Alternatively, the above verse could be rendered thus: "Is, perchance, he who worships . . . hoping for his Sustainer's grace, [equal to one who denies the truth]?"

16 This interpolation is justified by the fact that the possessive pronoun in the subsequent phrase "servants of Mine" obviously relates to God.

17 I.e., there is always a possibility of doing good and "migrating from evil unto God" – which is the permanent, spiritual connotation of the concept of *hijrah* implied here: see note 124 on 4 : 97.

Say: "God alone do I worship, sincere in my faith in Him alone ‹14› – and [it is up to you, O sinners, to] worship whatever you please instead of Him!"

Say: "Behold, the [true] losers will be they who shall have lost their own selves and their kith and kin on Resurrection Day:[18] for is not this, this, the [most] obvious loss? ‹15› Clouds of fire will they have above them, and [similar] clouds beneath them. . . ."

In this way does God imbue His servants with fear.[19]

O you servants of Mine! Be, then, conscious of Me ‹16› – seeing that for those who shun the powers of evil lest they [be tempted to] worship them,[20] and turn unto God instead, there is the glad tiding [of happiness in the life to come].[21]

Give, then, this glad tiding to [those of] My servants ‹17› who listen [closely] to all that is said, and follow the best of it:[22] [for] it is they whom God has graced with His guidance, and it is they who are [truly] endowed with insight! ‹18›

On the other hand,[23] could one on whom [God's] sentence of suffering has been passed [be rescued by man]? Couldst thou, perchance, save one who is [already, as it were,] in the fire?[24] ‹19›

قُلِ ٱللَّهَ أَعۡبُدُ مُخۡلِصٗا لَّهُۥ دِينِي ﴿١٤﴾ فَٱعۡبُدُواْ مَا شِئۡتُم مِّن دُونِهِۦۗ قُلۡ إِنَّ
ٱلۡخَٰسِرِينَ ٱلَّذِينَ خَسِرُوٓاْ أَنفُسَهُمۡ وَأَهۡلِيهِمۡ يَوۡمَ ٱلۡقِيَٰمَةِۗ أَلَا ذَٰلِكَ هُوَ
ٱلۡخُسۡرَانُ ٱلۡمُبِينُ ﴿١٥﴾ لَهُم مِّن فَوۡقِهِمۡ ظُلَلٞ مِّنَ ٱلنَّارِ وَمِن تَحۡتِهِمۡ
ظُلَلٞۚ ذَٰلِكَ يُخَوِّفُ ٱللَّهُ بِهِۦ عِبَادَهُۥۚ يَٰعِبَادِ فَٱتَّقُونِ ﴿١٦﴾ وَٱلَّذِينَ
ٱجۡتَنَبُواْ ٱلطَّٰغُوتَ أَن يَعۡبُدُوهَا وَأَنَابُوٓاْ إِلَى ٱللَّهِ لَهُمُ ٱلۡبُشۡرَىٰۚ فَبَشِّرۡ
عِبَادِ ﴿١٧﴾ ٱلَّذِينَ يَسۡتَمِعُونَ ٱلۡقَوۡلَ فَيَتَّبِعُونَ أَحۡسَنَهُۥٓۚ أُوْلَٰٓئِكَ ٱلَّذِينَ
هَدَىٰهُمُ ٱللَّهُۖ وَأُوْلَٰٓئِكَ هُمۡ أُوْلُواْ ٱلۡأَلۡبَٰبِ ﴿١٨﴾ أَفَمَنۡ حَقَّ عَلَيۡهِ كَلِمَةُ
ٱلۡعَذَابِ أَفَأَنتَ تُنقِذُ مَن فِي ٱلنَّارِ ﴿١٩﴾

Qulil-lāha ʾaʿbudu mukhliṣal-lahū dīnī. (14) Faʿbudū mā shiʾtum miñ-dūnih. Qul ʾinnal-khāsirīnal-ladhīna khasirūu ʾañfusahum wa ʾahlīhim Yawmal-Qiyāmah. ʾAlā dhālika huwal-khusrānul-mubīn. (15) Lahum-miñ-fawqihim ẓulalum-minan-nāri wa miñ-taḥtihim ẓulal. Dhālika yukhawwiful-lāhu bihī ʿibādah. Yā ʿibādi fattaqūn. (16) Wal-ladhīnaj-tanabuṭ-ṭāgūta ʾañy-yaʿbudūhā wa ʾanābūu ʾilal-lāhi lahumul-bushrā; fabashshir ʿibād. (17) ʾAladhīna yastamiʿūnal-qawla fayattabiʿūna ʾaḥsanah. ʾUlāaʾikal-ladhīna hadāhumul-lāhu wa ʾulāaʾika hum ʾulul-ʾalbāb. (18) ʾAfaman ḥaqqa ʿalayhi kalimatul-ʿadhābi ʾafaʾañta tuñqidhu mañ-fin-nār. (19)

18 Implying that on Resurrection Day they will be irretrievably separated from all whom they had loved, and all who had been close to them in this world. The "loss of one's own self" signifies, I think, the destruction of one's true identity and uniqueness as a human being, which is described in the next clause as "the most obvious loss" that man may be made to suffer in the life to come.

19 As in many other instances, the Qurʾān alludes in this phrase to the allegorical nature as well as to the real purpose of all descriptions of the suffering which awaits the sinners in the hereafter; cf. 74 : 35-36 – "that [hell-fire] is indeed one of the great [forewarnings]: a warning to mortal man".

20 For my rendering of *aṭ-ṭāghūt* as "powers of evil", see *sūrah* 2, note 250. In the present context, this term apparently circumscribes the seductive force of certain evil ambitions or desires – like striving after power for its own sake, acquisition of wealth by exploiting one's fellow-beings, social advancement by all manner of immoral means, and so forth – any of which may cause man to lose all spiritual orientation, and to be enslaved by his passions.

21 Cf. 10 : 62-64.

22 According to Rāzī, this describes people who examine every religious proposition (in the widest sense of this term) in the light of their own reason, accepting that which their mind finds to be valid or possible, and rejecting all that does not measure up to the test of reason. In Rāzī's words, the above verse expresses "a praise and commendation of following the evidence supplied by one's reason (*ḥujjat al-ʿaql*), and of reaching one's conclusions in accordance with [the results of] critical examination (*naẓar*) and logical inference (*istidlāl*)." A somewhat similar view is advanced, albeit in simpler terms, by Ṭabarī.

23 This, to my mind, is the meaning of the prefix *fa* in *fa-man* – stressing, by implication, the contrast between the glad tiding given to those who have attained to faith and the suffering which awaits those "who shall have lost their own selves" through sinning (verses 15-16).

24 In view of the repeated Qurʾanic statements that God always accepts a sinner's sincere repentance, provided it

لَٰكِنِ ٱلَّذِينَ ٱتَّقَوۡاْ رَبَّهُمۡ لَهُمۡ غُرَفٞ مِّن فَوۡقِهَا غُرَفٞ مَّبۡنِيَّةٞ تَجۡرِي مِن
تَحۡتِهَا ٱلۡأَنۡهَٰرُۖ وَعۡدَ ٱللَّهِۖ لَا يُخۡلِفُ ٱللَّهُ ٱلۡمِيعَادَ ﴿٢٠﴾ أَلَمۡ تَرَ أَنَّ ٱللَّهَ
أَنزَلَ مِنَ ٱلسَّمَآءِ مَآءٗ فَسَلَكَهُۥ يَنَٰبِيعَ فِي ٱلۡأَرۡضِ ثُمَّ يُخۡرِجُ بِهِۦ زَرۡعٗا
مُّخۡتَلِفًا أَلۡوَٰنُهُۥ ثُمَّ يَهِيجُ فَتَرَىٰهُ مُصۡفَرّٗا ثُمَّ يَجۡعَلُهُۥ حُطَٰمًاۚ إِنَّ فِي ذَٰلِكَ
لَذِكۡرَىٰ لِأُوْلِي ٱلۡأَلۡبَٰبِ ﴿٢١﴾ أَفَمَن شَرَحَ ٱللَّهُ صَدۡرَهُۥ لِلۡإِسۡلَٰمِ فَهُوَ
عَلَىٰ نُورٖ مِّن رَّبِّهِۦۚ فَوَيۡلٞ لِّلۡقَٰسِيَةِ قُلُوبُهُم مِّن ذِكۡرِ ٱللَّهِۚ أُوْلَٰٓئِكَ فِي
ضَلَٰلٖ مُّبِينٍ ﴿٢٢﴾ ٱللَّهُ نَزَّلَ أَحۡسَنَ ٱلۡحَدِيثِ كِتَٰبٗا مُّتَشَٰبِهٗا مَّثَانِيَ تَقۡشَعِرُّ
مِنۡهُ جُلُودُ ٱلَّذِينَ يَخۡشَوۡنَ رَبَّهُمۡ ثُمَّ تَلِينُ جُلُودُهُمۡ وَقُلُوبُهُمۡ إِلَىٰ ذِكۡرِ ٱللَّهِۚ

Lākinil-ladhīnat-taqaw Rabbahum lahum ghurafum-miñ-fawqihā ghurafum-mabniyyatuñ-tajrī miñ-taḥtihal-ʾanhār. Waʿdal-lāhi lā yukhliful-lāhul-mīʿād. (20) ʾAlam tara ʾannal-lāha añzala minas-samāaʾi māaʾañ-fasalakahū yanābīʿa fil-ʾarḍi thumma yukhriju bihī zarʿam-mukhtalifan ʾalwānuhū thumma yahīju fatarāhu muṣfarrañ-thumma yajʿaluhū ḥuṭāmā. ʾInna fī dhālika ladhikrā liʾulil-ʾalbāb. (21) ʾAfamañ-sharaḥal-lāhu ṣadrahū lilʾIslāmi fahuwa ʿalā nūrim-mir-Rabbih. Fawaylul-lilqāsiyati qulūbuhum-miñ-dhikril-lāh. ʾUlāaʾika fī ḍalālim-mubīn. (22) ʾAllāhu nazzala ʾaḥsanal-ḥadīthi Kitābam-mutashābiham-mathāniya taqshaʿirru minhu julūdul-ladhīna yakhshawna Rabbahum thumma talīnu julūduhum wa qulūbuhum ʾilā dhikril-lāh.

As against this,[25] they who of their Sustainer are conscious shall [in the life to come] have mansions raised upon mansions high, beneath which running waters flow: [this is] God's promise – [and] never does God fail to fulfil His promise. ‹20›

ART THOU NOT aware that it is God who sends down water from the skies, and then causes it to travel through the earth in the shape of springs? And then He brings forth thereby herbage of various hues; and then it withers, and thou canst see it turn yellow; and in the end He causes it to crumble to dust.[26]

Verily, in [all] this there is indeed a reminder to those who are endowed with insight! ‹21›

Could, then, one whose bosom God has opened wide with willingness towards self-surrender unto Him, so that he is illumined by a light [that flows] from his Sustainer, [be likened to the blind and deaf of heart]?

Woe, then, unto those whose hearts are hardened against all remembrance of God! They are most obviously lost in error! ‹22›

God bestows from on high[27] the best of all teachings in the shape of a divine writ fully consistent within itself, repeating each statement [of the truth] in manifold forms[28] – [a divine writ] whereat shiver the skins of all who of their Sustainer stand in awe: [but] in the end their skins and their hearts do soften at the remembrance of [the grace of] God. . . .

---

is proffered before the hour of death, His ineluctable "sentence of suffering" obviously relates to such as die *without* repentance, and hence find themselves, as it were, "*already* in the fire".

25 Lit., "But" (*lākin*), indicating a return to the theme of verses 17-18.

26 As in many other instances, the above Qurʾanic reference to the endless transformations and the miraculous cycle of life and death in all nature serves to emphasize God's almightiness and, specifically, His power to resurrect the dead – thus alluding, indirectly, to the statement at the end of the preceding verse that "never does God fail to fulfil His promise".

27 Lit., "has been bestowing from on high", i.e., step by step. The verbal form *nazzala* indicates both gradualness and continuity in the process of divine revelation and may, therefore, be appropriately rendered by the use of the present tense.

28 This is the most acceptable meaning, in this context, of the term *mathānī* (pl. of *mathnā*), as explained by Zamakhsharī in his commentary on the above verse. Another possible meaning, preferred by Rāzī, is "pairing its

Such is God's guidance: He guides therewith him that wills [to be guided][29] – whereas he whom God lets go astray can never find any guide.[30] ‹23›

Could, then, one who shall have nothing but his [bare] face to protect him[31] from the awful suffering [that will befall him] on Resurrection Day [be likened to the God-conscious]?

[On that Day,] the evildoers will be told: "Taste [now] what you have earned [in life]!" ‹24›

Those who lived before them did [too] give the lie to the truth – whereupon suffering befell them without their having perceived whence it came: ‹25› and thus God let them taste ignominy [even] in the life of this world.[32] Yet [how] much greater will be the [sinners'] suffering in the life to come – if they [who now deny the truth] but knew it! ‹26›

THUS, INDEED, have We propounded unto men all kinds of parables in this Qur'ān,[33] so that they might bethink themselves; [and We have revealed it] ‹27› as a discourse in the Arabic tongue, free of all deviousness,[34] so that they might become conscious of God. ‹28›

[To this end,] God sets forth a parable: A man who has for his masters several partners,[35] [all of them] at variance with

ذَٰلِكَ هُدَى ٱللَّهِ يَهْدِى بِهِۦ مَن يَشَآءُ ۚ وَمَن يُضْلِلِ ٱللَّهُ فَمَا لَهُۥ مِنْ
هَادٍ ﴿٢٣﴾ أَفَمَن يَتَّقِى بِوَجْهِهِۦ سُوٓءَ ٱلْعَذَابِ يَوْمَ ٱلْقِيَٰمَةِ ۚ وَقِيلَ
لِلظَّٰلِمِينَ ذُوقُوا۟ مَا كُنتُمْ تَكْسِبُونَ ﴿٢٤﴾ كَذَّبَ ٱلَّذِينَ مِن قَبْلِهِمْ فَأَتَىٰهُمُ
ٱلْعَذَابُ مِنْ حَيْثُ لَا يَشْعُرُونَ ﴿٢٥﴾ فَأَذَاقَهُمُ ٱللَّهُ ٱلْخِزْىَ فِى ٱلْحَيَوٰةِ
ٱلدُّنْيَا ۖ وَلَعَذَابُ ٱلْءَاخِرَةِ أَكْبَرُ ۚ لَوْ كَانُوا۟ يَعْلَمُونَ ﴿٢٦﴾ وَلَقَدْ ضَرَبْنَا
لِلنَّاسِ فِى هَٰذَا ٱلْقُرْءَانِ مِن كُلِّ مَثَلٍ لَّعَلَّهُمْ يَتَذَكَّرُونَ ﴿٢٧﴾ قُرْءَانًا
عَرَبِيًّا غَيْرَ ذِى عِوَجٍ لَّعَلَّهُمْ يَتَّقُونَ ﴿٢٨﴾ ضَرَبَ ٱللَّهُ مَثَلًا رَّجُلًا فِيهِ شُرَكَآءُ

Dhālika hudal-lāhi yahdī bihī mañy-yashāa'. Wa mañy-yuḍlilil-lāhu famā lahū min hād. (23) 'Afamañy-yattaqī biwajhihī sūu'al-ʿadhābi Yawmal-Qiyāmah. Wa qīla liẓẓālimīna dhūqū mā kuñtum taksibūn. (24) Kadhdhabal-ladhīna miñ-qablihim fa'atā-humul-ʿadhābu min ḥaythu lā yashʿurūn. (25) Fa'adhā-qahumul-lāhul-khizya fil-ḥayātid-dunyā wa laʿadhābul-'Ākhirati 'akbaru law kānū yaʿlamūn. (26) Wa laqad ḍarabnā linnāsi fī hādhal-Qur'āni miñ-kulli mathalil-laʿallahum yatadhakkarūn. (27) Qur'ānan ʿarabiyyan ghayra dhī ʿiwajil-laʿallahum yattaqūn. (28) Ḍarabal-lāhu mathalar-rajulañ-fīhi shurakāa'u

statements", i.e., referring to the polarity stressed in all Qur'anic teachings (e.g., command and prohibition, duties and rights, reward and punishment, paradise and hell, light and darkness, the general and the specific, and so forth). As regards the inner consistency of the Qur'ān, see also 4 : 82 and 25 : 32, as well as the corresponding notes.

29 Or: "He guides therewith whomever He wills", either of these two formulations being syntactically correct.

30 See note 4 on 14 : 4.

31 Lit., "who will protect himself with his face": an idiomatic phrase implying that the person concerned has nothing whatever with which to protect himself.

32 Cf. 16 : 26, which contains the additional sentence, "God visited with destruction all that they had ever built . . .", etc., which explains the present reference to their suffering and ignominy "in the life of this world".

33 As in many other passages of the Qur'ān, the use of the term "parable" (*mathal*) immediately or shortly after a description of men's condition – whether good or bad – in the hereafter is meant to remind us that all such descriptions relate to something that is "beyond the reach of a created being's perception" (*al-ghayb*), and cannot, therefore, be conveyed to man otherwise than by means of allegories or parables expressed in terms of human experience and therefore accessible, in a general sense, to human imagination.

34 Lit., "without any deviousness (*ʿiwaj*)", i.e., which could obscure its meaning: see note 1 on 18 : 1, where this term occurs in a slightly different phrasing. As regards the stress on the formulation of this divine writ "in the Arabic tongue", see 12 : 2, 13 : 37, 14 : 4 and 41 : 44, as well as the corresponding notes.

35 Lit., "with regard to whom there are [several] partners (*shurakā'*)", i.e., as masters: a metaphor for belief in a plurality of divine powers.

مُتَشَـٰكِسُونَ وَرَجُلًا سَلَمًا لِّرَجُلٍ هَلْ يَسْتَوِيَانِ مَثَلًا ٱلْحَمْدُ لِلَّهِ بَلْ
أَكْثَرُهُمْ لَا يَعْلَمُونَ (29) إِنَّكَ مَيِّتٌ وَإِنَّهُم مَّيِّتُونَ (30) ثُمَّ إِنَّكُمْ يَوْمَ
ٱلْقِيَـٰمَةِ عِندَ رَبِّكُمْ تَخْتَصِمُونَ (31) ۞ فَمَنْ أَظْلَمُ مِمَّن كَذَبَ عَلَى ٱللَّهِ
وَكَذَّبَ بِٱلصِّدْقِ إِذْ جَآءَهُۥٓ أَلَيْسَ فِى جَهَنَّمَ مَثْوًى لِّلْكَـٰفِرِينَ (32)
وَٱلَّذِى جَآءَ بِٱلصِّدْقِ وَصَدَّقَ بِهِۦٓ أُو۟لَـٰٓئِكَ هُمُ ٱلْمُتَّقُونَ (33) لَهُم
مَّا يَشَآءُونَ عِندَ رَبِّهِمْ ذَٰلِكَ جَزَآءُ ٱلْمُحْسِنِينَ (34) لِيُكَفِّرَ ٱللَّهُ
عَنْهُمْ أَسْوَأَ ٱلَّذِى عَمِلُوا۟ وَيَجْزِيَهُمْ أَجْرَهُم بِأَحْسَنِ ٱلَّذِى كَانُوا۟
يَعْمَلُونَ (35) أَلَيْسَ ٱللَّهُ بِكَافٍ عَبْدَهُۥ وَيُخَوِّفُونَكَ بِٱلَّذِينَ مِن دُونِهِۦ حزب 47 جزء 24

mutashākisūna wa rajulañ-salamal-lirajulin hal yastawiyāni mathalā. ʾAlḥamdu lillāhi bal ʾaktharuhum lā yaʿlamūn. (29) ʾInnaka mayyituñw-wa ʾinnahum-mayyitūn. (30) Thumma ʾinnakum Yawmal-Qiyāmati ʿiñda Rabbikum takhtaṣimūn. (31) ۞ Faman ʾaẓlamu mimmañ-kadhaba ʿalal-lāhi wa kadhdhaba biṣṣidqi ʾidh jāaʾah. ʾAlaysa fī jahannama mathwal-lilkāfirīn. (32) Wal-ladhī jāaʾa biṣṣidqi wa ṣaddaqa bihīi ʾulāaʾika humul-muttaqūn. (33) Lahum-mā yashāaʾūna ʿiñda Rabbihim; dhālika jazāaʾul-muḥsinīn. (34) Liyukaffiral-lāhu ʿanhum ʾaswaʾal-ladhī ʿamilū wa yajziyahum ʾajrahum biʾaḥsanil-ladhī kānū yaʿmalūn. (35) ʾAlaysal-lāhu bikāfin ʿabdah. Wa yukhawwifūnaka billadhīna miñ-dūnih.

one another, and a man depending wholly on one person: can these two be deemed equal as regards their condition?[36]
[Nay,] all praise is due to God [alone]: but most of them do not understand this. ‹29›
Yet, verily, thou art bound to die, [O Muḥammad,] and, verily, they, too, are bound to die: ‹30› and then, behold, on the Day of Resurrection you all shall place your dispute before your Sustainer. ‹31›
And who could be more wicked than he who invents lies about God,[37] and gives the lie to the truth as soon as it has been placed before him? Is not hell the [proper] abode for all who deny the truth?[38] ‹32›
But he who brings the truth, and he who wholeheartedly accepts it as true – it is they, they, who are [truly] conscious of Him! ‹33›
All that they have ever yearned for awaits them with their Sustainer: such will be the reward of the doers of good. ‹34› And to this end, God will efface from their record the worst that they ever did, and give them their reward in accordance with the best that they were doing [in life]. ‹35›

IS NOT God enough for His servant? And yet, they would frighten thee with those [imaginary divine powers which they worship] beside Him![39]

36 The term *mathal,* which is usually rendered by me as "parable" (e.g., at the beginning of this verse as well as in verse 27), primarily denotes a "likeness", i.e., of one thing to another; but sometimes it is used tropically as a synonym for *ṣifah* (the "quality", "intrinsic attribute" or "nature" of a thing) or *ḥālah* (its "state" or "condition"). In the present instance, the last-mentioned of these meanings is most appropriate, inasmuch as it alludes to man's condition arising from either of two contrasting attitudes: a belief in God's transcendental oneness and uniqueness, on the one hand, and a readiness to ascribe divine powers and qualities to a variety of created beings or supposed "incarnations" of God, on the other.

37 In this instance, the "inventing of lies about God" alludes to the attribution of a share in His divinity to anyone or anything beside Him, whether it be a belief in a plurality of deities, or in an imaginary "incarnation" of God in human form, or in saints allegedly endowed with semi-divine powers.

38 Lit., "Is not in hell an abode . . .", etc.: a rhetorical question indicating, firstly, that otherworldly suffering is the unavoidable destiny – symbolically, "an abode" – of all such sinners; and, secondly, that in the concept and picture of "hell" we are given an allegory of that self-caused suffering.

39 Or: "instead of Him". This relates not merely to false deities, but also to saints alive or dead, and even to certain abstract concepts which the popular mind endows with charismatic qualities – like wealth, power, social status, national or racial pre-eminence, the idea of man's "self-sufficiency", etc. – and, finally, to all false values which are allowed to dominate man's thoughts and desires. The godless always stress the supposed necessity of paying attention to all these imaginary forces and values, and frighten themselves and their fellow-men by the thought that a neglect to do so might have evil consequences in their practical life.

وَمَن يُضْلِلِ ٱللَّهُ فَمَا لَهُۥ مِنْ هَادٍ ﴿٣٦﴾ وَمَن يَهْدِ ٱللَّهُ فَمَا لَهُۥ مِن مُّضِلٍّ
أَلَيْسَ ٱللَّهُ بِعَزِيزٍ ذِى ٱنتِقَامٍ ﴿٣٧﴾ وَلَئِن سَأَلْتَهُم مَّنْ خَلَقَ ٱلسَّمَٰوَٰتِ
وَٱلْأَرْضَ لَيَقُولُنَّ ٱللَّهُ قُلْ أَفَرَءَيْتُم مَّا تَدْعُونَ مِن دُونِ ٱللَّهِ إِنْ أَرَادَنِىَ
ٱللَّهُ بِضُرٍّ هَلْ هُنَّ كَٰشِفَٰتُ ضُرِّهِۦٓ أَوْ أَرَادَنِى بِرَحْمَةٍ هَلْ هُنَّ مُمْسِكَٰتُ
رَحْمَتِهِۦ قُلْ حَسْبِىَ ٱللَّهُ عَلَيْهِ يَتَوَكَّلُ ٱلْمُتَوَكِّلُونَ ﴿٣٨﴾ قُلْ يَٰقَوْمِ
ٱعْمَلُوا۟ عَلَىٰ مَكَانَتِكُمْ إِنِّى عَٰمِلٌ فَسَوْفَ تَعْلَمُونَ ﴿٣٩﴾ مَن يَأْتِيهِ
عَذَابٌ يُخْزِيهِ وَيَحِلُّ عَلَيْهِ عَذَابٌ مُّقِيمٌ ﴿٤٠﴾ إِنَّآ أَنزَلْنَا عَلَيْكَ ٱلْكِتَٰبَ
لِلنَّاسِ بِٱلْحَقِّ فَمَنِ ٱهْتَدَىٰ فَلِنَفْسِهِۦ وَمَن ضَلَّ فَإِنَّمَا يَضِلُّ عَلَيْهَا
وَمَآ أَنتَ عَلَيْهِم بِوَكِيلٍ ﴿٤١﴾ ٱللَّهُ يَتَوَفَّى ٱلْأَنفُسَ حِينَ مَوْتِهَا وَٱلَّتِى

Wa mañy-yuḍlilil-lāhu famā lahū min hād. (36) Wa mañy-yahdil-lāhu famā lahū mim-muḍill. ᵓAlaysal-lāhu biᶜAzīziñ-Dhiñ-tiqām. (37) Wa laᵓiñ-saᵓaltahum-man-khalaqas-samāwāti wal-ᵓarḍa layaqūlunnal-lāh. Qul ᵓafaraᵓaytum-mā tadᶜūna miñ-dūnil-lāhi ᵓin ᵓarādaniyal-lāhu biḍurrin hal hunna kāshifātu ḍurrihīi ᵓaw ᵓarādanī biraḥmatin hal hunna mumsikātu raḥmatih. Qul ḥasbiyal-lāhu ᶜalayhi yatawakkalul-mutawakkilūn. (38) Qul yā qawmiᶜ-malū ᶜalā makānatikum ᵓinnī ᶜāmiluñ-fasawfa taᶜlamūna, (39) mañy-yaᵓtīhi ᶜadhābuñy-yukhzīhi wa yaḥillu ᶜalayhi ᶜadhābum-muqīm. (40) ᵓInnāa ᵓañzalnā ᶜalaykal-Kitāba linnāsi bilḥaqq. Famanih-tadā falinafsihī wa mañ-ḍalla faᵓinnamā yaḍillu ᶜalayhā; wa māa ᵓañta ᶜalayhim biwakīl. (41) ᵓAllāhu yatawaffal-ᵓañfusa ḥīna mawtihā wal-latī

But he whom God lets go astray can never find any guide, ‹36› whereas he whom God guides aright can never be led astray. Is not God almighty, an avenger of evil? ‹37›

And thus it is [with most people]: if[40] thou ask them, "Who is it that has created the heavens and the earth?" – they will surely answer, "God."[41]

Say: "Have you, then, ever considered what it is that you invoke instead of God? If God wills that harm should befall me, could those [imaginary powers] remove the harm inflicted by Him? Or, if He wills that grace should alight on me, could they withhold His grace [from me]?".

Say: "God is enough for me! In Him [alone] place their trust all who have trust [in His existence]." ‹38›

Say: "O my [truth-denying] people! Do yet all that may be within your power, [whereas] I, behold, shall labour [in God's way]: in time you will come to know ‹39› who it is that shall be visited [in this world] by suffering which will cover him with ignominy,[42] and upon whom long-lasting suffering shall alight [in the life to come]!" ‹40›

BEHOLD, from on high have We bestowed upon thee this divine writ, setting forth the truth for [the benefit of all] mankind. And whoever chooses to be guided [thereby], does so for his own good, and whoever chooses to go astray, goes but astray to his own hurt; and thou hast not the power to determine their fate.[43] ‹41›

It is God [alone that has this power – He] who causes all human beings to die at the time of their [bodily] death, and [causes to be as dead], during their sleep, those that

40 For this rendering of *laᵓin*, see *sūrah* 11, note 11.

41 See note 23 on 31 : 25.

42 Lit., "suffering (*ᶜadhāb*) that will disgrace him": implying that surrender to false values inevitably leads to man's spiritual decay and, if persisted in by many, to social catastrophes and widespread suffering.

43 Or: "thou art not responsible for their conduct" (see note 4 on 17 : 2).

have not yet died:[44] thus, He withholds [from life] those upon whom He has decreed death, and lets the others go free for a term set [by Him].

In [all] this, behold, there are messages indeed for people who think! ⟨42⟩

And yet,[45] they choose [to worship], side by side with God, [imaginary] intercessors![46]

Say: "Why – even though they have no power over anything, and no understanding?"[47] ⟨43⟩

Say: "God's alone is [the power to bestow the right of] intercession:[48] His [alone] is the dominion over the heavens and the earth; and, in the end, unto Him you will all be brought back." ⟨44⟩

And yet, whenever God alone is mentioned, the hearts of those who will not believe in the life to come contract with bitter aversion – whereas, when those [imaginary powers] are mentioned side by side with Him, lo, they rejoice![49] ⟨45⟩

Say: "O God! Originator of the heavens and the earth! Knower of all that is beyond the reach of a created being's perception, as well as of all that can be witnessed by a creature's senses or mind![50]

لَمْ تَمُتْ فِى مَنَامِهَا فَيُمْسِكُ ٱلَّتِى قَضَىٰ عَلَيْهَا ٱلْمَوْتَ وَيُرْسِلُ ٱلْأُخْرَىٰ إِلَىٰٓ أَجَلٍ مُّسَمًّى إِنَّ فِى ذَٰلِكَ لَءَايَٰتٍ لِقَوْمٍ يَتَفَكَّرُونَ ٤٢ أَمِ ٱتَّخَذُوا۟ مِن دُونِ ٱللَّهِ شُفَعَآءَ قُلْ أَوَلَوْ كَانُوا۟ لَا يَمْلِكُونَ شَيْـًٔا وَلَا يَعْقِلُونَ ٤٣ قُل لِّلَّهِ ٱلشَّفَٰعَةُ جَمِيعًا لَّهُۥ مُلْكُ ٱلسَّمَٰوَٰتِ وَٱلْأَرْضِ ثُمَّ إِلَيْهِ تُرْجَعُونَ ٤٤ وَإِذَا ذُكِرَ ٱللَّهُ وَحْدَهُ ٱشْمَأَزَّتْ قُلُوبُ ٱلَّذِينَ لَا يُؤْمِنُونَ بِٱلْءَاخِرَةِ وَإِذَا ذُكِرَ ٱلَّذِينَ مِن دُونِهِۦٓ إِذَا هُمْ يَسْتَبْشِرُونَ ٤٥ قُلِ ٱللَّهُمَّ فَاطِرَ ٱلسَّمَٰوَٰتِ وَٱلْأَرْضِ عَٰلِمَ ٱلْغَيْبِ وَٱلشَّهَٰدَةِ

lam tamut fī manāmihā fayumsikul-latī qaḍā ʿalayhal-mawta wa yursilul-ʾukhrāa ʾilāa ʾajalim-musammā. ʾInna fī dhālika laʾĀyātil-liqawmiñy-yatafakkarūn. ⟨42⟩ ʾAmit-takhadhū miñ-dūnil-lāhi shufaʿāaʾ. Qul ʾawa law kānū lā yamlikūna shayʾañw-wa lā yaʿqilūn. ⟨43⟩ Qul lillāhish-shafāʿatu jamīʿā. Lahū mulkus-samāwāti wal-ʾarḍi thumma ʾilayhi turjaʿūn. ⟨44⟩ Wa ʾidhā dhukiral-lāhu waḥdahush-maʾazzat qulūbul-ladhīna lā yuʾminūna bilʾĀkhirah. Wa ʾidhā dhukiral-ladhīna miñ-dūnihīi ʾidhā hum yastabshirūn. ⟨45⟩ Qulil-lāhumma Fāṭiras-samāwāti wal-ʾarḍi ʿĀlimal-ghaybi wash-shahādati

---

44 According to Rāzī, this passage connects allegorically with the preceding – the light of guidance being likened to life, and man's going astray, to death or, if it is not permanent, to death-like sleep followed by awakening. Beyond this, however, we have here a reminder – in tune with the subsequent passages – of God's almightiness, and especially of His exclusive power to create and to withdraw life. As to the operative verb *yatawaffā*, it primarily denotes "He takes [something] away in full"; and because death is characterized by a disappearance of all vital impulses (the "soul") from the once-living body – their being "taken away in full", as it were – this form of the verb has been used tropically, since time immemorial, in the sense of "causing to die", and (in its intransitive form) "dying" or (as a noun) "death": a usage invariably adhered to in the Qurʾān. The traditional likening of sleep to death is due to the fact that in both cases the body appears to be devoid of consciousness, partially and temporarily in the former case, and completely and permanently in the latter. (The popular translation of *anfus* – pl. of *nafs* – as "souls" is certainly inappropriate in the above context, since, according to the fundamental teaching of the Qurʾān, man's soul does not "die" at the time of his bodily death but, on the contrary, lives on indefinitely. Hence, the term *anfus* must be rendered here as "human beings".)

45 This is the meaning of the particle *am* in this context (Zamakhsharī), implying that despite all the evidence of God's almightiness, many people tend to disregard it.

46 I.e., intercessors who could act as such independently of God's permission – an assumption which the Qurʾān categorically denies (see *sūrah* 10, note 7).

47 A reference to the adoration of dead saints or their tombs or relics, as well as of inanimate representations of saints, of imaginary deities, etc.

48 Regarding the problem of intercession as such, see note 7 on 10 : 3.

49 Since a cognition of God must have a sense of moral responsibility as its correlate, the godless shrink from it, and joyfully turn to the "worship" – real or metaphoric – of imaginary powers which make no such moral demand.

50 See *sūrah* 6, note 65.

It is Thou who wilt judge between Thy servants [on Resurrection Day] with regard to all on which they were wont to differ!" ‹46›

But if those who are bent on evildoing possessed all that is on earth, and twice as much,[51] they would surely offer it as ransom from the awful suffering [that will befall them] on the Day of Resurrection:[52] for, something with which they had not reckoned before will [by then] have been made obvious to them by God;[53] ‹47› and obvious to them will have become the evil that they had wrought [in life]: and thus shall they be overwhelmed by the very truth which they were wont to deride.[54] ‹48›

NOW [thus it is:] when affliction befalls man, he cries out unto Us for help; but when We bestow upon him a boon by Our grace, he says [to himself], "I have been given [all] this by virtue of [my own] wisdom!"[55]

Nay, this [bestowal of grace] is a trial: but most of them understand it not! ‹49›

The same did say [to themselves many of] those who lived before their time; but of no avail to them was all that they had ever achieved: ‹50› for all the evil deeds that they had wrought fell [back] upon them. And [the same will happen to] people of the present time who are bent

أَنتَ تَحْكُمُ بَيْنَ عِبَادِكَ فِى مَا كَانُوا۟ فِيهِ يَخْتَلِفُونَ ﴿٤٦﴾ وَلَوْ أَنَّ لِلَّذِينَ ظَلَمُوا۟
مَا فِى ٱلْأَرْضِ جَمِيعًا وَمِثْلَهُۥ مَعَهُۥ لَٱفْتَدَوْا۟ بِهِۦ مِن سُوٓءِ ٱلْعَذَابِ يَوْمَ
ٱلْقِيَـٰمَةِ ۚ وَبَدَا لَهُم مِّنَ ٱللَّهِ مَا لَمْ يَكُونُوا۟ يَحْتَسِبُونَ ﴿٤٧﴾ وَبَدَا لَهُمْ سَيِّـَٔاتُ مَا
كَسَبُوا۟ وَحَاقَ بِهِم مَّا كَانُوا۟ بِهِۦ يَسْتَهْزِءُونَ ﴿٤٨﴾ فَإِذَا مَسَّ ٱلْإِنسَـٰنَ ضُرٌّ
دَعَانَا ثُمَّ إِذَا خَوَّلْنَـٰهُ نِعْمَةً مِّنَّا قَالَ إِنَّمَآ أُوتِيتُهُۥ عَلَىٰ عِلْمٍۭ ۚ بَلْ هِىَ فِتْنَةٌ وَلَـٰكِنَّ
أَكْثَرَهُمْ لَا يَعْلَمُونَ ﴿٤٩﴾ قَدْ قَالَهَا ٱلَّذِينَ مِن قَبْلِهِمْ فَمَآ أَغْنَىٰ عَنْهُم مَّا كَانُوا۟
يَكْسِبُونَ ﴿٥٠﴾ فَأَصَابَهُمْ سَيِّـَٔاتُ مَا كَسَبُوا۟ ۚ وَٱلَّذِينَ ظَلَمُوا۟ مِنْ هَـٰٓؤُلَآءِ

ʾAñta taḥkumu bayna ʿibādika fī mā kānū fīhi yakhtalifūn. ﴿46﴾ Wa law ʾanna lilladhīna ẓalamū mā fil-ʾarḍi jamīʿañw-wa mithlahū maʿahū laftadaw bihī miñ-sūuʾil-ʿadhābi Yawmal-Qiyāmah. Wa badā lahum-minal-lāhi mā lam yakūnū yaḥtasibūn. ﴿47﴾ Wa badā lahum sayyiʾātu mā kasabū wa ḥāqa bihim-mā kānū bihī yastahziʾūn. ﴿48﴾ Faʾidhā massal-ʾIñsāna ḍurruñ-daʿānā thumma ʾidhā khawwalnāhu niʿmatam-minnā qāla ʾinnamāa ʾūtītuhū ʿalā ʿilm. Bal hiya fitnatuñw-wa lākinna ʾaktharahum lā yaʿlamūn. ﴿49﴾ Qad qālahal-ladhīna miñ-qablihim famāa ʾaghnā ʿanhum-mā kānū yaksibūn. ﴿50﴾ Faʾaṣābahum sayyiʾātu mā kasabū. Wal-ladhīna ẓalamū min hāaʾulāaʾi

51 Lit., "and the like of it with it".

52 Cf. 3 : 91 and the corresponding note 71.

53 Lit., "will have become obvious to them (*badā lahum*) from God" – i.e., the fact that man's attitudes and actions in this world determine his state and further development in the hereafter: in other words, that happiness or suffering in the life to come (allegorically described as "paradise" or "hell", and "reward" or "chastisement") are but natural consequences of the use which man makes in this life of his capabilities, endowments and opportunities.

54 Lit., "that which they were wont to deride will enfold them" or "will have enfolded them": i.e., the reality of life after death and of the spiritual truths preached by God's prophets will overwhelm them.

55 Lit., "knowledge" – i.e., "my prosperity is due to my own ability and shrewdness": see the first sentence of 28 : 78 and the corresponding note. But whereas there this "saying" or thought is attributed to the legendary Qārūn, in the present instance – which is by far the earlier in the chronology of Qurʾanic revelation – it is said to be characteristic of *man as such* (see, e.g., 7 : 189-190, where this tendency is referred to in connection with the experience of parenthood).

on wrongdoing:[56] all the evil deeds that they have ever wrought will fall [back] upon them, and never will they be able to elude [God]! ‹51›
Are they, then, not aware that it is God who grants abundant sustenance, or gives it in scant measure, unto whomever He wills?
In this, behold, there are messages indeed for people who will believe! ‹52›

SAY: "[Thus speaks God:[57]] 'O you servants of Mine who have transgressed against your own selves! Despair not of God's mercy: behold, God forgives all sins[58] – for, verily, He alone is much-forgiving, a dispenser of grace!'" ‹53›
Hence, turn towards your Sustainer [alone] and surrender yourselves unto Him ere the suffering [of death and resurrection] comes upon you, for then you will not be succoured.[59] ‹54› And ere that suffering comes upon you of a sudden, without your being aware [of its approach], follow the most goodly [teaching] that has been revealed unto you by your Sustainer, ‹55› lest any human being[60] should say [on Judgment Day], "Alas for me for having been remiss in what is due to God, and for having been indeed one of those who scoffed [at the truth]!" ‹56› – or lest he should say, "If God had but guided me, I would surely have been among those who are conscious of Him!" ‹57› – or lest he should say, when he becomes aware of the suffering [that awaits him], "Would that

سَيُصِيبُهُمْ سَيِّـَٔاتُ مَا كَسَبُواْ وَمَا هُم بِمُعْجِزِينَ (51) أَوَلَمْ يَعْلَمُوٓاْ أَنَّ
ٱللَّهَ يَبْسُطُ ٱلرِّزْقَ لِمَن يَشَآءُ وَيَقْدِرُ ۚ إِنَّ فِى ذَٰلِكَ لَأَيَـٰتٍ لِّقَوْمٍ
يُؤْمِنُونَ (52) ۞ قُلْ يَـٰعِبَادِىَ ٱلَّذِينَ أَسْرَفُواْ عَلَىٰٓ أَنفُسِهِمْ لَا تَقْنَطُواْ مِن
رَّحْمَةِ ٱللَّهِ ۚ إِنَّ ٱللَّهَ يَغْفِرُ ٱلذُّنُوبَ جَمِيعًا ۚ إِنَّهُۥ هُوَ ٱلْغَفُورُ ٱلرَّحِيمُ (53)
وَأَنِيبُوٓاْ إِلَىٰ رَبِّكُمْ وَأَسْلِمُواْ لَهُۥ مِن قَبْلِ أَن يَأْتِيَكُمُ ٱلْعَذَابُ ثُمَّ لَا
تُنصَرُونَ (54) وَٱتَّبِعُوٓاْ أَحْسَنَ مَآ أُنزِلَ إِلَيْكُم مِّن رَّبِّكُم مِّن قَبْلِ أَن
يَأْتِيَكُمُ ٱلْعَذَابُ بَغْتَةً وَأَنتُمْ لَا تَشْعُرُونَ (55) أَن تَقُولَ نَفْسٌ يَـٰحَسْرَتَىٰ
عَلَىٰ مَا فَرَّطتُ فِى جَنۢبِ ٱللَّهِ وَإِن كُنتُ لَمِنَ ٱلسَّـٰخِرِينَ (56) أَوْ تَقُولَ لَوْ
أَنَّ ٱللَّهَ هَدَىٰنِى لَكُنتُ مِنَ ٱلْمُتَّقِينَ (57) أَوْ تَقُولَ حِينَ تَرَى ٱلْعَذَابَ لَوْ أَنَّ

ربع الحزب

sayuṣībuhum sayyiʾātu mā kasabū wa mā hum-bimuʿjizīn. (51) ʾAwalam yaʿlamūu ʾannal-lāha yabsuṭur-rizqa limañy-yashāaʾu wa yaqdir. ʾInna fī dhālika laʾĀyātil-liqawmiñy-yuʾminūn. (52) ◈ Qul yā ʿibādiyal-ladhīna ʾasrafū ʿalāa ʾañfusihim lā taqnaṭū mir-raḥmatil-lāh. ʾInnal-lāha yaghfirudh-dhunūba jamīʿā. ʾInnahū Huwal-Ghafūrur-Raḥīm. (53) Wa ʾanībūu ʾilā Rabbikum wa ʾaslimū lahū miñ-qabli ʾañy-yaʾtiyakumul-ʿadhābu thumma lā tuñṣarūn. (54) Wat-tabiʿūu ʾaḥsana māa ʾuñzila ʾilaykum-mir-Rabbikum miñ-qabli ʾañy-yaʾtiyakumul-ʿadhābu baghtatañw-wa ʾañtum lā tashʿurūn. (55) ʾAñ-taqūla nafsuñy-yā ḥasratā ʿalā mā farraṭtu fī jambil-lāhi wa ʾiñ-kuñtu laminas-sākhirīn. (56) ʾAw taqūla law ʾannal-lāha hadānī lakuñtu minal-muttaqīn. (57) ʾAw taqūla ḥīna taral-ʿadhāba law ʾanna

56 Lit., "those who are bent on wrongdoing (*alladhīna ẓalamū*) from among these here".

57 See note 16 on the opening words of verse 10 of this *sūrah*.

58 Sc., "whenever the sinner repents and turns to Him": cf., for instance, 6 : 54 – "Your Sustainer has willed upon Himself the law of grace and mercy – so that if any of you does a bad deed out of ignorance, and thereafter repents and lives righteously, He shall be [found] much-forgiving, a dispenser of grace"; or 4 : 110 – "he who does evil or [otherwise] sins against himself, and thereafter prays God to forgive him, shall find God much-forgiving, a dispenser of grace".

59 Cf. 4 : 18 – "repentance shall not be accepted from those who do evil deeds until their dying hour, and then say, 'Behold, I now repent'; nor from those who die as deniers of the truth".

60 Whenever there is no clear indication that the term *nafs* has another meaning, it signifies a "human being"; hence, the personal pronouns relating to this term (which is feminine in Arabic) are masculine in my rendering.

لِي كَرَّةً فَأَكُونَ مِنَ ٱلْمُحْسِنِينَ ﴿٥٨﴾ بَلَىٰ قَدْ جَآءَتْكَ ءَايَٰتِى فَكَذَّبْتَ
بِهَا وَٱسْتَكْبَرْتَ وَكُنتَ مِنَ ٱلْكَٰفِرِينَ ﴿٥٩﴾ وَيَوْمَ ٱلْقِيَٰمَةِ تَرَى
ٱلَّذِينَ كَذَبُوا۟ عَلَى ٱللَّهِ وُجُوهُهُم مُّسْوَدَّةٌ ۚ أَلَيْسَ فِى جَهَنَّمَ مَثْوًى
لِّلْمُتَكَبِّرِينَ ﴿٦٠﴾ وَيُنَجِّى ٱللَّهُ ٱلَّذِينَ ٱتَّقَوْا۟ بِمَفَازَتِهِمْ لَا يَمَسُّهُمُ ٱلسُّوٓءُ
وَلَا هُمْ يَحْزَنُونَ ﴿٦١﴾ ٱللَّهُ خَٰلِقُ كُلِّ شَىْءٍ ۖ وَهُوَ عَلَىٰ كُلِّ شَىْءٍ
وَكِيلٌ ﴿٦٢﴾ لَّهُۥ مَقَالِيدُ ٱلسَّمَٰوَٰتِ وَٱلْأَرْضِ ۗ وَٱلَّذِينَ كَفَرُوا۟ بِـَٔايَٰتِ
ٱللَّهِ أُو۟لَٰٓئِكَ هُمُ ٱلْخَٰسِرُونَ ﴿٦٣﴾ قُلْ أَفَغَيْرَ ٱللَّهِ تَأْمُرُوٓنِّىٓ أَعْبُدُ أَيُّهَا
ٱلْجَٰهِلُونَ ﴿٦٤﴾ وَلَقَدْ أُوحِىَ إِلَيْكَ وَإِلَى ٱلَّذِينَ مِن قَبْلِكَ لَئِنْ أَشْرَكْتَ

lī karratañ-fa'akūna minal-muḥsinīn. ﴿58﴾ Balā qad jāa'atka 'Āyātī fakadhdhabta bihā was-takbarta wa kuñta minal-kāfirīn. ﴿59﴾ Wa Yawmal-Qiyāmati taral-ladhīna kadhabū ʿalal-lāhi wujūhuhum muswaddah. 'Alaysa fī jahannama mathwal-lilmutakabbirīn. ﴿60﴾ Wa yunajjil-lāhul-ladhīnat-taqaw bimafāzatihim lā yamassuhumus-sūu'u wa lā hum yaḥzanūn. ﴿61﴾ 'Allāhu Khāliqu kulli shay'iñw-wa Huwa ʿalā kulli shay'iñw-Wakīl. ﴿62﴾ Lahū maqālīdus-samāwāti wal-'arḍ. Wal-ladhīna kafarū bi'Āyātil-lāhi 'ulāa'ika hu-mul-khāsirūn. ﴿63﴾ Qul 'afaghayral-lāhi ta'murūunnīi 'aʿbudu 'ayyuhal-jāhilūn. ﴿64﴾ Wa laqad 'ūḥiya 'ilayka wa 'ilal-ladhīna miñ-qablika la'in 'ashrakta

I had a second chance [in life], so that I could be among the doers of good!"[61] ‹58›

[But God will reply:] "Yea, indeed! My messages did come unto thee; but thou gavest them the lie, and wert filled with false pride, and wert among those who deny the truth!" ‹59›

And [so,] on the Day of Resurrection thou wilt see all who invented lies about God [with] their faces darkened [by grief and ignominy].[62] Is not hell the [proper] abode for all who are given to false pride?[63] ‹60›

But God will safeguard all who were conscious of Him, [and will grant them happiness] by virtue of their [inner] triumphs; no evil shall ever touch them, and neither shall they grieve. ‹61›

GOD is the Creator of all things, and He alone has the power to determine the fate of all things.[64] ‹62›

His are the keys [to the mysteries] of the heavens and the earth: and they who are bent on denying the truth of God's messages – it is they, they, who are the losers! ‹63›

Say: "Is it, then, something other than God that you bid me to worship, O you who are unaware [of right and wrong]?" ‹64›

And yet, it has already been revealed to thee [O man,][65] as well as to those who lived before thee, that if thou ever ascribe divine powers to aught but God,

61 Cf. 2 : 167 and 26 : 102, as well as 6 : 27-28 and the corresponding note 19.

62 The phrase *iswadda wajhuhu* (lit., "his face became black" or "dark") is used idiomatically to describe a face expressive of grief or ignominy (cf. 16 : 58), just as its opposite, *ibyaḍḍa wajhuhu* (lit., "his face became white" or "shining") describes a countenance expressive of happiness or justified pride: cf. 3 : 106 – "some faces will shine [with happiness] and some faces will be dark [with grief]". Apart from this, both phrases have also a tropical significance, namely, "he became [or "felt"] disgraced", resp. "honoured". – As regards the "inventing of lies about God" spoken of in this verse, see note 37 above.

63 See note 38 on the last sentence of verse 32 of this *sūrah*.

64 For the meaning of the term *wakīl* in this context, see note 4 on 17 : 2.

65 I.e., "it has been conveyed to thee through the divine messages revealed to the prophets". The assumption of almost all the classical commentators that this passage is addressed to Muḥammad does not make much sense in view of God's knowledge that neither he nor any of the prophets who came before him would ever commit the deadly sin (referred to in the sequence) of "ascribing divine powers to aught beside God". On the other hand, the above reminder becomes very cogent and relevant as soon as it is conceived as being addressed to man in general, irrespective of time and circumstance.

all thy works shall most certainly have been in vain: for [in the life to come] thou shalt most certainly be among the lost. «65»
Nay, but thou shalt worship God [alone], and be among those who are grateful [to Him]! «66»
And no true understanding of God have they [who worship aught beside Him], inasmuch as the whole of the earth will be as a [mere] handful to Him on Resurrection Day, and the heavens will be rolled up in His right hand:[66] limitless is He in His glory, and sublimely exalted above anything to which they may ascribe a share in His divinity! «67»
And [on that Day,] the trumpet [of judgment] will be sounded, and all [creatures] that are in the heavens and all that are on earth will fall down senseless, unless they be such as God wills [to exempt].[67]
And then it will sound again – and lo! standing [before the Seat of Judgment], they will begin to see [the truth]![68] «68»
And the earth will shine bright with her Sustainer's light.[69] And the record [of everyone's deeds] will be laid bare,[70] and all the prophets will be brought forward, and all [other] witnesses;[71] and judgment will be passed on them all in justice.

لَيَحْبَطَنَّ عَمَلُكَ وَلَتَكُونَنَّ مِنَ ٱلْخَـٰسِرِينَ ﴿٦٥﴾ بَلِ ٱللَّهَ فَٱعْبُدْ وَكُن مِّنَ
ٱلشَّـٰكِرِينَ ﴿٦٦﴾ وَمَا قَدَرُوا۟ ٱللَّهَ حَقَّ قَدْرِهِۦ وَٱلْأَرْضُ جَمِيعًا قَبْضَتُهُۥ يَوْمَ
ٱلْقِيَـٰمَةِ وَٱلسَّمَـٰوَٰتُ مَطْوِيَّـٰتٌۢ بِيَمِينِهِۦ ۚ سُبْحَـٰنَهُۥ وَتَعَـٰلَىٰ عَمَّا يُشْرِكُونَ ﴿٦٧﴾
وَنُفِخَ فِى ٱلصُّورِ فَصَعِقَ مَن فِى ٱلسَّمَـٰوَٰتِ وَمَن فِى ٱلْأَرْضِ إِلَّا مَن شَآءَ
ٱللَّهُ ۖ ثُمَّ نُفِخَ فِيهِ أُخْرَىٰ فَإِذَا هُمْ قِيَامٌ يَنظُرُونَ ﴿٦٨﴾ وَأَشْرَقَتِ ٱلْأَرْضُ بِنُورِ
رَبِّهَا وَوُضِعَ ٱلْكِتَـٰبُ وَجِا۟ىٓءَ بِٱلنَّبِيِّـۧنَ وَٱلشُّهَدَآءِ وَقُضِىَ بَيْنَهُم بِٱلْحَقِّ

layaḥbaṭanna ᶜamaluka wa latakūnanna minal-khāsirīn. ﴿65﴾ Balil-lāha faᶜbud wa kum-minash-shākirīn. ﴿66﴾ Wa mā qadarul-lāha ḥaqqa qadrihī wal-ᵓarḍu jamīᶜañ-qabḍatuhū Yawmal-Qiyāmati was-samāwātu maṭwiyyātum-biyamīnih. Subḥānahū wa taᶜālā ᶜammā yushrikūn. ﴿67﴾ Wa nufikha fiṣ-ṣūri faṣaᶜiqa mañ-fis-samāwāti wa mañ-fil-ᵓarḍi ᵓillā mañ-shāaᵓal-lāh. Thumma nufikha fīhi ᵓukhrā faᵓidhā hum qiyāmuñy-yañẓurūn. ﴿68﴾ Wa ᵓashraqatil-ᵓarḍu binūri Rabbihā wa wuḍiᶜal-Kitābu wa jīiᵓa bin-Nabiy-yīna wash-shuhadāaᵓi wa quḍiya baynahum bilḥaqqi

66 I.e., the whole universe is as nothing before Him: for this specific allegory of God's almightiness, see 21 : 104. There are many instances, in the Qurᵓān as well as in authentic *aḥādīth*, of the clearly metaphorical use of the term "hand" in allusions to God's absolute power and dominion. The particular reference, in the above, to the Day of Resurrection is due to the fact that it will be only on his own resurrection that a human being shall fully grasp the concept of God's almightiness, referred to in the subsequent words, "limitless is He in His glory (*subḥānahu*)".

67 As is evident from 27 : 89, the above is an allusion to the unbroken spiritual life in this world – and, therefore, happiness in the hereafter – of those who have attained to faith and have done righteous deeds. Cf. 21 : 103 – "the supreme awesomeness [of the Day of Resurrection] will cause them no grief".

68 Cf. 37 : 19.

69 I.e., with a clear revelation of His will. See also 14 : 48, where it is stated that on Resurrection Day "the earth shall be changed into another earth, as shall be the heavens". A further allusion to this transformation (and *not* annihilation) of the universe is found in 20 : 105-107

70 Cf. 17 : 13-14 (and the corresponding note 18); also 18 : 49.

71 See 4 : 41 and the corresponding note 52. Accordingly, the above phrase may well have the meaning of "all the prophets *as* witnesses", i.e., for or against those to whom they conveyed God's message. In all probability, however, the term *shuhadāᵓ* (or *ashhād* in 40 : 51) signifies here – as its singular *shahīd* obviously does in 50 : 21 – man's newly-awakened consciousness, which will compel him to bear witness against himself on Judgment Day (cf. 6 : 130, 17 : 14, 24 : 24, 36 : 65, 41 : 20 ff.).

وَهُمْ لَا يُظْلَمُونَ ﴿٦٩﴾ وَوُفِّيَتْ كُلُّ نَفْسٍ مَّا عَمِلَتْ وَهُوَ أَعْلَمُ بِمَا
يَفْعَلُونَ ﴿٧٠﴾ وَسِيقَ ٱلَّذِينَ كَفَرُوٓاْ إِلَىٰ جَهَنَّمَ زُمَرًا حَتَّىٰٓ إِذَا جَآءُوهَا
فُتِحَتْ أَبْوَٰبُهَا وَقَالَ لَهُمْ خَزَنَتُهَآ أَلَمْ يَأْتِكُمْ رُسُلٌ مِّنكُمْ يَتْلُونَ
عَلَيْكُمْ ءَايَٰتِ رَبِّكُمْ وَيُنذِرُونَكُمْ لِقَآءَ يَوْمِكُمْ هَٰذَا قَالُواْ بَلَىٰ
وَلَٰكِنْ حَقَّتْ كَلِمَةُ ٱلْعَذَابِ عَلَى ٱلْكَٰفِرِينَ ﴿٧١﴾ قِيلَ ٱدْخُلُوٓاْ
أَبْوَٰبَ جَهَنَّمَ خَٰلِدِينَ فِيهَا فَبِئْسَ مَثْوَى ٱلْمُتَكَبِّرِينَ ﴿٧٢﴾ وَسِيقَ
ٱلَّذِينَ ٱتَّقَوْاْ رَبَّهُمْ إِلَى ٱلْجَنَّةِ زُمَرًا حَتَّىٰٓ إِذَا جَآءُوهَا وَفُتِحَتْ أَبْوَٰبُهَا
وَقَالَ لَهُمْ خَزَنَتُهَا سَلَٰمٌ عَلَيْكُمْ طِبْتُمْ فَٱدْخُلُوهَا خَٰلِدِينَ ﴿٧٣﴾ وَقَالُواْ
ٱلْحَمْدُ لِلَّهِ ٱلَّذِى صَدَقَنَا وَعْدَهُۥ وَأَوْرَثَنَا ٱلْأَرْضَ نَتَبَوَّأُ مِنَ ٱلْجَنَّةِ
حَيْثُ نَشَآءُ فَنِعْمَ أَجْرُ ٱلْعَٰمِلِينَ ﴿٧٤﴾

wa hum lā yuẓlamūn. (69) **Wa wuffiyat kullu nafsim-mā ʿamilat wa Huwa ʾaʿlamu bimā yafʿalūn.** (70) **Wa sīqal-ladhīna kafarūu ʾilā jahannama zumarā. Ḥattāa ʾidhā jāaʾūhā futiḥat ʾabwābuhā wa qāla lahum khazanatuhāa ʾalam yaʾtikum Rusulum-miñkum yatlūna ʿalaykum ʾĀyāti Rabbikum wa yuñdhirūnakum liqāaʾa Yawmikum hādhā. Qālū balā wa lākin ḥaqqat kalimatul-ʿadhābi ʿalal-kāfirīn.** (71) **Qīlad-khulūu ʾabwāba jahannama khālidīna fīhā fabiʾsa mathwal-mutakabbirīn.** (72) **Wa sīqal-ladhīnat-taqaw Rabbahum ʾilal-jannati zumarā. Ḥattāa ʾidhā jāaʾūhā wa futiḥat ʾabwābuhā wa qāla lahum khazanatuhā salāmun ʿalaykum ṭibtum fadkhulūhā khālidīn.** (73) **Wa qālul-ḥamdu lillāhil-ladhī ṣadaqanā waʿdahū wa ʾawrathanal-ʾarḍa natabawwaʾu minal-jannati ḥaythu nashāaʾu faniʿma ʾajrul-ʿāmilīn.** (74)

And they will not be wronged, «69» for every human being will be repaid in full for whatever [good or evil] he has done:[72] and He is fully aware of all that they do. «70»

And those who were bent on denying the truth will be urged on in throngs towards hell till, when they reach it, its gates will be opened, and its keepers will ask them, "Have there not come to you apostles from among yourselves, who conveyed to you your Sustainer's messages and warned you of the coming of this your Day [of Judgment]?"

They will answer: "Yea, indeed!"

But the sentence of suffering will [already] have fallen due upon the deniers of the truth;[73] «71» [and] they will be told, "Enter the gates of hell, therein to abide!"

And how vile an abode for those who were given to false pride![74] «72»

But those who were conscious of their Sustainer will be urged on in throngs towards paradise till, when they reach it, they shall find its gates wide-open;[75] and its keepers will say unto them, "Peace be upon you! Well have you done: enter, then, this [paradise], herein to abide!" «73»

And they will exclaim: "All praise is due to God, who has made His promise to us come true, and has bestowed upon us this expanse [of bliss] as our portion,[76] so that we may dwell in paradise as we please!"

And how excellent a reward will it be for those who laboured [in God's way]! «74»

---

72 Cf. 99 : 7-8, "he who shall have done an atom's weight of good, shall behold it; and he who shall have done an atom's weight of evil, shall behold it".

73 I.e., as an ineluctable consequence of their unrepented sinning.

74 Sc., "and therefore refused to submit to the guidance offered them by God's apostles": cf. 96 : 6-7 – "man becomes grossly overweening whenever he believes himself to be self-sufficient". See also 16 : 22 and the corresponding note 15.

75 Lit., "and its gates have [or "will have"] been opened", i.e., before their arrival, as indicated by the particle *wa* (lit., "and"), which in this case denotes precedence in time (Zamakhsharī). Cf. in this connection 38 : 50 – "gardens of perpetual bliss, with gates wide-open to them".

76 Lit., "has made us heirs to this land", i.e., of paradise. According to all the classical commentators, the concept of "heritage" is used here metaphorically, to denote the rightful due, or portion, of the blessed. The term *arḍ* (lit., "earth" or "land") has also – especially in poetry – the connotation of "anything that is spread" (cf. Lane I, 48): hence my rendering of it, in the above context, as "expanse".

And thou wilt see the angels surrounding the throne of [God's] almightiness,[77] extolling their Sustainer's glory and praise. And judgment will have been passed in justice on all [who had lived and died], and the word will be spoken:[78] "All praise is due to God, the Sustainer of all the worlds!" ‹75›

وَتَرَى ٱلْمَلَٰٓئِكَةَ حَآفِّينَ مِنْ حَوْلِ ٱلْعَرْشِ يُسَبِّحُونَ بِحَمْدِ رَبِّهِمْ وَقُضِىَ بَيْنَهُم بِٱلْحَقِّ وَقِيلَ ٱلْحَمْدُ لِلَّهِ رَبِّ ٱلْعَٰلَمِينَ ﴿٧٥﴾

Wa taral-Malāaᵓikata ḥāaffīna min ḥawlil-ᶜarshi yusabbiḥūna biḥamdi Rabbihim wa quḍiya baynahum bilḥaqqi wa qīlal-ḥamdu lillāhi Rabbil-ᶜālamīn. ‹75›

77 Whenever the term *al-ᶜarsh* ("the throne [of God]") occurs in the Qurᵓān, it is used as a metaphor for His absolute dominion over all that exists: hence my rendering, "the throne of [God's] almightiness". (See also 7 : 54 and the corresponding note 43.) The mention of the "angels surrounding" it has, obviously, a metaphorical meaning: see note 4 on 40 : 7.

78 Lit., "it will be said".

The Fortieth Sūrah

Ghāfir (Forgiving)

Mecca Period

THE MAIN THEME of this *sūrah* is that false pride which often makes man think that he is the centre of the universe, and thus impels him to remain smugly satisfied with his own, empirically-acquired knowledge (verse 83), to worship all manner of imaginary forces and false values seemingly helpful to human aggrandizement – like wealth, power, or even the conceit of "progress" – and to deny validity to any truth, however obvious, which runs counter to his sense of self-importance. The arrogant assumption that man is self-sufficient – an illusion already touched upon in verses 6-7 of one of the earliest Qur'anic revelations (*sūrah* 96) – brings with it the conviction that he is above all need of divine guidance, implying a rejection of the belief in resurrection and of God's ultimate judgment on "the Day of Reckoning" (verse 27). The opening chord of this theme appears in the statement that "none but those who are *bent* on denying the truth would call God's messages in question" (verse 4), and is developed in many variations throughout the *sūrah*: thus, "in their hearts is nothing but overweening self-conceit, which they will never be able to satisfy" (verse 56); and "perverted are the minds of those who knowingly reject God's messages" (verse 63) – for "God sets a seal on every arrogant, self-exalting heart" (verse 35), condemning it to spiritual blindness in this world and, as a consequence, to suffering in the life to come.

As so often in the Qur'ān, these ideas are illustrated by references to the stories of earlier prophets, and to what happened in the end to deniers of the truth in bygone times (verses 21-22 and 82 ff.) – "such being the way of God that has always obtained for His creatures" (verse 85).

The key-word by which the *sūrah* is known has been taken from verse 3, where God is spoken of as *ghāfir adh-dhanb* ("forgiving sins"): but it has also been designated as *Al-Mu'min* ("The Believer"), alluding to the "believing man of Pharaoh's family" who tried to convince his erring compatriots of the truth of Moses' mission.

All authorities agree that the present and the six successive *sūrahs* (all of which are prefixed with the letter-symbols *Ḥā-Mīm*) belong to the later part of the middle Mecca period.

سورة غافر مكية -40-
وآياتها خمس وثمانون

IN THE NAME OF GOD, THE MOST GRACIOUS, THE DISPENSER OF GRACE:

Ḥā. Mīm.[1] ‹1›
THE BESTOWAL from on high of this divine writ issues from God, the Almighty, the All-Knowing, ‹2› forgiving sins and accepting repentance, severe in retribution, limitless in His bounty.
There is no deity save Him: with Him is all journeys' end. ‹3›

NONE BUT THOSE who are bent on denying the truth would call God's messages in question. But let it not deceive thee that they seem to be able to do as they please on earth: ‹4› to the truth gave the lie, before their time, the people of Noah and, after them, all those [others] who were leagued together [against God's message-bearers];[2] and each of those communities schemed against the apostle sent unto them,[3] aiming to lay hands on him; and they contended [against his message] with fallacious arguments, so as to render void the truth thereby: but then I took them to task – and how awesome was My retribution! ‹5›
And thus shall thy Sustainer's word come true against all who are bent on denying the truth: they shall find themselves in the fire [of hell]. ‹6›

بِسۡمِ ٱللَّهِ ٱلرَّحۡمَٰنِ ٱلرَّحِيمِ

نصف الحزب

حمٓ ﴿١﴾ تَنزِيلُ ٱلۡكِتَٰبِ مِنَ ٱللَّهِ ٱلۡعَزِيزِ ٱلۡعَلِيمِ ﴿٢﴾ غَافِرِ ٱلذَّنۢبِ
وَقَابِلِ ٱلتَّوۡبِ شَدِيدِ ٱلۡعِقَابِ ذِي ٱلطَّوۡلِۖ لَآ إِلَٰهَ إِلَّا هُوَۖ إِلَيۡهِ
ٱلۡمَصِيرُ ﴿٣﴾ مَا يُجَٰدِلُ فِيٓ ءَايَٰتِ ٱللَّهِ إِلَّا ٱلَّذِينَ كَفَرُواْ فَلَا يَغۡرُرۡكَ
تَقَلُّبُهُمۡ فِي ٱلۡبِلَٰدِ ﴿٤﴾ كَذَّبَتۡ قَبۡلَهُمۡ قَوۡمُ نُوحٖ وَٱلۡأَحۡزَابُ مِنۢ بَعۡدِهِمۡۖ
وَهَمَّتۡ كُلُّ أُمَّةِۭ بِرَسُولِهِمۡ لِيَأۡخُذُوهُۖ وَجَٰدَلُواْ بِٱلۡبَٰطِلِ لِيُدۡحِضُواْ بِهِ
ٱلۡحَقَّ فَأَخَذۡتُهُمۡۖ فَكَيۡفَ كَانَ عِقَابِ ﴿٥﴾ وَكَذَٰلِكَ حَقَّتۡ كَلِمَتُ
رَبِّكَ عَلَى ٱلَّذِينَ كَفَرُوٓاْ أَنَّهُمۡ أَصۡحَٰبُ ٱلنَّارِ ﴿٦﴾

Bismil-lāhir-Raḥmānir-Raḥīm.
Ḥā-Mīim. (1) Tañzīlul-Kitābi minal-lāhil-ʿAzīzil-ʿAlīm. (2) Ghāfiridh-dhambi wa qābilit-tawbi shadīdil-ʿiqābi dhiṭ-ṭawl. Lāa ʾilāha ʾillā Huwa ʾilayhil-maṣīr. (3) Mā yujādilu fīi ʾĀyātil-lāhi ʾillal-ladhīna kafarū falā yaghrurka taqallubuhum fil-bilād. (4) Kadhdhabat qablahum qawmu Nūḥiñw-wal-ʾaḥzābu mim-baʿdihim; wa hammat kullu ʾummatim-biRasūlihim liyaʾkhudhūh. Wa jādalū bilbāṭili liyudḥiḍū bihil-ḥaqqa faʾakhadhtuhum; fakayfa kāna ʿiqāb. (5) Wa kadhālika ḥaqqat Kalimatu Rabbika ʿalal-ladhīna kafarūu ʾannahum ʾaṣḥābun-nār. (6)

---

1 See Appendix II.
2 Cf. 38 : 12-14, where some of those who were "leagued together" (*al-aḥzāb*) are enumerated; also verses 30 ff. of this *sūrah*.
3 Lit., "each community schemed against their apostle".

THEY WHO BEAR [within themselves the knowledge of] the throne of [God's] almightiness, as well as all who are near it,[4] extol their Sustainer's limitless glory and praise, and have faith in Him, and ask forgiveness for all [others] who have attained to faith:

"O our Sustainer! Thou embracest all things within [Thy] grace and knowledge: forgive, then, their sins unto those who repent and follow Thy path, and preserve them from suffering through the blazing fire! ‹7›

"And, O our Sustainer, bring them into the gardens of perpetual bliss[5] which Thou hast promised them, together with the righteous from among their forebears, and their spouses, and their offspring – for, verily, Thou alone art almighty, truly wise ‹8› – and preserve them from [doing] evil deeds: for anyone whom on that Day [of Judgment] Thou wilt have preserved from [the taint of] evil deeds, him wilt Thou have graced with Thy mercy: and that, that will be the triumph supreme!" ‹9›

[But,] behold, as for those who are bent on denying the truth – [on that same Day] a voice will call out unto them:[6] "Indeed, greater than your [present] loathing of yourselves[7] was God's loathing of you [at the time] when you were called unto faith but went on denying the truth!"[8] ‹10›

ٱلَّذِينَ يَحْمِلُونَ ٱلْعَرْشَ وَمَنْ حَوْلَهُۥ يُسَبِّحُونَ بِحَمْدِ رَبِّهِمْ وَيُؤْمِنُونَ بِهِۦ
وَيَسْتَغْفِرُونَ لِلَّذِينَ ءَامَنُوا۟ رَبَّنَا وَسِعْتَ كُلَّ شَىْءٍ رَّحْمَةً وَعِلْمًا فَٱغْفِرْ
لِلَّذِينَ تَابُوا۟ وَٱتَّبَعُوا۟ سَبِيلَكَ وَقِهِمْ عَذَابَ ٱلْجَحِيمِ ﴿٧﴾ رَبَّنَا وَأَدْخِلْهُمْ
جَنَّـٰتِ عَدْنٍ ٱلَّتِى وَعَدتَّهُمْ وَمَن صَلَحَ مِنْ ءَابَآئِهِمْ وَأَزْوَٰجِهِمْ
وَذُرِّيَّـٰتِهِمْ إِنَّكَ أَنتَ ٱلْعَزِيزُ ٱلْحَكِيمُ ﴿٨﴾ وَقِهِمُ ٱلسَّيِّـَٔاتِ وَمَن تَقِ
ٱلسَّيِّـَٔاتِ يَوْمَئِذٍ فَقَدْ رَحِمْتَهُۥ وَذَٰلِكَ هُوَ ٱلْفَوْزُ ٱلْعَظِيمُ ﴿٩﴾ إِنَّ ٱلَّذِينَ
كَفَرُوا۟ يُنَادَوْنَ لَمَقْتُ ٱللَّهِ أَكْبَرُ مِن مَّقْتِكُمْ أَنفُسَكُمْ إِذْ تُدْعَوْنَ إِلَى
ٱلْإِيمَـٰنِ فَتَكْفُرُونَ ﴿١٠﴾

ʾAlladhīna yaḥmilūnal-ʿarsha wa man ḥawlahū yusabbiḥūna biḥamdi Rabbihim wa yuʾminūna bihī wa yastaghfirūna lilladhīna ʾāmanū. Rabbanā wasiʿta kulla shayʾir-raḥmatañw-wa ʿilmañ-faghfir lilladhīna tābū wat-tabaʿū sabīlaka wa qihim ʿadhābal-jaḥīm. ⟨7⟩ Rabbanā wa ʾadkhilhum jannāti ʿadninil-latī waʿattahum wa mañ-ṣalaḥa min ʾābāaʾihim wa ʾazwājihim wa dhurriyyātihim. ʾInnaka ʾAñtal-ʿAzīzul-Ḥakīm. ⟨8⟩ Wa qihimus-sayyiʾāti wa mañ-taqis-sayyiʾāti Yawmaʾidhiñ-faqad raḥimtahu wa dhālika huwal-fawzul-ʿaẓīm. ⟨9⟩ ʾInnal-ladhīna kafarū yunādawna lamaqtul-lāhi ʾakbaru mim-maqtikum ʾañfusakum ʾidh tudʿawna ʾilal-ʾīmāni fatakfurūn. ⟨10⟩

---

4 Lit, "around it": cf. Zamakhsharī's explanation of the expression *ḥawlahā* occurring in 27 : 8 in the sense of "near it". In his commentary on the verse which we are now considering, Bayḍāwi states explicitly that the "bearing" of God's throne of almightiness (*al-ʿarsh* – see note 43 on 7 : 54) must be understood in a metaphorical sense: "Their carrying it and surrounding it [or "being near it"]" is a metaphor of their being mindful of it and acting in accordance therewith (*majāz ʿan ḥifẓihim wa-tadbīrihim lahu*), or a metonym (*kināyah*) for their closeness to the Lord of the Throne, their dignity in His sight, and their being instrumental in the realization of His will." My rendering of the above verse reflects Bayḍāwī's interpretation. – As regards the beings which are said to be close to the throne of God's almightiness, most of the classical commentators – obviously basing their view on the symbolic image of "the angels surrounding the throne of [God's] almightiness" on the Day of Judgment (39 : 75) – think in this instance, too, exclusively of angels. But whereas it cannot be denied that the present verse refers *also* to angels, it does not follow that it refers *exclusively* to them. In its abstract connotation, the verb *ḥamala* frequently signifies "he bore [or "took upon himself"] the *responsibility* [for something]": and so it is evident that it applies here not only to angels but also to all human beings who are conscious of the tremendous implications of the concept of God's almightiness, and hence feel morally responsible for translating this consciousness into the reality of their own and their fellow-beings' lives.

5 See note 45 on 38 : 50.

6 Lit., "they will be called" or "summoned".

7 I.e., "on realizing, belatedly, your past sinfulness".

8 Since it is impossible to attribute to God a purely human emotion, "God's loathing" of those sinners is obviously a metonym for His rejection of them (Rāzī), similar to the metonymic use of the expression "God's wrath (*ghaḍab*)" in the sense of His condemnation (see first sentence of note 4 on 1 : 7).

قَالُوا۟ رَبَّنَآ أَمَتَّنَا ٱثْنَتَيْنِ وَأَحْيَيْتَنَا ٱثْنَتَيْنِ فَٱعْتَرَفْنَا بِذُنُوبِنَا فَهَلْ إِلَىٰ
خُرُوجٍ مِّن سَبِيلٍ ﴿11﴾ ذَٰلِكُم بِأَنَّهُۥٓ إِذَا دُعِىَ ٱللَّهُ وَحْدَهُۥ كَفَرْتُمْ ۖ وَإِن
يُشْرَكْ بِهِۦ تُؤْمِنُوا۟ ۚ فَٱلْحُكْمُ لِلَّهِ ٱلْعَلِىِّ ٱلْكَبِيرِ ﴿12﴾ هُوَ ٱلَّذِى يُرِيكُمْ
ءَايَٰتِهِۦ وَيُنَزِّلُ لَكُم مِّنَ ٱلسَّمَآءِ رِزْقًا ۚ وَمَا يَتَذَكَّرُ إِلَّا مَن يُنِيبُ ﴿13﴾
فَٱدْعُوا۟ ٱللَّهَ مُخْلِصِينَ لَهُ ٱلدِّينَ وَلَوْ كَرِهَ ٱلْكَٰفِرُونَ ﴿14﴾ رَفِيعُ
ٱلدَّرَجَٰتِ ذُو ٱلْعَرْشِ يُلْقِى ٱلرُّوحَ مِنْ أَمْرِهِۦ عَلَىٰ مَن يَشَآءُ مِنْ عِبَادِهِۦ
لِيُنذِرَ يَوْمَ ٱلتَّلَاقِ ﴿15﴾ يَوْمَ هُم بَٰرِزُونَ ۖ لَا يَخْفَىٰ عَلَى ٱللَّهِ مِنْهُمْ شَىْءٌ ۚ
لِّمَنِ ٱلْمُلْكُ ٱلْيَوْمَ ۖ لِلَّهِ ٱلْوَٰحِدِ ٱلْقَهَّارِ ﴿16﴾

[Whereupon] they will exclaim: "O our Sustainer! Twice hast Thou caused us to die, just as twice Thou hast brought us to life![9] But now that we have acknowledged our sins, is there any way out [of this second death]?" ‹11›
[And they will be told:] "This [has befallen you] because, whenever the One God was invoked, you denied this truth; whereas, when divinity was ascribed to aught beside Him, you believed [in it]! But all judgment rests with God, the Exalted, the Great!"[10] ‹12›

HE IT IS who shows you His wonders [in all nature], and sends down sustenance for you from the sky: but none bethinks himself [thereof] save those who are wont to turn to God. ‹13›
Invoke, then, God, sincere in your faith in Him alone, however hateful this may be to those who deny the truth! ‹14›
High above all orders [of being] is He, in almightiness enthroned.[11] By His own will does He bestow inspiration upon whomever He wills of His servants, so as to warn [all human beings of the coming] of the Day when they shall meet Him[12] ‹15› – the Day when they shall come forth [from death], with nothing of themselves hidden from God.
With whom will sovereignty rest on that Day?
With God, the One who holds absolute sway over all that exists! ‹16›

Qālū Rabbanāa ʾamattanath-natayni wa ʾaḥyaytanath-natayni faᶜtarafnā bidhunūbinā fahal ʾilā khurūjim-miñ-sabīl. (11) Dhālikum biʾannahūu ʾidhā duᶜiyal-lāhu waḥdahū kafartum wa ʾiñy-yushrak bihī tuʾminū; falḥukmu lillāhil-ᶜAliyyil-Kabīr. (12) Huwalladhī yurīkum ʾĀyātihī wa yunazzilu lakum-minas-samāaʾi rizqañw-wa mā yatadhakkaru ʾillā mañy-yunīb. (13) Fadᶜul-lāha mukhliṣīna lahud-dīna wa law karihal-kāfirūn. (14) Rafīᶜud-darajāti Dhul-ᶜarshi yulqir-Rūḥa min ʾamrihī ᶜalā mañy-yashāaʾu min ᶜibādihī liyuñdhira Yawmat-talāq. (15) Yawma hum bārizūna lā yakhfā ᶜalal-lāhi minhum shayʾ. Limanil-mulkul-Yawm. Lillāhil-Wāḥidil-Qahhār. (16)

9 I.e., "Thou hast brought us to life on earth, and then hast caused us to die; thereupon Thou hast resurrected us, and now hast condemned us to spiritual death in consequence of our wilful spiritual blindness on earth."

10 An answer to the sinners' question at the end of the preceding verse may be found in the following extremely well-authenticated, parabolic saying of the Prophet: "[On the Day of Judgment,] those who deserve paradise will enter paradise, and those who deserve the fire, the fire. Thereupon God, the Sublimely Exalted, will say, 'Take out [of the fire] everyone in whose heart there was as much of faith [or, in some versions, "as much of good"] as a grain of mustard seed!' And so they will be taken out of it, already blackened, and will be thrown into the River of Life; and then they will come to life [lit., 'sprout'] as a herb sprouts by the side of a stream: and didst thou not see how it comes out, yellow and budding?" (Bukhārī, on the authority of Abū Saᶜīd al-Khudrī, in *Kitāb al-Īmān* and *Kitāb Badʾ al-Khalq*; also Muslim, Nasāʾī and Ibn Ḥanbal.) The characterization as "yellow and budding" – i.e., tender and of light colour – indicates the freshness of new life in the pardoned sinner. This, of course, has nothing to do with the sinners' futile – because meaningless – request on Judgment Day to be given a "second chance" *on earth* (cf. 6 : 27-28 or 32 : 12). See also last but one sentence of 6 : 128 and the corresponding note 114.

11 Lit., "He of the throne of almightiness". For the meaning of the term *ᶜarsh*, see note 43 on 7 : 54.

12 Lit., "the Day of the Meeting". – For my rendering of *ar-rūḥ* as "inspiration", see note 2 on 16 : 2, as well as note 71 on 2 : 87.

ٱلْيَوْمَ تُجْزَىٰ كُلُّ نَفْسٍۭ بِمَا كَسَبَتْ ۚ لَا ظُلْمَ ٱلْيَوْمَ ۚ إِنَّ ٱللَّهَ سَرِيعُ
ٱلْحِسَابِ ﴿١٧﴾ وَأَنذِرْهُمْ يَوْمَ ٱلْءَازِفَةِ إِذِ ٱلْقُلُوبُ لَدَى ٱلْحَنَاجِرِ كَـٰظِمِينَ ۚ
مَا لِلظَّـٰلِمِينَ مِنْ حَمِيمٍ وَلَا شَفِيعٍ يُطَاعُ ﴿١٨﴾ يَعْلَمُ خَآئِنَةَ ٱلْأَعْيُنِ وَمَا تُخْفِى
ٱلصُّدُورُ ﴿١٩﴾ وَٱللَّهُ يَقْضِى بِٱلْحَقِّ ۖ وَٱلَّذِينَ يَدْعُونَ مِن دُونِهِۦ لَا يَقْضُونَ
بِشَىْءٍ ۗ إِنَّ ٱللَّهَ هُوَ ٱلسَّمِيعُ ٱلْبَصِيرُ ﴿٢٠﴾ ۞ أَوَلَمْ يَسِيرُوا۟ فِى ٱلْأَرْضِ
فَيَنظُرُوا۟ كَيْفَ كَانَ عَـٰقِبَةُ ٱلَّذِينَ كَانُوا۟ مِن قَبْلِهِمْ ۚ كَانُوا۟ هُمْ أَشَدَّ مِنْهُمْ قُوَّةً
وَءَاثَارًا فِى ٱلْأَرْضِ فَأَخَذَهُمُ ٱللَّهُ بِذُنُوبِهِمْ وَمَا كَانَ لَهُم مِّنَ ٱللَّهِ مِن
وَاقٍ ﴿٢١﴾ ذَٰلِكَ بِأَنَّهُمْ كَانَت تَّأْتِيهِمْ رُسُلُهُم بِٱلْبَيِّنَـٰتِ فَكَفَرُوا۟ فَأَخَذَهُمُ
ٱللَّهُ ۚ إِنَّهُۥ قَوِىٌّ شَدِيدُ ٱلْعِقَابِ ﴿٢٢﴾ وَلَقَدْ أَرْسَلْنَا مُوسَىٰ بِـَٔايَـٰتِنَا وَسُلْطَـٰنٍ
مُّبِينٍ ﴿٢٣﴾ إِلَىٰ فِرْعَوْنَ وَهَـٰمَـٰنَ وَقَـٰرُونَ فَقَالُوا۟ سَـٰحِرٌ كَذَّابٌ ﴿٢٤﴾ فَلَمَّا
جَآءَهُم بِٱلْحَقِّ مِنْ عِندِنَا قَالُوا۟ ٱقْتُلُوٓا۟ أَبْنَآءَ ٱلَّذِينَ ءَامَنُوا۟ مَعَهُۥ وَٱسْتَحْيُوا۟

ثلاثة ارباع الحزب

On that Day will every human being be requited for what he has earned: no wrong [will be done] on that Day: verily, swift in reckoning is God! ‹17›
Hence, warn them of that Day which draws ever nearer, when the hearts will chokingly come up to the throats: no loving friend will the evildoers have, nor any intercessor who would be heeded:[13] ‹18› [for] He is aware of the [most] stealthy glance, and of all that the hearts would conceal.[14] ‹19›
And God will judge in accordance with truth and justice, whereas those [beings] whom they invoke beside Him[15] cannot judge at all: for, verily, God alone is all-hearing, all-seeing. ‹20›
Have they, then, never journeyed about the earth and beheld what happened in the end to those [deniers of the truth] who lived before their time? Greater were they in power than they are, and in the impact which they left on earth: but God took them to task for their sins, and they had none to defend them against God: ‹21› this, because their apostles had come to them with all evidence of the truth, and yet they rejected it: and so God took them to task – for, verily, He is powerful, severe in retribution! ‹22›

THUS, INDEED, did We send Moses with Our messages and a manifest authority [from Us] ‹23› unto Pharaoh, and Hāmān, and Qārūn;[16] but they [only] said, "A spell-binder is he, a liar!" ‹24›
Now [as for Pharaoh and his followers,] when he came to them, setting forth the truth from Us, they said, "Slay the sons of those who share his beliefs,[17] and spare

ʾAlyawma tujzā kullu nafsim-bimā kasabat; lā ẓulmal-Yawma ʾinnal-lāha Sarīʿul-ḥisāb. (17) Wa ʾañdhirhum Yawmal-ʾazifati ʾidhil-qulūbu ladal-ḥanājiri kāẓimīn. Mā liẓẓālimīna min ḥamīmiñw-wa lā shafīʿiñy-yuṭāʿ. (18) Yaʿlamu khāaʾinatal-ʾaʿyuni wa mā tukhfiṣ-ṣudūr. (19) Wal-lāhu yaqḍī bilḥaqqi wal-ladhīna yadʿūna miñ-dūnihī lā yaqḍūna bishayʾ. ʾInnal-lāha Huwas-Samīʿul-Baṣīr. (20) ۞ ʾAwalam yasīrū fil-ʾarḍi fayañẓurū kayfa kāna ʿāqibatul-ladhīna kānū miñ-qablihim. Kānū hum ʾashadda minhum quwwatañw-wa ʾāthārañ-fil-ʾarḍi faʾakhadhahumul-lāhu bidhunūbihim wa mā kāna lahum-minal-lāhi miñw-wāq. (21) Dhālika biʾannahum kānat-taʾtīhim Rusuluhum bilbayyināti fakafarū faʾakhadhahumul-lāhu ʾinnahū Qawiyyuñ-Shadīdul-ʿiqāb. (22) Wa laqad ʾarsalnā Mūsā biʾĀyātinā wa sulṭānim-mubīn. (23) ʾIlā Firʿawna wa Hāmāna wa Qārūna faqālū sāḥiruñ-kadhdhāb. (24) Falammā jāaʾahum bilḥaqqi min ʿiñdinā qāluq-tulūu ʾabnāaʾal-ladhīna ʾāmanū maʿahū was-taḥyū

13 Regarding the problem of "intercession" (*shafāʿah*) and its meaning in the Qurʾān, see note 7 on 10 : 3.

14 God's omniscience is shown here as the reason why there can be no "intercession" with Him in the commonly-accepted sense of this term (cf. *sūrah* 10, note 27).

15 I.e., saints, whether real or imaginary, or angels. (The pronoun *alladhīna* is used only with reference to sentient beings endowed with reason.)

16 As regards Qārūn, who is said to have been a follower – and subsequently an opponent – of Moses, see 28 : 76 ff., as well as the corresponding note 84. For a discussion of the name "Hāmān", see note 6 on 28 : 6.

17 Lit., "those who have come to believe with him".

[only] their women!" – but the guile of those deniers of the truth could not lead to aught but failure. ⟨25⟩

And Pharaoh said: "Leave it to me to slay Moses – and let him invoke his [alleged] sustainer![18] Behold, I fear lest he cause you to change your religion, or lest he cause corruption to prevail in the land!" ⟨26⟩

But Moses said: "With [Him who is] my Sustainer as well as your Sustainer have I indeed found refuge from everyone who, immersed in false pride, will not believe in [the coming of] the Day of Reckoning!" ⟨27⟩

At that, a believing man of Pharaoh's family, who [until then] had concealed his faith,[19] exclaimed: "Would you slay a man because he says, 'God is my Sustainer' – seeing, withal, that he has brought you all evidence of this truth from your Sustainer? Now if he be a liar, his lie will fall back on him; but if he is a man of truth, something [of the punishment] whereof he warns you is bound to befall you: for, verily, God would not grace with His guidance one who has wasted his own self by lying [about Him].[20] ⟨28⟩

"O my people! Yours is the dominion today, [and] most eminent are you on earth: but who will rescue us from God's punishment, once it befalls us?"

Said Pharaoh: "I but want to make you see what I see myself;[21] and I would never make you follow any path but that of rectitude!" ⟨29⟩

Thereupon exclaimed he who had attained to faith: "O my people! Verily, I fear for you the like of what one day befell those others who were leagued together [against God's truth] ⟨30⟩ – the like of what happened to

نِسَآءَهُمْ وَمَا كَيْدُ ٱلْكَٰفِرِينَ إِلَّا فِى ضَلَٰلٍ ﴿٢٥﴾ وَقَالَ فِرْعَوْنُ ذَرُونِىٓ
أَقْتُلْ مُوسَىٰ وَلْيَدْعُ رَبَّهُۥٓ إِنِّىٓ أَخَافُ أَن يُبَدِّلَ دِينَكُمْ أَوْ أَن يُظْهِرَ فِى
ٱلْأَرْضِ ٱلْفَسَادَ ﴿٢٦﴾ وَقَالَ مُوسَىٰٓ إِنِّى عُذْتُ بِرَبِّى وَرَبِّكُم مِّن كُلِّ مُتَكَبِّرٍ
لَّا يُؤْمِنُ بِيَوْمِ ٱلْحِسَابِ ﴿٢٧﴾ وَقَالَ رَجُلٌ مُّؤْمِنٌ مِّنْ ءَالِ فِرْعَوْنَ يَكْتُمُ
إِيمَٰنَهُۥٓ أَتَقْتُلُونَ رَجُلًا أَن يَقُولَ رَبِّىَ ٱللَّهُ وَقَدْ جَآءَكُم بِٱلْبَيِّنَٰتِ مِن رَّبِّكُمْ
وَإِن يَكُ كَٰذِبًا فَعَلَيْهِ كَذِبُهُۥ وَإِن يَكُ صَادِقًا يُصِبْكُم بَعْضُ ٱلَّذِى
يَعِدُكُمْ إِنَّ ٱللَّهَ لَا يَهْدِى مَنْ هُوَ مُسْرِفٌ كَذَّابٌ ﴿٢٨﴾ يَٰقَوْمِ لَكُمُ ٱلْمُلْكُ
ٱلْيَوْمَ ظَٰهِرِينَ فِى ٱلْأَرْضِ فَمَن يَنصُرُنَا مِنۢ بَأْسِ ٱللَّهِ إِن جَآءَنَا قَالَ
فِرْعَوْنُ مَآ أُرِيكُمْ إِلَّا مَآ أَرَىٰ وَمَآ أَهْدِيكُمْ إِلَّا سَبِيلَ ٱلرَّشَادِ ﴿٢٩﴾ وَقَالَ
ٱلَّذِىٓ ءَامَنَ يَٰقَوْمِ إِنِّىٓ أَخَافُ عَلَيْكُم مِّثْلَ يَوْمِ ٱلْأَحْزَابِ ﴿٣٠﴾ مِثْلَ دَأْبِ

nisāaʾahum. Wa mā kaydul-kāfirīna ʾillā fī ḍalāl. ⟨25⟩
Wa qāla Firʿawnu dharūnīi ʾaqtul Mūsā wal-yadʿu
Rabbah. ʾInnīi ʾakhāfu ʾañy-yubaddila dīnakum ʾaw
ʾañy-yuẓhira fil-ʾarḍil-fasād. ⟨26⟩ Wa qāla Mūsāa ʾinnī
ʿudhtu biRabbī wa Rabbikum-miñ-kulli mutakabbi-
ril-lā yuʾminu biYawmil-Ḥisāb. ⟨27⟩ Wa qāla rajulum-
muʾminum-min ʾāli Firʿawna yaktumu ʾīmānahūu
ʾataqtulūna rajulan ʾañy-yaqūla Rabbiyal-lāhu wa
qad jāaʾakum bilbayyināti mir-Rabbikum. Wa ʾiñy-
yaku kādhibañ-faʿalayhi kadhibuh. Wa ʾiñy-ya-
ku ṣādiqañy-yuṣibkum-baʿḍul-ladhī yaʿidukum.
ʾInnal-lāha lā yahdī man huwa musrifuñ-kadhdhāb.
⟨28⟩ Yā qawmi lakumul-mulkul-yawma ẓāhirīna fil-
ʾarḍi famañy-yañṣurunā mim-baʾsil-lāhi ʾiñ-
jāaʾanā. Qāla Firʿawnu māa ʾurīkum ʾillā māa ʾarā
wa māa ʾahdīkum ʾillā sabīlar-rashād. ⟨29⟩ Wa
qālal-ladhīi ʾāmana yā qawmi ʾinnīi ʾakhāfu
ʿalaykum-mithla yawmil-ʾaḥzāb. ⟨30⟩ Mithla daʾbi

18 My interpolation of the word "alleged" is necessitated by the obvious sarcasm of Pharaoh's remark.

19 Cf. the parable of the believer in 36 : 20-27 and, in particular, the corresponding note 15.

20 Lit., "a liar". As regards my rendering of *musrif* as "one who wastes [or "has wasted"] his own self", see note 21 on the last sentence of 10 : 12. Thus, the anonymous believer spoken of here argues that the message brought by Moses is so convincing that, by itself, it is a proof of his *not* being "one who wastes his own self" – i.e., destroys himself spiritually – by a spurious claim to divine inspiration.

21 Thus alluding to the reasons underlying his intention to kill Moses, expressed in verse 26.

Noah's people, and to [the tribes of] ᶜĀd and Thamūd and those who came after them! And, withal, God does not will any wrong for His creatures.[22] ⟨31⟩

"And, O my people, I fear for you [the coming of] that Day of [Judgment – the Day when you will be] calling unto one another [in distress] ⟨32⟩ – the Day when you will [wish to] turn your backs and flee, having none to defend you against God: for he whom God lets go astray can never find any guide.[23] ⟨33⟩

"And [remember:] it was to you that Joseph came aforetime with all evidence of the truth; but you never ceased to throw doubt on all [the messages] that he brought you – so much so that when he died, you said, 'Never will God send any apostle [even] after him!'[24]

"In this way God lets go astray such as waste their own selves by throwing suspicion [on His revelations] ⟨34⟩ – such as would call God's messages in question without having any evidence therefor:[25] [a sin] exceedingly loathsome in the sight of God and of those who have attained to faith. It is in this way that God sets a seal on every arrogant, self-exalting heart."[26] ⟨35⟩

But Pharaoh said: "O Hāmān! Build me a lofty tower, that haply I may attain to the [right] means ⟨36⟩ – the means of approach to the heavens – and that [thus] I may have a look at the god of Moses:[27] for, behold, I am indeed certain that he is a liar!"

قَوْمِ نُوحٍ وَعَادٍ وَثَمُودَ وَٱلَّذِينَ مِنۢ بَعْدِهِمْ ۚ وَمَا ٱللَّهُ يُرِيدُ ظُلْمًا لِّلْعِبَادِ ﴿٣١﴾
وَيَـٰقَوْمِ إِنِّىٓ أَخَافُ عَلَيْكُمْ يَوْمَ ٱلتَّنَادِ ﴿٣٢﴾ يَوْمَ تُوَلُّونَ مُدْبِرِينَ مَا
لَكُم مِّنَ ٱللَّهِ مِنْ عَاصِمٍ ۗ وَمَن يُضْلِلِ ٱللَّهُ فَمَا لَهُۥ مِنْ هَادٍ ﴿٣٣﴾ وَلَقَدْ جَآءَكُمْ
يُوسُفُ مِن قَبْلُ بِٱلْبَيِّنَـٰتِ فَمَا زِلْتُمْ فِى شَكٍّ مِّمَّا جَآءَكُم بِهِۦ ۖ حَتَّىٰٓ إِذَا هَلَكَ
قُلْتُمْ لَن يَبْعَثَ ٱللَّهُ مِنۢ بَعْدِهِۦ رَسُولًا ۚ كَذَٰلِكَ يُضِلُّ ٱللَّهُ مَنْ هُوَ مُسْرِفٌ
مُّرْتَابٌ ﴿٣٤﴾ ٱلَّذِينَ يُجَـٰدِلُونَ فِىٓ ءَايَـٰتِ ٱللَّهِ بِغَيْرِ سُلْطَـٰنٍ أَتَىٰهُمْ ۖ كَبُرَ مَقْتًا
عِندَ ٱللَّهِ وَعِندَ ٱلَّذِينَ ءَامَنُوا۟ ۚ كَذَٰلِكَ يَطْبَعُ ٱللَّهُ عَلَىٰ كُلِّ قَلْبِ مُتَكَبِّرٍ
جَبَّارٍ ﴿٣٥﴾ وَقَالَ فِرْعَوْنُ يَـٰهَـٰمَـٰنُ ٱبْنِ لِى صَرْحًا لَّعَلِّىٓ أَبْلُغُ ٱلْأَسْبَـٰبَ ﴿٣٦﴾
أَسْبَـٰبَ ٱلسَّمَـٰوَٰتِ فَأَطَّلِعَ إِلَىٰٓ إِلَـٰهِ مُوسَىٰ وَإِنِّى لَأَظُنُّهُۥ كَـٰذِبًا ۚ

qawmi Nūḥiñw-wa ᶜĀdiñw-wa Thamūda wal-ladhīna mim-baᶜdihim wa mal-lāhu yurīdu ẓulmal-lilᶜibād. (31) Wa yā qawmi ʾinnīi ʾakhāfu ᶜalaykum Yawmat-tanād. (32) Yawma tuwallūna mudbirīna mā lakum-minal-lāhi min ᶜāṣim. Wa mañy-yuḍlilil-lāhu famā lahū min hād. (33) Wa laqad jāaʾakum Yūsufu miñ-qablu bil-bayyināti famā ziltum fī shakkim-mimmā jāaʾakum bihī ḥattāa ʾidhā halaka qultum lañy-yabᶜathal-lāhu mim-baᶜdihī Rasūlā. Kadhālika yuḍillul-lāhu man huwa musrifum-murtāb. (34) ʾAlladhīna yujādilūna fīi ʾĀyātil-lāhi bighayri sulṭānin ʾatāhum. Kabura maqtan ʿiñdal-lāhi wa ᶜiñdal-ladhīna ʾāmanū. Kadhālika yaṭbaᶜul-lāhu ᶜalā kulli qalbi mutakabbiriñ-jabbār. (35) Wa qāla Firᶜawnu yā Hāmānub-ni lī ṣarḥal-laᶜallīi ʾablughul-ʾasbāb. (36) ʾAsbābas-samāwāti faʾaṭṭaliᶜa ʾilāa ʾilāhi Mūsā wa ʾinnī laʾaẓunnuhū kādhibā.

22 I.e., those sinners were not *wronged* by what befell them in this world: they had deserved it. The next two verses refer to the Day of Judgment.

23 See note 152 on 7 : 186 and note 4 on 14 : 4.

24 Thus not only refusing to acknowledge Joseph's prophethood, but also denying the possibility of *any* prophet being sent by God (Zamakhsharī). It would seem that Joseph had been accepted in Egypt as a prophet only by the ruling class, the Hyksos, who were of Arab origin, spoke a language closely related to Hebrew (cf. *sūrah* 12, note 44), and were, therefore, emotionally and culturally predisposed towards the spirit of Joseph's mission, while the rest of the population was and remained hostile to the faith preached by him.

25 Lit., "without any authority [or "evidence"] having come to them": i.e., without having any cogent evidence that would support their "denial" of the fact of revelation. – The verb *jādala* primarily denotes "he argued"; followed by the particle *fī* ("with regard to" or "about") it has the meaning of "contesting" the truth of something, or "calling it in question".

26 Lit., "on the heart of every arrogant, self-exalting [person]". For an explanation of God's "sealing" an inveterate sinner's heart, see note 7 on 2 : 7.

27 See *sūrah* 28, notes 6 and 37.

وَكَذَٰلِكَ زُيِّنَ لِفِرْعَوْنَ سُوٓءُ عَمَلِهِۦ وَصُدَّ عَنِ ٱلسَّبِيلِ ۚ وَمَا كَيْدُ فِرْعَوْنَ
إِلَّا فِى تَبَابٍ ﴿٣٧﴾ وَقَالَ ٱلَّذِىٓ ءَامَنَ يَٰقَوْمِ ٱتَّبِعُونِ أَهْدِكُمْ سَبِيلَ
ٱلرَّشَادِ ﴿٣٨﴾ يَٰقَوْمِ إِنَّمَا هَٰذِهِ ٱلْحَيَوٰةُ ٱلدُّنْيَا مَتَٰعٌ وَإِنَّ ٱلْءَاخِرَةَ هِىَ
دَارُ ٱلْقَرَارِ ﴿٣٩﴾ مَنْ عَمِلَ سَيِّئَةً فَلَا يُجْزَىٰٓ إِلَّا مِثْلَهَا ۖ وَمَنْ عَمِلَ
صَٰلِحًا مِّن ذَكَرٍ أَوْ أُنثَىٰ وَهُوَ مُؤْمِنٌ فَأُو۟لَٰٓئِكَ يَدْخُلُونَ ٱلْجَنَّةَ يُرْزَقُونَ
فِيهَا بِغَيْرِ حِسَابٍ ﴿٤٠﴾ ۞ وَيَٰقَوْمِ مَا لِىٓ أَدْعُوكُمْ إِلَى ٱلنَّجَوٰةِ
وَتَدْعُونَنِىٓ إِلَى ٱلنَّارِ ﴿٤١﴾ تَدْعُونَنِى لِأَكْفُرَ بِٱللَّهِ وَأُشْرِكَ بِهِۦ مَا لَيْسَ لِى
بِهِۦ عِلْمٌ وَأَنَا۠ أَدْعُوكُمْ إِلَى ٱلْعَزِيزِ ٱلْغَفَّٰرِ ﴿٤٢﴾ لَا جَرَمَ أَنَّمَا تَدْعُونَنِىٓ حزب 48
إِلَيْهِ لَيْسَ لَهُۥ دَعْوَةٌ فِى ٱلدُّنْيَا وَلَا فِى ٱلْءَاخِرَةِ وَأَنَّ مَرَدَّنَآ إِلَى ٱللَّهِ وَأَنَّ
ٱلْمُسْرِفِينَ هُمْ أَصْحَٰبُ ٱلنَّارِ ﴿٤٣﴾ فَسَتَذْكُرُونَ مَآ أَقُولُ لَكُمْ ۚ وَأُفَوِّضُ
أَمْرِىٓ إِلَى ٱللَّهِ ۚ إِنَّ ٱللَّهَ بَصِيرٌۢ بِٱلْعِبَادِ ﴿٤٤﴾ فَوَقَىٰهُ ٱللَّهُ سَيِّـَٔاتِ مَا مَكَرُوا۟ ۖ
وَحَاقَ بِـَٔالِ فِرْعَوْنَ سُوٓءُ ٱلْعَذَابِ ﴿٤٥﴾

Wa kadhalika zuyyina liFirʿawna sūuʾu ʿamalihī wa ṣudda ʿanis-sabīl. Wa mā kaydu Firʿawna ʾillā fī tabāb. (37) Wa qālal-ladhīi ʾāmana yā qawmit-tabiʿūni ʾahdikum sabīlar-rashād. (38) Yā qawmi ʾinnamā hādhihil-ḥayātud-dunyā matāʿuñw-wa ʾinnal-ʾĀkhirata hiya dārul-qarār. (39) Man ʿamila sayyiʾatañ-falā yujzāa ʾillā mithlahā. Wa man ʿamila ṣāliḥam-miñ-dhakarin ʾaw ʾuñthā wa huwa muʾminuñ-faʾulāaʾika yadkhulūnal-jannata yurzaqūna fīhā bi-ghayri ḥisāb. (40) ۞ Wa yā qawmi mā līi ʾadʿūkum ʾilan-najāti wa tadʿūnanīi ʾilan-nār. (41) Tadʿūnanī liʾakfura billāhi wa ʾushrika bihī mā laysa lī bihī ʿilmuñw-wa ʾana ʾadʿūkum ʾilal-ʿAzīzil-Ghaffār. (42) Lā jarama ʾannamā tadʿūnanīi ʾilayhi laysa lahū daʿwatuñ-fid-dunyā wa lā fil-ʾĀkhirati wa ʾanna maraddanāa ʾilal-lāhi wa ʾannal-musrifīna hum ʾaṣḥābun-nār. (43) Fasatadhkurūna māa ʾaqūlu la-kum wa ʾufawwiḍu ʾamrīi ʾilal-lāh. ʾInnal-lāha Baṣīrum-bilʿibād. (44) Fawaqāhul-lāhu sayyiʾāti mā makarū wa ḥāqa biʾāli Firʿawna sūuʾul-ʿadhāb. (45)

And thus, goodly seemed unto Pharaoh the evil of his own doings, and so he was barred from the path [of truth]: and Pharaoh's guile did not lead to aught but ruin. ‹37›

Still, the man who had attained to faith went on: "O my people! Follow me: I shall guide you onto the path of rectitude! ‹38›

"O my people! This worldly life is but a brief enjoyment, whereas, behold, the life to come is the home abiding. ‹39› [There,] anyone who has done a bad deed will be requited with no more than the like thereof, whereas anyone, be it man or woman, who has done righteous deeds and is a believer withal – all such will enter paradise, wherein they shall be blest with good beyond all reckoning![28] ‹40›

"And, O my people, how is it[29] that I summon you to salvation, the while you summon me to the fire? ‹41› – [for] you call upon me to deny [the oneness of] God and to ascribe a share in His divinity to aught of which I cannot [possibly] have any knowledge,[30] the while I summon you to [a cognition of] the Almighty, the All-Forgiving! ‹42›

"There is no doubt that what you summon me to is something that has no claim to being invoked either in this world or in the life to come – as [there is no doubt] that unto God is our return, and that they who have wasted their own selves shall find themselves in the fire: ‹43› and at that time you will [have cause to] remember what I am telling you [now].

"But [as for me,] I commit myself unto God: for, verily, God sees all that is in [the hearts of] His servants." ‹44›

And God preserved him from the evil of their scheming, whereas suffering vile was to encompass Pharaoh's folk: ‹45›

---

28 I.e., beyond any earthly imagination. The concept of *rizq* (expressed in the verb *yurzaqūn*) has here its full significance of *all* that is good and of benefit to a living being, comprising things material as well as intellectual and spiritual; hence my rendering of *yurzaqūn* (lit., "they will be given sustenance") as "they shall be blest with good".

29 Lit., "what is the matter with me": an expression of astonishment at the incongruity of the two attitudes referred to in the sequence.

30 I.e., because there is no reality whatsoever in those supposedly "divine" beings or forces (Zamakhsharī).

the fire [of the hereafter – that fire] which they had been made to contemplate [in vain], morning and evening:[31] for on the Day when the Last Hour dawns [God will say], "Make Pharaoh's folk enter upon suffering most severe!" ‹46›

AND LO! They [who in life were wont to deny the truth] will contend with one another in the fire [of the hereafter]; and then the weak will say unto those who had gloried in their arrogance, "Behold, we were but your followers: can you, then, relieve us of some [of our] share of this fire?"[32] ‹47› – [to which] they who had [once] been arrogant will reply, "Behold, we are all in it [together]! Verily, God has judged between His creatures!" ‹48›
And they who are in the fire will say to the keepers of hell,[33] "Pray unto your Sustainer that He lighten, [though it be] for one day [only], this suffering of ours!" ‹49›
[But the keepers of hell] will ask, "Is it not [true] that your apostles came unto you with all evidence of the truth?" Those [in the fire] will reply, "Yea, indeed." [And the keepers of hell] will say, "Pray, then!"[34] – for the prayer of those who deny the truth cannot lead to aught but delusion. ‹50›

BEHOLD, We shall indeed succour Our apostles and those who have attained to faith, [both] in this world's life and on the Day when all the witnesses shall stand up[35] ‹51› – the Day when their excuses

ٱلنَّارُ يُعْرَضُونَ عَلَيْهَا غُدُوًّا وَعَشِيًّا ۖ وَيَوْمَ تَقُومُ ٱلسَّاعَةُ أَدْخِلُوٓا۟ ءَالَ فِرْعَوْنَ
أَشَدَّ ٱلْعَذَابِ ﴿٤٦﴾ وَإِذْ يَتَحَآجُّونَ فِى ٱلنَّارِ فَيَقُولُ ٱلضُّعَفَٰٓؤُا۟ لِلَّذِينَ
ٱسْتَكْبَرُوٓا۟ إِنَّا كُنَّا لَكُمْ تَبَعًا فَهَلْ أَنتُم مُّغْنُونَ عَنَّا نَصِيبًا مِّنَ ٱلنَّارِ ﴿٤٧﴾
قَالَ ٱلَّذِينَ ٱسْتَكْبَرُوٓا۟ إِنَّا كُلٌّ فِيهَآ إِنَّ ٱللَّهَ قَدْ حَكَمَ بَيْنَ ٱلْعِبَادِ ﴿٤٨﴾ وَقَالَ
ٱلَّذِينَ فِى ٱلنَّارِ لِخَزَنَةِ جَهَنَّمَ ٱدْعُوا۟ رَبَّكُمْ يُخَفِّفْ عَنَّا يَوْمًا مِّنَ ٱلْعَذَابِ ﴿٤٩﴾
قَالُوٓا۟ أَوَلَمْ تَكُ تَأْتِيكُمْ رُسُلُكُم بِٱلْبَيِّنَٰتِ ۖ قَالُوا۟ بَلَىٰ ۚ قَالُوا۟ فَٱدْعُوا۟ ۗ وَمَا
دُعَٰٓؤُا۟ ٱلْكَٰفِرِينَ إِلَّا فِى ضَلَٰلٍ ﴿٥٠﴾ إِنَّا لَنَنصُرُ رُسُلَنَا وَٱلَّذِينَ ءَامَنُوا۟ فِى
ٱلْحَيَوٰةِ ٱلدُّنْيَا وَيَوْمَ يَقُومُ ٱلْأَشْهَٰدُ ﴿٥١﴾ يَوْمَ لَا يَنفَعُ ٱلظَّٰلِمِينَ مَعْذِرَتُهُمْ ۖ

ʾAnnāru yuʿraḍūna ʿalayhā ghuduwwañw-wa ʿashiyyā. Wa Yawma taqūmus-Sāʿatu ʾadkhilūu ʾāla Firʿawna ʾashaddal-ʿadhāb. (46) Wa ʾidh yataḥāaj-jūna fin-nāri fayaqūluḍ-ḍuʿafāaʾu lilladhīnas-takbarūu ʾinnā kunnā lakum tabaʿañ-fahal ʾañtum-mughnūna ʿannā naṣībam-minan-nār. (47) Qālal-ladhīnas-takbarūu ʾinnā kulluñ-fīhāa ʾinnal-lāha qad ḥakama baynal-ʿibād. (48) Wa qālal-ladhīna fin-nāri likhazanati jahannamad-ʿū Rabbakum yukhaffif ʿannā yawmam-minal-ʿadhāb. (49) Qālūu ʾawalam taku taʾtīkum Rusulukum-bilbayyināti qālū balā. Qālū fadʿū wa mā duʿāaʾul-kāfirīna ʾillā fī ḍalāl. (50) ʾInnā lanañṣuru Rusulanā wal-ladhīna ʾāmanū fil-ḥayātid-dunyā wa Yawma yaqūmul-ʾashhād. (51) Yawma lā yañfaʿuẓ-ẓālimīna maʿdhiratuhum

31 I.e., of which they had been warned, day-in and day-out, by prophets and believers like the one spoken of in this passage.

32 Cf. 14 : 21 and the corresponding notes 28 and 29.

33 I.e., the angelic forces that are to watch over the suffering of the sinners in the hereafter: perhaps an allegory of the belated awakening of the latters' conscience.

34 According to the classical commentators, this answer implies no more than a refusal on the part of the "keepers of hell" to intercede for the doomed sinners, telling them, as it were, "Pray yourselves, if you can." It seems to me, however, that we have here an indirect allusion to the sinners' erstwhile, blasphemous devotion to false objects of worship and false values – the meaning being, "Pray now to those imaginary powers to which you were wont to ascribe a share in God's divinity, and see whether they can help you!" This interpretation finds support in the next sentence, which speaks of the delusion (*ḍalāl*) inherent in the prayers of "those who deny the truth", i.e., during their life on earth – for, obviously, on the Day of Judgment all such delusions will have disappeared.

35 See note 71 on 39 : 69.

وَلَهُمُ ٱللَّعْنَةُ وَلَهُمْ سُوٓءُ ٱلدَّارِ ﴿٥٢﴾ وَلَقَدْ ءَاتَيْنَا مُوسَى ٱلْهُدَىٰ وَأَوْرَثْنَا
بَنِىٓ إِسْرَٰٓءِيلَ ٱلْكِتَٰبَ ﴿٥٣﴾ هُدًى وَذِكْرَىٰ لِأُو۟لِى ٱلْأَلْبَٰبِ ﴿٥٤﴾
فَٱصْبِرْ إِنَّ وَعْدَ ٱللَّهِ حَقٌّ وَٱسْتَغْفِرْ لِذَنۢبِكَ وَسَبِّحْ بِحَمْدِ رَبِّكَ بِٱلْعَشِىِّ
وَٱلْإِبْكَٰرِ ﴿٥٥﴾ إِنَّ ٱلَّذِينَ يُجَٰدِلُونَ فِىٓ ءَايَٰتِ ٱللَّهِ بِغَيْرِ سُلْطَٰنٍ أَتَىٰهُمْ
إِن فِى صُدُورِهِمْ إِلَّا كِبْرٌ مَّا هُم بِبَٰلِغِيهِ فَٱسْتَعِذْ بِٱللَّهِ إِنَّهُۥ هُوَ ٱلسَّمِيعُ
ٱلْبَصِيرُ ﴿٥٦﴾ لَخَلْقُ ٱلسَّمَٰوَٰتِ وَٱلْأَرْضِ أَكْبَرُ مِنْ خَلْقِ ٱلنَّاسِ
وَلَٰكِنَّ أَكْثَرَ ٱلنَّاسِ لَا يَعْلَمُونَ ﴿٥٧﴾ وَمَا يَسْتَوِى ٱلْأَعْمَىٰ وَٱلْبَصِيرُ
وَٱلَّذِينَ ءَامَنُوا۟ وَعَمِلُوا۟ ٱلصَّٰلِحَٰتِ وَلَا ٱلْمُسِىٓءُ قَلِيلًا مَّا تَتَذَكَّرُونَ ﴿٥٨﴾

will be of no avail to the evildoers, seeing that their lot will be rejection from all that is good, and a woeful hereafter.[36] ‹52›
And, indeed, We bestowed aforetime [Our] guidance on Moses, and [thus] made the children of Israel heirs to the divine writ [revealed to him] ‹53› as a [means of] guidance and a reminder for those who were endowed with insight:[37] ‹54› hence, remain thou patient in adversity – for, verily, God's promise always comes true – and ask forgiveness for thy sins, and extol thy Sustainer's glory and praise by night and by day.[38] ‹55›
Behold, as for those who call God's messages in question without having any evidence therefor[39] – in their hearts is nothing but overweening self-conceit, which they will never be able to satisfy:[40] seek thou, then, refuge with God – for, verily, He alone is all-hearing, all-seeing! ‹56›
Greater indeed than the creation of man is the creation of the heavens and the earth:[41] yet most men do not understand [what this implies]. ‹57›
But [then,] the blind and the seeing are not equal; and neither [can] they who have attained to faith and do good works and the doers of evil [be deemed equal]. How seldom do you keep this in mind! ‹58›

wa lahumul-laʿnatu wa lahum sūuʾud-dār. (52) Wa laqad ʾātaynā Mūsal-hudā wa ʾawrathnā banīi ʾIsrāaʾīlal-Kitāb. (53) Hudanw-wa dhikrā liʾulil-ʾalbāb. (54) Faṣbir ʾinna waʿdal-lāhi ḥaqqunw-was-taghfir lidhambika wa sabbiḥ biḥamdi Rabbika bilʿashiyyi wal-ʾibkār. (55) ʾInnal-ladhīna yujādilūna fīi ʾĀyātil-lāhi bighayri sulṭānin ʾatāhum ʾin-fī ṣudūrihim ʾillā kibrum-mā hum bibālighīh. Fas-taʿidh billāhi ʾinnahū Huwas-Samīʿul-Baṣīr. (56) Lakhalqus-samāwāti wal-ʾarḍi ʾakbaru min khalqin-nāsi wa lākinna ʾaktharan-nāsi lā yaʿlamūn. (57) Wa mā yastawil-ʾaʿmā wal-baṣīru wal-ladhīna ʾāmanū wa ʿamiluṣ-ṣāliḥāti wa lal-musīiʾ. Qalīlam-mā tata-dhakkarūn. (58)

36 Lit., "the evil of the [otherworldly] abode". As regards the term *laʿnah*, its primary significance is "estrangement" or "rejection"; in Qurʾanic terminology it denotes "rejection from all that is good" (*Lisān al-ʿArab*) and, specifically, "estrangement from God's grace" (Zamakhsharī).

37 Sc., "and thus, too, have We bestowed Our revelation upon Muḥammad". This connects with the opening words of verse 51, "We shall indeed succour Our apostles and those who have attained to faith", thus explaining the purport of the preceding story of the believer who stood up for Moses. The reference to "those [of the children of Israel] who were endowed with insight" and therefore could benefit from the message of Moses, is undoubtedly meant to remind the followers of the Qurʾān that this divine writ, too, is for "those who are endowed with insight" (*ūlu 'l-albāb*), for "people who think" (*qawm yatafakkarūn*), and "people who use their reason" (*qawm yaʿqilūn*).

38 According to all classical commentators, the above passage is addressed in the first instance to the Prophet and, through him, to every believer. As regards the Prophet himself, see note 41 on the last sentence of 24 : 31.

39 See note 25 above.

40 Lit., "which they will never [be able to] reach" or "fulfil". This is a reference to the conceit which makes many agnostics think that man is "self-sufficient" and that, therefore, there are no limits to what he may yet achieve, and no need to assume that he is responsible to a higher Power. Cf. in this connection 96 : 6-7, which is one of the earliest Qurʾanic revelations: "Nay, verily, man becomes grossly overweening whenever he believes himself to be self-sufficient." And since this "self-sufficiency" is entirely illusory, those who build their world-view on it "will never be able to satisfy their overweening conceit". (Cf. also the reference to "arrogant, self-exalting hearts" in verse 35 above.)

41 I.e., of the universe as a whole. By stressing the fact that man is only a small, insignificant part of the universe, the Qurʾān points out the absurdity of the man-centred world-view alluded to in the preceding verse.

إِنَّ ٱلسَّاعَةَ لَأٓتِيَةٌ لَّا رَيۡبَ فِيهَا وَلَٰكِنَّ أَكۡثَرَ ٱلنَّاسِ لَا يُؤۡمِنُونَ ﴿٥٩﴾ وَقَالَ
رَبُّكُمُ ٱدۡعُونِيٓ أَسۡتَجِبۡ لَكُمۡۚ إِنَّ ٱلَّذِينَ يَسۡتَكۡبِرُونَ عَنۡ عِبَادَتِي سَيَدۡخُلُونَ
جَهَنَّمَ دَاخِرِينَ ﴿٦٠﴾ ٱللَّهُ ٱلَّذِي جَعَلَ لَكُمُ ٱلَّيۡلَ لِتَسۡكُنُواْ فِيهِ وَٱلنَّهَارَ
مُبۡصِرًاۚ إِنَّ ٱللَّهَ لَذُو فَضۡلٍ عَلَى ٱلنَّاسِ وَلَٰكِنَّ أَكۡثَرَ ٱلنَّاسِ لَا يَشۡكُرُونَ ﴿٦١﴾
ذَٰلِكُمُ ٱللَّهُ رَبُّكُمۡ خَٰلِقُ كُلِّ شَيۡءٖ لَّآ إِلَٰهَ إِلَّا هُوَۖ فَأَنَّىٰ تُؤۡفَكُونَ ﴿٦٢﴾
كَذَٰلِكَ يُؤۡفَكُ ٱلَّذِينَ كَانُواْ بِـَٔايَٰتِ ٱللَّهِ يَجۡحَدُونَ ﴿٦٣﴾ ٱللَّهُ ٱلَّذِي جَعَلَ
لَكُمُ ٱلۡأَرۡضَ قَرَارٗا وَٱلسَّمَآءَ بِنَآءٗ وَصَوَّرَكُمۡ فَأَحۡسَنَ صُوَرَكُمۡ وَرَزَقَكُم مِّنَ
ٱلطَّيِّبَٰتِۚ ذَٰلِكُمُ ٱللَّهُ رَبُّكُمۡۖ فَتَبَارَكَ ٱللَّهُ رَبُّ ٱلۡعَٰلَمِينَ ﴿٦٤﴾ هُوَ ٱلۡحَيُّ لَآ
إِلَٰهَ إِلَّا هُوَ فَٱدۡعُوهُ مُخۡلِصِينَ لَهُ ٱلدِّينَۗ ٱلۡحَمۡدُ لِلَّهِ رَبِّ ٱلۡعَٰلَمِينَ ﴿٦٥﴾ ۞ قُلۡ
إِنِّي نُهِيتُ أَنۡ أَعۡبُدَ ٱلَّذِينَ تَدۡعُونَ مِن دُونِ ٱللَّهِ لَمَّا جَآءَنِيَ ٱلۡبَيِّنَٰتُ مِن
رَّبِّي وَأُمِرۡتُ أَنۡ أُسۡلِمَ لِرَبِّ ٱلۡعَٰلَمِينَ ﴿٦٦﴾ هُوَ ٱلَّذِي خَلَقَكُم مِّن تُرَابٖ ثُمَّ

ربع الحزب

Verily, the Last Hour is sure to come: of this there is no doubt; yet most men will not believe it.[42] «59»
But your Sustainer says: "Call unto Me, [and] I shall respond to you![43] Verily, they who are too proud to worship Me will enter hell, abased!" «60»

IT IS GOD who has made the night for you, so that you might rest therein, and the day, to make [you] see.[44] Behold, God is indeed limitless in His bounty unto man – but most men are ungrateful. «61»
Such is God, your Sustainer, the Creator of all that exists: there is no deity save Him.
How perverted, then, are your minds![45] «62»
[For] thus it is: perverted are the minds of those who knowingly reject God's messages.[46] «63»
It is God who has made the earth a resting-place for you and the sky a canopy, and has formed you – and formed you so well[47] – and provided for you sustenance out of the good things of life.
Such is God, your Sustainer: hallowed, then, is God, the Sustainer of all the worlds! «64»
He is the Ever-Living; there is no deity save Him: call, then, unto Him [alone], sincere in your faith in Him. All praise is due to God, the Sustainer of all the worlds! «65»
Say: "Since all evidence of the truth has come to me from my Sustainer, I am forbidden to worship [any of] those beings whom you invoke instead of God; and I am bidden to surrender myself to the Sustainer of all the worlds." «66»
It is He who creates you out of dust,[48] and

ʾInnas-Sāʿata laʾātiyatul-lā rayba fīhā wa lākinna ʾaktharan-nāsi lā yuʾminūn. (59) Wa qāla Rabbukumud-ʿūnīi ʾastajib lakum. ʾInnal-ladhīna yastakbirūna ʿan ʿibādatī sayadkhulūna jahannama dākhirīn. (60) ʾAllāhul-ladhī jaʿala lakumul-layla litaskunū fīhi wan-nahāra mubṣirā. ʾInnal-lāha ladhū faḍlin ʿalan-nāsi wa lākinna ʾaktharan-nāsi lā yashkurūn. (61) Dhālikumul-lāhu Rabbukum Khāliqu kulli shayʾil-lāa ʾilāha ʾillā Huwa faʾannā tuʾfakūn. (62) Kadhālika yuʾfakul-ladhīna kānū biʾĀyātil-lāhi yajḥadūn. (63) ◈ ʾAllāhul-ladhī jaʿala lakumul-ʾarḍa qarārañw-was-samāaʾa binā aʾañw-wa ṣawwarakum faʾaḥsana ṣuwarakum wa razaqakum-minaṭ-ṭayyibāt. Dhālikumul-lāhu Rabbukum fatabārakal-lāhu Rabbul-ʿālamīn. (64) Huwal-Ḥayyu lāa ʾilāha ʾillā Huwa fadʿūhu mukhliṣīna lahud-dīn. ʾAlḥamdu lillāhi Rabbil-ʿālamīn. (65) Qul ʾinnī nuhītu ʾan ʾaʿbudal-ladhīna tadʿūna miñ-dūnil-lāhi lammā jāaʾaniyal-bayyinātu mir-Rabbī wa ʾumirtu ʾan ʾuslima liRabbil-ʿālamīn. (66) Huwal-ladhī khalaqakum-miñ-turābiñ-thumma

42 I.e., refuse to admit to themselves that the world as they know it could ever come to an end: which is another aspect of the "overweening conceit" spoken of in verse 56 above.

43 Cf. 2: 186.

44 See note 77 on 27 : 86.

45 Sc., "O you who deny this truth!" For my above rendering of *tuʾfakūn*, see note 90 on the last sentence of 5 : 75.

46 See *sūrah* 29, note 45.

47 I.e., in accordance with the exigencies of human life. See also note 9 on the first sentence of 7 : 11.

48 See note 4 on 23 : 12.

then out of a drop of sperm, and then out of a germ-cell; and then He brings you forth as children; and then [He ordains] that you reach maturity, and then, that you grow old – though some of you [He causes to] die earlier: – and [all this He ordains] so that you might reach a term set [by Him],[49] and that you might [learn to] use your reason. ‹67›
It is He who grants life and deals death; and when He wills a thing to be, He but says unto it, "Be" – and it is. ‹68›

ART THOU NOT aware of how far they who call God's messages in question have lost sight of the truth?[50] ‹69› – they who give the lie to this divine writ and [thus] to all [the messages] with which We sent forth Our apostles [of old]?[51]
But in time they will come to know [how blind they have been: they will know it on Judgment Day], ‹70› when they shall have to carry the shackles and chains [of their own making] around their necks,[52] and are dragged ‹71› into burning despair, and in the end become fuel for the fire [of hell].[53] ‹72›
And then they will be asked: "Where now are those [powers] to which you were wont to ascribe divinity ‹73› side by side with God?"
They will answer: "They have forsaken us – or, rather, what we were wont to invoke aforetime did not exist at all!"[54]
[And they will be told:] "It is thus that God lets the deniers of the truth go astray:[55] ‹74›

مِن نُّطْفَةٍ ثُمَّ مِنْ عَلَقَةٍ ثُمَّ يُخْرِجُكُمْ طِفْلًا ثُمَّ لِتَبْلُغُوٓا۟ أَشُدَّكُمْ ثُمَّ لِتَكُونُوا۟
شُيُوخًا ۚ وَمِنكُم مَّن يُتَوَفَّىٰ مِن قَبْلُ ۖ وَلِتَبْلُغُوٓا۟ أَجَلًا مُّسَمًّى وَلَعَلَّكُمْ
تَعْقِلُونَ ﴿٦٧﴾ هُوَ ٱلَّذِى يُحْىِۦ وَيُمِيتُ ۖ فَإِذَا قَضَىٰٓ أَمْرًا فَإِنَّمَا يَقُولُ لَهُۥ
كُن فَيَكُونُ ﴿٦٨﴾ أَلَمْ تَرَ إِلَى ٱلَّذِينَ يُجَـٰدِلُونَ فِىٓ ءَايَـٰتِ ٱللَّهِ أَنَّىٰ
يُصْرَفُونَ ﴿٦٩﴾ ٱلَّذِينَ كَذَّبُوا۟ بِٱلْكِتَـٰبِ وَبِمَآ أَرْسَلْنَا بِهِۦ رُسُلَنَا ۖ فَسَوْفَ
يَعْلَمُونَ ﴿٧٠﴾ إِذِ ٱلْأَغْلَـٰلُ فِىٓ أَعْنَـٰقِهِمْ وَٱلسَّلَـٰسِلُ يُسْحَبُونَ ﴿٧١﴾ فِى
ٱلْحَمِيمِ ثُمَّ فِى ٱلنَّارِ يُسْجَرُونَ ﴿٧٢﴾ ثُمَّ قِيلَ لَهُمْ أَيْنَ مَا كُنتُمْ تُشْرِكُونَ ﴿٧٣﴾
مِن دُونِ ٱللَّهِ ۖ قَالُوا۟ ضَلُّوا۟ عَنَّا بَل لَّمْ نَكُن نَّدْعُوا۟ مِن قَبْلُ شَيْـًٔا ۚ كَذَٰلِكَ
يُضِلُّ ٱللَّهُ ٱلْكَـٰفِرِينَ ﴿٧٤﴾

miñ-nuṭfatiñ-thumma min ʿalaqatiñ-thumma yukhrijukum ṭiflañ-thumma litablughūu ʾashuddakum thumma litakūnū shuyūkhā. Wa miñkum-mañy-yutawaffā miñ-qablu wa litablughūu ʾajalam-musammañw-wa laʿallakum taʿqilūn. (67) Huwalladhī yuḥyī wa yumīt. Faʾidhā qaḍāa ʾamrañ-faʾinnamā yaqūlu lahū kuñ-fayakūn. (68) ʾAlam tara ʾilalladhīna yujādilūna fīi ʾĀyātil-lāhi ʾannā yuṣrafūn. (69) ʾAlladhīna kadhdhabū bil-Kitābi wa bimāa ʾarsalnā bihī Rusulanā; fasawfa yaʿlamūn. (70) ʾIdhil-ʾaghlālu fīi ʾaʿnāqihim was-salāsilu yusḥabūna, (71) fil-ḥamīmi thumma fin-nāri yusjarūn. (72) Thumma qīla lahum ʾayna mā kuñtum tushrikūna, (73) miñ-dūnil-lāh. Qālū ḍallū ʿannā bal-lam nakuñ-nadʿū miñ-qablu shayʾā. Kadhālika yuḍillul-lāhul-kāfirīn. (74)

49 Or: "a term known [only to Him]" – cf. 6 : 2 and the corresponding note 2.

50 Lit., "how they are turned away" – i.e., from the truth: in this case, from all the observable evidence of God's almightiness and creative activity.

51 Since, as the Qurʾān so often points out, the fundamental truths set forth in all divine revelations are the same, a rejection of the last of them amounts to a rejection of all the preceding ones.

52 For an explanation of the allegory of "shackles" and "chains", see note 13 on 13 : 5, note 44 on the last but one sentence of 34 : 33, and notes 6 and 7 on 36 : 8.

53 Thus Mujāhid (as quoted by Ṭabarī) explains the verb *yusjarūn*. As regards my rendering of *ḥamīm* as "burning despair", see *sūrah* 6, note 62.

54 Lit., "we have not been invoking aforetime any [real] thing": thus realizing, belatedly, the intrinsic nothingness of all those imaginary powers and values – including the belief in man's alleged self-sufficiency and greatness – to which they paid homage in life.

55 I.e., by allowing them to pursue illusions and foolish fancies in consequence of their unwillingness to

this is an outcome of your having arrogantly exulted on earth without any [concern for what is] right, and of your having been so full of self-conceit! ‹75› Enter [now] the gates of hell, therein to abide: and how vile an abode for all who are given to false pride!" ‹76›

HENCE, remain thou patient in adversity – for, verily, God's promise always comes true. And whether We show thee [in this world] something of what We hold in store for those [deniers of the truth], or whether We cause thee to die [ere that retribution takes place – know that, in the end], it is unto Us that they will be brought back.[56] ‹77›
And, indeed, [O Muḥammad,] We sent forth apostles before thy time; some of them We have mentioned to thee,[57] and some of them We have not mentioned to thee. And it was not given to any apostle to bring forth a miracle other than by God's leave.[58]
Yet when God's will becomes manifest,[59] judgment will [already] have been passed in all justice, and lost will be, then and there, all who tried to reduce to nothing [whatever they could not understand].[60] ‹78›
It is God who [at all times works wonders for you:[61] thus, He] provides for you [all manner of] livestock, so that on some of them you may ride, and from some derive your food, ‹79› and find [yet other] benefits in them;[62] and that through them

ذَٰلِكُم بِمَا كُنتُمْ تَفْرَحُونَ فِى ٱلْأَرْضِ بِغَيْرِ ٱلْحَقِّ وَبِمَا كُنتُمْ
تَمْرَحُونَ ﴿٧٥﴾ ٱدْخُلُوٓا۟ أَبْوَٰبَ جَهَنَّمَ خَٰلِدِينَ فِيهَا ۖ فَبِئْسَ مَثْوَى
ٱلْمُتَكَبِّرِينَ ﴿٧٦﴾ فَٱصْبِرْ إِنَّ وَعْدَ ٱللَّهِ حَقٌّ ۚ فَإِمَّا نُرِيَنَّكَ بَعْضَ
ٱلَّذِى نَعِدُهُمْ أَوْ نَتَوَفَّيَنَّكَ فَإِلَيْنَا يُرْجَعُونَ ﴿٧٧﴾ وَلَقَدْ أَرْسَلْنَا رُسُلًا مِّن
قَبْلِكَ مِنْهُم مَّن قَصَصْنَا عَلَيْكَ وَمِنْهُم مَّن لَّمْ نَقْصُصْ عَلَيْكَ ۗ وَمَا
كَانَ لِرَسُولٍ أَن يَأْتِىَ بِـَٔايَةٍ إِلَّا بِإِذْنِ ٱللَّهِ ۚ فَإِذَا جَآءَ أَمْرُ ٱللَّهِ قُضِىَ
بِٱلْحَقِّ وَخَسِرَ هُنَالِكَ ٱلْمُبْطِلُونَ ﴿٧٨﴾ ٱللَّهُ ٱلَّذِى جَعَلَ لَكُمُ ٱلْأَنْعَٰمَ
لِتَرْكَبُوا۟ مِنْهَا وَمِنْهَا تَأْكُلُونَ ﴿٧٩﴾ وَلَكُمْ فِيهَا مَنَٰفِعُ وَلِتَبْلُغُوا۟ عَلَيْهَا

Dhālikum-bimā kuñtum tafraḥūna fil-ʾarḍi bighayril-ḥaqqi wa bimā kuñtum tamraḥūn. (75) ʾUdkhulūu ʾabwāba jahannama khālidīna fīhā fabiʾsa mathwal-mutakabbirīn. (76) Faṣbir ʾinna waʿdal-lāhi ḥaqq. Faʾimmā nuriyannaka baʿḍal-ladhī naʿiduhum ʾaw natawaffayannaka faʾilaynā yurjaʿūn. (77) Wa laqad ʾarsalnā Rusulam-miñ-qablika minhum mañ-qaṣaṣnā ʿalayka wa minhum-mal-lam naqṣuṣ ʿalayk. Wa mā kāna liRasūlin ʾañy-yaʾtiya biʾĀyatin ʾillā biʾidhnil-lāh. Faʾidhā jāaʾa ʾamrul-lāhi quḍiya bilḥaqqi wa khasira hunālikal-mubṭilūn. (78) ʾAllāhul-ladhī jaʿala lakumul-ʾanʿāma litarkabū minhā wa minhā taʾkulūn. (79) Wa lakum fīhā manāfiʿu wa litablughū ʿalayhā

acknowledge the self-evident truth of God's existence and uniqueness and of man's utter dependence on Him. For a discussion of the problem of God's "letting" a sinner go astray, see note 4 on 14 : 4.

56 See the almost identical passage in 10 : 46, as well as the corresponding notes 66 and 67.

57 I.e., in the Qurʾān.

58 See 6 : 109 – "Miracles are in the power of God alone" – and the corresponding note 94. Both passages (6 : 109 and the present one) relate to the futile demand of Muḥammad's opponents to be shown a miracle in proof of the divine origin of the Qurʾān – the implication being that it is *not* God's will to convince the deniers of the truth by means of what is commonly regarded as miracles".

59 Lit., "when God's command comes", i.e., whether it be in this world or on the Day of Judgment: a reference to the retribution spoken of in verse 77 above.

60 I.e., in this case, divine revelation as such. For the above rendering of *al-mubṭilūn*, see note 47 on the last sentence of 29 : 48.

61 I.e., by providing in a wondrous manner the means of man's subsistence, and by endowing him with the miracle of a creative intellect which enables him to make fruitful use of so many natural phenomena. (This passage connects with the statement implied in verse 78 that "miracles are in the power of God alone": see note 58.)

62 The "other benefits" are both concrete and abstract in their nature: concrete benefits like wool, skins, etc., and

you may attain to the fulfilment of [many] a heartfelt need:[63] for on them, as on ships, you are borne [through life]. ‹80›
And [thus] He displays His wonders before you: which, then, of God's wonders can you still deny? ‹81›

HAVE THEY, then, never journeyed about the earth and beheld what happened in the end to those [deniers of the truth] who lived before their time? More numerous were they, and greater in power than they are, and in the impact which they left on earth: but all that they ever achieved was of no avail to them ‹82› – for when their apostles came to them with all evidence of the truth, they arrogantly exulted in whatever knowledge they [already] possessed:[64] and [so, in the end,] they were overwhelmed by the very thing which they were wont to deride.[65] ‹83›
And then, when they [clearly] beheld Our punishment,[66] they said: "We have come to believe in the One God, and we have renounced all belief in that to which we were wont to ascribe a share in His divinity!"[67] ‹84›
But their attaining to faith after they had beheld Our punishment could not possibly benefit them[68] – such being the way of God that has always obtained for His creatures: – and so, then and there, lost were they who had denied the truth.[69] ‹85›

حَاجَةً فِى صُدُورِكُمْ وَعَلَيْهَا وَعَلَى ٱلْفُلْكِ تُحْمَلُونَ ﴿٨٠﴾ وَيُرِيكُمْ
ءَايَٰتِهِۦ فَأَىَّ ءَايَٰتِ ٱللَّهِ تُنكِرُونَ ﴿٨١﴾ أَفَلَمْ يَسِيرُوا۟ فِى ٱلْأَرْضِ
فَيَنظُرُوا۟ كَيْفَ كَانَ عَٰقِبَةُ ٱلَّذِينَ مِن قَبْلِهِمْ ۚ كَانُوٓا۟ أَكْثَرَ مِنْهُمْ وَأَشَدَّ
قُوَّةً وَءَاثَارًا فِى ٱلْأَرْضِ فَمَآ أَغْنَىٰ عَنْهُم مَّا كَانُوا۟ يَكْسِبُونَ ﴿٨٢﴾ فَلَمَّا
جَآءَتْهُمْ رُسُلُهُم بِٱلْبَيِّنَٰتِ فَرِحُوا۟ بِمَا عِندَهُم مِّنَ ٱلْعِلْمِ وَحَاقَ بِهِم مَّا
كَانُوا۟ بِهِۦ يَسْتَهْزِءُونَ ﴿٨٣﴾ فَلَمَّا رَأَوْا۟ بَأْسَنَا قَالُوٓا۟ ءَامَنَّا بِٱللَّهِ وَحْدَهُۥ
وَكَفَرْنَا بِمَا كُنَّا بِهِۦ مُشْرِكِينَ ﴿٨٤﴾ فَلَمْ يَكُ يَنفَعُهُمْ إِيمَٰنُهُمْ لَمَّا رَأَوْا۟
بَأْسَنَا ۖ سُنَّتَ ٱللَّهِ ٱلَّتِى قَدْ خَلَتْ فِى عِبَادِهِۦ ۖ وَخَسِرَ هُنَالِكَ
ٱلْكَٰفِرُونَ ﴿٨٥﴾

ḥājatañ-fī ṣudūrikum wa ʿalayhā wa ʿalal-fulki tuḥmalūn. ﴿80﴾ Wa yurīkum ʾĀyātihī faʾayya ʾĀyātil-lāhi tuñkirūn. ﴿81﴾ ʾAfalam yasīrū fil-ʾarḍi fayañẓurū kayfa kāna ʿāqibatul-ladhīna miñ-qablihim. Kānūu ʾakthara minhum wa ʾashadda quwwatañw-wa ʾāthārañ-fil-ʾarḍi famāa ʾaghnā ʿanhum-mā kānū yaksibūn. ﴿82﴾ Falammā jāaʾat-hum Rusuluhum bil-bayyināti fariḥū bimā ʿiñdahum-minal-ʿilmi wa ḥāqa bihim-mā kānū bihī yastahziʾūn. ﴿83﴾ Falammā raʾaw baʾsanā qālūu ʾāmannā billāhi waḥdahū wa kafarnā bimā kunnā bihī mushrikīn. ﴿84﴾ Falam yaku yañfaʿuhum ʾīmānuhum lammā raʾaw baʾsanā. Sunnatal-lāhil-latī qad khalat fī ʿibādihī wa khasira hunālikal-kāfirūn. ﴿85﴾

abstract ones like beauty (cf. 16 : 6-8, as well as Solomon's reverence for the God-created beauty of horses expressed in 38 : 31-33) or the all-time companionship of man and dog symbolized in the legend of the Men of the Cave (18 : 18 and 22).

63 Lit., "a need in your bosoms" [or "hearts"]: i.e., *a genuine* need.

64 I.e., they were fully satisfied with their own empirically or speculatively acquired or inherited knowledge; and so, in their arrogant conviction that man is "self-sufficient" and, therefore, not in need of any guidance by a Power beyond the reach of human perception, they rejected whatever ethical and spiritual truths were offered them by the prophets.

65 I.e., the idea of God's existence and inescapable judgment: see 6 : 10 and the corresponding note 9.

66 I.e., the God-willed, catastrophic breakdown of their society and civilization in consequence of their persistent rejection of all spiritual values.

67 This evidently includes their past belief in man's supposedly "unlimited possibilities" and the illusory conviction that one day he would achieve "mastery over nature".

68 I.e., firstly, because this belated faith could not unmake a reality which had already come into being, and, secondly, because it could not contribute to their spiritual growth inasmuch as it was not an outcome of free choice but had been, rather, forced on them by the shock of an irreversible calamity.

69 The "way of God" (*sunnat Allāh*) is the Qurʾanic term for the totality of natural laws instituted by the Creator: in this case, the law that faith has no spiritual value unless it arises out of a genuine, inner enlightenment.

سورة فصلت مكية

وآياتها أربع وخمسون

بِسْمِ ٱللَّهِ ٱلرَّحْمَٰنِ ٱلرَّحِيمِ

حمٓ تَنزِيلٌ مِّنَ ٱلرَّحْمَٰنِ ٱلرَّحِيمِ

كِتَٰبٌ فُصِّلَتْ ءَايَٰتُهُۥ

قُرْءَانًا عَرَبِيًّا لِّقَوْمٍ يَعْلَمُونَ

The Forty-First Sūrah

Fuṣṣilat (Clearly Spelled Out)

Mecca Period

REVEALED immediately after the preceding *sūrah,* this one continues the theme begun in the latter: man's reasoned acceptance or wilful rejection of divine revelations.

The title is derived from the verb *fuṣṣilat* occurring in verse 3, where it relates to the "clearly spelled-out" messages of the Qur᾽ān.

سورة فصلت مكية -41-
وآياتها أربع وخمسون

IN THE NAME OF GOD, THE MOST GRACIOUS, THE DISPENSER OF GRACE:

Ḥā. Mīm.[1] ‹1›
THE BESTOWAL from on high [of this revelation] issues from the Most Gracious, the Dispenser of Grace: ‹2› a divine writ, the messages whereof have been clearly spelled out as a discourse in the Arabic tongue[2] for people of [innate] knowledge, ‹3› to be a herald of glad tidings as well as a warning.
And yet, [whenever this divine writ is offered to men,] most of them turn away, so that they cannot hear [its message]:[3] ‹4›
and so they say, [as it were:] "Our hearts are veiled from whatever thou callest us to, [O Muḥammad,] and in our ears is deafness, and between us and thee is a

بِسۡمِ ٱللَّهِ ٱلرَّحۡمَٰنِ ٱلرَّحِيمِ

حمٓ ① تَنزِيلٌ مِّنَ ٱلرَّحۡمَٰنِ ٱلرَّحِيمِ ② كِتَٰبٌ فُصِّلَتۡ ءَايَٰتُهُۥ قُرۡءَانًا
عَرَبِيًّا لِّقَوۡمٍ يَعۡلَمُونَ ③ بَشِيرًا وَنَذِيرًا فَأَعۡرَضَ أَكۡثَرُهُمۡ فَهُمۡ لَا يَسۡمَعُونَ ④
وَقَالُواْ قُلُوبُنَا فِيٓ أَكِنَّةٖ مِّمَّا تَدۡعُونَآ إِلَيۡهِ وَفِيٓ ءَاذَانِنَا وَقۡرٞ وَمِنۢ بَيۡنِنَا وَبَيۡنِكَ

Bismil-lāhir-Raḥmānir-Raḥīm.
Ḥā-Mīim. ① Tañzīlum-minar-Raḥmānir-Raḥīm. ②
Kitābuñ-fuṣṣilat ᵓĀyātuhū Qurᵓānan ᶜarabiyyal-liqaw-
miñy-yaᶜlamūn. ③ Bashīrañw-wa Nadhīrañ-faᵓaᶜraḍa
ᵓaktharuhum fahum lā yasmaᶜūn. ④ Wa qālū
qulūbunā fii ᵓakinnatim-mimmā tadᶜūnāa ᵓilayhi wa
fii ᵓādhāninā waqruñw-wa mim-bayninā wa baynika

---

1 See Appendix II.

2 See 12 : 2 and the corresponding note 3.

3 The "people of [innate] knowledge" mentioned in the preceding verse are obviously those who understand the spiritual purport of this divine writ and, therefore, submit to its guidance: hence, it cannot he "most of *them*" who are referred to in the above phrase and in the next verse, but, on the contrary, people who are *devoid* of such knowledge and to whom, in consequence, the Qur'ān is meaningless. This elliptically implied differentiation – overlooked by almost all of the commentators (with perhaps the sole exception of Ibn Kathīr) – can only be brought out by means of an interpolation at the beginning of the sentence.

barrier.[4] Do, then, [whatever thou wilt, whereas,] behold, we shall do [as we have always done]!" ‹5›

Say thou, [O Prophet:] "I am but a mortal like you.[5] It has been revealed to me that your God is the One God: go, then, straight towards Him and seek His forgiveness!"

And woe unto those who ascribe divinity to aught beside Him, ‹6› [and] those who do not spend in charity: for it is they, they who [thus] deny the truth of the life to come![6] ‹7›

[But,] verily, they who have attained to faith and do good works shall have a reward unending! ‹8›

نصف الحزب

SAY: "Would you indeed deny Him who has created the earth in two aeons?[7] And do you claim that there is any power that could rival Him,[8] the Sustainer of all the worlds?" ‹9›

For He [it is who, after creating the earth,] placed firm mountains on it, [towering] above its surface, and bestowed [so many] blessings on it, and equitably apportioned[9] its means of subsistence to all who would seek it: [and all this He created] in four aeons.[10] ‹10›

And[11] He [it is who] applied His design to

حِجَابٌ فَٱعْمَلْ إِنَّنَا عَـٰمِلُونَ ۝٥ قُلْ إِنَّمَآ أَنَا۠ بَشَرٌ مِّثْلُكُمْ يُوحَىٰٓ إِلَىَّ
أَنَّمَآ إِلَـٰهُكُمْ إِلَـٰهٌ وَٰحِدٌ فَٱسْتَقِيمُوٓا۟ إِلَيْهِ وَٱسْتَغْفِرُوهُ ۗ وَوَيْلٌ
لِّلْمُشْرِكِينَ ۝٦ ٱلَّذِينَ لَا يُؤْتُونَ ٱلزَّكَوٰةَ وَهُم بِٱلْـَٔاخِرَةِ هُمْ كَـٰفِرُونَ ۝٧
إِنَّ ٱلَّذِينَ ءَامَنُوا۟ وَعَمِلُوا۟ ٱلصَّـٰلِحَـٰتِ لَهُمْ أَجْرٌ غَيْرُ مَمْنُونٍ ۝٨ ۞ قُلْ
أَئِنَّكُمْ لَتَكْفُرُونَ بِٱلَّذِى خَلَقَ ٱلْأَرْضَ فِى يَوْمَيْنِ وَتَجْعَلُونَ لَهُۥٓ أَندَادًا
ذَٰلِكَ رَبُّ ٱلْعَـٰلَمِينَ ۝٩ وَجَعَلَ فِيهَا رَوَٰسِىَ مِن فَوْقِهَا وَبَـٰرَكَ فِيهَا
وَقَدَّرَ فِيهَآ أَقْوَٰتَهَا فِىٓ أَرْبَعَةِ أَيَّامٍ سَوَآءً لِّلسَّآئِلِينَ ۝١٠ ثُمَّ ٱسْتَوَىٰٓ إِلَى

ḥijābuñ-faᶜmal ᵓinnanā ᶜāmilūn. ‹5› **Qul ᵓinnamāa ᵓana basharum-mithlukum yūḥāa ᵓilayya ᵓannamāa ᵓIlāhukum ᵓIlāhuñw-Wāḥiduñ fastaqīmūu ᵓilayhi was-taghfirūh. Wa waylul-lilmushrikīn.** ‹6› **ᵓAlladhīna lā yuᵓtūnaz-Zakāta wa hum-bilᵓĀkhirati hum kāfirūn.** ‹7› **ᵓInnal-ladhīna ᵓāmanū wa ᶜamiluṣ-ṣāliḥāti lahum ᵓajrun ghayru mamnūn.** ‹8› ۞ **Qul ᵓaᵓinnakum latakfurūna billadhī khalaqal-ᵓarḍa fī yawmayni wa tajᶜalūna lahūu ᵓañdādā. Dhālika Rabbul-ᶜālamīn.** ‹9› **Wa jaᶜala fīhā rawāsiya miñ-fawqihā wa bāraka fīhā wa qaddara fīhāa ᵓaqwātahā fīi ᵓarbaᶜati ᵓayyāmiñ-sawāaᵓal-lissāaᵓilīn.** ‹10› **Thummas-tawāa ᵓilas-**

4 For this rendering of the term *ḥijāb*, see note 36 on the first sentence of 7 : 46. See also 6 : 25. The "saying" of those who turn away from the message of the Qurᵓān is, of course, figurative, describing only their *attitude*.

5 Cf. 6 : 50 and the corresponding note 38.

6 Belief in God's oneness and charitableness towards one's fellow-men are two cardinal demands of Islam. Conversely, a deliberate offence against either of these two demands amounts to a denial of man's responsibility before God and hence, by implication, of a continuation of life in the hereafter. (For my rendering of *zakāh*, in this context, as "charity", see *sūrah* 2, note 34. It is to be borne in mind that the application of this term to the obligatory tax incumbent on Muslims dates from the Medina period, whereas the present *sūrah* is a Meccan revelation.)

7 For the above rendering of the term *yawm* (lit., "day"), as "aeon", see last third of note 43 on 7 : 54. As in so many verses of the Qurᵓān which relate to cosmic events, the repeated mention of the "six aeons" during which the universe was created – "two" of which, according to the above verse, were taken by the evolution of the inorganic universe, including the earth – has a purely allegorical import: in this case, I believe, an indication that the universe did not exist "eternally" but had a definite beginning in time, and that it required a definite time-lapse to evolve to its present condition.

8 Lit., "do you give Him compeers (*andād*)?" For an explanation, see note 13 on 2 : 22.

9 I.e., in accordance with divine justice, and not with human concepts of "equity" or "need".

10 Almost all the classical commentators agree in that these "four aeons" include the "two" mentioned in the preceding verse: hence my interpolation of the words "and all this He created". Together with the "two aeons" of verse 12, the entire allegorical number comes to six.

11 Whenever the particle *thumma* is used, as in the above instance, to link parallel statements – i.e., statements not necessarily indicating a sequence in time – it has the function of a simple conjunction, and may be rendered as "and".

the skies, which were [yet but] smoke;[12] and He [it is who] said to them and to the earth, "Come [into being], both of you, willingly or unwillingly!" – to which both responded, "We do come in obedience."[13] ‹11›
And He [it is who] decreed that they become seven heavens[14] in two aeons, and imparted unto each heaven its function. And We adorned the skies nearest to the earth with lights, and made them secure:[15] such is the ordaining of the Almighty, the All-Knowing. ‹12›

BUT IF they turn away,[16] say: "I warn you of [the coming of] a thunderbolt of punishment[17] like the thunderbolt [that fell upon the tribes] of ᶜĀd and Thamūd!"[18] ‹13›
Lo! There came unto them [God's] apostles, speaking of what lay open before them and what was [still] beyond their ken,[19] [and calling unto them,] "Worship none but God!"
They answered: "If our Sustainer had willed [us to believe in what you say],

ٱلسَّمَآءِ وَهِىَ دُخَانٌ فَقَالَ لَهَا وَلِلْأَرْضِ ٱئْتِيَا طَوْعًا أَوْ كَرْهًا قَالَتَآ أَتَيْنَا
طَآئِعِينَ (11) فَقَضَىٰهُنَّ سَبْعَ سَمَٰوَاتٍ فِى يَوْمَيْنِ وَأَوْحَىٰ فِى كُلِّ سَمَآءٍ أَمْرَهَا
وَزَيَّنَّا ٱلسَّمَآءَ ٱلدُّنْيَا بِمَصَٰبِيحَ وَحِفْظًا ذَٰلِكَ تَقْدِيرُ ٱلْعَزِيزِ ٱلْعَلِيمِ (12) فَإِنْ
أَعْرَضُوا۟ فَقُلْ أَنذَرْتُكُمْ صَٰعِقَةً مِّثْلَ صَٰعِقَةِ عَادٍ وَثَمُودَ (13) إِذْ جَآءَتْهُمُ
ٱلرُّسُلُ مِنۢ بَيْنِ أَيْدِيهِمْ وَمِنْ خَلْفِهِمْ أَلَّا تَعْبُدُوٓا۟ إِلَّا ٱللَّهَ قَالُوا۟ لَوْ شَآءَ رَبُّنَا

samāaʾi wa hiya dukhānuñ-faqāla lahā wa lilʾarḍiʾ-tiyā ṭawᶜan ʾaw karhañ-qālatāa ʾataynā ṭāaʾiᶜīn. (11) Faqaḍāhunna sabᶜa samāwātiñ-fī yawmayni wa ʾawḥā fī kulli samāaʾin ʾamrahā. Wa zayyannas-samāaʾad-dunyā bimaṣābīḥa wa ḥifẓā. Dhālika taqdīrul-ᶜAzīzil-ᶜAlīm. (12) Faʾin ʾaᶜraḍū faqul ʾañdhartukum ṣāᶜiqatam-mithla ṣāᶜiqati ᶜĀdiñw-wa Thamūd. (13) ʾIdh jāaʾat-humur-Rusulu mim-bayni ʾaydīhim wa min khalfihim ʾallā taᶜbudūu ʾillal-lāh. Qālū law shāaʾa Rabbunā

12 I.e., a gas – evidently hydrogen gas, which physicists regard as the primal element from which all material particles of the universe have evolved and still evolve. For the meaning of the term *samāʾ* ("sky" or "skies" or "heaven") in its cosmic connotation, see note 20 on 2 : 29.

13 Explaining this passage, Zamakhsharī observes: "The meaning of God's command to the skies and the earth to 'come', and their submission [to His command] is this: He willed their coming into being, and so they came to be as He willed them to be . . . : and this is the kind of metaphor (*majāz*) which is called 'allegory' (*tamthīl*). . . . Thus, the purport [of this passage] is but an illustration (*taṣwīr*) of the effect of His almighty power on all that is willed [by Him], and nothing else. . . ." (It is obvious that Zamakhsharī's reasoning is based on the oft-repeated Qurʾanic statement, "When God wills a thing to be, He but says unto it, 'Be' – and it is.") Concluding his interpretation of the above passage, Zamaksharī adds: "If I am asked about the meaning of [the words] 'willingly or unwillingly', I say that it is a figurative expression (*mathal*) indicating that His almighty will must inevitably take effect."

14 I.e., a multiplicity of cosmic systems (cf. note 20 on 2 : 29).

15 Cf. 15 : 16-18 and the corresponding notes 16 and 17; also 37 : 6 ff.

16 This connects with the opening sentence of verse 9 above: "Would you indeed deny Him who has created . . .", etc.

17 See note 40 on 2 : 55.

18 For the story of these two ancient tribes, see 7 : 65-79 and the corresponding notes, in particular 48 and 56; also 26 : 123-158.

19 Lit., "from between their hands and from behind them": i.e., reminding them of something that was known to them – namely, what happened to sinners like themselves who lived before their time – and warning them of what was bound to happen in the future to them, too, if they persisted in their denial of the truth (Al-Ḥasan al-Baṣrī, as quoted by Zamakhsharī). However, it is possible to understand the above phrase (which has been explained in note 247 on 2 : 255) in yet another, more direct way: God's message-bearers pointed out to those sinning communities something that should have been obvious to them (lit., "between their hands") – namely, their patently wrong attitude in their worldly, social concerns and moral concepts – as well as the unreasonableness of their denying something that was still beyond their ken (lit., "behind them"): namely, life after death and God's ltimate judgment.

He would have sent down angels [as His message-bearers][20]. As it is, behold, we deny that there is any truth in what you [claim to] have been sent with!" ‹14›
Now as for [the tribe of] ᶜĀd, they walked arrogantly on earth, [offending] against all right, and saying, "Who could have a power greater than ours?"
Why – were they, then, not aware that God, who created them, had a power greater than theirs?
But they went on rejecting Our messages; ‹15› and thereupon We let loose upon them a stormwind raging through days of misfortune,[21] so as to give them, in the life of this world, a foretaste of suffering through humiliation: but [their] suffering in the life to come will be far more humiliating, and they will have none to succour them. ‹16›
And as for [the tribe of] Thamūd, We offered them guidance, but they chose blindness in preference to guidance: and so the thunderbolt of shameful suffering fell upon them as an outcome of all [the evil] that they had wrought; ‹17› and We saved [only] those who had attained to faith and were conscious of Us. ‹18›

Hence, [warn all men of] the Day when the enemies of God shall be gathered together before the fire, and then shall be driven onward, ‹19› till, when they come close to it, their hearing and their sight and their [very] skins will bear witness against them, speaking of what they were doing [on earth]. ‹20›
And they will ask their skins, "Why did you bear witness against us?" – [and] these will reply: "God, who gives speech to all things, has given speech to us [as well]: for He [it is who] has created you in the first instance – and unto Him you are [now] brought back. ‹21› And you did not try to hide [your sins] lest your hearing or

لَأَنزَلَ مَلَٰٓئِكَةً فَإِنَّا بِمَآ أُرۡسِلۡتُم بِهِۦ كَٰفِرُونَ ﴿١٤﴾ فَأَمَّا عَادٌ
فَٱسۡتَكۡبَرُواْ فِي ٱلۡأَرۡضِ بِغَيۡرِ ٱلۡحَقِّ وَقَالُواْ مَنۡ أَشَدُّ مِنَّا قُوَّةًۖ أَوَلَمۡ
يَرَوۡاْ أَنَّ ٱللَّهَ ٱلَّذِي خَلَقَهُمۡ هُوَ أَشَدُّ مِنۡهُمۡ قُوَّةٗۖ وَكَانُواْ بِـَٔايَٰتِنَا
يَجۡحَدُونَ ﴿١٥﴾ فَأَرۡسَلۡنَا عَلَيۡهِمۡ رِيحٗا صَرۡصَرٗا فِيٓ أَيَّامٖ نَّحِسَاتٖ
لِّنُذِيقَهُمۡ عَذَابَ ٱلۡخِزۡيِ فِي ٱلۡحَيَوٰةِ ٱلدُّنۡيَاۖ وَلَعَذَابُ ٱلۡأٓخِرَةِ أَخۡزَىٰۖ
وَهُمۡ لَا يُنصَرُونَ ﴿١٦﴾ وَأَمَّا ثَمُودُ فَهَدَيۡنَٰهُمۡ فَٱسۡتَحَبُّواْ ٱلۡعَمَىٰ عَلَى
ٱلۡهُدَىٰ فَأَخَذَتۡهُمۡ صَٰعِقَةُ ٱلۡعَذَابِ ٱلۡهُونِ بِمَا كَانُواْ يَكۡسِبُونَ ﴿١٧﴾
وَنَجَّيۡنَا ٱلَّذِينَ ءَامَنُواْ وَكَانُواْ يَتَّقُونَ ﴿١٨﴾ وَيَوۡمَ يُحۡشَرُ أَعۡدَآءُ ٱللَّهِ إِلَى
ٱلنَّارِ فَهُمۡ يُوزَعُونَ ﴿١٩﴾ حَتَّىٰٓ إِذَا مَا جَآءُوهَا شَهِدَ عَلَيۡهِمۡ سَمۡعُهُمۡ
وَأَبۡصَٰرُهُمۡ وَجُلُودُهُم بِمَا كَانُواْ يَعۡمَلُونَ ﴿٢٠﴾ وَقَالُواْ لِجُلُودِهِمۡ لِمَ شَهِدتُّمۡ
عَلَيۡنَاۖ قَالُوٓاْ أَنطَقَنَا ٱللَّهُ ٱلَّذِيٓ أَنطَقَ كُلَّ شَيۡءٖۚ وَهُوَ خَلَقَكُمۡ أَوَّلَ مَرَّةٖ
وَإِلَيۡهِ تُرۡجَعُونَ ﴿٢١﴾ وَمَا كُنتُمۡ تَسۡتَتِرُونَ أَن يَشۡهَدَ عَلَيۡكُمۡ سَمۡعُكُمۡ وَلَآ

laʾañzala Malāaʾikatañ-faʾinnā bimāa ʾursiltum-bihī kāfirūn. (14) Faʾamma ᶜĀduñ-fastakbarū fil-ʾarḍi bighayril-ḥaqqi wa qālū man ʾashaddu minnā quwwah. ʾAwalam yaraw ʾannal-lāhal-ladhī khalaqahum Huwa ʾashaddu minhum quwwah. Wa kānū biʾĀyātinā yajḥadūn. (15) Faʾarsalnā ᶜalayhim rīḥañ-ṣarṣarañ-fīi ʾayyāmiñ-naḥisātil-linudhīqahum ᶜadhābal-khizyi fil-ḥayātid-dunyā wa laᶜadhābul-ʾĀkhirati ʾakhzā wa hum lā yuñṣarūn. (16) Wa ʾammā Thamūdu fahadaynāhum fastaḥabbul-ᶜamā ᶜalal-hudā faʾakhadhat-hum ṣāᶜiqatul-ᶜadhābil-hūni bimā kānū yaksibūn. (17) Wa najjaynal-ladhīna ʾāmanū wa kānū yattaqūn. (18) Wa Yawma yuḥsharu ʾaᶜdāaʾul-lāhi ʾilan-nāri fahum yūzaᶜūn. (19) Ḥattāa ʾidhā mā jāaʾūhā shahida ᶜalayhim samᶜuhum wa ʾabṣāruhum wa julūduhum-bimā kānū yaᶜmalūn. (20) Wa qālū lijulūdihim lima shahittum ᶜalaynā. Qālūu ʾañṭaqanal-lāhul-ladhīi ʾañṭaqa kulla shayʾiñw-wa Huwa khalaqakum ʾawwala marratiñw-wa ʾilayhi turjaᶜūn. (21) Wa mā kuñtum tastatirūna ʾañy-yashhada ᶜalaykum samᶜukum wa lāa

20 Cf. 6 : 8-9 and 15 : 7.
21 See 69 : 6-8.

your sight or your skins bear witness against you: nay, but you thought that God did not know much of what you were doing ‹22› – and that very thought which you thought about your Sustainer has brought you to perdition, and so now you find yourselves among the lost!" ‹23›

And then, [even] if they endure [their lot] in patience, the fire will still be their abode;[22] and if they pray to be allowed to make amends, they will not be allowed to do so:[23] ‹24› for [when they became oblivious of Us,] We assigned to them [their own evil impulses as their] other selves,[24] and these made appear goodly to them whatever lay open before them and whatever was beyond their ken.[25]

And so, the sentence [of doom] will have fallen due upon them together with the [other sinful] communities of invisible beings[26] and humans that passed away before their time: verily, they [all] will indeed be lost! ‹25›

NOW THOSE who are bent on denying the truth say [unto one another]: "Do not listen to this Qur᾽ān, but rather talk frivolously about it, so that you might gain the upper hand!"[27] ‹26›

أَبْصَٰرُكُمْ وَلَا جُلُودُكُمْ وَلَٰكِن ظَنَنتُمْ أَنَّ ٱللَّهَ لَا يَعْلَمُ كَثِيرًا مِّمَّا
تَعْمَلُونَ ﴿22﴾ وَذَٰلِكُمْ ظَنُّكُمُ ٱلَّذِى ظَنَنتُم بِرَبِّكُمْ أَرْدَىٰكُمْ فَأَصْبَحْتُم
مِّنَ ٱلْخَٰسِرِينَ ﴿23﴾ فَإِن يَصْبِرُوا۟ فَٱلنَّارُ مَثْوًى لَّهُمْ ۖ وَإِن يَسْتَعْتِبُوا۟ فَمَا
هُم مِّنَ ٱلْمُعْتَبِينَ ﴿24﴾ ۞ وَقَيَّضْنَا لَهُمْ قُرَنَآءَ فَزَيَّنُوا۟ لَهُم مَّا بَيْنَ أَيْدِيهِمْ
وَمَا خَلْفَهُمْ وَحَقَّ عَلَيْهِمُ ٱلْقَوْلُ فِىٓ أُمَمٍ قَدْ خَلَتْ مِن قَبْلِهِم مِّنَ ٱلْجِنِّ
وَٱلْإِنسِ ۖ إِنَّهُمْ كَانُوا۟ خَٰسِرِينَ ﴿25﴾ وَقَالَ ٱلَّذِينَ كَفَرُوا۟ لَا تَسْمَعُوا۟
لِهَٰذَا ٱلْقُرْءَانِ وَٱلْغَوْا۟ فِيهِ لَعَلَّكُمْ تَغْلِبُونَ ﴿26﴾

ثلاثة ارباع الحزب

ᵓabṣārukum wa lā julūdukum wa lākiñ-ẓanañtum
ᵓannal-lāha lā yaᶜlamu kathīram-mimmā taᶜmalūn.
22 Wa dhālikum ẓannukumul-ladhī ẓanañtum-
biRabbikum ᵓardākum faᵓaṣbaḥtum minal-khāsirīn.
23 Faᵓiñy-yaṣbirū fannāru mathwal-lahum. Wa ᵓiñy-
yastaᶜtibū famā hum minal-muᶜtabīn. 24 ۞ Wa
qayyaḍnā lahum quranāaᵓa fazayyanū lahum mā
bayna ᵓaydīhim wa mā khalfahum wa ḥaqqa
ᶜalayhimul-qawlu fii ᵓumamiñ-qad khalat miñ-
qablihim-minal-Jinni wal-ᵓIñsi ᵓinnahum kānū
khāsirīn. 25 Wa qālal-ladhīna kafarū lā tasmaᶜū
lihādhal-Qurᵓāni wal-ghaw fīhi laᶜallakum tagh-
libūn. 26

22 Sc., "unless God wills to reprieve them": see the last paragraph of 6 : 128 and the corresponding note 114; also the *ḥadīth* quoted in note 10 on 40 : 12.

23 Lit., "they will not be of those who are allowed to make amends": an allusion to the request of the doomed, on the Day of Judgment, to be granted a "second chance" on earth, and to God's refusal of this request (cf. 6 : 27-28 and 32 : 12).

24 Or: "soul-mates" (cf. 4 : 38). The verb *qarana*, from which the noun *qarīn* is derived, signifies "he linked" or "intimately associated" or "yoked together [one thing with another]". Cf. 43 : 36 – "as for anyone who chooses to remain blind to the remembrance of the Most Gracious, to him We assign an [enduring] evil impulse [lit., "a satan"], to become his other self".

25 Lit., "that which was between their hands and that which was behind them": i.e., their own evil impulses (which had become their "other selves", as it were) made alluring to them the unrestrained enjoyment, without any moral discrimination, of all the worldly attractions which lay open before them, causing them, at the same time, to dismiss as an illusion the idea of resurrection and of God's judgment – thus giving them a false sense of security with regard to something that was beyond their ken.

26 For this rendering – and the meaning – of the term *jinn*, see Appendix III.

27 This is an allusion to efforts aimed at discrediting the Qur᾽ān by describing it as "invented" by Muḥammad for his own – personal and political – ends, as a series of "misunderstood quotations" from earlier scriptures, as the result of "hallucinations", and so forth: all of which implies that the opponents of the Qur᾽anic message instinctively feel its force, realizing at the same time that it endangers their self-complacent, materialistic outlook on life and ought, therefore, to be combatted. This explains the statement, at the end of verse 28, that they "*knowingly* reject" God's messages.

But We shall most certainly give those who are [thus] bent on denying the truth a taste of suffering severe, and We shall most certainly requite them according to the worst of their deeds! ‹27› That requital of God's enemies will be the fire [of the hereafter]: in it will they have an abode of unmeasurable duration as an outcome of their having knowingly rejected Our messages.[28] ‹28›

And they who [in their life on earth] were bent on denying the truth will [thereupon] exclaim: "O our Sustainer! Show us those of the invisible beings and humans that have led us astray:[29] we shall trample them underfoot, so that they shall be the lowest of all!"[30] ‹29›

[But,] behold, as for those who say, "Our Sustainer is God," and then steadfastly pursue the right way – upon them do angels often descend, [saying:] "Fear not and grieve not, but receive the glad tiding of that paradise which has been promised to you! ‹30› We are close unto you in the life of this world and [will be so] in the life to come; and in that [life to come] you shall have all that your souls may desire, and in it you shall have all that you ever prayed for, ‹31› as a ready welcome from Him who is much-forgiving, a dispenser of grace!" ‹32›

And who could be better of speech than he who calls [his fellow-men] unto God, and does what is just and right, and says, "Verily, I am of those who have surrendered themselves to God"? ‹33›

But [since] good and evil cannot be equal, repel thou [evil] with something that is better[31] – and lo! he between whom and thyself was enmity [may then become] as though he had [always] been close [unto thee], a true friend! ‹34›

فَلَنُذِيقَنَّ ٱلَّذِينَ كَفَرُواْ عَذَابًا شَدِيدًا وَلَنَجْزِيَنَّهُمْ أَسْوَأَ ٱلَّذِى كَانُواْ
يَعْمَلُونَ ﴿27﴾ ذَٰلِكَ جَزَآءُ أَعْدَآءِ ٱللَّهِ ٱلنَّارُ لَهُمْ فِيهَا دَارُ ٱلْخُلْدِ جَزَآءَۢ
بِمَا كَانُواْ بِـَٔايَٰتِنَا يَجْحَدُونَ ﴿28﴾ وَقَالَ ٱلَّذِينَ كَفَرُواْ رَبَّنَآ أَرِنَا ٱلَّذَيْنِ
أَضَلَّانَا مِنَ ٱلْجِنِّ وَٱلْإِنسِ نَجْعَلْهُمَا تَحْتَ أَقْدَامِنَا لِيَكُونَا مِنَ
ٱلْأَسْفَلِينَ ﴿29﴾ إِنَّ ٱلَّذِينَ قَالُواْ رَبُّنَا ٱللَّهُ ثُمَّ ٱسْتَقَٰمُواْ تَتَنَزَّلُ عَلَيْهِمُ
ٱلْمَلَٰٓئِكَةُ أَلَّا تَخَافُواْ وَلَا تَحْزَنُواْ وَأَبْشِرُواْ بِٱلْجَنَّةِ ٱلَّتِى كُنتُمْ تُوعَدُونَ ﴿30﴾
نَحْنُ أَوْلِيَآؤُكُمْ فِى ٱلْحَيَوٰةِ ٱلدُّنْيَا وَفِى ٱلْءَاخِرَةِ وَلَكُمْ فِيهَا مَا تَشْتَهِىٓ
أَنفُسُكُمْ وَلَكُمْ فِيهَا مَا تَدَّعُونَ ﴿31﴾ نُزُلًا مِّنْ غَفُورٍ رَّحِيمٍ ﴿32﴾ وَمَنْ
أَحْسَنُ قَوْلًا مِّمَّن دَعَآ إِلَى ٱللَّهِ وَعَمِلَ صَٰلِحًا وَقَالَ إِنَّنِى مِنَ ٱلْمُسْلِمِينَ ﴿33﴾
وَلَا تَسْتَوِى ٱلْحَسَنَةُ وَلَا ٱلسَّيِّئَةُ ٱدْفَعْ بِٱلَّتِى هِىَ أَحْسَنُ فَإِذَا ٱلَّذِى
بَيْنَكَ وَبَيْنَهُۥ عَدَٰوَةٌ كَأَنَّهُۥ وَلِىٌّ حَمِيمٌ ﴿34﴾

Falanudhīqannal-ladhīna kafarū ᶜadhābañ-shadīdañw-wa lanajziyannahum ʾaswaʾal-ladhī kānū yaᶜmalūn. (27) Dhālika jazāaʾu ʾaᶜdāaʾil-lāhin-nār. Lahum fīhā dārul-khuldi jazāaʾam-bimā kānū biʾĀyātinā yajḥadūn. (28) Wa qālal-ladhīna kafarū Rabbanāa ʾarinal-ladhayni ʾaḍallānā minal-Jinni wal-ʾIñsi najᶜalhumā taḥta ʾaqdāminā liyakūnā minal-ʾasfalīn. (29) ʾInnal-ladhīna qālū Rabbunal-lāhu thummas-taqāmū tatanazzalu ᶜalayhimul-Malāaʾikatu ʾallā takhāfū wa lā taḥzanū wa ʾabshirū bil-jannatil-latī kuñtum tūᶜadūn. (30) Naḥnu ʾawliyāaʾukum fil-ḥayātid-dunyā wa fil-ʾĀkhirati wa lakum fīhā mā tashtahīi ʾañfusukum wa lakum fīhā mā taddaᶜūn. (31) Nuzulam-min Ghafūrir-Raḥīm. (32) Wa man ʾaḥsanu qawlam-mimmañ-daᶜāa ʾilal-lāhi wa ᶜamila ṣāliḥañw-wa qāla ʾinnanī minal-Muslimīn. (33) Wa lā tastawil-ḥasanatu wa las-sayyiʾah. ʾIdfaᶜ billatī hiya ʾaḥsanu faʾidhal-ladhī baynaka wa baynahū ᶜadāwatuñ-kaʾannahū waliyyun ḥamīm. (34)

28 For the above rendering of the verb *jaḥada*, see *sūrah* 29, note 45.

29 See 6 : 112 – "against every prophet We have set up as enemies the evil forces (*shayāṭīn*) from among humans as well as from among invisible beings" – and the corresponding note 98.

30 Cf. 7 : 38.

31 See note 44 on 13 : 22. In the present instance, the injunction to "repel [evil] with something that is better" relates to scurrilous objections to, and hostile criticism of, the Qurʾān. The whole of this passage (verses 33 ff.)

Yet [to achieve] this is not given to any but those who are wont to be patient in adversity: it is not given to any but those endowed with the greatest good fortune! ‹35›

Hence, if it should happen that a prompting from Satan stirs thee up [to blind anger], seek refuge with God: behold, He alone is all-hearing, all-knowing![32] ‹36›

Now among His signs are the night and the day, as well as the sun and the moon: [hence,] adore not the sun or the moon, but prostrate yourselves in adoration before God, who has created them – if it is Him whom you [really] worship.[33] ‹37›

And though some be too proud [to listen to this call], they who [in their hearts] are with thy Sustainer extol His limitless glory by night and by day, and never grow weary [thereof]. ‹38›

For among His signs is this: thou seest the earth lying desolate – and lo! when We send down water upon it, it stirs and swells [with life]! Verily, He who brings it to life can surely give life to the dead [of heart as well]: for, behold, He has the power to will anything.[34] ‹39›

VERILY, they who distort the meaning of Our messages are not hidden from Us: hence, which [of the two] will be in a better state – he that is [destined to be] cast into the fire, or he that shall come secure [before Us] on Resurrection Day? Do what you will: verily, He sees all that you do. ‹40›

وَمَا يُلَقَّىٰهَآ إِلَّا ٱلَّذِينَ صَبَرُواْ وَمَا يُلَقَّىٰهَآ إِلَّا ذُو حَظٍّ عَظِيمٍ ﴿٣٥﴾ وَإِمَّا
يَنزَغَنَّكَ مِنَ ٱلشَّيْطَٰنِ نَزْغٌ فَٱسْتَعِذْ بِٱللَّهِ إِنَّهُۥ هُوَ ٱلسَّمِيعُ ٱلْعَلِيمُ ﴿٣٦﴾
وَمِنْ ءَايَٰتِهِ ٱلَّيْلُ وَٱلنَّهَارُ وَٱلشَّمْسُ وَٱلْقَمَرُ لَا تَسْجُدُواْ لِلشَّمْسِ وَلَا
لِلْقَمَرِ وَٱسْجُدُواْ لِلَّهِ ٱلَّذِى خَلَقَهُنَّ إِن كُنتُمْ إِيَّاهُ تَعْبُدُونَ ﴿٣٧﴾ فَإِنِ
ٱسْتَكْبَرُواْ فَٱلَّذِينَ عِندَ رَبِّكَ يُسَبِّحُونَ لَهُۥ بِٱلَّيْلِ وَٱلنَّهَارِ وَهُمْ لَا السجدة
يَسْـَٔمُونَ ۩ ﴿٣٨﴾ وَمِنْ ءَايَٰتِهِۦٓ أَنَّكَ تَرَى ٱلْأَرْضَ خَٰشِعَةً فَإِذَآ أَنزَلْنَا
عَلَيْهَا ٱلْمَآءَ ٱهْتَزَّتْ وَرَبَتْ إِنَّ ٱلَّذِىٓ أَحْيَاهَا لَمُحْىِ ٱلْمَوْتَىٰٓ إِنَّهُۥ عَلَىٰ
كُلِّ شَىْءٍ قَدِيرٌ ﴿٣٩﴾ إِنَّ ٱلَّذِينَ يُلْحِدُونَ فِىٓ ءَايَٰتِنَا لَا يَخْفَوْنَ عَلَيْنَآ
أَفَمَن يُلْقَىٰ فِى ٱلنَّارِ خَيْرٌ أَم مَّن يَأْتِىٓ ءَامِنًا يَوْمَ ٱلْقِيَٰمَةِ ٱعْمَلُواْ مَا شِئْتُمْ
إِنَّهُۥ بِمَا تَعْمَلُونَ بَصِيرٌ ﴿٤٠﴾

Wa mā yulaqqāhāa ʾillal-ladhīna ṣabarū wa mā yulaqqāhāa ʾillā dhū ḥaẓẓin ᶜaẓīm. (35) Wa ʾimmā yañzaghannaka minash-Shayṭāni nazghuñ-fastaᶜidh billāhi ʾinnahū Huwas-Samīᶜul-ᶜAlīm. (36) Wa min ʾĀyātihil-laylu wan-nahāru wash-shamsu wal-qamar. Lā tasjudū lishshamsi wa lā lilqamari was-judū lillāhil-ladhī khalaqahunna ʾiñ-kuñtum ʾIyyāhu taᶜbudūn. (37) Faʾinis-takbarū falladhīna ᶜiñda Rabbika yusabbiḥūna lahū billayli wan-nahāri wa hum lā yasʾamūn. ۩ (38) Wa min ʾĀyātihīi ʾannaka taral-ʾarḍa khāshiᶜatañ-faʾidhāa ʾañzalnā ᶜalayhal-māaʾah-tazzat wa rabat. ʾInnal-ladhīi ʾaḥyāhā lamuḥyil-mawtā ʾinnahū ᶜalā kulli shayʾiñ-Qadīr. (39) ʾInnal-ladhīna yulḥidūna fīi ʾĀyātinā lā yakhfawna ᶜalaynā. ʾAfamañy-yulqā fin-nāri khayrun ʾammañy-yaʾtīi ʾāminañy-Yawmal-Qiyāmah. ʾIᶜmalū mā shiʾtum ʾinnahū bimā taᶜmalūna Baṣīr. (40)

connects with verse 26.

32 I.e., He alone sees what is in the hearts of men, and He alone understands the innermost motivations, of which they themselves are unconscious, of those who criticize the Qurʾān adversely. – See 7 : 199-200 and the corresponding notes, especially note 164.

33 This, according to Rāzī, connects with the phrase "calling [one's fellow-men] unto God" in verse 33 above. God is the sole cause and source of all that exists; and whatever exists is but a wondrous sign of His creative power. Hence, it is a blasphemy – apart from being unreasonable – to ascribe real power (which is the meaning of "adoration" in this context) to anything *created*, whether it be a concrete phenomenon, or an abstract force of nature, or a set of circumstances, or even an idea.

34 Although the allusion to the reviving earth often occurs in the Qurʾān as a parable of man's ultimate resurrection, in the present context (and in tune with the entire passage comprising verses 33-39) it appears to be an illustration of God's power to bestow spiritual life upon hearts that have hitherto remained closed to the truth of His existence and omnipotence. Hence, it implies a call to the believer never to abandon the hope that "those who deny the truth" may one day grasp the truth of the Qurʾanic message.

إِنَّ ٱلَّذِينَ كَفَرُوا۟ بِٱلذِّكْرِ لَمَّا جَآءَهُمْ ۖ وَإِنَّهُۥ لَكِتَـٰبٌ عَزِيزٌ ﴿٤١﴾ لَّا
يَأْتِيهِ ٱلْبَـٰطِلُ مِنۢ بَيْنِ يَدَيْهِ وَلَا مِنْ خَلْفِهِۦ ۖ تَنزِيلٌ مِّنْ حَكِيمٍ
حَمِيدٍ ﴿٤٢﴾ مَّا يُقَالُ لَكَ إِلَّا مَا قَدْ قِيلَ لِلرُّسُلِ مِن قَبْلِكَ ۚ إِنَّ رَبَّكَ لَذُو
مَغْفِرَةٍ وَذُو عِقَابٍ أَلِيمٍ ﴿٤٣﴾ وَلَوْ جَعَلْنَـٰهُ قُرْءَانًا أَعْجَمِيًّا لَّقَالُوا۟ لَوْلَا
فُصِّلَتْ ءَايَـٰتُهُۥٓ ۖ ءَا۬عْجَمِىٌّ وَعَرَبِىٌّ ۗ قُلْ هُوَ لِلَّذِينَ ءَامَنُوا۟ هُدًى وَشِفَآءٌ ۖ
وَٱلَّذِينَ لَا يُؤْمِنُونَ فِىٓ ءَاذَانِهِمْ وَقْرٌ وَهُوَ عَلَيْهِمْ عَمًى ۚ أُو۟لَـٰٓئِكَ يُنَادَوْنَ
مِن مَّكَانٍۭ بَعِيدٍ ﴿٤٤﴾ وَلَقَدْ ءَاتَيْنَا مُوسَى ٱلْكِتَـٰبَ فَٱخْتُلِفَ فِيهِ ۗ

ʾInnal-ladhīna kafarū bidh-Dhikri lammā jāaʾahum wa ʾinnahū laKitābun ʿazīz. (41) Lā yaʾtīhil-bāṭilu mim-bayni yadayhi wa lā min khalfihī tañzīlum-min Ḥakīmin Ḥamīd. (42) Mā yuqālu laka ʾillā mā qad qīla lirRusuli miñ-qablik. ʾInna Rabbaka ladhū maghfira-tiñw-wa dhū ʿiqābin ʾalīm. (43) Wa law jaʿalnāhu Qurʾānan ʾaʿjamiyyal-laqālū lawlā fuṣṣilat ʾĀyātuh. ʾĀʿjamiyyuñw-wa ʿarabiyy. Qul huwa lilladhīna ʾāmanū hudañw-wa shifāaʾ. Wal-ladhīna lā yuʾmi-nūna fīi ʾādhānihim waqruñw-wa huwa ʿalayhim ʿamā. ʾUlāaʾika yunādawna mim-makānim-baʿīd. (44) Wa laqad ʾātaynā Mūsal-Kitāba fakhtulifa fīh.

Verily, they who are bent on denying the truth of this reminder as soon as it comes to them – [they are the losers]: for, behold, it is a sublime divine writ: «41» no falsehood can ever attain to it openly, and neither in a stealthy manner,[35] [since it is] bestowed from on high by One who is truly wise, ever to be praised. «42»

[And as for thee, O Prophet,] nothing is being said to thee but what was said to all [of God's] apostles before thy time.[36]

Behold, thy Sustainer is indeed full of forgiveness – but He has also the power to requite most grievously! «43»

Now if We had willed this [divine writ] to be a discourse in a non-Arabic tongue, they [who now reject it] would surely have said, "Why is it that its messages have not been spelled out clearly?[37] Why – [a message in] a non-Arabic tongue, and [its bearer] an Arab?"

Say: "Unto all who have attained to faith, this [divine writ] is a guidance and a source of health; but as for those who will not believe – in their ears is deafness, and so it remains obscure to them: they are [like people who are] being called from too far away.[38] «44»

Thus, too, have We vouchsafed revelation unto Moses aforetime, and thereupon disputes arose about it.[39] And [then, as

---

35 Lit., "neither from between its hands, nor from behind it", i.e., it cannot be openly changed by means of additions or omissions (Rāzī), and neither surreptitiously, by hostile or deliberately confusing interpretations. The above is one of the Qurʾanic passages on which the great commentator Abū Muslim al-Iṣfahānī (as quoted by Rāzī) bases his absolute rejection of the theory of "abrogation" (for which see note 87 on 2 : 106). Since the "abrogation" of *any* Qurʾān-verse would have amounted to its *ibṭāl* – that is, to an open or implied declaration that it was henceforth to be regarded as null and void – the verse in question would have to be considered "false" (*bāṭil*) in the context of the Qurʾān as it is before us: and this, as Abū Muslim points out, would clearly contradict the above statement that "no falsehood (*bāṭil*) can ever attain to it".

36 This is an allusion to the allegation of the Prophet's opponents that he himself was the "author" of what he claimed to be a divine revelation, as well as to their demand that he should "prove" the truth of his prophetic mission by producing a miracle: a scornful attitude with which all the earlier prophets had been confronted at one time or another, and which is epitomized in the "saying" of the unbelievers mentioned in verse 5 of this *sūrah*.

37 Sc., "in a tongue which we can understand". Since the Prophet was an Arab and lived in an Arabian environment, his message *had* to be expressed in the Arabic language, which the people to whom it was addressed in the first instance could understand: see in this connection note 72 on the first sentence of 13 : 37, as well as the first half of 14 : 4 – "never have We sent forth any apostle otherwise than [with a message] in his own people's tongue, so that he might make [the truth] clear unto them". Had the message of the Qurʾān been formulated in a language other than Arabic, the opponents of the Prophet would have been justified in saying, "between us and thee is a barrier" (verse 5 of this *sūrah*).

38 Lit., "from a far-off place": i.e., they only hear the sound of the words, but cannot understand their meaning.

39 As was and is the case with the Qurʾān, some people accepted the divine message revealed to Moses, and

now,] had it not been for a decree that had already gone forth from thy Sustainer, all would indeed have been decided between them [from the outset].[40] As it is, behold, they [who will not believe in this divine writ] are in grave doubt, amounting to suspicion, about what it portends.[41] ‹45›

WHOEVER does what is just and right, does so for his own good; and whoever does evil, does so to his own hurt: and never does God do the least wrong to His creatures. ‹46›

In Him alone is vested the knowledge of when the Last Hour will come. And no fruit bursts forth from its calyx, and no female ever conceives, nor ever gives birth, save with His knowledge.

And so, on the Day when He shall call out to them, "Where, now, are those [alleged] partners of Mine?" – they will [surely] answer, "We confess unto Thee that none of us can bear witness [to anyone's having a share in Thy divinity]!" ‹47› And so, all that they were wont to invoke aforetime will have forsaken them; and they shall know for certain that there is no escape for them. ‹48›

MAN NEVER TIRES of asking for the good [things of life]; and if evil fortune touches him, he abandons all hope,[42] giving himself up to despair. ‹49›

Yet whenever We let him taste some of Our grace after hardship has visited him, he is sure to say, "This is but my due!" – and, "I do not think that the Last Hour will ever come:[43] but if [it should come, and] I should indeed be brought back unto

وَلَوْلَا كَلِمَةٌ سَبَقَتْ مِن رَّبِّكَ لَقُضِيَ بَيْنَهُمْ وَإِنَّهُمْ لَفِي شَكٍّ مِّنْهُ
مُرِيبٍ ﴿٤٥﴾ مَّنْ عَمِلَ صَٰلِحًا فَلِنَفْسِهِۦ وَمَنْ أَسَآءَ فَعَلَيْهَا وَمَا رَبُّكَ
بِظَلَّٰمٍ لِّلْعَبِيدِ ﴿٤٦﴾ ۞ إِلَيْهِ يُرَدُّ عِلْمُ ٱلسَّاعَةِ وَمَا تَخْرُجُ مِن ثَمَرَٰتٍ مِّنْ
أَكْمَامِهَا وَمَا تَحْمِلُ مِنْ أُنثَىٰ وَلَا تَضَعُ إِلَّا بِعِلْمِهِۦ وَيَوْمَ يُنَادِيهِمْ أَيْنَ
شُرَكَآءِى قَالُوٓا۟ ءَاذَنَّٰكَ مَا مِنَّا مِن شَهِيدٍ ﴿٤٧﴾ وَضَلَّ عَنْهُم مَّا كَانُوا۟
يَدْعُونَ مِن قَبْلُ وَظَنُّوا۟ مَا لَهُم مِّن مَّحِيصٍ ﴿٤٨﴾ لَّا يَسْـَٔمُ ٱلْإِنسَٰنُ مِن
دُعَآءِ ٱلْخَيْرِ وَإِن مَّسَّهُ ٱلشَّرُّ فَيَـُٔوسٌ قَنُوطٌ ﴿٤٩﴾ وَلَئِنْ أَذَقْنَٰهُ رَحْمَةً مِّنَّا مِنۢ
بَعْدِ ضَرَّآءَ مَسَّتْهُ لَيَقُولَنَّ هَٰذَا لِى وَمَآ أَظُنُّ ٱلسَّاعَةَ قَآئِمَةً وَلَئِن رُّجِعْتُ إِلَىٰ حزب 49
جزء 25

Wa lawlā kalimatuñ-sabaqat mir-Rabbika laquḍiya baynahum. Wa ʾinnahum lafī shakkim-minhu murīb. (45) Man ʿamila ṣaliḥañ-falinafsihī wa man ʾasāaʾa faʿalayhā. Wa mā Rabbuka biẓallāmil-lilʿabīd. (46) ۞ ʾIlayhi yuraddu ʿilmus-Sāʿah. Wa mā takhruju miñ-thamarātim-min ʾakmāmihā wa mā taḥmilu min ʾuñthā wa lā taḍaʿu ʾillā biʿilmih. Wa Yawma yunādīhim ʾayna shurakāaʾī qālūu ʾādhannāka mā minnā miñ-shahīd. (47) Wa ḍalla ʿanhum-mā kānū yadʿūna miñ-qablu wa ẓannū mā lahum-mim-maḥīṣ. (48) Lā yasʾamul-ʾIñsānu miñ-duʿāaʾil-khayri wa ʾim-massahush-sharru fayaʾūsuñ-qanūṭ. (49) Wa laʾin ʾadhaqnāhu raḥmatam-minnā mim-baʿdi ḍarrāaʾa massat-hu layaqūlanna hādhā lī wa māa ʾaẓunnus-Sāʿata qāaʾimatañw-wa laʾir-rujiʿtu ʾilā

some rejected it (Zamakhsharī, Rāzī), while others disagreed about the import and application of its tenets (Ṭabarī).

40 For an explanation of this passage, as well as of the above parallel between men's attitudes towards the earlier scriptures and the Qurʾān, see the second sentence of 10 : 19 and the corresponding note 29.

41 Lit., "about it", i.e., doubts as to whether the Qurʾanic approach to problems of man's spirit and body – and, in particular, its stress on the essential unity of these twin aspects of human life (cf. note 118 on the first sentence of 2 : 143) – is justified or not. In a wider sense, these doubts of the deniers of the truth relate to the question of whether religion as such is "beneficial" or "injurious" to human society – a question which is posed and answered by them with a strong bias *against* all religious faith.

42 See note 17 on 11 : 9.

43 I.e., man is, as a rule, so blinded by his love of this world that he cannot imagine its ever coming to an end.

my Sustainer, then, behold, the ultimate good awaits me with Him!"[44]
But [on the Day of Judgment] We shall most certainly give those who were bent on denying the truth[45] full understanding of all that they ever did, and shall most certainly give them [thereby] a taste of suffering severe.[46] ‹50›
And, too, when We bestow Our blessings upon man, he tends to turn aside and keep aloof [from remembering Us]; but as soon as evil fortune touches him, he is full of wordy prayers![47] ‹51›

رَبِّيٓ إِنَّ لِي عِندَهُۥ لَلۡحُسۡنَىٰۚ فَلَنُنَبِّئَنَّ ٱلَّذِينَ كَفَرُواْ بِمَا عَمِلُواْ وَلَنُذِيقَنَّهُم
مِّنۡ عَذَابٍ غَلِيظٖ ﴿٥٠﴾ وَإِذَآ أَنۡعَمۡنَا عَلَى ٱلۡإِنسَٰنِ أَعۡرَضَ وَنَـَٔا بِجَانِبِهِۦ
وَإِذَا مَسَّهُ ٱلشَّرُّ فَذُو دُعَآءٍ عَرِيضٖ ﴿٥١﴾ قُلۡ أَرَءَيۡتُمۡ إِن كَانَ مِنۡ عِندِ
ٱللَّهِ ثُمَّ كَفَرۡتُم بِهِۦ مَنۡ أَضَلُّ مِمَّنۡ هُوَ فِي شِقَاقِۭ بَعِيدٖ ﴿٥٢﴾ سَنُرِيهِمۡ ءَايَٰتِنَا
فِي ٱلۡأٓفَاقِ وَفِيٓ أَنفُسِهِمۡ حَتَّىٰ يَتَبَيَّنَ لَهُمۡ أَنَّهُ ٱلۡحَقُّۗ أَوَلَمۡ يَكۡفِ بِرَبِّكَ
أَنَّهُۥ عَلَىٰ كُلِّ شَيۡءٖ شَهِيدٌ ﴿٥٣﴾ أَلَآ إِنَّهُمۡ فِي مِرۡيَةٖ مِّن لِّقَآءِ رَبِّهِمۡۗ أَلَآ إِنَّهُۥ
بِكُلِّ شَيۡءٖ مُّحِيطُۢ ﴿٥٤﴾

HAVE YOU given thought [to how you will fare] if this be truly [a revelation] from God, the while you deny its truth? Who could be more astray than one who places himself [so] deeply in the wrong?[48] ‹52›
In time We shall make them fully understand[49] Our messages [through what they perceive] in the utmost horizons [of the universe] and within themselves,[50] so that it will become clear unto them that this [revelation] is indeed the truth. [Still,] is it not enough [for them to know] that thy Sustainer is witness unto everything?[51] ‹53›
Oh, verily, they are in doubt as to whether they will meet their Sustainer [on Judgment Day]!
Oh, verily, He encompasses everything! ‹54›

Rabbīi ʾinna lī ʿiñdahū lalḥusnā. Falanunabbiʾannal-ladhīna kafarū bimā ʿamilū wa lanudhīqannahum-min ʿadhābin ghalīẓ. ﴿50﴾ Wa ʾidhāa ʾanʿamnā ʿalal-ʾIñsāni ʾaʿraḍa wa naʾā bijānibihī wa ʾidhā massa-hush-sharru fadhū duʿāaʾin ʿarīḍ. ﴿51﴾ Qul ʾaraʾaytum ʾiñ-kāna min ʿiñdil-lāhi thumma kafartum-bihī man ʾaḍallu mimman huwa fī shiqāqim-baʿīd. ﴿52﴾ Sa-nurīhim ʾĀyātinā fil-ʾāfāqi wa fīi ʾañfusihim ḥattā ya-tabayyana lahum ʾannahul-ḥaqq. ʾAwa lam yakfi bi-Rabbika ʾannahū ʿalā kulli shayʾiñ-Shahīd. ﴿53﴾ ʾAlāa ʾinnahum fī miryatim-mil-liqāaʾi Rabbihim. ʾAlāa ʾinnahū bikulli shayʾim-Muḥīṭ. ﴿54﴾

Implied in this statement is a doubt as to whether there will really be an afterlife, and whether man will really be judged by God on resurrection.

44 Being fully convinced of his own merit (as expressed in the words, "This is but my due"), he is confident that – in case there should really be a life after death – his own flattering view of himself will be confirmed by God.

45 I.e., the truth of resurrection and of God's judgment.

46 I.e., the realization of the spiritual blindness in which they spent their life will *in itself* be a source of their suffering in the hereafter: cf. 17 : 72 – "whoever is blind [of heart] in this [world] will be blind in the life to come [as well]".

47 Lit., "wide [i.e., prolonged or diffuse] prayers".

48 According to Rāzī, this is an implied allusion to the attitude of people who – as mentioned in verses 4 and 5 of this *sūrah* – "turn away" from the message of the Qurʾān, saying, as it were: "Our hearts are veiled from whatever thou callest us to, [O Muḥammad,] and in our ears is deafness, and between us and thee is a barrier."

49 Lit., "We will show them" or "make them see".

50 I.e., through a progressive deepening and widening of their insight into the wonders of the universe as well as through a deeper understanding of man's own psyche – all of which points to the existence of a conscious Creator.

51 I.e., that He is almighty and all-seeing: a fundamental truth which, by itself, should be enough to remind man of his responsibility before Him.

The Forty-Second Sūrah

Ash-Shūrā (Consultation)

Mecca Period

THE BEGINNING and the end of this *sūrah* stress the reality of divine revelation, and the fact that all prophets, at all times, preached one and the same essential truth – namely, the existence and oneness of God – and the same ethical principles: either of which makes it imperative that *all* believers in the One God, whatever their historical "denomination", should regard themselves as "one single community" (see verse 13 and the corresponding note 14, as well as verse 15). Hence, all divisive speculations about the "nature" of God are "null and void in their Sustainer's sight" (verse 16), because "there is nothing like unto Him" (verse 11), and, therefore, nothing by which to define Him. And because God is undefinable and unfathomable, man cannot grasp even the real nature of His activity beyond the fact that He has imposed on all creation the law of cause and effect – so that in the life to come man will only harvest "what his own hands have wrought" in this world.

The key-word by which this *sūrah* has always been designated is derived from the phrase *shūrā baynahum* ("consultation among themselves") in verse 38, outlining one of the basic social principles which ought to characterize the community of true believers.

-42- سورة الشورى مكية
وآياتها ثلاث وخمسون

IN THE NAME OF GOD, THE MOST GRACIOUS, THE DISPENSER OF GRACE:

Ḥā. Mīm. ‹1› *ᶜAyn. Sīn. Qāf.*[1] ‹2›
THUS has God, the Almighty, the Wise, revealed [the truth] unto thee, [O Muḥammad,] and unto those who preceded thee:[2] ‹3›
His is all that is in the heavens and all that is on earth; and most exalted, tremendous is He. ‹4›
The uppermost heavens are well-nigh rent asunder [for awe of Him]; and the angels extol their Sustainer's limitless glory and praise, and ask forgiveness for all who are on earth.[3]
Oh, verily, God alone is truly-forgiving, a dispenser of grace! ‹5›

NOW AS FOR those who take aught beside Him for their protectors – God watches them, and thou art not responsible for their conduct. ‹6›
[Thou art but entrusted with Our message:] and so We have revealed unto thee a discourse in the Arabic tongue[4] in order that thou mayest warn the foremost of all cities and all who dwell around it[5] – to wit, warn [them] of the Day of the Gathering, [the coming of] which is beyond all doubt:

بِسۡمِ ٱللَّهِ ٱلرَّحۡمَٰنِ ٱلرَّحِيمِ

حمٓ (1) عٓسٓقٓ (2) كَذَٰلِكَ يُوحِيٓ إِلَيۡكَ وَإِلَى ٱلَّذِينَ مِن قَبۡلِكَ ٱللَّهُ
ٱلۡعَزِيزُ ٱلۡحَكِيمُ (3) لَهُۥ مَا فِي ٱلسَّمَٰوَٰتِ وَمَا فِي ٱلۡأَرۡضِۖ وَهُوَ
ٱلۡعَلِيُّ ٱلۡعَظِيمُ (4) تَكَادُ ٱلسَّمَٰوَٰتُ يَتَفَطَّرۡنَ مِن فَوۡقِهِنَّۚ وَٱلۡمَلَٰٓئِكَةُ
يُسَبِّحُونَ بِحَمۡدِ رَبِّهِمۡ وَيَسۡتَغۡفِرُونَ لِمَن فِي ٱلۡأَرۡضِۗ أَلَآ إِنَّ ٱللَّهَ هُوَ
ٱلۡغَفُورُ ٱلرَّحِيمُ (5) وَٱلَّذِينَ ٱتَّخَذُواْ مِن دُونِهِۦٓ أَوۡلِيَآءَ ٱللَّهُ حَفِيظٌ
عَلَيۡهِمۡ وَمَآ أَنتَ عَلَيۡهِم بِوَكِيلٖ (6) وَكَذَٰلِكَ أَوۡحَيۡنَآ إِلَيۡكَ قُرۡءَانًا
عَرَبِيّٗا لِّتُنذِرَ أُمَّ ٱلۡقُرَىٰ وَمَنۡ حَوۡلَهَا وَتُنذِرَ يَوۡمَ ٱلۡجَمۡعِ لَا رَيۡبَ فِيهِۚ

Bismil-lāhir-Raḥmānir-Raḥīm.
Ḥā-Mīim. (1) ᶜAyyn-Siin-Qāaf. (2) Kadhālika yūḥii ᵓilayka wa ᵓilal-ladhīna miñ-qablikal-lāhul-ᶜAzīzul-Ḥakīm. (3) Lahū mā fis-samāwāti wa mā fil-ᵓarḍi wa Huwal-ᶜAliyyul-ᶜAẓīm. (4) Takādus-samāwātu yatafaṭṭarna miñ-fawqihinna wal-Malāaᵓikatu yusabbiḥūna biḥamdi Rabbihim wa yastaghfirūna limañ-fil-ᵓarḍ. ᵓAlāa ᵓinnal-lāha Huwal-Ghafūrur-Raḥīm. (5) Wal-ladhīnat-takhadhū miñ-dūnihīi ᵓawliyāaᵓal-lāhu ḥafīẓun ᶜalayhim wa māa ᵓañta ᶜalayhim-biwakīl. (6) Wa kadhālika ᵓawḥaynāa ᵓilayka Qurᵓānan ᶜarabiyyal-lituñdhira ᵓummal-qurā wa man ḥawlahā wa tuñdhira Yawmal-Jamᶜi lā rayba fīh.

---

1 See Appendix II.

2 I.e., the basic truths propounded in the Qurᵓanic revelation – some of which are summarized in the sequence – are the same as those revealed to all the earlier prophets.

3 I.e., all human beings (as indicated by the relative pronoun *man*, which always refers to beings endowed with conscious intelligence). The implication is that whereas all humans – whether believers or unbelievers – are liable to err and to sin, God "is full of forgiveness unto men despite all their evildoing" (13 : 6). See also the first sentence of 10 : 11 and the corresponding note 17.

4 Cf. 14 : 4 – "never have We sent forth any apostle otherwise than [with a message] in his own people's tongue"; see also note 72 on the first sentence of 13 : 37.

5 I.e., all mankind (Ṭabarī, Baghawī, Rāzī). As regards the designation of Mecca as "the foremost of all cities", see note 75 on the identical phrase in 6 : 92.

[the Day when] some shall find themselves in paradise, and some in the blazing flame. ⟨7⟩

Now had God so willed, He could surely have made them all one single community:[6] none the less, He admits unto His grace him that wills [to be admitted][7] – whereas the evildoers shall have none to protect them and none to succour them [on Judgment Day]. ⟨8⟩

Did they, perchance, [think that they could] choose protectors other than Him? But God alone is the Protector [of all that exists], since it is He alone who brings the dead to life, and He alone who has the power to will anything. ⟨9⟩

AND ON WHATEVER you may differ, [O believers,] the verdict thereon rests with God.[8]

[Say, therefore:] "Such is God, my Sustainer: in Him have I placed my trust, and unto Him do I always turn!" ⟨10⟩

The Originator [is He] of the heavens and the earth. He has given you mates of your own kind[9] – just as [He has willed that] among the beasts [there be] mates – to multiply you thereby: [but] there is nothing like unto Him, and He alone is all-hearing, all-seeing.[10] ⟨11⟩

فَرِيقٌ فِي الْجَنَّةِ وَفَرِيقٌ فِي السَّعِيرِ ﴿٧﴾ وَلَوْ شَاءَ اللَّهُ لَجَعَلَهُمْ أُمَّةً
وَاحِدَةً وَلَٰكِن يُدْخِلُ مَن يَشَاءُ فِي رَحْمَتِهِ ۚ وَالظَّالِمُونَ مَا لَهُم مِّن
وَلِيٍّ وَلَا نَصِيرٍ ﴿٨﴾ أَمِ اتَّخَذُوا مِن دُونِهِ أَوْلِيَاءَ ۖ فَاللَّهُ هُوَ الْوَلِيُّ وَهُوَ
يُحْيِي الْمَوْتَىٰ وَهُوَ عَلَىٰ كُلِّ شَيْءٍ قَدِيرٌ ﴿٩﴾ وَمَا اخْتَلَفْتُمْ فِيهِ مِن شَيْءٍ
فَحُكْمُهُ إِلَى اللَّهِ ۚ ذَٰلِكُمُ اللَّهُ رَبِّي عَلَيْهِ تَوَكَّلْتُ وَإِلَيْهِ أُنِيبُ ﴿١٠﴾ فَاطِرُ
السَّمَاوَاتِ وَالْأَرْضِ ۚ جَعَلَ لَكُم مِّنْ أَنفُسِكُمْ أَزْوَاجًا وَمِنَ الْأَنْعَامِ
أَزْوَاجًا ۖ يَذْرَؤُكُمْ فِيهِ ۚ لَيْسَ كَمِثْلِهِ شَيْءٌ ۖ وَهُوَ السَّمِيعُ الْبَصِيرُ ﴿١١﴾

Farīquñ-fil-jannati wa farīquñ-fis-saʿīr. (7) **Wa law shāaʾal-lāhu lajaʿalahum ʾummatañw-wāḥidatañw-wa lākiñy-yudkhilu mañy-yashāaʾu fī raḥmatih. Waẓ-ẓālimūna mā lahum miñw-waliyyiñw-wa lā naṣīr.** (8) **ʾAmit-takhadhū miñ-dūnihīi ʾawliyāaʾ. Fallāhu Huwal-Waliyyu wa Huwa yuḥyil-mawtā wa Huwa ʿalā kulli shayʾiñ-Qadīr.** (9) **Wa makh-talaftum fīhi miñ-shayʾiñ-faḥukmuhūu ʾilal-lāh. Dhālikumul-lāhu Rabbī ʿalayhi tawakkaltu wa ʾilayhi ʾunīb.** (10) **Fāṭirus-samāwāti wal-ʾarḍ. Jaʿala lakum-min ʾañfusikum ʾazwājañw-wa minal-ʾanʿāmi ʾazwājañy-yadhraʾūkum fīh. Laysa kamithlihī shayʾuñw-wa Huwas-Samīʿul-Baṣīr.** (11)

6 The implication being, "but He has not willed it": see second paragraph of 5 : 48 and the corresponding notes 66 and 67; 16 : 93 and note 116; also note 29 on 10 : 19.

7 Or: "He admits whomever He wills unto His grace" – similar to the double meaning inherent in the oft-recurring phrase, *Allāhu yahdī man yashāʾu wa-yuḍillu man yashāʾu*, which can be understood either as "God guides whomever He wills and lets go astray whomever He wills", or, alternatively, as "God guides him that wills [to be guided] and lets go astray him that wills [to go astray]". See, in particular, Zamakhsharī's elaborate comment on this problem quoted in note 4 on the second half of 14 : 4.

8 This, connecting with the first sentence of verse 8 above, evidently relates to problems of faith and religious law (Baghawī, Zamakhsharī). The above verse has provided some of the great exponents of Islamic Law – Ibn Ḥazm among them – with one of the main arguments against the acceptance of deductions by analogy (*qiyās*) as a means to "establish" points of religious law not formulated as such in the *naṣṣ* – i.e., the self-evident (*ẓāhir*) wording of the Qurʾān and, by obvious implication, of the Prophet's commandments. This, as Rāzī points out, is the meaning of the phrase "on whatever you may differ, the verdict (*ḥukm*) thereon rests with God". (See in this connection note 120 on 5 : 101; also the section on "The Scope of Islamic Law"' in my *State and Government*, pp. 11-15.)

9 See note 81 on 16 : 72.

10 The preceding allusion to the God-willed function of sex and, hence, to the polarity and multiplicity evident in all animated nature – man and animal alike – is meant to stress the above statement of the oneness and absolute uniqueness of God. The phrase "there is nothing like unto Him" implies that He is fundamentally – and not merely in His attributes – "different" from anything that exists or could exist, or anything that man can conceive or imagine or

لَهُۥ مَقَالِيدُ ٱلسَّمَٰوَٰتِ وَٱلْأَرْضِ يَبْسُطُ ٱلرِّزْقَ لِمَن يَشَآءُ وَيَقْدِرُ إِنَّهُۥ
بِكُلِّ شَىْءٍ عَلِيمٌ ﴿١٢﴾ ۞ شَرَعَ لَكُم مِّنَ ٱلدِّينِ مَا وَصَّىٰ بِهِۦ نُوحًا وَٱلَّذِىٓ
أَوْحَيْنَآ إِلَيْكَ وَمَا وَصَّيْنَا بِهِۦٓ إِبْرَٰهِيمَ وَمُوسَىٰ وَعِيسَىٰٓ أَنْ أَقِيمُوا۟ ٱلدِّينَ
وَلَا تَتَفَرَّقُوا۟ فِيهِ كَبُرَ عَلَى ٱلْمُشْرِكِينَ مَا تَدْعُوهُمْ إِلَيْهِ ٱللَّهُ يَجْتَبِىٓ إِلَيْهِ
مَن يَشَآءُ وَيَهْدِىٓ إِلَيْهِ مَن يُنِيبُ ﴿١٣﴾ وَمَا تَفَرَّقُوٓا۟ إِلَّا مِنۢ بَعْدِ مَا جَآءَهُمُ
ٱلْعِلْمُ بَغْيًۢا بَيْنَهُمْ وَلَوْلَا كَلِمَةٌ سَبَقَتْ مِن رَّبِّكَ إِلَىٰٓ أَجَلٍ مُّسَمًّى

ربع الحزب

His are the keys of the heavens and the earth: He grants abundant sustenance, or gives it in scant measure, unto whomever He wills: for, behold, He has full knowledge of everything.[11] ⟨12⟩

In matters of faith,[12] He has ordained for you that which He had enjoined upon Noah – and into which We gave thee [O Muḥammad] insight through revelation[13] – as well as that which We had enjoined upon Abraham, and Moses, and Jesus: Steadfastly uphold the [true] faith, and do not break up your unity therein.[14]

[And even though] that [unity of faith] to which thou callest them appears oppressive to those who are wont to ascribe to other beings or forces a share in His divinity, God draws unto Himself everyone who is willing, and guides unto Himself everyone who turns unto Him. ⟨13⟩

And [as for the followers of earlier revelation,] they broke up their unity, out of mutual jealousy, only after they had come to know [the truth].[15] And had it not been for a decree that had already gone forth from thy Sustainer, [postponing all decision] until a term set [by Him], all

Lahū maqālīdus-samāwāti wal-ʾarḍi yabsuṭur-rizqa limañy-yashāaʾu wa yaqdir. ʾInnahū bikulli shayʾin ᶜAlīm. ⟨12⟩ ۞ Sharaᶜa lakum-minad-dīni mā waṣṣā bihī Nūḥañw-wal-ladhīi ʾawḥaynāa ʾilayka wa mā waṣṣaynā bihīi ʾIbrāhīma wa Mūsā wa ᶜĪsāa ʾan ʾaqīmud-dīna wa lā tatafarraqū fīh. Kabura ᶜalal-mushrikīna mā tadᶜūhum ʾilayh. ʾAllāhu yajtabīi ʾilayhi mañy-yashāaʾu wa yahdīi ʾilayhi mañy-yunīb. ⟨13⟩ Wa mā tafarraqūu ʾillā mim-baᶜdi mā jāaʾahumul-ᶜilmu baghyam-baynahum. Wa lawlā kalimatuñ-sabaqat mir-Rabbika ʾilāa ʾajalim-musammal-

define (see note 88 on 6 : 100); and since "there is nothing that could be compared with Him" (112 : 4), even the "how" of His being "different" from everything else is beyond the categories of human thought.

11 I.e., He knows not only what every human being "deserves", but also what is intrinsically – though not always perceptibly – good and necessary in the context of His plan of creation. Moreover, all that exists belongs to Him alone, and man is allowed no more than the *usufruct* of what is commonly regarded as "property".

12 See first paragraph of note 249 on 2 : 256. Since, as the sequence shows, the term *dīn* cannot apply in this context to "religion" in its widest connotation, including religious *laws* – which, by their very nature, have been different in each successive dispensation (cf. note 66 on 5 : 48) – it obviously denotes here only the ethical and spiritual *contents* of religion, i.e., "faith" in its most general sense. With this verse, the discourse returns to the theme sounded at the beginning of this *sūrah*, namely, the unchanging sameness of the spiritual and moral principles underlying all revealed religions.

13 Lit., "which We have revealed unto thee", implying that it was only through revelation that the Prophet Muḥammad came to know "that which God had enjoined upon Noah".

14 Cf. 3 : 19 – "the only [true] religion in the sight of God is [man's] self-surrender unto Him"; and 3 : 85 – "if one goes in search of a religion other than self-surrender unto God, it will never be accepted from him". Parallel with this principle, enunciated by all of God's apostles, is the categorical statement in 21 : 92 and 23 : 52 – "Verily, [O you who believe in Me,] this community of yours is one single community, since I am the Sustainer of you all". Most of the great commentators (e.g., Zamakhsharī, Rāzī, Ibn Kathīr) understand this as an unequivocal reference to the ecumenical unity of all religions based on belief in the One God, notwithstanding all the differences with regard to "the [specific] statutes and practices enjoined for the benefit of the various communities in accordance with their [time-bound] conditions (*ᶜalā ḥasab aḥwālihā*)", as expressed by Zamakhsharī in his comments on the verse under discussion.

15 Lit., "they did not break up their unity until after knowledge had come to them" – i.e., the knowledge that God is one, and that the teachings of all of His prophets were essentially the same. Cf. 2 : 213 and, more explicitly, 23 : 53,

would indeed have been decided between them [from the outset].[16] As it is, behold, they who have inherited their divine writ from those who preceded them[17] are [now] in grave doubt, amounting to suspicion, about what it portends.[18] ‹14›

Because of this, then,[19] summon [all mankind], and pursue the right course, as thou hast been bidden [by God]; and do not follow their likes and dislikes, but say:

"I believe in whatever revelation God has bestowed from on high; and I am bidden to bring about equity in your mutual views.[20] God is our Sustainer as well as your Sustainer. To us shall be accounted our deeds, and to you, your deeds. Let there be no contention between us and you: God will bring us all together – for with Him is all journeys' end." ‹15›

And as for those who would [still] argue about God[21] after He has been acknowledged [by them] – all their arguments are null and void in their Sustainer's sight, and upon them will fall [His] condemnation, and for them is suffering severe in store: ‹16› [for] it is God [Himself] who has bestowed revelation from on high, setting forth the truth, and [thus given man] a balance [wherewith to weigh right and wrong].[22]

And for all thou knowest, the Last Hour may well be near! ‹17›

لَقُضِيَ بَيْنَهُمْ ۚ وَإِنَّ ٱلَّذِينَ أُورِثُوا۟ ٱلْكِتَٰبَ مِنۢ بَعْدِهِمْ لَفِى شَكٍّ مِّنْهُ
مُرِيبٍ ﴿١٤﴾ فَلِذَٰلِكَ فَٱدْعُ ۖ وَٱسْتَقِمْ كَمَآ أُمِرْتَ ۖ وَلَا تَتَّبِعْ أَهْوَآءَهُمْ ۖ وَقُلْ
ءَامَنتُ بِمَآ أَنزَلَ ٱللَّهُ مِن كِتَٰبٍ ۖ وَأُمِرْتُ لِأَعْدِلَ بَيْنَكُمُ ۖ ٱللَّهُ رَبُّنَا
وَرَبُّكُمْ ۖ لَنَآ أَعْمَٰلُنَا وَلَكُمْ أَعْمَٰلُكُمْ ۖ لَا حُجَّةَ بَيْنَنَا وَبَيْنَكُمُ ۖ ٱللَّهُ
يَجْمَعُ بَيْنَنَا ۖ وَإِلَيْهِ ٱلْمَصِيرُ ﴿١٥﴾ وَٱلَّذِينَ يُحَآجُّونَ فِى ٱللَّهِ مِنۢ بَعْدِ مَا
ٱسْتُجِيبَ لَهُۥ حُجَّتُهُمْ دَاحِضَةٌ عِندَ رَبِّهِمْ وَعَلَيْهِمْ غَضَبٌ وَلَهُمْ
عَذَابٌ شَدِيدٌ ﴿١٦﴾ ٱللَّهُ ٱلَّذِىٓ أَنزَلَ ٱلْكِتَٰبَ بِٱلْحَقِّ وَٱلْمِيزَانَ ۗ وَمَا
يُدْرِيكَ لَعَلَّ ٱلسَّاعَةَ قَرِيبٌ ﴿١٧﴾

laquḍiya baynahum. Wa ʾinnal-ladhīna ʾūrithul-Kitāba mim-baᶜdihim lafī shakkim-minhu murīb. (14) Falidhālika fadᶜu was-taqim kamāa ʾumirta wa lā tattabiᶜ ʾahwāaʾahum. Wa qul ʾāmañtu bimāa ʾañzalal-lāhu miñ-Kitābiñw-wa ʾumirtu liʾaᶜdila baynakum. ʾAllāhu Rabbunā wa Rabbukum; lanāa ʾaᶜmālunā wa lakum ʾaᶜmālukum. Lā ḥujjata baynanā wa baynakum. ʾAllāhu yajmaᶜu baynanā wa ʾilayhil-maṣīr. (15) Wal-ladhīna yuḥāajjūna fil-lāhi mim-baᶜdi mas-tujība lahū ḥujjatuhum dāḥiḍatun ᶜiñda Rabbihim wa ᶜalayhim ghaḍabuñw-wa lahum ᶜadhābuñ-shadīd. (16) ʾAllāhul-ladhīi ʾañzalal-Kitāba bil-ḥaqqi wal-mīzān. Wa mā yudrīka laᶜallas-Sāᶜata qarīb. (17)

which comes immediately after the statement that "this community of yours is one single community" (see also note 30 on 23 : 53).

16 For an explanation of this passage, see note 29 on 10 : 19.

17 Lit., "who have become heirs to the divine writ after them": obviously referring to the Bible and its followers in later times.

18 Lit., "about it" – i.e., in doubt as to whether the relevant scripture has really been revealed by God, and, ultimately, as to whether there is any truth in the concept of "divine revelation" as such.

19 I.e., because of this breach of the original unity of men's faith in the One God.

20 Lit., "between you" – i.e., "to induce you to be more tolerant of one another": evidently an allusion to the bitterness which stands in the way of an understanding between the various sects and schools of thought in all revealed religions.

21 I.e., about His attributes and the "how" of His Being, all of which is beyond the grasp of the human mind.

22 The above two interpolations are based on 57 : 25, where the idea underlying this verse has been stated clearly. The implication is that since God Himself has given man, through successive revelations, a standard whereby to discern between right and wrong, it is presumptuous and futile to argue about the nature of His Being and His ultimate judgment: hence the reference, in the second half of this and the next verse, to the Last Hour and, thus, the Day of Judgment.

Those who do not believe in it [mockingly] ask for its speedy advent[23] – whereas those who have attained to faith stand in awe of it, and know it to be the truth.
Oh, verily, they who call the Last Hour in question have indeed gone far astray!
‹18›

GOD is most kind unto His creatures: He provides sustenance for whomever He wills – for He alone is powerful, almighty!
‹19›
To him who desires a harvest in the life to come, We shall grant an increase in his harvest; whereas to him who desires [but] a harvest in this world, We [may] give something thereof – but he will have no share in [the blessings of] the life to come.[24] ‹20›
Is it that they [who care for no more than this world] believe in forces supposed to have a share in God's divinity,[25] which enjoin upon them as a moral law something that God has never allowed?[26]
Now were it not for [God's] decree on the final judgment,[27] all would indeed have been decided between them [in this world]:[28] but, verily, grievous suffering awaits the evildoers [in the life to come].
‹21›

يَسْتَعْجِلُ بِهَا ٱلَّذِينَ لَا يُؤْمِنُونَ بِهَا ۖ وَٱلَّذِينَ ءَامَنُوا۟ مُشْفِقُونَ مِنْهَا وَيَعْلَمُونَ
أَنَّهَا ٱلْحَقُّ ۗ أَلَآ إِنَّ ٱلَّذِينَ يُمَارُونَ فِى ٱلسَّاعَةِ لَفِى ضَلَـٰلٍۭ بَعِيدٍ ﴿١٨﴾ ٱللَّهُ
لَطِيفٌۢ بِعِبَادِهِۦ يَرْزُقُ مَن يَشَآءُ ۖ وَهُوَ ٱلْقَوِىُّ ٱلْعَزِيزُ ﴿١٩﴾ مَن كَانَ يُرِيدُ
حَرْثَ ٱلْـَٔاخِرَةِ نَزِدْ لَهُۥ فِى حَرْثِهِۦ ۖ وَمَن كَانَ يُرِيدُ حَرْثَ ٱلدُّنْيَا نُؤْتِهِۦ
مِنْهَا وَمَا لَهُۥ فِى ٱلْـَٔاخِرَةِ مِن نَّصِيبٍ ﴿٢٠﴾ أَمْ لَهُمْ شُرَكَـٰٓؤُا۟ شَرَعُوا۟ لَهُم
مِّنَ ٱلدِّينِ مَا لَمْ يَأْذَنۢ بِهِ ٱللَّهُ ۚ وَلَوْلَا كَلِمَةُ ٱلْفَصْلِ لَقُضِىَ بَيْنَهُمْ ۗ وَإِنَّ
ٱلظَّـٰلِمِينَ لَهُمْ عَذَابٌ أَلِيمٌ ﴿٢١﴾

Yastaʿjilu bihal-ladhīna lā yuʾminūna bihā; wal-ladhīna ʾāmanū mushfiqūna minhā wa yaʿlamūna ʾannahal-ḥaqq. ʾAlāa ʾinnal-ladhīna yumārūna fis-Sāʿati lafī ḍalālim-baʿīd. (18) ʾAllāhu Laṭīfum-biʿibādihī yarzuqu mañy-yashāaʾu wa Huwal-Qawiyyul-ʿAzīz. (19) Mañ-kāna yurīdu ḥarthal-ʾĀkhirati nazid lahū fī ḥarthih. Wa mañ-kāna yurīdu ḥarthad-dunyā nuʾtihī minhā wa mā lahū fil-ʾĀkhirati miñ-naṣīb. (20) ʾAm lahum shurakāaʾu sharaʿū lahum-minad-dīni mā lam yaʾdham-bihil-lāh. Wa lawlā kalimatul-faṣli laquḍiya baynahum. Wa ʾinnaẓ-ẓālimīna lahum ʿadhābun ʾalīm. (21)

23 This is not merely a reference to the sarcastic demand of Muḥammad's opponents (mentioned several times in the Qurʾān) to bring about their "speedy chastisement" in proof of his being God's message-bearer, but also an oblique allusion to unbelievers of all times who, without having any "proof" either way, categorically reject the idea of resurrection and judgment.

24 I.e., whereas those who live righteously and turn their endeavours towards spiritual ends are sure to receive in the hereafter more than they are hoping for, those who strive *exclusively* after worldly rewards may – but not necessarily will – achieve something, and not necessarily all, of their aims, without having any reason to expect "a share in the blessings" that await the righteous in the hereafter.

25 Lit., "Is it that they have partners [of God]" – i.e., "do they believe that circumstantial phenomena like wealth, power, 'luck', etc., have something divine about them?" – the implication being that belief in such "forces" is usually at the root of men's pursuance of exclusively worldly ends. (For my above explanatory rendering of the term *shurakāʾ* – lit., "partners" or "associates" [of God] – see note 15 on 6 : 22.)

26 I.e., which cause them to abandon themselves with an almost religious fervour to something of which God disapproves – namely, the striving after purely materialistic goals and a corresponding disregard of all spiritual and ethical values. For my rendering of *dīn*, in this context, as "moral law", see note 3 on 109 : 6.

27 Lit., "word of decision", i.e., that His final judgment shall be postponed until the Day of Resurrection (see next note).

28 I.e., God would have made a clear-cut distinction, in this world, between those who look forward to the hereafter and those who care for no more than worldly success, by granting unlimited happiness to the former and causing the latter to suffer: but since it is only in the hereafter that man's life is to be truly fulfilled, God has willed to postpone this distinction until then.

[In that life to come,] thou wilt see the evildoers full of fear at [the thought of] what they have earned: for [now] it is bound to fall back upon them.

And in the flowering meadows of the gardens [of paradise thou wilt see] those who have attained to faith and done righteous deeds: all that they might desire shall they have with their Sustainer: [and] this, this is the great bounty ‹22› – that [bounty] whereof God gives the glad tiding to such of His servants as attain to faith and do righteous deeds.

Say [O Prophet]: "No reward do I ask of you for this [message] other than [that you should] love your fellow-men."[29]

For, if anyone gains [the merit of] a good deed, We shall grant him through it an increase of good: and, verily, God is much-forgiving, ever responsive to gratitude. ‹23›

DO THEY, perchance, say, "[Muḥammad] has attributed his own lying inventions to God"?

But then, had God so willed, He could have sealed thy heart [forever]: for God blots out all falsehood, and by His words proves the truth to be true.[30]

Verily, He has full knowledge of what is in the hearts [of men]; ‹24› and it is He who accepts repentance from His servants, and pardons bad deeds, and knows all that you do, ‹25› and responds unto all who attain to faith and do righteous deeds; and [it is He who, in the life to come,] will give them, out of His bounty, far more [than they will have deserved], whereas for the deniers of the truth there is [but] suffering severe in store. ‹26›

تَرَى ٱلظَّٰلِمِينَ مُشْفِقِينَ مِمَّا كَسَبُوا۟ وَهُوَ وَاقِعٌۢ بِهِمْ ۗ وَٱلَّذِينَ ءَامَنُوا۟
وَعَمِلُوا۟ ٱلصَّٰلِحَٰتِ فِى رَوْضَاتِ ٱلْجَنَّاتِ ۖ لَهُم مَّا يَشَآءُونَ عِندَ رَبِّهِمْ ۚ
ذَٰلِكَ هُوَ ٱلْفَضْلُ ٱلْكَبِيرُ ﴿٢٢﴾ ذَٰلِكَ ٱلَّذِى يُبَشِّرُ ٱللَّهُ عِبَادَهُ ٱلَّذِينَ
ءَامَنُوا۟ وَعَمِلُوا۟ ٱلصَّٰلِحَٰتِ ۗ قُل لَّآ أَسْـَٔلُكُمْ عَلَيْهِ أَجْرًا إِلَّا ٱلْمَوَدَّةَ فِى
ٱلْقُرْبَىٰ ۗ وَمَن يَقْتَرِفْ حَسَنَةً نَّزِدْ لَهُۥ فِيهَا حُسْنًا ۚ إِنَّ ٱللَّهَ غَفُورٌ شَكُورٌ ﴿٢٣﴾
أَمْ يَقُولُونَ ٱفْتَرَىٰ عَلَى ٱللَّهِ كَذِبًا ۖ فَإِن يَشَإِ ٱللَّهُ يَخْتِمْ عَلَىٰ قَلْبِكَ ۗ وَيَمْحُ
ٱللَّهُ ٱلْبَٰطِلَ وَيُحِقُّ ٱلْحَقَّ بِكَلِمَٰتِهِۦٓ ۚ إِنَّهُۥ عَلِيمٌۢ بِذَاتِ ٱلصُّدُورِ ﴿٢٤﴾
وَهُوَ ٱلَّذِى يَقْبَلُ ٱلتَّوْبَةَ عَنْ عِبَادِهِۦ وَيَعْفُوا۟ عَنِ ٱلسَّيِّـَٔاتِ وَيَعْلَمُ مَا
تَفْعَلُونَ ﴿٢٥﴾ وَيَسْتَجِيبُ ٱلَّذِينَ ءَامَنُوا۟ وَعَمِلُوا۟ ٱلصَّٰلِحَٰتِ وَيَزِيدُهُم
مِّن فَضْلِهِۦ ۚ وَٱلْكَٰفِرُونَ لَهُمْ عَذَابٌ شَدِيدٌ ﴿٢٦﴾

Taraẓ-ẓālimīna mushfiqīna mimmā kasabū wa huwa wāqiʿum-bihim. Wal-ladhīna ʾāmanū wa ʿamiluṣ-ṣāliḥāti fī rawḍātil-jannāti lahum-mā yashāaʾūna ʿiñda Rabbihim; dhālika huwal-faḍlul-kabīr. (22) Dhālikal-ladhī yubashshirul-lāhu ʿibādahul-ladhīna ʾāmanū wa ʿamiluṣ-ṣāliḥāt. Qul lāa ʾasʾalukum ʿalayhi ʾajran ʾillal-mawaddata fil-qurbā. Wa mañy-yaqtarif ḥasanatañ-nazid lahū fīhā ḥusnā. ʾInnal-lāha Ghafūruñ-Shakūr. (23) ʾAm yaqūlūnaf-tarā ʿalal-lāhi kadhibā. Faʾiñy-yashaʾil-lāhu yakhtim ʿalā qalbik. Wa yamḥul-lāhul-bāṭila wa yuḥiqqul-ḥaqqa biKalimātih. ʾInnahū ʿAlīmum-bidhātiṣ-ṣudūr. (24) Wa Huwal-ladhī yaqbalut-tawbata ʿan ʿibādihī wa yaʿfū ʿanis-sayyiʾāti wa yaʿlamu mā tafʿalūn. (25) Wa yastajībul-ladhīna ʾāmanū wa ʿamiluṣ-ṣāliḥāti wa yazīduhum-miñ-faḍlih. Wal-kāfirūna lahum ʿadhābuñ-shadīd. (26)

29 Lit., "love for those who are near (*al-qurbā*)". Some commentators take this to mean "those who are near to *me*", i.e., Muḥammad's kinsfolk: but quite apart from the objection that such a "personal" demand would conflict with the preceding assurance, "No reward do I ask of you", the deliberate omission of any possessive pronoun in respect of the term *al-qurbā* indicates that it is not limited to any personal relationship but, rather, alludes to a relationship common to *all* human beings: namely, the fellowship of man – a concept which implies the fundamental ethical postulate to care for one another's material and spiritual welfare.

30 See note 103 on 10 : 82.

نصف الحزب

۞ وَلَوْ بَسَطَ ٱللَّهُ ٱلرِّزْقَ لِعِبَادِهِۦ لَبَغَوْا۟ فِى ٱلْأَرْضِ وَلَـٰكِن يُنَزِّلُ بِقَدَرٍ
مَّا يَشَآءُ ۚ إِنَّهُۥ بِعِبَادِهِۦ خَبِيرٌۢ بَصِيرٌ ﴿٢٧﴾ وَهُوَ ٱلَّذِى يُنَزِّلُ ٱلْغَيْثَ مِنۢ بَعْدِ
مَا قَنَطُوا۟ وَيَنشُرُ رَحْمَتَهُۥ ۚ وَهُوَ ٱلْوَلِىُّ ٱلْحَمِيدُ ﴿٢٨﴾ وَمِنْ ءَايَـٰتِهِۦ خَلْقُ
ٱلسَّمَـٰوَٰتِ وَٱلْأَرْضِ وَمَا بَثَّ فِيهِمَا مِن دَآبَّةٍ ۚ وَهُوَ عَلَىٰ جَمْعِهِمْ إِذَا
يَشَآءُ قَدِيرٌ ﴿٢٩﴾ وَمَآ أَصَـٰبَكُم مِّن مُّصِيبَةٍ فَبِمَا كَسَبَتْ أَيْدِيكُمْ
وَيَعْفُوا۟ عَن كَثِيرٍ ﴿٣٠﴾ وَمَآ أَنتُم بِمُعْجِزِينَ فِى ٱلْأَرْضِ ۖ وَمَا لَكُم مِّن
دُونِ ٱللَّهِ مِن وَلِىٍّ وَلَا نَصِيرٍ ﴿٣١﴾ وَمِنْ ءَايَـٰتِهِ ٱلْجَوَارِ فِى ٱلْبَحْرِ
كَٱلْأَعْلَـٰمِ ﴿٣٢﴾ إِن يَشَأْ يُسْكِنِ ٱلرِّيحَ فَيَظْلَلْنَ رَوَاكِدَ عَلَىٰ ظَهْرِهِۦٓ ۚ

۞ Wa law basaṭal-lāhur-rizqa liʿibādihī labaghaw fil-ʾarḍi wa lākiñy-yunazzilu biqadarim-mā yashāaʾ. ʾInnahū biʿibādihī Khabīrum-Baṣīr. (27) Wa Huwal-ladhī yunazzilul-ghaytha mim-baʿdi mā qanaṭū wa yañshuru raḥmatah. Wa Huwal-Waliyyul-Ḥamīd. (28) Wa min ʾĀyātihī khalqus-samāwāti wal-ʾarḍi wa mā baththa fīhimā miñ-dāabbah. Wa Huwa ʿalā jamʿihim ʾidhā yashāaʾu Qadīr. (29) Wa māa ʾaṣābakum-mim-muṣībatiñ-fabimā kasabat ʾaydīkum wa yaʿfū ʿañ-kathīr. (30) Wa māa ʾañtum-bimuʿjizīna fil-ʾarḍi wa mā lakum miñ-dūnil-lāhi miñw-waliyyiñw-wa lā naṣīr. (31) Wa min ʾĀyātihil-jawāri fil-baḥri kalʾaʿlām. (32) ʾIñy-yashaʾ yuskinir-rīḥa fayaẓlalna rawākida ʿalā ẓahrih.

For, if God were to grant [in this world] abundant sustenance to [all of] His servants, they would behave on earth with wanton insolence:[31] but as it is, He bestows [His grace] from on high in due measure, as He wills: for, verily, He is fully aware of [the needs of] His creatures, and sees them all. ‹27›

And it is He who sends down rain after [men] have lost all hope, and unfolds His grace [thereby]:[32] for He alone is [their] Protector, the One to whom all praise is due. ‹28›

And among His signs is the [very] creation of the heavens and the earth, and of all the living creatures which He has caused to multiply throughout them:[33] and [since He has created them,] He has [also] the power to gather them [unto Himself] whenever He wills. ‹29›

Now whatever calamity may befall you [on Judgment Day] will be an outcome of what your own hands have wrought,[34] although He pardons much; ‹30› and you cannot elude Him on earth, and you will have none to protect you from God [in the life to come], and none to bring you succour. ‹31›

And among His signs[35] are the ships that sail like [floating] mountains through the seas: ‹32› if He so wills, He stills the wind, and then they lie motionless on the sea's

---

31 This passage connects with, and elucidates, the statement in the preceding verse that God "responds unto all who attain to faith and do righteous deeds" – a statement which, at first glance, seems to be contrary to the fact that whereas many wrongdoers prosper and are happy, many righteous people suffer hurt and deprivation. In reply to this objection, the above verse points elliptically to man's innate "greed for more and more" (see 102 : 1), which often causes him to become "grossly overweening whenever he believes himself to be self-sufficient" (96 : 6). To counteract this tendency, the Qurʾān stresses again and again that God's "response" to the righteous – as well as to wrongdoers – will become fully evident only in the life to come, and not necessarily in this world, which, after all, is only the first, short stage of man's existence.

32 This reference to the symbol of life-giving rain connects with the preceding statement that "He bestows [His grace] in due measure, as He wills", and is a preamble, as it were, to the statement in the next verse that all creation is but a visible "sign" or "revelation" of God's existence and purposeful activity, as well as of the God-willed continuation of all life in the hereafter.

33 Lit., "in both". In the Qurʾān, the expression "the heavens and the earth" invariably denotes the universe in its entirety.

34 This oft-recurring phrase is a Qurʾanic metonym for man's doings and conscious attitudes in this world, meant to bring out the fact that these doings or attitudes are the "harvest" of a person's spiritual character and have, therefore, a definite influence on the quality of his life in the hereafter. Since the latter is but an organic continuation of earthly life, man's subsequent spiritual growth and bliss or, alternatively, spiritual darkness and suffering – symbolically circumscribed as God's "reward" and "chastisement" or "paradise" and "hell" – depend on, and are a result of, what one has previously "earned".

35 As is evident from the sequence, in this instance the term *āyah* (lit., "sign" or "[divine] message") is used in the

surface – [and] herein, behold, there are messages indeed for all who are wholly patient in adversity and deeply grateful [to God]; «33» or else He may cause them to perish because of what they have wrought;[36] and [withal,] He pardons much. «34»
And let them know, those who call Our messages in question,[37] that for them there is no escape. «35»

AND [remember that] whatever you are given [now] is but for the [passing] enjoyment of life in this world – whereas that which is with God is far better and more enduring.
[It shall be given] to all who attain to faith and in their Sustainer place their trust; «36» and who shun the more heinous sins and abominations; and who, whenever they are moved to anger, readily forgive; «37» and who respond to [the call of] their Sustainer and are constant in prayer; and whose rule [in all matters of common concern] is consultation among themselves;[38] and who spend on others out of what We provide for them as sustenance;[39] «38» and who, whenever tyranny afflicts them, defend themselves. «39»
But [remember that an attempt at] requiting evil may, too, become an evil:[40]

إِنَّ فِي ذَٰلِكَ لَأٓيَٰتٖ لِّكُلِّ صَبَّارٖ شَكُورٍ ٣٣ أَوۡ يُوبِقۡهُنَّ بِمَا كَسَبُواْ
وَيَعۡفُ عَن كَثِيرٖ ٣٤ وَيَعۡلَمَ ٱلَّذِينَ يُجَٰدِلُونَ فِيٓ ءَايَٰتِنَا مَا لَهُم مِّن
مَّحِيصٖ ٣٥ فَمَآ أُوتِيتُم مِّن شَيۡءٖ فَمَتَٰعُ ٱلۡحَيَوٰةِ ٱلدُّنۡيَاۖ وَمَا عِندَ ٱللَّهِ خَيۡرٞ
وَأَبۡقَىٰ لِلَّذِينَ ءَامَنُواْ وَعَلَىٰ رَبِّهِمۡ يَتَوَكَّلُونَ ٣٦ وَٱلَّذِينَ يَجۡتَنِبُونَ كَبَٰٓئِرَ
ٱلۡإِثۡمِ وَٱلۡفَوَٰحِشَ وَإِذَا مَا غَضِبُواْ هُمۡ يَغۡفِرُونَ ٣٧ وَٱلَّذِينَ ٱسۡتَجَابُواْ
لِرَبِّهِمۡ وَأَقَامُواْ ٱلصَّلَوٰةَ وَأَمۡرُهُمۡ شُورَىٰ بَيۡنَهُمۡ وَمِمَّا رَزَقۡنَٰهُمۡ يُنفِقُونَ ٣٨
وَٱلَّذِينَ إِذَآ أَصَابَهُمُ ٱلۡبَغۡيُ هُمۡ يَنتَصِرُونَ ٣٩ وَجَزَٰٓؤُاْ سَيِّئَةٖ سَيِّئَةٞ مِّثۡلُهَاۖ

ʾInna fī dhālika laʾĀyātil-likulli ṣabbāriñ-shakūr. (33) ʾAw yūbiqhunna bimā kasabū wa yaʿfu ʿañ-kathīr. (34) Wa yaʿlamal-ladhīna yujādilūna fīi ʾĀyātinā mā lahum-mim-maḥīṣ. (35) Famāa ʾūtītum-miñ-shayʾiñ-famatāʿul-ḥayātid-dunyā. Wa mā ʿiñdal-lāhi khayruñw-wa ʾabqā lilladhīna ʾāmanū wa ʿalā Rabbihim yatawakkalūn. (36) Wal-ladhīna yajtanibūna kabāaʾiral-ʾithmi wal-fawāḥisha wa ʾidhā mā ghaḍibū hum yaghfirūn. (37) Wal-ladhīnas-tajābū liRabbihim wa ʾaqāmuṣ-Ṣalāta wa ʾamruhum shūrā baynahum wa mimmā razaqnāhum yuñfiqūn. (38) Wal-ladhīna ʾidhāa ʾaṣābahumul-baghyu hum yañtaṣirūn. (39) Wa jazāaʾu sayyiʾatiñ-sayyiʾatum-mithluhā.

sense of "parable". (See next note.)

36 I.e., because of the evil which they have committed. The above passage is, I believe, a parabolical allusion to the three possible alternatives in the life to come: spiritual progress and happiness (symbolized by ships that sail freely through the sea); spiritual stagnancy (ships that lie motionless on the sea's surface); and spiritual disaster and suffering (summarized in the concept of perdition). The second of these three alternatives seems to point to the condition of those *ʿala 'l-aʿrāf* spoken of in 7 : 46 f. and explained in the corresponding note 37.

37 For this rendering of *yujādilūn*, see note 25 on 40 : 35.

38 This particular qualification of true believers – regarded by the Prophet's Companions as so important that they always referred to this *sūrah* by the key-word "consultation" (*shūrā*) – has a double import: firstly, it is meant to remind all followers of the Qurʾān that they must remain united within one single community (*ummah*); and, secondly, it lays down the principle that all their communal business *must* be transacted in mutual consultation. (For the political implications of this principle, see *State and Government*, pp. 44 ff.).

39 See note 4 on 2 : 3. Following as it does immediately upon the call to communal unity and consultation, the "spending on others" bears here the general connotation of social justice.

40 Lit., "is [or "may be"] an evil like it". In other words, successful struggle against tyranny (which latter is the meaning of the noun *baghy* in the last sentence of the preceding verse) often tends to degenerate into a similarly tyrannical attitude towards the erstwhile oppressors. Hence, most of the classical commentators (e.g., Baghawī, Zamakhsharī, Rāzī, Bayḍāwī) stress the absolute prohibition of "going beyond what is right" (*iʿtidāʾ*) when defending oneself against tyranny and oppression. (Cf. the passage relating to fighting against "those who wage war against you" in 2 : 190 ff.)

hence, whoever pardons [his foe] and makes peace, his reward rests with God – for, verily, He does not love evildoers.[41] «40» Yet indeed, as for any who defend themselves after having been wronged – no blame whatever attaches to them: «41» blame attaches but to those who oppress [other] people and behave outrageously on earth, offending against all right: for them there is grievous suffering in store! «42» But withal, if one is patient in adversity and forgives – this, behold, is indeed something to set one's heart upon![42] «43»

AND [thus it is:] he whom God lets go astray[43] has henceforth no protector whatever: and so thou wilt see such evildoers[44] [on Judgment Day, and wilt hear how] they exclaim as soon as they behold the suffering [that awaits them], "Is there any way of return?"[45] «44»
And thou wilt see them exposed to that [doom], humbling themselves in abasement, looking [around] with a furtive glance – the while those who had attained to faith will say, "Verily, lost on [this] Day of Resurrection are they who have squandered their own and their followers' selves!"[46]
Oh, verily, the evildoers will fall into long-lasting suffering, «45» and will have no protector whatever to succour them against God: for he whom God lets go astray shall find no way [of escape]. «46»

فَمَنْ عَفَا وَأَصْلَحَ فَأَجْرُهُۥ عَلَى ٱللَّهِ إِنَّهُۥ لَا يُحِبُّ ٱلظَّٰلِمِينَ ﴿40﴾ وَلَمَنِ
ٱنتَصَرَ بَعْدَ ظُلْمِهِۦ فَأُو۟لَٰٓئِكَ مَا عَلَيْهِم مِّن سَبِيلٍ ﴿41﴾ إِنَّمَا ٱلسَّبِيلُ
عَلَى ٱلَّذِينَ يَظْلِمُونَ ٱلنَّاسَ وَيَبْغُونَ فِى ٱلْأَرْضِ بِغَيْرِ ٱلْحَقِّ أُو۟لَٰٓئِكَ
لَهُمْ عَذَابٌ أَلِيمٌ ﴿42﴾ وَلَمَن صَبَرَ وَغَفَرَ إِنَّ ذَٰلِكَ لَمِنْ عَزْمِ
ٱلْأُمُورِ ﴿43﴾ وَمَن يُضْلِلِ ٱللَّهُ فَمَا لَهُۥ مِن وَلِىٍّ مِّنۢ بَعْدِهِۦ وَتَرَى
ٱلظَّٰلِمِينَ لَمَّا رَأَوُا۟ ٱلْعَذَابَ يَقُولُونَ هَلْ إِلَىٰ مَرَدٍّ مِّن سَبِيلٍ ﴿44﴾ وَتَرَىٰهُمْ
يُعْرَضُونَ عَلَيْهَا خَٰشِعِينَ مِنَ ٱلذُّلِّ يَنظُرُونَ مِن طَرْفٍ خَفِىٍّ وَقَالَ ٱلَّذِينَ
ءَامَنُوٓا۟ إِنَّ ٱلْخَٰسِرِينَ ٱلَّذِينَ خَسِرُوٓا۟ أَنفُسَهُمْ وَأَهْلِيهِمْ يَوْمَ ٱلْقِيَٰمَةِ أَلَآ
إِنَّ ٱلظَّٰلِمِينَ فِى عَذَابٍ مُّقِيمٍ ﴿45﴾ وَمَا كَانَ لَهُم مِّنْ أَوْلِيَآءَ يَنصُرُونَهُم
مِّن دُونِ ٱللَّهِ وَمَن يُضْلِلِ ٱللَّهُ فَمَا لَهُۥ مِن سَبِيلٍ ﴿46﴾

Faman ʿafā wa ʾaṣlaḥa faʾajruhū ʿalal-lāh. ʾInnahū lā yuḥibbuẓ-ẓālimīn. (40) Wa lamaniñ-taṣara baʿda ẓulmihī faʾulāaʾika mā ʿalayhim-miñ-sabīl. (41) ʾInnamas-sabīlu ʿalal-ladhīna yaẓlimūnan-nāsa wa yabghūna fil-ʾarḍi bighayril-ḥaqq. ʾUlāaʾika lahum ʿadhābun ʾalīm. (42) Wa lamañ-ṣabara wa ghafara ʾinna dhālika lamin ʿazmil-ʾumūr. (43) Wa mañy-yuḍlilil-lāhu famā lahū miñw-waliyyim-mim-baʿdih. Wa taraẓ-ẓālimīna lammā raʾawul-ʿadhāba yaqūlūna hal ʾilā maraddim-miñ-sabīl. (44) Wa tarāhum yuʿraḍūna ʿalayhā khāshiʿīna minadh-dhulli yañẓurūna miñ-ṭarfin khafiyy. Wa qālal-ladhīna ʾāmanūu ʾinnal-khāsirīnal-ladhīna khasirūu ʾañfusahum wa ʾahlīhim Yawmal-Qiyāmah. ʾAlāa ʾinnaẓ-ẓālimīna fī ʿadhābim-muqīm. (45) Wa mā kāna lahum min ʾawliyāaʾa yañṣurūnahum miñ-dūnil-lāh. Wa mañy-yuḍlilil-lāhu famā lahū miñ-sabīl. (46)

41 I.e., in this context, such as succumb to the temptation of indulging in undue acts of revenge against their former oppressors.

42 Cf. 41 : 34-35, as well as note 44 on 13 : 22.

43 See note 4 on 14 : 4.

44 Although this is primarily a reference to "those who oppress [other] people and behave outrageously on earth, offending against all right" (verse 42 above), the meaning of the term is general, applying to *all* kinds of deliberate evildoers.

45 I.e., a "second chance" on earth: cf. 6 : 27-28.

46 The term *ahl* denotes primarily the "people" of one town, country or family, as well as the "fellow-members" of one race, religion, profession, etc. In its wider, ideological sense it is applied to people who have certain characteristics in common. e.g., *ahl al-ʿilm* ("people of knowledge", i.e., scholars), or who follow one and the same persuasion or belief, e.g., *ahl al-kitāb* ("the followers of [earlier] revelation"), *ahl al-Qurʾān* ("the followers of the Qurʾān"), and so forth. Since, as has been pointed out in note 44, the above passage refers primarily – though not exclusively – to the tyrants and oppressors spoken of in verse 42, the term *ahluhum* evidently connotes "their followers". Thus, the above

[Hence, O men,] respond to your Sustainer before there comes, at God's behest,[47] a Day on which there will be no turning back: [for] on that Day you will have no place of refuge, and neither will you be able to deny aught [of the wrong that you have done]. «47»

BUT IF they turn away [from thee, O Prophet, know that] We have not sent thee to be their keeper: thou art not bound to do more than deliver the message [entrusted to thee].

And, behold, [such as turn away from Our messages are but impelled by the weakness and inconstancy of human nature:[48] thus,] when We give man a taste of Our grace, he is prone to exult in it;[49] but if misfortune befalls [any of] them in result of what their own hands have sent forth, then, behold, man shows how bereft he is of all gratitude![50] «48»

God's alone is the dominion over the heavens and the earth. He creates whatever He wills: He bestows the gift of female offspring on whomever He wills, and the gift of male offspring on whomever He wills; «49» or He gives both male and female [to whomever He wills], and causes to be barren whomever He wills: for, verily, He is all-knowing, infinite in His power.[51] «50»

ٱسْتَجِيبُوا۟ لِرَبِّكُم مِّن قَبْلِ أَن يَأْتِىَ يَوْمٌ لَّا مَرَدَّ لَهُۥ مِنَ ٱللَّهِ ۚ مَا لَكُم مِّن
مَّلْجَإٍ يَوْمَئِذٍ وَمَا لَكُم مِّن نَّكِيرٍ ﴿٤٧﴾ فَإِنْ أَعْرَضُوا۟ فَمَآ أَرْسَلْنَٰكَ عَلَيْهِمْ
حَفِيظًا ۖ إِنْ عَلَيْكَ إِلَّا ٱلْبَلَٰغُ ۗ وَإِنَّآ إِذَآ أَذَقْنَا ٱلْإِنسَٰنَ مِنَّا رَحْمَةً فَرِحَ
بِهَا ۖ وَإِن تُصِبْهُمْ سَيِّئَةٌۢ بِمَا قَدَّمَتْ أَيْدِيهِمْ فَإِنَّ ٱلْإِنسَٰنَ كَفُورٌ ﴿٤٨﴾ لِّلَّهِ
مُلْكُ ٱلسَّمَٰوَٰتِ وَٱلْأَرْضِ ۚ يَخْلُقُ مَا يَشَآءُ ۚ يَهَبُ لِمَن يَشَآءُ إِنَٰثًا وَيَهَبُ
لِمَن يَشَآءُ ٱلذُّكُورَ ﴿٤٩﴾ أَوْ يُزَوِّجُهُمْ ذُكْرَانًا وَإِنَٰثًا ۖ وَيَجْعَلُ مَن يَشَآءُ
عَقِيمًا ۚ إِنَّهُۥ عَلِيمٌ قَدِيرٌ ﴿٥٠﴾

ʾIstajībū liRabbikum-miñ-qabli ʾañy-yaʾtiya Yawmul-lā maradda lahū minal-lāh. Mā lakum-mim-maljaʾiñy-Yawmaʾidhiñw-wa mā lakum-miñ-nakīr. (47) Faʾin ʾaʿraḍū famāa ʾarsalnāka ʿalayhim ḥafīẓan ʾin ʿalayka ʾillal-balāgh. Wa ʾinnāa ʾidhāa ʾadhaqnal-ʾIñsāna minnā raḥmatañ-fariḥa bihā; wa ʾiñ-tuṣibhum sayyiʾatum-bimā qaddamat ʾaydīhim faʾinnal-ʾIñsāna kafūr. (48) Lillāhi mulkus-samāwāti wal-ʾarḍi yakhluqu mā yashāaʾ. Yahabu limañy-yashāaʾu ʾināthañw-wa yahabu limañy-yashāaʾudh-dhukūr. (49) ʾAw yuzawwijuhum dhukrānañw-wa ʾināthañw-wa yajʿalu mañy-yashāaʾu ʿaqīman ʾinnahū ʿAlīmuñ-Qadīr. (50)

sentence implies that every kind of evildoing (*ẓulm*), and particularly the oppression of others, inevitably results in a spiritual injury to, and ultimately the self-destruction of, its perpetrators and/or their followers.

47 Lit., "from God".

48 This interpolation – necessary for a proper understanding of the context – is based on Rāzī's convincing explanation of how this passage connects with the preceding one. Man is, as a rule, absorbed in a pursuit of material goods and comforts, the achievement of which he identifies with "happiness"; hence, he pays but scant attention to spiritual aims and values, and the more so if he is called upon to abandon his selfish pursuits in favour of the – to him as yet hypothetical – life in the hereafter.

49 I.e., when God bestows on him a measure of material benefits, man tends to exult in this "success" as such, attributing it exclusively to his own ability and cleverness (cf. the first sentence of 41 : 50).

50 I.e., instead of remembering his past happiness with gratitude, he calls the very existence of God in question, arguing that if God did really exist, He "could not possibly have permitted" so much misfortune and unhappiness to prevail in the world: a fallacious argument inasmuch as it does not take the reality of the *hereafter* into account and is, moreover, based on a concept of God in terms of purely human feelings and expectations.

51 The purport of this passage is a re-affirmation of the fact that whatever happens to man is an outcome of God's unfathomable will: a fact which is illustrated in the sequence by the most common, recurrent phenomenon in man's life – the unpredictability of male or female births, as well as of barrenness: and so, too, God's bestowal of worldly happiness and unhappiness cannot be measured or predicted in terms of what man may regard as his "due".

ثلاثة ارباع الحزب

And it is not given to mortal man that God should speak unto him otherwise than through sudden inspiration,[52] or [by a voice, as it were,] from behind a veil, or by sending an apostle to reveal, by His leave, whatever He wills [to reveal]:[53] for, verily, He is exalted, wise. ‹51›

And thus, too,[54] [O Muḥammad,] have We revealed unto thee a life-giving message,[55] [coming] at Our behest.

[Ere this message came unto thee,] thou didst not know what revelation is, nor what faith [implies]:[56] but [now] We have caused this [message] to be a light, whereby We guide whom We will of Our servants: and, verily, [on the strength thereof] thou, too, shalt guide [men] onto the straight way ‹52› – the way that leads to God, to whom all that is in the heavens and all that is on earth belongs.

Oh, verily, with God is the beginning and the end of all things![57] ‹53›

۞ وَمَا كَانَ لِبَشَرٍ أَن يُكَلِّمَهُ ٱللَّهُ إِلَّا وَحْيًا أَوْ مِن وَرَآيِ حِجَابٍ أَوْ
يُرْسِلَ رَسُولًا فَيُوحِىَ بِإِذْنِهِۦ مَا يَشَآءُ ۚ إِنَّهُۥ عَلِىٌّ حَكِيمٌ ﴿51﴾ وَكَذَٰلِكَ
أَوْحَيْنَآ إِلَيْكَ رُوحًا مِّنْ أَمْرِنَا ۚ مَا كُنتَ تَدْرِى مَا ٱلْكِتَٰبُ وَلَا
ٱلْإِيمَٰنُ وَلَٰكِن جَعَلْنَٰهُ نُورًا نَّهْدِى بِهِۦ مَن نَّشَآءُ مِنْ عِبَادِنَا ۚ وَإِنَّكَ
لَتَهْدِىٓ إِلَىٰ صِرَٰطٍ مُّسْتَقِيمٍ ﴿52﴾ صِرَٰطِ ٱللَّهِ ٱلَّذِى لَهُۥ مَا فِى
ٱلسَّمَٰوَٰتِ وَمَا فِى ٱلْأَرْضِ ۗ أَلَآ إِلَى ٱللَّهِ تَصِيرُ ٱلْأُمُورُ ﴿53﴾

۞ **Wa mā kāna libasharin ʾañy-yukallimahul-lāhu ʾillā waḥyan ʾaw miñw-warāaʾi ḥijābin ʾaw yursila Rasūlañ-fayūḥiya biʾidhnihī mā yashāaʾu ʾinnahū ʿAliyyun Ḥakīm. (51) Wa kadhālika ʾawḥaynāa ʾilayka Rūḥam-min ʾamrinā. Mā kuñta tadrī mal-Kitābu wa lal-ʾīmānu wa lākiñ-jaʿalnāhu Nūrañ-nahdī bihī mañ-nashāaʾu min ʿibādinā. Wa ʾinnaka latahdīi ʾilā ṣirāṭim-mustaqīm. (52) Ṣirāṭil-lāhil-ladhī lahū mā fis-samāwāti wa mā fil-ʾarḍ. ʾAlāa ʾilal-lāhi taṣīrul-ʾumūr. (53)**

---

52 This is the primary meaning of *waḥy*, a term which combines the concepts of suddenness and inner illumination (Rāghib); in the usage of the Qurʾān, it is often, though by no means always, synonymous with "revelation". – The above passage connects with the first paragraph of verse 48, which speaks of the divine message entrusted to the Prophet.

53 Cf. 53 : 10.

54 I.e., in all the three ways mentioned in the preceding verse.

55 The term *rūḥ* (lit., "spirit" or "soul") has in the Qurʾān often the meaning of "divine inspiration" (see *sūrah* 16, note 2). In the present context, it evidently denotes the *contents* of the divine inspiration bestowed on the Prophet Muḥammad, i.e., the Qurʾān (Ṭabarī, Zamakhsharī, Rāzī, Ibn Kathīr), which is meant to lead man to a more intensive spiritual life: hence my above rendering.

56 I.e., that the very concept of "faith" implies man's complete self-surrender (*islām*) to God.

57 Lit., "unto God do all things (*al-umūr*) pursue their course": i.e., all things go back to Him as their source, and from His will depends the course which they take (Bayḍāwī).

The Forty-Third Sūrah

Az-Zukhruf (Gold)

Mecca Period

DERIVING its title from the incidental mention of the word *zukhruf* in verse 35, this *sūrah* is almost entirely devoted to the principle that to attribute divinity, in whatever form, to anyone or anything but God is not only spiritually destructive but also logically inadmissible. Furthermore, stress is laid on the fact that all such spiritual aberration is, as a rule, due to people's blind adherence to what they regard as the faith of their forebears: "Behold, we found our forefathers agreed on what to believe – and, verily, it is in their footsteps that we find our guidance" (verse 22 and, in a slightly modified form, verse 23).

-43-
سورة الزخرف مكية
وآياتها تسع وثمانون

IN THE NAME OF GOD, THE MOST GRACIOUS, THE DISPENSER OF GRACE:

Ḥā. Mīm.[1] ‹1›
CONSIDER this divine writ, clear in itself and clearly showing the truth:[2] ‹2› behold, We have caused it to be a discourse in the Arabic tongue, so that you might encompass it with your reason.[3] ‹3›
And, verily, [originating as it does] in the source, with Us, of all revelation,[4] it is indeed sublime, full of wisdom. ‹4›

[O YOU who deny the truth!] Should We, perchance, withdraw this reminder from you altogether, seeing that you are people bent on wasting your own selves?[5] ‹5›
And how many a prophet did We send to people of olden times! ‹6› But never yet came a prophet to them without their deriding him ‹7› – and so, [in the end,] We destroyed them [even though they were] of greater might than these:[6] and the [very] image of those people of old became a thing of the past. ‹8›
Yet thus it is [with most people]: if[7] thou ask them, "Who is it that has created the heavens and the earth?" – they will surely answer, "The Almighty, the All-Knowing has created them." ‹9›

بِسۡمِ ٱللَّهِ ٱلرَّحۡمَٰنِ ٱلرَّحِيمِ

حمٓ ﴿١﴾ وَٱلۡكِتَٰبِ ٱلۡمُبِينِ ﴿٢﴾ إِنَّا جَعَلۡنَٰهُ قُرۡءَٰنًا عَرَبِيّٗا لَّعَلَّكُمۡ
تَعۡقِلُونَ ﴿٣﴾ وَإِنَّهُۥ فِيٓ أُمِّ ٱلۡكِتَٰبِ لَدَيۡنَا لَعَلِيٌّ حَكِيمٌ ﴿٤﴾ أَفَنَضۡرِبُ
عَنكُمُ ٱلذِّكۡرَ صَفۡحًا أَن كُنتُمۡ قَوۡمٗا مُّسۡرِفِينَ ﴿٥﴾ وَكَمۡ أَرۡسَلۡنَا مِن نَّبِيّٖ فِي
ٱلۡأَوَّلِينَ ﴿٦﴾ وَمَا يَأۡتِيهِم مِّن نَّبِيٍّ إِلَّا كَانُواْ بِهِۦ يَسۡتَهۡزِءُونَ ﴿٧﴾
فَأَهۡلَكۡنَآ أَشَدَّ مِنۡهُم بَطۡشٗا وَمَضَىٰ مَثَلُ ٱلۡأَوَّلِينَ ﴿٨﴾ وَلَئِن سَأَلۡتَهُم مَّنۡ
خَلَقَ ٱلسَّمَٰوَٰتِ وَٱلۡأَرۡضَ لَيَقُولُنَّ خَلَقَهُنَّ ٱلۡعَزِيزُ ٱلۡعَلِيمُ ﴿٩﴾

Bismil-lāhir-Raḥmānir-Raḥīm.
Ḥā-Mīim. (1) Wal-Kitābil-mubīn. (2) ʾInnā jaʿalnāhu Qurʾānan ʿarabiyyal-laʿallakum taʿqilūn. (3) Wa ʾinnahū fii ʾummil-Kitābi ladaynā laʿaliyyun ḥakīm. (4) ʾAfanaḍribu ʿañkumudh-dhikra ṣafḥan ʾañ-kuñtum qawmam-musrifīn. (5) Wa kam ʾarsalnā miñ-Nabiyyiñ-fil-ʾawwalīn. (6) Wa mā yaʾtīhim-miñ-Nabiyyin ʾillā kānū bihī yastahziʾūn. (7) Faʾahlaknāa ʾashadda minhum-baṭshañw-wa maḍā mathalul-ʾawwalīn. (8) Wa laʾiñ-saʾaltahum-man khalaqas-samāwāti wal-ʾarḍa layaqūlunna khalaqahunnal-ʿAzīzul-ʿAlīm. (9)

---

1 See Appendix II.
2 Regarding this rendering of the term *mubīn*, see note 2 on 12 : 1.
3 See note 3 on 12 : 3.
4 Cf. last clause of 13 : 39 – "with Him (*ʿindahu*) is the source (*umm*) of all revelation". The term *umm* (lit., "mother") has often the idiomatic connotation of "origin" or "source" (*aṣl*), and sometimes – as in 3 : 7 – of "essence". In the present context, only the former meaning is applicable. See also note 11 on the last verse of *sūrah* 85.
5 For this rendering of the term *musrif*, see note 21 on the last sentence of 10 : 12. The above rhetorical question answers itself, of course, in the negative – implying that God never ceases to "remind" the sinner through His revelations, and always accepts repentance.
6 I.e., than the people addressed in verse 5 above.
7 See *sūrah* 30, note 45.

He it is who has made the earth a cradle for you, and has provided for you ways [of livelihood] thereon,[8] so that you might follow the right path. ‹10›
And He it is who sends down, again and again,[9] waters from the sky in due measure: and [as] We raise therewith dead land to life, even thus will you be brought forth [from the dead]. ‹11›
And He it is who has created all opposites.[10]
And He [it is who] has provided for you all those ships and animals whereon you ride, ‹12› in order that you might gain mastery over them,[11] and that, whenever you have mastered them, you might remember your Sustainer's blessings and say, "Limitless in His glory is He who has made [all] this subservient to our use – since [but for Him,] we would not have been able to attain to it. ‹13› Hence, verily, it is unto our Sustainer that we must always turn." ‹14›

AND YET,[12] they attribute to Him offspring from among some of the beings created by Him![13] Verily, most obviously bereft of all gratitude is man! ‹15›

ٱلَّذِى جَعَلَ لَكُمُ ٱلْأَرْضَ مَهْدًا وَجَعَلَ لَكُمْ فِيهَا سُبُلًا لَّعَلَّكُمْ
تَهْتَدُونَ ﴿١٠﴾ وَٱلَّذِى نَزَّلَ مِنَ ٱلسَّمَآءِ مَآءًۢ بِقَدَرٍ فَأَنشَرْنَا بِهِۦ بَلْدَةً مَّيْتًا
كَذَٰلِكَ تُخْرَجُونَ ﴿١١﴾ وَٱلَّذِى خَلَقَ ٱلْأَزْوَٰجَ كُلَّهَا وَجَعَلَ لَكُم مِّنَ
ٱلْفُلْكِ وَٱلْأَنْعَٰمِ مَا تَرْكَبُونَ ﴿١٢﴾ لِتَسْتَوُۥا۟ عَلَىٰ ظُهُورِهِۦ ثُمَّ تَذْكُرُوا۟
نِعْمَةَ رَبِّكُمْ إِذَا ٱسْتَوَيْتُمْ عَلَيْهِ وَتَقُولُوا۟ سُبْحَٰنَ ٱلَّذِى سَخَّرَ لَنَا هَٰذَا وَمَا
كُنَّا لَهُۥ مُقْرِنِينَ ﴿١٣﴾ وَإِنَّآ إِلَىٰ رَبِّنَا لَمُنقَلِبُونَ ﴿١٤﴾ وَجَعَلُوا۟ لَهُۥ مِنْ
عِبَادِهِۦ جُزْءًا ۚ إِنَّ ٱلْإِنسَٰنَ لَكَفُورٌ مُّبِينٌ ﴿١٥﴾

ʾAlladhī jaʿala lakumul-ʾarḍa mahdañw-wa jaʿala lakum fīhā subulal-laʿallakum tahtadūn. ﴿10﴾ Wal-ladhī nazzala minas-samāaʾi māaʾam-biqadariñ-faʾañsharnā bihī baldatam-maytañ-kadhālika tukh-rajūn. ﴿11﴾ Wal-ladhī khalaqal-ʾazwāja kullahā wa jaʿala lakum-minal-fulki wal-ʾanʿāmi mā tarkabūn. ﴿12﴾ Litastawū ʿalā ẓuhūrihī thumma tadhkurū niʿmata Rabbikum ʾidhas-tawaytum ʿalayhi wa taqūlū subḥānal-ladhī sakhkhara lanā hādhā wa mā kunnā lahū muqrinīn. ﴿13﴾ Wa ʾinnāa ʾilā Rabbinā lamuñqalibūn. ﴿14﴾ Wa jaʿalū lahū min ʿibādihī juzʾā. ʾInnal-ʾIñsāna lakafūrum-mubīn. ﴿15﴾

8 Cf. 20 : 53.
9 The grammatical form *nazzala* implies here recurrence: hence, "again and again".
10 Lit., "all pairs". Some commentators regard the term *azwāj* as synonymous in this context with "kinds" (Baghawī, Zamakhsharī, Bayḍāwī, Ibn Kathīr): i.e., they take the above phrase to mean no more than that God created *all kinds* of things, beings and phenomena. Others (e.g., Ṭabarī) see in it a reference to the *polarity* evident in all creation. Ibn ʿAbbās (as quoted by Rāzī) says that it denotes the concept of *opposites* in general, like "sweet and sour, or white and black, or male and female"; to which Rāzī adds that everything in creation has its complement, "like high and low, right and left, front and back, past and future, being and attribute", etc., whereas God – and He alone – is unique, without anything that could be termed "opposite" or "similar" or "complementary". Hence, the above sentence is an echo of the statement that "there is nothing that could be compared with Him" (112 : 4).
11 Lit., "over its backs" – i.e., according to all classical commentators, the "backs" of the above-mentioned animals and ships alike, the singular form of the pronoun ("its") relating to the collective entity comprised in the concept of "all whereon you ride" (*mā tarkabūn*): in other words, "all that you use or may use by way of transport". As regards my rendering of *li-tastaʾū* as "so that you might gain mastery", I should like to point out that the verb *istawā* (lit., "he established himself") has often the connotation adopted by me: see Jawharī, Rāghib and *Lisān al-ʿArab*, art. *sawā*; also Lane IV, 1478.
12 I.e., despite the fact that most people readily admit that God has *created* all that exists (verse 9 above), some of them tend to forget His uniqueness.
13 Lit., "attribute to Him a part out of [some of] His creatures (*ʿibād*)": cf. 6 : 100 and the corresponding notes. The noun *juzʾ* (lit., "part") evidently denotes here "a part of *Himself*", as implied in the concept of "offspring"; hence my rendering. If, on the other hand, *juzʾ* is understood in its literal sense, the above sentence could have (as Rāzī assumes) a more general meaning, namely, "they attribute a part *of His divinity* to some of the beings created by Him". However, in view of the sequence, which clearly refers to the blasphemous attribution of "offspring" to God, my rendering seems to be preferable.

Or [do you think], perchance, that out of all His creation He has chosen for Himself daughters, and favoured you with sons?[14] ‹16›

For [thus it is:] if any of them is given the glad tiding of [the birth of] what he so readily attributes to the Most Gracious,[15] his face darkens, and he is filled with suppressed anger: ‹17› "What! [Am I to have a daughter –] one who is to be reared [only] for the sake of ornament?"[16] – and thereupon he finds himself torn by a vague inner conflict.[17] ‹18›

And [yet] they claim that the angels – who in themselves are but beings created by the Most Gracious[18] – are females: [but] did they witness their creation?

This false claim of theirs[19] will be recorded, and they will be called to account [for it on Judgment Day]! ‹19›

Yet they say, "Had [not] the Most Gracious so willed, we would never have worshipped them!"

[But] they cannot have any knowledge of [His having willed] such a thing: they do nothing but guess.[20] ‹20›

Or have We, perchance, vouchsafed them, before this one, a revelation [to the contrary,] to which they are still holding fast?[21] ‹21›

أَمِ ٱتَّخَذَ مِمَّا يَخْلُقُ بَنَاتٍ وَأَصْفَىٰكُم بِٱلْبَنِينَ ﴿١٦﴾ وَإِذَا بُشِّرَ أَحَدُهُم
بِمَا ضَرَبَ لِلرَّحْمَٰنِ مَثَلًا ظَلَّ وَجْهُهُۥ مُسْوَدًّا وَهُوَ كَظِيمٌ ﴿١٧﴾ أَوَمَن
يُنَشَّؤُا۟ فِى ٱلْحِلْيَةِ وَهُوَ فِى ٱلْخِصَامِ غَيْرُ مُبِينٍ ﴿١٨﴾ وَجَعَلُوا۟ ٱلْمَلَٰٓئِكَةَ
ٱلَّذِينَ هُمْ عِبَٰدُ ٱلرَّحْمَٰنِ إِنَٰثًا ۚ أَشَهِدُوا۟ خَلْقَهُمْ ۚ سَتُكْتَبُ شَهَٰدَتُهُمْ
وَيُسْـَٔلُونَ ﴿١٩﴾ وَقَالُوا۟ لَوْ شَآءَ ٱلرَّحْمَٰنُ مَا عَبَدْنَٰهُم ۗ مَّا لَهُم بِذَٰلِكَ مِنْ
عِلْمٍ ۖ إِنْ هُمْ إِلَّا يَخْرُصُونَ ﴿٢٠﴾ أَمْ ءَاتَيْنَٰهُمْ كِتَٰبًا مِّن قَبْلِهِۦ فَهُم بِهِۦ
مُسْتَمْسِكُونَ ﴿٢١﴾

ʾAmit-takhadha mimmā yakhluqu banātiñw-wa ʾaṣfākum-bilbanīn. (16) Wa ʾidhā bushshira ʾaḥaduhum-bimā ḍaraba lir-Raḥmāni mathalañ-ẓalla wajhuhū muswaddañw-wa huwa kaẓīm. (17) ʾAwa mañy-yunashshaʾu fil-ḥilyati wa huwa fil-khiṣāmi ghayru mubīn. (18) Wa jaʿalul-Malāaʾikatal-ladhīna hum ʿibādur-Raḥmāni ʾināthā. ʾAshahidū khalqahum. Sa-tuktabu shahādatuhum wa yusʾalūn. (19) Wa qālū law shāaʾar-Raḥmānu mā ʿabadnāhum. Mā lahum-bidhālika min ʿilmin ʾin hum ʾillā yakhruṣūn. (20) ʾAm ʾātaynāhum Kitābam-miñ-qablihī fahum-bihī mustamsikūn. (21)

14 It should be remembered that the people thus addressed were the pagan Arabs, who believed that some of their goddesses, as well as the angels, were "God's daughters". In view of the fact that those pre-Islamic Arabs regarded daughters as a mere liability and their birth as a disgrace, this verse is obviously ironical. (Cf. in this connection 16 : 57-59.)

15 Lit., "what he postulates as a likeness of [or "as likely for"] the Most Gracious": i.e., female offspring, which implies a natural "likeness" to its progenitor.

16 I.e., one who, from the viewpoint of the pre-Islamic Arabs, would have no function other than "embellishing" a man's life.

17 Lit., "he finds himself in an invisible (*ghayr mubīn*) conflict" – i.e., an inner conflict which he does not quite admit to his consciousness: cf. 16 : 59 – "[he debates within himself:] Shall he keep this child despite the contempt [which he feels for it] – or shall he bury it in the dust?" (See also, in particular, the corresponding note 66.)

18 Or: "who are but worshippers [or "creatures"] (*ʿibād*) of the Most Gracious" – in either case stressing their having been *created* and, hence, not being divine.

19 Lit., "their testimony", i.e., regarding the "sex" of the angels, who are spiritual in nature (Rāzī) and, therefore, sexless.

20 I.e., they cannot have any "knowledge" of something that is devoid of all reality – because, far from having "willed" their sin, God had left it to their free will to make a moral choice between right and wrong. (See in this connection *sūrah* 6, note 143.)

21 I.e., a revelation which would allow man to worship other beings beside God, or to attribute "offspring" to Him: a rhetorical question implying its own negation.

Nay, but they say, "Behold, We found our forefathers agreed on what to believe – and, verily, it is in their footsteps that we find our guidance!" ‹22›
And thus it is: whenever We sent, before thy time, a warner to any community, those of its people who had lost themselves entirely in the pursuit of pleasures[22] would always say, "Behold, we found our forefathers agreed on what to believe – and, verily, it is but in their footsteps that we follow!"[23] ‹23›
[Whereupon each prophet] would say,[24] "Why, even though I bring you a guidance better than that which you found your forefathers believing in?" – [to which] the others would reply, "Behold, we deny that there is any truth in [what you claim to be] your messages!" ‹24›
And so We inflicted Our retribution on them: and behold what happened in the end to those who gave the lie to the truth! ‹25›

AND WHEN Abraham spoke to his father and his people, [he had this very truth in mind:[25]] "Verily, far be it from me to worship what you worship! ‹26› None [do I worship] but Him who has brought me into being: and, behold, it is He who will guide me!" ‹27›
And he uttered this as a word destined to endure among those who would come after him, so that they might [always] return [to it]. ‹28›

بَلْ قَالُوٓا۟ إِنَّا وَجَدْنَآ ءَابَآءَنَا عَلَىٰٓ أُمَّةٍ وَإِنَّا عَلَىٰٓ ءَاثَٰرِهِم مُّهْتَدُونَ ﴿٢٢﴾
وَكَذَٰلِكَ مَآ أَرْسَلْنَا مِن قَبْلِكَ فِى قَرْيَةٍ مِّن نَّذِيرٍ إِلَّا قَالَ مُتْرَفُوهَآ إِنَّا
وَجَدْنَآ ءَابَآءَنَا عَلَىٰٓ أُمَّةٍ وَإِنَّا عَلَىٰٓ ءَاثَٰرِهِم مُّقْتَدُونَ ﴿٢٣﴾ ۞ قَٰلَ أَوَلَوْ
جِئْتُكُم بِأَهْدَىٰ مِمَّا وَجَدتُّمْ عَلَيْهِ ءَابَآءَكُمْ قَالُوٓا۟ إِنَّا بِمَآ أُرْسِلْتُم بِهِۦ
كَٰفِرُونَ ﴿٢٤﴾ فَٱنتَقَمْنَا مِنْهُمْ فَٱنظُرْ كَيْفَ كَانَ عَٰقِبَةُ ٱلْمُكَذِّبِينَ ﴿٢٥﴾
وَإِذْ قَالَ إِبْرَٰهِيمُ لِأَبِيهِ وَقَوْمِهِۦٓ إِنَّنِى بَرَآءٌ مِّمَّا تَعْبُدُونَ ﴿٢٦﴾ إِلَّا ٱلَّذِى
فَطَرَنِى فَإِنَّهُۥ سَيَهْدِينِ ﴿٢٧﴾ وَجَعَلَهَا كَلِمَةًۢ بَاقِيَةً فِى عَقِبِهِۦ لَعَلَّهُمْ
يَرْجِعُونَ ﴿٢٨﴾ حزب 50

Bal qālūu ʾinnā wajadnāa ʾābāaʾanā ʿalāa ʾummatiñw-wa ʾinnā ʿalāa ʾāthārihim-muhtadūn. (22) Wa kadhālika māa ʾarsalnā miñ-qablika fī qaryatim-miñ-Nadhīrin ʾillā qāla mutrafūhāa ʾinnā wajadnāa ʾābāaʾanā ʿalāa ʾummatiñw-wa ʾinnā ʿalāa ʾāthārihim-muqtadūn. (23) ۞ Qāla ʾawa law jiʾtukum-biʾahdā mimmā wajattum ʿalayhi ʾābāaʾakum. Qālūu ʾinnā bimāa ʾursiltum-bihī kāfirūn. (24) Fañtaqamnā minhum fañẓur kayfa kāna ʿāqibatul-mukadhdhibīn. (25) Wa ʾidh qāla ʾIbrāhīmu liʾabīhi wa qawmihīi ʾinnanī barāaʾum-mimmā taʿbudūn. (26) ʾIllal-ladhī faṭaranī faʾinnahū sayahdīn. (27) Wa jaʿalahā kalimatam-bāqiyatañ-fī ʿaqibihī laʿallahum yarjiʿūn. (28)

22 For this rendering of the term *mutraf* (derived from the verb *tarafa*), see note 147 on 11 : 116.

23 Commenting on this passage, Rāzī says: "Had there been in the Qurʾān nothing but these verses, they would have sufficed to show the falsity of the principle postulating [a Muslim's] blind, unquestioning adoption of [another person's] religious opinions (*ibṭāl al-qawl bi't-taqlīd*): for, God has made it clear [in these verses] that those deniers of the truth had not arrived at their convictions by way of reason, and neither on the clear authority of a revealed text, but solely by blindly adopting the opinions of their forebears and predecessors; and all this God has mentioned in terms of blame and sharp disparagement."

24 Whereas in some of the readings of the Qurʾān the opening word of this verse is vocalized as an imperative, *qul* ("say"), the reading of Ḥafs ibn Sulaymān al-Asadī – on which this translation is based – gives the pronounciation *qāla* ("he said" or, since it is a repeated occurrence, "he would say").

25 Namely, the inadmissibility of blindly accepting the religious views sanctioned by mere ancestral tradition and thus prevalent in one's environment, and regarding them as valid even though they may conflict with one's reason and/or divine revelation. Abraham's search after truth is mentioned several times in the Qurʾān, and particularly in 6 : 74 ff. and 21 : 51 ff.

Now [as for those who did come after him,] I allowed them – as [I had allowed] their forebears – to enjoy their lives freely until the truth should come unto them through an apostle who would make all things clear:[26] «29» but now that the truth has come to them, they say, "All this is mere spellbinding eloquence[27] – and, behold, we deny that there is any truth in it!" «30»

And they say, too, "Why was not this Qurʾān bestowed from on high on some great man of the two cities?"[28] «31»

But is it they who distribute thy Sustainer's grace?

[Nay, as] it is We who distribute their means of livelihood among them in the life of this world, and raise some of them by degrees above others, to the end that they might avail themselves of one another's help – [so, too, it is We who bestow gifts of the spirit upon whomever We will]: and this thy Sustainer's grace is better than all [the worldly wealth] that they may amass. «32»

And were it not that [with the prospect of boundless riches before them] all people would become one [evil] community,[29] We might indeed have provided for those who [now] deny the Most Gracious roofs of silver for their houses, and [silver] stairways whereon to ascend, «33» and [silver] doors for their houses, and [silver] couches whereon to recline, «34» and gold [beyond count]. . . .[30]

بَلْ مَتَّعْتُ هَٰٓؤُلَآءِ وَءَابَآءَهُمْ حَتَّىٰ جَآءَهُمُ ٱلْحَقُّ وَرَسُولٌ مُّبِينٌ ٢٩
وَلَمَّا جَآءَهُمُ ٱلْحَقُّ قَالُوا۟ هَٰذَا سِحْرٌ وَإِنَّا بِهِۦ كَٰفِرُونَ ٣٠ وَقَالُوا۟ لَوْلَا
نُزِّلَ هَٰذَا ٱلْقُرْءَانُ عَلَىٰ رَجُلٍ مِّنَ ٱلْقَرْيَتَيْنِ عَظِيمٍ ٣١ أَهُمْ يَقْسِمُونَ
رَحْمَتَ رَبِّكَ نَحْنُ قَسَمْنَا بَيْنَهُم مَّعِيشَتَهُمْ فِى ٱلْحَيَوٰةِ ٱلدُّنْيَا وَرَفَعْنَا
بَعْضَهُمْ فَوْقَ بَعْضٍ دَرَجَٰتٍ لِّيَتَّخِذَ بَعْضُهُم بَعْضًا سُخْرِيًّا وَرَحْمَتُ
رَبِّكَ خَيْرٌ مِّمَّا يَجْمَعُونَ ٣٢ وَلَوْلَآ أَن يَكُونَ ٱلنَّاسُ أُمَّةً وَٰحِدَةً
لَّجَعَلْنَا لِمَن يَكْفُرُ بِٱلرَّحْمَٰنِ لِبُيُوتِهِمْ سُقُفًا مِّن فِضَّةٍ وَمَعَارِجَ عَلَيْهَا
يَظْهَرُونَ ٣٣ وَلِبُيُوتِهِمْ أَبْوَٰبًا وَسُرُرًا عَلَيْهَا يَتَّكِـُٔونَ ٣٤ وَزُخْرُفًا

Bal mattaʿtu hāaʾulāaʾi wa ʾābāaʾahum ḥattā jāaʾahumul-ḥaqqu wa Rasūlum-mubīn. (29) Wa lammā jāaʾahumul-ḥaqqu qālū hādhā siḥruñw-wa ʾinnā bihī kāfirūn. (30) Wa qālū lawlā nuzzila hādhal-Qurʾānu ʿalā rajulim-minal-qaryatayni ʿaẓīm. (31) ʾAhum yaqsimūna raḥmata Rabbik. Naḥnu qasamnā baynahum-maʿīshatahum fil-ḥayātid-dunyā. Wa rafaʿnā baʿḍahum fawqa baʿḍiñ-darajātil-liyattakhidha baʿḍuhum-baʿḍañ-sukhriyyā. Wa raḥmatu Rabbika khayrum-mimmā yajmaʿūn. (32) Wa lawlāa ʾañy-yakūnan-nāsu ʾummatañw-wāḥidatal-lajaʿalnā limañy-yakfuru bir-Raḥmāni libuyūtihim suqufam-miñ-fiḍḍatiñw-wa maʿārija ʿalayhā yaẓharūn. (33) Wa libuyūtihim ʾabwābañw-wa sururan ʿalayhā yattakiʾūn. (34) Wa zukhrufā.

26 I.e., God did not impose on them any moral obligations before making the meaning of right and wrong clear to them through a revealed message. Primarily, this is an allusion to the pagan contemporaries of the Prophet, and to the prosperity which they had been allowed to enjoy for a long time (cf. 21 : 44); in its wider sense, however, this passage implies that God would never call people to task for any wrong they may have done so long as they have not been clearly shown how to discriminate between good and evil (cf. 6 : 131-132).

27 See note 12 on 74 : 24, where this connotation of *siḥr* appears for the first time in the course of Qurʾanic revelation.

28 I.e., Mecca and Ṭāʾif – implying that if it were really a divine revelation it would have been bestowed on a person of "great standing", and not on Muḥammad, who had neither wealth nor a position of eminence in his native city.

29 Since "man has been created weak" (4 : 28), it is almost a "law of nature" that whenever he is exposed to the prospect of great wealth he is liable to lose sight of all spiritual and moral considerations, and to become utterly selfish, greedy and ruthless.

30 The primary meaning of the noun *zukhruf* is "gold"; its application to "ornaments" or (as in 10 : 24) to "artful adornment" is only secondary (*Tāj al-ʿArūs*).

وَإِن كُلُّ ذَٰلِكَ لَمَّا مَتَٰعُ ٱلْحَيَوٰةِ ٱلدُّنْيَا ۚ وَٱلْءَاخِرَةُ عِندَ رَبِّكَ لِلْمُتَّقِينَ ﴿٣٥﴾
وَمَن يَعْشُ عَن ذِكْرِ ٱلرَّحْمَٰنِ نُقَيِّضْ لَهُۥ شَيْطَٰنًا فَهُوَ لَهُۥ قَرِينٌ ﴿٣٦﴾
وَإِنَّهُمْ لَيَصُدُّونَهُمْ عَنِ ٱلسَّبِيلِ وَيَحْسَبُونَ أَنَّهُم مُّهْتَدُونَ ﴿٣٧﴾ حَتَّىٰٓ إِذَا
جَآءَنَا قَالَ يَٰلَيْتَ بَيْنِى وَبَيْنَكَ بُعْدَ ٱلْمَشْرِقَيْنِ فَبِئْسَ ٱلْقَرِينُ ﴿٣٨﴾
وَلَن يَنفَعَكُمُ ٱلْيَوْمَ إِذ ظَّلَمْتُمْ أَنَّكُمْ فِى ٱلْعَذَابِ مُشْتَرِكُونَ ﴿٣٩﴾ أَفَأَنتَ
تُسْمِعُ ٱلصُّمَّ أَوْ تَهْدِى ٱلْعُمْىَ وَمَن كَانَ فِى ضَلَٰلٍ مُّبِينٍ ﴿٤٠﴾ فَإِمَّا
نَذْهَبَنَّ بِكَ فَإِنَّا مِنْهُم مُّنتَقِمُونَ ﴿٤١﴾

Wa ʾiñ-kullu dhālika lammā matāʿul-ḥayātid-dunyā. Wal-ʾĀkhiratu ʿiñda Rabbika lilmuttaqīn. (35) Wa mañy-yaʿshu ʿañ-dhikrir-Raḥmāni nuqayyiḍ lahū Shayṭānañ-fahuwa lahū qarīn. (36) Wa ʾinnahum layaṣuddūnahum ʿanis-sabīli wa yaḥsabūna ʾannahum-muhtadūn. (37) Ḥattāa ʾidhā jāaʾanā qāla yā layta baynī wa baynaka buʿdal-mashriqayni fabiʾsal-qarīn. (38) Wa lañy-yañfaʿakumul-Yawma ʾiẓ-ẓalamtum ʾannakum fil-ʿadhābi mushtarikūn. (39) ʾAfaʾañta tusmiʿuṣ-ṣumma ʾaw tahdil-ʿumya wa mañ-kāna fī ḍalālim-mubīn. (40) Faʾimmā nadhhabanna bika faʾinnā minhum-muñtaqimūn. (41)

Yet all this would have been nothing but a [brief] enjoyment of life in this world – whereas [happiness in] the life to come awaits the God-conscious with thy Sustainer. ‹35›

But as for anyone who chooses to remain blind to the remembrance of the Most Gracious, to him We assign an [enduring] evil impulse, to become his other self:[31] ‹36› whereupon, behold, these [evil impulses] bar all such from the path [of truth], making them think that they are guided aright! ‹37›

But in the end,[32] when he [who has thus sinned] appears before us [on Judgment Day], he will say [to his other self], "Would that between me and thee there had been the distance of east and west!"[33] – for, evil indeed [has proved] that other self! ‹38›

On that Day it will not profit you in the least [to know] that, since you have sinned [together], you are now to share your suffering [as well].[34] ‹39›

CANST THOU, perchance, [O Muḥammad,] make the deaf hear, or show the right way to the blind or to such as are obviously lost in error?[35] ‹40›

But whether We do [or do not] take thee away [ere thy message prevails] – verily, We shall inflict Our retribution on them; ‹41›

31 Lit., "to him We assign a satan, and he becomes his other self (*qarīn*)": see note 24 on 41 : 25. For the psychological connotation of the term *shayṭān* as "evil impulse", see first half of note 16 on 15 : 17 as well as note 31 on 14 : 22.

32 Lit., "until".

33 Thus do most of the commentators interpret the above phrase which, literally, reads "the two easts" (*al-mashriqayn*). This interpretation is based on the idiomatic usage, not infrequent in classical Arabic, of referring to two opposites – or two conceptually connected entities – by giving them the designation of *one* of them in the dual form: e.g., "the two moons", denoting "sun and moon"; "the two Baṣrahs", i.e., Kūfah and Baṣrah; and so forth.

34 I.e., "you will not be consoled, as would have been the case in earthly suffering, by the knowledge that you are not to suffer alone" (Zamakhsharī, Rāzī, Bayḍāwī). Since this address is formulated in the plural and not in the dual, it evidently relates to *all* sinners who, in their lifetime, were impelled by their own evil impulses – their "other selves", as it were – to "remain blind to the remembrance of God". In its wider meaning, the above verse implies that all evil deeds, whenever and wherever committed, are but links of one chain, one evil ineluctably leading to another: cf. 14 : 49 – "on that Day thou wilt see those who were lost in sin linked together (*muqarranīn*) in fetters" – a phrase which has been explained in my corresponding note 64. It is noteworthy that the participle *muqarran* is derived from the same verbal root (*qarana*) as the term *qarīn* (rendered by me in verses 36 and 38 of this *sūrah* and in 41 : 25 as "other self"): and this, I believe, is a further indication, alluded to in the present verse, to the "togetherness" of all evil deeds.

35 This rhetorical question implies a negative answer: cf. 35 : 22 – "thou canst not make hear such as are [deaf of heart like the dead] in the graves".

and whether We show thee [or do not show thee in this world] the fulfilment of what We have promised them – verily, We have full power over them! ‹42›
So hold fast to all that has been revealed to thee: for, behold, thou art on a straight way; ‹43› and, verily, this [revelation] shall indeed become [a source of] eminence for thee and thy people:[36] but in time you all will be called to account [for what you have done with it].[37] ‹44›
Yet [above all else,] ask any of Our apostles whom We sent forth before thy time[38] whether We have ever allowed that deities other than the Most Gracious be worshipped! ‹45›

THUS, INDEED,[39] have We sent Moses with Our messages unto Pharaoh and his great ones; and he said: "Behold, I am an apostle of the Sustainer of all the worlds!" ‹46›
But as soon as he came before them with Our [miraculous] signs,[40] lo! they derided them, ‹47› although each sign that We showed them was weightier than the preceding one: and [each time] We took them to task through suffering, so that they might return [to Us].[41] ‹48›
And [every time] they exclaimed: "O thou sorcerer! Pray for us to thy Sustainer on the strength of the covenant [of prophethood] which He has made with thee: for, verily, we shall now follow the right way!" ‹49›

أَوْ نُرِيَنَّكَ ٱلَّذِى وَعَدْنَٰهُمْ فَإِنَّا عَلَيْهِم مُّقْتَدِرُونَ ﴿42﴾ فَٱسْتَمْسِكْ
بِٱلَّذِىٓ أُوحِىَ إِلَيْكَ ۖ إِنَّكَ عَلَىٰ صِرَٰطٍ مُّسْتَقِيمٍ ﴿43﴾ وَإِنَّهُۥ لَذِكْرٌ لَّكَ
وَلِقَوْمِكَ ۖ وَسَوْفَ تُسْـَٔلُونَ ﴿44﴾ وَسْـَٔلْ مَنْ أَرْسَلْنَا مِن قَبْلِكَ مِن رُّسُلِنَآ
أَجَعَلْنَا مِن دُونِ ٱلرَّحْمَٰنِ ءَالِهَةً يُعْبَدُونَ ﴿45﴾ وَلَقَدْ أَرْسَلْنَا مُوسَىٰ
بِـَٔايَٰتِنَآ إِلَىٰ فِرْعَوْنَ وَمَلَإِي۟هِۦ فَقَالَ إِنِّى رَسُولُ رَبِّ ٱلْعَٰلَمِينَ ﴿46﴾ فَلَمَّا
جَآءَهُم بِـَٔايَٰتِنَآ إِذَا هُم مِّنْهَا يَضْحَكُونَ ﴿47﴾ وَمَا نُرِيهِم مِّنْ ءَايَةٍ إِلَّا
هِىَ أَكْبَرُ مِنْ أُخْتِهَا ۖ وَأَخَذْنَٰهُم بِٱلْعَذَابِ لَعَلَّهُمْ يَرْجِعُونَ ﴿48﴾ وَقَالُوا۟
يَٰٓأَيُّهَ ٱلسَّاحِرُ ٱدْعُ لَنَا رَبَّكَ بِمَا عَهِدَ عِندَكَ إِنَّنَا لَمُهْتَدُونَ ﴿49﴾

ʾAw nuriyannakal-ladhī waʿadnāhum faʾinnā ʿalayhim-muqtadirūn. (42) Fastamsik billadhīi ʾūḥiya ʾilayka ʾinnaka ʿalā ṣirāṭim-mustaqīm. (43) Wa ʾinnahū ladhikrul-laka wa liqawmika wa sawfa tusʾalūn. (44) Was-ʾal man ʾarsalnā miñ-qablika mir-Rusulināa ʾajaʿalnā miñ-dūnir-Raḥmāni ʾālihatañy-yuʿbadūn. (45) Wa laqad ʾarsalnā Mūsā biʾĀyātināa ʾilā Firʿawna wa malaʾihī faqāla ʾinnī Rasūlu Rab-bil-ʿālamīn. (46) Falammā jāaʾahum-biʾĀyātināa ʾidhā hum-minhā yaḍḥakūn. (47) Wa mā nurīhim-min ʾĀyatin ʾillā hiya ʾakbaru min ʾukhtihā wa ʾakhadhnāhum-bilʿadhābi laʿallahum yarjiʿūn. (48) Wa qālū yāa ʾayyuhas-sāḥirud-ʿu lanā Rabbaka bimā ʿahida ʿiñdaka ʾinnanā lamuhtadūn. (49)

36 For the above rendering of *dhikr* as "[a source of] eminence", see first half of note 13 on 21 : 10.

37 The meaning is that on the Day of Judgment all prophets will be asked, metaphorically, as to what response they received from their people (cf. 5 : 109), and those who professed to follow them will be called to account for the spiritual and social use they made – or did not make – of the revelation conveyed to them: and thus, the "eminence" promised to the followers of Muḥammad, will depend on their actual behaviour and not on their mere profession of faith.

38 I.e., "look into the earlier revelations and ask thyself".

39 I.e., in pursuance of the principle, referred to above, that it is not permissible to worship anyone or anything but God.

40 See note 94 on the last sentence of 6 : 109.

41 The concept of "returning" to God implies that the instinctive ability to perceive His existence is inherent in human nature as such, and that man's "turning away" from God is only a consequence of spiritual degeneration, and not an *original* tendency or predisposition: cf. 7 : 172-173. – The "suffering" (*ʿadhāb*) mentioned above relates to the plagues with which the recalcitrant Egyptians were struck (see 7 : 130 ff.).

But whenever We removed the suffering from them, lo! they would break their word. ‹50›
And Pharaoh issued a call to his people, saying: "O my people! Does not the dominion over Egypt belong to me, since all these running waters flow at my feet?[42] Can you not, then, see [that I am your lord supreme]? ‹51› Am I not better than this contemptible man who can hardly make his meaning clear?[43] ‹52›
"And then – why have no golden armlets been bestowed on him?[44] – or why have no angels come together with him?" ‹53›
Thus he incited his people to levity, and they obeyed him: for, behold, they were people depraved! ‹54›
But when they continued to challenge Us, We inflicted Our retribution on them, and drowned them all: ‹55› and so We made them a thing of the past, and an example to those who would come after them. ‹56›

NOW WHENEVER [the nature of] the son of Mary is set forth as an example, [O Muḥammad,] lo! thy people raise an outcry on this score, ‹57› and say, "Which is better – our deities or he ?"[45]
[But] it is only in the spirit of dispute that they put this comparison before thee: yea, they are contentious folk![46] ‹58›

فَلَمَّا كَشَفْنَا عَنْهُمُ ٱلْعَذَابَ إِذَا هُمْ يَنكُثُونَ ﴿٥٠﴾ وَنَادَىٰ فِرْعَوْنُ فِى
قَوْمِهِۦ قَالَ يَٰقَوْمِ أَلَيْسَ لِى مُلْكُ مِصْرَ وَهَٰذِهِ ٱلْأَنْهَٰرُ تَجْرِى مِن
تَحْتِىٓ ۖ أَفَلَا تُبْصِرُونَ ﴿٥١﴾ أَمْ أَنَا۠ خَيْرٌ مِّنْ هَٰذَا ٱلَّذِى هُوَ مَهِينٌ وَلَا يَكَادُ
يُبِينُ ﴿٥٢﴾ فَلَوْلَآ أُلْقِىَ عَلَيْهِ أَسْوِرَةٌ مِّن ذَهَبٍ أَوْ جَآءَ مَعَهُ ٱلْمَلَٰٓئِكَةُ
مُقْتَرِنِينَ ﴿٥٣﴾ فَٱسْتَخَفَّ قَوْمَهُۥ فَأَطَاعُوهُ ۚ إِنَّهُمْ كَانُوا۟ قَوْمًا فَٰسِقِينَ ﴿٥٤﴾
فَلَمَّآ ءَاسَفُونَا ٱنتَقَمْنَا مِنْهُمْ فَأَغْرَقْنَٰهُمْ أَجْمَعِينَ ﴿٥٥﴾ فَجَعَلْنَٰهُمْ سَلَفًا
وَمَثَلًا لِّلْءَاخِرِينَ ﴿٥٦﴾ ۞ وَلَمَّا ضُرِبَ ٱبْنُ مَرْيَمَ مَثَلًا إِذَا قَوْمُكَ مِنْهُ
يَصِدُّونَ ﴿٥٧﴾ وَقَالُوٓا۟ ءَأَٰلِهَتُنَا خَيْرٌ أَمْ هُوَ ۚ مَا ضَرَبُوهُ لَكَ إِلَّا جَدَلًۢا ۚ بَلْ
هُمْ قَوْمٌ خَصِمُونَ ﴿٥٨﴾

ربع الحزب

Falammā kashafnā ᶜanhumul-ᶜadhāba ᵓidhā hum yañkuthūn. (50) Wa nādā Firᶜawnu fī qawmihī qāla yā qawmi ᵓalaysa lī mulku Miṣra wa hādhihil-ᵓanhāru tajrī miñ-taḥtī. ᵓAfalā tubṣirūn. (51) ᵓAm ᵓana khayrum-min hādhal-ladhī huwa mahīnuñw-wa lā yakādu yubīn. (52) Falawlāa ᵓulqiya ᶜalayhi ᵓaswiratum-miñ-dhahabin ᵓaw jāaᵓa maᶜahul-Malāaᵓikatu muqtarinīn. (53) Fastakhaffa qawmahū faᵓaṭāᶜūhu ᵓinnahum kānū qawmañ-fāsiqīn. (54) Falammāa ᵓāsafūnañ-taqamnā minhum faᵓaghraqnāhum ᵓajmaᶜīn. (55) Fajaᶜalnāhum salafañw-wa mathalal-lilᵓākhirīn. (56) ۞ Wa lammā ḍuribab-nu Maryama mathalan ᵓidhā qawmuka minhu yaṣiddūn. (57) Wa qālūu ᵓaᵓālihatunā khayrun ᵓam hū. Mā ḍarabūhu laka ᵓillā jadalam-bal hum qawmun khaṣimūn. (58)

42 Lit., "beneath me", i.e., "at my command": a reference to the imposing irrigation system originating in the Nile and controlled by royal power.

43 An allusion to the impediment in speech from which Moses suffered (cf. 20 : 27-28 and the corresponding note 17), or perhaps to the contents of his message, which to Pharaoh appeared unconvincing.

44 In ancient Egypt, golden armlets and necklaces were regarded as princely insignia (cf. Genesis xli, 42), or at least as evidence of high social dignity. This is apparently an echo of the pagan objection to Muḥammad, mentioned in verse 31 above: "Why was not this Qurᵓān bestowed from on high on some great man of the two cities?" The same is the case with the subsequent reference to the "absence of angels".

45 Objecting to the Qurᵓanic condemnation of their idolatrous worship of angels – whom they describe here as "our deities" – the pagan Quraysh pointed to the parallel Christian worship of Jesus as "the son of God", and even as "God incarnate", and argued more or less thus: "The Qurᵓān states that Jesus was purely human – and yet the Christians, whom the same Qurᵓān describes as 'followers of earlier revelation' (*ahl al-kitāb*), consider him divine. Hence, are we not rather justified in our worshipping angels, who are certainly superior to a mere human being?" The fallacy inherent in this "argument" is disposed of in the sequence.

46 Since the Qurᵓān condemns explicitly, and in many places, the deification of Jesus by the Christians, this unwarranted deification cannot be used as an argument in favour of the pagan worship of angels and, thus, against the Qurᵓān: in the words of Zamakhsharī, such an argument amounts to "applying a false analogy to a false proposition" (*qiyās bāṭil bi-bāṭil*).

[As for Jesus,] he was nothing but [a human being –] a servant [of Ours] whom We had graced [with prophethood], and whom We made an example for the children of Israel. ‹59› And had We so willed, [O you who worship angels,] We could indeed have made *you* into angels succeeding one another on earth![47] ‹60›

AND, BEHOLD, this [divine writ] is indeed a means to know [that] the Last Hour [is bound to come];[48] hence, have no doubt whatever about it, but follow Me: this [alone] is a straight way. ‹61› And let not Satan bar you [from it] – for, verily, he is your open foe! ‹62›

NOW WHEN Jesus came [to his people] with all evidence of the truth, he said: "I have now come unto you with wisdom,[49] and to make clear unto you some of that on which you are at variance:[50] hence, be conscious of God, and pay heed unto me. ‹63›
"Verily, God is my Sustainer as well as your Sustainer; so worship [none but] Him: this [alone] is a straight way!" ‹64›
But factions from among those [who came after Jesus] began to hold divergent views:[51] woe, then, unto those who are bent on evildoing – [woe] for the suffering [that will befall them] on a grievous Day! ‹65›

إِنْ هُوَ إِلَّا عَبْدٌ أَنْعَمْنَا عَلَيْهِ وَجَعَلْنَٰهُ مَثَلًا لِّبَنِىٓ إِسْرَٰٓءِيلَ ﴿٥٩﴾ وَلَوْ
نَشَآءُ لَجَعَلْنَا مِنكُم مَّلَٰٓئِكَةً فِى ٱلْأَرْضِ يَخْلُفُونَ ﴿٦٠﴾ وَإِنَّهُۥ لَعِلْمٌ
لِّلسَّاعَةِ فَلَا تَمْتَرُنَّ بِهَا وَٱتَّبِعُونِ هَٰذَا صِرَٰطٌ مُّسْتَقِيمٌ ﴿٦١﴾ وَلَا يَصُدَّنَّكُمُ
ٱلشَّيْطَٰنُ إِنَّهُۥ لَكُمْ عَدُوٌّ مُّبِينٌ ﴿٦٢﴾ وَلَمَّا جَآءَ عِيسَىٰ بِٱلْبَيِّنَٰتِ قَالَ قَدْ
جِئْتُكُم بِٱلْحِكْمَةِ وَلِأُبَيِّنَ لَكُم بَعْضَ ٱلَّذِى تَخْتَلِفُونَ فِيهِ فَٱتَّقُوا۟ ٱللَّهَ
وَأَطِيعُونِ ﴿٦٣﴾ إِنَّ ٱللَّهَ هُوَ رَبِّى وَرَبُّكُمْ فَٱعْبُدُوهُ هَٰذَا صِرَٰطٌ
مُّسْتَقِيمٌ ﴿٦٤﴾ فَٱخْتَلَفَ ٱلْأَحْزَابُ مِنۢ بَيْنِهِمْ فَوَيْلٌ لِّلَّذِينَ ظَلَمُوا۟ مِنْ
عَذَابِ يَوْمٍ أَلِيمٍ ﴿٦٥﴾

ʾIn huwa ʾillā ʿabdun ʾanʿamnā ʿalayhi wa jaʿalnāhu mathalal-libanīi ʾIsrāaʾīl. (59) Wa law nashāaʾu lajaʿalnā miñkum-Malāaʾikatañ-fil-ʾarḍi yakhlufūn. (60) Wa ʾinnahū laʿilmul-lis-Sāʿati falā tamtarunna bihā wat-tabiʿūni hādhā ṣirāṭum-mustaqīm. (61) Wa lā yaṣuddannakumush-Shayṭānu ʾinnahū lakum ʿaduwwum-mubīn. (62) Wa lammā jāaʾa ʿĪsā bil-bayyināti qāla qad jiʾtukum-bilḥikmati wa liʾubayyina lakum-baʿḍal-ladhī takhtalifūna fīhi fattaqul-lāha wa ʾaṭīʿūn. (63) ʾInnal-lāha Huwa Rabbī wa Rabbukum faʿbudūhu hādhā ṣirāṭum-mustaqīm. (64) Fakhtalafal-ʾaḥzābu mim-baynihim; fawaylul-lilladhīna ẓalamū min ʿadhābi Yawmin ʾalīm. (65)

47 Implying not only that Jesus was not a supernatural being, but that the angels, too, are mere created beings finite in their existence – as indicated by the phrase "succeeding one another" – and, therefore, utterly removed from the status of divinity (Bayḍāwī).

48 Whereas most of the commentators regard the pronoun *hu* in *innahu* as relating to Jesus and, consequently, interpret the above phrase as "he is indeed a means to know [i.e., an indication of the coming of] the Last Hour", some authorities – e.g., Qatādah, Al-Ḥasan al-Baṣrī and Saʿīd ibn Jubayr (all of them quoted by Ṭabarī, Baghawī and Ibn Kathīr) – relate the pronoun to the Qurʾān, and understand the phrase in the sense adopted in my rendering. The specific mention of the Last Hour in the above context is meant to stress man's ultimate responsibility before the Creator and, therefore, the fact that worship is due to Him alone: and so this parenthetic passage follows logically upon the mention of the false deification of Jesus.

49 I.e., with divine revelation.

50 According to Ṭabarī, the restrictive allusion to "*some* of that . . ." etc., bears on the realm of faith and morals alone, since it was not a part of Jesus' mission to deal with problems of his people's worldly life. This observation coincides with the image of Jesus forthcoming from the (admittedly fragmentary) description of his teachings available to us in the Synoptic Gospels.

51 Sc., regarding the nature of Jesus and the inadmissibility of worshipping anyone but God: an allusion to subsequent developments in Christianity.

ARE THEY [who are lost in sin] but waiting for the Last Hour – [waiting] that it come upon them of a sudden, without their being aware [of its approach]? ‹66›

On that Day, [erstwhile] friends will be foes unto one another[52] – [all] save the God-conscious. ‹67›

[And God will say:] "O you servants of Mine! No fear need you have today, and neither shall you grieve ‹68› – [O you] who have attained to faith in Our messages and have surrendered your own selves unto Us! ‹69› Enter paradise, you and your spouses, with happiness blest!" ‹70›

[And there] they will be waited upon with trays and goblets of gold; and there will be found all that the souls might desire, and [all that] the eyes might delight in.

And therein shall you abide, [O you who believe:] ‹71› for such will be the paradise which you shall have inherited by virtue of your past deeds: ‹72› fruits [of those deeds] shall you have in abundance, [and] thereof shall you partake! ‹73›

[But,] behold, they who are lost in sin shall abide in the suffering of hell:[53] ‹74› it will not be lightened for them; and therein they will be lost in hopeless despair. ‹75›

And it is not We who will be doing wrong unto them, but it is they who will have wronged themselves. ‹76›

And they will cry: "O thou [angel] who rulest [over hell]! Let thy Sustainer put an end to us!" – [whereupon] he will reply: "Verily, you must live on [in this state]. . . ." ‹77›

INDEED, [O you sinners,] We have conveyed the truth unto you; but most of you abhor the truth.[54] ‹78›

هَلْ يَنظُرُونَ إِلَّا ٱلسَّاعَةَ أَن تَأْتِيَهُم بَغْتَةً وَهُمْ لَا يَشْعُرُونَ (66) ٱلْأَخِلَّآءُ
يَوْمَئِذٍۭ بَعْضُهُمْ لِبَعْضٍ عَدُوٌّ إِلَّا ٱلْمُتَّقِينَ (67) يَٰعِبَادِ لَا خَوْفٌ عَلَيْكُمُ
ٱلْيَوْمَ وَلَآ أَنتُمْ تَحْزَنُونَ (68) ٱلَّذِينَ ءَامَنُوا۟ بِـَٔايَٰتِنَا وَكَانُوا۟
مُسْلِمِينَ (69) ٱدْخُلُوا۟ ٱلْجَنَّةَ أَنتُمْ وَأَزْوَٰجُكُمْ تُحْبَرُونَ (70) يُطَافُ
عَلَيْهِم بِصِحَافٍ مِّن ذَهَبٍ وَأَكْوَابٍ ۖ وَفِيهَا مَا تَشْتَهِيهِ ٱلْأَنفُسُ وَتَلَذُّ
ٱلْأَعْيُنُ ۖ وَأَنتُمْ فِيهَا خَٰلِدُونَ (71) وَتِلْكَ ٱلْجَنَّةُ ٱلَّتِىٓ أُورِثْتُمُوهَا بِمَا
كُنتُمْ تَعْمَلُونَ (72) لَكُمْ فِيهَا فَٰكِهَةٌ كَثِيرَةٌ مِّنْهَا تَأْكُلُونَ (73) إِنَّ
ٱلْمُجْرِمِينَ فِى عَذَابِ جَهَنَّمَ خَٰلِدُونَ (74) لَا يُفَتَّرُ عَنْهُمْ وَهُمْ فِيهِ مُبْلِسُونَ (75)
وَمَا ظَلَمْنَٰهُمْ وَلَٰكِن كَانُوا۟ هُمُ ٱلظَّٰلِمِينَ (76) وَنَادَوْا۟ يَٰمَٰلِكُ لِيَقْضِ
عَلَيْنَا رَبُّكَ ۖ قَالَ إِنَّكُم مَّٰكِثُونَ (77) لَقَدْ جِئْنَٰكُم بِٱلْحَقِّ وَلَٰكِنَّ
أَكْثَرَكُمْ لِلْحَقِّ كَٰرِهُونَ (78)

Hal yañẓurūna ʾillas-Sāʿata ʾañ-taʾtiyahum-baghtatañw-wa hum lā yashʿurūn. (66) ʾAlʾakhillāaʾu Yawmaʾidhim-baʿḍuhum libaʿḍin ʿaduwwun ʾillal-muttaqīn. (67) Yā ʿibādi lā khawfun ʿalaykumul-Yawma wa lāa ʾañtum taḥzanūn. (68) ʾAlladhīna ʾāmanū biʾĀyātinā wa kānū Muslimīn. (69) ʾUdkhulul-jannata ʾañtum wa ʾazwājukum tuḥbarūn. (70) Yuṭāfu ʿalayhim-biṣiḥāfim-miñ-dhahabiñw-wa ʾakwāb. Wa fīhā mā tashtahīhil-ʾañfusu wa taladhdhul-ʾaʿyunu wa ʾañtum fīhā khālidūn. (71) Wa tilkal-jannatul-latīi ʾūriththumūhā bimā kuñtum taʿmalūn. (72) Lakum fīhā fākihatuñ-kathīratum-minhā taʾkulūn. (73) ʾInnal-mujrimīna fī ʿadhābi jahannama khālidūn. (74) Lā yu-fattaru ʿanhum wa hum fīhi mublisūn. (75) Wa mā ẓalamnāhum wa lākiñ-kānū humuẓ-ẓālimīn. (76) Wa nādaw yā Māliku liyaqḍi ʿalaynā Rabbuka qāla ʾinnakum-mākithūn. (77) Laqad jiʾnākum-bilḥaqqi wa lākinna ʾaktharakum lilḥaqqi kārihūn. (78)

52 I.e., they will hate one another – those who realize that they have been led astray by their erstwhile friends, and the latter, because they see that they will be held responsible for the sins of those whom they have led astray.

53 I.e., for an unspecified period: see the last paragraph of 6 : 128 and the corresponding note 114, as well as the saying of the Prophet quoted in note 10 on 40 : 12, indicating that – in accordance with the Qurʾanic statement, "God has willed upon Himself the law of grace and mercy" (6 : 12 and 54) – the otherworldly suffering described as "hell" will not be of unlimited duration. Among the theologians who hold this view is Rāzī, who stresses in his comments on the above passage that the expression "they shall abide (*khālidūn*) in the suffering of hell" indicates only an indeterminate duration, but "does *not* convey the meaning of perpetuity" (*lā yafīdu 'd-dawām*).

54 As is evident from verses 81 ff. above, this is a reference to the truth of God's oneness and uniqueness, which

Why – can they [who deny the truth ever] determine what [the truth] should be?[55] [Nay,] for, behold, it is We who detemine [everything]. «79» Or do they, perchance, think that We do not hear their hidden thoughts and their secret confabulations?[56]

Yea, indeed, [We do,] and Our heavenly forces[57] are with them, recording [all]. «80»

Say [O Prophet]: "If the Most Gracious [truly] had a son, I would be the first to worship him!" «81»

Utterly remote, in His glory, is the Sustainer of the heavens and the earth – the Sustainer, in almightiness enthroned[58] – from all that they may attribute to Him by way of definition![59] «82»

But leave them to indulge in idle talk and play [with words][60] until they face that [Judgment] Day of theirs which they have been promised: «83» for [then they will come to know that] it is He [alone] who is God in heaven and God on earth, and [that] He alone is truly wise, all-knowing. «84»

And hallowed be He unto whom the dominion over the heavens and the earth and all that is between them belongs, and with whom the knowledge of the Last Hour rests, and unto whom you all shall be brought back! «85»

أَمْ أَبْرَمُوٓا۟ أَمْرًا فَإِنَّا مُبْرِمُونَ ﴿79﴾ أَمْ يَحْسَبُونَ أَنَّا لَا نَسْمَعُ سِرَّهُمْ
وَنَجْوَىٰهُم ۚ بَلَىٰ وَرُسُلُنَا لَدَيْهِمْ يَكْتُبُونَ ﴿80﴾ قُلْ إِن كَانَ لِلرَّحْمَـٰنِ وَلَدٌ
فَأَنَا۠ أَوَّلُ ٱلْعَـٰبِدِينَ ﴿81﴾ سُبْحَـٰنَ رَبِّ ٱلسَّمَـٰوَٰتِ وَٱلْأَرْضِ رَبِّ
ٱلْعَرْشِ عَمَّا يَصِفُونَ ﴿82﴾ فَذَرْهُمْ يَخُوضُوا۟ وَيَلْعَبُوا۟ حَتَّىٰ يُلَـٰقُوا۟ يَوْمَهُمُ
ٱلَّذِى يُوعَدُونَ ﴿83﴾ وَهُوَ ٱلَّذِى فِى ٱلسَّمَآءِ إِلَـٰهٌ وَفِى ٱلْأَرْضِ إِلَـٰهٌ ۚ وَهُوَ
ٱلْحَكِيمُ ٱلْعَلِيمُ ﴿84﴾ وَتَبَارَكَ ٱلَّذِى لَهُۥ مُلْكُ ٱلسَّمَـٰوَٰتِ وَٱلْأَرْضِ وَمَا
بَيْنَهُمَا وَعِندَهُۥ عِلْمُ ٱلسَّاعَةِ وَإِلَيْهِ تُرْجَعُونَ ﴿85﴾

ᵓAm ᵓabramūu ᵓamrañ-faᵓinnā mubrimūn. (79) ᵓAm yaḥsabūna ᵓannā lā nasmaᶜu sirrahum wa najwāhum. Balā wa Rusulunā ladayhim yaktubūn. (80) Qul ᵓiñ-kāna lirRaḥmāni waladuñ-faᵓana ᵓawwalul-ᶜābidīn. (81) Subḥāna Rabbis-samāwāti wal-ᵓarḍi Rab bil-ᶜarshi ᶜammā yaṣifūn. (82) Fadharhum yakhūḍū wa yalᶜabū ḥattā yulāqū Yawmahumul-ladhī yūᶜadūn. (83) Wa Huwal-ladhī fis-samāaᵓi ᵓIlāhuñw-wa fil-ᵓarḍi ᵓIlāhuñw-wa Huwal-Ḥakīmul-ᶜAlīm. (84) Wa tabārakal-ladhī lahū mulkus-samāwāti wal-ᵓarḍi wa mā baynahumā wa ᶜiñdahū ᶜilmus-Sāᶜati wa ᵓilayhi turjaᶜūn. (85)

those who believe in Jesus as "the son of God" refuse, as it were, to acknowledge: thus, the discourse returns here to the question of the "nature" of Jesus touched upon in verses 57-65.

55 The verb *barama* or *abrama* signifies, literally, "he twined" or "twisted [something] together", e.g., the strands that are to form a rope; or "he twisted [something] well" or "strongly". Tropically, it connotes the act of "establishing" or "determining" a thing, a proposition, a course of events, etc. (Jawharī). According to the *Lisān al-ᶜArab*, the phrase *abrama al-amr* has the meaning of "he determined (*aḥkama*) the case". In the present context, the term *amr*, having no definite article, signifies "anything" or – in its widest sense – "anything that should [or "could"] be": and so, taking the preceding verse into account, we arrive at the meaning of arbitrarily "determining what [the truth] should be" – i.e., in contradiction to what the Qurᵓān postulates as the truth.

56 This is most probably an allusion to the centuries-long subtle Christian controversies on the question as to whether or not Jesus was "the son of God" and, hence, divine. These controversies were often influenced by a subconscious leaning of some of the early Christian thinkers towards ancient, mostly Mithraistic, cults and concepts which were in the beginning strongly opposed by unitarian theologians, foremost among them Arius, Patriarch of Alexandria (about 280-336 C.E.). However, at the politically-motivated Council of Nicaea (325 C.E.), the Arian views – which until then had been shared by the overwhelming majority of articulate Christians – were condemned as "heretical", and the doctrine of Christ's divinity was officially formulated in the so-called Nicene Creed as the basis of Christian beliefs. (See also note 60 below).

57 Lit., "Our messengers", i.e., angels.

58 Cf. the last clause of *sūrah* 9 and the corresponding note 171.

59 See note 88 on the last sentence of 6 : 100.

60 Evidently an allusion to the verbal subtleties of the Nicene Creed, and particularly the statement, "Jesus Christ,

And those [beings] whom some invoke beside God[61] have it not in their power to intercede [on Judgment Day] for any but such as have [in their lifetime] borne witness to the truth, and have been aware [that God is one and unique].[62] ‹86›
Now if thou ask those [who worship any being other than God] as to who it is that has created them, they are sure to answer, "God." How perverted, then, are their minds! ‹87›
[But God has full knowledge of the true believer[63]] and of his [despairing] cry: "O my Sustainer! Verily, these are people who will not believe! ‹88›
Yet bear thou with them, and say, "Peace [be upon you]!" – for in time they will come to know [the truth]. ‹89›

وَلَا يَمْلِكُ ٱلَّذِينَ يَدْعُونَ مِن دُونِهِ ٱلشَّفَٰعَةَ إِلَّا مَن شَهِدَ بِٱلْحَقِّ وَهُمْ
يَعْلَمُونَ ﴿٨٦﴾ وَلَئِن سَأَلْتَهُم مَّنْ خَلَقَهُمْ لَيَقُولُنَّ ٱللَّهُ ۖ فَأَنَّىٰ يُؤْفَكُونَ ﴿٨٧﴾
وَقِيلِهِۦ يَٰرَبِّ إِنَّ هَٰٓؤُلَآءِ قَوْمٌ لَّا يُؤْمِنُونَ ﴿٨٨﴾ فَٱصْفَحْ عَنْهُمْ وَقُلْ
سَلَٰمٌ ۚ فَسَوْفَ يَعْلَمُونَ ﴿٨٩﴾

Wa lā yamlikul-ladhīna yadʿūna miñ-dūnihish-shafāʿata ʾillā mañ-shahida bilḥaqqi wa hum yaʿlamūn. (86) Wa laʾiñ-saʾaltahum-man khalaqahum layaqūlunnal-lāhu faʾannā yuʾfakūn. (87) Wa qīlihī yā Rabbi ʾinna hāaʾulāaʾi qawmul-lā yuʾminūn. (88) Faṣfaḥ ʿanhum wa qul salāmuñ-fasawfa yaʿlamūn. (89)

the Son of God, begotten, not made [i.e., not created], by the Father as His only Son, of the same substance as the Father, God of God . . .", etc.

61 A reference to falsely deified saints or prophets and, particularly (in view of the context), to Jesus.

62 For an explanation of the Qurʾanic concept of "intercession", see 10 : 3 – "There is none that could intercede with Him unless He grants leave therefor" – and the corresponding note 7. – My interpolation, at the end of the above verse, of the words "that God is one and unique" is based on Rāzī's interpretation of this passage, implying that a mere oral "bearing witness to the truth" is useless if it is not the outcome of an inner awareness of God's oneness and uniqueness.

63 Rāzī (on whose commentary the above interpolation is based), regards this as a reference to the Prophet Muḥammad. It seems, however, that the meaning is wider, embracing every believer, of whatever denomination, who is distressed at the blindness of people who attribute divinity or divine qualities to any being other than God Himself.

The Forty-Fourth Sūrah

Ad-Dukhān (Smoke)

Mecca Period

REVEALED at the same period as the other six chapters of the *Ḥā-Mīm* sequence – that is, in the later half of the middle Mecca period – this *sūrah* derives its customary title from the word *dukhān* occurring in verse 10.

سورة الدخان مكية -44-

وآياتها تسع وخمسون

IN THE NAME OF GOD, THE MOST GRACIOUS, THE DISPENSER OF GRACE:

Ḥā. Mīm.[1] ‹1›
CONSIDER this divine writ, clear in itself and clearly showing the truth![2] ‹2›
Behold, from on high have We bestowed it on a blessed night:[3] for, verily, We have always been warning [man].[4] ‹3›
On that [night] was made clear, in wisdom, the distinction between all things [good and evil][5] ‹4› at a behest from Ourselves: for, verily, We have always been sending [Our messages of guidance] ‹5›

بِسْمِ ٱللَّهِ ٱلرَّحْمَٰنِ ٱلرَّحِيمِ

حمٓ ① وَٱلْكِتَٰبِ ٱلْمُبِينِ ② إِنَّآ أَنزَلْنَٰهُ فِى لَيْلَةٍ مُّبَٰرَكَةٍ إِنَّا كُنَّا
مُنذِرِينَ ③ فِيهَا يُفْرَقُ كُلُّ أَمْرٍ حَكِيمٍ ④ أَمْرًا مِّنْ عِندِنَآ إِنَّا كُنَّا
مُرْسِلِينَ ⑤

Bismil-lāhir-Raḥmānir-Raḥīm.
Ḥā-Mīm. ① **Wal-Kitābil-mubīn.** ② **ʾInnāa ʾañzalnāhu fī laylatim-mubārakatin ʾinnā kunnā muñdhirīn.** ③ **Fīhā yufraqu kullu ʾamrin ḥakīm.** ④ **ʾAmram-min ʿiñdināa ʾinnā kunnā mursilīn.** ⑤

---

1 See Appendix II.

2 See note 2 on 12 : 1.

3 I.e., the night on which the revelation of the Qurʾān began: see *sūrah* 97.

4 The revelation of the Qurʾān is but a continuation and, indeed, the climax of all divine revelation which has been going on since the very dawn of human consciousness. Its innermost purpose has always been the warning extended by God to man not to abandon himself to mere material ambitions and pursuits and, thus, to lose sight of spiritual values.

5 Lit., "was made distinct everything wise", i.e., "wisely" or "in wisdom": a metonymical attribution of the adjective "wise" – which in reality relates to God, the maker of that distinction – to what has thus been made distinct (Zamakhsharī and Rāzī). The meaning is that the revelation of the Qurʾān, symbolized by that "blessed night" of its beginning, provides man with a standard whereby to discern between good and evil, or between all that leads to spiritual growth through an ever-deepening realization (*maʿrifah*) of God's existence, on the one hand, and all that results in spiritual blindness and self-destruction, on the other.

in pursuance of thy Sustainer's grace [unto man]. Verily, He alone is all-hearing, all-knowing, ‹6› the Sustainer of the heavens and the earth and all that is between them – if you could but grasp it with inner certainty![6] ‹7›
There is no deity save Him: He grants life and deals death: He is your Sustainer as well as the Sustainer of your forebears of old. ‹8›
Nay, but they [who lack inner certainty] are but toying with their doubts.[7] ‹9›

WAIT, THEN, for the Day when the skies shall bring forth a pall of smoke which will make obvious [the approach of the Last Hour], ‹10› enveloping all mankind, [and causing the sinners to exclaim:] "Grievous is this suffering! ‹11› O our Sustainer, relieve us of suffering, for, verily, we [now] believe [in Thee]!" ‹12›
[But] how shall this remembrance avail them [at the Last Hour], seeing that an apostle had previously come unto them, clearly expounding the truth, ‹13› whereupon they turned their backs on him and said, "Taught [by others] is he,[8] a madman"? ‹14›
[Still,] behold, We shall postpone[9] this suffering for a little while, although you are bound to revert [to your evil ways: but] ‹15› on the Day when We shall seize [all sinners] with a most mighty onslaught, We shall, verily, inflict Our retribution [on you as well]! ‹16›

رَحْمَةً مِّن رَّبِّكَ إِنَّهُۥ هُوَ ٱلسَّمِيعُ ٱلْعَلِيمُ ﴿6﴾ رَبِّ ٱلسَّمَٰوَٰتِ
وَٱلْأَرْضِ وَمَا بَيْنَهُمَآ إِن كُنتُم مُّوقِنِينَ ﴿7﴾ لَآ إِلَٰهَ إِلَّا هُوَ يُحْيِۦ
وَيُمِيتُ رَبُّكُمْ وَرَبُّ ءَابَآئِكُمُ ٱلْأَوَّلِينَ ﴿8﴾ بَلْ هُمْ فِى شَكٍّ يَلْعَبُونَ ﴿9﴾
فَٱرْتَقِبْ يَوْمَ تَأْتِى ٱلسَّمَآءُ بِدُخَانٍ مُّبِينٍ ﴿10﴾ يَغْشَى ٱلنَّاسَ هَٰذَا عَذَابٌ
أَلِيمٌ ﴿11﴾ رَّبَّنَا ٱكْشِفْ عَنَّا ٱلْعَذَابَ إِنَّا مُؤْمِنُونَ ﴿12﴾ أَنَّىٰ لَهُمُ
ٱلذِّكْرَىٰ وَقَدْ جَآءَهُمْ رَسُولٌ مُّبِينٌ ﴿13﴾ ثُمَّ تَوَلَّوْا۟ عَنْهُ وَقَالُوا۟ مُعَلَّمٌ
مَّجْنُونٌ ﴿14﴾ إِنَّا كَاشِفُوا۟ ٱلْعَذَابِ قَلِيلًا إِنَّكُمْ عَآئِدُونَ ﴿15﴾ يَوْمَ نَبْطِشُ
ٱلْبَطْشَةَ ٱلْكُبْرَىٰٓ إِنَّا مُنتَقِمُونَ ﴿16﴾

Raḥmatam-mir-Rabbika ʾinnahū Huwas-Samīʿul-ʿAlīm. (6) Rabbis-samāwāti wal-ʾarḍi wa mā baynahumāa ʾiñ-kuñtum-mūqinīn. (7) Lāa ʾilāha ʾillā Huwa yuḥyī wa yumīt. Rabbukum wa Rabbu ʾābāaʾikumul-ʾawwalīn. (8) Bal hum fī shakkiñy-yalʿabūn. (9) Fartaqib Yawma taʾtis-samāaʾu bidukhānim-mubīn. (10) Yaghshan-nāsa hādhā ʿadhābun ʾalīm. (11) Rabbanak-shif ʿannal-ʿadhāba ʾinnā muʾminūn. (12) ʾAnnā lahumudh-dhikrā wa qad jāaʾahum Rasūlum-mubīn. (13) Thumma tawallaw ʿanhu wa qālū muʿallamum-majnūn. (14) ʾInnā kāshiful-ʿadhābi qalīlan ʾinnakum ʿāaʾidūn. (15) Yawma nabṭishul-baṭshatal-kubrā ʾinnā muñtaqimūn. (16)

6 Lit., "if you had but inner certainty". According to Abū Muslim al-Iṣfahānī (as quoted by Rāzī), this means, "you would know it if you would but truly *desire* inner certainty and would pray for it".

7 Lit., "are toying in doubt": i.e., their half-hearted admission of the possibility that God exists is compounded of doubt and irony (Zamakhsharī) – doubt as to the proposition of God's existence, and an ironical amusement at the idea of divine revelation.

8 A reference to the allegation of the Prophet's opponents that someone else had "imparted" to him the ideas expressed in the Qurʾān (see 16 : 103 and the corresponding notes 129 and 130), or at least had "helped" him to compose it (cf. 25 : 4 and notes 5 and 6).

9 Lit., "remove". This is apparently said on the time-level of the present – i.e., *before* the coming of the Last Hour – so as to give the sinners an opportunity to repent.

نصف الحزب

AND, INDEED, [long] before their time did We try Pharaoh's people [in the same way]: for there came unto them a noble apostle, [who said:] ‹17› "Give in unto me, O God's bondmen![10] Verily, I am an apostle [sent] unto you, worthy of trust! ‹18›

"And exalt not yourselves against God: for, verily, I come unto you with a manifest authority [from Him]; ‹19› and, behold, it is with my Sustainer – and your Sustainer – that I seek refuge against all your endeavours to revile me.[11] ‹20› And if you do not believe me, [at least] stand away from me!" ‹21›

But then, [when they beset him with their enmity,] he called out to his Sustainer, "These are [indeed] people lost in sin!" ‹22›

And [God said]: "Go thou forth with My servants by night, for you will surely be pursued; ‹23› and leave the sea becalmed[12] [between thee and Pharaoh's men]: for, verily, they are a host destined to be drowned!" ‹24›

[And so they perished: and] how many gardens did they leave behind, and water-runnels, ‹25› and fields of grain, and noble dwellings, ‹26› and [all that] life of ease in which they used to delight! ‹27›

Thus it was. And [then] We made another people heirs [to what they had left], ‹28› and neither sky nor earth shed tears over them, nor were they allowed a respite.[13] ‹29›

And, indeed, We delivered the children of Israel from the shameful suffering ‹30›

۞ وَلَقَدْ فَتَنَّا قَبْلَهُمْ قَوْمَ فِرْعَوْنَ وَجَآءَهُمْ رَسُولٌ كَرِيمٌ ﴿١٧﴾ أَنْ أَدُّوٓاْ إِلَيَّ
عِبَادَ ٱللَّهِ إِنِّى لَكُمْ رَسُولٌ أَمِينٌ ﴿١٨﴾ وَأَن لَّا تَعْلُواْ عَلَى ٱللَّهِ إِنِّىٓ ءَاتِيكُم
بِسُلْطَٰنٍ مُّبِينٍ ﴿١٩﴾ وَإِنِّى عُذْتُ بِرَبِّى وَرَبِّكُمْ أَن تَرْجُمُونِ ﴿٢٠﴾ وَإِن لَّمْ
تُؤْمِنُواْ لِى فَٱعْتَزِلُونِ ﴿٢١﴾ فَدَعَا رَبَّهُۥٓ أَنَّ هَٰٓؤُلَآءِ قَوْمٌ مُّجْرِمُونَ ﴿٢٢﴾ فَأَسْرِ
بِعِبَادِى لَيْلًا إِنَّكُم مُّتَّبَعُونَ ﴿٢٣﴾ وَٱتْرُكِ ٱلْبَحْرَ رَهْوًا إِنَّهُمْ جُندٌ
مُّغْرَقُونَ ﴿٢٤﴾ كَمْ تَرَكُواْ مِن جَنَّٰتٍ وَعُيُونٍ ﴿٢٥﴾ وَزُرُوعٍ وَمَقَامٍ كَرِيمٍ ﴿٢٦﴾
وَنَعْمَةٍ كَانُواْ فِيهَا فَٰكِهِينَ ﴿٢٧﴾ كَذَٰلِكَ وَأَوْرَثْنَٰهَا قَوْمًا ءَاخَرِينَ ﴿٢٨﴾ فَمَا
بَكَتْ عَلَيْهِمُ ٱلسَّمَآءُ وَٱلْأَرْضُ وَمَا كَانُواْ مُنظَرِينَ ﴿٢٩﴾ وَلَقَدْ نَجَّيْنَا بَنِىٓ
إِسْرَٰٓءِيلَ مِنَ ٱلْعَذَابِ ٱلْمُهِينِ ﴿٣٠﴾

Wa laqad fatannā qablahum qawma Firʿawna wa jāaʾahum Rasūluñ-karīm. (17) ʾAn ʾaddūu ʾilayya ʿibādal-lāhi ʾinnī lakum Rasūlun ʾamīn. (18) Wa ʾal-lā taʿlū ʿalal-lāhi ʾinnīi ʾātīkum-bisulṭānim-mubīn. (19) Wa ʾinnī ʿudhtu biRabbī wa Rabbikum ʾañ-tarjumūn. (20) Wa ʾil-lam tuʾminū lī faʿtazilūn. (21) Fadaʿā Rabbahūu ʾanna hāaʾulāaʾi qawmum-mujrimūn. (22) Faʾasri biʿibādī laylan ʾinnakum-muttabaʿūn. (23) Wat-rukil-baḥra rahwan ʾinnahum juñdum-mughraqūn. (24) Kam tarakū miñ-jannātiñw-wa ʿuyūn. (25) Wa zurūʿiñw-wa maqāmiñ-karīm. (26) Wa naʿmatiñ-kānū fīhā fākihīn. (27) Kadhālika wa ʾawrathnāhā qawman ʾākharīn. (28) Famā bakat ʿalayhimus-samāaʾu wal-ʾarḍu wa mā kānū muñẓarīn. (29) Wa laqad najjaynā banīi ʾIsrāaʾīla minal-ʿadhābil-muhīn. (30)

10 Most of the classical commentators (e.g., Ṭabarī, Zamakhsharī, Rāzī, Bayḍāwī) point out that this phrase can be understood in either of two senses, namely: "Give in unto me, O God's bondmen (*ʿibād*)", implying a call to the Egyptians (since all human beings are "God's bondmen") to accept the divine message which Moses was about to convey to them; or, alternatively, "Give up to me God's servants", i.e., the children of Israel, who were kept in bondage in Egypt. Inasmuch as the vocalization *ʿibāda* is applicable to the vocative as well as the accusative case, either of these two interpretations is legitimate.

11 Lit., "lest you throw stones at me". It is to be noted that the verb *rajama* is used in the physical sense of "throwing stones" as well as, metaphorically, in the sense of "throwing aspersions" or "reviling".

12 Or: "cleft" – the expression *rahwan* having both these connotations (Jawharī, with especial reference to the above phrase). See also notes 33 and 35 on 26 : 63-66.

13 Sc., "to repent their sins".

[inflicted on them] by Pharaoh, seeing that he was truly outstanding among those who waste their own selves;[14] ‹31› and, indeed, We chose them knowingly above all other people,[15] ‹32› and gave them such signs [of Our grace] as would clearly presage a test.[16] ‹33›
[Now,] behold, these [people] say indeed:[17] ‹34› "That [which is ahead of us] is but our first [and only] death,[18] and we shall not be raised to life again. ‹35› So then, bring forth our forefathers [as witnesses], if what you claim is true!"[19] ‹36›
Are they, then, better than the people of Tubbaʿ and those before them, whom We destroyed because they were truly lost in [the same] sin?[20] ‹37›
For [thus it is:] We have not created the heavens and the earth and all that is between them in mere idle play:[21] ‹38›

مِن فِرْعَوْنَ ۚ إِنَّهُۥ كَانَ عَالِيًا مِّنَ ٱلْمُسْرِفِينَ ﴿31﴾ وَلَقَدِ ٱخْتَرْنَـٰهُمْ عَلَىٰ عِلْمٍ
عَلَى ٱلْعَـٰلَمِينَ ﴿32﴾ وَءَاتَيْنَـٰهُم مِّنَ ٱلْـَٔايَـٰتِ مَا فِيهِ بَلَـٰٓؤٌا۟ مُّبِينٌ ﴿33﴾ إِنَّ
هَـٰٓؤُلَآءِ لَيَقُولُونَ ﴿34﴾ إِنْ هِىَ إِلَّا مَوْتَتُنَا ٱلْأُولَىٰ وَمَا نَحْنُ بِمُنشَرِينَ ﴿35﴾
فَأْتُوا۟ بِـَٔابَآئِنَآ إِن كُنتُمْ صَـٰدِقِينَ ﴿36﴾ أَهُمْ خَيْرٌ أَمْ قَوْمُ تُبَّعٍ وَٱلَّذِينَ مِن
قَبْلِهِمْ ۚ أَهْلَكْنَـٰهُمْ ۖ إِنَّهُمْ كَانُوا۟ مُجْرِمِينَ ﴿37﴾ وَمَا خَلَقْنَا ٱلسَّمَـٰوَٰتِ
وَٱلْأَرْضَ وَمَا بَيْنَهُمَا لَـٰعِبِينَ ﴿38﴾

Miñ-Firʿawna ʾinnahū kāna ʿāliyam-minal-musrifīn.
(31) Wa laqadikh-tarnāhum ʿalā ʿilmin ʿalal-ʿālamīn.
(32) Wa ʾātaynāhum-minal-ʾĀyāti mā fīhi balāaʾum-
mubīn. (33) ʾInna hāaʾulāaʾi layaqūlūna, (34) ʾin hiya
ʾillā mawtatunal-ʾūlā wa mā naḥnu bimuñsharīn. (35)
Faʾtū biʾābāaʾināa ʾiñ-kuñtum ṣādiqīn. (36) ʾAhum
khayrun ʾam qawmu Tubbaʿiñw-wal-ladhīna miñ-
qablihim. ʾAhlaknāhum ʾinnahum kānū mujrimīn. (37)
Wa mā khalaqnas-samāwāti wal-ʾarḍa wa mā bayna-
humā lāʿibīn. (38)

14 For this rendering of the term *musrif*, see *sūrah* 10, note 21.

15 I.e., according to all commentators, above all people *of their time*, because at that time the children of Israel were the only people who worshipped the One God: which is the reason of the frequent Qurʾanic references to the story of their delivery from bondage. The stress on God's having "chosen them *knowingly*" alludes to His foreknowledge that in later times they would deteriorate morally and thus forfeit His grace (Zamakhsharī and Rāzī).

16 Lit., "as would have in them a manifest test": an allusion to the long line of prophets raised in their midst, as well as to the freedom and prosperity which they were to enjoy in the Promised Land. All this presaged a test of their sincerity with regard to the spiritual principles which in the beginning raised them "above all other people" and, thus, of their willingness to act as God's message-bearers to all the world. The formulation of the above sentence implies elliptically that they did *not* pass that test inasmuch as they soon forgot the spiritual mission for which they had been elected, and began to regard themselves as God's "chosen people" simply on account of their descent from Abraham: a notion which the Qurʾān condemns in many places. Apart from this, the majority of the children of Israel very soon lost their erstwhile conviction that the life in this world is but the first and not the final stage of human life, and – as their Biblical history shows – abandoned themselves entirely to the pursuit of material prosperity and power. (See next note.)

17 Although, on the face of it, by "these people" the Israelites are meant, the reference is obviously a general one, applying to all who hold the views expressed in the sequence, and in particular to the pagan contemporaries of the Prophet Muḥammad. Nevertheless, there is a subtle connection between this passage and the preceding allusion to the "test" with which the children of Israel were to be faced: for it is a historical fact that up to the time of the destruction of the Second Temple and their dispersion by the Roman emperor Titus, the priestly aristocracy among the Jews, known as the Sadducces, openly denied the concepts of resurrection, divine judgment and life in the hereafter, and advocated a thoroughly materialistic outlook on life.

18 I.e., "it is a final death, with nothing beyond it".

19 I.e., "bring our forefathers back to life and let them bear witness that there is a hereafter". This ironic demand accords with the saying of the unbelievers mentioned in 43 : 22 and 23, "We found our forefathers agreed on what to believe – and, verily, it is in their footsteps that we find our guidance!" Thus, in the last resort, the fact that their ancestors did not believe in a hereafter is to them as conclusive an argument against it as the fact that nobody has as yet come back to life to confirm the truth of resurrection.

20 "Tubbaʿ" was the title borne by a succession of powerful Ḥimyar kings who ruled for centuries over the whole of South Arabia, and were finally overcome by the Abyssinians in the fourth century of the Christian era. They are mentioned elsewhere in the Qurʾān (50 : 14) as having denied the truth of resurrection and God's judgment.

21 I.e., without meaning or purpose (cf. 21 : 16) – implying that if there were no hereafter, man's life on earth would be utterly meaningless, and thus in contradiction to the above as well as the subsequent statement, "none of all this have We created without [an inner] truth".

مَا خَلَقْنَٰهُمَآ إِلَّا بِٱلْحَقِّ وَلَٰكِنَّ أَكْثَرَهُمْ لَا يَعْلَمُونَ ﴿٣٩﴾ إِنَّ يَوْمَ
ٱلْفَصْلِ مِيقَٰتُهُمْ أَجْمَعِينَ ﴿٤٠﴾ يَوْمَ لَا يُغْنِى مَوْلًى عَن مَّوْلًى شَيْـًٔا وَلَا هُمْ
يُنصَرُونَ ﴿٤١﴾ إِلَّا مَن رَّحِمَ ٱللَّهُ إِنَّهُۥ هُوَ ٱلْعَزِيزُ ٱلرَّحِيمُ ﴿٤٢﴾ إِنَّ
شَجَرَتَ ٱلزَّقُّومِ ﴿٤٣﴾ طَعَامُ ٱلْأَثِيمِ ﴿٤٤﴾ كَٱلْمُهْلِ يَغْلِى فِى ٱلْبُطُونِ ﴿٤٥﴾
كَغَلْىِ ٱلْحَمِيمِ ﴿٤٦﴾ خُذُوهُ فَٱعْتِلُوهُ إِلَىٰ سَوَآءِ ٱلْجَحِيمِ ﴿٤٧﴾ ثُمَّ صُبُّوا۟
فَوْقَ رَأْسِهِۦ مِنْ عَذَابِ ٱلْحَمِيمِ ﴿٤٨﴾ ذُقْ إِنَّكَ أَنتَ ٱلْعَزِيزُ
ٱلْكَرِيمُ ﴿٤٩﴾ إِنَّ هَٰذَا مَا كُنتُم بِهِۦ تَمْتَرُونَ ﴿٥٠﴾ إِنَّ ٱلْمُتَّقِينَ فِى مَقَامٍ
أَمِينٍ ﴿٥١﴾ فِى جَنَّٰتٍ وَعُيُونٍ ﴿٥٢﴾ يَلْبَسُونَ مِن سُندُسٍ وَإِسْتَبْرَقٍ
مُّتَقَٰبِلِينَ ﴿٥٣﴾ كَذَٰلِكَ وَزَوَّجْنَٰهُم بِحُورٍ عِينٍ ﴿٥٤﴾

Mā khalaqnāhumāa ᵓillā bilḥaqqi wa lākinna ᵓaktharahum lā yaᶜlamūn. (39) ᵓInna Yawmal-Faṣli mīqātuhum ᵓajmaᶜīn. (40) Yawma lā yughnī mawlan ᶜam-mawlañ-shayᵓañw-wa lā hum yuñṣarūn. (41) ᵓIllā mar-raḥimal-lāhu ᵓinnahū Huwal-ᶜAzīzur-Raḥīm. (42) ᵓInna shajarataz-zaqqūmi, (43) ṭaᶜāmul-ᵓathīm. (44) Kalmuhli yaghlī fil-buṭūni, (45) kaghalyil-ḥamīm. (46) Khudhūhu faᶜtilūhu ᵓilā sawāaᵓil-jaḥīm. (47) Thumma ṣubbū fawqa raᵓsihī min ᶜadhābil-ḥamīm. (48) Dhuq ᵓinnaka ᵓañtal-ᶜazīzul-karīm. (49) ᵓInna hādhā mā kuñtum-bihī tamtarūn. (50) ᵓInnal-muttaqīna fī maqāmin ᵓamīn. (51) Fī jannātiñw-wa ᶜuyūn. (52) Yalbasūna miñ-suñdusiñw-wa ᵓistabraqim-mutaqābilīn. (53) Kadhālika wa zawwajnāhum-biḥūrin ᶜīn. (54)

none of this have We created without [an inner] truth:[22] but most of them understand it not. ‹39›

VERILY, the Day of Distinction [between the true and the false] is the term appointed for all of them:[23] ‹40› the Day when no friend shall be of the least avail to his friend, and when none shall be succoured ‹41› save those upon whom God will have bestowed His grace and mercy: for, verily, He alone is almighty, a dispenser of grace. ‹42›

Verily, [in the life to come] the tree of deadly fruit[24] ‹43› will be the food of the sinful:[25] ‹44› like molten lead will it boil in the belly, ‹45› like the boiling of burning despair.[26] ‹46›

[And the word will be spoken:] "Seize him, [O you forces of hell,] and drag him into the midst of the blazing fire: ‹47› then pour over his head the anguish of burning despair! ‹48› Taste it – thou who [on earth] hast considered thyself so mighty, so noble![27] ‹49› This is the very thing which you [deniers of the truth] were wont to call in question!"[28] ‹50›

[As against this –] verily, the God-conscious will find themselves in a state secure, ‹51› amid gardens and springs, ‹52› wearing [garments] of silk and brocade, facing one another [in love].[29] ‹53›

Thus shall it be. And We shall pair them with companions pure, most beautiful of eye.[30] ‹54›

---

22 See note 11 on 10 : 5.

23 See note 6 on 77 : 13.

24 See *sūrah* 37, note 22.

25 The term *al-athīm* (lit., "the sinful one") has here apparently a specific connotation, referring to a wilful denial of resurrection and of God's judgment: in other words, of all sense and meaning in man's existence.

26 For this tropical meaning of the term *ḥamīm*, see *sūrah* 6, note 62.

27 Lit., "for, behold, thou wert . . . ", etc. – thus alluding to the sin of arrogance due to disbelief in a continuation of life after death and, hence, in man's ultimate responsibility to God. (Cf. 96 : 6-7 – "Verily, man becomes grossly overweening whenever he believes himself to be self-sufficient" – and the corresponding note 4.)

28 I.e., the continuation of life after death.

29 For these particular allegories of life in paradise, see note 41 on 18 : 31.

30 For the rendering of *ḥūr ᶜīn* as "companions pure, most beautiful of eye", see *sūrah* 56, notes 8 and 13. It is to be noted that the noun *zawj* (lit., "a pair" or – according to the context – "one of a pair") applies to either of the two sexes, as does the transitive verb *zawaja*, "he paired" or "joined", i.e., one person with another.

In that [paradise] they shall [rightfully] claim all the fruits [of their past deeds],[31] resting in security; ‹55› and neither shall they taste death there after having passed through their erstwhile death.[32]
Thus will He have preserved them from all suffering through the blazing fire ‹56› – an act of thy Sustainer's favour:[33] and that, that will be the triumph supreme! ‹57›

THUS, THEN, [O Prophet,] have We made this [divine writ] easy to understand, in thine own [human] tongue, so that men might take it to heart.[34] ‹58›
So wait thou [for what the future will bring]: behold, they, too, are waiting.[35] ‹59›

يَدْعُونَ فِيهَا بِكُلِّ فَٰكِهَةٍ ءَامِنِينَ ﴿٥٥﴾ لَا يَذُوقُونَ فِيهَا ٱلْمَوْتَ إِلَّا
ٱلْمَوْتَةَ ٱلْأُولَىٰ ۖ وَوَقَىٰهُمْ عَذَابَ ٱلْجَحِيمِ ﴿٥٦﴾ فَضْلًا مِّن رَّبِّكَ ۚ ذَٰلِكَ هُوَ
ٱلْفَوْزُ ٱلْعَظِيمُ ﴿٥٧﴾ فَإِنَّمَا يَسَّرْنَٰهُ بِلِسَانِكَ لَعَلَّهُمْ يَتَذَكَّرُونَ ﴿٥٨﴾
فَٱرْتَقِبْ إِنَّهُم مُّرْتَقِبُونَ ﴿٥٩﴾

Yadᶜūna fīhā bikulli fākihatin ᵓāminīn. ﴿55﴾ Lā yadhūqūna fīhal-mawta ᵓillal-mawtatal-ᵓūlā wa waqāhum ᶜadhābal-jaḥīm. ﴿56﴾ Faḍlam-mir-Rabbika dhālika huwal-fawzul-ᶜaẓīm. ﴿57﴾ Faᵓinnamā yassarnāhu bilisānika laᶜallahum yatadhakkarūn. ﴿58﴾ Fartaqib ᵓinnahum-murtaqibūn. ﴿59﴾

31 Cf. 43 : 73.

32 Lit., "except [or "beyond"] the first [i.e., erstwhile] death" (cf. 37 : 58-59).

33 I.e., by His having offered them guidance, of which they availed themselves: thus, the attainment of ultimate felicity is the result of an interaction between God and man, and of man's communion with Him.

34 See note 81 on 19 : 97.

35 I.e., whether they know it or not, God's will shall be done.

The Forty-Fifth Sūrah

Al-Jāthiyah (Kneeling Down)

Mecca Period

THE DESIGNATION of this *sūrah* – revealed immediately after the preceding one – is based on a word which appears in verse 28 and refers to the humility with which all human beings will face, on resurrection, their final judgment.

سورة الجاثية مكية -45-
وآياتها سبع وثلاثون

IN THE NAME OF GOD, THE MOST GRACIOUS, THE DISPENSER OF GRACE:

Ḥā. Mīm.[1] ‹1›
THE BESTOWAL from on high of this divine writ issues from God, the Almighty, the Wise. ‹2›
Behold, in the heavens as well as on earth there are indeed messages for all who [are willing to] believe.[2] ‹3›
And in your own nature, and in [that of] all the animals which He scatters [over the earth] there are messages for people who are endowed with inner certainty.[3] ‹4›
And in the succession of night and day, and in the means of subsistence[4] which God sends down from the skies, giving life thereby to the earth after it had been life-

بِسْمِ ٱللَّهِ ٱلرَّحْمَٰنِ ٱلرَّحِيمِ

حمٓ ۝١ تَنزِيلُ ٱلْكِتَٰبِ مِنَ ٱللَّهِ ٱلْعَزِيزِ ٱلْحَكِيمِ ۝٢ إِنَّ فِى
ٱلسَّمَٰوَٰتِ وَٱلْأَرْضِ لَءَايَٰتٍ لِّلْمُؤْمِنِينَ ۝٣ وَفِى خَلْقِكُمْ وَمَا يَبُثُّ
مِن دَآبَّةٍ ءَايَٰتٌ لِّقَوْمٍ يُوقِنُونَ ۝٤ وَٱخْتِلَٰفِ ٱلَّيْلِ وَٱلنَّهَارِ وَمَآ
أَنزَلَ ٱللَّهُ مِنَ ٱلسَّمَآءِ مِن رِّزْقٍ فَأَحْيَا بِهِ ٱلْأَرْضَ بَعْدَ مَوْتِهَا

Bismil-lāhir-Raḥmānir-Raḥīm.
Ḥā-Mīim. (1) Tañzīlul-Kitābi minal-lāhil-ʿAzīzil Ḥakīm. (2) ʾInna fis-samāwāti wal-ʾarḍi laʾĀyātil-lilmuʾminīn. (3) Wa fī khalqikum wa mā yabuththu miñ dāabbatin ʾĀyātul-liqawmiñy-yūqinūn. (4) Wakh-tilāfil-layli wan-nahāri wa māa ʾañzalal-lāhu minas-samāaʾi mir-rizqiñ-faʾaḥyā bihil-ʾarḍa baʿda mawtihā

---

1 See Appendix II.

2 Cf. 2 : 164, where the term *āyāt* has been rendered by me in the same way, inasmuch as those visible signs of a consciously creative Power convey a spiritual message to man.

3 Cf. 7 : 185 and the corresponding note 151. – The intricate structure of human and animal bodies, and the life-preserving instincts with which all living creatures have been endowed, make it virtually impossible to assume that all this has developed "by accident"; and if we assume, as we must, that a creative *purpose* underlies this development, we must conclude, too, that it has been willed by a conscious Power which creates all natural phenomena "in accordance with an inner truth" (see note 11 on 10 : 5).

4 I.e., rain, with the symbolic connotation of physical and spiritual grace often attached to it in the Qurʾān.

less, and in the change of the winds: [in all this] there are messages for people who use their reason. ‹5›
These messages of God do We convey unto thee, setting forth the truth. In what other tiding, if not in God's messages,[5] will they, then, believe? ‹6›
Woe unto every sinful self-deceiver[6] ‹7› who hears God's messages when they are conveyed to him, and yet, as though he had not heard them, persists in his haughty disdain!
Hence, announce unto him grievous suffering ‹8› – for when he does become aware of any of Our messages, he makes them a target of his mockery!
For all such there is shameful suffering in store. ‹9› Hell is ahead of them; and all that they may have gained [in this world] shall be of no avail whatever to them, and neither shall any of those things which, instead of God, they have come to regard as their protectors:[7] for, awesome suffering awaits them. ‹10›
[To pay heed to God's signs and messages:] this is [the meaning of] guidance; on the other hand,[8] for those who are bent on denying the truth of their Sustainer's messages there is grievous suffering in store as an outcome of [their] vileness.[9] ‹11›

IT IS GOD who has made the sea subservient [to His laws, so that it be of use] to you[10] – so that ships might sail through it at His behest, and that you might seek to obtain [what you need] of His bounty, and that you might have cause to be grateful. ‹12›

وَتَصْرِيفِ ٱلرِّيَٰحِ ءَايَٰتٌ لِّقَوْمٍ يَعْقِلُونَ ﴿٥﴾ تِلْكَ ءَايَٰتُ ٱللَّهِ نَتْلُوهَا
عَلَيْكَ بِٱلْحَقِّ فَبِأَيِّ حَدِيثٍۭ بَعْدَ ٱللَّهِ وَءَايَٰتِهِۦ يُؤْمِنُونَ ﴿٦﴾ وَيْلٌ لِّكُلِّ
أَفَّاكٍ أَثِيمٍ ﴿٧﴾ يَسْمَعُ ءَايَٰتِ ٱللَّهِ تُتْلَىٰ عَلَيْهِ ثُمَّ يُصِرُّ مُسْتَكْبِرًا كَأَن لَّمْ
يَسْمَعْهَا فَبَشِّرْهُ بِعَذَابٍ أَلِيمٍ ﴿٨﴾ وَإِذَا عَلِمَ مِنْ ءَايَٰتِنَا شَيْـًٔا ٱتَّخَذَهَا
هُزُوًا أُو۟لَٰٓئِكَ لَهُمْ عَذَابٌ مُّهِينٌ ﴿٩﴾ مِّن وَرَآئِهِمْ جَهَنَّمُ وَلَا يُغْنِى عَنْهُم
مَّا كَسَبُوا۟ شَيْـًٔا وَلَا مَا ٱتَّخَذُوا۟ مِن دُونِ ٱللَّهِ أَوْلِيَآءَ وَلَهُمْ عَذَابٌ
عَظِيمٌ ﴿١٠﴾ هَٰذَا هُدًى وَٱلَّذِينَ كَفَرُوا۟ بِـَٔايَٰتِ رَبِّهِمْ لَهُمْ عَذَابٌ مِّن
رِّجْزٍ أَلِيمٌ ﴿١١﴾ ۞ ٱللَّهُ ٱلَّذِى سَخَّرَ لَكُمُ ٱلْبَحْرَ لِتَجْرِىَ ٱلْفُلْكُ فِيهِ
بِأَمْرِهِۦ وَلِتَبْتَغُوا۟ مِن فَضْلِهِۦ وَلَعَلَّكُمْ تَشْكُرُونَ ﴿١٢﴾

ثلاثة ارباع الحزب

wa taṣrīfir-riyāḥi ᵓĀyātul-liqawmiñy-yaᶜqilūn. (5) Tilka ᵓĀyātul-lāhi natlūhā ᶜalayka bil-ḥaqqi fabiᵓayyi ḥadīthim-baᶜdal-lāhi wa ᵓĀyātihī yuᵓminūn. (6) Waylul-likulli ᵓaffākin ᵓathīm. (7) Yasmaᶜu ᵓĀyātil-lāhi tutlā ᶜalayhi thumma yuṣirru mustakbirañ-kaᵓal-lam yasmaᶜhā fabashshirhu biᶜadhābin ᵓalīm. (8) Wa ᵓidhā ᶜalima min ᵓĀyātinā shayᵓanit-takhadhahā huzuwā. ᵓUlāaᵓika lahum ᶜadhābum-muhīn. (9) Miñw-warāaᵓihim jahannam. Wa lā yughnī ᶜanhum mā kasabū shayᵓañw-wa lā mat-takhadhū miñ-dūnil-lāhi ᵓawliyāaᵓa wa lahum ᶜadhābun ᶜaẓīm. (10) Hādhā hudā. Wal-ladhīna kafarū biᵓĀyāti Rabbihim lahum ᶜadhābum-mir-rijzin ᵓalīm. (11) ◈ ᵓAllāhul-ladhī sakhkhara lakumul-baḥra litajriyal-fulku fīhi biᵓamrihī wa litabtaghū miñ-faḍlihī wa laᶜallakum tashkurūn. (12)

5 Lit., "in what tiding after God and His messages".

6 The term *affāk*, which literally signifies a "liar" – and, particularly, a "habitual liar" – has here the connotation of "one who lies to himself" because he is *maᵓfūk*, i.e., "perverted in his intellect and judgment" (Jawharī).

7 I.e., anything to which they may attribute a *quasi*-divine influence on their lives, whether it be false deities or false values, e.g., wealth, power, social status, etc.

8 Lit., "and" or "but".

9 For an explanation of this rendering of the phrase *min rijzin*, see note 4 on 34 : 5.

10 For the reason of the above interpolation, see *sūrah* 14, note 46.

And He has made subservient to you, [as a gift] from Himself, all that is in the heavens and on earth:[11] in this, behold, there are messages indeed for people who think! ‹13›

Tell all who have attained to faith that they should forgive those who do not believe in the coming of the Days of God,[12] [since it is] for Him [alone] to requite people for whatever they may have earned. ‹14›

Whoever does what is just and right, does so for his own good; and whoever does evil, does so to his own hurt; and in the end unto your Sustainer you all will be brought back. ‹15›

AND, INDEED, [already] unto the children of Israel did We vouchsafe revelation, and wisdom, and prophethood;[13] and We provided for them sustenance out of the good things of life, and favoured them above all other people [of their time].[14] ‹16›

And We gave them clear indications of the purpose [of faith];[15] and it was only after all this knowledge had been vouchsafed to them that they began, out of mutual jealousy, to hold divergent views:[16] [but,] verily, thy Sustainer will judge between them on Resurrection Day regarding all whereon they were wont to differ. ‹17›

وَسَخَّرَ لَكُم مَّا فِى ٱلسَّمَٰوَٰتِ وَمَا فِى ٱلْأَرْضِ جَمِيعًا مِّنْهُ ۚ إِنَّ فِى ذَٰلِكَ
لَءَايَٰتٍ لِّقَوْمٍ يَتَفَكَّرُونَ ﴿١٣﴾ قُل لِّلَّذِينَ ءَامَنُوا۟ يَغْفِرُوا۟ لِلَّذِينَ لَا يَرْجُونَ
أَيَّامَ ٱللَّهِ لِيَجْزِىَ قَوْمًۢا بِمَا كَانُوا۟ يَكْسِبُونَ ﴿١٤﴾ مَنْ عَمِلَ صَٰلِحًا
فَلِنَفْسِهِۦ ۖ وَمَنْ أَسَآءَ فَعَلَيْهَا ۖ ثُمَّ إِلَىٰ رَبِّكُمْ تُرْجَعُونَ ﴿١٥﴾ وَلَقَدْ ءَاتَيْنَا بَنِىٓ
إِسْرَٰٓءِيلَ ٱلْكِتَٰبَ وَٱلْحُكْمَ وَٱلنُّبُوَّةَ وَرَزَقْنَٰهُم مِّنَ ٱلطَّيِّبَٰتِ
وَفَضَّلْنَٰهُمْ عَلَى ٱلْعَٰلَمِينَ ﴿١٦﴾ وَءَاتَيْنَٰهُم بَيِّنَٰتٍ مِّنَ ٱلْأَمْرِ ۖ فَمَا
ٱخْتَلَفُوٓا۟ إِلَّا مِنۢ بَعْدِ مَا جَآءَهُمُ ٱلْعِلْمُ بَغْيًۢا بَيْنَهُمْ ۚ إِنَّ رَبَّكَ يَقْضِى
بَيْنَهُمْ يَوْمَ ٱلْقِيَٰمَةِ فِيمَا كَانُوا۟ فِيهِ يَخْتَلِفُونَ ﴿١٧﴾

Wa sakhkhara lakum mā fis-samāwāti wa mā fil-ʾarḍi jamīʿam-minh. ʾInna fī dhālika laʾĀyātil-liqawmiñy-yatafakkarūn. (13) Qul lilladhīna ʾāmanū yaghfirū lilladhīna lā yarjūna ʾAyyāmal-lāhi liyajziya qawmam-bimā kānū yaksibūn. (14) Man ʿamila ṣāliḥañ-falinafsihī wa man ʾasāaʾa faʿalayhā; thumma ʾilā Rabbikum turjaʿūn. (15) Wa laqad ʾātaynā banīi ʾIsrāaʾīlal-Kitāba wal-ḥukma wan-Nubuwwata wa razaqnāhum minaṭ-ṭayyibāti wa faḍalnāhum ʿalal-ʿālamīn. (16) Wa ʾātaynāhum-bayyinātim-minal-ʾamri famakh-talafūu ʾillā mim-baʿdi mā jāaʾahumul-ʿilmu baghyam-baynahum. ʾInna Rabbaka yaqḍī baynahum Yawmal-Qiyāmati fīmā kānū fīhi yakhtalifūn. (17)

11 I.e., by endowing man, alone among all living beings, with a creative mind and, thus, with the ability to make conscious use of the nature that surrounds him and is within him.

12 Lit., "who do not hope for [i.e., expect] the Days of God", implying that they do not believe in them. As regards the meaning of "the Days of God", see *sūrah* 14, note 5.

13 Sc., "in the same way and for the same purpose as We now bestow this revelation of the Qurʾān" – thus stressing the fact of continuity in all divine revelation.

14 I.e., inasmuch as at that time they were the only truly monotheistic community (cf. 2 : 47).

15 This, I believe, is the meaning of the phrase *min al-amr* in the above context, although most of the classical commentators are of the opinion that *amr* signifies here "religion" (*dīn*), and interpret the whole phrase, accordingly, as "of what pertains to religion". Since, however, the common denominator in all the possible meanings of the term *amr* – e.g., "command", "injunction", "ordinance", "matter [of concern]", "event", "action", etc. – is the element of *purpose*, whether implied or explicit, we may safely assume that this is the meaning of the term in the above elliptic phrase, which obviously alludes to the purpose underlying all divine revelation and, consequently, man's faith in it. Now from the totality of the Qurʾanic teachings it becomes apparent that the innermost purpose of all true faith is, firstly, a realization of the existence of God and of every human being's responsibility to Him; secondly, man's attaining to a consciousness of his own dignity as a positive element – a *logically necessary* element – in God's plan of creation and, thus, achieving freedom from all manner of superstitions and irrational fears; and, lastly, making man aware that whatever good or evil he does is but done for the benefit, or to the detriment, of his own self (as expressed in verse 15 above).

16 See 23 : 53 and the corresponding note 30.

ثُمَّ جَعَلْنَٰكَ عَلَىٰ شَرِيعَةٍ مِّنَ ٱلْأَمْرِ فَٱتَّبِعْهَا وَلَا تَتَّبِعْ أَهْوَآءَ ٱلَّذِينَ لَا
يَعْلَمُونَ ﴿18﴾ إِنَّهُمْ لَن يُغْنُوا۟ عَنكَ مِنَ ٱللَّهِ شَيْـًٔا ۚ وَإِنَّ ٱلظَّٰلِمِينَ بَعْضُهُمْ
أَوْلِيَآءُ بَعْضٍ ۖ وَٱللَّهُ وَلِىُّ ٱلْمُتَّقِينَ ﴿19﴾ هَٰذَا بَصَٰٓئِرُ لِلنَّاسِ وَهُدًى وَرَحْمَةٌ
لِّقَوْمٍ يُوقِنُونَ ﴿20﴾ أَمْ حَسِبَ ٱلَّذِينَ ٱجْتَرَحُوا۟ ٱلسَّيِّـَٔاتِ أَن نَّجْعَلَهُمْ كَٱلَّذِينَ
ءَامَنُوا۟ وَعَمِلُوا۟ ٱلصَّٰلِحَٰتِ سَوَآءً مَّحْيَاهُمْ وَمَمَاتُهُمْ ۚ سَآءَ مَا يَحْكُمُونَ ﴿21﴾
وَخَلَقَ ٱللَّهُ ٱلسَّمَٰوَٰتِ وَٱلْأَرْضَ بِٱلْحَقِّ وَلِتُجْزَىٰ كُلُّ نَفْسٍۭ بِمَا
كَسَبَتْ وَهُمْ لَا يُظْلَمُونَ ﴿22﴾ أَفَرَءَيْتَ مَنِ ٱتَّخَذَ إِلَٰهَهُۥ هَوَىٰهُ وَأَضَلَّهُ ٱللَّهُ

Thumma jaʿalnāka ʿalā sharīʿatim-minal-ʾamri fat-tabiʿhā wa lā tattabiʿ ʾahwāaʾal-ladhīna lā yaʿlamūn. (18) ʾInnahum lañy-yughnū ʿañka minal-lāhi shayʾā. Wa ʾinnaẓ-ẓālimīna baʿḍuhum ʾawliyāaʾu baʿḍiñw-wal-lāhu Waliyyul-muttaqīn. (19) Hādhā baṣāaʾiru linnāsi wa hudañw-wa raḥmatul-liqaw-miñy-yūqinūn. (20) ʾAm ḥasibal-ladhīnaj-taraḥus-sayyiʾāti ʾan-najʿalahum kalladhīna ʾāmanū wa ʿamiluṣ-ṣāliḥāti sawāaʾam-maḥyāhum wa mamātuhum. Sāaʾa mā yaḥkumūn. (21) Wa khalaqal-lāhus-samāwāti wal-ʾarḍa bilḥaqqi wa litujzā kullu nafsim-bimā kasabat wa hum lā yuẓlamūn. (22) ʾAfaraʾayta manit-takhadha ʾilāhahū hawāhu wa ʾaḍallahul-lāhu

And, finally,[17] [O Muḥammad,] We have set *thee* on a way by which the purpose [of faith] may be fulfilled:[18] so follow thou this [way], and follow not the likes and dislikes of those who do not know [the truth].[19] ‹18› Behold, they could never be of any avail to thee if thou wert to defy the will of God[20] – for, verily, such evildoers are but friends and protectors of one another, whereas God is the Protector of all who are conscious of Him. ‹19›

This [revelation, then,][21] is a means of insight for mankind, and a guidance and grace unto people who are endowed with inner certainty. ‹20›

Now as for those who indulge in sinful doings – do they think that We place them, both in their life and their death, on an equal footing with those who have attained to faith and do righteous deeds?[22]

Bad, indeed, is their judgment: ‹21› for, God has created the heavens and the earth in accordance with [an inner] truth,[23] and [has therefore willed] that every human being shall be recompensed for what he has earned and none shall be wronged. ‹22›

HAST THOU ever considered [the kind of man] who makes his own desires his deity, and whom God has [thereupon] let go

17 Lit., "thereafter" or "in the end" (*thumma*) – i.e., after the failure of the earlier communities to realize the ideal purpose of faith in their actual mode of life.

18 Lit., "on a way of the purpose [of faith]": see note 15 above. It is to be borne in mind that the literal meaning of the term *sharīʿah* is "the way to a watering-place", and since water is indispensable for all organic life, this term has in time come to denote a "system of laws", both moral and practical, which shows man the way towards spiritual fulfilment and social welfare: hence, "religious law" in the widest sense of the term. (See in this connection note 66 on the second part of 5 : 48.)

19 I.e., who are not – or not primarily – motivated by God-consciousness and, hence, are swayed only by what they themselves regard as "right" in accordance with worldly, changing circumstances.

20 Lit., "against [i.e., "in defiance of"] God".

21 I.e., the Qurʾān, which unfolds to man the purpose of all faith.

22 The meaning is twofold: "that We consider them to be equal with those who . . .", etc., and "that We shall deal with them in the same manner as We deal with those who . . .", etc. The reference to the intrinsic difference between these two categories with regard to "their life and their death" points not merely to the moral quality of their worldly existence, but also, on the one hand, to the inner peace and tranquility with which a true believer faces life's tribulations and the moment of death, and on the other, to the nagging anxiety which so often accompanies spiritual nihilism, and the "fear of the unknown" at the time of dying.

23 See note 11 on 10 : 5. The implication is that without a differentiation between right and wrong – or true and false – there would be no "inner truth" in the concept of a divinely-planned creation.

astray, knowing [that his mind is closed to all guidance],[24] and whose hearing and heart He has sealed, and upon whose sight He has placed a veil?[25] Who, then, could guide him after God [has abandoned him]? Will you not, then, bethink yourselves? ‹23›

And yet they say: "There is nothing beyond our life in this world. We die as we come to life,[26] and nothing but time destroys us." But of this they have no knowledge whatever: they do nothing but guess. ‹24›

And [so,] whenever Our messages are conveyed to them in all their clarity, their only argument is this:[27] "Bring forth our forefathers [as witnesses], if what you claim is true!"[28] ‹25›

Say: "It is God who gives you life, and then causes you to die; and in the end He will gather you together on Resurrection Day, [the coming of] which is beyond all doubt – but most human beings understand it not." ‹26›

For, God's is the dominion over the heavens and the earth; and on the Day when the Last Hour dawns – on that Day will be lost all who [in their lifetime] tried to reduce to nothing [whatever they could not understand].[29] ‹27›

And [on that Day] thou wilt see all people kneeling down [in humility]: all people will be called upon to [face] their record: "Today you shall be requited for all that you ever did! ‹28› This Our record speaks of you in all truth: for, verily, We have caused to be recorded all that you ever did!" ‹29›

Now as for those who have attained to faith and done righteous deeds, their Sustainer will admit them to His grace: that, that will be [their] manifest triumph! ‹30›

عَلَىٰ عِلْمٍ وَخَتَمَ عَلَىٰ سَمْعِهِۦ وَقَلْبِهِۦ وَجَعَلَ عَلَىٰ بَصَرِهِۦ غِشَٰوَةً فَمَن
يَهْدِيهِ مِنۢ بَعْدِ ٱللَّهِ أَفَلَا تَذَكَّرُونَ ﴿٢٣﴾ وَقَالُوا۟ مَا هِىَ إِلَّا حَيَاتُنَا
ٱلدُّنْيَا نَمُوتُ وَنَحْيَا وَمَا يُهْلِكُنَآ إِلَّا ٱلدَّهْرُ وَمَا لَهُم بِذَٰلِكَ مِنْ عِلْمٍ إِنْ
هُمْ إِلَّا يَظُنُّونَ ﴿٢٤﴾ وَإِذَا تُتْلَىٰ عَلَيْهِمْ ءَايَٰتُنَا بَيِّنَٰتٍ مَّا كَانَ حُجَّتَهُمْ
إِلَّآ أَن قَالُوا۟ ٱئْتُوا۟ بِـَٔابَآئِنَآ إِن كُنتُمْ صَٰدِقِينَ ﴿٢٥﴾ قُلِ ٱللَّهُ يُحْيِيكُمْ ثُمَّ
يُمِيتُكُمْ ثُمَّ يَجْمَعُكُمْ إِلَىٰ يَوْمِ ٱلْقِيَٰمَةِ لَا رَيْبَ فِيهِ وَلَٰكِنَّ أَكْثَرَ
ٱلنَّاسِ لَا يَعْلَمُونَ ﴿٢٦﴾ وَلِلَّهِ مُلْكُ ٱلسَّمَٰوَٰتِ وَٱلْأَرْضِ وَيَوْمَ تَقُومُ
ٱلسَّاعَةُ يَوْمَئِذٍ يَخْسَرُ ٱلْمُبْطِلُونَ ﴿٢٧﴾ وَتَرَىٰ كُلَّ أُمَّةٍ جَاثِيَةً كُلُّ أُمَّةٍ
تُدْعَىٰٓ إِلَىٰ كِتَٰبِهَا ٱلْيَوْمَ تُجْزَوْنَ مَا كُنتُمْ تَعْمَلُونَ ﴿٢٨﴾ هَٰذَا كِتَٰبُنَا
يَنطِقُ عَلَيْكُم بِٱلْحَقِّ إِنَّا كُنَّا نَسْتَنسِخُ مَا كُنتُمْ تَعْمَلُونَ ﴿٢٩﴾ فَأَمَّا
ٱلَّذِينَ ءَامَنُوا۟ وَعَمِلُوا۟ ٱلصَّٰلِحَٰتِ فَيُدْخِلُهُمْ رَبُّهُمْ فِى رَحْمَتِهِۦ ذَٰلِكَ
هُوَ ٱلْفَوْزُ ٱلْمُبِينُ ﴿٣٠﴾

ʿalā ʿilmiñw-wa khatama ʿalā samʿihī wa qalbihī wa jaʿala ʿalā baṣarihī ghishāwatañ-famañy-yahdīhi mim-baʿdil-lāh. ʾAfalā tadhakkarūn. (23) Wa qālū mā hiya ʾillā ḥayātunad-dunyā namūtu wa naḥyā wa mā yuhlikunāa ʾillad-dahr. Wa mā lahum-bidhālika min ʿilmin ʾin hum ʾillā yaẓunnūn. (24) Wa ʾidhā tutlā ʿalayhim ʾĀyātunā bayyinātim-mā kāna ḥujjatahum ʾillāa añ-qālūʾ-tū biʾābāaʾināa ʾiñ-kuñtum ṣādiqīn. (25) Qulil-lāhu yuḥyīkum thumma yumītukum thumma yajmaʿukum ʾilā Yawmil-Qiyāmati lā rayba fīhi wa lākinna ʾaktharan-nāsi lā yaʿlamūn. (26) Wa lillāhi mulkus-samāwāti wal-ʾarḍ. Wa Yawma taqūmus-Sāʿatu Yawmaʾidhiñy-yakhsarul-mubṭilūn. (27) Wa tarā kullā ʾummatiñ-jāthiyah. Kullu ʾummatiñ-tudʿāa ʾilā Kitābihal-Yawma tujzawna mā kuñtum taʿmalūn. (28) Hādhā Kitābunā yañṭiqu ʿalaykum bilḥaqq. ʾInnā kunnā nastañsikhu mā kuñtum taʿmalūn. (29) Faʾammal-ladhīna ʾāmanū wa ʿamiluṣ-ṣāliḥāti fayudkhiluhum Rabbuhum fī raḥmatih. Dhālika huwal-fawzul-mubīn. (30)

24 Thus Rāzī, evidently reflecting the views of Zamakhsharī, which have been quoted at length in my note 4 on 14 : 4.

25 See note 7 on 2 : 7.

26 I.e., by accident, or as an outcome of blind forces of nature.

27 Lit., "their argument is nothing but that they say".

28 Cf. 44 : 36 and the corresponding note 19.

29 I.e., whatever they could not "prove" by direct observation or calculation. For the above rendering of *al-mubṭilūn*, see *sūrah* 29, note 47.

But as for those who were bent on denying the truth, [they will be told:] "Were not My messages conveyed to you? And withal, you gloried in your arrogance, and so you became people lost in sin: ‹31› for when it was said, 'Behold, God's promise always comes true, and there can be no doubt about [the coming of] the Last Hour' – you would answer, 'We do not know what that Last Hour may be: we think it is no more than an empty guess, and [so] we are by no means convinced!'" ‹32›

And [on that Day,] the evil of their doings will become obvious to them, and they will be overwhelmed by the very thing which they were wont to deride.[30] ‹33›

And [the word] will be spoken: "Today We shall be oblivious of you as you were oblivious of the coming of this your Day [of Judgment]; and so your goal is the fire, and you shall have none to succour you: ‹34› this, because you made God's messages the target of your mockery, having allowed the life of this world to beguile you!"[31]

On that Day, therefore, they will not be brought out of the fire,[32] nor will they be allowed to make amends. ‹35›

AND THUS, all praise is due to God, Sustainer of the heavens and Sustainer of the earth: the Sustainer of all the worlds! ‹36›

And His alone is all majesty in the heavens and on earth; and He alone is almighty, truly wise! ‹37›

وَأَمَّا ٱلَّذِينَ كَفَرُوٓاْ أَفَلَمۡ تَكُنۡ ءَايَٰتِي تُتۡلَىٰ عَلَيۡكُمۡ فَٱسۡتَكۡبَرۡتُمۡ وَكُنتُمۡ
قَوۡمٗا مُّجۡرِمِينَ (31) وَإِذَا قِيلَ إِنَّ وَعۡدَ ٱللَّهِ حَقّٞ وَٱلسَّاعَةُ لَا رَيۡبَ فِيهَا
قُلۡتُم مَّا نَدۡرِي مَا ٱلسَّاعَةُ إِن نَّظُنُّ إِلَّا ظَنّٗا وَمَا نَحۡنُ بِمُسۡتَيۡقِنِينَ (32)
وَبَدَا لَهُمۡ سَيِّـَٔاتُ مَا عَمِلُواْ وَحَاقَ بِهِم مَّا كَانُواْ بِهِۦ يَسۡتَهۡزِءُونَ (33)
وَقِيلَ ٱلۡيَوۡمَ نَنسَىٰكُمۡ كَمَا نَسِيتُمۡ لِقَآءَ يَوۡمِكُمۡ هَٰذَا وَمَأۡوَىٰكُمُ ٱلنَّارُ
وَمَا لَكُم مِّن نَّٰصِرِينَ (34) ذَٰلِكُم بِأَنَّكُمُ ٱتَّخَذۡتُمۡ ءَايَٰتِ ٱللَّهِ هُزُوٗا
وَغَرَّتۡكُمُ ٱلۡحَيَوٰةُ ٱلدُّنۡيَاۚ فَٱلۡيَوۡمَ لَا يُخۡرَجُونَ مِنۡهَا وَلَا هُمۡ يُسۡتَعۡتَبُونَ (35)
فَلِلَّهِ ٱلۡحَمۡدُ رَبِّ ٱلسَّمَٰوَٰتِ وَرَبِّ ٱلۡأَرۡضِ رَبِّ ٱلۡعَٰلَمِينَ (36) وَلَهُ
ٱلۡكِبۡرِيَآءُ فِي ٱلسَّمَٰوَٰتِ وَٱلۡأَرۡضِۖ وَهُوَ ٱلۡعَزِيزُ ٱلۡحَكِيمُ (37)

Wa ʾammal-ladhīna kafarūu ʾafalam takun ʾĀyātī tutlā ʿalaykum fastakbartum wa kuñtum qawmam-mujrimīn. (31) Wa ʾidhā qīla ʾinna waʿdal-lāhi ḥaqquñw-was-Sāʿatu lā rayba fīhā qultum-mā nadrī mas-Sāʿatu ʾin-naẓunnu ʾillā ẓannañw-wa mā naḥnu bimustayqinīn. (32) Wa badā lahum sayyiʾātu mā ʿamilū wa ḥāqa bihim mā kānū bihī yastahziʾūn. (33) Wa qīlal-Yawma nañsākum kamā nasītum liqāaʾa Yawmikum hādhā wa maʾwākumun-nāru wa mā lakum miñ-nāṣirīn. (34) Dhālikum-biʾannakumut-takhadhtum ʾĀyātil-lāhi huzuwañw-wa gharratkumul-ḥayātud-dunyā. FalYawma lā yukhrajūna minhā wa lā hum yustaʿtabūn. (35) Falillāhil-ḥamdu Rabbis-samāwāti wa Rabbil-ʾarḍi Rabbil-ʿālamīn. (36) Wa lahul-kibriyāaʾu fis-samāwāti wal-ʾarḍi wa Huwal-ʿAzīzul-Ḥakīm. (37)

30 Lit., "and that which they were wont to deride will have enfolded them".

31 Lit., "since the life of this world has beguiled you": implying that this self-abandonment to worldly pursuits was the *cause* of their scornful disregard of God's messages.

32 Lit., "out of it". Regarding the stress on the phrase, "*On that Day*", see note 114 on the last paragraph of 6 : 128, note 10 on 40 : 12 and note 59 on 43 : 74.

وَمَا بَيْنَهُمَآ إِلَّا بِٱلْحَقِّ وَأَجَلٍ مُّسَمًّى

وَٱلَّذِينَ كَفَرُوا عَمَّآ أُنذِرُوا

مُعْرِضُونَ ۝ قُلْ أَرَءَيْتُم مَّا

تَدْعُونَ مِن دُونِ ٱللَّهِ أَرُونِى

مَاذَا خَلَقُوا مِنَ ٱلْأَرْضِ أَمْ لَهُمْ

سورة الأحقاف مكية

بِسْمِ ٱللَّهِ ٱلرَّحْمَٰنِ ٱلرَّحِيمِ

حمٓ تَنزِيلُ ٱلْكِتَٰبِ مِنَ ٱللَّهِ ٱلْعَزِيزِ

ٱلْحَكِيمِ مَا خَلَقْنَا ٱلسَّمَٰوَٰتِ وَٱلْأَرْضَ

وآياتها خمس وثلاثون

The Forty-Sixth Sūrah

Al-ʾAḥqāf (The Sand-Dunes)

Mecca Period

THE KEY-WORD of this *sūrah* (the last of the *Ḥā-Mīm* series) is found in verse 21. It was most probably revealed at approximately the same time as *sūrah* 72, that is, about two years, or even less, before the Prophet's *hijrah* to Medina.

سورة الأحقاف مكية -46-
وآياتها خمس وثلاثون

حزب 51
جزء 26

IN THE NAME OF GOD, THE MOST GRACIOUS, THE DISPENSER OF GRACE:

Ḥā. Mīm.[1] ‹1›
THE BESTOWAL from on high of this divine writ issues from God, the Almighty, the Wise. ‹2›
We have not created the heavens and the earth and all that is between them otherwise than in accordance with [an inner] truth, and for a term set [by Us]:[2] and yet, they who are bent on denying the truth turn aside from the warning which has been conveyed unto them.[3] ‹3›
Say: "Have you [really] given thought to what it is that you invoke instead of God? Show me what these [beings or forces] have created anywhere on earth! Or had they, perchance, a share in [creating] the heavens? [If so,] bring me any divine writ

بِسْمِ ٱللَّهِ ٱلرَّحْمَٰنِ ٱلرَّحِيمِ

حمٓ ① تَنزِيلُ ٱلْكِتَٰبِ مِنَ ٱللَّهِ ٱلْعَزِيزِ ٱلْحَكِيمِ ② مَا خَلَقْنَا
ٱلسَّمَٰوَٰتِ وَٱلْأَرْضَ وَمَا بَيْنَهُمَآ إِلَّا بِٱلْحَقِّ وَأَجَلٍ مُّسَمًّى وَٱلَّذِينَ
كَفَرُوا۟ عَمَّآ أُنذِرُوا۟ مُعْرِضُونَ ③ قُلْ أَرَءَيْتُم مَّا تَدْعُونَ مِن دُونِ ٱللَّهِ أَرُونِى
مَاذَا خَلَقُوا۟ مِنَ ٱلْأَرْضِ أَمْ لَهُمْ شِرْكٌ فِى ٱلسَّمَٰوَٰتِ ٱئْتُونِى بِكِتَٰبٍ

Bismil-lāhir-Raḥmānir-Raḥīm.
Ḥā-Mīm. ① Tañzīlul-Kitābi minal-lāhil-ʿAzīzil-Ḥakīm. ② Mā khalaqnas-samāwāti wal-ʾarḍa wa mā baynahumāa ʾillā bilḥaqqi wa ʾajalim-musammā. Wal-ladhīna kafarū ʿammāa ʾuñdhirū muʿriḍūn. ③ Qul ʾaraʾaytum-mā tadʿūna miñ-dūnil-lāhi ʾarūnī mādhā khalaqū minal-ʾarḍi ʾam lahum shirkuñ-fis-samāwāt. ʾIʾtūnī bikitābim-

1 See Appendix II.

2 Regarding the expression "in accordance with [an inner] truth", see note 11 on 10 : 5. The reference to the "term" set by God to all creation is meant to stress the fact of its finality in time as well as in space, in contrast with His Own timelessness and infinity.

3 Lit., "from that whereof they have been warned": i.e., they refuse to heed the warning not to attribute divine qualities to any being or force beside God.

preceding this one, or any [other] vestige of knowledge[4] – if what you claim is true!" ‹4›

And who could be more astray than one who invokes, instead of God, such as will not respond to him either now or on the Day of Resurrection,[5] and are not even conscious of being invoked? ‹5› – such as, when all mankind is gathered [for judgment], will be enemies unto those [who worshipped them], and will utterly reject their worship?[6] ‹6›

But whenever Our messages are conveyed to them in all their clarity, they who are bent on denying the truth speak thus of the truth as soon as it is brought to them: "This is clearly nothing but spellbinding eloquence!"[7] ‹7›

Or do they say, "He has invented all this"? Say [O Muḥammad]: "Had I invented it, you would not be of the least help to me against God.[8] He is fully aware of that [slander] into which you so recklessly plunge: enough is He as a witness between me and you! And [withal,] He alone is truly-forgiving, a true dispenser of grace."[9] ‹8›

Say: "I am not the first of [God's] apostles;[10] and [like all of them,] I do not know what will be done with me or with you;[11] I only follow what is revealed to me: for I am nothing but a plain warner." ‹9›

مِّن قَبْلِ هَـٰذَآ أَوْ أَثَـٰرَةٍ مِّنْ عِلْمٍ إِن كُنتُمْ صَـٰدِقِينَ ﴿4﴾ وَمَنْ أَضَلُّ مِمَّن
يَدْعُواْ مِن دُونِ ٱللَّهِ مَن لَّا يَسْتَجِيبُ لَهُۥٓ إِلَىٰ يَوْمِ ٱلْقِيَـٰمَةِ وَهُمْ عَن
دُعَآئِهِمْ غَـٰفِلُونَ ﴿5﴾ وَإِذَا حُشِرَ ٱلنَّاسُ كَانُواْ لَهُمْ أَعْدَآءً وَكَانُواْ
بِعِبَادَتِهِمْ كَـٰفِرِينَ ﴿6﴾ وَإِذَا تُتْلَىٰ عَلَيْهِمْ ءَايَـٰتُنَا بَيِّنَـٰتٍ قَالَ ٱلَّذِينَ
كَفَرُواْ لِلْحَقِّ لَمَّا جَآءَهُمْ هَـٰذَا سِحْرٌ مُّبِينٌ ﴿7﴾ أَمْ يَقُولُونَ ٱفْتَرَىٰهُ قُلْ
إِنِ ٱفْتَرَيْتُهُۥ فَلَا تَمْلِكُونَ لِى مِنَ ٱللَّهِ شَيْـًٔا هُوَ أَعْلَمُ بِمَا تُفِيضُونَ فِيهِ
كَفَىٰ بِهِۦ شَهِيدًۢا بَيْنِى وَبَيْنَكُمْ وَهُوَ ٱلْغَفُورُ ٱلرَّحِيمُ ﴿8﴾ قُلْ مَا كُنتُ
بِدْعًا مِّنَ ٱلرُّسُلِ وَمَآ أَدْرِى مَا يُفْعَلُ بِى وَلَا بِكُمْ إِنْ أَتَّبِعُ إِلَّا مَا
يُوحَىٰٓ إِلَىَّ وَمَآ أَنَا۠ إِلَّا نَذِيرٌ مُّبِينٌ ﴿9﴾

miñ-qabli hādhāa ʾaw ʾathāratim-min ʿilmin ʾiñ-kuñtum ṣādiqīn. ‹4› Wa man ʾaḍallu mimmañy-yadʿū miñ-dūnil-lāhi mal-lā yastajību lahūu ʾilā Yawmil-Qiyāmati wa hum ʿañ-duʿāaʾihim ghāfilūn. ‹5› Wa ʾidhā ḥushiran-nāsu kānū lahum ʾaʿdāaʾañw-wa kānū biʿibādatihim kāfirīn. ‹6› Wa ʾidhā tutlā ʿalayhim ʾĀyātunā bayyinātiñ qālal-ladhīna kafarū lilḥaqqi lammā jāaʾahum hādhā siḥrum-mubīn. ‹7› ʾAm yaqūlūnaf-tarāh. Qul ʾinif-taraytuhū falā tamlikūna lī minal-lāhi shayʾā. Huwa ʾaʿlamu bimā tufīḍūna fīh. Kafā bihī Shahīdam-baynī wa baynakum. Wa Huwal-Ghafūrur-Raḥīm. ‹8› Qul mā kuñtu bidʿam-minar-Rusuli wa māa ʾadrī mā yufʿalu bī wa lā bikum. ʾIn ʾattabiʿu ʾillā mā yūḥāa ʾilayya wa māa ʾana ʾillā Nadhīrum-mubīn. ‹9›

4 Sc., "in support of your claim that there are other divine powers besides God".

5 Lit., "will not respond to him till the Day of Resurrection", i.e., never.

6 For this symbolic "enmity" of all false objects of worship, see note 13 on 35 : 14.

7 Lit., "sorcery": see note 12 on 74 : 24, where the term *siḥr* has been used, chronologically, for the first time in the above sense. As in that early instance, the truth referred to here is the message of the Qurʾān.

8 Sc., "then why should I have invented all this for your sake?"

9 The implication is, "May God forgive you, and grace you with His guidance" (Zamakhsharī).

10 Thus Ṭabarī, Baghawī, Rāzī, Ibn Kathīr, implying – as Rāzī, stresses – "I am but a human being like all of God's message-bearers who preceded me". Alternatively, the phrase may be rendered as "I am no innovator among the apostles" – i.e., "I am not preaching anything that was not already preached by all of God's apostles before me" (Rāzī and Bayḍāwī): which coincides with the Qurʾanic doctrine of the identity of the ethical teachings propounded by all of God's prophets.

11 I.e., "What will happen to all of us in this world" (Ṭabarī, quoting with approval this interpretation of Al-Ḥasan al-Baṣrī), or "both in this world and in the hereafter" (Bayḍāwī). Either of these two interpretations implies a denial on the Prophet's part of any foreknowledge of the future and, in a wider sense, any knowledge of "that which is beyond the reach of human perception" (*al-ghayb*): cf. 6 : 50 or 7 : 188.

Say: "Have you given thought [to how you will fare] if this be truly [a revelation] from God and yet you deny its truth? – even though a witness from among the children of Israel has already borne witness to [the advent of] one like himself,[12] and has believed [in him], the while you glory in your arrogance [and reject his message]? Verily, God does not grace [such] evil-doing folk with His guidance!" ‹10›
But they who are bent on denying the truth speak thus of those who have attained to faith: "If this [message] were any good, these [people] would not have preceded us in accepting it!"[13] And since they refuse to be guided by it, they will always say, "This[14] is [but] an ancient falsehood!" ‹11›
And yet, before this there was the revelation of Moses, a guide and a [sign of God's] grace; and this [Qurʾān] is a divine writ confirming the truth [of the Torah[15]] in the Arabic tongue, to warn those who are bent on evildoing, and [to bring] a glad tiding to the doers of good: ‹12› for, behold, all who say, "Our Sustainer is God", and thereafter stand firm [in their faith] – no fear need they have, and neither shall they grieve: ‹13› it is they who are destined for paradise, therein to abide as a reward for all that they have done. ‹14›

قُلْ أَرَءَيْتُمْ إِن كَانَ مِنْ عِندِ ٱللَّهِ وَكَفَرْتُم بِهِۦ وَشَهِدَ شَاهِدٌ مِّنۢ بَنِىٓ
إِسْرَٰٓءِيلَ عَلَىٰ مِثْلِهِۦ فَـَٔامَنَ وَٱسْتَكْبَرْتُمْ إِنَّ ٱللَّهَ لَا يَهْدِى ٱلْقَوْمَ
ٱلظَّٰلِمِينَ ﴿١٠﴾ وَقَالَ ٱلَّذِينَ كَفَرُوا۟ لِلَّذِينَ ءَامَنُوا۟ لَوْ كَانَ خَيْرًا مَّا
سَبَقُونَآ إِلَيْهِ وَإِذْ لَمْ يَهْتَدُوا۟ بِهِۦ فَسَيَقُولُونَ هَٰذَآ إِفْكٌ قَدِيمٌ ﴿١١﴾ وَمِن قَبْلِهِۦ
كِتَٰبُ مُوسَىٰٓ إِمَامًا وَرَحْمَةً وَهَٰذَا كِتَٰبٌ مُّصَدِّقٌ لِّسَانًا عَرَبِيًّا لِّيُنذِرَ
ٱلَّذِينَ ظَلَمُوا۟ وَبُشْرَىٰ لِلْمُحْسِنِينَ ﴿١٢﴾ إِنَّ ٱلَّذِينَ قَالُوا۟ رَبُّنَا ٱللَّهُ ثُمَّ
ٱسْتَقَٰمُوا۟ فَلَا خَوْفٌ عَلَيْهِمْ وَلَا هُمْ يَحْزَنُونَ ﴿١٣﴾ أُو۟لَٰٓئِكَ أَصْحَٰبُ ٱلْجَنَّةِ
خَٰلِدِينَ فِيهَا جَزَآءًۢ بِمَا كَانُوا۟ يَعْمَلُونَ ﴿١٤﴾

Qul ʾaraʾaytum ʾiñ-kāna min ʿiñdil-lāhi wa kafartum-bihī wa shahida shāhidum-mim-banīi ʾIsrāaʾīla ʿalā mithlihī faʾāmana was-takbartum. ʾInnal-lāha lā yahdil-qawmaẓ-ẓālimīn. (10) Wa qālal-ladhīna kafarū lilladhīna ʾāmanū law kāna khayram-mā sabaqūnāa ʾilayh. Wa ʾidh lam yahtadū bihī fasayaqūlūna hādhāa ʾifkuñ-qadīm. (11) Wa miñ-qablihī Kitābu Mūsāa ʾimāmañw-wa raḥmah. Wa hādhā Kitābum-muṣaddiqul-lisānan ʿarabiyyal liyuñdhiral-ladhīna ẓalamū wa bushrā lilmuḥsinīn. (12) ʾInnal-ladhīna qālū Rabbunal-lāhu thummas-taqāmū falā khawfun ʿalayhim wa lā hum yaḥzanūn. (13) ʾUlāaʾika ʾaṣḥābul-jannati khālidīna fīhā jazāaʾam-bimā kānū yaʿmalūn. (14)

12 I.e., a prophet like himself. The "witness" spoken of here is evidently Moses: cf. the two Biblical passages relating to the advent of the Prophet Muḥammad (Deuteronomy xviii, 15 and 18): "The Lord thy God will raise up unto thee a prophet from the midst of thee, *of thy brethren, like unto me*"; and "I will raise them up a prophet *from among thy brethren, like unto thee,* and will put My words in his mouth." (See in this connection note 33 on 2 : 42.)

13 Lit., "towards it". Almost all of the classical commentators assume that this refers, specifically, to the contempt with which the pagan Quraysh looked down upon the early followers of Muḥammad, most of whom came from the poorest, lowliest strata of Meccan society. However, the above "saying" has undoubtedly a timeless import inasmuch as the poor and lowly have always been among the first to follow a prophet. Moreover, it may also have a bearing on our times as well, inasmuch as the materially powerful nations, whom their technological progress has blinded to many spiritual verities, are increasingly contemptuous of the weakness of those civilizations in which religion still plays an important, albeit largely formalistic, role; and so, not realizing that this very formalism and the ensuing cultural sterility, and not religious faith as such, is the innermost cause of that weakness, they attribute it to the influence of religion *per se*, saying as it were, "If religion were any good, we would have been the first in holding on to it" – thus "justifying" their own materialistic attitude and their refusal to be guided by spiritual considerations.

14 I.e., the concept of divine revelation as such, as is evident from the subsequent reference to the revelation of Moses.

15 Sc., in its original, uncorrupted form.

NOW [among the best of the deeds which] We have enjoined upon man [is] goodness towards his parents.[16] In pain did his mother bear him, and in pain did she give him birth; and her bearing him and his utter dependence on her took thirty months.[17] And so, when he attains to full maturity and reaches forty years,[18] he [that is righteous] prays: "O my Sustainer! Inspire me so that I may forever be grateful for those blessings of Thine with which Thou hast graced me and my parents, and that I may do what is right [in a manner] that will meet with Thy goodly acceptance; and grant me righteousness in my offspring [as well]. Verily, unto Thee have I turned in repentance:[19] for, verily, I am of those who have surrendered themselves unto Thee!" ‹15›

It is [such as] these from whom We shall accept the best that they ever did,[20] and whose bad deeds We shall overlook: [they will find themselves] among those who are destined for paradise, in fulfilment of the true promise which they were given [in this world]. ‹16›

But [there is many a one] who says to his parents [whenever they try to imbue him with faith in God]: "Fie upon both of you! Do you promise me that I shall be brought forth [from the dead], although [so many] generations have passed away before me?"[21] And [while] they both pray for God's help [and say], "Alas for thee! Believe, for, behold, God's promise always comes true!" – he but answers, "All this is nothing but fables of ancient times!" ‹17›

وَوَصَّيْنَا ٱلْإِنسَٰنَ بِوَٰلِدَيْهِ إِحْسَٰنًا حَمَلَتْهُ أُمُّهُۥ كُرْهًا وَوَضَعَتْهُ كُرْهًا
وَحَمْلُهُۥ وَفِصَٰلُهُۥ ثَلَٰثُونَ شَهْرًا حَتَّىٰٓ إِذَا بَلَغَ أَشُدَّهُۥ وَبَلَغَ أَرْبَعِينَ سَنَةً قَالَ
رَبِّ أَوْزِعْنِىٓ أَنْ أَشْكُرَ نِعْمَتَكَ ٱلَّتِىٓ أَنْعَمْتَ عَلَىَّ وَعَلَىٰ وَٰلِدَىَّ وَأَنْ
أَعْمَلَ صَٰلِحًا تَرْضَىٰهُ وَأَصْلِحْ لِى فِى ذُرِّيَّتِىٓ إِنِّى تُبْتُ إِلَيْكَ وَإِنِّى مِنَ
ٱلْمُسْلِمِينَ ﴿١٥﴾ أُو۟لَٰٓئِكَ ٱلَّذِينَ نَتَقَبَّلُ عَنْهُمْ أَحْسَنَ مَا عَمِلُوا۟ وَنَتَجَاوَزُ
عَن سَيِّـَٔاتِهِمْ فِىٓ أَصْحَٰبِ ٱلْجَنَّةِ وَعْدَ ٱلصِّدْقِ ٱلَّذِى كَانُوا۟ يُوعَدُونَ ﴿١٦﴾
وَٱلَّذِى قَالَ لِوَٰلِدَيْهِ أُفٍّ لَّكُمَآ أَتَعِدَانِنِىٓ أَنْ أُخْرَجَ وَقَدْ خَلَتِ ٱلْقُرُونُ
مِن قَبْلِى وَهُمَا يَسْتَغِيثَانِ ٱللَّهَ وَيْلَكَ ءَامِنْ إِنَّ وَعْدَ ٱللَّهِ حَقٌّ فَيَقُولُ مَا
هَٰذَآ إِلَّآ أَسَٰطِيرُ ٱلْأَوَّلِينَ ﴿١٧﴾

Wa waṣṣaynal-ʾInsāna biwālidayhi ʾiḥsānā. Ḥamalat-hu ʾummuhū kurhañw-wa waḍaᶜat-hu kurhañw-wa ḥamluhū wa fiṣāluhū thalāthūna shahrā. Ḥattāa ʾidhā balagha ʾashuddahū wa balagha ʾarbaᶜīna sanatañ-qāla Rabbi ʾawziᶜnīi ʾan ʾashkura niᶜmatakal-latīi ʾanᶜamta ᶜalayya wa ᶜalā wālidayya wa ʾan ʾaᶜmala ṣāliḥañ-tarḍāhu wa ʾaṣliḥ lī fī dhurriyyatīi ʾinnī tubtu ʾilayka wa ʾinnī minal-Muslimīn. (15) ʾUlāaʾikal-ladhīna nataqabbalu ᶜanhum ʾaḥsana mā ᶜamilū wa natajāwazu ᶜañ-sayyiʾātihim fīi ʾaṣḥābil-jannati waᶜdaṣ-ṣidqil-ladhī kānū yūᶜadūn. (16) Wal-ladhī qāla liwālidayhi ʾuffil-lakumāa ʾataᶜidāninīi ʾan ʾukhraja wa qad khalatil-qurūnu miñ-qablī wa humā yastaghīthānil-lāha waylaka ʾāmin ʾinna waᶜdal-lāhi ḥaqquñ-fayaqūlu mā hādhāa ʾillāa ʾasāṭīrul-ʾawwalīn. (17)

16 Cf. 29 : 8 and 31 : 14. In the present instance, this connects with the reference to the "doers of good" at the end of verse 12 and in verses 13-14.

17 See note 14 on 31 : 14.

18 I.e., the age at which man is supposed to attain to full intellectual and spiritual maturity. It is to be borne in mind that the masculine noun *insān* ("man" or "human being") appearing in the first sentence of this verse applies to both sexes alike.

19 Sc., "of whatever sin I may have committed". See note 41 on the last sentence of 24 : 31.

20 I.e., "whom We shall reward in accordance with the best that they ever did": cf. 29 : 7.

21 Sc., "without any indication that anyone has been or will be resurrected". This parabolical "dialogue" is not only meant to illustrate the ever-recurring – and perhaps natural – conflict between older and younger generations, but also points to the transmission of religious ideas as the most important function of parenthood, and thus, in a wider sense, as the basic element of all social continuity.

ربع الحزب

أُوْلَٰٓئِكَ ٱلَّذِينَ حَقَّ عَلَيْهِمُ ٱلْقَوْلُ فِيٓ أُمَمٍ قَدْ خَلَتْ مِن قَبْلِهِم مِّنَ ٱلْجِنِّ
وَٱلْإِنسِ إِنَّهُمْ كَانُواْ خَٰسِرِينَ ﴿18﴾ وَلِكُلٍّ دَرَجَٰتٌ مِّمَّا عَمِلُواْ
وَلِيُوَفِّيَهُمْ أَعْمَٰلَهُمْ وَهُمْ لَا يُظْلَمُونَ ﴿19﴾ وَيَوْمَ يُعْرَضُ ٱلَّذِينَ كَفَرُواْ
عَلَى ٱلنَّارِ أَذْهَبْتُمْ طَيِّبَٰتِكُمْ فِي حَيَاتِكُمُ ٱلدُّنْيَا وَٱسْتَمْتَعْتُم بِهَا فَٱلْيَوْمَ
تُجْزَوْنَ عَذَابَ ٱلْهُونِ بِمَا كُنتُمْ تَسْتَكْبِرُونَ فِي ٱلْأَرْضِ بِغَيْرِ ٱلْحَقِّ
وَبِمَا كُنتُمْ تَفْسُقُونَ ﴿20﴾ ۞ وَٱذْكُرْ أَخَا عَادٍ إِذْ أَنذَرَ قَوْمَهُۥ
بِٱلْأَحْقَافِ وَقَدْ خَلَتِ ٱلنُّذُرُ مِنۢ بَيْنِ يَدَيْهِ وَمِنْ خَلْفِهِۦٓ أَلَّا تَعْبُدُوٓاْ إِلَّا
ٱللَّهَ إِنِّيٓ أَخَافُ عَلَيْكُمْ عَذَابَ يَوْمٍ عَظِيمٍ ﴿21﴾ قَالُوٓاْ أَجِئْتَنَا لِتَأْفِكَنَا
عَنْ ءَالِهَتِنَا فَأْتِنَا بِمَا تَعِدُنَآ إِن كُنتَ مِنَ ٱلصَّٰدِقِينَ ﴿22﴾

It is [such as] these upon whom the sentence [of doom] will fall due, together with the [other sinful] communities of invisible beings[22] and humans that have passed away before their time. Verily, they will be lost: ‹18› for, [in the life to come,] all shall have their degrees in accordance with whatever [good or evil] they did: and so,[23] He will repay them in full for their doings, and none shall be wronged. ‹19›

And on the Day when those who were bent on denying the truth will be brought within sight of the fire, [they will be told:] "You have exhausted your [share of] good things in your worldly life, having enjoyed them [without any thought of the hereafter]: and so today you shall be requited with the suffering of humiliation for having gloried on earth in your arrogance,[24] offending against all that is right, and for all your iniquitous doings!" ‹20›

AND REMEMBER that brother of [the tribe of] ʿĀd,[25] how – seeing that [other] warnings had already come and gone within his own knowledge as well as in times beyond his ken[26] – he warned his people [who lived] among those sand-dunes: "Worship none but God! Verily, I fear lest suffering befall you on an awesome day!" ‹21›

They answered: "Hast thou come to seduce us away from our gods? Bring, then, upon us that [doom] with which thou threatenest us, if thou art a man of truth!" ‹22›

ʾUlāaʾikal-ladhīna ḥaqqa ʿalayhimul-qawlu fīi ʾumamiñ-qad khalat miñ-qablihim minal-Jinni wal-ʾIñsi ʾinnahum kānū khāsirīn. (18) Wa likulliñ-darajātum-mimmā ʿamilū wa liyuwaffiyahum ʾaʿmālahum wa hum lā yuẓlamūn. (19) Wa Yawma yuʿraḍul-ladhīna kafarū ʿalan-nāri ʾadhhabtum ṭayyibātikum fī ḥayātikumud-dunyā was-tamtaʿtum-bihā fal-Yawma tujzawna ʿadhābal-hūni bimā kuñtum tastakbirūna fil-ʾarḍi bighayril-ḥaqqi wa bimā kuñtum tafsuqūn. (20) ۞ Wadh-kur ʾakhā ʿĀdin ʾidh ʾañdhara qawmahū bilʾaḥqāfi wa qad khalatin-nudhuru mim-bayni yadayhi wa min khalfihīi ʾallā taʿbudūu ʾillal-lāha ʾinnīi ʾakhāfu ʿalaykum ʿadhāba Yawmin ʿaẓīm. (21) Qālūu ʾajiʾtanā litaʾfikanā ʿan ʾālihatinā faʾtinā bimā taʿidunāa ʾiñ-kuñta minaṣ-ṣādiqīn. (22)

---

22 See Appendix III.

23 The particle *li* prefixed to the subsequent verb is evidently what the grammarians call a *lām al-ʿāqibah*: i.e., not an indication of intent ("so that") but simply of a *causal sequence*, which is best rendered as "and", "and so", or "hence".

24 I.e., for having arrogantly, without any objective justification, asserted that there is no life after death.

25 I.e., the Prophet Hūd (see *sūrah* 7, note 48). The mention of Hūd and the tribe of ʿĀd connects with the last sentence of the preceding verse, inasmuch as this tribe "transgressed all bounds of equity all over their lands" (89 : 11).

26 Lit.,"from between his hands and from behind him". This idiomatic phrase (explained in note 247 on 2 : 255) is evidently an allusion to the many warning messages, in Hūd's own time as well as in the almost forgotten past, which ought to have made – but did not make – the tribe of ʿĀd conscious of how far astray they had gone. We have here a subtle, parenthetic reminder that, apart from the revelations which He bestows upon His prophets, God offers His guidance to man through the many signs and warnings apparent in all nature as well as in the changing conditions of human society.

Said he: "Knowledge [of when it is to befall you] rests with God alone: I but convey unto you the message with which I have been entrusted; but I see that you are people ignorant [of right and wrong]!" ‹23›
And so, when they beheld it[27] in the shape of a dense cloud approaching their valleys, they exclaimed, "This is but a heavy cloud which will bring us [welcome] rain!"
[But Hūd said:] "Nay, but it is the very thing which you [so contemptuously] sought to hasten – a wind bearing grievous suffering, ‹24› bound to destroy everything at its Sustainer's behest!"
And then they were so utterly wiped out[28] that nothing could be seen save their [empty] dwellings: thus do We requite people lost in sin. ‹25›
And yet, We had established them securely in a manner in which We have never established you, [O people of later times;][29] and We had endowed them with hearing, and sight, and [knowledgeable] hearts:[30] but neither their hearing, nor their sight, nor their hearts were of the least avail to them, seeing that they went on rejecting God's messages; and [in the end] they were overwhelmed[31] by the very thing which they had been wont to deride. ‹26›
Thus have We destroyed many a [sinful] community living round about you;[32] and yet, [before destroying them,] We had given many facets to [Our warning] messages, so that they might turn back [from their evil ways]. ‹27›

قَالَ إِنَّمَا ٱلْعِلْمُ عِندَ ٱللَّهِ وَأُبَلِّغُكُم مَّآ أُرْسِلْتُ بِهِۦ وَلَٰكِنِّىٓ أَرَىٰكُمْ قَوْمًا
تَجْهَلُونَ ﴿٢٣﴾ فَلَمَّا رَأَوْهُ عَارِضًا مُّسْتَقْبِلَ أَوْدِيَتِهِمْ قَالُوا۟ هَٰذَا عَارِضٌ
مُّمْطِرُنَا بَلْ هُوَ مَا ٱسْتَعْجَلْتُم بِهِۦ رِيحٌ فِيهَا عَذَابٌ أَلِيمٌ ﴿٢٤﴾ تُدَمِّرُ كُلَّ
شَىْءٍۭ بِأَمْرِ رَبِّهَا فَأَصْبَحُوا۟ لَا يُرَىٰٓ إِلَّا مَسَٰكِنُهُمْ كَذَٰلِكَ نَجْزِى
ٱلْقَوْمَ ٱلْمُجْرِمِينَ ﴿٢٥﴾ وَلَقَدْ مَكَّنَّٰهُمْ فِيمَآ إِن مَّكَّنَّٰكُمْ فِيهِ وَجَعَلْنَا
لَهُمْ سَمْعًا وَأَبْصَٰرًا وَأَفْـِٔدَةً فَمَآ أَغْنَىٰ عَنْهُمْ سَمْعُهُمْ وَلَآ أَبْصَٰرُهُمْ وَلَآ
أَفْـِٔدَتُهُم مِّن شَىْءٍ إِذْ كَانُوا۟ يَجْحَدُونَ بِـَٔايَٰتِ ٱللَّهِ وَحَاقَ بِهِم مَّا كَانُوا۟
بِهِۦ يَسْتَهْزِءُونَ ﴿٢٦﴾ وَلَقَدْ أَهْلَكْنَا مَا حَوْلَكُم مِّنَ ٱلْقُرَىٰ وَصَرَّفْنَا
ٱلْءَايَٰتِ لَعَلَّهُمْ يَرْجِعُونَ ﴿٢٧﴾

Qāla ʾinnamal-ʿilmu ʿiñdal-lāhi wa ʾuballighukum māa ʾursiltu bihī wa lākinnīi ʾarākum qawmañ-tajhalūn. (23) Falammā raʾawhu ʿāriḍam-mustaqbila ʾawdiyatihim qālū hādhā ʿāriḍum-mumṭirunā. Bal huwa mas-taʿjaltum-bihī rīḥuñ-fīhā ʿadhābun ʾalīm. (24) Tudammiru kulla shayʾim-biʾamri Rabbihā faʾaṣbaḥū lā yurāa ʾillā masākinuhum; kadhālika najzil-qawmal-mujrimīn. (25) Wa laqad makkannāhum fīmāa ʾim-makkannākum fīhi wa jaʿalnā lahum samʿañw-wa ʾabṣārañw-wa ʾafʾidatañ-famāa ʾaghnā ʿanhum samʿuhum wa lāa ʾabṣāruhum wa lāa ʾafʾidatuhum miñ-shayʾin ʾidh kānū yajḥadūna biʾĀyātil-lāhi wa ḥāqa bihim mā kānū bihī yastahziʾūn. (26) Wa laqad ʾahlaknā mā ḥawlakum-minal-qurā wa ṣarrafnal-ʾĀyāti laʿallahum yarjiʿūn. (27)

27 I.e., when they beheld, without recognizing it as such, the approach of their doom.

28 Lit., "then they became so that . . .", etc. See 69 : 6-8, describing the sandstorm which destroyed the tribe of ʿĀd without leaving any trace of them.

29 This relates in the first instance to the pagan contemporaries of the Prophet, but applies to later generations as well. – The tribe of ʿĀd were the unchallenged lords in the vast region in which they lived (cf. 89 : 8 – "the like of whom has never been reared in all the land"). Moreover, the social conditions of their time were so simple and so free of the many uncertainties and dangers which beset people of higher civilizations that they could be regarded as more "securely established" on earth than people of later, more complex times.

30 I.e., intellect and feeling, both of which are comprised in the noun *fuʾād*.

31 Lit., "enfolded".

32 I.e., "close to you in space as well as in time". In its wider sense, this phrase denotes "all the rest of the world".

But, then, did those [beings] whom they had chosen to worship as deities beside God, hoping that they would bring them nearer [to Him],[33] help them [in the end]? Nay, they forsook them: for that [alleged divinity] was but an outcome of their self-delusion and all their false imagery.[34] ‹28›

AND LO![35] We caused a group of unseen beings to incline towards thee, [O Muḥammad,][36] so that they might give ear to the Qurʾān; and so, as soon as they became aware of it,[37] they said [unto one another], "Listen in silence!" And when [the recitation] was ended, they returned to their people as warners.[38] ‹29›
They said: "O our people! Behold, we have been listening to a revelation bestowed from on high after [that of] Moses, confirming the truth of whatever there still remains [of the Torah]:[39] it guides towards the truth, and onto a straight way. ‹30›
"O our people! Respond to God's call, and have faith in Him: He will forgive you [whatever is past] of your sins, and deliver you from grievous suffering [in the life to come]. ‹31› But he who does not respond to God's call can never elude [Him] on earth, nor can he have any protector against Him [in the life to come]: all such are most obviously lost in error."[40] ‹32›

فَلَوْلَا نَصَرَهُمُ ٱلَّذِينَ ٱتَّخَذُواْ مِن دُونِ ٱللَّهِ قُرْبَانًا ءَالِهَةَۢ بَلْ ضَلُّواْ عَنْهُمْ
وَذَٰلِكَ إِفْكُهُمْ وَمَا كَانُواْ يَفْتَرُونَ ﴿28﴾ وَإِذْ صَرَفْنَآ إِلَيْكَ نَفَرًا مِّنَ ٱلْجِنِّ
يَسْتَمِعُونَ ٱلْقُرْءَانَ فَلَمَّا حَضَرُوهُ قَالُوٓاْ أَنصِتُواْ فَلَمَّا قُضِىَ وَلَّوْاْ إِلَىٰ
قَوْمِهِم مُّنذِرِينَ ﴿29﴾ قَالُواْ يَٰقَوْمَنَآ إِنَّا سَمِعْنَا كِتَٰبًا أُنزِلَ مِنۢ بَعْدِ مُوسَىٰ
مُصَدِّقًا لِّمَا بَيْنَ يَدَيْهِ يَهْدِىٓ إِلَى ٱلْحَقِّ وَإِلَىٰ طَرِيقٍ مُّسْتَقِيمٍ ﴿30﴾ يَٰقَوْمَنَآ
أَجِيبُواْ دَاعِىَ ٱللَّهِ وَءَامِنُواْ بِهِۦ يَغْفِرْ لَكُم مِّن ذُنُوبِكُمْ وَيُجِرْكُم مِّنْ
عَذَابٍ أَلِيمٍ ﴿31﴾ وَمَن لَّا يُجِبْ دَاعِىَ ٱللَّهِ فَلَيْسَ بِمُعْجِزٍ فِى ٱلْأَرْضِ
وَلَيْسَ لَهُۥ مِن دُونِهِۦٓ أَوْلِيَآءُ أُوْلَٰٓئِكَ فِى ضَلَٰلٍ مُّبِينٍ ﴿32﴾

Falawlā naṣarahumul-ladhīnat-takhadhū miñ-dūnil-lāhi qurbānan ʾālihah. Bal ḍallū ʿanhum; wa dhālika ʾifkuhum wa mā kānū yaftarūn. (28) Wa ʾidh ṣarafnāa ʾilayka nafaram-minal-Jinni yastamiʿūnal-Qurʾāna falammā ḥaḍarūhu qālūu ʾañṣitū; falammā quḍiya wallaw ʾilā qawmihim-muñdhirīn. (29) Qālū yā qawmanāa ʾinnā samiʿnā Kitāban ʾuñzila mim-baʿdi Mūsā muṣaddiqal-limā bayna yadayhi yahdīi ʾilal-ḥaqqi wa ʾilā ṭarīqim-mustaqīm. (30) Yā qawmanāa ʾajībū dāʿiyal-lāhi wa ʾāminū bihī yaghfir lakum-miñ-dhunūbikum wa yujirkum-min ʿadhābin ʾalīm. (31) Wa mal-lā yujib dāʿiyal-lāhi falaysa bimuʿjiziñ-fil-ʾarḍi wa laysa lahū miñ-dūnihīi ʾawliyāaʾ. ʾUlāaʾika fī ḍalālim-mubīn. (32)

33 This clause gives the meaning of the expression *qurbānan*, which contains an allusion not merely to false deities but also to the deification of saints, living or dead, who allegedly act as mediators between man and the transcendental Supreme Being.

34 Lit., "that was their lie and all that they were wont to invent".

35 See *sūrah* 2, note 21. The connection between this passage and the preceding one apparently lies in the fact that whereas "those who are lost in sin" (of whom the tribe of ʿĀd is given as an example) refuse to heed God's messages, the "unseen beings" spoken of in the sequence immediately perceived their truth and accepted them.

36 The term *nafar* signifies a group of more than three and up to ten persons. The occurrence mentioned in this passage – said to have taken place in the small oasis of Nakhlah, on the way leading from Mecca to Ṭāʾif (Ṭabarī) – is evidently identical with that described in 72 : 1-15; for a tentative explanation, see note 1 on 72 : 1.

37 Lit., "as soon as they attended to it", i.e., to its recitation by the Prophet.

38 I.e., as preachers of the Qurʾanic creed. The expression "as warners" connects with the preceding references to "warning messages".

39 For an explanation of this rendering of the phrase *mā bayna yadayhi*, see *sūrah* 3, note 3. – As pointed out in note 1 on 72 : 1, this reference to the Qurʾān as revealed "after Moses", omitting any mention of Jesus, seems to indicate that the speakers were followers of the Jewish faith; hence my interpolation of the words "of the Torah".

40 See note 11 on 72 : 15.

ARE, THEN, they [who deny the life to come] not aware that God, who has created the heavens and the earth and never been wearied by their creation,[41] has [also] the power to bring the dead back to life? Yea, verily, He has the power to will anything! ‹33›

And so, on the Day when those who were bent on denying the truth will be brought within sight of the fire [and will be asked], "Is not this the truth?" – they will answer, "Yea, by Our Sustainer!"

[And] He will say: "Taste, then, this suffering as an outcome of your denial of the truth!" ‹34›

REMAIN, then, [O believer,] patient in adversity, just as all of the apostles, endowed with firmness of heart, bore themselves with patience. And do not ask for a speedy doom of those [who still deny the truth]: on the Day when they see [the fulfilment of] what they were promised,[42] [it will seem to them] as though they had dwelt [on earth] no longer than one hour of [an earthly] day![43]

[This is Our] message. Will, then, any be [really] destroyed save iniquitous folk?[44] ‹35›

أَوَلَمْ يَرَوْا۟ أَنَّ ٱللَّهَ ٱلَّذِى خَلَقَ ٱلسَّمَٰوَٰتِ وَٱلْأَرْضَ وَلَمْ يَعْىَ بِخَلْقِهِنَّ
بِقَٰدِرٍ عَلَىٰٓ أَن يُحْۦِىَ ٱلْمَوْتَىٰ ۚ بَلَىٰٓ إِنَّهُۥ عَلَىٰ كُلِّ شَىْءٍ قَدِيرٌ ﴿٣٣﴾ وَيَوْمَ
يُعْرَضُ ٱلَّذِينَ كَفَرُوا۟ عَلَى ٱلنَّارِ أَلَيْسَ هَٰذَا بِٱلْحَقِّ ۖ قَالُوا۟ بَلَىٰ وَرَبِّنَا ۚ
قَالَ فَذُوقُوا۟ ٱلْعَذَابَ بِمَا كُنتُمْ تَكْفُرُونَ ﴿٣٤﴾ فَٱصْبِرْ كَمَا صَبَرَ أُو۟لُوا۟
ٱلْعَزْمِ مِنَ ٱلرُّسُلِ وَلَا تَسْتَعْجِل لَّهُمْ ۚ كَأَنَّهُمْ يَوْمَ يَرَوْنَ مَا يُوعَدُونَ لَمْ
يَلْبَثُوٓا۟ إِلَّا سَاعَةً مِّن نَّهَارٍۭ ۚ بَلَٰغٌ ۚ فَهَلْ يُهْلَكُ إِلَّا ٱلْقَوْمُ ٱلْفَٰسِقُونَ ﴿٣٥﴾

ʾAwalam yaraw ʾannal-lāhal-ladhī khalaqas-samāwāti wal-ʾarḍa wa lam yaʿya bikhalqihinna biqādirin ʿalāa ʾañy-yuḥyiyal-mawtā. Balāa ʾinnahū ʿalā kulli shayʾiñ-Qadīr. (33) Wa Yawma yuʿraḍul-ladhīna kafarū ʿalan-nāri ʾalaysa hādhā bil-ḥaqq. Qālū balā wa Rabbinā. Qāla fadhūqul-ʿadhāba bimā kuñtum takfurūn. (34) Faṣbir kamā ṣabara ʾulul-ʿazmi minar-Rusuli wa lā tastaʿjil-lahum. Kaʾannahum Yawma yarawna mā yūʿadūna lam yalbathūu ʾillā sāʿatam-min-nahār. Balāghuñ-fahal yuhlaku ʾillal-qawmul-fāsiqūn. (35)

41 This is apparently an allusion to the Qurʾanic doctrine that God's creative activity is continuous and unending.

42 I.e., the reality of life after death.

43 In this parabolic manner the Qurʾān points to the illusory concept of "time" as experienced by the human mind – a concept which has no bearing on the ultimate reality to be unfolded in the hereafter.

44 Cf. the last sentence of 6 : 47 and the corresponding note 37.

The Forty-Seventh Sūrah

Muḥammad

Medina Period

THIS IS undoubtedly one of the earliest revelations – perhaps *the* earliest – of the Medina period; as pointed out in note 11 below, verse 13 may have been revealed during the Prophet's *hijrah*. The view of Aḍ-Ḍaḥḥāk and Saʿīd ibn Jubayr (cited by Zamakhsharī) that it is a Meccan *sūrah* lacks both internal and external evidence, and cannot be accepted.

The title is based on the mention of the name of the Prophet Muḥammad in verse 2; but since the *sūrah* deals prominently with various aspects of fighting (*qitāl*) in God's cause, it was often designated by the Prophet's Companions and their immediate successors as *Sūrat al-Qitāl.*

-47-
سورة محمد مدنية
وآياتها ثمان وثلاثون

IN THE NAME OF GOD, THE MOST GRACIOUS, THE DISPENSER OF GRACE:

AS FOR THOSE who are bent on denying the truth and on barring [others] from the path of God – all their [good] deeds will He let go to waste;[1] ‹1› whereas those who have attained to faith and do righteous deeds, and have come to believe in what has been bestowed from on high on Muḥammad – for it is the truth from their Sustainer – [shall attain to God's grace:] He will efface their [past] bad deeds, and will set their hearts at rest.[2] ‹2›

This, because they who are bent on denying the truth pursue falsehood, whereas they who have attained to faith pursue [but] the truth [that flows] from their Sustainer.

In this way does God set forth unto man the parables of their true state.[3] ‹3›

NOW WHEN you meet [in war] those who are bent on denying the truth,[4] smite their

بِسْمِ ٱللَّهِ ٱلرَّحْمَٰنِ ٱلرَّحِيمِ

ٱلَّذِينَ كَفَرُوا۟ وَصَدُّوا۟ عَن سَبِيلِ ٱللَّهِ أَضَلَّ أَعْمَٰلَهُمْ ﴿١﴾ وَٱلَّذِينَ
ءَامَنُوا۟ وَعَمِلُوا۟ ٱلصَّٰلِحَٰتِ وَءَامَنُوا۟ بِمَا نُزِّلَ عَلَىٰ مُحَمَّدٍ وَهُوَ ٱلْحَقُّ
مِن رَّبِّهِمْ كَفَّرَ عَنْهُمْ سَيِّـَٔاتِهِمْ وَأَصْلَحَ بَالَهُمْ ﴿٢﴾ ذَٰلِكَ بِأَنَّ ٱلَّذِينَ
كَفَرُوا۟ ٱتَّبَعُوا۟ ٱلْبَٰطِلَ وَأَنَّ ٱلَّذِينَ ءَامَنُوا۟ ٱتَّبَعُوا۟ ٱلْحَقَّ مِن رَّبِّهِمْ كَذَٰلِكَ
يَضْرِبُ ٱللَّهُ لِلنَّاسِ أَمْثَٰلَهُمْ ﴿٣﴾ فَإِذَا لَقِيتُمُ ٱلَّذِينَ كَفَرُوا۟ فَضَرْبَ

Bismil-lāhir-Raḥmānir-Raḥīm.
ʾAlladhīna kafarū wa ṣaddū ᶜañ-sabīlil-lāhi ʾaḍalla ʾaᶜmālahum. (1) Wal-ladhīna ʾāmanū wa ᶜamiluṣ-ṣāliḥāti wa ʾāmanū bimā nuzzila ᶜalā Muḥammadiñw-wa huwal-ḥaqqu mir-Rabbihim kaffara ᶜanhum sayyiʾātihim wa ʾaṣlaḥa bālahum. (2) Dhālika biʾannal-ladhīna kafarut-tabaᶜul-bāṭila wa ʾannal-ladhīna ʾāmanut-tabaᶜul-ḥaqqa mir-Rabbihim. Kadhālika yaḍribul-lāhu linnāsi ʾamthālahum. (3) Faʾidhā laqītumul-ladhīna kafarū faḍarbar-

---

1 I.e., whatever good deeds they may do will be so completely outweighed by the above-mentioned sin that they will amount to nothing on the Day of Judgment. (But see also note 9 below.) The above verse connects with the last sentence of the preceding *sūrah*, "Will, then, any be [really] destroyed save iniquitous folk?"

2 Lit., "will set aright their hearts" or "their minds", inasmuch as one of the several meanings of the term *bāl* is the "heart" or "mind" of man (Jawharī).

3 Lit., "their parables" (*amthālahum*). This, according to some of the most outstanding commentators, relates to the parabolic expressions in the above three verses: the "going to waste" – in consequence of their deliberate "pursuance of falsehood" – of the good deeds of those who deny the truth, as well as the "effacement of the bad deeds" of the true believers in consequence of their "pursuance of the truth" (Baghawī, Zamakhsharī, Rāzī, Bayḍāwī). In a broader perspective, this interpretation takes into account the parabolic nature not only of the above sentence but also of many other Qurʾanic statements relating to men's spiritual conditions and destinies in this world as well as in the life to come.

4 Sc., "and on barring [others] from the path of God" – thus connecting with verse 1 and laying down the fundamental condition which alone justifies physical warfare: namely, a defence of the Faith and of freedom (cf. in this connection note 167 on 2 : 190). In other words, when "those who are bent on denying the truth" try to deprive the Muslims of their social and political liberty and thus to make it impossible for them to live in accordance with the principles of their faith, a just war (*jihād*) becomes allowable and, more than that, a duty. The whole of the above verse relates to war *actually in progress* (cf. note 168 on the first part of 2 : 191); and there is no doubt that it was revealed *after* 22 : 39-40, the earliest Qurʾanic reference to physical warfare.

نصف الحزب

necks until you overcome them fully, and then tighten their bonds;[5] but thereafter [set them free,] either by an act of grace or against ransom, so that the burden of war may be lifted:[6] thus [shall it be].

And [know that] had God so willed, He could indeed punish them [Himself]; but [He wills you to struggle] so as to test you [all] by means of one another.[7]

And as for those who are slain in God's cause, never will He let their deeds go to waste: ‹4› He will guide them [in the hereafter as well], and will set their hearts at rest, ‹5› and will admit them to the paradise which He has promised them. ‹6›

O you who have attained to faith! If you help [the cause of] God, He will help you, and will make firm your steps; ‹7› but as for those who are bent on denying the truth, ill fortune awaits them, since He will let all their [good] deeds go to waste: ‹8› this, because they hate [the very thought of] what God has bestowed from on high[8] – and thus He causes all their deeds to come to nought![9] ‹9›

Have they, then, never journeyed about the earth and beheld what happened in the end to those [wilful sinners] who lived before their time? God destroyed them utterly: and the like thereof awaits all who deny the truth.[10] ‹10›

This, because God is the Protector of all who have attained to faith, whereas they who deny the truth have no protector. ‹11›

ٱلرِّقَابِ حَتَّىٰٓ إِذَآ أَثۡخَنتُمُوهُمۡ فَشُدُّواْ ٱلۡوَثَاقَ فَإِمَّا مَنَّۢا بَعۡدُ وَإِمَّا فِدَآءً
حَتَّىٰ تَضَعَ ٱلۡحَرۡبُ أَوۡزَارَهَاۚ ذَٰلِكَۖ وَلَوۡ يَشَآءُ ٱللَّهُ لَٱنتَصَرَ مِنۡهُمۡ وَلَٰكِن
لِّيَبۡلُوَاْ بَعۡضَكُم بِبَعۡضٖۗ وَٱلَّذِينَ قُتِلُواْ فِي سَبِيلِ ٱللَّهِ فَلَن يُضِلَّ
أَعۡمَٰلَهُمۡ ٤ سَيَهۡدِيهِمۡ وَيُصۡلِحُ بَالَهُمۡ ٥ وَيُدۡخِلُهُمُ ٱلۡجَنَّةَ عَرَّفَهَا
لَهُمۡ ٦ يَٰٓأَيُّهَا ٱلَّذِينَ ءَامَنُوٓاْ إِن تَنصُرُواْ ٱللَّهَ يَنصُرۡكُمۡ وَيُثَبِّتۡ
أَقۡدَامَكُمۡ ٧ وَٱلَّذِينَ كَفَرُواْ فَتَعۡسٗا لَّهُمۡ وَأَضَلَّ أَعۡمَٰلَهُمۡ ٨ ذَٰلِكَ
بِأَنَّهُمۡ كَرِهُواْ مَآ أَنزَلَ ٱللَّهُ فَأَحۡبَطَ أَعۡمَٰلَهُمۡ ٩ ۞ أَفَلَمۡ يَسِيرُواْ فِي
ٱلۡأَرۡضِ فَيَنظُرُواْ كَيۡفَ كَانَ عَٰقِبَةُ ٱلَّذِينَ مِن قَبۡلِهِمۡۖ دَمَّرَ ٱللَّهُ عَلَيۡهِمۡۖ
وَلِلۡكَٰفِرِينَ أَمۡثَٰلُهَا ١٠ ذَٰلِكَ بِأَنَّ ٱللَّهَ مَوۡلَى ٱلَّذِينَ ءَامَنُواْ وَأَنَّ
ٱلۡكَٰفِرِينَ لَا مَوۡلَىٰ لَهُمۡ ١١

riqābi ḥattāa ʾidhāa ʾathkhañtumūhum fashuddul-wathāqa faʾimmā mannam-baᶜdu wa ʾimmā fidāaʾan ḥattā taḍaᶜal-ḥarbu ʾawzārahā. Dhālika wa law yashāaʾul-lāhu lañtaṣara minhum wa lākil-liyabluwa baᶜḍakum-bibaᶜḍ. Wal-ladhīna qutilū fī sabīlil-lāhi falañy-yuḍilla ʾaᶜmālahum. (4) Sayah-dīhim wa yuṣliḥu bālahum. (5) Wa yudkhiluhumul-jannata ᶜarrafahā lahum. (6) Yāa ʾayyuhal-ladhīna ʾāmanūu ʾiñ-tañṣurul-lāha yañṣurkum wa yuthabbit ʾaqdāmakum. (7) Wal-ladhīna kafarū fataᶜsal-lahum wa ʾaḍalla ʾaᶜmālahum. (8) Dhālika biʾannahum karihū māa ʾañzalal-lāhu faʾaḥbaṭa ʾaᶜmālahum. (9) ۞ ʾAfalam yasīrū fil-ʾarḍi fayañẓurū kayfa kāna ᶜāqibatul-ladhīna miñ-qablihim. Dammaral-lāhu ᶜalayhim wa lilkāfirīna ʾamthāluhā. (10) Dhālika biʾannal-lāha Mawlal-ladhīna ʾāmanū wa ʾannal-kāfirīna lā mawlā lahum. (11)

5 Lit., "tighten the bond". According to almost all the commentators, this expression denotes the taking of prisoners of war. In addition, it may also refer to any sanctions or safeguards which would make it unlikely that the aggression could be resumed in the foreseeable future.

6 Lit., "so that (*ḥattā*) the war may lay down its burdens". The term "ransom" comprises also, in this context, a mutual exchange of prisoners of war (Zamakhsharī, quoting an opinion of Imām Ash-Shāfiᶜī).

7 I.e., so as to enable the believers to prove by actual deeds the depth of their faith and their readiness for self-sacrifice, and to enable the aggressors to realize how wrong they have been, and thus to bring them closer to the truth.

8 Namely, the revelation relating to man's moral responsibility to a Supreme Being.

9 The particle *fa* ("and thus") at the beginning of this clause connotes a *consequence*: in other words, it is their rejection of the idea of moral responsibility, inherent in all divine revelation, that deprives the deeds of "those who are bent on denying the truth" – even such deeds as might be termed "good" – of all moral value. This law of inner causality explains fully the phrase "He will let all their [good] deeds go to waste" occurring in verses 1 and 8.

10 Cf. 6 : 10 and the corresponding note 9.

Verily, God will admit all who attain to faith and do righteous deeds into gardens through which running waters flow, whereas they who are bent on denying the truth shall have – even though they may enjoy their life [in this world] and eat as cattle eat – the fire [of the hereafter] for their abode. ‹12›
And how many a community[11] of greater power than this thy community which has driven thee out, [O Muḥammad,] have We destroyed, with none to succour them! ‹13›

CAN, THEN, he who takes his stand on a clear evidence from his Sustainer be likened unto one[12] to whom the evil of his own doings [always] seems goodly, and unto such as would follow but their own lusts? ‹14›
[And can] the parable of the paradise which the God-conscious are promised[13] – [a paradise] wherein there are rivers of water which time does not corrupt, and rivers of milk the taste whereof never alters, and rivers of wine delightful to those who drink it,[14] and rivers of honey of all impurity cleansed, and the enjoyment[15] of all the fruits [of their good deeds] and of forgiveness from their Sustainer: – can this [parable of paradise] be likened unto [the parable of the recompense of[16]] such as are to abide in the fire and be given waters of burning despair[17] to drink, so that it will tear their bowels asunder? ‹15›

إِنَّ ٱللَّهَ يُدْخِلُ ٱلَّذِينَ ءَامَنُوا۟ وَعَمِلُوا۟ ٱلصَّٰلِحَٰتِ جَنَّٰتٍ تَجْرِى مِن
تَحْتِهَا ٱلْأَنْهَٰرُ ۖ وَٱلَّذِينَ كَفَرُوا۟ يَتَمَتَّعُونَ وَيَأْكُلُونَ كَمَا تَأْكُلُ ٱلْأَنْعَٰمُ
وَٱلنَّارُ مَثْوًى لَّهُمْ ﴿١٢﴾ وَكَأَيِّن مِّن قَرْيَةٍ هِىَ أَشَدُّ قُوَّةً مِّن قَرْيَتِكَ ٱلَّتِىٓ
أَخْرَجَتْكَ أَهْلَكْنَٰهُمْ فَلَا نَاصِرَ لَهُمْ ﴿١٣﴾ أَفَمَن كَانَ عَلَىٰ بَيِّنَةٍ مِّن
رَّبِّهِۦ كَمَن زُيِّنَ لَهُۥ سُوٓءُ عَمَلِهِۦ وَٱتَّبَعُوٓا۟ أَهْوَآءَهُم ﴿١٤﴾ مَّثَلُ ٱلْجَنَّةِ ٱلَّتِى
وُعِدَ ٱلْمُتَّقُونَ ۖ فِيهَآ أَنْهَٰرٌ مِّن مَّآءٍ غَيْرِ ءَاسِنٍ وَأَنْهَٰرٌ مِّن لَّبَنٍ لَّمْ يَتَغَيَّرْ
طَعْمُهُۥ وَأَنْهَٰرٌ مِّنْ خَمْرٍ لَّذَّةٍ لِّلشَّٰرِبِينَ وَأَنْهَٰرٌ مِّنْ عَسَلٍ مُّصَفًّى ۖ وَلَهُمْ
فِيهَا مِن كُلِّ ٱلثَّمَرَٰتِ وَمَغْفِرَةٌ مِّن رَّبِّهِمْ ۖ كَمَنْ هُوَ خَٰلِدٌ فِى ٱلنَّارِ
وَسُقُوا۟ مَآءً حَمِيمًا فَقَطَّعَ أَمْعَآءَهُمْ ﴿١٥﴾

ʾInnal-lāha yudkhilul-ladhīna ʾāmanū wa ᶜamiluṣ-ṣāliḥāti jannātiñ-tajrī miñ-taḥtihal-ʾanhār. Wal-ladhīna kafarū yatamattaᶜūna wa yaʾkulūna kamā taʾkulul-ʾanᶜāmu wan-nāru mathwal-lahum. ﴿١٢﴾ Wa kaʾayyim-miñ-qaryatin hiya ʾashaddu quwwatam-miñ-qaryatikal-latīi ʾakhrajatka ʾahlaknāhum falā nāṣira lahum. ﴿١٣﴾ ʾAfamañ-kāna ᶜalā bayyinatim-mir-Rabbihī kamañ-zuyyina lahū sūuʾu ᶜamalihī wat-tabaᶜūu ʾahwāaʾahum. ﴿١٤﴾ Mathalul-jannatil-latī wuᶜidal-muttaqūn. Fīhāa ʾanhārum-mim-māaʾin ghayri ʾāsiñw-wa ʾanhārum-mil-labanil-lam yataghayyar ṭaᶜmuhu wa ʾanhārum-min khamril-ladhdhatil-lishshāribīna wa ʾanhārum-min ᶜasalim-muṣaffā. Wa lahum fīhā miñ-kullith-thamarāti wa maghfiratum-mir-Rabbihim. Kaman huwa khāliduñ-fin-nāri wa suqū māaʾan ḥamīmañ-faqaṭṭaᶜa ʾamᶜāaʾahum. ﴿١٥﴾

11 See note 116 on 6 : 131. It is said that this verse was revealed on the first night of the Prophet's *hijrah* from Mecca to Medina (Ṭabarī, on the authority of Ibn ᶜAbbās).

12 Lit., "Is, then, one who takes his stand . . . like one . . .", etc.

13 My rendering of this verse is based in its entirety on the grammatical construction given to it by Zamakhsharī and supported by Rāzī. In this construction, the parabolic description of paradise – beginning with the phrase "wherein there are rivers . . .", etc., and ending with the words "and forgiveness from their Sustainer" – is a parenthetic passage (*jumlah muᶜtariḍah*). As for the term "parable" (*mathal*) itself, it is undoubtedly meant to impress upon those who read or listen to the Qurʾān that its descriptions of life in the hereafter are purely allegorical: see in this connection Zamakhsharī's explicit remarks cited in note 65 on 13 : 35.

14 Cf. 37 : 45-47, especially verse 47: "no headiness will there be in it, and they will not get drunk thereon".

15 Lit., "and wherein they [i.e., the God-conscious] will have . . .", etc.

16 This interpolation reproduces literally Zamakhsharī's explanation of the above ellipticism.

17 Lit., "exceedingly hot [or "boiling"] water". For an explanation of this metaphor, see note 62 on 6 : 70.

Now among those [hapless sinners] are such as [pretend to] listen to thee, [O Muḥammad,][18] and then, as soon as they leave thy presence, speak [with scorn] unto those who have understood [thy message]:[19] "What is it that he has said just now?"

It is such as these whose hearts God has sealed because they [always] followed but their own lusts[20] ‹16› – just as for those who are [willing to be] guided, He increases their [ability to follow His] guidance and causes them to grow in God-consciousness.[21] ‹17›

Are, then, they [whose hearts are sealed] waiting for the Last Hour – [waiting] that it come upon them of a sudden? But it has already been foretold![22] And what will their remembrance [of their past sins] avail them, once it has come upon them?[23] ‹18›

Know, then, [O man,] that there is no deity save God, and [while there is yet time,] ask forgiveness for thy sins and for [the sins of] all other believing men and women: for God knows all your comings and goings as well as your abiding [at rest].[24] ‹19›

NOW THOSE who have attained to faith say, "Would that a revelation [allowing us to fight] were bestowed from on high!"[25]

وَمِنْهُم مَّن يَسْتَمِعُ إِلَيْكَ حَتَّىٰٓ إِذَا خَرَجُوا۟ مِنْ عِندِكَ قَالُوا۟ لِلَّذِينَ
أُوتُوا۟ ٱلْعِلْمَ مَاذَا قَالَ ءَانِفًا ۚ أُو۟لَـٰٓئِكَ ٱلَّذِينَ طَبَعَ ٱللَّهُ عَلَىٰ قُلُوبِهِمْ
وَٱتَّبَعُوٓا۟ أَهْوَآءَهُمْ ﴿١٦﴾ وَٱلَّذِينَ ٱهْتَدَوْا۟ زَادَهُمْ هُدًى وَءَاتَىٰهُمْ
تَقْوَىٰهُمْ ﴿١٧﴾ فَهَلْ يَنظُرُونَ إِلَّا ٱلسَّاعَةَ أَن تَأْتِيَهُم بَغْتَةً ۖ فَقَدْ جَآءَ
أَشْرَاطُهَا ۚ فَأَنَّىٰ لَهُمْ إِذَا جَآءَتْهُمْ ذِكْرَىٰهُمْ ﴿١٨﴾ فَٱعْلَمْ أَنَّهُۥ لَآ إِلَـٰهَ
إِلَّا ٱللَّهُ وَٱسْتَغْفِرْ لِذَنۢبِكَ وَلِلْمُؤْمِنِينَ وَٱلْمُؤْمِنَـٰتِ ۗ وَٱللَّهُ يَعْلَمُ
مُتَقَلَّبَكُمْ وَمَثْوَىٰكُمْ ﴿١٩﴾ وَيَقُولُ ٱلَّذِينَ ءَامَنُوا۟ لَوْلَا نُزِّلَتْ سُورَةٌ ۖ

Wa minhum mañy-yastamiᶜu ᵓilayka ḥattāa ᵓidhā kharajū min ᶜiñdika qālū lilladhīna ᵓūtul-ᶜilma mādhā qāla ᵓānifā. ᵓUlāaᵓikal-ladhīna ṭabaᶜal-lāhu ᶜalā qulūbihim wat-tabaᶜūu ᵓahwāaᵓahum (16) Walladhīnah-tadaw zādahum hudañw-wa ᵓātāhum taqwāhum. (17) Fahal yañẓurūna ᵓillas-Sāᶜata ᵓañtaᵓtiyahum-baghtah. Faqad jāaᵓa ᵓashrāṭuhā. Faᵓannā lahum ᵓidhā jāaᵓat-hum dhikrāhum. (18) Faᶜlam ᵓannahū lāa ᵓilāha ᵓillal-lāhu was-taghfir lidhambika wa lilmuᵓminīna wal-muᵓmināt. Wallāhu yaᶜlamu mutaqallabakum wa mathwākum. (19) Wa yaqūlul-ladhīna ᵓāmanū lawlā nuzzilat sūrah.

18 Cf. 6 : 25 and 10 : 42-43.

19 Lit., "unto those who have been given knowledge", sc., "of the truth" or "of thy message": i.e., the believers. The people spoken of in the above are the hypocrites among the contemporaries of the Prophet as well as all people, at all times, who pretend to approach the Qurᵓanic message with a show of "reverence" but are in their innermost unwilling to admit that there is any sense in it.

20 I.e., the "sealing" of their hearts (for an explanation of which see note 7 on 2 : 7) is a *consequence* of their "following but their own lusts".

21 Lit., "and gives them their God-consciousness (*taqwāhum*)".

22 Lit., "its indications have already come": a reference to the many Qurᵓanic predictions of its inevitability, as well as to the evidence, accessible to every unprejudiced mind, of the temporal finality of all creation.

23 I.e., "of what benefit will be to them, when the Last Hour comes, their dawning awareness of having sinned, and their belated repentance?"

24 I.e., "He knows all that you do and all that you fail to do".

25 I am rendering the term *sūrah* here and in the next sentence as "a revelation", for whereas there is no *sūrah* as such which deals *exclusively* with questions of war, there are numerous references to it in various *sūrahs;* and this is evidently the meaning of this term in the present context as well as in 9 : 86. – There is no doubt that this verse *precedes* the revelation, in the year 1 H., of 22 : 39, which states categorically – and for the first time – that the believers are allowed to wage war whenever "war is wrongfully waged" against them (see in this connection note 57 on 22 : 39).

But now that a revelation clear in and by itself,[26] mentioning war, has been bestowed from on high, thou canst see those in whose hearts is disease looking at thee, [O Muḥammad,] with the look of one who is about to faint for fear of death! And yet, far better for them would be ‹20› obedience [to God's call] and a word that could win [His] approval:[27] for, since the matter has been resolved [by His revelation], it would be but for their own good to remain true to God. ‹21›

[Ask them:] "Would you, perchance, after having turned away [from God's commandment, prefer to revert to your old ways, and] spread corruption on earth, and [once again] cut asunder your ties of kinship?"[28] ‹22›

It is such as these whom God rejects, and whom He makes deaf [to the voice of truth], and whose eyes He blinds [to its sight]![29] ‹23›

Will they not, then, ponder over this Qurʾān? – or are there locks upon their hearts? ‹24›

VERILY, those who turn their backs [on this message] after guidance has been made clear to them, [do it because] Satan has embellished their fancies and filled them with false hopes: ‹25› [they do turn their backs on it] inasmuch as[30] they are wont to say unto those who abhor all that God has revealed, "We will comply with your views on some points."[31]

But God knows their secret thoughts: ‹26›

فَإِذَآ أُنزِلَتْ سُورَةٌ مُّحْكَمَةٌ وَذُكِرَ فِيهَا ٱلْقِتَالُ رَأَيْتَ ٱلَّذِينَ فِى قُلُوبِهِم
مَّرَضٌ يَنظُرُونَ إِلَيْكَ نَظَرَ ٱلْمَغْشِىِّ عَلَيْهِ مِنَ ٱلْمَوْتِ فَأَوْلَىٰ لَهُمْ ﴿20﴾
طَاعَةٌ وَقَوْلٌ مَّعْرُوفٌ فَإِذَا عَزَمَ ٱلْأَمْرُ فَلَوْ صَدَقُوا۟ ٱللَّهَ لَكَانَ خَيْرًا
لَّهُمْ ﴿21﴾ فَهَلْ عَسَيْتُمْ إِن تَوَلَّيْتُمْ أَن تُفْسِدُوا۟ فِى ٱلْأَرْضِ وَتُقَطِّعُوٓا۟
أَرْحَامَكُمْ ﴿22﴾ أُو۟لَٰٓئِكَ ٱلَّذِينَ لَعَنَهُمُ ٱللَّهُ فَأَصَمَّهُمْ وَأَعْمَىٰٓ
أَبْصَٰرَهُمْ ﴿23﴾ أَفَلَا يَتَدَبَّرُونَ ٱلْقُرْءَانَ أَمْ عَلَىٰ قُلُوبٍ أَقْفَالُهَآ ﴿24﴾ إِنَّ
ٱلَّذِينَ ٱرْتَدُّوا۟ عَلَىٰٓ أَدْبَٰرِهِم مِّنۢ بَعْدِ مَا تَبَيَّنَ لَهُمُ ٱلْهُدَى ٱلشَّيْطَٰنُ
سَوَّلَ لَهُمْ وَأَمْلَىٰ لَهُمْ ﴿25﴾ ذَٰلِكَ بِأَنَّهُمْ قَالُوا۟ لِلَّذِينَ كَرِهُوا۟ مَا نَزَّلَ ٱللَّهُ
سَنُطِيعُكُمْ فِى بَعْضِ ٱلْأَمْرِ وَٱللَّهُ يَعْلَمُ إِسْرَارَهُمْ ﴿26﴾

Faʾidhāa ʾuñzilat sūratum-muḥkamatuñw-wa dhukira fīhal-qitālu raʾaytal-ladhīna fī qulūbihim-maraḍuñy-yañẓurūna ʾilayka naẓaral-maghshiyyi ʿalayhi minal-mawti faʾawlā lahum. (20) Ṭāʿatuñw-wa qawlum-maʿrūf. Faʾidhā ʿazamal-ʾamru falaw ṣadaqul-lāha lakāna khayral-lahum. (21) Fahal ʿasaytum ʾiñ-tawallaytum ʾañ-tufsidū fil-ʾarḍi wa tuqaṭṭiʿūu ʾarḥāmakum. (22) ʾUlāaʾikal-ladhīna laʿanahumul-lāhu faʾaṣammahum wa ʾaʿmāa ʾabṣārahum. (23) ʾAfalā yatadabbarūnal-Qurʾāna ʾam ʿalā qulūbin ʾaqfāluhā. (24) ʾInnal-ladhīnar-taddū ʿalāa ʾadbārihim-mim-baʿdi mā tabayyana lahumul-hudash-Shayṭānu sawwala lahum wa ʾamlā lahum. (25) Dhālika biʾannahum qālū lilladhīna karihū mā nazzalal-lāhu sanuṭīʿukum fī baʿḍil-ʾamri wal-lāhu yaʿlamu ʾisrārahum. (26)

26 This is a reference to 22 : 39-40. For an explanation of the expression *muḥkamah* ("clear in and by itself"), see note 5 on 3 : 7. (As in the preceding sentence, the term *sūrah* has been rendered here, exceptionally, as "revelation".)

27 I.e., an expression of readiness to fight in His cause: which is obviously the meaning of *qawl maʿrūf* in this context.

28 The above interpolations are in tune with the explanation of this passage advanced by almost all of the classical commentators, who regard this rhetorical "question" as an allusion to the chaotic conditions of pre-Islamic Arabia, its senseless internecine wars, and the moral darkness from which Islam had freed its followers. Nevertheless, this verse has, like the whole of the passage of which it forms a part, a timeless import as well.

29 Cf. the reference to God's "sealing" the hearts of stubborn wrongdoers in 2 : 7.

30 Lit., "this, because . . .", etc.

31 Lit., "in some [or "parts of"] the matter": i.e., "although we cannot agree with you [atheists] as regards your denial of God, or of resurrection, or of the fact of revelation as such, we do agree with you that Muḥammad is an impostor and that the Qurʾān is but his invention" (Rāzī). By "those who turn their backs [on this message] after guidance has been vouchsafed to them" are meant, in the first instance, the hypocrites and half-hearted followers of

hence, how [will they fare] when the angels gather them in death, striking their faces and their backs?[32] ‹27› This, because they were wont to pursue what God condemns, and to hate [whatever would meet with] His goodly acceptance:[33] and so He has caused all their [good] deeds to come to nought. ‹28›

Or do they in whose hearts is disease think, perchance, that God would never bring their moral failings to light?[34] ‹29›

Now had We so willed, We could have shown them clearly to thee, so that thou wouldst know them for sure as by a visible mark:[35] but [even so,] thou wilt most certainly recognize them by the tone of their voice.[36]

And God knows all that you do, [O men;] ‹30› and most certainly We shall try you all, so that We might mark out[37] those of you who strive hard [in Our cause] and are patient in adversity: for We shall put to a test [the truth of] all your assertions.[38] ‹31›

Verily, they who are bent on denying the truth and on barring [others] from the path of God, and [who thus] cut themselves off from the Apostle[39] after guidance has been vouchsafed to them, can in no wise harm God; but He will cause all their deeds to come to nought. ‹32›

فَكَيْفَ إِذَا تَوَفَّتْهُمُ ٱلْمَلَٰٓئِكَةُ يَضْرِبُونَ وُجُوهَهُمْ وَأَدْبَٰرَهُمْ ﴿٢٧﴾ ذَٰلِكَ
بِأَنَّهُمُ ٱتَّبَعُوا۟ مَآ أَسْخَطَ ٱللَّهَ وَكَرِهُوا۟ رِضْوَٰنَهُۥ فَأَحْبَطَ أَعْمَٰلَهُمْ ﴿٢٨﴾ أَمْ
حَسِبَ ٱلَّذِينَ فِى قُلُوبِهِم مَّرَضٌ أَن لَّن يُخْرِجَ ٱللَّهُ أَضْغَٰنَهُمْ ﴿٢٩﴾ وَلَوْ
نَشَآءُ لَأَرَيْنَٰكَهُمْ فَلَعَرَفْتَهُم بِسِيمَٰهُمْ وَلَتَعْرِفَنَّهُمْ فِى لَحْنِ ٱلْقَوْلِ وَٱللَّهُ
يَعْلَمُ أَعْمَٰلَكُمْ ﴿٣٠﴾ وَلَنَبْلُوَنَّكُمْ حَتَّىٰ نَعْلَمَ ٱلْمُجَٰهِدِينَ مِنكُمْ
وَٱلصَّٰبِرِينَ وَنَبْلُوَا۟ أَخْبَارَكُمْ ﴿٣١﴾ إِنَّ ٱلَّذِينَ كَفَرُوا۟ وَصَدُّوا۟ عَن سَبِيلِ
ٱللَّهِ وَشَآقُّوا۟ ٱلرَّسُولَ مِنۢ بَعْدِ مَا تَبَيَّنَ لَهُمُ ٱلْهُدَىٰ لَن يَضُرُّوا۟ ٱللَّهَ شَيْـًٔا
وَسَيُحْبِطُ أَعْمَٰلَهُمْ ﴿٣٢﴾

Fakayfa ʾidhā tawaffat-humul-Malāaʾikatu yaḍribūna wujūhahum wa ʾadbārahum. (27) Dhālika biʾannahumut-tabaʿū māa ʾaskhaṭal-lāha wa karihū riḍwānahū faʾaḥbaṭa ʾaʿmālahum. (28) ʾAm ḥasibal-ladhīna fī qulūbihim-maraḍun ʾallañy-yukhrijal-lāhu ʾaḍghānahum. (29) Wa law nashāaʾu laʾaraynākahum falaʿaraftahum-bisīmāhum. Wa lataʿrifannahum fī laḥnil-qawli wal-lāhu yaʿlamu ʾaʿmālakum. (30) Wa lanabluwannakum ḥattā naʿlamal-mujāhidīna miñkum waṣ-ṣābirīna wa nabluwa ʾakhbārakum. (31) ʾInnal-ladhīna kafarū wa ṣaddū ʿañ-sabīlil-lāhi wa shāaqqur-Rasūla mim-baʿdi mā tabayyana lahumul-hudā lañy-yaḍurrul-lāha shayʾañw-wa sayuḥbiṭu ʾaʿmālahum. (32)

Islam at the time of the Prophet who refused to fight in defence of the Faith; in a wider sense, however, this definition applies to all people, at all times, who are impressed by the teachings of the Qurʾān but nevertheless refuse to accept it as God-inspired and, therefore, morally binding.

32 See note 55 on 8 : 50.

33 See first clause of verse 3 of this *sūrah*, which speaks of the "pursuit of falsehood". In the present instance, "that which would meet with His goodly acceptance" is the believer's readiness to sacrifice, if necessary, his life in the defence of the Faith.

34 The noun *ḍighn* (of which *aḍghān* is the plural) denotes, primarily, "rancour" or "hate"; in its wider sense it signifies a person's "disposition", "inclination" or "leaning", especially in its negative aspects (Jawharī): hence, a "moral defect" or "failing".

35 Lit., "by their marks": implying, elliptically, that God does *not* grant to anyone a clear insight, as by a visible mark, into another human being's heart or mind.

36 Lit., "the tone (*laḥn*) of speech": indicating that a true believer recognizes hypocrisy even without a "visible mark" (*sīmā*).

37 Cf. 3 : 140, where the verb *ʿalama* has been rendered in the same way.

38 Lit., "your announcements" – i.e., all assertions relating to belief. The "test" consists in one's readiness to undergo any sacrifice – and, since most of this *sūrah* deals with the problem of a just war (*jihād*) in God's cause – even the sacrifice of one's life.

39 For the above rendering of *shāqqū*, see note 16 on 8 : 13. The "cutting oneself off" from the Apostle signifies, of course, a rejection of his message, and, in this particular context, a refusal to follow the Qurʾanic call to fight in a just cause, i.e., in defence of the Faith or of freedom (see note 167 on 2 : 190).

يَٰٓأَيُّهَا ٱلَّذِينَ ءَامَنُوٓا۟ أَطِيعُوا۟ ٱللَّهَ وَأَطِيعُوا۟ ٱلرَّسُولَ وَلَا تُبْطِلُوٓا۟
أَعْمَٰلَكُمْ ﴿٣٣﴾ إِنَّ ٱلَّذِينَ كَفَرُوا۟ وَصَدُّوا۟ عَن سَبِيلِ ٱللَّهِ ثُمَّ مَاتُوا۟ وَهُمْ
كُفَّارٌ فَلَن يَغْفِرَ ٱللَّهُ لَهُمْ ﴿٣٤﴾ فَلَا تَهِنُوا۟ وَتَدْعُوٓا۟ إِلَى ٱلسَّلْمِ وَأَنتُمُ
ٱلْأَعْلَوْنَ وَٱللَّهُ مَعَكُمْ وَلَن يَتِرَكُمْ أَعْمَٰلَكُمْ ﴿٣٥﴾ إِنَّمَا ٱلْحَيَوٰةُ ٱلدُّنْيَا
لَعِبٌ وَلَهْوٌ ۚ وَإِن تُؤْمِنُوا۟ وَتَتَّقُوا۟ يُؤْتِكُمْ أُجُورَكُمْ وَلَا يَسْـَٔلْكُمْ
أَمْوَٰلَكُمْ ﴿٣٦﴾ إِن يَسْـَٔلْكُمُوهَا فَيُحْفِكُمْ تَبْخَلُوا۟ وَيُخْرِجْ
أَضْغَٰنَكُمْ ﴿٣٧﴾

ثلاثة ارباع الحزب

Yāa ʾayyuhal-ladhīna ʾāmanūu ʾaṭīʿul-lāha wa ʾaṭīʿur-Rasūla wā lā tubṭilūu ʾaʿmālakum. (33) ʾInnal-ladhīna kafarū wa ṣaddū ʿañ-sabīlil-lāhi thumma mātū wa hum kuffāruñ-falañy-yaghfiral-lāhu lahum. (34) Falā tahinū wa tadʿūu ʾilas-salmi wa ʾañtumul-ʾaʿlawna wal-lāhu maʿakum wa lañy-yatirakum ʾaʿmālakum. (35) ʾInnamal-ḥayātud-dunyā laʿibuñw-wa lahw. Wa ʾiñ-tuʾminū wa tattaqū yuʾtikum ʾujūrakum wa lā yasʾalkum ʾamwālakum. (36) ʾIñy-yasʾalkumūhā fayuḥfikum tabkhalū wa yukhrij ʾaḍghānakum. (37)

O you who have attained to faith! Pay heed unto God, and pay heed unto the Apostle, and let not your [good] deeds come to nought! ‹33›
Verily, as for those who are bent on denying the truth and on barring [others] from the path of God, and then die as deniers of the truth – indeed, God will not grant them forgiveness! ‹34›

AND SO, [when you fight in a just cause,] do not lose heart and [never] beg for peace: for, seeing that God is with you, you are bound to rise high [in the end];[40] and never will He let your [good] deeds go to waste. ‹35›
The life of this world is but a play and a passing delight: but if you believe [in God] and are conscious of Him, He will grant you your deserts.
And withal, He does not demand of you [to sacrifice in His cause all of] your possessions:[41] ‹36› [for,] if He were to demand of you all of them, and urge you,[42] you would niggardly cling [to them], and so He would [but] bring out your moral failings.[43] ‹37›

40 I.e., even if the fortunes of war go against them, the consciousness of having fought in the cause of truth and justice is bound to enhance the inner strength of the believers and, thus, to become a source of their future greatness: cf. 3 : 139.

41 Although the life of this world is "but a play and a passing delight", God does not want to deprive the believers of its rightful enjoyment: and so He expects them to sacrifice only a small part of their possessions in His cause. This passage evidently foreshadows the imposition of the obligatory annual tax called *zakāh* ("the purifying dues"), amounting to about $2^1/2$ percent of a Muslims's income and property, as pointed out by most of the classical commentators in connection with the above verse (hence my interpolation). The proceeds of this tax are to be utilized in what the Qurʾān describes as "the cause [lit., "way"] of God", i.e., for the defence and propagation of the Faith and the welfare of the community; and its spiritual purpose is the "purification" of a Muslim's possessions from the blemish of greed and selfishness. (It is to be noted that the payment of *zakāh* was made obligatory at the very beginning of the Medina period, that is, at approximately the same time as the revelation of the present *sūrah*.)

42 Sc., "to divest yourselves of all your possessions".

43 For my rendering of *aḍghān* as "moral failings", see note 34. In the present context this term has more or less the same meaning as the term *fujūr* in 91 : 8. The implication is that since "man has been created weak" (4 : 28), the imposition of too great a burden on the believers would be self-defeating inasmuch as it might result not in an increase of faith but, rather, in its diminution. This passage illustrates the supreme realism of the Qurʾān, which takes into account human nature as it is, with all its God-willed complexity and its inner contradictions, and does not, therefore, postulate *a priori* an impossible ideal as a norm of human behaviour. (Cf. 91 : 8, which speaks of man's personality as "imbued with moral failings as well as consciousness of God" – a phrase which is explained in the corresponding note 6.)

هَٰٓأَنتُمْ هَٰٓؤُلَآءِ تُدْعَوْنَ لِتُنفِقُوا۟ فِى سَبِيلِ ٱللَّهِ فَمِنكُم مَّن يَبْخَلُ ۖ وَمَن
يَبْخَلْ فَإِنَّمَا يَبْخَلُ عَن نَّفْسِهِۦ ۚ وَٱللَّهُ ٱلْغَنِىُّ وَأَنتُمُ ٱلْفُقَرَآءُ ۚ وَإِن تَتَوَلَّوْا۟
يَسْتَبْدِلْ قَوْمًا غَيْرَكُمْ ثُمَّ لَا يَكُونُوٓا۟ أَمْثَٰلَكُم ﴿38﴾

Hāa᾿añtum hāa᾿ulāa᾿i tudᶜawna lituñfiqū fī sabīlil-lāhi famiñkum-mañy-yabkhalu wa mañy-yabkhal fa᾿innamā yabkhalu ᶜañ-nafsih. Wal-lāhul-Ghaniyyu wa ᾿añtumul-fuqarāa᾿. Wa ᾿iñ-tatawallaw yastabdil qawman ghayrakum thumma lā yakūnūu ᾿amthālakum. ﴿38﴾

Behold, [O believers,] it is you who are called upon to spend freely in God's cause: but [even] among you are such as turn out to be niggardly! And yet, he who acts niggardly [in God's cause] is but niggardly towards his own self: for God is indeed self-sufficient, whereas you stand in need [of Him]; and if you turn away [from Him], He will cause other people to take your place, and they will not be the likes of you! ‹38›

The Forty-Eighth Sūrah

Al-Fatḥ (Victory)

Medina Period

TOWARDS the end of the sixth year of the *hijrah*, the Prophet decided to perform, accompanied by his followers, the "lesser pilgrimage" or "pious visit" (*ᶜumrah*) to Mecca. Although for nearly six years there had been a more or less permanent state of war between the Muslim community at Medina and the pagan oligarchy of Mecca, the Prophet did not anticipate any hostilities on that occasion, since the month of Dhu 'l-Qaᶜdah, in which he intended to reach Mecca, was one of the four "sacred months" during which, in accordance with time-honoured Arabian custom, all warfare was outlawed, and particularly so in and around the Holy City. A call was issued to some of the allied bedouin tribes in the vicinity of Medina to join the Prophet on this pilgrimage, but most of them excused themselves on some pretext or other (see note 10 on verse 11 of this *sūrah*). Thus, the Prophet's party which set out for Mecca consisted of only 1400-1500 men, all of them dressed in the pilgrim's garb (*iḥrām*) and, apart from their sheathed swords, unarmed.

On learning of the Prophet's approach, the Meccans decided – against all Arabian tradition – to oppose the entry of the pilgrims by force of arms. A detachment of two hundred horsemen under the command of Khālid ibn al-Walīd (who was destined to embrace Islam less than two years later) was sent out to intercept the Prophet's party, while several thousand heavily-armed men took up positions around Mecca. Since the Prophet was neither inclined nor in a position to give battle, he turned westwards from Bīr ᶜUsfān (a place about one day's journey from Mecca) and alighted on the plain of Al-Ḥudaybiyyah, where he and his followers remained for the next few days. There and then negotiations were opened between the Muslims and the Meccan oligarchy. After some preliminary discussions conducted by various emissaries of both parties, the Prophet sent ᶜUthmān ibn ᶜAffān (who belonged to one of the most influential Meccan clans) as his envoy. Shortly after ᶜUthmān's arrival in Mecca, a rumour that he had been murdered reached the Muslim camp at Ḥudaybiyyah. Thereupon the Prophet, expecting a treacherous attack by the Meccans, assembled his followers and, sitting under a wild acacia tree, took, amid scenes of the greatest enthusiasm, a pledge from each one of his followers that they would remain steadfast and fight unto death; and after the revelation of verse 18 of this *sūrah*, this "Pledge of the Tree" became known to history as *Bayᶜat ar-Riḍwān* ("the Pledge of [God's] Goodly Acceptance").

When a few days later the rumour of ᶜUthmān's death proved false and he himself returned to Ḥudaybiyyah, it became clear that the Meccans were prepared to conclude a truce. A treaty was drawn up, stipulating, among other provisions, that all warfare between Mecca and Medina should be suspended for ten years, and that the Prophet and his followers should refrain from entering Mecca that year, but would be free to do so the following year. The Prophet also agreed that if a Meccan minor or any other person under guardianship should go over to the Muslims without the permission of his guardian, he would be returned to the latter; but should any follower of the Prophet – whether minor or of age – go over to the Quraysh of his own free will, he or she would not be returned. Although this last stipulation appeared at first glance to be disadvantageous to the Muslims, it is obvious that the Prophet agreed to it in pursuance of the principle that "there shall be no coercion in matters of faith" (2 : 256).

The Truce of Ḥudaybiyyah was to prove of the greatest importance to the future of Islam. For the first time in six years peaceful contacts were established between Mecca and Medina, and thus the way was opened to the penetration of Islamic ideas into the citadel of Arabian paganism. The Meccans who had occasion to visit the Muslim camp at Ḥudaybiyyah returned deeply impressed by the spirit and the unity of Muḥammad's followers, and many of them began to waver in their hostility towards the faith preached by him. As soon as the perennial warfare came to an end and people of both sides could meet freely, new converts rallied around the Prophet, first in tens, then in hundreds, then in thousands – so much so that when the pagan Quraysh broke the truce two years after its conclusion, the Prophet could and did occupy Mecca almost without resistance. Thus, in fact if not in appearance, the Truce of Ḥudaybiyyah ushered in the moral and political victory of Islam over all Arabia.

In the consensus of all the authorities, the *sūrah* commemorating this victory was revealed during the Prophet's return march from Ḥudaybiyyah to Medina.

سورة الفتح مدنية

-48-

وآياتها تسع وعشرون

IN THE NAME OF GOD, THE MOST GRACIOUS, THE DISPENSER OF GRACE:

بِسْمِ ٱللَّهِ ٱلرَّحْمَٰنِ ٱلرَّحِيمِ

VERILY, [O Muḥammad,] We have laid open before thee a manifest victory,[1] «1» so that God might show His forgiveness of all thy faults, past as well as future,[2] and [thus] bestow upon thee the full measure of His blessings, and guide thee on a straight way,[3] «2» and [show] that God will succour thee with [His] mighty succour. «3»

It is He who from on high has bestowed inner peace upon the hearts of the believers,[4] so that – seeing that God's are all the forces of the heavens and the earth, and that God is all-knowing, truly wise – they might grow yet more firm in their faith.[5] «4» [and] that He might admit the believers, both men and women, into gardens through which running waters flow, therein to abide, and that He might efface their [past] bad deeds: and that is, in the sight of God, indeed a triumph supreme! «5»

And [God has willed] to impose suffering [in the life to come] on the hypocrites, both men and women, and on those who ascribe divinity to aught beside Him,

إِنَّا فَتَحْنَا لَكَ فَتْحًا مُّبِينًا ﴿١﴾ لِّيَغْفِرَ لَكَ ٱللَّهُ مَا تَقَدَّمَ مِن ذَنۢبِكَ وَمَا
تَأَخَّرَ وَيُتِمَّ نِعْمَتَهُۥ عَلَيْكَ وَيَهْدِيَكَ صِرَٰطًا مُّسْتَقِيمًا ﴿٢﴾ وَيَنصُرَكَ ٱللَّهُ
نَصْرًا عَزِيزًا ﴿٣﴾ هُوَ ٱلَّذِىٓ أَنزَلَ ٱلسَّكِينَةَ فِى قُلُوبِ ٱلْمُؤْمِنِينَ
لِيَزْدَادُوٓا۟ إِيمَٰنًا مَّعَ إِيمَٰنِهِمْ ۗ وَلِلَّهِ جُنُودُ ٱلسَّمَٰوَٰتِ وَٱلْأَرْضِ ۚ وَكَانَ ٱللَّهُ
عَلِيمًا حَكِيمًا ﴿٤﴾ لِّيُدْخِلَ ٱلْمُؤْمِنِينَ وَٱلْمُؤْمِنَٰتِ جَنَّٰتٍ تَجْرِى مِن
تَحْتِهَا ٱلْأَنْهَٰرُ خَٰلِدِينَ فِيهَا وَيُكَفِّرَ عَنْهُمْ سَيِّـَٔاتِهِمْ ۚ وَكَانَ ذَٰلِكَ عِندَ
ٱللَّهِ فَوْزًا عَظِيمًا ﴿٥﴾ وَيُعَذِّبَ ٱلْمُنَٰفِقِينَ وَٱلْمُنَٰفِقَٰتِ وَٱلْمُشْرِكِينَ

Bismil-lāhir-Raḥmānir-Raḥīm.

ʾInnā fataḥnā laka fatḥam-mubīnā. (1) Liyaghfira lakal-lāhu mā taqaddama miñ-dhambika wa mā taʾakhkhara wa yutimma niᶜmatahū ᶜalayka wa yahdiyaka ṣirāṭam-mustaqīmā. (2) Wa yañṣurakal-lāhu naṣran ᶜazīzā. (3) Huwal-ladhīi ʾañzalas-sakīnata fī qulūbil-muʾminīna liyazdādūu ʾīmānam-maᶜa ʾīmānihim. Wa lillāhi junūdus-samāwāti wal-ʾarḍi wa kānal-lāhu ᶜAlīman Ḥakhīmā. (4) Liyudkhilal-muʾminīna wal-muʾmināti jannātiñ-tajrī miñ-taḥtihal-ʾanhāru khālidīna fīhā wa yukaffira ᶜanhum sayyiʾātihim; wa kāna dhālika ᶜiñdal-lāhi fawzan ᶜaẓīmā. (5) Wa yuᶜadhdhibal-munāfiqīna wal-munāfiqāti wal-mushrikīna

---

1 Namely, the moral victory achieved by the Truce of Ḥudaybiyyah which opened the doors to the subsequent triumph of Islam in Arabia (see introductory note, which explains many allusions to this historic event found in the subsequent verses).

2 Lit., "so that God might forgive thee all that is past of thy sins and all that is yet to come" – thus indicating elliptically that freedom from faults is an exclusive prerogative of God, and that every human being, however exalted, is bound to err on occasion.

3 Sc., "to a fulfilment of thy mission", which the Truce of Ḥudaybiyyah clearly presaged.

4 I.e., endowed them, although they were few and practically unarmed, with calm courage in the face of the much more powerful forces of the enemy.

5 Lit., "so that they might add faith to their faith, seeing that God's are . . .", etc. Since the latter is obviously a parenthetic clause, I have transposed it in my rendering in order to make the meaning clear.

both men and women: all who entertain evil thoughts about God.[6] Evil encompasses them from all sides, and God's condemnation rests upon them; and He has rejected them [from His grace], and has readied hell for them: and how evil a journey's end! ‹6›
For, God's are all the forces of the heavens and the earth; and God is indeed almighty, truly wise! ‹7›

VERILY, [O Muḥammad,] We have sent thee as a witness [to the truth], and as a herald of glad tidings and a warner ‹8› – so that you [O men] might believe in God and His Apostle, and might honour Him, and revere Him, and extol His limitless glory from morn to evening.[7] ‹9›
Behold, all who pledge their allegiance to thee pledge their allegiance to God: the hand of God is over their hands.[8] Hence, he who breaks his oath, breaks it only to his own hurt; whereas he who remains true to what he has pledged unto God, on him will He bestow a reward supreme. ‹10›
Those of the bedouin who stayed behind[9] will say unto thee: "[The need to take care of] our chattels and our families kept us busy: do then, [O Prophet,] ask God to forgive us!" [Thus,] they will utter with their tongues something that is not in their hearts.[10]

وَٱلْمُشْرِكَٰتِ ٱلظَّآنِّينَ بِٱللَّهِ ظَنَّ ٱلسَّوْءِ ۚ عَلَيْهِمْ دَآئِرَةُ ٱلسَّوْءِ ۖ وَغَضِبَ ٱللَّهُ
عَلَيْهِمْ وَلَعَنَهُمْ وَأَعَدَّ لَهُمْ جَهَنَّمَ ۖ وَسَآءَتْ مَصِيرًا ﴿6﴾ وَلِلَّهِ جُنُودُ
ٱلسَّمَٰوَٰتِ وَٱلْأَرْضِ ۚ وَكَانَ ٱللَّهُ عَزِيزًا حَكِيمًا ﴿7﴾ إِنَّآ أَرْسَلْنَٰكَ شَٰهِدًا
وَمُبَشِّرًا وَنَذِيرًا ﴿8﴾ لِّتُؤْمِنُوا۟ بِٱللَّهِ وَرَسُولِهِۦ وَتُعَزِّرُوهُ وَتُوَقِّرُوهُ وَتُسَبِّحُوهُ
بُكْرَةً وَأَصِيلًا ﴿9﴾ إِنَّ ٱلَّذِينَ يُبَايِعُونَكَ إِنَّمَا يُبَايِعُونَ ٱللَّهَ يَدُ ٱللَّهِ فَوْقَ
أَيْدِيهِمْ ۚ فَمَن نَّكَثَ فَإِنَّمَا يَنكُثُ عَلَىٰ نَفْسِهِۦ ۖ وَمَنْ أَوْفَىٰ بِمَا عَٰهَدَ عَلَيْهُ
ٱللَّهَ فَسَيُؤْتِيهِ أَجْرًا عَظِيمًا ﴿10﴾ سَيَقُولُ لَكَ ٱلْمُخَلَّفُونَ مِنَ ٱلْأَعْرَابِ
شَغَلَتْنَآ أَمْوَٰلُنَا وَأَهْلُونَا فَٱسْتَغْفِرْ لَنَا ۚ يَقُولُونَ بِأَلْسِنَتِهِم مَّا لَيْسَ فِى قُلُوبِهِمْ ۚ

wal-mushrikātiẓ-ẓāannīna billāhi ẓannas-sawᵓ. ᶜAlayhim dāaᵓiratus-sawᵓi wa ghaḍibal-lāhu ᶜalayhim wa laᶜanahum wa ᵓaᶜadda lahum jahannama wa sāaᵓat maṣīrā. (6) Wa lillāhi junūdus-samāwāti wal-ᵓarḍi wa kānal-lāhu ᶜAzīzan Ḥakīmā. (7) ᵓInnāa ᵓarsalnāka Shāhidañw-wa Mubashshirañw-wa Nadhīrā. (8) Lituᵓminū billāhi wa Rasūlihī wa tuᶜazzirūhu wa tuwaqqirūhu wa tusabbiḥūhu bukratañw-wa ᵓaṣīlā. (9) ᵓInnal-ladhīna yubāyiᶜūnaka ᵓinnamā yubāyiᶜūnal-lāha yadul-lāhi fawqa ᵓaydīhim. Famañnakath faᵓinnamā yañkuthu ᶜalā nafsih. Wa man ᵓawfā bimā ᶜāhada ᶜalayhul-lāha fasayuᵓtīhi ᵓajran ᶜaẓīmā. (10) Sayaqūlu lakal-mukhallafūna minal-ᵓaᶜrābi shaghalatnāa ᵓamwālunā wa ᵓahlūnā fastaghfir lanā. Yaqūlūna biᵓalsinatihim-mā laysa fī qulūbihim.

6 I.e., who deny His existence or man's responsibility to Him, or offend against the concept of His oneness.

7 Lit., "at morn and evening", i.e., at all times.

8 This refers, in the first instance, to the pledge of faith and allegiance (*bayᶜat ar-riḍwān*) which the Muslims assembled at Ḥudaybiyyah gave to the Prophet (see introductory note). Beyond this historical allusion, however, the above sentence implies that as one's faith in God's message-bearer is to all intents and purposes synonymous with a declaration of faith in God Himself, so does one's willingness to obey God necessarily imply a willingness to obey His message-bearer. – The phrase "the hand of God is over their hands" does not merely allude to the hand-clasp with which all of the Prophet's followers affirmed their allegiance to him, but is also a metaphor for His being a witness to their pledge.

9 Lit., "who were left behind": i.e., the bedouin belonging to the tribes of Ghifār, Muzaynah, Juhaynah, Ashjaᶜ, Aslam and Dhayl, who, although allied with the Prophet and outwardly professing Islam, refused under various pretexts to accompany him on his march to Mecca (which resulted in the Truce of Ḥudaybiyyah), since they were convinced that the Meccans would give battle and destroy the unarmed Muslims (Zamakhsharī). The excuses mentioned in the sequence were made after the Prophet's and his followers' successful return to Medina; hence the future tense, *sayaqūl*.

10 Implying that the excuses which they would proffer would be purely hypocritical.

Say: "Who, then, has it in his power to avert from you aught that God may have willed,[11] whether it be His will to harm you or to confer a benefit on you? Nay, but God is fully aware of what you do! ‹11›

Nay, you thought that the Apostle and the believers would never return to their kith and kin: and this seemed goodly to your hearts.[12] And you entertained [such] evil thoughts because you have always been people devoid of all good!" ‹12›

Now as for those who will not believe in God and His Apostle – verily, We have readied a blazing flame for all [such] deniers of the truth! ‹13›

But God's is the dominion over the heavens and the earth: He forgives whomever He wills, and imposes suffering on whomever He wills – and [withal,] He is indeed much-forgiving, a dispenser of grace.[13] ‹14›

As soon as you [O believers] are about to set forth on a war that promises booty,[14] those who stayed behind [aforetime] will surely say, "Allow us to go with you" – [thus showing that] they would like to alter the Word of God.[15]

Say: "By no means shall you go with us: God has declared aforetime[16] [to whom all spoils shall belong].

Thereupon they will [surely] answer, "Nay, but you begrudge us [our share of booty]!" Nay, they can grasp but so little of the truth! ‹15›

قُلْ فَمَن يَمْلِكُ لَكُم مِّنَ ٱللَّهِ شَيْـًٔا إِنْ أَرَادَ بِكُمْ ضَرًّا أَوْ أَرَادَ بِكُمْ
نَفْعًۢا ۚ بَلْ كَانَ ٱللَّهُ بِمَا تَعْمَلُونَ خَبِيرًۢا ﴿11﴾ بَلْ ظَنَنتُمْ أَن لَّن يَنقَلِبَ
ٱلرَّسُولُ وَٱلْمُؤْمِنُونَ إِلَىٰٓ أَهْلِيهِمْ أَبَدًا وَزُيِّنَ ذَٰلِكَ فِى قُلُوبِكُمْ وَظَنَنتُمْ
ظَنَّ ٱلسَّوْءِ وَكُنتُمْ قَوْمًۢا بُورًا ﴿12﴾ وَمَن لَّمْ يُؤْمِنۢ بِٱللَّهِ وَرَسُولِهِۦ فَإِنَّآ
أَعْتَدْنَا لِلْكَٰفِرِينَ سَعِيرًا ﴿13﴾ وَلِلَّهِ مُلْكُ ٱلسَّمَٰوَٰتِ وَٱلْأَرْضِ ۚ يَغْفِرُ
لِمَن يَشَآءُ وَيُعَذِّبُ مَن يَشَآءُ ۚ وَكَانَ ٱللَّهُ غَفُورًا رَّحِيمًا ﴿14﴾ سَيَقُولُ
ٱلْمُخَلَّفُونَ إِذَا ٱنطَلَقْتُمْ إِلَىٰ مَغَانِمَ لِتَأْخُذُوهَا ذَرُونَا نَتَّبِعْكُمْ ۖ يُرِيدُونَ أَن
يُبَدِّلُوا۟ كَلَٰمَ ٱللَّهِ ۚ قُل لَّن تَتَّبِعُونَا كَذَٰلِكُمْ قَالَ ٱللَّهُ مِن قَبْلُ ۖ فَسَيَقُولُونَ
بَلْ تَحْسُدُونَنَا ۚ بَلْ كَانُوا۟ لَا يَفْقَهُونَ إِلَّا قَلِيلًا ﴿15﴾

Qul famañy-yamliku lakum-minal-lāhi shayʾan ʾin ʾarāda bikum ḍarran ʾaw ʾarāda bikum nafʿā. Bal kānal-lāhu bimā taʿmalūna Khabīrā. (11) Bal ẓanañtum ʾal-lañy-yañqalibar-Rasūlu wal-muʾminūna ʾilāa ʾahlīhim ʾabadañw-wa zuyyina dhālika fī qulūbikum wa ẓanañtum ẓannas-sawʾi wa kuñtum qawmam-būrā. (12) Wa mal-lam yuʾmim-billāhi wa Rasūlihī faʾinnāa ʾaʿtadnā lilkāfirīna saʿīrā. (13) Wa lillāhi mulkus-samāwāti wal-ʾarḍ. Yaghfiru limañy-yashāaʾu wa yuʿadhdhibu mañy-yashāaʾu wa kānal-lāhu Ghafūrar-Raḥīmā. (14) Sayaqūlul-mukhallafūna ʾidhañ-ṭalaqtum ʾilā maghānima litaʾkhudhūhā dharūnā nattabiʿkum; yurīdūna ʾañy-yubaddilū kalāmal-lāh. Qul lañ-tattabiʿūnā kadhālikum qālal-lāhu miñ-qabl. Fasayaqūlūna bal taḥsudūnanā; bal kānū lā yafqahūna ʾillā qalīlā. (15)

11 Lit., "has anything in his power [that could be obtained] in your behalf from God": a construction which, in order to become meaningful in translation, necessitates a paraphrase.

12 Implying that the real sympathies of those bedouin were with the pagan Quraysh rather than with the Muslims.

13 Implying that He may forgive even the most hardened sinners if they truly repent and mend their ways: an allusion to what the Prophet was to say according to verse 16.

14 Lit., "set forth to take booty": i.e., any expedition other than against the Quraysh of Mecca, with whom the Prophet had just concluded a truce. This is generally taken as an allusion to the forthcoming war against the Jews of Khaybar (in the year 7 H.), but the meaning may well be more general.

15 Evidently a reference to 8 : 1 – "All spoils of war belong to God and the Apostle" – which, as pointed out in note 1 on that verse, implies that no individual warrior can have any *claim* to the booty obtained in war. Moreover, fighting for the sake of booty contravenes the very principle of a "war in God's cause", which may be waged only in defence of faith or liberty (cf. *sūrah* 2, note 167), "until there is no more oppression and all worship is devoted to God alone" (see 2 : 193 and the corresponding note 170). It is to these principles, too, that the Prophet's anticipated answer, mentioned in the sequence, refers.

16 I.e., in the first verse of *Al-Anfāl*, which was revealed in the year 2 H. (see preceding note).

Say unto those bedouin who stayed behind: "In time you will be called upon [to fight] against people of great prowess in war:[17] you will have to fight against them [until you die] or they surrender. And then, if you heed [that call], God will bestow on you a goodly reward; but if you turn away as you turned away this time,[18] He will chastise you with grievous chastisement." ‹16›

No blame attaches to the blind, nor does blame attach to the lame, nor does blame attach to the sick [for staying away from a war in God's cause];[19] but whoever heeds [the call of] God and His Apostle [in deed or in heart[20]], him will He admit into gardens through which running waters flow; whereas him who turns away will He chastise with grievous chastisement. ‹17›

52 حزب

INDEED, well-pleased was God with the believers when they pledged their allegiance unto thee [O Muḥammad] under that tree,[21] for He knew what was in their hearts; and so He bestowed inner peace upon them from on high, and rewarded them with [the glad tiding of] a victory soon to come[22] ‹18› and [of] many war-gains which they would achieve: for God is indeed almighty, wise. ‹19›

[O you who believe!] God has promised you many war-gains which you shall yet achieve; and He has vouchsafed you these [worldly gains] well in advance,[23] and has stayed from you the hands of [hostile]

قُل لِّلْمُخَلَّفِينَ مِنَ ٱلْأَعْرَابِ سَتُدْعَوْنَ إِلَىٰ قَوْمٍ أُو۟لِى بَأْسٍ شَدِيدٍ
تُقَٰتِلُونَهُمْ أَوْ يُسْلِمُونَ ۖ فَإِن تُطِيعُوا۟ يُؤْتِكُمُ ٱللَّهُ أَجْرًا حَسَنًا ۖ وَإِن تَتَوَلَّوْا۟
كَمَا تَوَلَّيْتُم مِّن قَبْلُ يُعَذِّبْكُمْ عَذَابًا أَلِيمًا ﴿١٦﴾ لَّيْسَ عَلَى ٱلْأَعْمَىٰ حَرَجٌ
وَلَا عَلَى ٱلْأَعْرَجِ حَرَجٌ وَلَا عَلَى ٱلْمَرِيضِ حَرَجٌ ۗ وَمَن يُطِعِ ٱللَّهَ وَرَسُولَهُۥ
يُدْخِلْهُ جَنَّٰتٍ تَجْرِى مِن تَحْتِهَا ٱلْأَنْهَٰرُ ۖ وَمَن يَتَوَلَّ يُعَذِّبْهُ عَذَابًا
أَلِيمًا ﴿١٧﴾ ۞ لَّقَدْ رَضِىَ ٱللَّهُ عَنِ ٱلْمُؤْمِنِينَ إِذْ يُبَايِعُونَكَ تَحْتَ ٱلشَّجَرَةِ
فَعَلِمَ مَا فِى قُلُوبِهِمْ فَأَنزَلَ ٱلسَّكِينَةَ عَلَيْهِمْ وَأَثَٰبَهُمْ فَتْحًا قَرِيبًا ﴿١٨﴾
وَمَغَانِمَ كَثِيرَةً يَأْخُذُونَهَا ۗ وَكَانَ ٱللَّهُ عَزِيزًا حَكِيمًا ﴿١٩﴾ وَعَدَكُمُ ٱللَّهُ
مَغَانِمَ كَثِيرَةً تَأْخُذُونَهَا فَعَجَّلَ لَكُمْ هَٰذِهِۦ وَكَفَّ أَيْدِىَ ٱلنَّاسِ عَنكُمْ

Qul lilmukhallafīna minal-ʾaʿrābi satudʿawna ʾilā qawmin ʾulī baʾsiñ-shadīdiñ-tuqātilūnahum ʾaw yuslimūn. Faʾiñ-tuṭīʿū yuʾtikumul-lāhu ʾajran ḥasanā. Wa ʾiñ-tatawallaw kamā tawallaytum-miñ-qablu yuʿadhdhibkum ʿadhāban ʾalīmā. (16) Laysa ʿalal-ʾaʿmā ḥarajuñw-wa lā ʿalal-ʾaʿraji ḥarajuñw-wa lā ʿalal-marīḍi ḥaraj. Wa mañy-yuṭiʿil-lāha wa Rasūlahū yudkhilhu jannātiñ-tajrī miñ-taḥtihal-ʾanhāru wa mañy-yatawalla yuʿadhdhibhu ʿadhāban ʾalīmā. (17)
◈ Laqad raḍiyal-lāhu ʿanil-muʾminīna ʾidh yubāyiʿūnaka taḥtash-shajarati faʿalima mā fī qulūbihim faʾañzalas-sakīnata ʿalayhim wa athābahum fatḥañ-qarībā. (18) Wa maghānima kathīratañy-yaʾkhudhūnahā. Wa kānal-lāhu ʿAzīzan Ḥakīmā. (19) Waʿadakumul-lāhu maghānima kathīratañ-taʾkhudhūnahā faʿajjala lakum hādhihī wa kaffa ʾaydiyan-nāsi ʿañkum

17 This is evidently a prophecy relating to the future wars against Byzantium and Persia.

18 Lit., "before", i.e., at the time of the expedition which resulted in the Truce of Ḥudaybiyyah.

19 These three categories circumscribe metonymically *all* kinds of infirmities or disabilities which may prevent a person from actively participating in a war in God's cause.

20 This latter applies, by obvious implication, to such as are unable to participate in the fighting physically, but are in their hearts with those who fight.

21 I.e., at Ḥudaybiyyah (see introductory note).

22 Most of the commentators assume that this relates to the conquest of Khaybar, which took place a few months after the Truce of Ḥudaybiyyah. It is probable, however, that the implication is much wider than that – namely, a prophecy of the almost bloodless conquest of Mecca in the year 8 H., the victorious establishment of Islam in all of Arabia and, finally, the tremendous expansion of the Islamic Commonwealth under the Prophet's immediate successors.

23 Se., "of what is to come to you in the hereafter".

people, so that this [your inner strength] may become a symbol to the believers [who will come after you[24]], and that He may guide you all on a straight way. «20»
And there are yet other [gains] which are still beyond your grasp,[25] [but] which God has already encompassed [for you]: for God has the power to will anything. «21»
And [now,] if they who are bent on denying the truth should fight against you, they will indeed turn their backs [in flight], and will find none to protect them and none to bring them succour:[26] «22» such being God's way which has ever obtained in the past – and never wilt thou find any change in God's way![27] «23»
And He it is who, in the valley of Mecca, stayed their hands from you, and your hands from them, after He had enabled you to vanquish them; and God saw indeed what you were doing.[28] «24»
[It was not for your enemies' sake that He stayed your hands from them:[29] for] it was they who were bent on denying the truth, and who debarred you from the Inviolable House of Worship[30] and prevented your offering from reaching its destination.[31] And had it not been for the believing men and believing women [in Mecca], whom you might have unwittingly trampled underfoot,[32] and on whose account you might have become guilty, without knowing it,

وَلِتَكُونَ ءَايَةً لِّلْمُؤْمِنِينَ وَيَهْدِيَكُمْ صِرَٰطًا مُّسْتَقِيمًا ﴿٢٠﴾ وَأُخْرَىٰ لَمْ
تَقْدِرُوا۟ عَلَيْهَا قَدْ أَحَاطَ ٱللَّهُ بِهَا ۚ وَكَانَ ٱللَّهُ عَلَىٰ كُلِّ شَىْءٍ قَدِيرًا ﴿٢١﴾
وَلَوْ قَٰتَلَكُمُ ٱلَّذِينَ كَفَرُوا۟ لَوَلَّوُا۟ ٱلْأَدْبَٰرَ ثُمَّ لَا يَجِدُونَ وَلِيًّا وَلَا نَصِيرًا ﴿٢٢﴾
سُنَّةَ ٱللَّهِ ٱلَّتِى قَدْ خَلَتْ مِن قَبْلُ ۖ وَلَن تَجِدَ لِسُنَّةِ ٱللَّهِ تَبْدِيلًا ﴿٢٣﴾ وَهُوَ ٱلَّذِى
كَفَّ أَيْدِيَهُمْ عَنكُمْ وَأَيْدِيَكُمْ عَنْهُم بِبَطْنِ مَكَّةَ مِنۢ بَعْدِ أَنْ أَظْفَرَكُمْ
عَلَيْهِمْ ۚ وَكَانَ ٱللَّهُ بِمَا تَعْمَلُونَ بَصِيرًا ﴿٢٤﴾ هُمُ ٱلَّذِينَ كَفَرُوا۟ وَصَدُّوكُمْ عَنِ
ٱلْمَسْجِدِ ٱلْحَرَامِ وَٱلْهَدْىَ مَعْكُوفًا أَن يَبْلُغَ مَحِلَّهُۥ ۚ وَلَوْلَا رِجَالٌ مُّؤْمِنُونَ
وَنِسَآءٌ مُّؤْمِنَٰتٌ لَّمْ تَعْلَمُوهُمْ أَن تَطَـُٔوهُمْ فَتُصِيبَكُم مِّنْهُم مَّعَرَّةٌۢ بِغَيْرِ عِلْمٍ ۖ

wa litakūna ʾāyatal-lilmuʾminīna wa yahdiyakum ṣirāṭam-mustaqīmā. (20) Wa ʾukhrā lam taqdirū ᶜalayhā qad ʾaḥāṭal-lāhu bihā; wa kānal-lāhu ᶜalā kulli shayʾiñ-Qadīrā. (21) Wa law qātalakumul-ladhīna kafarū lawallawul-ʾadbāra thumma lā yajidūna waliyyañw-wa lā naṣīrā. (22) Sunnatal-lāhil-latī qad khalat miñ-qablu wa lañ-tajida lisunnatil-lāhi tabdīlā. (23) Wa Huwal-ladhī kaffa ʾaydiyahum ᶜañkum wa ʾaydiyakum ᶜanhum-bibaṭni Makkata mim-baᶜdi ʾan ʾaẓfarakum ᶜalayhim; wa kānal-lāhu bimā taᶜmalūna Baṣīrā. (24) Humul-ladhīna kafarū wa ṣaddūkum ᶜanil-Masjidil-Ḥarāmi wal-hadya maᶜkūfan ʾañy-yablugha maḥillah. Wa lawlā rijālum-muʾminūna wa nisāaʾum-muʾminātul-lam taᶜlamūhum ʾañ-taṭaʾūhum fatuṣībakum-minhum-maᶜarratum-bighayri ᶜilm.

24 Thus Rāzī.

25 I.e., the achievement of final bliss in the life to come.

26 This divine promise was fulfilled in the unbroken sequence of Muslim victories after the Truce of Ḥudaybiyyah, ultimately leading to the establishment of an empire which extended from the Atlantic Ocean to the confines of China. – For the *conditional* nature of the above promise, see note 82 on 3 : 111.

27 This reference to "God's way" (*sunnat Allāh*) is twofold: on the one hand, "you are bound to rise high if you are [truly] believers" (3 : 139), and, on the other, "God does not change men's condition unless they change their inner selves" (13 : 11), in both the positive and negative connotations of the concept of "change".

28 Shortly before the Truce of Ḥudaybiyyah was concluded, a detachment of Quraysh warriors – variously estimated at between thirty and eighty men – attacked the Prophet's camp, but his practically unarmed followers overcame them and took them prisoner; after the signing of the treaty the Prophet released them unharmed (Muslim, Nasāʾī, Ṭabarī).

29 This interpolation is based on Rāzī's explanation of the connection between this and the preceding verse.

30 I.e., the Kaᶜbah, which, until the year 7 H., the Muslims were not allowed to approach.

31 See *sūrah* 2, note 175.

32 I.e., killed. After the Prophet's and his followers' exodus to Medina, a number of Meccans – both men and women – had embraced Islam, but had been prevented by the pagan Quraysh from emigrating (Ṭabarī, Zamakhsharī). Their identities were not generally known to the Muslims of Medina.

لِّيُدْخِلَ ٱللَّهُ فِى رَحْمَتِهِۦ مَن يَشَآءُ ۚ لَوْ تَزَيَّلُوا۟ لَعَذَّبْنَا ٱلَّذِينَ كَفَرُوا۟ مِنْهُمْ
عَذَابًا أَلِيمًا ﴿٢٥﴾ إِذْ جَعَلَ ٱلَّذِينَ كَفَرُوا۟ فِى قُلُوبِهِمُ ٱلْحَمِيَّةَ حَمِيَّةَ
ٱلْجَٰهِلِيَّةِ فَأَنزَلَ ٱللَّهُ سَكِينَتَهُۥ عَلَىٰ رَسُولِهِۦ وَعَلَى ٱلْمُؤْمِنِينَ وَأَلْزَمَهُمْ كَلِمَةَ
ٱلتَّقْوَىٰ وَكَانُوٓا۟ أَحَقَّ بِهَا وَأَهْلَهَا ۚ وَكَانَ ٱللَّهُ بِكُلِّ شَىْءٍ عَلِيمًا ﴿٢٦﴾ لَّقَدْ صَدَقَ
ٱللَّهُ رَسُولَهُ ٱلرُّءْيَا بِٱلْحَقِّ ۖ لَتَدْخُلُنَّ ٱلْمَسْجِدَ ٱلْحَرَامَ إِن شَآءَ ٱللَّهُ ءَامِنِينَ

Liyudkhilal-lāhu fī raḥmatihī mañy-yashāaʾ. Law tazayyalū laʿadhdhabnal-ladhīna kafarū minhum ʿadhāban ʾalīmā. (25) ʾIdh jaʿalal-ladhīna kafarū fī qulūbihimul-ḥamiyyata ḥamiyyatal-jāhiliyyati faʾañzalal-lāhu sakīnatahū ʿalā Rasūlihī wa ʿalal-muʾminīna wa ʾalzamahum kalimatat-taqwā wa kānūu ʾaḥaqqa bihā wa ʾahlahā. Wa kānal-lāhu bikulli shayʾin ʿAlīmā. (26) Laqad ṣadaqal-lāhu Rasūlahur-ruʾyā bil-ḥaqq. Latadkhulun-nal-Masjidal-Ḥarāma ʾiñ-shāaʾal-lāhu ʾāminīna

of a grievous wrong: – [had it not been for this, you would have been allowed to fight your way into the city: but you were forbidden to fight[33]] so that [in time] God might admit to His grace whomever He wills.[34] Had they [who deserve Our mercy and they whom We have condemned] been clearly discernible [to you],[35] We would indeed have imposed grievous suffering [at your hands] on such of them as were bent on denying the truth. ‹25›

Whereas they who are bent on denying the truth harboured a stubborn disdain in their hearts – the stubborn disdain [born] of ignorance[36] – God bestowed from on high His [gift of] inner peace upon His Apostle and the believers, and bound them to the spirit of God-consciousness:[37] for they were most worthy of this [divine gift], and deserved it well. And God has full knowledge of all things. ‹26›

Indeed, God has shown the truth in His Apostle's true vision:[38] most certainly shall you enter the Inviolable House of Worship, if God so wills, in full security,

33 Thus Zamakhsharī, supported by Rāzī, Ibn Kathīr, and other commentators.

34 I.e., so that the believers might be spared, and that in time many a pagan Meccan might embrace Islam, as actually happened.

35 Lit., "had they been separated from one another": i.e., the believers and the pagans among the Meccans. In its wider sense, the above implies that man never really knows whether another human being deserves God's grace or condemnation.

36 Although this reference to the "stubborn disdain" (*ḥamiyyah*) on the part of the pagan Quraysh may have been characteristic of their over-all attitude towards the Prophet and his mission, it is probable – as Zamakhsharī points out – that its special mention here relates to an incident which occurred at Ḥudaybiyyah during the truce negotations between the Prophet and the emissary of the Meccans, Suhayl ibn ʿAmr. The Prophet began to dictate to ʿAlī ibn Abī Ṭālib the text of the proposed agreement: "Write down, 'In the name of God, the Most Gracious, the Dispenser of Grace'"; but Suhayl interrupted him and said: "We have never heard of [the expression] 'the Most Gracious'; write down only what *we* know." Whereupon the Prophet said to ʿAlī: "Write, then, 'In Thy name, O God'." ʿAlī wrote as he was told; and the Prophet continued: "This is what has been agreed upon between Muḥammad, God's Apostle, and the people of Mecca . . .". But Suhayl interrupted again: "If thou wert [really] an apostle of God, [this would be an admission on our part that] we have been doing wrong to thee; write, therefore, as *we* understand it." And so the Prophet dictated to ʿAlī: "Write thus: 'This is what has been agreed upon between Muḥammad, the son of ʿAbd Allāh, son of ʿAbd al-Muṭṭalib, and the people of Mecca . . .'." (This story is recorded in many versions, among others by Nasaʾī, Ibn Ḥanbal and Ṭabarī.)

37 Lit., "the word of God-consciousness" (*kalimat at-taqwā*): implying that their consciousness of God and of His all-pervading power enabled them to bear the "stubborn disdain" of their enemies with inner calm and serenity.

38 Shortly before the expedition which ended at Ḥudaybiyyah, the Prophet had a dream in which he saw himself and his followers entering Mecca as pilgrims. This dream-vision was destined to be fulfilled a year later, in 7 H., when the Muslims were able to perform their first peaceful pilgrimage to the Holy City.

with your heads shaved or your hair cut short,[39] without any fear: for He has [always] known that which you yourselves could not know.[40] And He has ordained [for you], besides this, a victory soon to come.[41] ‹27›
He it is who has sent forth His Apostle with the [task of spreading] guidance and the religion of truth, to the end that He make it prevail over every [false] religion; and none can bear witness [to the truth] as God does.[42] ‹28›

مُحَلِّقِينَ رُءُوسَكُمْ وَمُقَصِّرِينَ لَا تَخَافُونَ فَعَلِمَ مَا لَمْ تَعْلَمُوا۟ فَجَعَلَ مِن
دُونِ ذَٰلِكَ فَتْحًا قَرِيبًا 27 هُوَ ٱلَّذِىٓ أَرْسَلَ رَسُولَهُۥ بِٱلْهُدَىٰ وَدِينِ
ٱلْحَقِّ لِيُظْهِرَهُۥ عَلَى ٱلدِّينِ كُلِّهِۦ وَكَفَىٰ بِٱللَّهِ شَهِيدًا 28 مُّحَمَّدٌ رَّسُولُ
ٱللَّهِ وَٱلَّذِينَ مَعَهُۥٓ أَشِدَّآءُ عَلَى ٱلْكُفَّارِ رُحَمَآءُ بَيْنَهُمْ تَرَىٰهُمْ رُكَّعًا سُجَّدًا
يَبْتَغُونَ فَضْلًا مِّنَ ٱللَّهِ وَرِضْوَٰنًا سِيمَاهُمْ فِى وُجُوهِهِم مِّنْ أَثَرِ ٱلسُّجُودِ
ذَٰلِكَ مَثَلُهُمْ فِى ٱلتَّوْرَىٰةِ وَمَثَلُهُمْ فِى ٱلْإِنجِيلِ كَزَرْعٍ أَخْرَجَ شَطْـَٔهُۥ فَـَٔازَرَهُۥ
فَٱسْتَغْلَظَ فَٱسْتَوَىٰ عَلَىٰ سُوقِهِۦ يُعْجِبُ ٱلزُّرَّاعَ لِيَغِيظَ بِهِمُ ٱلْكُفَّارَ

MUHAMMAD is God's Apostle; and those who are [truly] with him are firm and unyielding[43] towards all deniers of the truth, [yet] full of mercy towards one another.[44] Thou canst see them bowing down, prostrating themselves [in prayer], seeking favour with God and [His] goodly acceptance: their marks are on their faces, traced by prostration.[45]
This is their parable in the Torah as well as their parable in the Gospel:[46] [they are] like a seed that brings forth its shoot, and then He strengthens it, so that it grows stout, and [in the end] stands firm upon its stem, delighting the sowers. . . .
[Thus will God cause the believers to grow in strength,] so that through them He might confound[47] the deniers of the truth.

muḥalliqīna ruʾūsakum wa muqaṣṣirīna lā takhāfūn. Faʿalima mā lam taʿlamū fajaʿala miñ-dūni dhālika fatḥañ-qarībā. 27 Huwal-ladhīi ʾarsala Rasūlahū bilhudā wa dīnil-ḥaqqi liyuẓhirahū ʿalad-dīni kullihī wa kafā billāhi Shahīdā. 28 Muḥammadur-Rasūlul-lāh. Wal-ladhīna maʿahūu ʾashiddāaʾu ʿalal-kuffāri ruḥamāaʾu baynahum. Tarāhum rukkaʿañ-sujjadañy-yabtaghūna faḍlam-minal-lāhi wa riḍwānā. Sīmāhum fī wujūhihim-min ʾatharis-sujūd. Dhālika mathaluhum fit-Tawrāti wa mathaluhum fil-ʾIñjīli kazarʿin ʾakhraja shaṭʾahū faʾāzarahū fastaghlaẓa fastawā ʿalā sūqihī yuʿjibuz-zurrāʿa liyaghīẓa bihimul-kuffār.

39 Male pilgrims usually shave or (which is the meaning of the conjunctive *wa* in this context) cut their hair short before assuming the pilgrim's garb (*iḥrām*) for it is not permitted to do so while in the state of pilgrimage. A repetition of the same act marks the completion of the pilgrimage (cf. 2 : 196).

40 Namely, the future.

41 See note 22.

42 Sc., "through the revelations which He grants to His prophets". See also 3 : 19 – "the only [true] religion in the sight of God is [man's] self-surrender unto Him": from which it follows that any religion (in the widest sense of this term) which is not based on the above principle is, *eo ipso*, false.

43 This composite gives, I believe, the full meaning of the term *ashiddāʾ* (sing. *shadīd*) in the above context.

44 Lit., "among themselves". Cf. 5 : 54 – "humble towards the believers, proud towards all who deny the truth".

45 The infinitive noun *sujūd* ("prostration") stands here for the innermost consummation of faith, while its "trace" signifies the spiritual reflection of that faith in the believer's manner of life and even in his outward aspect. Since the "face" is the most expressive part of man's personality, it is often used in the Qurʾān in the sense of one's "whole being".

46 Regarding the significance of the term *Injīl* ("Gospel") as used in the Qurʾān, see *sūrah* 3, note 4.

47 Lit., "infuse with wrath".

[But] unto such of them as may [yet] attain to faith and do righteous deeds, God has promised forgiveness and a reward supreme.[48] ‹29›

وَعَدَ ٱللَّهُ ٱلَّذِينَ ءَامَنُوا۟ وَعَمِلُوا۟ ٱلصَّـٰلِحَـٰتِ مِنْهُم مَّغْفِرَةً وَأَجْرًا عَظِيمًۢا ﴿٢٩﴾

Waᶜadal-lāhul-ladhīna ᵓāmanū wa ᶜamiluṣ-ṣāliḥāti minhum maghfiratañw-wa ᵓajran ᶜaẓīmā. ﴿٢٩﴾

48 Whereas most of the classical commentators understand the above sentence as alluding to believers in general, Rāzī relates the pronoun in *minhum* ("of them" or "among them") explicitly to the deniers of the truth spoken of in the preceding sentence – i.e., to those of them who *might yet* attain to faith and thus achieve God's forgiveness: a promise which was fulfilled within a few years after the revelation of this verse, inasmuch as most of the Arabian enemies of the Prophet embraced Islam, and many of them became its torchbearers. But in a wider sense, this divine promise remains open until Resurrection Day (Ṭabarī), relating to everybody, at all times and in all cultural environments, who might yet attain to the truth and live up to it.

The Forty-Ninth Sūrah

Al-Ḥujurāt (The Private Apartments)

Medina Period

REVEALED, in the consensus of most of the authorities, in the year 9 H., this *sūrah* deals predominantly with social ethics. Beginning with the reverence due to the Prophet and – by implication – to the righteous leaders of the community after him, the discourse culminates in the principle of the brotherhood of all believers (verse 10) and, in its widest sense, the brotherhood of all mankind (verse 13). The concluding passage (verses 14 ff.) points out the difference between true faith and a mere outward observance of religious formalities.

The title is derived from the mention of the word *al-ḥujurāt* in verse 4.

سورة الحجرات مدنية -49-
وآياتها ثماني عشرة

IN THE NAME OF GOD, THE MOST GRACIOUS, THE DISPENSER OF GRACE:

O YOU who have attained to faith! Do not put yourselves forward[1] in the presence of [what] God and His Apostle [may have ordained], but remain conscious of God: for, verily, God is all-hearing, all-knowing! ‹1›

O you who have attained to faith! Do not raise your voices above the voice of the Prophet,[2] and neither speak loudly to him, as you would speak loudly to one another,[3] lest all your [good] deeds come to nought without your perceiving it. ‹2›

بِسۡمِ ٱللَّهِ ٱلرَّحۡمَٰنِ ٱلرَّحِيمِ

يَٰٓأَيُّهَا ٱلَّذِينَ ءَامَنُواْ لَا تُقَدِّمُواْ بَيۡنَ يَدَيِ ٱللَّهِ وَرَسُولِهِۦۖ وَٱتَّقُواْ ٱللَّهَۚ إِنَّ
ٱللَّهَ سَمِيعٌ عَلِيمٞ ١ يَٰٓأَيُّهَا ٱلَّذِينَ ءَامَنُواْ لَا تَرۡفَعُوٓاْ أَصۡوَٰتَكُمۡ فَوۡقَ
صَوۡتِ ٱلنَّبِيِّ وَلَا تَجۡهَرُواْ لَهُۥ بِٱلۡقَوۡلِ كَجَهۡرِ بَعۡضِكُمۡ لِبَعۡضٍ أَن
تَحۡبَطَ أَعۡمَٰلُكُمۡ وَأَنتُمۡ لَا تَشۡعُرُونَ ٢

ربع الحزب

Bismil-lāhir-Raḥmānir-Raḥīm.

Yāa ʾayyuhal-ladhīna ʾāmanū lā tuqaddimū bayna yadayil-lāhi wa Rasūlihī wat-taqul-lāh. ʾInnal-lāha Samīʿun ʿAlīm. ① Yāa ʾayyuhal-ladhīna ʾāmanū lā tarfaʿūu ʾaṣwātakum fawqa ṣawtin-Nabiyyi wa lā tajharū lahū bilqawli kajahri baʿḍikum libaʿḍin ʾañ taḥbaṭa ʾaʿmālukum wa ʾañtum lā tashʿurūn. ②

---

1 I.e., "do not allow your own desires to have precedence".

2 This has both a literal and a figurative meaning: literal in the case of the Prophet's Companions, and figurative for them as well as for believers of later times – implying that one's personal opinions and predilections must not be allowed to overrule the clear-cut legal ordinances and/or moral stipulations promulgated by the Prophet (cf. 4 : 65 and the corresponding note 84).

3 I.e., address him, or (in later times) speak of him, with unbecoming familiarity.

Behold, they who lower their voices in the presence of God's Apostle – it is they whose hearts God has tested [and opened] to consciousness of Himself; [and] theirs shall be forgiveness and a reward supreme. ‹3›

Verily, [O Prophet,] as for those who call thee from without thy private apartments[4] – most of them do not use their reason: ‹4› for, if they had the patience [to wait] until thou come forth to them [of thine own accord], it would be for their own good. Still, God is much forgiving, a dispenser of grace. ‹5›

O YOU who have attained to faith! If any iniquitous person comes to you with a [slanderous] tale, use your discernment,[5] lest you hurt people unwittingly and afterwards be filled with remorse for what you have done.[6] ‹6›

And know that God's Apostle is among you:[7] were he to comply with your inclinations in each and every case,[8] you would be bound to come to harm [as a community]. But as it is, God has caused [your] faith to be dear to you, and has given it beauty in your hearts, and has made hateful to you all denial of the truth, and all iniquity, and all rebellion [against what is good].

Such indeed are they who follow the right course ‹7› through God's bounty and favour; and God is all-knowing, truly wise. ‹8›

إِنَّ ٱلَّذِينَ يَغُضُّونَ أَصْوَٰتَهُمْ عِندَ رَسُولِ ٱللَّهِ أُو۟لَٰٓئِكَ ٱلَّذِينَ ٱمْتَحَنَ ٱللَّهُ
قُلُوبَهُمْ لِلتَّقْوَىٰ لَهُم مَّغْفِرَةٌ وَأَجْرٌ عَظِيمٌ ﴿٣﴾ إِنَّ ٱلَّذِينَ يُنَادُونَكَ مِن
وَرَآءِ ٱلْحُجُرَٰتِ أَكْثَرُهُمْ لَا يَعْقِلُونَ ﴿٤﴾ وَلَوْ أَنَّهُمْ صَبَرُوا۟ حَتَّىٰ تَخْرُجَ
إِلَيْهِمْ لَكَانَ خَيْرًا لَّهُمْ وَٱللَّهُ غَفُورٌ رَّحِيمٌ ﴿٥﴾ يَٰٓأَيُّهَا ٱلَّذِينَ ءَامَنُوٓا۟ إِن
جَآءَكُمْ فَاسِقٌۢ بِنَبَإٍ فَتَبَيَّنُوٓا۟ أَن تُصِيبُوا۟ قَوْمًۢا بِجَهَٰلَةٍ فَتُصْبِحُوا۟ عَلَىٰ مَا
فَعَلْتُمْ نَٰدِمِينَ ﴿٦﴾ وَٱعْلَمُوٓا۟ أَنَّ فِيكُمْ رَسُولَ ٱللَّهِ لَوْ يُطِيعُكُمْ فِى كَثِيرٍ
مِّنَ ٱلْأَمْرِ لَعَنِتُّمْ وَلَٰكِنَّ ٱللَّهَ حَبَّبَ إِلَيْكُمُ ٱلْإِيمَٰنَ وَزَيَّنَهُۥ فِى قُلُوبِكُمْ
وَكَرَّهَ إِلَيْكُمُ ٱلْكُفْرَ وَٱلْفُسُوقَ وَٱلْعِصْيَانَ أُو۟لَٰٓئِكَ هُمُ ٱلرَّٰشِدُونَ ﴿٧﴾
فَضْلًا مِّنَ ٱللَّهِ وَنِعْمَةً وَٱللَّهُ عَلِيمٌ حَكِيمٌ ﴿٨﴾

ʾInnal-ladhīna yaghuḍḍūna ʾaṣwātahum ʿiñda Rasūlil-lāhi ʾulāaʾikal-ladhīnam-taḥanal-lāhu qulūbahum littaqwā. Lahum-maghfiratuñw-wa ʾajrun ʿaẓīm. (3) ʾInnal-ladhīna yunādūnaka miñw-warāaʾil-ḥujurāti ʾaktharuhum lā yaʿqilūn. (4) Wa law ʾannahum ṣabarū ḥattā takhruja ʾilayhim lakāna khayral-lahum; wal-lāhu Ghafūrur-Raḥīm. (5) Yāa ʾayyuhal-ladhīna ʾāmanūu ʾiñ-jāaʾakum fāsiqum-binabaʾiñ-fatabayyanūu añ-tuṣībū qawmam-bijahālatiñ-fatuṣbiḥū ʿalā mā faʿaltum nādimīn. (6) Waʿ-lamūu ʾanna fīkum Rasūlal-lāh. Law yuṭīʿukum fī kathīrim-minal-ʾamri laʿanittum wa lākinnal-lāha ḥabbaba ʾilaykumul-ʾīmāna wa zayyanahū fī qulūbikum wa karraha ʾilaykumul-kufra wal-fusūqa wal-ʿiṣyān. ʾUlāaʾika humur-rāshidūn. (7) Faḍlam-minal-lāhi wa niʿmah. Wal-lāhu ʿAlīmun Ḥakīm. (8)

4 While this relates in the first instance to the Prophet, it may also be taken to apply to any supreme leader of the community (*amīr al-muʾminīn*) who acts as the Prophet's successor (*khalīfah*) and rules in his name, i.e., under the aegis of Islamic Law. (As regards the Prophet himself, the above exhortation to reverent behaviour implies, in the view of many outstanding Islamic thinkers, a prohibition to "call out to him" when visiting his tomb.)

5 I.e., verify the truth before giving credence to any such report or rumour. The tale-bearer is characterized as "iniquitous" because the very act of spreading unsubstantiated rumours affecting the reputation of other persons constitutes a spiritual offence.

6 Thus, after laying stress in the preceding verses on the reverence due to God's message-bearer – and, by implication, to every righteous leader of the community – the discourse turns to the moral imperative of safeguarding the honour and reputation of every member of the community, man and woman alike. This principle is taken up, more explicitly, in verse 12.

7 Sc., "and he ought to be an example for you as regards your behaviour towards one another": i.e., *he* would not accept rashly a hearsay tale affecting the honour of third persons, but would either refuse to listen to it altogether or, should a clarification become necessary in the interests of the community, would insist on ascertaining the truth objectively.

8 Lit., "in many a case (*amr*)": the implication being that, more often than not, man is prone to give credence to

Hence, if two groups of believers fall to fighting,[9] make peace between them; but then, if one of the two [groups] goes on acting wrongfully towards the other, fight against the one that acts wrongfully until it reverts to God's commandment;[10] and if they revert, make peace between them with justice, and deal equitably [with them]: for verily, God loves those who act equitably! «9»

All believers are but brethren.[11] Hence, [whenever they are at odds,] make peace between your two brethren, and remain conscious of God, so that you might be graced with His mercy. «10»

O YOU who have attained to faith! No men shall deride [other] men: it may well be that those [whom they deride] are better than themselves; and no women [shall deride other] women: it may well be that those [whom they deride] are better than themselves.[12] And neither shall you defame one another, nor insult one another by [opprobrious] epithets: evil is all imputation of iniquity after [one has attained to] faith;[13] and they who [become guilty thereof and] do not repent – it is they, they who are evildoers! «11»

O you who have attained to faith! Avoid most guesswork [about one another][14] – for, behold, some of [such] guesswork is [in itself] a sin; and do not spy upon one another, and neither allow yourselves to speak ill of one another behind your backs. Would any of you like to eat the flesh of his dead brother? Nay, you would loathe it!

وَإِن طَآئِفَتَانِ مِنَ ٱلْمُؤْمِنِينَ ٱقْتَتَلُوا۟ فَأَصْلِحُوا۟ بَيْنَهُمَا ۖ فَإِنۢ بَغَتْ
إِحْدَىٰهُمَا عَلَى ٱلْأُخْرَىٰ فَقَـٰتِلُوا۟ ٱلَّتِى تَبْغِى حَتَّىٰ تَفِىٓءَ إِلَىٰٓ أَمْرِ ٱللَّهِ ۚ فَإِن فَآءَتْ
فَأَصْلِحُوا۟ بَيْنَهُمَا بِٱلْعَدْلِ وَأَقْسِطُوٓا۟ ۖ إِنَّ ٱللَّهَ يُحِبُّ ٱلْمُقْسِطِينَ ﴿٩﴾ إِنَّمَا
ٱلْمُؤْمِنُونَ إِخْوَةٌ فَأَصْلِحُوا۟ بَيْنَ أَخَوَيْكُمْ ۚ وَٱتَّقُوا۟ ٱللَّهَ لَعَلَّكُمْ
تُرْحَمُونَ ﴿١٠﴾ يَـٰٓأَيُّهَا ٱلَّذِينَ ءَامَنُوا۟ لَا يَسْخَرْ قَوْمٌ مِّن قَوْمٍ عَسَىٰٓ أَن
يَكُونُوا۟ خَيْرًا مِّنْهُمْ وَلَا نِسَآءٌ مِّن نِّسَآءٍ عَسَىٰٓ أَن يَكُنَّ خَيْرًا مِّنْهُنَّ ۖ وَلَا
تَلْمِزُوٓا۟ أَنفُسَكُمْ وَلَا تَنَابَزُوا۟ بِٱلْأَلْقَـٰبِ ۖ بِئْسَ ٱلِٱسْمُ ٱلْفُسُوقُ بَعْدَ
ٱلْإِيمَـٰنِ ۚ وَمَن لَّمْ يَتُبْ فَأُو۟لَـٰٓئِكَ هُمُ ٱلظَّـٰلِمُونَ ﴿١١﴾ يَـٰٓأَيُّهَا ٱلَّذِينَ ءَامَنُوا۟
ٱجْتَنِبُوا۟ كَثِيرًا مِّنَ ٱلظَّنِّ إِنَّ بَعْضَ ٱلظَّنِّ إِثْمٌ ۖ وَلَا تَجَسَّسُوا۟ وَلَا يَغْتَب
بَّعْضُكُم بَعْضًا ۚ أَيُحِبُّ أَحَدُكُمْ أَن يَأْكُلَ لَحْمَ أَخِيهِ مَيْتًا فَكَرِهْتُمُوهُ

**Wa ʾiñ-ṭāaʾifatāni minal-muʾminīnaq-tatalū faʾaṣ-
liḥū baynahumā. Faʾim-baghat ʾiḥdāhumā ʿalal-
ʾukhrā faqātilul-latī tabghī ḥattā tafiiʾa ʾilāa ʾamril-
lāh. Faʾiñ-fāaʾat faʾaṣliḥū baynahumā bilʿadli wa
ʾaqsiṭūu ʾinnal-lāha yuḥibbul-muqsiṭīn. (9) ʾInnamal-
muʾminūna ʾikhwatuñ-faʾaṣliḥū bayna ʾakhaway-
kum. Wat-taqul-lāha laʿallakum turḥamūn. (10) Yāa
ʾayyuhal-ladhīna ʾāmanū lā yaskhar qawmum-miñ-
qawmin ʿasāa ʾañy-yakūnū khayram-minhum wa lā
nisāaʾum-miñ-nisāaʾin ʿasāa ʾañy-yakunna khay-
ram-minhunn. Wa lā talmizūu ʾañfusakum wa lā
tanābazū bilʾalqāb. Biʾsal-ismul-fusūqu baʿdal-
ʾīmān. Wa mal-lam yatub faʾulāaʾika humuẓ-
ẓālimūn. (11) Yāa ʾayyuhal-ladhīna ʾāmanuj-tanibū
kathīram-minaẓ-ẓanni ʾinna baʿḍaẓ-ẓanni ʾithm. Wa
lā tajassasū wa lā yaghtab-baʿḍukum-baʿḍā.
ʾAyuḥibbu ʾaḥadukum ʾañy-yaʾkula laḥma ʾakhīhi
maytañ-fakarihtumūh.**

---

malicious rumours devoid of any real evidence.

9 The expression "fighting" comprises in this context all modes of discord and contention, both in word and deed, evidently as a consequence of the slanderous rumours spoken of in verse 6 above.

10 I.e., that the believers should act as brethren (see next verse).

11 The plural noun *ikhwah* ("brethren" or "brotherhood") has here, of course, a purely ideological connotation, comprising men and women alike; the same applies to the subsequent mention of "your two brethren".

12 The implication is that believers, whether men or women, shall never deride one another (Zamakhsharī, Bayḍāwī).

13 This applies no less to the faith of the one who insults than to that of the insulted (Rāzī): cf. 6 : 82 – "[those] who have not obscured their faith by wrongdoing".

14 I.e., guesswork that may lead to unfounded suspicion of another person's motives: see note 22 on 24 : 19.

نصف الحزب

And be conscious of God. Verily, God is an acceptor of repentance, a dispenser of grace! ‹12›

O men! Behold, We have created you all out of a male and a female,[15] and have made you into nations and tribes, so that you might come to know one another.[16] Verily, the noblest of you in the sight of God is the one who is most deeply conscious of Him. Behold, God is all-knowing, all-aware. ‹13›

THE BEDOUIN say, "We have attained to faith."

Say [unto them, O Muḥammad]: "You have not [yet] attained to faith; you should [rather] say, 'We have [outwardly] surrendered' – for [true] faith has not yet entered your hearts.[17] But if you [truly] pay heed unto God and His Apostle, He will not let the least of your deeds[18] go to waste: for, behold, God is much-forgiving, a dispenser of grace." ‹14›

[Know that true] believers are only those who have attained to faith in God and His Apostle and have left all doubt behind,[19] and who strive hard in God's cause with their possessions and their lives: it is they, they who are true to their word! ‹15›

وَٱتَّقُوا۟ ٱللَّهَ إِنَّ ٱللَّهَ تَوَّابٌ رَّحِيمٌ ﴿١٢﴾ يَٰٓأَيُّهَا ٱلنَّاسُ إِنَّا خَلَقْنَٰكُم مِّن ذَكَرٍ
وَأُنثَىٰ وَجَعَلْنَٰكُمْ شُعُوبًا وَقَبَآئِلَ لِتَعَارَفُوٓا۟ إِنَّ أَكْرَمَكُمْ عِندَ ٱللَّهِ أَتْقَىٰكُمْ
إِنَّ ٱللَّهَ عَلِيمٌ خَبِيرٌ ﴿١٣﴾ ۞ قَالَتِ ٱلْأَعْرَابُ ءَامَنَّا قُل لَّمْ تُؤْمِنُوا۟ وَلَٰكِن
قُولُوٓا۟ أَسْلَمْنَا وَلَمَّا يَدْخُلِ ٱلْإِيمَٰنُ فِى قُلُوبِكُمْ وَإِن تُطِيعُوا۟ ٱللَّهَ
وَرَسُولَهُۥ لَا يَلِتْكُم مِّنْ أَعْمَٰلِكُمْ شَيْـًٔا إِنَّ ٱللَّهَ غَفُورٌ رَّحِيمٌ ﴿١٤﴾ إِنَّمَا
ٱلْمُؤْمِنُونَ ٱلَّذِينَ ءَامَنُوا۟ بِٱللَّهِ وَرَسُولِهِۦ ثُمَّ لَمْ يَرْتَابُوا۟ وَجَٰهَدُوا۟
بِأَمْوَٰلِهِمْ وَأَنفُسِهِمْ فِى سَبِيلِ ٱللَّهِ أُو۟لَٰٓئِكَ هُمُ ٱلصَّٰدِقُونَ ﴿١٥﴾

Wat-taqul-lāha ʾinnal-lāha Tawwābur-Raḥīm. (12) Yāa ʾayyuhan-nāsu ʾinnā khalaqnākum-miñ-dhakariñw-wa ʾuñthā wa jaᶜalnākum shuᶜūbañw-wa qabāaʾila litaᶜārafū. ʾInna ʾakramakum ᶜiñdal-lāhi ʾatqākum. ʾInnal-lāha ᶜAlīmun Khabīr. (13) ۞ Qālatil-ʾaᶜrābu ʾāmannā; qul lam tuʾminū wa lākiñ-qūlūu ʾaslamnā wa lammā yadkhulil-ʾīmānu fī qulūbikum. Wa ʾiñ-tuṭīᶜul-lāha wa Rasūlahū lā yalitkum-min ʾaᶜmālikum shayʾā. ʾInnal-lāha Ghafūrur-Raḥīm. (14) ʾInnamal-muʾminūnal-ladhīna ʾāmanū billāhi wa Rasūlihī thumma lam yartābū wa jāhadū biʾamwālihim wa ʾañfusihim fī sabīlil-lāh. ʾUlāaʾika humuṣ-ṣādiqūn. (15)

15 I.e., "We have created every one of you out of a father and a mother" (Zamakhsharī, Rāzī, Bayḍāwī) – implying that this equality of biological origin is reflected in the equality of the human dignity common to all.

16 I.e., know that all belong to one human family, without any inherent superiority of one over another (Zamakhsharī). This connects with the exhortation, in the preceding two verses, to respect and safeguard each other's dignity. In other words, men's evolution into "nations and tribes" is meant to foster rather than to diminish their mutual desire to understand and appreciate the essential human oneness underlying their outward differentiations; and, correspondingly, all racial, national or tribal prejudice (*ᶜaṣabiyyah*) is condemned – implicitly in the Qurʾān, and most explicitly by the Prophet (see second half of note 15 on 28 : 15). In addition, speaking of people's boasting of their national or tribal past, the Prophet said: "Behold, God has removed from you the arrogance of pagan ignorance (*jāhiliyyah*) with its boast of ancestral glories. Man is but a God-conscious believer or an unfortunate sinner. All people are children of Adam, and Adam was created out of dust." (Fragment of a *ḥadīth* quoted by Tirmidhī and Abū Dāʾūd, on the authority of Abū Hurayrah.)

17 Inasmuch as this is evidently an allusion to the intense tribalism of the bedouin and their "pride of descent" (Rāzī), the above verse connects with the preceding condemnation of all tribal preferences and prejudices, and with the call for their abandonment as a prerequisite of true faith. Primarily, this relates to the bedouin contemporaries of the Prophet, but its import is general and timeless.

18 I.e., "your own deeds, in distinction from the supposed 'glorious deeds' of your ancestors, which count for nothing in His sight".

19 Lit., "and thereafter have had no doubt".

Say: "Do you, perchance, [want to] inform God of [the nature of] your faith[20] – although God knows all that is in the heavens and all that is on earth? Indeed, God has full knowledge of everything!" ‹16›

Many people[21] think that they have bestowed a favour upon thee [O Prophet] by having surrendered [to thee].[22] Say thou: "Deem not your surrender a favour unto me: nay, but it is God who bestows a favour upon you by showing you the way to faith – if you are true to your word!" ‹17›

Verily, God knows the hidden reality of the heavens and the earth; and God sees all that you do. ‹18›

قُلْ أَتُعَلِّمُونَ ٱللَّهَ بِدِينِكُمْ وَٱللَّهُ يَعْلَمُ مَا فِى ٱلسَّمَـٰوَٰتِ وَمَا فِى ٱلْأَرْضِ ج
وَٱللَّهُ بِكُلِّ شَىْءٍ عَلِيمٌ ﴿16﴾ يَمُنُّونَ عَلَيْكَ أَنْ أَسْلَمُوا۟ صلے قُل لَّا تَمُنُّوا۟ عَلَىَّ
إِسْلَـٰمَكُم صلے بَلِ ٱللَّهُ يَمُنُّ عَلَيْكُمْ أَنْ هَدَىٰكُمْ لِلْإِيمَـٰنِ إِن كُنتُمْ
صَـٰدِقِينَ ﴿17﴾ إِنَّ ٱللَّهَ يَعْلَمُ غَيْبَ ٱلسَّمَـٰوَٰتِ وَٱلْأَرْضِ ج وَٱللَّهُ بَصِيرٌۢ بِمَا
تَعْمَلُونَ ﴿18﴾

Qul ʾatuʿallimūnal-lāha bidīnikum wal-lāhu yaʿlamu mā fis-samāwāti wa mā fil-ʾarḍi wal-lāhu bikulli shayʾin ʿAlīm. (16) Yamunnūna ʿalayka ʾan ʾaslamū. Qul lā tamunnū ʿalayya ʾislāmakum; balil-lāhu yamunnu ʿalaykum ʾan hadākum lilʾīmāni ʾin-kuntum ṣādiqīn. (17) ʾInnal-lāha yaʿlamu ghaybas-samāwāti wal-ʾarḍi wal-lāhu Baṣīrum-bimā taʿmalūn. (18)

20 Like the preceding passage, this, too, is addressed in the first instance to certain contemporaries of the Prophet, but its meaning extends to all people, at all times, who think that their mere profession of faith and outward adherence to its formalities makes them "believers".

21 Lit., "They" (see preceding note).

22 I.e., "by professing to be thy followers".

The Fiftieth Sūrah

Qāf

Mecca Period

KNOWN only by the letter-symbol *q* (*qāf*) preceding the first verse, this *sūrah* appears to have been revealed in the fourth year of the Prophet's mission. Commencing and ending with a reference to the Qurʾān, it is devoted in its entirety to the twin problems of death and resurrection.

-50-

سورة ق مكية

وآياتها خمس وأربعون

IN THE NAME OF GOD, THE MOST GRACIOUS, THE DISPENSER OF GRACE:

Qāf.[1]
CONSIDER this sublime Qurʾān! ‹1›
But nay – they deem it strange that a warner should have come unto them from their own midst;[2] and so these deniers of the truth are saying, "A strange thing is this! ‹2› Why – [how could we be resurrected] after we have died and become mere dust? Such a return seems far-fetched indeed!" ‹3›
Well do We know how the earth consumes their bodies,[3] for with Us is a record unfailing. ‹4› Nay, but they [who refuse to believe in resurrection] have been wont to give the lie to this truth whenever it was proffered to them; and so they are in a state of confusion.[4] ‹5›

بِسْمِ ٱللَّهِ ٱلرَّحْمَٰنِ ٱلرَّحِيمِ

قٓ وَٱلْقُرْءَانِ ٱلْمَجِيدِ ﴿١﴾ بَلْ عَجِبُوٓا۟ أَن جَآءَهُم مُّنذِرٌ مِّنْهُمْ فَقَالَ
ٱلْكَٰفِرُونَ هَٰذَا شَىْءٌ عَجِيبٌ ﴿٢﴾ أَءِذَا مِتْنَا وَكُنَّا تُرَابًا ذَٰلِكَ رَجْعٌۢ
بَعِيدٌ ﴿٣﴾ قَدْ عَلِمْنَا مَا تَنقُصُ ٱلْأَرْضُ مِنْهُمْ وَعِندَنَا كِتَٰبٌ حَفِيظٌۢ ﴿٤﴾
بَلْ كَذَّبُوا۟ بِٱلْحَقِّ لَمَّا جَآءَهُمْ فَهُمْ فِىٓ أَمْرٍ مَّرِيجٍ ﴿٥﴾

Bismil-lāhir-Raḥmānir-Raḥīm.
Qāaf; wal-Qurʾānil-majīd. (1) Bal ʿajibūu ʾañ-jāaʾahum-muñdhirum-minhum faqālal-kāfirūna hādhā shayʾun ʿajīb. (2) ʾAʾidhā mitnā wa kunnā turābañ-dhālika rajʿum-baʿīd. (3) Qad ʿalimnā mā tañquṣul-ʾarḍu minhum; wa ʿiñdanā Kitābun ḥafīẓ. (4) Bal kadhdhabū bil-ḥaqqi lammā jāaʾahum fahum fīi ʾamrim-marīj. (5)

---

1 Chronologically, the above is the second occurrence (after *sūrah* 68) of one of the disjointed letter-symbols which precede some of the Qurʾanic *sūrahs*. For the theories relating to these symbols, see Appendix II. As regards my rendering of the adjurative particle *wa* which opens the next sentence as "Consider", see first half of note 23 on 74 : 32, where this adjuration appears for the first time in the chronological order of revelation.

2 This is the earliest Qurʾanic mention – repeated again and again in other places – of people's "deeming it strange" that a purportedly divine message should have been delivered by someone "from their own midst", i.e., a mortal like themselves. Although it is undoubtedly, in the first instance, a reference to the negative attitude of the Meccan pagans to Muḥammad's call, its frequent repetition throughout the Qurʾān has obviously an implication going far beyond that historical reference: it points to the tendency common to many people, at all stages of human development, to distrust any religious statement that is devoid of all exoticism inasmuch as it is enunciated by a person sharing the social and cultural background of those whom he addresses, and because the message itself relies exclusively – as the Qurʾān does – on an appeal to man's reason and moral sense. Hence, the Qurʾān explicitly mentions people's "objections" to a prophet "who eats food [like ordinary mortals] and goes about in the market-places" (25 : 7; see also note 16 on 25 : 20).

3 Lit., "what the earth diminishes of them" – implying that God's promise of resurrection takes the fact of the dead bodies' decomposition fully into account. Consequently, resurrection will be like "a new creation" (cf. 10 : 4, 21 : 104, 30 : 11, 85 : 13, etc.), recalling the recurrent process of creation and re-creation visible in all organic nature (cf. 10 : 34, 27 : 64, 30 : 27).

4 Since they reject *a priori* all thought of life after death, they are perplexed by the lack of any answer to the "why" and "what for" of man's life, by the evident inequality of human destinies, and by what appears to them as a senseless, blind cruelty of nature: problems which can be resolved only against the background of a belief in a continuation of life after bodily "death" and, hence, in the existence of a purpose and a plan underlying all creation.

Do they not look at the sky above them – how We have built it and made it beautiful and free of all faults?[5] ‹6›
And the earth – We have spread it wide, and set upon it mountains firm, and caused it to bring forth plants of all beauteous kinds, ‹7› thus offering an insight and a reminder unto every human being who willingly turns unto God. ‹8›
And We send down from the skies water rich in blessings, and cause thereby gardens to grow, and fields of grain, ‹9› and tall palm-trees with their thickly-clustered dates, ‹10› as sustenance apportioned to men; and by [all] this We bring dead land to life: [and] even so will be [man's] coming-forth from death. ‹11›
[Long] before those [who now deny resurrection] did Noah's people give the lie to this truth, and [so did] the folk of Ar-Rass,[6] and [the tribes of] Thamūd ‹12› and ʿĀd, and Pharaoh, and Lot's brethren,[7] ‹13› and the dwellers of the wooded dales [of Madyan], and the people of Tubbaʿ:[8] they all gave the lie to the apostles – and thereupon that whereof I had warned [them] came true. ‹14›
Could We, then, be [thought of as being] worn out by the first creation?[9]
Nay – but some people[10] are [still] lost in doubt about [the possibility of] a new creation! ‹15›

NOW, VERILY, it is We who have created man, and We know what his innermost self whispers within him: for We are closer to him than his neck-vein. ‹16› [And so,]

أَفَلَمْ يَنظُرُوٓا۟ إِلَى ٱلسَّمَآءِ فَوْقَهُمْ كَيْفَ بَنَيْنَٰهَا وَزَيَّنَّٰهَا وَمَا لَهَا مِن
فُرُوجٍ ﴿٦﴾ وَٱلْأَرْضَ مَدَدْنَٰهَا وَأَلْقَيْنَا فِيهَا رَوَٰسِىَ وَأَنۢبَتْنَا فِيهَا مِن
كُلِّ زَوْجٍۭ بَهِيجٍ ﴿٧﴾ تَبْصِرَةً وَذِكْرَىٰ لِكُلِّ عَبْدٍ مُّنِيبٍ ﴿٨﴾ وَنَزَّلْنَا مِنَ
ٱلسَّمَآءِ مَآءً مُّبَٰرَكًا فَأَنۢبَتْنَا بِهِۦ جَنَّٰتٍ وَحَبَّ ٱلْحَصِيدِ ﴿٩﴾ وَٱلنَّخْلَ
بَاسِقَٰتٍ لَّهَا طَلْعٌ نَّضِيدٌ ﴿١٠﴾ رِّزْقًا لِّلْعِبَادِ ۖ وَأَحْيَيْنَا بِهِۦ بَلْدَةً مَّيْتًا ۚ
كَذَٰلِكَ ٱلْخُرُوجُ ﴿١١﴾ كَذَّبَتْ قَبْلَهُمْ قَوْمُ نُوحٍ وَأَصْحَٰبُ ٱلرَّسِّ
وَثَمُودُ ﴿١٢﴾ وَعَادٌ وَفِرْعَوْنُ وَإِخْوَٰنُ لُوطٍ ﴿١٣﴾ وَأَصْحَٰبُ ٱلْأَيْكَةِ وَقَوْمُ
تُبَّعٍ ۚ كُلٌّ كَذَّبَ ٱلرُّسُلَ فَحَقَّ وَعِيدِ ﴿١٤﴾ أَفَعَيِينَا بِٱلْخَلْقِ ٱلْأَوَّلِ ۚ بَلْ هُمْ
فِى لَبْسٍ مِّنْ خَلْقٍ جَدِيدٍ ﴿١٥﴾ وَلَقَدْ خَلَقْنَا ٱلْإِنسَٰنَ وَنَعْلَمُ مَا تُوَسْوِسُ
بِهِۦ نَفْسُهُۥ ۖ وَنَحْنُ أَقْرَبُ إِلَيْهِ مِنْ حَبْلِ ٱلْوَرِيدِ ﴿١٦﴾

ʾAfalam yanẓurūu ʾilas-samāaʾi fawqahum kayfa banaynāhā wa zayyannāhā wa mā lahā miñ-furūj. (6) Wal-ʾarḍa madadnāhā wa ʾalqaynā fīhā rawāsiya wa ʾambatnā fīhā miñ-kulli zawjim-bahīj. (7) Tabṣiratañw-wa dhikrā likulli ʿabdim-munīb. (8) Wa nazzalnā minas-samāaʾi māaʾam-mubārakañ-faʾambatnā bihī jannātiñw-wa ḥabbal-ḥaṣīd. (9) Wannakhla bāsiqātil-lahā ṭalʿuñ-naḍīd. (10) Rizqal-lilʿibādi wa ʾaḥyaynā bihī baldatam-maytā. Kadhālikal-khurūj. (11) Kadhdhabat qablahum qawmu Nūḥiñw-wa ʾaṣḥābur-Rassi wa Thamūd. (12) Wa ʿĀduñw-wa Firʿawnu wa ʾikhwānu Lūṭ. (13) Wa ʾaṣḥābul-ʾAykati wa qawmu Tubbaʿiñ-kulluñ-kadhdhabar-Rusula faḥaqqa waʿīd. (14) ʾAfaʿayīnā bilkhalqil-ʾawwal. Bal hum fī labsim-min khalqiñ-jadīd. (15) Wa laqad khalaqnal-ʾIñsāna wa naʿlamu mā tuwaswisu bihī nafsuh. Wa Naḥnu ʾaqrabu ʾilayhi min ḥablil-warīd. (16)

5 Lit., "and it has no gaps [or "breaks"] whatever".

6 See note 33 on 25 : 38.

7 The term "brethren" (*ikhwān*) is used here metonymically, denoting a group of people who share the same views or, alternatively, the same environment. Since the people referred to formed Lot's social environment (cf. 7 : 83 or 11 : 77-83), they are described as his "brethren" although his moral concepts and inclinations were entirely different from theirs.

8 Regarding "the people of Tubbaʿ", see 44 : 37 and the corresponding note. The "dwellers of the wooded dales" are the people of Madyan (the Biblical Midian), as is evident from 26 : 176 ff. Their story is found in the Qurʾān in several places; for the most detailed version, see 11 : 84-95.

9 I.e., by the creation of the universe or, more specifically, of man.

10 Lit., "they".

whenever the two demands [of his nature] come face to face, contending from the right and from the left,[11] ‹17› not even a word can he utter but there is a watcher with him, ever-present.[12] ‹18›
And [then,] the twilight of death brings with it the [full] truth[13] – that [very thing, O man,] from which thou wouldst always look away! ‹19› – and [in the end] the trumpet [of resurrection] will be blown: that will be the Day of a warning fulfilled. ‹20›
And every human being will come forward with [his erstwhile] inner urges and [his] conscious mind,[14] ‹21› [and will be told:] "Indeed, unmindful hast thou been of this [Day of Judgement]; but now We have lifted from thee thy veil, and sharp is thy sight today!" ‹22›
And one part[15] of him will say: "This it is that has been ever-present with me!"[16] ‹23›

إِذْ يَتَلَقَّى ٱلْمُتَلَقِّيَانِ عَنِ ٱلْيَمِينِ وَعَنِ ٱلشِّمَالِ قَعِيدٌ ﴿17﴾ مَّا يَلْفِظُ مِن
قَوْلٍ إِلَّا لَدَيْهِ رَقِيبٌ عَتِيدٌ ﴿18﴾ وَجَآءَتْ سَكْرَةُ ٱلْمَوْتِ بِٱلْحَقِّ ذَٰلِكَ
مَا كُنتَ مِنْهُ تَحِيدُ ﴿19﴾ وَنُفِخَ فِى ٱلصُّورِ ذَٰلِكَ يَوْمُ ٱلْوَعِيدِ ﴿20﴾
وَجَآءَتْ كُلُّ نَفْسٍ مَّعَهَا سَآئِقٌ وَشَهِيدٌ ﴿21﴾ لَّقَدْ كُنتَ فِى غَفْلَةٍ مِّنْ
هَٰذَا فَكَشَفْنَا عَنكَ غِطَآءَكَ فَبَصَرُكَ ٱلْيَوْمَ حَدِيدٌ ﴿22﴾ وَقَالَ قَرِينُهُۥ
هَٰذَا مَا لَدَىَّ عَتِيدٌ ﴿23﴾

ʾIdh yatalaqqal-mutalaqqiyāni ʿanil-yamīni wa ʿanish-shimāli qaʿīd. (17) Mā yalfiẓu miñ-qawlin ʾillā ladayhi raqībun ʿatīd. (18) Wa jāaʾat sakratul-mawti bil-ḥaqq. Dhālika mā kuñta minhu taḥīd. (19) Wa nu-fikha fiṣ-ṣūri dhālika Yawmul-waʿīd. (20) Wa jāaʾat kullu nafsim-maʿahā sāaʾiquñw-wa shahīd. (21) Laq-ad kuñta fī ghaflatim-min hādhā fakashafnā ʿañka ghiṭāaʾaka fabaṣarukal-Yawma ḥadīd. (22) Wa qāla qarīnuhū hādhā mā ladayya ʿatīd. (23)

11 The first part of the above sentence – i.e., the phrase *yatalaqqā al-mutalaqqiyān* – may be understood in either of two senses: "the two that are meant to receive do receive", or "the two that aim at meeting each other do meet". The classical commentators adopt, as a rule, the first sense and, consequently, interpret the passage thus: ". . . the two angels that are charged with recording man's doings do record them, sitting on his right and on his left". In my opinion, however, the second of the two possible meanings ("the two that aim at meeting each other") corresponds better with the preceding verse, which speaks of what man's innermost self (*nafs*) "whispers within him", i.e., voices his subconscious desires. Thus, "the two that aim at meeting" are, I believe, the two demands of, or, more properly, the two fundamental motive forces within man's nature: his primal, instinctive urges and desires, both sensual and non-sensual (all of them comprised in the modern psychological term "libido"), on the one side, and his reason, both intuitive and reflective, on the other. The "sitting (*qāʿid*) on the right and on the left" is, to my mind, a metaphor for the conflicting nature of these two forces which strive for predominance within every human being: hence, my rendering of *qāʿid* as "contending". This interpretation is, moreover, strongly supported by the reference, in verse 21, to man's appearing on Judgment Day with "that which drives and that which bears witness" – a phrase which undoubtedly alludes to man's instinctive urges as well as his conscious reason (see note 14 below).

12 I.e., his conscience. The "uttering of a word" is conceptually connected with the "whispering" within man's psyche spoken of in the preceding verse.

13 I.e., full insight into one's own self.

14 Lit., "with that which drives (*sāʾiq*) and that which bears witness (*shahīd*)". While the former term evidently circumscribes man's primal urges – and particularly those which drive him into unrestrained self-indulgence and, thus, into sin – the term *shahīd* (rendered by me as "conscious mind") alludes here to the awakening of the deeper layers of man's consciousness, leading to a sudden perception of his own moral reality – the "lifting of the veil" referred to in the next verse – which forces him to "bear witness" against himself (cf. 17 : 14, 24 : 24, 36 : 65, 41 : 20 ff.).

15 Lit., "his intimate companion" (*qarīnuhu*). The term *qarīn* denotes something that is "connected", "linked" or "intimately associated" with another thing (cf. 41 : 25 and 43 : 36, where *qarīn* is rendered as "[one's] other self"). In the present instance – read together with verse 21 – the term apparently denotes "one part" of man, namely, his awakened moral consciousness.

16 I.e., the sinner's reason will plead that he had always been more or less conscious, and perhaps even critical, of the urges and appetites that drove him into evildoing: but, as is shown in the sequence, this belated and, therefore, morally ineffective rational cognition does not diminish but, rather, enhances the burden of man's guilt.

ثلاثة ارباع الحزب

أَلْقِيَا فِي جَهَنَّمَ كُلَّ كَفَّارٍ عَنِيدٍ ﴿24﴾ مَّنَّاعٍ لِّلْخَيْرِ مُعْتَدٍ مُّرِيبٍ ﴿25﴾
ٱلَّذِي جَعَلَ مَعَ ٱللَّهِ إِلَٰهًا ءَاخَرَ فَأَلْقِيَاهُ فِي ٱلْعَذَابِ ٱلشَّدِيدِ ﴿26﴾ ۞
قَالَ قَرِينُهُۥ رَبَّنَا مَآ أَطْغَيْتُهُۥ وَلَٰكِن كَانَ فِي ضَلَٰلٍۭ بَعِيدٍ ﴿27﴾ قَالَ لَا
تَخْتَصِمُوا۟ لَدَىَّ وَقَدْ قَدَّمْتُ إِلَيْكُم بِٱلْوَعِيدِ ﴿28﴾ مَا يُبَدَّلُ ٱلْقَوْلُ لَدَىَّ
وَمَآ أَنَا۠ بِظَلَّٰمٍ لِّلْعَبِيدِ ﴿29﴾ يَوْمَ نَقُولُ لِجَهَنَّمَ هَلِ ٱمْتَلَأْتِ وَتَقُولُ هَلْ
مِن مَّزِيدٍ ﴿30﴾ وَأُزْلِفَتِ ٱلْجَنَّةُ لِلْمُتَّقِينَ غَيْرَ بَعِيدٍ ﴿31﴾ هَٰذَا مَا
تُوعَدُونَ لِكُلِّ أَوَّابٍ حَفِيظٍ ﴿32﴾ مَّنْ خَشِيَ ٱلرَّحْمَٰنَ بِٱلْغَيْبِ وَجَآءَ
بِقَلْبٍ مُّنِيبٍ ﴿33﴾

[Whereupon God will command:] "Cast, cast[17] into hell every [such] stubborn enemy of the truth, ⟨24⟩ [every] withholder of good [and] sinful aggressor [and] fomentor of distrust [between man and man – everyone] ⟨25⟩ who has set up another deity beside God:[18] cast him, then, cast him into suffering severe!" ⟨26⟩

Man's other self[19] will say: "O our Sustainer! It was not I that led his conscious mind[20] into evil – [nay,] but it had gone far astray [of its own accord]!"[21] ⟨27⟩

[And] He will say: "Contend not before Me, [O you sinners,] for I gave you a forewarning [of this Day of Reckoning]. ⟨28⟩ The judgment passed by Me shall not be altered; but never do I do the least wrong unto My creatures!" ⟨29⟩

On that Day We will ask hell, "Art thou filled?" – and it will answer, "[Nay,] is there yet more [for me]?" ⟨30⟩

And [on that Day] paradise will be brought within the sight of[22] the God-conscious, and will no longer be far away; [and they will be told:] ⟨31⟩ "This is what you were promised – [promised] unto everyone who was wont to turn unto God and to keep Him always in mind ⟨32⟩ – [everyone] who stood in awe of the Most Gracious although He is beyond the reach of human perception, and who has come [unto Him] with a heart full of contrition.[23] ⟨33⟩

ʾAlqiyā fī jahannama kulla kaffārin ʿanīd. (24) Mannāʿil-lilkhayri muʿtadim-murīb. (25) ʾAlladhī jaʿala maʿal-lāhi ʾilāhan ʾākhara faʾalqiyāhu fil-ʿadhābish-shadīd. (26) ۞ Qāla qarīnuhū Rabbanā māa ʾaṭghaytuhū wa lākiñ-kāna fī ḍalālim-baʿīd. (27) Qāla lā takhtaṣimū ladayya wa qad qaddamtu ʾilaykum-bilwaʿīd. (28) Mā yubaddalul-qawlu ladayya wa māa ʾAna biẓallāmil-lilʿabīd. (29) Yawma naqūlu lijahannama halim-talaʾti wa taqūlu hal mim-mazīd. (30) Wa ʾuzlifatil-jannatu lilmuttaqīna ghayra baʿīd. (31) Hādhā mā tūʿadūna likulli ʾawwābin ḥafīẓ. (32) Man khashiyar-Raḥmāna bilghaybi wa jāaʾa biqalbim-munīb. (33)

17 In this instance, as well as in verse 26, the imperative "cast" has the dual form (*alqiyā*). As many classical philologists (and almost all of the commentators) point out, this is linguistically permissible for the sake of special stress, and is equivalent to an emphatic *repetition* of the imperative in question. Alternatively, the dual form may be taken as indicative of an *actual* duality thus addressed: namely, the two manifestations within man's psyche alluded to in verse 17 and described in verse 21 as *sāʾiq* and *shahīd* (see note 14 above), both of which, in their interaction, are responsible for his spiritual downfall and, hence, for his suffering in the life to come.

18 This relates not merely to the veneration of real or imaginary beings or forces to which one ascribes divine qualities, but also to the "worship" of false values and immoral concepts to which people often adhere with an almost religious fervour.

19 Lit., as in verse 23, "his intimate companion" (*qarīn*): but whereas there it may be taken as denoting man's moral consciousness or reason (cf. note 15 above), in the present instance the "speaker" is obviously its counterpart, namely, the complex of the sinner's instinctive urges and inordinate, unrestrained appetitites summarized in the term *sāʾiq* ("that which drives") and often symbolized as *shayṭān* ("satan" or "satanic force": see Rāzī's remarks quoted in note 31 on 14 : 22.) In this sense, the term *qarīn* has the same connotation as in 41 : 25 and 43 : 36.

20 Lit., "him" or "it" – referring to man's faculty of conscious, controlling reason (*shahīd*).

21 I.e., man's evil impulses and appetites cannot gain ascendancy unless his conscious mind goes astray from moral verities: and this explains the purport, in the present context, of verses 24-25 above.

22 Lit., "brought near to".

23 See last sentence of 24 : 31 and the corresponding note 41.

Enter this [paradise] in peace; this is the Day on which life abiding begins!"[24] ‹34›
In that [paradise] they shall have whatever they may desire – but there is yet more with Us. ‹35›

AND HOW MANY a generation have We destroyed before those [who now deny the truth][25] – people of greater might than theirs: – but [when Our chastisement befell them,] they became wanderers on the face of the earth, seeking no more than a place of refuge.[26] ‹36›
In this, behold, there is indeed a reminder for everyone whose heart is wide-awake[27] – that is, [everyone who] lends ear with a conscious mind[28] ‹37› – and [who knows that] We have indeed created the heavens and the earth and all that is between them in six aeons, and [that] no weariness could ever touch Us.[29] ‹38›

HENCE, [O believer,] bear thou with patience whatever they may say,[30] and extol thy Sustainer's limitless glory and praise before the rising of the sun and before its setting;[31] ‹39› and in the night, too, extol His glory, and at every prayer's end.[32] ‹40›

ٱدْخُلُوهَا بِسَلَٰمٍ ذَٰلِكَ يَوْمُ ٱلْخُلُودِ ﴿٣٤﴾ لَهُم مَّا يَشَآءُونَ فِيهَا وَلَدَيْنَا
مَزِيدٌ ﴿٣٥﴾ وَكَمْ أَهْلَكْنَا قَبْلَهُم مِّن قَرْنٍ هُمْ أَشَدُّ مِنْهُم بَطْشًا فَنَقَّبُوا۟ فِى
ٱلْبِلَٰدِ هَلْ مِن مَّحِيصٍ ﴿٣٦﴾ إِنَّ فِى ذَٰلِكَ لَذِكْرَىٰ لِمَن كَانَ لَهُۥ قَلْبٌ أَوْ
أَلْقَى ٱلسَّمْعَ وَهُوَ شَهِيدٌ ﴿٣٧﴾ وَلَقَدْ خَلَقْنَا ٱلسَّمَٰوَٰتِ وَٱلْأَرْضَ وَمَا
بَيْنَهُمَا فِى سِتَّةِ أَيَّامٍ وَمَا مَسَّنَا مِن لُّغُوبٍ ﴿٣٨﴾ فَٱصْبِرْ عَلَىٰ مَا يَقُولُونَ
وَسَبِّحْ بِحَمْدِ رَبِّكَ قَبْلَ طُلُوعِ ٱلشَّمْسِ وَقَبْلَ ٱلْغُرُوبِ ﴿٣٩﴾ وَمِنَ ٱلَّيْلِ
فَسَبِّحْهُ وَأَدْبَٰرَ ٱلسُّجُودِ ﴿٤٠﴾

ʾUdkhulūhā bisalāmiñ-dhālika Yawmul-khulūd. (34) Lahum-mā yashāaʾūna fīhā wa ladaynā mazīd. (35) Wa kam ʾahlaknā qablahum-miñ-qarnin hum ʾashaddu minhum-baṭshañ-fanaqqabū fil-bilādi hal mim-maḥīṣ. (36) ʾInna fī dhālika ladhikrā limañ-kāna lahū qalbun ʾaw ʾalqas-samʿa wa huwa shahīd. (37) Wa laqad khalaqnas-samāwāti wal-ʾarḍa wa mā baynahumā fī sittati ʾayyāmiñw-wa mā massanā millughūb. (38) Faṣbir ʿalā mā yaqūlūna wa sabbiḥ biḥamdi Rabbika qabla ṭulūʿish-shamsi wa qablal-ghurūb. (39) Wa minal-layli fasabbiḥhu wa ʾadbāras-sujūd. (40)

24 Lit., "the Day of Abiding".

25 This connects with verses 12-14 above. It should be borne in mind that in ancient Arabic usage the term *qarn* – here rendered as "generation" – often denotes "a period of time succeeding another": hence, a "century", or "people of one and the same period" and, finally, a "civilization" in the historical sense of this word. That this last significance is intended here becomes evident from the sequence.

26 Lit., "they wandered searching (*naqqabū*) in the lands: Is there any place of refuge?" – implying that after the destruction of their civilization they could do no more than strive for bare survival.

27 Thus Zamakhsharī; literally, the phrase reads, "who has a heart".

28 Lit., "or lends ear and is withal a witness (*wa-huwa shahīd*)", which latter phrase Zamakhsharī explains as meaning "is present with his intellect", i.e., with a conscious mind. (Cf. the same use of the term *shahīd* in verse 21.) The conjunctive particle "or" (*aw*) which precedes the above clause does not signify an alternative but has – as is often the case in Qurʾanic usage – an *explanatory* function, similar to phrases like "that is'" or "in other words", followed by an amplification of what was said before.

29 The whole of this passage (verses 36-38) stresses God's omnipotence, which can be perceived by "anyone whose heart is wide-awake". The above reference to God's having created the universe "in six aeons" is the oldest in the chronology of Qurʾanic revelation. In this connection it is to be noted that in ancient Arabic usage the term *yawm* does not always denote the twenty-four hours of the earthly "day", but is also applied to *any* period of time, however long or short. In the cosmic sense in which it is used here and elsewhere in the Qurʾān, the plural *ayyām* is best rendered as "aeons". The mention of the impossibility of God's ever being "wearied" by the process of creation connects the present passage with verse 15 of this *sūrah* and, thus, alludes to God's power to resurrect the dead.

30 Sc., "regarding the alleged 'impossibility' of resurrection".

31 I.e., "remember His almightiness at all times of day".

32 Lit., "at the ends (*adbār*) of prostration".

And [always] listen for the day when He who issues the call [of death] shall call [thee] from close-by;[33] «41» [and bethink thyself, too, of] the Day on which all [human beings] will in truth hear the final blast – that Day of [their] coming-forth [from death]. «42»
Verily, it is We who grant life and deal death; and with Us will be all journeys' end «43» on the Day when the earth is riven asunder all around them as they hasten forth [towards God's judgment]: that gathering will be easy for Us [to encompass]. «44»
Fully aware are We of what they [who deny resurrection] do say; and thou canst by no means force them [to believe in it]. Yet none the less, remind, through this Qurʾān, all such as may fear My warning. «45»

وَٱسْتَمِعْ يَوْمَ يُنَادِ ٱلْمُنَادِ مِن مَّكَانٍ قَرِيبٍ ﴿41﴾ يَوْمَ يَسْمَعُونَ ٱلصَّيْحَةَ
بِٱلْحَقِّ ذَٰلِكَ يَوْمُ ٱلْخُرُوجِ ﴿42﴾ إِنَّا نَحْنُ نُحْيِۦ وَنُمِيتُ وَإِلَيْنَا
ٱلْمَصِيرُ ﴿43﴾ يَوْمَ تَشَقَّقُ ٱلْأَرْضُ عَنْهُمْ سِرَاعًا ذَٰلِكَ حَشْرٌ عَلَيْنَا
يَسِيرٌ ﴿44﴾ نَحْنُ أَعْلَمُ بِمَا يَقُولُونَ وَمَآ أَنتَ عَلَيْهِم بِجَبَّارٍ فَذَكِّرْ
بِٱلْقُرْءَانِ مَن يَخَافُ وَعِيدِ ﴿45﴾

Was-tamiʿ Yawma yunādil-munādi mim-makāniñ-qarīb. (41) Yawma yasmaʿūnaṣ-ṣayḥata bilḥaqqi dhālika Yawmul-khurūj. (42) ʾInnā Naḥnu nuḥyī wa numītu wa ʾilaynal-maṣīr. (43) Yawma tashaqqaqul-ʾarḍu ʿanhum sirāʿañ-dhālika ḥashrun ʿalaynā yasīr. (44) Naḥnu ʾaʿlamu bimā yaqūlūna wa māa ʾañta ʿalayhim-bijabbāriñ-fadhakkir bilQurʾāni mañy-yakhāfu waʿīd. (45)

33 Lit., "from a place nearby" – i.e., from within man himself: an echo of verse 16, "We are closer to him than his neck-vein". The "call" spoken of here is evidently the call of death, for which man should always be prepared.

The Fifty-First Sūrah

Adh-Dhāriyāt (The Dust-Scattering Winds)

Mecca Period

THE TITLE of this *sūrah* – revealed, according to Suyūṭī, about two years before the Prophet's exodus to Medina – is based on the adjectival participle *adh-dhāriyāt* occurring in the first verse.

-51-

سورة الذاريات مكية

وآياتها ستون

IN THE NAME OF GOD, THE MOST GRACIOUS, THE DISPENSER OF GRACE:

بِسۡمِ ٱللَّهِ ٱلرَّحۡمَٰنِ ٱلرَّحِيمِ

CONSIDER the winds that scatter the dust far and wide, ‹1›
and those that carry the burden [of heavy clouds], ‹2›
and those that speed along with gentle ease, ‹3›
and those that apportion [the gift of life] at [God's] behest![1] ‹4›
Verily, that which you are promised[2] is true indeed, ‹5› and, verily, judgment is bound to come! ‹6›

CONSIDER the firmament full of starry paths![3] ‹7›

وَٱلذَّٰرِيَٰتِ ذَرۡوٗا ﴿١﴾ فَٱلۡحَٰمِلَٰتِ وِقۡرٗا ﴿٢﴾ فَٱلۡجَٰرِيَٰتِ يُسۡرٗا ﴿٣﴾
فَٱلۡمُقَسِّمَٰتِ أَمۡرًا ﴿٤﴾ إِنَّمَا تُوعَدُونَ لَصَادِقٞ ﴿٥﴾ وَإِنَّ ٱلدِّينَ لَوَٰقِعٞ ﴿٦﴾
وَٱلسَّمَآءِ ذَاتِ ٱلۡحُبُكِ ﴿٧﴾

Bismil-lāhir-Raḥmānir-Raḥīm.
Wadh-dhāriyāti dharwā. (1) Fal-ḥāmilāti wiqrā. (2) Fal-jāriyāti yusrā. (3) Fal-muqassimāti ʾamrā. (4) ʾInnamā tūʿadūna laṣādiq. (5) Wa ʾinnad-dīna lawāqiʿ. (6) Was-samāaʾi dhātil-ḥubuk. (7)

---

1 These symbolical epithets, consisting of adjectival participles without any mention of the nouns which they qualify, have been variously interpreted by the early commentators; but since there is a consensus of opinion regarding the first of these participles – *adh-dhāriyāt* – as denoting "dust-scattering winds", we may assume that the other three relate to different phases or manifestations of the same phenomenon (Rāzī) – namely, to the life-giving function of the combination of wind, clouds and rain – pointing, symbolically, to the miraculous creation of *life as such* and, thus, to the existence of a conscious, purposeful Creator.

2 I.e., life after death.

3 I.e., "think of the Creator of this great universe and, hence, of your responsibility to Him".

Verily, [O men,] you are deeply at variance as to what to believe:[4] ‹8› perverted in his views thereon is he who would deceive himself![5] ‹9›
They but destroy themselves,[6] they who are given to guessing at what they cannot ascertain[7] ‹10› – they who blunder along, in ignorance lost ‹11› – they who [mockingly] ask, "When is that Day of Judgment to be?" ‹12›
[It will be] a Day when they will be sorely tried by the fire,[8] ‹13› [and will be told:] "Taste this your trial! It is this that you were so hastily asking for!"[9] ‹14›
[But,] behold, the God-conscious will find themselves amid gardens and springs, ‹15› enjoying all that their Sustainer will have granted them [because], verily, they were doers of good in the past:[10] ‹16› they would lie asleep during but a small part of the night, ‹17› and would pray for forgiveness from their innermost hearts;[11] ‹18› and [would assign] in all that they possessed a due share unto such as might ask [for help] and such as might suffer privation.[12] ‹19›

AND ON EARTH there are signs [of God's existence, visible] to all who are endowed with inner certainty, ‹20› just as [there are signs thereof] within your own selves:[13] can you not, then, see? ‹21›

إِنَّكُمْ لَفِى قَوْلٍ مُّخْتَلِفٍ ﴿٨﴾ يُؤْفَكُ عَنْهُ مَنْ أُفِكَ ﴿٩﴾ قُتِلَ
ٱلْخَرَّٰصُونَ ﴿١٠﴾ ٱلَّذِينَ هُمْ فِى غَمْرَةٍ سَاهُونَ ﴿١١﴾ يَسْـَٔلُونَ أَيَّانَ يَوْمُ
ٱلدِّينِ ﴿١٢﴾ يَوْمَ هُمْ عَلَى ٱلنَّارِ يُفْتَنُونَ ﴿١٣﴾ ذُوقُوا۟ فِتْنَتَكُمْ هَـٰذَا ٱلَّذِى
كُنتُم بِهِۦ تَسْتَعْجِلُونَ ﴿١٤﴾ إِنَّ ٱلْمُتَّقِينَ فِى جَنَّـٰتٍ وَعُيُونٍ ﴿١٥﴾ ءَاخِذِينَ
مَآ ءَاتَىٰهُمْ رَبُّهُمْ إِنَّهُمْ كَانُوا۟ قَبْلَ ذَٰلِكَ مُحْسِنِينَ ﴿١٦﴾ كَانُوا۟ قَلِيلًا مِّنَ
ٱلَّيْلِ مَا يَهْجَعُونَ ﴿١٧﴾ وَبِٱلْأَسْحَارِ هُمْ يَسْتَغْفِرُونَ ﴿١٨﴾ وَفِىٓ أَمْوَٰلِهِمْ حَقٌّ
لِّلسَّآئِلِ وَٱلْمَحْرُومِ ﴿١٩﴾ وَفِى ٱلْأَرْضِ ءَايَـٰتٌ لِّلْمُوقِنِينَ ﴿٢٠﴾ وَفِىٓ
أَنفُسِكُمْ أَفَلَا تُبْصِرُونَ ﴿٢١﴾

ʾInnakum lafī qawlim-mukhtalif. (8) Yuʾfaku ʿanhu man ʾufik. (9) Qutilal-kharrāṣūn. (10) ʾAlladhīna hum fī ghamratiñ-sāhūn. (11) Yasʾalūna ʾayyāna Yawmud-dīn. (12) Yawma hum ʿalan-nāri yuftanūn. (13) Dhūqū fitnatakum hādhal-ladhī kuñtum bihī tastaʿjilūn. (14) ʾInnal-muttaqīna fī jannātiñw-wa ʿuyūn. (15) ʾĀkhidhīna māa ʾātāhum Rabbuhum; ʾinnahum kānū qabla dhālika muḥsinīn. (16) Kānū qalīlam-minal-layli mā yahjaʿūn. (17) Wa bilʾasḥāri hum yastaghfirūn. (18) Wa fīi ʾamwālihim ḥaqqul-lissāaʾili wal-maḥrūm. (19) Wa fil-ʾarḍi ʾĀyātul-lilmūqinīn. (20) Wa fīi ʾañfusikum ʾafalā tubṣirūn. (21)

4 Lit., "you are indeed in a discordant opinion (*qawl*)", i.e., as to whether or not there is life after death, whether God exists, whether there is any truth in divine revelation, and so forth.

5 Lit., "perversely turned away from this [truth] is he who is made to lie" – or, according to the *Tāj al-ʿArūs*, "he who is perverted in his reason and opinion", i.e., who is *a priori* disposed to deceive himself: implying that belief in God and, hence, in life after death is inherent in man's mind and feeling, and that, therefore, a departure from this belief is but an outcome of intellectual perversion.

6 For this rendering of the expression *qutila*, see note 9 on 74 : 19.

7 Thus the *Tāj al-ʿArūs*, explaining the deeper meaning of *al-kharrāṣūn*. "That which they cannot ascertain" is, in this context, synonymous with *al-ghayb*, "the reality which is beyond the reach of human perception".

8 This "trial (*fitnah*) by the fire" is in tune with several Qurʾanic allusions to the effect that the otherworldly suffering described as "hell" is not to be eternal: see in this connection note 114 on 6 : 128, note 10 on 40 : 12 and note 53 on 43 : 74.

9 A reference to their one-time sarcastic demand that they should be punished for their rejection of the Qurʾanic message: cf. 6 : 57-58 and 8 : 32.

10 Lit., "before that [Day]".

11 See note 10 on 3 : 17.

12 Sc., "but could not beg" – and this applies to all living creatures, whether human beings or mute animals (Rāzī), irrespective of whether the need is of a physical or an emotional nature.

13 See note 3 on 45 : 4.

And in heaven is [the source of] your sustenance [on earth][14] and [of] all that you are promised [for your life after death]: ⟪22⟫ for, by the Sustainer of heaven and earth, this [life after death] is the very truth – as true as that you are endowed with speech![15] ⟪23⟫

AND HAS the story of Abraham's honoured guests ever come within thy ken?[16] ⟪24⟫
When those [heavenly messengers] came unto him and bade him peace, he answered, "[And upon you be] peace!" – [saying to himself,] "They are strangers."[17] ⟪25⟫
Then he turned quietly to his household, and brought forth a fat [roasted] calf, ⟪26⟫ and placed it before them, saying, "Will you not eat?" ⟪27⟫
[And when he saw that the guests would not eat,] he became apprehensive of them;[18] [but] they said, "Fear not" – and gave him the glad tiding of [the birth of] a son who would be endowed with deep knowledge.[19] ⟪28⟫
Thereupon his wife approached [the guests] with a loud cry, and struck her face [in astonishment] and exclaimed: "A barren old woman [like me]!" ⟪29⟫
They answered: "Thus has thy Sustainer decreed; and, verily, He alone is truly wise, all-knowing!" ⟪30⟫
Said [Abraham]: "And what [else] may you have in view, O you [heavenly] messengers?" ⟪31⟫

وَفِى ٱلسَّمَآءِ رِزْقُكُمْ وَمَا تُوعَدُونَ ﴿22﴾ فَوَرَبِّ ٱلسَّمَآءِ وَٱلْأَرْضِ إِنَّهُۥ
لَحَقٌّ مِّثْلَ مَآ أَنَّكُمْ تَنطِقُونَ ﴿23﴾ هَلْ أَتَىٰكَ حَدِيثُ ضَيْفِ إِبْرَٰهِيمَ
ٱلْمُكْرَمِينَ ﴿24﴾ إِذْ دَخَلُوا۟ عَلَيْهِ فَقَالُوا۟ سَلَٰمًا ۖ قَالَ سَلَٰمٌ قَوْمٌ
مُّنكَرُونَ ﴿25﴾ فَرَاغَ إِلَىٰٓ أَهْلِهِۦ فَجَآءَ بِعِجْلٍ سَمِينٍ ﴿26﴾ فَقَرَّبَهُۥٓ إِلَيْهِمْ قَالَ
أَلَا تَأْكُلُونَ ﴿27﴾ فَأَوْجَسَ مِنْهُمْ خِيفَةً ۖ قَالُوا۟ لَا تَخَفْ ۖ وَبَشَّرُوهُ بِغُلَٰمٍ
عَلِيمٍ ﴿28﴾ فَأَقْبَلَتِ ٱمْرَأَتُهُۥ فِى صَرَّةٍ فَصَكَّتْ وَجْهَهَا وَقَالَتْ عَجُوزٌ
عَقِيمٌ ﴿29﴾ قَالُوا۟ كَذَٰلِكِ قَالَ رَبُّكِ ۖ إِنَّهُۥ هُوَ ٱلْحَكِيمُ ٱلْعَلِيمُ ﴿30﴾ ۞
قَالَ فَمَا خَطْبُكُمْ أَيُّهَا ٱلْمُرْسَلُونَ ﴿31﴾

حزب 53
جزء 27

Wa fis-samāaʾi rizqukum wa mā tūʿadūn. (22) Fawa-Rabbis-samāaʾi wal-ʾarḍi ʾinnahū laḥaqqum-mithla māa ʾannakum tanṭiqūn. (23) Hal ʾatāka ḥadīthu ḍayfi ʾIbrāhīmal-mukramīn. (24) ʾIdh dakhalū ʿalayhi faqālū salāmañ-qāla salāmuñ-qawmum-muñkarūn. (25) Farāgha ʾilāa ʾahlihī fajāaʾa biʿijliñ-samīn. (26) Faqarrabahūu ʾilayhim qāla ʾalā taʾkulūn. (27) Faʾawjasa minhum khīfatañ-qālū lā takhaf; wa bashsharūhu bighulāmin ʿalīm. (28) Faʾaqbalatim-raʾatuhū fī ṣarratiñ-faṣakkat wajhahā wa qālat ʿajūzun ʿaqīm. (29) Qālū kadhāliki qāla Rabbuki ʾinnahū Huwal-Ḥakīmul-ʿAlīm. (30) ۞ Qāla famā khaṭbukum ʾayyuhal-Mursalūn. (31)

14 I.e., both physical (rain) and spiritual (truth and guidance).

15 Lit., "even as you speak" or "are able to speak": an allusion to man's ability to think conceptually and to express himself – that is, to something of which man is absolutely, axiomatically conscious.

16 This story (as well as the subsequent mention of what happened to Lot's people and to the tribes of ʿĀd and Thamūd, of Moses and Pharaoh's people, and of Noah's people) is connected with the preceding references to the "signs", visible and conceptual, of God's existence and almightiness and the inflexible moral causality apparent in what the Qurʾān describes as "the way of God" (*sunnat Allāh*). The story of Abraham's angelic guests appears also in 11 : 69 ff. and – in a somewhat shorter version – in 15 : 51 ff. as well.

17 Lit., "unknown people" – i.e., not realizing that they were angels.

18 See note 101 on 11 : 70.

19 I.e., with prophethood (cf. 15 : 53).

They answered: "Behold, we have been sent unto a people lost in sin,[20] ‹32› to let loose upon them stone-hard blows of chastisement,[21] ‹33› marked out in thy Sustainer's sight for [the punishment of] such as have wasted their own selves."[22] ‹34›

And in the course of time[23] We brought out [of Lot's city] such [few] believers as were there: ‹35› for apart from one [single] house[24] We did not find there any who had surrendered themselves to Us. ‹36›

And so We left therein[25] a message for those who fear the grievous suffering [which awaits all evildoers]. ‹37›

AND IN [the story of Pharaoh and] Moses, too, [We left the same message:[26] for] when We sent him unto Pharaoh with [Our] manifest authority, ‹38› and he turned away in [the pride of] his power and said, "A sorcerer [is this Moses], or a madman!" ‹39› – We seized him and his hosts, and cast them all into the sea: and [none but Pharaoh] himself was to blame [for what happened].[27] ‹40›

And [you have the same message] in [what happened to the tribe of] ᶜĀd when We let loose against them that life-destroying wind ‹41› which spared nothing of what it came upon, but caused [all of] it to become like bones dead and decayed.[28] ‹42›

And in [the story of the tribe of] Thamūd, too, when they were told, "You shall enjoy your life for [but] a little while,"[29] ‹43›

قَالُوٓاْ إِنَّآ أُرۡسِلۡنَآ إِلَىٰ قَوۡمٖ مُّجۡرِمِينَ ﴿٣٢﴾ لِنُرۡسِلَ عَلَيۡهِمۡ حِجَارَةٗ مِّن
طِينٖ ﴿٣٣﴾ مُّسَوَّمَةً عِندَ رَبِّكَ لِلۡمُسۡرِفِينَ ﴿٣٤﴾ فَأَخۡرَجۡنَا مَن كَانَ فِيهَا مِنَ
ٱلۡمُؤۡمِنِينَ ﴿٣٥﴾ فَمَا وَجَدۡنَا فِيهَا غَيۡرَ بَيۡتٖ مِّنَ ٱلۡمُسۡلِمِينَ ﴿٣٦﴾ وَتَرَكۡنَا
فِيهَآ ءَايَةٗ لِّلَّذِينَ يَخَافُونَ ٱلۡعَذَابَ ٱلۡأَلِيمَ ﴿٣٧﴾ وَفِي مُوسَىٰٓ إِذۡ أَرۡسَلۡنَٰهُ
إِلَىٰ فِرۡعَوۡنَ بِسُلۡطَٰنٖ مُّبِينٖ ﴿٣٨﴾ فَتَوَلَّىٰ بِرُكۡنِهِۦ وَقَالَ سَٰحِرٌ أَوۡ مَجۡنُونٞ ﴿٣٩﴾
فَأَخَذۡنَٰهُ وَجُنُودَهُۥ فَنَبَذۡنَٰهُمۡ فِي ٱلۡيَمِّ وَهُوَ مُلِيمٞ ﴿٤٠﴾ وَفِي عَادٍ إِذۡ أَرۡسَلۡنَا
عَلَيۡهِمُ ٱلرِّيحَ ٱلۡعَقِيمَ ﴿٤١﴾ مَا تَذَرُ مِن شَيۡءٍ أَتَتۡ عَلَيۡهِ إِلَّا جَعَلَتۡهُ
كَٱلرَّمِيمِ ﴿٤٢﴾ وَفِي ثَمُودَ إِذۡ قِيلَ لَهُمۡ تَمَتَّعُواْ حَتَّىٰ حِينٖ ﴿٤٣﴾

Qālūu ᵓinnāa ᵓursilnāa ᵓilā qawmim-mujrimīn. (32) Linursila ᶜalayhim ḥijāratam-miñ-ṭīn. (33) Musawwamatan ᶜiñda Rabbika lilmusrifīn. (34) Faᵓakhrajnā mañ-kāna fīhā minal-muᵓminīn. (35) Famā wajadnā fīhā ghayra baytim-minal-Muslimīn. (36) Wa taraknā fīhāa ᵓāyatal-lilladhīna yakhāfūnal-ᶜadhābal-ᵓalīm. (37) Wa fī Mūsāa ᵓidh ᵓarsalnāhu ᵓilā Firᶜawna bisulṭānim-mubīn. (38) Fatawallā biruknihī wa qāla sāḥirun ᵓaw majnūn. (39) Faᵓakhadhnāhu wa junūdahū fanabadhnāhum fil-yammi wa huwa mulīm. (40) Wa fī ᶜĀdin ᵓidh ᵓarsalnā ᶜalayhimur-rīḥal-ᶜaqīm. (41) Mā tadharu miñ-shayᵓin ᵓatat ᶜalayhi ᵓillā jaᶜalat-hu karramīm. (42) Wa fī Thamūda ᵓidh qīla lahum tamattaᶜū ḥattā ḥīn. (43)

20 I.e., Lot's people.

21 Lit., "stones of clay" – the noun "clay" (*ṭīn*) is, according to Zamakhsharī, identical with the term *sijjīl* mentioned in 11 : 82 and tentatively explained in the corresponding note 114 as signifiying "chastisement pre-ordained".

22 For an explanation of this rendering of the term *musrifīn*, see note 21 on 10 : 12.

23 Lit., "And then", i.e., after the events described in 11 : 77 ff. and 15 : 61 ff.

24 I.e., Lot's family.

25 I.e., in the utter destruction of Sodom and Gomorrah.

26 The above interpolations are based on the consensus of most of the classical commentators regarding the phrase "And in Moses, too".

27 This is an illustration of the Qurᵓanic doctrine that the suffering which is bound to befall an evildoer in this world or in the life to come, or in both, is but a consequence of his own doings.

28 See 69 : 6-8. For the story of the tribe of ᶜĀd as such, see second half of note 48 on 7 : 65.

29 Cf. 11 : 65. An outline of the story of the Thamūd is given in 7 : 73-79.

after they had turned with disdain from their Sustainer's commandment – whereupon the thunderbolt of punishment overtook them while they were [helplessly] looking on: ‹44› for they were unable even to rise, and could not defend themselves. ‹45›
And [thus, too, We destroyed] Noah's people aforetime: for they were iniquitous folk. ‹46›

AND IT IS We who have built the universe[30] with [Our creative] power; and, verily, it is We who are steadily expanding it.[31] ‹47›
And the earth have We spread out wide – and how well have We ordered it![32] ‹48›
And in everything have We created opposites,[33] so that you might bear in mind [that God alone is One].[34] ‹49›
And so, [O Muḥammad, say unto them:] "Flee unto God [from all that is false and evil]! Verily, I am a plain warner to you from Him! ‹50› And do not ascribe divinity to aught[35] side by side with God: verily, I am a plain warner to you from Him!" ‹51›
[But] thus it is: never yet came any apostle to those who lived before their time but they said, "A spellbinder[36] [is he], or a madman!" ‹52› Have they, perchance, handed down this [way of thinking] as a legacy unto one another?
Nay, they are people filled with overweening arrogance! ‹53›
Turn, then, away from them, and thou shalt incur no blame; ‹54› yet go on reminding [all who would listen]: for, verily, such a reminder will profit the believers. ‹55›

فَعَتَوْا۟ عَنْ أَمْرِ رَبِّهِمْ فَأَخَذَتْهُمُ ٱلصَّٰعِقَةُ وَهُمْ يَنظُرُونَ ﴿44﴾ فَمَا
ٱسْتَطَٰعُوا۟ مِن قِيَامٍ وَمَا كَانُوا۟ مُنتَصِرِينَ ﴿45﴾ وَقَوْمَ نُوحٍ مِّن قَبْلُ إِنَّهُمْ
كَانُوا۟ قَوْمًا فَٰسِقِينَ ﴿46﴾ وَٱلسَّمَآءَ بَنَيْنَٰهَا بِأَيْي۟دٍ وَإِنَّا لَمُوسِعُونَ ﴿47﴾
وَٱلْأَرْضَ فَرَشْنَٰهَا فَنِعْمَ ٱلْمَٰهِدُونَ ﴿48﴾ وَمِن كُلِّ شَىْءٍ خَلَقْنَا زَوْجَيْنِ
لَعَلَّكُمْ تَذَكَّرُونَ ﴿49﴾ فَفِرُّوٓا۟ إِلَى ٱللَّهِ إِنِّى لَكُم مِّنْهُ نَذِيرٌ مُّبِينٌ ﴿50﴾ وَلَا
تَجْعَلُوا۟ مَعَ ٱللَّهِ إِلَٰهًا ءَاخَرَ إِنِّى لَكُم مِّنْهُ نَذِيرٌ مُّبِينٌ ﴿51﴾ كَذَٰلِكَ مَآ أَتَى
ٱلَّذِينَ مِن قَبْلِهِم مِّن رَّسُولٍ إِلَّا قَالُوا۟ سَاحِرٌ أَوْ مَجْنُونٌ ﴿52﴾ أَتَوَاصَوْا۟
بِهِۦ بَلْ هُمْ قَوْمٌ طَاغُونَ ﴿53﴾ فَتَوَلَّ عَنْهُمْ فَمَآ أَنتَ بِمَلُومٍ ﴿54﴾ وَذَكِّرْ فَإِنَّ
ٱلذِّكْرَىٰ تَنفَعُ ٱلْمُؤْمِنِينَ ﴿55﴾

Faᶜataw ᶜan ᵓamri Rabbihim faᵓakhadhat-humuṣ-ṣāᶜiqatu wa hum yañẓurūn. (44) Famas-taṭāᶜū miñ-qiyāmiñw-wa mā kānū muñtaṣirīn. (45) Wa qawma Nūḥim-miñ-qablu ᵓinnahum kānū qawmañ-fāsiqīn. (46) Was-samāaᵓa banaynāhā biᵓaydiñw-wa ᵓinnā lamūsiᶜūn. (47) Wal-ᵓarḍa farashnāhā faniᶜmal-māhidūn. (48) Wa miñ-kulli shayᵓin khalaqnā zawjayni laᶜallakum tadhakkarūn. (49) Fafirrūu ᵓilal-lāhi ᵓinnī lakum-minhu Nadhīrum-mubīn. (50) Wa lā tajᶜalū maᶜal-lāhi ᵓilāhan ᵓākhara ᵓinnī lakum minhu Nadīrum-mubīn. (51) Kadhālika māa ᵓatal-ladhīna miñ-qablihim-mir-Rasūlin ᵓillā qālū sāḥirun ᵓaw majnūn. (52) ᵓAtawāṣaw bih. Bal hum qawmuñ-ṭāghūn. (53) Fatawalla ᶜanhum famāa ᵓañta bimalūm. (54) Wa dhakkir faᵓinnadh-dhikrā tañfaᶜul-muᵓminīn. (55)

30 Lit., "the sky" or "the heaven", which in the Qurᵓān often has the connotation of "universe" or, in the plural ("the heavens"), of "cosmic systems".

31 See note 38 on the first part of 21 : 30. The phrase *innā la-mūsiᶜūn* clearly foreshadows the modern notion of the "expanding universe" – that is, the fact that the cosmos, though finite in extent, is continuously expanding in space.

32 I.e., in accordance with the requirements of the living organisms that were to – and did – develop on it.

33 Lit., "of every thing have We created pairs" – a phrase which is explained in note 18 on 36 : 36.

34 Cf. 89 : 3 and the corresponding note 2.

35 Lit., "do not set up any other deity".

36 Lit., "sorcerer".

And [tell them that] I have not created the invisible beings[37] and men to any end other than that they may [know and] worship Me.[38] ‹56› [But withal,] no sustenance do I ever demand of them, nor do I demand that they feed Me: ‹57› for, verily, God Himself is the Provider of all sustenance, the Lord of all might, the Eternal! ‹58›
And, verily, they who are bent on doing evil shall have their share [of evil] like unto the share of their fellows [of old]:[39] so let them not ask Me to hasten [their doom]! ‹59›
For, woe unto those who are bent on denying the truth – [woe] on the Day which they have been promised! ‹60›

وَمَا خَلَقْتُ ٱلْجِنَّ وَٱلْإِنسَ إِلَّا لِيَعْبُدُونِ ﴿٥٦﴾ مَآ أُرِيدُ مِنْهُم مِّن رِّزْقٍ
وَمَآ أُرِيدُ أَن يُطْعِمُونِ ﴿٥٧﴾ إِنَّ ٱللَّهَ هُوَ ٱلرَّزَّاقُ ذُو ٱلْقُوَّةِ ٱلْمَتِينُ ﴿٥٨﴾
فَإِنَّ لِلَّذِينَ ظَلَمُوا۟ ذَنُوبًا مِّثْلَ ذَنُوبِ أَصْحَـٰبِهِمْ فَلَا يَسْتَعْجِلُونِ ﴿٥٩﴾ فَوَيْلٌ
لِّلَّذِينَ كَفَرُوا۟ مِن يَوْمِهِمُ ٱلَّذِى يُوعَدُونَ ﴿٦٠﴾

Wa mā khalaqtul-Jinna wal-ʾIñsa ʾillā liyaʿbudūn.
(56) Māa ʾurīdu minhum-mir-rizqiñw-wa māa ʾurīdu ʾañy-yuṭʿimūn. (57) ʾInnal-lāha Huwar-Razzāqu Dhul-quwwatil-Matīn. (58) Faʾinna lilladhīna ẓalamū dhanū-bam-mithla dhanūbi ʾaṣḥābihim falā yastaʿjilūn. (59)
Fawaylul-lilladhīna kafarū miñy-Yawmihimul-ladhī yūʿadūn. (60)

---

37 For a full discussion of the term *jinn* ("invisible beings"), see Appendix III. As pointed out by most of the philologists – and stressed by Rāzī in his comments on the above verse – this term includes also the angels, since they, too, are beings or forces "concealed from man's senses".

38 Thus, the innermost purpose of the creation of all rational beings is their cognition (*maʿrifah*) of the existence of God and, hence, their conscious willingness to conform their own existence to whatever they may perceive of His will and plan: and it is this twofold concept of cognition and willingness that gives the deepest meaning to what the Qurʾān describes as "worship" (*ʿibādah*). As the next verse shows, this spiritual call does not arise from any supposed "need" on the part of the Creator, who is self-sufficient and infinite in His power, but is designed as an instrument for the inner development of the worshipper, who, by the act of his conscious self-surrender to the all-pervading Creative Will, may hope to come closer to an understanding of that Will and, thus, closer to God Himself.

39 Implying that every act of evildoing bears the seed of its own retribution either in this world or in the hereafter.

The Fifty-Second Sūrah

Aṭ-Ṭūr (Mount Sinai)

Mecca Period

THIS *SŪRAH*, revealed most probably in the later half of the Mecca period (according to some authorities, immediately after *sūrah* 32), takes its designation from the mention of Mount Sinai (*aṭ-ṭūr*) in verse 1.

-52-

سورة الطور مكية

وآياتها تسع وأربعون

IN THE NAME OF GOD, THE MOST GRACIOUS, THE DISPENSER OF GRACE:

CONSIDER Mount Sinai![1] ‹1›
Consider [God's] revelation, inscribed ‹2› on wide-open scrolls.[2] ‹3›
Consider the long-enduring house [of worship]![3] ‹4›
Consider the vault [of heaven] raised high! ‹5›
Consider the surf-swollen sea![4] ‹6›

VERILY, [O man,] the suffering decreed by thy Sustainer [for the sinners] will indeed come to pass: ‹7› there is none who could avert it. ‹8›

بِسْمِ ٱللَّهِ ٱلرَّحْمَٰنِ ٱلرَّحِيمِ

وَٱلطُّورِ ﴿١﴾ وَكِتَٰبٍ مَّسْطُورٍ ﴿٢﴾ فِى رَقٍّ مَّنشُورٍ ﴿٣﴾ وَٱلْبَيْتِ
ٱلْمَعْمُورِ ﴿٤﴾ وَٱلسَّقْفِ ٱلْمَرْفُوعِ ﴿٥﴾ وَٱلْبَحْرِ ٱلْمَسْجُورِ ﴿٦﴾ إِنَّ
عَذَابَ رَبِّكَ لَوَٰقِعٌ ﴿٧﴾ مَّا لَهُۥ مِن دَافِعٍ ﴿٨﴾

Bismil-lāhir-Raḥmānir-Raḥīm.
Waṭ-Ṭūr. ① Wa Kitābim-masṭūr. ② Fī raqqim-
mañshūr. ③ Wal-Baytil-maᶜmūr. ④ Was-saqfil-
marfūᶜ. ⑤ Wal-baḥril-masjūr. ⑥ ᵓInna ᶜadhāba
Rabbika lawāqiᶜ. ⑦ Mā lahū miñ-dāfiᶜ. ⑧

---

1 For my rendering of the adjurative particle *wa* as "Consider", see first half of note 23 on 74 : 32. The expression *aṭ-ṭūr* (lit., "the mountain") is used in the Qurᵓān exclusively to denote Mount Sinai, on which Moses received his decisive revelation. In the present context it signifies, metonymically, revelation as such, to which the next verse calls attention.

2 I.e., always open to man's understanding (Rāzī).

3 This is a metonym for the fact that ever since the dawn of human consciousness men have persistently – although often but dimly – realized the existence of God and have tried, spurred on by the continuous, direct revelation granted to His prophets, to come closer to Him through worship. Hence, Bayḍāwī regards the expression *al-bayt al-maᶜmūr* as a metaphor for the heart of the believer.

4 I.e., "Consider the immensity and wonderful configuration of the visible universe as an evidence of a conscious Creator."

[It will come to pass] on the Day when the skies will be convulsed in [a great] convulsion, ‹9› and the mountains will move with [an awesome] movement. ‹10›
Woe, then, on that Day to all who give the lie to the truth ‹11› – all those who [throughout their lives] but idly played with things vain ‹12› – on the Day when they shall be thrust into the fire with [an irresistible] thrust, [and will be told:] ‹13›
"This is the fire which you were wont to call a lie! ‹14› Was it, then, a delusion[5] – or is it that you failed to see [its truth]? ‹15› Endure it [now]! But [whether you] bear yourselves with patience or without patience, it will be the same to you: you are but being requited for what you were wont to do."[6] ‹16›
[But,] verily, the God-conscious will find themselves [on that Day] in gardens and in bliss, ‹17› rejoicing in all that their Sustainer will have granted them: for their Sustainer will have warded off from them all suffering through the blazing fire. ‹18›
[And they will be told:] "Eat and drink with good cheer as an outcome of what you were wont to do, ‹19› reclining on couches [of happiness] ranged in rows !"[7]
And [in that paradise] We shall mate them with companions pure, most beautiful of eye.[8] ‹20›
And as for those who have attained to faith and whose offspring will have followed them in faith, We shall unite them with their offspring; and We shall not let aught of their deeds go to waste:[9] [but] every human being will be held in pledge for whatever he has earned.[10] ‹21›

يَوْمَ تَمُورُ ٱلسَّمَآءُ مَوْرًا ﴿٩﴾ وَتَسِيرُ ٱلْجِبَالُ سَيْرًا ﴿١٠﴾ فَوَيْلٌ يَوْمَئِذٍ
لِّلْمُكَذِّبِينَ ﴿١١﴾ ٱلَّذِينَ هُمْ فِى خَوْضٍ يَلْعَبُونَ ﴿١٢﴾ يَوْمَ يُدَعُّونَ إِلَىٰ نَارِ
جَهَنَّمَ دَعًّا ﴿١٣﴾ هَـٰذِهِ ٱلنَّارُ ٱلَّتِى كُنتُم بِهَا تُكَذِّبُونَ ﴿١٤﴾ أَفَسِحْرٌ هَـٰذَآ أَمْ
أَنتُمْ لَا تُبْصِرُونَ ﴿١٥﴾ ٱصْلَوْهَا فَٱصْبِرُوٓا۟ أَوْ لَا تَصْبِرُوا۟ سَوَآءٌ عَلَيْكُمْ
إِنَّمَا تُجْزَوْنَ مَا كُنتُمْ تَعْمَلُونَ ﴿١٦﴾ إِنَّ ٱلْمُتَّقِينَ فِى جَنَّـٰتٍ وَنَعِيمٍ ﴿١٧﴾
فَـٰكِهِينَ بِمَآ ءَاتَىٰهُمْ رَبُّهُمْ وَوَقَىٰهُمْ رَبُّهُمْ عَذَابَ ٱلْجَحِيمِ ﴿١٨﴾ كُلُوا۟
وَٱشْرَبُوا۟ هَنِيٓـًٔا بِمَا كُنتُمْ تَعْمَلُونَ ﴿١٩﴾ مُتَّكِـِٔينَ عَلَىٰ سُرُرٍ مَّصْفُوفَةٍ
وَزَوَّجْنَـٰهُم بِحُورٍ عِينٍ ﴿٢٠﴾ وَٱلَّذِينَ ءَامَنُوا۟ وَٱتَّبَعَتْهُمْ ذُرِّيَّتُهُم بِإِيمَـٰنٍ
أَلْحَقْنَا بِهِمْ ذُرِّيَّتَهُمْ وَمَآ أَلَتْنَـٰهُم مِّنْ عَمَلِهِم مِّن شَىْءٍ كُلُّ ٱمْرِئٍۭ بِمَا
كَسَبَ رَهِينٌ ﴿٢١﴾

Yawma tamūrus-samāaʾu mawrā. (9) Wa tasīrul-jibālu sayrā. (10) Fawayluñy-Yawmaʾidhil-lilmukadhdhibīn. (11) ʾAlladhīna hum fī khawḍiñy-yalʿabūn. (12) Yawma yudaʿʿūna ʾilā nāri jahannama daʿʿā. (13) Hādhihin-nārul-latī kuñtum-bihā tukadhdhibūn. (14) ʾAfasiḥrun hādhāa ʾam ʾañtum lā tubṣirūn. (15) ʾIṣlawhā faṣbirūu ʾaw lā taṣbirū sawāaʾun ʿalaykum; ʾinnamā tujzawna mā kuñtum taʿmalūn. (16) ʾInnal-muttaqīna fī jannātiñw-wa naʿīm. (17) Fākihīna bimāa ʾātāhum Rabbuhum wa waqāhum Rabbuhum ʿadhābal-jaḥīm. (18) Kulū wash-rabū hanīiʾam-bimā kuñtum taʿmalūn. (19) Muttakiʾīna ʿalā sururim-maṣfūfatiñw-wa zawwajnāhum biḥūrin ʿīn. (20) Walladhīna ʾāmanū wat-tabaʿat-hum dhurriyyatuhum biʾīmānin ʾalḥaqnā bihim dhurriyyatahum wa māa ʾalatnāhum-min ʿamalihim-miñ-shayʾ. Kullumriʾim-bimā kasaba rahīn. (21)

5 This is obviously the meaning of the term *siḥr* in the present context (see *sūrah* 74, note 12).

6 I.e., "you will have to endure it in either case, for it is but a consequence of your own doings and attitudes": a subtle allusion to the fact that the "punishments" and "rewards" in the life to come are but allegories of the logical *consequences* of the manner in which one acts or behaves in this life.

7 As explained by Rāzī in his comments on the above verse as well as on 18 : 31 and 55 : 54, the "reclining on couches" or "on carpets" in paradise is a symbol of inner fulfilment and peace of mind; and he points out that this is also alluded to in the identity of the verbal root *sarra* ("he was [or "became"] happy") in both the nouns *surūr* ("happiness") and *sarīr* ("couch").

8 For an explanation of the expression *ḥūr ʿīn*, see *sūrah* 56, note 8.

9 Implying that the righteousness of their children increases the merit of the parents.

10 I.e., the righteousness of the parents cannot absolve their offspring from individual responsibility.

And We shall bestow on them fruit and meat in abundance – whatever they may desire: ‹22› and in that [paradise] they shall pass on to one another a cup which will not give rise to empty talk, and neither incite to sin.[11] ‹23›

And they will be waited upon by [immortal] youths,[12] [as if they were children] of their own,[13] [as pure] as if they were pearls hidden in their shells. ‹24›

And they [who are thus blest] will turn to one another, asking each other [about their past lives].[14] ‹25›

They will say: "Behold, aforetime – when we were [still living] in the midst of our kith and kin – we were full of fear [at the thought of God's displeasure]:[15] ‹26› and so God has graced us with His favour, and has warded off from us all suffering through the scorching winds [of frustration]. ‹27› Verily, we did invoke Him [alone] ere this: [and now He has shown us[16]] that He alone is truly benign, a true dispenser of grace!" ‹28›

EXHORT, then, [O Prophet, all men:] for, by thy Sustainer's grace, thou art neither a soothsayer nor a madman. ‹29›

Or do they say, "[He is but] a poet – let us await what time will do unto him"?[17] ‹30›

وَأَمْدَدْنَٰهُم بِفَٰكِهَةٍ وَلَحْمٍ مِّمَّا يَشْتَهُونَ ﴿22﴾ يَتَنَٰزَعُونَ فِيهَا كَأْسًا لَّا
لَغْوٌ فِيهَا وَلَا تَأْثِيمٌ ﴿23﴾ ۞ وَيَطُوفُ عَلَيْهِمْ غِلْمَانٌ لَّهُمْ كَأَنَّهُمْ لُؤْلُؤٌ
مَّكْنُونٌ ﴿24﴾ وَأَقْبَلَ بَعْضُهُمْ عَلَىٰ بَعْضٍ يَتَسَآءَلُونَ ﴿25﴾ قَالُوٓا۟ إِنَّا كُنَّا
قَبْلُ فِىٓ أَهْلِنَا مُشْفِقِينَ ﴿26﴾ فَمَنَّ ٱللَّهُ عَلَيْنَا وَوَقَىٰنَا عَذَابَ ٱلسَّمُومِ ﴿27﴾
إِنَّا كُنَّا مِن قَبْلُ نَدْعُوهُ إِنَّهُۥ هُوَ ٱلْبَرُّ ٱلرَّحِيمُ ﴿28﴾ فَذَكِّرْ فَمَآ أَنتَ
بِنِعْمَتِ رَبِّكَ بِكَاهِنٍ وَلَا مَجْنُونٍ ﴿29﴾ أَمْ يَقُولُونَ شَاعِرٌ نَّتَرَبَّصُ بِهِۦ
رَيْبَ ٱلْمَنُونِ ﴿30﴾

ربع الحزب

Wa ʾamdadnāhum bifākihatiñw-wa laḥmim-mimmā yashtahūn. 22 Yatanāzaʿūna fīhā kaʾsal-lā laghwuñ-fīhā wa lā taʾthīm. 23 ۞ Wa yaṭūfu ʿalayhim ghilmānul-lahum kaʾannahum luʾluʾum-maknūn. 24 Wa ʾaqbala baʿḍuhum ʿalā baʿḍiñy-yatasāaʾalūn. 25 Qālūu ʾinnā kunnā qablu fīi ʾahlinā mushfiqīn. 26 Famannal-lāhu ʿalaynā wa waqānā ʿadhābas-samūm. 27 ʾInnā kunnā miñ-qablu nadʿūhu ʾinnahū Huwal-Barrur-Raḥīm. 28 Fadhakkir famāa ʾañta biniʿmati Rabbika bikāhiniñw-wa lā majnūn. 29 ʾAm yaqūlūna shāʿiruñ-natarabbaṣu bihī raybal-manūn. 30

11 Cf. 37 : 47 – "no headiness will there be in it, and they will not get drunk thereon"; and 56 : 19 – "by which their minds will not be clouded, and which will not make them drunk": an allegory of conscious, joyful elation. As regards the preceding reference to "fruit and meat in abundance – whatever they may desire", Rāzī observes that this symbolic "abundance" of sensual satisfaction will not lead to satiety but, rather, to a pleasurable desire which – contrary to what is man's lot in this world – can always be gratified.

12 See note 6 on 56 : 17-18.

13 Thus Rāzī, explaining the selfless devotion implied in the pronoun *lahum* (lit., "for them", i.e., "of their own").

14 This symbolic "asking one another about their past lives" is meant to bring out the fact, often stressed in the Qurʾān, that man's individual consciousness invariably survives his bodily death, to continue unbroken in the life to come.

15 Thus do all classical commentators – without, to my knowledge, any exception – interpret the above verse.

16 Sc., "through our own, actual experience". This interpolation is based on the reading of the subsequent word as *annahu* ("that He is"), according to the Medina school, in contrast with the more conventional Kūfah and Baṣrah reading *innahu* ("verily, He is"). As Ṭabarī stresses, either of these two readings is correct; I have chosen for my rendering the former inasmuch as it points to the overwhelming, direct insight which will be granted to the blessed on resurrection.

17 Lit., "let us await for him the evil happenings of time", i.e., brought about by time: this is the meaning given by Jawharī and Zamakhsharī (in the *Asās*) to the expression *rayb al-manūn* (which latter word is, according to these two authorities, a synonym of *dahr*, "time"). In the present context, the phrase obviously denotes the expectation of the Prophet's detractors that time would prove his teachings to have been false or, at best, a delusion.

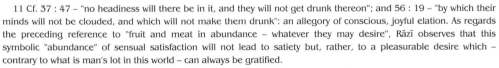

Say thou: "Wait, [then,] hopefully; behold, I, too, shall hopefully wait with you!"[18] ‹31›
Is it their minds that bid them [to take] this [attitude] – or are they [simply] people filled with overweening arrogance?[19] ‹32›
Or do they say, "He himself has composed this [message]"?
Nay, but they are not willing to believe! ‹33›
But then, [if they deem it the work of a mere mortal,] let them produce another discourse like it – if what they say be true! ‹34›
[Or do they deny the existence of God?[20]] Have they themselves been created without anything [that might have caused their creation]?[21] – or were they, perchance, their own creators? ‹35› [And] have they created the heavens and the earth?[22]
Nay, but they have no certainty of anything! ‹36›
[How could they?] Are thy Sustainer's treasures with them?[23] Or are they in charge [of destiny]? ‹37› Or have they a ladder by which they could [ascend to ultimate truths and] listen [to what is beyond the reach of human perception]? Let, then, any of them who has listened [to it] produce a manifest proof [of his knowledge]! ‹38›
Or, [if you believe in God, how can you believe that] He has [chosen to have] daughters, whereas you yourselves would have [only] sons?[24] ‹39›
Or is it that [they who reject thy message, O Muḥammad, fear lest] thou ask of them a reward, so that they would be burdened with debt [if they should listen to thee]? ‹40›

قُلْ تَرَبَّصُوا۟ فَإِنِّى مَعَكُم مِّنَ ٱلْمُتَرَبِّصِينَ ﴿٣١﴾ أَمْ تَأْمُرُهُمْ أَحْلَٰمُهُم
بِهَٰذَآ ۚ أَمْ هُمْ قَوْمٌ طَاغُونَ ﴿٣٢﴾ أَمْ يَقُولُونَ تَقَوَّلَهُۥ ۚ بَل لَّا يُؤْمِنُونَ ﴿٣٣﴾
فَلْيَأْتُوا۟ بِحَدِيثٍ مِّثْلِهِۦٓ إِن كَانُوا۟ صَٰدِقِينَ ﴿٣٤﴾ أَمْ خُلِقُوا۟ مِنْ غَيْرِ شَىْءٍ
أَمْ هُمُ ٱلْخَٰلِقُونَ ﴿٣٥﴾ أَمْ خَلَقُوا۟ ٱلسَّمَٰوَٰتِ وَٱلْأَرْضَ ۚ بَل لَّا
يُوقِنُونَ ﴿٣٦﴾ أَمْ عِندَهُمْ خَزَآئِنُ رَبِّكَ أَمْ هُمُ ٱلْمُصَۜيْطِرُونَ ﴿٣٧﴾ أَمْ لَهُمْ
سُلَّمٌ يَسْتَمِعُونَ فِيهِ ۖ فَلْيَأْتِ مُسْتَمِعُهُم بِسُلْطَٰنٍ مُّبِينٍ ﴿٣٨﴾ أَمْ لَهُ ٱلْبَنَٰتُ
وَلَكُمُ ٱلْبَنُونَ ﴿٣٩﴾ أَمْ تَسْـَٔلُهُمْ أَجْرًا فَهُم مِّن مَّغْرَمٍ مُّثْقَلُونَ ﴿٤٠﴾

Qul tarabbaṣū faʾinnī maʿakum-minal-mutarabbiṣīn. (31) ʾAm taʾmuruhum ʾaḥlāmuhum bihādhāa ʾam hum qawmuñ-ṭāghūn. (32) ʾAm yaqūlūna taqawwalah. Bal-lā yuʾminūn. (33) Falyaʾtū biḥadīthim-mithlihīi ʾiñ-kānū ṣādiqīn. (34) ʾAm khuliqū min ghayri shayʾin ʾam humul-khāliqūn. (35) ʾAm khalaqus-samāwāti wal-ʾarḍ. Bal-lā yūqinūn. (36) ʾAm ʿiñdahum khazāaʾinu Rabbika ʾam humul-musayṭirūn. (37) ʾAm lahum sullamuñy-yastamiʿūna fīh. Falyaʾti mustamiʿuhum bisulṭānim-mubīn. (38) ʾAm lahul-banātu wa lakumul-banūn. (39) Am tasʾaluhum ʾajrañ-fahum-mim-maghramim-muthqalūn. (40)

18 I.e., "Whereas you are waiting for my message to be proved false, I am awaiting its fulfilment!"

19 The meaning is: Have they any reasoned objection to the contents of this message – or do they simply reject the truth because their false pride in man's supposed "self-sufficiency" (cf. 96 : 6-7) prevents them from accepting the notion of responsibility before a Supreme Being?

20 I.e., implicitly, by denying the fact of His revelation.

21 I.e., by "spontaneous generation", as it were.

22 This is a *reductio ad absurdum* of their unwillingness to admit the existence of a conscious Primary Cause underlying all creation.

23 I.e., the treasures of His infinite knowledge and power.

24 This is addressed specifically to the pagan contemporaries of the Prophet, implying that "you not only

Or [do they think] that the hidden reality [of all that exists] is almost within their grasp, so that [in time] they can write it down?[25] ‹41›
Or do they want to entrap [thee in contradictions]? But they who are bent on denying the truth – it is they who are truly entrapped![26] ‹42›
Have they, then, any deity other than God? Utterly remote is God, in His limitless glory, from anything to which men may ascribe a share in His divinity! ‹43›

AND YET, if they [who refuse to see the truth] were to see part of the sky falling down, they would [only] say, "[It is but] a mass of clouds!" ‹44›
Hence, leave them alone until they face that [Judgment] Day of theirs, when they will be stricken with terror: ‹45› the Day when none of their scheming will be of the least avail to them, and they will receive no succour. . . . ‹46›
But, verily, for those who are bent on doing evil, there is suffering in store [even] closer at hand than that [supreme suffering in the hereafter]:[27] but most of them are not aware of it. ‹47›
And so, await in patience thy Sustainer's judgment, for thou art well within Our sight.[28] And extol thy Sustainer's limitless glory and praise whenever thou risest up, ‹48› and extol His glory at night, and at the time when the stars retreat. ‹49›

أَمْ عِندَهُمُ ٱلْغَيْبُ فَهُمْ يَكْتُبُونَ ﴿٤١﴾ أَمْ يُرِيدُونَ كَيْدًا فَٱلَّذِينَ كَفَرُوا۟
هُمُ ٱلْمَكِيدُونَ ﴿٤٢﴾ أَمْ لَهُمْ إِلَٰهٌ غَيْرُ ٱللَّهِ سُبْحَٰنَ ٱللَّهِ عَمَّا
يُشْرِكُونَ ﴿٤٣﴾ وَإِن يَرَوْا۟ كِسْفًا مِّنَ ٱلسَّمَآءِ سَاقِطًا يَقُولُوا۟ سَحَابٌ
مَّرْكُومٌ ﴿٤٤﴾ فَذَرْهُمْ حَتَّىٰ يُلَٰقُوا۟ يَوْمَهُمُ ٱلَّذِى فِيهِ يُصْعَقُونَ ﴿٤٥﴾ يَوْمَ لَا
يُغْنِى عَنْهُمْ كَيْدُهُمْ شَيْـًٔا وَلَا هُمْ يُنصَرُونَ ﴿٤٦﴾ وَإِنَّ لِلَّذِينَ ظَلَمُوا۟ عَذَابًا
دُونَ ذَٰلِكَ وَلَٰكِنَّ أَكْثَرَهُمْ لَا يَعْلَمُونَ ﴿٤٧﴾ وَٱصْبِرْ لِحُكْمِ رَبِّكَ فَإِنَّكَ
بِأَعْيُنِنَا وَسَبِّحْ بِحَمْدِ رَبِّكَ حِينَ تَقُومُ ﴿٤٨﴾ وَمِنَ ٱلَّيْلِ فَسَبِّحْهُ وَإِدْبَٰرَ
ٱلنُّجُومِ ﴿٤٩﴾

ʾAm ʿiñdahumul-ghaybu fahum yaktubūn. (41) ʾAm yurīdūna kaydā. Falladhīna kafarū humul-makīdūn. (42) ʾAm lahum ʾilāhun ghayrul-lāh. Subḥānal-lāhi ʿammā yushrikūn. (43) Wa ʾiñy-yaraw kisfam-minas-samāaʾi sāqiṭañy-yaqūlū saḥābum-markūm. (44) Fadharhum ḥattā yulāqū Yawmahumul-ladhī fīhi yuṣʿaqūn. (45) Yawma lā yughnī ʿanhum kayduhum shayʾañw-wa lā hum yuñṣarūn. (46) Wa ʾinna lilladhīna ẓalamū ʿadhābañ-dūna dhālika wa lākinna ʾaktharahum lā yaʿlamūn. (47) Waṣ-bir liḥukmi Rabbika faʾinnaka biʾaʿyuninā wa sabbiḥ biḥamdi Rabbika ḥīna taqūm. (48) Wa minal-layli fasabbiḥhu wa ʾidbāran-nujūm. (49)

blaspheme by ascribing progeny to God, but you intensify your blasphemy by ascribing to Him something that you yourselves despise, i.e., female offspring": cf. 16 : 57-59 and the corresponding notes.

25 For an explanation, see note 26 on the identical passage in 68 : 47.

26 I.e., it is they who constantly lose themselves in contradictions, whereas the message of the Qurʾān is free thereof (cf. 4 : 82 and the corresponding note).

27 As in 32 : 21, the Qurʾān stresses here the fact that every evil deed is bound to react in some way or other, even in this world, against him who commits it – either by depriving him of the affection of those who surround him and, thus, deepening his inner loneliness, or, more directly, by creating circumstances which make the achievement of real happiness and satisfaction increasingly impossible.

28 I.e., "under Our protection".

The Fifty-Third Sūrah

An-Najm (The Unfolding)

Mecca Period

IT IS generally assumed that this is a comparatively early Meccan *sūrah*, revealed shortly after *sūrah* 112. However, some parts of it undoubtedly belong to a later period – especially verses 13-18, which allude to the Prophet's mystic experience of an ascension to heaven (*mi^crāj*), about one year before his exodus to Medina (see Appendix IV).

The title – explained in note 1 on the following page – is taken from the word *an-najm* at the beginning of the first verse.

-53-

سورة النجم مكية

وآياتها اثنتان وستون

IN THE NAME OF GOD, THE MOST GRACIOUS, THE DISPENSER OF GRACE:

CONSIDER this unfolding [of God's message], as it comes down from on high![1] ‹1›

This fellow-man of yours has not gone astray, nor is he deluded,[2] ‹2› and neither does he speak out of his own desire: ‹3› that [which he conveys to you] is but [a divine] inspiration with which he is being inspired ‹4› – something that a very mighty one[3] has imparted to him: ‹5› [an angel] endowed with surpassing power, who in time manifested himself in his true shape and nature, ‹6› appearing in the horizon's loftiest part,[4] ‹7› and then drew near, and came close, ‹8› until he was but two bow-lengths away, or even nearer.[5] ‹9›

And thus did [God] reveal unto His servant whatever He deemed right to reveal.[6] ‹10›

بِسْمِ ٱللَّهِ ٱلرَّحْمَٰنِ ٱلرَّحِيمِ

وَٱلنَّجْمِ إِذَا هَوَىٰ (1) مَا ضَلَّ صَاحِبُكُمْ وَمَا غَوَىٰ (2) وَمَا يَنطِقُ
عَنِ ٱلْهَوَىٰٓ (3) إِنْ هُوَ إِلَّا وَحْيٌ يُوحَىٰ (4) عَلَّمَهُۥ شَدِيدُ ٱلْقُوَىٰ (5)
ذُو مِرَّةٍ فَٱسْتَوَىٰ (6) وَهُوَ بِٱلْأُفُقِ ٱلْأَعْلَىٰ (7) ثُمَّ دَنَا فَتَدَلَّىٰ (8)
فَكَانَ قَابَ قَوْسَيْنِ أَوْ أَدْنَىٰ (9) فَأَوْحَىٰٓ إِلَىٰ عَبْدِهِۦ مَآ أَوْحَىٰ (10)

Bismil-lāhir-Raḥmānir-Raḥīm.

Wan-najmi ʾidhā hawā. (1) Mā ḍalla ṣāḥibukum wa mā ghawā. (2) Wa mā yañṭiqu ʿanil-hawā. (3) ʾIn huwa ʾillā waḥyuñy-yūḥā. (4) ʿAllamahū shadīdul-quwā. (5) Dhū mirratiñ-fastawā. (6) Wa huwa bilʾufuqil-ʾaʿlā. (7) Thumma danā fatadallā. (8) Fakāna qāba qawsayni ʾaw ʾadnā. (9) Faʾawḥāa ʾilā ʿabdihī māa ʾawḥā. (10)

---

1 Or: "Consider the star when it sets" – an interpretation which for some reason has the preference of the majority of the commentators. However, almost all of them admit that the term *najm* – derived from the verb *najama*, "it appeared", "began", "ensued", or "proceeded" – denotes also the "unfolding" of something that comes or appears gradually, as if by instalments. Hence, this term has from the very beginning been applied to each of the gradually-revealed parts (*nujūm*) of the Qurʾān and, thus, to the *process* of its gradual revelation, or its "unfolding", as such. This was, in fact, the interpretation of the above verse given by ʿAbd Allāh ibn ʿAbbās (as quoted by Ṭabarī); in view of the sequence, this interpretation is regarded as fully justified by Rāghib, Zamakhsharī, Rāzī, Bayḍāwī, Ibn Kathīr and other authorities. Rāghib and Ibn Kathīr, in particular, point to the phrase *mawāqiʿ an-nujūm* in 56 : 75, which undoubtedly refers to the step-by-step revelation of the Qurʾān. – As regards my rendering of the adjurative particle *wa* as "Consider", see *sūrah* 74, note 23.

2 See note 150 on 7 : 184.

3 I.e., the Angel of Revelation, Gabriel.

4 Cf. 81 : 23 and the corresponding note 8. According to the Qurʾān and the testimony of authentic Traditions, the Prophet had no more than twice in his lifetime a vision of this angelic force "manifested in its true shape and nature" (which, as pointed out by Zamakhsharī, is the meaning of the expression *istawā* in this context): once after the period called *fatrat al-waḥy* (see introductory note to *sūrah* 74), and another time, as alluded to in verses 13-18, in the course of his mystic vision known as the "Ascension" (see Appendix IV).

5 This graphic "description" of the angel's approach, based on an ancient Arabian figure of speech, is meant to convey the idea that the Angel of Revelation became a clearly perceptible, almost tangible, presence.

6 Lit., "whatever He revealed": an allusion to the exceptional manifestation of the angel "in his true shape and nature" as well as to the contents of divine revelation as such. In its deeper sense the above phrase implies that even to His chosen prophets God does not *entirely* unveil the ultimate mysteries of existence, of life and death, of the purpose for which He has created the universe, or of the nature of the universe itself.

The [servant's] heart did not give the lie to what he saw:[7] ‹11› will you, then, contend with him as to what he saw?[8] ‹12›
And, indeed, he saw him[9] a second time ‹13› by the lote-tree of the farthest limit,[10] ‹14› near unto the garden of promise, ‹15› with the lote-tree veiled in a veil of nameless splendour. . . .[11] ‹16›
[And withal,] the eye did not waver, nor yet did it stray: ‹17› truly did he see some of the most profound of his Sustainer's symbols.[12] ‹18›

HAVE YOU, then, ever considered [what you are worshipping in] Al-Lāt and Al-ʿUzzā, ‹19› as well as [in] Manāt, the third and last [of this triad]'?[13] ‹20›
Why – for yourselves [you would choose only] male offspring, whereas to Him [you assign] female:[14] ‹21› that, lo and behold, is an unfair division! ‹22›

مَا كَذَبَ ٱلْفُؤَادُ مَا رَأَىٰ (11) أَفَتُمَٰرُونَهُۥ عَلَىٰ مَا يَرَىٰ (12) وَلَقَدْ رَءَاهُ
نَزْلَةً أُخْرَىٰ (13) عِندَ سِدْرَةِ ٱلْمُنتَهَىٰ (14) عِندَهَا جَنَّةُ ٱلْمَأْوَىٰٓ (15)
إِذْ يَغْشَى ٱلسِّدْرَةَ مَا يَغْشَىٰ (16) مَا زَاغَ ٱلْبَصَرُ وَمَا طَغَىٰ (17) لَقَدْ رَأَىٰ
مِنْ ءَايَٰتِ رَبِّهِ ٱلْكُبْرَىٰٓ (18) أَفَرَءَيْتُمُ ٱللَّٰتَ وَٱلْعُزَّىٰ (19) وَمَنَوٰةَ
ٱلثَّالِثَةَ ٱلْأُخْرَىٰٓ (20) أَلَكُمُ ٱلذَّكَرُ وَلَهُ ٱلْأُنثَىٰ (21) تِلْكَ إِذًا قِسْمَةٌ
ضِيزَىٰٓ (22)

Mā kadhabal-fuʾādu mā raʾā. (11) ʾAfatumārūnahū ʿalā mā yarā. (12) Wa laqad raʾāhu nazlatan ʾukhrā. (13) ʿIñda sidratil-muñtahā. (14) ʿIñdahā jannatul-maʾwā. (15) ʾIdh yaghshas-sidrata mā yaghshā. (16) Mā zāghal-baṣaru wa mā ṭaghā. (17) Laqad raʾā min ʾĀyāti Rabbihil-kubrā. (18) ʾAfaraʾaytumul-Lāta wal-ʿUzzā. (19) Wa Manātath-thālithatal-ʾukhrā. (20) ʾAlakumudh-dhakaru wa lahul-ʾuñthā. (21) Tilka ʾidhañ-qismatuñ-ḍīzā. (22)

---

7 Inasmuch as the Prophet was fully aware of the *spiritual* character of his experience, there was no conflict between his conscious mind and his intuitive perception (the "vision of the heart") of what is normally not perceptible.

8 Thus the Qurʾān makes it clear that the Prophet's vision of the angel was not a delusion but a true spiritual experience: but precisely because it was purely spiritual in nature, it could be conveyed to others only by means of symbols and allegories, which sceptics all too readily dismiss as fancies, "contending with him as to what he saw".

9 I.e., he saw the angel "manifested in his true shape and nature".

10 I.e., on the occasion of his mystic experience of the "Ascension" (*miʿrāj*). Explaining the vision conveyed in the expression *sidrat al-muntahā*, Rāghib suggests that owing to the abundance of its leafy shade, the *sidr* or *sidrah* (the Arabian lote-tree) appears in the Qurʾān as well as in the Traditions relating to the Ascension as a symbol of the "shade" – i.e., the spiritual peace and fulfilment – of paradise. One may assume that the qualifying term *al-muntahā* ("of the utmost [or "farthest"] limit") is indicative of the fact that God has set a definite limit to all knowledge accessible to created beings, as pointed out in the *Nihāyah*: implying, in particular, that human knowledge, though potentially vast and penetrating, can never – not even in paradise (the "garden of promise" mentioned in the next verse) – attain to an understanding of the ultimate reality, which the Creator has reserved for Himself (cf. note 6 above).

11 Lit., "when the lote-tree was veiled with whatever veiled [it]": a phrase deliberately vague (*mubham*), indicative of the inconceivable majesty and splendour attaching to this symbol of paradise "which no description can picture and no definition can embrace" (Zamakhsharī).

12 Lit., "[some] of the greatest of his Sustainer's symbols (*āyāt*)". For this specific rendering of the term *āyah*, see note 2 on 17 : 1, which refers to the same mystic experience, namely, the Ascension. In both these Qurʾanic allusions the Prophet is said to have been "made to see" (i.e., given to understand) some, but not all, of the ultimate truths (cf. also 7 : 187-188); and this, too, serves to explain the idea expressed in verse 10 above.

13 After pointing out that the Prophet was granted true insight into some of the most profound verities, the Qurʾān draws our attention to the "false symbols" which men so often choose to invest with divine qualities or powers: in this instance – by way of example – to the blasphemous imagery of the Prophet's pagan contemporaries epitomized in the triad of Al-Lāt, Manāt and Al-ʿUzzā. These three goddesses – regarded by the pagan Arabs as "God's daughters" side by side with the angels (who, too, were conceived of as females) – were worshipped in most of pre-Islamic Arabia, and had several shrines in the Ḥijāz and in Najd. The worship of Al-Lāt was particularly ancient and almost certainly of South-Arabian origin; she may have been the prototype of the Greek semi-goddess Leto, one of the wives of Zeus and mother of Apollo and Artemis.

14 In view of the contempt which the pagan Arabs felt for their female offspring (cf. 16 : 57-59 and 62, as well as the corresponding notes), their attribution of "daughters" to God was particularly absurd and self-contradictory: for, quite apart from the blasphemous belief in God's having "offspring" of any kind, their ascribing to Him what they

These [allegedly divine beings] are nothing but empty names which you have invented – you and your forefathers – [and] for which God has bestowed no warrant from on high.[15] They [who worship them] follow nothing but surmise and their own wishful thinking[16] – although right guidance has now indeed come unto them from their Sustainer. ‹23›
Does man imagine that it is his due to have[17] all that he might wish for, ‹24› despite the fact that [both] the life to come and this present [one] belong to God [alone]'?[18] ‹25›
For, however many angels there be in the heavens, their intercession can be of no least avail [to anyone] – except after God has given leave [to intercede] for whomever He wills and with whom He is well-pleased.[19] ‹26›
Behold, it is [only] such as do not [really] believe in the life to come that regard the angels as female beings;[20] ‹27› and [since] they have no knowledge whatever thereof,[21] they follow nothing but surmise: yet, behold, never can surmise take the place of truth. ‹28›

إِنْ هِيَ إِلَّآ أَسْمَآءٌ سَمَّيْتُمُوهَآ أَنتُمْ وَءَابَآؤُكُم مَّآ أَنزَلَ ٱللَّهُ بِهَا مِن سُلْطَٰنٍ
إِن يَتَّبِعُونَ إِلَّا ٱلظَّنَّ وَمَا تَهْوَى ٱلْأَنفُسُ وَلَقَدْ جَآءَهُم مِّن رَّبِّهِمُ
ٱلْهُدَىٰٓ (23) أَمْ لِلْإِنسَٰنِ مَا تَمَنَّىٰ (24) فَلِلَّهِ ٱلْءَاخِرَةُ وَٱلْأُولَىٰ (25) ۞
وَكَم مِّن مَّلَكٍ فِى ٱلسَّمَٰوَٰتِ لَا تُغْنِى شَفَٰعَتُهُمْ شَيْـًٔا إِلَّا مِنۢ بَعْدِ أَن
يَأْذَنَ ٱللَّهُ لِمَن يَشَآءُ وَيَرْضَىٰٓ (26) إِنَّ ٱلَّذِينَ لَا يُؤْمِنُونَ بِٱلْءَاخِرَةِ
لَيُسَمُّونَ ٱلْمَلَٰٓئِكَةَ تَسْمِيَةَ ٱلْأُنثَىٰ (27) وَمَا لَهُم بِهِۦ مِنْ عِلْمٍ إِن يَتَّبِعُونَ
إِلَّا ٱلظَّنَّ وَإِنَّ ٱلظَّنَّ لَا يُغْنِى مِنَ ٱلْحَقِّ شَيْـًٔا (28)

نصف الحزب

ʾIn hiya ʾillāa ʾasmāaʾuñ-sammaytumūhāa ʾañtum wa ʾābāaʾukum-māa ʾañzalal-lāhu bihā miñ-sulṭān. ʾIñy-yattabiʿūna ʾillaẓ-ẓanna wa mā tahwal-ʾañfusu wa laqad jāaʾahum-mir-Rabbihimul-hudā. (23) ʾAm lilʾIñsāni mā tamannā. (24) Falillāhil-ʾĀkhiratu wal-ʾūlā. (25) ◈ Wa kam-mim-Malakiñ-fis-samāwāti lā tughnī shafāʿatuhum shayʾan ʾillā mim-baʿdi ʾañy-yaʾdhanal-lāhu limañy-yashāaʾu wa yarḍā. (26) ʾInnal-ladhīna lā yuʾminūna bilʾĀkhirati layusammūnal-Malāaʾikata tasmiyatal-ʾuñthā. (27) Wa mā lahum bihī min ʿilm. ʾIñy-yattabiʿūna ʾillaẓ-ẓanna wa ʾinnaẓ-ẓanna lā yughnī minal-ḥaqqi shayʾā. (28)

themselves despised gave the lie to their alleged "reverence" for Him whom they, too, regarded as the Supreme Being – a point which is stressed with irony in the next sentence.

15 Cf. 12 : 40.

16 An allusion to the pagan idea that those goddesses, as well as the angels, would act as "mediators" between their worshippers and God: a wishful idea which lingers on even among adherents of higher religions in the guise of a veneration of saints and deified persons.

17 Lit., "Is it for man to have . . .", etc.

18 I.e., despite the fact (which is the meaning of the particle *fa* in this context) that God is omnipotent and omniscient and does not, therefore, require any "mediator" between Himself and His creatures.

19 For an explanation of the Qurʾanic concept of "intercession", see note 7 on 10 : 3, as well as notes 26 and 27 on 10 : 18.

20 Lit., "that name the angels with a female name" – i.e., think of them as being endowed with sex and/or as being "God's daughters". As the Qurʾān points out in many places, the people spoken of in this context do believe in life after death, inasmuch as they express the hope that the angels and the imaginary deities which they worship will "mediate" between them and God, and will "intercede" for them. However, their belief is far too vague to make them realize that the quality of man's life in the hereafter does not depend on such outside factors but is causally, and directly, connected with the manner of his life in *this* world: and so the Qurʾān declares that their attitude is, for all practical purposes, not much different from the attitude of people who reject the idea of a hereafter altogether.

21 Namely, of the real nature and function of the category of beings spoken of in the Qurʾān as angels, inasmuch as they belong to the realm of *al-ghayb*, "that which is beyond the reach of human perception". Alternatively, the pronoun in *bihi* may relate to God, in which case the phrase could be rendered as "they have no knowledge whatever of Him" – implying that both the attribution of "progeny" to Him and the belief that His judgment depends on, or could be influenced by, "mediation" or "intercession" is the result of an anthropomorphic concept of God and, therefore, far removed from the truth.

Avoid thou, therefore, those who turn away from all remembrance of Us and care for no more than the life of this world, ‹29› which, to them, is the only thing worth knowing.[22] Behold, thy Sustainer is fully aware as to who has strayed from His path, and fully aware is He as to who follows His guidance. ‹30›

Indeed, unto God belongs all that is in the heavens and all that is on earth: and so He will reward those who do evil in accordance with what they did, and will reward those who do good with ultimate good.[23] ‹31›

As for those who avoid the [truly] grave sins and shameful deeds – even though they may sometimes stumble[24] – behold, thy Sustainer is abounding in forgiveness.

He is fully aware of you[25] when He brings you into being out of dust,[26] and when you are still hidden in your mothers' wombs: do not, then, consider yourselves pure – [for] He knows best as to who is conscious of Him.[27] ‹32›

HAST THOU, then, ever considered him who turns away [from remembering Us, and cares for no more than the life of this world], ‹33› and gives so little [of himself for the good of his soul], and so grudgingly?[28] ‹34›

Does he [claim to] have knowledge of something that is beyond the reach of human perception, so that he can see [it clearly]?[29] ‹35›

فَأَعْرِضْ عَن مَّن تَوَلَّىٰ عَن ذِكْرِنَا وَلَمْ يُرِدْ إِلَّا ٱلْحَيَوٰةَ ٱلدُّنْيَا ﴿٢٩﴾ ذَٰلِكَ
مَبْلَغُهُم مِّنَ ٱلْعِلْمِ إِنَّ رَبَّكَ هُوَ أَعْلَمُ بِمَن ضَلَّ عَن سَبِيلِهِۦ وَهُوَ أَعْلَمُ
بِمَنِ ٱهْتَدَىٰ ﴿٣٠﴾ وَلِلَّهِ مَا فِى ٱلسَّمَٰوَٰتِ وَمَا فِى ٱلْأَرْضِ لِيَجْزِىَ
ٱلَّذِينَ أَسَٰٓـُٔوا۟ بِمَا عَمِلُوا۟ وَيَجْزِىَ ٱلَّذِينَ أَحْسَنُوا۟ بِٱلْحُسْنَى ﴿٣١﴾ ٱلَّذِينَ
يَجْتَنِبُونَ كَبَٰٓئِرَ ٱلْإِثْمِ وَٱلْفَوَٰحِشَ إِلَّا ٱللَّمَمَ إِنَّ رَبَّكَ وَٰسِعُ ٱلْمَغْفِرَةِ
هُوَ أَعْلَمُ بِكُمْ إِذْ أَنشَأَكُم مِّنَ ٱلْأَرْضِ وَإِذْ أَنتُمْ أَجِنَّةٌ فِى بُطُونِ
أُمَّهَٰتِكُمْ فَلَا تُزَكُّوٓا۟ أَنفُسَكُمْ هُوَ أَعْلَمُ بِمَنِ ٱتَّقَىٰٓ ﴿٣٢﴾ أَفَرَءَيْتَ ٱلَّذِى
تَوَلَّىٰ ﴿٣٣﴾ وَأَعْطَىٰ قَلِيلًا وَأَكْدَىٰٓ ﴿٣٤﴾ أَعِندَهُۥ عِلْمُ ٱلْغَيْبِ فَهُوَ يَرَىٰٓ ﴿٣٥﴾

Fa'a'riḍ 'am-mañ-tawallā 'añ-dhikrinā wa lam yurid
'illal-ḥayātad-dunyā. (29) Dhālika mablaghuhum-
minal-'ilm. 'Inna Rabbaka Huwa 'a'lamu bimañ-
ḍalla 'añ-sabīlihī wa Huwa 'a'lamu bimanih-tadā.
(30) Wa lillāhi mā fis-samāwāti wa mā fil-'arḍi liyaj-
ziyal-ladhīna 'asāa'ū bimā 'amilū wa yajziyal-
ladhīna 'aḥsanū bilḥusnā. (31) 'Alladhīna yajta-
nibūna kabāa'iral-'ithmi wal-fawāḥisha 'illal-lamam.
'Inna Rabbaka Wāsi'ul-maghfirah. Huwa 'a'lamu bi-
kum 'idh 'añsha'akum-minal-'arḍi wa 'idh 'añtum
'ajinnatuñ-fī buṭūni 'ummahātikum. Falā tuzakkūu
'añfusakum; Huwa 'a'lamu bimanit-taqā. (32) 'Afa-
ra'aytal-ladhī tawallā. (33) Wa 'a'ṭā qalīlañw-wa
'akdā. (34) 'A'iñdahū 'ilmul-ghaybi fahuwa yarā. (35)

---

22 Lit., "that is their sum-total [or "goal"] of knowledge".

23 I.e., whereas good deeds will be rewarded with far more than their merits may warrant, evil will be recompensed with no more than its equivalent (cf. 6 : 160); and either will be decided by the Almighty without the need of "mediation" or "intercession".

24 Lit., "save for a touch [thereof]": a phrase which may be taken to mean "an occasional stumbling into sin" – i.e., not deliberately – followed by sincere repentance (Baghawī, Rāzī, Ibn Kathīr).

25 Sc., "and of your inborn weakness" – an implied echo of the statement that "man has been created weak" (4 : 28) and, therefore, liable to stumble into sinning.

26 Lit., "out of the earth": see second half of note 47 on 3 : 59, as well as note 4 on 23 : 12.

27 I.e., "never boast about your own purity", but remain humble and remember that "it is God who causes whomever He wills to remain pure" (4 : 49).

28 My rendering of the above two verses (together with the two interpolations between brackets) is based on Rāzī's convincing interpretation of this passage as a return to the theme touched upon in verses 29-30.

29 I.e., "How can he be so sure that there is no life in the hereafter, and no judgment?"

Or has he never yet been told of what was [said] in the revelations of Moses, ‹36›
and of Abraham, who to his trust was true:[30] ‹37›
that no bearer of burdens shall be made to bear another's burden;[31] ‹38›
and that nought shall be accounted unto man but what he is striving for;[32] ‹39›
and that in time [the nature of] all his striving will be shown [to him in its true light],[33] ‹40› whereupon he shall be requited for it with the fullest requital; ‹41›
and that with thy Sustainer is the beginning and the end [of all that exists];[34] ‹42›
and that it is He alone who causes [you] to laugh and to weep; ‹43›
and that it is He alone who deals death and grants life; ‹44›
and that it is He who creates the two kinds – the male and the female ‹45› – out of a [mere] drop of sperm as it is poured forth, ‹46› and that [therefore] it is within His power to bring about a second life;[35] ‹47›
and that it is He alone who frees from want and causes to possess; ‹48›

أَمْ لَمْ يُنَبَّأْ بِمَا فِى صُحُفِ مُوسَىٰ (36) وَإِبْرَٰهِيمَ ٱلَّذِى وَفَّىٰٓ (37) أَلَّا تَزِرُ
وَازِرَةٌ وِزْرَ أُخْرَىٰ (38) وَأَن لَّيْسَ لِلْإِنسَٰنِ إِلَّا مَا سَعَىٰ (39) وَأَنَّ
سَعْيَهُۥ سَوْفَ يُرَىٰ (40) ثُمَّ يُجْزَىٰهُ ٱلْجَزَآءَ ٱلْأَوْفَىٰ (41) وَأَنَّ إِلَىٰ رَبِّكَ
ٱلْمُنتَهَىٰ (42) وَأَنَّهُۥ هُوَ أَضْحَكَ وَأَبْكَىٰ (43) وَأَنَّهُۥ هُوَ أَمَاتَ وَأَحْيَا (44)
وَأَنَّهُۥ خَلَقَ ٱلزَّوْجَيْنِ ٱلذَّكَرَ وَٱلْأُنثَىٰ (45) مِن نُّطْفَةٍ إِذَا تُمْنَىٰ (46) وَأَنَّ
عَلَيْهِ ٱلنَّشْأَةَ ٱلْأُخْرَىٰ (47) وَأَنَّهُۥ هُوَ أَغْنَىٰ وَأَقْنَىٰ (48)

ʾAm lam yunabbaʾ bimā fī ṣuḥufi Mūsā. (36) Wa ʾIbrāhīmal-ladhī waffā. (37) ʾAllā taziru wāziratuñw-wizra ʾukhrā. (38) Wa ʾal-laysa lilʾIñsāni ʾillā mā saʿā. (39) Wa ʾanna saʿyahū sawfa yurā. (40) Thumma yujzāhul-jazāaʾal-ʾawfā. (41) Wa ʾanna ʾilā Rabbikal-muñtahā. (42) Wa ʾannahū Huwa ʾaḍḥaka wa ʾabkā. (43) Wa ʾannahū Huwa ʾamāta wa ʾaḥyā. (44) Wa ʾannahū khalaqaz-zawjaynidh-dhakara wal-ʾuñthā. (45) Miñ-nuṭfatin ʾidhā tumnā. (46) Wa ʾanna ʿalayhin-nashʾatal-ʾukhrā. (47) Wa ʾannahū Huwa ʾaghnā wa ʾaqnā. (48)

30 Cf. 2 : 124 and the corresponding note 100. It is obvious that the names of Abraham and Moses are cited here only by way of example, drawing attention to the fact that all through human history God has entrusted His elect, the prophets, with the task of conveying certain unchangeable ethical truths to man.

31 This basic ethical law appears in the Qurʾān five times – in 6 : 164, 17 : 15, 35 : 18, 39 : 7, as well as in the above instance, which is the oldest in the chronology of revelation. Its implication is threefold: firstly, it expresses a categorical rejection of the Christian doctrine of the "original sin" with which every human being is allegedly burdened from birth; secondly, it refutes the idea that a person's sins could be "atoned for" by a saint's or a prophet's redemptive sacrifice (as evidenced, for instance, in the Christian doctrine of Jesus' vicarious atonement for mankind's sinfulness, or in the earlier, Persian doctrine of man's vicarious redemption by Mithras); and, thirdly, it denies, by implication, the possibility of any "mediation" between the sinner and God.

32 Cf. the basic, extremely well-authenticated saying of the Prophet, "Actions will be [judged] only according to the conscious intentions [which prompted them]; and unto everyone will be accounted only what he consciously intended", i.e., while doing whatever he did. This Tradition is quoted by Bukhārī in seven places – the first one as a kind of introduction to his *Ṣaḥīḥ* – as well as by Muslim, Tirmidhī, Abū Dāʾūd, Nasāʾī (in four places), Ibn Mājah, Ibn Ḥanbal, and several other compilations. In this connection it is to be noted that in the ethics of the Qurʾān, the term "action" (*ʿamal*) comprises also a deliberate *omission* of actions, whether good or bad, as well as a deliberate voicing of beliefs, both righteous and sinful: in short, everything that man consciously aims at and expresses by word or deed.

33 Lit., "his striving will be seen", i.e., on the Day of Judgment, when – as the Qur'ān states in many places – God "will make you [truly] understand all that you were doing [in life]".

34 Lit., "the utmost limit" or "goal", circumscribing the beginning and the end of the universe both in time and in space, as well as the source from which everything proceeds and to which everything must return.

35 Lit., "that upon Him rests the other [or "second"] coming to life (*nashʾah*)", i.e., resurrection.

السجدة

and that it is He alone who sustains the brightest star;[36] ‹49›
and that it is He who destroyed the ancient [tribes of] ᶜĀd ‹50› and Thamūd, leaving no trace [of them],[37] ‹51› as well as the people of Noah before them – [since,] verily, they all had been most wilful in their evildoing and most overweening ‹52› – just as He thrust into perdition those cities that were overthrown ‹53› and then covered them from sight forever.[38] ‹54›
About which, then, of thy Sustainer's powers canst thou [still] remain in doubt?[39] ‹55›

THIS IS a warning like those warnings of old:[40] ‹56› that [Last Hour] which is so near draws ever nearer, ‹57› [although] none but God can unveil it. . . . ‹58›
Do you, perchance, find this tiding strange? ‹59› And do you laugh instead of weeping, ‹60› and divert yourselves all the while? ‹61›
[Nay,] but prostrate yourselves before God, and worship [Him alone]! ‹62›

وَأَنَّهُۥ هُوَ رَبُّ ٱلشِّعْرَىٰ ﴿٤٩﴾ وَأَنَّهُۥٓ أَهْلَكَ عَادًا ٱلْأُولَىٰ ﴿٥٠﴾ وَثَمُودَا۟ فَمَآ
أَبْقَىٰ ﴿٥١﴾ وَقَوْمَ نُوحٍ مِّن قَبْلُ ۖ إِنَّهُمْ كَانُوا۟ هُمْ أَظْلَمَ وَأَطْغَىٰ ﴿٥٢﴾
وَٱلْمُؤْتَفِكَةَ أَهْوَىٰ ﴿٥٣﴾ فَغَشَّىٰهَا مَا غَشَّىٰ ﴿٥٤﴾ فَبِأَىِّ ءَالَآءِ رَبِّكَ
تَتَمَارَىٰ ﴿٥٥﴾ هَٰذَا نَذِيرٌ مِّنَ ٱلنُّذُرِ ٱلْأُولَىٰٓ ﴿٥٦﴾ أَزِفَتِ ٱلْءَازِفَةُ ﴿٥٧﴾
لَيْسَ لَهَا مِن دُونِ ٱللَّهِ كَاشِفَةٌ ﴿٥٨﴾ أَفَمِنْ هَٰذَا ٱلْحَدِيثِ تَعْجَبُونَ ﴿٥٩﴾
وَتَضْحَكُونَ وَلَا تَبْكُونَ ﴿٦٠﴾ وَأَنتُمْ سَٰمِدُونَ ﴿٦١﴾ فَٱسْجُدُوا۟ لِلَّهِ
وَٱعْبُدُوا۟ ۩ ﴿٦٢﴾

Wa ᵓannahū Huwa Rabbush-shiᶜrā. ‹49› Wa ᵓannahūu
ᵓahlaka ᶜĀdanil-ᵓūlā. ‹50› Wa Thamūda famāa ᵓabqā
‹51› Wa qawma Nūḥim-miñ-qablu ᵓinnahum kānū hum
ᵓaẓlama wa ᵓaṭghā. ‹52› Wal-muᵓtafikata ᵓahwā. ‹53›
Faghashshāhā mā ghashshā. ‹54› Fabiᵓayyi ᵓālāaᵓi
Rabbika tatamārā. ‹55› Hādhā Nadhīrum-minan-
Nudhuril-ᵓūlā. ‹56› ᵓAzifatil-ᵓĀzifah. ‹57› Laysa lahā
miñ-dūnil-lāhi kāshifah. ‹58› ᵓAfamin hādhal-ḥadīthi
taᶜjabūn. ‹59› Wa taḍḥakūna wa lā tabkūn. ‹60› Wa
ᵓañtum sāmidūn. ‹61› Fasjudū lillāhi waᶜ-budū. ۩ ‹62›

36 Lit., "who is the Sustainer of Sirius (*ash-shiᶜrā*)", a star of the first magnitude, belonging to the constellation Canis Major. Because it is the brightest star in the heavens, it was widely worshipped in pre-Islamic Arabia. Idiomatically, the phrase *rabb ash-shiᶜrā* is used as a metonym for the Creator and Upholder of the universe.

37 For the story of the tribe of ᶜĀd see second half of note 48 on 7 : 65; for that of the Thamūd, note 56 on 7 : 73.

38 Lit., "so that there covered them that which covered": a reference to Sodom and Gomorrah, the cities of "Lot's people" (see, in particular, 11 : 77-83).

39 This rhetorical question is evidently addressed to the type of man spoken of in verses 33-35. – For the reason of my rendering of *alāᵓ* (lit., "blessings" or "bounties") as "powers", see second half of note 4 on 55 : 13.

40 Lit., "a warning of [or "from among"] the warnings of old" – implying that the revelation granted to Muḥammad does not aim at establishing a "new" religion but, on the contrary, continues and confirms the basic message entrusted to the earlier prophets – in this particular instance alluding to the certainty of the coming of the Last Hour and of God's ultimate judgment.

The Fifty-Fourth Sūrah

Al-Qamar (The Moon)

Mecca Period

AS RĀZĪ points out, the first verse of this *sūrah* appears almost like a continuation of the last verses of the preceding one, especially 53 : 57 – "that [Last Hour] which is so near draws ever nearer": – and so we may assume that both were revealed at approximately the same time, i.e., towards the end of the early part (perhaps the fourth year) of Muḥammad's prophethood.

سورة القمر مكية
-54-
وآياتها خمس وخمسون

IN THE NAME OF GOD, THE MOST GRACIOUS, THE DISPENSER OF GRACE:

THE LAST HOUR draws near, and the moon is split asunder![1] ‹1›
But if they [who reject all thought of the Last Hour] were to see a sign [of its approach], they would turn aside and say, "An ever-recurring delusion!" ‹2› – for they are bent on giving it the lie,[2] being always wont to follow their own desires.
Yet everything reveals its truth in the

بِسْمِ اللَّهِ الرَّحْمَٰنِ الرَّحِيمِ

اقْتَرَبَتِ السَّاعَةُ وَانشَقَّ الْقَمَرُ ﴿١﴾ وَإِن يَرَوْا آيَةً يُعْرِضُوا وَيَقُولُوا
سِحْرٌ مُّسْتَمِرٌّ ﴿٢﴾ وَكَذَّبُوا وَاتَّبَعُوا أَهْوَاءَهُمْ وَكُلُّ أَمْرٍ مُّسْتَقِرٌّ ﴿٣﴾

Bismil-lāhir-Raḥmānir-Raḥīm.
ʾIqtarabatis-Sāʿatu wañ-shaqqal-qamar. (1) Wa ʾiñy-yaraw ʾĀyatañy-yuʿriḍū wa yaqūlū siḥrum-mustamirr. (2) Wa kadhdhabū wat-tabaʿūu ʾahwāaʾahum. Wa kullu ʾamrim-mustaqirr. (3)

---

1 Most of the commentators see in this verse a reference to a phenomenon said to have been witnessed by several of the Prophet's contemporaries. As described in a number of reports going back to some Companions, the moon appeared one night as if split into two distinct parts. While there is no reason to doubt the *subjective* veracity of these reports, it is possible that what actually happened was an unusual kind of partial lunar eclipse, which produced an equally unusual optical illusion. But whatever the nature of that phenomenon, it is practically certain that the above Qurʾān-verse does not refer to it but, rather, to a *future* event: namely, to what will happen when the Last Hour approaches. (The Qur'ān frequently employs the past tense to denote the future, and particularly so in passages which speak of the coming of the Last Hour and of Resurrection Day; this use of the past tense is meant to stress the certainty of the happening to which the verb relates.) Thus, Rāghib regards it as fully justifiable to interpret the phrase *inshaqqa 'l-qamar* ("the moon is split asunder") as bearing on the cosmic cataclysm – the end of the world as we know it – that will occur before the coming of Resurrection Day (see art. *shaqq* in the *Mufradāt*). As mentioned by Zamakhsharī, this interpretation has the support of some of the earlier commentators; and it is, to my mind, particularly convincing in view of the juxtaposition, in the above Qurʾān-verse, of the moon's "splitting asunder" and the approach of the Last Hour. (In this connection we must bear in mind the fact that none of the Qurʾanic allusions to the "nearness" of the Last Hour and the Day of Resurrection is based on the *human* concept of "time".)

2 Lit., "they have given [it] the lie": an allusion to the prediction of the Last Hour and the Day of Resurrection. The use of the past tense indicates conscious intent or determination (cf. *sūrah* 2, note 6). For my rendering of *siḥr* as "delusion", see *sūrah* 74, note 12.

وَلَقَدْ جَآءَهُم مِّنَ ٱلْأَنۢبَآءِ مَا فِيهِ مُزْدَجَرٌ ﴿٤﴾ حِكْمَةٌۢ بَٰلِغَةٌۖ فَمَا تُغْنِ
ٱلنُّذُرُ ﴿٥﴾ فَتَوَلَّ عَنْهُمْۘ يَوْمَ يَدْعُ ٱلدَّاعِ إِلَىٰ شَىْءٍ نُّكُرٍ ﴿٦﴾ خُشَّعًا
أَبْصَٰرُهُمْ يَخْرُجُونَ مِنَ ٱلْأَجْدَاثِ كَأَنَّهُمْ جَرَادٌ مُّنتَشِرٌ ﴿٧﴾ مُّهْطِعِينَ إِلَى
ٱلدَّاعِۖ يَقُولُ ٱلْكَٰفِرُونَ هَٰذَا يَوْمٌ عَسِرٌ ﴿٨﴾ ۞ كَذَّبَتْ قَبْلَهُمْ قَوْمُ نُوحٍ
فَكَذَّبُوا۟ عَبْدَنَا وَقَالُوا۟ مَجْنُونٌ وَٱزْدُجِرَ ﴿٩﴾ فَدَعَا رَبَّهُۥٓ أَنِّى مَغْلُوبٌ فَٱنتَصِرْ ﴿١٠﴾
فَفَتَحْنَآ أَبْوَٰبَ ٱلسَّمَآءِ بِمَآءٍ مُّنْهَمِرٍ ﴿١١﴾ وَفَجَّرْنَا ٱلْأَرْضَ عُيُونًا فَٱلْتَقَى
ٱلْمَآءُ عَلَىٰٓ أَمْرٍ قَدْ قُدِرَ ﴿١٢﴾ وَحَمَلْنَٰهُ عَلَىٰ ذَاتِ أَلْوَٰحٍ وَدُسُرٍ ﴿١٣﴾
تَجْرِى بِأَعْيُنِنَا جَزَآءً لِّمَن كَانَ كُفِرَ ﴿١٤﴾

ثلاثة ارباع الحزب

end.[3] ‹3›
And withal, there has come unto them many a tiding that should have restrained [their arrogance]:[4] ‹4› far-reaching wisdom [was held out to them]: but [since] all warnings have been of no avail, ‹5› turn thou away from them.
On the Day when the Summoning Voice will summon [man] unto something that the mind cannot conceive,[5] ‹6› they will come forth from their graves, with their eyes downcast, [swarming about] like locusts scattered [by the wind], ‹7› running in confusion towards the Summoning Voice; [and] those who [now] deny the truth will exclaim, "Calamitous is this Day!" ‹8›

[LONG] BEFORE those [who now deny resurrection] did Noah's people call it a lie; and they gave the lie to Our servant and said, "Mad is he!" – and he was repulsed.[6] ‹9›
Thereupon he called out to his Sustainer, "Verily, I am defeated; come Thou, then, to my succour!" ‹10›
And so We caused the gates of heaven to open with water pouring down in torrents, ‹11› and caused the earth to burst forth with springs, so that the waters met for a purpose pre-ordained: ‹12› but him We bore on that [vessel] made of [mere] planks and nails, ‹13› and it floated under Our eyes:[7] a recompense for him who had been rejected with ingratitude. ‹14›

Wa laqad jāaʾahum-minal-ʾambāaʾi mā fīhi muzda-
jar. ﴿4﴾ Ḥikmatum-bālighatuñ-famā tughnin-nudhur.
﴿5﴾ Fatawalla ʿan-hum. Yawma yadʿud-dāʿi ʾilā
shayʾiñ-nukur. ﴿6﴾ Khushshaʿan ʾabṣārahum yakh-
rujūna minal-ʾajdāthi kaʾannahum jarādum-
muñtashir. ﴿7﴾ Muhṭiʿīna ʾilad-dāʿi yaqūlul-kāfirūna
hādhā Yawmun ʿasir. ﴿8﴾ ۞ Kadhdhabat qablahum
qawmu Nūḥiñ-fakadhdhabū ʿabdanā wa qālū
majnūnuñw-waz-dujir. ﴿9﴾ Fadaʿā Rabbahūu ʾannī
maghlūbuñ-fañtaṣir. ﴿10﴾ Fafataḥnāa ʾabwābas-
samāaʾi bimāaʾim-munhamir. ﴿11﴾ Wa fajjarnal-ʾarḍa
ʿuyūnañ-faltaqal-māaʾu ʿalāa ʾamriñ-qad qudir. ﴿12﴾
Wa ḥamalnāhu ʿalā dhāti ʾalwāḥiñw-wa dusur. ﴿13﴾
Tajrī biʾaʿyuninā jazāaʾal-limañ-kāna kufir. ﴿14﴾

3 Lit., "everything is settled in its [own] being": i.e., everything has an intrinsic reality (*ḥaqīqah*) of its own, and is bound to reveal that reality either in this world or in the next (Baghawī, on the authority of Al-Kalbī); hence, everything must have a purpose or "goal" of its own (Zamakhsharī). These two – mutually complementary – interpretations reflect the repeated Qurʾanic statement that everything that exists or happens has a meaning and a purpose: cf. 3 : 191, 10 : 5 and 38 : 27 (particularly, see note 11 on 10 : 5). In the present context, the phrase relates both to the truth referred to in the preceding verses and to its rejection by those who are "wont to follow [but] their own desires".

4 Lit., "in which there was a restraint": i.e., many an indication, in observable nature, of God's creative and re-creative power, as well as many a tiding, through God-inspired prophets, of a continuation of life after bodily death and, therefore, of the fact that a person's attitudes and doings in this world must have definite *consequences* in the life to come.

5 Lit., "something not known (*nukur*)" – that is, "something that human beings cannot know [i.e., visualize] because they have never met with anything like it" (Zamakhsharī).

6 See 11 : 25-48, where the story of Noah and the Flood is given in greater detail.

7 I.e., "under Our protection". The reference to Noah's ark as "made of mere planks and nails" is meant to stress the frailty of this – as well as any other – human contrivance.

And, indeed, We have caused such [floating vessels] to remain forever a sign [of Our grace unto man]:[8] who, then, is willing to take it to heart?[9] ‹15›
And how severe is the suffering which I inflict when My warnings are disregarded![10] ‹16›
Hence, indeed, We made this Qur᾽ān easy to bear in mind:[11] who, then, is willing to take it to heart? ‹17›

TO THE TRUTH gave the lie [the tribe of] ᶜĀd: and how severe was the suffering which I inflicted when My warnings were disregarded! ‹18›
Behold, We let loose upon them a raging stormwind on a day of bitter misfortune: ‹19› it swept the people away as though they were palm-trunks uprooted:[12] ‹20› for, how severe is the suffering which I inflict when My warnings are disregarded! ‹21›
Hence, indeed, We made this Qur᾽ān easy to bear in mind: who, then, is willing to take it to heart? ‹22›

[AND the tribe of] Thamūd gave the lie to all [Our] warnings; ‹23› and they said: "Are we to follow one single mortal, one from among ourselves?[13] In that case, behold, we would certainly sink into error and folly! ‹24› Why – on him alone from among all of us should a [divine] reminder have been bestowed? Nay, but he is a boastful liar!" ‹25›

وَلَقَد تَّرَكْنَٰهَآ ءَايَةً فَهَلْ مِن مُّدَّكِرٍ (15) فَكَيْفَ كَانَ عَذَابِى
وَنُذُرِ (16) وَلَقَدْ يَسَّرْنَا ٱلْقُرْءَانَ لِلذِّكْرِ فَهَلْ مِن مُّدَّكِرٍ (17) كَذَّبَتْ
عَادٌ فَكَيْفَ كَانَ عَذَابِى وَنُذُرِ (18) إِنَّآ أَرْسَلْنَا عَلَيْهِمْ رِيحًا صَرْصَرًا فِى
يَوْمِ نَحْسٍ مُّسْتَمِرٍّ (19) تَنزِعُ ٱلنَّاسَ كَأَنَّهُمْ أَعْجَازُ نَخْلٍ مُّنقَعِرٍ (20)
فَكَيْفَ كَانَ عَذَابِى وَنُذُرِ (21) وَلَقَدْ يَسَّرْنَا ٱلْقُرْءَانَ لِلذِّكْرِ فَهَلْ مِن
مُّدَّكِرٍ (22) كَذَّبَتْ ثَمُودُ بِٱلنُّذُرِ (23) فَقَالُوٓا۟ أَبَشَرًا مِّنَّا وَٰحِدًا نَّتَّبِعُهُۥٓ
إِنَّآ إِذًا لَّفِى ضَلَٰلٍ وَسُعُرٍ (24) أَءُلْقِىَ ٱلذِّكْرُ عَلَيْهِ مِنۢ بَيْنِنَا بَلْ هُوَ كَذَّابٌ
أَشِرٌ (25)

Wa laqat-taraknāhāa ᵓĀyatañ-fahal mim-muddakir. (15) Fakayfa kāna ᶜadhābī wa nudhur. (16) Wa laqad yassarnal-Qurᵓāna lidhdhikri fahal mim-muddakir. (17) Kadhdhabat ᶜĀduñ-fakayfa kāna ᶜadhābī wa nudhur. (18) ᵓInnāa ᵓarsalnā ᶜalayhim rīḥañ-ṣarṣarañ-fī yawmi naḥsim-mustamirr. (19) Tañziᶜun-nāsa kaᵓannahum ᵓaᶜjāzu nakhlim-muñqaᶜir. (20) Fakayfa kāna ᶜadhābī wa nudhur. (21) Wa laqad yassarnal-Qurᵓāna lidhdhikri fahal mim-muddakir. (22) Kadhdhabat Thamūdu binnudhur. (23) Faqālūu ᵓabasharam-minnā wāḥidañ-nattabiᶜuhūu ᵓinnāa ᵓidhal-lafī ḍalāliñw-wa suᶜur. (24) ᵓAᵓulqiyadh-Dhikru ᶜalayhi mim-bayninā bal huwa kadhdhābun ᵓashir. (25)

8 See 36 : 41-42 and the corresponding notes 22 and 23. Literally, the above phrase reads, "We have left them [or "such"] as a sign . . .", etc. According to Ibn Kathīr, the pronoun *hā* in *taraknāhā* relates to "ships in a generic sense" (*jins as-sufun*), and quotes in this connection the above-mentioned passage (36 : 41-42); hence my interpolation, between brackets, of the words "floating vessels". The "sign" spoken of here alludes to God's having endowed man's mind with inventiveness and, thus, with the ability to widen the scope of his life through conscious effort.

9 Lit., "And is there any that will . . .", etc. The above sentence recurs several times, like a refrain, in this *sūrah*.

10 Lit., "how was My [causing] suffering (*ᶜadhābī*) and My warnings" – i.e., *after* the warnings. Although this sentence is phrased in the past tense, its purport is evidently timeless.

11 The noun *dhikr* primarily denotes "remembrance", or – as defined by Rāghib – the "presence [of something] in the mind". Conceptually, and as used in the above context as well as in verses 22, 32 and 40, this term comprises the twin notions of understanding *and* remembering, i.e., bearing something in mind.

12 As mentioned in 69 : 6-8, this wind – obviously an exceptionally violent sandstorm – raged without break for seven nights and eight days. For particulars of the tribe of ᶜĀd, see second half of note 48 on 7 : 65.

13 For the general implication of this rhetorical question, see note 2 on 50 : 2. For the story of the tribe of

[And God said:] "On the morrow[14] they will come to know who the boastful liar is! ⟨26⟩ Behold, [O Ṣāliḥ,] We are letting loose this she-camel as a test for them;[15] and thou but watch them, and contain thyself in patience. ⟨27⟩ And let them know that the water [of their wells] is to be divided between them,[16] with each share of water equitably apportioned." ⟨28⟩

But they summoned their [boldest] companion, and he ventured [upon the evil deed], and cruelly slaughtered [the animal]:[17] ⟨29⟩ and how severe was the suffering which I inflicted when My warnings were disregarded! ⟨30⟩

Behold, We let loose upon them one single blast [of Our punishment],[18] and they became like the dried-up, crumbling twigs of a sheepfold. ⟨31⟩

Hence, indeed, We made this Qurᵓān easy to bear in mind: who, then, is willing to take it to heart? ⟨32⟩

LOT'S PEOPLE [too] gave the lie to all [Our] warnings: ⟨33⟩ [and so,] behold, We let loose upon them a deadly tempest;[19] and only Lot's kinsfolk did We save at the break of dawn, ⟨34⟩ as a blessing from Us: thus do We reward all who are grateful. ⟨35⟩

For he had truly warned them of Our punishing might; but they stubbornly cast doubt on these warnings, ⟨36⟩ and even demanded that he give up his guests [to them]:[20] whereupon We deprived them of

سَيَعۡلَمُونَ غَدٗا مَّنِ ٱلۡكَذَّابُ ٱلۡأَشِرُ ﴿٢٦﴾ إِنَّا مُرۡسِلُواْ ٱلنَّاقَةِ فِتۡنَةٗ لَّهُمۡ
فَٱرۡتَقِبۡهُمۡ وَٱصۡطَبِرۡ ﴿٢٧﴾ وَنَبِّئۡهُمۡ أَنَّ ٱلۡمَآءَ قِسۡمَةُۢ بَيۡنَهُمۡۖ كُلُّ شِرۡبٖ
مُّحۡتَضَرٞ ﴿٢٨﴾ فَنَادَوۡاْ صَاحِبَهُمۡ فَتَعَاطَىٰ فَعَقَرَ ﴿٢٩﴾ فَكَيۡفَ كَانَ عَذَابِي
وَنُذُرِ ﴿٣٠﴾ إِنَّآ أَرۡسَلۡنَا عَلَيۡهِمۡ صَيۡحَةٗ وَٰحِدَةٗ فَكَانُواْ كَهَشِيمِ ٱلۡمُحۡتَظِرِ ﴿٣١﴾
وَلَقَدۡ يَسَّرۡنَا ٱلۡقُرۡءَانَ لِلذِّكۡرِ فَهَلۡ مِن مُّدَّكِرٖ ﴿٣٢﴾ كَذَّبَتۡ قَوۡمُ لُوطِۢ
بِٱلنُّذُرِ ﴿٣٣﴾ إِنَّآ أَرۡسَلۡنَا عَلَيۡهِمۡ حَاصِبًا إِلَّآ ءَالَ لُوطٖۖ نَّجَّيۡنَٰهُم
بِسَحَرٖ ﴿٣٤﴾ نِّعۡمَةٗ مِّنۡ عِندِنَاۚ كَذَٰلِكَ نَجۡزِي مَن شَكَرَ ﴿٣٥﴾ وَلَقَدۡ
أَنذَرَهُم بَطۡشَتَنَا فَتَمَارَوۡاْ بِٱلنُّذُرِ ﴿٣٦﴾ وَلَقَدۡ رَٰوَدُوهُ عَن ضَيۡفِهِۦ فَطَمَسۡنَآ

Sayaᶜlamūna ghadam-manil-kadhdhābul-ᵓashir. (26) ᵓInnā mursilun-nāqati fitnatal-lahum fartaqibhum waṣ-ṭabir. (27) Wa nabbiᵓhum ᵓannal-māaᵓa qismatum-baynahum; kullu shirbim-muḥtaḍar. (28) Fanādaw ṣāḥibahum fataᶜāṭā faᶜaqar. (29) Fakayfa kāna ᶜadhābī wa nudhur. (30) ᵓInnāa ᵓarsalnā ᶜalayhim ṣayḥatañw-wāḥidatañ-fakānū kahashīmil-muḥtaẓir. (31) Wa laqad yassarnal-Qurᵓāna lidhdhikri fahal mim-muddakir. (32) Kadhdhabat qawmu Lūṭim-binnudhur. (33) ᵓInnāa ᵓarsalnā ᶜalayhim ḥāṣiban ᵓillāa ᵓāla Lūṭiñ-najjaynāhum bisaḥar. (34) Niᶜmatam-min ᶜiñdinā; kadhālika najzī mañ-shakar. (35) Wa laqad ᵓañdharahum-baṭshatanā fatamāraw binnudhur. (36) Wa laqad rāwadūhu ᶜañ-ḍayfihī faṭamasnāa

Thamūd, their prophet Ṣāliḥ, and the incident of the she-camel, see 7 : 73-79, 11 : 61-68, 26 : 141-158, and the corresponding notes.

14 I.e., soon. In classical Arabic, the term *ghadan* ("tomorrow") often applies to a *relatively* near future, signifying "tomorrow" (in its literal sense) as well as "in time" or "soon". Hence – as pointed out by all authorities – it may have been used in the above context with reference to the Last Hour, which in the first verse of this very *sūrah* is spoken of as having "drawn near".

15 For this and other Qurᵓanic references to the she-camel that was to be "let loose as a test" for the Thamūd, see *sūrah* 7, note 57. God's "letting her loose" is in this context evidently synonymous with "allowing her to become" a test.

16 I.e., between their own herds and the ownerless she-camel: see 26 : 155 and the corresponding note 67.

17 For the above rendering of *ᶜaqara*, see note 61 on 7 : 77.

18 See note 98 on 11 : 67.

19 Sc., "of chastisement": see 11 : 82 and the corresponding note 114. – The story of Lot and the people among whom he dwelt is mentioned in several places, most extensively in 11 : 69-83.

20 See 11 : 77-79 and the corresponding notes.

their sight [and thus told them, as it were]:[21] "Taste, then, the suffering which I inflict when My warnings are disregarded!" ⟨37⟩
And, indeed, abiding suffering did befall them early on the morrow: ⟨38⟩ "Taste, then, the suffering which I inflict when My warnings are disregarded!" ⟨39⟩
Hence, indeed, We made this Qurʾān easy to bear in mind: who, then, is willing to take it to heart? ⟨40⟩
Now surely, unto Pharaoh's folk [too] came such warnings; ⟨41⟩ they, too, gave the lie to all Our messages: and thereupon We took them to task as only the Almighty, who determines all things, can take to task.[22] ⟨42⟩

ARE, THEN, those of you who [now] deny the truth[23] better than those others – or have you, perchance, [been promised] immunity in the [ancient] books of [divine] wisdom?[24] ⟨43⟩
Or do they say, "We are a group united, [and therefore] bound to prevail"?[25] ⟨44⟩
[Yet] the hosts [of those who deny the truth] shall be routed, and they shall turn their backs [in flight]![26] ⟨45⟩

أَعْيُنَهُمْ فَذُوقُوا۟ عَذَابِى وَنُذُرِ ﴿٣٧﴾ وَلَقَدْ صَبَّحَهُم بُكْرَةً عَذَابٌ
مُّسْتَقِرٌّ ﴿٣٨﴾ فَذُوقُوا۟ عَذَابِى وَنُذُرِ ﴿٣٩﴾ وَلَقَدْ يَسَّرْنَا ٱلْقُرْءَانَ لِلذِّكْرِ فَهَلْ
مِن مُّدَّكِرٍ ﴿٤٠﴾ وَلَقَدْ جَآءَ ءَالَ فِرْعَوْنَ ٱلنُّذُرُ ﴿٤١﴾ كَذَّبُوا۟ بِـَٔايَـٰتِنَا كُلِّهَا
فَأَخَذْنَـٰهُمْ أَخْذَ عَزِيزٍ مُّقْتَدِرٍ ﴿٤٢﴾ أَكُفَّارُكُمْ خَيْرٌ مِّنْ أُو۟لَـٰٓئِكُمْ أَمْ
لَكُم بَرَآءَةٌ فِى ٱلزُّبُرِ ﴿٤٣﴾ أَمْ يَقُولُونَ نَحْنُ جَمِيعٌ مُّنتَصِرٌ ﴿٤٤﴾ سَيُهْزَمُ
ٱلْجَمْعُ وَيُوَلُّونَ ٱلدُّبُرَ ﴿٤٥﴾

ʾaʿyunahum fadhūqū ʿadhābī wa nudhur. (37) Wa laqad ṣabbaḥahum bukratan ʿadhābum-mustaqirr. (38) Fadhūqū ʿadhābī wa nudhur. (39) Wa laqad yassarnal-Qurʾāna lidhdhikri fahal mim-muddakir. (40) Wa laqad jāaʾa ʾāla Firʿawnan-nudhur. (41) Kadhdhabū biʾĀyātinā kullihā faʾakhadhnāhum ʾakhdha ʿAzīzim-Muqtadir. (42) ʾAkuffārukum khayrum-min ʾulāaʾikum ʾam lakum barāaʾatuñ-fiz-Zubur. (43) ʾAm yaqūlūna naḥnu jamīʿum-muñtaṣir. (44) Sayuhzamul-jamʿu wa yuwallūnad-dubur. (45)

21 According to Ibn ʿAbbās (as quoted by Rāzī), the expression *ṭams al-ʿayn* ("deprivation of sight") denotes here a "veiling [of something] from one's consciousness" (*ḥajb ʿan al-idrāk*). Hence, the phrase *ṭamasnā aʿyunahum* may be understood to mean that God deprived them, in consequence of their evil propensities, of all moral insight (cf. 36 : 66 and the corresponding notes), and thus made them liable – as the sequence shows – to undergo bitter suffering in this world and in the next.

22 Lit., "We gripped them with the grip of an almighty . . .", etc. The special – and concluding – mention of "Pharaoh's folk" is due to the fact that the Egyptians were the most highly developed and powerful nation in the antiquity to which this and the preceding passages refer.

23 Lit., "your deniers of the truth".

24 See *sūrah* 21, note 101.

25 The reasoning which underlies this thought may be summed up thus: "We who reject these so-called divine revelations represent a very large body of opinion; and because our views are held by so many, they are obviously right and, therefore, bound to triumph in the end." In other words, the people characterized as "deniers of the truth" draw their assurance from the mere fact of their being representative of the "majority opinion" – a self-delusion based on a purely materialistic outlook on life.

26 The fact that the Prophet recited this verse just before the battle of Badr (see note 10 on 8 : 10) has caused most of the commentators to assume that it had been revealed as a specific prophecy of the future victory of the Muslims over the pagan Quraysh. While this is possible, I believe, nevertheless, that the above passage has the much wider, timeless meaning explained in the preceding note. This view finds strong support in the subsequent verses, which speak of the evil otherworldly consequences of deliberate sinning, quite apart from the social and moral defeat, in this world, of the sinful community as a whole.

But nay – the Last Hour is the time when they shall truly meet their fate;[27] and that Last Hour will be most calamitous, and most bitter: ‹46› for, behold, those who are lost in sin [will at that time come to know that it is they who] were sunk in error and folly![28] ‹47›
On the Day when they shall be dragged into the fire on their faces,[29] [they will be told:] "Taste now the touch of hell-fire!" ‹48›

بَلِ ٱلسَّاعَةُ مَوْعِدُهُمْ وَٱلسَّاعَةُ أَدْهَىٰ وَأَمَرُّ ﴿46﴾ إِنَّ ٱلْمُجْرِمِينَ فِى ضَلَٰلٍ
وَسُعُرٍ ﴿47﴾ يَوْمَ يُسْحَبُونَ فِى ٱلنَّارِ عَلَىٰ وُجُوهِهِمْ ذُوقُوا۟ مَسَّ سَقَرَ ﴿48﴾
إِنَّا كُلَّ شَىْءٍ خَلَقْنَٰهُ بِقَدَرٍ ﴿49﴾ وَمَآ أَمْرُنَآ إِلَّا وَٰحِدَةٌ كَلَمْحٍۭ بِٱلْبَصَرِ ﴿50﴾
وَلَقَدْ أَهْلَكْنَآ أَشْيَاعَكُمْ فَهَلْ مِن مُّدَّكِرٍ ﴿51﴾ وَكُلُّ شَىْءٍ فَعَلُوهُ فِى
ٱلزُّبُرِ ﴿52﴾ وَكُلُّ صَغِيرٍ وَكَبِيرٍ مُّسْتَطَرٌ ﴿53﴾ إِنَّ ٱلْمُتَّقِينَ فِى جَنَّٰتٍ وَنَهَرٍ ﴿54﴾
فِى مَقْعَدِ صِدْقٍ عِندَ مَلِيكٍ مُّقْتَدِرٍۭ ﴿55﴾

BEHOLD, everything have We created in due measure and proportion; ‹49› and Our ordaining [a thing and its coming into being] is but one [act], like the twinkling of an eye.[30] ‹50›
Thus, indeed, did We destroy people like you [in the past]: who, then, is willing to take it to heart? ‹51›
[They were truly guilty] because all [the evil] that they ever did had been [revealed to them as such] in the [ancient] books of [divine] wisdom;[31] ‹52› and everything [that man does], be it small or great, is recorded [with God]. ‹53›
[Hence, too,] behold, the God-conscious will find themselves in [a paradise of] gardens and running waters, ‹54› in a seat of truth, in the presence of a Sovereign who determines all things. . . . ‹55›

Balis-Sāᶜatu mawᶜiduhum was-Sāᶜatu ᵓadhā wa ᵓamarr. (46) ᵓInnal-mujrimīna fī ḍalāliñw-wa suᶜur. (47) Yawma yusḥabūna fin-nāri ᶜalā wujūhihim dhūqū massa saqar. (48) ᵓInnā kulla shayᵓin khalaqnāhu biqadar. (49) Wa māa ᵓamrunāa ᵓillā wāḥidatuñ-kalamḥim-bilbaṣar. (50) Wa laqad ᵓahlaknāa ᵓashyāᶜakum fahal mim-muddakir. (51) Wa kullu shayᵓiñ-faᶜalūhu fiz-Zubur. (52) Wa kullu ṣaghīriñw-wa kabīrim-mustaṭar. (53) ᵓInnal-muttaqīna fī jannātiñw-wa nahar. (54) Fī maqᶜadi ṣidqin ᶜiñda Malīkim-Muqtadir. (55)

27 Lit., "the time appointed for them" (*mawᶜiduhum*).

28 See verse 24 above.

29 See note 83 on 33 : 66 as well as note 30 on 25 : 34.

30 I.e., there is no time lag and no conceptual difference between God's "willing" the creation of a thing and His "creating" it, for "when He wills a thing to be, He but says unto it, 'Be' – and it is" (2 : 117, 3 : 47, 16 : 40, 19 : 35, 36 : 82 and 40 : 68). The comparison with the "twinkling of an eye" is, of course, merely idiomatic, i.e., based on the *human* concept of something instantaneous. In the present context this is – as the sequence shows – an allusion to the rapidity with which God can, if He so wills, destroy a sinful community.

31 I.e., the ancient revealed scriptures (*az-zubur*) had made the meaning of good and evil absolutely clear to them, but they wilfully disregarded or even consciously rejected that teaching. The above verse implies, firstly, that the basic ethical teachings of all revealed religions are essentially identical, and, secondly, that God "would never destroy a community for [its] wrongdoing so long as its people are still unaware [of the meaning of right and wrong]" (see 6 : 131-132, 15 : 4, 26 : 208-209, and the corresponding notes).

The Fifty-Fifth Sūrah

Ar-Raḥmān (The Most Gracious)

Period Uncertain

ALTHOUGH most of the commentators regard this *sūrah* as a Meccan revelation, Zamakhsharī and (among the later scholars) Suyūṭī ascribe it to the Medina period. Bayḍāwī leaves the question open, and adds that parts of it may have been revealed before and parts after the Prophet's *hijrah* to Medina. Some authorities are of the opinion that it followed immediately upon *sūrah* 13 ("Thunder"): an opinion which is not very helpful since that *sūrah*, too, cannot be assigned to either of the two periods with any degree of certainty.

-55-

سورة الرحمن مدنية

وآياتها ثمان وسبعون

حزب 54

IN THE NAME OF GOD, THE MOST GRACIOUS, THE DISPENSER OF GRACE:

THE MOST GRACIOUS ‹1› has imparted this Qur'ān [unto man]. ‹2›
He has created man: ‹3› He has imparted unto him articulate thought and speech.[1] ‹4›
[At His behest] the sun and the moon run their appointed courses;[2] ‹5› [before Him] prostrate themselves the stars and the trees. ‹6›

بِسۡمِ ٱللَّهِ ٱلرَّحۡمَٰنِ ٱلرَّحِيمِ

ٱلرَّحۡمَٰنُ ﴿١﴾ عَلَّمَ ٱلۡقُرۡءَانَ ﴿٢﴾ خَلَقَ ٱلۡإِنسَٰنَ ﴿٣﴾ عَلَّمَهُ
ٱلۡبَيَانَ ﴿٤﴾ ٱلشَّمۡسُ وَٱلۡقَمَرُ بِحُسۡبَانٖ ﴿٥﴾ وَٱلنَّجۡمُ وَٱلشَّجَرُ
يَسۡجُدَانِ ﴿٦﴾

Bismil-lāhir-Raḥmānir-Raḥīm.
ʾArraḥmān. ‹1› ʿAllamal-Qurʾān. ‹2› Khalaqal-ʾInsān. ‹3› ʿAllamahul-bayān. ‹4› ʾAshshamsu wal-qamaru biḥusbān. ‹5› Wan-najmu wash-shajaru yasjudān. ‹6›

1 The term *al-bayān* – denoting "the means whereby a thing is [intellectually] circumscribed and made clear" (Rāghib) – applies to both thought and speech inasmuch as it comprises the faculty of making a thing or an idea apparent to the mind and conceptually distinct from other things or ideas, as well as the power to express this cognition clearly in spoken or written language (*Tāj al-ʿArūs*): hence, in the above context, "articulate thought and speech", recalling the "knowledge of all the names" (i.e., the faculty of conceptual thinking) with which man is endowed (see 2 : 31 and the corresponding note 23).

2 Lit., "according to a definite reckoning".

And the skies has He raised high, and has devised [for all things] a measure,[3] ‹7› so that you [too, O men,] might never transgress the measure [of what is right]: ‹8› weigh, therefore, [your deeds] with equity, and cut not the measure short! ‹9›
And the earth has He spread out for all living beings, ‹10› with fruit thereon, and palm trees with sheathed clusters [of dates], ‹11› and grain growing tall on its stalks, and sweet-smelling plants. ‹12›
Which, then, of your Sustainer's powers can you disavow?[4] ‹13›
He has created man out of sounding clay, like pottery,[5] ‹14› whereas the invisible beings He has created out of a confusing flame of fire.[6] ‹15› Which, then, of your Sustainer's powers can you disavow? ‹16›
[He is] the Sustainer of the two farthest points of sunrise, and the Sustainer of the two farthest points of sunset.[7] ‹17› Which, then, of your Sustainer's powers can you disavow? ‹18›
He has given freedom to the two great bodies of water, so that they might meet: ‹19› [yet] between them is a barrier which they may not transgress.[8] ‹20› Which, then, of your Sustainer's powers can you disavow? ‹21›
Out of these two [bodies of water] come forth pearls, both great and small. ‹22›

وَٱلسَّمَآءَ رَفَعَهَا وَوَضَعَ ٱلْمِيزَانَ ﴿7﴾ أَلَّا تَطْغَوْا۟ فِى ٱلْمِيزَانِ ﴿8﴾ وَأَقِيمُوا۟
ٱلْوَزْنَ بِٱلْقِسْطِ وَلَا تُخْسِرُوا۟ ٱلْمِيزَانَ ﴿9﴾ وَٱلْأَرْضَ وَضَعَهَا
لِلْأَنَامِ ﴿10﴾ فِيهَا فَٰكِهَةٌ وَٱلنَّخْلُ ذَاتُ ٱلْأَكْمَامِ ﴿11﴾ وَٱلْحَبُّ ذُو
ٱلْعَصْفِ وَٱلرَّيْحَانُ ﴿12﴾ فَبِأَىِّ ءَالَآءِ رَبِّكُمَا تُكَذِّبَانِ ﴿13﴾ خَلَقَ
ٱلْإِنسَٰنَ مِن صَلْصَٰلٍ كَٱلْفَخَّارِ ﴿14﴾ وَخَلَقَ ٱلْجَآنَّ مِن مَّارِجٍ مِّن
نَّارٍ ﴿15﴾ فَبِأَىِّ ءَالَآءِ رَبِّكُمَا تُكَذِّبَانِ ﴿16﴾ رَبُّ ٱلْمَشْرِقَيْنِ وَرَبُّ
ٱلْمَغْرِبَيْنِ ﴿17﴾ فَبِأَىِّ ءَالَآءِ رَبِّكُمَا تُكَذِّبَانِ ﴿18﴾ مَرَجَ ٱلْبَحْرَيْنِ
يَلْتَقِيَانِ ﴿19﴾ بَيْنَهُمَا بَرْزَخٌ لَّا يَبْغِيَانِ ﴿20﴾ فَبِأَىِّ ءَالَآءِ رَبِّكُمَا
تُكَذِّبَانِ ﴿21﴾ يَخْرُجُ مِنْهُمَا ٱللُّؤْلُؤُ وَٱلْمَرْجَانُ ﴿22﴾

**Was-samāaʾa rafaʿahā wa waḍaʿal-mīzān. (7) ʾAllā
taṭghaw fil-mīzān. (8) Wa ʾaqimul-wazna bilqisṭi
wa lā tukhsirul-mīzān. (9) Wal-ʾarḍa waḍaʿahā
lilʾanām. (10) Fīhā fākihatuñw-wan-nakhlu dhātul-
ʾakmām. (11) Wal-ḥabbu dhul-ʿasfi war-rayḥān. (12)
Fabiʾayyi ʾālāaʾi Rabbikumā tukadh-dhibān. (13)
Khalaqal-ʾIñsāna miñ-ṣalṣāliñ-kalfakhkhār. (14) Wa
khalaqal-Jāanna mim-mārijim-miñ-nār. (15) Fabiʾayyi
ʾālāaʾi Rabbikumā tukadhdhibān. (16) Rabbul-mash-
riqayni wa Rabbul-maghribayn. (17) Fabiʾayyi ʾālāaʾi
Rabbikumā tukadhdhibān. (18) Marajal-baḥrayni yal
taqiyān. (19) Baynahumā barzakhul-lā yabghiyān.
(20) Fabiʾayyi ʾālāaʾi Rabbikumā tukadhdhibān. (21)
Yakhruju minhumal-luʾluʾu wal-marjān. (22)**

3 The noun *mīzān*, usually denoting a "balance", has here the more general connotation of "measure" or "measuring" by any means whatsoever (Zamakhsharī), in both the concrete and abstract senses of the word. (Cf. also the parabolic use of the term *mīzān* in 42 : 17 and 57 : 25.)

4 The majority of the classical commentators interpret the dual form of address appearing in this phrase – *rabbikumā* ("the Sustainer of you two") and *tukadhdhibān* ("do you [or "can you"] two disavow") – as relating to the worlds of men and of the "invisible beings" (*jinn* – see Appendix III); but the most obvious explanation (mentioned, among others, by Rāzī) is that it refers to the two categories of *human* beings, men and women, to both of whom the Qurʾān is addressed. The plural noun *ālāʾ*, rendered by me as "powers", signifies literally "blessings" or "bounties"; but as the above refrain, which is repeated many times in this *sūrah*, bears not only on the bounties which God bestows on His creation but, more generally, on *all* manifestations of His creativeness and might, some of the earliest commentators – e.g., Ibn Zayd, as quoted by Ṭabarī – regard the term *ālāʾ*, in this context, as synonymous with *qudrah* ("power" or "powers").

5 See 15 : 26 and the corresponding note 24.

6 Cf. 15 : 27 – "the fire of scorching winds (*nār as-samūm*)" – thus stressing their non-corporeal origin and composition. The significance of the term *jinn* ("invisible beings") has been touched upon briefly in note 86 on 6 : 100 and note 67 on 37 : 158; for a more detailed explanation, see Appendix III.

7 I.e., of the extreme points of sunrise and sunset in summer and in winter (see 37 : 5 and 70 : 40), including "all that is between them": a metonym for God's being the Ultimate Cause of the orbital movement within the universe.

8 See 25 : 53 and the corresponding notes 41 and 42.

Which, then, of your Sustainer's powers can you disavow? ‹23›
And His are the lofty ships that sail like [floating] mountains through the seas.[9] ‹24› Which, then, of your Sustainer's powers can you disavow? ‹25›
All that lives on earth or in the heavens[10] is bound to pass away: ‹26› but forever will abide thy Sustainer's Self,[11] full of majesty and glory. ‹27› Which, then, of your Sustainer's powers can you disavow? ‹28›
On Him depend all creatures[12] in the heavens and on earth; [and] every day He manifests Himself in yet another [wondrous] way. ‹29› Which, then, of your Sustainer's powers can you disavow? ‹30›

فَبِأَيِّ ءَالَآءِ رَبِّكُمَا تُكَذِّبَانِ ﴿23﴾ وَلَهُ ٱلْجَوَارِ ٱلْمُنشَـَٔاتُ فِى ٱلْبَحْرِ
كَٱلْأَعْلَـٰمِ ﴿24﴾ فَبِأَيِّ ءَالَآءِ رَبِّكُمَا تُكَذِّبَانِ ﴿25﴾ كُلُّ مَنْ عَلَيْهَا فَانٍ ﴿26﴾
وَيَبْقَىٰ وَجْهُ رَبِّكَ ذُو ٱلْجَلَـٰلِ وَٱلْإِكْرَامِ ﴿27﴾ فَبِأَيِّ ءَالَآءِ رَبِّكُمَا
تُكَذِّبَانِ ﴿28﴾ يَسْـَٔلُهُۥ مَن فِى ٱلسَّمَـٰوَٰتِ وَٱلْأَرْضِ ۚ كُلَّ يَوْمٍ هُوَ فِى
شَأْنٍ ﴿29﴾ فَبِأَيِّ ءَالَآءِ رَبِّكُمَا تُكَذِّبَانِ ﴿30﴾ سَنَفْرُغُ لَكُمْ أَيُّهَ
ٱلثَّقَلَانِ ﴿31﴾ فَبِأَيِّ ءَالَآءِ رَبِّكُمَا تُكَذِّبَانِ ﴿32﴾ يَـٰمَعْشَرَ ٱلْجِنِّ
وَٱلْإِنسِ إِنِ ٱسْتَطَعْتُمْ أَن تَنفُذُوا۟ مِنْ أَقْطَارِ ٱلسَّمَـٰوَٰتِ وَٱلْأَرْضِ
فَٱنفُذُوا۟ ۚ لَا تَنفُذُونَ إِلَّا بِسُلْطَـٰنٍ ﴿33﴾ فَبِأَيِّ ءَالَآءِ رَبِّكُمَا تُكَذِّبَانِ ﴿34﴾
يُرْسَلُ عَلَيْكُمَا شُوَاظٌ مِّن نَّارٍ وَنُحَاسٌ فَلَا تَنتَصِرَانِ ﴿35﴾ فَبِأَيِّ ءَالَآءِ
رَبِّكُمَا تُكَذِّبَانِ ﴿36﴾

[ONE DAY] We shall take you to task,[13] O you sin-laden two![14] ‹31› Which, then, of your Sustainer's powers can you disavow? ‹32›
O you who live in close communion with [evil] invisible beings and humans![15] If you [think that you] can pass beyond the regions of the heavens and the earth,[16] pass beyond them! [But] you cannot pass beyond them, save by a sanction [from God]![17] ‹33› Which, then, of your Sustainer's powers can you disavow? ‹34›
A flash of fire will be let loose upon you, and smoke, and you will be left without succour! ‹35› Which, then, of your Sustainer's powers can you disavow? ‹36›

Fabiʾayyi ʾālāaʾi Rabbikumā tukadhdhibān. (23) Wa lahul-jawāril-muñshaʾātu fil-baḥri kalʾaʿlām. (24) Fabiʾayyi ʾālāaʾi Rabbikumā tukadhdhibān. (25) Kullu man ʿalayhā fān. (26) Wa yabqā Wajhu Rabbika Dhul-jalāli wal-ʾikrām. (27) Fabiʾayyi ʾālāaʾi Rabbikumā tukadhdhibān. (28) Yasʾaluhū mañ-fis-samāwāti wal-ʾarḍi kulla yawmin Huwa fī shaʾn. (29) Fabiʾayyi ʾālāaʾi Rabbikumā tukadhdhibān. (30) Sanafrughu lakum ʾayyuhath-thaqalān. (31) Fabiʾayyi ʾālāaʾi Rabbikumā tukadhdhibān. (32) Yā maʿsharal-Jinni wal-ʾIñsi ʾinis-taṭaʿtum ʾañ-tañfudhū min ʾaqṭāris-samāwāti wal-ʾarḍi fañfudhū; lā tañfudhūna ʾillā bi-sulṭān. (33) Fabiʾayyi ʾālāaʾi Rabbikumā tukadhdhibān. (34) Yursalu ʿalaykumā shuwāẓum-miñ-nāriñw-wa nuḥāsuñ-falā tañtaṣirān. (35) Fabiʾayyi ʾālāaʾi Rabbikumā tukadhdhibān. (36)

9 Lit., "in the sea like mountains". The reference to ships as "belonging to God" is meant to stress the God-given nature of man's intelligence and inventiveness – a reflection of God's creative powers – which expresses itself in all that man is able to produce. (See also 42 : 32-34 and the corresponding notes.)

10 Lit., "Everyone who is upon it", i.e., on earth and/or, according to Ibn Kathīr, in the heavens – since the pronoun in *ʿalayhā* apparently relates to the whole universe.

11 Lit., "face", or "countenance", a term used metonymically in classical Arabic to denote the "self" or "whole being" of a person – in this case, the essential Being, or Reality, of God. Cf. also 28 : 88, "Everything is bound to perish, save His [eternal] Self".

12 Lit., "Him does ask [or "of Him does beg"] whoever is . . .", etc.: i.e., all depend on Him for their safety and sustenance.

13 Lit., "We shall apply Ourselves to you".

14 I.e., "you sin-laden men and women" (see note 4 above). According to an interpretation quoted by Rāzī, the designation *thaqalān* (the dual form of *thaqal*, "a thing of weight") signifies that both these categories of human beings are liable to, and therefore burdened with, sinning.

15 For an explanation of this rendering of *maʿshar al-jinn wa-'l-ins*, see note 112 on the first paragraph of 6 : 128.

16 I.e., in order to escape God's judgment and chastisement.

17 I.e., "unless He wills to reprieve you": cf. the last paragraph of 6 : 128 and the corresponding note 114.

فَإِذَا ٱنشَقَّتِ ٱلسَّمَآءُ فَكَانَتْ وَرْدَةً كَٱلدِّهَانِ ﴿37﴾ فَبِأَىِّ ءَالَآءِ رَبِّكُمَا
تُكَذِّبَانِ ﴿38﴾ فَيَوْمَئِذٍ لَّا يُسْـَٔلُ عَن ذَنۢبِهِۦٓ إِنسٌ وَلَا جَآنٌّ ﴿39﴾ فَبِأَىِّ
ءَالَآءِ رَبِّكُمَا تُكَذِّبَانِ ﴿40﴾ يُعْرَفُ ٱلْمُجْرِمُونَ بِسِيمَٰهُمْ فَيُؤْخَذُ
بِٱلنَّوَٰصِى وَٱلْأَقْدَامِ ﴿41﴾ فَبِأَىِّ ءَالَآءِ رَبِّكُمَا تُكَذِّبَانِ ﴿42﴾ هَٰذِهِۦ
جَهَنَّمُ ٱلَّتِى يُكَذِّبُ بِهَا ٱلْمُجْرِمُونَ ﴿43﴾ يَطُوفُونَ بَيْنَهَا وَبَيْنَ حَمِيمٍ
ءَانٍ ﴿44﴾ فَبِأَىِّ ءَالَآءِ رَبِّكُمَا تُكَذِّبَانِ ﴿45﴾ وَلِمَنْ خَافَ مَقَامَ رَبِّهِۦ
جَنَّتَانِ ﴿46﴾ فَبِأَىِّ ءَالَآءِ رَبِّكُمَا تُكَذِّبَانِ ﴿47﴾ ذَوَاتَآ أَفْنَانٍ ﴿48﴾ فَبِأَىِّ
ءَالَآءِ رَبِّكُمَا تُكَذِّبَانِ ﴿49﴾

And when the sky is rent asunder and becomes red like [burning] oil[18] ‹37› – which, then, of your Sustainer's powers can you disavow? ‹38›
For on that Day neither man nor invisible being will be asked about his sins.[19] ‹39›
Which, then, of your Sustainer's powers can you disavow? ‹40›
All who were lost in sin shall by their marks be known, and shall by their forelocks and their feet be seized![20] ‹41›
Which, then, of your Sustainer's powers can you disavow? ‹42›
This will be the hell which those who are lost in sin [now] call a lie: ‹43› between it and [their own] burning-hot despair will they wander to and fro![21] ‹44› Which, then, of your Sustainer's powers can you disavow? ‹45›

BUT FOR THOSE who of their Sustainer's Presence stand in fear, two gardens [of paradise are readied][22] ‹46› – which, then, of your Sustainer's powers can you disavow? ‹47› – [two gardens] of many wondrous hues.[23] ‹48› Which, then, of your Sustainer's powers can you disavow? ‹49›

Faʾidhañ-shaqqatis-samāaʾu fakānat wardatañ-kad-
dihān. (37) Fabiʾayyi ʾālāaʾi Rabbikumā tukadh-
dhibān. (38) FaYawmaʾidhil-lā yusʾalu ʿañ-dhambihīi
ʾIñsuñw-wa lā Jāann. (39) Fabiʾayyi ʾālāaʾi Rabbiku-
mā tukadhdhibān. (40) Yuʿraful-mujrimūna bisī-
māhum fayuʾkhadhu binnawāṣī wal-ʾaqdām. (41)
Fabiʾayyi ʾālāaʾi Rabbikumā tukadhdhibān. (42)
Hādhihī jahannamul-latī yukadhdhibu bihal-mujri-
mūn. (43) Yaṭūfuna baynahā wa bayna ḥamīmin ʾān.
(44) Fabiʾayyi ʾālāaʾi Rabbikumā tukadhdhibān. (45)
Wa liman khāfa maqāma Rabbihī jannatān. (46)
Fabiʾayyi ʾālāaʾi Rabbikumā tukadhdhibān. (47)
Dhawātāa ʾafnān. (48) Fabiʾayyi ʾālāaʾi Rabbikumā
tukadhdhibān. (49)

---

18 This is one of several legitimate interpretations of the term *dihān* (see Ṭabarī); another is "freshly tanned [or "red"] leather", synonymous with *adīm* (Zamakhsharī); and yet another, "dregs of olive-oil" (Rāghib). All these interpretations have one idea in common – namely, the sudden and surprising change (or changes) of colour to which the sky will be subject at the Last Hour.

19 I.e., the sinners "will find all that they ever wrought [now] facing them" (18 : 49), and "their own tongues and hands and feet will bear witness against them by [recalling] all that they did" (24 : 24).

20 This is an allusion to their utter humiliation and disgrace. When the ancient Arabs wanted to stress someone's subjection to another person, they would say, "His forelock is in the hand of so-and-so." (See also 96 : 15-16 and the corresponding note 8.)

21 For my rendering of *ḥamīm* as "burning despair", see note 62 on the last sentence of 6 : 70. The allegorical nature of all Qurʾanic descriptions of "rewards" and "punishments" in the hereafter is clearly hinted at in the phrasing of the above verse, which speaks of the sinners' "wandering to and fro" *between* hell and burning despair (*baynahā wa-bayna ḥamīm*) – i.e., tossed between factual suffering and the despair of vain regrets.

22 I.e., two *kinds* of paradise, to be experienced simultaneously. Various interpretations are advanced on this score by the classical commentators: e.g., "a paradise for their doing of good deeds, and another paradise for their avoidance of sins" (Zamakhsharī); or a paradise that "will comprise both spiritual and physical joys, [so that it will seem] as if it were two paradises" (Rāzī). Finally, one might conclude that the pointed reference to the "*two* gardens" of paradise contains – like the preceding reference to the sinners' "wandering *between* hell and burning despair" – a pointed allusion to the allegorical character of all descriptions of the life to come, as well as to the inexpressible intensity (or multiplication) of all imaginable and unimaginable sensations in that afterlife. The subsequent descriptions of the joys of paradise must be understood in the same symbolic light.

23 According to Ṭabarī, the noun *fann* (lit., "mode" or "manner") is in this case synonymous with *lawn* ("colour" or "hue"). *Afnān* is a double plural, and hence denotes "*many* hues"; and since – as pointed out in the *Tāj al-ʿArūs* – one of the several accepted meanings of *fann* is "a wonderful thing", *afnān* can also be understood as "many wonderful

In [each of] these two [gardens] two springs will flow.[24] ‹50› Which, then, of your Sustainer's powers can you disavow? ‹51›

In [each of] these two will two kinds of every fruit be [found].[25] ‹52› Which, then, of your Sustainer's powers can you disavow? ‹53›

[In such a paradise the blest will dwell,] reclining upon carpets lined with rich brocade;[26] and the fruit of both these gardens will be within easy reach. ‹54› Which, then, of your Sustainer's powers can you disavow? ‹55›

In these [gardens] will be mates of modest gaze, whom neither man nor invisible being will have touched ere then.[27] ‹56› Which, then, of your Sustainer's powers can you disavow? ‹57›

[When you are promised splendours] as though [of] rubies and [of] pearls ‹58› – which, then, of your Sustainer's powers can you disavow? ‹59› Could the reward of good be aught but good? ‹60› Which, then, of your Sustainer's powers can you disavow? ‹61›

And besides those two will be yet two [other] gardens[28] ‹62› – which, then, of your Sustainer's powers can you disavow? ‹63›

فِيهِمَا عَيْنَانِ تَجْرِيَانِ ﴿٥٠﴾ فَبِأَيِّ ءَالَآءِ رَبِّكُمَا تُكَذِّبَانِ ﴿٥١﴾ فِيهِمَا
مِن كُلِّ فَـٰكِهَةٍ زَوْجَانِ ﴿٥٢﴾ فَبِأَيِّ ءَالَآءِ رَبِّكُمَا تُكَذِّبَانِ ﴿٥٣﴾
مُتَّكِـِٔينَ عَلَىٰ فُرُشٍ بَطَآئِنُهَا مِنْ إِسْتَبْرَقٍ وَجَنَى ٱلْجَنَّتَيْنِ دَانٍ ﴿٥٤﴾
فَبِأَيِّ ءَالَآءِ رَبِّكُمَا تُكَذِّبَانِ ﴿٥٥﴾ فِيهِنَّ قَـٰصِرَٰتُ ٱلطَّرْفِ لَمْ
يَطْمِثْهُنَّ إِنسٌ قَبْلَهُمْ وَلَا جَآنٌّ ﴿٥٦﴾ فَبِأَيِّ ءَالَآءِ رَبِّكُمَا تُكَذِّبَانِ ﴿٥٧﴾
كَأَنَّهُنَّ ٱلْيَاقُوتُ وَٱلْمَرْجَانُ ﴿٥٨﴾ فَبِأَيِّ ءَالَآءِ رَبِّكُمَا تُكَذِّبَانِ ﴿٥٩﴾ هَلْ
جَزَآءُ ٱلْإِحْسَـٰنِ إِلَّا ٱلْإِحْسَـٰنُ ﴿٦٠﴾ فَبِأَيِّ ءَالَآءِ رَبِّكُمَا تُكَذِّبَانِ ﴿٦١﴾
وَمِن دُونِهِمَا جَنَّتَانِ ﴿٦٢﴾ فَبِأَيِّ ءَالَآءِ رَبِّكُمَا تُكَذِّبَانِ ﴿٦٣﴾

Fīhimā ʿaynāni tajriyān. (50) Fabiʾayyi ʾālāaʾi Rabbikumā tukadhdhibān. (51) Fīhimā miñ-kulli fākihatiñ-zawjān. (52) Fabiʾayyi ʾālāaʾi Rabbikumā tukadhdhibān. (53) Muttakiʾīna ʿalā furushim-baṭāaʾinuhā min ʾistabraqiñw-wa janal-jannatayni dān. (54) Fabiʾayyi ʾālāaʾi Rabbikumā tukadhdhibān. (55) Fīhinna qāṣirātuṭ-ṭarfi lam yaṭmithhunna ʾIñsuñ-qablahum wa lā Jāann. (56) Fabiʾayyi ʾālāaʾi Rabbikumā tukadhdhibān. (57) Kaʾannahunnal-yāqūtu wal-marjān. (58) Fabiʾayyi ʾālāaʾi Rabbikumā tukadhdhibān. (59) Hal jazāaʾul-ʾiḥsāni ʾillal-ʾiḥsān. (60) Fabiʾayyi ʾālāaʾi Rabbikumā tukadhdhibān. (61) Wa miñ-dūnihimā jannatān. (62) Fabiʾayyi ʾālāaʾi Rabbikumā tukadhdhibān. (63)

things". The rendering adopted by me combines both these interpretations. – As regards the indescribable nature of what is termed "paradise", see 32 : 17 and the corresponding note 15.

24 The "two springs" of paradise call to mind the "two seas" spoken of in 18 : 60-61, which, according to Bayḍāwī, symbolize the two sources or streams of knowledge accessible to man: the one obtained through the observation and intellectual analysis of external phenomena (*ʿilm aẓ-ẓāhir*), and the other through inward, mystic insight (*ʿilm al-bāṭin*).

25 Zamakhsharī: "a kind that is known and a kind that is strange (*gharīb*)" – i.e., cognitions or sensations that are imaginable on the basis of our experiences in the present life, and such as are, as yet, unimaginable to us, and can, therefore, be only hinted at by means of symbols or allegories. Regarding the concept of "allegory" as such, see 3 : 7 and the corresponding note 8.

26 Cf. 18 : 31 and the corresponding note 41. The "reclining upon carpets" (or "upon couches" in 18 : 31) is a symbol of utter restfulness and peace of mind. The mention of the "carpets" of paradise being *lined* with rich brocade is perhaps meant to convey the idea that – just as the lining of a carpet is, as a rule, invisible – the beauty of paradise has nothing to do with outward show, being of an inner, spiritual nature (Rāzī). This concept appears already in an earlier interpretation, quoted by Zamakhsharī, according to which the "carpets" spoken of here consist of *light*.

27 See 56 : 35-36 and the corresponding note 14. As regards the expression *qāṣirāt aṭ-ṭarf* (lit., "such as restrain their gaze"), see note 46 on 38 : 52, the earliest Qurʾanic instance of this expression.

28 Most of the commentators assume – not very convincingly – that the "two other gardens" are those to which believers of lesser merit will attain. As against this weak and somewhat arbitrary interpretation, it seems to me that the juxtaposition of "two other gardens" with the "two" previously mentioned is meant to convey the idea of *infinity* in

– two [gardens] of the deepest green.[29] ‹64› Which, then, of your Sustainer's powers can you disavow? ‹65›

In [each of] these two [gardens] will two springs gush forth. ‹66› Which, then, of your Sustainer's powers can you disavow? ‹67›

In both of them will be [all kinds of] fruit, and date-palms and pomegranates. ‹68› Which, then, of your Sustainer's powers can you disavow? ‹69›

In these [gardens] will be [all] things most excellent and beautiful. ‹70› Which, then, of your Sustainer's powers can you disavow? ‹71›

[There the blest will live with their] companions pure[30] and modest, in pavillions [splendid] ‹72› – which, then, of your Sustainer's powers can you disavow? ‹73› – [companions] whom neither man nor invisible being will have touched ere then. ‹74› Which, then, of your Sustainer's powers can you disavow? ‹75›

[In such a paradise will they dwell,] reclining upon meadows green and carpets rich in beauty. ‹76› Which, then, of your Sustainer's powers can you disavow? ‹77›

HALLOWED be thy Sustainer's name, full of majesty and glory! ‹78›

مُدْهَآمَّتَانِ (64) فَبِأَيِّ ءَالَآءِ رَبِّكُمَا تُكَذِّبَانِ (65) فِيهِمَا عَيْنَانِ
نَضَّاخَتَانِ (66) فَبِأَيِّ ءَالَآءِ رَبِّكُمَا تُكَذِّبَانِ (67) فِيهِمَا فَٰكِهَةٌ وَنَخْلٌ
وَرُمَّانٌ (68) فَبِأَيِّ ءَالَآءِ رَبِّكُمَا تُكَذِّبَانِ (69) فِيهِنَّ خَيْرَٰتٌ حِسَانٌ (70)
فَبِأَيِّ ءَالَآءِ رَبِّكُمَا تُكَذِّبَانِ (71) حُورٌ مَّقْصُورَٰتٌ فِى ٱلْخِيَامِ (72)
فَبِأَيِّ ءَالَآءِ رَبِّكُمَا تُكَذِّبَانِ (73) لَمْ يَطْمِثْهُنَّ إِنسٌ قَبْلَهُمْ وَلَا
جَآنٌّ (74) فَبِأَيِّ ءَالَآءِ رَبِّكُمَا تُكَذِّبَانِ (75) مُتَّكِـِٔينَ عَلَىٰ رَفْرَفٍ
خُضْرٍ وَعَبْقَرِىٍّ حِسَانٍ (76) فَبِأَيِّ ءَالَآءِ رَبِّكُمَا تُكَذِّبَانِ (77) تَبَٰرَكَ
ٱسْمُ رَبِّكَ ذِى ٱلْجَلَٰلِ وَٱلْإِكْرَامِ (78)

Mud-hāammatān. (64) Fabiʾayyi ʾālāaʾi Rabbikumā tukadhdhibān. (65) Fīhimā ʿaynāni naḍḍākhatān. (66) Fabiʾayyi ʾālāaʾi Rabbikumā tukadhdhibān. (67) Fīhimā fākihatuñw-wa nakhluñw-wa rummān. (68) Fabiʾayyi ʾālāaʾi Rabbikumā tukadhdhibān. (69) Fīhinna khayrātun ḥisān. (70) Fabiʾayyi ʾālāaʾi Rabbikumā tukadhdhibān. (71) Ḥūrum-maqṣūratuñ fil-khiyām. (72) Fabiʾayyi ʾālāaʾi Rabbikumā tukadhdhibān. (73) Lam yaṭmithhunna ʾInsuñ-qablahum wa lā Jāann. (74) Fabiʾayyi ʾālāaʾi Rabbikumā tukadhdhibān. (75) Muttakiʾīna ʿalā rafrafin khuḍriñw-wa ʿabqariyyin ḥisān. (76) Fabiʾayyi ʾālāaʾi Rabbikumā tukadhdhibān. (77) Tabārakas-mu Rabbika Dhil-jalāli wal-ʾikrām. (78)

connection with the concept of paradise as such: gardens beyond gardens beyond gardens in an endless vista, slightly varying in description, but all of them symbols of supreme bliss.

29 I.e., by reason of abundant watering (*Tāj al-ʿArūs*). It is to be noted that the adjective "green" is often used in the Qurʾān to indicate ever-fresh life: e.g., the "green garments" which the inmates of paradise will wear (18 : 31 and 76 : 21), or the "green meadows" upon which they will recline (cf. verse 76 of the present *sūrah*).

30 For this rendering of the plural noun *ḥūr* (which is both masculine and feminine), see note 8 on 56 : 22, the earliest occurrence of this term in the Qurʾān; also note 13 on 56 : 34.

The Fifty-Sixth Sūrah

*Al-Wāqi*ᶜ*ah* (That Which Must Come to Pass)

Mecca Period

ACCORDING to all available evidence, this *sūrah* was revealed about seven years before the Prophet's *hijrah.*

سورة الواقعة مكية
-56-
وآياتها ست وتسعون

ربع الحزب

IN THE NAME OF GOD, THE MOST GRACIOUS, THE DISPENSER OF GRACE:

WHEN THAT which must come to pass[1] [at last] comes to pass, ‹1› there will be nought that could give the lie to its having come to pass, ‹2› abasing [some], exalting [others]! ‹3›

When the earth is shaken with a shaking [severe], ‹4› and the mountains are shattered into [countless] shards, ‹5› so that they become as scattered dust ‹6› – [on that Day,] then, shall you be [divided into] three kinds. ‹7›

Thus, there shall be such as will have attained to what is right:[2] oh, how [happy] will be they who have attained to what is right! ‹8›

And there shall be such as will have lost themselves in evil:[3] oh, how [unhappy] will be they who have lost themselves in evil! ‹9›

بِسۡمِ ٱللَّهِ ٱلرَّحۡمَٰنِ ٱلرَّحِيمِ

إِذَا وَقَعَتِ ٱلۡوَاقِعَةُ ﴿1﴾ لَيۡسَ لِوَقۡعَتِهَا كَاذِبَةٌ ﴿2﴾ خَافِضَةٞ رَّافِعَةٌ ﴿3﴾
إِذَا رُجَّتِ ٱلۡأَرۡضُ رَجّٗا ﴿4﴾ وَبُسَّتِ ٱلۡجِبَالُ بَسّٗا ﴿5﴾ فَكَانَتۡ هَبَآءٗ
مُّنۢبَثّٗا ﴿6﴾ وَكُنتُمۡ أَزۡوَٰجٗا ثَلَٰثَةٗ ﴿7﴾ فَأَصۡحَٰبُ ٱلۡمَيۡمَنَةِ مَآ أَصۡحَٰبُ
ٱلۡمَيۡمَنَةِ ﴿8﴾ وَأَصۡحَٰبُ ٱلۡمَشۡـَٔمَةِ مَآ أَصۡحَٰبُ ٱلۡمَشۡـَٔمَةِ ﴿9﴾

Bismil-lāhir-Raḥmānir-Raḥīm.
ᵓIdhā waqaᶜatil-Wāqiᶜah. (1) **Laysa liwaqᶜatihā kā-**
dhibah. (2) **Khāfiḍatur-rāfiᶜah.** (3) **ᵓIdhā rujjatil-**
ᵓarḍu rajjā. (4) **Wa bussatil-jibālu bassā.** (5)
Fakānat habāaᵓam-mumbaththā. (6) **Wa kuñtum**
ᵓazwājañ-thalāthah. (7) **Faᵓaṣḥābul-maymanati māa**
ᵓaṣḥābul-maymanah. (8) **Wa ᵓaṣḥābul-mashᵓamati**
māa ᵓaṣḥābul-mashᵓamah. (9)

---

1 I.e., the Last Hour and Resurrection.

2 Lit., "those [or "the people"] of the right side": see note 25 on 74 : 39.

3 Lit., "those [or "the people"] of the left side". Similarly to the use of the expression *maymanah* as a metonym for "attaining to what is right", the term *mashᵓamah* is used to denote "losing oneself in evil" (e.g., in 90 : 19). The origin of both these metonyms is based on the belief of the pre-Islamic Arabs that future events could be predicted by observing the direction of the flight of birds at certain times: if they flew to the right, the event in question promised

But the foremost shall be [they who in life were] the foremost [in faith and good works]: ‹10› they who were [always] drawn close unto God! ‹11› In gardens of bliss [will they dwell] ‹12› – a good many of those of olden times, ‹13› but [only] a few of later times.[4] ‹14›
[They will be seated] on gold-encrusted thrones of happiness, ‹15› reclining upon them, facing one another [in love].[5] ‹16›
Immortal youths will wait upon them ‹17› with goblets, and ewers, and cups filled with water from unsullied springs[6] ‹18› by which their minds will not be clouded and which will not make them drunk; ‹19› and with fruit of any kind that they may choose, ‹20› and with the flesh of any fowl that they may desire.[7] ‹21›
And [with them will be their] companions pure, most beautiful of eye,[8] ‹22› like unto pearls [still] hidden in their shells. ‹23›
[And this will be] a reward for what they did [in life]. ‹24› No empty talk will they hear there, nor any call to sin, ‹25› but only the tiding of inner soundness and peace.[9] ‹26›

وَٱلسَّٰبِقُونَ ٱلسَّٰبِقُونَ ﴿10﴾ أُوْلَٰٓئِكَ ٱلۡمُقَرَّبُونَ ﴿11﴾ فِي جَنَّٰتِ
ٱلنَّعِيمِ ﴿12﴾ ثُلَّةٞ مِّنَ ٱلۡأَوَّلِينَ ﴿13﴾ وَقَلِيلٞ مِّنَ ٱلۡأٓخِرِينَ ﴿14﴾ عَلَىٰ سُرُرٖ
مَّوۡضُونَةٖ ﴿15﴾ مُّتَّكِـِٔينَ عَلَيۡهَا مُتَقَٰبِلِينَ ﴿16﴾ يَطُوفُ عَلَيۡهِمۡ وِلۡدَٰنٞ
مُّخَلَّدُونَ ﴿17﴾ بِأَكۡوَابٖ وَأَبَارِيقَ وَكَأۡسٖ مِّن مَّعِينٖ ﴿18﴾ لَّا يُصَدَّعُونَ عَنۡهَا
وَلَا يُنزِفُونَ ﴿19﴾ وَفَٰكِهَةٖ مِّمَّا يَتَخَيَّرُونَ ﴿20﴾ وَلَحۡمِ طَيۡرٖ مِّمَّا يَشۡتَهُونَ ﴿21﴾
وَحُورٌ عِينٞ ﴿22﴾ كَأَمۡثَٰلِ ٱللُّؤۡلُوِٕ ٱلۡمَكۡنُونِ ﴿23﴾ جَزَآءَۢ بِمَا كَانُواْ
يَعۡمَلُونَ ﴿24﴾ لَا يَسۡمَعُونَ فِيهَا لَغۡوٗا وَلَا تَأۡثِيمًا ﴿25﴾ إِلَّا قِيلٗا سَلَٰمٗا
سَلَٰمٗا ﴿26﴾

Was-sābiqūnas-sābiqūn. (10) ʾUlāaʾikal-muqarrabūn. (11) Fī jannātin-naʿīm. (12) Thullatum-minal-ʾawwalīn. (13) Wa qalīlum-minal-ʾākhirīn. (14) ʿAlā sururim-mawḍūnah. (15) Muttakiʾīna ʿalayhā mutaqābilīn. (16) Yaṭūfu ʿalayhim wildānum-mukhalladūna, (17) bi-ʾakwābiñw-wa ʾabārīqa wa kaʾsim-mim-maʿīn. (18) Lā yuṣaddaʿūna ʿanhā wa lā yuñzifūn. (19) Wa fākihatim-mimmā yatakhayyarūn. (20) Wa laḥmi ṭayrim-mimmā yashtahūn. (21) Wa ḥūrun ʿīn. (22) Kaʾamthālil-luʾluʾil-maknūn. (23) Jazāaʾam-bimā kānū yaʿmalūn. (24) Lā yasmaʿūna fīhā laghwañw-wa lā taʾthīmā. (25) ʾIllā qīlañ-salāmañ-salāmā. (26)

to be auspicious; if to the left, the contrary. This ancient belief was gradually absorbed by linguistic usage, so that "right" and "left" became more or less synonymous with "auspicious" and "inauspicious". In the idiom of the Qurʾān, these two concepts have been deepened into "righteousness" and "unrighteousness", respectively.

4 The above stress on the "many" and the "few" contains an allusion to the progressive diminution, in the historical sense, of the element of excellence in men's faith and ethical achievements. (See also note 16 on verses 39-40.)

5 See note 34 on 15 : 47 which explains the symbolism of the above two verses.

6 This is evidently a symbolic allusion to the imperishable quality – the eternal youthfulness, as it were – of all the experiences in the state described as "paradise". (See also next two notes.)

7 Regarding this and any other Qurʾanic description of the joys of paradise, see 32 : 17 and, in particular, the corresponding note 15. The famous *ḥadīth* quoted in that note must be kept in mind when reading any Qurʾanic reference to the state or quality of human life in the hereafter.

8 The noun *ḥūr* – rendered by me as "companions pure" – is a plural of both *aḥwar* (masc.) and *ḥawrāʾ* (fem.), either of which describes "a person distinguished by *ḥawar*", which latter term primarily denotes "intense whiteness of the eyeballs and lustrous black of the iris" (*Qāmūs*). In a more general sense, *ḥawar* signifies simply "whiteness" (*Asās*) or, as a moral qualification, "purity" (cf. Ṭabarī, Rāzī and Ibn Kathīr in their explanations of the term *ḥawāriyyūn* in 3 : 52). Hence, the compound expression *ḥūr ʿīn* signifies, approximately, "pure beings [or, more specifically, "companions pure"], most beautiful of eye" (which latter is the meaning of *ʿīn*, the plural of *aʿyan*). In his comments on the identical expression in 52 : 20, Rāzī observes that inasmuch as a person's eye reflects his soul more clearly than any other part of the human body, *ʿīn* may be understood as "rich of soul" or "soulful". As regards the term *ḥūr* in its more current, feminine connotation, quite a number of the earliest Qurʾān-commentators – among them Al-Ḥasan al-Baṣrī – understood it as signifying no more and no less than "the righteous among the women of the human kind" (Ṭabarī) – "[even] those toothless old women of yours whom God will resurrect as new beings" (Al-Ḥasan, as quoted by Rāzī in his comments on 44 : 54). See in this connection also note 46 on 38 : 52.

9 Lit., "only the saying, 'Peace, peace' (*salām*)!" Regarding this latter term, see note 48 on 19 : 62, as well as note 29 on 5 : 16.

NOW AS FOR those who have attained to righteousness – what of those who have attained to righteousness?[10] ‹27›
[They, too, will find themselves] amidst fruit-laden lote-trees,[11] ‹28› and acacias flower-clad, ‹29› and shade extended,[12] ‹30› and waters gushing, ‹31› and fruit abounding, ‹32› never-failing and never out of reach. ‹33›
And [with them will be their] spouses, raised high:[13] ‹34› for, behold, We shall have brought them into being in a life renewed, ‹35› having resurrected them as virgins,[14] ‹36› full of love, well-matched ‹37› with those who have attained to righteousness:[15] ‹38› a good many of olden times, ‹39› and a good many of later times.[16] ‹40›

BUT AS FOR those who have persevered in evil – what of those who have persevered in evil?[17] ‹41›

وَأَصۡحَٰبُ ٱلۡيَمِينِ مَآ أَصۡحَٰبُ ٱلۡيَمِينِ ﴿٢٧﴾ فِي سِدۡرٖ مَّخۡضُودٖ ﴿٢٨﴾ وَطَلۡحٖ
مَّنضُودٖ ﴿٢٩﴾ وَظِلّٖ مَّمۡدُودٖ ﴿٣٠﴾ وَمَآءٖ مَّسۡكُوبٖ ﴿٣١﴾ وَفَٰكِهَةٖ كَثِيرَةٖ ﴿٣٢﴾
لَّا مَقۡطُوعَةٖ وَلَا مَمۡنُوعَةٖ ﴿٣٣﴾ وَفُرُشٖ مَّرۡفُوعَةٍ ﴿٣٤﴾ إِنَّآ أَنشَأۡنَٰهُنَّ إِنشَآءٗ ﴿٣٥﴾
فَجَعَلۡنَٰهُنَّ أَبۡكَارًا ﴿٣٦﴾ عُرُبًا أَتۡرَابٗا ﴿٣٧﴾ لِّأَصۡحَٰبِ ٱلۡيَمِينِ ﴿٣٨﴾ ثُلَّةٞ مِّنَ
ٱلۡأَوَّلِينَ ﴿٣٩﴾ وَثُلَّةٞ مِّنَ ٱلۡأٓخِرِينَ ﴿٤٠﴾ وَأَصۡحَٰبُ ٱلشِّمَالِ مَآ أَصۡحَٰبُ
ٱلشِّمَالِ ﴿٤١﴾

Wa ʾaṣḥābul-yamīni māa ʾaṣḥābul-yamīn. (27) Fī sidrim-makhḍūd. (28) Wa ṭalḥim-mañḍūd. (29) Wa ẓillim-mamdūd. (30) Wa māaʾim-maskūb. (31) Wa fākihatiñ-kathīrah. (32) Lā maqṭūʿatiñw-wa lā mamnūʿah. (33) Wa furushim-marfūʿah. (34) ʾInnāa ʾañshaʾnāhunna ʾiñshāaʾā. (35) Fajaʿalnāhunna ʾabkārā. (36) ʿUruban ʾatrābā. (37) Liʾaṣḥābil-yamīn. (38) Thullatum-minal-ʾawwalīn. (39) Wa thullatum-minal-ʾākhirīn. (40) Wa ʾaṣḥābush-shimāli māa ʾaṣḥābush-shimāl. (41)

10 Lit., "those on the right hand". According to some commentators, it is those who had not always been "foremost in faith and good works", but have gradually, after erring and sinning, attained to righteousness (Rāzī). However, though they may not have been as perfect in life as the "foremost", their ultimate achievement brings them to the same state of spiritual fulfilment as those others.

11 See note 10 on 53 : 14.

12 See note 74 on 4 : 57.

13 Or: "[they will rest on] couches raised high". The rendering adopted by me is regarded as fully justified by some of the most outstanding commentators (e.g., Baghawī, Zamakhsharī, Rāzī, Bayḍāwī, etc.), and this for two reasons: firstly, because in the classical Arabic idiom, the term *firāsh* (lit., "bed" or "couch") is often used tropically to denote "wife" or "husband" (Rāghib; also *Qāmūs, Tāj al-ʿArūs*, etc.), and, secondly, because of the statement in the next verse that God "shall have brought them (*hunna*) into being in a life renewed". (In the context of this interpretation, Zamakhsharī quotes also 36 : 56, which thus refers to the inmates of paradise: ". . . in happiness will *they and their spouses* on couches recline". There is no doubt that the "spouses raised high" – i.e., to the status of the blest – are identical with the *ḥūr* mentioned in verse 22 above as well as in 44 : 54, 52 : 20 and 55 : 72.

14 Lit., "and We shall have made them virgins". According to a number of authentic Traditions (quoted in full by Ṭabarī and Ibn Kathīr), the Prophet stated on several occasions that all righteous women, however old and decayed they may have been on earth, will be resurrected as virginal maidens and will, like their male counterparts, remain eternally young in paradise.

15 I.e., equal in dignity with all other inmates of paradise. As regards the term *atrāb* (sing. *tirb*), rendered above – as well as in 38 : 52 and 78 : 33 – as "well-matched", there is no doubt that it primarily denotes "[persons] of equal age" (a meaning adopted by most of the commentators); however, as pointed out by all philological authorities, this term is also used in the sense of "[persons] equal in *quality*", that is, "well-matched": a significance which, to my mind, is eminently appropriate here inasmuch as it is meant to stress the equal excellence of all who have attained to righteousness, whether they be men or women, or, alternatively, the equal attraction towards one another and, thus, a mutual fulfilment of their spiritual and emotional needs; or both of the above meanings.

16 In contrast with "the foremost", who have always been "drawn close unto God" – and of whom there are less and less as time goes on (see note 4 above) – there will always be many of those who attain to righteousness after initial stumbling and sinning (see note 10).

17 I.e., until their death. Literally, the phrase reads, "those on the left hand" (see note 3 above).

[They will find themselves] in the midst of scorching winds, and burning despair,[18] ‹42› and the shadows of black smoke ‹43› – [shadows] neither cooling nor soothing. ‹44›

For, behold, in times gone by they were wont to abandon themselves wholly to the pursuit of pleasures,[19] ‹45› and would persist in heinous sinning, ‹46› and would say, "What! After we have died and become mere dust and bones, shall we, forsooth, be raised from the dead? ‹47› – and perhaps, too, our forebears of old?" ‹48›

Say: "Verily, those of olden times and those of later times ‹49› will indeed be gathered together at an appointed time on a Day known [only to God]: ‹50› and then, verily, O you who have gone astray and called the truth a lie, ‹51› you will indeed have to taste of the tree of deadly fruit,[20] ‹52› and will have to fill your bellies therewith, ‹53› and will thereupon have to drink [many a draught] of burning despair ‹54› – drink it as the most insatiably thirsty camels drink!" ‹55›

Such will be their welcome on Judgment Day! ‹56›

IT IS WE who have created you, [O men:] why, then, do you not accept the truth? ‹57›

Have you ever considered that [seed] which you emit?[21] ‹58› Is it you who create it – or are We the source of its creation? ‹59›

We have [Indeed] decreed that death shall be [ever-present] among you: but there is nothing to prevent Us ‹60› from changing the nature of your existence[22] and bringing you into being [anew] in a manner [as yet] unknown to you. ‹61›

فِي سَمُومٍ وَحَمِيمٍ ﴿٤٢﴾ وَظِلٍّ مِّن يَحْمُومٍ ﴿٤٣﴾ لَّا بَارِدٍ وَلَا كَرِيمٍ ﴿٤٤﴾
إِنَّهُمْ كَانُوا قَبْلَ ذَٰلِكَ مُتْرَفِينَ ﴿٤٥﴾ وَكَانُوا يُصِرُّونَ عَلَى الْحِنثِ
الْعَظِيمِ ﴿٤٦﴾ وَكَانُوا يَقُولُونَ أَئِذَا مِتْنَا وَكُنَّا تُرَابًا وَعِظَامًا أَإِنَّا
لَمَبْعُوثُونَ ﴿٤٧﴾ أَوَآبَاؤُنَا الْأَوَّلُونَ ﴿٤٨﴾ قُلْ إِنَّ الْأَوَّلِينَ وَالْآخِرِينَ ﴿٤٩﴾
لَمَجْمُوعُونَ إِلَىٰ مِيقَاتِ يَوْمٍ مَّعْلُومٍ ﴿٥٠﴾ ثُمَّ إِنَّكُمْ أَيُّهَا الضَّالُّونَ
الْمُكَذِّبُونَ ﴿٥١﴾ لَآكِلُونَ مِن شَجَرٍ مِّن زَقُّومٍ ﴿٥٢﴾ فَمَالِئُونَ مِنْهَا الْبُطُونَ ﴿٥٣﴾
فَشَارِبُونَ عَلَيْهِ مِنَ الْحَمِيمِ ﴿٥٤﴾ فَشَارِبُونَ شُرْبَ الْهِيمِ ﴿٥٥﴾ هَٰذَا
نُزُلُهُمْ يَوْمَ الدِّينِ ﴿٥٦﴾ نَحْنُ خَلَقْنَاكُمْ فَلَوْلَا تُصَدِّقُونَ ﴿٥٧﴾ أَفَرَأَيْتُم مَّا
تُمْنُونَ ﴿٥٨﴾ أَأَنتُمْ تَخْلُقُونَهُ أَمْ نَحْنُ الْخَالِقُونَ ﴿٥٩﴾ نَحْنُ قَدَّرْنَا
بَيْنَكُمُ الْمَوْتَ وَمَا نَحْنُ بِمَسْبُوقِينَ ﴿٦٠﴾ عَلَىٰ أَن نُّبَدِّلَ أَمْثَالَكُمْ
وَنُنشِئَكُمْ فِي مَا لَا تَعْلَمُونَ ﴿٦١﴾

Fī samūmiñw-wa ḥamīm. (42) Wa ẓillim-miñy-yaḥmūm. (43) Lā bāridiñw-wa lā karīm. (44) ʾInnahum kānū qabla dhālika mutrafīn. (45) Wa kānū yuṣirrūna ʿalal-ḥiñthil-ʿaẓīm. (46) Wa kānū yaqūlūna ʾaʾidhā mitnā wa kunnā turābañw-wa ʿiẓāman ʾaʾinnā lamabʿūthūn. (47) ʾAwa ʾābāaʾunal-ʾawwalūn. (48) Qul ʾinnal-ʾawwalīna wal-ʾākhirīna, (49) lamajmuʿūna ʾilā mīqāti Yawmim-maʿlūm. (50) Thumma ʾinnakum ʾayyuhaḍ-ḍāalūnal-mukadhdhibūna, (51) laʾākilūna miñ-shajarim-miñ-zaqqūm. (52) Famāliʾūna minhal-buṭūn. (53) Fashāribūna ʿalayhi minal-ḥamīm. (54) Fashāribūna shurbal-hīm. (55) Hādhā nuzuluhum Yawmad-Dīn. (56) Naḥnu khalaqnākum falawlā tuṣaddiqūn. (57) ʾAfaraʾaytum-mā tumnūn. (58) ʾAʾañtum takhluqūnahūu ʾam Naḥnul-Khāliqūn. (59) Naḥnu qaddarnā baynakumul-mawta wa mā Naḥnu bimasbūqīna, (60) ʿalāa ʾañ-nubaddila ʾamthālakum wa nuñshiʾakum fī mā lā taʿlamūn. (61)

18 For this rendering of *ḥamīm*, see *sūrah* 6, note 62.

19 I.e., to the exclusion of all moral considerations. For the meaning of the term *mutraf*, see *sūrah* 11, note 147.

20 See note 22 on 37 : 62.

21 This refers to both the male semen and the female ovum, and thus, by implication, to the awe-inspiring, complex phenomenon of procreation as such.

22 Lit., "changing your likenesses (*amthāl*)". However, the term *mathal* signifies also, tropically, the state, condition and the qualities (*ṣifāt*) of a thing or person – in brief, "the nature of his [or its] existence".

And [since] you are indeed aware of the [miracle of your] coming into being in the first instance – why, then, do you not bethink yourselves [of Us]? «62»
Have you ever considered the seed which you cast upon the soil? «63» Is it you who cause it to grow – or are We the cause of its growth? «64» [For,] were it Our will, We could indeed turn it into chaff, and you would be left to wonder [and to lament], «65» "Verily we are ruined! «66» Nay, but we have been deprived [of our livelihood]!" «67»
Have you ever considered the water which you drink? «68» Is it you who cause it to come down from the clouds – or are We the cause of its coming down? «69» [It comes down sweet – but] were it Our will, We could make it burningly salty and bitter: why, then, do you not give thanks [unto Us]? «70»
Have you ever considered the fire which you kindle? «71» Is it you who have brought into being the tree that serves as its fuel[23] – or are We the cause of its coming into being? «72»
It is We who have made it a means to remind [you of Us],[24] and a comfort for all who are lost and hungry in the wilderness [of their lives].[25] «73»
Extol, then, the limitless glory of thy Sustainer's mighty name! «74»

وَلَقَدْ عَلِمْتُمُ ٱلنَّشْأَةَ ٱلْأُولَىٰ فَلَوْلَا تَذَكَّرُونَ ﴿٦٢﴾ أَفَرَءَيْتُم مَّا تَحْرُثُونَ ﴿٦٣﴾
ءَأَنتُمْ تَزْرَعُونَهُۥٓ أَمْ نَحْنُ ٱلزَّٰرِعُونَ ﴿٦٤﴾ لَوْ نَشَآءُ لَجَعَلْنَٰهُ حُطَٰمًا فَظَلْتُمْ
تَفَكَّهُونَ ﴿٦٥﴾ إِنَّا لَمُغْرَمُونَ ﴿٦٦﴾ بَلْ نَحْنُ مَحْرُومُونَ ﴿٦٧﴾ أَفَرَءَيْتُمُ
ٱلْمَآءَ ٱلَّذِى تَشْرَبُونَ ﴿٦٨﴾ ءَأَنتُمْ أَنزَلْتُمُوهُ مِنَ ٱلْمُزْنِ أَمْ نَحْنُ
ٱلْمُنزِلُونَ ﴿٦٩﴾ لَوْ نَشَآءُ جَعَلْنَٰهُ أُجَاجًا فَلَوْلَا تَشْكُرُونَ ﴿٧٠﴾ أَفَرَءَيْتُمُ
ٱلنَّارَ ٱلَّتِى تُورُونَ ﴿٧١﴾ ءَأَنتُمْ أَنشَأْتُمْ شَجَرَتَهَآ أَمْ نَحْنُ ٱلْمُنشِـُٔونَ ﴿٧٢﴾
نَحْنُ جَعَلْنَٰهَا تَذْكِرَةً وَمَتَٰعًا لِّلْمُقْوِينَ ﴿٧٣﴾ فَسَبِّحْ بِٱسْمِ رَبِّكَ
ٱلْعَظِيمِ ﴿٧٤﴾

Wa laqad ʿalimtumun-nashʾatal-ʾūlā falawlā tadhakkarūn. (62) ʾAfaraʾaytum-mā taḥruthūn. (63) ʾAʾañtum tazraʿūnahūu ʾam Naḥnuz-zāriʿūn. (64) Law nashāaʾu lajaʿalnāhu ḥuṭāmañ-faẓaltum tafakkahūn. (65) ʾInnā lamughramūn. (66) Bal naḥnu maḥrūmūn. (67) ʾAfaraʾaytumul-māaʾal-ladhī tashrabūn. (68) ʾAʾañtum ʾañzaltumūhu minal-muzni ʾam Naḥnul-muñzilūn. (69) Law nashāaʾu jaʿalnāhu ʾujājañ-falawlā tashkurūn. (70) ʾAfaraʾaytumun-nāral-latī tūrūn. (71) ʾAʾañtum ʾañshaʾtum shajaratahāa ʾam Naḥnul-muñshiʾūn. (72) Naḥnu jaʿalnāhā tadhkiratañw-wa matāʿal-lilmuqwīn. (73) Fasabbiḥ bismi Rabbikal-ʿAẓīm. (74)

23 Lit., "its tree": a metonym pointing to the plant-origin, direct or indirect, of almost all the known fuels, including mineral fuels like coal, which is but petrified wood, or petroleum, which is a liquefied residue of plant-nourished organisms buried in the earth for millions of years.

24 Inasmuch as "fire" (in the widest sense of this word) is the source of all light known to man, it is apt to remind him that "God is the light of the heavens and the earth" (see 24 : 35 and the corresponding notes).

25 The participial noun *muqw* is derived from the verb *qawiya*, "it became deserted" or "desolate". From the same root is derived the noun *qawāʾ* (or *qiwāʾ*), which signifies "desert", "wilderness" or "wasteland" as well as "hunger" or "starvation". Hence, *muqw* denotes "one who is hungry" as well as "one who is lost [or "who wanders"] in a deserted place". In the above verse this expression is evidently used tropically, for it is difficult to imagine that, as some commentators assume, it relates merely to "wayfarers in the desert". My composite rendering of *al-muqwīn* as "all who are lost and hungry in the wilderness", on the other hand, is literal and tropical at the same time, inasmuch as it describes people who are lonely, unfortunate and confused, and who hunger after human warmth and spiritual light.

نصف الحزب

NAY, I call to witness the coming-down in parts [of this Qurʾān][26] ‹75› – and, behold, this is indeed a most solemn affirmation, if you but knew it! ‹76› Behold, it is a truly noble discourse, ‹77› [conveyed unto man] in a well-guarded divine writ ‹78› which none but the pure [of heart] can touch:[27] ‹79› a revelation from the Sustainer of all the worlds! ‹80›

Would you, now, look down with disdain on a tiding like this,[28] ‹81› and make it your daily bread [as it were] to call the truth a lie? ‹82›

Why, then,[29] when [the last breath] comes up to the throat [of a dying man], ‹83› the while you are [helplessly] looking on ‹84› – and while We are closer to him than you, although you see [Us] not: ‹85› – why, then, if [you think that] you are not truly dependent [on Us], ‹86› can you not cause that [ebbing life] to return – if what you claim is true? ‹87›

[ALL OF YOU are destined to die.] Now if one happens to be of those who are drawn close unto God,[30] ‹88› happiness [awaits him in the life to come], and inner fulfilment, and a garden of bliss. ‹89›

And if one happens to be of those who have attained to righteousness,[31] ‹90› [he, too, will be welcomed into paradise with the words,] "Peace be unto thee [that art] of those who have attained to righteousness!" ‹91›

فَلَآ أُقۡسِمُ بِمَوَٰقِعِ ٱلنُّجُومِ ﴿٧٥﴾ وَإِنَّهُۥ لَقَسَمٞ لَّوۡ تَعۡلَمُونَ عَظِيمٌ ﴿٧٦﴾ إِنَّهُۥ
لَقُرۡءَانٞ كَرِيمٞ ﴿٧٧﴾ فِي كِتَٰبٖ مَّكۡنُونٖ ﴿٧٨﴾ لَّا يَمَسُّهُۥٓ إِلَّا ٱلۡمُطَهَّرُونَ ﴿٧٩﴾
تَنزِيلٞ مِّن رَّبِّ ٱلۡعَٰلَمِينَ ﴿٨٠﴾ أَفَبِهَٰذَا ٱلۡحَدِيثِ أَنتُم مُّدۡهِنُونَ ﴿٨١﴾
وَتَجۡعَلُونَ رِزۡقَكُمۡ أَنَّكُمۡ تُكَذِّبُونَ ﴿٨٢﴾ فَلَوۡلَآ إِذَا بَلَغَتِ ٱلۡحُلۡقُومَ ﴿٨٣﴾
وَأَنتُمۡ حِينَئِذٖ تَنظُرُونَ ﴿٨٤﴾ وَنَحۡنُ أَقۡرَبُ إِلَيۡهِ مِنكُمۡ وَلَٰكِن لَّا
تُبۡصِرُونَ ﴿٨٥﴾ فَلَوۡلَآ إِن كُنتُمۡ غَيۡرَ مَدِينِينَ ﴿٨٦﴾ تَرۡجِعُونَهَآ إِن كُنتُمۡ
صَٰدِقِينَ ﴿٨٧﴾ فَأَمَّآ إِن كَانَ مِنَ ٱلۡمُقَرَّبِينَ ﴿٨٨﴾ فَرَوۡحٞ وَرَيۡحَانٞ وَجَنَّتُ
نَعِيمٖ ﴿٨٩﴾ وَأَمَّآ إِن كَانَ مِنۡ أَصۡحَٰبِ ٱلۡيَمِينِ ﴿٩٠﴾ فَسَلَٰمٞ لَّكَ مِنۡ أَصۡحَٰبِ
ٱلۡيَمِينِ ﴿٩١﴾

Falāa ʾuqsimu bimawāqiʿin-nujūm. (75) Wa ʾinnahū laqasamul-law taʿlamūna ʿaẓīm. (76) ʾInnahu laQurʾānuñ-karīm. (77) Fī Kitābim-maknūn. (78) Lā yamassuhūu ʾillal-muṭahharūn. (79) Tañzīlum-mir-Rabbil-ʿālamīn. (80) ʾAfabihādhal-ḥadīthi ʾañtum-mud-hinūn. (81) Wa tajʿalūna rizqakum ʾannakum tukadhdhibūn. (82) Falawlāa ʾidhā balaghatil-ḥulqūm. (83) Wa ʾañtum ḥīnaʾidhiñ-tañẓurūn. (84) Wa naḥnu ʾaqrabu ʾilayhi miñkum wa lākil-lā tubṣirūn. (85) Falawlāa ʾiñ-kuñtum ghayra madīnīna, (86) tarjiʿūnahāa ʾiñ-kuñtum ṣādiqīn. (87) Faʾammāa ʾiñ-kāna minal-muqarrabīna, (88) farawḥuñw-wa rayḥānuñw-wa jannatu naʿīm. (89) Wa ʾammāa ʾiñ-kāna min ʾaṣḥābil-yamīni, (90) fasalāmul-laka min ʾaṣḥābil-yamīn. (91)

26 Or: "the setting [or "orbiting"] of the stars". The term *mawqiʿ* (of which *mawāqiʿ* is the plural) denotes the "time [or "place" or "manner"] at which something comes down". Although many of the commentators think that the phrase *mawāqiʿ an-nujūm* relates to the break-up of the stars at the Last Hour, Ibn ʿAbbās, ʿIkrimah and As-Suddī were definitely of the opinion, strongly supported by the subsequent verses, that this phrase refers to the step-by-step revelation – or "coming-down in parts (*nujūm*)" – of the Qurʾān (cf. Ṭabarī, and Ibn Kathīr; see also note 1 on 53 : 1). By "calling to witness" the gradual manner of its revelation, the Qurʾān points implicitly to the astounding fact that it has remained free of all inconsistencies and inner contradictions (cf. 4 : 82 and the corresponding note 97) despite all the dramatic changes in the Prophet's life during the twenty-three years of the "unfolding" of the divine writ: and this explains, too, the subsequent parenthetic clause (verse 76).

27 I.e., which only the pure of heart can truly understand and derive benefit from. As for the preceding reference to "a well-guarded [i.e., incorruptible] divine writ" (*kitāb maknūn*), see 85 : 21-22 and the corresponding note 11.

28 I.e., the message of resurrection and judgment.

29 The elliptic implication is: "If, then, as you claim, you are really independent of any Supreme Power, why do you not . . .", etc., thus connecting with verses 57-74.

30 I.e., the "foremost" spoken of in verses 10-11 of this *sūrah*.

31 See note 10 on verse 27.

But if one happens to be of those who are wont to call the truth a lie, and [thus] go astray, ‹92› a welcome of burning despair [awaits him in the life to come,] ‹93› and the heat of a blazing fire! ‹94›
Verily, this is indeed the truth of truths ![32] ‹95›
Extol, then, the limitless glory of thy Sustainer's mighty name! ‹96›

وَأَمَّآ إِن كَانَ مِنَ ٱلْمُكَذِّبِينَ ٱلضَّآلِّينَ ﴿٩٢﴾ فَنُزُلٌ مِّنْ حَمِيمٍ ﴿٩٣﴾
وَتَصْلِيَةُ جَحِيمٍ ﴿٩٤﴾ إِنَّ هَٰذَا لَهُوَ حَقُّ ٱلْيَقِينِ ﴿٩٥﴾ فَسَبِّحْ بِٱسْمِ رَبِّكَ
ٱلْعَظِيمِ ﴿٩٦﴾

Wa ʾammāa ʾiñ-kāna minal-mukadhdhibīnaḍ-ḍāal-līina, (92) fanuzulum-min ḥamīm. (93) Wa taṣliyatu jaḥīm. (94) ʾInna hādhā lahuwa ḥaqqul-yaqīn. (95) Fasabbiḥ bismi Rabbikal-ᶜAẓīm. (96)

32 Lit., "a truth of certainty", i.e., a truth most certain. The pronoun "this" in the above sentence relates not merely to the announcement of resurrection and life after death, but also – and primarily – to the stress on man's utter dependence on God.

The Fifty-Seventh Sūrah

Al-Ḥadīd (Iron)

Medina Period

THE MENTION in verse 25 of "iron" and all that this word implies (see note 42 below) so impressed the contemporaries and successors of the Prophet that this *sūrah* has always been known as "the *sūrah* in which iron is mentioned" (Ṭabarī). From the reference to the conquest of Mecca (*al-fatḥ*) in verse 10 it is obvious that the earliest date of its revelation would be the end of the year 8 H.

سورة الحديد مدنية -57-

وآياتها تسع وعشرون

IN THE NAME OF GOD, THE MOST GRACIOUS, THE DISPENSER OF GRACE:

ALL THAT IS in the heavens and on earth extols God's limitless glory: for He alone is almighty, truly wise! ⟨1⟩

His is the dominion over the heavens and the earth; He grants life and deals death; and He has the power to will anything. ⟨2⟩

He is the First and the Last,[1] and the Outward as well as the Inward:[2] and He has full knowledge of everything. ⟨3⟩

بِسۡمِ ٱللَّهِ ٱلرَّحۡمَٰنِ ٱلرَّحِيمِ

سَبَّحَ لِلَّهِ مَا فِي ٱلسَّمَٰوَٰتِ وَٱلۡأَرۡضِۖ وَهُوَ ٱلۡعَزِيزُ ٱلۡحَكِيمُ ١ لَهُۥ

مُلۡكُ ٱلسَّمَٰوَٰتِ وَٱلۡأَرۡضِۖ يُحۡيِۦ وَيُمِيتُۖ وَهُوَ عَلَىٰ كُلِّ شَيۡءٖ قَدِيرٌ ٢

هُوَ ٱلۡأَوَّلُ وَٱلۡأٓخِرُ وَٱلظَّٰهِرُ وَٱلۡبَاطِنُۖ وَهُوَ بِكُلِّ شَيۡءٍ عَلِيمٌ ٣

Bismil-lāhir-Raḥmānir-Raḥīm.

Sabbaḥa lillāhi mā fis-samāwāti wal-ʾarḍi wa Huwal-ʿAzīzul-Ḥakīm. (1) Lahū mulkus-samāwāti wal-ʾarḍi yuḥyī wa yumītu wa Huwa ʿalā kulli shayʾiñ-Qadīr. (2) Huwal-ʾAwwalu wal-ʾĀkhiru waẓ-Ẓāhiru wal-Bāṭinu wa Huwa bikulli shayʾin ʿAlīm. (3)

---

1. I.e., His Being is eternal, without anything preceding His existence and without anything outlasting its infinity: an interpretation given by the Prophet himself, as recorded in several well-authenticated Traditions. Thus, "time" itself – a concept beyond man's understanding – is but God's creation.

2 I.e., He is the transcendental Cause of all that exists and, at the same time, immanent in every phenomenon of His creation – cf. the oft-repeated Qurʾanic phrase (e.g., in verse 5), "all things go back unto God [as their source]"; in the words of Ṭabarī, "He is closer to everything than anything else could be". Another – perhaps supplementary – rendering could be, "He is the Evident as well as the Hidden": i.e., "His existence is evident (*ẓāhir*) in the effects of His activity, whereas He Himself is not perceptible (*ghayr mudrak*) to our senses" (Zamakhsharī).

He it is who has created the heavens and the earth in six aeons, and is established on the throne of His almightiness.[3]

He knows all that enters the earth, and all that comes out of it, as well as all that descends from the skies, and all that ascends to them.[4]

And He is with you wherever you may be; and God sees all that you do. ⟨4⟩

His is the dominion over the heavens and the earth; and all things go back unto God [as their source]. ⟨5⟩

He makes the night grow longer by shortening the day, and makes the day grow longer by shortening the night; and He has full knowledge of what is in the hearts [of men]. ⟨6⟩

BELIEVE in God and His Apostle, and spend on others out of that of which He has made you trustees:[5] for, those of you who have attained to faith and who spend freely [in God's cause] shall have a great reward. ⟨7⟩

And why should you not believe in God, seeing that the Apostle calls you to believe in [Him who is] your Sustainer, and [seeing that] He has taken a pledge from you?[6] [Why should you not believe in Him] if you are able to believe [in anything]?[7] ⟨8⟩

It is He who bestows from on high clear messages unto [this] His servant, to lead you out of the deep darkness into the light: for, behold, God is most compassionate towards you, a dispenser of grace. ⟨9⟩

هُوَ ٱلَّذِى خَلَقَ ٱلسَّمَٰوَٰتِ وَٱلْأَرْضَ فِى سِتَّةِ أَيَّامٍ ثُمَّ ٱسْتَوَىٰ عَلَى ٱلْعَرْشِ يَعْلَمُ مَا يَلِجُ فِى ٱلْأَرْضِ وَمَا يَخْرُجُ مِنْهَا وَمَا يَنزِلُ مِنَ ٱلسَّمَاءِ وَمَا يَعْرُجُ فِيهَا وَهُوَ مَعَكُمْ أَيْنَ مَا كُنتُمْ وَٱللَّهُ بِمَا تَعْمَلُونَ بَصِيرٌ ۝ لَّهُ مُلْكُ ٱلسَّمَٰوَٰتِ وَٱلْأَرْضِ وَإِلَى ٱللَّهِ تُرْجَعُ ٱلْأُمُورُ ۝ يُولِجُ ٱلَّيْلَ فِى ٱلنَّهَارِ وَيُولِجُ ٱلنَّهَارَ فِى ٱلَّيْلِ وَهُوَ عَلِيمٌ بِذَاتِ ٱلصُّدُورِ ۝ ءَامِنُوا۟ بِٱللَّهِ وَرَسُولِهِ وَأَنفِقُوا۟ مِمَّا جَعَلَكُم مُّسْتَخْلَفِينَ فِيهِ فَٱلَّذِينَ ءَامَنُوا۟ مِنكُمْ وَأَنفَقُوا۟ لَهُمْ أَجْرٌ كَبِيرٌ ۝ وَمَا لَكُمْ لَا تُؤْمِنُونَ بِٱللَّهِ وَٱلرَّسُولُ يَدْعُوكُمْ لِتُؤْمِنُوا۟ بِرَبِّكُمْ وَقَدْ أَخَذَ مِيثَٰقَكُمْ إِن كُنتُم مُّؤْمِنِينَ ۝ هُوَ ٱلَّذِى يُنَزِّلُ عَلَىٰ عَبْدِهِ ءَايَٰتٍ بَيِّنَٰتٍ لِّيُخْرِجَكُم مِّنَ ٱلظُّلُمَٰتِ إِلَى ٱلنُّورِ وَإِنَّ ٱللَّهَ بِكُمْ لَرَءُوفٌ رَّحِيمٌ ۝

Huwal-ladhī khalaqas-samāwāti wal-ʾarḍa fī sittati ʾayyāmiñ-thummas-tawā ʿalal-ʿarsh. Yaʿlamu mā yaliju fil-ʾarḍi wa mā yakhruju minhā wa mā yañzilu minas-samāaʾi wa mā yaʿruju fīhā; wa Huwa maʿakum ʾayna mā kuñtum. Wal-lāhu bimā taʿmalūna Baṣīr. ۝ Lahū mulkus-samāwāti wal-ʾarḍi wa ʾilal-lāhi turjaʿul-ʾumūr. ۝ Yūlijul-layla fin-nahāri wa yūlijun-nahāra fil-layli wa Huwa ʿAlīmum-bidhātiṣ-ṣudūr. ۝ ʾĀminū billāhi wa Rasūlihī wa ʾañfiqū mimmā jaʿalakum mustakhlafīna fīh. Fal-ladhīna ʾāmanū miñkum wa ʾañfaqū lahum ʾajruñ-kabīr. ۝ Wa mā lakum lā tuʾminūna billāhi war-Rasūlu yadʿūkum lituʾminū biRabbikum wa qad ʾakhadha mīthāqakum ʾiñ-kuñtum-muʾminīn. ۝ Huwal-ladhī yunazzilu ʿalā ʿabdihī ʾĀyātim-bay-yinātil-liyukhrijakum-minaẓ-ẓulumāti ʾilan-nūr. Wa ʾinnal-lāha bikum laRaʾūfur-Raḥīm. ۝

---

3 Cf. the identical phrase in 7 : 54 and the corresponding note 43.

4 See note 1 on 34 : 2.

5 Implying that all that man "possesses" is but held in trust from God, since "all that is in the heavens and on earth belongs to Him", whereas man is allowed only its usufruct.

6 God's "taking a pledge" is a metonymic allusion to the faculty of *reason* with which He has endowed man, and which ought to enable every sane person to grasp the evidence of God's existence by observing the effects of His creativeness in all nature and by paying heed to the teachings of His prophets (Zamakhsharī). See in this connection 7 : 172 and the corresponding note 139.

7 Lit., "if you are believers": implying, according to Rāzī, "if you can believe in anything on the basis of sound evidence".

And why should you not spend freely in the cause of God, seeing that God's [alone] is the heritage of the heavens and the earth?[8]
Not equal are those of you who spent and fought [in God's cause] before the Victory[9] [and those who did not do so]: they are of a higher rank than those who would spend and fight [only] after it – although God has promised the ultimate good to all [who strive in His cause].[10] And God is aware of all that you do. ‹10›

WHO IS IT that will offer up unto God a goodly loan, which He will amply repay?[11]
For, such [as do so] shall have a noble reward ‹11› on the Day when thou shalt see all believing men and believing women, with their light spreading rapidly before them and on their right,[12] [and with this welcome awaiting them:] "A glad tiding for you today: gardens through which running waters flow, therein to abide! This, this is the triumph supreme!" ‹12›
On that Day shall the hypocrites, both men and women,[13] speak [thus] unto those who have attained to faith: "Wait for us! Let us have a [ray of] light from your light!" [But] they will be told: "Turn back, and seek a light [of your own]!"[14]
And thereupon a wall will be raised between them [and the believers], with a gate in it: within it will be grace and mercy, and against the outside thereof, suffering.[15] ‹13›

وَمَا لَكُمْ أَلَّا تُنفِقُوا۟ فِى سَبِيلِ ٱللَّهِ وَلِلَّهِ مِيرَٰثُ ٱلسَّمَٰوَٰتِ وَٱلْأَرْضِ
لَا يَسْتَوِى مِنكُم مَّنْ أَنفَقَ مِن قَبْلِ ٱلْفَتْحِ وَقَٰتَلَ أُو۟لَٰٓئِكَ أَعْظَمُ دَرَجَةً
مِّنَ ٱلَّذِينَ أَنفَقُوا۟ مِنۢ بَعْدُ وَقَٰتَلُوا۟ وَكُلًّا وَعَدَ ٱللَّهُ ٱلْحُسْنَىٰ وَٱللَّهُ بِمَا
تَعْمَلُونَ خَبِيرٌ ﴿١٠﴾ مَّن ذَا ٱلَّذِى يُقْرِضُ ٱللَّهَ قَرْضًا حَسَنًا فَيُضَٰعِفَهُۥ لَهُۥ
وَلَهُۥٓ أَجْرٌ كَرِيمٌ ﴿١١﴾ يَوْمَ تَرَى ٱلْمُؤْمِنِينَ وَٱلْمُؤْمِنَٰتِ يَسْعَىٰ نُورُهُم بَيْنَ
أَيْدِيهِمْ وَبِأَيْمَٰنِهِم بُشْرَىٰكُمُ ٱلْيَوْمَ جَنَّٰتٌ تَجْرِى مِن تَحْتِهَا ٱلْأَنْهَٰرُ
خَٰلِدِينَ فِيهَا ذَٰلِكَ هُوَ ٱلْفَوْزُ ٱلْعَظِيمُ ﴿١٢﴾ يَوْمَ يَقُولُ ٱلْمُنَٰفِقُونَ
وَٱلْمُنَٰفِقَٰتُ لِلَّذِينَ ءَامَنُوا۟ ٱنظُرُونَا نَقْتَبِسْ مِن نُّورِكُمْ قِيلَ ٱرْجِعُوا۟
وَرَآءَكُمْ فَٱلْتَمِسُوا۟ نُورًا فَضُرِبَ بَيْنَهُم بِسُورٍ لَّهُۥ بَابٌۢ بَاطِنُهُۥ فِيهِ
ٱلرَّحْمَةُ وَظَٰهِرُهُۥ مِن قِبَلِهِ ٱلْعَذَابُ ﴿١٣﴾

Wa mā lakum ʾallā tuñfiqū fī sabīlil-lāhi wa lillāhi mīrāthus-samāwāti wal-ʾarḍ. Lā yastawī miñkum-man ʾañfaqa miñ-qablil-fatḥi wa qātal. ʾUlāaʾika ʾaʿẓamu darajatam-minal-ladhīna ʾañfaqū mim-baʿdu wa qātalū. Wa kullañw-waʿadal-lāhul-ḥusnā; wal-lāhu bimā taʿmalūna Khabīr. (10) Mañ-dhal-ladhī yuqriḍul-lāha qarḍan ḥasanañ-fayuḍāʿifahū lahū wa lahūu ʾajruñ-karīm. (11) Yawma taral-muʾminīna wal-muʾmināti yasʿā nūruhum bayna ʾaydīhim wa biʾaymānihim bushrākumul-Yawma jannātuñ-tajrī miñ-taḥtihal-ʾanhāru khālidīna fīhā. Dhālika huwal-fawzul-ʿaẓīm. (12) Yawma yaqūlul-munāfiqūna wal-munāfiqātu lilladhīna ʾāmanuñ-ẓurūnā naqtabis miñ-nūrikum qīlar-jiʿū warāaʾakum faltamisū nūrañ-faḍuriba baynahum-bisūril-lahū bābum-bāṭinuhū fīhir-raḥmatu wa ẓāhiruhū miñ-qibalihil-ʿadhāb. (13)

8 I.e., "that to God *belongs* all that is . . .", etc.: see note 5 above; also note 22 on 15 : 23.

9 I.e., before the conquest of Mecca in 8 H., when the Muslims were still weak and their future uncertain.

10 The above principle applies, of course, to the relative merits of believers of all times who strive in God's cause before and/or after success has been achieved.

11 See note 234 on the identical phrase in 2 : 245. In the present instance the meaning is apparently wider, applying to *all* that man may do selflessly, for the sake of God alone.

12 See note 25 on the expression *aṣḥāb al-yamīn* ("those on the right hand") in 74 : 39. In many instances, the metaphor of "the right hand" or "right side" is used in the Qurʾan to denote "righteousness" and, therefore, "blessedness", symbolized in the present context by the "light spreading rapidly" before and on the right side of the believers as a result of their "cognition of God, and their high morality, and their freedom from ignorance and blameworthy traits" (Rāzī).

13 Meant here are, apparently, not only outright "hypocrites" (in the connotation given to this term in Western languages), but also people who, being shaky in their beliefs and uncertain in their moral convictions, are inclined to deceive *themselves* (see note 7 on 29 : 11).

14 I.e., "you *should have* sought light while you lived on earth".

15 The stress on there being a *gate* in the wall separating true believers and hypocrites (or the weak of faith) points

They [who will remain without] will call out to those [within], "Were we not with you?" – [to which] the others will answer: "So it was! But you allowed yourselves to succumb to temptation,[16] and you were hesitant [in your faith[17]], and you were doubtful [of resurrection]; and your wishful thinking beguiled you until God's command came to pass:[18] for, [indeed, your own] deceptive thoughts about God deluded you![19] ‹14›
"And so, no ransom[20] shall be accepted today from you, and neither from those who were [openly] bent on denying the truth. Your goal is the fire: it is your [only] refuge[21] – and how evil a journey's end!" ‹15›

IS IT NOT time that the hearts of all who have attained to faith should feel humble at the remembrance of God and of all the truth that has been bestowed [on them] from on high,[22] lest they become like those who were granted revelation aforetime,[23] and whose hearts have hardened with the passing of time so that many of them are [now] depraved?[24] ‹16›
[But] know that God gives life to the earth after it has been lifeless![25]
We have indeed made Our messages clear unto you, so that you might use your reason. ‹17›

يُنَادُونَهُمْ أَلَمْ نَكُن مَّعَكُمْ ۖ قَالُوا۟ بَلَىٰ وَلَـٰكِنَّكُمْ فَتَنتُمْ أَنفُسَكُمْ وَتَرَبَّصْتُمْ
وَٱرْتَبْتُمْ وَغَرَّتْكُمُ ٱلْأَمَانِىُّ حَتَّىٰ جَآءَ أَمْرُ ٱللَّهِ وَغَرَّكُم بِٱللَّهِ ٱلْغَرُورُ ﴿١٤﴾
فَٱلْيَوْمَ لَا يُؤْخَذُ مِنكُمْ فِدْيَةٌ وَلَا مِنَ ٱلَّذِينَ كَفَرُوا۟ ۚ مَأْوَىٰكُمُ ٱلنَّارُ ۖ هِىَ
مَوْلَىٰكُمْ ۖ وَبِئْسَ ٱلْمَصِيرُ ﴿١٥﴾ ۞ أَلَمْ يَأْنِ لِلَّذِينَ ءَامَنُوٓا۟ أَن تَخْشَعَ
قُلُوبُهُمْ لِذِكْرِ ٱللَّهِ وَمَا نَزَلَ مِنَ ٱلْحَقِّ وَلَا يَكُونُوا۟ كَٱلَّذِينَ أُوتُوا۟
ٱلْكِتَـٰبَ مِن قَبْلُ فَطَالَ عَلَيْهِمُ ٱلْأَمَدُ فَقَسَتْ قُلُوبُهُمْ ۖ وَكَثِيرٌ مِّنْهُمْ
فَـٰسِقُونَ ﴿١٦﴾ ٱعْلَمُوٓا۟ أَنَّ ٱللَّهَ يُحْىِ ٱلْأَرْضَ بَعْدَ مَوْتِهَا ۚ قَدْ بَيَّنَّا لَكُمُ
ٱلْـَٔايَـٰتِ لَعَلَّكُمْ تَعْقِلُونَ ﴿١٧﴾

ثلاثة ارباع الحزب

Yunādūnahum ʾalam nakum-maʿakum qālū balā wa lākinnakum fatañtum ʾañfusakum wa tarabbaṣtum war-tabtum wa gharratkumul-ʾamāniyyu ḥattā jāaʾa ʾamrul-lāhi wa gharrakum bil-lāhil-gharūr. (14) Fal-Yawma lā yuʾkhadhu miñkum fidyatuñw-wa lā mi-nal-ladhīna kafarū. Maʾwākumun-nāru hiya maw-lākum wa biʾsal-maṣīr. (15) ۞ ʾAlam yaʾni lilladhīna ʾāmanūu ʾañ-takhshaʿa qulūbuhum lidhikril-lāhi wa mā nazala minal-ḥaqqi wa lā yakūnū kalladhīna ʾūtul-Kitāba miñ-qablu faṭāla ʿalayhimul-ʾamadu fa-qasat qulūbuhum; wa kathīrum-minhum fāsiqūn. (16) ʾIʿlamūu ʾannal-lāha yuḥyil-ʾarḍa baʿda mawtihā. Qad bayyannā lakumul-ʾĀyāti laʿallakum taʿqilūn. (17)

to the possibility of the latters' redemption: cf. the famous *ḥadīth* quoted in note 10 on 40 : 12. Mujāhid (as quoted by Ṭabarī) identifies the "wall" spoken of here with the "barrier" (*ḥijāb*) mentioned in 7 : 46.

16 Sc., "by the prospect of worldly gains" or "by fear for your personal safety" – both of which characterize the half-hearted as well as the hypocrites.

17 Thus Ibn Zayd (quoted by Ṭabarī), explaining the verb *tarabbaṣtum*.

18 I.e., "until your death".

19 See note 30 on the last sentence of 31 : 33.

20 I.e., belated repentance.

21 Lit., "your friend" (*mawlākum*) – i.e., "the only thing by which you may hope to be purified and redeemed": cf, the saying of the Prophet mentioned in note 10 on 40 : 12; see also note 15 above.

22 I.e., "Should not the remembrance of God and His revelation make them humble rather than proud?" This is an emphatic warning against all smugness, self-righteousness and false pride at having "attained to faith" – a failing which only too often attains to such as consider themselves "pious".

23 This is apparently an allusion to the spiritually arrogant among the Jews, who regard themselves as "God's chosen people" and, therefore, as predestined for His acceptance.

24 I.e., so that now they act contrary to the ethical precepts of their religion: implying that the purpose of all true faith is to make man humble and God-conscious rather than self-satisfied, and that a loss of that spiritual humility invariably results in moral degeneration.

25 According to most of the commentators – and, particularly, Zamakhsharī, Rāzī and Ibn Kathīr – this is a

إِنَّ ٱلْمُصَّدِّقِينَ وَٱلْمُصَّدِّقَـٰتِ وَأَقْرَضُوا۟ ٱللَّهَ قَرْضًا حَسَنًا يُضَـٰعَفُ لَهُمْ
وَلَهُمْ أَجْرٌ كَرِيمٌ ﴿18﴾ وَٱلَّذِينَ ءَامَنُوا۟ بِٱللَّهِ وَرُسُلِهِۦٓ أُو۟لَـٰٓئِكَ هُمُ
ٱلصِّدِّيقُونَ ۖ وَٱلشُّهَدَآءُ عِندَ رَبِّهِمْ لَهُمْ أَجْرُهُمْ وَنُورُهُمْ ۖ وَٱلَّذِينَ كَفَرُوا۟
وَكَذَّبُوا۟ بِـَٔايَـٰتِنَآ أُو۟لَـٰٓئِكَ أَصْحَـٰبُ ٱلْجَحِيمِ ﴿19﴾ ٱعْلَمُوٓا۟ أَنَّمَا ٱلْحَيَوٰةُ
ٱلدُّنْيَا لَعِبٌ وَلَهْوٌ وَزِينَةٌ وَتَفَاخُرٌۢ بَيْنَكُمْ وَتَكَاثُرٌ فِى ٱلْأَمْوَٰلِ وَٱلْأَوْلَـٰدِ ۖ
كَمَثَلِ غَيْثٍ أَعْجَبَ ٱلْكُفَّارَ نَبَاتُهُۥ ثُمَّ يَهِيجُ فَتَرَىٰهُ مُصْفَرًّا ثُمَّ يَكُونُ
حُطَـٰمًا ۖ وَفِى ٱلْـَٔاخِرَةِ عَذَابٌ شَدِيدٌ وَمَغْفِرَةٌ مِّنَ ٱللَّهِ وَرِضْوَٰنٌ ۚ وَمَا ٱلْحَيَوٰةُ
ٱلدُّنْيَآ إِلَّا مَتَـٰعُ ٱلْغُرُورِ ﴿20﴾

Verily, as for the men and women who accept the truth as true,[26] and who [thus] offer up unto God a goodly loan, they will be amply repaid,[27] and shall have a noble reward [in the life to come]. ‹18›
For, they who have attained to faith in God and His Apostles – it is they, they who uphold the truth, and they who bear witness [thereto] before their Sustainer:[28] [and so] they shall have their reward and their light! But as for those who are bent on denying the truth and on giving the lie to Our messages – it is they who are destined for the blazing fire! ‹19›

ᵓInnal-muṣṣaddiqīna wal-muṣṣaddiqāti wa ᵓaqraḍul-lāha qarḍan ḥasanañy-yuḍāᶜafu lahum wa lahum ᵓajruñ-karīm. (18) Wal-ladhīna ᵓāmanū billāhi wa Rusulihīi ᵓulāaᵓika humuṣ-ṣiddīqūna wash-shuhadāaᵓu ᶜiñda Rabbihim lahum ᵓajruhum wa nūruhum. Wal-ladhīna kafarū wa kadhdhabū biᵓĀyātināa ᵓulāaᵓika ᵓaṣḥābul-jaḥīm. (19) ᵓIᶜlamūu ᵓannamal-ḥayātud-dunyā laᶜibuñw-wa lahwuñw-wa zīnatuñw-wa tafākhurum-baynakum wa takāthuruñ-fil-ᵓamwāli wal-ᵓawlād. Kamathali ghaythin ᵓaᶜjabal-kuffāra nabātuhū thumma yahīju fatarāhu muṣfarrañ-thumma yakūnu ḥuṭāmā. Wa fil-ᵓĀkhirati ᶜadhābuñ-shadīduñw-wa maghfiratum-minal-lāhi wa riḍwān. Wa mal-ḥayātud-dunyāa ᵓillā matāᶜul-ghurūr. (20)

KNOW [O men] that the life of this world is but a play and a passing delight, and a beautiful show, and [the cause of] your boastful vying with one another, and [of your] greed for more and more riches and children.[29]
Its parable is that of[30] [life-giving] rain: the herbage which it causes to grow delights the tillers of the soil;[31] but then it withers, and thou canst see it turn yellow; and in the end it crumbles into dust.
But [the abiding truth of man's condition will become fully apparent] in the life to come: [either] suffering severe, or[32] God's forgiveness and His goodly acceptance: for the life of this world is nothing but an enjoyment of self-delusion. ‹20›

---

parabolic allusion to the effect of a re-awakening of God-consciousness in hearts that had become deadened by self-satisfaction and false pride.

26 Or: "who give in charity" – depending on the vocalization of the consonants *ṣād* and *dāl*. In view of the sequence, the sense given in my rendering seems preferable (and is, indeed, stressed by Zamakhsharī), although in the reading of Hafṣ ibn Sulaymān al-Asadī, on which this translation is based, the relevant nouns appear in the spelling *muṣṣaddiqīn* and *muṣṣaddiqāt*, "men and women who give in charity".

27 See verse 11 above.

28 I.e., by their readiness for any sacrifice.

29 Commenting at length on this passage, Rāzī makes it clear that life *as such* is not to be despised, inasmuch as it has been created by God: cf. 38 : 27 – "We have not created heaven and earth and all that is between them without meaning and purpose"; and 23 : 115 – "Did you think that We have created you in mere idle play?" But whereas life in itself is a positive gift of God and – as Rāzī points out – the potential source of all blessings, it loses this positive quality if it is indulged in recklessly, blindly and with disregard of spiritual values and considerations: in brief, if it is indulged in without any thought of the hereafter.

30 Lit., "[It is] like the parable of . . .", etc.

31 This is the sole instance in the Qurᵓān where the participial noun *kāfir* (in its plural form *kuffār*) has its original meaning of "tiller of the soil". For the etymology of this meaning, see note 4 on 74 : 10, where the term *kāfir* (in the sense of "denier of the truth") appears for the first time in the sequence of Qur'anic revelation.

32 According to Ṭabarī, the conjunction *wa* has here the meaning of *aw* ("or").

[Hence,] vie with one another in seeking to your Sustainer's forgiveness,[33] and [thus] to a paradise as vast as the heavens and the earth, which has been readied for those who have attained to faith in God and His Apostles:[34] such is the bounty of God which He grants unto whomever He wills – for God is limitless in His great bounty. ‹21›

NO CALAMITY can ever befall the earth, and neither your own selves,[35] unless it be [laid down] in Our decree before We bring it into being: verily, all this[36] is easy for God. ‹22› [Know this,] so that you may not despair over whatever [good] has escaped you nor exult [unduly] over whatever [good] has come to you:[37] for, God does not love any of those who, out of self-conceit, act in a boastful manner[38] ‹23› – those who are niggardly [with God's bounty] and bid others to be niggardly![39]
And he who turns his back [on this truth[40] ought to know that], verily, God alone is self-sufficient, the One to whom all praise is due! ‹24›
Indeed, [even aforetime] did We send forth Our apostles with all evidence of [this] truth; and through them[41] We bestowed revelation from on high, and [thus gave you] a balance [wherewith to weigh right and wrong], so that men might behave with equity; and We bestowed [upon you] from on high [the ability to make use of] iron, in which there is awesome power as

سَابِقُوٓا۟ إِلَىٰ مَغْفِرَةٍ مِّن رَّبِّكُمْ وَجَنَّةٍ عَرْضُهَا كَعَرْضِ ٱلسَّمَآءِ وَٱلْأَرْضِ
أُعِدَّتْ لِلَّذِينَ ءَامَنُوا۟ بِٱللَّهِ وَرُسُلِهِۦ ذَٰلِكَ فَضْلُ ٱللَّهِ يُؤْتِيهِ مَن يَشَآءُ
وَٱللَّهُ ذُو ٱلْفَضْلِ ٱلْعَظِيمِ ﴿٢١﴾ مَآ أَصَابَ مِن مُّصِيبَةٍ فِى ٱلْأَرْضِ وَلَا
فِىٓ أَنفُسِكُمْ إِلَّا فِى كِتَٰبٍ مِّن قَبْلِ أَن نَّبْرَأَهَآ إِنَّ ذَٰلِكَ عَلَى ٱللَّهِ
يَسِيرٌ ﴿٢٢﴾ لِّكَيْلَا تَأْسَوْا۟ عَلَىٰ مَا فَاتَكُمْ وَلَا تَفْرَحُوا۟ بِمَآ ءَاتَىٰكُمْ وَٱللَّهُ
لَا يُحِبُّ كُلَّ مُخْتَالٍ فَخُورٍ ﴿٢٣﴾ ٱلَّذِينَ يَبْخَلُونَ وَيَأْمُرُونَ ٱلنَّاسَ
بِٱلْبُخْلِ وَمَن يَتَوَلَّ فَإِنَّ ٱللَّهَ هُوَ ٱلْغَنِىُّ ٱلْحَمِيدُ ﴿٢٤﴾ لَقَدْ أَرْسَلْنَا
رُسُلَنَا بِٱلْبَيِّنَٰتِ وَأَنزَلْنَا مَعَهُمُ ٱلْكِتَٰبَ وَٱلْمِيزَانَ لِيَقُومَ ٱلنَّاسُ

Sābiqūu ʾilā maghfiratim-mir-Rabbikum wa jannatin ʿarḍuhā kaʿarḍis-samāaʾi wal-ʾarḍi ʾuʿiddat lilladhīna ʾāmanū billāhi wa Rusulih. Dhālika faḍlul-lāhi yuʾtīhi mañy-yashāaʾu wal-lāhu Dhul-faḍlil-ʿaẓīm. (21) Māa ʾaṣāba mim-muṣībatiñ-fil-ʾarḍi wa lā fii ʾañfusikum ʾillā fī Kitābim-miñ-qabli ʾan-nabraʾahā. ʾInna dhālika ʿalal-lāhi yasīr. (22) Likaylā taʾsaw ʿalā mā fātakum wa lā tafraḥū bimāa ʾātākum. Wal-lāhu lā yuḥibbu kulla mukhtāliñ-fakhūr. (23) ʾAlladhīna yabkhalūna wa yaʾmurūnan-nāsa bilbukhl. Wa mañy-yatawalla faʾinnal-lāha Huwal-Ghaniyyul-Ḥamīd. (24) Laqad ʾarsalnā Rusulanā bil-bayyināti wa ʾañzalnā maʿahumul-Kitāba wal-mīzāna liyaqūman-nāsu

33 Sc., "rather than in striving for glory and worldly possessions": implying elliptically that no man is free from faults and transgressions, and hence everyone is in need of God's forgiveness. (Cf. note 41 on 24 : 31.)

34 For a further qualification of the humility which characterizes true believers, see 3 : 133-135.

35 I.e., "the earth or mankind as a whole, or any of you individually": an allusion to natural as well as man-made catastrophes, and to individual suffering through illness, moral or material deprivation, etc.

36 I.e., God's decreeing an event and bringing it into being.

37 Thus, the knowledge that whatever has happened *had* to happen – and could not have *not* happened – because, obviously, it had been willed by God in accordance with His unfathomable plan, ought to enable a true believer to react with conscious equanimity to whatever good or ill comes to him.

38 I.e., attributing their good fortune to their own merit or "luck".

39 Cf. last sentence of 4 : 36 and the whole of verse 37.

40 I.e., does not want to admit that whatever has happened must have been willed by God.

41 Lit., "with them".

بِٱلْقِسْطِ ۖ وَأَنزَلْنَا ٱلْحَدِيدَ فِيهِ بَأْسٌ شَدِيدٌ وَمَنَٰفِعُ لِلنَّاسِ وَلِيَعْلَمَ ٱللَّهُ
مَن يَنصُرُهُۥ وَرُسُلَهُۥ بِٱلْغَيْبِ ۚ إِنَّ ٱللَّهَ قَوِىٌّ عَزِيزٌ ﴿25﴾ وَلَقَدْ أَرْسَلْنَا نُوحًا
وَإِبْرَٰهِيمَ وَجَعَلْنَا فِى ذُرِّيَّتِهِمَا ٱلنُّبُوَّةَ وَٱلْكِتَٰبَ ۖ فَمِنْهُم مُّهْتَدٍ ۖ وَكَثِيرٌ
مِّنْهُمْ فَٰسِقُونَ ﴿26﴾ ثُمَّ قَفَّيْنَا عَلَىٰٓ ءَاثَٰرِهِم بِرُسُلِنَا وَقَفَّيْنَا بِعِيسَى ٱبْنِ
مَرْيَمَ وَءَاتَيْنَٰهُ ٱلْإِنجِيلَ وَجَعَلْنَا فِى قُلُوبِ ٱلَّذِينَ ٱتَّبَعُوهُ رَأْفَةً وَرَحْمَةً
وَرَهْبَانِيَّةً ٱبْتَدَعُوهَا مَا كَتَبْنَٰهَا عَلَيْهِمْ إِلَّا ٱبْتِغَآءَ رِضْوَٰنِ ٱللَّهِ فَمَا رَعَوْهَا حَقَّ

bilqisṭi wa ʾañzalnal-ḥadīda fīhi baʾsuñ-shadīduñw-wa manāfiʿu linnāsi wa liyaʿlamal-lāhu mañy-yañṣuruhū wa Rusulahū bil-ghayb. ʾInnal-lāha Qawiyyun ʿAzīz. (25) Wa laqad ʾarsalnā Nūḥañw-wa ʾIbrāhīma wa jaʿalnā fī dhurriyyatihiman-Nubuwwata wal-Kitāba faminhum-muhtadiñw-wa kathīrum-minhum fāsiqūn. (26) Thumma qaffaynā ʿalāa ʾāthārihim biRusulinā wa qaffaynā biʿĪsab-ni Maryama wa ʾātaynāhul-ʾIñjīla wa jaʿalnā fī qulūbil-ladhīnat-tabaʿūhu raʾfatañw-wa raḥmatañw-wa rahbāniyyatanib-tadaʿūhā mā katabnāhā ʿalayhim ʾillab-tighāaʾa riḍwānil-lāhi famā raʿawhā ḥaqqa

well as [a source of] benefits for man:[42] and [all this was given to you] so that God might mark out those who would stand up for Him and His Apostles,[43] even though He [Himself] is beyond the reach of human perception.[44]
Verily, God is powerful, almighty! ‹25›
And, indeed, [to the same end[45]] We sent forth Noah and Abraham [as Our message-bearers], and established prophethood and revelation among their descendants; and some of them were on the right way, but many were iniquitous. ‹26›
And thereupon We caused [other of] Our apostles to follow in their footsteps; and [in the course of time] We caused them to be followed by Jesus, the son of Mary, upon whom We bestowed the Gospel;[46] and in the hearts of those who [truly] followed him We engendered compassion and mercy. But as for monastic asceticism[47] – We did not enjoin it upon them: they invented it themselves out of a desire for God's goodly acceptance.[48] But then, they did not [always] observe it as it ought to

42 Side by side with enabling man to discriminate between right and wrong (which is the innermost purpose of all divine revelation), God has endowed him with the ability to convert to his use the natural resources of his earthly environment. An outstanding symbol of this ability is man's skill, unique among all animated beings, in making *tools*; and the primary material for all tool-making – and, indeed, for all human technology – is iron: the one metal which is found abundantly on earth, and which can be utilized for beneficial as well as destructive ends. The "awesome power" (*baʾs shadīd*) inherent in iron manifests itself not merely in the manufacture of weapons of war but also, more subtly, in man's ever-growing tendency to foster the development of an increasingly complicated technology which places the *machine* in the foreground of all human existence and which, by its inherent – almost irresistible – dynamism, gradually estranges man from all inner connection with nature. This process of growing mechanization, so evident in our modern life, jeopardizes the very structure of human society and, thus, contributes to a gradual dissolution of all moral and spiritual perceptions epitomized in the concept of "divine guidance". It is to warn man of this danger that the Qurʾān stresses – symbolically and metonymically – the potential evil (*baʾs*) of "iron" if it is put to wrong use: in other words, the danger of man's allowing his technological ingenuity to run wild and thus to overwhelm his spiritual consciousness and, ultimately, to destroy all possibility of individual and social happiness.

43 Lit., "those who succour Him and His Apostles", i.e., those who stand up for the *cause* of God and His Apostles. The meaning is that only they who put God's spiritual and material gifts to right use can be described as "true believers".

44 See note 3 on 2 : 3.

45 I.e., to give man a balance wherewith to weigh right and wrong, and so to enable him to behave with equity (see preceding verse).

46 See *sūrah* 3, note 4.

47 The term *rahbāniyyah* combines the concepts of monastic life with an exaggerated asceticism, often amounting to a denial of any value in the life of this world – an attitude characteristic of early Christianity but disapproved of in Islam (cf. 2 : 143 – "We have willed you to be a community of the middle way" – and the corresponding note 118).

48 Or: "they invented it themselves, [for] We did not enjoin it upon them: [We enjoined upon them] only the seeking of God's goodly acceptance". Both these interpretations are equally legitimate, and are accepted as such by

have been observed:[49] and so We granted their recompense unto such of them as had [truly] attained to faith, whereas many of them became iniquitous.[50] ⟨27⟩

O YOU who have attained to faith![51] Remain conscious of God, and believe in His Apostle, [and] He will grant you doubly of His grace, and will light for you a light wherein you shall walk, and will forgive you [your past sins]: for God is much-forgiving, a dispenser of grace. ⟨28⟩

And the followers of earlier revelation should know[52] that they have no power whatever over any of God's bounty,[53] seeing that all bounty is in God's hand [alone]: He grants it unto whomever He wills – for God is limitless in His great bounty. ⟨29⟩

رِعَايَتِهَا فَـَٔاتَيْنَا ٱلَّذِينَ ءَامَنُوا۟ مِنْهُمْ أَجْرَهُمْ وَكَثِيرٌ مِّنْهُمْ فَـٰسِقُونَ ﴿٢٧﴾ يَـٰٓأَيُّهَا
ٱلَّذِينَ ءَامَنُوا۟ ٱتَّقُوا۟ ٱللَّهَ وَءَامِنُوا۟ بِرَسُولِهِۦ يُؤْتِكُمْ كِفْلَيْنِ مِن رَّحْمَتِهِۦ
وَيَجْعَل لَّكُمْ نُورًا تَمْشُونَ بِهِۦ وَيَغْفِرْ لَكُمْ ۚ وَٱللَّهُ غَفُورٌ رَّحِيمٌ ﴿٢٨﴾ لِّئَلَّا
يَعْلَمَ أَهْلُ ٱلْكِتَـٰبِ أَلَّا يَقْدِرُونَ عَلَىٰ شَىْءٍ مِّن فَضْلِ ٱللَّهِ ۙ وَأَنَّ ٱلْفَضْلَ
بِيَدِ ٱللَّهِ يُؤْتِيهِ مَن يَشَآءُ ۚ وَٱللَّهُ ذُو ٱلْفَضْلِ ٱلْعَظِيمِ ﴿٢٩﴾

riᶜāyatihā. Faᵓātaynal-ladhīna ᵓāmanū minhum ᵓajrahum wa kathīrum-minhum fāsiqūn. (27) Yāa ᵓayyuhal-ladhīna ᵓāmanut-taqul-lāha wa ᵓāminū bi-Rasūlihī yuᵓtikum kiflayni mir-raḥmatihī wa yajᶜal lakum nūrañ-tamshūna bihī wa yaghfir lakum. Wal-lāhu Ghafūrur-Raḥīm. (28) Liᵓallā yaᶜlama ᵓahlul-Kitābi ᵓallā yaqdirūna ᶜalā shayᵓim-miñ-faḍlil-lāhi wa ᵓannal-faḍla biyadil-lāhi yuᵓtīhi mañy-yashāaᵓ. Wal-lāhu Dhul-faḍlil-ᶜaẓīm. (29)

most of the classical commentators. The rendering adopted by me corresponds to the interpretation given by Saᶜīd ibn Jubayr and Qatādah (both of them cited by Ṭabarī and Ibn Kathīr).

49 I.e., not *all* of them observed it in the right spirit (Ṭabarī, Zamakhsharī, Ibn Kathīr), inasmuch as in the course of time many of them – or, rather, many of those who came after the early ascetics (Ṭabarī) – corrupted their devotions by accepting the ideas of Trinity and of God's incarnation in Jesus, and by lapsing into empty formalism (Rāzī).

50 Sc., "and were deprived of Our grace".

51 As is evident from the preceding passage as well as from verse 29, the people thus addressed are the followers of earlier revelation (*ahl al-kitāb*), and in particular the true – i.e., unitarian – followers of Jesus.

52 Lit., "so that the followers of earlier revelation [i.e., the Bible] may know".

53 I.e., that they have no exclusive *claim* to any of God's bounty – which latter term relates, in the present context, to a bestowal of divine revelation. This is addressed in the first instance to the Jews, who reject the revelation granted to Muḥammad in the belief that the office of prophethood is an exclusive "preserve" of the children of Israel, as well as to the Christians who, as followers of the Bible, implicitly accept this unwarranted claim.

The Fifty-Eighth Sūrah

Al-Mujādalah (The Pleading)

Medina Period

BEGINNING with an allusion to the wrongs done to woman in pre-Islamic times, followed by a divine *reductio ad absurdum* – and thus, a prohibition – of the pagan method of divorce known as *ẓihār* (see note 1 on the following page, as well as a fuller explanation in note 3 on 33 : 4), the *sūrah* proceeds to questions of faith and its absence as well as their repercussions on man's social life, to the problem of hypocrisy, and ends with a discussion of the attitude which believers should adopt towards non-believers.

The date of revelation may be placed at the beginning of the year 5 H. or, possibly, towards the end of 4 H. The customary title of this *sūrah* is based on the mention of "her who pleads" in its first verse.

سورة المجادلة مدنية -58- وآياتها اثنتان وعشرون

IN THE NAME OF GOD, THE MOST GRACIOUS, THE DISPENSER OF GRACE:

بِسْمِ ٱللَّهِ ٱلرَّحْمَـٰنِ ٱلرَّحِيمِ

GOD has indeed heard the words of her who pleads with thee concerning her husband, and complains unto God.[1]

And God does hear what you both have to say:[2] verily, God is all-hearing, all-seeing. ⟨1⟩

As for those of you who [henceforth] separate themselves from their wives by saying, "Thou art as unlawful to me as my mother",[3] [let them bear in mind that] they can never be [as] their mothers: none are their mothers save those who gave them birth: and so, behold, they but utter a saying that runs counter to reason,[4] and is [therefore] false.

But, behold, God is indeed an absolver of sins, much-forgiving: ⟨2⟩ hence, as for those who would separate themselves from their wives by saying, "Thou art as

قَدْ سَمِعَ ٱللَّهُ قَوْلَ ٱلَّتِى تُجَـٰدِلُكَ فِى زَوْجِهَا وَتَشْتَكِىٓ إِلَى ٱللَّهِ وَٱللَّهُ يَسْمَعُ
تَحَاوُرَكُمَآ ۚ إِنَّ ٱللَّهَ سَمِيعٌۢ بَصِيرٌ ﴿١﴾ ٱلَّذِينَ يُظَـٰهِرُونَ مِنكُم مِّن نِّسَآئِهِم
مَّا هُنَّ أُمَّهَـٰتِهِمْ ۖ إِنْ أُمَّهَـٰتُهُمْ إِلَّا ٱلَّـٰٓـِٔى وَلَدْنَهُمْ ۚ وَإِنَّهُمْ لَيَقُولُونَ مُنكَرًا
مِّنَ ٱلْقَوْلِ وَزُورًا ۚ وَإِنَّ ٱللَّهَ لَعَفُوٌّ غَفُورٌ ﴿٢﴾ وَٱلَّذِينَ يُظَـٰهِرُونَ مِن نِّسَآئِهِمْ

Bismil-lāhir-Raḥmānir-Raḥīm.

Qad samiʿal-lāhu qawlal-latī tujādiluka fī zawjihā wa tashtakīi ʾilal-lāhi wal-lāhu yasmaʿu taḥāwurakumā. ʾInnal-lāha Samīʿum-Baṣīr. (1) ʾAlladhīna yuẓāhirūna miñkum-miñ-nisāaʾihim-mā hunna ʾummahātihim; ʾin ʾummahātuhum ʾillal-lāaʾī waladnahum; wa ʾinnahum layaqūlūna muñkaram-minal-qawli wa zūrā. Wa ʾinnal-lāha laʿAfuwwun-Ghafūr. (2) Wal-ladhīna yuẓāhirūna miñ-nisāaʾihim

حزب 55
جزء 28

---

1 According to the classical commentators, this is a reference to the case of Khawlah (or Khuwaylah) bint Thaʿlabah, whose husband Aws ibn aṣ-Ṣāmit divorced her by pronouncing the arbitrary pre-Islamic oath known as *ẓihār* (explained in note 3 on 33 : 4). When she pleaded before the Prophet against this divorce – which deprived her of all her marital rights and, at the same time, made it impossible for her to remarry – the iniquitous custom of *ẓihār* was abolished by the revelation of verses 2-4 of this *sūrah*. – In view of the sequence, as well as of several Traditions to this effect, there is no doubt that the above verse alludes, in the first instance, to the divine condemnation of *ẓihār*. However, the deliberately unspecified reference to "her who pleads concerning her husband" seems to point to *all* cases where a wife has reason to complain against her husband: that is to say, not merely to an appeal against an unjustified or cruel divorce, but also to a wife's demand for release from an unbearable marriage. Such a dissolution of the marriage-tie at the wife's instance – termed *khulʿ* – is fully sanctioned by the *sharīʿah* on the basis of 2 : 229 and a number of extremely well-authenticated Traditions. (For a fuller discussion of this problem, see note 218 on the second paragraph of 2 : 229.)

2 Lit., "does hear the mutual contentions of both of you (*taḥāwurakumā*)", i.e., of husband and wife alike, embracing with His infinite wisdom and justice the innermost motivations of both. Alternatively – if the above verse is understood as referring specifically to the case of Khawlah – the second person indicated by the suffix *kumā* ("both of you") may relate to the Prophet, who, before the revelation of this *sūrah*, thought that a divorce through *ẓihār* was valid and, therefore, repeatedly told Khawlah, "Thou art now indeed unlawful to him" (Ṭabarī). This opinion was subsequently – almost immediately – reversed by the divine prohibition of *ẓihār* expressed in verses 2 ff.

3 For this explanatory rendering of the verb *yuẓāhirūn*, see *sūrah* 33, note 3. My interpolation of the word "henceforth" is necessary in view of the fact that the custom of *ẓihār* – in its sense of a definitive act of divorce – had been abolished by verses 2-4 of the present *sūrah*.

4 For this particular rendering of the term *munkar*, see *sūrah* 16, note 109.

ثُمَّ يَعُودُونَ لِمَا قَالُوا۟ فَتَحْرِيرُ رَقَبَةٍ مِّن قَبْلِ أَن يَتَمَآسَّا ذَٰلِكُمْ تُوعَظُونَ
بِهِۦ وَٱللَّهُ بِمَا تَعْمَلُونَ خَبِيرٌ ﴿٣﴾ فَمَن لَّمْ يَجِدْ فَصِيَامُ شَهْرَيْنِ مُتَتَابِعَيْنِ
مِن قَبْلِ أَن يَتَمَآسَّا فَمَن لَّمْ يَسْتَطِعْ فَإِطْعَامُ سِتِّينَ مِسْكِينًا ذَٰلِكَ
لِتُؤْمِنُوا۟ بِٱللَّهِ وَرَسُولِهِۦ وَتِلْكَ حُدُودُ ٱللَّهِ وَلِلْكَٰفِرِينَ عَذَابٌ أَلِيمٌ ﴿٤﴾
إِنَّ ٱلَّذِينَ يُحَآدُّونَ ٱللَّهَ وَرَسُولَهُۥ كُبِتُوا۟ كَمَا كُبِتَ ٱلَّذِينَ مِن قَبْلِهِمْ
وَقَدْ أَنزَلْنَآ ءَايَٰتٍۭ بَيِّنَٰتٍ وَلِلْكَٰفِرِينَ عَذَابٌ مُّهِينٌ ﴿٥﴾ يَوْمَ يَبْعَثُهُمُ
ٱللَّهُ جَمِيعًا فَيُنَبِّئُهُم بِمَا عَمِلُوٓا۟ أَحْصَىٰهُ ٱللَّهُ وَنَسُوهُ وَٱللَّهُ عَلَىٰ كُلِّ شَىْءٍ
شَهِيدٌ ﴿٦﴾

thumma yaᶜūdūna limā qālū fataḥrīru raqabatim-miñ-qabli ᵓañy-yatamāassā; dhālikum tūᶜaẓūna bihī wal-lāhu bimā taᶜmalūna Khabīr. (3) Famal-lam yajid faṣiyāmu shahrayni mutatābiᶜayni miñ-qabli ᵓañy-yatamāassā; famal-lam yastaṭiᶜ faᵓiṭᶜāmu sittīna miskīnā. Dhālika lituᵓminū billāhi wa Rasūlihī wa tilka ḥudūdul-lāh. Wa lilkāfirīna ᶜadhābun ᵓalīm. (4) ᵓInnal-ladhīna yuḥāaddūnal-lāha wa Rasūlahū kubitū kamā kubital-ladhīna miñ-qablihim wa qad ᵓañzalnāa ᵓĀyātim-bayyināt. Wa lilkāfirīna ᶜadhābum-muhīn. (5) Yawma yabᶜathuhumul-lāhu jamīᶜañ-fayunabbiᵓuhum bimā ᶜamilū; ᵓaḥṣāhul-lāhu wa nasūhu wal-lāhu ᶜalā kulli shayᵓiñ-Shahīd. (6)

unlawful to me as my mother", and thereafter would go back on what they have said, [their atonement] shall be the freeing of a human being from bondage[5] before the couple may touch one another again: this you are [hereby] exhorted to do – for God is fully aware of all that you do.[6] ‹3›

However, he who does not have the wherewithal shall fast [instead] for two consecutive months[7] before the couple may touch one another again; and he who is unable to do it shall feed sixty needy ones:[8] this, so that you might prove your faith in God and His Apostle.[9]

Now these are the bounds set by God; and grievous suffering [in the life to come] awaits all who deny the truth. ‹4›

Verily, those who contend against God and His Apostle shall be brought low even as those [evildoers] who lived before them were brought low after We had bestowed [on them] clear messages from on high.[10]

And [so,] for those who deny the truth there will be shameful suffering in store ‹5› on the Day when God will raise them all from the dead and will make them truly understand all that they did [in life]: God will have taken [all of] it into account, even though they [themselves] may have forgotten it – for God is witness unto everything. ‹6›

5 I.e., the freeing or purchasing the freedom of a slave or captive. In modern times, when slavery is more or less non-existent, the concept of *taḥrīr raqabah* may, I believe, be legitimately extended to the redeeming of a human being from the bondage of debt or of great poverty.

6 Cf. 2 : 225 – "God will not take you to task for oaths which you may have uttered without thought, but will take you to task [only] for what your hearts have conceived [in earnest]".

7 I.e., in the manner prescribed for fasting during the month of Ramaḍān (see 2 : 183-187). As regards the phrase "he who does not find the wherewithal (*lam yajid*)", it may indicate either a lack of financial means or the impossibility of finding anyone else who could be redeemed from factual or figurative bondage (see note 5 above). According to many Islamic scholars of our times (e.g., Rashīd Riḍāᵓ, commenting on 4 : 92), this relates, in the first instance, to circumstances in which "slavery will have been abolished in accordance with the aim of Islam" (*Manār* V, 337).

8 Or, alternatively, one needy person for sixty days. The inability to fast for two consecutive months may be due either to ill-health or to really compelling external circumstances (for instance, the necessity of performing labours which require great physical and/or mental vigour and alertness).

9 Sc., "by showing that you have renounced the practices of the Time of Ignorance" (Rāzī). In other words, the pronouncement of *ẓihār* is not to be considered a divorce, as was the case in pre-Islamic times, but solely as a reprehensible act which must be atoned for by a sacrifice.

10 Sc., "which they chose to disregard". Thus, proceeding from the particular to the general, the present passage connects with the reference, at the end of verse 4, to "all who deny the truth", i.e., of divine revelation.

ART THOU NOT aware that God knows all that is in the heavens and all that is on earth? Never can there be a secret confabulation between three persons without His being the fourth of them, nor between five without His being the sixth of them; and neither between less than that, or more, without His being with them wherever they may be. But in the end, on Resurrection Day, He will make them truly understand what they did: for, verily, God has full knowledge of everything. ‹7›

Art thou not aware of such as have been forbidden [to intrigue through] secret confabulations,[11] and yet [always] revert to that which they have been forbidden, and conspire with one another with a view to sinful doings, and aggressive conduct, and disobedience to the Apostle?[12] Now whenever such [people] approach thee, [O Muḥammad,][13] they salute thee with a greeting which God has never countenanced;[14] and they say to themselves, "Why does not God chastise us for what we are saying?"[15] Hell shall be their allotted portion: they shall [indeed] enter it – and how vile a journey's end! ‹8›

أَلَمْ تَرَ أَنَّ ٱللَّهَ يَعْلَمُ مَا فِى ٱلسَّمَٰوَٰتِ وَمَا فِى ٱلْأَرْضِ مَا يَكُونُ مِن
نَّجْوَىٰ ثَلَٰثَةٍ إِلَّا هُوَ رَابِعُهُمْ وَلَا خَمْسَةٍ إِلَّا هُوَ سَادِسُهُمْ وَلَآ أَدْنَىٰ مِن
ذَٰلِكَ وَلَآ أَكْثَرَ إِلَّا هُوَ مَعَهُمْ أَيْنَ مَا كَانُوا۟ ثُمَّ يُنَبِّئُهُم بِمَا عَمِلُوا۟ يَوْمَ
ٱلْقِيَٰمَةِ إِنَّ ٱللَّهَ بِكُلِّ شَىْءٍ عَلِيمٌ ﴿٧﴾ أَلَمْ تَرَ إِلَى ٱلَّذِينَ نُهُوا۟ عَنِ ٱلنَّجْوَىٰ
ثُمَّ يَعُودُونَ لِمَا نُهُوا۟ عَنْهُ وَيَتَنَٰجَوْنَ بِٱلْإِثْمِ وَٱلْعُدْوَٰنِ وَمَعْصِيَتِ ٱلرَّسُولِ
وَإِذَا جَآءُوكَ حَيَّوْكَ بِمَا لَمْ يُحَيِّكَ بِهِ ٱللَّهُ وَيَقُولُونَ فِىٓ أَنفُسِهِمْ لَوْلَا
يُعَذِّبُنَا ٱللَّهُ بِمَا نَقُولُ حَسْبُهُمْ جَهَنَّمُ يَصْلَوْنَهَا فَبِئْسَ ٱلْمَصِيرُ ﴿٨﴾

ʾAlam tara ʾannal-lāha yaʿlamu mā fis-samāwāti wa mā fil-ʾarḍ. Mā yakūnu miñ-najwā thalāthatin ʾillā Huwa rābiʿuhum wa lā khamsatin ʾillā Huwa sādisuhum wa lāa ʾadnā miñ-dhālika wa lāa ʾakthara ʾillā Huwa maʿahum ʾayna mā kānū; thumma yunabbiʾuhum bimā ʿamilū Yawmal-Qiyāmah. ʾInnal-lāha bikulli shayʾin ʿAlīm. (7) ʾAlam tara ʾilal-ladhīna nuhū ʿanin-najwā thumma yaʿūdūna limā nuhū ʿanhu wa yatanājawna bilʾithmi wal-ʿudwāni wa maʿṣiyatir-Rasūli wa ʾidhā jāaʾūka ḥayyawka bimā lam yuḥayyika bihil-lāhu wa yaqūlūna fii ʾañfusihim lawlā yuʿadhdhibunal-lāhu bimā naqūl. Ḥasbuhum jahannamu yaṣlawnahā fabiʾsal-maṣīr. (8)

11 The prohibition referred to here arises from the Qurʾanic statement, "No good comes, as a rule, out of secret confabulations – save those which are devoted to enjoining charity, or equitable dealings, or setting things to rights between people" (see 4 : 114 and the corresponding note 138). Although there is no doubt that, as the classical commentators point out, the "secret confabulations" spoken of in this passage relate to intrigues aimed against the Prophet and his followers by some of their unbelieving contemporaries, there is no doubt, either, that the passage has a general import, and is, therefore, valid for all times.

12 I.e., in the wider sense, disobedience to the Apostle's ethical teachings.

13 The reference to "approaching" the Prophet has here a twofold meaning, relating literally to his unbelieving contemporaries, and figuratively to an intellectual "approach" to his person and his teachings by hostile critics of all later times. The same observation is valid with regard to the next clause as well.

14 Lit., "with which God has never saluted thee". Historically, this is an allusion to the hostile attitude of the Jews of Medina towards the Prophet. It is recorded that instead of pronouncing the traditional greeting "Peace be upon thee" when encountering him, some of them used to mumble the word *salām* ("peace") in such a way as to make it indistinguishable from *sām* ("death"); and they employed the same scurrilous play of words with regard to the Prophet's Companions as well. (The relevant *aḥādīth* are quoted in full, with indication of the sources, by Ṭabarī and Ibn Kathīr in their commentaries on the above verse.) But see also the preceding note.

15 Sc., "if Muḥammad is truly a prophet".

[Hence,] O you who have attained to faith, when you do hold secret confabulations, do not conspire with one another with a view to sinful doings, and aggressive conduct, and disobedience to the Apostle,[16] but [rather] hold counsel in the cause of virtue and God-consciousness: and [always] remain conscious of God, unto whom you all shall be gathered. ‹9›
[All other kinds of] secret confabulations are but of Satan's doing, so that he might cause grief to those who have attained to faith; yet he cannot harm them in the least, unless it be by God's leave:[17] in God, then, let the believers place their trust! ‹10›

O YOU who have attained to faith! When you are told, "Make room for one another in your collective life",[18] do make room: [and in return,] God will make room for you [in His grace].[19]
And whenever you are told, "Rise up [for a good deed]", do rise up;[20] [and] God will exalt by [many] degrees those of you who have attained to faith and, [above all,] such as have been vouchsafed [true] knowledge:[21] for God is fully aware of all that you do. ‹11›

يَٰٓأَيُّهَا ٱلَّذِينَ ءَامَنُوٓاْ إِذَا تَنَٰجَيۡتُمۡ فَلَا تَتَنَٰجَوۡاْ بِٱلۡإِثۡمِ وَٱلۡعُدۡوَٰنِ
وَمَعۡصِيَتِ ٱلرَّسُولِ وَتَنَٰجَوۡاْ بِٱلۡبِرِّ وَٱلتَّقۡوَىٰۖ وَٱتَّقُواْ ٱللَّهَ ٱلَّذِيٓ إِلَيۡهِ
تُحۡشَرُونَ ۝٩ إِنَّمَا ٱلنَّجۡوَىٰ مِنَ ٱلشَّيۡطَٰنِ لِيَحۡزُنَ ٱلَّذِينَ ءَامَنُواْ
وَلَيۡسَ بِضَآرِّهِمۡ شَيۡـًٔا إِلَّا بِإِذۡنِ ٱللَّهِۚ وَعَلَى ٱللَّهِ فَلۡيَتَوَكَّلِ ٱلۡمُؤۡمِنُونَ ۝١٠
يَٰٓأَيُّهَا ٱلَّذِينَ ءَامَنُوٓاْ إِذَا قِيلَ لَكُمۡ تَفَسَّحُواْ فِي ٱلۡمَجَٰلِسِ فَٱفۡسَحُواْ
يَفۡسَحِ ٱللَّهُ لَكُمۡۖ وَإِذَا قِيلَ ٱنشُزُواْ فَٱنشُزُواْ يَرۡفَعِ ٱللَّهُ ٱلَّذِينَ ءَامَنُواْ
مِنكُمۡ وَٱلَّذِينَ أُوتُواْ ٱلۡعِلۡمَ دَرَجَٰتٖۚ وَٱللَّهُ بِمَا تَعۡمَلُونَ خَبِيرٞ ۝١١

Yāa ʾayyuhal-ladhīna ʾāmanūu ʾidhā tanājaytum falā tatanājaw bilʾithmi wal-ʿudwāni wa maʿṣiyatir-Rasūli wa tanājaw bilbirri wat-taqwā; wat-taqul-lāhal-ladhīi ʾilayhi tuḥsharūn. (9) ʾInnaman-najwā minash-Shayṭāni liyaḥzunal-ladhīna ʾāmanū wa laysa biḍāarrihim shayʾan ʾillā biʾidhnil-lāhi wa ʿalal-lāhi falyatawakkalil-muʾminūn. (10) Yāa ʾayyuhal-ladhīna ʾāmanūu ʾidhā qīla lakum tafassaḥū fil-majālisi fafsaḥū yafsaḥil-lāhu lakum. Wa ʾidhā qīlañ-shuzū fañshuzū yarfaʿil-lāhul-ladhīna ʾāmanū miñkum wal-ladhīna ʾūtul-ʿilma darajāt. Wal-lāhu bimā taʿmalūna Khabīr. (11)

16 See note 12.

17 I.e., in and by itself, the force of evil epitomized in the concept of "Satan" has no power whatever: cf. 14 : 22 – "I had no power at all over you: I but called you – and you responded unto me. Hence, blame not me, but blame yourselves." (See also Rāzī's views quoted in my note 31 on the above-mentioned verse.) As regards the problem of God's "letting" or "allowing" a person to go astray (implied in the phrase "unless it be by God's leave"), see note 4 on 14 : 4.

18 Lit., "in the assemblies (*al-majālis*)". Although it is frequently assumed that this refers to the assemblies held by the Prophet, when his followers would throng around him in their eagerness the better to hear what he had to say, or – more generally – to congregations in mosques, etc., in later times, I am (with Rāzī) of the opinion that the plural noun *majālis* is used here in a tropical or metaphorical sense, denoting the totality of men's social life. Taken in this sense, the "making room for one another" implies the mutual providing of opportunities for a decent life to all – and especially to the needy or handicapped – members of the community. See also next note.

19 Commenting on this passage, Rāzī says: "This verse indicates that if one widens the means (*abwāb*) of happiness and well-being of God's creatures (*ʿibād*), God will widen for him all that is good in this life and in the hereafter. Hence, no reasonable person (*al-ʿāqil*) could ever restrict [the purport of] this verse to merely making room for one another in an [actual] assembly."

20 The interpretation implied in the words "for a good deed" interpolated by me above is analogous to that offered by most of the classical commentators, and most explicitly by Ṭabarī; in the words of Qatādah (*ibid.*), "Whenever you are called upon to do a good deed, respond to this call."

21 Cf. the saying of the Prophet: "The superiority of a learned man (*ʿālim*) over a [mere] worshipper (*ʿābid*) is like the superiority of the moon on the night when it is full over all other stars" (Ibn Ḥanbal, Abū Dāʾūd, Tirmidhī, Nasāʾī, Ibn Mājah and Dārimi).

O YOU who have attained to faith! Whenever you [intend to] consult the Apostle, offer up something in charity on the occasion of your consultation:[22] this will be for your own good, and more conducive to your [inner] purity. Yet if you are unable to do so,[23] [know that,] verily, God is much-forgiving, a dispenser of grace. ‹12›
Do you, perchance, fear lest [you may be sinning if] you cannot offer up anything in charity on the occasion of your consultation [with the Apostle]? But if you fail to do it [for lack of opportunity], and God turns unto you in His mercy, remain but constant in prayer and render [no more than] the purifying dues,[24] and [thus] pay heed unto God and His Apostle: for God is fully aware of all that you do. ‹13›

ART THOU NOT aware of those who would be friends with people whom God has condemned?[25] They are neither of you [O believers] nor of those [who utterly reject the truth]: and so they swear to a falsehood the while they know [it to be false]. ‹14›

يَٰٓأَيُّهَا ٱلَّذِينَ ءَامَنُوٓاْ إِذَا نَٰجَيۡتُمُ ٱلرَّسُولَ فَقَدِّمُواْ بَيۡنَ يَدَيۡ نَجۡوَىٰكُمۡ
صَدَقَةٗۚ ذَٰلِكَ خَيۡرٞ لَّكُمۡ وَأَطۡهَرُۚ فَإِن لَّمۡ تَجِدُواْ فَإِنَّ ٱللَّهَ غَفُورٞ رَّحِيمٌ ﴿١٢﴾
ءَأَشۡفَقۡتُمۡ أَن تُقَدِّمُواْ بَيۡنَ يَدَيۡ نَجۡوَىٰكُمۡ صَدَقَٰتٖۚ فَإِذۡ لَمۡ تَفۡعَلُواْ وَتَابَ
ٱللَّهُ عَلَيۡكُمۡ فَأَقِيمُواْ ٱلصَّلَوٰةَ وَءَاتُواْ ٱلزَّكَوٰةَ وَأَطِيعُواْ ٱللَّهَ وَرَسُولَهُۥۚ
وَٱللَّهُ خَبِيرُۢ بِمَا تَعۡمَلُونَ ﴿١٣﴾ ۞ أَلَمۡ تَرَ إِلَى ٱلَّذِينَ تَوَلَّوۡاْ قَوۡمًا غَضِبَ ٱللَّهُ
عَلَيۡهِم مَّا هُم مِّنكُمۡ وَلَا مِنۡهُمۡ وَيَحۡلِفُونَ عَلَى ٱلۡكَذِبِ وَهُمۡ يَعۡلَمُونَ ﴿١٤﴾

ربع الحزب

Yāa ʾayyuhal-ladhīna ʾāmanūu ʾidhā nājaytumur-Rasūla faqaddimū bayna yaday najwākum ṣadaqah. Dhālika khayrul-lakum wa ʾaṭhar. Faʾil-lam tajidū faʾinnal-lāha Ghafūrur-Raḥīm. (12) ʾAʾashfaqtum ʾañ-tuqaddimū bayna yaday najwākum ṣadaqāt. Faʾidh lam tafʿalū wa tābal-lāhu ʿalaykum faʾaqīmuṣ-Ṣalāta wa ʾātuz-Zakāta wa ʾaṭīʿul-lāha wa Rasūlah. Wal-lāhu Khabīrum-bimā taʿmalūn. (13) ۞ ʾAlam tara ʾilal-ladhīna tawallaw qawman ghaḍibal-lāhu ʿalayhim-mā hum-miñkum wa lā minhum wa yaḥlifūna ʿalal-kadhibi wa hum yaʿlamūn. (14)

22 This call to an exercise of charity on every occasion (*bayna yaday*) of one's "consultation" with God's Apostle has been widely misunderstood as applying only to factual consultations with him, i.e., in his lifetime, supposedly with a view to lessening the encroachments on his time by some of his too-eager followers. This misunderstanding, together with the qualified dispensation from the above-mentioned injunction expressed in the next verse, has given rise to the unwarranted contention by some of the commentators that this injunction has been "abrogated". But apart from the fact that the theory of "abrogation" as such is entirely untenable (see 2 : 106 and the corresponding note 87), the above verse reveals its true meaning as soon as we realize that the term "the Apostle" (*ar-rasūl*) is used in the Qur'ān not merely to designate the unique *person* of the Prophet Muḥammad but also the sum-total of the *teachings* conveyed by him to the world. This is evident from the many Qurʾanic exhortations, "Pay heed unto God and the Apostle", and, more specifically (in 4 : 59), "if you are at variance over any matter, refer it unto God [i.e., the Qurʾān] and the Apostle [i.e., his *sunnah*]", which latter is but meant to elucidate the former. Taken in this sense, the above reference to a "consultation with the Apostle" obviously applies not only to his person and his contemporaries, but rather to his teachings in general and to believers of all times and environments. In other words, every believer is exhorted to "offer up something in charity" – whether it be material alms to a needy person, or the imparting of knowledge to such as may be in need of enlightenment, or even a mere word of kindness to a weak human being – whenever he intends to immerse himself in a study of the Apostle's teachings or, as the Qurʾān phrases it, to "consult" him who has conveyed the divine writ to us.

23 Lit., "if you do not find", sc., anyone on whom to bestow charity at that particular moment, or have – for whatever reason – no opportunity to exercise it.

24 I.e., the obligatory tax (*zakāh*) which is meant to purify a believer's possessions and income from the taint of selfishness: implying that one's inability to do more by way of charity does not constitute a sin.

25 For the meaning of "God's condemnation", see note 4 on the last verse of *Al-Fātiḥah*. In this particular context, the ones "who would be friends with people whom God has condemned" are the half-hearted who – while dimly perceiving the truth of God's existence and self-revelation – are nevertheless unwilling to surrender themselves to this truth for fear of estranging themselves from their God-denying environment and, thus, of losing what they regard as the material advantages of a spiritually uncommitted life: and it is this moral falsehood to which the last sentence of this verse refers. (See also the last verse of *sūrah* 60.)

أَعَدَّ ٱللَّهُ لَهُمْ عَذَابًا شَدِيدًا إِنَّهُمْ سَآءَ مَا كَانُوا۟ يَعْمَلُونَ ﴿15﴾ ٱتَّخَذُوٓا۟
أَيْمَـٰنَهُمْ جُنَّةً فَصَدُّوا۟ عَن سَبِيلِ ٱللَّهِ فَلَهُمْ عَذَابٌ مُّهِينٌ ﴿16﴾ لَّن تُغْنِىَ
عَنْهُمْ أَمْوَٰلُهُمْ وَلَآ أَوْلَـٰدُهُم مِّنَ ٱللَّهِ شَيْـًٔا ۚ أُو۟لَـٰٓئِكَ أَصْحَـٰبُ ٱلنَّارِ ۖ هُمْ
فِيهَا خَـٰلِدُونَ ﴿17﴾ يَوْمَ يَبْعَثُهُمُ ٱللَّهُ جَمِيعًا فَيَحْلِفُونَ لَهُۥ كَمَا يَحْلِفُونَ
لَكُمْ ۖ وَيَحْسَبُونَ أَنَّهُمْ عَلَىٰ شَىْءٍ ۚ أَلَآ إِنَّهُمْ هُمُ ٱلْكَـٰذِبُونَ ﴿18﴾ ٱسْتَحْوَذَ
عَلَيْهِمُ ٱلشَّيْطَـٰنُ فَأَنسَىٰهُمْ ذِكْرَ ٱللَّهِ ۚ أُو۟لَـٰٓئِكَ حِزْبُ ٱلشَّيْطَـٰنِ ۚ أَلَآ إِنَّ
حِزْبَ ٱلشَّيْطَـٰنِ هُمُ ٱلْخَـٰسِرُونَ ﴿19﴾ إِنَّ ٱلَّذِينَ يُحَآدُّونَ ٱللَّهَ وَرَسُولَهُۥٓ
أُو۟لَـٰٓئِكَ فِى ٱلْأَذَلِّينَ ﴿20﴾ كَتَبَ ٱللَّهُ لَأَغْلِبَنَّ أَنَا۠ وَرُسُلِىٓ ۚ إِنَّ ٱللَّهَ قَوِىٌّ
عَزِيزٌ ﴿21﴾ لَّا تَجِدُ قَوْمًا يُؤْمِنُونَ بِٱللَّهِ وَٱلْيَوْمِ ٱلْـَٔاخِرِ يُوَآدُّونَ مَنْ حَآدَّ
ٱللَّهَ وَرَسُولَهُۥ وَلَوْ كَانُوٓا۟ ءَابَآءَهُمْ أَوْ أَبْنَآءَهُمْ أَوْ إِخْوَٰنَهُمْ أَوْ عَشِيرَتَهُمْ

ʾAʿaddal-lāhu lahum ʿadhābañ-shadīdan ʾinnahum sāaʾa mā kānū yaʿmalūn. (15) ʾIttakhadhūu ʾaymānahum junnatañ-faṣaddū ʿañ-sabīlil-lāhi falahum ʿadhābum-muhīn. (16) Lañ-tughniya ʿanhum ʾamwāluhum wa lāa ʾawlāduhum-minal-lāhi shayʾā. ʾUlāaʾika ʾaṣḥābun-nāri hum fīhā khālidūn. (17) Yawma yabʿathuhumul-lāhu jamīʿañ-fayaḥlifūna lahū kamā yaḥlifūna lakum wa yaḥsabūna ʾannahum ʿalā shayʾ. ʾAlāa ʾinnahum humul-kādhibūn. (18) ʾIstaḥwadha ʿalayhimush-Shayṭānu faʾañsāhum dhikral-lāh. ʾUlāaʾika ḥizbush-Shayṭān. ʾAlāa ʾinna ḥizbash-Shayṭāni humul-khāsirūn. (19) ʾInnal-ladhīna yuḥāaddūnal-lāha wa Rasūlahūu ʾulāaʾika fil-ʾadhallīn. (20) Katabal-lāhu laʾaghlibanna ʾAna wa Rusulīi ʾinnal-lāha Qawiyyun ʿAzīz. (21) Lā tajidu qawmañy-yuʾminūna billāhi wal-Yawmil-ʾĀkhiri yuwāaddūna man ḥāaddal-lāha wa Rasūlahū wa law kānūu ʾābāaʾahum ʾaw ʾabnāaʾahum ʾaw ʾikhwānahum ʾaw ʿashīratahum.

God has readied for them suffering severe [in the life to come]. Behold, evil indeed is what they are wont to do: ‹15› they have made their oaths a cover [for their falseness], and thus they turn others away from the path of God:[26] hence, shameful suffering awaits them. ‹16›

Neither their worldly possessions nor their offspring will be of the least avail to them against God: it is they who are destined for the fire, therein to abide! ‹17›

On the Day when God will raise them all from the dead, they will swear before Him as they [now] swear before you, thinking that they are on firm ground [in their assumptions].[27]

Oh, verily, it is they, they who are the [greatest] liars![28] ‹18› Satan has gained mastery over them, and has caused them to remain oblivious of the remembrance of God.

Such as these are Satan's partisans: oh, verily, it is they, the partisans of Satan, who will truly be the losers! ‹19›

Verily, those who contend against God and His Apostle – it is they who [on Judgment Day] shall find themselves among the most abject. ‹20› [For] God has thus ordained: "I shall most certainly prevail, I and My apostles!"

Verily, God is powerful, almighty! ‹21›

Thou canst not find people who [truly] believe in God and the Last Day and [at the same time] love anyone who contends against God and His Apostle – even though they be their fathers, or their sons, or their brothers, or [others of] their kindred.[29]

---

26 I.e., by sowing doubts in other people's hearts.

27 Namely, that their preference of worldly benefits to a spiritual commitment is "reasonable" and, therefore, morally "justified". It is to this flagrant self-deception that the next sentence refers.

28 The definite article *al* prefixed to the participial noun *kādhibūn* indicates that the people thus characterized have reached the utmost degree of self-deception; hence my interpolation of the adjective "greatest" in consonance with Zamakhsharī's interpretation of the above phrase.

29 The operative phrase of this passage is contained in the words, "anyone who contends against (*man ḥādda*) God and His Apostle": i.e., anyone who is engaged in *active hostility* against God's message and the person or the teachings of His Apostle. As regards relations with non-believers who are *not* actively hostile to Islam, the Qurʾān explicitly permits and implicitly ordains in many places (e.g., in 60 : 8-9) kindness and friendliness towards them.

[As for the true believers,] it is they in whose hearts He has inscribed faith, and whom He has strengthened with inspiration from Himself,[30] and whom [in time] He will admit into gardens through which running waters flow, therein to abide. Well-pleased is God with them, and well-pleased are they with Him. They are God's partisans: oh, verily, it is they, the partisans of God, who shall attain to a happy state! ‹22›

أُوْلَـٰٓئِكَ كَتَبَ فِي قُلُوبِهِمُ ٱلْإِيمَـٰنَ وَأَيَّدَهُم بِرُوحٍ مِّنْهُ ۖ وَيُدْخِلُهُمْ جَنَّـٰتٍ
تَجْرِي مِن تَحْتِهَا ٱلْأَنْهَـٰرُ خَـٰلِدِينَ فِيهَا ۚ رَضِيَ ٱللَّهُ عَنْهُمْ وَرَضُوا۟ عَنْهُ ۚ
أُوْلَـٰٓئِكَ حِزْبُ ٱللَّهِ ۚ أَلَآ إِنَّ حِزْبَ ٱللَّهِ هُمُ ٱلْمُفْلِحُونَ ﴿٢٢﴾

ᵓUlāaᵓika kataba fī qulūbihimul-ᵓīmāna wa ᵓayyadahum birūḥim-minh. Wa yudkhiluhum jannātiñ-tajrī miñ-taḥtihal-ᵓanhāru khālidīna fīhā. Raḍiyal-lāhu ᶜanhum wa raḍū ᶜanh. ᵓUlāaᵓika ḥizbul-lāh. ᵓAlāa ᵓinna ḥizbal-lāhi humul-mufliḥūn. ⟨22⟩

30 For my rendering of *rūḥ* as "inspiration" or, occasionally, as "divine inspiration", see note 2 on 16 : 2. As pointed out by Zamakhsharī, the pronominal suffix in *minhu* may relate either to God – as in my rendering – or to the believers' faith, in which latter case the phrase could be rendered as "strengthened with inspiration [flowing] therefrom".

The Fifty-Ninth Sūrah

Al-Ḥashr (The Gathering)

Medina Period

MOST of this *sūrah* (i.e., verses 2-17) refers, directly or indirectly, to the conflict between the Muslim community and the Jewish tribe of Banu 'n-Naḍīr of Medina, and to the subsequent banishment of the latter. Shortly after his and his followers' exodus from Mecca to Medina, the Prophet concluded a treaty with the Banu 'n-Naḍīr according to which they pledged themselves to neutrality in the hostilities between the Muslims and the pagan Quraysh. After the Muslim victory in the battle of Badr, in the year 2 H., the leaders of that Jewish tribe spontaneously declared that Muḥammad was indeed the prophet whose coming had been predicted in the Torah; but one year later, after the near-defeat of the Muslims at Uḥud (see *sūrah* 3, note 90), the Banu 'n-Naḍīr treacherously broke their compact with the Prophet Muḥammad and entered into an alliance with the Meccan Quraysh with a view to destroying the Muslim community once and for all. Thereupon the Prophet placed before them an alternative: either war or departure from Medina with all their possessions. If they accepted this latter proposition, they would be allowed to return every year to gather the produce of their date groves, which would thus remain their property. Ostensibly agreeing to the second alternative, the Banu 'n-Naḍīr asked for – and were granted – ten days of respite. In the meantime they secretly conspired with the hypocrites among the Arabs of Medina, led by ᶜAbd Allāh ibn Ubayy, who promised them armed support by two thousand warriors in case they decided to remain in their fortified settlements on the outskirts of the town: "Hence, do not leave your homes; if the Muslims fight against you, we shall fight side by side with you; and if they should succeed in driving you away, we shall leave Medina together with you." The Banu 'n-Naḍīr followed this advice, defied the Prophet and took up arms. In the ensuing conflict, their forts were besieged by the Muslims – though without actual fighting – for twenty-one days; but when the promised help of ᶜAbd Allāh ibn Ubayy's followers did not materialize, the Naḍīr surrendered in the month of Rabīᶜ al-Awwal, 4 H., and sued for peace. This they were granted on condition that they would leave Medina, taking with them all their movable properties, but not their arms. Most of them emigrated to Syria in a caravan of about six hundred camels; only two families chose to settle in the oasis of Khaybar, while a few individuals went as far as Al-Ḥīrah in lower Mesopotamia. As shown in verses 7-8 of this *sūrah*, their fields and plantations were forfeited; most of them were divided among needy Muslims, and the remainder was reserved for the requirements of the Islamic community as a whole.

As always in the Qurʾān, these historical references serve to illustrate a spiritual truth: in this case, the lesson that believers – even if they are inferior in numbers, wealth and equipment – are bound to triumph over their opponents so long as they remain truly conscious of God: for, as the opening and closing verses of this *sūrah* declare, "He alone is almighty, truly wise".

The date of revelation is the year 4 H. The conventional title of the *sūrah* echoes the mention of the "gathering [for war]" in verse 2, although some of the Prophet's Companions – e.g., Ibn ᶜAbbās – used to refer to it as *Sūrat Bani 'n-Naḍīr* (Ṭabarī).

سورة الحشر مدنية -59-
وآياتها أربع وعشرون

IN THE NAME OF GOD, THE MOST GRACIOUS, THE DISPENSER OF GRACE:

بِسۡمِ ٱللَّهِ ٱلرَّحۡمَٰنِ ٱلرَّحِيمِ

ALL THAT IS in the heavens and all that is
on earth extols God's limitless glory: for
He alone is almighty, truly wise. ‹1›
He it is who turned out of their homes, at
the time of [their] first gathering [for war],
such of the followers of earlier revelation
as were bent on denying the truth.[1]
You did not think [O believers] that they
would depart [without resistance] – just as
they thought that their strongholds would
protect them against God: but God came
upon them in a manner which they had
not expected,[2] and cast terror into their
hearts; [and thus] they destroyed their
homes by their own hands as well as the
hands of the believers.[3]
Learn a lesson, then, O you who are endowed with insight! ‹2›
And had it not been for God's having
ordained banishment for them, He would
indeed have imposed [yet greater] suffering on them in this world: still, in the life
to come there awaits them suffering
through fire: ‹3› this, because they cut
themselves off from God and His Apostle:[4]

سَبَّحَ لِلَّهِ مَا فِي ٱلسَّمَٰوَٰتِ وَمَا فِي ٱلۡأَرۡضِۖ وَهُوَ ٱلۡعَزِيزُ ٱلۡحَكِيمُ ﴿١﴾
هُوَ ٱلَّذِيٓ أَخۡرَجَ ٱلَّذِينَ كَفَرُواْ مِنۡ أَهۡلِ ٱلۡكِتَٰبِ مِن دِيَٰرِهِمۡ لِأَوَّلِ
ٱلۡحَشۡرِۚ مَا ظَنَنتُمۡ أَن يَخۡرُجُواْۖ وَظَنُّوٓاْ أَنَّهُم مَّانِعَتُهُمۡ حُصُونُهُم مِّنَ
ٱللَّهِ فَأَتَىٰهُمُ ٱللَّهُ مِنۡ حَيۡثُ لَمۡ يَحۡتَسِبُواْۖ وَقَذَفَ فِي قُلُوبِهِمُ ٱلرُّعۡبَۚ
يُخۡرِبُونَ بُيُوتَهُم بِأَيۡدِيهِمۡ وَأَيۡدِي ٱلۡمُؤۡمِنِينَ فَٱعۡتَبِرُواْ يَٰٓأُوْلِي
ٱلۡأَبۡصَٰرِ ﴿٢﴾ وَلَوۡلَآ أَن كَتَبَ ٱللَّهُ عَلَيۡهِمُ ٱلۡجَلَآءَ لَعَذَّبَهُمۡ فِي ٱلدُّنۡيَاۖ
وَلَهُمۡ فِي ٱلۡأٓخِرَةِ عَذَابُ ٱلنَّارِ ﴿٣﴾ ذَٰلِكَ بِأَنَّهُمۡ شَآقُّواْ ٱللَّهَ وَرَسُولَهُۥۖ

Bismil-lāhir-Raḥmānir-Raḥīm.
Sabbaḥa lillāhi mā fis-samāwāti wa mā fil-ʾarḍi wa
Huwal-ʿAzīzul-Ḥakīm. ⟨1⟩ Huwal-ladhīi ʾakhrajal-
ladhīna kafarū min ʾahlil-Kitābi miñ-diyārihim liʾaw-
walil-ḥashr. Mā ẓanañtum ʾañy-yakhrujū wa ẓannūu
ʾannahum-māniʿatuhum ḥuṣūnuhum-minal-lāhi
faʾatāhumul-lāhu min ḥaythu lam yaḥtasibū wa qa-
dhafa fī qulūbihimur-ruʿb. Yukhribūna buyūtahum
biʾaydīhim wa ʾaydil-muʾminīna faʿtabirū yāa ʾulil-
ʾabṣār. ⟨2⟩ Wa lawlāa ʾañ-katabal-lāhu ʿalayhimul-
jalāaʾa laʿadhdhabahum fid-dunyā; wa lahum fil-
ʾĀkhirati ʿadhābun-nār. ⟨3⟩ Dhālika biʾannahum
shāaqqul-lāha wa Rasūlah.

---

1 For this and the subsequent historical references, see the introductory note to this *sūrah.* The tribe of Banu 'n-Naḍīr – who, as Jews, are naturally termed *ahl al-kitāb* ("followers of earlier revelation") – are characterized as "such as were bent on denying the truth" (*alladhīna kafarū,* see note 6 on 2 : 6) because they treacherously turned against the Prophet despite their earlier admission that he was truly the bearer of God's message announced in their own holy scriptures (Deuteronomy xviii, 15 and 18).

2 Lit., "from whence they had not thought [it possible]": an allusion to the last-minute, unexpected failure of ʿAbd Allāh ibn Ubayy to come to their aid.

3 As mentioned in the introductory note, the Banu 'n-Naḍīr had originally concluded a treaty of mutual non-interference with the Muslim community, and were to live at Medina as its friendly neighbours; and even later, when their hostility to the Muslims had become apparent and they were ordered to emigrate, they were to be allowed to retain ownership of their plantations. Subsequently, however, they forfeited by their treachery both their citizenship and the rights to their landed property, and thus "destroyed their homes by their own hands".

4 For this condemnation of the Banu 'n-Naḍīr see note 1 above. As regards my rendering of the verb *shāqqū* as "they cut themselves off", see note 16 on 8 : 13.

and as for him who cuts himself off from God – verily, God is severe in retribution! ‹4›

Whatever [of their] palm trees you may have cut down, [O believers,] or left standing on their roots, was [done] by God's leave,[5] and in order that He might confound the iniquitous. ‹5›

Yet [remember:] whatever [spoils taken] from the enemy[6] God has turned over to His Apostle, you did not have to spur horse or riding-camel for its sake:[7] but God gives His apostles mastery over whomever He wills – for God has the power to will anything. ‹6›

Whatever [spoils taken] from the people of those villages God has turned over to His Apostle – [all of it] belongs to God and the Apostle,[8] and the near of kin [of deceased believers], and the orphans, and the needy, and the wayfarer,[9] so that it may not be [a benefit] going round and round among such of you as may [already] be rich. Hence, accept [willingly] whatever the Apostle[10] gives you [thereof], and refrain from [demanding] anything that he withholds from you; and remain conscious of God: for, verily, God is severe in retribution. ‹7›

[Thus, part of such war-gains shall be given] to the poor among those who have

وَمَن يُشَآقِّ ٱللَّهَ فَإِنَّ ٱللَّهَ شَدِيدُ ٱلْعِقَابِ ﴿٤﴾ مَا قَطَعْتُم مِّن لِّينَةٍ أَوْ تَرَكْتُمُوهَا
قَآئِمَةً عَلَىٰٓ أُصُولِهَا فَبِإِذْنِ ٱللَّهِ وَلِيُخْزِىَ ٱلْفَـٰسِقِينَ ﴿٥﴾ وَمَآ أَفَآءَ ٱللَّهُ عَلَىٰ
رَسُولِهِۦ مِنْهُمْ فَمَآ أَوْجَفْتُمْ عَلَيْهِ مِنْ خَيْلٍ وَلَا رِكَابٍ وَلَـٰكِنَّ ٱللَّهَ يُسَلِّطُ
رُسُلَهُۥ عَلَىٰ مَن يَشَآءُ وَٱللَّهُ عَلَىٰ كُلِّ شَىْءٍ قَدِيرٌ ﴿٦﴾ مَّآ أَفَآءَ ٱللَّهُ عَلَىٰ رَسُولِهِۦ
مِنْ أَهْلِ ٱلْقُرَىٰ فَلِلَّهِ وَلِلرَّسُولِ وَلِذِى ٱلْقُرْبَىٰ وَٱلْيَتَـٰمَىٰ وَٱلْمَسَـٰكِينِ وَٱبْنِ
ٱلسَّبِيلِ كَىْ لَا يَكُونَ دُولَةًۢ بَيْنَ ٱلْأَغْنِيَآءِ مِنكُمْ وَمَآ ءَاتَىٰكُمُ ٱلرَّسُولُ فَخُذُوهُ
وَمَا نَهَىٰكُمْ عَنْهُ فَٱنتَهُوا۟ وَٱتَّقُوا۟ ٱللَّهَ إِنَّ ٱللَّهَ شَدِيدُ ٱلْعِقَابِ ﴿٧﴾ لِلْفُقَرَآءِ

Wa mañy-yushāaqqil-lāha faʾinnal-lāha shadīdul-ʿiqāb. ‹4› Mā qaṭaʿtum-mil-līnatin ʾaw taraktumūhā qāaʾimatan ʿalāa ʾuṣūlihā fabiʾidhnil-lāhi wa liyukhziyal-fāsiqīn. ‹5› Wa mā ʾafāaʾal-lāhu ʿalā Rasūlihī minhum famāa ʾawjaftum ʿalayhi min khayliñw-wa lā rikābiñw-wa lākinnal-lāha yusalliṭu Rusulahū ʿalā mañy-yashāaʾ. Wal-lāhu ʿalā kulli shayʾiñ-Qadīr. ‹6› Māa ʾafāaʾal-lāhu ʿalā Rasūlihī min ʾahlil-qurā falillāhī wa lirRasūli wa lidhil-qurbā wal-yatāmā wal-masākīni wab-nis-sabīli kay lā yakūna dūlatam-baynal-ʾaghniyāaʾi miñkum. Wa māa ʾātākumur-Rasūlu fakhudhūhu wa mā nahākum ʿanhu fañtahū. Wattaqul-lāha ʾinnal-lāha Shadīdul-ʿiqāb. ‹7› Lilfuqarāaʾil-

5 I.e., to facilitate the military operations against the strongholds of the Banu 'n-Naḍīr (ʿAbd Allāh ibn Masʿūd, as quoted by Zamakhsharī *et al.*). It should, however, be noted that apart from such stringent military exigencies, all destruction of enemy property – and, in particular, of trees and crops – had been and continued to be prohibited by the Prophet (Ṭabarī, Baghawī, Zamakhsharī, Rāzī, Ibn Kathīr), and has thus become an integral part of Islamic Law.

6 Lit., "from them": i.e., from the Banu 'n-Naḍīr

7 I.e., "you did not have to fight for it, since the enemy surrendered without giving battle". The term *fayʾ* (a noun derived from the verb *fāʾa*, "he returned [something]" or "turned [it] over") is applied in the Qurʾān and the Traditions exclusively to war-gains – whether consisting of lands, or tribute, or indemnities – which are obtained, as a condition of peace, from an enemy who has laid down arms before actual fighting has taken place (*Tāj al-ʿArūs*).

8 Sc., and not to individual Muslim warriors. As so often in the Qurʾān, the expression "God and the Apostle" is here a metonym for the Islamic cause, resp. for a government that rules in accordance with the laws of the Qurʾān and the teachings of the Prophet.

9 Cf. 8 : 41, which relates to booty acquired in *actual warfare*, out of which only one-fifth is to be reserved for the above five categories (see note 41 on 8 : 41). In distinction from all such booty, the gains obtained through *fayʾ* are to be utilized in their *entirety* under these five headings. As regards the term *ibn as-sabīl* ("wayfarer"), see *sūrah* 2, note 145.

10 Respectively, in later times, the head of an Islamic state, who has to decide – in the light of the exigencies – how the share of "God and His Apostle" is to be utilized for the common weal.

forsaken the domain of evil:[11] those who have been driven from their homelands and their possessions, seeking favour with God and [His] goodly acceptance, and who aid [the cause of] God and His Apostle: it is they, they who are true to their word! «8»
And [it shall be offered, too, unto the poor from among] those who, before them,[12] had their abode in this realm and in faith – [those] who love all that come to them in search of refuge, and who harbour in their hearts no grudge for whatever the others may have been given, but rather give them preference over themselves, even though poverty be their own lot:[13] for, such as from their own covetousness are saved – it is they, they that shall attain to a happy state![14] «9»
And so, they who come after them[15] pray: "O our Sustainer! Forgive us our sins, as well as those of our brethren who preceded us in faith, and let not our hearts entertain any unworthy thoughts or feelings against [any of] those who have attained to faith. O our Sustainer! Verily, Thou art compassionate, a dispenser of grace!" «10»

ART THOU NOT aware of how those who would always dissemble [their real feelings][16] speak to their truth-denying brethren from among the followers of earlier revelation:[17] "If you are driven away, we shall most certainly go forth with you,

ٱلْمُهَٰجِرِينَ ٱلَّذِينَ أُخْرِجُوا۟ مِن دِيَٰرِهِمْ وَأَمْوَٰلِهِمْ يَبْتَغُونَ فَضْلًا مِّنَ
ٱللَّهِ وَرِضْوَٰنًا وَيَنصُرُونَ ٱللَّهَ وَرَسُولَهُۥٓ ۚ أُو۟لَٰٓئِكَ هُمُ ٱلصَّٰدِقُونَ ﴿٨﴾
وَٱلَّذِينَ تَبَوَّءُو ٱلدَّارَ وَٱلْإِيمَٰنَ مِن قَبْلِهِمْ يُحِبُّونَ مَنْ هَاجَرَ إِلَيْهِمْ
وَلَا يَجِدُونَ فِى صُدُورِهِمْ حَاجَةً مِّمَّآ أُوتُوا۟ وَيُؤْثِرُونَ عَلَىٰٓ أَنفُسِهِمْ وَلَوْ
كَانَ بِهِمْ خَصَاصَةٌ ۚ وَمَن يُوقَ شُحَّ نَفْسِهِۦ فَأُو۟لَٰٓئِكَ هُمُ ٱلْمُفْلِحُونَ ﴿٩﴾
وَٱلَّذِينَ جَآءُو مِنۢ بَعْدِهِمْ يَقُولُونَ رَبَّنَا ٱغْفِرْ لَنَا وَلِإِخْوَٰنِنَا ٱلَّذِينَ
سَبَقُونَا بِٱلْإِيمَٰنِ وَلَا تَجْعَلْ فِى قُلُوبِنَا غِلًّا لِّلَّذِينَ ءَامَنُوا۟ رَبَّنَآ إِنَّكَ
رَءُوفٌ رَّحِيمٌ ﴿١٠﴾ ۞ أَلَمْ تَرَ إِلَى ٱلَّذِينَ نَافَقُوا۟ يَقُولُونَ لِإِخْوَٰنِهِمُ
ٱلَّذِينَ كَفَرُوا۟ مِنْ أَهْلِ ٱلْكِتَٰبِ لَئِنْ أُخْرِجْتُمْ لَنَخْرُجَنَّ مَعَكُمْ

نصف الحزب

muhājirīnal-ladhīna ʾukhrijū miñ-diyārihim wa ʾamwālihim yabtaghūna faḍlam-minal-lāhi wa riḍwānañw-wa yañṣurūnal-lāha wa Rasūlahūu ʾulāaʾika humuṣ-ṣādiqūn. (8) Wal-ladhīna tabawwaʾud-dāra wal-ʾīmāna miñ-qablihim yuḥibbūna man hājara ʾilayhim wa lā yajidūna fī ṣudūrihim ḥājatam-mimmāa ʾūtū wa yuʾthirūna ʿalāa ʾañfusihim wa law kāna bihim khaṣāṣah. Wa mañy-yūqa shuḥḥa nafsihī faʾulāaʾika humul-mufliḥūn. (9) Wal-ladhīna jāaʾū mim baʿdihim yaqūlūna Rabbanagh-fir lanā wa liʾikhwāninal-ladhīna sabaqūnā bilʾīmāni wa lā tajʿal fī qulūbinā ghillal-lilladhīna ʾāmanū Rabbanāa ʾinnaka Raʾūfur-Raḥīm. (10) ۞ ʾAlam tara ʾilal-ladhīna nāfaqū yaqūlūna liʾikhwānihimul-ladhīna kafarū min ʾahlil-Kitābi laʾin ʾukhrijtum lanakhrujanna maʿakum

11 For this rendering of the term *muhājirūn* ("emigrants"), see *sūrah* 2, note 203.

12 I.e., before the coming to them of "those who have forsaken the domain of evil" (see next note).

13 This relates, in the first instance, to the historical *anṣār* ("helpers") of Medina, who had embraced Islam before the Prophet's and his Meccan followers' coming to them, and who received the refugees with utmost generosity, sharing with them like brethren their own dwellings and all their possessions. In a wider sense, the above refers also to all true believers, at all times, who live in freedom and security within the realm of Islam, and are prepared to receive with open arms anyone who is compelled to leave his homeland in order to be able to live in accordance with the dictates of his faith.

14 Thus, greed, niggardliness and covetousness are pointed out here as the main obstacles to man's attaining to a happy state in this world and in the hereafter (cf. *sūrah* 102).

15 I.e., all who attain to a belief in the Qurʾān and its Prophet (Rāzī).

16 I.e., the hypocrites of Medina (see introductory note as well as next note).

17 The Banu 'n-Naḍīr. From the construction of the next verse it appears that the whole of this passage (verses 11-14) was revealed *before* the actual advance of the Muslims against the Naḍīr strongholds: verses 12-14 might be of a prophetic nature, predicting what was yet to happen (Zamakhsharī). Alternatively, the passage may be under-

and shall never pay heed to anyone against you; and if war is waged against you, we shall most certainly come to your succour."

But God bears witness that they are most flagrantly lying: «11» [for] if those [to whom they have pledged themselves] are indeed driven away, they will not go forth with them; and if war is waged against them, they will not come to their succour; and even if they [try to] succour them, they will most certainly turn their backs [in flight], and in the end will [themselves] find no succour. «12»

Nay, [O believers,] you arouse in their bosoms a fear more intense than [even their fear of] God: this, because they are people who fail to grasp the truth.[18] «13»

Never will they fight you, [even] in unison, otherwise than from within fortified strongholds or from behind walls.[19] Severe is their warlike discord among themselves: thou wouldst think that they are united, whereas [in fact] their hearts are at odds [with one another]: this, because they are people who will not use their reason.[20] «14»

[To both kinds of your enemies,[21] O believers, is bound to happen] the like of [what happened to] those who, a short while before them, had to taste the evil that came from their own doings,[22] with

وَلَا نُطِيعُ فِيكُمْ أَحَدًا أَبَدًا وَإِن قُوتِلْتُمْ لَنَنصُرَنَّكُمْ وَٱللَّهُ يَشْهَدُ إِنَّهُمْ
لَكَـٰذِبُونَ ﴿١١﴾ لَئِنْ أُخْرِجُوا۟ لَا يَخْرُجُونَ مَعَهُمْ وَلَئِن قُوتِلُوا۟ لَا
يَنصُرُونَهُمْ وَلَئِن نَّصَرُوهُمْ لَيُوَلُّنَّ ٱلْأَدْبَـٰرَ ثُمَّ لَا يُنصَرُونَ ﴿١٢﴾ لَأَنتُمْ
أَشَدُّ رَهْبَةً فِى صُدُورِهِم مِّنَ ٱللَّهِ ۚ ذَٰلِكَ بِأَنَّهُمْ قَوْمٌ لَّا يَفْقَهُونَ ﴿١٣﴾ لَا
يُقَـٰتِلُونَكُمْ جَمِيعًا إِلَّا فِى قُرًى مُّحَصَّنَةٍ أَوْ مِن وَرَآءِ جُدُرٍۭ ۚ بَأْسُهُم
بَيْنَهُمْ شَدِيدٌ ۚ تَحْسَبُهُمْ جَمِيعًا وَقُلُوبُهُمْ شَتَّىٰ ۚ ذَٰلِكَ بِأَنَّهُمْ قَوْمٌ لَّا
يَعْقِلُونَ ﴿١٤﴾ كَمَثَلِ ٱلَّذِينَ مِن قَبْلِهِمْ قَرِيبًا ۖ ذَاقُوا۟ وَبَالَ أَمْرِهِمْ وَلَهُمْ

wa lā nuṭīᶜu fīkum ʾaḥadan ʾabadañw-wa ʾiñ-qūtiltum lanañṣurannakum. Wal-lāhu yashhadu ʾinnahum lakādhibūn. (11) Laʾin ʾukhrijū lā yakhrujūna maᶜahum wa laʾiñ-qūtilū lā yañṣurūnahum wa laʾiñ-naṣarūhum layuwallunnal-ʾadbāra thumma lā yuñṣarūn. (12) Laʾañtum ʾashaddu rahbatañ-fī ṣudūrihim-minal-lāh. Dhālika biʾannahum qawmul lā yafqahūn. (13) Lā yuqātilūnakum jamīᶜan ʾillā fī quram-muḥaṣṣanatin ʾaw miñw-warāaʾi judur. Baʾsuhum-baynahum shadīd. Taḥsabuhum jamīᶜañw-wa qulūbuhum shattā; dhālika biʾannahum qawmul-lā yaᶜqilūn. (14) Kamathalil-ladhīna miñ-qablihim qarībañ-dhāqū wabāla ʾamrihim wa lahum

stood in a wider, timeless sense, applying to the falsity and futility inherent in all "alliances" between, on the one hand, people who openly deny the truth and, on the other, half-hearted waverers who have neither the will to commit themselves to a spiritual proposition nor the moral courage to declare openly their lack of belief.

18 Inasmuch as they do not – or, at best, only half-heartedly – believe in God, the tangible, material dangers facing them in this world arouse in them a far greater fear than the thought of His ultimate judgment.

19 The meaning is: "Even if they were able – which they are not – to put forth against you a truly unified front, they will always fight you only from what they regard as well-established 'positions of strength'."

20 Sc., "with a view to achieving what is good for themselves": implying that people who have no real faith and no definite moral convictions can never attain to true unity among themselves, but are always impelled to commit acts of aggression against one another.

21 This interpolation – relating as it does to both the outright deniers of the truth and the hypocrites – is justified by the occurrence of the dual form in verse 17.

22 In the first instance, this is apparently an allusion to the fate of the pagan Quraysh at the battle of Badr (Zamakhsharī) or, according to some authorities (quoted by Ṭabarī), to the treachery and subsequent expulsion from Medina, in the month of Shawwāl, 2 H., of the Jewish tribe of Banū Qaynuqāᶜ. But in a wider perspective – strongly suggested by the next two verses – the meaning is general and not restricted to any particular time or historical occurrence.

[yet more] grievous suffering awaiting them [in the life to come]: ‹15› the like of [what happens] when Satan says unto man, "Deny the truth!" – but as soon as [man] has denied the truth, [Satan] says, "Behold, I am not responsible for thee: behold, I fear God, the Sustainer of all the worlds!"[23] ‹16›
Thus, in the end, both [the deniers of the truth and the hypocrites][24] will find themselves in the fire, therein to abide: for such is the recompense of evildoers. ‹17›

O YOU who have attained to faith! Remain conscious of God; and let every human being look to what he sends ahead for the morrow!
And [once again]: Remain conscious of God, for God is fully aware of all that you do; ‹18› and be not like those who are oblivious of God, and whom He therefore causes to be oblivious of [what is good for] their own selves: [for] it is they, they who are truly depraved![25] ‹19›
Not equal are those who are destined for the fire and those who are destined for paradise: those who are destined for paradise – it is they, they [alone] who shall triumph [on Judgment Day]! ‹20›

HAD WE bestowed this Qurʾān from on high upon a mountain, thou wouldst indeed see it humbling itself, breaking asunder for awe of God. . . .[26]
And [all] such parables We propound unto men, so that they might [learn to] think. ‹21›

GOD IS HE save whom there is no deity: the One who knows all that is beyond the reach of a created being's perception, as

عَذَابٌ أَلِيمٌ ﴿15﴾ كَمَثَلِ ٱلشَّيْطَٰنِ إِذْ قَالَ لِلْإِنسَٰنِ ٱكْفُرْ فَلَمَّا كَفَرَ
قَالَ إِنِّى بَرِىٓءٌ مِّنكَ إِنِّىٓ أَخَافُ ٱللَّهَ رَبَّ ٱلْعَٰلَمِينَ ﴿16﴾ فَكَانَ
عَٰقِبَتَهُمَآ أَنَّهُمَا فِى ٱلنَّارِ خَٰلِدَيْنِ فِيهَا ۚ وَذَٰلِكَ جَزَٰٓؤُا۟ ٱلظَّٰلِمِينَ ﴿17﴾
يَٰٓأَيُّهَا ٱلَّذِينَ ءَامَنُوا۟ ٱتَّقُوا۟ ٱللَّهَ وَلْتَنظُرْ نَفْسٌ مَّا قَدَّمَتْ لِغَدٍ ۖ وَٱتَّقُوا۟ ٱللَّهَ ۚ
إِنَّ ٱللَّهَ خَبِيرٌۢ بِمَا تَعْمَلُونَ ﴿18﴾ وَلَا تَكُونُوا۟ كَٱلَّذِينَ نَسُوا۟ ٱللَّهَ فَأَنسَىٰهُمْ
أَنفُسَهُمْ ۚ أُو۟لَٰٓئِكَ هُمُ ٱلْفَٰسِقُونَ ﴿19﴾ لَا يَسْتَوِىٓ أَصْحَٰبُ ٱلنَّارِ وَأَصْحَٰبُ
ٱلْجَنَّةِ ۚ أَصْحَٰبُ ٱلْجَنَّةِ هُمُ ٱلْفَآئِزُونَ ﴿20﴾ لَوْ أَنزَلْنَا هَٰذَا ٱلْقُرْءَانَ عَلَىٰ
جَبَلٍ لَّرَأَيْتَهُۥ خَٰشِعًا مُّتَصَدِّعًا مِّنْ خَشْيَةِ ٱللَّهِ ۚ وَتِلْكَ ٱلْأَمْثَٰلُ نَضْرِبُهَا
لِلنَّاسِ لَعَلَّهُمْ يَتَفَكَّرُونَ ﴿21﴾ هُوَ ٱللَّهُ ٱلَّذِى لَآ إِلَٰهَ إِلَّا هُوَ ۖ عَٰلِمُ ٱلْغَيْبِ

ᶜadhābun ʾalīm. ﴿15﴾ Kamathalish-Shayṭāni ʾidh qāla lilʾInsānik-fur falammā kafara qāla ʾinnī bariīʾum-miñka ʾinnii ʾakhāful-lāha Rabbal-ᶜālamīn. ﴿16﴾ Fakāna ᶜāqibatahumāa ʾannahumā fin-nāri khālidayni fīhā. Wa dhālika jazāaʾuẓ-ẓālimīn. ﴿17﴾ Yāa ʾayyuhal-ladhīna ʾāmanut-taqul-lāha wal-tañẓur nafsum-mā qaddamat lighad. Wat-taqul-lāha ʾinnal-lāha Khabīrum-bimā taᶜmalūn. ﴿18﴾ Wa lā takūnū kalladhīna nasul-lāha faʾañsāhum ʾañfusahum; ʾulāaʾika humul-fāsiqūn. ﴿19﴾ Lā yastawīi ʾaṣḥābun-nāri wa ʾaṣḥābul-jannah. ʾAṣḥābul-jannati humul-fāaʾizūn. ﴿20﴾ Law ʾañzalnā hādhal-Qurʾāna ᶜalā jabalil-laraʾaytahū khāshiᶜam-mutaṣaddiᶜam-min khashyatil-lāh. Wa tilkal-ʾamthālu naḍribuhā linnāsi laᶜallahum yatafakkarūn. ﴿21﴾ Huwal-lāhul-ladhī lāa ʾilāha ʾillā Huwa ᶜAlimul-ghaybi

23 Cf. 8 : 48; also 14 : 22 and the corresponding notes.

24 Lit., "the end (*ᶜāqibah*) of both will be that both . . .", etc.

25 I.e., by having made a deliberately wrong use of the faculty of reason with which God has endowed man, and – by remaining oblivious of Him – having wasted their own spiritual potential.

26 I.e., in contrast with those who, by remaining oblivious of God and all moral imperatives, are spiritually more dead than an inert mountain.

well as all that can be witnessed by a creature's senses or mind:[27] He, the Most Gracious, the Dispenser of Grace. ‹22›
God is He save whom there is no deity: the Sovereign Supreme, the Holy, the One with whom all salvation rests,[28] the Giver of Faith, the One who determines what is true and false,[29] the Almighty, the One who subdues wrong and restores right,[30] the One to whom all greatness belongs!
Utterly remote is God, in His limitless glory, from anything to which men may ascribe a share in His divinity! ‹23›
He is God, the Creator, the Maker who shapes all forms and appearances![31]
His [alone] are the attributes of perfection.[32] All that is in the heavens and on earth extols His limitless glory: for He alone is almighty, truly wise! ‹24›

وَٱلشَّهَٰدَةِ هُوَ ٱلرَّحْمَٰنُ ٱلرَّحِيمُ ﴿٢٢﴾ هُوَ ٱللَّهُ ٱلَّذِى لَآ إِلَٰهَ إِلَّا هُوَ
ٱلْمَلِكُ ٱلْقُدُّوسُ ٱلسَّلَٰمُ ٱلْمُؤْمِنُ ٱلْمُهَيْمِنُ ٱلْعَزِيزُ ٱلْجَبَّارُ ٱلْمُتَكَبِّرُ
سُبْحَٰنَ ٱللَّهِ عَمَّا يُشْرِكُونَ ﴿٢٣﴾ هُوَ ٱللَّهُ ٱلْخَٰلِقُ ٱلْبَارِئُ ٱلْمُصَوِّرُ لَهُ
ٱلْأَسْمَآءُ ٱلْحُسْنَىٰ يُسَبِّحُ لَهُۥ مَا فِى ٱلسَّمَٰوَٰتِ وَٱلْأَرْضِ وَهُوَ ٱلْعَزِيزُ
ٱلْحَكِيمُ ﴿٢٤﴾

wash-shahādati Huwar-Raḥmānur-Raḥīm. ﴿22﴾ Huwal-lāhul-ladhī lāa ᵓilāha ᵓillā Huwal-Malikul-Quddūsus-Salāmul-Muᵓminul-Muhayminul-ᶜAzīzul-Jabbārul-Mutakabbir. Subḥānal-lāhi ᶜammā yushrikūn. ﴿23﴾ Huwal-lāhul-Khāliqul-Bāriᵓul-Muṣawwiru lahul-ᵓAsmāaᵓul-Ḥusnā. Yusabbiḥu lahū mā fis-samāwāti wal-ᵓarḍi wa Huwal-ᶜAzīzul-Ḥakīm. ﴿24﴾

---

27 See note 65 on the second paragraph of 6 : 73.

28 Lit., "the Salvation" (*as-salām*): see *sūrah* 5, note 29.

29 For this rendering of *muhaymin*, see 5 : 48 – where this term is applied to the Qurᵓān – and the corresponding note 64.

30 Since the verb *jabara* – from which the noun *jabbār* is derived – combines the concepts of "setting right" or "restoring" (e.g., from a state of brokenness, ill-health, or misfortune) and of "compelling" or "subduing [someone or something] to one's will", I believe that the term *al-jabbār*, when applied to God, is best rendered as above.

31 Thus Bayḍāwī. The two terms *al-bāriᵓ* ("the Maker") and *al-muṣawwir* ("the Shaper", i.e., of all forms and appearances) evidently constitute here one single unit.

32 For this rendering of *al-asmāᵓ al-ḥusnā*, see *sūrah* 7, note 145.

هُوَ ٱللَّهُ ٱلَّذِى لَآ إِلَٰهَ إِلَّا هُوَ ٱلْمَلِكُ
ٱلْقُدُّوسُ ٱلسَّلَٰمُ ٱلْمُؤْمِنُ ٱلْمُهَيْمِنُ
ٱلْعَزِيزُ ٱلْجَبَّارُ ٱلْمُتَكَبِّرُ سُبْحَٰنَ ٱللَّهِ عَمَّا
يُشْرِكُونَ هُوَ ٱللَّهُ ٱلْخَٰلِقُ ٱلْبَارِئُ
ٱلْمُصَوِّرُ لَهُ ٱلْأَسْمَآءُ ٱلْحُسْنَىٰ

The Sixtieth Sūrah

Al-Mumtaḥanah (The Examined One)

Medina Period

THE KEY-WORD by which this *sūrah* has been known from earliest times is based on the injunction "examine them" in verse 10. Revealed some months after the conclusion of the Truce of Ḥudaybiyyah (see introductory note to *sūrah* 48) – that is, not earlier than the year 7 H and probably as late as the beginning of 8 H. – *Al-Mumtaḥanah* is in its entirety devoted to the problem of the believers' relations with unbelievers. Although, as was quite natural, most of the Prophet's Companions visualized these problems under the aspect of the historical events of which they were witnesses, the import of the injunctions laid down in this *sūrah* cannot be restricted to that particular historical situation but has, as always in the Qur'ān, a definite bearing on how believers of all times should behave.

سورة الممتحنة مدنية -60- وآياتها ثلاث عشرة

IN THE NAME OF GOD, THE MOST GRACIOUS, THE DISPENSER OF GRACE:

O YOU who have attained to faith! Do not take My enemies – who are your enemies as well[1] – for your friends, showing them affection even though they are bent on denying whatever truth has come unto you, [and even though] they have driven the Apostle and yourselves away, [only] because you believe in God, your Sustainer![2]

If [it be true that] you have gone forth [from your homes] to strive in My cause, and out of a longing for My goodly acceptance, [do not take them for your friends,] inclining towards them in secret affection: for I am fully aware of all that you may conceal as well as of all that you do openly. And any of you who does this has already strayed from the right path.[3] ‹1›

If they could but overcome you, they would [still] remain your foes, and would stretch forth their hands and tongues against you with evil intent: for they desire that you [too] should deny the truth. ‹2›

But [bear in mind that] neither your kinsfolk nor [even] your own children will be of any benefit to you on Resurrection Day, [for then] He will decide between you [on your merit alone]: and God sees all that you do. ‹3›

بِسْمِ ٱللَّهِ ٱلرَّحْمَٰنِ ٱلرَّحِيمِ

يَٰٓأَيُّهَا ٱلَّذِينَ ءَامَنُواْ لَا تَتَّخِذُواْ عَدُوِّى وَعَدُوَّكُمْ أَوْلِيَآءَ تُلْقُونَ إِلَيْهِم
بِٱلْمَوَدَّةِ وَقَدْ كَفَرُواْ بِمَا جَآءَكُم مِّنَ ٱلْحَقِّ يُخْرِجُونَ ٱلرَّسُولَ
وَإِيَّاكُمْ أَن تُؤْمِنُواْ بِٱللَّهِ رَبِّكُمْ إِن كُنتُمْ خَرَجْتُمْ جِهَٰدًا فِى سَبِيلِى
وَٱبْتِغَآءَ مَرْضَاتِى تُسِرُّونَ إِلَيْهِم بِٱلْمَوَدَّةِ وَأَنَا۠ أَعْلَمُ بِمَآ أَخْفَيْتُمْ وَمَآ
أَعْلَنتُمْ وَمَن يَفْعَلْهُ مِنكُمْ فَقَدْ ضَلَّ سَوَآءَ ٱلسَّبِيلِ ﴿1﴾ إِن يَثْقَفُوكُمْ
يَكُونُواْ لَكُمْ أَعْدَآءً وَيَبْسُطُوٓاْ إِلَيْكُمْ أَيْدِيَهُمْ وَأَلْسِنَتَهُم بِٱلسُّوٓءِ وَوَدُّواْ
لَوْ تَكْفُرُونَ ﴿2﴾ لَن تَنفَعَكُمْ أَرْحَامُكُمْ وَلَآ أَوْلَٰدُكُمْ يَوْمَ ٱلْقِيَٰمَةِ
يَفْصِلُ بَيْنَكُمْ وَٱللَّهُ بِمَا تَعْمَلُونَ بَصِيرٌ ﴿3﴾

Bismil-lāhir-Raḥmānir-Raḥīm.

Yāa ʾayyuhal-ladhīna ʾāmanū lā tattakhidhū ʿaduwwī wa ʿaduwwakum ʾawliyāaʾa tulqūna ʾilayhim bil-mawaddati wa qad kafarū bimā jāaʾakum minal-ḥaqqi yukhrijūnar-Rasūla wa ʾiyyākum ʾañ-tuʾminū billāhi Rabbikum ʾiñ-kuñtum kharajtum jihādañ-fī sabīlī wab-tighāaʾa marḍātī. Tusirrūna ʾilayhim bil-mawaddati wa ʾAna ʾaʿlamu bimāa ʾakhfaytum wa māa ʾaʿlañtum. Wa mañy-yafʿalhu miñkum faqad ḍalla sawāaʾas-sabīl. (1) ʾIñy-yathqafūkum yakūnū lakum ʾaʿdāaʾañw-wa yabsuṭūu ʾilaykum ʾaydiyahum wa ʾalsinatahum bissūuʾi wa waddū law takfurūn. (2) Lañ-tañfaʿakum ʾarḥāmukum wa lāa ʾawlādukum; Yawmal-Qiyāmati yafṣilu baynakum; wal-lāhu bimā taʿmalūna Baṣīr. (3)

---

1 Lit., "and your enemies" – implying that people who deliberately reject God's messages are *ipso facto* inimical to those who believe in them.

2 Historically, this is a reference to the forced emigration of the Prophet and his followers from Mecca to Medina. In a more general sense, however, it is an allusion to the potential persecution of believers of all times by "those who are bent on denying the truth", i.e., those who are averse to religious beliefs as such.

3 As is shown in verses 7-9, this prohibition of taking unbelievers for friends relates only to such of them as are *actively hostile* towards the believers (cf. 58 : 22 and the corresponding note 29).

ثلاثة ارباع الحزب

Indeed, you have had a good example in Abraham and those who followed him, when they said unto their [idolatrous] people: "Verily, we are quit of you and of all that you worship instead of God: we deny the truth of whatever you believe; and between us and you there has arisen enmity and hatred, to last until such a time[4] as you come to believe in the One God!"

The only exception was[5] Abraham's saying to his father, "I shall indeed pray for [God's] forgiveness for thee,[6] although I have it not in my power to obtain anything from God in thy behalf."

[And Abraham and his followers prayed:] "O our Sustainer! In Thee have we placed our trust, and unto Thee do we turn: for unto Thee is all journeys' end. ‹4› O our Sustainer! Make us not a plaything[7] for those who are bent on denying the truth! And forgive us our sins, O our Sustainer: for Thou alone art almighty, truly wise!" ‹5›

In them, indeed, you have a good example for everyone who looks forward [with hope and awe[8]] to God and the Last Day. And if any turns away, [let him know that] God is truly self-sufficient, the One to whom all praise is due. ‹6›

[But] it may well be that God will bring about [mutual] affection between you [O believers] and some of those whom you [now] face as enemies: for, God is infinite in His power – and God is much-forgiving, a dispenser of grace. ‹7›

قَدْ كَانَتْ لَكُمْ أُسْوَةٌ حَسَنَةٌ فِيٓ إِبْرَٰهِيمَ وَٱلَّذِينَ مَعَهُۥٓ إِذْ قَالُواْ لِقَوْمِهِمْ
إِنَّا بُرَءَٰٓؤُاْ مِنكُمْ وَمِمَّا تَعْبُدُونَ مِن دُونِ ٱللَّهِ كَفَرْنَا بِكُمْ وَبَدَا بَيْنَنَا
وَبَيْنَكُمُ ٱلْعَدَٰوَةُ وَٱلْبَغْضَآءُ أَبَدًا حَتَّىٰ تُؤْمِنُواْ بِٱللَّهِ وَحْدَهُۥٓ إِلَّا قَوْلَ
إِبْرَٰهِيمَ لِأَبِيهِ لَأَسْتَغْفِرَنَّ لَكَ وَمَآ أَمْلِكُ لَكَ مِنَ ٱللَّهِ مِن شَيْءٍ رَّبَّنَا
عَلَيْكَ تَوَكَّلْنَا وَإِلَيْكَ أَنَبْنَا وَإِلَيْكَ ٱلْمَصِيرُ ۝٤ رَبَّنَا لَا تَجْعَلْنَا فِتْنَةً
لِّلَّذِينَ كَفَرُواْ وَٱغْفِرْ لَنَا رَبَّنَآ إِنَّكَ أَنتَ ٱلْعَزِيزُ ٱلْحَكِيمُ ۝٥ لَقَدْ كَانَ
لَكُمْ فِيهِمْ أُسْوَةٌ حَسَنَةٌ لِّمَن كَانَ يَرْجُواْ ٱللَّهَ وَٱلْيَوْمَ ٱلْءَاخِرَ وَمَن يَتَوَلَّ
فَإِنَّ ٱللَّهَ هُوَ ٱلْغَنِيُّ ٱلْحَمِيدُ ۝٦ ۞ عَسَى ٱللَّهُ أَن يَجْعَلَ بَيْنَكُمْ وَبَيْنَ
ٱلَّذِينَ عَادَيْتُم مِّنْهُم مَّوَدَّةً وَٱللَّهُ قَدِيرٌ وَٱللَّهُ غَفُورٌ رَّحِيمٌ ۝٧

Qad kānat lakum ʾuswatun ḥasanatuñ-fīi ʾIbrāhīma wal-ladhīna maʿahūu ʾidh qālū liqawmihim ʾinnā buraʾāaʾu miñkum wa mimmā taʿbudūna miñ-dūnil-lāhi kafarnā bikum wa badā baynanā wa baynakumul-ʿadāwatu wal-baghḍāaʾu ʾabadan ḥattā tuʾminū billāhi waḥdahuū ʾillā qawla ʾIbrāhīma liʾabīhi laʾastaghfiranna laka wa māa ʾamliku laka minal-lāhi miñ-shayʾ. Rabbanā ʿalayka tawakkalnā wa ʾilayka ʾanabnā wa ʾilaykal-maṣīr. ‹4› Rabbanā lā tajʿalnā fitnatal-lilladhīna kafarū wagh-fir lanā Rabbanā; ʾinnaka ʾAñtal-ʿAzīzul-Ḥakīm. ‹5› Laqad kāna lakūm fīhim ʾuswatun ḥasanatul-limañ-kāna yarjul-lāha wal-Yawmal-ʾĀkhir. Wa mañy-yatawalla faʾinnal-lāha Huwal-Ghaniyyul-Ḥamīd. ‹6› ۞ ʿAsal-lāhu ʾañy-yajʿala baynakum wa baynal-ladhīna ʿādaytum-minhum-mawaddatañw-wal-lāhu Qadīr. Wal-lāhu Ghafūrur-Raḥīm. ‹7›

4 Since the adverb *abadan* is immediately followed by the particle *ḥattā* ("until such a time as . . ."), it is obviously erroneous to give it the meaning of "forever", as has been hitherto done in all translations of the Qurʾān into Western languages. In view of the original connotation of the noun *abad* as "time" or "long time", i.e., of indefinite duration (Jawharī, Zamakhsharī's *Asās*, *Mughnī*, etc.), *abadan* is best rendered in the present context as "to last [until] . . .", etc.

5 Lit., "Except for": i.e., an exception from Abraham's statement, "between us and you there has arisen enmity and hatred, to last . . .", etc. In other words, his filial love prevented Abraham from including his father in his declaration of "enmity and hatred", although later – after his father had died as an idolater – Abraham could not but disavow him (cf. 9 : 114).

6 Cf. 19 : 47-48.

7 Lit., "temptation to evil" (*fitnah*): cf. 10 : 85, where the term *fitnah* has the same meaning as in the present instance.

8 As in the similar phrase in 33 : 21, this double connotation is implied in the verb *rajawa* and all the noun-forms derived from it.

As for such [of the unbelievers] as do not fight against you on account of [your] faith, and neither drive you forth from your homelands, God does not forbid you to show them kindness and to behave towards them with full equity:[9] for, verily, God loves those who act equitably. ⟨8⟩
God only forbids you to turn in friendship towards such as fight against you because of [your] faith, and drive you forth from your homelands, or aid [others] in driving you forth: and as for those [from among you] who turn towards them in friendship, it is they, they who are truly wrongdoers! ⟨9⟩

O YOU who have attained to faith! Whenever believing women come unto you, forsaking the domain of evil,[10] examine them, [although only] God is fully aware of their faith;[11] and if you have thus ascertained that they are believers, do not send them back to the deniers of the truth, [since] they are not [any longer] lawful to their erstwhile husbands,[12] and these are [no longer] lawful to them. None the less, you shall return to them whatever they have spent [on their wives by way of dower];[13]

لَا يَنْهَىٰكُمُ ٱللَّهُ عَنِ ٱلَّذِينَ لَمْ يُقَـٰتِلُوكُمْ فِى ٱلدِّينِ وَلَمْ يُخْرِجُوكُم مِّن
دِيَـٰرِكُمْ أَن تَبَرُّوهُمْ وَتُقْسِطُوٓا۟ إِلَيْهِمْ ۚ إِنَّ ٱللَّهَ يُحِبُّ ٱلْمُقْسِطِينَ ﴿٨﴾ إِنَّمَا
يَنْهَىٰكُمُ ٱللَّهُ عَنِ ٱلَّذِينَ قَـٰتَلُوكُمْ فِى ٱلدِّينِ وَأَخْرَجُوكُم مِّن دِيَـٰرِكُمْ
وَظَـٰهَرُوا۟ عَلَىٰٓ إِخْرَاجِكُمْ أَن تَوَلَّوْهُمْ ۚ وَمَن يَتَوَلَّهُمْ فَأُو۟لَـٰٓئِكَ هُمُ
ٱلظَّـٰلِمُونَ ﴿٩﴾ يَـٰٓأَيُّهَا ٱلَّذِينَ ءَامَنُوٓا۟ إِذَا جَآءَكُمُ ٱلْمُؤْمِنَـٰتُ مُهَـٰجِرَٰتٍ
فَٱمْتَحِنُوهُنَّ ۖ ٱللَّهُ أَعْلَمُ بِإِيمَـٰنِهِنَّ ۖ فَإِنْ عَلِمْتُمُوهُنَّ مُؤْمِنَـٰتٍ فَلَا تَرْجِعُوهُنَّ
إِلَى ٱلْكُفَّارِ ۖ لَا هُنَّ حِلٌّ لَّهُمْ وَلَا هُمْ يَحِلُّونَ لَهُنَّ ۖ وَءَاتُوهُم مَّآ أَنفَقُوا۟ ۚ

Lā yanhākumul-lāhu ᶜanil-ladhīna lam yuqātilūkum fid-dīni wa lam yukhrijūkum-miñ-diyārikum ᵓañ-tabarrūhum wa tuqsiṭūu ᵓilayhim; ᵓinnal-lāha yuḥibbul-muqsiṭīn. ⟨8⟩ ᵓInnamā yanhākumul-lāhu ᶜanil-ladhīna qātalūkum fid-dīni wa ᵓakhrajūkum-miñ-diyārikum wa ẓāharū ᶜalāa ᵓikhrājikum ᵓañ-tawallawhum. Wa mañy-yatawallahum faᵓulāaᵓika humuẓ-ẓālimūn. ⟨9⟩ Yāa ᵓayyuhal-ladhīna ᵓāmanū ᵓidhā jāaᵓakumul-muᵓminātu muhājirātiñ-famtaḥinūhunn. ᵓAllāhu ᵓaᶜlamu biᵓīmānihinna faᵓin ᶜalimtumūhunna muᵓminātiñ-falā tarjiᶜūhunna ᵓilal-kuffār. Lā hunna ḥillul-lahum wa lā hum yaḥillūna lahunna wa ᵓātūhum-māa ᵓañfaqū.

9 The expression "God does not forbid you" implies in this context a positive exhortation (Zamakhsharī). See also note 29 on 58 : 22.

10 Lit., "as emigrants" (*muhājirāt*). For an explanation of my rendering this term as above, see *sūrah* 2, note 203.

11 Under the terms of the Truce of Ḥudaybiyyah, concluded in the year 6 H. between the Prophet and the pagan Quraysh of Mecca, any Meccan minor or other person under guardianship who went over to the Muslims without the permission of his or her guardian was to be returned to the Quraysh (see introductory note to *sūrah* 48). The Quraysh took this stipulation to include also married women, whom they considered to be under the "guardianship" of their husbands. Accordingly, when several Meccan women embraced Islam against the will of their husbands and fled to Medina, the Quraysh demanded their forcible return to Mecca. This the Prophet refused on the grounds that married women did not fall within the category of "persons under guardianship". However, since there was always the possibility that some of these women had gone over to the Muslims not for reasons of faith but out of purely worldly considerations, the believers were enjoined to make sure of their sincerity; and so, the Prophet asked each of them: "Swear before God that thou didst not leave because of hatred of thy husband, or out of a desire to go to another country, or in the hope of attaining to worldly advantages: swear before God that thou didst not leave for any reason save the love of God and His Apostle" (Ṭabarī). Since God alone knows what is in the heart of a human being, a positive response of the woman concerned was to be regarded as the only humanly attainable – and, therefore, legally sufficient – proof of her sincerity. The fact that God alone is really aware of what is in a human being's heart is incorporated in the *sharᶜī* principle that any adult person's declaration of faith, in the absence of any evidence to the contrary, makes it mandatory upon the community to accept that person – whether man or woman – as a Muslim on the basis of this declaration alone.

12 Lit., "to them". Thus, if a wife embraces Islam while her husband remains outside its pale, the marriage is considered, from the Islamic point of view, to have been automatically annulled.

13 Such an annulment is to be subject to the same conditions as a *khulᶜ* (dissolution of marriage, at the wife's

وَلَا جُنَاحَ عَلَيْكُمْ أَن تَنكِحُوهُنَّ إِذَآ ءَاتَيْتُمُوهُنَّ أُجُورَهُنَّ وَلَا تُمْسِكُوا۟
بِعِصَمِ ٱلْكَوَافِرِ وَسْـَٔلُوا۟ مَآ أَنفَقْتُمْ وَلْيَسْـَٔلُوا۟ مَآ أَنفَقُوا۟ ذَٰلِكُمْ حُكْمُ ٱللَّهِ
يَحْكُمُ بَيْنَكُمْ وَٱللَّهُ عَلِيمٌ حَكِيمٌ ﴿١٠﴾ وَإِن فَاتَكُمْ شَىْءٌ مِّنْ أَزْوَٰجِكُمْ
إِلَى ٱلْكُفَّارِ فَعَاقَبْتُمْ فَـَٔاتُوا۟ ٱلَّذِينَ ذَهَبَتْ أَزْوَٰجُهُم مِّثْلَ مَآ أَنفَقُوا۟
وَٱتَّقُوا۟ ٱللَّهَ ٱلَّذِىٓ أَنتُم بِهِۦ مُؤْمِنُونَ ﴿١١﴾ يَـٰٓأَيُّهَا ٱلنَّبِىُّ إِذَا جَآءَكَ
ٱلْمُؤْمِنَـٰتُ يُبَايِعْنَكَ عَلَىٰٓ أَن لَّا يُشْرِكْنَ بِٱللَّهِ شَيْـًٔا وَلَا يَسْرِقْنَ وَلَا يَزْنِينَ وَلَا

Wa lā junāḥa ʿalaykum ʾañ-tañkiḥūhunna ʾidhāa ʾātaytumūhunna ʾujūrahunn. Wa lā tumsikū biʿiṣamil-kawāfirī was-ʾalū māa ʾañfaqtum wal-yasʾalū māa ʾañfaqū. Dhālikum ḥukmul-lāhi yaḥkumu baynakum; wal-lāhu ʿAlīmun Ḥakīm. (10) Wa ʾiñ-fātakum shayʾum-min ʾazwājikum ʾilal-kuffāri faʿāqabtum faʾātul-ladhīna dhahabat ʾazwājuhum mithla māa ʾañfaqū. Wat-taqul-lāhal-ladhīi ʾañtum bihī muʾminūn. (11) Yāa ʾayyuhan-Nabiyyu ʾidhā jāaʾakal-muʾminātu yubāyiʿnaka ʿalāa ʾallā yushrikna billāhi shayʾañw-wa lā yasriqna wa lā yaznīna wa lā

and [then, O believers,] you will be committing no sin if you marry them after giving them their dowers.

On the other hand, hold not to the marriage-tie with women who [continue to] deny the truth,[14] and ask but for [the return of] whatever you have spent [by way of dower] – just as they [whose wives have gone over to you] have the right to demand[15] [the return of] whatever they have spent.

Such is God's judgment: He judges between you [in equity] – for God is all-knowing, wise. ‹10›

And if any of your wives should go over to the deniers of the truth, and you are thus afflicted in turn,[16] then give unto those whose wives have gone away the equivalent of what they had spent [on their wives by way of dower],[17] and remain conscious of God, in whom you believe! ‹11›

O Prophet! Whenever believing women come unto thee to pledge their allegiance to thee,[18] [pledging] that [henceforth] they would not ascribe divinity, in any way, to aught but God, and would not steal,[19] and would not commit adultery, and would not

instance, from her Muslim husband – see note 218 on the second paragraph of 2 : 229): that is to say, since the non-Muslim former husband is presumed to have been innocent of any breach of his marital obligations as such, the wife is to be considered the contract-breaking party and has, therefore, to refund the dower (*mahr*) which she received from him at the time of concluding the marriage. In case of her inability to do so, the Muslim *community* is obliged to indemnify the erstwhile husband: hence the plural form in the imperative "you shall return" (lit., "give").

14 I.e., such of the pagan wives of Muslim converts as refuse to abandon their beliefs and their non-Muslim environment, in which case the Muslim husband is to regard the marriage as null and void. As for Muslim wives who, abandoning their husbands, go over to the unbelievers and renounce their faith, see verse 11.

15 Lit., "and let them demand . . .", etc.

16 Lit., "and you are thus taking your turn", i.e., like the unbelievers whose wives have gone over to the Muslims and renounced their erstwhile faith.

17 Since, as a rule, the unbelievers cannot really be expected to indemnify a husband thus deserted, the Muslim community as a whole is bound to undertake this obligation. As a matter of fact, there were only six such cases of apostasy in the lifetime of the Prophet (all of them before the conquest of Mecca in 8 H.); and in each case the Muslim husband was awarded by the communal treasury, on orders of the Prophet, the equivalent of the dower originally paid by him (Baghawī and Zamakhsharī).

18 This connects with verse 10 above, and particularly with the words, "examine them . . . and if you have thus ascertained that they are believers . . .", etc. (see note 11). Thus, after having "ascertained" their belief as far as is humanly possible, the Prophet – or, in later times, the head of the Islamic state or community – is empowered to accept their pledge of allegiance (*bayʿah*), which concludes, as it were, the "examination". It should be noted that this pledge does not differ essentially from that of a male convert.

19 In this context, according to Rāzī, the term "stealing" comprises also all acquisition of gains through cheating or other unlawful means.

kill their children,[20] and would not indulge in slander, falsely devising it out of nothingness,[21] and would not disobey thee in anything [that thou declarest to be] right – then accept their pledge of allegiance, and pray to God to forgive them their [past] sins: for, behold, God is much-forgiving, a dispenser of grace. ‹12›

O YOU who have attained to faith! Be not friends with people whom God has condemned![22] They [who would befriend them] are indeed bereft of all hope of a life to come[23] – just as those deniers of the truth are bereft of all hope of [ever again seeing] those who are [now] in their graves.[24] ‹13›

يَقْتُلْنَ أَوْلَٰدَهُنَّ وَلَا يَأْتِينَ بِبُهْتَٰنٍ يَفْتَرِينَهُۥ بَيْنَ أَيْدِيهِنَّ وَأَرْجُلِهِنَّ وَلَا
يَعْصِينَكَ فِى مَعْرُوفٍ فَبَايِعْهُنَّ وَٱسْتَغْفِرْ لَهُنَّ ٱللَّهَ إِنَّ ٱللَّهَ غَفُورٌ رَّحِيمٌ ﴿١٢﴾
يَٰٓأَيُّهَا ٱلَّذِينَ ءَامَنُوا۟ لَا تَتَوَلَّوْا۟ قَوْمًا غَضِبَ ٱللَّهُ عَلَيْهِمْ قَدْ يَئِسُوا۟ مِنَ
ٱلْءَاخِرَةِ كَمَا يَئِسَ ٱلْكُفَّارُ مِنْ أَصْحَٰبِ ٱلْقُبُورِ ﴿١٣﴾

yaqtulna ʾawlādahunna wa lā yaʾtīna bibuhtāniñy-yaftarīnahū bayna ʾaydīhinna wa ʾarjulihinna wa lā yaʿṣīnaka fī maʿrūfiñ-fabāyiʿhunna was-tagfir lahunnal-lāh. ʾInnal-lāha Ghafūrur-Raḥīm. ⑫ Yāa ʾayyuhal-ladhīna ʾāmanū lā tatawallaw qawman ghaḍibal-lāhu ʿalayhim qad yaʾisū minal-ʾĀkhirati kamā yaʾisal-kuffāru min ʾaṣḥābil-qubūr. ⑬

20 Sc., "as the pagan Arabs often did, burying their unwanted female offspring alive" (see also note 147 on 6 : 151).

21 Lit., "between their hands and their feet": i.e., by their own effort, the "hands" and "feet" symbolizing all human activity.

22 Cf. 58 : 14 and the corresponding note 25, which explains the reference to those "who would be friends with people whom God has condemned".

23 I.e., only people without any real belief in a life to come can remain "neutral" between right and wrong.

24 I.e., because they utterly reject the idea of resurrection.

The Sixty-First Sūrah

Aṣ-Ṣaff (The Ranks)

Medina Period

THE TITLE of this *sūrah* has been derived from the expression *ṣaffan* ("in [solid] ranks") occurring in verse 4. The central idea, first enunciated in verse 2 and developed in the subsequent passages, is "Why do you say one thing and do another?" Thus, it is essentially a call to unity between professed belief and actual behaviour.

The date of revelation cannot be established with absolute certainty, but it is probable that it was revealed shortly after the near-defeat of the Muslims in the battle of Uḥud – that is, towards the end of the year 3 or the beginning of 4 H.

سورة الصف مدنية
-61-
وآياتها أربع عشرة

IN THE NAME OF GOD, THE MOST GRACIOUS, THE DISPENSER OF GRACE:

ALL THAT IS in the heavens and all that is on earth extols God's limitless glory: for He alone is almighty, truly wise! ‹1›

O YOU who have attained to faith! Why do you say one thing and do another?[1] ‹2› Most loathsome is it in the sight of God that you say what you do not do! ‹3› Verily, God loves [only] those who fight in His cause in [solid] ranks,[2] as though they were a building firm and compact. ‹4› Now when Moses spoke to his people, [it was this same truth that he had in mind:] "O my people! Why do you cause me grief,[3] the while you know that I am an apostle of God sent unto you?" And so, when they swerved from the right way, God let their hearts swerve from the truth:[4] for God does not bestow His guidance upon iniquitous folk. ‹5› And [this happened, too,] when Jesus, the son of Mary, said: "O children of Israel! Behold, I am an apostle of God unto you, [sent] to confirm the truth of whatever there still remains[5] of the Torah,

بِسْمِ ٱللَّهِ ٱلرَّحْمَٰنِ ٱلرَّحِيمِ

سَبَّحَ لِلَّهِ مَا فِى ٱلسَّمَٰوَٰتِ وَمَا فِى ٱلْأَرْضِ ۖ وَهُوَ ٱلْعَزِيزُ ٱلْحَكِيمُ ﴿١﴾
يَٰٓأَيُّهَا ٱلَّذِينَ ءَامَنُوا۟ لِمَ تَقُولُونَ مَا لَا تَفْعَلُونَ ﴿٢﴾ كَبُرَ مَقْتًا عِندَ ٱللَّهِ
أَن تَقُولُوا۟ مَا لَا تَفْعَلُونَ ﴿٣﴾ إِنَّ ٱللَّهَ يُحِبُّ ٱلَّذِينَ يُقَٰتِلُونَ فِى سَبِيلِهِۦ
صَفًّا كَأَنَّهُم بُنْيَٰنٌ مَّرْصُوصٌ ﴿٤﴾ وَإِذْ قَالَ مُوسَىٰ لِقَوْمِهِۦ يَٰقَوْمِ لِمَ
تُؤْذُونَنِى وَقَد تَّعْلَمُونَ أَنِّى رَسُولُ ٱللَّهِ إِلَيْكُمْ ۖ فَلَمَّا زَاغُوٓا۟ أَزَاغَ ٱللَّهُ
قُلُوبَهُمْ ۚ وَٱللَّهُ لَا يَهْدِى ٱلْقَوْمَ ٱلْفَٰسِقِينَ ﴿٥﴾ وَإِذْ قَالَ عِيسَى ٱبْنُ مَرْيَمَ
يَٰبَنِىٓ إِسْرَٰٓءِيلَ إِنِّى رَسُولُ ٱللَّهِ إِلَيْكُم مُّصَدِّقًا لِّمَا بَيْنَ يَدَىَّ مِنَ ٱلتَّوْرَىٰةِ

Bismil-lāhir-Raḥmānir-Raḥīm.
Sabbaḥa lillāhi mā fis-samāwāti wa mā fil-ʾarḍi
wa Huwal-ʿAzīzul-Ḥakīm. (1) Yāa ʾayyuhal-ladhīna
ʾāmanū lima taqūlūna mā lā tafʿalūn. (2) Kabura
maqtan ʿiñdal-lāhi ʾañ-taqūlū mā lā tafʿalūn. (3)
ʾInnal-lāha yuḥibbul-ladhīna yuqātilūna fī sabīlihī
ṣaffañ-kaʾannahum bunyānum-marṣūṣ. (4) Wa ʾidh
qāla Mūsā liqawmihī yā qawmi lima tuʾdhūnanī wa
qat-taʿlamūna ʾannī Rasūlul-lāhi ʾilaykum. Falamma
zāghūu ʾazāghal-lāhu qulūbahum. Wal-lāhu lā yah-
dil-qawmal-fāsiqīn. (5) Wa ʾidh qāla ʿĪsab-nu Marya-
ma yā banīi ʾIsrāaʾīla ʾinnī Rasūlul-lāhi ʾilaykum-
muṣaddiqal-limā bayna yadayya minat-Tawrāti

---

1 Lit., "Why do you say what you do not do?" In the first instance, this may be an allusion to such of the Prophet's Companions as had retreated in disorder from their battle stations at Uḥud (see *sūrah* 3, note 90) despite their previous assertions that they were ready to lay down their lives in the cause of God and His Apostle. In a wider sense, the passage is addressed to all those who claim that they are willing to live up to anything that the divine writ declares to be desirable, and then fall short of this determination.

2 I.e., in unison, with their deeds corresponding to their assertions of faith. This moral necessity is further illustrated – by its opposite – in the subsequent reference to Moses and the recalcitrant among his followers.

3 Sc., "by admitting that I speak in the name of God, and acting contrary to this your assertion": an allusion to the many instances of the contrariness and rebelliousness of the children of Israel evident from their own scriptures.

4 Thus, persistence in wrong actions is bound to react on man's beliefs as well. As regards God's "letting their hearts swerve from the truth", see *sūrah* 14, note 4. Cf. also the oft-recurring reference to God's "sealing" a sinner's heart explained in note 7 on 2 : 7.

5 Lit., "whatever there is between my hands" – a phrase explained in *sūrah* 3, note 3.

and to give [you] the glad tiding of an apostle who shall come after me, whose name shall be Aḥmad."[6]

But when he [whose coming Jesus had foretold] came unto them[7] with all evidence of the truth, they said: "This [alleged message of his] is [nothing but] spellbinding eloquence!"[8] ‹6›

And who could be more wicked than one who invents [such] a lie about [a message from] God, seeing that he is [but] being called to self-surrender unto Him?

But God does not bestow His guidance upon evildoing folk. ‹7› They aim to extinguish God's light with their utterances:[9] but God has willed to spread His light in all its fullness, however hateful this may be to all who deny the truth. ‹8›

He it is who has sent forth His Apostle with [the task of] spreading guidance and the religion of truth, to the end that He make it prevail over all [false] religion,[10] however hateful this may be to those who ascribe divinity to aught but God. ‹9›

O YOU who have attained to faith! Shall I point out to you a bargain that will save you from grievous suffering [in this world and in the life to come]?[11] ‹10›

وَمُبَشِّرًۢا بِرَسُولٍ يَأْتِي مِنۢ بَعْدِي ٱسْمُهُۥٓ أَحْمَدُ ۖ فَلَمَّا جَآءَهُم بِٱلْبَيِّنَٰتِ
قَالُوا۟ هَٰذَا سِحْرٌ مُّبِينٌ ﴿٦﴾ وَمَنْ أَظْلَمُ مِمَّنِ ٱفْتَرَىٰ عَلَى ٱللَّهِ ٱلْكَذِبَ وَهُوَ
يُدْعَىٰٓ إِلَى ٱلْإِسْلَٰمِ ۚ وَٱللَّهُ لَا يَهْدِي ٱلْقَوْمَ ٱلظَّٰلِمِينَ ﴿٧﴾ يُرِيدُونَ
لِيُطْفِـُٔوا۟ نُورَ ٱللَّهِ بِأَفْوَٰهِهِمْ وَٱللَّهُ مُتِمُّ نُورِهِۦ وَلَوْ كَرِهَ ٱلْكَٰفِرُونَ ﴿٨﴾
هُوَ ٱلَّذِيٓ أَرْسَلَ رَسُولَهُۥ بِٱلْهُدَىٰ وَدِينِ ٱلْحَقِّ لِيُظْهِرَهُۥ عَلَى ٱلدِّينِ
كُلِّهِۦ وَلَوْ كَرِهَ ٱلْمُشْرِكُونَ ﴿٩﴾ يَٰٓأَيُّهَا ٱلَّذِينَ ءَامَنُوا۟ هَلْ أَدُلُّكُمْ عَلَىٰ
تِجَٰرَةٍ تُنجِيكُم مِّنْ عَذَابٍ أَلِيمٍ ﴿١٠﴾

wa mubashshiram-biRasūliñy-yaʾtī mim-baᶜdis-muhūu ʾAḥmad. Falammā jāaʾahum bil-bayyināti qālū hādhā siḥrum-mubīn. (6) Wa man ʾaẓlamu mimmanif-tarā ᶜalal-lāhil-kadhiba wa huwa yudᶜāa ʾilal-ʾIslām. Wal-lahu lā yahdil-qawmaẓ-ẓālimīn. (7) Yurīdūna liyuṭfiʾū nūral-lāhi biʾafwāhihim wal-lāhu mutimmu nūrihī wa law karihal-kāfirūn. (8) Huwal-ladhīi ʾarsala Rasūlahū bil-hudā wa dīnil-ḥaqqi liyuẓhirahū ᶜalad-dīni kullihī wa law karihal-mushrikūn. (9) Yāa ʾayyuhal-ladhīna ʾāmanū hal ʾadullukum ᶜalā tijāratiñ-tuñjīkum-min ᶜadhābin ʾalīm. (10)

6 This prediction is supported by several references in the Gospel of St. John to the *Paráklētos* (usually rendered as "Comforter") who was to come after Jesus. This designation is almost certainly a corruption of *Períklytos* ("the Much-Praised"), an exact Greek translation of the Aramaic term or name *Mawḥamana.* (It is to be borne in mind that Aramaic was the language used in Palestine at the time of, and for some centuries after, Jesus, and was thus undoubtedly the language in which the original – now lost – texts of the Gospels were composed.) In view of the phonetic closeness of *Períklytos* and *Paráklētos* it is easy to understand how the translator – or, more probably, a later scribe – confused these two expressions. It is significant that both the Aramaic *Mawḥamana* and the Greek *Períklytos* have the same meaning as the two names of the Last Prophet, *Muḥammad* and *Aḥmad,* both of which are derived from the verb *ḥamida* ("he praised") and the noun *ḥamd* ("praise"). An even more unequivocal prediction of the advent of the Prophet Muḥammad – mentioned by name, in its Arabic form – is said to be forthcoming from the so-called Gospel of St. Barnabas, which, though now regarded as apocryphal, was accepted as authentic and was read in the churches until the year 496 of the Christian era, when it was banned as "heretical" by a decree of Pope Gelasius. However, since the original text of that Gospel is not available (having come down to us only in an Italian translation dating from the late sixteenth century), its authenticity cannot be established with certainty.

7 I.e., to the later followers of the Bible.

8 Alluding to the Qurʾān (see 74 : 24-25 and the corresponding note 12).

9 Lit., "with their mouths" – i.e., by describing God's message as "nothing but spellbinding eloquence" on the part of Muḥammad.

10 Cf. 3 : 19 – "the only [true] religion in the sight of God is [man's] self-surrender unto Him".

11 Cf. 9 : 111 – "God has bought of the believers their lives and their possessions, promising them paradise in return" – which explains the metaphor of a "bargain" (*tijārah*). My interpolation, between brackets, of the phrase "in this world and in the life to come" is justified by the subsequent verses 12 and 13, one of which relates to the here-

You are to believe in God and His Apostle, and to strive hard in God's cause with your possessions and your lives: this is for your own good – if you but knew it! ‹11›
[If you do so,] He will forgive you your sins, and [in the life to come] will admit you into gardens through which running waters flow, and into goodly mansions in [those] gardens of perpetual bliss:[12] that [will be] the triumph supreme! ‹12›
And [withal, He will grant you] yet another thing that you dearly love: succour from God [in this world], and a victory soon to come:[13] and [thereof, O Prophet,] give thou a glad tiding to all who believe. ‹13›

تُؤْمِنُونَ بِاللَّهِ وَرَسُولِهِ وَتُجَاهِدُونَ فِي سَبِيلِ اللَّهِ بِأَمْوَالِكُمْ وَأَنفُسِكُمْ
ذَٰلِكُمْ خَيْرٌ لَّكُمْ إِن كُنتُمْ تَعْلَمُونَ ﴿١١﴾ يَغْفِرْ لَكُمْ ذُنُوبَكُمْ
وَيُدْخِلْكُمْ جَنَّاتٍ تَجْرِي مِن تَحْتِهَا الْأَنْهَارُ وَمَسَاكِنَ طَيِّبَةً فِي
جَنَّاتِ عَدْنٍ ذَٰلِكَ الْفَوْزُ الْعَظِيمُ ﴿١٢﴾ وَأُخْرَىٰ تُحِبُّونَهَا نَصْرٌ مِّنَ اللَّهِ
وَفَتْحٌ قَرِيبٌ وَبَشِّرِ الْمُؤْمِنِينَ ﴿١٣﴾ يَا أَيُّهَا الَّذِينَ آمَنُوا كُونُوا أَنصَارَ
اللَّهِ كَمَا قَالَ عِيسَى ابْنُ مَرْيَمَ لِلْحَوَارِيِّينَ مَنْ أَنصَارِي إِلَى اللَّهِ قَالَ
الْحَوَارِيُّونَ نَحْنُ أَنصَارُ اللَّهِ فَآمَنَت طَّائِفَةٌ مِّن بَنِي إِسْرَائِيلَ
وَكَفَرَت طَّائِفَةٌ فَأَيَّدْنَا الَّذِينَ آمَنُوا عَلَىٰ عَدُوِّهِمْ فَأَصْبَحُوا
ظَاهِرِينَ ﴿١٤﴾

O YOU who have attained to faith! Be helpers [in the cause] of God – even as Jesus, the son of Mary, said unto the white-garbed ones,[14] "Who will be my helpers in God's cause?" – whereupon the white-garbed [disciples] replied, "We shall be [thy] helpers [in the cause] of God!"
And so [it happened that] some of the children of Israel came to believe [in the apostleship of Jesus], whereas others denied the truth.[15] But [now] We have given strength against their foes unto those who have [truly] attained to faith:[16] and they have become the ones that shall prevail. ‹14›

Tuʾminūna billāhi wa Rasūlihī wa tujāhidūna fī sabīlil-lāhi biʾamwālikum wa ʾañfusikum; dhālikum khayrul-lakum ʾiñ-kuñtum taʿlamūn. (11) Yaghfir lakum dhunūbakum wa yudkhilkum jannātiñ-tajrī miñ-taḥtihal-ʾanhāru wa masākina ṭayyibatañ-fī jannāti ʿadn. Dhālikal-fawzul-ʿaẓīm. (12) Wa ʾukhrā tuḥibbūnahā; naṣrum-minal-lāhi wa fatḥuñ-qarīb. Wa bashshiril-muʾminīn. (13) Yāa ʾayyuhal-ladhīna ʾāmanū kūnūu ʾañṣāral-lāhi kamā qāla ʿĪsab-nu Maryama lilḥawāriyyīna man ʾañṣārīi ʾilal-lāh. Qālal-ḥawāriyyūna naḥnu ʾañṣārul-lāhi faʾāmanaṭ-ṭāaʾifatum-mim-banīi ʾIsrāaʾīla wa kafaraṭ-ṭāaʾifah. Faʾayyadnal-ladhīna ʾāmanū ʿalā ʿaduwwihim faʾaṣbaḥū ẓāhirīn. (14)

after, and the other to this world.

12 For this rendering of *ʿadn*, see note 45 on 38 : 50.

13 Some of the commentators see in this promise of victory a prediction of actual, warlike conquests by the Muslims. It is, however, much more probable that it relates to a spiritual victory of the Qurʾanic message, and its spread among people who had not previously understood it.

14 For this rendering of *al-ḥawāriyyūn*, see *sūrah* 3, note 42.

15 I.e., some of them recognized him as a prophet – and, therefore, as no more than a created, human being – whereas others denied this truth in the course of time by regarding him as "the son of God" – and, therefore, as "God incarnate" – while still others rejected him and his message altogether. The fact that the earliest followers of Jesus regarded him as purely human is evident from the many theological controversies which persisted during the first three or four centuries of the Christian era. Thus, some renowned theologians, like Theodotus of Byzantium, who lived towards the end of the second century, and his followers – among them Paul of Samosata, Bishop of Antioch in the year 260 – maintained that the "sonship of God" mentioned in the then-existing texts of the Gospels was purely symbolic, denoting no more than that Jesus was a human being *exalted* by God. The originally widespread teachings of Bishop Arius (280-326) centred in the concept of Jesus as a mortal man *chosen* by God for a specific task, and in the concept of God as absolutely One, unknowable, and separate from every created being; this doctrine, however, was ultimately condemned by the Councils of Nicaea (325) and Constantinople (381), and gradually ceased to have any influence on the Christian masses.

16 I.e., all who truly believe in Jesus as God's Apostle and, thus, as a forerunner of the Last Prophet, Muḥammad, whose message confirms and expands the true message of Jesus.

The Sixty-Second Sūrah

Al-Jumuᶜah (The Congregation)

Medina Period

REVEALED in the early part of the Medina period, this *sūrah* takes its name from verses 9-10, which ordain the obligatory congregational prayer on Friday.

-62-

سورة الجمعة مدنية

وآياتها إحدى عشرة

حزب 56

IN THE NAME OF GOD, THE MOST GRACIOUS, THE DISPENSER OF GRACE:

ALL THAT IS in the heavens and all that is on earth extols the limitless glory of God, the Sovereign Supreme, the Holy, the Almighty, the Wise! ‹1›
He it is who has sent unto the unlettered people an apostle from among themselves,[1] to convey unto them His messages, and to cause them to grow in purity, and to impart unto them the divine writ as well as wisdom – whereas before that they were indeed, most obviously, lost in error; ‹2› – and [to cause this message to spread] from them unto other people as soon as they come into contact with them:[2] for He alone is almighty, truly wise! ‹3›

بِسْمِ ٱللَّهِ ٱلرَّحْمَـٰنِ ٱلرَّحِيمِ

يُسَبِّحُ لِلَّهِ مَا فِى ٱلسَّمَـٰوَٰتِ وَمَا فِى ٱلْأَرْضِ ٱلْمَلِكِ ٱلْقُدُّوسِ ٱلْعَزِيزِ
ٱلْحَكِيمِ ① هُوَ ٱلَّذِى بَعَثَ فِى ٱلْأُمِّيِّـۧنَ رَسُولًا مِّنْهُمْ يَتْلُوا۟ عَلَيْهِمْ
ءَايَـٰتِهِۦ وَيُزَكِّيهِمْ وَيُعَلِّمُهُمُ ٱلْكِتَـٰبَ وَٱلْحِكْمَةَ وَإِن كَانُوا۟ مِن قَبْلُ
لَفِى ضَلَـٰلٍ مُّبِينٍ ② وَءَاخَرِينَ مِنْهُمْ لَمَّا يَلْحَقُوا۟ بِهِمْ ۚ وَهُوَ ٱلْعَزِيزُ
ٱلْحَكِيمُ ③

Bismil-lāhir-Raḥmānir-Raḥīm.
Yusabbiḥu lillāhi mā fis-samāwāti wa mā fil-ᵓarḍil-Malikil-Quddūsil-ᶜAzīzil-Ḥakīm. ① Huwal-ladhī baᶜatha fil-ᵓummiyyīna Rasūlam-minhum yatlū ᶜalayhim ᵓĀyātihī wa yuzakkīhim wa yuᶜallimuhumul-Kitāba wal-ḥikmata wa ᵓiñ-kānū miñ-qablu lafī ḍalālim-mubīn. ② Wa ᵓākharīna minhum lammā yalḥaqū bihim; wa Huwal-ᶜAzīzul-Ḥakīm. ③

1 The term "unlettered people" (*ummiyūn*) denotes a nation or community who had not previously had a revealed scripture of their own (Rāzī). The designation of the Prophet as a man "from among themselves" is meant, in this context, to stress the fact that he, too, was unlettered (*ummī*) in the *primary* sense of this word (cf. 7 : 157 and 158), and could not, therefore, have "invented" the message of the Qurᵓān or "derived" its ideas from earlier scriptures.

2 I.e., to cause the message of the Qurᵓān to reach people of other environments and of future times through the medium of the Arabs and their language: thus stressing the universality and timeless validity of all that has been revealed to Muḥammad.

Such is God's bounty: He grants it to anyone who is willing [to receive it]:[3] for God is limitless in His great bounty. ‹4›

THE PARABLE of those who were graced with the burden of the Torah, and thereafter failed to bear this burden,[4] is that of an ass that carries a load of books [but cannot benefit from them].

Calamitous is the parable of people who are bent on giving the lie to God's messages – for God does not bestow His guidance upon such evildoing folk! ‹5›

Say: "O you who follow the Jewish faith![5] If you claim that you [alone] are close to God, to the exclusion of all other people, then you should be longing for death – if what you say is true!"[6] ‹6›

But never will they long for it, because [they are aware] of what their hands have wrought in this world;[7] and God has full knowledge of evildoers. ‹7›

Say: "Behold, the death from which you are fleeing[8] is bound to overtake you – and then you will be brought back unto Him who knows all that is beyond the reach of a created being's perception as well as all that can be witnessed by a creature's senses or mind,[9] whereupon He will make you truly understand all that you were doing [in life]." ‹8›

ذَٰلِكَ فَضْلُ ٱللَّهِ يُؤْتِيهِ مَن يَشَآءُ ۚ وَٱللَّهُ ذُو ٱلْفَضْلِ ٱلْعَظِيمِ ﴿٤﴾ مَثَلُ
ٱلَّذِينَ حُمِّلُوا۟ ٱلتَّوْرَىٰةَ ثُمَّ لَمْ يَحْمِلُوهَا كَمَثَلِ ٱلْحِمَارِ يَحْمِلُ أَسْفَارًۢا ۚ
بِئْسَ مَثَلُ ٱلْقَوْمِ ٱلَّذِينَ كَذَّبُوا۟ بِـَٔايَـٰتِ ٱللَّهِ ۚ وَٱللَّهُ لَا يَهْدِى ٱلْقَوْمَ
ٱلظَّـٰلِمِينَ ﴿٥﴾ قُلْ يَـٰٓأَيُّهَا ٱلَّذِينَ هَادُوٓا۟ إِن زَعَمْتُمْ أَنَّكُمْ أَوْلِيَآءُ لِلَّهِ مِن
دُونِ ٱلنَّاسِ فَتَمَنَّوُا۟ ٱلْمَوْتَ إِن كُنتُمْ صَـٰدِقِينَ ﴿٦﴾ وَلَا يَتَمَنَّوْنَهُۥٓ أَبَدًۢا
بِمَا قَدَّمَتْ أَيْدِيهِمْ ۚ وَٱللَّهُ عَلِيمٌۢ بِٱلظَّـٰلِمِينَ ﴿٧﴾ قُلْ إِنَّ ٱلْمَوْتَ ٱلَّذِى
تَفِرُّونَ مِنْهُ فَإِنَّهُۥ مُلَـٰقِيكُمْ ۖ ثُمَّ تُرَدُّونَ إِلَىٰ عَـٰلِمِ ٱلْغَيْبِ وَٱلشَّهَـٰدَةِ
فَيُنَبِّئُكُم بِمَا كُنتُمْ تَعْمَلُونَ ﴿٨﴾

Dhālika faḍlul-lāhi yu'tīhi mañy-yashāa'u wal-lāhu Dhul-faḍlil-ʿaẓīm. (4) Mathalul-ladhīna ḥummilut-Tawrāta thumma lam yaḥmilūhā kamathalil-ḥimāri yaḥmilu 'asfārā. Bi'sa mathalul-qawmil-ladhīna kadhdhabū bi'Āyātil-lāh. Wal-lāhu lā yahdil-qawmaẓ-ẓālimīn. (5) Qul yāa 'ayyuhal-ladhīna hādūu 'iñ-zaʿamtum 'annakum 'awliyāa'u lillāhi miñ-dūnin-nāsi fatamannawul-mawta 'iñ-kuñtum ṣādiqīn. (6) Wa lā yatamannawnahūu 'abadam-bimā qaddamat 'aydīhim. Wal-lāhu ʿAlīmum-biẓẓālimīn. (7) Qul 'innal-mawtal-ladhī tafirrūna minhu fa'innahū mulāqīkum thumma turaddūna 'ilā ʿĀlimil-ghaybi wash-shahādati fayunabbi'ukum-bimā kuñtum taʿmalūn. (8)

3 Or: "He grants it unto whomever He wills". Both these formulations are syntactically correct; but since the bounty of God referred to in this passage relates to the divine guidance granted to man through the medium of the revelation bestowed upon God's Apostle, the construction chosen by me seems to be more appropriate, expressing as it does the idea that the bounty of God's guidance is always available to one who sincerely desires it.

4 Connecting with the idea – implied in the preceding passage – that God's revelation is a sacred trust as well as a bounty, the discourse turns now to the problem of man's betrayal of this trust, exemplified by the Jews of post-Biblical times. They had been entrusted by God with the task of carrying the message of His oneness and uniqueness to all the world: but they failed in this task inasmuch as they came to believe that they were "God's chosen people" because of their descent from Abraham, Isaac and Jacob, and that, therefore, the divine message was meant for them alone and not for people of other nations. Hence, too, they came to deny the possibility of prophethood being bestowed on anyone who did not belong to the children of Israel (cf. 2 : 90 and 94, and the corresponding notes 75 and 79), and so they summarily rejected the idea of Muḥammad's prophethood despite the clear predictions of his advent in the Torah itself (see note 33 on 2 : 42). By thus corrupting the innermost purport of the divine writ bestowed on Moses, they themselves became unable to derive any real spiritual benefit from it, and to live up to its teachings.

5 I.e., in its *present* form, estranged from the original purport of the Torah.

6 For this and the next verse, cf. 2 : 94-95.

7 Lit., "of what their hands have sent ahead".

8 An allusion to what is said in 2 : 96.

9 See *sūrah* 6, note 65.

O YOU who have attained to faith! When the call to prayer is sounded on the day of congregation,[10] hasten to the remembrance of God, and leave all worldly commerce: this is for your own good, if you but knew it. ‹9› And when the prayer is ended, disperse freely on earth[11] and seek to obtain [something] of God's bounty; but remember God often, so that you might attain to a happy state! ‹10›

Yet [it does happen that] when people[12] become aware of [an occasion for] worldly gain[13] or a passing delight, they rush headlong towards it, and leave thee standing [and preaching].[14]

Say: "That which is with God is far better than all passing delight and all gain! And God is the best of providers!" ‹11›

يَـٰٓأَيُّهَا ٱلَّذِينَ ءَامَنُوٓا۟ إِذَا نُودِىَ لِلصَّلَوٰةِ مِن يَوْمِ ٱلْجُمُعَةِ فَٱسْعَوْا۟ إِلَىٰ
ذِكْرِ ٱللَّهِ وَذَرُوا۟ ٱلْبَيْعَ ۚ ذَٰلِكُمْ خَيْرٌ لَّكُمْ إِن كُنتُمْ تَعْلَمُونَ ﴿٩﴾ فَإِذَا
قُضِيَتِ ٱلصَّلَوٰةُ فَٱنتَشِرُوا۟ فِى ٱلْأَرْضِ وَٱبْتَغُوا۟ مِن فَضْلِ ٱللَّهِ وَٱذْكُرُوا۟
ٱللَّهَ كَثِيرًا لَّعَلَّكُمْ تُفْلِحُونَ ﴿١٠﴾ وَإِذَا رَأَوْا۟ تِجَـٰرَةً أَوْ لَهْوًا ٱنفَضُّوٓا۟
إِلَيْهَا وَتَرَكُوكَ قَآئِمًا ۚ قُلْ مَا عِندَ ٱللَّهِ خَيْرٌ مِّنَ ٱللَّهْوِ وَمِنَ ٱلتِّجَـٰرَةِ ۚ وَٱللَّهُ
خَيْرُ ٱلرَّٰزِقِينَ ﴿١١﴾

Yāa ʾayyuhal-ladhīna ʾāmanūu ʾidhā nūdiya liṣ-Ṣalāti miñy-yawmil-Jumuᶜati fasᶜaw ʾilā dhikril-lāhi wa dharul-bayᶜ. Dhālikum khayrul-lakum ʾiñ-kuñtum taᶜlamūn. ⁽⁹⁾ Faʾidhā quḍiyatiṣ-Ṣalātu fañtashirū fil-ʾarḍi wab-taghū miñ-faḍlil-lāhi wadh-kurul-lāha kathīral-laᶜallakum tufliḥūn. ⁽¹⁰⁾ Wa ʾidhā raʾaw tijāratan ʾaw lahwaniñ-faḍḍūu ʾilayhā wa tarakūka qāaʾimā. Qul mā ᶜiñdal-lāhi khayrum-minal-lahwi wa minat-tijārati wal-lāhu Khayrur-rāziqīn. ⁽¹¹⁾

10 I.e., on Friday, when the congregational prayer at noon is obligatory. Nevertheless, as the sequence shows, Friday is not a day of compulsory rest in Islamic Law.

11 I.e., "you may devote yourselves to worldly pursuits".

12 Lit., "they".

13 Lit., "trade" or "a bargain".

14 Sc., "O Prophet" – thus alluding to an historical incident, when most of the congregation, on hearing that a long-expected trade caravan had come from Syria, rushed out of the mosque in the midst of the Prophet's Friday-sermon. In a wider, timeless sense, the above verse contains an allusion to an all-too-human weakness against which even true believers are not always immune: namely, the tendency to overlook religious obligations for the sake of a transitory, worldly advantage.

The Sixty-Third Sūrah

Al-Munāfiqūn (The Hypocrites)

Medina Period

THE MAIN PART of this *sūrah* – most of which was revealed shortly after the battle of Uḥud (see *sūrah* 3, note 90), that is to say, towards the end of the year 3 or the beginning of 4 H. – is devoted to the problem of hypocrisy as it faced the Prophet and his followers during the early years after their exodus from Mecca to Medina. Nevertheless, the Qurʾanic treatment of this problem renders its lessons applicable to all times and circumstances.

-63-

سورة المنافقون مدنية

وآياتها إحدى عشرة

IN THE NAME OF GOD, THE MOST GRACIOUS, THE DISPENSER OF GRACE:

WHEN THE HYPOCRITES come unto thee, they say, "We bear witness that thou art indeed God's Apostle!" But God knows that thou art truly His Apostle; and He bears witness that the hypocrites are indeed false [in their declaration of faith]. ‹1›

They have made their oaths a cover [for their falseness], and thus they turn others away from the path of God.[1] Evil, indeed, is all that they are wont to do: ‹2› this, because [they profess that] they have attained to faith, whereas[2] [inwardly] they deny the truth – and so, a seal has been set on their hearts, so that they can no longer understand [what is true and what false].[3] ‹3›

بِسْمِ اللَّهِ الرَّحْمَٰنِ الرَّحِيمِ

إِذَا جَاءَكَ الْمُنَافِقُونَ قَالُوا نَشْهَدُ إِنَّكَ لَرَسُولُ اللَّهِ ۗ وَاللَّهُ يَعْلَمُ إِنَّكَ
لَرَسُولُهُ وَاللَّهُ يَشْهَدُ إِنَّ الْمُنَافِقِينَ لَكَاذِبُونَ ﴿1﴾ اتَّخَذُوا أَيْمَانَهُمْ
جُنَّةً فَصَدُّوا عَن سَبِيلِ اللَّهِ ۚ إِنَّهُمْ سَاءَ مَا كَانُوا يَعْمَلُونَ ﴿2﴾ ذَٰلِكَ
بِأَنَّهُمْ آمَنُوا ثُمَّ كَفَرُوا فَطُبِعَ عَلَىٰ قُلُوبِهِمْ فَهُمْ لَا يَفْقَهُونَ ﴿3﴾

Bismil-lāhir-Raḥmānir-Raḥīm.

ʾIdhā jāaʾakal-munāfiquna qālū nashhadu ʾinnaka laRasūlul-lāhi wal-lāhu yaʿlamu ʾinnaka laRasūluhū wal-lāhu yashhadu ʾinnal-munāfiqīna lakādhibūn. (1) **ʾIttakhadhūu ʾaymānahum junnatañ-faṣaddū ʿañ-sabīlil-lāhi ʾinnahum sāaʾa mā kānū yaʿmalūn.** (2) **Dhālika biʾannahum ʾāmanū thumma kafarū faṭubiʿa ʿalā qulūbihim fahum lā yafqahūn.** (3)

---

1 See note 26 on the identical sentence in 58 : 16.

2 The particle *thumma* ("and then") has often the same function as the simple conjunctive *wa* ("and"), which in this case may be properly rendered as "whereas".

3 See *sūrah* 2, note 7.

وَإِذَا رَأَيْتَهُمْ تُعْجِبُكَ أَجْسَامُهُمْ وَإِن يَقُولُوا تَسْمَعْ لِقَوْلِهِمْ كَأَنَّهُمْ
خُشُبٌ مُّسَنَّدَةٌ يَحْسَبُونَ كُلَّ صَيْحَةٍ عَلَيْهِمْ هُمُ الْعَدُوُّ فَاحْذَرْهُمْ قَاتَلَهُمُ
اللَّهُ أَنَّىٰ يُؤْفَكُونَ ﴿٤﴾ وَإِذَا قِيلَ لَهُمْ تَعَالَوْا يَسْتَغْفِرْ لَكُمْ رَسُولُ اللَّهِ
لَوَّوْا رُءُوسَهُمْ وَرَأَيْتَهُمْ يَصُدُّونَ وَهُم مُّسْتَكْبِرُونَ ﴿٥﴾ سَوَاءٌ عَلَيْهِمْ
أَسْتَغْفَرْتَ لَهُمْ أَمْ لَمْ تَسْتَغْفِرْ لَهُمْ لَن يَغْفِرَ اللَّهُ لَهُمْ إِنَّ اللَّهَ لَا يَهْدِي
الْقَوْمَ الْفَاسِقِينَ ﴿٦﴾ هُمُ الَّذِينَ يَقُولُونَ لَا تُنفِقُوا عَلَىٰ مَنْ عِندَ رَسُولِ اللَّهِ
حَتَّىٰ يَنفَضُّوا وَلِلَّهِ خَزَائِنُ السَّمَاوَاتِ وَالْأَرْضِ وَلَٰكِنَّ الْمُنَافِقِينَ لَا
يَفْقَهُونَ ﴿٧﴾ يَقُولُونَ لَئِن رَّجَعْنَا إِلَى الْمَدِينَةِ لَيُخْرِجَنَّ الْأَعَزُّ مِنْهَا الْأَذَلَّ

Wa ʾidhā raʾaytahum tuʿjibuka ʾajsāmuhum; wa ʾiñy-yaqūlū tasmaʿ liqawlihim; kaʾannahum khushubum-musannadah. Yaḥsabūna kulla ṣayḥatin ʿalayhim. Humul-ʿaduwwu faḥdharhum. Qātalahumul-lāhu ʾannā yuʾfakūn. (4) Wa ʾidhā qīla lahum taʿālaw yastaghfir lakum Rasūlul-lāhi lawwaw ruʾūsahum wa raʾaytahum yaṣuddūna wa hum-mustakbirūn. (5) Sawāaʾun ʿalayhim ʾastaghfarta lahum ʾam lam tastaghfir lahum lañy-yaghfiral-lāhu lahum. ʾInnal-lāha lā yahdil-qawmal-fāsiqīn. (6) Humul-ladhīna yaqūlūna lā tuñfiqū ʿalā man ʿiñda Rasūlil-lāhi ḥattā yañfaḍḍū. Wa lillāhi khazāaʾinus-samāwāti wal-ʾarḍi wa lākinnal-munāfiqīna lā yafqahūn. (7) Yaqūlūna laʾir-rajaʿnāa ʾilal-Madīnati layukhrijannal-ʾaʿazzu minhal-ʾadhall.

ربع الحزب

Now when thou seest them, their outward appearance may please thee; and when they speak, thou art inclined to lend ear to what they say.[4] [But though they may seem as sure of themselves] as if they were timbers [firmly] propped up, they think that every shout is [directed] against them.
They are the [real] enemies [of all faith], so beware of them. [They deserve the imprecation,] "May God destroy them!"[5]
How perverted are their minds![6] ‹4› – for, when they are told, "Come, the Apostle of God will pray [unto God] that you be forgiven", they turn their heads away, and thou canst see how they draw back in their false pride. ‹5› As for them, it is all the same whether thou dost pray that they be forgiven or dost not pray for them: God will not forgive them – for, behold, God does not bestow His guidance upon such iniquitous folk.[7] ‹6›
It is they who say [to their compatriots[8]], "Do not spend anything on those who are with God's Apostle, so that they [may be forced to] leave."[9]
However, unto God belong the treasures of the heavens and the earth: but this truth the hypocrites cannot grasp. ‹7›
[And] they say, "Indeed, when we return to the City,[10] [we,] the ones most worthy of honour, will surely drive out therefrom those most contemptible ones!"

4 Lit., "thou dost give ear to their words": i.e., hypocrisy has usually a plausible outward aspect inasmuch as it is *meant* to deceive.

5 Regarding my interpolation of the phrase "They deserve the imprecation", see note 45 on the identical sentence at the end of 9 : 30.

6 See *sūrah* 5, note 90.

7 Cf. 9 : 80 and the corresponding note 111.

8 I.e., to the people of Medina in general, and to the *anṣār* in particular (see next note).

9 The leader of the hypocrites of Medina, ʿAbd Allāh ibn Ubayy, never forgave the Prophet for having overshadowed him who previously had been unquestioningly recognized by the people of Medina as their most outstanding leader. Since the Prophet's political strength depended mainly on the Meccan Muslims who followed him in his *hijrah* to Medina, Ibn Ubayy tried to persuade his compatriots – many of whom were supporting the newcomers with all the means at their disposal – to withdraw this material support and thereby force the *muhājirūn*, most of whom were very poor, to leave Medina: a stratagem which, if successful, would have greatly weakened the Prophet's position. This suggestion of the leader of the hypocrites was, of course, rejected by the *anṣār*.

10 I.e., Medina, the "City of the Prophet" (*Madīnat an-Nabī*), as the town previously called Yathrib began to be known after the *hijrah*. Since – as is established through several *aḥādīth* – the subsequent saying was uttered by ʿAbd

However, all honour belongs to God, and [thus] to His Apostle and those who believe [in God]: but of this the hypocrites are not aware.[11] ‹8›

O YOU who have attained to faith! Let not your worldly goods or your children make you oblivious of the remembrance of God: for if any behave thus – it is they, they who are the losers! ‹9›

And spend on others out of what We have provided for you as sustenance,[12] ere there come a time when death approaches any of you, and he then says, "O my Sustainer! If only Thou wouldst grant me a delay for a short while,[13] so that I could give in charity and be among the righteous!" ‹10›

But never does God grant a delay to a human being when his term has come; and God is fully aware of all that you do. ‹11›

وَلِلَّهِ ٱلۡعِزَّةُ وَلِرَسُولِهِۦ وَلِلۡمُؤۡمِنِينَ وَلَٰكِنَّ ٱلۡمُنَٰفِقِينَ لَا يَعۡلَمُونَ ﴿٨﴾
يَٰٓأَيُّهَا ٱلَّذِينَ ءَامَنُواْ لَا تُلۡهِكُمۡ أَمۡوَٰلُكُمۡ وَلَآ أَوۡلَٰدُكُمۡ عَن ذِكۡرِ ٱللَّهِۚ
وَمَن يَفۡعَلۡ ذَٰلِكَ فَأُوْلَٰٓئِكَ هُمُ ٱلۡخَٰسِرُونَ ﴿٩﴾ وَأَنفِقُواْ مِن مَّا
رَزَقۡنَٰكُم مِّن قَبۡلِ أَن يَأۡتِيَ أَحَدَكُمُ ٱلۡمَوۡتُ فَيَقُولَ رَبِّ لَوۡلَآ أَخَّرۡتَنِيٓ
إِلَىٰٓ أَجَلٖ قَرِيبٖ فَأَصَّدَّقَ وَأَكُن مِّنَ ٱلصَّٰلِحِينَ ﴿١٠﴾ وَلَن يُؤَخِّرَ ٱللَّهُ
نَفۡسًا إِذَا جَآءَ أَجَلُهَاۚ وَٱللَّهُ خَبِيرُۢ بِمَا تَعۡمَلُونَ ﴿١١﴾

Wa lillāhil-ʿizzatu wa liRasulihī wa lilmuʾminīna wa lākinnal-munāfiqīna lā yaʿlamūn. (8) Yāa ʾayyuhal-ladhīna ʾāmanū lā tulhikum ʾamwālukum wa lāa ʾawlādukum ʿañ-dhikril-lāh. Wa mañy-yafʿal dhālika faʾulāaʾika humul-khāsirūn. (9) Wa ʾañfiqū mimmā razaqnākum-miñ-qabli ʾañy-yaʾtiya ʾaḥadakumul-mawtu fayaqūla Rabbi lawlāa ʾakhkhartanīi ʾilāa ʾajaliñ-qarībiñ-faʾaṣṣaddaqa wa ʾakum-minaṣ-ṣāliḥīn. (10) Wa lañy-yuʾakhkhiral-lāhu nafsan ʾidhā jāaʾa ʾajaluhā; wal-lāhu Khabīrum-bimā taʿmalūn. (11)

Allāh ibn Ubayy during the campaign against the tribe of Banū Muṣṭaliq in 5 H., it is obvious that verses 7 and 8 were revealed at the same date or a little later.

11 It is in these two Qurʾanic statements – "unto God belong the treasures . . .", etc., and "all honour belongs to God . . .", etc. – that the real, lasting purport of the above historical allusions is to be found.

12 See *sūrah* 2, note 4.

13 Lit., "for (*ilā*) a term close-by".

The Sixty-Fourth Sūrah

At-Taghābun (Loss and Gain)

Period Uncertain

THE MAJORITY of the commentators regard this *sūrah* as belonging to the Medina period, but many others are of the opinion that it is a late Meccan revelation.

The expression *taghābun,* occurring in verse 9, has become the key-word by which this *sūrah* is designated.

-64-
سورة التغابن مدنية
وآياتها ثماني عشرة

IN THE NAME OF GOD, THE MOST GRACIOUS, THE DISPENSER OF GRACE:

ALL THAT IS in the heavens and all that is on earth extols God's limitless glory: His is all dominion, and to Him all praise is due; and He has the power to will anything. ‹1›
He it is who has created you: and among you are such as deny this truth, and among you are such as believe [in it].[1] And God sees all that you do. ‹2›
He has created the heavens and the earth in accordance with [an inner] truth,[2] and has formed you – and formed you so well;[3] and with Him is your journey's end. ‹3›

بِسْمِ ٱللَّهِ ٱلرَّحْمَٰنِ ٱلرَّحِيمِ

يُسَبِّحُ لِلَّهِ مَا فِي ٱلسَّمَٰوَٰتِ وَمَا فِي ٱلْأَرْضِ لَهُ ٱلْمُلْكُ وَلَهُ ٱلْحَمْدُ وَهُوَ
عَلَىٰ كُلِّ شَيْءٍ قَدِيرٌ ﴿١﴾ هُوَ ٱلَّذِي خَلَقَكُمْ فَمِنكُمْ كَافِرٌ وَمِنكُم
مُّؤْمِنٌ وَٱللَّهُ بِمَا تَعْمَلُونَ بَصِيرٌ ﴿٢﴾ خَلَقَ ٱلسَّمَٰوَٰتِ وَٱلْأَرْضَ بِٱلْحَقِّ
وَصَوَّرَكُمْ فَأَحْسَنَ صُوَرَكُمْ وَإِلَيْهِ ٱلْمَصِيرُ ﴿٣﴾

Bismil-lāhir-Raḥmānir-Raḥīm.
Yusabbiḥu lillāhi mā fis-samāwāti wa mā fil-ʾarḍi lahul-mulku wa lahul-ḥamdu wa Huwa ʿalā kulli shayʾiñ-Qadīr. (1) Huwal-ladhī khalaqakum famiñkum kāfiruñw-wa miñkum muʾmin. Wal-lāhu bimā taʿmalūna Baṣīr. (2) Khalaqas-samāwāti wal-ʾarḍa bil-ḥaqqi wa ṣawwarakum faʾaḥsana ṣuwarakum wa ʾilayhil-maṣīr. (3)

1 The above construction, pointing to man's acceptance or denial of the truth of God's creative activity, is in accord with Ṭabarī's interpretation of this passage, as well as with that of Az-Zajjāj (quoted by Rāzī). According to Zamakhsharī, those who deny this truth are mentioned first because they are more numerous and possess greater influence than those who consciously believe in God. A further implication appears to be this: Since all human beings are endowed with the instinctive ability to perceive the existence of the Creator (cf. 7 : 172 and the corresponding note 139), one man's denial of this truth and another's belief in it is, in the last resort, an outcome of free choice.

2 See *sūrah* 10, note 11.

3 I.e., in accordance with the exigencies of human life. See also note 9 on 7 : 11.

He knows all that is in the heavens and on earth; and He knows all that you keep secret as well as all that you bring into the open: for God has full knowledge of what is in the hearts [of men]. ‹4›

HAVE THE STORIES of those who, in earlier times, refused to acknowledge the truth never yet come within your ken? [They denied it –] and so they had to taste the evil outcome of their own doings,[4] with [more] grievous suffering awaiting them [in the life to come]: ‹5› this, because time and again there came unto them their apostles[5] with all evidence of the truth, but they [always] replied, "Shall mere mortal men be our guides?"[6] And so they denied the truth and turned away.
But God was not in need [of them]: for God is self-sufficient, ever to be praised. ‹6›
They who are bent on denying the truth claim that they will never be raised from the dead![7]
Say: "Yea, by my Sustainer! Most surely will you be raised from the dead, and then, most surely, will you be made to understand what you did [in life]! For, easy is this for God!" ‹7›
Believe, then, [O men,] in God and His Apostle, and in the light [of revelation] which We have bestowed [on you] from on high! And God is fully aware of all that you do. ‹8›
[Think of[8]] the time when He shall gather you all together unto the Day of the [Last] Gathering – that Day of Loss and Gain!

يَعْلَمُ مَا فِى ٱلسَّمَـٰوَٰتِ وَٱلْأَرْضِ وَيَعْلَمُ مَا تُسِرُّونَ وَمَا تُعْلِنُونَ ۚ وَٱللَّهُ عَلِيمٌۢ
بِذَاتِ ٱلصُّدُورِ ﴿٤﴾ أَلَمْ يَأْتِكُمْ نَبَؤُا۟ ٱلَّذِينَ كَفَرُوا۟ مِن قَبْلُ فَذَاقُوا۟ وَبَالَ
أَمْرِهِمْ وَلَهُمْ عَذَابٌ أَلِيمٌ ﴿٥﴾ ذَٰلِكَ بِأَنَّهُۥ كَانَت تَّأْتِيهِمْ رُسُلُهُم بِٱلْبَيِّنَـٰتِ
فَقَالُوٓا۟ أَبَشَرٌ يَهْدُونَنَا فَكَفَرُوا۟ وَتَوَلَّوا۟ ۚ وَّٱسْتَغْنَى ٱللَّهُ ۚ وَٱللَّهُ غَنِىٌّ حَمِيدٌ ﴿٦﴾
زَعَمَ ٱلَّذِينَ كَفَرُوٓا۟ أَن لَّن يُبْعَثُوا۟ ۚ قُلْ بَلَىٰ وَرَبِّى لَتُبْعَثُنَّ ثُمَّ لَتُنَبَّؤُنَّ بِمَا عَمِلْتُمْ ۚ
وَذَٰلِكَ عَلَى ٱللَّهِ يَسِيرٌ ﴿٧﴾ فَـَٔامِنُوا۟ بِٱللَّهِ وَرَسُولِهِۦ وَٱلنُّورِ ٱلَّذِىٓ أَنزَلْنَا ۚ وَٱللَّهُ
بِمَا تَعْمَلُونَ خَبِيرٌ ﴿٨﴾ يَوْمَ يَجْمَعُكُمْ لِيَوْمِ ٱلْجَمْعِ ۖ ذَٰلِكَ يَوْمُ ٱلتَّغَابُنِ ۗ

Yaʿlamu mā fis-samāwāti wal-ʾarḍi wa yaʿlamu mā tusirrūna wa mā tuʿlinūn. Wal-lāhu ʿAlīmum-bidhātiṣ-ṣudūr. (4) ʾAlam yaʾtikum nabaʾul-ladhīna kafarū miñ-qablu fadhāqū wabāla ʾamrihim wa lahum ʿadhābun ʾalīm. (5) Dhālika biʾannahū kānat-taʾtīhim Rusuluhum bilbayyināti faqālūu ʾabasharuñy-yahdūnanā fakafarū wa tawallaw. Was-taghnal-lāhu wal-lāhu Ghaniyyun Ḥamīd. (6) Zaʿamal-ladhīna kafarūu ʾal-lañy-yubʿathū. Qul balā wa Rabbī latubʿathunna thumma latunabbaʾunna bimā ʿamiltum. Wa dhālika ʿalal-lāhi yasīr. (7) Faʾāminū billāhi wa Rasūlihī wan-Nūril-ladhīi ʾañzalnā. Wal-lāhu bimā taʿmalūna Khabīr. (8) Yawma yajmaʿukum liYawmil-Jamʿi dhālika Yawmut-Taghābun.

4 This is an allusion to the disasters and the suffering which, as history shows, inevitably befall every community or nation bent on rejecting the basic ethical truths and, thus, all standards of morality.

5 I.e., apostles from their own midst, entrusted with divine messages specifically meant for them. The expression "time and again" is conditioned by the phrase *kānat taʾtīhim*, which implies repetition and duration.

6 Lit., "guide us". This negative response is characteristic of people who, in result of their own estrangement from all moral standards, are instinctively, and deeply, distrustful of all things human and cannot, therefore, accept the idea that a divine message could manifest itself through mere human beings that have nothing "supernatural" about them.

7 Their refusal to believe in resurrection and a life to come implies a conviction that no one will be called upon, after death, to answer for what he did in life.

8 This or a similar interpolation is necessary in view of the *manṣūb* form of the subsequent noun, *yawma* (lit., "day"), which I am rendering in this context as "the time".

For, as for him who shall have believed in God and done what is just and right, He will [on that Day] efface his bad deeds, and will admit him into gardens through which running waters flow, therein to abide beyond the count of time: that will be a triumph supreme! ‹9›
But as for those who are bent on denying the truth and on giving the lie to Our messages – they are destined for the fire, therein to abide: and how vile a journey's end! ‹10›

NO CALAMITY can ever befall [man] unless it be by God's leave: hence, whoever believes in God guides his [own] heart [towards this truth];[9] and God has full knowledge of everything. ‹11›
Pay heed, then, unto God, and pay heed unto the Apostle; and if you turn away, [know that] Our Apostle's only duty is a clear delivery of this message: ‹12› God – there is no deity save Him![10]
In God, then, let the believers place their trust. ‹13›

O YOU who have attained to faith! Behold, some of your spouses[11] and your children are enemies unto you: so beware of them![12] But if you pardon [their faults], and forbear, and forgive – then, behold, God will be much-forgiving, a dispenser of grace. ‹14›

وَمَن يُؤْمِنۢ بِٱللَّهِ وَيَعْمَلْ صَٰلِحًا يُكَفِّرْ عَنْهُ سَيِّـَٔاتِهِۦ وَيُدْخِلْهُ جَنَّٰتٍ
تَجْرِى مِن تَحْتِهَا ٱلْأَنْهَٰرُ خَٰلِدِينَ فِيهَآ أَبَدًا ۚ ذَٰلِكَ ٱلْفَوْزُ ٱلْعَظِيمُ ﴿٩﴾
وَٱلَّذِينَ كَفَرُوا۟ وَكَذَّبُوا۟ بِـَٔايَٰتِنَآ أُو۟لَٰٓئِكَ أَصْحَٰبُ ٱلنَّارِ خَٰلِدِينَ فِيهَا
وَبِئْسَ ٱلْمَصِيرُ ﴿١٠﴾ مَآ أَصَابَ مِن مُّصِيبَةٍ إِلَّا بِإِذْنِ ٱللَّهِ ۗ وَمَن يُؤْمِنۢ
بِٱللَّهِ يَهْدِ قَلْبَهُۥ ۚ وَٱللَّهُ بِكُلِّ شَىْءٍ عَلِيمٌ ﴿١١﴾ وَأَطِيعُوا۟ ٱللَّهَ وَأَطِيعُوا۟
ٱلرَّسُولَ ۚ فَإِن تَوَلَّيْتُمْ فَإِنَّمَا عَلَىٰ رَسُولِنَا ٱلْبَلَٰغُ ٱلْمُبِينُ ﴿١٢﴾ ٱللَّهُ لَآ إِلَٰهَ
إِلَّا هُوَ ۚ وَعَلَى ٱللَّهِ فَلْيَتَوَكَّلِ ٱلْمُؤْمِنُونَ ﴿١٣﴾ يَٰٓأَيُّهَا ٱلَّذِينَ ءَامَنُوٓا۟ إِنَّ مِنْ
أَزْوَٰجِكُمْ وَأَوْلَٰدِكُمْ عَدُوًّا لَّكُمْ فَٱحْذَرُوهُمْ ۚ وَإِن تَعْفُوا۟ وَتَصْفَحُوا۟
وَتَغْفِرُوا۟ فَإِنَّ ٱللَّهَ غَفُورٌ رَّحِيمٌ ﴿١٤﴾

Wa mañy-yuʾmim-billāhi wa yaʿmal ṣāliḥañy-yukaffir ʿanhu sayyiʾātihī wa yudkhilhu jannātiñ-tajrī miñ-taḥtihal-ʾanhāru khālidīna fīhāa ʾabadā. Dhālikal-fawzul-ʿaẓīm. (9) Wal-ladhīna kafarū wa kadhdhabū biʾĀyātināa ʾulāaʾika ʾaṣḥābun-nāri khālidīna fīhā wa biʾsal-maṣīr. (10) Māa ʾaṣāba mim-muṣībatin ʾillā biʾidhnil-lāh. Wa mañy-yuʾmim-billāhi yahdi qalbahū wal-lāhu bikulli shayʾin ʿAlīm. (11) Wa ʾaṭīʿul-lāha wa ʾaṭīʿur-Rasūl. Faʾiñ-tawallaytum faʾinnamā ʿalā Rasūlinal-balāghul-mubīn. (12) ʾAllāhu lāa ʾilāha ʾillā Huwa wa ʿalal-lāhi falyatawakkalil-muʾminūn. (13) Yāa ʾayyuhal-ladhīna ʾāmanūu ʾinna min ʾazwājikum wa ʾawlādikum ʿaduwwal-lakum faḥdharūhum. Wa ʾiñ-taʿfū wa taṣfaḥū wa taghfirū faʾinnal-lāha Ghafūrur-Raḥīm. (14)

9 I.e., in the words of Rāzī, "towards self-surrender to God's will . . . [and so] towards gratitude in times of ease, and patience in times of misfortune". It is also possible – as some of the commentators do – to understand the phrase in another sense, namely, "if anyone believes in God, He [i.e., God] guides his heart". However, the rendering adopted by me seems to be preferable inasmuch as it stresses the idea that conscious belief in God impels man's *reason* to control and direct his emotions and inclinations in accordance with all that this belief implies.

10 The above construction of this passage makes it clear, firstly, that a realization of God's existence, oneness and almightiness is the innermost purport – and, thus, the beginning and the end – of God's message to man; and, secondly, that His prophets can do no more than deliver and expound this message, leaving it to man's reason and free choice to accept or reject it.

11 I.e., "*sometimes*, your spouses . . .", etc. Since, in the teachings of the Qurʾān, all moral duties are binding on women as well as on men, it is obvious that the term *azwājikum* must not be rendered as "your wives", but is to be understood – according to classical Arabic usage – as applying equally to both the male and the female partners in a marriage.

12 Love of his or her family may sometimes tempt a believer to act contrary to the demands of conscience and faith; and, occasionally, one or another of the loved ones – whether wife or husband or child – may consciously try to *induce* the person concerned to abandon some of his or her moral commitments in order to satisfy some real or

Your worldly goods and your children are but a trial and a temptation,[13] whereas with God there is a tremendous reward. ‹15›
Remain, then, conscious of God as best you can, and listen [to Him], and pay heed. And spend in charity for the good of your own selves: for, such as from their own covetousness are saved – it is they, they that shall attain to a happy state![14] ‹16›
If you offer up to God a goodly loan, He will amply repay you for it, and will forgive you your sins: for God is ever responsive to gratitude, forbearing, ‹17› knowing all that is beyond the reach of a created being's perception as well as all that can be witnessed by a creature's senses or mind[15] – the Almighty, the Wise! ‹18›

إِنَّمَآ أَمۡوَٰلُكُمۡ وَأَوۡلَٰدُكُمۡ فِتۡنَةٞۚ وَٱللَّهُ عِندَهُۥٓ أَجۡرٌ عَظِيمٞ ﴿١٥﴾ فَٱتَّقُواْ ٱللَّهَ
مَا ٱسۡتَطَعۡتُمۡ وَٱسۡمَعُواْ وَأَطِيعُواْ وَأَنفِقُواْ خَيۡرٗا لِّأَنفُسِكُمۡۗ وَمَن يُوقَ شُحَّ
نَفۡسِهِۦ فَأُوْلَٰٓئِكَ هُمُ ٱلۡمُفۡلِحُونَ ﴿١٦﴾ إِن تُقۡرِضُواْ ٱللَّهَ قَرۡضًا حَسَنٗا
يُضَٰعِفۡهُ لَكُمۡ وَيَغۡفِرۡ لَكُمۡۚ وَٱللَّهُ شَكُورٌ حَلِيمٌ ﴿١٧﴾ عَٰلِمُ ٱلۡغَيۡبِ
وَٱلشَّهَٰدَةِ ٱلۡعَزِيزُ ٱلۡحَكِيمُ ﴿١٨﴾

ʾInnamāa ʾamwālukum wa ʾawlādukum fitnah. Wal-lāhu ᶜin̄dahūu ʾajrun ᶜaẓīm. (15) Fattaqul-lāha mas-taṭaᶜtum was-maᶜū wa ʾaṭīᶜū wa ʾan̄fiqū khayral-liʾan̄fusikum. Wa man̄y-yūqa shuḥḥa nafsihī faʾulāa-ʾika humul-mufliḥūn. (16) ʾIn̄-tuqriḍul-lāha qarḍan ḥasanan̄y-yuḍāᶜifhu lakum wa yaghfir la-kum; wal-lāhu Shakūrun Ḥalīm. (17) ᶜĀlimul-ghaybi wash-shahādatil-ᶜAzīzul-Ḥakīm. (18)

imaginary "family interest", and thus becomes the other's spiritual "enemy". It is to this latter eventuality that the next sentence alludes.

13 For an explanation, see note 28 on 8 : 28, which is almost identical with the present passage.

14 Cf. last sentence of 59 : 9 and the corresponding note 14.

15 See *sūrah* 6, note 65.

The Sixty-Fifth Sūrah

Aṭ-Ṭalāq (Divorce)

Medina Period

THE WHOLE of this *sūrah* (revealed about the middle of the Medina period) is devoted to one particular aspect of the problem of divorce, namely, to ordinances relating to the waiting-period which divorced women must undergo before the marriage is finally dissolved and they are allowed to remarry – thus amplifying and elucidating verses 228-233 of *Al-Baqarah*.

سورة الطلاق -65- مدنية
وآياتها اثنتا عشرة

IN THE NAME OF GOD, THE MOST GRACIOUS, THE DISPENSER OF GRACE:

بِسۡمِ ٱللَّهِ ٱلرَّحۡمَٰنِ ٱلرَّحِيمِ

O PROPHET! When you[1] [intend to] divorce women, divorce them with a view to the waiting-period appointed for them,[2] and reckon the period [carefully], and be conscious of God, your Sustainer.

نصف الحزب

Do not expel them from their homes;[3] and neither shall they [be made to] leave[4] unless they become openly guilty of immoral conduct.[5]

يَٰٓأَيُّهَا ٱلنَّبِيُّ إِذَا طَلَّقۡتُمُ ٱلنِّسَآءَ فَطَلِّقُوهُنَّ لِعِدَّتِهِنَّ وَأَحۡصُواْ ٱلۡعِدَّةَۖ وَٱتَّقُواْ ٱللَّهَ
رَبَّكُمۡۖ لَا تُخۡرِجُوهُنَّ مِنۢ بُيُوتِهِنَّ وَلَا يَخۡرُجۡنَ إِلَّآ أَن يَأۡتِينَ بِفَٰحِشَةٖ مُّبَيِّنَةٖۚ

Bismil-lāhir-Raḥmānir-Raḥīm.
Yāa ʾayyuhan-Nabiyyu ʾidhā ṭallaqtumun-nisāaʾa fa̱ṭalliqūhunna liʿiddatihinna wa ʾaḥṣul-ʿiddatata wat-taqul-lāha Rabbakum. Lā tukhrijūhunna mim-buyūtihinna wa lā yakhrujna ʾillāa ʾañy-yaʾtīna bifāḥishatim-mubayyinah.

---

1 The plural "you" indicates that the whole community is thus addressed.

2 See 2 : 228 and the corresponding notes, especially note 215. – Most of the great jurists hold the view that the required *three* pronouncements of divorce, which make it final and irrevocable (cf. first paragraph of 2 : 229), must be made singly, i.e., spaced over the waiting-period of three months, so as to give the husband time to reconsider his intention, and thus to prevent a hasty act which might be subsequently regretted. This provision is in tune with the well-authenticated saying of the Prophet, "In the sight of God, the most hateful of all things allowed (*abghaḍ al-ḥalāli*) is divorce" (Abū Dāʾūd, on the authority of ʿAbd Allāh ibn ʿUmar). In other words, divorce is just barely permissible, and must not be resorted to unless it is absolutely evident that nothing can save the marriage from utter hopelessness.

3 I.e., during the waiting-period. As shown in verse 6 below, during that period the husband is fully responsible for the maintenance of the wife whom he is divorcing in accordance with the standard of living observed during their married life.

4 E.g., by their husbands' failure to provide for their maintenance. (This particular injunction does *not* imply a prohibition of a divorced woman's leaving her home of her own free will.)

5 Implying that in such a case she *may* be lawfully turned out of her marital home. Regarding the term *fāḥishah* ("immoral conduct"), see *sūrah* 4, note 14.

وَتِلْكَ حُدُودُ ٱللَّهِ ۚ وَمَن يَتَعَدَّ حُدُودَ ٱللَّهِ فَقَدْ ظَلَمَ نَفْسَهُۥ ۚ لَا تَدْرِى لَعَلَّ ٱللَّهَ
يُحْدِثُ بَعْدَ ذَٰلِكَ أَمْرًا ﴿١﴾ فَإِذَا بَلَغْنَ أَجَلَهُنَّ فَأَمْسِكُوهُنَّ بِمَعْرُوفٍ
أَوْ فَارِقُوهُنَّ بِمَعْرُوفٍ وَأَشْهِدُوا۟ ذَوَىْ عَدْلٍ مِّنكُمْ وَأَقِيمُوا۟ ٱلشَّهَٰدَةَ لِلَّهِ ۚ
ذَٰلِكُمْ يُوعَظُ بِهِۦ مَن كَانَ يُؤْمِنُ بِٱللَّهِ وَٱلْيَوْمِ ٱلْـَٔاخِرِ ۚ وَمَن يَتَّقِ ٱللَّهَ
يَجْعَل لَّهُۥ مَخْرَجًا ﴿٢﴾ وَيَرْزُقْهُ مِنْ حَيْثُ لَا يَحْتَسِبُ ۚ وَمَن يَتَوَكَّلْ عَلَى
ٱللَّهِ فَهُوَ حَسْبُهُۥٓ ۚ إِنَّ ٱللَّهَ بَٰلِغُ أَمْرِهِۦ ۚ قَدْ جَعَلَ ٱللَّهُ لِكُلِّ شَىْءٍ قَدْرًا ﴿٣﴾
وَٱلَّٰٓـِٔى يَئِسْنَ مِنَ ٱلْمَحِيضِ مِن نِّسَآئِكُمْ إِنِ ٱرْتَبْتُمْ فَعِدَّتُهُنَّ ثَلَٰثَةُ
أَشْهُرٍ وَٱلَّٰٓـِٔى لَمْ يَحِضْنَ ۚ وَأُو۟لَٰتُ ٱلْأَحْمَالِ أَجَلُهُنَّ أَن يَضَعْنَ حَمْلَهُنَّ ۚ
وَمَن يَتَّقِ ٱللَّهَ يَجْعَل لَّهُۥ مِنْ أَمْرِهِۦ يُسْرًا ﴿٤﴾ ذَٰلِكَ أَمْرُ ٱللَّهِ أَنزَلَهُۥٓ

Wa tilka ḥudūdul-lāhi wa mañy-yataʿadda ḥudūdal-lāhi faqad ẓalama nafsah. Lā tadrī laʿallal-lāha yuḥdithu baʿda dhālika ʾamrā. (1) Faʾidhā balaghna ʾajalahunna faʾamsikūhunna bimaʿrūfin ʾaw fāriqūhunna bimaʿrūfiñw-wa ʾashhidū dhaway ʿadlim-miñkum wa ʾaqīmush-shahādata lillāh. Dhālikum yūʿaẓu bihī mañ-kāna yuʾminu billāhi wal-Yawmil-ʾĀkhir. Wa mañy-yattaqil-lāha yajʿal lahū makhrajā. (2) Wa yarzuqhu min ḥaythu lā yaḥtasib. Wa mañy-yatawakkal ʿalal-lāhi faHuwa ḥasbuh. ʾInnal-lāha bālighu ʾamrih. Qad jaʿalal-lāhu likulli shayʾiñ-qadrā. (3) Wal-lāaʾī yaʾisna minal-maḥīḍi miñ-nisāaʾikum ʾinir-tabtum faʿiddatuhunna thalāthatu ʾashhuriñw-wal-lāaʾī lam yaḥiḍn. Wa ʾulātul-ʾaḥmāli ʾajaluhunna ʾañy-yaḍaʿna ḥamlahunn. Wa mañy-yattaqil-lāha yajʿal-lahū min ʾamrihī yusrā. (4) Dhālika ʾamrul-lāhi ʾañzalahūu

These, then, are the bounds set by God – and he who transgresses the bounds set by God does indeed sin against himself: [for, O man, although] thou knowest it not, after that [first breach] God may well cause something new to come about.[6] «1»
And so, when they are about to reach the end of their waiting-term, either retain them in a fair manner or part with them in a fair manner. And let two persons of [known] probity from among your own community[7] witness [what you have decided]; and do yourselves bear true witness before God:[8] thus are admonished all who believe in God and the Last Day.
And unto everyone who is conscious of God, He [always] grants a way out [of unhappiness], «2» and provides for him in a manner beyond all expectation;[9] and for everyone who places his trust in God, He [alone] is enough.
Verily, God always attains to His purpose: [and] indeed, unto everything has God appointed its [term and] measure. «3»
Now as for such of your women as are beyond the age of monthly courses, as well as for such as do not have any courses,[10] their waiting-period – if you have any doubt [about it] – shall be three [lunar] months; and as for those who are with child, the end of their waiting-term shall come when they deliver their burden. And for everyone who is conscious of God, He makes it easy to obey His commandment:[11] «4» [for] all this is God's commandment, which He has bestowed

6 According to Ibn ʿAbbās (as quoted by Rāzī) and several other authorities (see Ibn Kathīr), this is an allusion to the possibility of reconciliation and, hence, a resumption of marital relations before the divorce becomes final (see *sūrah* 2, second part of verse 228 and first paragraph of 229).

7 Lit., "from yourselves": i.e., persons who are sufficiently acquainted with the circumstances of the case.

8 Sc., that the relevant decision has not been made in a frivolous spirit.

9 Lit., "whence he does not expect". It is to be noted that the relative pronoun *man* ("whoever" or "everyone who") – although grammatically requiring the use of the masculine gender in the verbs or pronouns to which it relates – applies to *persons of either sex*, as is evidenced by innumerable passages in the Qurʾān: hence, the present passage, too, including the sentence that follows, must be understood as relating to the women as well as to the men in question; and the same holds good of verses 5 and 11 below.

10 I.e., for any physiological reason whatever.

11 Lit., "He grants ease out of his condition" – i.e., makes his condition easy: the implication being that God-consciousness makes it easy for the believer to submit gladly to whatever God may decree.

upon you from on high. And unto everyone who is conscious of God will He pardon [some of] his bad deeds, and will grant him a vast reward. ‹5›

[Hence,] let the women [who are undergoing a waiting-period] live in the same manner as you live yourselves,[12] in accordance with your means; and do not harass them with a view to making their lives a misery. And if they happen to be with child, spend freely on them until they deliver their burden; and if they nurse your offspring [after the divorce has become final], give them their [due] recompense; and take counsel with one another in a fair manner [about the child's future]. And if both of you find it difficult [that the mother should nurse the child],[13] let another woman nurse it on behalf of him [who has begotten it].[14] ‹6›

[In all these respects,] let him who has ample means spend in accordance with[15] his amplitude; and let him whose means of subsistence are scanty spend in accordance with what God has given him: God does not burden any human being with more than He has given him – [and it may well be that] God will grant, after hardship, ease. ‹7›

AND HOW MANY a community has turned with disdain from the commandment of its Sustainer and His apostles![16] – whereupon We called them all to account with an accounting severe, and caused them to suffer with a suffering unnameable: ‹8› and thus they had to taste the evil outcome of their own doings:[17] for, [in this world,] the end of their doings was ruin, ‹9› [the while] God has readied for them [yet more] suffering severe [in the life to come].

إِلَيْكُمْ ۚ وَمَن يَتَّقِ ٱللَّهَ يُكَفِّرْ عَنْهُ سَيِّـَٔاتِهِۦ وَيُعْظِمْ لَهُۥٓ أَجْرًا ﴿٥﴾
أَسْكِنُوهُنَّ مِنْ حَيْثُ سَكَنتُم مِّن وُجْدِكُمْ وَلَا تُضَآرُّوهُنَّ لِتُضَيِّقُوا۟
عَلَيْهِنَّ ۚ وَإِن كُنَّ أُو۟لَـٰتِ حَمْلٍ فَأَنفِقُوا۟ عَلَيْهِنَّ حَتَّىٰ يَضَعْنَ حَمْلَهُنَّ ۚ فَإِنْ
أَرْضَعْنَ لَكُمْ فَـَٔاتُوهُنَّ أُجُورَهُنَّ ۖ وَأْتَمِرُوا۟ بَيْنَكُم بِمَعْرُوفٍ ۖ وَإِن تَعَاسَرْتُمْ
فَسَتُرْضِعُ لَهُۥٓ أُخْرَىٰ ﴿٦﴾ لِيُنفِقْ ذُو سَعَةٍ مِّن سَعَتِهِۦ ۖ وَمَن قُدِرَ عَلَيْهِ
رِزْقُهُۥ فَلْيُنفِقْ مِمَّآ ءَاتَىٰهُ ٱللَّهُ ۚ لَا يُكَلِّفُ ٱللَّهُ نَفْسًا إِلَّا مَآ ءَاتَىٰهَا ۚ سَيَجْعَلُ
ٱللَّهُ بَعْدَ عُسْرٍ يُسْرًا ﴿٧﴾ وَكَأَيِّن مِّن قَرْيَةٍ عَتَتْ عَنْ أَمْرِ رَبِّهَا وَرُسُلِهِۦ
فَحَاسَبْنَـٰهَا حِسَابًا شَدِيدًا وَعَذَّبْنَـٰهَا عَذَابًا نُّكْرًا ﴿٨﴾ فَذَاقَتْ وَبَالَ
أَمْرِهَا وَكَانَ عَـٰقِبَةُ أَمْرِهَا خُسْرًا ﴿٩﴾ أَعَدَّ ٱللَّهُ لَهُمْ عَذَابًا شَدِيدًا

ʾilaykum; wa mañy-yattaqil-lāha yukaffir ᶜanhu sayyiʾātihī wa yuᶜẓim lahūu ʾajrā. (5) ʾAskinūhunna min ḥaythu sakañtum-miñw-wujdikum wa lā tuḍāarrūhunna lituḍayyiqū ᶜalayhinn. Wa ʾiñ-kunna ʾulāti ḥamliñ-faʾañfiqū ᶜalayhinna ḥattā yaḍaᶜna ḥamlahunn. Faʾin ʾarḍaᶜna lakum faʾātūhunna ʾujūrahunna waʾ-tamirū baynakum bimaᶜrūf. Wa ʾiñ-taᶜāsartum fasaturḍiᶜu lahūu ʾukhrā. (6) Liyuñfiq dhū saᶜatim-miñ-saᶜatihī wa mañ-qudira ᶜalayhi rizquhū falyuñfiq mimmāa ʾātāhul-lāh. Lā yukalliful-lāhu nafsan ʾillā māa ʾātāhā. Sayajᶜalul-lāhu baᶜda ᶜusriñy-yusrā. (7) Wa kaʾayyim-miñ-qaryatin ᶜatat ᶜan ʾamri Rabbihā wa Rusulihī faḥāsabnāhā ḥisābañ-shadīdañw-wa ᶜadhdhabnāhā ᶜadhābañ-nukrā. (8) Fadhāqat wabāla ʾamrihā wa kāna ᶜāqibatu ʾamrihā khusrā. (9) ʾAᶜaddal-lāhu lahum ᶜadhābañ-shadīdañ-

12 Lit., "let them dwell wherever you dwell" – i.e., tropically, "let them share fully your standard of living".

13 E.g., for reasons of her health, or because she intends to remarry, etc.

14 I.e., at the father's expense: see 2 : 233 and the corresponding notes 219 and 220.

15 Lit., "out of".

16 This connects with, and stresses, the fact that all the preceding injunctions are divinely ordained.

17 See note 4 on 64 : 5.

Hence, remain conscious of God, O you who are endowed with insight – [you] who have attained to faith!
God has indeed bestowed on you a reminder from on high: ⟨10⟩ [He has sent] an apostle who conveys unto you God's clear messages, so that He might lead those who have attained to faith and do righteous deeds out of the depths of darkness into the light.
And whoever believes in God and does what is right and just, him will He admit into gardens through which running waters flow, therein to abide beyond the count of time: indeed, a most goodly provision will God have granted him! ⟨11⟩

GOD is He who has created seven heavens,[18] and, like them, [the many aspects] of the earth. Through all of them flows down from on high, unceasingly, His [creative] will,[19] so that you might come to know that God has the power to will anything, and that God encompasses all things with His knowledge. ⟨12⟩

فَٱتَّقُوا۟ ٱللَّهَ يَٰٓأُو۟لِى ٱلْأَلْبَٰبِ ٱلَّذِينَ ءَامَنُوا۟ ۚ قَدْ أَنزَلَ ٱللَّهُ إِلَيْكُمْ
ذِكْرًا ﴿10﴾ رَّسُولًا يَتْلُوا۟ عَلَيْكُمْ ءَايَٰتِ ٱللَّهِ مُبَيِّنَٰتٍ لِّيُخْرِجَ ٱلَّذِينَ
ءَامَنُوا۟ وَعَمِلُوا۟ ٱلصَّٰلِحَٰتِ مِنَ ٱلظُّلُمَٰتِ إِلَى ٱلنُّورِ ۚ وَمَن يُؤْمِنۢ بِٱللَّهِ
وَيَعْمَلْ صَٰلِحًا يُدْخِلْهُ جَنَّٰتٍ تَجْرِى مِن تَحْتِهَا ٱلْأَنْهَٰرُ خَٰلِدِينَ فِيهَآ
أَبَدًا ۖ قَدْ أَحْسَنَ ٱللَّهُ لَهُۥ رِزْقًا ﴿11﴾ ٱللَّهُ ٱلَّذِى خَلَقَ سَبْعَ سَمَٰوَٰتٍ وَمِنَ
ٱلْأَرْضِ مِثْلَهُنَّ يَتَنَزَّلُ ٱلْأَمْرُ بَيْنَهُنَّ لِتَعْلَمُوٓا۟ أَنَّ ٱللَّهَ عَلَىٰ كُلِّ شَىْءٍ
قَدِيرٌ وَأَنَّ ٱللَّهَ قَدْ أَحَاطَ بِكُلِّ شَىْءٍ عِلْمًۢا ﴿12﴾

fattaqul-lāha yāa ʾulil-ʾalbābil-ladhīna ʾāmanū. Qad ʾañzalal-lāhu ʾilaykum Dhikrā. (10) Rasūlañy-yatlū ʿalaykum ʾĀyātil-lāhi mubayyinātil-liyukhrijal-ladhīna ʾāmanū wa ʿamiluṣ-ṣāliḥāti minaẓ-ẓulumāti ʾilan-nūr. Wa mañy-yuʾmim-billāhi wa yaʿmal ṣāliḥañy-yudkhilhu jannātiñ-tajrī miñ-taḥtihal-ʾanhāru khālidīna fīhāa ʾabadā. Qad ʾaḥsanal-lāhu lahū rizqā. (11) ʾAllāhul-ladhī khalaqa sabʿa samāwātiñw-wa minal-ʾarḍi mithlahunna yatanazzalul-ʾamru baynahunna litaʿlamūu ʾannal-lāha ʿalā kulli shayʾiñ-Qadīruñw-wa ʾannal-lāha qad ʾaḥāṭa bikulli shayʾin ʿilmā. (12)

18 See *sūrah* 2, note 20.
19 Lit., "the command". The verbal form *yatanazzalu* implies recurrence and continuity; its combination with the noun *al-amr* reflects the concept of God's unceasing creative activity.

The Sixty-Sixth Sūrah

At-Taḥrīm (Prohibition)

Medina Period

REVEALED in the second half of the Medina period – probably in 7 H. – this *sūrah* has been occasionally designated as "The *Sūrah* of the Prophet" (Zamakhsharī) inasmuch as the first half of it deals with certain aspects of his personal and family life.

سورة التحريم مدنية -66-
وآياتها اثنتا عشرة

ثلاثة ارباع الحزب

IN THE NAME OF GOD, THE MOST GRACIOUS, THE DISPENSER OF GRACE:

O PROPHET! Why dost thou, out of a desire to please [one or another of] thy wives, impose [on thyself] a prohibition of something that God has made lawful to thee?[1]
But God is much-forgiving, a dispenser of grace: ⟨1⟩ God has already enjoined upon you [O believers] the breaking and expiation of [such of] your oaths [as may run counter to what is right and just]:[2] for, God is your Lord Supreme, and He alone is all-knowing, truly wise. ⟨2⟩

بِسْمِ ٱللَّهِ ٱلرَّحْمَٰنِ ٱلرَّحِيمِ

يَٰٓأَيُّهَا ٱلنَّبِيُّ لِمَ تُحَرِّمُ مَآ أَحَلَّ ٱللَّهُ لَكَ تَبْتَغِى مَرْضَاتَ أَزْوَٰجِكَ وَٱللَّهُ
غَفُورٌ رَّحِيمٌ ﴿١﴾ قَدْ فَرَضَ ٱللَّهُ لَكُمْ تَحِلَّةَ أَيْمَٰنِكُمْ وَٱللَّهُ مَوْلَىٰكُمْ
وَهُوَ ٱلْعَلِيمُ ٱلْحَكِيمُ ﴿٢﴾

Bismil-lāhir-Raḥmānir-Raḥīm.
Yāa ʾayyuhan-Nabiyyu lima tuḥarrimu māa ʾaḥallal-lāhu lak. Tabtaghī marḍāta ʾazwājik. Wal-lāhu Ghafūrur-Raḥīm. ⟨1⟩ Qad faraḍal-lāhu lakum taḥillata ʾaymānikum; wal-lāhu mawlākum wa Huwal-ʿAlīmul-Ḥakīm. ⟨2⟩

---

1 There are several essentially conflicting – and, therefore, in their aggregate, not very trustworthy – reports as to the exact reason or reasons why, at some time during the second half of the Medina period, the Prophet declared on oath that for one month he would have no intercourse with any of his wives. Still, while the exact reason cannot be established with certainty, it is sufficiently clear from the above-mentioned *aḥādīth* that this emotional, temporary renunciation of marital life was caused by a display of mutual jealousy among some of the Prophet's wives. In any case, the purport of the above Qurʾanic allusion to this incident is not biographical but, rather, intended to bring out a moral lesson applicable to all human situations: namely, the inadmissibility of regarding as forbidden (*ḥarām*) anything that God has made lawful (*ḥalāl*), even if such an attitude happens to be motivated by the desire to please another person or other persons. Apart from this, it serves to illustrate the fact – repeatedly stressed in the Qurʾān – that the Prophet was but a human being, and therefore subject to human emotions and even liable to commit an occasional mistake (which in his case, however, was invariably pointed out to him, and thus rectified, through divine revelation).

2 See 2 : 224 and the corresponding note 212, which shows that in certain circumstances an oath *should* be broken and then atoned for: hence the above phrase, "God has *enjoined* upon you the breaking and expiation" (with the term *taḥillah* comprising both these concepts).

And lo![3] [It so happened that] the Prophet told something in confidence to one of his wives; and when she thereupon divulged it, and God made this known to him, he acquainted [others] with some of it and passed over some of it.[4] And as soon as he let her know it, she asked, "Who has told thee this?"[5] – [to which] he replied, "The All-Knowing, the All-Aware has told me." ‹3›

[Say, O Prophet:[6]] "Would that you two turn unto God in repentance, for the hearts of both of you have swerved [from what is right]![7] And if you uphold each other against him [who is God's message-bearer, know that] God Himself is his Protector, and [that,] therefore,[8] Gabriel, and all the righteous among the believers, and all the [other] angels will come to his aid." ‹4›

[O wives of the Prophet!] Were he to divorce [any of] you, his Sustainer might well give him in your stead spouses better than you – women who surrender themselves unto God, who truly believe, devoutly obey His will, turn [unto Him] in repentance [whenever they have sinned], worship [Him alone], and go on and on [seeking His goodly acceptance][9] – be they women previously married or virgins.[10] ‹5›

وَإِذْ أَسَرَّ ٱلنَّبِىُّ إِلَىٰ بَعْضِ أَزْوَٰجِهِۦ حَدِيثًا فَلَمَّا نَبَّأَتْ بِهِۦ وَأَظْهَرَهُ ٱللَّهُ
عَلَيْهِ عَرَّفَ بَعْضَهُۥ وَأَعْرَضَ عَنۢ بَعْضٍ ۖ فَلَمَّا نَبَّأَهَا بِهِۦ قَالَتْ مَنْ أَنۢبَأَكَ
هَٰذَا ۖ قَالَ نَبَّأَنِىَ ٱلْعَلِيمُ ٱلْخَبِيرُ ﴿٣﴾ إِن تَتُوبَآ إِلَى ٱللَّهِ فَقَدْ صَغَتْ
قُلُوبُكُمَا ۖ وَإِن تَظَٰهَرَا عَلَيْهِ فَإِنَّ ٱللَّهَ هُوَ مَوْلَىٰهُ وَجِبْرِيلُ وَصَٰلِحُ
ٱلْمُؤْمِنِينَ ۖ وَٱلْمَلَٰٓئِكَةُ بَعْدَ ذَٰلِكَ ظَهِيرٌ ﴿٤﴾ عَسَىٰ رَبُّهُۥٓ إِن طَلَّقَكُنَّ أَن
يُبْدِلَهُۥٓ أَزْوَٰجًا خَيْرًا مِّنكُنَّ مُسْلِمَٰتٍ مُّؤْمِنَٰتٍ قَٰنِتَٰتٍ تَٰٓئِبَٰتٍ
عَٰبِدَٰتٍ سَٰٓئِحَٰتٍ ثَيِّبَٰتٍ وَأَبْكَارًا ﴿٥﴾

Wa ʾidh ʾasarran-Nabiyyu ʾilā baʿḍi ʾazwājihī ḥadīthañ-falammā nabbaʾat bihī wa ʾaẓharahul-lāhu ʿalayhi ʿarrafa baʿḍahū wa ʾaʿraḍa ʿam-baʿḍ. Falammā nabbaʾahā bihī qālat man ʾambaʾaka hādhā. Qāla nabbaʾaniyal-ʿAlīmul-Khabīr. (3) ʾIñ-tatūbāa ʾilal-lāhi faqad ṣaghat qulūbukumā; wa ʾiñ-taẓāharā ʿalayhi faʾinnal-lāha Huwa Mawlāhu wa Jibrīlu wa ṣāliḥul-muʾminīna wal-Malāaʾikatu baʿda dhālika ẓahīr. (4) ʿAsā Rabbuhūu ʾiñ-ṭallaqakunna ʾañy-yubdilahūu ʾazwājan khayram-miñkunna Muslimātim-muʾminātiñ-qānitātiñ-tāaʾibātin ʿābidātiñ-sāaʾiḥātiñ-thayyibātiñw-wa ʾabkārā. (5)

3 See *sūrah* 2, note 21.

4 Lit., "he turned aside from [or "avoided"] some of it". There is no reliable Tradition as to the subject of that confidential information. Some of the early commentators, however, connect it with the Prophet's veiled prediction that Abū Bakr and ʿUmar ibn al-Khaṭṭāb would succeed him as leaders of the Muslim community; the recipient of the information is said to have been Ḥafṣah, the daughter of ʿUmar, and the one to whom she disclosed it, ʿĀʾishah, the daughter of Abū Bakr (Baghawī, on the authority of Ibn ʿAbbās and Al-Kalbī; also Zamakhsharī). If this interpretation is correct, it would explain why the Prophet "acquainted [others] with some of it and passed over some of it": for, once his confidential prediction had been divulged, he saw no point in withholding it any longer from the community; nevertheless, he alluded to it in deliberately vague terms – possibly in order not to give to the succession of Abū Bakr and ʿUmar the appearance of an "apostolic sanction" but to leave it, rather, to a free decision of the community in pursuance of the Qurʾanic principle *amruhum shūrā baynahum* (see 42 : 38).

5 I.e., that she had broken the Prophet's confidence.

6 Although in the sequence the Prophet is referred to in the third person, it is obvious that it is he who is commanded through revelation to speak thus to his wives Ḥafṣah and ʿĀʾishah (see note 4); hence my above interpolation.

7 Referring to Ḥafṣah, who betrayed the Prophet's confidence, and to ʿĀʾishah, who by listening contributed to this betrayal (see note 4 above).

8 Lit., "after that", i.e., in consequence of the fact that God Himself protects him.

9 For this rendering of the expression *sāʾiḥāt*, see note 147 on 9 : 112, where the same expression occurs in the masculine gender relating to both men and women.

10 I.e., like the actual wives of the Prophet, one of whom (ʿĀʾishah) was a virgin when she married him, one (Zaynab bint Jaḥsh) had been divorced, while the others were widows. This allusion, together with the fact that the

O YOU who have attained to faith! Ward off from yourselves and those who are close to you[11] that fire [of the hereafter] whose fuel is human beings and stones:[12] [lording] over it are angelic powers awesome [and] severe,[13] who do not disobey God in whatever He has commanded them, but [always] do what they are bidden to do.[14] ‹6›

[Hence,] O you who are bent on denying the truth, make no [empty] excuses today:[15] [in the life to come] you shall be but recompensed for what you were doing [in this world]. ‹7›

O you who have attained to faith! Turn unto God in sincere repentance:[16] it may well be that your Sustainer will efface from you your bad deeds, and will admit you into gardens through which running waters flow, on a Day on which God will not shame the Prophet and those who share his faith:[17] their light will spread rapidly before them, and on their right;[18] [and] they will pray: "O our Sustainer! Cause this our light to shine for us forever,[19] and forgive us our sins: for, verily, Thou hast the power to will anything!" ‹8›

يَٰٓأَيُّهَا ٱلَّذِينَ ءَامَنُوا۟ قُوٓا۟ أَنفُسَكُمْ وَأَهْلِيكُمْ نَارًا وَقُودُهَا ٱلنَّاسُ
وَٱلْحِجَارَةُ عَلَيْهَا مَلَٰٓئِكَةٌ غِلَاظٌ شِدَادٌ لَّا يَعْصُونَ ٱللَّهَ مَآ أَمَرَهُمْ
وَيَفْعَلُونَ مَا يُؤْمَرُونَ ﴿6﴾ يَٰٓأَيُّهَا ٱلَّذِينَ كَفَرُوا۟ لَا تَعْتَذِرُوا۟ ٱلْيَوْمَ إِنَّمَا
تُجْزَوْنَ مَا كُنتُمْ تَعْمَلُونَ ﴿7﴾ يَٰٓأَيُّهَا ٱلَّذِينَ ءَامَنُوا۟ تُوبُوٓا۟ إِلَى ٱللَّهِ تَوْبَةً
نَّصُوحًا عَسَىٰ رَبُّكُمْ أَن يُكَفِّرَ عَنكُمْ سَيِّـَٔاتِكُمْ وَيُدْخِلَكُمْ جَنَّٰتٍ
تَجْرِى مِن تَحْتِهَا ٱلْأَنْهَٰرُ يَوْمَ لَا يُخْزِى ٱللَّهُ ٱلنَّبِىَّ وَٱلَّذِينَ ءَامَنُوا۟
مَعَهُۥ نُورُهُمْ يَسْعَىٰ بَيْنَ أَيْدِيهِمْ وَبِأَيْمَٰنِهِمْ يَقُولُونَ رَبَّنَآ أَتْمِمْ لَنَا نُورَنَا
وَٱغْفِرْ لَنَآ إِنَّكَ عَلَىٰ كُلِّ شَىْءٍ قَدِيرٌ ﴿8﴾

Yāa ʾayyuhal-ladhīna ʾāmanū qūu ʾañfusakum wa ʾahlīkum nārañw-waqūduhan-nāsu wal-ḥijāratū ʿalayhā Malāaʾikatun ghilāẓuñ-shidādul-lā yaʿṣūnal-lāha māa ʾamarahum wa yafʿalūna mā yuʾmarūn. ‹6› Yāa ʾayyuhal-ladhīna kafarū lā taʿtadhirul-Yawma ʾinnamā tujzawna mā kuñtum taʿmalūn. ‹7› Yāa ʾayyuhal-ladhīna ʾāmanū tūbūu ʾilal-lāhi tawbatañ-naṣūḥān ʿasā Rabbukum ʾañy-yukaffira ʿañkum sayyiʾātikum wa yudkhilakum jannātiñ-tajrī miñ-taḥtihal-ʾanhāru Yawma lā yukhzil-lāhun-Nabiyya wal-ladhīna ʾāmanū maʿah. Nūruhum yasʿā bayna ʾaydīhim wa biʾaymānihim yaqūlūna Rabbanāa ʾatmim lanā nūranā wagh-fir lanāa ʾinnaka ʿalā kulli shayʾiñ-Qadīr. ‹8›

Prophet did *not* divorce any of his wives, as well as the purely hypothetical formulation of this passage, shows that it is meant to be an indirect admonition to the Prophet's wives, who, despite their occasional shortcomings – unavoidable in human beings – did possess the virtues referred to above. On a wider plane, it seems to be an admonition to *all* believers, men and women alike: and this explains the subsequent change in the discourse.

11 Lit., "your families" or "your people"; however, the term *ahl* denotes also people who share one's race, religion, occupation, etc., as well as "dependants" in the most comprehensive sense of this word (Jawharī, Rāghib; also *Mughnī*).

12 See *sūrah* 2, note 16.

13 See 74 : 27 ff. and the corresponding notes, particularly notes 15 and 16, in which I have tried to explain the allegorical meaning of that passage.

14 I.e., these angelic powers are subject to the God-willed law of cause and effect which dominates the realm of the spirit no less than the world of matter.

15 I.e., "do not try to rationalize your deliberate denial of the truth" – the element of conscious intent being implied in the past-tense phrase *alladhīna kafarū* (see note 6 on 2 : 6).

16 Se., "since no human being, however imbued with faith, can ever remain entirely free from faults and temptations".

17 The implication is that He will not only "not shame" the Prophet and his followers but will, on the contrary, *exalt* them: an idiomatic turn of phrase similar to sayings like "I shall let you know something that will not be to your detriment" – i.e., "something that will *benefit* you".

18 Cf. 57 : 12 and the corresponding note 12.

19 Lit., "Complete for us our light", i.e., by making it permanent.

O PROPHET! Strive hard against the deniers of the truth and the hypocrites, and be adamant with them.[20] And [if they do not repent,] their goal shall be hell – and how vile a journey's end! ⟨9⟩

For those who are bent on denying the truth God has propounded a parable in [the stories of] Noah's wife and Lot's wife: they were wedded to two of Our righteous servants, and each one betrayed her husband;[21] and neither of the two [husbands] will be of any avail to these two women when they are told [on Judgment Day], "Enter the fire with all those [other sinners] who enter it!"[22] ⟨10⟩

And for those who have attained to faith God has propounded a parable in [the story of] Pharaoh's wife[23] as she prayed, "O my Sustainer! Build Thou for me a mansion in the paradise [that is] with Thee, and save me from Pharaoh and his doings, and save me from all evildoing folk!" ⟨11⟩

And [We have propounded yet another parable of God-consciousness in the story of] Mary, the daughter of ᶜImrān,[24] who guarded her chastity, whereupon We breathed of Our spirit into that [which was in her womb],[25] and who accepted the truth of her Sustainer's words – and [thus,] of His revelations[26] – and was one of the truly devout. ⟨12⟩

يَٰٓأَيُّهَا ٱلنَّبِيُّ جَٰهِدِ ٱلْكُفَّارَ وَٱلْمُنَٰفِقِينَ وَٱغْلُظْ عَلَيْهِمْ وَمَأْوَىٰهُمْ جَهَنَّمُ
وَبِئْسَ ٱلْمَصِيرُ ﴿9﴾ ضَرَبَ ٱللَّهُ مَثَلًا لِّلَّذِينَ كَفَرُوا۟ ٱمْرَأَتَ نُوحٍ
وَٱمْرَأَتَ لُوطٍ كَانَتَا تَحْتَ عَبْدَيْنِ مِنْ عِبَادِنَا صَٰلِحَيْنِ فَخَانَتَاهُمَا فَلَمْ
يُغْنِيَا عَنْهُمَا مِنَ ٱللَّهِ شَيْـًٔا وَقِيلَ ٱدْخُلَا ٱلنَّارَ مَعَ ٱلدَّٰخِلِينَ ﴿10﴾
وَضَرَبَ ٱللَّهُ مَثَلًا لِّلَّذِينَ ءَامَنُوا۟ ٱمْرَأَتَ فِرْعَوْنَ إِذْ قَالَتْ رَبِّ ٱبْنِ لِى
عِندَكَ بَيْتًا فِى ٱلْجَنَّةِ وَنَجِّنِى مِن فِرْعَوْنَ وَعَمَلِهِۦ وَنَجِّنِى مِنَ ٱلْقَوْمِ
ٱلظَّٰلِمِينَ ﴿11﴾ وَمَرْيَمَ ٱبْنَتَ عِمْرَٰنَ ٱلَّتِىٓ أَحْصَنَتْ فَرْجَهَا فَنَفَخْنَا فِيهِ
مِن رُّوحِنَا وَصَدَّقَتْ بِكَلِمَٰتِ رَبِّهَا وَكُتُبِهِۦ وَكَانَتْ مِنَ ٱلْقَٰنِتِينَ ﴿12﴾

Yāa ʾayyuhan-Nabiyyu jāhidil-kuffāra wal-munāfiqīna wagh-luẓ ᶜalayhim. Wa maʾwāhum jahannamu wa biʾsal-maṣīr. (9) Ḍarabal-lāhu mathalal-lilladhīna kafarum-raʾata Nūḥiñw-wam-raʾata Lūṭ. Kānatā taḥta ᶜabdayni min ᶜibādinā ṣāliḥayni fakhānatāhumā falam yughniyā ᶜanhumā minal-lāhi shayʾañw-wa qīlad-khulan-nāra maᶜad-dākhilīn. (10) Wa ḍarabal-lāhu mathalal-lilladhīna ʾāmanum-raʾata Firᶜawna ʾidh qālat Rabbib-ni lī ᶜiñdaka baytañ-fil-jannati wa najjinī miñ-Firᶜawna wa ᶜamalihī wa najjinī minal-qawmiẓ-ẓālimīn. (11) Wa Maryamab-nata ᶜImrānal-latīi ʾaḥṣanat farjahā fanafakhnā fīhi mirrūḥinā wa ṣaddaqat biKalimāti Rabbihā wa Kutubihī wa kānat minal-qānitīn. (12)

20 See note 101 on 9 : 73, which is identical with the above verse.

21 Lit., "and both betrayed them", i.e., their respective husbands. The story of Lot's wife and her spiritual betrayal of her husband is mentioned in the Qurʾān in several places; see, in particular, note 66 on 7 : 83 and note 113 on 11 : 81. As regards Noah's wife, the above is the only explicit reference to her having betrayed her husband; it would seem, however, that the qualification of "those on whom [God's] sentence has already been passed" in 11 : 40 applies to her no less than to her son (whose story appears in 11 : 42-47).

22 The "parable" (*mathal*) of these two women implies, firstly, that even the most intimate relationship with a truly righteous person – even though he be a prophet – cannot save an unrepentant sinner from the consequences of his sin; and, secondly, that a true believer must cut himself off from any association with "those who are bent on denying the truth" even if they happen to be those nearest and dearest to him (cf. 11 : 46).

23 Cf. 28 : 8-9.

24 I.e., a descendant of the *House* of ᶜImrān (cf. the last third of note 22 on 3 : 33).

25 I.e., into the as yet unborn child (Rāzī, thus explaining the pronoun in *fīhi*). For an explanation of the much-misunderstood allegorical phrase, "We breathed of Our spirit into it", see note 87 on 21 : 91.

26 For the meaning of God's "words" (*kalimāt*), see note 28 on 3 : 39.

The Sixty-Seventh Sūrah

Al-Mulk (Dominion)

Mecca Period

THE FUNDAMENTAL idea running through the whole of this *sūrah* is man's inability ever to encompass the mysteries of the universe with his earthbound knowledge, and, hence, his utter dependence on guidance through divine revelation.

Best known by the key-word *al-mulk* ("dominion") taken from its first verse, the *sūrah* has sometimes been designated by the Companions as "The Preserving One" (*Al-Wāqiyah*) or "The Saving One" (*Al-Munjiyah*) inasmuch as it is apt to save and preserve him who takes its lesson to heart from suffering in the life to come (Zamakhsharī).

-67- سورة الملك مكية وآياتها ثلاثون

IN THE NAME OF GOD, THE MOST GRACIOUS, THE DISPENSER OF GRACE:

HALLOWED be He in whose hand all dominion rests, since He has the power to will anything: ‹1› He who has created death as well as life,[1] so that He might put you to a test [and thus show] which of you is best in conduct, and [make you realize that] He alone is almighty, truly forgiving. ‹2›

[Hallowed be] He who has created seven heavens in full harmony with one another:[2] no fault wilt thou see in the creation of the Most Gracious. And turn thy vision [upon it] once more: canst thou see any flaw? ‹3›

Yea, turn thy vision [upon it] again and yet again: [and every time] thy vision will fall back upon thee, dazzled and truly defeated. . . .[3] ‹4›

And, indeed, We have adorned the skies nearest to the earth with lights,[4] and have made them the object of futile guesses for the evil ones [from among men]:[5] and for them have We readied suffering through a blazing flame ‹5› – for, suffering in hell awaits all who are [thus] bent on blaspheming against their

بِسۡمِ ٱللَّهِ ٱلرَّحۡمَٰنِ ٱلرَّحِيمِ

تَبَٰرَكَ ٱلَّذِى بِيَدِهِ ٱلۡمُلۡكُ وَهُوَ عَلَىٰ كُلِّ شَىۡءٖ قَدِيرٌ ﴿١﴾ ٱلَّذِى خَلَقَ
ٱلۡمَوۡتَ وَٱلۡحَيَوٰةَ لِيَبۡلُوَكُمۡ أَيُّكُمۡ أَحۡسَنُ عَمَلٗاۚ وَهُوَ ٱلۡعَزِيزُ
ٱلۡغَفُورُ ﴿٢﴾ ٱلَّذِى خَلَقَ سَبۡعَ سَمَٰوَٰتٖ طِبَاقٗاۖ مَّا تَرَىٰ فِى خَلۡقِ
ٱلرَّحۡمَٰنِ مِن تَفَٰوُتٖۖ فَٱرۡجِعِ ٱلۡبَصَرَ هَلۡ تَرَىٰ مِن فُطُورٖ ﴿٣﴾ ثُمَّ
ٱرۡجِعِ ٱلۡبَصَرَ كَرَّتَيۡنِ يَنقَلِبۡ إِلَيۡكَ ٱلۡبَصَرُ خَاسِئٗا وَهُوَ حَسِيرٞ ﴿٤﴾
وَلَقَدۡ زَيَّنَّا ٱلسَّمَآءَ ٱلدُّنۡيَا بِمَصَٰبِيحَ وَجَعَلۡنَٰهَا رُجُومٗا لِّلشَّيَٰطِينِۖ حزب 57
وَأَعۡتَدۡنَا لَهُمۡ عَذَابَ ٱلسَّعِيرِ ﴿٥﴾ وَلِلَّذِينَ كَفَرُواْ بِرَبِّهِمۡ عَذَابُ جَهَنَّمَۖ جزء 29

Bismil-lāhir-Raḥmānir-Raḥīm.

Tabārakal-ladhī biyadihil-mulku wa Huwa ʿalā kulli shayʾiñ-Qadīr. (1) ʾAlladhī khalaqal-mawta wal-ḥayāta liyabluwakum ʾayyukum ʾaḥsanu ʿamalañ-wa Huwal-ʿAzīzul-Ghafūr. (2) ʾAlladhī khalaqa sabʿa samāwātiñ-ṭibāqam-mā tarā fī khalqir-Raḥmāni miñ-tafāwut. Farjiʿil-baṣara hal tarā miñ-fuṭūr. (3) Thummar-jiʿil-baṣara karratayni yañqalib ʾilaykal-baṣaru khāsiʾañw-wa huwa ḥasīr. (4) Wa laqad zayyannas-samāaʾad-dunyā bimaṣābīḥa wa jaʿalnāhā rujūmal-lish-Shayāṭīni wa ʾaʿtadnā lahum ʿadhābas-saʿīr. (5) Wa lilladhīna kafarū biRabbihim ʿadhābu jahannama

---

1 Since what is termed "death" is stated here to have been *created*, it cannot be identical with "non-existence", but obviously must have a positive reality of its own. To my mind, it connotes, firstly, the inanimate state of existence preceding the emergence of life in plants or animated beings; and, secondly, the state of transition from life as we know it in this world to the – as yet to us unimaginable – condition of existence referred to in the Qurʾān as "the hereafter" or "the life to come" (*al-ākhirah*).

2 Or: "conforming [with one another]", this being the primary significance of *tibāq* (sing. *tabaq*). For the meaning of the "seven heavens"', see *sūrah* 2, note 20.

3 Sc., in its endeavour to encompass the mysteries of the universe.

4 Lit., "lamps" – i.e., stars: cf. 37 : 6, "We have adorned the skies nearest to the earth with the beauty of stars".

5 For the wider meaning of *shayāṭīn* – a term which in this context points specifically to "the satans from among mankind, that is, the astrologers" (Bayḍāwī) – see *sūrah* 15, note 16. As regards the term *rajm* (pl. *rujūm*), which literally denotes the "throwing [of something] like a stone" – i.e., at random – it is often used metaphorically in the sense of "speaking conjecturally" or "making [something] the object of guesswork" (Jawharī, Rāghib – the latter

Sustainer:[6] and how vile a journey's end! ‹6›

When they are cast into that [hell], they will hear its breath indrawing as it boils up, ‹7› well-nigh bursting with fury; [and] every time a host [of such sinners] is flung into it, its keepers will ask them, "Has no warner ever come to you?" ‹8›

They will reply: "Yea, a warner did indeed come unto us, but we gave him the lie and said, 'Never has God sent down anything [by way of revelation]! You [self-styled warners] are but lost in a great delusion!'"[7] ‹9›

And they will add: "Had we but listened [to those warnings], or [at least] used our own reason, we would not [now] be among those who are destined for the blazing flame!"[8] ‹10›

Thus will they come to realize their sins: but [by that time,] remote will have become all good from those who are destined for the blazing flame. ‹11›

[As against this,] behold, for those who stand in awe of their Sustainer although He is beyond the reach of their perception,[9] there is forgiveness in store and a great reward. ‹12›

AND [know, O men, that] whether you keep your beliefs[10] secret or state them openly, He has full knowledge indeed of all that is in [your] hearts.[11] ‹13›

وَبِئْسَ ٱلْمَصِيرُ ﴿٦﴾ إِذَآ أُلْقُواْ فِيهَا سَمِعُواْ لَهَا شَهِيقًا وَهِىَ تَفُورُ ﴿٧﴾
تَكَادُ تَمَيَّزُ مِنَ ٱلْغَيْظِ كُلَّمَآ أُلْقِىَ فِيهَا فَوْجٌ سَأَلَهُمْ خَزَنَتُهَآ أَلَمْ يَأْتِكُمْ
نَذِيرٌ ﴿٨﴾ قَالُواْ بَلَىٰ قَدْ جَآءَنَا نَذِيرٌ فَكَذَّبْنَا وَقُلْنَا مَا نَزَّلَ ٱللَّهُ مِن شَىْءٍ
إِنْ أَنتُمْ إِلَّا فِى ضَلَٰلٍ كَبِيرٍ ﴿٩﴾ وَقَالُواْ لَوْ كُنَّا نَسْمَعُ أَوْ نَعْقِلُ مَا كُنَّا
فِىٓ أَصْحَٰبِ ٱلسَّعِيرِ ﴿١٠﴾ فَٱعْتَرَفُواْ بِذَنۢبِهِمْ فَسُحْقًا لِّأَصْحَٰبِ ٱلسَّعِيرِ ﴿١١﴾
إِنَّ ٱلَّذِينَ يَخْشَوْنَ رَبَّهُم بِٱلْغَيْبِ لَهُم مَّغْفِرَةٌ وَأَجْرٌ كَبِيرٌ ﴿١٢﴾ وَأَسِرُّواْ
قَوْلَكُمْ أَوِ ٱجْهَرُواْ بِهِۦٓ إِنَّهُۥ عَلِيمٌۢ بِذَاتِ ٱلصُّدُورِ ﴿١٣﴾

wa biʾsal-maṣīr. (6) **ʾIdhāa ʾulqū fīhā samiʿū lahā shahīqañw-wa hiya tafūr.** (7) **Takādu tamayyazu minal-ghayẓu kullamāa ʾulqiya fīhā fawjuñ-saʾalahum khazanatuhāa ʾalam yaʾtikum Nadhīr.** (8) **Qālū balā qad jāaʾanā Nadhīruñ-fakadhdhabnā wa qulnā mā nazzalal-lāhu miñ-shayʾin ʾin ʾañtum ʾillā fī ḍalāliñ-kabīr.** (9) **Wa qālū law kunnā nasmaʿu ʾaw naʿqilu mā kunnā fīi ʾaṣḥābis-sāʿīr.** (10) **Faʿtarafū bidhambihim fasuḥqal-liʾaṣḥābis-saʿīr.** (11) **ʾInnal-ladhīna yakhshawna Rabbahum bilghaybi lahum maghfiratuñw-wa ʾajruñ-kabīr.** (12) **Wa ʾasirrū qawlakum ʾawij-harū bihīi ʾinnahū ʿalīmum-bidhātiṣ-ṣudūr.** (13)

connecting this metaphor explicitly with the above verse –, *Lisān al-ʿArab, Qāmūs, Tāj al-ʿArūs,* etc.). Cf. also 37 : 6-10.

6 I.e., by presuming to know what will happen in the future – a knowledge which rests with God alone. This connects with the statement in verse 4 that man can never truly unravel the mysteries of cosmic space ("the heavens"), which in its turn implies that he should not presume to foretell terrestrial events from the position and the aspects of the stars. Since only God knows "that which is beyond the reach of a created being's perception" (*al-ghayb*), any such attempt is a blasphemy (*kufr*).

7 Lit., "You are in nothing but a great error (*ḍalāl*)" – thus denying the reality of divine revelation as such.

8 Reason, properly used, must lead man to a cognition of God's existence and, thus, of the fact that a definite *plan* underlies all His creation. A logical concomitant of that cognition is the realization that certain aspects of the divine plan touching upon human life – in particular, the distinction between right and wrong – are being continuously disclosed to man through the medium of the revelation which God bestows on His chosen message-bearers, the prophets. This innate "bond with God" (referred to in 2 : 27 and explained in the corresponding note 19) may be broken only at the expense of man's spiritual future, with suffering in the life to come as the inevitable alternative.

9 For this rendering of the expression *bi'l-ghayb*, see *sūrah* 2, note 3.

10 While the primary significance of the noun *qawl* is "a saying" or "an utterance", it is often used tropically in the sense of "a statement", i.e., of a belief, an opinion, a teaching, a doctrine, etc. In the present context it evidently relates to man's beliefs in general, be they affirmative or negative: hence the plural form in my rendering of this term.

11 I.e., He knows *why* one person believes in Him and another rejects this belief; hence, He takes man's innermost motivations, abilities and inabilities fully into account.

How could it be that He who has created [all] should not know [all]?[12]
Yea, He alone is unfathomable [in His wisdom], all-aware![13] ‹14›
He it is who has made the earth easy to live upon:[14] go about, then, in all its regions, and partake of the sustenance which He provides: but [always bear in mind that] unto Him you shall be resurrected. ‹15›
Can you ever feel secure that He who is in heaven[15] will not cause the earth to swallow you up when, lo and behold, it begins to quake? ‹16›
Or can you ever feel secure that He who is in heaven will not let loose against you a deadly stormwind,[16] whereupon you would come to know how [true] My warning was? ‹17›
And, indeed, [many of] those who lived aforetime[17] did give the lie [to My warnings]: and how awesome was My rejection [of them]! ‹18›
Have they, then, never beheld the birds above them, spreading their wings and drawing them in? None but the Most Gracious upholds them: for, verily, He keeps all things in His sight. ‹19›
[And] is there any, besides the Most Gracious, that could be a shield[18] for you, and could succour you [against danger]? They who deny this truth are but lost in self-delusion! ‹20›
Or is there any that could provide you with sustenance if He should withhold His provision [from you]?

أَلَا يَعْلَمُ مَنْ خَلَقَ وَهُوَ ٱللَّطِيفُ ٱلْخَبِيرُ ﴿١٤﴾ هُوَ ٱلَّذِى جَعَلَ لَكُمُ
ٱلْأَرْضَ ذَلُولًا فَٱمْشُوا۟ فِى مَنَاكِبِهَا وَكُلُوا۟ مِن رِّزْقِهِۦ ۖ وَإِلَيْهِ
ٱلنُّشُورُ ﴿١٥﴾ ءَأَمِنتُم مَّن فِى ٱلسَّمَآءِ أَن يَخْسِفَ بِكُمُ ٱلْأَرْضَ فَإِذَا هِىَ
تَمُورُ ﴿١٦﴾ أَمْ أَمِنتُم مَّن فِى ٱلسَّمَآءِ أَن يُرْسِلَ عَلَيْكُمْ حَاصِبًا ۖ فَسَتَعْلَمُونَ
كَيْفَ نَذِيرِ ﴿١٧﴾ وَلَقَدْ كَذَّبَ ٱلَّذِينَ مِن قَبْلِهِمْ فَكَيْفَ كَانَ
نَكِيرِ ﴿١٨﴾ أَوَلَمْ يَرَوْا۟ إِلَى ٱلطَّيْرِ فَوْقَهُمْ صَٰٓفَّٰتٍ وَيَقْبِضْنَ ۚ مَا
يُمْسِكُهُنَّ إِلَّا ٱلرَّحْمَٰنُ ۚ إِنَّهُۥ بِكُلِّ شَىْءٍۭ بَصِيرٌ ﴿١٩﴾ أَمَّنْ هَٰذَا
ٱلَّذِى هُوَ جُندٌ لَّكُمْ يَنصُرُكُم مِّن دُونِ ٱلرَّحْمَٰنِ ۚ إِنِ ٱلْكَٰفِرُونَ
إِلَّا فِى غُرُورٍ ﴿٢٠﴾ أَمَّنْ هَٰذَا ٱلَّذِى يَرْزُقُكُمْ إِنْ أَمْسَكَ رِزْقَهُۥ

ʾAlā yaʿlamu man khalaq wa Huwal-Laṭīful-Khabīr. (14) Huwal-ladhī jaʿala lakumul-ʾarḍa dhalūlañ-famshū fī manākibihā wa kulū mir-rizqihī wa ʾilayhin-nushūr. (15) ʾAʾamiñtum-mañ-fis-samāaʾi ʾañy-yakhsifa bikumul-ʾarḍa faʾidhā hiya tamūr. (16) ʾAm ʾamiñtum-mañ-fis-samāaʾi ʾañy-yursila ʿalaykum ḥāṣibañ-fasataʿlamūna kayfa nadhīr. (17) Wa laqad kadhdhabal-ladhīna miñ-qablihim fakayfa kāna nakīr. (18) ʾAwalam yaraw ʾilaṭ-ṭayri fawqahum ṣāaffātiñw-wa yaqbiḍn. Mā yumsikuhunna ʾillar-Raḥmān. ʾInnahū bikulli shayʾim-Baṣīr. (19) ʾAmman hādhal-ladhī huwa juñdul-lakum yañṣurukum-miñ-dūnir-Raḥmān. ʾInil-kāfirūna ʾillā fī ghurūr. (20) ʾAmman hādhal-ladhī yarzuqukum ʾin ʾamsaka rizqah.

12 Lit., "Does He not know, [He] who has created?"

13 See *sūrah* 6, note 89.

14 Lit., "who has made the earth submissive (*dhalūlan*) to you": i.e., yielding to the intelligence with which He has endowed man.

15 This expression is, of course, purely metaphorical since God is limitless in space as well as in time. Its use here is apparently meant to stress the unfathomable quality of His existence and power, which penetrates, and reveals itself in, every aspect of His cosmic creativeness, symbolized in the term "heaven".

16 Lit., "a stormwind that raises stones".

17 Lit., "before them" (*min qablihim*). This personal pronoun relates – as does the whole of the passage beginning with verse 13 – to people of *all* times, who are herewith reminded of what happened to deniers of the truth in earlier times; hence my rendering of *min qablihim* as "aforetime".

18 Lit., "an army".

بَل لَّجُّوا۟ فِى عُتُوٍّ وَنُفُورٍ ﴿٢١﴾ أَفَمَن يَمْشِى مُكِبًّا عَلَىٰ وَجْهِهِۦٓ أَهْدَىٰٓ
أَمَّن يَمْشِى سَوِيًّا عَلَىٰ صِرَٰطٍ مُّسْتَقِيمٍ ﴿٢٢﴾ قُلْ هُوَ ٱلَّذِىٓ أَنشَأَكُمْ وَجَعَلَ
لَكُمُ ٱلسَّمْعَ وَٱلْأَبْصَٰرَ وَٱلْأَفْـِٔدَةَ ۖ قَلِيلًا مَّا تَشْكُرُونَ ﴿٢٣﴾ قُلْ هُوَ
ٱلَّذِى ذَرَأَكُمْ فِى ٱلْأَرْضِ وَإِلَيْهِ تُحْشَرُونَ ﴿٢٤﴾ وَيَقُولُونَ مَتَىٰ هَٰذَا
ٱلْوَعْدُ إِن كُنتُمْ صَٰدِقِينَ ﴿٢٥﴾ قُلْ إِنَّمَا ٱلْعِلْمُ عِندَ ٱللَّهِ وَإِنَّمَآ أَنَا۠ نَذِيرٌ
مُّبِينٌ ﴿٢٦﴾ فَلَمَّا رَأَوْهُ زُلْفَةً سِيٓـَٔتْ وُجُوهُ ٱلَّذِينَ كَفَرُوا۟ وَقِيلَ هَٰذَا ٱلَّذِى
كُنتُم بِهِۦ تَدَّعُونَ ﴿٢٧﴾ قُلْ أَرَءَيْتُمْ إِنْ أَهْلَكَنِىَ ٱللَّهُ وَمَن مَّعِىَ أَوْ رَحِمَنَا
فَمَن يُجِيرُ ٱلْكَٰفِرِينَ مِنْ عَذَابٍ أَلِيمٍ ﴿٢٨﴾ قُلْ هُوَ ٱلرَّحْمَٰنُ ءَامَنَّا بِهِۦ
وَعَلَيْهِ تَوَكَّلْنَا ۖ فَسَتَعْلَمُونَ مَنْ هُوَ فِى ضَلَٰلٍ مُّبِينٍ ﴿٢٩﴾

Bal-lajjū fī ʿutuwwiñw-wa nufūr. (21) ʾAfamañy-yamshī mukibban ʿalā wajhihīi ʾahdāa ammañy-yamshī sawiyyan ʿalā ṣirāṭim-mustaqīm. (22) Qul Huwal-ladhīi ʾañshaʾakum wa jaʿala lakumus-samʿa wal-ʾabṣāra wal-ʾafʾidata qalīlam-mā tashkurūn. (23) Qul Huwal-ladhī dharaʿakum fil-ʾarḍi wa ʾilayhi tuḥsharūn. (24) Wa yaqūlūna matā hādhal-waʿdu ʾiñ-kuñtum ṣādiqīn. (25) Qul ʾinnamal-ʿilmu ʿiñdal-lāhi wa ʾinnamāa ʾana Nadhīrum-mubīn. (26) Falammā raʾawhu zulfatañ-sīiʾat wujūhul-ladhīna kafarū wa qīla hādhal-ladhī kuñtum bihī taddaʿūn. (27) Qul ʾaraʾaytum ʾin ʾahlakaniyal-lāhu wa mam-maʿiya ʾaw raḥimanā famañy-yujīrul-kāfirīna min ʿadhābin ʾalīm. (28) Qul Huwar-Raḥmānu ʾāmannā bihī wa ʿalayhi tawakkalnā; fasataʿlamūna man huwa fī ḍalālim-mubīn. (29)

Nay, but they [who are bent on denying the truth] stubbornly persist in their disdain [of God's messages] and in their headlong flight [from Him]! ‹21›
But then, is he that goes along with his face close to the ground[19] better guided than he that walks upright on a straight way? ‹22›

SAY: "[God is] He who has brought you [all] into being, and has endowed you with hearing, and sight, and hearts:[20] [yet] how seldom are you grateful!" ‹23›
Say: "It is He who has multiplied you on earth; and it is unto Him that you shall be gathered [on resurrection]." ‹24›
But they [only] ask, "When is this promise to be fulfilled? [Answer this, O you who believe in it,] if you are men of truth!" ‹25›
Say thou, [O Prophet:] "Knowledge thereof rests with God alone; and I am only a plain warner." ‹26›
Yet in the end, when they shall see that [fulfilment] close at hand, the faces of those who were bent on denying the truth will be stricken with grief; and they will be told, "This it is that you were [so derisively] calling for!" ‹27›

SAY [O Prophet]: "What do you think? Whether God destroys me and those who follow me, or graces us with His mercy[21] – is there anyone that could protect [you] deniers of the truth from grievous suffering [in the life to come]?" ‹28›
Say: "He is the Most Gracious: we have attained to faith in Him, and in Him have we placed our trust; and in time you will come to know which of us was lost in manifest error." ‹29›

19 Lit., "prone upon his face" – i.e., seeing only what is immediately beneath his feet, and utterly unaware of the direction into which his path is taking him: a metaphor of the spiritual obtuseness which prevents a person from caring for anything beyond his immediate, worldly concerns, and thus makes him resemble an earthworm that "goes along prone upon its face".

20 I.e., with the faculty of feeling as well as of rational thinking.

21 I.e., "Whether we succeed in spreading God's message or not, what have you unbelievers to gain?"

Say [unto those who deny the truth]: "What do you think? If of a sudden all your water were to vanish underground, who [but God] could provide you with water from [new] unsullied springs?"[22] ⟨30⟩

قُلْ أَرَءَيْتُمْ إِنْ أَصْبَحَ مَآؤُكُمْ غَوْرًا فَمَن يَأْتِيكُم بِمَآءٍ مَّعِينٍ ﴿٣٠﴾

Qul ʾaraʾaytum ʾin ʾaṣbaḥa māaʾukum ghawrañ-famañy-yaʾtīkum bimāaʾim-maʿīn. ﴿30﴾

22 Apart from a further reminder of God's providential power (thus continuing the argument touched upon in verses 19-21), the above verse has a parabolic significance as well. Just as water is an indispensable element of all organic life, so is a constant flow of moral consciousness an indispensable prerequisite of all spiritual life and stability: and who but God could enable man to regain that consciousness after all the older ethical stimuli have dried up and "vanished underground"?

The Sixty-Eighth Sūrah

Al-Qalam (The Pen)

Mecca Period

IN THE chronological order of revelation, this *sūrah* most probably occupies the third place. Some authorities – among them Suyūṭī – incline to the view that it was revealed immediately after the first five verses of *sūrah* 96 ("The Germ-Cell"); this, however, is contradicted by some of the best-authenticated Traditions, according to which most of *sūrah* 74 came second in the order of revelation (see introductory note to that *sūrah*). In any case, "The Pen" is undoubtedly one of the oldest parts of the Qur'ān.

سورة القلم مكية
-68-
وآياتها اثنتان وخمسون

ربع الحزب

IN THE NAME OF GOD, THE MOST GRACIOUS, THE DISPENSER OF GRACE:

Nūn.[1]
CONSIDER the pen, and all that they write [therewith]![2] ‹1›
Thou art not, by thy Sustainer's grace, a madman![3] ‹2› And, verily, thine shall be a reward never-ending ‹3› – for, behold, thou keepest indeed to a sublime way of life;[4] ‹4› and [one day] thou shalt see, and they [who now deride thee] shall see, ‹5› which of you was bereft of reason. ‹6›
Verily, thy Sustainer alone is fully aware as to who has strayed from His path, just as He alone is fully aware of those who have found the right way. ‹7›
Hence, defer not to [the likes and dislikes of] those who give the lie to the truth: ‹8›

بِسْمِ ٱللَّهِ ٱلرَّحْمَٰنِ ٱلرَّحِيمِ

نٓ وَٱلْقَلَمِ وَمَا يَسْطُرُونَ ﴿١﴾ مَآ أَنتَ بِنِعْمَةِ رَبِّكَ بِمَجْنُونٍ ﴿٢﴾ وَإِنَّ
لَكَ لَأَجْرًا غَيْرَ مَمْنُونٍ ﴿٣﴾ وَإِنَّكَ لَعَلَىٰ خُلُقٍ عَظِيمٍ ﴿٤﴾ فَسَتُبْصِرُ
وَيُبْصِرُونَ ﴿٥﴾ بِأَييِّكُمُ ٱلْمَفْتُونُ ﴿٦﴾ إِنَّ رَبَّكَ هُوَ أَعْلَمُ بِمَن ضَلَّ
عَن سَبِيلِهِۦ وَهُوَ أَعْلَمُ بِٱلْمُهْتَدِينَ ﴿٧﴾ فَلَا تُطِعِ ٱلْمُكَذِّبِينَ ﴿٨﴾

Bismil-lāhir-Raḥmānir-Raḥīm.
Nūun. Wal-qalami wa mā yasṭurūn. (1) Māa ᵓañta
biniᶜmati Rabbika bimajnūn. (2) Wa ᵓinna laka
laᵓajran ghayra mamnūn. (3) Wa ᵓinnaka laᶜalā khu-
luqin ᶜaẓīm. (4) Fasatubṣiru wa yubṣirūn. (5) Biᵓay-
yikumul-maftūn. (6) ᵓInna Rabbaka Huwa ᵓaᶜlamu
bimañ-ḍalla ᶜañ-sabīlihī wa Huwa ᵓaᶜlamu bilmuh-
tadīn. (7) Falā tuṭiᶜil-mukadhdhibīn. (8)

---

1 Chronologically, this is the first appearance of any of the "disjointed" [i.e., single] letters (*al-muqaṭṭaᶜāt*) which precede a number of the *sūrahs* of the Qurᵓān; for the various theories relating to these letters, see Appendix II. The supposition of some of the early commentators (extensively quoted by Ṭabarī) that the letter *n*, pronounced *nūn*, represents here an abbreviation of the identically-pronounced noun which signifies both "great fish" and "inkwell" has been convincingly rejected by some of the most outstanding authorities (e.g., Zamakhsharī and Rāzī) on grammatical grounds.

2 For the meaning of the adjurative particle *wa* at the beginning of this sentence, see the first half of note 23 on 74 : 32. The mention of "the pen" is meant to recall the earliest Qurᵓanic revelation, namely, the first five verses of *sūrah* 96 ("The Germ-Cell"), and thus to stress the fact of Muḥammad's prophethood. As regards the symbolic significance of the concept of "the pen", see 96 : 3-5 and the corresponding note 3.

3 This is an allusion to the taunt with which most of Muḥammad's contemporaries greeted the beginning of his preaching, and with which they continued to deride him for many years. In its wider sense, the above passage relates – as is so often the case in the Qurᵓān – not merely to the Prophet but also to all who followed or will follow him: in this particular instance, to all who base their moral valuations on their belief in God and in life after death.

4 The term *khuluq*, rendered by me as "way of life", describes a person's "character", "innate disposition" or "nature" in the widest sense of these concepts, as well as "habitual behaviour" which becomes, as it were, one's "second nature" (*Tāj al-ᶜArūs*). My identification of *khuluq* with "way of life" is based on the explanation of the above verse by ᶜAbd Allāh ibn ᶜAbbās (as quoted by Ṭabarī), stating that this term is here synonymous with *dīn*: and we must remember that one of the primary significances of the latter term is "a way [or "manner"] of behaviour" or "of acting" (*Qāmūs*). Moreover, we have several well-authenticated Traditions according to which Muḥammad's widow ᶜĀᵓishah, speaking of the Prophet many years after his death, repeatedly stressed that "his way of life (*khuluq*) was the Qurᵓān" (Muslim, Ṭabarī and Ḥākim, on the authority of Saᶜīd ibn Hishām; Ibn Ḥanbal, Abū Dāᵓūd and Nasāᵓī, on the authority of Al-Ḥasan al-Baṣrī; Ṭabarī, on the authority of Qatādah and Jubayr ibn Nufayl; and several other compilations).

they would like thee to be soft [with them], so that they might be soft [with thee].[5] ‹9›
Furthermore,[6] defer not to the contemptible swearer of oaths, ‹10› [or to] the slanderer that goes about with defaming tales, ‹11› [or] the withholder of good, [or] the sinful aggressor, ‹12› [or] one who is cruel, by greed possessed,[7] and, in addition to all this, utterly useless [to his fellow-men].[8] ‹13›
Is it because he is possessed of worldly goods and children ‹14› that, whenever Our messages are conveyed to him, such a one says, "Fables of ancient times"?[9] ‹15›
[For this] We shall brand him with indelible disgrace![10] ‹16›
[As for such sinners,] behold, We [but] try them[11] as We tried the owners of a certain garden who vowed that they would surely harvest its fruit on the morrow, ‹17› and made no allowance [for the will of God]:[12] ‹18› whereupon a visitation from thy Sustainer came upon that [garden] while they were asleep, ‹19› so that by the morrow it became barren and bleak. ‹20›
Now when they rose at early morn, they called unto one another, ‹21› "Go early to your tilth if you want to harvest the fruit!" ‹22›

وَدُّوا۟ لَوْ تُدْهِنُ فَيُدْهِنُونَ ۝٩ وَلَا تُطِعْ كُلَّ حَلَّافٍ مَّهِينٍ ۝١٠ هَمَّازٍ
مَّشَّآءٍۭ بِنَمِيمٍ ۝١١ مَّنَّاعٍ لِّلْخَيْرِ مُعْتَدٍ أَثِيمٍ ۝١٢ عُتُلٍّۭ بَعْدَ ذَٰلِكَ زَنِيمٍ ۝١٣
أَن كَانَ ذَا مَالٍ وَبَنِينَ ۝١٤ إِذَا تُتْلَىٰ عَلَيْهِ ءَايَٰتُنَا قَالَ أَسَٰطِيرُ
ٱلْأَوَّلِينَ ۝١٥ سَنَسِمُهُۥ عَلَى ٱلْخُرْطُومِ ۝١٦ إِنَّا بَلَوْنَٰهُمْ كَمَا بَلَوْنَآ أَصْحَٰبَ
ٱلْجَنَّةِ إِذْ أَقْسَمُوا۟ لَيَصْرِمُنَّهَا مُصْبِحِينَ ۝١٧ وَلَا يَسْتَثْنُونَ ۝١٨ فَطَافَ
عَلَيْهَا طَآئِفٌ مِّن رَّبِّكَ وَهُمْ نَآئِمُونَ ۝١٩ فَأَصْبَحَتْ كَٱلصَّرِيمِ ۝٢٠
فَتَنَادَوْا۟ مُصْبِحِينَ ۝٢١ أَنِ ٱغْدُوا۟ عَلَىٰ حَرْثِكُمْ إِن كُنتُمْ صَٰرِمِينَ ۝٢٢

Waddū law tud-hinu fayud-hinūn. (9) Wa lā tuṭiʿ kulla ḥallāfim-mahīn. (10) Hammāzim-mashshāaʾim-binamīm. (11) Mannāʿil-lilkhayri muʿtadin ʾathīm. (12) ʿUtullim-baʿda dhālika zanīm. (13) ʾAñ-kāna dhā māliñw-wa banīn. (14) ʾIdhā tutlā ʿalayhi ʾĀyātunā qāla ʾasāṭīrul-ʾawwalīn. (15) Sanasimuhū ʿalal-khurṭūm. (16) ʾInnā balawnāhum kamā balawnāa ʾaṣḥābal-jannati ʾidh ʾaqsamū layaṣrimunnahā muṣbiḥīn. (17) Wa lā yastathnūn. (18) Faṭāfa ʿalayhā ṭāaʾifum-mir-Rabbika wa hum nāaʾimūn. (19) Faʾaṣbaḥat kaṣṣarīm. (20) Fatanādaw muṣbiḥīna, (21) ʾanigh-dū ʿalā ḥarthikum ʾiñ-kuñtum ṣārimīn. (22)

5 I.e., "they would like thee to be conciliatory in the matter of ethical principles and moral valuations, whereupon they would reciprocate and desist from actively opposing thee".

6 Lit., "And". The subsequently enumerated types of moral deficiency are, of course, mentioned only as *examples* of the type of man to whose likes or dislikes no consideration whatever should be shown.

7 The term *ʿutul* – derived from the verb *ʿatala*, "he dragged [someone or something] in a rough and cruel manner" – is used to describe a person combining within himself the attributes of cruelty and greed; hence the composite rendering adopted by me.

8 The commentators give the most divergent interpretations to the term *zanīm*, which is evidently derived from the noun *zanamah*, denoting either of the two wattles, or fleshy skin protuberances, hanging below the ears of a goat. Since these wattles do not seem to have any physiological function, the term *zanīm* has come to signify "someone [or "something"] not needed" (*Tāj al-ʿArūs*): in other words, redundant or useless. It is, therefore, logical to assume that in the above context this term describes a person who is entirely useless in the social sense.

9 The term *banūn* (lit., "children" or "sons") is often used in the Qurʾān metonymically, denoting "popular support" or "many adherents"; in conjunction with the term *māl* ("worldly goods") it is meant to illustrate a certain mentality which attributes a pseudo-religious significance to wealth and influence, and regards these visible signs of worldly success as a *post-factum* evidence of the "righteousness" of the person concerned and, hence, of his not being in need of further guidance.

10 Lit., "We shall brand him on the snout" (*khurṭūm*)". All commentators point out that this idiomatic phrase has a strictly metaphorical meaning, namely, "We shall stigmatize him with indelible disgrace" (cf. Lane II, 724, quoting both Rāghib and *Tāj al-ʿArūs*).

11 I.e., by bestowing on them affluence out of all proportion to their moral deserts.

12 I.e., they resolved upon their objective without the reservation, "if God so wills": which points to the first lesson to be derived from this parable, as well as to its connection with the rhetorical question in verses 14-15 above.

فَٱنطَلَقُواْ وَهُمْ يَتَخَٰفَتُونَ ﴿٢٣﴾ أَن لَّا يَدْخُلَنَّهَا ٱلْيَوْمَ عَلَيْكُم
مِّسْكِينٌ ﴿٢٤﴾ وَغَدَوْاْ عَلَىٰ حَرْدٍ قَٰدِرِينَ ﴿٢٥﴾ فَلَمَّا رَأَوْهَا قَالُوٓاْ إِنَّا
لَضَآلُّونَ ﴿٢٦﴾ بَلْ نَحْنُ مَحْرُومُونَ ﴿٢٧﴾ قَالَ أَوْسَطُهُمْ أَلَمْ أَقُل لَّكُمْ
لَوْلَا تُسَبِّحُونَ ﴿٢٨﴾ قَالُواْ سُبْحَٰنَ رَبِّنَآ إِنَّا كُنَّا ظَٰلِمِينَ ﴿٢٩﴾ فَأَقْبَلَ
بَعْضُهُمْ عَلَىٰ بَعْضٍ يَتَلَٰوَمُونَ ﴿٣٠﴾ قَالُواْ يَٰوَيْلَنَآ إِنَّا كُنَّا طَٰغِينَ ﴿٣١﴾
عَسَىٰ رَبُّنَآ أَن يُبْدِلَنَا خَيْرًا مِّنْهَآ إِنَّآ إِلَىٰ رَبِّنَا رَٰغِبُونَ ﴿٣٢﴾ كَذَٰلِكَ
ٱلْعَذَابُ وَلَعَذَابُ ٱلْءَاخِرَةِ أَكْبَرُ لَوْ كَانُواْ يَعْلَمُونَ ﴿٣٣﴾ إِنَّ لِلْمُتَّقِينَ
عِندَ رَبِّهِمْ جَنَّٰتِ ٱلنَّعِيمِ ﴿٣٤﴾ أَفَنَجْعَلُ ٱلْمُسْلِمِينَ كَٱلْمُجْرِمِينَ ﴿٣٥﴾

Fañṭalaqū wa hum yatakhāfatūna, (23) ᵓallā yadkhu-lannahal-yawma ᶜalaykum-miskīn. (24) Wa ghadaw ᶜalā ḥardiñ-qādirīn. (25) Falammā raᵓawhā qālūu ᵓinnā laḍāallūn. (26) Bal naḥnu maḥrūmūn. (27) Qāla ᵓawsaṭuhum ᵓalam ᵓaqul-lakum lawlā tusabbiḥūn. (28) Qālū subḥāna Rabbināa ᵓinnā kunnā ẓālimīn. (29) Faᵓaqbala baᶜḍuhum ᶜalā baᶜḍiñy-yatalāwamūn. (30) Qālū yā waylanāa ᵓinnā kunnā ṭāghīn. (31) ᶜAsā Rab-bunāa ᵓañy-yubdilanā khayram-minhāa ᵓinnāa ᵓilā Rabbinā rāghibūn. (32) Kadhālikal-ᶜadhābu wa la-ᶜadhābul-ᵓĀkhirati ᵓakbaru law kānū yaᶜlamūn. (33) ᵓInna lilmuttaqīna ᶜiñda Rabbihim jannātin-naᶜīm. (34) ᵓAfanajᶜalul-Muslimīna kalmujrimīn. (35)

Thus they launched forth, whispering unto one another, ‹23› "Indeed, no needy person shall enter it today [and come] upon you [unawares]!"[13] ‹24› – and early they went, strongly bent upon their purpose. ‹25›
But as soon as they beheld [the garden and could not recognize] it, they exclaimed, "Surely we have lost our way!" ‹26› – [and then,] "Nay, but we have been rendered destitute!" ‹27›
Said the most right-minded among them: "Did I not tell you, 'Will you not extol God's limitless glory?'"[14] ‹28›
They answered: "Limitless in His glory is our Sustainer! Verily, we were doing wrong!" ‹29› – and then they turned upon one another with mutual reproaches. ‹30›
[In the end] they said: "Oh, woe unto us! Verily, we did behave outrageously! ‹31› [But] it may be that our Sustainer will grant us something better instead:[15] for, verily, unto our Sustainer do we turn with hope!" ‹32›

SUCH is the suffering [with which We try some people in this world];[16] but greater by far will be the suffering [which sinners shall have to bear] in the life to come - if they but knew it! ‹33›
For, behold, it is the God-conscious [alone] whom gardens of bliss await with their Sustainer: ‹34› or should We, perchance, treat those who surrender themselves unto Us[17] as [We would treat] those who remain lost in sin? ‹35›

13 Ever since Biblical times it has been understood that the poor have a right to a share in the harvest of the fields and gardens owned by their more fortunate fellow-men (cf. 6 : 141 – "give [unto the poor] their due on harvest-day"). The determination of the "owners of the garden" to deprive the poor of this right is the second type of sin to which the above parable points: and inasmuch as it is a *social* sin, it connects with verses 10-13.

14 This is obviously a reference to their failure to realize that nothing can come about unless the Almighty so wills (verse 18).

15 Namely, His forgiveness.

16 This connects with the first clause of verse 17 above, which, in its turn, contains an allusion to the mentality spoken of in verses 14-15.

17 This is the earliest occurrence of the term *muslimūn* (sing. *muslim*) in the history of Qurᵓanic revelation. Throughout this work, I have translated the terms *muslim* and *islām* in accordance with their original connotations, namely, "one who surrenders [or "has surrendered"] himself to God", and "man's self-surrender to God"; the same holds good of all forms of the verb *aslama* occurring in the Qurᵓān. It should be borne in mind that the

مَا لَكُمْ كَيْفَ تَحْكُمُونَ ﴿36﴾ أَمْ لَكُمْ كِتَٰبٌ فِيهِ تَدْرُسُونَ ﴿37﴾ إِنَّ
لَكُمْ فِيهِ لَمَا تَخَيَّرُونَ ﴿38﴾ أَمْ لَكُمْ أَيْمَٰنٌ عَلَيْنَا بَٰلِغَةٌ إِلَىٰ يَوْمِ ٱلْقِيَٰمَةِ
إِنَّ لَكُمْ لَمَا تَحْكُمُونَ ﴿39﴾ سَلْهُمْ أَيُّهُم بِذَٰلِكَ زَعِيمٌ ﴿40﴾ أَمْ لَهُمْ
شُرَكَآءُ فَلْيَأْتُوا۟ بِشُرَكَآئِهِمْ إِن كَانُوا۟ صَٰدِقِينَ ﴿41﴾ يَوْمَ يُكْشَفُ عَن
سَاقٍ وَيُدْعَوْنَ إِلَى ٱلسُّجُودِ فَلَا يَسْتَطِيعُونَ ﴿42﴾ خَٰشِعَةً أَبْصَٰرُهُمْ
تَرْهَقُهُمْ ذِلَّةٌ وَقَدْ كَانُوا۟ يُدْعَوْنَ إِلَى ٱلسُّجُودِ وَهُمْ سَٰلِمُونَ ﴿43﴾ فَذَرْنِى
وَمَن يُكَذِّبُ بِهَٰذَا ٱلْحَدِيثِ سَنَسْتَدْرِجُهُم مِّنْ حَيْثُ لَا يَعْلَمُونَ ﴿44﴾
وَأُمْلِى لَهُمْ إِنَّ كَيْدِى مَتِينٌ ﴿45﴾

Mā lakum kayfa taḥkumūn. (36) ʾAm lakum kitābuñ-fīhi tadrusūna, (37) ʾinna lakum fīhi lamā takhayyarūn. (38) ʾAm lakum ʾaymānun ʿalaynā bālighatun ʾilā Yawmil-Qiyāmati ʾinna lakum lamā taḥkumūn. (39) Salhum ʾayyuhum bidhālika zaʿīm. (40) ʾAm lahum shurakāaʾu falyaʾtū bishurakāaʾihim ʾiñ-kānū ṣādiqīn. (41) Yawma yukshafu ʿañ-sāqiñw-wa yudʿawna ʾilas-sujūdi falā yastaṭīʿūn. (42) Khāshiʿatan ʾabṣāruhum tarhaquhum dhillatuñw-wa qad kānū yudʿawna ʾilas-sujūdi wa hum sālimūn. (43) Fadharnī wa mañy-yukadhdhibu bihādhal-ḥadīthi sanastadrijuhum-min ḥaythu lā yaʿlamūn. (44) Wa ʾumlī lahum; ʾinna kaydī matīn. (45)

What is amiss with you?[18] On what do you base your judgment [of right and wrong]? «36» Or have you, perchance, a [special] divine writ which you study, «37» and in which you find all that you may wish to find?[19] «38»

Or have you received a solemn promise, binding on Us till Resurrection Day, that yours will assuredly be whatever you judge [to be your rightful due]? «39»

Ask them which of them is able to vouch for this! «40» Or have they, perchance, any sages to support their views?[20]

Well, then, if they are sincere in this their claim, let them produce those supporters of theirs «41» on the Day when man's very being shall be bared to the bone,[21] and when they [who now deny the truth] shall be called upon to prostrate themselves [before God],[22] and shall be unable to do so: «42» downcast will be their eyes, with ignominy overwhelming them – seeing that they had been called upon [in vain] to prostrate themselves [before Him] while they were yet sound [and alive]. «43»

Hence, leave Me alone with such as give the lie to this tiding.[23] We shall bring them low, step by step, without their perceiving how it has come about:[24] «44» for, behold, though I may give them rein for a while, My subtle scheme is exceedingly firm![25] «45»

"institutionalized" use of these terms – that is, their exclusive application to the followers of the Prophet Muḥammad – represents a definitely post-Qurʾanic development and, hence, must be avoided in a translation of the Qurʾān.

18 Sc., "O you sinners".

19 Lit., "so that in it you [may] have all that you choose [to have]" – i.e., a moral justification of the claim that whatever is considered "expedient" is *eo ipso* right.

20 Lit., "Or have they any associates?" – i.e., wise people (*ʿuqalāʾ*) who would share their views and their way of life (Zamakhsharī and Rāzī). Accordingly, the expression *shurakāʾuhum* in the next sentence has been rendered as "those supporters of theirs".

21 Lit., "when the shin[-bone] shall be bared": i.e., when man's innermost thoughts, feelings and motivations will be laid bare. The implication is that their erstwhile claim that whatever is "expedient" is morally justifiable (see note 19 above), shall be revealed in all its nakedness – namely, as something indefensible and spiritually destructive.

22 I.e., willingly, gladly humbling themselves before Him.

23 I.e., to divine revelation in general, and to the tiding of resurrection and judgment, in particular – the implication being that God alone has the right to decide whether or how to chastise them.

24 Lit., "without their knowing whence [it comes]". The above sentence, as well as the next (verse 45), are found in exactly the same formulation in 7 : 182-183.

25 The term "subtle scheme" (*kayd*) evidently circumscribes here God's unfathomable plan of creation of which man can glimpse only isolated fragments and never the totality: a plan in which every thing and happening has a definite function, and nothing is accidental. (See in this connection note 11 on 10 : 5 – "None of this has God created

Or is it that [they fear lest] thou ask them for a reward, [O Prophet,] so that they would be burdened with debt [if they listened to thee]? «46»
Or [do they think] that the hidden reality [of all that exists] is within their grasp, so that [in time] they can write it down?[26] «47»

BEAR, THEN, with patience thy Sustainer's will, and be not like him of the great fish, who cried out [in distress] after having given in to anger.[27] «48» [And remember:] had not grace from his Sustainer reached him,[28] he would indeed have been cast forth upon that barren shore in a state of disgrace:[29] «49» but [as it was,] his Sustainer had elected him and placed him among the righteous. «50»
Hence, [be patient,] even though they who are bent on denying the truth would all but kill thee with their eyes whenever they hear this reminder, and [though] they say, "[As for Muḥammad,] behold, most surely he is a madman!" «51»
[Be patient:] for this is nought else but a reminder [from God] to all mankind. «52»

أَمْ تَسْـَٔلُهُمْ أَجْرًا فَهُم مِّن مَّغْرَمٍ مُّثْقَلُونَ ﴿46﴾ أَمْ عِندَهُمُ ٱلْغَيْبُ فَهُمْ
يَكْتُبُونَ ﴿47﴾ فَٱصْبِرْ لِحُكْمِ رَبِّكَ وَلَا تَكُن كَصَاحِبِ ٱلْحُوتِ إِذْ
نَادَىٰ وَهُوَ مَكْظُومٌ ﴿48﴾ لَّوْلَآ أَن تَدَٰرَكَهُۥ نِعْمَةٌ مِّن رَّبِّهِۦ لَنُبِذَ بِٱلْعَرَآءِ
وَهُوَ مَذْمُومٌ ﴿49﴾ فَٱجْتَبَٰهُ رَبُّهُۥ فَجَعَلَهُۥ مِنَ ٱلصَّٰلِحِينَ ﴿50﴾ وَإِن يَكَادُ
ٱلَّذِينَ كَفَرُوا۟ لَيُزْلِقُونَكَ بِأَبْصَٰرِهِمْ لَمَّا سَمِعُوا۟ ٱلذِّكْرَ وَيَقُولُونَ إِنَّهُۥ
لَمَجْنُونٌ ﴿51﴾ وَمَا هُوَ إِلَّا ذِكْرٌ لِّلْعَٰلَمِينَ ﴿52﴾

ʾAm tasʾaluhum ʾajrañ-fahum-mim-maghramim-muthqalūn. ﴿46﴾ ʾAm ᶜiñdahumul-ghaybu fahum yaktubūn. ﴿47﴾ Faṣbir liḥukmi Rabbika wa lā takuñ-kaṣāḥibil-ḥūt. ʾIdh nādā wa huwa makẓūm. ﴿48﴾ Lawlāa ʾañ-tadārakahū niᶜmatum-mir-Rabbihī lanubidha bilᶜarāaʾi wa huwa madhmūm. ﴿49﴾ Fajtabāhu Rabbuhū fajaᶜalahū minaṣ-ṣāliḥīn. ﴿50﴾ Wa ʾiñy-yakādul-ladhīna kafarū layuzliqūnaka biʾabṣārihim lammā samiᶜudh-Dhikra wa yaqūlūna ʾinnahū lamajnūn. ﴿51﴾ Wa mā huwa ʾillā Dhikrul-lilᶜālamīn. ﴿52﴾

without [an inner] truth".) Indirectly, the above passage alludes to the question as to the reason why God allows so many evil persons to enjoy their lives to the full, while so many of the righteous are allowed to suffer: the answer being that during his life in this world man cannot really understand where apparent happiness and unhappiness *ultimately* lead to, and what role they play in God's "subtle scheme" of creation.

26 Sc., "and that, therefore, they need not listen to divine revelation". For the real significance of the term *al-ghayb* – of which the above is undoubtedly the earliest instance in the chronology of Qurʾanic revelation – see *sūrah* 2, note 3. Its use in the above context is meant to elucidate and further develop the idea already touched upon in 96 : 6 – "man becomes grossly overweening whenever he believes himself to be self-sufficient". More particularly, the present passage points to the fallacy of the arrogant belief that the solution of all the mysteries of the universe is "just around the corner" and that man-centred science – epitomized in the reference to its being "written down" – can and will teach its adepts how to "conquer nature" and to attain to what they regard as the good life.

27 This is a reference to the Prophet Jonah – see 21 : 87 and the corresponding notes 82 and 83. As mentioned in 37 : 140, "he fled like a runaway slave" from the task with which he had been entrusted by God, because his people did not all at once accept his preaching as valid: and so Muḥammad is exhorted not to give in to despair or anger at the opposition shown to him by most of his contemporaries in Mecca, but to persevere in his prophetic mission.

28 Cf. 37 : 143 – "had he not been of those who [even in the deep darkness of their distress are able to] extol God's limitless glory": i.e., who always remember God and pray for His forgiveness.

29 Lit., "while he was still blameworthy", i.e., burdened with sin and unredeemed by repentance: implying that but for God's grace he would have died as a sinner.

The Sixty-Ninth Sūrah

Al-Ḥāaqqah (The Laying-Bare of the Truth)

Mecca Period

REVEALED shortly after *sūrah* 67 (*Al-Mulk*), i.e., about three or four years before the Prophet's exodus to Medina.

سورة الحاقة مكية -69-
وآياتها ثنتان وخمسون

نصف الحزب

IN THE NAME OF GOD, THE MOST GRACIOUS, THE DISPENSER OF GRACE:

OH, THE LAYING-BARE of the truth![1] ‹1›
How awesome that laying-bare of the truth! ‹2›
And what could make thee conceive what that laying-bare of the truth will be?[2] ‹3›

THE LIE gave [the tribes of] Thamūd and ᶜĀd to [all tidings of] that sudden calamity![3] ‹4›
Now as for the Thamūd – they were destroyed by a violent upheaval [of the earth];[4] ‹5› and as for the ᶜĀd – they were destroyed by a stormwind furiously raging, ‹6› which He willed against them for seven nights and eight days without

بِسْمِ ٱللَّهِ ٱلرَّحْمَٰنِ ٱلرَّحِيمِ

ٱلْحَآقَّةُ (1) مَا ٱلْحَآقَّةُ (2) وَمَآ أَدْرَىٰكَ مَا ٱلْحَآقَّةُ (3) كَذَّبَتْ ثَمُودُ
وَعَادٌۢ بِٱلْقَارِعَةِ (4) فَأَمَّا ثَمُودُ فَأُهْلِكُوا۟ بِٱلطَّاغِيَةِ (5) وَأَمَّا عَادٌ فَأُهْلِكُوا۟
بِرِيحٍ صَرْصَرٍ عَاتِيَةٍ (6) سَخَّرَهَا عَلَيْهِمْ سَبْعَ لَيَالٍ وَثَمَٰنِيَةَ أَيَّامٍ حُسُومًا

Bismil-lāhir-Raḥmānir-Raḥīm.
ᵓAlḥāaqqah. (1) Mal-ḥāaqqah. (2) Wa māa ᵓadrāka
mal-ḥāaqqah. (3) Kadhdhabat Thamūdu wa ᶜĀdum-
bilqāriᶜah. (4) Faᵓammā Thamudu faᵓuhlikū biṭ-
ṭāghiyah. (5) Wa ᵓammā ᶜĀduñ-faᵓuhlikū birīḥiñ-
ṣarṣarin ᶜātiyah. (6) Sakhkharahā ᶜalayhim sabᶜa
layāliñw-wa thamāniyata ᵓayyāmin ḥusūmañ-

---

1 I.e., the Day of Resurrection and Judgment, on which man will become fully aware of the quality of his past life and, freed from all self-deception, will see himself as he really was, with the innermost meaning of all his past doings – and thus of his destiny in the hereafter – blindingly revealed. (Cf. 37 : 19, the last sentence of 39 : 68, and 50 : 21-22.)

2 Implying that this sudden perception of the ultimate reality will be beyond anything that man can anticipate or imagine: hence, no answer is given to the above rhetorical question.

3 I.e., the Last Hour (see note 1 on 101 : 1). For particulars of the pre-Islamic tribes of ᶜĀd and Thamūd, see 7 : 65-79 and the corresponding notes.

4 Cf. 7 : 78.

فَتَرَى ٱلْقَوْمَ فِيهَا صَرْعَىٰ كَأَنَّهُمْ أَعْجَازُ نَخْلٍ خَاوِيَةٍ (7) فَهَلْ تَرَىٰ لَهُم مِّنۢ
بَاقِيَةٍ (8) وَجَآءَ فِرْعَوْنُ وَمَن قَبْلَهُۥ وَٱلْمُؤْتَفِكَٰتُ بِٱلْخَاطِئَةِ (9) فَعَصَوْا۟
رَسُولَ رَبِّهِمْ فَأَخَذَهُمْ أَخْذَةً رَّابِيَةً (10) إِنَّا لَمَّا طَغَا ٱلْمَآءُ حَمَلْنَٰكُمْ فِى
ٱلْجَارِيَةِ (11) لِنَجْعَلَهَا لَكُمْ تَذْكِرَةً وَتَعِيَهَآ أُذُنٌ وَٰعِيَةٌ (12) فَإِذَا نُفِخَ فِى
ٱلصُّورِ نَفْخَةٌ وَٰحِدَةٌ (13) وَحُمِلَتِ ٱلْأَرْضُ وَٱلْجِبَالُ فَدُكَّتَا دَكَّةً
وَٰحِدَةً (14) فَيَوْمَئِذٍ وَقَعَتِ ٱلْوَاقِعَةُ (15) وَٱنشَقَّتِ ٱلسَّمَآءُ فَهِىَ يَوْمَئِذٍ
وَاهِيَةٌ (16) وَٱلْمَلَكُ عَلَىٰٓ أَرْجَآئِهَا وَيَحْمِلُ عَرْشَ رَبِّكَ فَوْقَهُمْ يَوْمَئِذٍ
ثَمَٰنِيَةٌ (17)

fataral-qawma fīhā ṣarʿā kaʾannahum ʾaʿjāzu nakhlin khāwiyah. (7) Fahal tarā lahum-mim-bāqiyah. (8) Wa jāaʾa Firʿawnu wa mañ-qablahū wal-muʾtafikātu bilkhāṭiʾah. (9) Faʿaṣaw Rasūla Rabbihim faʾakhadhahum ʾakhdhatar-rābiyah. (10) ʾInnā lammā ṭaghal-māaʾu ḥamalnākum fil-jāriyah. (11) Linajʿalahā lakum tadhkiratañw-wa taʿiyahāa ʾudhunuñw-wāʿiyah. (12) Faʾidhā nufikha fiṣ-ṣūri nafkhatuñw-wāḥidah. (13) Wa ḥumilatil-ʾarḍu wal-jibālu fadukkatā dakkatañw-wāḥidah. (14) FaYawmaʾidhiñw-waqaʿatil-wāqiʿah. (15) Wañ-shaqqatis-samāaʾu fahiya Yawmaʾidhiñw-wāhiyah. (16) Wal-Malaku ʿalāa ʾarjāaʾihā; wa yaḥmilu ʿarsha Rabbika fawqahum Yawmaʾidhiñ-thamāniyah. (17)

cease, so that in the end thou couldst see those people laid low [in death], as though they were so many [uprooted] trunks of hollow palm trees: ‹7› and dost thou now see any remnant of them? ‹8›

And there was Pharaoh, too, and [many of] those who lived before him, and the cities that were overthrown[5] – [all of them] indulged in sin upon sin ‹9› and rebelled against their Sustainer's apostles: and so He took them to task with a punishing grasp exceedingly severe! ‹10›

[And] behold: when the waters [of Noah's flood] burst beyond all limits, it was We who caused you[6] to be borne [to safety] in that floating ark, ‹11› so that We might make all this[7] a [lasting] reminder to you all, and that every wide-awake ear might consciously take it in. ‹12›

Hence, [bethink yourselves of the Last Hour,] when the trumpet [of judgment] shall be sounded with a single blast, ‹13› and the earth and the mountains shall be lifted up and crushed with a single stroke! ‹14›

And so, that which must come to pass[8] will on that Day have come to pass; ‹15› and the sky will be rent asunder[9] – for, frail will it have become on that Day; ‹16› – and the angels [will appear] at its ends,[10] and, above them, eight will bear aloft on that Day the throne of thy Sustainer's almightiness. . . .[11] ‹17›

---

5 I.e., Sodom and Gomorrah, the cities of Lot's people (see 11 : 69-83).

6 I.e., metonymically (in the consensus of all classical commentators), "your ancestors".

7 Alluding to the punishment of evildoers and the saving grace bestowed upon the righteous.

8 I.e., the end of the world as we know it, followed by resurrection and the Last Judgment.

9 The term *as-samāʾ* may denote here "the sky" or "skies", i.e., the visible firmament, or "heaven" in its allegorical sense, or the aggregate of cosmic systems comprised in the concept of "the universe" (cf. *sūrah* 2, note 20). Its being "rent asunder" is perhaps a metaphor for a total breakdown of the cosmic order.

10 Or: "at its sides".

11 Since God is infinite in space as well as in time, it is obvious that His "throne" (*ʿarsh*) has a purely metaphorical connotation, circumscribing His absolute, unfathomable sway over all that exists or possibly could exist (cf. note 43 on 7 : 54). Hence, too, the "bearing aloft" of the throne of His almightiness cannot be anything but a metaphor – namely, an allusion to the full *manifestation* of that almightiness on the Day of Judgment. The Qurʾān is silent as to who or what the "eight" are on whom this manifestation rests. Some of the earliest commentators assume that they are eight angels; others, that they are eight *ranks* of angels; while still others frankly admit that it is impossible to say whether "eight" or "eight thousand" are meant (Al-Ḥasan al-Baṣrī, as quoted by Zamakhsharī). Possibly, we have here an allusion to eight (unspecified) attributes of God or aspects of His creation; but, as the Qurʾān states elsewhere, "none save God knows its final meaning" (see 3 : 7 and the corresponding note 8).

On that Day you shall be brought to judgment: not [even] the most hidden of your deeds will remain hidden. ‹18›
Now as for him whose record shall be placed in his right hand,[12] he will exclaim: "Come you all! Read this my record! ‹19› Behold, I did know that [one day] I would have to face my account!"[13] ‹20›
And so he will find himself in a happy state of life, ‹21› in a lofty paradise, ‹22› with its fruits within easy reach. ‹23›
[And all who are thus blest will be told:] "Eat and drink with good cheer in return for all [the good deeds] that you have sent ahead in days gone by!" ‹24›
But as for him whose record shall be placed in his left hand,[14] he will exclaim: "Oh, would that I had never been shown this my record, ‹25› and neither known this my account! ‹26› Oh, would that this [death of mine] had been the end of me! ‹27› Of no avail to me is all that I have [ever] possessed, ‹28› [and] all my power of argument has died away from me!"[15] ‹29›
[Thereupon the command will go forth:] "Lay hold of him, and shackle him,[16] ‹30› and then let him enter hell, ‹31› and then thrust him into a chain [of other sinners like him[17] – a chain] the length whereof is seventy cubits:[18] ‹32› for, behold, he did not believe in God, the Tremendous, ‹33›

يَوْمَئِذٍ تُعْرَضُونَ لَا تَخْفَىٰ مِنكُمْ خَافِيَةٌ ﴿18﴾ فَأَمَّا مَنْ أُوتِيَ كِتَٰبَهُۥ بِيَمِينِهِۦ فَيَقُولُ هَآؤُمُ ٱقْرَءُواْ كِتَٰبِيَهْ ﴿19﴾ إِنِّي ظَنَنتُ أَنِّي مُلَٰقٍ حِسَابِيَهْ ﴿20﴾ فَهُوَ فِي عِيشَةٍ رَّاضِيَةٍ ﴿21﴾ فِي جَنَّةٍ عَالِيَةٍ ﴿22﴾ قُطُوفُهَا دَانِيَةٌ ﴿23﴾ كُلُواْ وَٱشْرَبُواْ هَنِيٓـَٔۢا بِمَآ أَسْلَفْتُمْ فِي ٱلْأَيَّامِ ٱلْخَالِيَةِ ﴿24﴾ وَأَمَّا مَنْ أُوتِيَ كِتَٰبَهُۥ بِشِمَالِهِۦ فَيَقُولُ يَٰلَيْتَنِي لَمْ أُوتَ كِتَٰبِيَهْ ﴿25﴾ وَلَمْ أَدْرِ مَا حِسَابِيَهْ ﴿26﴾ يَٰلَيْتَهَا كَانَتِ ٱلْقَاضِيَةَ ﴿27﴾ مَآ أَغْنَىٰ عَنِّي مَالِيَهْ ﴿28﴾ هَّلَكَ عَنِّي سُلْطَٰنِيَهْ ﴿29﴾ خُذُوهُ فَغُلُّوهُ ﴿30﴾ ثُمَّ ٱلْجَحِيمَ صَلُّوهُ ﴿31﴾ ثُمَّ فِي سِلْسِلَةٍ ذَرْعُهَا سَبْعُونَ ذِرَاعًا فَٱسْلُكُوهُ ﴿32﴾ إِنَّهُۥ كَانَ لَا يُؤْمِنُ بِٱللَّهِ ٱلْعَظِيمِ ﴿33﴾

Yawmaʾidhiñ-tuʿraḍūna lā takhfā miñkum khāfiyah. (18) Faʾammā man ʾūtiya kitābahū biyamīnihī fayaqūlu hāaʾumuq-raʾū kitābiyah. (19) ʾInnī ẓanañtu ʾannī mulāqin ḥisābiyah. (20) Fahuwa fī ʿīshatir-rāḍiyah. (21) Fī jannatin ʿāliyah. (22) Quṭūfuhā dāniyah. (23) Kulū wash-rabū hanīiʾam-bimāa ʾaslaftum fil-ʾayyāmil-khāliyah. (24) Wa ʾammā man ʾūtiya kitābahū bishimālihī fayaqūlu yā laytanī lam ʾūta kitābiyah. (25) Wa lam ʾadri mā ḥisābiyah. (26) Yā laytahā kānatil-qāḍiyah. (27) Māa ʾaghnā ʿannī māliyah. (28) Halaka ʿannī sulṭāniyah. (29) Khudhūhu faghullūh. (30) Thummal-jaḥīma ṣallūh. (31) Thumma fī silsilatiñ-dharʿuhā sabʿūna dhirāʿañ-fasluküh. (32) ʾInnahū kāna lā yuʾminu billāhil-ʿAẓīm. (33)

12 I.e., whose record shows that he was righteous in his life on earth: cf. 17 : 71, as well as the symbolic expression "those on the right hand" in 74 : 39. The linguistic origin of the symbolism of "right" and "left" as "righteous" and "unrighteous" is explained in note 3 on 56 : 8-9.

13 Implying that he had always been conscious of resurrection and judgment, and had tried to behave accordingly.

14 Thus signifying that he had been unrighteous in his earthly life, in contrast with those "whose record will be placed in their right hand" (see verse 19 and note 12 above).

15 The term *sulṭān*, which primarily signifies "power" or "authority", has here – as in many other places in the Qurʾān – evidently the meaning of "argument", synonymous with *ḥujjah* (Ibn ʿAbbās, ʿIkrimah, Mujāhid, Aḍ-Ḍaḥḥāk, all of them quoted by Ṭabarī): in this case, an argument or arguments against the idea of life after death and, hence, of divine judgment.

16 For an explanation of the allegory of "shackles", see note 13 on 13 : 5, note 44 on the last but one sentence of 34 : 33, and notes 6 and 7 on 36 : 8.

17 See 14 : 49 – "on that Day thou wilt see all who were lost in sin (*al-mujrimīn*) linked together in fetters" – and the corresponding note 64, which explains my above interpolation of the phrase, "of other sinners like him".

18 I.e., a chain exceedingly long – the number "seventy" being used here metonymically, as is often done in classical Arabic, in the sense of "very many" (Zamakhsharī); hence "of a measure the length whereof is known only to God" (Ṭabarī; also (Al-Ḥasan as quoted by Rāzī).

وَلَا يَحُضُّ عَلَىٰ طَعَامِ ٱلْمِسْكِينِ ﴿٣٤﴾ فَلَيْسَ لَهُ ٱلْيَوْمَ هَـٰهُنَا حَمِيمٌ ﴿٣٥﴾
وَلَا طَعَامٌ إِلَّا مِنْ غِسْلِينٍ ﴿٣٦﴾ لَّا يَأْكُلُهُۥٓ إِلَّا ٱلْخَـٰطِـُٔونَ ﴿٣٧﴾ فَلَآ أُقْسِمُ
بِمَا تُبْصِرُونَ ﴿٣٨﴾ وَمَا لَا تُبْصِرُونَ ﴿٣٩﴾ إِنَّهُۥ لَقَوْلُ رَسُولٍ كَرِيمٍ ﴿٤٠﴾
وَمَا هُوَ بِقَوْلِ شَاعِرٍ قَلِيلًا مَّا تُؤْمِنُونَ ﴿٤١﴾ وَلَا بِقَوْلِ كَاهِنٍ قَلِيلًا مَّا
تَذَكَّرُونَ ﴿٤٢﴾ تَنزِيلٌ مِّن رَّبِّ ٱلْعَـٰلَمِينَ ﴿٤٣﴾ وَلَوْ تَقَوَّلَ عَلَيْنَا بَعْضَ
ٱلْأَقَاوِيلِ ﴿٤٤﴾ لَأَخَذْنَا مِنْهُ بِٱلْيَمِينِ ﴿٤٥﴾ ثُمَّ لَقَطَعْنَا مِنْهُ ٱلْوَتِينَ ﴿٤٦﴾
فَمَا مِنكُم مِّنْ أَحَدٍ عَنْهُ حَـٰجِزِينَ ﴿٤٧﴾ وَإِنَّهُۥ لَتَذْكِرَةٌ لِّلْمُتَّقِينَ ﴿٤٨﴾
وَإِنَّا لَنَعْلَمُ أَنَّ مِنكُم مُّكَذِّبِينَ ﴿٤٩﴾ وَإِنَّهُۥ لَحَسْرَةٌ عَلَى ٱلْكَـٰفِرِينَ ﴿٥٠﴾
وَإِنَّهُۥ لَحَقُّ ٱلْيَقِينِ ﴿٥١﴾ فَسَبِّحْ بِٱسْمِ رَبِّكَ ٱلْعَظِيمِ ﴿٥٢﴾

Wa lā yaḥuḍḍu ᶜalā ṭaᶜāmil-miskīn. (34) Falaysa lahul-Yawma hāhunā ḥamīm. (35) Wa lā ṭaᶜāmun ˀillā min ghislīn. (36) Lā yaˀkuluhū ˀillal-khāṭiˀūn. (37) Falāa ˀuqsimu bimā tubṣirūna, (38) wa mā lā tubṣirūna, (39) ˀinnahū laqawlu Rasūliñ-karīm. (40) Wa mā huwa bi-qawli shāᶜiriñ-qalīlam-mā tuˀminūn. (41) Wa lā biqawli kāhiniñ-qalīlam-mā tadhakkarūn. (42) Tañzīlum-mir-Rabbil-ᶜālamīn. (43) Wa law taqawwala ᶜalaynā baᶜḍal-ˀaqāwīli, (44) laˀakhadhnā minhu bilyamīn. (45) Thumma laqaṭaᶜnā minhul-watīn. (46) Famā miñkum-min ˀaḥadin ᶜanhu ḥājizīn. (47) Wa ˀinnahū latadhkiratul-lilmuttaqīn. (48) Wa ˀinnā lanaᶜlamu ˀanna miñkum-mukadhdhibīn. (49) Wa ˀinnahū laḥasratun ᶜalal-kāfirīn. (50) Wa ˀinnahū laḥaqqul-yaqīn. (51) Fasabbiḥ bismi Rabbikal-ᶜAẓīm. (52)

and did not feel any urge[19] to feed the needy: ⟨34⟩ and so, no friend has he here today, ⟨35⟩ nor any food save the filth ⟨36⟩ which none but the sinners eat!"[20] ⟨37⟩

BUT NAY! I call to witness all that you can see, ⟨38⟩ as well as all that you cannot see![21] ⟨39⟩

Behold, this [Qurˀān] is indeed the [inspired] word of a noble Apostle, ⟨40⟩ and is not – however little you may [be prepared to] believe it – the word of a poet; ⟨41⟩ and neither is it – however little you may [be prepared to] take it to heart – the word of a soothsayer: ⟨42⟩ [it is] a revelation from the Sustainer of all the worlds. ⟨43⟩

Now if he [whom We have entrusted with it] had dared to attribute some [of his own] sayings unto Us, ⟨44⟩ We would indeed have seized him by his right hand,[22] ⟨45⟩ and would indeed have cut his life-vein, ⟨46⟩ and none of you could have saved him! ⟨47⟩

And, verily, this [Qurˀān] is a reminder to all the God-conscious.[23] ⟨48⟩

And, behold, well do We know that among you are such as will give the lie to it: ⟨49⟩ yet, behold, this [rejection] will indeed become a source of bitter regret for all who deny the truth [of God's revelation] ⟨50⟩ – for, verily, it is truth absolute! ⟨51⟩

Extol, then, the limitless glory of thy Sustainer's mighty name! ⟨52⟩

---

19 Lit., "did not urge", i.e., himself.

20 The noun *ghislīn*, which appears in the Qurˀān only in this one instance, has been variously – and very contradictorily – explained by the early commentators. Ibn ᶜAbbās, when asked about it, frankly answered, "I do not know what *ghislīn* denotes" (Rāzī). The term "filth" used by me contains an allusion to the "devouring" of all that is abominable in the spiritual sense: cf. its characterization in the next verse as "[that] which none but the sinners eat" – i.e., (metaphorically) in this world and, consequently, in the hereafter as well.

21 The phrase "all that you can see" comprises all the observable phenomena of nature – including man himself and the organic conditions of his own existence – as well as the configuration of human society and the perceptible rules of its growth and decay in the historical sense; whereas "that which you cannot see" relates to the intangible spiritual verities accessible to man's intuition and instinct, including the voice of his own conscience: all of which "bears witness", as it were, to the fact that the light which the divine writ (spoken of in the sequence) casts on the innermost realities and interrelations of all that exists objectively – or, as the case may be, manifests itself subjectively in man's own psyche – *must* be an outcome of genuine revelation, inasmuch as it goes far beyond anything that unaided human intellect could ever achieve.

22 I.e., deprived him of all ability to act – the "right hand" symbolizing power.

23 Sc., "who believe in [the existence of] that which is beyond the reach of human perception": cf. 2 : 2-3.

The Seventieth Sūrah

Al-Maʿārij (The Ways of Ascent)

Mecca Period

THUS CALLED after the word *al-maʿārij* appearing in verse 3, this *sūrah* belongs to the middle of the Mecca period. It is mainly devoted to the challenge which unbelief – or, rather, unwillingness to believe – offers to faith, both of them being conditioned by the restlessness inherent in human nature.

سورة المعارج مكية -70-
وآياتها أربع وأربعون

IN THE NAME OF GOD, THE MOST GRACIOUS, THE DISPENSER OF GRACE:

ONE who is minded to ask might ask[1] about the suffering which [in the hereafter] is bound to befall ‹1› those who deny the truth.[2]
[Know, then, that] nothing can ward it off, ‹2› [since it will come] from God, unto whom there are many ways of ascent:[3] ‹3› all the angels and all the inspiration [ever granted to man] ascend unto Him[4] [daily,] in a day the length whereof is [like] fifty thousand years. . . .[5] ‹4›

بِسْمِ ٱللَّهِ ٱلرَّحْمَـٰنِ ٱلرَّحِيمِ

سَأَلَ سَآئِلُۢ بِعَذَابٍ وَاقِعٍ ﴿١﴾ لِّلْكَـٰفِرِينَ لَيْسَ لَهُۥ دَافِعٌ ﴿٢﴾ مِّنَ ٱللَّهِ
ذِى ٱلْمَعَارِجِ ﴿٣﴾ تَعْرُجُ ٱلْمَلَـٰٓئِكَةُ وَٱلرُّوحُ إِلَيْهِ فِى يَوْمٍ كَانَ مِقْدَارُهُۥ
خَمْسِينَ أَلْفَ سَنَةٍ ﴿٤﴾

Bismil-lāhir-Raḥmānir-Raḥīm.
Saʾala sāaʾilum-biʿadhābiñw-wāqiʿ. ① Lilkāfirīna laysa lahū dāfiʿ. ② Minal-lāhi Dhil-maʿārij. ③ Taʿrujul-Malāaʾikatu war-rūḥu ʾilayhi fī yawmiñ-kāna miqdāruhū khamsīna ʾalfa sanah. ④

---

1 Lit., "An inquirer inquired" or "might inquire".

2 In view of the fact that many of "those who deny the truth" – and, by implication, do evil in consequence of that deliberate denial – prosper in this world, a doubter might well ask whether or when this state of affairs will really be reversed and the values adjusted in accord with divine justice. An answer to the "whether" is given in the second paragraph of verse 2; and to the "when", elliptically, at the end of verse 4.

3 Lit., "He of the [many] ascents": a metonymical phrase implying that there are many ways by which man can "ascend" to a comprehension of God's existence, and thus to spiritual "nearness" to Him – and that, therefore, it is up to each human being to avail himself of any of the ways leading towards Him (cf. 76 : 3).

4 For my rendering of *rūḥ* as "inspiration", see *sūrah* 16, note 2. The "ascent" of the angels and of all inspiration may be understood in the same sense as the frequently-occurring phrase "all things go back to God [as their source]" (Rāzī).

5 The very concept of "time" is meaningless in relation to God, who is timeless and infinite: cf. note 63 on the last sentence of 22 : 47 – "in thy Sustainer's sight a day is like a thousand years of your reckoning": in other words, a day, or an aeon, or a thousand years, or fifty thousand years are alike to Him, having an apparent reality only within the *created* world and none with the Creator. And since in the hereafter time will cease to have a meaning for man as well, it is irrelevant to ask as to "when" the evildoers will be chastised and the righteous given their due.

Therefore, [O believer, endure all adversity with goodly patience: ‹5› behold, men[6] look upon that [reckoning] as something far away ‹6› – but We see it as near! ‹7›
[It will take place] on a Day when the sky will be like molten lead, ‹8› and the mountains will be like tufts of wool, ‹9› and [when] no friend will ask about his friend, ‹10› though they may be in one another's sight: [for,] everyone who was lost in sin will on that Day but desire to ransom himself from suffering at the price of his own children, ‹11› and of his spouse, and of his brother, ‹12› and of all the kinsfolk who ever sheltered him, ‹13› and of whoever [else] lives on earth, all of them – so that he could but save himself. ‹14›
But nay! Verily, all [that awaits him] is a raging flame, ‹15› tearing away his skin! ‹16›
It will claim all such as turn their backs [on what is right], and turn away [from the truth], ‹17› and amass [wealth] and thereupon withhold [it from their fellow-men]. ‹18›

VERILY, man is born with a restless disposition.[7] ‹19›
[As a rule,] whenever misfortune touches him, he is filled with self-pity;[8] ‹20› and whenever good fortune comes to him, he selfishly withholds it [from others]. ‹21›
Not so, however, those who consciously turn towards God in prayer,[9] ‹22› [and] who incessantly persevere in their prayer; ‹23›

فَٱصْبِرْ صَبْرًا جَمِيلًا ﴿٥﴾ إِنَّهُمْ يَرَوْنَهُۥ بَعِيدًا ﴿٦﴾ وَنَرَىٰهُ قَرِيبًا ﴿٧﴾ يَوْمَ
تَكُونُ ٱلسَّمَآءُ كَٱلْمُهْلِ ﴿٨﴾ وَتَكُونُ ٱلْجِبَالُ كَٱلْعِهْنِ ﴿٩﴾ وَلَا يَسْـَٔلُ
حَمِيمٌ حَمِيمًا ﴿١٠﴾ يُبَصَّرُونَهُمْ يَوَدُّ ٱلْمُجْرِمُ لَوْ يَفْتَدِى مِنْ عَذَابِ
يَوْمِئِذٍۭ بِبَنِيهِ ﴿١١﴾ وَصَٰحِبَتِهِۦ وَأَخِيهِ ﴿١٢﴾ وَفَصِيلَتِهِ ٱلَّتِى تُـْٔوِيهِ ﴿١٣﴾
وَمَن فِى ٱلْأَرْضِ جَمِيعًا ثُمَّ يُنجِيهِ ﴿١٤﴾ كَلَّآ إِنَّهَا لَظَىٰ ﴿١٥﴾ نَزَّاعَةً
لِّلشَّوَىٰ ﴿١٦﴾ تَدْعُوا۟ مَنْ أَدْبَرَ وَتَوَلَّىٰ ﴿١٧﴾ وَجَمَعَ فَأَوْعَىٰٓ ﴿١٨﴾ ۞ إِنَّ
ٱلْإِنسَٰنَ خُلِقَ هَلُوعًا ﴿١٩﴾ إِذَا مَسَّهُ ٱلشَّرُّ جَزُوعًا ﴿٢٠﴾ وَإِذَا مَسَّهُ ٱلْخَيْرُ
مَنُوعًا ﴿٢١﴾ إِلَّا ٱلْمُصَلِّينَ ﴿٢٢﴾ ٱلَّذِينَ هُمْ عَلَىٰ صَلَاتِهِمْ دَآئِمُونَ ﴿٢٣﴾

ثلاثة ارباع الحزب

Faṣbir ṣabrañ-jamīlā. (5) ʾInnahum yarawnahū baᶜīdā.
(6) Wa narāhu qarībā. (7) Yawma takūnus-samāaʾu
kalmuhl. (8) Wa takūnul-jibālu kalᶜihn. (9) Wa lā
yasʾalu ḥamīmun ḥamīmā. (10) Yubaṣṣarū-nahum;
yawaddul-mujrimu law yaftadī min ᶜadhābi Yaw-
miʾidhim-bibanīh. (11) Wa ṣāḥibatihī wa ʾakhīh. (12)
Wa faṣīlatihil-latī tuʾwīh. (13) Wa mañ-fil-ʾarḍi jamīᶜañ-
thumma yuñjīh. (14) Kallāa ʾinnahā laẓā. (15) Naz-
zāᶜatal-lishshawā. (16) Tadᶜū man ʾadbara wa tawa-
llā. (17) Wa jamaᶜa faʾawᶜā. (18) ۞ ʾInnal-ʾIñsāna
khuliqa halūᶜā. (19) ʾIdhā massahush-sharru jazūᶜā.
(20) Wa ʾidhā massahul-khayru manūᶜā. (21) ʾIllal-
muṣallīn. (22) ʾAlladhīna hum ᶜalā Ṣalātihim dāa-
ʾimūn. (23)

6 Lit., "they".

7 Lit., "man has been created restless (*halūᶜan*)" – that is, endowed with an inner restlessness which may equally well drive him to fruitful achievement or to chronic discontent and frustration. In other words, it is the manner in which man utilizes this God-willed endowment that determines whether it shall have a positive or a negative character. The subsequent two verses (20 and 21) allude to the latter, while verses 22-25 show that only true spiritual and moral consciousness can mould that inborn restlessness into a positive force, and thus bring about inner stability and abiding contentment.

8 The participle *jazūᶜ* – derived from the verb *jaziᶜa* – combines the concepts of "lacking patience" and "lamenting over one's misfortune", and is therefore the contrary of *ṣabr* (Jawharī).

9 This, I believe, is the meaning of the expression *al-muṣallīn* (lit., "the praying ones"), which evidently does not relate here to the mere *ritual* of prayer but, rather, as the next verse shows, to the attitude of mind and the spiritual need underlying it. In this sense it connects with the statement in verse 19 that "man is born with a restless disposition" which, when rightly used, leads him towards conscious spiritual growth, as well as to freedom from all self-pity and selfishness.

and in whose possessions there is a due share, acknowledged [by them], ‹24› for such as ask [for help] and such as are deprived [of what is good in life];[10] ‹25›
and who accept as true the [coming of the] Day of Judgment; ‹26›
and who stand in dread of their Sustainer's chastisement ‹27› – for, behold, of their Sustainer's chastisement none may ever feel [wholly] secure;[11] ‹28›
and who are mindful of their chastity,[12] ‹29› [not giving way to their desires] with any but their spouses – that is, those whom they rightfully possess [through wedlock]:[13] – for then, behold, they are free of all blame, ‹30› whereas such as seek to go beyond that [limit] are truly transgressors; ‹31›
and who are faithful to their trusts and to their pledges; ‹32›
and who stand firm whenever they bear witness; ‹33›
and who guard their prayers [from all worldly intent]. ‹34›
These it is who in the gardens [of paradise] shall be honoured! ‹35›

WHAT, THEN, is amiss with such as are bent on denying the truth, that they run about confusedly to and fro before thee, ‹36› [coming upon thee] from the right and from the left, in crowds?[14] ‹37›

وَٱلَّذِينَ فِىٓ أَمْوَٰلِهِمْ حَقٌّ مَّعْلُومٌ ﴿24﴾ لِّلسَّآئِلِ وَٱلْمَحْرُومِ ﴿25﴾ وَٱلَّذِينَ
يُصَدِّقُونَ بِيَوْمِ ٱلدِّينِ ﴿26﴾ وَٱلَّذِينَ هُم مِّنْ عَذَابِ رَبِّهِم مُّشْفِقُونَ ﴿27﴾
إِنَّ عَذَابَ رَبِّهِمْ غَيْرُ مَأْمُونٍ ﴿28﴾ وَٱلَّذِينَ هُمْ لِفُرُوجِهِمْ حَـٰفِظُونَ ﴿29﴾
إِلَّا عَلَىٰٓ أَزْوَٰجِهِمْ أَوْ مَا مَلَكَتْ أَيْمَـٰنُهُمْ فَإِنَّهُمْ غَيْرُ مَلُومِينَ ﴿30﴾ فَمَنِ
ٱبْتَغَىٰ وَرَآءَ ذَٰلِكَ فَأُو۟لَـٰٓئِكَ هُمُ ٱلْعَادُونَ ﴿31﴾ وَٱلَّذِينَ هُمْ لِأَمَـٰنَـٰتِهِمْ
وَعَهْدِهِمْ رَٰعُونَ ﴿32﴾ وَٱلَّذِينَ هُم بِشَهَـٰدَٰتِهِمْ قَآئِمُونَ ﴿33﴾ وَٱلَّذِينَ هُمْ عَلَىٰ
صَلَاتِهِمْ يُحَافِظُونَ ﴿34﴾ أُو۟لَـٰٓئِكَ فِى جَنَّـٰتٍ مُّكْرَمُونَ ﴿35﴾ فَمَالِ ٱلَّذِينَ
كَفَرُوا۟ قِبَلَكَ مُهْطِعِينَ ﴿36﴾ عَنِ ٱلْيَمِينِ وَعَنِ ٱلشِّمَالِ عِزِينَ ﴿37﴾

**Wal-ladhīna fīi ͗amwālihim ḥaqqum-ma ͨlūm. ﴾24﴿
Lissāa ͗ili wal-maḥrūm. ﴾25﴿ Wal-ladhīna yuṣaddiqūna
biYawmid-Dīn. ﴾26﴿ Wal-ladhīna hum-min ͨadhābi
Rabbihim mushfiqūn. ﴾27﴿ ͗Inna ͨadhāba Rabbihim
ghayru ma ͗mūn. ﴾28﴿ Wal-ladhīna hum lifurūjihim
ḥāfiẓūna, ﴾29﴿ ͗illā ͨalāa ͗azwājihim ͗aw mā malakat
͗aymānuhum fa ͗innahum ghayru malūmīn. ﴾30﴿
Famanib-taghā warāa ͗a dhālika fa ͗ulāa ͗ika humul-
ͨādūn. ﴾31﴿ Wal-ladhīna hum li ͗amānātihim wa
ͨahdihim rā ͨūn. ﴾32﴿ Wal-ladhīna hum bishahādātihim
qāa ͗imūn. ﴾33﴿ Wal-ladhīna hum ͨalā Ṣalātihim yuḥāfiẓūn. ﴾34﴿ ͗Ulāa ͗ika fī jannātim-mukramūn. ﴾35﴿
Famālil-ladhīna kafarū qibalaka muhṭi ͨīn. ﴾36﴿ ͨAnil-
yamīni wa ͨanish-shimāli ͨizīn. ﴾37﴿**

---

10 Sc., "but do not or cannot beg": see Rāzī's comments on a similar phrase in 51 : 19, quoted in my corresponding note 12.

11 This warning against pharisaic self-righteousness implies that however "good" a person may be, there is always a possibility of his or her having done a moral wrong (e.g., an injury to a fellow-being) and then conveniently "forgotten" this sin. Elliptically, this warning contains a call to increasing *consciousness* in all one's doings – for, "temptation to evil (*fitnah*) does not befall only those who are bent on evildoing" (8 : 25), but may also befall people who are otherwise righteous.

12 Lit., "who guard their private parts".

13 See the identical passage in 23 : 5-7, as well as the corresponding note 3, in which I have fully explained the reasons for my rendering of the phrase *aw mā malakat aymānuhum* as "that is, those whom they rightfully possess [through wedlock]". As regards this interpretation, see also Rāzī's comments on 4 : 24, as well as one of the alternative interpretations of that verse advanced by Ṭabarī on the authority of Ibn ͨAbbās and Mujāhid.

14 This, again, connects with the statement in verse 19, "man is born with a restless disposition" (see note 7 above). People who do not *want* to see the truth of God's existence and have, therefore, no solid basis on which to build their world-view, are, by the same token, unable to conceive any definite standards of personal and social ethics. Hence, whenever they are confronted with anyone's positive assertion of faith, they "run about to and fro" in spiritual confusion, trying, in order to justify themselves intellectually, to demolish the premises of that faith by means of many-sided, contradictory arguments – an endeavour depicted in the metaphor, "coming upon thee from the right

Does every one of them hope to enter [by this means] a garden of bliss?[15] ‹38›
Never! For, behold, We have created them out of something that they know [only too well]![16] ‹39›
But nay! I call to witness [Our being] the Sustainer of all the points of sunrise and sunset:[17] verily, well able are We ‹40› to replace them with [people] better than they are; for there is nothing to prevent Us [from doing what We Will].[18] ‹41›
Hence, leave them to indulge in idle talk and play [with words][19] until they face that [Judgment] Day of theirs which they have been promised ‹42› – the Day when they shall come forth in haste from their graves, as if racing towards a goal-post, ‹43› with downcast eyes, with ignominy over-whelming them: that Day which they were promised again and again. . . .[20] ‹44›

أَيَطْمَعُ كُلُّ آمْرِيٍ مِّنْهُمْ أَن يُدْخَلَ جَنَّةَ نَعِيمٍ ﴿٣٨﴾ كَلَّآ إِنَّا خَلَقْنَٰهُم
مِّمَّا يَعْلَمُونَ ﴿٣٩﴾ فَلَآ أُقْسِمُ بِرَبِّ ٱلْمَشَٰرِقِ وَٱلْمَغَٰرِبِ إِنَّا لَقَٰدِرُونَ ﴿٤٠﴾
عَلَىٰٓ أَن نُّبَدِّلَ خَيْرًا مِّنْهُمْ وَمَا نَحْنُ بِمَسْبُوقِينَ ﴿٤١﴾ فَذَرْهُمْ يَخُوضُوا۟
وَيَلْعَبُوا۟ حَتَّىٰ يُلَٰقُوا۟ يَوْمَهُمُ ٱلَّذِى يُوعَدُونَ ﴿٤٢﴾ يَوْمَ يَخْرُجُونَ مِنَ
ٱلْأَجْدَاثِ سِرَاعًا كَأَنَّهُمْ إِلَىٰ نُصُبٍ يُوفِضُونَ ﴿٤٣﴾ خَٰشِعَةً أَبْصَٰرُهُمْ
تَرْهَقُهُمْ ذِلَّةٌ ذَٰلِكَ ٱلْيَوْمُ ٱلَّذِى كَانُوا۟ يُوعَدُونَ ﴿٤٤﴾

ᵓAyaṭmaᶜu kullum-riᵓim-minhum ᵓañy-yudkhala jannata naᶜīm. (38) Kallāa ᵓinnā khalaqnāhum-mimmā
yaᶜlamūn. (39) Falāa ᵓuqsimu biRabbil-mashāriqi wal-
maghāribi ᵓinnā laqādirūna, (40) ᶜalāa ᵓan-nubaddila
khayram-minhum wa mā Naḥnu bimasbūqīn. (41)
Fadharhum yakhūḍū wa yalᶜabū ḥattā yulāqū Yawmahumul-ladhī yūᶜadūn. (42) Yawma yakhrujūna
minal-ᵓajdāthi sirāᶜañ-kaᵓannahum ᵓilā nuṣubiñy-
yūfiḍūn. (43) Khāshiᶜatan ᵓabṣāruhum tarhaquhum
dhillatuñ-dhālikal-Yawmul-ladhī kānū yūᶜadūn. (44)

---

and from the left"; and since they derive all their strength from a conformity with shallow mass-opinions, they can do this only "in crowds".

15 I.e., "Do they hope to achieve inner peace and fulfilment by 'disproving' another person's faith?"

16 Namely, out of "dust" – i.e., out of the same primitive organic and inorganic substances as are found in and on the earth: the implication being that only spiritual consciousness and endeavour can raise man above the mere material form of his existence, and thus enable him to achieve the inner fulfilment metaphorically described here as "a garden of bliss".

17 I.e., of all the variation, throughout the solar year, of the points at which the sun "rises" and "sets": thus stressing the fact that He is the Ultimate Cause of all orbital movement in the universe and, hence, its Creator (cf. 37 : 5 and 55 : 17).

18 The implication is that it is *not* His will to replace "those who are bent on denying the truth", in this world, by believers, inasmuch as such a "replacement" would not be in accord with His design of multiform human existence, in which faith is always challenged and tested by unbelief, and *vice versa*.

19 I.e., their philosophizing about a supposedly "uncreated" world and a hypothetical "self-generation" of life, as well as their blatant "denial", unsupported by any factual evidence, of a life after death or even of the existence of God.

20 The concept of "again and again" – i.e., by a succession, through the ages, of prophetic revelations – is implied in the auxiliary verb *kānū*, which usually connotes repetition and/or duration.

The Seventy-First Sūrah

Nūḥ (Noah)

Mecca Period

DEVOTED in its entirety to Noah's preaching to his erring fellow-men, this *sūrah* depicts symbolically every conscious believer's struggle against blind materialism and the resulting lack of all spiritual values. The story of Noah as such is mentioned in several places in the Qurʾān, and particularly in 11 : 25 ff.

-71-
سورة نوح مكية
وآياتها ثمان وعشرون

IN THE NAME OF GOD, THE MOST GRACIOUS, THE DISPENSER OF GRACE:

BEHOLD, We sent Noah unto his people, [saying:] "Warn thy people ere grievous suffering befall them!" ‹1›
[And Noah] said: "O my people! I am but a plain warner to you, [sent to tell you] ‹2› that you should worship God [alone] and be conscious of Him.
"Now do pay heed unto me, ‹3› so that He may forgive you some of your sins, and grant you respite until a term known [to Him alone]:[1] but, behold, when the term appointed by God does come, it can never be put back – if you but knew it!" ‹4›

بِسْمِ ٱللَّهِ ٱلرَّحْمَٰنِ ٱلرَّحِيمِ

إِنَّآ أَرْسَلْنَا نُوحًا إِلَىٰ قَوْمِهِۦٓ أَنْ أَنذِرْ قَوْمَكَ مِن قَبْلِ أَن يَأْتِيَهُمْ عَذَابٌ
أَلِيمٌ ﴿١﴾ قَالَ يَٰقَوْمِ إِنِّى لَكُمْ نَذِيرٌ مُّبِينٌ ﴿٢﴾ أَنِ ٱعْبُدُوا۟ ٱللَّهَ وَٱتَّقُوهُ
وَأَطِيعُونِ ﴿٣﴾ يَغْفِرْ لَكُم مِّن ذُنُوبِكُمْ وَيُؤَخِّرْكُمْ إِلَىٰٓ أَجَلٍ مُّسَمًّى ۚ إِنَّ
أَجَلَ ٱللَّهِ إِذَا جَآءَ لَا يُؤَخَّرُ ۖ لَوْ كُنتُمْ تَعْلَمُونَ ﴿٤﴾

Bismil-lāhir-Raḥmānir-Raḥīm.
ʾInnāa ʾarsalnā Nūḥan ʾilā qawmihīi ʾan ʾañdhir qawmaka miñ-qabli ʾañy-yaʾtiyahum ʿadhābun ʾalīm. ‹1›
Qāla yā qawmi ʾinnī lakum Nadhīrum-mubīn. ‹2›
ʾAniʿ-budul-lāha wat-taqūhu wa ʾaṭīʿūni, ‹3› **yaghfir lakum-miñ-dhunūbikum wa yuʾakhkhirkum ʾilāa ʾajalim-musammā. ʾInna ʾajalal-lāhi ʾidhā jāaʾa lā yuʾakhkharu law kuñtum taʿlamūn.** ‹4›

---

1 Namely, until the end of each person's life – implying that although they might be forgiven all sins committed *before* their postulated change of heart, they would henceforth, until their death, be held fully accountable for their behaviour in the light of that new-found faith. Cf. 4 : 18 – "repentance shall not be accepted from those who do evil deeds until their dying hour and then say, 'Behold, I now repent'".

[And after a time, Noah] said: "O my Sustainer! Verily, I have been calling unto my people night and day, ‹5› but my call has only caused them to flee farther and farther away [from Thee].[2] ‹6› And, behold, whenever I called unto them with a view to Thy granting them forgiveness, they put their fingers into their ears, and wrapped themselves up in their garments [of sin],[3] and grew obstinate, and became [yet more] arrogant in their false pride. ‹7›

"And, behold, I called unto them openly; ‹8› and, behold, I preached to them in public; and I spoke to them secretly, in private; ‹9› and I said:

"Ask your Sustainer to forgive you your sins – for, verily, He is all-forgiving! ‹10› He will shower upon you heavenly blessings abundant,[4] ‹11› and will aid you with worldly goods and children, and will bestow upon you gardens, and bestow upon you running waters.[5] ‹12›

"What is amiss with you that you cannot look forward to God's majesty,[6] ‹13› seeing that He has created [every one of] you in successive stages?[7] ‹14›

"'Do you not see how God has created seven heavens in full harmony with one another,[8] ‹15› and has set up within them the moon as a light [reflected], and set up the sun as a [radiant] lamp?[9] ‹16›

قَالَ رَبِّ إِنِّى دَعَوْتُ قَوْمِى لَيْلًا وَنَهَارًا ﴿5﴾ فَلَمْ يَزِدْهُمْ دُعَآءِىٓ إِلَّا
فِرَارًا ﴿6﴾ وَإِنِّى كُلَّمَا دَعَوْتُهُمْ لِتَغْفِرَ لَهُمْ جَعَلُوٓا۟ أَصَٰبِعَهُمْ فِىٓ ءَاذَانِهِمْ
وَٱسْتَغْشَوْا۟ ثِيَابَهُمْ وَأَصَرُّوا۟ وَٱسْتَكْبَرُوا۟ ٱسْتِكْبَارًا ﴿7﴾ ثُمَّ إِنِّى دَعَوْتُهُمْ
جِهَارًا ﴿8﴾ ثُمَّ إِنِّىٓ أَعْلَنتُ لَهُمْ وَأَسْرَرْتُ لَهُمْ إِسْرَارًا ﴿9﴾ فَقُلْتُ
ٱسْتَغْفِرُوا۟ رَبَّكُمْ إِنَّهُۥ كَانَ غَفَّارًا ﴿10﴾ يُرْسِلِ ٱلسَّمَآءَ عَلَيْكُم مِّدْرَارًا ﴿11﴾
وَيُمْدِدْكُم بِأَمْوَٰلٍ وَبَنِينَ وَيَجْعَل لَّكُمْ جَنَّٰتٍ وَيَجْعَل لَّكُمْ
أَنْهَٰرًا ﴿12﴾ مَّا لَكُمْ لَا تَرْجُونَ لِلَّهِ وَقَارًا ﴿13﴾ وَقَدْ خَلَقَكُمْ
أَطْوَارًا ﴿14﴾ أَلَمْ تَرَوْا۟ كَيْفَ خَلَقَ ٱللَّهُ سَبْعَ سَمَٰوَٰتٍ طِبَاقًا ﴿15﴾
وَجَعَلَ ٱلْقَمَرَ فِيهِنَّ نُورًا وَجَعَلَ ٱلشَّمْسَ سِرَاجًا ﴿16﴾

Qāla Rabbi ʾinnī daʿawtu qawmī laylañw-wa nahārā. (5) Falam yazid-hum duʿāaʾīi ʾillā firārā. (6) Wa ʾinnī kullamā daʿawtuhum litaghfira lahum jaʿalūu ʾaṣābiʿahum fīi ʾādhānihim was-taghshaw thiyābahum wa ʾaṣarrū was-takbarus-tikbārā. (7) Thumma ʾinnī daʿawtuhum jihārā. (8) Thumma ʾinnīi ʾaʿlañtu lahum wa ʾasrartu lahum ʾisrārā. (9) Faqultus-taghfirū Rabbakum ʾinnahū kāna Ghaffārā. (10) Yursilis-samāaʾa ʿalaykum-midrārā. (11) Wa yumdidkum-biʾamwāliñw-wa banīna wa yajʿal-lakum jannātiñw-wa yajʿal-lakum ʾanhārā. (12) Mā lakum lā tarjūna lillāhi waqārā. (13) Wa qad khalaqakum ʾaṭwārā. (14) ʾAlam taraw kayfa khalaqal-lāhu sabʿa samāwātiñ-ṭibāqā. (15) Wa jaʿalal-qamara fīhinna nūrañw-wa jaʿalash-shamsa sirājā. (16)

2 Lit., "has not increased them in anything but flight".

3 For the reason of the above interpolation – which endows the concept of "garments" with a metaphorical meaning – see note 2 on 74 : 4; cf. also the expression "garment of God-consciousness" (*libās at-taqwā*) in 7 : 26.

4 Lit., "He will let loose the sky over you with abundance" (but see also note 76 on 11 : 52).

5 The two last-mentioned blessings are an allusion to the state of happiness in the hereafter, symbolized in the Qurʾān as "gardens through which running waters flow".

6 I.e., "that you refuse to *believe* in God" (Zamakhsharī). Some authorities (e.g., Jawharī) give to the above phrase the meaning, "that you will not *fear* God's majesty", which, too, implies lack of belief in Him.

7 I.e., by a process of gradual evolution, in the mother's womb, from a drop of sperm and a fertilized germ-cell (the female ovum), up to the point where the embryo becomes a new, self-contained human entity (cf. 22 : 5): all of which points to the existence of a plan and a purpose and, hence, to the existence of a conscious Creator.

8 Cf. 67 : 3 and the corresponding note 2.

9 See 10 : 5, where the sun is described as "a [source of] radiant light" (*ḍiyāʾ*) and the moon as "light [reflected]" (*nūr*); both these interpolations are explained in note 10 on 10 : 5.

"'And God has caused you to grow out of the earth in [gradual] growth;[10] and thereafter He will return you to it [in death]: ‹17› and [then] He will bring you forth [from it] in resurrection.[11] ‹18›

"'And God has made the earth a wide expanse for you, ‹19› so that you might walk thereon on spacious paths.'"[12] ‹20›

[And] Noah continued: "O my Sustainer! Behold, they have opposed me [throughout], for they follow people whose wealth and children lead them increasingly into ruin,[13] ‹21› and who have devised a most awesome blasphemy [against Thee], ‹22› inasmuch as they said [to their followers], 'Do not ever abandon your gods: abandon neither Wadd nor Suwāʿ, and neither Yaghūth nor Yaʿūq nor Nasr!'[14] ‹23›

"And so they have led many a one astray: hence, ordain Thou not that these evildoers stray but farther and farther away [from all that they may desire]!"[15] ‹24›

And so, because of their sins, they were drowned [in the great flood], and were doomed to suffer the fire [of the hereafter];[16] and they found none who could succour them against God. ‹25›

وَٱللَّهُ أَنۢبَتَكُم مِّنَ ٱلْأَرْضِ نَبَاتًا ﴿17﴾ ثُمَّ يُعِيدُكُمْ فِيهَا وَيُخْرِجُكُمْ
إِخْرَاجًا ﴿18﴾ وَٱللَّهُ جَعَلَ لَكُمُ ٱلْأَرْضَ بِسَاطًا ﴿19﴾ لِّتَسْلُكُواْ مِنْهَا
سُبُلًا فِجَاجًا ﴿20﴾ قَالَ نُوحٌ رَّبِّ إِنَّهُمْ عَصَوْنِى وَٱتَّبَعُواْ مَن لَّمْ يَزِدْهُ
مَالُهُۥ وَوَلَدُهُۥٓ إِلَّا خَسَارًا ﴿21﴾ وَمَكَرُواْ مَكْرًا كُبَّارًا ﴿22﴾ وَقَالُواْ لَا
تَذَرُنَّ ءَالِهَتَكُمْ وَلَا تَذَرُنَّ وَدًّا وَلَا سُوَاعًا وَلَا يَغُوثَ وَيَعُوقَ وَنَسْرًا ﴿23﴾
وَقَدْ أَضَلُّواْ كَثِيرًا ۖ وَلَا تَزِدِ ٱلظَّٰلِمِينَ إِلَّا ضَلَٰلًا ﴿24﴾ مِّمَّا خَطِيٓـَٔـٰتِهِمْ
أُغْرِقُواْ فَأُدْخِلُواْ نَارًا فَلَمْ يَجِدُواْ لَهُم مِّن دُونِ ٱللَّهِ أَنصَارًا ﴿25﴾

Wal-lāhu ʾambatakum-minal-ʾarḍi nabātā. (17) Thumma yuʿīdukum fīhā wa yukhrijukum ʾikhrājā. (18) Wal-lāhu jaʿala lakumul-ʾarḍa bisāṭā. (19) Litaslukū minhā subulañ-fijājā. (20) Qāla Nūḥur-Rabbi ʾinnahum ʿaṣawnī wat-tabaʿū mal-lam yazid-hu māluhū wa waladuhūu ʾillā khasārā. (21) Wa makarū makrañ-kubbārā. (22) Wa qālū lā tadharunna ʾālihatakum wa lā tadharunna Waddañw-wa lā Suwāʿañw-wa lā Yaghūtha wa Yaʿūqa wa Nasrā. (23) Wa qad ʾaḍallū kathīrañw-wa lā tazidiẓ-ẓālimīna ʾillā ḍalālā. (24) Mimmā khaṭīiʾātihim ʾughriqū faʾudkhilū nārañ-falam yajidū lahum-miñ-dūnil-lāhi ʾañṣārā. (25)

10 This phrase has a twofold meaning. In the first instance, it alludes to the evolution of the individual human body out of the same substances – both organic and inorganic – as are found in and on the earth as well: and in this sense it enlarges upon the creation of the human individual "in successive stages" referred to in verse 14 above. Secondly, it alludes to the evolution of the human *species*, which, starting from the most primitive organisms living on earth, has gradually ascended to ever higher stages of development until it has finally reached that complexity of body, mind and soul evident in the human being.

11 Lit., "with a [final] bringing-forth".

12 I.e., "He has provided you with all facilities for a good life on earth" – the unspoken implication being, "Will you not, then, acknowledge Him and be grateful to Him?"

13 Lit., "and have followed him whose wealth and children do not increase him in aught but loss": i.e., people whose propensity and power only enhance their false pride and arrogance, and thus lead them to spiritual ruin. Beyond this, we have here a subtle allusion to the fact that an *exclusive* devotion to material prosperity must of necessity, in the long run, destroy all moral values and, thus, the very fabric of society.

14 As is evident from early sources, these five gods were among the many worshipped by the pre-Islamic Arabs as well (see the small but extremely valuable work by Hishām ibn Muḥammad al-Kalbī, *Kitāb al-Asnām*, ed. Aḥmad Zakī, Cairo 1914). Their cult had probably been introduced into Arabia from Syria and Babylonia, where it seems to have existed in earliest antiquity.

15 Lit., "increase Thou not the evildoers in aught but in straying-away", i.e., from an achievement of their worldly goals (Rāzī).

16 Lit., "and were made to enter the fire" – the past tense indicating the *inevitability* of the suffering yet to come (Zamakhsharī).

And Noah prayed: "O my Sustainer! Leave not on earth any of those who deny the truth: ‹26› for, behold, if Thou dost leave them, they will [always try to] lead astray those who worship Thee, and will give birth to nothing but wickedness and stubborn ingratitude.[17] ‹27›

"O my Sustainer! Grant Thy forgiveness unto me and unto my parents, and unto everyone who enters my house as a believer, and unto all believing men and believing women [of later times]; and grant Thou that the doers of evil shall increasingly meet with destruction!"[18] ‹28›

وَقَالَ نُوحٌ رَّبِّ لَا تَذَرْ عَلَى ٱلْأَرْضِ مِنَ ٱلْكَـٰفِرِينَ دَيَّارًا ﴿٢٦﴾ إِنَّكَ
إِن تَذَرْهُمْ يُضِلُّوا۟ عِبَادَكَ وَلَا يَلِدُوٓا۟ إِلَّا فَاجِرًا كَفَّارًا ﴿٢٧﴾ رَّبِّ ٱغْفِرْ لِى
وَلِوَٰلِدَىَّ وَلِمَن دَخَلَ بَيْتِىَ مُؤْمِنًا وَلِلْمُؤْمِنِينَ وَٱلْمُؤْمِنَـٰتِ وَلَا تَزِدِ
ٱلظَّـٰلِمِينَ إِلَّا تَبَارًۢا ﴿٢٨﴾

Wa qāla Nūḥur-Rabbi lā tadhar ᶜalal-ᵓarḍi minal-kāfirīna dayyārā. (26) ᵓInnaka ᵓin-tadharhum yuḍillū ᶜibādaka wa lā yalidūu ᵓillā fājiran-kaffārā. (27) Rabbigh-fir lī wa liwālidayya wa limañ-dakhala baytiya muᵓminañw-wa lilmuᵓminīna wal-muᵓmināti wa lā tazidiẓ-ẓālimīna ᵓillā tabārā. (28)

17 Lit., "to such as are wicked (*fājir*), stubbornly ingrate (*kaffār*)": but since no one – and particularly not a prophet – is ever justified in assuming that the progeny of evildoers must of necessity be evil, it is obvious that the terms *fājir* and *kaffār* are used here metonymically, denoting qualities or attitudes, and not persons.

18 Lit., "increase Thou not the evildoers in aught but destruction" – i.e., destruction of their aims and, thus, of evil as such.

The Seventy-Second Sūrah

Al-Jinn (The Unseen Beings)

Mecca Period

REVEALED not later than during the last two years of the Prophet's sojourn in Mecca, this *sūrah* takes its name from the plural noun *al-jinn* in the first verse.

سورة الجن مكية -72-
وآياتها ثمان وعشرون

حزب 58

IN THE NAME OF GOD, THE MOST GRACIOUS, THE DISPENSER OF GRACE:

SAY: "It has been revealed to me that some of the unseen beings gave ear [to this divine writ],[1] and thereupon said [unto their fellow-beings]:
"'Verily, we have heard a wondrous discourse, ‹1› guiding towards consciousness of what is right; and so We have come to believe in it. And we shall never ascribe divinity to anyone beside our Sustainer, ‹2› for [we know] that sublimely exalted is our Sustainer's majesty: no consort has He ever taken unto Himself, nor a son! ‹3›

بِسْمِ ٱللَّهِ ٱلرَّحْمَٰنِ ٱلرَّحِيمِ

قُلْ أُوحِيَ إِلَيَّ أَنَّهُ ٱسْتَمَعَ نَفَرٌ مِّنَ ٱلْجِنِّ فَقَالُوٓاْ إِنَّا سَمِعْنَا قُرْءَانًا
عَجَبًا ﴿١﴾ يَهْدِىٓ إِلَى ٱلرُّشْدِ فَـَٔامَنَّا بِهِۦ ۖ وَلَن نُّشْرِكَ بِرَبِّنَآ أَحَدًا ﴿٢﴾
وَأَنَّهُۥ تَعَٰلَىٰ جَدُّ رَبِّنَا مَا ٱتَّخَذَ صَٰحِبَةً وَلَا وَلَدًا ﴿٣﴾

Bismil-lāhir-Raḥmānir-Raḥīm.
Qul ʾūḥiya ʾilayya ʾannahus-tamaʿa nafarum-minal-Jinni faqālūu ʾinnā samiʿnā Qurʾānan ʿajabā. ‹1› Yahdīi ʾilar-rushdi faʾāmannā bihī wa lañ-nushrika biRabbināa ʾaḥadā. ‹2› Wa ʾannahū taʿālā jaddu Rabbinā mat-takhadha ṣāḥibatañw-wa lā waladā. ‹3›

---

1 I.e., had heard and *accepted* it: this being the meaning, in the above context, of the verbal form *istamaʿa*. – As regards the various meanings attributable to the plural noun *jinn* (rendered by me here as "unseen beings"), see Appendix III. As pointed out there, the *jinn* are referred to in the Qurʾān in many connotations. In a few cases – e.g., in the present instance and in 46 : 29-32 – this expression may possibly signify "*hitherto* unseen beings", namely, strangers who had never before been seen by the people among and to whom the Qurʾān was then being revealed. From 46 : 30 (which evidently relates to the same occurrence as the present one) it transpires that the *jinn* in question were followers of the Mosaic faith, inasmuch as they refer to the Qurʾān as "a revelation bestowed from on high after [that of] Moses", thus pointedly omitting any mention of the intervening prophet, Jesus, and equally pointedly (in verse 3 of the present *sūrah*) stressing their rejection of the Christian concept of the Trinity. All this leads one to the assumption that they may have been Jews from distant parts of what is now the Arab world, perhaps from Syria or even Mesopotamia. (Ṭabarī mentions in several places that the *jinn* referred to in this *sūrah* as well as in 46 : 29 ff. hailed from Naṣībīn, a town on the upper reaches of the Euphrates.) I should, however, like to stress that my explanation of this occurrence is purely tentative.

"'And [now we know] that the foolish among us were wont to say outrageous things about God,[2] ⟨4⟩ and that [we were mistaken when] we thought that neither man nor [any of] the invisible forces would ever tell a lie about God.[3] ⟨5⟩ Yet [it has always happened] that certain kinds of humans would seek refuge with certain kinds of [such] invisible forces:[4] but these only increased their confusion ⟨6⟩ – so much so that they came to think, as you [once] thought, that God would never [again] send forth anyone [as His apostle].[5] ⟨7⟩

"'And [so it happened] that we reached out towards heaven:[6] but we found it filled with mighty guards and flames,[7] ⟨8⟩ notwithstanding that we were established in positions [which we had thought well-suited] to listening to [whatever secrets might be in] it:[8] and anyone who now [or ever] tries to listen will [likewise] find a flame lying in wait for him![9] ⟨9⟩

وَأَنَّهُۥ كَانَ يَقُولُ سَفِيهُنَا عَلَى ٱللَّهِ شَطَطًا ﴿٤﴾ وَأَنَّا ظَنَنَّآ أَن لَّن تَقُولَ
ٱلْإِنسُ وَٱلْجِنُّ عَلَى ٱللَّهِ كَذِبًا ﴿٥﴾ وَأَنَّهُۥ كَانَ رِجَالٌ مِّنَ ٱلْإِنسِ
يَعُوذُونَ بِرِجَالٍ مِّنَ ٱلْجِنِّ فَزَادُوهُمْ رَهَقًا ﴿٦﴾ وَأَنَّهُمْ ظَنُّوا۟ كَمَا ظَنَنتُمْ
أَن لَّن يَبْعَثَ ٱللَّهُ أَحَدًا ﴿٧﴾ وَأَنَّا لَمَسْنَا ٱلسَّمَآءَ فَوَجَدْنَٰهَا مُلِئَتْ حَرَسًا
شَدِيدًا وَشُهُبًا ﴿٨﴾ وَأَنَّا كُنَّا نَقْعُدُ مِنْهَا مَقَٰعِدَ لِلسَّمْعِ ۖ فَمَن يَسْتَمِعِ
ٱلْـَٔانَ يَجِدْ لَهُۥ شِهَابًا رَّصَدًا ﴿٩﴾

Wa ʾannahū kāna yaqūlu safīhunā ʿalal-lāhi shaṭaṭā. (4) Wa ʾannā ẓanannāa ʾal-lañ-taqūlal-ʾIñsu wal-Jinnu ʿalal-lāhi kadhibā. (5) Wa ʾannahū kāna rijālum-minal-ʾIñsi yaʿūdhūna birijālim-minal-Jinni fazādūhum rahaqā. (6) Wa ʾannahum ẓannū kamā ẓanañtum ʾal-lañy-yabʿathal-lāhu ʾaḥadā. (7) Wa ʾannā lamasnas-samāaʾa fawajadnāhā muliʾat ḥarasañ-shadīdañw-wa shuhubā. (8) Wa ʾannā kunnā naqʿudu minhā maqāʿida lissamʿi famañy-yastamiʿil-ʾāna yajid lahū shihābar-raṣadā. (9)

2 If we accept the supposition that the beings spoken of here were Jewish strangers, the "outrageous things" (*shaṭaṭ*) which they mention would appear to be an allusion to the deep-set belief of the Jews that they were "God's chosen people" – a belief which the Qurʾān consistently rejects, and of which the new converts now divested themselves.

3 In this and the next verse, the term *jinn* (rendered here as "invisible forces") apparently refers to what is described as "occult powers" or, rather, to a person's preoccupation with them (see Appendix III). Irrespective of whether these "forces" are real or mere products of human imagination, they "tell lies about God" inasmuch as they induce their devotees to conceive all manner of fantastic, arbitrary notions about the "nature" of His Being and of His alleged relations with the created universe: notions exemplified in all mystery-religions, in the various gnostic and theosophical systems, in cabalistic Judaism, and in the many medieval offshoots of each of them.

4 Lit., "that men (*rijāl*) from among the humans used to (*kāna*) seek refuge with men from among the *jinn*". Since the reference to "the humans" (*al-ins*) applies to men *and* women, the expression *rijāl* is obviously used here – as so often in the Qurʾān – in the sense of "some persons" or "certain kinds" of people. "Seeking refuge is synonymous with seeking help, protection or the satisfaction of physical or spiritual needs; in the context of the above passage, this is evidently an allusion to the hope of "certain kinds of humans" that the occult powers to which they have turned would successfully guide them through life, and thus make it unnecessary for them to look forward to the coming of a new prophet.

5 Thus Ṭabarī (on the authority of Al-Kalbī) and Ibn Kathīr. The overwhelming majority of the Jews were convinced that no prophet would be raised after those who were explicitly mentioned in the Old Testament: hence their rejection of Jesus and, of course, Muḥammad, and their "reaching out towards heaven" (see next verse) in order to obtain a direct insight into God's plan of creation.

6 The above may be understood as alluding not only, metaphorically, to the arrogant Jewish belief in their being "God's chosen people", but also, more factually, to their old inclination to, and practice of, astrology as a means to foretell the future. Apart from this – and in a more general sense – their "reaching out towards heaven" may be a metaphorical description of a state of mind which causes man to regard himself as "self-sufficient" and to delude himself into thinking that he is bound to achieve mastery over his own fate.

7 See notes 16 and 17 on 15 : 17-18.

8 I.e., "we failed notwithstanding our status as descendants of Abraham, and despite all our ability and learning".

9 As the sequence shows (and as has been pointed out in note 17 on 15 : 18), this relates to all attempts at predicting the future by means of astrology or esoteric calculations, or at influencing the course of future events by means of "occult sciences".

وَأَنَّا لَا نَدْرِىٓ أَشَرٌّ أُرِيدَ بِمَن فِى ٱلْأَرْضِ أَمْ أَرَادَ بِهِمْ رَبُّهُمْ رَشَدًا (10)
وَأَنَّا مِنَّا ٱلصَّٰلِحُونَ وَمِنَّا دُونَ ذَٰلِكَ ۖ كُنَّا طَرَآئِقَ قِدَدًا (11) وَأَنَّا ظَنَنَّآ
أَن لَّن نُّعْجِزَ ٱللَّهَ فِى ٱلْأَرْضِ وَلَن نُّعْجِزَهُۥ هَرَبًا (12) وَأَنَّا لَمَّا سَمِعْنَا
ٱلْهُدَىٰٓ ءَامَنَّا بِهِۦ ۖ فَمَن يُؤْمِنۢ بِرَبِّهِۦ فَلَا يَخَافُ بَخْسًا وَلَا رَهَقًا (13)
وَأَنَّا مِنَّا ٱلْمُسْلِمُونَ وَمِنَّا ٱلْقَٰسِطُونَ ۖ فَمَنْ أَسْلَمَ فَأُو۟لَٰٓئِكَ تَحَرَّوْا۟
رَشَدًا (14) وَأَمَّا ٱلْقَٰسِطُونَ فَكَانُوا۟ لِجَهَنَّمَ حَطَبًا (15) وَأَلَّوِ ٱسْتَقَٰمُوا۟
عَلَى ٱلطَّرِيقَةِ لَأَسْقَيْنَٰهُم مَّآءً غَدَقًا (16) لِّنَفْتِنَهُمْ فِيهِ ۚ وَمَن يُعْرِضْ عَن
ذِكْرِ رَبِّهِۦ يَسْلُكْهُ عَذَابًا صَعَدًا (17)

Wa ᵓannā lā nadrīi ᵓasharrun ᵓurīda bimañ-fil-ᵓarḍi ᵓam ᵓarāda bihim Rabbuhum rashadā. (10) Wa ᵓannā minnaṣ-ṣāliḥuna wa minnā dūna dhālika kunnā ṭarāaᵓiqa qidadā. (11) Wa ᵓannā ẓanannāa ᵓal-lañ-nuᶜjizal-lāha fil-ᵓarḍi wa lañ-nuᶜjizahū harabā. (12) Wa ᵓannā lammā samiᶜnal-hudāa ᵓāmannā bih. Famañy-yuᵓmim-biRabbihī falā yakhāfu bakhsañw-wa lā rahaqā. (13) Wa ᵓannā minnal-Muslimūna wa minnal-qāsiṭūna faman ᵓaslama faᵓulāaᵓika taḥarraw rashadā. (14) Wa ᵓammal-qāsiṭūna fakānū lijahannama ḥaṭabā. (15) Wa ᵓallawis-taqāmū ᶜalaṭ-ṭarīqati laᵓasqaynāhum-māaᵓan ghadaqā. (16) Linaftinahum fīh. Wa mañy-yuᶜriḍ ᶜañ-dhikri Rabbihī yasluk-hu ᶜadhābañ-ṣaᶜadā. (17)

"'And [now we have become aware] that we [created beings] may not know whether evil fortune is intended for [any of] those who live on earth, or whether it is their Sustainer's will to endow them with consciousness of what is right:[10] ‹10› just as [we do not know how it happens that] some from among us are righteous, while some of us are [far] below that: we have always followed widely divergent paths. ‹11›

"'And, withal, we have come to know that we can never elude God [while we live] on earth, and that we can never elude Him by escaping [from life]. ‹12› Hence, as soon as we heard this [call to His] guidance, we came to believe in it: and he who believes in his Sustainer need never have fear of loss or injustice. ‹13›

"'Yet [it is true] that among us are such as have surrendered themselves to God – just as there are among us such as have abandoned themselves to wrongdoing. Now as for those who surrender themselves to Him – it is they that have attained to consciousness of what is right; ‹14› but as for those who abandon themselves to wrongdoing – they are indeed but fuel for [the fires of] hell!'"[11] ‹15›

[KNOW,] THEN, that if they [who have heard Our call] keep firmly to the [right] path, We shall certainly shower them with blessings abundant,[12] ‹16› so as to test them by this means: for he who shall turn away from the remembrance of his Sustainer, him will He cause to undergo suffering most grievous.[13] ‹17›

---

10 Thus, as in verses 2 and 21 of this *sūrah*, "consciousness of what is right" (*rashad* or *rushd*) is equated with the opposite of evil fortune, i.e., with happiness.

11 With this assertion ends, according to all classical commentators, the "confession of faith" of the beings described at the beginning of this passage as *jinn*. Whatever be the real meaning of this term in the present instance – whether it signifies "unseen beings" of a nature unknown to man or, alternatively, a group of humans from distant lands – matters little, for the context makes it abundantly clear that the "speech" of those beings is but a parable of the guidance which the Qurᵓān offers to a mind intent on attaining to "consciousness of what is right".

12 Lit., "water abundant": a metaphor of happiness, echoing the allegorical reference, so frequently occurring in the Qurᵓān, to the "running waters" of paradise (Abū Muslim, quoted by Rāzī).

13 I.e., God's bestowal of blessings is not just a "reward" of righteousness but, rather, a test of man's remaining conscious of, and therefore grateful to, Him.

And [know] that all worship[14] is due to God [alone]: hence, do not invoke anyone side by side with God! ‹18› Yet [thus it is] that whenever a servant of God stands up in prayer to Him, they [who are bent on denying the truth] would gladly overwhelm him with their crowds.[15] ‹19›

Say: "I invoke my Sustainer alone, for I do not ascribe divinity to anyone beside Him." ‹20›

Say: "Verily, it is not in my power to cause you harm or to endow you with consciousness of what is right." ‹21›

Say: "Verily, no one could ever protect me from God, nor could I ever find a place to hide from Him ‹22› if I should fail to convey[16] [to the world whatever illumination comes to me] from God and His messages."

Now as for him who rebels against God and His Apostle – verily, the fire of hell awaits him, therein to abide beyond the count of time.[17] ‹23›

[Let them, then, wait] until the time when they behold that [doom] of which they were forewarned:[18] for then they will come to understand which [kind of man] is more helpless and counts for less![19] ‹24›

Say: "I do not know whether that [doom] of which you were forewarned is near, or whether my Sustainer has set for it a distant term." ‹25›

وَأَنَّ ٱلْمَسَٰجِدَ لِلَّهِ فَلَا تَدْعُوا۟ مَعَ ٱللَّهِ أَحَدًا ﴿١٨﴾ وَأَنَّهُۥ لَمَّا قَامَ عَبْدُ ٱللَّهِ
يَدْعُوهُ كَادُوا۟ يَكُونُونَ عَلَيْهِ لِبَدًا ﴿١٩﴾ قُلْ إِنَّمَآ أَدْعُوا۟ رَبِّى وَلَآ أُشْرِكُ
بِهِۦٓ أَحَدًا ﴿٢٠﴾ قُلْ إِنِّى لَآ أَمْلِكُ لَكُمْ ضَرًّا وَلَا رَشَدًا ﴿٢١﴾ قُلْ إِنِّى لَن
يُجِيرَنِى مِنَ ٱللَّهِ أَحَدٌ وَلَنْ أَجِدَ مِن دُونِهِۦ مُلْتَحَدًا ﴿٢٢﴾ إِلَّا بَلَٰغًا مِّنَ
ٱللَّهِ وَرِسَٰلَٰتِهِۦ وَمَن يَعْصِ ٱللَّهَ وَرَسُولَهُۥ فَإِنَّ لَهُۥ نَارَ جَهَنَّمَ خَٰلِدِينَ
فِيهَآ أَبَدًا ﴿٢٣﴾ حَتَّىٰٓ إِذَا رَأَوْا۟ مَا يُوعَدُونَ فَسَيَعْلَمُونَ مَنْ أَضْعَفُ نَاصِرًا
وَأَقَلُّ عَدَدًا ﴿٢٤﴾ قُلْ إِنْ أَدْرِىٓ أَقَرِيبٌ مَّا تُوعَدُونَ أَمْ يَجْعَلُ لَهُۥ رَبِّىٓ
أَمَدًا ﴿٢٥﴾

Wa ʾannal-masājida lillāhi falā tadʿū maʿal-lāhi ʾaḥadā. (18) Wa ʾannahū lammā qāma ʿabdul-lāhi yadʿūhu kādū yakūnūna ʿalayhi libadā. (19) Qul ʾinnamāa ʾadʿū Rabbī wa lāa ʾushriku bihīi ʾaḥadā. (20) Qul ʾinnī lāa ʾamliku lakum ḍarrañw-wa lā rashadā. (21) Qul ʾinnī lañy-yujīranī minal-lāhi ʾaḥaduñw-wa lan ʾajida miñ-dūnihī multaḥadā. (22) ʾIllā balāgham-minal-lāhi wa Risālātih. Wa mañy-yaʿṣil-lāha wa Rasūlahū faʾinna lahū nāra jahannama khālidīna fīhāa ʾabadā. (23) Ḥattāa ʾidhā raʾaw mā yūʿadūna fasayaʿlamūna man ʾaḍʿafu nāṣirañw-wa ʾaqallu ʿadadā. (24) Qul ʾin ʾadrīi ʾaqarībum-mā tūʿadūna ʾam yajʿalu lahū Rabbīi ʾamadā. (25)

14 Lit., "the places of worship" (*al-masājid*): i.e., worship as such.

15 Lit., "would almost be upon him in crowds (*libad*, sing. *libdah*)" – i.e., with a view to extinguishing God's [guiding] light" (Ṭabarī, evidently alluding to 9 : 32). Most of the commentators assume that the above verse refers to the Prophet Muḥammad and the hostility shown to him by his pagan contemporaries. While this may have been so in the first instance, it is obvious that the passage has a general import as well, alluding to the hostility shown by the majority of people, at all times and in all societies, to a minority or an individual who stands up for a self-evident – but unpopular – moral truth. (In order to be understood fully, the above verse should be read in conjunction with 19 : 73-74 and the corresponding notes.)

16 Lit., "except through an announcement" (*illā balāghan*). In this instance, however, the particle *illā* is evidently a contraction of *in lā* ("if not"): thus, the above phrase signifies "if I do not [or "if I should fail to"] convey. . .", etc. (Ṭabarī, Zamakhsharī, Rāzī).

17 This obviously relates to "those who are bent on denying the truth" – i.e., consciously – and thus destroy their own spiritual identity. The people alluded to in this particular instance are those who "would gladly overwhelm God's servant with their crowds" (verse 19).

18 I.e., on the Day of Judgment. Cf. the second paragraph of 19 : 75, which is similarly phrased.

19 Lit., "is weaker as to helpers and less in numbers" – i.e., less significant *despite* its greater numbers.

He [alone] knows that which is beyond the reach of a created being's perception, and to none does He disclose aught of the mysteries of His Own unfathomable knowledge,[20] ⟨26⟩ unless it be to an apostle whom He has been pleased to elect [therefor]:[21] and then He sends forth [the forces of heaven] to watch over him in whatever lies open before him and in what is beyond his ken[22] ⟨27⟩ – so as to make manifest that it is indeed [but] their Sustainer's messages that these [apostles] deliver: for it is He who encompasses [with His knowledge] all that they have [to say],[23] just as He takes count, one by one, of everything [that exists]. ⟨28⟩

عَٰلِمُ ٱلْغَيْبِ فَلَا يُظْهِرُ عَلَىٰ غَيْبِهِۦٓ أَحَدًا ﴿٢٦﴾ إِلَّا مَنِ ٱرْتَضَىٰ مِن رَّسُولٍ
فَإِنَّهُۥ يَسْلُكُ مِنۢ بَيْنِ يَدَيْهِ وَمِنْ خَلْفِهِۦ رَصَدًا ﴿٢٧﴾ لِّيَعْلَمَ أَن قَدْ أَبْلَغُوا۟
رِسَٰلَٰتِ رَبِّهِمْ وَأَحَاطَ بِمَا لَدَيْهِمْ وَأَحْصَىٰ كُلَّ شَىْءٍ عَدَدًۢا ﴿٢٨﴾

ᶜĀlimul-ghaybi falā yuẓhiru ᶜalā ghaybihīi ᵓaḥadā. ⟨26⟩ ᵓIllā manir-taḍā mir-Rasūliñ-faᵓinnahū yasluku mim-bayni yadayhi wa min khalfihī raṣadā. ⟨27⟩ Liyaᶜlama ᵓañ-qad ᵓablaghū Risālāti Rabbihim wa ᵓaḥāṭa bimā ladayhim wa ᵓaḥṣā kulla shayᵓin ᶜadadā. ⟨28⟩

20 The possessive pronoun "His" in the phrase *ᶜalā ghaybihi* evidently indicates God's exclusive *knowledge* of "that which is beyond the perception of any created being" (*al-ghayb*): hence the above, somewhat free, rendering of this truly untranslatable phrase.

21 Cf. 3 : 179 – "And it is not God's will to give you insight into that which is beyond the reach of human perception: but [to that end] God elects whomsoever He wills from among His apostles".

22 For an explanation of this rendering of the phrase *min bayni yadayhi wa-min khalfihi* (lit., "from between his hands and from behind him"), see note 247 on 2 : 255. In the present context the phrase implies that the very fact of his being graced by divine revelation protects every apostle, spiritually, in all concerns of his life, irrespective of whether these concerns are obvious to him or are beyond his ken.

23 Lit., "all that is with them", i.e., of knowledge and wisdom.

The Seventy-Third Sūrah

Al-Muzzammil (The Enwrapped One)

Mecca Period

THIS *SŪRAH* is almost certainly the fourth in the order of revelation. Although some of its verses may have come at a slightly later date, the whole of it belongs to the earliest Mecca period. The contention of some authorities that verse 20 was revealed at Medina lacks all substance, as is pointed out in note 13 below.

سورة المزمل مكية -73-
وآياتها عشرون

IN THE NAME OF GOD, THE MOST GRACIOUS, THE DISPENSER OF GRACE:

O THOU enwrapped one![1] ‹1›
Keep awake [in prayer] at night, all but a small part ‹2› of one-half thereof[2] – or make it a little less than that, ‹3› or add to it [at will]; and [during that time] recite the Qur᾽ān calmly and distinctly, with thy mind attuned to its meaning.[3] ‹4›

بِسْمِ ٱللَّهِ ٱلرَّحْمَٰنِ ٱلرَّحِيمِ

يَٰٓأَيُّهَا ٱلْمُزَّمِّلُ ﴿١﴾ قُمِ ٱلَّيْلَ إِلَّا قَلِيلًا ﴿٢﴾ نِّصْفَهُۥٓ أَوِ ٱنقُصْ مِنْهُ
قَلِيلًا ﴿٣﴾ أَوْ زِدْ عَلَيْهِ وَرَتِّلِ ٱلْقُرْءَانَ تَرْتِيلًا ﴿٤﴾

Bismil-lāhir-Raḥmānir-Raḥīm.
Yāa ᾽ayyuhal-muzzammilu, (1) qumil-layla ᾽illā qalīlā. (2) Niṣfahūu ᾽awin-quṣ minhu qalīlā. (3) ᾽Aw zid ᶜalayhi wa rattilil-Qur᾽āna tartīlā. (4)

---

1 The expression *muzzammil* has a meaning similar to that of *muddaththir*, which occurs at the beginning of the next *sūrah*: namely, "one who is covered [with anything]", "enwrapped" or "enfolded [in anything]"; and, like that other expression, it may be understood in a concrete, literal sense – i.e., "wrapped up in a cloak" or "blanket" – as well as metaphorically, i.e., "wrapped up in sleep" or even "wrapped up in oneself". Hence, the commentators differ widely in their interpretations of the above apostrophe, some of them preferring the literal connotation, others the metaphorical; but there is no doubt that irrespective of the linguistic sense in which the address "O thou enwrapped one" is understood, it implies a call to heightened consciousness and deeper spiritual awareness on the part of the Prophet.

2 Thus Zamakhsharī, relating the phrase *illā qalīlan* ("all but a small part") to the subsequent word *niṣfahu* ("one-half thereof", i.e., of the night).

3 This, I believe, is the closest possible rendering of the phrase *rattil al-qur᾽āna tartīlan*. The term *tartīl* primarily denotes "the putting [of something] together distinctly, in a well-arranged manner, and without any haste" (Jawharī, Bayḍāwī; also *Lisān al-ᶜArab, Qāmūs*). When applied to the recitation of a text, it signifies a calm, measured utterance with thoughtful consideration of the *meaning* to be brought out. A somewhat different significance attaches to a variant of this phrase in 25 : 32, applying to the manner in which the Qur᾽ān was revealed.

Behold, We shall bestow upon thee a weighty message ‹5› – [and,] verily, the hours of night impress the mind most strongly and speak with the clearest voice,[4] ‹6› whereas by day a long chain of doings is thy portion. ‹7› But [whether by night or by day] remember thy Sustainer's name, and devote thyself unto Him with utter devotion. ‹8›

The Sustainer of the east and the west [is He]: there is no deity save Him: hence, ascribe to Him alone the power to determine thy fate,[5] ‹9› and endure with patience whatever people may say [against thee], and avoid them with a comely avoidance. ‹10›

And leave Me alone [to deal] with those who give the lie to the truth[6] – those who enjoy the blessings of life [without any thought of God] – and bear thou with them for a little while: ‹11› for, behold, heavy fetters [await them] with Us, and a blazing fire, ‹12› and food that chokes, and grievous suffering[7] ‹13› on the Day when the earth and the mountains will be convulsed, and the mountains will [crumble and] become like a sand-dune on the move![8] ‹14›

BEHOLD, [O men,] We have sent unto you an apostle who shall bear witness to the truth before you, even as We sent an

إِنَّا سَنُلْقِى عَلَيْكَ قَوْلًا ثَقِيلًا ﴿5﴾ إِنَّ نَاشِئَةَ ٱلَّيْلِ هِىَ أَشَدُّ وَطْـًٔا وَأَقْوَمُ
قِيلًا ﴿6﴾ إِنَّ لَكَ فِى ٱلنَّهَارِ سَبْحًا طَوِيلًا ﴿7﴾ وَٱذْكُرِ ٱسْمَ رَبِّكَ وَتَبَتَّلْ إِلَيْهِ
تَبْتِيلًا ﴿8﴾ رَّبُّ ٱلْمَشْرِقِ وَٱلْمَغْرِبِ لَآ إِلَـٰهَ إِلَّا هُوَ فَٱتَّخِذْهُ وَكِيلًا ﴿9﴾
وَٱصْبِرْ عَلَىٰ مَا يَقُولُونَ وَٱهْجُرْهُمْ هَجْرًا جَمِيلًا ﴿10﴾ وَذَرْنِى وَٱلْمُكَذِّبِينَ أُو۟لِى
ٱلنَّعْمَةِ وَمَهِّلْهُمْ قَلِيلًا ﴿11﴾ إِنَّ لَدَيْنَآ أَنكَالًا وَجَحِيمًا ﴿12﴾ وَطَعَامًا ذَا
غُصَّةٍ وَعَذَابًا أَلِيمًا ﴿13﴾ يَوْمَ تَرْجُفُ ٱلْأَرْضُ وَٱلْجِبَالُ وَكَانَتِ ٱلْجِبَالُ
كَثِيبًا مَّهِيلًا ﴿14﴾ إِنَّآ أَرْسَلْنَآ إِلَيْكُمْ رَسُولًا شَـٰهِدًا عَلَيْكُمْ كَمَآ أَرْسَلْنَآ

ʾInnā sanulqī ʿalayka qawlañ-thaqīlā. ‹5› ʾInna nāshiʾatal-layli hiya ʾashaddu waṭʾañw-wa ʾaqwamu qīlā. ‹6› ʾInna laka fin-nahāri sabḥañ-ṭawīlā. ‹7› Wadh-kuris-ma Rabbika wa tabattal ʾilayhi tabtīlā. ‹8› Rabbul-mashriqi wal-maghribi lāa ʾilāha ʾillā Huwa fattakhidhhu Wakīlā. ‹9› Waṣ-bir ʿalā mā yaqūlūna wah-jurhum hajrañ-jamīlā. ‹10› Wa dharnī wal-mukadhdhibīna ʾulin-naʿmati wa mahhilhum qalīlā. ‹11› ʾInna ladaynāa ʾañkālañw-wa jaḥīmā. ‹12› Wa ṭaʿāmañ-dha ghuṣṣatiñw-wa ʿadhāban ʾalīmā. ‹13› Yawma tarjuful-ʾarḍu wal-jibālu wa kānatil-jibālu kathībam-mahīlā. ‹14› ʾInnāa ʾarsalnāa ʾilaykum Rasūlañ-shāhidan ʿalaykum kamāa ʾarsalnāa

4 Lit., "are strongest of tread and most upright of speech".

5 For this rendering of the term *wakīl*, see *sūrah* 17, note 4.

6 Cf. 74 : 11 and the last sentence of the corresponding note 5.

7 Explaining this symbolism of torment in the hereafter, Rāzī says: "These four conditions may well be understood as denoting the spiritual consequences [of one's doings in life]. As regards the 'heavy fetters', they are a symbol of the soul's remaining shackled to its [erstwhile] physical attachments and bodily pleasures . . . : and now that their realization has become impossible, those fetters and shackles prevent the [resurrected] human personality (*an-nafs*) from attaining to the realm of the spirit and of purity. Subsequently, those spiritual shackles generate spiritual 'fires', inasmuch as one's strong inclination towards bodily concerns, together with the impossibility of attaining to them, give rise, spiritually, to [a sensation of] severe burning . . . : and this is [the meaning of] 'the blazing fire' (*al-jaḥīm*). Thereupon [the sinner] tries to swallow the choking agony of deprivation and the pain of separation [from the objects of his desire]: and this is the meaning of the words, 'and food that chokes'. And, finally, because of these circumstances, he remains deprived of all illumination by the light of God, and of all communion with the blessed ones: and this is the meaning of the words 'and grievous suffering'. . . . But [withal,] know that I do not claim to have exhausted the meaning of these [Qurʾān-]verses by what I have stated [above]. . . ."

8 See the first part of 14 : 48, and the corresponding note 63, as well as note 90 on 20 : 105-107.

apostle unto Pharaoh:[9] ‹15› and Pharaoh rebelled against the apostle, whereupon We took him to task with a crushing grip. ‹16›
How, then, if you refuse to acknowledge the truth, will you protect yourselves on that Day which shall turn the hair of children grey,[10] ‹17› [the Day] on which the skies shall be rent asunder, [and] His promise [of resurrection] fulfilled? ‹18›
This, verily, is a reminder: let him who wills, then, set out on a way to his Sustainer! ‹19›

إِلَىٰ فِرْعَوْنَ رَسُولًا ﴿١٥﴾ فَعَصَىٰ فِرْعَوْنُ ٱلرَّسُولَ فَأَخَذْنَٰهُ أَخْذًا وَبِيلًا ﴿١٦﴾
فَكَيْفَ تَتَّقُونَ إِن كَفَرْتُمْ يَوْمًا يَجْعَلُ ٱلْوِلْدَٰنَ شِيبًا ﴿١٧﴾ ٱلسَّمَآءُ مُنفَطِرٌۢ
بِهِۦ ۚ كَانَ وَعْدُهُۥ مَفْعُولًا ﴿١٨﴾ إِنَّ هَٰذِهِۦ تَذْكِرَةٌ ۖ فَمَن شَآءَ ٱتَّخَذَ إِلَىٰ رَبِّهِۦ
سَبِيلًا ﴿١٩﴾ ۞ إِنَّ رَبَّكَ يَعْلَمُ أَنَّكَ تَقُومُ أَدْنَىٰ مِن ثُلُثَىِ ٱلَّيْلِ وَنِصْفَهُۥ وَثُلُثَهُۥ
وَطَآئِفَةٌ مِّنَ ٱلَّذِينَ مَعَكَ ۚ وَٱللَّهُ يُقَدِّرُ ٱلَّيْلَ وَٱلنَّهَارَ ۚ عَلِمَ أَن لَّن تُحْصُوهُ
فَتَابَ عَلَيْكُمْ ۖ فَٱقْرَءُوا۟ مَا تَيَسَّرَ مِنَ ٱلْقُرْءَانِ ۚ عَلِمَ أَن سَيَكُونُ مِنكُم
مَّرْضَىٰ ۙ وَءَاخَرُونَ يَضْرِبُونَ فِى ٱلْأَرْضِ يَبْتَغُونَ مِن فَضْلِ ٱللَّهِ ۙ وَءَاخَرُونَ
يُقَٰتِلُونَ فِى سَبِيلِ ٱللَّهِ ۖ فَٱقْرَءُوا۟ مَا تَيَسَّرَ مِنْهُ ۚ وَأَقِيمُوا۟ ٱلصَّلَوٰةَ وَءَاتُوا۟

ربع الحزب

ʾilā Firᶜawna Rasūlā. 15 Faᶜaṣā Firᶜawnur-Rasūla faʾakhadhnāhu ʾakhdhañw-wabīlā. 16 Fakayfa tattaqūna ʾiñ-kafartum Yawmañy-yajᶜalul-wildāna shībā. 17 ʾAssamāaʾu muñfaṭirum-bih. Kāna waᶜduhū mafᶜūlā. 18 ʾInna hādhihī tadhkiratañ-famañ-shāaʾat-takhadha ʾilā Rabbihī sabīlā. 19 ◆ ʾInna Rabbaka yaᶜlamu ʾannaka taqūmu ʾadnā miñ-thuluthayil-layli wa niṣfahū wa thuluthahū wa ṭāaʾifatum-minal-ladhīna maᶜak. Wal-lāhu yuqaddirul-layla wan-nahār. ᶜAlima ʾal-lañ-tuḥṣūhu fatāba ᶜalaykum. Faqraʾū mā tayassara minal-Qurʾān. ᶜAlima ʾañ-sayakūnu miñkum-marḍā wa ʾākharūna yaḍribūna fil-ʾarḍi yabtaghūna miñ-faḍlil-lāhi wa ʾākharūna yuqātilūna fī sabīlil-lāh. Faqraʾū mā tayassara minh. Wa ʾaqīmuṣ-Ṣalāta wa ʾātuz-

BEHOLD, [O Prophet,] thy Sustainer knows that thou keepest awake [in prayer] nearly two-thirds of the night, or one-half of it, or a third of it, together with some of those who follow thee.[11] And God, who determines the measure of night and day, is aware that you would never grudge it:[12] and therefore He turns towards you in His grace.
Recite, then, as much of the Qurʾān as you may do with ease. He knows that in time there will be among you sick people, and others who will go about the land in search of God's bounty, and others who will fight in God's cause.[13] Recite, then, [only] as much of it as you may do with ease, and be constant in prayer, and spend

9 This is probably the oldest Qurʾanic reference to the earlier prophets, to the historic continuity in mankind's religious experience, and, by implication, to the fact that the Qurʾān does not institute a "new" faith but represents only the final, most comprehensive statement of a religious principle as old as mankind itself: namely, that "in the sight of God, the only [true] religion is [man's] self-surrender unto Him" (3 : 19), and that "if one goes in search of a religion other than self-surrender unto God, it will never be accepted from him" (3 : 85).

10 In ancient Arabian usage, a day full of terrifying events was described metaphorically as "a day on which the locks of children turn grey"; hence the use of this phrase in the Qurʾān. Its purely metaphorical character is obvious since, according to the teachings of the Qurʾān, children are considered sinless – i.e., not accountable for their doings – and will, therefore, remain untouched by the ordeals and terrors of the Day of Judgment (Rāzī).

11 Lit., "of those who are with thee". With this concluding passage, the discourse returns to the theme of the opening verses, namely, the great spiritual value of praying at night.

12 Lit., "count it", i.e., the length of your vigil.

13 This reference to "fighting in God's cause" has induced many commentators to assume that the whole of verse 20 was revealed at Medina, that is, years after the rest of the *sūrah*: for, the principle of "fighting in God's cause" (*jihād*) was introduced only after the Prophet's *hijrah* from Mecca to Medina. This assumption must, however, be dismissed as unwarranted. Although there is no doubt that *jihād* was first sanctioned during the Medina period, the sentence in question is clearly expressed in the *future* tense: "in time there *will be*" (*sayakūn*) – and must, therefore, as Ibn Kathīr points out, be understood as a prediction of future circumstances. With all this, the above passage stresses the necessity of avoiding all exaggeration, even in one's devotions.

in charity,[14] and [thus] lend unto God a goodly loan: for whatever good deed you may offer up in your own behalf, you shall truly find it with God – yea, better, and richer in reward.
And [always] seek God's forgiveness: behold, God is much-forgiving, a dispenser of grace! ‹20›

ٱلزَّكَوٰةَ وَأَقۡرِضُواْ ٱللَّهَ قَرۡضًا حَسَنًاۚ وَمَا تُقَدِّمُواْ لِأَنفُسِكُم مِّنۡ خَيۡرٖ تَجِدُوهُ عِندَ ٱللَّهِ هُوَ خَيۡرٗا وَأَعۡظَمَ أَجۡرٗاۚ وَٱسۡتَغۡفِرُواْ ٱللَّهَۖ إِنَّ ٱللَّهَ غَفُورٞ رَّحِيمُۢ ﴿20﴾

Zakāta wa ʾaqriḍul-lāha qarḍan ḥasanā. Wa mā tuqaddimū liʾañfusikum-min khayriñ-tajidūhu ʿiñdal-lāhi huwa khayrañw-wa ʾaʿẓama ʾajrā. Was-taghfirul-lāha ʾinnal-lāha Ghafūrur-Raḥīm. ﴿20﴾

14 For an explanation of the term *zakāh* – of which the above is the earliest Qurʾanic instance – see *sūrah* 2, note 34.

The Seventy-Fourth Sūrah

Al-Muddaththir (The Enfolded One)

Mecca Period

AFTER the Prophet's earliest revelation – consisting of the first five verses of *sūrah* 96 ("The Germ-Cell") – a period elapsed during which he received no revelation at all. The length of this break in revelation (*fatrat al-waḥy*) cannot be established with certainty; it may have been as little as six months or as much as three years. It was a time of deepest distress for the Prophet: the absence of revelation almost led him to believe that his earlier experience in the cave of Mount Ḥirā᾿ (see introductory note to *sūrah* 96) was an illusion; and it was only due to the moral support of his wife Khadījah and her undaunted faith in his prophetic mission that he did not entirely lose his courage and hope. At the end of this intermission the Prophet had a vision of the Angel Gabriel, "sitting between heaven and earth". Almost immediately afterwards, the present *sūrah* was revealed; and from then on, in Muḥammad's own words, "revelation became intense and continuous" (Bukhārī, *Bad᾿ al-Waḥy* and *Kitāb at-Tafsīr*; also Muslim).

Although some verses of this *sūrah* may have been revealed at a slightly later time, there is no doubt that all of it belongs to the earliest part of the Mecca period, that is, to the very beginning of Muḥammad's mission. But in spite of its early origin and its brevity, the *sūrah* outlines almost all the fundamental concepts to which the Qur᾿ān as a whole is devoted: the oneness and uniqueness of God, resurrection and ultimate judgment; life after death and the allegorical nature of all descriptions relating to it; man's weakness and utter dependence on God, his proneness to false pride, greed and selfishness; each human being's responsibility for his own behaviour and doings; "paradise" and "hell" as natural *consequences* of one's earthly life, and not as arbitrary rewards or punishments; the principle of the historical continuity of all true religious experience; and various other ideas and concepts which were to be more fully developed in later revelations.

-74-
سورة المدثر مكية
وآياتها ست وخمسون

IN THE NAME OF GOD, THE MOST GRACIOUS, THE DISPENSER OF GRACE:

O THOU [in thy solitude] enfolded![1] ‹1›
Arise and warn! ‹2›
And thy Sustainer's greatness glorify! ‹3›
And thine inner self purify![2] ‹4›
And all defilement shun! ‹5›
And do not through giving seek thyself to gain,[3] ‹6› but unto thy Sustainer turn in patience. ‹7›
And [warn all men that] when the trumpet-call [of resurrection] is sounded, ‹8› that very Day shall be a day of anguish, ‹9› not of ease, for all who [now] deny the truth![4] ‹10›

بِسْمِ ٱللَّهِ ٱلرَّحْمَٰنِ ٱلرَّحِيمِ

يَٰٓأَيُّهَا ٱلْمُدَّثِّرُ ﴿١﴾ قُمْ فَأَنذِرْ ﴿٢﴾ وَرَبَّكَ فَكَبِّرْ ﴿٣﴾ وَثِيَابَكَ
فَطَهِّرْ ﴿٤﴾ وَٱلرُّجْزَ فَٱهْجُرْ ﴿٥﴾ وَلَا تَمْنُن تَسْتَكْثِرُ ﴿٦﴾ وَلِرَبِّكَ فَٱصْبِرْ ﴿٧﴾
فَإِذَا نُقِرَ فِى ٱلنَّاقُورِ ﴿٨﴾ فَذَٰلِكَ يَوْمَئِذٍ يَوْمٌ عَسِيرٌ ﴿٩﴾ عَلَى ٱلْكَٰفِرِينَ
غَيْرُ يَسِيرٍ ﴿١٠﴾

Bismil-lāhir-Raḥmānir-Raḥīm.
Yāa ʾayyuhal-muddaththiru. (1) **qum faʾañdhir.** (2)
Wa Rabbaka fakabbir. (3) **Wa thiyābaka faṭahhir.** (4)
War-rujza fahjur. (5) **Wa lā tamnuñ-tastakthir.** (6)
Wa liRabbika faṣbir. (7) **Faʾidhā nuqira fin-nāqūri,**
(8) **fadhālika Yawmaʾidhiñy-Yawmun ʿasīr.** (9) **ʿAlal-kāfirīna ghayru yasīr.** (10)

---

1 The expression *muddaththir* (an abbreviated form of *mutadaththir*) signifies "one who is covered [with something]" or "enfolded [in something]"; and all philologists point out that the verb *dathara*, from which the above participial noun is derived, may equally well have a concrete or abstract connotation. Most of the commentators understand the phrase "O thou enfolded one" in its literal, concrete sense, and assume that it refers to the Prophet's habit of covering himself with a cloak or blanket when he felt that a revelation was about to begin. Rāzī, however, notes that this apostrophe may well have been used metaphorically, as an allusion to Muḥammad's intense desire for solitude before the beginning of his prophetic mission (cf. introductory note to *sūrah* 96): and this, according to Rāzī, would explain his being thus addressed in connection with the subsequent call, "Arise and warn" – i.e., "Give now up thy solitude, and stand up before all the world as a preacher and warner."

2 Lit., "thy garments (*thiyāb*) purify": but almost all the classical commentators point out that the noun *thawb* and its plural *thiyāb* is often metonymically applied to that which a garment encloses, i.e., a person's "body" or, in a wider sense, his "self" or his "heart", or even his "spiritual state" or "conduct" (*Tāj al-ʿArūs*). Thus, commenting on the above verse, Zamakhsharī draws the reader's attention to the well-known idiomatic phrases *ṭāhir ath-thiyāb* (lit., "one who is clean in his garments") and *danis ath-thiyāb* ("one who is filthy in his garments"), and stresses their tropical significance of "free from faults and vices" and "vicious and perfidious", respectively. Rāzī states with approval that "according to most of the [earlier] commentators, the meaning [of this verse] is, 'purify thy heart of all that is blameworthy'".

3 Lit., "and do not bestow favours to obtain increase".

4 Since this is the earliest Qurʾānic occurrence of the expression *kāfir* (the above *sūrah* having been preceded only by the first five verses of *sūrah* 96), its use here – and, by implication, in the whole of the Qurʾān – is obviously determined by the meaning which it had in the speech of the Arabs *before* the advent of the Prophet Muḥammad: in other words, the term *kāfir* cannot be simply equated, as many Muslim theologians of post-classical times and practically all Western translators of the Qurʾān have done, with "unbeliever" or "infidel" in the specific, restricted sense of one who rejects the system of doctrine and law promulgated in the Qurʾān and amplified by the teachings of the Prophet – but must have a wider, more general meaning. This meaning is easily grasped when we bear in mind that the root verb of the participial noun *kāfir* (and of the infinitive noun *kufr*) is *kafara*, "he [or "it"] covered [a thing]":

LEAVE Me alone [to deal] with him whom I have created alone,[5] ‹11› and to whom I have granted resources vast, ‹12› and children as [love's] witnesses, ‹13› and to whose life I gave so wide a scope:[6] ‹14› and yet, he greedily desires that I give yet more! ‹15›
Nay, verily, it is against Our messages that he knowingly, stubbornly sets himself[7] ‹16› – [and so] I shall constrain him to endure a painful uphill climb![8] ‹17›
Behold, [when Our messages are conveyed to one who is bent on denying the truth,] he reflects and meditates [as to how to disprove them] ‹18› – and thus he destroys himself,[9] the way he meditates: ‹19› yea, he destroys himself, the way he meditates! ‹20› – and then he looks [around for new arguments], ‹21›

ذَرْنِي وَمَنْ خَلَقْتُ وَحِيدًا ﴿11﴾ وَجَعَلْتُ لَهُۥ مَالًا مَّمْدُودًا ﴿12﴾ وَبَنِينَ
شُهُودًا ﴿13﴾ وَمَهَّدتُّ لَهُۥ تَمْهِيدًا ﴿14﴾ ثُمَّ يَطْمَعُ أَنْ أَزِيدَ ﴿15﴾ كَلَّآ إِنَّهُۥ
كَانَ لِءَايَٰتِنَا عَنِيدًا ﴿16﴾ سَأُرْهِقُهُۥ صَعُودًا ﴿17﴾ إِنَّهُۥ فَكَّرَ وَقَدَّرَ ﴿18﴾
فَقُتِلَ كَيْفَ قَدَّرَ ﴿19﴾ ثُمَّ قُتِلَ كَيْفَ قَدَّرَ ﴿20﴾ ثُمَّ نَظَرَ ﴿21﴾

Dharnī wa man khalaqtu waḥīdā. (11) Wa jaᶜaltu lahū mālam-mamdūdā. (12) Wa banīna shuhūdā. (13) Wa mahhattu lahū tamhīdā. (14) Thumma yaṭmaᶜu ʾan ʾazīd. (15) Kallāa ʾinnahū kāna liʾĀyātinā ᶜanīdā. (16) Saʾurhiquhū ṣaᶜūdā. (17) ʾInnahū fakkara wa qad-dar. (18) Faqutila kayfa qaddar. (19) Thumma qutila kayfa qaddar. (20) Thumma naẓar. (21)

thus, in 57 : 20 the tiller of the soil is called (without any pejorative implication) *kāfir,* "one who covers", i.e., the sown seed with earth, just as the night is spoken of as having "covered" (*kafara*) the earth with darkness. In their abstract sense, both the verb and the nouns derived from it have a connotation of "concealing" something that exists or "denying" something that is true. Hence, in the usage of the Qurʾān – with the exception of the one instance (in 57 : 20) where this participial noun signifies a "tiller of the soil" – a *kāfir* is "one who denies [or "refuses to acknowledge"] the truth" in the widest, spiritual sense of this latter term: that is, irrespective of whether it relates to a cognition of the supreme truth – namely, the existence of God – or to a doctrine or ordinance enunciated in the divine writ, or to a self-evident moral proposition, or to an acknowledgment of, and therefore gratitude for, favours received. (Regarding the expression *alladhīna kafarū,* implying conscious intent, see *sūrah* 2, note 6.)

5 Or: ". . . whom I alone have created". The above sentence can be understood in either of these two senses, depending on whether one relates the expression "alone" (*waḥīd*) to God – thus stressing His uniqueness as Creator – or to this particular object of His creation, man, who begins and ends his life in a state of utter loneliness (cf. 6 : 94 and 19 : 80 and 95). In either case, our attention is drawn to the fact of man's inescapable dependence on God. Beyond that, the phrase in question carries a further meaning, namely, "Leave it to Me alone to decide what to do with him who forgets that I am his Creator and Sustainer" – thus forbidding any *human* punishment of "those who deny the truth".

6 Lit., "for whom I have spread [all] out in a [wide] spread" – i.e., "whom I have endowed with potentialities far beyond those open to other living beings".

7 Lit., "he is wont (*kāna*) to set himself". The noun *ᶜanīd,* derived from the verb *ᶜanada,* denotes "one who opposes or rejects something that is true, *knowing* it to be true" (*Lisān al-ᶜArab*). The element of human contrariness and stubbornness is implied in the use of the auxiliary verb *kāna,* which indicates here a permanently recurring phenomenon despite its past-tense formulation. I am, therefore, of the opinion that verses 18-25, although ostensibly formulated in the past tense, must also be rendered in the present tense.

8 In combination with the verb *urhiquhu* ("I shall constrain him to endure") the term *ṣaᶜūd* (lit., "ascent" or "climb") has the tropical connotation of something extremely difficult, painful or distressing. In the above context, it is an allusion to the loss of all instinctive innocence – and, hence, to the individual and social suffering – which unavoidably follows upon man's wilful neglect of moral and spiritual truths ("God's messages") in this world, and bars his spiritual development in the life to come.

9 The expression *qutila* reads, literally, "he has been killed" or, as an imprecation, "may he be killed". Since a literal rendering of this expression – whether conceived as a statement of fact or an imprecation – would be meaningless here, many commentators (Ṭabarī among them) understand it as signifying "he is rejected from God's grace" (*luᶜina*), i.e., "killed" spiritually by his own action or attitude; hence my rendering, "he destroys himself".

and then he frowns and glares,[10] ‹22› and in the end he turns his back [on Our message], and glories in his arrogance,[11] ‹23› and says, "All this is mere spellbinding eloquence handed down [from olden times]![12] ‹24› This is nothing but the word of mortal man!" ‹25›
[Hence,] I shall cause him to endure hell-fire [in the life to come]![13] ‹26›
And what could make thee conceive what hell-fire is? ‹27›
It does not allow to live, and neither leaves [to die], ‹28› making [all truth] visible to mortal man.[14] ‹29›
Over it are nineteen [powers].[15] ‹30›
For We have caused none but angelic powers to lord over the fire [of hell];[16]

ثُمَّ عَبَسَ وَبَسَرَ (22) ثُمَّ أَدْبَرَ وَٱسْتَكْبَرَ (23) فَقَالَ إِنْ هَـٰذَآ إِلَّا
سِحْرٌ يُؤْثَرُ (24) إِنْ هَـٰذَآ إِلَّا قَوْلُ ٱلْبَشَرِ (25) سَأُصْلِيهِ سَقَرَ (26)
وَمَآ أَدْرَىٰكَ مَا سَقَرُ (27) لَا تُبْقِى وَلَا تَذَرُ (28) لَوَّاحَةٌ لِّلْبَشَرِ (29)
عَلَيْهَا تِسْعَةَ عَشَرَ (30) وَمَا جَعَلْنَآ أَصْحَـٰبَ ٱلنَّارِ إِلَّا مَلَـٰٓئِكَةً

Thumma ʿabasa wa basar. (22) Thumma ʾadbara was-takbar. (23) Faqāla ʾin hādhāa ʾillā siḥruñy-yuʾthar. (24) ʾIn hādhāa ʾillā qawlul-bashar. (25) Saʾuṣlīhi saqar. (26) Wa māa ʾadrāka mā saqar. (27) Lā tubqī wa lā tadhar. (28) Lawwāḥatul-lilbashar. (29) ʿAlayhā tisʿata ʿashar. (30) Wa mā jaʿalnāa ʾaṣḥāban-nāri ʾillā Malāaʾikatañw-

10 I.e., he becomes emotionally involved because he suspects in his heart that his arguments are weak (Rāzī).

11 See 96 : 6-7.

12 The term *siḥr*, which usually denotes "sorcery" or "magic", primarily signifies "the turning of something from its proper [or "natural"] state of being into another state"; hence, it is often applied to the fascination or enchantment caused by exceptional, "spellbinding" eloquence (*Tāj al-ʿArūs*). In its pejorative sense – as used by deniers of the truth to describe a divine message – it has also the connotation of "wilful deception" or "delusion".

13 This is unquestionably the earliest instance of the term *saqar* ("hell-fire"), one of the seven metaphorical names given in the Qurʾān to the concept of the suffering in the hereafter which man brings upon himself by sinning and deliberately remaining blind and deaf, in this world, to spiritual truths (cf. *sūrah* 15, note 33). The allegorical character of this and all other Qurʾanic descriptions of man's condition and destiny in the hereafter is clearly alluded to in the subsequent verse as well as in verses 28 ff.

14 Most of the commentators interpret the above elliptic phrase in the sense of "changing the appearance of man" or "scorching the skin of man". The rendering adopted by me, on the other hand, is based on the primary significance of the verb *lāḥa* – "it appeared", "it shone forth" or "it became visible". Hence, the primary meaning of the intensive participial noun *lawwāh* is "that which makes [something] visible". In the above context, it relates to the sinner's belated cognition of the truth, as well as to his distressing insight into his own nature, his past failings and deliberate wrongdoings, and the realization of his own responsibility for the suffering that is now in store for him: a state neither of life nor of death (cf. 87 : 12-13).

15 Whereas most of the classical commentators are of the opinion that the "nineteen" are the angels that act as keepers or guardians of hell, Rāzī advances the view that we may have here a reference to the physical, intellectual and emotional powers *within man himself*: powers which raise man potentially far above any other creature, but which, if used wrongly, bring about a deterioration of his whole personality and, hence, intense suffering in the life to come. According to Rāzī, the philosophers (*arbāb al-ḥikmah*) identify these powers or faculties with, firstly, the seven organic functions of the animal – and therefore also human – body (gravitation, cohesion, repulsion of noxious foreign matter, absorption of beneficent external matter, assimilation of nutrients, growth, and reproduction); secondly, the five "external" or physical senses (sight, hearing, touch, smell and taste); thirdly, the five "internal" or intellectual senses, defined by Ibn Sīnā – on whom Rāzī apparently relies – as (1) perception of isolated sense-images, (2) conscious apperception of ideas, (3) memory of sense-images, (4) memory of conscious apperceptions, and (5) the ability to correlate sense-images and higher apperceptions; and, lastly, the emotions of desire or aversion (resp. fear or anger), which have their roots in both the "external" and "internal" sense-categories – thus bringing the total of the powers and faculties which preside over man's spiritual fate to nineteen. In their aggregate, it is these powers that confer upon man the ability to think *conceptually*, and place him, in this respect, even above the angels (cf. 2 : 30 ff. and the corresponding notes; see also the following note).

16 Since it is by virtue of his powers of conscious perception and conceptual thinking that man can arrive at a discriminating cognition of good and evil and, thus, rise to great spiritual heights, these powers are described here as "angelic" (lit., "angels" – this being the earliest occurrence of the term *malak* in the history of Qurʾanic revelation). On

and We have not caused their number to be aught but a trial for those who are bent on denying the truth[17] – to the end that they who have been granted revelation aforetime might be convinced [of the truth of this divine writ];[18] and that they who have attained to faith [in it] might grow yet more firm in their faith; and that [both] they who have been granted the earlier revelation and they who believe [in this one] might be freed of all doubt; and that they in whose hearts is disease[19] and they who deny the truth outright might ask, "What does [your] God mean by this parable?"[20]
In this way God lets go astray him that wills [to go astray], and guides aright him that wills [to be guided].[21]
And none can comprehend thy Sustainer's forces save Him alone: and all this[22] is but a reminder to mortal man. «31»

NAY, but consider the moon![23] «32»
Consider the night when it departs, «33»
and the morn when it dawns! «34»

وَمَا جَعَلْنَا عِدَّتَهُمْ إِلَّا فِتْنَةً لِّلَّذِينَ كَفَرُوا۟ لِيَسْتَيْقِنَ ٱلَّذِينَ أُوتُوا۟
ٱلْكِتَـٰبَ وَيَزْدَادَ ٱلَّذِينَ ءَامَنُوٓا۟ إِيمَـٰنًا ۙ وَلَا يَرْتَابَ ٱلَّذِينَ أُوتُوا۟ ٱلْكِتَـٰبَ
وَٱلْمُؤْمِنُونَ ۙ وَلِيَقُولَ ٱلَّذِينَ فِى قُلُوبِهِم مَّرَضٌ وَٱلْكَـٰفِرُونَ مَاذَآ أَرَادَ ٱللَّهُ
بِهَـٰذَا مَثَلًا ۚ كَذَٰلِكَ يُضِلُّ ٱللَّهُ مَن يَشَآءُ وَيَهْدِى مَن يَشَآءُ ۚ وَمَا يَعْلَمُ
جُنُودَ رَبِّكَ إِلَّا هُوَ ۚ وَمَا هِىَ إِلَّا ذِكْرَىٰ لِلْبَشَرِ ﴿٣١﴾ كَلَّا وَٱلْقَمَرِ ﴿٣٢﴾
وَٱلَّيْلِ إِذْ أَدْبَرَ ﴿٣٣﴾ وَٱلصُّبْحِ إِذَآ أَسْفَرَ ﴿٣٤﴾

wa mā jaʿalnā ʿiddatahum ʾillā fitnatal-lilladhīna kafarū liyastayqinal-ladhīna ʾūtul-Kitāba wa yazdādal-ladhīna ʾāmanūu ʾīmānañw-wa lā yartābal-ladhīna ʾūtul-Kitāba wal-muʾminūna wa liyaqūlal-ladhīna fī qulūbihim maraḍuñw-wal-kāfirūna mādhāa ʾarādal-lāhu bihādhā mathalā. Kadhālika yuḍillul-lāhu mañy-yashāaʿu wa yahdī mañy-yashāaʾ. Wa mā yaʿlamu junūda Rabbika ʾillā Hū. Wa mā hiya ʾillā dhikrā lilbashar. (31) Kallā wal-qamar. (32) Wal-layli ʾidh ʾadbar. (33) Waṣ-ṣubḥi ʾidhāa ʾasfar. (34)

the other hand, since a neglect or a deliberately wrong use of these angelic powers is at the root of all sinning on the part of man and, therefore, of his suffering in the hereafter, they are spoken of as "the lords (*aṣḥāb*) of the fire [of hell]", which complements the expression "over it" in the preceding verse.

17 This is apparently an allusion to the allegorical character of this passage, which "those who are bent on denying the truth" are unwilling to recognize as such and, hence, fail to grasp its real purport. By speculating on the reasons which allegedly induced Muḥammad – whom they regard as the "author" of the Qurʾān – to lay stress on one particular number, they tend to take the allegory in a literal sense, thus missing its point entirely.

18 Namely, by being enabled, through an understanding of the above allegory, to appreciate the rational approach of the Qurʾān to all questions of faith. The reference to "those who have been granted revelation aforetime" is the earliest statement outlining the principle of continuity in mankind's religious experience.

19 I.e., in this instance, the half-hearted ones who, despite their ability to discern between right and wrong, incline towards unbelief.

20 Cf. the identical phrase in 2 : 26, together with the corresponding note 18. My interpolation, in both these passages, of the word "your" between brackets is necessitated by the fact that it is the *unbelievers* who ask this question.

21 Or: "God lets go astray whomever He wills, and guides aright whomever He wills" (see *sūrah* 14, note 4). The stress on the allegorical nature of the above passage, spoken of as a "parable" (*mathal*), has here the same purpose as in 2 : 26 – namely, to prevent the followers of the Qurʾān from attaching a *literal* meaning to its eschatological descriptions – a purpose that is unmistakably expressed in the concluding sentence of this passage: "All this is but a reminder to mortal man". (See also next note.)

22 Lit., "it" or "these" – depending on whether the personal pronoun *hiya* is taken to denote a singular – in which case it would refer to the feminine noun *saqar*, "hell-fire" (Ṭabarī, Zamakhsharī, Baghawī, Ibn Kathīr) – or a plural, referring to what Rāzī pinpoints as "those [Qurʾanic] verses dealing with these allegories (*hādhihi 'l-mutashābihāt*)": hence my compromise rendering "all this".

23 This is the earliest Qurʾanic instance of the adjurative particle *wa* used in the sense of a solemn, oathlike assertion – a calling to witness, as it were – meant (as in the expression "by God!") to give weight to a subsequently

Verily, that [hell-fire] is indeed one of the great [forewarnings] ‹35› – a warning to mortal man ‹36› – to every one of you, whether he chooses to come forward or to hang back![24] ‹37›
[On the Day of Judgment,] every human being will be held in pledge for whatever [evil] he has wrought ‹38› – save only those who shall have attained to righteousness:[25] ‹39› [dwelling] in gardens [of paradise], they will inquire ‹40› of those who were lost in sin: ‹41› "What has brought you into hell-fire?" ‹42›
They will answer: "We were not among those who prayed,[26] ‹43› and neither did we feed the needy; ‹44› and we were wont to indulge in sinning together with all [the others] who indulged in it; ‹45› and the Day of Judgment we were wont to call a lie ‹46› – until certainty came upon us [in death]." ‹47›
And so, of no benefit to them could be the intercession of any that would intercede for them.[27] ‹48›

WHAT, THEN, is amiss with them[28] that they turn away from all admonition ‹49› as though they were terrified asses ‹50› fleeing from a lion? ‹51›
Yea, every one of them claims that he [himself] ought to have been given revelations unfolded![29] ‹52›

إِنَّهَا لَإِحۡدَى ٱلۡكُبَرِ ﴿٣٥﴾ نَذِيرٗا لِّلۡبَشَرِ ﴿٣٦﴾ لِمَن شَآءَ مِنكُمۡ أَن يَتَقَدَّمَ
أَوۡ يَتَأَخَّرَ ﴿٣٧﴾ كُلُّ نَفۡسِۭ بِمَا كَسَبَتۡ رَهِينَةٌ ﴿٣٨﴾ إِلَّآ أَصۡحَٰبَ ٱلۡيَمِينِ ﴿٣٩﴾
فِي جَنَّٰتٖ يَتَسَآءَلُونَ ﴿٤٠﴾ عَنِ ٱلۡمُجۡرِمِينَ ﴿٤١﴾ مَا سَلَكَكُمۡ فِي سَقَرَ ﴿٤٢﴾
قَالُواْ لَمۡ نَكُ مِنَ ٱلۡمُصَلِّينَ ﴿٤٣﴾ وَلَمۡ نَكُ نُطۡعِمُ ٱلۡمِسۡكِينَ ﴿٤٤﴾ وَكُنَّا
نَخُوضُ مَعَ ٱلۡخَآئِضِينَ ﴿٤٥﴾ وَكُنَّا نُكَذِّبُ بِيَوۡمِ ٱلدِّينِ ﴿٤٦﴾ حَتَّىٰٓ أَتَىٰنَا
ٱلۡيَقِينُ ﴿٤٧﴾ فَمَا تَنفَعُهُمۡ شَفَٰعَةُ ٱلشَّٰفِعِينَ ﴿٤٨﴾ فَمَا لَهُمۡ عَنِ ٱلتَّذۡكِرَةِ
مُعۡرِضِينَ ﴿٤٩﴾ كَأَنَّهُمۡ حُمُرٞ مُّسۡتَنفِرَةٞ ﴿٥٠﴾ فَرَّتۡ مِن قَسۡوَرَةِۭ ﴿٥١﴾ بَلۡ
يُرِيدُ كُلُّ ٱمۡرِيٕٖ مِّنۡهُمۡ أَن يُؤۡتَىٰ صُحُفٗا مُّنَشَّرَةٗ ﴿٥٢﴾

ʾInnahā laʾiḥdal-kubar. (35) Nadhīral-lilbashar. (36) Limañ-shāaʾa miñkum ʾañy-yataqaddama ʾaw yataʾakhkhar. (37) Kullu nafsim-bimā kasabat rahīnatun, (38) ʾillāa ʾaṣḥābal-yamīn. (39) Fī jannātiñy-yatasāaʾalūna, (40) ʿanil-mujrimīna, (41) mā salakakum fī saqar. (42) Qālū lam naku minal-muṣallīn. (43) Wa lam naku nuṭʿimul-miskīn. (44) Wa kunnā nakhūḍu maʿal-khāaʾiḍīn. (45) Wa kunnā nukadhdhibu biYawmid-Dīn (46) Ḥattāa ʾatānal-yaqīn. (47) Famā tañfaʿuhum shafāʿatush-shāfiʿīn. (48) Famā lahum ʿanit-tadhkirati muʿriḍīn. (49) Kaʾannahum ḥumurum-mustañfirah. (50) Farrat miñ-qaswarah. (51) Bal yurīdu kullum-riʾim-minhum ʾañy-yuʾtā ṣuḥufam-munashsharah. (52)

stated truth or evidence of the truth: hence, I am rendering it here and elsewhere as "consider". In the present case, the truth thus to be stressed is the implied statement that just as the changing phases of the moon and the alternation of night and day are the outcome of God-given, natural laws, so, too, a sinner's suffering in the hereafter is but a *natural outcome* of his deliberate wrongdoing in this world. (See also note 7 on 2 : 7.)

24 Lit., "any of you who chooses . . .", etc. – i.e., irrespective of whether one has chosen to follow or to disregard the divine call: implying that even true believers may stumble into sinning, and hence need to be warned.

25 Lit., "those [or "the people"] on the right hand" (*aṣḥāb al-yamīn*), an expression based on the tropical significance of *yamīn* as "righteous" or "righteousnes" and, consequently, "blessedness". The above is probably the oldest Qurʾanic incidence of this expression, which evidently comprises all those whose conduct in life will have earned them God's forgiveness of whatever sins they may have committed.

26 In view of the fact that at the time of the revelation of this very early *sūrah* the canonical prayer (*ṣalāh*) had not yet been made obligatory on the followers of the Qurʾān, it is reasonable to assume that in the above context this term is used in its widest sense, namely, conscious belief in God.

27 Lit., "the intercession of intercessors" – implying that there would be none to intercede for them with God. As regards the much-misunderstood Islamic concept of "intercession", see 10 : 3 – "there is none that could intercede with Him unless He grants His leave therefor" – and the corresponding note 7.

28 I.e., with so many people who refuse to listen to the truth.

29 Lit., "every one of them wants to be given wide-open scriptures", or "scriptures unfolded" (i.e., open to

Nay, but they do not [believe in and, hence, do not] fear the life to come. ‹53›
Nay, verily, this is an admonition ‹54› – and whoever wills may take it to heart. ‹55›
But they [who do not believe in the life to come] will not take it to heart unless God so wills:[30] [for] He is the Fount of all God-consciousness, and the Fount of all forgiveness. ‹56›

كَلَّا ۖ بَل لَّا يَخَافُونَ ٱلْـَٔاخِرَةَ ﴿٥٣﴾ كَلَّآ إِنَّهُۥ تَذْكِرَةٌ ﴿٥٤﴾ فَمَن شَآءَ
ذَكَرَهُۥ ﴿٥٥﴾ وَمَا يَذْكُرُونَ إِلَّآ أَن يَشَآءَ ٱللَّهُ ۚ هُوَ أَهْلُ ٱلتَّقْوَىٰ وَأَهْلُ
ٱلْمَغْفِرَةِ ﴿٥٦﴾

Kallā bal lā yakhāfūnal-ʾĀkhirah. (53) Kallāa ʾinnahū tadhkirah. (54) Famañ-shāaʾa dhakarah. (55) Wa mā yadhkurūna ʾillāa ʾañy-yashāaʾal-lāh. Huwa ʾAhlut-taqwā wa ʾAhlul-maghfirah. (56)

everyone's understanding): cf. 2 : 118 – "Why does not God speak unto us, nor is a message conveyed to us?" – i.e., directly, without the intervention of a prophet. The above is the earliest illustration of the "arrogance" or "false pride" to which the Qurʾān so often refers.

30 Namely, unless He bestows His grace on them by making their minds and hearts receptive to the truth, so that they are compelled – from within themselves, as it were – to make the right choice. (See also note 11 on 81 : 28-29, as well as note 4 on 14 : 4.)

The Seventy-Fifth Sūrah

Al-Qiyāmah (Resurrection)

Mecca Period

REVEALED during the first third of the Mecca period, this *sūrah* is devoted almost entirely (with the exception of the parenthetic passage in verses 16-19) to the concept of resurrection, on which its traditional "title" is based.

سورة القيامة مكية -75-
وآياتها أربعون

نصف الحزب

IN THE NAME OF GOD, THE MOST GRACIOUS, THE DISPENSER OF GRACE:

NAY! I call to witness the Day of Resurrection![1] ‹1› But nay! I call to witness the accusing voice of man's own conscience![2] ‹2›

Does man think that We cannot [resurrect him and] bring his bones together again? ‹3› Yea indeed, We are able to make whole his very finger-tips! ‹4›

None the less, man chooses to deny what lies ahead of him, ‹5› asking [derisively], "When is that Resurrection Day to be?" ‹6›

But [on that Day,] when the eyesight is by fear confounded, ‹7›

and the moon is darkened, ‹8›

and the sun and the moon are brought together[3] ‹9›

– on that Day will man exclaim, "Whither to flee?" ‹10›

But nay: no refuge [for thee, O man]! ‹11›

بِسۡمِ ٱللَّهِ ٱلرَّحۡمَٰنِ ٱلرَّحِيمِ

لَآ أُقۡسِمُ بِيَوۡمِ ٱلۡقِيَٰمَةِ ١ وَلَآ أُقۡسِمُ بِٱلنَّفۡسِ ٱللَّوَّامَةِ ٢ أَيَحۡسَبُ
ٱلۡإِنسَٰنُ أَلَّن نَّجۡمَعَ عِظَامَهُۥ ٣ بَلَىٰ قَٰدِرِينَ عَلَىٰٓ أَن نُّسَوِّيَ بَنَانَهُۥ
٤ بَلۡ يُرِيدُ ٱلۡإِنسَٰنُ لِيَفۡجُرَ أَمَامَهُۥ ٥ يَسۡـَٔلُ أَيَّانَ يَوۡمُ
ٱلۡقِيَٰمَةِ ٦ فَإِذَا بَرِقَ ٱلۡبَصَرُ ٧ وَخَسَفَ ٱلۡقَمَرُ ٨ وَجُمِعَ
ٱلشَّمۡسُ وَٱلۡقَمَرُ ٩ يَقُولُ ٱلۡإِنسَٰنُ يَوۡمَئِذٍ أَيۡنَ ٱلۡمَفَرُّ ١٠ كَلَّا لَا
وَزَرَ ١١

Bismil-lāhir-Raḥmānir-Raḥīm.
Lāa ʾuqsimu biYawmil-Qiyāmah. (1) Wa lāa ʾuqsimu binnafsil-lawwāmah. (2) ʾAyaḥsabul-ʾIñsānu ʾallañ-najmaʿa ʿiẓāmah. (3) Balā qādirīna ʿalāa ʾañ-nusawwiya banānah. (4) Bal yurīdul-ʾIñsānu liyafjura ʾamāmah. (5) Yasʾalu ʾayyāna Yawmul-Qiyāmah. (6) Faʾidhā bariqal-baṣar. (7) Wa khasafal-qamar. (8) Wa jumiʿash-shamsu wal-qamar. (9) Yaqūlul-ʾIñsānu Yawmaʾidhin ʾaynal-mafarr. (10) Kallā lā wazar. (11)

---

1 By "calling it to witness", i.e., by speaking of the Day of Resurrection as if it had already occurred, the above phrase is meant to convey the *certainty* of its coming.

2 Lit., "the [self-]reproaching soul": i.e., man's subconscious awareness of his own shortcomings and failings.

3 I.e., in their loss of light, or in the moon's colliding with the sun.

With thy Sustainer, on that Day, the journey's end will be! ‹12›
Man will be apprised, on that Day, of what he has done and what he has left undone:[4] ‹13› nay, but man shall against himself be an eye-witness, ‹14› even though he may veil himself in excuses.[5] ‹15›

MOVE NOT thy tongue in haste, [repeating the words of the revelation:][6] ‹16› for, behold, it is for Us to gather it [in thy heart,] and to cause it to be read [as it ought to be read].[7] ‹17›
Thus, when We recite it, follow thou its wording [with all thy mind]:[8] ‹18› and then, behold, it will be for Us to make its meaning clear.[9] ‹19›

NAY, but [most of] you love this fleeting life, ‹20› and give no thought to the life to come [and to Judgment Day]! ‹21›
Some faces will on that Day be bright with happiness, ‹22› looking up to their Sustainer; ‹23› and some faces will on that Day be overcast with despair, ‹24› knowing that a crushing calamity is about to befall them. ‹25›

إِلَىٰ رَبِّكَ يَوْمَئِذٍ ٱلْمُسْتَقَرُّ ﴿١٢﴾ يُنَبَّؤُا۟ ٱلْإِنسَٰنُ يَوْمَئِذٍۭ بِمَا قَدَّمَ
وَأَخَّرَ ﴿١٣﴾ بَلِ ٱلْإِنسَٰنُ عَلَىٰ نَفْسِهِۦ بَصِيرَةٌ ﴿١٤﴾ وَلَوْ أَلْقَىٰ مَعَاذِيرَهُۥ ﴿١٥﴾
لَا تُحَرِّكْ بِهِۦ لِسَانَكَ لِتَعْجَلَ بِهِۦٓ ﴿١٦﴾ إِنَّ عَلَيْنَا جَمْعَهُۥ وَقُرْءَانَهُۥ ﴿١٧﴾
فَإِذَا قَرَأْنَٰهُ فَٱتَّبِعْ قُرْءَانَهُۥ ﴿١٨﴾ ثُمَّ إِنَّ عَلَيْنَا بَيَانَهُۥ ﴿١٩﴾ كَلَّا بَلْ
تُحِبُّونَ ٱلْعَاجِلَةَ ﴿٢٠﴾ وَتَذَرُونَ ٱلْءَاخِرَةَ ﴿٢١﴾ وُجُوهٌ يَوْمَئِذٍ نَّاضِرَةٌ ﴿٢٢﴾
إِلَىٰ رَبِّهَا نَاظِرَةٌ ﴿٢٣﴾ وَوُجُوهٌ يَوْمَئِذٍۭ بَاسِرَةٌ ﴿٢٤﴾ تَظُنُّ أَن يُفْعَلَ بِهَا
فَاقِرَةٌ ﴿٢٥﴾

ʾIlā Rabbika Yawmaʾidhinil-mustaqarr. (12) Yunab-baʾul-ʾIñsānu Yawmaʾidhim-bimā qaddama wa ʾakhkhar. (13) Balil-ʾIñsānu ʿalā nafsihī baṣīrah. (14) Wa law ʾalqā maʿādhīrah. (15) Lā tuḥarrik bihī lisānaka litaʿjala bih. (16) ʾInna ʿalaynā jamʿahū wa qurʾānah. (17) Faʾidhā qaraʾnāhu fattabiʿ qurʾānah. (18) Thumma ʾinna ʿalaynā bayānah. (19) Kallā bal tuḥibbūnal-ʿājilah. (20) Wa tadharūnal-ʾĀkhirah. (21) Wujūhuñy-Yawmaʾidhiñ-nāḍirah. (22) ʾIlā Rabbihā nāẓirah. (23) Wa wujūhuñy-Yawmaʾidhim-bāsirah. (24) Taẓunnu ʾañy-yufʿala bihā fāqirah. (25)

4 Lit., "what he has sent ahead and left behind", i.e., whatever good and bad deeds he committed or omitted (Zamakhsharī).

5 Cf. 24 : 24, 36 : 65 or 41 : 20-22.

6 Lit., "Move not thy tongue therewith so that thou might hasten it" – the pronoun undoubtedly referring to the contents of revelation. In order to understand this parenthetic passage (verses 16-19) more fully, one should read it side by side with the related passage in 20 : 114, together with the corresponding note 101. Both these passages are in the first instance addressed to the Prophet, who is said to have been afraid that he might forget some of the revealed words unless he repeated them at the very moment of revelation; but both have also a wider import inasmuch as they apply to every believer who reads, listens to or studies the Qurʾān. In 20 : 114 we are told not to draw hasty – and therefore potentially erroneous – conclusions from isolated verses or statements of the Qurʾān, since only the study of the *whole* of its message can give us a correct insight. The present passage, on the other hand, lays stress on the need to imbibe the divine writ slowly, patiently, to give full thought to the meaning of every word and phrase, and to avoid the kind of haste which is indistinguishable from mechanical glibness, and which, moreover, induces the person who reads, recites or listens to it to remain satisfied with the mere beautiful sound of the Qurʾanic language without understanding – or even paying adequate attention to – its message.

7 I.e., "it is for Us to make thee remember it and to cause it to be read with mind and heart". As pointed out in the preceding note, the Qurʾān can be understood only if it is read thoughtfully, as one integral whole, and not as a mere collection of moral maxims, stories or disjointed laws.

8 Lit., "follow thou its recitation", i.e., its message as expressed in words. Since it is God who reveals the Qurʾān and bestows upon man the ability to understand it, He attributes its "recitation" to Himself.

9 I.e., if the Qurʾān is read "as it ought to be read" (see note 7 above), it becomes – as stressed by Muḥammad ʿAbduh – "its own best commentary".

NAY, but when [the last breath] comes up to the throat [of a dying man], ‹26› and people ask, "Is there any wizard [that could save him]?"[10] ‹27› – the while he [himself] knows that this is the parting, ‹28› and is enwrapped in the pangs of death:[11] ‹29› – at that time towards thy Sustainer does he feel impelled to turn![12] ‹30›

[Useless, though, will be his repentance:[13]] for [as long as he was alive] he did not accept the truth, nor did he pray [for enlightenment], ‹31› but, on the contrary, he gave the lie to the truth and turned away [from it], ‹32› and then went arrogantly back to what he had come from.[14] ‹33›

[And yet, O man, thine end comes hourly] nearer unto thee, and nearer ‹34› – and ever nearer unto thee, and nearer! ‹35›

DOES MAN, then, think that he is to be left to himself, to go about at will?[15] ‹36›

Was he not once a [mere] drop of sperm that had been spilt, ‹37› and thereafter became a germ-cell – whereupon He created and formed [it] in accordance with what [it] was meant to be,[16] ‹38› and fashioned out of it the two sexes, the male and the female? ‹39›

Is not He, then, able to bring the dead back to life? ‹40›

كَلَّآ إِذَا بَلَغَتِ ٱلتَّرَاقِىَ ﴿٢٦﴾ وَقِيلَ مَنْۜ رَاقٍ ﴿٢٧﴾ وَظَنَّ أَنَّهُ ٱلْفِرَاقُ ﴿٢٨﴾
وَٱلْتَفَّتِ ٱلسَّاقُ بِٱلسَّاقِ ﴿٢٩﴾ إِلَىٰ رَبِّكَ يَوْمَئِذٍ ٱلْمَسَاقُ ﴿٣٠﴾ فَلَا
صَدَّقَ وَلَا صَلَّىٰ ﴿٣١﴾ وَلَٰكِن كَذَّبَ وَتَوَلَّىٰ ﴿٣٢﴾ ثُمَّ ذَهَبَ إِلَىٰٓ أَهْلِهِۦ
يَتَمَطَّىٰٓ ﴿٣٣﴾ أَوْلَىٰ لَكَ فَأَوْلَىٰ ﴿٣٤﴾ ثُمَّ أَوْلَىٰ لَكَ فَأَوْلَىٰٓ ﴿٣٥﴾ أَيَحْسَبُ
ٱلْإِنسَٰنُ أَن يُتْرَكَ سُدًى ﴿٣٦﴾ أَلَمْ يَكُ نُطْفَةً مِّن مَّنِىٍّ يُمْنَىٰ ﴿٣٧﴾ ثُمَّ كَانَ
عَلَقَةً فَخَلَقَ فَسَوَّىٰ ﴿٣٨﴾ فَجَعَلَ مِنْهُ ٱلزَّوْجَيْنِ ٱلذَّكَرَ وَٱلْأُنثَىٰٓ ﴿٣٩﴾
أَلَيْسَ ذَٰلِكَ بِقَٰدِرٍ عَلَىٰٓ أَن يُحْـِۧىَ ٱلْمَوْتَىٰ ﴿٤٠﴾

Kallāa ᵓidhā balaghatit-tarāqī. (26) Wa qīla man, rāq. (27) Wa ẓanna ᵓannahul-firāq. (28) Wal-taffatis-sāqu bissāq. (29) ᵓIlā Rabbika Yawmaᵓidhinil-masāq. (30) Falā ṣaddaqa wa lā ṣallā. (31) Wa lākiñ-kadhdhaba wa tawallā. (32) Thumma dhahaba ᵓilāa ᵓahlihī yatamaṭṭā. (33) ᵓAwlā laka faᵓawlā. (34) Thumma ᵓawlā laka faᵓawlā. (35) ᵓAyaḥsabul-ᵓIñsānu ᵓañy-yutraka sudā. (36) ᵓAlam yaku nuṭfatam-mim-maniyyiñy-yumnā. (37) Thumma kāna ᶜalaqatañ-fakhalaqa fasawwā. (38) Fajaᶜala minhuz-zawjaynidh-dhakara wal-ᵓuñthā. (39) ᵓAlaysa dhālika biqādirin ᶜalāa ᵓañy-yuḥyiyal-mawtā. (40)

10 Lit., "Who is a wizard [or "a charmer"]?" A similar construction is found in 28 : 71 and 72.

11 Lit., "when shank is wrapped around shank" – an idiomatic phrase denoting "the affliction of the present state of existence . . . combined with that of the final state" (Lane IV, 1471, quoting both the *Qāmūs* and the *Tāj al-ᶜArūs*). As pointed out by Zamakhsharī, the noun *sāq* (lit., "shank") is often used metaphorically in the sense of "difficulty", "hardship" or "vehemence" (*shiddah*); hence the well-known phrase, *qāmat al-ḥarb ᶜalā sāq*, "the war broke out with vehemence" (*Tāj al-ᶜArūs*).

12 Lit., "towards thy Sustainer will be the driving", i.e., with belated repentance (see next three verses). The phrase rendered above as "at the time" reads, literally, "on that day"; but the term *yawm* is often used idiomatically in the sense of "time" regardless of its duration.

13 This interpolation, necessary for a full understanding of the sequence, is based on 4 : 17-18, which has a definite bearing on the above passage.

14 Lit., "to his people": i.e., to the arrogant belief, rooted in the materialism of his social environment, that man is "self-sufficient" and, therefore, not in need of any divine guidance (cf. 96 : 6).

15 I.e., without being held morally responsible for his doings.

16 For this rendering of *sawwā*, see note 1 on 87 : 2 and note 5 on 91 : 7. The stress on God's creating man *after* he had been a germ-cell is a metonym for His endowing the (originally) lowly organism with what is described as a "soul".

The Seventy-Sixth Sūrah

Al-ʾIñsān (Man)

Period Uncertain

THE OPINIONS of the earliest commentators are divided as to whether this *sūrah* – also called *Ad-Dahr* ("Time" or "Endless Time") after a word occurring in the first verse – belongs to the Mecca or the Medina period. Many authorities of the second generation – among them Mujāhid, Qatādah, Al-Ḥasan al-Baṣrī and ʿIkrimah (all of them quoted by Baghawī) – hold the view that it was revealed at Medina.

سورة الإنسان مدنية
-76-
وآياتها إحدى وثلاثون

IN THE NAME OF GOD, THE MOST GRACIOUS, THE DISPENSER OF GRACE:

HAS THERE [not] been an endless span of time[1] before man [appeared – a time] when he was not yet a thing to be thought of?[2] ‹1›
Verily, it is We who have created man out of a drop of sperm intermingled,[3] so that We might try him [in his later life]: and therefore We made him a being endowed with hearing and sight. ‹2›
Verily, We have shown him the way:[4] [and it rests with him to prove himself] either grateful or ungrateful. ‹3›

بِسۡمِ ٱللَّهِ ٱلرَّحۡمَٰنِ ٱلرَّحِيمِ

هَلۡ أَتَىٰ عَلَى ٱلۡإِنسَٰنِ حِينٞ مِّنَ ٱلدَّهۡرِ لَمۡ يَكُن شَيۡـٔٗا مَّذۡكُورًا ﴿١﴾ إِنَّا
خَلَقۡنَا ٱلۡإِنسَٰنَ مِن نُّطۡفَةٍ أَمۡشَاجٖ نَّبۡتَلِيهِ فَجَعَلۡنَٰهُ سَمِيعَۢا بَصِيرًا ﴿٢﴾ إِنَّا
هَدَيۡنَٰهُ ٱلسَّبِيلَ إِمَّا شَاكِرٗا وَإِمَّا كَفُورًا ﴿٣﴾

Bismil-lāhir-Raḥmānir-Raḥīm.
Hal ʾatā ʿalal-ʾIñsāni ḥīnum-minad-dahri lam yakuñ-shayʾam-madhkūrā. ‹1› ʾInnā khalaqnal-ʾIñsāna min-nuṭfatin ʾamshājiñ-nabtalīhi fajaʿalnāhu samīʿam-baṣīrā. ‹2› ʾInnā hadaynāhus-sabīla ʾimmā shākirañw-wa ʾimmā kafūrā. ‹3›

---

1 Implying, according to all the classical commentators, "there has indeed been an immensely long [or "endless"] span of time" – the interrogative particle *hal* having here the positive meaning of *qad*. However, this meaning can be brought out equally well by interpolating the word "not".

2 Lit., "a thing mentioned" or "mentionable" – i.e., non-existent even as a hypothetical concept. The purport of this statement is a refutation of the blasphemous "anthropocentric" world-view, which postulates man as he exists – and not any Supreme Being – as the centre and ultimate reality of all life.

3 Sc., "with the female ovum": cf. 86 : 6-7.

4 I.e., God has not only endowed man with "hearing and sight", i.e., with reason and the instinctive ability to discern between right and wrong, good and evil (cf. 90 : 10), but He also actively guides him by means of the revelation bestowed on the prophets.

[Now,] behold, for those who deny the truth[5] We have readied chains and shackles, and a blazing flame[6] ‹4› – [whereas,] behold, the truly virtuous shall drink from a cup flavoured with the calyx of sweet-smelling flowers:[7] ‹5› a source [of bliss] whereof God's servants shall drink, seeing it flow in a flow abundant.[8] ‹6›

[The truly virtuous are] they [who] fulfil their vows,[9] and stand in awe of a Day the woe of which is bound to spread far and wide, ‹7› and who give food – however great be their own want of it[10] – unto the needy, and the orphan, and the captive,[11] ‹8› [saying, in their hearts,] "We feed you for the sake of God alone: we desire no recompense from you, nor thanks: ‹9› behold, we stand in awe of our Sustainer's judgment[12] on a distressful, fateful Day! ‹10›

And so, God will preserve them from the woes of that Day, and will bestow on them brightness and joy, ‹11› and will reward them for all their patience in adversity with a garden [of bliss] and with [garments of] silk.[13] ‹12›

In that [garden] they will on couches recline, and will know therein neither [burning] sun nor cold severe, ‹13›

إِنَّآ أَعۡتَدۡنَا لِلۡكَٰفِرِينَ سَلَٰسِلَاْ وَأَغۡلَٰلٗا وَسَعِيرًا ﴿٤﴾ إِنَّ ٱلۡأَبۡرَارَ
يَشۡرَبُونَ مِن كَأۡسٖ كَانَ مِزَاجُهَا كَافُورًا ﴿٥﴾ عَيۡنٗا يَشۡرَبُ بِهَا عِبَادُ ٱللَّهِ
يُفَجِّرُونَهَا تَفۡجِيرٗا ﴿٦﴾ يُوفُونَ بِٱلنَّذۡرِ وَيَخَافُونَ يَوۡمٗا كَانَ شَرُّهُۥ
مُسۡتَطِيرٗا ﴿٧﴾ وَيُطۡعِمُونَ ٱلطَّعَامَ عَلَىٰ حُبِّهِۦ مِسۡكِينٗا وَيَتِيمٗا وَأَسِيرًا ﴿٨﴾
إِنَّمَا نُطۡعِمُكُمۡ لِوَجۡهِ ٱللَّهِ لَا نُرِيدُ مِنكُمۡ جَزَآءٗ وَلَا شُكُورًا ﴿٩﴾ إِنَّا
نَخَافُ مِن رَّبِّنَا يَوۡمًا عَبُوسٗا قَمۡطَرِيرٗا ﴿١٠﴾ فَوَقَىٰهُمُ ٱللَّهُ شَرَّ ذَٰلِكَ ٱلۡيَوۡمِ
وَلَقَّىٰهُمۡ نَضۡرَةٗ وَسُرُورٗا ﴿١١﴾ وَجَزَىٰهُم بِمَا صَبَرُواْ جَنَّةٗ وَحَرِيرٗا ﴿١٢﴾
مُّتَّكِـِٔينَ فِيهَا عَلَى ٱلۡأَرَآئِكِ لَا يَرَوۡنَ فِيهَا شَمۡسٗا وَلَا زَمۡهَرِيرٗا ﴿١٣﴾

ʾInnāa ʾaᶜtadnā lilkāfirīna salāsila wa ʾaghlālañw-wa saᶜīrā. (4) ʾInnal-ʾabrāra yashrabūna miñ-kaʾsiñ-kāna mizājuhā kāfūrā. (5) ᶜAynañy-yashrabu bihā ᶜibādul-lāhi yufajjirūnahā tafjīrā. (6) Yūfūna bin-nadhri wa yakhāfūna Yawmañ-kāna sharruhū mustaṭīrā. (7) Wa yuṭᶜimūnaṭ-ṭaᶜāma ᶜalā ḥubbihī miskīnañw-wa yatīmañw-wa ʾasīrā. (8) ʾInnamā nuṭᶜimukum liwajhil-lāhi lā nurīdu miñkum jazāaʾañw-wa lā shukūrā. (9) ʾInnā nakhāfu mir-Rabbinā Yawman ᶜabūsañ-qamṭarīrā. (10) Fawaqāhumul-lāhu sharra dhālikal-Yawmi wa laqqāhum naḍratañw-wa surūrā. (11) Wa jazāhum bimā ṣabarū jannatañw-wa ḥarīrā. (12) Muttakiʾīna fīhā ᶜalal-ʾarāaʾiki lā yarawna fīhā shamsañw-wa lā zamharīrā. (13)

5 In this context, the "denial of the truth" (*kufr*) apparently relates to man's deliberate suppression of his inborn cognition of God's existence (cf. 7 : 172 and the corresponding note 139) as well as to his disregard of his own instinctive perceptions of good and evil.

6 Sc., "of despair". For the metaphor of "shackles and chains" – i.e., the consequence of the sinners' blind surrender to their own passions and to false values, and the resulting enslavement of their spirit – see *sūrah* 34, note 44; also Rāzī's elaborate comments (quoted in note 7 on 73 : 12-13) on this allegory of suffering in the hereafter.

7 The *Lisān al-ᶜArab* gives "the calyx (*kimm*) of the grape before its flowering" as the primary significance of *kāfūr*; according to other lexicologists (e.g., *Tāj al-ᶜArūs*), it denotes "the calyx of *any* flower"; Jawharī applies it to the "spathe of a palm tree". Hence, this – and not "camphor" – is evidently the meaning of *kāfūr* in the above context: an allusion to the sweet, extremely delicate fragrance of the symbolic "drink" of divine knowledge (cf. 83 : 25-28 and the corresponding notes 8 and 9).

8 Lit., "making [or "letting"] it flow . . .", etc.: i.e., having it always at their disposal.

9 I.e., the spiritual and social obligations arising from their faith.

10 Or, as in 2 : 177, "however much they themselves may cherish [i.e., "need"] it"; cf. also 90 : 14-16. It is to be noted that in this context the concept of "giving food" comprises every kind of help and care, both material and moral.

11 The term *asīr* denotes anyone who is a "captive" either literally (e.g., a prisoner) or figuratively, i.e., a captive of circumstances which render him helpless; thus, the Prophet said, "Thy debtor is thy captive; be, therefore, truly kind to thy captive" (Zamakhsharī, Rāzī, *et al.*). The injunction of kindness towards all who are in need of help – and therefore "captive" in one sense or another – applies to believers and non-believers alike (Ṭabarī, Zamakhsharī), and apparently also to animals dependent on man.

12 Lit., "we fear our Sustainer".

13 For this allegory, see first half of note 41 on 18 : 31.

وَدَانِيَةً عَلَيْهِمْ ظِلَٰلُهَا وَذُلِّلَتْ قُطُوفُهَا تَذْلِيلًا (14) وَيُطَافُ عَلَيْهِم
بِـَٔانِيَةٍ مِّن فِضَّةٍ وَأَكْوَابٍ كَانَتْ قَوَارِيرَا۠ (15) قَوَارِيرَا۠ مِن فِضَّةٍ قَدَّرُوهَا
تَقْدِيرًا (16) وَيُسْقَوْنَ فِيهَا كَأْسًا كَانَ مِزَاجُهَا زَنجَبِيلًا (17) عَيْنًا فِيهَا
تُسَمَّىٰ سَلْسَبِيلًا (18) ۞ وَيَطُوفُ عَلَيْهِمْ وِلْدَٰنٌ مُّخَلَّدُونَ إِذَا رَأَيْتَهُمْ
حَسِبْتَهُمْ لُؤْلُؤًا مَّنثُورًا (19) وَإِذَا رَأَيْتَ ثَمَّ رَأَيْتَ نَعِيمًا وَمُلْكًا كَبِيرًا (20)
عَٰلِيَهُمْ ثِيَابُ سُندُسٍ خُضْرٌ وَإِسْتَبْرَقٌ وَحُلُّوٓا أَسَاوِرَ مِن فِضَّةٍ وَسَقَىٰهُمْ
رَبُّهُمْ شَرَابًا طَهُورًا (21) إِنَّ هَٰذَا كَانَ لَكُمْ جَزَآءً وَكَانَ سَعْيُكُم
مَّشْكُورًا (22)

ثلاثة ارباع الحزب

Wa dāniyatan ʿalayhim ẓilāluhā wa dhullilat quṭūfuhā tadhlīlā. (14) Wa yuṭāfu ʿalayhim biʾāniyatim-miñ-fiḍḍatiñw-wa ʾakwābiñ-kānat qawārīra. (15) Qawārīra miñ-fiḍḍatiñ-qaddarūhā taqdīrā. (16) Wa yusqawna fīhā kaʾsañ-kāna mizājuhā zañjabīlā. (17) ʿAynañ-fīhā tusammā salsabīlā. (18) ۞ Wa yaṭūfu ʿalayhim wildānum-mukhalladūna ʾidhā raʾaytahum ḥasibtahum luʾluʾam-mañthūrā. (19) Wa ʾidhā raʾayta thamma raʾayta naʿīmañw-wa mulkañ-kabīrā. (20) ʿĀliyahum thiyābu suñdusin khuḍruñw-wa ʾistabraq. Wa ḥullūu ʾasāwira miñ-fiḍḍatiñw-wa saqāhum Rabbuhum sharābañ-ṭahūrā. (21) ʾInna hādhā kāna lakum jazāaʾañw-wa kāna saʿyukum-mashkūrā. (22)

since its [blissful] shades will come down low over them,[14] and low will hang down its clusters of fruit, most easy to reach.[15] ‹14›

And they will be waited upon with vessels of silver and goblets that will [seem to] be crystal ‹15› – crystal-like, [but] of silver – the measure whereof they alone will determine.[16] ‹16›

And in that [paradise] they will be given to drink of a cup flavoured with ginger, ‹17› [derived from] a source [to be found] therein, whose name is "Seek Thy Way".[17] ‹18›

And immortal youths will wait upon them:[18] when thou seest them, thou wouldst deem them to be scattered pearls; ‹19› and when thou seest [anything that is] there, thou wilt see [only] bliss and a realm transcendent. ‹20›

Upon those [blest] will be garments of green silk and brocade; and they will be adorned with bracelets of silver.[19] And their Sustainer will give them to drink of a drink most pure.[20] ‹21›

[And they will be told:] "Verily, all this is your reward, since your endeavour [in life] has met with [God's] goodly acceptance!" ‹22›

14 Regarding the allegorical implication of the term "shades" (*ẓilāl*), see note 74 on 4 : 57. It is to be noted that the existence of shade presupposes the existence of *light* (Jawharī), which latter is one of the characteristics implicit in the concept of "paradise".

15 Lit., "in all humility".

16 I.e., partaking of as much as they may desire.

17 This is how ʿAlī ibn Abī Ṭālib – as quoted by Zamakhsharī and Rāzī – explains the (obviously compound) word *salsabīlan*, dividing it into its two components, *sal sabīlan* ("ask [or "seek"] the way"): namely, "seek thy way to paradise by means of doing righteous deeds". Although Zamakhsharī does not quite agree with this interpretation, it is, in my opinion, very convincing inasmuch as it contains an allusion to the highly allegorical character of the concept of "paradise" as a spiritual *consequence* of one's positive endeavours in this world. That its delights are not of a material nature is also evident from their varying descriptions – i.e., "a cup flavoured with ginger" in verse 17, and "flavoured with the calyx of sweet-smelling flowers" in verse 5; or "they will be waited upon with trays and goblets of gold" in 43 : 71, and "vessels of silver and goblets that will [seem to] be crystal – crystal-like, [but] of silver", in verses 15-16 of this *sūrah*; and so forth.

18 See note 6 on 56 : 17-18.

19 See 18 : 31 (where "bracelets of gold" are mentioned) and the corresponding note 41.

20 Implying that God *Himself* will slake their spiritual thirst by purifying their inner selves "of all envy, and rancour, and malice, and all that leads to harm, and all that is base in man's nature" (Ibn Kathīr, quoting ʿAlī ibn Abī Ṭālib), and by allowing them to "drink" of His Own Light (Rāzī).

VERILY, [O believer,] it is We who have bestowed from on high this Qurʾān upon thee, step by step[21] – truly a bestowal from on high! ‹23›
Await, then, in all patience thy Sustainer's judgment,[22] and pay no heed to any of them who is a wilful sinner or an ingrate; ‹24› and bear in mind thy Sustainer's name[23] at morn and evening ‹25› and during some of the night,[24] and prostrate thyself before Him, and extol His limitless glory throughout the long night.[25] ‹26›
Behold, they [who are unmindful of God] love this fleeting life, and leave behind them [all thought of] a grief-laden Day. ‹27›
[They will not admit to themselves that] it is We who have created them and strengthened their make[26] – and [that], if it be Our will, We can replace them entirely with others of their kind.[27] ‹28›

VERILY, all this is an admonition: whoever, then, so wills, may unto his Sustainer find a way. ‹29›
But you cannot will it unless God wills [to show you that way]:[28] for, behold, God is indeed all-knowing, wise. ‹30›
He admits unto His grace everyone who wills [to be admittedl];[29] but as for the evildoers – for them has He readied grievous suffering [in the life to come]. ‹31›

إِنَّا نَحْنُ نَزَّلْنَا عَلَيْكَ ٱلْقُرْءَانَ تَنزِيلًا (23) فَٱصْبِرْ لِحُكْمِ رَبِّكَ وَلَا
تُطِعْ مِنْهُمْ ءَاثِمًا أَوْ كَفُورًا (24) وَٱذْكُرِ ٱسْمَ رَبِّكَ بُكْرَةً
وَأَصِيلًا (25) وَمِنَ ٱلَّيْلِ فَٱسْجُدْ لَهُۥ وَسَبِّحْهُ لَيْلًا طَوِيلًا (26) إِنَّ
هَٰٓؤُلَآءِ يُحِبُّونَ ٱلْعَاجِلَةَ وَيَذَرُونَ وَرَآءَهُمْ يَوْمًا ثَقِيلًا (27) نَّحْنُ
خَلَقْنَٰهُمْ وَشَدَدْنَآ أَسْرَهُمْ ۖ وَإِذَا شِئْنَا بَدَّلْنَآ أَمْثَٰلَهُمْ تَبْدِيلًا (28) إِنَّ
هَٰذِهِۦ تَذْكِرَةٌ ۖ فَمَن شَآءَ ٱتَّخَذَ إِلَىٰ رَبِّهِۦ سَبِيلًا (29) وَمَا تَشَآءُونَ إِلَّآ
أَن يَشَآءَ ٱللَّهُ ۚ إِنَّ ٱللَّهَ كَانَ عَلِيمًا حَكِيمًا (30) يُدْخِلُ مَن يَشَآءُ فِى
رَحْمَتِهِۦ ۚ وَٱلظَّٰلِمِينَ أَعَدَّ لَهُمْ عَذَابًا أَلِيمًۢا (31)

ʾInnā Naḥnu nazzalnā ʿalaykal-Qurʾāna tañzīlā. (23) Faṣbir liḥukmi Rabbika wa lā tuṭiʿ minhum ʾāthiman ʾaw kafūrā. (24) Wadh-kuris-ma Rabbika bukratañw-wa ʾaṣīlā. (25) Wa minal-layli fasjud lahū wa sabbiḥhu laylañ-ṭawīlā. (26) ʾInna hāaʾulāaʾi yuḥibbūnal-ʿājilata wa yadharūna warāaʾahum Yawmañ-thaqīlā. (27) Naḥnu khalaqnāhum wa shadadnāa ʾasrahum. Wa ʾidhā shiʾnā baddalnāa ʾamthalahum tabdīlā. (28) ʾInna hādhihī tadhkirah. Famañ-shāaʾat-takhadha ʾilā Rabbihī sabīlā. (29) Wa mā tashāaʾūna ʾillāa ʾañy-yashāaʾal-lāh. ʾInnal-lāha kāna ʿAlīman Ḥakīmā. (30) Yudkhilu mañy-yashāaʾu fī raḥmatih. Waẓ-ẓālimīna ʾaʿadda lahum ʿadhāban ʾalīmā. (31)

---

21 The gradualness of Qurʾanic revelation is implied in the verbal form *nazzalnā*.

22 This connects with the preceding mention of the life to come, in which the righteous will meet with bliss, and the evildoers with suffering.

23 I.e., His "attributes" as they manifest themselves in His creation – since the human mind can grasp only the fact of His existence and the *manifestation* of those "attributes", but never the "how" of His Reality (Rāzī).

24 I.e., at all times of wakefulness.

25 I.e., "whenever unhappiness oppresses thee and all seems dark around thee".

26 I.e., endowed their bodies and minds with the ability to *enjoy* "this fleeting life".

27 I.e., with other human beings who would have the same powers of body and mind, but would put them to better use.

28 See note 11 on 81 : 28-29. The perplexity of some of the commentators at the apparent "contradiction" between those two verses – as well as between verses 29-30 of the present *sūrah* – has been caused by their elliptic formulation, which, I believe, is resolved in my rendering. In the present instance, in particular, there is a clear connection between the above two verses and verse 3 of this *sūrah*: "We have shown him the way: [and it rests with him to prove himself] either grateful or ungrateful". (Cf. also 74 : 56.)

29 Or: "whomever He wills" – either of these two formulations being syntactically justified.

The Seventy-Seventh Sūrah

Al-Mursalāt (Those Sent Forth)

Mecca Period

TAKING its name from the word *al-mursalāt* which appears in the first verse (and which obviously refers to the gradual revelation of the Qurʾān), this *sūrah* may be placed chronologically between *sūrahs* 104 (*Al-Humazah*) and 50 (*Qāf*), i.e., almost certainly in the fourth year of the Prophet's mission.

-77-

سورة المرسلات مكية

وآياتها خمسون

IN THE NAME OF GOD, THE MOST GRACIOUS, THE DISPENSER OF GRACE:

CONSIDER these [messages,] sent forth in waves[1] ‹1›
and then storming on with a tempest's force! ‹2›
Consider these [messages] that spread [the truth] far and wide, ‹3›
thus separating [right and wrong] with all clarity,[2] ‹4›
and then giving forth a reminder, ‹5›
[promising] freedom from blame or [offering] a warning![3] ‹6›

BEHOLD, all that you are told to expect[4] will surely come to pass. ‹7›
Thus, [it will come to pass] when the stars are effaced, ‹8›

بِسْمِ ٱللَّهِ ٱلرَّحْمَٰنِ ٱلرَّحِيمِ

وَٱلْمُرْسَلَٰتِ عُرْفًا ﴿١﴾ فَٱلْعَٰصِفَٰتِ عَصْفًا ﴿٢﴾ وَٱلنَّٰشِرَٰتِ نَشْرًا ﴿٣﴾
فَٱلْفَٰرِقَٰتِ فَرْقًا ﴿٤﴾ فَٱلْمُلْقِيَٰتِ ذِكْرًا ﴿٥﴾ عُذْرًا أَوْ نُذْرًا ﴿٦﴾ إِنَّمَا
تُوعَدُونَ لَوَٰقِعٌ ﴿٧﴾ فَإِذَا ٱلنُّجُومُ طُمِسَتْ ﴿٨﴾

Bismil-lāhir-Raḥmānir-Raḥīm.
Wal-mursalāti ʿurfā. (1) Falʿāṣifāti ʿaṣfā. (2) Wan-
nāshirāti nashrā. (3) Falfāriqāti farqā. (4) Falmul-
qiyāti dhikrā. (5) ʿUdhran ʾaw nudhrā. (6) ʾInnamā
tūʿadūna lawāqiʿ. (7) Faʾidhan-nujūmu ṭumisat. (8)

---

1 I.e., one after another: an allusion to the gradual, step-by-step revelation of the Qurʾān. By contrast, the next clause (verse 2) obviously relates to the impact of the divine writ *as a whole*. For my rendering of the adjurative particle *wa* as "Consider", see *sūrah* 74, first half of note 23.

2 Lit., "with [all] separation" (*farqan*). Cf. 8 : 29 and the corresponding note; also note 38 on 2 : 53.

3 I.e., showing what *leads to* freedom from blame – in other words, the principles of right conduct – and what is ethically reprehensible and, therefore, to be avoided.

4 Lit., "that which you are promised", i.e., resurrection.

and when the sky is rent asunder, ‹9›
and when the mountains are scattered like dust, ‹10›
and when all the apostles are called together at a time appointed. . . .[5] ‹11›
For what day has the term [of all this] been set? ‹12›
For the Day of Distinction [between the true and the false]![6] ‹13›
And what could make thee conceive what that Day of Distinction will be? ‹14›
Woe on that Day unto those who give the lie to the truth! ‹15›
Did We not destroy [so many of] those [sinners] of olden days? ‹16› And We shall let them be followed by those of later times:[7] ‹17› [for] thus do We deal with such as are lost in sin. ‹18›
Woe on that Day unto those who give the lie to the truth! ‹19›
Did We not create you out of a humble fluid, ‹20› which We then let remain in [the womb's] firm keeping ‹21› for a term pre-ordained? ‹22›
Thus have We determined [the nature of man's creation]: and excellent indeed is Our power to determine [what is to be]![8] ‹23›
Woe on that Day unto those who give the lie to the truth! ‹24›
Have We not caused the earth to hold within itself ‹25› the living and the dead?[9] ‹26› – and have We not set on it proud, firm mountains, and given you sweet water to drink?[10] ‹27›

وَإِذَا ٱلسَّمَآءُ فُرِجَتْ ﴿9﴾ وَإِذَا ٱلْجِبَالُ نُسِفَتْ ﴿10﴾ وَإِذَا ٱلرُّسُلُ
أُقِّتَتْ ﴿11﴾ لِأَىِّ يَوْمٍ أُجِّلَتْ ﴿12﴾ لِيَوْمِ ٱلْفَصْلِ ﴿13﴾ وَمَآ أَدْرَىٰكَ مَا
يَوْمُ ٱلْفَصْلِ ﴿14﴾ وَيْلٌ يَوْمَئِذٍ لِّلْمُكَذِّبِينَ ﴿15﴾ أَلَمْ نُهْلِكِ ٱلْأَوَّلِينَ ﴿16﴾
ثُمَّ نُتْبِعُهُمُ ٱلْءَاخِرِينَ ﴿17﴾ كَذَٰلِكَ نَفْعَلُ بِٱلْمُجْرِمِينَ ﴿18﴾ وَيْلٌ يَوْمَئِذٍ
لِّلْمُكَذِّبِينَ ﴿19﴾ أَلَمْ نَخْلُقكُّم مِّن مَّآءٍ مَّهِينٍ ﴿20﴾ فَجَعَلْنَٰهُ فِى قَرَارٍ
مَّكِينٍ ﴿21﴾ إِلَىٰ قَدَرٍ مَّعْلُومٍ ﴿22﴾ فَقَدَرْنَا فَنِعْمَ ٱلْقَٰدِرُونَ ﴿23﴾ وَيْلٌ
يَوْمَئِذٍ لِّلْمُكَذِّبِينَ ﴿24﴾ أَلَمْ نَجْعَلِ ٱلْأَرْضَ كِفَاتًا ﴿25﴾ أَحْيَآءً
وَأَمْوَٰتًا ﴿26﴾ وَجَعَلْنَا فِيهَا رَوَٰسِىَ شَٰمِخَٰتٍ وَأَسْقَيْنَٰكُم مَّآءً
فُرَاتًا ﴿27﴾

**Wa ʾidhas-samāaʾu furijat. (9) Wa ʾidhal-jibālu nusi-
fat. (10) Wa ʾidhar-Rusulu ʾuqqitat. (11) Liʾayyi yawmin
ʾujjilat. (12) LiYawmil-Faṣl. (13) Wa māa ʾadrāka mā
Yawmul-Faṣl. (14) Wayluñy-Yawmaʾidhil-lilmukadhdhibīn. (15) ʾAlam nuhlikil-ʾawwalīn. (16) Thumma nut-
biʿuhumul-ʾākhirīn. (17) Kadhālika nafʿalu bilmujrimīn. (18) Wayluñy-Yawmaʾidhil-lilmukadhdhibīn. (19)
ʾAlam nakhlukkum-mim-māaʾim-mahīn. (20) Fajaʿalnāhu fī qarārim-makīn. (21) ʾIlā qadarim-maʿlūm. (22)
Faqadarnā faniʿmal-qādirūn. (23) Wayluñy-Yawmaʾidhil-
lilmukadhdhibīn. (24) ʾAlam najʿalil-ʾarḍa kifātā. (25)
ʾAḥyāaʾañw-wa ʾamwātā. (26) Wa jaʿalnā fīhā
rawāsiya shāmikhātiñw-wa ʾasqaynākum-māaʾañ-
furātā. (27)**

5 Sc., to bear witness for or against those to whom they conveyed God's message (cf. 4 : 41–42, 5 : 109, 7 : 6 or 39 : 69).

6 This is chronologically the earliest occurrence of the expression *yawm al-faṣl*, which invariably relates to the Day of Resurrection (cf. 37 : 21, 44 : 40, 78 : 17, as well as verse 38 of the present *sūrah*): an allusion to the oft-repeated Qurʾanic statement that on resurrection man will gain a perfect, unfailing insight into himself and the innermost motivation of his past attitudes and doings (cf. 69 : 1 and the corresponding note 1).

7 The use of the conjunction *thumma* – which in this case has been rendered as "And" – implies that suffering in the hereafter is *bound* to befall the sinners "of later times" (*al-ākhirūn*) even if God, in His unfathomable wisdom, wills to spare them in this world.

8 The process of man's coming into being (illustrated, for instance, in 23 : 12-14) clearly points to God's creative activity and, hence, to His existence. Consequently, lack of gratitude on man's part amounts to what the Qurʾān describes as "giving the lie to the truth".

9 This refers not merely to the fact that the earth is an abode for living and dead human beings and animals, but is also an allusion to the God-willed, cyclic recurrence of birth, growth, decay and death in all organic creation – and thus an evidence of the existence of the Creator who "brings forth the living out of that which is dead, and brings forth the dead out of that which is alive" (3 : 27, 6 : 95, 10 : 31 and 30 : 19).

10 Parallel with the preceding, this verse refers to God's creation of *inanimate* matter, and thus rounds off the

وَيْلٌ يَوْمَئِذٍ لِّلْمُكَذِّبِينَ (28) ٱنطَلِقُوٓا۟ إِلَىٰ مَا كُنتُم بِهِۦ تُكَذِّبُونَ (29)
ٱنطَلِقُوٓا۟ إِلَىٰ ظِلٍّ ذِى ثَلَٰثِ شُعَبٍ (30) لَّا ظَلِيلٍ وَلَا يُغْنِى مِنَ ٱللَّهَبِ (31)
إِنَّهَا تَرْمِى بِشَرَرٍ كَٱلْقَصْرِ (32) كَأَنَّهُۥ جِمَٰلَتٌ صُفْرٌ (33) وَيْلٌ يَوْمَئِذٍ
لِّلْمُكَذِّبِينَ (34) هَٰذَا يَوْمُ لَا يَنطِقُونَ (35) وَلَا يُؤْذَنُ لَهُمْ فَيَعْتَذِرُونَ (36)
وَيْلٌ يَوْمَئِذٍ لِّلْمُكَذِّبِينَ (37) هَٰذَا يَوْمُ ٱلْفَصْلِ جَمَعْنَٰكُمْ وَٱلْأَوَّلِينَ (38)
فَإِن كَانَ لَكُمْ كَيْدٌ فَكِيدُونِ (39) وَيْلٌ يَوْمَئِذٍ لِّلْمُكَذِّبِينَ (40) إِنَّ
ٱلْمُتَّقِينَ فِى ظِلَٰلٍ وَعُيُونٍ (41) وَفَوَٰكِهَ مِمَّا يَشْتَهُونَ (42) كُلُوا۟ وَٱشْرَبُوا۟
هَنِيٓـًٔا بِمَا كُنتُمْ تَعْمَلُونَ (43) إِنَّا كَذَٰلِكَ نَجْزِى ٱلْمُحْسِنِينَ (44) وَيْلٌ
يَوْمَئِذٍ لِّلْمُكَذِّبِينَ (45)

Wayluñy-Yawmaʾidhil-lilmukadhdhibīn. (28) ʾIñṭaliqūu
ʾilā mā kuñtum bihī tukadhdhibūn. (29) ʾIñṭaliqūu
ʾilā ẓilliñ-dhī thalāthi shuʿab. (30) Lā ẓalīliñw-wa lā
yughnī minal-lahab. (31) ʾInnahā tarmī bisharariñ-
kalqaṣr. (32) Kaʾannahū jimālatuñ-ṣufr. (33) Wayluñy-
Yawmaʾidhil-lilmukadhdhibīn. (34) Hādhā Yawmu lā
yañṭiqūn. (35) Wa lā yuʾdhanu lahum fayaʿtadhirūn.
(36) Wayluñy-Yawmaʾidhil-lilmukadhdhibīn. (37) Hādhā
Yawmul-Faṣli jamaʿnākum wal-ʾawwalīn. (38) Faʾiñ-
kāna lakum kayduñ-fakīdūn. (39) Wayluñy-Yaw-
maʾidhil-lilmukadhdhibīn. (40) ʾInnal-muttaqīna fī
ẓilāliñw-wa ʿuyūn. (41) Wa fawākiha mimmā yash-
tahūn. (42) Kulū wash-rabū hanīʾam-bimā kuñtum
taʿmalūn. (43) ʾInnā kadhālika najzil-muḥsinīn. (44)
Wayluñy-Yawmaʾidhil-lilmukadhdhibīn. (45)

Woe on that Day unto those who give the
lie to the truth! ‹28›

GO ON towards that [resurrection] which
you were wont to call a lie! ‹29›
Go on towards the threefold shadow[11]
‹30› that will offer no [cooling] shade and
will be of no avail against the flame ‹31›
which – behold! – will throw up sparks like
[burning] logs, ‹32› like giant fiery
ropes![12] ‹33›
Woe on that Day unto those who give the
lie to the truth ‹34› – that Day on which
they will not [be able to] utter a word, ‹35›
nor be allowed to proffer excuses! ‹36›
Woe on that Day unto those who give the
lie to the truth ‹37› – that Day of Distinction [between the true and the false, when
they will be told]: "We have brought you
together with those [sinners] of olden
times; ‹38› and if you [think that you]
have a subterfuge left, try to outwit Me!"
‹39›
Woe on that Day unto those who give the
lie to the truth! ‹40›

[AS AGAINST this,] behold, the God-
conscious shall dwell amidst [cooling]
shades and springs, ‹41› and [partake of]
whatever fruit they may desire; ‹42› [and
they will be told:] "Eat and drink in good
cheer in return for what you did [in life]!"[13]
‹43›
Thus, behold, do We reward the doers of
good; ‹44› [but] woe on that Day unto
those who give the lie to the truth! ‹45›

---

statement that He is the Maker of the universe in all its manifestations, both organic and inorganic.

11 I.e., of death, resurrection and God's judgment, all three of which cast dark shadows, as it were, over the sinners' hearts.

12 Lit., "like yellow twisted ropes", yellow being "the colour of fire" (Baghawī). The conventional rendering of *jimālāt* (also spelt *jimālat* and *jimālah*) as "camels", adopted by many commentators and, until now, by all translators of the Qurʾān, must be rejected as grossly anomalous; see in this connection note 32 on the second part of 7 : 40 – "they shall not enter paradise any more than a twisted rope can pass through a needle's eye". In the above verse, too, the plural noun *jimālah* (or *jimālāt*) signifies "twisted ropes" or "giant ropes" – a connotation that has been forcefully stressed by Ibn ʿAbbās, Mujāhid, Saʿīd ibn Jubayr and others (cf. Ṭabarī, Baghawī, Rāzī, Ibn Kathīr; also Bukhārī, *Kitāb at-Tafsīr*). Moreover, our observation of the trajectory of shooting stars fully justifies the rendering "giant fiery ropes". Similarly, my rendering of *qaṣr*, in this context, as "[burning] logs" – instead of the conventional (and utterly meaningless) "castles", "palaces", etc. – goes back to all of the above-mentioned authorities.

13 For this symbolism of the joys of paradise, see Appendix I.

EAT [your fill] and enjoy your life for a little while, O you who are lost in sin![14] ‹46› [But] woe on that Day unto those who give the lie to the truth, ‹47› and when they are told, "Bow down [before God]", do not bow down: ‹48› woe on that Day unto those who give the lie to the truth! ‹49›

In what other tiding, then, will they, after this, believe? ‹50›

كُلُوا۟ وَتَمَتَّعُوا۟ قَلِيلًا إِنَّكُم مُّجْرِمُونَ ﴿٤٦﴾ وَيْلٌ يَوْمَئِذٍ لِّلْمُكَذِّبِينَ ﴿٤٧﴾
وَإِذَا قِيلَ لَهُمُ ٱرْكَعُوا۟ لَا يَرْكَعُونَ ﴿٤٨﴾ وَيْلٌ يَوْمَئِذٍ لِّلْمُكَذِّبِينَ ﴿٤٩﴾
فَبِأَىِّ حَدِيثٍۭ بَعْدَهُۥ يُؤْمِنُونَ ﴿٥٠﴾

Kulū wa tamattaʿū qalīlan ʾinnakum-mujrimūn. (46) Wayluñy-Yawmaʾidhil-lilmukadhdhibīn. (47) Wa ʾidhā qīla lahumur-kaʿū lā yarkaʿūn. (48) Wayluñy-Yawmaʾidhil-lilmukadhdhibīn. (49) Fabiʾayyi ḥadīthim-baʿdahū yuʾminūn. (50)

14 Lit., "behold, you are lost in sin (*mujrimūn*)".

The Seventy-Eighth Sūrah

An-Nabaʾ (The Tiding)

Mecca Period

THE THEME of this undoubtedly late Meccan *sūrah* (Suyūṭī) is the continuation of human life after bodily death, i.e., resurrection and God's ultimate judgment. Its conventional title is derived from the word *nabaʾ* appearing in the second verse.

-78-

سورة النبأ مكية

وآياتها أربعون

حزب 59

جزء 30

IN THE NAME OF GOD, THE MOST GRACIOUS, THE DISPENSER OF GRACE:

ABOUT WHAT do they [most often] ask one another? ⟨1⟩ About the awesome tiding [of resurrection], ⟨2⟩ on which they [so utterly] disagree.[1] ⟨3⟩

Nay, but in time they will come to understand [it]! ⟨4⟩

And once again:[2] Nay, but in time they will come to understand! ⟨5⟩

بِسْمِ ٱللَّهِ ٱلرَّحْمَٰنِ ٱلرَّحِيمِ

عَمَّ يَتَسَآءَلُونَ ﴿١﴾ عَنِ ٱلنَّبَإِ ٱلْعَظِيمِ ﴿٢﴾ ٱلَّذِى هُمْ فِيهِ مُخْتَلِفُونَ ﴿٣﴾

كَلَّا سَيَعْلَمُونَ ﴿٤﴾ ثُمَّ كَلَّا سَيَعْلَمُونَ ﴿٥﴾

Bismil-lāhir-Raḥmānir-Raḥīm.

ʿAmma yatasāaʾalūn. (1) ʿAnin-nabaʾil-ʿaẓīm. (2) ʾAlladhī hum fīhi mukhtalifūn. (3) Kallā sayaʿlamūn. (4) Thumma kallā sayaʿlamūn. (5)

---

1 The question which preoccupies man above all others – the question as to whether there is life after death – has been variously answered throughout the ages. It is, of course, impossible to describe the innumerable variations of those answers; nevertheless, a few main lines of thought are clearly discernible, and their mention may be useful for a better understanding of the Qurʾanic treatment of this problem. Some people – probably a minority – seem to be convinced that bodily death amounts to total and irreversible extinction, and that, therefore, all talk about a hereafter is but an outcome of wishful thinking. Others are of the opinion that after individual death the human "life-essence" returns to the supposed source of its origin – conceived as the "universal soul" – and merges with it entirely. Some believe in a successive transmigration of the individual soul, at the moment of death, into another body, human or animal, but without a continuation of individual consciousness. Others, again, think that only the soul, and not the entire human "personality", continues to live after death – that is, in a purely spiritual, disembodied form. And, lastly, some believe in an undiminished survival of the individual personality and consciousness, and regard death and resurrection as the twin stages of a positive act of re-creation of the *entire* human personality, in whatever form this may necessarily involve: and this is the Qurʾanic view of the life to come.

2 For this rendering of the particle *thumma*, see *sūrah* 6, note 31.

HAVE WE NOT made the earth a resting-place [for you], «6» and the mountains [its] pegs?[3] «7»
And We have created you in pairs;[4] «8» and We have made your sleep [a symbol of] death[5] «9» and made the night [its] cloak «10» and made the day [a symbol of] life.[6] «11»
And We have built above you seven firmaments,[7] «12» and have placed [therein the sun,] a lamp full of blazing splendour. «13»
And from the wind-driven clouds We send down waters pouring in abundance, «14» so that We might bring forth thereby grain, and herbs, «15» and gardens dense with foliage.[8] «16»

VERILY, the Day of Distinction [between the true and the false][9] has indeed its appointed time: «17» the Day when the trumpet [of resurrection] is sounded and you all come forward in multitudes; «18» and when the skies are opened and become [as wide-flung] gates,[10] «19» and when the mountains are made to vanish as if they had been a mirage.[11] «20»

أَلَمْ نَجْعَلِ ٱلْأَرْضَ مِهَـٰدًا ﴿6﴾ وَٱلْجِبَالَ أَوْتَادًا ﴿7﴾ وَخَلَقْنَـٰكُمْ
أَزْوَٰجًا ﴿8﴾ وَجَعَلْنَا نَوْمَكُمْ سُبَاتًا ﴿9﴾ وَجَعَلْنَا ٱلَّيْلَ لِبَاسًا ﴿10﴾
وَجَعَلْنَا ٱلنَّهَارَ مَعَاشًا ﴿11﴾ وَبَنَيْنَا فَوْقَكُمْ سَبْعًا شِدَادًا ﴿12﴾ وَجَعَلْنَا
سِرَاجًا وَهَّاجًا ﴿13﴾ وَأَنزَلْنَا مِنَ ٱلْمُعْصِرَٰتِ مَآءً ثَجَّاجًا ﴿14﴾ لِّنُخْرِجَ
بِهِۦ حَبًّا وَنَبَاتًا ﴿15﴾ وَجَنَّـٰتٍ أَلْفَافًا ﴿16﴾ إِنَّ يَوْمَ ٱلْفَصْلِ كَانَ
مِيقَـٰتًا ﴿17﴾ يَوْمَ يُنفَخُ فِى ٱلصُّورِ فَتَأْتُونَ أَفْوَاجًا ﴿18﴾ وَفُتِحَتِ ٱلسَّمَآءُ
فَكَانَتْ أَبْوَٰبًا ﴿19﴾ وَسُيِّرَتِ ٱلْجِبَالُ فَكَانَتْ سَرَابًا ﴿20﴾

ʾAlam najʿalil-ʾarḍa mihādā. (6) Wal-jibāla ʾawtādā. (7) Wa khalaqnākum ʾazwājā. (8) Wa jaʿalnā nawmakum thubātā. (9) Wa jaʿalnal-layla libāsā. (10) Wa jaʿalnan-nahāra maʿāshā. (11) Wa banaynā fawqakum sabʿañ-shidādā. (12) Wa jaʿalnā sirājañw-wahhājā. (13) Wa ʾañzalnā minal-muʿṣirāti māaʾañ-thajjājā. (14) Linukhrija bihī ḥabbañw-wa nabātā. (15) Wa jannātin ʾalfāfā. (16) ʾInna Yawmal-Faṣli kāna mīqātā. (17) Yawma yuñfakhu fiṣ-ṣūri fataʾtūna ʾafwājā. (18) Wa futiḥatis-samāaʾu fakānat ʾabwābā. (19) Wa suyyiratil-jibālu fakānat sarābā. (20)

3 See 16 : 15 – "He has placed firm mountains on earth, lest it sway with you" – and the corresponding note 11, which explains the reference to mountains as "pegs". – The whole of this passage (verses 6-16) is meant to illustrate God's almightiness and creativeness, as if to say, "Is not He who has created the universe equally able to resurrect and re-create man in whatever form He deems necessary?"

4 I.e., "with the same creative power We have created the miraculous polarity of the two sexes in you and in other animated beings". The phenomenon of polarity, evident throughout the universe (see 36 : 36 and the corresponding note 18), is further illustrated in verses 9-11.

5 Thus Zamakhsharī, stressing the primary significance of *subāt* as "cutting-off" (*qaṭʿ*), i.e., "death"; also the famous second-century philologist Abū ʿUbaydah Maʿmar ibn al-Muthannā, who (as quoted by Rāzī) explains the above Qurʾanic phrase as an "analogue (*shibh*) of death".

6 According to Zamakhsharī, the term *maʿāsh* ("that whereby one lives") is here synonymous with "life". In the polarity of sleep (or "death") and wakefulness (or "life") we see the allusion to bodily death and subsequent resurrection already touched upon in 6 : 60.

7 Lit., "seven firm ones", indicating the multiplicity of cosmic systems (see *sūrah* 2, note 20).

8 Implying that the overwhelming evidence of purpose and plan in all observable nature points to the existence of a conscious Creator who has "not created [anything of] this without meaning and purpose" (3 : 191), and who – as is stressed in the sequence – will one day pronounce His judgment on every human being's willingness or unwillingness to live up to the standards of morality made clear to him through inborn instinct as well as through divine revelation.

9 See note 6 on 77 : 13. This passage connects with verses 4-5.

10 Allegorically, "its mysteries will be opened to man's understanding" – thus further amplifying the concept of "the Day of Distinction between the true and the false".

11 See note 90 on 20 : 105-107, as well as note 63 on 14 : 48.

[On that Day,] verily, hell will lie in wait [for those who deny the truth] ‹21› – a goal for all who are wont to transgress the bounds of what is right! ‹22›

In it shall they remain for a long time.[12] ‹23› Neither coolness shall they taste therein nor any [thirst-quenching] drink ‹24› – only burning despair and ice-cold darkness:[13] ‹25› a meet requital [for their sins]! ‹26›

Behold, they were not expecting to be called to account, ‹27› having given the lie to Our messages one and all: ‹28› but We have placed on record every single thing [of what they did]. ‹29›

[And so We shall say:] "Taste, then, [the fruit of your evil doings,] for now We shall bestow on you nothing but more and more suffering!"[14] ‹30›

[But,] verily, for the God-conscious there is supreme fulfilment in store:[15] ‹31› luxuriant gardens and vineyards, ‹32› and splendid companions well-matched,[16] ‹33› and a cup [of happiness] overflowing. ‹34› No empty talk will they hear in that [paradise], nor any lie. ‹35›

إِنَّ جَهَنَّمَ كَانَتْ مِرْصَادًا ﴿٢١﴾ لِّلطَّٰغِينَ مَـَٔابًا ﴿٢٢﴾ لَّٰبِثِينَ فِيهَآ
أَحْقَابًا ﴿٢٣﴾ لَّا يَذُوقُونَ فِيهَا بَرْدًا وَلَا شَرَابًا ﴿٢٤﴾ إِلَّا حَمِيمًا وَغَسَّاقًا ﴿٢٥﴾
جَزَآءً وِفَاقًا ﴿٢٦﴾ إِنَّهُمْ كَانُوا۟ لَا يَرْجُونَ حِسَابًا ﴿٢٧﴾ وَكَذَّبُوا۟ بِـَٔايَٰتِنَا
كِذَّابًا ﴿٢٨﴾ وَكُلَّ شَىْءٍ أَحْصَيْنَٰهُ كِتَٰبًا ﴿٢٩﴾ فَذُوقُوا۟ فَلَن نَّزِيدَكُمْ إِلَّا
عَذَابًا ﴿٣٠﴾ إِنَّ لِلْمُتَّقِينَ مَفَازًا ﴿٣١﴾ حَدَآئِقَ وَأَعْنَٰبًا ﴿٣٢﴾ وَكَوَاعِبَ
أَتْرَابًا ﴿٣٣﴾ وَكَأْسًا دِهَاقًا ﴿٣٤﴾ لَّا يَسْمَعُونَ فِيهَا لَغْوًا وَلَا كِذَّٰبًا ﴿٣٥﴾

ʾInna jahannama kanat mirṣādā. (21) Liṭṭāghīna maʾābā. (22) lābithīna fīhāa ʾaḥqābā. (23) Lā yadhūqūna fīhā bardañw-wa lā sharābā. (24) ʾIllā ḥamīmañw-wa ghassāqā. (25) Jazāaʾañw-wifāqā. (26) ʾInnahum kānū lā yarjūna ḥisābā. (27) Wa kadhdhabū biʾĀyātinā kidhdhābā. (28) Wa kulla shayʾin ʾaḥṣaynāhu Kitābā. (29) Fadhūqū falañ-nazīdakum ʾillā ʿadhābā. (30) ʾInna lilmuttaqīna mafazā. (31) Ḥadāaʾiqa wa ʾaʿnābā. (32) Wa kawāʿiba ʾatrābā. (33) Wa kaʾsañ-dihāqā. (34) Lā yasmaʿūna fīhā laghwañw-wa lā kidhdhābā. (35)

12 I.e., not forever, since the term *ḥuqb* or *ḥiqbah* (of which *aḥqāb* is the plural) denotes no more than "a period of time" or "a long time" (Jawharī) – according to some authorities, "eighty years", according to others, "a year" or simply "years" (*Asās, Qāmūs, Lisān al-ʿArab*, etc.). But however one defines this term, it is obvious that it signifies a *limited* period of time, and not eternity: and this is in tune with many indications in the Qurʾān to the effect that the suffering described as "hell" is not eternal (see note 114 on the last paragraph of 6 : 128), as well as with several authentic sayings of the Prophet (e.g., the one quoted in note 10 on 40 : 12).

13 For my rendering of *ḥamīm* as "burning despair", see *sūrah* 6, note 62. The meaning of *ghassāq* is explained in note 47 on 38 : 57-58.

14 Lit., "We shall not increase you in anything but suffering": i.e., until the sins committed in this world are atoned for by commensurate suffering in the hereafter – for "whoever shall come [before God] with an evil deed will be requited with no more than the like thereof; and none shall be wronged" (6 : 160).

15 I.e., the fulfilment of all that a human being may ever desire (Rāzī), symbolized by the "luxuriant gardens", etc., of the sequence.

16 For the above rendering of *atrāb*, see *sūrah* 56, note 15. As regards my rendering of *kawāʿib* as "splendid companions", it is to be remembered that the term *kaʿb* – from which the participle *kāʿib* is derived – has many meanings, and that one of these meanings is "prominence", "eminence" or "glory" (*Lisān al-ʿArab*); thus, the verb *kaʿba,* when applied to a person, signifies "he made [another person] prominent", "glorious" or "splendid" (*ibid*). Based on this tropical meaning of both the verb *kaʿba* and the noun *kaʿb*, the participle *kāʿib* has often been used, in popular parlance, to denote "a girl whose breasts are becoming prominent" or "are budding": hence, many commentators see in it an allusion to some sort of youthful "female companions" who would entertain the (presumably male) inmates of paradise. But quite apart from the fact that all Qurʾanic allegories of the joys of paradise invariably apply to men and women alike, this interpretation of *kawāʿib* overlooks the purely *derivative* origin of the above popular usage – which is based on the tropical connotation of "prominence" inherent in the noun *kaʿb* – and substitutes for this obviously figurative sense the literal meaning of something that is *physically* prominent: and this, in my opinion, is utterly unjustified. If we bear in mind that the Qur'anic descriptions of the blessings

[All this will be] a reward from thy Sustainer, a gift in accordance with [His Own] reckoning[17] ‹36› – [a reward from] the Sustainer of the heavens and the earth and all that is between them, the Most Gracious!

[And] none shall have it in their power to raise their voices unto Him ‹37› on the Day when all [human] souls[18] and all the angels will stand up in ranks: none will speak but he to whom the Most Gracious will have given leave; and [everyone] will say [only] what is right.[19] ‹38›

That will be the Day of Ultimate Truth:[20] whoever wills, then, let him take the path that leads towards his Sustainer! ‹39›

Verily, We have warned you of suffering near at hand – [suffering] on the Day when man shall [clearly] see what his hands have sent ahead, and when he who has denied the truth shall say, "Oh, would that I were mere dust . . . !"[21] ‹40›

جَزَآءً مِّن رَّبِّكَ عَطَآءً حِسَابًا ﴿٣٦﴾ رَّبِّ ٱلسَّمَٰوَٰتِ وَٱلْأَرْضِ وَمَا
بَيْنَهُمَا ٱلرَّحْمَٰنِ لَا يَمْلِكُونَ مِنْهُ خِطَابًا ﴿٣٧﴾ يَوْمَ يَقُومُ ٱلرُّوحُ
وَٱلْمَلَٰٓئِكَةُ صَفًّا لَّا يَتَكَلَّمُونَ إِلَّا مَنْ أَذِنَ لَهُ ٱلرَّحْمَٰنُ وَقَالَ
صَوَابًا ﴿٣٨﴾ ذَٰلِكَ ٱلْيَوْمُ ٱلْحَقُّ فَمَن شَآءَ ٱتَّخَذَ إِلَىٰ رَبِّهِۦ مَـَٔابًا ﴿٣٩﴾ إِنَّآ
أَنذَرْنَٰكُمْ عَذَابًا قَرِيبًا يَوْمَ يَنظُرُ ٱلْمَرْءُ مَا قَدَّمَتْ يَدَاهُ وَيَقُولُ ٱلْكَافِرُ
يَٰلَيْتَنِى كُنتُ تُرَٰبًۢا ﴿٤٠﴾

Jazāa'am-mir-Rabbika ʿaṭāa'an ḥisābā. (36) Rabbis-samāwāti wal-'arḍi wa mā baynahumar-Raḥmāni lā yamlikūna minhu khiṭābā. (37) Yawma yaqūmur-rūḥu wal-Malāa'ikatu ṣaffā. Lā yatakallamūna 'illā man 'adhina lahur-Raḥmānu wa qāla ṣawābā. (38) Dhālikal-Yawmul-Ḥaqq. Famañ-shāa'at-takhadha 'ilā Rabbihī ma'ābā. (39) 'Innāa 'añdharnākum ʿadhābañ-qarībañy-Yawma yañẓurul-mar'u mā qaddamat yadāhu wa yaqūlul-kāfiru yā laytanī kuñtu turābā. (40)

---

of paradise are *always* allegorical, we realize that in the above context the term *kawāʿib* can have no other meaning than "glorious [or "splendid"] beings", without any definition of sex; and that, in combination with the term *atrāb*, it denotes, "splendid companions well-matched" – thus alluding to the relations of the blest with one another, and stressing the absolute mutual compatibility and equal dignity of all of them. See also note 13 on 56 : 34.

17 I.e., not merely in accordance with their good deeds but far in excess of them, in accordance with God's unlimited bounty.

18 Lit., "the soul", in the singular but implying a plural. This is, according to Ibn ʿAbbās, Qatādah and Al-Ḥasan (all of them quoted by Ṭabarī), the meaning of *ar-rūḥ* in the above context.

19 This includes the symbolic right of the prophets to "intercede" for the sinners on Judgment Day (see 10 : 3 – "There is none that could intercede with Him unless He grants leave therefor" – and the corresponding note 7, which makes it clear that such "intercession" implies God's *a-priori* acceptance of the sinner's repentance). In a wider sense, the statement that he whom God will allow to speak "will say [only] what is right" implies the impossibility of anyone's being untruthful on Judgment Day.

20 Cf. 69 : 1 and the corresponding note 1. Objectively, it will be the moment when the ultimate reality of human life and its purpose will become fully accessible to man's understanding.

21 Cf. 69 : 27.

The Seventy-Ninth Sūrah

An-Nāziᶜāt (Those That Rise)

Mecca Period

THIS late Meccan *sūrah*, revealed shortly after the preceding one, takes its name from the word *an-nāziᶜāt* in the first verse.

سورة النازعات مكية -79-
وآياتها ست وأربعون

IN THE NAME OF GOD, THE MOST GRACIOUS, THE DISPENSER OF GRACE:

بِسۡمِ ٱللَّهِ ٱلرَّحۡمَٰنِ ٱلرَّحِيمِ

CONSIDER those [stars] that rise only to set,[1] ‹1›
and move [in their orbits] with steady motion,[2] ‹2›
and float [through space] with floating serene, ‹3›
and yet overtake [one another] with swift overtaking:[3] ‹4›

وَٱلنَّٰزِعَٰتِ غَرۡقٗا ﴿١﴾ وَٱلنَّٰشِطَٰتِ نَشۡطٗا ﴿٢﴾ وَٱلسَّٰبِحَٰتِ سَبۡحٗا ﴿٣﴾
فَٱلسَّٰبِقَٰتِ سَبۡقٗا ﴿٤﴾

Bismil-lāhir-Raḥmānir-Raḥīm.
Wan-nāziᶜāti gharqā. ‹1› Wan-nāshiṭāti nashṭā. ‹2›
Was-sābiḥāti sabḥā. ‹3› Fas-sābiqāti sabqā. ‹4›

---

1 For my rendering of the adjurative particle *wa* as "Consider", see the first half of note 23 on 74 : 32. – The early commentators differ widely in their explanations of verses 1-5 of this *sūrah*. The most popular interpretation is based on the view that the descriptive participles *an-nāziᶜāt, an-nāshiṭāt, as-sābiḥāt, as-sābiqāt* and *al-mudabbirāt* refer to angels and their activities with regard to the souls of the dying: an interpretation categorically rejected by Abū Muslim al-Iṣfahānī, who – as mentioned by Rāzī – points out that the angels are never referred to in the Qur'ān in the female gender, as is the case in the above five participles, and that the present passage cannot be an exception. Almost equally unconvincing – because somewhat laboured – are the explanations which link those five participles to the souls of the dying, or to warriors engaged in holy war, or to war-mounts, and so forth. The clearest and simplest interpretation is that advanced by Qatādah (as quoted by Ṭabarī and Baghawī) and Al-Ḥasan al-Baṣrī (quoted by Baghawī and Rāzī), who maintain that what is meant in this passage are the *stars* – including the sun and the moon – and their movements in space: and this interpretation is fully in tune with many other passages in the Qur'ān in which the harmony of those celestial bodies in their multiform orbits and graded speeds is cited as an evidence of God's planning and creativeness. In accordance with this interpretation, the participle *an-nāziᶜāt* occurring in the first verse denotes the daily "ascending" or "rising" of the stars, while their subsequent "setting" is indicated by the expression *gharqan*, which comprises the two concepts of "drowning" (i.e., disappearing) and, tropically, of the "completeness" of this daily phenomenon (Zamakhsharī).

2 I.e., passing from constellation to constellation (Zamakhsharī).

3 This is apparently an allusion to the different speeds of the orbiting stars (Al-Ḥasan and Abū ᶜUbaydah, as quoted by Rāzī), as well as to the extent of their orbits in relation to one another.

and thus they fulfil the [Creator's] behest! ‹5›

[HENCE,[4] think of] the Day when a violent convulsion will convulse [the world], ‹6› to be followed by further [convulsions]! ‹7›
On that Day will [men's] hearts be throbbing, ‹8› [and] their eyes downcast. . . . ‹9›
[And yet,] some say, "What! Are we indeed to be restored to our former state ‹10› – even though we may have become [a heap of] crumbling bones?" ‹11› [And] they add, "That, then, would be a return with loss!"[5] ‹12›
[But,] then, that [Last Hour] will be [upon them of a sudden, as if it were] but a single accusing cry ‹13› – and then, lo, they will be fully awakened [to the truth]! ‹14›

HAS THE STORY of Moses ever come within thy ken?[6] ‹15›
Lo! His Sustainer called out to him in the twice-hallowed valley:[7] ‹16›
"Go unto Pharaoh – for, verily, he has transgressed all bounds of what is right ‹17› – and say [unto him], 'Art thou desirous of attaining to purity? ‹18› [If so,] then I shall guide thee towards [a cognition of] thy Sustainer, so that [henceforth] thou wilt stand in awe [of Him].'"[8] ‹19›
And thereupon he [went to Pharaoh and] made him aware of the great wonder [of God's grace].[9] ‹20›

فَٱلْمُدَبِّرَٰتِ أَمْرًا ﴿5﴾ يَوْمَ تَرْجُفُ ٱلرَّاجِفَةُ ﴿6﴾ تَتْبَعُهَا ٱلرَّادِفَةُ ﴿7﴾
قُلُوبٌ يَوْمَئِذٍ وَاجِفَةٌ ﴿8﴾ أَبْصَٰرُهَا خَٰشِعَةٌ ﴿9﴾ يَقُولُونَ أَءِنَّا
لَمَرْدُودُونَ فِى ٱلْحَافِرَةِ ﴿10﴾ أَءِذَا كُنَّا عِظَٰمًا نَّخِرَةً ﴿11﴾ قَالُوا۟ تِلْكَ إِذًا
كَرَّةٌ خَاسِرَةٌ ﴿12﴾ فَإِنَّمَا هِىَ زَجْرَةٌ وَٰحِدَةٌ ﴿13﴾ فَإِذَا هُم بِٱلسَّاهِرَةِ ﴿14﴾
هَلْ أَتَىٰكَ حَدِيثُ مُوسَىٰٓ ﴿15﴾ إِذْ نَادَىٰهُ رَبُّهُۥ بِٱلْوَادِ ٱلْمُقَدَّسِ
طُوًى ﴿16﴾ ٱذْهَبْ إِلَىٰ فِرْعَوْنَ إِنَّهُۥ طَغَىٰ ﴿17﴾ فَقُلْ هَل لَّكَ إِلَىٰٓ أَن
تَزَكَّىٰ ﴿18﴾ وَأَهْدِيَكَ إِلَىٰ رَبِّكَ فَتَخْشَىٰ ﴿19﴾ فَأَرَىٰهُ ٱلْءَايَةَ ٱلْكُبْرَىٰ ﴿20﴾

Fal-mudabbirāti ʾamrā. (5) Yawma tarjufur-rājifah.
(6) Tatbaʿuhar-rādifah. (7) Qulūbuñy-Yawmaʾidhiñw-
wājifah. (8) ʾAbṣāruhā khāshiʿah. (9) Yaqūlūna
ʾaʾinnā lamardūdūna fil-ḥāfirah. (10) ʾAʾidhā kunnā
ʿiẓāmañ-nakhirah. (11) Qālū tilka ʾidhañ-karratun
khāsirah. (12) Faʾinnamā hiya zajratuñw-wāḥidah. (13)
Faʾidhā hum bissāhirah. (14) Hal ʾatāka ḥadīthu
Mūsā. (15) ʾIdh nādāhu Rabbuhū bilwādil-muqaddasi
Ṭuwā. (16) ʾIdhhab ʾilā Firʿawna ʾinnahū ṭaghā. (17)
Faqul hal-laka ʾilāa ʾañ-tazakkā. (18) Wa ʾahdiyaka
ʾilā Rabbika fatakhshā. (19) Faʾarāhul-ʾĀyatal-kubrā.
(20)

4 I.e., upon realizing the above-mentioned evidence of God's almightiness and, therefore, of man's subjection to His ultimate judgment.

5 Implying derisively (Zamakhsharī) that in such a case they would be proved wrong in what they now consider a "reasonable" assumption.

6 Connecting with the preceding passage, the story of Moses (which appears in much greater detail in 20 : 9-98) is cited here as an illustration of the fact that everyone will have to answer on Judgment Day for whatever he did in life, and that it is the main function of every prophet to make man aware of this responsibility.

7 See note 9 on 20 : 12. – For the meaning of the particle *idh* at the beginning of this sentence, rendered by me as "Lo!", see *sūrah* 2, note 21.

8 Implying that so long as man is not fully aware of the existence of God, he cannot really discern between what is morally right or wrong; and since God is just, He does not punish anyone who has not yet attained to such a discernment (or, as expressed in the preceding sentence, "to [moral] purity"): cf. 6 : 131 – "thy Sustainer would never destroy a community for its wrongdoing so long as its people are still unaware [of the meaning of right and wrong]".

9 Lit., "showed him the great wonder", i.e., of the guidance which God, in His measureless grace, offers even to the most recalcitrant sinner.

But [Pharaoh] gave him the lie and rebelliously rejected [all guidance], ‹21› and brusquely turned his back [on Moses]; ‹22› and then he gathered [his great ones], and called [unto his people], ‹23› and said, "I am your Lord All-Highest!"[10] ‹24›

And thereupon God took him to task, [and made him] a warning example in the life to come as well as in this world.[11] ‹25›

In this, behold, there is a lesson indeed for all who stand in awe [of God]. ‹26›

[O MEN!] Are you more difficult to create than the heaven which He has built?[12] ‹27›

High has He reared its vault and formed it in accordance with what it was meant to be;[13] ‹28› and He has made dark its night and brought forth its light of day. ‹29›

And after that, the earth: wide has He spread its expanse, ‹30› and has caused its waters to come out of it, and its pastures,[14] ‹31› and has made the mountains firm: ‹32› [all this] as a means of livelihood for you and your animals.[15] ‹33›

AND SO, when the great, overwhelming event [of resurrection] comes to pass ‹34› – on that Day man will [clearly] remember all that he has ever wrought; ‹35› and the blazing fire [of hell] will be laid open before all who [are destined to] see it.[16] ‹36›

فَكَذَّبَ وَعَصَىٰ (21) ثُمَّ أَدْبَرَ يَسْعَىٰ (22) فَحَشَرَ فَنَادَىٰ (23) فَقَالَ أَنَا
رَبُّكُمُ ٱلْأَعْلَىٰ (24) فَأَخَذَهُ ٱللَّهُ نَكَالَ ٱلْأٓخِرَةِ وَٱلْأُولَىٰٓ (25) إِنَّ فِى
ذَٰلِكَ لَعِبْرَةً لِّمَن يَخْشَىٰٓ (26) ءَأَنتُمْ أَشَدُّ خَلْقًا أَمِ ٱلسَّمَآءُ ۚ بَنَىٰهَا (27) رَفَعَ
سَمْكَهَا فَسَوَّىٰهَا (28) وَأَغْطَشَ لَيْلَهَا وَأَخْرَجَ ضُحَىٰهَا (29) وَٱلْأَرْضَ بَعْدَ
ذَٰلِكَ دَحَىٰهَآ (30) أَخْرَجَ مِنْهَا مَآءَهَا وَمَرْعَىٰهَا (31) وَٱلْجِبَالَ
أَرْسَىٰهَا (32) مَتَٰعًا لَّكُمْ وَلِأَنْعَٰمِكُمْ (33) فَإِذَا جَآءَتِ ٱلطَّآمَّةُ
ٱلْكُبْرَىٰ (34) يَوْمَ يَتَذَكَّرُ ٱلْإِنسَٰنُ مَا سَعَىٰ (35) وَبُرِّزَتِ ٱلْجَحِيمُ
لِمَن يَرَىٰ (36)

Fakadhdhaba wa ʿaṣā. (21) Thumma ʾadbara yasʿā.
(22) Faḥashara fanādā. (23) Faqāla ana Rabbukumul-
ʾaʿlā. (24) Faʾakhadhahul-lāhu nakālal-ʾĀkhirati wal-
ʾūlā. (25) ʾInna fī dhālika laʿibratal-limañy-yakhshā.
(26) ʾAʾañtum ʾashaddu khalqan ʾamis-samāaʾu
banāhā. (27) Rafaʿa samkahā fasawwāhā. (28) Wa
ʾaghṭasha laylahā wa ʾakhraja ḍuḥāhā. (29) Wal-ʾarḍa
baʿda dhālika daḥāhā. (30) ʾAkhraja minhā māaʾahā
wa marʿāhā. (31) Wal-jibāla ʾarsāhā. (32) Matāʿal-
lakum wa liʾanʿāmikum. (33) Faʾidhā jāaʾatiṭ-ṭāam-
matul-kubrā. (34) Yawma yatadhakkarul-ʾIñsānu mā
saʿā. (35) Wa burrizatil-jaḥīmu limañy-yarā. (36)

---

10 Cf. 28 : 38 and the corresponding note 36. Pharaoh's claim to divine status is the cardinal sin whereby "he has transgressed all bounds of what is right" (verse 17 above).

11 Lit., "in the first [life]". See last sentence of 7 : 137 – "We utterly destroyed all that Pharaoh and his people had wrought, and all that they had built" – and the corresponding note 100.

12 Lit., "or the heaven . . .", etc. The "heaven" is here, as in many other places in the Qurʾān, a metonym for "cosmic system" (cf. note 20 on 2 : 29). The above verse is an echo of an earlier, more explicit passage – namely, 40 : 56-57, which should be read together with the corresponding notes 40 and 41. Both these passages refute the "man-centred" view of the universe by pointing out man's insignificance as compared with the vastness and complexity of the whole God-created universe.

13 See 87 : 2, which is the earliest instance, in the chronology of Qurʾanic revelation, of the use of the verb *sawwā* in the above sense.

14 The term "pasture" (*marʿā*) connotes here, metonymically, all herbal produce suitable for consumption by man or animal (Rāzī).

15 Implying (as in 80 : 24-32) that man ought to be grateful to God, and should always be conscious of His being the Provider: hence the subsequent return of the discourse to the theme of resurrection and ultimate judgment.

16 Cf. 26 : 91 – "will be laid open before those who had been lost in grievous error": thus reminding man that suffering in the hereafter ("hell") is the inevitable consequence of spiritual self-destruction through deliberate wrongdoing.

For, unto him who shall have transgressed the bounds of what is right, ‹37› and preferred the life of this world [to the good of his soul], ‹38› that blazing fire will truly be the goal! ‹39›

But unto him who shall have stood in fear of his Sustainer's Presence, and held back his inner self from base desires, ‹40› paradise will truly be the goal! ‹41›

THEY WILL ASK thee [O Prophet] about the Last Hour: "When will it come to pass?" ‹42›

[But] how couldst thou tell anything about it,[17] ‹43› [seeing that] with thy Sustainer alone rests the beginning and the end [of all knowledge] thereof?[18] ‹44› Thou art but [sent] to warn those who stand in awe of it. ‹45›

On the Day when they behold it, [it will seem to them] as if they had tarried [in this world] no longer than one evening or [one night, ending with] its morn![19] ‹46›

فَأَمَّا مَن طَغَىٰ ﴿37﴾ وَءَاثَرَ ٱلْحَيَوٰةَ ٱلدُّنْيَا ﴿38﴾ فَإِنَّ ٱلْجَحِيمَ هِىَ
ٱلْمَأْوَىٰ ﴿39﴾ وَأَمَّا مَنْ خَافَ مَقَامَ رَبِّهِۦ وَنَهَى ٱلنَّفْسَ عَنِ ٱلْهَوَىٰ ﴿40﴾
فَإِنَّ ٱلْجَنَّةَ هِىَ ٱلْمَأْوَىٰ ﴿41﴾ يَسْـَٔلُونَكَ عَنِ ٱلسَّاعَةِ أَيَّانَ مُرْسَىٰهَا ﴿42﴾
فِيمَ أَنتَ مِن ذِكْرَىٰهَآ ﴿43﴾ إِلَىٰ رَبِّكَ مُنتَهَىٰهَآ ﴿44﴾ إِنَّمَآ أَنتَ مُنذِرُ مَن
يَخْشَىٰهَا ﴿45﴾ كَأَنَّهُمْ يَوْمَ يَرَوْنَهَا لَمْ يَلْبَثُوٓا۟ إِلَّا عَشِيَّةً أَوْ ضُحَىٰهَا ﴿46﴾

Faᵓammā mañ-ṭaghā. (37) Wa ᵓātharal-ḥayātad-dunyā, (38) faᵓinnal-jaḥīma hiyal-maᵓwā. (39) Wa ᵓammā man khāfa maqāma Rabbihī wa nahan-nafsa ᶜanil-hawā, (40) faᵓinnal-jannata hiyal-maᵓwā. (41) Yasᵓalūnaka ᶜanis-Sāᶜati ᵓayyāna mursāhā. (42) Fīma ᵓañta miñ-dhikrāhā. (43) ᵓIlā Rabbika muñtahāhā. (44) ᵓInnamāa ᵓañta Muñdhiru mañy-yakhshāhā. (45) Kaᵓannahum Yawma yarawnahā lam yalbathūu ᵓillā ᶜashiyyatan ᵓaw ḍuḥāhā. (46)

17 Lit., "wherein [or "whereon"] art thou with regard to stating it (*min dhikrāhā*)?"

18 Lit., "its utmost limit", i.e., the beginning and the end of all that can be known about it. Cf. 7 : 187 and the corresponding note 153.

19 As in many other places in the Qurᵓān (e.g., in 2 : 259, 17 : 52, 18 : 19, 20 : 103-104, 23 : 112-113, 30 : 55, etc.), this is a subtle indication of the illusory, earthbound nature of man's concept of "time" – a concept which, we are told, will lose all its meaning in the context of the ultimate reality comprised in the term "hereafter" (*al-ākhirah*).

The Eightieth Sūrah

ᶜ*Abasa* (He Frowned)

Mecca Period

REVEALED at a very early stage of the Prophet's mission, this *sūrah* has always been designated by the predicate with which its first sentence opens. The immediate cause of the revelation of the first ten verses was an incident witnessed by a number of the Prophet's contemporaries (see verses 1-2 and the corresponding note 1 below).

-80-

سورة عبس مكية

وآياتها اثنتان وأربعون

IN THE NAME OF GOD, THE MOST GRACIOUS, THE DISPENSER OF GRACE:

HE FROWNED and turned away ⟨1⟩ because the blind man approached him![1] ⟨2⟩

Yet for all thou didst know, [O Muḥammad,] he might perhaps have grown in purity, ⟨3⟩ or have been reminded [of the truth], and helped by this reminder. ⟨4⟩

بِسۡمِ ٱللَّهِ ٱلرَّحۡمَٰنِ ٱلرَّحِيمِ

عَبَسَ وَتَوَلَّىٰٓ ① أَن جَآءَهُ ٱلۡأَعۡمَىٰ ② وَمَا يُدۡرِيكَ لَعَلَّهُۥ يَزَّكَّىٰٓ ③

أَوۡ يَذَّكَّرُ فَتَنفَعَهُ ٱلذِّكۡرَىٰٓ ④

ربع الحزب

Bismil-lāhir-Raḥmānir-Raḥīm.

ᶜAbasa wa tawallāa, ① ᵓañ-jāaᵓahul-ᵓaᶜmā. ②
Wa mā yudrīka laᶜallahū yazzakkā. ③ ᵓAw yadh-
dhakkaru fatañfaᶜahudh-dhikrā. ④

---

1 One day, as recorded in many well-authenticated Traditions, the Prophet was engrossed in a conversation with some of the most influential chieftains of pagan Mecca, hoping to convince them – and, through them, the Meccan community at large – of the truth of his message. At that point, he was approached by one of his followers, the blind ᶜAbd Allāh ibn Shurayḥ – known after his grandmother's name as Ibn Umm Maktūm – with the request for a repetition or elucidation of certain earlier passages of the Qurᵓān. Annoyed by this interruption of what he momentarily regarded as a more important endeavour, Muḥammad "frowned and turned away" from the blind man – and was immediately, there and then, reproved by the revelation of the first ten verses of this *sūrah*. In later years he often greeted Ibn Umm Maktūm with these words of humility: "Welcome unto him on whose account my Sustainer has rebuked me (*ᶜātabanī*)!"

Indirectly, the sharp Qurᵓanic rebuke (stressed, in particular, by the use of the third-person form in verses 1-2) implies, firstly, that what would have been a minor act of discourtesy on the part of an ordinary human being, assumed the aspect of a major sin, deserving a divine rebuke, when committed by a prophet; and, secondly, it illustrates the objective nature of the Qurᵓanic revelation: for, obviously, in conveying God's reproof of him to the world at large, the Prophet "does not speak out of his own desire" (cf. 53 : 3).

Now as for him who believes himself to be self-sufficient[2] ‹5› – to him didst thou give thy whole attention, ‹6› although thou art not accountable for his failure to attain to purity;[3] ‹7› but as for him who came unto thee full of eagerness ‹8› and in awe [of God] ‹9› – him didst thou disregard! ‹10›

NAY, VERILY, these [messages] are but a reminder:[4] ‹11› and so, whoever is willing may remember Him ‹12› in [the light of His] revelations blest with dignity, ‹13› lofty and pure, ‹14› [borne] by the hands of messengers ‹15› noble and most virtuous. ‹16›

[But only too often] man destroys himself:[5] how stubbornly does he deny the truth! ‹17›

[Does man ever consider] out of what substance [God] creates him? ‹18›

Out of a drop of sperm He creates him, and thereupon determines his nature,[6] ‹19› and then makes it easy for him to go through life;[7] ‹20› and in the end He causes him to die and brings him to the grave; ‹21› and then, if it be His will, He shall raise him again to life. ‹22›

Nay, but [man] has never yet fulfilled what He has enjoined upon him![8] ‹23›

أَمَّا مَنِ ٱسْتَغْنَىٰ ﴿٥﴾ فَأَنتَ لَهُۥ تَصَدَّىٰ ﴿٦﴾ وَمَا عَلَيْكَ أَلَّا يَزَّكَّىٰ ﴿٧﴾
وَأَمَّا مَن جَآءَكَ يَسْعَىٰ ﴿٨﴾ وَهُوَ يَخْشَىٰ ﴿٩﴾ فَأَنتَ عَنْهُ تَلَهَّىٰ ﴿١٠﴾ كَلَّآ
إِنَّهَا تَذْكِرَةٌ ﴿١١﴾ فَمَن شَآءَ ذَكَرَهُۥ ﴿١٢﴾ فِى صُحُفٍ مُّكَرَّمَةٍ ﴿١٣﴾ مَّرْفُوعَةٍ
مُّطَهَّرَةٍۭ ﴿١٤﴾ بِأَيْدِى سَفَرَةٍ ﴿١٥﴾ كِرَامٍۭ بَرَرَةٍ ﴿١٦﴾ قُتِلَ ٱلْإِنسَٰنُ مَآ
أَكْفَرَهُۥ ﴿١٧﴾ مِنْ أَىِّ شَىْءٍ خَلَقَهُۥ ﴿١٨﴾ مِن نُّطْفَةٍ خَلَقَهُۥ فَقَدَّرَهُۥ ﴿١٩﴾ ثُمَّ
ٱلسَّبِيلَ يَسَّرَهُۥ ﴿٢٠﴾ ثُمَّ أَمَاتَهُۥ فَأَقْبَرَهُۥ ﴿٢١﴾ ثُمَّ إِذَا شَآءَ أَنشَرَهُۥ ﴿٢٢﴾ كَلَّا
لَمَّا يَقْضِ مَآ أَمَرَهُۥ ﴿٢٣﴾

ʾAmmā manis-taghnā. (5) faʾañta lahū taṣaddā. (6) Wa mā ᶜalayka ʾallā yazzakkā. (7) Wa ʾammā mañ-jāaʾaka yasᶜā, (8) wa huwa yakhshā, (9) faʾañta ᶜanhu talahhā. (10) Kallāa ʾinnahā tadhkirah. (11) Famañ-shāaʾa dhakarah. (12) Fī Ṣuḥufim-mukarramah. (13) Marfūᶜatim-muṭahharah. (14) Biʾaydī safarah. (15) Kirāmim-bararah. (16) Qutilal-ʾIñsānu māa ʾakfarah. (17) Min ʾayyi shayʾin khalaqah. (18) Miñ-nuṭfatin khalaqahū faqaddarah. (19) Thummas-sabīla yassarah. (20) Thumma ʾamātahū faʾaqbarah. (21) Thumma ʾidhā shāaʾa ʾañsharah. (22) Kallā lammā yaqḍi māa ʾamarah. (23)

2 I.e., who does not feel the need of divine guidance: a reference to the arrogant pagan chieftains with whom the Prophet was conversing.

3 Lit., "it is not upon thee (*ᶜalayka*) that he does not attain to purity".

4 Sc., of the existence and omnipotence of God. The Qurʾān is described here, as in many other places, as "a reminder" because it is meant to bring man's instinctive – though sometimes hazy or unconscious – realization of God's existence into the full light of consciousness. (Cf. 7 : 172 and the corresponding note 139.)

5 For my rendering of *qutila* as "he destroys himself", see *sūrah* 74, note 9.

6 I.e., in accordance with the organic functions which man's body and mind are to fulfil, and the natural conditions to which he will have to adapt himself. Verses 18-22, although formulated in the past tense, obviously describe a recurrent phenomenon.

7 Lit., "He makes easy the way for him". This is an allusion to man's being endowed with the intellectual equipment enabling him to discern between good and evil and to make fruitful use of the opportunities offered to him by his earthly environment.

8 In other words, man has failed to make adequate use of the intellectual and spiritual endowment referred to in verse 20. Whereas some commentators are of the opinion that this relates only to the type of man spoken of in verse 17 above, others maintain, with greater plausibility, that it is a reference to man in general – thus: "No human being has ever fulfilled all that was imposed on him as a [moral] duty" (Mujāhid, as quoted by Ṭabarī, with a similar statement attributed by Baghawī to Al-Ḥasan al-Baṣrī); or "From the time of Adam to this time, no human being has ever been free of shortcomings" (Zamakhsharī, Bayḍawī). This is in tune with the Qurʾanic doctrine that perfection is an attribute of God alone.

Let man, then, consider [the sources of] his food: ⟨24⟩ [how it is] that We pour down water, pouring it down abundantly; ⟨25⟩ and then We cleave the earth [with new growth], cleaving it asunder, ⟨26⟩ and thereupon We cause grain to grow out of it, ⟨27⟩ and vines and edible plants, ⟨28⟩ and olive trees and date-palms, ⟨29⟩ and gardens dense with foliage, ⟨30⟩ and fruits and herbage, ⟨31⟩ for you and for your animals to enjoy.[9] ⟨32⟩

AND SO,[10] when the piercing call [of resurrection] is heard ⟨33⟩ on a Day when every- one will [want to] flee from his brother, ⟨34⟩ and from his mother and father, ⟨35⟩ and from his spouse and his children: ⟨36⟩ on that Day, to every one of them will his own state be of sufficient concern. ⟨37⟩

Some faces will on that Day be bright with happiness, ⟨38⟩ laughing, rejoicing at glad tidings. ⟨39⟩

And some faces will on that Day with dust be covered, ⟨40⟩ with darkness over-spread: ⟨41⟩ these, these will be the ones who denied the truth and were immersed in iniquity! ⟨42⟩

فَلْيَنظُرِ ٱلْإِنسَٰنُ إِلَىٰ طَعَامِهِۦٓ ﴿24﴾ أَنَّا صَبَبْنَا ٱلْمَآءَ صَبًّا ﴿25﴾ ثُمَّ شَقَقْنَا
ٱلْأَرْضَ شَقًّا ﴿26﴾ فَأَنۢبَتْنَا فِيهَا حَبًّا ﴿27﴾ وَعِنَبًا وَقَضْبًا ﴿28﴾ وَزَيْتُونًا
وَنَخْلًا ﴿29﴾ وَحَدَآئِقَ غُلْبًا ﴿30﴾ وَفَٰكِهَةً وَأَبًّا ﴿31﴾ مَّتَٰعًا لَّكُمْ
وَلِأَنْعَٰمِكُمْ ﴿32﴾ فَإِذَا جَآءَتِ ٱلصَّآخَّةُ ﴿33﴾ يَوْمَ يَفِرُّ ٱلْمَرْءُ مِنْ
أَخِيهِ ﴿34﴾ وَأُمِّهِۦ وَأَبِيهِ ﴿35﴾ وَصَٰحِبَتِهِۦ وَبَنِيهِ ﴿36﴾ لِكُلِّ ٱمْرِئٍ مِّنْهُمْ
يَوْمَئِذٍ شَأْنٌ يُغْنِيهِ ﴿37﴾ وُجُوهٌ يَوْمَئِذٍ مُّسْفِرَةٌ ﴿38﴾ ضَاحِكَةٌ
مُّسْتَبْشِرَةٌ ﴿39﴾ وَوُجُوهٌ يَوْمَئِذٍ عَلَيْهَا غَبَرَةٌ ﴿40﴾ تَرْهَقُهَا قَتَرَةٌ ﴿41﴾
أُو۟لَٰٓئِكَ هُمُ ٱلْكَفَرَةُ ٱلْفَجَرَةُ ﴿42﴾

Falyañẓuril-ʾIñsānu ʾilā ṭaʿāmih. (24) ʾAnnā ṣabab-nal-māaʾa ṣabbā. (25) Thumma shaqaqnal-ʾarḍa shaqqā. (26) Faʾambatnā fīhā ḥabbā. (27) Wa ʿinabañw-wa qaḍbā. (28) Wa zaytūnañw-wa nakhlā. (29) Wa ḥadāaʾiqa ghulbā. (30) Wa fākihatañw-wa ʾabbā. (31) Matāʿal-lakum wa liʾanʿāmikum. (32) Faʾidhā jāaʾatiṣ-Ṣāakhkhah. (33) Yawma yafirrul-marʾu min ʾakhīh. (34) Wa ʾummihī wa ʾabīh. (35) Wa ṣāḥibatihī wa banīh. (36) Likullim-riʾim-minhum Yaw-maʾidhiñ-shaʾnuñy-yughnīh. (37) Wujūhuñy-Yawma-ʾidhim-musfirah. (38) Ḍāḥikatum-mustabshirah. (39) Wa wujūhuñy-Yawmaʾidhin ʿalayhā ghabarah. (40) Tarhaquhā qatarah. (41) ʾUlāaʾika humul-kafaratul-fajarah. (42)

9 The implication is that man ought to be grateful for all this God-given bounty, but as a rule is not: and this connects with the subsequent evocation of the Day of Resurrection, already hinted at in the reference to the recurring phenomenon of life-renewal.

10 I.e., as God is able to bring forth new life out of a seemingly dead earth, so is He able to resurrect the dead.

The Eighty-First Sūrah

At-Takwīr (Shrouding in Darkness)

Mecca Period

THE conventional designation of this very early *sūrah* (most probably the seventh in the order of revelation) is derived from the verb *kuwwirat,* which occurs in the first verse and introduces the symbolic image of the Last Hour and, hence, of man's resurrection.

سورة التكوير مكية -81-
وآياتها تسع وعشرون

IN THE NAME OF GOD, THE MOST GRACIOUS, THE DISPENSER OF GRACE:

WHEN THE SUN is shrouded in darkness, ‹1› and when the stars lose their light, ‹2›
and when the mountains are made to vanish,[1] ‹3›
and when she-camels big with young, about to give birth, are left untended, ‹4›
and when all beasts are gathered together,[2] ‹5›
and when the seas boil over, ‹6›
and when all human beings are coupled [with their deeds],[3] ‹7›
and when the girl-child that was buried alive is made to ask ‹8› for what crime she had been slain,[4] ‹9›

بِسْمِ ٱللَّهِ ٱلرَّحْمَٰنِ ٱلرَّحِيمِ

إِذَا ٱلشَّمْسُ كُوِّرَتْ ﴿١﴾ وَإِذَا ٱلنُّجُومُ ٱنكَدَرَتْ ﴿٢﴾ وَإِذَا ٱلْجِبَالُ
سُيِّرَتْ ﴿٣﴾ وَإِذَا ٱلْعِشَارُ عُطِّلَتْ ﴿٤﴾ وَإِذَا ٱلْوُحُوشُ حُشِرَتْ ﴿٥﴾
وَإِذَا ٱلْبِحَارُ سُجِّرَتْ ﴿٦﴾ وَإِذَا ٱلنُّفُوسُ زُوِّجَتْ ﴿٧﴾ وَإِذَا ٱلْمَوْءُۥدَةُ
سُئِلَتْ ﴿٨﴾ بِأَىِّ ذَنۢبٍ قُتِلَتْ ﴿٩﴾

Bismil-lāhir-Raḥmānir-Raḥīm.
ʾIdhash-shamsu kuwwirat. (1) Wa ʾidhan-nujūmuñ-kadarat. (2) Wa ʾidhal-jibālu suyyirat. (3) Wa ʾidhal-ʿishāru ʿuṭṭilat. (4) Wa ʾidhal-wuḥūshu ḥushirat. (5) Wa ʾidhal-biḥāru sujjirat. (6) Wa ʾidhan-nufūsu zuwwijat. (7) Wa ʾidhal-mawʾūdatu suʾilat. (8) Biʾayyi dhambiñ-qutilat. (9)

---

1 See 20 : 105-107 and the corresponding note 90; also note 63 on 14 : 48.

2 I.e., when they crowd together in terror of the manifestation of the Last Hour, or – as Muʿtazilī commentators maintain – in order to be indemnified by God for man's cruelty to them (Rāzī). It is also said that the animals which were loved by human beings will live in the hereafter together with those who loved them (Zamakhsharī). This interpretation is evidently based on 6 : 38 – "there is no beast that walks on earth and no bird that flies on its two wings which is not [God's] creature like yourselves" – followed almost immediately by the words, "Unto their Sustainer shall they [all] be gathered."

3 I.e., when none will be able to divest himself of responsibility for his past deeds.

4 The barbaric custom of burying female infants alive seems to have been fairly widespread in pre-Islamic Arabia, although perhaps not to the extent as has been commonly assumed. The motives were twofold: the fear that an increase of female offspring would result in economic burdens, as well as fear of the humiliation frequently caused by

and when the scrolls [of men's deeds] are unfolded, ‹10›
and when heaven is laid bare, ‹11›
and when the blazing fire [of hell] is kindled bright, ‹12›
and when paradise is brought into view: ‹13›
[on that Day] every human being will come to know what he has prepared [for himself]. ‹14›

BUT NAY! I call to witness the revolving stars, ‹15›
the planets that run their course and set, ‹16›
and the night as it darkly falls, ‹17›
and the morn as it softly breathes: ‹18›
behold, this [divine writ] is indeed the [inspired] word of a noble Apostle,[5] ‹19›
with strength endowed, secure with Him who in almightiness is enthroned;[6] ‹20›
[the word of] one to be heeded, and worthy of trust! ‹21›
For, this fellow-man of yours is not a madman:[7] ‹22› he truly beheld [the angel – beheld] him on the clear horizon;[8] ‹23›
and he is not one to begrudge others the knowledge [of whatever has been revealed to him] out of that which is beyond the reach of human perception.[9] ‹24›

وَإِذَا ٱلصُّحُفُ نُشِرَتْ ﴿١٠﴾ وَإِذَا ٱلسَّمَآءُ كُشِطَتْ ﴿١١﴾ وَإِذَا ٱلْجَحِيمُ
سُعِّرَتْ ﴿١٢﴾ وَإِذَا ٱلْجَنَّةُ أُزْلِفَتْ ﴿١٣﴾ عَلِمَتْ نَفْسٌ مَّآ أَحْضَرَتْ ﴿١٤﴾
فَلَآ أُقْسِمُ بِٱلْخُنَّسِ ﴿١٥﴾ ٱلْجَوَارِ ٱلْكُنَّسِ ﴿١٦﴾ وَٱلَّيْلِ إِذَا
عَسْعَسَ ﴿١٧﴾ وَٱلصُّبْحِ إِذَا تَنَفَّسَ ﴿١٨﴾ إِنَّهُۥ لَقَوْلُ رَسُولٍ كَرِيمٍ ﴿١٩﴾
ذِى قُوَّةٍ عِندَ ذِى ٱلْعَرْشِ مَكِينٍ ﴿٢٠﴾ مُّطَاعٍ ثَمَّ أَمِينٍ ﴿٢١﴾ وَمَا
صَاحِبُكُم بِمَجْنُونٍ ﴿٢٢﴾ وَلَقَدْ رَءَاهُ بِٱلْأُفُقِ ٱلْمُبِينِ ﴿٢٣﴾ وَمَا هُوَ عَلَى
ٱلْغَيْبِ بِضَنِينٍ ﴿٢٤﴾

Wa ᵓidhaṣ-ṣuḥufu nushirat. (10) Wa ᵓidhas-samāaᵓu kushiṭat. (11) Wa ᵓidhal-jaḥīmu suᶜirat. (12) Wa ᵓidhal-jannatu ᵓuzlifat. (13) ᶜAlimat nafsum-māa ᵓaḥḍarat. (14) Falāa ᵓuqsimu bilkhunnas. (15) ᵓAljawāril-kunnas. (16) Wal-layli ᵓidhā ᶜasᶜas. (17) Waṣ-ṣubḥi ᵓidhā tanaffas. (18) ᵓInnahū laqawlu Rasūliñ-karīm. (19) Dhī quwwatin ᶜiñda Dhil-ᶜarshi makīn. (20) Muṭāᶜiñ-thamma ᵓamīn. (21) Wa mā ṣāḥibukum-bimajnūn. (22) Wa laqad raᵓāhu bilᵓufuqil-mubīn. (23) Wa mā huwa ᶜalal-ghaybi biḍanīn. (24)

girls being captured by a hostile tribe and subsequently preferring their captors to their parents and brothers. Before Islam, one of the foremost opponents of this custom was Zayd ibn ᶜAmr ibn Nufayl, a cousin of ᶜUmar ibn al-Khaṭṭāb and spiritually a precursor of Muḥammad (cf. Bukhārī, *Faḍāᵓil Aṣḥāb an-Nabī*, on the authority of ᶜAbd Allāh ibn ᶜUmar); he died shortly before Muḥammad's call to prophethood (*Fatḥ al-Bārī* VII, 112). Another man, Ṣaᶜṣaᶜah ibn Nājiyah at-Tamīmī – grandfather of the poet Farazdaq – achieved equal fame as a saviour of infants thus condemned to death; he later embraced Islam. Ibn Khallikān (II, 197) mentions that Ṣaᶜṣaᶜah saved about thirty girls by paying ransom to their parents.

5 By "calling to witness" certain natural phenomena which are familiar to man because of their permanent recurrence, attention is drawn to the fact that what we call "laws of nature" are but the observable elements of God's plan of creation – a plan in which His revelations (referred to in this and the subsequent verses) play a decisive role: and so, by implication, the divine writ granted to Muḥammad is as intrinsically "natural" as any other phenomenon, concrete or abstract, in the realm of God's creation.

6 Lit., "with Him of the throne of almightiness". It is to be noted that the Qurᵓanic term *ᶜarsh* – of which the above is the earliest occurrence in the order of revelation – invariably signifies God's absolute sovereignty and almightiness (cf. note 43 on 7 : 54).

7 See *sūrah* 68, note 3. The characterization of Muḥammad as "this fellow-man of yours" is meant to stress his absolute humanness, and thus to counteract any possibility on the part of his followers to deify him. (See also note 150 on 7 : 184.)

8 This is evidently a reference to the Prophet's vision of the Angel Gabriel which ended the break in revelation (*fatrat al-waḥy*) mentioned in the introductory note to *sūrah* 74. See also 53 : 5 ff. and the corresponding notes.

9 Sc., "and so he conveys this revelation to you".

Nor is this [message] the word of any satanic force accursed.[10] ‹25›
Whither, then, will you go? ‹26›
This [message] is no less than a reminder to all mankind ‹27› – to every one of you who wills to walk a straight way. ‹28›
But you cannot will it unless God, the Sustainer of all the worlds, wills [to show you that way].[11] ‹29›

وَمَا هُوَ بِقَوْلِ شَيْطَـٰنٍ رَّجِيمٍ ﴿٢٥﴾ فَأَيْنَ تَذْهَبُونَ ﴿٢٦﴾ إِنْ هُوَ إِلَّا ذِكْرٌ لِّلْعَـٰلَمِينَ ﴿٢٧﴾ لِمَن شَآءَ مِنكُمْ أَن يَسْتَقِيمَ ﴿٢٨﴾ وَمَا تَشَآءُونَ إِلَّآ أَن يَشَآءَ ٱللَّهُ رَبُّ ٱلْعَـٰلَمِينَ ﴿٢٩﴾

Wa mā huwa biqawli Shayṭānir-rajīm. ‹25› Faʾayna tadhhabūn. ‹26› ʾIn huwa ʾillā dhikrul-lilʿālamīn. ‹27› Limañ-shāaʾa miñkum ʾañy-yastaqīm. ‹28› Wa mā tashāaʾūna ʾillāa ʾañy-yashāaʾal-lāhu Rabbul-ʿālamīn. ‹29›

10 For my occasional rendering of *shayṭān* as "satanic force", see first half of note 16 on 15 : 17.

11 I.e., "you can will it only because *God has willed* to show you the right way by means of the positive instincts which He has implanted in you, as well as through the revelations which He has bestowed on His prophets": implying that the choice of the right way is open to everyone who is willing to avail himself of God's universal guidance. (Cf. a similar passage in 76 : 29-30.)

The Eighty-Second Sūrah

Al-Iñfiṭār (The Cleaving Asunder)

Mecca Period

ALTHOUGH some authorities assign this *sūrah* to the early part of the Mecca period, others regard it as more probable that it belongs to the last group of Meccan revelations.

سورة الانفطار مكية -82- وآياتها تسع عشرة

IN THE NAME OF GOD, THE MOST GRACIOUS, THE DISPENSER OF GRACE:

WHEN THE SKY is cleft asunder,[1] ‹1›
and when the stars are scattered, ‹2›
and when the seas burst beyond their bounds, ‹3›
and when the graves are overturned ‹4›
– every human being will [at last] comprehend what he has sent ahead and what he has held back [in this world].[2] ‹5›

O MAN! What is it that lures thee away from thy bountiful Sustainer,[3] ‹6› who has created thee, and formed thee in accordance with what thou art meant to be,[4] and shaped thy nature in just

بِسْمِ ٱللَّهِ ٱلرَّحْمَٰنِ ٱلرَّحِيمِ

إِذَا ٱلسَّمَآءُ ٱنفَطَرَتْ (1) وَإِذَا ٱلْكَوَاكِبُ ٱنتَثَرَتْ (2) وَإِذَا ٱلْبِحَارُ
فُجِّرَتْ (3) وَإِذَا ٱلْقُبُورُ بُعْثِرَتْ (4) عَلِمَتْ نَفْسٌ مَّا قَدَّمَتْ وَأَخَّرَتْ (5)
يَٰٓأَيُّهَا ٱلْإِنسَٰنُ مَا غَرَّكَ بِرَبِّكَ ٱلْكَرِيمِ (6) ٱلَّذِى خَلَقَكَ فَسَوَّىٰكَ

نصف الحزب

Bismil-lāhir-Raḥmānir-Raḥīm.
ʾIdhas-samāaʾuñ-faṭarat. (1) Wa ʾidhal-kawākibuñ-tatharat. (2) Wa ʾidhal-biḥāru fujjirat. (3) Wa ʾidhal-qubūru buʿthirat. (4) ʿAlimat nafsum-mā qaddamat wa ʾakhkharat. (5) Yāa ʾayyuhal-ʾIñsānu mā gharraka biRabbikal-Karīm. (6) ʾAlladhī khalaqaka fasawwāka

---

1 An allusion to the Last Hour, when the world as known to man will come to an end and the ultimate reality of the hereafter will begin.

2 I.e., what he has done and what he has omitted to do. An alternative rendering would be, "what he has placed forward and what he has placed behind", i.e., what he prized more and what less in his erstwhile, subjective valuation. Thus, at the moment of resurrection man will suddenly understand the true motivations and moral implications of whatever he did – or consciously refrained from doing – during his life in this world: and this applies to all the good deeds he did and the sins he refrained from, as well as to all the sins he committed and the good deeds he failed to do.

3 A rhetorical question implying that no human being is ever entirely immune against "that temptation to evil (*fitnah*) which does not befall only those among you who are bent on denying the truth" (see 8 : 25 and the corresponding note 25). The answer is given in verse 9 below.

4 I.e., "endowed thee with all the qualities and abilities relevant to the exigencies of thy individual life and thy environment".

proportions,[5] ‹7› having put thee together in whatever form He willed [thee to have]? ‹8›

Nay, [O men,] but you [are lured away from God whenever you are tempted to] give the lie to [God's] Judgment![6] ‹9›

And yet, verily, there are ever-watchful forces over you, ‹10› noble, recording, ‹11› aware of whatever you do![7] ‹12›

Behold, [in the life to come] the truly virtuous will indeed be in bliss, ‹13› whereas, behold, the wicked will indeed be in a blazing fire ‹14› – [a fire] which they shall enter on Judgment Day, ‹15› and which they shall not [be able to] evade. ‹16›

And what could make thee conceive what that Judgment Day will be? ‹17›

And once again: What could make thee conceive what that Judgment Day will be?[8] ‹18›

[It will be] a Day when no human being shall be of the least avail to another human being: for on that Day [it will become manifest that] all sovereignty is God's alone. ‹19›

فَعَدَلَكَ ﴿٧﴾ فِيٓ أَيِّ صُورَةٖ مَّا شَآءَ رَكَّبَكَ ﴿٨﴾ كَلَّا بَلۡ تُكَذِّبُونَ
بِٱلدِّينِ ﴿٩﴾ وَإِنَّ عَلَيۡكُمۡ لَحَٰفِظِينَ ﴿١٠﴾ كِرَامٗا كَٰتِبِينَ ﴿١١﴾ يَعۡلَمُونَ
مَا تَفۡعَلُونَ ﴿١٢﴾ إِنَّ ٱلۡأَبۡرَارَ لَفِي نَعِيمٖ ﴿١٣﴾ وَإِنَّ ٱلۡفُجَّارَ لَفِي جَحِيمٖ ﴿١٤﴾
يَصۡلَوۡنَهَا يَوۡمَ ٱلدِّينِ ﴿١٥﴾ وَمَا هُمۡ عَنۡهَا بِغَآئِبِينَ ﴿١٦﴾ وَمَآ أَدۡرَىٰكَ مَا يَوۡمُ
ٱلدِّينِ ﴿١٧﴾ ثُمَّ مَآ أَدۡرَىٰكَ مَا يَوۡمُ ٱلدِّينِ ﴿١٨﴾ يَوۡمَ لَا تَمۡلِكُ نَفۡسٞ لِّنَفۡسٖ
شَيۡـٔٗاۖ وَٱلۡأَمۡرُ يَوۡمَئِذٖ لِّلَّهِ ﴿١٩﴾

faᶜadalak. (7) Fii ʾayyi ṣūratim-mā shāaʾa rakkabak. (8) Kallā bal tukadhdhibūna biddīn. (9) Wa ʾinna ᶜalaykum laḥāfiẓīn. (10) Kirāmañ-kātibīn. (11) Yaᶜlamūna mā tafᶜalūn. (12) ʾInnal-ʾabrāra lafī naᶜīm. (13) Wa ʾinnal-fujjāra lafī jaḥīm. (14) Yaṣlawnahā Yawmad-Dīn. (15) Wa mā hum ᶜanhā bighāaʾibīn. (16) Wa māa ʾadrāka mā Yawmud-Dīn. (17) Thumma māa ʾadrāka mā Yawmud-Dīn. (18) Yawma lā tamliku nafsul-linafsiñ-shayʾañw-wal-ʾamru Yawmaʾidhil-lillāh. (19)

5 Lit., "made thee proportionate", i.e., a being subject to physical needs and emotional urges, and at the same time endowed with intellectual and spiritual perceptions: in other words, a being in whom there is no *inherent* conflict between the demands of "the spirit and the flesh", since both these aspects of the human condition are – as stressed in the next verse – God-willed and, therefore, morally justified.

6 In view of the fact that the whole of this passage is addressed to "man" or "men" in general, and not merely to deniers of the truth, I believe that the expression "you give the lie" does not, in this context, necessarily imply a conscious *denial* of God's ultimate judgment but, rather, a tendency inherent in most human beings to close one's mind – occasionally or permanently, as the case may be – to the prospect of having to answer before God for one's doings: hence my rendering, "you are *tempted* to give the lie".

7 The classical commentators are of the opinion that we have here a reference to the guardian angels who record, allegorically, all of men's deeds. However, another explanation has been suggested by me in my rendering of 50 : 16-23 and elaborated in the corresponding notes 11-16. In consonance with that interpretation, the "watchful force" (*ḥāfiẓ*) set over every human being is *his own conscience*, which "records" all his motives and actions in his subconscious mind. Since it is the most precious element in man's psyche, it is described in verse 11 as "noble".

8 For my rendering of *thumma* at the beginning of this verse as "And once again", see *sūrah* 6, note 31. The repetition of this rhetorical question is meant to indicate that man's intellect and imagination cannot possibly answer it, since what is described as the Day of Judgment will usher in a reality which as yet is wholly outside our human experience and, therefore, cannot be grasped conceptually: hence, only allegory – and our own emotional response to it – can give us an inkling of what that reality might be.

The Eighty-Third Sūrah

Al-Muṭaffifīn (Those Who Give Short Measure)

Period Uncertain

MANY AUTHORITIES – among them Suyūṭī – regard this *sūrah* as the last Meccan revelation. However, a number of authentic Traditions make it clear that at least the first four verses were revealed shortly after the Prophet's arrival at Medina (cf. Ṭabarī, Baghawī, Ibn Kathīr): some commentators go even further and ascribe the whole of the *sūrah* to the Medina period. If we take all the available evidence into account and disregard all speculations based on no more than theme and style, we may assume that the main body of this *sūrah* indeed represents the very last Meccan revelation, while the opening passage (to which the above-mentioned Traditions explicitly refer) belongs to the earliest Medina period. Thus, the *sūrah* as a whole stands – like *sūrah* 29 (*Al-ᶜAnkabūt*) – on the threshold between these two periods.

سورة المطففين مكية -83- وآياتها ست وثلاثون

IN THE NAME OF GOD, THE MOST GRACIOUS, THE DISPENSER OF GRACE:

بِسۡمِ ٱللَّهِ ٱلرَّحۡمَٰنِ ٱلرَّحِيمِ

WOE UNTO THOSE who give short measure: ‹1› those who, when they are to receive their due from [other] people, demand that it be given in full ‹2› – but when they have to measure or weigh whatever they owe to others, give less than what is due![1] ‹3›

Do they not know that they are bound to be raised from the dead ‹4› [and called to account] on an awesome Day ‹5› – the Day when all men shall stand before the Sustainer of all the worlds? ‹6›

NAY, VERILY, the record of the wicked is indeed [set down] in a mode inescapable![2] ‹7›

And what could make thee conceive what that mode inescapable will be? ‹8›

A record [indelibly] inscribed! ‹9›

Woe on that Day unto those who give the lie to the truth ‹10› – those who give the lie to the [coming of] Judgment Day: ‹11› for, none gives the lie to it but such as are wont to transgress against all that is right [and are] immersed in sin:[3] ‹12› [and so,] whenever Our messages are conveyed to them, they but say, "Fables of ancient times!" ‹13›

وَيۡلٞ لِّلۡمُطَفِّفِينَ (1) ٱلَّذِينَ إِذَا ٱكۡتَالُواْ عَلَى ٱلنَّاسِ يَسۡتَوۡفُونَ (2)
وَإِذَا كَالُوهُمۡ أَو وَّزَنُوهُمۡ يُخۡسِرُونَ (3) أَلَا يَظُنُّ أُوْلَٰٓئِكَ أَنَّهُم
مَّبۡعُوثُونَ (4) لِيَوۡمٍ عَظِيمٖ (5) يَوۡمَ يَقُومُ ٱلنَّاسُ لِرَبِّ ٱلۡعَٰلَمِينَ (6)
كَلَّآ إِنَّ كِتَٰبَ ٱلۡفُجَّارِ لَفِي سِجِّينٖ (7) وَمَآ أَدۡرَىٰكَ مَا سِجِّينٞ (8)
كِتَٰبٞ مَّرۡقُومٞ (9) وَيۡلٞ يَوۡمَئِذٖ لِّلۡمُكَذِّبِينَ (10) ٱلَّذِينَ يُكَذِّبُونَ بِيَوۡمِ
ٱلدِّينِ (11) وَمَا يُكَذِّبُ بِهِۦٓ إِلَّا كُلُّ مُعۡتَدٍ أَثِيمٍ (12) إِذَا تُتۡلَىٰ عَلَيۡهِ
ءَايَٰتُنَا قَالَ أَسَٰطِيرُ ٱلۡأَوَّلِينَ (13)

Bismil-lāhir-Raḥmānir-Raḥīm.
Waylul-lilmuṭaffifīn. (1) ᵓAlladhīna ᵓidhak-tālū ᶜalan-nāsi yastawfūn. (2) Wa ᵓidhā kālūhum ᵓaw-wazanūhum yukhsirūn. (3) ᵓAlā yaẓunnu ᵓulāaᵓika ᵓannahum-mabᶜūthūna, (4) liYawmin ᶜaẓīm. (5) Yawma yaqūmun-nāsu liRabbil-ᶜālamīn. (6) Kallāa ᵓinna kitābal-fujjāri lafī sijjīn. (7) Wa māa ᵓadrāka mā sijjīn. (8) Kitābum-marqūm. (9) Wayluñy-Yawma-ᵓidhil-lilmukadhdhibīn. (10) ᵓAlladhīna yukadhdhibūna biYawmid-Dīn. (11) Wa mā yukadhdhibu bihiī ᵓillā kullu muᶜtadin ᵓathīm. (12) ᵓIdhā tutlā ᶜalayhi ᵓĀyātunā qāla ᵓasāṭīrul-ᵓawwalīn. (13)

---

1 This passage (verses 1-3) does not, of course, refer only to commercial dealings but touches upon every aspect of social relations, both practical and moral, applying to every individual's rights and obligations no less than to his physical possessions.

2 According to some of the greatest philologists (e.g., Abū ᶜUbaydah, as quoted in the *Lisān al-ᶜArab*), the term *sijjīn* is derived from – or even synonymous with – the noun *sijn*, which signifies "a prison". Proceeding from this derivation, some authorities attribute to *sijjīn* the tropical meaning of *dāᵓim*, i.e., "continuing" or "lasting" (*ibid.*). Thus, in its metaphorical application to a sinner's "record", it is evidently meant to stress the latter's *inescapable quality*, as if its contents were lastingly "imprisoned", i.e., set down indelibly, with no possibility of escaping from what they imply: hence my rendering of the phrase *fī sijjīn* as "[set down] in a mode inescapable". This interpretation is, to my mind, fully confirmed by verse 9 below.

3 Implying that a denial of ultimate responsibility before God – and, hence, of His judgment – is invariably

سكتة لطيفة على اللام

كَلَّا بَلْ رَانَ عَلَىٰ قُلُوبِهِم مَّا كَانُوا يَكْسِبُونَ (14) كَلَّا إِنَّهُمْ عَن رَّبِّهِمْ
يَوْمَئِذٍ لَّمَحْجُوبُونَ (15) ثُمَّ إِنَّهُمْ لَصَالُوا الْجَحِيمِ (16) ثُمَّ يُقَالُ هَٰذَا
الَّذِي كُنتُم بِهِ تُكَذِّبُونَ (17) كَلَّا إِنَّ كِتَابَ الْأَبْرَارِ لَفِي عِلِّيِّينَ (18)
وَمَا أَدْرَاكَ مَا عِلِّيُّونَ (19) كِتَابٌ مَّرْقُومٌ (20) يَشْهَدُهُ الْمُقَرَّبُونَ (21)
إِنَّ الْأَبْرَارَ لَفِي نَعِيمٍ (22) عَلَى الْأَرَائِكِ يَنظُرُونَ (23) تَعْرِفُ فِي
وُجُوهِهِمْ نَضْرَةَ النَّعِيمِ (24) يُسْقَوْنَ مِن رَّحِيقٍ مَّخْتُومٍ (25) خِتَامُهُ مِسْكٌ

Nay, but their hearts are corroded by all [the evil] that they were wont to do![4] ‹14›
Nay, verily, from [the grace of] their Sustainer shall they on that Day be debarred; ‹15› and then, behold, they shall enter the blazing fire ‹16› and be told: "This is the [very thing] to which you were wont to give the lie!" ‹17›

NAY, VERILY, the record of the truly virtuous is [set down] in a mode most lofty![5] ‹18›
And what could make thee conceive what that mode most lofty will be? ‹19›
A record [indelibly] inscribed, ‹20› witnessed by all who have [ever] been drawn close unto God.[6] ‹21›
Behold, [in the life to come] the truly virtuous will indeed be in bliss: ‹22› [resting] on couches, they will look up [to God]:[7] ‹23› upon their faces thou wilt see the brightness of bliss. ‹24›
They will be given a drink of pure wine whereon the seal [of God] will have been set, ‹25› pouring forth with a fragrance of musk.[8]

Kallā bal, rāna ᶜalā qulūbihim-mā kānū yaksibūn. (14) **Kallāa ᵓinnahum ᶜar-Rabbihim Yawmaᵓidhil-lamaḥjūbūn.** (15) **Thumma ᵓinnahum laṣālul-jaḥīm.** (16) **Thumma yuqālu hādhal-ladhī kuñtum-bihī tukadhdhibūn.** (17) **Kallāa ᵓinna kitābal-ᵓabrāri lafī ᶜilliyyīn.** (18) **Wa māa ᵓadrāka mā ᶜilliyyūn.** (19) **Kitābum-marqūm.** (20) **Yashhaduhul-muqarrabūn.** (21) **ᵓInnal-ᵓabrāra lafī naᶜīm.** (22) **ᶜAlal-ᵓarāaᵓiki yañẓurūn.** (23) **Taᶜrifu fī wujūhihim naḍratan-naᶜīm.** (24) **Yusqawna mir-raḥīqim-makhtūm.** (25) **Khitāmuhū misk.**

conducive to sinning and to transgression against all moral imperatives. (Although this and the next verse are formulated in the singular, I am rendering them in the plural inasmuch as this plurality is idiomatically indicated by the word *kull* before the descriptive participles *muᶜtad* and *athīm*, as well as by the use of a straight plural in verses 14 ff.)

4 Lit., "that which they were earning has covered their hearts with rust": implying that their persistence in wrongdoing has gradually deprived them of all consciousness of moral responsibility and, hence, of the ability to visualize the fact of God's ultimate judgment.

5 I.e., in contrast to the record of the wicked (see verse 7 above). As regards the term *ᶜilliyyūn*, it is said to be the plural of *ᶜillī* or *ᶜilliyyah* ("loftiness") or, alternatively, a plural which has no singular (*Qāmūs*, *Tāj al-ᶜArūs*); in either case it is derived from the verb *ᶜalā*, which signifies "[something] was [or "became"] high" or "lofty" or – tropically – "exalted": thus in the well-known idiomatic phrase, *huwa min ᶜilliyyat qawmihi*, "he is among the [most] exalted of his people". In view of this derivation, the plural *ᶜilliyyūn* has evidently the intensive connotation of "loftiness upon loftiness" (*Tāj al-ᶜArūs*) or "a mode most lofty".

6 I.e., by the prophets and saints of all times as well as by the angels.

7 Cf. 75 : 23. As elsewhere in the Qur'ān, the "couches" of the virtuous in paradise symbolize complete restfulness and inner fulfilment.

8 Lit., "the end whereof (*khitāmuhu*) will be musk". My rendering of the above phrase reflects the interpretation given to it by several authorities of the second generation of Islam, and by Abū ᶜUbaydah ibn al-Muthannā (all of them quoted by Rāzī). The "pure wine" (*raḥīq*) of the hereafter – which, contrary to the wine of this world, will carry "the seal" (i.e., the sanction) of God because "no headiness will be in it, and they will not get drunk thereon" (37 : 47) – is another symbol of paradise, alluding, by means of comparisons with sensations that can be experienced by man, to the otherworldly sensations of joy which, in a form intensified beyond all human imagination, are in store for the righteous. Some of the great Muslim mystics (e.g., Jalāl ad-Dīn Rūmī) see in that "pure wine" an allusion to a spiritual vision of God: an interpretation which, I believe, is fully justified by the sequence.

To that [wine of paradise], then, let all such aspire as [are willing to] aspire to things of high account: ‹26› for it is composed of all that is most exalting[9] ‹27› – a source [of bliss] whereof those who are drawn close unto God shall drink.[10] ‹28›

BEHOLD, those who have abandoned themselves to sin are wont to laugh at such as have attained to faith;[11] ‹29› and whenever they pass by them, they wink at one another [derisively]; ‹30› and whenever they return to people of their own kind,[12] they return full of jests; ‹31› and whenever they see those [who believe,] they say, "Behold, these [people] have indeed gone astray!" ‹32›
And, withal, they have no call to watch over [the beliefs of] others. . . .[13] ‹33›
But on the Day [of Judgment], they who had attained to faith will [be able to] laugh at the [erstwhile] deniers of the truth:[14] ‹34› [for, resting in paradise] on couches, they will look on [and say to themselves]: ‹35› "Are these deniers of the truth being [thus] requited for [aught but] what they were wont to do?" ‹36›

وَفِي ذَٰلِكَ فَلْيَتَنَافَسِ ٱلْمُتَنَٰفِسُونَ ﴿26﴾ وَمِزَاجُهُۥ مِن تَسْنِيمٍ ﴿27﴾ عَيْنًا
يَشْرَبُ بِهَا ٱلْمُقَرَّبُونَ ﴿28﴾ إِنَّ ٱلَّذِينَ أَجْرَمُوا۟ كَانُوا۟ مِنَ ٱلَّذِينَ ءَامَنُوا۟
يَضْحَكُونَ ﴿29﴾ وَإِذَا مَرُّوا۟ بِهِمْ يَتَغَامَزُونَ ﴿30﴾ وَإِذَا ٱنقَلَبُوٓا۟ إِلَىٰٓ
أَهْلِهِمُ ٱنقَلَبُوا۟ فَكِهِينَ ﴿31﴾ وَإِذَا رَأَوْهُمْ قَالُوٓا۟ إِنَّ هَٰٓؤُلَآءِ
لَضَآلُّونَ ﴿32﴾ وَمَآ أُرْسِلُوا۟ عَلَيْهِمْ حَٰفِظِينَ ﴿33﴾ فَٱلْيَوْمَ ٱلَّذِينَ ءَامَنُوا۟
مِنَ ٱلْكُفَّارِ يَضْحَكُونَ ﴿34﴾ عَلَى ٱلْأَرَآئِكِ يَنظُرُونَ ﴿35﴾ هَلْ ثُوِّبَ
ٱلْكُفَّارُ مَا كَانُوا۟ يَفْعَلُونَ ﴿36﴾

Wa fī dhālika falyatanāfasil-mutanāfisūn. ﴿26﴾ Wa mizājuhū miñ-tasnīm. ﴿27﴾ ᶜAynañy-yashrabu bihal-muqarrabūn. ﴿28﴾ ᵓInnal-ladhīna ᵓajramū kānū minal-ladhīna ᵓāmanū yaḍḥakūn. ﴿29﴾ Wa ᵓidhā marrū bihim yataghāmazūn. ﴿30﴾ Wa ᵓidhañ-qalabūu ᵓilāa ᵓahli-himuñ-qalabū fakihīn. ﴿31﴾ Wa ᵓidhā raᵓawhum qālūu ᵓinna hāaᵓulāaᵓi laḍāallūn. ﴿32﴾ Wa māa ᵓursilū ᶜalayhim ḥāfiẓīn. ﴿33﴾ Fal-Yawmal-ladhīna ᵓāmanū minal-kuffāri yaḍḥakūn. ﴿34﴾ ᶜAlal-ᵓarāaᵓiki yañẓurūn. ﴿35﴾ Hal thuwwibal-kuffāru mā kānū yafᶜalūn. ﴿36﴾

9 Whereas most of the classical commentators regard the infinitive noun *tasnīm* as the proper name of one of the allegorical "fountains of paradise", or, alternatively, refrain from any definition of it, it seems to me that the derivation of *tasnīm* from the verb *sannama* – "he raised [something]" or "made [it] lofty" – points, rather, to the *effect* which the "wine" of divine knowledge will have on those who "drink" of it in paradise. Hence, the *tābiᶜī* ᶜIkrimah (as quoted by Rāzī) equates *tasnīm* with *tashrīf*, "that which is ennobling" or "exalting".

10 Cf. 76 : 5-6 and the corresponding notes.

11 In the original, verses 29-33 are in the past tense, as if viewed from the time-level of Judgment Day. However, since the preceding and the following passages (i.e., verses 18-28 and 34-36) are formulated in the future tense, verses 29-33 (which relate to life in this world) may be adequately rendered in the present tense.

12 Lit., "to their [own] people".

13 Lit., "they have not been sent as watchers over them" – implying that none who is devoid of faith has the right to criticize the faith of any of his fellow-men.

14 Speaking of the righteous, the Qurᵓān repeatedly stresses that on the Day of Judgment God "shall have removed whatever unworthy thoughts or feelings (*ghill*) may have been [lingering] in their bosoms" (7 : 43 and 15 : 47). Since an expression of vengeful joy on the part of the blest at the calamity which in the hereafter will befall the erstwhile sinners would certainly fall within the category of "unworthy feelings", their "laughing" can only have a metaphorical meaning, denoting no more than a realization of their own good fortune.

The Eighty-Fourth Sūrah

Al-Inshiqāq (The Splitting Asunder)

Mecca Period

IN THE chronological order, this *sūrah* comes immediately after *sūrah* 82 (*Al-Infiṭār*) and, hence, is probably one of the last Meccan revelations.

سورة الانشقاق مكية -84-
وآياتها خمس وعشرون

ثلاثة ارباع الحزب

IN THE NAME OF GOD, THE MOST GRACIOUS, THE DISPENSER OF GRACE:

WHEN THE SKY is split asunder,[1] ‹1› obeying its Sustainer, as in truth it must; ‹2› and when the earth is levelled,[2] ‹3› and casts forth whatever is in it, and becomes utterly void,[3] ‹4› obeying its Sustainer, as in truth it must: ‹5› – [then,] O man – thou [that] hast, verily, been toiling towards thy Sustainer in painful toil[4] – then shalt thou meet Him! ‹6› And as for him whose record shall be placed in his right hand,[5] ‹7› he will in time be called to account with an easy accounting, ‹8› and will [be able to] turn joyfully to those of his own kind.[6] ‹9›

بِسۡمِ ٱللَّهِ ٱلرَّحۡمَٰنِ ٱلرَّحِيمِ

إِذَا ٱلسَّمَآءُ ٱنشَقَّتۡ ﴿١﴾ وَأَذِنَتۡ لِرَبِّهَا وَحُقَّتۡ ﴿٢﴾ وَإِذَا ٱلۡأَرۡضُ مُدَّتۡ ﴿٣﴾
وَأَلۡقَتۡ مَا فِيهَا وَتَخَلَّتۡ ﴿٤﴾ وَأَذِنَتۡ لِرَبِّهَا وَحُقَّتۡ ﴿٥﴾ يَٰٓأَيُّهَا ٱلۡإِنسَٰنُ إِنَّكَ
كَادِحٌ إِلَىٰ رَبِّكَ كَدۡحٗا فَمُلَٰقِيهِ ﴿٦﴾ فَأَمَّا مَنۡ أُوتِيَ كِتَٰبَهُۥ بِيَمِينِهِۦ ﴿٧﴾
فَسَوۡفَ يُحَاسَبُ حِسَابٗا يَسِيرٗا ﴿٨﴾ وَيَنقَلِبُ إِلَىٰٓ أَهۡلِهِۦ مَسۡرُورٗا ﴿٩﴾

Bismil-lāhir-Raḥmānir-Raḥīm.
ʾIdhas-samāaʾuñ-shaqqat. (1) Wa ʾadhinat liRabbihā wa ḥuqqat. (2) Wa ʾidhal-ʾarḍu muddat. (3) Wa ʾalqat mā fīhā wa takhallat. (4) Wa ʾadhinat liRabbihā wa ḥuqqat. (5) Yāa ʾayyuhal-ʾIñsānu ʾinnaka kādiḥun ʾilā Rabbika kadḥañ-famulāqīh. (6) Faʾammā man ʾūtiya kitābahū biyamīnihī, (7) fasawfa yuḥāsabu ḥisābañy-yasīrā. (8) Wa yañqalibu ʾilāa ʾahlihī masrūrā. (9)

---

1 I.e., at the coming of the Last Hour and the beginning of a new reality, both in fact and in man's perception.

2 See 20 : 105-107.

3 I.e., loses all its reality.

4 An allusion to the fact that in man's earthly life – irrespective of whether one is consciously aware of it or not – sorrow, pain, drudgery and worry by far outweigh the rare moments of true happiness and satisfaction. Thus, the human condition is described as "painful toiling towards the Sustainer" – i.e., towards the moment when one meets Him on resurrection.

5 I.e., whose behaviour in life characterizes him as "righteous": see note 12 on 69 : 19.

6 Lit., "his people" – i.e., those who, like him, were righteous in life.

But as for him whose record shall be given to him behind his back,[7] ‹10› he will in time pray for utter destruction: ‹11› but he will enter the blazing flame. ‹12›
Behold, [in his earthly life] he lived joyfully among people of his own kind[8] ‹13› – for, behold, he never thought that he would have to return [to God]. ‹14›
Yea indeed! His Sustainer did see all that was in him! ‹15›

BUT NAY! I call to witness the sunset's [fleeting] afterglow, ‹16›
and the night, and what it [step by step] unfolds, ‹17›
and the moon, as it grows to its fullness:[9] ‹18›
[even thus, O men,] are you bound to move onward from stage to stage.[10] ‹19›
What, then, is amiss with them that they will not believe [in a life to come]?[11] ‹20› – and [that] when the Qurʾān is read unto them, they do not fall down in prostration?[12] ‹21›
Nay, but they who are bent on denying the truth give the lie [to this divine writ]! ‹22›
Yet God has full knowledge of what they conceal [in their hearts].[13] ‹23›
Hence, give them the tiding of grievous suffering [in the life to come] ‹24› – unless it be such [of them] as [repent, and] attain to faith, and do good works: for theirs shall be a reward unending! ‹25›

السجدة

وَأَمَّا مَنْ أُوتِيَ كِتَٰبَهُۥ وَرَآءَ ظَهْرِهِۦ ﴿١٠﴾ فَسَوْفَ يَدْعُوا۟ ثُبُورًا ﴿١١﴾
وَيَصْلَىٰ سَعِيرًا ﴿١٢﴾ إِنَّهُۥ كَانَ فِىٓ أَهْلِهِۦ مَسْرُورًا ﴿١٣﴾ إِنَّهُۥ ظَنَّ أَن لَّن
يَحُورَ ﴿١٤﴾ بَلَىٰٓ إِنَّ رَبَّهُۥ كَانَ بِهِۦ بَصِيرًا ﴿١٥﴾ فَلَآ أُقْسِمُ بِٱلشَّفَقِ ﴿١٦﴾
وَٱلَّيْلِ وَمَا وَسَقَ ﴿١٧﴾ وَٱلْقَمَرِ إِذَا ٱتَّسَقَ ﴿١٨﴾ لَتَرْكَبُنَّ طَبَقًا
عَن طَبَقٍ ﴿١٩﴾ فَمَا لَهُمْ لَا يُؤْمِنُونَ ﴿٢٠﴾ وَإِذَا قُرِئَ عَلَيْهِمُ ٱلْقُرْءَانُ
لَا يَسْجُدُونَ ۩ ﴿٢١﴾ بَلِ ٱلَّذِينَ كَفَرُوا۟ يُكَذِّبُونَ ﴿٢٢﴾ وَٱللَّهُ أَعْلَمُ بِمَا
يُوعُونَ ﴿٢٣﴾ فَبَشِّرْهُم بِعَذَابٍ أَلِيمٍ ﴿٢٤﴾ إِلَّا ٱلَّذِينَ ءَامَنُوا۟ وَعَمِلُوا۟
ٱلصَّٰلِحَٰتِ لَهُمْ أَجْرٌ غَيْرُ مَمْنُونٍ ﴿٢٥﴾

Wa ʾammā man ʾūtiya kitābahū warāaʾa ẓahrihī, ‹10› fasawfa yadʿū thubūrā. ‹11› Wa yaṣlā saʿīrā. ‹12› ʾInnahū kāna fii ʾahlihī masrūrā. ‹13› ʾInnahū ẓanna ʾal-lañy-yaḥūr. ‹14› Balāa ʾinna Rabbahū kāna bihī Baṣīrā. ‹15› Falāa ʾuqsimu bishshafaq. ‹16› Wal-layli wa mā wasaq. ‹17› Wal-qamari ʾidhat-tasaq. ‹18› Latarkabunna ṭabaqan ʿañ-ṭabaq. ‹19› Famā lahum lā yuʾminūn. ‹20› Wa ʾidhā quriʾa ʿalayhimul-Qurʾānu lā yasjudūn. ۩ ‹21› Balil-ladhīna kafarū yukadhdhibūn. ‹22› Wal-lāhu ʾaʿlamu bimā yūʿūn. ‹23› Fabashshirhum biʿadhābin ʾalīm. ‹24› ʾIllal-ladhīna ʾāmanū wa ʿamiluṣ-ṣāliḥāti lahum ʾajrun ghayru mamnūn. ‹25›

7 At first glance, this seems to contrast with 69 : 25, where it is stated that the record of the unrighteous "shall be placed in his left hand". In reality, however, the present formulation alludes to the sinner's horror at his record, and his wish that he had never been shown it (69 : 25-26): in other words, his *not wanting to see it* is symbolized by its appearance "behind his back".

8 Lit., "his people" – i.e., people of the same sinful inclinations. (Cf. note 14 on 75 : 33.)

9 Thus God "calls to witness" the fact that nothing in His creation is ever at a standstill, since everything moves unceasingly from one state of being into another, at every moment changing its aspect and its condition: a phenomenon aptly described by the Greek philosopher Heraclitus by the phrase *panta rhei* ("everything is in flux").

10 Or: "from one state to another state" (Zamakhsharī): i.e., in an unceasing progression – conception, birth, growth, decline, death and, finally, resurrection.

11 Since the inexorable movement of all that exists from stage to stage or from one condition into another corresponds to a fundamental law evident in all creation, it is unreasonable to assume that man alone should be an exception, and that *his* onward movement should cease at the moment of his bodily death, not to be followed by a change-over into another state of being.

12 I.e., seeing how consistently it stresses the divine law of unceasing change and progression in all that exists.

13 Namely, their unwillingness to admit their responsibility to a Supreme Being.

The Eighty-Fifth Sūrah

Al-Burūj (The Great Constellations)

Mecca Period

REVEALED after *sūrah* 91 ("The Sun").

سورة البروج مكية -85-

وآياتها ثنتان وعشرون

IN THE NAME OF GOD, THE MOST GRACIOUS, THE DISPENSER OF GRACE:

بِسۡمِ ٱللَّهِ ٱلرَّحۡمَٰنِ ٱلرَّحِيمِ

CONSIDER the sky full of great constellations, ‹1›
and [then bethink thyself of] the promised Day,[1] ‹2›
and [of] Him who witnesses [all], and [of] that unto which witness is borne [by Him] [2] ‹3›

THEY DESTROY [but] themselves,[3] they who would ready a pit ‹4› of fire fiercely burning [for all who have attained to faith]![4] ‹5›

وَٱلسَّمَآءِ ذَاتِ ٱلۡبُرُوجِ ١ وَٱلۡيَوۡمِ ٱلۡمَوۡعُودِ ٢ وَشَاهِدٖ وَمَشۡهُودٖ ٣
قُتِلَ أَصۡحَٰبُ ٱلۡأُخۡدُودِ ٤ ٱلنَّارِ ذَاتِ ٱلۡوَقُودِ ٥

Bismil-lāhir-Raḥmānir-Raḥīm.
Was-samāaʾi dhātil-burūj. 1 **Wal-Yawmil-mawʿūd.**
2 **Wa shāhidiñw-wa mashhūd.** 3 **Qutila ʾaṣḥābul-ʾukhdūd.** 4 **ʾAnnāri dhātil-waqūd.** 5

---

1 I.e., the Day of Resurrection.

2 By creating the universe, God "bears witness", as it were, to His Own almightiness and uniqueness: cf. 3 : 18 – "God [Himself] bears witness that there is no deity save Him" – and the corresponding note 11.

3 For an explanation of this rendering of *qutila*, see note 9 on 74 : 19-20.

4 Lit., "those responsible (*aṣḥab*) for the pit of fire abounding in fuel". In order to explain this parabolic passage the commentators interpret it – quite unnecessarily – in the past tense, and advance the most contradictory legends meant to "identify" those evildoers in historical terms. The result is a medley of stories ranging from Abraham's experiences with his idolatrous contemporaries (cf. 21 : 68-70) to the Biblical legend of Nebuchadnezzar's attempt to burn three pious Israelites in a fiery furnace (The Book of Daniel iii, 19 ff.), or the persecution, in the sixth century, of the Christians of Najrān by the King of Yemen, Dhū Nawās (who was a Jew by religion), or the entirely apocryphal story of a Zoroastrian king who burnt to death those of his subjects who refused to accept his dictum that a marriage of brother and sister was "permitted by God"; and so forth. None of these legends needs, of course, to be seriously considered in this context. As a matter of fact, the very anonymity of the evildoers referred to in the above Qurʾanic

Lo! [With glee do] they contemplate that [fire], ‹6› fully conscious of what they are doing to the believers.[5] ‹7› whom they hate for no other reason than that they believe in God, the Almighty, the One to whom all praise is due, ‹8› [and] to whom the dominion of the heavens and the earth belongs.

But God is witness unto everything! ‹9›

Verily, as for those who persecute believing men and believing women, and thereafter do not repent, hell's suffering awaits them: yea, suffering through fire awaits them![6] ‹10›

[But,] verily, they who attain to faith and do righteous deeds shall [in the life to come] have gardens through which running waters flow – that triumph most great![7] ‹11›

VERILY, thy Sustainer's grip is exceedingly strong! ‹12›

Behold, it is He who creates [man] in the first instance, and He [it is who] will bring him forth anew. ‹13›

And He alone is truly-forgiving, all-embracing in His love, ‹14› in sublime almightiness enthroned,[8] ‹15› a sovereign doer of whatever He wills. ‹16›

HAS IT ever come within thy ken the story of the [sinful] hosts ‹17› of Pharaoh, and of [the tribe of] Thamūd?[9] ‹18›

And yet, they who are bent on denying the truth persist in giving it the lie: ‹19›

إِذْ هُمْ عَلَيْهَا قُعُودٌ ﴿٦﴾ وَهُمْ عَلَىٰ مَا يَفْعَلُونَ بِٱلْمُؤْمِنِينَ شُهُودٌ ﴿٧﴾ وَمَا
نَقَمُوا۟ مِنْهُمْ إِلَّآ أَن يُؤْمِنُوا۟ بِٱللَّهِ ٱلْعَزِيزِ ٱلْحَمِيدِ ﴿٨﴾ ٱلَّذِى لَهُۥ مُلْكُ
ٱلسَّمَـٰوَٰتِ وَٱلْأَرْضِ ۚ وَٱللَّهُ عَلَىٰ كُلِّ شَىْءٍ شَهِيدٌ ﴿٩﴾ إِنَّ ٱلَّذِينَ فَتَنُوا۟
ٱلْمُؤْمِنِينَ وَٱلْمُؤْمِنَـٰتِ ثُمَّ لَمْ يَتُوبُوا۟ فَلَهُمْ عَذَابُ جَهَنَّمَ وَلَهُمْ عَذَابُ
ٱلْحَرِيقِ ﴿١٠﴾ إِنَّ ٱلَّذِينَ ءَامَنُوا۟ وَعَمِلُوا۟ ٱلصَّـٰلِحَـٰتِ لَهُمْ جَنَّـٰتٌ
تَجْرِى مِن تَحْتِهَا ٱلْأَنْهَـٰرُ ۚ ذَٰلِكَ ٱلْفَوْزُ ٱلْكَبِيرُ ﴿١١﴾ إِنَّ بَطْشَ رَبِّكَ
لَشَدِيدٌ ﴿١٢﴾ إِنَّهُۥ هُوَ يُبْدِئُ وَيُعِيدُ ﴿١٣﴾ وَهُوَ ٱلْغَفُورُ ٱلْوَدُودُ ﴿١٤﴾ ذُو
ٱلْعَرْشِ ٱلْمَجِيدُ ﴿١٥﴾ فَعَّالٌ لِّمَا يُرِيدُ ﴿١٦﴾ هَلْ أَتَىٰكَ حَدِيثُ
ٱلْجُنُودِ ﴿١٧﴾ فِرْعَوْنَ وَثَمُودَ ﴿١٨﴾ بَلِ ٱلَّذِينَ كَفَرُوا۟ فِى تَكْذِيبٍ ﴿١٩﴾

ʾIdh hum ʿalayhā quʿūd. (6) Wa hum ʿalā mā yafʿalūna bilmuʾminīna shuhūd. (7) Wa mā naqamū minhum ʾillāa ʾañy-yuʾminū billāhil-ʿAzīzil-Ḥamīd. (8) ʾAlladhī lahū mulkus-samāwāti wal-ʾarḍi wallāhu ʿalā kulli shayʾiñ-Shahīd. (9) ʾInnal-ladhīna fatanul-muʾminīna wal-muʾmināti thumma lam yatūbū falahum ʿadhābu jahannama wa lahum ʿadhābul-ḥarīq. (10) ʾInnal-ladhīna ʾāmanū wa ʿamiluṣ-ṣāliḥāti lahum jannātuñ-tajrī miñ-taḥtihal-ʾanhāru dhālikal-fawzul-kabīr. (11) ʾInna baṭsha Rabbika lashadīd. (12) ʾInnahū Huwa yubdiʾu wa yuʿīd. (13) Wa Huwal-Ghafūrul-Wadūd. (14) Dhul-ʿarshil-Majīd. (15) Faʿʿālul-limā yurīd. (16) Hal ʾatāka ḥadīthul-junūd. (17) Firʿawna wa Thamūd. (18) Balil-ladhīna kafarū fī takdhīb. (19)

passage shows that we have here a *parable* and not an allusion to "historical" or even legendary events. The persecutors are people who, having no faith whatsoever, hate to see faith in others (see verse 8 below); the "pit of fire" is a metaphor for the persecution of the latter by the former: a phenomenon not restricted to any particular time or to a particular people but recurring in many forms and in varying degrees of intensity throughout recorded history.

5 Lit., "as they sit over it, the while they witness all that they are doing . . .", etc.

6 Lit., "through burning".

7 This is almost certainly the earliest Qurʾanic reference to "gardens through which running waters flow" as an allegory of the bliss which awaits the righteous in the hereafter.

8 Lit., "He of the sublime throne of almightiness (*al-ʿarsh al-majīd*)". For my rendering of *al-ʿarsh* as "the throne of almightiness", see 7 : 54 and the corresponding note 43.

9 Sc., "both of which were destroyed because of their sins". The story of Pharaoh and his forces, and their destruction by drowning, is referred to many times in the Qur'ān; for the story of the Thamūd see, in particular, 7 : 73 ff. and the corresponding notes 56-62.

but all the while God encompasses them [with His knowledge and might] without their being aware of it.[10] ‹20›
Nay, but this [divine writ which they reject] is a discourse sublime, ‹21› upon an imperishable tablet [inscribed].[11] ‹22›

وَٱللَّهُ مِن وَرَآئِهِم مُّحِيطٌۢ ﴿٢٠﴾ بَلْ هُوَ قُرْءَانٌ مَّجِيدٌ ﴿٢١﴾ فِى لَوْحٍ مَّحْفُوظٍۭ ﴿٢٢﴾

Wal-lāhu miñw-warāa'ihim muḥīṭ. (20) Bal huwa Qur'ānum-majīd. (21) Fī lawḥim-maḥfūẓ. (22)

10 Lit., "from behind them", an idiomatic phrase denoting a happening imperceptible to those whom it closely concerns.

11 Lit., "upon a well-guarded tablet (*lawḥ maḥfūẓ*)" – a description of the Qur'ān to be found only in this one instance. Although some commentators take it in its literal sense and understand by it an actual "heavenly tablet" upon which the Qur'ān is inscribed since all eternity, to many others the phrase has always had a metaphorical meaning: namely, an allusion to the *imperishable quality* of this divine writ. This interpretation is pointedly mentioned as justified by, e.g., Ṭabarī, Baghawī, Rāzī or Ibn Kathīr, all of whom agree that the phrase "upon a well-guarded tablet" relates to God's promise that the Qur'ān would never be corrupted, and would remain free of all arbitrary additions, diminutions and textual changes. See in this connection also 15 : 9 and the corresponding note 10.

The Eighty-Sixth Sūrah

Aṭ-Ṭāriq (That Which Comes in the Night)

Mecca Period

REVEALED at a comparatively early date (probably in the fourth year of the Prophet's mission), the *sūrah* takes its name from the noun *aṭ-ṭāriq* in its first verse.

-86-

سورة الطارق مكية

وآياتها سبع عشرة

IN THE NAME OF GOD, THE MOST GRACIOUS, THE DISPENSER OF GRACE:

بِسۡمِ ٱللَّهِ ٱلرَّحۡمَٰنِ ٱلرَّحِيمِ

CONSIDER the heavens and that which comes in the night![1] ‹1›
And what could make thee conceive what it is that comes in the night? ‹2›
It is the star that pierces through [life's] darkness: ‹3›
[for] no human being has ever been left unguarded.[2] ‹4›

وَٱلسَّمَآءِ وَٱلطَّارِقِ ﴿١﴾ وَمَآ أَدۡرَىٰكَ مَا ٱلطَّارِقُ ﴿٢﴾ ٱلنَّجۡمُ
ٱلثَّاقِبُ ﴿٣﴾ إِن كُلُّ نَفۡسٖ لَّمَّا عَلَيۡهَا حَافِظٞ ﴿٤﴾

Bismil-lāhir-Raḥmānir-Raḥīm.
Was-samāa'i waṭ-ṭāriq. (1) Wa māa 'adrāka maṭ-ṭāriq. (2) 'Annajmuth-thāqib. (3) 'Iñ-kullu nafsil-lammā ʿalayhā ḥāfiẓ. (4)

---

1 Some commentators assume that what is described here as *aṭ-ṭāriq* ("that which comes in the night") is the morning-star, because it appears towards the end of the night; others – like Zamakhsharī or Rāghib – understand by it "*the* star" in its generic sense. Now if we analyze the origin of this noun, we find that it is derived from the verb *ṭaraqa*, which primarily means "he beat [something]" or "knocked [at something]"; hence, *ṭaraqa 'l-bāb*, "he knocked at the door". Tropically, the noun signifies "anything [or "anyone"] that comes in the night", because a person who comes to a house by night is expected to knock at the door (*Tāj al-ʿArūs*). In the Qur'anic mode of expression, *aṭ-ṭāriq* is evidently a metaphor for the heavenly solace which sometimes comes to a human being lost in the deepest darkness of affliction and distress; or for the sudden, intuitive enlightenment which disperses the darkness of uncertainty; or, finally, for divine revelation, which knocks, as it were, at the doors of man's heart, and thus fulfils the functions of both solace and enlightenment. (For my rendering of the adjurative *wa* as "Consider", see *sūrah* 74, first half of note 23.)

2 Lit., "there is no human being without a guardian [or "without a watch being kept"] over it". See in this connection note 7 on 82 : 10-12.

LET MAN, then, observe out of what he has been created: ‹5› he has been created out of a seminal fluid ‹6› issuing from between the loins [of man] and the pelvic arch [of woman].[3] ‹7› Now, verily, He [who thus creates man in the first instance] is well able to bring him back [to life] ‹8› on the Day when all secrets will be laid bare, ‹9› and [man] will have neither strength nor helper! ‹10›
Consider[4] the heavens, ever-revolving, ‹11› and the earth, bursting forth with plants! ‹12›

فَلْيَنظُرِ ٱلْإِنسَٰنُ مِمَّ خُلِقَ ﴿5﴾ خُلِقَ مِن مَّآءٍ دَافِقٍ ﴿6﴾ يَخْرُجُ مِنۢ
بَيْنِ ٱلصُّلْبِ وَٱلتَّرَآئِبِ ﴿7﴾ إِنَّهُۥ عَلَىٰ رَجْعِهِۦ لَقَادِرٌ ﴿8﴾ يَوْمَ تُبْلَى
ٱلسَّرَآئِرُ ﴿9﴾ فَمَا لَهُۥ مِن قُوَّةٍ وَلَا نَاصِرٍ ﴿10﴾ وَٱلسَّمَآءِ ذَاتِ
ٱلرَّجْعِ ﴿11﴾ وَٱلْأَرْضِ ذَاتِ ٱلصَّدْعِ ﴿12﴾ إِنَّهُۥ لَقَوْلٌ فَصْلٌ ﴿13﴾ وَمَا
هُوَ بِٱلْهَزْلِ ﴿14﴾ إِنَّهُمْ يَكِيدُونَ كَيْدًا ﴿15﴾ وَأَكِيدُ كَيْدًا ﴿16﴾ فَمَهِّلِ
ٱلْكَٰفِرِينَ أَمْهِلْهُمْ رُوَيْدًۢا ﴿17﴾

BEHOLD, this [divine writ] is indeed a word that cuts between truth and falsehood,[5] ‹13› and is no idle tale. ‹14›
Behold, they [who refuse to accept it] devise many a false argument[6] [to disprove its truth]; ‹15› but I shall bring all their scheming to nought.[7] ‹16›
Let, then, the deniers of the truth have their will: let them have their will for a little while! ‹17›

Falyañẓuril-ʾIñsānu mimma khuliq. ﴿5﴾ Khuliqa mim-māaʾiñ-dāfiq. ﴿6﴾ Yakhruju mim-bayniṣ-ṣulbi wat-tarāaʾib. ﴿7﴾ ʾInnahū ᶜalā rajᶜihī laqādir. ﴿8﴾ Yawma tublas-sarāaʾir. ﴿9﴾ Famā lahū miñ-quwwatiñw-wa lā nāṣir. ﴿10﴾ Was-samāaʾi dhātir-rajᶜ. ﴿11﴾ Wal-ʾarḍi dhātiṣ-ṣadᶜ. ﴿12﴾ ʾInnahū laqawluñ-faṣl. ﴿13﴾ Wa mā huwa bilhazl. ﴿14﴾ ʾInnahum yakīdūna kaydā. ﴿15﴾ Wa ʾakīdu kaydā. ﴿16﴾ Famahhilil-kāfirīna ʾamhilhum ruwaydā. ﴿17﴾

3 The plural noun *tarāʾib*, rendered by me as "pelvic arch", has also the meaning of "ribs" or "arch of bones"; according to most of the authorities who have specialized in the etymology of rare Qurʾanic expressions, this term relates specifically to *female* anatomy (*Tāj al-ᶜArūs*).

4 Sc., "And, finally, in order to grasp more fully God's power of creation and re-creation, consider . . .", etc.

5 Lit., "a decisive word", or "word of distinction", i.e., between the true and the false – in this case, belief in a continuation of life after "death", on the one hand, and a denial of its possibility, on the other. (Cf. 37 : 21, 44 : 40, 77 : 13 and 38, and 78 : 17, where Resurrection Day is spoken of as "the Day of Distinction"; see also note 6 on 77 : 13)

6 Lit., "devise [many] an artful scheme (*kayd*)": see note 41 on 34 : 33, where the almost synonymous term *makr* is used in the same sense.

7 Lit., "I shall devise a [yet more subtle] scheme", sc., "to bring theirs to nought". The paraphrase adopted by me gives, according to all the authorities, the meaning of the above sentence.

The Eighty-Seventh Sūrah

Al-ᵓAᶜlā (The All-Highest)

Mecca Period

THIS IS most probably the eighth *sūrah* in the chronology of revelation. The key-word by which it has always been known appears in the first verse.

سورة الأعلى مكية -87-
وآياتها تسع عشرة

حزب 60

IN THE NAME OF GOD, THE MOST GRACIOUS, THE DISPENSER OF GRACE:

EXTOL the limitless glory of thy Sustainer's name: [the glory of] the All-Highest, ‹1›
who creates [every thing], and thereupon forms it in accordance with what it is meant to be,[1] ‹2›
and who determines the nature [of all that exists],[2] and thereupon guides it [towards its fulfilment], ‹3›
and who brings forth herbage, ‹4› and thereupon causes it to decay into rust-brown stubble![3] ‹5›

WE SHALL teach thee, and thou wilt not forget [aught of what thou art taught], ‹6›
save what God may will [thee to forget][4] – for, verily, He [alone] knows all that is open to [mans] perception as well as all

بِسۡمِ ٱللَّهِ ٱلرَّحۡمَٰنِ ٱلرَّحِيمِ

سَبِّحِ ٱسۡمَ رَبِّكَ ٱلۡأَعۡلَى ١ ٱلَّذِي خَلَقَ فَسَوَّىٰ ٢ وَٱلَّذِي قَدَّرَ
فَهَدَىٰ ٣ وَٱلَّذِيٓ أَخۡرَجَ ٱلۡمَرۡعَىٰ ٤ فَجَعَلَهُۥ غُثَآءً أَحۡوَىٰ ٥
سَنُقۡرِئُكَ فَلَا تَنسَىٰٓ ٦ إِلَّا مَا شَآءَ ٱللَّهُۚ إِنَّهُۥ يَعۡلَمُ ٱلۡجَهۡرَ وَمَا

Bismil-lāhir-Raḥmānir-Raḥīm.
Sabbiḥis-ma Rabbikal-ᵓAᶜlā. (1) ᵓAlladhī khalaqa fasawwā. (2) Wal-ladhī qaddara fahadā. (3) Wal-ladhīi ᵓakhrajal-marᶜā. (4) Fajaᶜalahū ghuthāa-ᵓan ᵓaḥwā. (5) Sanuqriᵓuka falā tañsā. (6) ᵓIllā mā shāaᵓal-lāhu ᵓinnahū yaᶜlamul-jahra wa mā

---

1 I.e., He endows it with inner coherence and with qualities consistent with the functions which it is meant to perform, and thus adapts it *a priori* to the exigencies of its existence.

2 Cf. the last sentence of 25 : 2 and the corresponding note 3; also 20 : 50 and note 31.

3 I.e., metonymically, "who brings forth life and deals death".

4 The classical commentators assume that the above words are addressed specifically to the Prophet, and that, therefore, they relate to his being *taught the Qurᵓān* and being promised that he would not forget anything thereof, "save what God may will [thee to forget]". This last clause has ever since given much trouble to the commentators,

that is hidden [from it]:[5] ‹7› – and [thus] shall We make easy for thee the path towards [ultimate] ease.[6] ‹8›

REMIND, THEN, [others of the truth, regardless of] whether this reminding [would seem to] be of use [or not]:[7] ‹9› in mind will keep it he who stands in awe [of God], ‹10› but aloof from it will remain that most hapless wretch ‹11› – he who [in the life to come] shall have to endure the great fire ‹12› wherein he will neither die nor remain alive.[8] ‹13›

To happiness [in the life to come] will indeed attain he who attains to purity [in this world], ‹14› and remembers his Sustainer's name, and prays [unto Him]. ‹15›

But nay, [O men,] you prefer the life of this world, ‹16› although the life to come is better and more enduring. ‹17›

Verily, [all] this has indeed been [said] in the earlier revelations ‹18› – the revelations of Abraham and Moses.[9] ‹19›

يَخْفَىٰ ﴿٧﴾ وَنُيَسِّرُكَ لِلْيُسْرَىٰ ﴿٨﴾ فَذَكِّرْ إِن نَّفَعَتِ ٱلذِّكْرَىٰ ﴿٩﴾
سَيَذَّكَّرُ مَن يَخْشَىٰ ﴿١٠﴾ وَيَتَجَنَّبُهَا ٱلْأَشْقَى ﴿١١﴾ ٱلَّذِى يَصْلَى ٱلنَّارَ
ٱلْكُبْرَىٰ ﴿١٢﴾ ثُمَّ لَا يَمُوتُ فِيهَا وَلَا يَحْيَىٰ ﴿١٣﴾ قَدْ أَفْلَحَ مَن تَزَكَّىٰ ﴿١٤﴾
وَذَكَرَ ٱسْمَ رَبِّهِۦ فَصَلَّىٰ ﴿١٥﴾ بَلْ تُؤْثِرُونَ ٱلْحَيَوٰةَ ٱلدُّنْيَا ﴿١٦﴾ وَٱلْـَٔاخِرَةُ
خَيْرٌ وَأَبْقَىٰٓ ﴿١٧﴾ إِنَّ هَٰذَا لَفِى ٱلصُّحُفِ ٱلْأُولَىٰ ﴿١٨﴾ صُحُفِ إِبْرَٰهِيمَ
وَمُوسَىٰ ﴿١٩﴾

yakhfā. (7) Wa nuyassiruka lilyusrā. (8) Fadhakkir ʾiñ-nafaʿatidh-dhikrā. (9) Sayadhdhakkaru mañy-yakhshā. (10) Wa yatajannabuhal-ʾashqā. (11) ʾAlladhī yaṣlan-nāral-kubrā. (12) Thumma lā yamūtu fīhā wa lā yaḥyā. (13) Qad ʾaflaḥa mañ-tazakkā. (14) Wa dhakaras-ma Rabbihī faṣallā. (15) Bal tuʾthirūnal-ḥayātad-dunyā. (16) Wal-ʾĀkhiratu khayruñw-wa ʾabqā. (17) ʾInna ḥādhā lafiṣ-ṣuḥufil-ʾūlā. (18) Ṣuḥufi ʾIbrāhīma wa Mūsā. (19)

inasmuch as it is not very plausible that He who has revealed the Qurʾān to the Prophet should cause him to forget *anything* of it. Hence, many unconvincing explanations have been advanced from very early times down to our own days, the least convincing being that last refuge of every perplexed Qurʾān-commentator, the "doctrine of abrogation" (refuted in my note 87 on 2 : 106). However, the supposed difficulty of interpretation disappears as soon as we allow ourselves to realize that the above passage, though ostensibly addressed to the Prophet, is directed at *man in general*, and that it is closely related to an earlier Qurʾanic revelation – namely, the first five verses of *sūrah* 96 ("The Germ-Cell") and, in particular, verses 3-5, which speak of God's having "taught man what he did not know". In note 3 on those verses I have expressed the opinion that they allude to mankind's cumulative acquisition of empirical and rational knowledge, handed down from generation to generation and from one civilization to another: and it is to this very phenomenon that the present passage, too, refers. We are told here that God, who has formed man in accordance with what he is meant to be and has promised to guide him, will enable him to acquire (and thus, as it were, "impart" to him) elements of knowledge which mankind will accumulate, record and collectively "remember" – except what God may cause man to "forget" (in another word, to abandon) as having become redundant by virtue of his new experiences and his acquisition of wider, more differentiated elements of knowledge, empirical as well as deductive or speculative, including more advanced, empirically acquired skills. However, the very next sentence makes it clear that all knowledge arrived at through our observation of the external world and through speculation, though necessary and most valuable, is definitely limited in scope and does not, therefore, in itself suffice to give us an insight into ultimate truths.

5 I.e., all that is intrinsically beyond the reach of human perception (*al-ghayb*): the implication being that, since human knowledge must forever remain imperfect, man cannot really find his way through life without the aid of divine revelation.

6 I.e., towards an ease of the mind and peace of the spirit.

7 Thus Baghawī, as well as Rāzī in one of his alternative interpretations of this phrase.

8 I.e., *in consequence* of having remained aloof from the divine reminder. (Cf. 74 : 28-29.)

9 These two names are given here only as *examples* of earlier prophetic revelations, thus stressing, once again, the twofold fact of continuity in mankind's religious experiences and of the identity of the basic truths preached by all the prophets. (Cf. also 53 : 36 ff.) The noun *ṣuḥuf* (sing. *ṣaḥīfah*), which literally denotes "leaves [of a book]" or "scrolls", is synonymous with *kitāb* in all the senses of this term (Jawharī): hence, in the above context, "revelations".

The Eighty-Eighth Sūrah

Al-Ghāshiyah (The Overshadowing Event)

Mecca Period

REVEALED most probably about the middle of the Mecca period, this *sūrah* derives its title from the participial noun *al-ghāshiyah* in the first verse.

-88-

سورة الغاشية مكية

وآياتها ست وعشرون

IN THE NAME OF GOD, THE MOST GRACIOUS, THE DISPENSER OF GRACE:

HAS THERE COME unto thee the tiding of the Overshadowing Event?[1] ‹1›
Some faces will on that Day be downcast, ‹2› toiling [under burdens of sin], worn out [by fear], ‹3› about to enter a glowing fire, ‹4› given to drink from a boiling spring. ‹5›
No food for them save the bitterness of dry thorns, ‹6› which gives no strength and neither stills hunger.[2] ‹7›
[And] some faces will on that Day shine with bliss, ‹8› well-pleased with [the fruit of] their striving, ‹9› in a garden sublime, ‹10› wherein thou wilt hear no empty talk. ‹11›

بِسْمِ ٱللَّهِ ٱلرَّحْمَـٰنِ ٱلرَّحِيمِ

هَلْ أَتَىٰكَ حَدِيثُ ٱلْغَـٰشِيَةِ ﴿1﴾ وُجُوهٌ يَوْمَئِذٍ خَـٰشِعَةٌ ﴿2﴾ عَامِلَةٌ
نَّاصِبَةٌ ﴿3﴾ تَصْلَىٰ نَارًا حَامِيَةً ﴿4﴾ تُسْقَىٰ مِنْ عَيْنٍ ءَانِيَةٍ ﴿5﴾ لَّيْسَ لَهُمْ
طَعَامٌ إِلَّا مِن ضَرِيعٍ ﴿6﴾ لَّا يُسْمِنُ وَلَا يُغْنِى مِن جُوعٍ ﴿7﴾ وُجُوهٌ يَوْمَئِذٍ
نَّاعِمَةٌ ﴿8﴾ لِّسَعْيِهَا رَاضِيَةٌ ﴿9﴾ فِى جَنَّةٍ عَالِيَةٍ ﴿10﴾ لَّا تَسْمَعُ فِيهَا
لَـٰغِيَةً ﴿11﴾

Bismil-lāhir-Raḥmānir-Raḥīm.
Hal ᵓatāka ḥadīthul-Ghāshiyah. ﴿1﴾ Wujūhuñy-Yaw-
maᵓidhin khāshiᶜah. ﴿2﴾ ᶜĀmilatuñ-nāṣibah. ﴿3﴾ Taṣlā
nāran ḥāmiyah. ﴿4﴾ Tusqā min ᶜaynin ᵓāniyah. ﴿5﴾
Laysa lahum ṭaᶜāmun ᵓillā miñ-ḍarīᶜ. ﴿6﴾ Lā yusmi-
nu wa lā yughnī miñ-jūᶜ. ﴿7﴾ Wujūhuñy-Yawma-
ᵓidhiñ-nāᶜimah. ﴿8﴾ Lisaᶜyihā rāḍiyah. ﴿9﴾ Fī jannatin
ᶜāliyah. ﴿10﴾ Lā tasmaᶜu fīhā lāghiyah. ﴿11﴾

---

1 I.e., the Day of Resurrection.

2 According to Al-Qiffāl (as quoted by Rāzī), this kind of hellish drink and food is a metonym for utter hopelessness and abasement. As regards the noun *ḍarīᶜ* – which is said to be a bitter, thorny plant in its dried state (Jawharī) – it is to be borne in mind that it is derived from the verb *ḍaraᶜa* or *ḍariᶜa*, which signifies "he [or "it"] became abject" or "abased" (*ibid.*): hence my rendering of this (obviously metaphorical) expression as "the bitterness of dry thorns". A similarly metaphorical meaning attaches to the expression "a boiling spring" in verse 5, which recalls the term *ḥamīm* so often mentioned in the Qurᵓān (see note 62 on the last sentence of 6 : 70).

Countless springs[3] will flow therein, ‹12› [and] there will be thrones [of happiness] raised high,[4] ‹13› and goblets placed ready, ‹14› and cushions ranged, ‹15› and carpets spread out. . . . ‹16›

DO, THEN, they [who deny resurrection] never gaze at the clouds pregnant with water, [and observe] how they are created?[5] ‹17›
And at the sky, how it is raised aloft? ‹18›
And at the mountains, how firmly they are reared? ‹19›
And at the earth, how it is spread out? ‹20›
And so, [O Prophet,] exhort them; thy task is only to exhort: ‹21› thou canst not compel them [to believe].[6] ‹22›
However, as for him who turns away, being bent on denying the truth, ‹23› him will God cause to suffer the greatest suffering [in the life to come]: ‹24› for, behold, unto Us will be their return, ‹25› and, verily, it is for Us to call them to account. ‹26›

فِيهَا عَيْنٌ جَارِيَةٌ (12) فِيهَا سُرُرٌ مَّرْفُوعَةٌ (13) وَأَكْوَابٌ مَّوْضُوعَةٌ (14)
وَنَمَارِقُ مَصْفُوفَةٌ (15) وَزَرَابِيُّ مَبْثُوثَةٌ (16) أَفَلَا يَنظُرُونَ إِلَى ٱلْإِبِلِ
كَيْفَ خُلِقَتْ (17) وَإِلَى ٱلسَّمَآءِ كَيْفَ رُفِعَتْ (18) وَإِلَى ٱلْجِبَالِ
كَيْفَ نُصِبَتْ (19) وَإِلَى ٱلْأَرْضِ كَيْفَ سُطِحَتْ (20) فَذَكِّرْ إِنَّمَآ
أَنتَ مُذَكِّرٌ (21) لَّسْتَ عَلَيْهِم بِمُصَيْطِرٍ (22) إِلَّا مَن تَوَلَّىٰ وَكَفَرَ (23)
فَيُعَذِّبُهُ ٱللَّهُ ٱلْعَذَابَ ٱلْأَكْبَرَ (24) إِنَّ إِلَيْنَآ إِيَابَهُمْ (25) ثُمَّ إِنَّ عَلَيْنَا
حِسَابَهُم (26)

Fīhā ʿaynuñ-jāriyah. (12) Fīhā sururum-marfūʿah. (13) Wa ʾakwābum-mawḍūʿah. (14) Wa namāriqu maṣfūfah. (15) Wa zarābiyyu mabthūthah. (16) ʾAfalā yañẓurūna ʾilal-ʾibili kayfa khuliqat. (17) Wa ʾilas-samāaʾi kayfa rufiʿat. (18) Wa ʾilal-jibāli kayfa nuṣibat. (19) Wa ʾilal-ʾarḍi kayfa suṭiḥat. (20) Fadhakkir ʾinnamāa ʾañta mudhakkir. (21) Lasta ʿalayhim bimuṣayṭir. (22) ʾIllā mañ-tawallā wa kafar. (23) Fayuʿadhdhibuhul-lāhul-ʿadhābal-ʾakbar. (24) ʾInna ʾilaynāa ʾiyābahum. (25) Thumma ʾinna ʿalaynā ḥisābahum. (26)

3 Lit., "a spring" – but, as Zamakhsharī and Ibn Kathīr point out, the singular form has here a *generic* import, implying "a multitude of springs". This metaphor of the life-giving element is analogous to that of the "running waters" (*anhār*) frequently mentioned in Qurʾanic descriptions of paradise.

4 See note 34 on 15 : 47.

5 Implying that a denial of resurrection and life in the hereafter renders the concept of a conscious Creator utterly meaningless; hence my interpolation of the words "who deny resurrection" in the first part of this verse. – As regards the noun *ibil*, it denotes, as a rule, "camels": a generic plural which has no singular form. But one must remember that it also signifies "clouds bearing rain-water" (*Lisān al-ʿArab, Qāmūs, Tāj al-ʿArūs*) – a meaning which is preferable in the present context. If the term were used in the sense of "camels", the reference to it in the above verse would have been primarily – if not exclusively – addressed to the Arabian contemporaries of the Prophet, to whom the camel was always an object of admiration on account of its outstanding endurance, the many uses to which it could be put (riding, load-bearing, and as a source of milk, flesh and fine wool) and its indispensability to people living amid deserts. But precisely because a reference to "camels" would restrict its significance to people of a particular environment and a particular time (without even the benefit of a historical allusion to past events), it must be ruled out here, for the Qurʾanic appeals to observe the wonders of the God-created universe are invariably directed at people of all times and all environments. Hence, there is every reason to assume that the term *ibil* relates here not to camels but to "clouds pregnant with water": the more so as such an allusion to the miraculous, cyclic process of the evaporation of water, the skyward ascension of vapour, its condensation and, finally, its precipitation over the earth is definitely more in tune with the subsequent mention (in verses 18-20) of sky, mountains and earth, than would be a reference to "camels", however admirable and noteworthy these animals may be.

6 Lit., "thou hast no power over them".

The Eighty-Ninth Sūrah

Al-Fajr (The Daybreak)

Mecca Period

THE DESIGNATION of this *sūrah* – the tenth in the order of revelation – is based on the mention of "the daybreak" in the first verse.

سورة الفجر مكية -89-
وآياتها ثلاثون

IN THE NAME OF GOD, THE MOST GRACIOUS, THE DISPENSER OF GRACE:

بِسْمِ ٱللَّهِ ٱلرَّحْمَٰنِ ٱلرَّحِيمِ

CONSIDER the daybreak ‹1› and the ten nights![1] ‹2›
Consider the multiple and the One![2] ‹3›
Consider the night as it runs its course![3] ‹4›
Considering all this – could there be, to anyone endowed with reason, a [more] solemn evidence of the truth?[4] ‹5›

وَٱلْفَجْرِ ﴿١﴾ وَلَيَالٍ عَشْرٍ ﴿٢﴾ وَٱلشَّفْعِ وَٱلْوَتْرِ ﴿٣﴾ وَٱلَّيْلِ إِذَا
يَسْرِ ﴿٤﴾ هَلْ فِى ذَٰلِكَ قَسَمٌ لِّذِى حِجْرٍ ﴿٥﴾

Bismil-lāhir-Raḥmānir-Raḥīm.
Wal-fajr. (1) Wa layālin ᶜashr. (2) Wash-shafᶜi wal-watr. (3) Wal-layli ᵓidhā yasr. (4) Hal fī dhālika qasa-mul-lidhī ḥijr. (5)

---

1 The "daybreak" (*fajr*) apparently symbolizes man's spiritual awakening; hence, the "ten nights" is an allusion to the last third of the month of Ramaḍān, in the year 13 before the *hijrah*, during which Muḥammad received his first revelation (see introductory note to *sūrah* 96) and was thus enabled to contribute to mankind's spiritual awakening.

2 Lit., "the even and the odd" or "the one": i.e., the multiplicity of creation as contrasted with the oneness and uniqueness of the Creator (Baghawī, on the authority of Saᶜīd ibn al-Khudrī, as well as Ṭabarī in one of his alternative interpretations of the above phrase). The concept of the "even number" implies the existence of *more than one* of the same kind: in other words, it signifies every thing that has a counterpart or counterparts and, hence, a definite relationship with other things (cf. the term *azwāj* in 36 : 36, referring to the polarity evident in all creation). As against this, the term *al-watr* – or, in the more common (Najdī) spelling, *al-witr* – primarily denotes "that which is single" or "one" and is, hence, one of the designations given to God – since "there is nothing that could be compared with Him" (112 : 4) and "nothing like unto Him" (42 : 11).

3 An allusion to the night of spiritual darkness which is bound to "run its course" – i.e., to disappear – as soon as man becomes truly conscious of God.

4 Lit., "a [more] solemn affirmation" (*qasam*): i.e., a convincing evidence of the existence and oneness of God.

ART THOU NOT aware of how thy Sustainer has dealt with [the tribe of] ʿĀd,[5] ‹6› [the people of] Iram the many-pillared, ‹7› the like of whom has never been reared in all the land? ‹8› – and with [the tribe of] Thamūd,[6] who hollowed out rocks in the valley? ‹9› – and with Pharaoh of the [many] tent-poles?[7] ‹10›
[It was they] who transgressed all bounds of equity all over their lands, ‹11› and brought about great corruption therein: ‹12› and therefore thy Sustainer let loose upon them a scourge of suffering: ‹13› for, verily, thy Sustainer is ever on the watch! ‹14›

أَلَمْ تَرَ كَيْفَ فَعَلَ رَبُّكَ بِعَادٍ ﴿٦﴾ إِرَمَ ذَاتِ ٱلْعِمَادِ ﴿٧﴾ ٱلَّتِى لَمْ يُخْلَقْ
مِثْلُهَا فِى ٱلْبِلَٰدِ ﴿٨﴾ وَثَمُودَ ٱلَّذِينَ جَابُوا۟ ٱلصَّخْرَ بِٱلْوَادِ ﴿٩﴾ وَفِرْعَوْنَ
ذِى ٱلْأَوْتَادِ ﴿١٠﴾ ٱلَّذِينَ طَغَوْا۟ فِى ٱلْبِلَٰدِ ﴿١١﴾ فَأَكْثَرُوا۟ فِيهَا ٱلْفَسَادَ ﴿١٢﴾
فَصَبَّ عَلَيْهِمْ رَبُّكَ سَوْطَ عَذَابٍ ﴿١٣﴾ إِنَّ رَبَّكَ لَبِٱلْمِرْصَادِ ﴿١٤﴾ فَأَمَّا
ٱلْإِنسَٰنُ إِذَا مَا ٱبْتَلَىٰهُ رَبُّهُۥ فَأَكْرَمَهُۥ وَنَعَّمَهُۥ فَيَقُولُ رَبِّىٓ أَكْرَمَنِ ﴿١٥﴾
وَأَمَّآ إِذَا مَا ٱبْتَلَىٰهُ فَقَدَرَ عَلَيْهِ رِزْقَهُۥ فَيَقُولُ رَبِّىٓ أَهَٰنَنِ ﴿١٦﴾ كَلَّا ۖ بَل
لَّا تُكْرِمُونَ ٱلْيَتِيمَ ﴿١٧﴾ وَلَا تَحَٰٓضُّونَ عَلَىٰ طَعَامِ ٱلْمِسْكِينِ ﴿١٨﴾ وَتَأْكُلُونَ
ٱلتُّرَاثَ أَكْلًا لَّمًّا ﴿١٩﴾ وَتُحِبُّونَ ٱلْمَالَ حُبًّا جَمًّا ﴿٢٠﴾

BUT AS FOR man,[8] whenever his Sustainer tries him by His generosity and by letting him enjoy a life of ease, he says, "My Sustainer has been [justly] generous towards me";[9] ‹15› whereas, whenever He tries him by straitening his means of livelihood, he says, "My Sustainer has disgraced me!"[10] ‹16›
But nay, nay, [O men, consider all that you do and fail to do:] you are not generous towards the orphan, ‹17› and you do not urge one another to feed the needy,[11] ‹18› and you devour the inheritance [of others] with devouring greed, ‹19› and you love wealth with boundless love! ‹20›

ʾAlam tara kayfa faʿala Rabbuka biʿĀd. (6) ʾIrama dhātil-ʿimād. (7) ʾAllatī lam yukhlaq mithluhā fil-bilād. (8) Wa Thamūdal-ladhīna jābuṣ-ṣakhra bilwād. (9) Wa Firʿawna dhil-ʾawtād. (10) ʾAlladhīna ṭaghaw fil-bilād. (11) Faʾaktharū fīhal-fasād. (12) Faṣabba ʿalayhim Rabbuka sawṭa ʿadhāb. (13) ʾInna Rabbaka labilmirṣād. (14) Faʾammal-ʾIñsānu ʾidhā mab-talāhu Rabbuhū faʾakramahū wa naʿʿamahū fayaqūlu Rabbīi ʾakraman. (15) Wa ʾammāa ʾidhā mab-talāhu faqadara ʿalayhi rizqahu fayaqūlu Rabbīi ʾahānan. (16) Kallā bal lā tukrimūnal-yatīm. (17) Wa lā taḥāaḍḍūna ʿalā ṭaʿāmil-miskīn. (18) Wa taʾkulūnat-turātha ʾaklal-lammā. (19) Wa tuḥibbūnal-māla ḥubbañ-jammā. (20)

5 See 7 : 65-72, and particularly the second half of note 48 on 7 : 65. Iram, mentioned in the next verse, seems to have been the name of their legendary capital, now covered by the sands of the desert of Al-Aḥqāf.

6 See *sūrah* 7, notes 56 and 59. The "valley" referred to in the sequence is the Wādi 'l-Qurā, situated north of Medina on the ancient caravan route from South Arabia to Syria.

7 For an explanation of this epithet, see *sūrah* 38, note 17.

8 The above phrase, introduced by the particle *fa-ammā* ("But as for . . ."), obviously connects with the reference to the "solemn evidence of the truth" in verse 5 – implying that man does not, as a rule, bethink himself of the hereafter, being concerned only with this world and what promises to be of immediate advantage to him (Zamakhsharī, Rāzī, Bayḍawī).

9 I.e., he regards God's bounty as something *due* to him (Rāzī).

10 I.e., he regards the absence or loss of affluence not as a trial, but as an evidence of divine "injustice" – which, in its turn, may lead to a denial of God's existence.

11 I.e., "you *feel* no urge to feed the needy" (cf. 107 : 3).

Nay, but [how will you fare on Judgment Day,] when the earth is crushed with crushing upon crushing, ‹21› and [the majesty of] thy Sustainer stands revealed,[12] as well as [the true nature of] the angels, rank upon rank? ‹22›

And on that Day hell will be brought [within sight]; on that Day man will remember [all that he did and failed to do]: but what will that remembrance avail him? ‹23›

He will say, "Oh, would that I had provided beforehand for my life [to come]!" ‹24›

For, none can make suffer as He will make suffer [the sinners] on that Day, ‹25› and none can bind with bonds like His.[13] ‹26›

[But unto the righteous God will say,] "O thou human being that hast attained to inner peace! ‹27› Return thou unto thy Sustainer, well-pleased [and] pleasing [Him]: ‹28› enter, then, together with My [other true] servants ‹29› – yea, enter thou My paradise!" ‹30›

كَلَّآ إِذَا دُكَّتِ ٱلْأَرْضُ دَكًّا دَكًّا ﴿٢١﴾ وَجَآءَ رَبُّكَ وَٱلْمَلَكُ صَفًّا
صَفًّا ﴿٢٢﴾ وَجِاْىٓءَ يَوْمَئِذٍۭ بِجَهَنَّمَ ۚ يَوْمَئِذٍ يَتَذَكَّرُ ٱلْإِنسَـٰنُ وَأَنَّىٰ لَهُ
ٱلذِّكْرَىٰ ﴿٢٣﴾ يَقُولُ يَـٰلَيْتَنِى قَدَّمْتُ لِحَيَاتِى ﴿٢٤﴾ فَيَوْمَئِذٍ لَّا يُعَذِّبُ
عَذَابَهُۥٓ أَحَدٌ ﴿٢٥﴾ وَلَا يُوثِقُ وَثَاقَهُۥٓ أَحَدٌ ﴿٢٦﴾ يَـٰٓأَيَّتُهَا ٱلنَّفْسُ ٱلْمُطْمَئِنَّةُ ﴿٢٧﴾
ٱرْجِعِىٓ إِلَىٰ رَبِّكِ رَاضِيَةً مَّرْضِيَّةً ﴿٢٨﴾ فَٱدْخُلِى فِى عِبَـٰدِى ﴿٢٩﴾ وَٱدْخُلِى
جَنَّتِى ﴿٣٠﴾

Kallāa ʾidhā dukkatil-ʾarḍu dakkañ-dakkā. (21) Wa jāaʾa Rabbuka wal-Malaku ṣaffañ-ṣaffā. (22) Wa jīiʾa Yawmaʾidhim-bijahannam. Yawmaʾidhiñy-yatadhakkarul-ʾIñsānu wa ʾannā lahudh-dhikrā. (23) Yaqūlu yā laytanī qaddamtu liḥayātī. (24) Fa Yawmaʾidhil-lā yuʿadhdhibu ʿadhābahūu ʾaḥad. (25) Wa lā yūthiqu wathāqahūu ʾaḥad. (26) Yāa ʾayyatuhan-nafsul-muṭmaʾinnah. (27) ʾIrjiʿīi ʾilā Rabbiki rāḍiyatam-marḍiyyah. (28) Fadkhulī fī ʿibādī. (29) Wad-khulī jannatī. (30)

12 Lit., "[when] thy Sustainer comes", which almost all of the classical commentators understand as the revelation (in the abstract sense of this word) of God's transcendental majesty and the manifestation of His judgment.

13 See note 7 on 73 : 12-13.

The Ninetieth Sūrah

Al-Balad (The Land)

Mecca Period

ALTHOUGH Suyūṭī places this *sūrah* in the middle of the Mecca period (after *sūrah* 50), it is most probable that it belongs to the earliest years of Muḥammad's prophethood.

سورة البلد مكية -٩٠-
وآياتها عشرون

IN THE NAME OF GOD, THE MOST GRACIOUS, THE DISPENSER OF GRACE:

NAY! I call to witness this land ‹1› – this land in which thou art free to dwell[1] ‹2› – and [I call to witness] parent and offspring:[2] ‹3›
Verily, We have created man into [a life of] pain, toil and trial.[3] ‹4›
Does he, then, think that no one has power over him? ‹5›

بِسْمِ ٱللَّهِ ٱلرَّحْمَٰنِ ٱلرَّحِيمِ

لَآ أُقْسِمُ بِهَٰذَا ٱلْبَلَدِ ﴿١﴾ وَأَنتَ حِلٌّۢ بِهَٰذَا ٱلْبَلَدِ ﴿٢﴾ وَوَالِدٍ وَمَا
وَلَدَ ﴿٣﴾ لَقَدْ خَلَقْنَا ٱلْإِنسَٰنَ فِى كَبَدٍ ﴿٤﴾ أَيَحْسَبُ أَن لَّن يَقْدِرَ عَلَيْهِ
أَحَدٌ ﴿٥﴾

ربع الحزب

Bismil-lāhir-Raḥmānir-Raḥīm.
Lāa ʾuqsimu bihādhal-balad. (1) Wa ʾan̄ta ḥillum-
bihādhal-balad. (2) Wa wālidin̄w-wa mā walad. (3)
Laqad khalaqnal-ʾIn̄sāna fī kabad. (4) ʾAyaḥsabu
ʾal-lan̄y-yaqdira ʿalayhi ʾaḥad. (5)

---

1 Lit., "while thou art dwelling in this land". The classical commentators give to the term *balad* the connotation of "city", and maintain that the phrase *hadha 'l-balad* ("this city") signifies Mecca, and that the pronoun "thou" in the second verse refers to Muḥammad. Although this interpretation is plausible in view of the fact that the sacredness of Mecca is repeatedly stressed in the Qurʾān, the sequence – as well as the tenor of the whole *sūrah* – seems to warrant a wider, more general interpretation. In my opinion, the words *hadha 'l-balad* denote "this land of *man*", i.e., the earth (which latter term is, according to all philologists, one of the primary meanings of *balad*). Consequently, the "thou" in verse 2 relates to man in general, and that which is metaphorically "called to witness" is his earthly environment.

2 Lit., "the begetter and that which he has begotten". According to Ṭabarī's convincing explanation, this phrase signifies "every parent and all their offspring" – i.e., the human race from its beginning to its end. (The masculine form *al-wālid* denotes, of course, both male and female parents.)

3 The term *kabad*, comprising the concepts of "pain", "distress", "hardship", "toil", "trial", etc., can be rendered only by a compound expression like the one above.

He boasts, "I have spent wealth abundant!"[4] ‹6›
Does he, then, think that no one sees him?[5] ‹7›
Have We not given him two eyes, ‹8› and a tongue, and a pair of lips,[6] ‹9› and shown him the two highways [of good and evil]? ‹10›
But he would not try to ascend the steep uphill road. . . . ‹11›
And what could make thee conceive what it is, that steep uphill road? ‹12›
[It is] the freeing of one's neck [from the burden of sin],[7] ‹13› or the feeding, upon a day of [one's own] hunger, ‹14› of an orphan near of kin, ‹15› or of a needy [stranger] lying in the dust ‹16› – and being, withal, of those who have attained to faith, and who enjoin upon one another patience in adversity, and enjoin upon one another compassion. ‹17›
Such are they that have attained to righteousness;[8] ‹18› whereas those who are bent on denying the truth of Our messages – they are such as have lost themselves in evil, ‹19› [with] fire closing in upon them.[9] ‹20›

يَقُولُ أَهْلَكْتُ مَالًا لُّبَدًا ﴿6﴾ أَيَحْسَبُ أَن لَّمْ يَرَهُۥٓ أَحَدٌ ﴿7﴾ أَلَمْ
نَجْعَل لَّهُۥ عَيْنَيْنِ ﴿8﴾ وَلِسَانًا وَشَفَتَيْنِ ﴿9﴾ وَهَدَيْنَٰهُ ٱلنَّجْدَيْنِ ﴿10﴾
فَلَا ٱقْتَحَمَ ٱلْعَقَبَةَ ﴿11﴾ وَمَآ أَدْرَىٰكَ مَا ٱلْعَقَبَةُ ﴿12﴾ فَكُّ رَقَبَةٍ ﴿13﴾ أَوْ
إِطْعَٰمٌ فِى يَوْمٍ ذِى مَسْغَبَةٍ ﴿14﴾ يَتِيمًا ذَا مَقْرَبَةٍ ﴿15﴾ أَوْ مِسْكِينًا ذَا
مَتْرَبَةٍ ﴿16﴾ ثُمَّ كَانَ مِنَ ٱلَّذِينَ ءَامَنُوا۟ وَتَوَاصَوْا۟ بِٱلصَّبْرِ وَتَوَاصَوْا۟
بِٱلْمَرْحَمَةِ ﴿17﴾ أُو۟لَٰٓئِكَ أَصْحَٰبُ ٱلْمَيْمَنَةِ ﴿18﴾ وَٱلَّذِينَ كَفَرُوا۟ بِـَٔايَٰتِنَا
هُمْ أَصْحَٰبُ ٱلْمَشْـَٔمَةِ ﴿19﴾ عَلَيْهِمْ نَارٌ مُّؤْصَدَةٌۢ ﴿20﴾

Yaqūlu ʾahlaktu mālal-lubadā. (6) ʾAyaḥsabu ʾal-lam yarahūu ʾaḥad. (7) ʾAlam najʿal lahū ʿaynayn. (8) Wa lisānañw-wa shafatayn. (9) Wa hadaynāhun-najdayn. (10) Falaq-taḥamal-ʿaqabah. (11) Wa māa ʾadrāka mal-ʿaqabah. (12) Fakku raqabah. (13) ʾAw ʾiṭʿāmuñ-fī yawmiñ-dhī masghabah. (14) Yatīmañ-dhā maqrabah. (15) ʾAw miskīnañ-dhā matrabah. (16) Thumma kāna minal-ladhīna ʾāmanū wa tawāṣaw bißṣabri wa tawāṣaw bilmarḥamah. (17) ʾUlāaʾika ʾaṣḥābul-maymanah. (18) Wal-ladhīna kafarū biʾĀyātinā hum ʾaṣḥābul-mashʾamah. (19) ʿAlayhim nārum-muʾṣadah. (20)

4 Implying that his resources – and, therefore, his possibilities – are inexhaustible. We must remember that the term "man" is used here in the sense of "human race": hence, the above boast is a metonym for the widespread belief – characteristic of all periods of religious decadence – that there are no limits to the power to which man may aspire, and that, therefore, his worldly "interests" are the only criteria of right and wrong.

5 I.e., "Does he think that he is responsible to none but himself?"

6 I.e., to recognize and to voice the truth of God's existence or, at least, to ask for guidance.

7 Thus ʿIkrimah, as quoted by Baghawī; also Rāzī. Alternatively, the phrase *fakk raqabah* may be rendered as "the freeing of a human being from bondage" (cf. note 146 on 2 : 177), with the latter term covering all those forms of subjugation and exploitation – social, economic or political – which can be rightly described as "slavery".

8 Lit., "people (*aṣḥāb*) of the right side": see note 25 on 74 : 39.

9 I.e., the fires of despair in the life to come "rising over the [sinners'] hearts" and "closing in upon them": cf. 104 : 6-8 and the corresponding note 5. The phrase rendered by me as "such as have lost themselves in evil" reads, literally, "people of the left side (*al-mashʾamah*)".

The Ninety-First Sūrah

Ash-Shams (The Sun)

Mecca Period

THE KEY-WORD by which this *sūrah* has always been identified occurs in its first verse. It is generally assumed that it was revealed shortly after *sūrah* 97 (*Al-Qadr*).

سورة الشمس مكية
-91-
وآياتها خمس عشرة

IN THE NAME OF GOD, THE MOST GRACIOUS, THE DISPENSER OF GRACE:

CONSIDER the sun and its radiant brightness, ‹1› and the moon as it reflects the sun![1] ‹2›
Consider the day as it reveals the world,[2] ‹3› and the night as it veils it darkly! ‹4›
Consider the sky and its wondrous make,[3] ‹5› and the earth and all its expanse! ‹6›

بِسْمِ اللَّهِ الرَّحْمَٰنِ الرَّحِيمِ

وَالشَّمْسِ وَضُحَاهَا ﴿١﴾ وَالْقَمَرِ إِذَا تَلَاهَا ﴿٢﴾ وَالنَّهَارِ إِذَا جَلَّاهَا ﴿٣﴾
وَاللَّيْلِ إِذَا يَغْشَاهَا ﴿٤﴾ وَالسَّمَاءِ وَمَا بَنَاهَا ﴿٥﴾ وَالْأَرْضِ وَمَا
طَحَاهَا ﴿٦﴾

Bismil-lāhir-Raḥmānir-Raḥīm.
Wash-shamsi wa ḍuḥāhā. ‹1› Wal-qamari ᵓidhā talāhā. ‹2› Wan-nahāri ᵓidhā jallāhā. ‹3› Wal-layli ᵓidhā yaghshāhā. ‹4› Was-samāaᵓi wa mā banāhā. ‹5› Wal-ᵓarḍi wa mā ṭaḥāhā. ‹6›

---

1 Lit., "as it follows it (*talāhā*)", i.e., the sun. According to the great philologist Al-Farrāᵓ, who lived in the second century after the *hijrah*, "the meaning is that the moon derives its light from the sun" (quoted by Rāzī). This is also Rāghib's interpretation of the above phrase.

2 Lit., "it" – a pronoun apparently indicating "the world" or "the earth" (Zamakhsharī). It is to be noted that verses 1-10 stress the polarity – both physical and spiritual – inherent in all creation and contrasting with the oneness and uniqueness of the Creator.

3 Lit., "and that which has built it" – i.e., the wondrous qualities which are responsible for the harmony and coherence of the visible cosmos (which is evidently the meaning of the term *samāᵓ* in this context). Similarly, the subsequent reference to the earth, which reads literally, "that which has spread it out", is apparently an allusion to the qualities responsible for the beauty and variety of its expanse.

Consider the human self,[4] and how it is formed in accordance with what it is meant to be,[5] ‹7› and how it is imbued with moral failings as well as with consciousness of God![6] ‹8›
To a happy state shall indeed attain he who causes this [self] to grow in purity, ‹9› and truly lost is he who buries it [in darkness]. ‹10›

وَنَفْسٍ وَمَا سَوَّىٰهَا ﴿٧﴾ فَأَلْهَمَهَا فُجُورَهَا وَتَقْوَىٰهَا ﴿٨﴾ قَدْ أَفْلَحَ مَن
زَكَّىٰهَا ﴿٩﴾ وَقَدْ خَابَ مَن دَسَّىٰهَا ﴿١٠﴾ كَذَّبَتْ ثَمُودُ بِطَغْوَىٰهَآ ﴿١١﴾ إِذِ
ٱنۢبَعَثَ أَشْقَىٰهَا ﴿١٢﴾ فَقَالَ لَهُمْ رَسُولُ ٱللَّهِ نَاقَةَ ٱللَّهِ وَسُقْيَـٰهَا ﴿١٣﴾
فَكَذَّبُوهُ فَعَقَرُوهَا فَدَمْدَمَ عَلَيْهِمْ رَبُّهُم بِذَنۢبِهِمْ فَسَوَّىٰهَا ﴿١٤﴾ وَلَا يَخَافُ
عُقْبَـٰهَا ﴿١٥﴾

TO [THIS] TRUTH gave the lie, in their overweening arrogance, [the tribe of] Thamūd,[7] ‹11› when that most hapless wretch from among them rushed forward [to commit his evil deed], ‹12› although God's apostle had told them, "It is a she-camel belonging to God, so let her drink [and do her no harm]!"[8] ‹13›
But they gave him the lie, and cruelly slaughtered her[9] – whereupon their Sustainer visited them with utter destruction for this their sin, destroying them all alike: ‹14› for none [of them] had any fear of what might befall them.[10] ‹15›

Wa nafsiñw-wa mā sawwāhā. (7) Faʾalhamahā fujūrahā wa taqwāhā. (8) Qad ʾaflaḥa mañ-zakkāhā. (9) Wa qad khāba mañ-dassāhā. (10) Kadhdhabat Thamūdu biṭaghwāhā. (11) ʾIdhim-baʿatha ʾashqāhā. (12) Faqāla lahum Rasūlul-lāhi nāqatal-lāhi wa suqyāhā. (13) Fakadhdhabūhu faʿaqarūhā fadamdama ʿalayhim Rabbuhum bidhambihim fasawwāhā. (14) Wa lā yakhāfu ʿuqbāhā. (15)

4 As in so many other instances, the term *nafs*, which has a very wide range of meanings (see first sentence of note 1 on 4 : 1), denotes here the human self or personality as a whole: that is, a being composed of a physical body and that inexplicable life-essence loosely described as "soul".

5 Lit., "and that which has made [or "formed"] it (*sawwāhā*) in accordance with . . .", etc. For this particular connotation of the verb *sawwā*, see note 1 on 87 : 2, which represents the oldest Qurʾanic instance of its use in the above sense. The reference to man and that which constitutes the "human personality", as well as the implied allusion to the extremely complex phenomenon of a life-entity in which bodily needs and urges, emotions and intellectual activities are so closely intertwined as to be indissoluble, follows organically upon a call to consider the inexplicable grandeur of the universe – so far as it is perceptible and comprehensible to man – as a compelling evidence of God's creative power.

6 Lit., "and [consider] that which has inspired it with its immoral doings (*fujūrahā*) and its God-consciousness (*taqwāhā*)" – i.e., the fact that man is equally liable to rise to great spiritual heights as to fall into utter immorality is an essential characteristic of human nature as such. In its deepest sense, man's ability to act wrongly is a concomitant to his ability to act rightly: in other words, it is this inherent polarity of tendencies which gives to every "right" choice a value and, thus, endows man with moral free will (cf. in this connection note 16 on 7 : 24-25).

7 For the story of the tribe of Thamūd, given here as an illustration of man's potential wickedness, see 7 : 73-79 and the corresponding notes.

8 Regarding this "she-camel belonging to God", see *sūrah* 7, note 57. For the particular reference to the injunction, "Let her drink", see 26 : 155 and the corresponding note 67. The formulation of this passage shows that the legend of the she-camel was well known in pre-Islamic Arabia.

9 For this rendering of *ʿaqarūhā*, see note 61 on 7 : 77.

10 Implying that their total lack of compassion for God's creatures showed that they did not fear His retribution and, hence, did not really believe in Him.

The Ninety-Second Sūrah

Al-Layl (The Night)

Mecca Period

UNANIMOUSLY regarded as one of the very early revelations – most probably the ninth in the chronological order – the *sūrah* derives its name from the mention of "the night" in the first verse.

سورة الليل مكية -92- وآياتها إحدى وعشرون

IN THE NAME OF GOD, THE MOST GRACIOUS, THE DISPENSER OF GRACE:

CONSIDER the night as it veils [the earth] in darkness, ‹1› and the day as it rises bright! ‹2›
Consider the creation of the male and the female![1] ‹3›
Verily, [O men,] you aim at most divergent ends ![2] ‹4›
Thus, as for him who gives [to others] and is conscious of God, ‹5› and believes in the truth of the ultimate good[3] ‹6› – for him shall We make easy the path towards [ultimate] ease.[4] ‹7›
But as for him who is niggardly, and thinks that he is self-sufficient,[5] ‹8›

بِسۡمِ ٱللَّهِ ٱلرَّحۡمَٰنِ ٱلرَّحِيمِ

وَٱلَّيۡلِ إِذَا يَغۡشَىٰ ١ وَٱلنَّهَارِ إِذَا تَجَلَّىٰ ٢ وَمَا خَلَقَ ٱلذَّكَرَ
وَٱلۡأُنثَىٰٓ ٣ إِنَّ سَعۡيَكُمۡ لَشَتَّىٰ ٤ فَأَمَّا مَنۡ أَعۡطَىٰ وَٱتَّقَىٰ ٥
وَصَدَّقَ بِٱلۡحُسۡنَىٰ ٦ فَسَنُيَسِّرُهُۥ لِلۡيُسۡرَىٰ ٧ وَأَمَّا مَنۢ بَخِلَ
وَٱسۡتَغۡنَىٰ ٨

Bismil-lāhir-Raḥmānir-Raḥīm.
Wal-layli ʾidhā yaghshā. (1) Wan-nahāri ʾidhā tajal-
lā. (2) Wa mā khalaqadh-dhakara wal-ʾunthā. (3)
ʾInna saʿyakum lashattā. (4) Faʾammā man ʾaʿṭā
wat-taqā. (5) Wa ṣaddaqa bilḥusnā. (6) Fasanuyas-
siruhū lilyusrā. (7) Wa ʾammā mam-bakhila was-
taghnā. (8)

---

1 Lit., "Consider that which has created [or "creates"] the male and the female", i.e., the elements which are responsible for the *differentiation* between male and female. This, together with the symbolism of night and day, darkness and light, is an allusion – similar to the first ten verses of the preceding *sūrah* – to the polarity evident in all nature and, hence, to the dichotomy (spoken of in the next verse) which characterizes man's aims and motives.

2 I.e., at good and bad ends (cf. note 6 on 91 : 8) – sc., "and so the *consequences* of your doings are, of necessity, divergent".

3 I.e., in moral values independent of time and social circumstance and, hence, in the absolute validity of what may be described as "the moral imperative".

4 See note 6 on 87 : 8.

5 Cf. 96 : 6-7.

and calls the ultimate good a lie ‹9› – for him shall We make easy the path towards hardship: ‹10› and what will his wealth avail him when he goes down [to his grave]?[6] ‹11›

BEHOLD, it is indeed for Us to grace [you] with guidance; ‹12› and, behold, Ours is [the dominion over] the life to come as well as [over] this earlier part [of your life]:[7] ‹13›
and so I warn you of the raging fire ‹14› – [the fire] which none shall have to endure but that most hapless wretch ‹15› who gives the lie to the truth and turns away [from it]. ‹16›
For, distant from it shall remain he who is truly conscious of God: ‹17› he that spends his possessions [on others] so that he might grow in purity ‹18› – not as payment for favours received,[8] ‹19› but only out of a longing for the countenance of his Sustainer, the All-Highest: ‹20› and such, indeed, shall in time be well-pleased. ‹21›

وَكَذَّبَ بِٱلْحُسْنَىٰ ﴿9﴾ فَسَنُيَسِّرُهُۥ لِلْعُسْرَىٰ ﴿10﴾ وَمَا يُغْنِى عَنْهُ مَالُهُۥٓ
إِذَا تَرَدَّىٰٓ ﴿11﴾ إِنَّ عَلَيْنَا لَلْهُدَىٰ ﴿12﴾ وَإِنَّ لَنَا لَلْءَاخِرَةَ وَٱلْأُولَىٰ ﴿13﴾
فَأَنذَرْتُكُمْ نَارًا تَلَظَّىٰ ﴿14﴾ لَا يَصْلَىٰهَآ إِلَّا ٱلْأَشْقَى ﴿15﴾ ٱلَّذِى كَذَّبَ
وَتَوَلَّىٰ ﴿16﴾ وَسَيُجَنَّبُهَا ٱلْأَتْقَى ﴿17﴾ ٱلَّذِى يُؤْتِى مَالَهُۥ يَتَزَكَّىٰ ﴿18﴾ وَمَا
لِأَحَدٍ عِندَهُۥ مِن نِّعْمَةٍ تُجْزَىٰٓ ﴿19﴾ إِلَّا ٱبْتِغَآءَ وَجْهِ رَبِّهِ ٱلْأَعْلَىٰ ﴿20﴾
وَلَسَوْفَ يَرْضَىٰ ﴿21﴾

Wa kadhdhaba bilḥusnā. ﴿9﴾ Fasanuyassiruhū lil-
ᶜusrā. ﴿10﴾ Wa mā yughnī ᶜanhu māluhūu ʾidhā ta-
raddā. ﴿11﴾ ʾInna ᶜalaynā lalhudā. ﴿12﴾ Wa ʾinna lanā
lalʾĀkhirata wal-ʾūlā. ﴿13﴾ Faʾan̄dhartukum nāran̄-
talaẓẓā. ﴿14﴾ Lā yaṣlāhāa ʾillal ʾashqā. ﴿15﴾ ʾAlladhī
kadhdhaba wa tawallā. ﴿16﴾ Wa sayujannabuhal-
ʾatqā. ﴿17﴾ ʾAlladhī yuʾtī mālahū yatazakkā. ﴿18﴾ Wa
mā liʾaḥadin ᶜin̄dahū min̄-niᶜmatin̄-tujzā. ﴿19﴾ ʾIllab-
tighāaʾa wajhi Rabbihil-ʾAᶜlā. ﴿20﴾ Wa lasawfa
yarḍā. ﴿21﴾

6 Or (as a statement): "of no avail will be to him his wealth when he. . .", etc.

7 This statement is meant to stress the fact that man's life in this world and in the hereafter are but two stages of one continuous entity.

8 Lit., "no one having with him any favour to be repaid". In its widest sense, projected towards the future, the phrase implies also the *expectation* of a reward.

The Ninety-Third Sūrah

Aḍ-Ḍuḥā (The Bright Morning Hours)

Mecca Period

IT IS SAID that after *sūrah* 89 (*Al-Fajr*) was revealed, some time elapsed during which the Prophet did not receive any revelation, and that his opponents in Mecca taunted him on this score, saying, "Thy God has forsaken and scorned thee!" – whereupon the present *sūrah* was revealed. Whether or not we accept this somewhat doubtful story, there is every reason to assume that the *sūrah* as such, although in the first instance addressed to the Prophet, has a far wider purport: it concerns – and is meant to console – every faithful man and woman suffering from the sorrows and bitter hardships which so often afflict the good and the innocent, and which sometimes cause even the righteous to question God's transcendental justice.

-93-
سورة الضحى مكية
وآياتها إحدى عشرة

IN THE NAME OF GOD, THE MOST GRACIOUS, THE DISPENSER OF GRACE:

بِسۡمِ ٱللَّهِ ٱلرَّحۡمَٰنِ ٱلرَّحِيمِ

CONSIDER the bright morning hours, ‹1›
and the night when it grows still and dark.[1] ‹2›
Thy Sustainer has not forsaken thee, nor does He scorn thee:[2] ‹3› for, indeed, the life to come will be better for thee than this earlier part [of thy life]! ‹4›
And, indeed, in time will thy Sustainer grant thee [what thy heart desires], and thou shalt be well-pleased. ‹5›

وَٱلضُّحَىٰ (1) وَٱلَّيۡلِ إِذَا سَجَىٰ (2) مَا وَدَّعَكَ رَبُّكَ وَمَا قَلَىٰ (3)
وَلَلۡأٓخِرَةُ خَيۡرٞ لَّكَ مِنَ ٱلۡأُولَىٰ (4) وَلَسَوۡفَ يُعۡطِيكَ رَبُّكَ فَتَرۡضَىٰٓ (5)

Bismil-lāhir-Raḥmānir-Raḥīm.
Waḍ-ḍuḥā. (1) **Wal-layli ᵓidhā sajā.** (2) **Mā waddaᶜaka Rabbuka wa mā qalā.** (3) **Wa lalᵓĀkhiratu khayrul-laka minal-ᵓūlā.** (4) **Wa lasawfa yuᶜṭīka Rabbuka fatarḍā.** (5)

---

1 The expression "bright morning hours" apparently symbolizes the few and widely-spaced periods of happiness in human life, as contrasted with the much greater length of "the night when it grows still and dark", i.e., the extended periods of sorrow or suffering that, as a rule, overshadow man's existence in this world (cf. 90 : 4). The further implication is that, as sure as morning follows night, God's mercy is bound to lighten every suffering, either in this world or in the life to come – for God has "willed upon Himself the law of grace and mercy" (6 : 12 and 54).

2 Se., "as the thoughtless might conclude in view of the suffering that He has willed thee to bear".

Has He not found thee an orphan, and given thee shelter?[3] ‹6›
And found thee lost on thy way, and guided thee? ‹7›
And found thee in want, and given thee sufficiency? ‹8›
Therefore, the orphan shalt thou never wrong, ‹9›
and him that seeks [thy] help shalt thou never chide,[4] ‹10›
and of thy Sustainer's blessings shalt thou [ever] speak.[5] ‹11›

أَلَمْ يَجِدْكَ يَتِيمًا فَـَٔاوَىٰ ﴿٦﴾ وَوَجَدَكَ ضَآلًّا فَهَدَىٰ ﴿٧﴾ وَوَجَدَكَ
عَآئِلًا فَأَغْنَىٰ ﴿٨﴾ فَأَمَّا ٱلْيَتِيمَ فَلَا تَقْهَرْ ﴿٩﴾ وَأَمَّا ٱلسَّآئِلَ فَلَا تَنْهَرْ ﴿١٠﴾
وَأَمَّا بِنِعْمَةِ رَبِّكَ فَحَدِّثْ ﴿١١﴾

ʾAlam yajidka yatīmañ-faʾāwā. (6) Wa wajadaka
ḍāallañ-fahadā. (7) Wa wajadaka ʿāaʾilañ-faʾaghnā.
(8) Faʾammal-yatīma falā taqhar. (9) Wa ʾammas-
sāaʾila falā tanhar. (10) Wa ʾammā biniʿmati Rabbika
faḥaddith. (11)

---

3 Possibly an allusion to the fact that Muḥammad was born a few months after his father's death, and that his mother died when he was only six years old. Apart from this, however, every human being is an "orphan" in one sense or another, inasmuch as everyone is "created in a lonely state" (cf. 6 : 94), and "will appear before Him on Resurrection Day in a lonely state" (19 : 95).

4 The term *sāʾil* denotes, literally, "one who asks", which signifies not only a "beggar" but anyone who asks for help in a difficult situation, whether physical or moral, or even for enlightenment.

5 Sc., "rather than of thy suffering".

The Ninety-Fourth Sūrah

Ash-Sharḥ (The Opening-Up of the Heart)

Mecca Period

THIS *sūrah,* revealed almost immediately after the preceding one, appears to be a direct continuation of the latter. Indeed, some renowned scholars of the first century after the *hijrah* – e.g., Ṭāʾūs ibn Kaysān, or the Caliph ᶜUmar ibn ᶜAbd al-ᶜAzīz (known as "the Second ᶜUmar") – regarded *Aḍ-Ḍuḥā* and *Ash-Sharḥ* as one *sūrah,* and used to recite them in prayer accordingly, that is, without separating the one from the other by a second invocation "In the name of God" (Rāzī). Whether this view is accepted or not, there is no doubt that the present *sūrah,* like the preceding one, is addressed in the first instance to the Prophet and, through him, to every true follower of the Qurʾān.

-94-
سورة الشرح مكية
وآياتها ثمان

نصف الحزب

IN THE NAME OF GOD, THE MOST GRACIOUS, THE DISPENSER OF GRACE:

HAVE WE NOT opened up thy heart,[1] ‹1› and lifted from thee the burden ‹2› that had weighed so heavily on thy back?[2] ‹3› And [have We not] raised thee high in dignity?[3] ‹4›
And, behold, with every hardship comes ease: ‹5› verily, with every hardship comes ease! ‹6›
Hence, when thou art freed [from distress], remain steadfast, ‹7› and unto thy Sustainer turn with love. ‹8›

بِسْمِ ٱللَّهِ ٱلرَّحْمَٰنِ ٱلرَّحِيمِ

أَلَمْ نَشْرَحْ لَكَ صَدْرَكَ ﴿١﴾ وَوَضَعْنَا عَنكَ وِزْرَكَ ﴿٢﴾ ٱلَّذِىٓ أَنقَضَ
ظَهْرَكَ ﴿٣﴾ وَرَفَعْنَا لَكَ ذِكْرَكَ ﴿٤﴾ فَإِنَّ مَعَ ٱلْعُسْرِ يُسْرًا ﴿٥﴾ إِنَّ مَعَ
ٱلْعُسْرِ يُسْرًا ﴿٦﴾ فَإِذَا فَرَغْتَ فَٱنصَبْ ﴿٧﴾ وَإِلَىٰ رَبِّكَ فَٱرْغَب ﴿٨﴾

Bismil-lāhir-Raḥmānir-Raḥīm.
ʾAlam nashraḥ laka ṣadrak. (1) Wa waḍaᶜnā ᶜañka wizrak. (2) ʾAlladhīi ʾañqaḍa ẓahrak. (3) Wa rafaᶜnā laka dhikrak. (4) Faʾinna maᶜal-ᶜusri yusrā. (5) ʾInna maᶜal-ᶜusri yusrā. (6) Faʾidhā faraghta fañṣab. (7) Wa ʾilā Rabbika farghab. (8)

---

1 Lit., "thy breast" or "bosom".

2 I.e., "the burden of thy past sins, which are now forgiven" (Ṭabarī, on the authority of Mujāhid, Qatādah, Aḍ-Ḍaḥḥāk and Ibn Zayd). In the case of Muḥammad, this relates apparently to mistakes commited before his call to prophethood (*ibid.*), and is obviously an echo of 93 : 7 – "Has He not found thee lost on thy way, and guided thee?"

3 Or: "raised high thy renown". The primary meaning of the term *dhikr* is "reminder" or "remembrance"; and, secondarily, "that *by which* something [or "someone"] is remembered", i.e., with praise: hence, it signifies "fame" or "renown", and, tropically – as in the present context – "eminence" or "dignity".

The Ninety-Fifth Sūrah

At-Tīn (The Fig)

Mecca Period

REVEALED after *sūrah* 85 ("The Great Constellations"), the present *sūrah* formulates a fundamental moral verity, stressing the fact that it is common to all true religious teachings. The "title" – or, rather, the key-word by which it is known – is derived from the mention of the fig (i.e., fig tree) in the first verse.

-95-

سورة التين مكية

وآياتها ثمان

IN THE NAME OF GOD, THE MOST GRACIOUS, THE DISPENSER OF GRACE:

بِسۡمِ ٱللَّهِ ٱلرَّحۡمَٰنِ ٱلرَّحِيمِ

CONSIDER the fig and the olive, ‹1› and Mount Sinai, ‹2› and this land secure![1] ‹3›

وَٱلتِّينِ وَٱلزَّيۡتُونِ ﴿١﴾ وَطُورِ سِينِينَ ﴿٢﴾ وَهَٰذَا ٱلۡبَلَدِ ٱلۡأَمِينِ ﴿٣﴾

Bismil-lāhir-Raḥmānir-Raḥīm.
Wat-tīni waz-zaytūn. (1) Wa Ṭūri Sīnīn. (2) Wa hādhal-baladil-ʾamīn. (3)

---

1 The "fig" and the "olive" symbolize, in this context, the *lands* in which these trees predominate: i.e., the countries bordering on the eastern part of the Mediterranean, especially Palestine and Syria. As it was in these lands that most of the Abrahamic prophets mentioned in the Qurʾān lived and preached, these two species of tree may be taken as metonyms for the *religious teachings* voiced by the long line of those God-inspired men, culminating in the person of the last Judaic prophet, Jesus. "Mount Sinai", on the other hand, stresses specifically the apostleship of Moses, inasmuch as the religious law valid before, and up to, the advent of Muḥammad – and in its essentials binding on Jesus as well – was revealed to Moses on a mountain of the Sinai Desert. Finally, "this land secure" signifies undoubtedly (as is evident from 2 : 126) Mecca, where Muḥammad, the Last Prophet, was born and received his divine call. Thus, verses 1-3 draw our attention to the fundamental ethical unity underlying the teachings – the *genuine* teachings – of all the three historic phases of monotheistic religion, metonymically personified by Moses, Jesus and Muḥammad. The *specific* truth to be considered here is referred to in the next three verses.

Verily, We create man in the best conformation,[2] ‹4› and thereafter We reduce him to the lowest of low[3] ‹5› – excepting only such as attain to faith and do good works: and theirs shall be a reward unending! ‹6›
What, then, [O man,] could henceforth cause thee to give the lie to this moral law?[4] ‹7›
Is not God the most just of judges? ‹8›

لَقَدْ خَلَقْنَا ٱلْإِنسَٰنَ فِىٓ أَحْسَنِ تَقْوِيمٍ ﴿4﴾ ثُمَّ رَدَدْنَٰهُ أَسْفَلَ
سَٰفِلِينَ ﴿5﴾ إِلَّا ٱلَّذِينَ ءَامَنُوا۟ وَعَمِلُوا۟ ٱلصَّٰلِحَٰتِ فَلَهُمْ أَجْرٌ غَيْرُ
مَمْنُونٍ ﴿6﴾ فَمَا يُكَذِّبُكَ بَعْدُ بِٱلدِّينِ ﴿7﴾ أَلَيْسَ ٱللَّهُ بِأَحْكَمِ
ٱلْحَٰكِمِينَ ﴿8﴾

Laqad khalaqnal-ʾInsāna fīi ʾaḥsani taqwīm. ﴿4﴾ Thumma radadnāhu ʾasfala sāfilīn. ﴿5﴾ ʾIllal-ladhīna ʾāmanū wa ʿamiluṣ-ṣāliḥāti falahum ʾajrun ghayru mamnūn. ﴿6﴾ Famā yukadhdhibuka baʿdu biddīn. ﴿7﴾ ʾAlaysal-lāhu biʾAḥkamil-ḥākimīn. ﴿8﴾

2 I.e., endowed with all the positive qualities, physical as well as mental, corresponding to the functions which this particular creature is meant to perform. The concept of "the best conformation" is related to the Qurʾanic statement that everything which God creates, including the human being or self (*nafs*), is "formed in accordance with what it is meant to be" (see 91 : 7 and the corresponding note 5, as well as – in a more general sense – 87 : 2 and note 1). This statement does not in any way imply that all human beings have the *same* "best conformation" in respect of their bodily or mental endowments: it implies simply that irrespective of his natural advantages or disadvantages, each human being is endowed with the ability to make the, for him, best possible use of his inborn qualities and of the environment to which he is exposed. (See in this connection 30 : 30 and the corresponding notes, especially 27 and 28.)

3 This "reduction to the lowest of low" is a consequence of man's betrayal – in another word, corruption – of his original, positive disposition: that is to say, a consequence of man's own doings and omissions. Regarding the attribution, by God, of this "reduction" to His Own doing, see note 7 on 2 : 7.

4 I.e., to the validity of the moral law – which, to my mind, is the meaning of the term *dīn* in this context – outlined in the preceding three verses. (For this specific significance of the concept of *dīn*, see note 3 on 109 : 6.) The above rhetorical question has this implication: Since the moral law referred to here has been stressed in the teachings of all monotheistic religions (cf. verses 1-3 and note 1 above), its truth ought to be self-evident to any unprejudiced person; its negation, moreover, amounts to a negation of all freedom of moral choice on man's part and, hence, of justice on the part of God, who, as the next verse points out, is – by definition – "the most just of judges".

The Ninety-sixth Sūrah

Al-ᶜAlaq (The Germ-Cell)

Mecca Period

THERE IS no doubt that the first five verses of this *sūrah* represent the very beginning of the revelation of the Qurʾān. Although the exact date cannot be established with certainty, all authorities agree in that these five verses were revealed in the last third of the month of Ramaḍān, thirteen years before the *hijrah* (corresponding to July or August, 610, of the Christian era). Muḥammad was then forty years old. At that period of his life "solitude became dear unto him, and he used to withdraw into seclusion in a cave of Mount Ḥirāʾ [near Mecca] and there apply himself to ardent devotions" consisting of long vigils and prayers (Bukhārī). One night, the Angel of Revelation suddenly appeared to him and said, "Read!" Muḥammad at first thought that he was expected to read actual script, which, being unlettered, he was unable to do; and so he answered, "I cannot read" – whereupon, in his own words, the angel "seized me and pressed me to himself until all strength went out of me; then he released me and said, 'Read!' I answered, 'I cannot read. . . .' Then he seized me again and pressed me to himself until all strength went out of me; then he released me and said, 'Read!' – to which I [again] answered, 'I cannot read. . . .' Then he seized me and pressed me to himself a third time; then he released me and said, 'Read in the name of thy Sustainer, who has created – created man out of a germ-cell! Read – for thy Sustainer is the Most Bountiful One . . .'": and so Muḥammad understood, in sudden illumination, that he was called upon to "read", that is, to receive and understand, God's message to man.

The above excerpts are quoted from the third Tradition of the section *Badʾ al-Waḥy,* which forms the introductory chapter of Bukhārī's *Ṣaḥīḥ;* almost identical versions of this Tradition are found in two other places in Bukhārī as well as in Muslim, Nasāʾī and Tirmidhī.

Verses 6-19 of this *sūrah* are of a somewhat later date.

سورة العلق مكية -96-
وآياتها تسع عشرة

IN THE NAME OF GOD, THE MOST GRACIOUS, THE DISPENSER OF GRACE:

READ[1] in the name of thy Sustainer, who has created ‹1› – created man out of a germ-cell![2] ‹2›
Read – for thy Sustainer is the Most Bountiful One ‹3› who has taught [man] the use of the pen ‹4› – taught man what he did not know![3] ‹5›
Nay, verily, man becomes grossly overweening ‹6› whenever he believes himself to be self-sufficient: ‹7› for, behold, unto thy Sustainer all must return.[4] ‹8›

بِسْمِ ٱللَّهِ ٱلرَّحْمَٰنِ ٱلرَّحِيمِ

ٱقْرَأْ بِٱسْمِ رَبِّكَ ٱلَّذِى خَلَقَ ﴿١﴾ خَلَقَ ٱلْإِنسَٰنَ مِنْ عَلَقٍ ﴿٢﴾ ٱقْرَأْ
وَرَبُّكَ ٱلْأَكْرَمُ ﴿٣﴾ ٱلَّذِى عَلَّمَ بِٱلْقَلَمِ ﴿٤﴾ عَلَّمَ ٱلْإِنسَٰنَ مَا لَمْ
يَعْلَمْ ﴿٥﴾ كَلَّآ إِنَّ ٱلْإِنسَٰنَ لَيَطْغَىٰٓ ﴿٦﴾ أَن رَّءَاهُ ٱسْتَغْنَىٰٓ ﴿٧﴾ إِنَّ إِلَىٰ
رَبِّكَ ٱلرُّجْعَىٰٓ ﴿٨﴾

Bismil-lāhir-Raḥmānir-Raḥīm.
ʾIqraʾ bismi Rabbikal-ladhī khalaq. (1) Khalaqal-ʾInsāna min ʿalaq. (2) ʾIqraʾ wa Rabbukal-ʾAkram. (3) ʾAlladhī ʿallama bilqalam. (4) ʿAllamal-ʾInsāna mā lam yaʿlam. (5) Kallāa ʾinnal-ʾInsāna layaṭghāa, (6) ʾar-raʾāhus-taghnā. (7) ʾInna ʾilā Rabbikar-rujʿā. (8)

---

1 Sc., "this divine writ". The imperative *iqrāʾ* may be rendered as "read" or "recite". The former rendering is, to my mind, by far the preferable in this context inasmuch as the concept of "reciting" implies no more than the oral delivery – with or without understanding – of something already laid down in writing or committed to memory, whereas "reading" primarily signifies a conscious taking-in, with or without an audible utterance but with a view to understanding them, of words and ideas received from an outside source: in this case, the message of the Qurʾān.

2 The past tense in which the verb *khalaqa* appears in these two verses is meant to indicate that the act of divine creation (*khalq*) has been and is being continuously repeated. It is also noteworthy that this very first Qurʾanic revelation alludes to man's embryonic evolution out of a "germ-cell" – i.e., out of a fertilized female ovum – thus contrasting the primitiveness and simplicity of his biological origins with his intellectual and spiritual potential: a contrast which clearly points to the existence of a conscious design and a purpose underlying the creation of life.

3 "The pen" is used here as a symbol for the art of writing or, more specifically, for all knowledge recorded by means of writing: and this explains the symbolic summons "Read!" at the beginning of verses 1 and 3. Man's unique ability to transmit, by means of written records, his thoughts, experiences and insights from individual to individual, from generation to generation, and from one cultural environment to another endows all human knowledge with a cumulative character; and since, thanks to this God-given ability, every human being partakes, in one way or another, in mankind's continuous accumulation of knowledge, man is spoken of as being "taught by God" things which the single individual does not – and, indeed, cannot – know by himself. (This double stress on man's utter dependence on God, who creates him as a biological entity and implants in him the will and the ability to acquire knowledge, receives its final accent, as it were, in the next three verses.) Furthermore, God's "teaching" man signifies also the act of His revealing, through the prophets, spiritual truths and moral standards which cannot be unequivocally established through human experience and reasoning alone: and, thus, it circumscribes the phenomenon of divine revelation as such.

4 Lit., "is the return (*ar-rujʿā*)". This noun has here a twofold implication: "everyone will inescapably be brought before God for judgment", as well as "everything that exists goes back to God as its source". In ultimate analysis, the statement expressed in verses 6-8 rejects as absurd the arrogant idea that man could ever be self-sufficient and, hence, "master of his own fate"; furthermore, it implies that all moral concepts – that is, all discrimination between good and evil, or right and wrong – are indissolubly linked with the concept of man's responsibility to a Supreme Power: in other words, without such a feeling of responsibility – whether conscious or subconscious – the concept of "morality" as such loses all its meaning.

أَرَءَيْتَ ٱلَّذِى يَنْهَىٰ ﴿9﴾ عَبْدًا إِذَا صَلَّىٰٓ ﴿10﴾ أَرَءَيْتَ إِن كَانَ عَلَى
ٱلْهُدَىٰٓ ﴿11﴾ أَوْ أَمَرَ بِٱلتَّقْوَىٰٓ ﴿12﴾ أَرَءَيْتَ إِن كَذَّبَ وَتَوَلَّىٰٓ ﴿13﴾ أَلَمْ
يَعْلَم بِأَنَّ ٱللَّهَ يَرَىٰ ﴿14﴾ كَلَّا لَئِن لَّمْ يَنتَهِ لَنَسْفَعًۢا بِٱلنَّاصِيَةِ ﴿15﴾ نَاصِيَةٍ
كَـٰذِبَةٍ خَاطِئَةٍ ﴿16﴾ فَلْيَدْعُ نَادِيَهُۥ ﴿17﴾ سَنَدْعُ ٱلزَّبَانِيَةَ ﴿18﴾ كَلَّا
لَا تُطِعْهُ وَٱسْجُدْ وَٱقْتَرِب ۩ ﴿19﴾

ʾAraʾaytal-ladhī yanhā, (9) ʿabdan ʾidhā ṣallā. (10) ʾAraʾayta ʾiň-kāna ʿalal-hudā. (11) ʾAw ʾamara bit-taqwā. (12) ʾAraʾayta ʾiň-kadhdhaba wa tawallā. (13) ʾAlam yaʿlam biʾannal-lāha yarā. (14) Kallā laʾil-lam yañtahi lanasfaʿam-binnāṣiyah. (15) Nāṣiyatiň-kādhibatin khāṭiʾah. (16) Falyadʿu nādiyah. (17) Sanadʿuz-zabāniyah. (18) Kallā lā tuṭiʿhu was-jud waq-tarib. ۩ (19)

السجدة

HAST THOU ever considered him who tries to prevent ‹9› a servant [of God] from praying?[5] ‹10›

Hast thou considered whether he is on the right way, ‹11› or is concerned with God-consciousness?[6] ‹12›

Hast thou considered whether he may [not] be giving the lie to the truth and turning his back [upon it]?[7] ‹13›

Does he, then, not know that God sees [all]? ‹14›

Nay, if he desist not, We shall most surely drag him down upon his forehead[8] ‹15› – the lying, rebellious forehead! ‹16› – and then let him summon [to his aid] the counsels of his own [spurious] wisdom,[9] ‹17› [the while] We shall summon the forces of heavenly chastisement! ‹18›

Nay, pay thou no heed to him, but prostrate thyself [before God] and draw close [unto Him]! ‹19›

---

5 Lit., "who forbids a servant [of God] when he prays", implying an *attempt* at preventing. Since this seems to refer to praying *in public*, most of the classical commentators see in this passage (which was revealed at least a year later than the first five verses) an allusion to Abū Jahl, the Prophet's bitterest opponent in Mecca, who persistently tried to prevent Muḥammad and his followers from praying before the Kaʿbah. However, there is no doubt that the purport of the above passage goes far beyond any historical incident or situation inasmuch as it applies to all attempts, at all times, to deny to religion (symbolized in the term "praying") its legitimate function in the shaping of social life – attempts made either in the conviction that religion is every individual's "private affair" and, therefore, must not be allowed to "intrude" into the realm of social considerations, or, alternatively, in the pursuit of the illusion that man is above any need of metaphysical guidance.

6 Lit., "or enjoins God-consciousness (*taqwā*)" – i.e., whether his aim is to deepen his fellow-men's *God-consciousness* by insisting that religion is a purely personal matter: the obvious implication being that this is not his aim, and that he is not on the right way in thinking and acting as he does. – Throughout this work, the term *taqwā* – of which the present is the earliest instance in the chronology of Qurʾanic revelation – has been rendered as "God-consciousness", with the same meaning attaching to the verbal forms from which this noun is derived. (See also *sūrah* 2, note 2.)

7 Sc., "because in his arrogance he cannot face it".

8 Lit., "by his forelock" – an ancient Arabian expression denoting a person's utter subjection and humiliation (see 11 : 56 and the corresponding note 80). However, as Rāzī points out, the term "forelock" (*nāṣiyah*) is here used metonymically for the *place* on which the forelock grows, i.e., the forehead (cf. also *Tāj al-ʿArūs*).

9 Lit., "his council". According to the commentators who tend to interpret verses such as this in purely historical terms, this may be a reference to the traditional council of elders (*dār annadwah*) in pagan Mecca; but more probably, I think, it is an allusion to the arrogance which so often deludes man into regarding himself as "self-sufficient" (verses 6-7 above).

The Ninety-Seventh Sūrah

Al-Qadr (Destiny)

Mecca Period

OPENING with a reference to the revelation of the first five verses of the preceding *sūrah* – that is, to the beginning of Muḥammad's prophetic mission – *Al-Qadr* undoubtedly belongs to a very early part of the Mecca period.

سورة القدر مكية -97- وآياتها خمس

IN THE NAME OF GOD, THE MOST GRACIOUS, THE DISPENSER OF GRACE:

BEHOLD, from on high have We bestowed this [divine writ] on the Night of Destiny.[1] ‹1›
And what could make thee conceive what it is, that Night of Destiny? ‹2›
The Night of Destiny is better than a thousand months:[2] ‹3›
in hosts descend in it the angels,[3] bearing divine inspiration[4] by their Sustainer's leave;
from all [evil] that may happen ‹4› does it make secure,[5] until the rise of dawn. ‹5›

بِسْمِ ٱللَّهِ ٱلرَّحْمَـٰنِ ٱلرَّحِيمِ

إِنَّآ أَنزَلْنَـٰهُ فِى لَيْلَةِ ٱلْقَدْرِ ﴿١﴾ وَمَآ أَدْرَىٰكَ مَا لَيْلَةُ ٱلْقَدْرِ ﴿٢﴾ لَيْلَةُ
ٱلْقَدْرِ خَيْرٌ مِّنْ أَلْفِ شَهْرٍ ﴿٣﴾ تَنَزَّلُ ٱلْمَلَـٰٓئِكَةُ وَٱلرُّوحُ فِيهَا بِإِذْنِ
رَبِّهِم مِّن كُلِّ أَمْرٍ ﴿٤﴾ سَلَـٰمٌ هِىَ حَتَّىٰ مَطْلَعِ ٱلْفَجْرِ ﴿٥﴾

Bismil-lāhir-Raḥmānir-Raḥīm.
ʾInnāa ʾañzalnāhu fī Laylatil-Qadr. ‹1› Wa māa ʾadrāka mā Laylatul-Qadr. ‹2› Laylatul-Qadri khay-rum-min ʾalfi shahr. ‹3› Tanazzalul-Malāaʾikatu war-rūḥu fīhā biʾidhni Rabbihim miñ-kulli ʾamr. ‹4› Salāmun hiya ḥattā maṭlaʿil-fajr. ‹5›

---

1 Or: "of Almightiness" or "of Majesty" – thus describing the night on which the Prophet received his first revelation (see introductory note to the preceding *sūrah*). On the basis of several Traditions it may be assumed that it was one of the last ten nights – probably the twenty-seventh – of the month of Ramaḍān, thirteen years before the Prophet's emigration to Medina.

2 Sc., "in which there was no similar night" (Rāzī).

3 The grammatical form *tanazzalu* implies repetition, frequency or multitude; hence – as suggested by Ibn Kathīr – "descending in hosts".

4 Lit., "and [divine] inspiration". For this rendering of *rūḥ*, see first sentence of 16 : 2 and the corresponding note 2. The present instance is undoubtedly the earliest example of the Qurʾanic use of this term in the sense of "divine inspiration".

5 Lit., "it is salvation" (*salām*, see *sūrah* 5, note 29) – i.e., it makes the believer secure from all *spiritual* evil: thus Mujāhid (as quoted by Ibn Kathīr), evidently implying that a conscious realization of the sanctity of this night acts as a shield against unworthy thoughts and inclinations.

The Ninety-Eighth Sūrah

Al-Bayyinah (The Evidence of the Truth)

Period Uncertain

WHEREAS some of the authorities are of the opinion that this *sūrah* belongs to the Medina period, many others regard it as a late Meccan revelation. The key-word by which it is designated is found at the end of the first verse.

-98-

سورة البينة مدنية

وآياتها ثمان

IN THE NAME OF GOD, THE MOST GRACIOUS, THE DISPENSER OF GRACE:

IT IS NOT [conceivable] that such as are bent on denying the truth – [be they] from among the followers of earlier revelation or from among those who ascribe divinity to aught beside God[1] – should ever be abandoned [by Him] ere there comes unto them the [full] evidence of the truth: ‹1› an apostle from God, conveying [unto them] revelations blest with purity, ‹2› wherein there are ordinances of ever-true soundness and clarity.[2] ‹3›

بِسْمِ ٱللَّهِ ٱلرَّحْمَـٰنِ ٱلرَّحِيمِ

لَمْ يَكُنِ ٱلَّذِينَ كَفَرُوا۟ مِنْ أَهْلِ ٱلْكِتَـٰبِ وَٱلْمُشْرِكِينَ مُنفَكِّينَ حَتَّىٰ تَأْتِيَهُمُ ٱلْبَيِّنَةُ ﴿١﴾ رَسُولٌ مِّنَ ٱللَّهِ يَتْلُوا۟ صُحُفًا مُّطَهَّرَةً ﴿٢﴾ فِيهَا كُتُبٌ قَيِّمَةٌ ﴿٣﴾

Bismil-lāhir-Raḥmānir-Raḥīm.
Lam yakunil-ladhīna kafarū min ʾahlil-Kitābi wal-mushrikīna muñfakkīna ḥattā taʾtiyahumul bayyinah. ⟨1⟩ Rasūlum-minal-lāhi yatlū ṣuḥufam-muṭahharah. ⟨2⟩ Fīhā Kutubuñ-qayyimah. ⟨3⟩

---

1 I.e., idol-worshippers or animists (in the anthropological sense of this word) who have never had any revealed scripture to fall back upon.

2 This aggregate connotation is inherent in the adjective *qayyimah* as used here (Rāzī). – The above passage has caused some difficulties to the classical commentators on account of the participle *munfakkīn* occurring in the first verse. It is generally assumed that this participle, in combination with the phrase *lam yakun* at the beginning of the verse, denotes "they did not [or "could not"] give up" or "separate themselves from" – i.e., supposedly, from their erroneous beliefs – "until there came to them the evidence of the truth" in the person of the Prophet Muḥammad and in the revelation of the Qurʾān: implying that after the evidence came, they did give up those false beliefs. This assumption is, however, deficient on two counts: firstly, it is well-known that not all of the erring ones from among the *ahl al-kitāb* and the *mushrikīn* accepted the message of the Qurʾān when it was conveyed to them; and, secondly, the *ahl al-kitāb* are spoken of in verse 4 as having "broken their unity [of faith]" – i.e., offended against the fundamental principles of that faith – *after* "the evidence of the truth" had come to them. This apparent contradiction has been convincingly resolved by no less an authority than Ibn Taymiyyah (see *Tafsīr Sitt Suwar*, pp. 391 ff.); and it is his interpretation that I have followed in my rendering of the above three verses. According to Ibn Taymiyyah, the pivotal phrase *lam yakun munfakkīn* does not denote "they did not give up" or "separate themselves from", but, rather, "they are not *abandoned*" – i.e., condemned by God – unless and until they have been *shown* the right way by a

Now those who have been vouchsafed revelation aforetime[3] did break up their unity [of faith] after such an evidence of the truth had come to them.[4] ‹4›
And withal, they were not enjoined aught but that they should worship God, sincere in their faith in Him alone, turning away from all that is false;[5] and that they should be constant in prayer; and that they should spend in charity:[6] for this is a moral law endowed with ever-true soundness and clarity.[7] ‹5›
Verily, those who [despite all evidence] are bent on denying the truth[8] – [be they] from among the followers of earlier revelation or from among those who ascribe divinity to aught beside God – will find themselves in the fire of hell, therein to abide: they are the worst of all creatures. ‹6›
[And,] verily, those who have attained to faith and do righteous deeds – it is they, they who are the best of all creatures. ‹7›
Their reward [awaits them] with God: gardens of perpetual bliss, through which running waters flow, therein to abide beyond the count of time; well-pleased is God with them, and well-pleased are they with Him: all this awaits him who of his Sustainer stands in awe! ‹8›

وَمَا تَفَرَّقَ ٱلَّذِينَ أُوتُوا۟ ٱلْكِتَـٰبَ إِلَّا مِنۢ بَعْدِ مَا جَآءَتْهُمُ ٱلْبَيِّنَةُ ﴿4﴾
وَمَآ أُمِرُوٓا۟ إِلَّا لِيَعْبُدُوا۟ ٱللَّهَ مُخْلِصِينَ لَهُ ٱلدِّينَ حُنَفَآءَ وَيُقِيمُوا۟ ٱلصَّلَوٰةَ
وَيُؤْتُوا۟ ٱلزَّكَوٰةَ ۚ وَذَٰلِكَ دِينُ ٱلْقَيِّمَةِ ﴿5﴾ إِنَّ ٱلَّذِينَ كَفَرُوا۟ مِنْ أَهْلِ
ٱلْكِتَـٰبِ وَٱلْمُشْرِكِينَ فِى نَارِ جَهَنَّمَ خَـٰلِدِينَ فِيهَآ ۚ أُو۟لَـٰٓئِكَ هُمْ شَرُّ
ٱلْبَرِيَّةِ ﴿6﴾ إِنَّ ٱلَّذِينَ ءَامَنُوا۟ وَعَمِلُوا۟ ٱلصَّـٰلِحَـٰتِ أُو۟لَـٰٓئِكَ هُمْ خَيْرُ
ٱلْبَرِيَّةِ ﴿7﴾ جَزَآؤُهُمْ عِندَ رَبِّهِمْ جَنَّـٰتُ عَدْنٍ تَجْرِى مِن تَحْتِهَا ٱلْأَنْهَـٰرُ
خَـٰلِدِينَ فِيهَآ أَبَدًا ۖ رَّضِىَ ٱللَّهُ عَنْهُمْ وَرَضُوا۟ عَنْهُ ۚ ذَٰلِكَ لِمَنْ خَشِىَ رَبَّهُۥ ﴿8﴾

Wa mā tafarraqal-ladhīna ʾūtul-Kitāba ʾillā mimbaʿdi mā jāaʾat-humul bayyinah. (4) Wa māa ʾumirūu ʾillā liyaʿbudul-lāha mukhliṣīna lahud-dīna ḥunafāaʾa wa yuqīmuṣ-Ṣalāta wa yuʾtuz-Zakāh. Wa dhālika dīnul-qayyimah. (5) ʾInnal-ladhīna kafarū min ʾahlil-Kitābi wal-mushrikīna fī nāri jahannama khālidīna fīhā. ʾUlāaʾika hum sharrul-bariyyah. (6) ʾInnal-ladhīna ʾāmanū wa ʿamiluṣ-ṣāliḥāti ʾulāaʾika hum khayrul-bariyyah. (7) Jazāaʾuhum ʿiñda Rabbihim jannātu ʿadniñ-tajrī miñ taḥtihal-ʾanhāru khālidīna fīhāa ʾabadā. Raḍiyal-lāhu ʿanhum wa raḍū ʿanh. Dhālika liman khashiya Rabbah. (8)

God-sent prophet, and thereupon have consciously refused to follow it: and this is in accord with repeated statements in the Qurʾān to the effect that God does not take anyone to task for wrong beliefs and wrong actions unless the true meaning of right and wrong has previously been made clear to him (cf. 6 : 131-132 and the second paragraph of 17 : 15, as well as the corresponding notes). Hence, the above reference to "the evidence of the truth" does not relate only to the Qurʾān and the Prophet Muḥammad but to all the earlier prophets and revelations as well (cf. 42 : 13 and the corresponding notes 12-14) – just as the "ordinances of ever-true soundness and clarity" (spelled out in verse 5 below) are common to *all* God-inspired messages, of which the Qurʾān is the final, most perfect expression.

3 This definition is general, comprising the followers of all religious teachings revealed before the advent of the Prophet Muḥammad (Ibn Kathīr), and not – as some commentators assume – only the Jews and the Christians. (See also notes 12 and 13 on 3 : 19.)

4 I.e., most of them strayed from the teachings of the prophets sent to them, all of whom had preached the same fundamental truths (see next verse and note 6 below).

5 For this rendering of *ḥunafāʾ* (sing. *ḥanīf*), see *sūrah* 2, note 110.

6 Since the term *zakāh* has here obviously a wider meaning than the obligatory tax incumbent on Muslims (which, as its name indicates, is meant to purify their income and their possessions from the taint of selfishness), I am rendering the above phrase in the more general sense of "spending in [i.e., practicing] charity".

7 As regards the connotation of "moral law" in the term *dīn*, see note 3 on 109 : 6; the qualifying noun *al-qayyimah* (in the genitive case) has here the same meaning as the adjective *qayyimah* at the end of verse 3. The above definition of moral law outlines, in a condensed form, all the basic demands of true religion: a cognition of God's oneness and uniqueness and, implicitly, of man's responsibility to Him; a turning-away from all false concepts, values and dubious beliefs, all over-estimation of oneself, and all superstition; and, finally, kindness and charity towards all of God's creatures.

8 Namely, the self-evident principles formulated in the preceding verse as the beginning and the end of all moral law.

The Ninety-Ninth Sūrah

Az-Zalzalah (The Earthquake)

Period Uncertain

MOST PROBABLY revealed in the early part of the Medina period (*Itqān*), although some authorities regard it as a Meccan revelation.

سورة الزلزلة مدنية -٩٩-
وآياتها ثمان

IN THE NAME OF GOD, THE MOST GRACIOUS, THE DISPENSER OF GRACE:

بِسۡمِ ٱللَّهِ ٱلرَّحۡمَٰنِ ٱلرَّحِيمِ

إِذَا زُلۡزِلَتِ ٱلۡأَرۡضُ زِلۡزَالَهَا ۝١ وَأَخۡرَجَتِ ٱلۡأَرۡضُ أَثۡقَالَهَا ۝٢ وَقَالَ
ٱلۡإِنسَٰنُ مَا لَهَا ۝٣ يَوۡمَئِذٖ تُحَدِّثُ أَخۡبَارَهَا ۝٤ بِأَنَّ رَبَّكَ أَوۡحَىٰ
لَهَا ۝٥ يَوۡمَئِذٖ يَصۡدُرُ ٱلنَّاسُ أَشۡتَاتٗا لِّيُرَوۡاْ أَعۡمَٰلَهُمۡ ۝٦ فَمَن يَعۡمَلۡ
مِثۡقَالَ ذَرَّةٍ خَيۡرٗا يَرَهُۥ ۝٧ وَمَن يَعۡمَلۡ مِثۡقَالَ ذَرَّةٖ شَرّٗا يَرَهُۥ ۝٨

WHEN THE EARTH quakes with her [last] mighty quaking, ‹1›
and [when] the earth yields up her burdens,[1] ‹2›
and man cries out, "What has happened to her?" ‹3›
– on that Day will she recount all her tidings, ‹4› as thy Sustainer will have inspired her to do.[2] ‹5›
On that Day will all men come forward, cut off from one another,[3] to be shown their [past] deeds. ‹6›
And so, he who shall have done an atom's weight of good, shall behold it; ‹7›
and he who shall have done an atom's weight of evil, shall behold it. ‹8›

Bismil-lāhir-Raḥmānir-Raḥīm.
ʾIdhā zulzilatil-ʾarḍu zilzālahā. (1) Wa ʾakhrajatil-ʾarḍu ʾathqālahā. (2) Wa qālal-ʾIñsānu mā lahā. (3) Yawmaʾidhiñ-tuḥaddithu ʾakhbārahā, (4) biʾanna Rabbaka ʾawḥā lahā. (5) Yawmaʾidhiñy-yaṣdurun-nāsu ʾashtatañ-liyuraw ʾaʿmālahum. (6) Famañy-yaʿmal mithqāla dharratin khayrañy-yarah. (7) Wa mañy-yaʿmal mithqāla dharratiñ-sharrañy-yarah. (8)

---

1 I.e., all that was hitherto hidden in it, including the bodies – or the remnants – of the dead.

2 I.e., on the Day of Judgment the earth will bear witness, as it were, to all that has ever been done by man: an explanation given by the Prophet, according to a Tradition on the authority of Abū Hurayrah (quoted by Ibn Ḥanbal and Tirmidhī).

3 Lit., "as separate entities" (*ashtātan*). Cf. 6 : 94 – "And now, indeed, you have come unto Us in a lonely state, even as We created you in the first instance": thus stressing the individual, untransferable responsibility of every human being.

The Hundredth Sūrah

Al-ʿĀdiyāt (The Chargers)

Mecca Period

REVEALED after *sūrah* 103. For an explanation of the symbolism of "the chargers", see note 2 below.

سورة العاديات مكية -100- وآياتها إحدى عشرة

IN THE NAME OF GOD, THE MOST GRACIOUS, THE DISPENSER OF GRACE:

OH,[1] the chargers that run panting, ‹1›
sparks of fire striking, ‹2›
rushing to assault at morn, ‹3›
thereby raising clouds of dust, ‹4›
thereby storming [blindly] into any host![2] ‹5›

بِسْمِ ٱللَّهِ ٱلرَّحْمَٰنِ ٱلرَّحِيمِ

وَٱلْعَٰدِيَٰتِ ضَبْحًا ﴿١﴾ فَٱلْمُورِيَٰتِ قَدْحًا ﴿٢﴾ فَٱلْمُغِيرَٰتِ صُبْحًا ﴿٣﴾
فَأَثَرْنَ بِهِۦ نَقْعًا ﴿٤﴾ فَوَسَطْنَ بِهِۦ جَمْعًا ﴿٥﴾

Bismil-lāhir-Raḥmānir-Raḥīm.
Wal-ʿādiyāti ḍabḥā. (1) Fal-mūriyāti qadḥā. (2) Fal-mughīrāti ṣubḥā. (3) Faʾatharna bihī naqʿā. (4) Fa-wasaṭna bihī jamʿā. (5)

---

1 Since the subsequent clauses refer to a parabolic, imaginary situation, the adjurative particle *wa* is more suitably rendered here as "Oh", instead of the rendering "Consider" usually adopted by me, or the adjuration "By" appearing in most other translations.

2 I.e., blinded by clouds of dust and not knowing whether their assault aims at friend or foe. The metaphoric image developed in the above five verses is closely connected with the sequence, although this connection has never been brought out by the classical commentators. The term *al-ʿādiyāt* undoubtedly denotes the war-horses, or chargers, employed by the Arabs from time immemorial down to the Middle Ages (the feminine gender of this term being due to the fact that, as a rule, they preferred mares to stallions). But whereas the conventional explanation is based on the assumption that "the chargers" symbolize here the believers' fight in God's cause (*jihād*) and, therefore, represent something highly commendable, it takes no account whatever of the discrepancy between so positive an imagery and the *condemnation* expressed in verses 6 ff., not to speak of the fact that such a conventional interpretation does not provide any logical link between the two parts of the *sūrah*. But since such a link *must* exist, and since verses 6-11 are undoubtedly condemnatory, we must conclude that the first five verses, too, have the same – or, at least, a similar – character. This character becomes at once obvious if we dissociate ourselves from the preconceived notion that the imagery of "the chargers" is used here in a laudatory sense. In fact, the opposite is the case. Beyond any doubt, "the chargers" symbolize the erring human soul or self – a soul devoid of all spiritual direction, obsessed and ridden by all manner of wrong, selfish desires, madly, unseeingly rushing onwards, unchecked by conscience or reason, blinded by the dust-clouds of confused and confusing appetites, storming into insoluble situations and, thus, into its own spiritual destruction.

ثلاثة أرباع الحزب

VERILY, towards his Sustainer man is most ungrateful[3] ‹6› – and to this, behold, he [himself] bears witness indeed: ‹7› for, verily, to the love of wealth is he most ardently devoted. ‹8›

But does he not know that [on the Last Day,] when all that is in the graves is raised and brought out, ‹9› and all that is [hidden] in men's hearts is bared ‹10› – that on that Day their Sustainer [will show that He] has always been fully aware of them? ‹11›

إِنَّ ٱلۡإِنسَٰنَ لِرَبِّهِۦ لَكَنُودٞ ٦ وَإِنَّهُۥ عَلَىٰ ذَٰلِكَ لَشَهِيدٞ ٧ وَإِنَّهُۥ
لِحُبِّ ٱلۡخَيۡرِ لَشَدِيدٌ ٨ ۞ أَفَلَا يَعۡلَمُ إِذَا بُعۡثِرَ مَا فِي ٱلۡقُبُورِ ٩
وَحُصِّلَ مَا فِي ٱلصُّدُورِ ١٠ إِنَّ رَبَّهُم بِهِمۡ يَوۡمَئِذٖ لَّخَبِيرُۢ ١١

ʾInnal-ʾInsāna liRabbihī lakanūd. (6) Wa ʾinnahū ᶜalā dhālika lashahīd. (7) Wa ʾinnahū liḥubbil-khayri lashadīd. (8) ۞ ʾAfalā yaᶜlamu ʾidhā buᶜthira mā fil-qubūr. (9) Wa ḥuṣṣila mā fiṣ-ṣudūr. (10) ʾInna Rabbahum bihim Yawmaʾidhil-laKhabīr. (11)

3 I.e., whenever he surrenders to his appetites, symbolized by the madly storming chargers, he forgets God and his own responsibility to Him.

The Hundred-First Sūrah

Al-Qāriᶜah (The Sudden Calamity)

Mecca Period

AN early Meccan *sūrah*, most probably revealed after *sūrah* 95 (*At-Tīn*).

سورة القارعة مكية -101- وآياتها إحدى عشرة

IN THE NAME OF GOD, THE MOST GRACIOUS, THE DISPENSER OF GRACE:

OH, the sudden calamity![1] ‹1› How awesome the sudden calamity! ‹2›
And what could make thee conceive what that sudden calamity will be? ‹3›
[It will occur] on the Day when men will be like moths swarming in confusion, ‹4› and the mountains will be like fluffy tufts of wool. . . . ‹5›
And then, he whose weight [of good deeds] is heavy in the balance ‹6› shall find himself in a happy state of life; ‹7›
whereas he whose weight is light in the balance ‹8› shall be engulfed by an abyss.[2] ‹9›
And what could make thee conceive what that [abyss] will be? ‹10›
A fire hotly burning![3] ‹11›

بِسْمِ ٱللَّهِ ٱلرَّحْمَٰنِ ٱلرَّحِيمِ

ٱلْقَارِعَةُ (1) مَا ٱلْقَارِعَةُ (2) وَمَآ أَدْرَىٰكَ مَا ٱلْقَارِعَةُ (3) يَوْمَ يَكُونُ
ٱلنَّاسُ كَٱلْفَرَاشِ ٱلْمَبْثُوثِ (4) وَتَكُونُ ٱلْجِبَالُ كَٱلْعِهْنِ
ٱلْمَنفُوشِ (5) فَأَمَّا مَن ثَقُلَتْ مَوَٰزِينُهُۥ (6) فَهُوَ فِى عِيشَةٍ رَّاضِيَةٍ (7)
وَأَمَّا مَنْ خَفَّتْ مَوَٰزِينُهُۥ (8) فَأُمُّهُۥ هَاوِيَةٌ (9) وَمَآ أَدْرَىٰكَ مَا هِيَهْ (10)
نَارٌ حَامِيَةٌۢ (11)

Bismil-lāhir-Raḥmānir-Raḥīm.
ᵓAlqāriᶜatu, (1) mal-qāriᶜah. (2) Wa māa ᵓadrāka mal-qāriᶜah. (3) Yawma yakūnun-nāsu kalfarāshil-mabthūth. (4) Wa takūnul-jibālu kalᶜihnil-mañfūsh. (5) Faᵓammā mañ-thaqulat mawāzīnuhū, (6) fahuwa fī ᶜīshatir-rāḍiyah. (7) Wa ᵓammā man khaffat mawāzīnuhū, (8) faᵓummuhū hāwiyah. (9) Wa māa ᵓadrāka mā hiyah. (10) Nārun ḥāmiyah. (11)

---

1 I.e., the coming of the Last Hour, which will involve a terrifying transformation of the world (see note 63 on 14 : 48 and note 90 on 20 : 105-107).

2 Lit., "his mother [i.e., goal] will be an abyss", sc., of suffering and despair. The term "mother" (*umm*) is used idiomatically to denote something that embraces or enfolds.

3 Lit., "hot fire", the adjective meant to *stress* the essential quality of fire. It should be borne in mind that all Qurᵓanic descriptions of the sinner's suffering in the hereafter are metaphors or allegories relating to situations and conditions which can be understood only by means of comparisons with physical phenomena lying within the range of human experience (see Appendix I).

The Hundred-Second Sūrah

At-Takāthur (Greed for More and More)

Mecca Period

THIS early Meccan *sūrah* is one of the most powerful, prophetic passages of the Qurʾān, illuminating man's unbounded greed in general, and, more particularly, the tendencies which have come to dominate all human societies in our technological age.

سورة التكاثر مكية -102-
وآياتها ثمان

IN THE NAME OF GOD, THE MOST GRACIOUS, THE DISPENSER OF GRACE:

بِسۡمِ ٱللَّهِ ٱلرَّحۡمَٰنِ ٱلرَّحِيمِ

أَلۡهَىٰكُمُ ٱلتَّكَاثُرُ ﴿1﴾ حَتَّىٰ زُرۡتُمُ ٱلۡمَقَابِرَ ﴿2﴾ كَلَّا سَوۡفَ تَعۡلَمُونَ ﴿3﴾
ثُمَّ كَلَّا سَوۡفَ تَعۡلَمُونَ ﴿4﴾ كَلَّا لَوۡ تَعۡلَمُونَ عِلۡمَ ٱلۡيَقِينِ ﴿5﴾ لَتَرَوُنَّ
ٱلۡجَحِيمَ ﴿6﴾ ثُمَّ لَتَرَوُنَّهَا عَيۡنَ ٱلۡيَقِينِ ﴿7﴾ ثُمَّ لَتُسۡـَٔلُنَّ يَوۡمَئِذٍ عَنِ ٱلنَّعِيمِ ﴿8﴾

YOU ARE OBSESSED by greed for more and more ‹1› until you go down to your graves.[1] ‹2›

Nay, in time you will come to understand! ‹3›

And once again:[2] Nay, in time you will come to understand! ‹4›

Nay, if you could but understand [it] with an understanding [born] of certainty, ‹5› you would indeed, most surely, behold the blazing fire [of hell]![3] ‹6›

In the end you will indeed, most surely, behold it with the eye of certainty:[4] ‹7›

and on that Day you will most surely be called to account for [what you did with] the boon of life! ‹8›

Bismil-lāhir-Raḥmānir-Raḥīm.
ᵓAlhākumut-takāthuru, ﴿1﴾ ḥattā zurtumul-maqābir. ﴿2﴾ Kallā sawfa taᶜlamūn. ﴿3﴾ Thumma kallā sawfa taᶜlamūn. ﴿4﴾ Kallā law taᶜlamūna ᶜilmal-yaqīn. ﴿5﴾ Latarawunnal-jaḥīm. ﴿6﴾ Thumma latarawunnahā ᶜaynal-yaqīn. ﴿7﴾ Thumma latusᵓalunna Yawmaᵓidhin ᶜanin-naᶜīm. ﴿8﴾

1 The term *takāthur* bears the connotation of "greedily striving for an increase", i.e., in benefits, be they tangible or intangible, real or illusory. In the above context it denotes man's obsessive striving for more and more comforts, more material goods, greater power over his fellow-men or over nature, and unceasing technological progress. A passionate pursuit of such endeavours, to the exclusion of everything else, bars man from all spiritual insight and, hence, from the acceptance of any restrictions and inhibitions based on purely *moral* values – with the result that not only individuals but whole societies gradually lose all inner stability and, thus, all chance of happiness.

2 See *sūrah* 6, note 31.

3 Sc., "in which you find yourselves *now*" – i.e., the "hell on earth" brought about by a fundamentally wrong mode of life: an allusion to the gradual destruction of man's natural environment, as well as to the frustration, unhappiness and confusion which an overriding, unrestrained pursuit of "economic growth" is bound to bring – and has, indeed, brought in our time – upon a mankind that is about to lose the remnants of all spiritual, religious orientation.

4 I.e., in the hereafter, through a direct, unequivocal insight into the real nature of one's past doings, and into the inescapability of the suffering which man brings upon himself by a wrong, wasteful use of the boon of life (*an-naᶜīm*).

سورة العصر مكية

بِسۡمِ ٱللَّهِ ٱلرَّحۡمَٰنِ ٱلرَّحِيمِ

وَٱلۡعَصۡرِ إِنَّ ٱلۡإِنسَٰنَ لَفِي خُسۡرٍ

إِلَّا ٱلَّذِينَ ءَامَنُواْ وَعَمِلُواْ ٱلصَّٰلِحَٰتِ

وآياتها ثلاث

The Hundred-Third Sūrah

Al-ʿAṣr (The Flight of Time)

Mecca Period

REVEALED shortly after *sūrah* 94.

-103-

سورة العصر مكية

وآياتها ثلاث

IN THE NAME OF GOD, THE MOST GRACIOUS, THE DISPENSER OF GRACE:

CONSIDER the flight of time![1] ⟨1⟩
Verily, man is bound to lose himself ⟨2⟩
unless he be of those[2] who attain to faith,
and do good works,
and enjoin upon one another the keeping to truth,
and enjoin upon one another patience in adversity. ⟨3⟩

بِسْمِ ٱللَّهِ ٱلرَّحْمَـٰنِ ٱلرَّحِيمِ

وَٱلْعَصْرِ ﴿١﴾ إِنَّ ٱلْإِنسَـٰنَ لَفِى خُسْرٍ ﴿٢﴾ إِلَّا ٱلَّذِينَ ءَامَنُوا۟ وَعَمِلُوا۟
ٱلصَّـٰلِحَـٰتِ وَتَوَاصَوْا۟ بِٱلْحَقِّ وَتَوَاصَوْا۟ بِٱلصَّبْرِ ﴿٣﴾

Bismil-lāhir-Raḥmānir-Raḥīm.
Wal-ʿaṣr. ⟨1⟩ ʾInnal-ʾInsāna lafī khusr. ⟨2⟩ ʾIllal-ladhīna ʾāmanū wa ʿamiluṣ-ṣāliḥāti wa tawāṣaw bil-ḥaqqi wa tawāsaw biṣṣabr. ⟨3⟩

---

1 The term *ʿaṣr* denotes "time" that is measurable, consisting of a succession of periods (in distinction from *dahr*, which signifies "unlimited time", without beginning or end: i.e., "time absolute"). Hence, *ʿaṣr* bears the connotation of the passing or the flight of time – time which can never be recaptured.

2 Lit., "man is indeed in [a state of] loss, except those . . .", etc.

The Hundred-Fourth Sūrah

Al-Humazah (The Slanderer)

Mecca Period

TAKING its conventional name from a noun occurring in the first verse, this *sūrah* seems to have been revealed towards the end of the third year of Muḥammad's prophethood – probably after *sūrah* 75 ("Resurrection").

سورة الهمزة مكية
-104-
وآياتها تسع

IN THE NAME OF GOD, THE MOST GRACIOUS, THE DISPENSER OF GRACE:

WOE unto every slanderer, fault-finder![1] ⟨1⟩

[Woe unto him[2]] who amasses wealth and counts it a safeguard, ⟨2⟩ thinking that his wealth will make him live forever![3] ⟨3⟩

Nay, but [in the life to come such as] he shall indeed be abandoned to crushing torment![4] ⟨4⟩

And what could make thee conceive what that crushing torment will be? ⟨5⟩

A fire kindled by God, ⟨6⟩ which will rise over the [guilty] hearts:[5] ⟨7⟩

verily, it will close in upon them ⟨8⟩ in endless columns![6] ⟨9⟩

بِسۡمِ ٱللَّهِ ٱلرَّحۡمَٰنِ ٱلرَّحِيمِ

وَيۡلٞ لِّكُلِّ هُمَزَةٖ لُّمَزَةٍ ١ ٱلَّذِي جَمَعَ مَالٗا وَعَدَّدَهُۥ ٢ يَحۡسَبُ أَنَّ مَالَهُۥٓ
أَخۡلَدَهُۥ ٣ كَلَّاۖ لَيُنۢبَذَنَّ فِي ٱلۡحُطَمَةِ ٤ وَمَآ أَدۡرَىٰكَ مَا ٱلۡحُطَمَةُ ٥
نَارُ ٱللَّهِ ٱلۡمُوقَدَةُ ٦ ٱلَّتِي تَطَّلِعُ عَلَى ٱلۡأَفۡـِٔدَةِ ٧ إِنَّهَا عَلَيۡهِم
مُّؤۡصَدَةٞ ٨ فِي عَمَدٖ مُّمَدَّدَةِۭ ٩

Bismil-lāhir-Raḥmānir-Raḥīm
Waylul-likulli humazatil-lumazah. (1) **ʾAlladhī jamaʿa**
mālañw-wa ʿaddadah. (2) **Yaḥsabu ʾanna mālahūu**
ʾakhladah. (3) **Kallā layumbadhanna fil-ḥuṭamah.**
(4) **Wa māa ʾadrāka mal-ḥuṭamah.** (5) **Nārul-lāhil-**
mūqadah. (6) **ʾAllatī taṭṭaliʿu ʿalal-ʾafʾidah.** (7) **ʾIn-**
nahā ʿalayhim-muʾṣadah. (8) **Fī ʿamadim-mumad-**
dadah. (9)

---

1 I.e., everyone who maliciously tries to uncover real or imaginary faults in others.

2 This repetitive interpolation is necessary because the blameworthy attitude spoken of in verses 2-3 obviously belongs to a category entirely different from the two mentioned in verse 1.

3 This is a metonym for the tendency to attribute an almost "religious" value to the acquisition and possession of material goods and facilities – a tendency which precludes man from giving any real importance to spiritual considerations (cf. note 1 on 102 : 1). My rendering of *ʿaddadahu* in the preceding verse as "[he] counts it a safeguard" is based on Jawharī's explanation of this term.

4 *Al-ḥuṭamah* – one of several metaphors for the otherworldly suffering comprised within the concept of "hell" (see note 33 on 15 : 43-44).

5 I.e., originating *in* their hearts – thus clearly alluding to the spiritual nature of the "fire" in the sinners' belated realization of their guilt.

6 Lit., "in extended columns", i.e., overwhelming with despair.

The Hundred-Fifth Sūrah

Al-Fīl (The Elephant)

Mecca Period

TAKING its name from the mention of the "Army of the Elephant" in the first verse, this *sūrah* alludes to the Abyssinian campaign against Mecca in the year 570 of the Christian era. Abrahah, the Christian viceroy of the Yemen (which at that time was ruled by the Abyssinians), erected a great cathedral at Sanᶜāᵓ, hoping thus to divert the annual Arabian pilgrimage from the Meccan sanctuary, the Kaᶜbah, to the new church. When this hope remained unfulfilled, he determined to destroy the Kaᶜbah; and so he set out against Mecca at the head of a large army, which included a number of war elephants as well, and thus represented something hitherto unknown and utterly astounding to the Arabs: hence the designation of that year, by contemporaries as well as historians of later generations, as "the Year of the Elephant". Abrahah's army was totally destroyed on its march (see Ibn Hishām; also Ibn Saᶜd I/1, 55 f.) – probably by an extremely virulent outbreak of smallpox or typhus (see note 2 below) – and Abrahah himself died on his return to Sanᶜāᵓ.

-105-

سورة الفيل مكية
وآياتها خمس

IN THE NAME OF GOD, THE MOST GRACIOUS, THE DISPENSER OF GRACE:

ART THOU NOT aware of how thy Sustainer dealt with the Army of the Elephant?[1] ‹1›
Did He not utterly confound their artful planning? ‹2›
Thus, He let loose upon them great swarms of flying creatures ‹3› which smote them with stone-hard blows of chastisement pre-ordained,[2] ‹4› and caused them to become like a field of grain that has been eaten down to stubble[3] – ‹5›

بِسْمِ ٱللَّهِ ٱلرَّحْمَٰنِ ٱلرَّحِيمِ

أَلَمْ تَرَ كَيْفَ فَعَلَ رَبُّكَ بِأَصْحَٰبِ ٱلْفِيلِ (1) أَلَمْ يَجْعَلْ كَيْدَهُمْ فِى
تَضْلِيلٍ (2) وَأَرْسَلَ عَلَيْهِمْ طَيْرًا أَبَابِيلَ (3) تَرْمِيهِم بِحِجَارَةٍ مِّن
سِجِّيلٍ (4) فَجَعَلَهُمْ كَعَصْفٍ مَّأْكُولٍ (5)

Bismil-lāhir-Raḥmānir-Raḥīm.
ʾAlam tara kayfa faʿala Rabbuka biʾaṣḥābil-fīl. (1)
ʾAlam yajʿal kaydahum fī taḍlīl. (2) Wa ʾarsala
ʿalayhim ṭayran ʾabābīl. (3) Tarmīhim biḥijāratim-
min-sijjīl. (4) Fajaʿalahum kaʿaṣfim-maʾkūl. (5)

---

1 Lit., "the companions (*aṣḥāb*) of the elephant" – see introductory note.

2 Lit., "with stones of *sijjīl*". As explained in note 114 on 11 : 82, this latter term is synonymous with *sijill*, which signifies "a writing" and, tropically, "something that has been decreed [by God]": hence, the phrase *ḥijārah min sijjīl* is a metaphor for "stone-hard blows of chastisement pre-ordained", i.e., in God's decree (Zamakhsharī and Rāzī, with analogous comments on the same expression in 11 : 82). As already mentioned in the introductory note, the particular chastisement to which the above verse alludes seems to have been a sudden epidemic of extreme virulence: according to Wāqidī and Muḥammad ibn Isḥāq – the latter as quoted by Ibn Hishām and Ibn Kathīr – "this was the first time that spotted fever (*ḥaṣbah*) and smallpox (*judarī*) appeared in the land of the Arabs". It is interesting to note that the word *ḥaṣbah* – which, according to some authorities, signifies also typhus – primarily means "pelting [or smiting"] with stones" (*Qāmūs*). – As regards the noun *ṭāʾir* (of which *ṭayr* is the plural), we ought to remember that it denotes any "flying creature", whether bird or insect (*Tāj al-ʿArūs*). Neither the Qurʾān nor any authentic Tradition offers us any evidence as to the nature of the "flying creatures" mentioned in the above verse; and since, on the other hand, all the "descriptions" indulged in by the commentators are purely imaginary, they need not be seriously considered. If the hypothesis of an epidemic is correct, the "flying creatures" – whether birds or insects – may well have been the carriers of the infection. One thing, however, is clear: whatever the nature of the doom that overtook the invading force, it was certainly miraculous in the true sense of this word – namely, in the sudden, totally unexpected rescue which it brought to the distressed people of Mecca.

3 This passage is evidently continued in the next *sūrah*, which, according to some authorities, is part of the present one (see introductory note to *sūrah* 106).

The Hundred-Sixth Sūrah

Quraysh

Mecca Period

ACCORDING to some of the Companions of the Prophet and several learned men of the next generation, this *sūrah* and the preceding one form, in fact, one entity. Thus, in the Qur'ān-copy owned by Ubayy ibn Kaᶜb, *Al-Fīl* and *Quraysh* were written as one *sūrah* i.e., without the customary invocation "In the name of God" intervening between them (Baghawī and Zamakhsharī). We must remember that side by side with Zayd ibn Thābit and ᶜAlī ibn Abī Ṭālib, Ubayy ibn Kaᶜb was one of the foremost authorities on whom both Abū Bakr and ᶜUthmān relied for the final recension of the text of the Qur'ān; and it is probably for this reason that Ibn Ḥajar al-ᶜAsqalānī regards the evidence of Ubayy's Qur'ān-copy as fairly conclusive (*Fatḥ al-Bārī* VIII, 593). Moreover, it is established that, when leading the congregational prayer, ᶜUmar ibn al-Khaṭṭāb used to recite the two *sūrahs* as one (Zamakhsharī and Rāzī). But whether *Al-Fīl* and *Quraysh* are one *sūrah* or two separate ones, there is hardly any doubt that the latter is a continuation of the former, implying that God destroyed the Army of the Elephant "so that the Quraysh might remain secure" (see verse 1 on the following page and the corresponding note).

-106-
سورة قريش مكية
وآياتها أربع

IN THE NAME OF GOD, THE MOST GRACIOUS, THE DISPENSER OF GRACE:

SO THAT the Quraysh might remain secure,[1] ‹1› secure in their winter and summer journeys.[2] ‹2›
Let them, therefore, worship the Sustainer of this Temple,[3] ‹3› who has given them food against hunger, and made them safe from danger.[4] ‹4›

بِسْمِ ٱللَّهِ ٱلرَّحْمَٰنِ ٱلرَّحِيمِ

لِإِيلَٰفِ قُرَيْشٍ ۝١ إِۦلَٰفِهِمْ رِحْلَةَ ٱلشِّتَآءِ وَٱلصَّيْفِ ۝٢ فَلْيَعْبُدُوا۟
رَبَّ هَٰذَا ٱلْبَيْتِ ۝٣ ٱلَّذِىٓ أَطْعَمَهُم مِّن جُوعٍ وَءَامَنَهُم مِّنْ
خَوْفٍۭ ۝٤

Bismil-lāhir-Raḥmānir-Raḥīm.
**Li˒īlāfi Quraysh. (1) ˒Īlāfihim riḥlatash-shitāa˒i
waṣ-ṣayf. (2) Falya˓budū Rabba hādhal-Bayt. (3)
˒Alladhīi ˒aṭ˓amahum-miñ-jū˓iñw-wa ˒āmanahum-
min khawf. (4)**

---

1 Lit., "for the safeguarding of the Quraysh", i.e., as the custodians of the Ka˓bah and the tribe in the midst of which the Last Prophet, Muḥammad, was to appear. Thus, the "security of the Quraysh" is a metonym for the security of the Ka˓bah, the focal point of the Faith based on the concept of God's oneness, for the sake of which the army of Abrahah was destroyed (see introductory note as well as preceding *sūrah*).

2 I.e., the two annual trade caravans – to the Yemen in winter and to Syria in summer – on which the prosperity of Mecca depended.

3 I.e., the Ka˓bah (see note 102 on 2 : 125).

4 Cf. Abraham's prayer, "O my Sustainer! Make this a land secure, and grant its people fruitful sustenance" (2 : 126).

The Hundred-Seventh Sūrah

Al-Mā ᶜūn (Assistance)

Mecca Period

THE NAME of this *sūrah*, which was revealed in the early years of the Prophet's mission (probably after *sūrah* 102), is derived from the word *al-mā ᶜūn* occurring in the last verse. The view of some commentators that verses 4-7 were revealed at Medina lacks all historical or textual evidence and may, therefore, be disregarded.

سورة الماعون مكية -107-
وآياتها سبع

IN THE NAME OF GOD, THE MOST GRACIOUS, THE DISPENSER OF GRACE:

بِسْمِ ٱللَّهِ ٱلرَّحْمَٰنِ ٱلرَّحِيمِ

HAST THOU ever considered [the kind of man] who gives the lie to all moral law?[1] ‹1›
Behold, it is this [kind of man] that thrusts the orphan away, ‹2›
and feels no urge[2] to feed the needy. ‹3›
Woe, then, unto those praying ones ‹4›
whose hearts from their prayer are remote[3] ‹5›
– those who want only to be seen and praised, ‹6›
and, withal, deny all assistance [to their fellow-men]![4] ‹7›

أَرَءَيْتَ ٱلَّذِى يُكَذِّبُ بِٱلدِّينِ ۝١ فَذَٰلِكَ ٱلَّذِى يَدُعُّ ٱلْيَتِيمَ ۝٢ وَلَا
يَحُضُّ عَلَىٰ طَعَامِ ٱلْمِسْكِينِ ۝٣ فَوَيْلٌ لِّلْمُصَلِّينَ ۝٤ ٱلَّذِينَ هُمْ عَن
صَلَاتِهِمْ سَاهُونَ ۝٥ ٱلَّذِينَ هُمْ يُرَآءُونَ ۝٦ وَيَمْنَعُونَ ٱلْمَاعُونَ ۝٧

Bismil-lāhir-Raḥmānir-Raḥīm.

ᵓAraᵓaytal-ladhī yukadhdhibu biddīn. ۝1 Fadhālikal-ladhī yaduᶜᶜul-yatīm. ۝2 Wa lā yaḥuḍḍu ᶜalā ṭaᶜāmil-miskīn. ۝3 Fawaylul-lilmuṣallīn, ۝4 ᵓalladhīna hum ᶜan-ṣalātihim sāhūn. ۝5 ᵓAlladhīna hum yurāaᵓūn. ۝6 Wa yamnaᶜūnal-māᶜūn. ۝7

1 I.e., who denies that there is any objective validity in religion *as such* and, thus, in the concept of moral law (which is one of the primary connotations of the term *dīn* – cf. note 3 on 109 : 6). Some commentators are of the opinion that in the above context *dīn* signifies "judgment", i.e., the Day of Judgment, and interpret this phrase as meaning "who calls the Day of Judgment a lie".

2 Lit., "does not urge", i.e., himself.

3 Lit., "who are [knowingly] unmindful of their prayers".

4 The term *al-mā ᶜūn* comprises the many small items needed for one's daily use, as well as the occasional acts of kindness consisting in helping out one's fellow-men with such items. In its wider sense, it denotes "aid" or "assistance" in any difficulty.

The Hundred-Eighth Sūrah

Al-Kawthar (Good in Abundance)

Period Uncertain

WHEREAS most of the authorities assign this *sūrah* to the early part of the Mecca period, Ibn Kathīr considers it most probable that it was revealed at Medina. The reason for this assumption (shared by many other scholars) is to be found in an authentic *ḥadīth* on the authority of Anas ibn Mālik, who narrates – with a good deal of circumstantial detail – how the *sūrah* was revealed "while the Apostle of God was *among us in the mosque*" (Muslim, Ibn Ḥanbal, Abū Dā᾽ūd, Nasā᾽ī). The "mosque" referred to by Anas can only have been the mosque of Medina: for, on the one hand, Anas – a native of that town – had never met the Prophet before the latter's exodus to Medina (at which time Anas was barely ten years old); and, on the other hand, there had been no mosque – i.e., a public place of congregational worship – available to the Muslims at Mecca before their conquest of that city in 8 H.

The three verses of the *sūrah* are addressed, in the first instance, to the Prophet and, through him, to every believing man and woman.

سورة الكوثر مكية -108- وآياتها ثلاث

IN THE NAME OF GOD, THE MOST GRACIOUS, THE DISPENSER OF GRACE:

BEHOLD, We have bestowed upon thee good in abundance:[1] ‹1› hence, pray unto thy Sustainer [alone], and sacrifice [unto Him alone]. ‹2›
Verily, he that hates thee has indeed been cut off [from all that is good]![2] ‹3›

بِسْمِ ٱللَّهِ ٱلرَّحْمَٰنِ ٱلرَّحِيمِ

إِنَّآ أَعْطَيْنَٰكَ ٱلْكَوْثَرَ ﴿١﴾ فَصَلِّ لِرَبِّكَ وَٱنْحَرْ ﴿٢﴾ إِنَّ شَانِئَكَ هُوَ ٱلْأَبْتَرُ ﴿٣﴾

Bismil-lāhir-Raḥmānir-Raḥīm.
᾽Innāa ᾽aᶜṭaynākal-kawthar. ﴿1﴾ Faṣalli liRabbika wan-ḥar. ﴿2﴾ ᾽Inna shāni᾽aka huwal-᾽abtar. ﴿3﴾

---

1 The term *kawthar* is an intensive form of the noun *kathrah* (Zamakhsharī), which, in its turn, denotes "copiousness", "multitude" or "abundance"; it also occurs as an adjective with the same connotation (*Qāmūs, Lisān al-ᶜArab*, etc.). In the above context, which is the sole instance of its use in the Qur᾽ān, *al-kawthar* obviously relates to the abundant bestowal on the Prophet of all that is good in an abstract, spiritual sense, like revelation, knowledge, wisdom, the doing of good works, and dignity in this world and in the hereafter (Rāzī); with reference to the believers in general, it evidently signifies the *ability* to acquire knowledge, to do good works, to be kind towards all living beings, and thus to attain to inner peace and dignity.

2 Lit., "it is he that is cut off (*abtar*)". The addition, between brackets, of the phrase "from all that is good" is based on an explanation forthcoming from the *Qāmūs*.

The Hundred-Ninth Sūrah

Al-Kāfirūn (Those Who Deny the Truth)

Mecca Period

REVEALED shortly after *sūrah* 107.

-109-
سورة الكافرون مكية
وآياتها ست

IN THE NAME OF GOD, THE MOST GRACIOUS, THE DISPENSER OF GRACE:

SAY: "O you who deny the truth! ⟨1⟩
"I do not worship that which you worship, ⟨2⟩ and neither do you worship that which I worship.[1] ⟨3⟩
"And I will not worship that which you have [ever] worshipped, ⟨4⟩ and neither will you [ever] worship that which I worship.[2] ⟨5⟩
"Unto you, your moral law, and unto me, mine!"[3] ⟨6⟩

بِسْمِ ٱللَّهِ ٱلرَّحْمَٰنِ ٱلرَّحِيمِ

قُلْ يَٰٓأَيُّهَا ٱلْكَٰفِرُونَ ﴿١﴾ لَآ أَعْبُدُ مَا تَعْبُدُونَ ﴿٢﴾ وَلَآ أَنتُمْ عَٰبِدُونَ
مَآ أَعْبُدُ ﴿٣﴾ وَلَآ أَنَا۠ عَابِدٌ مَّا عَبَدتُّمْ ﴿٤﴾ وَلَآ أَنتُمْ عَٰبِدُونَ مَآ
أَعْبُدُ ﴿٥﴾ لَكُمْ دِينُكُمْ وَلِىَ دِينِ ﴿٦﴾

Bismil-lāhir-Raḥmānir-Raḥīm.
Qul yāa ʾayyuhal-kāfirūn. ⟨1⟩ **Lāa ʾaʿbudu mā taʿbudūn.** ⟨2⟩ **Wa lāa ʾantum ʿābidūna māa ʾaʿbud.** ⟨3⟩ **Wa lāa ʾana ʿābidum-mā ʿabattum.** ⟨4⟩ **Wa lāa ʾantum ʿābidūna māa ʾaʿbud.** ⟨5⟩ **Lakum dīnukum wa liya dīn.** ⟨6⟩

---

1 In the above rendering, the particle *mā* ("that which") alludes, on the one hand, to all positive concepts and ethical values – e.g., belief in God and the believer's self-surrender to Him – and, on the other, to false objects of worship and false values, such as man's belief in his own supposed "self-sufficiency" (cf. 96 : 6-7), or his overriding, almost compulsive "greed for more and more" (*sūrah* 102).

2 Sc., "so long as you are unwilling to abandon the false values which cause you to deny the truth".

3 Lit., "unto me, my moral law". The primary significance of *dīn* is "obedience"; in particular, obedience to a law or to what is conceived as a system of established – and therefore binding – usages, i.e., something endowed with moral authority: hence "religion", "faith" or "religious law" in the widest sense of these terms (cf. first half of note 249 on 2 : 256); or simply "moral law", as in the above instance as well as in 42 : 21, 95 : 7, 98 : 5 or 107 : 1.

The Hundred-Tenth Sūrah

An-Naṣr (Succour)

Medina Period

REVEALED at Minā during the Prophet's Farewell Pilgrimage in the month of Dhu 'l-Ḥijjah, 10 H. – that is, a little over two months before his death – this is unquestionably the last complete *sūrah* conveyed by him to the world. It was preceded one day earlier (on Friday, the 9th of Dhu 'l-Ḥijjah) by the revelation of the words, "Today have I perfected your religious law for you, and bestowed upon you the full measure of My blessings, and willed that self-surrender unto Me (*al-islām*) shall be your religion" (5 : 3); and since those words were almost immediately followed by the present *sūrah*, some of the Prophet's Companions concluded that his mission was fulfilled, and that he was about to die (Bukhārī). As a matter of fact, the only revelation which the Prophet received after *An-Naṣr* was verse 281 of *Al-Baqarah*.

-110-

سورة النصر مدنية

وآياتها ثلاث

IN THE NAME OF GOD, THE MOST GRACIOUS, THE DISPENSER OF GRACE:

WHEN GOD'S SUCCOUR comes, and victory, ‹1› and thou seest people enter God's religion[1] in hosts, ‹2› extol thy Sustainer's limitless glory, and praise Him, and seek His forgiveness: for, behold, He is ever an acceptor of repentance.[2] ‹3›

بِسۡمِ ٱللَّهِ ٱلرَّحۡمَٰنِ ٱلرَّحِيمِ

إِذَا جَآءَ نَصۡرُ ٱللَّهِ وَٱلۡفَتۡحُ ﴿١﴾ وَرَأَيۡتَ ٱلنَّاسَ يَدۡخُلُونَ فِي دِينِ ٱللَّهِ
أَفۡوَاجٗا ﴿٢﴾ فَسَبِّحۡ بِحَمۡدِ رَبِّكَ وَٱسۡتَغۡفِرۡهُۚ إِنَّهُۥ كَانَ تَوَّابَۢا ﴿٣﴾

Bismil-lāhir-Raḥmānir-Raḥīm.
ʾIdhā jāaʾa naṣrul-lāhi wal-fatḥ. (1) Wa raʾaytan-nāsa yadkhulūna fī Dīnil-lāhi ʾafwājā. (2) Fasabbiḥ biḥamdi Rabbika was-taghfirhu ʾinnahū kāna Taw-wābā. (3)

---

1 I.e., the religion of self-surrender to God: cf. 3 : 19 – "the only [true] religion in the sight of God is [man's] self-surrender unto Him".

2 Implying that even if people *should* embrace the true religion in great numbers, a believer ought not to grow self-complacent but should, rather, become more humble and more conscious of his own failings. Moreover, the Prophet is reported to have said, "Behold, people have entered God's religion in hosts – and in time they will leave it in hosts" (Ibn Ḥanbal, on the authority of Jābir ibn ʿAbd Allāh; a similar Tradition, on the authority of Abū Hurayrah, is found in the *Mustadrak*).

The Hundred-Eleventh Sūrah

Al-Masad (The Twisted Strands)

Mecca Period

THIS very early *sūrah* – the sixth in the order of revelation – derives its name from its last word. It relates to the bitter hostility always shown to the Prophet's message by his uncle Abū Lahab: a hostility rooted in his inborn arrogance, pride in his great wealth, and a dislike of the idea, propounded by Muḥammad, that all human beings are equal before God and will be judged by Him on their merits alone (Ibn Zayd, as quoted by Ṭabarī in his commentary on the first verse of this *sūrah*).

As reported by several unimpeachable authorities – Bukhārī and Muslim among them – the Prophet ascended one day the hillock of Aṣ-Ṣafā in Mecca and called together all who could hear him from among his tribe, the Quraysh. When they had assembled, he asked them: "O sons of ᶜAbd al-Muṭṭalib! O sons of Fihr! If I were to inform you that enemy warriors are about to fall upon you from behind that hill, would you believe me?" They answered: "Yes, we would." Thereupon he said: "Behold, then, I am here to warn you of the coming of the Last Hour!" At that, Abū Lahab exclaimed: "Was it for this purpose that thou hast summoned us? May thou be doomed!" And shortly afterwards this *sūrah* was revealed.

سورة المسد مكية -111-
وآياتها خمس

IN THE NAME OF GOD, THE MOST GRACIOUS, THE DISPENSER OF GRACE:

DOOMED are the hands of him of the glowing countenance,[1] and doomed is he! ‹1›
What will his wealth avail him, and all that he has gained? ‹2›
[In the life to come] he shall have to endure a fire fiercely glowing,[2] ‹3› together with his wife, that carrier of evil tales,[3] ‹4› [who bears] around her neck a rope of twisted strands![4] ‹5›

بِسْمِ ٱللَّهِ ٱلرَّحْمَٰنِ ٱلرَّحِيمِ

تَبَّتْ يَدَآ أَبِى لَهَبٍ وَتَبَّ ﴿1﴾ مَآ أَغْنَىٰ عَنْهُ مَالُهُۥ وَمَا كَسَبَ ﴿2﴾
سَيَصْلَىٰ نَارًا ذَاتَ لَهَبٍ ﴿3﴾ وَٱمْرَأَتُهُۥ حَمَّالَةَ ٱلْحَطَبِ ﴿4﴾ فِى
جِيدِهَا حَبْلٌ مِّن مَّسَدٍۭ ﴿5﴾

Bismil-lāhir-Raḥmānir-Raḥīm.
Tabbat yadāa ᵓAbī Lahabiñw-wa tabb. ﴾1﴿ Māa ᵓaghnā ᶜanhu māluhū wa mā kasab. ﴾2﴿ Sayaṣlā nārañ-dhāta lahab. ﴾3﴿ Wam-raᵓatuhu ḥammālatal-ḥaṭab. ﴾4﴿ Fī jīdihā ḥablum-mim-masad. ﴾5﴿

---

1 The real name of this uncle of the Prophet was ᶜAbd al-ᶜUzzā. He was popularly nicknamed Abū Lahab (lit., "He of the Flame") on account of his beauty, which was most notably expressed in his glowing countenance (Baghawī, on the authority of Muqātil; Zamakhsharī and Rāzī *passim* in their comments on the above verse; *Fatḥ al-Bārī* VIII, 599). Since this nickname, or *kunyah*, appears to have been applied to him even before the advent of Islam, there is no reason to suppose that it had a pejorative significance. – The expression "hands" in the above clause is, in accordance with classical Arabic usage, a metonym for "power", alluding to Abū Lahab's great influence.

2 The expression *nār dhāt lahab* is a subtle play upon the meaning of the nickname Abū Lahab.

3 Lit., "carrier of firewood", a well-known idiomatic expression denoting one who surreptitiously carries evil tales and slander from one person to another "so as to kindle the flames of hatred between them" (Zamakhsharī; see also ᶜIkrimah, Mujāhid and Qatādah, as quoted by Ṭabarī). The woman's name was Arwā umm Jamīl bint Ḥarb ibn Umayyah; she was a sister of Abū Sufyān and, hence, a paternal aunt of Muᶜāwiyah, the founder of the Umayyad dynasty. Her hatred of Muḥammad, and his followers was so intense that she would often, under the cover of darkness, scatter thorns before the Prophet's house with a view to causing him hurt; and she employed her great eloquence in persistently slandering him and his message.

4 The term *masad* signifies anything that consists of twisted strands, irrespective of the material (*Qāmūs, Mughnī, Lisān al-ᶜArab*). In the abstract sense in which it is evidently used here, the above phrase seems to have a double connotation: it alludes to the woman's twisted, warped nature, as well as to the spiritual truth that "every human being's destiny is tied to his neck" (see 17 : 13 and, in particular, the corresponding note 17) – which, together with verse 2, reveals the general, timeless purport of this *sūrah*.

The Hundred-Twelfth Sūrah

Al-ʾIkhlāṣ (The Declaration of [God's] Perfection)

Mecca Period

AS REPORTED in a great number of authentic Traditions, the Prophet was wont to describe this *sūrah* as "equivalent to one-third of the whole Qurʾān" (Bukhārī, Muslim, Ibn Ḥanbal, Abu Dāʾūd, Nasāʾī, Tirmidhī, Ibn Mājah). It seems to have been revealed in the early part of the Mecca period.

سورة الإخلاص مكية -112-
وآياتها أربع

IN THE NAME OF GOD, THE MOST GRACIOUS, THE DISPENSER OF GRACE:

بِسْمِ ٱللَّهِ ٱلرَّحْمَٰنِ ٱلرَّحِيمِ

SAY: "He is the One God: ‹1›
"God the Eternal, the Uncaused Cause of All That Exists."[1] ‹2›
"He begets not, and neither is He begotten; ‹3›
"and there is nothing that could be compared with Him."[2] ‹4›

قُلْ هُوَ ٱللَّهُ أَحَدٌ ﴿١﴾ ٱللَّهُ ٱلصَّمَدُ ﴿٢﴾ لَمْ يَلِدْ وَلَمْ يُولَدْ ﴿٣﴾ وَلَمْ يَكُن
لَّهُۥ كُفُوًا أَحَدٌۢ ﴿٤﴾

Bismil-lāhir-Raḥmānir-Raḥīm.
Qul Huwal-lāhu ʾAḥad. ‹1› ʾAllāhuṣ-Ṣamad. ‹2› Lam yalid wa lam yūlad. ‹3› Wa lam yakul-lahū kufuwan ʾAḥad. ‹4›

---

1 This rendering gives no more than an approximate meaning of the term *aṣ-ṣamad*, which occurs in the Qurʾān only once, and is applied to God alone. It comprises the concepts of Primary Cause and eternal, independent Being, combined with the idea that everything existing or conceivable goes back to Him as its source and is, therefore, dependent on Him for its beginning as well as for its continued existence.

2 Cf. note 2 on 89 : 3, as well as *sūrah* 19, note 77. The fact that God is one and unique in every respect, without beginning and without end, has its logical correlate in the statement that "there is nothing that could be compared with Him" – thus precluding any possibility of describing or defining Him (see note 88 on the last sentence of 6 : 100). Consequently, the *quality* of His Being is beyond the range of human comprehension or imagination: which also explains why any attempt at "depicting" God by means of figurative representations or even abstract symbols must be qualified as a blasphemous denial of the truth.

The Hundred-Thirteenth Sūrah

Al-Falaq (The Rising Dawn)

Period Uncertain

WHEREAS most of the commentators assign this and the next *sūrah* to the early part of the Mecca period, some authorities (e.g., Rāzī, Ibn Kathīr) consider them to have been revealed at Medina, while yet others (e.g., Baghawī, Zamakhsharī, Bayḍāwī) leave the question open. On the basis of the scant evidence available to us it appears probable that both these *sūrahs* are of early Meccan origin.

سورة الفلق مكية -113- وآياتها خمس

IN THE NAME OF GOD, THE MOST GRACIOUS, THE DISPENSER OF GRACE:

SAY: "I seek refuge with the Sustainer of the rising dawn,[1] ‹1›
"from the evil of aught that He has created, ‹2›
"and from the evil of the black darkness whenever it descends,[2] ‹3›
"and from the evil of all human beings bent on occult endeavours,[3] ‹4›

بِسْمِ ٱللَّهِ ٱلرَّحْمَٰنِ ٱلرَّحِيمِ

قُلْ أَعُوذُ بِرَبِّ ٱلْفَلَقِ ﴿١﴾ مِن شَرِّ مَا خَلَقَ ﴿٢﴾ وَمِن شَرِّ غَاسِقٍ إِذَا
وَقَبَ ﴿٣﴾ وَمِن شَرِّ ٱلنَّفَّٰثَٰتِ فِى ٱلْعُقَدِ ﴿٤﴾

Bismil-lāhir-Raḥmānir-Raḥīm.
Qul ᵓaᶜūdhu biRabbil-falaq. (1) Miñ-sharri mā khalaq. (2) Wa miñ-sharri ghāsiqin ᵓidhā waqab. (3) Wa miñ-sharrin-naffāthāti fil-ᶜuqad. (4)

---

1 The term *al-falaq* ("the light of dawn" or "the rising dawn") is often used tropically to describe "the emergence of the truth after [a period of] uncertainty" (*Tāj al-ᶜArūs*): hence, the appellation "Sustainer of the rising dawn" implies that God is the source of all cognition of truth, and that one's "seeking refuge" with Him is synonymous with striving after truth.

2 I.e., the darkness of despair, or of approaching death. In all these four verses (2-5), the term "evil" (*sharr*) has not only an objective but also a subjective connotation – namely, *fear* of evil.

3 Lit., "of those that blow (*an-naffāthāt*) upon knots": an idiomatic phrase current in pre-Islamic Arabia and, hence, employed in classical Arabic to designate all supposedly occult endeavours; it was probably derived from the practice of "witches" and "sorcerers" who used to tie a string into a number of knots while blowing upon them and murmuring magic incantations. The feminine gender of *naffāthāt* does not, as Zamakhsharī and Rāzī point out, necessarily indicate "women", but may well relate to "human beings" (*anfus*, sing. *nafs*, a noun that is grammatically feminine). In his explanation of the above verse, Zamakhsharī categorically rejects all belief in the reality and effectiveness of such

"and from the evil of the envious when he envies."[4] ‹5›

وَمِن شَرِّ حَاسِدٍ إِذَا حَسَدَ ﴿٥﴾

Wa miñ-sharri ḥāsidin ʾidhā ḥasad. ﴿5﴾

practices, as well as of the concept of "magic" as such. Similar views have been expressed – albeit in a much more elaborate manner, on the basis of established psychological findings – by Muḥammad ʿAbduh and Rashīd Riḍāʾ (see *Manār* I, 398 ff.). The reason why the believer is enjoined to "seek refuge with God" from such practices despite their palpable irrationality is – according to Zamakhsharī – to be found in the inherent *sinfulness* of such endeavours (see *sūrah* 2. note 84), and in the mental danger in which they may involve their author.

4 I.e., from the effects – moral and social – which another person's envy may have on one's life, as well as from succumbing oneself to the evil of envy. In this connection, Zamakhsharī quotes a saying of the Caliph ʿUmar ibn ʿAbd al-ʿAzīz (called "the Second ʿUmar" on account of his piety and integrity): "I cannot think of any wrongdoer (*ẓālim*) who is more likely to be the wronged one (*maẓlūm*) than he who envies another."

The Hundred-Fourteenth Sūrah

An-Nās (Men)

Period Uncertain

SEE introductory note to the preceding *sūrah*, with which this one is closely connected.

سورة الناس مكية -114-
وآياتها ست

IN THE NAME OF GOD, THE MOST GRACIOUS, THE DISPENSER OF GRACE:

SAY: "I seek refuge with the Sustainer of men, ‹1›
"the Sovereign of men, ‹2›
"the God of men, ‹3›
"from the evil of the whispering, elusive tempter ‹4›
"who whispers in the hearts of men[1] ‹5›
– "from all [temptation to evil by] invisible forces as well as men."[2] ‹6›

بِسْمِ ٱللَّهِ ٱلرَّحْمَٰنِ ٱلرَّحِيمِ

قُلْ أَعُوذُ بِرَبِّ ٱلنَّاسِ ﴿١﴾ مَلِكِ ٱلنَّاسِ ﴿٢﴾ إِلَٰهِ ٱلنَّاسِ ﴿٣﴾ مِن شَرِّ
ٱلْوَسْوَاسِ ٱلْخَنَّاسِ ﴿٤﴾ ٱلَّذِى يُوَسْوِسُ فِى صُدُورِ ٱلنَّاسِ ﴿٥﴾ مِنَ
ٱلْجِنَّةِ وَٱلنَّاسِ ﴿٦﴾

Bismil-lāhir-Raḥmānir-Raḥīm.
Qul ʾaʿūdhu biRabbin-nās. ‹1› Malikin-nās. ‹2› ʾIlāhin-nās. ‹3› Miñ-sharril-waswāsil-khannās. ‹4› ʾAlladhī yuwaswisu fī ṣudūrin-nās. ‹5› Minal-Jinnati wan-nās. ‹6›

1 I.e., "Satan" in the widest meaning of this designation, as pointed out by Rāzī (quoted in *sūrah* 14, note 31).

2 The above is perhaps the oldest Qurʾanic mention of the term and concept of *al-jinnah* (synonymous with *al-jinn*), which has been tentatively explained in Appendix III. In the above context, the term probably denotes the intangible, mysterious forces of nature to which man's psyche is exposed, and which sometimes make it difficult for us to discern between right and wrong. However, in the light of this last verse of the last *sūrah* of the Qurʾān it is also possible to conclude that the "invisible forces" from which we are told to seek refuge with God are the temptations to evil emanating from the blindness of our own hearts, from our gross appetites, and from the erroneous notions and false values that may have been handed down to us by our predecessors.

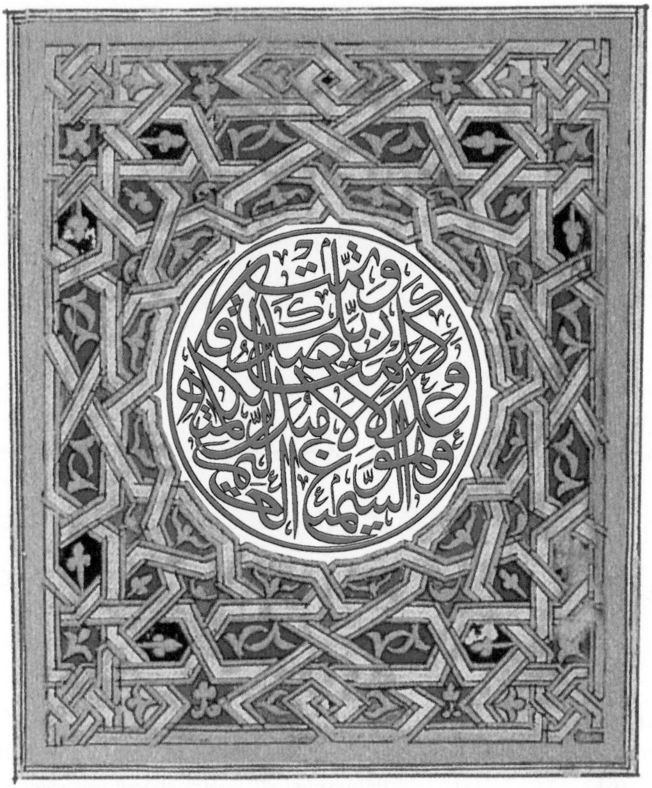

Wa tammat Kalimatu Rabbika ṣid-qañw-wa ʿadlā. Lā mubaddila liKa-limātihī wa Huwas-Samīʿul-ʿAlīm.

وَتَمَّتْ كَلِمَتُ رَبِّكَ صِدْقًا وَعَدْلًا لَّا
مُبَدِّلَ لِكَلِمَٰتِهِۦ وَهُوَ ٱلسَّمِيعُ ٱلْعَلِيمُ

– for, truly and justly has thy Sustainer's promise been fulfilled. There is no power that could alter [the fulfilment of] His promises: and He alone is all-hearing, all-knowing.

Sūrah 6, *verse* 115. *Volume* 2, *page* 217

Appendix I

Symbolism and Allegory in the Qur'ān

WHEN studying the Qur'ān, one frequently encounters what may be described as "key-phrases" – that is to say, statements which provide a clear, concise indication of the idea underlying a particular passage or passages: for instance, the many references to the creation of man "out of dust" and "out of a drop of sperm", pointing to the lowly biological origin of the human species; or the statement in the ninety-ninth *sūrah* (*Az-Zalzalah*) that on Resurrection Day "he who shall have done an atom's weight of good, shall behold it; and he who shall have done an atom's weight of evil, shall behold it" – indicating the ineluctible afterlife consequences of, and the responsibility for, all that man consciously does in this world; or the divine declaration (in 38 : 27), "We have not created heaven and earth and all that is between them without meaning and purpose (*bāṭilan*), as is the surmise of those who are bent on denying the truth."

Instances of such Qur'anic key-phrases can be quoted almost *ad infinitum*, and in many varying formulations. But there is one fundamental statement in the Qur'ān which occurs only once, and which may be qualified as "the key-phrase of all its key-phrases": the statement in verse 7 of *Āl ʿImrān* to the effect that the Qur'ān "contains messages that are clear in and by themselves (*āyāt muḥkamāt*) as well as others that are allegorical (*mutashābihāt*)". It is this verse which represents, in an absolute sense, a key to the understanding of the Qur'anic message and makes the whole of it accessible to "people who think" (*li-qawmin yatafakkarūn*).

In my notes on the above-mentioned verse of *Āl ʿImrān* I have tried to elucidate the meaning of the expression *āyāt muḥkamāt* as well as the general purport of what is termed *mutashābih* ("allegorical" or "symbolic"). Without a proper grasp of what is implied by this latter term, much of the Qur'ān is liable to be – and, in fact, has often been – grossly misunderstood both by believers and by such as refuse to believe in its divinely-inspired origin. However, an appreciation of what is meant by "allegory" or "symbolism" in the context of the Qur'ān is, by itself, not enough to make one fully understand its world-view: in order to achieve this we must relate the Qur'anic use of these terms to a concept touched upon almost at the very beginning of the divine writ – namely, the existence of "a realm which is beyond the reach of human perception" (*al-ghayb*). It is this concept that constitutes the basic premise for an understanding of the call of the Qur'ān, and, indeed, of the principle of religion – every religion – as such: for all truly religious cognition arises from and is based on the fact that only a small segment of reality is open to man's perception and imagination, and that by far the larger part of it escapes his comprehension altogether.

However, side by side with this clear-cut metaphysical concept we have a not less clear-cut finding of a psychological nature: namely, the finding that the human mind (in which term we comprise conscious thinking, imagination, dream-life, intuition, memory, etc.) can operate only on the basis of perceptions previously experienced by that very mind either in their entirety or in some of their constituent elements: that is to say, it cannot visualize, or form an idea of, something that lies entirely *outside* the realm of previously realized experiences. Hence, whenever we arrive at a seemingly "new" mental image or idea, we find, on closer examination, that even if it is new as a composite entity, it is not really new as regards its component *elements*, for these are invariably derived from previous – and sometimes quite disparate – mental experiences which are now but brought together in a new combination or series of new combinations.

Now as soon as we *realize* that the human mind cannot operate otherwise than on the basis of previous experiences – that is to say, on the basis of apperceptions and cognitions already recorded in that mind – we are faced by a weighty question: Since the metaphysical ideas of religion relate, by virtue of their nature, to a realm beyond the reach of human perception or experience – how can they be successfully conveyed to us? How can we be expected to grasp ideas which have no counterpart, not even a fractional one, in any of the apperceptions which we have arrived at empirically?

The answer is self-evident: By means of *loan-images* derived from our actual – physical or mental – experiences; or, as Zamakhsharī phrases it in his commentary on 13 : 35, "through a parabolic illustration, by means of something which we know from our experience, of something that is beyond the reach of our perception" (*tamthīlan li-mā ghāba ʿannā bi-mā nushāhid*). And this is the innermost purport of the term and concept of *al-mutashābihāt* as used in the Qurʾān.

Thus, the Qurʾān tells us clearly that many of its passages and expressions *must* be understood in an allegorical sense for the simple reason that, being intended for human understanding, they could not have been conveyed to us in any other way. It follows, therefore, that if we were to take every Qurʾanic passage, statement or expression in its outward, literal sense and disregard the possibility of its being an allegory, a metaphor or a parable, we would be offending against the very spirit of the divine writ.

Consider, for instance, some of the Qurʾanic references to God's Being – a Being indefinable, infinite in time and space, and utterly beyond any creature's comprehension. Far from being able to imagine Him, we can only realize what He is *not*: namely, not limited in either time or space, not definable in terms of comparison, and not to be comprised within any category of human thought. Hence, only very generalized metaphors can convey to us, though most inadequately, the idea of His existence and activity.

And so, when the Qurʾān speaks of Him as being "in the heavens" or "established on His throne (*al-ʿarsh*)", we cannot possibly take these phrases in their literal senses, since then they would imply, however vaguely, that God is limited in space: and since such a limitation would contradict the concept of an Infinite Being, we know immediately, without the least doubt, that the "heavens" and the "throne" and God's being "established" on it are but linguistic vehicles meant to convey an idea which is outside all human experience, namely, the idea of God's almightiness and absolute sway over all that exists. Similarly, whenever He is described as "all-seeing", "all-hearing" or "all-aware", we know that these descriptions have nothing to do with the phenomena of physical seeing or hearing but simply circumscribe, in terms understandable to man, the fact of God's eternal Presence in all that is or happens. And since "no human vision can encompass Him" (Qurʾān 6 : 103), man is not expected to realize His existence otherwise than through observing the effects of His unceasing activity within and upon the universe created by Him.

But whereas our belief in God's existence does not – and, indeed, could not – depend on our grasping the unfathomable "how" of His Being, the same is not the case with problems connected with *man's own* existence, and, in particular, with the idea of a life in the hereafter: for, man's psyche is so constituted that it cannot accept any proposition relating to himself without being given a clear exposition of its purport.

The Qur'ān tells us that man's life in this world is but the first stage – a very short stage – of a life that continues beyond the hiatus called "death"; and the same Qur'ān stresses again and again the principle of man's moral responsibility for all his conscious actions and his behaviour, and of the continuation of this responsibility, in the shape of inescapable *consequences*, good or bad, in a person's life in the hereafter. But how could man be made to understand the nature of these consequences and, thus, of the quality of the life that awaits him? – for, obviously, inasmuch as man's resurrection will be the result of what the Qur'ān describes as "a new act of creation", the life that will follow upon it must be entirely different from anything that man can and does experience in this world.

This being so, it is not enough for man to be told, "If you behave righteously in this world, you will attain to happiness in the life to come", or, alternatively, "If you do wrong in this world, you will suffer for it in the hereafter". Such statements would be far too general and abstract to appeal to man's imagination and, thus, to influence his behaviour. What is needed is a more direct appeal to the intellect, resulting in a kind of "visualization" of the consequences of one's conscious acts and omissions: and such an appeal can be effectively produced by means of metaphors, allegories and parables, each of them stressing, on the one hand, the absolute *dissimilarity* of all that man will experience after resurrection from whatever he did or could experience in this world; and, on the other hand, establishing means of *comparison* between these two categories of experience.

Thus, explaining the reference to the bliss of paradise in 32 : 17, the Prophet indicated the essential difference between man's life in this world and in the hereafter in these words: "God says, 'I have readied for My righteous servants what no eye has ever seen, and no ear has ever heard, and no heart of man has ever conceived'" (Bukhārī, Muslim, Tirmidhī). On the other hand, in 2 : 25 the Qur'ān speaks thus of the blessed in paradise: "Whenever they are granted fruits therefrom as their appointed sustenance, they will say, 'It is this that in days of yore was granted to us as our sustenance' – for they shall be given something which will recall that [past]": and so we have the image of gardens through which running waters flow, blissful shade, spouses of indescribable beauty, and many other delights infinitely varied and unending, and yet somehow comparable to what may be conceived of as most delightful in this world.

However, this possibility of an intellectual comparison between the two stages of human existence is to a large extent limited by the fact that all our thinking and imagining is indissolubly connected with the concepts of finite time and finite space: in other words, we cannot imagine infinity in either time or space – and therefore cannot imagine a state of existence *independent* of time and space – or, as the Qur'ān phrases it with reference to a state of happiness in afterlife, "a paradise as vast as the heavens and the earth" (3 : 133): which expression is the Qur'anic synonym for the entire created universe. On the other hand, we know that every Qur'anic statement is directed to man's reason and must, therefore, be comprehensible either in its literal sense (as in the case of the *āyāt muḥkamāt*) or allegorically (as in the *āyāt mutashābihāt*); and since, owing to the constitution of the human mind, neither infinity nor eternity are comprehensible to us, it follows that the reference to the infinite "vastness" of paradise cannot relate to anything but the *intensity of sensation* which it will offer to the blest.

By obvious analogy, the principle of a "comparison through allegory" applied in the Qur'ān to all references to paradise – i.e., a state of unimaginable happiness in afterlife – must be extended to all descriptions of otherworldly suffering – i.e., hell – in respect of its utter dissimilarity from all earthly experiences as well as its unmeasurable intensity. In both cases the descriptive method of the Qur'ān is the same. We are told, as it were: "Imagine the most joyous sensations, bodily as well as emotional, accessible to man: indescribable beauty, love physical and spiritual, consciousness of fulfilment, perfect peace and harmony; and imagine these sensations intensified beyond anything imaginable in this world – and at the same time entirely *different* from anything imaginable: and you have an inkling, however vague, of what is meant by 'paradise'." And, on the other hand: "Imagine the greatest suffering, bodily as well as spiritual, which man may experience: burning by fire, utter loneliness and bitter desolation, the torment of unceasing frustration, a condition of neither living nor dying; and imagine this pain, this darkness and this despair intensified beyond anything imaginable in this world – and at the same time entirely *different* from anything imaginable: and you will know, however vaguely, what is meant by 'hell'."

Side by side with these allegories relating to man's life after death we find in the Qur'ān many symbolical expressions referring to the evidence of God's activity. Owing to the limitations of human language – which, in their turn, arise from the inborn limitations of the human mind – this activity can only be circumscribed and never really described. Just as it is impossible for us to imagine or define God's Being, so the true nature of His creativeness – and, therefore, of His plan of creation – must remain beyond our grasp. But since the Qur'ān aims at conveying to us an ethical teaching based, precisely, on the concept of God's purposeful creativeness, the latter must be, as it were, "translated" into categories of thought accessible to man. Hence the use of expressions which at first sight have an almost anthropomorphic hue, for instance, God's "wrath" (*ghaḍab*) or "condemnation"; His "pleasure" at good deeds or "love" for His creatures; or His being "oblivious" of a sinner who was oblivious of Him; or "asking" a wrongdoer on Resurrection Day about his wrongdoing; and so forth. All such verbal "translations" of God's activity into human terminology are unavoidable as long as we are expected to conform to ethical principles revealed to us by means of a human language; but there can be no greater mistake than to think that these "translations" could ever enable us to define the Undefinable.

And, as the Qur'ān makes it clear in the seventh verse of *Āl ʿImrān*, only "those whose hearts are given to swerving from the truth go after that part of the divine writ which has been expressed in allegory, seeking out [what is bound to create] confusion, and seeking [to arrive at] its final meaning [in an arbitrary manner]: but none save God knows its final meaning."

Appendix II

Al-Muqaṭṭaᶜāt

ABOUT one-quarter of the Qurʾanic *sūrahs* are preceded by mysterious letter-symbols called *muqaṭṭaᶜāt* ("disjointed letters") or, occasionally, *fawātiḥ* ("openings") because they appear at the beginning of the relevant *sūrahs*. Out of the twenty-eight letters of the Arabic alphabet, exactly one-half – that is, fourteen – occur in this position, either singly or in varying combinations of two, three, four or five letters. They are always pronounced singly, by their designations and not as mere sounds – thus: *alif lām mīm*, or *ḥā mīm*, etc.

The significance of these letter-symbols has perplexed the commentators from the earliest times. There is no evidence of the Prophet's having ever referred to them in any of his recorded utterances, nor of any of his Companions having ever asked him for an explanation. None the less, it is established beyond any possibility of doubt that all the Companions – obviously following the example of the Prophet – regarded the *muqaṭṭaᶜāt* as integral parts of the *sūrahs* to which they are prefixed, and used to recite them accordingly: a fact which disposes effectively of the suggestion advanced by some Western orientalists that these letters may be no more than the initials of the scribes who wrote down the individual revelations at the Prophet's dictation, or of the Companions who recorded them at the time of the final codification of the Qurʾān during the reign of the first three Caliphs.

Some of the Companions as well as some of their immediate successors and later Qurʾān-commentators were convinced that these letters are abbreviations of certain words or even phrases relating to God and His attributes, and tried to "reconstruct" them with much ingenuity: but since the possible combinations are practically unlimited, all such interpretations are highly arbitrary and, therefore, devoid of any real usefulness. Others have tried to link the *muqaṭṭaᶜāt* to the numerological values of the letters of the Arabic alphabet, and have "derived" by this means all manner of esoteric indications and prophecies.

Yet another, perhaps more plausible interpretation, based on two sets of facts, has been advanced by some of the most outstanding Islamic scholars throughout the centuries:

Firstly, all words of the Arabic language, without any exception, are composed of either one letter or a combination of two, three, four or five letters, and never more than five: and, as already mentioned, these are the forms in which the *muqaṭṭaᶜāt* appear.

Secondly, all *sūrahs* prefixed by these letter-symbols open, directly or obliquely, with a reference to revelation, either in its generic sense or its specific manifestation, the Qurʾān. At first glance it might appear that three *sūrahs* (29, 30 and 68) are exceptions to this rule; but this assumption is misleading. In the opening verse of *sūrah* 29 (*Al-ᶜAnkabūt*), a reference to revelation is obviously implied in the saying, "We have attained to faith" (*amannā*), i.e., in God and His messages. In *sūrah* 30 (*Ar-Rūm*), divine revelation is unmistakably stressed in the prediction of Byzantine victory in verses 2-4. In verse 1 of *sūrah* 68 (*Al-Qalam*) the phenomenon of revelation is clearly referred to in the evocative mention of "the pen" (see note 2 on the first verse of that *sūrah*). Thus, there are no "exceptions" in the *sūrahs* prefixed by one or more of the *muqaṭṭaᶜāt*: each of them opens with a reference to divine revelation.

This, taken together with the fact that the *muqaṭṭaᶜāt* mirror, as it were, all word-forms of the Arabic language, has led scholars and thinkers like Al-Mubarrad, Ibn Ḥazm, Zamakhsharī, Rāzī, Bayḍāwī, Ibn Taymiyyah, Ibn Kathīr – to mention only a few of them – to the conclusion that the *muqaṭṭaᶜāt* are meant to illustrate the inimitable, wondrous nature of Qurᵓanic revelation, which, though originating in a realm beyond the reach of human perception (*al-ghayb*), can be and is conveyed to man by means of the very sounds (represented by letters) of ordinary human speech.

However, even this very attractive interpretation is not entirely satisfactory inasmuch as there are many *sūrahs* which open with an explicit reference to divine revelation and are nevertheless not preceded by any letter-symbol. Secondly – and this is the most weighty objection – the above explanation, too, is based on no more than conjecture: and so, in the last resort, we must content ourselves with the finding that a solution of this problem still remains beyond our grasp. This was apparently the view of the four Right-Guided Caliphs, summarized in these words of Abū Bakr: "In every divine writ (*kitāb*) there is [an element of] mystery – and the mystery of the Qurᵓān is [indicated] in the openings of [some of] the *sūrahs*."

Appendix III

On the Term and Concept of *Jinn*

IN ORDER to grasp the purport of the term *jinn* as used in the Qurʾān, we must dissociate our minds from the meaning given to it in Arabian folklore, where it early came to denote all manner of "demons" in the most popular sense of this word. This folkloristic image has somewhat obscured the original connotation of the term and its highly significant – almost self-explanatory – verbal derivation. The root-verb is *janna*, "he [or "it"] concealed" or "covered with darkness": cf. 6 : 76, which speaks of Abraham "when the night overshadowed him with its darkness (*janna ʿalayhi*)". Since this verb is also used in the intransitive sense ("he [or "it"] was [or "became"] concealed", resp. "covered with darkness"), all classical philologists point out that *al-jinn* signifies "intense [or "confusing"] darkness" and, in a more general sense, "that which is concealed from [man's] senses", i.e., things, beings or forces which cannot normally be perceived by man but have, nevertheless, an objective reality, whether concrete or abstract, of their own.

In the usage of the Qurʾān, which is certainly different from the usage of primitive folklore, the term *jinn* has several distinct meanings. The most commonly encountered is that of spiritual forces or beings which, precisely because they have no corporeal existence, are beyond the perception of our corporeal senses: a connotation which includes "satans" and "satanic forces" (*shayāṭīn* – see note 16 on 15 : 17) as well as "angels" and "angelic forces", since all of them are "concealed from our senses" (Jawharī, Rāghib). In order to make it quite evident that these invisible manifestations are not of a corporeal nature, the Qurʾān states parabolically that the *jinn* were created out of "the fire of scorching winds" (*nār as-samūm*, in 15 : 27), or out of "a confusing flame of fire" (*mārij min nār*, in 55 : 15), or simply "out of fire" (7 : 12 and 38 : 76, in these last two instances referring to the Fallen Angel, Iblīs). Parallel with this, we have authentic *aḥādīth* to the effect that the Prophet spoke of the angels as having been "created out of light" (*khuliqat min nūr*: Muslim, on the authority of ʿĀʾishah) – light and fire being akin, and likely to manifest themselves within and through one another (cf. note 7 on verse 8 of *sūrah* 27).

The term *jinn* is also applied to a wide range of phenomena which, according to most of the classical commentators, indicate certain *sentient organisms* of so fine a nature and of a physiological composition so different from our own that they are not normally accessible to our sense-perception. We know, of course, very little as to what can and what cannot play the role of a living organism; moreover, our inability to discern and observe such phenomena is by no means a sufficient justification for a denial of their existence. The Qurʾān refers often to "the realm which is beyond the reach of human perception" (*al-ghayb*), while God is frequently spoken of as "the Sustainer of all the worlds" (*rabb al-ʿālamīn*): and the use of the plural clearly indicates that side by side with the "world" open to our observation there are other "worlds" as well – and, therefore, other forms of life, different from ours and presumably from one another, and yet subtly interacting and perhaps even permeating one another in a manner beyond our ken. And if we assume, as we must, that there are living organisms whose biological premises are entirely different from our own, it is only logical to assume that our physical senses can establish contact with them only under very exceptional circumstances: hence the description of them as "invisible beings". Now that occasional, very rare crossing of paths between their life-mode and ours may well give rise to strange – because unexplainable – manifestations, which man's primitive fantasy has subsequently interpreted as ghosts, demons and other such "supernatural" apparitions.

Occasionally, the term *jinn* is used in the Qur'ān to denote those elemental forces of nature – including human nature – which are "concealed from our senses" inasmuch as they manifest themselves to us only in their effects but not in their intrinsic reality. Instances of this connotation are found, e.g., in 37 : 158 ff. (and possibly also in 6 : 100), as well as in the earliest occurrence of this concept, namely, in 114 : 6.

Apart from this, it is quite probable that in many instances where the Qur'ān refers to *jinn* in terms usually applied to organisms endowed with reason, this expression either implies a symbolic "personification" of man's *relationship* with "satanic forces" (*shayāṭīn*) – an implication evident, e.g., in 6 : 112, 7 : 38, 11 : 119, 32 : 13 – or, alternatively, is a metonym for a person's preoccupation with what is loosely described as "occult powers", whether real or illusory, as well as for the resulting practices as such, like sorcery, necromancy, astrology, soothsaying, etc.: endeavours to which the Qur'ān invariably refers in condemnatory terms (cf. 2 : 102 and the corresponding note 84; also 6 : 128 and 130, or 72 : 5-6).

In a few instances (e.g., in 46 : 29-32 and 72 : 1-15) the term *jinn* may conceivably denote beings not invisible in and by themselves but, rather, "*hitherto unseen beings*" (see note 1 on 72 : 1).

Finally, references to *jinn* are sometimes meant to recall certain legends deeply embedded in the consciousness of the people to whom the Qur'ān was addressed in the first instance (e.g., in 34 : 12-14, which should be read in conjunction with note 77 on 21 : 82) – the purpose being, in every instance, not the legend as such but the illustration of a moral or spiritual truth'.

Appendix IV

The Night Journey

THE PROPHET'S "Night Journey" (*isrā'*) from Mecca to Jerusalem and his subsequent "Ascension" (*miʿrāj*) to heaven are, in reality, two stages of one mystic experience, dating almost exactly one year before the exodus to Medina (cf. Ibn Saʿd I/1, 143). According to various well-documented Traditions – extensively quoted and discussed by Ibn Kathīr in his commentary on 17 : 1, as well as by Ibn Ḥajar in *Fatḥ al-Bārī* VII, 155 ff. – the Apostle of God, accompanied by the Angel Gabriel, found himself transported by night to the site of Solomon's Temple at Jerusalem, where he led a congregation of many of the earlier, long since deceased prophets in prayer; some of them he afterwards encountered again in heaven. The Ascension, in particular, is important from the viewpoint of Muslim theology inasmuch as it was in the course of this experience that the five daily prayers were explicitly instituted, by God's ordinance, as an integral part of the Islamic Faith.

Since the Prophet himself did not leave any clear-cut explanation of this experience, Muslim thinkers – including the Prophet's Companions – have always widely differed as to its true nature. The great majority of the Companions believed that both the Night Journey and the Ascension were *physical* occurrences – in other words, that the Prophet was borne bodily to Jerusalem and then to heaven – while a minority were convinced that the experience was purely spiritual. Among the latter we find, in particular, the name of ʿĀ'ishah, the Prophet's widow and most intimate companion of his later years, who declared emphatically that "he was transported only in his spirit (*bi-rūḥihi*), while his body did not leave its place" (cf. Ṭabarī, Zamakhsharī and Ibn Kathīr in their commentaries on 17 : 1); the great Al-Ḥasan al-Baṣrī, who belonged to the next generation, held uncompromisingly to the same view (*ibid.*). As against this, the theologians who maintain that the Night Journey and the Ascension were physical experiences refer to the corresponding belief of most of the Companions – without, however, being able to point to a single Tradition to the effect that the Prophet himself described it as such. Some Muslim scholars lay stress on the words *asrā bi-ʿabdihi* ("He transported His servant by night") occurring in 17 : 1, and contend that the term *ʿabd* ("servant") denotes a living being in its entirety, i.e., a combination of body and soul. This interpretation, however, does not take into account the probability that the expression *asrā bi-ʿabdihi* simply refers to the *human quality* of the Prophet, in consonance with the many Qur'anic statements to the effect that he, like all other apostles, was but a mortal *servant* of God, and was not endowed with any supernatural qualities. This, to my mind, is fully brought out in the concluding words of the above verse – "verily, He alone is all-hearing, all-seeing" – following upon the statement that the Prophet was shown *some* of God's symbols (*min āyātinā*), i.e., given insight into some, but by no means all, of the ultimate truths underlying God's creation.

The most convincing argument in favour of a spiritual interpretation of both the Night Journey and the Ascension is forthcoming from the highly allegorical descriptions found in the authentic Traditions relating to this double experience: descriptions, that is, which are so obviously symbolic that they preclude any possibility of interpreting them literally, in "physical" terms. Thus, for instance, the Apostle of God speaks of his encountering at Jerusalem, and subsequently in heaven, a number of the earlier prophets, all of whom had undoubtedly passed away a long time before. According to one Tradition (quoted by Ibn Kathīr on the authority of Anas), he visited Moses *in his grave*, and found him praying. In another Tradition, also on the authority of Anas (cf. *Fatḥ al-Bārī* VII, 158), the Prophet describes how, on his Night Journey, he encountered an old woman, and was thereupon told by Gabriel, "This old woman is the mortal world (*ad-dunyā*)". In the words of yet another Tradition, on the authority of Abū Hurayrah (*ibid.*), the Prophet "passed by people who were sowing and harvesting; and every time they completed their harvest, [the grain] grew up again. Gabriel said, 'These are the fighters in God's cause (*al-mujāhidūn*).' Then they passed by people whose heads were being shattered by rocks; and every time they were shattered, they became whole again. [Gabriel] said, 'These are they whose heads were oblivious of prayer.' . . . Then they passed by people who were eating raw, rotten meat and throwing away cooked, wholesome meat. [Gabriel] said, 'These are the adulterers.'"

In the best-known Tradition on the Ascension (quoted by Bukhārī), the Prophet introduces his narrative with the words: "While I lay on the ground next to the Kaᶜbah [lit., "in the *ḥijr*"], lo! there came unto me an angel, and cut open my breast and took out my heart. And then a golden basin *full of faith* was brought unto me, and my heart was washed [therein] and was filled [with it]; then it was restored to its place. . . ." Since "faith" is an abstract concept, it is obvious that the Prophet himself regarded this prelude to the Ascension – and therefore the Ascension itself and, *ipso facto*, the Night Journey to Jerusalem – as purely spiritual experiences.

But whereas there is no cogent reason to believe in a "bodily" Night Journey and Ascension, there is, on the other hand, no reason to doubt the objective *reality* of this event. The early Muslim theologians, who could not be expected to possess adequate psychological knowledge, could visualize only two alternatives: either a physical happening or a dream. Since it appeared to them – and rightly so – that these wonderful occurrences would greatly lose in significance if they were relegated to the domain of mere dream, they instinctively adopted an interpretation in physical terms and passionately defended it against all contrary views, like those of ᶜĀʾishah, Muᶜāwiyah or Al-Ḥasan al-Baṣrī. In the meantime, however, we have come to know that a dream-experience is not the *only* alternative to a physical occurrence. Modern psychical research, though still in its infancy, has demonstrably proved that not every spiritual experience (that is, an experience in which none of the known organs of man's body has a part) must necessarily be a mere subjective manifestation of the "mind" – whatever this term may connote – but that it may, in special circumstances, be no less real or "factual" in the objective sense of this word than anything that man can experience by means of his physiological organism. We know as yet very little about the quality of such exceptional psychic activities, and so it is well-nigh impossible to reach definite conclusions as to their nature. Nevertheless, certain observations of modern psychologists have confirmed the possibility – claimed from time immemorial by mystics of all persuasions – of a temporary "independence" of man's spirit from his living body. In the event of such a temporary independence, the spirit or soul appears to be able freely to traverse time and space, to embrace within its insight occurrences and phenomena belonging to otherwise widely separated categories of reality, and to condense them within symbolical perceptions of great intensity, clarity and comprehensiveness. But when it comes to communicating such "visionary" experiences (as we are constrained to call them for lack of a better term) to people who have never experienced anything of the kind, the person concerned – in this case, the Prophet – is obliged to resort to figurative expressions: and this would account for the allegorical style of all the Traditions relating to the mystic vision of the Night Journey and the Ascension.

At this point I should like to draw the reader's attention to the discussion of "spiritual Ascension" by one of the truly great Islamic thinkers, Ibn al-Qayyim (Zād al-Maᶜād II, 48 f.):

"ᶜĀʾishah and Muᶜāwiyah maintained that the [Prophet's] Night Journey was performed by his soul (*bi-rūḥihi*), while his body did not leave its place. The same is reported to have been the view of Al-Ḥasan al-Baṣrī. But it is necessary to know the difference between the saying, 'the Night Journey took place in dream (*manāman*)', and the saying, 'it was [performed] by his soul without his body'. The difference between these two [views] is tremendous. . . . What the dreamer sees are mere reproductions (*amthāl*) of forms already existing in his mind; and so he dreams [for example] that he ascends to heaven or is transported to Mecca or to [other] regions of the world, while [in reality] his spirit neither ascends nor is transported. . . .

"Those who have reported to us the Ascension of the Apostle of God can be divided into two groups – one group maintaining that the Ascension was in spirit *and* in body, and the other group maintaining that it was performed by his spirit, while his body did not leave its place. But these latter [also] do *not* mean to say that the Ascension took place in a dream: they merely mean that it was his soul itself which actually went on the Night Journey and ascended to heaven, and that the soul witnessed things which it [otherwise] witnessses after death [lit., *mufāraqah*, "separation"]. Its condition on that occasion was similar to the condition [of the soul] after death. . . . But that which the Apostle of God experienced on his Night Journey was superior to the [ordinary] experiences of the soul after death, and, of course, was far above the dreams which one sees in sleep. . . . As to the prophets [whom the Apostle of God met in heaven], it was but their souls which had come to dwell there after the separation from their bodies, while the soul of the Apostle of God ascended there in his lifetime."

It is obvious that this kind of spiritual experience is not only not inferior, but, on the contrary, vastly superior to anything that bodily organs could ever perform or record; and it goes without saying, as already mentioned by Ibn al-Qayyim, that it is equally superior to what we term "dream-experiences", inasmuch as the latter have no objective existence outside the subject's mind, whereas spiritual experiences of the kind referred to above are not less "real" (that is, objective) than anything which could be experienced "in body". By assuming that the Night Journey and the Ascension were spiritual and not bodily, we do not diminish the extraordinary value attaching to this experience of the Prophet. On the contrary, it appears that the fact of his having had such an experience by far transcends any miracle of bodily ascension, for it presupposes a personality of tremendous spiritual perfection – the very thing which we expect from a true Prophet of God. However, it is improbable that we ordinary human beings will ever be in a position fully to comprehend spiritual experiences of this kind. Our minds can only operate with elements provided by our consciousness of time and space; and everything that extends beyond this particular set of conceptions will always defy our attempts at a clear-cut definition.

In conclusion, it should be noted that the Prophet's Night Journey from Mecca to Jerusalem, immediately preceding his Ascension, was apparently meant to show that Islam is not a *new* doctrine but a continuation of the same divine message which was preached by the prophets of old, who had Jerusalem as their spiritual home. This view is supported by Traditions (quoted in *Fatḥ al-Bārī* VII, 158), according to which the Prophet, during his Night Journey, also offered prayers at Yathrib, Sinai, Bethlehem, etc. His encounters with other prophets, mentioned in this connection, symbolize the same idea. The well-known Traditions to the effect that on the occasion of his Night Journey the Prophet led a prayer in the Temple of Jerusalem, in which all other prophets ranged themselves behind him, expresses in a figurative manner the doctrine that Islam, as preached by the Prophet Muḥammad, is the fulfilment and perfection of mankind's religious development, and that Muḥammad, was the last and the greatest of God's message-bearers.

In humility and obedience the incapable servant has completed his work in explaining the eternal words of His Lord. All praise is due to God – there is no deity save Him; and blessing and peace be on the unlettered Arab prophet [Muḥammad] after whom there is no other prophet.

وَتَمّتْ خشُوعًا وخُضوعًا
كَلِمَة العبد العَاجز
فى تفسير كَلِمَات ربّه الخَالدة
والحمدُ لله الذى لا إلهَ إلّا هوَ
والصّلاة والسّلام
علىٰ النبيّ الأمّيّ العربيّ
الذى لا نبيَّ بعده

Muhammad Asad

محمّد أسد

General Index✧

Aaron [*Hārūn*], 4:163; 6:84. ***the House** of, 2:248; 19:28. ***as helper** to Moses, 5:25; 7:122, 142; 10:75; 19:53; 20:29-35, 70; 21:48; 23:45-48; 25:35-36; 26:13-16, 48; 28:34-35; 37:114-122. ***and the golden calf**, 7:150-151; 20:90-94. (See Moses.)

Ablution, 5:6; see *Tayammum*.

Abraham [*ʾIbrāhīm*]: the House of, 3:33; 11:73. ***fulfilled** God's commands, 2:124; 16:120; 53:37. ***and the Kaʿbah**, 2:125, 127; 3:96-97. ***his creed**, *ḥanīf*, 2:130-133, 135, 140; 3:67, 95; 4:125; 6:79, 161; 16:120, 123; 26:77-82. ***neither a Jew** nor a Christian, 2:135, 160; 3:65-67. ***rejects** worship of celestial bodies, 6:76-79. ***argues** with king, 2:258. ***argues** with his father and his people against idolatry, 6:74; 19:41-50; 21:51-56, 66-67; 26:69-77; 29:16-18, 25; 37:83-98. ***and resurrection** of the dead, 2:260; 26:81. ***preaches** to his people, 6:80-83; 19:49-50. ***asks God's forgiveness** for his father, 9:114; 19:47; 26:86-87; 60:4. ***the sacrifice** of his son, 37:102-111. ***the angels** announce birth of his son, 11:69-74; 15:51-55; 29:31; 37:112; 51:24-29. ***intercedes** for Lot's people, 11:74-76; 29:31-32. ***his prayers**, 2:126-130; 14:35-41; 26:83-89; 37:100; 60:4-5. ***as a model**, 9:114; 11:75; 16:120-123; 60:4-6. ***saved** from the fire, 21:69; 26:98. ***revelation** of, 2:136; 3:84; 53:36-54; 87:18-19. ***his example** in dealing with unbelievers, 60:4-8. ***forefather** of the believers, 3:68; 22:78.

Abrogation: of earlier revelations, 2:106; 13:38-39; 16:101. ***unfounded** with regard to the Qurʾān, 2:85; 17:86; 18:27; 41:41-42.

Abū Bakr (alluded to), 9:40.

Abū Lahab, 111:1-5.

Acceptance (**God's goodly**) [*marḍāti-llāh; riḍwāna-llāh*], 47:21; 94:7-8. ***those who seek**, 2:207, 265; 3:162, 174; 4:114; 5:2, 16; 9:109; 20:84; 48:29; 57:27; 59:8; 60:1. ***as reward in** Paradise, 3:15; 5:119; 9:20-21, 72, 100; 57:20; 89:27-30; 98:8. ***those with whom** God is pleased, 21:28; 39:7; 48:18; 53:26; 58:22. ***those who** disdain, 4:108; 9:62; 47:28; 58:8.

ʿĀd (people of Hūd), 7:65-72; 11:50-60; 25:38; 26:123-140; 29:38-39; 41:15-16; 46:21-26; 51:41-42; 54:18-21; 69:4-8; 89:6-14.

Adam: creation of, 2:30; 7:11. ***his fall**, 2:35-39; 7:19-25; 20:117, 121, 123-124. ***his two sons**, 5:27-31. ***children of**, 7:172; see Man. ***tempted** by Satan, 17:62-65; 20:120-121.

Adoption: see Children: adopted; Marriage: with ex wives of adopted children.

Adornment: see Beauty; Deception.

Adultery, 17:32, 64; 24:2-3, 26; 25:68-69; 60:12. ***accusation** of, 24:4-26. (See Conduct (Immoral); Fornication; Punishment; Slaves.)

Affliction: see Misfortune.

Aggression, 9:12-15; 22:39-40, 72; 33:26; 68:12. ***do not commit**, 2:190. ***respond only** with like thereof, 2:194; 16:126; 22:60; see Self-defence.

Agony: see Death: its agony, or nearness of.

Aḥmad (name of Prophet Muḥammad), 61:6; see Muḥammad: mentioned by name.

Aid, 2:45, 153; 9:40; see Succour (God's).

ʿĀʾishah (wife of Prophet Muḥammad; not named), 66:4. ***calumny** against, 24:11-19.

Alcoholic drinks [*khamr*], 2:219; 5:90-91; 16:67. ***drunkenness**, 4:43. ***their effects** described by negation, 37:45-47; 52:23; 56:17-19. ***wine** in Paradise: see Paradise: food and drink.

Alms: see Charity; Spending on others.

Al-Yasaʾ: see Elisha.

Angels [*malak*; pl., *malāʾika*], 3:87; 4:166; 6:146; 7:20; 16:49-50; 43:60; 89:22. ***and the creation** of Adam, 2:30-33; 38:69. ***prostrate** before Adam, 2:34; 7:11; 15:29-30; 17:61; 18:50; 20:116; 38:71-73. ***Gabriel** and Michael, 2:97-98. ***sent only** in accordance with the truth, 15:7-8. ***sent** with Revelation, 2:97; 16:2; 19:64; see Revelation: the angels of. ***as 'heavenly** forces', 9:26, 40; 37:173; 43:80; 48:4, 7; 74:30-31; 96:18. ***on Day of Judgement**, 25:22, 25. ***message-bearers** with wings, 35:1. ***ask God's forgiveness** for those on earth, 42:5. ***their prayer** for the believers, 40:7-9. ***and divine** inspiration, 70:4; 97:3-4. ***ever-watchful guardians** of men, 6:61; 10:21; 43:80; 72:27; 82:10-12; 86:4. ***the host on high**, 37:8; 38:69. ***announce** the birth of Jesus, 3:42-49. ***announce** the birth of John, 3:39-41. ***sent to reaffirm** and strengthen the believers, 3:124-125; 8:9-12; 9:40; 41:30-32. ***regarded** as God's daughters by pagans, 53:27; see Attributing to God: sons and daughters. ***the deniers** of truth demand that they be sent down to them, 6:8-9; 11:12; 15:7; 17:92, 94-95; 25:7, 21; 43:53. ***angel of death**, 6:61; 32:11. ***guardians** of Hell: see Hell: guardians of. (See Abraham: the angels announce birth of his son; intercedes for Lot's people; Gabriel; Invisible beings; Michael; Revelation: angels of; Servants of God: angels as.)

Animals, 5:1-4; 6:146; 11:40; 24:45; 25:49; 81:5. ***subservient** to man's needs, 16:5-8, 80; 22:27-28, 36-37; 36:71-73; 39:6; 40:79-80. ***ass**, 2:259; 16:8; 31:19; 62:5; 74:49-51. ***crow**, 5:31. ***dog**, 7:176; 18:18-22. ***fish**, 7:163; 18:61-63. ***frog**, 7:133. ***goat**, 6:143. ***quail**, 2:57; 7:160; 20:80. ***lion**, 74:51. ***monkey**, 2:65; 5:60; 7:166. ***mule**, 16:8. ***sheep**, 6:143, 146; 20:18; 21:78; 38:23-24. ***snake**, 7:107; 20:20; 26:32; 27:10; 28:31. ***swine**, 2:173; 5:3, 60; 6:145; 16:115. ***whale** (great fish), 37:142, 144; 68:48. ***wolf**, 12:13-17. (See Birds; Camels; Cattle; Cows; Horses; Insects; Language: animals endowed with speech.)

Apostasy, 2:217; 3:82-83, 86, 90, 106; 4:115; 5:54; 6:71; 9:66, 74; 16:106; 33:14-15; 47:25-34; see Faith: followed by apostasy.

Apostles (Prophets): their mission, 2:213; 6:48, 130;

✧ This Index has been compiled by Abdur-Razzaq Pérez Fernández

18:56; 72:26-28. *solemn pledge of the prophets, 3:81-86; 33:7-8. *their duty is only to deliver their message, 2:119; 5:92; 16:35; 29:18; 36:17. *sent to their peoples, 10:74; 14:4; 30:47. *in every community, 10:47; 16:36; 35:24; 39:71. *entrusted with a like message, 7:59, 65, 73, 85; 11:50, 61, 84; 21:25; 23:23, 32, 51-52; 26:196; 42:13; 43:45; 53:36-54; 87:18-19. *are human beings, 3:144; 5:75; 10:2; 13:38; 14:11; 16:43-44; 21:7-8, 34; 22:75; 25:20; 64:6. *invested with authority, 4:59, 64, 79-80; 11:96; 12:56; 23:45; 28:35; 33:66; 40:23; 44:19; 51:38; 81:19-21; see Leave (God's): and the authority of the Apostles; Muḥammad: obedience due to; Obedience. *some more favoured by God than others, 2:253; 17:55; 72:26-27. *the Qur'ān mentions some, not others, 4:164; 6:34; 40:78. *ask no salary or reward, 10:72; 11:29, 51; 26:109, 127, 145, 164, 180; 36:21; 38:86. *cannot force people to believe, 10:99-100; 11:28; 18:29; 39:41; 50:45; see Coercion. *believers accept all of them, without distinction, 2:285; 4:152. *rejection of, 2:87; 4:150-151; 14:9, 13; 40:26; 41:43. *derided, 6:10; 13:32; 15:10-11; 18:56; 25:7-8; 36:30; 43:52-53. *given the lie, 3:184; 6:34; 12:110; 23:33-39, 44, 47-48; 29:18; 34:45; 35:25; 40:5. *branded as liars, 5:70; 7:66; 11:27; 12:110; 23:25-26, 38-39, 44, 47-48; 26:117; 28:38; 34:8; 36:15; 38:4-7; 40:37; 42:24; 54:9; 67:9; *-as madmen, 11:54; 23:70; 26:27; 34:8; 37:36; 51:39, 52; 54:9, 24; see Muḥammad: accused of madness. *-as sorcerers: see Sorcery: prophets are accused of. *God has set up enemies against them, 6:112; 22:52; 25:31. *some were murdered by the Jews, 2:61, 87, 91; 3:112, 181, 183; 4:155; 5:70. *witnesses on Day of Judgement, 4:41; 5:109; 7:6; 16:84, 89; 39:69; 77:11. *in one line of descent (Adam-Noah-Abraham-ʿImrān), 3:33-34; 4:163-164; 6:84-87; 19:58; 57:26-27. *distinction between apostles and prophets, 22:52. *angels as message-bearers, 6:61; 22:75; see Angels; Revelation: angels of. (See Knowledge: given to prophets; Prophethood; Servants of God: apostles and prophets described as. Truth: the apostles are sent with the.)

Arabic: as language of the Qur'ān, 12:2; 13:37; 14:4; 16:103; 19:97; 20:113; 26:193-195, 199; 39:28; 41:3, 44; 42:7; 43:3; 44:58; 46:12; App. II; see Qur'ān.

ʿArafāt, 2:198-200; 22:32; see Pilgrimage.

Arguments: see Proof.

Ark (Noah's), 7:64; 11:37-44; 17:3; 23:27-30; 29:15; 54:13.

Arrogance (Haughtiness; Insolence; Pride), 2:118, 206; 10:23; 14:15, 21; 16:29, 49-50; 17:4; 23:75-77; 34:31-35; 37:30; 39:72; 40:47-48, 76; 42:27, 42; 53:50-52; 68:29-31; 74:52; 96:6-7. *of Iblīs (Satan), 2:34; 7:12-13; 38:72-76. *Pharaoh and his dignitaries, archetypes of, 7:133; 10:75, 90; 23:45-47; 28:4, 39, 76; 29:39; 40:27; 51:39. *leads to denial of truth, 2:87, 90; 4:172-173; 5:64, 68, 93; 7:36, 40, 75-76, 88; 11:59; 16:22-24; 17:60; 23:66-67; 27:13-14; 31:7; 35:42-43; 37:35; 38:2; 39:59-60; 40:82-83; 41:15; 45:7-8, 31-32; 46:10-11, 20; 51:53; 52:32-33; 54:2-4; 63:5; 71:7; 74:23-24; 75:32-33; 91:11. *God leads the arrogant astray, 2:14-15; 6:110; 7:146, 186; 10:11; 40:34-35, 74-75. (See Evil: powers of; Injustice; Oppression; Virtue: humbleness.)

Ascension: see Night Journey.

Ascribing divinity to other than God (Idolatry) [*shirk*], 2:165; 4:117; 6:1, 22-23, 136-137; 7:189-190; 10:28-29, 34-35, 66, 104-106; 12:106; 13:33; 16:27, 53-57, 86; 18:52; 19:81-82; 26:92-93, 97-98; 28:62-64, 71-75; 30:28, 40, 42; 34:27; 39:45; 40:73-74; 42:21; 46:28. *something He has never sanctioned: see Leave (God's): what God has never sanctioned. *divine prohibition of, 4:36; 16:51-52; 17:39; 18:110; 26:213; 28:87-88; 29:8; 31:13, 15; 72:18. *an offence which God does not forgive, 4:48, 116. *its punishment, 5:72; 7:138-139; 22:71-72; 30:42; 50:24, 26. *deification of angels, prophets, rabbis, monks, etc., 3:64, 79-80; 7:30; 9:30-31; 22:12-13; 24:3; 25:17-19; 39:3; see Desires (Worldly): made into a deity. *not to marry idolaters, 2:221; 24:3; 60:10. (See Ascribing to God; Deities (False); God: Only God; there is no deity save Him; Invisible beings: to whom divinity is ascribed...; Jesus.)

Astray (**to go**), 1:7; 2:108, 198; 3:69; 4:113, 115-116, 136-137, 160, 167; 5:12, 60, 77, 105; 6:56, 117, 122, 140, 153; 7:30, 146, 149; 10:45; 13:33; 14:3, 18, 30; 15:56; 16:36, 94, 125; 17:15, 72, 97; 19:75; 22:11-13; 23:73-74, 106; 25:9, 27, 34, 42-44; 26:96-98; 27:60, 92; 28:50; 30:53; 31:11; 34:24, 32, 50; 38:26; 39:41; 40:37; 41:22-23; 42:18, 46; 43:37, 40; 46:32; 51:10-12; 53:2, 30; 54:47; 60:1; 61:5; 62:2; 67:22; 68:7; 96:9-12. *to take error in exchange for guidance, 2:16, 175; 3:90; 4:44; 7:175; 9:9; 13:11. *guidance is now distinct from error, 2:256; 10:32, 108; 33:36; 41:52. *prophets and believers accused of being, 4:51; 7:60-61; 8:49; 34:7-8; 36:47; 54:24; 83:32. *Adam and Eve, 20:121. *the people of Abraham, 6:74; 21:54; 26:86. *following in their forefathers' steps, 2:170; 20:63; 26:69-76, 136-138; 27:43; 37:69-71; 51:52-53; see Forefathers. *those who abandon all remembrance of God, 18:101; 25:18; 39:22. *those who call truth a lie, 6:31; 7:146; 10:45; 23:33; 56:51, 92; 82:6-9. *those who take unbelievers as friends, 3:100; 25:28-29; 60:1. (See Desires (Worldly).)

Astray (**to lead**), 4:27, 113, 167; 5:77; 6:116, 119, 144; 7:38, 44-45, 86; 8:36, 47; 9:34, 37; 10:88; 11:18-19; 14:2-3; 16:88; 20:16; 22:8-9; 25:28-29; 28:87; 29:12; 31:6; 39:8; 41:29; 47:1, 32, 34; 58:16; 63:2; 71:26-27. *God lets evildoers go, 2:15, 26; 4:88, 115; 143; 6:39, 110, 125; 7:146, 155, 178, 186; 10:11; 11:34; 13:27, 33; 14:4; 14:27; 16:37, 93; 17:97; 18:17; 27:4; 30:29; 35:8; 39:23, 36-37; 40:33-34, 74; 42:44, 46; 45:23; 61:5; 74:31. *some followers of the Bible want to lead the Muslims astray: see Jews and Christians. *Satan, 4:60, 117-120; 7:175; 22:3-4; 27:24; 28:15; 36:62. *Pharaoh, 10:88; 11:97-98; 20:79; 28:41; 40:29, 41. *leaders and thinkers, 11:59; 14:28-30; 26:96-99; 28:62-63; 33:67; 34:31-33; 38:6-8; 40:23-24; 71:21-24; see Pharaoh. *the **Samaritan**, 20:85. *false objects of worship, 5:56; 14:35-36; 18:51; 25:17, 42-43; 46:5-6; see Ascribing divinity to other than God; Deities (False).

Atonement: for killing another believer by mistake, 4:92. ***for breaking** an oath, 5:89; 66:2. ***for hunting** during pilgrimage, 5:95. ***for pronouncing** *aẓ-ẓihār*, 58:3-4. ***secret charity** as A. for sins, 2:271. ***forgoing** due retribution as A. for sins, 4:92; 5:45.

Attributes of God's perfection [*al-ʾasmāʾu 'l-ḥusnā*], 7:180; 20:8; 59:24. ***the Most Merciful** [*ar-Raḥmān*], 1:1, 3; 2:163; 17:110; 19:88-92; 20:90, 108-109; 21:36, 42, 112; 25:60; 55:1-2; 78:37. ***the Dispenser** of Grace [*ar-Raḥīm*], 1:1, 3; 52:28; 59:22. ***the Sovereign** Supreme [*al-Malik*], 20:114, 23:116; 59:23; 62:1. ***the Holy** [*al-Quddūs*], 59:23; 62:1. ***the One** with whom all salvation rests [*as-Salām*], 59:23. ***the Giver** of Faith [*al-Muʾmin*], 59:23. ***the One who determines** what is true or false [*al-Muhaimin*], 59:23. ***the Almighty** [*al-ʿAzīz*], 3:6; 14:1; 34:6; 39:5; 85:8. ***the One who subdues** wrong and restores right [*al-Jabbār*], 59:23. ***the One** to whom all greatness belongs [*al-Mutakabbir*], 59:23. ***the Creator** [*al-Khāliq*], 6:102; 36:81; 59:24. ***the Maker** [*al-Bāriʾ*], 59:24. ***the One who shapes** all forms [*al-Muṣawwir*], 59:24. ***the All-Forgiving** [*al-Ghaffār*], 38:66; 39:5; 40:42. ***the One who holds** absolute sway over all that exists [*al-Qahhār*], 12:39; 14:48; 38:65; 39:4. ***the Giver** of Gifts [*al-Wahhāb*], 3:8; 38:9, 35. ***the Provider** of all sustenance [*ar-Razzāq*], 51:58. ***the One who opens** all truth [*al-Fattāḥ*], 34:26. ***the All-Knowing** [*al-ʿAlīm*], 6:96; 34:26; 36:38; 40:2; 66:3. ***the All-Hearing** [*as-Samīʿ*], 5:76; 6:13; 40:20; 42:11. ***the All-Seeing** [*al-Baṣīr*], 17:1; 22:61; 40:20, 56; 42:11. ***the Unfathomable** [*al-Laṭīf*], 6:103; 67:14. ***the All-Aware** [*al-Khabīr*], 6:18, 103; 34:1; 66:3; 67:14. ***the Tremendous** [*al-ʿAẓīm*], 2:255; 42:4; 69:33. ***the Truly-Forgiving** [*al-Ghafūr*], 18:58; 85:14. ***the Exalted** [*al-ʿAlī*], 2:255; 22:62; 31:30; 40:12. ***the Truly-Great** [*al-Kabīr*], 13:9; 22:62; 31:30; 40:12. ***the Most Bountiful** [*al-ʾAkram*], 96:3. ***the One who keeps watch** over everything [*ar-Raqīb*], 4:1; 5:117; 33:52. ***the Truly Wise** [*al-Ḥakīm*], 3:6, 18, 126; 27:9; 34:27; 39:1; 42:3; 45:2; 46:2; 62:1; 64:18. ***the All-Embracing** in His love [*al-Wadūd*], 85:14. ***the Ultimate Truth** [*al-Ḥaqq*], 10:32; 13:14; 18:44; 20:114; 22:6, 62; 23:116; 24:25; 31:30; 78:39. ***the Powerful** [*al-Qawī*], 11:66; 42:19. ***the Eternal** [*al-Matīn*], 51:58. ***the Protector** [*al-Walī*], 42:9, 28. ***the One** to whom all praise is due [*al-Ḥamīd*], 14:1; 22:24; 31:26; 34:6; 35:15; 85:8. ***the Ever-Living** [*al-Ḥayy*], 2:255; 3:2; 20:111; 25:58. ***the Self-Subsisting** Fount of All Being [*al-Qayyūm*], 2:255; 3:2; 20:111. ***the One** [*al-Wāḥid; al-ʾAḥad*], 12:39; 14:48; 38:65; 39:4; 112:1. ***the Eternal**, Uncaused Cause of All That Exists [*aṣ-Ṣamad*], 112:2. ***the First** [*al-ʾAwwal*], 57:3. ***the Last** [*al-ʾĀkhir*], 57:3. ***the Outward** [*aẓ-Ẓāhir*], 57:3. ***the Inward** [*al-Bāṭin*], 57:3. ***the One** above everything [*al-Mutaʿalī*], 13:9. ***the All-Highest** [al-ʾAʿlā], 87:1; 92:20. ***the Truly Benign** [*al-Barr*], 52:28. ***the Acceptor of Repentance** [*at-Tawwāb*], 2:37, 54, 160; 9:104, 118; 42:25. ***the Lord Supreme** [*al-Mawlā*], 2:286; 3:150; 6:62; 8:40; 9:51; 10:30; 22:78; 66:2. ***the Giver** of Succour [*an-Naṣīr*], 8:40; 22:78. ***the Originator** of the heavens and the earth [*Badīʿu 's-samāwāti wa 'l-ʾarḍ*], 2:117; 6:14, 101; 42:11. ***Lord** of almightiness [*Rabbu 'l-ʿizzah*], 37:180. ***Lord** of all dominion [*Maliku 'l-mulk*], 3:26. ***the Self-Sufficient** [*al-Ghanī*], 10:68; 22:64; 47:38. ***the Light** of the heavens and the earth [*Nūru 's-samāwāti wa 'l-arḍ*], 24:35. ***the Upholder** of Equity [*Qāʾimun bi 'l-qisṭ*], 3:18.

Attributing to God: the origin of pagan practices, 5:103; 6:136-140, 143-144, 148, 150; 7:28, 71; 12:40; 16:35; 43:20-21; 53:23. ***sons and daughters**, 2:116; 4:171; 6:100-101; 9:30; 10:68; 16:57, 62; 17:40; 18:4-5; 19:88-92; 21:26; 37:149-159; 43:15-16; 53:22-23. ***false** inventions, 3:24, 78, 94; 4:48-50; 5:103; 6:21, 24, 93-94, 137, 144; 7:37, 53; 10:17, 30, 59-60, 68-69; 11:18, 21; 13:33; 14:46; 16:56, 116; 17:73; 18:15; 28:75; 29:68; 39:32; 43:20; 46:28; 61:7; 69:44-47. (v. Ascribing divinity to other than God; Leave (God's): what God has never sanctioned.)

Authority: see Apostles: invested with authority; Proof.

Avarice: see Niggardliness.

Awliyāʾ Allāh (Those who are close to God; Those who are drawn close unto God), 10:62-63; 83:20-21, 28. ***the angels** as, 34:40-41; 39:75; 40:7. (See God: is near unto men....)

Āyah: of Light [*āyatu 'n-nūr*], 24:35; -of the Sword [*āyatu 's-saif*], 9:5; **-of the Throne** [*āyatu 'l-kursī*], 2:255; see Throne. (See Messages of God)

Āzar (father of Abraham), 6:74; see Abraham: argues with his father...; asks God's forgiveness for his father.

Baal, 37:125.

Babylon, 2:102.

Badr (Battle of), 3:13, 123, 165; 8:5-19, 41-48; 9:25.

Bakkah (Mecca), 3:96; see Mecca.

Balance (Scales): as a standard to discern between true and false, 42:17; 57:25; see Judgement (Sound). ***in the Day** of Judgement, 7:8-9; 21:47; 23:102-103; 101:6-9 (See Commerce.)

Banu 'n-Naḍīr (not named), 59:2-5, 11-14.

Banū Quraiẓa (not named), 33:26-27.

Barrier [*ḥijāb*], 7:46; 18:52; 23:100; 33:53; 57:13. ***veiling** the unbelievers, 6:25; 17:45-46; 26:200-201, 212; 27:43; 30:59; 36:9; 41:5; 50:22. ***excluding** the doomed, 25:22; 34; 34:54; 83:15. ***against** Gog and Magog, 18:94. ***between** the two great bodies of water, 25:53; 27:61; 55:17-19.

Beast (creature of the Last Hour), 27:82; see Animals.

Beauty (Adornment), 7:31-32; 10:24; 16:5-6, 8, 13; 18:46; 33:52; 37:6; 41:12; 50:6; 67:5. ***as a test** for mankind, 18:7; 20:131. ***in jewels** and clothes, 7:26; 16:14; 35:12. (See Deception; Heaven: adorned; Heavens (the seven): adorned.)

Bedouins [*al-aʿrāb*], 9:90, 97-106, 120; 48:11-16; 49:14-17.

Bees, 16:68-69; see Insects.

Behaviour (**Right**): see Manners; Virtue.

Believers [*al-muʾminūn; alladhīna ʾāmanū*], 2:253; 4:51, 147; 5:53; 7:32, 87, 188; 8:62-64, 72; 9:124; 10:2, 98-100; 11:29, 36, 40, 120; 13:28, 31; 19:73; 22:17; 28:3; 29:51; 38:28; 40:58; 45:21; 51:55; 59:10; 66:11-12; 71:28; 83:34-36; 90:17; 98:7. ***descriptions of** the, 2:2-5, 121, 165, 177; 3:134-135; 4:125, 162; 5:54-56; 6:82; 8:2-4, 74-75; 9:20, 44, 71, 112; 13:20-22; 17:19; 22:41; 23:1-9, 57-61; 24:51-52, 62; 25:63-68, 72-77; 26:227; 32:15-16; 42:36-39; 48:29; 49:10, 14-15; 57:19; 70:22-35. ***are called** to God-consciousness and righteousness, 2:153-157, 208, 278-281; 3:92, 102-105, 120, 122, 133, 139, 142, 160, 200; 4:135-136; 5:1-2, 8-11, 35, 93; 7:87; 8:1, 29; 9:51, 119; 24:56; 29:56; 33:9, 41-42, 69-71; 34:37; 39:10; 42:43; 46:13, 35; 47:38; 49:1-5; 50:40-42; 57:16, 28; 59:18-19; 63:9-10; 64:13-17; 65:10; 66:6, 8. ***warnings** and commands addressed to, 2:104, 172-173, 178-185, 221, 254, 264-274, 282-283; 3:100-101, 118, 130-136, 149, 156; 4:19-43, 36, 39, 58-59, 71-76, 84-86, 94, 101-104, 144; 5:1-7, 35, 51, 54, 57, 87-96, 101-102, 106-108; 8:15-28, 45-47; 9:16, 23-24, 28-29, 38-41, 113, 122-123; 11:120; 14:11-12, 31; 16:90-91; 17:22-39; 22:77-78; 24:3, 12-17, 21-22, 27-31, 56, 58, 63; 28:86-88; 33:6, 36, 49, 53-54, 56, 59; 42:10; 45:14; 47:33, 35, 38; 49:6-12; 58:9, 11-13; 60:10-11; 61:2-4, 10-11, 14; 62:9-10. ***bear witness** to the truth, 2:26, 143-144, 285; 5:83-84; 6:114; 7:75; 12:57; 22:78; 28:53; 33:22-23; 42:18; 43:86; 46:30; 47:3; see Knowledge: those endowed with K. bear witness to the truth; Truth. ***God guides**, helps and strengthens the, 2:213-214, 257; 3:68, 124-126, 139, 160, 164, 171-172; 4:26-28, 141; 6:34; 7:52, 203; 8:12; 9:26, 61; 10:9, 103; 11:120; 12:111; 14:27; 16:64, 89, 102; 18:14; 22:23-24, 37-38, 54; 27:53; 30:4-5, 47; 31:5; 33:9, 25-27, 43; 40:51; 41:44; 47:2, 7, 11; 48:4, 18-21, 24, 26-28; 61:13; 64:11; 65:10-11; see Victory. ***their faith** put to the test, 2:214; 3:140-143; 9:16; 29:2-5, 11; 33:11; see Trials. ***reward** promised to those of them who do good, 2:3-5, 25, 82, 218, 277; 3:57, 107, 136, 157-158; 4:57, 74, 95-96, 122, 124, 152, 162, 175; 5:9; 7:32, 42-43; 9:20-22, 72, 120-121; 10:4, 9-10, 62-64; 11:23; 13:29; 14:23; 16:96-97; 17:9, 19; 18:2-3, 30-31, 107-108; 19:60-63, 96; 20:82; 22:14, 23-24, 50, 56; 24:55; 25:24, 70, 74-76; 28:67, 80; 29:6-7, 9, 58; 30:15, 45; 31:8-9; 32:17, 19; 33:35, 47; 34:37; 35:7; 39:10; 40:40; 41:8; 42:22-23, 26, 36; 43:68-73; 45:30; 46:13-14; 47:12, 35-36; 48:5, 18-21, 29; 52:21-28; 57:7, 11-12, 19, 21, 28; 58:11; 61:10-13; 65:11; 66:8; 70:35; 84:25; 85:11; 95:6; 98:7-8. ***prayer of the angels** and the righteous for the, 14:41; 40:7-9; 71:28. ***God's bond** with them, 3:103; 5:7; 9:111; 16:91. ***had God** willed it, all mankind would be, 6:35; 10:99-100; 26:4; 32:13; see Guidance. ***among the** invisible beings, 46:29-32; 72:1-15. ***among** Jews and Christians, 2:62; 3:110, 113-114; 4:55, 173; 5:69; 22:40; 57:26-27; 61:14. ***Satan** has no power over them, 16:99; 17:65; 34:21; 58:10. ***mockery**, deception and malice against the, 2:8-20, 76, 105, 212; 3:69, 99-100, 118-120, 175; 5:57-59; 8:49; 9:47, 79, 98, 107; 10:65; 20:16; 23:110; 24:19; 25:63; 29:12; 33:48, 58; 46:11; 58:10; 60:1-2, 9; 83:29-33; 85:4-8, 10. ***enemies of the**, 3:111; 4:44-45, 88-91, 101-104, 144; 5:105; 8:60-62, 65-66, 73; 9:8-16, 36, 123; 48:22-25, 29; 59:11-17; 60:1-9, 13; 63:4. (See Denying the truth; Faith; Messages or signs of God: for people who will believe; Muslims.)

Betting: see Games of chance.

Beyond human perception (**that which is**) (the Hidden Reality; the Unseen) [*al-ghaib*], 2:3; 3:179; 12:81; 19:61, 78; 20:15; 34:14, 41, 53; 52:38, 41; 53:35; 68:47; 81:24; App. I and III. ***only God** knows all, 2:33; 3:5; 5:109, 116; 6:59, 73; 9:78, 94, 105; 10:20; 11:123; 13:9; 16:77; 18:26; 23:92; 27:25, 65, 75; 31:16; 32:6; 34:3, 48; 35:38; 36:45; 39:46; 49:18; 59:22; 62:8; 64:18; 67:14; 72:26-27; 87:7; see Hearts; Hour (the Last): knowledge of it rests with God alone; Knowledge; Manifest and Hidden. ***the Prophet** does not know, 6:50; 7:187-188; 11:31; 21:109. ***those who fear God** although He is, 5:94; 21:49; 35:18; 36:11; 50:33; 57:25; 67:12. ***accounts revealed** to the Prophet from, 3:44; 11:49; 12:102.

Birds, 2:260; 6:38; 22:31; 27:16-17, 20; 56:21. ***God alone** holds them aloft, 16:79; 67:19. ***glorify** God, 24:41; 27:16, 20. ***join David** in praising God, 21:79; 34:10; 38:18-19. ***hoopoe**: see Solomon: and the hoopoe. ***crow**, 5:31.

Blame (Reproach), 3:75; 5:54, 59; 12:32. ***those who** are free of, 2:262-264; 7:164; 9:91-92; 12:92; 23:5-7; 24:61; 33:37-38; 42:41; 48:17; 51:54-55; 70:29-31. ***those who** rightly deserve, 9:93; 17:29, 39 ; 42:41-42. (See Fighting: those exempt from; those who refuse to fight.)

Blood, 7:133; 12:18; 16:66; 22:37. ***ties of kinship**, 4:1; 23:101; 25:54; see Children; Parents; Relatives. ***-shedding**, 2:30, 84-85. ***-money** [*diyyah*]: see Homicide: indemnity for; Retribution (Just). (See Food and Drink: forbidden kinds of; Murder; Uterus.)

Booty, 4:94; 8:1, 67-69; 33:27; 48:15, 19-20. ***distribution of**, 8:41; 59:7-9. (See Fighting.)

Bounds: set by God, 2:187, 229-230; 4:13-14; 9:112; 58:4; 65:1. ***of truth** in religious beliefs, do not overstep, 4:171; 5:77. ***of what is right**, transgression of, 2:61, 178; 3:112; 5:78, 87, 94, 107; 6:119; 9:10; 10:74; 26:166; 38:55; 78:22. ***of equity**, transgression of, 17:33; 20:24, 43, 45, 81; 79:17, 37; 89:11.

Bribery (offered to judges), 2:188.

Bronze: see Metals.

Byzantines, 30:2-5.

Calendar (**Islamic**): lunar, 2:189; 10:5. ***months in**, 9:36-37.

Calf: the golden, 2:51, 54, 92-93; 4:153; 7:148, 152; 20:85-97. ***Abraham offers** the heavenly messengers a roasted, 11:69-70; 51:26-27.

Calumny, 4:112; 24:10-25; 33:58; 60:12; 104:1. ***its punishment**, 24:4-5, 19, 23-25. ***the hypocrites** malign Prophet Muḥammad, 9:61, 64-66, 74. ***uttered by the Jews** against Mary, 4:156. (See ʿĀʾishah: calumny against.)

Camels, 6:144; 56:55; 59:6. ***the she-camel** of Thamūd, 7:73, 77; 11:64-65; 17:59; 26:155-157; 54:27-29; 91:13-14.

Captives, 2:85; 76:8. ***prisoners** of war, 8:67-70; 9:5; 33:26; 47:4. (See Slaves.)

Cattle, 3:14; 5:1; 6:142, 146; 7:179; 10:24; 16:5-8, 10, 66, 80; 20:54; 22:30; 23:21-22; 25:44; 26:133; 32:27; 35:28; 36:71-73; 39:6; 40:79-80; 42:11; 43:12-13; 47:12; 79:33; 80:32. ***sacrificial** animals, 5:2; 22:28, 34, 36-37. ***idolatrous** practices related to, 4:119; 5:103; 6:136, 138-139, 143-144. (See Animals; Cows; Sacrifices.)

Cave (the Men of the), 18:9-26.

Certainty, 56:95; 69:51; 102:7. ***of the life** to come, 2:4, 46, 249; 13:2; 27:3; 31:4; 51:23; 74:47. ***inner**, 2:265; 32:24; 44:7. ***people endowed** with inner, 2:118; 5:50; 6:75; 45:4, 20; 51:20. ***do not be disquieted** by people devoid of, 30:60. ***the unbelievers** lack inner, 44:9; 52:36. ***of punishment**, 41:48; 102:6-7; see Punishment: evildoers cannot escape.

Challenges: to God's apostles, 11:32; 13:6; 15:7; 22:47; see Punishment: unbelievers ask for it to be hastened on. ***of God** to the Jews, 2:94; 62:6-7. ***of the prophets** to their unbelieving peoples, 7:195; 10:71; 11:55, 93. ***of God** to the unbelievers, 2:23-24; 28:49-50; 77:38-39; see Proof: God's challenges to the unbelievers; Qurʾān: its inimitability as proof of its divine origin.

Charity [*ṣadaqah; zakāh*], 2:196, 271, 280; 4:92; 7:156; 9:75; 22:28; 30:38-39; 33:35; 41:7; 57:18; 58:12-13; 63:10; 76:7-10. ***linked** to prayer, 2:3, 43, 83, 277; 4:162; 5:12; 8:3; 9:18; 19:31, 55; 21:73; 22:41; 27:3; 31:4; 35:29; 42:38; 70:22-25; 73:20; 98:5. (See Atonement; Purifying dues; Spending on others.)

Chastity, 12:32; 19:20; 21:91; 23:5-7; 24:30-31, 33; 33:35; 66:12; 70:29-31. (See Virtue.)

Children (Offspring; Progeny), 3:61; 4:11-12, 23; 7:189-190; 9:24; 16:72; 17:40; 24:31; 31:33; 33:55; 37:149; 42:49-50; 43:16; 58:22; 70:11; 74:11-13; 80:34-36. ***linked** to wealth, 3:14; 8:28; 9:55, 69, 85; 17:6, 64; 18:34, 39, 46; 19:77; 23:55-56; 26:88, 133; 34:35, 37; 57:20; 58:17; 63:9; 68:14-15; 71:12, 21; 74:11-13; see Wealth. ***as trial** and temptation, 8:28; 63:9; 64:14-15; 71:21. ***killing** one's own, 6:137, 140, 151; 16:59; 17:31; 60:12; 81:8-9. ***and riches**, of no avail against God, 3:10, 116; 26:88; 31:33; 34:35, 37; 58:17; 60:3. ***born** as miraculous sign, 3:38-41, 45-47; 11:71-74; 15:53-55; 19:5-33; 21:91; 51:28-30. ***kindness** towards parents, 6:151; 17:23-24; 29:8; 31:14-15; 46:15. ***nursing**, 2:233; 31:14; 46:15. ***daughters**, 4:23; 11:78-79; 15:71; 16:57-59; 28:27; 33:50, 59; 42:49-50; 43:16-18; 81:8-9. ***adopted**, 33:4-5, 37. ***attributing** sons and daughters to God: see Attributing to God. (See Enemies.)

Christ (**the**) [*al-masīḥ*], 3:45; 4:157, 171-172; 5:17, 72, 75; 9:30-31; see Jesus.

Christianity, 4:171-173. ***God** is not the Christ, 5:17, 72. ***do not say**, '[God is] a trinity', 4:171; 5:73. (See Christ; Crucifixion; Gospel; Jesus; Monasticism.)

Christians, 2:62, 140; 5:14-16, 18-19, 47; 9:29-35; 22:17. ***closest** in affection to the Muslims, 5:82-85. ***claim that only they** will enter Paradise; are rightly guided, 2:111, 135. ***accuse** Jews of lacking a valid base for their beliefs, and vice-versa, 2:113. ***their deification** of Jesus, 4:171; 5:17, 72; 9:30-31; 61:14. ***challenged** to a trial through prayer, 3:58-61. ***severe warnings** to, 4:171; 5:77, 115; 18:4-5; 19:37-39. ***salvation** of, 2:62; 5:83-85. ***they alter** and contradict the teachings of Jesus, 2:146, 159-160, 129, 174-176; 3:71, 78-80; 5:72-77; 15:90. (See Jesus; Jews and Christians.)

Clothes: see Dress.

Clouds, 2:164; 7:57; 13:12-13; 24:43; 30:48; 35:9; 56:69; 78:14; 88:17; see Rain; Resurrection: as God's bringing dead land to life; Water; Wind.

Coercion: not in matters of faith, 2:256; 6:149; 11:28; 18:29; 26:4; 32:13; 50:45.

Commerce, 2:198, 275, 282-283; 9:24; 17:12; 24:37; 34:18-19; 35:12; 62:11; 73:20; 106:2. ***just dealings** in, 4:29; 6:152; 17:35; 26:181-183. ***supreme bargain** with God, 2:207; 4:74; 9:111; 35:29-30; 61:10-12. (See Debts; Deception; Justice; Usury.)

Communities (Nations): mankind as a single C., 2:213; 5:48; 10:19; 11:118; 16:93; 42:8. ***destroyed** or passed away, 2:134, 141; 7:34; 11:100-102, 117; 13:30; 18:55; 28:58. ***destroyed** or punished only after having received, and rejected, God's Revelation, 3:137-138; 6:131; 7:4-5, 94-95; 9:115; 10:47; 15:4, 10-13, 73-84; 17:15-17, 58; 18:55, 58-59; 21:6-9, 11-15, 74, 95-97; 23:44; 26:208-209; 28:59; 40:5, 21-22; 41:17; 43:23-25; 46:27; 47:13; 58:5; 65:8-9; 98:1-6. ***each community** has had an apostle, 10:47; 15:10; 16:36, 63; 23:44; 25:51; 35:24. ***witnesses** against them on Day of Judgement, 4:41; 16:84, 89; 28:75. ***the believers** form a single, 21:92; 23:52. ***different rituals**, laws and ways of life for each of them, 2:148; 5:48; 6:108; 22:67. ***should compete** with each other in doing good works, 2:148; 5:48. ***their powerful and corrupt ones** reject the prophets, 34:34-35; 43:23-24, 52-53. ***to learn** from their destruction, 3:137-138; 15:73-77; 20:128; 32:26; 43:55-56. ***of invisible** beings, 41:25.

Community (**the Muslim**), 3:102-104; 8:72-75. ***that of all** the prophets, 2:128; 6:84-90; 21:92; 42:13. ***of the middle way**, 2:143. ***God declares** it to be the best ever brought forth for mankind, 3:110. ***enjoins doing what is right** and forbids what is wrong, 3:104, 110; see Muslims: to enjoin what is right.

Competing: see Good deeds: compete amongst yourselves in doing; Communities: should compete with each other in doing good deeds; Forgiveness (God's): vie with each other for.

Conduct (Immoral), 4:15, 19, 25; 33:30.

Confabulations (Secret), 4:114; 58:8-10. *God is present in them; knows them, 9:78; 43:80; 58:7.

Conjectures, 2:78; 4:157; 6:116, 148; 10:36, 59, 66; 17:36; 43:20; 45:24; 51:10-11. *can never be a substitute for truth, 10:36; 53:27-28. *about others, to be avoided, 49:12.

Consciousness (God-) [*at-taqwā*], 2:2; 2:66, 103, 180, 212, 224, 237, 241; 3:125, 130; 5:2, 8, 27, 93; 6:51, 69, 72; 8:29; 9:108-109; 19:97; 21:48; 22:32-33, 37; 24:34; 47:17; 48:26; 49:13; 65:2, 4-5; 69:48; 91:7-8; 92:5; 96:11-12. *God, fount of all, 74:56. *divine ordinances seek to promote and support, 2:179, 183, 187; 6:51, 153; 7:63, 171; 20:113; 39:27-28. *calls to, 2:21, 41, 63, 103, 194, 196-197, 203, 206, 223, 231, 233, 281-283; 3:50, 102, 125, 130, 200; 4:1, 131; 5:2, 8, 35, 100, 112; 8:1, 29; 9:119; 10:31-32; 16:2; 22:1; 23:52; 26:*passim*; 31:33; 33:1, 70; 49:12; 51:55-56; 52:29; 57:28; 59:18; 64:16; 65:2, 4-5, 10. *man's nobility, proportionate to his, 49:13. *the best of all provisions, 2:197. *the garment of, 7:26-27; 21:80. *men are to co-operate in furthering, 5:2; 58:9. *description of the God-conscious, 2:177, 189; 3:133-135; 6:32; 7:169-170; 12:57, 109; 39:33; 50:31-35; 51:15-19; 92:17-21. *God loves the God-conscious; is with them, 2:194; 3:76; 9:4, 7, 36, 123; 16:128; 45:19. *reward of the God-conscious, 3:15, 133, 172, 179, 198; 4:77; 7:128, 156, 169-170; 8:29; 10:63-64; 11:49; 13:35; 15:45-48; 16:30-32; 19:63, 72, 85; 20:132; 24:52; 25:15-16; 26:90; 28:83; 38:28, 49-50; 39:20, 33-35, 61, 73-74; 43:35; 44:51-57; 47:15; 50:31-35; 52:17-20; 54:54-55; 65:5; 68:34; 77:41-44; 78:31-37; 92:17-21. (See Righteousness.)

Considering: see Oaths: divine O. and calls to reflection; Thought: calls to reflection; have you ever considered...?

Constellations: see Heaven (the nearest): adorned ...; Heavens (the seven): adorned ....

Consultation: in matters of public concern, 3:159; 42:38. *personal C. with the Prophet, 58:12. *with followers of earlier revelations, 10:94; 16:43; 17:101; 21:7; 43:45.

Contract, 5:1; 17:34. *commercial, 2:282-283. *matrimonial: see Marriage.

Corruption: see Injustice.

Corruption of revealed texts, 2:42, 75, 79; 3:78; 4:46; 5:13, 41; 15:90-91. (See Attributing to God: false inventions; Christians; Israel (children of); Revelation.)

Countenance (God's), 2:115. *those who, through righteousness, seek, 2:272; 6:52; 13:22; 18:28; 30:38-39; 92:17-21; see Acceptance (God's goodly); Love: doing good for God's sake. *everything perishes except, 28:88; 55:26-27. (See God.)

Covenant (Bond with God), 3:76, 103, 112; 6:152; 16:91, 95; 7:172-173; 13:20-21; 16:91-91; 19:78, 87. *solemn pledge of the prophets, 2:124; 3:81-86; 33:7-8. *those who break or barter away their, 2:26-27; 3:77; 13:25; 16:95. *the deniers of truth invoke God's C. with the prophets, 7:134; 43:49. (See Israel (children of): God's covenant with; Promises; Uterus: what God has bidden to be joined.)

Covenants (Bonds; Treaties), 3:112; 4:89-90, 92; 8:56-58, 72: 9:1, 4, 7-13. (See Covenant; Ḥudaybiyyah; Promises.)

Cows (Bovine cattle), 6:144, 146; 39:6; see Cattle. *yellow cow of the children of Israel, 2:67-71. *in Pharaoh's dream, 12:43-49. (See Calf.)

Creation, 6:1-2; 7:54; 14:32-33; 15:21-23; 21:30; 27:60, 64; 29:19-20; 31:10-11; 35:1-3; 41:9-12; 50:6-11; 51:47-48; 52:35-36; 55:1-15; 65:12; 67:1-5; 79:27-33; 88:17-20. *God creates what He wills, 3:47; 5:17; 24:45; 28:68; 30:54; 35:1; 42:49-50; see Will (God's): God does what He wills. *easy for God, 19:21; 29:19; 30:27. *God commands, 'Be' -and it is, 2:117; 3:47; 6:73; 36:82; 40:68; 54:50. *those endowed with insight reflect on, 3:190-191. *with meaning and purpose, 3:191; 10:5; 38:27. *messages in, 2:164; 10:6; 13:3; 16:11-13, 79; 27:86; 29:44; 45:3-6M; see Messages. *of mankind out of a single living entity, 4:1; 6:98; 7:189; 39:6. *in six aeons, 7:54; 10:3; 11:7; 25:59; 32:4; 50:38; 57:4. *of the earth in two aeons, 41:9. *without witnesses, 18:51; 37:150. *not as idle play, 21:16; 23:115; 44:38. *all created in pairs, or opposites, 13:3; 36:36; 43:12; 51:49; see Pairs. *perfect, 27:88; 32:7; 54:49; 64:3; 67:3-4. *variety in, 16:13; 35:27-28. *it does not tire Him, 46:33; 50:15, 38. *of the heavens and the earth in accordance with truth [*bil-ḥaqq*], 6:73; 10:5; 14:19; 15:85; 16:3; 29:44; 30:8; 39:5; 44:39; 45:22; 46:3; 64:2-3. *everything created in due measure and proportion, 32:7; 54:49; 64:3; 67:3-4. *of the heavens and the earth, greater than that of man, 40:57; 79:27. *pagans recognising God as the Creator, 39:38; 43:9, 87. *everything on earth created for man, 2:29; 16:5-18; see Man. *all living things created from water, 21:30; 24:45; 25:54. (See Earth; God: creates in the first instance and then brings forth anew; Heavens; Man.)

Crops, 6:141; 13:3; 16:11; 18:32; 26:148; 32:27; 39:21; 44:26; 56:63-64; see Plants and Trees. *as a metaphor of human endeavours, 2:205; 42:20. *'your wives are your tilth', 2:223.

Crucifixion: of Jesus, denied, 4:157-158; see Jesus. *of the magicians by Pharaoh, 7:124; 20:71; 26:49. *of those who oppose God and His apostle, 5:33. (See Punishment.)

Crying, 9:92;12:16, 84-86; 44:29. *God causes you to laugh and to weep, 53:43. *when hearing God's messages, 5:83; 17:107-109; 19:58; 53:59-61. *in Hell, 9:82; 11:106.

Darkness: see Light.

David [*Dāwūd*], 5:78; 34:13. *God's favour upon, 2:251; 4:163; 6:84; 17:55; 21:78-80; 27:15-16; 34:10-11; 38:17-20, 25-26. *sentence passed by David and Solomon, 21:78-79. *and the two litigants, 38:21-24.

Day [*yawm*], 3:72; 7:98, 163; 9:36; 24:58; 55:29; 69:24. *of Judgement, 50:41; 64:9; 77:12-13; see

Day of Resurrection. *and ritual prayer, 4:103; 11:114; 17:78; 20:130; 62:9; see Prayer: times of the. *as daylight time, 10:67; 27:86; 36:37; 40:61; 79:29; 91:3; 92:2; 93:1. *as a measure of time, 2:80; 3:24; 9:108; 18:19; 25:47; 26:38, 155; 35:11; 36:40, 68; 40:49; 69:6-7; 70:4; 73:20; see Time. *as a fixed term, 2:184, 185, 196, 203, 234; 3:41; 5:89; 11:65; 19:10; 22:28. *as the event of a battle, 3:155, 166-167; 8:16, 41-42; 9:25. *as a joyful occasion, 3:140; 9:3; 12:92; 19:15, 33; 20:59; 30:4-5. *as a woeful occasion, 3:140; 11:77; 14:18; 15:2. *days of God's punishment, 10:102; 16:27; 26:135, 156, 189; 41:16; 46:21; 54:19; 74:9-10. (See Night and Day; Time: its perception after resurrection.)

Day of Resurrection (Day of Judgement; That Day), [*yawm al-qiyāmah; yawm ad-dīn; yawmuʾiḍ*], 2:85; 7:14, 25; 11:103-105; 14:41; 18:99-101; 19:85-87; 20:100-112; 30:43; 32:5; 34:40-42; 37:20-33; 39:67-75; 44:40-42; 45:26-37; 50:43-44; 51:10-14; 56:1-14; 69:13-37; 77:7-15; 78:17-40; 79:34-41; 80:33-42; 82:9-19; 83:15-17, 34-36; 99:6. ***God**, Lord of, 1:4; 6:62, 73; 40:16; 82:19. ***the meeting** with God, 2:223; 6:31, 154; 10:7, 45; 13:2; 14:21, 48; 18:48, 105, 110; 25:21; 29:5; 30:8; 32:10; 33:44; 40:15; 41:54; 79:40; 83:6; 84:6. ***certainty** of its coming, 3:9, 25; 4:87; 6:12; 13:2; 30:43; 42:7; 45:26; 51:5-6. ***its term is set**, but known only to God, 11:103-104; 15:36-38; 17:99; 34:30; 38:81; 41:47; 56:50; 78:17; 85:2. ***as the Last Day**, belief in, 2:8, 62, 126, 177, 228, 232, 264; 3:114; 4:38-39, 59, 136; 4:162; 5:69; 9:44-45, 99; 24:2; 58:22; 60:6; 65:2. ***cataclysmic** changes and portents signalling the, 14:48; 18:47; 20:105-107; 21:104; 25:25; 27:88; 36:51; 39:67; 52:9-10; 56:4-6; 69:13-17; 70:8-9; 73:14, 17-18; 75:8-9; 77:7-10; 78:19-20; 79:6-7; 81:1-14; 84:1-5; 89:21-22; 99:1-4; 101:4-5. ***the trumpet** of the, 18:99; 20:102; 23:101; 27:87; 39:68; 50:20; 69:13; 74:8; 78:18. ***the Summoning Voice**, 20:108; 54:6-8. ***the final blast**, 36:53; 37:19-20; 50:42; 80:33; see Punishment: blast of. ***a distressful, fateful Day** for all who deny the truth, 14:41-51; 19:37-39; 25:22-29; 54:6-8; 70:6-14, 42-44; 76:7, 10, 27; 77:28-47; 83:4-12; 101:1-5. ***the righteous** will be spared the terror of, 21:103; 27:87, 89; 33:44; 39:68; 43:68-69; 76:7-12. ***God's final** judgement, 2:113, 281; 4:141, 172-173; 7:6-9; 14:21; 16:84-89, 111; 17:34, 36, 71-72; 18:47-49; 19:68-72; 22:14-18, 55-57; 25:17-19; 27:83-90. ***every human being** will appear alone, 6:94; 18:48; 19:80, 95; 42:8; 99:6. ***witnesses** from each community, 4:41, 159; 5:109; 11:18; 16:84, 89; 28:74-75; 39:69; 40:51; 44:12-13. ***witnessing** borne on that Day, 4:159; 5:116-118; 6:130; 17:13-14; 24:24; 36:65, 70; 41:20-22, 47; 55:39; 75:14; 99:1-5; 102:8. ***clarification** of every matter or discrepancy, 2:113; 3:55; 5:14, 105; 6:159; 10:93; 16:39, 92, 124; 22:17, 67-69; 24:25, 64; 29:8; 32:25; 34:26; 39:3, 46; 41:50; 45:17; 53:40; 58:6-7; 64:7; 78:40; 86:9; 100:9-11. ***man will see** all his good and bad actions, 3:30; 10:30; 45:33; 69:18-27; 75:13-15; 79:35; 89:23; 99:6-8. ***some faces will be** bright with happiness, others veiled with darkness, 3:106-107; 10:26-27; 11:105; 39:60; 75:22-25; 80:38-42; 83:22-24; 88:2-3, 8-10. ***the record** of human actions, 17:13-14, 71; 18:49; 23:62; 39:69; 40:16; 45:28-29; 54:53; 69:18-26; 78:29; 81:10; 83:7-9, 18-21; 84:7-12. ***belated repentance** of evildoers, 2:167; 4:62; 6:27-28; 7:53; 14:44; 16:28, 87; 23:107; 25:27-29; 32:12, 29; 33:66; 34:51-52; 39:56-58; 40:11; 42:44; 43:38; 67:10-11; 89:24. ***reward** and punishment, 2:165-166, 174; 3:56-57, 77, 105-107, 185, 194-195; 4:173; 5:119; 6:15-16; 7:32; 10:26-27; 14:49-51; 16:25-29, 88; 18:105-108; 19:85-87; 20:74-76; 22:55-57; 25:22-24; 27:89-90; 30:14-16, 43-45; 32:14; 34:54; 40:46, 70-72; 46:20; 52:11-28; 57:11-15; 64:9-10; 69:18-37; 101:6-11; see Paradise; Hell. ***none** shall be wronged, 2:281; 3:25, 161, 182; 4:40, 124; 6:160; 10:54; 16:111; 17:71; 18:49; 20:112; 21:47; 22:9-10; 24:25; 36:54; 39:69-70; 40:17, 20; 50:29; 53:41; see Injustice: God does not wrong anyone in the least. ***intercession**, 2:48, 254; 4:109; 10:3; 19:87; 20:109; 21:28; 30:13; 32:4; 34:23; 40:18; 43:86; 74:48; 78:38; see Intercession. ***no-one will speak** but with His leave, 11:105; 20:109; 78:37-38; see Leave (God's). ***wealth and children** will be of no use, 3:10, 116; 26:88; 58:17; 60:3. ***no ransom or amends** will be accepted from evildoers, 2:123, 254; 3:91; 5:36; 6:70; 10:54; 13:18; 14:31; 30:57; 31:33; 34:42; 39:47; 41:24; 44:41-42; 45:35; 57:15. ***evildoers will blame** each other, 7:38-39; 14:21; 26:96-99; 29:25; 33:67-68; 34:31-33; 37:27-32; 38:59-64; 39:31; 41:29; 43:38, 67; 50:21-29.

Other names of: -the Last Day [*yawm al-ākhir*]: see Day of Resurrection: as the Last Day, belief in; **-Days of God** [*ayyām Allāh*], 14:5; 45:14; **-Day of the Final Decision** [*yawm al-fatḥ*], 32:29; **-Day of Distinction** [*yawm al-faṣl*], 37:21; 44:40; 77:13-14, 38; 78:17; **-Day of Reckoning** [*yawm al-ḥisāb*], 14:41; 38:16, 26, 53; 40:27; **-Day of Regrets** [*yawm al-ḥasrah*], 19:39; **-Day of Loss and Gain** [*yawm at-taghābun*], 64:9; **-Day of the Gathering** [*yawm al-jamᶜ*], 42:7; 64:9; **-Day of Ultimate Truth** [*yawm al-ḥaqq*], 78:39; **-Day of the Meeting** [*yawm at-talāq*], 40:15. (See Deities (False); Hell; Intercession; Paradise; Resurrection.)

Days of God: see Day of Resurrection: Other names of.

Death, 2:28, 73, 94, 132-133, 180; 3:102, 143, 145, 154-158, 168-169, 193; 4:15, 97, 100; 6:162; 7:25; 8:6; 15:99; 22:58; 23:37; 25:3; 31:34; 33:23; 35:22; 37:58-59; 44:35, 56; 45:21, 24; 62:6-8; 67:2; 74:47; 77:25-26; 78:9; 102:1-2. ***God grants life** and deals, 2:258; 3:27, 145, 156; 6:95; 7:158; 9:116; 10:31, 56, 104; 15:23; 16:70; 22:66; 23:80; 26:81; 30:19, 40; 39:42; 40:11, 68; 44:8; 45:26; 50:43; 53:44; 57:2; 80:21. ***inevitability** of, 3:154, 168, 185; 4:78; 6:61; 21:34-35; 23:15; 29:57; 33:16; 39:30; 56:60; 62:8. ***of prophets** and apostles, 3:55, 144; 5:75, 117; 10:46; 12:101; 13:40; 19:15, 33; 21:8, 34-35; 26:81; 29:57; 34:14; 35:24; 39:30; 40:34, 77. ***death, resurrection** and spiritual regeneration, 2:28, 56, 259-260; 3:49; 5:110; 6:36, 60, 122;

10:34; 19:15, 33; 22:6, 66; 23:16; 26:81; 30:19, 40, 50; 38:34; 41:39; 45:26; 57:16-17; 80:22; see Sleep: and awakening...; Rain: with which God brings dead land back to life; Resurrection: as a metaphor. ***fear of**, 2:19, 243; 4:84; 8:65; 33:16, 19; 47:20; 62:8. ***agony**, or nearness of, 2:133, 180; 4:18, 159; 5:106; 6:93; 10:90; 23:99; 31:32; 33:19; 50:19, 41; 56:83-87; 63:10-11; 75:26-30; see Ships: the faith of people confronted with great danger. ***angels of**, 4:97; 6:61, 93; 7:37; 8:50; 16:28, 32; 47:27. ***the doomed in hell** will not live nor die, 14:17; 20:74; 35:36; 74:28; 87:13. ***as extinction** beseeched by the doomed, 4:42; 14:17; 20:74; 25:13-14; 35:36; 43:77; 69:27; 74:28; 78:40; 84:11; 87:13. (See Martyrs; Term set by God.)

Debts, 9-60; 2:282. ***cancelling**, 2:280. ***to be settled** before sharing out an inheritance, 4:11-12. (See Commerce; Contract.)

Deception (Fraud), 3:196; 40:4; 83:1-3. ***those who would deceive** God and the believers, 2:8-9, 10; 3:78; 4:142; 5:49; 8:62; 25:33. ***self-deception**, 2:9; 6:23-24, 113; 13:33; 15:3; 23:90; 26:221-226; 30:55; 31:33; 35:5, 40; 39:3; 40:50; 45:7-8, 35; 46:28; 51:8-9; 57:14; 67:20; 82:6-9. ***false arguments** against God's messages, 10:21; 34:33; 86:15-16. ***inconceivable** in prophets, 3:161; 38:86. ***God's apostles** accused of: see Apostles: given the lie; accused of lying about God. ***branding truth** as, 8:49; 11:7; 28:48: 33:12; 52:14-15; 53:2; 54:2; 67:9; see Denying the truth: labelling it as 'fables of ancient times'. ***do not use** your oaths to deceive one another, 16:92, 94. ***in measure** and weight, 11:84-85; 26:181-183; see Commerce; Justice. ***of Pharaoh's** magicians, 7:117; 26:45; see Pharaoh: and his magicians. ***evil made** to appear goodly, 35:8; 40:37; 41:25; see Evil: seems goodly to evildoers. ***the D. of Satan** and the forces of evil, 4:119-121; 6:112-113, 128-129; 7:21-22; 14:22; 17:64; see Satan: makes evil doings seem goodly; his guile is weak. (See Attributing to God: false inventions; Life: The life of this world: the deception of; Lying.)

Decree (God's), 7:156. ***which God** has willed upon Himself, 6:12, 54; 10:103; 16:38; 21:104; 30:47; 32:13; 56:60; see Promises: God's. ***encompasses** everything, 6:38, 59; 7:37; 8:75; 9:36; 10:61; 11:6; 17:58; 20:52; 27:75; 33:6; 34:3; 35:11; 57:22; 68:48. ***a decree** already gone forth, which postpones punishment, 8:68; 10:19; 11:110; 20:129; 41:45; 42:14, 21. ***of divine** punishment, 7:167; 10:24; 11:40, 43, 58, 66, 76, 82, 94, 101; 15:66; 19:68-72; 23:27. (See Will, God's.)

Deities (False), 3:80; 7:190; 16:51, 54-57, 86-87; 17:42; 18:52; 21:21-22, 43; 22:12-13; 23:91, 117; 26:213; 31:30; 43:45; 72:18. ***taken as lords** beside God, 3:64, 80; 6:14; 7:3, 30; 9:31; 12:30-40; 18:50-52. ***worshipped** as intercessors, 39:3, 43-44; 46:28. ***worshipped** as a source of strength, protection, etc., 13:11; 18:102; 19:81; 29:25; 36:74-75; 42:6; 45:10. ***only names** invented by men, 6:100-101; 7:71; 12:40; 30:13; 53:23. ***their total** impotence, 6:71; 7:148, 191-198; 10:34-35, 106; 11:101; 13:14-16; 16:17, 20-21, 73; 17:56-57; 20:88-89; 21:43; 22:12, 73; 25:3, 55; 28:71-72; 29:41; 30:40; 34:22; 35:13-14; 36:23; 39:38, 43; 45:10; 46:4-5. ***absent from the Day** of Judgement, 6:22-23; 16:27; 18:52; 26:92-93; 28:62-64; 40:73-74. ***will disavow** their cults and devotees, 2:216; 19:82; 25:17-19; 28:62-63; 29:25; 34:40-41; 35:14; 46:5-6. ***forces of evil** [*aṭ-ṭāghūt*], 2:256-257; 4:51, 60, 76; 5:60; 16:36; 39:17; see Evil. ***do not offend** against, 6:108. ***of pagan** Arabs, 53:19-23. ***of Noah's** people, 71:22-24. ***of Abraham's** people, 37:85-96. (See Ascribing divinity to other than God; Lying: idolatry gives visible shape to a lie; Desires (Worldly); Rabbis and Monks.)

Denying the truth (**those who are bent on**) [*kufr; al-kāfirūn; alladhīna kafarū*], 2:6-7, 257; 3:176-179; 4:140, 167, 170; 5:3; 6:1, 5, 7, 25-26; 8:38; 9:37; 10:38-39; 13:33; 24:55; 25:55, 77; 35:39; 38:27; 46:3; 52:34-42; 60:10-11; 74:31. ***descriptions of**, 2:26-28, 212; 4:150-151; 11:5; 13:25; 14:2-3; 16:106-109; 19:73; 53:29-30; 64:7; 70:36-39; 72:19; 74:18-25. ***parables of**, 2:17-20, 171; 7:177; 66:10; see Parables. ***advice** to the believers with regard to, 3:100-101, 149, 156, 176; 6:31-36; 8:73; 31:23; 60:1-9; 68:51-52. ***God gives** them free rein for a while, 3:178, 196-197; 8:59; 10:11; 13:32; 14:42; 15:3; 19:83-84; 21:44; 22:44, 48; 24:57; 25:18; 31:24; 39:8; 40:4; 44:15; 47:12; 68:45; 86:15-17. ***among Jews** and Christians, 2:8-20, 85-91, 105; 3:19-25, 55-56, 70-71, 86-91, 112; 4:153-156, 160-161; 5:41-44, 57-65, 72-74, 78-81, 110; 9:29-30; 18:102-106; 44:34-36; 46:10; 59:2-4, 11; 62:5; 98:1-6. ***divine** challenges to, 2:23; 11:13-14; 52:30-38; see Challenges. ***do not understand**, nor reason, 2:26, 171; 5:103; 6:39; 7:179; 8:21-23, 65; 10:100; 11:91; 12:109; 16:41-42; 23:114-115; 25:44; 27:61; 34:9; 53:27-28. ***contend against** God's messages, 8:31-32; 11:7; 13:27, 43; 18:56-57; 21:38; 22:42-43; 25:4-11; 27:68-72; 30:58; 34:3-5, 43-45; 36:45-48; 40:4, 35, 56; 45:32; 46:7-11. see Questions: posed by unbelievers. ***loathsome evil** that God lays upon evildoers, 6:107; 7:71; 10:100. ***dismiss the truth** as 'fables of ancient times', 6:25; 8:31; 16:24; 23:81-83; 25:4-5; 27:67-68; 46:11, 17; 68:14-15; 73:23-24; 83:12-13. ***want** to extinguish God's light: see Light: the unbelievers want to extinguish... ***reject** even the most obvious, 2:28-29; 6:109-111; 10:96-97; 13:12-31, 31; 21:30-33; 23:84-90; 43:78; 46:7. ***their plots** and antagonism, 3:54; 8:30, 36; 14:13; 21:36; 22:72; 25:4-11, 32-33, 60; 32:3; 34:5, 7-8, 31-38; 35:42-44; 38:2-8; 40:4-5; 41:26; 52:42. ***follow in their** forefathers' footsteps, 2:170; 5:103-104; 6:148; 9:30; 11:87, 109; 21:52-54; 23:81-83; 31:20-21; 34:43; 43:22-24; 51:52-53; see Forebears: those who reject truth following in their F. footsteps. ***are allies** of one another, 8:73; 9:36. ***the worst** of all creatures before God, 8:22-23, 55; 9:12, 28, 95; 35:39; 40:10; 98:6; see Evil: archetypes of. ***duty** to fight them, 4:76, 84-85; 8:39; 9:29; 25:52; see Fighting. ***God** does not guide them, 2:26, 258, 264; 3:86; 4:137, 168; 5:67;

6:109-111, 144; 9:19, 37; 16:36-37, 104, 107; 18:57; 27:4; 28:50; 30:59; 46:10; 61:7-8. *witnesses against them on Day of Judgement, 4:41-42; 16:84, 89. *their good works rendered void, 3:21-22, 116-117; 18:103-106; 24:39-40; 47:1, 32; see Good deeds: done by unbelievers.... *wealth and children will avail them not, 3:10, 91, 116; 5:36-37; 34:35-38; 111:2. *their mutual reproaches on Day of Judgement, 34:31-33; 41:29: see Day of Resurrection: evildoers will blame each other. *punishment of, 1:7; 2:24, 39, 161-162, 257; 3:10-12, 56, 86-91, 151, 176-178; 4:56, 168-169; 5:10, 86; 6:27-31; 8:35-38, 50-52; 9:3, 26, 90; 10:4; 13:31, 34; 16:85-88; 21:39-40, 97; 22:19-22, 25, 55, 57; 25:12-14, 34-42; 33:64; 34:38, 51-54; 35:36; 40:6, 10-12; 47:8-10; 70:42-44; 88:23-26; 98:6; see Hell; Punishment: evildoers cannot escape. (See Ascribing divinity to other than God; Astray: God lets evildoers go; Attributing to God: false inventions;.)

Desires (**Worldly**) (Likes and Dislikes; Passions; Whims) [*ash-shahawāt; al-hawā; al-amaniyyah*], 2:87; 3:14; 23:71; 25:52; 42:15; 45:18. *do not follow, 4:135; 13:37; 38:26; 79:40. *made into a deity, 24:3; 25:43; 45:23; see Ascribing divinity to other than God. *as Satan instigation, 4:119, 121. *lead to evil, 4:135; 5:80; 6:71; 38:26. *those who only follow their own, 4:27; 7:176; 18:28; 19:59; 20:16; 28:50; 30:29; 47:14, 16; 54:3. *Muḥammad does not speak out of [his own] desire, 53:2-3. (See Play.)

Despair, 5:3; 12:110; 25:27; 29:23, 67; 30:12; 60:13; 75:24. *do not despair of God's mercy, 2:214; 12:87; 15:55-56; 39:53; 68:48. *in misfortune, 6:44; 11:9; 17:83; 30:36; 41:49. *neither despair nor exultation, 57:23. *as punishment in the life to come, 6:70; 10:4; 22:19; 37:67; 38:57; 40:72; 43:75; 44:46-48; 47:15; 55:44; 56:42, 54, 93; 78:25. (See Hardship and Ease; Misfortune; Patience; Trials.)

Destiny (Fate; Fortune; Luck) [*ṭā'ir*]: God alone determines, 13:31; 17:2; 18:45; 27:47; 27:47; 33:38; 39:41-42, 62; 73:9. *man as maker of his own, 39:41; 42:30; 45:15. *of every human being: tied to his neck, 13:15; 17:13; 36:19. *Jesus and the D. of the Israelites, 3:49; 5:110. *the Night of, 44:3-4; 97:1-5.

Devils: see Satan: satanic forces; as evil impulses.

Dhu 'l-Kifl (he who has pledged himself [unto God]), 21:85; 38:48.

Dhu 'l-Qarnayn: see Two-Horned One (the).

Discernment (Discrimination; Insight), 7:46-48; 8:29; 36:66-67; 49:6. *in the Revelation: see Revelation: as a means of insight. *of right and wrong: see Judgement (Sound): of right and wrong. *those endowed with insight [*ulū al-albāb*], 2:179, 197, 269; 3:7, 190-191; 5:100; 12:111; 13:19-22; 14:52; 20:104; 38:29, 43; 39:9, 17-18, 21; 40:53-54; 59:2; 65:9-10. *in war, 4:94; 48:25. *people without awareness [of right and wrong], 6:91; 7:138; 11:29; 27:55. (See Judgement (Sound); Knowledge; Reason; Thought.)

Disciples: see Jesus: disciples of.

Discrepancies, 2:213; 10:19; 11:118-119; 16:92-93; 22:67-69; 42:10; 51:8; 78:1-5; 92:4. *Revelation resolves all, 16:64; 27:76; 43:63. *after Revelation, 2:213; 3:19, 105; 10:93; 45:17. *of Jews and Christians, 2:213, 253; 4:157; 5:14; 6:159; 11:110; 16:124; 19:34-39; 23:53; 27:76; 39:3-4; 42:14-17, 15; 43:63-65; 98:4-5. *God, supreme judge in all, 2:113; 3:55; 5:48; 6:164; 10:93; 16:39, 124; 22:69; 32:25; 39:3, 46. *believers must submit to the ordinances of the Prophet all their, 4:59, 65; see Muḥammad: judge in all D. (See Day of Resurrection: clarification of every matter; Envy; Manners; Sects.)

Discrimination: see Discernment.

Divination, 5:90; 67:5; see Divining arrows; Sorcery.

Divining arrows (to draw lots) [*al-azlām; al-aqlām*], 3:44; 5:3, 90; 37:141.

Divorce, 2:226-232, 236-237, 241; 4:19-21, 35, 130; 58:2; 60:10; 65:1-7; 66:5. *at the wife's instance [*khul'*], 2:229. * ***ʿiddah*** (waiting-period), 2:228, 231-232, 234-235; 33:49; 65:1-7. *and suckling, 2:233; 65:6-7; see Suckling. ****ẓihār*** (pagan form of divorce), 33:4; 58:2-4.

Doubt (Hesitation; Suspicion), 4:88; 10:71; 11:109; 50:24-25. *do not doubt truth; nor Revelation, 2:2, 147; 3:60, 114; 7:2; 10:37, 94; 11:17; 18:21; 22:5; 32:23; 40:59; 43:61; 49:15; 74:31. *the Day about which there is no doubt: see Day of Resurrection: certainty of its coming. *when drawing up a contract, or a will, 2:282; 5:106. *concerning the waiting-period [*ʿiddah*], 33:49; 65:4. *of those who deny the truth; of hypocrites, 2:23; 4:143, 157; 6:2-3; 9:45; 10:104; 11:62, 110; 14:9-10; 15:63-64; 22:55; 24:50; 27:66; 29:48; 34:21, 54; 38:8; 40:34-35; 41:45, 54; 42:14; 44:9, 50; 45:32; 50:15; 53:55; 54:36; 57:14. (See Certainty; Conjectures.)

Dowry, 2:229; 4:4, 19-21, 24-25; 5:5; 33:50; 60:10. *when marriage not consummated, 2:236-237. *its return, in case of divorce, 2:229; 4:20-21; 60:10-11. (See Divorce; Marriage.)

Dreams (Visions), 21:5; App. IV. *in the story of Joseph, 12:4-6, 36-37, 41, 43-49, 100. *of Abraham, 37:102, 104-106. *of the Prophet, 8:43; 17:60; 48:27. (See Night Journey)

Dress (Clothes; Garments), 7:26; 11:5; 24:58; 16:81; 71:7; 73:1; 74:1. *garments of God-consciousness, 7:26-27; 21:80. *in women, 24:31, 60; 33:59. *of Jesus' disciples, 3:52; 5:111-112; 61:14. *protective clothing, 16:81; 21:80. *clothing the needy as atonement, 5:89. *with metaphoric meaning, 2:187; 14:50; 22:19; 25:47; 74:1, 4. (See Paradise: garments and jewels.)

Earth, 2:251; 3:196; 6:6; 7:168; 8:73; 10:24; 11:44; 13:3-4, 41; 16:61; 17:37, 95; 18:7-8; 19:40; 21:44; 22:63-65; 23:71, 79; 24:35; 26:7; 30:25; 35:38, 41; 36:36; 40:4; 43:60; 50:7-8; 55:10-12, 33; 88:20. *God's sovereignty over the heavens and the, 2:107, 116-117, 255, 284; 3:83, 109, 189; 4:131-132; 5:17; 6:12; 7:128; 20:6; 39:63; 42:12; 43:84-85; 48:4, 7; 57:4-5; 64:1. *creation of the, 10:3; 11:7; 15:85;

16:3; 18:51; 21:30; 25:59; 29:44; 30:8; 32:4; 39:5; 40:57; 41:9-11; 46:33; 50:38; 57:4; 65:12. ***created with purpose**, 3:191; 21:16; 38:27; 44:38-39; 46:3. ***extols** God's infinite glory, 17:44; 57:1; 59:1. ***has been** well ordered, 7:56, 85; 51:48. ***refused** the trust, together with the heavens and the mountains, 33:72. ***in it there are** clear messages, 2:164; 3:190-191; 10:6; 12:105; 13:4; 16:65; 26:7-8; 34:9; 42:29; 45:3-6; 50:7-8; 51:20; 86:12. ***prepared** for man, 2:22, 30, 36; 6:165; 7:10, 24-25; 15:19-20; 16:13-16; 20:53-55; 21:31; 22:65; 23:18-20; 27:61; 31:10, 20; 43:10; 45:13; 50:7-11; 67:15; 71:19-20; 77:25-27; 78:6-16; 79:30-33; 80:24-32. ***man**, created and grown out of, 20:55; 22:5; 71:17-18; see Man: his creation. ***has been made** spacious for man, 9:25, 118; 29:56; 50:7; 51:48; 71:19-20; 79:30; 91:6. ***is vast**, to flee from oppression, 4:97, 100; 29:56; 39:10; 51:48-50. ***the righteous** shall inherit the, 21:105; 24:55. ***how God** brings dead land back to life, 22:5; 25:48-49; see Rain. ***on the Last Hour** and on Day of Resurrection, 7:187; 14:48; 18:47; 27:82; 39:67-69; 56:4-6; 69:14; 73:14; 84:3-5; 89:21; 99:1-5. (See Creation; Injustice: spreading corruption on earth; Travel on the earth.)

Ease: see Hardship.

Egypt, 2:61; 12:21, 56, 99; 43:51.

Elephant (**Army of the**), 105:1-5.

Elijah, 6:85; 37:123-132.

Elisha, 6:86; 38:48.

Enemies, 2:36; 7:24; 20:123; 28:8; 43:67. ***of God**, 2:98; 8:60; 9:114; 20:39; 41:19, 28; 60:1. ***set up** by God against every prophet, 6:112; 20:39; 22:52; 25:31. ***of the believers**, 2:217; 3:118-120; 4:101; 5:82; 20:80; 60:1-2, 4-5, 9; 63:4. ***turned** into brothers, 3:103; 15:47; 41:34; 60:7. ***some of your spouses** and children are your, 64:14-15. ***God**, enemy of all who deny the truth, 2:98; see Denying the truth: the worst of all creatures before God. ***Satan**, an open foe to man, 7:22; 17:53; see Satan.

Enjoyment in this world (Blessings; Pleasure), 4:4, 24; 10:22; 18:28; 22:11; 28:77; 33:51; 39:45; 56:45-46; 66:1; 74:43-45. ***as blessings** bestowed, or promised, to the believers, 1:7; 8:69; 10:98; 11:3, 52; 37:148; 71:10-12; 72:16. ***the fleeting E.** of this life, 2:36; 3:14, 185; 6:128; 7:24; 9:24; 13:26; 17:18; 20:131; 24:33; 28:60; 29:64; 33:16, 28; 42:36; 43:29, 33-35; 44:25-27; 47:36; 57:20; 80:24-32; 89:15-16; 102:8. ***is but brief**, 4:77; 9:38; 10:69-70; 16:55, 117; 26:205-207; 30:34; 31:24; 40:39. ***God allows evil-doers** to enjoy life for a while, 2:126; 3:196-197; 6:6, 44; 9:69; 10:23; 11:48, 65; 14:30; 15:3; 21:44; 25:18; 28:61; 29:66; 39:8; 46:20; 47:12; 51:43; 73:11; 77:46; see Denying the truth: God gives them free rein for a while. ***indulgence in pleasures** corrupts human beings, 11:116; 17:16; 21:13; 23:33, 64; 34:34; 43:23; 56:45-46; 74:43-45. (See Life: The life of this world; Paradise; Prohibitions: do not forbid what God has made lawful; Victory.)

Enmity, 5:2, 8, 91; 41:34; 49:10. ***between** man and Satan, 2:36; 7:16-17, 20-22, 27; 20:117; 35:6. ***between** followers of the Bible, 2:85; 5:14, 64. ***of the Jews** towards the Muslims, 5:82.

Environment (**Destruction of the**), 6:47; 13:31; 30:30, 41; see Earth: has been well ordered; Injustice: spreading corruption on earth.

Envy (Mutual jealousy), 7:42-43; 12:5; 15:47; 16:90; 59:10; 113:5. ***of the followers** of earlier revelation, 2:90, 109; 4:54. ***discrepancies** caused by mutual jealousy, 2:213; 3:19; 42:14; 45:17; see Discrepancies.

Evil, 2:81, 169, 181, 216, 286; 3:30, 120, 180; 4:17-18, 25, 110, 123, 149; 5:2; 6:54, 70; 7:188; 9:102, 122; 11:54, 113-114; 12:24, 51; 13:6, 10-11; 14:26; 16:28, 59-61, 119; 17:22-39; 21:35; 22:30; 25:70; 27:11, 46-47, 62; 36:18; 39:48; 40:9, 58; 42:40; 48:6; 58:15; 63:2; 113:*passim*; 114:4-6. ***a consequence** of human action, 3:155, 165; 4:78-79; 13:31; 27:52; 30:36; 39:51; 42:30, 48. ***seems goodly** to evildoers, 6:112, 122, 129; 9:37; 27:4; 35:8; 40:37; 47:14. ***to be repelled** with good, 13:22; 23:96; 28:54; 41:34-35; 42:40. ***protection** against, 113:1-5; 114:1-6. ***turns against** its doer, 2:6-20, 57; 3:69; 4:111, 113; 6:123-124; 7:160; 10:23; 16:34, 94; 17:4-8; 30:10; 35:43; 39:51; 41:46; 45:15; 48:10; 51:59; 59:15; 64:5; 65:9. ***rewarded** with the like thereof, 6:160; 10:27; 28:84; 40:40; 53:31. ***man's inner self** incites, or is prone, to, 4:128; 12:53. ***not to be mentioned** openly, 4:148-149. ***archetypes of**, 8:21-23, 55; 9:12, 67; 16:60; 25:77; 28:4, 41-42; 35:39; 98:6; 111:1-5. ***powers of**, [*aṭ-ṭāghūt*], 2:256-257; 4:51, 60, 76; 5:60; 6:112; 16:36; 39:17; v. Satán. (See Good and Evil; Good deeds; Injustice; Misfortune.)

Examples (Models), 43:56. ***models** proposed as: **-Muḥammad**, 33:21; **-Abraham**, 60:4-6; **-Jesus**, 43:57-59; **-the wife** of Pharaoh, 66:11; **-Mary**, 66:12. ***the Muslims** as E. for mankind, 2:143; 3:110; 22:78. ***the Israelites**, by God's favour, 28:5. ***archetypes** of evil, 9:12; 16:60; 28:39-41; 43:54-56; see Evil: archetypes of.

Exemption tax [*jizyah*], 9:29.

Expressions: see Words.

Ezra [*ʿUzayr*]: so-called 'son of God', 9:30.

Faith (Belief), 2:3-4, 13, 136-137, 177, 285; 3:84-85, 193; 4:136; 8:2-4; 10:105; 11:36; 30:30-43; 42:15, 52; 47:2-3; 48:9; 49:14-17; 52:21; 57:8; 58:22; 59:9-10; 61:10-13; 64:11; 84:20, 25. ***believes only** whoever God wills, 10:99-100; 13:31; 28:56; 36:7-10; 49:7; 59:23; see Believers: had God willed it, all mankind would be; Denying the truth: loathsome evil that God lays upon evildoers; Guidance: God guides whoever He wills,...; had God so willed, He would have guided you all aright. ***messages** for people who will believe: see Messages. ***with certainty**, 49:15; see Certainty. ***no coercion** in matters of, 2:256; 10:99-100; 26:4; 32:13; 50:45. ***in misfortune**, or danger: see Misfortune: man invokes God in; Ships: the faith of people confronted with great danger. ***belated belief** of the doomed, useless, 6:158; 10:51-52, 90-91, 96-97; 32:12-14;

34:51-53; 38:3; 40:84-85; 44:10-14. ***strengthened** in danger, 3:173; 48:4. ***and good** works, 4:124, 173; 5:55, 69, 93; 6:158; 9:53-54; 16:96-97; 18:88; 24:55; 31:22; 40:40, 58; 57:7; 90:12-17; 103:3; see Good deeds. ***followed** by apostasy, 3:167, 177; 4:137; 5:54; 9:66, 74; 10:32; 16:106; 33:14-15; 47:22; see Apostasy. (See Believers.)

Falsehood: see Deception; Lying.

Fasting: in Ramadhān, 2:183-185, 187. ***as expiation**, 2:196; 4:92; 5:89, 95; 58:4. ***abstinence** from speech, 19:26. ***reward** of, 33:35.

Fear, 2:114; 3:151; 4:9; 6:65; 10:83; 13:12; 16:112; 17:100; 20:77; 28:6; 30:24, 28; 33:72; 42:22; 75:7. ***fear nothing** but God, 2:150; 3:175; 5:3, 44, 54; 9:13, 18; 16:51; 33:37, 39. ***replaced** with security, 24:55; 28:32; 48:27. ***the believers** who do righteous deeds need not fear God's judgement, 2:38, 62, 112, 262, 274, 277; 4:39; 5:69; 6:48; 7:35; 10:62; 20:112; 27:10-11; 43:68-69; 46:13; 72:13. ***of death**, 2:19, 243; 4:84; 8:65; 10:22; 47:20. ***of poverty**, 2:268; 6:151; 9:28; 17:31. ***of fighting**, 2:243; 3:175; 4:77, 84; 8:65; 29:10; 59:13. ***as the root** of hypocrisy, 9:56-57, 64; 29:10-11; see Hypocrisy. ***as excuse** to reject divine guidance, 5:52; 24:50; 28:57; 52:40; 68:46. ***Satan arouses** in you the fear of poverty; of his allies, 2:268; 3:175.

Fear of God, 7:154, 205; 11:103; 13:21; 14:14; 20:3; 21:28, 49; 22:35; 23:57-60; 24:37, 52; 35:18, 28; 36:11; 39:23; 51:37; 52:26; 55:46; 59:13, 21; 67:12; 76:10; 79:19, 26, 45; 80:8-9; 98:8. ***tested** by God, 5:94. ***God imbues fear** in His servants, 17:59-60; 39:16; 74:35-39. ***in the angels**, 13:13; 16:49-50. ***call upon God** with longing and, 7:56; 21:90; 32:16. ***rocks** which crumble from, 2:74. ***Satan declares** himself fearful of God, 8:48; 59:16. (See Consciousness, God-.)

Fighting in God's cause, 3:13, 146-147, 165-172; 4:94-96, 101-104; 8:5-26; 9:8, 81-83, 86-88, 90-96; 33:9-27; 47:4-11, 35; 48:15-25; 57:10. ***divine commands** and calls to, 2:216-218, 243-245; 3:142-143; 4:71-78, 84-85; 8:38-39; 9:5, 12-16, 24, 29, 38-52, 73, 111; 47:20-21; 66:9. ***in self-defence**, 2:190-194, 251; 4:89-91; 22:39-40; see Self-defence. ***in defence** of the oppressed, 4:75, 85. ***as striving** in God's cause, 2:218; 3:142; 4:95; 8:72, 74-75; 9:41, 81; 16:110; 25:52; 49:15; 61:10-11. ***combatants** helped by God, 3:121-127; 8:9-12; 33:9. ***twenty of them** will defeat two-hundred; a hundred will defeat a thousand, 8:65. ***a hundred of them** will defeat two-hundred; a thousand will defeat two-thousand, 8:66. ***unity** in combat, 8:15-16, 45-46, 73; 9:36; 61:4. ***reward** promised to the fighters, 3:157-158; 4:74; 9:88-89; 2451-52, 55; 29:69; 47:4-7; 48:17. ***martyrs** are alive, 2:154; 3:169-172; see Martyrs. ***fighting** among believers, 49:9-10. ***and the people** of Moses, 2:246, 249-251; 5:21-24. ***those exempt** from, 9:91-92; 48:17. ***desertion**, 3:155; 48:17. ***those who** refuse, 9:81-90, 93-96; 24:53; 33:12-20; 47:20-24; 48:16-17. (See Badr; Banu 'n-Naḍīr; Booty; Captives; Ḥunayn; Trench; Uḥud.)

Fire: God's gift, 36:80; 56:71-73. ***Moses' mystical**, 20:10; 27:7-8; 28:29. ***in the parable** of God's Light, 24:35. ***the parable of people** who kindle a, 2:17-18. ***invisible beings** [*jinn*], created from, 15:27; 55:15. ***Iblīs**, created from, 7:12; 38:76. (See Hell.)

Firmness: see Steadfastness.

Food and drink, 2:57-61, 168, 172; 5:4-5, 87-88, 96; 6:118, 141-142; 16:14, 66-69, 114; 22:28-29; 23:51; 35:12; 47:12; 77:46; 80:24-32. ***forbidden** kinds of, 2:173; 5:1, 3; 6:119, 121, 145; 16:115; 22:29; see Prohibitions. ***extreme need** suspends some prohibitions, 2:173; 5:3; 6:119, 145; 16:115. ***and the God-conscious**, 5:93. ***superstitions** related to, 6:136, 138-140, 143-144, 148, 150; 10:59-60. ***in Paradise**, 2:25; 37:40-47; 38:51; 47:15; 52:19, 22-24; 55:50-52, 54, 66-68; 56:17-21, 28-33; 69:23-24; 76:21; 77:42-43; 83:25-28; App. I; see Paradise. ***in Hell**, 37:65-66; 44:43-46; 47:15; 56:52-55; 69:36-37; see Hell. (See Alcoholic drinks; Prohibitions: do not forbid what God has made lawful.)

Forebears (Ancestors; Forefathers), 6:91; 15:24; 24:34; 26:26, 184; 35:42; 37:126; 44:8. ***the righteous** amongst your, 4:26; 6:87; 12:38; 13:23; 22:78; 40:8; 57:26-27. ***those gone astray** amongst your, 6:148; 8:52, 54; 15:10-13; 17:59; 18:55; 21:44; 23:68; 25:18; 28:36, 43-45; 34:45; 36:6; 37:16-18; 43:6-8, 29-30; 46:18. ***those who reject** truth following in their F. footsteps, 2:170; 5:104; 7:28, 70-71, 95, 172-173; 10:78; 11:62, 87, 109; 12:40; 14:10; 16:35-36; 18:4-5; 20:63; 21:52-54; 23:24; 26:72-76, 136-138; 29:25; 31:21; 34:43; 37:69-73, 167-169; 38:6-7; 43:22-24; 44:35-36; 45:25; 51:52-53; 53:23; 56:47-48; see Astray (to go). (See ᶜĀd; Communities; Denying the truth: labelling it as 'fables of ancient times'; follow in their forefathers' footsteps; Madyan; Thamūd; Travel on earth: and behold what happened to those who denied the truth.)

Forerunners in the Faith (the First; the Foremost), 6:14, 162-163; 7:143; 9:100; 11:116; 23:57-61; 24:36-38; 25:74; 26:51; 28:5; 35:32; 39:11-12; 56:10-14; See *Awliyāʾ Allāh*; Consciousness (God-); Good deeds: compete amongst yourselves in doing; Righteous (the): the truly virtuous; Righteousness: those who have attained to.

Forgetting (Oblivion), 2:237, 286; 6:41; 12:80; 18:24, 61, 73; 19:23; 20:88; 28:77. ***caused** by God, 2:106; 59:19; 87:6-7. ***God** and His messages, 2:44; 5:13-14; 6:44; 7:165; 9:67; 11:92; 20:126; 23:71, 110; 25:18; 58:19; 59:19; see Remembrance of God. ***the Day** of Judgement, 7:51; 32:14; 38:26. ***God does** not forget, 19:64; 20:52; 58:6. ***man is** prone to forgetfulness, 11:9; 18:57; 20:115; 36:78; 39:8. ***caused** by Satan, 6:68; 12:42; 18:63. (See Remembering.)

Forgiveness (God's), 2:175, 221, 268; 3:31, 136, 157; 4:43, 99; 5:9; 8:4, 70; 11:11; 13:6; 14:10; 16:110; 22:50; 24:26; 33:35, 71; 34:4; 35:7; 36:11, 27; 42:30, 34; 46:31; 47:15; 48:5, 29; 49:3; 57:20, 28; 61:12; 64:17; 65:5; 67:12; 71:4; 74:56. ***God forgives** all sins, 20:82; 39:53; 40:3;

42:25. *to whoever He wants, 2:284; 3:129; 4:48; 5:18, 40; 41:43; 48:14; see Will (God's). *to those who avoid the greater sins, 4:31; 53:32; see Sin: God effaces lesser sins if the great ones are avoided. *to those who strive in God's cause, 3:195; 4:95-96; 8:74; 16:110; 61:10-12. *to the Prophet, 9:43; 48:2. *to inspire gratitude, 2:52; see Gratitude: divine favour as stimulus to. *after repentance, 2:58, 160; 3:89; 4:64; 6:54; 16:119; 17:25; 20:82. *vie with each other for, 3:133; 57:21. *those who will not obtain, 4:48, 116, 137, 168; 9:80; 47:34; 63:6. (See Mercy; Repentance.)

Asking God's forgiveness, 2:199, 285-286; 3:16-17, 135, 147, 193; 4:64, 110; 5:74; 11:3, 52, 61, 90; 23:109, 118; 27:46; 40:55; 41:6; 42:5; 47:19; 51:18; 59:10; 66:8; 71:10; 73:20; 110:3. *Adam and Eve, 7:23. *Noah, 11:47; 71:28. *Abraham, 14:41; 26:82; 60:5. *Moses, 7:151, 155; 28:16. *David, 38:24-25. *Solomon, 38:34-35. *Jonah, 21:87. *the children of Israel, 2:58; 7:149, 161. *the sorcerers of Pharaoh, 20:73; 26:50-51. *Abraham for his father, 9:114; 14:41; 19:47-48; 26:86-87; 60:4. *Jacob for his children, 12:97-98. *Joseph for his brothers, 12:92. *the Prophet for the believers, 3:159; 4:64; 9:103; 24:62; 60:12. *the angels and the righteous for the believers, 40:7-9; 71:28. *for the believers, 59:10. *for hypocrites and unbelievers, is wrong and useless, 9:80, 113; 11:37, 46-47; 23:27; 63:5-6.

Forgiving others, 2:109; 3:134, 159; 4:149; 5:13; 15:85; 24:22; 42:40, 43. *partial, in case of homicide, 2:178. *relatives, 24:22; 64:14. *readily, after being angry, 42:37. *those who deny the truth, 2:109; 45:14. *repel evil with good, 13:22; 23:96; 28:54; 41:34-36; 42:40.

Fornication, 4:24-25; 5:5. (See Adultery; Conduct, immoral.)

Forsaking the domain of evil (Migration unto God) [*hijrah; al-muhājirūn; alladhīna hājarū*], 2:218; 3:195; 4:89, 100; 8:72, 74-75; 9:20, 100, 117; 16:41, 110; 22:58; 24:22; 29:26; 51:50. *the earth is wide enough to, 4:97; 29:56; 39:10. *Muslims not responsible for those who do not migrate, 8:72. *the migrants, beneficiaries of booty, 59:8. *in case of women who migrate, examine their faith, 60:10. *the Prophet's *hijrah*, 9:40.

Fraud: see Deception.

Freedom of choice (Free will), 2:256; 3:154, 178; 4:115; 6:137, 149; 10:99; 11:118-119; 13:31; 16:9, 35; 18:29; 28:68; 36:66-67; 43:20; 53:24-25; 75:36; 95:7. *everything prostrates to God, willingly or unwillingly, 13:15; 22:18. *and believers, 4:65; 33:36. (See Destiny; Responsibility.)

Friday (prayer of), 62:9-11.

Fruits, 14:24-25. *for your sustenance, 2:22, 126, 267; 14:32, 37; 16:67; 20:53-54; 23:19-20; 28:57; 36:33-35; 55:11-12; 80:24-32; see Plants and trees. *product of man's labour, 2:155; 18:34; 68:17-22. *assigned to false deities, 6:136. *as consequences, good or bad, 42:20; -in Paradise, 2:25; 13:35; 37:41-42; 38:51; 43:72-73; 44:55; 47:15; 52:22; 55:52, 54, 68; 56:20, 28, 32-33; 69:23-24; 76:14; 77:42-43; App. I; see Paradise; -those from righteous deeds are eternal [*al-bāqiyātu aṣ-ṣāliḥāt*], 18:46; 19:76; -in Hell, 37:62-66; 44:43-46; 56:52-53.

Gabriel (Angel), 2:97-98; 53:5-9, 13-18; 66:4; 81:23; App. IV.

Games of chance [*al-maysir*], 2:219; 5:90-91.

Garden: see Paradise.

Ghaib (*al-*): see Beyond human perception.

God [*subḥānahu wa-taʿāla*]: Limitless is He in His glory, and sublimely exalted above anything to which men may ascribe a share in His divinity, 7:190; 9:31; 10:18; 16:1, 3; 17:43; 20:114; 23:92, 116; 27:63; 28:68; 30:40; 39:67; 52:43; 59:23. *He is indefinable, for there is nothing like unto Him and nothing can be compared to Him, 6:100, 103; 13:33; 16:74; 19:65; 21:22; 23:91; 37:159, 180; 42:11; 112:4. *Only God, 2:163; 6:19; 16:22; 37:4; 112:1. *there is no deity save Him, 2:163, 255; 3:2, 6, 18, 62; 4:87; 5:73; 6:102, 106; 7:59, 65, 73, 85, 158; 9:31, 129: 10:90; 11:14, 50, 61, 84; 13:30; 16:2; 20:8, 14, 98; 21:25, 87; 23:23, 32, 91, 116; 27:26; 28:70, 88; 35:3; 37:35; 38:65; 39:6; 40:3, 62, 65; 44:8; 47:19; 52:43; 59:22-23; 64:13; 73:9. *the Lord Supreme: see Attributes of God's perfection. *proof of His uniqueness, 17:42; 21:22; 23:91; 30:28. *Creator: see Creation; Earth; Heavens; Man. *His command -'Be': see Creation: God commands, 'Be' -and it is. *omnipotence of, 2:165, 255, 284; 3:26, 189; 4:133; 5:120; 6:17-18, 61, 65; 10:65; 13:13, 31, 41; 22:6; 24:45; 31:5, 10; 46:33; 57:2; 60:7; 64:1; 65:12; 67:1; 85:9. *unto Him belongs all that is in the heavens and all that is on earth, 2:255, 284; 3:189; 4:126; 5:120; 6:12-13; 10:55; 22:64; 31:26; 34:1; 42:53; 48:7; 53:24-25; 55:24, 29. *sovereign doer of whatever He wills, 2:253; 3:40, 47; 11:107; 14:27; 22:14, 18; 46:33; 57:2; 85:14-16; see Will (God's): God does what He wills. *beginning and end of all things, 42:53; 53:42. *God's unchangeable way [*sunnat Allāh*], 6:35; 17:76-77; 33:38, 60-62; 34:36; 35:43; 40:85; 48:22-23. *all things go back to Him, 3:109; 8:44; 10:4, 56; 11:123; 22:76, 48; 28:70; 35:4, 18; 40:3; 57:5; 60:4; 96:8. *omniscience of: see Knowledge; Hour (the Last): knowledge of it rests with God alone. *He knows all that is beyond human perception, 2:33, 255; 5:109, 116; 6:59, 73; 9:78; 13:9; 23:92; 32:6; 34:3; see Beyond human perception. *encompasses everything, 3:120; 4:126; 6:80; 7:89; 32:5; 41:54; 65:12; 72:28. *Sustainer: -of all the worlds, 1:2; 2:131; 5:28; 6:45, 71, 162; 7:54, 61, 67, 104, 121-122; 10:10, 37; 26:16, 23, 47-48, 77, 98, 109, 192; 27:8, 44; 28:30; 32:2; 37:87, 182; 39:75; 40:64-65; 41:9; 43:46; 45:36; 56:80; 59:16; 69:43; 81:29; 83:6; -of the heavens and the earth, 13:16; 17:102; 18:14; 19:65; 21:56; 26:24; 37:5; 38:66; 43:82; 44:7; 45:36; 51:23; 78:37; -of the seven heavens, 23:86; -of the east and the west, 2:115; 26:28; 73:9; -of all the points of sunrise and of sunset, 37:5; 55:17; 70:40; -of rising dawn, 113:1; -of this City (Mecca), 27:91; -of this Temple (the Kaʿbah), 106:3;

-**of Sirius**, 53:49; -**enthroned** in omnipotence, 9:129; 23:86, 116; 40:15; see Throne. ***Limitless is He** in His glory [*subḥānahu*], 6:100; 10:10, 68; 19:35; 21:26; 39:4. ***all things and beings** prostrate before, 13:15; 22:18; 55:6; see Surrender to God. ***everything** in creation extols His limitless glory, 17:44; 21:79; 37:166; 57:1; 59:1, 24; 61:1; 64:1; see Birds: glorify God; Mountains: glorify God.... ***all praise is due** to Him alone, 1:2; 6:1, 45; 7:43; 10:10; 16:75; 18:1; 23:28; 27:15, 59, 93; 28:70; 29:63; 30:18; 31:25; 34:1; 35:1; 37:182; 39:75; 64:1. ***worship** only Him, 1:5; 2:21, 138, 152; 3:51; 4:36; 5:72, 117; 6:102, 162; 7:59; 10:3; 11:2, 50, 123; 13:14-15; 16:36; 17:22-23; 19:36; 21:92; 22:77; 29:16-17, 56; 39:2-3, 11, 66; 40:14; 53:62; 109:2-5; see Supplications: do not invoke other than God. ***remembrance** of: see Remembrance of God. ***God's countenance**: see Countenance (God's). ***is true** to His promise, 2:80; 3:9, 152, 171-172, 194; 4:122; 7:137; 9:111; 10:55; 11:45; 13:31; 17:108; 18:98; 19:61; 22:47; 30:6; 31:33; 39:20, 74; 40:55, 77. ***none is** as worthy of trust as, 4:81, 132, 171; 17:65; 33:3, 48. ***believers must** place their trust in: see Trust in God. ***God's goodly** acceptance: see Acceptance (God's goodly). ***is near** unto men; unto the believers, 2:186, 257; 3:68; 11:61; 34:50; 50:16; 57:4; 58:7. ***is not unaware** of what you do, 2:74, 85, 140, 144, 149; 3:99; 6:131-132; 11:123; 14:42; 27:93; 41:22-23. ***sends down** the Revelation: see Revelation. ***His words** are inexhaustible, 18:109; 31:27. ***signs** or messages of: see Messages. ***mercy of**: see Mercy. ***the most just** of all judges, 10:109; 11:45; 21:47; 95:8. ***does not wrong** His creatures in the least, 3:108, 117, 182; 4:40; 8:51; 10:44; 22:10; 26:208-209; 40:31; 41:46; 50:29. ***God describes** Himself, 2:255; 3:26-27; 6:12, 54, 95-103; 17:111; 25:2-3, 6; 32:4-7; 40:2-3; 43:84-85; 53:42-54; 57:1-6; 59:22-24; 85:12-16; 112:1-4; see Attributes of God's perfection. ***the face of**: see Countenance (God's). ***the eye of**, 11:37; 20:39; 23:27; 52:48; 54:13-14. ***the hand of**, 3:26, 73; 5:64; 38:75; 39:67; 48:10; 57:29. ***names of**: see Attributes of God's perfection. ***forbearing**, 2:225, 263; 3:155; 4:12; 22:59. ***much-forgiving**, 2:225; 3:155; 22:60; 58:2. ***most generous** in giving, 3:74; 10:60; 27:40; 57:29; 82:6. ***creates in** the first instance and then brings forth anew, 10:4, 34; 21:104; 30:11; 85:13; see Resurrection. ***determines** all things, 18:45; 54:42, 55; 65:3. ***rewards** good: see Good deeds: rewarded. ***responds** to all invocations, 2:186; 11:61; 14:34; see Supplications: God's response to. ***infinite**, 2:115; 3:73; 24:32. ***witness** unto everything, 5:117; 10:61; 13:33; 22:17; 41:53; 58:6; 85:3, 9. ***grants life** and deals death, 2:258; 3:156; 7:158; 9:116; 10:56, 104; 15:23; 22:66; 23:80; 53:44; 57:2; 80:18-22; see Death. ***brings forth** the living out of the dead, and vice versa, 3:27; 6:95; 10:31; 30:19; see Resurrection. ***causes** [you] to laugh and to weep, 53:43. ***most compassionate**, 2:143, 207; 3:30; 9:117; 16:7; 24:20. ***absolver** of sins, 22:60; 58:2. ***most kind**, 42:19. ***guides** onto a straight way, 22:54; 25:31; see Guidance. ***ever-responsive** to gratitude, 35:30, 34; 42:23; 64:17. ***tests** men: see Trials. ***has neither sons** nor daughters, nor consort, 6:100-101; 16:57; 17:111; 37:149-157; 43:16-17, 81; 112:3; see Attributing to God. (See Ascribing divinity to other than God; Attributes of God's perfection; Consciousness (God-); Countenance (God's); Creation; Day of Resurrection; Earth; Fear of; Forgiveness; Heavens; Leave (God's); Love; Man; Mercy; Messages of; Remembrance of; Revelation; Supplications; Throne; Will (God's).)

Gog and Magog, 18:94; 21:96.

Gold, 3:14, 91; 9:34; 43:35, 53. ***as ornament** in Paradise, 18:31; 22:23; 35:33; 43:71. (See Metals.)

Goliath [*Jālūt*], 2:249-251.

Good and Evil, 2:286; 3:30; 4:78-79, 85, 149; 7:146; 10:11, 26-27; 11:10, 114; 17:7, 11; 21:35; 24:11; 41:46; 45:15; 70:20-21; 90:10; 99:7-8. ***to repel** evil with good, 13:22; 23:96; 25:63; 28:54; 41:34-36. ***there is no** comparison between, 5:100; 41:34. (See; Community (the Muslim): enjoins doing what is right and forbids what is wrong; Evil; Ways: of good and ways of evil.)

Good deeds, 2:62, 83, 184, 197, 215, 224; 3:26, 57, 104; 4:114, 127; 29:69; 45:15. ***their fruits** are eternal [*al-bāqiyātu aṣ-ṣāliḥāt*], 11:86; 18:46; 19:76. ***drive away** evil deeds, 11:114. ***compete** amongst yourselves in doing, 2:148; 3:114, 133; 5:48; 21:90; 23:61. ***good is** its own reward, 2:110, 184, 272; 4:85, 170-171; 6:104; 9:41, 74; 10:26, 108; 17:7, 15; 24:55; 27:40, 89, 92; 29:6; 31:12; 35:18; 39:10, 34-35, 41; 41:46; 45:15; 47:21; 53:31; 55:60; 61:11; 62:9; 64:16; 73:20. ***rewarded**, 2:261-262, 274; 3:115; 4:32, 85, 114, 162; 5:32, 85; 6:84; 7:161, 170; 9:20-22, 120-121; 11:11, 115; 12:22, 56, 90; 16:30-32, 111; 24:55; 28:14, 54; 29:7; 33:29; 39:70; 40:40; 47:2; 48:10; see Believers: reward promised to; Striving (in God's cause): reward of. ***-with double**, 28:54; 33:31; 34:37; 57:28. ***-ten times**, 6:160. ***increased**, 4:40; 27:89; 28:84; 39:10; 42:23; 64:17. ***done to be seen** by others [*riʾāʾa an-nās*], 2:264; 4:38, 142; 107:4-6. ***done by** unbelievers, idolaters, apostates or hypocrites, rendered void by God, 2:217, 264; 3:90-91, 117; 5:5, 53; 6:88; 7:139, 147; 9:17, 54, 69; 11:15-16; 14:18; 18:103-105; 24:39-40; 25:22-23; 33:19; 39:65; 47:1, 8-9, 28, 32-33. (See Evil; Virtue: doing good.)

Gospel, 3:3-4, 65; 5:46; 9:111. ***imparted** to Jesus, 3:48; 5:110; 57:27. ***calls** to its followers, 4:171-172; 5:47, 65-66, 68-69, 77. ***Prophet** Muḥammad mentioned in, 7:157; 61:6. ***parable** of Muḥammad's followers in the, 48:29. *[**Allusions** to the Gospels in notes: 2:n.48; 3:nn.4, 28, 32, 52, 60; 4:n.171; 5:nn.14, 30, 84, 133; 7:nn.32, 125; 19:n.2; 43:n.50; 61:nn.6, 15] (See Jesus.)

Government (**Islamic**): guidelines of, 3:159; 4:59; 33:36; 42:38; 49:10; see Community (the Muslim); Muslims; Revelation: duty to judge according to.

Gratitude (Thanks-giving) [*shukr*], 25:62; 39:7; 76:2-3, 9. ***divine favour** as stimulus to, 2:52, 56; 3:123; 5:6, 89; 8:26; 14:37; 16:14, 78; 22:36; 27:19; 28:73;

30:46; 35:12; 45:12. ***calls** to, 2:152, 172, 185; 7:144; 16:114; 29:17; 31:12, 14; 34:15; 36:33-35, 71-73; 39:66; 56:68-70. ***rewarded**, 3:144-145; 6:53; 7:58; 14:7; 54:33-35. ***God is** ever responsive to, 4:147; 35:29-30, 33-34; 42:23; 64:17. ***promises** of future gratitude, 6:63; 7:189; 10:22. ***of the apostles** and the righteous, 14:5; 16:120-121; 17:3; 27:19, 40; 31:31; 34:19; 42:33; 46:15. ***ingratitude** of human beings, 2:276; 7:10, 17; 10:60; 11:9; 12:38; 14:34; 16:54-55; 17:27; 21:80; 22:38; 23:78; 25:50; 27:73; 29:65-66; 30:33-34; 31:12, 32; 32:9; 34:13; 39:3; 40:61; 43:15; 54:14; 67:23; 71:27; 76:24; 100:6-8; see Man: ingratitude of. ***ingratitude** punished, 14:7; 16:112; 17:69; 34:16-17; 35:36.

Guidance (**Divine**), 1:6-7; 2:5, 26, 38, 142-143, 159, 185, 213, 256-257; 3:101, 103; 4:26, 68, 175; 5:15-16, 108; 6:71, 77, 84-91, 149, 161; 7:30, 43, 178; 8:53; 9:18, 115; 10:9, 35, 108; 13:7, 27; 14:4, 12; 16:9, 36; 17:2, 94; 19:58, 76; 20:50; 22:24, 37, 54; 23:49; 25:31; 26:78; 27:63; 28:50, 85; 29:69; 31:5; 37:118; 39:3, 18; 40:53-54; 42:13; 47:5; 48:20; 49:7-8; 53:23, 30; 64:11; 67:22; 72:13; 87:3; 92:12. ***essence of**, 3:73; 6:125; 7:158; 22:16; 39:23, 33; 42:52-53; 45:11. ***promised** to Adam, 2:37-38; 20:122-123. ***to bring mankind** out of darkness and into the light, 2:257; 5:15-16; 6:122; 14:1, 5; 24:40; 33:43; 57:9; 65:11. ***the Kaᶜbah**, a [source of] G. unto all the worlds, 3:96. ***is the only** true guidance, 2:120; 6:71; 7:43, 178, 186; 11:34; 16:9; 17:97; 18:17; 24:40; 33:4; 39:23; 45:23. ***God guides whoever He wills**, or whoever wills to be guided, 2:142, 213, 272; 6:39; 7:155; 10:25; 16:93; 22:16; 24:35, 46; 28:56-57; 35:8; 42:52; 47:17; 62:2-4; 74:31, 56. ***had God so willed**, He would have guided you all aright, 6:35, 149; 10:99-100; 13:31; 16:9; 32:13; 81:27-29; see Faith: no coercion in matters of. ***exchanged** for error, 2:16, 175; 4:44, 115; 7:175-176. ***rejection** of, 6:140; 18:57; 41:13-14, 17; 47:25, 32; 53:23; see Denying the truth. ***those whom** God does not grace with His, 4:88; 7:146; 9:24, 80, 109; 12:52; 13:11; 27:4; 40:28; 61:5, 7; 63:6; see Denying the truth: God does not guide them. (See Astray (to lead): God lets evildoers go; Qurʾān: guidance,...; Revelation: as guidance; Supplications: asking for God's guidance.)

Hafsah (wife of the Prophet; not named), 66:4.

Hāmān, 28:6, 8, 38; 29:39; 40:23-24, 36.

Ḥanīf (whoever turns away from all that is false), 10:105; 22:31; 30:30; 98:5; see Abraham: his creed.

Happiness: the believers who do good will attain to, 2:5, 201-202; 3:104; 4:57; 7:8, 157; 9:88; 11:108; 13:29; 23:1-11, 102; 24:51-52; 30:15, 38; 31:5; 39:61; 58:22; 59:9; 64:16; 92:17-21. ***remember God**, remain conscious of Him and do good works, so that you might attain to, 2:189; 3:130, 200; 5:35, 90, 100; 7:69; 18:2-3; 20:130; 22:77; 24:31; 28:67; 62:10. ***some faces**, on that Day, will be bright with, 3:106-107; 11:105; 36:55-58; 75:22-23; 80:38-39; 88:8-16. ***in Paradise**, 9:72; 10:9-10; 15:47-48; 28:83; 39:74; 43:68-70; 52:17-18; 56:88-89; 76:19-20; 84:7-9, 22-24; 87:14; 91:9; see Paradise. ***evildoers will** never attain to, 6:135; 9:69; 10:17, 69; 16:116; 23:117; 28:37, 82.

Hardship and Ease, 2:45; 9:41-42, 49; 18:88; 34:18-19; 65:6-7; 84:7-14; 87:8; 90:4; 92:5-11; 94:5-6. ***God does** not want H. for His servants, 2:185, 187; 4:26-28; 5:6, 101-102; 19:97; 22:78; 44:58; 67:15. ***God does not burden** man with more than he is well able to bear, 2:220, 233, 286; 6:152; 7:42; 8:66; 23:62; 65:7. see Man: not burdened by God with more...; Responsibility. ***extreme need** suspends some prohibitions: see Food and Drink. ***the steep** uphill road (*al-ᶜaqabah*), 90:11-17. ***ease** in the Qurʾān: see Qurʾān. (See Misfortune.)

Hārūt and Mārūt, 2:102.

Hatred, 2:85; 5:91; 26:55-56; 59:9. ***do not let H.** of people lead you to injustice, 5:2, 8. ***among the** followers of the Bible, 5:14, 64. ***of those who** deny the truth towards the believers, 3:118; 60:4; 68:51. (See Enemies; Enmity.)

Haughtiness: see Arrogance.

Hearts, 2:118; 3:17; 7:42-43; 8:24; 9:117-118; 26:193-195; 33:53; 34:23; 50:37; 53:11. ***God alone** can unite the, 3:103; 8:63. ***the Qurʾān**, a cure for, 10:57; 25:32; see Qurʾān: guidance, mercy and cure. ***find their rest** in the remembrance of God, 13:28; 39:23. ***strengthened** by God, 18:14; 28:10; 47:2, 5; 48:4. ***God knows** what is in the, 3:15, 29; 5:7; 29:10; 42:24; 57:6; 64:4; 67:13. ***that tremble** of fear, 22:35; 23:60; 79:8. ***surrendered** to God, 22:54. ***in which God** has inscribed faith, 58:22. ***hardened**, of the children of Israel, 2:74; 5:13. ***sealed** by God, 2:7; 4:155; 6:46; 7:100-101; 9:87, 93, 127; 10:74; 16:108; 30:59; 40:35; 42:24; 45:23; 47:16. ***in which there is** disease, 2:10; 5:52; 8:49; 9:125; 16:22; 22:53; 24:50; 33:12, 32, 60; 47:20, 29; 74:31. ***which God** is not willing to cleanse, 2:174; 3:77; 5:41. ***veiled**, 6:25, 110; 17:46; 18:57; 83:14. ***veiled** to the Revelation, 26:200; 41:5; 63:3. ***hardened**, 6:43; 22:53; 39:22; 57:16. ***it is not the eyes** that become blind, but the, 22:46.

Heaven (**the nearest**): its creation, 21:30, 32-33. ***adorned** by God, 37:6; 41:12; 50:6; 67:5. ***protected** against satanic forces, 15:16-18; 37:7-10.

Heavens (**the seven**): their creation, 2:29; 7:54; 10:3; 11:7; 21:30; 23:17; 25:59; 32:4; 41:11-12; 51:47; 65:12; 67:3. ***their creation**, greater than that of man, 37:11; 40:57; 79:27. ***not created** without purpose, 3:191; 21:16; 44:38. ***raised** without visible supports, 13:2; 30:25; 31:10; 35:41. ***their perfect** harmony, 67:3-4; 71:15; 86:11. ***in their** creation there are clear messages, 2:164; 3:190; 29:44; see Messages: in the heavens. ***their creation** and maintenance do not tire Him, 2:255; 46:33; 50:38. ***God alone** knows all that is in the, 2:33; 5:97; 11:123; 16:77; 18:26; 27:74-75; 29:52; 31:16; 34:3. ***adorned** by God, 15:16; 25:61; 71:16. ***will be rolled up** in His right hand, 21:104; 39:67. ***their destruction** in the Last Day, 25:25; 52:9; 69:16; 73:18; 77:9. ***are well-nigh rent** asunder for awe of Him, 19:88-92; 42:5. ***impossible** to pass beyond their regions without God's leave, 55:33. ***protected** against satanic forces, 15:17-18. (See Creation: of the heavens and the earth in accordance with truth.)

Hell (Fire) [*jahannam*], 2:206; 3:12, 162, 197; 4:93, 97, 115, 121, 140, 169; 7:18, 41, 179; 8:16, 36-37; 9:49, 63, 68, 73, 81, 95, 109; 11:119; 13:18; 14:28-29; 15:43-44; 16:29; 17:8, 18, 39; 18:100-106; 19:68-72, 86; 21:98-102; 25:34, 65-66; 26:94-95; 28:41; 29:54-55; 32:13-14; 35:36; 38:85; 39:32, 60, 71-72; 40:60, 76; 43:74-77; 45:10; 50:24-30; 54:48; 55:43-44; 58:8; 67:5-11; 74:26-31; 78:21-22; 89:23; 98:6. ***warnings** of, 3:131; 4:14; 17:60, 63; 20:74; 21:29; 22:72; 29:68; 32:13; 35:36; 36:63-64; 38:27, 55-58; 39:16; 48:6; 66:6, 9; 72:23-25; 74:35-37; 85:10. ***mutual wrangling** of the doomed, 7:38-39; 26:96-102; 35:37; 38:59-64; 40:47-50; 41:29; 50:27-29; 67:9-11. ***guardians of**, 39:71; 40:49-50; 43:77; 66:6; 67:8; 74:30-31. ***fuel of**, 2:24; 3:10; 21:98; 40:72; 66:6; 72:15. ***talk** and arguments of its inmates, 7:44, 50; 23:103-108; 33:66-68; 35:37; 40:73-76; 74:43-47; 89:24. ***torments in**, 4:10, 56; 9:35; 14:15-17; 17:97; 18:29; 21:100; 22:19-22; 23:103-104; 35:36; 37:62-67; 38:57-58; 47:15; 69:30-37; 70:15-16; 73:12-13; 74:26-29; 76:4; 78:21-30; 87:12-13; 88:3-7; see Death: as extinction beseeched by the doomed.

Other names of: -'**fire**' [*nār*], 2:24, 39, 80-81, 126, 167, 175, 201, 221, 275; 3:16, 24, 185, 191-192; 4:14, 145; 5:37, 72; 6:27; 7:38; 8:14; 11:16, 98, 106; 13:5, 35; 18:29; 24:57; 27:90; 32:20; 34:42; 38:27; 39:8; 40:6, 41, 46, 72; 41:24, 28; 45:34-35; 47:12, 15; 57:15; 66:6; 72:23; 85:10; 87:12-13; 90:20; 101:11; 111:3; -'**blazing fire**' [*jaḥīm*], 2:119; 5:10, 86; 9:113; 22:51; 26:91; 37:22-23, 55, 64, 68, 163; 40:7; 44:47, 56; 52:18; 56:93-94; 57:19; 73:12; 79:36, 39; 81:12; 82:14-16; 83:16-17; 88:4; 102:6; -'**blazing flame**' [*saʿīr*], 4:10; 17:97; 22:4; 25:11-14; 31:21; 35:6; 48:13; 67:5, 10-11; 76:4; -'**hell-fire**' [*saqar*], 74:26-29, 42-43; -'**raging flame**' [*laẓā*], 70:15-16; 92:14-16; -'**crushing torment**' [*ḥuṭamah*], 104:4-9. (See Food and drink: in Hell; Life: The life to come: punishment in; Punishment; Tree: of deadly fruit.)

Hidden: see Manifest and Hidden.

Hijrah: see Forsaking the domain of evil.

Holy Land (Palestine), 5:21-26; 7:137; 17:1; 21:71, 81; 34:18.

Homicide, 2:84-85, 178; 4:29; 5:27-32; 6:151; 17:33; 18:74; 25:68. ***of children**, 6:140, 151; 17:31; 60:12; see Children. ***indemnity** for, 2:178; 4:92-93. ***punishment** for: see Punishment; Retribution (Just). ***committed** by Moses, 20:40; 28:15-19, 33; see Moses: kills a man. (See Blood: -shedding; Man: his life is sacred; Murder.)

Homosexuality: condemned, 7:80-81; 11:77-79; 15:67-72; 21:74; 26:165-168; 27:54-55; 29:28-29.

Honey: health for man in, 16:69. ***in Paradise**, 47:15.

Horses, 3:14; 8:60; 16:8; 17:64; 59:6. ***Solomon** and his, 38:31-33.

Hour (**the Last**), 6:40-41; 19:75; 21:49; 25:11; 27:82; 30:12-16, 55; 40:46; 42:17-18; 44:10-11; 45:27; 53:57-58; 54:1-3, 46; 69:13-14; 79:13-14; 81:1-14; 82:1-5; 84:1-6; 101:1-5. ***knowledge** of it rests with God alone, 7:187; 31:34; 33:63; 41:47; 43:85; 79:42-44. ***comes** suddenly, 6:31; 12:107; 16:77; 21:40; 22:55; 43:66; 47:18; 101:1-3. ***certainty of**, 15:85; 18:21; 20:15-16; 22:7; 34:3; 40:59; 43:61. ***terror** of the, 22:1-2; 34:23. ***denied**, 18:36; 34:3; 41:50; 45:32; 54:2-3. ***the unbelievers** demand its speedy advent, 42:18; see Punishment: unbelievers ask for it to be hastened on. (See Day of Resurrection.)

House of worship, 2:114, 187; 22:40. ***the Inviolable**: see Kaʿbah. ***the Remote** (Solomon's Temple), 17:1, 5, 7; 34:13. ***built by the** hypocrites, 9:107-110. (See Temple.)

Hūd, 7:65-72; see ʿĀd.

Ḥudaybiyyah, 48:18-25. ***Truce** of, 48:1-3.

Human nature, 3:59; 11:24; 45:4; 50:17-18. ***innate** and established by God, 2:27; 13:25; 20:50; 25:2; 77:23; 80:18-20; 82:6-8; 87:1-3. ***its weakness**, 7:199; 20:115; 21:37; see Man: has been created weak; ... ***God can** change, 36:66-67; 56:60-61. (See Man: his natural disposition; Mankind.)

Humbleness: see Virtue: humbleness.

Ḥunayn (Battle of), 9:25-26.

Hunting: forbidden in the sanctuary of Mecca, 2:125. ***forbidden** while on pilgrimage, 5:1-2, 94-96; see Atonement: for hunting during pilgrimage. ***animals** trained for, 5:4.

Hypocrites, 2:8-20; 4:60-68, 88-91; 8:49; 9:61-70, 73-87, 101, 107-110; 33:1, 4, 24, 48; 59:11-12; 63:1-8. ***linked** to unbelievers, 4:140; 9:68, 73; 33:1, 48, 73; 48:6; 57:15; 59:11, 17; 66:9. ***description** of, 2:8-13, 17-20; 4:72-73, 81-83, 105, 137-139; 5:51-53; 9:62-67, 74-79, 93-98; 29:10-11; 47:20-24; 59:11-14; 63:1-5. ***their appearance** and discourse are deceiving, 2:204-206; 63:4. ***use** their oaths as cover, 58:16; 63:2. ***always** wavering, 4:137, 143; 9:45; 57:14. ***should be** admonished, 4:63. ***to strive** hard against, 4:89; 9:73; 66:9. ***God** does not forgive them, 4:137-138; 9:80; 48:6; 63:6. ***punishment** of, 4:137-146; 9:101; 33:60-62, 73; 48:6; 57:13-15; 58:14-20. ***at** Uḥud, 3:167-168. ***at the battle** of the Trench, 33:12-20. ***and the expedition** to Khaybar, 48:15. ***and the expedition** to Tabūk, 9:38-59. (See Good deeds: done to be seen by others; done by unbelievers; House of worship.)

Iblīs (name of Satan), 7:11-18; 15:30-44; 26:94-95; 38:73-85. ***his arrogance** and rebellion, 2:34; 7:11-12; 17:61; 18:50; 20:116; 38:73-76. ***his mission**, 15:39-41; 17:62-65; 34:20-21; 38:82-83. ***created** from fire, 7:12; 38:76. (See Invisibles beings: created from fire; Satan.)

Idolatry: see Ascribing divinity to other than God; Deities (False].

Idrīs, 19:56-57; 21:85-86.

ʿImrān (**the House of**), 3:33-36; 66:12.

Ingratitude: see Gratitude: ingratitude of human beings.

Inheritance, 4:7-13, 19, 33, 176. ***wills**, 2:180-182. ***witnesses**, 5:106-108. ***bequests**, 2:180, 240; 4:11-12.

Injustice (Corruption; Wrongdoing), 2:182; 21:64; 53:21-22. ***God wills no wrong** for His creation, 3:108; 40:31; 45:22. ***do not wrong** one another, 2:188, 278-279; 4:29-30, 85; 11:85; 18:87; 26:183; 28:59, 83; 29:36; 38:22-24; 93:9. ***those who** suffer, 4:148; 17:33; 22:39-40, 60; 26:227; 42:39-41. ***God does not wrong** anyone in the least, 2:272; 3:182; 4:49, 77; 8:50-51, 60; 10:47; 19:60; 23:62; 24:50; 26:208-209; 41:46; 46:19; 72:13; see Day of Resurrection: none shall be wronged. ***God does not** wrong evildoers, it is they who wrong themselves, 3:117; 9:70; 10:44; 11:100-101; 16:33, 118; 24:50; 29:40; 30:9-10; 43:76. ***wrongdoers sin** against themselves, 2:270; 3:117, 135; 4:64, 110-111; 5:39; 7:23; 14:45; 16:113; 27:44; 29:14, 49; 35:32; 37:113; 39:53. ***those who act wrongfully**, offending against all right [*bi-ghairi 'l-ḥaqq*], 2:61; 3:21, 112, 181; 4:155, 161; 5:62; 9:34; 10:23; 40:74-75; 41:15; 42:41-42; 46:20; 83:12. ***duty** to fight against, 2:251; 4:85; 8:73; 11:116-117; 42:41; 49:9. ***spreading corruption** on earth, 2:11-13, 26-27, 30, 60, 205-206, 220; 3:63; 5:32-33, 64; 7:55-56, 74, 85-86, 103, 142; 10:40, 81-82, 91; 12:73; 13:25; 16:88; 17:4-8; 18:94; 26:150-152; 27:14; 28:77; 29:30; 38:28; 40:26; 47:22; 89:6-12; see Bounds; Environment; Evil: archetypes of; Pharaoh: his great cruelty. (See Justice; Light: and darkness; Oppression; Orphans: strict fairness towards the wealth of.)

Ink, 18:109; 31:27; see Pen.

Insects: bees, 16:68-69. ***spider**, 29:41. ***woodworm**, 34:14. ***ants**, 27:18-19. ***locusts**, 7:133; 54:7. ***fly**, 22:73. ***gnat**, 2:26. ***lice**, 7:133. ***moths**, 101:4.

Insight: see Discernment.

Insolence: see Arrogance.

Inspiration: holy, 11:37; 16:102; 23:27; 70:4; 97:4. ***Jesus** strengthened with holy inspiration, 2:87, 253; 5:110. ***divine**, 16:2; 17:85; 70:4; 97:4. ***the believers** strengthened with divine I., 16:102; 58:22. ***as life-giving** message, 42:52. ***conveying** a divine command, 7:117, 160; 16:68, 123; 20:77; 23:27; 26:63; 28:7; 38:42, 44. (See Revelation; Spirit.)

Intercession: in the Day of Resurrection, 2:48, 123, 254; 4:109; 6:51, 70; 7:53; 17:86; 26:100; 32:4; 40:18; 43:86; 74:48. ***only** with God's leave, 2:255; 10:3; 11:105; 19:87; 20:109; 21:28; 34:23; 39:44; 53:26; 78:37-38; see Leave (God's). ***of Abraham**, 11:74-76. ***of Moses**, 7:155. ***of Jesus**, 5:117-118. ***imaginary** intercessors, 6:94; 10:18; 30:13; 36:23; 39:43; 43:86. (See Day of Resurrection: intercession.)

Invisible beings, or forces [*jinn*], 17:88; 18:50; 51:56; 114:6; App. III. ***created** from fire, 15:27; 55:15. ***a group of them** listen to the Qur'ān and believe, 46:29-32; 72:1-15. ***to whom divinity** is ascribed beside God, 6:100; 34:41; 37:158; see Ascribing divinity to other than God. ***closely associated** with human beings in evil pursuits, 6:128-130; 55:33. ***subjected** to Solomon, 21:82; 27:17, 39; 34:12-14. ***the sinful among** them, and their punishment, 6:112; 7:38, 179; 11:119; 32:13; 41:25, 29; 46:18.

Iram (capital of the people of ʿĀd), 89:6-8; see ʿĀd.

Iron, 17:50; 18:96; 22:21; 57:25; see Metals.

Isaac [*ʾIsḥāq*], 2:133-140; 3:84; 4:163; 6:84; 11:71; 12:6, 38; 14:39; 19:49-50; 21:72-73; 29:27; 37:112-113; 38:45.

Ishmael [*ʾIsmāʿīl*], 2:133, 136, 140; 3:84; 4:163; 6:86; 19:54-55; 21:85-86; 38:48. ***and Abraham**, 2:125-129; 14:37, 39; 37:100-108.

Islam (Al-): see Surrender to God.

Israel (Jacob), 3:93; 19:58; see Israel (children of); Jacob.

Israel (**Children of**) (Jews; Judaism), 2:40-103, 132-134, 211; 4:153-162; 5:12-13, 15-16, 20-26, 32, 41-45, 70-82, 110; 27:76; 33:26-27; 44:30-33; 59:2-4, 11-14; 61:14. ***God's favour to**, 2:40, 47, 49-54, 56-58, 60, 63-64, 72-73, 122; 4:54; 5:12, 20-21, 70; 7:137-138, 141, 160-161; 10:90, 93; 20:80; 26:59; 28:5-6; 37:115-118; 45:16-17. ***admonitions** addressed to, 2:40-46, 48, 83-85, 122-124; 7:171; 17:4-8; 20:81. ***God's covenant** with, 2:40-43, 63, 83-84, 93; 3:76-77, 81-82, 112, 187-188; 4:154-155; 5:12-13, 70; 7:169; 20:80-81. ***His promise to**, 7:128-129, 137; 17:104. ***have received** Revelation, 2:136, 211; 3:23, 48-51, 84, 199; 4:163-164; 5:44-47; 17:2, 4; 32:23; 40:53-54; 45:16; 62:5; see Jesus: sent to the children of Israel; Moses: receives the divine writ; the tablets of the Law. ***God appointed** leaders for them, 2:246-251; 21:72-73; 32:24. ***many of their learned men** have recognised the Qur'ān as true, 26:197. ***the true believers** among them, 2:62, 121; 3:110, 113-115, 199; 4:55, 162; 5:66; 7:159, 164, 168; 57:26. ***rebelliousness**, perversity and arrogance of, 2:55, 59, 61, 63-66, 74, 80, 87-93, 97-103, 246-247; 3:23-24, 52, 181-184; 4:49-54, 153-161; 5:24-26, 32, 41-43, 58-66, 70-71, 78-81; 7:129, 138, 162-166, 169; 17:4-8; 33:69; 57:26; 61:6; 62:5. ***killed** some of their prophets, 2:61, 87, 91; 3:112, 181, 183; 4:155. ***story of the cow**, 2:67-73. ***have altered** and concealed the revealed texts, 2:41-42, 75-76, 79, 140, 146-147, 159-160, 174, 211; 3:71, 78, 187-188; 4:46, 50; 5:13, 41, 44; 6:91; 15:90. ***claim that only them** will enter Paradise; are on the right path, 2:94, 111, 135; 62:6-7; see Jews and Christians. ***dietary restrictions** imposed on, 3:50, 93-94; 4:160; 6:146; 16:118; see Prohibitions. ***the most eager** to cling to this life, 2:96; 62:8. ***envious of**, and hostile to the Muslims, 2:90, 109; 4:54; 5:82. ***their punishment**, 2:61, 86, 90; 4:160-161; 5:13, 26; 7:167-168; 17:4-8. (See Banu 'n-Naḍīr; Banu Quraiẓa; Calf (the golden); Israel; Jesus; Jews and Christians; Moses; Prophethood; Revelation; Sabbath; Torah.)

Iʿyāz: see Qur'ān: its inimitability as proof of its divine origin.

Jacob (Israel) [*Yaʿqūb*], 2:132-133, 136, 140; 3:84; 4:163; 6:84; 11:71; 12:*passim*; 19:6, 49; 21:72-73; 29:27; 38:45-47. (See Israel.)

Jealousy (**Mutual**): see Envy.

Jesus [*ᶜĪsā*], 2:136; 3:49-62, 84; 4:159, 163, 171-172; 5:17, 46, 72-78, 110-118; 6:85; 19:16-37; 33:7; 42:13; 43:57-59, 63-64; 57:27. ***annunciation** and birth of, 3:45-49; 19:16-26. ***his nature**, 3:59; 19:34. ***only** an apostle of God, 4:171; 5:75; 43:59, 63-64; 61:6. ***sent** to the children of Israel, 2:87; 3:49-51; 43:59; 61:6. ***he is neither God** nor the son of God, 4:171; 5:17, 72; 9:30; 16:35; 19:34-36. ***message** and miracles of, 3:49-51; 5:110, 114, 116-117; 19:30-33, 36; 25:2. ***strengthened** with holy inspiration, 2:87, 253; 4:163; 5:110. ***Gospel** of, 5:46, 110; 57:27; see Gospel. ***announces** the advent of Prophet Muḥammad, 61:6. ***disciples** of, 3:52-53; 5:111-115; 61:14. ***as a symbol** and an example, 19:21; 21:91; 23:50; 43:57-59. ***was not crucified**, 4:157-158; 5:110. (See Christ; Christians; Mary.)

Jews: see Israel (children of); Jews and Christians.

Jews and Christians (followers of earlier revelations) [*ᵓahl al-kitāb*], 2:105-106, 146, 253; 3:19-20, 64-89, 98-99, 110-115; 4:44-55, 123-125, 159; 5:12-19, 48-51, 57-66, 68-86; 6:114; 9:29-35; 16:43; 21:7; 22:17; 29:46-47; 42:14; 98:1-6. ***some of them** believe and follow a right course, 2:62; 3:110, 113-115, 199; 4:55, 162; 5:66; 22:40; 29:47. ***some** have believed in Muḥammad, 26:197; 28:52-55; 29:47. ***Abraham and his descendants** were neither 'Jews' nor 'Christians', 2:140; 3:67. ***claim to be God's children** and His beloved ones, 3:187-188; 5:18; 57:29. ***attribute sons** to God: see Attributing to God: sons and daughters. ***accuse each other** of groundless beliefs, 2:113. ***claim that only they** will enter Paradise; are on the right path, 2:111, 135. ***do not take them** as allies, 5:51, 57. ***they are allies** of one another, 5:51. ***they would love** to lead the Muslims astray, 2:109, 120; 3:69, 99-100; 4:44; 5:49. (See Abraham; Ascribing divinity to other than God; Christians; Denying the truth: among Jews and Christians; Israel (children of).)

Jihād: see Fighting; Self-defence; Striving.

Jinn: see Invisible beings.

Jizyah: see Exemption tax.

Job [*ᵓAyyūb*], 4:163; 6:84. ***affliction** and patience of, 21:83-84; 38:41-44.

John (the Baptist) [*Yaḥyā*], 3:39; 6:85; 19:2-15; 21:89-90; see Sabians.

Jonah [*Yūnus*], 4:163; 6:86. ***his people**, 10:98; 37:147-148. ***flight** and repentance of, 21:87-88; 37:139-148; 68:48-50.

Joseph [*Yūsuf*], 6:84; 12:*passim*; 40:34.

Judgement: see Day of Resurrection.

Judgement (**Sound**): given to prophets, 3:79; 6:89; 21:74, 79. ***given** to the God-conscious, 8:29. ***the standard** to discern true from false [*al-furqān*], 2:53, 185; 3:4; 21:48; 25:1; 42:17; 57:25; 86:13-14. (v. Balance; Discernment.)

Jūdī (**Mount**), 11:44.

Justice, 4:65. ***duty to judge** in accordance with what God has revealed, 4:105; 5:44-50, 68; 57:25; see Revelation: duty to judge according to. ***be just**, 4:58, 135; 5:8, 42; 7:29; 16:90; 49:9; 57:25; 60:8. ***divine**, 4:141; 6:57, 132; 7:87; 9:106; 10:47, 54; 13:41; 14:51; 17:71; 21:112; 22:56; 27:78; 39:69-70, 75; 40:20, 48, 78; 60:10; see Injustice. ***fairness** to women and orphans, 4:3, 127-129; see Orphans. ***in all dealings**, 2:188; 6:152; 11:84-85; 17:35. ***God**, the most just of all judges, 7:87; 10:109; 11:45; 12:80; 21:47; 95:8; see Day of Resurrection: none shall be wronged. ***capital** punishment in the pursuit of: see Punishment. (See Commerce; Day of Resurrection; Injustice; Relatives; Retribution (Just); Virtue.)

Kaᶜbah (**al-**): the Inviolable House of Worship [*al-Masjid al-Ḥarām*]; the Temple [*al-Bait*]; the Most Ancient Temple [*al-Bait al-ᶜAtīq*]; the Inviolable Temple [*al-Bait al-Ḥarām*], 2:125, 127, 144, 149-150, 158, 191, 196, 217; 3:96-97; 5:2, 95, 97; 8:34-35; 9:7, 19, 28; 14:37; 17:1; 22:25-29, 33; 48:25, 27; 106:3. ***as a sanctuary** secure, 28:57; 29:67.

Khaḍir (**al-**) (not named), 18:60-82.

Khaybar (alluded to), 48:15, 18-19.

Knowledge: exclusive of God, of five things, 13:8; 31:34; 41:47. ***God's omniscience**, 2:29, 231, 255; 3:5, 29; 4:108; 5:97; 6:59; 10:18, 61; 12:76; 13:33; 14:38; 20:98; 21:28, 47, 81; 31:16; 34:2-3; 54:53; 57:4; 67:13-14; 72:26-27; see Attributes of God's perfection: the All-Knowing; the Truly Wise. ***God knows**, whereas you do not know, 2:140, 216, 232; 3:66; 16:74. ***of the Last Hour**, 7:187; 33:63; 43:85; 79:44. ***those endowed** with K. bear witness to the truth, 3:7, 18; 16:27; 17:107; 22:54; 29:49; 30:56; 34:6; 35:28. ***linked** to fear of Him, 35:28. ***imparted** to the prophets, 2:31, 251; 3:48; 4:113; 5:110; 12:6, 21-22, 37, 68, 76, 86, 96, 101; 18:65-68; 19:12, 43; 21:74, 79-80; 27:15-16, 42; 28:14; 72:26-28. ***the value** of wisdom, 2:269; see Wisdom. ***the search** for, 18:60; 22:46; 29:20; see Travel on earth: and behold what happened to those who denied the truth. ***human K. is** very limited, 12:105; 16:8; 17:44, 85; 30:7; 34:9; 45:24; 53:28-30. ***they know** only whatever God wills, 2:255; 5:4; 7:26; 57:25; 96:4-5. ***supplication for** increase of, 20:114. ***of right** and wrong, 17:22-39; 90:10; see Discernment; Good and Evil; Judgement (Sound). ***occult** pursuits, 2:102; 5:90; 15:17-18; 37:8-10; 72:6-9; 113:4; see Sorcery. (See Beyond human perception; Certainty; Discernment; Reason; Wisdom.)

Koran: see Qurᵓān.

Kufr: see Denying the truth.

Language, 15:26, 28, 33; 41:20-22; 51:23. ***imparted to man** by God, 2:31-33; 55:3-4. ***its diversity**, 30:22. ***every prophet** brings a message to his people in their, 14:4; 19:97. ***animals** endowed with speech, 27:16, 18-19, 21-28. (See Arabic; Qurᵓān: revealed in Arabic; Thought; Words.)

Last Day (**the**): see Day of Resurrection: as the Last Day: belief in.

Lāt (al-) (pagan deity of Arabia), 53:19-23.

Leave (God's) (Permission) [*ʾidn Allāh; sulṭān*], 4:91; 21:44; 24:36; 40:35, 56; 55:33; 89:15; see Denying the truth: God gives them free rein... ***whatever happens** is by, 2:213; 3:145; 7:58; 10:22, 98; 14:23-25; 22:65; 24:36; 34:12; 35:32; 59:5. ***what God has** never sanctioned, 3:151; 4:108; 6:81; 7:33, 71; 12:40; 22:71; 30:35; 42:21; 43:45; 53:23. ***and the descent** of Revelation and divine inspiration, 2:97; 42:51; 97:3-4. ***as necessary** pre-requisite for faith, 2:221; 10:99-100; see Believers: had God willed it, all mankind would be; Faith: believes only whoever God wills; Guidance: God guides whoever He wills,...; had God so willed.... ***and the authority** of the Apostles, 4:64; 9:33; 14:1; 33:46. ***miracles** happen only by, 3:49; 5:110; 13:38; 14:11; 40:78; see Miracles. ***to intercede**, 2:255; 10:3; 11:105; 20:109; 34:23; 53:26; 78:38; see Intercession. ***in both victory** and defeat, 2:249, 251; 3:152, 166; 8:66; 48:24; see Fighting; Self-defence: divine sanction to fight in; Victory: divine promise of; by God's succour. ***"O our Sustainer!** Do not allow...", 10:85; 59:10; 60:5. ***what God** will not allow 4:141; 9:32; 16:84; 18:1; 30:57; 41:24; 45:35; 77:35-36. ***calamities** happen with, 2:102; 58:10; 64:11; see Misfortune: happens with God's knowledge... (See Knowledge: God's omniscience; Decree (God's); Will (God's).)

Left (**Side, or hand**), 7:17; 16:48; 18:17-18; 34:15; 50:17-18; 70:36-37. ***those who** have persevered in evil: [*aṣḥābu al-mashʾamah; aṣḥābu ash-shimāl*: lit., people of the *left side*], 56:9, 41-48; 90:19-20. ***those whose record** shall be placed in their left hand, 69:25-26; 84:10-15; see Day of Resurrection: the record of human actions. (See Right side.)

Letters (disjointed): see *Muqaṭṭaʿāt.*

Life: human, 35:37; 90:4; 102:8; see God: brings forth the living out of the dead,...; creates in the first instance...; grants life.... ***human life** is sacred: see Man: his life is sacred. ***this life / the life to come**, 2:28, 94, 200-201, 217, 219-220; 3:14-15, 22, 45, 56, 145, 148, 152; 4:77, 134; 5:33, 41; 6:32; 7:156, 169; 8:67; 9:38; 11:15-16; 12:101; 13:26, 34; 14:3, 27; 16:96, 107, 117, 122; 17:18-21, 72; 22:11, 15; 23:115; 24:14, 19, 23; 28:60, 77; 29:20, 27, 64; 30:7; 39:26; 40:39, 43; 41:16, 31; 42:20, 36; 43:35; 53:24-25; 57:20; 59:3; 75:20-21; 87:16-17; 89:24; 92:13; 93:4; App. I.

The life of this world: the reality of, 3:14, 185; 4:77; 6:32; 9:38; 18:46; 26:205-207; 29:64; 40:39; 43:35; 47:36; 57:20. ***parables of**, 10:24; 18:45; 57:20. ***those who** only desire, 2:204; 3:152; 4:134; 10:7, 23; 11:15; 13:26; 14:3; 16:107; 17:18; 18:104; 28:79; 42:20; 53:29-30; 75:20-21; 76:27; 79:38; 87:16. ***those who buy it** at the price of the life to come, 2:86; 16:95-96. ***the deception of**, 6:70, 130; 7:51; 35:5; 45:35; 57:20. ***clinging to**, 2:96, 212; 9:38. ***reward in**, 2:130; 3:145, 148; 10:64; 14:27; 16:41, 97; 29:27. ***punishment in**, 2:85, 114; 5:33, 41; 9:55, 74, 85, 101; 10:98; 13:34; 28:42; 33:57; 39:25-26; 41:16; 68:17-33; see Punishment. (See Enjoyment.)

The life to come: belief in and certainty of, 2:4, 45-46; 6:92; 27:3; 31:4; 42:20; 51:5-6, 22-23. ***is the best**, 6:32; 7:169; 12:57, 109; 16:95-96; 17:21; 29:64; 87:17; 93:4. ***those who** believe in, 6:92; 42:20. ***those who give** this life in exchange for, 2:207; 4:74; see Martyrs. ***as purifying** remembrance, 23:33; 38:46. ***human knowledge** does not reach, 27:65-66; 30:7. ***reward in**, 2:130; 3:145, 148; 4:74; 7:170; 8:67; 9:88-89; 10:64; 14:27; 16:41, 96-97; 17:19; 28:83; 29:27; 43:35; see Paradise. ***punishment in**, 2:96, 102, 114; 3:77, 85-88, 176-178, 188; 5:5, 33, 41; 6:70; 9:74, 101, 128; 11:20-22, 103; 13:34; 16:109; 20:127; 24:19; 27:5; 33:57; 39:26; 41:16; 68:33; see Hell. ***those who deny**, 6:29, 113, 150; 7:44-45, 147; 11:18-19; 12:37; 16:22, 60; 17:10, 45; 23:33, 35-37, 73-74; 27:4; 30:16; 34:8; 39:45; 41:7; 53:27; 60:13; 74:53. (See Day of Resurrection.)

Light, 39:69. ***spiritual L.**, source of guidance, 4:174; 5:15-16, 44, 46; 6:91; 7:157; 21:48; 24:40; 33:46; 42:52; 64:8. ***the parable** of God's, 24:35. ***assigned** to the believers, 6:122; 39:22; 57:12-13, 19, 28; 39:22; 66:8. ***and darkness**, 2:17, 257; 5:15-16; 6:1, 122; 13:16; 14:1, 5; 24:40; 33:43; 35:20; 57:9; 65:11; 86:3-4; 91:3-4; see Night and Day. ***the unbelievers** want to extinguish God's, 9:32; 61:8. ***from** sky luminaries, 10:5; 28:71-73; 36:37; 71:16; 79:29; 81:2; 91:1-2. (See Guidance.)

Likes and Dislikes: see Desires (Worldly).

Lot [*Lūṭ*], 6:86; 7:80-84; 21:71, 74-75; 29:26; 37:133-138; 51:35-36. ***the people of**, 11:89; 22:43; 38:13; 50:13; 51:31-37. ***and the heavenly** messengers, 11:70, 77-83; 15:58-77; 29:33-34; 51:31-33. ***warns** his people, 26:160-175; 27:54-58; 29:28-35; 54:33-39. ***the wife** of, 7:83; 11:81; 15:59-60; 26:171; 27:57; 29:33; 37:135; 66:10.

Lote-tree, 34:16; 53:14-16; 56:28; see Plants and Trees.

Love [*ḥubb*], 3:119; 7:79, 189; 11:90; 12:30; 20:39; 28:56; 29:25; 30:21; 38:32; 42:23; 61:13; 85:14. ***of God**, 2:165; 3:31; 5:54; 9:24. ***doing good** for God's sake, 9:34, 79, 103-104; 76:9; see Acceptance (God's goodly); Countenance (God's). ***for the faith** and for the believers, 42:23; 49:7; 59:9-10. ***those whom** God loves, 2:195, 222; 3:31, 76, 134, 146-148, 159; 4:125; 5:13, 42, 54, 93; 9:4, 7, 108; 19:96; 49:9; 60:8; 61:4. ***for the life** of this world, 2:93, 216; 14:2-3; 75:20-21; 76:27; 89:20; 100:8; see Wealth: intense love for; Life: The life of this world. ***those whom** God loves <u>not</u>, 2:190, 205, 276; 3:32, 56-57, 140; 4:36-38, 107; 5:64, 87; 6:141; 7:31, 55; 8:58; 16:23-24; 22:38; 28:76-77; 30:45; 31:18; 42:40; 57:23.

Luqmān, 31:12-19.

Lying (Falsehood), 2:42; 3:71; 5:48; 6:57; 8:8; 10:32; 12:74; 13:17; 17:81; 21:18; 22:62; 27:27; 28:75; 29:52, 67; 31:30; 34:48-49; 40:5, 78; 42:24; 47:3; 78:35. ***inventing lies** about God, 3:75, 78, 93-94; 7:169; 11:50; 18:4-5; 39:60; 40:28; 72:5; see Attributing to God: false inventions; Apostles: branded as liars. ***those who deny** the truth and the hypocrites, described as liars, 2:9-10; 5:42; 6:28, 116, 148;

7:152; 9:42-43, 77, 107; 10:66; 11:93; 16:62; 20:61; 23:90; 26:221-226; 29:2-3, 12-13; 37:151-153; 39:3; 43:20; 58:18; 59:11; 63:1-3; 96:15-17. ***in accusations** of adultery, 24:6-9, 11-13; see Calumny. ***branding** truth as lies, 6:31; 15:90-91; 23:33; 32:20; 34:42; 37:21; 42:24; 46:11; 52:14-15; 55:43; 67:18; 69:48-49; 74:46; 77:29; 83:16-17; 92:8-10; see Astray (to go): those who call truth a lie; Denying the truth: labelling it as 'fables of ancient times'. ***idolatry** gives visible shape to a lie, 7:71; 12:40; 29:17; 37:85-86, 95; 53:23; see Deities (False). (See Bounds: of truth in religious beliefs, do not overstep; Deception: self-deception; branding truth as; Muḥammad: accused of forging his message; Truth: God crushes falsehood with the.)

Madyan (Shuᶜayb's people), 7:85-93; 9:70; 11:84-95; 15:78-79; 22:44; 26:176-191; 28:45; 29:36-37; 38:13; 50:14. ***Moses in**, 20:40; 28:22-28.

Man (children of Adam), 2:24; 3:137-138, 195; 4:79, 165; 7:26-36, 172-173; 12:53; 16:69; 17:13-15; 20:1-4; 30:20-23; 33:4, 72; 35:28; 53:24-25, 39; 64:11; 66:6; 75:2-6, 36; 76:1; 79:35; 80:17-32; 84:18-19; 90:4; 114:1-6. ***his creation**, 2:28; 3:59, 195; 4:1; 6:2; 7:12, 189; 15:26-29; 16:4; 17:61; 18:37; 19:67; 23:12, 115; 25:54; 29:20; 30:20-21; 32:7; 36:66-68; 38:71-72, 75-76; 39:6; 40:57, 67-68; 50:16; 53:32; 55:3-4, 14; 56:57-58, 62; 74:11; 78:8; 79:27; 82:6-8; 91:7-8; 92:3. ***God breaths** into him of His spirit, 15:29; 32:9; 38:72. ***evolution** of human species, 15:16; 71:17. ***stages in man's life-cycle** (from conception to death), 3:6; 7:189; 16:78; 18:37; 22:5; 23:13-15; 31:14; 32:7-9; 35:11; 36:77-79; 39:6; 40:67; 46:15; 49:13; 56:58; 71:14; 75:37-39; 76:2; 77:20-23; 80:18-19; 84:18-19; 86:5-7; 96:1-2. ***diversity** of races, tongues and colours, 30:22; 35:28; 49:13. ***divine promise** of guidance to, 2:38; 20:122-123. ***favoured** by God, 2:243; 17:70; 27:73; 40:61-64; 74:11-15; 80:20, 24-32; 90:8-10; 96:4-5. ***some more favoured** than others, 17:21; 43:32. ***created** in the best conformation, 40:64; 76:28; 82:7-8; 91:7; 95:4. ***his purpose** and duty, 2:21; 4:1, 36; 11:7; 17:23-39; 23:115; 29:8; 30:30-31; 31:14; 46:15; 51:56-58; 80:23. ***God has made him** to inherit the earth [*khalīfah*], 2:30; 6:165; 24:55; 27:62; 35:39. ***his natural** disposition [*fiṭrah*], 7:172; 30:30. ***endowed with the power** to think and to argue, 2:31-33; 16:4; 36:77; 55:4. ***his conscience**, 50:16-18; 75:2; 82:10-12; 86:4. ***his knowledge** is very limited, 2:255; 16:8; 17:44, 85; 20:110; 30:7-8; 34:9; 36:36; 53:28. ***has been created** weak, restless, argumentative, etc., 4:28; 13:13; 18:54; 30:54; 42:48; 70:19-21; 74:15-25; 91:8. ***not burdened by God** with more than he is well able to bear, 2:286; 6:152; 7:42; 11:88; 18:88; 23:57-62; 47:36-37; 65:7; see Hardship and Ease. ***all around him** either created for, or subservient to him, 2:22, 29; 14:32-33; 16:5-18; 31:20; 36:71-73; 40:61-64; 45:12-13; 67:15; 79:27-33; 80:24-32. ***his life** is sacred, 5:32; 6:151; 17:33; 18:74; 25:68. ***his sustenance**, given in due measure, 13:26; 29:62; 30:37; 39:52; 42:27; 43:32-35. ***human models** of righteousness, 16:120-121; 24:36-38; 33:23, 35; 57:18-19; 70:19-35; 76:7-10; 79:40-41; 90:12-18; 92:5-7; see Example; Righteous; Virtue. ***his love** for the delights of this fleeting life, 3:14-15; 4:2; 11:15; 13:26; 14:3; 41:49; 57:20; 76:27; 89:19-20; 100:8; 102:1-2; 104:2-3; see Life: The life of this world: those who only desire...; those who buy it.... ***descriptions** of wrongdoing by, 10:21-23; 17:83, 89-94, 100; 18:54; 30:41; 31:6-7, 20-21; 33:72; 36:45-48; 39:8; 41:49-51; 42:48; 51:8-12; 70:20-21; 72:6; 74:16-25; 89:15-20; 90:5-7; 96:6-14; 100:6-8. ***God knows well** what is in the heart of, 3:15; 5:7; 39:7; 42:24; 47:26; 57:6; 64:4; 67:13-14. ***tested by God**, 2:155-157; 3:186; 6:53; 17:60; 18:7-8; 23:30; 29:2-4; 47:31; 57:25; see Trials. ***opposite kinds of**, 2:204-207; 3:162-163; 6:122; 11:15-24; 13:19-25; 16:75-76; 17:18-21; 18:32-44; 19:73-75; 22:18-23; 28:61; 35:19-22, 32; 39:8-9, 29; 40:58; 45:21-22; 47:14-17; 67:22; 72:14-15; 74:38-47; 90:17:20; 92:4-11. ***warned** of Satan's enmity, 7:22; 12:5; 17:53; 25:29; 28:15; see Satan: an open foe to man. ***ungrateful**, 2:243; 7:189-190; 10:12; 11:9-11; 14:34; 17:67-69; 21:80; 22:66; 23:78; 25:50; 27:73; 30:33-34; 32:9; 34:13; 39:7; 40:61; 41:51; 42:48; 43:15; 67:23; 100:6; see Gratitude. ***despairs** in misfortune, 30:36; 41:49; 42:28; see Despair. ***wrongs himself**, 3:117; 7:23; 9:70; 10:44; 27:44; 29:40; 30:9-10; 35:32; 80:17; see Injustice. ***prays for** bad things; is prone to be hasty, foolish, 17:11; 21:37; 33:72. ***bound** to lose himself, except those who believe and do good, 103:2-3. (See Adam; Creation; Evil: man's inner self incites to, or is prone to; Freedom; Language; Mankind; Responsibility; Servants of God: all men and women are; Soul.)

Manāt (pagan deity of Arabia), 53:20-23.

Manifest and Hidden, 2:235, 271, 274; 5:52; 6:120, 151; 7:33; 13:22; 14:31; 16:75; 35:29; 69:18; 72:27. ***God knows all** that is, 2:33, 77, 235, 255, 284; 3:29, 118, 154; 167; 4:148-149; 5:61, 99; 6:3; 9:78; 11:5; 13:9-11; 14:38; 16:19, 23; 20:7, 110; 21:3-4, 28, 110; 22:76; 24:29; 25:6; 27:25, 74-75; 28:69; 33:54; 35:29; 36:45, 76; 41:40; 43:80; 47:26; 60:1; 64:4; 84:23; 100:9-11; see Beyond human perception: God knows all; God: He knows all that is beyond human perception; Hearts: God knows what is in the. (See Evil: not to be mentioned openly; God: omniscience of; Secret.)

Mankind, 2:189, 219; 3:96, 110, 137-138; 4:1; 5:32, 97; 9:3; 14:19-21; 17:60, 88-89, 94; 22:2, 78; 25:37; 27:82; 30:20; 35:16; 43:33-35; 44:10-11. ***as a single** community, 2:213; 10:19; 11:118. ***divine** guidance for all, 2:124, 159, 185, 187, 221; 3:3-4; 6:90-91; 12:104; 14:52; 17:89; 18:54; 20:113, 122-124; 28:51, 68; 42:17; 68:52; 81:27-28. ***Muḥammad** sent to all, 4:79, 170; 7:158; 9:128; 10:2; 14:1; 16:44; 27:92; 34:28; 38:87; 39:41. ***symbols** unto, 19:21; 21:91; 29:15. ***gathered** on Day of Judgement, 3:9; 14:21; 18:99; 46:6. (See Guidance; Man.)

Manna, 2:57; 7:160; 20:80.

Manners (Etiquette; Right behaviour), 8:53; 11:117; 13:11; 17:36-37; 28:59; 49:10, 13. ***with the Qur'ān**: see Qur'ān: recitation of. ***when calling people** to Islam, 7:199; 9:6; 16:125. ***when arguing**, 7:200-202; 16:126-127; 29:46. ***in a discrepancy** among believers, 4:59, 65; 24:47-52, 62; 33:36. ***entering** houses, 24:27-29. ***at home**, 24:58-61. ***in the Prophet's** houses, 33:53. ***greeting** the Prophet, 33:56. ***greetings**, 4:86, 94; 11:69; 15:51-52; 24:27, 61; 58:8. ***do not offend God**, nor His Apostle, nor the believers, 5:2; 33:53, 57-58; 49:1-5. ***verify a report** before acting on it, 49:6. ***do not mention** evil openly, 4:148. ***do not deride**, spy or defame one another, 49:11-12; 17:36. ***in your collective** life, 58:11. ***do not revile** their false deities, 6:108. (See Commerce: just dealings in; Justice: in all dealings; Virtue.)

Marriage, 2:187, 223, 230, 232; 4:3-4, 19-25; 5:5; 16:72; 23:6; 24:32-33; 25:54; 30:21; 70:30. ***forbidden** unions, 4:22-24; 33:53. ***to Christian** or Jewish women, 5:5. ***not to marry pagans**, 2:221; 24:3; 60:10-11. ***with slave girls**, 4:3, 25. ***with orphan girls**, 4:3-4, 127. ***with ex wives** of adopted sons, 33:37. ***responsibility** and authority of husband, 4:34. ***duty** of the wife, 4:34. ***crisis** in, 4:34, 128-130. ***of Moses**, 28:27-28. ***of Prophet Muḥammad**, 33:37-39, 50-52. ***some spouses** are enemies unto you, 64:14. ***waiting-period** of widows, 2:234-235. (See Divorce; Dowry; Paradise: their companions in; Spouses.)

Martyrs, 3:156-157; 33:23; 47:4-6. ***are alive**, not dead, 2:154; 3:169. ***joy** and plenitude of, 3:170-171, 195; 22:58-59. (See Fighting.)

Mary [*Maryam*] (mother of Jesus), 5:17, 75, 110, 116; 19:27-29, 32; 21:91; 23:50; 66:12. ***her birth**, 3:35-37. ***guarded** her chastity, 3:47; 19:20; 21:91; 66:12. ***annunciation** of Jesus, 3:42-49; 4:171; 19:16-21. ***birth** of Jesus, 19:22-26. ***calumny** uttered against, 4:156. (See Jesus.)

Meaning (Sense), 2:213; 18:1; 73:4; 75:18-19. ***everything created** with, 3:190-191; 38:27; see Creation: with meaning and purpose; everything created in due measure and proportion; of the heavens and the earth in accordance with truth; Heavens: not created without purpose. ***final** or ultimate, 3:7; 7:53; 10:39; 12:6, 21, 101; 18:78-82; 29:43-44. ***of dreams**: see Dreams: in the story of Joseph. ***the deniers** of truth do not understand: see Denying the truth: they do not understand, nor reason; they reject even the most obvious. ***those who distort** the Revelation, 3:78; 4:46; 5:13, 41; 7:180; 41:40; see Christians: alter and contradict...; Corruption of revealed texts; Israel (children of): have altered and concealed.... (See Discrepancies; Messages of God: for people who reason, who reflect; clearly spelled out; Parables; Qur'ān: expounded with clarity; easy to understand; Thought: clear messages for people who reflect; calls to reflection.)

Mecca, 2:191; 3:96; 6:92; 27:91; 34:18; 42:7; 48:24; 90:1-2. ***as a sanctuary** secure, 2:125-126; 14:35; 28:57; 29:67; 95:3. (See Ka'bah; Victory.)

Medina [*Yathrib*], 9:120; 33:13-14, 60; 63:8. ***siege** of, 33:9-27. (See Yathrib.)

Meeting with God: see Day of Resurrection: the meeting with God.

Mercy and Grace (God's) [*raḥmah*], 2:178; 3:107, 159; 4:26-27, 83, 96, 113; 9:106; 11:9; 18:98; 23:75; 24:10, 14, 20-21; 28:73; 33:17; 35:2; 36:44; 40:9; 42:48; 43:32; 44:42; 57:13; 58:13; 73:20. ***overspreads** everything, 7:156; 40:7. ***God has willed** upon Himself the law of, 6:12, 54. ***God, the Most Merciful** [*ar-Raḥmān*], 13:30; 17:110; 19:18, 58, 96; 55:1; **-the Dispenser of Grace** [***ar-Raḥīm***], 27:30; 34:2; 41:2; 59:22; **-the most merciful** of the merciful [*arḥamu 'r-rāḥimīn*], 7:151; 12:64, 92; 21:83; 23:118; **-the truest bestower** of mercy [*khairu 'r-rāḥimīn*], 23:109, 118; **-limitless** in His grace [*dhū raḥmah*], 6:133, 147; 18:58. ***God grants** it to whoever He wills, 3:74; 9:15, 27; 29:21; 42:8; 48:25; 76:31. ***do not despair of**, 12:87; 15:56; 29:23; 39:53. ***it is better** than all [the wealth] they amass, 3:157-158; 43:32. ***supplications** for: see Supplications: for God's mercy and grace. ***Prophet Muḥammad** is a grace to believers; to all mankind, 9:61; 21:107; 28:46. ***Jesus** is a grace from God, 19:21. ***Revelation as**, 6:154, 157; 7:52, 154, 203; 10:57-58; 11:17; 12:111; 16:64, 89; 17:82; 27:77; 28:43; 44:5-6; 46:12; see Qur'ān. ***that which** earns, 2:218; 3:132; 4:17, 175; 6:155; 7:56, 63, 204; 9:20-21, 71, 99, 117-118; 21:75, 84, 86; 24:56; 27:46; 33:73; 36:45; 45:30; 49:10; 58:11. ***of the Prophet** towards the believers, 9:128. ***engendered by God** in the hearts of Christians, 57:27.

Messages of God (Signs) [*āyāt*], 2:106, 129, 151, 187, 219-221; 3:49-50, 58-59, 96-97, 101, 103, 108, 113, 164, 199; 6:42; 7:26, 35, 146, 156; 8:2; 10:2, 71, 75; 12:7; 13:1; 14:5; 15:1, 75-77; 17:1, 101; 18:9; 19:58; 20:134; 21:37; 23:58; 24:46; 25:73; 27:12, 81-82; 28:35, 47, 59, 87; 29:24; 30:53; 32:15, 24, 26; 33:34, 39; 34:19; 37:1-3; 39:52; 43:68-69; 45:6; 57:9; 62:2; 65:11; 77:1-6. ***in the heavens**, on earth, in creation and in man, 2:164; 3:190; 6:95-99; 10:6, 67, 101; 13:3-4; 16:79; 20:53-54; 27:86; 29:44; 30:20-24; 36:33-44; 41:53; 42:32-35; 45:3-5, 13; 51:20-21. ***as divine portents**, or wonders, 6:157-158; 20:22-23; 30:20-25, 46; 31:31; 40:13, 79-81; 79:20; see Miracles. ***for people** who use their reason; who reflect, 2:164, 242, 266; 10:24; 13:3-4; 16:10-16; 20:53-54, 128; 23:30; 30:21, 24, 28; 38:29; 39:42; 45:13; 57:17; see Reason; Thought. ***for people who** will believe, 6:99; 16:79; 27:86; 29:24; 30:37; 39:52; see Believers. ***in the Revelation**, 2:99; 22:16; 24:1, 34; 26:1; 27:1; 28:2; 29:49; 31:2; 38:29; 41:2-4; 80:11-14. ***clear** and allegorical, 3:7; App. I. ***clearly** spelled out, 5:75, 89; 6:46, 55, 65, 97-98, 105, 126; 7:32, 174; 9:11; 10:5; 11:1; 12:1; 13:2; 22:52; 24:18, 58-59, 61; 26:1; 41:3, 44; 46:27; 57:17. ***corruption of**, 2:211; 41:40; see Corruption of revealed texts. ***rejected**, or treated with frivolity or malice, 2:41, 61, 231; 3:70, 98; 4:140; 5:44; 6:4-5, 21, 33, 46, 68, 150, 157; 7:36; 8:31-32; 9:9, 65; 10:15, 17, 21, 101;

16:82, 104-105; 18:56-57, 106; 19:73; 20:56; 22:51, 72; 23:66, 105; 25:36; 27:13-14, 83-84; 29:47, 49; 31:32; 34:33, 38, 43; 36:46; 40:4, 56, 63, 69-70; 41:44; 43:47-48; 45:8-9, 25, 31, 35; 46:7; 62:5; 68:15; 74:16-25; 78:28; 83:13. ***consequences** of rejecting them, 2:39; 3:4, 11, 21, 112; 4:56, 155; 5:10, 86; 6:39, 49, 93, 124, 157; 7:9, 36-37, 40, 147, 175-176, 182; 8:52, 54; 10:7-8, 73, 95, 101-102; 11:59; 17:97-98; 18:103-106; 19:77-80; 20:126-127; 22:57; 29:23; 30:10, 16; 31:7; 32:22; 34:5; 39:63, 71; 40:34-35; 41:15-16, 28; 42:35; 45:7-11; 46:26; 54:42; 57:19; 58:5; 64:10; 90:19-20. (See *Āyah*; Revelation.)

Metals, 13:17. ***bronze**, 18:96-97. ***copper**, 34:12-13; 70:8. ***lead**, 18:29; 61:4. (See Gold; Iron; Silver.)

Michael (**Angel**), 2:98.

Migration: see Forsaking the domain of evil.

Milk, 16:66; 23:21; 36:73. ***in Paradise**, 47:15. (See Suckling.)

Miracles (Portents; Miraculous signs), 2:118; 17:59; 26:153-156. ***are in the power** of God alone, 6:109; 7:143; 8:17; 13:38; 29:50; 40:78. ***demanded** of Muḥammad, 3:183; 6:37, 109-111; 7:203; 10:20; 13:7, 27; 17:59, 90-93; 20:133; 21:5; 29:50-51. ***given to Moses**, 2:60; 7:106-108, 117; 17:101-102; 20:20-23; 27:10, 12; 43:47-48; **-to Jesus**, 3:49; 5:110; **-to Muḥammad**, 8:17; 29:50-51. ***dismissed** as sorcery, 5:110; 6:7; 7:132; 15:14-15; 17:101; 27:13; see Sorcery. (See Messages of God: as divine portents....)

Misfortune (Adversity; Affliction; Calamity), 3:140-142, 165; 4:72, 78-79; 6:17; 9:50, 98; 10:107; 16:53-54, 127; 20:2, 117, 123; 22:11; 23:75, 106; 39:38, 51; 42:30, 48; 54:19. ***happens** with God's knowledge and His leave, 57:22; 64:11; see Leave (God's). ***as test** from God, 3:152-154; 6:42-43; 7:94-95; 21:35; 23:76; 89:15-16. ***attitude of the believers** when afflicted by, 2:156, 177, 214; 6:34; 9:51-52; 11:10-11; 12:18; 21:83-84, 87-88; 22:35; see Muslims: should not be grieved.... ***despair** in, 6:44; 11:9; 17:83; 30:36; 41:49; 57:23; see Despair. ***man** invokes God in, 2:214; 6:40-41; 10:12; 16:53; 30:33; 39:8, 49; 41:51; see Ships; Supplications. ***on Day** of Resurrection, 4:62; 11:105-106; 16:27; 28:47; 42:30; 47:8; 87:11-12; 92:14-15. (See Evil; Hardship and Ease; Patience; Trials.)

Models: see Examples.

Modesty: walk on earth with, 17:37; 25:63; 31:18-19. ***in speech**, 31:19. ***mates of modest gaze** in Paradise, 37:48-49; 38:52; 55:56, 70-72. ***in dress**: see Dress. (See Virtue: humbleness.)

Monastic asceticism: not enjoined by God, 57:27.

Monks, 5:82; 9:31, 34. (See Monastic asceticism; Rabbis and Monks.)

Months, 2:189; 9:36-37. ***the sacred**, 2:194, 217; 5:2, 97; 9:36. (See Fasting: in Ramadhān; Pilgrimage.)

Moon, 6:77, 96; 7:54; 12:4; 13:2; 21:33; 22:18; 25:61; 29:61; 31:29; 35:13; 36:39-40; 39:5; 41:37; 54:1; 55:5; 71:16; 74:32; 75:8-9; 84:18-19; 91:2. ***subservient** to man, 10:5; 14:33; 16:12. ***new moon**, 2:189; 36:39. (See Calendar; Months; Sun.)

Moses [*Mūsā*], 2:49-55, 60-61, 67-74, 87, 92, 108; 3:84; 5:20-26; 6:84; 7:103-157; 10:75-89; 11:96-97; 14:5-8; 17:101-102; 19:51-53; 20:9-98; 23:45-49; 26:10-68; 27:7-14; 28:3-50; 29:39; 37:114-122; 40:23-28, 37, 53-54; 42:13; 43:46-56; 51:38-40; 79:15-26. ***God speaks with**, 4:164; 7:143-145; 20:11-48, 83-85; 25:36; 26:10-17; 27:9-12; 28:30-35; 79:15-19. ***receives** the divine writ, 6:91, 154; 11:17, 110; 17:2; 21:48-49; 23:49; 25:35; 32:23; 37:117; 41:45; 46:12, 30; 53:36; 87:18-19; see Torah. ***the tablets** of the Law, 7:145, 150, 154. ***miracles of**, 2:60; 7:107-108, 117, 160; 26:63. ***the House of**, 2:248. ***insolence** of the Israelites toward, 2:55, 67-71, 108; 4:153; 5:24; 7:138-140; 33:69; 61:5. ***accused** of sorcery, 7:109-110, 132; 10:76; 17:101; 20:57, 63, 71; 26:34-35; 27:13; 28:36; 40:23-24; 43:49; 51:39. ***kills** a man, 20:40; 26:14, 19-21; 28:15-21, 33. ***in Madyan**, 20:40; 28:22-28. ***and al-Khaḍir**, 18:60-82. (See Aaron; Israel (children of); Pharaoh: and Moses; Revelation; Torah.)

Mother: see Parents.

Mountains, 13:3; 15:19; 16:15, 81; 17:37; 21:31; 22:18; 27:61; 31:10; 33:72; 35:27; 41:10; 50:7; 59:21; 77:27; 78:6-7, 20; 79:32; 88:19. ***rhetorical** reference to, 13:31; 14:46; 19:90. ***their cataclysmic transformation** on the Last Day, 18:47; 20:105-107; 27:88; 52:10; 56:5-6; 69:14; 70:9; 73:14; 77:10; 81:3; 101:5. ***glorify** God, together with prophet David, 21:79; 34:10; 38:18. (See Sinai; Jūdī, mount.)

Muḥammad (God's blessings and peace be upon him): some passages alluding to, 2:4, 23, 143-152, 252; 3:20, 121-129, 152-153, 159; 4:64; 5:48-49; 8:1, 17, 33, 41, 62-65; 9:*passim*; 11:12, 49; 13:40; 16:43-44; 24:63; 28:44-47; 30:47; 32:23; 33:1-3, 7, 13, 36-40, 60; 35:22-25; 36:3, 69; 38:29, 65-70; 39:30; 40:78; 42:3, 51-52; 43:40-45; 45:18-19; 46:29; 47:13, 20; 48:1-3, 18; 58:12-13; 60:12; 66:9; 73:1-10, 20; 74:1-7; 94:*passim*. ***mentioned** by name, 3:144; 33:40; 47:2; 48:29; 61:6. ***announced** in earlier revelations, 7:157; 20:133; 48:29; 61:6. ***Apostle of God**, 2:252; 5:15; 7:158; 13:30; 33:40; 48:29. ***inspired** with Revelation, 4:113, 163-166; 5:67; 6:19; 11:12; 12:2-3, 102; 16:44, 64, 89; 17:105-106; 18:1; 26:192-195; 29:45, 47-48; 33:2; 34:50; 39:41; 41:6; 42:52; 43:44; 53:1-10; 69:40, 43; 81:19; see Qur'ān. ***does not know** what is beyond man's perception (*al-ghaib*), 6:50; 7:187-188; 11:49; 12:102; 38:69-70; 46:9. ***follows only** that which is revealed to him, 6:50; 7:203; 10:15, 109; 46:9. ***the unlettered Prophet**, 7:157-158; 12:3; 29:48; 42:52; 62:2. ***his mission**, 2:119, 129; 5:15-16, 19, 67; 7:157-158; 9:33; 13:30; 16:44, 64; 17:105-106; 19:97; 22:49; 24:54; 26:192-195; 27:91-92; 32:3; 33:45-46; 34:28; 35:23-24; 42:48, 52; 48:8-9, 28; 51:50-51, 55; 61:9; 88:21-22. ***only** a messenger; a herald of glad tidings and warner, 3:144; 5:92, 99; 7:184, 188; 11:2, 12; 15:89; 16:82; 17:93; 25:56; 33:45; 34:28; 46:9; 48:8; 64:12-13; 74:1-2; 79:45. ***not responsible** for the conduct of his people, nor can he determine their fate, 2:119; 3:128; 4:80; 6:52, 66, 104, 107; 10:41, 108; 17:54; 25:43; 26:216; 42:48. *__witness__, 2:143; 4:41-42; 22:78; 33:7-8, 45. *__sent__ to all mankind, 4:79, 170, 174; 6:90; 7:158; 9:128; 10:2; 12:104; 14:1; 16:44; 17:106; 27:92; 34:28; 38:87; 39:41; 62:3; 74:31. *__obedience__ due to, 3:32, 132; 4:13-14, 42, 59, 69, 80; 5:92; 7:157; 8:1, 20-21, 24, 46; 24:54, 63; 33:56; 47:33; 48:10, 18. *__his message__ is the same as that of all prophets, 4:163-165; 21:24-25; 42:3, 13; 43:45; 53:56. *__is a human being__, a mortal, like all other apostles, 3:144; 13:40; 17:94; 18:110; 21:34-35; 39:30; 41:6; 50:2. *__to call people__ with wisdom and kindness, 7:199; 16:125-128; 29:46. *__should not grieve__ over the rejection of his message, 5:68; 16:127; 18:6; 27:70; 31:23; 35:8. *__his testimony__, 10:104, 108; 11:2-4; 12:108; 13:30, 36; 39:11-15; 41:6. *__asks__ no reward, 6:90; 12:104; 23:72; 25:57; 34:47; 38:86; 42:23; 52:40; 68:46. *__the Seal of all Prophets__, 33:40. *__and Abraham__, 2:129; 3:68; 6:161; 16:123; 22:78. *__his exalted__ position and character, 4:113; 9:24; 33:6, 56; 34:45; 43:44; 68:4; 81:19-21. *__a mercy__ of God to all mankind, 8:33; 21:107; 28:46. *__God's mercy and favour__ to the believers, 3:164; 9:61. *__full of compassion and mercy__ towards the believers, 3:159; 9:128; 15:85; 26:215. *__a model__, 33:21. *__devoted__ to prayer, 17:78-79; 73:1-8, 20. *__respect__ due to, 2:104; 4:46; 33:53-57; 49:1-5. *__bless him__, 33:56. *__his wives__ and family, 24:11-17; 33:6, 28-34, 37-38, 50-55, 59, 66:1-5. *__and the blind man__, 80:1-10. *__judge__ in all discrepancies among believers, 4:59, 65; 24:47-52; 33:36. *__opposition__ to his message, 3:20, 183-184; 4:42; 5:64, 68; 6:5-11, 25-26; 7:195; 8:13, 30-40; 9:13, 38-66, 81-87, 107-110; 13:43; 15:10-15; 17:47-48, 73-76, 90-93; 21:3-6, 36, 41; 22:42, 47; 25:4-8, 41-42, 60; 28:48-50; 34:29-31, 43-45; 35:4, 25; 41:4-5, 43; 46:7-11; 47:13; 58:5, 20-22; 59:4; 68:51. *__plots__ against, 4:81, 113; 8:30; 9:40, 48; 13:42; 17:76; 58:8. *__accused__ of forging his message, 10:38; 11:13, 35; 12:111; 16:103; 21:5; 25:4-5; 32:3; 34:8, 43; 42:24; 46:8; 52:30-33; 53:3-4; 74:25; __-of madness__, 7:184; 15:6; 17:47; 25:8; 34:8, 46; 40:14; 51:52-53; 52:29; 53:2; 68:2, 51; 81:22; __-of sorcery__, 6:7; 10:2; 34:43; 46:7; 51:52; 52:29; 69:42; 74:24; see Sorcery; __-of being a poet__, 21:5; 36:69; 52:30, 33; 69:41. *__arrogant demands__ addressed to, 2:104, 108; 4:153; 6:8; 7:203; 10:15; 11:12; 13:7, 27, 31-32; 17:90-93; 20:133; 25:32; 29:50-54; 42:17-18. (See Apostles; Miracles; Night Journey; Qurʾān; Revelation; *Sunnah*; Wives.)

Muqaṭṭaᶜāt (*al-*) (the disjointed letters that precede some sūrahs), **Alif. Lām. Mīm.*, 2:1; 3:1; 29:1; 30:1; 31:1; 32:1. **Alif. Lām. Mīm. Rā.*, 13:1. **Alif. Lām. Mīm. Ṣād.*, 7:1. **Alif. Lām. Rā.*, 10:1; 11:1; 12:1; 14:1; 15:1. **ᶜAīn. Sīn. Qāf.*, 42:2. **Ḥā. Mīm.*, 40:1; 41:1; 42:1; 43:1; 44:1; 45:1; 46:1. **Kāf. Hā. Yā. ᶜAin. Ṣād.*, 19:1. **Nūn.*, 68:1. **Qāf.*, 50:1. **Ṣād.*, 38:1. **Ṭā. Sīn.*, 27:1. **Ṭā. Sīn. Mīm.*, 26:1; 28:1. **Ṭā. Hā.*, 20:1. **Yā. Sīn.*, 36:1. (See App. II.)

Murder, 2:178; 4:93; 5:27-32; 6:151; 17:33. *__of prophets__ and people who enjoin equity, 3:21; see Israel (children of): killed some of their prophets. (See Children: killing one's own; Homicide; Man: his life is sacred; Punishment: for murder; for homicide.)

Muslims (those who have surrendered to God) [*al-muslimūn; alladhīna aslamū*], 3:19-20; 4:125; 6:14, 161-162; 22:78; 31:22; 33:35; 39:12, 22; 46:15; 48:29; 49:14; 72:14. *__description of__: see Believers: descriptions of. *__duty of__, 2:136, 143, 165, 177, 190-195; 3:104, 142, 200; 17:22-39; 22:77-78; see Believers: warnings and commands addressed to. *__called__ to unity, 3:103, 105; 8:73; see Sects: among Muslims. *__what they must__ abstain from, or shun, 2:188; 4:36-38, 104-107; 5:90, 95, 101; 6:56, 119, 151-152; 15:88; 16:90; 17:23, 26-27, 29, 31-39; 24:3; 25:67-68, 72; 49:11-12; 51:51; 58:22; 60:9; see Prohibitions. *__should not be grieved__ by the behaviour and sayings of unbelievers, 3:176; 5:41, 68; 6:33-35; 10:65; 15:88; 16:127; 27:70; 31:23; 35:8; 36:76. *__to enjoin what is right__ and forbid what is wrong, 3:104, 110; 7:199; 9:71, 112; 22:41. *__must keep__ their promises, 2:177, 283; 16:91-95; 17:34; 19:54; 23:8; 70:32. *__are brothers__, 3:103; 49:10. *__friends and protectors__ of one another, 3:103; 5:54-55; 8:72-75; 9:71; 15:88; 48:29. *__make peace between them__, if they fight amongst themselves, 49:9-10. *__friendship__ and alliances with non-Muslims, 3:28, 118-120, 149; 5:2, 51-53, 57; 60:7-9. *__conquests of__, 33:27; 48:18-28; see Fighting; Victory. *__enemies of the__, 3:118-120; 5:54, 82; 60:7; see Believers: enemies of. (See Believers; Community (the Muslim); Surrender to God.)

Names of God: see Attributes of God's perfection; Justice; Mercy.

Nasr (deity of Noah's people), 71:23.

Needy (the), 2:177, 215, 271-273; 4:6, 135; 17:26; 18:79; 24:22, 32; 30:38; 69:34; 74:44; 76:8; 89:18; 90:14-16; 93:8; 107:3. *__kindness to__, 2:83, 262-264; 4:8-9, 36; 17:28; 22:28, 36; 24:22. *__feeding__ or dressing them, as atonement, 2:184; 5:89, 95; 58:4. *__at harvest time__, give them their due, 6:141; 68:21-25. *__beneficiaries__ of *zakāh* and booty, 8:41; 9:60; 59:7-9. (See Charity; Poverty; Spending on others.)

Niggardliness (Greed), 2:195, 270; 3:180; 4:37; 9:75-76; 17:29, 100; 47:37-38; 53:34; 57:24; 68:23-24; 70:18, 21; 92:8-11. *__happy are those__ who are saved from their own covetousness, 59:9. *__Satan__ bids you to be niggardly, 2:268. (See Charity; Purifying dues; Spending (on others): those who refuse.)

Night, 2:187; 6:76; 7:4, 97, 142; 17:1; 19:10-11; 21:78; 23:67; 24:58; 84:17; 86:1-4; 89:4. *__prayer__ in the, 3:113; 11:114; 17:78-79; 20:130; 21:20; 25:64; 32:16; 39:9; 40:55; 41:38; 50:40; 51:17-18; 52:49; 73:2-6, 20; 76:26. *__of Destiny__ [*lailatu 'l-qadr*], 44:3-4; 97:1-5. *__intrigues__ in the, 4:81, 108; 27:49; 34:33.

Night and Day, 2:274; 6:13, 60; 10:24, 50; 13:10; 19:11, 62; 21:20, 33, 42; 28:71-73; 30:23; 34:18, 33; 36:37, 40; 40:55; 41:37-38; 71:5; 73:6-7; 74:33-34; 79:29; 81:17-18; 89:1-2; 91:3-4; 92:1-2; 93:1-2.

*functions of, 6:96; 10:67; 25:47; 27:86; 28:72-73; 40:61; 78:10-11. *subservient to man, 14:33; 16:12. *succession of, 2:164; 3:27, 190; 7:54; 10:6; 13:3; 22:61; 23:80; 24:44; 25:62; 31:29; 35:13; 39:5; 45:5; 57:6; 73:20. *as symbols, or signs, 17:12; 36:37; 41:37; 78:9-11. (See Day; Time.)

Night Journey [*al-isrā*ʾ], 17:1, 60; 53:13-18; App. IV.

Noah [*Nūḥ*], 3:33-34; 4:163; 6:84; 7:69; 17:17; 19:58; 21:76-77; 22:42; 23:23-30; 25:37; 33:7-8; 37:75-82; 42:13; 57:26. *his people reject his message, 7:59-64; 9:70; 10:71-74; 11:25-34, 89; 14:9; 26:105-121; 29:14; 38:12; 40:5, 31; 50:12; 51:46; 53:52; 54:9-10; 71:*passim*. *the Ark, 7:64; 10:73; 11:36-41, 44, 48; 17:3; 23:27-30; 26:119; 29:15; 54:13-15. *his wife, 66:10. *and his son, 11:42-43, 45-47. *the Deluge, 11:40, 44; 23:28; 29:14; 54:11-12; 71:25.

Oaths, 2:224-227; 4:33; 5:89; 9:12-13; 16:91-92, 94; 24:6-9; 38:44; 66:2. *of witnesses, 5:106-108. *pledge of allegiance to the Prophet, 48:10, 18; 60:12. *divine O. and calls to reflection, 36:2; 37:1-3; 38:1; 43:2; 44:2; 50:2; 51:1-7; 52:1-6; 53:1; 56:75-76; 68:2; 69:38-39; 70:40-41; 74:32-34; 75:1-2; 77:1-6; 79:1-5; 81:15-21; 84:16-19; 85:1-3; 86:1, 11-12; 89:1-5; 90:1-4; 91:1-8; 92:1-3; 93:1-2; 95:1-3; 103:1. *of hypocrites and unbelievers, 6:109; 9:12-13, 42, 56, 62, 74, 95-96, 107; 14:44; 16:38; 24:53; 27:49; 35:42; 58:14-18; 63:2-3; 68:10, 17-18. *of Satan, 38:82-83; see Satan: declares his mission before God.

Obedience, 4:34; 5:7; 16:52, 120; 23:34; 65:4; 84:2, 5. *to God and to His apostles, 2:285; 3:32, 50, 132; 4:13-14, 46, 59, 64, 69, 80-81; 5:92; 8:1, 20, 46; 9:71; 20:90; 24:47, 51-56; 26:108, 110, 126, 131, 144, 150, 163, 179; 33:31, 33, 66, 71; 43:63; 47:20-21, 33; 48:16-17; 49:14; 58:13; 60:12; 64:12, 16; 66:5; 81:21; see Muḥammad: obedience due to. *to evildoers: warnings against, 3:100, 149; 6:116, 121; 11:97; 16:100; 18:28; 33:67; 43:54; 47:26; 76:24; 96:19. (See Surrender to God: all creation surrendered to God; Will (God's): all things obey God's will.)

Oblivion: see Forgetting; Remembering.

Old age, 17:23-24; 30:54; 35:11; 36:68; 40:67.

Olive tree: see Plants and Trees: Olive tree.

Opinions (Views), 6:152; 18:21; 27:32; 34:20. *errant views, 2:120, 176; 5:48-49, 77; 6:56, 119, 150; 35:40; 68:41; see Thought: wrong, unworthy or evil thoughts. (See Words.)

Opposites: see Pairs.

Oppression (Tyranny), 2:177; 4:97; 7:33; 20:1-2; 28:19. *is even worse than killing, 2:191, 217. *examples of tyranny, 10:23; 28:4; 41:15; 46:20; 89:6-12. *of Pharaoh on the children of Israel: see Arrogance: Pharaoh and his dignitaries, archetypes of; Pharaoh: his great cruelty. *duty to fight against, 2:190-194; 4:75, 89, 91; 8:39, 73; 22:39-40; 42:39-42. (See Arrogance; Bounds: of equity, transgression of; Coercion; Forsaking the domain of evil; Injustice; Persecution, religious.)

Orphans, 18:82; 93:6; 107:2. *good treatment of, 2:83, 220; 4:36, 127; 89:17; 93:9. *strict fairness towards their wealth, 4:2-3, 5-10; 6:152; 17:34. *charity to, 2:177, 215; 76:8; 90:14-15. *marriage with orphan girls, 4:3, 127. *beneficiaries of booty, 8:41; 59:7.

Pairs (Opposites), 35:19-22. *everything created in, 13:3; 26:7; 31:10; 36:36; 42:11; 43:12; 51:49; 89:3. *in the human species, 4:1; 7:189; 30:21; 35:11; 39:6; 42:11; 53:45-46; 78:8. (See Good and Evil; Hardship and Ease; Life: this life / the life to come; Light: and darkness; Man: opposite kinds of; Night and Day.)

Palm tree, 6:99; 50:10; 55:11. *Mary and the, 19:23-25. *date-palm gardens, 2:266; 17:91; 18:32; 23:19; 36:34. (See Plants and Trees.)

Parables [*mathal*; pl., *ʾamthāl*]: that God propounds unto men, 2:26; 14:45; 18:54; 24:34-35; 29:43; 30:58; 39:27; 47:3; 59:21; 66:10; 74:31. *people who kindle a fire, 2:17-18. *a violent cloudburst, 2:19-20. *the shepherd's cry, 2:171. *the town in ruins, 2:259. *the grain out of which grow seven ears, 2:261. *the smooth rock, 2:264. *the fertile garden, 2:265. *the garden scorched by fire, 2:266. *the icy wind, 3:117. *the panting dog, 7:175-177. *the building on a crumbling river-bank, 9:109-110. *the life of this world is like the rain, 10:24; 18:45; 57:20. *the one who stretches his hands towards water, 13:14. *the scum carried along by the stream, 13:17-18. *the paradise promised to the God-conscious, 13:35; 47:15. *ashes which the wind blows about, 14:18. *the good tree and the bad, 14:24-27. *the powerless slave and the rich free man, 16:75. *the powerless dumb and the righteous man, 16:76. *the woman who untwists the yarn she has spun, 16:92. *the city that was prosperous, but ungrateful, 16:112-113. *the Men of the Cave, 18:9-26. *two men, one arrogant and the other God-conscious, 18:32-44. *he who falls from the sky and the birds, or the wind, carry him away, 22:31. *the fly, 22:73. *divine Light, 24:35. *the mirage, 24:39. *depths of darkness upon an abysmal sea, 24:40. *the spider's house, 29:41. *taking slaves as partners, 30:28. *the people of a township who rejected God's message-bearers, 36:13-29. *the servant with several masters, 39:29. *the seed that brings forth its shoot, 48:29. *the Qurʾān and the mountain, 59:10. *the ass loaded with books, 62:5. *if all your water will vanish underground, 67:30. *the owners of a certain garden, 68:17-33.

Paradise (Garden), 2:111, 214, 221; 3:133, 185; 7:46-50; 26:90; 36:26; 37:40-62; 39:73-74; 41:30-32; 42:7; 55:46-78; 56:10-40; 59:20; 66:8, 11; 69:21-23; 76:5-22; 81:13; App. I. *promise of, 2:82; 3:15, 133-136; 4:122, 124; 5:12; 7:42-43; 9:72, 111-112; 10:26; 13:35; 19:60-63; 25:15-16, 24; 29:58-59; 31:8-9; 32:17; 38:49-54; 40:40; 41:30; 42:22-23; 46:13-14, 16; 47:4-6, 15; 50:31-35; 57:21. *as reward, 2:112; 3:136, 195; 5:85; 7:43; 18:30-31; 20:76; 25:75; 29:58; 34:37; 39:74; 46:14; 76:22; 78:36; 98:8. *that which rests with God; good deeds the fruit thereof endures forever [*al-bāqiyātu aṣ-*

ṣāliḥāt], 11:86; 16:95-96; 18:46; 19:76; 42:36; 64:15; 73:20. ***to whom** it is reserved, 3:142, 195; 9:20-22, 88-89, 100; 11:23, 108; 13:19-24, 35; 16:30-32; 18:107; 19:60-63; 20:75-76; 23:1-11; 25:70-76; 29:58-59; 34:37; 50:32-33; 51:15-19; 56:88-91; 70:22-35; 76:7-12; 79:40-41. ***to whom** it will be denied, 5:72; 7:40. ***peace**, happiness and plenitude of its indwellers, 4:57; 7:42-43, 49; 10:10; 13:22-24; 14:23; 15:45-48; 18:108; 19:62; 25:16, 75; 35:35; 36:55-58; 37:58-59; 39:74; 41:31-32; 42:22; 43:68-71; 44:51-56; 50:34-35; 52:17-18; 54:54-55; 56:24-33, 88-89; 69:21-23; 76:13-14; 78:31-35; 83:22-24; 88:8-11; see Happiness. ***they will obtain** God's goodly acceptance and forgiveness, 3:15, 136; 5:119; 9:21, 72; 48:5; 58:22; 89:27-30; 98:8. ***their companions** in, 2:25; 3:15; 4:57; 13:23; 36:56; 37:44, 48-49; 38:52; 40:8; 43:70; 44:53-54; 52:20-21, 24; 55:56, 58, 70-74; 56:16-17, 22-23, 34-38; 76:19; 78:33. ***food** and drink in, 2:25; 37:41-42, 45-47; 38:51; 43:71, 73; 47:15; 52:19, 22-23; 55:50-52, 54, 66-68; 56:17-21; 69:23-24; 76:5-6, 17-18, 21; 78:34; 83:25-28. ***garments** and jewels in, 18:31; 22:23; 35:33; 44:53; 76:12, 21. ***delights** and magnificence of, 3:133; 9:72; 25:10; 43:71-72; 55:54, 76; 56:15; 76:15-16, 20; 88:12-16. ***utterances** of its indwellers, 7:43-44, 50-51; 10:10; 35:34-35; 37:50-60; 52:25-28; 74:40-42; 83:35-36.

Other names of: -'**gardens** through which running waters flow', 2:25; 3:15, 136, 195, 198; 4:13, 57, 122; 5:12, 85, 119; 9:89, 100; 13:35; 14:23; 16:31; 18:31; 22:14, 23; 25:10; 47:12; 48:5, 17; 57:12; 58:22; 61:12; 64:9; 65:11; 85:11; 98:8; -'**gardens** of perpetual bliss' [*jannātu ʿadn*], 9:72; 13:23; 16:31; 18:31; 19:61; 20:76; 35:33; 38:50; 40:8; 61:12; 98:8; -'**gardens** of bliss' [*jannātu 'n-naʿīm*], 5:65; 10:9; 22:56; 26:85; 31:8; 37:42-43; 56:11-12, 89; 70:38; -'**paradise** of life abiding' [*jannātu 'l-khuldi*], 25:15; -'**garden** of delight' [*rawḍa*], 30:15; -'**gardens** of paradise' [*jannātu 'l-firdaws*], 18:107; -'**gardens** of rest, or of promise' [*jannātu 'l-maʾawā*], 32:19; 53:15. (See Fruits: in Paradise; Victory: Paradise as supreme triumph.)

Parents, 4:7, 33; 9:113; 31:33; 58:22; 60:3-4; 80:34-35; 90:3. ***kindness** to, 2:83, 215; 4:36; 17:23-24; 29:8; 31:14-15; 46:15, 17. ***the mother**, 16:78; 31:14; 39:6; 46:15; 53:32; 58:2. (See Forebears; Relatives; Supplications: for our parents.)

Passions: see Desires (Worldly).

Patience, 2:155-157, 177, 250; 3:17, 142; 7:126, 128; 12:18, 83, 90; 14:5, 12; 16:41-42, 110, 126-127; 18:28; 22:35; 29:58-59; 31:31; 32:24; 34:19; 37:102; 38:44; 41:35; 42:33, 43; 47:31; 50:39; 68:48; 90:17; 103:3. ***God is with** those who are patient, 2:153, 249; 3:146; 8:46, 66. ***source of aid** and protection, 2:45, 153; 3:120, 125; 6:34; 8:65-66. ***calls to**, 3:186, 200; 4:25; 7:87; 10:109; 11:49, 115; 20:130; 25:20; 30:60; 31:17; 38:17; 40:55, 77; 46:35; 49:5; 52:48; 68:51-52; 70:5; 73:10; 74:7; 76:24. ***reward of**, 7:137; 11:11; 13:22; 16:96; 23:111; 25:75; 28:54, 80; 33:35; 39:10; 76:12. (See Virtue: patience.)

Peace, 2:224; 4:114; 11:48; 19:15, 33, 62; 20:47; 25:63; 27:59; 42:40; 56:26. ***greeting of**, 4:86, 94; 6:54; 7:46; 11:69; 13:23-24; 15:52; 19:47; 28:55; 43:89; 51:25. ***inner**, 2:248; 3:97; 9:26, 40; 21:69; 48:4, 18, 26. ***abode of**, 6:127; 10:25; 23:50. ***the greeting** in Paradise, 10:10; 14:23; 15:46; 16:32; 25:75; 33:44; 36:58; 39:73; 50:34; 56:91. ***greeting** to the prophets, 37:79, 109, 120, 130, 181. ***and war**, 4:83, 90-91; 8:61; 47:35. ***agreements**, 4:90, 92; 8:56-58, 72; 9:1-13; see Covenants; Ḥudaybiyyah. (See Salvation.)

Pearls, 55:22. ***as jewels** in Paradise, 22:23; 35:33. ***hidden or scattered**, a metaphor for the companions in Paradise, 52:24; 56:22-23; 76:19.

Pen, 31:27; 68:2; 96:3-5; see Ink.

Permission: see Leave (God's).

Persecution (**Religious**), 2:191, 193, 214, 217, 286; 3:146-147; 7:82; 12:110; 16:41; 27:56; 40:25-26; 59:8; 60:1-2, 5, 8-9; 85:4-10; see Pharaoh. ***against** the Prophet, 8:30; 17:76; 60:1. ***fear** of, 8:26; 10:83-86; 29:10. ***helping believers** that suffer, 8:72. ***among** Christians, 5:14. (See Self-defence.)

Pharaoh, 3:11; 8:52, 54; 10:75; 38:12; 50:12-13; 54:41-42; 69:9; 79:15-26; 85:17-18; 89:10. ***his great** cruelty, 2:49; 7:124, 127, 141; 14:6; 20:71; 26:49; 28:4. ***and Moses**, 7:103-137; 10:75-92; 11:96-97; 17:101-103; 20:24, 39, 43-52, 56-63; 22:44; 23:45-49; 26:10-68; 27:12-14; 28:3-13, 32-42; 40:23-46; 43:46-56; 44:17-31; 51:38-40; 73:15-16; 79:15-26. ***and his sorcerers**, 7:111-126; 10:79-81; 20:60-73; 26:36-51. ***a believer** from his family, 40:28-46. ***his wife**, a pious woman, 28:8-9; 66:11. ***declares** himself god, 26:29; 28:38; 79:24. ***orders** a high tower to be built, 28:38; 40:36-37. ***the plagues**, 7:130-135. ***drowns** together with his army, 2:50; 7:136; 17:103; 20:78; 26:66; 28:40; 43:55. ***belated** conversion of, 10:90-91. ***his body** rescued from the sea, 10:92. (See Moses.)

Pilgrimage [*ḥajj*], 2:158, 189, 196-203; 3:97; 5:2, 97; 9:19; 22:26-37. ***pious** visit [*ʿumrah*], 2:158, 196. ***no hunting** while on, 5:1-2, 94-96. ***the Greatest**, 9:3.

Plague: as divine punishment, 2:59; 7:162. ***plagues** of Egypt, 7:130-135.

Plants and Trees (Vegetation), 7:57-58; 13:3; 18:45; 20:53; 22:5; 31:10; 37:146; 57:20; 78:15-16; 80:24-32; 86:12. ***God** makes them grow, 6:95, 99; 56:63-65. ***acacia**, 56:29. ***garlic**, 2:61. ***aromatic plants** and spices, 2:61; 55:12; 76:5. ***lote-tree**, 34:16; 53:14-16; 56:28. ***onion**, 2:61. ***cereals**, 2:261; 6:95, 99; 12:43, 46-48; 13:4; 16:11; 18:32; 26:148; 36:33; 44:26; 48:29; 50:9; 55:12; 78:15; 80:27. ***thorns**, 88:6. ***pomegranate**, 6:99, 141; 55:68. ***herbage**, 16:10; 32:27; 39:21; 79:31; 80:31-32. ***fig tree** (fig), 95:1. ***vegetables**, 2:61; 80:28. ***ginger**, 76:17. ***lentils**, 2:61. ***manna**, 2:57; 7:160; 20:80. ***mustard**, 21:47; 31:16. ***olive tree**, 6:99, 141; 16:11; 23:20; 24:35; 80:29; 95:1. ***date-palm**, 2:266; 6:99, 141; 13:4; 16:11, 67; 17:91; 18:32; 19:23-25; 20:71; 23:19; 26:148; 36:34; 50:10; 55:11, 68; 59:5; 80:29; see Palm-tree. ***cucumber**,

2:61. *tamarisk, 34:16. *vines (grapes), 2:266; 6:99; 16:11, 67; 80:28; see Vineyards. *in Paradise, 53:14-16; 55:68; 56:28-29; 76:5, 17. (See Crops; Fruits: for your sustenance; Tree.)

Play, 23:115; 43:83; 44:9, 38; 47:36; 52:12. ***those who make** play their religion, or make their religion a mere play, 5:57-58; 6:70; 7:51; 31:6.

Pleasure: see Enjoyment.

Pledges: see Promises.

Poets, 26:224-226. ***Muḥammad** branded as a poet, 21:5; 36:69; 37:36; 52:30; 69:40-41.

Polygamy, 4:3, 129.

Poverty, 17:29; 59:9. ***fear of**, 9:28. ***Satan** threatens you with, 2:268. ***do not kill** your children for fear of, 6:151; 17:31. (See Needy.)

Praise of God: see God: everything in creation extols His limitless glory; all praise is due to Him alone.

Prayer, 2:3; 4:103; 9:18; 14:31; 17:107-111; 19:31, 55, 59; 20:14, 132; 21:73; 22:26, 41, 78; 23:9; 24:37; 39:9; 48:29. ***turning** to God, 7:125; 9:59; 11:75, 88; 13:27; 17:25; 26:50-51; 30:31, 33; 31:15; 38:17, 19, 30, 44; 39:8, 17, 54; 40:13-14; 42:10, 13; 43:14, 48; 50:7-8, 32-33; 60:4; 68:32; 70:22-23; see Repentance. ***due only** to God, 1:5; 7:206; 13:14-15; 72:18-20; see Supplications: do not invoke other than God. ***source** of help, 1:5; 2:45, 153; see Aid; Succour. ***restrains** man from loathsome deeds, 29:45. ***linked** to charity: see Charity. ***direction of** [*qiblah*], 2:142-150. ***times of the**, 4:103; 7:205; 11:114; 17:78-79; 20:130; 30:17-18; 50:39-40; 52:48-49; 73:1-8, 20; 76:25-26. ***Friday's**, 62:9-10. ***when travelling** or in danger, 2:239; 4:101-102. ***ablution** for the, 4:43; 5:6. ***correct form** and attitude in, 2:238; 7:29, 205; 17:110; 23:1-2. ***do not pray** in a state of drunkenness or ritual impurity, 4:43. ***supplications**: see Supplications. ***of hypocrites**, 4:142. ***for dead unbelievers**, 9:113-114. ***of the unbelievers**, 8:35; 13:14; 40:50. (See Forgiveness; Night: prayer in the; Prostration; Remembrance of God; Supplications.)

Pride: see Arrogance.

Priests (Christian), 5:82; see Monks; Rabbis and Monks.

Prisoners of war, 8:67-71; 9:5; 33:26; 47:4. (See Captives; Slaves.)

Prohibitions, 2:85, 275; 3:64, 187; 4:2, 6, 29-32, 89-90, 161; 5:2; 6:28, 141-142, 150-153; 7:3, 20, 22, 32-33, 50, 85-86, 157, 166; 8:20-21, 27, 46-47; 9:29, 37; 10:105-106; 11:46-47, 62, 84-85, 113; 16:90-92, 94-95; 22:30; 24:33; 26:181-183; 28:86-88; 30:31-32; 31:13; 33:32-33; 40:66; 42:13; 46:35; 58:8; 60:8-9; 66:1. ***believers forbid** doing what is wrong, 3:104, 110, 114; 9:71, 112; 22:41; 31:17. ***do not forbid** what God has made lawful, 5:5, 87; 6:140; 7:32; 10:59; 16:116. ***what was forbidden** only to the Jews, 3:50, 93; 4:160; 6:146; 16:118; see Sabbath. ***declared by** unbelievers and hypocrites, 6:143-144, 148; 9:67; 10:59; 15:70; 16:35, 116; 48:25. (See Alcoholic drinks; Believers: warnings and commands...; Food and Drink; Marriage: forbidden unions; Muslims: what they must abstain from....)

Promises (Pledges; Word), 2:270; 4:21; 7:135; 9:114, 119; 12:66, 80. ***God's**, 2:124; 3:194-195; 4:95-96, 122, 124, 162, 171, 175; 5:48; 6:34, 115, 134; 7:44, 137; 9:111-112; 10:4, 33, 64, 96, 103; 11:119; 14:7, 13-14, 47; 17:108; 18:2-3, 27, 98; 19:61; 20:86; 21:105; 22:38, 55; 25:15-16; 28:7-13, 61; 30:4-6, 47; 31:8-9; 33:35; 38:84-85; 39:20; 40:6, 55; 46:16-17; 48:29; 53:15; 68:39; see Words: as God's promises; Victory: divine promise of. ***of resurrection** and judgement, 10:48; 13:31; 14:47-48; 16:38; 17:104; 18:21; 21:38, 97, 104; 27:71-72; 30:60; 31:33; 35:5; 40:77; 45:32; 46:17; 67:25; 73:18. ***believers** must fulfil all their, 2:177; 5:89; 9:4; 13:20; 16:91-92, 94-95; 19:54; 22:38; 23:8; 70:32. ***you will be called** to account for all your, 17:34; 33:15. ***broken** by the Jews, 2:100; 4:155; 5:13; 20:86-87. ***Satan's** deluding, 4:120; 14:22; 17:64. (See Covenants; Oaths; Paradise: promise of; Responsibility; Uterus: what God has bidden to be joined.)

Proof (Arguments; Authority), 2:76, 145; 6:80-83, 149; 10:59; 14:10-11; 18:15, 22; 20:133; 23:117; 30:35; 37:156-157; 58:1. ***the Revelation** as clear, 2:87, 92; 20:133; 57:25; 98:1-3. ***God's challenges** to the unbelievers, 2:111; 6:148-150; 21:24; 27:64; 28:49-50; 30:28; 35:40; 37:151-157; 46:4; 68:36-42. ***false arguments** against God's messages, 6:148; 10:21; 16:35, 127; 18:56; 23:24; 27:70; 34:33, 43-44; 35:41-43; 36:77-79; 40:4-5; 41:14; 42:15-18; 43:20; 45:24-27; 74:18-25; 86:15-16. ***lack of arguments** of the doomed, 6:94; 28:65-66, 74-75; 69:25-29. (See God: proof of His uniqueness; Qurʾān: its inimitability, as proof of its divine origin; Leave (God's): what God has never sanctioned...)

Prophethood, 7:35-36; 22:75. ***need for**, 4:165; 6:130-132; 15:4; 26:208-209; 28:46-47. ***spiritual** dignity of, 2:253; 4:64, 69. ***among the descendants** of Noah, Abraham, Isaac and Jacob, 4:54; 6:84-89; 29:27; 57:26. ***among** the children of Israel, 4:163-164; 5:44; 45:16; see Israel (children of): have received Revelation. ***of Jesus**, 3:79; 43:59; see Jesus. (See Apostles; Revelation.)

Prophets: see Apostles; Prophethood.

Prostitution, 24:33.

Prostration, 2:125; 3:43, 113; 9:112; 15:98; 22:26; 25:63-64, 219; 38:24; 39:9; 48:29; 76:25-26. ***everything** in creation prostrates before God, 13:15; 16:48-50; 22:18; 55:5-6. ***God commands** angels to prostrate to Adam, 2:34; 7:11-12; 15:28-33; 17:61; 18:50; 20:116; 38:71-75. ***verses** of P. during Qurʾān recitation, 7:206; 13:15; 16:49-50; 17:107-109; 19:58; 22:18, 77; 25:60; 27:25-26; 32:15; 41:37; 53:62; 84:20-21; 96:19. ***in the story** of Joseph, 12:4, 100. ***of Pharaoh's** magicians, 7:120-121; 20:70; 26:46-48. ***those who refuse** to prostrate, 68:42-43. (See Prayer; Shadows.)

Provision (God's) (Material and spiritual sustenance), 2:164; 3:37-38; 4:130; 6:151; 7:10, 32; 8:26; 9:28; 10:59, 93; 11:88; 15:20-22; 16:75, 112; 17:31, 70; 18:19; 22:34-35; 23:18-22; 28:57; 50:9-11; 65:2-3; see Fruits: for your sustenance. ***spiritual** provision,

6:154; 10:31; 18:16; 19:76; 27:64; 34:24; 35:3; 40:13; 43:32; 45:16; 51:22; see Guidance; Mercy and Grace (God's). ***all sustenance** comes only from God, 11:6; 16:56, 72-73; 20:131-132; 26:132-134; 29:17, 60; 40:64, 79-80; 51:57-58; 67:21, 30. ***God-consciousness** is the best, 2:197; see Consciousness (God-). ***comes down** in due measure, 15:21; 42:27; 65:3. ***God provides** abundantly, or in scant measure, whomever He wills, 2:212; 3:27, 37; 13:26; 16:71; 17:30-31; 24:38; 28:82; 29:62-63; 30:37; 34:36, 39; 39:52; 42:11-12, 19. ***eat of the good** things which God has provided for you, 2:60-61, 172; 5:96; 6:141-142; 16:114; 20:81; 22:28; 34:15; 67:15. ***supplications** for, 2:126, 201; 3:38; 5:114; 14:37. ***in the life** to come, 2:201; 3:169; 7:32, 50; 8:4, 74; 19:62-63; 22:50, 58-59; 24:26, 38; 30:44; 33:31; 34:4; 37:40-44; 38:49-54; 42:20, 22-23; 51:22; 52:17-23; 65:11; 89:24; see Life: The life to come; Paradise. ***God, the best** of providers, 5:114; 20:131; 22:58; 23:72; 34:39; 62:11. ***as God's** bounty, 2:198; 4:32; 17:12; 24:22, 32; 28:73; 30:46; 35:12; 39:8, 49; 42:22-23; 45:12; 57:29; 62:10; 73:20. ***spend** on others out of what We provide for you, 2:3, 254; 4:39; 6:141; 8:3; 22:35; 24:33; 32:16; 35:29; 76:7-9; see Charity; Purifying dues; Spending on others. ***its abundance** does not denote God's favour, 19:73-75, 77-80; 23:55-56; 28:61, 82; 34:34-37; 39:49-52; 43:32-35; 74:11-17. (See Ships; Wealth.)

Punishment, 21:46. ***warning** against, 8:38; 17:15-17; 20:134; 26:206-209; 28:58-59. ***blast** of, 11:67, 94; 15:73-74, 83; 23:41; 29:40; 36:29, 49-50, 53; 38:15; 54:31. ***thunderbolt** of, 2:55; 4:153; 13:13; 41:13, 17; 51:44. ***God's punishing** grasp, 11:102; 13:32; 16:61; 18:58; 22:44, 48; 23:64; 28:40; 29:40; 35:26; 40:5, 21-22; 43:48; 51:40; 54:42; 69:10; 73:16; 79:25; 89:25-26. ***in the life to come**: see Life: The life to come: punishment in. ***comes** suddenly, 6:44, 47; 7:95; 12:107; 16:26, 45-46; 22:55; 26:201-202; 29:53; 39:54-55. ***unbelievers** ask for it to be hastened on, 6:57; 8:32; 10:50-51; 11:8; 13:6; 22:47; 26:187, 204; 29:29, 53-54; 37:176; 42:18. ***for making war** on God and His apostle, 2:190-191; 5:33. ***for adultery**, 4:25; 24:2; 25:68-69. ***for murder**, 4:53; 5:32; 17:33; 18:74. ***for homicide**, 2:178; 4:92; 5:45. ***for desecration**, 5:94-95. ***for spreading** corruption on earth, 5:32-33; 7:103; 13:25; 16:88-89; 17:4-5; 27:14; 29:36-37; 89:11-13. ***for immoral** conduct, 4:15-16, 25; 33:30; 68:17-33. ***for theft**, 5:38. ***for calumny**, 24:4-5, 23-25. ***commensurate** with the offence, 10:27. ***capital**, 5:32-33; 6:151; 17:33; 18:74; 25:68-69. ***postponed**, 14:42-44; 16:61; 19:84; 21:111; 35:45. ***God** grants a respite to Iblīs, 7:14-15; 15:36-38; 17:62-63; 38:79-81. ***protection** against, 8:33-34. ***exemplary**, 2:66; 3:137-138; 43:55-56. ***evildoers** cannot escape, 3:188; 4:42; 6:134; 8:59; 9:2-3; 10:52-53; 11:8, 20, 32-33, 43; 12:110; 13:11, 34; 14:21; 16:45-46; 18:53; 20:97, 108; 22:22; 24:57; 25:19; 29:4, 21-22, 39-40; 33:16-17; 34:51; 38:3; 39:19, 51; 41:40, 48; 42:31, 35; 46:32; 72:12; 75:10-12; 82:14-16. ***so that men** might mend their ways, 6:42-43, 65; 7:168; 30:41; 32:21; 43:48; 49:9. ***no bearer of burdens** shall be made to bear another's burden, 6:164; 17:15; 29:12-13; 35:18; 39:7; 53:38. (See Communities: destroyed or punished...; Denying the truth: punishment of; Hell.)

Purification (Purity), 2:129, 132, 232; 3:42; 7:82; 11:78; 18:81; 19:12-13, 19; 23:4; 27:56; 53:32; 56:79; 80:3-7, 13-14; 98:2-3. ***God purifies** whomever He wills, 4:49; 24:21. ***calls** to, 2:222; 24:28, 30; 33:53; 35:18; 58:12; 74:4-5; 79:17-19. ***God wants** to purify the believers, 2:151; 3:164; 5:6; 8:11; 9:103, 108; 12:24; 24:21; 33:33; 38:46; 62:2. ***recompense** of all who attain to, 16:32; 20:76; 87:14; 91:9; 92:17-18. ***purity** of the people of Paradise, 2:25; 3:15; 4:57; 7:43; 15:47; 44:54; 52:20; 55:70-72; 56:22-23. ***those** whom God does not purify, 2:174; 3:77; 5:41. (See Ablution; Chastity; Purifying dues.)

Purifying dues [*az-zakāh*], 2:110, 177; 4:77; 5:55; 9:5, 11; 10:71; 22:78; 24:56; 33:33; 41:7; 58:13. ***beneficiaries** of *zakāh*, 9:60. (See Charity; Niggardliness.)

Purity: see Purification.

Qiblah, 2:115, 142-145, 149-150, 177; 3:96-97.

Questions, 2:186; 16:56; 18:70, 76; 25:59; 70:1-2. ***God's**, 4:39, 41; 5:109; 7:22, 32, 172; 16:72-73; 19:77-78; 24:50; 25:17; 27:59-64; 33:8; 34:40; 36:60-62; 37:62. ***"they will ask thee** [oh Prophet,] ...", 2:189, 215, 217, 219-220, 222; 5:4; 7:187; 8:1; 10:53; 17:85; 18:83; 20:105-107; 33:63; 79:42-44. ***do not ask** about unspoken matters which might cause you hardship, 5:101-102. ***addressed** to the believers, 3:52, 165; 4:88; 9:38; 16:30. ***to the followers** of earlier revelations, 2:139-140, 211; 3:20; 4:51-54; 7:163-164; 10:94; 16:43; 18:22; 21:7; 43:45. ***to those** who deny the truth, 2:28, 210; 5:50; 6:143-144, 148; 7:184-185; 9:65; 10:32, 35, 50-52; 13:16, 33; 16:23-24; 19:66-67; 23:68-70; 26:69-76; 27:84, 86; 28:62, 65-66, 74; 29:61-63; 30:40; 31:25; 37:11; 39:38; 43:9, 87; 55:13, *passim*; 56:57-64, 68-73, 81-87; see Thought: Have you ever considered...? ***God's rhetorical questions**, 2:138; 4:87, 125; 5:50; 13:19, 33; 18:6; 19:65; 24:50; 27:60; 28:50; 29:10; 38:28; 39:9, 15, 19, 22, 24, 29, 32, 36-37, 52, 60; 83:36; 95:8. ***posed by** the deniers of truth, 2:118, 142; 6:53; 9:124; 10:20, 48, 53; 17:49-51; 19:66-67; 21:38; 25:32, 60; 27:71; 34:28-29; 37:16-17, 51-53; 51:12; 67:25; 74:31; 75:5-6, 26-29; 78:1-3. ***on the Last Day**, 7:48; 20:125; 23:101; 34:23; 41:19-21; 50:30; 55:39; 70:10-11; 81:8-9. ***of the blessed** ones in Paradise, 37:50-59; 52:25; 74:39-44. ***asked by God** and the angels to the inmates of Hell, 4:97; 23:105-106, 112-115; 26:92-93; 27:90; 37:24-25; 39:71; 46:34; 67:7-8.

Quraish (tribe of Mecca): their unbelief, 54:43-47, 51. ***God's favour** and call to, 106:1-4.

Qurʾān, 4:174; 5:48; 6:92; 10:2, 15-16; 13:1; 14:1; 15:87; 16:101; 17:85-89, 105-109; 20:133; 22:54; 26:192-196; 27:6; 29:45, 47-49, 51; 31:2-3; 35:31-

32; 36:2; 38:87-88; 42:3, 51-52; 43:43-44; 44:2-3; 53:10; 59:21; 80:11-16; 97:1. *divine message, 4:82, 166; 6:114; 10:37; 11:17; 12:111; 20:4; 26:192; 28:85-87; 32:2-3; 39:1-2; 40:2; 41:2; 45:2; 46:2; 55:1-2; 57:77-80; 69:40-43; 76:23. *description of, 15:1; 18:1-2; 19:96-97; 26:2; 27:1-2; 28:2; 31:2-3; 35:31-32; 36:69-70; 43:2-4; 44:58; 54:17; 69:51; 86:13-14. *the imperishable tablet [*al-lauḥ al-maḥfūẓ*], 85:21-22; see Revelation: [*ʾumm al-kitāb*] the source, or essence, of all. *its purpose, 2:185; 4:26; 6:19, 38, 92, 155-157; 7:2-3; 16:64, 102; 17:9-10; 18:2-4; 19:97; 20:2-3, 113; 27:76; 39:27-28, 55-58; 42:7; 98:1-3. *guidance, criterion, mercy and cure, 2:2, 97, 185; 5:15-16; 7:52, 203; 10:57; 11:17; 12:111; 16:89, 102; 17:82, 105; 27:1-2, 77; 29:51; 31:3; 39:41; 41:44; 45:20; 46:30. *revealed for all mankind, 12:104; 16:44; 17:89; 18:54; 39:41; 68:52; 74:31; 81:27-28. *as confirmation of earlier revelations, 2:41; 3:3; 5:48; 6:92; 10:37; 12:111; 26:196; 35:31; 46:12, 30. *its inimitability [*iʿyāz*], as proof of its divine origin, 2:23-24; 10:37-38; 11:13-14; 12:111; 17:88; 28:49-50; 53:33-34. *some messages clear by themselves, others allegorical, 3:7; App. I. *came down gradually, 3:3; 6:114; 16:89, 101-102; 17:82, 106; 25:32-33; 56:75-76; 76:23. *revealed in Arabic, 12:2; 13:37; 16:103; 19:97; 20:113; 26:193-195, 198-199; 41:3, 44; 42:7; 43:3; 44:58. *protected by God, 15:9; 56:77-79; 75:16-17; 85:21-22. *fully consistent within itself, free from contradictions and falsehood, 2:2; 4:82; 25:32; 39:23, 27-28; 41:41-42. *expounded with clarity, 11:1; 12:1-3, 111; 17:12, 41; 18:1-2; 25:33; 28:85; 29:49; 39:23; 41:3; 43:2. *easy to understand; to remember, 19:97; 44:58; 54:17, 22, 32, 40; 75:19. *recitation of, 7:204-205; 16:98; 17:45, 78; 20:114; 33:34; 46:29; 73:4, 20; 75:16-18. *as a reminder and admonition, 12:104; 16:44; 20:99; 21:10, 50; 29:51; 38:1; 50:45; 65:10; 69:48; 74:54; 80:11-12; 81:27-28. *to meditate upon it, 4:82; 38:29; 47:24. *considered irrelevant, 25:30. *rejection of, and objections raised by unbelievers, 15:90-91; 16:101, 103-105; 17:41, 45-46, 82-83, 94; 20:99-100; 21:2-6; 23:71; 25:4-9; 26:197-201; 28:48; 29:49; 30:58; 32:3; 34:8, 43; 38:7-8; 41:4-5; 42:24; 43:30-31; 46:7-8, 11; 47:25-26; 52:29-33; 68:51; 69:48-49; 74:18-25; 84:21-22. (See Abrogation; Prostration: verses of P. during Qurʾān recitation; Revelation.)

Rabbis and monks, 5:44, 63, 82; 9:34. *taken as lords beside God, 3:64; 9:30-31; see Ascribing divinity to other than God. (See Monastic asceticism.)

Rain, 2:265; 4:102; 11:52; 15:22; 31:34; 56:68-70; 88:17. *life-giving, 2:22, 164; 6:99; 7:57; 14:32; 16:10-11; 20:53; 22:63; 23:18-19; 27:60; 31:10; 35:27; 39:21; 42:28; 50:9; 78:14-16; 80:25. *with which God brings dead land to life, 16:65; 22:5; 25:48-49; 29:63; 30:24, 48-50; 32:27; 41:39; 43:11; 59:9-11. *sent down with due measure, 23:18; 43:11. *as a parable of the life of this world, 10:24; 18:45; 57:20. *in the parable of the Resurrection, 22:5; 30:48-50; 32:27; 36:33; 41:39; 43:11; 50:9-11. *in the parable of truth and falsehood, 13:17. *at Badr, 8:11. *of destruction, 7:84; 26:173; 27:58; 46:24-25; see Noah: the Deluge. (See Water.)

Ramadhān, 2:185; see Fasting.

Rass (ar-), 25:38; 50:12.

Reason, 12:108; 16:125; 33:72; 49:4. *messages for people who use their, 2:164; 13:4; 16:12-13, 67; 29:34-35; 30:24, 28; 45:5. *the Revelation as stimulus and criterion for, 2:73, 242; 3:118; 6:151; 12:2; 24:61; 40:67; 43:2-3; 57:17. *God forbids all that runs counter to, 16:90; 24:21; 29:45; 58:2. *Will you not use your reason?, 2:44, 76; 3:65; 6:32; 7:169; 10:16; 11:51; 12:109; 21:10, 67; 23:80; 36:62, 68; 37:133-138. *those who deny the truth will not use their, 2:170-171; 5:58, 103; 8:22; 10:42, 100; 12:39; 18:15; 25:44; 26:28; 27:60; 29:60, 63; 59:14; 67:10. (See Discernment; Messages of God: for people who use their reason…; Thought.)

Record of human actions: see Day of Resurrection: the record of human actions.

Reflection: see Thought.

Relatives, 2:180; 4:1, 7-8, 33; 8:41; 9:113; 35:18; 58:22; 59:7; 60:3; 70:11-13. *kind treatment to, 2:83, 177, 215; 4:8, 36; 16:90; 17:26; 24:22; 30:38; 42:23; 90:14-15. *duty to warn them, 20:132; 26:214; 66:6. *to be just, even against one's, 4:135; 5:106; 6:152; see Justice. (See Blood: ties of kinship; Parents.)

Remembering, 6:68; 12:15, 45, 85, 89; 18:83; 19:64; 25:73; 37:13; 38:32, 46; 50:7-8, 23, 32; 51:49; 54:17, 22, 32, 40; 56:71-73; 69:11-12; 87:9-11. *God's blessings and favour, 2:40, 47-61, 122-124, 231; 3:103; 5:7, 11, 20, 110; 7:69, 74, 86; 8:26; 14:6-7; 33:9; 35:3; 43:13. *calls to, 2:63, 200, 221, 269; 3:7; 6:80, 152; 7:3, 26, 57, 171; 8:38; 13:19; 16:90; 20:128; 24:1, 27; 28:51; 32:26; 33:34; 38:1; 39:9; 40:58; 87:9-10. *the Revelation as a reminder, 6:70; 11:114, 120; 15:6, 9; 16:44; 20:99; 21:2, 10, 24, 48-50; 23:71; 38:49; 80:11-12. *the example of the apostles, 19:2, 16, 41, 51-57; 21:84; 37:78-79, 108-109, 119-120, 129-130; 38:17, 41, 43, 45-49; 46:21. *in the Day of Judgement, 40:43-44; 44:13; 47:18; 75:13-15; 79:35; 89:2-3; 99:7-8. (See Forgetting; Remembrance of God.)

Remembrance of God, 2:114, 198-203; 5:4; 7:69, 201, 205; 8:2; 11:114; 24:36-38; 38:32; 57:16; 80:11-12; 87:14-15. *calls to the, 2:152, 203, 238-239; 20:14; 33:41-42; 51:55; 62:9-10; 63:9; 73:8; 76:25-26. *the greatest [good], 29:45. *houses raised for the, 2:114; 22:40; 24:36. *after sinning, or forgetting oneself, 3:135; 18:24. *in it hearts find rest, 13:28; 39:23. *frequent and abundant, 3:41; 7:205; 18:28; 20:33-34, 42; 26:227; 30:17-18; 33:21, 35, 41-42; 62:10. *in the night, 3:113; 25:64; 76:26. *in combat, 8:45. *standing, sitting and lying down, 3:191; 4:103; 25:64. *those negligent with the; those who are oblivious of, 4:142; 18:101; 20:124; 21:42; 23:110; 25:18;

39:22, 45; 41:51; 43:36; 53:29, 33; 58:19; 59:19; 72:17; 87:9-13. *Satan wants to turn you away from the, 5:91; 58:19. (See Prayer; Remembering.)

Repentance (Turning to God), 2:160, 222; 3:89; 7:143; 9:112; 17:25; 19:60; 21:95-97; 24:31; 25:70-71; 28:67; 34:9; 38:24, 34; 66:4-5; 75:29-31. ***calls to**, 2:54; 5:74; 11:3, 52; 61:90; 66:8. ***acceptable** to God, 2:160; 4:17; 5:39; 16:119. ***and God's pardon**, 3:89; 6:54; 7:153; 17:25; 20:82; 40:7. ***God** accepts, 2:37, 54; 4:16, 64; 5:71; 9:104, 118; 20:122: 40:3; 42:25; 49:12; 110:3; see Attributes of God's Perfection: the Acceptor of Repentance. ***unacceptable** at the hour of death, 4:18; 10:90-92; 23:99-100; 63:10-11; 75:28-31; see Death: agony, or nearness of. (See Day of Resurrection: belated repentance; Forgiveness (God's): after repentance; Supplications: for forgiveness.)

Reproach: see Blame.

Responsibility, 2:234, 240, 284; 5:105; 6:68-69; 7:6; 8:72; 14:4; 16:56, 93; 17:34-36; 21:23; 33:15; 75:36; 83:4-6; 102:8. ***the trust** accepted by man [*al-ʾamānah*], 8:27; 33:72. ***God does not burden** man with more than he is well able to bear: see Hardship and Ease. ***each one accountable** only for his/her actions, 2:134, 139, 141; 4:84; 6:70, 164; 24:11; 26:216; 28:55; 34:25; 42:15. ***no-one shall be made** to bear another's burden, 6:164; 17:15; 35:18; 39:7; 53:38. ***prophets** not sent as keepers of their peoples, 2:119; 4:80; 6:52, 66, 104, 107, 159; 10:41, 108; 11:86; 25:43; 42:6, 48; 80:7; see Apostles. ***whoever leads others astray**, is responsible for their errors, 11:98; 16:25; 29:13; 11:98. ***men shall take** full care of women, 4:34. (See Freedom of choice.)

Resurrection of the dead, 2:28, 259; 7:25; 10:4; 16:21; 17:50-51, 99; 21:21; 22:5-7, 66; 23:16; 28:85; 29:19-20; 29:19; 30:11, 40, 50; 31:28; 36:12, 48-53; 46:33; 50:20-22; 53:47; 67:15; 75:37-40; 80:22; 83:4-6; 85:13; 86:8. ***easy** for God, 29:19; 30:27; 50:44; 64:7. ***as God's bringing** dead land back to life, 7:57; 22:5; 30:19, 48-50; 32:27; 35:9; 48-50; 32:27; 41:39; 43:11; 50:9-11. ***by the divine** command -'Be', 16:39-40; 36:81-82. ***and Abraham**, 2:260. ***rejected** by unbelievers, 6:29; 11:7; 13:5; 16:38-40; 17:49-52, 98; 23:35-37, 81-83; 27:67-68; 32:10; 34:7; 36:48; 37:16-20; 44:34-36; 45:24-25; 46:17; 50:3-5; 56:47-50; 60:13; 64:7; 75:3-4. ***as miraculous sign** given to Jesus, 3:49; 5:110. ***as a metaphor**, 2:56; 6:60, 122; 57:16-17. (See Day of Resurrection; Death: death, resurrection and spiritual regeneration; Promises: of resurrection and judgement; Rain: in the parable of the Resurrection; Sleep: and awakening....)

Retaliation, 5:45; see Retribution (Just).

Retribution (Just) [*qiṣāṣ*], 2:178-179, 194; 16:126; 17:33; 22:60; 42:40-43; see Self-Defence.

Revelation [*al-kitāb; al-wāhy; āyātu-l·lāh*], 2:105-106, 129, 151, 213, 231; 3:44, 48, 79, 101; 4:51, 54, 153; 5:101, 110; 9:64, 86; 10:94; 11:17, 49; 12:102; 15:1; 17:85; 19:30; 21:45, 108; 28:51; 39:1-2, 23; 41:2; 42:15-17, 51-52; 52:2-3. *[***ʾUmm al-kitāb***] **the source**, or essence, of all, 3:7; 13:39; 43:4. ***must be accepted** in its entirety, 2:41, 91, 121, 177, 285; 3:7, 81, 84, 119; 4:47, 136, 162; 5:59, 66; 6:114; 11:17; 7:3; 29:46; 42:15. ***always confirms** earlier ones, 2:41, 89-91, 97, 101; 3:3; 4:47; 5:46, 48; 6:92; 10:37; 35:31; 43:45. ***purpose of**, 3:73; 4:165; 7:2, 203; 20:134; 39:55-58; 41:4. ***to be conveyed** to men, 2:42, 76, 146; 3:71, 187; 10:16; 11:12; 16:125; 18:27; 29:45. ***as guidance**, mercy and reminder, 3:3-4, 73; 5:44, 46; 6:88, 154; 7:52, 154, 203; 11:17; 14:1; 17:2; 21:2, 48-50; 23:49; 28:43; 40:53-54; 45:20; 46:12; see Remembering: the Revelation as a reminder. ***as a means** of insight, 6:104; 7:203; 17:102; 28:43; 45:20. ***entrusted** to the prophets, 2:213; 4:163-165; 20:13; 21:7, 25; 42:13, 51; 43:45; 57:25-27; 72:26-28. ***the angels** of, 2:97; 16:2, 102; 19:17, 64; 26:192-194; 53:5-9; 97:4. ***continuity of**, 3:84; 4:163; 5:44-48; 6:83-92; 11:17; 13:38-39; 16:43-44; 21:48-50; 26:196; 29:27; 32:23; 41:43; 42:3, 13; 46:12; 53:36-56; 57:25-27; 87:18-19. ***duty to judge** according to, 2:213; 4:105; 5:44-45, 47-50; 6:114; 9:29; 24:47. ***the Prophet** follows only what is revealed to him, 6:50, 106; 7:203; 10:15, 109; 33:2; 46:9. ***abrogation** of earlier revelations, 2:106; 13:39; see Abrogation. ***rejection of**, 2:89-91, 101, 144-146, 170, 176; 3:4, 19-20, 70, 72-73, 98, 184; 5:64, 68; 6:89-91; 10:15; 18:29; 21:45; 30:56; 34:31, 43-45; 35:25; 36:15; 39:59; 40:35, 56; 41:4-5, 45; 67:9. (See Corruption of revealed texts; Gospel; Inspiration; Israel (children of); Jews and Christians; Judgement (Sound); Messages of God; Moses: receives the divine writ; Muḥammad: inspired with Revelation; Qurʾān; Torah; Truth: the Revelation sets forth and confirms the.)

Revelations (Earlier, followers of): see Jews and Christians.

Reward: see Believers: reward promised to; Day of Resurrection: reward and punishment; Good Deeds; Life; Paradise; Patience; Striving (for God's sake): reward of.

Righteous (the) [*aṣ-ṣāliḥūn*], 3:21; 4:69; 5:84; 7:181, 196; 9:75; 12:101; 13:23; 29:9; 40:8; 63:10; 65:11; 66:4; 72:11. ***endowed** with insight: see Discernment. ***the truly** virtuous: see Virtue. ***prophets** described as of, 2:130; 3:39, 46; 6:85; 16:122; 21:75, 86; 26:83; 27:19; 29:27; 37:100, 112; 66:10; 68:50. ***description of**, 3:113-114; 7:159, 181; 11:116; 13:19-22; 33:35; 90:11-18. ***will inherit** the earth, 21:105. (See Forerunners; Righteousness; Virtue.)

Righteousness, 18:66; 21:51. ***those who have** attained to: [*aṣḥābul-maymanah; aṣḥābul-yamīn*: lit., people of the *right side*], 56:7-8, 27-40, 90-91; 74:38-40; 90:17-18. ***those who do** what is right and just, 23:51; 28:80; 33:31; 34:37; 41:33, 46; 45:15; 65:11. ***the path** of, 7:146; 9:100; 38:22, 26; 72:14. (See Muslims: to enjoin what is right...; Right; Righteous (the); Straight Way (the); Supplications: for rectitude; Virtue; Ways: of good and ways of evil.)

Right (Side, or hand), 7:17; 16:48; 18:17-18; 20:17, 69; 34:15; 37:28, 93; 50:17-18; 57:12; 66:8; 69:44-47; 70:36-37. ***people** of *the right side*: see Righteousness: those who have attained to. ***those whose** record shall be placed in their R. hand, 17:71; 69:19; 84:7-9; see Day of Resurrection: the record of human actions. ***the right-hand slope** of Mount Sinai, 19:52; 20:80; 28:30; see Sinai. (See God: the hand of; Left-side.)

Sabbath, 4:154. ***ordained only** for those who disagreed about Abraham, 16:124. ***the Sabbath-breakers**, 2:65-66; 4:47; 7:163-166.
Sabians (followers of John the Baptist), 2:62; 5:69; 22:17.
Sacrifices, 5:2; 22:27-37. ***neither their flesh** nor their blood reach God, 22:37. ***those offered** to other than God, loathsome, 2:173; 5:3, 90; 6:145; 16:115; 22:30; see Ascribing divinity to other than God. (See Abraham.)
Ṣafā and Marwah, 2:158.
Ṣāliḥ, 7:73-79; see Thamūd.
Salvation [*as-salām*], 5:15-16; 59:23. ***faith and** righteousness lead to, 2:38, 62, 112, 262, 274, 277; 4:39-40; 5:69; 6:48; 7:35; 10:62-64; 16:96-97; 20:112; 43:68-70; 46:13. (See Paradise.)
Samaritan (the), 20:85-98.
Samuel (prophet; not named), 2:246-248.
Sarah (wife of Abraham: not named), 11:71-73; 51:29-30.
Satan (Devils), 4:83, 117-120; 5:90-91; 6:68; 7:175; 19:44; 37:65. ***declares his mission** before God, 4:117-118; 7:16-17; 15:39-40; 17:62; 38:82-83. ***and the Fall** of Adam and Eve, 2:36; 7:20-22, 27; 20:120. ***his guile** and deceit, 2:168-169, 275; 3:155; 4:60, 119-120; 5:90-91; 6:68; 7:21-22; 14:22; 22:52-53. ***an open foe** to man, 2:168-169, 208; 6:142; 7:22; 12:5; 17:53; 18:50; 20:117; 28:15; 35:6; 36:60; 43:62. ***to seek** God's protection against, 3:36; 7:200-202; 16:98; 23:97-98; 41:36; 114:*passim*. ***threatens with poverty** and bids you to be niggardly, 2:268. ***seeking God's** protection against, 3:36; 7:200-202; 16:98; 23:97-98; 41:36; 114:*passim*. ***his guile** is weak, 4:76. ***makes evil doings** seem goodly, 6:43; 8:48; 16:63; 27:24; 29:38; 41:25; 47:25. ***he abandons those** he has lead astray, and declares himself God-fearing, 8:48; 59:16. ***has no real power** over men, 14:22; 15:42; 16:99-100; 17:65; 34:20-21; 58:10. ***tries to sow discord** and hatred among men, 5:91; 17:53; 58:10. ***is close to** those who deny the truth, 4:38, 119; 7:27, 30; 16:63; 19:45. ***as evil impulses**, 2:14; 7:30, 200-202; 22:53; 23:97-98; 41:25; 43:36-39. ***his party**, hosts and tribe, 3:175; 4:38; 7:18, 27; 17:64; 18:50; 19:44-45; 26:94-95; 35:6; 58:19. ***as evil forces**, evil spirits or satanic forces, 6:112, 128; 7:27; 15:17; 19:83; 22:3; 26:210-212, 221-223; 37:7; 38:37-38; 67:5; 81:25; see Deities (False): forces of evil. (See Fear of God: Satan declares himself fearful of God; Iblīs; Promises: Satan's deluding; Ways: the footsteps of Satan.)
Saul [*Ṭālūt*], 2:246-251.
Sayings: see Words.
Scheming: by unbelievers, 6:123-124; 7:123; 10:21; 11:55; 14:46; 16:26, 45; 27:48-50; 34:33; 35:10, 43; 40:45; 71:22-23; 86:15-17. ***against** Jesus, 3:54. ***against** Muḥammad, 4:81, 108; 7:195; 8:30; 9:48; 58:8-10. ***God's**, 3:54; 7:99, 182-183; 8:30; 10:21; 12:76, 100; 13:42; 27:50. ***of the brothers** of Joseph, 12:5, 102.
Sea (Ocean): travelling by, 10:22; 16:14; 31:31-32; 42:32-33; 45:12; see Ships. ***food and** ornaments from the, 16:14; 35:12. (See Water: the two great bodies of.)
Secret, 4:83; 5:52; 7:187; 20:62; 66:3; 69:18; 72:26-27; 86:9. ***love-companions**, 4:25; 5:5. (See Manifest and Hidden.)
Sects, 21:92-93; 30:32. ***among Jews** and Christians, 3:105; 6:159; 19:37; 43:63-65; 45:17. ***among Muslims**, 6:159; 23:53. ***believers** to remain united, 3:103-105; 21:92; 23:52-54. (See Day of Resurrection: clarification of every matter; Discrepancies; Satan: an open foe to man; tries to sow discord....)
Self-Defence, 16:126. ***God helps** those fighting in, 9:13-15; 17:33; 22:60. ***as deterrent** to corruption and oppression, 2:251; 8:73; 22:40; 42:39-42; see Injustice: duty to fight against. ***divine sanction** to fight in, 2:190-195; 4:91; 9:12-15; 22:39-40; 26:227. (See Aggression; Fighting.)
Servants of God, 3:35. ***all men** and women are, 2:186, 207, 221; 3:15; 4:118; 5:118; 6:61, 88; 7:128; 9:104; 10:107; 14:11, 31; 15:49; 17:5, 17, 53; 19:61, 93; 20:77; 23:109; 26:52; 27:15; 29:56; 30:48; 34:9, 13, 39; 35:45; 37:167-169; 39:7, 10, 16, 36, 46, 53; 40:44; 42:25, 27, 52; 44:18, 23; 72:19; 96:9-10. ***apostles** and prophets described as, 2:23, 90; 4:172; 8:41; 12:24; 16:2; 17:1, 3; 18:1; 19:2, 30; 20:40-41; 25:1; 27:59; 37:79-81, 109-111, 120-124, 130-132, 171-172; 38:17, 30, 41, 44-45; 40:15; 43:59; 53:10; 54:9; 57:9; 66:10. ***the true**, 15:40; 17:65; 18:65; 19:63; 21:105; 25:63, 72; 27:19; 35:28, 31-32; 37:40-42, 74, 127-128, 159-160; 38:82-83; 39:17-18; 42:23; 43:68-70; 76:6; 89:28-30. ***the angels** as honoured, 4:172; 21:19-20, 26.
Shadows (Shade), 2:57, 210; 7:160, 171; 25:45-46; 28:24; 31:32; 35:19-21. ***prostrate** to God in submission, 13:15; 16:48. ***blissful** shade of Paradise, 4:57; 13:35; 56:28-30; 76:14; 77:41. ***dark S.** of punishment, 56:42-44; 77:29-31. ***darkness** will overshadow the faces of evildoers, 10:26-27; 75:24; 80:40-41. (See Light: and darkness.)
Sheba, 34:15-19. ***the queen** of, 27:22-44.
Ships (Boats), 2:164; 6:97; 16:14, 16; 17:70; f23:22; 27:63; 36:41-42; 40:80; 42:32-33; 55:24. ***made subservient** to man's needs, 14:32; 17:66; 22:65; 30:46; 31:31; 35:12; 43:12-14; 45:12. ***the faith of people** confronted with great danger, 6:63; 10:22; 17:66-70; 29:65; 31:32; 36:43-44. ***and Al-Khaḍir**, 18:71, 79. ***and Jonah**, 37:139-142. ***Noah's Ark**: see Ark.

Shu^cayb, 7:85-93; 11:84-95; 26:176-191; 29:36-37; see Madyan.

Signs (Marks; Signals; Tokens), 2:273; 7:46-48; 12:35; 24:33; 33:59; 48:29. ***of God** for mankind, 2:259; 10:92; 21:30-33; 30:50; 36:33-44; 41:37, 39; 42:29, 32-33; 54:15; see Messages of God: as divine portents, or wonders; Miracles. ***that God** grants to His apostles, 3:41; 5:114; 7:73, 104-108, 132-133; 11:64; 19:10; 26:153-156; 28:31-32; see Miracles. ***for the believers**; for those who use their reason, etc., 2:118; 3:13, 118; 15:75-77; 29:34-35; 48:20; 51:20-21. ***for the children** of Israel, 2:248; 44:30-33. ***of the Last** Hour, 47:18; 54:1-2. ***marks of the blessed**; of the doomed, 3:106-107; 55:39-41; 75:22-25; 80:38-42; 83:22-24. ***of hypocrites**, 2:204-206; 3:166-168; 4:137, 142-143; 47:30; 63:2, 4. ***those who** would not believe though they may see every sign of the truth, 6:25; 7:146; 10:96-97; 12:105; see Denying the truth: they reject even the most obvious. ***idolatrous** cattle ear-marking, 4:119; 5:103. (See Messages of God.)

Silence, 7:204; 17:110; 19:26; 46:29.

Silver, 3:14; 9:34; 43:33-34; 76:15-16, 21; see Metals.

Sin, 4:20, 29-32, 107-112; 5:2, 29; 6:31, 120; 7:33; 11:89; 19:83; 24:11; 25:77; 28:78; 33:57-58; 40:35; 42:37; 49:12; 58:8-9; 74:42-47. ***which God** does not forgive, 4:48, 116. ***injustice** and wrong only to oneself, 2:57; 4:97, 111; 7:160, 177; 9:36; 18:35; 28:16; 29:40; 34:19; 39:53; see Injustice. ***cause** of all affliction; of the destruction of communities, 3:155; 5:49; 6:6, 45, 164; 7:4-5, 100; 8:52-54; 29:40; 40:21; 69:9-10; 71:25; 77:16-18; 91:14; see Communities: destroyed or punished.... ***direct witnesses** of man's, 36:65; 41:20-23. ***of men**, nobody knows it like God, 4:108; 17:17; 25:58; 31:16; 41:22-23. ***charity** as atonement for, 2:271; 5:45. ***the most abominable** sins, 2:278-279; 4:50-52; 7:33; 8:15-16; 9:93; 17:31-33; 31:13; 33:57; 42:37; 56:46. ***God effaces** lesser sins if the great ones are avoided, 4:31; 53:32. ***those who lead others astray** promising them to take upon themselves their sins, 29:12-13; see Astray (to lead). (See Atonement; Evil; Forgiveness; Punishment; Responsibility.)

Sinai (Mount), 23:20; 52:1; 95:2. ***Moses sees a fire** on the slope of, 20:10; 27:7; 28:29-30. ***Moses' appointment** on, 2:51; 7:142-143; 19:52; 20:80; 28:44, 46; see Moses: God speaks with. ***raised over the heads** of the Israelites, 2:63, 93; 4:154; 7:171.

Sirius (brightest star), 53:49.

Slaves, 2:178; 12:30; 16:75; 37:139-140. ***freeing them** as atonement, pious action and allocation of *zakāh*, 2:177; 4:92; 5:89; 9:60; 58:3; 90:12-13. ***manumission** of, 24:33. ***marriage** with slave-girls, 4:3, 25; 24:32. ***good treatment** to, 4:36; 16:71. ***do not force** slave-girls into prostitution, 24:33. ***punishment halved** to slave-girls for adultery, 4:25. ***slavery** of the children of Israel, 23:47; 26:22; 37:114-115. (See Captives.)

Sleep, 7:4, 97; 30:23; 51:17; 68:19. ***neither slumber** nor S. overtake God, 2:255. ***and awakening**, as symbols of death and resurrection, 25:47; 39:42; 78:9; see Death: death, resurrection and spiritual regeneration; Resurrection: as a metaphor. ***the Men** of the Cave, 18:11-12, 18-19. (See Night; Night and Day.)

Sodom and Gomorrah (not named): destruction of, 11:81-82; 15:61-77; 29:31-34; 37:133-138. (See Homosexuality.)

Solomon, 2:102; 4:163; 6:84; 21:78-82; 27:15-44; 38:30-40. ***God's favour upon**, 21:81-82; 27:15-16, 19; 34:12-13; 38:34-40. ***his wisdom**, 21:78-79. ***and the ants**, 27:17-19. ***and the hoopoe**, 27:20-29. ***and the queen** of Sheba, 27:22-44. ***and his horses**, 38:31-33. ***death of**, 34:14. (See David; Temple: of Jerusalem.)

Sorcery (Magic; Spellbinding eloquence), 2:102; 7:116; 20:69; 113:4. ***prophets** are accused of, 5:110; 6:7; 7:132; 10:2, 76-77; 17:101; 20:57-58, 63-71; 21:3; 26:34-35, 49; 28:36; 38:4; 40:24; 43:49; 51:39, 52. ***truth** dismissed as, 10:76-77; 11:7; 15:14-15; 27:13; 34:43; 37:14-15; 43:30; 46:7; 52:15; 61:6; 74:23-24. (See Knowledge: occult pursuits; Pharaoh: sorcerers of.)

Soul (Human being; Inner self) [*nafs* (pl. *anfus*); *rūḥ*]: as the totality of human being, 2:223; 3:30; 4:1; 6:93; 9:55, 85, 118; 16:111; 21:35; 50:17-23; 74:38; 78:38; see Man: not burdened by God with more than he is well able to bear. ***that incites** to evil, 4:128; 5:80; 12:53; 50:16; 79:40. ***self-reproaching**, 75:2. ***serene** and pleased in Paradise, 21:101-102; 41:31; 43:71; 89:27-30; see Paradise. (See Evil: turns against its doers; Good deeds: good is its own reward; Injustice: wrongdoers sin against themselves; Inspiration; Spirit.)

Soundness: see Steadfastness.

Spending on others, 2:3, 43, 83, 177, 215, 261-274, 276-277; 3:92; 4:8, 162; 5:12; 8:2-3; 13:22; 16:90; 17:26-29; 22:35; 25:67; 27:3; 28:54; 30:39; 32:16; 42:38; 51:19; 57:7, 10; 63:10; 64:16; 70:24-25; 73:20; 92:5-7, 17-21; 98:5. ***in God's cause**, 2:195, 219, 254, 261-274; 3:17; 4:97; 8:60; 9:79, 98-99, 121; 14:31; 35:29; 47:38; 57:10. ***in times of plenty** and in times of need, 3:134; 76:8; 90:13-16. ***God always** replaces it, 34:39. ***a goodly loan** offered unto God, 2:245; 57:11, 18; 64:17; 73:20. ***as a means** of purification, 9:103; 92:17-21. ***to speak kindly**, when one is unable to give, 2:263; 17:28. ***offerings** given for the sake of God (*ṣadaqāt*), 9:58-60. ***Satan** bids you to be niggardly, 2:268. ***to be seen** and praised by men, 2:264; 4:38-39. ***to lead** others astray, 8:36. ***those** who refuse, 16:71; 36:47; 41:6-7; 47:38; 63:7; see Niggardliness. ***by hypocrites**, rejected, 9:53-54; see Good deeds: done to be seen by others. (See Charity; Good deeds; Niggardliness; Purifying dues.)

Spider, 29:41; see Insects.

Spirit (God's): breathed into man, 15:29; 32:9; 38:72. ***breathed** into Mary, 21:91; 66:12. ***Jesus**, a S. created by God, 4:171. ***as holy** inspiration, 2:87; 16:102; 17:85; see Inspiration.

Spouses (Mates), 2:102, 226-237; 16:72; 23:6; 30:21; 40:8; 58:3-4; 64:14; 70:11-12, 30; 80:36; see Wives.

Standard of right and wrong (the): see Judgement (Sound).
Steadfastness (Firmness; Soundness), 3:152; 16:94; 20:115. ***a support** most unfailing, 2:256; 3:101; 31:22. ***God gives** firmness to the believers, 8:12; 11:120; 14:24-27; 17:74; 22:41; 47:7. ***calls to**, 4:135-136; 5:8; 8:45; 10:105; 19:65; 30:30, 43; 46:13, 35; 48:29; 68:8-13; 70:32-33; 72:16; 94:7-8. ***supplications** for, 2:250; 3:147. ***the Revelation**, a source of, 16:102; 74:31. ***inner soundness** in Paradise, 19:62; 56:25-26.
Straight Way (the) [*aṣ-ṣirāṭ al-mustaqīm*], 1:6-7; 2:150, 186; 5:105; 7:16; 10:35; 17:9; 18:13; 23:49, 73-74; 28:22; 32:3; 43:10, 49; 46:30; 82:27-29. ***the way** of your Sustainer is straight, 3:51; 6:125-126, 153; 11:56; 15:39-42; 19:36; 36:60-61; 43:61-62, 64. ***only God** guides to, 2:142, 198, 213, 272; 4:66-68, 175; 5:15-16; 6:39, 87, 153, 161; 7:43; 10:25, 35, 43; 14:12; 16:9, 37, 104, 121; 17:97; 18:17; 19:76; 22:54; 24:46; 29:69; 33:4; 34:50; 36:3-5, 66; 37:117-118; 42:52-53; 48:2, 20. ***those** who are on, 2:137, 156-157; 3:20, 101; 6:56, 82; 10:89; 16:76; 20:82; 22:67; 24:54; 34:24; 41:30; 42:15; 43:43; 57:26-27; 67:22; 68:7; 72:16. ***follow it**, for your own good, 10:108; 17:15; 27:92. ***those who go**, or lead others, astray: see Astray, (to go); (to lead). (See Guidance; Jews and Christians: claim that only they are on the right path; Righteousness: the path of; Ways.)
Striving (for God's sake), 3:186; 31:17; 42:43; 53:39-41; 80:23; 90:11-18. ***in God's cause**, 4:95; 8:72; 9:20, 41, 81; 22:78; 49:15; 61:11; 94:7-8; see Fighting: as striving in God's cause; Forsaking the domain of evil. ***for the life** to come, 3:133-136; 17:19. ***only according** to one's capacity: see Man: not burdened by God with more than he is well able to bear. ***reward of**, 3:136, 195; 4:95-96; 17:19, 21; 18:30; 20:15; 29:69; 39:74; 53:40-41; 88:9-10.
Succour (God's): see Aid; Believers: God guides, helps...; Fighting; Patience; Victory. ***those who** will not obtain, 3:21-22, 56; 13:33-34; 86:10.
Suckling, 22:2; 31:14; 46:15. ***and divorced** mothers, 2:233; 65:6. ***of Moses**, 20:40; 28:7-12.
Suicide, 2:195.
Sun, 2:258; 6:78, 96; 7:54; 10:5; 12:4; 13:2; 18:17, 86, 90; 21:33; 22:18; 25:45; 29:61; 31:29; 35:13; 36:38, 40; 37:5; 39:5; 41:37; 55:5, 17; 70:40; 71:16; 75:9; 78:13; 81:1; 91:1. ***subservient** to man, 14:33; 16:12. ***indicates** the times of prayer, 11:114; 17:78; 20:130; 11:114; 50:39. ***-worship**, 27:24; 41:37.
Sunnah: see Example; Wisdom: the prophetic *sunnah* as 'the wisdom'.
Sunnat Allāh: see God: God's unchangeable way.
Supplications to God, 3:26-27, 190-195; 4:32; 7:189; 9:129; 10:22; 14:38; 31:32; 37:143-144; 39:8; 40:13-14, 60. ***how to supplicate**, 3:17; 7:29, 55-56; 11:46-47; 17:110-111; 51:18; see Forgiveness: Asking God's forgiveness: for hypocrites and unbelievers, is wrong and useless. ***do not invoke** other than God, 10:106-107; 13:14; 22:12-13; 25:68; 26:213; 28:88; 29:17; 40:14; 72:18. ***for forgiveness**, 2:285-286; 3:16, 147, 193; 7:23, 151; 11:47; 14:41; 23:28, 109, 118; 28:16; 40:7-9; 59:10; 60:5; 66:8; 71:28; see Repentance. ***for God's mercy** and grace, 2:286; 3:8; 7:56-57, 151, 155; 18:10; 23:109, 118. ***for His acceptance** and favour, 2:127-128; 5:83-84; 14:40; 27:19; 46:15. ***for protection** against punishment, 2:201, 286; 3:16, 191-192; 7:47; 23:93-94; 25:65-66. ***for succour** against those who deny the truth, 2:250, 286; 3:147; 10:85-86; 21:112; 23:26, 39; 26:169; 28:21; 29:30; 54:10; 60:5; 66:11. ***for rectitude**, 18:10, 24; 46:15. ***for patience**, 2:250; 7:126. ***for firmness** and strength, 2:250; 3:147; 17:80. ***for knowledge**, 20:114. ***upon entering or leaving** a situation, or a course of action, 17:80. ***for the good** in this life and the Hereafter, 2:201; 7:156; 28:24. ***for the Paradise** promised, 3:194; 40:8. ***for a death** like that of the righteous; in surrender to God, 3:193; 7:126; 12:101. ***asking** for God's guidance, 1:6-7; 2:129; 3:8; 6:77; 14:35-36; 23:29. ***for our parents**, 14:41; 17:24; 71:28. ***for rightly-guided** wives and children, 3:38; 7:189; 14:35, 40; 25:74; 37:100; 46:15. ***for God's** provision: see Provision. ***when starting** on a journey, 43:13-14. ***of gratitude**, 14:39; 23:28; 27:19; 46:15. ***against oppression**, 4:75. ***against evil** impulses, 7:200-202; 23:97-98; 41:36. ***against evil**, 113:1-5. ***against Satan**, 3:36; 114:1-6; see Satan: seeking God's protection against. ***of Adam** and Eve, 7:23. ***of Noah** 11:41, 45, 47; 23:26, 28-29; 26:117-118; 54:10; 71:26-28. ***of Abraham**, 2:126-129; 14:35-41; 26:83-89; 37:100; 60:4-5. ***of Lot**, 26:169; 29:30. ***of Job**, 21:83; 38:41-42. ***of Jonah**, 21:87. ***of Joseph**, 12:33, 101. ***of Shuʿayb**, 7:89. ***of Moses**, 5:25; 7:151, 155-156; 10:88; 20:25-35; 28:16-17, 21-22, 24. ***of Pharaoh's wife**, 66:11. ***of Pharaoh's** magicians, 7:126. ***of Solomon**, 27:19; 38:35. ***of Zachariah**, 3:38; 19:4-6; 21:89. ***of Jesus**, 5:114, 118. ***of Jesus'** disciples, 3:53. ***of Muḥammad**, 9:129. ***of angels** for the believers, 40:7-9. ***of believers** in the Day of Judgement, 66:8. ***in misfortune**, or danger, 19:18; see Misfortune: man invokes God in; Ships: the faith of people confronted with great danger. ***God's response** to, 2:186; 3:195; 6:63; 7:156-157; 8:9, 12; 10:89; 11:61; 12:34; 14:34, 39; 19:4; 21:84, 88, 90; 27:62; 28:16; 38:36-40, 42; 42:25-26. (See Prayer: turning to God.)
Surrender to God [*al-islām*], 2:112, 128, 208; 3:64, 80, 102; 4:125; 6:14, 71, 163; 7:126; 9:74; 11:14; 12:101; 16:81, 89, 102; 21:108; 22:34, 78; 27:31, 38, 42, 44, 81, 91; 28:53; 29:46; 30:53; 31:22; 33:22, 35, 56; 37:103; 39:12, 22, 54; 40:66; 41:33; 43:69; 46:15; 49:14; 51:36; 61:7; 66:5; 68:35; 72:14. ***only** religion before God, 3:19-20, 85; 5:3; 6:125. ***religion** of all prophets, 2:131-133, 136; 3:67, 84; 5:44; 10:72, 84; 42:13. ***proffered by early** Christians, 3:52; 5:111. ***belated**, of the doomed, 10:90; 15:2; 16:28, 87; 37:26-27. ***all creation** surrendered to God, 2:116; 3:83; 13:15; 16:48-50;

22:18; 27:87; 30:26; see God: all things and beings prostrate before. (See Muslims.)

Suspicion: see Conjectures.

Sustainer: see God: Sustainer: ....

Sustenance: see Provision (God's).

Suwāᶜ (deity of Noah's people), 71:23.

Tabūk (Expedition to), 9:38-59, 81-99, 117-122.

Ṭāghūt: see Evil: forces of.

Tax: see Exemption tax; Purifying dues.

Tayammum (ablution with pure dust), 4:43; 5:6.

Temple, see Kaᶜbah. ***Temple** of Jerusalem, 17:1, 7; see Solomon. (See House of worship.)

Term set by God, 6:67; 9:4; 17:99; 18:98; 22:5; 30:8; 44:40; 46:3; 77:12. ***of life** for His creatures, 3:145; 6:2, 60, 98, 128; 7:185; 11:3, 6; 14:10; 16:61; 20:129; 22:33; 29:5; 35:37; 39:42; 40:67; 63:10-11; 71:4. ***each community** has its, 7:34; 10:49; 15:5; 23:43. ***punishment** postponed for a, 3:178; 7:182-183; 10:11; 11:8, 103-104; 18:58-59; 29:53; 35:45; 42:14; 68:44-45; 72:25. ***for the orbits** of sun and moon, 13:2; 31:29; 35:13; 39:5.

Thamūd (Ṣāliḥ's people), 7:73-79; 9:70; 11:61-68, 95; 14:9; 17:59; 22:42; 25:38; 26:141-158; 27:45-53; 29:38; 38:13; 40:31; 41:13-18; 50:12; 51:43-45; 53:51; 54:23-31; 69:4-5; 85:17-18; 89:6-13; 91:11-15. (See Camels.)

Thought (Considering; Reflection), 2:225; 5:89; 20:44; 25:62; 35:37; 40:13. ***imparted** by God to man, 16:4; 36:77; 55:1-4; see Language. ***the Revelation** as stimulus and criterion for, 2:219, 266; 7:176; 14:24-25, 52; 16:44; 17:41; 25:50; 26:46; 28:43; 38:29; 39:27; 44:58; 59:21. ***clear messages** for people who reflect, 10:24; 13:3; 16:10-13, 69; 23:30; 30:21; 39:42; 45:13. ***a most** purifying, 21:49; 23:60; 38:46. ***calls to**, 4:82; 6:50; 7:184-185; 10:3; 11:24, 30; 16:17, 76; 23:85; 27:62; 30:8; 32:4; 34:46; 36:1-2; 37:86-87, 151-155; 39:29; 41:52; 43:2; 46:4, 10; 47:24; 56:62; 69:40-42; 81:24; see Oaths: divine O. and calls to reflection; Parables. ***Have you** ever considered...?, 10:50, 59-60; 16:48, 79; 19:77; 25:43-44; 26:7, 75-76, 205-207; 28:71-72; 35:40; 39:38; 45:23; 53:19-20, 33-34; 56:58-59, 63-64, 68-69, 71-72; 107:1-3. ***God knows** your most secret thoughts, 9:78; 13:10; 43:80; 47:26. ***divine** punishment as stimulus to, 7:130; 8:57; see Punishment: so that men might mend their ways. ***wrong**, unworthy or evil thoughts, 3:154, 169; 5:52, 70-71; 7:30, 43; 11:92; 14:42, 47; 15:47; 21:3, 87; 25:30; 28:39; 33:10; 36:78; 41:22-23; 48:12; 51:52-53; 59:10; 72:4-7; 74:18-20; 84:13-14; see Opinions: errant views. (See Discernment; Inspiration; Messages of God: for people who reason; who reflect; Reason.)

Throne: of God's omnipotence [*al-ᶜarsh*], 7:54; 10:3; 11:7; 9:129; 13:2; 20:5; 23:86, 116; 25:59; 32:4; 39:75; 40:7; 57:4; 69:17; 81:20; 85:15-16; see *Āyah*. ***Solomon's**, 38:34. ***of the queen** of Sheba, 27:23, 38-42.

Time, 45:24; 76:1. ***reckoning of**, 2:189; 6:96; 10:5; 14:33; 16:12; 17:12; 55:5. ***a day in God's sight** is like a thousand years; like fifty thousand years, 22:47; 70:4. ***taken in the creation** of the heavens and the earth, 7:54; 10:3; 11:7; 25:59; 32:4; 41:9; 50:38; 57:4. ***the flight of**, 23:114; 76:27; 103:1. ***an instant**; the smallest fraction of, 7:34; 10:49; 16:61, 77; 27:39-40; 34:30; 38:15. ***its perception** after resurrection, 2:259; 10:45; 17:52; 20:102-104; 23:112-114; 30:55; 46:35; 79:46. (See Day; Denying the truth: God gives them free rein for a while; Months; Term set by God.)

Torah, 3:3-4, 65, 93; 5:43-46, 66, 68; 9:111; 46:30; 48:29; 61:6; 62:5. ***and Jesus**, 3:48, 50; 5:110; 61:6. ***Prophet Muḥammad** described in the, 7:157. (See Abrogation; Israel (children of); Moses.)

Transactions: see Commerce; Justice.

Travel on the earth, 9:121; 22:46; 29:20; 34:18-19; 67:15; 71:19-20. ***and behold** what happened to those who denied the truth, 3:137; 6:11; 12:109; 16:36; 27:69; 30:9, 42; 35:44; 40:21, 82; 47:10. ***shortening** prayers, 4:101.

Tree, 16:68; 27:60; 28:30; 31:27; 36:80; 48:18; 55:6; 56:72. ***forbidden** to Adam and Eve, 2:35; 7:19-22; 20:120. ***parable** of the good tree and the bad, 14:24-26. ***of deadly fruit**, 17:60; 37:62-66; 44:43-46; 56:52-53. (See Plants and Trees.)

Trench (Battle of the), 33:9-27.

Trials (Tests from God; Temptation), 2:143, 155-156, 214; 3:140-141, 186; 5:48, 94; 6:165; 7:155, 163, 168; 8:17; 9:49, 126; 10:14; 11:7; 16:92; 23:30; 27:47; 29:2-3, 10; 33:11; 34:21; 44:17-18; 47:31; 49:3; 57:25; 67:2; 68:17-18, 33; 74:31; 76:2-3; 90:4. ***as purification**, 3:140-142, 154. ***beauty** created as a test, 18:7; 20:131. ***with blessings** and afflictions, 7:94-95, 168; 21:35; 23:76; 39:49-52; 72:16-17; 89:15-16. ***defeat as**, 3:152-154. ***wealth** and children are a, 8:28; 17:64; 18:7; 20:131; 64:15. ***God tests men** through one another, 6:53; 25:20; 47:4. ***Abraham's**, 2:124; 37:102-106. ***Moses'**, 20:40. ***of the children** of Israel, 2:49, 249; 7:141; 14:6; 20:85; 44:30-33. ***Joseph's**, 12:23-24. ***David's**, 38:24. ***Solomon's**, 27:40; 38:34. (See Persecution (Religious); Satan: declares his mission before God.)

Trinity: see Christianity.

Trust [*ʾamānah*]: see Responsibility.

Trust in God [*tawakkul*], 7:89; 9:129; 11:56, 88, 13:30; 39:38; 42:10; 60:4; 67:29. ***believers** are called to, 3:122, 159-160; 4:81; 5:11, 23; 8:49, 64; 9:51; 10:84-85; 11:123; 12:67; 14:11-12; 16:42, 99; 25:58; 26:217; 27:79; 33:3, 48; 42:36; 58:10; 64:13; 65:3.

Truth [*al-ḥaqq*], 2:71, 109; 3:86; 7:159, 169, 181; 8:5-6; 9:48; 12:51; 13:17; 15:8; 19:34; 23:71; 25:33; 38:84-85; 48:27; 50:42; 57:16; 103:3. ***the T. that** comes from your Sustainer, 2:146-147, 149, 170; 3:60; 4:170; 10:94, 108; 11:17; 18:29; 22:54; 28:48, 53; 47:2-3. ***as fulfilment** of God's will, 6:73; 14:22; 15:55, 64. ***God bears** witness to the, 3:59-60, 62; 27:79; 32:3; 33:4; 41:53; 51:23; 56:95; 69:51. ***as justice**, 6:57; 7:8, 89; 21:112; 34:26; 38:22, 26; 39:69, 75; 40:20, 78.

*the apostles are sent with the, 2:119; 4:170; 7:43, 53, 104-105; 11:120; 13:1, 19; 17:105; 23:70; 34:6; 35:24; 37:37; 43:29. *God proves the T. to be true, 7:118; 8:7-8; 10:82; 42:24. *the religion of, 9:29, 33; 48:28; 61:9. *the Revelation sets forth and confirms the, 2:41, 176, 213, 252; 3:3, 108; 4:105; 5:27, 48; 6:114; 16:102; 28:3; 35:31; 37:37; 39:2, 41; 42:17; 45:6. *The Day of Ultimate, 6:30; 7:44; 28:75; 43:89; 46:34; 69:1-3; 78:39. *God crushes falsehood with the, 17:81; 21:18; 34:48-49. *conjecture can never be a substitute for, 10:35-36; 53:28. *rejection of, 2:42, 91, 146-147; 3:71; 6:4-5, 66, 93; 8:32; 10:32; 18:56; 21:24; 23:70, 90; 24:49; 29:68; 40:5, 25; 43:78-79; 50:5, 19; 60:1; see Sorcery: truth dismissed as. (See Attributes of God's Perfection: the Ultimate Truth.; Believers: bear witness to the truth; Bounds: in religious belief, do not overstep; Creation: of the heavens and the earth in accordance with truth; Denying the truth.)

Tubba^c (Ḥimyar kings of S. Arabia), 44:37; 50:14.

Two-horned one (the) [*Dhu 'l-Qarnayn*], 18:83-98.

Tyranny: see Oppression.

Uḥud (Battle of), 3:121-128, 140-180.

ʿUmrah: see Pilgrimage.

Unbelievers: see Denying the truth.

Unseen (the): see Beyond human perception.

Usury [*ribā*]: condemned, 2:275-280; 3:130; 4:161; 30:39.

Uterus [*raḥm*], 2:228; 3:6; 4:1; 13:8; 22:5; 23:12-14; 31:34; 35:11; 77:20-22. *what God has bidden to be joined, 2:27; 13:20-21, 25; 47:22; see Injustice: spreading corruption on earth. (See Blood: ties of kinship; Man: stages in man's life-cycle.)

ʿUzair: see Ezra.

ʿUzzā (al-) (pagan deity of Arabia), 53:19-23.

Vegetation: see Plants and Trees.

Victory, 2:89; 4:73-74; 5:23; 8:19; 30:2-5; 48:1-3, 24; 54:44-45; 61:14. *divine promise of, 8:7-8, 65-66; 14:13-15; 22:40-41; 23:111; 24:55; 28:35; 37:171-173; 47:7; 48:18-21, 27-28; 54:45; 58:21; 61:13; 110:1. *by God's succour, 3:123-127, 160; 8:9-12; 9:25-26; 12:90; 17:6; 30:4-5; 33:25-27; 37:114-116; 40:51. *it is the God-conscious, His partisans, who will achieve, 5:56; 24:52; 33:71; 37:172-173. *conquest of Mecca, 48:24-27; 57:10. *Paradise as supreme triumph, 3:185; 4:13; 5:119; 6:16; 9:20-22; 9:72, 89, 100, 111-112; 10:64; 37:58-61; 40:8-9; 44:55-57; 45:30; 48:5; 57:12; 59:20; 61:12; 64:9; 85:11. *Satan falsely promises, 8:48. (See Fighting in God's cause.)

Views: see Opinions.

Vineyards, 2:266; 6:99; 13:4; 18:32-43; 23:19; 36:34; 78:32; see Plants and Trees: vines.

Virtue, 2:177, 232; 3:92; 33:70-71. *the truly virtuous, 3:193, 198; 4:34; 76:5-10; 80:13-16; 82:13; 83:18-28. *the steep uphill road [*al-ʿaqabah*], 90:11-17. *gratitude to God: see Gratitude. *doing good, 2:83, 110, 195, 197, 215; 3:134, 146-148; 4:36, 127-128, 149; 5:13, 93; 7:56; 10:26; 16:90, 128; 17:7, 23-24; 22:37, 77; 28:77; 29:69; 31:3-5, 22; 34:11; 39:58; 46:12; 51:15-19; 73:20; see Believers: reward promised ...; Faith: and good works; Good deeds: rewarded. *charity: see Charity; Orphans: charity to; Spending (on others). *chastity, 23:5-7; 24:30-31, 33; 33:35; see Chastity. *trust in God, 3:122, 159-160; 4:81; 8:49; see God: believers must place their...; Trust in God. *faithfulness to promises and trusts: see Promises: believers must fulfil all their. *honesty, 2:283; 3:75; 4:58; 23:8. *hospitality, 9:6; 11:69, 78; 15:68-70; 17:26; 59:9. *humbleness, 2:45; 4:154; 5:54, 82; 6:42-43; 7:55, 94, 161; 11:23, 112; 16:69; 17:24, 37, 109; 19:13-14, 31-32; 21:90; 22:34-35, 54; 23:2, 76-77; 31:18-19; 32:15; 33:35; 49:1-5; 57:16. *justice: see Justice; Relatives: to be just, even against one's. *moderation, 3:147; 7:31; 16:126; 17:26-27, 29; 22:60; 25:67. *modesty: see Modesty. *to enjoin what is right and forbid what is wrong: see Muslims: to enjoin what is right. *patience: see Patience. *forgiveness: see Forgiveness: forgiving others. *righteousness: see Righteousness; Straight Way (the). *to hold anger in check, 3:134; 7:200-202; 41:36. *repel evil with good, 13:22; 19:46-47; 23:96; 25:63; 28:54; 33:70; 41:34-35; 42:40. *forbearance, 5:13; 7:199; 24:22; 43:89; 64:14. *truthfulness, 5:119; 22:30-31; 25:72; 29:3; 33:23-24, 70; 49:15. (See Consciousness (God-); Manners.)

Visions: see Dreams.

Wadd (deity of Noah's people), 71:23.

War: see Captives; Fighting in God's cause; Self-defence.

Water, 2:249; 8:11; 13:4, 14; 18:41; 23:18-19; 38:42; 39:21; 56:68-70; 67:30; 77:27. *God's throne rests upon the, 11:7. *all living things created from, 21:30; 24:45; 25:54. *sent down in due measure, 23:18; 43:11. *the two great bodies of, 25:53; 27:61; 35:12; 55:19-22. (See Rain; Sea.)

Wayfarer [*ibn as-sabīl*]: assistance due to, 2:177, 215; 17:26; 30:38. *kindness to, 4:36. *beneficiary of booty and *zakāh*, 8:41; 9:60; 59:7. (See Travel on the earth.)

Ways (Paths; Roads), 4:100; 15:76, 79; 20:77; 37:22-23; 39:21; 71:19-20; 76:17-18. ****fī sabīli-llāh*** (lit., in God's *way*), 38:26; see Fighting: in God's cause; Striving: in God's cause. *Revelation as a means of insight: see Revelation. *that God has traced out for His creation, 16:15-16, 69; 20:53; 21:31. *of good and ways of evil, 1:6-7; 4:22, 98, 115, 150-151; 5:15-16, 46; 6:55-56, 129; 7:142, 145-146, 159, 181; 12:108; 14:1-2; 16:125; 17:32, 42, 48, 84; 19:43; 20:135; 22:24; 25:57; 29:29, 69; 31:15, 32; 34:6; 35:32; 36:66-67; 38:22; 40:7, 38; 45:18; 49:17; 70:3-4; 72:11; 73:19; 76:3, 29-30; 87:8; 90:10; 92:5-10; see Good and evil. *the footsteps of Satan, 2:168, 208; 4:83; 6:142; 24:21. (See Astray (to go), (to lead); Righteousness: the path of; Straight Way (the).)

Wealth (Possessions), 2:180, 247; 7:188; 9:103; 17:64; 18:46; 27:35-36; 34:47; 59:8. ***as God's blessing** and favour, 2:36; 7:24; 9:28, 74-76; 24:33; 28:60; 33:27; 43:32; 71:11-12. ***strict fairness** towards the W. of orphans, 6:152; 17:34; see Orphans: good treatment of. ***do not devour**, nor covet, other people's possessions, 4:29, 32, 161; 15:88; 30:39. ***intense** love for, 7:48, 169; 9:24, 34-35, 76; 10:58; 28:76-79; 57:20; 63:9; 70:18; 89:19-20; 90:6; 92:8-11; 100:6-8; 104:2-3. ***as trial** and temptation, 2:155; 3:186; 8:28; see Trials. ***is the cause** of many going astray, 8:36; 9:69; 10:88; 11:87; 28:58, 61; 34:35-37; 43:33-35; 48:11; 74:11-15; 111:1-2. (See Children: linked to wealth; and riches, of no avail against God; Fighting: in God's cause; Provision; Spending: in God's cause; Striving: in God's cause.)

Whispering, 6:112; 19:98; 20:102-103; 50:16. ***Satan's**, 6:121; 7:20; 8:11; 20:120; 114:1-6.

Widows: maintenance of, 2:240. ***inheritance** of, 4:12. ***waiting-period** [*ʿiddah*], 2:234-235.

Will of God, 2:73, 185; 3:179; 4:26-28, 48-49, 116; 11:44; 16:120; 17:18; 23:93-94; 28:5-6; 33:24, 37-38; 37:103-108; 45:19; 66:5; 68:17-18; 72:10; 80:22. ***all things** obey, 2:116; 30:26; see Surrender to God: all creation surrendered to God. ***heavens** and earth subject to, 6:96; 36:38; 41:12; 65:12. ***"-if God so wills"**; "-except as God may please", 2:70; 6:41; 7:188; 9:28; 10:49; 11:107; 12:99; 17:54; 18:23-24, 39, 69; 27:87; 28:27; 37:102; 39:68; 48:27; 74:56; 76:29-30; 87:6-7. ***God does** what He wills, 2:105, 247, 255, 261, 269, 284; 3:13, 40, 73-74, 128-129; 5:1, 17-18, 54; 6:133; 7:128; 9:15, 27; 11:73, 107; 13:13, 38-39; 14:27; 16:2; 22:14, 18; 24:21; 29:21; 30:48; 35:1, 22; 40:15; 42:32-33, 49-52; 57:29; 59:6; see Creation: God creates what He wills. ***had God so willed...**, 2:20, 220, 253; 4:50; 5:17, 48; 6:107, 112, 137; 7:100, 155, 176; 11:118; 12:110; 16:93; 17:86; 21:9, 17; 25:45, 51; 26:4; 34:9; 36:66-67; 39:4; 42:8, 24; 43:60; 47:4, 29-30; 48:25; 56:63-65, 68-70; see Believers: had God willed it, all mankind would be; Faith: believes only whoever God wills; Guidance: had God so willed... ***when God** shall make manifest His, 2:109; 9:24, 48; 40:78. ***nothing** can frustrate, 4:47; 5:17; 6:34, 115; 8:59; 10:64; 11:57; 12:21, 100; 13:11, 41; 18:27; 28:13; 33:17, 38; 35:2, 44; 48:11; 56:60-61; 65:3; 70:40-41. ***regarding** punishment of evildoers, 3:176; 5:49; 8:7; 9:55, 85; 11:34; 17:16. (See Guidance: God guides whoever He wills...; Leave (God's); Provision: God provides abundantly, ...)

Wills, 2:180-182, 240; 5:106-108. (See Inheritance; Witnesses.)

Wind, 2:164; 14:18; 15:27; 18:45; 22:31; 45:5; 51:1-4. ***as glad tiding** of God's coming grace, 7:57; 25:48; 27:63; 30:46. ***and rain**, 7:57; 15:22; 25:48-49; 30:46, 48-49; 35:9; 51:4; 78:14-16. ***and ships** at sea, 10:22; 30:46; 42:33. ***subjected** to Solomon, 21:81; 34:12; 38:36. ***of destruction**, 3:117; 30:51; 33:9; 41:16; 46:24-25; 51:41-42; 54:19-20; 69:6-7. ***Hell's scorching** winds, 52:27; 56:42.

Wine: see Alcoholic drinks.

Wisdom, 2:251, 269; 3:48; 10:39; 15:53; 16:125; 19:12; 22:46; 26:197; 31:12; 38:20; 39:49; 43:63; 51:28; 68:41; 96:17-18. ***in Revelation**, 3:58, 184; 4:163; 10:2; 16:44; 17:55; 21:105; 26:196; 31:2; 35:25; 36:2; 43:2-4; 54:4-5, 43, 52. ***divine**, 4:166; 11:14; 13:13; 22:63; 27:78; 31:16; 33:34; 67:14. ***only God** is truly wise, 2:32, 129, 209, 220, 228, 240, 260; 3:62; 4:11, 17, 24, 26, 56, 92, 104, 111, 130, 158, 165, 170; 5:38, 118; 6:18, 73, 83, 128, 139; 8:10, 49, 63, 67, 71; 9:15, 28, 40, 60, 71, 97, 106, 110; 11:1; 12:6, 86, 100; 14:4; 15:25; 16:60; 22:52; 24:10, 18, 58-59; 27:6; 29:26, 42; 30:27; 31:8-9, 27; 33:1; 34:1; 35:2; 40:8; 41:42; 42:51; 43:84; 45:37; 48:4, 7, 19; 49:7-8; 51:30; 57:1; 59:1, 24; 60:5, 10; 61:1; 62:3; 66:2; 76:30; see Attributes of God's perfection: the Truly Wise; God: He knows all that is beyond...; Hour (the Last): knowledge of it rest with God alone; Knowledge: God's omniscience. ***the prophetic *sunnah*** as 'the wisdom', 2:129, 151, 231; 3:81, 164; 4:54, 113; 5:110; 33:34; 45:16; 62:2. ***Luqmān** advises his son: see Luqmān. ***the story of al-Khaḍir**: see Khaḍir. (See Discernment; Knowledge; Reason; Solomon: wisdom of.)

Witnesses, 4:6, 135; 5:8; 25:72; 70:33. ***to the solemn pledge** of the prophets, 3:81. ***the Apostle** and the believers, bear witness to the truth, 2:143; 22:78; 43:86; see Believers: bear witness to the truth. ***when making** a bequest, 5:106-108. ***in a commercial** contract, 2:282-283. ***in case of immoral conduct** or adultery, 4:15; 24:4-9, 13. ***in case of divorce**, 65:2. ***of punishment** for adultery, 24:2. (See Creation: without witnesses. Day of Resurrection: witnesses; witnessing borne on. God: witness unto everything.)

Wives, 2:102, 187, 223; 4:19-21, 129; 9:24; 25:74; 26:165-166; 60:10-11; 70:11-12; 80:34-36; 111:4. ***rights** and duties of, 2:228; 4:34. ***of some** prophets, 2:35; 7:19-25, 83; 11:71-73, 81; 13:38; 15:60; 19:5, 8; 20:117; 21:90; 26:171; 27:57; 29:32-33; 51:29; 66:10. ***of Prophet** Muḥammad, 24:11-26; 33:6, 28-34, 37, 50-55, 59; 66:1-5; see ʿĀʾiša; Hafsa; Zaynab. ***in Paradise**, 2:25; 3:15; 4:57; 13:23; 36:56; 43:70; 44:54; 52:20; 56:22-23, 34-38. (See Divorce; Dowry; Inheritance: bequests; Marriage; Spouses; Women.)

Women, 2:49, 178, 282; 3:14, 34-36, 40, 42, 61; 4:1, 34, 43, 75, 98, 127-128; 5:5, 6; 6:139; 7:81, 127, 141, 189; 12:21, 23-34, 50-51; 14:6; 16:58-59; 24:23, 26; 27:55; 28:4; 40:25; 43:17-18; 49:11, 13; 60:10-12; 66:10-12; 86:7. ***equal to men** in dignity, reward and punishment, 3:195; 4:15-16, 32, 124; 16:97; 24:2-3; 33:35-36, 58, 73; 40:40; 48:6; 57:18. ***conduct** and dress, 4:34; 24:31, 60; 33:33, 59. ***monthly courses**, 2:222, 228; 65:4. ***inheritance** of, 4:7, 11; see Inheritance. ***those guilty** of immoral conduct, 4:15-16; 24:2-3; see Adultery; Conduct (Immoral); Fornication. ***their awesome** guile, 12:28. ***proposed** as models, 66:11-12: **-Mary**, mother of Jesus: see Mary; **-the wife** of Pharaoh, 28:8-9; 66:11; **-the mother** of Moses, 20:38-40;

28:7-13; -**the queen** of Sheba, 27:23-24, 29-44. ***the daughters** of Jethro, 28:23-28. (See Divorce; Dowry; Marriage; Uterus; Wives.)

Words (Expressions; Sayings), 3:77; 18:93; 19:34; 20:27-28, 109; 43:52, 88; 55:17-18; 58:1; 63:4; 69:44-48; 74:23-25; 75:16-17; 77:34-36; 78:37-38; 81:25. ***the revealed** 'word' of God, 2:37, 75-76; 7:158; 9:6; 18:27, 109; 23:68; 28:51; 31:27; 36:70; 48:15; 69:40-43; 81:19; 86:13. ***God's**, 6:73; 10:82; 16:40; 21:27; 42:24; see Creation: God commands, 'Be' -and it is. ***as God's** promises, 3:39, 45; 4:171; 6:146; 8:7; 10:33, 96-97; 11:119; 27:82, 85; 28:63; 32:13; 36:7, 55-58; 37:31, 171-173; 39:74; 40:6; 66:12; see Promises: God's. ***as promise** or bond, 2:177; 3:17; 7:135; 9:119; 33:24, 35; 43:50; 49:17; see Covenant: those who break...; Covenants; Promises. ***parable** of the good W. and the bad, 14:24-27. ***kind, true**, good, 2:235, 263; 3:64; 6:152; 19:34; 33:70; 35:10; 41:33; 43:26-28; 47:20-21. ***speak unto** people in a kindly manner, 2:83, 235, 262-264; 4:5, 8; 16:125; 17:28, 53; 20:44; 29:46; 43:89. ***to distort** the meaning of revealed, 4:46; 5:13, 41; see Christians: alter and contradict...; Corruption of revealed texts; Israel (children of): have altered and concealed.... ***offensive** or blasphemous, 3:181; 6:33, 68; 9:32, 74; 18:5; 33:48; 61:7-8. ***false**, idle talk; play with, 6:91; 13:33; 22:30; 23:99-100; 31:6; 33:4; 43:83; 70:42. (See Language; Opinions; Promises.)

Wrong: see Injustice.

Yagūth (deity of Noah's people), 71:23.

Yathrib, 33:13; App. IV. ***alluded to**, 33:6, 50.

Yaᶜūq (deity of Noah's people), 71:23.

Zachariah [*Zakariyya*] (father of John the Baptist), 3:37-41; 6:85; 19:2-11; 21:89-90; see Supplications: of Zachariah.

Zakāh: see Purifying dues; Charity.

Zayd (adopted son of the Prophet), 33:37.

Zaynab (wife of the Prophet; not named), 33:37.

Zoroastrians (*al-majūs*), 22:17.

ٱلْإِنسَٰنَ مِنْ عَلَقٍ

ٱقْرَأْ وَرَبُّكَ ٱلْأَكْرَمُ

ٱلَّذِى عَلَّمَ بِٱلْقَلَمِ

عَلَّمَ ٱلْإِنسَٰنَ مَا لَمْ يَعْلَمْ